the

N E W

INTERNATIONAL DICTIONARY OF PENTECOSTAL AND CHARISMATIC MOVEMENTS

REVISED AND EXPANDED EDITION

STANLEY M. BURGESS, Editor

and EDUARD M. VAN DER MAAS, Associate Editor

ZONDERVAN™

GRAND RAPIDS, MICHIGAN 49530 USA

ZONDERVAN™

The New International Dictionary of Pentecostal and Charismatic Movements
Copyright © 2002 by Stanley M. Burgess and Eduard M. van der Maas

Requests for information should be addressed to:

Zondervan, *Grand Rapids, Michigan 49530*

Library of Congress Cataloging-in-Publication Data

The new international dictionary of Pentecostal and charismatic movements.—Rev. and
   expanded / Stanley M. Burgess, editor; Eduard M. van der Maas, associate editor.
      p.   cm.
   Rev. ed. of: Dictionary of Pentecostal and charismatic movements.
   Includes bibliographic references.
   ISBN 0-310-22481-0 (hardcover)
   1. Pentecostalism—Dictionaries. 2. Pentecostal churches—Dictionaries. I. Burgess,
   Stanley M., 1937 –   II. van der Maas, Ed M. III. Dictionary of Pentecostal and charismatic
   movements.

   BR1644 .D53 2001
   270.8'2'03—dc21   2001023554

Interior design by Sherri L. Hoffman

Printed in the United States of America

02 03 04 05 06 07 08 /❖ DC/ 10 9 8 7 6 5 4 3 2

Contents

List of Articles vi

Preface xv

Introduction xvii

Editors and Contributors xxv

Abbreviations and Acronyms xxix

Part I: Global Survey 1

Part II: Global Statistics 283

Part III: Dictionary 303

Timeline 1227

Picture Sources 1235

Indexes 1237

List of Articles

Part I: Global Survey 1

Afghanistan 3
Africa, Central (Survey) 3
Africa, East (Survey) 4
Africa, North, and the
    Middle East (Survey) 6
Africa, West (Survey) 11
Albania 21
Algeria 21
American Samoa 21
Andorra 21
Angola 21
Anguilla 22
Antigua 23
Argentina 23
Armenia 26
Aruba .26
Australia 26
Austria 29
Azerbaijan 29
Bahamas 29
Bahrain 31
Bangladesh 31
Barbados 31
Belgium 32
Belize .33
Belorussia 33
Benin .33
Bermuda 33
Bhutan 34
Bolivia 34
Bosnia-Herzegovina 35
Botswana 35
Bougainville 35
Brazil .35
Britain 42
British Indian Ocean 46
British Virgin Islands 46
Brunei 46
Bulgaria 46
Burkina Faso 46
Burma 46
Burundi 47
Cambodia 47
Cameroon 47
Canada 48

Cape Verde 51
Caribbean Islands (Survey) 51
Cayman Islands 53
Central African Republic 53
Chad 54
Channel Islands 54
Chile 55
China .58
Christmas Island 65
Cocos (Keeling) Islands 65
Colombia 65
Comoros 66
Congo, Democratic
    Republic of 67
Congo, Republic of the
    (Brazzaville) 75
Cook Islands 76
Costa Rica 77
Croatia 77
Cuba 77
Cyprus 80
Czech Republic 80
Denmark 80
Djibouti 81
Dominica 81
Dominican Republic 81
Ecuador 83
Egypt .84
El Salvador 84
Equatorial Guinea 84
Eritrea 84
Estonia 85
Ethiopia 85
Europe, Eastern (Survey) 88
Europe, Western (Survey) 96
Faeroe Islands 99
Falkland Islands 99
Fiji 99
Finland 103
France 105
French Guiana 107
French Polynesia 107
Gabon 108
Gambia 108
Georgia 108
Germany 109
Ghana 111

Gibraltar 111
Greece 112
Greenland 112
Grenada 112
Guadeloupe 112
Guam 112
Guatemala 112
Guinea, Republic of 113
Guinea-Bissau 115
Guyana 115
Haiti .115
Honduras 117
Hungary 117
Iceland 117
India .118
Indonesia 126
Iran 132
Iraq 132
Ireland 132
Isle of Man 132
Israel .132
Italy 132
Ivory Coast 141
Jamaica (I) 141
Jamaica (II) 146
Japan .147
Jordan 150
Kazakhstan 150
Kenya 150
Kirghizia 156
Kiribati 156
Kuwait 156
Laos .156
Latin America (Survey) 157
Latvia 168
Lebanon 168
Lesotho 168
Liberia 168
Libya .168
Liechtenstein 168
Lithuania 168
Luxembourg 168
Macedonia 168
Madagascar 168
Malawi 169
Malaysia 170
Maldives 173

Mali .173
Malta 173
Marshall Islands 173
Martinique 175
Mauritania 175
Mauritius 175
Mayotte 175
Mexico 175
Micronesia, Federated
  States of 178
Middle East 179
Moldavia 179
Monaco 179
Mongolia 179
Montserrat 179
Morocco 179
Mozambique 180
Myanmar 181
Namibia 183
Nauru 184
Nepal 184
Netherlands, the 184
Netherlands Antilles 186
New Caledonia (Kanaky) 186
New Zealand 187
Nicaragua 192
Niger .192
Nigeria 192
Niue Island 192
Norfolk Island 192
North Korea 192
Northern Cyprus 192
Northern Mariana Islands 192
Norway 193
Oman 194
Pacific Islands (Survey) 194
Pakistan 196
Palau 196
Palestine 196
Panama 197
Papua New Guinea 197
Paraguay 198
Peru .198
Philippines 201
Pitcairn Island 207
Poland 207
Portugal 208
Puerto Rico 209
Qatar 211
Réunion 211
Romania 212
Russia 217

Rwanda 219
Sahara 221
Saint Helena 221
Saint Kitts and Nevis 221
Saint Lucia 221
Saint Pierre and Miquelon 221
Saint Vincent 221
Samoa (Western Samoa) 221
San Marino 222
Sao Tome and Principe 222
Saudi Arabia 222
Scandinavia (Survey) 222
Senegal 222
Seychelles 223
Sierra Leone 223
Singapore 223
Slovakia 225
Slovenia 226
Solomon Islands 226
Somalia 227
Somaliland 227
South Africa 227
South Korea 239
Spain 247
Spanish North Africa 247
Sri Lanka 248
Sudan 253
Suriname 253
Svalbard and Jan Mayen 255
Swaziland 255
Sweden 255
Switzerland 257
Syria .259
Taiwan 259
Tajikistan 264
Tanzania 264
Thailand 269
Timor 271
Togo .271
Tokelau Islands 271
Tonga 271
Trinidad and Tobago 272
Tunisia 273
Turkey 273
Turkmenistan 273
Turks and Caicos Islands 273
Tuvalu 273
Uganda 273
Ukraine 277
United Arab Emirates 277
United Kingdom 277
United States of America 277

Uruguay 277
Uzbekistan 278
Vanuatu 279
Venezuela 279
Viet Nam 281
Virgin Islands of the U.S. 281
Wallis and Futuna Islands 281
Western Samoa 281
Yemen 281
Yugoslavia 281
Zambia 282
Zimbabwe 283

Part II: Global Statistics 283

Part III: Dictionary 303
  Abraham, K. E. 305
  Abrams, Minnie F. 305
  Acts 29 Ministries 306
  Adams, John A. D. 308
  Adini-Abala, Alexander 308
  African Independent Churches 309
  African Initiated Churches
    (AICs) in Diaspora—Europe 309
  Ahn (Kim), Seen Ok 309
  Alamo, Tony and Susan 310
  Allen, Asa Alonso 311
  Alliance of Christian Churches 312
  Alpha Course 312
  American Baptist Charismatic
    Renewal 312
  American Evangelistic
    Association 313
  Anderson, Paul R. 313
  Anderson, Robert Mapes 313
  Andersson, Axel 314
  Angelus Temple 314
  Anglican Renewal Ministries . .315
  Animism and Pentecostalism:
    A Case Study 315
  Anointing with Oil 318
  Apostle, Office of 318
  Apostolic Assembly of Faith
    in Jesus Christ, Inc. 321
  Apostolic Christian Assembly
    (India) 322
  Apostolic Church 322
  Apostolic Church of Faith in
    Jesus Christ 323
  Apostolic Church of God of
    Romania, The 324

Apostolic Church of Pentecost
of Canada 325
Apostolic Faith (Baxter
Springs, KS) 326
Apostolic Faith Mission
(Portland, OR) 327
Apostolic Faith Movement,
Origins 327
Apostolic Overcoming Holy
Church of God 329
Archival Resources 329
Argue, Andrew Harvey 331
Argue, Watson 331
Argue, Zelma 331
Arguinzoni, Sonny 331
Arnold, R. Louis 332
Arnott, John 332
Aschoff, Friedrich 332
Assemblea Cristiana 333
Assemblies of God 333
Assemblies of God in Great
Britain and Ireland 340
Assemblies of God in Mexico . .341
Assemblies of the Lord
Jesus Christ 342
Assembly of Christian Churches 342
Association of Faith Churches
and Ministries 342
Association of International
Mission Services 342
Atkinson, Maria W. 343
Awakened 343
Awrey, Daniel P. 344
Azusa Street Revival 344
Bada, Alexander Adebayo
Abiodun 351
Baker, Elizabeth V. 351
Baker, H. A. 352
Bakker, James Orsen ("Jim") . . .352
Ball, Henry Cleophas 354
Baptism in the Holy Spirit 354
Baptist Pentecostals and
Charismatics 363
Barnes, Leanore O. ("Mother
Mary") 364
Barr, Edmond S. and
Rebecca 364
Barratt, Thomas Ball 365
Bartleman, Frank 366
Basham, Don Wilson 367
Baumert, Norbert 367
Baxter, W. J. E. ("Ern") 367

Bazán, Demetrio 368
Bázan, Manuelita (Nellie)
Treviño 368
Beall, James Lee 368
Beall, Myrtle D. 368
Bell, Eudorus N. 369
Bennett, Dennis Joseph
and Rita 369
Berg, Daniel 369
Berlin Declaration 371
Bertolucci, John 371
Bettex, Paul 371
Bhengu, Nicholas Bhekinkosi
Hepworth 372
Bible Institutes, Colleges,
Universities 372
Bible Institutes,
Spanish-Speaking. 380
Bible Quizzing 381
Bible Way Churches of Our Lord
Jesus Christ World Wide 382
Bibliography and Historiography
of Pentecostalism in the
United States 382
Bibliography and Historiography
of Pentecostalism Outside
North America 405
Bickle, Mike 417
Bilby, Ian 417
Biolley, Hélène 417
Bittlinger, Arnold 418
Björk, Olov Leonard 418
Bjorner, Anna Larssen 419
Black Holiness Pentecostalism .419
Black Theology 428
Blaisdell, Francisca D. 432
Blasphemy against the Holy
Spirit 432
Blessed Trinity Society 435
Bloch-Hoell, Nils Egede 435
Bloomfield, Ray 435
Blumhofer, Edith 436
Bochian, Pavel 436
Boddy, Alexander Alfred 436
Boddy, Mary 437
Bonnie Brae Street Cottage . . .437
Bonnke, Reinhard Willi
Gottfried 438
Bosworth, Fred Francis 439
Bradford, George Crain
("Brick") 440
Branding, Harry W. 440

Branham, William Marrion . . .440
Braxton, S. Lee 441
Bredesen, Harald 441
Brewster, Percy Stanley 442
Brittain, Blanche Elizabeth 442
Britton, Bill 443
Britton, Francis Marion 443
Brotherhood of the Cross
and Star 443
Brown, James H. 444
Brown, Robert 444
Brown, Vin R. 445
Brownsville Revival 445
Brumback, Carl 447
Bruner, Frederick Dale 447
Bryant, John 447
Buchanan, William Alexander
(Alex) 447
Buckingham, James William II
("Jamie") 448
Buffum, Herbert 448
Bundy, David Dale 448
Buntain, Daniel Mark 449
Buntain, Daniel Newton 449
Burciaga, Cesáreo 450
Burgess, John Harry 450
Burnett, Bill 450
Burning Bush Movement 451
Burton, William Frederick
Padwick 451
Byrd, Vernon 451
Calvary Chapel 453
Calver, Clive 453
Campbell, Ivey Glenshaw 454
Cantalamessa, Raniero 454
Cantel, Margaret 454
Cantú, Benjamín 455
Capps, Charles Emmitt 455
Carlson, Glen 455
Carlson, Guy Raymond 455
Carter, Alfred Howard 456
Carter, John H. 456
Cashwell, Gaston Barnabas . . .457
Cathcart, William 458
Catholic Apostolic Church 459
Catholic Charismatic Renewal .460
Catholic Fraternity of Charismatic
Covenant Communities and
Fellowships 467
Celestial Church of Christ 467
Cerullo, Morris 472
Chambers, George Augustus . .472

Chambers, Stanley Warren 472
Charisma in Missions 472
Charismatic Communities 473
Charismatic Episcopal Church
  (CEC) 476
Charismatic Movement 477
Charismatic Renewal Services
  (CRS) 519
Charisms 520
Chavda, Mahesh 520
Chawner, C. Austin 520
Chernoff, David L. 521
Cherokee County (NC)
  Revival 521
Chesser, H. L. 521
Chi Alpha 521
Cho, David (Paul) Yonggi 521
Choi, Ja-Sil 522
Christenson, Laurence Donald
  ("Larry") 522
Christ for the Nations Institute
  (CFNI) 523
Christian and Missionary
  Alliance 523
Christian Church of North
  America 525
Christian City Churches
  International 527
Christian Growth Ministries . .528
Christian Outreach Centres . . .528
Christian Worker's Union 528
Christ's Church Fellowship . . .528
Church Membership 529
Church of God
  (Cleveland, TN) 530
Church of God (Cleveland, TN)
  in Canada 534
Church of God (Original) 535
Church of God by Faith 535
Church of God in Christ 535
Church of God in Christ
  (White) 535
Church of God in the Republic of
  Mexico (Iglesia de Dios en la
  República Mexicana) 537
Church of God, Jerusalem Acres 538
Church of God of Prophecy 539
Church of God of Prophecy in
  Canada 542
Church of God of the Mountain
  Assembly 543

Church of Our Lord Jesus Christ
  of the Apostolic Faith 543
Church of the Living God,
  Christian Workers for
  Fellowship 543
Church of the Lord Jesus Christ
  of the Apostolic Faith 544
Church, Theology of the 544
Clark, Ian George 551
Clark, Randy 552
Clark, Stephen B. 552
Clarke, Charles J. 552
Classical Pentecostalism 553
Clemmons, Ithiel Conrad 555
Coady, A. Ron 556
Coates, Gerald 556
Coe, Jack 556
Communion of Evangelical
  Episcopal Churches
  (CEEC) 557
Conatser, Howard 557
Concilio Latino-Americano de
  Iglesias Cristianas 557
Concilio Latino-Americano de
  la Iglesia de Dios Pentecostal
  de New York 557
Congregational Holiness
  Church 557
Conn, Charles William 558
Convergence Movement 558
Cook, Glenn A. 559
Cook, Ralph G. 560
Cook, Robert F. 560
Cooley, Robert Earl 561
Coombs, Barnabas 561
Copeland, Kenneth 562
Correll, Norman Leigh 562
Cortese, Aimee García 562
Corvin, Raymond Othel 563
Cotton, Emma L. 563
Courtney, Howard Perry 563
Cousen, Cecil 564
Crawford, Florence Louise 564
Crawford, Raymond Robert . . .565
Cross, Milo Parks 565
Crouch, Andrae 565
Crouch, Paul Franklin 565
Crumpler, Ambrose Blackman .566
Cruz, Nicky 566
Culpepper, Richard Weston . . .567
Cummings, Robert Wallace . . .567
Cunningham, Loren 567

Cursillo Movement 567
Dake, Finis Jennings 569
Dallière, Louis 569
Dallimore, A. H. 570
Damascus Christian Churches,
  Inc. 570
Dancing in the Spirit 570
Daugherty, Billy Joe 571
David J. du Plessis Center for
  Christian Spirituality 572
Dawson, John 573
Dayton, Donald Wilber 573
De la Cruz, Marcial 573
Deeper Christian Life Mission
  (International) 574
Denny, Richard (Dick) 574
Derstine, Gerald 574
Dialogue, Reformed–
  Pentecostal 575
Dialogue, Roman Catholic and
  Classical Pentecostal 576
DiOrio, Ralph A. 582
Discernment of Spirits,
  Gift of 582
Dispensationalism 584
Donald Gee Centre 586
Door of Faith Churches
  of Hawaii 586
Dowie, John Alexander 586
Draper, Minnie Tingley 587
Duffield, Guy Payson 588
Duncan, Susan A. 588
Dunk, Gilbert T. S. 588
Du Plessis, David Johannes . . .589
Du Plessis, Justus Telo 593
DuPree, Sherry Sherrod 593
Durasoff, Steve 593
Durham, William H. 594
Dye, Colin. 595
Eastman, Dick 596
Ecclesiastical Polity 596
Edvardsen, Aril 598
Elim Fellowship 598
Elim Pentecostal Church 598
Epiclesis (Epiklesis) 599
Episcopal Renewal Ministries .600
Erickson, Elmer C. 600
Ervin, Howard Matthew 600
Eschatology, Pentecostal
  Perspectives on 601
Escobedo, Modesto 605

Ethics in the Classical
  Pentecostal Tradition 605
European Pentecostal
  Theological Association
  (EPTA) 610
European Pietist Roots of
  Pentecostalism 610
Evangelicalism 613
Evangelism 617
Evangelists 620
Evangelization Society, The . . .623
Evans, William Irvin 623
Ewart, Frank J. 623
Exorcism 624
Faith, Gift of 629
Faith Churches 630
Faith Homes 630
Faricy, Robert 632
Farrow, Lucy F. 632
Fasting 633
Fauss, Oliver F. 635
Fee, Gordon Donald 635
Fellowship of Christian
  Assemblies 636
Fields of the Wood 636
Fierro, Robert Felix 637
Finished Work Controversy . . .638
Finkenbinder, Frank O. 639
Finkenbinder, Paul Edwin
  ("Hermano Pablo") 640
Fire-Baptized Holiness Church .640
First Church of Jesus Christ . . .641
Fisher, Elmer Kirk 641
Flattery, George Manford 641
Flores, Samuel Joachín 641
Flower, Joseph James Roswell
  and Alice Reynolds 642
Flower, Joseph Reynolds 644
Follette, John Wright 644
Ford, Josephine Massyngbaerde 645
Ford, Louis Henry 645
Forrest, Tom 645
Forster, Roger T. 645
Fountain Trust 646
Foursquare Gospel Church
  of Canada 646
Francescon, Luigi 646
Frangipane, Francis 646
Frodsham, Arthur W. 647
Frodsham, Stanley Howard . . .647
Froen, Hans-Jacob 648
Fruit of the Spirit 648

Fullam, Everett L. ("Terry") . . .652
Fuller, William E. 652
Full Gospel Baptist Church
  Fellowship 653
Full Gospel Business
  Men's Fellowship
  International 653
Full Gospel Church of God in
  Southern Africa 654
Full Gospel Evangelistic
  Association 654
Fulton, Charles B., Jr. 655
Fundamentalism 655
Gaines, Margaret 659
García Peraza, Juanita ("Mita") .659
Garlock, Henry Bruce 659
Garr, Alfred Goodrich, Sr. 660
Garrigus, Alice Belle 661
Garr Memorial Church 661
Gause, Rufus Hollis 661
Gaxiola, Manuel Jesús 662
Gee, Donald 662
Gelpi, Donald L. 663
Gereja Bethel Indonesia 664
Gibson, Christine Amelia 664
Gifts of the Spirit 664
Gifts of the Spirit: Natural
  and Supernatural 667
Gimenez, John and Anne 668
Glad Tidings Missionary
  Society 668
Glad Tidings Tabernacle 669
Global University of the
  Assemblies of God 669
Glossolalia 670
Glossolalia: An Outsider's
  Perspective 676
Glossolalia, Manual. 677
González, Eusebio (Aarón)
  Joaquín 678
Gospel Publishing House 678
Goss, Howard Archibald 679
Gourley, Thomas Hampton . . .679
Grace Ministries 680
Graves, Frederick A. 680
Green, Lynn 680
Greenway, Alfred L. 680
Greenwood, Charles Lewis 681
Gregory Thaumaturgus 681
Guerra, Elena. 682
Guillén, Miguel 682
Gunstone, John 682

Guti, Ezekiel H. 682
Gypsies 683
Hagin, Kenneth E. 687
Hall, Homer Richard 687
Hall, Jimmie Louis 688
Hammond, Hattie Philletta
  Ludy 688
Hanson, Carl M. 689
Hargrave, Vessie D. 689
Harper, Michael Claude 689
Harrell, David Edwin, Jr. 690
Harris, Leo Cecil 690
Harris, Thoro 691
Harrison, Alda B. 691
Harvey, Esther Bragg 692
Hayford, Jack Williams, Jr. 692
Haywood, Garfield Thomas . . .693
Healing, Gift of 694
Healing in the Christian
  Church 698
Hebden, James and Ellen K. . . .711
"Hermano Pablo" 712
Hezmalhalch, Thomas 712
Hickey, Marilyn Sweitzer 712
Hicks, Roy H. 712
Hicks, Tommy 713
Hildegard of Bingen 713
Hinn, Benedict ("Benny") 713
Hispanic Pentecostalism 715
Hite, Benjamin Harrison 723
Hocken, Peter Dudley 723
Hodges, Melvin Lyle 724
Hodgson, Edmund ("Teddy") . .725
Hogan, James Philip 725
Holiness Church of North
  Carolina 726
Holiness Movement 726
Hollenweger, Walter Jacob 729
Holmes, Nickels John 730
Holy Spirit, Doctrine of:
  The Ancient Fathers 730
Holy Spirit, Doctrine of:
  The Medieval Churches 747
Holy Spirit, Doctrine of:
  Reformation Traditions 763
Holy Spirit Teaching Mission . .769
Holy Trinity Brompton 770
Hoover, Willis Collins 770
Hope Chapel 771
Hornshuh, Fred 771
Horton, Harold Lawrence
  Cuthbert 772

Horton, Stanley Monroe 772
Horton, Wade Henry 773
House Church Movement 773
Houston, Frank 774
Howard-Browne, Rodney M. ..774
Hughes, Ray Harrison 775
Humbard, Alpha Rex
    Emmanuel and Maude Aimee 775
Humburg, Emil 775
Hurst, Wesley Robinson 776
Iglesia de Cristo Misionera 777
Iglesia de Dios Pentecostal de
    Puerto Rico 777
Ilunga, Ngoi wa Mbuya
    Kalulwa (Jonathan) 777
Independent Assemblies of
    God International 778
Independent Evangelical
    Church 778
Independent Pentecostal
    Evangelical Church
    Movement 778
Indian Pentecostal Church
    of God 778
Indigenous Churches 779
Ingram, James Henry 784
Initial Evidence 784
Integrity Communications 791
Interdenominational Christian
    Church 791
International Catholic
    Charismatic Renewal
    Services 792
International Charismatic
    Consultation on World
    Evangelization 792
International Church of the
    Foursquare Gospel 793
International Convention of Faith
    Churches and Ministers 794
International Correspondence
    Institute 795
International Evangelism
    Crusades 795
International Ministerial
    Association 795
International Pentecostal-
    Charismatic Scholarly
    Associations 795
International Pentecostal
    Church of Christ 797

International Pentecostal
    Council 798
International Pentecostal Holiness
    Church 798
International Pentecostal Press
    Association 801
Interpretation of Tongues,
    Gift of 801
Irish, Charles Manning 802
Irving, Edward 803
Irwin, Benjamin Hardin 804
Irwin, David Kent 805
Italian Pentecostal Church
    of Canada 805
Jackson, Ray, Sr. 806
Jacobs, Cindy 806
Jacobs, Sam G. 806
Jakes, Thomas D., Sr. 806
Jaramillo, Diego 807
Jeffreys, George 807
Jeffreys, Stephen 808
Jenkins, Leroy 809
Jernigan, John C. 809
Jesus Only 809
Jeyaraj, Yesudian 809
John XXIII 810
John Paul II and the Catholic
    Charismatic Renewal 810
Johnson, Bernhard, Jr. 812
Johnson, Joseph J. 813
Jones, Bryn 813
Jones, Charles Edwin 813
Jones, Ozro Thurston, Sr. 813
Jones, Thea F. 814
Joyner, Rick 814
Jungkuntz, Theodore 814
Junk, Thomas 814
Juster, Daniel C. 814
Kansas City Conference 816
Kansas City Fellowship 816
Kansas City Prophets 816
Kaseman, Jim 817
Kayembe, Michel 817
Kellar, Nancy 817
Keller, Otto C. and Marian 818
Kendrick, Graham 818
Kendrick, Klaude 818
Kennedy, Mildred ("Minnie") ..819
Kenyon, Essek William 819
Kerr, Cecil and Myrtle 820
Kerr, Daniel Warren 820

Keswick Higher Life
    Movement 820
Ketcham, Maynard L. 821
King, Joseph Hillery 822
Knight, Cecil Brigham 823
Knight, Giles N. 823
Knowledge, Word of 823
Kollins, Kim Catherine-Marie .825
Kramar, Marilynn 825
Kuhlman, Kathryn 826
Kuzmič, Peter 827
Lake, John Graham 828
Lancaster, Sarah Jane (Jeannie) 828
Latin American District
    Council of the Assemblies
    of God in the
    U.S.A. 829
Latter Rain Movement 830
Laurentin, René 833
Lauster, Herman 833
Law, Terry 833
Lawrence, Bennett Freeman ...834
Laying on of Hands 834
Lea, Larry 836
Lebeau, Paul 837
Lee, Flavius Josephus 837
Lee, Yong-Do 837
Lensch, Rodney 838
Leonard, Thomas King 838
Lewer, Alfred 838
Lewis, Gayle F. 839
Lidman, Sven 839
L.I.F.E. Bible College 839
Life in the Spirit Seminars 840
Light of the World Church ..840
Lindsay, Gordon and
    Freda Theresa 841
Litwiller, Nelson 842
Llorente, Francisco 843
Logos International Fellowship,
    Inc. 843
Lopez, Abundio L. and Rosa ..844
Luce, Alice Eveline 844
Lugo, Juan L. 845
Lukusa, Luvungu Albert 846
Lum, Clara E. 846
Lupton, Levi Rakestraw 846
Lutheran Charismatics 847
McAlister, Harvey 852
McAlister, Robert Edward 852
McCauley, Ray 852
McClain, Samuel C. 852

McDonnell, Kilian 853
Macedo, Edir 853
McGee, Gary Blair 854
McKenna, Briege 855
McKinney, Claude Adams 855
MacKnight, James
   Montgomery 855
MacNutt, Francis Scott 855
McPherson, Aimee Semple . . .856
McPherson, Rolf Kennedy 859
Mainse, David 859
Malachuk, Daniel 859
Mallory, Arenia Cornelia 859
Maranatha Campus Ministries,
   International 860
March for Jesus 860
Marshall, Sarah Catherine
   Wood 860
Martin, R. Francis 861
Martin, Ralph 861
Marxism and Pentecostalism . .862
Mary and the Holy Spirit 863
Mascarenhas, Fiorello 864
Mason, Charles Harrison 865
Mattsson-Boze, Joseph D. 867
Mead, Samuel J. and Ardella . .867
Meares, John L. 868
Melodyland Christian Center . .868
Memphis Miracle 869
Mennonite Charismatics 869
Menzies, William Watson 871
Messianic Judaism 871
Metro Christian Fellowship . . .874
Metropolitan Church
   Association (Burning Bush). .874
Meyer, Joyce 875
Miracles, Gift of 875
Miranda, Jesse 876
Mirly, Herbert H. 876
Missiology: Pentecostal and
   Charismatic 877
Missionary Church of Christ . .880
Missionary Conference, The . . .885
Missions, Overseas (North
   American Pentecostal) 885
"Mita" Congregation, Inc. 901
Mitchell, Robert Bryant 901
Mitton, Michael 902
Mjorud, Herbert 902
Mohan, David 902
Moise, Mary Gill ("Mother") . .902
Monot, Ronald Jean 903

Montague, George T. 903
Montanism 903
Montgomery, Carrie Judd 904
Montgomery, Granville
   Harrison 906
Moore, Jennie Evans 906
Moorhead, Max Wood 907
Morgan, Arthur Theodore 907
Morgan Howard, Concepción
   (Chonita) 907
Morrow, Peter and Anne 908
Morton, Paul S., Jr. 908
Morton, Tony 908
Moss, Virginia E. 909
Mount Sinai Holy Church of
   America 909
Mühlen, Heribert 910
Mülheim Association 910
Mulungo, Laurentino 910
Mumford, Bernard C., Jr. (Bob) .911
Murray, George A. and Annie .911
Music, Pentecostal and
   Charismatic 911
Myerscough, Thomas 920
Myland, David Wesley 920
Naickomparambil, Mathew . . .922
National Association of
   Evangelicals 922
National Gay Pentecostal
   Alliance 925
National Service Committee
   (NSC). 926
Native American Pentecostals .926
Nava, Antonio Castañeda 927
Nelson, Peter Christopher 927
Neocharismatics 928
Neo-Pentecostals 928
New Apostolic Church 928
New Apostolic Reformation . . .930
New Churches 930
Nichol, John Thomas 930
Nickel, Thomas Roy 931
Nikoloff, Nicholas 931
Nondenominational Pentecostal
   and Charismatic Churches . . .932
North American Congresses
   on the Holy Spirit and
   World Evangelization 935
North American Renewal
   Service Committee 935
Norton, Albert 935
O'Connor, Edward Dennis 936

Olazábal, Francisco 936
Oneness Pentecostalism 936
Ongman, John 944
Ongman, Paul 945
Open Bible Standard
   Churches, Inc. 945
Opperman, Daniel Charles
   Owen 946
Ordinances, Pentecostal 947
Örebro Mission and Örebro
   Mission School 949
Orozco, Rodolfo O. 949
Ortiz, Francisco D. 949
Ortiz, Juan Carlos 950
Osborn, Tommy Lee 950
Oschoffa, Samuel Bileóu
   Joseph 951
Osteen, John Hillery 951
Ottolini, Pietro 951
Ozman, Agnes Nevada 952
Pacifism 953
Parham, Charles Fox 955
Parish Renewal Council 957
Parr, John Nelson 957
Pathway Press 957
Patterson, Gilbert Earl 957
Paul, Jonathan Anton
   Alexander 958
Paulk, Earl Pearly, Jr. 958
Pawson, David 959
Payne, Leanne 959
Pearlman, Myer 959
Pearson, Carlton Demetrius . . .959
Pederson, W. Dennis 960
Pendleton, William H. 960
Pensacola Revival 960
Pentecost, Feast of 960
Pentecostal Assemblies of
   Canada 961
Pentecostal Assemblies of Jesus
   Christ 964
Pentecostal Assemblies of
   Newfoundland 964
Pentecostal Assemblies of the
   World 965
Pentecostal/Charismatic
   Churches of North America . .965
Pentecostal Church,
   Incorporated 965
Pentecostal Church of God . . .965
Pentecostal Coalition for
   Human Rights 966

Pentecostal Community of the
Congo 967
Pentecostal Conference of
North American Keralites . . .967
Pentecostal Fellowship of
North America 968
Pentecostal Fire-Baptized
Holiness Church of God
of the Americas 969
Pentecostal Free-Will Baptist
Church 969
Pentecostal Holiness Church . .969
Pentecostal Holiness Church
of Canada 969
Pentecostal Mission in South
and Central Africa 970
Pentecostal Missionary Union .970
Pentecostal World Conference .971
Periodicals 974
Perkin, Noel 982
Perry, Samuel Clement 982
Perry, Troy Deroy 983
Persecution 983
Peterson, Paul Bernhard 985
Pethrus, Petrus Lewi 986
Petts, David 987
Phair, Robert 987
Philippines for Jesus Movement .988
Phillips, Everett L. 988
Pike, John Martin 988
Pinson, Mack M. 989
Piper, William Hamner 989
Pisgah Home Movement 990
Plymire, Victor Guy 991
Polhill, Cecil H. 991
Polman, Gerrit Roelof 992
Positive Confession Theology . .992
Post, Ansel Howard 994
Prange, Erwin 994
Prayer Mountains 994
Prayer Towers 994
Presbyterian and Reformed
Charismatics 995
Price, Charles Sydney 997
Price, Frederick Kenneth Cercie .998
Pridgeon, Charles Hamilton . . .998
Prince, Peter Derek V. 999
Prophecy, Gift of 999
Pulkingham, William Graham 1013
Purdie, James Eustace 1013
Pytches, David 1013
Quakers (Society of Friends) .1014

Quebedeaux, Richard Anthony1014
Radio 1015
Ramabai, Sarasvati Mary
(Pandita) 1016
Ranaghan, Kevin Mathers
and Dorothy 1018
Restorationism in Classical
Pentecostalism 1019
Rhema Ministerial Association
International 1021
Richey, John R. and
Louise H. 1021
Richey, Raymond Theodore . .1021
Riggs, Ralph Meredith 1022
Robeck, Cecil Melvin, Jr. 1023
Roberts, Granville Oral 1024
Roberts, H. V. (Harry) 1025
Roberts, Henry 1026
Roberts, Richard 1026
Roberts, Thomas 1027
Robertson, Marion Gordon
("Pat") 1027
Robinson, Albert Ernest 1028
Robinson, Ida 1028
Robison, James 1028
Rosado, Leoncia Rosseau
("Mama Leo") 1029
Rossin, Delbert 1029
Rowlands, John Frances 1029
Ruesga, David 1030
Rumsey, Mary 1031
Russian and Eastern European
Mission 1031
Sacraments 1033
Salmon, John 1036
Salter, James 1036
Samuel, Saint 1036
Sanders, Anna 1037
Sandford, Frank 1037
Sandidge, Jerry L. 1038
Sandru, Trandafir 1038
Sanford, Agnes Mary 1039
Savelle, Jerry 1039
Scadden, Cecil C. H. 1039
Scandinavian Missions to Latin
America 1040
Scanlan, Michael 1041
Schaepe, John G. 1042
Schlink, Basilea 1042
Schmidt, Gustav Herbert 1042
Schoonmaker, Christian H. . .1043
Scofield Reference Bible 1044

Scott, Douglas R. 1045
Seminaries and Graduate
Schools 1045
Semple, Robert James 1050
Sepúlveda, Carlos 1051
Seraphim of Sarov 1051
Serpent Handling 1052
Seymour, William Joseph 1053
Shakarian, Demos 1058
Shakers 1058
Sharing of Ministries Abroad .1059
Shepherding Movement, The .1060
Sherrill, John Lewis and
Elizabeth 1062
Shields, Ann Elizabeth 1062
Shlemon-Ryan, Barbara Leahy1062
Siberian Seven 1063
Signs and Wonders 1063
Simpson, Albert Benjamin . . .1069
Simpson, Charles Vernon 1070
Simpson, William Wallace . . .1070
Sinclair, John Chalmers 1071
Sisson, Elizabeth 1071
Sizelove, Rachel Artamissie . .1072
Slain in the Spirit 1072
Smail, Thomas A. 1074
Smale, Joseph 1074
Small, Franklin 1075
Smith, Campbell Bannerman .1075
Smith, Charles ("Chuck") 1075
Smith, Frank W. 1076
Snake Handling 1076
Social Justice and the
Pentecostal/Charismatic
Movement 1076
Society for Pentecostal Studies 1079
Sociology of British Pentecostal
and Charismatic Movements .1080
Sociology of World
Pentecostalism 1083
Spencer, Ivan Carlton 1091
Spencer, Ivan Quay 1091
Spiritual Warfare: A
Neocharismatic Perspective .1091
Spirituality, Pentecostal and
Charismatic 1096
Spittler, Russell Paul 1102
Squire, Frederick Henry 1104
Stanphill, Ira 1104
Stark, Edmond F. 1105
Steelberg, Wesley Rowland . . .1105
Steidel, Florence 1105

Steiner, Leonhard 1106
Stephanou, Eusebius A. 1106
Stewart, Leon Otto 1107
Strang, Stephen Edward 1107
Straton, Warren Badenoch . . .1108
Studd, George B. 1108
Suenens, Léon-Joseph 1108
Sullivan, Francis A. 1109
Sumrall, Lester Frank 1109
Sunshine Revival 1110
Swaggart, Jimmy Lee 1111
Sweet, Henry Charles 1111
Symeon the New Theologian .1112
Synan, Harold Vinson 1112
Synan, Joseph Alexander 1113
Tabernacle Pentecostal Church1114
Taitinger, Robert W. 1114
Tañon, Ricardo 1114
Tanusaputra, Abraham Alex . .1114
Tardif, Emilien 1114
Tate, Mary Magdalena 1115
Taylor, George Floyd 1115
Taylor, William 1116
Teen Challenge 1116
Television 1118
Theology, Pentecostal 1120
Third Wave 1141
Thistlethwaite, Lilian T. 1141
Thompson, Frank Charles . . .1142
Tinney, James Steven 1142
Tomlinson, Ambrose Jessup . .1142
Tomlinson, Homer Aubrey . . .1145
Tomlinson, Milton Ambrose .1147
Topeka Revival 1147
Toppi, Francesco 1149
Toronto Blessing 1149
Trasher, Lillian Hunt 1153
Trask, Thomas E. 1154
Triplett, Loren Otis, Jr. 1154
Tucker, J. W. 1154
Tugwell, Simon 1154
Turney, Henry Michael 1155
Tyson, Tommy 1155
Underwood, B. E. 1156
Union De Prière 1156
Union of Messianic Jewish
    Congregations 1156
United Church of Christ,
    Fellowship of Charismatic
    Christians in the 1157
United Holy Church of
    America 1157

United House of Prayer for All
    People, Church on the Rock
    the Apostolic Church 1158
United Methodist
    Charismatics 1158
United Pentecostal Church,
    International 1160
Universal Church of the
    Kingdom of God. 1165
Universal Fellowship of
    Metropolitan Community
    Churches 1166
Upper Room Mission 1166
Urquhart, Colin 1167
Urshan, Andrew David 1167
Urshan, Nathaniel Andrew . . .1167
Utterbach, Clinton and Sarah .1168
Vaagenes, Morris G. C., Jr. . . .1169
Valdez, A. C., Sr. 1169
Valenzuela, Romanita
    Carbajal de 1169
Van Cleave, Nathaniel Moore .1170
Van Dusen, Henry Pitney 1170
Van Eyk, Frederick Barnabas .1170
Vassar, Theodore Roosevelt . .1171
Vatican II 1171
Verhoef, W. W. 1174
Vernaud, Jacques 1174
Victory Outreach International1175
Viens et Vois 1175
Villafañe, Eldin 1176
Villanueva, Eddie C. 1177
Vineyard Christian Fellowship 1177
Vingren, Adolf Gunnar 1177
Vinyard, Richard 1178
Virgo, Terry 1178
Voice of Healing 1178
Volf, Miroslav 1179
Voronaev, Ivan Efimovich 1179
Vouga, Oscar 1180
Wacker, Grant 1181
Wagner, Charles Peter 1181
Waldvogel, Hans R. 1181
Walkem, Charles William . . .1182
Walker, John. Herbert, Jr. 1182
Walker, John Herbert, Sr. 1183
Walker, Paul Haven 1183
Walker, Paul Laverne 1183
Walker, Robert Alander 1183
Wallis, Arthur R. 1184
Walton, John 1184

Wannenmacher, Joseph Paul
    and Helen 1184
Ward, Charles Morse 1185
Ware, R. Kenneth 1185
Warner, Wayne Earl 1185
Watson, David C. K. 1186
Weiner, Robert Thomas 1186
Welch, John William 1187
Welsh Revival 1187
Wesleyan Holiness Charismatic
    Fellowship 1188
West of Scotland Revival 1189
Weston, Edward (Ned) R. . . .1192
Wheaton, Elizabeth Ryder . . .1193
Wheeler, Rob 1193
Whetstone, Ross 1194
White, Kent 1194
Whitehead, Charles 1194
Wierwille, Victor Paul 1194
Wigglesworth, Smith 1195
Wilkerson, David Ray 1195
Wilkerson, Ralph A. 1196
Willans, Jean Stone 1197
Williams, Ernest Swing 1197
Williams, J. Rodman 1198
Williams, Ralph Darby 1199
Wilson, Frederick A. 1199
Wimber, John 1199
Winsett, Roger Emmet 1200
Wisdom, Word of 1200
Witherspoon, William
    Thomas 1202
Women, Role of 1203
Women's Aglow Fellowship
    International 1209
Wongsak, Joseph C. 1211
Woodworth-Etter, Maria Beulah 1211
Woon Mong Ra 1213
World Council of Churches . .1213
Worley, A. S. 1217
Worrell, Adolphus Spalding . .1217
Worship 1217
Wright, James Elwin 1220
Wyatt, Thomas 1221
Yeomans, Lilian Barbara 1222
Yoakum, Finis Ewing 1222
Youth With A Mission 1223
Zaire Evangelistic Mission . . .1225
Zimmerman, Thomas Fletcher1225
Zion City 1226
Zion Evangelistic Fellowship .1226
Zopfi, Jakob 1226

Preface

The *New International Dictionary of Pentecostal and Charismatic Movements* is intended not only to increase the self-understanding of those inside the pentecostal, charismatic, and neocharismatic movements, but also to introduce the broader religious community to the inner life and thought of a modern religious phenomenon that has had a significant impact on Christianity worldwide. The editors have sought to avoid apologetic and polemical approaches, and they have made every effort to present a balanced overview of the many perspectives that have grown out of a genuinely diverse set of traditions. Included among the contributors are classical pentecostals, charismatics representing a wide variety of denominational affiliations, neocharismatics from independent churches and groups, and others who are not participants in the renewal. Opinions expressed in this volume are intended to represent the diversity within the movements but are not necessarily those of the editors or of the publisher.

This volume is divided into three sections.

Part I (Global Survey) introduces the reader to the emergence and expansion of pentecostalism in specific countries and regions of the world, with demographic data for each country. The entries are arranged in alphabetical order.

Due to space limitations (and in some cases lack of available information) only statistical information is provided for a number of countries. In other cases (e.g., North Africa and the Middle East), a number of countries are covered in a single survey article.

The country articles do not conform to a single pattern or perspective. Rather, the articles in their variety show that the study of pentecostal, charismatic, and neocharismatic movements is a multiperspectival enterprise that must make appropriate use of the various disciplines of the social sciences. (An illustration is the entry "Jamaica," which consists of two complementary articles.)

The statistics at the end of each entry in Part I are (even as the statistics in Part II) based on the *World Christian Encyclopedia* (2001), ed. David B. Barrett et al. These statistics may in some cases differ from the numbers cited in the text of a country article. The introductory and methodological sections of Part II show that statistical variations may be due to different definitions of the parameters of the groups in question.

Part II (Global Statistics) details growth patterns of the three waves of pentecostal renewal. It includes data for each of the seven continents and projections for future growth.

The terms *pentecostal, neo-pentecostal, charismatic,* and *neocharismatic* are lower-cased in this dictionary. The exception is Part II, where careful distinctions are made between *pentecostal* and *Pentecostal, charismatic* and *Charismatic, neocharismatic* and

Neocharismatic. A proper understanding and interpretation of the statistical data provided in this section hinges on an understanding of these distinctions. The reader is therefore urged to read the introductory and methodological sections of Part II before moving on to the data.

Part III (Dictionary) contains topical and biographical entries arranged in alphabetical order. Articles on books of the Bible, included in the original *Dictionary of Pentecostal and Charismatic Movements,* have been eliminated to provide room for additional historical and descriptive entries.

No Internet addresses (URLs) are provided in the dictionary, since these are subject to rapid change. Instead, the reader is referred to www.google.com for locating current web addresses.

The *New International Dictionary* introduces readers to worldwide pentecostalism in its many forms. The vastness of these movements, however, precludes complete coverage in a single volume. Treatment is necessarily uneven because academic scholarship of classical pentecostal and charismatic movements is just now flowering, and as a rule the independent and indigenous churches and groups of the "third wave" have been examined episodically by social scientists but have not yet been studied from within.

An additional difficulty is that, in many countries, classical pentecostal scholars do not even recognize the existence of other groups in the renewal. The result is that treatment is more adequate for the classical pentecostals and charismatics than for the neocharismatics, who outnumber the first two waves combined.

The reader will note that the story in countries where participants in the renewal are under persecution does not include current information on centers of strength and the identity of leaders. The recounting of their spirituality and heroism is best reserved for the future when such dangers are past.

Introduction

The 20th century witnessed the emergence and phenomenal growth of the pentecostal, charismatic, and neocharismatic movements. These three waves of pentecostalism, which constitute one of Christianity's greatest renewals, have impacted every segment of the church in virtually all countries of the world with new vitality and fervor. Participants in this renewal share exuberant worship, an emphasis on subjective religious experience and spiritual gifts, claims of supernatural miracles, signs, and wonders—including a language of experiential spirituality rather than of theology—and mystical "life in the Spirit" by which they daily live out the will of God.

The *Dictionary of Pentecostal and Charismatic Movements*, published in 1988, was limited in its coverage, both temporally and spatially. It emphasized 20th-century developments in the U.S. and Western Europe, where white pentecostal historians have traditionally placed the origins of these movements. In reality, however, modern pentecostalism did not begin on Jan. 1, 1901, in Topeka, KS. More recent scholarship has demonstrated convincingly that pentecostal outpourings occurred in other parts of the world—notably Africa, England, Finland, Russia, India, and Latin America—well before the 20th century. Indeed, we now know that pentecostal phenomena, especially prophecy, healings, and signs and wonders, never disappeared completely from the church after the first century of the Christian era, as traditional pentecostal historians have argued (Burgess, 1989, 1997). What is new in 20th-century pentecostalism is its spectacular growth and its impact on the larger Christian world.

The *New International Dictionary of Pentecostal and Charismatic Movements* not only includes a wealth of information on pre-20th-century pentecostalism, it also places special emphasis on these movements outside the U.S. and Western Europe. Indeed, it is in these other nations and regions that modern movements of the Spirit have experienced their most phenomenal growth. The country with the greatest renewal population is Brazil. The United States is second, but no other country in North America or Europe ranks in the top 10 (except for Mexico, which is 9th).

In 1988, when the *Dictionary of Pentecostal and Charismatic Movements* was published, it was fashionable to categorize groups in the renewal as part of either the first wave (classical pentecostals), the second wave (charismatics in the historic mainline churches), or the third wave (nonpentecostal, noncharismatic, mainstream church renewal) (Burgess, McGee, Alexander, 1988). Subsequently, however, the amazing growth of independent and postdenominational groups throughout the world has required a revision in this classification scheme (Hollenweger, 1997; Barrett et al., 2001).

In this volume the so-called "third wave" will be broadened and relabeled "neocharismatic"; it will include the vast numbers of independent and indigenous churches and groups that cannot be classified as either pentecostal or charismatic. These are Christian bodies with pentecostal-like experiences that have no traditional pentecostal or charismatic denominational connections. Barrett discovered that the neocharismatics actually outnumber all pentecostals and charismatics combined (see Part II, Global Statistics, pp. 281–302). Their greatest concentrations of strength are in the prophetic African independent churches (variously called the "Banta separatist churches," "Aladura," "Spirit churches," and "Zionist churches"); in Asia, especially the House Church Movement in China; and in Latin American countries, especially Brazil.

The terms *pentecostal* and *charismatic* are often used interchangeably. Indeed, they do have many features in common, and even for the expert it is frequently difficult to draw a dividing line. When points of delineation are determined and connected, the resulting line is invariably crooked, perhaps broken, and sometimes split into various branches. For one venturing into the field of pentecostal and charismatic studies for the first time, a brief historical overview and some help in differentiating between the terms *pentecostal* and *charismatic* in particular is indispensable.

I. A Brief Historical Survey.

A. Classical Pentecostals.

Historians often trace the origins of pentecostalism in the United States to a revival that began on Jan. 1, 1901, at Charles F. Parham's Bethel Bible School in Topeka, KS. With the identification of speaking in tongues as the evidence of baptism in the Holy Spirit, Parham and his students made a vital theological connection that has remained essential to much of classical pentecostalism. While the immediate impact of this event was limited, Parham's ministry gained more acceptance several years later in a revival conducted outside Houston, TX. From there William J. Seymour, a black Holiness preacher who had become convinced of the truth of Parham's teaching on Spirit baptism, traveled to Los Angeles, CA, to preach the new message. The ensuing revival at the Azusa Street Mission (1906–9) represented an anomaly on the American religious scene. Blacks, whites, and Hispanics worshiped together. Men and women shared leadership responsibilities. The barrier between clergy and laity vanished, since participants believed that the endowment with spiritual power for ministry was intended to be received by all. The gifts of the Holy Spirit (1 Cor. 12), understood by most denominations as having ceased at the end of the first century, had been restored.

From Los Angeles, news of the "outpouring of the Holy Spirit" spread across the nation and around the world by word of mouth and the printed page. Before long, pentecostal revivals could be found in Canada, England, Scandinavia, Germany, India, China, Africa, and South America.

Theological issues soon began to divide the movement, however. Questions concerning the nature of sanctification, the gift of tongues, and the Trinity generated tensions that have remained. The racial harmony of Azusa Street waned within a few months, and as a result, pentecostalism remains racially divided with very limited progress toward reconciliation. While in the early years women enjoyed considerable freedom in ministry, often surpassing that of women in the established Protestant denominations, their prominence has declined with but few exceptions.

Although several Holiness denominations in the southeastern part of the United States accepted pentecostal theology, many participants in the new movements were rejected by their parent groups and were therefore skeptical of ecclesiastical organizations. Even with these reservations, however, pentecostal mission agencies, "fellowships," and denominations began to evolve shortly thereafter. By 1950 pentecostals were outstripping most other Christian bodies in their rate of growth. This phenomenon only accelerated in the last half of the 20th century. During the period 1970–90 pentecostals tripled in number.

B. The Charismatic Movement.

While early pentecostalism was often associated with the lower socioeconomic classes and relegated to the fringe of evangelical Christianity, the desire for spiritual renewal in the historic and more affluent mainline churches unexpectedly resulted in an increased interest in spiritual gifts, including glossolalia, prophecy, and physical healing. News of this renewal in the U.S. began to surface on the national level in 1960 with the publicity surrounding remarkable happenings in the ministry of Dennis Bennett, an Episcopal rector in Van Nuys, CA. As the movement grew, it spread to other Protestant churches, the Roman Catholic Church, and finally also to the Orthodox churches.

Part of the groundwork for charismatic renewal, reflecting its deep roots in the pentecostal movement, had been laid by the ministries of Oral Roberts, David J. du Plessis, and Demos Shakarian and the Full Gospel Business Men's Fellowship International. It quickly became apparent that this renewal, which also sought after the dynamic power of the Spirit, flowed out of what many believed to be a vacuum in the religious life in the U.S., as well as a longing to return to the essence of NT Christianity within one's particular church tradition.

The renewal in the Roman Catholic Church, which can in part be traced to the monumental changes ushered in by the Second Vatican Council, spread around the world and was experienced by both prelates and laity. Officially, the movement began in 1967, simultaneously at Duquesne University in Pittsburgh, PA, and in Bogota, Columbia. Charismatic splinter groups began even earlier, including the Legion of Mary (Legio Mariae) in Kenya (1962).

The charismatic renewal represents a transdenominational movement of Christians who emphasize a "life in the Spirit" and the importance of exercising extraordinary gifts of the Spirit, including but not limited to glossolalia, both in private prayer and in public worship. In recent years charismatics also have explored their newfound experiences within their own traditions. Without roots in some of the extremes of the Holiness movement, they have typically been more overtly supernaturalistic and culture-affirming in their perspective on the Christian life than classical pentecostals. As time passed, most of the renewal movements found a degree of recognition and approval within their denominational structures.

C. Neocharismatics.

The rapid growth of pentecostalism in its various forms also brought a considerable variety of worship patterns, cultural attitudes, ecclesiastical structures, and methods of evangelism. Wide differences in forms of spirituality and theology become even more apparent when indigenous neocharismatic groups are examined.

"Neocharismatic" is a catch-all category that comprises 18,810 independent, indigenous, postdenominational denominations and groups that cannot be classified as either pentecostal or charismatic but share a common emphasis on the Holy Spirit, spiritual gifts, pentecostal-like experiences (*not* pentecostal terminology), signs and wonders, and power encounters. In virtually every other way, however, they are as diverse as the world's cultures they represent.

Neocharismatics include such groups as the New Apostolic Churches, the Legion of Mary (an independent Catholic church beginning in Kenya), the Kimbanguist Church and the Église de Jésus Christ sur la terre d'après le prophète Simon Kimbangu (Zaire), Mana Egreja Crista (Portugal-based), True Jesus Church (indigenous Oneness church from China), and the Celestial Church of Christ (indigenous church originating in Ghana).

In Africa, spiritual experiences among the independent churches are pentecostal in nature, but the rest of their theology, which tends to vary greatly from group to group, is often characterized by a high level of doctrinal ambiguity and local cosmology. They usually lack institutional structure and organization. While many of these groups have emerged in the past 20 years, others are quite old, even predating the traditional birth of pentecostalism. African indigenous churches have been known to exist in an organized fashion since 1815, and many became charismatic beginning in 1864. Barrett suggests that the adherents of these African churches may have numbered as many as 900,000 in 1900, the year *before* the "official birth date" of pentecostalism!

These neocharismatic African churches generally accept and practice faith healing, prophetic visions, fervent ecstatic prayer, and glossolalia. This notwithstanding, they usually have been castigated by both classical pentecostals and charismatic churches as harbingers of demons and evil spirits because they retain an African cosmology that includes the world of spirits and ancestors, the reality of witchcraft, and predestination.

In China, the house-church movement and two other indigenous groups that began earlier—the Assembly Hall Churches (Little Flock) and the True Jesus Church—now comprise nearly 65% of the over 78 million Christians. Perhaps because all Chinese Christians continue to suffer persecution, classical pentecostals and charismatics have been less inclined to condemn these neocharismatics, despite the third-wave attacks on denominationalism and their frequently extreme spiritual manifestations. Other Asian countries with rapid neocharismatic growth include South Korea, India, the Philippines, Indonesia, and Japan.

Latin America continues to be the most pentecostalized continent, with rapid growth in all three waves of renewal. There has been minimal cooperation or acceptance between pentecostals, charismatics, and neocharismatics, however. It is not uncommon to find individuals from each wave denying the very existence of the other two, or at the least rejecting the notion that the hand of God may be present in the other two. Typically, Latin American neocharismatics tend to be more progressive, both socially and politically, than either their Catholic charismatic or classical pentecostal neighbors, and the movement incorporates large numbers of economically disadvantaged people in common socioeconomic causes.

Brazil—where numbers in the renewal are staggering—is the country of pentecostalism's greatest strength, yet neocharismatics actually outnumber pentecostals there. Among the more important neocharismatic groups are the Legio Mariae (Legion of Mary from Kenya) and the Igreja Maná (from Portugal). Peter Wagner points out that during the past 20 years the great megachurches begun in virtually every metropolitan area of Latin America are those pastored by individuals with no connection to foreign missionaries or mission-initiated institutions (Wagner, 17).

II. Pentecostals and Charismatics.

A. Pentecostal-Charismatic Differences.

There are two approaches to differentiating between *pentecostal* and *charismatic,* one theological, the other ecclesiastical. A theological differentiation can be found especially in the doctrine concerning Spirit baptism (also called the baptism in, or of, the Holy Spirit). It is oversimplified, but perhaps useful, to say that pentecostals subscribe to a work of grace subsequent to conversion, in which Spirit baptism is evidenced by glossolalia (speaking in tongues); for some, this baptism must also follow another act of grace, namely, sanctification. Charismatics, on the other hand, do not always advocate either the necessity of a second work of grace or the evidence of glossolalia as an affirmation of Spirit baptism. Yet both emphasize the present work of the Spirit through gifts in the life of the individual and the church.

Ecclesiastical differentiation is based on denominational affiliation. Thus, *pentecostals* refers to those participating in classical pentecostal denominations, such as the Assemblies of God, the Church of God (Cleveland, TN), the Church of God in Christ, the United Pentecostal Church, and the International Church of the Foursquare Gospel. *Charismatics,* on the other hand, refers to persons outside these classical pentecostal denominations but with connections to mainline denominations. *Neocharismatics* are participants in independent, postdenominational, nondenominational, or indigenous groups or organizations, such as the Vineyard Christian Fellowship.

Obviously, neither the theological nor the ecclesiastical differentiation is entirely adequate. The former overlooks the natural denominational lines drawn by history, while the strictly ecclesiastical approach ignores the tremendous theological diversity among and within denominational and independent groups. For example, Roman Catholic charismatics express their understanding of Spirit baptism in a wide variety of ways, ranging from an almost pentecostal "second stage" understanding to a perspective that rejects any notion of a second work of grace. Likewise, some within classical pentecostalism are uncomfortable with denominational insistence that Spirit baptism is subsequent to salvation and must be accompanied by the "initial physical evidence" of speaking in tongues.

B. Pentecostal-Charismatic Tensions.

From a separation that fed on rejection and its own early tendency toward isolation and intolerant exclusiveness, classical pentecostalism has, since WWII, become interactive with Protestant evangelicalism and, in certain cases, even with the broader ecumenical Christian community. In many countries the result has been a relatively higher level of acceptance and respectability—which pentecostals now share with nonseparatist charismatics who never suffered as high a level of rejection. Because many pentecostals, fearing compromise of basic tenets that might lead to a loss of distinctiveness, are not yet entirely comfortable with this entrance into the mainstream of American Christianity, the movement tends to be divided between those who identify with the past and those who relish their newfound identification with the larger church world.

Growing pains became evident with the emergence of the charismatic movement. Pentecostals, who by the middle of the 20th century were identifying closely with mainstream evangelicals, initially applauded the movement. But when many charismatics remained in their own churches rather than shifting to classical pentecostalism, more provincial pentecostals became frustrated with them. Dually aligned to their own church traditions and to the historic people of the Spirit, charismatics have tended to recognize the ebb and flow of fervent spirituality in Christian history and have found their identity as part of the latest wave of renewal.

Nevertheless, in the 1980s and 1990s many pentecostals recognized that the Holy Spirit was accomplishing a new work and sensed an affinity with it. The charismatic renewal brought pressure on the pentecostals to broaden their identification within the universal church to groups previously considered apostate. In this regard, the untiring efforts of the late David J. du Plessis (1905–87), one-time secretary of the Pentecostal World Conference, proved to be particularly instrumental in building bridges between pentecostals and charismatics. Through such efforts, the early ideal of ecumenism among the Spirit-baptized has extended beyond the Pentecostal World Conference, primarily made up of classical pentecostals, to the recent North American Congresses on the Holy Spirit and World Evangelization (meeting annually since 1986, now scheduled through 2002), which have encompassed all stripes of classical pentecostals, together with charismatic Baptists, Episcopalians, Lutherans, Mennonites, Messianic Jews, Methodists, Presbyterians, Reformed, Greek Orthodox, and Roman Catholics. These events rank among the most important modern gatherings of Christians because of their size as well as their theological significance. Viewed with suspicion by both pentecostals and charismatics as the new wave on the shore, neocharismatics—by their very nature independent and resistant to ecclesiastical connection—have yet to be integrated in significant numbers into these ecumenical dialogues.

■ **Bibliography:** A. H. Anderson and W. J. Hollenweger, eds., *Pentecostals after a Century: Global Perspectives on a Movement in Transition* (1999) ▮ G. Anderson, *Biographical Dictionary of Christian Missions* (1998) ▮ R. Anderson, *Vision of the Disinherited: The Making of American Pentecostalism* (1979) ▮ D. Barrett, *Schism and Renewal in Africa: An Analysis of Six Thousand Contemporary Move-*

ments (1968) ▓ D. B. Barrett, G. Kurian, and T. Johnson, *World Christian Encyclopedia* (2001) ▓ J. Burdick, "What Is the Color of the Holy Spirit?" *Latin American Research Review* 34 (1999): 109–31 ▓ S. Burgess, G. McGee, and P. Alexander, *Dictionary of Pentecostal and Charismatic Movements* (1988) ▓ S. Burgess, *The Holy Spirit: Eastern Christian Traditions* (1989) ▓ idem, *The Holy Spirit: Medieval Roman Catholic and Reformation Traditions* (1997) ▓ A. Droogers et al., *Popular Power in Latin American Religions* (1991) ▓ S. Hayes, *Black Charismatic Anglicans* (1990) ▓ W. Hollenweger, *Pentecostalism* (1997) ▓ idem, *The Pentecostals* (1972) ▓ C. Jones, *Guide to the Study of the Pentecostal Movement*, 2 vols. (1983) ▓ idem, *The Charismatic Movement: A Guide to the Study of Neo-Pentecostalism with Emphasis on Anglo-American Sources*, 2 vols (1995) ▓ F. Kamsteeg, *Prophetic Pentecostalism in Chile: A Case Study on Religion and Development Policy* (1995) ▓ R. Kydd, *Healing through the Centuries* (1998) ▓ K. Poewe, ed., *Charismatic Christianity as a Global Culture* (1994) ▓ J. Ruthven, *On the Cessation of the Charismata: The Protestant Polemic on Postbiblical Miracles* (1993) ▓ J. Sepúlveda, "Pentecostalism as Popular Religion," *International Review of Mission* (1989): 80–88 ▓ D. Stoll, *Is Latin America Turning Protestant? The Politics of Evangelical Growth* (1990) ▓ C. P. Wagner, *The New Apostolic Churches* (1998) ▓ B. Yoo, *Korean Pentecostalism: Its History and Theology* (1988).

Editors and Contributors

EDITOR

Stanley M. Burgess Ph.D., University of Missouri–Columbia. Professor of Religious Studies, Southwest Missouri State University, Springfield, Missouri.

ASSOCIATE EDITOR

Eduard M. van der Maas Th.M., Dallas Theological Seminary, Dallas, Texas. President, Open Range Editorial.

CONTRIBUTORS

Afe Adogame Ph.D., University of Bayreuth. Professor of Religious Studies, University of Lagos, Lagos, Nigeria.

Lauri Ahonen D.Miss., Biola University. Project manager, Center for Continuing Education, University of Helsinki, Finland.

Patrick Alexander M.A., Gordon-Conwell Theological Seminary. Publishing Director, Brill Academic Publishers, Boston, Massachusetts.

Delton L. Alford Ph.D., Florida State University. Director of Music, Pathway Press, Cleveland, Tennessee.

Paul Anderson M.Div., Luther Theological Seminary. Director, International Lutheran Renewal, St. Paul, Minnesota.

Chris R. Armstrong Ph.D. candidate, Duke University, Durham, North Carolina.

French L. Arrington Ph.D., Saint Louis University. Professor of New Testament Greek and Exegesis, Church of God Theological Seminary, Cleveland, Tennessee.

William H. Barnes Th.D., Harvard Divinity School. Associate Professor of Bible, Southeastern College of the Assemblies of God, Lakeland, Florida.

David B. Barrett Ph.D., Columbia University. Research Professor of Missiometrics and Global Evangelization, School of Divinity, Regent University, Virginia Beach, Virginia.

Daniel H. Bays Ph.D., University of Michigan. Professor of History and Director of the East Asian Studies Program, Calvin College, Grand Rapids, Michigan.

Courtney N. Bender Ph.D., Princeton University. Associate Professor of Religion, Columbia University, New York.

Frances Bixler Ph.D., University of Arkansas-Fayetteville. Freelance writer, Springfield, Missouri.

Edith L. Blumhofer Ph.D., Harvard University. Professor of History and Director, Institute for the Study of American Evangelicals, Wheaton College, Wheaton, Illinois.

Joyce Booze M.S., Delta State University, Cleveland, Mississippi; M.S. Ed., Southwest Missouri State University, Springfield, Missouri. Freelance writer, Ridgedale, Missouri.

David D. Bundy Cand. Doctorate en Philologie et Histoire Orientale, Université Catholique de Louvain; Cand. Doctorate in Church History, University of Uppsala. Librarian and Associate Professor of Church History, Christian Theological Seminary, Indianapolis, Indiana.

Ruth Vassar Burgess Ph.D., University of Missouri–Columbia. Professor, School of Teacher Education, Southwest Missouri State University, Springfield, Missouri.

Stanley M. Burgess Ph.D., University of Missouri–Columbia. Professor of Religious Studies, Southwest Missouri State University, Springfield, Missouri.

Jeffrey Carter Ph.D., University of Chicago. Director, Castle Rock Institute, Brevard College, Brevard, North Carolina.

Desmond W. Cartwright MrA., Sheffield University. Official historian emeritus, Elim Pentecostal Church. Archivist, Donald Gee Research Centre, Mattersey Hall, U.K.

Augustus Cerillo Jr. Ph.D., Northwestern University. Professor of History, California State University–Long Beach.

Barry Chant Ph.D., Macquarie University, Sydney, Australia. President, Tabor College, Sydney.

Larry Christenson B.Th., Luther Theological Seminary. Former Director, International Lutheran Renewal Center, St. Paul, Minnesota.

Ithiel C. Clemmons† D.Min, Union Seminary and New York Theological Seminary. Bishop for the Armed Forces and Institutional Chaplaincy, Church of God in Christ; Pastor, Wells Memorial Church of God in Christ, Greensboro, North Carolina; and Pastor, First Church of God in Christ, Brooklyn, New York.

Marcel Codreanu M.Div., Assemblies of God Theological Seminary, Springfield, Missouri. Director of Studies, Elim Evangelical Theological Seminary, Timisoara, Romania.

Joseph Colletti Ph.D., University of Birmingham. Executive Director, Institute for Urban Research and Development, Pasadena, California; Adjunct Professor, Fuller Theological Seminary, Pasadena, California.

Charles W. Conn Litt.D., Lee College. Author and church historian, Cleveland, Tennessee.

Donald Dayton Ph.D., University of Chicago. Professor of Historical Theology and Church History, Drew University, Madison, New Jersey.

Douglas B. Debolt B.A., University of North Florida. Vice President for Communication for ACTS 29 Ministries and Editor of *Acts 29* magazine, Atlanta, Georgia.

David Dorries Ph.D., University of Aberdeen. Assistant Professor of Church History, Oral Roberts Unversity, Tulsa, Oklahoma.

Sherry Sherrod Dupree Ed.S, University of Michigan. Librarian, Santa Fe Community College, Gainesville, Florida.

Steve Durasoff Ph.D., New York University. Former Professor of Theology, Oral Roberts University, Tulsa, Oklahoma; former President, Continental Theological Seminary, Brussels, Belgium.

George Edgerly Parsons College, Fairfield, Iowa. Pastor, First Pentecostal Assemblies of God, Ottumwa, Iowa.

Yeol Soo Eim D. Miss., Fuller Theological Seminary. President, Gospel Theological Seminary, Taejon, Korea; Professor of Mission and Director of D.Min. Korean Program, Oral Roberts University, Tulsa, Oklahoma.

David Embree M.A., Southwest Missouri State University. Instructor in Religious Studies, Southwest Missouri State University, Springfield, Missouri.

Manfred Ernst Dr.Phil., University of Hamburg, Germany. Lecturer in Church and Society, Pacific Theological College, Suva, Fiji Islands.

Gaston Espinosa Ph.D., University of California–Santa Barbara. Assistant Professor of Religious Studies, Westmont College, Santa Barbara, California.

Josephine Massyngbaerde Ford Ph.D., University of Nottingham. Professor of Theology, University of Notre Dame, South Bend, Indiana.

David J. Garrard Ph.D., Aberdeen University. Mattersey Hall, Assemblies of God Bible College, Mattersey, Doncaster, England.

Edward J. Gitre M.A.T.S., Assemblies of God Theological Seminary, Springfield, Missouri. Chi Alpha Ministries, University of Chicago, Chicago, Illinois.

James R. Goff Jr. Ph.D., University of Arkansas–Fayetteville. Associate Professor in History, Appalachian State University, Boone, North Carolina.

Glenn W. Gohr M.Div., Assemblies of God Theological Seminary. Assistant Archivist, Assemblies of God Archives, Springfield, Missouri.

R. Marie Griffith Ph.D., Harvard University. Lecturer in the Department of Religion and Associate Director of the Center for the Study of Religion, Princeton University.

Ian R. Hall Ph.D., University of Leeds. President, Elim Evangelical Theological Seminary, Timisoara, Romania.

J. L. Hall M.A., Emporia State University. Editor-in-Chief of Publications, United Pentecostal Church International, Hazelwood, Missouri.

Daniel J. Hedges D.Min., McCormick Theological Seminary. Assistant Dean for Doctoral Studies and Associate Professor of Practical Theology, Oral Roberts University, Tulsa, Oklahoma.

Roger E. Hedlund D.Miss., Fuller Theological Seminary. Professor of Mission Studies (Research), Serampore College, Serampore, W. Bengal, India.

James Allen Hewett Ph.D., University of Manchester. Pastor, United Methodist Church, Chaquota, Oklahoma.

Irving Hexham Ph.D., Bristol University. Professor, Department of Religious Studies, University of Calgary, Calgary, Canada.

Peter D. Hocken Ph.D., University of Birmingham. Historian and theologian, Bishop's House, Northampton, England.

Walter J. Hollenweger Th.D., University of Zurich. Professor (emeritus) of Mission, University of Birmingham.

Stephen Hopkins B.A., Southwest Missouri State University, Springfield, Missouri. Freelance writer, Fort Benning, Georgia.

Stanley M. Horton Th.D., Central Baptist Theological Seminary. Distinguished Professor of Bible and Theology, Assemblies of God Theological Seminary, Springfield, Missouri.

Harold D. Hunter Ph.D., Fuller Theological Seminary. Director of Archives and Research Center, International Pentecostal Holiness Church, Oklahoma City, Oklahoma.

Larry W. Hurtado Ph.D., Case Western Reserve University. Professor and Chair, Department of New Testament Language, Literature, and Theology, University of Edinburgh, Edinburgh, Scotland.

Mark Hutchinson Ph.D., University of New South Wales. Head of Church History Discipline, Southern Cross College, Macquarie, NSW Australia.

David Hymes Th.M., Princeton University. Professor, Central Bible College, Tokyo, Japan.

Charles M. Irish B.D., Bexley Hall Divinity School. Former National Coordinator, Episcopal Renewal Ministries, Fairfax, Virginia.

Todd M. Johnson Ph.D., William Carey International University. Adjunct Professor, Trinity Evangelical Divinity School, Deerfield, Illinois; Director, World Evangelization Research Center.

Charles Edwin Jones Ph.D., University of Wisconsin. Historian and bibliographer, Oklahoma City, Oklahoma.

Daniel C. Juster Th.D., New Covenant International Seminary, New Zealand. Past President, The Union of Messianic

Jewish Congregations; Director of Tikkun International, Gaithersburg, Maryland.

Veli-Matti Kärkkäinen Dr.Theol., University of Helsinki. Professor of Theology, Fuller Theological Seminary, Pasadena, California.

William K. Kay Ph.D., History; Ph.D., Education; London University. Senior Research Fellow, Centre for Theology and Education, Trinity College, Carmarthen, England.

Chin Do Kham D. Min., Oral Roberts University; Ph.D., Trinity Evangelical University, Deerfield, Illinois. Dean of Students, Asia Pacific Theological Seminary, Boggio, Philippines.

William Kostlevy Ph.D., University of Notre Dame. Archivist and special collections librarian, Asbury Theological Seminary.

Brett Knowles Ph.D., University of Otago, Dunedin, New Zealand. National Training Coordinator, Elim Church of New Zealand. Faculty, University of Otago and Tawangmangu Theological College, Central Java, Indonesia.

Charles Kraft Ph.D., Hartford Seminary Foundation. Sun-Hee Kwak Professor of Anthropology and Intercultural Communications, Fuller Theological Seminary, Pasadena, California.

Ronald A. N. Kydd Ph.D., University of St. Andrews. Assistant priest, St. Peters Anglican Church, Cobourg, Ontario, Canada.

Young-Hoon Lee Ph.D., Temple University, Philadelphia, Pennsylvania. Director, International Theological Institute, Yoido Full Gospel Church, Seoul, Korea.

Elisabeth Leembruggen-Kallberg Ed.D., Boston University. Lecturer, Azusa Theologische Hogeschool, Lunteren, the Netherlands.

Paul Lewis Ph.D., Baylor Universaity. Faculty in Theology, Asia Pacific Theological Seminary, Baguio City, Philippines.

Leonard Lovett Ph.D., Emory University. Chief Executive Officer, Seminex Ministries, Alexandria, Virginia.

Julie Ma Ph.D., Fuller Theological Seminary. Lecturer in Intercultural Studies, Asia Pacific Theological Seminary, Baguio City, Philippines.

Wonsuk Ma Ph.D., Fuller Theological Seminary. Academic Dean, Asia Pacific Theological Seminary, Baguio City, Philippines.

Frank D. Macchia D.Theol., University of Basel. Associate Professor of Theology, Vanguard University, Costa Mesa, California.

Francis Martin S.S.D., Pontifical Institute. New Testament scholar and theologian, Mother of God Community, Gaithersburg, Maryland, and Professor of Biblical Theology, John Paul II Institute for Studies on Marriage and Family, Washington, D.C.

L. Grant Mcclung Jr. D.Miss., Fuller Theological Seminary. Field Director for the Church of God (Cleveland, TN) in Western Europe/Mediterranean/Middle East, and Associate Professor of Missions and Church Growth at the Church of God Theological Seminary, Cleveland, Tennessee.

Thomson Matthew D.Min., Oral Roberts University; Ed.D., Oklahoma State University, Stillwater, Oklahoma. Dean, School of Theology and Mission, Oral Roberts University, Tulsa, Oklahoma.

Gary B. McGee Ph.D., St. Louis University. Professor of Church History and Pentecostal Studies, Assemblies of God Theological Seminary, Springfield, Missouri.

J. Ramsey Michaels Th.D., Harvard University. Professor Emeritus of Religious Studies, Southwest Missouri State University, Springfield, Missouri.

Jesse Miranda D.Min., Fuller Theological Seminary, Pasadena, California. Associate Director for Urban and Multicultural Affairs of the C. P. Haggard School of Theology at Asuza Pacific University, Asuza, California.

David J. Moore Ph.D., University of Arizona. Director, Intercultural Ministries; Home Missions Administrator, Assemblies of God, Springfield, Missouri.

S. David Moore D.Min., Regent University. Senior Pastor, Covenant Christian Fellowship—Foursquare Gospel Church, Manteca, California.

Louis Morgan B.A., Lee University, Cleveland, Tennessee. Archivist, Dixon Pentecostal Research Center, Cleveland, Tennessee.

Charles Nienkirchen Ph.D., University of Waterloo. Professor, Canadian Nazarene University College, Calgary, Alberta.

Douglass P. Norwood Th.M., Princeton Theological Seminary. International Director, Cornerstone Ministries, Prince Edward Island, Canada.

Jacob K. Olupona Ph.D., Boston University. Director, African American and African Studies; Director, Religious Studies; University of California, Davis.

Michael Palmer Ph.D., Marquette University. Chair, Department of Biblical Studies and Philosophy, Evangel University, Springfield, Missouri.

Karla Poewe-Hexham Ph.D., University of New Mexico. Professor of Anthropology, University of Calgary, Alberta, Canada

Margaret Poloma Ph.D., Case Western Reserve University. Professor Emeritus, University of Akron.

Timothy Powell Ph.D., Fuller Theological Seminary. Pastor, Fresno Christian Life Assembly, Fresno, California.

Craig Prentiss Ph.D., University of Chicago. Assistant Professor, Theology and Religious Studies Department, Rockhurst College, Kansas City, Missouri.

David A. Reed Ph.D., Boston University. Associate Professor of Pastoral Theology, Wycliffe College, University of Toronto, Canada.

Frank M. Reynolds B.S., Cornell University. Freelance writer, Springfield, Missouri.

Richard M. Riss M.C.S., Regent College. Zarephath Bible Institute, Zarephath, New Jersey.

Cecil M. Robeck Jr. Ph.D., Fuller Theological Seminary. Director, David du Plessis Center for Christian Spirituality and Professor of Church History and Ecumenics, School of Theology, Fuller Theological Seminary, Pasadena, California.

Elizabeth B. Robinson   Ph.D., Ohio State University. Catholic Community Services, Canton, Ohio.

Darrin J. Rodgers   M.A., Assemblies of God Theological Seminary, Springfield, Missouri. Freelance writer and historian, Grand Forks, North Dakota.

David G. Roebuck   Ph.D., Vanderbilt University, Nashville, Tennessee. Director, Hal Bernard Dixon Jr. Pentecostal Research Center, Lee University, Cleveland, Tennessee.

Murray A. Rubinstein   Ph.D., New York University. Professor of History, Baruch College, City University of New York; Chair, Taiwan Studies Group, Association of Asian Studies.

Jerry L. Sandidge†   Ph.D., Catholic University of Leuven.

Scott Shemeth   M.Div., Assemblies of God Theological Seminary, Springfield, Missouri. Senior Pastor, Christian Life Church, Kensington, Connecticut.

Jerry W. Shepperd   Ph.D., University of Texas–Austin. Assistant Dean and Professor of Sociology, Austin Community College, Austin, Texas.

JoAnn Smith   Ph.D., Regent University. Carlstrom Deaf Studies Department Chair, North Central University, Minneapolis, Minnesota.

Russell P. Spittler   Ph.D., Harvard University. Provost/Vice President of Academic Affairs and Professor of New Testament, Fuller Theological Seminary, Pasadena, California.

George R. Stotts   Ph.D., Texas Tech University, Lubbock, Texas. Dean, School of Graduate Studies, ICI University, Irving, Texas.

B. Maurice Stout   Th.M., Harvard University. Military Chaplain, Fort Sill, Oklahoma.

Stephen Strang   B.S., University of Florida. President, Strang Communications Company, Lake Mary, Florida.

Francis A. Sullivan, S.J.   S.T.D., Pontifical Gregorian University. Professor Emeritus, Gregorian University; Adjunct Professor of Theology, Boston College.

Helen V. Sullivan   M.Th., Bethel Bible Seminary, Dehra Dun, India. Freelance writer, Teague, Texas.

H. Vinson Synan   Ph.D., University of Georgia. Dean, Regent University, Virginia Beach, Virginia. Chair, North American Renewal Service Committee.

Derek Tan   Th.M., Regent College, Vancouver, Canada. Academic Dean, Theological Center for Asia, Singapore.

T. Paul Thigpen   Ph.D., Emory University. Fellow in Theology, College of St. Thomas Moore, Fort Worth, Texas.

Sherry L. Thomas   B.A., Southwest Missouri State University. Freelance writer, Kansas City, Missouri.

James S. Tinney†   Ph.D., Howard University.

John F. Tipei   Ph.D., University of Sheffield. President, Institutul Teologic Penticostal, Bucuresti, Romania.

Giovanni Traettino   Ph.D., University of Naples. President, Chiesa Evangelica della Riconciliazione. Co-Chair of Charismatic Consultation of Italy.

Harold Dean Trulear   Ph.D., Drew University. Director of Research Projects, Public/Private Ventures, Philadelphia, Pennsylvania.

Cornelis van der Laan   Ph.D., University of Birmingham. President, Azusa Theologische Hogeschool, Lunteren, the Netherlands.

Grant Wacker   Ph.D., Harvard University. Associate Professor of the History of Religion in America, Duke Divinity School, Durham, North Carolina.

C. Peter Wagner   Ph.D., University of Southern California. Senior Professor of Church Growth, School of World Mission, Fuller Theological Seminary, Pasadena, California.

Steven L. Ware   Ph.D., Drew University. Associate Registrar and Assistant Professor of History, Nyack College, Manhattan Center, New York, New York.

Wayne E. Warner   Diploma in Ministerial Course, Eugene Bible College. Director, Assemblies of God Archives, Springfield, Missouri

William Wedenoja   Ph.D., University of California–San Diego. Professor of Sociology and Anthropology, Southwest Missouri State University, Springfield, Missouri.

J. Rodman Williams   Ph.D., Columbia University. Professor of Systematic Theology, Regent University School of Divinity, Virginia Beach, Virginia.

Dwight J. Wilson   Ph.D., University of California–Santa Cruz. Professor of History, Bethany Bible College, Santa Cruz, California.

Everett A. Wilson   Ph.D., Stanford University. President and Professor of History, Bethany Bible College, Santa Cruz, California.

Lewis F. Wilson   Ph.D. University of California–Berkeley. Professor Emeritus of History, Vanguard University, Costa Mesa, California.

Daniel Woods   Ph.D., University of Mississippi. Associate Proffessor of History, Ferrum College, Ferrum, Virginia.

James R. Zeigler   M.A., Gordon-Conwell Theological Seminary. Freelance writer and historian, Broken Arrow, Oklahoma.

†Deceased.

Abbreviations

AB	Anchor Bible	IB	The Interpreter's Bible
AF	The Apostolic Faith	IBMR	International Bulletin of Missionary Research
AFM	Apostolic Faith Mission		
AG/AOG	Assemblies of God	ICC	International Critical Commentary
AJPS	Asian Journal of Pentecostal Studies	ICCRO	International Catholic Charismatic Renewal Office
AGH	Assemblies of God Heritage		
ANET	Ancient Near Eastern Texts	IDB	The Interpreter's Bible Dictionary
ANF	The Ante-Nicene Fathers	ISBE	The International Standard Bible Encyclopedia
Antiq.	Josephus, Antiquities		
AuPS	Australian Pentecostal Studies	JBL	Journal of Biblical Literature
Az	Azusa	JEPTA	Journal of the European Pentecostal Theological Association
BAGD	Bauer, Arndt, Gingrich, and Danker, Greek-English Lexicon of the New Testament		
		JETS	Journal of the Evangelical Theological Society
		JHLT	Journal of Hispanic/Latino Theology
BDB	Brown, Driver, and Briggs, Hebrew and English Lexicon of the Old Testament	JNES	Journal of Near Eastern Studies
		JPT	Journal of Pentecostal Theology
BETS	Bulletin of the Evangelical Theological Society	JRT	Journal of Religious Thought
		JSPS	Pneuma—Journal of the Society for Pentecostal Studies
Bib	Biblica		
CA Herald	Christ's Ambassador Herald	JSSR	Journal for the Scientific Study of Religion
CBQ	Catholic Biblical Quarterly	JTS	Journal of Theological Studies
CBQMS	Catholic Biblical Quarterly Monograph Series	LJ	Logos Journal
		LRE	Latter Rain Evangel
CCL	Classics of Christian Literature	LSJ	Liddel, Scott, and Jones, Greek-English Lexicon
CGE	Church of God Evangel		
CT	Christianity Today	LThK	Lexicon für Theologie und Kirche
DCPM	Dictionary of Pentecostal and Charismatic Movements (1988)	LXX	Septuagint
		MM	Moulton and Milligan, The Vocabulary of the Greek New Testament
DThC	Dictionaire de Théologie Catholique		
EBC	Expositors Bible Commentary	MMD	Miracles and Missions Digest
EDBibT	Evangelical Dictionary of Biblical Theology	MRW	Missionary Review of the World
EDT	Evangelical Dictionary of Theology	NBD	The New Bible Dictionary
EPTA Bulletin	European Pentecostal Theological Association Bulletin	NCBC	New Century Bible Commentary
		NIC	New International Commentary
EQ	Evangelical Quarterly	NICNT	New International Commentary of the New Testament
ET	Evangelische Theologie		
ExpT	Expository Times	NIDCC	New International Dictionary of the Christian Church
FGMH	Full Gospel Missionary Herald		
Fuller	Fuller Theological Seminary	NIDNTT	New International Dictionary of New Testament Theology
HMM	History of Methodist Missions		
HNTC	Harper's New Testament Commentary	NIGTC	New International Greek Testament Commentary
HTKNT	Herder's Theologischer Kommentar zum Neuen Testament		
		NSHERK	New Schaff-Herzog Encyclopedia of Religious Knowledge
HTR	Harvard Theological Review		

NTS	*New Testament Studies*	*TDNT*	*Theological Dictionary of the New Testament*
Nº	*Numéro*	*TF*	*Triumphs of Faith*
NovT	*Novum Testamentum*	*TR*	*Theological Renewal*
ODCC	*Oxford Dictionary of the Christian Church*	*TS*	*Theological Studies*
PE	*Pentecostal Evangel*	*VT/VetTest*	*Vetus Testamentum*
PG	*Patrologia Graeca*	*WBC*	*Wycliffe Bible Commentary*
PL	*Patrologia Latina*	*WE*	*World Evangelism*
Pn	*Pneumatikoi*	*WTJ*	*Westminster Theological Journal*
RGG	*Die Religion in Geschichte und Gegenwart*	*ZAW*	*Zeitschrift für die alttestamentliche Wissenschaft*
SBK	Strack and Billerbeck, *Kommentar zum Neuen Testament aus Talmud und Midrash*	*ZNW*	*Zeitschrift für die neutestamentliche Wissenschaft*
SBL	*Society of Biblical Literature*	*ZPEB*	*Zondervan Pictorial Encyclopedia of the Bible*
SC	*The Spirit and the Church* (Korea)		
SJT	*Scottish Journal of Theology*		

Abbreviations for States, Provinces, and Countries

United States

AL	Alabama
AK	Alaska
AZ	Arizona
AR	Arkansas
CA	California
CO	Colorado
CT	Connecticut
DE	Delaware
FL	Florida
GA	Georgia
HI	Hawaii
ID	Idaho
IL	Illinois
IN	Indiana
IA	Iowa
KS	Kansas
KY	Kentucky
LA	Louisiana
ME	Maine
MD	Maryland
MA	Massachusetts
MI	Michigan
MN	Minnesota
MS	Mississippi
MO	Missouri
MT	Montana
NE	Nebraska
NV	Nevada
NH	New Hampshire
NJ	New Jersey
NM	New Mexico
NY	New York
NC	North Carolina
ND	North Dakota
OH	Ohio
OK	Oklahoma
OR	Oregon
PA	Pennsylvania
RI	Rhode Island
SC	South Carolina
SD	South Dakota
TN	Tennessee
TX	Texas
UT	Utah
VT	Vermont
VA	Virginia
WA	Washington
WV	West Virginia
WI	Wisconsin
WY	Wyoming
DC	District of Columbia

Canada

Alta.	Alberta
B.C.	British Columbia
Man.	Manitoba
N.B.	New Brunswick
Nfld.	Newfoundland
N.W.T.	Northwest Territories
N.S.	Nova Scotia
Ont.	Ontario
P.E.I.	Prince Edward Island
Que.	Quebec
Sask.	Saskatchewan
Y.T.	Yukon Territory

Countries

N.Z.	New Zealand
S.A.	South Africa
U.K.	United Kingdom
U.S.	United States of America

Old Testament

Ge	Genesis	2Ch	2 Chronicles	Da	Daniel
Exod	Exodus	Ez	Ezra	Hos	Hosea
Lev	Leviticus	Ne	Nehemiah	Joel	Joel
Nu	Numbers	Est	Esther	Am	Amos
Dt	Deuteronomy	Job	Job	Ob	Obadiah
Jos	Joshua	Ps(s)	Psalm(s)	Jnh	Jonah
Jdg	Judges	Pr	Proverbs	Mic	Micah
Ru	Ruth	Eccl	Ecclesiastes	Na	Nahum
1Sa	1 Samuel	SS	Song of Songs	Hab	Habakkuk
2Sa	2 Samuel	Isa	Isaiah	Zep	Zephaniah
1Ki	1 Kings	Jer	Jeremiah	Hag	Haggai
2Ki	2 Kings	La	Lamentations	Zec	Zechariah
1Ch	1 Chronicles	Eze	Ezekiel	Mal	Malachi

New Testament

Mt	Matthew	Eph	Ephesians	Heb	Hebrews
Mk	Mark	Phil	Philippians	Jas	James
Lk	Luke	Col	Colossians	1Pe	1 Peter
Jn	John	1Th	1 Thessalonians	2Pe	2 Peter
Ac	Acts	2Th	2 Thessalonians	1Jn	1 John
Ro	Romans	1Ti	1 Timothy	2Jn	2 John
1Co	1 Corinthians	2Ti	2 Timothy	3Jn	3 John
2Co	2 Corinthians	Tit	Titus	Jude	Jude
Gal	Galatians	Phm	Philemon	Rev	Revelation

PART I

Global Survey

AFGHANISTAN

■ Pentecostals 48 (2%)   ■ Charismatics 267 (12%)   ■ Neocharismatics 1,985 (86%)   ■ Total Renewal: 2,300

See AFRICA, NORTH, AND THE MIDDLE EAST.

AFRICA, CENTRAL (Survey)

1. Origins of Pentecostalism in Central Africa.

The origins of pentecostalism in Central Africa date back to the missionary emphasis arising from the post–Azusa Street spread of the pentecostal experience in both North America and Europe. Pentecostals of different persuasions believed that they had to preach the gospel to the unsaved, so that within a very short period after the introduction of pentecostalism on both of these continents—and in some cases even before recognized denominations or fellowships had been formed—missionaries were being sent to Central and Southern Africa.

Most of the earliest pentecostals who evangelized and planted churches in Central Africa were from the early pentecostal denominations and associations in North America and Europe. For reasons of transport and communications, the majority of the earliest pentecostal missionaries to the southern area of the region traveled there via South Africa (S.A.) and had contacts with pentecostalism in the south of the continent. This is important because links were (and are still today) generally maintained with the same denominations or other sympathetic pentecostals in S.A. The S.A. influence should never be neglected in any study on Central African pentecostalism, especially with regard to the anglophone countries (Zimbabwe, Zambia, Malawi). Included in this block of countries, which has always had strong links with S.A., is the French-speaking Katanga/Shaba province of Congo/Zaire, and the Portuguese-speaking nation of Mozambique. All of these countries were linked by rail and road to the South, and even today they have close trade and economic ties.

2. The Problem of Numbers.

There is great confusion over the accuracy of statistics in this entire region. Many groups do not keep accurate statistics, which means that the numbers are estimates. Statistics recorded in works such as *Operation World, World Churches Handbook,* and *World Christian Encyclopedia* vary considerably and often do not include all the groups we have found. While pentecostal/charismatic groups in some countries tended to exaggerate their statistics, in others (Congo-Kinshasa, for example), for political reasons, all Protestant groups underestimated their membership by as much as 50%. Most African groups do not include the unbaptized in their membership numbers, but they may include them under the total number of adherents. Pedobaptists include children, while most pentecostals do not. Under churches we include all gatherings of believers. However, there are many (often the majority) that do not have their own buildings.

3. Regions.

a. The English-Speaking Bloc. Zimbabwe, Zambia, and Malawi. This region was initially introduced to pentecostalism by pentecostals who had links with the Apostolic Faith Mission and the other major pentecostal groups in South Africa such as the Full Gospel Church. Most of the first pentecostals in Zimbabwe and Zambia were whites who lived in Zimbabwe or who worked in the mines of the copper belt in Zambia. Small groups of pentecostal believers established churches that were, for the most part, for whites. These groups of white pentecostals were not, at least initially, very concerned with evangelism among the African nationals. As late as the 1970s the separatist attitudes of southern Africa meant that many of these pentecostal churches were still segregated, and because many whites, especially in Zambia, were leaving the country, the churches in towns like Lusaka, Kitwe, and Ndola were decreasing in numbers. For this reason it was only at the introduction of the pentecostal mission efforts from outside the region that pentecostals had a clear opportunity to evangelize the nationals and introduce to them the pentecostal message.

b. The Portuguese-Speaking Bloc. Mozambique and Angola.

c. The French-Speaking Bloc. The Democratic Republic of Congo (formerly Congo-Kinshasa and Congo-Zaire), Rwanda, Burundi, The People's Republic of Congo (Brazzaville), Gabon, and Central African Republic.

See articles on individual countries: ANGOLA; BURUNDI; CENTRAL AFRICAN REPUBLIC; CONGO, DEMOCRATIC REPUBLIC OF (CONGO-ZAIRE); CONGO, PEOPLE'S REPUBLIC OF (CONGO-BRAZZAVILLE); GABON; MALAWI; MOZAMBIQUE; RWANDA.

■ **Bibliography:**

Books and Articles. Action Africa, *The African Experience* (1997) ■ *Apostolic Church: Year Book 1989–90* ■ D. B. Barrett, ed., *World Christian Encyclopedia* (1982) ■ E. M. Braekman, *Histoire du Protestantisme au Congo* (1961) ■ P. Brierley, ed., *World Churches Handbook* (1997) ■ W. F. P. Burton, *God Working with Them* (1933) ■ idem, *Rosalie Hegi: Winning the Wild Wabembe to Christ* (1971) ■ P. Calzada,

Racontez ses merveilles: 40 ans de Mission (1997) ▪ M. Chavda, *Only Love Can Make a Miracle* (1990) ▪ J. R. Crawford, *Protestant Missions in Congo 1878–1969* (n.d.) ▪ R. Dayton, ed., *Mission Handbook*, 11th ed. (1976) ▪ C. G. Enerson, *Venture into Faith* (1993) ▪ M. Froibe, ed., *World Christianity: South Central Africa* (1991) ▪ D. J. Garrard, "The History of the Zaire Evangelistic Mission/Communauté Pentecôtiste au Zaïre from 1915 to 1982" (diss., U. of Aberdeen, 1983) ▪ B. L. Goddard, ed., *The Encyclopedia of Modern Christian Missions* (1967) ▪ K. G. Grubb, ed., *World Christian Handbook* (1949) ▪ J. P. Hogan, *The Growth of the Assemblies of God Worldwide* (1997) ▪ W. J. Hollenweger, *Pentecostalism: Origins and Developments Worldwide* (1997) ▪ idem, *The Pentecostals* (1972) ▪ C. Irvine, *The Church of Christ in Zaire: A Handbook of Protestant Churches, Missions and Communities, 1878–1978* (1978) ▪ P. Johnstone, *Operation World* (1998) ▪ G. G. Kulbeck, *What God Hath Wrought: A History of the Pentecostal Assemblies of Canada* (1958) ▪ D. J. Maxwell, "A Social and Conceptual History of North-East Zimbabwe, 1890–1990" (diss., Oxford, 1994) ▪ R. Prosén et al., *CEPZa miaka 60, 1921–1981: Kitabu cha ukumbusho* [Community of Pentecostal Churches of Zaire: 60 years, 1921–1981: Book of Remembrance] (1981) ▪ M. Söderlund, *Pingstmission i Kongo och Ruanda-Urundi* (1995) ▪ R. Steele, *Plundering Hell* (1984) ▪ G. Suckling, *Kachongu Sesa-Mbinga* (1997) ▪ G. R. Upton, *The Miracle of Mozambique* (1980) ▪ P. Watt, *From Africa's Soil: The Story of the Assemblies of God in Southern Africa* (1992) ▪ H. Womersley, *Congo Miracle: Fifty Years of God's Working in Congo (Zaire)* (1974) ▪ J. E. Worsfold, *The Origins of the Apostolic Church in Great Britain* (1991) ▪ Zimbabwe National Evangelism Task (Net) Committee, *Target 2000: Congress on Church Planting* (1992).

Periodicals. *Contact-Congo* (Zaire/Congo Evangelistic Mission; formerly known as *Report from Bros. Burton and Salter, Report from Bro. W. F. P. Burton;* from issue no. 21, *Congo Evangelistic Mission;* from Sept. 1921, *Congo Evangelistic Mission: Report of the Work;* from Jan. 1972, *The Zaire Evangelistic Mission Report;* from Feb. 1980, *Contact with Zaire Evangelistic Mission;* from Jan. 1996 until June 1997, *Contact-Zaire*) ▪ *Elim Evangel* (Elim–U.K.) ▪ *En Mission Avec Eux* ("Action Missionnaire," AG–France) ▪ *Pentecôte* (AG–France) ▪ *Redemption Tidings* (now called *Joy;* AG–U.K.) ▪ *Serviteur de Dieu* (AG–France).

Archives. Dossier PM.XIV 26/10/1922, Archives Africain, Brussels ▪ D. J. Garrard, unpub. private papers ▪ Donald Gee Centre, Mattersey Hall, Mattersey, U.K.

Private Communications (Letters, E-mail, and Interviews). C. W. Beardsmore (retired AG–U.K. missionary to Congo/Kinshasa) ▪ G. S. Bialik (former AG–U.S. Angolan missionary in Portugal) ▪ B. Burr and S. Burr (regional missions overseers for Central and Southern Africa, AG–U.S.) ▪ P. Calzada (missions secretary/director, AG–France) ▪ D. Corbin (missions overseer for Africa, AG–U.S.) ▪ M. Cornelius (missionary director for Central and Southern Africa, PAOC) ▪ T. Deuschle (pastor, Hear the Word Ministries, Harare, Zimbabwe) ▪ G. A. Dickinson (AG–U.S. missionary to Congo/Brazzaville) ▪ B. Dodzweit (missions director, Elim–U.S.) ▪ Bengt Halldorf (Svenska Fria Missionen missionary to Burundi) ▪ Daniel Halldorf (regional coordinator for francophone Central Africa, Svenska Fria Missionen) ▪ Walter J. Hollenweger (prof. emeritus, U. of Birmingham, U.K.) ▪ Bruno Kondabéka (AG–U.K. pastor; citizen of Congo/Brazzaville) ▪ David Laity (former PAOC missionary to Zambia) ▪ M. Lines (retired AG–France missionary to both Congos) ▪ J.-P. Mary (Wycliffe translator, Congo-Brazzaville) ▪ Freddie Massa (AG–U.K. pastor; citizen of Congo/Kinshasa) ▪ Gordon McKillop (CEM missionary, Congo/Kinshasa) ▪ Bill Mercer (PAOC missionary to Mozambique) ▪ Ronald Jean Monot (pastor AG–Switzerland; formerly CEM missionary to Congo/Kinshasa) ▪ Claude Moser (administrator, Coopération Evangélique dans le Monde [missionary branch of La Porte Ouverte] France) ▪ Simon Pierre Nzubahimana (pastor; citizen of Rwanda) ▪ Heinz Ramseier (Schweizerische Pfingstmission missionary in Bangui, Central African Republic) ▪ Edgar Reed (AG–U.S. missionary to Congo/Brazzaville) ▪ Bill Riley (AG–U.S. missionary to Angola) ▪ Edmund Rowlands (pastor, AG–U.K.; former CEM missionary to Congo/Kinshasa) ▪ Margit Söderlund (Svenka Fria Missionen missionary to Burundi) ▪ Sven Stenberg (Svenska Fria Missionen missionary to Burundi) ▪ Paul Stevens (Elim–U.K. Missions Dept.) ▪ Sylvia Turner (AG–U.S. missionary to Congo/Kinshasa) ▪ Magnus Udd (Independent AG missionary to Malawi) ▪ Jacques Vernaud (AG–U.S. missionary to Congo/Kinshasa) ▪ Judith Wall (member, "Hear the Word Ministries," Harare, Zimbabwe).

▪ D. J. GARRARD

AFRICA, EAST (Survey)

East Africa was included in the regions of the continent divided up at the Berlin Conference in 1884. Kenya and Uganda were taken over by the British not long after the European rush for colonies. Many British people moved to Kenya and Uganda to farm and for trading purposes. Although Kenya and Uganda lie on the equator, much of their territory is on a plateau nearly a mile high, which gives the highlands, inland from the coast, an ideal climate. Geographically, Tanzania is very similar and benefits from the huge inland water resources of Lake Tanganyika.

When the British decided to construct the railway from Mombassa to Uganda, they brought in thousands of workers from India to do the building; many stayed and added to the mix of peoples in this part of the continent. Many of these were Hindus, but there were also quite a number of Muslims. This part of Africa, including Tanzania, had long been used to seeing slave trains from the interior making their way to the coast. With the discoveries of Livingstone, Burton, and Speake, it was not long before missionaries began to evangelize this vast hinterland of what was then known as the Dark Continent.

Even the earliest pentecostals were relatively late on the scene compared to the Anglicans (1860s) and the Moravians (from the 1890s). There is still much to be done in terms of evangelism and teaching, but it is most likely that missions in this region need to reappraise their role, as needs have changed greatly during the last 100 years. If East Africa is going to be reached for Christ, it will not be the missions that will make the difference—it will be East Africans.

East Africa was originally considered to include Kenya, Uganda, and Tanzania (then Tanganyika). After WWI Britain was the colonial power responsible for the entire region. The British administration imposed its stamp on the basic infrastructure, from the way trade was carried out to the emphases in primary, secondary, and postsecondary education. Many of the larger companies that operated in all three countries often had a central administration with their head office in one of the three. For example, instead of having a separate airline company for each country, East African Airways served the entire area. Each country was administered by the colonial office in London, with a governor over each. This meant that the churches found a certain amount of uniformity of practice and similarity in the rules for registration of denominations and the acquisition of land, the involvement in primary school education, medical work, and so on. There was bureaucracy, but it was not as cumbersome as in the French, Portuguese, or Belgian colonies. It was likely also less biased than Roman Catholic governments of the French, Portuguese, and Belgians in terms of which church traditions were granted rights to evangelism within its borders.

Ethiopia, Eritrea, and Somalia are geographically part of East Africa, but they never linked in any official regional agreements with Kenya, Uganda, or Tanzania. Prior to the independence of the East African countries, there was not a great deal of communication between Ethiopia, Somalia, and its southern neighbors. This is generally still true, although there are open corridors for air traffic.

Although many Britons moved to East Africa before and after WWII, there never were as many as there had been in South Africa or in Zimbabwe. Many of them left Kenya at the time of the Mau Mau uprising, and they were never as numerous in Uganda as in Kenya. This is important, because the influence of white residential expatriate pentecostals was considerable in the south of the continent. There is no indication that this influence was as marked in East Africa, although pentecostal missionaries were certainly important in the expansion of the charismatic message to this region.

See articles on individual countries: ERITREA, ETHIOPIA, KENYA, SOMALIA, TANZANIA, UGANDA.

■ **Bibliography:**

Books. D. B. Barrett, ed., *World Christian Encyclopedia* (1982) ▨ P. Brierley, ed., *World Churches Handbook: Based on the Operation World Database by Patrick Johnstone WEC International, 1993* (1997) ▨ E. Hilpinen, ed., *Suomen Vapaa Ulkolähetys 70 vuotta: Finnish Free Foreign Mission 70 years* (Finnish and English; Finnish Free Foreign Mission, 1997) ▨ G. G. Kulbeck, *What God Hath Wrought: A History of the Pentecostal Assemblies of Canada* (1958) ▨ H. Ros, *"Weiszer Mann, geh heim!" Missionsarbeit unter den Iteso und Langi in Uganda von 1966 bis 1986* (1990) ▨ M. Söderlund, *Pingstmission i Kongo och Ruanda-Urundi* (1995).

Periodicals. *Elim Evangel* (Elim Church–U.K.) ▨ *Elim Year Book* (1964–95; Elim Church–U.K.) ▨ *Evangelii Härold* (Swedish Free Churches) ▨ *Field Focus* (AG–U.S. Division of Foreign Missions) ▨ *Final Frontiers* (Association of International Mission Services [AIMS]) ▨ *Harvest Messenger* (Africa Harvest 2000) ▨ *Leader's Touch* (AG–U.S. Division of Foreign Missions) ▨ Nairobi Pentecostal Bible College (Newsletter, Aug. 1998) ▨ *Pentecostal Evangel* (AG–U.S.) ▨ *The Pentecostal Testimony* (PAOC) ▨ *Resource* (PAOC Overseas Missions Department, 1986).

Archives. Assemblies of God, Division of Foreign Missions, Springfield, MO ▨ Donald Gee Centre, Mattersey Hall, Mattersey, UK ▨ Pentecostal Assemblies of Canada, Mississauga, Ont., Canada.

Private Communications and Interviews. Maud Andersson (missionary of the SFM and Legal Representative for Kenya) ▨ Rasmus Ayot (pastor, Maranatha Church Kenya) ▨ Fred A. Brannen (former Church of God [CG, Cleveland, TN] missionary to Kenya; field representative for CG) ▨ Darren Gingras (PAOC missionary in Ethiopia) ▨ Merja Hakala (Finnish Free Church Mission) ▨ Jan-Edy Johannesson (SFM School of Mission, Kaggeholm, Sweden) ▨ Martin K. Michael (Tanzanian student at Mattersey Hall; member Tanzanian Field Outreach) ▨ William Muturi (Kenyan student at Mattersey Hall; member KAG) ▨ Les Norman (The DCI Trust, Colston Bassett, England) ▨ Fred Nyman, (SFM missionary from Tanzania; vice secretary general of the PCAT 1993–98) ▨ Carin Nyström (SFM missionary from Tanzania) ▨ Alan Perry (AG–U.K. missionary in Kenya) ▨ Ron Posein (PAOC missionary in Tanzania) ▨ Alan Renshaw (retired Elim–U.K. missionary from Tanzania) ▨ Herbert Ros, (retired Volksmission [Germany] missionary from Kenya and Uganda; now pastoring in Germany) ▨ Brian Rutten (PAOC missionary in Ethiopia) ▨ Gary M. Skinner (PAOC missionary in Uganda) ▨ Paul K. H. Song (pastor of Brixton Full Gospel Church, London, U.K.; missionary of Yoido Full Gospel Church, Seoul, Korea and part of the oversight of East Africa work) ▨ Hilary Tumusiime (New Life Church of Uganda).   ■ D. J. GARRARD

AFRICA, NORTH, AND THE MIDDLE EAST (Survey)

I. North Africa
   A. Egypt
   B. Sudan
   C. Libya, Tunisia, Algeria, Morocco, Mauritania
   D. Israel
   E. Jordan
   F. Lebanon

II. The Arabian Peninsula

III. Iran and Iraq
   A. Iran
   B. Iraq

IV. Syria, Turkey, Pakistan, and Afghanistan
   A. Syria
   B. Turkey
   C. Pakistan
   D. Afghanistan

The region of the world labeled North Africa and the Middle East is a hostile place to share the gospel. In nations ruled by Islam, Christian missionaries, especially those from the West, are not welcome. Yet pentecostal believers are working in Islamic countries in greater numbers than ever before. Of necessity, their ministry must be adapted to the Arab culture, and they live with some degree of risk constantly. Yet the Spirit of God is moving across the Muslim world. Hundreds of Muslims, and in some places thousands, are coming to Christ. This movement to the cross is backed by a worldwide prayer fellowship of more than 100,000 people.

The list of nations that make up the region designated North Africa and the Middle East varies from one writer to another. This article includes the Arab nations of North Africa (Mauritania, Morocco, Algeria, Tunisia, Libya, Egypt, and Sudan), those on the Arabian Peninsula, and eastward across Iran to Pakistan and Afghanistan. This region is one of the least evangelized in the world, with evangelical Christians constituting less than 5% of the total population.

Three major world religions—Judaism, Christianity, and Islam—began in this area. Although all three religions claim spiritual descent from Abraham, their differences have spawned intense political and cultural rivalry. Except for Israel, Islam is the dominant religion in all North African and Middle Eastern countries.

I. NORTH AFRICA.

By the end of the first century, the message of Christianity had been preached in most of North Africa. According to tradition, John Mark founded the church in Alexandria, Egypt. It quickly became a center of early Christian activity. Christianity flourished across North Africa in the second and third centuries, producing leaders such as Augustine and Tertullian. When Christians were persecuted in the Roman Empire, numerous North African believers faced death rather than recant their faith. The strength of their commitment to Christ is immortalized by the story of Perpetua, a young mother condemned to death for her faith. She was thrown to the beasts in the arena at Carthage in A.D. 203.

During the fourth and fifth centuries, however, the church in North Africa became divided by doctrinal issues. A quest for political power replaced its former evangelistic zeal. These factors helped set the stage for the aggressive expansion of Islam immediately after Mohammed's death in 632.

The Coptic Orthodox Church, centered in Alexandria, Egypt, had broken ties with Rome and Constantinople over doctrinal matters. When Islam began its spread across Egypt in 640, many members embraced the new religion. The Coptic tradition survived, however, and has endured through the centuries, especially in Ethiopia and Egypt. Today Copts represent about 5% of Egypt's population, making the Coptic Church the largest Christian body in North Africa.

A. Egypt.

A man from Egypt received the Holy Spirit at the ⸬Azusa Street revival in California and wrote to his relatives, telling them about his experience. They responded by asking that a pentecostal missionary come to Egypt. G. S. Brelsford, a minister who had received the Holy Spirit about two years earlier, responded. He arrived in Assiout, Egypt, in Mar. 1909, where he founded Egypt's first pentecostal church. The following year ⸬Ansel H. Post, a Baptist minister who had experienced the pentecostal blessing, came to Alexandria, and H. E. Randall, a Canadian Holiness missionary baptized in

Assemblies of God church in Cairo, Egypt. Note the low wall separating women and men.

Ordained ministers of the Egypt District Council of the AG in 1943. Their number (12) equals the number of Christ's apostles.

the Holy Spirit while on furlough, returned to Cairo and opened a pentecostal church. These three men laid the foundation for Egypt's pentecostal community. In 1912, the Crouch family began missionary ministry in Egypt, with some part of the family continuing to work there for nearly 50 years. The C. W. Doneys arrived in 1913 to start long-term service.

Two women also pioneered pentecostal ministries in Egypt. In 1910 ▸Lillian Trasher went to Egypt as a "faith" missionary without the backing of any organized missions board. Early the next year, a dying mother gave Lillian her baby. This was the beginning of the Lillian Trasher Memorial Orphanage in Assiout. For 50 years, until her death in 1961, "Mama" Lillian took in thousands of needy children and widows, providing them a home, food, clothing, medical care, education, and spiritual instruction. The orphanage, which continues to serve needy children, recently received the Egyptian government's highest award for humanitarian service. It is the largest Christian social institution in the entire North African region.

Mabel Dean arrived in Egypt in 1924 when she was 40 years old and lived there the rest of her life. From her mission station in Minia, she founded a chain of strong indigenous churches. When she died at age 77, she left 45 active pentecostal congregations with leaders she had trained.

Numerous other pentecostal missionaries have participated in building a strong fellowship in Egypt. In a Protestant community of approximately half a million, pentecostals and charismatics number about 100,000, by far the largest group of pentecostals in any nation in North Africa and the Middle East. Egyptian pentecostals report growing churches despite intense persecution. Signs and wonders, especially miracles of healing and deliverance, draw both Muslims and Copts to a personal relationship with Christ. A move of the Holy Spirit in the Coptic Church has created a charismatic element within that ancient tradition.

B. Sudan.

In Sudan, the only other North African nation with a pentecostal constituency of more than a few hundred, Christians experience brutal violence. The largest nation in Africa, Sudan is divided between two peoples and two identities. Northern Sudan is mostly populated by Muslim Arabs who dominate the political and military structure of the nation. Southern Sudan is inhabited by black Africans whose religious life is a mixture of tribal animism and Christianity.

This division is magnified by a 10-year civil war that has taken more than a million lives. Christian villages often are plundered. Men are killed, women and children are taken as slaves. The war has disrupted farming, and famine is prevalent in the south. Yet Western aid is prevented from reaching the imperiled.

The tremendous hostility and hardship have forged Christians into a resilient group. Some barriers to the gospel have broken down as people move from place to place to avoid the conflict. Mainline denominations are experiencing a move of the Holy Spirit, and Sudanese pentecostal churches are growing. Conditions prevent accurate reporting, but Christian refugees tell stories of divine protection, as do pentecostals from Kenya who minister in south Sudan.

C. Libya, Tunisia, Algeria, Morocco, Mauritania.

In the other five nations of North Africa, evangelical Christians usually make up less than 1% of the population, of which pentecostals and charismatics comprise a fraction. Small pentecostal house churches exist in some cities. The few workers who live in these nations do so as tentmakers. Most evangelism is through distribution of Scriptures, correspondence courses, videos, and broadcast media.

Opposition to the gospel in these nations is intense, and missions must be done creatively. In one city a pentecostal worker assembled printing equipment in his garage. He translated the Gospel of Mark, planning to print copies and distribute them discreetly. However, he realized that the noise of the press could create a problem. If neighbors or a passerby became suspicious and reported him to the police, the entire project and possibly his life would be in jeopardy. He stopped printing and prayed. The next morning, he awoke to the roar of motors and clang of machinery. Looking out the window, he saw that the city was repaving his street. Hurriedly he resumed printing. The noise from the paving project allowed him to finish his work.

Two recent approaches to evangelism hold promise. High unemployment in North Africa has caused thousands of Muslims to seek work in Europe. Each August, Europe takes a summer holiday, and these workers head back to their homes for a visit. They travel south through France to the little city of Algeciras, Spain, where they wait, sometimes for days, for a ferry to take them across the Strait of Gibraltar to their North African homeland.

Since 1995, teams from the ˒Assemblies of God (AG) and other pentecostals have ministered on the streets in Algeciras, offering literature and friendship to these travelers. In one month as many as 300,000 copies of the New Testament in Arabic and 75,000 copies of the Jesus film are distributed.

Another evangelism approach is thorough television. Although Christian programs are not allowed in these nations, people can buy a small satellite dish for about $100, enabling them to view programs from London, Hong Kong, or San Francisco. Among the choices is a Christian satellite channel that blankets the entire Arabic-speaking world with the good news of Jesus' love. For the first time in history, it is possible to enter the privacy of Muslim homes across North Africa and much of the Middle East and speak to millions of people all at once with the Good News.

As these avenues of ministry expand, the Holy Spirit is touching Muslim hearts. Some see visions and are spoken to by angels. Some seekers experience dreams that direct them to people who can tell them the way of salvation. After years of sowing seed without seeing much response, dedicated workers are seeing signs of a harvest that earlier missionaries could only dream of. If Jesus tarries, North Africa may once again be a center for New Testament Christianity.

D. Israel.

The history of pentecostal ministries in Israel and Jordan goes back to one woman, Elizabeth Brown. She went to Jerusalem in 1895 under a nonpentecostal mission board. After being baptized in the Holy Spirit in 1908, she established a pentecostal work. While home on furlough during WWI, she was accepted as a missionary with the AG. Her work was primarily among the Arab population, since Jews were only a small minority of Israel's population then. However, when Israel became a nation and Jerusalem was divided, her mission property, located in the State of Israel, became a center for ministries to Jews.

Miss Brown died in 1940, but since then numerous missionaries from various pentecostal denominations have worked in Israel. Some primarily minister to Jews while others work among the Arab population. In a few pentecostal congregations, Jews and Arabs now worship together. At least 40 Jewish ˒Messianic assemblies meet in various parts of Israel.

The AG operates a bookstore in Jerusalem that stocks Bibles in some 30 languages. Christian literature, extremely important due to the multiplicity of languages spoken by immigrants, also is available. In the Haifa area, pentecostals from Russia are active in evangelism. Both Arab and Messianic Jewish converts are being discipled through correspondence courses and Bible schools.

Although pentecostals and charismatics are the fastest-growing sector of Protestant Christianity in Israel, their number remains under 8,000.

E. Jordan.

The pentecostal message was preached in Jordan by missionary Laura Radford in the 1920s, and a church was opened at Es Salt. After a fruitful ministry, she returned to the U.S. in 1947. In the following years, missionary activities in Jordan were limited because of sensitive religious and political situations. AG missionaries returned to Jordan in 1966. A few churches were established, but in spite of dedicated missionaries and national Christians, growth was minimal.

As a result of the Persian Gulf crisis, questions about the relevance and truth of Islam have resulted in unprecedented openness among Jordanians and Iraqi refugees. The loving, effective aid given to refugees by Jordanian Christians, including pentecostals, has been a major factor in opening new opportunities to witness.

Young leadership has brought renewed zeal and enthusiasm for evangelism to pentecostal groups. Media outreaches are especially effective in the Jordanian culture. The Jesus film has been seen by a half million people with hundreds of responses. Yet persecution is intense. While Jordan's constitution promotes the free exercise of religious belief, it prohibits Muslims from changing religions. Pentecostal adherents probably number fewer than 3,000.

F. Lebanon.

Lebanon has the largest Christian population in the Middle East. The overwhelming majority belong to Catholic or Orthodox traditions. Earlier in this century, Lebanon was admired as a land of peace and prosperity and became a center for Christian agencies seeking to evangelize the Arab world. Pentecostals worked in Lebanon to establish churches, Bible schools, and literature ministries.

The scene changed in 1975 when the fragile governing coalition of Christians and Muslims collapsed and thrust the nation into the agony of a 16-year civil war. By the time an uneasy peace was reached in 1992, parts of the nation were destroyed and the economy was in ruins. Church outreaches were severely hampered. Non-Christian factions are for the most part unable to separate the real Jesus from the political rhetoric of their nominally Christian foes.

The decline of resident missionaries in Lebanon and the emigration of national church leaders have left evangelical and pentecostal groups, whose membership is estimated to be about 2,500, without adequate pastoral care. Some pentecostal missionaries have returned to strengthen the remnants of the church. Although a few nominal Christians and Muslims have come to faith in Jesus, a significant move of the

Holy Spirit is needed to bring revival to this suffering, fragmented part of the body of Christ.

II. THE ARABIAN PENINSULA.

The nations of Saudi Arabia, Yemen, Oman, Kuwait, Qatar, Bahrain, and United Arab Emirates share not only the Arab Peninsula but also a culture that is almost totally closed to Christianity. As in North Africa, most of the Arab population in these nations have never heard the gospel, seen a Bible, or known anyone who truly believes in and lives for Jesus.

One of the few avenues of Christian witness in these nations is through the influx of workers from Asia. Pentecostals from South Korea, Sri Lanka, and the Philippines have been among those imported to work in service positions. Stifling legal controls and differences in language and culture have limited the effectiveness of their witness. However, whatever underground church exists in these countries is largely the product of the witness of these Third World workers who have courageously testified about Jesus to their Muslim Arab employers.

In some of these nations, the New Testament in Arabic, the Jesus film, and other Christian videos and literature are in surreptitious circulation. In most of these nations, people who confess Christ must remain secret believers or risk losing their lives. Even secret gatherings are risky.

Pentecostals and other evangelical missions agencies use radio, literature, and television to take the gospel message into these areas. However, only a work of God's Spirit, such as took place in the former Soviet Union, can break down barriers and open these nations to the preaching of the gospel. In the meantime, the strength of any pentecostal movement in this region is known only to God.

A river baptism in Rezaieh, Iran, in 1961.

III. IRAN AND IRAQ.

A. Iran.

The pentecostal message came to Iran in 1909. A group of Assyrian pentecostals from Chicago who had experienced the infilling of the Holy Spirit went to northwestern Iran. As they told friends and relatives about the spiritual outpouring taking place in the U.S., revival broke out. Over the next few months, several hundred believers were filled with the Spirit.

At first most pentecostals were from the traditionally Christian Armenian and Assyrian minority groups. As Muslims heard the gospel and converted, persecution increased.

The pentecostal constituency in Iran, which is reported to exceed 50,000 Spirit-filled believers, is the largest in this area. But this growth has not come without price. In the last decade, five pentecostal pastors have been martyred.

Christian workers in Iran faced personal hardships in their efforts to plant the church. In 1969, missionaries Mark and Gladys Bliss were in a highway accident that took the lives of their three children. Traveling with them was Haik Hovsepian Mehr, a young national pastor, and his family. The Hovsepians' baby son also was killed. Twenty-five years later Haik, by then the leader of the nation's pentecostal churches, was martyred. Four other pastors also have given their lives. All pentecostal pastors in Iran suffer harassment, arrests, frequent interrogation, and threats against their lives.

But opposition has not stopped pentecostals from witnessing nor their churches from growing. Recent reports tell of hundreds of Muslims coming to Christ. Though some are secret believers, many take an open stand for their Lord in the face of economic loss and personal danger.

B. Iraq.

In Iraq, the Persian Gulf War hampered efforts by Western pentecostals to establish a foothold for ministry. However, changes are taking place, and more Iraqis are showing interest in hearing the gospel and reading the Bible. The Jesus film has been widely shown, with the result that house churches, some of them pentecostal, are growing in major cities.

Iraqi refugees in Jordan have shown some response to the gospel. Also, pentecostal outreaches to the Kurds in Iraq's northern mountains have resulted in a few believers. While Orthodox and Catholic groups in Iraq have more than a half million members, pentecostals and charismatics probably number fewer than 2,000 in a population of 22 million.

IV. SYRIA, TURKEY, PAKISTAN, AND AFGHANISTAN.

A. Syria.

Syria became a stronghold of the gospel in New Testament times. In Damascus, the Syrian capital, a visitor can still walk down "the street called Straight" where Saul of Tarsus received his sight and a call to missions. But almost nothing of the 1st century faith that Paul preached has survived.

Christian minorities, which make up about 8% of the population, are mostly Catholic and Orthodox. Protestant churches are small but slowly growing, and pentecostal groups are estimated to have a following of about 3,000 believers. The government treats Christians moderately well in order to assure their political loyalty, and allows each group the freedom to worship and witness within its own community. Conversions from Islam are rare.

Missionaries are not allowed to reside in Syria. Some are permitted to enter for limited pastoral visits. Christian professionals working in the nation are one of the few means of maintaining a gospel witness. The Jesus film on videocassette is widely circulated. Bibles and Christian literature have been available in the major languages for the last decade, but several minorities have no Christian witness. The only known pentecostals in Syria are a few house groups that meet for worship.

B. Turkey.

Turkey is among the largest unreached nations in the Middle East. Few of its more than 65 million Muslims have heard the gospel. The Christian population has declined throughout this century. A history of wars with "Christian" European nations make conversion appear as an act of treason. The few Christians who remain are mostly non-Turkish.

The pentecostal message came to Turkey sometime in the early 1960s when a few Spirit-filled evangelists visited. Mostly, they held small-group meetings among Armenians living in Turkey. Then a sovereign move of the Holy Spirit among an evangelical group ministering in Turkey brought a charismatic influence into nonpentecostal house churches. AG missionaries arrived in 1976 and assumed leadership of a small group of Muslim converts whose former leader had to leave the country.

Today pentecostal missionaries work in close fellowship with other evangelicals in Turkey. Church growth has been slow, but continued prayer and outreach efforts are yielding fruit. Although the number of Spirit-filled believers is small, many barriers have been broken down, and signs of progress are apparent. With the translation of the Scriptures into modern Turkish, requests for Bibles and Bible correspondence courses have escalated, and national leadership is developing in the church. A pentecostal revival among Turks and Turkish-speaking ▸Gypsies living in Bulgaria may be a means of a stronger gospel witness in Turkey, as it has been in the Turkic republics of Central Asia, where thousands of Muslims have come to Christ.

C. Pakistan.

When Great Britain gave India independence, Pakistan was partitioned off as a homeland for Muslims. Civil war between Hindus and Muslims followed, claiming an estimated 6 million lives. A half century later much tension and animosity remains. The Christians of Pakistan, mostly converts from the lowest castes of Hinduism, are as despised by the Pakistani Muslim majority today as they once were by the higher-cast Hindu majority when still living in India.

As a Muslim state, Pakistan has adopted Islamic *Sharia* law. Christians are not allowed to defend themselves or give testimony in Muslim courts on important matters. This makes the Muslim blasphemy law (showing disrespect to the prophet Mohammed) a powerful weapon in the hands of Islamic fundamentalists. Beatings, imprisonment, and loss of property have left Christians gripped with fear and dismay. Since 1988 persecution has increased. Christians, barred from some professions, are often legally marginalized by being given only token political representation under Pakistani law.

Various mainline denominations have had missionaries in Pakistan for more than 150 years. Most converts are from the Hindu minorities. Pentecostal missionaries arrived during the mid 1900s. Poverty, illiteracy, and opposition from non-Christian religions have kept church growth at a minimum. Pentecostals and charismatics number about 150,000 in a population of 135 million.

D. Afghanistan.

Landlocked Afghanistan, one of the world's least developed countries, is also one of the least evangelized by Christianity. It is 99% Muslim. The only church building ever erected in Afghanistan was constructed in 1960 and bulldozed to the ground by the government several years later. Today Afghanistan has 48,000 mosques but not one visible church.

The invasion by the Soviet Union in 1979 to prop up a communist regime resulted in a flood of refugees into Pakistan. After the Soviets withdrew in 1990, guerrilla factions, representing various Islamic sects, continued the warfare. This "holy war" has destroyed most of the nation's infrastructure, and the countryside is littered with land mines that continue to maim and kill.

Neither prolonged national misery nor prohibitions against evangelizing Muslims have silenced the gospel witness. Tentmakers, often working in the medical and humanitarian relief professions, minister Christ's love. One pentecostal couple has spent more than 20 years among an Afghan people group because they asked God to send them to "a hard place where no one else wants to go." Through their love for the Afghan people and their servant ministry to them, the gospel has been planted among several extended families of this language group.

The dedication of such missionaries, the fervent prayers of God's people, and the blood of Afghan martyrs are bearing fruit. Several thousand believers now live in Afghanistan. It is estimated that more than half of them are pentecostal.

Refugee camps in Iran and Pakistan, home to more than 6 million Afghans, have opened another avenue for ministry.

Through humanitarian programs, international Christian groups offer help and a very cautious witness in this hostile environment. Some refugees have responded to the gospel, but open professions of Christianity often have led to death. At least three Christian aid workers have been killed, and the number of Afghan martyrs is unknown.

From where the waters of the Atlantic Ocean wash the shores of Morocco to the turbulent mountainous nations of Afghanistan and Pakistan, the wind of the Spirit is softly blowing. Strong Christians with servant hearts have heard a word of prophecy that, from across these nations dominated by Islam, the Holy Spirit is orchestrating the greatest people movement to the foot of the cross the world has ever seen. Pentecostals and charismatics are working with the Spirit to see it happen.   ■ J. BOOZE

AFRICA, WEST (Survey)

   I.   Prophetic Independent Churches

  II.   Pentecostal-Charismatic Churches

 III.   Prophetic and Charismatic Churches and Gender

 IV.   Conclusion

The study of the history of Christianity in West Africa has produced a rich and important literature. Three general lines of research have been pursued, the first being conventional histories about the emergence of Christian missions and the growth of the established churches in Africa. A few scholars among this group have also provided critical analysis of the religious evolution and transformation that occurred in the late 19th and early 20th centuries as a result of missionary and colonial intervention in the affairs of West African people (Agbeti, 1986; Ajayi, 1965; Ayandele, 1966; Ekechi, 1978; Kalu, 1978; Sanneh, 1983).

A second line of research is ethnographies of missions, analyzing how Christian missions shaped and were shaped by the local cultural conditions. While, on the one hand, these works analyze how the church acquired local idioms and identity (Omoyajowo, 1987; Peel, 1968; Webster, 1964), they also show how in some instances colonial Christianity became the dominant symbol system for thought and practice among the new converts.

Third, and currently the area of greatest growth, is the study of the prophetic independent churches (Crumbley, 1992; Omoyajowo, 1987; Peel, 1968; Turner, 1967) and the pentecostal-charismatic movements (Gifford, 1994; Haliburton, 1973; Marshal, 1991; Meyer, 1992; Ojo, 1988; Webster, 1964). The assumption that these movements are new and genuinely African in origin and character has led to their being studied widely, and it propels scholars' continuing interest in them.

This article focuses on the third area, the prophetic independent churches and the pentecostal-charismatic movements in West Africa. The prophetic independent churches include a diverse group of churches, begun by African charismatic men and women who claimed that they were called by God through visions and prophetic utterances to begin a spiritual church. The founders emphasized the efficacy and sufficiency of prayer alone as a panacea for all human needs and as a solution to life's problems. Unlike the Western colonial churches before them, the prophetic churches were initially primarily ethnic. The mission of their founders was first directed at their immediate local communities, though several of these churches later spread to other regions.

The beliefs and practices of the pentecostal African churches are highly indigenized. In addition to the use of the Bible, they borrow heavily from African religious idioms and cultural elements, especially those with deeply held symbolic meanings. Prayers, songs, sermons, and the use of time and space reflect deep African spirituality.

The pentecostal-charismatic churches are also mainly African-initiated, although some were established through foreign agencies. From their inception, most of the pentecostal-charismatic churches have had a more cosmopolitan, transethnic appeal than the prophetic independent churches. When placed along a historical continuum, prophetic churches began shortly after the turn of the century as an African alternative to the mission churches, whereas the pentecostal-charismatic churches began mainly in the 1970s, becoming fully established in the 1980s. Both the prophetic African churches and the pentecostal-charismatics emerge out of similar cultural matrices and religious attitudes. Both are culturally bound and indigenously oriented, and both incorporate aspects of African religious worldviews and realities.

I will provide a general survey of the nature and character of these churches and movements and will examine their historical, symbolic, and social significance and their contributions to the growth and identity of Christianity in the region. My approach will be phenomenological and cultural, focusing on doctrine and theology only when these will elucidate the overall picture of the phenomenon. Even though some scholars of African Christianity make a distinction between the prophetic African churches and the pentecostal-charismatic movement, such a distinction is very artificial.

It is important to examine both the prophetic African churches and the charismatic movements that came into prominence in the last two decades, rather than limiting discussion to the latter. For, as Irving Hexlam and Karla Poewe point out, African charismatic Christianity encompasses "the Independent African churches, the pentecostal and charismatic movements and global charismatic networks, and lay ministries" (1994, 58).

There is continuity between prophetic African churches and the pentecostal-charismatics. Both churches are engaged in what we could term the African primal quest for the sacred and the transcendent: the quest for healing, well-being, material success, and long life. Both establish some degree of religious independence in that, unlike the mission churches before them, they are not under a larger foreign mission. Both groups of churches also derive their success from their appeal, however unacknowledged, to African spiritual sensibilities. For example, African prophetic churches and pentecostal-charismatic churches, while both condemning African ritual practices such as divination, ancestor veneration, traditional medicine, and healing, paradoxically share other aspects of indigenous religious orientation, such as visions, dreams, healing, "spirit" possession, and divine revelation.

Also, as Harvey Cox revealed in a seminal essay, the independent African churches manifest various qualities of pentecostal spirituality in addition to holding their own distinct qualities: "Pentecost is everywhere in the history and theology of the African indigenous churches" (1995, 245, 250). Cox emphasizes that, in style, the African churches show the same characteristics as pentecostal churches in the rest of the world: oral theology, ritual performances, and the active role of dreams, trances, and healing in their community. Another shared characteristic is the central role of the Holy Spirit in the life of the churches. In addition to this, the obvious influence of American and European pentecostal traditions is not necessarily the cause but often rather the catalyst that sparks the indigenous Christian responses to the working of the Spirit (1995, 243–62).

I. PROPHETIC INDEPENDENT CHURCHES.

Prophetic churches, often labeled the Independent African Churches (IACs), are the largest and the most numerous of the Christian groups in Africa. They are often referred to by their local names in each country, which generally signify a central theme in their theology. In West Africa, especially in Nigeria, these churches are called Aladura (referring to prayer people); in Ghana they are called Spirit Churches, and in South Africa they are called Zionist Churches—the largest being the Zulu Zionist Church, which has thousands of members. Even though there are significant differences among these prophetic churches, in large part they all accept and practice faith healing, prophetic visions, fervent ecstatic prayer, and glossolalia. The central distinguishing element of these churches is that they take the African cosmological worldview seriously, including the reality of witchcraft, predestination, the

world of spirits and ancestors, and so on. In their liturgical practices and social ethics as well, they often combine elements of Christian tradition with indigenous African culture.

The African prophetic churches were founded by African charismatic men and women who felt themselves called by God to be prophets, to begin a new mission of prayer, healing, and prophecy among their own people. In spite of the divine call of their founders, the rise and growth of these churches, especially the older ones, took place within the context of the colonial and missionary enterprise in early-20th-century West Africa. Several of the churches were founded by evangelists, catechists, and laypersons who had been connected with the mission churches and who wanted to achieve spiritual independence from them. Often in their quest for religious independence these African church founders accused the mission churches of being unwilling to accommodate African spiritual and existential needs. As these churches attracted more and more followers, many of their leaders clashed with colonial governments, who were often nervous about the possible disruption of public peace that they believed these movements might cause. Prophet Harris of Ivory Coast, for example, was jailed by the French colonial government because of his popularity among his followers.

Of central importance in the emergence of African prophetic churches is the quest for spiritual independence. Although their founders were not so much concerned with political liberation or nationalist issues as the Ethiopian African churches that preceded them, the African Independent churches advocated for spiritual liberation from the mission churches whose "foreign" religious teachings did not encourage African indigenous spiritual heritage. No wonder some of these churches, which were quite active during the colonial era, had altercations with the colonial administrations, some with dire consequences.

A. Prophetic Charismatic Leadership.

At the center of the African prophetic churches is the role of the charismatic founders and leaders. The visions, prophecies, utterances, and actual practices of these leaders help define the identity and character of their churches and of the pentecostal African movement in general. A few examples will suffice here. The founder of the ʼCelestial Church of Christ, ʼSamuel Bileóu Oschoffa, was born in Dahomey (renamed the Republic of Benin in 1975), though his grandfather migrated from Nigeria. His polygamous father gave birth to several female children, and in dire need of a male child, he requested one from God, vowing to dedicate himself to God in the manner of Hannah (a barren woman who asked God to give her a child) in the OT. His son, Oschoffa, was born in 1901 and was given the Christian name Samuel and the African name Bileóu. Both the biblical and the African names are significant. In Yoruba culture, *Bileóu* is a name given to children who die young and are believed to be reborn on a recurring basis. Samuel, the name given to Hannah's son, signifies that she has dedicated him to the service of God. So from the beginning, Oschoffa carried the double sacred identity of biblical prophet and sacred personality in the African culture. Oschoffa was first raised in the compound of a Methodist superintendent in Porto Novo, Benin, and later by a European bishop based in Benin.

Oschoffa's prophetic career began on May 24, 1947, when, on his way to purchase planks in a village, there was a total eclipse and he heard a voice calling him to prophesy. It was in response to this visionary experience that Oschoffa started the nucleus of the Celestial Church of Christ in Porto Novo. With another prophecy calling him to "go out, the work that you are assigned is for the whole world, not for one particular place," Oschoffa moved to Lagos, where his church blossomed and rose to become the largest West African prophetic church during the 1970s.

A second example is William Wade Harris, who was born in Liberia but whose movement became quite influential in the francophone colony of Ivory Coast. Prophet Harris was born in 1865 in the Southeast Liberia village of Graway (Walker, 1979, 87). Like Oschoffa, Harris was baptized and raised as a Christian by a Methodist minister in Liberia. In spite of his local upbringing, he had a limited exposure to life outside his immediate environment when he was employed as a crewman on British ships sailing the West African coast. When he returned to Liberia, he became a lay preacher and teacher, and he also worked as a government interpreter. Harris had his first encounter with the colonial government when he was arrested for his involvement in an alleged coup plot against the government. In prison he had a revelation in a vision: the archangel Gabriel appeared to him, informing him that he had been chosen to be his prophet and to convert people to Christ. Once out of jail, Harris became an evangelist, preaching to his people. Like Oschoffa, Harris traveled from his home in Liberia to the Ivory coast, a more accepting environment, where his mission became quite

Women preparing food for Yako convention in Upper Volta (now Burkina Faso).

established. As Harris and his small group of women followers moved from place to place in Liberia and the Ivory Coast, a large crowd of people would gather around him to hear his message and to accept his baptism and anointing.

Because he did not establish a church, his converts were encouraged to join the local mission churches. The mission churches had different religious objectives, however, and this created problems for several of these followers. Harris's teachings were both religious and social. He asked for a total conversion to a new spiritual life, enjoining the believers to leave behind all vestiges of traditional religious practices. He warned of dire consequences for those who abandoned the faith. He preached against such social vices as alcoholism, laziness, and the oppression of women, including traditional practices that discriminated against women, such as enforced mourning rituals for widows and the ostracizing of menstruating women. Though he did not encourage the practice of polygamy, he advocated equal treatment of wives in polygamous homes. Harris's social and religious reforms angered the French colonial government. He was repatriated to his home in Liberia, where his converts continued to seek him out until he died.

B. Prophetic Independent Church Identity.

The prophetic movements are very loosely organized, and in the early stages of their establishment are not structured at all. Unlike the mission churches that are established according to a clearly articulated plan, the prophetic churches vary greatly in their organizational structures. Nevertheless, certain common features are discernible. Several of the churches have groups of church elders (patriarchs) and a youth brigade. The patriarchs are often responsible for spiritual and administrative matters, while the youth brigades take charge of conduct and order both within and outside the church. The sole authority of the movement, however, lies with the founders, whose utterances, instructions, and pronouncements, often backed up by revelations and visions, are considered to be divinely inspired and therefore cannot be questioned. The founders are in every sense charismatic leaders.

In spite of their spiritual independence, several of the churches continue to make use of some of the liturgical resources of the old mission churches, though they also accommodate local preferences, adapting their songs to melodies suitable for dancing, for instance. Several elements from the old missions liturgical calendar also remain: daily and weekly worship and annual festivals such as All Saints' Day, Christmas, and harvest thanksgiving (Omoyajowo, 1987; Clarke, 1978). In spite of this borrowing, the prophetic churches are in general innovative and more indigenized than were those of their mission forebears.

The most significant characteristic of the prophetic churches is faith healing. At the time of their emergence in the colonial period in West Africa, their popularity surged when, with the outbreak of influenza in the region in 1918, Western hospitals and Western medicine appeared incapable of stopping the epidemic. A prayer band formed within the old Anglican Church, led by J. B. Shadare and Sophia Odulami. They had great success in healing, using a combination of ordinary water consecrated into holy water and fervent prayer. They attracted a large number of followers, which caused them to clash with the colonial administrators. They later affiliated with the Faith Tabernacle Church in Philadelphia and became the nucleus of Christ Apostolic Church.

An important feature of Aladura prophet churches is their preoccupation with holiness. In order to maintain purity of body and soul, which is considered a precondition for the efficacy of their prayers and supplications, a number of prohibitions and taboos are maintained in places of worship and in places consecrated for prayer and healing rituals. For example, menstruating women are prohibited from entering the sanctuary of God. Couples must undergo ritual bathing after sexual intercourse before entering the church. Certain animals considered unclean, such as pigs, are prohibited. Some hills and mountains are considered holy grounds to which followers withdraw periodically for special prayer rituals such as fasting and night vigils. In some of the churches such as the Celestial Church of Christ, local streams are reserved for ritual cleansing of their members and those who seek assistance for healing. For the prophetic churches, fervent prayers carry the weight of divine power. They are compulsive rather than persuasive, as in most mission churches. The use during prayers of holy (often Hebrew) names of God and of prayer tangibles such as water and candles gives church members extra confidence that their fervent prayers will be answered. As a further mark of their holiness, a number of these churches require their members to wear a white robe in worship, which they consider the cloth of the Spirit, as distinct from ordinary clothes of the body. Such distinct attire demarcates them from those outside the sacred canopy of their churches.

One of the most distinguishing marks of prophetic independent African churches is the adaptation of African liturgical practices in their churches. As a reaction to the mission churches' foreign liturgical practices, their founders embarked on the indigenization of church worship. African ritual symbols such as water, holy oil, and palm fronds are used in worship and other ritual practices. Although in more recent times a number of churches have adopted modern musical instruments such as xylophones, bugles, and trumpets, for a long period most of these churches used African musical instruments such as drums and gongs.

The prophetic churches maintain an ambivalent relationship with African religion and culture. The churches explicitly reject African beliefs and religious practices, labeling them as pagan, though they surreptitiously employ cultural symbols from the very traditions they condemn. Some of the founders of the movements set fires on shrines during moments of evangelical fervor and employ other ritual practices from native religions. They also accept the reality of indigenous cosmology and adopt some of its approaches in healing. Forms of spirituality manifested in dreams, visions, spirit possession, and prophetic experiences are closely related to African indigenous religions. For example, the founder of the Celestial Church of Christ, Samuel Biléou Oschoffa, selectively used elements from both the African and the Christian cosmologies to establish one of the largest prophetic churches in West Africa. In his conversion stories, he drew from the events of his birth and early life, which were embedded in both traditional Yoruba and biblical worldviews in ways that provided an essential paradigm for the new church (Olupona, 1987). Celestial church members identified with these stories, cognitively appropriated the founder's experiences, and relied on the prophetic church's newly integrated paradigmatic truth as the pattern on which to reorder their worldview.

II. PENTECOSTAL-CHARISMATIC CHURCHES.

A more recent development in West African Christianity is the pentecostal-charismatic movement, whose phenomenal rise in numbers and membership has taken scholars by total surprise. Charismatic churches are evangelical churches founded by African leaders who have adopted radical spiritual conversion, often called "born again," through baptism of the Holy Spirit, recalling the Day of the Pentecost. As in the prophetic independent African churches before them, the charismatic churches emphasize speaking in tongues, divine healing, and miracles. In addition, they profess that the material success and prosperity of their members are signs of divine grace and benevolence. Unlike the founders of the prophetic African churches, who are in general semi-literate, the founders of the charismatic churches are generally well educated, most being college graduates. Indeed, the origins of several of the churches have been partly traced to the college and university student ministries of these leaders (Ojo, 1988).

One major distinction between the charismatics and the prophetic churches is that whereas the latter use prayer tangibles, the charismatics are characterized by the use of literature—tracts, magazines, and Bible commentaries. Most of these are written and published by the founders. In addition to the above, signs bearing the identity of members are exhibited. Car stickers and T-shirts, on which are inscribed important messages of the group such as "Jesus Is Lord," "Are You Saved?" and "The Blood of Jesus," adorn their homes, cars, and places of work. Members can also be seen distributing tracts to coworkers and strangers on public buses in the hope of converting them. Large cloth and paper posters with biblical passages and spiritual words can be seen on university campuses and in strategic places in the cities, announcing the place and time of worship and revival meetings. A central part of the ministry of the charismatic churches is the emphasis placed on crusades, revival meetings, and open-air preaching. Although these meetings are primarily organized by their members, thousands of Christians across denominational lines troop to revival pavilions to participate in the witnessing, healing, and miracle activities carried out by these churches.

Perhaps the most central theological position of the charismatic churches is their position on the devil (Satan) and evil spirits. There is a general assumption that the world is inhabited by satanic power that causes misfortunes for believers. Evil spirits are viewed as the major cause of life's problems and crises. Brigid Meyer, who has written on this issue, has described the concern with "the image of the devil and the imagination of evil" as a popular cultural belief found among all pentecostal churches in West Africa (1995, 237). Meyer further observed that such strong belief in the existence of evil, especially witchcraft, satanic riches, and demon belief, is not a product of "false consciousness," as scholars often theorize; neither is it a belief system derived from premodern archaic spirituality. Rather, it is constructed as real by its members and as having significant impact and consequences on their daily life (Meyer, 1995).

Like the pentecostal African churches, charismatic churches reject indigenous African religions, which they construe as harbingers of demons and evil spirits.

A. Globalization and Transnationalism.

As a reference to their international status, several of these churches use words like *global, international,* and *continental* to qualify their titles (Peil and Asare, 1994, 201). The churches share the view that African churches, which were for over a century targets of European and American missionaries, have now come of age, possessing authentic Christian spirituality, and are able to engage in a reverse mission to Western society. The churches are generally small, which facilitates the development of a sense of community. Paradoxically, the spread of the African churches overseas is taking place at a time when American evangelical churches are also making unprecedented inroads into Africa. Indeed, the writings of some European and American evangelicals and charismatics such as Billy Graham, T. L. Osborn, Oral Roberts, and Robert Schuller are valuable resources the African charismatic churches tap into for their own growth and development. It is too soon to determine whether the African churches are lured to Europe and the U.S. by the prosperity gospel preached by some of the American fundamentalist churches in Africa, or whether they are simply moving independently to evangelize Europeans and Americans, as they generally claim. We know that there is a flow of economic resources from the more affluent Western societies to the mother churches in Africa. Paradoxically, unlike the

mission churches before them, for whom overseas headquarters meant a drain on local resources, the pentecostal churches benefit from their outpost stations, which send money to their mother church in West Africa. Whichever way it goes, Hexham and Poewe caution against overemphasizing the foreign (and especially the American) influence on African charismatics (1994, 59). Certainly the exportation of charismatics from Africa to Europe and America is an indication that the movement is a two-way street.

B. The Nature of the Pentecostal-Charismatic Movement.

What is the nature of the pentecostal-charismatic movement, and what are its distinguishing features? A major problem for scholars doing research on the pentecostal-charismatic movement in Africa is the lack of reliable statistics to document assertions in the literature and the press that it is the fastest-growing church in West Africa. This is partly due to inadequate census figures, which in particular neglect religious affiliation. Judging from the number of pentecostal buildings and the large number of people who come to pentecostal assemblies, it is probably true that the pentecostals are the fastest-growing movement in West Africa. Nevertheless, the old prophetic churches are also quite popular and are still growing. Some, such as Christ Apostolic Church and Cherubim and Seraphim, have spawned numerous splinter groups, some of which have adopted the style and organizational skills of the charismatic churches.

The origin of the charismatic movement has generally been placed in the 1970s, a decade after the period when most African countries obtained independence from the colonial government. The charismatics are not in any way unified in their beliefs, practices, and identity, but they manifest certain traits and features that are commonly seen in the entire West African region. My examples are drawn from the charismatic movement in the two major countries where they have large followings, Nigeria and Ghana, although references will also be made to other parts of Africa.

The origin of the charismatic movement in West Africa is very complex, and no single theory explains its rise and growth. We can locate the beginning of the charismatics in the contemporary West African region from within and outside the continent. Both factors combine to give the charismatic movement its legal tone and identity. One key element in the origin of several of the groups were college and university student ministries in the 1970s (Ojo, 1988)—the Student Christian Movement, Scripture Union, and Campus Christian Fellowship are notable examples. As some of the leaders of the groups graduated from college, they formed house prayer groups, ministering to youth and adults alike. Some of these house churches expanded into full-time ministries in urban centers. The Deeper Christian Life ministry of William F. Kumuyi typifies this form of charismatic group in Nigeria.

A few of the charismatic groups have their origins in foreign countries, especially the U.S. They were established as national branches of international religious groups, but they very quickly assumed the identity of their respective countries. A classic example is the Full Gospel Business Men's Fellowship International. Others, on the other hand, originating in Africa, very quickly established linkages with overseas countries. They also spread their evangelical activities to the entire West African region by recruiting new converts, training a selected group of followers in evangelical methods, and sending them out as disciples to other nations and places. The late Archbishop Benson Idahosa, by far the most successful pentecostal preacher in Africa, typified this approach. Shortly after its beginning, Idahosa's Church of God Mission International spread to other West African countries. Some of the disciples he trained and ordained form the nucleus of a group of charismatic speakers active in places like Ghana and Ivory Coast. Nicholas Duncan Williams of the Christian Action Faith Ministry International and Charles Agyin Asare of the World Miracle Bible Church in Tamale, Ghana, are Idahosa's protégés and successful charismatic leaders (Gifford, 1994).

In the early period, one of the major traits of West African charismatics was a concern for holiness that presented a radical challenge to the established churches—especially the Roman Catholic and the Anglican churches—about perceived attitudes toward Christian spirituality. I mention this because some of the scholarship on the pentecostals understates the evangelical profile of the mainline churches and portrays a lack of historical understanding of the Christian history in the region. Scholars who affirm that the mission churches totally lacked prophetic and pentecostal spirit demonstrate a lack of understanding of events during this period. Undoubtedly, evangelism was very limited. Like Sufism in Islam, it was seen as something reserved for the most pious and committed Christians. Besides, the tenor of the liturgy and the spiritual practice, which the church inherited from mother churches in Europe and America, speaks against emotional, high-pitched spirituality. A good example from my own upbringing in the Anglican mission house would illustrate this. A popular evangelical Yoruba (Nigeria) lyric we all learned for morning prayers in the 1960s says, "Say openly to the unbeliever that Jesus is the Lord and King; Tell them [unbelievers] in a gentle voice that Jesus is Lord and King; The Devil is at work, yet the gospel grows in abundance. Herald the victory of Jesus Christ." While this popular folk song will fit perfectly well into the modern-day charismatic hymnals, the third stanza clearly shows that the established churches prefer the "gentle voice" to the shouting of the charismatic; the song lacks the aggressive, high-pitched tone of contemporary charismatic lyrics. Some of the founders of the pentecostals were once staunch members of the mainline churches and the independent African churches.

What the new movement represents, as David Lehmann has remarked, is "more brazen, more of an affront to the established ways of being Christian" (Lehmann, 1996, 122).

C. Charismatic Christian Identity.

Perhaps the most fundamental claim of the charismatics is that they have experienced a renewed life in Christ and have been born again. The charismatics are very exclusivistic and regard Christians outside their churches as nominal Christians for whom Christian living is far from being a way of life. It is in this context that I have labeled the church the Christian *umma* in the manner of Islam (Olupona, 1997). By presenting a life of holiness, members of the charismatics distinguish themselves from other Christians, noncharismatics, for example. Pastor Kumuyi of the Deeper Life prescribed the day-to-day lifestyle of its members, including what to wear and style of hairdo. In its early days, any form of luxury, such as watching television, was forbidden (Ojo, 1988). But as Ojo clearly shows, such legalistic proscription and exclusivism, which stem from the thinking of the Deeper Life's Apostolic Faith background, faced serious objections from other evangelical groups and has threatened the viability of the Deeper Life itself (Ojo, 1988).

The liturgical practice and worship mode of the charismatics are major identity markers. Unlike the relatively quiet services of the mainline churches, the charismatics' worship services are characterized by "raising a loud shout to God in praise" (see Ps. 95). Christian lyrics and songs, with instrumental accompaniment provided by accordions, brass bands, guitars, and trumpets are used in most churches. Whereas written doctrine (articles of faith) plays a significant role in the order and ritual practices of the mainline churches, charismatics such as the African prophetic churches depend mainly on the oral theology, sayings, deeds, and instructions of their founders. These utterances become paradigmatic sources for the core activities of the movements. As such, prophecy, dreams, visions, and Holy Spirit–possession play central roles in their theology and worship activities. The impact of this on faith and practice is enormous.

For example, several years ago my late father, an Anglican archdeacon, faced a serious crisis that pitted his Anglican intellectualist approach against the emotional and popular stance of a few charismatics in his congregation. A popular woman and church member who had just died was accused of witchcraft by several people in the church, and they asked the priest (my father) not to bury her body in the church cemetery or even to bring her body into the church for the funeral service. Seriously objecting to this proposal, my father brought out his Anglican prayer book to read to the young charismatics the passage that stipulates the ordinance of burial. He pointed out to these young men that only suicides are forbidden from Anglican Christian burial and that the Anglican prayer book does not mention witchcraft. Besides, he argued, the children of the deceased woman, who were highly placed in Lagos, could sue the church if their mother was denied a proper burial in a church where she was an active member for several years. This particular episode rocked the local Anglican church to its very foundation. The young men were not convinced by either argument. What was of interest to me was the comment of one of the young men that the pentecostal churches would not bury witches in their church cemeteries. The statement indicates that there is a great divide between mainline churches and pentecostal and charismatic churches. The latter recognizes the reality of African cosmology and belief systems, while the former denies it and prefers the European secular mind-set.

D. Charismatic Theology.

Essential to charismatic theology are three aspects of charismatic belief and practices—demons, healing, and glossolalia.

The most emphasized aspect of charismatic theology is belief in the existence of demons and evil spirits in society and the world at large. Belief in demons covers a wide range of cultural beliefs and activities and social ills: witchcraft, mediums, divination, sorcery, secret societies, ancestor veneration, even traditional healing methods and apparatus. Fringe religious traditions such as the Amorc and the Hare Krishna are also included. Anything essential to traditional religion is considered demonic by the charismatics. Personal and communal crises are blamed on demons. Demons are the cause of illnesses, misfortune such as childlessness, bad harvests, and even political oppression. A charismatic leader recently characterized Nigeria's military dictatorship as the work of the devil.

The pervasive presence of demons in the pentecostal and charismatic movement is captured by David Lehmann (1996, 139), who observed that "the Devil's presence is doctrinal, practical and ritual." In the West African context, it is doctrinal in that it is an unwritten article of faith "to proclaim the power of Jesus to liberate individuals from the power of the devil and from possession by the devil." Second, because the devil is ever-present and constitutes a "permanent presence or threat . . . in individuals' lives and indeed in their bodies," members are regularly enjoined to be on guard. Third, regular prayer rituals of expulsion of devils take place (Lehmann, 1996, 139).

As a result of the pervasive belief in demons, substantial time and space are devoted to the exorcising of the disturbing spirits. Casting out demons is normally the climax of revival meetings, open-air services, and private prayer meetings.

A linkage exists between the pentecostal understanding of demons and the social construction of evil in special places. In a recent essay, Paul Gifford remarked that when he asked a number of Ghanaian charismatics how their concept of demons differs from that of the Nigerian charismatics, they responded that they considered Nigerians' account of demonic powers to be too exaggerated, "frightening," bizarre, and possibly untrue (Gifford, 1994, 255). This view is supported by Peil and Opoku's study that in Ghana, witchcraft and other forms of mystical principles and power are not commonly emphasized in sermons (Peil and Opoku, 1994). Given the fact that the main source for charismatics' imagination and construction of the demons is indigenous religions, it is not surprising that the Nigerians' charismatic imagination of demons is in direct proportion to the country's social ills.

Healing is at the core of the charismatic ministry. Most churches emphasize a holistic attitude toward healing, encompassing spiritual, physical, and emotional healing. The charismatic understanding of healing is quite wide, and so are the programs of action put in place to carry them out. As with other aspects of their theology, there is no coherent idea about healing in charismatic churches; it is conceived primarily as a gift of the Holy Spirit, in principle not limited to the pastor but rather a gift that every born-again Christian can have. In practice, however, it is mainly the prerogative of the leader and those with special spiritual gifts to practice the ritual of anointing and laying on of hands that normally precedes healing. Certain days of the week are devoted to special healing sessions in which the congregation gathers and fervent prayers are offered for healing. The "corporate" style of the healing ministry has been suggested as a positive element in the charismatic movement's approach to healing (Richards, 1984). Interestingly, one of the criticisms of the Western approach to healing has been its individualism and emphasis on a personal approach, in contrast to the African traditional method, which is hailed as corporate-, group-, and community-based (Appiah-Kubi, 1981). Because of the emphasis the church places on healing, charismatic revival meetings are always large, because healing and exorcism are often included. Several of the posters and radio-television announcements of such gatherings promise deliverance and miracles. A large number of those who come to the revival pavilions (variously called miracle centers, healing centers, or Daniel's courtyard) are people with various infirmities and disabilities.

A third commonly observed phenomenon, glossolalia, is the most visible sign of divine possession in charismatic churches. Most churches rely on Acts 2 to defend the practice of glossolalia, although this biblical passage is given different interpretations. In West Africa it is viewed variously as a form of Holy Spirit possession or as prophetic utterances, signs of divine revelation, and a divine gift from God. Not all charismatic churches encourage its use in worship, although none normally condemn it when it occurs.

E. Literature and Pastoral Training.

The most important source of authority for the charismatic movement is the Bible. Regarded as a divine revelation, the Bible is understood literally, and members quote from it repeatedly to support their practices and belief. Although the New Testament is more commonly used than the Old Testament, many references are made to the latter, especially to the inspirational words in the book of Psalms. As the most authoritative source of their theology, biblical stories provide the paradigmatic pattern for beliefs, conduct, and practices. Members are encouraged to read the Bible regularly, to bring their Bibles to church, and to follow the reading of the cited texts along with the minister. At times the minister himself calls on members to read aloud passages selected by him during sermons. During smaller gatherings such as house prayer meetings, Bible study meetings, and counseling sessions, Bible reading forms part of the program.

It is not uncommon for a church to invite guest preachers, usually from fellow charismatic ministries in other parts of the country. Members look forward to such visits, especially when the visitor is famous for his or her ecstatic sermons. But it is in biblical interpretation and contexualization that the charismatic leaders are most creative. They relate their texts to religious, political, and economic situations in African culture and society, often telling tales of mystical supernatural beings in African society only to condemn them. Indigenous mythological and fictitious characters prominently occur in sermons. Tales of witchcraft and sorcery are common; corruption in high places, especially in oil-rich but poverty-ridden Nigeria, abounds. Such tales are punctuated with exclamations like "Shout Allelujah," or "The Bible says," to which the congregation responds in thunderous tones. Charismatic preachers seize every opportunity to connect major political events with biblical passages. In Nigeria, for example, the sudden death of a military dictator prompted comparisons with the death of the biblical pharaoh, who held the Israelites in bondage until he perished with his soldiers in the Red Sea. Seeing the hand of God in Nigerian history, one of the charismatic leaders warned the military leadership that only democratic freedom for Nigeria would save the military from divine judgment.

To enhance the quality of ministerial work of the church, the charismatic centers encourage proper training of people aspiring to be ministers. It is not sufficient to rely on a divine calling, though a sizable number of charismatics consider that essential; training must be provided in evangelism and theology (Peil and Opoku, 1994). Biblical schools have sprung up all over West Africa to train the new generation of preachers and to gain respectability for their churches paralleling that of mainline churches with established theological seminaries. The aim of charismatic Bible colleges is not to produce theologians but to train new ministers in evangelism. Some of the larger training schools for the aspiring clergy are jointly owned by a number of churches. For example, the Church of the Pentecost Bible Training Center serves pentecostal church branches in West Africa, while the Good News Training Institute is sponsored by the Pentecostal Association of Ghana and the Lutheran Church (ibid.). A diverse curriculum is encouraged in several of the charismatic seminaries. Courses such as pastoral counseling, biblical studies, preaching, evangelism, finance, Islam, world religions, and African traditional religion provide well-rounded training.

Charismatic churches distribute an abundance of literature, most of which is written and published by the ministries. These pamphlets are the major sources for the beliefs and practices of the church. Rev. Kumuyi of the Deeper Life has written on various themes such as the Holy Spirit, demons, and Christian marriage, presenting his church's doctrine and interpretation of the Bible. The abundance of pamphlets reflects the higher literacy rate among the members of the charismatic churches than is common in the prophetic African churches. Such publications also allow the church to maintain a high profile in a society where book knowledge is highly esteemed. Other publications, such as weekly or monthly magazines and pamphlets, cover topics such as prayer readings, marriage counseling, health and wellness, witchcraft, infidelity, and how to keep a Christian home.

F. The Charismatic Movement and Modernity.

One of the appeals of the charismatic movement is its ability to respond to the existential and pragmatic needs faced by modern, urban congregations, including domestic and economic problems. In addition to healing the soul, these ministries promise to heal the body. Various outreach programs, such as prison and hospital ministries, counseling for women, welfare programs, and child ministry are organized (Gifford, 1994, 243). Lauren MacLean recently tried to explain the neocharismatic churches' emergence in Ghana in the 1980s as a "reconfiguration of the moral economy" of the traditional society. That is, in response to the economic crisis in Ghana, the charismatic churches "extend a community to its members," and this helps to alleviate their material needs during the crisis period (MacLean, 1997).

Undoubtedly, charismatic churches reformulate traditional values of communal aid and self-help, especially with the World Bank's structural adjustment policy, which has created economic woes and further lowered the living standard of the ordinary people. It is argued that this situation has intensified the phenomenal rise in the membership of the churches in the last twenty years or so, although the problems associated with urbanism undoubtedly play a large role as well. With the migration of a large number of people from rural to urban areas, the new urbanites are more ethnically heterogeneous and better educated than the urban dwellers in the post-independent period. The charismatic churches appeal to the new urban dwellers, especially those whom ethnically oriented prophetic African churches cannot accommodate. The ethos of the charismatic movements, especially their emphasis on individuality, high achievement, individual success, and prosperity, has great appeal for the new urbanites. Because of this new appeal, the influence of African prophetic and charismatic churches has increased dramatically as they have spread to other regions of the globe. Not only have they crossed their national boundaries to establish branches in other parts of West Africa; in the last ten years a large number of them have appeared in Europe, Asia, and America, ministering to Africa's immigrant populations in those regions.

G. Charismatic Churches and Civil Society.

One of the major concerns of the charismatic churches in the last few years is their role in the public sphere. The attitude of the charismatic churches to political development is very vague; they manifest both functional and dysfunctional characteristics, depending on circumstances and situations. Some of the churches have been largely docile and have occasionally become tools in the hands of states that value their involvement because of their sheer numerical strength. In such cases, they have unpretentiously played active roles in supporting governments considered tyrannical and even illegitimate. For example, in Ghana, the largest of the charismatic churches, the Christian Faith Ministries International of Nicholas Duncan Williams, plays an active role in state-sponsored religious functions. On the occasion of the National Thanksgiving Service marking the anniversary of the beginning of the Republic, Duncan Williams was one of the key clergymen invited by the president, Jerry Rawlings (Gilford, 1994, 242), even when some of the mainline churches have chosen not to support this state-sponsored church service. On the other hand, pentecostal churches have increasingly been critical of the Nigerian state for its failure to institutionalize a democratic civic and moral order that would lead to a healthy nation. The Nigerian state's tendency is to favor Islam. The state's desire to make Islam an official religion is evidenced by the state's recommendation that the nation adopt the *Sharia* (Muslim judicial system) as part of the nation's judicial process, thereby surreptitiously taking Nigeria into the Organization of the Islamic Conference. This, in part, led to the formation of the Christian Association of Nigeria, an umbrella ecumenical association of Nigerian churches, whose goal is to counter what is perceived as the government's plan to Islamize Nigeria. The charismatic church plays a significant role in the formation and maintenance of this body.

A recent development in the role of the charismatic churches in civil society is the attempt some are making to play a key role in nation building, especially in spheres where the state has been very negligent in promoting good governance and citizenship. This is the sphere where religious "fundamentalist" groups have been most active in several societies. A recent example in Nigeria is the decision of the Living Water Unlimited Church in Lagos to posthumously reward dead policemen who were victims of the Maitasine riot in a Lagos suburb on May 28, 1998. Maitasine is a millenarian Islamic fundamentalist who has been provoking civil strife in the last ten years in Nigeria. Neither the Nigerian army nor the police have succeeded in solving this ongoing crisis. When the group struck on May 28, they left more than 20 people dead, and properties worth millions of naira were destroyed. The decision of the church to give a "posthumous award for selfless service" to the police victims of the riot came as a welcome surprise to a number of people.

To justify the necessity of such an award, which he claimed would be presented to the families of the dead policemen on the last day of the church's four-day crusade, the leader of the Living Water Unlimited Church, Pastor Ladi Thompson, said that the award was in response to the call of the Nigerian head of state, General Abubakar, "for all to cooperate towards charting a new direction for the country." The church leader took the occasion to ascertain that "the contemptuous attitude of greed in many Nigerians will be curbed or wiped out if people know that their honest services will not only be appreciated but also rewarded" (*Post Express Wired,* Jul. 12, 1998).

This episode has many ramifications. First, it indicates the role of charismatic churches in a new arena: social ethics. It also shows their desire to step into the vacuum of the promotion of patriotism, which the government has totally neglected. And it is an indirect indictment of the state, whose poor attitude toward the spirit of patriotism and selfless service has led to low morale among voluntary agencies and the police force. Finally, it underlies the unique power of the charismatic church to carve a new niche for itself and create a new vision for public service unmatched by other religious bodies.

III. PROPHETIC AND CHARISMATIC CHURCHES AND GENDER.

The role of women in the prophetic and pentecostal churches in Africa has aroused some debate and scholarly discussion (Jules-Rosette, 1979; Walker, 1979). The scholarly debate is focused mainly between those who argue that women are highly marginalized in the prophetic and pentecostal churches and those who argue the contrary. The latter argue that these churches provide a significant avenue for women's empowerment, as well as room to play a major role in a religious capacity, a role they are denied in the mission churches.

This is one of the most critical issues in the profile of the prophetic and charismatic movements in West Africa, not only because women constitute a large majority of its membership, but also because a number of churches were established by women. Evangelist Bola Are of the Christ Apostolic Church; Bola Odeleke, the founder of Power Pentecost

Church; and Prophet Ogunranti, the founder of the Christ Apostolic Church, Bethel, are notable examples in southwestern Nigeria.

Prophetic and pentecostal churches normally support strict gender separation, and they acknowledge gender differences. The ideal role for women, as professed by the churches, is to serve as wives and mothers in their communities. Yet the churches maintain that women have specific roles to play in the movement as prophets, visionaries, and ceremonial leaders.

Two of the churches that splintered from the Prophet Harris Movement were begun by women: The Deima Church of Marie Lalou, Ivory Coast, and the Church of the Twelve Apostles in southwestern Ghana, begun by Grace Thannie (Walker, 1979, 87). Also, one of the largest Aladura churches in West Africa, the Cherubim and Seraphim, was started partly through divine revelation received by a female prophet, Abidun Emmanuel, who indeed became the head of the worldwide movement in spite of the opposition of the male members. The lives and ministries of these remarkable women and church founders are quite fascinating. Several of them were propelled into their new careers after receiving divine revelations in the form of dreams and visions. In their prophecy, they addressed broadly based social concerns, especially the conditions of women in their churches. They also did much to alleviate the sufferings of women, decreeing changes in the social and cultural conditions that cause women's low status and power, such as polygamy, levirate marriage, and widowhood.

In general, women are excluded from political leadership and decision-making processes in the predominantly malefounded churches. The assigned roles may not be different from the roles women play in traditional societies, where women's spiritual power is recognized as vital to the existence of the group.

Jules-Rosette has underscored the importance of the role of women in an interactive power context (1979, 128). By this she means women's ceremonial leadership role in nonpolitical spheres, where they serve as healers, mediums, and musicians (women formulate and lead songs in church services). But in spite of the denial of political leadership roles, women, nevertheless, in ritual context, surreptitiously express their displeasure at males' wrongdoing (Jules-Rosette, 1979, 130). Rituals constitute a powerful domain for cultural resistance in pentecostal and prophetic churches in African societies.

Another form of gender separation is evolving in pentecostal-charismatic movements: women-only churches, formed to evangelize only women and to minister purely to women's needs. A good example is the Nigerian Jesus Women Prayer and Ministry, founded by evangelist Eunice Osagiede in Benin City, Nigeria. Their motto, "We Have Seen Jesus" (John 20:25), indicates that Jesus women, as members are called, can have direct access to Christ without men as intermediaries.

IV. CONCLUSION.

This essay has outlined many features of the prophetic and pentecostal-charismatic churches. Although we lack reliable statistics to be able to determine the percentage of their members in the West African region, and it is difficult to determine the percentage of mainline churches that have assumed charismatic characteristics, prophetic and pentecostal-charismatic churches are emerging in contemporary Africa. Undoubtedly, the 21st century will be an exciting period in the history of these churches and in African Christianity in general.

■ **Bibliography:** J. K. Agbeti, *West African Church History* (1986) ■ J. A. Ajayi, *Christian Missions in Nigeria 1841–1891: The Making of a New Elite* (1965) ■ K. Appiah-Kubi, *Man Cures, God Heals: Religion and Medical Practice among the Akan of Ghana* (1981) ■ M. Assimeng, *Saints and Social Structures* (1986) ■ E. Ayandele, *The Missionary Impact on Modern Nigeria, 1842–1914: A Political and Social Analysis* (1966) ■ P. B. Clarke, *West Africa and Christianity* (1986) ■ H. Cox, *Fire from Heaven: The Rise of Pentecostal Spirituality and the Reshaping of Religion in the Twenty-First Century* (1995) ■ D. H. Crumbley, "Impurity and Power: Women in Aladura Church," *Africa* 62 (4, 1992) ■ R. T. Curley, "Dreams of Power: Social Process in a West African Religious Movement," *Africa* 53 (3, 1988) ■ F. Ekechi, *Missionary Enterprise and Rivalry in Ipboland, 1857–1914* (1972) ■ P. Gifford, "'Africa Shall Be Saved': An Appraisal of Reinhard Bonnke's Pan-African Crusade," *Journal of Religion in Africa* 17 (1, 1987) ■ idem, "Ghana's Charismatic Churches," *Journal of Religion in Africa* 24 (3, 1994) ■ R. I. J. Hackett, ed., *New Religious Movements in Nigeria* (1987) ■ G. M. Haliburton, *The Prophet Harris: A Study of an African Prophet and His Mass Movement in the Ivory Coast and the Gold Coast, 1913–1915.* (1973) ■ H. Harold, *African Independent Church: The Life and Faith of the Church of the Lord* [Aladura] (1967) ■ idem, *History of an African Independent Church*, vols. 1 and 2 (1967) ■ I. Hexham and K. Poewe, "Charismatic Churches in South Africa: A Critique of Criticisms and Problems of Bias," in *Charismatic Christianity as a Global Culture*, ed. K. Poewe (1994) ■ B. Jules-Rosette, ed., *The New Religions of Africa* (1979) ■ O. A. Kalu, *The History of Christianity in West Africa* (1980) ■ D. Lehmann, *Struggle for the Spirit: Religious Transformation and Popular Culture in Brazil and Latin America* (1996) ■ L. M. MacLean, "The Moral Economy of the Urban Middle Class: The Rise of Charismatic Churches in Ghana Since the 1980s" (African Traditional Religions seminar paper, U. of California–Davis, 1997) ■ R. Marshall, "Power in the Name of Jesus," *Review of African Political Economy* 52 (1991) ■ B. Meyer, "Delivered from the Powers of Darkness: Confessions of Satanic Riches in Christian Ghana," *Africa* 65 (2, 1995) ■ idem, "If You Are a Devil, You Are a Witch and If You Are a Witch, You Are a Devil: The Integration of 'Pagan' Ideas into the Conceptual Universe of

Ewe Christians in Southeastern Ghana," *Journal of Religion in Africa* 22 (2, 1992) ▌ M. A. Ojo, " The Contextual Significance of the Charismatic Movements in Independent Nigeria," *Africa* 58 (2, 1988) ▌ idem, "Deeper Christian Life Ministry: A Case Study of the Charismatic Movements in Western Nigeria," *Journal of Religion in Africa* 18 (2, 1988) ▌ J. K. Olupona, "The Celestial Churches in Ondo: A Phenomenological Perspective," in *New Religious Movements in Nigeria*, ed. R. I. J. Hackett (1987) ▌ idem, "Prophetic Movements: Western Africa," in *The Encyclopedia of Africa South of the Sahara*, ed. John Middleton (1997) ▌ J. A. Omoyajowo, *Cherubim and Seraphim* (1987) ▌ J. D. Y. Peel, *Aladura: A Religious Movement among the Yoruba* (1968) ▌ M. Peil with K. A. Opoku, "The Development and Practice of Religion in an Accra Suburb." *Journal of Religion in Africa* 24 (3, 1994) ▌ K. Poewe, ed., *Charismatic Christianity as a Global Culture* (1994) ▌ L. Sanneh, *West African Christianity: The Religious Impact* (1983) ▌ N. R. Toulis, *Believing Identity: Pentecostalism and the Mediation of Jamaican Ethnicity and Gender in England* (1997) ▌ S. S. Walker, "Women in the Harris Movement," in *The New Religions of Africa*, ed. B. Jules-Rosette (1979) ▌ J. B. Webster, *The African Churches among the Yoruba 1888–1922* (1964) ▌ R. S. Wyllie, *Spiritism in Ghana: A Study of New Religious Movements* (1990).   ▌ J. K. OLUPONA

ALBANIA

▪ Pentecostals 2,868 (3%)   ▪ Charismatics 40,946 (41%)   ▪ Neocharismatics 56,186 (56%)   ▪ Total Renewal: 100,000

ALGERIA

▪ Pentecostals 0 (0%)   ▪ Charismatics 1,736 (3%)   ▪ Neocharismatics 53,264 (97%)   ▪ Total Renewal: 55,000

See AFRICA, NORTH, AND THE MIDDLE EAST.

AMERICAN SAMOA

▪ Pentecostals 3,570 (36%)   ▪ Charismatics 5,527 (56%)   ▪ Neocharismatics 803 (8%)   ▪ Total Renewal: 9,900

ANDORRA

▪ Pentecostals 0 (0%)   ▪ Charismatics 758 (90%)   ▪ Neocharismatics 82 (10%)   ▪ Total Renewal: 840

ANGOLA

▪ Pentecostals 414,526 (20%)   ▪ Charismatics 783,776 (38%)   ▪ Neocharismatics 846,698 (41%)   ▪ Total Renewal: 2,045,000

For a general introduction to Central Africa and bibliography, see AFRICA, CENTRAL.

The first pentecostal missionaries to work in Angola were ►Edmond and Pearl Mabel Stark from the Church of God (CG, Cleveland, TN), who arrived from the U.S. in Angola in May 1938 to commence the Pentecostal Mission. After nine months Edmond died as the result of malaria, but not before winning the first convert, a man called Bembua; Pearl went home to the U.S. in Sept. 1939, and Bembua died in 1941. WWII was on, and it was not possible for the CG to send anyone to Angola.

After the war the Angolan authorities made it very difficult for anyone to enter the colony. A new missionary party from the CG who requested admission to Portugal to learn the language were denied entry. (Angola was a Portuguese colony until 1951, and a Portuguese overseas province until 1975, when it gained independence.) Eventually the CG agreed to send Pearl Stark back to Angola on her own; she arrived in Feb. 1948. She was not allowed to start a mission, so she worked alongside Brethren missionaries of the Chitau mission in Andula Bié for about a year. The problem was that in 1940 Portugal had signed a concordat with the Vatican, according to which all Portuguese colonies became the monopoly of the Roman Catholic Church. All Protestants came under increasing pressure in an effort to oust them from Angola (the same was true in Mozambique).

In 1949 Pearl Stark moved to the coast at Benguela and after a few months was joined by Joaquim Antonio Cartaxo Martins and his family from the Assemblies of God (AG) in Portugal. Because Martins was Portuguese, he obtained legal permission in 1952 to do missionary work under an organization he registered as Missão Evangélica de Vista Alegre (Evangelical Mission of Vista Alegre). Vista Alegre was the name of the place where they had settled. From this base the missionaries branched out as far as they were permitted under the legal restrictions placed on them as Protestants. As a result, many were converted and baptized.

During Stark's furlough, T. D. Mooneyham went to Angola under the CG but was only able to obtain a visitor's visa of limited duration. At the same time, Martins' elder brother, Manuel, joined them to help in the school that had been established. While Joaquim and Stark were out of the country, the authorities, at the urging of the Roman Catholic Church, rescinded the permit the mission had originally been granted. When Joaquim and Stark eventually did return, severe restrictions were placed on their activities. In spite of this, the work grew so much that there were more than 50 localities where there were preaching points and churches. This growth so riled the Catholics that by 1957 they ordered the closure of Vista Alegre and told the Martins brothers that they were no longer allowed to perform any missionary activities at all. It is estimated that at that time there were at least 80 regular preaching places and over 5,000 regular adherents in the pentecostal churches that had sprung up. The AG–Portugal was asked for help with the work and became responsible for its consolidation. The Portuguese believed that the evangelicals were a cover for the independence movements. During the 1960s, the young church forged ahead despite the lack of trained leadership and the persecution and even martyrdom of many believers. This was the foundation for the pentecostal churches that later came into existence. In 1970–4, the final years of the colonial government, several Portuguese missionaries from the AG were in Angola. They all withdrew before or at independence in 1975.

The pentecostal group founded by the Starks (CG) and the Portuguese AG was named the Assembleia de Deus Pentecostal de Angola (ADPA, Pentecostal Assembly of God of Angola); it claims over 700,000 adherents (although even one of their own missionaries believes this number is somewhat inflated) and is represented in all 18 provinces of the country. Its main strength is in Kwanza Sul Province (between Luanda and Lobito), where Pearl Stark began. A large AG church can be found in every village in this province. In the town of Gabela, where Stark lived for some time and where Portuguese missionary Reganho Pereira worked, there are 20,000 adult members in the many congregations of the town.

In 1983 the ADPA invited Billy Burr and Morris Williams, representatives of the AG–U.S. Missions Department, to establish a Bible college on the outskirts of Luanda at Kicolo. A campus was constructed, and the Gordon S. Bialiks were the first resident AG–U.S. missionaries to move to Angola in July 1986. They were joined by Bill and Dickie Riley, who are still in Luanda and teach at the Bible college; they are the only AG–U.S. missionaries resident in Angola at present, although three families from the Brazilian AG are working in Angola. The first national general superintendent of the ADPA was Carlos Prado; the present general superintendent is Fernando Panzo. Most ADPA churches are organized so that each central church is responsible for from 24 to 36 daughter congregations. In Luanda alone there are 13 central churches with from 100 to 150 congregations. They do not operate on the cell principle, but house groups are used to plant new churches in unevangelized areas.

During the years of persecution, both prior to independence and during the Civil War, the church grew. Divisions in the ADPA gave birth to the Igreja Evangélica Pentecostal de Angola (IEPA, Evangelical Pentecostal Church of Angola) with 20,000-plus adherents, and the Missão Evangélica Pentecostal de Angola (MEPA, Evangelical Pentecostal Mission of Angola). The war, which lasted for more than 30 years in this country, led to great spiritual hunger. People pack into churches of all denominations throughout the country. The pentecostal movement has grown by leaps and bounds without very much outside help. Pentecostals from Congo/Kinshasa have also been involved in evangelizing in Angola. Missionaries may have been among the first to plant the pentecostal church in this country, but it is not a missionary church. Conditions have been such that the very few expatriate missionaries were not able to greatly influence the flavor and direction of what was happening in the churches. The result has to be attributed to the moving of the Holy Spirit and the participation of the Angolans who have evangelized and planted the majority of churches. The many thousands of unknown believers are the unsung heroes of what we find in the Angolan pentecostal churches today.

■ D. J. GARRARD

ANGUILLA

■ Pentecostals 0 (0%) ■ Charismatics 1,040 (100%) ■ Neocharismatics 0 (0%) ■ Total Renewal: 1,040

See CARIBBEAN ISLANDS.

ANTIGUA

■ Pentecostals 2,249 (27%)   ■ Charismatics 5,280 (63%)   ■ Neocharismatics 891 (11%)   ■ Total Renewal: 8,420

See CARIBBEAN ISLANDS.

ARGENTINA

■ Pentecostals 1,612,606 (19%)   ■ Charismatics 4,763,302 (57%)   ■ Neocharismatics 2,024,092 (24%)
■ Total Renewal: 8,400,000

1. The Beginnings of Pentecostalism in Argentina.

The earliest pentecostal missions to Argentina came from Norway and Canada. Berger Johnson of Norway and Alice Wood, a Canadian Methodist Holiness woman, arrived in Argentina in early 1909. Wood had joined the Christian and Missionary Alliance (CMA) and served as an independent Holiness missionary in Venezuela with G. Bially. The cooperation between Wood and Johnson ended when he came out against the involvement of women in ministry. In 1914 she united with the Assemblies of God (AG) and eventually took over (1917) leadership of an already existing independent pentecostal congregation that she pastored until her return to North America just before her death in 1951. Through letters from ►Willis Hoover published in the Norwegian pentecostal periodical edited by ►T. B. Barratt, *Korsets Seier,* Johnson made contact with the Chilean pentecostal church. Unlike Methodists in Chile, Argentine Methodists were more English and North American in orientation and more ethnically isolated. Therefore, there was no split in the Methodist church of Argentina. Johnson, having read about the pentecostal revival in Chile, wrote to Hoover asking about the availability of Spanish-language pentecostal literature. Hoover commented, "Do you see how we get bound up together with each other?" Italian pentecostal missionaries, Luis Francesconi, Giácomo Lombardi, and Lucía Menna, arrived in Argentina on Oct. 9, 1909, to found the Iglesia Asamblea Cristiana. Danish pentecostal missionaries arrived in 1913, followed by Norwegian pentecostal missionaries. Swedish pentecostal missionaries began work in Argentina in 1920. Other ethnically based pentecostal denominations were established among the immigrants from Bulgaria, Poland, Russia, and the Ukraine.

In 1917 North American missionaries F. L. Ryder and Lucy Leatherman began evangelistic efforts in Argentina under the auspices of the Church of God (CG, Cleveland, TN). However, when they returned to the U.S. in 1923, they left no organized congregations behind. This changed when an Italian immigrant, Marcus Mazzucco, was converted and began a church in his home. In 1928 he associated his congregation with the mission of the Swedish pentecostal churches (Svenska Fria Mission). A church building was constructed (1936), but in 1940 he separated from the Swedish pentecostal mission to establish the Iglesia Evangélica Pentecostal.

In the mid 1940s, during a visit of CG mission theorist and diplomat ►J. H. Ingram to Buenos Aires, Mazzucco led his denomination into affiliation with that denomination. By 1960 the mother church of the denomination had more than 3,000 members. Mission by this denomination into the hinterlands of Argentina led to contact with a Mennonite mission to the Toba, a native tribe. The Toba had experienced contacts with pentecostalism as early as 1935. Other sources give credit to Juan Richard Lagar of the Iglesia Evangélica Pentecostal, who in 1946 enabled the conversion of 3,800 Toba to pentecostalism in one day. A pentecostal revival broke out among them in 1962, resulting in the majority of the tribe forming the Iglesia Evangélica Unia Toba. The remainder of the tribe joined the Iglesia Evangélica Pentecostal de Argentina, which eventually put into filial relationship with the CG.

Pentecostal ecumenism brought several churches together (1948) to form the Unión des las Asambleas de Dios (UAD), the largest of which were the mission churches of the AG–U.S. and the Pentecostal Assemblies of Canada (PAOC). Of the latter group, M. Wortman is perhaps the best-known missionary.

In addition to the Scandinavian, Italian, and North American missionary presence, the role of Chilean pentecostal missionaries to Argentina was important in the pre-1950s period and deserves significant research. Among the Chilean

Annual conference of the Assemblies of God in Buenos Aires, July 1941.

missions that established a presence during the early period were the Corporación Evangélica de Vitacura, Iglesia de Dios Pentecostal, Iglesia Evangélica Pentecostal, Iglesia Misión San Pablo, Iglesia Wesleyana Nacional, and the Misión Iglesia Pentecostal. These made major contributions to the indigenization of the older mission groups.

2. The Tommy Hicks Revivals and the Aftermath.

The events of Apr. 14–June 12, 1954, changed Argentine pentecostal history. These fall months saw the transformation of small groups of religious dissidents into a national movement and provided an identity in the popular mind. The process began with the visit of AG missionary pastor Louie B. Stokes to the ►T. L. Osborn evangelistic campaigns in Chile. When it became clear that Osborn was unavailable to lead a similar crusade in Argentina, Stokes and his associates turned to ►Tommy Hicks. The Atlanta Football Stadium of Buenos Aires, with a capacity of 45,000, was rented. Pastors from churches throughout the city were invited to cooperate. Enthusiastic participation in the "Great Salvation-Healing Campaign" resulted in a type of evangelical ecumenism under the leadership of the pentecostals throughout Argentina. Among those who devoted people and resources to the campaign were Baptists (under the leadership of Pastor Cristi), the CMA, and the UAD (under the leadership of superintendent E. Fazzini). When it was clear that the meetings were a national success, the Methodists sought to participate.

A story that does not make it into most sources is told by R. E. Miller about conversations of Hicks with Argentine president Juan Perón. These visits apparently resulted in the healing of Perón from a skin disease (eczema). Perón then gave permission for the revivalists to hold the crusade without government interference, have access to radio, and rent stadiums sufficient to hold the crowds. Paul Sorenson served as interpreter for the 8,000 who attended the first evening. Each evening the crowds increased. People from all social classes attended, but the vast majority of participants and converts came from the lower laboring classes. They persisted through rain and bone-chilling cold nights. By mid-May, over 100,000 persons packed into the Atlanta Stadium every night, with thousands more gathered outside. On Saturday, May 22, the campaign was moved to the 100,000-seat Huracán Stadium. Buenos Aires newspapers were soon estimating attendance at over 200,000. At each service thousands were healed and converted. New congregations were established throughout the country, but especially in Buenos Aires. Of special importance were the ecumenical relationships established among pentecostals but also between pentecostals and the other churches, especially the CMA, the Baptists, and the Methodists.

There is some evidence that the growth of the pentecostal churches after the campaign was less than expected. Louie B. Stokes reported numbers at a meeting of AG–U.S.-dominated Latin American pentecostal denominations in Santiago, Chile, in Jan. 1961. The minutes of the meeting were published as *Bolletin de la Confraternidad de Las Asembleas de Dios de Sud America, Zona Sur*. Stokes allowed that the Unión de las Asambleas de Dios de Argentina had 3,000 members and 2,000 additional adherents in 100 congregations. No mention was made of the Hicks campaigns in the historical summary. However, growth did begin. The Unión de las Asambleas de Dios had 32 congregations in 1954, 65 in 1955, and by 1957 had about 100.

A few years later Hollenweger estimated the pentecostals churches to have 60,000 adult baptized members. Half of these, including many Toba, were members of the Iglesia Evangélica Pentecostal de Argentina. Another 18,000 members were part of the churches related to the Svenska Fria Mission. The UAD had 5,000 members. The rest were divided between another 10 denominations and missions. There were probably more than three times that many "adherents" who were not members. The UAD established daily radio broadcasts in Buenos Aires from 1957 on, and other denominations soon followed suit. The churches have continued to grow. Demographer David Barrett and his collaborators estimate that at the beginning of the new millennium there were more than 1.6 million pentecostals in Argentina.

3. The Independent Pentecostal Revivals.

The 1970s saw the development of a more radical pentecostal revivalism that again changed public perceptions of pentecostal and charismatic life in Argentina. Already, large Baptist churches had become functionally pentecostal after the Hicks campaign. They adopted pentecostal understandings of spirituality, healing, and theology. However, these churches, for example, First Baptist Church pastored by Pablo Deiros, have remained Baptist. The new ministries began as local congregations that developed ministries outside the established pentecostal churches. Three of the major founders of the "new paradigm" churches in Argentina were the Argentine pentecostal/charismatic evangelists Omar Cabrera (Fondación Visión de Futuro), Héctor Aníbal Giménez (Ondas de Amor y Paz), and Carlos Annacondia (Asociación Evangelísta Mensaje de Salvacón). All of these have had a significant influence in Argentine religious and cultural life; all of these ministries, despite oblique roots in other traditions, are indigenous Argentine expressions of pentecostalism.

The movement resulting from the ministry of Omar Cabrera (born 1936) began in 1972 as the Ministrio de Fe, becoming in 1986 the Fondación Visión de Futuro, which is juridically linked to the Asociación Iglesia de Dios Argentina, but is know widely as Iglesia Visión de Futuro. The theological orientation of the group is toward a "gospel ... of prosperity." Baptized Catholic, Cabrera became a member of the UAD. He studied in the U.S. at Holmes Bible College (NC) and at Franklin Springs College (GA), worked with ʳMorris Cerullo in California, and received a mail-order doctorate from an institution in Orlando. His wife serves as Latin American coordinator for ʳWomen's Aglow, and his children have studied at Oral Roberts University, ʳChrist for the Nations (Dallas), and Christ for All Nations (ʳReinhard Bonnke) in Wiesbaden. The ideas and individuals encountered in these contexts provide the theological basis for his work and the model for ministry. The theology is conservative, even fundamentalistic, the ethics holiness, the style entrepreneurial and prosperity gospel (ʳPositive Confession). The ministry has ebbed and flowed. Adherence in the movement surged to a high of 145,000 in 1985 and declined by nearly 40% by 1989, when the adherents numbered 85,000.

The second evangelist was Héctor Aníbal Giménez (born 1957) who is the founder and leader of the organization Ondas de Amor y Paz (Waves of Love and Peace). Having been formed among the less-than-privileged of Buenos Aires, this organization uses sites for its ministry that make persons from those backgrounds more comfortable while attending the vibrant evangelistic meetings. The meetings take place in cinemas and theaters with modern music. Giménez has a significant radio and television ministry. Most of the ministry associates are his age or slightly younger. His wife, Irma, is a copastor and plays an important role in the ministry. Because of his unusual style and his socioeconomic background, he is not accepted by the other pentecostal organizations, despite the fact that his theology is certainly pentecostal. Ondas de Amor y Paz had 24 preaching centers in Argentina in 1989 and 70 in 1991. It has spread (1999) to Uruguay, Brazil, Chile, and the U.S. (Miami).

The third, and probably most influential evangelist outside Argentina, is Carlos Annocondia (born 1944), who is the leader of La Asociación Evangélistica Mensaje de Salvación, a parachurch evangelistic association. After two decades as a successful businessman, Annocondia felt called to ministry in 1981. He has developed a ministry of carefully organized evangelistic campaigns that cooperate with local congregations, modeled on the Hicks campaigns but with less attention to healing. Campaigns have also been held in Brazil, Paraguay, Mexico, the U.S., Russia, Finland, Switzerland, Spain, and Singapore.

On the basis of these models numerous revival ministries have arisen that are having an impact around the world. These revivalists have been allowed to speak beyond Argentina in the volume edited by Peter Wagner and Pablo Deiros, *The Rising Revival: Firsthand Accounts of the Incredible Argentine Revival—And How It Can Spread around the World* (1998). These charismatic or neocharismatic (ʳthird wave) ministries have again changed public perceptions of the nature of the pentecostal churches and of the pentecostal religious experience, since it has reached across traditional religious boundaries with more alacrity than the earlier revivals.

4. The Other Pentecostal Churches.

In addition to the denominations mentioned above, there are a large number of denominational and independent pentecostal ministries. These include: Asamblea Cristiana Cultural; Asamblea Cristiana de Argentina; Asamblea Cristiana; Asamblea de Dios, Iglesia de Dios Cristiana Pentecostal; Iglesia de Dios de la Profecia; Iglesia del Evangelio Cuadrangular; Iglesia Evangélica Pentecostal Argentina; Iglesia Evangélica Pentecostal Apostolica Argentina; Iglesia Evangélica Pentecostal de Chile; Iglesia Evangélica Unida Toba; Iglesia Santa Pentecostes; Iglesia Pentecostal de Argentina; Mission Pentecostal; as well as at least 20 other groups. The Iglesia Pentecostal Unida de Argentina is related to the ʳUnited Pentecostal Church (UPC). It traces its beginnings to the arrival of the first UPC missionaries, John and Ruby Klemin, in 1967. This church claims (1999) 6,860 members, 78 licensed ministers, and 159 congregations and preaching points.

■ **Bibliography:** D. B. Barrett, G. T. Kurian, and T. M. Johnson, *World Christian Encyclopedia* (2001) ■ D. D. Bundy, "Pentecostalism in Argentina," *Pneuma* 20 (Spring 1998) ■ D. L. Burk, ed., *Foreign Missions Insight: A Digest of Foreign Missions Faces, Facts, Fields and Figures* (1999), 130 ■ A. W. Enns, *Man, Milieu and Mission in Argentina: A Close Look at Church Growth* (1971) ■ A. Frigerio, ed. *Ciencias sociales y religión en el Cono Sur* (1993) ■ idem, ed., *Nuevos movimientos religiosos y ciencias sociales*, 2 vols. (1993) ■ idem, ed., *El Pentecostalismo en la Argentina* (1994) ■ W. J. Hollenweger, *Handbuch der Pfingstbewegung* (diss., Zurich, 1967), 855–64 [para. 02b.01] ■ L. Jeter de Walker, *Siembre y consecha. Vol. 2: Reseña histórica de las Asambleas de Dios en Argentina, Boliva, Chile, Paraguay, Perú y Uruguay* (1992) ■ R. E. Miller, *The Flaming Flame: Ezekiel 20:47* (1973) ■ idem, *Thy God Reigneth: The Story of the Revival in Argentina* (1964) ■ E. Miller, "Pentecostalism among the Argentine Toba" (diss., U. of Pittsburgh, 1967) ■ O. Nilsen, *Ut i all Verden: Pinsevennenes ytre misjon i 75 år* (1984) ■ P. A. Pedersen, "Argentina," in *Til Jordens Ender: Norsk pinsemisjon gjennom 50 år*, ed. Kåre Juul (1960), 271–78 ■ W. D. Reyburn and M. F. Reyburn, "Toba Caciqueship and the Gospel," *International Review of Mission* 45(1956) ■ N. Saracco, *Argentine Pentecostalism: Its History and Theology* (diss., U. of Birmingham, 1989) ■ G. E. Söderholm, *Den Svenska Pingstväckelsens spridning utom och inom Sverige* ■ Supplement till de Svenska Pingstväckelsens Historia *(1933)* ■ L. B. Stokes, *Historia del Movimiento Pentecostal en la Argentina* (1968) ■ idem, *The Great Revival in Buenos Aires* (n.d.) ■ A. Sundstedt, *Pingstväckelsen*, 5 vols. (1969–73) ■ I. M. Witzøe, *De Aapene døre: Norges Frie Evangeliske Hedningemissions arbeider og virke gjennom 10 aar* (1925) ■ H. H. Wynarczyk, *Perfíl sociológico Pentecostal* (1994) ■ idem, *Tres evangelistas carismáticos: Omar Cabrera, Annacondia, Giménez* (unpub. ms., 1989) ■ H. H. Wynarczyk, P. Semán, and M. de Majo, *Panorama actual del campo Evangélico en Argentina. Un Estudio sociológico* (1995).   ■ D. D. Bundy

ARMENIA

■ Pentecostals 0 (0%)   ■ Charismatics 59,228 (77%)   ■ Neocharismatics 17,672 (23%)   ■ Total Renewal: 76,900

See Russia.

ARUBA

■ Pentecostals 2,550 (30%)   ■ Charismatics 4,668 (55%)   ■ Neocharismatics 1,232 (15%)   ■ Total Renewal: 8,450

See Caribbean Islands.

AUSTRALIA

■ Pentecostals 146,247 (6%)   ■ Charismatics 1,776,680 (72%)   ■ Neocharismatics 532,073 (22%)   ■ Total Renewal: 2,455,000

1. Origins.

To some degree, pentecostalism in Australia has suffered from the public perception that it is an American import. The evidence, however, suggests that it is an indigenous development, influenced by first British and then American literature and itinerant evangelism. Chant traces the first outbreaks to Victoria, with instances of tongues in Portland (Joseph Marshall, 1870) and Melbourne (John Coombe, 1908). There is strong oral evidence of tongues among Methodist prayer groups in the 1890s.

In Australia, as elsewhere, there was a groundswell of increasing interest in intense faith experiences and "victorious Christian living" (▶Keswick movement), which provided the ground for a sort of common expectation that "something would happen." Higher Life teaching was transplanted to Australia in 1891 by the formation of the Geelong Convention. Geelong Keswick soon spawned a series of offspring and emulators, including Belgrave Heights, Eltham, and Katoomba. The same circles supported and prospered with the huge impact of the Torrey-Alexander and Chapman-Alexander crusades in 1902 and 1905. It is not too much to say that such institutions created an ongoing intensification of the Christian experience that was essential to the creation of a sphere of plausibility for the reimplementation of such church practices as speaking in tongues, prophecy, and healing. It was, for example, at the Eltham conference grounds in 1909 that the news of the 1905 Mukti revival in India provoked an outbreak of tongues-speaking that divided the mainstream community. Into this mixture flowed the influence of ▶John Alexander Dowie, whose ministries in South Australia, Sydney, and Melbourne provided an interest in healing and a cohort of disciples who later blended easily with the early pentecostal movement. Many of those who were converted at his rallies later entered pentecostal congregations, and among those influenced directly or indirectly were such important early Australian pentecostals as C. L. Greenwood, Maxwell Armstrong, and R. A. Mintern.

Dowie's influence on ▶Aimee Semple McPherson, ▶Fred Van Eyk, Kelso Glover, and ▶Donald Gee later fed back into Australia through teaching and evangelistic visits.

The best claimant to the title of "founder" of Australian pentecostalism is a woman ▶Jeannie ("Mother") Lancaster, who was born in 1858 as Sarah Jane Murrell. An active Methodist, she began to search intensely for the power promised to Christians in the book of Acts after an old man challenged her in 1902 to explain why healing was no longer taught in the church. When in 1906 she received literature from England that told of "back to Pentecost" experiences, she began to seek "the baptism" earnestly. This culminated in a Gethsemane experience in 1908, which was followed after some time by ecstatic tongues. Gathering a number of people around her, Lancaster bought an old temperance hall in 1909, which she and her followers transformed into Good News Hall (GNH), Australia's first permanent pentecostal congregation. The GNH publication, *Good News,* eventually circulated to more than 3,000 people all over Australia and was a key element in the spread of early pentecostalism in Australia. Its theology, however, isolated it from the broader Wesleyan-experiential movement, and when significant growth in the movement occurred, it was from the Southern Evangelical Mission of former Methodist minister Robert Horne.

The visits of ▶Smith Wigglesworth and Aimee Semple McPherson in 1921 won the hearts of many in the mainstream to an acceptance of the need for a "fuller Gospel" than they were receiving in their traditional churches. While McPherson won the mainline clergy over, along with thousands of converts to evangelical Protestantism, who retained a positive image of pentecostalism as a result, Wigglesworth polarized opinion. His prophecy and ministry of healing in William Lamb's large Darlinghurst Baptist Church led to the ejection of such important early pentecostals as R. H. Fallon and Fred and Phillip Duncan from the Baptist communion. Such excommunications of pentecostals became more frequent through the 1920s and '30s as the pentecostal message began to take hold in Australia, leading to the formation of the earliest protodenominational pentecostal structures, such as journals, Bible schools, annual conferences, etc.

An overseas visitor who made less of an impact on the Australian public at large, but who was probably more important for the internal life of the movement, was ►A. C. Valdez Sr., who arrived in 1925. In 1916, the same year in which the Apostolic Church was established in Wales, ►Charles Greenwood, a former Church of Christ convert who had heard about the baptism in the Holy Spirit through a adherent of Dowie follower ►John G. Lake and had been baptized in the Spirit in 1913, began revival prayer meetings in his house at Sunshine, Melbourne. Within a few weeks, Valdez had the Sunshine Hall packed with people of all denominations; hundreds received the baptism, hundreds more received healing or simple conversion. Someone wrote, "Trains running from Melbourne to Sunshine were crowded with people attending the meetings. As they journeyed, they sang favorite hymns such as 'Joy Unspeakable.' Some were converted on the train before they arrived at the meeting." The news spread around the country, and people such as the Duncans, father and son, came down from Sydney, while others traveled from Western Australia, Queensland, and South Australia. They in turn went back and founded new works. The meetings continued, moving to the larger Prahran Town Hall, and then to the purchased Richmond Theatre, which became that still-thriving powerhouse of Australian pentecostalism, Richmond Temple. In the twelve months since he had begun ministering in Melbourne, Valdez had brought about an important change in the nature of pentecostalism in Australia—the movement had clearly moved from being a mission to being a church. In part this was due to the need to institutionalize the gains of the revival. Valdez chose and ordained people as elders, and the Pentecostal Church of Australia (PCA) was organized to act as a framework for continued cooperation by the people from around the country who had been through the fires of revival together.

In part, increased organization was also prompted by the sudden influx of hundreds of new supporters, whose leaving mainstream churches caused negative reactions among the clergy and in the popular press. A similar, though somewhat more muted, reaction occurred when Valdez's son, A. C. Valdez Jr., visited Australia in 1952, and again, but more virulently, with the orchestrated vandalism associated with the ►Oral Roberts crusade in 1956.

A brief listing of the commencement dates of the major pentecostal groupings in Australia demonstrate this process of variegation and formalization. Good News Hall was founded in 1909, the mission in which the Southern Evangelical Mission had its roots in 1911. In 1926 Frederick Van Eyk organized a number of congregations (including Good News Hall) into a loose grouping called the Apostolic Faith Mission, some of which was a reaction to the formation in

the same year of the Valdez and Greenwood–inspired PCA. This latter was a name that was clearly interchangeable for many with that of the Assemblies of God. To unite these works under a common name and constitution, an All Australia Conference was held in 1937 in the Duncans' church in Redfern, and the largely East Coast movement took the name of the Assemblies of God in Australia (AG). In short order the movement developed its own training institutions, which mediated the influence in particular of British pentecostals such as Henry Wiggins and Donald Gee. The emphasis on orthodoxy in the early institutions also foreshadowed the use of training institutions as a means by which ministerial discipline could be enforced through the issuing of licenses dependent on education. The loose-knit nature of the movement has undermined this to some degree, and there has been a proliferation of Bible or ministerial training institutions, and even of institutions within institutions (the Christian Life Centres, begun by Frank Houston, are an example of this sort of centripetal force within the AG). These necessarily appeal to the charismatic leadership and congregational nature of the movement and undermine central discipline, while competing with "official" institutions of the movement such as Commonwealth Bible College. Nevertheless, the AG has grown to be the largest pentecostal denomination in Australia, with some 117,000 members.

Shortly before the national convention that united the AG, two other groupings began to take hold in the still loosely defined pentecostal world. In 1929 Frederick Van Eyk was forced out of the Apostolic Faith Mission and (on his way back to South Africa) linked up with Albert Banton. Their campaign resulted in the formation of the first Four-Square Church, in Cessnock. By 1932 there were six such assemblies scattered up and down the East Coast, and, as someone put it, others were "opening up faster than we can supply pastors," prompting the formation of a council and formal organization. In 1930 the Wales-based Apostolic Church (AC) was virtually founded in Australia by the advent of ►William Cathcart, though formal organization cannot really be said to have taken place until 1932–33, when the movement's formal office holders (in the form of apostles and prophets as well as evangelists) were in place and headquarters had been established in Melbourne. Out of the AG and AC movements came ►Leo Cecil Harris, who, after being converted to ►British Israelitism in 1941, came to blows with the older movements over their theology and ecclesiology. Harris returned to Australia to found the National Revival Crusade (which had already been founded in New Zealand) in 1945, which was later renamed the Commonwealth Revival Crusade and then the Christian Revival Crusade (CRC), which took the Bible as its only constitution and local church autonomy and British Israelitism as some of its distinctives.

The two largest denominational groupings of Australian pentecostalism were, therefore, founded before 1950. After that, the pattern was influenced by the internationalization of Australian and world culture following WWII, and pentecostalism was affected by the same sort of splintering that was typical of American pentecostalism. In 1952 ˒Ray Jackson came to Australia, essentially founding the Associated Mission Churches (or Latter Rain) movement in this country. Two years later the ˒United Pentecostal Church, the ˒Oneness breakaway from the AG–U.S., began operations under the leadership of Glen Bogue. In 1958 state rivalry prompted two Melbourne congregations to separate from the CRC's search for a more formal organizational structure, and these became the nucleus for the Revival Centre movement. In 1963 the Full Gospel Church began as a fellowship for independent pentecostal groups. In 1976 the American Church of God (CG, Cleveland, TN) opened up operations under the pastorship of Billie McAlpin. They were followed to this country by their alter ego, the Church of God of Prophecy. A more homegrown and successful product has been that of Clark Taylor's ˒Christian Outreach Centres, which began in his Queensland home in 1974 and grew rapidly, so that within the decade the Brisbane church numbered over 2,500 and there were 31 other associated churches, mostly in Queensland and northern New South Wales. Since then numerous groups, such as the New Testament Church of God, the Calvary Life Assemblies, ˒Christian City Churches, and dozens of small parachurch missions have proliferated.

2. The Charismatic Movement.

Paul Freston has talked of the myth that the charismatic movement began with ˒Dennis Bennett, noting that charismatic teaching and experience was commonplace in South America in the 1950s. While not as "commonplace" in Australia, the return of missionaries from the East Africa Revival, China, and Pakistan meant that there was a significant bank of charismatic experience and activity, even in such ecclesiastically conservative areas as Sydney. The healing meetings of J. M. Hickson in 1923 and the Order of St. Luke among Anglicans also maintained a continuing level of interest in healing among the mainstream denominations.

Significant figures among the mainline churches began to be touched by charismatic renewal from the mid 1950s onward—Baptist evangelist John Ridley had a significant experience under the ministry of Phillip Duncan that nearly destroyed his career, while Jim Glennon, who went on to found one of the largest cathedral healing services in the world, received the gift of tongues at the hands of ˒Agnes Sanford in 1959. Oral accounts seem to suggest that these experiences increased in frequency through the early 1960s, with the work of important linking institutions such as Camps Farthest Out, ˒Youth With A Mission, and the ˒Full Gospel

Business Men's Fellowship International. Barry Hobart, an Anglican baptized in the office of his boarding-school house master, AG minister Doug Moody, lived a double life as leader of the AG youth movement in New South Wales and teacher at St. Andrews Cathedral School. As founding president of the Full Gospel Business Men's Fellowship in Sydney, he deliberately steered the organization away from domination by classical pentecostals, thus creating an open environment for interaction with mainline denominations. In later years Hobart was to chair the meetings that featured speakers like ˒David du Plessis and ˒Michael Harper.

The role of missionaries continued to be important. Future Christian City Church leader Ian Jagelman's reading of a "steady diet" of missionary biographies in New Guinea in the early 1960s led him to ask, "Lord, if you can use them, why can't you use me?" Doug McCraw, an ordained Anglican minister from Sydney working as a missionary pilot with Missionary Aviation Fellowship, gave Jagelman two prepentecostal classics: John McNeill's *The Spirit-Filled Life,* and R. A. Torrey's *The Person and Work of the Holy Spirit.* In 1967 prominent Methodist evangelist Alan Walker returned from South America and spoke publicly about the "thrilling story of Methodist-pentecostal progress in South America," though some charismatics felt that he "appeared quite unable to relate it to the church in Australia." The next year, Walker inspired a convention at the Wesley Centre, Sydney, called "Rediscovering the Holy Spirit," seen by some as marking a new openness to charismatic renewal. One person involved in this conference was John Blacker, who went on to build the largest charismatic congregation in the Uniting Church, at Sunshine in Victoria. Likewise, it was out of a missionary conference in Picton, New South Wales, that the first major public outbreak of charismatic phenomena was experienced under the leadership of local Anglican rector Barry Scholfield. Greg Blaxland, a missionary in South America, furthered some of this influence in the Anglican Church through his leadership of the South American Missionary Society.

Following a period of mass immigration and unsettled social relationships in Australia, by the end of the 1960s there were dozens of clergy and laypersons, many tired and dispirited in their ministries in a variety of denominations, who were prepared to think about the charismatic option. In Jan. 1969 Alex Reichel, associate professor of mathematics at the University of Sydney, returned from a sabbatical in the U.S. with news of the Catholic renewal there. With the permission of Cardinal Gilroy, he introduced the new practices in prayer meetings at St. Michael's College and then later at St. Francis parish church, Surrey Hills. News of the renewal spread quickly, in part through visitors, and sometimes simply accounts of renewal in Sydney were sufficient to spark outbreaks of renewal in places like Bardon, Queensland, and Melbourne. Within two years it was in every capital city in Australia, and prayer groups were manifold. A 1973 questionnaire by the New

South Wales Methodist conference found that over 600 Methodists in the state were in some way involved in charismatic renewal and about 10% of the clergy, with wider reactions from clergy ranging from "enriching" to "satanic."

These movements in mainline denominations were formalized with the formation of the Temple Trust by Alan Langstaff and others in 1971. Modeled on Michael Harper's ▸Fountain Trust, the Temple Trust brought classical pentecostals and charismatics from all traditions into contact with one another through nondenominational conferences. The attendance at these conferences was large by Australian standards, rising to some 15,000 in the great 1979 Randwick Racecourse meeting. In that year, however, the Trust imploded, with Alan Langstaff declaring the charismatic renewal to be "dead" and moving to the U.S. The Trust became Vision Ministries and eventually declined under Harry Westcott through the influence of American-based prosperity doctrines (▸Positive Confession). Through the 1980s the leadership of mainstream charismatic activity was maintained by denominational organizations such as Anglican Renewal Ministries Australia (ARMA) and by nondenominational ones such as House of Tabor (now Tabor College), whose bold yet balanced perspective was reflected in its United Charismatic Conventions that attracted thousands of delegates from all churches, featuring notable speakers such as ▸Reinhard Bonnke and ▸Paul Yonggi Cho. These were reinforced by the speaking tours of ▸John Wimber, John White, and Ken Blue. Many, however, felt that the ability of the movement to maintain a presence in the mainstream denominations had declined, and thousands transferred out of traditional churches into pentecostal or independent charismatic churches. These fueled the development of the megachurch in Australia, as transfer and new-conversion growth fed into the development of large churches such as the Christian City Church and the Christian Life Centre movement in Sydney and Melbourne, the Waverley Christian Family Centre in Melbourne, the Christian Outreach Centre in Brisbane, and the like. Figures from the Australian AG across the period 1993–95 suggested that this flow from mainline denominations was slowing, though it still had significant life in it. Growth of nonaligned charismatic churches, which form by moving whole congregations out of an existing mainstream denomination, such as Grace Christian Fellowship in Canberra, seemed to be gathering strength, particularly in those denominations that experienced significant internal friction over debates such as homosexuality among the clergy and the ordination of women. The shape of the charismatic renewal was clearly changing, and the waning of revivalistic phenomena such as the ▸Toronto Blessing and the continued growth of neocharismatic churches such as the ▸Vineyard movement presented profound challenges to classical pentecostal, mainstream, and independent charismatic churches alike.

■ **Bibliography:** L. Averill, *Go North Young Man* (1992) ■ B. Chant, *Heart of Fire: The Story of Australian Pentecostalism* (1973, 1984) ■ E. Dearn, *Christ and Charism* (1982) ■ M. Hutchinson, "Is Anglican Renewal Dead?" (ARMA national conference, 1993) ■ M. Hutchinson and J. Hull, "Healing and Hurting: Mainline Relationships with Australian Pentecostalism, and the 1952 Valdez Crusade" (CSAC Working Papers, no. 8, 1992) ■ Oral History Project interviews, Archives, Centre for the Study of Australian Christianity ■ S. Piggin, *Evangelical Christianity in Australia: Spirit, Word and World* (1996) ■ D. and G. Smith, *A River Is Flowing: A History of the Assemblies of God in Australia* (1987).   ■ M. HUTCHINSON

AUSTRIA

■ Pentecostals 17,316 (6%)   ■ Charismatics 269,594 (90%)   ■ Neocharismatics 11,590 (4%)   ■ Total Renewal: 298,500

See EUROPE, WESTERN.

AZERBAIJAN

■ Pentecostals 0 (0%)   ■ Charismatics 6,259 (63%)   ■ Neocharismatics 3,741 (37%)   ■ Total Renewal: 10,000

See RUSSIA.

BAHAMAS

■ Pentecostals 28,127 (57%)   ■ Charismatics 10,937 (22%)   ■ Neocharismatics 9,936 (20%)   ■ Total Renewal: 49,000

The first pentecostal believers in the Bahamas were perhaps ▸Rebecca and Edmund S. Barr, who had experienced the baptism in the Holy Spirit during a visit to the U.S., at Pleasant Grove Campground near Durant, FL, in early 1909. They were members of an African-Bahamian Holiness congregation. The first pentecostal missionaries to the Bahamas were apparently R. M. and Ida V. Evans and the youthful Carl M. Padgett. Evans was born in 1847, the son of Holiness Methodists, and died at Live Oak, FL, on Oct. 12, 1924. He served as pastor of the Methodist Episcopal Church, South, in 1872–1906 and was involved in Holiness camp meetings and related activities. After his retirement he came into contact with the pentecostals at Pleasant Grove Campground and experienced the baptism in the Holy Spirit. He was ordained as a minister in the ›Church of God (CG, Cleveland, TN) on May 30, 1909, by ›A. J. Tomlinson.

Feeling a burden for missions, Evans sailed to Nassau, Bahamas, on Dec. 31, 1909. There he joined with the Barrs. Together they began a ministry primarily among the black Bahamians. There were numerous converts, who were organized into self-supporting, self-governing congregations. He cooperated with Padgett, and Bahamian converts did evangelistic work in the markets. Among the first converts were W. V. and Arabella Eneas, who suffered extensive persecution. The organization was basically organized as a faith mission. The mission program of the CG was not yet organized, and thus there was no standardized supervision from the U.S., nor were resources available. Some offerings came from the U.S., but no salaries were paid, and no foreign funds were used to build the first churches. A number of U.S. visitors came, including an evangelistic tour led by A. J. Tomlinson, founder of the CG, and J. W. Buckalew. During the first decades of the CG, numerous articles about the mission work in the Bahamas were published in *The Evening Light and Church of God Evangel*, which later became the *Church of God Evangel*. Evans remained in the Bahamas until Jan. 1913, when his funds were depleted.

During WWI, American missionaries could not be in the Bahamas, and so William R. Franks was made overseer.

Franks was converted in 1913, licensed to preach in 1915, and appointed overseer in 1918. He bore the brunt of extensive persecution but established congregations throughout the islands. Padgett returned to the Bahamas as a missionary and eventually became overseer of the CG interests. He remained in the Bahamas until 1926. Franks, however, had a long-term, significant ministry of about 60 years.

When Tomlinson was impeached as general overseer of the CG and founded the Church of God of Prophecy (CGP) in 1923, most of the Bahamian churches joined the new denomination. This denomination has grown to include more than 42 congregations with about 3,000 members (1999). After this split, only ten self-supporting congregations remained with the CG. Various leaders of the CG made evangelistic and diplomatic tours to the Bahamas to reestablish the viability of that tradition there. Until 1928 there were separate organizations for black and white congregations. In 1928 W. V. Eneas, who had initially participated in the founding of the CGP, but who had returned to the CG, was elected overseer. This self-direction by the Bahamians was short-lived, and since 1931—until recently—a white overseer was appointed from the U.S. church. During the 1930s, missionary statesman J. H. Ingram visited the Bahamas and significantly influenced the churches. In 1999 the church reported more than 70 congregations with over 5,000 members.

The ›Assemblies of God (AG–U.S.) also established a presence in the Bahamas with the 1928 founding of First AG in Nassau in 1928 under the leadership of S. B. Pinder. The main interest, however, came during WWII, when missionaries were sent after a congregation that split off from the CG asked to join the AG. The Bahamian Council of the AG was organized in 1955 with Early W. Weech as superintendent. By 1956, 356 members in 9 churches were reported; in 1976, 397 "baptized members" and 2,000 "other believers" in 16 congregations were announced. The number increased to about 2,500 in 25 congregations by 1990. In 1999 the AG–U.S. claimed 5,000 "members and adherents" in 26 churches.

The ›United Pentecostal Church sent missionaries, apparently during the 1970s. They claim 2,500 constituents in nine churches and preaching points (1999). The Church of God in Christ also has a number of congregations and has supported missionaries. In 1985 they reported about 1,500 members.

Large church group in the Bahamas, probably 1910s or 1920s (Church of God [Cleveland, TN] photo).

■ **Bibliography:** D. Bryan, "Personal Perspectives on Ministry to Bahamian Youth," (thesis, Church of God School of

Theology, 1983) ▪ D. L. Burk, ed., *Foreign Missions Insight: A Digest of Foreign Missions Faces, Facts, Fields and Figures* (1999), 71–72 ▪ C. W. Conn, *Like a Mighty Army: A History of the Church of God* (1955; rev. 1977) ▪ idem, *Where the Saints Have Trod: A History of Church of God Missions* (1959) ▪ J. E. Cossey, *R. M. Evans: "The First of a Kind"* (n.d.) ▪ Division of Foreign Missions [AG], *1999 Annual Statistics* ▪ A. S. Ferguson, *History of the Church of God of Prophecy in the Bahamas* (1976) ▪ S. M. Hodges, *Look on the Fields: A Survey of the Assemblies of God in Foreign Lands* (1956) ▪ W. J. Hollenweger, *Handbuch der Pfingstbewegung* (diss., Zurich, 1967), 865–67 [para. 02b.02] ▪ P. Humphrey, *J. H. Ingram, Missionary Dean* (1966) ▪ J. H. Ingram, *Around the World with Gospel Light* (1938) ▪ [H. McCracken], *History of Church of God Missions* (1943) ▪ E. L. Simmons, *History of the Church of God* (1938).   ▪ D. D. Bundy

BAHRAIN

▪ Pentecostals 0 (0%)   ▪ Charismatics 2,372 (8%)   ▪ Neocharismatics 26,028 (92%)   ▪ Total Renewal: 28,400

See AFRICA, NORTH, AND THE MIDDLE EAST.

BANGLADESH

▪ Pentecostals 17,556 (4%)   ▪ Charismatics 28,804 (6%)   ▪ Neocharismatics 433,639 (90%)   ▪ Total Renewal: 479,999

BARBADOS

▪ Pentecostals 31,428 (64%)   ▪ Charismatics 10,732 (22%)   ▪ Neocharismatics 6,740 (14%)   ▪ Total Renewal: 48,900

Church of England (Anglican) clergyman James H. Marshall, who had experienced pentecostal spirituality, apparently established the first pentecostal church in Barbados as early as 1911. Evangelist James A. Joseph from Monserrat established another early ministry. Joseph had, before 1917, established a pentecostal Mission at Bridgetown, Barbados. No other details of the earliest history are known. In 1917 ▸Church of God (CG, Cleveland, TN) evangelist F. L. Ryder went to Barbados and met with Joseph, who united with the CG. Ryder and Joseph cooperated in evangelism, and four congregations with a membership of 80 were established by the fall of 1917, when Joseph died en route to attend a CG annual assembly in the U.S. The CG did not work with Joseph's successors, and the people appear to have joined the churches initiated by Marshall.

Missionaries also came from the ▸Pentecostal Assemblies of Canada. Robert and Elizabeth Jamieson at first sent missionaries from the Bible School in Trinidad (from 1935) and then moved to Barbados, where they lived and evangelized with the Pentecostal Assemblies of the West Indies until Robert's death in 1961.

In 1935 the peripatetic CG missionary statesman ▸James H. Ingram visited Bridgetown, Barbados, and met with J. H. Marshall. As a result of that visit, Marshall's church began to study the possibility of joining the CG. A year later, in 1936, Ingram made a return visit. A significant number of clergy and congregations joined the CG, and Marshall was appointed overseer. The fledgling CG in Barbados received an important infusion of members and leadership in 1938. That year Rose B. Hawkins led her independent congregation in Bank Hall, Bethelite Mission, into the denomination. At that point, her congregation was the largest, most visible, and most vital pentecostal ministry in Barbados. After Marshall's death in 1943, a Canadian missionary, J. B. Winter, was appointed overseer of Barbados. The resultant church, the New Testament Church of God, is the largest pentecostal denomination in Barbados.

Other pentecostal churches active in Barbados include the ▸Church of God of Prophecy and the ▸Pentecostal Assemblies of the World.

▪ **Bibliography:** C. W. Conn, *Like a Mighty Army: A History of the Church of God* (rev. ed., 1977) ▪ idem, *Where the Saints Have Trod: A History of Church of God Missions* (1959) ▪ W. J. Hollenweger, *Handbuch der Pfingstbewegung* (diss, Zurich, 1967), 1066–71 (para. 02b.21) ▪ P. Humphrey, *J. H. Ingram, Missionary Dean* (1966) ▪ J. H. Ingram, *Around the World with Gospel Light* (1938) ▪ [H. McCracken], *History of Church of God Missions* (1943) ▪ T. W. Miller, *Canadian Pentecostals: A History of the Pentecostal Assemblies of Canada* (1994) ▪ E. L. Simmons, *History of the Church of God* (1938) ▪ I. A. Whitt, "Developing a Pentecostal Missiology in the Canadian Context (1867–1944): The Pentecostal Assemblies of Canada" (diss., Fuller, 1994).   ▪ D. D. Bundy

BELGIUM

■ Pentecostals 13,310 (4%)　　■ Charismatics 267,136 (88%)　　■ Neocharismatics 22,054 (7%)　　■ Total Renewal: 302,500

Belgium, although it has its own national identity, is divided into two parts by language: the southern part speaks French, the northern part, Flemish (a close relative of Dutch). Because of the linguistic continuity between Flemish Belgium and the Netherlands, the history of the pentecostal and charismatic movements in Flemish Belgium and the Netherlands is somewhat intertwined. This article focuses on Flemish Belgium.

1. The Pentecostal Movement in Flemish Belgium.

a. Inception. The first pentecostal witness in Belgium was Mrs. Ada Esselbach-Whiting (1867–1927) from England. Before her marriage in 1904 to Frederik Esselbach (1848–1925), a German, she had been a Church Army Mission worker in England. In Aug. 1904 the couple took charge of the International Sailors' Rest in Antwerp. In Apr. 1909 Mrs. Esselbach-Whiting received the Spirit baptism in Amsterdam and from then on became a witness to the pentecostal message in Belgium. She remained in close contact with ►Gerrit Polman of the Netherlands, who for some years organized pentecostal meetings in Antwerp (1920–24).

Cornelis T. Potma (1861–1929), born in the Netherlands, had been an evangelist among the blacks in Virginia and probably stayed for some years in South Africa before he settled in Belgium in 1920. Initially he cooperated with Ralph C. Norton, founder of the Belgian Gospel Mission. Since Norton did not agree with Potma's pentecostal convictions, Potma ended up as an independent itinerant evangelist supported by the British ►Elim churches. In 1926 a pentecostal revival campaign with ►George Jeffreys resulted in 18 people being baptized in the public bath in Antwerp. In 1929 Potma died and was succeeded by the Rietdijks, a Dutch couple. Johannes Rietdijk (1901–86) and Anke van Hoften (1874–1975) met in Belgium, where Johan was enrolled at Norton's Flemish Bible School. Because Anke was 27 years older, Norton disapproved of the marriage and dismissed Rietdijk from the school in 1925. Rietdijk joined Potma and received the Spirit baptism. Unlike Potma, who seems never to have established an assembly, Rietdijk founded the Evangelische Kerk Pniël in Kiel, near Antwerp, in 1930—the first pentecostal assembly in Flanders. Other assemblies came and went.

b. Growth. The pentecostal movement in Flanders remained small and did not begin to grow somewhat stronger until after WWII. Important Flemish leaders were Francois L. De Meester (1908–84) and Johan Van Kesteren (1905–81). Missionaries from the Netherlands, England, Scandinavia, the U.S., and South Africa worked independently of one another, making it difficult to find a national identity.

Since 1969 annual meetings of pentecostal assemblies have been held, out of which grew the Broederschap van Vlaamse Pinkstergemeenten (Brotherhood of Flemish Pentecostal Churches). In 1979 Michael Williams of Antwerp formed the Belgische Christelijke Pinkstergemeenschap Elim (Belgian Christian Pentecostal Fellowship Elim) as an umbrella organization for several assemblies in and around Antwerp. The two groups merged in 1993 in the Verbond van Vlaamse Pinkstergemeenten (Union of Flemish Pentecostal Churches). With 39 assemblies and 2,500 members, the Verbond represents a strong segment of the Flemish pentecostal movement. Of the remaining local assemblies, three have ties with the Dutch Full Gospel Assemblies and two with Johan Maasbach's Wereldzending, while the rest are independent. Recently many migrant churches, often pentecostal, have emerged in the larger cities. Altogether the Flemish pentecostal movement comprises 75 assemblies with 5,000 to 6,000 members.

2. The Charismatic Movement in Flemish Belgium.

The ►Catholic charismatic renewal (CCR) in Flanders started in the 1970s. Fr. Jos Biesbrouck had already received the Spirit baptism through the prayer of ►David du Plessis at a ►Full Gospel Business Men's meeting in Utrecht, Holland, in May 1965. Gradually Biesbrouck would become one of the initiators of the CCR in Flanders. In Dec. 1971 Biesbrouck started the first charismatic prayer group in Harelbeke. He further promoted the CCR by organizing lectures about the charismatic renewal and by publishing the first charismatic periodical, *Pinksternieuws* (1973), together with Ludo van Galoen from Brugge.

Meanwhile, independent of Biesbrouck, more charismatic groups emerged, often through individual contact with the CCR in other countries (esp. the U.S., Canada, and France).

Of great importance for the CCR was the contribution of Cardinal ►Léon-Joseph Suenens, Catholic archbishop and primate of Belgium (1961–79). During a trip through the U.S. in 1972, Suenens had become personally involved in the CCR. In 1975 he was asked by Pope Paul VI to see to the integration of the renewal into the heart of the Catholic Church. At Suenens' invitation, the International Catholic Renewal Office was established in Brussels (now moved to Rome). Suenens organized theological consultations at Mechelen (Malines), which resulted in a series of publications, *Documents of Mechelen*.

The Jesuit Walter Smet, personally touched by the CCR, published two books on the CCR and started a charismatic prayer group in Antwerp in 1973. As more and more prayer groups emerged, Smet and his fellow Jesuit Paul Vrancken helped to provide a structure by establishing a service center for the CCR in Antwerp in 1977, which publishes the monthly *Goed Nieuws (Good News)*, later renamed *Jezus Leeft (Jesus Lives)*. Since 1992 the center is situated in Zoersel–St. Antonius near Antwerp.

Today there are about 100 charismatic prayer groups; group attendance varies from 15 to 80. Every diocese has a team responsible for promoting unity among the charismatic groups. An interdiocese team is responsible for the annual conventions and training courses.

See also THE NETHERLANDS.

■ **Bibliography:** D. D. Bundy, "Charismatic Renewal in Belgium: A Bibliographical Essay," *EPTA Bulletin 5* (3, 1986) ■ I. Demaerel, "Tachtig jaar pinksterbeweging in Vlaanderen (1909–1989)" (thesis, Universitaire Faculteit voor Protestantse Godgeleerdheid, Brussels, 1990) ■ J. L. Sandidge, "The Origin and Development of the Catholic Charismatic Movement in Belgium" (thesis, Katholieke Universiteit, Leuven, 1976). ■ C. van der Laan

BELIZE

■ Pentecostals 7,082 (23%)   ■ Charismatics 20,089 (64%)   ■ Neocharismatics 4,229 (13%)   ■ Total Renewal: 31,400

See LATIN AMERICA

BELORUSSIA

■ Pentecostals 63,842 (67%)   ■ Charismatics 22,035 (23%)   ■ Neocharismatics 9,123 (10%)   ■ Total Renewal: 95,000

See RUSSIA.

BENIN

■ Pentecostals 84,306 (25%)   ■ Charismatics 104,526 (31%)   ■ Neocharismatics 153,168 (45%)   ■ Total Renewal: 342,000

See AFRICA, WEST

BERMUDA

■ Pentecostals 2,421 (18%)   ■ Charismatics 8,335 (62%)   ■ Neocharismatics 2,644 (20%)   ■ Total Renewal: 13,400

The first pentecostal missionary in the Bermudas was ˃J. H. Ingram, who arrived in Hamilton in early 1921. Recently converted and with no financial or moral support, Ingram worked as a plumber's assistant to make enough money to survive. His family had remained in the U.S. A few converts were made, and eventually Ingram rented a hall for evangelistic services. After 18 months Bermuda authorities refused to renew his visa and he was forced to return home. As a result of his work, several independent congregations were established, which received some support from other pentecostal groups in the U.S. but not from the Church of God (CG, Cleveland, TN), which was distracted and weakened by its own ethical and power struggles in the U.S. Ingram returned in 1925 and opened a mission in Hamilton. Family obligations, however, once again forced him to return to the U.S.

Ingram returned to Bermuda in 1938. This time he worked with the Bermuda pentecostal clergy, including people converted during his earlier visits. He encouraged them to join forces with the CG, and at that point the leadership of the church was taken over by CG missionaries from the U.S. The resultant church, the New Testament Church of God, is the largest pentecostal denomination in Bermuda, with more than 3,500 adherents.

Other pentecostal missionaries came from Canada in 1938. Under the leadership of R. J. Jamieson and the efforts of Trinidad pentecostals, extensive evangelistic work was undertaken in Bermuda. This resulted in the Pentecostal Assemblies of the West Indies, which claims more than 1,000 adherents. Another U.S. denomination, the ˃United Holy Church of America, also has a significant presence.

■ **Bibliography:** C. W. Conn, *Like a Mighty Army: A History of the Church of God* (rev. ed., 1977) ■ idem, *Where the Saints Have Trod: A History of Church of God Missions* (1959) ■ W. J. Hollenweger, *Handbuch der Pfingstbewegung* (diss, Zurich, 1967), 1066–71 (para. 02b.21) ■ P. Humphrey, *J. H. Ingram, Missionary Dean* (1966) ■ J. H. Ingram, *Around the World with Gospel Light* (1938) ■ "Bermuda Mission," *Church of God Evangel* 29 (July 29, 1938) ■ idem, "News from Bermuda," *Church of God Evangel* 12 (June 4, 1921) ■ [H. McCracken], *History of Church of God Missions* (1943) ■ T. W. Miller, *Canadian Pentecostals: A History of the Pentecostal Assemblies of Canada* (1994) ■ E. L. Simmons, *History of the Church of God* (1938) ■ I. A. Whitt, "Developing a Pentecostal Missiology in the Canadian Context (1867–1944): The Pentecostal Assemblies of Canada" (diss., Fuller, 1994). ■ D. D. Bundy

BHUTAN

■ Pentecostals 231 (4%)   ■ Charismatics 304 (6%)   ■ Neocharismatics 4,965 (90%)   ■ Total Renewal: 5,500

BOLIVIA

■ Pentecostals 146,912 (12%)   ■ Charismatics 948,882 (78%)   ■ Neocharismatics 119,206 (10%)   ■ Total Renewal: 1,215,000

1. Early History.

The first pentecostal missionary to visit Bolivia of whom a record is preserved was Earl W. Clark, a Holiness pentecostal missionary in Chile, who briefly visited Argentina and Oruro, Bolivia. In 1914 Howard W. and Clara Cragin, who had worked in Peru and then in Ecuador, began work in La Paz, Bolivia. They worked primarily among the Aymara. Catharine Cragin, mother of Howard and his younger brother, Paul, came to Bolivia about 1916 and established a small congregation among the Quechua.

During the 1920s, Swedish pentecostal missionaries came to Bolivia. Gustav Flood, Axel and Ruth Severin, Kristian and Ruth Nilsén, Albin and Fanny Gustafsson, and Karl and Maria Fredriksson, as well as the Norwegian pentecostal Birger Johnson, worked in Bolivia for varying lengths of time. They established congregations in Cochabamba, Rio Tercero, Santa Cruz, La Paz, and other cities, despite significant persecution by Catholic clergy. Some of these missionaries were supported by the ▸Örebro Mission.

The ▸International Church of the Foursquare Gospel (ICFG) began missionary work in Bolivia in 1928, when Thomas and Fannie Anderson and their four children joined the church. They had already served five years in Bolivia as independent missionaries. They located in Trinidad, Bolivia, where they worked among the Sirionos Indians. From this beginning the Iglesia del Evangelio Cuadrangular spread throughout Bolivia.

2. After World War II.

After WWII, missionaries of the U.S. ▸Assemblies of God began to arrive in large numbers. They established missions in the same cities where successful evangelization by the Swedish missionaries had already taken place. Thus churches were initially established in Cochabamba, Santa Cruz, and La Paz. Since that time the Asambleas de Dios de Bolivia has spread throughout the country. Hodges (1956) reported 900 members. Barrett reported in 1982 that there were about 10,000 members and 20,000 adherents. The Assemblies of God reported 38,552 baptized members in 1999.

The post WWII period also saw increased mission work in Bolivia by persons related to the ICFG. From its initial position near the Brazilian border it grew significantly. In 1999 the Iglesia del Evangelio Cuadrangular claims 6,452 members, with perhaps as many as 12,000 additional adherents.

In 1953 the Norwegian Pinsevennenes Ytre Misjon began work in Bolivia with the arrival of Leonard and Ragna Pettersen from Brazil. They established a work in La Paz before their retirement. They were replaced by Marita and Erling Andreassen, who focused their efforts in Puerto Gonzalo Moreno. They cooperated with the Swedish missionaries from the Svensk Fria Mission related to the Swedish Filadelfia Church movement. The Swedish missionaries undertook an extensive program of evangelistic work, beginning in 1955 with the arrival of 15 missionaries whose only task was evangelism. Swedish pentecostals have also made significant contributions in other areas. For example, they have been active in educational and community/economic development work in Bolivia. The Iglesia Pentecostal Sueca has a membership of about 6,000 (with perhaps 13,000 adherents), but the influence in Bolivia has been greater than that number indicates. The Scandinavians insisted on "self-supporting," self-governing, self-propagating churches from the beginning.

Also present in Bolivia are missionaries of both the Finnish Free Pentecostal Mission (11 in 1989) and the Finlands Svensk Pingstmission. Both groups of Finnish missionaries have established congregations and have worked in various ways to support the ministries of already existing congregations and denominations.

The first ▸United Pentecostal Church (UPC) residential missionaries, Vondas and Leah Smith, came to Bolivia in Dec. 1974. The Iglesia Pentecostal Unida claims 2,850 "constituents" and 23 licensed ministers with 32 congregations (1999). The UPC supports a Bible school in Cochabamba.

Throughout Bolivia, the teachings of the pentecostal churches have been accepted by the indigenous peoples. Significant research has been undertaken relative to the interaction of pentecostal Christian culture and the indigenous cultures, especially with regard to how values are prioritized.

3. Other Pentecostal Churches.

Bolivia has been influenced not only by U.S. and Scandinavian missionaries, but also by missionaries from Brazil, Chile, Argentina, Peru, and several other countries. Among the other denominations are the Iglesia Asamblea de Dios Boliviana, Iglesia Ekklesía, Iglesia de Dios (Church of God, Cleveland, TN; since 1959), Iglesia Evangélica Pentecostal de Chile (since 1935), and the Iglesia Pentecostal Brasilera. There are a number of indigenous independent congregations and small but significant charismatic movements in other churches.

■ **Bibliography:** X. Albo, "La experiencia religiosa aymara," in M. Mazal, ed., *Rostos indios de Dios* (1992) ■ J. Å. Alvarsson, *Är Indianerna dödsdömda?* (1981) ■ idem, *Bolivia indianland* (1980) ■ idem, *Dela som Syskon: Att förmedla evangeliet över kulturgränserna* (1992) ■ idem, *Får drömmen leva? Möten med sydamerikanska indianledare* (1984) ■ idem, *Ny hopp. Nu har vi ett hem!* (1988) ■ idem, *Skola för de allra fattigaste? Utvärdering av gymnasieskolan Buenas Nuevas i Cochabamba, Bolivia* (Forskningsrapporter i missionsvetenskap, missionshistoria och missionsantropologi, 5; 1989) ■ idem, *Ved Indianerbålet*, trans. I. Aas (1982) ■ idem, *Yo soy weenhayek: Una monografía breve de la cultura de los Mataco-Noctenes de Bolivia* (1992) ■ Anon., *Bolivia* (Springfield, MO, c. 1960) ■ D. B. Barrett, *World Christian Encyclopedia* (1982), 180–84 ■ D. Bundy, "Pentecostal Missions to Brazil: The Case of the Norwegian G. L. Pettersen," *Norsk tidsskrift for misjon* 47(1993) ■ D. L. Burk, ed., *Foreign Missions Insight: A Digest of Foreign Missions Faces, Facts, Fields and Figures* (1999), 131–32 ■ A. Herberts, *I Kärlekens Tjänst. Finlands Svenska Pingstmission under 70 ar* (1994) ■ S. M. Hodges, *Look on the Fields. A Survey of the Assemblies of God in Foreign Lands* (1956), 153–54 ■ W. J. Hollenweger, *Handbuch der Pfingstbewegung* (diss., Zurich, 1967), 870–72 (para. 02b. 04) ■ L. Jeter de Walker, *Siembre y cosecha*, vol. 2 (1992) ■ R. Kanto, *Pingströrelsen i Svenskfinland* (1994) ■ O. Nilsen, *Ut i all Verden: Pinsevennenes ytre misjon i 75 år* (1984) ■ P. A. Pedersen, "Bolivia," in *Til Jordens Ender: Norsk pinsemisjon gjennom 50 år* (1960) ■ G. L. Pettersen, *Pinse over grensene* (Oslo, 1989) ■ A. Ruuth, "Aspectos sociales de las fiesta andinas: Experiencias pentecostales en Bolivia," in *El Pentecostalismo en America Latina: Entre tradición y globalización*, ed. A. Pollak-Eltz and Y. Salas (1998) ■ R. L. Segata, "Cambio religioso y desetnificación: la expansión evangélica en los Andes Centrales de Argentina," *Religiones Latinoamericanas* 1 (1991) ■ G. E. Söderholm, *Den Svenska Pingstväckelsens spridning utom och inom Sverige* ■ *Supplement till de Svenska Pingstväckelsens Historia* (1933) ■ A. Sundstedt, *Pingstväckelsen*, 5 vols. (1969–73) ■ N. M. Van Cleve, *The Vine and the Branches: A History of the International Church of the Foursquare Gospel* (1992) ■ C. P. Wagner, *The Protestant Movement in Bolivia* (1972). ■ D. D. Bundy

BOSNIA-HERZEGOVINA

■ Pentecostals 479 (1%)   ■ Charismatics 31,631 (98%)   ■ Neocharismatics 290 (1%)   ■ Total Renewal: 32,400

See EUROPE, EASTERN.

BOTSWANA

■ Pentecostals 29,479 (6%)   ■ Charismatics 26,639 (5%)   ■ Neocharismatics 478,882 (90%)   ■ Total Renewal: 535,000

BOUGAINVILLE

■ Pentecostals 0 (0%)   ■ Charismatics 6,658 (72%)   ■ Neocharismatics 2,642 (28%)   ■ Total Renewal: 9,300

BRAZIL

■ Pentecostals 24,810,921 (31%)   ■ Charismatics 33,970,683 (42%)   ■ Neocharismatics 21,168,395 (26%)
■ Total Renewal: 79,949,999

I. The Antecedents of Brazilian Pentecostalism
   A. Brazil's Social Uniqueness
   B. The Colonial Legacy
   C. Tensions between Spiritists and Scientists
   D. Brazilian Spirituality
II. A Profile of Brazilian Pentecostalism
   A. The Size and Scope of the Brazilian
      Movement

   B. Explanations for Pentecostal Growth in Brazil
   C. The Emergence of National Pentecostal
      Movements
III. Brazilian Pentecostalism as a Popular Social
   Movement
   A. The Fertile Soil of Brazilian Spirituality
   B. The Diverse Structures of Brazilian Pentecostalism

    C. *The Catholic Charismatics*

IV. The Future of Brazilian Pentecostalism
    A. *Pentecostalism and Social Progress*
    B. *Perils and Paradoxes*

I. THE ANTECEDENTS OF BRAZILIAN PENTECOSTALISM.

A. Brazil's Social Uniqueness.

Brazil is Portuguese-speaking, with its own dialect, culture, and nationality, and with a population more than three times the rest of the Portuguese-speaking world combined (Portugal, Angola, Mozambique, São Tomé, and Príncipe). Because of its ethnic mixture and characteristic tolerance, Brazil has sometimes been referred to as a "racial democracy." About one-half of the population is European, with large Portuguese and Spanish minorities dispersed throughout the country, and notable concentrations of immigrants from Italy and Germany in the south-central and southern states of São Paulo, Paraná, Santa Catarina, and Rio Grande do Sul. At least 15% of all Brazilians are considered to be of African descent, and perhaps as many as a third of all Brazilians are mulatto. The northern state of Bahia, the cultural heartland of traditional Brazil—e.g., the cradle of Brazilian cuisine, religion, and folklore, and an important port of entry for the massive (3.5 million) slave trade in the colonial era—is overwhelmingly African in its culture. Small but significant populations of native peoples still maintain their way of life in the interior regions of the Amazon, and large numbers of Asians—notably Okinawans—have established themselves in the south-central states.

Brazil's national character was set early as Portugal's New World empire was used, like Australia by the British, mainly for dumping convicts and religious dissidents, including Jews. Brazilians were early characterized as being nonconformists, an often charming, virile, and unruly people who scoffed at authority. Portugal left the feudal *donatarios* (grantees) undisturbed in a policy of "salutary neglect"; and with the expulsion in 1763 of the Jesuits, the most unifying and constructive force in colonial Brazil, Brazilians developed a "softened, lyric" Christianity, unlike the dramatic Catholicism of Castile. Mystical and pliant, this unique form of Catholicism served also as the basis for Brazilian unity, providing cohesion and character in national life.

B. The Colonial Legacy.

Colonized by the Portuguese, beginning in 1500, Brazil developed a feudal system of large holdings run by regional bosses and a cismontane (more loyal to the crown rather than to the papacy) hierarchy heading a church whose practices were those of folk Catholicism. These features have persisted, despite the sweeping social changes of the 20th century. The decentralization of political power, along with marked racial diversity, administrative continuities that survived separation from Portugal, the get-rich-quick nature of Brazil's economic development, extremes of social stratification, and the country's isolation from both Europe and its Hispanic American neighbors all have contributed to Brazil's unique religious development.

Brazil occupies half of the South American continent. It is separated from the adjacent countries by the Amazon basin on the north, the Andes mountains on the west, and the Chaco desert on the south. Dense population settlement is found only along the Atlantic shore in a shallow strip that extends inland only 200 miles. Until the 20th century, Brazil's vast hinterlands to the north and west—the *sertao*—were settled only thinly by a "moving frontier" of cowboys *(vaqueiros)*, mixed-blood peasants, communities of former slaves, miners, and Amazon rubber harvesters. These *caboclos,* whose worldview was essentially medieval, lived in isolated settlements. The substratum of Brazilian society, the caboclos have been described as "imbued with fanaticism, [they are] strong, honest, revengeful, primitive, and refractory to modern ideas and life." In the 1890s the national army was called in to put down an insurgency centered in Canudos, 300 miles northwest of the colonial capital of Salvador da Bahia. Led for 35 years by a high-priest/king who worked miracles and took paternalistic care of his subjects, the rebels formed a theocratic state within Brazil. Their religion was a mixture of Catholicism, fetishism, and a millenarian faith called Sebastianism, based on the belief that a medieval king of Portugal who was killed in a crusade against the Muslim Moors would someday return in triumph. The insurgents held out against federal troops for three years before they were overrun. The rebels' faith and fanatical resistance were immortalized in the classic *Os Sertoes* by Eucides da Cunha, an engineer who saw in the Canudos resistance an expression of the mystical soul of the Brazilian people. Numerous 20th-century political

A river baptism in Brazil.

messiahs and the persistence of traditional beliefs and practices make Brazil fertile soil for popular religious movements.

C. Tensions between Spiritists and Scientists.

Religion in modern Brazil is thus deeply rooted in the nation's history, the emergence of a diverse, fiercely independent, and imaginative people. When Portugal was overrun by Napoleon in 1803, the emperor and the Portuguese court simply withdrew to Brazil and continued to govern the Portuguese empire from the colony. After the emperor returned to Portugal, his heir, Pedro I, declared Brazil's independence. In 1831 Pedro I returned to Portugal and left the government of Brazil in the hands of a regency until his young son came of age. Given internal conflicts in the country, Brazilians called on Pedro II to assume the leadership of the country in 1840, when he was only 19 years old. The second Pedro reigned as a benevolent monarch until 1889, when Brazil joined the other American states in becoming a republic. But the long period of relative peace and tranquillity contrasted sharply with the rancor and civil upheaval that "balkanized" the other South American countries at Independence. These continuities also ensured that Brazil would keep its religiously relaxed system.

Pedro II was open to Protestantism and the advanced scientific thinking of the era. Moreover, the state was much stronger than the church, and the latter had to acquiesce in its subordinate role. There was a shortage of priests, and clerical morals were notoriously loose. Moreover, the first candidate to be put forward under the new regime as the bishop of Rio de Janeiro advocated the abolition of clerical celibacy. When in 1864 Pope Pius IX denounced the Masonic Order—which in Brazil, unlike in Europe, was more a fraternal than an anticlerical organization—a priest in Rio de Janeiro who like many churchmen was also a Mason was required by his bishop to sever his connections with Freemasonry or suffer suspension. Eventually the bishop himself was convicted of violating the constitution and was sentenced to four years in prison. Politically, regalism—the power of the emperor over the church hierarchy—triumphed over attempts to discipline Brazilians in matters of religious faith.

Modernizing change during the 19th century had an impact on religious thought. The quickening pace of economic changes; the growth of cities (from 1840 to the end of the empire, Rio de Janeiro grew from 140,000 to 550,000); the concentration of ever greater wealth with the rapid growth of coffee exports and industrialization; the increasing consumer demands of a growing urban middle class; and confidence in science and the positivistic philosophy of August Comte all helped to shape religion in modern Brazil. In recognition of this quest for utopia, the Brazilian flag displays a globe with the legend *Ordem e progresso* (order and progress). The rationalizing of national life under the aegis of positivist philosophy tended to support both liberal and conservative ideas, which were represented by, respectively, the equality of the races and the inherent superiority of anything European.

Although Brazil was left the only country in the American hemisphere to retain slavery after the end of the U.S. Civil War (1865), by 1871 children born to slave mothers were declared free. Slavery was abolished entirely in 1889. Positivism—scientific progress—was the basis for wanting to encourage European immigration. Both on the sugar plantations of the north and the coffee plantations of the south-central states, free labor tended to replace slave labor without legislation. To induce desirable European immigrants, however, the government had to advertise guarantees of religious freedom. German immigrants, about one-half of whom were Protestants, arrived in the southern states in the 19th century, along with a large number of Italians who settled in São Paulo and Paraná.

D. Brazilian Spirituality.

Spiritism (often referred to as "high spiritism," in contrast to folk spiritism of caboclo or African origin), gained support in Brazil in the last half of the 19th century. Its main form was based on the doctrines of Alan Kardec, which had been imported from France. Kardec accepted reincarnation and the communication with spirits through mediums. His teachings had wide influence, finding a following in a variety of forms throughout Brazilian society. Kardec rejected some principal tenets of Christianity, including heaven and hell, the Trinity, the deity of Christ, and the divine origins of miracles. His writings, however, embraced Christian morality—such as moral purity, unselfishness, and benevolent acts. Kardicist "disobsession" is a kind of exorcism of evil from practitioners of the movement. Spiritism in Brazil has many devotees in all walks of life. This proclivity is found in the generally held belief that the spirits of the dead continue to remain with the living. "Spirits," says David Hess, "are therefore a part of *brasilidade* (Brazilianness)," that elusive amalgam of symbols and feelings that constitutes national identity. That Kardec's grand scheme of wedding Catholicism, Protestantism, science, and mysticism found a welcome home in Brazil reveals much about the fertile syncretistic soil Brazil provided for pentecostalism. More important, however, was the freedom given for the emergence of African religion, once practiced clandestinely or at least within the general framework of folk Catholicism.

Afro-Brazilian religion, in contrast to Kardicism, is often called "low spiritism." During the colonial period, Afro-Brazilian religion developed regionally: Candomblé in Bahia, Xangó in Pernambuco, and Macumba in Rio de Janeiro. African influence also altered Brazilian Catholicism, making it less severe and contributing festive dances and dramas. Although these practices were considered barbarian and the practitioners were sometimes persecuted by the authorities, nevertheless, various African cults were well established by the turn of the century. These consisted in the main of spirit possession groups led by a practitioner who directed initiates dressed in white outfits in dances and singing. With the gradual breakdown of *African religioes das nacoes* (tribal religion imported more or less intact), Macumba emerged in the early part of the century. The shift occurred as the practitioners of folk religion syncretistically commingled traditional African folk practices with Brazilian Catholic cultural traits. Eventually, this process of adaptation produced Umbanda in the 1920s.

Umbanda was the result of a revelation to Zelio de Moraes, son of a Kardicist, who received a vision for the formation of a new religion that would bring together both the *Pretos Velhos* (the African patriarchs) and the caboclos, the spiritual wisdom of the Brazilian natives. By 1941 Umbanda had its first congress in Rio de Janeiro. Kardicism was too intellectual and refined, and Macumba retained too many of the traditional practices, like animal sacrifices, to satisfy the emerging urban groups. Umbanda became popular, claiming to be rooted in the ancient mysticisms of Egypt, India, Peru, and Mexico, as well as those of Africa. Moreover, it claimed to combine the three sources of Brazilian population, those of Africa, Europe, and America, into a single national entity. It purges the black magic of traditional African religion and replaces it with a more palatable nationalistic belief in good spirits. Umbanda, say some practitioners, means *uma banda,* one single group, to indicate the unifying nature and distinctly Brazilian character of their religion.

II. A PROFILE OF BRAZILIAN PENTECOSTALISM.

A. The Size and Scope of the Brazilian Movement.

Brazil, the world's largest Roman Catholic country (with a population of 170 million, of whom an estimated 90% are baptized Catholics), also has the largest number of Protes-

Major Brazilian Pentecostal/Neo-Pentecostal Churches

Church	Congregations	Members	Community
Assembleias de Deus	85,000	6,000,000	14,000,000
Igreja Universal do Reino de Deus	10,000	2,000,000	4,000,000
Congregacao Cristia	15,294	1,560,000	3,120,000
Deus é Amor	3,200	1,600,000	2,670,000
Brasil para Cristo	5,000	1,000,000	2,000,000
Igreja Foursquare	2,641	389,266	607,567
Totals (less double counting)	121,135	11,000,000	23,475,000

Source: Patrick Johnstone, *Operation World* (1996).

tant pentecostals. Presently pentecostals in Brazil are approaching 25 million members (15% of the population; the national census of 1991 officially identified 8.98% as Protestant), of which the Assembleias de Deus is the largest group. Begun about 1910 simultaneously in both the north (Belém) and the south-central (São Paulo) regions, pentecostal groups have spread throughout the country. A Jan. 1995 *National Geographic* article noted that on the Amazon River all villages tended to look the same: "one or two roads, a Roman Catholic church, and an Assemblies of God church, a small market, stacks of beer crates, boys playing soccer." Besides the main pentecostal denominations, there are several large neocharismatic groups, namely, the Igreja Universal do Reino de Deus (the Universal Church of the Kingdom of God), Deus é Amor (God Is Love), and Brasil para Cristo (Brazil for Christ), which together make up at least a third of all pentecostal adherents. With 85% of Brazil's Protestants—and still growing—the pentecostals have been investigated frequently by students of social change. Moreover, Catholic charismatic cells have emerged in many Brazilian parishes alongside ecclesial base communities (CEBs), another example of local lay initiative. As well as revealing the nature of Brazilian pentecostalism, these studies inform our understanding of the struggles for recognition of the emerging popular sectors in 20th-century Brazil.

B. Explanations for Pentecostal Growth in Brazil.

The pentecostal phenomenon in Brazil, unique in many respects even among the Latin American churches, is highly dynamic and especially suited to the nation's culture. Berg and Pretiz (1996) offer an explanation for the growth not only of pentecostal and charismatic groups but of other grassroots religious movements. According to their analysis, colonial Brazil produced a mixture of European Catholicism and African religion, including the latter's familiarity with the spirit world. The Roman Catholic Church, according to Berg and Pretiz, was able to live with religious syncretism, but Protestants rejected this hybrid "cultural matrix." While the early-20th-century pentecostals, like other Protestants, denied animistic beliefs, they affirmed the reality of the spiritual realm and asserted their superiority in it. Charismatic teaching in the 1960s divided the historic Protestants between those churches that ignored the Brazilian worldview and those sensitive to the spiritual sensibilities of the people.

The explanations of most scholars are more prosaic. Social scientists relate the emergence of pentecostalism to the secular process of industrialization and the rationalization of the agricultural sectors—both of which contributed to anxiety-producing demographic shifts from rural and village communities to large cities, replacement of the traditionally secure personal relationships with impersonal contractual arrangements, and social protest by the marginal sectors. According to sociologist Emilio Willems, "Conversion to Protestantism … constitutes one of the many ways in which hostility and rebellion against a decaying social structure may be expressed." In this conceptualization pentecostalism has a progressive social function, a view held by other scholars, including Rowan Ireland. Burdick (1999) argues as well that pentecostalism in Brazil, often believed to have undermined African culture, has offered a range of ideas and practices that nourish rather than corrode black identity.

Hoffnagel (1980), however, along with d'Pinay and Sabastián, among others, takes exception to this view. She sees the Brazilian pentecostals as a reactionary social force that tends to strengthen rather than weaken traditional hierarchical social organization. According to her interpretation, pentecostal organization bears a striking resemblance to the traditional plantation society where support is never lacking in crisis and unlimited power is given to the *patrão*, the head of the patriarchal community. Individuals in the past would attach themselves to some powerful family and submit to the authority of the *patrão* in return for physical and economic security. The *pastor-presidente,* the spiritual and administrative head of a regional pentecostal church, according to Hoffnagel, governs in the place of the landowning *patrão,* and the church, made up of people whose world is in bewildering transition, reconstitutes the mutually dependent and authoritarian culture of the plantation.

C. The Emergence of National Pentecostal Movements.

The initial pentecostal efforts in Brazil were undertaken by missionaries and evangelists whose doctrines and practices represented pentecostalism as it emerged at the beginning of the century, with emphasis on experience and demonstrations of divine power. Rather than presenting a well-defined and rationally explained theology, pentecostalism was suited to Brazilians for whom religion was fluid, often eclectic, and often mystical. The movement's steady growth from 1909, when Luis Francescon, an Italian immigrant, took the message to São Paulo, and Swedish immigrants Gunnar Vingren and Daniel Berg introduced pentecostalism to Belém, in the northern state of Pará, corresponds to a period when the Brazilian masses struggled for a secure place in national life. Within several months the two efforts had given rise to congregations that were the beginnings of national movements, the Congregação Cristã and the Assembleias de Deus (a name adopted only after the group had been in existence for a decade; the group initially referred to itself as A Fe Apostólica—The Apostolic Faith). Although the name corresponded to that of the North American Assemblies of God (AG) organized in 1914—and some North American missionaries made strategic contributions after WWII—the Brazilian group was initially mentored almost exclusively by Swedish pentecostals and

emulates their "mother-church" polity and approaches, rather than those found typically in the AG–U.S.

The resources, personnel, vision, energy, and tenacity necessary to develop the movement were, however, clearly Brazilian. The Swedish pentecostals, still a small group at the time, although with highly effective leadership in the person of ▸Lewi Pethrus, could offer little more than vision, encouragement, and some overseas missionaries. As events demonstrated, even the styles of the church were so thoroughly Brazilian that later investigators developed a theory of atavistic regression, as pentecostals appeared in some respects to be more Brazilian and less adaptable to foreign or modernizing influences—reflected in legalistic codes of dress and conduct—than were other Protestants. By 1921 the group had already ordained its first national pastors, and in 1930 it held its first national conference attended by 16 pastors, Berg, Vingren, and several other Swedish missionaries. Already, however, these pastores-presidentes were not simply local leaders but autocratic heads of a central church with a network of dependent satellite congregations. The 16 pastors accounted for 300 congregations and 13,000 adherents. The entire pentecostal community in 1930 was reported to number 40,000 persons.

III. BRAZILIAN PENTECOSTALISM AS A POPULAR SOCIAL MOVEMENT.

A. The Fertile Soil of Brazilian Spirituality.

The appearance of the first pentecostal churches in the "drought zone" of northern Brazil, the area identified with the *caboclo* culture of the interior with its struggle for existence in a hostile environment—which periodically produced massive southward migrations—directly ties the growth of Brazilian pentecostalism to the throes of national formation. Spiritually sensitive, sensual, mystical Brazil, the home of Afro-Brazilian Umbanda, as well as the "high" spiritualism of Alan Kardec, persistent indigenous religious practices, and spiritually directed protest movements apparently offered considerable opportunity for the introduction of pentecostalism. Specifically, a study in 1932 left little doubt about the group's rapid spread and grassroots effectiveness. The authors mentioned the northern states of Para, Pernambuco, and Rio Grande do Norte, and also the Amazon, where, they say, there were "few villages where some Protestant is not living and possibly working in his way for the advancement of the Kingdom."

Until the 1980s it could be said that the Brazilian pentecostals were largely recruited from the marginal social sectors. Anthropologist Charles Wagley concluded in a classic survey of Brazil that "conversion to Protestantism is generally a result and concomitant of social mobility. Baptists and pentecostals, he observed, "seem to attract people of mixed racial ancestry and lower-class origins." Brazilian pentecostals are concerned with power. "It is obvious that the people are simple, but they speak with the confidence and the authority of heaven," wrote an observer of the early movement. It is telling that presently many nonpentecostal evangelicals practice and believe much as the pentecostals do themselves. Prayer for the sick, expressiveness in worship, belief in spirit possession, features often if not universally associated with pentecostals, are found in greater or lesser frequency among most other Brazilian Protestant denominations.

B. The Diverse Structures of Brazilian Pentecostalism.

Moreover, the Brazilian pentecostal groups are diverse and highly institutionalized. Often rigid, legalistic, and demanding, the discipline required of members of the traditional denominational groups cannot be easily exaggerated. The stress on hard work and abstention from drinking, gambling, and extramarital sex, Charles Wagley points out, leads to the breaking of kinship ties as well as those with the traditional church. "The strong in-group feelings of local churches ... provides them with a new, highly personalized social milieu in which their new values and achievements are given prestige." As early as 1939 the Assembleias de Deus church in Rio de Janeiro had a benevolence program for the aged and for disabled ministers, and sustained a missionary program to the Indians of the interior. The Congregação Cristã, on the other hand, with an unpaid clergy, used its resources almost entirely for benevolence programs and the construction of new churches. Increasingly, however, the Congregação Cristã is considered outside the main pentecostal stream because of its adherence to traditional practices (like veils for women worshipers, the use of wine at Communion, and strict formulas for prayer) and the members' unwillingness to associate with other pentecostals.

Presently the Brazilian pentecostals have emerged as a recognized force in national life. Not only are 85% of all Protestants pentecostal, but these groups, despite their humble origins, increasingly are recognized as a desirable religious option. The emergence of neocharismatic groups, especially, has given Brazilian pentecostals considerable visibility. The home church of the Brasil para Cristo movement in São Paulo meets in a church building that is believed to be the largest in the hemisphere, designed to seat 15,000 but accommodating up to 30,000 on occasion. Founded by Manoel de Mello, who conducted meetings in a tent in the 1950s, the church has a record of social service, political involvement, and education for the poor. Bitterly opposed by Roman Catholics at the beginning of his rise to recognition, de Mello also alienated many evangelicals by his ecumenism and progressive social programs. After the founder's death in 1970, the leadership of the church was assumed by his son Lutero, who moderated some of his father's emphases without changing the essential character of the church.

The Deus é Amor church meets in a former factory in São Paulo, a building that often seats more than the 10,000 worshipers for which it was originally intended. Women are seated on one side and the men on the other, like most pentecostal congregations, but unlike the more progressive Brasil para Cristo. In these churches the typically strict dress codes of the more traditional pentecostal denominations are relaxed. The struggle against spiritual oppression is a motif of this church. Founded by David Miranda, the brother-in-law of Manoel de Mello, the Deus é Amor has spread to other parts of Latin America and has congregations in the United States.

The Igreja Universal del Reino de Deus (IURD), which has especially emphasized prosperity teaching, was founded by the enterprising Edir Macedo, who currently lives in New York City. Even more flamboyant than the other neocharismatics, the IURD has acquired huge assets, including a major-market TV channel in São Paulo and a highly rated AM frequency in Rio de Janeiro. The use of sacred objects (blessed oil, fig paste for healing poultices, water bottled from the Jordan River) are part of the IURD's artifacts. Charges brought against Macedo for his business dealings have further heightened the controversy surrounding his work.

C. Catholic Charismatics.

In Brazil, Catholic charismatic renewal groups (often referred to as CCRs) have also become an important source of grassroots religious initiative. Throughout Latin America these groups have received the support of an international network of priests, nuns, and lay leaders as part of the Catholic renewal in the U.S. that began in 1967. Nevertheless, the movement in Brazil has taken on a distinctly national character. Observers point out that in the 1970s, preceding the formation of local Catholic charismatic groups, the People's Church movement (*comunidades ecclesiales de base*— ecclesial base communities, or CEBs) in support of liberation theology had gained a considerable following and had the support of many priests. Estimates at the movement's peak

Inauguration of Assemblies of God church in Camargos, Brazil.

rose to as many as 100,000 groups with the number of active members in each averaging perhaps 20 persons. To these CEBs in the 1980s were added in many parishes CCRs that further generated and channeled the religious energies of laypersons. Mario de Theije compares the two movements, CEBs and the CCRs, as they actually operate at the grassroots level. She points out that while the two lay movements appear antithetical ideologically—CEBs are community focused, emphasizing social programs, while CCRs are individualistic, emphasizing one's subjective experience—the two local groups may be made up in part of the same persons and may often work to realize similar agendas.

Since lay movements within the church are an important part of Brazilian Catholicism and other kinds of preconciliar, lay-driven organizations like the Legião de Maria (Legion of Mary) and the Apostolado da Oração (The Apostolate of Prayer) are widespread, Theije sees the CCRs as simply another expression of grassroots initiative in Brazilian religion. Although priests are less likely to encourage the CCRs than the CEBs, according to Theije, some priests concede that the CCRs produce highly committed Catholics. Moreover, CCRs offer an alternative to parishioners who are attracted to the features of non-Catholic religious practices. By reaching out to embrace pentecostal phenomena, the Roman Catholic

Assemblies of God church in São Paulo, Brazil.

Church obviates the need for the faithful to supplement their spiritual life from sources outside the church.

IV. THE FUTURE OF BRAZILIAN PENTECOSTALISM.

A. Pentecostalism and Social Progress.

Pentecostalism in Brazil, for some interpreters, represents the empowering and mobilization of the emergent social classes. Symbolic of this progressive view is the attention given to Benadita da Silva, a former member of the Assembleias de Deus who served in the national Chamber of Deputies as a vocal advocate of the poor. But in-depth studies of pentecostal participation in politics are inconclusive, since many pentecostals refrain from involvement, while others, given the corruption of public life, avoid direct church support of party candidates and platforms. The tendency for many pastors to use their influence politically, however, appears to make increased activity inevitable.

Meanwhile, most pentecostals still subscribe to the fairly rigid standards of conduct and association traditional in their sectarian churches. Viewed often as a constructive social force, this personal discipline and commitment to traditional values has been celebrated by investigators like Cecial Mariz, who argues that pentecostalism has led to the strengthening of the nuclear family and the larger community, as well as confidence for forging a better life for the common people. Even Professor Mariz, however, acknowledges that social progress within (as opposed to between) generations is limited.

B. Perils and Paradoxes.

Although political and business leaders recognize that Brazilian pentecostalism has become one of the major forces in the country, critics point out paradoxes and inconsistencies. As elsewhere in Latin America, pentecostals are unlikely to vote consistently and uniformly in a bloc, diffusing their political influence. Despite their effective mobilization of the popular sectors, with its implied commitment to improving their position, pentecostals at critical junctures have adopted reactionary positions. But whether pentecostals can retain their moral influence and still participate in public life is questionable, especially since there have been notable cases of pentecostal politicians who seem to have sold out their integrity for personal gain.

Within traditional pentecostal groups, as well, problems are apparent. Rigidity has led to the loss to the neocharismatic churches of many younger members and many new converts from the business and professional classes. Even admirers of the traditional pentecostals are likely to point out that institutional growth continues without the spontaneity and conviction that has usually marked the highly committed membership. There are also concerns about tensions within the movement. Besides growing differences between the poor and the affluent as more pentecostals are recruited from the middle sectors and the children of pentecostal families have access to education and other social opportunities, the autocratic organization of the major church jurisdictions has resulted in competing efforts, outdated authoritarianism, flagrant nepotism, heightened sectarianism, and personality conflicts. Whether the intensity of the early movement can be maintained despite these impediments remains to be seen. The greatest hope appears to lie in the inherent adaptability of the pentecostals, whose creativity and resilience have been repeatedly demonstrated.

Undoubtedly, however, Brazilian pentecostalism represents some of the best features that the global movement has to offer. Its enormous size, extensive influence, and penetration into many areas of national life makes it formidable. Having incorporated large numbers of the common people in a common cause, its spiritual vitality has been and continues to be impressive.

■ **Bibliography:** C. L. Berg and P. Pretiz, *Spontaneous Combustion: Grass Roots Christianity, Latin American Style* (1996) ■ J. Burdick, "What Is the Color of the Holy Spirit?" *Latin American Research Review* 34 (1999) ■ R. A. Chestnut, *Born Again in Brazil: The Pentecostal Boom and the Pathogens of Poverty* (1997) ■ E. L. Cleary, "Pentecostals, Prominence, and Politics," in E. L. Cleary and H. W. S. Gambino, eds., *Power, Politics, and Pentecostals in Latin America* (1997) ■ A. Corten, *Pentecostalism in Brasil: Emotion of the Poor and Theological Romanticism* (1999) ■ M. De Theije, "CEBs and Catholic Charismatics in Brazil," in C. Smith and J. Prokopy, eds., *Latin American Religion in Motion* (1999) ■ A. Droogers, "Paradoxical Views on a Paradoxical Religion: Models for the Explanation of Pentecostal Expansion in Brazil and Chile," in B. Boudewijnse, A. Droogers, and F. Kamsteeg, eds., *More Than Opium: An Anthropological Approach to Latin American and Caribbean Pentecostal Praxis* (1998) ■ J. C. Hoffnagel, "Pentecostalism: A Revolutionary or Conservative Movement?" in S. D. Glazier, ed., *Perspectives on Pentecostalism: Case Studies from the Caribbean and Latin America* (1980) ■ D. Hess, *Spirits and Scientists: Ideology, Spiritism, and Brazilian Culture* (1991) ■ R. Ireland, *Kingdoms Come: Religion and Politics in Brazil* (1991) ■ C. L. Mariz, *Coping with Poverty: Pentecostals and Christian Base Communities in Brazil* (1994) ■ E. Willems, *Followers of the New Faith: Culture Change and the Rise of Protestantism in Brazil and Chile* (1967). ■ E. A. Wilson

BRITAIN

■ Pentecostals 277,128 (5%)   ■ Charismatics 4,089,776 (70%)   ■ Neocharismatics 1,453,096 (25%)
■ Total Renewal: 5,820,000

1. Classification.

The elements in the pentecostal and charismatic movement in the U.K. can be thought of as belonging to a spectrum. At one end are the classical pentecostal denominations whose foundation documents and constitutions include reference to spiritual gifts and some or all of the ministry gifts of Eph. 4. The distinctiveness of these churches rests in their traditional emphasis on manifestations of the Holy Spirit. In the middle are the traditional churches, Anglican, Roman Catholic, Baptist, and so on, whose historical identities may date back to the Reformation and whose welcoming of spiritual gifts from the 1960s onward was dependent on local enthusiasm and theology. At the other end are the New Churches, founded for the most part in the 1970s and 1980s. Their acceptance of spiritual gifts was never in question, but their distinctiveness usually lies in flexible church structures built around relationships with authoritative preachers who are almost invariably seen as embodying apostolic ministry.

2. Social Background.

Within the U.K., as within much of Europe, there has been steady decline in religious observance, a rise in living standards, an increase in the size and variety of non-Christian groups, and near-zero population growth. Against this background the pentecostal and charismatic churches have managed to run counter to the general religious trend and to grow.

They have done so by taking advantage of modern means of communication, by church planting, by appealing to young people, and by making use of the transformation within British society that has turned it from an elite system of higher education to a mass system of higher education. Nearly all the classical and New Church groups have their own training programs by which new ministers are prepared for service (▸Sociology of British Pentecostal and Charismatic Movements).

3. Theological Factors.

The Evangelical Alliance has provided an interdenominational framework that offers accommodation to nearly the whole pentecostal and charismatic movement. This is particularly important in the case of the New Churches, which, by and large, have tended to avoid hammering out doctrinal bases of faith and yet see the importance of general affiliation in the cause of the gospel. Interestingly, the Evangelical Alliance in Britain is headed by Joel Edwards, a black pentecostal from the Church of God.

Other evidences of underlying unity within these churches are to be found in the prevalence of the ▸Toronto Blessing that swept through many of them in the mid 1990s and in attendance at common residential events, the largest of which is Spring Harvest, which caters to some 80,000 people a year in various venues. Spring Harvest has a deliberate policy of providing both charismatic and noncharismatic speakers, thus allowing its visitors to choose the kind of worship and teaching they prefer, while at the same time expressing a shared evangelical faith.

This sense of unity, however, is not reflected in a uniform acceptance of ›spiritual warfare (sometimes understood as prayer and exorcism and at other times identified with ›Marches for Jesus). Similarly, the legitimacy of women's preaching ministry and, to a lesser extent, counseling according to secular psychological models are issues over which unanimity is not always found.

4. Classical Pentecostals.

All the classical pentecostals—›Apostolic Church (AC), ›Assemblies of God in Great Britain and Ireland (AGGBI), (New Testament) Church of God (CG), and the ›Elim Pentecostal Church (EPC)—have been influenced by the charismatic movement and the New Churches. Some of the influence has been in terms of style, and in other cases theology and structure have also been affected. Alongside these changes there has been development, as a consequence of the factors identified above, in the areas of education, media ministry, church planting, and interdenominational cooperation. (See also individual articles on each of these four churches.)

a. Apostolic Church. The AC has 115-plus congregations with 76 pastors and workers. It has upgraded its educational provision but retains its traditional form of apostolic governance. Within the British Isles, AC has probably been the least affected among all the classical pentecostal churches by theological and social developments elsewhere.

b. Assemblies of God in Great Britain and Ireland. The AGGBI has 670-plus congregations with 900-plus ordained ministers. Since the 1980s AGGBI has adopted a composite structure. Local congregations are autonomous, but there are regional and general superintendents. The tension between autonomy and superintendence gives rise to ambiguities that are probably incapable of complete resolution. Autonomy is often identified with theological stress on ministry gifts; superintendence is urged on the grounds that ministers themselves need to be cared for and that national cohesiveness cannot be achieved without a formal translocal structure. Nevertheless, these issues have not reduced the impact of the Holy Spirit beyond the denomination through, for example, the Sunderland Christian Centre's part in the spread of the Toronto Blessing and revivalism. And, since AG's educational provision now covers the full range of academic degrees, there is an interdenominational aspect to this work. Moreover, in the midst of constitutional changes, missionary work has been reorganized to allow greater freedom to individual directors.

c. (New Testament) Church of God. The CG has 100-plus congregations and 250-plus ministers and, in England, is mainly Afro-Caribbean. It has made no recent changes to

what is basically an episcopal structure of government or to its doctrines, but its ongoing commitment to social responsibility has led to modifications in relation to the ministry of women, their admission to debate in the General Assembly, and a removal of the ban on divorcees, provided they are the innocent party in a marriage break-up, from ordination.

d. Elim Pentecostal Church. The EPC has 580-plus congregations and 600-plus ministers. During the 1980s regionalization was introduced, and in 1994 there was a streamlining of Fundamental Truths, which removed reference to the millennium on the grounds that such a truth cannot be properly regarded as fundamental. Educational provision for ministers now offers the full range of degrees. The influence of Kensington Temple (KT), which is by far the largest congregation in the fellowship, is likely to grow, especially as, with its satellite churches, KT will probably come to about a quarter of the size of the rest of the fellowship combined.

5. Denominational Charismatics.

a. Anglican Charismatics. Initially, Anglican charismatics were serviced by the ›Fountain Trust (founded in 1964), which helped shape their theology and style of worship, primarily by the publication of *Renewal* magazine and by arranging high-profile conferences. Later ›Anglican Renewal Ministries (from 1980) used similar methods, though its emphasis included topics like "prayer combat" and the Jewish and Celtic roots of spirituality. It also worked through diocesan renewal groups and developed teaching materials suitable for one-day conferences. Charismatic teaching and events were publicized through the magazine *Anglicans for Renewal.* It serves the whole Anglican church, evangelical as well as Anglo-Catholic. Up to 20% of Anglican churches have been positively affected by the charismatic movement, an influence most noticeable in music for worship and the rise of lay ministry. This influence is more pronounced in urban areas.

The flagship congregations for charismatic activity within Anglicanism have been ›Holy Trinity Brompton (HTB), which initiated the Alpha courses for young Christians (more than 3,000 people in HTB alone in 1997) and St. Andrew's Chorleywood (SAC). HTB retains liturgical services that follow the prayer book for its noncharismatic attendees, but during its other services it is more informal and emphasizes applied Bible teaching. Mark Stibbe, presently ministering at SAC, has turned attention to the intellectual implications of charismatic functioning and has argued that theology itself may be renewed by the present move of the Spirit (Stibbe, 1993).

HTB is a thriving, well-financed congregation involved in church planting, youth work, home groups, training, prison ministry, and so on. It operates within the Anglican episcopal and diocesan structure yet was instrumental in the spread of the Toronto Blessing cross-denominationally.

b. Catholic Charismatics. The Catholic charismatic movement in the U.K. is diffuse and was also, at its inception, influenced by the Fountain Trust, though perhaps more by North American sources. In the 1970s it generated great excitement and was spread through days of renewal that resulted in the formation of the National Service Committee (1973), a group neither appointed by bishops nor elected. With regard to their church, Catholic charismatics found themselves in a position different from that of many narrower Protestant denominations. At an official level the Catholic Church never took a negative view of Catholic charismatics and, unless particular local situations were especially discouraging, prayer groups and charismatic-style eucharists provided suitable expressions of faith and opportunities to grow.

Theologically, the decision to accept the nurture of the Catholic Church was made easier by the distinction, expressed in a number of Catholic theologians, that the Holy Spirit was received at infant baptism but released through baptism in the Spirit (Tugwell). This had the effect of safeguarding the validity of infant baptism.

In contrast to the Anglican communion, however, Catholic charismatic congregations and parishes did not come into existence. In the 1980s the second wave of Catholic charismatics were attracted to communities that were especially important in reaching young people (➤Charismatic Communities).

About 3,000 copies of the Catholic charismatic newsletter *Good News* are circulated every two months, though this represents a small percentage of the 2.2 million who attend mass weekly. Additionally, charismatic renewal is fostered by camps, retreats, and conferences; and Catholic teachers are able to draw on the rich resources of Catholic scholarship in their understanding of charismatic phenomena.

c. Baptist Charismatics. An estimate that 20% of all Baptist churches in Britain are sympathetic to the charismatic movement is probably too cautious. Douglas McBain suggests that the majority of younger ministers are positively influenced by charismatic doctrine and worship (McBain, 1997, 1998). He also points out that some Baptist churches have dual loyalty, both to New Frontiers International (see below) and to the Baptist Union. A movement that started in the 1970s in the churches of the Baptist Union, Mainstream, has been one of the key agencies of renewal.

d. Methodist Charismatics. The best available figures (Haley, 1999) show that almost exactly 10% of Methodist Circuit Ministers in the U.K. think that speaking in tongues in public worship should be encouraged and that approximately a quarter of Methodist ministers would describe themselves as charismatic. The spread of charismatic renewal within the Methodist Church, however, has been hindered by the circuit system, which moves ministers on after a set period of time and gives a minister charge over several congregations, while requiring him or her to work with local preachers who reflect the overall theological diversity within the denomination. The dynamic link between minister and congregation that might lead to the establishment of a charismatically empowered congregation is thus absent. Continuity in charismatic teaching was, however, provided by *Dunamis,* a magazine widely distributed among Methodists and sympathetic to the charismatic movement that ran from the early 1970s to the mid 1990s. Moreover, attendance at annual charismatically influenced events could attract up to 12,000 Methodist worshipers.

6. New Churches.

The origins of the New Churches (also known as ➤House Churches or ➤Restorationists) are to be found in a complex set of factors discussed by Hocken (1984, 1998) and Walker (1985, 1992). These include the nonhierarchical ecclesiology of Brethrenism, a distaste for the mechanics of denominational structures, an unwillingness, in some instances, to accept tongues or "signs following" as initial evidence of the baptism in the Spirit, and a tendency toward amillennialism. Yet the New Churches share much with pentecostals and charismatics, particularly in their understanding of the manifestations of the Holy Spirit, and are willing, to a greater or lesser extent, to see these manifestations as being logically and theologically linked with the emergence of the ministries of apostle, prophet, pastor, evangelist, and teacher. In their style of worship, these churches may be indistinguishable from the freer pentecostal and charismatic congregations.

The size of these groups of churches is difficult to estimate, partly because they are continually growing and partly because there have been tendencies for sets of churches to break away from one apostolic figure and attach themselves to another. Moreover, nearly all these groups engage in missionary work overseas, which means that resources are deployed in unpredictable ways. The best available figures (Francis and Brierley, 1997) suggest that the New Churches are larger than (perhaps twice the numerical size of) the older pentecostal churches.

a. Bugbrooke. In 1969 a Baptist church in Northamptonshire under the leadership of Noel Stanton became a Christian community practicing simplicity of life. Its early members were bikers, hippies, and others engaged in the counterculture. By 1996 the community had grown to 60 large houses and 20 smaller ones, distributed across the whole of the U.K. Membership exists at various levels, and any finances people bring when they join may be taken again if they decide to leave. The Jesus Army, the community's evangelistic arm, is aggressive but effective in areas of urban poverty.

b. Cornerstone Ministries. Cornerstone Ministries, now known as c.net, was founded in 1982. Its team leader is ►Tony Morton. A group of 35 churches operate in the U.K., and more than twice this number overseas. Apostolic ministry from several nations emphasizes both contemporary charismatic life and practical initiatives (e.g., pregnancy counseling and Christian schools). The major priorities, however, are church planting and training.

c. Covenant Ministries International. CMI came into existence when Harvest Time changed its name in 1989. Its two leading figures are the brothers ►Bryn and Keri Jones. A group of 35 churches operate in the U.K. and a roughly equal number overseas.

d. Ichthus. The Ichthus Fellowship in south London is made up of about 2,000 people in more than 25 congregations. Founded in 1974 by Roger and Faith Forster, it has been marked by an emphasis on the Holy Spirit, persistent evangelism, a concern for social action (Jesus Action), the ministry of women on an equal basis with that of men, an outlook that welcomes interdenominational cooperation, and a plurality of leadership through elders.

e. Kingsway International Christian Centre. KICC works mainly in London, particularly among the African and Asian communities. Its senior pastor is Matthew Ashimolowo, a Nigerian of Islamic origin. The total number of adherents is approximately 7,000 (in 1998). Their planned northeast London auditorium, seating 5,000, will be able to accommodate the largest single congregation in the U.K.

f. New Frontiers International (NFI). NFI, the largest of the New Church networks, was founded by ►Terry Virgo in Sept. 1980. The reformed theology to which Virgo is strongly attracted and his teaching ministry have produced a fellowship of around 200 congregations in the U.K., with an income of over £2 million in 1995. Considerable efforts are put into church planting and training, and the overall vision is to restore the church to New Testament Christianity. The Stoneleigh Bible Week attracts some 20,000 people from 40 nations; similar conferences are held in India, South Africa, the U.S., and Mexico.

g. Pioneer. ►Gerald Coates, the leading figure, characterizes Pioneer's more than 100 congregations as standing for "revival, relationships, and relevance." High-profile events have attracted people and publicity nationally. For example, Pioneer and Gerald Coates, along with Ichthus/YWAM, are cofounders of the International March for Jesus. They were also instrumental, along with Patrick Dixon, in launching ACET (Age Care Education in Training), the largest

provider of home care in the U.K. for those suffering with AIDS. Though the network is centered in North East Surrey just outside of southwest London, it has a regional structure that gives responsibility to regional team directors.

h. Salt and Light. A community church in Basingstoke under the leadership of Barney Coombs is the center of this network. Approximately 70 congregations in the U.K. are linked to Salt and Light apostolic teams, though each is governed by its own elders. Christian schools have been established in Britain and abroad, and an annual conference is held, usually at Harrogate.

i. Other Groups. Other apostolic networks (e.g., Plumbline, founded by Simon Matthews in 1985, with eight congregations in the U.K.; and Ground Level, led by Stuart Bell, with 40 church leaders) and numerous independent charismatic churches of various sizes and theologies can be found in the U.K. London has large numbers of African pentecostal churches, some independent, some loosely affiliated to each other.

7. Reflection.

The New Churches, which have made such an impact on the British scene, have yet to face the transition of authority and ministry from their founding generation to the next. Whether they will be able in the course of time to replace their key apostolic ministries smoothly remains to be seen. The constitutional solution to this problem used by the classical pentecostal churches has been shown to work reasonably well. But the New Churches see constitutions as inimical to personal relationships and part of the denominational package they reject.

Each set of churches along the pentecostal and charismatic spectrum has its own recognized training programs for producing ministers with valid credentials. The perpetuation of group identity is protected by this process. The problem for the denominational charismatics is different, because they must try to ensure that the charismatic element in congregations is preserved when there is no administrative or hierarchical procedure to guarantee this. Their training and induction programs must be broad enough to admit non-charismatics to ministry. They must therefore rely on special charismatic agencies within their denominational systems and on charismatic interdenominational conferences for revitalization.

The impact of the charismatic movement on the older denominations (Anglican, Baptist, Methodist, and, to an extent, Roman Catholic) has been seen most obviously in style of worship and heard in music. Songs by New Church ministers (e.g., ►Graham Kendrick, Noel Richards, and Dave Fellingham) have been very influential in Britain, but they have also been translated and sung all over the world. Theologically, the impact is more difficult to measure, but the impression of many commentators is that trainees for the ministry usually contain a large proportion of those for whom the charismatic movement has been a positive influence.

One issue that concerns pentecostal and charismatic churches particularly, but also applies in some measure to denominational churches, is the question of what exactly a church is. The arrival of "cell theology" suggests that a church is any Christian group that is capable of reproducing itself. Yet, in practical terms, pentecostal churches have often been thought of as groups capable of supporting a full-time minister. If it is true that the continued exercise of charismatic gifts within a group of congregations depends on ministerial life and activity, then cell churches must ensure that ministers remain able to function in the power of the Holy Spirit.

■ **Bibliography:** G. Coates, *An Intelligent Fire* (1991) ▋ L. J. Francis and P. W. Brierley, "The Changing Face of the British Churches: 1975–1995," in W. Shaffir, ed., *Leaving Religion and Religious Life:* *Patterns and Dynamics* (1997) ▋ L. J. Francis and D. W. Lankshear, "The Influence of the Charismatic Movement on Local Church Life: A Comparative Study among Anglican Rural, Urban and Suburban Churches, *Journal of Contemporary Religion* (1998) ▋ J. Gunstone, *Pentecostal Anglicans* (1982) ▋ J. M. Haley, "Methodist Circuit Ministers' Survey" (diss., U. of Wales, 1999) ▋ P. D. Hocken, "Baptised in the Spirit: The Origins and Early Development of the Charismatic Movement in Great Britain" (diss., U. of Birmingham, U.K., 1984) ▋ idem, *Streams of Renewal,* 2d ed. (1998) ▋ D. McBain, *Fire over the Waters* (1998) ▋ idem, "Mainstream Charismatics: Some Observations of Baptist Renewal," in S. Hunt, M. Hamilton, and T. Walter, eds., *Charismatic Christianity: Sociological Perspectives* (1997) ▋ M. W. G. Stibbe, "The Theology of Renewal and the Renewal of Theology, *JPT* 3 (1993) ▋ S. Tugwell, *Did You Receive the Spirit?* (1971) ▋ A. Walker, *Beyond the Kingdom* (1992) ▋ idem, *Restoring the Kingdom* (1985). ■ W. K. Kay

BRITISH INDIAN OCEAN

■ Pentecostals 0   ■ Charismatics 0   ■ Neocharismatics 0   ■ Total Renewal: 0

BRITISH VIRGIN ISLANDS

■ Pentecostals 705 (26%)   ■ Charismatics 1,607 (60%)   ■ Neocharismatics 359 (13%)   ■ Total Renewal: 2,671

See CARIBBEAN ISLANDS.

BRUNEI

■ Pentecostals 0 (0%)   ■ Charismatics 2,509 (28%)   ■ Neocharismatics 6,341 (72%)   ■ Total Renewal: 8,850

BULGARIA

■ Pentecostals 55,894 (40%)   ■ Charismatics 3,778 (3%)   ■ Neocharismatics 80,328 (57%)   ■ Total Renewal: 140,000

See EUROPE, EASTERN.

BURKINA FASO

■ Pentecostals 635,430 (75%)   ■ Charismatics 151,853 (18%)   ■ Neocharismatics 56,717 (7%)   ■ Total Renewal: 844,000

See AFRICA, WEST.

BURMA
See MYANMAR.

BURUNDI

■ Pentecostals 497,639 (64%)   ■ Charismatics 257,824 (33%)   ■ Neocharismatics 19,537 (3%) Total Renewal: 775,000

For a general introduction to Central Africa and bibliography, see
AFRICA, CENTRAL.

The same ethnic tensions between Tutsi and Hutu that exist in neighboring Rwanda exist also in Burundi. This has created difficulties within the churches, especially at the leadership level. In 1934 the governor of Burundi at Bujumbura was approached by the Mission Libre Suédoise (MLS—the name given to the Svenska Fria Missionen [Swedish Free Mission] in the French-speaking countries of Central Africa). He encouraged them to find an area that was not occupied by other missions. At first they considered the region of Gitega, but there were already other missions located there. In May 1934 Gosta Palmertz and Julius Aspelind from the Democratic Republic of Congo visited the territory of Bururi, where they were granted two parcels of land for the MLS; one was at Kayogoro in the province of Mabanda and the other at Kiremba in the province of Bururi.

The first missionaries to reside in Burundi came in 1935, when Almaa Andersson and Alice Kjellberg settled at Kayogoro. They were soon followed by Alda Holmström and Thomas and Anna Winberg, all of whom had previously worked at Uvira in Congo-Kinshasa. The second group began the work at Kiremba. Gösta and Viola Werlinder then arrived to reinforce the work of Andersson and Kjellberg, who were due for furlough. The first baptismal service was held on Sept. 13, 1936, at Kiremba, with four candidates. This was followed by two more baptismal services within eight months and the addition of 44 more believers. The Kiremba church has grown faster than any of the churches that have been planted, and with its branch churches *(chapelles)* had 72,118 members by the end of 1997. This church is pastored by Abed-Nego Madengo (born c. 1931). The pastor of Kayogoro is Lazaro Samiye (born 1927).

The churches that were founded by the MLS (SFM) constitute the largest Protestant group in the country. The direction of the churches was given to the national leadership in 1960. By nature the churches are independent, but they collaborate under the name La Communauté des Eglises de Pentecôte au Burundi (CEPBU, The Community of Pentecostal Churches of Burundi); the present legal representative of this grouping is Meshac Kabwa; Mpangaje Nathanael is the assistant legal representative. The CEPBU has 15 major churches that are considered mother churches and over 600 congregations (*chapelles*, which would also be considered churches in non-Swedish terms) and 280,863 members by the end of 1997. They have been active in primary education and evangelism. In 1997 alone there were 24,400 baptisms of adult believers. The combined number of those attending Sunday school in the CEPBU churches in 1997 was 129,326.

The Pentecostal Evangelistic Fellowship of Africa (PEFA—see Kenya) was recognized by the government in 1975 and has had considerable growth. Its legal representative and general overseer is François Ntigahera, and the vice general overseer is Etienne Nahimana. Since the introduction of multiparty democracy in the country in 1992, several new pentecostal groups have been formed. One of these is Elim–U.K., which has been involved in supporting ministry in Burundi since 1993, when Simeon Nzishura and his church were accepted under the Elim Church International (ECI—the international grouping of Elim–U.K.) umbrella. Eight churches have been founded with 815 adult members. The chairman is Abeli Gashagiri, and the secretary general is Eliki Bucamupaka.

The Eglise Unie du Saint-Esprit (The United Church of the Holy Spirit) has been present in Burundi for three years, and the Eglise Vivante (Living Church) has also attracted some members from existing pentecostal churches. These newer groups do not enjoy fellowship with the established pentecostal churches. Some independent pentecostals hold to a "Jesus Only" (⁎Oneness) doctrine. The doctrine of rebaptism for those who have been baptized using the trinitarian formula has caused some concern among pastors of the CEPBU. Many charismatics can be found in the Anglican churches, especially in the dioceses of Bujumbura and Matana. Other noncharismatic denominations also experience a charismatic renewal.   ■ D. J. Garrard

CAMBODIA

■ Pentecostals 1,187 (2%)   ■ Charismatics 2,716 (5%)   ■ Neocharismatics 52,097 (93%)   ■ Total Renewal: 56,000

CAMEROON

■ Pentecostals 99,499 (10%)   ■ Charismatics 554,497 (57%)   ■ Neocharismatics 326,004 (33%)   ■ Total Renewal: 980,000

See AFRICA, WEST.

CANADA

■ Pentecostals 504,551 (11%) ■ Charismatics 2,596,361 (59%) ■ Neocharismatics 1,324,088 (30%)
■ Total Renewal: 4,425,000

Perhaps the most striking feature of Christian experience in the 20th century has been the global moving of the Spirit. It could be argued that there have been two major pulses of the Spirit. The first, early in the century, produced what has come to be known as pentecostalism; the second was felt at midcentury and came to be known as the charismatic renewal. The two movements have constantly interacted with each other with indebtedness and influence passing back and forth freely.

None of this has passed Canada by. The interactions have been diverse and at times intense. Those Canadians who prayed for an "outpouring of the Spirit" or a "new Pentecost" might have anticipated that if it came it would challenge existing church structures and practices just as the first Pentecost did. The story of the pentecostal and charismatic movements in Canada has been one of innovation, testing, disappointment, and jubilation. New wine was poured into old wineskins twice in the century, and the results were remarkable. The discussion of these movements will fall into three chronological sections.

1. 1906–50.

Pentecost arrived in Canada in 1906. Some had traveled to the Apostolic Faith Mission on ʾAzusa St. in Los Angeles and had been baptized in the Spirit, but the first recorded outbreak in Canada took place in a mission operated by Ellen and ʾJames Hebden in Toronto. By the end of the decade the movement had spread from what is now the east coast of Canada to the west. Important centers were St. John's, Nfld.; Toronto, Ont.; Winnipeg, Man.; Swift Current, Sask.; and Vancouver, B.C. From the outset, aggressive evangelism and a passion for world missions characterized pentecostalism.

Women and men worked side by side in establishing pentecostalism. Important names include American ʾAlice Garrigus, the Hebdens, ʾR. E. McAlister, ʾG. A. Chambers, Alice Wood, ʾA. H. Argue, and ʾFranklin Small. They also include Hugh Cadwalder, ʾFlorence Crawford, and ʾGarfield Haywood, Americans who came north for longer or shorter periods of time to help the emerging movement. These leaders and those who worked with them played a crucial role in defining Canadian pentecostalism. With an eye always cocked toward the U.S. and informed by their own experiences, they determined how pentecostals would worship and what they would believe.

The early decades of their existence were difficult for Canadian pentecostals. Along with the questions of identity, they struggled, first with the impulse to organize and then

with the "Jesus Only" doctrine (ʾOneness Pentecostalism). When these two issues came together around 1920, the result was the first major split within the young movement with the Apostolic Church of Pentecost (ACOP) breaking off from the Pentecostal Assemblies of Canada (PAOC). They had wanted to avoid structural and theological controversy, but it had come anyway, and now the bloom was off the rose.

In the 1920s several clergymen from older denominations made their way into pentecostal groups. ʾD. N. Buntain came from Methodism, ʾH. C. Sweet and T. T. Latto from Presbyterianism, and ʾJ. Eustace Purdie from Anglicanism. They shared a spiritual longing with others already in the movement, and they embraced pentecostal worship and practice, soon moving into leadership. Their training and experience recommended them for pastorates in major churches and for positions as superintendents of districts and teachers in newly founded Bible schools. Quite purposely they applied what they had learned in their previous denominations, contributing to the growth, stability, and institutionalization of pentecostalism. Officially, the older denominations treated those leaving to join the burgeoning movement respectfully, in spite of the disparaging comments pentecostals made about their organizational sophistication and their "deadness."

Canadian pentecostalism surged into the 1930s. The country as a whole, and especially the West, was plunged into drought and depression, but pentecostalism enjoyed the second-fastest decade of growth in the whole of its history in Canada. While others left the "dust bowl" of the prairies, pentecostals—often pairs of single women such as Madge Black and Bessie Wood—found ways to make do and to stay. In fact, new pentecostal groups were established as "missionaries" came north from the U.S. to work in various parts of the country. A prime example of this activity was given by the Church of God (CG, Cleveland, TN). In fact, ʾC. W. Conn once pointed out that for a short period Canada was listed in the foreign missions records of the CG.

The last decade of this period, the 1940s, was dominated by the outbreak of the ʾLatter Rain movement. As numbers, stability, and ministerial training among pentecostals grew, so did a sense of loss. People began to feel a waning in spontaneity and eagerness for God. This crystallized in North Battleford, Sask., in 1948. A small prairie city became the center of a movement within a movement, and the new movement spun off the old. Led by George Hawtin and Percy Hunt, many individuals and assemblies who left came to be known as the "Latter Rain," emphasizing among other things the reappearance of New Testament gifts and offices.

2. 1950–75.

Growth—institutional and social as well as numerical—continued during this second period. The PAOC refined their organizational structure, while the Foursquare Gospel Church of Canada (FGCOC) redefined its relationship with its parent body in the U.S. Two even amalgamated. In 1949 the Evangelical Churches of Pentecost (ECOP) and the ACOP began to discuss merger, finally consummating the union in 1953.

There is strong evidence of improving socioeconomic conditions among the various groups. Like the homes of some of their members, some churches became larger and more architecturally elaborate. This was dramatically the case with the PAOC. A social conscience began to appear. The PAOC founded a hospital and built residences for seniors. Several pentecostals went into politics at the local, provincial, and national levels, representing political parties from the right to the left. One, Sam Jenkins, even became the head of a trade union.

Some pentecostals began to reach across barriers that had gone up between them and other evangelicals. This was difficult because the "tyranny of small differences" was at work here and rivalry was often intense. In spite of this, through the efforts of pentecostal Dr. J. Harry Faught, the Evangelical Fellowship of Canada was born.

Alongside these developments, the old values were being preserved. All pentecostal groups emphasized giving to missions and the expansion of missionary programs. Evangelism remained a priority. Saturday nights found groups of believers in parks and towns holding street meetings in attempts to win the lost.

This was also the period when the second pulse of the Spirit, the charismatic renewal, was felt. In the early 1960s, reports circulated regarding a fresh move among nonpentecostals in the U.S. Canadians began to hear about the experiences of Episcopalians like ʾDennis Bennett and Presbyterians like ʾJames Brown. These were people from the "mainline" who had begun to act like pentecostals. They caught the attention of the media and provided a social validation for pentecostal behavior. Phenomena associated with the movements, such as glossolalia, soon attracted scholarly interest.

The renewal appeared north of the border with the same kind of diversity as it had in the U.S. In the absence of an established taxonomy, I will identify three branches: denominational, nondenominational, and the "Jesus People." The first was composed of those who embraced the vitality of experiences of the Spirit but wished to remain within the older denominations in which they had grown up. The second welcomed people who had distanced themselves from any previously existing Christian groups. Many of these had been pentecostals, and a significant part of the leadership of

this branch had been active in the Latter Rain in the late 1940s and early 1950s. The third was largely made up of those who had been converted out of the drug culture of the 1960s in a movement that began in California and then spread north and east.

These three branches interacted intensely with each other and with older pentecostal groups. They shared conferences, speakers, audio- and videotapes, literature, ideas, music, and most of all, a spirituality. They were leaving the colorlessness and emptiness of old lives, whether in pentecostal or liturgical churches or in the counterculturalism of the 1960s, to find new hope through the experience of the Spirit. They met in venues as different as parks where the scent of "pot" hung heavy and neogothic Anglican churches.

The contact between Canadian pentecostals and the charismatics was complex. In parts of the country, Anglican and Catholic priests were invited into chapels and churches to share their experiences of Christ and the Spirit. In Quebec, however, the pentecostals, who had begun to grow rapidly as a result of initiatives from English-speaking Canada, were confused. They saw prayer groups forming throughout the province and large crowds, made up primarily of Catholics, gathering to worship like pentecostals, or Jesus People. But these worshipers were not leaving their Catholic parishes; they were "blooming where they were planted." They were finding ways to assimilate pentecostal experience and priorities into the sacramental system and Marian devotion, and they were becoming more active in their Catholic parishes as a result. Some pentecostals applauded and attempted to support the charismatics; others criticized emotional excesses and doctrinal naiveté. Some attended conferences, bought tapes, and joyfully embraced ideas such as "shepherding," while others attempted to guide congregations with increasingly divided loyalties. The soft-rock worship styles of the Jesus People found an acceptance that transcended the many differences among the groups.

The older denominations, looking on from the outside, determined to respond to the new pulse of the Spirit carefully. The 1975 General Assembly of the Presbyterian Church in Canada received the reports of no fewer than three committees that had been studying the renewal. The Anglican Church began to see the renewal within itself in 1962, and in 1973 the General Synod passed a resolution requesting bishops and delegates to do everything possible to "enable and support" it, and in 1974 it invited a pentecostal to lead a workshop focusing on the charismatic renewal at a ministerial conference.

The strongest positive response, however, came from the Catholic Church. In a statement issued by Canadian bishops in 1975, the renewal was characterized as "a hymn of wholehearted trust in the all-powerful presence of the Spirit in the world." The bishops also repeated an earlier call for the best possible communications to be maintained between charismatics and their home dioceses across Canada.

3. 1975–2000.

With some midcourse adjustments, trajectories established earlier have continued into the last quarter of the century. The renewal persists within the Catholic Church. Annual conferences are held in almost every diocese in Canada; prayer groups serve thousands throughout Canada (there are 186 groups in the province of Ontario alone, with approximately 5,800 persons attending); ˒Life in the Spirit seminars, characteristic of the Catholic renewal for several decades, are held frequently, usually at the invitation of parish pastors; an increasing number of priests and laypeople are being baptized in the Spirit, and lines of communication between charismatics and diocesan officials tend to be strong. The bishops in Quebec are concerned, but outside that province episcopal support of the renewal is high. An increasing number of bishops have themselves been baptized in the Spirit.

Research done in the early 1990s in the Anglican Church showed that 20% of the active clergy had been significantly influenced by the charismatic movement as had 30% of parishes. In the mid 1990s, charismatic Anglicans forged a coalition with evangelicals and liturgical-reform supporters in that communion to attempt to hold the mother church in traditional positions doctrinally and liturgically. Some clergy who have had charismatic experiences have also risen to the episcopal level.

During the same period, Canadian pentecostalism has continued to evolve. In metropolitan areas, particularly in the east, congregations have become dramatically multiracial. Some of the older pentecostal groups, which minister primarily to immigrant populations from the Caribbean, have become predominantly African-Canadian and have drawn leadership from that community. In most parts of the country, pentecostal growth is occurring to a large extent not only within Caribbean but also among other ethnic groupings. Somali, Ethiopian, Tamil, and Korean churches are the most prominent in this respect. It is among the same population groups that Catholic charismatic prayer groups are most common in Montreal.

Some of the older pentecostal denominations continue to refine and reposition themselves structurally and educationally. Following Canadian political trends and economic decentralizing, some services and programs previously provided by a national office are being reassigned to district jurisdictions in hopes of greater efficiency and effectiveness. In worship, patterns arising out of the Jesus People are almost universal as conscious attempts are made to respond to the tastes of the wider society. In fact, the strongest influence the charismatic movement has had on pentecostalism in Canada has not been in theology or pastoral practice, but in music.

There are 13 long-established Canadian pentecostal groups: The Apostolic Church in Canada, The ˒Apostolic Church of Pentecost, The Church of God, The Church of God of Prophecy in Canada, The Elim Fellowship of Evangelical Churches and Ministers, The Foursquare Gospel Church of Canada, ˒The Independent Assemblies of God–Canada, The ˒Italian Pentecostal Church of Canada, The Open Bible Standard Church of Canada, The ˒Pentecostal Assemblies of Canada, The ˒Pentecostal Assemblies of Newfoundland, The ˒Pentecostal Holiness Church of Canada, and the ˒United Pentecostal Church.

Standing beside these, but more a part of them than of any of the branches of the charismatic movement, are a number of new pentecostal fellowships or networks, for example, the Association for Education and Evangelism, the ˒Fellowship of Christian Assemblies, and the Open Bible Faith Fellowship. These have tended to come out of the ministries of individuals who have found older pentecostal groups structurally or liturgically restrictive. They speak respectfully of the older groups, but they have first gathered assemblies and then created loosely bound networks of their own. These networks serve to provide a means of recognizing, or credentialing, clergy and of placing in ministry graduates of Bible institutes with which the networks may be associated. Within these networks, overriding emphasis is placed on the "leading of the Spirit" and spontaneity.

These new groupings have tended to be successful in the same ethnic populations as the older pentecostals. Assessing numerical strength is extraordinarily difficult. One of the newer fellowships in Ontario, the Open Bible Faith Fellowship, operates a Bible institute with 200 full-time students. World Impact Ministries, led by Peter Youngrin and George Woodward, accepted an invitation to ally with the older Open Bible Faith Fellowship, and the number of credentialholders under the name of the older organization jumped from 19 to 230 in less than three years. There are grounds for assuming that the total numbers of churches and adherents within these newer pentecostal networks would reach into the hundreds and the tens of thousands, respectively. As the century closes, they constitute a segment of Canadian pentecostalism that cannot be overlooked.

All of these—the new pentecostal networks, the older pentecostal denominations, and the charismatics—are dealing with a new challenge as the 1990s close—the ˒Toronto Blessing. This phenomenon appeared in early 1994 at the airport assembly of the ˒Vineyard Fellowship. Along with calls for deeper Christian commitment and promises of refreshing, it gave place to unusual physical behavior and then developed a sharpened focus on prophecies related to the end times. A significant division of opinion among pentecostals and charismatics exists over the authenticity of its teachings and practices.

4. Conclusion.

As one commentator has put it, the 20th century has been "the era of the Spirit." It is safe to say that during this period the church at large has become more aware of the presence and reality of the Spirit than at any other point in its history. It has not been an easy voyage. Stresses of various kinds have arisen, and this is as true for Canada as for anywhere else.

Canada has seen the appearance of perhaps 20 Christian bodies that were not in existence in 1900. Early pentecostals, with their penchant for independence, could not have imagined this. They thought that for the Spirit to move freely there could be no "man-made" organizations. It has also led to the reevaluation of the spiritual life, worship, and theology on the part of some of the older Canadian denominations. All of this has laid challenges before the Christian community in Canada. What does one do when the Spirit moves? How does one discern that it truly is the Holy Spirit that is moving? The questions are difficult, but they insist on answers just as they did after the first Pentecost.

■ **Bibliography:** M. Di Giacomo, "Les assemblées de la Pentecôte du Canada: leur origine, leur évolution, leur théologie distinctive" (thesis, Université Laval, 1994) ■ C. J. Jaenen, "The Pentecostal Movement" (thesis, U. of Manitoba, 1950) ■ B. K. Janes, "Floods upon the Dry Ground: A History of the Pentecostal Assemblies of Newfoundland, 1910–39" (thesis, Memorial U. of Newfoundland, 1991) ■ D. T. Klan, "Pentecostal Assemblies of Canada Church Growth in British Columbia from Origins to 1953" (thesis, Regent College [Vancouver, B.C.], 1979) ■ R. A. N. Kydd, "Canadian Pentecostalism and the Evangelical Impulse," in *Aspects of the Canadian Evangelical Experience,* ed. G. A. Rawlyk (1997), 289–300, 491–95 ■ idem, "The Impact of the Charismatic Renewal in Classical Pentecostalism in Canada," *Pneuma* 18 (1996) ■ idem, "Pentecostals, Charismatics and the Canadian Denominations," *Église et Théologie* 13 (1982) ■ idem, "A Retrospectus/Prospectus on Physical Phenomena Centred on the 'Toronto Blessing,'" *JPT* 12 (1998) ■ R. A. Larden, *Our Apostolic Heritage* (1971) ■ T. W. Miller, *Canadian Pentecostals: A History of the Pentecostal Assemblies of Canada,* ed. W. A. Griffin (1994).
■ R. A. N. Kydd

CAPE VERDE

■ Pentecostals 499 (2%)   ■ Charismatics 17,621 (56%)   ■ Neocharismatics 13,580 (43%)   ■ Total Renewal: 31,700

CARIBBEAN ISLANDS (Survey)

The Caribbean Islands have a complex history. Although colonial and economic exploitation played a major role, it is only part of the story. The Islands have also been a meeting ground for cultures of the world, which they have absorbed and yet made distinctively their own. The result is a complex reality from nearly every point of view.

This is true of pentecostalism. One can interpret significant parts of the pentecostal evangelization and organization as another period of colonization, but throughout the area, the Caribbean pentecostals have made the tradition their own and have established their juridical and economic independence. This independence of faith and mind is frequently seen in the theological and liturgical paradigms of the movements. Although often small in number, the churches have generally found diverse, appropriate, and affordable structures for accomplishing educational and formational goals.

From the published sources, a number of themes can be seen that set the Caribbean pentecostal experience apart from that of other areas of Latin America. The first is the important mission role and national experience of the Pentecostal Assemblies of Canada (PAOC). They have remained remarkably nonpolitical and have focused, as has the Canadian government, on the well-being of the islands. Second,

although it is hard to document given the present state of research, the North American African-American pentecostal churches, especially the Church of God in Christ, the Pentecostal Assemblies of the World, and the United Holy Church, have had an extensive influence. This influence extends far beyond the membership and influence of the daughter churches of the Caribbean to Great Britain, Central and South America, and Mexico, as well as to the U.S.

Third, the African ethnic churches of the Caribbean have been involved in an emigration paradigm that has seen thousands of believers (especially, but not exclusively among the "Oneness" churches) move to Great Britain. There they have transmitted their cultural values to succeeding generations and have been active in evangelism among other branches of the African diaspora in England as well as to Africa. This African connection, both of the emigration and of the occasional juridical identification with indigenous African churches by Caribbean groups, needs additional research.

Finally, except in Trinidad, there has been little influence historically and no current presence of the Scandinavian pentecostal churches. Even in Trinidad that involvement was short-term and deliberately connected to the newly arrived missionaries of the Open Bible Standard Church (OBSC). In other areas, such as Mexico and the larger countries of South America, the Scandinavian pentecostal churches have maintained a significant, often defining, presence.

Other themes are congruent with the experience of the rest of Latin America. First, there is the importance throughout the region of the Holiness and pentecostal churches, especially the Pilgrim Holiness Church (now Wesleyan Church) and the Church of God (Anderson, IN). This has provided not just the language and theological framework, but also frequently personnel, such as especially R. J. Jamieson. This base has without doubt contributed to another regional phenomenon, the fact that the Church of God (CG, Cleveland, TN) and in some areas the Church of God of Prophecy (CGP) are frequently the largest pentecostal churches on certain islands. There are numerous reasons for this preeminence, but the work of 'J. H. Ingram is certainly a primary reason. He worked tirelessly to bring independent congregations into cooperative relationships under the leadership of the CG.

A third remarkable feature is inter-island evangelism. Especially significant are the efforts of missionaries from Puerto Rico and Trinidad throughout the region from 1917 onward. Individuals and congregations on other islands, as well as from Mexico, have been heavily involved in mission within the region as well. The Trinidad missionaries worked especially under the aegis of the Pentecostal Assemblies of the West Indies (PAWI). The PAWI were never controlled by the sponsoring PAOC, and so the results of the mission work were quickly established as indigenous churches. Sometimes Puerto Rican missionaries cooperated with or served under boards from the U.S., especially the Assemblies of God–U.S. or the CG. Often they were involved in initial efforts to achieve independence from the North American churches. More recently they have provided economic and ecumenical leadership. It would be hard to overstate the role of the Puerto Rican missionaries in the definition of pentecostalism in the Caribbean.

The geography and demography of the Caribbean, as well as the complex histories of the pentecostal and charismatic churches on the larger islands, has required a two-part approach. This article discusses some of the smaller islands or those with less-complicated pentecostal histories, while the larger islands have received their own treatments. A list of cross-references is provided below.

In addition to the larger islands, to which separate articles are devoted, there are three groups of Caribbean Islands. The ABC Islands include Aruba, Bonaire, and Curaçao. The Leeward Islands include the British Virgin Islands, the U.S. Virgin Islands, Anguilla, Antigua, Montserrat, St. Kitts, Nevis, St. Barts, St. Martin, and the Netherlands Antilles Islands of Eustatius and Saba. The Windward Islands include Dominica, Guadeloupe, Martinique, St. Lucia, St. Vincent, Barbados (see article), and Grenada. The histories of the pen-

tecostal denominations and congregations on the smaller islands are often unrecorded. Some are the result of mission efforts from other Caribbean Islands or from the U.S., Canada, or England; others are indigenous. An effort is made here to provide some data about these churches, but additional research is needed.

Initial pentecostal evangelistic efforts were made on St. Vincent and St. Lucia by J. H. Marshall of Bridgetown, Barbados, during the 1930s. Other Barbadian evangelists and J. H. Ingram also spent time on the islands that decade. These early efforts were thwarted, however, by the Catholic Church. Finally, in 1940 a Barbadian woman evangelist, L. W. Green, established a permanent CG mission and then congregations at four villages, including Biabou, St. Vincent. Her successor, Gladys Priam, a convert of Green on St. Vincent, continued to found congregations. This denomination is probably the largest on both islands, followed by the CGP and PAWI. The OBSC claims (1995) 220 members in two congregations on St. Vincent. There are several small independent congregations, ministries, and missions.

In 1938 another woman, Thelma A. Griffith, established a CG congregation in Dominica, where after 1963 there was also a CGP presence. In Dec. 1940 Griffith founded a CG congregation in Castries, St. Lucia. The largest pentecostal denomination on St. Lucia, however, is probably the United Holy Church of America. Other churches on Dominica include the PAWI and the CGP.

PAOC missionaries Ruth Pemberton and Clara Siemens arrived on St. Kitts in 1918 and established a church. St. Kitts was also evangelized by A. C. Lewis, a Barbadian evangelist, but the work of establishing a congregation was made by Caroline R. Halstead, who in 1943 affiliated with the CG. The two major denominations on St. Kitts–Nevis are the CGP and the CG, followed by the PAWI.

On Grenada Edward D. Hasmatali visited from Trinidad and established a congregation of the CG on Nov. 2, 1958, at St. George. Missionaries of the PAWI have also established congregations on Grenada. The Open Standard Bible Churches, beginning with evangelistic teams from Trinidad, have been active since the 1960s, with resident missionaries beginning in 1971, and claim (1995) four congregations with 400 members and one Bible school. By 1959 there was a CG congregation on Aruba founded from Grenada. There are also CGP congregations on Aruba. The AG–U.S., is a more recent arrival on the island.

On Antigua there are about 10 congregations of the CGP (since 1946), which have about 500 members. The PAWI, founded and influenced by Canadian missionaries of the PAOC is the largest denomination on Montserrat. Founded in 1912 by Robert and Elizabeth Jamieson, former missionaries of the Pilgrim Holiness Church, it claims more than 600 members and about 1,200 adherents. Also on Montserrat are several congregations of the CGP. In the Netherlands

Antilles the CG and the CGP have a small presence. Apparently the only pentecostal presence on the British Virgin Islands is a CG congregation.

The CG was established in the U.S. Virgin Islands on St. Thomas on June 20, 1917, by F. L. Ryder and on St. Croix a few weeks later. Most of this mission opted for the CGP (1926), which has more than 8,000 members and adherents (1999), although the CG remains vital with more than 1,000 participants. The United Pentecostal Church claims (1999) about 1,000 "constituents." Also active on these islands are the Church of God in Christ and the Pentecostal Assemblies of the World. R. J. Jamieson founded congregations of the Pilgrim Holiness Church on St. Croix from 1906 before his conversion to pentecostalism. Converts from this period formed the base of the PAWI in the U.S. Virgin Islands.

Most of the pentecostal churches on these islands have been decimated by emigration to Great Britain, where branches of these churches have been established. The United Pentecostal Church maintains missions in the ABC Islands, the Windward Islands, and the Leeward Islands and claims (1999) 1,285 members, 20 clergy, and 19 congregations on these islands.

See also BAHAMAS, BARBADOS, BERMUDA, CUBA, DOMINICAN REPUBLIC, HAITI, JAMAICA, PUERTO RICO, TRINIDAD AND TOBAGO.

■ **Bibliography:** D. B. Barrett, *World Christian Encyclopedia* (1982) ▌ M. A. Bryant, *My Commitment to God* [CGP–Aruba] (thesis, Church of God School of Theology, 1982) ▌ D. L. Burk, ed., *Foreign Missions Insight: A Digest of Foreign Missions Faces, Facts, Fields and Figures* (1999) ▌ C. W. Conn, *Like a Mighty Army: A History of the Church of God* (rev. ed., 1995) ▌ idem, *Where the Saints Have Trod: A History of Church of God Missions* (1959) ▌ J. H. Henney, "Spirit-Possession Belief and Trance Behavior in a Religious Group in St. Vincent" (diss., Ohio State U., 1968) ▌ idem, "Spirit-Possession Belief and Trance Behavior in Two Fundamentalistic Groups in St. Vincent," in F. Goodman, J. Henney, and E. Pressel, *Trance, Healing and Hallucination* (1974) ▌ W. J. Hollenweger, *Handbuch der Pfingstbewegung* (diss., Zurich, 1967) ▌ P. Humphrey, *J. H. Ingram, Missionary Dean* (1966) ▌ J. H. Ingram, *Around the World with Gospel Light* (1938) ▌ [H. McCracken], *History of Church of God Missions* (1943) ▌ T. W. Miller, *Canadian Pentecostals: A History of the Pentecostal Assemblies of Canada,* ed. W. A. Griffin (1994) ▌ R. B. Mitchell and L. M. Mitchell, *Heritage and Harvest: The History of the International Ministries of the Open Bible Standard Churches* (1995) ▌ E. L. Simmons, *History of the Church of God* (1938) ▌ J. D. Spencer, *Black Women in the Church: Historical Highlights and Profiles,* ed. Celia T. Marcelle and Catherine J. Robinson (1986) ▌ N. M. Van Cleve, *The Vine and the Branches: A History of the International Church of the Foursquare Gospel* (1992) ▌ I. A. Whitt, "Developing a Pentecostal Missiology in the Canadian Context (1867–1944): The Pentecostal Assemblies of Canada" (diss., Fuller, 1994).

■ D. D. Bundy

CAYMAN ISLANDS
■ Pentecostals 601 (9%)   ■ Charismatics 3,683 (57%)   ■ Neocharismatics 2,216 (34%)   ■ Total Renewal: 6,500

CENTRAL AFRICAN REPUBLIC
■ Pentecostals 103,705 (21%)   ■ Charismatics 123,870 (26%)   ■ Neocharismatics 257,425 (53%)   ■ Total Renewal: 485,000

For a general introduction to Central Africa and bibliography, see AFRICA, CENTRAL.

The Central African Republic (C.A.R.) was part of French Equatorial Africa from 1905. In 1960 it gained independence from France. Since 1966 it has been mostly a military dictatorship. It was known as The Empire until 1979.

In 1927 a Norwegian Baptist missionary, Oscar Berntz-Lanz, arrived from Congo (Kinshasa). He settled at Alindao in the Basse-Kotto region. From this work has grown the group known as l'Union des Eglises Evangéliques Elim en République Centrafricaine (The Union of Elim Evangelical Churches in the Central African Republic). The name Eglise Evangélique du Réveil (The Evangelical Revival Church), which is found in some dictionaries, is not the correct appellation for l'Union des Eglises Evangéliques Elim en République Centrafricane. (This is the only group in affiliation with the Elim Mission and the SPM). Although Berntz-Lanz was originally Baptist, he founded an independent movement that, because of contacts through his Swiss wife, gradually became the responsibility of the Schweizerische Pfingstmission (Swiss Pentecostal Mission, SPM). Most of the approximately 200 churches belonging to this movement are in the east of the country (Basse-Kotto); there are approximately 50,000 members. They are involved in various areas of social work, including an agricultural school, basic health care, rehabilitation of the blind, translation, and the teaching of reading and writing in the Sango language.

The Elim mission has a Bible institute, the Institut Biblique Elim (Elim Bible Institute) with 54 students, a medical clinic, a maternity ward, and a small print shop. Presently 13 missionaries and their families from the SMP work in this mission. A few missionaries from other Swiss missions—Eglise de Réveil (Revival Church), Eglise Luthérienne Charismatique (Charismatic Lutheran Church), and Eglises Apostoliques Suisse (Swiss Apostolic Churches)—have been seconded to work in the C.A.R., but all of them are under the direction of the SPM.

There are two other large pentecostal denominations in the country: Coopération Evangélique Centrafricaine (Central African Evangelical Cooperation), and Action Apostolique Africaine (AAA, African Apostolic Action). The first is the result of the ministry of an existing group of independent believers and missionaries of La Porte Ouverte (PO, The Open Door), also known as Coopération Evangélique dans le Monde (Evangelical Cooperation in the World), a pentecostal association in France. Gabriel Yerima is the president of this group. The first missionaries from PO went to the C.A.R. in 1961 and worked with churches that were newly founded and without fixed ecclesiastical structures. In 1987 autonomy was granted to the churches. They have approximately 250 churches and 30,000 members. Philippe Monod of PO was involved with the evangelization of the Pygmies in the equatorial forest from 1970. Many churches with their own workers and a system of preparation for leadership now exist. Since 1985 efforts have been made to evangelize the nomadic Fulbhe (Fulani) people, who are mostly Muslims. The second large denomination, Action Apostolique (Apostolic Action), is linked with Pierre Truschel and l'Eglise du Chandelier (The Church of the Candlestick) in Grenoble, France. Clément Guerekozoungbo is its president.

Among some of the smaller yet significant pentecostal denominations are the Foursquare Church, which has come from Nigeria in the past few years; L'Eglise du Réveil (Revival Church), which is independent of any mission attachments (and not related to the church of the same name in Switzerland); L'Eglise Evangélique de Pentecôte (The Evangelical Church of Pentecost), which is the result of the work of a former Elim pastor; Eglise de la Fraternité Apostolique (Church of the Apostolic Brotherhood), which has come out of the AAA; Eglises de la Fraternité Evangélique (Churches of the Evangelical Brotherhood); Eglise du Chemin vers Jésus (Church of the Way to Jesus); and the Eglise du Christ (Church of Christ). Approximately six churches in Bangui have taken the name Assemblées de Dieu (AG) and are lead by Hulem Felix. These churches are led by C.A.R. citizens who have been primarily influenced by AG in Kinshasa. They have contacts with AG–France and AG–U.S. but have no binding affiliation at present. AG–U.S. is contemplating the possibility of sending missionaries to work in the C.A.R. in the near future, although they are not committed to any group at present. Billy Burr (AG–U.S.) has visited there a few times in 1997–98 in anticipation of future cooperation between some of these independent churches and the AG–U.S.

Other groups call themselves pentecostal but do not give evidence of pentecostal practice: the Eglises Baptistes (Baptist Churches), which came from the Mission Suèdoise Örebro (Swedish Mission of Örebro), calls itself the Eglises des Baptistes de l'Ouest (EBO, The Baptist Churches of the West), where "West" signifies the geographical area within the C.A.R. Their head office is at Berberati among the Gbaya people. They call themselves pentecostal, but there is some question as to their understanding of the word, since it would likely be thought by evangelicals that their meetings reflect more Baptist than pentecostal liturgy. The Comité Baptiste (Baptist Committee), which split from the Baptist Mid Mission in 1956, for reasons that are unclear but were likely mostly ethnic and political, had its leadership trained by the Mission Coopération Evangélique (Porte Ouverte). Despite this link with pentecostalism and its use of the name, it is not evident that there is any depth of pentecostal commitment in this grouping.

A relatively high number of evangelicals live in this country. The single language, Sango, facilitates the communication of the gospel, yet there is a considerable problem with formalism among second-generation believers and a great divide between charismatics and noncharismatics. Some pentecostal churches evidence a new visitation of the Holy Spirit and efforts at reconciliation between churches after the three mutinies by the military during 1996 and 1997. Many believers recognize that they are responsible for the evangelization of the neglected or underevangelized groups, including the Arabs, Pygmies, and Foulbhes (Fulani, of Berber or Ethiopian origin). ■ D. J. Garrard

CHAD

■ Pentecostals 17,107 (7%) ■ Charismatics 149,905 (60%) ■ Neocharismatics 82,988 (33%) ■ Total Renewal: 250,000

CHANNEL ISLANDS

■ Pentecostals 1,419 (17%) ■ Charismatics 6,981 (83%) ■ Neocharismatics 0 (0%) ■ Total Renewal: 8,400

CHILE

■ Pentecostals 90,791 (2%)   ■ Charismatics 1,635,173 (30%)   ■ Neocharismatics 3,811,036 (69%)   ■ Total Renewal: 5,537,000

1. Pentecostal Prehistory.

The prehistory of pentecostalism in Chile is closely related to, but not dependent on, that of Peru and Bolivia. The peripatetic Methodist-Episcopal evangelist ►William Taylor, who had arrived in Chile initially on a fact-finding trip from Oct. 1877 until June 1878, returned to Chile to establish congregations in various cities, including Valparaiso, Conceptión, and Coquimbo, as well as Iquique, Peru, which would be ceded to Chile during the war. At both Coquimbo and Iquique he built the first church buildings with his own hands. After his return to the U.S., where he had first achieved fame as a "street preacher" in San Francisco (1849–56) and from the publication of his books on Latin America (*Our Latin American Cousins,* 1878) and on mission theory (*Pauline Missions,* 1879), dozens of missionaries came to Chile. Known as "Taylor missionaries" or "self-supporting missionaries," these independent Holiness/ Methodist missionaries came to Chile without the approval of the Mission Society of the Methodist Episcopal Church. Taylor's "Pauline" concept that the role of missionaries was to establish self-supporting, self-determining, and self-propagating churches made a strong impression in Chile as it had in other areas of the world. He insisted on inclusion of non-missionaries in the decision-making process of mission and the immediate transfer of the leadership of congregations and denominations to the converts. Taylor was an active participant in the Wesleyan/Holiness movement in the U.S. and around the world. He was a good friend of Phoebe and Walter Palmer, as well as of other Holiness advocates within the Methodist Episcopal Church. Among the William Taylor missionaries were ►Willis Hoover and Mary Louise Hoover.

2. Willis Hoover and the Beginnings of the Pentecostal Revival.

The Hoovers were assigned initially to Iquique, where Willis had charge of the Collegio Ingles and where he became pastor of the first successful Methodist Spanish-language congregation in Chile. He was transferred to Valparaiso in 1903. There he experienced increasing frustration as the Methodist Episcopal Church Mission Board worked to gain control of the churches in Chile and to decrease the influence of the women missionaries, the Chilean Methodist Episcopal pastors, and the "Taylor" missionaries. In the midst of the struggle, Mary Louise Hoover's friend from her days at Chicago Evangelistic Training School, Anna Abrams, sent her a copy of her book published in India, *The Baptism of the Holy Ghost and Fire* (2d ed., 1906). ►Minnie Abrams had gone to India as a missionary of the Methodist Episcopal Church but had withdrawn to work with ►Pandita Ramabai.

This treatise formalized the theological questions and gave direction to the spiritual crisis provoked by the conflict over mission praxis in Chile. Three weeks after Easter 1909, after seeking for it with the encouragement of Chilean laity from his congregation, Willis Hoover experienced pentecostal glossolalia. Almost immediately the revival took on nationalist and liberationist overtones. On Sept. 12, 1909, the first groups were forced from the Methodist churches in Valparaiso and Santiago. The revival was ecumenical in its outreach as the movement spread throughout the country, partly through the agency of women prophets and evangelists. As Hoover sought to understand the implications of this experience for ministry in Chile, one of his correspondents was ►T. B. Barratt.

Eventually (1910), Hoover, whom ►A. B. Simpson called "the most successful missionary in Chile," was forced to resign from the Methodist ministry. At the request of the Chilean believers, he organized the fledgling pentecostal churches into a Chilean, national, independent, self-supporting, self-governing, and self-propagating church, the Iglesia Metodista Pentecostal (IMP). The particular pentecostal development of a popular revivalistic religious style, attuned to Chilean nationalist sentiment and to Chilean culture, drew significant numbers of converts, especially among the lower classes of society. Doctrinally, Chilean pentecostalism was different from the majority of North American pentecostal churches in that there was no doctrine of "initial evidence."

3. The Beginnings of Pentecostalism in Chile.

The period 1910–32 was a period of continuing development for the pentecostal movements of Chile. Although not officially incorporated until 1929, the IMP, led by Hoover and associates already from 1910, provided an organizational umbrella for those forced from the Methodist Episcopal Church and other denominations. The IMP was self-supporting in the tradition of the Taylor mission. Women had central roles in the establishment of the movement's identity, although they were supplanted as the movement grew. Worship was enthusiastic, but no musical instruments were used. Order was maintained through the use of a bell rung by the worship leader. In Oct. 1913, after conflict over liturgy and leadership, the Iglesia del Señor, led by Carlos del Campo, was established. Another conflict about leadership resulted in the formation of the Iglesia Evangélica de los Hermanos Penteostales, centered in Santiago.

Until 1925, when the constitutional separation of church and state occurred, pentecostals were persecuted by the government at the behest of the Catholic Church. Thereafter, Catholic persecution continued as efforts were made to isolate the pentecostals from the mainstream of Chilean society. Feuding among pentecostals caused even more problems. The major problems began in the early 1930s. In 1933, after several years feeling frustrated at Hoover's leadership, Manuel Umaña Salinas used manipulative accusations, illegal meetings, and character assassination to remove Hoover from both the congregation in Valparaiso and the superintendency of the IMP. He then established himself as the absolute power in the IMP. Umaña promoted himself to bishop, survived exposés in the secular press about his embezzlement of funds, his extramarital affairs and illegitimate children, personal ownership of church property after having established rules against such practices, and other abuses of power, to die as bishop of the IMP in 1964. Hoover and his supporters struggled to retain their properties (settled in 1943) but in April organized what became the Iglesia Evangélica Pentecostal (IEP), with Guillermo Castillo as assistant superintendent. Hoover died on May 27, 1936. The denomination achieved government recognition in 1940. Both the IMP and IEP have continued to grow.

4. The Proliferation of Denominations.

Since about 1930, the pentecostal churches have continued to split and diversify. New ones unrelated to the older churches have been created. Most of the divisions have occurred, not over theological but over ethical issues and liturgy. Some were forced to leave their churches. For example, Enrique Chávez Campos was expelled from the IMP for insisting on honest fiscal reporting and other reforms in 1946. Chávez and most of his congregation in Curicó joined him in founding the Iglesia Pentecostal de Chile, which joined the World Council of Churches (WCC) in 1962. Also joining the WCC in 1962 was the Misión Iglesia Pentecostal, led by Victor Pavéz Jr., which was organized in 1952 by a group that withdrew from the IEP.

Other churches, according to Kessler (1967, 316), split from the Iglesia del Señor: Iglesia del Señor Apostólica (1930), Misión Iglesia del Señor, and Iglesia del Señor la cual El ganó con su Sangre (1941); from this last organization came Iglesia del Señor Jesús as well as Corporación Iglesia del Señor. From the IEP came others: Iglesia Cristiana de la Fe Apostólica (1932), Iglesia Cristiana ganada con su Sangre (1936), Iglesia de Dios Pentecostal (1951), Misión Iglesia Pentecostal (1952), Corporación Evangélica Pentecostal (1956), Iglesia Pentecostal Apostólica, and the Iglesia Evangélica de la Nueva Jerusalem. From the IMP also came the Corporación Evangélica de Vitacura (1933); Iglesia Pentecostal de Chile Austral (1933); Iglesia Evangélica Cristiana (1936); Ejército Evangélico de Chile (1937), from which came the Ejército Evangélico Nacional (1942), which in turn produced the Movimiento Evangélico Nacional (1960); the Iglesia Misionera de Cristo (1947); the Ejército Evangélico Pentecostal; the Iglesia Pentecostal Apostólica, which pro-

duced the Iglesia Pentecostal Apostólica Libre (1943); the Misión Cristiana Apostólica; Iglesia Cristiana Pentecostal; Iglesia Evangélica el Pesebre Humilde de Cristo (1943); Iglesia Pentecostal de Chile; Iglesia de Cristo Evangélica Nacional; and the Iglesia Evangélica Metodista Pentecostal Reunida en el Nombre de Jesús (1950), from which came the Misión Cristiana Evangélica Pentecostal (1953).

Other churches have no such relationships with the IMP or its descendants. One of the churches is the Misión Wesleyana National, founded through the efforts of Víctor Manuel Mora (b. 1884). Mora grew up in the Methodist Episcopal Church and, after studies at a Presbyterian seminary (1921–23), served as a Methodist Episcopal pastor until 1931. He eventually began a ministry among the miners, some of whom had been influenced by pentecostal worship. Conflict within the congregation and with the Methodist district superintendents led to the establishment of an independent church. There are perhaps another 70 or so denominations of varying sizes and histories in this category.

Also important are the mass conversions among the Native American tribes, the Mapuche in the South of Chile and the Aymara in the North. The conversions from nominal Catholicism with foreign clergy to Chilean-led pentecostal congregations have been interpreted as cultural destruction as well as recovery and cultural transformation of indigenous pre-Columbian structures.

Among the pentecostal mission agencies that have either planted churches, aided churches, or joined together with established churches are the Norwegian Pentecostal Mission, Swedish Pentecostal Mission, Philadelfia Bewegung, Die Vereinigten Missionsfreunde, Church of God (CG, Cleveland, TN), Church of God of Prophecy, Asambleas de Dios Autónomas, Iglesia Evangélica Foursquare, Pentecostal Holiness Church, AG–U.S. (which claimed 194 congregations and 15,983 adherents in 1999), the Apostolic Faith (Portland, OR), and the United Pentecostal Church (27 churches, 2,000 constituents [1999]). Missionaries have also come from countries such as Argentina, Brazil, Australia, New Zealand, and Canada.

The charismatic renewal has had a significant impact on the Roman Catholic Church in Chile. This has resulted in the circulation of extensive literature promoting Catholic versions of charismatic/pentecostal theology, as well as research on the traditions by charismatic Catholic scholars. There appear to be no reliable statistics, but observers place the numbers of adherents in the hundreds of thousands. Other Protestant churches have also adapted elements of pentecostal spirituality as well as liturgical innovations to compete with the tradition for adherents.

5. Allende, Pinochet, and the Pentecostals.

When Allende was elected president of Chile, it was hoped that a new period of social justice and economic development would ensue. However, land and political reform efforts provoked a backlash, political polarization, and civic unrest. It was to the initial relief of many Catholics, Protestants, and pentecostals alike that Pinochet took control of the government in a military coup on Sept. 11, 1973. The brutality of the military government soon manifested itself, however, and the Catholic Church refused to bless the government in the traditional Te Deum. Pinochet was invited to the inauguration of the new IMP Jotabecche Cathedral, an invitation accepted on the condition that the IMP celebrate his first year in power with a pentecostal Te Deum. This was done in Dec. 1974 and annually thereafter. Pinochet rewarded the supportive pentecostal leaders with recognition, gifts, travel, and limited access to persons of power. At the same time, as documented by Kamsteeg and others, many pentecostals resisted the excesses of the Pinochet regime. Pentecostal youth, especially the intelligentsia, were forced into exile, primarily in Europe; others disappeared, killed by the Pinochet military. The Misión Iglesia Pentecostal, which worked in the poorest areas of the cities and had connections to the WCC, was especially targeted. Since the removal of Pinochet from power, IMP churches are still suspect in some areas for their support of the repressive regime.

6. Pentecostalism as Popular Religion and a Theological Tradition.

Because of the success of pentecostalism in Chile (about 13% of the population attending church in 1992), and because of its general identification with the poor, it has been interpreted primarily as a sociological tradition. An extensive literature defines pentecostalism as "popular religion," assuming that theological decisions among the converts essentially serve sociological needs. From Hoover onward, however, there has been a tradition of theological reflection in the periodicals, occasional books, testimonies, and preaching of the pentecostals. Most recently Juan Sepúlveda has become an internationally recognized interpreter of the phenomenon. He recognizes both the sociological and theological aspects of pentecostal life. Of particular importance in this process of theological definition is the work of Carmen Galilea W.

■ **Bibliography:**

General. D. B. Barrett, *World Christian Encyclopedia* (1982), 226–30 ■ M. M. Castro D., "Metodistas y pentecostales," in *Unidos en la diversidad* (1992) ■ T. A. Fontaine and H. Beyer, "Retrato del movimiento evangélico a la luz de las encuestas de opinión pública," *Estudios Públicos* 44 (1991) ■ C. Galilea W., *El Predicador Pentecostal* (Centro Bellarmino–CISOC; Santiago, 1991) ■ idem, *El Pentecostal: Testimonio y experiencia de Dios* (1990) ■ W. J. Hollenweger, *Handbuch der Pfingstbewegung* (diss., Zurich, 1967), 941–1003 (para. 02b.08) ■ J. A. B. Kessler, *A Study of the Older Protestant Missions and Churches in Peru and Chile, with Special Reference to the Problems of Division, Nationalism and Native Ministry* (1967).

Pre-History to Revival. G. Arms, *History of the Self-Supporting Missions in South America* (1921) ■ D. Bundy, "Bishop William Taylor and Methodist Mission: A Study in Nineteenth-Century Social History," *Methodist History* 27 (July 4, 1989) and 28 (Oct. 1, 1989) ■ idem, "William Taylor, 1821–1902: Entrepreneurial Maverick for the Indigenous Church," in *Mission Legacies: Biographical Studies of Leaders of the Modern Missionary Movement*, ed. G. Anderson et al. (1994) ■ W. Taylor, *Our South American Cousins* (1878) ■ idem, *Pauline Methods of Missionary Work* (1879) ■ idem, *The Story of My Life* (1895).

Hoover and the Beginnings of the Pentecostal Revival. D. Bundy, "Unintended Consequences: The Methodist Episcopal Missionary Society and the Beginnings of Pentecostalism in Norway and Chile," *Missiology* 27 (1999) ■ J. T. Copplestone, *Twentieth-Century Perspectives: The Methodist Episcopal Church, 1896–1939* (1973) ■ W. Taylor (1878; 1879; 1895 [see above]).

The Beginnings of Pentecostalism in Chile. M. L. H. [Mary Louise Hoover] to Mrs. Boddy, dated 24 Mar. 1909, published as "South America: A Congregation Hungry for God," *Confidence* [Supplement] 2 (June 6, 1909) ■ M. L. Hoover, "Pentecost in Chile, South America," *The Upper Room* 1 (Jan. 6, 1910) ■ W. C. Hoover, *Historia del Avivamiento Pentecostal en Chile* (1934; repr. 1948), repr. in *Historia del Avivamiento, origen y desarrollo de la Iglesia Evangélica Pentecostal* (1977) ■ idem, *History of the Pentecostal Movement in Chile*, trans. M. G. Hoover (2000) ■ idem, "Apostolic Power Brings Apostolic Persecution: How God Exonerated His Servants under Trial," *LRE* (Feb. 1921) ■ idem, "Ecclesia—Church. Needed: A Complete Purification of Pastors and People," *LRE* (May 1921) ■ idem, "Pentecost in Chile," *PE* (July 16, 1932) ■ idem, "The Pentecostal Revival in Chile," *PE* (July 22 and Aug. 5, 1922) ■ idem, "A Phenomenal Self-supporting Native Work: Transformed from Professional Rogues to Preachers of the Gospel," *LRE* (Jan. 1921) ■ idem, "Raised from the Dead," *PE* (Mar. 14, 1936) ■ idem, "The Remarkable Spread of Pentecost in Chile," *PE* (Jan. 5, 1918) ■ idem, "'Send Me Where You Need Me,'" *LRE* (Dec. 1921) ■ idem, "Through Perils and Hardships to Crowning Days: The Outpouring of the Spirit in Chile," *LRE* 6 (June 1914) ■ idem, "The Wonderful Works of God in Chile," *LRE* 3 (Apr. and July 1911) ■ idem, "Work in Chile," *Word and Work* (July 1911) ■ A. R. Schick and D. H. Talbert, *La Iglesia Metodista Pentecostal, ayer y hoy*, 2 vols. (1987) ■ E. del Carmen Salazar Sanzana, *"Todas seriamos rainhas. Historia do pentecostalismo chileno da perspectiva da mulher, 1909–1935* (thesis, Instituto Metodista de Ensino Superior, São Bernardo do Campo, SP, Brasil, 1995).

The Proliferation of Denominations. C. Álvarez et al., *Historia de la Iglesia Pentecostal de Chile* (n.d.) ■ D. L. Burk, ed., *Foreign Missions Insight: A Digest of Foreign Missions Faces, Facts, Fields and Figures* (1999), 135–36 ■ C. Galilea W., *Catolicos Carismaticos y Protestantes Pentecostales. Análisis comparativo de sus vivencias religiosas* (1992) ■ B. Guerrero, *"A Dios Rogando…." Los pentecostales en la sociedad aymara del norte grande de Chile* (diss., Free U. Amsterdam, 1994) ■ L. Jeter Walker, *Siembra y cosecha* (1992), 2:57–89 ■ K. G. O'Brien, *El rol de ecumenismo protestante como possible solución al impasse de las relaciones* entre la Iglesia Catolica y la communidad Pentecostal (1992) ▪ M. Ossa, *Espiritualidad popular y accion politica: El Pastor Victor Mora y la Misión Wesleyana Nacional: 40 años de historia religiosa y social (1928–1969)* (1990) ▪ J. Sepúlveda, *The Andean Highlands: An Encounter with Two Forms of Christianity* (1997).

Allende, Pinochet, and the Pentecostals. E. Erdtman, "Identidad penticostal y religiosidad popular protestante en Santiago de Chile," in *Iglesia y sociedad en Chile 500 años despues de Colon y dos años despues de Pinochet,* ed. C. F. Hallencreutz (1993) ▪ F. Kamsteeg, *Prophetic Pentecostalism in Chile: A Case Study on Religion and Development Policy* (diss., Free U. of Amsterdam, 1995; pub. 1998) ▪ H. Lagos and A. Chacón, *La crisis de la hegemonia en Chile y la función de las Iglesias Evangélicos* (1984) ▪ A. M. Vidal, "El Pentecostal y 'su actitud socio politica en el Chile'" (1986).

Pentecostalism as Popular Religion and a Theological Tradition. M. Canales, S. Palma, and H. Villela, eds., *En Tierra Extraña II. Para una socoiología de la religiosidad popular protestante* (1991) ▪ H. Lagos and A. Chacón, *Los Evangélicos en Chile: Una lectura sociológica* (1987)

▪ C. Lalive d'Epinay, *El Refugio de las masas: estudio sociológico del protestantismo chileno* (1968) ▪ idem, *Réligion, dynamique social et dépendence: les mouvements protestantes en Argentine et au Chile* (1975) ▪ M. Ossa, *Lo ajeno y lo propio. Identidad Pentecostal y trabajo* (1991) ▪ I. Palma, ed., *En Tierra Extraña. Itinerario del Pueblo Pentecostal Chileno* (1988) ▪ F. Sampedro N., *Pentecostalismo, Sectas y Pastoral* (1989) ▪ J. Sepúlveda, "Born Again: Baptism and the Spirit. A Pentecostal Perspective," in *Pentecostal Movements as an Ecumenical Challenge,* ed. J. Moltmann and K. J. Kuschel (1996) ▪ idem, "Pentecostalism as Popular Religion," *International Review of Mission* (1989) ▪ idem, "Reflexiones sobre el aporte pentecostal a la misión de la Iglesia en Chile," in *Pentecostalismo, Sectas y Pastoral,* ed. F. Sampedro (1989) ▪ idem, "Theological Characteristics of an Indigenous Pentecostalism: The Case of Chile," in *In the Power of the Spirit: The Pentecostal Challenge to the Historic Churches in Latin America,* ed. B. F. Gutiérrez and D. Smith (1996) ▪ H. Tennekes, *El movimiento pentecostal en las sociedad chilena* (1985).   ▪ D. D. Bundy

CHINA

▪ Pentecostals 47,686 (0%) ▪ Charismatics 629,491 (1%) ▪ Neocharismatics 53,597,823 (99%) ▪ Total Renewal: 54,275,000

I. China 1907–49
  A. The Chinese Context
  B. The First Pentecostal Missionaries
  C. The Impact of Pentecostalism on Protestant China Missions
  D. The Contours of Missionary Pentecostalism Until 1949
  E. Native Chinese Pentecostal Movements

II. China After 1949

I. CHINA 1907–49.

Pentecostal currents flowing directly from the North American pentecostal revivals of 1906–7 had a substantial impact on Christian missions and the Protestant movement in China. Originally the pentecostal pioneers in China, as in other places in the world, hoped to transform the entire mission enterprise and to empower it, not just to form another missionary agency. Eventually, by about 1915, most established denominational missions in China rejected pentecostalism, and pentecostals formed their own separate mission structures. However, pentecostal ideas and practices profoundly affected several of the major independent or indigenous Chinese churches of the early 20th century; several of these are still in existence and quite influential today. This article discusses the milieu into which the early pentecostals came, their activities and the reaction to them, and the pattern of the pentecostal presence until the Chinese Communist party set up a new government in 1949 and a new era began for all Chinese Christians.

A. The Chinese Context.

In the early 1900s, Protestant missions in China had, after more than 60 years of development, achieved an impressive presence. They were a few thousand strong and had built not only churches but many other institutions, such as schools and hospitals. Moreover, despite their denominational diversity, foreign missions had maintained considerable unity. They continued to share a common evangelical theological foundation, and all missionary bodies were represented at the major all-China missionary conferences of 1877, 1890, and 1907.

Nevertheless, by the early 1900s several factors were visible that would be the cause of future fissures in the Protestant world. The fundamentalist-modernist split would not erupt openly until the 1920s, but the issue of soul-winning versus social amelioration, for example, was increasingly fractious. And a rapid proliferation of new, small-scale missions efforts during the 1890s and early 1900s, many of them freelance "faith missions," brought new missionaries to the field who were fired by a premillennial urgency and less inclined to cooperate with the established missions. Many of these were laypersons, often products of the new Bible schools, such as Moody or Nyack, and often from a lower socioeconomic background and status than that of ordained missionaries of earlier decades.

Thus, when the first pentecostals came to China, there were as yet no open splits in Protestant unity, but that unity was clearly fraying. Its theological and social underpinnings were eroding with the arrival of new mission groups and divergent emphases among social reformers and those stressing personal regeneration. At the same time, Protestantism was growing rapidly after 1900. Many new converts were being made, new missionaries were arriving from both old and new mission bodies, and institutional growth, especially of schools, was accelerating even more. Onto this dynamic and already unstable scene came the first pentecostal currents from North America.

B. The First Pentecostal Missionaries.

Most of the earliest pentecostals in China had a direct link to the ▸Azusa Street revival. However, the first couple, Mr. and Mrs. T. J. McIntosh of North Carolina, did not. They arrived in Hong Kong in Aug. 1907 and immediately went on to nearby Macao, where they met several missionaries, some vacationing from inland South China. Two of the latter, Mr. Hamill and Miss Edwards of the ▸Christian and Missionary Alliance (CMA), and a local Macao missionary named Fannie Winn, had a pentecostal experience. This was the beginning of the complex relationship that developed over the next decade between the China stations of the CMA and pentecostal ideas and practices.

A more or less permanent pentecostal community in Hong Kong began with the arrival of ▸Alfred G. Garr and his wife, Lillian, from India in early Oct. 1907. The Garrs had received Spirit baptism at Azusa Street in June 1906, after which they had gone to India. They were soon joined in Hong Kong by a group of pentecostals, also inspired by Azusa Street, who came directly across the Pacific by way of Washington State. This group was led by M. L. Ryan, originally of Salem, OR, who had founded an Apostolic Assembly in Spokane, WA, 15 of whom set off for Asia in Sept. 1907. Several of the Ryan party stopped off in Tokyo, but May Law and Rosa Pittman, both single women, proceeded directly to Hong Kong, where they arrived just three days after the Garrs arrived from India. Thus was constituted the first Hong Kong group of four pentecostals. None could speak Chinese, although Lillian Garr had earlier been convinced, in 1906 in Los Angeles, that she could speak both Chinese and Tibetan.

The four pentecostals went to the American Board of Commissioners for Foreign Missions (ABCFM; Congregationalist) compound, where they were welcomed by C. R. Hager. Fortuitously, the chapel of the ABCFM was not being used, and Hager turned it over to Garr. Garr began meetings immediately, preaching in English with translation by a talented Chinese deacon of the ABCFM church, Mok Lai Chi. Mok soon received Spirit baptism and the gift of tongues, as did several other Chinese members of the church. After several weeks of pentecostal meetings and what was clearly a stormy split in the ABCFM congregation over the use of tongues, Hager took away the use of the chapel, and the pentecostals had to find other facilities. Some of the friction between the pentecostals and other missionaries was evident in an article in the major missionary journal in China, the *Chinese Recorder*, which portrayed Garr's group as "attacking the methods of other Christian missionaries."

The small pentecostal group labored on, in effect led by Mok rather than by Garr, who could still speak no Chinese. Mok spearheaded the founding of the first pentecostal newspaper in China, *Pentecostal Truths* (90% in Chinese) in Jan. 1908. This paper was an important vehicle for pentecostal ideas in China. By late 1909 Mok claimed that 6,000 copies were being printed and mailed nationwide. The paper was published until at least Apr. 1917, with 39 issues appearing by that date.

In 1908–9 the foreign contingent in Hong Kong almost disappeared with Garr's departure and the severe sickness of Law and Pittman. But by 1909–10 others had arrived, including Bertha Milligan and Cora Fritsch from the M. L. Ryan group, and Robert and Aimee Semple (later ▸Aimee Semple McPherson).

After Hong Kong, the next pentecostal base in China was established on the North China plain. Bernt Berntsen, a faith missionary in North China, somehow got access to an early copy of *The Apostolic Faith*, the publication of the Azusa

Crowd attending the 1935 dedication of the Mukden (Shenyang) Gospel Tabernacle, in Manchuria, China.

Street mission, in late 1906. He was so intrigued that he sailed back across the Pacific in the early fall of 1907 to visit Azusa Street, where he was baptized in the Spirit. He then gathered a small group, including Mr. and Mrs. Roy Hess and Mr. and Mrs. George Hanson and their families, and returned to North China, where in early 1908 they established a new mission in Zhengding, Hebei Province. This group soon scattered (some went to Shanghai, for example), but Berntsen himself remained in Zhengding for several years and became the primary pentecostal activist in North China, traveling over several provinces with the pentecostal message. In 1912 Berntsen also founded the second major pentecostal Chinese-language paper, *Popular Gospel Truth*.

Other early pentecostal missionaries with Azusa Street connections were Mr. and Mrs. ›Thomas Junk, who went to Shandong Province in North China in mid 1908, and Hector and Sigrid McLean, who had been in China since 1901 with the China Inland Mission (CIM), and who after visiting Azusa Street returned to China in 1909 as independent Apostolic Faith missionaries. In 1910 they joined ›Cecil Polhill's fledgling ›Pentecostal Missionary Union (PMU), a loose network of British faith missionaries.

Besides Hong Kong and the North China plain, the other major pentecostal base that developed by 1910 was Shanghai. Between 1908 and 1910 there arrived in Shanghai the Hess and Hanson families from Berntsen's North China group, Antoinette Moomau, a former Presbyterian, and Mrs. H. L. Lawler and her daughter Beatrice (the entire H. L. Lawler family had been part of the original M. L. Ryan group of 1907).

After 1910 the ranks of pentecostal missionaries were increased both by new arrivals from North America and the U.K. and by defections from some of the established mission bodies in China. A directory of foreign missionaries in China of late 1915 indicates that there may have been as many as 150 pentecostals scattered over nearly 30 sites. Pentecostals were in China to stay, although they were hardly well organized or firmly established institutionally. After the organization of the Assemblies of God (AG) in 1914, increasing numbers of North American pentecostals in China affiliated with that group, and most British pentecostals with the PMU, which was absorbed by the ›AG in Great Britain and Ireland in 1926.

C. The Impact of Pentecostalism on Protestant China Missions.

What was the nature of the relationship between these pentecostal pioneers in China and the earlier mission bodies? On the whole, missionaries from the traditional denominational societies rejected the pentecostals' message, although a handful from these missions joined the new movement. Many more in the faith-missions sector, especially from the CIM and the CMA, were attracted.

In 1907 T. J. McIntosh in Macao induced Mr. Hamill and Miss Edwards of the CMA to adopt the new doctrines of Spirit baptism and speaking in tongues, and they in turn carried them back to their inland stations in South China, where several more missionaries and Chinese converts took them up. But in Hong Kong, Alfred G. Garr's group seems to have had unremitting failure in convincing other missionaries. Garr wrote in Jan. 1908, "It is a hard fight here at times. . . . There is not one missionary standing with us in Hong Kong." Likewise, Bernt Berntsen in North China enjoyed very little success in convincing missionaries already in the field to take the new pentecostal doctrines seriously.

It is not surprising that, on the other hand, some in the CIM and the CMA were receptive to pentecostalism. Both of these faith mission enterprises were characterized by evangelical zeal and a strong millenarian cast, and many in both organizations ardently hoped for revival and renewal in the church as well as the imminent second coming of Christ. Many also believed in the idea of the baptism of the Holy Spirit. There were eruptions of pentecostal activity at the Missionary Training Institute in Nyack, NY, beginning in 1906, and in some CMA missions overseas, including India as well as China.

The failure of pentecostals to convince for the most part even their most sympathetic hearers among the established China missions is shown by the experience of R. A. Jaffray of the CMA. Jaffray was an old China hand, having been there since the 1890s. He was one of several at the CMA station in Wuzhou, South China, who received the baptism of the Spirit and spoke in tongues in the fall of 1907. But a year and a half later, in Mar. 1909, Jaffray contributed an important article to the CMA journal in which he carefully delineated both the positive and negative features of pentecostalism. While acknowledging the validity of the baptism of the Spirit and tongues, he forcefully argued that tongues could not be considered "evidence" of the baptism, and that many had overemphasized tongues to the detriment of a healthy faith. Moreover, he blasted the foolishness of certain independent missionaries who had come and were still coming to China or Japan claiming to speak the language instantly and supernaturally.

At the same time that Jaffray was reaching these conclusions in China, A. B. Simpson, founder of the CMA, was coming to the same position for the organization as a whole. Shortly after 1910 it had become clear that any CMA missionary who took the position that tongues were required as evidence of the baptism of the Spirit would have to leave the organization. Several did so, one of the most prominent of whom was ›W. W. Simpson, who was forced to resign in 1914.

The CIM also experienced several years of debate, controversy, and internal tensions over pentecostalism between about 1907 and 1915. This reflected the fact that several

CIM missionaries were attracted to the new ideas. Finally, in 1914–15, the CIM ruling council at Shanghai conducted extensive deliberations and consultations on the issue. In Apr. 1915 the council adopted a long statement condemning the pentecostal movement both for doctrinal errors and for behaviors involving "disorder . . . mental derangement and maniacal ravings."

In the end, what were the essentials of the indictment brought against pentecostalism? There was not a great deal of opposition to pentecostal ideas about the baptism or infilling of the Spirit, the "latter rain," using the book of Acts as a primitivist model, and so forth. There was, however, great opposition to declaring tongues to be "evidence" that was in effect required. There was also resentment at the self-assurance with which many early pentecostal missionaries denounced or denigrated the methods and achievements of established missions. And there was absolute outrage at the newcomers' claims to be able to speak Chinese without having studied it. Finally, the pentecostals were resented because they tended to evangelize other missionaries and Chinese Christians as much as the unconverted. They badgered other missionaries, ignored long-established comity boundaries, and also recruited valuable Chinese workers away from other missions.

Gate of the Truth Bible Institute (AG) in Beijing, China. The large characters read "Behold, I have set before thee an open door, and no man shall shut it."

By about 1915 the result was the drawing of clear lines between other missions and pentecostals. The latter, having come to China in hopes of transforming the entire missionary enterprise, ended up studying the Chinese language just like other missionaries did, forming their own separate agencies and institutions, and behaving much like any other denomination on the mission field—except that a greater number of pentecostal missionaries remained independent, stubbornly unaffiliated with any organization.

D. The Contours of Missionary Pentecostalism Until 1949.

From approximately 1915 to the establishment of the People's Republic of China, pentecostal missionaries coalesced into a few mission bodies scattered over several sites. A 1936 survey of the missionary body in China confirmed that the AG–U.S. was by far the largest pentecostal mission body, with 75 foreign missionaries in 29 stations and about 6,200 Chinese adherents. The next largest was the former PMU, now part of the AG in Great Britain and Ireland, with 19 missionaries in 10 stations. The South China Peniel Holiness Missionary Society, based in Los Angeles, had 11 missionaries in Hong Kong. The Pentecostal Holiness Mission, representing the ▸Pentecostal Holiness Church (Franklin Springs, GA), also had 11 missionaries in Hong Kong. The ▸Pentecostal Assemblies of Canada mission in China had seven members. There were at least another 30 pentecostals with essentially independent mission status around the country.

Thus in the mid 1930s there were nearly 150 pentecostal missionaries altogether—about the same number as 20 years earlier, constituting perhaps 3% of the overall Protestant missionary body. Insofar as we can estimate numbers of converts, the total of Chinese Christians affiliated with pentecostal missions was probably no more than 10,000, which was likewise 3% or less of the nearly 400,000 Protestants. Pentecostal missions remained focused on evangelism, with very little in the way of schools, hospitals, or other institutions; some mission stations had schools for basic education or orphanages, however, and by the late 1940s there was an AG Bible school in South China.

The chaos of the war against Japan after 1937, followed by civil war between the nationalists and the communists in the late 1940s, makes it very difficult to ascertain statistics on the eve of the Communist victory in China. However, a directory based on a survey by the National Christian Council and published in early 1950 indicated that the China AG, an amalgamation of at least some of the AG missions of earlier years and by far the largest pentecostal group linked with foreign missions in China, had about 150 churches and 12,000 converts nationwide. This would be about 1.6% of the 750,000 Protestants in China. Adding converts from other pentecostal mission groups, including independents, would probably put the figure at over 2% of Protestants. This was a small number, to be sure, but it does not take into account the impact of pentecostalism on other mission groups and especially on several independent (that is, nonmission) Chinese Protestant groups.

A feature of pentecostalism that could function as a "bridge" to other Christian groups was its intimate association with revivalism. Just as the origins of pentecostalism in the West are associated with the strong revivalism from the 1880s until the early 1900s and with the hopes of many evangelical Christians for an experience like the great Welsh revival of 1904, in the same way pentecostal currents tended to quicken whenever revivalism appeared in denominational missions in China. For example, the American Presbyterians (North) in Shandong Province had roundly rejected pentecostal influences in the late 1910s. But in the context of the famous Shandong Revival of the late 1920s and early 1930s, these same Presbyterians at first were quite tolerant of the openly pentecostal activities, including speaking in tongues, of several of their Chinese pastors. Likewise, the U.S. Southern Baptists, also strong participants in the Shandong Revival, were for a time enthusiastic about the revival and its practices, which were clearly pentecostal in nature (though Baptist reports never used the term directly). Both mission groups backed off from their support and eventually denounced the "excesses" of the movement, but the attraction of pentecostalism in the context of revivalism was clear.

E. Native Chinese Pentecostal Movements.

The most important product of pentecostalism in 20th-century China was a number of native Chinese Protestant movements. At least one of these indigenous Chinese pentecostal groups was far larger in size than the AG mission, and some of them survive today as an important part of the Christian scene in China.

Pentecostalism facilitated the emergence and growth of indigenous churches in at least three ways. First, pentecostal ideas and practices, with their stress on the miraculous and the supernatural, made a better fit with traditional Chinese folk religiosity than did the increasingly institutionalized older denominational missions. As a result, many if not most of the indigenous Protestant churches and movements of the 20th century, especially those centered in the countryside, have been pentecostal in orientation.

Second, pentecostal missionary operations were often considerably less structured and less centralized than those of other missions, and there was more scope for talented Chinese coworkers to rise faster and to have more responsibility than in the established

missions. Faith missionaries seldom had the two full years necessary to learn Chinese well, with the result that many remained handicapped linguistically and very dependent on their Chinese helpers and colleagues. This gave capable Chinese scope for rapid advancement and the ability to gain valuable experience in the mission, after which they sometimes left to work on their own.

Third, the very nature of pentecostalism, especially its egalitarianism and making available God's direct revelation to all in dramatic fashion through the gifts of the Spirit, facilitated the emergence of independent Chinese churches. Any Chinese believer could have the same access to God and the gifts of the Spirit that foreign missionaries had. Capable ones could and did organize their own pentecostal churches.

The most important Chinese pentecostal church of the 20th century has been the True Jesus Church. The True Jesus Church developed between 1917 and 1919 in North China, in the corridor between Beijing, Tianjin, and Shandong Province. Of its Chinese founders, one (Paul Wei) came from a London Missionary Society (Congregational) mission, and several others were of Presbyterian background. The True Jesus Church adopted basic pentecostal beliefs and combined them with a "Jesus Only" (▸Oneness) formula for baptism and with the practice of seventh-day Sabbath worship, which it picked up from early Seventh-day Adventist missions and publications in China. From the early 1920s on, the True Jesus Church grew very rapidly throughout China, especially in the rural areas and small towns of Central China. The church was often antiforeign and had contentious relations with foreign missions, who often accused the church of stealing their converts. There was some truth in this, for the True Jesus Church was acutely conscious of its total independence of any foreign direction. It was also quite exclusivist—that is,

The Church of God on Kwan Ye Cha at Lsiuaufu Shautun, China, c. 1920. Photo taken in the yard of the Church of God missionary's house.

it insisted that its converts renounce any former Christian affiliations and acknowledge the unique legitimacy of the True Jesus Church and its doctrines.

The True Jesus Church was the largest of all the Chinese independent churches; by the late 1940s it had over 100,000 adherents. In the early 1950s the church, at that time under the leadership of Isaac Wei, son of founder Paul Wei, was dissolved as counterrevolutionary by the new Communist government, and its leaders were jailed. But prior to this the movement had firmly established itself in Taiwan, where its international headquarters remain. The True Jesus Church is still active around the world today and has congregations on every continent, wherever there are Chinese communities. The church has also reemerged in China since the 1980s and has become strong enough for local governments and religious affairs offices to recognize its legitimacy and to give it the right to use its own name in many places.

The other independent Chinese pentecostal movement that has had a long-lasting impact is the Jesus Family. This was a communitarian church started in rural Shandong Province about 1927 by a Methodist convert, Jing Dianying. In later years other Jesus Family communities were founded as offshoots of the original "family," mainly in North and Central China. They were all in rural or semirural areas. In each community of up to several hundred members, the believers lived and worked together and held property in common, under the direction of the "family head." There were well over 100 of these communities by 1949, with a total of several thousand members. The Jesus Family was intensely millenarian and thoroughly pentecostal, basing its worship and behavior on spiritual gifts, including tongues and receiving divine revelation while in a trance. All the Jesus Family communities were disbanded in 1953, but today many former adherents are active members and leaders in local Chinese Christian communities. Since the 1980s some Jesus Family groups have reappeared, but they are technically illegal and often persecuted by the authorities. Unlike the True Jesus Church, the Jesus Family did not relocate outside of mainland China.

Thus the pentecostal message was brought to China by foreign missionaries beginning in 1907, and some small pentecostal groups of Chinese converts coalesced around the missions before 1949. However, the largest growth of pentecostalism was in entirely Chinese groups, and it is these indigenous groups, especially the True Jesus Church, that have probably had the deeper long-range influence in making pentecostalism a permanent part of the Chinese Protestant scene both before 1949 and in the recent past.

II. CHINA AFTER 1949.

From the perspective of the atheistic Communist revolution of 1949 it would be hard to imagine China 50 years later containing more pentecostals and charismatics than any single country in the world except for Brazil and the U.S. The Communist persecution, beginning with the expulsion of all foreign missionaries and culminating in the repressive decade of the Cultural Revolution, would further seem to leave little hope for Christian influence in the world's most populous nation. In fact, nascent Catholic, Protestant, Independent, Orthodox, and Anglican churches all declined in the 1950s and 1960s. The pentecostal/charismatic renewal movement had reached an apex of over 500,000 by 1949, then steadily declined to only about 150,000 by 1970.

This decline was partially the result of the organization of the Three-Self Reform Movement (TSRM) in 1951, led by YMCA executive Y. T. Wu, which set itself the task of helping churches to rid themselves of imperialism, feudalism, and bourgeois thinking. This was carried out through denunciation meetings, with attacks on both former missionaries and Chinese church leaders, and through study sessions concerning Communist doctrine. The net effect of this practice was the gradual decline of denominational structures and of religious activities in general. With the outbreak of the Great Proletarian Cultural Revolution in Aug. 1966, a spontaneous attack led by Red Guard youth groups was directed against all visible forms of religion as part of their assault on the "Four Olds" (old habits, old customs, old ideas, old culture). For 10 years, until the death of Mao Tse-tung, Christians were subject to brutal treatment. To the most informed observers, institutional Christianity was on the road to extinction.

An unexpected but most significant development for Chinese Christianity in general and for renewal in particular was the rise of the House Church Movement. Although prayer and worship meetings in China were common long before 1949, Communist repression made houses the only viable meeting place for most Christians. Nonetheless, house meetings were highly dangerous, and groups had to remain very small to avoid detection. Independent churches from the beginning met in homes, emphasizing personal evangelism and grassroots cell groups. Witness Lee's Local Church, typifying these churches, would find its congregations shouting in unison, "Denominationalism is a sin." These churches were better prepared for the repression of the Cultural Revolution and remained quietly active from 1950 to 1980.

With the death of Mao Tse-tung and the subsequent rise of Deng Xiaoping, religious groups were gradually given more freedom. Deng's economic modernization policy inadvertently brought about increased openness to the outside world in the social, cultural, and religious landscape of China. By the spring of 1979 a series of conferences within the Chinese government led to open resumption of religious activities. This change in policy was first felt in the coastal provinces, with their greater accessibility to tourists, businessmen, and most importantly, Chinese Christians from Hong Kong and other overseas locations. Religious persecution was still experienced by Christians but was most intense in inland provinces, far away from Western eyes. The TSRM and the government-related Catholic Church experienced modest growth in this period, but it was the House Church Movement that mushroomed. By the time of the student uprising at Tiananmen Square in Beijing in June 1989, profound changes had already taken place in the Chinese church. However, talk of abolishing the TSRM and of reducing the government's control in the churches, mirroring the democracy movement in Chinese society, was abruptly halted, and a new period of repression, continuing to the present day, began. Independents, Protestants, and Catholics have all reported renewed persecution and harassment.

From 1970 to 1995 the Chinese church as a whole grew from about 1.5 million to over 78 million. The government has maintained the fiction that there are only 5 million or so professing Christians in China, which merely leads to the other 70 million being described as crypto-Christians. Whereas in 1970 only 10% of the Christians were pentecostal or charismatic, by 1995 nearly 65% were in the renewal (called independents, postdenominationalists, or neocharismatics). The explosive growth of the House Church Movement is largely responsible for this increase. The emphasis in these cell groups on informality, spontaneity, and personal experience paved the way for the outpouring of the Holy Spirit. Nearly all Chinese Christians believe in the power of specific prayer for healing. Although many extreme manifestations exist, such as violent exorcisms resulting in deaths or messianic prophets misleading young believers, most of the house churches remain committed to an orthodox Christian faith. Visits to China after 1980 by Western and non-Western pentecostals and charismatics brought news to the outside world of this phenomenon but also injected corrections in theology and practice into the strategic locations they visited. As an example, a 1993 visit from overseas Chinese resulted in thousands of new neocharismatics across the land.

Another critical factor in the growth of Christianity in China was Christian broadcasting. The typical Chinese believer will tune in to any broadcast he or she can find, and many Chinese Christians have come to faith as a result of radio programs alone. Christian television has also had a surprisingly effective role in evangelization in China. But video presentations, such as the Jesus film, have had an enormous evangelistic impact. Not surprisingly, pentecostals/charismatics have been quick to utilize these tools for the spread of the renewal. In addition, print media, such as Scripture and literature distribution, have contributed to rapid church and pentecostal/charismatic growth.

The renewal in China is not limited to the House Church Movement. Two of the earliest indigenous movements, Assembly Hall Churches (Little Flock) and the True Jesus Church, each number over a million members in mainland China. Roman Catholic charismatics number over a million

and are found in the open and clandestine Catholic Church as well as in the government-controlled Chinese Catholic Patriotic Association. Another significant aspect of the renewal is the many ethnic minority churches outside of the Han majority. Some of these, such as the Lisu church, have been in existence for more than 100 years and have a long history of pentecostal and charismatic experience. These churches collectively have over a million members today. Also significant is the recent inclusion of pentecostals and charismatics from both Hong Kong and Macau. These churches have had extensive contacts with the rest of the world and may provide somewhat of a bridge between Chinese Christians and the global Christian community in the coming decades.

The renewal in China has a bright and promising future. It is likely that by 2025 there will be over 90 million Christians in the renewal in China. If current trends continue in the 21st century, it is entirely possible that no country in the world will have more pentecostals and charismatics than China. This fact will certainly bring with it a fundamental redefinition to the maturing renewal movement as it pulls further away from Western theological direction and control in the third millennium.

■ **Bibliography:**
China 1907–47. D. H. Bays, "Indigenous Protestant Churches in China, 1900–1937: A Pentecostal Case Study," in *Indigenous Responses to Western Christianity,* ed. S. Kaplan (1995) ■ C. L. Boynton and C. D. Boynton, eds., *1936 Handbook of the Christian Movement in China under Protestant Auspices* (1936) ■ *Bridegroom's Messenger* (1907–8) ■ Mok Lai Chi, "Good News from the Land of Sinim," *LRE* (Dec. 1909) ■ M. Crawford, *The Shantung Revival* (1933) ■ H. and A. Fritsch, *Letters from Cora* (1987) ■ R. A. Jaffray, "'Speaking in Tongues'—Some Words of Kindly Counsel," *The Christian and Missionary Alliance* 31 (24, 1909) ■ E. M. Law, *Pentecostal Mission Work in South China* (1915) ■ S. McLean, *Over Twenty Years in China* (1987) ■ National Christian Council of China, *Revised Directory of the Protestant Christian Movement in China* (1950) ■ D. V. Rees, *The "Jesus Family" in Communist China* (1959) ■ T. M. Sung, "The Story of My Conversion: History of the Hong Kong Pentecostal Mission," *LRE* (June 1938) ■ W. A. Ward, *The Trailblazer: Dr A. G. Garr* (n.d.) ■ *Yearbook of Apostolic Assembly of Spokane, Washington* (1907).

China After 1947. D. B. Barrett, G. T. Kurian, and T. M. Johnson, *World Christian Encyclopedia* (2001) ■ D. H. Bays, ed., *Christianity in China: From the Eighteenth Century to the Present* (1996) ■ J. Chao and R. van Houten, *Wise as Serpents, Harmless as Doves* (1988) ■ R. R. Covell, *The Liberating Gospel in China: The Christian Faith among China's Minority Peoples* (1995) ■ T. Lambert, *The Resurrection of the Chinese Church* (1991) ■ E. Tang and J. Wiest, *The Catholic Church in Modern China: Perspectives* (1993).
■ D. H. Bays (China 1907–49);
T. M. Johnson (China after 1949)

CHRISTMAS ISLAND

■ Pentecostals 0   ■ Charismatics 0   ■ Neocharismatics 0   ■ Total Renewal: 0

COCOS (Keeling) ISLANDS

■ Pentecostals 0   ■ Charismatics 0   ■ Neocharismatics 0   ■ Total Renewal: 0

COLOMBIA

■ Pentecostals 512,397 (4%)   ■ Charismatics 11,522,127 (92%)   ■ Neocharismatics 550,476 (4%)
■ Total Renewal: 12,585,000

1. The Beginnings of Pentecostalism in Colombia.

The first recorded ministry of pentecostal evangelists in Colombia appears to be the arrival of Adah Winger Wegner and Edward Wegner on Oct. 12, 1932. Adah Winger Wegner had worked as a missionary in Venezuela together with G. F. Bender before her marriage to Wegner in 1931. After discussion with Presbyterian missionaries in Bogotá, they settled at Sogamoso. They began by distributing biblical texts with the assistance of the Bible Society. In an attempt to achieve a level of self-support and to establish credibility in a hostile environment, the Collegio Americano, a school for children, especially the poor, was established at Sogamoso. Adah Wegner educated her converts to be evangelists and pastors in the tradition of Bender, and preaching points and then congregations were begun throughout the region. Colombian convert Benito Vega offered his home as the first meeting place. By Aug. 1940 a second chapel had been constructed in Sogamoso. The ministry united with the Assemblies of God (AG), U.S., in 1942. More missionaries arrived from the U.S., and the Istituto Bíblico Bereano was established in 1943 to provide more formal education for clergy. On June 27, 1944, Adah Wegner died.

The growth of the AG in Colombia was soon eclipsed by another pentecostal church that began in 1936 with the arrival of missionary Verner Larsen. Larsen was Danish by birth but had immigrated to Canada, where he joined the ►Pentecostal Assemblies of Jesus Christ, a ►Oneness pentecostal denomination. After language study, the family moved in 1938 to Bucaramanga, where Larsen's first wife died giving birth to their second child. He stayed there, developed a small congregation, and in 1940 married an independent pentecostal missionary from the U.S.

2. The Development of the Two Churches Named Iglesia Pentecostal Unida.

Larsen's mission theory was like that of ►William Taylor and ►T. B. Barratt. He empowered the converts to develop ministries of their own. Since there was no money to do otherwise, he did not subsidize the salaries of pastors or evangelists. They were dependent on the people they served for their sustenance, or they worked in the local economy to earn their livelihoods. In addition, he was not afraid to minister to those who, with the collaboration of the government and church, were dispossessed by the oligarchy and flooded the cities. Most of the converts, and therefore most of the clergy, were from this segment of society. The church grew quickly under the leadership of these preachers and evangelists. The people provided the meeting places, were involved in the selection of clergy, and assembled significant financial resources for the sustenance of the common ministry.

Gustavo Quiroga preaching in a Sunday morning open air service: "Wherever stones are thrown, there we will raise up a church!"

As the church reached out to the poor and dispossessed, the persecutions began in earnest. Pentecostal clergy and other "liberals" were hunted down and killed. The Catholic Church organized pogroms against the churches. With the support of local governments and the wealthy, the priests undertook the burning of homes, churches, and Bibles, as well as killing church members. Few pentecostal churches in the world have withstood such systematic long-term, unlimited persecution. Only after ˒Vatican II did this begin to moderate, but the social conditions remain difficult, complicated now by the drug trade and the problems posed by globalization of Western business interests. However, despite these problems, the church has flourished.

The Pentecostal Assemblies of Jesus Christ (Canada) merged into the U.S. ˒United Pentecostal Church (UPC) (1945). In Colombia the new denomination was called the Iglesia Pentecostal Unida. UPC missionaries began to arrive from the U.S. who did not share the self-supporting, self-theologizing, self-governing mission model of Larsen. After a while the Canadian church withdrew from the union, and the mission fields were divided among the two. The UPC–U.S. received Colombia. This increased tensions between the Canadian Larsen and the other missionaries. The Colombian pastors were also increasingly disenfranchised. In 1965 the Colombian pastors presented a petition to the UPC mission board requesting nationalization of the church. Nothing happened, but the Colombians continued forming pastors as before and even sent missionaries to Peru, Bolivia, and Ecuador. At the UPC–Colombia convention, the church voted to nationalize and establish a radio station (1967). The protocol made the Colombian church independent, relegated U.S. missionaries to an advisory position, and forbade the UPC to send additional missionaries. In June 1969 the U.S. missionaries refused to compromise with the Colombians and the church split. This church, the largest pentecostal denomination in Colombia, now claims about 200,000 adherents.

The missionaries and about 5% of the Colombians of the UPC started a competitor church that is controlled by the mission organization. The newer church is also called the Iglesia Pentecostal Unida. It claims (1999) 16,410 "constituents," 276 clergy, and 769 churches and preaching points.

3. The Iglesia del Evangelio Cuadrangular.
The beginnings of the ˒International Church of the Foursquare Gospel in Colombia can be traced to the ministry of English missionaries John and Joanna Firth, who arrived in Colombia in 1938 and worked in the area of Bogotá. In 1944 (some sources say 1942), Paul Anderson and Glen Martin and their families arrived as Foursquare missionaries. They installed themselves in Barrancabermeja, and in 1947 they dedicated the large Templo Evangélico there. The ministry spread to other cities, and persecution increased with the success of the churches. Catholic priests succeeded in convincing municipal authorities to close the Barrancabermeja church for eight months in 1951. This happened again in 1953. However, the threats, demonstrations, imprisonment, and bodily harm only increased interest among the poor. In 1953 it was again necessary to build a larger building to handle the crowds that averaged about 1,000 persons. In 1952 John Firth brought his ministry into the Foursquare Church and moved with his family to Barranquilla, where he started another congregation. By 1980 this Colombian church claimed about 70,000 adherents in 353 congregations.

4. The Other Pentecostal Churches.
Colombia has attracted missionaries from several other Latin American countries, including Chile, Peru, and Venezuela. In addition, there are a number of indigenous denominations and independent congregations that do not claim origins or administrative/financial relationships with North American or European pentecostal churches. Among these are Iglesia Cristiana Pentecostés; Iglesia Cruzada Evangélica Colombiana; Iglesia de Cristo Pentecostal; Iglesia de Dios en Colombia; Iglesia Evangélica Cristiana Casa de Oración; Iglesia Evangélica Cristiana Independiente; Iglesia Evangélica Pentecostal; Misión Cristiana La Fe; as well as at least 25 other, generally smaller, denominations and groups. A significant presence of the charismatic movement can also be found in the Catholic Church. It is interesting to note that the Catholic charismatic movement first appeared in two locations in 1967: Duquesne University in Pittsburgh, PA, and in Bogota, Colombia.

■ **Bibliography:** D. B. Barrett, *World Christian Encyclopedia* (1982), 240–44 ■ D. L. Burk, ed., *Foreign Missions Insight: A Digest of Foreign Missions Faces, Facts, Fields and Figures* (1999), 140–41 ■ E. Capina, S.J., *Breve Reseña historica con un estudio especial de la llamada "persecución religiosa"* (1954) ■ R. Domínguez, *Pioneros de Pentecostes en el mundo de habla Hispana*, vol. 3, *Venezuela y Columbia* (1990) ■ C. B. Flora, *Pentecostalism in Colombia: Baptism by Fire and Spirit* (1976) ■ W. J. Hollenweger, "Handbuch der Pfingstbewegung" (diss., Zurich, 1967), 1059–65 (para. 02b.20) ■ F. Ordóñez, *Historia del Cristianismo Evangélico en Colombia* (1956) ■ A. Winger Wegner, *Think: What about South America. God's Proved Faithfulness* (1941).   ■ D. D. Bundy

COMOROS

■ Pentecostals 0 (0%) ■ Charismatics 198 (35%) ■ Neocharismatics 362 (65%) ■ Total Renewal: 560

CONGO, DEMOCRATIC REPUBLIC OF

■ Pentecostals 78,344 (0%)   ■ Charismatics 2,780,182 (16%)   ■ Neocharismatics 14,891,474 (84%)   ■ Total Renewal: 17,750,000

For a general introduction to Central Africa and bibliography, see AFRICA, CENTRAL.

I.   South-Central Region (Katanga/Shaba; Kasai)

II. The Northeastern Region (Kivu, Maniema, Upper-Congo, Equator)

III. Northwestern Region

IV. General Trends throughout the Congo

The Democratic Republic of the Congo was the Belgian Congo until June, 30, 1960, when it became independent. It was called The Democratic Republic of Congo-Kinshasa until 1971, and the Republic of Zaire until May 1997. (The Republic of the Congo, which was formerly part of French Equatorial Africa, lies west of the Democratic Republic of the Congo.)

Prior to Independence in 1960, the CPC, Conseil Protestant du Congo (Congo Protestant Council) served as an advisory body to all Protestant groups working in Congo and maintained contact with the predominantly Catholic Belgian authorities on their behalf. The CPC also attempted to direct new missions to areas of the Congo that were not being evangelized by any other Protestant group to avoid duplication of effort. This policy held throughout the colonial period but broke down after Independence. It accounts for the reason why most pentecostal groups were originally evenly scattered throughout the country and did not overlap. This is now no longer the case, although the individual groups are still predominant in their original areas. In the early 1970s the CPC changed its name to the Eglise du Christ au Congo (Church of Christ in Congo, COC), and by government legislation all Protestant groups were forced to join this one umbrella movement if they wished to remain free to evangelize. The names of the churches were all changed to *Communautés* (Communities) and accorded a number to signify which community they were within the COC. Since 1991 some groups have been recognized by the government without joining the COC. Because of the size of the country (approximately 25% of the land mass of continental U.S.) we will divide the country into three regions for this article: south-central, northeastern, and northwestern.

I. SOUTH-CENTRAL REGION (KATANGA/SHABA; KASAI).

A. The Congo Evangelistic Mission.

The Congo Evangelistic Mission (CEM) was the first bearer of the pentecostal message in this region. George Bowie from Bethel Pentecostal Assembly in Newark, NJ, had started an association that was registered in South Africa as the Pentecostal Mission of Central and South Africa. This mission had sent a reconnoitering party from South Africa by boat to East Africa in 1914, but while they were in German East Africa (Tanzania), WWI broke out and they had to flee to the (then Belgian) Congo. One of their party (Richardson) died, and the other two (Bowie and Ulyate) made their way through the Kivu to the upper reaches of the Zaire/Congo River. On their way south they visited Mwanza in the Katanga and felt that this was where they should establish a mission post. Of that party only Bowie survived; the others died of malaria.

The first group of pentecostals intent on settling in the Belgian Congo in 1915 was the direct result of this initial journey. It included a group of two Englishmen, ►W. F. P. Burton and ►James Salter, from Preston Lancashire; Joseph Blakeney, an American who had worked in South Africa for two years among the Zulu; and an older man, George Armstrong, a South African who was called "Daddy." Burton and Salter were not members of the Pentecostal Mission but agreed to work under their umbrella until their work was established, whereupon they planned to move to their own area. Burton was the only French speaker among them; consequently he became the spokesman for the party as well as being implicated legally in establishing the Pentecostal Mission in the country, even though he was not officially a member. Armstrong died of malaria on the way to Mwanza, and J. Blakeney withdrew in Oct. 1915 to South Africa. Blakeney later returned to the Congo (at Gombari near Isiro), north of Kisangani (formerly Stanleyville), under the auspices of the AG–U.S. in 1921. From these beginnings sprang the CEM, as the work under the leadership of Burton and Salter later became known.

The outstanding visible healing of a cripple, Tentami, upon the arrival of the first missionaries at their station, as well as a number of remarkable healings of unbelievers, was undoubtedly one of the reasons for the later success. On one occasion Burton and Salter were given food containing poison to eat but after prayer suffered no ill effects. The first convert was Abulahama Nyuki of Mwanza-Sope in Dec. 1915. He won many of his family and friends to Christ, and these became the nucleus of the church at Mwanza. Nyuki pioneered many assemblies. Mission stations were begun throughout the area on the left bank of the Lualaba (upper reaches of the Congo/Zaire) River; this area extended from the coal-mining town of Luena in the southeast to Kongolo in the northeast, and from Kinkondja in the east to Kipushya in the west (an area approximately the size of England and Wales).

This area was added to after Independence in 1960, when evangelism by traveling pentecostals meant that many of the larger cities and towns that had been off-limits to Protestants during the Belgian era became fair game for all. Pentecostals working in the copper mines in Lubumbashi, Likasi, and Kolwezi started their own churches, because they were not welcome in other denominations. Early pioneers planted mission stations from which evangelization of the surrounding area was carried out. From the earliest days new believers were incorporated in the evangelization of their own areas, and this was the key to the spread of the gospel.

In spite of a number of early conversions, it was not until Jan. 1920 that there was what Burton called a "Luban Pentecost" (the people were Luba), when approximately 160 people were filled with the Holy Spirit at Mwanza. Some spoke in German, Dutch, English, and other recognizable languages. This was followed by confession and the restitution of stolen goods. Many of those filled with the Holy Spirit volunteered to be sent to evangelize difficult areas. After this, when Axel Oman found only a few converts at Kabondo-Dianda, he held special meetings for teaching concerning the Holy Spirit. Consequently, 19 people were filled with the Holy Spirit. An unbeliever by the name of Mateo attempted to destroy the newly built church but was stopped and struck down by an unseen force. He was immediately converted and baptized in the Holy Spirit. This resulted in the conversion of over 60 people and the baptism in the Spirit of another 25. This sort of behavior seems to have set the pattern for many years after that in the evangelism of new areas: extreme opposition followed by acceptance of the Christian message, confession of sins, signs, and spiritual gifts. Prior to Independence in 1960, the major task of the CEM was expansion with limited personnel and financial resources. Evangelism resulted in the planting of 15 centers of outreach supervised by missionaries.

One remarkable intervention and aid in the initial evangelization of Katanga and Kasai was the arrival at Mwanza of a band of former slaves who had been captured and taken to Angola to be sent overseas. However, emancipation was announced, and they were free to return to their own countries. Meanwhile, they had been converted in the Bie district, where missionaries of the American Board of Commissioners for Foreign Missions, the Board of Mission of the Presbyterian Church of Canada, and the Brethren Mission were resident. The first party to leave was led by Shalumbo, a Songye (from the Kasai), who had been taken captive as a youth. They spoke only Kimbundu. The second group came from Kisamba and had spent two years with the United Methodists at Kapanga (on the western border with Angola). They came to inquire about the whereabouts of their homes. Many of these former slaves found their way to Mwanza, where they were filled with the Holy Spirit before returning to their homes or becoming involved in evangelism else-

where. They became church planters and greatly facilitated the growth of the pentecostal church in the Katanga as well as in the Kasai. Notable in this group were Shalumbo, who helped pioneer at Kipushya in the Kasai; Ngoloma, who worked at Kipamba; Shambelo, at Kisanga; Sukié, at Kalui; Musoka, at Katompe; and Zwao, at Kamungu. Mutombo Kusomba Shimioni pioneered among the cannibals at Madia; he became senior overseer and then station overseer of Kabongo station until he retired in 1972.

Prior to Independence in 1960, the CEM missionaries decided that it was time for the administration to be handed over to the national leaders. At a conference of all the national leaders and missionaries held at Kabondo-Dianda, two candidates for office were proposed: Ephraim Kayumba and ▸Jonathan Ilunga. The latter was chosen and has been the head executive of the national church now called the Communauté Pentecôtiste du Congo (Pentecostal Community of Congo, N°30, CEPCO) from 1960 to the present (2000).

Kayumba later left to start his own denomination; today, after several splits, it is called the Communauté Evangélique de Pentecôte au Shaba (Evangelical Pentecostal Community of Shaba, N°45, CEPS) and is led by Mulongo Ndombe.

In 1960–64 civil war raged in Congo. The majority of missionaries were forced to leave the country, and people were not free to move about at will. After this period there was sudden and dramatic growth in numbers. Many stories from this period mirror the miraculous intervention and keeping power of God over his people. However, there are also stories of great persecution and loss. It was in 1960, not long after the declaration of Independence, that Elton Knauff (New Zealand) and Teddy Hodgson (U.K.), both CEM missionaries, were martyred while attempting to take medical supplies to one of the stations. Estimated numbers of adherents in CEPCO is 500,000. Since the 1980s there have been numerous splits, and various new churches have sprung from the original pentecostal body founded by the CEM missionaries. Exact numbers are difficult to come by, but it is estimated that there are between 2,000 and 3,000 assemblies in CEPCO, not including the various other groups in the area.

Altogether, 230 missionaries from pentecostal groups (Apostolic Church New Zealand, AG–U.S., AG–U.K., AG–S.A., AG–N.Z., Elim–U.K., PAOC, AFM [S.A.], and others) have worked with the CEM/ZEM since its inception, but most have been British pentecostals.

From the early 1980s various sections of the pentecostal community began to voice discontent over what was understood as autocratic government by the leaders of CEPCO. From that point there were some splits resulting in the group called Communauté Pentecôtiste du Nord Shaba (The Pentecostal Community of North Shaba; this group is not part of the COC), led by Umba Kiloba and Banza Mulwani Wakutompwa. This group included most of the churches in the Kabongo zone as well as that of Kamina, which had previously been part of CEPCO. In the East Kasai, the pentecostal churches claimed autonomy from Shaba/Katanga and are presently led by Kitengie Kifwame; in the West Kasai many split off after Mbulu Lowo was excluded by Kalombo Muela (from Mbuji Mayi), the leader imposed on the churches of the entire Kasai by Jonathan Ilunga. A new grouping calling itself Eglise Pentecôtiste du Congo (The Pentecostal Church of Congo, EPCO; not part of the COC) is now recognized by the government. Mbulu Lowo is the executive director as well as director of the Bible college at Kananga. The main assembly, Jésus la Porte (Jesus the Door), of which Mbulu is pastor, has grown to 1,260 members within three years. Other leaders split off from the original CEPCO and joined existing pentecostal groups that were present elsewhere in the country but had not been working in Shaba/Katanga. These groups included the AG (N°37) from Kinshasa; Communauté des Eglises de Pentecôte en Afrique Centrale (the Community of Pentecostal Churches, N°8, CEPAC), started by the Swedish Free Mission in the Kivu; Communautés des Eglises Libres de Pentecôte (the Community of Free Churches in Congo, N°5, CELP), started by the Norwegian Free Churches; and others.

Most of the pastors in the pentecostal churches have not had the means nor the occasion to attend Bible schools. Since 1964, however, when a two-year Bible institute was started by Harold Womersley, Horace Butler, and Joe Robinson at Kamina, and a four-year course was introduced at Kamina II by David Womersley in 1974, many of the new generation have had the means to attend Bible training centers. Branch Bible schools have been established in most of the area serviced by the pentecostal churches, so that all who have desired to attend are able to do so. The best students are sent to the central institute at Kamina for the final years. The lack of Bible training has resulted in a variety of syncretistic practices in many of the assemblies. Official doctrinal positions are held by the churches but are not always understood by pastors or by members.

In 1986 the Institut Supérieur de Théologie Evangélique a Lubumbashi (Advanced School of Theology) was started at Lubumbashi by David Garrard and Gordon Stewart. This college granted the equivalent of an undergraduate degree in theology. It graduated one group at the master's level, but logistic difficulties caused the discontinuation of this course. Its graduates have been accepted for postgraduate work in the U.S., in ACTEA colleges in Kenya, and for doctoral work in Britain. Today this college is under the leadership of Congolese teachers who have postgraduate degrees, mostly from outside the country, and some from outside the continent. Kabila Mukombi is the director.

The Pentecostal Community of Congo is divided into 70 stations, each of which is under a station pastor or superintendent. Stations vary in size depending on the locality. The Lubumbashi station has more than 70 churches.

B. Other Pentecostals in This Region.

Since Independence there has been a proliferation of pentecostal groups in this region. Some of them are registered and recognized by the government, but the majority are small and are not recognized. The larger ones include Communauté Evangélique de Pentecôte au Shaba (Evangelical Pentecostal Community of Shaba, N°45, CEPS) and the extensions of the other recognized groups from other regions including the Assemblées de Dieu (AG), the Community of Pentecostal Churches (N°8, CEPAC), and the Community of Free Churches in Congo (N°5, CELP). Other smaller groups include Réveil (Revival) and numerous independent churches that may only have one or two congregations. The Apostolic Faith Mission (S.A.) has a few extensions in Shaba, but since the ethnic cleansing of the mid 1990s, most have been replanted in the Kasai provinces. The Apostolic Church in Zambia has also planted some churches in the Katanga and for a time had a missionary family resident in Lubumbashi. Nzambe Malamu (FEPACO) has churches throughout Katanga and the Kasai. The PAOC are involved in supporting the work of a former student who attended their college in Kitwe Zambia and who is now church planting in Katanga.

II. THE NORTHEASTERN REGION (KIVU, MANIEMA, UPPER-CONGO, EQUATOR).

The first pentecostal missions in this region were the AG–U.S., the Norwegian and Swiss Free Churches, and the AG–U.K. (not to be confused with the CEM in the Katanga).

A. Assemblies of God–U.S.

Today the Assemblies of God have two autonomous bodies within the country that should not be confused: the northeastern Isiro branch (N°12), and the western branch with its headquarters at Kinshasa (N°37).

Joseph Blakeney (CEM) led a party to Gombari near Isiro in the area north of Stanleyville in 1921 (see above). From this center the AG evangelized the entire area. Outreach stations were planted at Andudu and Ndeya in 1937, but these were closed in 1954 and relocated in Biodi among the Azande due to population movements. Emphasis was also given to the evangelization among the army camps, and since 1950 three leprosariums have been opened. The area was divided up so that each station was responsible for its own territory. Isiro, formerly known as Paulis, became the administrative center for this work. In the early 1960s, AG evangelist Lorne Fox held an evangelistic crusade in Isiro, where crowds of over 8,000 attended nightly. A number of healings took place, greatly impacting the local population. This was not long before AG missionary Jay W. Tucker was killed during the Simba uprising in Congo in 1964, just before he could be rescued by a UN-backed Katangese army at Paulis. By 1949 there were 34 full-time national workers and 45,000 adherents in this field. Today there are an estimated 100,000 adherents. Due to the pillaging of the entire country by Mobutu's troops during the takeover by Laurent Kabila (Oct. 1996–May 1997), all expatriate personnel were forced to leave this area. Still there are no AG missionary personnel in this region, although Billy Burr, AG overseer for Central and Southern Africa, makes periodic visits to this region to maintain contact with the national leadership. The church in this area is called the Communauté Assemblée de Dieu au Congo (Community of the Assembly of God in Congo, N°12); Ggyuwu Mbwanga is the president of the fellowship.

B. Assemblies of God–U.K.

The work established by the AG–U.K. is in the area immediately influenced by the Arab slave traders pursued by David Livingstone; the first missionaries followed the same route taken by him on his way to the Congo/Lualaba in the west. It was and still is one of the most Islamized areas in Congo.

The Arthur Richardsons from Britain entered the Belgian Congo in 1920 from Tanzania. They arrived at Baraka on Lake Tanganyika and settled at Kalembelembe among the Wabembe people. They were later joined by Maggie G. Noad, Mary Anderson, and, in 1921, by Frank Adams and Garfield Vale. Mission stations were established at Baraka, Nundu, Kisochi, and Lwata. Lulimba replaced Kalembelembe in 1952. Later Makombo was opened under the charge of Idris Parry. *Douglas Scott, who is better known for his church planting in France, was in Congo in 1939–45. From these centers the surrounding territories were evangelized and churches planted at Kabambare. Some have suggested that because this mission was surrounded by other Protestants, it could not grow. It was greatly limited by the lack of finance and shortage of personnel so that parts of the area were surrendered to other Protestant missions. There was considerable competition for resources between this AG–U.K. field and the CEM to the south; both drew most of their support from the same churches in the U.K.

The missionaries made it a policy to use Swahili rather than learn the local languages, because they worked among several language groups. Because there were never many missionaries, the work soon became independent. In 1964, after Independence, the J. W. Beardsmores, C. Crosses, G. Hawksleys, and J. Liddles, as well as K. Lucas and A. Brereton were held hostage with their families and threatened by the Mulele/Simba rebels for 129 days (June 10–Oct. 4) at Lulimba before being liberated by the national army. After this liberation there was a massacre of Christians by the rebels during which superintendent Petro Amisi and his son were killed and hundreds of villages were burnt to the ground.

Since that time there have been no resident missionaries in this entire area, because until 1987 the greater part of the region remained under the control of antigovernment rebels. In the 1950s and later, Eliya Yuma Lupande was the leader of this work. It has experienced a number of splits since the 1970s due to power struggles over leadership. It has churches in this entire area and as far south as Kalemie in the Katanga. The church is called the Communauté Assemblée de Dieu à l'Est du Congo (Community of the Assembly of God in the East of Congo, CADECO) and claims more than 500 churches. Muhasanya Lubunga is its president and legal representative, while Yuma Lupande, who was general superintendent until his death (1960–90), has been replaced by Mulongecha M'molecha. Because this area is very isolated, it has not been encroached upon by other pentecostal groups.

C. Norwegian Free Churches Missions.

There was close collaboration between the Swedish and Norwegian Free Churches Missions at the beginning of their work in Congo. Gunnerius Tollefsen from Norway and Axel B. Lindgren from the Philadelphia Assembly in Stockholm first traveled together to the Kivu from East Africa. On several occasions the Belgian administration, abetted by the Catholic Church, hindered them from finding a place to settle. Eventually a station was opened at Nya-Kaziba for the Norwegians. This later became important as a hospital and medical center. By 1928 a second station was opened at Moganga by John Brynhildsen. Both of these stations were among the Nyabongo people. In 1941 centers of evangelism were started at Kalambi and in 1946 at Kitutu among the Rega people. The WWII period was especially difficult because the Norwegians were cut off from their homeland and support and Norway was occupied by the Germans. After the war more stations were opened at Bideka (1949) and Bagira (1956). This work has spread to the Maniema and elsewhere in the Kivu, so that in many areas they are alongside the work established by the Swedish Free Church Mission and vice versa. The churches founded by the Norwegians have followed the pattern of the Free Churches in the homelands, where each local church is considered autonomous in terms of its government. However, like the Swedish Free churches, local churches will found new groups of believers that remain under their control until such time as the new groups are considered to be in a position to govern themselves properly. These groups gather in what are generally called *chapelles* (chapels). The Norwegians are responsible for the founding of the group now known as the Communauté des Eglises Libres de Pentecôte (The Community of Pentecostal Free Churches, N°5, CELP). This group has over 200,000 adult members, and Totoro Baraghine has been its leader for many years. They have a Bible school at Mugnaga, a hospital, a clinic for outpatients, and a children's home at Kaziba. They also have a teachers' training college.

D. Swedish Free Churches Mission.

Axel Lingren eventually established a mission station at Muchumbi for the Swedish Mission. The first baptismal service was held on Pentecost Sunday in 1923, when the first five converts were baptized in Lake Tanganyika. One of the most difficult tests of the period took place over Christmas 1923 when three missionaries died within five days. It was thought that they had been poisoned. New recruits volunteered to replace them, and stations were opened at Lemera among the Fuliro (1927) as well as at Uvira (1927), Walikale (1931), Ntoto (1932), Pinga (1935), Bukavu, (1948), Kavumu (1955), and Ndofia (1955). After the uprisings of the 1960s the majority of the missionary work was centered on Bukavu and the hospital at Lemera. Some of the other stations, however, were kept open. In Bukavu a print shop was opened, and weekly programs are aired on Radio Bukavu. Since the 1960s considerable sums of money have been made available by the Swedish government through its policy of foreign aid being administered by Swedish nationals overseas; this policy has benefited the medical and educational projects of the Swedish Free Mission in Congo, Rwanda, and Burundi.

The Finnish Free Foreign Mission (FFFM) has cooperated with the Swedish Free Mission by providing personnel. The first Finnish missionary in Congo to work with the SFM in the 1930s and 1940s was Hanna Ihalainen. The present pentecostal church that resulted from this early mission estimates its membership at 450,000 adults (1998). They have a theological college at Bukavu called the Institut Supérieur de théologie évangélique du Kivu (Evangelical School of Advanced Theology in the Kivu), begun by Daniel Halldorf in 1985 and directed at present by Kuye Ndondo, who is also assistant legal representative of the denomination. Ruhigita Ndagora, who had been legal representative during the entire post-Independence period, died in 1995. The present legal representative is Menhe Mushunganya. The churches founded by this mission are called the Communauté des Eglises de Pentecôte en Afrique Centrale (Community of Pentecostal Churches in Central Africa, N°8, CEPAC). The AG–U.S. seconded Arthur and Anna Berg to work with the SFM from 1922 until 1926. The FFFM has also been active in planting pentecostal churches through Ugandan refugees who escaped from Uganda to Congo during the uprisings of Amin and Obote. They invited Åke Söderlund (see article on Uganda) to teach them the Bible. Söderlund was able to do this during many visits to the Democratic Republic of Congo. There was a revival during which many churches were planted in the Kisangani, Bunia, and Beni areas, with 12,000 believers by 1995.

Since the first establishment of pentecostal churches in this region there have been a number of independent pentecostal groups that have become involved in church planting. Since the Tutsi-Hutu uprising in Rwanda (1994) and the Banyamulenge uprising (1996–97) that brought President Kabila to power, a number of ethnic Tutsi have begun churches in the Kivu. The Elim–U.K. have been involved with some of those who returned to Congo from the refugee camps in Ngara, Tanzania, after Dec. 1996. These returning Tutsi, under the leadership of Dunia Eba Mikongo, who attended the Elim Bible school at Tanga in Tanzania, have founded seven churches with over 800 adult members and are mostly in the Uvira area north of Lake Tanganyika. This group is involved in looking after 120 orphans from the conflict in the region.

E. Other Pentecostal Groups.

In the early 1980s Ralph and Shirley Hagemeier, who had previously worked in Tanzania under appointment with the AG–U.S., moved to the lakeside center of Kalemie, where they erected a large tent and began meetings. Hagemeier has mostly been involved in the training of people from all evangelical and pentecostal groups within the COC. Since this is a Swahili-speaking region, all instruction is given in that language. The number of personnel involved in this project has grown as the "Agape" ministry has developed. Although Hagemeier works independently of any existing group, he is recognized by the regional synod of the COC in Katanga. There are a growing number of independent groups within the northeastern region, but not nearly as many as there are in the south-central area.

III. NORTHWESTERN REGION.

The northwestern region was the last to be evangelized by pentecostal missions, because it was the exclusive domain of the Roman Catholic churches and other Protestant denominations during the colonial era.

A. Communauté Assemblée de Dieu au Congo.

In 1965, during the civil war that followed Independence, most of the country was engulfed in chaos, except the capital itself at Kinshasa (then Leopoldville). ▸Jacques Vernaud, a Swiss missionary working with the French AG in Brazzaville, was invited by Alphonse Futa, an elder in a Baptist church in Kinshasa, to hold meetings. Futa had come into Pentecost through the healing of one of his children. Vernaud made frequent crossings from Brazzaville to Kinshasa, and as the work in Kinshasa grew, he decided to move permanently. At that point the French AG felt that they were no longer able to support Vernaud, since they did not want to start a work in Congo/Kinshasa. Vernaud and Futa worked together and traveled widely, holding crusades and opening new pentecostal churches. The crowds had not heard the gospel message, nor of healing, but many were healed. In 1969 ▸Tommy L. Osborn was invited by Vernaud for a crusade. Osborn visited Kinshasa and held meetings organized by Vernaud Feb. 14–Mar. 9. Vernaud acted as

Osborn's interpreter. There were many healings, and the crusade had a great impact on Kinshasa. From this time on the pentecostal work in Kinshasa really began to grow. So great was the response that Vernaud continued holding meetings for another two weeks in order to do follow-up and to make sure that the converts were introduced to a local church. Six new churches were opened across the city. Since that time the pentecostal message has had a great impact on many churches and other denominations.

Vernaud continued to evangelize in a big tent he took to many different places for crusades. The Church of God (Cleveland, TN) invited Vernaud to join them, but this never materialized. Eventually Vernaud and the churches he had started—Communauté Assemblée de Dieu au Congo (The Community of the Assemblies of God in Congo, N°37)—transferred to the AG–U.S. in 1970, but he still keeps close contact with the AG–France. Since 1984 Vernaud has devoted most of his time to the establishment of the largest AG congregation in Africa, the French-speaking assembly at La Borne, with a membership of between 10,000 and 15,000. During the sacking of the city by Mobutu's troops (prior to Kabila's takeover), and following the coup d'état in Brazzaville (1997), Vernaud was one of the few missionaries who remained in Kinshasa and the only AG missionary in the entire country who remained. All other AG mission centers throughout Congo/Zaire were completely destroyed by Mobutu's rampaging army. In recent years Vernaud has had 90 minutes each week on both radio and TV to preach the gospel. This broadcast covers Kinshasa (population over 5 million) as well as the Atlantic port of Matadi and the towns of Tshikapa, Mbandaka, Kisangani, and neighboring Brazzaville north of the river. Johanna Vernaud, a qualified nurse, is the coordinator of the social work of the church, which has its own schools and a medical center with qualified doctors and nurses. Young people from this church are being trained, and a number of these have been sent to the AG graduate school in Lome Togo. Some are teaching in the AG college in Kinshasa, and others are in pastoral work.

Although the churches planted in Kinshasa were under the auspices of the AG, the work was set up as autonomous because Kinshasa was so far removed from the administration in Kisangani and Isiro, and it has always maintained this status, even within the COC. The present legal representative and executive leader of the church is Tshisungu Mawambe. Not only has the AG evangelized the entire Kinshasa area, it is now also involved elsewhere in the country, so that it is also found in areas that were at one time the exclusive domain of the CEM or the Swedish pentecostals. AG missionaries have been involved in the translation of Scriptures in their own areas. The AG have a Bible college in Kinshasa and also one that serves the Isiro area. Vernaud estimates the number of believers at 250,000 in the entire AG work in the Democratic Republic of the Congo. The AG–France has participated in the work of the AG in Congo. The Bernard Lines were resident there from 1979 until 1986. French missionary evangelists Jean Ollé and Michel Maréchal, as well as others, have made valuable contributions. More recently the many national pastors and evangelists have contributed to the overall growth and impact of the AG on the city of Kinshasa, as well as on the entire northwestern region. From Kinshasa the gospel has been taken to neighboring zones as well as to neighboring countries.

B. Fraternité Evangélique Pentecôte en Afrique du Congo

▸Alexander Adini-Abala, who had been converted in Kenya, was working with Jacques Vernaud by the time of the Osborn crusade (1969). However, he was also, unbeknown to Vernaud, being supported by the Elim Fellowship of Lima, NY. After the Kinshasa crusade he left to commence his own movement with the involvement of Arthur Dodzweit (Elim [NY]), a missionary from Tanzania. This church is best known by its nickname, Nzambe Malamu, a name from the Lingala language meaning "God is good," T. L. Osborn's crusade war cry. Properly the group is called the Fraternité Evangélique Pentecôte en Afrique du Congo (The Pentecostal Evangelical Brotherhood in Africa: Congo, FEPACO) and has recently been granted government recognition apart from the COC. It has an estimated 350 churches in Kinshasa and 4,000 throughout the republic (the latter number may in actuality be lower). This grouping has a Bible college in Kinshasa with outside help from the Elim (NY) Fellowship. Since Alexander's death in 1997, his son Pefa is now responsible for this movement, which has churches in six other African, as well as five European, countries. Other pentecostal groups regard the FEPACO with some suspicion because of its unusual forms of worship, the supreme place of its leader, and what is seen as questionable theology.

C. Other Groups in the Northwestern Region.

As in other areas of the Democratic Republic of Congo, a proliferation of pentecostal churches have been established in this region and especially in the capital at Kinshasa. Most of them consist of one congregation, but in some cases several come under the authority of one individual. Some very successful crusades have been held in this city during the last 25 years. One of the most successful was that of T. L. Osborn (see above). ▸Mahesh Chavda from the U.S. visited Kinshasa in June 1985, and some phenomenal miracles accompanied that crusade, including the raising from the dead of Katshinyi, son of Mulamba Manikai, a six-year-old boy who had been pronounced dead for eight hours. This miracle resulted in crowds of over 100,000 gathering to hear the gospel preached.

IV. GENERAL TRENDS THROUGHOUT THE CONGO.

A. Education and Health Care.

Most of the missions in Congo during the colonial period were involved in primary-school education. The government relied on missions (both Catholic and Protestant) for the education and health care of the population. Schools became important instruments in the evangelization of the areas in which the missions were based. The majority of pastors and leaders in the pentecostal churches had been brought up in the mission school system. These schools continue to be run by the national churches they have founded, although the costs for running the schools are subsidized by the state. Secondary schooling was not a major focus until after 1960, when a limited number of institutions were established by the missions to serve their members. In addition to education, primary health care became the responsibility of missions. All had clinics that were subsidized by the government if the criteria established by the Belgian government were met. All the pentecostals had clinics and maternity facilities. Hospitals often functioned without doctors; qualified nurses were responsible for the work doctors do in the Western world. Budgets were always limited and facilities very basic. The Swedish and Norwegian missions were later able to benefit from their governments' overseas aid programs to finance educational and medical facilities and constructed schools and hospitals in the Kivu, Rwanda, and Burundi. The AG–U.S., AG–U.K., and the CEM/ZEM did not have that financial help. Except for a short period (Dr. Scherer Penny, 1953–54), the CEM/ZEM did not have a full-time doctor until 1991 (Dr. Andy Ostins-Kipushya and Dr. Illunga Baba-Lwamba).

B. Opposition to Pentecostals and Their Message.

Opposition to the pentecostal (and other Protestant) missions in Congo during the colonial period came from three quarters: The traditional leaders represented by some of the chiefs and the religious secret societies; the Roman Catholic Church; and the colonial government, which for the most part was under strong influence of the Roman Catholic Church (until the Liberal government came to power in Belgium in 1948). After Independence, and especially during the Mobutu years (1965–97), the one-party state, Mouvement Populaire de la Révolution (Popular Movement for the Revolution, MPR), was afraid that the churches would become hotbeds of discontent against its policies and limited the churches' freedom by legislation.

Protestant missions were continually in conflict with the Catholic Belgian colonial government. The granting of civil recognition was in some cases withheld from pentecostal missions for as much as 20 years. This meant that they could not legally purchase land nor build with permanent materials.

The Foursquare mission, which attempted to evangelize the area bordering on CEM territory in the East Kasai Province, was forced out of the country by the Belgians in 1944, accused of disturbing the peace. The Belgians did not like the pentecostals because they claimed that their doctrine encouraged xenophobia among the Africans and the tendency to rebellion against authority.

During the colonial period, many of the pentecostal missions appeared to have played down their pentecostal emphasis because of pressure from the government. This was in spite of an initial manifestation of charismatic gifts during the planting stage. With the arrival of new mission personnel after WWII, there was once again greater emphasis given to the importance of the Holy Spirit among the British pentecostals, although the Swedish pentecostals tended to tread softly in this area and as late as the 1980s were still hesitant to put emphasis on the work of the Holy Spirit for fear that the African tendency toward "things spiritual" would be exaggerated. This is likely the reason for the rapid growth of many independent pentecostal groups, some of which have incorporated distinct traditional religious practices into their doctrine and practice. They have interpreted the lack of willingness on the part of some missionaries to mean a lack of availability of "power" in the white man's version of Christianity. In some cases this has resulted in the spawning of numerous "prophet movements," which have similarities with Christianity, because the Bible is claimed to be the authority, but which in many cases are syncretistic and reduce the Holy Spirit to an impersonal power to be manipulated at one's will.

C. Pentecostals and Training of Pastors.

Most of the pentecostal missions during the colonial period did not emphasize the formal training of its African pastors. Most of the pentecostal missionaries came from churches that did not stress such training in their homelands. Indeed, most of the earlier missionaries had not had the benefit of such training themselves. After 1960, however, there was great demand on the part of the national churches for formal Bible training. Nevertheless, there has often been considerable suspicion on the part of the older generation of pastors for all those graduating from Bible schools and colleges. It is not uncommon to hear older pastors say that they have the "Holy Spirit" and that is all that is necessary. Not all graduates from existing schools and colleges have been eagerly readmitted to ministry after graduation. This may be one reason why a number have started their own churches. Some of the most successful pastors in the larger cities have never had any formal Bible training. One disadvantage is that leaders tend to follow the latest trends without being aware of the dangers. All the groups belonging to the COC have Bible training centers at one level or another.

D. Emergence of Prayer Groups.

The phenomenon of prayer groups is of great importance when we look at what is taking place in the pentecostal/charismatic realm in the Congo now. Since the mid 1980s, and especially since Mobutu's liberalization in 1991, prayer groups *(groupes de prière)* or prayer cells *(cellules de prière)* have made an appearance in the majority of large cities and centers throughout the country. These groups start when members of an existing congregation or denomination start additional services in their homes or in erected shelters in their gardens outside normal meeting hours. They may continue this way, but often when the numbers increase, they split off from the church and become independent. Many of these groups grow to be as big as the churches from which they split. Some of them continue to function alongside the existing churches. These groups or cells differ from established churches in that their members come from different churches. In many cases they are not organized by churches, and the person who is in charge need not be recognized as an elder or deacon in his or her own church. In the cities there are often more prayer-cell churches than recognized churches. Most of these cells are charismatic to varying degrees. Even those started by noncharismatics tend to be charismatic because of the influence of charismatic members. In a good number of these groups there is considerable syncretistic practice, just as there is in many of the recognized pentecostal/charismatic denominations. Exact statistics are not available, but it is probably not an exaggeration to say that because of these groups, there are more pentecostal/charismatic Christians in Congo than there are in all the other denominations combined (not counting the Roman Catholics). Many of the prayer cells include a good percentage of Catholics.

►The Full Gospel Business Men's Fellowship in Congo has grown rapidly in the large centers of Congo during the last ten years. ►Michel Kayembe wa Dikonda has been the major force in the growth of this movement. It has had a great deal of influence on those who are financially better off in the society, as well as those of political and intellectual position. As a result, many who have previously had no contact with the gospel—from many backgrounds, including Roman Catholics—have become charismatic believers. This group has been responsible for the integration of many governors and military people into the pentecostal and charismatic churches.

E. Government Control of Churches and the Politicizing of the Eglise du Christ au Congo.

Since government legislation forced all Protestant denominations to belong to the COC (under the leadership of Bishop Bokeleale), many of the activities of the recognized denominations have been politicized. As a consequence, relationships between missions and national church leaders have often deteriorated to the extent that missionaries, including pentecostal missionaries, have been expelled from the country. Many of the pentecostal missions in the country have lived through soul-searching times when they have wondered whether or not they would remain. In the case of at least one pentecostal mission, the government opposed the order of national church leaders to expel the majority of their missionaries because the government realized the important role they played. Much of this politicized attitude has been a direct result of the Mobutu program Le Retour à l'Authenticité (Return to Authenticity) that was promoted during the 1970s. This plan was originally meant to have all expatriates leave the country by 1980. The plan resulted in financial chaos and eventually fell through, but the anti-missionary attitudes are still felt in many quarters. Not only has Bokeleale attempted to manipulate what has gone on in the missions and denominations, he has made every effort to exclude the growth of independent groups and churches that did not belong to the official COC. Since 1991 and the change in Mobutu's political exclusivism, which eventually led to his own downfall, there has been considerable relaxation on the part of the state authorities toward the denominations. This has meant that a number of groups have received government recognition outside the COC and many independent churches, including many that are pentecostal/charismatic, have been ignored and left to worship freely.

Since the number of unregistered pentecostal/charismatic churches (some are denominations, some individual churches) was more than 1,500 in the region of Katanga alone in 1980, the number throughout the country is considerable.

E. Kimbanguism (Simon Kimbangu).

The failure to include Kimbanguism in this survey is by design and not by omission. The reason is that, although Kimbanguists have been included in other world surveys, it is questionable that they should be regarded as a pentecostal/charismatic group. National pentecostal (and other Protestant) church leaders do not regard the Kimbanguist position as biblically justifiable. They have been accepted within the WCC, but since the adherents of this movement have elevated Simon Kimbangu to the place of the Black Messiah, their practice as well as their theology is unorthodox. In spite of any attempts by the official spokesmen for Kimbanguism to present themselves as a bona fide Christian denomination, it is not possible to regard such a group as meeting the biblical criterion that Jesus Christ is the only Savior of humankind. Kimbanguists would put Kimbangu, at best, on an even footing with Christ and more often would regard Christ as inferior when it comes to the salvation of the black man. Their estimated statistic of more than 6 million adherents is suspect.   ■ D. J. Garrard

CONGO, REPUBLIC OF THE (Brazzaville)

■ Pentecostals 53,479 (9%) ■ Charismatics 195,925 (33%) ■ Neocharismatics 339,595 (58%) ■ Total Renewal: 588,999

For a general introduction to Central Africa and bibliography, see AFRICA, CENTRAL.

The Republic of the Congo, formerly part of French Equatorial Africa, lies west of the Democratic Republic of the Congo (the former Belgian Congo). It was colonized under the French, who kept a tight reign on the presence of Protestants and favored the Roman Catholic Church. Throughout the colonial period the AG–France was the only official pentecostal grouping within the French Congo. In 1958 the Congo declared itself an autonomous republic, which resulted in tribal warfare. Since gaining independence from France (1960), the country has gone through numerous revolutions. In 1968 the pro-Marxist party of Marian Ngouabi was in power. He was followed by President Sassou who, like his predecessor, was Marxist and opposed the churches. Sassou was voted out in an election but during a coup d'état regained power in 1997. His anti-Christian stance appears to have mellowed considerably.

▸Jacques and Johanna Vernaud of the French AG arrived from Gabon in May 1961; they were the first pentecostal missionaries to go to Congo. They were installed at Brazzaville in 1962, where they stayed until 1965 when, because of the unsettled state of the country and the fact that they could not get recognized status for the church, they decided to leave. The response to the gospel on the Kinshasa side of the Congo River, in the Democratic Republic of the Congo (the former Belgian Congo), and a clear call from God directed them there. During the intervening years believers from the newly planted AG churches in Kinshasa (Democratic Republic of the Congo) began to testify of their experiences to the people of Congo/Brazzaville. This testimony, together with the preaching of Itoua Lucien at his home village of M'bekanga, resulted in the first assembly at Gambona in the center of the country in 1970.

Other groups that were open to the pentecostal experience at Brazzaville contacted the missions department of the AG–France (known as Action Missionnaire [Missionary Action]). As a result, Roger Albert, who had worked in Ivory Coast and Gabon, together with Jean Ollé, who was secretary of the French AG missions department at the time, made an exploratory journey in 1972 to visit with this group. They found that there were those who were desirous of being led by the Spirit of God, but some of the influential members were unable to distinguish between the work of the Spirit and demonic manifestations. Roger Albert spent two months teaching on the biblical basis for the gifts and Christian living, after which those who wished to follow the Bible had to decide what they would do. Those who did not want to make a break with their past split from their former

partners. From that time the French AG has cooperated with the members of the group that wanted to serve the Lord. Jean Ollé spent periods of time in 1973 and again in 1974 teaching and evangelizing in the Congo.

Land was acquired in Brazzaville on which buildings could be erected, and special meetings were held with Jean Ollé. Two men from Kinshasa, pastors Mambu and Djuruwa, also participated. A number of healings and deliverances from demonic possession took place. Within a very short time the church grew. Spontaneous testimonies, healings, and the work of the Spirit of God resulted in the burning of witchcraft paraphernalia and fetishes. In 1975 Aimé Cizeron came to hold evangelistic campaigns. This was at a difficult time, because Marxism was already in place and there was considerable antagonism against all churches. In one area of Brazzaville, Bacongo, about 15 lame people threw away their crutches when they were healed. Within four weeks 81 people were baptized and added to the church. This church came under the leadership of the French missionary Réaux. In August and September of the same year, Cizeron held crusades at Pointe Noire on the coast. Again many healings resulted in 150 people being baptized and the call going out to missionary Bernard Lines to pastor this group. From 1975 to 1978 both Réaux and Lines spent the majority of their time instructing the eldership.

In 1978 a religious sect was blamed for the assassination of President Ngouabi. This resulted in immediate expulsion of most Protestant denominations and personnel. Some say that this was due to direct intervention of the government, while others say that national church leaders were behind it. This brought to an end the direct missionary work of the French pentecostal missions until the AG–U.S. became involved in May 1990. At Brazzaville, Réaux was taken to the airport in chains for deportation within 24 hours, and Lines was given 12 days to leave the Congo with his family. The believers were ordered to join the Evangelical Church, which was one of the two Protestant groups recognized by the government. Some did join the Evangelical Church, but many continued to pray in groups in their homes and the homes of friends. They also continued to evangelize and baptize. In 1980 a law was passed granting more religious freedom, and churches were encouraged to register for recognition. Some of those who had been part of the work that was started in 1973 attempted to register under the name Eglises de Dieu du Congo (Church of God of Congo, EDC). Others called themselves Communauté des Assemblées du Plein Evangile (Community of Full Gospel Assemblies in Congo, CAPEC). The Congo government administration kept these groups waiting without answer.

In 1985 new contacts were established between former pentecostal leaders and the French missions department. In 1985 Michel Maréchal was able to preach publicly to 400 people in Brazzaville; many were healed, including a blind woman and two deaf people. In June 1986 Bernard Lines, who was by this time working in Kinshasa, was able to return to Brazzaville to find more than 1,000 believers in four assemblies. In 1987 the government authorized a crusade that was held on government land. An evangelist from Kinshasa preached to thousands who gathered to hear the Word of God. In 1987 Jean Ollé made another journey to Brazzaville to meet with leaders and visit the assemblies. He noted that by that time there were seven assemblies in different parts of the capital, each with 300 to 400 people. It was not until Bob Herndon of the AG–U.S. was granted a residency visa in 1990 that any pentecostal missionary was able to return full time to the country.

The story of the pentecostal church in Congo is one of splits and intrigue. After the initial planting of pentecostal churches by the French AG, numerous groups sprang up. Many of them have syncretistic tendencies and questionable practices (from the orthodox pentecostal perspective). Others, however, accept traditional pentecostal/charismatic doctrine and practice. Some of these (as seen above) formed the Eglise de Dieu (Church of God). Jean Baptiste Bafoungissa, one of the earliest converts of the French AG in 1973, has served as its president since the early 1980s. Some confusion over names exists, because there was already a local pentecostal church of the same name. Itoua Lucien, who had been part of the Church of God, split from them and now has his base in the plateau region with his headquarters at Mbekanga. He leads the CAPEC.

Another important factor in the growth of the pentecostal churches in Congo is related to government policy during the Marxist years. Students were sent to the Eastern bloc for education. A number of those sent were contacted by the underground church. Some even married and returned with their Russian or Ukrainian brides to Congo. Many of those who were converted began to plant churches upon their return. One such is Gustave Koukola, who originally trained in the former USSR as a dentist. He is president of the Fédération des Eglises de Réveil (Federation of Revival Churches) in Pointe Noire. This is part of the wider grouping known as Fédération des Assemblées de Réveil (Federation of the Revival Assemblies, FAR) but not to be confused with it. The latter was formed by independent pentecostal/charismatic churches in order to present a unified front to the government. The reason for this was that the authorities were confused as to the identity of these "Revival Churches." Jean Baptiste Bafoungissa is the current president of this organization, which has a high profile in Brazzaville; in 1997, prior to the overthrow of the government, it held meetings with politicians and officials in the capital.

There is at present a grassroots movement in Congo with over 500 churches called the Assemblées de Dieu de Pentecôte (Assemblies of God of Pentecost). The AG–U.S. began to work in Congo in May 1990. Since July 1991 the church has been recognized by the government. The first missionaries were Bob and Linda Herndon, who were joined in 1993 by Gary and Janice Dickinson. Initially they worked with a loose grouping of pentecostal churches, including those led by Itoua Lucien and pastors Buka and Malonga (CAPEC). Due to difficulties over doctrine and practice, in 1995 Buka, who had previously been in fellowship with Nzambe Malamu (see ▸Alexander Adini-Abala), and Malongo left this grouping but kept the name. The AG–U.S. missionaries initiated discussions between the EDC and CAPEC and now work with both of these groups. There has been considerable coming and going of members and individual churches between these two major groupings. The AG–U.S. is involved in Bible teaching and plans to open a Bible school in Brazzaville under the leadership of Edgar and Janora Reed. In 1995 AG–U.S. opened a Bible institute at Pointe Noire where all the pastors in the city attend. The AG–U.S. has approximately 120 churches in fellowship. There are many hundreds more of various independent pentecostal groups that have sprung up between 1990 and 1996. In the civil war that raged for five months and ended in Oct. 1997, between 10,000 and 15,000 were killed; many of the inhabitants of Brazzaville fled the city for their home villages. This has meant that at present (May 1998) many of the churches in the capital are nearly empty, as it still is considered unsafe to live there.   ■ D. J. Garrard

---

COOK ISLANDS

■ Pentecostals 1,278 (41%)   ■ Charismatics 1,816 (59%)   ■ Neocharismatics 6 (0%)   ■ Total Renewal: 3,100

For general introduction and bibliography, see PACIFIC ISLANDS.

The 15 islands that make up the Cook Islands are an internally self-governing state in free association with New Zealand. The main island is Rarotonga, located 1,900 mi (3,000 km) northeast of Auckland. Most of the islands are coral atolls. Some islands in the south are of volcanic origin and more elevated, with mountains up to 2100 ft (650 m).

The Cook Islanders are Polynesian Maori. Several tribes trace their ancestry back to Samoa or Tahiti. There are also some lines connecting them with New Zealand.

The total population in 1990 was about 18,300. Of those, 10,000 live on the island of Rarotonga and in the administrative center Avarua alone. Migration to New Zealand is easy, and the rate of migrants high. It is estimated that today more Cook Islanders live in New Zealand than on the home islands.

The Cook Islands Christian Church, which was established by the London Missionary Society in the middle of the 19th century, is still the dominant church, to which approximately 60% of the population belonged in 1992. Since that time support has steadily weakened and the Christian population has become increasingly fragmented into a variety of denominations. Second in terms of adherents is the Roman Catholic Church (approximately 17%), followed by the Seventh-day Adventists (7.6%) and the Mormons (6%). The only major pentecostal/charismatic presence is the Assemblies of God (AG). In 1998 the AG claimed 7 churches and 2 preaching points, 56 ministers, and about 700 adherents (3.8%). The AG also runs a Bible school in the Cook Islands with 70 students enrolled in 1998.

■ M. Ernst

COSTA RICA

■ Pentecostals 223,063 (45%)   ■ Charismatics 199,841 (40%)   ■ Neocharismatics 71,095 (14%)   ■ Total Renewal: 493,999

See LATIN AMERICA.

CROATIA

■ Pentecostals 2,909 (2%)   ■ Charismatics 119,765 (94%)   ■ Neocharismatics 5,146 (4%)   ■ Total Renewal: 127,820

See EUROPE, EASTERN.

CUBA

■ Pentecostals 68,215 (12%)   ■ Charismatics 366,011 (64%)   ■ Neocharismatics 136,774 (24%)   ■ Total Renewal: 571,000

The first known pentecostal evangelist in Cuba appears to have been Sam C. Perry, who was in Cuba in 1910. Despite the proximity to the U.S. and the developing cultural connections, there appears to have been little pentecostal activity in Cuba during the first two decades of the movement. This may be explained in part by the fact that American Protestant missions here did not begin until after 1898. The missionaries of the mainline U.S. churches were no longer related to the Holiness movement, and so the kind of pre-pentecostal mission seen in other countries was not present in Cuba. The revolution of 1959 ruptured official relationships with the U.S. denominations, but the pentecostals, more perhaps than some other churches, had a Cuban clergy and lay leaders able and willing to give leadership to the churches. Only among Santeria was there a comparable depth of competent indigenous Cuban leadership. Pentecostals had deep roots among the African diaspora and the poor, which positioned them well to minister in Cuba after 1959; they had both rural and urban connections.

1. The Asambleas de Dios and the Iglesia Evangélica Pentecostal de Cuba.

The second documented presence of pentecostal missionaries was May Kelty and her mother, Harriet Kelty, who arrived in Havana in 1920 after serving in Argentina with Alice Wood. They returned to the U.S. in 1922 to work in a Bible school with ▸Henry Ball. In 1931, however, May Kelty came again to Cuba, accompanied by Mrs. Anna Sanders; Kelty stayed in Cuba until 1957. The two women experienced significant persecution from the Catholic Church in their work, especially during the early days of the movement. Esther and Francisco Rodríguez, a Puerto Rican pastoral couple from New York, joined them in 1933. Francisco became pastor in Havana, and Kelty and Sanders moved to El Moro. Then came Catalina and Teodoro Bueno from Venezuela in Jan. 1935.

Until 1936 the Assemblies of God (AG) work in Cuba was considered juridically to be part of the U.S. Latin American District of the AG. In May 1936 the Cuba mission was placed under the direction of the AG Department of Foreign Missions. Superintendents included Lawrence Perrault (1936–38; see also Dominican Republic and Haiti), Louis Stokes (1938–40; see Argentina), and Hugh Jeter (1942–52).

In Jan. 1940 ▸Noel Perkin visited Cuba and organized an "executive commission" to direct the churches in Cuba, composed of Perrault, Francisco Rodríguez, and Enrique Rodríguez. Later that year a schism developed. Francisco Rodríguez and Roberto Reyes and most of the members withdrew from the Asambleas de Dios, which was left with only 10 congregations and preaching points and less than 200 members. It is unclear what the issues were, but it appears that control from the U.S. was a major concern of the Cuban pastors. In 1948 ›Melvin Hodges arrived and for two months toured the island, urging the churches of the Iglesia Evangélica Pentecostal de Cuba to become self-sustaining, self-governing, and self-propagating. This ameliorated the situation and provided a decade of preparation for the sudden departure of missionaries.

The greatest prerevolutionary expansion of pentecostalism came through the evangelistic and healing campaigns of ›T. L. Osborn hosted by Luis Ortiz, Dennis Valdez, Hugo Jeter, and Ezequiel Álvarez, among others. From Mar. 1950 until late 1951, Osborn and other evangelists crisscrossed the nation. Mass meetings were held in the stadium at Guarina as well as in Havana (Amphitheater of Marianao), Holguín, Palma Soriano, Sancti Spíritus, and Santiago de Cuba. Many churches, including nonpentecostal churches, cooperated with the campaigns that were vigorously opposed by the Catholic Church. About 50,000 persons made professions of faith and were channeled into congregations. Several pentecostal congregations increased significantly. Luiz Ortiz and Avelino González left the Iglesia Evangélica Pentecostal de Cuba in about 1958 and established an independent indigenous ministry.

A radio ministry was developed by Perrault, who also founded Cuban Bible Institute, which had an enrollment of 70 by 1958. In 1956, S. Hodges listed 25 congregations, 250 "outstations," and 4,000 members. In 1959 the AG (U.S.) claimed 25 "organized churches," 143 "outstations," 130 "national workers," 2,600 members, and a Sunday school enrollment of 12,590. After the revolution, Cuban and U.S. diplomatic relations deteriorated. However, even after the breaking of diplomatic relations and the beginning of the embargo in Jan. 1961, AG (U.S.), missionaries stayed until 1963. On Mar. 17, 1963, the Bible school was sacked and ordered closed. AG missionaries Floyd and Millie Woodworth, Ramón Nieves, and Kerry González and their families were initially placed under arrest in a hotel in Havana. Then Floyd Woodworth and Kerry González were placed in a maximum security prison in solitary confinement. The Red Cross secured their release and repatriation. Others were harassed in other ways. During the next four years, all of the missionaries and not a few Cuban clergy dispersed throughout Latin America, Spain, and the U.S.

The Pentecostal Assemblies of Canada (PAOC) became active in Cuba when it was no longer possible for the U.S. AG to be involved because of U.S. opposition to the Cuban revolution. Relationships continued with select pentecostal congregations and organizations in Cuba. The PAOC has not sought to establish congregations and has resisted efforts of Cuban churches to establish juridical or formal ties.

In the meantime, by all accounts the Iglesia Evangélica Pentecostal has prospered since the years 1959–63. Louisa Jeter de Walker claimed (1995) 610 clergy, 1,400 *iglesias/anexos,* and 35,000 adherents. In 1999 the AG–U.S. Department of Foreign Missions claimed 82,700 "members and adherents." In each of these cases, it is difficult to ascertain who and what is being counted as Asambleas de Dios.

2. Primera Iglesia Pentecostal de Cuba and the Iglesia del Evangelio Cuadrangular.

In 1940 Francisco Rodríguez, a Puerto Rican missionary, and Roberto Reyes, with most of the members, withdrew from the Iglesia Evangélica Pentecostal de Cuba to form the Iglesia Pentecostal en Cuba. From 1946 until 1951 they made common cause with the ›International Church of the Foursquare Gospel and changed their name to Iglesia del Evangelio Cuadrangualar. However, in 1951 they broke relations with the Los Angeles–based church of ›Aimee Semple McPherson and returned to the original name. Later, in 1957, Fermín Curí and some groups that did not remain in the Primera Iglesia Pentecostal de Cuba established an Iglesia del Evangelio Cuadrangular at Pinar del Río.

3. La Iglesia de Dios, known as the Iglesia de Dios del Evangelio Completo (Full Gospel Church of God).

Despite the early presence of ›Sam Perry, it was not until 1938 that the ›Church of God (CG, Cleveland, TN) missionary statesman visited Cuba where he held discussions with a former Catholic priest, Alberto Blanco. The first CG missionaries, Hoye and Mildred Case, arrived in Cuba in Jan. 1943 and settled in Santiago de Cuba. Blanco and his family joined the fledgling congregation and became involved in evangelistic work. The Catholic Church, both priests and educators, severely persecuted those who expressed interest in the new tradition, including their children. At a revival in 1944 the first group experienced pentecostal baptism of the Holy Spirit, including Blanco and the American evangelist's translator, Esperanza Estevens. Blanco was supervisor of the mission from 1948 to 1950. He was replaced by the U.S. missionaries Edward L. McLean (1950–55) and Hoyle Case (1955–59). They were joined by Puerto Rican missionary Sixto Molina, who became superintendent of the congregations on the western end of the island, including Havana, where he planted churches (1953–56). Barrett (1982) reported 636 members and adherents.

3. La Iglesia de la Biblia Abierta de Cuba.

This church is the result, initially, of mission efforts by the ›Open Bible Standard Churches. These began when Luther and Hazel Adams arrived in Cuba in Nov. 1944. They went, as invited, to work with independent pentecostal missionary Sidney Correll on a mission farm at Cabanas Bay. Paul and LaVon Lakin Hartman came in 1945. They developed a small congregation, built missionary residences, and started a Bible school. The Hartmans began work in Guayabel (about 1946), then Rancho Grande, and eventually Ceiba del Agua (1950). At Cieba they organized the Open Bible Institute of Cuba in 1951. The Revolution required the exit of all missionaries, although filial relations have continued. The first completely Cuban council of the church was held on May 20, 1960. Since that time, several individuals were elected superintendent, the church has grown, and a process of theological education has been implemented. In Jan. 1995 the church reported 13 congregations, 12 clergy, and 1,040 members.

4. La Iglesia Cristiana Pentecostal de Cuba.

This church is also a schism from the Iglesia Evangélica Pentecostal. After the Osborn campaigns Luis Ortiz, a Puerto Rican missionary and pastor of the church at Santiago de Cuba, became increasingly uneasy with the limitations imposed by the AG–U.S. on the Cuban denomination and with the second-class status of nonwhite pastors and missionaries. He withdrew in 1956 to establish an independent denomination. This church has 3,500 members in 38 congregations, with 20 ordained and 53 lay workers (González, 1986). The church is a member of the Latin American Council of Churches (CLAI), the Caribbean Council of Churches (CCC), and the Encuentro Pentecostal Latin Americano (EPLA), and has a partnership with the U.S. Disciples of Christ and the United Church of Christ.

5. Iglesia Pentecostal Unida.

It is unclear when the ►United Pentecostal Church (UPC) began mission work in Cuba. Cuba was the destination for some missionaries of the Pentecostal Assemblies of the World as early as 1930, but it is less than certain as to the results of those efforts. The UPC claims 33 congregations, 32 clergy, and "approximately 5,600 constituents" (1999). Ministerial education is conducted through correspondence courses and a continuing series of seminars.

6. Churches in 1967 and 1982 and in the Cuban Council of Churches.

In 1967 Hollenweger identified the following pentecostal denominations as active in Cuba: Assemblies of God, Church of God (Cleveland, TN), Church of God (Holiness), Church of God of Prophecy, Church of the Apostolic Faith (Portland, OR), International Pentecostal Assemblies, Pentecostal Holiness Church, Elim Missionary Churches, Church of the Foursquare Gospel, Pentecostal Church of God, Open Bible Standard Churches, Pentecostal Evangelical Church (related to the AG–U.S.), as well as the Full Gospel Business Men's Fellowship International.

In 2001 Barrett listed the Asambleas de Dios, Iglesia Apostólica de Jesucristo (related to the church in Mexico), Iglesia Congregacional Pentecostal (formerly related to the Congregational Holiness Church, U.S.), Iglesia Cristiana Pentecostal de Cuba (schism from Asambleas de Dios, 1956), Iglesia de Dios (formerly related to the Church of God [Cleveland, TN]), Iglesia de Dios de Profecía, Iglesia de Dios Pentecostal, Iglesia del Evangelio Cuadrangular, Iglesia Evangélica Pentecostal de Cuba (formerly related to the AG–U.S.), Iglesia Santa Pentecostés (formerly related to the International Pentecostal Holiness Church), Iglesias Biblicas (formerly related to the Open Bible Standard Churches), Iglesias de la Fe Apostólica (Portland, OR), Iglesias Elim, and at least 12 indigenous pentecostal denominations.

The pentecostal churches in Cuba that are part of the Council of Churches of Cuba (Consejo de Iglesias de Cuba) include La Iglesia de Dios en Cuba, Iglesia Cristiana Pentecostal, Iglesia Santa Pentecostés, Iglesia Evangélica Bethel, Iglesia Apostolica de Jesucristo, and the Iglesia Congregacional Pentecostal. Those with observer status (1997) include La Hermandad Agraria de Cuba, Iglesia Getsemaní, Iglesia de la Biblia Abierta, Iglesia Evangélica Libre, and the Movimiento Apostólico de la Iglesia de Dios en Cristo Jésus.

■ **Bibliography:** Anon., *Cuba* (Springfield, MO, c. 1958) ■ Anon., *Normas y constitución de la Iglesia Evangélica Pentecostal de Cuba* (1957) ■ D. B. Barrett, *World Christian Encyclopedia* (1982), 252–55 ■ A. Blanco, "Revival in Cuba," *Church of God Evangel* (Nov. 4, 1944) ■ D. L. Burk, ed., *Foreign Missions Insight: A Digest of Foreign Missions Faces, Facts, Fields and Figures* (1999) ■ C. W. Conn, *Where the Saints Have Trod: A History of Church of God Missions* (1959) ■ A. González, "La Iglesia Cristiana Pentecostal de Cuba como misionera y misionada," in *La herencia misionera en Cuba*, ed. Rafael Cepeda (1986) ■ S. M. Hodges, *Look on the Fields: A Survey of the Assemblies of God in Foreign Lands* (1956) ■ W. J. Hollenweger, *Handbuch der Pfingstbewegung* (diss., Zurich, 1967), 1066–71 (para. 02b.21) ■ P. Humphrey, *J. H. Ingram, Missionary Dean* (1966) ■ J. H. Ingram, "News Flashes from the Mission Field," *Church of God Evangel* (Apr. 30, 1938) ■ C. W. Lynn, "The Living Church in Cuba," *The Pentecostal Testimony* (Jan. 1977) ■ D. A. McGavern et al., *Church Growth in Mexico* (1963) ■ E. F. McLean, "History of the Church of God in Cuba" (unpub., n.d.) ■ T. W. Miller, *Canadian Pentecostals: A History of the Pentecostal Assemblies of Canada*, ed. W. A. Griffin (1994) ■ R. B. Mitchell and L. M. Mitchell, *Heritage and Harvest: The History of the International Ministries of the Open Bible Standard Churches* (1995) ■ T. L. Osborn, *Revival Fires Sweep Cuba* ■ *Miracles of Healing* (n.d.) ■ R. A. Valentín and M. Quintero, ed., *Carismatismo en Cuba* (1997). N. M. Van Cleve, *The Vine and the Branches: A History of the International Church of the Foursquare Gospel* (1992).

■ D. D. Bundy

CYPRUS

■ Pentecostals 1,398 (44%)   ■ Charismatics 1,543 (48%)   ■ Neocharismatics 260 (8%)   ■ Total Renewal: 3,201

CZECH REPUBLIC

■ Pentecostals 9,451 (4%)   ■ Charismatics 155,059 (61%)   ■ Neocharismatics 91,490 (36%)   ■ Total Renewal: 256,000

See EUROPE, EASTERN.

DENMARK

■ Pentecostals 27,390 (13%)   ■ Charismatics 141,621 (69%)   ■ Neocharismatics 36,989 (18%)   ■ Total Renewal: 206,000

The pentecostal movement reached Denmark in 1907 when Norwegian pastor ►T. B. Barratt visited Copenhagen. He ministered in close fellowship with the members of the Methodist Church, Salvation Army, Home Mission Union, and the Lutheran State Church. The meetings were covered favorably by the press until one of the most well-known actresses of the time, Anna Larsen, was baptized with the Holy Spirit and relinquished her career in the theater. Barratt visited Denmark frequently between 1907 and 1913.

The early pentecostals did not regard themselves as a new denomination, but rather as a revival movement that had a message for the body of Christ at large. The first pentecostal church was established in Copenhagen in 1912. Subsequently, a few more local churches were established. These independent churches formed a loosely organized fellowship. While the Danish churches had close ties with the other pentecostal bodies in Scandinavia, the pentecostal movement did not prosper in Denmark as it had in Norway and Sweden.

A split occurred among the pentecostals of Denmark in 1924. The main issue was the form of church government. A well-known pentecostal leader, Sigur Bjørner, was appointed at the Apostolic Church (AC) convention in Wales as the apostle of Denmark. As a result, Bjørner's home church in Copenhagen and nine other churches joined the AC. Only eight churches, comprising some 200 members, remained in the fellowship of churches calling themselves the Pentecostal Revival. All of the missionaries remained in fellowship with the latter group, which created the extraordinary situation that there were more missionaries working abroad than there were salaried ministers in the homeland.

I. APOSTOLIC CHURCH (APOSTOLSK KIRKE).

Employing such methods of evangelism as literature mission, tent meetings, and social work, the workers of the Apostolic Church started 10 new assemblies in the decade 1924–34. By 1933 five apostles, one prophet, nine evangelists, two missionaries, and 30 elders were serving in the ranks of the Apostolic Church. The leading figure was Sigur Bjørner, and the

church in Copenhagen acted as a mother church for the new developing communities of believers.

Some 25 new assemblies were founded in 1935–49. The period was characterized by decentralization as the church became a more coherent fellowship and was no longer dependent on the mother church of Copenhagen. In 1949 there were 40 churches and the membership stood at 2,000.

The period 1950–74 was characterized by construction activities while new church buildings were being erected. The growth was mostly from within as the children of the pentecostal families joined the churches. The Apostolic Church had about 2,800 members in 1974.

In 1998 there were 40 congregations with a total of 2,340 members and some 2,000 adherents (e.g., children of pentecostal families). The number of missionaries is relatively high, as 30 missionaries are currently serving in 10 countries, mainly in Africa, but also in Eastern Europe, Greenland, Colombia, and China. The church publishes the monthly magazine *Evangeliebladet*. The International Apostolic Bible College, founded in 1939, is located in Kolding. Between 80 and 90 students are enrolled; they come from different denominations and from 15 nations in Europe, Africa, and other continents.

Recently the Apostolic Church has experienced trying times, as the "Word of Faith" doctrine has caused conflicts in the churches.

II. THE PENTECOSTAL REVIVAL (PINSEVAEKKELSEN).

The pentecostal revival (PR) of Denmark is firmly anchored in the pentecostal revival of Sweden. When the PR magazine *Maran Atha* was founded in 1925, a number of articles were published on the scriptural pattern of church government. The sovereignty of the local churches was emphasized; the local church was independent and not subject to a mission secretary or any form of national leadership. This was probably due to the need to make a clear distinction between the PR and the AC, which was centrally governed. The PR has depended on the fellowship model of organization, which is largely kept together through ties of friendship among pastors.

After the split, the PR reestablished itself under the spiritual leadership of A. Endersen and H. P. Rosenving, and in 1948 the membership stood at 3,200. But in the years that followed there was not much growth. In 1974 there were 24 churches with 3,400 members. At about that time, a new period of growth was initiated as the Jesus Movement and the charismatic renewal helped the churches to regain their evangelistic vision.

The human catalyst in this renewal was Alfred Lorenzen, pastor of a church in Copenhagen and a respected leader both within and outside pentecostal circles. In addition, Paul Conrad initiated the "pioneer mission" in 1970, through which young people were organized for evangelistic outreach campaigns that ultimately resulted in the founding of new churches. Indeed, considerable resources are directed toward church planting, and for the most part growth has occurred in the new churches. In 1997 there were 57 churches with 5,012 members. The work force is rather young. At present there are some 65 pastors, most of which are under 40 years of age and have begun their ministries since 1980. Two workers' conferences are held annually. One is specifically for the pastors and preachers, the other is designated for the church leaders at large.

When the split occurred in 1924, all the missionaries remained in fellowship with PR. This led to an extraordinary situation: there were more missionaries working abroad than there were salaried ministers in the homeland. In 1936, 26 missionaries were working in China, South Africa, Zaire, Israel, Argentina, and France. At present there are 20 missionaries, the majority of which are working in East Africa. Other fields include Argentina, Paraguay, Peru, Ireland, Greenland, and Japan.

The PR has a Bible school and four other schools in Mariager. The annual summer conference, attended by some 3,000 participants, is also held in Mariager. Other ministries include broadcasting and TV (TV-Inter, IBRA-radio); a publishing house; a magazine, *KE*, which appears twice a month; and five rehabilitation centers for alcoholics and drug addicts.

After seeking reconciliation, the AC and PR fully restored their broken relationship in 1998.

See also SCANDINAVIAN MISSIONS TO LATIN AMERICA; BIBLIOGRAPHY AND HISTORIOGRAPHY OUTSIDE NORTH AMERICA.

■ **Bibliography:** T. B. Barratt, *Själlvbiografi* (1942) ■ N. Bloch-Hoel, *Pinsebevægelsen: en undersøgelse af Pinsebevegelsens tilblivelse, utvikling og særpreg med særlig henblikk på bevegelsens utformning i Norge* (1956) ■ S. Bjørner, *Den Apostolske kirkes sejrsgang* (1933) ■ N. Neiiendam, *Frikirker og sekter?* 3d ed. (1948) ■ S. Østergaard, *Menighedsetablering i spænding mellem tradition og kontekst* (1998) ■ A. Sundstedt, *Pingstväckelsen*, vol. 5 (1973).

■ T. Jacobsen; J. E. Jacobsen; L. Ahonen

DJIBOUTI

■ Pentecostals 0 (0%)   ■ Charismatics 984 (98%)   ■ Neocharismatics 16 (2%)   ■ Total Renewal: 1,000

DOMINICA

■ Pentecostals 1,202 (24%)   ■ Charismatics 2,355 (47%)   ■ Neocharismatics 1,443 (29%)   ■ Total Renewal: 5,000

See CARIBBEAN ISLANDS.

DOMINICAN REPUBLIC

■ Pentecostals 169,018 (16%)   ■ Charismatics 770,066 (74%)   ■ Neocharismatics 96,916 (9%)   ■ Total Renewal: 1,036,000

1. Beginnings.

The earliest stages of pentecostalism in the Dominican Republic are to be found in the stories of Puerto Rican missionaries. The first effort began in Mar. 1917, when Salomón Feliciano Quiñones and his wife arrived in the Dominican Republic from Ponce, Puerto Rico. He and a friend, ʾJuan Lugo, had experienced the pentecostal baptism of the Holy Spirit during a revival in Hawaii in June 1913. Both returned to the Caribbean via San Francisco and Los Angeles, where they visited pentecostal ministries. The early days were difficult. There were no foreign-support funds, and it was difficult to find work. Salomón established a mission in the city of San Pedro de Macorís. He became well known for preaching in the streets and marketplaces. He built a large congregation at Jarabacoa, despite intense persecution by the Catholic Church.

Another influential Puerto Rican pentecostal missionary was Francisco Hernández González. He initially visited the

Dominican Republic in 1928, but finally he and his wife, Victoria, arrived as faith missionaries on Sept. 2, 1930. He began work in Santo Domingo before proceeding to San Pedro de Macorís, where he teamed up with the Clemente Figueroa family, expatriate Puerto Rican pentecostals working in the area. Their efforts were quite successful, and from there the revival spread throughout the nation. In 1934 Andrea Rosario founded the church in La Romana. That same year Juan Críspulo Rivero initiated a congregation in El Seybo and would also eventually start works in Guaymate, Eneas, and Arroyo Grande. Eloísa Feliciano established a house church in 1937 that grew into an active congregation in Guaymate, and Jimiro Feliciano founded a congregation in another part of the city that same year. Roberto Martín and Ángel Betancourt began a congregation in Santiago in 1939. Eduardo Vázquez initiated (1945) the church in San Juan de la Maguana the same year that Rafael Muñoz established the church at Baní. The church at Barahona was begun sometime before 1949 by Alejo Mercedes.

2. Church of God (Cleveland, TN).

The first missionary of the Church of God (CG, Cleveland, TN) was George L. Silvestre, a Bahamian layperson who was born in Castries, St. Lucia. Silvestre had immigrated to the Bahamas in 1928 and was converted there. He was appointed as a missionary to the Dominican Republic in Jan. 1939. He arrived on June 7, 1939, and began preaching on Aug. 7 in Ciudad Trujillo. His work was supported with a stipend from the U.S. Silvestre reported successful efforts at founding churches in four cities. The mission executives in Cleveland did not trust him and sent John P. Kluzit, an American missionary in Haiti, to inspect the work. This encounter led to a severe misunderstanding or disagreement over the use of mission funds and the personal ethics of the clergy appointed by Silvestre. The problem was complicated by the fact that Kluzit understood no Spanish and was totally ignorant of Spanish-African culture. He surreptitiously sought information from independent pentecostal pastors about Silvestre. Silvestre then resigned from the CG, and the four congregations he had initiated declined radically.

Despite this struggle the denomination continued. Pedro Cabrera, a convert of Salomón Feliciano, initially became the de facto leader of the CG. He founded a congregation in Ciudad Trujillo in 1942. Kluzit was sent to the Dominican Republic (1940–44) but appears to have had little influence. He was primarily interested in Haiti. More influential were J. W. Aucher and C. F. French, who established modest but effective educational programs for clergy. Also influential was evangelist and pastor Francisco de Castro y Hernández, who brought his independent congregation into the CG. By 1959 the church claimed 700 members and 3,000 adherents in 13 congregations and 7 missions. Until 1978 (except for a time during the 1960s) the overseers were always North Americans. As more indigenous leadership has been allowed, the church has grown rapidly. In 1980 it reported 6,003 members in 140 congregations; in 1996 it reported 22,077 members, and to that number can probably be added an additional 20,000 children and adherents in 372 congregations.

3. Assemblies of God.

The initial efforts of the Puerto Rican missionaries were taken over by the U.S. Assemblies of God (AG) in 1941. Lawrence and Jessie Perrault arrived as the first AG missionaries. A large number of missionaries followed (50 by 1997). Extensive funding and effort were devoted to mass evangelism. A Bible school was opened in 1945. Since 1965 Dominican leadership has prevailed, although not until 1977 did Jimiro Feliciano become director of the Instituto Bíblico, to be followed by Manuel Bello, Julio Sánchez, Darío Mateo, and others. In 1994, Louisa Jeter de Walker claimed 49,753 "adherents"; the AG–U.S. Division of Foreign Missions claimed 63,029 "members and adherents" in 1998.

4. Other Denominations.

Among the other pentecostal churches in the Dominican Republic are two denominations founded by Puerto Rican missionaries: the Iglesia de Dios Pentecostal (c. 1945) and the Asamblea de Iglesias Cristianas (1939). Others were founded by U.S. missionaries: Iglesia de Dios de la Profecía (1940), the Iglesia de la Fe Apostólica (founded from Portland, OR), the Iglesia de Dios en Cristo, and the Iglesia del Evangelio Cuadrangular. Missionary Glen Smith of the United Pentecostal Church founded a congregation in the Dominican Republic in 1965. The resulting Iglesia Pentecostal Unida claims (1999) 1,750 constituents, 59 ministers, and 48 congregations.

■ **Bibliography:** J. F. Amparo, *El Cincuentenario del Concilio Asambleas de Dios en la República Dominicana* (1995) ■ AG (U.S.) Division of Foreign Missions, *1999 Annual Statistics* (1999) ■ D. B. Barrett, *World Christian Encyclopedia* (1982), 268–70 ■ F. de Castro y Hernández, "La Iglesia de Dios en la República Dominicana," *El Evangelico de la Iglesia de Dios* (Oct. 1946), 16 ■ C. W. Conn, *Like a Mighty Army: A History of the Church of God* (rev. ed., 1977) ■ idem, *Where the Saints Have Trod: A History of Church of God Missions* (1959) ■ V. J. Cruz, "Los Comienzos de la Iglesia de Dios en la República Dominicana" (paper, CG School of Theology, 1996) ■ R. Domínguez, *Pioneros de Pentecostés* (1990), 1:317–24 ■ *Foreign Missions Insight: A Digest of Foreign Missions Faces, Facts, Fields and Figures*, ed. Dorsey L. Burk (1999), 73–74 ■ S. M. Hodges, *Look on the Fields: A Survey of the Assemblies of God in Foreign Lands* (1956), 183–85 ■ W. J. Hollenweger, "Handbuch der Pfingstbewegung" (diss., Zurich, 1967), 1007–21 (para. 02b.10) ■ P. Humphrey, *J. H. Ingram, Missionary Dean* (1966) ■ J. H. Ingram, *Around the World with Gospel Light* (1938) ■ [H. McCracken], *History of Church of God Missions* (1943) ■ *Profile of the Dominican Republic* (1985) ■ G. L. Sylvestre, "Notices from the Dominican Republic," *Church of God Evangel*

(Jan. 13, 1940) ▪ P. H. Walker, "Church of God Enters Dominican Republic," *Church of God Evangel* (Sept. 30, 1939), 6 ▪ L. Jeter de Walker, *Siembra y Cosecha*, vol. 3 (1996) ▪ V. G. Woods, "The Cultural Concept of Missions: A Cultural View of the Dominican Republic" (paper, CG School of Theology, 1986).

▪ D. D. Bundy

ECUADOR

▪ Pentecostals 129,230 (9%)   ▪ Charismatics 1,218,821 (86%)   ▪ Neocharismatics 61,949 (4%)   ▪ Total Renewal: 1,410,000

The earliest pentecostal missionaries to Ecuador were probably Howard and Clara Cragin, who were there briefly between 1912 and 1914. Nothing of their work appears to have survived. They returned in late 1918 and established the Misión Evangélica Quichua in Agato but returned to Peru in 1922. Not until the 1950s was there an influx of pentecostal missionaries.

In 1956 the *International Church of the Foursquare Gospel established a presence in Ecuador under the leadership of the Arthur Gadberry family. They pioneered in Guayaquil, and by 1962 two congregations had been established. They were reinforced by the Aguirre family, who earlier served in Panama. The Gadberrys moved to Quito to establish a church there. Revival meetings in the "bull ring" in Guayaquil, led by Robert Espinosa from California, drew as many as 40,000 persons during the six-week campaign. Claims of healing led to published newspaper reports of the meetings. By the close of the meetings, 1,500 had been baptized and more than 600 members added to the Guayaquil congregations. Innovative ministries, including education for children of prisoners, were developed. The Henry Davis family developed orphanages, "Houses of Happiness," that attracted national attention, resulting in a medal presented to the Davises by the president of Ecuador. The Iglesia del Evangelio Cuadrangular is arguably the largest pentecostal denomination in Ecuador. It claims 40,469 members (1999).

The Assemblies of God (AG) was started by Peruvian evangelist Fernando Moroco in 1956. The denomination began in Guayaquil and developed under the leadership of Héctor Chávez Yépez, who made contact with the AG–U.S. and affiliated the Ecuadorian church with them. In 1962–63 mass evangelism campaigns created an image for the church throughout the country. A Bible school was established, and considerable resources were devoted to radio ministry. The AG claims 8,500 baptized members (1999).

The Church of God (CG, Cleveland, TN) began missionary work in Ecuador in 1971. CG converts have been active in the national government, especially with regard to social justice issues. A seminary has been established in Quito, which serves the denomination throughout Latin America.

Refugees from civil strife in Colombia brought the Iglesia Pentecostal Unida to Ecuador in 1957. The first *United Pentecostal Church (UPC) missionary to Ecuador, Lucile Farmer arrived in 1964. The church has grown rapidly and is probably the second-largest pentecostal church in Ecuador. In 1999 the UPC claimed about 15,000 "constituents," 300 congregations, 250 preaching points, and 137 "licensed workers." A Bible school is maintained by the church in Quito.

Indigenous pentecostal churches are quite numerous in Ecuador. Some of these have established virtual or actual

Tract ministry in Guayaquilinos, Ecuador.

Baptism of Dr. Luis Flores from Quito, Ecuador.

denominations. They include Asamblea del Señor, Iglesia de Cristo Jesus, Iglesia del Espiritu Santo, Iglesia Evangélica Cristo Rey, Iglesia Independiente Nacional, Iglesia Independiente Universal de Cristo, Iglesia La Voz de Cristo, and about 40 other indigenous denominations and congregations of note. There is also the congregation founded in 1971 by followers of William Branham, Voz de Aclamación. The Iglesia Evangélica Bereana was founded in Guaranda in 1958. Finnish Free Foreign Mission missionaries are also at work in the country, often in cooperation with other churches.

Throughout Ecuador, the teachings of the pentecostal churches have been accepted by the indigenous peoples. Significant research has been undertaken relative to the interaction of pentecostal Christian culture and the indigenous cultures, especially with regard to how concepts and values are prioritized and reprioritized in the changing of religious cultures.

■ **Bibliography:** L. K. Ahonen, *Suomen Helluntaiherätyksen Historia* (1994) ■ S. Andrade, "Del Paganismo al Protestantismo: Algunos spuntes sobre el proceso de reinterpretación de lo sagrado en los indígenas de Chimborazo-Ecuador," in *El Pentecostalismo en America Latina: Entre Tradición y Globalización,* ed. A. Pollak-Elze and Y. Salas (1998) ■ Anon., *Equador* (Springfield, MO, c. 1960) ■ D. B. Barrett, *World Christian Encyclopedia* (1982), 270–73 ■ D. L. Burk, ed., *Foreign Missions Insight: A Digest of Foreign Missions Faces, Facts, Fields and Figures* (1999), 136–37 ■ L. Farmer, "Lucile Farmer," *Profiles of Pentecostal Missionaries* (1986) ■ A. Hämäläinen, *Kaikkeen Maailmaan, 1929–1989. 60 vuotta helluntaiseurakuntien lähetystyötä* (1989), 36 ■ W. J. Hollenweger, *Handbuch der Pfingstbewegung* (diss., Zurich, 1967), 1022–23 [para. 02b. 11] ■ M. Loudermilk, *A Willing Heart: The Story of Lucile Farmer* (n.d.) ■ N. M. Van Cleve, *The Vine and the Branches: A History of the International Church of the Foursquare Gospel* (1992) ■ L. Jeter de Walker, *Siembre y cosecha,* vol. 3 (1992).   ■ D. D. Bundy

EGYPT

■ Pentecostals 165,338 (22%)   ■ Charismatics 422,795 (56%)   ■ Neocharismatics 164,868 (22%)   ■ Total Renewal: 753,001

See AFRICA, NORTH, AND THE MIDDLE EAST.

EL SALVADOR

■ Pentecostals 368,891 (25%)   ■ Charismatics 446,544 (30%)   ■ Neocharismatics 664,565 (45%)   ■ Total Renewal: 1,480,000

See LATIN AMERICA.

EQUATORIAL GUINEA

■ Pentecostals 3,323 (13%)   ■ Charismatics 10,597 (43%)   ■ Neocharismatics 10,980 (44%)   ■ Total Renewal: 24,900

See AFRICA, WEST.

ERITREA

■ Pentecostals 0 (0%)   ■ Charismatics 34,452 (91%)   ■ Neocharismatics 3,348 (9%)   ■ Total Renewal: 37,800

For general introduction to East Africa and bibliography, see AFRICA, EAST.

In 1889 Eritrea was colonized by the Italians, but it was occupied by Allied forces and governed by Britain between 1941 and 1952. Until May 24, 1993, Eritrea was officially part of Ethiopia, which had annexed the region in 1962. After a long and violent war that lasted for about 30 years, Eritrea was finally granted independence. However, relations between Eritrea and Ethiopia remain hostile. The population is almost evenly divided between Christians and Muslims, and individuals living there have freedom of choice to worship as they desire.

It is difficult to know with precision the identity of the first pentecostals to visit Asmara. Some reports say that two Ethiopians preached the pentecostal message in Asmara and that from this contact a few individuals were converted and received the infilling of the Holy Spirit. From those beginnings the nucleus of the Full Gospel Church was formed.

This contact only took place, however, about 1965, and we know that the capital city of Asmara was evangelized by the Finnish Free Foreign Mission (FFFM; see also article on Ethiopia) before that time. In 1961 Paavo and Meeri Virtanen were involved in evangelism and education in this city. The FFFM sent a number of individuals to work in Asmara when it was still part of Ethiopia. Due to the efforts of the Roininen family, which remained in Asmara throughout the years of the Marxist government, the pentecostal church was able to maintain a limited amount of freedom, and the Christian school continued to function throughout the period; in fact, it was the only school of any mission organization that was never nationalized by the communists. In 1989 the elementary and secondary schools in Asmara moved to new facilities built by funds from the Lähetyksen Kehitysapu (LKA, the FFFM aid association). Today this complex is a joint project run in cooperation between the LKA and the Ministry of Education of Eritrea. The Full Gospel Church of Eritrea, the offshoot of the FFFM missionary work, has over 700 members. During the years of communist rule in Ethiopia/Eritrea, the church was forced to meet secretly in cell groups, and many of its members worshiped with other, recognized, churches. The figures do not tell all, however, because in the church at Asmara alone, 2,000 attend the services in four congregations.

In 1967 two American pentecostal women visited Asmara for ministry. Contact was made with the original group, which was to become the Full Gospel Church of Eritrea. The group was encouraged and began meeting in homes. After the fall of the Dirge (the communist regime; also written *Deurg* or *Durge*), the AG–U.S. became involved in Eritrea after contacts between representatives of the AG–U.S. and members of the Full Gospel Church of Eritrea. By 1997 Jerry and Maxine Falley were involved in the School of Leadership Training, an in-service program designed to help in the preparation of those involved in church planting, teaching, evangelism, and pastoral duties.

Documents from both the AG–U.S. and the FFFM make claims of being responsible for the existence of the Full Gospel Church of Eritrea. Since the FFFM was the first pentecostal group in Eritrea and in Asmara and had representatives in Asmara throughout the years when no other pentecostals were living there, its role should not be minimized; however, it is likely that due to the nature of events since the 1990s, both have had a role to play in the established structure of the national church.

Pentecostals and charismatics can be found in the churches started by the Sudan Interior Mission (now SIM) as well as within the Orthodox Church. The Full Gospel Church cooperates with all the evangelical groups in the country.   ■ D. J. Garrard

ESTONIA

■ Pentecostals 6,488 (11%)   ■ Charismatics 18,862 (31%)   ■ Neocharismatics 34,650 (58%)   ■ Total Renewal: 60,000

See RUSSIA.

ETHIOPIA

■ Pentecostals 1,095,426 (27%)   ■ Charismatics 2,229,221 (55%)   ■ Neocharismatics 741,353 (18%)   ■ Total Renewal: 4,066,000

For general introduction and bibliography to East Africa, see AFRICA, EAST.

[Note: due to variations in the transliteration from Amharic script, the spelling of some church names varies in written English. For example, *Hewot* is also written *Hiwot, Heywet,* and sometimes *Yehewot; Guenet* is also written *Ghenet* or *Genet.*]

Ethiopia was a monarchy until the overthrow of Emperor Haile Selassie in 1974, when Mengistu Haile Miriam became the country's Marxist president. Regional droughts and uprisings led to the failure of the regime in 1991, when Mengistu fled to Zimbabwe for refuge. Ethiopia claims to have been a Christian nation from the fourth century. Its form of Coptic Christianity was represented by the Ethiopian Orthodox Church, which was the state church until the revolution. Since 1991, however, there has been considerable freedom of religious expression in spite of vigorous antievangelical activities on the part of the Orthodox Church and Islam. Islam is strongest in the North, in the East along the border with Somalia, and in the Southeast.

The Finnish Free Foreign Mission (FFFM) became involved in Ethiopia when in 1951 Anna-Liisa and Sanfrid Mattsson became the first pentecostal missionaries to Ethiopia. They were granted 80 hectares of land in Wolmara by Haile Selassie in order to construct a mission station. Conditions imposed by the government for the FFFM missionary work required that all evangelization had to be accompanied by social work. This the FFFM did by founding clinics, schools, and children's homes. The mission extended itself to Sidamo, Kaffa, and Asmara (now in Eritrea but then part of Ethiopia) in the North.

After the 1974 revolution, nearly all missionaries were eventually forced to leave in 1978. Only the school at Asmara continued to function with Kyösti and Aino Roininen in residence. Ethiopian believers continued to be responsible for the administration and outreach of the churches. From the work of the Finnish Mission the Sefer Guenet was born (alternate spelling: *Sefer Ghenet* or *Sefer Genet;* English: Guenet Church of Ethiopia). This church has been autonomous and nationally run since 1967. During the years of persecution, from 1974 on, much of the work continued underground. Prior to the Marxist revolution there had been 65 churches and 900 believers, but there was a great revival during the years of persecution, and by 1991 there were 127 churches and 19,000 believers. The revival continues until the present, and by 1997 the Guenet Church of Ethiopia had 211 local churches and subchurches with 38,000 believers. In Addis Ababa alone the Guenet Church has seven local churches.

Many of the leaders of the major pentecostal/charismatic denominations in the country have been raised up from the original work started by the FFFM. It is estimated that there are 900,000 believers within the largest pentecostal groups alone. The FFFM has close collaboration with all of these denominations, especially in the area of pastoral training. The Lähetyksen Kehitysapu, the aid association of the FFFM, is presently engaged in five development projects in the country. The Holeta Health Centre is involved in community health care and has provided basic treatment for over 20,000 patients each year. It is also responsible for drilling wells that ensure safe drinking water throughout the region. There are similar centers at Shebe and Wotera as well as a training institute for health science at Jimma. The emphasis in the churches at present is on evangelism and church planting. The FFFM would like to see the establishment of a full-time Bible school for those in ministry in Ethiopia.

The Svenska Fria Missionen (SFM, Swedish Free Mission) was admitted to Ethiopia in 1960 when it became involved in the Southern town of Awasa. This work was originally started by a Kenyan evangelist who went to Ethiopia and began proclaiming the gospel and the work of the Holy Spirit. A major revival broke out in the Sidaama region, an area still regarded as the center of pentecostalism and the beginning of what is today known as the Hewot Berhan (also spelled *Hiwot, Heywet,* or *Yehewot; Berhan* or *Birhane;* English: Ethiopian Hewot Berhan Church [EHBC]), with 950 churches throughout the country. Great outpourings of the Holy Spirit took place in the beginning in Awasa itself. These outpourings were followed by the repression of the communist era, which caused the church to go underground for 17 years. The national leader of EHBC is Yenneneh Worku.

The Mulu Wengel (also known as Full Gospel Believers Church) has roots similar to those of the EHBC. It experienced exceptional growth among university students in Addis Ababa. It has never been part of a foreign church mission and is entirely an autonomous, indigenous church movement. The majority of its members are converts from the Ortho-dox Church who have become pentecostal. They were severely persecuted in 1972–75 as a result of collusion between the Orthodox Church, which opposed them, and the Marxist government of the day. More than 300 members were imprisoned under false charges of treason or immorality. Mulu Wengel is led by Solomon Regassa.

Because of the government's restrictions, open evangelism was limited, but many opportunities were made available through social work. It was by means of this channel that the Pentecostal Assemblies of Canada (PAOC) was first invited to become fully involved in Ethiopia. During the early days after the breakup of the communist regime, Emergency Relief and Development Overseas (ERDO), the social arm of the PAOC, was involved in the distribution of grain in Ethiopia in cooperation with the Canada Foodgrains Bank. The donations, which were made without any preconditions, led to an invitation to become further involved at the missionary level. Don Raymer, who was PAOC director of ERDO, and Gerald Morrison, the PAOC missions overseer for East and West Africa, had made several visits to Addis Ababa to deal with the food distribution before it was decided that the PAOC should become directly involved with the pentecostal churches. An agreement was worked out between themselves and the missionaries of the SFM who had been present in Ethiopia for many years. The PAOC sent Brian and Val Rutten to Addis Ababa in 1992 (from Kitwe, Zambia), where they have been up until the present.

When the Ruttens arrived they found that the pastors had never had the opportunity to benefit from any form of training. Not long after their arrival, a program entitled "Mission Ethiopia" was launched. The goal was to train 50 men for a year and send them to 50 new areas. In addition, Rutten has gained the confidence of many of the independent pentecostal groups, which have asked for help with the training of their leadership. The Pentecostal Training Centre (PTC) in Addis Ababa is the hub of all the training programs. From this center extension courses are taught in night schools in strategic towns throughout the nation. Teachers are sent out from PTC to teach series of extension courses over a limited period of time. As of Apr. 1998 these were being taught at Awasa, Jimma, Bahirdar, Zeway, and Shashemane, as well as in night classes in Addis Ababa itself. The Elders' Training Program is concerned with training thousands of lay church leaders throughout rural Ethiopia. Graduates from the PTC courses, as well as other guest teachers, present the materials to the candidates using the local language of any given area. Teachers have been involved in instruction, coordination of social work, seminars, and evangelism. A special focus is children's ministries, since in the past children have been greatly neglected in Ethiopia. Children's workers are being shown in practical workshop classes how to develop materials for children's work in evangelism, publishing, and printing. It is anticipated that there may well be a full college program in the future for the training of children's workers in the country.

The PAOC together with the other pentecostal groups in the country are also attempting to reach out to the growing "Ortho-Pentecostal" movement. The Ethiopian Orthodox Church has 35 million members and has in the past been responsible for much persecution against Protestants and pentecostals. Within the Orthodox Church now, however, there are many Spirit-filled believers who are eager to know more about the work of the Spirit. They are requesting help and training. Amharic is the main language of much of Ethiopia, which means that there is an ongoing need for instructional materials. This has led to a project to translate and print good materials from English, which will eventually help in the growth of the national church.

Hundreds of training centers are scattered around the country, and a projected correspondence program will allow for an initial enrollment of 2,000 students. Val Rutten is involved with a program called Child Care Plus, which is a child sponsorship program operating in Ethiopia and designed to assist children who come from families devastated by the war and strife that tore this country apart until so recently. Through this program children are supplied with the basic necessities of life and given the education necessary to enable them to become self-supporting. Through Child Care Plus many children have already become Christians and gone on to lead their parents to Christ.

The U.S. Assemblies of God (AG–U.S.) first entered Ethiopia in 1975 with the purpose of helping in the area of the education of youth. A breakdown in relations between the U.S. and Ethiopian governments resulted in them leaving within a year. After the fall of Mengistu, Duane and Sylvia Stewart were able to transfer to Ethiopia in 1992. The AG then sent two other missionary couples, Jim and Patsy Macauley and Paul and Lisa York, to cooperate with existing national pentecostal groups within the country. Their major emphasis has been in the area of Bible college work and the training of national church leaders. This training is undertaken in cooperation with the other pentecostal missions in Ethiopia. Currently there are eight AG–U.S. missionaries in Ethiopia.

The Elim Fellowship (Lima, NY) has been in Ethiopia since 1956. The International Church of the Foursquare Gospel has two churches and an estimated 970 adherents. The Christian Missionary Fellowship has 55 assemblies and an estimated 16,600 adherents. The Church of God (Cleveland, TN) is represented in Ethiopia by Hiruy Tsige.

The Kenyan branch of the International Pentecostal Holiness Church has recently become involved in evangelism in Ethiopia. They have one Ethiopian couple planting churches. Other pentecostal groups include the Apostolic Church, with 11 congregations and 7,000 adherents, and the United Pentecostal Church (U.S.), with a reported 1,600 churches and 280,000 adherents.

The neo-pentecostals are charismatics who are still attached to their denominations. They mostly are found in the Lutheran Church and the Bethel Evangelical Church of Ethiopia, which merged with the Evangelical Church Mekane Yesu in 1975.

Evangelical missions, which usually are regarded as being unsympathetic to the pentecostal/charismatic movement, have found that in spite of the normal mission stance, many of their leaders and members have become pentecostal/charismatic in their practice. This means that many of the members of the Meserete Kristos Church (started by the Mennonites), presently led by Solomon Kebede, as well as those of the Kali Hewot (started by the SIM), are pentecostal, even though their own missionaries are taking steps to oppose this trend. The majority of pentecostal/charismatic groups in the country, including 97% of all evangelical churches in Ethiopia, belong to the Evangelical Fellowship of Churches in Ethiopia.

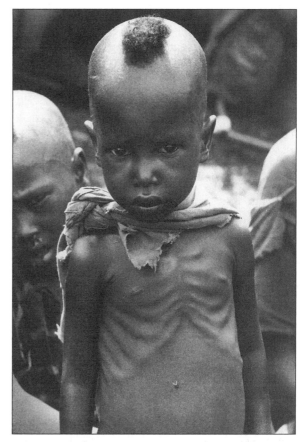

Child at Food Relief Station, Ebnet, Gonder Province, Ethiopia, in 1982.

This means that there is much collaboration between all evangelicals within the country.

The new freedom from the repression of communism has made it possible for the church to grow at a rate previously unknown. A number of missiologists claim that Ethiopia is home to the fastest growing church in all of Africa. It is estimated that there are between 6 and 12 million evangelicals in Ethiopia and that the majority of them are pentecostal/charismatic in faith and practice. However, there are now many new believers who are not grounded in the Word of God. They are susceptible to heresy, schism, and leadership power struggles. Although there is considerable cooperation between the major pentecostal/charismatic groups, there is also the emergence of many new, independent groups that are not accountable to anyone. The great challenge is to train leadership in all the churches, and this is the major emphasis of the pentecostal missions presently working within the country.

One of the troubling tendencies is that many of the new groups springing up have, since the years of greater liberty, taken on the materialistic attitudes of the West. Churches are fighting and splitting over such things as church buildings and the size of congregations. It is not uncommon to hear Christians voice the opinion that they would be better off spiritually were they to return to the state of affairs that existed under the Dirge (the communist regime; also written *Deurg* or *Durge*), when Christians were persecuted for their faith, many were imprisoned, and numbers were executed. At that time the church worked secretly, but all believers prioritized their faith in God and their reliance on the Holy Spirit. That was also when the power of God was most evident and miracles were part of daily living for the Christians.

It is apparent from the testimonies of those involved in the growing churches that one of the reasons for the rapid growth of the pentecostal/charismatic churches is the work of the Holy Spirit in the lives of many individuals. All pentecostal groups report continual outpourings of the Holy Spirit with great numbers of new believers being added all over the country. There are constant reports of small churches being founded where many are saved, delivered, and healed by the power of God. Aden and Kuno Halake, Ethiopians who had fled to Kenya during the Marxist years, graduated from Nairobi Pentecostal Bible College before returning to Ethiopia in late 1996; in a little over a year they had already planted six new churches with the addition of 867 members by Aug. 1998. This is only one example and is not in any way out of the ordinary. It is merely indicative of a trend that is taking place throughout the country. It is not unusual to find open-air gatherings of believers at countryside conferences with over 25,000 believers attending.

There is a general involvement of all believers in evangelism and church life, since the divide between clergy and laity only exists to a limited extent, although those with spiritual gifts are allowed to function within the area of their gifting. This has helped to accelerate church growth, because every believer understands that it is not only normal but expected that he or she be involved in evangelism.

While the numbers are encouraging, many of the more than 90 people groups in Ethiopia are virtually unreached (estimates vary, but 41 is a number often quoted). It is likely that they will have to be reached by Ethiopians.

■ D. J. Garrard

EUROPE, EASTERN (Survey)

I. ORIGINS.

The origins of the pentecostal movement in Eastern Europe may be traced to the intensive period of spiritual awakening with which the 20th century opened. Although the ▸Welsh Revival (1904–6) is the best-known example, in reality every nation where the Christian church was located was blessed by a visitation of God's Spirit, bringing a fresh impulse of spiritual life and power. As J. Edwin Orr commented, "It was the most extensive Evangelical Awakening of all time."

A noticeable feature of this period of spiritual awakening was the preoccupation with the person and work of the Holy Spirit, a hitherto largely neglected aspect of Christian teaching. This renewed emphasis coalesced with the rising tide of spiritual fervor to prepare an atmosphere in which pentecostal manifestations could and did occur. At first sporadic and

occasional, affecting small groups of revived believers as far apart as the U.S. and India, pentecostalism quickly spread among those influenced by the awakening, until by the end of the first decade every continent and almost every country touched by the revival had its "apostolic (faith)" or "pentecostal" fellowship. Several of the prominent leaders of the evangelical awakening, such as ▸Thomas B. Barratt of Norway, ▸Lewi Pethrus of Sweden, ▸Jonathan Paul of Germany, and William Fetler of Russia and the Baltic states, also embraced the pentecostal faith.

Throughout Central and Eastern Europe the revival movement in both its evangelical and pentecostal aspects affected the scattered German ethnic communities earlier and more extensively than any other ethnic group. The primary reason for this was the long history of Pietism among the German Lutherans, which with its emphasis on heartfelt

(Pektoral) religion and its practice of meeting in small groups *(Klassis)* for mutual encouragement and personal prayer, provided fertile ground for a fresh encounter with God through the Holy Spirit. Those renewed by the spiritual awakening gathered in fellowship groups *(Gemeinschaften).* These groups were informally linked by the ministry of itinerant preachers, such as Jakob Vetter from Mülheim (the pre WWI center of German pentecostalism), founder of the German Tent Mission; the evangelist Dr. Frederick Baedeker, who worked primarily along the eastern edge of the Austro-Hungarian Empire; the English Lord Grenville Radstock; and William Fetler, the German-Lettish graduate of Spurgeon's College in London who, together with his brother Robert, founded the Russian Missionary Society (RMS) and traveled extensively throughout western imperial Russia and the Baltic region. The news of each fresh move of the Spirit easily spread from one area to another.

Although the outbreak of hostilities in 1914 ended the ministry of such itinerants, the population movements that accompanied the conflict helped spread the awakening further. For example, the revival that swept the Plock area of Poland from 1913 onward spread to the Volga region of imperial Russia in 1915 when the Russians deported the German ethnic population to that area. A German-Polish pastor from Plock, August Dreher, was conscripted into the Russian Army and used the opportunity to evangelize and promote spiritual awakening among the German and other ethnic communities in Russia. The Romanian conscript Nitu Constantin came into contact with these Russian pentecostals while serving in the Russian imperial army and in 1918, on returning to his home, Vicovul de Sus in Bukovina laid the foundation of a pentecostal work there. By 1920 his wife, Justina, was renowned for her prophetic ministry throughout the area.

While the end of the war permitted the return of many of the deportees to their homes, the Russian revolution scattered others touched by the revival across the newly emerging Soviet Union. Throughout the 1920s, the communist authorities, despite their official atheism, permitted and even encouraged the growth of evangelical and pentecostal groups in an effort to break the power of the formerly state-sponsored Orthodox Church. In return, the pentecostal and evangelical Christians supported the communist state that had liberated them from the bondage of Orthodox persecution, until the Stalinist regime brought a return of the earlier repression.

Pentecostalism in prerevolutionary Russia may be traced not only to the influence of the revival movement that affected mainly the German ethnic minority and, to a lesser degree, the Russian ethnic majority, but also to Scandinavian and Finnish influences in the Northwest and to native Russian and Armenian movements in the South. Pentecostalism arrived in Scandinavia early in its history through Barratt of Norway and quickly spread across the Baltic Sea, penetrating Finland through those affected by the Laestadtian revival movement. Until 1918 Finland was under Russian control and provided a natural conduit for pentecostal influences into the Baltic states and imperial Russia itself. In 1906 the first pentecostal church in Lithuania was established in Birzai. By 1910 pentecostal congregations were flourishing throughout the area. Pentecostal literature was being printed in both Finland and Norway.

The following year, 1911, Barratt conducted a very successful evangelistic crusade in St. Petersburg that resulted in the establishment of a large pentecostal church there. The same year Persian pentecostal missionary ▸Andrew Urshan visited Helsinki, Finland, en route for Persia and led N. P. Smorodin and N. I. Ivanov, the leaders of the Russian Evangelical Christians Church, into the pentecostal baptism. They in turn returned to St. Petersburg and established another pentecostal work there—the Evangelical Christians in the Apostolic Spirit, later known as *Smorodintsy.* Urshan's adoption of Jesus Only, or ▸Oneness, theology in 1916, inspired Smorodin and Ivanov and their rapidly spreading pentecostal fellowship of churches to follow suit.

The movement in southern Russia actually predates the modern pentecostal movement and may be traced back to medieval charismatic and prophetic sects, such as the Paulicians (▸Holy Spirit, Doctrine of: Medieval). A succession of historical revivals reinforced the popularity and strength of

A former Jewish synagogue bought and renovated by the Pentecostal Church in Osijek, Yugoslavia, where Dr. Peter Kuzmič served as pastor.

the various Holy Spirit groups, such as the Spiritual Christians of Biblical Faith in Bessarabia, the Ukraine, and Crimea and the Molokane and Sakharovtsy in Russian Armenia, Georgia, and the Ural Mountain region, providing fertile ground for the development of an indigenous pentecostal movement. The Turkish persecution of Armenian Christians (1895–1915) prompted an Armenian diaspora and further reinforced the work in the area between the Black Sea and the Caspian Sea, despite systematic attempts by the Orthodox church to eliminate it. The eastward trek to California under prophetic direction by these early Armenian pentecostals spread the pentecostal faith across southern Russia and beyond to the farthest reaches of the empire.

Those who fled westward to escape the persecution of the Orthodox Church, which continued in southern Russia despite Czar Nicolas's edicts of toleration in 1905 and 1906, strengthened the revival movements in the Balkans and Central Europe. Although most of those involved in the revival movements preferred simply to be known as Evangelical Christians, in practice and experience they were thoroughly pentecostal. When the first news of the pentecostal movement elsewhere reached them, they readily and almost to the last person identified themselves with it.

The displacement of population noted above in relation to Poland was not limited to the German-Russian area, but also affected the Austro-Hungarian Hapsburg Empire. Pentecostal phenomena had been apparent among the Transylvanian Saxons (Germans) of the Siebenburgen along the border with Wallachia (Southern Romania). The region around Hermannstadt (modern Sibiu) and Medias was especially affected. Three ethnic German ladies visiting Berlin prior to WWI were baptized in water and in the Holy Spirit there and on their return began to spread the pentecostal message. By the end of that war an indigenous pentecostal movement, later known as Christians Baptized with the Holy Spirit, was well established in southern Transylvania.

When in 1917 the Brenkus family was deported from Slovakia to a farm near Medias, they came into contact with Spirit-filled farmers and were touched by the pentecostal message. On their return six months later to Nove Sady, a village near Kosice, Slovakia, they took their pentecostal faith with them, establishing the first Slovakian pentecostal fellowship there.

In addition to the national and regional movements resulting from spiritual awakenings and population movements, the news of the emergence of modern pentecostalism reported in the Christian press—not always favorably—did inspire zealous local Christian groups to seek God for a restoration of the apostolic faith and experience. Many like the Evangelical Christians of southern Russia and the Balkans, and the Baptists of northern Russia, the Baltic states, and Poland simply and largely identified themselves with the new movement.

Others were influenced by returning emigrants who came back to the old country to share their newly found pentecostal faith with their countrymen. For example, the pentecostal movement in Slovakia was augmented by the return of Juraj Zelman and Jan Balca, who had experienced the Holy Spirit baptism in the U.S. and Norway respectively. Similarly, in Yugoslavia the earliest pentecostal work among the German ethnic population spread to the Slavic inhabitants when in 1933 Calvary Assembly of God in Milwaukee, WI, pastored by the Hungarian-Romanian emigrant ►Joseph Wannenmacher, sponsored another Hungarian emigrant, Ernest Mihok, and his Slovenian wife, Mary, to return for ministry to Hungary and Slovenia (northeastern Yugoslavia). From their first meetings in Vescica in the home of the assistant mayor, Josef Novak, came the first Slavic pentecostal church in the country, which in turn sponsored other pentecostal churches in Sulinci and in Nuskova, where the pastor for over 40 years was Leopold Kuzmič, father of ►Peter Kuzmič, currently president of the (pentecostal) Evangelical Church of Croatia and of the Evangelical Theological Seminary in Osijek, Croatia, and one of the leading theologians of the former communist world. The pentecostal work in northern Romania was reinforced in 1918 by the return to Udesti, Bukovina, of Filaret Rotaru, who had been healed and baptized in the Holy Spirit while in the U.S.

The development of pentecostalism in Romania, which until the end of WWI had been confined almost entirely to the German and Hungarian ethnic minorities, spread into the Romanian ethnic population in the early 1920s. In 1919 a German pentecostal fellowship had been established in the Carpathian mountain village of Dirlos near Sibiu through a German-American pentecostal, Sister Konerth. In July 1921 a local outpouring of the Spirit in Dirlos and nearby Curei brought into existence the first predominantly Romanian ethnic pentecostal fellowship, under the leadership of Pastors Kast and Helmut Telman. A year later, in Sept. 1922, the western region of Transylvania saw the formation of another Romanian pentecostal work, under the name Pentecostal Church of God, in the village of Paulis near Arad. A report of the healing ministry of Sister ►Aimee Semple McPherson came into the hands of a Baptist, Gheorghe Bradin, whose wife, Persida, was consequently healed of tuberculosis, resulting in a local spiritual awakening. Subsequent correspondence regarding the pentecostal faith between Bradin and McPherson's Foursquare Gospel organization, the Church of God Publishing House in Cleveland, TN, and the Assemblies of God (AG) in Springfield, MO, resulted in Pavel Budeanu, a Romanian immigrant to the U.S. and AG evangelist, returning to his homeland to set the work in order.

Further outpourings of the Spirit in 1923 in Bukovina in the Northeast, along the Ukrainian border, in Moldavian Kischiniev (modern Chisinau), and in Iassy (modern Iasi) in the East, reinforced the pentecostal work. In 1926 David Raroha, a Hungarian pentecostal evangelist working with RMS in Hungary, was encouraged to visit Timisoara in Banat to set in order the pentecostal work among the Hungarian and German ethnic minorities there. This resulted in a growing "Apostolic Faith" work that later spread to the Romanian ethnic population. When Raroha teamed up with the newly formed ›Russian and Eastern European Mission (REEM) shortly afterward, the work in Banat became a natural bridge between the Apostolic Faith work in Hungary and the growing pentecostal movement in Bulgaria. Despite intense opposition and persecution from the Orthodox Church, the scattered pentecostal churches survived, and in Feb. 1929 many of those in the West formally united under the leadership of Bradin with the name The Apostolic Church of God. Working loosely with this body was yet another group, The Disciples of the Lord, led by Ioan Jiloveanu, which had originated in the late 1920s partially through the ministry of Ioan Bododea of Braila, a former Baptist pastor and national representative to the Baptist World Alliance, who was renowned as an author and a skillful apologist for pentecostalism; he was to be the editor of the first pentecostal journals and the first pentecostal hymnal.

Immediately following WWI several pentecostal emigrant families were sponsored by the AG–U.S. to return to Eastern Europe to assist the indigenous work, notably Dionissy and Olga Zaplishny to Bulgaria; Ivan Efimovich and Katharina Varonaeff to Bulgaria and later to the Ukraine and Russia; Gustav Herbert and Carrie Schmidt to Russia and Poland; and ›Nicholas and Martha Nikoloff to Bulgaria and later to Poland. ›Vinson Synan has called them "missionaries of the one-way ticket," since they would lay down their lives for the pentecostal message in those lands.

While those who returned under the auspices of a Western pentecostal denomination had had some basic theological and ministerial training, most of the national workers in Eastern Europe had no such opportunities. A major problem in the Slavic lands was the behavior of extremist fanatics who, claiming to be led by the Spirit, advocated unbiblical practices and doctrines. These threatened to destroy the work or at least bring it into disrepute and so vitiate its witness. Some Western-supported mission-

aries like Schmidt sponsored Eastern Europeans to attend the Pentecostal Missionary Union Bible School in Hampton, England, but the cost was prohibitive. The solution was to be found in the opening of a Bible training institute in Eastern Europe.

The opening of this institute was made possible by the formation of REEM in Chicago in 1927 by Schmidt; Paul Peterson, a former worker with RMS; and C. W. Swanson, a California businessman who had provided funds for the publication of Schmidt's journal, *The Gospel Call of Russia*, which became the official magazine of REEM. On his return to Poland, while awaiting funds to commence the school, Schmidt traveled extensively throughout Europe, teaching intensive Bible courses. Once the Bible institute became a reality, those who had attended these courses became a ready recruiting source for the student body.

By 1929 the funds were available and property was secured in the Free City of Danzig (modern Gdansk) for the first pentecostal Bible school in Eastern Europe. Its opening coincided with the enforcing of antireligious laws in Soviet Russia and the arrest of some 800 pentecostal pastors, many of whom, after "show trials," were exiled to Siberia. The first class of 25 was selected from Russia, the Ukraine, Poland, and Bulgaria. Although REEM worked closely with the AG–U.S. until 1940, primarily because its principals held credentials with that organization, several of the teachers at the Danzig Bible Institute were from other European pentecostal denominations, such as ›Donald Gee from the British Assemblies of God, ›John Nelson Parr from Full Gospel Testimony in England, Len Jones from the British Elim Foursquare Gospel Alliance, and Nicholas Nikoloff from Bulgaria's

A graduating class of the Danzig (modern Gdansk) Bible Institute before WWII. (Second row) Gustav H. Schmidt (third from left), Donald Gee, Nicholas Nikoloff, and Gustav Kinderman; Martha Nikoloff (second from right).

Evangelical Pentecostal Churches. Despite the brevity of the school's existence, its influence was enormous. From its ranks came many of the leaders of Eastern European pentecostalism, such as Oskar Jeske of Poland, ▸Pavel Bochian of Romania, Eugenie Bodor of Romania, Haralan Popov of Bulgaria, and John Vinnichek of Poland (later of Argentina).

In 1931, at the insistent plea of Pavel Budeanu, the Romanian-American evangelist working with the Apostolic Church of God in Romania, REEM became extensively involved in the pentecostal work there. Earlier contacts with the predominantly German ethnic work around Medias and with the mainly Hungarian work in Timisoara, however, made these more natural centers for their activity, especially as a spiritual awakening during Raroha's evangelistic meetings in Timisoara in 1928 had resulted in a substantial influx of Romanians into the Apostolic Church there. This led to the establishment of a separate Romanian fellowship under the leadership of Alexandru Izbasa, which identified itself eventually with The Christians Baptized with the Holy Spirit of Transylvania and The Disciples of the Lord based in Bucharest rather than with The Apostolic Church of God.

Undoubtedly, the influence of REEM itself was greatest in Poland, since its European field office was established in Danzig. The arrest and imprisonment or exile of all its missionaries in the Soviet Union in 1930, as a result of the antireligious legislation of the previous year, effectively ended its activities there until after WWII. It did, however, continue to pour missionaries and funds into the Balkans, especially Bulgaria, until the rising pro-Nazi sentiments and the outbreak of hostilities caused the suspension of all foreign missionary activities.

In addition to the work of those missionaries associated with REEM, several Western pentecostal denominations also had missionaries working in Eastern Europe between the two World Wars; for example, the American AG had a separate missionary force from the mid 1920s on under the supervision of Gustav Kinderman. The Swedish pentecostal churches supported several missionaries, such as Georg Stehn and the Swiss Leonhard Steiner.

Complete and accurate statistics for the pentecostal movement in Eastern Europe up to the end of WWI are impossible to obtain, partly because Spirit-filled believers were usually part of larger "revival fellowships" within existing denominations and partly because the large population displacement and immigration to the Americas that resulted from religious and civil persecution and from the war caused rapid fluctuations. Of the more than 100,000 evangelical Christians within the Soviet Union at its beginning, the majority were pentecostal in experience, according to Mikhail Zhidkov, the son of one of the leaders of the evangelical Christians in the post-Stalinist period. Similarly, the pentecostal work in Poland was at first part of the larger revival

movement in the Polish Lutheran Church and was estimated at about 3,000 believers when Fetler visited eastern Poland in 1918. A similar number was estimated for both Latvia and Estonia according to early accounts in Finnish pentecostal journals and reports from itinerant pentecostal teachers like Barratt and Gee.

The decade following WWI saw considerable pentecostal growth throughout Eastern Europe as distinctly pentecostal fellowships were established and Western-supported missionaries reported on the progress of the work to their sending agencies. The *Pentecostal Evangel* of the AG–U.S. recounted Varonaeff's report of 500 pentecostal assemblies with some 75,000 spirit-filled believers in 1928, double what he had reported two years before. In 1932 Gee estimated more than 30 assemblies, plus other preaching points, with more than 5,000 members in Bulgaria; 10 main assemblies and between 3,500 and 4,000 believers in Estonia; about 90 assemblies with 2,600 members in Hungary; about 30 assemblies in Yugoslavia; and "hundreds of meeting places" and some 7,000 believers in Romania. Swanson of REEM estimated that in 1930 there were 130 pentecostal churches in Romania, more than 500 pentecostal assemblies in Poland, and more than 700 assemblies in Russia.

On the eve of WWII the pentecostal work in many Eastern European lands had achieved its maximum growth for a generation or more. Bulgaria had about 8,500 members meeting in some 175 assemblies and another 60 preaching points; Hungary, 4,000 believers in 150 assemblies; Yugoslavia, 2,000 believers in 25 assemblies; Poland, 24,000 believers in 700 assemblies, at least 500 of which were in the Polish National Pentecostal Fellowship; Romania, 5,000 to 6,000 believers in 300 assemblies; Czechoslovakia, about 2,000 believers; Estonia, about 3,000 believers; Latvia about 1,500 believers; and Lithuania, about 500 believers.

II. THE IMPACT OF POLITICAL REGIMES.

The outbreak of WWII heralded a half-century of political oppression for the pentecostal movement, first under the Nazi regimes and, after the war, under atheistic communism. The attitude of the political authorities varied considerably from country to country and according to local officials' prejudices. The antipathy of the Nazi regimes toward the pentecostals, whom they considered to be mentally unstable, resulted in the destruction or confiscation of pentecostal churches and the extermination of many of the believers in the Nazi death camps. The pentecostal movement in Germany and in occupied countries such as Belgium, Bulgaria, Czechoslovakia, France, Greece, Holland, and Yugoslavia was virtually eliminated.

Following the example of the Soviet Union in the 1920s, some communist regimes allowed greater freedom to groups like the pentecostals in an attempt to break the power of the former state church, usually Roman Catholic in the North or Orthodox in the South and East. This gave the pentecostals opportunities to organize and evangelize as never before. In Romania, for the first time, the main body of the pentecostals, the Apostolic Church of God, was granted provisional recognition in 1946. Since the Romanian communist government was not willing to recognize more than one pentecostal group, by 1950 both The Christians Baptized in the Holy Spirit and The Disciples of the Lord were compelled to join forces with the larger group under the name The Pentecostal Church—the Apostolic Church of God in order to receive full government approval.

The pentecostals in most of the Soviet bloc countries were, however, not legally recognized as denominations and were compelled either to amalgamate with other evangelical denominations, to disband, or to function without government approval as an "underground" or dissident church. Many pentecostal believers who were members of recognized denominations secretly attended dissident church meetings, where there was greater freedom to enjoy distinctively pentecostal practices. In 1945 in the Soviet Union, the majority of The Christians of Evangelical Faith (the pentecostal branch of the Evangelical Christians) were absorbed into the All-Union Council of Evangelical Christians—Baptists (AUCECB). A substantial group, about 100,000 strong, rejected this union and established a separate, unregistered Council of Christians of the Evangelical Faith, often referred to as Initiativniki. Although periodically these pentecostals unsuccessfully applied for government recognition because of the restrictions placed on their distinctively pentecostal manifestations, the continued presence of pentecostals in the AUCECB enabled them to present a united evangelical front to the non-Christian world and to share their pentecostal experience with fellow evangelicals, leading to a gradual "pentecostalizing" of the denomination, especially in regard to divine healing. In the early 1970s some of the Initiativniki outside the AUCECB were permitted to register with the government but were subject to strict controls and stringent supervision by government agencies.

Similarly in Poland the compulsory amalgamation of the pentecostals with other evangelical groups in the United Evangelical Church of Poland not only enabled them to survive despite the intense opposition of the former state church (the Roman Catholic Church) but also to cooperate with Baptist, Christian Brethren, and Methodist evangelicals in witnessing to the gospel. In Czechoslovakia the surviving pentecostals became part of the Union of Free Congregational Churches.

Despite the restrictions placed on all evangelistic (and many of the distinctively pentecostal) activities, some pentecostal groups were able to maintain themselves and even grow. Part of the growth may be attributed to demograph-

ics—the pentecostals generally opposed all forms of birth control and thus had larger families. In Romania, for example, a family of 10 children was not considered unusual among pentecostals. But they also grew because they were seen as a legitimate vehicle of protest against the communist regime, even though to identify publicly with the pentecostals could mean the loss of opportunities for higher education, job advancement, quality housing, and even the right to raise one's own children. The fortitude of their martyrs under interrogation, torture, and imprisonment inspired their children, fellow prisoners, and often their oppressors to adopt the same faith and follow in their footsteps. Particularly in the Soviet Union the practice of sentencing dissidents, including pentecostals, to internal exile helped spread their influence throughout the union, even to areas to which voluntary travel would not have been permitted. A further factor in the growth of the pentecostal movement was the strong emphasis on prayer and miraculous healing. Since direct evangelism was not possible, prayer became the primary means of advancing the gospel, as well as of providing a refuge from government pressure and persecution. Also, because medical care was available through government channels only, many pentecostals were fearful of what might happen to them in a government medical facility, so they simply trusted God for healing. The resulting testimonies proved a powerful attraction, especially among the poor and physically hopeless.

Although government pressure on the recognized pentecostal groups throughout the communist bloc sought to limit their growth and to ensure that compliant individuals were elevated to positions of leadership, it is a testimony to the creativity of the local church leaders and even some of the denominational leaders that they were able to sustain the work. When ▸Pavel Bochian succeeded Bradin as the president of the Romanian Pentecostal Church in 1962, there were some 35,000 believers. By 1969 that number had increased to 50,000; a decade later (1979) it had doubled in size; and it doubled yet again in the next decade to 200,000, meeting in 795 churches, the strongest pentecostal work in the Eastern bloc outside the Soviet Union.

The Apostolic Church in Czechoslovakia, despite its early beginnings, found itself struggling for its existence in a hostile environment. At the end of WWII it briefly recouped its losses, growing to about 2,500 members and adherents, but the communist government refused to recognize it as a separate entity until 1977, by which time it had declined to 700 members. Although it took four years to clear the final hurdles to full government recognition, the fortunes of the church began to improve almost immediately, and from 1983 on the church was permitted to organize Bible courses, evangelistic outreach, and mission activities, leading to the establishment of several new churches and the doubling of church membership to 1,400 by 1989.

Similarly, the reorganizing of the Pentecostal Church of Poland as a separate legal body in Feb. 1987, with 82 churches and about 6,000 members, provided increased opportunities for pentecostal witness, including publishing, Bible training courses, and even youth and children's ministry.

Other national fellowships were not able to sustain such growth, and some were barely able to keep themselves in existence. The Apostolic Church in Hungary, also known as the Primitive Christian Brethren, simply maintained itself with about 3,000 members as did the Christ Pentecostal Church (Kristova Pentekostna Crkva) of Yugoslavia.

It is noteworthy that the growth of the pentecostal movement during this era was achieved with little help from outside missionary organizations. Some Western churches did appoint a representative or committee to oversee relations with the Eastern-bloc churches to provide encouragement and obtain an accurate picture of the current situation there; e.g., the AG–U.S. in 1968 appointed Robert Mackish, a veteran missionary from Texas, as its European liaison, who for the next 20 years traveled from capital to capital, keeping the lines of communication open. From Germany, Waldemar Sardaczuk and the Action Committee for Persecuted Christians (Aktionskomitee für Verfolgte Christen [AVC]) and the Nehemia Christian Aid Service (Nehemia Christenhilfsdienst) provided both spiritual and material help and encouragement, especially among the German ethnic minorities. The British pentecostal churches cooperated in supporting the Slavic and European Evangelistic Society (in the mid 1960s the word *Slavic* was dropped), which took up much of the work formerly done by REEM, since that organization adopted an increasingly anti-pentecostal stance after it severed its ties with the AG–U.S. in 1940, despite the continuing leadership of Peterson until the late 1970s. The openness of the more Western-looking communist countries, such as Poland, Hungary, and Yugoslavia, enabled expatriates to return home for visits and to bring needed support. In Yugoslavia the AG–U.S. was able to establish a Bible school, first in Zagreb and later in Osijek under the leadership of a Western-educated Yugoslav national, ▸Peter Kuzmič, which was able to provide theological education for pentecostals and other evangelicals throughout Eastern Europe.

III. RECENT DEVELOPMENTS.

By 1989, the epochal year that marked the end of the communist regimes in most of Eastern Europe, it was obvious that pentecostalism was an established feature of the religious landscape, despite the opposition and even outright persecution by government authorities and the former state churches. The fall of European communism brought radical changes throughout the former Eastern-bloc countries and opened the door to Western missionary involvement to a degree that had been impossible for half a century. In some countries, because of the compromised position of much of the denominational administration, the first months after the downfall of the communist regimes saw sweeping changes in national leadership resulting in the emergence of young and relatively inexperienced leaders who struggled to balance the long-established traditions of the churches with the new openness to fresh ideas and opportunities. Other countries were able to weather the storm much more easily because either the national leaders were relatively new or were widely respected for their resistance to the former government authorities; in Czechoslovakia, for example, Jozef Brenkus had succeeded to the leadership of the Apostolic Church on the death of Milan Bednar in Jan. 1989.

The influx of missionary personnel and funds from the West has had both positive and negative results. On the one hand, it has enabled the Eastern churches to establish Bible schools; build churches; engage in evangelism; develop ministries in radio, television, and publishing; and provide ministries for youth and children, thus helping to satisfy the intense spiritual hunger apparent throughout the region. But on the other hand, the unexpected rapid growth has often overwhelmed the capacity of the national leadership to cope, leading to a destabilizing of many of the existing pentecostal unions. The breakup of the old government-orchestrated unions was frequently encouraged by Western denominational agencies and personnel and by ambitious nationals, who seized the opportunity to establish distinctive works under their own name and reflecting their own cultural and doctrinal perspectives. This in turn soured the enthusiastic welcome initially given to Western missionaries within the national churches, leading to further alienation and independence of action by the missionaries and their national fellow workers.

Both within the older pentecostal unions and in the newer, Western-created fellowships, the closing decade of the 20th century was a time of unprecedented growth. The Pentecostal Union in Romania, for example, grew from 795 to 2,153 sovereign churches and about 1,000 other preaching points, with more than 500,000 baptized adult members, and a further 126 churches with some 5,000 members outside the union in the AG Association of Romania, the Nehemia (German-supported) fellowship, Pentecostal Holiness Churches, and independent charismatic churches. The former Romanian region of Moldavia, annexed by the Soviet Union in 1944, has witnessed similar growth and now has more than 120 churches and 12,000 members in its Pentecostal Union. The Pentecostal Church of Poland has also grown from 86 churches and 7,000 members to 172 churches and 20,000 members, which was the same membership reported 60 years ago at the outbreak of WWII.

The Bulgarian Evangelical Pentecostal Union survived the opposition of one of the most virulently antireligious regimes in Eastern Europe to face the new opportunities with about 100 churches and 10,000 members. The next five years of spiritual awakening saw the number of churches grow to about

350, with at least 30,000 members, before the Bulgarian Orthodox Church combined its efforts with those of the former communist Bulgarian Socialist Party to pressure the government to halt the growth of evangelicalism by some of the most repressive legislation in Europe. A vitriolic media campaign against pentecostals and nonpentecostal evangelicals alike has fed the increasing religious intolerance, resulting in spasmodic outbreaks of government-sanctioned violence, despite which, partly due to the astute leadership of Victor Virchev, the church is continuing to grow. There is also a small unregistered Church of God (Cleveland, TN) fellowship.

The political disintegration and ensuing wars in the former Yugoslavia meant that the pentecostal church had to reorganize itself in accordance with the new national boundaries, resulting in the establishing of the Pentecostal Union of Slovenia, the Evangelical Church of Croatia, the Evangelical Church of Bosnia, the Evangelical Church of Macedonia, and the continuing Christ Pentecostal Church of Yugoslavia (Serbia and Montenegro). Under the influence of Kuzmič and the Evangelical Theological Seminary of Osijek, Croatia, the churches in the former Yugoslav republics of Croatia, Bosnia, and Macedonia have steadily moved away from a specifically pentecostal orientation toward a more general evangelical position, as their adopted names suggest. The exception is the church in Slovenia, the former national stronghold of pentecostalism, where there are 16 churches and about 1,500 members in the Pentecostal Union and 3 independent charismatic churches with about 60 members. There is also a small Church of God (Cleveland, TN) fellowship of 4 churches and some 60 members in Croatia.

The separation of the former Czechoslovak republic into two independent political units also necessitated the division of the Apostolic Church. The Apostolic Churches in both the Czech and Slovak republics have shown healthy growth with some 30 churches, 80 preaching points, and 3,000 members in the former, and 24 churches, 30 preaching points, and another 3,000 members in the latter, with a further 9 churches and 1,000 members in the charismatic Christian Fellowship of Slovakia, which was formed in 1994.

The pentecostal movement in the former Soviet Union, later known as the CIS, has shown phenomenal growth, despite internal divisions and external opposition from the Russian Orthodox Church and the former communist party. In 1991 the previously registered as well as unregistered pentecostals agreed to form an All-Union Congress of Pentecostals. Despite initial prospects of cooperation, however, 45 of the more Western-oriented churches, under the influence of American pentecostal missionaries, had separated within a short time to form the Russian Union of Christians of the Evangelical Faith (RUCEF) under the leadership of Sergei Ryakhovsky, leaving the original union to represent the more traditionally minded believers. Since then the RUCEF, with

extensive Western support and missionaries, has grown to over 1,300 churches and is fast approaching the size of the national Pentecostal Union. The third major group of churches is the Charismatic Association of Christian Churches of Russia, led by Igor Nikitin, composed of those influenced by the many independent Western charismatic preachers who have flooded into Russia since *glasnost* (openness) began and those preferring a more exuberant form of worship than was possible in the existing unions.

Although the Baltic states received the pentecostal message early in the history of the movement, the devastation of war, the deportation of much of the original population, and the intensive reeducation process of the communist era hindered the growth of pentecostalism. Lithuania, for example, entered the new era with only three functioning churches, but with the support of the AG–U.S. a Bible school has been established and the number of churches has expanded to about 30.

A major factor in the growth of the pentecostal movement in the postcommunist era has undoubtedly been the establishing of Bible schools and other centers for theological education. The Apostolic Churches in the Czech and the Slovak republics jointly sponsored a Bible school in Kolin, near Prague. The Slovak Apostolic Church, together with four other evangelical denominations, also formed the Faculty of Evangelical Theology and Missions within the state University of Banska Bystrica in central Slovakia. The small Bible school established by the Bulgarian pentecostals in Ruse in 1991 was moved to Sofia the next year and has exercised an increasing influence on the movement, despite the surrounding opposition.

Similarly the Bible College in Budapest, established by the Evangelical Pentecostal Fellowship of Hungary under the leadership of Attila Fabian, has played a prominent role in the aggressive evangelistic program that has seen approximately 18 new churches planted each year since 1989. In 1997 the first steps were taken toward the establishing of an accrediting association, the Euro-Asian Theological Association, for the more than 120 Bible schools between the Atlantic and the Pacific Oceans.

The collapse of the communist governments throughout the Eastern bloc exposed the appalling economic situation resulting from the pervasive mismanagement of the natural and industrial resources of the nations. The transition to a market economy, combined with escalating inflation, plunged most of the population into poverty. This, together with the devastation of the internecine conflicts in the former Yugoslavia, provided the pentecostals an unprecedented opportunity to show the love of Christ in a tangible way through a variety of compassion ministries, such as the Agape Ministries of the AG–U.S., led by Kuzmič of Croatia, which has resulted in a greater openness to the gospel among the sufferers.

The complete results of a century of pentecostal witness in Eastern Europe can only be told in eternity, but the more than 20 million pentecostal believers in these former communist countries stand as a testimony to what God has accomplished and to what might yet be accomplished in the new millennium by his power.

[Note: Apart from Poland, Romania, Slovakia, and Slovenia, no national pentecostal movements or international pentecostal missions agencies provided official statistics regarding the work in Eastern Europe. All statistics are therefore based on published accounts and eyewitness estimates.]

■ **Bibliography:**

Books. G. Atter, *The Third Force* (1970) ■ T. B. Barratt, *When the Fire Fell* (1927) ■ R. E. Davies, *I Will Pour Out My Spirit* (1992) ■ S. Durasoff, *Bright Wind of the Spirit* (1972) ■ idem, *Pentecost behind the Iron Curtain* (1972) ■ S. H. Frodsham, *With Signs Following* (1946) ■ D. Gee, *Upon All Flesh* (1935) ■ idem, *Wind and Flame* (1967) ■ W. J. Hollenweger, *The Pentecostals* (1972) ■ O. Jeske, *Revival or Revolution* (1973) ■ G. B. McGee, *This Gospel Shall Be Preached* (1986) ■ J. E. Orr, *The Flaming Tongue* (1973) ■ P. B. Peterson, *History of the First Fifty Years (1927–1977) of the Eastern European Mission* (n.d.) ■ T. Sandru, *The Pentecostal Apostolic Church of God of Romania* (1982) ■ D. Shakarian, *The Happiest People in the World* (1975) ■ H. V. Synan, *In the Latter Days* (1984) ■ idem, *The Holiness-Pentecostal Tradition* (1997) ■ C. C. Whittaker, *Great Revivals* (1984).

Articles, monographs, and reports. M. Codreanu, "'The Forgotten Chapter' in the History of Romanian Pentecostalism during the Inter-War Years (1917–1941)" (thesis, Assembly of God Theol. Sem., n.d.) ■ E. Czajko, "Poland" (unpub.) ■ A. Higgins, "Macedonia" (privately pub.) ■ J. Kusnierik, "Evangelicals in Central Europe" (1997) ■ P. Kuzmič, "Agape Ministries" (privately pub.) ■ J. Tipei, "The Apostolic Church of God of Romania" (unpub.) ■ various news reports in *Charisma, Christianity Today, The Eurasian, The Gospel Call (of Russia), Mountain Movers,* and *PE.*

Correspondence. J. Brenkus (Slovakia) to I. R. Hall ■ D. Campbell (Slovenia) to I. R. Hall ■ C. Gornold-Smith (Slovakia) to I. R. Hall ■ B. Schaffner (Poland) to I. R. Hall ■ P. B. Peterson (REEM) to N. Perkins (1939) ■ and S. H. Frodsham (1940).

■ I. R. Hall

EUROPE, WESTERN (Survey)

1. Background.

As in America, the main background to the pentecostal movement in Europe is to be found in the Holiness movements of the late 19th century. The European Holiness currents, already evident in the writings of the Irish Methodist William Arthur, were intensified by the visits to Britain and Germany of Robert Pearsall Smith, aided by the British campaign of D. L. Moody, which all led to the annual ▸Keswick conventions held in northwestern England each July from 1875 on. The same period saw the revitalization of Pietist cells *(Gemeinschaften)* in the state churches of Germany. A European tour by R. A. Torrey in 1903 spread the concept of a postconversion baptism in the Spirit as an empowerment for ministry and service.

Significant differences did exist, however, between the European and American Holiness groups. For example, while the Keswick conventions did teach and encourage the expectation of an experiential coming of the Holy Spirit to give the Christian a breakthrough in the struggle against temptation, they gave greater emphasis to the ongoing faith proclamation of Jesus' victory. A second difference was that Keswick and German circles rejected the view, widespread in the U.S., of Christian perfection as the eradication of the flesh by nature, and proclaimed instead an ongoing victory over temptation, with slogans such as "the victorious life" and "the overcomer." Of the American Holiness teachers, European Holiness leaders felt most at home with the circles associated with ▸A. B. Simpson and D. L. Moody. And third, there was less Wesleyan-Methodist influence on the European than on the American Holiness movements. Holiness teaching in Europe was mostly Calvinistic (among many Anglican evangelicals at Keswick and among Welsh Calvinistic Methodists) or Lutheran (as in much of the Gemeinschaftsbewegung, the Holiness movement within the Protestant state churches in Germany).

Holiness currents were equally present in pentecostal origins in Europe and in America though in general less visibly in the former. The advent of glossolalia was more immediately divisive in America, where it disrupted newly formed Holiness denominations, than in Europe, except for Germany, with its rejection by the Gemeinschaftsbewegung in the ▸Berlin Declaration. Early pentecostal teachings in Europe are suffused with Holiness teaching on the victorious, overcoming life, e.g., with ▸Mary Boddy and ▸Jonathan Paul. The influence of the Welsh revival (1904–6) was more marked in Europe, with some pentecostal pioneers visiting Wales during the period of intense revival.

2. Origins.

The pentecostal movement in Europe developed from the ministry of ▸Thomas Ball Barratt, a naturalized Norwegian of English birth, who was baptized in the Spirit in New York in Nov. 1906. On his return to Oslo (then Christiania) the following month, Barratt held meetings in a large gymnasium to preach the pentecostal message. These meetings received extensive publicity, so that many flocked to hear Barratt, including ▸Alexander Boddy from England (Mar. 1907) and Jonathan Paul from Germany (Apr. 1907).

All countries in Western Europe (except Holland and Italy) in which the pentecostal movement became established before WWI received the message from Norway: Sweden in early 1907 (a Barratt visit expanded the small beginnings sparked by Andrew G. Johnson, a Swedish American baptized in the Spirit at ▸Azusa Street); Great Britain in Mar. 1907 (Boddy's return, boosted by Barratt's Sunderland mission in Sept. 1907); Germany in the spring of 1907 (two Norwegian visitors from Oslo); Denmark in June 1907 (Barratt's first visit); Switzerland in the summer of 1907 (visit of the same Norwegian visitors, followed by a Barratt visit in 1908); and Finland in the fall of 1911 (visit by Barratt).

Although there were small pockets of pentecostal believers before WWI in Belgium, France, the Baltic states, and Russia, these assemblies did not form a nucleus for the movement, which grew later from new roots. In Amsterdam, Holland, ▸Gerrit and Wilhelmina Polman heard of Azusa Street through receiving the *Apostolic Faith* magazine. Wilhelmina was baptized in the Spirit in Holland in 1907, some months before her husband received the baptism in England. In Italy the movement's beginnings in 1908 came through Italian-American missionaries bringing the message from the U.S. to their homeland.

The factors contributing most to the expansion of the pentecostal movement in Northern Europe before WWI were (in probable order of importance):

a. Personal witness. From the beginning, the movement was strongly evangelistic, with pentecostal people proclaiming their experience to all who would listen. While newcomers were frequently baptized in the Spirit at pentecostal meetings, the witness of pentecostal believers was often the initial attraction.

b. Literature. In five countries (Britain, Norway, Germany, Holland, and Switzerland) leaders were producing pentecostal monthlies by 1908–9, within two years of the movement's arrival. All reported the worldwide spread of the movement and were augmented by an array of pamphlets, joined before long by magazines and bulletins issuing from other pentecostal sources.

c. Annual conferences. Annual conferences were held in such pentecostal centers as Sunderland, England; Mülheim, Germany; and Örebro, Sweden. Other major conferences were held in Hamburg (1908) and Oslo (1911). Sunderland in particular attracted speakers and participants from other lands, emphasizing the international character of the pentecostal movement.

d. Press coverage. In some places the pentecostal outbreak drew comment in the secular press, usually skeptical and sometimes derisive. Though the pentecostals were presented as credulous fanatics, such publicity—e.g., in Norway and Britain—often produced more interested inquirers. Hostile comment in Christian journals tended to be more damaging to the movement, such as the controversy surrounding the negative Berlin Declaration of 1909 in Germany.

e. Travels by major figures. The early pentecostal leaders, such as Barratt, Boddy, Polman, and Paul, all visited each other, with closer links between Britain, Holland, and Germany than between these and Norway. These leaders undertook regular preaching tours, though Paul traveled less than the other three.

A group attending a Sunderland (U.K.) Convention in 1912, including the leading European pentecostals of the time. (Front row, left to right) Smith Wigglesworth, T. Hackett, Gerrit Polman, Jonathan Paul, Thomas B. Barratt, Emil Humburg, a Mr. Schilling, and A. A. Boddy; (center) John Leech, a Mr. Techner, J. H. King, Stanley Frodsham, and T. Moggs; (back row) Cecil Polhill and W. H. Sandwith.

f. Visitors from the U.S. Many American pentecostal pioneers made trips around the world, often visiting Europe on their way home. These included ➤Frank Bartleman, ➤Joseph Hillery King, Daniel Awrey, ➤A. H. Post, and ➤Elizabeth Sisson. They do not, however, seem to have contributed significantly to the European beginnings.

3. European Dimensions.

In the first decade of the movement, contacts between pentecostal leaders in different European countries were closer than in subsequent years. The major leaders regularly attended and spoke at each other's conventions and kept up frequent correspondence. These bonds were formalized in the ➤International Pentecostal Council, formed in 1912, which, while welcoming some leaders from America, was in effect a European council.

These bonds of fellowship were disrupted by WWI, which restricted travel and communications. After the war the degree of closeness was never recovered, despite the international conference held in Amsterdam in 1921. The 1920s were years of denominationalization, a process that inevitably introduced rivalries and led to the term "movement"—preferred by pentecostals to church terminology—becoming applied to particular denominations. Nonetheless, the common experience of baptism in the Holy Spirit with signs following was distinctive enough for the whole pentecostal movement in Europe to retain a sense of its particular identity even amid diminished international contacts. This sense was enhanced in the 1920s and '30s by the evangelistic campaigns of ➤Smith Wigglesworth, who was not aligned with any one pentecostal denomination, and the developing teaching ministry of ➤Donald Gee, which was valued in all strands of the movement.

Gee was the prime mover in an attempt to gather pentecostals from European groups into one conference, which was finally held in Stockholm in June 1939. This conference was the only occasion in pentecostal history when doctrinal and theological issues have been openly debated between delegates from a variety of allegiances. Here was manifest a problem that bedeviled subsequent attempts at pentecostal unity: the clash between those emphasizing the sovereignty of the local church (notably the Scandinavian pentecostals, but also the French AG) and those with an element of denominational centralization. The former were deeply suspicious of all attempts to form any kind of pentecostal organization, whether at a national, continental, or worldwide level.

Collaboration across national boundaries was reinforced after WWII by the inauguration of ➤Pentecostal World Conferences (PWC), the first of which was held in Zurich, Switzerland, in 1947. It was at the Paris PWC in 1949 that the organizational issue caused another confrontation. The desire to form some kind of pentecostal world organization was vehemently opposed by the Scandinavians. It was agreed simply to hold the PWC together with five advisors, with the secretary's responsibility limited to contacts in view of the next PWC. Rumblings among the Scandinavians continued for several years, as they were fearful of the secretary (then ➤David du Plessis) being seen as a spokesman for the whole movement. Gee did much to assuage fears and keep international communications open.

No specifically European pentecostal groupings came about until the 1960s. In 1966 the European Pentecostal Fellowship (EPF) was formed in Rome, bringing together pentecostal denominations with national organizations. Initially comprising mostly AG-type denominations, EPF was later joined by the Church of God (Germany) and Elim (Britain). Congregational-type pentecostals began in 1949 to hold Pentecostal European Conferences (PEC), initially on a small scale in Sweden, but from 1972 on every three years in various European centers. In 1987 the European fellowship that had been sought for so long became a reality when the EPF and PEC amalgamated to form the Pentecostal European Fellowship (PEF).

From discussions at the PEC in The Hague, Netherlands, in 1978, the ➤European Pentecostal Theological Association (EPTA) was formed in 1979. EPTA has been primarily an association of those engaged in administration and teaching at pentecostal Bible colleges. The annual conferences have had a strongly practical as well as an academic character. The EPTA Education Board has helped Bible colleges in several countries obtain national accreditation. In 1989 an East Europe Committee was formed to assist pentecostal education in the former communist bloc, and every third annual conference has been held in Eastern Europe.

Less frequent academic conferences on Pentecostal and Charismatic Research in Europe have been held since 1980, first convened by ➤David Bundy and ➤Jerry Sandidge in Leuven, Belgium. This group, which later adopted the formal title of European Pentecostal-Charismatic Research Association (EPCRA) in 1993, has been strongly supported by Professor ➤Walter Hollenweger and his doctoral students researching pentecostal and charismatic topics. Until 1992 there was a close link between these scholars and the *EPTA Bulletin,* during the editorship of Jean-Daniel Plüss, a founder of EPCRA. Since 1993 the *EPTA Bulletin,* which has since become *The Journal of the European Pentecostal Theological Association,* has become what its new name indicates.

■ **Bibliography:** P. Branco, *Pentecostes un Desafío al Mundo* (1984) ■ D. D. Bundy, "Early European Scholarly Perspectives on Pentecostalism," *EPTA Bulletin* 5 (1986) ■ idem, "Historical Perspectives on the Development of The European Pentecostal Theological Association, *Pneuma* 2 (1980) ■ D. Gee, *Upon All Flesh* (1947) ■ idem, *Wind and Flame* (1967) ■ W. J. Hollenweger, *Pentecostalism* (1997) ■ idem, *The Pentecostals* (1972) ■ idem, ed., *Die Pfingstkirchen* (1971) ■ L. Steiner, *Mit Folgenden Zeichen* (1954).

■ P. D. Hocken

FAEROE ISLANDS

■ Pentecostals 691 (23%)   ■ Charismatics 1,940 (65%)   ■ Neocharismatics 349 (12%)   ■ Total Renewal: 2,980

FALKLAND ISLANDS

■ Pentecostals 0   ■ Charismatics 0   ■ Neocharismatics 0   ■ Total Renewal: 0

FIJI

■ Pentecostals 65,206 (35%)   ■ Charismatics 35,740 (19%)   ■ Neocharismatics 84,054 (45%)   ■ Total Renewal: 185,000

For general introduction and bibliography, see PACIFIC ISLANDS.

Of the countries of the South Pacific region, Fiji is the second largest in population (after Papua New Guinea), and the fourth largest in land area (after Papua New Guinea, the Solomon Islands, and New Caledonia). The Fiji group consists of about 332 islands that vary in size from 3,800 mi² (10,000 km²) to tiny islets a few yards in circumference. About a hundred of these islands are usually inhabited, while those remaining islands that are sufficiently large in area are used for temporary residence or for occasional plantation. The principal islands are Viti Levu (Big Fiji) and Vanua Levu (Big Land), which together constitute 87% of the total land area of Fiji (6,151 mi² [15,923 km²] out of a total of 7,055 mi² [18,272 km²]).

The capital is Suva, located on the southeast side of Viti Levu. Suva has 180,000 inhabitants out of the total population of 800,000 in 1995. Fiji's population is multiethnic. The two major groups are the indigenous Melanesian population, referred to as Fijians, and those who are of Indian descent, referred to as Indians. Apart from Fijians and Indians, there are small groups of Europeans, part-Europeans, Chinese, and other Pacific Islanders.

1. Assemblies of God.

The first pentecostal missionary couple to Fiji was Albert T. and Lou Page, who arrived in Suva in May 1913, a year before the ►Assemblies of God (AG) was organized in the U.S. But there was no immediate success, and one year later Page wrote in a letter, "The Spirit has not yet fallen, except on one" (Larson, 1994). The AG started officially in Fiji in 1926, when Rev. Adrian Heeterby and his wife, Charlotte, arrived. Three years later the first AG church was organized in Suva. From the very beginning there was little financial support from the U.S. headquarters, and the opposition from the already established Methodist Church was strong. Mainly for these reasons, the AG did not have a great impact until the 1960s. In 1966 the number of adherents was still under 3,000. But from that time on, the AG has been the fastest-growing religious group in Fiji.

The first converts were mainly Europeans and Indians. This picture has changed completely, so that today the vast majority of adherents of the AG in Fiji are indigenous Fijians. From its early beginnings, the AG of Fiji have been very mission-oriented. As documented by Larson (1994), the AG in Vanuatu, the Solomons, and Tonga, for example, were established by missionaries from Fiji. Since 1966 the AG in Fiji has been an independent fellowship within the worldwide structure of the AG church. There are still a few missionaries from the U.S., but since that date they have worked under the auspices of the local leaders and the General Council. The AG belongs to the very few churches in Fiji that are practically independent in terms of finances too. Locally raised income from tithes, offerings, and donations covers the cost of salaries, programs, and the maintenance of church properties. Only in the case of new church buildings does some support come from the AG overseas. By the end of 1997 the total number of adherents was 56,349, reflecting rapid growth compared to the 2,763 adherents in 1966. Today there are 1,287 credentialed national ministers and 1,274 lay ministers. Besides the 143 churches, there are 224 preaching points.

Since its inception in 1966, the South Pacific Bible College at Wainadoi, near Suva, has trained hundreds of church workers and ministers from the South Pacific Region for the ministry. In 1997, 200 students were enrolled to study for their diplomas or bachelor's degrees. The AG college is also the site for a master's degree extension program of the Far East Advanced School of Theology in Manila. Besides the Bible school, the AG–Fiji runs a primary as well as a secondary school. In Suva the AG runs the Assembly Press, which prints religious literature in several languages and dialects of the region. Plans are underway for the construction of new headquarters, which will cost F$1.2 million (1998 equiv. US $580,000) if realized.

Close cooperation exists between the AG and other religious groups that subscribe to a similar theological self-understanding of being born-again Christians (Brethren Church, Bible Society, Baptist Convention, World Vision,

Campus Crusade for Christ, etc.). Being the strongest of all these groups, the AG has taken the lead in building up structures for evangelical/fundamentalist and born-again individuals and religious groups. This became evident in the establishment of the Evangelical Fellowship of the South Pacific, whose president is a minister of an AG church in Suva and the majority of whose members are from the AG.

2. Christian Outreach Centre.

The ›Christian Outreach Centre (COC) has been successful in Fiji, where activities started in 1987–88. Today there are nine centers (Ba, Nadi, Lautoka, Labasa, Nausori, Navua, Rakiraki, Levuka, and Suva). The number of adherents in Fiji, according to the COC headquarters in Suva, is about 1,100, including children. Fifty percent of the adherents are new converts from the not-religious or not-religious–nonpracticing section of the society. The meetings take place in private homes or rented buildings. All services are held in English, because the COC does not want to separate the races on the basis of their different cultural backgrounds. In 1993 there were 14 pastors, called workers, who were paid by the church. The national chairman of the COC in Fiji is an Australian pastor. The COC cooperates in Fiji mainly with other charismatic/pentecostal religious groups, especially with Every Home for Christ, the Apostles Gospel Outreach Fellowship International, and the AG.

3. Church of God (Cleveland, TN).

In Fiji the ›Church of God (CG) was registered officially in May 1990, after some years of mission activities. The CG claims to have about 1,100 members. In 1992 the CG made an application to the Fiji Council of Churches to become an affiliated member. The application was turned down because the CG did not meet the requirement that a church has to be established over a period of several years before an application will be considered.

4. United Pentecostal Church International.

Compared to the AG, the ›United Pentecostal Church International (UPC) is a quite small, new religious group in the contemporary religious setting of the Pacific Islands. There are only about 5,000 UPC adherents in the Pacific Islands. One of the reasons for this is that the UPC did not start work in the Pacific until 1972, when a missionary from the U.S. arrived in Fiji. Today the UPC claims to have about 2,200 adherents, 33 churches (meeting places), and 66 ministers in Fiji.

The growing importance of the South Pacific region for the UPC was underlined when, for the first time, a subregional conference was held in Suva, with about 200 participants from the region as well as some from Australia, New Zealand, the Philippines, and the U.S. One of the prominent speakers at the conference was the current director of the Foreign Missions Division, Harry E. Scism.

Apostles Gospel Outreach Fellowship International, Fiji. (Courtesy Manfred Ernst.)

Major developments over the last five years include the building of a new Bible college and dormitories. An average of 35 to 40 students enroll in the Bible college each year. The annual conference in 1998 was held in the National Stadium, with 6,000 in attendance. In 1998 there were five missionaries from overseas in Fiji, one full-time or career missionary family, and two volunteers. The full-time missionary is Richard S. Carver, who is also the general superintendent of the UPC in Fiji.

Small congregations of the UPC, sometimes under another name (Apostolic Church International), with no more than 50 to 200 adherents, are established in the Solomon Islands, Vanuatu, Chuuk, Pohnpei, American Samoa, and the Cook Islands.

5. Apostles Gospel Outreach Fellowship International.

The Apostles Gospel Outreach Fellowship International (AGOFI) started as a breakaway group from the AG in Fiji. It is an autonomous, indigenous, evangelical/charismatic new religious group with no support from or links to any other church or group in Fiji or overseas. The name goes back to an AG prayer group of five men who started to meet in 1972 and called themselves "apostles." Because of differences with the leadership of the AG, the group decided in June 1988 to leave. These differences were caused mainly by the fact that the apostles wanted to preach the gospel and evangelize beyond any ethnic or national boundaries; they disagreed with the existence within the AG of so-called "ethnic councils."

The AGOFI started in 1988 with just 26 people (including some children), meeting in the living room of Pastor

Mata, who became the leader and first general superintendent. A few weeks later the group needed more space. It rented the Girmit Centre in Lautoka, and on the first Sunday there 150 people turned up. By Dec. 1988 about 500 people came to the services in the Centre. When the group continued to grow in 1989, it was decided to decentralize. One group was set up in Nadi, one in Suva, and one remained in Lautoka. In Suva, Pastor Mata started in 1990 with only 15 people in the Raiwai Youth Centre, but from early 1991 until now the group has rented the National Gymnasium, which seats about 1,000. At the end of 1992, four years after organizing themselves as a new church, the AGOFI claimed to have about 3,000 members; about 80% of these, according to Pastor Mata, have come from the Methodist Church.

The main purpose of the founders of the AGOFI was not to establish a new denomination, but to help people "to become better Christians." But now, established and registered, they are what they did not want to be, a new denomination in the religious setting of Fiji. Baptisms (by immersion), marriages, funerals, and communion services are led by AGOFI ministers. Besides worship on Sundays, Bible lessons are held daily in the Civic Centre in Suva, and training courses or camps for adherents are organized throughout the country.

6. Every Home for Christ/Christian Mission Fellowship.

According to Roberts and Siewert (1989), Every Home for Christ (EHC) is an evangelical, interdenominational, evangelistic service agency of independent tradition, engaged in evangelism, correspondence courses, literature production, literature distribution, and support of national workers. The EHC is in close fellowship with some well-known personalities and the organizations behind them, such as Billy Graham, Ted W. Engstrom, ˒Pat Robertson, and Luis Palau.

In their zeal to reach every person in every nation with the gospel, EHC sponsors, wherever it is active, nationwide, evangelistic outreaches called Every Home Crusades. In a typical crusade two evangelistic booklets, one for children and another for adults, are personally and systematically delivered by Christian nationals from house to house in every city and village. Statistics of their activities are kept and published. EHC in Fiji, for instance, claims to have already visited 51,229 homes. They have also recorded 20,511 professions of faith, and 7,246 students are enrolled in Bible correspondence courses of the EHC in Fiji.

The EHC started in the Pacific region in 1984, first in Fiji, where, until 1988, it worked very closely with the Methodist Church and, to a lesser extent, with the AG and the Anglican Church. In 1990 the EHC decided to continue the work by establishing a new church under the name of Christian Mission Fellowship (CMF). The EHC still claims that it never intended to form its own church, because the stated policy of the EHC is to work with and alongside the established churches. In Fiji, however, circumstances have led to the EHC continuing as an independent parachurch organization with a special and very close relationship to the CMF. Today the CMF claims to have 60 churches in Fiji with 21 ordained ministers. The number of adherents is about 12,000, most of them converts from the Methodist Church. In Dec. 1992 the headquarters, previously in Labasa, were moved to Suva, mainly for administrative purposes. In Labasa, EHC runs its Bible school and training center for missionaries and pastors, with 55 students enrolled in 1993. These students come from Papua New Guinea, the Solomon Islands, Vanuatu, and Fiji. The school is recognized by the World Evangelical Fellowship.

The EHC was and is still active in other Pacific Islands where they started in the late 1980s. They have 40 volunteers working in Papua New Guinea, 40 in Vanuatu, and about 50 in the Solomon Islands (in close cooperation with the South Sea Evangelical Church). Sixty volunteers have been trained by the EHC in Kiribati, where there is close cooperation between the Kiribati Protestant Church (KPC) and EHC. The EHC has also trained volunteers in the Cook Islands in cooperation with the Cook Islands Christian Church (CICC) and the AG. The work there today is in the hands of the respective churches. In Fiji the EHC has about 150 volunteers doing field work.

7. Evangelical Fellowship of Fiji.

The Evangelical Fellowship of Fiji (EFF) was established in 1989 by a small group of individuals, churches, and church organizations who subscribe to the statement of faith in the

Meeting of Every Home for Christ, Fiji. (Courtesy Manfred Ernst.)

Evangelical Fellowship's constitution, which is basically fundamentalist in theology, stating for instance that "the Holy Scriptures as originally given by God, (are) divinely inspired, infallible, entirely trustworthy, and the supreme authority in all matters of faith and conduct." All members of the EEF consider themselves born-again Christians—in fact, to be "born again" is a precondition of membership.

Driving forces in the establishment of the EFF of Fiji have been the AG, the Brethren Church (Fiji Gospel Churches), the Fiji Baptist Convention, and, last but not least, Ratu Inoke Kubuabola, a Baptist who is a former general secretary of the Bible Society, former president of the Fiji Council of Churches, and a prominent member of the nationalistic Taukei movement, who after the military coup in 1987 made a considerable career in politics.

In 1991 a small group of three individuals separated from the EFF and formed the Evangelical Alliance of Fiji (EA) because of personal problems between the former general secretary and the majority of members.

In 1993 the EFF had 30 members, most of them AG ministers but also at least two Methodist ministers. Organizational members are the AG, the Brethren Church, the Covenant Evangelical Church, and the CG. Close relations exist between the EFF and ›Youth With A Mission and EHC.

On the regional level, the EFF was one of the founding members of the Evangelical Fellowship of the South Pacific in Honiara, Solomon Islands, in Apr. 1992. The Evangelical Fellowship is also present in Western Samoa, New Zealand, and Australia. On the international level, the Evangelical Fellowship of Fiji and the South Pacific is affiliated with the World Evangelical Fellowship (WEF).

The Evangelical Alliance of Fiji and the South Pacific operates at present on a low level with a small budget. It is limited basically to its members and has not been able to attract great numbers of evangelicals/fundamentalists within other religious groups. Although the Evangelical Fellowship has no full-time staff and no office of its own yet, it has the potential for future development as an umbrella organization for evangelicals/fundamentalists across all denominational borders and as a kind of counteragency to the Pacific Conference of Churches.

8. Full Gospel Business Men's Fellowship International.

The ›Full Gospel Business Men's Fellowship International (FGBMFI) is a nondenominational, charismatic/pentecostal parachurch organization of U.S. origin. It includes mainline Protestant and Catholic charismatics. It was founded, organized, and initially funded by ›Demos Shakarian, a wealthy Armenian-American dairy processor, in Los Angeles in 1951.

The FGBMFI is not visibly organized in the Pacific Islands. Although there is a loosely organized group of members in Fiji, there are neither headquarters nor offices. Usually business people get in contact with the FGBMFI during business trips to the U.S., Australia, or New Zealand. After they have returned, some of them become members and start to organize small prayer groups or meetings. Some join already existing charismatic groups. The FGBMFI encourages its members to be witnesses to others but at the same time to stay within their own churches.

In Fiji, for example, the former president and general secretary of the Methodist Church, Isireli Caucau, is a member of the FGBMFI, as is the well-known local businessman and minister for finance Jim Ah Koy. At meetings sporadically organized by the FGBMFI in Suva, one can find members of parliament, senators, ministers, and businesspeople, as well as Prime Minister Sitiveni Rabuka, who is a lay preacher of the Methodist Church and known to be sympathetic to the organization.

The influence of the FGBMFI is not to be measured by the number of its members in the Pacific Islands, which is quite low, but more by the informal network of charismatic/pentecostal born-again Christians who hold key positions in the government, the economy, or military of the respective countries.

9. Other Organizations.

Other organizations in the Fiji Islands include Child Evangelism, Campus Crusade, ›Youth With A Mission, and World Vision (the latter focuses on community development projects). Some but not all of these organizations have fellowship with one another (some have a distinctly nonpentecostal/noncharismatic theology), and some are in competition because they have similar target groups and objectives. In their self-understanding the members of these groups have in common that they are born-again Christians. Usually they see themselves as the true defenders of the gospel against suspected liberal and modern influences, and they have a strong zeal for evangelism. These parachurch organizations all have in common that they are newcomers on the religious scene in Fiji, having become active there in the last quarter-century.

■ M. Ernst

FINLAND

■ Pentecostals 73,741 (11%)　■ Charismatics 513,445 (77%)　■ Neocharismatics 79,813 (12%)　■ Total Renewal: 666,999

‣Thomas Ball Barratt of Norway brought the pentecostal movement to Finland in the fall of 1911. Charismatic manifestations had been apparent among Finnish Christians, however, long before Barratt's visit. In fact, the Lutheran revivalistic movement called ‣Awakened (*Heränneet*) began in 1796 as the result of a sudden outpouring of the Holy Spirit, which was accompanied by such observable signs as visions and speaking in tongues. In time the charismatic gifts were widely accepted, and speaking in tongues continued on into the 20th century. Likewise, glossolalia has occasionally occurred among the members of another Lutheran group, the Laestadians *(Laestadiolaiset)*. In 1889–99, a Laestadian group experienced an outpouring of the Holy Spirit in the city of Narva in Northern Estonia, with manifestations of visions and prophecies. The group became known as the Narvaitic Laestadians. Furthermore, a few years before Barratt's visit, two Swedish-speaking Baptist pastors, J. A. Lindkvist and A. A. Herrmans, and several church members had experienced the baptism of the Holy Spirit.

The Narvaitic Laestadians invited Barratt to Finland. Meetings in Helsinki started on Sept. 17, 1911, and continued for two weeks. During this journey, Barratt visited several major cities in Finland as well as St. Petersburg, Russia. When Barratt returned to Norway, he left behind a number of Christians who shared the same understanding of the charismata. These Christians from various denominations gathered informally, and the spiritual manifestations continued. The prayer meetings were held on the Laestadian premises in the home of Miss Hanna Castren, a school principal. Missionary Emil Danielsson was regarded as the leader of this emerging pentecostal group.

In Jan. 1912 Barratt's magazine, *Korsets Seier,* was issued in the Finnish language under the name *Ristin Voitto* (Victory of the Cross). In addition, the Christian journal *Toivon Tähti (Star of Hope)* became a pentecostal organ under the editorship of Pekka Brofeldt. Soon after Barratt's visit, Gerhard Smidt, another Norwegian pentecostal, came to minister in Finland. In the spring of 1912 a genuine spiritual revival with charismatic manifestations broke out. This revival furthered the pentecostal movement as a number of ministers from various denominations joined the movement. In addition to the Laestadians, Christians from the Methodist Church, the Free Church, the Finnish Missionary Society, the Baptist Church, and the Salvation Army accepted the pentecostal message. Pentecostal summer gatherings were initiated in 1912, and the first baptismal services were held during the summer of that year. The first pentecostal missionary, Emil Danielsson, was consecrated in July 1912. The name Helluntaiherätys (Pente-

costal Revival [PR]) was first used for the Finnish pentecostals in 1913. Barratt visited Finland again in 1912 and 1913.

Before WWI the pentecostal message had been introduced in most parts of the country. Furthermore, pentecostal pastors and evangelists ministered in Estonia and in the Finnish-speaking regions of Russia, as well as among the immigrants of North America. Pentecostal ministers and lay leaders began to hold annual conventions *(veljespäivät)* and the Pentecostal Alliance of Brethren *(Veljesliitto)* was formed in 1914. The first local church, Siloam, was founded in Helsinki in May 1915 by the Baptist sector of the pentecostals. The other pentecostals, however, continued to gather informally. WWI and the Civil War of 1918 unfortunately hindered growth for many years.

In 1919–20 a division occurred over the doctrine of the autonomy of the local church and closed versus open communion. The advocates of open communion and informal fellowship took the name Helluntaiystävät (Pentecostal Friends [PF]), while those who embraced the doctrine of the autonomy of the local church adopted the name Helluntaiherätys (PR). Smidt, who worked in Finland during 1912–14 and 1920–25, played a part in the split. In the 1920s, the two groups were equally strong. During that decade, the adherents of PR set up more than 40 local assemblies. In addition, the first common associations were established to sustain publishing efforts and missionary outreaches. At the end of the 1920s, the total number of pentecostals was estimated at 10,000. By the end of the 1930s, the PR had become the main branch of pentecostalism in Finland. At the end of that decade, the number of local churches numbered 90 and the total number of pentecostals stood at over 20,000.

Finland's involvement in WWII caused very heavy losses, and the Christian work was seriously disrupted. The churches were left without pastors as a number of ministers served in the army. The district of Karelia was lost to Russia, and 14 pentecostal churches had to be evacuated from that region. Moreover, the war years were plagued by internal conflicts relating to unarmed military service and the mode of cooperation among the churches belonging to PR. Although Finland survived as an independent nation, it took years to recover from the material and spiritual losses.

After WWII, the membership of the PF began to diminish, and they ceased to function in the 1990s. On the other hand, the PR experienced a period of growth. A number of churches were founded and church buildings erected. In 1960 the combined membership of local churches reached 26,000. But in the early '60s another split took place when an influential pastor, Vilho Soininen, started a group called Vapaa Helluntaiherätys (Free Pentecostal Revival; this group reunited with the PR in 1985). In 1964 the seventh ˃Pentecostal World Conference was held in Helsinki.

In the late 1970s and early '80s a revival occurred as a result of the healing ministry of Niilo Yli-Vainio. The meetings were attended by thousands, and the ministry attracted much press coverage, mostly favorable. Before Yli-Vainio's death in 1982, the ministry had gained a worldwide reputation.

At present, the pentecostals form the third-largest religious entity in Finland (after the Lutheran and Orthodox churches). The PR has two branches, one consisting of Finnish-speaking churches, the other of churches for Swedish-speaking Finns. At the end of 1996 there were 223 Finnish-speaking churches, with a total membership of 46,300. The Swedish-speaking churches numbered 32, with a membership of 2,700. Thus, total PR membership was 49,000 in 255 churches. Together with adherents (e.g., the children of pentecostal families), the number is now estimated between 55,000 and 60,000. The largest local church is Saalem of Helsinki, with a membership of 3,169 at the end of 1997.

In addition, there are a few independent pentecostal churches that do not belong to the PR (e.g. Siiloan and Helsingin Helluntaiseurakunta). The estimated membership of these groups is about 1,000.

In 1912 the first pentecostal missionary, Emil Danielsson, was sent to Kenya, where he worked at the mission station of Kima in Kisumu. He returned to Finland in 1919. Pastor Pekka Nuutinen ministered in Estonia from 1914 until 1925, when he moved to North America to work among the Finnish and Estonian immigrants there. Nikolai Pöysti, a former Methodist missionary to Manchuria, was instrumental in the founding of the Finnish Free Foreign Mission (FFFM) in 1927. At that time the doctrine of the autonomy of the local church was strongly emphasized; since it was feared that a mission agency would encroach on the churches' autonomy, the operations of the FFFM were suspended in 1929. The local churches took over responsibility for equipping and sending out missionaries. The first missionaries, Martta and Nikolai Pöysti, together with their children and Toimi Yrjölä, were sent to Manchuria in the fall of 1929. In the 1930s Manchuria became the main mission field. However, a number of missionaries were sent to new fields, including India, Burma (Myanmar), Tanzania, South Africa, and Argentina.

WWII brought numerous obstructions for the missionary work at large, and no new missionaries were sent out from the homeland. After the war there was an upsurge of missionary enthusiasm, and the local churches, in increasing numbers, assumed responsibility for sending out new missionaries. Furthermore, it was realized that a missionary association was needed in order to coordinate the expanding work. Thus, in 1950, the FFFM was resurrected as a common mission board for the independent churches. The local assemblies are now responsible for sending out and supporting missionaries, and the mission board acts as an official representative in ventures abroad. Since the 1970s, development work and humanitarian aid have become important branches of the FFFM. At the end of 1997 there were 458 missionaries working in more than 40 countries. The largest concentrations were in Thailand (43), Japan (34), Tanzania (29), Russia (28), Spain (27), Papua New-Guinea (25), Ethiopia (21), Bolivia (19), Uganda (17), Austria (13), and Taiwan (13).

Conforming to the Scandinavian pattern, the PR of Finland is distinctly a lay movement. The board of elders is in charge of church government, and although the churches normally employ one or more full-time pastors, administrative responsibilities are carried out collectively. Nevertheless, the board of elders is accountable to the congregation, and church members are consulted on major issues. Thus, the form of church government is a mixture of congregational and presbyterian practices. Because of the emphasis on the autonomy of the local churches, PR is not registered as a denomination according to Finnish law. The churches are, however, in voluntary fellowship with one another and form a united front. Conventions of pastors and lay leaders are held twice a year, both nationally and in the provinces. The churches depend on voluntary associations for the coordination of mutual interests. The fellowship has a common publishing house, mission board, humanitarian aid agency, home mission fund, Bible college, broadcasting company, rehabilitation centers for alcoholics and drug addicts, and other related associations.

˃T. B. Barratt and Gerhard Smidt played prominent roles in bringing the pentecostal movement to Finland. A number of Finnish ministers also joined the movement in its initial stages, and pentecostalism began to develop under indigenous leadership, especially since the outbreak of WWI, when foreigners had to leave the country. In the early years, editor Pekka Brofeldt, Pekka Lattu, Pekka Nuutinen, Pekka Sahib, Akseli Puhakainen, and missionary Vilho Pylkkänen were influential pioneers. After the split of 1919–20, the latter became the leader of the PF. Among the PR, pastors Väinö Pfaler, Eino Heinonen, and Eino Manninen held prominent positions after the 1920s. In later years, Eino Ahonen became a recognized leader. Manninen and Ahonen have been the most talented leaders among the PR of Finland in terms of leadership skills. The evangelistic ministry of Niilo Yli-Vainio achieved world renown in the late 1970s and early '80s. The most influential foreigners, as far as theology is concerned, have been T. B. Barratt, ˃Lewi Pethrus, and ˃Donald Gee.

Finnish pentecostalism has a number of distinctive features. The proportion of missionaries is very high: approximately 1 missionary for every 100 members. The activity of women as evangelists is also notable: more than 600 female evangelists have taken their place in the ranks of pentecostal workers; more than 100 of these later entered missionary service abroad. Another distinctive feature is the annual pentecostal conference. The event is usually held in mid-summer, with an attendance of around 30,000. It is the largest annual pentecostal gathering in Europe and one of the largest in the world. The meetings are held, camp-meeting style, in huge tents.

See also BIBLIOGRAPHY AND HISTORIOGRAPHY OUTSIDE NORTH AMERICA; SCANDINAVIAN MISSIONS TO LATIN AMERICA.

■ **Bibliography:** L. Ahonen, *Missions Growth: A Case Study on Finnish Free Foreign Mission* (1982) ▤ idem, *Suomen helluntaiherätyksen historia* (1994) ▤ K. Antturi, J. Kuosmanen, and V. Luoto, *Helluntaiherätys tänään* (1986) ▤ N. Bloch-Hoell, *The Pentecostal Movement* (1964) ▤ P. Brofeldt, *Helluntai-herätys Suomessa* (1932) ▤ E. Helander, *Naiset eivät vaienneet* (1987) ▤ N. Holm, *Pingströrelsen: En religionvetenskapling studie av pingströrelsen on Svenskfinland* (1978) ▤ J. Kuosmanen, *Herätyksen historia* (1979) ▤ A. Pietilä, *Helluntailiike* (1913) ▤ W. Schmidt, *Die Pfingstbewegung in Finland* (1935).   ■ L. Ahonen

FRANCE

■ Pentecostals 161,535 (11%)   ■ Charismatics 1,114,446 (76%)   ■ Neocharismatics 191,019 (13%)
■ Total Renewal: 1,467,000

When one speaks of pentecostalism in France, one must speak for the most part of the Assemblies of God (AG) of France. Through the efforts of a young evangelist, Douglas Scott, and his wife, Clarice, pentecostalism was brought to the shores of the country of Voltaire. Scott in his wisdom refused to permit the fledgling AG–France to become a part of its British counterpart; rather, he insisted that the newborn movement be left to develop in accordance with French mentality, including its organizational structure. What follows is a précis of an extraordinary movement of God's Spirit in a land known for its culture and education.

The dawn of the 20th century brought the almost simultaneous upsurge of pentecostalism to America, England, and Wales. Pentecostals, also derisively known as Apostolics, Holy Rollers, Hallelujahs, and the "tongues movement," made inroads into Scandinavia, penetrated German Lutheranism, found a toehold in Greece, and made headway in Italy. The U.S. had its ►Parham and its ►Seymour, England its ►Boddy, and Scandinavia its ►Barratt. France, it seemed, was left out.

The exact origins of French pentecostalism lie buried in those unheralded but dedicated pioneers who braved obstacles to evangelize the country. Donald Gee, in his general history of pentecostalism, mentions that in 1909 Paris had a small hall where meetings were held for those seeking the baptism of the Holy Spirit. Leonhard Steiner, a Swiss historian of pentecostalism, says that from 1909 on there were small individual groups of pentecostal believers, such as those in Paris and Le Havre. ►Bloch-Hoell has remarked that T. B. Barratt had a proselyte in France in 1907—a Dutchman who in 1907 had frequented Barratt's meetings in Norway. ►Frank Bartleman, a self-styled world evangelist and a product of the ►Azusa Street Mission in Los Angeles, remarked that while in France in 1912 he had visited a Brother Michael Mast who had a little pentecostal mission at Rosny sous Bois, some 10 miles from Paris. He had visited that mission in 1910. In 1912

Bartleman preached a one-week meeting in the mission. He also noted that he had held a meeting in the heart of Paris in Mast's tailoring establishment with about 30 present. Bartleman concluded that it was very difficult to get people to attend a gospel meeting in Paris. He noted that he knew of a pentecostal mission in Le Havre. Whatever the importance of the few isolated cells of pentecostalism in France for the future of the movement there, the major surge, prior to 1939, originated from two sources. One specific source was ►Hélène Biolley's temperance hotel, the Ruban Bleu, in Le Havre, which was to become in time the center of pentecostal activity. A more general source was a revivalistic spirit, comparable to that existing simultaneously in Wales, that captivated the minds of not a few French Christians.

The Welsh revival of 1904–5 made a deep impression in orthodox circles both in the British Isles and in France. Henri Bois, a French historian of the Welsh revival, stated that many French people earnestly sought God for an outpouring of his Spirit upon France. Sometime after 1906, a Scotsman, H. E. Alexander, himself influenced by the Welsh Revival, founded L'Action biblique, a narrow fundamentalist group that placed great emphasis on the power of the Holy Spirit in an individual's life. In England in 1908 a group of pentecostals formed the Apostolic Faith Church—a group that held extreme ideas on being led by the Holy Spirit plus other eccentricities. The upshot of such extravagances caused a more moderate group to withdraw in 1916 to form the Apostolic Church of Wales. This group sent missionaries to France, one of whom was the young Welshman ►Thomas Roberts, who before his death in the late 1980s was deeply involved with the Roman Catholic and Protestant charismatic renewal in France. In 1926 Roberts established a mission in Paris that soon became a thriving group of pentecostal converts.

Important as Roberts's mission was for pentecostalism in France, the most important river of pentecostalism flowed from Hélène Biolley's Ruban Bleu, the temperance hotel she established in Le Havre in 1909. Born, reared, and educated in Switzerland, she belonged to the "Pure Hearts," a mystical Swiss sect that placed emphasis on examining one's motives: "Are my thoughts pure?" "Have I treated my neighbor right?" Although a cultivated and refined lady of no mean ability, she wanted to work among the dregs of society and to lift up the down-and-outers. The Ruban Bleu became a combination temperance hotel and religious center.

Many foreign missionaries on their way to French-speaking West Africa stopped at the Ruban Bleu to perfect their French or just to have a few days of rest. Many of those who spent time at the Ruban Bleu had heard of pentecostalism or were themselves pentecostal. Their conversations aroused her curiosity about this new move of God. Biolley invited the well-known English evangelist ►Smith Wigglesworth to Le Havre, where he held a number of meetings. In 1920 she invited Dutch pentecostal preacher ►G. R. Polman to give studies on divine healing and the baptism of the Holy Spirit. The meetings of these evangelists contributed to an ardent desire in Biolley's spirit to have prayer meetings for a move of God's Spirit in France.

Romanian-born Christo Domoutchief is another person who played an important role both in Biolley's Ruban Bleu and in the pentecostal movement. Yet another foreigner, Ove Falg from Denmark, was a major player in the early days of the pentecostal movement in France. In 1925 he visited Paris, where he chanced to meet a group of young English pentecostals. In this group was Thomas Roberts. The encounter with this youth group so altered Falg's spiritual mentality that he became a convinced follower of the pentecostal way.

Thus Hélène Biolley and the Ruban Bleu provided the focus for the future success of pentecostalism in France, for it was here that intercession for revival began and that the young Englishman and his bride, Douglas and Clarice Scott, would land on Jan. 1, 1930, to bring the message of Pentecost to France. (The story of the Scotts' arrival and the meetings they held in Le Havre are detailed in *Le Pentecôtisme au Pays de Voltaire*.)

Toward the end of 1930, the message of Pentecost preached at Le Havre had spread among Protestant circles, particularly among Baptist churches in the north of France. From Le Havre the message also spread south to Rouen, which itself became a stronghold of pentecostalism, as did Dieppe on the coast near the Belgian border. What Scott was to Le Havre, Domoutchief was to Paris. The spread of pentecostalism knew no national borders; it reached into southern Belgium and Switzerland by means of healing missions.

Important to understanding the spread of pentecostalism is the effect the message had on Baptist churches in Northern France and on the French Reformed Church. Many of the Baptist churches, anticipating a spiritual movement, accepted pentecostalism as that which they were seeking. In

the camp of the French Reformed, Ax Bernoulli, pastor of the French Reformed Church at St. Chamond, Loire, expressed the sentiments of many Reformed ministers when he stated that "our churches need revival and we hope that many of the pastors and church officials of France will stretch out a fraternal hand to our brothers of the pentecostal movement." Scott had a close collaboration with many French Reformed pastors and was asked on a number of occasions to address consistories of the Reformed Church on the subject of the Holy Spirit and pentecostalism. By 1935 the pentecostal message had spread all over France, with the exception of eastern France, which would not be "pentecostalized" until after the war.

Scott had no intention of forming a new denomination. His intention was to bring the pentecostal message to France. By 1932, however, it became apparent that new wine could not be put in old bottles. So it was in Feb. 1932 in Le Havre that the AG–France was formed. It should be noted that this organization has no organic relationship with the AG–U.S. Any relationship is purely fraternal. Following Scott's intense evangelization and his belief that God desires miracles of healing to take place, pastors in France, even today, are intensely evangelistic and are strong proponents of God's divine intervention, such as healing.

The AG–France has a national convention, which is divided into two regional conventions, north and south. Each convention is divided into sections. The movement maintains its own radio and TV department, a publishing house, a monthly journal, and overseas missions outreach. The movement also operates a Bible school, an organization to help former communist-bloc countries, and homes for the aged, and it is particularly well known for its summer youth camps. There are over 600 meeting places presided over by 400 pastors and their *stagiaires* ("apprentices").

The AG–France is by far the fastest-growing and most widespread of all pentecostal groups in France, yet it should be mentioned that other foreign-based pentecostal denominations have established a few congregations in some of the larger cities. Of importance are the many ethnic groups in France, particularly the Portuguese and Africans, among whom pentecostalism has had a wide reach. The charismatic movement among Protestants and Catholics has been strong. Of considerable importance is the impact pentecostalism has had among the ►Gypsies. It is of interest that, for the most part, Americans who have come to France as missionaries have had little success, except among those ethnic groups that have maintained their ethnicity.

Leaving aside the ethnic pentecostal groups, the AG–France faces a dilemma: either to continue to let the wind of the Spirit blow through the movement or to allow an accumulation of nearly 67 years of tradition dictate its future. As Douglas Scott said, "Then there will no longer be a movement, but a monument."

■ **Bibliography:** *Dictionnaire du Monde Religieux dans la France Contemporaine: Les Protestants* (1993) ■ D. Jeter, "Le Retour a une foi simple" (diss., Paris IV–Sorbonne, 1993) ■ J. L. Hurlbut, *L'Histoire de l'Eglise chrétienne* (1988), chap. 25 ■ *Annuaire des Assemblées de Dieu de France* (lists addresses of AG in France, pastors' names and addresses, plus information on French AG activities) ■ *Pentecôte* (official monthly magazine of the AG of France) ■ R. Pfister, *Soixante ans de pentecôtisme en Alsace (1930–1990)* (1995) ■ G. R. Stotts, *Le Pentecôtisme au Pays de Voltaire* (1978). The works of both Jeter and Stotts have extensive bibliographies.

■ G. R. Stotts

FRENCH GUIANA

■ Pentecostals 2,116 (20%)   ■ Charismatics 6,509 (63%)   ■ Neocharismatics 1,775 (17%)   ■ Total Renewal: 10,400

FRENCH POLYNESIA

■ Pentecostals 1,374 (6%)   ■ Charismatics 20,188 (81%)   ■ Neocharismatics 3,238 (13%)   ■ Total Renewal: 24,800

For general introduction and bibliography, see PACIFIC ISLANDS.

French Polynesia consists of 118 islands that form 5 archipelagoes scattered across some 2 million mi² (5 million km²) of ocean—although the total land area is only 1,255 mi² (3,251 km²). Tahiti, the biggest island, is 548 mi² (1,420 km²). The 118 islands can be divided into two groups: islands of volcanic origin and low coral islands.

There are currently some 200,000 residents in French Polynesia, approx. 160,000 on Tahiti. The growth rate of the population is high, at 3%.

1. Pentecostal and charismatic movements.

The pentecostal movement started within the Evangelical Church, mainly in the Chinese Bethel parish (known today as Jourdan parish), and has split into different groups. The first step was taken in 1967 with the setting up of a wel-

fare fellowship, called Alleluia, by four deacons of the Chinese parish of Bethel. This rapidly turned into a breakaway, and the separation became effective when the Alleluia church built its chapel at Faariipiti and asked Pastor Vinubah, a French Army chaplain originally from Viet Nam, to minister to them. Later they spread into the Tahitian community, and they confirmed their pentecostal direction by calling upon ministers from the Assemblies of God (AG) overseas. During the next few years the pentecostals split up into different groups. The biggest group became affiliated with the AG in France and another directly with the AG–U.S. The total number of adherents of the AG in 1997 is about 700. The Alleluia church today has only about 45 adherents, all Chinese. The services are held in the Cantonese dialect, and the small community has been pastored since 1985 by a minister from Malaysia who was formerly affiliated with the Philadelphia Fellowship in the U.S.

2. Confederation of Reformed Churches of French Polynesia.

The Confederation was formed in 1982 by a former minister responsible for the youth work of the Evangelical Church. This minister came into contact with ▶Youth With A Mission and was influenced by its emphases. The decision to leave the Evangelical Church was also influenced by disagreement with the church leadership and the handling of money on the local level. The founder and current president of the confederation stated in 1992 that he believes he is leading a badly needed renewal movement. The theological orientation is clearly evangelical-fundamentalist. With 4 ordained ministers and 4 churches, including 10 parishes and a total of about 1,100 adherents, the Confederation of Reformed Churches has become to some

Alleluia Church in Papeete, Tahiti.

extent an *omnium gatherum* for all those who disagree with the polity, structure, administration, financial practices, or theological direction of the Evangelical Church.

An interesting phenomenon is the near-complete absence of all evangelical-fundamentalist parachurch organizations that are very active in most of the other Pacific Islands. But this could change rapidly. During field research on other Pacific Islands, several groups, including Every Home for Christ, the ▸United Pentecostal Church, and the ▸Christian Outreach Centre, explained to the author that they are planning to extend their activities to French Polynesia in the near future.

■ M. Ernst

GABON

■ Pentecostals 12,144 (14%) ■ Charismatics 41,662 (47%) ■ Neocharismatics 35,694 (40%) ■ Total Renewal: 89,500

For a general introduction and bibliography to Central Africa, see AFRICA, CENTRAL.

Gabon, like the Republic of the Congo (Congo-Brazzaville), was a former French colony until its independence in 1960. Gaston Vernaud had worked with the French Reform Church Mission (Paris Evangelical Missionary Society) in Gabon since 1930. He was baptized in the Holy Spirit in 1934 through the ministry of George Jeffreys. In 1936 Vernaud was used of God in a pentecostal revival in Gabon where many were baptized in the Holy Spirit and spoke in tongues. There were also numerous healings. Because of this, he was forced to leave the French Reformed Church Mission in 1937 and returned to Switzerland. He was soon contacted by the AG–France and sent out as their very first missionary to found the Mission Evangélique de Pentecôte (MEP, Pentecostal Evangelical Mission) in 1939.

The first church was started at Owendo, where a Bible school was opened in the same year. In 1943 a mission station was founded at Medouneu. Gabonese pastors were consecrated by the end of the 1940s, and the assemblies were properly constituted. One of the most important was that at Abelogo, which was under the leadership of Pastors Oguisi and Oyembo, who had been part of the original revival in 1936. From these first churches, Georges Ndjongue became the first president of the Eglise Evangélique de Pentecôte in Gabon (Pentecostal Evangelical Church). These churches are also called the Assemblées de Dieu du Gabon (AG–Gabon). [Note: M. Demba Esaïe, who came from Congo/Brazzaville and is considered a false prophet by mainline pentecostals, has also used the name Assemblées de Dieu. This causes some confusion.]

Other churches were planted in the East-Ogooué and Mid-Ogooué regions. In 1967 two French missionaries were sent to help encourage evangelism within the country. Campaigns were held at Libreville and Port-Gentil. Many miracles took place during these meetings, with lame, paralyzed, deaf, and mute people being healed. By the seventh day of the meetings, more than 16,000 were in attendance. In one meeting alone, 47 paralyzed people were healed. Following this time of blessing there was considerable spiritual division. By the end of 1969, the work started by the AG mission separated itself from the AG–France and all French missionaries withdrew; however, visits from Jean Ollé and Michel Maréchal, who have held evangelistic campaigns in various places, help to maintain the important link between AG–France and AG–Gabon. Between 1969 and 1989 there was not much growth in the churches, nor was there much in the way of church planting in new areas. The pentecostal movement remained relatively unknown and insignificant. By 1989 there was evidence of new enthusiasm and the appearance of new assemblies at Libreville and elsewhere in the country. The current president of the Eglise Evangélique de Pentecôte is Jude Benjamin N'gouwa, who in 1990 began to publish and distribute a magazine called *Pentecôte Gabonaise* (*Gabonese Pentecost*). The Centre de Formation Biblique (Center of Biblical Instruction) opened in 1982 at Port Gentil and is directed by Jean de Dieu Ntiwini Igana. There are an estimated 10,000 adherents and 20 congregations in the pentecostal churches and another 9,000 pentecostals and charismatics in other groups throughout the country.

■ D. J. Garrard

GAMBIA

■ Pentecostals 197 (2%) ■ Charismatics 1,618 (15%) ■ Neocharismatics 9,185 (84%) ■ Total Renewal: 11,000

See AFRICA, WEST.

GEORGIA

■ Pentecostals 0 (0%) ■ Charismatics 20,609 (69%) ■ Neocharismatics 9,391 (31%) ■ Total Renewal: 30,000

See RUSSIA.

GERMANY

■ Pentecostals 145,957 (6%)   ■ Charismatics 1,904,070 (73%)   ■ Neocharismatics 549,974 (21%)   ■ Total Renewal: 2,600,001

The emergence and growth of pentecostalism in Germany can be divided into different phases of development. The earliest phase is rooted in the impact of the Holiness movement in late 19th-century Europe, an era that was characterized by the resurgence of Pietism within the German Lutheran churches. Since this resurgence, known as the *Gemeinschaftsbewegung* (GB) or *Heiligungsbewegung,* took place within the structure of German evangelical Protestantism, their teaching on holiness was largely influenced by the Lutheran tradition.

The GB was also influenced by its members who attended pentecostal conferences in England and elsewhere during the first decade of the 20th century. The Deutscher Evangelischer Verband für Gemeinschaftspflege und Evangelisation, better known as the Gnadauer Verband (GV; after Gnadau, the place where it was initiated in 1888; it was formally organized in 1897), received some impetus from this conference. Their main emphasis was on personal salvation and holiness, the second coming of Jesus Christ, as well as seeing the church as the body of Christ. Early pentecostal teachings were thus suffused with holiness teaching on the victorious, overcoming life. In 1906 R. A. Torrey was invited to the annual conference of the Evangelische Allianz in Blankenburg. He gave a sermon on the baptism in the Holy Spirit, which was believed to have awakened the thirst for a "revival" and for the "reception of the Holy Spirit" in many participants. Consequently, the GV conference held at Brieg/Schlesien in 1907 was claimed to have been well attended by those who anticipated a great spiritual revival.

The development of the pentecostal movement was further enhanced through influences from Scandinavia. In 1907 the Oslo Pentecostal Conference was held in Norway under the auspices of the Scandinavian Methodist pastor ►Thomas Ball Barratt's ministry. Barratt received the baptism in the Holy Spirit in New York in Nov. 1906. On his return to Oslo he inaugurated meetings in which he started to preach the pentecostal message. These meetings received wide publicity and drew participants from several West European countries, including Germany. Among the German delegation to the Oslo Conference were ►Jonathan Paul and Emil Mayer (Hamburg). In that same year, two pentecostal missionaries from Norway, Dagmar Gregerson and Agnes Telle, who had plans for missionary work in Africa, came to Hamburg through the invitation of preacher and evangelist Heinrich Dallmayer. These Norwegian women participated in evangelical meetings in Kassel on July 7–Aug. 2, 1906, which was the birthplace of what later came to be known as the Kasseler Zungenbewegung (Kassel tongues movement). Some reported that what began as an impressive spiritual experience for those present ended as a "big religious scandal," with controversial prophecies, visions, and "uncontrolled" spiritual outbursts (i.e., glossolalia). The meetings were brought to an abrupt end by the police on Aug. 2.

This event marked the beginning of the pentecostal movement in Germany—and of schisms within the GB. The GB was split between those who were favorably disposed toward these pentecostal influences, those who partially accepted them, and those who were in total opposition. However, at another pentecostal conference held in Hamburg on Dec. 8–11, 1908, those in attendance resolved to continue with their action plans for evangelism. On July 14–16, 1909, a pentecostal conference was held in Mühlheim/Ruhr under the leadership of ►Emil Humburg. It was attended by about 1,700 participants.

Major opposition to the German pentecostal movement came from the GB. On Sept. 15, 1909, the *Berliner Erklärung* (►Berlin Declaration) utterly condemned the pentecostal teaching and experiences emanating from the new group as "demonic spiritualism." The meeting in Berlin at which the declaration was drawn up was summoned by about 56 leading members of the GV. One remarkable statement in the declaration is the reference to the baptism of the Holy Spirit within the pentecostal movements as *nicht von oben, sondern von unten* (not from on high, but from below). The opposition claimed that evil spirits, not the Holy Spirit, were at work in the pentecostal movement to lead many people astray.

One consequence of this opposition was the isolation and exclusion of pentecostal groups from the German Protestant churches. The *Berliner Erklärung* reinforced the pressure already put on all members of the GB by vehemently condemning the new group as belonging to the evil spirit. Though this had a far-reaching impact on the growth of the pentecostal movement, by this time the pentecostal teaching had had an impact on some members of the GB and others in the German state churches. The second Mühlheimer conference was organized by Jonathan Paul two weeks after the Berlin Declaration (Sept. 28–Oct. 1). It came as a direct reaction to the *Berliner Erklärung*. This conference had a larger turnout than the first one—about 2,500 people. Several healing miracles were claimed to have occurred during this revival.

The body called the *Hauptbrüdertag* (leadership committee) was formed, with the inaugural meeting held in Berlin. Date and venue of subsequent meetings were to rotate annually. One of the foremost leaders of the pentecostal movement in Germany was Jonathan Paul (1853–1931). He was an active member of the GV until 1907, when he claimed to have experienced the baptism of the Holy Spirit through his visit to the Oslo pentecostal conference. He formed the Mühlheimer Verband (MV) with some of his followers. He laid emphasis in his sermons and writings on "full salvation" for all Christians. This teaching appears to be a direct influence from the Pietist tradition. In 1911 the MV witnessed schism with the exit of some staunch members like E. Meyer (Hamburg), Maute (Obertürkheim), Schilling (Berlin), Gensichen (Berlin), and Sturner (Calw). Many left due to disagreements with the leadership. H. Viether (Ulm), an itinerant preacher in Southern Germany, also left the movement on the grounds that it had overwhelming Scandinavian pentecostal influence. Schilling established two independent communities in Berlin and by 1920 had started to produce his own spiritual magazine, *Wort und Geist (Word and Spirit)*. All attempts at reconciliation between the leadership of the MV and the members who left proved abortive.

In 1919 the first post-WWI conference was again held in Mühlheim, with about 3,200 participants. It was the second post-war meeting in 1928 that marked a turning point in the history of the German pentecostal movement. C. O. Voget (1879–1936) became a leading figure in the MV. He is said to have had a vision of a new holiness movement. Though Voget went back to take church leadership in Stapelmoor/Ostfriesland, his pietistic influence remained with the MV and to a large extent determined it. Other independent pen-

Two prominent German Pentecostal leaders: Emil Humburg (left), first president of the Mühlheim Association, and Jonathan Paul (right), a founder of the association and a prolific writer. In the center is H. Schober.

tecostal communities existed side by side with the MV. The Zeltmission Berlin-Lichterfelde was established in 1921. In 1926 the Christengemeinde Elim was founded in Hamburg-Barmbek with R. Rabe and H. Dittert. Through their evangelistic activities, many Elim communities were founded in Saxony and East Prussia. A mission house and a Bible school were established at their headquarters in Lauter/Erzgebirge. Their spiritual magazine, *Der Glaubensweg (The Way of Faith)*, reached a distribution of 37,000 copies.

In the 1930s the pentecostal movement met with repression and proscription under the Nazi regime. The insistence by Hitler's regime on one German "Unified Church" led to the change of name in 1938 from Deutsche Pfingstbewegung to Christlicher Gemeinschaftsverband Mühlheim/Ruhr, in order to avoid any association with the Nazi-friendly Glaubensbewegung Deutscher Christen. WWII also had an adverse effect on the growth of the pentecostal movement in Germany. It is estimated that 41 preachers, 11 female workers, and 7,000 members lost their lives during the war.

WWII marked the end of the first phase of German pentecostalism, as well as the beginning of a new phase. In the post-WWII era, pentecostalism started to gain prominence again, especially with the emergence of the German Free Pentecostal Churches. Their rapid growth is linked to a large extent to the refugee influx from Eastern Europe, where German communities had become familiar with pentecostal revivalism. While pentecostalism appeared to be thriving in former West Germany in the post-WWII period, it remained to a large extent illegal in East Germany (DDR) until the unification of Germany in the 1990s. One of the pioneer founders and leaders among the Pentecostal Free Churches was Erwin Lorenz (1906–85). In 1934 he took over the leadership of the pentecostal communities in Berlin. Due to political pressure, the Elim-Bewegung merged with the Bund Evangelisch-Freikirchlicher Gemeinden (BEF). In 1937 the Berliner Gemeinde (Steglitz) was proscribed by the Nazi Regime.

In May 1947 a joint conference in Stuttgart created the forum for the unification of the Free Pentecostal movements. In Sept. 1948 a greater initiative for unity among the pentecostal groups came up with the Einheitskonferenz der Freien Christengemeinden in Deutschland. The participants included Elim-Brüder, Freie Christengemeinden, Internationale Volksmission, Vereinigte Missionsfreunde Velbert, Elim-Brüder in der Ost-Zone, Freie Pfingstmission, and others. Most of these new groups, called Free Churches, were greatly influenced by Scandinavian, British, and American pentecostalism. Greater emphasis was placed on the baptism of the Spirit with signs following. Though not all pentecostal groups participated in the "Unity Conference," one consequence of the meeting was nevertheless the establishment of an umbrella association of pentecostal churches. In 1954 they drafted a legal constitution with which they formally registered with the German state as Arbeitsgemeinschaft der Christengemeinden in Deutschland (ACD). In 1974 the ACD was formally granted legal status (*Körperschaft des öffentlichen Rechtes*) in the region of Hessen. The foundation of the Forum Freikirchlicher Pfingstgemeinden in Deutschland (FFP) was laid in 1979 by five groups: the ACD, Gemeinde Gottes (GeGo), Volksmission, Apostolische Kirche-Urchristliche Mission, and Christlicher Gemeinschaftsverband. In 1982 the ACD changed its name to Bund Freikirchlicher Pfingstgemeinden (BFP). By 1998 the FFP had enlarged its membership to include ten different groups. It now comprises the Christlicher Gemeinschaftsverband, Mühlheim/Ruhr; Bund Freikirchlicher Pfingstgemeinden; Volksmission Entschiedener Christen; GeGo; Apostolische Kirche-Urchristliche Mission; Vereinigte Missionsfreunde Freudenthal; Jugend-, Missions- und Sozialwerk Altensteig; Gemeinde der Christen Ecclesia Solingen; and more recently the Freikirchliches Evangelisches Gemeindewerk in Deutschland and the Christliches Zentrum, Berlin.

From the 1960s on there has been a gradual proliferation of neo-pentecostal churches, especially from America, Britain, and Africa. Pentecostal evangelists such as ▸Oral Roberts, ▸Tommy Hicks, ▸Gordon Lindsay, ▸William Branham, and ▸Tommy L. Osborn have visited Germany at different times for evangelistic campaigns. Such campaigns have had immense impact on the development of pentecostalism in Germany. German pentecostal evangelists such as Hermann Zaiss and ▸Reinhard Bonnke have also extended their evangelical and healing ministries to Africa and elsewhere. A number of neo-pentecostal groups has also emerged since the 1970s, with a pentecostal mission but without the intent of founding new communities or denominations. Pentecostal groups, youth organizations, and centers were founded, such as the Wort des Glaubens (München), Gemeinde auf dem Weg (formerly Filadelfia-Gemeinde, Berlin), Christliche Gemeinde (Köln), Christliche Glaubensgemeinde (Stuttgart), Full Gospel Business Men's Fellowship International, the Church of God, Jugend mit einer Mission, Jesus Haus Düsseldorf, and the Glaubenszentrum Bad Gandersheim. A concurrent development is the proliferation of charismatic (renewal) movements, both from within and independently of the German state churches.

The pentecostal movement in Germany, as elsewhere, needs to be seen as a complex phenomenon rather than as a simple, homogeneous "confessional" group. Its complexity must be understood in terms of situational differences, cultural, and church background. A basic feature that runs through all the pentecostal groups is the common spiritual experience of baptism in the Holy Spirit with charismatic manifestations. All pentecostal movements accept and teach the baptism of the Holy Spirit, the existence of spiritual gifts, and the efficacy of healing. However, the use and interpretation of these charismatic experiences, such as glossolalia, prophecy, and visions, vary from one movement to another. One remarkable difference between the pentecostal movements of the first phase, i.e., the Mühlheimer Verband, and the Free Pentecostal Churches of the second phase is that while the latter emerged and developed independently of the German state churches, the former remains within the structures of the Lutheran (Protestant) Church, from where they exhibit their pentecostal experience and convictions. The MV has continued the holiness teaching of the GB. They do not include the phenomenon of glossolalia as "initial evidence" of spiritual rebirth in their teaching. Glossolalia is a central constituent and necessary starting point in the process of spiritual regeneration of members within many pentecostal movements. Due to the opposition from the German Protestant/evangelical churches, the pentecostal groups were in relative isolation at their infancy. However, due to increasing ecumenical activities, there seems to be growing cooperation among the various pentecostal movements, as well as between the pentecostal movements and some evangelical/charismatic movements in Germany.

■ **Bibliography:** P. Fleisch, *Die Pfingstbewegung in Deutschland* (1957) ▨ idem, *Geschichte der Pfingstbewegung in Deutschland von 1900–1950*, Marburg (1983) ▨ E. Giese, *Und flicken die Netze. Dokumente zur Erweckungsgeschichte des 20. Jahrhunderts* (1988) ▨ W. J. Hollenweger, *enthusiastisches Christentum. Die Pfingstbewegung in Geschichte und Gegenwart*, Zurich (1969), 201–51 ▨ C. Krust, *50 Jahre Deutsche Pfingstbewegung* (1958) ▨ H. Reimer, *"Die Pfingstlerischen Bewegungen,"* in *Orientierungen und Berichte* 20 (5, 1994) ▨ Forum Freikirchlicher Pfingstgemeinden in Deutschland, *90 Jahre Pfingstgemeinden in Deutschland* (1997).

■ A. Adogame

GHANA

■ Pentecostals 858,349 (19%)   ■ Charismatics 889,035 (20%)   ■ Neocharismatics 2,732,617 (61%)   ■ Total Renewal: 4,480,001

See AFRICA, WEST.

GIBRALTAR

■ Pentecostals 0 (0%)   ■ Charismatics 3,900 (100%)   ■ Neocharismatics 0 (0%)   ■ Total Renewal: 3,900

GREECE

■ Pentecostals 3,157 (3%)   ■ Charismatics 104,249 (85%)   ■ Neocharismatics 14,594 (12%)   ■ Total Renewal: 122,000

GREENLAND

■ Pentecostals 2,206 (39%)   ■ Charismatics 3,277 (59%)   ■ Neocharismatics 117 (2%)   ■ Total Renewal: 5,600

GRENADA

■ Pentecostals 5,684 (40%)   ■ Charismatics 5,656 (40%)   ■ Neocharismatics 2,861 (20%)   ■ Total Renewal: 14,201

See CARIBBEAN ISLANDS.

GUADELOUPE

■ Pentecostals 4,294 (19%)   ■ Charismatics 18,236 (80%)   ■ Neocharismatics 281 (1%)   ■ Total Renewal: 22,811

See CARIBBEAN ISLANDS.

GUAM

■ Pentecostals 2,410 (24%)   ■ Charismatics 6,694 (68%)   ■ Neocharismatics 797 (8%)   ■ Total Renewal: 9,901

GUATEMALA

■ Pentecostals 698,717 (28%)   ■ Charismatics 921,741 (37%)   ■ Neocharismatics 869,542 (35%)   ■ Total Renewal: 2,490,000

See LATIN AMERICA.

Pentecostal congregation in Cakechiguel, Guatemala.

GUINEA, REPUBLIC OF

■ Pentecostals 8,646 (14%)   ■ Charismatics 11,841 (19%)   ■ Neocharismatics 41,913 (67%)   ■ Total Renewal: 62,400

Guinea is a former French colony and was formerly part of French Africa. It gained independence in 1958. The first president was Sékou Touré, a Marxist who involved the communists in much of his country's building and philosophy. He involved Chinese and others from the former Eastern bloc in road building and the planning behind the country's infrastructure. In 1968 a coup against him was attempted, for which he blamed the Catholics; the result was the expulsion of all Christian groups for a time. Only some Christian Missionary Alliance (CMA) personnel were permitted to remain at the pastors' training school at Télékoro near Kissidougou, because Paul Ellenberger (CMA), who had been a boyhood friend of Sékou Touré, requested leniency for the missionaries in that service.

After Sékou Touré's death, General Lansana Conté became president. He was reelected to another five-year term in 1998. He is fairly tolerant of Christianity and has rejected requests from the Arab League to make Guinea a Muslim State and to eject all Christian missionaries. At present over 83% of the population is Muslim. Because of the civil wars in Liberia, Guinea-Bissau, and Sierra Leone, there are considerable numbers of refugees living in Guinea. Many of these are English speaking, and a good number of the pentecostal churches are primarily concerned with providing for the spiritual needs of these refugees, to the neglect of the indigenous Guinean, French-speaking population. The danger is that if and when the refugees return to their own countries, the churches will be seen as primarily for "foreigners."

There is much misunderstanding on the part of Muslims as to the distinctives of Christians. The majority of Protestants are perceived in the light of Roman Catholic doctrine and practice because of the association of most Guineans with Christianity and the French colonials who were Catholics—the only form of Christianity known to the majority of the population.

1. Pentecostal and Charismatic Groups.

Evidence shows that the U.S. Assemblies of God (AG–U.S.) sent itinerant missionaries to Guinea as early as 1922. The Harry Wrights from Burkina Fasso planned to settle in Guinea, but there is no record of them ever being established there. In 1922 the Pierre Duprets, who later joined the AG–France, had visited in Senegal, Ivory Coast, and Guinea before becoming residents in Burkina Fasso.

The first recognized pentecostal mission in Guinea was that of the AG–France. Daniel Monbuleau arrived from Ivory Coast in 1985 and settled in Conakry. At about the same time Eli Chirelli of the Pentecostal Assemblies of Canada (PAOC) settled in Conakry. The original plan was that the Canadians and the French AG collaborate, but due

to personal differences between Monbuleau and Chirelli, this did not happen. Monbuleau set out to establish the Assemblées de Dieu de Guinée (AG–Guinea) while Chirelli established the group that is now known as Eglise Pentecôtiste Alleluia (Pentecostal Hallelujah Church [the word "Hallelujah" is associated with Protestant churches in Guinea]). The AG–Guinea church now has 29 churches throughout the country, with about 3,000 members. The majority of the churches are in the forest area bordering Sierra Leone and Liberia, where many of the converts are from the non-Islamic, animist background of the Forest Peoples. Indeed, most of the pentecostal churches in the Gueckédou-N'zérékoré area are made up of refugees who have fled the wars in Sierra Leone and Liberia. In Conakry there are two growing AG assemblies whose membership includes French-speaking Guineans and English-speaking natives of Sierra Leone, Liberia, and other West African countries. All services are interpreted so that both French and English are current in the meetings. Where English is not used as the second language, all services are interpreted from French to Soussou, the predominant language of the Conakry area. The Conseiga Abel family are missionaries, supported by the AG–Burkina Fasso, who work with the AG–Guinea in Conakry.

The densely populated interior of the country, where mostly Muslim Fulbhe (Fulani) and Malenke (Maninka) live, are still hardly touched as far as the Christian message is concerned. Presently there are only three pentecostal missionaries in the entire hinterland: the Ken Herschell family from AG–Australia at Pita, Carlo Frutiger from Alpha Mission in Switzerland at Mamou, and the Noufé Sambou family, working with AG–Guinea, from Ivory Coast, at Kankan. There are towns of over 20,000 without any Christian witness (neither Catholic nor Protestant). The Swedish Svenska Fria Missionen (SFM, Swedish Free Mission) has had Gunnar and Osalena Nimmersjö, missionaries seconded to the AG at Daboula, but they are no longer resident there. Most of the Swedish emphasis has been in the area of social work financed by the Swedish government, which works with PMU Interlife and cooperates with ASDI (Agence Suédoise pour le Développement International—Swedish Agency for International Development). The AG–Guinea is governed by its annual conference and executive. The president is Emile Honomou, pastor in N'Zérékoré; the vice president is Hubert Gbenakou, who pastors the Taouyah assembly in Conakry.

The Pentecostal Halleluja Church now has two PAOC families (The Bill Farands and La Chance) working in Conakry with two local assemblies in the capital; it has planted three churches in the interior (Boffa, Kankan, and Tokounou). The majority of the members in Conakry are

English-speaking expatriates, but efforts are being made to evangelize French-speaking Guineans. In Conakry, Pastor Mahomet, who grew up in Sierra Leone but is from the Malenke (Maninka) people, is the head of the work. He trained at the AG Bible college in Dakar (Senegal).

The group known as Eglise Shekina (Shekina Church) originated under Apostle Williams, a Liberian who lives in Nigeria. Pastor Janvier, who was from Benin, planted the first Shekina church in Conakry about 1991. A number of remarkable healings took place, which resulted in considerable growth of the church. In early 1992 many healings occurred during a revival. Hadja Djedoua Kourouma, who had been minister of education under Sékou Touré, was healed from terminal illness and became a member of Shekina. The church grew rapidly so that today it has about 20 congregations in Guinea. The first lady of Guinea also attended this group and was responsible for the invitation to ▸Reinhard Bonnke to come to Conakry at the end of 1992. During the highly successful crusade, many healings and conversions took place. The Muslim leaders opposed the visit because of the impact it had on the population, and as a result, Bonnke has never been able to make a return visit. The Shekina Church suffered several splits when Janvier, along with Victor Okafor, was expelled from the country at the instigation of the first lady. After this expulsion Jadja Djedoua Kourouma became its leader. Another influential member of Shekina, Mama Touré, who had started out with AG, had joined Shekina prior to this time. But after the expulsion of Janvier, Mama Touré and Afrique Williams, both of whom had become leaders in the church, left Shekina and joined L'Eglise l'Amour de Dieu (The Church of the Love of God), which had been started by Jacques Lamah and Koulewondy. Things did not work out between them, so that Jacques Lamah and Koulewondy were left with what is known as Eglise l'Amour de Dieu Chemin de Fer (The Church of the Love of God at the Railway), while Touré and Lamah started a new group by the same name, which, to avoid confusion, is known as Eglise l'Amour de Dieu Mission (The Church of the Love of God Mission), or Church of the Love of God Number Two. Other pentecostal churches in Guinea, mostly in Conakry, include Vie Profonde (Deeper Life) from Nigeria, where Pastor Moril is the leader and sanctification is the main emphasis. Janvier, formerly with Shekina, eventually came back to Guinea about 1995 and started the Rhema Church (there is no direct link between this church and others outside the country bearing the same name). Victor Okafor, also previously with Shekina, is now with Béthel. A charismatic church of Arian faith (Jesus is only a creature) is Baptiste Oeuvre Mission (Baptist Mission Work), which originates from Ivory Coast and has Dion Robert as its founder.

The Bible Overte (Open Bible Church) was started by the Tom Moores at Boké among the Baga people. It has one church in Conakry. The Church of Pentecost from Ghana has also started working in Guinea but mostly among the English-speaking expatriate population. Eglise Béthel (Bethel Church) is from Bethel World Outreach in the U.S. and was started by Siafa Getaway, a Liberian. It started working in Guinea in 1993 and has four churches. In 1994 the Mission Kalima was started by Achim Eichorn from Munich (associated with the German pentecostals); it is involved in Bible School work and has a medical clinic at Kankan. It has not planted any churches but works with all existing Protestant churches. Eglise Mission Alpha (Church Mission Alpha) was started by Alpha Oumarbarry, a Fulbhe man who was sent to Switzerland by Sékou Touré on a grant to study. He was converted there and knew that he could not return to Guinea while Sékou Touré was alive. He started a mission in Burkina Fasso in 1982 but in 1987 was able to return to Guinea. There are two Mission Alpha churches in Conakry and one in Mamou. In 1994 a Congolese from Kinshasa started a Nzambe Malamu church in Conakry. The Eglise Pentecôtiste du Réveil (Pentecostal Revival Church) from the Central African Republic has planted a church of which Pastor Pascal is the head.

Pentecostal churches associated with the Association of Evangelical Churches and Missions of Guinea (Association des Eglises et Missions Evangélique de Guinea, AEMEG) include the Assemblées de Dieu de Guinée (AG–Guinea; associated with the French, Australian, Ivory Coast, and Burkina Fasso AGs and the Swedish Free Mission); the Eglise Pentecôtiste Alleluia (The Pentecostal Allelujah Church, associated with the PAOC); the Mission Kalimatou'llah (Kilima Mission—German Pentecostal Mission); Mission et Eglise Protestante Bible Overte (Open Bible Church and Mission-Pentecostal Church USA); and the Mission Alpha (Alpha Mission, Switzerland). The Eglise Evangélique Shekina (Shekina Evangelical Church) has not yet been admitted to the AEMEG due to questions over some of its practices.

2. Contemporary Challenges for the Church.

The pentecostal churches in Guinea are relatively new. The entire Protestant witness has not had a significant impact on this predominantly Muslim country where there are less than 50,000 believers in the entire country of over 8 million. Even in the capital of Conakry, the majority of members within the pentecostal and Protestant community are from the non-Muslim Forest peoples. Again, in the mountainous Futa Jalon (Mid-Guinea), which is home to the majority of the Fulbhe people, and in Upper Guinea, home to the Malenke (Maninka), both of whom are Muslim peoples, the churches have a majority of Forest peoples as members. Greater effort needs to be made to reach the Muslims as distinctive people groups.

The 1992 Bonnke crusade did much for Protestantism as a whole. Prior to that time the Guinean government only recognized the Catholics as representatives of Christianity when Christians were to be consulted on any issue; since that time Protestants have come to be seen as a separate body, distinct from Catholics.

Pentecostals need to make sure that they are not seen as representatives of "foreigners" in Guinea by adjusting the format of their services so that French speakers and members of the majority peoples of any area do not feel that they are excluded during worship and the preaching of the gospel by the predominance of languages that are not their own. At present this lack of sensitivity is apparent in many pentecostal services.

Special approaches to reach the Muslim population are needed. Traditional services are not going to draw them. Bridge building and friendship evangelism, together with an emphasis on the need for the work and gifts of the Holy Spirit are the only solution to this dilemma. Muslims have a mind-set that is directly opposed to the presuppositions of Christians, and only the power of the Holy Spirit will bring about the changes necessary for conversion. This means that concerted and consistent prayer is necessary to bring about the salvation of Guinea.

Because of the antagonism and vociferous opposition of some Muslim groups—as in Kankan, where the mayor has been pressured by the Islamic League not to allow any open-air preaching of the gospel nor the showing of the Jesus film (Campus Crusade for Christ)—a number of Protestant missionaries have become almost apologetic in their approach to evangelism. Pentecostals need to be bold in the presentation of the gospel, while relying on the power of the Holy Spirit

and his wisdom in times of conflict. In the Futa Jalon, home to the Fulbhe, open-air evangelism on market days and the showing of the Jesus film have been profitable, even where there has been some opposition.

[Note: The Fulbhe people are described variously in ethnic studies. Fulbhe is the name they ascribe to themselves. In French-speaking countries they are described as Peuls, Peuhls, or Peules; in English literature they are described as Fulani or Fula. They are an ethnic grouping of over 18 million, which reaches from Senegal in the west of the Sahel of Africa to Sudan and the Central African Republic in the East. Their language is Pular or Fula and has regional variations. The Fulbhe are Muslim and of Berber/Arab origin.]

■ **Bibliography:** Assemblées de Dieu, *75è Anniversaire des Assemblées de Dieu du Burkina Faso 1921–1996, Célébration du 12–15 Décembre 1996 à Ouagadougou* ■ P. Calzada, *Racontez ses merveilles: 40 ans de mission* [Viens et Vois] *(1997)* ■ P. Ellenberger, "Histoire de l'Oeuvre Missionnaire en Guinée," in *Premier Congrés National sur l'Evangélisation de la Guinée, Tenu du 25 au 29 avril 1988 à Télékoro,* ed. J. M. Koivogi (1988) ■ Interviews: Timothy Faya (pastor, AG–Guinea, Gueckédou, 1998); Michel Freyd (missionary, AG–France, Conakry, 1998); Carlo Frutiger (missionary, Mission Alpha, Mamou, Guinea, 1998); Hubert Gbenakou (vice president, AG–Guinea, Conakry, 1998); Kenneth Herschell (missionary, AG–Australia, Pita, Guinea, 1998) ■ Jérémie Kamano (pastor, AG–Guinea, Daboula, 1988); Philippe (pastor, Eglise Pentecôtiste Alleluia, Kankan, Guinea, 1998); Noufe Sambou (missionary, AG–Ivory Coast, Kankan, Guinea, 1998).   ■ D. J. Garrard

GUINEA-BISSAU

■ Pentecostals 347 (1%)   ■ Charismatics 4,928 (14%)   ■ Neocharismatics 29,025 (85%)   ■ Total Renewal: 34,300

See Africa, West.

GUYANA

■ Pentecostals 76,242 (61%)   ■ Charismatics 28,351 (23%)   ■ Neocharismatics 21,407 (17%)   ■ Total Renewal: 126,000

HAITI

■ Pentecostals 327,903 (22%)   ■ Charismatics 973,804 (65%)   ■ Neocharismatics 194,293 (13%)   ■ Total Renewal: 1,496,000

Pentecostalism in Haiti has a complex history and has played an interesting role in the interaction between African religious traditions, Creole Haitian traditions, and centuries of Catholic culture. The beginnings of pentecostalism in Haiti are apparently unknowable. It is reasonably certain that it was either an anonymous plant from the U.S. or an indigenous

interaction of Haitians with pentecostal ideas. It was not due to mission efforts of the North American denominations. The first known pentecostal evangelist was apparently Paulceus Joseph, a Haitian pastor converted to pentecostalism under the aegis of the Church of God in Christ (COGIC) in the U.S. He returned to Haiti in 1929 and established a mission in Port-au-Prince. One convert was Jacques Vital Herne (spelled various ways in the sources).

1. L'Eglise de Dieu.

In 1933 Vital Herne contacted Church of God (CG, Cleveland, TN) mission executives after he developed unresolvable conflicts with Joseph and other pentecostal pastors in Haiti. The CG general overseer, S. W. Latimer, visited Haiti in 1934 and officially accepted Vital Herne into the denomination. With the infusion of financial assistance, new chapels were opened in several towns outside Port-au-Prince. When Vital Herne attended the CG General Assembly in 1936, he reported 30 congregations.

In Jan. 1938 Herne was found guilty, apparently of doctrinal differences, and forced from the CG. At that point, two newly arrived independent pentecostal missionaries from the U.S., John and Stephanie Kluzit, were accepted into the church and appointed superintendents of the mission in Haiti under the direction of ►J. H. Ingram. Stephanie Kluzit was Haitian Creole and played a major part in the restoration and development of the mission. They began again with only 20 congregations, but by Dec. 1940 there were 37 congregations and 62 preaching stations.

In Aug. 1941 the president of Haiti was angered by derogatory comments made by a visiting CG pastor or executive from the U.S. He ordered the CG-related churches closed. The African Methodist Episcopal Church gave many congregations permission to worship on their premises. Not until 1943 was the ban lifted. At that time only 1,032 members of the earlier 3,214 remained. Others returned, however, and the history since has been one of steady growth. Particularly significant were the Bible-school work and youth educational efforts of James M. and Virginia Beaty. Haitian evangelists were empowered and developed powerful ministries, including Rémus Arbouet, Jules Deshommes Bernard Lacombe, Robert Marthurin, and Domany Rubens. By 1959 the CG in Haiti, the Eglise de Dieu, reported about 10,000 members, 30,000 adherents, and 140 congregations. By 1980 there were more than 20,000 members and 40,000 adherents in 390 congregations. The Eglise de Dieu is probably the largest pentecostal ministry in Haiti.

2. L'Eglise de Dieu de Prophétie.

The Church of God of Prophecy began work in Haiti in the 1930s and has grown significantly. In 1980 the Eglise de Dieu de Prophétie reported more than 16,000 members, 34,000 adherents, and 249 congregations.

3. Les Assemblées de Dieu.

Lawrence Perrault, who would later serve in the Dominican Republic, first attempted, unsuccessfully, missionary work in Haiti in 1945. He was, however, contacted in 1957 by some churches disenchanted with other mission agencies. Robert and Arletta Turnbull were transferred from the

Baby in mother's arms in Haitian Pentecostal country church (September 22, 1974).

Dominican Republic in Jan. 1959. Robert Turnbull became the first Assemblies superintendent. At Petionville, 8 miles from Port-au-Prince, Turnbull founded a church, Turnbull Memorial Bible School, and residences for missionaries. Missionaries Homer and Dorothy Specter worked (1960–64) to establish a congregation in Port-au-Prince. By 1962 there were 8 congregations and 15 "outstations." The denomination counts 57,000 "members and adherents," among which are 14,500 "baptized adults" (1999).

4. Other Pentecostal Churches.

Other churches with North American connections include the Eglise de Dieu en Christ, the Pentecostal Assemblies of the World, and the United Pentecostal Church (UPC). The latter established the Eglise Pentecôtiste Unie, which claims 24,698 members in 288 congregations (1998). The UPC in Haiti was founded by Glen Smith in 1968. The first resident UPC missionaries did not arrive until 1978. The denomination has been quite indigenous from the beginning, which may in part account for its rapid growth.

The charismatic evangelists from the U.S. have had an important influence in Haiti ever since the early 1960s. Crusades by the "healing evangelists" were particularly successful. In addition, there are a large number of foreign-based independent pentecostal and charismatic ministries in Haiti that provide food, orphanages, education, and ministerial education. Missionaries have come from various European countries, especially France, Belgium, and Switzerland. Prominent among the ministries extended from the U.S. has been ►Christ for the Nations (which maintains a Bible school in Haiti) and related ministries.

■ **Selected Bibliography:** Anon., "Een Opwekking in Haiti," *De Pinksterboodschap* 1 (5, Sept. 1960) ■ Anon., *Haiti* (Springfield, MO, c. 1960) ■ D. B. Barrett, *World Christian Encyclopedia* (1982), 348–51 ■ D. L. Burk, ed., *Foreign Missions Insight: A Digest of For-*

eign Missions Faces, Facts, Fields and Figures (1999), 78–79 ■ M. J.C. Calley, *God's People: West Indian Pentecostal Sects in London* (1965) ■ C. W. Conn, *Like a Mighty Army: A History of the Church of God* (1955; rev. 1977) ■ idem, *Where the Saints Have Trod: A History of Church of God Missions* (1959) ■ J. F. Conway, "Pentecostalism in the Context of Haitian Religion and Health Practices" (diss., American U., 1978) ■ Division of Foreign Missions [AG], *1999 Annual Statistics* (1999) ■ L. E. Frazier, "The Missionary Role in the Church of God with Emphasis on Roles in Haiti" (paper, CG School of Theology, 1986) ■ J. V. Herne, "Haiti Convention," *Church of God Evangel* (Sept. 29, 1934), 8 ■ W. J. Hol-

lenweger, "Handbuch der Pfingstbewegung" (diss., Zurich, 1967), 1045–52 (para. 02b.16) ■ P. Humphrey, *J. H. Ingram, Missionary Dean* (1966) ■ J. H. Ingram, *Around the World with Gospel Light* (1938) ■ G. Lindsay, "Native Church Crusade Sparks Evangelism in Haiti," *Voice of Healing* (June 1964) ■ [H. McCracken], *History of Church of God Missions* (1943) ■ E. L. Simmons, *History of the Church of God* (1938) ■ J. H. Walker Jr. et al., *L'Eglise de Dieu: enseignements et organisations* (1949) ■ J. H. Walker Jr. and L. Walker, *Haiti: Its Land, Its People, Its Religion and the History of the Church of God in Haiti* (1950).   ■ D. D. Bundy

HONDURAS

■ Pentecostals 199,438 (23%)   ■ Charismatics 531,984 (62%)   ■ Neocharismatics 128,578 (15%)   ■ Total Renewal: 860,000

See LATIN AMERICA.

HUNGARY

■ Pentecostals 11,202 (2%)   ■ Charismatics 514,103 (75%)   ■ Neocharismatics 164,694 (24%)   ■ Total Renewal: 689,999

See EUROPE, EASTERN.

ICELAND

■ Pentecostals 878 (4%)   ■ Charismatics 18,109 (79%)   ■ Neocharismatics 4,013 (17%)   ■ Total Renewal: 23,000

▶Thomas B. Barratt introduced pentecostalism to Iceland in 1920. His ministry was followed up by other Norwegian and Swedish evangelists who visited the country from 1920 to 1936.

The largest pentecostal church in Iceland, Filadelfia in Reykjavik, was founded in 1936 with Eric Ericsson as the first pastor. Later the church was served by Asmundur Eiriksson, Einar Gislason, and Haflidi Kristinsson. The present pastor is Vördur Levi Traustason. In 1957 a sanctuary was built that seats 500. Membership stood at about 600 in 1997.

Currently, the pentecostal movement is the third-largest religious movement in Iceland and comprises 6 independent churches and 12 auxiliary churches with a total membership of 1,200. These churches have outreach ministries in numerous locations around the island. The churches are governed collectively by a board of elders. Laymen are actively involved in the church ministry. While the movement has no central committee, the pastors of the six independent churches (ordained, with credentials recognized by the government) form an administrative council that represents the movement as a whole. The annual meeting is held in March.

The Pentecostal Church of Iceland (PCI) is involved in diverse mission activities and evangelistic work. The church has supported missionary work for several decades and has sent missionaries to England, Hungary, and Africa. These

missionaries act as representatives of the Icelandic church while working in close affiliation with other missionary societies in Scandinavia and Canada.

Most of the evangelistic outreach efforts are geared toward founding churches in new locations. The new groups of believers come under the pastoral care of the nearest pentecostal church until leaders are found who can take care of the work for a minimum of two years.

A Christian nonprofit organization, Samhjalp, was established in 1973, based on a Swedish model pioneered by the ▶Lewi Pethrus Foundation. Samhjalp operates a treatment facility for alcoholics and drug abusers and participates in a wide range of medical and social relief work. The program is carried out under the National Health Service of Iceland. Although Samhjalp is governed independently, it is an integral part of the Filadelfia Church of Reykjavik.

Radio Lindin, a nonprofit Christian radio station, was established in Mar. 1995. The ministry began under the leadership of Mike and Sheila Fitzgerald, Assemblies of God missionaries to Iceland. Lindin broadcasts to 75% of Iceland's population 24 hours a day, 7 days a week. In 1996 some 14,000 prayer requests were received from listeners.

A Bible school is held each year for a three-month period. This short-term theological education has become very popular, since it is both practical and economical. The program is arranged in cooperation with the World Horizon Mission.

The school has an international flavor, since a number of students come from foreign countries. The lectures are given jointly by Icelandic and foreign teachers, and occasionally training courses are held abroad. In addition, students gain practical experience in mission trips, which are conducted in collaboration with the local pentecostal congregations.

The PCI have a conference center in Kirkjulækjarkot, in the southern part of Iceland. The center offers accommodations for 120 participants, dining facilities for 300, and an assembly hall for 70 to 80. A large assembly hall with a seating capacity of 6,000 was erected in 1996. All pentecostal conferences are held at Kirkjulækjarkot, and the Bible school, when in Iceland, is also conducted there.

The pentecostal movement in Iceland broadcasts meetings over the Internet. In addition, the churches are known for their effective work with young people. Some of the churches are operating preschools as a means of furthering children's evangelism. The first preschool was started in Akureyri in 1988.

■ L. Ahonen with T. Birgisson

INDIA

■ Pentecostals 1,263,041 (4%) ■ Charismatics 5,032,741 (15%) ■ Neocharismatics 27,234,219 (81%)
■ Total Renewal: 33,530,001

I. Pentecostal and Pentecostal-Like Movements (1860–1910)
  A. Tirunelveli and Travancore (1860–80)
  B. Revivals Across India (1905–6)
  C. Pentecostalism Across India (1906–10)

II. Development and Growth of Pentecostalism in India (1910–60)
  A. South India
  B. North India

III. The Second and Third Waves of Renewal (1960–Present)
  A. The Catholic Charismatic Movement
  B. The Neocharismatics
  C. Persecution

I. PENTECOSTAL AND PENTECOSTAL-LIKE MOVEMENTS (1860–1910).

Pentecostal and pentecostal-like movements in India preceded the development of 20th-century pentecostalism in North America and Europe by at least 40 years. Apart from the revival under Edward Irving in the U.K. in the early 1830s, the most prominent revivals of the 19th century characterized by the charismatic gifts of the Holy Spirit occurred in India. When modern pentecostalism began there in 1906, it developed independently from the influence of similar revivals in the West.

A. Tirunelveli and Travancore (1860–80).

Major revivals marked by restoration of the charismatic gifts, other paranormal or "pentecostal" phenomena, indigenous leadership, and evangelism, were reported in Tirunelveli (in present-day Tamil Nadu state) in 1860–61 and neighboring Travancore (in present-day Kerala state) in 1874–75.

The seeds of these movements can be traced to the pietistic influences of missionaries such as Wilhelm T. Ringeltaube, Carl T. E. Rhenius, Anthony Norris Groves, and many others. The Church Missionary Society (CMS) sent Rhenius (a Prussian missionary) out in 1814; Anthony Norris Groves, an independent missionary from England, arrived in 1833. Rhenius emphasized the principles of self-support and self-propagation for the Indian churches, and he ordained Indian catechists, which led to his discharge from the CMS. With Groves came instruction in the millennial eschatology and other teachings of the Plymouth Brethren (e.g., the imminent coming of Christ, hope for the outpouring of the Holy Spirit, spiritual gifts, and an egalitarian concept of ministry). He also pioneered the use of simpler "apostolic methods" in missions.

The awakening of 1860 in Tirunelveli began after news reached South India of revivals in the United States, England, and Ulster in 1857–59. The leader, John Christian Aroolappen, had been trained as an Anglican catechist by Rhenius and had been an understudy of Groves. The phenomena in the revival included prophecy, glossolalia, glossographia, and interpretation of tongues, as well as intense conviction of sin among nominal Christians, dreams, visions, signs in the heavens, and people falling down and/or shaking. Other noted features were restoration of the offices of apostle and prophet, evangelism, conversions of unbelievers, prayer for the sick, and concern for the poor. The appearance of the gifts of the Holy Spirit in the ministry of Aroolappen clearly indicated an open-ended expectation of the miraculous, based on expectancy of the outpouring of the Holy Spirit as predicted for the end times by the OT prophet Joel. The revival not only attracted Indian Christians, but British soldiers stationed in the region as well.

From the outset, the revival took an indigenous course. Missionaries and Western money had little or no influence. Evangelistic outreach involved men and women, the latter representing unmistakable evidence of pentecostal anticipation: daughters and female servants would prophesy (Joel 2:28–29; Acts 21:9). Evangelists, following the pattern of NT apostles and evangelists as modeled by Aroolappen, traveled "on faith" (without pledged support) and set their own itineraries.

Not surprisingly, the traditional control of "native" churches and clergy by paternalistic missionary societies left little room for such dispensing of authority as came with the Spirit's gifts (e.g., leadership [1 Cor. 12:28]). On one occasion, missionaries complained of believers who contended that they had received visions that revealed the names of 12 persons to be appointed as apostles and evangelists, and 7 as prophets; names of missionaries, however, did not appear. From the ethnocentric perspectives of many missionaries, Indian Christians required extended tutelage before they could assume control of their churches. Thus, missionaries believed that a sound English-language education in Western culture and theology must precede any attempt to evangelize in the vernacular. Only then could the door be opened to mass conversions and a Christian civilization in India. Little wonder, then, that they were unprepared for the evangelizing initiatives taken by Indian Christians affected by the revival. The subsequent number of conversions amazed the missionaries, some of whom approved the revival and its phenomena and then became disillusioned with its indigenous character. Others had condemned it from the beginning.

Through the influence of the Aroolappen family and their followers, the movement spread westward a decade later into nearby Travancore among CMS congregations and those of the Syrian Church of Malabar and met with considerable success. Prominent leaders there included two prophets, Kudarapallil Thommen and the Brahmin convert Justus Joseph, whose entire family had been converted under the ministry of CMS missionary Joseph Peet. Justus Joseph formed the Revival Church in 1875, which became known as the "Six Years Party" (also called the "Five and a Half Years Party"), because of a prophecy that Christ would return in 1881.

Like the previous one in Tirunelveli, this revival was indigenous in nature; notable highlights included the negation of caste and the composition of music by Indian believers. At first, missionaries applauded what they viewed as positive aspects but then questioned the appearance of glossolalia and other related spiritual phenomena. They also detected lingering traces of heathen culture in the lack of emotional restraint among participants. Complaints ranged from criticisms of independent and unordained clergy, the establishment of the prophetic office, the pronouncing of controversial predictions, to the growth of schismatic congregations. The Revival Church continued into the 20th century, though discredited and in considerably diminished proportions. By the time of the next awakening in 1905, evangelists and prophets such as John Christian Aroolappen and Justus Joseph had been largely forgotten or simply dismissed as misguided enthusiasts.

B. Revivals across India (1905–6).

Toward the close of the 19th century, radical evangelicals, noting the slow pace of conversions in the mission lands and awaiting the imminent return of Jesus Christ, wondered how the world could be evangelized in the time remaining. Told of the immensity of the mission task in India, the 1898 ▸Keswick Convention in England responded to the personal appeal of ▸Pandita Sarasvati Ramabai , one of India's foremost Christians, and prayed that God would raise up 200,000 Indian male and female evangelists to travel across the subcontinent sharing the gospel message. In late 1897 leaders of various mission agencies in India issued a special call to prayer for the conversion of the country, which became an annual call.

The growing popularity of Wesleyan Holiness and Higher Life teachings among many missionaries and Indian Christians across the country contributed to the spiritual awakening that began in 1905. For example, Methodist missionaries had gained inspiration from the holiness preaching of John S. Inskip and other leaders of the National Camp Meeting Association for the Promotion of Holiness as they toured in 1880–82. In conferences for college and university students in the mid 1890s, Robert P. Wilder, a founder of the Student Volunteer Movement for Foreign Missions and traveling secretary of the Indian Young Men's Christian Association (YMCA), accentuated the Higher Life view of the baptism in the Holy Spirit and called his listeners to seek for "power from on high" (Luke 24:49) to evangelize non-Christians.

Cook preparing chappatis at Junnar Boys Home, Junnar, India.

When revival fires burned in Wales in 1904, many interpreted this as the start of the worldwide outpouring of the Spirit as predicted in Joel 2:28–29. The revival immediately gained notoriety for public confessions of sin, prayer in concert, seeking the baptism in the Holy Spirit, vibrant singing, and remarkable changes in the moral behavior of tens of thousands of converts. Missionaries in India paid close attention to these reports and to those of other revivals. In Jan. 1905 the Methodist Press in Madras published a booklet in English on the awakening in Wales entitled *The Great Revival,* with translations in Tamil, Telugu, and (later) Kannada. Through newspapers, booklets, journals, and other mission periodicals, missionaries and Christians of major language groups kept abreast of the events.

In Mar. 1905 the earliest stirrings of revival occurred among tribal peoples in the Khassia Hills in the northeast, at Welsh Presbyterian mission stations. Believers there began confessing their sins in "prayer-storms" (hours spent in fervent and loud prayer) that pushed aside the traditional Western order of worship. Expectancy had also grown at Pandita Ramabai's Mukti Mission at Kedgaon in South India. In one of the most celebrated moments of the revival (in a story that underwent several redactions), the matron of a girls' dormitory rushed to the quarters of ʾMinnie F. Abrams, an administrator at the mission and sometime Methodist missionary, at 3:30 A.M. on June 29. Declaring that one of the girls had been baptized in the Holy Spirit and with "fire" (Matt. 3:11), she related how flames had engulfed the screaming girl and how she had run across the room for a pail of water, only to discover that the girl was not actually on fire. This "purifying flame" prompted confessions of sin and repentance among the other girls, and soon Mukti became a chief center of revival activity.

Mission publications carried stories of similar developments across India, providing coverage for an awakening that came to encompass Anglicans (CMS); Baptists; Danish Lutherans; members of the Christian and Missionary Alliance (CMA), London Missionary Society, Church of Scotland, Young Men's and Women's Christian Associations, and Poona and Indian Village Mission; Methodists; Open Brethren; Presbyterians; Reformed; Wesleyan Methodists (U.K.); and others. Along with confessions of sin and prayer-storms (the most striking features), other wonders and pentecostal-like phenomena captured attention: dreams, visions, signs in the heavens, reception of the "burning" work of the Holy Spirit, accounts of visible "tongues of fire," prophecies, and even miraculous provisions of food.

Child widows at Mukti Mission, India, rescued by Pandita Ramabai.

Two of the best-known publicists of the revival were J. Pengwern Jones and Minnie F. Abrams, a Presbyterian and a Methodist. Jones observed firsthand the events in the Khassia Hills and in the course of two years published many widely read reports. In May 1906 Abrams penned the first edition of her influential book, *Baptism in the Holy Ghost and Fire,* a popular exposition combining holiness and "Higher Life" teachings that urged Christians to seek for the post-conversionary baptism in the Holy Spirit for purification and empowerment in Christian witness. Two major Christian newspapers, the *Bombay Guardian* (Mumbai) and *Christian Patriot* (Chennai), as well as the Methodist periodical, *Indian Witness* (Lucknow and Calcutta), serialized it.

C. Pentecostalism across India (1906–10).

Though pentecostal-like phenomena had been present from the early months of the revival and there had been some discussion about the restoration of the gift of tongues, stories of believers speaking in tongues came later. Unrelated to pentecostal happenings in North America (e.g., ʾTopeka Revival [1901], ʾAzusa Street Revival [1906–9]), incidents of tongues took place two and three months after a CMS conference in Aurangabad in Apr. 1906, where Abrams had been the guest speaker. The testimony of a "pupil teacher" who returned home in June to the Zenana Bible and Medical Mission orphanage at Manmad sparked a revival where one or two girls likely spoke in tongues. The best-known episode, however, transpired in early July, when other girls returned from Aurangabad to a CMS boarding school in Bombay. Their enthusiasm stirred the students to prayer and confession of sins. Several girls spoke in tongues, including a nine-year-old named Sarah. Canon R. S. Heywood, thinking it might be analogous to the glossolalia on the Day of Pentecost, found someone who could interpret Sarah's words and who then announced that she was interceding in prayer for the conversion of Libya. This incident and probably others caused Maud Weist to editorialize in the Sept. 1906 issue of the *India Alliance* (CMA) that the gifts of the Holy Spirit, including that of tongues, had become prominent features in the revival.

Events at Manmad and Bombay were followed by reports of tongues at the Mukti Mission in late Dec. 1906. Having read about the Los Angeles revival in the pages of the *Apostolic Faith* (Los Angeles), Ramabai and Abrams acknowledged that this deeper work of the Holy Spirit had not yet been received at the mission. Before Christmas, seekers claiming divine enablement reportedly spoke for the first time in languages they had never studied, among them English, Kannada, and Sanskrit. Unintelligible or "unknown" tongues could also be heard. Several girls acquired the gifts of interpretation and prophecy and gifts of healings. Abrams herself testified to speaking in Hebrew; Ramabai did not speak in tongues but warmly commended the experience.

It is significant that pentecostalism emerged in India with important differences from the movement in the West. This becomes especially obvious in Abrams' second edition of her *Baptism in the Holy Ghost and Fire* (Dec. 1906), which mentions the restoration of tongues yet makes no reference to their utility for missionary preaching or their being required as evidence of baptism in the Holy Spirit, both of which were hallmarks of the classical pentecostal theology taught by the American pentecostal leader ›Charles F. Parham and his understudy ›William J. Seymour.

The arrival in Calcutta of ›Alfred G. ("A. G.") and Lillian Garr, missionaries from the Azusa Street revival, at the turn of 1907, changed the direction of the pentecostal movement in India. Alfred Garr believed that God had bestowed on him the Bengali language when baptized in the Holy Spirit, and Lillian thought she had received Tibetan and Mandarin. Both anticipated preaching in these languages. Their visit coincided with the end of a missionary conference in the city that featured two well-known "Higher Life" teachers, Otto Stockmayer and R. J. Ward. The gathering offered the Garrs the opportunity they wanted to tell of the recent happenings in Los Angeles. At the same time, they discovered that glossolalia among Indian Christians had preceded them. At the invitation of Pastor C. H. Hook, Garr then began to hold services at the historic Carey Baptist Chapel in Lal Bazaar, Calcutta. There he taught the pentecostal doctrine of tongues as conceived by Parham, stating unequivocally that without tongues one had not received the baptism in the Holy Spirit and could not be considered pentecostal.

Conflict naturally grew over his claim to speak in Bengali, insistence on tongues as necessary evidence of Spirit baptism, and his tolerance of what appeared to be unrestrained emotionalism in the services. Editorials and articles in the Methodist *Indian Witness* sharply condemned his claims and the meetings. Within a few weeks Garr modified Parham's doctrine on the utility of tongues but retained tongues as the indispensable sign of baptism in the Holy Spirit. Though still the "tongues of men and of angels" (1 Cor. 13:1), their function now centered on praise and intercessory prayer in the Spirit to God.

Prominent recipients of tongues in the services included Susan C. Easton, a veteran missionary with the Woman's Union Missionary Society of America for Heathen Lands, and ›Max Wood Moorhead, a Presbyterian missionary serving with the YMCA in Sri Lanka. The influence of the

revival in Calcutta continued to spread as Garr traveled across the country holding services and presenting the classical pentecostal doctrine of baptism in the Holy Spirit. Moorhead contributed by publishing *Cloud of Witnesses to Pentecost in India* (1907–c. 1910) and *World Wide Pentecost* (1907–?) to make his readership aware of the worldwide growth of the movement, report on developments in India, and correct the view on tongues held by missionaries such as Minnie F. Abrams and others, who objected to their absolute indispensability for Spirit baptism.

In the fall of 1907 the ministries of Garr and Moorhead, as well as the credibility of the pentecostal movement, received even greater criticism when they endorsed and promoted the prophecy of a Sri Lankan Christian woman who predicted on Sept. 23, 1907, that Colombo, Ceylon (Sri Lanka), would be destroyed by an earthquake on Oct. 17; this then would precede the complete destruction and disappearance of the island 10 months later. Understood as a seismic portent of the coming wrath upon unbelievers, some saw it as a parallel to the successful prediction of the San Francisco earthquake of 1906. As a result, approximately 2,600 people fled Colombo, with many seeking refuge in the interior of the country. Despite the embarrassment of the failed prophecy, the movement continued to grow.

Across the subcontinent, pentecostal revivals continued among missionaries and Indian believers affiliated with at least 15 mission agencies: CMS, American Baptist Mission, English Baptist Mission, Mukti Mission, Peniel Mission, Open Brethren, Salvation Army, Scandinavian Alliance, American Presbyterian, Woman's Foreign Missionary Union, Thibetan Mission, Poona and Indian Village Mission, Latter Rain Mission, Industrial and Evangelical Mission, and Young Women's Christian Association. The CMA may have been the agency most impacted, since 20 of its missionaries experienced glossolalia.

Approximately 1,000 people scattered across the country testified to speaking in tongues, including 60 missionaries serving at 28 mission stations. Significantly, the largest number of veteran missionaries in any one country to embrace the pentecostal gift of tongues lived in India. As a group, their level of professional training ranked above that of most pentecostals in other parts of the world. Prominent among them were Minnie F. Abrams, Max Wood Moorhead, ›Albert and Walter Norton, Kate Knight, Laura Gardner, ›Christian H. Schoonmaker, Maud Orlebar, Eveline A. Luce (later ›Alice E. Luce), Laura Radford, and Agnes Hill, among many others.

Women made notable contributions that included theological and missiological reflection. For example, Kate Knight (CMA) became an outspoken apologist for the movement; as a result, the Brethren writer G. H. Lang centered his *Modern Gift of Tongues: Whence Is It?* (1913) on condemning her beliefs. While Abrams also contributed to such reflection, she recruited six new women missionaries while on a promotional tour in the U.S. for the Mukti Mission to evangelize unreached peoples at Uska Bazar near the border of Nepal. To facilitate their endeavor, she organized the party as the Bezaleel Evangelistic Mission (Ex. 31:2–3) in about 1910, perhaps the only women's missionary society founded by pentecostals.

Most of the missionaries, however, remained with their agencies, possibly due to an unwillingness to accept the classical pentecostal view of tongues and/or lose their current missionary status. However, new pentecostal missionaries, convinced of the essential value of tongues for Spirit baptism and zealous to accomplish the evangelization of India, soon arrived from North America and Western Europe. Among the earliest from the U.S. was George E. Berg in 1908, a former missionary to India with connections to the Church of God (Holiness) and baptized in the Holy Spirit at Azusa Street. During these initial years, both veterans and newcomers gathered for special conferences to promote fellowship and spiritual renewal; one of the most noteworthy convened at Faizabad in 1910.

Although historians of the pentecostal movement have sometimes referred to the occurrence of tongues at the Mukti Mission in Dec. 1906, most have wrongly credited the Calcutta revival as the real beginning of pentecostalism in India. As a result, the earlier movement led in large part by Minnie F. Abrams became invisible.

II. DEVELOPMENT AND GROWTH OF PENTECOSTALISM IN INDIA (1910–60).

A. South India.

It is not surprising that South India has been more responsive than the North to pentecostalism. According to the 4th-century historian Eusebius, Christianity was planted there as early as the time of St. Thomas in A.D. 57. A strong Christian presence followed, with Marthoma (Mar Thoma) Syrian and Assyrian branches coexisting until the arrival of Roman Catholicism in 1600. In addition, the people of Travancore (later Kerala) were the most educated in all of India, and with the absence of adequate reading material in any language, they were eager to read early Malayalam and English pentecostal literature. The seedbed had been prepared for modern pentecostal awakenings.

George E. Berg, an independent American missionary of German descent, went to India in 1901 and returned to the U.S. in 1908. He attended the Azusa Street Mission, where he received the baptism in the Holy Spirit and spoke in tongues. Since he had already lived in India, he identified some of the languages spoken at the Azusa Street Mission as legitimate Indian languages. In 1908 he returned to India and lived in Bangalore, using it as a center for his work.

The first Assemblies of God (AG) missionary to South India was the veteran missionary to Africa, Mary Weems

Chapman. She traveled extensively, holding meetings in Bombay, Mukti, Dhond, and Bangalore, and finally settled in Madras in 1915, founding the pentecostal work there. While in Madras, a delegation from Travancore requested that she come there. This she did periodically, finally moving to Trivandrum after hearing of a disastrous flood in Travancore. In 1922 Spencer May from Wales, a British AG missionary, came to Trivandrum to join with Mrs. Chapman. Together they published the first Malayalam pentecostal magazine, the *Pentecostal Trumpet,* with a circulation in South Africa, the Gulf States, Ceylon, and Malaysia, as well as India.

▸Robert F. Cook received Spirit baptism at the Azusa Street Mission in 1908 while praying for his wife's healing. At that time he also felt called to India. He arrived in Bangalore as an independent missionary in 1913. While working with George E. Berg, Cook joined the AG and began working at Kottarakkara, Travancore. According to George P. Alexander, several years later Cook moved to Chengannur, where he founded Mt. Zion Bible Institute in June 1927 (Cook later claimed it was founded in 1922, when he began giving classes in his house).

When Robert Cook went on furlough to the U.S. in 1923, William M. Faux, foreign mission secretary of the AG, came to Travancore to conduct revival meetings. Recognizing the need for additional missionaries and Indian workers, Faux commissioned ▸John H. Burgess to begin a Bible college. Burgess founded Bethel Bible Institute (later College) in Mavelikara in June 1927, the year after his arrival in Travancore. It was the first permanent AG Bible college established outside the U.S. Shortly after Burgess's arrival in Mavelikara, Mary Chapman died, leaving him with the additional responsibility of her work. Missionaries Mildred Ginn and Lydia Graner, and later Ernest Sorbo, also served at Bethel. Bethel was relocated to Punalur in 1949.

In 1929 Robert Cook and Indian pastor ▸K. E. Abraham left the AG, choosing to work independently. Abraham separated from Cook in 1930, forming the Indian Pentecostal Church (IPC). Cook's congregations were known as the Malankara Full Gospel Church. Cook surrounded himself with a group of Indian missionaries who moved into Tamil-speaking Madras. From there the Malankara work spread to Telegu-speaking Mysore and Hindu-speaking regions to the north.

The Great Depression led Cook once again to consider affiliation with an American organization for support. In 1936 he joined with the Church of God (CG, Cleveland, TN), bringing those churches that were under his supervision with him.

Early pentecostal missionaries focused most of their attention on evangelistic work, but George Berg did establish five schools for children, each connected with a local church. Four such schools also were established by Robert

Cook. In general, however, most of the South Indian missionaries did not consider such charitable work as effective as direct evangelism coupled with the training of Indian evangelists and pastors.

Converts from other Christian groups, such as the Jacobites and Mar-Thomites, proved to be very useful as native pastors because they already had an understanding of the Scriptures. One of the earliest among this group was K. E. Abraham, who was training for ministry in one of the Syrian Christian churches when he received the baptism in the Holy Spirit under George Berg's ministry. Those who worked with John Burgess included A. J. John (from the Church of God, Anderson, IN), P. V. John (a Syrian Christian), C. Kunjummen (one of the first teachers at Bethel Bible Institute), and A. C. Samuel (the first Indian to lead the South India District of the AG).

At present the IPC is the largest pentecostal denomination in Kerala, with a total number of churches reaching 1,000 (over 4,400 throughout India). IPC has two ministerial training centers, Hebron Bible College and Salem Bible School. Beginning in 1953, the IPC suffered a split caused by disagreement over administrative matters. The new denomination was the Sharon Fellowship Church, centered at Tiruvalla, and led by P. J. Thomas; it emphasizes the education and feeding of abandoned and orphaned children.

Unlike other pentecostal groups, Ceylon Pentecostal Mission is an exclusivist group that has no relationship with other pentecostal groups or other Christian churches. Founded in Colombo by Paul Ramankutty in 1924, it has spread throughout Kerala establishing "faith homes." It has more women workers than men—perhaps because it demands clerical celibacy.

Elizabeth Simat, a missionary of the ‣United Pentecostal Church (UPC), came to Punalur, Kerala, from the U.S. in 1942. After the arrival of Ellis L. Scism and his family in 1949, UPC headquarters was moved to Adur, where the work flourished and a Bible College was established. At present the UPC headquarters for South India is located at Kodaikanal, Madras State (now Tamil Nadu).

Pentecostalism came to Madras State in 1907 when ‣Thomas Ball Barratt of Norway held revival meetings in the hill station, Coonoor. Shortly thereafter, Mary Weems Chapman and a colleague, "Sister Rodebaugh," began the work in Madras before Chapman moved to Travancore. Constance Swinfen Eady, at first an independent missionary before joining the newly formed AG, began pentecostal services in Yercaud in the Shevaroy Hills and in Bangalore, where she ran a missionary home and worked among the Tamils there. In 1948 Tamil Bible Institute was opened in Madura. In July 1951 Alfred Cawston inaugurated Southern Asia Bible Institute (later College) in Bangalore. Robert and Doris Maloney Edwards began a highly successful Industrial

School at Shencottah. W. E. Davis opened up the pentecostal work in the Malabar area.

After lagging behind neighboring Kerala for several decades, Tamil pentecostalism has experienced enormous growth during the past two decades. Leading the way has been New Life Assembly of God in Chennai (formerly Madras), led by ‣David Mohan. This congregation now has grown to over 15,000, with impressive outreach ministries including a "national highway scheme"—the planting of churches in towns and villages along national highway #45, stretching from Chennai to Cape Comorin (Kanniya Kumari).

Pentecostalism first came to the Marathi district (now Maharastra) in June 1905 at Pandita Ramabai's girls' orphanage at Mukti, where a pentecostal revival broke out, spreading from the orphanage to various parts of India and the world. The first pentecostal missionary to the Marathi was a Scotsman, Thomas Stoddart, who in about 1923 left North India and located in the city of Poona (Pune). There Stoddard joined the AG and ministered to Parsees, followers of Zoroaster, and British soldiers stationed there. Carl Holleman and ‣Ted and Estelle Vassar joined Stoddart in Poona in 1934. The Vassars took charge of the boys' orphanage and school at Junnar in 1947.

The Pentecostal Holiness Church first sent missionary Hobert Howard into Andra Pradesh in 1956, followed by Kenneth G. Donald, who arrived in Maruter in 1958 to work among the Telegus. In 1973 this work spread southward to Madras in Tamil Nadu. The Advanced Ministerial Training Program and a Bible College were established in Hydrabad to serve pastors from both North and South India.

The pentecostal churches in South India, particularly in Kerala, are sending missionaries to all parts of India and to Western countries, including the U.S., where Keralans have attempted to evangelize the Indian population. The most active group is the ‣Indian Pentecostal Church of God.

Minnie Abrams and coworkers engaged in evangelistic work, rescuing women and children in famine.

B. North India.

As we have observed, individual pentecostal missionaries, such as Alfred and Josephine Garr, came to North India shortly after the outbreak of revival at the Azusa Street Mission in Los Angeles, CA. The Garrs arrived in Calcutta in Jan. 1907 and began holding services. At about the same time a pentecostal revival broke out in the Elliot Road Orphanage in Calcutta under the ministry of Fannie Simpson, a Methodist missionary. Eventually Simpson was recalled by her bishop. She returned to India as an independent pentecostal missionary about 1915, establishing the girls' orphanage at Purulia.

These independent pentecostal missionaries purchased properties and opened mission stations in the larger cities along the railroad lines to facilitate their evangelism. Some of these early missionaries became associated with the AG when it was organized in 1914. But early missionary efforts in North India proved that the area was one of the world's hardest mission fields. While missionaries in the South experienced considerable growth, those in the North saw little fruit for their labors, and there seemed slight hope of establishing indigenous churches. More recently, missionaries have made concerted efforts to reach the larger cities.

Because of difficulties faced in evangelizing North India, early pentecostal missionaries turned to establishing institutions such as orphanages, industrial schools, elementary schools, correspondence schools, radio programs, leper asylums, and dispensaries. The AG has the most extensive system of institutional works (centered in the Gangetic plain), including an orphanage and girls' school at Bettiah; a girls' orphanage at Purulia; the James Harvey boys' school at Nawabganj; a leper work at Uska Bazar, begun in 1911 by Minnie Abrams; a coeducational Bible school at Hardoi; the "Baby Fold" at Rupaidiha; a girls' industrial school at Siswa Bazar; a men's Bible school at Laheria Sarai; and Childers Lodge, a Himalayan hill station operated as a missionary rest facility and revival center.

During the time that Fanny Simpson was in the U.S. after having been recalled by her Methodist bishop, she traveled as an evangelist. During a meeting at a Methodist church in Eastport, Long Island, she prophesied, laying hands on the head of a five-year-old boy, Maynard Ketcham, who later opened the AG work in the Bengali section of Eastern India, including the vast "swampland" now called Bangladesh.

By far the best-known AG work in all of India has been that of ▸Mark and Huldah Buntain in Calcutta. Beginning in 1953 with the "Mission of Mercy," which now feeds over 20,000 hungry mouths each day, the Buntains' work has expanded to a hospital, a school of nursing, a junior college, a vocational school, six village clinics, a hostel for destitute youth, a drug prevention program, and 12 schools that provide instruction for 6,000 children.

▸Fire-Baptized Holiness missionary Daniel Awrey visited India in 1910–11 with ▸Frank Bartleman (the chronicler of pentecostal origins in Los Angeles). In 1911 ▸J. H. King also visited India, receiving independent missionaries R. E. Massey and D. S. McHaffey into the ▸Pentecostal Holiness Church (PHC). A permanent PHC work was begun in 1920 under the leadership of J. M. Turner. Orphanages were established in Jasidih, Giridih and Jha Jha (boys), and Madhupur (girls). Later PHC missionaries moved into West Bengal, Orissa, and Uttar Pradesh. They also have begun works among the Paharia, Ho, Bihor, Munda, Oroan, and Kharia tribes.

The Church of God (CG, Cleveland, TN), established in South India in 1936, expanded into Central and Northern India in 1954 under the leadership of William Pospisil and T. M. Varghese. Churches also were established around Delhi and near Calcutta.

In 1959 Harry Scism, son of Ellis Scism, opened a work for the United Pentecostal Church (UPC) in Bhopal. Stanley Scism, son of Harry, now serves as a missionary in Delhi. At present Harry Scism is general director of the UPC Foreign Missions Board.

III. THE SECOND AND THIRD WAVES OF RENEWAL (1960–PRESENT).

A. The Catholic Charismatic Movement.

In 1972 Minoo Engineer, a young Parsi civil engineer who had been studying at Fordham University and had been converted to Catholicism through his involvement with charismatics, brought the Catholic charismatic renewal to India. In that same year, two Jesuit priests, Fr. Fuster and Fr. Bertie Phillips, who had been in the U.S. for studies and research, returned to India as charismatics. These early leaders formed prayer groups. The first of these began in Bombay (Mumbai) with only four members present. The movement spread to Bandra, encouraged by the Medical Mission Sisters of the Holy Family Hospital. The largest group was at St. Andrew's, led by Terence and Beryl Fonn and Sr. Bernadine. Other prayer groups were formed in Vile Parle and Juhu. The first of four groups formed in Byculla was in the Institute of Deaf Mutes in Mazagaon. There was a very active group in Mahim in the Presentation Convent with Sr. Basil and Margare D'souza. Fr. Fuster and Fr. Phillips started the ▸Life in the Spirit Seminars and prayer groups at St. Xavier's College.

Shortly thereafter the renewal spread to Poona (now called Pune) and to Goa. Then prayer groups emerged in Gauhati in Assam in the Air Force Colony (an interdenominational prayer group). The charismatic movement then came to Delhi, with prayer groups developing at St. Thomas's Parish and St. Dominic's Parish. Soon small prayer groups had spread throughout all of India.

In 1974–75 a group of 30 Catholic charismatic leaders met in Bombay to hold the first National Charismatic Convention; to begin a journal, *Charisindia,* to serve the renewal; to print the first edition of the *Praise the Lord* hymnal; and to nominate a service team for Bombay. The National Service Team is the apex body of national leaders with the threefold task of discernment, prophetic ministry, and service to the movement.

The leading Indian Catholic charismatic leader is ►Mathew Naickomparambil, a healing evangelist from Kerala, who was baptized in the Spirit in the early 1970s. In 1978 the first healing occurred through his ministry. In 1990 the Vincential order, to which he belongs, purchased a hospital in Muringoor near Chalakudy to form the Divine Retreat Center. Large crowds flock to Muringoor to attend weeklong programs led by Naickomparambil and his associates. In 1992 he first visited the U.S. and has ministered since at healing conferences there.

B. The Neocharismatics.

Among the largest renewal groups in India are the ►third wave or ►neocharismatics. With few exceptions, these are indigenous bodies. The largest is the New Apostolic Church founded in 1969, with adherents totaling 1,448,209 in 1995. This group established a Kenya mission in 1973. Already described above is the second largest, the IPC (founded in 1924), with about 900,000 adherents throughout India and 10 other countries. Others include the New Life Fellowship (founded in 1968), now with about 480,000 adherents; the Manna Full Gospel churches and ministries (with origins c. 1968 and connections to Portugal), now with 275,000; the Nagaland Christian Revival Churches (1952, pentecostal splits from Nagaland Baptists), now with 260,000; Christ Groups (c. 1970, known for literature campaigns) with 233,000; Omega Full Gospel Assembly (c. 1960, in Karnataka) with 230,000; Believers Church in India (founded by K. P. Yohanan c. 1960) with 200,000; and 40 other independent ►Oneness bodies, many with U.S. connections, with 200,000 adherents. The total of Indian believers in the Neocharismatic denominations is 15,345,340. Millions more are in older independent Christian churches, such as the Mar Thoma Syrian Church, or are nonbaptized believers in Christ. Unfortunately, most of these groups are so new and independent that they have not yet been adequately studied. Typically, scholars have not risen in their ranks, and they have been treated by outsiders merely as "Indian indigenous churches."

C. Persecution.

Indian Christians of all varieties, especially the more aggressive Pentecostals and Catholic charismatics, have experienced

Ernest Komanapalli, the neocharismatic founder of Mana Church in Andra Pradesh, India.

severe persecution by radical Hindu groups in recent years. Atrocities have ranged from the beheading of Catholic priests and the raping of nuns to the destruction of churches, the exhuming of Christian bodies from cemeteries, the beating of AG believers in Annaipalayan, the burning of Bibles, and the parading of Christians naked through towns and villages. In response, virtually all Christian groups have united in the formation of an "All India United Christian Voice" to conduct mass rallies and to issue joint press releases.

Sadly, this spirit of cooperation has only emerged under duress and shows little signs of permanence. India may well have been the first country to experience the modern pentecostal outpouring. Indian pentecostalism has been weakened, however, by frequent divisions and by noncooperation between various Christian groups as well as between missionaries and Indian leaders. Notwithstanding, modest growth continues, especially among charismatic and independent pentecostal groups.

■ Bibliography:

I. Pentecostal and Pentecostal-like Movements (1860–1910). ***A. Tirunelveli and Travancore.*** C. M. Agur, *Church History of Travancore* (1903) ■ E. B. Bromley, *They Were Men Sent from God* (1937) ■ A. N. Groves, *Memoir of Anthony Norris Groves,* 3d ed. (1869) ■ J. C. Kurundamannil, "Yuomayam: A Messianic Movement in Kerala, India" (diss., Fuller, 1978) ■ G. H. Lang, *The History and Diaries of an Indian Christian (J. C. Aroolappen)* (1939) ■ J. E. Orr, *Evangelical Awakenings in India* (1970) ■ "The Religious Awakening in Travancore," *Indian Evangelical Review* 4 (Apr. 1874): 397–410 ■ W. J. Richards, "The 'Six Year's Party' in Travancore," *Church Missionary Intelligencer and Record* (Nov. 1882), 660–67.

B. Revivals and Pentecostalism across India (1905–10). M. F. Abrams, *Baptism of the Holy Ghost and Fire,* 2d ed. (1906) ■ idem, "Brief History of the Latter Rain Revival of 1910," *Word and Work* (May 1910), 138–41 ■ idem, "Mukti Mission," *Mukti Prayer-Bell* (Sept. 1907), 17–23 ■ H. S. Dyer, comp., *Revival in India, 1905–1906* (1907) ■ "The Fyzabad [Faizabad] Conference," *Cloud of Witnesses to Pentecost in India* (July 1910), 10–14 ■ B. F. Lawrence, *The Apostolic Faith Restored* (1916) ■ G. B. McGee, "' Latter Rain' Falling in the East: Early-Twentieth-Century Pentecostalism in India and the Debate over Speaking in Tongues," *Church History* 68 (Sept. 1999) ■ idem, "Pentecostal Phenomena and Revivals in India: Implications for Indigenous Church Leadership," *International Bulletin of Missionary Research* 20 (July 1996).

II. Development and Growth of Pentecostalism in India (1910–60). ***A. South India.*** K. E. Abraham, *Yesucristhuvinte Eliya Dasan Athava Pastor K. E. Abraham* (1965) ■ G. P. Alexander, "Development of the Church of God in India" (unpub. paper, 1980) ■ J. H. Burgess, personal papers and unpub. history of pentecostalism in South India ■ C. W. Conn, *Like a Mighty Army: A History of the Church of God* (1996) ■ idem, *Where the Saints Have Trod: A History of Church of God Missions* (1959) ■ R. Cook, *Half a Century of Divine Leading and 37 Years of Apostolic Achievements in South India* (1955) ■ E. Holley, *Apostolic Sentinel* (Texas District of the UPC) 10 (10, Dec. 1966) ■ P. D. Johnson, *Promise Fulfilled* (n.d.) ■ M. Kumar, *This Is Our South India (Pentecostal Holiness Church)* (1983) ■ T. Stoddart, "Pentecostal Blessings in South India," *PE* (May 7, 1932) ■ M. A. Thomas, *An Outline History of Christian Churches and Denominations in Kerala* (1977) ■ H. G. Varghese, *K. E. Abraham: An Apostle from Modern India* (1974) ■ T. P. Varghese, *A Historical Analysis of the Growth and Development of the Pentecostal Churches in Kerala with Special Reference to the Church of God (Full Gospel) in India* (1982) ■ T. Vassar, personal papers (1934–75).

B. North India. Anon., "Pentecostal Holiness Church in India" (n.d.) ■ H. Howard, *A Brief History of the India Work* (1999) ■ H. Hunter, "International Pentecostal Holiness Church," *Acts of Pentecost* (Seoul, 1998) ■ J. Mueller, *With Our Missionaries in North India* (1937).

III. The Second and Third Waves of Renewal (1960–Present).
A. Catholic Charismatic Movement. J. Duin, "India's 'Billy Graham' Is Catholic," *Charisma* (Nov. 1994).

B. Neocharismatics. R. Hedlund, "Indian Christians of Indigenous Origin and Their Solidarity with Original Groups," *Journal of Dharma* 24 (1, 1999) ■ idem., "Indian Instituted Churches: Indigenous Christianity Indian Style," *Mission Studies* 16 (Jan. 13, 1999) ■ idem, "Subaltern Movements and Indian Churches of Indigenous Origins," *Journal of Dharma* 23 (1, 1998).

C. Persecution. *Times of India, Bangalore* (Nov. 8, 1998).

■ G. B. McGee (1860–1910);
S. M. Burgess (1910–present)

INDONESIA

■ Pentecostals 1,395,797 (15%)   ■ Charismatics 971,415 (10%)   ■ Neocharismatics 7,082,789 (75%)   ■ Total Renewal: 9,450,001

From its humble beginnings in 1921, the pentecostal movement has grown to become a dominant force in Christianity in Indonesia. Accurate data on the actual size of the pentecostal denominations is difficult to obtain, since most churches in Indonesia are reluctant to publicize accurate data on their growth for fear of reprisals from the dominant religion or reaction from the government. According to David Barrett, there were 1,959,000 members in the pentecostal denominations he listed in 1980. These statistics are very conservative. Even if the totals were accurate, at least 10 pentecostal denominations were not listed. Also significant is the continued growth of the pentecostal/charismatic churches over the last decade. For example, the Gereja Sidang Jemaat Allah (Assemblies of God) has more than doubled in the last 10 years. A new church that grew out of the ▸Full Gospel Business Men's Fellowship, Gereja Betani (not mentioned by Barrett), now has congregations of more than 10,000 in several cities on Java. From my observation the pentecostal denominations are by and large the fastest-growing churches in Indonesia, constituting perhaps more than half of all evangelical Christians in Indonesia.

1. A Brief History of Christianity in Indonesia.

Pentecostals were rather late arrivers in Indonesia. The first known missionaries associated with the pentecostal movement arrived in Indonesia in 1921, 400 years after Portuguese sailors brought the message of Christianity to the Spice Islands, the Moluccas. (There is a speculation that Nestorian merchants brought Christianity to the island of Sumatra as early as the 8th century, but very little evidence remains to suggest that there was a community of believers that continued into the following centuries.)

Van den End divides the history of Christianity in Indonesia into three main periods. The first period was 1522–1800. During this period, two colonial governments, first the Portuguese and then the Dutch, played a major role in both the propagation of Christianity as well as church government. Although the Portuguese priests and Dutch chaplains represented radically different streams of Christianity, there are interesting similarities in their approach to propagating Christianity among "the natives." Both saw their main task as the spiritual care of the European colonialist. The Christianization of the "natives" was merely an afterthought for most of these early missionaries (with some notable exceptions, such as Francis Xavier). It is thus not surprising that the church that took root in this period was heavily dominated by European culture. What is astonishing is that Christianity became a dominant force in the Malucca Islands and was introduced throughout the coastal areas of the eastern end of the Indonesian archipelago.

The church in Indonesia entered a new era around the year 1800. Several political and religious changes had great impact on Christianity. There was a transfer of power in Dutch colonial government with the dissolution of the Vereenigde Oost-Indische Compagnie (United East India Company) in 1799. The king of Holland (and then, in 1864, the parliament) began to exercise direct rule over the colonies. Hence, political currents in Europe had a direct effect on Indonesia. Most significant for the church was the effect of the Enlightenment (Van den End, 1987, 145). The government began to take a neutral stance toward religion, and government support of religious workers declined. In many regions pastoral care diminished as Dutch missionaries returned to the Netherlands. However, new mission structures emerging in Europe as a result of the Pietistic revival began sending missionaries to Indonesia. One of the most influential of these was the Nederlandsch Zendelinggenootschap (Dutch Missionary Society), which sent more than 95 workers to Indonesia in 1813–94.

New structures, new methods of evangelism, and new life in the church began with the coming of a new breed of missionaries who had experienced the "fire" of the revival in Europe (Van den End, 1989, 142). Christianity made new inroads among animistic people groups in North Sumatra, Borneo (Kalimantan), North Celebes (Sulawesi), and the remainder of the islands of Eastern Indonesia.

Ironically, Islam also gained new strength and dominance in the 19th century. Opposition to Dutch rule spread. Islam became the rallying point for those opposed to foreign dominance, and resistance to Christianity in the areas that were predominantly Islamic increased. In order to insure peace—and productivity—the Dutch colonial government prevented missionary activity among adherents to Islam. This policy, which also applied to the Hindus of Bali, resulted in much of Sumatra, Java, Madura, Lombok, and southern Celebes being virtually "off-limits" to evangelism until the 20th century.

The third main period of Indonesian church history began in the 1930s. This new chapter was marked by significant changes in church leadership structure. The older Protestant churches became self-governing. A centralized hierarchy was exchanged for a presbyterian system. More importantly, Christianity began to break out of its traditional geographic boundaries. Churches sprang up even in the more Islamic regions, making Christianity one of the national religions of Indonesia.

The 1930s also marked a new trend in the missionary personnel being sent to Indonesia. European sending agencies began to decline, while North American–based mission societies intensified their efforts to place workers in Indonesia. American evangelicalism began to be a dominant outside force that changed the personality of Christianity in Indonesia. The majority of the rapidly increasing number of denominations and church organizations during this period trace their roots back to North American missions and church agencies. In general, the growth rate of these evangelical churches has surged since the 1930s, while the more traditional Protestant denominations dating back to the 19th century have grown at a more moderate rate.

2. Early Pentecostal Missions.

For at least 14 years prior to the arrival of the first pentecostals in Indonesia, those impacted by the pentecostal message in North America had begun to propagate their teaching in other countries. According to Gary McGee, over 185 pentecostal missionaries from North America alone had traveled overseas by 1910 (McGee, 612). Most of them were in some way linked to the revival at the ►Azusa Street Mission in Los Angeles that took place from 1906 to 1908. A deep burden for the lost and a powerful sense of urgency characterized the testimonies of the thousands that came under the influence of the early pentecostal movement. Pentecostal historian L. Grant McClung Jr. writes, "Motivation for lost souls and the preaching of the gospel to all the world flowed from a life in the Spirit and the literal instruction and modeling of Scripture, particularly the book of Acts" (McClung, 8). From its inception the pentecostal movement was a missionary movement.

There were several distinct groups among these early pentecostal missionaries. Some were veterans formerly serving with other mission agencies. Others were graduates of the Bible institutes associated with the pentecostal movement that began appearing throughout the U.S. Probably the majority of those early pentecostal missionaries ventured abroad with very limited financial resources, little preparation, and almost no knowledge of the language and culture of the people they were attempting to evangelize. Most could testify to a supernatural vision or revelation of their call and place of service. Many believed that God would supernaturally give them fluency in the language of their hearers (xenolalia). Their zeal was astounding, but their success ratio was rather low, especially before 1920 (McGee, 613).

3. The Beginnings of the Pentecostal Movement in Indonesia.

In Mar. 1921 two missionary families arrived in Jakarta aboard the ship *Suwa Maxu*: Cornelis and Marie Groesbeek and Dirkrichard and Stien van Klaveren. Details about them are rather sketchy, but we do know that they were in their early-to-mid-40s when they arrived in Indonesia. They were born in Holland but apparently had lived for some time in the Seattle, WA, area. As officers in the Salvation Army, they came in contact with the pentecostal message at a tent-revival meeting in 1919 near Seattle. A year later God spoke to them in a vision and said they were to go to Java, where they would pioneer a work that would become the center for a great harvest of souls (Sumual, 44). It is probable that they had some contact with Indonesia, due to the fact that it was still under Dutch rule and there were thousands of Dutch families here.

The Groesbeeks and Van Klaverens were sent out by Bethel Temple in Seattle, a thriving independent pentecostal church pastored by an Englishman named W. H. Offiler. When Pastor Offiler heard about the calling of these Dutch families who were former Salvation Army officers, he committed to help sponsor them. Offiler and Bethel Temple played a significant role in pentecostal missions in Indonesia, because eventually at least six other missionaries would be sent to Indonesia by this same church (Sumual, 45).

Upon arriving in Jakarta, the Groesbeeks and Van Klaverens immediately booked passage to Bali. In Denpasar, Bali, they rented a dilapidated building that had been used as a copra warehouse (copra is dried coconut meat from which coconut oil is derived). It served both as housing for the two families and as a meeting hall for their evangelistic efforts. The facilities were rather simple, with plywood walls installed as a partition for bedrooms and a small kitchen. The roof leaked, and the only way to reach the building was walking along a muddy path through a rice field.

The missionaries employed a Dutch-speaking Balinese man, who began helping them translate the gospel of Luke into Balinese. He also served as an interpreter for the evangelistic services they promptly began to hold in the copra warehouse.

From the outset the emphasis in their preaching was Jesus the Healer. Apparently the Balinese were interested in this strange new teaching, because they began to attend the evangelistic meetings. (We don't have exact figures as to how many actually attended, but the fact that they had any response at all is amazing, since traditionally the Balinese have been very resistant to the gospel. For example, the first Dutch missionary to Bali had one convert after 17 years of ministry. Then, in 1881, that missionary was murdered by his convert.) Many sick were brought to the services and prayed for by the evangelists. On one occasion a leper was brought to the meetings; and to the horror of the Balinese, the missionaries began washing his wounds. Apparently they didn't know it was actually leprosy. He was then anointed with oil and prayed for and was completely healed.

Opposition developed from the Balinese neighbors near the copra warehouse toward these strange foreigners, although it appears that on several occasions divine intervention silenced the opposition. There is no evidence that the efforts of these early pentecostal missionaries resulted in a congregation of believers. Had they been permitted to stay in Bali, they undoubtedly could have started a church, but in Jan. 1922, just 10 months after their arrival, the Groesbeeks and Van Klaverens were ordered by the Dutch government to leave Bali. (It is doubtful that they ever had official permission to serve in Bali, since the government forbade all Christian evangelistic activity on Bali.) The large city of Surabaya on the northeast coast of Java became their next target of ministry.

Upon arriving in Surabaya, the pentecostal missionaries began to fellowship with some of the Dutch evangelical Christians who were associated with an organization called Bond van Evangelisatie (Alliance for Evangelism). They were well received by this group and were even asked to preach. After several months in Surabaya the two families separated. The Van Klaverens moved to the town of Lawang in the mountains south of Surabaya, while the Lord opened a door for the Groesbeeks to start a church in the town of Cepu, about 200 kilometers east of Surabaya. Once again a miraculous healing was the impetus for an open door of ministry. Groesbeek was

instrumental in healing a woman who a few days later approached the Groesbeeks and requested them to accompany her to meet her son, George Van Gessel, who was employed by a large Dutch oil company in Cepu. This led to an invitation for the Groesbeeks to lead a weekly meeting in the home of the Van Gessels in Cepu. The nucleus of a church was formed, starting with about 10 people and growing to about 40 by the end of the year. The majority of those attending were Dutch, some were Indo (a mixture of Dutch and Indonesian), but apparently a couple of Dutch-speaking Indonesians were impacted by the meetings in the Van Gessel home. Many experienced encounters with the power of the Holy Spirit, resulting in glossolalia. Manifestations of the gifts of the Spirit were common in the meetings, and several miraculous healings took place. Probably the most significant result of this period of Groesbeek's ministry in Cepu was an imparting of his vision to others who had come in contact with his pentecostal doctrine. At least 10 people who had been involved in the Cepu meetings eventually became active in some type of ministry (among them were the Van Gassels, the Van Loons, the Lumoindongs, the Hornungs, and A. E. Siwi, who were all instrumental in carrying the pentecostal message to different parts of Indonesia).

In Mar. of 1923 Groesbeek led 13 people from his new congregation into water baptism by immersion. Most had been sprinkled as infants in the Dutch Reformed Church, but Groesbeek insisted that believer's baptism by immersion is the only valid biblical pattern. The baptismal formula was also important to Groesbeek. They were baptized "in the name of the Father, the Son, and the Holy Spirit, that is the Lord Jesus Christ," a formula reflecting the "Jesus Only" or ▸Oneness Pentecostalism espoused by Offiler's Bethel Temple in Seattle, WA.

Toward the end of 1923 Groesbeek returned to Surabaya. The pastoral leadership of the Cepu congregation was turned over to Van Gessel. Groesbeek then concentrated his evangelistic ministry in a storefront building in an area called Tunjungan in Surabaya. The Van Klaverens also returned to Surabaya and began holding services in the Sindunegara area. They continued to witness miracles, especially in healing the sick.

On one occasion the police were sent to investigate this "new religion." The policeman arrived at the service with pen and notebook in hand. His heart began to be stirred by the enthusiastic singing and the vibrant testimonies. At the end of the sermon he repented of his sins and trusted Christ as Savior. When he returned to the police station he turned in this succinct report on the pentecostal church service: *"Alles is goed"* ("All is well").

Between 1924 and 1926 a number of Indonesian young people came to Christ through the evangelistic efforts of the pentecostal missionaries. Young men by the names of Runkat, Lesnusa, Rantung, Jokom, and Mamahit experienced powerful conversions during this period. These and many others who were impacted by the pentecostal message during these years eventually became the backbone of leadership of the pentecostal movement, especially when the missionaries were interned during the Japanese occupation in WWII.

4. The Spread of Pentecostalism.

Within a decade of the establishing of the small, predominantly Dutch congregation in the small town of Cepu, the pentecostal message was disseminated throughout the areas of Indonesia that had previously been influenced by Christianity. Pentecostal congregations sprang up throughout the archipelago, first through the network of the Dutch who had attended the Cepu meetings, then through the Indonesians who had come to Christ in Surabaya.

Wenink Van Loon began propagating divine healing in Bandung, West Java, in 1926. A congregation was then established with Van Loon as pastor. An elderly couple named Hortsman, who lived in Temanggung in Central Java, opened their home to Groesbeek. When he preached there, many received the baptism of the Holy Spirit. Among them was M. A. Alt, a single female missionary serving in the nearby area of Gambangwalu. The Hortsmans' son Han, who at that time was a university student, was also among them and became ignited with a passion to preach the gospel. He then became the pastor of the Temanggung congregation and eventually moved to Malang, where he pastored one of the larger pentecostal churches.

Indonesian young people consumed with an evangelistic zeal were sent out to North Sumatra, North Sulawesi, Ambon, and Timor. Pentecostal churches were planted in all these areas by 1930. Even in cities like Bukittinggi and Pelembang (Central and West Sumatra), where the Christian presence was small, they experienced great responsiveness to their gospel message accompanied by "signs and wonders."

In the late 1920s pentecostalism also began to be received among the Chinese. Ong Ngo Tjwan was converted in Surabaya. After his training and discipleship at a Bible study lead by Van Gessel (who had moved to Surabaya in 1926), he began holding evangelistic crusades in Surabaya that were attended by thousands (mostly Chinese) The Lord used him powerfully in miracles of healing. There were reports of blind people receiving their sight, the deaf hearing, and lame people walking. Broken homes were mended, and many people were baptized into the faith (Sumual, 65).

Even more influential than Ong Ngo Tjwan in reaching large numbers of Chinese was a young evangelist from China by the name of John Sung. Upon the invitation of the pentecostals in Surabaya, he came to Indonesia in 1939. He held large crusades in the major cities throughout Java as well as in Udjung Pandang (Sulawesi) and Ambon. Thousands came to hear him preach with great fervor. He prayed for the sick, but he is most noted for his altar calls. He would quote specific sins that he felt the listeners had committed. Great con-

viction would fall on the hearers, and many would repent. He was in Indonesia only three months, but his impact was significant. Perhaps his greatest legacy is the number of young Indonesian evangelists he inspired to reap the harvest through mass evangelism (Willem, 1987).

There is no record of great receptivity toward pentecostalism among the Javanese during this early period. We can assume that some Javanese attended the evangelistic meetings in Surabaya. We know for certain that Miss Alt pastored several large Javanese congregations in the Gambangwalu area of Central Java. Her pentecostal experience at the Hortsmans' home was undoubtedly communicated to the believers under her care.

5. Pentecostal Training Institutions.

The early pentecostals were quick to realize the need for some method of discipling new converts and training workers for the harvest. Van Gessel turned over his congregation in Cepu to Lumoindong in 1926 and moved to Surabaya, where he started a Bible training program for the young people coming to Christ in that city. Many of the young evangelists who began carrying the pentecostal message to the outer islands in the early 1930s had spent time in the training sessions with Van Gessel.

In 1932 W. W. Patterson from Bethel Temple arrived in Bajarmasin, Kalimantan. After studying Bahasa Indonesia, he moved to Surabaya to open the first pentecostal Bible school. From its inception the emphasis of the school was a basic understanding of doctrine and a practical application of biblical truth. The course lasted less than a year, and then graduates were quickly thrust into full-time ministry. This school eventually moved to Lawang and then to Beji (near the city of Batu), where they continue to emphasize a practical, short-term approach to ministerial training. Every year they graduate about 600 students who then either immediately plant a church or go through further training under the tutelage of a local pastor. As of 1980 this school, along with 10 other Gereja Pantekosta Di Indonesia training institutions throughout Indonesia, have graduated over 7,500 workers.

6. Organization and Proliferation of Pentecostal Groups.

In 1924 the pentecostals were officially registered with the Dutch East Indies government under the name De Pinkster Gemeente in Nederlandsch Indie (The Pentecostal Church in Dutch East India). In 1942 the name was Indonesianized to Gereja Pentekosta di Indonesia (GPDI Pentecostal Church of Indonesia). The chairman of the new organization was Weenink Van Loon. They were given status as a church body with the right to receive members, ordain clergy, etc.

In 1925 Sister Alt was made secretary of the church, but tensions arose on two issues. One was ˻Oneness theology (which rejects the doctrine of the Trinity). The other issue was the role of women in ministry. Influential leaders such as Van Gessel were uncomfortable with women as pastors. Sister Alt felt restricted in her pulpit ministry in this new pentecostal denomination. In 1931 she resigned De Pinkster Gemeente in Nederlandsch Indie and started a new organization called De Pinkster Zending (The Pentecostal Mission). This became the first of many splits in the original pentecostal denomination—there are now more than 40 pentecostal denominations in Indonesia.

One year later (1932) Pastor Thiesen resigned from the original organization to form De Pinkster Beweging (The Pentecostal Movement), which later became the Gereja Gerakan Pantekosta. He, like Sister Alt, felt the doctrine of the Trinity was a bit shaky in the original organization.

In 1941 one of the early Batak leaders, Pastor D. Sinaga, pulled out of the GPDI and formed Gereja Pantekosta Sumatra Utara (The Pentecostal Church of North Sumatra). On this occasion the conflict was a cultural issue. Batak culture involves ritual meals in which blood is eaten. The GPDI forbade Christians to eat blood, based on a literal application of the decision reached at the Jerusalem Council (Acts 15). This prohibition created tension for Bataks who wanted to become pentecostals, especially since other Christian Batak churches did not apply this prohibition literally. Sinaga's group no longer made an issue of Christians who eat blood. (In 1948 Pastor Renatus Siburian left the GPDI over the same issue and started yet another pentecostal church in North Sumatra.)

During the ensuing years, other schisms occurred, not because of doctrinal differences, but because of personality clashes among those in leadership. Strong charismatic national leaders began to emerge, especially when the Japanese occupation (1942–45) required Indonesians to take over the leadership positions formerly held by Westerners. (Westerners, including missionaries, fled Indonesia or were interned during WWII; many including Van Klaveren died while in internment.) The leadership structure of the local church contributed to this schismatic tendency. In the GPDI the pastor is *raja* (king). He is the *bapak* (father), who in most cases not only rules the church, but owns it. The church properties are in his name or under an independent board of which he is the chairman.

New denominations were formed out of the GPDI with reasons such as, "We were not given freedom to work in an organized manner" (the reason given by Tan Hok Tjwan when he formed the Gereja Isa Almasih [Church of the Savior] in 1946), or "We wanted to stand on our own." The latter was the explanation given by Van Gessel when he resigned from the GPDI and formed the Gereja Bethel Injil Sepenuh (Bethel Full Gospel Church) in 1952; this church in turn has split into six different denominations since then. One of the six is the ›Geraja Bethel Indonesia; another is the Geraja Bethel Indonesia–Bethany, which reaches the middle class of society through music ministry; still another is the Geraja

Bethel Tabernakel (Bethel Tabernacle Church), founded in 1957. In 1959 Pastor Ishak Law pulled out of the GPDI because of a dispute over Bible school properties in Surabaya. His church, the Gereja Pantekosta Pusat Surabaya (Pentecostal Church, Headquarters Surabaya) now has several hundred congregations scattered throughout Indonesia.

This tragic tale of schism pervades the brief history of the pentecostal movement in Indonesia. While we must denounce as sin the motivation behind many of these divisions in the body of Christ, most of these 40-odd denominations have continued to grow at a phenomenal rate.

7. Gereja Sidang-Sidang Jemkat Allah.

Not all the pentecostal churches in Indonesia have a direct link to the ministry of Groesbeek and Van Klaveren in the 1920s. The Gereja Sidang-Sidang Yemaat Allah (literally, The Assemblies of the Congregation of God) reflects its historical ties with the Assemblies of God (AG) in the U.S.

In 1936 another American pentecostal missionary family, the Devins, arrived in Indonesia under the auspices of Bethel Temple in Seattle. Ralpli Devin owned a large office supply company in the Seattle area when he felt the call to serve in Indonesia. He approached the Christian and Missionary Alliance about the possibility of serving with their mission but was told that he and his wife "were too old, had too many children [five], and would never be able to learn the language" (Warner, 12). He was determined to fulfill his call, so he sold his company and briefly associated himself with Bethel Temple, having learned of their ties with the mission in the Dutch East Indies. They sailed to the island of Ambon in the Maluccas.

The following year Raymond Busby and his wife sailed from Seattle to Medan, North Sumatra, to join the pentecostal missionaries sent out from Bethel Temple. The Busbys and Devins, who had rather loose ties with Bethel Temple (they actually never received support from Bethel Temple), decided to form a new mission. In 1940 the Bethel Indies Mission received official government recognition from the Dutch East Indies government. The following year both families escaped Indonesia and returned the U.S. when the Japanese invaded Southeast Asia.

During the war years, the Devins and Busbys joined the AG and were received into the Northwest District Council. Following the war, the Devins returned to Ambon, and the Busbys located in Jakarta, where they opened a Bible school to train national pastors. The Busbys also maintained ties with a group of pentecostal believers in Medan, where they eventually opened another Bible school. Meanwhile the Devins started a Bible school in Ambon that produced workers who began to plant churches throughout the Maluccas. These churches, along with those started in Medan and Jakarta, identified themselves with the Assemblies of God of Indonesia.

Other AG missionaries soon joined the Devins and the Busbys. The Tinsmans, Carlblooms, Skoogs, Lamphears, and Margret Brown all began serving in Indonesia before 1950. The work expanded to North Sulawesi, Kalimantan, and other parts of Java. In 1951 the national pastors and missionaries gathered in Jakarta for the first General Council of the Assemblies of God of Indonesia. Ten ordained national pastors were present.

In 1952 the name of the church was changed to Gereja Sidang-Sidang Jemaat Allah (GSSJA). At that time six churches affiliated with the Gereja Utusan Pantekosta (formerly the Pinkster Zending that had been started by Sister Alt in 1931) joined the GSSJA. The leader of that church, Sumardi Stefanus, also joined and later (1959) became the first general superintendent of the GSSJA (Devin, 1991).

Currently, the church has a membership of 70,000, with about 700 congregations throughout almost every province of Indonesia. The denomination has nine Bible schools and one of the best Christian publishing houses in Indonesia.

8. Other Churches.

In addition to the churches already mentioned (Geraja Pantekosta di Indonesia, Geraja Bethel Injil Sepenuh, Geraja Bethel Indonesia, Geraja Bethel Indonesia–Bethany, Geraja Bethel Tabernakel, Geraja Isa Almasih, Geraja Penetckosta Pusat Surabaya, and Geraja Sidang-Sidang Jemaar Allah) other churches have nationwide ministries. One is the Geraja Utusan Pantekosta di Indonesia (Sending Pentecostal Churches in Indonesia), founded in 1935 by the Pinkster Gemeente van Holland (Pentecostal Church of Holland); its headquarters are in Solo, Central Java. Another is the Geraja Pantekosta Serikat (United Pentecostal Church), founded in 1939, with headquarters in Semarang, Java.

9. The Pentecostal Contribution.

During the 70 years since the pentecostal movement first entered Indonesia, it has influenced the nature and character of the church in Indonesia.

a. Ever since Groesbeek's and Van Klaveren's evangelistic meetings in Bali in 1921, prayer for the sick has been common to pentecostals in Indonesia. Culturally, Indonesians can relate to a supernatural worldview in which spirits exercise influence over humans, causing illness, misfortune, and even demonic bondage. Pentecostal theology addresses the dimension of the supernatural. This power-encounter approach in evangelism has created an openness and responsiveness to the gospel even among resistant peoples. Almost every testimony from those who have been converted to Christianity from a Muslim background involves some kind of miracle (healing, deliverance, dream, etc.). This emphasis on "power evangelism" is certainly not unique to pentecostals, but the pentecostal movement provided an example of it long before the current emphasis on the theology of the kingdom.

b. While evangelistic crusades are not unique to pentecostals, pentecostals have been most effective in using this means of reaching the lost in Indonesia. Since John Sung's crusade in 1939, large crowds have gathered in soccer stadiums, theaters, and public halls to hear pentecostal evangelists. Western pentecostal evangelists like ›Oral Roberts, ›T. L. Osborn, ›Morris Cerillo, and most recently ›Reinhard Bonnke have drawn the largest crowds (Bonnke's crusade in Jakarta in May 1991 had over 100,000 people in attendance each night). The anticipation of witnessing a miracle draws many who attend, creating something of a "circus atmosphere." Yet many repent at these meetings and are grafted into local churches.

c. Just as in many Western countries, pentecostals (and charismatics) in Indonesia have introduced a style of worship that has been incorporated to some degree in all evangelical churches. Hand clapping, lively music, and simple worship choruses have brought new life into many staid congregations.

d. Pentecostal Bible schools have produced few theologians yet have proven effective in turning out church planters and pastors. As in the West, the trend is toward higher theological degrees for ministerial candidates. However, most of the pentecostal Bible schools continue to place an emphasis on practical ministry in their curriculum.

e. Both in rural and urban areas pentecostals have disregarded the traditional boundaries of comity long established by other churches or mission agencies (Van den End, 1989, 257). Even if other Protestant churches are present, pentecostals have not been reluctant to start a home fellowship or rent a hall and begin holding evangelistic meetings with the goal of starting a new church. It is no wonder that from its humble beginnings in 1921 the pentecostal movement has produced thousands of new churches throughout Indonesia.

■ **Bibliography:** D. B. Barrett, ed., *World Christian Encyclopedia* (1982) ▪ S. M. Burgess and G. B. McGee, eds., *Dictionary of Pentecostal and Charismatic Movements* (1988) ▪ R. M. Devin, "Information on the Assemblies of God Work in Indonesia" (unpub. ms., Jan. 29, 1991) ▪ L. G. McClung Jr., ed., *Azusa Street and Beyond* (1986) ▪ W. W. Menzies, *Anointed to Serve: The Story of the Assemblies of God* (1971) ▪ N. J. Sumual, "Pantekosta Indonesia: Satu Sejarah" (unpub. paper on the history of pentecostals in Indonesia, 1980) ▪ F. Ukur and F. L. Cooley, *Jerih dan Juang* (*Hard Work and Struggle: A Survey of Churches in Indonesia*, 1979) ▪ Th. van den End, *Ragi Carita: Sejarah Gereja Di Indonesia Vol. I: 1500–1860* (1987) ▪ idem, *Ragi Carita: Sejarah Gereja Di Indonesia Vol. II: 1860 an–Sekarang* (1989) ▪ W. Warner, "The Evangel Crosses the Pacific," *AGH* 9 (3, Fall 1989) ▪ F. D. Willem, *John Sung: Riwayat Hidup Singkat Tokot-Tokot Dalam Sejarah Gereja* (1987).

Most of the information on the early history of the AG in Indonesia was obtained through personal interviews with the son of R. M. Devin, Morris Devin, who with his wife, Joyce, has served in Indonesia since 1952.   ■ P. Lewis

IRAN

■ Pentecostals 5,070 (7%)   ■ Charismatics 3,967 (5%)   ■ Neocharismatics 66,963 (88%)   ■ Total Renewal: 76,000

See AFRICA, NORTH, AND THE MIDDLE EAST.

IRAQ

■ Pentecostals 340 (0%)   ■ Charismatics 9,050 (3%)   ■ Neocharismatics 255,610 (96%)   ■ Total Renewal: 265,000

See AFRICA, NORTH, AND THE MIDDLE EAST.

IRELAND

■ Pentecostals 3,056 (1%)   ■ Charismatics 466,998 (95%)   ■ Neocharismatics 19,946 (4%)   ■ Total Renewal: 490,000

ISLE OF MAN

■ Pentecostals 181 (3%)   ■ Charismatics 5,625 (94%)   ■ Neocharismatics 194 (3%)   ■ Total Renewal: 6,000

ISRAEL

■ Pentecostals 2,692 (3%)   ■ Charismatics 17,668 (17%)   ■ Neocharismatics 84,640 (81%)   ■ Total Renewal: 105,000

See AFRICA, NORTH, AND THE MIDDLE EAST.

ITALY

■ Pentecostals 310,802 (3%)   ■ Charismatics 3,430,092 (82%)   ■ Neocharismatics 439,106 (11%)   ■ Total Renewal: 4,180,000

I. The Pentecostal Movement
   A. *Political and Social Context*
   B. *Origins: The Assemblea Christiana of Chicago*
   C. *Classical Pentecostals*
   D. *New Churches and Groupings*
   E. *Parachurch Organizations*
   F. *Promotion of Dialogue between Pentecostals*

II. The Catholic Charismatic Movement
   A. *Beginnings in Italy*
   B. *Developments in Italy*
   C. *Rinnovamento nello Spirito Santo*
   D. *Other Groupings*

III. Some Observations
   A. *Italy—A Special Case*
   B. *The Future*

The pentecostal/charismatic movement in Italy has two main branches: the evangelical pentecostal movement and the Catholic charismatic movement. The evangelical pentecostal movement is a varied archipelago of churches united by an evangelical theology and the baptism in the Holy Spirit. They can be subdivided into two main sections: *classical pentecostals* (denominations deriving directly from the Italian pentecostal movement of the early 1900s—or in any case, from either the ᐅAzusa Street revival or the ᐅWelsh revival of 1904–6) and *new groups and churches,* started mainly in the 1970s and '80s, which, while retaining the general ethos of classical pentecostalism, have opened up to the influence of neo-pentecostals and charismatics or are the fruit of these movements. This varied landscape, which is still evolving, is the most dynamic and lively branch of the Italian Protestant world.

The second branch is the Catholic charismatic movement, which, flowing from a common origin, includes various spiritual emphases and is organized into different movements, of which the largest in Italy is the Rinnovamento nello Spirito Santo (Renewal in the Holy Spirit).

Sadly absent are charismatic movements within the historic Protestant churches and other evangelical denominations, which elsewhere—e.g., in the U.K. and U.S.—have occupied the "middle ground" and have been important theological and spiritual mediators. This is one of the unusual features of the Italian situation.

I. THE PENTECOSTAL MOVEMENT.

A. Political and Social Context.

Protestantism in Italy is characterized by grassroots movements. At the beginning of the 20th century the Italian evangelical minority, numbering about 100,000 in all (mainly Waldensian, Methodist, Baptist, and Brethren) consisted largely of peasant farmers, workers, and artisans.

1. Emigration.

The Italian pentecostal movement took root in the political and social climate of the early 1900s, when great waves of emigrants left the poorest areas (408,000 between 1890 and 1905 alone, and continuing right up to the 1950s). These, mainly farmhands and peasants from the South, moved at first to South and North America, later to Australia and northern European countries. This background is vital for an understanding of the development of pentecostalism in Italy. Particularly in the U.S., the experience (shared by other southern European immigrants) of discrimination and poverty and the effects of the language barrier resulted in a cultural isolation that contributed to the strongly nationalistic character of the first Italian pentecostals.

2. Isolation.

When some of these emigrants returned to Italy with the pentecostal message, they frequently met with coldness from their families, hostility from the local community, and (for doctrinal reasons) suspicion and rejection from other evangelicals. In addition they were persecuted for over 30 years, had to live under the shadow of the monolithic Church of Rome, were cut off from communication with their mother churches in the U.S. in 1935–43, and for at least the first two generations suffered the effects of their openly declared hostility toward education and culture. Add to this the lack of contact with later pentecostal and charismatic revival movements in the English-speaking world (such as Latter Rain, the 1950s healing evangelists, the Jesus People, the various Protestant and Catholic charismatic movements, etc.), and one can begin to understand their often closed and defensive mentality. Obviously, theological justifications can be found for such attitudes, but theology is often colored by history and experience. Only at the end of the 20th century (1998) has there been even a tentative attempt at dialogue between Waldensians and some of the Italian classical pentecostal churches. The Assemblee di Dio in Italia (ADI, Italian Assemblies of God), however, remain closed to any dialogue, not only with the Protestants, but even with other pentecostal churches.

3. Persecution.

Like other evangelicals—indeed, perhaps more so—pentecostals faced scorn and hostility. Especially from 1929 on (the year of the Lateran Pacts and the Concordat between the Italian state and the Church of Rome), intolerance grew into authentic religious and political persecution.

Rome Crusade with Hal Herman in the Brancaccio Theater in September 1961.

The year 1929 was difficult and crucial for all Italian Protestants. It brought to an end the secular and liberal state of the Risorgimento era (1860–1929) that had as its slogan "A free church in a free state." Religious freedom was the first victim of the Concordat, fruit of the compromise between Mussolini's fascism (which needed to consolidate its power) and Roman clericalism. The pentecostal movement became the litmus test of the new illiberal and authoritarian Italian state.

On the legal front, persecution developed in two phases:

a. 1929–1935: Period of Tolerance. Under the Law on Permitted Faiths minority religions were "tolerated" but subjected to increasing hostility.

b. 1935–1955: Period of Persecution. Particularly of the pentecostals. This phase began with the infamous Buffarini-Guidi circular, which declared that pentecostal worship "can no longer be permitted in the Kingdom ... because it manifests itself in religious practices contrary to the social order and harmful to the physical and mental welfare of the race." This period may be subdivided into three phases:

(1) 1935–43. Organized persecution and systematic repression, with prefect, parish priest, and bishop acting in perfect agreement.

(2) 1943–48. A period of greater freedom and growth for the pentecostal movement, thanks to the presence of the Allied forces.

(3) 1948–55. Return to a climate of hostility and discrimination, for two main reasons: (1) despite the fall of fascism, its legal and police machinery remained intact (the Buffarini-Guidi circular was not annulled until Apr. 16, 1955); (2) social and cultural conditions remained unchanged.

4. Religious Freedom.

Industrial development and the modernization of the country, a maturing democracy, and the gradual (though still incomplete) declericalization of the state took a long time. Today—thanks to, among other factors, the changes resulting from Vatican II—there is complete de facto freedom. It is of the utmost significance that the ADI have obtained an "agreement" *(Intesa)* with the state; other pentecostal churches are in the process of requesting and obtaining the same. (The 1948 Republican Constitution of Italy, alongside the Concordat with the Roman Catholic Church, provides for agreements *[Intese]* with other religious confessions. To date such agreements have been signed with Waldensians, Jews, Seventh-day Adventists, Lutherans, Assemblies of God in Italy [ADI], Baptists, Buddhists, and Jehovah's Witnesses.) There remains, however, a disparity of treatment sanctioned by articles 7 and 8 of the Constitution; the deeply illiberal and unconstitutional 1929 Law on Permitted Faiths has still not been repealed; the law still provides for Catholic religious teaching in schools; and 50 years after the establishment of the republic, Parliament is still drafting a law on religious liberty.

B. Origins: The Assemblea Cristiana of Chicago.

The pentecostal movement among Italians began in Chicago, IL, with a small group of immigrants who had left the First Italian Presbyterian Church (Waldensian) because they had come to believe in the necessity of baptism by immersion. They took the name of ▸Assemblea Cristiana and were structured along lines similar to the Plymouth Brethren. In Apr. 1907, through ▸Luigi Francescon (1866–1964), they came into contact with ▸William H. Durham (1873–1912), who was preaching the pentecostal message at North Avenue Mission and became the father of the "baptist type" of pentecostalism. The interest of the group was aroused, and on Sept. 15, 1907, the entire fellowship experienced an extraordinary baptism in the Holy Spirit. The life of the fellowship was revolutionized, and thus the Italian pentecostal movement was born. The key to understanding much of Italian pentecostalism is to be found in the enthusiasm and the characteristics (cultural, theological, and ecclesiastical) of this fellowship and some of its leaders.

1. Mission.

The pioneers—Luigi Francescon, ▸Pietro Ottolini (1870–1962), Giacomo Lombardi (1862–1934), and others—went out from Chicago as missionaries to win families and groups of Italians in the U.S. and Canada, South America, and in their country of birth. Luigi Francescon, who founded pentecostal movements among Italians in Argentina and Brazil (1908–10), visited Italy a number of times from 1910 on, promoting a congregational approach. Pietro Ottolini worked among Italians in New York State (1908), in Italy (1910–1914), and thereafter in St. Louis, MO. Giacomo Lombardi, however, is recognized as the real founder of the movement in Italy, beginning in 1908.

2. Growth.

The first 40 years saw spontaneous growth without organization. By 1910 there were 4 churches; by 1920, 14; by 1930, 149; and by 1940 an additional 25. A large number of small, independent churches, especially in the South, grew up around charismatic men (or, rarely, women) and progressively lost contact with their Italian-American origins during the years 1929–43 as they entered the dark tunnel of isolation and persecution. Up to 1943 the movement presents a homogeneous appearance, though there were debates over ecclesiology, and differing types of spirituality were emerging (e.g., that of Giuseppe Petrelli).

C. Classical Pentecostals.

Between 1943 and 1947 the majority (some say only half) of Italian pentecostals decided to come together as the Assemblee di Dio in Italia (ADI)—mainly to meet the need for official recognition by the state in light of their recent experience of persecution.

Shortly after this the Congregazioni Cristiane Pentecostali (Pentecostal Christian Congregations) were formed, espousing the radical congregationalism of the early days. At the same time, a number of churches in Piedmont, Calabria, the province of Foggia, Sicily, and the valley of the River Sele in Campania joined forces around the magazine *Il Regno di Dio (The Kingdom of God)* and the teachings of Giuseppe Petrelli to form a "petrellian" movement. A number of churches remained independent, while the Zaccardians (named after Giuseppe Zaccardi), who were also known as the Santissimi (Holiest Ones), had distanced themselves from the rest as early as 1935; they were characterized by their strict approach to dress, ethics, doctrine, and their episcopal form of church government. In addition, the Chiesa Apostolica in Italia (Apostolic Church), born out of the 1904–6 Welsh revival, has been represented in Italy since 1928.

1. Assemblee di Dio in Italia (Assemblies of God in Italy).

The Assemblee di Dio in Italia (ADI) is currently the largest Protestant denomination in the country and the most successful attempt at organization within the pentecostal movement. They are present in 92 of the 102 provincial capitals and have a total of 1,089 churches (363 of them fully constituted), groups, and preaching stations. They have a total of 150,000 adherents and a ministerial body of 482 (101 pastors). The form of government is a presbyterian/congregational hybrid, with a strong role for the president: the first was Umberto Nello Gorietti (1947–77); the second is ►Francesco Toppi (still in office). The local churches are autonomous, but the buildings are owned by the denomination, and ministers are nominated by the General Council of the Churches.

The Istituto Biblico Italiano (Italian Bible Institute, founded in 1954) plays a strategic role in the training of pastors, and much energy has been invested in it by some of the most significant figures of the first generation of the ADI, such as Roberto Bracco (d. 1983)—a broad-minded theologian and key prophetic personality—and the current president. They publish the monthly *Risveglio Pentecostale (Pentecostal Revival,* circulation 6,350), the fortnightly *Cristiani oggi (Christians Today,* 3,500), and the quarterly *Sunday School Study Manual* (21,000). There are also three social welfare centers—Betania Emmaus (Torlupara Mentana, near Rome), Eben Ezer (Corato, Bari), and Betesda (Macchia di Giarre, Catania)—and several conference centers.

The denomination was officially founded in Naples in 1947, following an "exclusively spiritual" agreement of affiliation with the U.S. Assemblies of God (AG), at the same time strongly asserting its "complete autonomy." The founders would have preferred an association with the Christian Churches of North America, to whom they were historically and culturally closer and with whom they still had

fellowship, but for legal reasons they accepted the offer of affiliation to the AG, taking care, however, to assert their "differences" and affirming the strongly "national" character of the new denomination. This characteristic has been constantly maintained and jealously defended: "The Italian Pentecostal Movement is characterized by being totally free from foreign influence" (Womack and Toppi).

The intervening decades have witnessed a clear progressive institutionalization of the ADI. From 1959, when they obtained legal recognition, through the decade 1967–77, which was decisive for the definition of their internal structure *(Regolamento interno 1967),* they finally arrived at the agreement with the Italian state, signed on Dec. 29, 1986.

2. Congregazioni Cristiane Pentecostali (Pentecostal Christian Congregations).

The Congregazioni Cristiane Pentecostali (CCP) has 57 churches, mainly in Sicily, with others in friendly relations. There are no precise membership statistics; estimates range from 5,000 to 10,000. The CCP has suffered various splits over the years. They trace their origins to the teaching, ecclesiology, and practice of the first 20 years of pentecostalism in Italy, claiming continuity with what was deliberated at the first Convention (Niagara Falls, NY, 1927) of Italian Pentecostal Churches in the U.S., which significantly decided to call itself Assembly of Unorganized Italian Churches. All the resolutions of that convention were adopted the following year at the "Elders' Convention" held in Rome (Oct. 19–20, 1928).

When the ADI was formed, these churches rejected the move toward centralized organization, and at the Convention at Vittoria (Ragusa) in 1958 they reaffirmed "their determination to keep their congregational character and to live free and independent, to be known as Congregazioni Cristiane Pentecostali." They believe in the autonomy of the local churches in the choice of leaders and the exercise of ministry and administration; in the principle of collegiate government and administration of the local church; in promoting unity between sister churches; in the principle of liberty as regards fellowship "with all Christian congregations whose doctrine conforms to the Bible," collaboration "with all organisms promoting initiatives in accordance with the Word of God," and the equality of all believers, without distinction of dignity or hierarchy, before God.

3. Chiesa Cristiana Pentecostale Italiana (Italian Pentecostal Christian Church).

The Chiesa Cristiana Pentecostale Italiana (CCPI) was founded in 1997 and numbers 35 churches. The governing bodies are the Convegno Generale (general convention), in which the churches have equal representation, and a coordinating body, the Servizio Nazionale di Coordinamento, whose president is the national coordinator.

This is a fellowship of autonomous churches that refer back to the historical heritage and original doctrine of Italian pentecostalism with its congregational orientation. They emphasize the importance of cultivating the particular values of Italian pentecostalism in a world context. An urgent need is felt for launching projects for pastoral, diaconal, educational, and liturgical training. Giacomo Loggia, pastor of the church in Gela (Sicily) and current national coordinator (who was for many years a leading figure in the CCP), has had an important part in the formation of this fellowship of churches.

4. Chiese Evangeliche della Valle del Sele (Sele Valley Evangelical Churches)

There are 20 established churches and 10 missions and delegations in more than 30 communities in the provinces of Avellino, Salerno, and Potenza. The movement is led by an apostolic coordinator (Romolo Ricciardiello), supported by a college of the Sele Valley pastors. The local fellowships are administratively autonomous. There are over 2,000 members.

This movement was born from the testimony of emigrants returning from Buenos Aires and Chicago in the 1920s. During the 1930s and '40s they suffered persecution from fascism and Roman Catholicism and were ostracized by other evangelicals in the area. In 1946–50, with the greater freedom of the postwar period, the first churches were founded in the valley (Caposele, Contursi Terme, and Oliveto Citra), mainly due to the evangelistic efforts of Pasquale Albano, a pioneer and founding leader of the movement.

During the 1960s, revival broke out over the whole area and churches came out into the open or were newly formed in Upper Irpinia and the Ofanto Valley. Some joined the ADI; others chose to remain independent. Pasquale Albano and his helpers turned to the Sele Valley, which they completely evangelized, founding new churches and reaching as far as Salerno, Avellino, and Potenza, while also developing links with the province of Matera, Calabria, Sicily, and as far

Giovanni Traettino leading praise and worship at the Consultazione Carismatica Italiana in Bari, Italy, in 2000.

as Tuscany, Piedmont, and Lombardy through believers who emigrated north. The "theologian" of the movement was for many years Giuseppe Petrelli, who lived permanently in the U.S., a prolific writer characterized by a profound mysticism. Antonio Bernabei has been the most prominent representative of the Italian *petrelliani*. Their magazine was *Il granel di senape (The Grain of Mustard Seed)*.

Since 1968 Romolo Ricciardiello has been the key figure in the movement, bringing it out of isolation and working determinedly toward spiritual, ecclesiological, and cultural renewal. At the national level he is committed to working toward fellowship with and unity among all Italian evangelicals. His is one of the most important experiments in the renewal of Italian classical pentecostalism, similar in many ways to the revivals in Argentina and North America.

5. Chiesa Apostolica in Italia (Apostolic Church in Italy).

The Chiesa Apostolica in Italia (CAI) was founded in 1928 through contacts between Alfredo Del Rosso (Baptist) of Civitavecchia (Rome) and missionaries of the Apostolic Church, first from Denmark and then from the U.K. (George Evans and William Roger Thomas, 1933); it is part of the family of churches born of the Welsh revival (1904–6). Like its sister church in the U.K., it has a pentecostal theology and an apostolic form of government.

Found in all parts of the country, it has a distance-learning Bible school; its principal is Edoardo Labanchi. The most notable figures in its history were William Thomas (1909–93) and Iorwerth Howells (1928–94), apostle and for many years president of the Italian church, later international president of the Apostolic Church. The movement feels the need at this time for a profound renewal, growth, and expansion. One sign of this is new projects for evangelism both in Italy and on the mission field (Malta, Argentina, Albania). The Apostolic Church adheres to the Italian Evangelical Alliance and has opened proceedings for stipulating an agreement with the Italian State.

There are 82 churches and 52 groups, 56 pastors (members of the *consiglio nazionale*), and around 5,000 members. The CAI, with headquarters in Grossetto, is governed by a national leadership team and a national council. The president of the national council is currently Elia Landi. The CAI has its own publishing house, Ricchezze di grazia (Riches of Grace), and publishes a magazine, *L'Araldo Apostolico (The Apostolic Herald)*, and a quarterly theological journal, *Riflessioni (Reflections)*.

6. Chiesa Apostolica Italiana (Italian Apostolic Church).

Founded by Mario Affuso, a former pastor of the CAI, it consists of four churches and belongs to the Federazione delle Chiese Evangeliche in Italia (FCEI, Federation of Evangelical Churches in Italy). It publishes the magazine *Fedeltà (Faithfulness)*.

7. Chiesa di Dio (Church of God).

Present in Italy since 1963 through the work of Pastor De Fino, superintendent in Italy until 1970, it is in fellowship with the Church of God (Cleveland, TN). It belongs to the family of Wesleyan Holiness pentecostal churches. The national office is in Rome, and the current superintendent is Brownlow Lamar. There are 16 fellowships, mostly in Sicily, with about 2,000 members.

8. Independent Pentecostal Churches.

Included among the Italian classical pentecostals are scores of churches spread over the whole country for which no precise statistics are available. These are mostly the fruit, over decades, of groups leaving the ADI or the congregational bodies, or of missionary activity by Italian Americans. Listed here are a few that are significant from a historical or numerical point of view:

- Churches (6) that grew up around the ministry of Cannavò (Messina).
- Churches (6) in fellowship with Lucio Tommasello (Palermo), for many years a leading representative of the petrellian stream.
- About 40 churches grouped together as Chiese pentecostali autonome di Roma e del Lazio (Autonomous Pentecostal Churches in Rome and Lazio).
- Independent churches (92) having legal status as part of the interdenominational Missione Italiana per l'Evangelo (MIE, Italian Gospel Mission).
- Particular mention should be made of a movement started to the north of Naples in the early 1970s: Le Chiese Cristiane Pentecostali (Pentecostal Christian Churches). The key figures in this work are the brothers Michele and Antonio Romeo, pastors of the two largest churches at Secondigliano and Giugliano. The movement began in 1975 with Gennaro Alvino, formerly of the ADI. After his death in 1982, his assistant Michele Romeo took charge of the work. A strong evangelistic movement spread rapidly through the northern suburbs of Naples. The work grew, initially around the "mother church" in Secondigliano (a common pattern in the Italian pentecostal movement), later also around the church in Giugliano. There are now 10 churches with more than 2,000 members. Since 1991 they hold an annual summer camp, Eben-Ezer, at Lioni (Avellino).
- La Missione "Nuova Pentecoste" (New Pentecost Mission). Founded by Remo Cristallo (a former Air Force NCO), one-time pastor in the ADI and disciple of Pastor Alvino. There are 9 churches with about 1,000 adherents. The church in Aversa (Caserta) has grown mainly through street evangelism, a television ministry, and literature. Here too the "mother church model" has produced a network of churches, mainly in the province of Caserta. They have a publishing house, La Nuova Pentecoste, a television studio, and plans for a large printing press.

9. Chiese Elim in Italia (Italian Elim Churches).

Founded in Milan in 1993, these churches are in fellowship with the British Elim Pentecostal Churches. They total 50 churches, 25 of which are African churches in Italy affiliated through the Ghanaian Church of Pentecost (also in fellowship with Elim–UK). Spread throughout Italy, they have 11 pastors and 5,000 to 6,000 adherents. The headquarters are in Milan; the founder and president is Giuseppe Piccolo (formerly of the ADI), well known nationally for his connections with ministries such as ▶David Yonggi Cho, ▶Reinhard Bonnke, and ▶Peter Wagner, which are controversial and not accepted by the ADI, and more recently with the ▶Brownsville (Pensacola, FL) revival. The form of government is congregational; the local churches, though in fellowship in regard to faith and doctrine, have complete administrative, financial, and spiritual independence. Noteworthy as a new departure for Italian classical pentecostals, the Declaration of Faith does not mention tongues as proof of the baptism in the Spirit; all ministries, including apostle and prophet, are acknowledged, and faith in the physical return of Jesus is stated without an explicit affirmation of the ▶dispensationalist position. These aspects confirm the growing openness of this church to the charismatic wing of the pentecostal movement. The publishing house, Publielim, reflects this openness.

D. New Churches and Groupings.

Since the early 1970s, new groupings have emerged alongside (in some cases from) classical pentecostalism. They are distinguished from earlier pentecostalism by such characteristics as the desire to revitalize church culture and practices; the search for a more flexible and charismatic structure; a greater openness to the influence of the charismatic and neocharismatic movements of the 1950s and later decades; a more modern approach; an emphasis on worship; the desire for greater collaboration between denominations; a recognition of the ministry today of apostles, prophets, evangelists, pastors, and teachers; the importance of teamwork; and the emergence of authoritative leaders—usually recognized as apostolic ministers—around which men and movements converge.

1. Chiesa Evangelica Internazionale (International Evangelical Church).

Founded by John McTernan, a pastor of the International Evangelical Church (U.S.). A complex personality, broadminded and open to dialogue, he worked for unity among

Italian evangelicals and toward bringing together the independent pentecostals. He brought his church into the World Council of Churches in 1972 and was a promoter and member of the ˃Dialogue between pentecostals and Catholics. For a time he successfully brought together a number of different independent pentecostal churches.

Silvano Lilli succeeded him as leader of the church in Rome and president of the denomination. From the start this church was noted among pentecostals as being different and particularly able to dialogue with other Christians and with the world. The church in Rome was for many years a port of call for a number of the most important and open-minded personalities of the international pentecostal and charismatic world.

More recently, the work has grown largely due to the joining of churches from Sicily and Campania, part of a network of churches formed around the Comunità Cristiana "La Parola della Grazia" (Word of Grace Christian Fellowship) in Palermo. This church was formed in the early 1980s by a charismatic leader, Lirio Porrello. To date this is the largest and fastest-growing pentecostal church in Italy (around 2,000 members). Over the years a further seven churches have joined it. The movement is characterized by a strong emphasis on faith (the "Faith movement" [˃Positive Confession]), the supernatural, prosperity, centrality of the church, and spiritual authority. The church claims about 15,000 members in 30 churches spread throughout the country.

2. Chiesa Evangelica della Riconciliazione (Evangelical Reconciliation Church).

A charismatic evangelical movement with a pioneer calling, begun in the late 1970s by a group of ministers from different backgrounds (Baptist, Pentecostal, Plymouth Brethren, Anglican) with a vision for unity and the theological and spiritual renewal of the whole body of Christ. Through its magazine, *Tempi di Restaurazione* (*Restoration Times,* founded 1980, circulation 1000+), and conferences, it has pioneered the renewal of worship, pastoral care, and the recovery of apostolic and prophetic ministry and has worked for the unity of both pentecostals and evangelicals. Since 1992 it has taken the lead in dialogue and reconciliation with the Catholic charismatic movement. For some years the Istituto di studi storici e teologici "G. F. Alois" (G. F. Alois Historical and Theological Study Center) has been operating in Caserta, encouraging dialogue and confrontation with leading figures in Italian culture: philosophers, historians, theologians, churchmen, and thinkers, both Italian and foreign.

The movement has a presence in some 40 localities from north to south, including 18 established churches and 16 groups, with around 2,500 adherents. There are 31 ordained ministers (elders and deacons). The form of government is apostolic/episcopal. Its national leader is Giovanni Traettino, who has been leading a national team of ministers since 1979. Its publishing house is Edizioni Koinonia.

3. Chiese Cristiane "Gesú Cristo è il Signore" ("Jesus Christ Is Lord" Churches).

Begun in Catania in the early 1970s by British missionary Philip Wiles, who for many years had worked with the ADI, this group holds to the more classical style of pentecostalism. It has grown considerably and has widespread influence. Pastor Wiles, the charismatic leader of the movement, is a nationally recognized leadership figure. The group's 35 churches with about 3,000 adherents have an apostolic form of government.

4. Chiesa Cristiana "Gesú Cristo è il Signore" ("Jesus Christ Is Lord" Church).

Historically connected to Pastor Wiles. Its leader, Gilberto Perri (a former policeman), started a new work in Reggio Calabria, which has grown considerably and has offshoots in several other Italian cities. It has about 1,000 adherents.

5. Missione del Pieno Evangelo (Full Gospel Mission).

Started in 1966 by Dutch missionaries, it now numbers six churches and groups in the provinces of Bari, Potenza, and Matera. Since 1973 it has published a magazine, *Pensieri dall'Alto (Thoughts from On High),* edited mainly by Giuseppe Ronchi and Arend Booy, leading figures in the movement. The conference/camp center Il Rifugio has been active since 1988.

E. Parachurch Organizations.

Christ Is the Answer is an evangelistic movement that was founded by Bill Lowery in the U.S. in the 1970s as an outgrowth of the Jesus People movement. As of 1999 two teams are operating in Italy, led by Clark Slone and Vittorio Fiorese. Other teams have been formed in Italy and have gone to evangelize in other countries. Since the 1970s they have been an important factor in broadening the horizons of Italian pentecostalism. Moving their tents from one place to another, they have introduced a new style of worship, revivalist preaching, and—especially in the early days—an almost "Jesus People" lifestyle, influencing all branches of Italian pentecostalism and bringing in a breath of fresh air and sometimes even revival. Recently they have moved close to the Brownsville (Pensacola, FL) revival.

F. Promotion of Dialogue between Pentecostals.

In 1983 Bruno Crociani (Rome) initiated a project to promote fellowship and dialogue among pentecostals (the ADI, closed to any form of dialogue, did not take part). The result was the Coordinamento Nazionale dei Ministri Pentecostali (National Coordination of Pentecostal Ministries), which played an important role in drawing together various streams of Italian pentecostalism. In 1997 the "Coordinamento" changed its name to "Comunione delle Chiese Evangeliche Pentecostali" (Fellowship of Pentecostal Evangelical Churches) and evolved toward a more structured organization. More recently (2000), it has organized itself into a Federazione Chiese Pentecostali, FCP (Federation of Pentecostal Churches).

II. THE CATHOLIC CHARISMATIC MOVEMENT.

A. Beginnings in Italy.

The Catholic charismatic movement has its roots in pentecostalism but dates its origins specifically from the "Duquesne Weekend" in Feb. 1967 in Pittsburgh, PA. During a spiritual retreat with pentecostals and Protestant charismatics, a few Catholic students and professors who had read *The Cross and the Switchblade* by David Wilkerson and *They Speak with Other Tongues* by John Sherrill sought and received the baptism in the Holy Spirit and charismatic gifts.

The first prayer group in Italy, called Lumen Christi, began in 1971 at the Gregorian University in Rome and was English-speaking. Participants included the founder, ▸Fr. Francis Sullivan, and Fr. Carlo Maria Martini, now Cardinal Archbishop of Milan. This group's later involvement in ecumenism had international impact. The first Italian-speaking group was started in 1973 at San Mauro Pascoli, in Romagna, by the French-Canadian Fr. Valerien Gaudet, who had experienced the Holy Spirit at the University of Notre Dame in South Bend, IN.

A key year for the acceptance of the movement by the Catholic Church and its development in Italy was 1975. A large International Catholic Charismatic Congress was held in Rome, introducing the renewal for the first time to many who subsequently became leaders in the movement in Italy. During this congress, Pope Paul VI received the participants in audience and declared the movement "an opportunity for the Church and for the world." Six years later Pope John Paul II confirmed his predecessor's judgment and entrusted the Catholic Charismatic Renewal to the spiritual guidance of ▸Cardinal Suenens of Belgium; he held office until 1982 as episcopal advisor to the International Office (ICCRO), the movement's international coordination and consultation center (in 1993 renamed ▸International Catholic Charismatic Renewal Services, ICCRS). The current president of ICCRS (2000) is Alan Panozza (Australia); the director is the Italian Oreste Pesare. Throughout these years the Catholic charismatic movement has been enriched by the contributions of theologians such as Suenens, Ratzinger, Martini, Cantalamessa, Congar, Von Balthasar, Muhlen, Laurentin, Sullivan, Beck, Cultrera, Forte, Panciera, Baruffo, and Bentivegna.

B. Developments in Italy.

Like the pentecostal movement, the Catholic charismatic movement embraces different streams or spiritual families. The main stream in Italy is organized as an association called Rinnovamento nello Spirito Santo (Renewal in the Holy Spirit).

From 1975 on there was a period of growth and consolidation with an increasing acceptance of the movement within the Catholic Church. Both the vocabulary and the theology of the movement were more carefully defined, especially in regard to the baptism in the Holy Spirit. Groups began to take shape and relate to one another; among these, the Gruppo Maria (Mary Group), founded by Alfredo and Jacqueline Ancellotti, emphasized its Catholic nature and was less open to ecumenism. In 1978 a Comitato Nazionale di Servizio (National Service Committee) was formed and the first Convocazione Nazionale (National Convocation) was held in Rimini.

C. Rinnovamento nello Spirito Santo (Renewal in the Holy Spirit, RNS).

The RNS traces its roots to the early 1970s and is recognized as a private association of the faithful at work in the church within the stream known worldwide as the Catholic charismatic renewal movement. It numbers about 1,600 groups and communities with a total of c. 250,000 adherents. It publishes the official monthly *Rinnovamento nello Spirito Santo* (circulation c. 12,000) and the quarterly organ of the communities, *Venite e Vedrete* (*Come and You Will See*, c. 1,500 copies). The RNS is led nationally by the Comitato Nazionale di Servizio (CNS), which has nine members and is presided over by a national coordinator, currently Salvatore Martinez. The national spiritual advisor is Mgr. Dino Foglio, who was coordinator for the previous 20 years. At the regional level there are the Comitati Regionali di Servizio (CRS, Regional Service Committees) presided over by regional coordinators.

The prayer group is the basic unit of the movement. Locally each group is presided over by a "pastoral service

Giovanni Traettino (Protestant) and Matteo Calisi (Roman Catholic), co-chairs of the Consultazione Carismatica Italiana in Bari, Italy.

group," with responsibility for its leadership and activities. The theological/pastoral profile (1983) states that the RNS consists of "Christian groups that pray and seek in prayer, for each of its members, a new outpouring of the Holy Spirit, whereby to the grace of Christian initiation is added a new awareness of the Lordship of Christ, a new experience of the gifts and charisms of the Spirit, and a new willingness to use all the talents and gifts which God has given them in the service of their brothers." Alongside the groups, but remaining within the RNS, are also communities with differing spiritualities (covenant communities, residential communities, and monastic communities).

In the history of the Italian renewal movement, special mention must be made of the annual National Convocation in Rimini. First held in 1978, it grew from 5,000 participants to 40,000 and even 60,000 in the following years and became a spiritual event that has marked all the main milestones in the life of the movement. Particularly noteworthy was an event at the 1996 meeting, which had "Christian unity" as its theme, when Mgr. Foglio, followed by the National Service Committee and by bishops and a cardinal who was present, publicly asked forgiveness of the Italian pentecostals for the persecutions and discriminations of the past.

Alongside the national convention, regional convocations and meetings for prayer and healing have grown up, which attract thousands of people.

D. Other Groupings.

No longer under the umbrella of the RNS because of differing emphases or because they are centered around a particular strong or charismatic leader, other groupings with their own organizations have emerged. The most significant are:

- The Comunità Maria, started in 1976, with some 90 fellowships and about 3,500 adherents. National representative is Carlo Febbraio.
- The Comunità Vita Nuova (New Life Fellowship), based at Peschiera del Garda (Verona), was founded in 1982 and counts some 300 *cenacoli* (cell groups) and 2,000 adherents. Led by a layman, Luciano de Pieri (also responsible for the Italian branch of the Full Gospel Business Men's Fellowship International, founded in 1997), it publishes a monthly magazine, *Ruah* (Hebrew for "Spirit," circulation 5,000), and has an active publishing house, Editrice Il Dono.
- The Koinonia Giovanni Battista (John the Baptist Fellowship), started in 1978 by Fr. Riccardo Argagnaraz, numbers six residential communities in Italy with about 800 adherents.
- The Comunità Gesú Risorto (Risen Jesus Fellowship), started in 1987, now numbers 160 communities and about 12,000 adherents. National representative is Paolo Serafini. Since 1994 they publish a quarterly magazine, *Gesú Risorto* (*Risen Jesus*, circulation 4,200).

- The Rinnovamento Carismatico Servi di Cristo Vivo (Charismatic Renewal "Servants of the Living Christ"), started in 1987, has six local communities and about 100 groups with about 3,000 adherents. The charismatic leader is Fr. Michele Vassallo; they publish the quarterly *La Voce* (*The Voice*, distributed free).
- The Comunità Gesú Amore ("Jesus' Love" Community), started in 1990, numbers 20 groups with 600 adherents. National representative is Don Serafino Falvo, one of the founding leaders of the Italian renewal movement.
- The Comunità Gesú Ama ("Jesus Loves" Community), started in 1992, numbers about 20 local groups with 600 adherents. National representative is Laura Nardi.
- The Comunità Nuova Pentecoste (New Pentecost Community), started in 1996, numbers about 300 adherents led by Maria Manni.

In 1996 many of these groupings came together in a loose association and began an annual convention (Convegno di Comunione nel RCC) at Fiuggi (Roma), aimed at encouraging fellowship and interchange between their movements and fellowships.

III. SOME OBSERVATIONS.

A. Italy—A Special Case.

It is curious that in Italy—traditionally Catholic but now deeply secularized—there should be at the beginning of the new millennium two streams in the Catholic and evangelical worlds, similar in size and spirituality but with little history of brotherly relationships. Yet the pentecostal who happens to attend a Catholic charismatic meeting would be surprised by the extraordinary similarity of the songs, the testimonies, and the preaching—and vice versa. For years now there have been contacts, dialogues, conferences, joint studies, and research at an international level, but little awareness of this has penetrated Italy. The reasons for this lack of communication are obviously to be found in the particular history of the country. But this difficulty could become a historic opportunity for dialogue between Christians.

In 1992 a pentecostal pastor, during a charismatic convention at Bari, washed the feet of a Franciscan friar. This gesture of reconciliation opened a significant breach in the wall of separation that divides the two camps. From this came the Consultazione Carismatica Italiana, one of whose objectives was to organize an annual retreat, Ritiri per un Dialogo Fraterno (Brotherly Dialogue Retreats). Since then similar initiatives have been taken at the local level (Caserta, Bari, Calabria, Milan, Turin), with opportunities for dialogue and reconciliation. Men such as ►Raniero Cantalamessa, ►Gary McGee, ►Kilian McDonnell, ►Vinson Synan, ►Walter Hollenweger, Peter D. Hocken, and Stanley M. Burgess have been involved in this process. At Rimini in 1996, during the

Convocation on Christian Unity, the president of the RNS, together with bishops and a cardinal, publicly asked forgiveness of their pentecostal "brethren" for the persecution they had suffered in Italy. A new hope was born. Perhaps Italy could become a kind of laboratory for reconciliation between the children of the one Father.

B. The Future.

Some important issues for the future are:
- Relations with the state: a defining element in the life of religious minorities in Italy, where the theme of religious freedom is always hovering in the background, and a factor encouraging the formation of groupings and alliances among them.
- Relations between movements and denominations: the historic isolationism of the ADI and the resulting spiritual climate among other groups.
- Relations with the style and culture of the new groupings.
- Relationships with the global village: broadening of horizons of the Italian pentecostal world; dialogue between Christians, between the different traditions present within the pentecostal world and the different traditions that have been touched by the pentecostal message (David du Plessis).

- Relationship between fundamentalism and evangelicalism: the challenge of academic theology.

Finally, the influx of Third World immigrants in recent years includes a considerable number of pentecostals and other evangelical Christians (in 1998 estimated at 150,000), who have formed their own churches, worshiping in their native languages, all over Italy (especially in the North). As these immigrants and their children become integrated into Italian society, cooperation, cross-fertilization, and integration with the Italian churches will become a major issue.

■ **Bibliography:** L. Berzano and M. Introvigne, *La sfida infinita* (1994) ■ G. Bouchard, *Chiese e movimenti evangelici del nostro tempo* (1992) ■ R. Bracco, *Il Risveglio Pentecostale in Italia* (1956) ■ M. Calisi, "Carismatici cattolici: chi sono?" in *Tempi di Restaurazione* 13 (1994) ■ M. Introvigne, ed., *La sfida pentecostale* (1996) ■ M. Introvigne, M. Calisi, and G. Traettino, *Aspettando la Pentecoste* (1996) ■ W. J. Hollenweger, *El Pentecostalismo* (1976) ■ G. Peyrot, *La Circolare Buffarini—Guidi e i pentecostali* (1955) ■ G. Rochat, *Regime fascista e chiese evangeliche* (1990) ■ G. Spini, *Studi sull'evangelismo italiano tra Otto e Novecento* (1994), 119–57, 235–50 ■ E. Stretti, *Il Movimento Pentecostale, le Assemblee di Dio in Italia* (1999) ■ G. Traettino, *Il Movimento Pentecostale in Italia (1908–1959)* (diss., U. of Naples, 1971) ■ D. A. Womack and F. Toppi, *Le radici del Movimento Pentecostale* (1989).   ■ G. Traettino

IVORY COAST

■ Pentecostals 216,484 (18%)   ■ Charismatics 191,221 (16%)   ■ Neocharismatics 807,294 (66%)   ■ Total Renewal: 1,214,999

See AFRICA, WEST.

JAMAICA (I)

Jamaica is a very religious, overwhelmingly Protestant, country. Indeed, it is far more religious and has many more churches per capita than the U.S. (which regularly sends evangelists and missionaries to Jamaica). The main religious groups of the 19th century were the Anglican, Baptist, Congregationalist, Moravian, and Presbyterian churches, along with the indigenous, African-Christian religions of Myalism and Zion Revival. The 20th century saw the introduction of a number of new religions, chief among them the Seventh-day Adventists and several pentecostal churches, which have grown steadily at the expense of the earlier churches. The most spectacular growth has been in the pentecostal churches, which claimed 29% of the population in the 1991 census, making them the most popular faith on the island—all of the older churches listed above combined accounted for only 21%.

The following provides a brief description of the beliefs and practice of pentecostalism in Jamaica, placing it in its sociocultural and historical contexts, and attempts to explain

the growth of pentecostalism and the decline of the orthodox churches. The information is based on ethnographic research on religion (chiefly Zion Revival) carried out by this author in Jamaica intermittently since 1972, as well as on a study of pentecostalism in Jamaica by Diane Austin-Broos (1997) and a study of a Jamaican congregation of the New Testament Church of God by Nicole Rodriguez Toulis (1997).

1. The Evolution of Creole Religion.

Jamaica was originally inhabited by perhaps 60,000 Indians, whom archaeologists refer to as Tainos. Columbus "discovered" the island on his second voyage to the New World in 1494 and claimed it for Spain, which governed Jamaica until the English invasion of 1655, by which time the native population no longer existed. In the late 1600s an economy based on the production of sugar cane on relatively large estates or plantations, using enslaved African labor, began to take shape. Jamaica soon became a society of black slaves, ruled over by a small and often abusive white minority, generally intent on returning to England as rich men. This hellish state continued until the emancipation of slaves in 1838, at which time some of the freedmen remained as wage laborers on the plantations, others moved to the towns to become merchants, craftsmen, or laborers, and others became peasants in the mountainous interior.

As one missionary remarked, the slaves were left largely "in heathen darkness." The Anglican Church was supported by the state but existed to serve the (generally dissolute) plantocracy. The slaves developed their own religion, known as Myalism, in the 18th century. Myalism offered to protect individuals from Obeah or sorcery. It specialized in healing the sick, particularly from illnesses due to spirits. And it supplied spiritual fortification in numerous slave revolts.

The Moravians were the first missionaries to come to Jamaica (in 1754), but they initially had little success. Then in 1784 a free black minister by the name of George Lisle came from Georgia and established a church commonly known as the Black Baptists. Some of his followers mixed his teachings with those of Myalism to create a Creole (syncretic, African-European) religion known as the Native Baptists.

Missionaries were sent out to Jamaica by British Methodists in 1789, British Baptists in 1814, and the Church of Scotland in 1819. The Baptists focused on estate slaves and built on the foundation laid by Lisle, quickly becoming the most popular mission in Jamaica. The Methodists and the Presbyterians, on the other hand, built chapels in the towns and found support particularly among the small "free colored" sector. Some lay leaders in the Baptist missions were behind an abortive strike that turned into an uprising in 1831, known as the Baptist War. The reprisals against the missions by island whites were so shocking that Parliament was finally compelled to pass an Act of Emancipation. The missions, particularly the Baptists, received much credit from the slaves for their freedom, as well as for guiding them in the creation of "free villages" of freedmen, but this embracing of the missions was short-lived.

The 1840s and 1850s were decades of despair caused by droughts, epidemics, and low prices for produce. The suffering of the people was generally blamed on Obeah and led to a revival of the slave cult of Myalism, which claimed to use the guidance of angels to find and combat Obeah and Obeahmen. The disheartened missionaries sought to revive their work and combat Myalism through a revival campaign in 1860. It proved to be too successful, however. When the missionaries tried to discourage the Myalist practices that entered into the Great Revival, many of the followers left to create a new Creole religion, Zion Revival, which mingled the beliefs and practices of missionary Christianity with that of the Myalists and Native Baptists. One problem with Zion Revival is that it has never been sanctioned by the state. Its ministers are not licensed to perform marriages, and the churches cannot be incorporated. So a pattern of dual affiliation developed in which Revivalists maintained a nominal membership in a Christian denomination while participating actively in a Revival congregation.

Several lessons can be learned from this brief history, lessons that are pertinent to an understanding of pentecostalism in Jamaica. First, a Creole religion has been evolving in Jamaica for several hundred years (see Wedenoja [1988] for more details). The main dynamic in this religious evolution is the accommodation of African and European beliefs and traditions. Jamaicans have been very adept at taking Western ideas and practices and fitting them into an African and

Church service in Montego Bay, Jamaica.

increasingly Jamaican worldview. Pentecostalism is the latest example of this. Indeed, I would argue that it is the successor to Revival and to orthodox Christianity. It is, as Austin-Broos argues, a reconciliation of the ethical rationalism and moral discipline of orthodox European Christianity with the "eudemonic" enthusiasm of African and Revival ritual and healing. American pentecostalism was an easy "sell" in Jamaica. It fit in well with indigenous beliefs and practices. It offered a bridge between two disparate strands of the culture. Being American, it was more prestigious than Revival and perhaps the orthodox churches. And, unlike Revival, churches could be incorporated and ministers could be licensed. Nonetheless, pentecostalism built on Revival. It was "Jamaicanized," made Creole. Just as Myalism was mixed with orthodox Christianity to make Revival, so pentecostalism has been mixed with Revival—and vice versa. The whole ethos of religion in Jamaica has become imbued with pentecostalism, with both Revival churches and orthodox churches adopting elements of it and all three coming closer together. Indeed, it is getting increasingly more difficult to distinguish a Revival church from a pentecostal church.

2. The Introduction and Growth of Pentecostalism.

Pentecostalism was introduced to Jamaica shortly after the turn of the century, took root in the 1920s and 1930s, but didn't really begin its rapid growth until the 1940s. According to Austin-Broos, an evangelist by the name of J. Wilson Bell was sent to Jamaica in 1918 by the ›Church of God (CG, Cleveland, TN) but left the church several months later. His work was continued by a Jamaican farmer, Rudolph Smith, and two of Smith's converts, Henry Hudson and Percival Graham, who established several churches in rural areas. Following a split in the CG, Hudson was appointed the Jamaican overseer of the New Testament Church of God in 1935, and in the same year Smith was appointed overseer of what later came to be called the ›Church of God of Prophecy. These have become the most popular pentecostal denominations in Jamaica. The other major pentecostal church in Jamaica is the ›United Pentecostal Church, which came to Jamaica in 1947 and absorbed the Pentecostal Ministerial Alliance, a local organization dating back to 1933. A popular indigenous pentecostal church, City Mission, dates to 1924. There are a number of other prominent indigenous pentecostal denominations, including the Shiloah Apostolic Church and the Pentecostal Gospel Temple. The largest pentecostal denomination in the world, the Assemblies of God (AG), did not establish a mission in Jamaica until 1941 and has not grown as fast as the CG. This brief overview indicates how quickly black Jamaicans appropriated these white American organizations and branched out to form their own versions. All of the congregations I am familiar with are in the hands of Jamaican pastors, although they do receive visitors, funds, and literature from the U.S.

In the 1943 census, 4% of Jamaicans claimed affiliation with a pentecostal church. This increased to 13% in the 1960 census, 20% in the 1970 census, 24% in the 1982 census, and 29% (663,224) in the 1991 census. At the same time, those stating an affiliation with an orthodox church (Anglican, Baptist, Methodist, Moravian, Catholic, Presbyterian, and Congregationalist) declined from 82% in 1943 to 25% (577,632) in 1991. The 57-point decline of the orthodox churches is even more remarkable than the 25-point rise of the pentecostal churches. Another remarkable change in religious affiliation is that the percentage of those who claim no religious affiliation rose from 4% in 1943 to 25% (564,564) in 1991.

Throughout this century, Jamaicans have been emigrating in large numbers to other countries, chiefly in the pursuit of more profitable employment. Thousands, for example, worked as laborers in the construction of the Panama Canal, and many of their descendants still live in Panama. But the largest migrations have been to England in the 1950s, Canada in the 1960s, and the U.S. in the 1970s. Today about half a million Jamaicans live in the U.K. and at least that many in North America. Emigrants to the U.K. never felt comfortable or welcome in British churches, so they quickly established their own congregations, which for the most part seem to be pentecostal. Two fine studies of these congregations have been conducted, a very early one by Malcolm Calley (1965) and a recent one by Toulis (1997). Anecdotal evidence indicates that Jamaicans have established many pentecostal congregations in North America as well.

3. The Practice of Pentecostalism in Jamaica.

Jamaicans generally have an extensive knowledge of the Bible and, regardless of religious affiliation, take it literally, as the word of God. God is a remote figure in Revival, whose followers rely on the intercession of angels. This role is played by Jesus in pentecostalism, which is markedly Jesucentric and emphasizes the New Testament over the Old. Pentecostal churches fall into two categories, the "apostolic" churches, which baptize in the name of Jesus (and are commonly referred to as "Jesus-Onlys"), and the Trinitarian churches, which baptize in the name of the Trinity. The Holy Spirit is at home both in Revival and in pentecostal churches, but this power is expressed principally in glossolalia in pentecostal churches, while many other manifestations of the Spirit are also recognized by Revivalists. Both religions practice adult baptism by immersion. Healing figures prominently in both pentecostalism and Revival; it is restricted largely to prayer and the laying on of hands in the former but includes many other techniques, including baths, in the latter. Both religions also emphasize the holiness life of abstention from alcohol, drugs, tobacco, gambling, cursing, cosmetics, jewelry, and revealing clothes. These are all things "of the world," which is morally lax, ungodly, unclean, corrupt, and full of lost souls (Toulis, 175).

Pentecostal services include readings from the Bible, prayer, testimonies from members (typically presenting illnesses or other problems), sermons, altar calls, and the laying on of hands. But the main emphasis seems to be on singing, dancing, and ecstasy, as the "saints" definitely make "a joyful noise unto the Lord." This is also the case in Revival, where a service builds gradually to the point of ecstasy—manifested in "trance" or "possession" states. These services, in both faiths, are typically exciting, entertaining, and participatory events, which perhaps compensate for the restrictions "saints" must follow "in the world."

Pentecostals consider themselves to be "children of God," who is the head of their "family," and they naturally refer to each other as "brothers" and "sisters." A congregation is often a close-knit group, where members rely on each other for support and close themselves off from the unsaved. Indeed, the church should come before work and even family (Toulis, 191). It also tends to take up a lot of time and often money. The church can, therefore, be a refuge from the world, an alternative community. Joining this community sets one apart from, and above, those outside the church. But within the church there is relative equality. So long as you are "saved," nothing else matters—not wealth, power, education, occupation, or family. Perhaps this *communitas* is what enables the congregation to be close-knit.

4. "Getting Saved."

In order to become a "saint," one must become "saved." This rite of passage involves a mystical transformation of the self, resulting in a new person who speaks, dresses, looks, and acts differently (Toulis, 187). Salvation is the central concern of Jamaican pentecostalism. It begins with the recognition that the world is evil and ruled by the devil. One must then become convinced of one's own sinfulness, repent, and accept Jesus as one's personal Savior, in which case one will be cleansed by his blood and be reborn. This conviction is acknowledged by a (generally festive) public baptism. The convert must then live the sanctified life of a Christian, being kind, loving, nurturing, humble, and just (Toulis, 135), avoid the "things of the world," show sexual restraint, and keep his or her body morally pure. Speaking in tongues is clear proof of sanctification, because the Holy Ghost would not enter an impure person (Austin-Broos, 18).

According to Toulis, becoming a Christian transcends other identities, including being Jamaican, West Indian, poor, illegitimate, a single mother, and particularly being black, all of which are stigmatized in the racially antagonistic environment of Jamaicans in the U.K. It also provides a basis for integration with people of different colors and nationalities. Perhaps this is also a reflection of the transnational world that most Jamaicans now find themselves in, where they and their family members live and work in the U.K., Canada, and the U.S., as well as Jamaica.

5. Gender and Pentecostalism.

In almost every church on the island, women are in the majority. According to the 1991 census, the percentage of men indicating affiliation with a denomination ranged from 42% of pentecostals to 47% of Moravians. The gender ratio at an actual service is generally more skewed in favor of women. In contrast, 63% of those who claimed no religion were male. This "feminization" of religion is most evident in pentecostal churches. Indeed, Austin-Broos (203) notes that pentecostal services often become "celebrations of feminine community."

Notwithstanding the above, men generally hold most if not all of the highest positions of authority in pentecostal as well as in orthodox churches (whereas women often become leaders in Revival churches). The church is a community of women, seemingly led by men. Women do most of the inconspicuous work of the church, while men take center stage.

Pentecostal women are taught that they are the weaker sex. They are told to be helpful, passive, supportive, subservient, and submissive wives (Toulis, 227). Nonetheless, many are single women, often with children, or married to men who are unreliable and/or not pentecostal. They seem to find compensatory satisfaction in their holy "marriage" to the church, as a "bride of Christ," who is commonly spoken of as an intimate and dependable companion. Indeed, I have heard more than one woman remark, "Christ is enough husband for me."

Although men are formal leaders, their role is mainly performative in pentecostal churches, where women have considerable informal power. Women assume many lower-level positions, such as evangelist. And because they are free to testify, prophesy, speak in tongues, and occasionally preach, they often seize the stage (from men). Women also engage in more glossolalia and other ecstatic acts than men. Toulis (230) suggests that the power of women in the church is based on the strong role of mothers in Jamaican society (see Wedenoja, 1989). As mothers (in an abstract if not literal sense), they are empowered to "teach, admonish, and discipline" others.

Lower-class men are commonly portrayed (by pentecostals and women in general) as irresponsible, disorderly, unreliable, promiscuous, drinkers, smokers, and gamblers. And, indeed, drinking, smoking, gambling, and promiscuity are ways in which poor young men establish reputations as "men." A male convert has to renounce this male subculture and undergo symbolic feminization to be "saved." He has to embrace the expectations of women and play the role of a good son or a faithful husband. Basically, men have to give up much more than women do to become a "saint." At the same time, it also offers a socially acceptable "out" or alternative to the "rumshop" life that some may want to escape.

6. Sex and Pentecostalism in Jamaica.

As Austin-Broos (156) sees it, the principal focus of Jamaican pentecostalism is the avoidance of fornication. Sin is virtually synonymous with the casual sex and concubinage that prevail in the lower class, which encompasses most Jamaicans. The main concern of the church, particularly the male leadership, is to protect the women of the church from this "sweetheart life." The main job of the pastor is to "preach sin," that is, to warn women of the dangers of sex, which is held to be the downfall of society as well as of women. The burden of sexual restraint seems to fall exclusively on women. Nonetheless, the pentecostal churches are also in the business of refurbishing tarnished souls. Unlike the orthodox churches, they will accept single mothers and wash their sins away. And they also offer respectability to the single working woman, which, according to the middle-class values promoted by the orthodox churches, could only be gained by getting married and becoming a housewife.

7. Modernization and Pentecostalism.

In the preceding sections, I have emphasized aspects of Jamaican pentecostalism that may be unique to the culture. But pentecostalism is, of course, sweeping the world, particularly the so-called Third World. There must be some more-or-less universal factors to explain its broad appeal. Earlier (Wedenoja, 1980) I associated the rise of pentecostalism in Jamaica with the process of modernization, including the transition from an agrarian to an industrial society, migration from rural to urban areas (and abroad) in search of wage labor employment, economic expansion, a rising standard of living, commercialization, materialism, social mobility and the growth of a middle-class, and the emergence of a democratic, national political system to replace colonial rule. In this context, new and greater expectations for the future are raised, as well as new and probably greater anxieties. It is clear that the old order is waning, but the shape of the new order is still uncertain. People are living in dislocation from their home and relatives in the company of strangers. They need to acquire more education and show more initiative and self-reliance to get ahead. In short, modernization requires the development of new attitudes, new values, new abilities, new personality traits, and a new sense of self, including individualism, personal discipline, and initiative. Religion is probably the most effective way to accomplish this, particularly on a mass scale, in which case anthropologists refer to it as a "revitalization movement" (Wallace, 1956). Pentecostalism is often criticized as a conservative force that supports free-market capitalism and American hegemony. However, it does seem to be realistic for Jamaicans to embrace American capitalism. Particularly after the fall of communism and socialism, it has become the only game in town. The only alternative is to try and get out of the game entirely, which is the course the Rastafarians have followed.

8. The Appeals of Pentecostalism.

I am not a religious person, much less a pentecostal, but having lived for extended periods of time in peasant and lower-class communities in Jamaica, I can readily appreciate the attractions of pentecostalism. One common way people find their way to a pentecostal church is through a need for healing. Their suffering may be physical in cause, but it is more commonly spiritual (or, if preferred, psychological). They find a shelter from the world with warm, supportive, concerned people who come to be a "family." They become engaged in a process of identity transformation that allows them to turn from the past and look to the future. In doing so, they earn the respect of others and feel better about themselves. They find many opportunities to get involved in the church and gain offices. They learn to stand in front of hundreds of people and speak or sing to them, and they are praised for doing so. They feel blessed that God has chosen them as a vehicle for his Holy Spirit. And they are given many opportunities, in services, to demonstrate the fact that they have been chosen. They find a sense of connectedness or place. And they can sing and dance joyously for hours each week. Finally, and perhaps most controversially, they ally with a movement that is closely associated with the U.S., the dominant power in the world today, a nation that has been an icon of hope, prosperity, and upward mobility for decades, a country to which many yearn to emigrate for those very reasons.

For statistics, see beginning of next article.

■ **Bibliography:** D. J. Austin-Broos, *Ja'maica Genesis: Religion and the Politics of Moral Orders* (1997) ■ M. J. C. Calley, *God's People: West Indian Pentecostal Sects in England* (1965) ■ N. R. Toulis, *Believing Identity: Pentecostalism and the Mediation of Jamaican Ethnicity and Gender in England* (1997) ■ A. F. C. Wallace, "Revitalization Movements," *American Anthropologist* 58:264–81 ■ W. Wedenoja, "Modernization and the Pentecostal Movement in Jamaica," in *Perspectives on Pentecostalism: Case Studies from the Caribbean and Latin America*, ed. S. D. Glazier (1980) ■ idem, "Mothering and the Practice of 'Balm' in Jamaica," in *Women as Healers: Cross-Cultural Perspectives*, ed. C. S. McClain (1989) ■ idem, "The Origins of Revival, a Creole Religion in Jamaica," in *Culture and Christianity: The Dialectics of Transformation*, ed. G. R. Saunders (1988).

■ W. Wedenoja

JAMAICA (II)

■ Pentecostals 169,902 (44%)   ■ Charismatics 63,604 (17%)   ■ Neocharismatics 151,494 (39%)   ■ Total Renewal: 385,000

The beginnings of pentecostalism in Jamaica go back to the early 20th century. By 1917 a number of independent pentecostal churches were on the island. Most appear to have been the result either of the efforts of independent missionaries who went to Jamaica before the organization of pentecostal mission boards or of immigrants to the U.S. who returned to bring the message of pentecostalism to Jamaica. Scholars have generally been more interested in the current social realities of pentecostalism than in its history and theology. It is known that one of the early pentecostal evangelists was J. Wilson Bell, who in 1917 contacted the Church of God (CG, Cleveland, TN) and proposed an affiliation. Bell was imprisoned and his ministry destroyed because he did not seek medical attention for one of his children who became ill and died. U.S. mission executive J. S. Llewellyn went to Jamaica in Apr. 1918 and organized a church from Bell's former congregation. J. M. Parkinson was appointed pastor. The denomination grew quickly but elicited strong persecution. Considerable dissension among the pentecostals themselves evolved, both in Jamaica and in the U.S.

Therefore, little additional contact was made until 1924. E. E. Simmons of Florida went to Jamaica in 1925. He was succeeded by T. A. Sears. Sears, however, was convicted of immorality, and Z. R. Thomas was appointed overseer of the eight CG congregations in Jamaica in 1928. By 1935, when Thomas retired, there were 53 churches and 1,595 members. Evangelistic work was then undertaken in the Turk Islands, where congregations were established, as they were on Jamaica. The British colonial authorities forced the missionaries to leave during WWII, and supervision was loosely organized from the U.S. After the war, the missionaries returned, and efforts were made to establish a Bible school. Since 1950 there has been a CG Bible school in Kingston. Numerical growth continued apace. By 1959 the CG reported 189 congregations, with 11,218 members and 30,000 adherents, for the New Testament Church of God in Jamaica. In 1980, 32,218 members and 50,000 adherents were claimed by the church.

The United Pentecostal Church (UPC) was influenced in its earlier development in Jamaica by the Pentecostal Assemblies of the World (PAOW), which was established in Jamaica as early as 1914. One of the converts was Nina Ryan Russell (1888–1952), a Jamaican, who experienced baptism in the Holy Spirit in 1920. She had early contact with ▸Andrew Ursham and did evangelistic work throughout Jamaica. At Russell's invitation, ▸William T. Witherspoon of Columbus, OH, went to Jamaica in 1934 to establish the UPC. Nina Ryan Russell became a popular legend throughout the country, beyond pentecostal circles, and had a major role in defining pentecostalism in Jamaica. By 1980 the UPC claimed about 16,000 adherents in 62 congregations. In 1999 the UPC in Jamaica claimed 31,000 "constituents" in 218 "churches and preaching points."

Cyril Darell-Huckerby, born on Grenada to medical missionary parents, experienced the pentecostal baptism of the Holy Spirit in Vancouver, B.C., in 1934. Feeling called to Jamaica, he arrived in Spanish Town in Feb. 1937. By 1940 he was corresponding with the U.S. ▸Assemblies of God (AG) mission department, and he was appointed a missionary of that organization in late 1942. Through his work other independent congregations also decided to unite with the AG. On Aug. 1, 1943, the first annual conference of the Jamaican AG was held, with 400 in attendance, representing six congregations. By 1944 there were 13 congregations; by late 1945, 22; by 1977 there were 44 congregations and 5,568 "believers." In 1999 the Assemblies of God–U.S. mission statistics reported 12,800 "members and adherents."

The ▸Open Bible Standard Church was invited to Jamaica by the president of the Jamaican House of Representatives, S. A. Black, on July 23, 1948, at First Church of the Open Bible, Des Moines, IA. Ivan and Kay Morton were appointed missionaries to Jamaica in May 1949. A church was dedicated on Apr. 29, 1952, in Montego Bay, and a Bible school was established in Newport in 1953. In May 1974 the 25th anniversary of the church was held, and a totally Jamaican administration under the leadership of Pervis Gordon was elected. The North American church continues to supply occasional evangelists, seminars on spirituality, and hurricane recovery aid as needed. The Jamaican church has supported missionaries in the Cayman Islands, India, Pakistan, England, Nigeria, Venezuela, and the U.S. The church claims 38 congregations, 6,000 members, and one Bible school (1995). There are perhaps another 12,000 adherents.

Other pentecostal denominations in Jamaica include the assorted Apostolic Churches, Apostolic Church of God in Christ, ▸Apostolic Church of Pentecost (Canada), Assemblies of the First-Born, Church of God Fellowship, ▸Church of God in Christ, ▸Church of God of Prophecy, Church of God Pentecostal, ▸International Church of the Foursquare Gospel, International City Mission, ▸Pentecostal Assemblies of the World, and the ▸Pentecostal Church of God. In addition to the U.S. mission-related churches, there are many indigenous congregations and small denominations. There are also churches with connections to the U.K., including the Apostolic Church (Wales), as well as connections to emigrants to the U.K. who have founded branches of Jamaican traditions there. The Nigerian Aladura Church, the Church of the Lord (Aladura), also has a presence in Jamaica. Many independent mission groups, such as ▸Christ for the Nations (CFN), are present. CFN maintains a Bible school in Montego Bay, Jamaica, which works closely with the numerous independent charismatic congregations of the English-speaking Caribbean.

■ **Bibliography:** D. B. Barrett, *World Christian Encyclopedia* (1982), 416–19 ▪ L. E. Barrett, "Africa Roots of Jamaican Indigenous Religion," *Journal of Religious Thought* 35 (1978) ▪ I. Campbell, "Church of God Jamaican Experience: From Pocomaniasm to Pentecostalism" (paper, CG School of Theol., 1984) ▪ C. W. Conn, *Where the Saints Have Trod: A History of Church of God Missions* (1959) ▪ Division of Foreign Missions [AG–U.S.], *1999 Annual Statistics* (1999) ▪ *Foreign Missions Insight: A Digest of Foreign Missions Faces, Facts, Fields and Figures,* ed. D. L. Burk (1999), 80 ▪ S. M. Hodges, *Look on the Fields: A Survey of the Assemblies of God in Foreign Lands* (1956), 186–88 ▪ W. J. Hollenweger, *Handbuch der Pfingstbewegung* (diss., Zurich, 1967), 1027–39 [para. 02b.13] ▪ J. B. Hopkins, "Music in the Jamaican Pentecostal Churches" (thesis, Harvard, 1974) ▪ [H. McCracken], *History of Church of God Missions* (1943) ▪ D. A. McGavern, *Church Growth in Jamaica* (1962) ▪ R. B. Mitchell and L. M. Mitchell, *Heritage and Harvest: The History of the International Ministries of the Open Bible Standard Churches* (1995) ▪ F. E. Olsen, "Church of God Jamaica School of Theology," *Church of God Evangel* (Feb. 23, 1957) ▪ R. V. Reynolds, "Nina Ryan Russell," in *Profiles of Pentecostal Missionaries* (1986) ▪ E. L. Simmons, *History of the Church of God* (1938) ▪ W. Wedenoja, "Modernization and the Pentecostal Movement in Jamaica," in *Perspectives on Pentecostalism: Case Studies from the Caribbean and Latin America,* ed. S. D. Glazier (1980) ▪ idem, "Religion and Adaptation in Rural Jamaica" (diss., U. of Calif.–San Diego, 1978) ▪ C. A. Wilson, "The Religious Education Programme in Jamaica and the Need to Contextualize" (paper, CG School of Theol., 1985).   ■ D. D. Bundy

JAPAN

■ Pentecostals 55,740 (3%)   ■ Charismatics 152,234 (9%)   ■ Neocharismatics 1,552,026 (88%)   ■ Total Renewal: 1,760,000

I. Pentecostalism

II. The Charismatic Movement

III. Indigenous Pentecostal Churches

I. PENTECOSTALISM.

A. Pre–World War II Pentecostal Works.

Pentecostalism first arrived in Japan on Aug. 11, 1913, in the person of Carl F. Jeurgensen and family. Although their first years were difficult, by 1927 he was able to purchase property and establish the longest-lasting pentecostal church in Takinogawa, Tokyo. By 1914 the Jeurgensens were strengthened by the arrival of B. S. Moore and his wife, who were the first officially sent Assemblies of God (AG) missionaries to Japan. The first pentecostal experiences by Japanese believers reportedly took place in 1918–19. The pentecostal movement in Japan was most influenced by Kiyoma Yumiyama, who became interested in pentecostalism through the ministry of C. F. Jeurgensen's son, John. It was Yumiyama who in 1930 became pastor of the Takinogawa, Shinshou Church. To raise ministers, Yumiyama, established the Holy Spirit Bible Institute (Seirei Shingakuin) in 1931. During this period, pentecostal churches were added through the combined efforts of the institute graduates, transfer ministers, and missionaries from the U.S., Canada, and Great Britain. By 1940 the AG had many missionaries, about 20 Japanese pastors, and 15 churches. In 1941, however, the fellowship joined what was known as Block 10 of the Kyodan, the war-times United Church.

Another pentecostal work that has its roots in prewar Japan is that of the British layman turned missionary, L. W. Coots. He and his son established a Bible school in Ikoma in 1929. The work was closed during World War II but was reopened in 1950. Although for a time the work was considered ▸Oneness, it is presently considered Trinitarian.

B. Post–World War II Era.

The Japan AG reestablished itself in 1949, with the presence of missionaries and 16 Japanese ministers. Kiyoma Yumiyama was elected as the first superintendent. He was to be followed in the next 50 years by R. Kikuchi, A. Ito, M. Safu, and K. Kikuyama. In 1950 the Bible institute that had

Evangelistic crusade in Tokyo, Japan.

been started in 1931 was relocated and began to produce ministers not only for the AG, but for other pentecostal denominations and independent works.

The AG increased from 16 ministers and 4 church buildings to about 200 churches in 1999 (12,576 members in 1997). They account for almost half of the classical pentecostal population in Japan.

The postwar era, however, brought in many new pentecostal organizations into Japan. A recent study (Trevor, 1993) lists the following organizations as being pentecostal/charismatic: Japan AG; Sanbi Kyodan; Japan Open Bible Church; Japan Foursquare Gospel Kyodan; The Flock of the Gospel of Jesus Christ; Pentecostal Church of God in Japan; Japan Pentecostal Kyodan; Family of God Christian Church; Philadelphia Church Mission; Japan Evangelical Church; Japan Church of God; Calvary United Churches of Christ; Next Towns Crusade in Japan; Zion Mission; Missions to Japan, Inc.; Bethany Christian Assemblies; Full Gospel Tokyo Church; Christian Evangelistic Church; Independent Pentecostal Churches Fellowship; Finland Free Overseas Missionary Society; Total Christian Church; Independent Pentecostal Churches; Japan Gospel Mission, Inc.; Christian Fellowship of Japan; Ie no Kyokai; Apostolic Faith Mission; Japan Faith Mission; Japan Evangelical Church of Christ; Zama Christ Church. Others that could be listed are Jiyu Kurisuchan Dendo Dan, Tokyo Chuo Church, and Japan Christian Evangelistic Assemblies.

Of special note is the Full Gospel Church in Japan under the leadership of David (Paul) Yonggi Cho. The work was started when the Korean Yoido Church sent a worker to Tokyo in 1974. Since then 34 churches and a Bible school have been established. The total number of members is not known. From 1992 through 1997, a figure of 6,751 has been reported *(1999 Christian Yearbook)*. This is doubtful, however, since the number of churches reported in 1992 was 21, while in 1997, 34 are listed. It has also been pointed out that in the larger churches approximately two-thirds of the congregation were Koreans, while only one-third were Japanese.

The pentecostal movement in Japan received its first official evangelical recognition in 1988 when the Japan AG became a member of the Japan Evangelical Association (JEA). The prominent role of pentecostal/charismatics at the Lausanne II conference combined with the advent of the so-called *third wave movement caused a series of debates in the JEA. First, in 1991, pneumatology was debated, ultimately allowing for a pentecostal understanding. Power evangelism was then debated in 1994 with the result that some charismatics found it necessary to establish a parallel organization, the Nippon Revival Association (NRA), in 1996. The NRA has as its goal to establish a ministerial membership of 1,000, which would include those who consider themselves third wave, charismatic, or classical pentecostal. In 1998, 10 pentecostal organizations established a Pentecostal Coalition.

Included in this loose fellowship are Japan Open Bible Church, The Flock of the Gospel of Jesus Christ, Japan Church of God, Zion Mission, Family of God Christian Church, Japan Pentecostal Kyodan, Calvary United Churches of Christ, Japan Foursquare Gospel Kyodan, Japan AG, and Independent Pentecostal Churches Fellowship.

II. THE CHARISMATIC MOVEMENT.

The Catholic charismatic movement began in Japan in 1972 when Hiroshi Yoshiyama of the Japan AG was invited to the Hatsudai Catholic Church in Shibuya, Tokyo, for a Holy Spirit Seminar. The seminar was attended by 20 to 30 people: priests and believers, professors and seminarians. By the end of the two-month seminar, attendees received the Spirit baptism and a Catholic charismatic work was begun. In 1974 David du Plessis was invited to minister at a series of Holy Spirit Seminars that have continued since then. It is estimated that there are about 200 Catholic charismatic prayer groups today.

The name Yoshiyama continues to play a significant role in the Protestant charismatic movement also. Beginning from an initial series of meetings by *Ja-Sil Choi, David (Paul) Yonggi Cho's mother-in-law, focusing on prayer and fasting in preparation for the 1964 Tokyo Olympics, a connection was made with Korean pentecostalism that would not be unraveled. In 1968 Cho came to minister for Yoshiyama at his

Evangelistic center, Tokyo, Japan.

church, Koiwa Christ Church. Although it was not until 1977 that Cho would be part of an annual Tokyo Gospel Crusade, the bond with Yoshiyama sealed the future of the Protestant charismatic movement. Cho continued to minister for the next 15 to 16 years at the annual crusades. In 1978 Cho set the agenda in the charismatic mass meetings, where the goal of the salvation of 10 million Japanese souls was established. This tie to Korean pentecostalism is probably one of the unique characteristics of the Japanese charismatic movement.

A second parallel trajectory was that of a North American connection. First, the Canadian Lester Pritchard was invited to Japan for a Holy Spirit Revival in 1970. From this initial seminar, such names as ˃Bob Mumford, Dick Drisco, and others came and ministered to both pentecostals and evangelicals alike. At the 1971 Kanto Holy Spirit Revival Seminar, evangelicals and non-Japanese Catholic priests who had experienced charismatic services before gathered together. In this same vein in 1976 Pat Boone was invited; however, foreshadowing Cho's ministry in Japan, the charismatic service was transformed into evangelistic meetings.

During the mid 1980s, this trend toward evangelism over against charismatic manifestations played a strong role in mass meetings. It was not until 1990 that a renewed emphasis on signs and wonders began to change the tenor of the mass meetings. In 1992 lay minister Carlos Anacondia from Argentina began a trend that was followed by Claudio Frazen and others. At about the same time, the silent Japan Full Gospel Business Men's Fellowship sponsored Benny Hinn and others.

Beginning in the late 1980s, Japan was introduced to the so-called third wave through the teachings of Peter Wagner, his former students from Fuller Theological Seminary, and Vineyard Fellowship music.

III. INDIGENOUS PENTECOSTAL CHURCHES.

Japan has produce quite a few indigenous pentecostal groups. These include the Glorious Gospel Christian Church (1936), the Living Christ One Ear of Wheat Church (1939), Christian Canaan Church (1940), Japan Ecclesia of Christ (1940), the Spirit of Jesus Church (1941), Holy Ecclesia of Jesus (1946), the Sanctifying Christ Church (1948), and the Original Gospel Movement (1948) (Mullins, 1998). The three most prominent have been the Original Gospel Movement, the Spirit of Jesus Church, and the Holy Ecclesia of Jesus.

A. Original Gospel Movement.

The Original Gospel movement (Genshi Fukuin), sometimes referred to as the Tabernacle (Makuya) movement, is a split from the indigenous Nonchurch movement (Mukyoukai) founded by Kanzou Uchimura. Beginning in 1948, Ikurou Tejima (1910–73) and his followers began to experience tongues.

The core teachings of the Original Gospel movement have been taken from the teachings of the Nonchurch move-

ment, which include an independence from Western-based traditions, nonsacramentalism, emphasis on studying the Bible in Greek and Hebrew, and a ˃House-Church tradition (Mullins, 1998). In an attempt to be more biblically based, Tejima also began to teach and practice faith healing and prophesying. However, he also includes walking on coals (begun in 1958) and water ablutions, both adaptations from Japanese folk religions.

An important characteristic of the Original Gospel movement is its Old Testament or Zionist leaning. This can be seen in the use of the menorah as symbolizing the living Christ, the sending of trainees to Israel to learn Hebrew and Jewish culture, promoting annual pilgrimages to Israel, and publishing both popular and scholarly works related to the Hebrew language and Jewish origins. Practices have been affected to the point of sabbath observances, the use of Jewish folk music, and the celebration of bar mitzvahs.

The Original Gospel movement's unique combination of emphasis on a Jewish (Messianic) gospel, pentecostal experiences, and Japanese folk religions has fostered a strong nationalistic ideology emphasizing early Japanese mythologies and a glorification of the Japanese spirit.

It is difficult to establish the total adherence to the Original Gospel movement since they are a House-Church based movement that has not kept attendance records. They claim to distribute 25,000 copies of their monthly publications; however, in 1993 the movement gave a far more conservative figure of only 10,000 members.

B. Spirit of Jesus Church.

A second indigenous pentecostal movement is the Spirit of Jesus Church (Ieus no Mitama Kyoukai). Its founder, Jun Murai, upon experiencing tongues during a personal crisis in 1918, began to seek a different type of Christianity than that which he had experienced as a Methodist preacher's child. Murai aligned himself with the first pentecostal group that would ultimately become the Japan AG. He pastored the Nishisugamo Church beginning in 1933. In 1941, however, upon invitation from the True Jesus Church, he traveled to Taiwan, where he revised his teachings and formed a new church. The church was called the "Spirit of Jesus Christ" in response to a revelatory experience his wife Suwa Murai received.

Doctrinally, Murai modified his early AG-style pentecostal teaching with an explicit statement that both water and spirit baptism are necessary for salvation, that the Saturday sabbath was to be observed along with footwashing, that members were to adhere to the oneness doctrine, and that baptisms could be done on behalf of the dead. A Bible school was established in 1952 to promote this new movement.

In 1993 the Spirit of Jesus Christ claimed 433,108 members and 203 churches; however, only 143 of the churches are in Japan, while the practice of baptisms for the dead artificially inflates the membership figures. It is estimated that a more realistic figure would be anywhere between 5,000 and 10,000 (Trevor, 1993).

C. Holy Ecclesia of Jesus.

The Holy Ecclesia of Jesus was begun through a series of revelations to Takeji Otsuki, who had served as a Holiness missionary in China and had reportedly had a hand in 8,000 healings. It was in 1946 that Otsuki received a revelation to start a new church that would emphasize an apostolic Christianity. Building on the doctrines of the Holiness minister Juuji Nakada, which included the necessity for Israel to be restored, Otsuki added spirit baptism and the teaching that it was normative for Christians to receive revelations from God. Further revelations to Otsuki involved an understanding of "calling on the name(s) of God" as being salvific. This led to chanting the "names of God," which is similar to Buddhist-based chanting (Mullins, 1998).

The Holy Ecclesia of Jesus puts much emphasis on healing. Churches and homes will normally have flasks of oil or handkerchiefs for healing prayer. Recently a "Mary Spring" has been the focus of healing pilgrimages or water distribution. Along with the above use of visual aids like oil, handkerchiefs, and healing water, the Holy Ecclesia of Jesus utilizes other symbols, which is a form of contextualization of the gospel to the Japanese setting. This has included much borrowing from Catholicism and Japanese ritual traditions.

The Holy Ecclesia of Jesus continues the heritage of Juuji Nakada and the prayer for Israel. Although this has not taken the form of evangelization, like the Original Gospel movement, it has attempted to foster a positive image of Judaism and social-political relations with Israel. This has also lead to the incorporation of a Jewish element into its worship and religious calendar.

The Holy Ecclesia of Jesus has a seminary, the Logos Theological Seminary, which matriculates ministers who were single upon entry and who have now established 104 churches with a reported membership of 6,525 people.

■ **Bibliography:** *1999 Christian Yearbook* ■ C. Caldarola, *Christianity the Japanese Way* (1979) ■ Y. Ikegami, "Okinawan Shamansim and Charismatic Christianity," *The Japan Christian Review* 59 (1993) ■ Japan Assemblies of God Historical Committee, *Mitama ni Michibikarete* (Lead by the Holy Spirit, 1979) ■ M. R. Mullins, *Christianity Made in Japan: A Study of Indigenous Movements* (1998) ■ H. Trevor, *Japan's Post-War Protestant Churches* (1993).

■ D. Hymes

JORDAN

■ Pentecostals 2,653 (3%)　■ Charismatics 8,467 (10%)　■ Neocharismatics 76,879 (87%)　■ Total Renewal: 87,999

See AFRICA, NORTH, AND THE MIDDLE EAST.

KAZAKHSTAN

■ Pentecostals 0 (0%)　■ Charismatics 43,986 (54%)　■ Neocharismatics 38,014 (46%)　■ Total Renewal: 82,000

See RUSSIA.

KENYA

■ Pentecostals 2,077,689 (25%)　■ Charismatics 1,730,553 (21%)　■ Neocharismatics 4,541,758 (54%)
■ Total Renewal: 8,350,000

For general introduction to East Africa and bibliography, see AFRICA, EAST.

Kenya was a British colony before Independence in 1963. The population is roughly 45% Protestant. The government is not antagonistic to the church; many politicians and government officials in Kenya would identify themselves as Christians because they were educated in mission schools. In spite of its times of discontent, Kenya, along with Tanzania, is regarded as one of the most politically stable countries on the African continent. There is a relatively high ratio of Protestant missionaries to believers in Kenya, with over 2,300 foreign missionaries in the country in 1993, of whom 140 were pentecostals. The number of pentecostal missionaries has been reduced since that time. It is said that Kenya is one of the most evangelized of all African countries. Today most of the churches, including the pentecostal denominations, are under the authority of national church bodies and led by Kenyans.

1. Earliest Beginnings.

The first record of a pentecostal missionary in Kenya is that of Emil Danielsson, who went from Finland to Kenya in 1912, before there were any organized pentecostal churches in Finland. Next are the Witticks, who had first worked as missionaries at Utigi, Tanzania (then Tanganyika). After the death of Karl Wittick and Clarence Grothaus, Marion Wittick remained in Tanzania until her furlough. Shortly after her return to East Africa she married Otto Keller. Immigration restrictions prevented their reentering Tanzania, so in 1918 they turned their attention to Kenya. Eight miles from Kisumu, on Lake Victoria in Western Kenya at Nyang'ori, land was purchased; a church, a school, a workshop, student dormitories, and a home for the missionaries were erected. The colonial government insisted that in order for the mission to receive recognition, it had to have the backing of a chartered organization that would guarantee its stability and permanence. At that point Keller approached the PAOC concerning affiliation with the Kenya mission. In 1924 the PAOC accepted Kenya as one of its mission fields, and for many years Nyang'ori was considered the center of the PAOC missions outreach in Kenya. This was the beginning of what is today known as the Pentecostal Assemblies of God (PAG) in Kenya.

2. Pentecostal Assemblies of Canada.

In 1929 a great revival broke out on the mission stations with the result that many were converted and filled with the Holy Spirit. Twelve different ethnic groups, including the Maragoli, the Luo, the Bunoyore, the Tiriki, and the Nyang'ori peoples were touched during this revival, and this necessitated the training of many more Kenyan workers.

Because of the inability of the majority of the population to read, the missionaries found it was not possible to encourage the study of the Bible by the new believers. As in most mission areas in Africa, it was therefore necessary to become involved in educational programs to teach the people to read. Primary schooling was an integral part of this outreach. Initially, someone who could read was made responsible for the reading of the Bible in the daily worship meetings. Scriptures were often read in unison and memorized. By 1929 Nellie Henderson from Winnipeg began to teach pedagogy to the more advanced students who were also given Bible instruction. She became founder and principal of the Teacher Training School at Kisumu and also taught later in the Bethel Bible Institute of Kenya. The colonial government was so impressed with the educational initiatives of the Canadian missionaries that they agreed to subsidize the salaries of the Kenyan teachers in the mission schools.

A number of the earlier PAOC missionaries to Kenya were involved in educational work. The James Skinners (see articles on Zimbabwe and Zambia) were one such couple; they arrived in Kenya in 1936. During their time in Kenya, all the PAOC schools in Kenya were recognized by the colonial authorities. Others who started out in the educational system in Kenya but later became more involved in church activities and evangelism included the Fred Clarkes, who

arrived in Kenya in 1936 and worked at Goibei, where by 1958 there were 100 churches planted, and the John McBrides, who arrived at the beginning of WWII; the latter eventually moved to Nairobi to be in charge of the churches in that area. McBride became chairman of the Kenya Conference of the PAOC churches.

Through the Canadian evangelist Willard Cantelon, a link had been forged between the German Volksmission and the PAOC, so that from 1956 to the present they have collaborated in missionary work in East Africa. The first Volksmission missionary to join the PAOC work in their East African field was Heinz Battermann. Since that time more than 28 missionaries from the Volksmission have worked as part of the PAG team in Kenya, Uganda, and Tanzania. Battermann was first installed at Vihiga in western Kenya; he was also the person to launch the printing press at Nyang'ori and later went on to minister among the Masai and to teach in the Bible school at Nyang'ori.

The schools were seen as a means to evangelism. The PAOC began to plant churches starting from the areas where the schools were founded. All those who were involved in education were at the same time planting churches. Converts were taught that it was the responsibility of each believer to evangelize. The PAOC work in Kenya, Uganda, and Tanzania was originally united under the Pentecostal Assemblies of East Africa. With the breakup of the East African federation (Kenya, Uganda, and Tanganyika), the name Pentecostal Assemblies of God (PAG) was taken by the church in each of those countries. By 1958 there were more than 40,000 adult members in the PAG, and by 1967 an estimated 98,000. The missionary body grew significantly after WWII, but this was reduced to a minimum in the 1970s. By 1975 there were 1,600 congregations in the PAG–Kenya with over 190,000 adult members. There are now more than 5,000 PAG churches.

One of the notable things about the PAOC/PAG mission is the number of outstanding women who have been involved in education, medical work, and church planting. Starting with Marion Wittick, the list includes Nellie Hendrickson, Marion Munro, Renata Siemens, Irene Boris, Kathryn Roth, June Deacon, Mary Elder, Jean Meikle, Margaret Cantwell, Pauline Vaters, Iris Scheel, Marilyn Bush, and a number of others. Included in this group are several from the Volksmission: Adele Hilgert (née Bohlender); Margarete Mayer, who started out in nursing but found her niche in the national women's ministry; Bärbel zum Felde; Elisabeth Mast (née Hinger); Cornelia Frey; Elsbeth Meyer (Swiss Pentecostal); and numbers of others through whom sterling work has been accomplished in Kenya.

Churches have been planted in all areas of the country by the PAOC, which handed over responsibility to capable national leaders in 1965. Successive general superintendents include Charles Gungu, Shem Irangi, Michael Otang, and since June 1998 Salomo Salamba. Other outstanding leaders were Matia Alungwa, Dawde Chole, Stephen Umwari, Albert Owino, and Richard Odongo. Mark Kidula served as general secretary for 19 years until his death in Sept. 1993 and was also responsible for the missions outreach of the PAG within Kenya. Another man of considerable ability is Richard Odeng, who presently serves on the World Pentecostal Advisory Board.

The 1950s were very difficult years when, prior to Independence, the Mau Mau movement called for the expulsion of all whites. Much blood was shed in a brutal campaign, primarily by the Kikuyu and their allies, to wrest power from the British. The Kikuyu, Embu, and Meru peoples were involved in this uprising, which did not extend to all of the country. At this time Bahati, in Nairobi, was chosen to be the location of a new PAOC church; Bahati was the most troubled and terrorized location in Nairobi. One of the reasons for the Mau Mau success was that Kenya was being saturated by anti-Christian and communist propaganda.

In 1952 the Evangel Press (EP) was established at Nyang'ori by the PAOC to produce gospel literature. This press was later moved to Nairobi, where it shares the grounds of the Pan African Christian College (which grants a four-year B.A. degree), founded by the PAOC. It has become one of the largest evangelical publishers in East Africa. A number of missionaries from the Volksmission have been involved in the EP since its inception; these include Heinz Battermann, who was the first to launch the project at Nyang'ori; Ernst and Denise Spengler; and Richard and Frida Schaaf). Between the German, Canadian, and Kenyan personnel, this press continues to make a considerable contribution to the entire evangelical outreach in East Africa.

The largest pentecostal church in Nairobi is Valley Road Pentecostal Church, belonging to PAG. This church seats approximately 3,500 people and is filled three times every Sunday. Valley Road has been pastored by a number of missionaries, but for the past decade Dennis White, a missionary who is the fruit of PAOC missionary work in the Caribbean, has been the pastor. Recently, however, he has handed over this church to a Kenyan pastor and plans to plant churches in the city. Elmer and Sherry Komont, who pioneered a large church among the Muslims at Mombassa, have recently handed this work over to national leaders.

Evangelism has always been emphasized by the PAOC in Kenya. Willard Cantelon, a Canadian PAOC evangelist, together with Alfred Garr, a former Hollywood singer, held evangelistic campaigns in Nairobi in 1955. David Forest, missionary evangelist of the PAOC, has also held campaigns in several African countries including Kenya.

3. Pentecostal Evangelistic Fellowship of Africa.

The Pentecostal Evangelistic Fellowship of Africa (PEFA), established by Elim Fellowship of Lima, NY, is today an independent, self-supporting, African Pentecostal association. Bud Sickler went in 1944 from Elim to Kenya, where he settled and still lives in Mombasa. Sickler was aware that there were many independent pentecostal churches in Kenya that were not recognized by the government. He created the structure that has since become the PEFA, which is more an association of independent pentecostal churches than it is a denomination with an homogenous doctrinal and practical position to uphold. This means that the majority of PEFA churches have a great deal of autonomy and hold to their own distinctive theological emphases. PEFA, in its early days, invited ►T. L. Osborn to hold a crusade in Kenya in 1960; great healings and miracles took place, and PEFA grew enormously as a result. It now has about 1,400 churches throughout Kenya. PEFA is run by a council of elders. The general overseer is Erastus Otteno. By 1964 PEFA had 725 churches and a membership of 70,000. By 1982 this number had grown to 150,000 members, and in 1995 there were an estimated 310,000 adherents in 2,130 churches.

4. The Full Gospel Churches of Kenya.

The Full Gospel Churches of Kenya (FGCK) were founded by the Finnish Free Foreign Mission (FFFM). In 1949 the FFFM sent Alma and Eeva Taatikainen and Paavo and Vieno Kusmin to Kenya. They began their ministry in the western part of the country. Mauri Viksten, who followed in 1953, was known as the "Spiritual Seer" of the FFFM Kenyan mission, and was accepted as a well-respected Bible teacher. After 1965 many Finnish missionaries came to Kenya, which meant that it became the main FFFM mission field for a good number of years. During its time of greatest involvement, the FFFM had over 70 missionaries working in Kenya. Today, however, the work is totally indigenous and the missionaries assist only in special projects. By 1997 there were about 150,000 baptized adult members in the FGCK. The FGCK organizes its churches in the same way as the Swedish Free Mission (see below), so that there were 150 fully autonomous churches with about 2,000 subchurches still under the direction of a mother assembly. The chairman of the FGCK is Stephen Kiguru. Since 1960 the Koru Bible School has trained hundreds of workers who showed signs of a divine call and were already active in ministry. The Bible school has various streams and courses, including an elementary course, extension courses on different topics, a three-year diploma, and a child and youth ministry training program; it is also involved in holding regional seminars. Although it is partially self-sufficient, this school is also supported by the Finnish pentecostal churches. An important radio ministry is responsible for the broadcasting of nearly 800 programs in 13 different languages on a regular basis. Pioneering work among the Turkana and Pokot peoples was started through the Kapeddo Medical Clinic. The LKA Finnish aid project joined in the support of this program, and it was expanded to provide educational and health care projects with preschoolers, elementary and secondary schooling, a hospital, and medical clinics. These projects are all under national direction, although the LKA still supports them financially. As early as 1965 the Finnish missionaries were involved in looking after orphans at Homa Bay. Priority is now given to those who are orphaned due to the AIDS epidemic.

5. The Free Pentecostal Fellowship in Kenya.

The Svenska Fria Missionen (SFM—Swedish Free Mission) sent Gustav Struble to Kenya in 1961. He settled at Menegai in Nakuru, where he ran Bible courses for young people who later became the church planters of pentecostal churches.

The Pinsevennes Ytre Misjon (PYM, Pentecostal Foreign Mission of Norway) has been involved in Kenya since 1950. Walter Olsen, who belonged to this Norwegian mission, was partly supported by independent groups in Norway, and the churches he started in Kenya are therefore not regarded as solely the offspring of the PYM. His work became what is today known as the East Africa Pentecostal Churches. Most of its churches are in the Mount Kenya area. An estimate of the number of members is 30,000 in several hundred churches. The Arvid Bustgaards were sent to Kenya by the PYM in 1955. They went to Muhoroni, some 40 miles from Kisumu, where a farm called Thessalia was purchased from a Greek farmer; this farm later became the Norwegian mission's biggest station, with a school, an orphanage, a medical clinic, and a local church. This was also the place where training courses were held and where the Norwegian missionaries had a school for missionary children. From 1957 the Bustgaards were joined by Olaug Stenersby, who was a nurse and started a medical work. Between 1963 and 1965, the Linds and the Gjervoldstads (Sr.) were added, and from that time the number of missionaries gradually increased. A new mission was planted near Ukwala at Nyambare Hill in 1966. However, initially the Luo and Louya peoples were resistant to the gospel; it was only when a health clinic and maternity services were established that there was a clear change in their attitude and many turned to Christ. After that centers were opened at Nyamira, Kiptere, and Ouygis.

Discussions began during the 1970s between the Norwegian (PYM) and the Swedish (SFM) missions, who eventually agreed to merge their work in Kenya. The merger was completed by 1984. Consequently, the name of the national church was changed to the Free Pentecostal Fellowship in Kenya (FPFK). The FPFK now has 100 fully recognized local assemblies as well as 400 branch churches that are not autonomous. The membership is 50,000. The churches belonging to this grouping are in the Rift Valley, the eastern coastal region, the central area, and also in western Kenya. The national leaders of FPFK include the general secretary, Julius B. Gagaka; the chairman, Patrick Gikonyo; and the treasurer, Solomon Mwalili, all of whom were elected by the national conference in 1997 for a period of four years. The FPFK is responsible for Karen Bible School in Nairobi. This training center has a three-year diploma course with approximately 35 students. In western Kenya there are two dispensaries and a large preschool program supported by the PMU InterLife (the social arm of the SFM in Sweden) and funds from SIDA, the Swedish government foreign aid department. The PMU InterLife has also been involved in the construction of as many as eight schools and was previously responsible for a mobile health-care program that is not operating presently. There is also a program aimed at training the entire leadership of the FPFK regionally and nationally as well as providing the scholarships necessary for this training. Centers for teaching short courses to youth can also be found in various places. The FPFK runs Kindaruma Guesthouse in Nairobi. The Keswick Bookshop in Nairobi is the largest Christian bookshop in East Africa and supplies most of the theological colleges, schools, churches, and missionaries with materials from over 200 publishers in Europe and the U.S. Missionaries were very influential in the decision making of FPFK up until 1997, when a new constitution was passed during the annual general meeting, which placed Kenyans in all leadership positions.

6. The Kenya Assemblies of God.

In 1967 Dale Brown went to Kenya as an independent pentecostal missionary. He was primarily engaged in evangelism among the Kikuyu people. In 1969 he registered his work with the government under the name of Kenya Assemblies of God (KAG). Within a short time numbers of independent pentecostal churches requested that they be permitted to join this association. Brown made an appeal for help to the Division of Foreign Missions of the AG–U.S. Del Kinsriter, who had been a missionary in Malawi, was transferred to Kenya in 1972. This is the year that is normally regarded as the beginning of the AG–U.S. involvement in Kenya, even though the start of KAG goes back to 1967. The first general council of the KAG was held at Kisumu, Kenya, in July 1973 with more than 200 members attending. A Bible school was started at Kisumu in 1975 to train leaders. In 1979 the East African School of Theology (EAST) was opened in Nairobi as a college-level school. This college runs its program based on ICI courses and leads to a four-year degree. EAST also offers a three-year diploma course. Within 10 years of its first general council, the KAG experienced 400% growth in churches and a tenfold increase in the number of members. KAG has a large congregation that meets in rented facilities in Ufungamano House, Nairobi, but has purchased property and plans to build. The present congregation, which started in 1984, numbers about 700. It has organized house groups to facilitate ministry to the spiritual and physical needs of the members. KAG has its own missions program, with all of its missionaries either wholly or partially supported. In Dec. 1997 AG–U.S. reported there were 29 AG–U.S. missionaries working in Kenya with 1,400 churches in KAG and an estimated 350,000 baptized adult members and 560,000 adherents. A total of 400,000 are said to have been baptized in the Holy Spirit (this number appears to be high, however, when compared with statistics elsewhere).

The AG–U.K. are presently involved in a supporting role in Kenya. Cyril Cross left the Kelembelembe field in the Democratic Republic of Congo during the civil war in the 1960s and was waiting in Kenya to see how God would lead him. During this time, Cross met Samuel Mwatha of the Pentecostal Evangelistic Fellowship of Africa (PEFA) and Paul Johansson of Elim Fellowship (Lima, NY). They agreed to found a Bible college in Nairobi. After six months the Geoff Hawksleys joined Cyril and Barbara Cross in Nairobi in order to start the Nairobi Pentecostal Bible College (NPBC). Cyril Cross was the first principal, and the college operated from a rented house. In 1971 the AG–U.K. purchased land and built new facilities. NPBC was run mainly by the AG–U.K. with British trustees; the Overseas Mission Council of AG–U.K. appointed the principals. There was, however, also considerable participation by Elim–NY and PEFA. In 1989 the first Kenyan principal was appointed. Teachers have previously come from the U.K., Kenya, and Elim–NY. By 1998 all staff at NPBC were Kenyan. The principal is Reuben Ngume. Clive and Mary Beckenham (AG–U.K.) left NPBC in 1991 and started New Life Home in Nairobi. This work now comes under Barnabas Ministries, which was founded in 1989 to provide for those living in deprivation and suffering. This ministry is especially concerned with helping children, particularly those who have been orphaned due to AIDS. These are the only two areas in which the British AG are directly involved.

7. Elim Pentecostal Church of Kenya.

From 1949 the T. Johnstons, who worked for the British colonial government in Kenya, were recognized tentmakers in Kenya with the Elim Foursquare Gospel Alliance–U.K. (with the title "honorary Elim missionaries"). They were involved in ministry in various pentecostal churches, mostly in the vicinity of Nairobi. They did not plant any Elim churches. It was only in 1994 that a group in Kenya contacted Elim and expressed the desire to join. Alan Renshaw, who had spent most of his missionary career in Tanzania and Zimbabwe, was the liaison with the group represented by Simon Githigi, who today is the chairman of this work; a constitution was submitted to the government for official recognition and accepted in 1994. Presently 21 churches are linked to Elim in Kenya, most of them in the Nyahururu and Othaya districts and at Kitali. They have approximately 1,200 members. All groups like this, which affiliate with Elim–U.K., become part of what is outside the country called Elim Church International (ECI).

8. The New Testament Church of God.

The Church of God (CG, Cleveland, TN) first became involved in Kenya after A. W. Brummett, the superintendent for Africa, stopped over in Nairobi on a flight to South Africa. He met some local street preachers who invited him to send them a missionary. In confirmation of this call to work in Kenya, Frances Thayer, a CG pastor's wife in Michigan, dreamed that she had seen the places and faces of people in Kenya. As a result, Claude and Frances Thayer went to Kenya in 1978 to pioneer the CG work. Frances Brannen had a similar experience; at least two years before Brannens went to Kenya, God gave Frances Brannen three unusual dreams. Each conveyed the clear meaning that God wanted to saturate the country with his Word and send a revival that would result in believers reaching into the surrounding countries of East Africa.

The CG missionaries wanted to use the name Church of God, but this had already been used by the Church of God (Anderson, IN). The work was therefore given the name Church of God World Mission. The Thayers left Kenya due to Frances's ill health. They were replaced by Dr. David Morgan, who was overseer from 1980 until 1982 and was succeeded by Jack B. Morris (1982–90). During his tenure, it was perceived that many were confusing the name of the church in Kenya with Herbert W. Armstrong's Worldwide Church of God. For this reason the name was changed to the New Testament Church of God (NTCG). Between 1990 and 1998 the NTCG grew from 23 churches and 5 missions to 125 churches and 80 missions. (In the CG–Kenya new groups of believers that have not been in existence for long are required to report for six consecutive months to an immediate superior, who verifies their progress before they are regarded as being fully established churches. While in this probationary state, the groups are called missions.) The CG has an estimated 1,000 members and 2,500 adherents. All pastors are nationals, except for Jim Womble, who also serves as assistant in the accounts department of the national office in Kenya. The newly appointed overseer is David Mills, a missionary evangelist, pastor, state council member, and state youth and Christian education director in the CG–U.S.

9. Other Churches.

The International Pentecostal Holiness Church (IPHC) has its headquarters in Nairobi and its main church at Riara Ridge (Nairobi). This group was started by Philip List and has been in Kenya for more than 10 years. Apart from ministry in Kenya, IPHC has sent missionaries to pioneer church planting in Ethiopia.

The Redeemed Gospel Church (RGC) was started by Bishop Arthur Gitonga. It has a large assembly of 5,000 adherents at Huruma, Nairobi, of which Gitonga is pastor. Another group belonging to the same organization meets in the Nairobi city hall and is pastored by John Obonyo. This group uses the cell principle. Wilfred Lai, who also belongs to the RGC, is located in Mombassa, where he has what is likely the largest church in the country, called the Jesus Celebration Centre. This church has a reported 15,000 to 16,000 adherents

Jerry Savelle Ministries International, which is part of the Word of Faith movement, has a church in Nairobi pastored by Wade and Karla Porter, called Victory Faith Christian Centre. The church gathered at first in the University Hall, but the members have since procured their own land and hope to build. This group too, has been operating on the cell principle. Jerry Savelle visits Nairobi each year and holds conferences together with other guest speakers.

There are many smaller groups, such as Christ Pentecostal Church, founded by Gabriel Otieno, which has about five small churches in the slum areas of Nairobi and a few elsewhere in the country.

The Light House Church, pastored by an American, Don Matheney, meets in the City Stadium in Nairobi. It has about 3,000 adherents, most of whom are young people. This church functions on the cell principle.

Recently, ►Paul Yonggi Cho's ministry from Yoido Full Gospel Church, Seoul, Korea, has become involved in Kenya. Their missionary is Yun Kyo Chung, who has been in Kenya for 14 years. Their work is called the Full Gospel Mission and is based at Thika, Nairobi. This group has over 600 members and emphasizes the need for all-night prayer meetings each week; it also teaches the importance of the gifts of the Holy Spirit. The members attribute their present growth to their stance on these issues. They are involved in a training center and also have a church at Muranga.

The United Pentecostal Church International began work in Kenya in 1971; this Oneness group has its headquarters in Nairobi. It reports 230 churches in 1995 with 18,000 adherents. The Church of God of Prophecy reports 110 churches with 3,070 members and 7,680 adherents. The International Church of the Foursquare Gospel has 73 churches, 2,260 members, and 3,770 adherents. The Open Bible Standard Church has 70 churches, 5,110 members, and 10,200 adherents. (The numbers for the last three groups are 1995 statistics.)

►Reinhard Bonnke has held several crusades throughout Kenya with considerable success and many healings. However, unlike Zambia and Malawi, it is not always easy to evaluate how many people have been added to the churches as a result of these crusades. T. L. Osborn held crusades in the 1960s that most certainly had great impact upon church life as they inspired the founding of many new pentecostal churches. Paul Yonggi Cho has held crusades in Nairobi within the last two years, but again, the long-term benefit is difficult to appraise even though his meetings were well attended.

10. Observations.

Within the independent pentecostal churches, there is a tendency for leadership to be autocratic and the leader's word

to be final. Where there are church boards (or councils) in the newer churches, they are mostly understood as the means of legitimizing and executing the will of the person in charge. It is only in groups such as PAG, KAG, FPFK, AG, and the established pentecostal denominations that there are conferences with valid voting leading to the election of church officers. Elsewhere, autocratic leaders emphasize their particular style and understanding of certain biblical truths, so that the churches and the members who adhere to their doctrines tend to be very legalistic.

A major trend toward schism and division exists among the newer groups. Those in established pentecostal churches agree that there is a great need for emphasis to be given to Bible teaching and the training of leaders in Bible schools or in bona fide discipleship programs. The pentecostal churches emphasize the place of some of the charismata, but there is greater need for understanding the other areas of work of the Holy Spirit and the gifts of Christ to the church in the various ministries. The place of the gifts and miracles have had considerable influence on the development of the pentecostal churches in the country.

Some of the more recent groups in the country have experienced considerable growth in the number of churches affiliated with them. This is not, however, always through church planting and evangelism, but rather through the addition of already existing, independent pentecostal churches that have transferred to them. The trend is likely the result of Kenyan government legislation that requires all churches to belong to a recognized and registered church group. If the affiliation of independent churches to existing, recognized churches brings about greater cohesion among pentecostal/charismatic groups and at the same time maintains the impetus behind evangelism, which some will accuse the older denominations of having lost, this will prove positive.

There is no overall pentecostal fellowship in Kenya, which is surprising considering the number of those who claim to be pentecostal or charismatic. Pentecostals appear to continue to be suspicious of each other. As in many countries in the region, there is a need for greater cooperation and collaboration between pentecostals at every level, since many ministries and services are duplicated. In the area of leadership training, for example, at least three pentecostal denominations with similar doctrine and practice are working in the vicinity of Kisumu, but each has its own pastoral training facilities there. Pentecostals need to learn to collaborate more in evangelism and church planting.

Kenya, unlike a number of other Central and East African countries, does not appear to suffer from serious divisions along ethnic lines. Ethnic groups from throughout the country appear to mix well in pentecostal churches and worship together without any difficulty. Perhaps they could pass on their secret to the others who find great difficulty in this area.   ■ D. J. Garrard

KIRGHIZIA

■ Pentecostals 4,008 (23%)   ■ Charismatics 6,042 (34%)   ■ Neocharismatics 7,750 (44%)   ■ Total Renewal: 17,800

See RUSSIA.

KIRIBATI

■ Pentecostals 4,246 (33%)   ■ Charismatics 7,005 (55%)   ■ Neocharismatics 1,449 (11%)   ■ Total Renewal: 12,700

For general introduction and bibliography, see PACIFIC ISLANDS.

Kiribati was under British administration and known as the Gilbert Islands until it became independent on July 12, 1979. The country, a member of the Commonwealth of Nations, consists of three major archipelagos—the Gilberts proper, the Phoenix Islands, and the Line Islands—all together 33 coral atolls scattered across some 1.2 million mi² (3 million km²) of sea but with only 312 mi² (810 km²) of land. With the atoll terrain, the coral rock is covered with only some 8 ft (2.5 m) of hard sand and scanty soil. There are no rivers, but most islands enclose a lagoon. The thin layer of soil on the atolls supports little growth apart from seaside scrub, panadanus, and coconut. Native land fauna is limited to the Polynesian rat and two species of lizard. Sea life is considerably richer with its birds, fish, and coral.

The people, known as I-Kiribati, are Micronesians. In 1995 the total population was about 72,000 people, with about one-third of the population living in Tarawa, the capital. The I-Kiribati are very much people of the sea. Traditional skills include cultivating taro, fishing, and making and sailing canoes. Outer island life is essentially affluent-subsistence, with cash income from copra and some remittances from several hundred Kiribati men crewing overseas ships.

More than 1,000 men used to be employed in the phosphate workings in Nauru.

About 97 % of the population are considered to be Christians. Until WWII there were only two main churches, the Roman Catholic Church and the Kiribati Protestant Church (KPC), both more or less equally strong in numbers. By 1973 the Catholics had overtaken the Protestants, and in 1978 for the first time more than half of the population claimed Catholic adherence for themselves and their children.

Beginning with the Seventh-day Adventist Mission in 1947, other churches established centers in Kiribati: the Church of God (CG, Cleveland, TN) in 1957, the Baha'is in 1967, the Mormons in 1975, and the Assemblies of God (AG) in the early 1980s. With the exception of the Baha'i, all these newcomers have grown fast and steadily, basically at the expense of the KPC, which—according to an insider—has experienced a considerable erosion of membership (Ieuti, 1992).

According to Johnstone, the CG had about 2,000 adherents in 1995. In 1998 the AG claimed a total of 17 national ministers, joined by one missionary from overseas, and an unknown number of preaching points (rented places or private homes). The AG also runs a local Bible school with an average of 25 students enrolled annually.

■ M. Ernst

KUWAIT

■ Pentecostals 0 (0%)   ■ Charismatics 7,493 (11%)   ■ Neocharismatics 60,507 (89%)   ■ Total Renewal: 68,000

See AFRICA, NORTH, AND THE MIDDLE EAST.

LAOS

■ Pentecostals 0 (0%)   ■ Charismatics 3,178 (6%)   ■ Neocharismatics 46,822 (94%)   ■ Total Renewal: 50,000

LATIN AMERICA (Survey)

I. A Profile of Latin American Pentecostals
   A. *The Relative Size of the Latin American Pentecostal Church*
   B. *Pentecostals As a Percentage of the National Population in the Latin American Republics, Ranked by Size (1995)*
   C. *Descriptive Features of Latin American Pentecostals/Charismatics/Neocharismatics*
   D. *Prominent Latin American Pentecostal/Charismatic/Neocharismatic Movements*

II. The Dynamic Characteristics of Latin American Pentecostals
   A. *Functional Analysis of Latin American Pentecostals*
      1. Crisis
      2. Community
      3. Expressiveness
      4. Power
      5. Participation
      6. Moralism
      7. Versatility
   B. *Pentecostals Groups as Self-Initiating and Self-Sustaining Movements*

III. Country Profiles of Latin American Pentecostals
   A. *Argentina*
   B. *Belize*
   C. *Bolivia*
   D. *Brazil*
   E. *Chile*
   F. *Colombia*
   G. *Costa Rica*
   H. *Cuba*
   I. *Dominican Republic*
   J. *Ecuador*
   K. *El Salvador*
   L. *Guatemala*
   M. *Honduras*
   N. *Mexico*
   O. *Nicaragua*
   P. *Panama*
   Q. *Paraguay*
   R. *Peru*
   S. *Uruguay*
   T. *Venezuela*

IV. Assessments of Latin American Pentecostals
   A. *The Early Emergence of Latin American Pentecostals*
   B. *The Authenticity of Latin American Pentecostalism*
   C. *The Institutional Independence of Latin American Pentecostals*
   D. *The Institutionalization of Latin American Pentecostal Movements*
   E. *Pentecostals and Social Change*
   F. *Pentecostal Social Programs*
   G. *Pentecostals and Politics*

V. The Future of the Latin American Pentecostals

While Latin American Protestantism was once considered essentially a foreign faith introduced by northern European immigrants and numbers of evangelical missions to culturally unassimilated Indians, it is now seen as a mass movement, a religious alternative for growing numbers of people from various social sectors who face an uncertain future. Only recently, however, have scholars identified pentecostalism as a primary motif of the region's changing religious landscape. Although a similar conclusion was published in 1980 by Stephen D. Glazier, only with the publication of seminal, book-length studies by David Martin (1990) and David Stoll (1990) did the Latin American pentecostals suddenly gain the attention of large numbers of secular and religious scholars. A subsequent symposium (B. Doudewijnse et al., 1991), and investigations by Jean Pierre Bastian, José Míguez Bonino, Virginia Garrard-Burnett (1993), Edward L. Cleary, and Hannah Stewart Gambino (1997), among others, reinforced the view that these movements resulted from deeply rooted, secular impulses in societies that reflected the frustrations and aspirations of their longsuffering peoples. Harvey Cox (1994) similarly represented widely ranging, versatile pentecostalism as a profoundly spiritual phenomenon of global proportions. No longer was pentecostalism seen primarily as the "old-time religion" gone overseas, the product of massive investment of foreign personnel and resources; it was rather an authentic cultural expression of the peoples who embraced it, a primal scream from the stirring soul of the previously voiceless masses.

I. A PROFILE OF LATIN AMERICAN PENTECOSTALS.

A. The Relative Size of the Latin American Pentecostal Church.

The implication of this Latin American religious revolution is revealed in the statistics published in the World Christian Encyclopedia (2001). From two-thirds to three-fourths of the region's 40 million evangelical Christians are considered pentecostal, and of the estimated 66 million classical pentecostals worldwide, 33 million are found in Latin America. Moreover, Brazil, the world's largest Roman Catholic country, is also the nation with the largest number of pentecostals/charismatics/neocharismatics, estimated to number more than

79 million adherents. In addition, in all but five of these Spanish- or Portuguese-speaking republics—numbering 21 with Belize—pentecostals/charismatics/neocharismatics constitute the largest grouping of evangelicals.

Since Latin American pentecostalism developed at the beginning of the century, simultaneously with similar movements in North America, it has deep roots and its own emphases, some of which have little to do directly with pentecostal traditions elsewhere. Moreover, the indigenousness of some pentecostal or pentecostal-like movements make them difficult to categorize. A few are even suspect with respect to the historical Christian faith. Despite their burgeoning growth and heightened visibility only since the end of WWII when the region opened wide to outside influences, these movements are distinctly Latin American.

B. Pentecostals/Charismatics/ Neocharismatics as a Percentage of the National Population in the Latin American Republics, Ranked by Size (1995).

See table this page.

C. Descriptive Features of Latin American Pentecostals/Charismatics/Neocharismatics.

Among the generic traits that observers of the pentecostals have identified are their enthusiasm, social cohesion, moral idealism, home-grown leadership, spontaneity of expression, and extensive networks of like-minded men and women. Characteristically, pentecostals form tightly knit associations of believers that are not unlike extended families. These groups sometimes affirm rather than deny features of the traditional culture, such as gender roles and respect for authority, often giving their movements a conservative cast.

Social scientists find this form of community remarkably adaptable to a variety of cultures, ethnic groups, and social strata. In the terminology of Luther Gerlach, pentecostalism is "segmentary, a movement composed of semi-autonomous cells, decentralized, polycephalous, and reticulate, a network of overlapping membership by the sharing of a common ideology, common cause, and common opposition." Pentecostalism, according to Gerlach, resists "effective suppression or cooptation of the total movement through its redundancy, multiplicity of leadership, and self-sufficiency of local groups." Elsewhere he concludes that "the very characteristics of ecstatic religious behavior—ceremonial disassociation, decentralized structure, unconventional ideology, opposition to established structures—which might appear to be marks of a sect of misfits and dropouts, are indeed the features which combine to make Pentecostalism a growing, expanding, evangelistic religious movement of change."

Despite their generic similarities, however, Latin American pentecostals are considered individualistic, volatile, and inclined to local adaptations and schismatic fragmentation. They are, for instance, characteristically divided by their respective national origins, as well as by sectarian emphases and local cultures. This diversity is seen in the

Pentecostals/Charismatics/Neocharismatics as a Percentage of the National Population in the Latin American Republics, Ranked by Size (1995)

Country	Population	% Evangelicals	% Pentecostals/ charismatics/ neocharismatics
Mexico and the Caribbean			
Mexico	99,000,000	1.8	13.2
Cuba	11,200,000	1.2	5.1
Dominican Repub.	8,500,000	3.1	12.2
Puerto Rico	3,900,000	9.0	26.5
Central America			
Guatemala	11,400,000	10.4	21.9
El Salvador	6,300,000	6.7	23.6
Honduras	6,500,000	4.8	13.3
Belize	240,000	7.1	13.0
Nicaragua	5,000,000	8.8	14.2
Costa Rica	4,000,000	7.0	12.3
Panama	2,900,000	9.2	17.2
Andean Countries			
Venezuela	24,200,000	1.3	15.2
Colombia	42,300,000	1.4	29.7
Ecuador	12,600,000	2.3	11.2
Peru	25,700,000	4.4	13.4
Bolivia	8,300,000	4.5	14.6
Southern Cone and Brazil			
Chile	15,200,000	1.6	36.4
Argentina	37,000,000	5.3	22.7
Uruguay	3,300,000	1.9	9.1
Paraguay	5,500,000	2.9	4.4
Brazil	170,000,000	16.3	47.0

Source: Barrett et al., *World Christian Encyclopedia* (2001)

customs and growth patterns that differ widely between, for example, the large Chilean Pentecostal Methodist grouping and the Brazilian Assembléias de Deus, or between indigenous (Indian) movements with pentecostal features, such as the Otomí of central Mexico or the Toba of the Argentine Chaco, and socially more inclusive churches like the neopentecostal Verbo Church with which former Guatemalan president José Efaín Ríos Montt was affiliated during his political ascendancy in the early 1980s. In addition, denominational differences further divide the Latin American pentecostal groupings, for example, the Mexican Iglesia Apostólica de la Fe en Cristo Jesús, a ˟Oneness organization, and the Iglesia de Dios, a movement found in the Central American countries that is loosely affiliated with the Church of God, Cleveland, TN (CG).

Moreover, marked differences divide the urban churches, which are sometimes large, prominent, and progressive, from the rural and barrio churches, which are usually small, traditional, and conservative. Increasingly, large urban churches have broken away from the rigid codes respecting dress and customs that have kept them the exclusive domain of the marginal sectors, while at the other end of the spectrum pressures to conform to the larger society often provide the basis for a schismatic movement, usually under the aegis of a charismatic leader committed to traditional cultural forms. In Guatemala, pentecostalism has grown notably among both the Maya and Ladino (Europeanized) popular sectors, each of which has its own distinctive customs and concerns, despite their similarities. Everywhere, however, pentecostal groups are made up largely of displaced, poor, and aspiring peoples.

D. Prominent Latin American Pentecostal/Charismatic/Neocharismatic Movements.

See table this page.

II. THE DYNAMIC CHARACTERISTICS OF LATIN AMERICAN PENTECOSTALS.

A. Functional Analysis of Latin American Pentecostals.

In analyzing the growth of these groups, the question arises: If these movements originate among the least-favored social sectors, how does one explain their unusual vitality and resourcefulness? One of the earliest students of Latin American pentecostalism, Eugene Nida (1974), emphasized the pentecostals' spontaneous, grassroots character. Referring to them as "indigenous Protestants," Nida saw the movements that exhibited pentecostal-like features—tongues, fervent prayer, and evidence of spirit possession—as having deep roots in the local cultures. In addition, he adopted the anthropologists' functional explanations that related religious beliefs and practices to the needs of the people who embraced the

movement. Other writers, such as Christian Lalive d'Epinay (1968), Emilio Willems (1967), and coauthors Mike Berg and Paul Pretiz (1996), have followed Nida's functionalist explanations. They see the emergence of pentecostalism as a response to the search of people, caught in social and economic transition, to structure their disoriented lives, specifically to form community, obtain a distinctive identity, and find a basis for traditional standards of conduct and piety. A schematic representation of pentecostal development is

Prominent Latin American Pentecostal/ Charismatic/Neocharismatic Movements

Organization	Communicants	Community
Assembléias de Deus no Brasil	14,400,000	22,000,000
Igreja Universal do Reino de Deus (Brazil)	2,000,000	4,000,000
Congregação Crista do Brasil	1,560,000	3,120,000
Asambleas de Dios (excluding Mexico and Brazil)	1,062,000	2,829,000
Igreja Pentecostal Deus é Amor (Brazil)	1,600,000	2,670,000
O Brasil para Cristo	1,000,000	2,000,000
Iglesia Metodista Pentecostal (Chile)	520,000	720,000
Igreja Cuadrangular (Brazil)	389,000	607,000
Iglesia Evangélica Pentecostal de Chile	400,000	571,000
Asambleas de Dios (Mexico)	350,000	570,000
Iglesia de Dios (in 12 Spanish-language republics)	206,470	528,500
Iglesia Pentecostal de Chile	150,000	400,000
Cuban Pentecostals/Independent Charismatics	132,000	252,000
Elim (Guatemala, El Salvador)	122,000	314,000
Iglesia Cuadrangular (exclusive of Brazil)	117,000	307,600
Príncipe de Paz (Guatemala, El Salvador)	122,000	305,000
Visión del Futuro (Argentina)	95,000	190,000
Iglesia de la Fe en Cristo Jesús (Mexico, El Salvador)	83,000	176,000
Iglesia de Dios de la Profesía (in 4 republics)	44,360	124,500
Iglesia de Dios Pentecostal (Puerto Rico)	67,000	112,000
Movimiento Evangélico Pentecostal Independiente (Mexico)	47,000	85,000
Iglesia Pentecostal de la Santidad (Costa Rica)	7,000	16,000

Source: Barrett et al., *World Christian Encyclopedia* (2001)

included in the compilation edited by Daniel R. Miller (1994). Here pentecostals are portrayed as encouraging a succession of highly dynamic personal emphases that tend to ensure the growth and development of their communities. These begin with the movements' appropriateness for responding to personal crises and their adherents' willingness to seek new solutions to their problems.

1. Crisis.

Pentecostalism has usually flourished in the anomic situations of Latin American social upheaval, where new paradigms of community organization are welcome. "The Pentecostal creed," according to Emilio Willems, "is … almost ideally adapted to the aspirations and needs of the lower classes." The appeal of a society where the marginal groups could control their own lives and live according to their own values was developed by David Martin in his concept of "free space," as opposed to the imposed norms of traditional society. According to this assessment, hope, rather than despair, motivates pentecostals. Eugene Nida found something similar when he found pentecostals to be a "creative minority" among the upper-lower and lower-middle sectors, groups with the potential for "reshaping" Latin American life from the grassroots.

2. Community.

Pentecostal churches offer new converts inclusion in a structured community. They reconstitute the social solidarity recently lost in massive migrations and the breakup of family and community structures. "Where traditional social organization is breaking up, evangelical churches constitute new, more flexible groups … which are therefore more adaptable to rapidly changing conditions," concludes David Stoll. Bryan Roberts observes also that "[pentecostal] groups are visible and available forms of association. The doors of the … churches are always open."

3. Expressiveness.

Another feature characteristic of pentecostal communities is their subjective experience, including sometimes boisterous, emotional demonstrations, lively music, and freedom of expression. Bryan Wilson has observed that "Pentecostal teaching legitimized the expression of intense feelings for which there was so little opportunity otherwise." Similarly, sociologist Emilio Willems finds that the term *gozo* ("joy") recurs with frequency among Latin Americans within these new religious movements.

4. Power.

In addition, pentecostals provide and legitimize forms of power, initially in the sense of personal worth and effectiveness—spiritual filling and anointing—but extending to power over sickness, unfavorable circumstances, and various adversaries. Christian Lalive d'Epinay, along with other observers, concludes that many pentecostal conversions have followed physical healing. Pentecostals, unusually confident and sometimes presumptuous, extend this empowerment even to social dimensions, from a gospel of prosperity to political action.

5. Participation.

Pentecostals are generally recognized as activists whose energies are channeled by their beliefs and practices to numerous evangelistic activities. "The strength of the structure," concluded Nida, "is the participation of everyone." Sociologist Emilio Willems found similarly that "Pentecostal sects [find] means and ways to mobilize their vast human resources to the last man." Since women predominate in these groups, Willems's use of the masculine gender (1967) must be considered figurative, not literal. In fact, pentecostal churches are the one place where women do find forms of empowerment usually not available elsewhere.

6. Moralism.

While the acquisition of new community responsibilities may channel the energies and resources of pentecostal adherents into constructive activities, the groups' moralistic demands eventually define—and perhaps repel—some prospective or recent converts. Bryan Roberts found that "[pentecostal] groups are effective moral communities [that] stress the importance of their moral code." Emphasizing that among these groups status is achieved, not attributed, Bryan Wilson concluded that "a person's Christian quality is certified by changes which occur in his moral life rather than by his doctrinal loyalty." Not surprisingly, not all converts are willing to accept the churches' demanding codes of conduct and withdraw. Most church communities include some spouses or marginal adherents who never fulfill the members' ideals or advance to the highest levels of participation.

7. Versatility.

Still another characteristic of these groups is their remarkable versatility. William Read concluded in his study of evangelicals in Brazil that "the genius of Pentecost is to be free to find new methods … to adopt and adapt practices which reflect their cultural heritage." Similarly, Emilio Castro found that "freedom implicit in the Spirit's gifts confirms them in exercising individual freedom that a rigid confessional orthodoxy could never countenance." While not all of these features are found in every pentecostal group, they constitute a generic formula that is widespread and is identifiable where these movements remain dynamic.

B. Pentecostals Groups as Self-Initiating and Self-Sustaining Movements.

Despite the widespread diffusion of pentecostalism in the region, these groups remain a small, usually marginal minority in their respective republics. Only in three mainland areas of concentration—Brazil, Chile, and Central America—are pentecostals sufficiently strong to have gained social and political significance, although the movement in Mexico, the world's largest Spanish-speaking country, acquires importance because of its tenacity and its cultural leadership in the hemisphere. The emergence of pentecostalism in Puerto Rico, because of the group's proportional growth, also provides an important example of how these movements have penetrated society and influenced a given culture.

While it may be argued that the veritable explosion of growth was based essentially on the massification of Latin American society, including the creation of large rural and urban proletarian sectors, it is also apparent that these churches did not simply come into being as aggregations of displaced, anomic individuals, or as entirely new formations without precedent. The pentecostal communities, made up of a wide range of organizational types, theologies, and social sectors, have tended to form versatile, resilient social structures, much as military units fill out their cadres of experienced noncommissioned officers with new recruits. In the case of the pentecostals, however, the new recruits assume places of responsibility in the developing organizations, sometimes in a surprisingly short time.

III. COUNTRY PROFILES OF THE LATIN AMERICAN PENTECOSTALS.

A. Argentina.

In a country with a largely European population and strong Roman Catholic traditions, Argentina's Protestantism until recently consisted mainly of immigrant populations in historic churches, with only modest growth among pentecostals. After Argentina's defeat in the Falklands War (1982), however, dismay and disillusionment resulted in self-doubts and religious reflection. Revivals broke out spontaneously, producing many local leaders, new churches, and charismatic national figures, among them Omar Cabrera—distinctive for his atypical clerical collar—Carlos Annacondia and Claudio Freidzon, and their "third wave" or neo-pentecostal colleague, Ed Silvoso. From one of the more resistant countries in the region, Argentina has become a center of evangelical activity, with an estimated 2 million Protestants, of which 80% are pentecostal.

B. Belize.

Belize (formerly British Honduras), since 1964 a self-governing republic, has a record of considerable public support for evangelical Christianity. Anglicans, Methodists, and Mennonites, along with the country's largest group, the Seventh-day Adventists, make up 60% of the nation's 50,000 Protestants. Of this community, only 20% is pentecostal. In large part, pentecostalism in Belize is a Latin phenomenon,

having grown along with recent substantial immigration from the neighboring Spanish-speaking republics.

C. Bolivia.

Landlocked, largely indigenous, Bolivia reports a Protestant population of 12%, of which 40% is pentecostal. The existence of distinct cultural divisions between the Aymara, the Quechua, and the Guaraní populations and the highland (La Paz, Cochabamba) and lowland (Santa Cruz) regions have resulted in the emergence of several separate pentecostal movements, even where a degree of sectarian unity exists.

D. Brazil.

The territorial, political, and economic giant of the South American continent, Brazil also has the largest pentecostal population, an estimated 34 million people, 87% of the entire Protestant community. Two of these groups, the Assembléias de Deus (22 million adherents) and the Congregacao Crista (3.1 million) were established early in the century. Three more recent churches, the Igreja Universal do Reino de Deus (Universal Church of the Kingdom of God; 4 million), Deus é Amor (God Is Love; 2.7 million), and O Brasil para Cristo (Brazil for Christ; 2 million), have received considerable attention because of their social and political impact.

While these numbers are impressive, they are put in perspective when compared with the numbers of adherents of various popular spiritist groups, which may constitute as much as 60% of the entire Brazilian population (or over 100 million). These groups include "low spiritists" (whose members may often also be considered practicing Roman Catholics), who belong to African (or Afro-Brazilian) religions that are essentially animistic or rely on some spiritual intermediary to achieve what the devotee wants. These religions, which include Umbanda, Candomblé, and Macumba, have increasingly become Brazilianized by using Portuguese rather than African tribal languages, so that now Umbanda is the major "low" spiritist movement. "High spiritism" refers to Kardecism, a movement identified with Alain Kardec, a 19th-century French spiritist whose teachings found strong support among Brazilian elites at the beginning of the 20th century. These practitioners wanted to distance themselves from the African cults and so called themselves "high spiritists." More recently (after WWII) middle-class adherents have bought into the movement and made it a cult of physical healing (and of power in other respects) as opposed to the original healing of the spirit emphasized by Kardec. It could be argued that pentecostalism encountered a general openness to spirituality that stems from these forms of spritism.

E. Chile.

Chile's unique Pentecostal Methodist tradition has made a strong impact on the country and shaped the nature of Chilean evangelicalism. These groups account for 95% of all Chilean Protestants and almost a quarter of the entire national population. Highly fragmented, authoritarian, and restricted by tradition, these groups are not always considered models of spiritual maturity. Moreover, nominalism is found among the second, third, and fourth generations of Chilean pentecostals, unlike other national pentecostal movements where recent growth, social ostracism, and high standards of piety have more frequently tended to purge purely nominal adherents from the ranks.

F. Colombia.

A country that has always been deeply divided geographically and politically, Colombia has a tradition of pride and traditionalism that has resisted rapid pentecostal growth. Evangelicals claim only 3%—1 million of the national population of 35 million—of which more than two-thirds are pentecostal. Pentecostal growth has taken place under sometimes intense persecution and hardship, as during the post-WWII period, 1947–63, known in Colombian history as "La Violencia," and during the recent decades of drug wars.

G. Costa Rica.

A country that is proud of its European heritage and strong tradition of democracy, politically open and socially accessible Costa Rica has received substantial numbers of Protestant missionaries since the 1920s. In recent decades, however, pentecostal groups such as the Asambleas de Dios (Assemblies of God [AG]), the Iglesia de Dios (Church of God, Cleveland, TN [CG]), the Iglesia Pentecostal de la Santidad (Pentecostal Holiness), and the Iglesia International del Evangelio Cuadrangular (Church of the Foursquare Gospel), have tended to dominate the evangelical movement, accounting for two-thirds of all Protestants.

H. Cuba.

While all religious activity in Cuba has been restricted since the 1960s, the Christian churches had registered an impressive resurgence by the time of the Jan. 1998 visit of Pope John Paul II. Various pentecostal groups, led by the Assemblies of God, make up half of all Protestants. Typically, these congregations meet in houses and conduct multiple Sunday services to accommodate the churchgoers. U.S. journalists have portrayed Cuban evangelicals, including the pentecostals, as stalwart believers who are gaining converts rapidly, despite government-imposed or -encouraged obstacles.

I. Dominican Republic.

In this Caribbean republic that shares its island home with Haiti, two-thirds of the Dominicans are people of Afro-Caribbean origin. Pentecostals, who make up less than half of all Protestants, constitute about 3% of the entire population. These churches have been influenced appreciably by the mainland denominations (AG, CG, Pentecostal Holiness Church) and the Puerto Rican missions (Defensores de la Fe/Defenders of the Faith). Authoritarianism and legalism often characterize these churches, which reflect the prevail-

ing mores of the rural population. Consequently, these groups appear less attractive to the professional and business classes than is the case with more progressive pentecostal groups in several of the other republics. As elsewhere in the Caribbean, it is believed that as many as half of all Dominicans are involved informally in occult practices.

J. Ecuador.

Ecuador, a country made up of several distinct regions, has been exposed to considerably less Protestant influence than its Andean neighbors. Divided geographically into coastal (Guayaquil) and highland (Quito, Cuenca) regions, as well as lowland territory fronting on the Amazon basin, Ecuador has remained relatively isolated and traditional, without the influence of large numbers of Protestant immigrants. Where pentecostalism has found acceptance, it has been largely under the auspices of North American missions. Accordingly, the pentecostal groups are fairly new and less well established than, for example, in neighboring Peru.

K. El Salvador.

Pentecostalism in El Salvador grew as a primarily rural, peasant phenomenon until the 1950s, when churches were established in San Salvador, the political capital and the dominant social and economic center. Although both the Asambleas de Dios and the Iglesia de Dios (CG) have been strong, the development of a self-governing church by the initiative of the Salvadorans themselves made the Salvadoran church a model for the AG elsewhere. With little recognition until the 1980s, the church grew not only in the countryside but in the cities as well. Entrance into the ranks of the professional and business classes has led to the establishment of some strong pentecostal congregations even in the affluent districts of the capital city. Meanwhile, other strong pentecostal churches have emerged, including the ▸Oneness organization Los Apóstoles y Profetas (The Apostles and Prophets) movement, and the Príncipe de Paz and Elim groups that originated in neighboring Guatemala.

L. Guatemala.

The evangelical rise in Guatemala, a country that is 50% Mayan Indian, has attracted considerable attention. Although various historic groups such as the Presbyterians and the Central American Mission founded by C. I. Scofield established a strong evangelical foundation in Guatemala, the pentecostals now make up two-thirds of the total. These Protestants, in the aggregate, make up a quarter of the national population. Although divided, the evangelical community acquired a strong representative in the form of General José Efraín Ríos Montt, who was placed in office by a military coup in 1982. Ríos Montt, though not without his supporters, soon alienated powerful political elements. His overthrow left in doubt the possibility of an evangelical political reformation of Guatemala, especially after his evangel-

ical successor was driven into exile by accusations of malfea-
sance in office. Increasingly, the pentecostal movement is led
by neo-pentecostal groups whose greater accommodation to
modern life makes them attractive to the children of pentecostal parents, as well as to new converts from the middle
sectors.

M. Honduras.

Until recently Honduras has remained a largely rural, traditional country outside the mainstream of economic development that has brought considerable change to several of
the other Central American republics. Foreign influence has
centered on the Atlantic north coast region surrounding the
cities of San Pedro Sula and La Ceiba. The Iglesia de Dios
and the Asambleas de Dios have both attracted substantial
followings in the towns and cities. The country has received
much direct foreign missionary influence, as well as evangelistic efforts from neighboring Guatemala and El Salvador.

N. Mexico.

Pentecostalism has deep roots in Mexico, having grown
as part of the same movement that brought into being pentecostal churches in the United States. One of these, the
Iglesia Apostólica de la Fe en Cristo Jesus, a Oneness group,
has an unaffiliated North American Latin counterpart, the
Apostolic Church of the Faith in Jesus' Name. As well, the
Asambleas de Dios was an intregal part of the North American AG until separation occurred in the early 1920s. In
addition, however, a strong pentecostal church developed
early under the aegis of Scandinavian missionaries, and
strong pentecostal groups unaffiliated with foreign denominations have persisted. Nevertheless, the simultaneous
course of the anti-foreign Mexican Revolution (1910–17)
and subsequent strong nationalistic sentiments, some
observers believe, have worked against the emergence of
popular evangelical movements such as occurred in Brazil
and Chile. Increasingly, the various pentecostal groups have
been established as a force in national life, benefiting from
recent legislation that guarantees previously restricted religious freedom. The Asambleas de Dios, with a community
estimated to be as large as 700,000 adherents distributed
throughout the entire national territory, now has emerged as
Mexico's largest evangelical denomination.

O. Nicaragua.

Pentecostalism arrived in Nicaragua early in the century
under the influence of North American missionaries. Deep
animosities against 19th-century North American political
intrusion, notably by the filibuster William Walker, as well as
unsatisfactory relationships with some early missionaries,
however, tended to make Nicaraguan pentecostals extremely
nationalistic. During the Sandinista era (1982–91), however,
a strong pentecostal movement began to emerge, with some
progressive elements participating in national politics. This

growth has continued unabated amid severe economic and
social problems that increase the misery of a great part of the
population.

P. Panama.

The cosmopolitan character of Panama—West Indian,
East Indian, Asian, North American, and Amerindian—has
given that republic its own religious texture. Pentecostalism
has grown among most of these groups, which have been
absorbed to a notable degree in a mixed national culture. The
prominent Afro-Caribbean minority, with Protestant leanings, however, has contributed significantly to Panama's
openness to evangelical Christianity and has provided many
leaders of that country's pentecostal movement.

Q. Paraguay.

Pentecostalism has been slow to find acceptance in
Paraguay, with significant proportional growth occurring only
in recent years. Landlocked and isolated, and with a tragic
history of two genocidal wars that decimated the male population, Paraguay has a unique bilingual culture (Guaraní and
Spanish), based until the 1980s on a paternalistic-exploita-
tive state system. The largest Protestant groups in the country are found among colonies of European immigrants.

R. Peru.

Pentecostalism in Peru, with a reported community of
360,000 communicants, began early in the century and has
become deeply entrenched in parts of the Andean regions
and in the Amazon, as well as in Lima and other major cities.
In the 1980s pentecostals in the highlands, as a group that
had the confidence of many peasants, clashed with the
Maoist Sendero Luminoso (Shining Path), suffering both
numerous casualties and displays of deep commitment that
have brought pentecostal adherents respect. Although pentecostal groups are represented by groups affiliated with the
CG and the Church of God of Prophecy, by far the largest
denominational grouping is the Peruvian Asambleas de Dios,
a group that throughout its existence has shown strong independence from foreign control and has often suffered disruptive internal disputes.

S. Uruguay.

Despite its Roman Catholic heritage, the Republic of
Uruguay adopted a secular constitution in 1918 and is now
considered to be by far the most secular country in Latin
America. While spiritism has spread widely through the
working classes in neighboring Brazil and agnosticism has
long been part of the culture of the Latin American educated
classes, Uruguay, a largely middle-class society, has both spiritists and agnostics in large proportions. Pentecostals, including the Iglesia de Dios (CG) and the Asambleas de Dios,
presently make up more than half of all evangelicals. Even
including the numerous Protestant European immigrants,

Protestant Christians of all communions account for only about 3% of the population.

T. Venezuela.

Pentecostalism has not enjoyed the reception in Venezuela that it has received in some other Latin American republics. While as a grouping the pentecostals are larger than any other single Protestant denomination than the Seventh-day Adventists, they remain relatively small and marginal. Several, like the Brazil-based Congregacao Crista, are of foreign origin. The largest denomination, the Asambleas de Dios, reported a community of only 60,000 in a national population of 22 million in the mid 1990s, and Caracas in 1993 was reported to have only 25,000 evangelicals in a city of 3.6 million. Strong nationalistic feeling and a tendency toward legalism have been cited as reasons for the slower growth of evangelicals in Venezuela.

IV. ASSESSMENTS OF LATIN AMERICAN PENTECOSTALS.

The foregoing discussion of the origins of the Latin American pentecostal groups serves as the basis for an assessment of their resources and character. Beyond treating the groups' characteristics and the circumstantial reasons for their emergence, some scholars have attempted speculative or theoretical projections of their probable evolution and course of action. Such discussions, however, have often produced stereotypical treatments emphasizing one or another model of religious or social movements. Nevertheless, taken in the aggregate these discussions cast considerable light on the various pentecostal groups.

A. The Early Emergence of Latin American Pentecostals.

The notion persists that, since pentecostal groups have grown rapidly since WWII, the movement is relatively recent. In fact, while recent rapid growth has been termed "explosive," the infrastructure of pentecostal churches emerged contemporaneously with the pentecostal movement in North America and elsewhere. The dates given for the first pentecostal churches in these republics are Brazil, 1910; Chile, 1910; Argentina, 1910; Peru, 1911; Nicaragua, 1912; Mexico, 1914; Guatemala, 1916; and Puerto Rico, 1916. Some Latin American groups, such as the Brazilian and Argentine movements that nominally are related to the AG–U.S., came into existence under other names before that group was organized in 1914. Even after the proliferation of new groups, the vast majority of Latin American pentecostals still belong to denominational groupings that have had an existence of a half century or longer. It may be useful to investigate the institutional development of the missions of these agencies. On the face of it, as late as 1940 these groups were hardly able to undertake more than token efforts to work in the various countries of Latin America. Moreover, early on their efforts were directed at leadership training, especially in the conducting of Bible institutes.

A profile of the missionary staff, moreover, is instructive. Mission agencies usually list all adults as missionaries, without distinguishing whether they are single persons working singly or as part of a team, married couples working together, and whether they are men or women. This gives the impression of a larger number of discrete "work units" than is actually in the field. Also, missionary statistics often do not reflect the fact that there are all different kinds of missionaries doing many different kinds of work, and probationary or neophyte missionaries can hardly be compared with someone who knows the language and culture and has become established in his or her work. Finally, since missionaries usually have some kind of periodic furlough and new missionaries may have to spend some time raising support prior to taking up their overseas work, perhaps only 80% of the personnel are deployed overseas at any given time, while increasingly support personnel remain at home.

All this tends to highlight the tentativeness of much missionary effort, while the large proportion of personnel devoted to largely routine administrative or technical support tasks diminishes the proportion of the staff dedicated to aggressive work. Even when these are factored in, they omit the proportion of the missionary personnel who are inexperienced probationers or are superannuated. In other words, the indices used for evaluating missionary work, largely quantitative, simply are inadequate for assessing effectiveness. The Assembléias de Deus no Brasil, for instance, has 100,000 pastors and a half million recognized lay leaders. Yet the North American church in the early 1990s supported only seven couples for work in that country, of which only four had permanent residence in Brazil. Moreover, three of the seven were sons of immigrants or of expatriate missionaries who were not required to acculturate to Brazilian life or learn Portuguese as adults.

B. The Authenticity of Latin American Pentecostalism.

The notion also persists that Latin American pentecostals are an institutional extension of North American revivalist efforts. Despite the easy identification of Latin American pentecostals with the North American revivalist tradition, the largest movements have had the least North American influence. The models of Protestantism that were available at the outset were most often Lutheran, Anglican, and Methodist, reproductions of European and North American mainline denominations. Moreover, 20th-century pentecostals are not organizationally very similar to their putative founders. The Chilean pentecostals, with a community of as many as a quarter of the entire national population, retain a Methodist Episcopal polity and practice infant baptism, while most of their U.S. pentecostal cousins, especially those that later sent missionaries south, organized around congregational polity and only baptize adults. The Brazilian pentecostals, likewise, tend to have polities, styles, and customs that show little resemblance to any of the major U.S. pentecostal denominations, despite the similarity of the name of the largest grouping, the Assembléias de Deus, with the name of the largest North American pentecostal denomination, the AG. The two movements—and their respective names—derived independently and never represented any organic relationship, despite the ongoing, congenial, fraternal relationship between the two.

What may be even more important is the strong influence Europeans have played in Latin American pentecostalism. Brazilian pentecostals trace their origins to two different sets of European "founding fathers." Gunnar Vingren and ►Daniel Berg, Swedish immigrants to the U.S., took the movement to northern Brazil in 1910. Simultaneously, ►Luigi Francescon, an Italian immigrant to the U.S. who had previously been a Presbyterian, introduced the movement in the south of Brazil. Moreover, the Argentine Asambleas de Dios, a merger between existing groups, trace their origins to Swedish missionaries in 1910. Similarly, one of the important pentecostal groups in Mexico was pioneered in 1919 by ►Axel and Ester Andersson, supported by the Swedish Philadelphia pentecostal churches. Pentecostal scholar ►David Bundy concludes that "the heritage of much of Latin American pentecostals is generally to be traced to Sweden and Norway. The heritage of Latin American Pentecostalism is as much European as from the U.S.A."

C. The Institutional Independence of Latin American Pentecostals.

Still another assumption about these groups is that they are largely sustained by foreign financial and personnel resources. This dependency thesis quickly breaks down upon scrutiny. While North American and European pentecostals have long contributed personnel and funds to these churches, the numbers of missionaries and amounts of funding have proportionally little to do with their growth. Moreover, several North American pentecostal missions have merely adopted—not developed—overseas churches. Two vital considerations are whether national leaders receive salaries or substantial operational budgets from overseas sources, and whether property is held in the names of an overseas agency. Neither is in fact the case. Most pentecostal groups emphasize the need for national control and support of a given church, despite their contribution to capital projects like school construction. While Latin American pentecostals are appreciative of the assistance they have received, they would be the first to assert their autonomy and would smile at the suggestion that they are patronized by North Americans. They believe that they, not North Americans or Europeans, are the vanguard and the true representatives of the pentecostal movement. Ultimately, the region's pentecostals may represent the most independent, self-initiated popular move-

ment to be found in Latin America. Perhaps precisely because it lacks precedent and has emerged without reliance on foreign religious leadership, Latin American pentecostalism has not been well understood. Apart from the early origins and popular character of the vast majority of the Latin American pentecostal groups, their independent existence can be demonstrated by their relationship with the denominations with which they have been identified. If the CG, the AG, the Church of God of Prophecy, the Pentecostal Assemblies of Canada, the International Church of the Foursquare Gospel, and other pentecostal groups have engaged in missionary effort in Latin America, the total of their financial and personnel support would be an index of their control or excessive influence. In these respects David Stoll's logic is compelling. Asked what dollar amounts were invested annually in Latin America by the largest pentecostal mission, the Assemblies of God, Stoll learned that the amount totaled an estimated $20 million (roughly one-fifth of the annual denominational missions budget of $100 million). Then obtaining the probably undercounted total of 10 million members that the annual budget was expected to sustain, the average annual investment of $2.00 per member per year appeared to be inadequate to explain a rapidly growing movement. "If evangelical churches were really built on handouts," concluded Stoll, "they would be spiritless patronage structures, not vital, expanding grass-roots institutions."

D. The Institutionalization of Latin American Pentecostal Movements.

The notion also persists that pentecostals are too volatile and undisciplined to be institutionally sound. It was not until sociologists examined pentecostal structures more closely that they began to appreciate their organizational strength. While these groups appeared tenuous associations of marginal peoples, their organizations are remarkably resilient and durable. These cellular, polycephalous and reticulate, semiautonomous, and decentralized but interconnected segments, according to Luther Gerlach, tend to suggest the need for the tightening of command structures, eliminating duplication, and otherwise the need for rationalization. Gerlach reports that research led to the conclusion that such an organization was "highly adapted for exponential growth." Pentecostals may seem fragmented and unstable, but they are remarkably resilient and adaptive to new circumstances—an ingenious system of mobilizing the already mobile and tenuous popular groups.

While it is true that many more converts begin rather than remain with these churches, new arrivals find an organizational base and mechanisms that permit them to function effectively as members of an association, not merely as isolated believers. In societies where social class, gender, family name, profession, and other attributed statuses determine one's life chances, the existence of an option where status is acquired by personal merit is remarkable. The survival of these groups over a period of several decades suggests that these features are significant.

The formation of as many as 200,000 separate congregational communities, most of them tiny and inconspicuous, also belies the notion that the pentecostals are organizationally tenuous. On the contrary, they have provided a means by which the grassroots participants can gain control of their own lives and begin the structuring of an effectively organized community. The majority of pentecostal congregations have the *persona juridica* (articles of incorporation), by which the people from the poor and marginal sectors become legal entities and establish a basis for participation in civil life. Moreover, probably many more than half—some cases indicate more like three-quarters—own some real estate, a further indication of a foothold in the life of the larger society.

E. Pentecostals and Social Change.

Latin American pentecostals have been particularly offended by the pejorative term *sect* that has been applied to them. They are largely in the mainstream of conservative Christianity, affirming the doctrines, beliefs, and values that are promulgated by the historic groups. The many studies of these groups treat them generically, as though they were largely a single movement, despite their many internal differences. They do, in fact, constitute a single grouping, one that, should constituents wish to combine their efforts, could come under one broad denominational umbrella. Thus, they are not based on esoteric doctrines or under the influence of a single dominant leader, and thus hardly qualify as cults. But Latin Americans are remarkably intense and committed to their faith. They study theology and, as avid biblicists, tend to adhere to the principal Protestant doctrines. Their idealism regarding personal conduct—often considered a form of popular religious legalism—is offset by a sense of personal piety and conscientiousness. Even very humble people seem to distinguish between Mormons, Baptists, and Seventh-day Adventists. Their intellectual idealism and tradition of rote learning make them concerned with precision. In a culture where often large discrepancies are expected between what people believe and what they practice, these groups have turned not only to religion, but to rectitude, a sense of personal worth and integrity, what anthropologist Frank Manning has identified as "reputation." The bottom line is that Latin American pentecostals are in the vanguard—not at the margins—of the evangelical movement in Latin America. Despite social slights, the worth and achievements of these groups are now increasingly recognized.

F. Pentecostal Social Programs.

One of the best indications that Latin American pentecostals do have a strong foothold in their respective societies is the body of literature that is developing around the pentecostals' social impact. Although these groups have been accused of being socially passive, "other-worldly," or "on social strike," their character belies these characterizations. They regularly are described, for instance, as activist rather than contemplative. Their energetic efforts, their self-imposed sacrifices, and the hard work required to advance their movements, as well as their sometime uninhibited boldness in promoting their faith, all indicate the inadequacy of the stereotype of passivity. Moreover, the harassment, ostracism, and obstacles that the members of these groups have endured—including physical assaults and even jailings at least into the 1950s—suggest considerable assertiveness and tenacity in the face of stiff opposition. Investigations by Douglas Petersen (1996) and Everett Wilson (1993), as well as many other studies, demonstrate the inadequacy of the "social strike" theory.

While virtually all pentecostal groups maintain some self-help social programs, often sharing their meager resources with the less fortunate among them, the issue that has received the most attention has been their effectiveness in combating the Latin American cultural tendency to machismo, exaggerated male dominance.

A number of scholars have researched the inherent feminism of pentecostalism, which is based on belief in the equality of all believers. According to sociologists Elizabeth Brusco, Cecilia Mariz, and Cornelia Butler Flora, Latin American women typically help themselves by asserting their leadership in local congregations. Despite the appearance of male domination, the congregations are usually made up disproportionately of single women. While the pastor is only occasionally a woman, women tend to dominate policies and participate widely in congregational activities. Brusco's City University of New York dissertation studies these tendencies in depth and has given rise to several other dissertations on the subject. Her thesis is that pentecostal women are armed with an improved self-image based on their subjective religious experience and their full acceptance by the congregational community. As a result, they tend to respond in a more controlled and constructive manner in their relationships with their male partners. In turn, these men either leave or themselves adapt, accepting the values of the group even if they do not convert. The atmosphere in the home and the relationship between women and their men tends to make the evangelical home more stable, pleasant, and focused on hard work and its improvement. As women marry within the congregation or convert their husbands, the congregation benefits from these changes, as does the entire local community.

G. Pentecostals and Politics.

These changing profiles of Latin American pentecostals have also given rise to the potential of grassroots Protestants to alter Latin American society. Articles in *Forbes* (Oct. 15, 1990) and *Business Week* (June 4, 1990), for example, were based on the thesis that pentecostal growth would likely bring about a broader participation of the working classes in the region's economic and political life. While the study of these groups continues, and while some early forays into national politics have proved inconclusive—and in some cases disastrous—there is ample indication that pentecostals are prepared when it is to their advantage to engage in temporal as well as eternal concerns. The studies published by Edward Cleary and Hannah Stewart-Gambino (1997) simply document and analyze what was becoming increasingly clear—that pentecostals harbor a larger agenda than simply "saving souls." Since they are already involved in social projects, there is no reason to believe that they will not in the future pragmatically involve themselves in politics, despite their disclaimers about focusing solely on transcendent concerns.

V. THE FUTURE OF LATIN AMERICAN PENTECOSTALS.

What is the future of the Latin American pentecostals? Despite predictions that these groups will either simply taper off as they lose enthusiasm or will fragment themselves into oblivion, neither alternative seems to be in the immediate offing. While rates of growth have diminished for some national movements or denominational groups, and while the high demands of these communities has resulted in the steady exodus of large numbers of new converts, as well as of the members' own children, their net growth appears far from declining. In fact, their effectiveness in extending their faith into the middle classes and the rise of large urban congregations appears to leave the groups stronger than ever. Moreover, in countries like Argentina, Ecuador, and Mexico, where the pentecostals remain deeply sectarian, the pentecostals appear to be on the threshold of new growth and social influence.

There are many reasons, however, to assume that the Latin American pentecostals will not remain static. As concentrations of resources and as effective infrastructures, they are increasingly a preemptive target for programs and purposes other than those for which they came into being. Accordingly, while they may long survive, their form and direction may be greatly altered as they have to live with a measure of success and acceptance. Some observers discern the pentecostals' temptation to enter the political arena, to redirect their efforts to economic schemes, or to grow rigid and sectarian. According to Edward Cleary, the pragmatic pentecostals are clearly versatile, but they are hardly predictable.

Moreover, the rise of neo-pentecostal groups that provide many of the rewards of the movement without the demands on conduct and attitudes or the exclusivity of the early pentecostal movements apparently attracts converts who have progressive tendencies. While the pentecostals retain many features of traditional culture, which suggests resistance to change, they also appear to be building bridges to the future, which even more than their conservatism may ensure their continued influence in Latin American life.

■ **Bibliography:** S. Annis, *God and Production in a Guatemalan Town* (1987) ▨ D. B. Barrett, G. T. Kurian, and T. M. Johnson, *World Christian Encyclopedia* (2001) ▨ M. Berg and P. Pretiz, *Spontaneous Combustion: Grass Roots Christianity, Latin American Style* (1996) ▨ E. Brusco, *Machismo* (1989) ▨ J. Burdick, *Looking for God in Brazil: The Progressive Catholic Church in Brazil's Political Arena* (1993) ▨ E. Cleary and H. W. Stewart-Gambino, *Power, Politics, and Pentecostals in Latin America* (1997) ▨ H. Cox, *Fire from Heaven* (1994) ▨ B. Doudewijnse, A. Droopers, and F. Kamsteeg, eds., *Algo Más que Opio: una lectura antropológica del pentecostalismo latinoamericano y caribeno* (1991) ▨ V. Garrard-Burnett and D. Stoll, *Rethinking Protestantism in Latin America* (1993) ▨ L. Gerlach and V. H. Hine, *People, Power, Change: Movements of Social Transformation* (1970) ▨ S. D. Glazier, ed., *Perspectives on Pentecostalism: Case Studies from the Caribbean and Latin America* (1980) ▨ M. G. Hoover, ed., *Willis Collins Hoover: History of the Pentecostal Revival in Chile* (2000) ▨ R. Ireland, *Kingdoms Come: Religion and Politics in Brazil* (1991) ▨ P. Johnstone, *Operation World* (1993) ▨ C. Lalive d'Epinay, *Haven of the Masses* (1968) ▨ F. E. Manning, "Pentecostalism: Christianity and Reputation," in *Perspectives on Pentecostalism: Case Studies from the Caribbean and Latin America*, ed. Stephen D. Glazier (1980) ▨ C. L. Maríz, *Coping with Poverty: Pentecostals and Christian Base Communities in Brazil* (1994) ▨ D. Martin, *Tongues of Fire: The Explosion of Protestantism in Latin America* (1990) ▨ D. R. Miller, *Coming of Age, Protestantism in Contemporary Latin America* (1994) ▨ E. A. Nida, *Understanding Latin Americans* (1974) ▨ D. Petersen, *Not by Might, Nor by Power: A Pentecostal Theology of Social Concern in Latin America* (1996) ▨ B. Roberts, *The New Social Policies in Latin America* (1995) ▨ D. Stoll, *Is Latin America Turning Protestant?* (1990) ▨ idem, "Is There a Latin American Protestant Reformation?" *Christian Century* (Jan. 17, 1990) ▨ E. Willems, *Followers of the New Faith: Culture Change and the Rise of Protestantism in Brazil and Chile* (1967) ▨ B. Wilson, *Religion in Sociological Perspective* (1982) ▨ E. A. Wilson, "Challenging the Stereotypes of Latin American Pentecostal Passivity," *Transformation* (Jan. 1993) ▨ idem, "Passion and Power: A Profile of Emergent Latin American Pentecostalism," in *Called and Empowered: Global Mission in Pentecostal Perspective*, ed. M. Dempster, B. D. Klaus, and D. Petersen (1991).

■ E. A. Wilson

LATVIA
■ Pentecostals 9,698 (11%) ■ Charismatics 73,574 (82%) ■ Neocharismatics 6,728 (7%) ■ Total Renewal: 90,000

See RUSSIA.

LEBANON
■ Pentecostals 1,059 (1%) ■ Charismatics 61,267 (37%) ■ Neocharismatics 104,674 (63%) ■ Total Renewal: 167,000

See AFRICA, NORTH, AND THE MIDDLE EAST.

LESOTHO
■ Pentecostals 25,102 (7%) ■ Charismatics 68,896 (20%) ■ Neocharismatics 248,003 (73%) ■ Total Renewal: 342,001

LIBERIA
■ Pentecostals 152,946 (29%) ■ Charismatics 48,602 (9%) ■ Neocharismatics 318,452 (61%) ■ Total Renewal: 520,000

See AFRICA, WEST.

LIBYA
■ Pentecostals 0 (0%) ■ Charismatics 4,731 (26%) 13,269 ■ Neocharismatics 13,269 (74%) ■ Total Renewal: 18,000

See AFRICA, NORTH, AND THE MIDDLE EAST.

LIECHTENSTEIN
■ Pentecostals 0 (0%) ■ Charismatics 763 (95%) ■ Neocharismatics 37 (5%) ■ Total Renewal: 800

LITHUANIA
■ Pentecostals 3,197 (6%) ■ Charismatics 35,829 (70%) ■ Neocharismatics 12,274 (24%) ■ Total Renewal: 51,300

See RUSSIA.

LUXEMBOURG
■ Pentecostals 223 (1%) ■ Charismatics 17,652 (89%) ■ Neocharismatics 1,925 (10%) ■ Total Renewal: 19,800

MACEDONIA
■ Pentecostals 221 (3%) ■ Charismatics 2,171 (28%) ■ Neocharismatics 5,308 (69%) ■ Total Renewal: 7,700

MADAGASCAR
■ Pentecostals 15,252 (2%) ■ Charismatics 467,847 (64%) ■ Neocharismatics 251,901 (34%) ■ Total Renewal: 735,000

MALAWI

■ Pentecostals 130,999 (7%)   ■ Charismatics   346,922 (18%)   ■ Neocharismatics 1,462,079 (75%)
■ Total Renewal: 1,940,000

For a general introduction to Central Africa and Bibliography, see AFRICA, CENTRAL.

Initially, pentecostalism was introduced to Malawi through migrant workers from that country who went to seek employment in the gold mines of the Rand in South Africa (S.A.). The mines had need of vast numbers of personnel to keep them in operation. Apart from those who were drawn from the nationals of S.A., the majority of the external labor force came from Mozambique and to a lesser extent from Malawi, Zimbabwe, and Zambia. As their contracts terminated and they returned to their home countries, a good number of those who had been evangelized in the pentecostal churches of the Rand took their pentecostal faith with them.

One such person was Lyton (also spelled Laiton) E. R. Kalambule from Ntcheu, Malawi, who walked to S.A. in search of work in 1929. At the time he was a member of the Zambezi Mission but not a Christian believer. He heard Alexander Haig Cooper of the Full Gospel Church preach the gospel on the street in Durban and was converted and baptized in the Holy Spirit. He returned to Malawi (then Nyasaland) in 1931. His zeal soon resulted in vigorous opposition from the mainline denominations. As a result, Kalambule was thrown in jail at Ntcheu Boma (a government post), where many were converted. (It was at this time that the Watchtower Society was being strongly opposed in Malawi, and it is likely that he was accused of being one of their members.) He established the Full Gospel Church of Nyasaland. Fred Burke, who had originally been a member of the Full Gospel Church in Witbank, S.A., but later worked with the AG–U.S., was sent to help him in 1933. Burke made periodic visits from S.A. but was not able to continue these visits during the war years. In 1947 Kalambule linked up with the AG–U.S. Disagreements over the question of how to handle new believers in polygamous marriages resulted in Kalambule leaving the AG in 1945; in 1958 he formed the Independent Assemblies of God (IAG). He was joined by Magnus and Hazel Udd (formerly AG–U.S.) in 1948. The IAG in Malawi joined in fellowship with the AG–S.A. under the leadership of ►Nicholas Bhengu. This did not last, however, as the chairman under Bhengu, Stevenson Phiri, attempted to wrest the movement in Malawi from Kalambule and Udd. That brought the fellowship with AG–S.A. to an end. The IAG have over 3,000 adherents.

The AG–U.S. work in Malawi dates from its contacts with Kalambule and Burke's visits in 1933. It was not, however, until the end of WWII that a significant number of churches were established when new personnel, including Magnus and Ragnar Udd and their families, settled in the country. The first AG–U.S. missionaries to reside in Malawi were Ragnar E. and Alice Udd, who entered the country on a survey trip in 1943 and then settled at Mubula in the north in 1944. By 1949 the AG had 50 places of worship throughout the country and an estimated 3,000 Christians with 80 national workers. Today there are more than 310 congregations with over 31,100 adherents.

Robert Chinguwo brought the Apostolic Faith Mission (AFM) from S.A. in 1933. Moody Wright was the first AFM white missionary to contact Chinguwo in Malawi. He made periodic trips to encourage the work. Edward Wendland later came from Germany, and today Sigi Bongartz and his wife live in Lilongwe and work with AFM, which today has 83 congregations and 16,700 adherents. The Pentecostal Holiness Association entered the country in 1932. They have more than 95 congregations and over 5,700 adherents.

Other pentecostal groups in Malawi include the Church of God (Full Gospel Church of God), which started in 1970 (165 congregations and 13,400 adherents; David Le Page is the superintendent for East Africa and resides in Lilongwe).

Elim–U.K. sent John Potter to Zomba in 1978. Elim–U.K. collaborates with Elim–New Zealand and Elim Church International. At present the H. Thoms are their missionaries in the country. Trevor Mackreill, formerly of Blantyre Christian Centre, is also involved in this work. The superintendent of the Elim Pentecostal Church was Moffet S. Maunde, who lives in Limbe but recently decided to start his own group; the conference has not yet elected his successor. Pastor Phiri is the general secretary.

The Velberter mission is involved in Bible college ministry as well as in aid and development projects. The Finnish Free Foreign Mission collaborates with the Velberter Mission and has the Ulf Strohbehns involved in teaching at their Bible college. The Apostolic Church has also established a solid work with many churches in the country; its national office is in Blantyre. The Apostolic Church of Pentecost of Canada (Saskatoon, Sask.), now called the Apostolic Church of Pentecost of Malawi, started its work in Malawi in 1947. It has over 157 congregations and 4,000 adherents. The Pentecostal Church of Malawi invited the Pentecostal Assemblies of Canada to work with it in the late 1970s. They have churches in Lilongwe and Blantyre and are pioneering among the Muslim Yao. They have a Bible college in Lilongwe. The present general superintendent is Stephen Chatepa. Blantyre Christian Centre was pioneered by Barbara Tippett, who had been healed at Rhema in Randburg,

S.A. Jim Lapka, formerly of the Apostolic Church of Pentecost of Canada, is now pastor of the Blantyre Christian Centre. Bishop Lewis Chikhwaza leads Bible Faith Ministries at Limbe Christian Centre.

Many Malawians have started ministries of their own. One such is pastor Ndovie of Living Waters, who has two services on a Sunday and fills a 2,000-seat auditorium in each service. In 1978 the pentecostals in the country formed a coordinating body called the Pentecostal Fellowship of Malawi. Generally, the pentecostal churches have not had the growth experienced by the same denominations in other countries of this region, and the percentage of pentecostals compared to other Protestant denominations is very low or an estimated total of 195,000 adherents.

Those missions involved in Bible college training include PAOC (Lilongwe); AFM (Blantyre); AG (Dedza); the Vel-berter Mission (Blantyre). The AG–U.S. have had a printing press in Limbe since 1954. Evangelism has played an important role in the spread of the pentecostal/charismatic message. ►Reinhard Bonnke has held at least two crusades in the country. The police estimated the crowds at Chichiri in Limbe to be over 180,000. Ernest Ainsley of Akron, OH, held crusades in 1997 and 1998. Ralph Mahoney of World Map, Burbank, CA, has made a significant contribution to leadership training when those from various denominations have attended seminars. His *ACTS* magazine is published by Emmanuel Press at White River, S.A. Ane Vanderbijl (better known as Brother Andrew) sponsored a "Love Africa Congress" at Blantyre in May 1978, attended by 350 hand-picked leaders from 40 African countries. ►Christ for the Nations (Dallas) has collaborated in the supplying of finances for roofing church buildings.   ■ D. J. Garrard

MALAYSIA

■ Pentecostals 51,215 (9%)   ■ Charismatics 328,689 (61%)   ■ Neocharismatics 160,096 (30%)   ■ Total Renewal: 540,000

1. Pentecostals.

The earliest pentecostal ministry in the Malay Peninsula (apart from work started in 1928 in Singapore) was among the migrant workers from India and Ceylon (Sri Lanka) in the early 1930s. The Ceylon Pentecostal Mission (CPM), founded in 1927 in Ceylon, arrived in the 1930s and registered with the Malaysian government as the Pentecostal Church of Malaya (PCM). The first pastor was Pastor V. V. Samuel of India, who started churches in Kuala Lumpur and Ipoh among the Tamil and Malayalam workers. With a strong emphasis on salvation, baptism of the Holy Spirit, and healing, the PCM made converts from among nonbelievers as well as other Christian denominations (Roman Catholics, Anglicans, Methodists, and others). Later, works were established in Penang and Seremban during the 1960s; Johore Bahru in 1970; Kuala Lipis in 1971; and Alor Star in 1974. By 1978 the PCM had eight churches with a membership of about 1,000. Most of the churches are bilingual (Tamil and Malayalam) with predominantly Tamil workers and members.

Three independent pentecostal churches were also started in the 1930s. These three churches were splinter groups from the CPM, and their work was primarily among the poor laboring class, Indian Tamils from the different rubber plantations. (1) The church in Ipoh was founded in 1935 by Pastor P. C. John, a former member of the Ceylon Pentecostal Church and later of the Indian Pentecostal Mission in India. The church, though related to the latter, has no strict organizational ties with it and works independently. (2) Pastor John Rose, who came from the CPM in India, founded the church in Kuala Lumpur in 1935. In the early 1960s the church experienced a split, and many of its members left to join the AG. The church experienced very little growth and had only a few faithful members. (3) Pastor Koilpitchai founded the church in Port Dickson in the 1930s. He left the CPM to begin independent work among the plantation workers.

In 1978 the combined membership of these three churches was 150. The CPM and its splinter groups were among the earliest pentecostal groups that ministered primarily among the Tamil and Malayalam community from Indian and Ceylon.

The AG began its work in Malaysia in 1934, after earlier efforts in Singapore in 1928 among the Chinese community. Carrie P. Anderson, a former missionary to China, started a Cantonese work in her bungalow in Kuala Lumpur. Her first converts were two young men,

The fishing village of Kuala Sunger Pinang, Malaysia, an early focus of Assemblies of God evangelism.

Ng Kam Foh and Lee Charn Yew. In 1935 a paid worker, Miss Leong Shik Ngon from Hong Kong, came to assist her. They moved to a rented house in the Pudu area, 381 Lorong Brunei. The church was named Jalan Brunei Chapel (later the name was changed to Assembly of God Church).

The work was taken over by Rev. and Mrs. Sandhal when Miss Anderson returned to the U.S. on furlough in 1936. From 1937 to 1949, the Sandhals were assisted by Tsang Toh Hang, Paul Lim, and two Bible Women, Lee Siew Leng and Lee Sau Lan, all paid workers from Hong Kong. Sometime in 1937 or 1938, an evangelistic meeting was attended by over 100 people. There were a number of conversions. Such evangelistic meetings added converts to the church over the years. In 1940, during a visit of Lawrence O. McKinney, the church was officially affiliated with the AG. Lulu Ashmore took over the work later that year when the Sandhals left on furlough. In Dec. 1941, when the Japanese invaded Malaya, Miss Ashmore left for Singapore, and the work was left in the charge of Mr. Yap and his wife, Wong Ching Lan. They also left a few days later, and the church facilities were lost as a place of worship.

During the Japanese occupation, the AG congregation was scattered. A few leaders visited members whenever it was possible, and irregular Bible study and prayer meetings were conducted in homes. After the liberation in 1945, the church committee, Miss Lee Yoke Ang, and Brother Choo provided leadership. Soon attempts were made to gather back the old and missing members. Regular services resumed in borrowed facilities, and Sunday schools were conducted in various parts of town. Two years later the Sandhals returned to assume the pastorate of the church. The church grew, purchased property, and built a building by 1955. Three hundred people were in attendance at the dedication service of the new building in Dec. 1955.

Another AG church was planted in Penang with the arrival of Evelyn Iris Hatchett in Mar. 1953. Having been a missionary to China, she started the church by conducting English and Cantonese Sunday school in her home. When young people and adults began to attend, she started a bilingual worship service. To help with the Chinese-speaking church, she engaged four Chinese workers from Hong Kong, which allowed the services to be conducted in their vernacular. Soon two congregations emerged. The Chinese work was primarily pastored by paid pastors from Hong Kong, the English congregation by U.S. missionaries. The church also witnessed a rapid turnover of leadership in the first seven years. By 1960 the church, Penang First Assembly, purchased property at 286 Macalister Road, and the separation of the English and Chinese congregations took place. Luke Koo from Hong Kong led the Chinese congregation, and David H. Baker led the English congregation. Two other churches were also planted in Ipoh and Raub in the late 1950s. Missionaries from Britain started

the church in Malacca in the 1960s. By the mid 1970s all AG churches were pastored by nationals.

The spiritual breakthrough for the AG came in Aug. 1957 at the Youth Camp in Port Dickson, where some 70 to 80 youths attended and 20 of them were baptized in the Holy Spirit. Before this event, according to Rev. Guynes, who came in 1954, the AG churches could hardly be identified as pentecostal. When *Howard Carter came to Singapore and Kuala Lumpur for special teaching on the Holy Spirit, more than 40 were filled in Kuala Lumpur. The youth camps became the focus for spiritual renewal and Holy Spirit baptism. Great emphasis was placed on full-time service. That led many to respond to the call of God and to enter Bible school. By the 1960s, attendance at the camps averaged between 200 to 300, in the 1970s, between 400 and 600.

In 1960 the AG established the Bible Institute of Malaya in Petaling Jaya, and 12 young men and women from Penang, Raub, Kuala Lumpur, and Singapore formed the first class of students. H. C. Osgood served as the first principal. While in Bible school, the students were involved in pioneering churches around Kuala Lumpur. Of the 12 enrolled in the first class, seven graduated three years later and formed the earliest group of national pastors to serve in Malaya and Singapore. In 1972 Chris D. Thomas (who served as the first dean of students at the Bible Institute of Malaya in 1960) founded the Malaysia Tamil Bible Institute to train workers in the Tamil language. The growth of the AG can be attributed to the graduates from the two Bible schools. Soon every city and town in the Malay Peninsula had an AG church or outreach. The 1960s record 20 new churches, the 1970s, 44 new churches. By 1980 the AG had about 75 churches, and by 1987 the AG had about 200 churches and outreaches in both West and East Malaysia. In 1999 there were 292 churches and over 40,168 adherents.

2. Charismatics.

Prior to the charismatic renewal, nonpentecostals witnessed and experienced the movement of the Holy Spirit through the ministry of John Sung in the 1930s and Madam Kong Mui Yee in the early 1960s (see article on Singapore). The charismatic renewal came to Malaysia in the 1970s. Peter Young, an Anglican pastor who was then general secretary of the Scripture Union of Malaysia, received the baptism of the Holy Spirit in a hotel room in Malacca in 1973. He shared his experience with his own congregation, St. Gabriel Church, Kuala Lumpur. The church was slow to accept his experience; primarily the young adults were open to it. Only in their prayer meetings was there full expression of charismatic praise and worship. Young later formed a renewal committee, which included among others Tan Jin Huat and Joy Seevaratnam, to organize renewal seminars patterned after the renewal conference of Britain. The first seminar was held in Trinity Methodist Church, Petaling Jaya, sometime in the late 1970s. Because of Young's national role with Scripture Union, the seminar attracted a cross-section of Anglicans, Methodists, Baptists, Lutherans, and others. Around 250 to 300 packed the church hall. Other seminars were planned. However, the charismatic movement generally received a cool response from the mainline denominations. To the Anglicans it appeared as a threat to traditional church structures and authority, undermining the unique authority of priests and bishops and threatening the valued Anglican liturgical heritage. In 1987, in a renewal seminar for the clergy and laity, the Anglicans relaxed their earlier resistance to charismatic expression, in part to retain charismatic adherents who were leaving for charismatic churches. Other mainline churches also took this approach. Some, however, left and formed new charismatic churches.

The ▸Full Gospel Business Men's Fellowship (FGBMF) has played an important role in spreading the charismatic experience among both Roman Catholic and Protestant believers. At the height of the movement, the FGBMF attracted hundreds of believers and nonbelievers to their monthly meetings in various cities. Many who received the charismatic experience had difficulty reintegrating into their churches and either found their way into pentecostal churches or started their own fellowships, which soon turned into churches. By the early 1980s the FGBMF lost favor with some pentecostal and charismatic churches when its leadership started their own church and began to "advertise" their services in the meetings.

One of the charismatic churches that sprung up during this period was Full Gospel Assembly. The founders, Spirit-baptized Brethren who were not accepted by the Brethren church, started having meetings in the home of Dr. and Mrs. Koh Eng Kiat on Apr. 8, 1979, with about 40 people. The church grew by leaps and bounds; by 1983 attendance stood at 800, and the church took over a cinema in Taman Goodwood. The church continued to be one of the fastest-growing churches, and membership reached 5,000 in 1990. Other Full Gospel Assemblies were started in major towns such as Ipoh, Penang, Malacca, Johore Baru, and Singapore.

Other independent charismatic churches were founded due to an inability to integrate with pentecostal groups or to a unique focus and vision. One such group is the Latter Rain Church of Malaysia. Founded by Dexter Low in 1975, this church was born out of a vision he received. By 1984 they had 25 branches and a membership of 1,200. Differences between the leaders and the founding pastor, however, resulted in a secession of eight branches, reducing membership to 650 in 1985. Within a year they recovered and had 23 churches. Over the years, church splits have hampered their progress.

Another independent church is Tabernacle of Glory, founded by Raymond Row; at its height it had over 1,000 in attendance. Initially this church had some relationship with the AG but later decided to be independent.

The largest charismatic constituency in Malaysia is the Catholic charismatic renewal (CCR). Roman Catholics constitute 60% of Malaysian Christians and form the largest group in the charismatic renewal. In the early days they were seen attending pentecostal and charismatic conferences and FGBMF. The Catholic Church responded to the popularity of the renewal movement by adopting it into the mainstream of its churches. While the archbishop discouraged Catholics from attending non-Catholic pentecostal meetings, he organized full-time officials to "manage" the renewal at parish level. Regular charismatic meetings were conducted for its members, interwoven as part of the total life of the church. The emphasis at these meetings was on healing and deliverance; speaking in tongues was a private experience, and prophecies were not often uttered.

In East Malaysia (on the Island of Borneo) a charismatic revival broke out among the Kelabits, a small tribe in Sarawak, in 1973 at a traditional Easter convention when an Indonesian evangelist, Petrus Octavanius, preached. There were signs and wonders in his ministry. Many were truly converted, and a number received healing, while others found new zeal to share the revival with others. Among those present were a group of secondary-school students from Bario. Greatly impacted, they met regularly for prayer. In October of that year, at the close of their regular prayer meetings in Bario, the Holy Spirit fell upon the place. They began to confess their sins and weep in repentance. Many stayed all night in prayer, and others joined them. The meeting lasted a few days until it spread to the whole village. There were miracles and manifestations of gifts, and many were converted and baptized in the Holy Spirit.

The Bario revival soon spread to neighboring tribes. In December of that year, at the church in Ba Kelalan, the Holy Spirit came upon the church, and suddenly members started falling under the power of the Holy Spirit and a number spoke in tongues—revival had come to the Lun Bawang tribe. As the Bario revival waned, the Ba Kelalan revival increased in power. In a spectacular series of signs and wonders throughout 1984–85, the Ba Kelalan received national coverage in the national press. The *New Strait Times* reported the "Sarawak Sightings" for two days in Dec. 1985. The central figure of the Ba Kelalan revival of 1984–85 was Pa Agung Bangau, a powerful prophet, whose ministry was filled with signs and wonders. He exercised the gifts of knowledge, wisdom, workings of miracles, and prophecy. The Ba Kelalan revival impacted the Sidang Injil Borneo church (SIB) with whom Agung worked closely. The SIB church has a network of 45,000 members among the tribes of East Malaysia, among whom many were touched by the ministry of Agung. Agung passed away in 1992, an anointed prophet of God who brought revival to God's people in Ba Kelalan and in the SIB. This charismatic revival continued on within the SIB churches.

The movement of the Holy Spirit is still very much evident in churches in Malaysia, as evidenced by a number of charismatic churches that started in the 1990s and have experienced tremendous growth.

See also SINGAPORE.

■ **Bibliography:** C. Choo, *The Ba Kelalan Revival of East Malaysia* (1994) ■ R. Hunt et al., *Christianity in Malaysia: A Denominational History* (1992) ■ M. Northcott, "A Survey of the Rise of Charismatic Christianity in Malaysia," *Asia Journal of Theology* (1990) ■ J. W. Roxborough, *A Short Introduction to Malaysian Church History* (1986) ■ C. D. Thomas, *Diaspora Indians: Church Growth among Indians in West Malaysia* (1978). ■ D. Tan

MALDIVES

■ Pentecostals 0 (0%)　■ Charismatics 29 (58%)　■ Neocharismatics 21 (42%)　■ Total Renewal: 50

MALI

■ Pentecostals 1,599 (5%)　■ Charismatics 12,156 (42%)　■ Neocharismatics 15,444 (53%)　■ Total Renewal: 29,199

See AFRICA, WEST.

MALTA

■ Pentecostals 523 (1%)　■ Charismatics 95,811 (99%)　■ Neocharismatics 666 (1%)　■ Total Renewal: 97,000

MARSHALL ISLANDS

■ Pentecostals 19,189 (64%)　■ Charismatics 7,434 (25%)　■ Neocharismatics 3,577 (12%)　■ Total Renewal: 30,200

For general introduction and bibliography, see PACIFIC ISLANDS.

The Marshall Islands consist entirely of atolls (19 inhabited and 10 uninhabited) and reef islands (4 inhabited and 1 uninhabited). The largest atoll is Kwajalein, made up of about 90 islets around a lagoon 75 mi (120 km) long and 15 mi (24 km) wide. The total land area is only about 70 mi² (180 km²). The atolls and islets are distributed into two groups, the eastern *Ratak* (Sunrise) and the western *Ralik* (Sunset) chains, dispersed over a huge ocean area of 750,000 mi² (1,942,500 km²) in the Central Pacific.

No island is more than a few feet above sea level. The highest point is on Likiep, 33 ft (10 m) above sea level. The soil is generally poor. While coconut, pandanus, and breadfruit grow easily, the production of even basic crops requires persistence.

Today the administrative center and capital is Majuro Atoll. The total population in 1992 was about 56,000, with approximately 21,000 (42%) of the population living in Majuro. Although the influence of the U.S., especially in Majuro and Kwajalein, where more than 60% of the population lives, has affected customs, social behavior, and diet, traditional chiefs still command respect, and their importance has been acknowledged by the constitution.

Over the last three decades the population has been growing rapidly. The annual average growth rate of 4.2% in 1980–

Building a Bible school in the Marshall Islands.

Bible school class, meeting under thatched roof in the Marshall Islands.

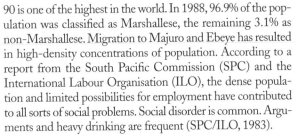

90 is one of the highest in the world. In 1988, 96.9% of the population was classified as Marshallese, the remaining 3.1% as non-Marshallese. Migration to Majuro and Ebeye has resulted in high-density concentrations of population. According to a report from the South Pacific Commission (SPC) and the International Labour Organisation (ILO), the dense population and limited possibilities for employment have contributed to all sorts of social problems. Social disorder is common. Arguments and heavy drinking are frequent (SPC/ILO, 1983).

1. Assemblies of God.

Officially the ᐧAssemblies of God (AG) started in 1964 when a missionary couple received an appointment. But the first time the pentecostal message reached the islands is recorded as being WWII, through U.S. servicemen based in the Marshalls. Prayer meetings were held, and one of the servicemen, Tom Fox, who had no knowledge of the Marshallese language, is reported to have delivered a message in fluent Marshallese when he was moved by the Holy Spirit.

When the servicemen left, the prayer meetings ended. Later, in 1961, an AG couple came to the Marshalls to teach in one of the high schools of the United Church of Christ (UCC). When they started to share their beliefs wherever possible and to organize meetings, they were fired. While the woman returned to Guam, her husband continued to preach. The UCC asked for the intervention of the government, but the missionary was able to organize considerable support so that several influential people, including one island chief, petitioned for his case, and he continued until an official appointment was made in 1964. In the same year the Calvary Bible Institute was established with 36 students. The AG grew very quickly in the first years, when healings and miracles took place. After reaching a plateau, the church grew more slowly but still steadily up to the present level of an estimated 10,000 adherents.

In 1997 there were 38 churches served by 110 ministers. An average of 25 students was enrolled in the AG Bible school, with approximately 10 graduates each year (1997 data). The AG in the Marshall Islands have their own local superintendent and executive committee; the church is to a large extent independent organizationally and financially. Two foreign missionaries assist and advise the local leaders in specific areas.

Bukot Non Jesus Church in Majuro, Marshall Islands. (Courtesy Manfred Ernst.)

In 1988 the AG experienced a major breakaway when a pastor who was disciplined was approached by the ›United Pentecostal Church International (UPC) and given their financial support to establish the Bukot Non Jesus (Looking for Jesus) Church in Majuro.

According to the principal of the AG Bible school, the success of the AG is related to a widespread desire of the people for a different style of worship as well as to the dissatisfaction of UCC members with the direction the UCC has taken recently. He admitted that many conversions have taken place on a very emotional basis.

Today the AG is represented on nearly every atoll. The majority of adherents is clearly concentrated in the fast-grow-ing urban centers, such as Majuro, where the AG have eight churches, two of which have about 1,000 adherents each.

2. Bukot Non Jesus Church.

The Bukot Non Jesus Church broke away from the AG in 1985 after a pastor was suspended from his work because of claims that he committed adultery. Together with this pastor a group of people left the AG, became affiliated with the UPC, and established the present church. Bukot Non Jesus has two main churches, one in Majuro and another in Kwajalein. Some members also live on other islands and atolls. The estimated number of adherents is about 2,400.

■ M. Ernst

MARTINIQUE

■ Pentecostals 4,579 (30%)   ■ Charismatics 9,080 (59%)   ■ Neocharismatics 1,741 (11%)   ■ Total Renewal: 15,400

See CARIBBEAN ISLANDS.

MAURITANIA

■ Pentecostals 0 (0%)   ■ Charismatics 154 (7%)   ■ Neocharismatics 1,946 (93%)   ■ Total Renewal: 2,100

See AFRICA, NORTH, AND THE MIDDLE EAST.

MAURITIUS

■ Pentecostals 112,576 (38%)   ■ Charismatics 180,422 (61%)   ■ Neocharismatics 3,002 (1%)   ■ Total Renewal: 296,000

MAYOTTE

■ Pentecostals 0 (0%)   ■ Charismatics 86 (43%)   ■ Neocharismatics 114 (57%)   ■ Total Renewal: 200

MEXICO

■ Pentecostals 680,408 (5%)   ■ Charismatics 10,243,667 (78%)   ■ Neocharismatics 2,125,925 (16%)
■ Total Renewal: 13,050,000

1. The Beginnings of Mexican Apostolic Pentecostalism.

The beginnings of pentecostalism in Mexico are tied to the origins of the tradition at the ›Azusa Street revival, where Mexican participation was significant in the early period. One of the immigrants to Los Angeles converted at the mission was ›Romana de Valenzuela, or Romanita as she became known. In 1914 she returned to Mexico. Assisted by her nephew Miguel García, she converted her family. It was the beginning of the Iglesia Apostólica. The first ordained pastor was the Holiness Methodist pastor and convert Rúben Ortega. Apparently de Valenzuela had been in contact with the ›Oneness version of pentecostalism in California, and, at her insistence, Ortega baptized the new converts "in Jesus' name." The church grew slowly under the leadership of Romanita and her protégés. She returned to the U.S. to die in 1918.

There is some evidence that during these early decades of the tradition there was close interaction with the Pentecostal Assemblies of the World (PAOW). Certainly African-American missionaries and pastors such as Manuel Walker had significant influence in the development of the tradition. There was also PAOW-recognized Francisco Lorente (some sources use Llorente), who served as the official representative in Mexico of the Mexican branch of the church. The church was reorganized as the Iglesia Apostólica de la Fe en Cristo Jesús.

The first doctrinal controversy (1925) had to do with the authority of prophecy. Two of the prophets called themselves Saúl and Silas. Among the converts was Eusebio Joaquín. After a dispute with church leaders about a year after his conversion, Joaquín went to Guadalajara in 1926 to establish a church of his own, which evolved into a denomination, Luz del Mundo. He changed his name to Aarón, and therefore his church members were referred to as Aaronistas. This work would later produce (1942) another denomination established under the leadership of José Maria Gonzalez, Le Buen Pastor.

This same conflict over authority eventually led to the schism from the Apostolic Church led by Francisco Borrego. With others, especially Ireneo Rojas, Borrego founded the Iglesia Evangélica del Consejo Espirituel Méxicano, which became the Iglesia Evangélica Cristiana Espirituel, with headquarters at Monterrey. Leaders and parishioners floated back and forth between the two churches, and efforts to reconcile became a dominant theme of the 1920s and '30s. To complicate matters, converts in Baja California and along the U.S. border affiliated with the California Apostolic Church. A significant number of the early leaders came from the Methodist Episcopal Church, having become disaffected by the post-Holiness mission approach of the 1920s and '30s among the Methodists. All of these churches that resulted from the work of Romanita have remained Apostolic or "Oneness" in doctrine and in international connections. All have been active in missions throughout Latin America (especially Nicaragua, Costa Rica, Panama) and the Caribbean, as well as in the U.S. and Spain.

Alejandro Portugal Jr. with members of the Church of God (Cleveland, TN) in Oaxaco, Mexico. The women wear traditional dress.

2. The Beginnings of the Assemblies of God and Related Denominations.

The Assembleas de Dios de México (ADM) can trace its origins to the work of Texas Holiness Methodist pastor ▸Henry C. Ball, who affiliated with the Assemblies of God (AG) in 1914. Together with ▸Alice E. Luce, a former Anglican missionary to India who received her pentecostal spirituality under the leadership of ▸Pandita Ramabai of Mukti, Ball did mission work in Mexico and Texas. By 1922 there were 22 indigenous Mexican congregations. Among the early leaders were Daniel Gómez Díaz, Cesário Burciaga Rubio, Rubén Arévalo, José Ibarra Hernández, Juan Rivas, and Evaristo Acevedo.

In 1922, after the AG–U.S. refused to allow the Mexican churches more autonomy, a significant group under the leadership of ▸Francisco Olazábal withdrew to form the Concilio Latino-Americano de Iglesias Cristianas, which soon had congregations in the U.S. and Puerto Rico as well as Mexico. This led to the establishment in 1929 of the ADM at Monterrey under the leadership of ▸David Ruesga and ▸Anna Sanders. Ruesga withdrew about a year later to found the Iglesia Cristiana Nacional, part of which eventually united with the Church of God (CG, Cleveland, TN), and another part of which became the Iglesia Cristiana Nacional de las Asambleas de Dios. From the beginnings through the 1960s, persecution of varying degrees of seriousness plagued the evangelistic efforts, as has occasional social unrest. Some persecution came as a result of governmental policies against all of the churches. In many instances, priests of the Catholic Church gave leadership to persecutory efforts, and hostile, demeaning Catholic apologetic tracts and comic books are still issued (1999) against the pentecostals.

The ADM has continued to grow under the leadership of ▸Rodolfo Orozco (1930–40), Rubén Arévalo (1940–44), Juan Orozco (1944–60), and their successors, including Fidel Amaya, Abel de la Cruz Calderón, and Julio César Pérez. Beginning with the Instituto Bíblico Elim, established in 1931 in Mexico City, efforts at formation of clergy have been continuous. By 1990 there were some 30 Bible schools. Jeter states that in 1990 the ADM counted some 570,000 adherents in 3,100 congregations. The actual numbers are probably higher.

3. Axel and Ester Andersson and the Swedish Pentecostal Mission.

Scandinavian mission interest in Mexico began early. H. A. Johnson did evangelism in Guanajuato and wrote a report published by ▸T. B. Barratt in the

Swedish language *Korsets Seger* (2 [Feb. 1912], 11–12). After studies at the Örebro Mission School in Sweden, ▸Axel and Ester Andersson moved to Mexico in 1919. Andersson ministered there until his death in 1981, after which Ester Andersson and some of the children remained in Mexico City. There was extensive persecution during those early years and martyrs among the converts. A Bible school on the Scandinavian model was started in Mexico City (c. 1924). In 1926 Andersson began to publish the periodical *Luz y Restauración*, which circulated thousands of copies throughout Latin America and the Caribbean as well as Spain and the Canary Islands.

By 1930 Andersson was pastoring three churches and loosely supervising 10 other mission centers and training a team of Mexican evangelists. The Anderssons were joined in 1930 by Ella Gustafsson, who worked as an evangelist among Indian tribes and in cities in southern Mexico. Over the next decades the growth of churches related to Andersson's efforts grew at phenomenal rates. It is said that from his work came more than 15,000 congregations and missions in Mexico. One of the results of this ministry was the Iglesia Cristiana Independiente Pentecostés, which had more than 1,500 established churches and 400,000 adherents by 1985. The leadership of Andrés Ornales Martínez was formative for its growth and development.

Other groups evolved in relationship to Andersson and the churches inspired by Swedish pentecostalism, or from splits in the fellowship. Thus, there are also the Iglesia Evangélical Independientes; the Iglesia Christiana Interdenominacional, led by Josue Mechia (who was also influenced by the Holiness movement in the Methodist Church); the Unión de Iglesia Evangelicas Mexicanas; and the Fraternidad Pentecostal Independientes. The Unión de Iglesias Evangelicas Independientes has more than 400,000 members, primarily among the Otomi Indians.

4. The Missions of the Church of God—the Iglesia de Dios and Related Churches.

The presence of the CG in Mexico is derivative of the story of ▸Maria Atkinson (1879–1963). Born into a well-to-do, very pious Catholic family, Maria Rivera received an excellent education and later worked as a teacher and nurse. In 1900 she married Dionisio Chomina. Her husband was transferred to Douglas, AZ, where he died in 1903. Maria was healed through the prayers of a Native American Holiness woman in 1907, and about 1908 she experienced the baptism in the Holy Spirit. In 1920 she married an Ameri-

can, M. W. Atkinson. She began to evangelize in Arizona. Shortly thereafter, she began missionary work back in her home state of Sonora, among both Native Americans and Mexicans, where she established four congregations by 1931.

That year CG missionary statesman ▸J. H. Ingram contacted her. Atkinson continued her work and established a congregation in Ciudad Obregón, Sonora. Ingram visited Sonora in 1932 and officially established the Iglesia de Dios (Evangelio Completo). Baptisms during this period were of necessity conducted in secret. Persecution by government regulations and then by Catholic clergy was intense. By 1936 governmental restrictions were lifted, and the church began to grow under the leadership of persons such as Fernando González, Uriel Aviléz, and Alejandro Portugal.

Efforts to unite with the Iglesia Cristiana Nacional led by David Ruesga during the periods 1939–41 and 1943–46 were frustrating for all involved and eventually led to very complicated relationships between some of the pentecostal churches. Persecution was fierce throughout Mexico during the early 1940s. It was especially so in La Gloria, Veracruz, where a priest led a mob against Church of God members and adherents in their homes (May 14, 1944). The government made efforts to restore religious liberty.

Growth continued, and by 1948 there were 148 congregations with 5,262 members. In 1958 there were 379 congregations and 14,737 members. Barrett reported 827 congregations, 28,179 members, and 50,000 adherents about 1980. Splits have produced denominations such as the Iglesia Cristiana Bethel.

5. Other Pentecostal Denominations and the Charismatic Movement.

There are more than 150 pentecostal denominations in Mexico. Among those related to North American Churches are the Iglesia de Dios de la Profecia (Church of God of

Mexican believers worshiping in Faith, Hope, and Love Center, Mexico City.

Prophecy, 1944), Iglesia de Dios en Cristo (Church of God in Christ, 1933), Iglesia de Dios Pentecostal (Pentecostal Church of God, 1942), Iglesia del Evangelio Cuadrangular (Church of the Foursquare Gospel, 1943), and the Iglesia Santa Pentecostés Mexicana (International Pentecostal Holiness Church, 1931). The United Pentecostal Church claims (1999) 260 congregations and 19,135 "constituents" in the Iglesia Pentecostal Unida de México. Another hundred or so churches are part of the Asociación Fraternal Pentecostés. These churches are generally indigenous and unaffiliated with foreign denominations. The association includes national, regional, and local juridical units. Among them are the Iglesia Cristiana Unida, Iglesia de Dios en Cristo por el Espiritu Santo, Iglesia de Dios en la República Mexicana, Iglesia Evangélica del Consejo Espiritual Mexicano, Iglesia Misionera Mexicana, Iglesia Libre Pentecostés, Iglesia Universal de Jesucristo, and Comunión de Iglesia Pentecostales Libres.

There is an active charismatic movement in the Catholic Church in Mexico, as well as in some of the classical Protestant denominations. The ►Full Gospel Business Men's Fellowship International has had an important influence, as have independent ministries related to the North American healing movement, such as ►Christ for the Nations in Dallas, TX.

■ **Bibliography:** Åke Boberg, *Svensk Pingstmission: Kortfattad beskrivning av de svenska mingstförsamlinggarnas mission och om dokumentation och utvärdering av den* (1990) ■ D. D. Bundy, "Swedish Pentecostal Missions: The Case of Axel Andersson in Mexico," in *To the Ends of the Earth* (SPS, 1993) ■ D. L. Burk, ed., *Foreign Missions Insight: A Digest of Foreign Missions Faces, Facts, Fields and Figures* (1999), 81–84 ■ R. Casillas, "Las Disidencias Cristianas y la democracia: Lo nuevo con lo viejo," in *Religión, iglesias y democracia,* ed. R. J. Blancarte (1995) ■ *Constitución de la Iglesia Cristiana de "Las Asambleas e Dios" en la República Mexicana* (1946) ■ C. Díaz de la Serna, *El movimiento de la renovación carismática como un proceso de socialización adulta* (1984) ■ R. Domínguez, *Pioneros de Pentecostés. Vol. II: México y Centroamérica* (1990), 13–156 ■ W. W. Elliot, "Sociocultural Change in a Pentecostal Group: A Case Study in Education and Culture of the Church of God in Sonora, Mexico" (diss., U. of Tennessee, 1971) ■ M. Gaxiola Lopez, *Historia de la Iglesia Apostólica de la Fe en Cristo Jesús* (1964) ■ M. J. Gaxiola y Gaxiola, *La serpiente y la paloma: Historia Teología y análisis de la Iglesia Apostólica de la Fe en Cristo Jesús (1914–1968)* (1970) ■ idem, *La serpiente y la paloma: Historia Teología y análisis de la Iglesia Apostólica de la Fe en Cristo Jesús (1914–1994)* (1994) ■ idem, ed., *Iglesias y grupos religiosos en México* (1984) ■ K. D. Gill, *Toward a Contextualized Theology for the Third World: The Emergence and Development of Jesus' Name Pentecostalism in Mexico* (1994) ■ O. T. Hargrave, "A History of the Church of God in Mexico" (thesis, Trinity U., 1958) ■ V. D. Hargrave, *The Church of God in the Americas (South of the Rio Bravo)* (1954) ■ A. Hernández et al., *Historia de la Iglesia Cristiana Evangélica Espiritual* (1992) ■ W. J. Hollenweger, "Handbuch der Pfingstbewegung" (diss., Zurich, 1967), 1072–89 [para. 02b.22] ■ P. Humphrey, *Mária Atkinson—La Madre de México: No Doubts Here* (1967) ■ L. Jeter Walker, *Siembra y cosecha* (1990), 2:13–61 ■ F. Jiménez Arias, "La Cuidad de México: Disafios y alternativas de la Iglesia Metropolitana" (paper, CG School of Theol., 1990) ■ M. Leyva Avilez, "Crecimiento de la Iglesia de Dios en el Noroeste de México" (paper, CG School of Theol., 1988) ■ E. López Cortés, *Pentecostalismo y milenarisom. La Iglesia Apostólica de la Fe en Cristo Jesús* (1990) ■ D. A. McGavern et al., *Church Growth in Mexico* (1963) ■ J. Manrique López, "Educación Teológica por Extensión en México (ETEMEX)" (paper, CG School of Theol., 1994) ■ P. A. Molina, "Historia de la Iglesia de Dios (Evangelio Completo) en México. Origenes en Sonora, 1926–1950" (thesis, Seminario Bautista de México, 1982) ■ I. Montgomery, "Historia, Desarrollo y Análisis de la Iglesia de Dios en el Noroeste de México" (paper, CG School of Theol., 1985) ■ J. Ortega Aguilar, *Historia de la Asamblea Apostólica de la Fe en Cristo Jesús* (1966) ■ P. Rivera, *Institucíones Protestantes de México* (1992) ■ R. R. Rodriguez, "Systematization of the Process of Discipleship in the Local Church: A Project for the Mexican Bible Seminary" (paper, CG School of Theol., 1998) ■ L. Scott, *Salt of the Earth: A Socio-Political History of Mexico City Evangelicals, 1964–1991* (1991) ■ G. E. Söderholm, *Den Svenska Pingstväckelsens spridning utom och inom Sverige* ■ Supplement till de Svenska Pingstväckelsens Historia *(1933)* ■ A. Sundstedt, *Pingstväckelsen* 5 vols. (1969–73).

■ D. D. Bundy

MICRONESIA, FEDERATED STATES OF

■ Pentecostals 1,081 (12%)   ■ Charismatics 7,480 (80%)   ■ Neocharismatics 839 (9%)   ■ Total Renewal: 9,400

For general introduction and bibliography, see PACIFIC ISLANDS.

The Federated States of Micronesia constitute one of four island states that are collectively also known as Micronesia. The others are the Marshall Islands, the Mariana Islands, and Palau. The four states combined have a land area of 752 mi² (1,950 km²), spread over an area of 2.7 million mi² (7 million km², approx. three-fourths the size of the U.S.). The Federated States of Micronesia have a population of about 120,000 (1995).

Pacific Missionary Aviation (PMA) is a nondenominational service agency engaged in aviation, church planting, programs for the handicapped, literature production, medical work, and youth programs. It was founded by a former missionary of the German-based Liebenzell Mission, Rev. Edmund Kalau, in 1975, and today has activities in Micronesia and the Philippines.

The PMA is part of the "Restoration Movement," which consists of a multitude of charismatic ministries and churches and can be seen as a newer dynamic and expanding fringe of American evangelicalism. There are no firm traditions or higher authorities except God. Restoration charismatics are fundamentalists who hold to the absolute inerrancy and literal truth of the Bible. An important difference from some other fundamentalists is that Restoration charismatics, like Edmund Katau, do not preach separation from the world and to some extent tolerate doctrinal differences. This brand of fundamentalist Christian is quite political and tries to help knit together the religious right in any given local context.

PMA planes provide emergency medical evacuations, airsea search and rescue operations, medicine and food drops, church support, evangelistic outreach, and interisland passenger and cargo transport. A floating medical clinic operates in Micronesia as well as a mobile eye clinic and a mobile dentistry clinic.

Besides these basic activities, Christian literature in 12 languages of Micronesia and the Philippines is produced by the Good News Press, the biggest company of its kind in the Federated States of Micronesia, and one that also undertakes some commercial printing for the government. Together with the Wycliffe Bible Translators, PMA has a team working in Bible translation in the Ulithi Islands in western Micronesia. In 1992 there was a huge building project on the way in Kolonia, from where PMA is planning to make radio and TV broadcasts for Micronesia, with 50% religious programs.

PMA is incorporated as a nonprofit Christian mission organization by the government of Guam. It is governed by a board of trustees and a U.S. advisory board. The president is Edmund Kalau.

While the business office is located at Guam, there is also an administrative office in Lahr, Germany, and a field office in Pohnpei, where Kalau is based. In the Philippines, PMA is registered under the name Flying Medical Samaritans (FMS). ■ M. Ernst

MIDDLE EAST

See AFRICA, NORTH, AND THE MIDDLE EAST.

MOLDAVIA

■ Pentecostals 16,451 (34%)   ■ Charismatics 31,334 (64%)   ■ Neocharismatics 1,214 (2%)   ■ Total Renewal: 48,999

See RUSSIA.

MONACO

■ Pentecostals 0 (0%)   ■ Charismatics 1,060 (100%)   ■ Neocharismatics 0 (0%)   ■ Total Renewal: 1,060

MONGOLIA

■ Pentecostals 0 (0%)   ■ Charismatics 3,093 (31%)   ■ Neocharismatics (69%)   ■ Total Renewal: 9,900

MONTSERRAT

■ Pentecostals 1,654 (47%)   ■ Charismatics 777 (22%)   ■ Neocharismatics 1,109 (31%)   ■ Total Renewal: 3,540

See CARIBBEAN ISLANDS.

MOROCCO

■ Pentecostals 89 (0%)   ■ Charismatics 801 (1%)   ■ Neocharismatics 149,110 (99%)   ■ Total Renewal: 150,000

See AFRICA, NORTH, AND THE MIDDLE EAST.

MOZAMBIQUE

■ Pentecostals 684,668 (29%)   ■ Charismatics 241,992 (10%)   ■ Neocharismatics 1,398,340 (60%)   ■ Total Renewal: 2,325,000

For a general introduction to Central Africa and bibliography, see AFRICA, CENTRAL.

Mozambique was a Portuguese colony for 470 years until Independence in 1975. Prior to 1975 there were some 250,000 Portuguese settlers living in Mozambique. As with Malawi, there were numbers of ex-miners from the Rand, in South Africa, who returned to Mozambique with their pentecostal faith. Some had been converted and filled with the Holy Spirit under the ministry of Charles and Emma Chawner and their son ►C. Austin Chawner. Charles W. Chawner was the first missionary of the Pentecostal Assemblies of Canada (PAOC) to Africa in 1908. The first known pentecostal in Mozambique was Paolo Xhosa, a convert of C. Austin Chawner. He began to evangelize in 1911. This was the start of the Evangelical Assemblies of God of Mozambique. In 1938 the PAOC commenced a work in former Lorenço Marques (today Maputo). Ingrid Lokken from the Norwegian pentecostals had been attempting to gain permission to reside in Mozambique but was continually rebuffed by the authorities. Eventually after more than 30 return journeys to Maputo, she was given a permit. C. Austin Chawner (PAOC), who had been attempting since 1937 to evangelize in Mozambique from across the border in the Transvaal, and Ingrid Lokken were married and moved to Maputo. In spite of great opposition from the Catholic Portuguese colonial government, over a period of 15 years, 200 churches with 6,000 believers were established. So great was the pentecostal impact that the government, under pressure from the Catholic Church, attempted to curtail all Protestant churches in the territory. However, indigenous principles had been applied from the beginning, so that even though the missionaries were restricted in their activities, the national evangelists and pastors continued the work. The Chawners continued to live in Maputo and evangelize among the white Portuguese.

By 1958 five full-time Portuguese workers were evangelizing throughout the country. One of the best known was Jose Augusto Pina, who went on to work among the Portuguese population living in Zimbabwe; another was J. Do Cerro Guerreiro who was a member of the AG–Portugal but who moved to Maputo in 1947. Do Cerro eventually moved to South Africa when Frelimo (the national independence party) took power. Eighteen districts of the country were evangelized and had churches, although the far northeastern coast was never reached (it is now). The printing press provided by Austin Chawner (located first at Shingwedzi and then in Nelspruit, South Africa) was moved to White River in the Transvaal. Under the direction of David Newington (AG–U.K.; formerly of Congo Evangelistic Mission), this press has been responsible for producing vast quantities of literature in the languages of the region, including those of Mozambique. From 1975 on, there were severe restrictions on religious literature during the time of President Samora Machel, but this position was relaxed somewhat after 1982, when Machel called for collaboration from the missions to rebuild the country. In June 1988 buildings that had been confiscated from the churches in 1975 were officially returned.

During the post-Independence war, PAOC had the Don Krohns and Bill Mercers working at the central church in Changana, Maputo, which also had a Bible college; since the death of Don Krohn (1997), Reinhard and Sieglinde Mattheis of the Volksmission have reinforced the numbers of missionary teaching personnel. Initially courses were held in the evenings so as to enable the greatest number of students to attend. The first courses ran for two years, but there is now also a three-year course in the Portuguese language. This church has become the largest Protestant and pentecostal church in the entire country and bears the name Evangelica Assembleia de Deus de Moçambique (The Evangelical Assemblies of God of Mozambique). ►Laurentino Mulungo of Maputo is part of this denomination, which has more than 600 congregations and 150,000 adherents. He is pastor of the Changana Assembly, with over 38,000 members and more than 106 cell groups. God has used many other men greatly, including Henrique Mugabe and Dino Amande; the latter leads the Portuguese-speaking assembly in Maputo with 6,000 members in 40 cell groups. Pastor Inguana is the present general superintendent. Since the end of the civil war, there is much more liberty for evangelization in the outlying districts of the country. The Apostolic Faith Mission (Missão da Fé Apostólica) has 6,000 adherents, and the Full Gospel Church (Igreja do Evangelho Completo de Deus), which was planted about 1931, has affiliations with the AG–Portugal as well as the Full Gospel Churches of South Africa and the Church of God (Cleveland, TN). This grouping has 149 congregations and 51,800 adherents. ZAOGA from Zimbabwe operates in Mozambique under the name of Assemblia de Deus, African (ADDA). It has made great strides since the mid 1960s and claims 120 congregations and over 50,000 adherents. The International AG (Missão da Assembleia de Deus Internacional) has over 400 congregations and 20,000 adherents. The AG–U.S. (Missão da Assembleia de Deus) estimates that it has over 300 congregations and 226,000 adherents. The Pentecostal Holiness Church has over 8,000 adherents. Other pentecostal missions working in Mozambique include the Norwegian pentecostals; Volksmission (AG–Germany); the Velberter Mission (Germany), represented by Patricia Fenken, who is involved in primary education at Chimoio; the Church of God of Prophecy; the Church of the Foursquare Gospel; the AG–U.K., which has one missionary in a support role at Quelimane in the North; Elim–U.K., which has seconded the D. W. Pates to Africa Inland Mission at Pemba in the North. They are also involved in various ministries within the country, although most of the personnel is based in Zimbabwe. Global Literature Lifeline is active in Mozambique. "Jesus Alive" ministries of Peter Pretorius (South Africa) are engaged in evangelism and relief in the country; they have been responsible for flying in essential aid to the areas of greatest need. Recently pentecostal churches have begun to become more aware of the need for theological education and training. This is taking place through Bible school programs and seminars.   ■ D. J. GARRARD

MYANMAR

■ Pentecostals 298,025 (31%)   ■ Charismatics 249,765 (26%)   ■ Neocharismatics 412,210 (43%)   ■ Total Renewal: 960,000

Myanmar, formerly called Burma, is the largest country in mainland Southeast Asia, with a land area of over 260,000 mi^2 (674,000 km^2). It is bordered to the northwest by Bangladesh and India, to the north and northeast by China (and Tibet), and to the southeast and south by Laos and Thailand. The highland areas are inhabited by the hill peoples of Myanmar, of which the largest groups are the Kachin, Chin, Shan, and Karen. The Burmans are extensively settled in the lowlands.

Of a population of 46 million, 87% are Buddhists, 3.8% Muslims, 1.1% Animists, 0.5% Hindus, 6.5% Christians (Protestants 5.2%) (Johnstone). The form of Buddhism embraced by the majority in Myanmar is called Theravada, distinct from the practice of Buddhism in Tibet, China, Korea, and Japan. Since Buddhism has permeated the whole of Myanmar society, it has not been easy to break Buddhist strongholds.

Myanmar was united in the 11th century. Its history is divided into five periods: monarchy; a complex period of colonialism versus nationalism; independence from British colonialism (1948); socialism; and since 1988, military control.

The first Roman Catholic (Portuguese) soldiers came to Myanmar in 1551, and their chaplains joined them in 1554. Adoniram Judson (1788–1850), who landed at Yangon on July 13, 1813, was the outstanding Protestant pioneer missionary to Myanmar. It was said that the American Baptist Mission Board was born as a result of Judson's letter concerning his missionary work in Myanmar. He laid a solid foundation for all of the Christian missions that have followed. He became known as "the apostle to Burma." Today the Baptists are the largest Christian group in Myanmar.

1. Pioneers of the Pentecostal Movement in Myanmar.

The first pentecostal witness to Myanmar nationals came in 1921. An English missionary, Ada Buchwalter (who later married Leonard Bolton), was a missionary to Southwest China. She made a trip to Pen Kai village on the Mekong River and had contact with some Lisu tribesmen from the northern part of Myanmar and was able to witness among them. The first Assemblies of God (AG) missionaries to set foot on the soil of Myanmar were Leonard and Olive Bolton, who sailed from England and landed in Yangon (Rangoon) in Sept. 1924 in preparation for their trip to the Salwin Valley of southwest China. Their ministry in southwest China was always linked with the ministry among the Lisu in Myanmar. Bolton was hosted and guided by David Ho, a Lisu preacher, using gestures, signs, and smiles as their way of communication.

In 1927 J. Clifford Morrison and his family escaped the communist revolt in China and came to Kachin state in Myanmar, crossing high mountains and sharing the gospel primarily among the Lisu tribe in the highland along the China/Myanmar border. As the Lisu converts on the China side began to witness to the Rawang tribesmen and the Marus, strong congregations were established by new believers. Thus, the work of the AG, which had started in China, began to extend into Myanmar. The AG church was officially established among the Lisus in 1931. Other missionaries joined the Morrisons and the Boltons in later years, and the ministry that had begun in northern Myanmar among hill tribes spread to other parts of the country, as far south as the capital city, Yangon. The AG work in Kachin state, which

Burmese church near Putao, Myanmar (c. 1960).

was accompanied by a great revival, was the earliest pentecostal work in Myanmar

Pentecostal missionaries from Sweden, Finland, and the Go Ye Fellowship labored in Myanmar prior to WWII. For a few years the Open Bible Standard Churches had a few workers in Myanmar. However, none of these groups returned to Myanmar after the war, and thus there was no continuing work. Walter Erola from Finland, who had worked in Myanmar before WWII with the Finnish Pentecostal Mission, returned in 1951 with his wife, Lucille, to central Myanmar under the AG–U.S. and settled in the city of Mogok.

In spite of war and the absence of missionaries, the AG showed great progress under the leadership of indigenous pioneers. The Holy Spirit anointed their labor so that the number of pentecostal believers increased from 700 before the war to 2,600 after the war. Of these, about 2,000 had been filled with the Holy Spirit. By 1960 there were 89 full-time pastors and lay preachers in 55 churches and 81 outstations, with a total of 18,108 pentecostal believers in the whole country. Potao, in Kachin state, became the general council headquarters.

Glenn and Kathleen Stafford, AG–U.S. missionaries, arrived in Yangon in July 1957. Then, in Aug. 1961, Ray and Bethany Trask arrived to relieve the Staffords in the Yangon Evangelistic Center during their furlough. In 1963 a Bible school for national workers was opened in Myitkyina by Trask.

A short-term Bible school was opened in Yangon by Stafford in 1963. Through this school many lay preachers were trained and sent back to their respective areas for evangelism with pentecostal conviction.

2. Pentecostal and Charismatic Churches in Myanmar Today.

Today the majority of pentecostal and charismatic churches in Myanmar are the AG, the ›United Pentecostal

Duet by girls at Vacation Bible School, Yangon, Myanmar.

Church (UPC), the Foursquare Church (FC), ›Church of God (CG, Cleveland, TN), and independent charismatic churches.

a. Assemblies of God of Myanmar. Since all foreign missionaries in Myanmar were asked to leave the country by Apr. 12, 1966, the AG missionaries arranged to hand over leadership offices to the national church leaders. Elected for the next four years were, among others, Samuel Fish (general superintendent), John Wadam (assistant superintendent), and Khong Dai (secretary/treasurer). On Mar. 25, 1966, ›Maynard Ketcham, the AG–U.S. field director for Far East Asia, came to Yangon to wind things up in transfer of leadership responsibilities to national church leaders.

God raised up national leaders to take over the challenges of leadership. When all missionaries had to leave in 1966, Myo Chit, a Burmese minister who had been nurtured and taught in the Word of God by missionary Glenn Stafford, assumed the pastorate of Evangel Church in Yangon, which became the largest pentecostal church in Yangon, with a weekly attendance of over 2,000. Myo Chit is now the general superintendent of the AG and is considered the most prominent pentecostal and evangelical leader in Myanmar.

In 1966 Walter Myo Aung became the principal of Evangel Bible Institute in Myitkyina in the place of Ray Trask. Later Joseph became the principal of the Bible school. Although the missionaries had left, the work of the Lord did not stop. In 1970 the total number of AG churches in Myanmar stood at 200, with a total membership of 25,000. Today the AG of Myanmar is by far the largest pentecostal church in the country, with 800 churches and a total membership of 82,000. In addition, affiliated membership is 41,000. Most members are from Kachin and Chin states. They have 956 full-time ministers (ordained and licensed) and over 1,000 with a worker's certificate. They have four Bible colleges offering a bachelor of theology degree: Evangel Bible College, Maranatha Bible College, Evangel Bible Institute, and Bethel Bible College, with a total enrollment of 520 full-time students today. The schools have 24 full-time faculty members, of whom 2 have earned doctorate degrees and 16 hold master's degrees.

Another individual who made a significant contribution to the pentecostal movement in Myanmar was the late Hau Lian Kham (1944–95) from Chin state. He was a Baptist minister who was excommunicated by his local church due to his pentecostal experience and conviction in 1973. He started conducting open-air crusades and seminars with pentecostal teaching. Thousands came to Christ and were baptized in the Holy Spirit through his ministry.

b. United Pentecostal Church of Myanmar. The UPC of Myanmar was formed in 1966 in a small village (Saikah, Thantlang township, Chin state) only two miles from the

India/Myanmar border. The first person who embraced the ＞Oneness pentecostal message was Lo Riak. In 1967 another group of people with the same faith migrated from India to Kanan, Tamu township, in Sagaing division. These groups had been members of the UPC of India; they met in 1970 and formed a fellowship, which was organized formally in Mar. 1972. Ral Buai has been the leader of this movement since then. Most of the members are from the Chin tribe. They now have 15,000 adherents and 200 licensed preachers with 150 churches. Since 1983 they also have a four-year Bible college, with an enrollment of 30 and 6 faculty members with master's degrees.

c. The Foursquare Church of Myanmar. The FC of Myanmar was started in Oct. 1988 by Philip Ahone, a former pastor of the AG. The FC now has 22 churches, 3,000 members, 15 full-time ministers (ordained and licensed), and 13 Christian workers. Most members are Chin, in the northern part of the country. They are affiliated with the ＞International Church of the Foursquare Gospel in the U.S.

d. The Church of God (Cleveland, TN) of Myanmar. The CG in Myanmar was founded in 1980 by L. Naw San, a former AG minister. He started with a handful of Spirit-filled believers in Kachin state, in the northern part of the country. After his death, Zau Ba was elected to the position of leadership. By 1984 they became officially affiliated with the CG in the U.S. Today they have 17 churches with 2,000 members, most of them in Kachin state; 13 full-time ministers (ordained and licensed), and 11 exhorters. They have one Bible School, Missionary Evangel Bible School, founded in Myitkyina, Kachin state, in 1990, but moved to Yangon in 1993. Sixty students have graduated from the Bible school with a diploma in theology.

e. Charismatic Churches. Even though there are pockets of charismatic individuals and small groups in different parts of Myanmar, most of them are among the Chin Christians. Since the early 1980s, the charismatic movement has swept across denominations among the Chin people. Especially in the 1990s, many Baptists received the gift of speaking in tongues, which caused them to be excommunicated. Many of those joined AG churches, but some of them formed independent churches.

The Chin people came from an animistic background. They were called "head hunters" until they experienced a great revival in the 1970s, which continues until today. The gospel has transformed Chin society, and now 90% are Christians. It has been said that "some Chin Baptist believers are more pentecostal than the pentecostals." They sing and worship the Lord with ＞dancing in the Spirit. Some Christians from mainline denominations who went abroad and experienced charismatic gifts came back and testified among their fellow believers. The charismatic movement is impacting many churches in Myanmar today.

One outstanding independent charismatic church in Yangon is the Full Gospel Assembly, a former AG church. Due to, among other things, the desire to have more freedom in worship and prayer, this church was founded on Sept. 13, 1987, with five people by Dam Suan Mung, a son of a Methodist pastor. They put a strong emphasis on prayer, praise, and worship. The first 10 days of every month are days of fasting and prayer in the church. On those days they sing and pray from 9:00 A.M. to 3:00 P.M. Every Saturday there is evangelistic outreach in Buddhist neighborhoods, where they have seen new Buddhist converts every week. The local church, which has a weekly attendance of over 1,000, has six mission outstations. It has 50 full-time workers as well as a nine-month Bible school with over 100 full-time students. It is the fastest-growing charismatic church in Myanmar today.

■ **Bibliography:** *The Assemblies of God in Foreign Lands* (1984) ■ L. Bolton, *China Call* (1984) ■ M. Chit, *A Brief History of the Assemblies of God Church in Burma (Myanmar)* (unpub. ms., n.d.) ■ D. Dakhum, *The History of Assemblies of God in Burma* (in Myanmar language; unpub. ms., n.d.) ■ S. Z. Go, *The Brief History of Pentecostal/Charismatic Revival in Zogam* (unpub. ms., n.d.) ■ J. M. Hull, *Judson the Pioneer* (1913) ■ P. Johnstone, *Operation World* (1993) ■ C. K. Khai, *Cross Amidst Pagodas* (1995) ■ G. D. Stafford, *A Brief History of the Assemblies of God of Burma* (paper, Central Bible College, 1977) ■ J. Walker, "The Message Came 50 Years Ago," *Mountain Movers* (1981). Interviews with Mrs. Philip Ahone (assistant pastor, Calvary Foursquare Church, Yangon); Zau Ba (superintendent, Church of God of Myanmar); Ral Buai (general superintendent, UPC of Myanmar); Myo Chit (general superintendent, AG of Myanmar); Dam Suan Mung (pastor, Full Gospel Assembly, Yangon).   ■ C. D. Kham

NAMIBIA

■ Pentecostals 23,749 (10%)   ■ Charismatics 87,174 (38%)   ■ Neocharismatics 119,077 (52%)   ■ Total Renewal: 230,000

See AFRICA, WEST.

NAURU

◼ Pentecostals 0 (0%)   ◼ Charismatics 708 (64%)   ◼ Neocharismatics 392 (36%)   ◼ Total Renewal: 1,100

See PACIFIC ISLANDS.

NEPAL

◼ Pentecostals 4,865 (1%)   ◼ Charismatics 1,318 (0%)   ◼ Neocharismatics 501,817 (99%)   ◼ Total Renewal: 508,000

NETHERLANDS

◼ Pentecostals 52,390 (5%)   ◼ Charismatics 537,922 (52%)   ◼ Neocharismatics 449,688 (43%)   ◼ Total Renewal: 1,040,000

I. THE PENTECOSTAL MOVEMENT IN THE NETHERLANDS.

A. Beginnings (1906–30).

Pentecostalism in the Netherlands began as an ecumenical revival movement. The intention was not to build a new church, but rather to be a blessing to the existing churches. Gradually the movement developed into separate denominations, consisting of loosely organized local assemblies with a more or less congregational structure.

The beginning lies with a small circle of believers in Amsterdam who were searching for more power in their spiritual lives. This group consisted largely of former Salvation Army members and was started in Jan. 1906 by ˈGerrit Polman (1868–1932) and his wife, Wilhelmine (1878–1961). The Polmans had been officers of the Salvation Army and had had contact with ˈJohn Dowie's Christian Catholic Church in Zion, IL. Through the *Apostolic Faith* paper they received news of the Azusa Street revival in Los Angeles (1906). In the course of 1907 the same manifestations penetrated Europe as well, in Norway, Germany, England, and Switzerland. In Oct. 1907 Mrs. Polman was the first of the prayer circle to receive the baptism with the Holy Spirit. Many others soon followed.

In Apr. 1908 Polman started the publication of *Spade Regen (Latter Rain)*; in 1915 followed by *Klanken des Vredes (Sounds of Peace)*. The pentecostal message gradually spread from Amsterdam across the country. In 1912 Emmanuel Hall was erected. Many believers from surrounding countries traveled to Amsterdam to receive the Spirit baptism in this center, which also housed a training school for missionaries.

Under the dynamic and charismatic leadership of the Polmans, the Dutch movement kept close contact with pentecostals from neighboring countries. During and after WWI, Polman played a significant mediating role between the German and British pentecostals, which culminated in the international conference in Amsterdam in 1921, where German and British pentecostals met again for the first time after the war.

In the eyes of Polman, the purpose of the pentecostal movement was not the building of a new church but the building up of the existing churches. Nevertheless, clergy of various churches stigmatized pentecostals as false or even demonic. The ˈBerlin Declaration of 1909, in which 56 leaders of the German *Gemeinschaftsbewegung* condemned pentecostalism as demonic, had prejudiced many in the Netherlands. In the end Polman failed morally, which led to his withdrawal in 1930 and caused many to turn away from the pentecostal movement.

B. Reconstruction (1930–50).

Three new leaders came to the fore: Peter van der Woude (1895–1978), Piet Klaver (1890–1970), and Nico Vetter (1890–1945). Klaver and Vetter had been trained by Polman. Both returned from the mission field, Klaver from China and the Dutch East Indies, Vetter from Venezuela. Van der Woude, on the other hand, never met Polman. After a long stay in England, where he had been converted and had become assistant pastor of the pentecostal assembly of Summer Road Chapel at Peckham, London, he returned to Holland in 1932.

The war years brought the pentecostals closer together. The Vereenigde Pinkstergemeenten in Nederland (United Pentecostal Assemblies in the Netherlands), founded in 1941, changed its name in 1944 to Pinkstergemeenten in Nederland (Pentecostal Assemblies in the Netherlands), and in 1947 it became the Volle Evangelie Gemeenten (Full Gospel Assemblies). A mission fund for the training of evangelists, pastors, and missionaries was founded. Selected candidates were sent to the International Bible Training Institute (IBTI) that had just started at Leamington Spa, England. In 1952 a new start was made with the foundation of the Broederschap van Volle Evangelie Gemeenten (Brotherhood of Full Gospel Assemblies). The *Volle Evangelie Koerier (Full Gospel Courier)* became its official paper.

C. Growth and Fragmentation Since 1950.

The growth of the present pentecostal movement dates from the 1950s. The visits of foreign healing evangelists

(Herman Zaiss from Germany and ‣T. L. Osborn from the U.S.), missionaries from Sweden, repatriates from the Dutch East Indies, and the rise of Stromen van Kracht (Streams of Power), a national revival movement led by Karel Hoekendijk, were very influential. After the 1958 Osborn crusade, developments began to move faster. The ministry of itinerant evangelist Johan Maasbach expanded greatly, and under the inspiring leadership of businessman Peter van den Dries, the Volle Evangelie Zakenlieden (‣Full Gospel Business Men's Fellowship) organized mass meetings called *Vreugdedagen* (Joy Days). Annual conferences at the Beukenstein mansion in Driebergen were held from 1960 to 1968. This same period saw the rise of the periodical *Kracht van Omhoog (Power from on High)*, which had been founded by Klaver in 1937 and now, under J. E. van den Brink, sought to provide a doctrinal foundation for the pentecostal experience. This led to the Kracht van Omhoog movement, an important branch of Dutch pentecostalism.

Part of the pentecostal assemblies, organized as the Broederschap van Pinkstergemeenten (Brotherhood of Pentecostal Assemblies) established a Bible school (now called Azusa Theologische Hogeschool) and affiliated with the Assemblies of God. Other assemblies organized themselves as Volle Evangelie Gemeenschap (Full Gospel Fellowship). The "One Way Day" youth rallies and the annual camp meetings of Stichting Opwekking (Revival Foundation) held around Pentecost (a national holiday in the Netherlands) drew thousands of people. But with growth, fragmentation also increased.

D. Recent Developments.

Since about 1980 several new groups have sprung up, some of which are connected with foreign organizations: De Deur (The Door), connected with the Potter's House Christian Center of Wayman Mitchell in Preston, AZ; Rafael Nederland, connected with the ‣International Church of the Foursquare Gospel; Berea Gemeenschap (formerly Kracht van Omhoog); Vineyard Assemblies, connected with the ‣Vineyard Christian Fellowship; Capitol Worship Center, connected with International Prophetic Ministries of the South African Ashley McGuicken, based in Belgium.

Another phenomenon is the rise of migrant churches. Cities such as Amsterdam and Rotterdam host dozens of African (Zairese, Ghanese), Latin American, and Asian pentecostal assemblies. A growing number of these join the Broederschap van Pinkstergemeenten.

Since 1986 the boards of the Volle Evangelie Gemeenten and the Broederschap van Pinkstergemeenten meet on a regular basis for prayer and consultation. Since 1989 this platform has also included representatives of the Volle Evangelie Bethel Kerk and Kracht van Omhoog, and since 1991 also Rafael Nederland. In 1994 the platform was incorporated. Membership is open to national operating denominations.

Recently the Bethel Pentecostal Temple Fellowship Nederland and Berea were added to the platform.

In 1994 the platform joined some of the smaller Reformed churches, Baptists, and the Evangelical Alliance in a successful effort to establish television rights. For this purpose the Stichting Zendtijd voor de Kerken was founded.

Initially, outsiders considered pentecostalism to be sectarian and of a temporary nature. Today pentecostals are increasingly recognized as legitimate. Their growth has attracted the interest of academic researchers. Recent sociological research has shown that pentecostals in the Netherlands are above average in income and education. The pentecostal faith is no longer limited to one class of the population but is found in all layers of society.

In 1998 there were 85,000 pentecostal believers in the Netherlands in more than 600 assemblies. The majority of Dutch pentecostal assemblies are independent and do not fall under any of the above-mentioned fellowships. The principle of the autonomy of the local church makes many averse to any kind of national organization. This fragmentation entails a great variety in doctrine, spirituality, structure, and liturgy.

II. THE CHARISMATIC MOVEMENT IN THE NETHERLANDS.

A. Charismatische Werkgemeenschap Nederland.

Initially there was very little contact between the pentecostal movement and the historic churches. This changed in the 1950s, when the historic churches showed a growing interest in the message of divine healing. Visits from Elaine Richards, Hermann Zaiss, and T. L. Osborn stirred many. Karel Hoekendijk (Stromen van Kracht) drew a great number of church people to his meetings, where many received the Spirit baptism. However, when Hoekendijk started to baptize church members by immersion, the Reformed churches turned against him. For this reason Wim Verhoef, vicar in the Reformed *(hervormde)* church, left Stromen van Kracht and started the publication *Vuur (Fire)* in 1957. Verhoef wanted to integrate the pentecostal message into the historic churches without challenging the practice of infant baptism. Under Verhoef's editorship, *Vuur* developed into a broadly charismatic and ecumenical periodical. Bible study weekends were started, followed by the publication of books and brochures. In the meantime other ministries with a more or less charismatic emphasis emerged, such as the Order of St. Luke, the Oase healing ministry of K. J. Kraan and W. C. van Dam, and the Near East Mission. In 1972 most groups joined forces in the Charismatische Werkgemeenschap Nederland (CWN; Charismatic Work Fellowship the Netherlands). *Vuur* became the organ of CWN. The bi-annual, five-day national conventions average 1,000 participants, the large majority of which come from the Reformed churches.

In 1978 CWN started publication of *Bulletin voor Charismatische Theologie,* a scholarly quarterly for theological reflection, edited by Martin Parmentier and Wim Verhoef. Since 1992 M. F. G. Parmentier (Old Catholic Church) occupies the chair for the theology of the charismatic renewal established at the Free University of Amsterdam by CWN, together with Bouwen aan een Nieuwe Aarde (see below).

B. Bouwen aan een Nieuwe Aarde.

The Catholic charismatic renewal (CCR) in the Netherlands had a modest beginning in the early 1960s, when individual Roman Catholics experienced the Spirit baptism through contacts with the renewal in other churches. Several small prayer groups started. In 1964 J. H. Horsthuis became the first Catholic on the editorial board of *Vuur*. In the 1970s the CCR began to grow rapidly. Fr. André Beijersbergen became the evangelist of the renewal. The periodical *Bouwen aan de nieuwe aarde (Helping build the new earth),* which he already edited, became the organ of the new movement. Beijersbergen received help from Ed and Karin Arons, who had been in touch with the renewal in New Zealand. In Jan. 1974 the CWN organized a meeting in Breda for Roman Catholics and Old Catholics from the Netherlands and Flanders. By the end of 1974 there were 40 charismatic prayer groups; today this number has grown to 160. A service center for the CCR that also functioned as a community was established in Eindhoven in 1974. In 1976 the CCR became organized in the foundation Bouwen aan de Nieuwe Aarde. More communities were established, and in the 1980s the CCR became more and more accepted and integrated into the official church structures. In 1988 the "Episcopal Declaration on the Roman Catholic Charismatic Renewal in the Netherlands" was issued. The service center moved from Eindhoven to Helmond in 1992. The bi-monthly *Bouwen aan de nieuwe aarde* is the official organ of the CCR in the Netherlands and is published in cooperation with the CCR in Flanders.

See also BELGIUM.

■ **Bibliography:** D. D. Bundy, "Charismatic Renewal in Belgium: A Bibliographical Essay," *EPTA Bulletin* 5 (3, 1986) ▌ I. Demaerel, "Tachtig jaar pinksterbeweging in Vlaanderen (1909–1989)" (thesis, Universitaire Faculteit voor Protestantse Godgeleerdheid, Brussels, 1990) ▌ R. van Kooij, *Spelen met vuur* (1995) ▌ C. van der Laan, *Sectarian against His Will* (1991) ▌ idem, "Discerning the Body," in *Pentecost, Mission and Ecumenism,* ed. J. A. B. Jongeneel (1992) ▌ C. van der Laan and P. N. van der Laan, *Pinksteren in beweging* (1982) ▌ P. N. van der Laan, "In Search of the Pentecostal Challenge," in *Experiences of the Spirit,* ed. J. A. B. Jongeneel (1991) ▌ idem, "The Question of Spiritual Unity" (diss., U. of Birmingham, 1988) ▌ J. L. Sandidge, "The Origin and Development of the Catholic Charismatic Movement in Belgium" (thesis, Katholieke Universiteit, Leuven, 1976) ▌ K. Slijkerman, ed., *25 jaar Katholieke Charismatische Vernieuwing* (1992) ▌ W. Smet, *Ik maak alles nieuw: Charismatische vernieuwing in de kerk* (2d ed., 1974) ▌ L. J. Suenens, *Een nieuw Pinksteren?* (1974) ▌ idem, *Oecumene en charismatische vernieuwing* (1979) ▌ H. H. Zegwaart, "Pinksterkerken in Nederland: een culturele lappendeken" (paper, Nederlandse Zendingsraad, 1998).

■ C. van der Laan

NETHERLANDS ANTILLES

■ Pentecostals 3,229 (32%)   ■ Charismatics 5,172 (51%)   ■ Neocharismatics 1,798 (18%)   ■ Total Renewal: 10,199

See CARIBBEAN ISLANDS.

NEW CALEDONIA (Kanaky)

■ Pentecostals 3,936 (33%)   ■ Charismatics 4,618 (39%)   ■ Neocharismatics 3,246 (28%)   ■ Total Renewal: 11,800

For general introduction and bibliography, see PACIFIC ISLANDS.

Known as La Grande Terre, the Caledonian mainland is about 250 mi (400 km) long and 30 mi (50 km) wide. With an area of about 6,500 mi² (16,750 km²), it is the largest island in the South Pacific after New Zealand. Some smaller islands contribute to the total land area of 7,375 mi² (19,103 km²).

The capital, Noumea, has about 88,000 inhabitants (1995) and is situated at the southwest tip of the main island. The total population is about 178,000 people (1995). Of the population, 37% are European (settlers), 45% are Melanesians, and the rest are from other, mainly French-speaking, Pacific Islands (13%), or Asians (5%).

The indigenous people of New Caledonia are Melanesians. The more than 30 Kanak dialects spoken reflect different ethnic origins, but the official language is French. Since its annexation in 1853, New Caledonia is a French colony (French overseas territory). In a 1998 referendum on independence the majority of the population voted for independence from France. The terms for independence are presently (1998) being discussed and finalized between France and Kanak representatives of the independence movement. The country has immense mineral resources. Apart from nickel and chrome, there are large deposits of iron, manganese, and cobalt.

The religious landscape is very similar to that of other Pacific islands. There are two historic mainline church groups, Roman Catholics (62%) and Protestants (23.6%). The Protestants are divided into two main denominations, the Evangelical Church of New Caledonia and a breakaway group known as the Free Evangelical Church. Over the last decades, newer religious groups, such as the Mormons, Seventh-day Adventists, and the Assemblies of God (AG), experienced fast growth, mainly at the expense of the established churches. There is also a substantial Muslim community (3.5%). In the last census, 7.8% of the population, mainly French, declared itself to be "non-religious."

The main Pentecostal denomination is the AG. The AG–France did some work before and during WWII, but with little impact. The present AG church came into being when an American couple, Ronald and Joy Killingbeck, went to New Caledonia in 1967 as approved AG ministers working overseas. Other expatriate missionaries followed. While the beginnings were slow, the AG experienced steady and fast growth since the first nationals of the country began to pastor their own churches. The nationalization started in 1972 when a Caledonian man, Loulou Manwo, a graduate of the South Pacific Bible College in Fiji, returned to New Caledonia. By the end of 1997 there were 25 AG churches and 30 preaching points, mainly in the urban areas. The 3,500 adherents were served by 18 ministers and 2 expatriate missionaries, and 35 students were enrolled in the national Bible school.   ■ M. Ernst

NEW ZEALAND

■ Pentecostals 37,262 (6%)   ■ Charismatics 419,689 (71%)   ■ Neocharismatics 133,049 (23%)   ■ Total Renewal: 590,000

1. The Pentecostal Movement.

a. Prehistory. Although classical pentecostalism did not arrive in New Zealand (N.Z.) until the 1920s, sporadic outbreaks of revivalism prepared the way for its appearance. These were a feature of religious life in this country in the late 19th century, especially among rural communities influenced by the Brethren movement (Jackson, 48–76). Visiting revivalists from overseas also sought to "spread the fire" in the towns. The most significant of these evangelists were two young Salvation Army officers who arrived in 1883 and had gained more than 3,000 converts by the end of their first year in N.Z. Revivalism also provided a background for the visit of ▸John Alexander Dowie in 1888. Dowie's emphasis on divine healing reinforced a prior interest in nontraditional forms of healing. This generalized belief had some of the characteristics of a "folk-religion" and provided the foundation on which the healing campaigns of ▸Smith Wigglesworth and others were later able to build.

b. Early Pentecostalism. The campaigns of Smith Wigglesworth in 1922 and 1923–24 were the first large-scale pentecostal meetings in this country and marked the emergence of the pentecostal movement in N.Z. (Ireton, 1984; Roberts; Worsfold). These campaigns formed part of a wider, multiform movement characterized by healing and revivalism. Their success reflected the renewed public interest in various forms of healing resulting in part from the massive mortality of WWI and of the 1918 influenza epidemic (Ireton, 1986). Wigglesworth was only one of a number of healers who ministered in N.Z. during the 1920s. Nevertheless, his campaigns were significant in that they led to the establishment of pentecostalism there.

The Pentecostal Church of New Zealand (PCNZ) was formed in Dec. 1924—partly through the influence of ▸A.

C. Valdez Sr. who was then also ministering in N.Z.—to consolidate the results of Wigglesworth's campaigns. However, controversy and schism characterized the early history of this group of churches. In particular, there was much disagreement over the movement's governmental structure, and this led to several secessions in 1926. A number of the seceding congregations affiliated with the Assemblies of God (AG) early the following year, and this provided the new movement with a ready-made constituency upon which to build. Despite early success, the AG was also to suffer the effects of schism, and a further realignment took place when the Apostolic Church (AC) arrived in N.Z. six years later. The emphasis of the AC on an organized and ordained hierarchy of leadership provided a stability that appealed to disaffected members of other pentecostal groups, many of whom transferred their membership to the AC. Nevertheless, there still remained a number of independent pentecostal groups (such as the "Revival Fire" churches associated with ▸A. H. Dallimore) that did not form links with the three main pentecostal churches. Other pentecostal groups continued to emerge in the late 1930s and 1940s, such as an independent group with an emphasis on Bible prophecy, which began in Wellington in 1939. Its emphasis on Britain's destiny as the successor to the lost 10 tribes of Israel (▸British Israelitism) secured it a hearing in the years immediately preceding WWII. This group linked up with ▸Leo Harris's Australian-based Christian Revival Crusade (CRC) in 1941, and adopted the latter group's name.

The PCNZ suffered a final blow in early 1946 when controversy arose as the result of the teaching of "baptism in 'the Name'" (▸Oneness Pentecostalism). This doctrine was introduced by three U.S. pastors from W. H. Offiler's Bethel Temple in Seattle, WA, who had arrived the previous year to work with the PCNZ. A substantial schism occurred, and many members of the movement's congregations left with the three Americans to form a new independent group. The PCNZ disbanded in 1952. Its remnants formed links with the Elim Church of Great Britain and reconstituted themselves as the Elim Church of New Zealand (ECNZ). The breakaway wing of the movement, led by ▸Ray Jackson, became associated with the ▸Latter Rain movement of North Battleford, Canada, in 1948. This provided it with its characteristic blend of Bethel Temple Bible teaching, based on the imaginative use of allegory and typology, and its church polity, which reflected the radical independence of the Latter Rain movement. This group in later years adopted a variety of titles, of which Indigenous Churches of New Zealand was used most frequently. Since 1988, its official name has been New Life Churches of New Zealand (Knowles, 1988, 1994).

Thus, by the mid 1950s, there were four pentecostal denominations in N.Z.: the ECNZ, the AG, the AC, and the CRC. There were also a number of smaller groups, not all of which identified themselves by a collective name. These included the Revival Fire churches, the forerunners of the New Life Churches, the highly sectarian Church of Christ N.Z. in Mount Roskill, Auckland, and numbers of independent pentecostal assemblies. All these groups and denominations were small, restricted in outlook, and sectarian in mentality. There were only 54 pentecostal churches in N.Z. in 1960, with about 10,000 adherents (Nichol, 179), and only the Auckland Queen Street Assembly of God, the "flagship" of the movement, had a membership of more than 100. The small size of the movement reflected its sectarian status, although this was to change markedly beginning in the late 1950s.

c. Pentecostal Expansion in the 1960s and Beyond. The postwar period was marked by evangelism and expansion for the mainstream churches in N.Z. The building of new churches and the expansion of older ones reflected the increasing suburbanization of the country. Baptist and Presbyterian churches were prominent in this evangelism, which culminated in the six-day Billy Graham Crusade in 1959, which resulted in 17,493 conversions. However, smaller groups such as the pentecostal churches did not immediately share in this expansion. This was due in part to their restricted outlook but also to opposition from other churches.

By 1957 this pentecostal isolationism was beginning to change. The earliest, although isolated, instance of this was the revivalist meetings of AG evangelists ▸Ray Bloomfield and ▸Frank Houston among rural Maori at Waiomio, near Kawa Kawa in Northland (Houston, 1989). The visit of U.S. evangelist ▸Tommy Hicks to N.Z. in late 1957 provided the inspiration for a new surge of healing-evangelism ministry in this country. Independent evangelist ▸Rob Wheeler was among the early pioneers of this form of pentecostal evangelism, which was consciously modeled on the U.S. tent cru-

sades of ▸Oral Roberts and used large tents as mobile churches. Other evangelists who were similarly inspired were Norman and Gilbert White of the AC and independent pentecostal campaigners Ian Hunt, Graeme Jacks, and Mike Bensley.

Early successes included the remote East Coast area of the North Island among rural Maori. By 1960, however, Wheeler and other evangelists were also having some successes in towns. The most significant of these was the five-week healing campaign conducted in Timaru, on the South Island, by U.S. pentecostal evangelist A. S. Worley (Grice; Henderson). This campaign resulted in over 600 conversions and the establishing of an independent pentecostal church that became the launch pad for further expansion on the South Island. Worley was joined in the latter part of this campaign by Paul Collins, ▸Ron Coady, and ▸Peter Morrow, and these men (and others) continued the momentum of what Worley had begun. Ron Coady was particularly successful, and his aggressive style of evangelism helped shape the new movement of independent Latter Rain type churches, which eventually became the New Life Churches of N.Z. Rob Wheeler claimed that at the height of this expansion he and Coady were, between the two of them, opening one new church every two weeks. By 1965 this new movement numbered some 60 churches, most of which had been formed within the previous five years (Knowles, 1988). A distinguishing feature of this movement, traceable to its Latter Rain antecedents, was an emphasis on "singing in the Spirit." This represented the reviving of a practice that, although prominent in early pentecostalism, had fallen into disuse. Rob Wheeler and others passed this on to David and Dale Garrett, whose "Scripture in Song" renditions of Scripture had a worldwide influence on the worship of the charismatic movement (Riss, 144).

Other pentecostal churches were also beginning to expand in 1960s, in particular the AG under the superintendency of Frank Houston (Houston, 1989). This expansion was in part due to the influence of the 1959 Billy Graham Crusade, which had created a constituency for evangelicalism, and thus also for campaigns such as those conducted by pentecostal healing evangelists. Of more significance, however, was the emphasis on healing, which tapped into the generalized interest in nontraditional forms of healing in the country. A further factor, and one that was more applicable to the later 1960s, was the "internalization of authority" produced by the youth movement. This rejected external, institutional forms of authority and stressed personal experience and the search for spiritual "values." These social factors found religious parallels in the pentecostal movement and thus enhanced its appeal (Knowles, 1992).

By 1972 the pentecostal movement was becoming a significant force in N.Z. Christianity. This process was reinforced by the 1972 ▸March for Jesus, organized as moralist protests at declining standards of public morality and the rise of the permissive society. The Jesus Marches were modeled on the 1971 British Festival of Light and shared the overall theme "Righteousness Exalts a Nation." They were also a spontaneous celebration of Jesus and fostered an informal conservative Christian ecumenism that furthered the development of the pentecostal and charismatic movements in the 1970s (Shaw). The influence of the charismatic movement strengthened this new ecumenism and helped to reinforce the erosion of sectarian attitudes in the pentecostal churches.

The visits of ►Ern Baxter in 1974 and ►Jack Hayford in 1975 were also significant catalysts for change. Hayford was keynote speaker at the 1975 Pastors' Conference in Snell's Beach, Auckland, which resulted in the creation of the Associated Pentecostal Churches of N.Z. (APCNZ). The twin themes of this conference were the reconciliation of differences among the pentecostal churches and the necessity of working together to express a common concern at social changes, such as sex education in schools. The first act of the APCNZ was to send two delegations to Wallace Rowling, the prime minister, and to Robert Muldoon, the leader of the opposition, expressing concern over social and moral issues. In part, moralist concern and a growing sense of political "clout" provided the motivation for the formation of the APCNZ. This reflected the changing sociological realities of the pentecostal movement, which had become much larger and more "upwardly mobile" than it had been before.

Over the 10-year period following the formation of the APCNZ, pentecostal churches provided much of the support for moralist activism in N.Z. Examples include the introduction of private Christian schools and the 1977 "Save Our Homes" campaign, organized by Anne Morrow in response to what was seen as destructive radical feminism. The most significant action was the marshalling of opposition to the 1985 Homosexual Law Reform Bill, introduced to legalize homosexuality. Petitions against the bill gathered more than 815,000 signatures—nearly a quarter of N.Z.'s population of just over 3 million. The rejection of this petition by Parliament and the passing of the bill represented a defeat of almost apocalyptic proportions for the moralist movement, which never recovered its former vigor. As a result, pentecostal activism was redirected into the political field. A number of pentecostals, including Pastor Rob Wheeler, unsuccessfully stood for Parliament in the 1987 elections (Rudman; Stratford), and the pentecostal churches provided strong support for the two Christian political parties set up in the 1990s.

d. Pentecostalism Today. The pentecostal movement has continued to grow. By 1984 pentecostal weekly adult attendance stood at more than 40,000, and the pentecostal worshiping community was already larger than the Baptist and Methodist churches and almost as large as the Presbyterian

Church. This represented a shift in the religious center of gravity over the previous 15 years, and pentecostalist and fundamentalist traditions were becoming the mainstream of N.Z. Christianity (Galvin, 99). This expansion appears to have continued, although not with the same rapidity, in the later 1980s, and estimated pentecostal adherence had reached almost 54,000 by 1990 (DAWN Strategy, 12). This figure, if accurate, would make the pentecostal churches the largest Protestant grouping in the country in terms of attendance.

This growth reflects both the adoption of a "church-planting" approach—particularly by the AG—and the growing diversity of the movement. A number of new pentecostal groups emerged in the 1980s and '90s to join the "big five" (Elim, New Life, AC, AG, and CRC). These new groups included the ►Rhema and ►Vineyard churches, the Christian Life Centre, ►Christian Outreach Centre, ►Christian City Churches, the Associated Fellowships, the South Pacific churches, and a number of other independent groups. An indication of the relative size of these churches is provided by the listings in the APCNZ *1997 Directory*. These show that, out of a total of 906 pentecostal pastors in N.Z., 34% are AG, 22% New Life, 15% AC, 10% Elim, while less than 2% belong to each of the other pentecostal groups. Since many larger churches are served by a multipastor staff, the total number of pentecostal churches in N.Z. would appear to be about 500 to 600.

In summary, the pentecostal movement in N.Z. has grown from humble and somewhat divisive beginnings in the 1920s to become a major force in N.Z. Christianity. The beginnings of the movement's expansion came in the 1960s, and since then the movement has grown exponentially and become more middle class and mainstream. It has contributed to, and benefited from, the emergence of the charismatic movement and has had a significant influence upon the moralist movement of the 1970s and 1980s. The pentecostal movement is now linked with the historic churches in a Decade of Evangelism and continues to be influential in the life of the N.Z. church.

2. The Charismatic Movement.

a. The Period of the Pioneers (before 1971). Although the charismatic movement did not emerge in N.Z. until 1965, its foundations had been laid earlier by Campbell McAlpine and ►Arthur Wallis. McAlpine had arrived in N.Z. in 1959 and was widely accepted as a preacher and conference speaker in Baptist and Brethren circles and in interdenominational groups such as Youth for Christ. He had received the baptism of the Spirit in South Africa in the late 1950s, however, and his acceptability in the Brethren assemblies began to wane when this became known. Nevertheless, he remained influential in preparing the way for the charismatic movement (Lineham).

Wallis built upon the foundation that McAlpine had laid. He also had great acceptability in Brethren and wider evangelical circles, and he was able to create an informal network of early participants in the charismatic movement. His most significant contribution, however, was his organizing of a conference at Massey University, Palmerston North, in Aug. 1964, which brought together participants in the charismatic and pentecostal movements for testimony and teaching. The Massey conference set the pattern for further annual transdenominational conferences that did much to spread the influence of the charismatic movement over the next decade. It helped to forge links between the early participants in the charismatic movement as well as between them and the classical pentecostal groups.

These personal, rather than organizational, links reflected the considerable influence that some pentecostals had on the early charismatic movement. Examples of this personal influence include AG pastors Frank Houston and Trevor Chandler in Lower Hutt, the campaigns of pentecostal evangelists throughout the country, and the ministry of Peter Morrow in Christchurch. The interchurch conferences organized by Des Short at Faith Bible College in Tauranga were also important, as was the involvement of AC pastors in their local ministers' fraternals (ministerial associations). There were also overseas influences, such as the activities of the ►Full Gospel Business Men's Fellowship International and ►Women's Aglow and the seminal effect of publications such as ►David Wilkerson's *The Cross and the Switchblade*. The charismatic movement in N.Z. therefore had no one source and no single manifestation. The visits of overseas speakers ►David du Plessis and ►Dennis Bennett in 1966 and ►Michael Harper in 1967 reinforced, rather than created, its expansion.

When the charismatic renewal (CR) emerged, it did so in different places and in different ways. In Palmerston North, the Awapuni Baptist Church seceded from the Baptist Union in 1965, becoming an independent charismatic assembly and creating a focal point for charismatics in the city. Several months later the Anglican chaplain at Massey University, Fr. Ray Muller, was influential in bringing a considerable number of university students into the baptism of the Spirit (Brown, 105; Neil, 88). This is generally regarded as the beginning of the CR in the Anglican Church in N.Z. Other early centers of the renewal in the Anglican Church included St. Paul's Anglican Church in Auckland (Merritt, 1981) and a number of Anglican parishes in Christchurch.

Pentecostal influence was more direct in Christchurch than elsewhere, and Peter Morrow and several other pentecostal pastors played significant roles in the beginning of the CR there. Morrow's church had opened a coffee bar named Adullam's Cave to reach young people off the streets. This coffee bar was also used for teaching meetings, where many denominational people came to receive teaching on the baptism of the Spirit and took it back to their churches over the next three years. Adullam's Cave became the early center of the charismatic renewal in Christchurch, and its success owed much to the open attitude shown by Morrow and his colleagues to the denominational churches.

In its initial stages the CR appears to have been largely limited to Protestants. After 1968 it began to emerge in the Catholic Church also, largely due to Morrow's influence on three Redemptorist priests who became leaders in the Catholic CR after 1970 (Knowles, 1994, 120; Loryman; Reidy and Richardson). The emergence of the CR in the denominational churches was not without its problems. The opposition faced by early participants in the renewal resulted in a migration, stimulated by the Bible teaching ethos of pentecostalism, into the pentecostal movement. Some charismatic groups found themselves in something of an uncomfortable limbo between the pentecostal and denominational churches.

b. The Time of Ingathering (1971–79). After 1971 the CR gathered momentum and began to move away from a dependence on its pentecostal mentors to establish an independent identity (Neil, 131). Several factors contributed to this distancing process. The introduction of programs such as the ►Life in the Spirit Seminars provided the nascent movement with tools that the pentecostals had never developed. A more important factor was the launching of Christian Advance Ministries in 1972. This parachurch organization—and particularly its 1973 Summer School, which became the model for further annual transdenominational conferences—created a new sense of charismatic identity. These summer schools contributed toward a shift from a predominantly pentecostal hermeneutic to a more theologically nuanced interpretation of charismatic experience. This new sense of identity was paralleled by the expansion of the renewal throughout the 1970s. It was common for combined charismatic gatherings to attract four-figure attendances, while a range of interdenominational renewal agencies sprang up and a "renewal jet-set" of very capable teachers emerged. As Battley observes, the 1970s were "heady and exhausting days" (Battley, 49).

Denominational participation in, and responses to, the charismatic movement varied. The Anglican Church set up a representative commission, which investigated the movement and came out with a broadly sympathetic report. Christchurch and Auckland were the main centers for Anglican renewal, with at least 40% of the clergy in Auckland and 30% in Christchurch open to the experience in 1974 (Brown, 105).

The charismatic movement in the Catholic Church was also centered in Auckland and Christchurch, but with groups in Wellington, Dunedin, Invercargill, Hamilton, and elsewhere. In contrast to its Anglican counterpart, the Catholic renewal was led by laypeople rather than by clergy, and women were more prominent in leadership.

In the Presbyterian Church the renewal was centered on Christchurch and especially Leeston in its early stages but later became more widespread. While few parishes became dominantly charismatic, about 20% of Presbyterian churches had been affected to some degree by the early 1980s. By the mid 1980s a majority of Presbyterian ordinands at Knox Theological Hall had some charismatic associations.

The Methodist Church—the most liberal of the mainstream N.Z. churches—was the one least affected by the charismatic movement. There was, however, significant and widespread growth in Christchurch and in Hawkes Bay, Northland, and other areas.

Other smaller denominations found that their experience of the charismatic renewal was often accompanied by disruption, particularly in the Brethren movement and the Baptist Union. Nevertheless, it is estimated that a quarter of the ministers in the Baptist Union had been baptized in the Spirit by 1975 (Brown, 105–8).

c. Consolidation (after 1980). The charismatic movement peaked at the end of the 1970s and entered a consolidation phase in the 1980s. Factors that led to this change of focus include the hardening of institutional attitudes toward the renewal, theological tensions, pastoral damage, the counterproductive effect of media attention, and above all, increasing "burn-out" among committed charismatics. This led to the development of a "siege mentality" among those charismatics who remained in denominational churches, with the result that pentecostal and evangelical groups reaped a harvest of migrating charismatic church members (Battley, 49). These factors were reinforced by the creation of denominational agencies for renewal, such as Anglican Renewal Ministries, Catholic Charismatic Renewal Services, the Methodist Aldersgate Fellowship, and the Presbyterian Paraclete Trust. The formation of these "in-house" agencies reflected a "narrowing of horizons" and paralleled the denominational churches' rejection of the ecumenical unity proposed in the National Council of Churches' *1971 Plan for Union.* This compartmentalization nullified one of the major driving forces of the charismatic movement, namely, the informal ecumenism across denominational boundaries that had characterized the earlier days of the movement.

A recent study of the Australian charismatic movement has suggested that the increasing secularization of society has meant that there were fewer people in the churches to be affected by the renewal. Consequently, the movement quickly reached its "market saturation point," with the resultant "drying up" of sources of new members (Hutchinson). This analysis may also be applicable in the N.Z. context. The continuing vitality of pentecostal churches in both Australia and N.Z., however, is an indication that not too much weight should

be placed on the secularization process as a factor. It is more likely that a transfer of constituency has taken place and that the pentecostal churches have been the ultimate beneficiaries of the charismatic movement. For their part, the denominational churches appear to have entered a "postcharismatic" phase in which the renewal has become somewhat domesticated. While parachurch groups such as Full Gospel Business Men's Fellowship International and Women's Aglow continue to attract support, their focus is now more on the maintenance, rather than the expansion, of the renewal. Nevertheless, the charismatic movement has contributed much to the life of the N.Z. churches.

■ **Bibliography:** Associated Pentecostal Churches of N.Z., *1997 Directory* ▪ D. Battley, *"Charismatic Renewal: A View from Inside,"* Ecumenical Review *38 (Jan. 1986)* ▪ C. Brown, "How Significant Is the Charismatic Movement?" in *Religion in New Zealand Society,* ed. B. Colless and P. Donovan (2d ed., 1985) ▪ DAWN Strategy New Zealand, *1990 Church Survey Report* ▪ R. Galvin, "Learning from the Sects," in *Towards an Authentic New Zealand Theology,* ed. J. M. Ker and K. J. Sharpe (1984) ▪ R. E. Grice, *Apostle to the Nations: An Authorized Biography of A. S. Worley, a Man of Faith and Miracles* (1990) ▪ M. Henderson, *From Glory to Glory: A History of the Timaru New Life Centre 1960–1980* (1980) ▪ H. Houston, *Being Frank: The Frank Houston Story* (1989) ▪ M. Hutchinson, "Is Anglican Renewal Dead?" *Cyberjournal for Pentecostal-Charismatic Research,* 2 (1997) ▪ D. Ireton, "'O Lord, How Long?': A Revival Movement in New Zealand 1920–1933" (thesis, Massey U., 1986) ▪ idem, "A Time to Heal: The Appeal of Smith Wigglesworth in New Zealand 1922–24" (thesis, Massey U., 1984) ▪ H. R. Jackson, *Churches and People in Australia and New Zealand 1860–1930* (1987) ▪ B. Knowles, *The History of a New Zealand Pentecostal Movement: The New Life Churches of New Zealand from 1946 to 1979* (1999; N.Z. ed.: *New Life: A History of the New Life Churches of New Zealand 1942–1979* [1999]) ▪ idem, "For the Sake of the Name: A History of the 'New Life Churches' from 1942 to 1965" (thesis, U. of Otago, 1988) ▪ idem, "Some Aspects of the History of the New Life Churches of New Zealand, 1960–1990" (diss., U. of Otago, 1994) ▪ idem, "Vision of the Disinherited? The Growth of the Pentecostal Movement in the 1960s, with Particular Reference to the New Life Churches of New Zealand," in *"Be Ye Separate": Fundamentalism and the New Zealand Experience,* ed. B. Gilling (1992) ▪ P. J. Lineham, "Tongues Must Cease: The Brethren and the Charismatic Movement in New Zealand," *Christian Brethren Review Journal* 34 (Nov. 1983) ▪ G. Loryman, "Growth of the Pentecostal Movement: A New Relationship with Christ," *Christchurch Star* (Oct. 27, 1973) ▪ N. F. H. Merritt, *To God Be the Glory: The First 10-1/2 Years of the Charismatic Renewal in St. Pauls* (1981) ▪ A. G. Neil, "Institutional Churches and the Charismatic Renewal: A Study of the Charismatic Renewal in the Anglican Church and the Roman Catholic Church in New Zealand" (thesis, Joint Board of Theol. Studies, 1974) ▪ J. T. Nichol, *The Pentecostals* (rev. ed. of *Pentecostalism,* 1971) ▪ M. T. V. Reidy and J. T. Richardson, "Roman Catholic Neo-

Pentecostalism: The New Zealand Experience," *Australia and New Zealand Journal of Sociology* 14 (1978) ■ R. M. Riss, *Latter Rain: The Latter Rain Movement of 1948 and the Mid-Twentieth-Century Evangelical Awakening* (1987) ■ H. V. Roberts, *New Zealand's Greatest Revival under Smith Wigglesworth* (1951) ■ B. Rudman, "For God and National," *New Zealand Listener* (Mar. 28, 1987) ■ T. R. Shaw, comp., *The Jesus Marchers 1972* (1972) ■ S. Stratford, "Christians, Awake! Join the National Party, Save New Zealand," *Metro* (Nov. 1986) ■ J. E. Worsfold, *A History of the Charismatic Movements in New Zealand* (1974).   ■ B. Knowles

NICARAGUA

■ Pentecostals 366,439 (51%) ■ Charismatics 253,949 (35%) ■ Neocharismatics 99,612 (14%) ■ Total Renewal: 720,000

See LATIN AMERICA.

NIGER

■ Pentecostals 526 (2%) ■ Charismatics 2,087 (8%) ■ Neocharismatics 24,387 (90%) ■ Total Renewal: 27,000

See AFRICA, WEST.

NIGERIA

■ Pentecostals 3,034,330 (8%) ■ Charismatics 9,793,479 (27%) ■ Neocharismatics 23,057,191 (64%) ■ Total Renewal: 35,885,000

See AFRICA, WEST.

NIUE ISLAND

■ Pentecostals 0 ■ Charismatics 0 ■ Neocharismatics 0 ■ Total Renewal: 0

NORFOLK ISLAND

■ Pentecostals 0 ■ Charismatics 0 ■ Neocharismatics 0 ■ Total Renewal: 0

NORTH KOREA

■ Pentecostals 0 (0%) ■ Charismatics 715 (0%) ■ Neocharismatics 449,285 (100%) ■ Total Renewal: 450,000

See SOUTH KOREA.

NORTHERN CYPRUS

■ Pentecostals 0 (0%) ■ Charismatics 0 (0%) ■ Neocharismatics 2,180 (100%) ■ Total Renewal: 2,180

NORTHERN MARIANA ISLANDS

■ Pentecostals 983 (12%) ■ Charismatics 6,232 (75%) ■ Neocharismatics 1,085 (13%) ■ Total Renewal: 8,300

NORWAY

■ Pentecostals 70,742 (6%)   ■ Charismatics 1,031,297 (83%)   ■ Neocharismatics 146,961 (12%)   ■ Total Renewal: 1,249,000

The Scandinavian pentecostal movement began with the charismatic experience of ▸Thomas Ball Barratt, a Norwegian Methodist minister of British descent. While on a fundraising tour in the U.S., he received the baptism of the Holy Spirit in New York on Nov. 15, 1906. At the time he spoke and sang in foreign languages for four hours.

Barratt was an editor of the Christian magazine *Byposten,* and he informed the readers about this event. When he returned to Norway soon afterwards, a number of people wanted to hear his personal testimony about the pentecostal movement and the manifestations of the Spirit. The first meeting was held in Oslo on Dec. 23, 1906, and by Dec. 29 some 10 persons had received the baptism of the Holy Spirit.

In early 1907 a pentecostal revival exploded in Oslo. "The meetings had such an enormous attendance that the police had to regulate the queue outside the premises." Word of the revival spread across the continent, and visitors from all over Europe came to witness the Norwegian Pentecost. One such visitor, ▸Alexander Boddy, an Anglican vicar who had witnessed the Welsh revival, exclaimed, "I stood with Evan Roberts in Tonypandy, but have never witnessed such scenes as those in Norway." The revival took on an interdenominational character as Christians from various churches participated in the meetings. A great number of people were baptized with the Holy Spirit. Significantly, a number of pastors joined the fledgling pentecostal movement.

Initially the pentecostal movement was not organized as a church or a denomination but expanded as a spontaneous spiritual awakening. The pentecostal message was spread far and wide by Spirit-inspired pentecostal pastors and evangelists. In 1908 a Baptist pastor, C. M. Seehuus, founded the first local pentecostal church in Skien. In the same year, churches were also established in Notodden and Lårdal. All three churches were located in the county of Telemark.

Today nearly 300 independent local churches form a pentecostal fellowship with a total membership of 32,000 baptized believers (45,000 including adherents, such as children of baptized believers). The fellowship is called Pinsebevegelsen (Pentecostal Revival, PR). The number of pentecostal workers is estimated at 300.

Pentecostal missionary efforts started in 1910 when Dagmar Gregersen (Engstrøm) and Agnes Telle (Beckdal) were sent to India. That same year, Parley Gulbrandsen ventured to China, and Anna Østreng started work in South Africa. A missions board was launched in 1915 (Norwegian Evangelical Mission among Heathen). Later, when increasing emphasis was placed on the autonomy of the local church, the missions agency was dissolved (1931). The local churches then assumed responsibility for the 35 missionaries working overseas at that time. Since then missionary efforts have expanded considerably, and at present there are about 300 missionaries serving in more than 30 countries.

Although a number of the pastors who joined the early pentecostal movement had a formal theological education, no extensive Bible training was provided during the early decades. The local churches were seen as the main training centers. Each fall an intensive training course, lasting four or five weeks, was arranged in the larger churches—most often in the Filadelfia Church of Oslo. More recently, the pentecostal Christians have started a Bible school and two folk high schools (the equivalent of high school plus approximately two years of college in the U.S.). A conference and training center has been established at Hedmarktoppen in Hamar, where the largest annual conferences are held.

In addition to schools, the Norwegian pentecostals are engaged in worldwide radio and TV broadcasting (IBRA and TV Inter). The social concern of pentecostal Christians is reflected in the medical and social work among the elderly. Furthermore, a rehabilitation center (Evangeliesenter) has been established for alcoholics and drug abusers. The Samspar Bank operates in affiliation with the Swedish pentecostal movement. A gospel ship, mainly sponsored by the Filadelfia Church of Oslo, sails in the coastal waters of Norway.

See also BIBLIOGRAPHY AND HISTORIOGRAPHY OUTSIDE NORTH AMERICA; SCANDINAVIAN MISSIONS TO LATIN AMERICA.

■ **Bibliography:** T. B. Barratt, *Erindringer* (1941) ■ idem, *When the Fire Fell and an Outline of My Life* (1927) ■ N. Bloch-Hoell, *The Pentecostal Movement* (1964) ■ T. E. Dahl, *Fra seier til nederlag: Pinsebevegelsen I Norge* (1978) ■ D. Gee, *The Pentecostal Movement* (1949) ■ S. B. Lange, *T. B. Barratt: Et Herrens sendebud* (1962) ■ O. Nilsen, *Pinseprofiler* (1975) ■ *Pinsebevegelsen I Norge 75 år* (1982) ■ *Pinsevekkelsen gjennom 30 år* (1937) ■ M. Ski, *T. B. Barratt: Døpt I Ånd og ild* (1979) ■ A. Sundstedt, *Pingstväckelsen,* vol. 1 (1969).

■ O. Nilsen; L. Ahonen

OMAN

■ Pentecostals 0 (0%)   ■ Charismatics 7,139 (15%)   ■ Neocharismatics 39,861 (85%)   ■ Total Renewal: 47,000

See AFRICA, NORTH, AND THE MIDDLE EAST

PACIFIC ISLANDS (Survey)

The "liquid continent," as some writers refer to the South Pacific, consists of thousands of islands and tiny atolls. The cultures are so diverse that even anthropologists have problems in classifying them. According to Campbell (1989), the degree of difference is "proportional to distance." A common way of starting to explain the diversities is to subdivide the huge area into three subregions: Melanesia in the west, Polynesia in the east, and Micronesia in the north of the South Pacific.

The *Melanesians* to the west, less dispersed than the rest of the Pacific Islanders, occupy a string of islands stretching from Papua New Guinea to New Caledonia. The majority of people live on islands of considerable dimensions. Melanesia is known as a rich field for linguistic studies, with its estimated 1,200 spoken languages (about one-fourth of the languages spoken in the world). The Melanesian peoples range in stature from tall to short and in skin color from light brown to deep black.

The *Polynesians* live in the eastern half of the ocean. Since the time of the discoveries by James Cook and others in the late 18th century, the people have usually been described as outstandingly friendly and good-looking. They have light brown skin. Polynesian societies are much more homogeneous in their organizational structure and in the languages they speak than the Melanesian groups (Grenfell Price, 1983).

North of the equator we find the *Micronesians,* with their homes on tiny atolls, sometimes no bigger than a couple of rugby fields. Most scholars today assume that the Micronesians are a blend of Polynesians and Asian influences, which becomes quite obvious in their stature and features. Culturally, the Micronesians are much more heterogeneous than the Polynesians, though less so than the Melanesians.

Traditional Melanesian societies are often described as "classless" in sharp distinction to Micronesian and Polynesian societies, which usually have several different classes and a strong hierarchical order. Social rituals, law, religion, settlement patterns, economy, and values showed far greater diversity in the pre-Christian period than people outside the region usually expect.

1. The Arrival of the Gospel.

The first Christians who came to the Pacific Islands were of Spanish origin and Roman Catholics, coming with the expeditions of, for example, Magellan in 1521, Mendana in 1567–68, or Quiros in 1595 and 1605–6. But these first visits did not play any part in the introduction of Christianity.

Organized mission work started first in 1668, when Spanish-Jesuit missionaries moved from the Philippines to Guam and from there northward to the islands known today as the Marianas. Looking at the South Pacific as a whole, these early Spanish Catholic attempts can be seen as "isolated incidents," because, according to Lange (1992), "these events did not lead on in any way to the spreading of Christianity into other parts of the Pacific." As in many other parts of the world, Christianity took root in the South Pacific in the very late 18th century and especially in the 19th century. After the discoveries of James Cook and others and the beginnings of contact and trade, the ground was prepared for the subsequent Christianization that took its course parallel to the new economic and political developments. By the end of the 19th century, most of the Pacific Islands had been taken under the control of various colonial powers (Great Britain, France, Germany, U.S.).

According to Forman (1982) a durable and organized mission work in the Pacific Islands started with the arrival of missionaries from the interdenominational London Missionary Society (LMS) in Tahiti in 1797. Subsequently, the LMS established congregationally structured churches, which today are predominant in Tahiti, the Cook Islands, Samoa, Tokelau, Niue, and Tuvalu.

The first Methodist missionaries arrived in the Pacific in 1822, and long-term mission work started in 1826. In the following decades Methodism took root mainly in Tonga and Fiji, where the Methodists are still dominant today. The predominant Presbyterian Church in Vanuatu traces its beginnings back to the work of John Geddie, who started the Presbyterian Mission in 1848.

A little later came the Anglican Melanesian Mission, started by Bishop Selwyn of New Zealand. The Anglican Church is predominant in the Solomon Islands today.

The Boston-based American Board of Commissioners for Foreign Missions (ABCFM), another Congregational body, was responsible for the establishment of Christianity in the 1850s in Micronesia (Marshall Islands, northern Kiribati, and what is known today as the Federated States of Micronesia).

Roman Catholic missions developed a strong rivalry with the Protestant missions. While already established in the Marianas and Guam, the Catholic mission work in the rest of the Pacific began in Hawaii in 1827.

With its mission work carried out by different missionary orders, Catholicism spread over the whole South Pacific and became predominant in New Caledonia, Wallis and

Futuna, and recently Kiribati, while in the rest of the region the Catholic Church is usually in second place after the previously established Protestant denominations.

The development of Christianity in the Pacific Islands as described so far can be seen as the first big wave of mission. Between 1844 and 1930, new religious groups from the U.S., such as the Mormons, Seventh-day Adventists, Assemblies of God, and Jehovah's Witnesses reached out to the Pacific Islands. With the exception of the Mormons in Polynesia, they were not able to convert large numbers of people until the 1960s. Breakaway groups from the respective Protestant mainline churches had led to a considerable diversification of religion in the South Pacific, which continues to be the case until today. But the newest development of Christianity is the emergence and rapid growth of pentecostal-charismatic movements in the Pacific Islands.

Besides Christianity, other world religions are also present in the South Pacific, especially Hinduism and Islam, which were introduced mainly through the importation of laborers from India to the Fiji sugar cane plantations at the end of the 19th century by the British colonial administration. Since WWII the Baha'i Faith, a reformist movement of Islam, has been gaining momentum in the South Pacific Islands.

2. Recent Developments in Specific Countries.

This is the Pacific Christian background in very broad historical strokes, on the basis of which it will be possible to take a closer look at recent developments in the religious situation in selected countries of the region (see individual articles on Cook Islands, Fiji, French Polynesia, Kiribati, Marshall Islands, Micronesia, New Caledonia, Papua New Guinea, Solomon Islands, Tonga, Vanuatu, and Western Samoa; not covered separately are the Marianas, Guam, and Hawaii). The information provided in these articles is based on a completely revised and updated version of parts of a major research project on rapidly growing religious groups in the Pacific Islands carried out by the author (Ernst, 1994).

The reader should be aware that, although close to 100 percent of all existing pentecostal-charismatic movements in the South Pacific are mentioned in these articles, it definitely will not be possible to cover all groups because of constant changes. New groups are established year by year, while others that are not successful disappear.

The articles attempt to cover major pentecostal and charismatic movements, namely, the ›Assemblies of God (AG), which is by far the biggest and most widespread pentecostal denomination within the region; the ›Christian Outreach Centre; ›Church of God (CG, Cleveland, TN); ›United Pentecostal Church International; Apostles Gospel Outreach Fellowship International; ›Rhema Church; Christian Mission Fellowship/Every Home for Christ; ›Full Gospel Business Men's Fellowship International; and Pacific Missionary Aviation.

3. Summary and Conclusion.

As recent research has shown (Ernst, 1994), there is clear evidence that especially pentecostal-charismatic movements have experienced rapid growth in the Pacific Islands during the past three decades. This has led to an ongoing reshaping of the religious landscape in the different island nations. Through the concomitant changes in religious affiliation, this has also led to an unprecedented diversity of Christian denominations in the region.

The causes for the growth and increasing number of adherents of a steadily growing number of pentecostal-charismatic movements are multifaceted. There is a clear correlation between the rise of pentecostal-charismatic movements and the occurrence of fundamental transformation in Pacific Islands' societies and cultures. Rapid changes in society, for example, were caused by WWII, with its sudden availability of an abundance of goods for the army, modern technology, and new ideas of equality and self-determination; the economic boom in the 1960s and the forced implementation of the Western capitalist system from the 1960s to the present; and the rapid urbanization and displacement of people. All these contributed to fundamental social changes: cultural values that were not compatible with those of the Western world disappeared; a cash and wages system replaced the subsistence and barter system; traditional social and political structures collapsed; social mobilization and urbanization broke up families, clans, and villages; the collapse of traditional social control gave way to criminality, alcoholism, domestic violence, etc. All of these social changes impinge on people in such a way that they feel uprooted from their traditions and confused about their future. They suffer the anonymity of the towns and long for a community to which they can belong (Ernst, 1994). The resulting search for a new social community very often ends in one of the pentecostal-charismatic groups. Those in need of clarity and orientation find personal answers in the simple doctrine, conservative interpretation of the Bible, and clear ethical principles taught by pentecostals or charismatics.

Apart from this sociopsychological explanation, some cultural aspects specific to the Pacific Islands have definitely contributed to the successful spread of pentecostal and charismatic movements in the region, since these groups fit to some extent easily within traditional belief patterns, as has been demonstrated in numerous publications (Trompf, 1977, 1987; Garrett, 1982). For example, Pacific Islanders have always believed in the presence of spirits endowed with extraordinary powers. They have also believed that somebody can be possessed by these spirits and be given the same power as well. Phenomena such as ecstasy, trance, speaking in tongues, and divination were common in traditional religions too and attributed to the presence of spirits, especially the spirits of ancestors. Pacific Islanders, especially Melanesians, have always placed importance on good relationships as being essential for health and healing, not only for individuals but for the whole community. Pentecostal and charismatic movements are also well known for the emotional involvement of participants in their services: dramatic baptisms by immersion of the Spirit, powerful confrontation between the power of God and evil, emotional public confessions and testimonies, rhythms and songs full of enthusiasm. All these are attractive to people whose traditional religious experience was also characterized by dramatic initiation forms, powerful singing, emotional mourning, and exciting mythical dances. Millennial expectations—beliefs in a coming age that will be morally just and equitable for all—have also been part of the Pacific Islanders in the past. The historic Protestant mainline churches usually repressed these millennial aspirations by teaching a rational view of human progress and development and by postponing ad infinitum the final coming of God's kingdom. Dreams and visions have been the most common link in the traditional societies between the living and the dead, between the people and all kinds of spirits. In spite of dreams and visions being present in the Bible too, they tend to be dismissed as unscientific by historic mainline churches. The apocalyptic sections of the Bible are not very fashionable within the mainline Protestant denominations. But especially charismatics make great use of that kind of literature.

Because of the continuation of the different external and internal sociopsychological factors that contributed to the emergence and growth of pentecostal-charismatic movements in the Pacific, and of the cultural background as briefly outlined above, it is very likely that the pentecostal-charismatic movements in the Pacific Islands will continue to grow fast in the foreseeable future.

See also COOK ISLANDS, FIJI, FRENCH POLYNESIA, KIRIBATI, MARSHALL ISLANDS, MICRONESIA, NEW CALEDONIA, PAPUA NEW GUINEA, SOLOMON ISLANDS, TONGA, VANUATU, AND WESTERN SAMOA.

■ **Bibliography:** I. C. Campbell, *A History of the Pacific Islands* (1989) ■ R. W. Dayton and J. A. Siewert, eds., *Mission Handbook: USA Canada Protestant Ministries Overseas,* 14th ed. (1989) ■ N. and N. Douglas, *Pacific Islands Yearbook* (1989) ■ M. Ernst, *Winds of Change: Rapidly Growing Religious Groups in the Pacific Islands* (1994) ■ M. Finau, "The Emergence of the Maamafo'ou Movement from the Free Wesleyan of Tonga," in C. W. Forman, ed., *Island Churches: Challenge and Change* (1992) ■ C. W. Forman, *The Island Churches of the South Pacific* (1982) ■ J. Garrett, *To Live among the Stars: Christian Origins in Oceania* (1982) ■ General Council of the Assemblies of God, Division of Foreign Missions, *Annual Statistics* (1997) ■ A. Grenfell Price, *Captain James Cook—Entdeckungsfahrten im Pazifik: Die Logbücher der Reisen von 1768–1779* (1983) ■ K. Hovey, "Pentecostal Churches in Papua New Guinea," *Catalyst: Social Pastoral Magazine for Melanesia* 20 (1, 1990) ■ T. Ieuti, "The Kiribati Protestant Church and the New Religious Movements," in C. W. Forman, ed., *Island Churches: Challenge and Change* (1992) ■ P. Johnstone, *Operation World* (1993) ■ R. T. Lange, "Christianity in the Pacific," *Exchange: Journal of Missiological and Ecumenical Research* 21 (1992) ■ L. R. Larson, *The Spirit in Paradise: The History of the Assemblies of God in Fiji and Its Outreaches to Other Island Countries throughout the South Pacific* (1997) ■ Republic of Kiribati, *Report on the 1978 Census of Population and Housing,* vol. 3 (1983) ■ Republic of the Marshall Islands, *Census of Population and Housing, 1988, Final Report* (1988) ■ Republic of the Marshall Islands, *National Population Policy* (1990) ■ J.-L. Saquet, *The Tahiti Handbook* (1990) ■ South Pacific Commission and International Labour Organisation, *Migration, Employment and Development in the South Pacific, Country Report No. 4, Fiji* (1983) ■ idem, *Migration, Employment and Development in the South Pacific, Country Report No. 22, Western Samoa* (1983) ■ G. Trompf, ed., *The Gospel Is Not Western* (1987) ■ idem, *Prophets of Melanesia* (1977) ■ D. Vincent, "Documentation on the Churches in P.N.G.—Reflections upon the 1990 National Census," *Catalyst* 23 (1, 1993).
■ M. Ernst

PAKISTAN

■ Pentecostals 77,920 (9%)   ■ Charismatics 292,012 (33%)   ■ Neocharismatics 520,068 (58%)   ■ Total Renewal: 890,000

See NORTH AFRICA AND THE MIDDLE EAST.

PALAU

■ Pentecostals 243 (19%)   ■ Charismatics 900 (71%)   ■ Neocharismatics 127 (10%)   ■ Total Renewal: 1,270

See PACIFIC ISLANDS.

PALESTINE

■ Pentecostals 1,665 (2%)   ■ Charismatics 3,857 (4%)   ■ Neocharismatics 101,478 (95%)   ■ Total Renewal: 107,000

See AFRICA, NORTH, AND THE MIDDLE EAST.

PANAMA

■ Pentecostals 225,235 (46%)   ■ Charismatics 207,163 (42%)   ■ Neocharismatics 57,602 (12%)   ■ Total Renewal: 490,000

See LATIN AMERICA.

PAPUA NEW GUINEA

■ Pentecostals 238,141 (32%)   ■ Charismatics 310,063 (41%)   ■ Neocharismatics 202,796 (27%)   ■ Total Renewal: 751,000

For general introduction and bibliography, see PACIFIC ISLANDS.

Papua New Guinea (P.N.G.) is an independent state (since 1975) and a member of the Commonwealth. It consists of the eastern half of the island of New Guinea (Indonesia's province of Irian Jaya occupies the western half) and many offshore islands, including New Britain, New Ireland, and Bougainville. The central core of the main island of New Guinea is a massive cordillera, 1,550 mi (2,500 km) long, that stretches from one end of the island to the other and forms one of the world's greatest mountain systems. Dense jungles are a striking characteristic of a large part of P.N.G. In most areas, from sea level to 3,200 ft (980 m), the rain forests grow in profusion. Port Moresby, the national capital, is 2,400 mi (3,900 km) north of Sydney.

The inhabitants include a large diversity of types. There had been much mixing of people groups long before Europeans made their first contacts, and the indigenous people of P.N.G. can be considered to be related to those other Melanesians who occupy the greater part of the Western Pacific. The population of 4.5 million (1995) is scattered widely throughout the country, but the greatest concentration are in the highland provinces. There are numerous tribal groups, more than half of which number under 1,000. Another characteristic that made the country a favorite destination for anthropologists, as well as Bible translators and missionaries, is the large number of languages (about 700 to 800). Today 96% of the population claim to be Christian, belonging to one of the more than 80 different denominations with activities in the country. The largest denominations in terms of members are the Roman Catholic Church, with an estimated 1.2 million adherents, and the Evangelical Lutheran Church of P.N.G., with about 550,000 adherents (1995).

An assessment, or even a description, of the pentecostal and charismatic segment of Christianity in P.N.G. is difficult, basically because of the denominational complexity— about 20 pentecostal denominations have been represented in one way or another at different times. "Probably no other part of Christianity in P.N.G. has seen as many denominational splits and amalgamations, or as much movement of workers or even congregations between one denomination and another" (Hovey, 1990).

The first wave of pentecostal missions to P.N.G. came from Australia and the U.S. in the first decade after WWII. Since there was little urbanization in P.N.G. at that time, these missionaries worked mostly in rural areas. Their rural involvement made them sensitive to the needs of the community at large, and this led to the establishment of literacy, medical, trading, or educational programs on their first mission stations. Emphasis was also placed on the development of national leaders with the aim of handing over responsibility to them.

A second wave of pentecostal churches, which added missionaries from the Netherlands, Sweden, and Finland, began in the 1970s. They were predominantly urban-based and followed the more "typical" pattern of pentecostal mission in the South Pacific by using urban churches as a base for church planting in both urban and rural areas.

While the first missionaries cooperated closely with other evangelical churches through initial agreements, it was different with the "second"-wave missionaries, who were moving into areas where other churches already existed. At least initially, there was often much conflict. In 1979 the National Council of Pentecostal Churches (NCPC) was formed, but the aim of reaching better cooperation and liaison between pentecostal and charismatic bodies was not always easy to reach because of the underlying conflicts that resulted from different churches working in the same locations with very similar church-planting goals.

The pentecostal churches in P.N.G. are today a significant part of the P.N.G. Christian landscape. This is evident from their current numerical strength, growth rates, and impact. Accurate statistics, even on the number of Christian churches in P.N.G., are not available, and consequently there is no reliable reformation on the number of adherents of the different pentecostal churches. There is no doubt that the pentecostal and charismatic movement is growing very fast, with an estimated annual increase of approximately 18% (Vincent, 1990). There is also some evidence that Patrick Johnstone (1992), with his estimate of 10.4% of P.N.G.'s population belonging to the wider pentecostal-charismatic movement, is quite close to the current situation.

■ M. Ernst

PARAGUAY

■ Pentecostals 76,990 (32%) ■ Charismatics 107,312 (44%) ■ Neocharismatics 57,698 (24%) ■ Total Renewal: 242,000

Norwegian pentecostal missionaries of the Pinsevennenes Ytre Misjon first worked in Paraguay among the indigenous populations along the Bolivian border from 1938. Then in 1952 Bergliot Nordmoen began a multidimensional ministry among the rural Guarani Indian poor in Paraguay. She was joined in 1957 by Gunvor Johansen and Ruth Kjellås. The three women purchased in 1958 an estate at Paso Cadena to serve as a mission center that would address various aspects of the local economic problems as well as serve as a center for evangelization. By 1984 more than 27 Norwegian missionaries were working or had worked in Paraguay. The Iglesia Evangélica Filadelfia has grown out of their work, claiming about 1,000 members (1984).

As far as can be ascertained, the first non-Indian pentecostals in Paraguay were refugees from Russia, Poland, and Germany who fled to South America during and immediately after WWII. These established small congregations, but there was severe persecution by the government at the insistence of the Catholic Church. The U.S. ʾAssemblies of God (AG) assigned Raymond Stawinski to work among the refugees in 1945; he settled at Encarnación. Shortly thereafter a church was started in Asunción. Hodges (1956) claimed 5 congregations and 200 members. Barrett reported 545 members and 2,000 adherents (1982). The AG reports 61 congregations and 8,120 "baptized members" with another 19,500 "attending" adults and children (1999). The AG established Paraguay Bible Institute in 1959.

The Iglesia de Dios en el Paraguay (ʾChurch of God [Cleveland, TN]) traces its roots to the German colony at Colonia Independencia. Converts contacted José Minay, a Chilean missionary, who in 1954 established connections with the U.S. denomination in negotiations with ʾVessie D. Hargrave. A Spanish-language congregation was established by Minay in Asunción, and missions were begun among the Guarani Indians. In 1957–59 there was extensive persecution of believers and leaders of the churches, but at the end of 1959 there were 11 congregations, 8 missions, and about 500 members. By the late 1980s there were about 4,000 members and adherents.

The Iglesia del Evangelio Cuadrangular was started by members of the ʾInternational Church of the Foursquare Gospel of Brazil in 1983. There are 13 congregations in Paraguay with 987 members and perhaps 3,000 additional adherents (1999).

The Iglesia Pentecostal Unida (ʾUnited Pentecostal Church [UPC]) began mission work in 1973 and claims about 1,000 "constituents," 11 ministers, and 26 congregations (1999). The UPC maintains a Bible school in Asunción. Other pentecostal denominations include the Iglesia Evangélica Gracia y Gloria, Iglesia Evangélica Plenitud, and Iglesia Pentecostal de Chile, as well as a number of indigenous congregations.

■ **Bibliography:** Anon., *Paraguay* (Springfield, MO, c. 1960) ▌ D. B. Barrett, *World Christian Encyclopedia* (1982), 555–58 ▌ D. L. Burk, ed., *Foreign Missions Insight: A Digest of Foreign Missions Faces, Facts, Fields and Figures* (1999), 137–38 ▌ C. W. Conn, *Like a Mighty Army: A History of the Church of God* (1955; rev. 1977, 1995) ▌ idem, *Where the Saints Have Trod: A History of Church of God Missions* (1959) ▌ S. M. Hodges, *Look on the Fields: A Survey of the Assemblies of God in Foreign Lands* (1956) ▌ W. J. Hollenweger, "Handbuch der Pfingstbewegung" (diss., Zurich, 1967), 1095–97 (para. 02b.25) ▌ L. Jeter de Walker, *Siembra y cosecha*, vol. 2 (1992) ▌ G. L. Johansen, "Paraguay," in *Til Jordens Ender: Norsk pinsemisjon gjennom 50 år* (1960) ▌ O. Nilsen, *Ut i all Verden: Pinsevennenes ytre misjon i 75 år* (1984) ▌ A. Sundstedt, *Pingstväckelsen*, 5 vols. (1969–73).

■ D. D. Bundy

PERU

■ Pentecostals 426,905 (12%) ■ Charismatics 2,647,604 (77%) ■ Neocharismatics 365,491 (11%) ■ Total Renewal: 3,440,000

The prehistory of pentecostalism in Peru is closely related to, but not dependent on, that of Chile. The peripatetic Methodist-Episcopal evangelist ʾWilliam Taylor arrived in Peru, initially on a fact-finding trip, in 1877. He returned to Peru to establish congregations in Callao and Iquique. At Iquique he built the first church building with his own hands; the congregation would later be served by Holiness Methodist missionary ʾWillis Hoover after the transfer of the city to Chile. More important, Taylor's "Pauline" concept—that the role of missionaries was to establish self-supporting, self-determining, and self-propagating churches—made a strong impression in Peru as it had in other areas of the world. He insisted on inclusion of nonmissionaries in the decision-making process of a mission and on the immediate transfer of the leadership of congregations and denominations to the converts.

Iquique was lost to Chile in war, but the ideas were spread widely through the Protestant communities of Peru and established a set of expectations among Peruvians as to the structure of non-Catholic mission and church work. Initial Protestant evangelistic efforts in Peru were hampered by legislation that outlawed non-Catholic worship. After the initial removal of legal restrictions on dissident religious traditions, missionaries, including some pentecostals, arrived in Peru.

1. The Beginnings of Pentecostalism in Peru.

It would appear that the first pentecostal missionaries to Peru were Howard W. and Clara Cragin. They came as independent missionaries to Callao on Feb. 12, 1911. Correspondence between Cragin and Willis Hoover in Chile was published in the periodical *Chile Pentecostal*. Cragin was not well received by the established churches and moved to Quito, Equador, in 1911, and on to La Paz, Bolivia, in 1914 before returning to Peru. There was little positive interest in early pentecostalism among the established mission denominations in Peru, probably due to the difficulties the early revival in Chile posed for the older churches. Therefore, the initial founding of congregations in Peru required more missionary involvement than in Chile or Argentina. Two U.S. Assemblies of God (AG) missionary couples, the J. R. Hurlburts and Forrest and Ethel Barker, arrived in Peru in 1922. The Hurlburts planted a congregation in Callao in 1922. In doing so they broke the standard "mainline" Protestant missionary comity principle, which involved the agreement of accepting assignments and working only in those areas in Peru where other denominations were not active. Other pentecostal churches were started in Huancayo, Callejón, and Carás. These were joined in 1925 by independent U.S. missionaries Leif and Florence Erickson, who spent a few months in Chile with Willis Hoover but disagreed with Hoover on infant baptism. The Ericksons accepted the invitation of Cragin to join ministry efforts in Peru.

The first baptismal service, scheduled for Huaraz on Feb. 27, 1927, was a disaster. Encouraged by Catholic priests, local mobs attacked the missionaries. Cragin and Erickson were both severely wounded but were saved from death by Peruvian converts. The experience of baptism of the Holy Spirit soon followed for several Peruvians. The use of tribal languages in the liturgy attracted large crowds.

Willis Hoover was invited from Chile to lead what turned out to be highly successful revival campaigns in Callao and Lima. This campaign had lasting influence throughout the country. From the immediate results of Hoover's visit came at least three congregations pastored by Peruvians. Thus, the first generation of pentecostal believers were well acquainted with the narratives and mission methods of William Taylor and Hoover. Persecution was intense during this period, especially at Huaraz. The Catholic bishop of Huaraz took an active part in the harassment of the fledgling pentecostal congregations in his diocese. The persecution led to growth, and in 1932 a Bible school was started at Huaraz by Erickson and Cragin. It was built on the Scandinavian model: inexpensive, short-term, nonresidential, and based on indigenous resources. It was rejected as insufficient by the AG mission program and was replaced by the program at Miraflores (see below). Pentecostals were also involved in the national fight for religious liberty. Particularly influential in this process were Emiliano Béjar and Rupert Villanueva.

2. The Struggles for Independence, 1936–56.

Two female AG missionaries, Ruth Couchman and Olga Pitt, arrived in Peru in 1928. They were apparently the first fully funded and supported denominational pentecostal missionaries to arrive. In 1936 they initiated a residential Bible school at Miraflores, a suburb of Lima. The graduates became paid employees of the AG–U.S. mission board. Couchman and Pitt controlled the distribution of these funds. This institution proved effective in preparing the first generation of Peruvian leadership in the pentecostal churches, but it also built in patterns of dependency. The increased power of the U.S. missionaries over the Peruvians led to the radicalization of many Peruvian pastors regarding nationalism. Some left the AG for other denominations, but others began the process of founding indigenous Peruvian denominations.

The first significant break came with the establishment of La Iglesia Evangélica de Cristo del Perú (1936). Couchman and Pitt were instrumental in the expulsion of most of the youth from the Callao AG church on May 31, 1936. The 26 youth organized a congregation, and from that beginning the denomination has spread throughout Peru. The second division occurred with the establishment of La Iglesia Evangélica Pentecostal Independiente. The first congregation to rebel was the church in Huaráz, founded by Howard and Clara Cragin. Cragin believed in the self-supporting, self-determining, self-theologizing "Pauline Holiness" concept of William Taylor and Willis Hoover and did not believe that clergy and missionaries should be paid and controlled by foreign funds. He himself worked as a mining engineer to support the mission efforts. When during the 1930s the AG–U.S. missionaries used a Peruvian economic crisis to attempt to extend their financial control over the Peruvian clergy who had been ordained before the arrival of Couchman and Pitt, the church felt obliged to withdraw.

The third split began with the establishment of La Avanzada Pentecostal, which became the Iglesia Evangélica Pentecostal Misionera (1946; in some sources, 1943 and 1945). This church started because of conflict between pentecostal youth evangelists and the U.S. missionaries. The youth of a Lima congregation had organized their own leadership and were heavily involved in evangelistic activity. They were summoned by the AG missionaries and told to desist from independent activities not expressly sanctioned in advance by the missionaries. Under the leadership of Severo Zamora, Carlos Landeo, Juan Sánchez, and Eulogio Cárdenas, they withdrew from the AG. Many youth from other congregations, both pentecostal and nonpentecostal, joined in solidarity with them.

Another denomination founded during this difficult period (1948) by Peruvian Dionicio Carrasco, in the district of San Agustín de Cajas, was the Iglesia Apostólica, which united dissidents throughout the country into a denomination. The central issue was control of polity and ministry by the foreign missionaries. After 1951 the tradition was influenced by William L. Hunter, a missionary who had come to Peru under the auspices of the AG–U.S. but withdrew quickly from that organization. This denomination changed its name to the Iglesia Autónoma Pentecostal del Perú. Later, Swedish pentecostal missionaries Peter and Brito Andreas came to work with this church, which would later merge/separate to form other groups; the name of the main church is now La Iglesia Evangélica Pentecostal de Jesucristo.

Couchman and Pitt achieved near absolute juridical and financial power over the Peruvian AG. After Pitt committed what may be described as sexual indiscretions, she was criticized by Erickson. With unwavering support from the U.S. mission program, she and Couchman remained in power and were successful in keeping Erickson from returning to Peru as an AG–U.S. missionary. This and other abuses of power eventually led to a visit to Peru by *Melvin Hodges, missionary secretary of the AG–U.S., in 1956. He turned power in the Asambleas de Dios del Perú over to the Peruvians and withdrew most of the U.S. missionaries from Peru. One more split occurred that was set up by decisions of the American missionaries and the expectations of the new leadership: La Iglesia Evangélica Pentecostal de Perú (1958); here the issue was the control of property.

3. Growth and Diversification.

After 1956 the diversification of pentecostalism in Peru continued and the growth rate increased. Other North American denominations sent missionaries. As a result of a periodical fascicle from *El Evangelio* found by Peruvian Christians, contacts between independent congregations and representatives of the *Church of God (CG, Cleveland, TN) were established. This led to the founding of the Iglesia de Dios del Peru (1947). The effort was boosted by the decision of Arthur and Emma Erickson to work with the new denomination. The Iglesia de Dios de la Profecia (1954) and the Iglesia Pentecostal Unida (1960) also found adherents in Peru. The latter, a mission of the *United Pentecostal Church, had 12,063 adherents in 317 congregations in Peru in 1999.

Missionaries also came from Chile, resulting in the Iglesia Metodista Pentecostal, and from Sweden, resulting in the Iglesia Pentecostal Sueca. The Peru-Mission, based in Switzerland, worked to support the ministries of various pentecostal and nonpentecostal denominations. Among the other more recently organized indigenous denominations are:

Misión Evangélica Pentecostal, Iglesias Pentecostales Autónomas, Iglesia Aposento Alto Paulista, Iglesia de Dios Movimiento Internacional, Movimiento Misionero Pentecostés Primitiva, Iglesia Pentecostal, Iglesia Evangélica Misionera Pentecostés, Iglesia Pentecostés Monte Calvario, and the Iglesia Pentecostal Elim. In total there are at least 55 pentecostal denominations in Peru.

Under Peruvian leadership, the Asambleas de Dios continued to grow and is said to comprise roughly 80% of Peruvian pentecostalism. As in Brazil and Chile, pentecostalism has established a major national presence in Peru, despite sporadic persecution by Catholic churchmen and writers. One of the most significant developments in the Asambleas de Dios has been the development of a committed, erudite pentecostal intelligentsia. The Peruvian churches have produced a number of published historians and theologians, including Alfonso Mora, Santiago Aquilino Huaman Pumayallim, and Rubén Zavala Hidalgo. The best known on an international level is probably Bernardo Campos, author of a number of books, including *De la Reforma Protestante a la Pentecostalidad de la Iglesia. Debate sobre el Pentecostalismo en América Latina* (1997).

■ **Bibliography:** D. B. Barrett, *World Christian Encyclopedia* (1982), 240–44 ▧ D. D. Bundy, "Bishop William Taylor and Methodist Mission: A Study in Nineteenth-Century Social History," *Methodist History* 27 (4, July 1989) and 28 (1, Oct. 1989) ▧ idem, "William Taylor, 1821–1902: Entrepreneurial Maverick for the Indigenous Church," in *Mission Legacies: Biographical Studies of Leaders of the Modern Missionary Movement,* ed. G. Anderson et al. (1994) ▧ D. L. Burk, ed., *Foreign Missions Insight: A Digest of Foreign Missions Faces, Facts, Fields and Figures* (1999), 140–41 ▧ W. J. Hollenweger, "Handbuch der Pfingstbewegung" (diss., Zurich, 1967), 1098–1105 (para. 02b.26) ▧ J. A. B. Kessler, *Historia del Evangelización en el Perú* (1987) ▧ idem, *A Study of the Older Protestant Missions and Churches in Peru and Chile, with Special Reference to the Problems of Division, Nationalism and Native Ministry* (1967) ▧ S. A. Huamán P., *La Primera Historia del Movimiento Pentecostal en el Perú* (1982) ▧ H. Meza, *Historia de Las Asambleas de Dios del Perú* (1971) ▧ A. Mora, *Trasfondo Histórico de Las Asambleas de Dios* (1984) ▧ E. Ríos, *Historia de las Asambleas de Dios del Perú* (1959) ▧ L. Steiner, "Mission in Peru," *Verheissung des Vaters* 57 (7, July 1964) ▧ H. R. Stutz, "Ein neues Missionswerk in Südamerika," *Verheissung des Vaters* 56 (12, Dec. 1963) ▧ W. Taylor, *Our South American Cousins* (1878) ▧ idem, *Pauline Methods of Missionary Work* (1879) ▧ idem, *The Story of My Life* (1895) ▧ L. J. Walker, *Peruvian Gold* (1985; Spanish version: *Oro Peruano* [1987]) ▧ idem, *Siembra y consecha* (1992), 2:90–137 ▧ R. Zavala Hidalgo, *Historia de las Asambleas de Dios del Perú* (1989).   ■ D. D. Bundy

PHILIPPINES

■ Pentecostals 765,813 (4%)   ■ Charismatics 11,659,457 (58%)   ■ Neocharismatics 7,624,730 (38%)
■ Total Renewal: 20,050,000

As the three-and-a-half-century-old Spanish rule (1566–1898) ended with the defeat of the Spanish fleet by the U.S. at Manila Bay, a floodgate was suddenly opened for Protestant mission, mainly from the U.S. As the Philippines celebrated the centennial of Protestant mission in 1998, the pentecostal churches, charismatic groups, and pentecostal-type churches were flourishing all over the tropical archipelago. This survey divides the pentecostal/charismatic churches and fellowships into three groups. Most of the classical pentecostal denominations belong to the Philippine Council of Evangelical Churches (PCEC), and the majority of independent charismatic fellowships/churches are under the Philippines for Jesus Movement (PJM). However, this categorization is not entirely accurate, since some independent charismatic groups have membership in the PCEC and at least one classical pentecostal group is part of PJM.

1. Pentecostal Denominations.

When the pentecostal movement was born in the U.S., the Philippine islands had already received the initial wave of missionaries from the mainline denominations. Thus, by the time pentecostals set foot in the country, missionary work was well under way, with a comity agreement among the mission groups. In a sense, pentecostals arrived when there was no area left for them to work in. For this reason it was important that Filipino pentecostals in the U.S. returned to their country to preach the pentecostal message.

Four pioneering groups began their work in the 1940s; all but one became major pentecostal denominations, while one remains primarily regional. The 1970s and '80s showed a surge in the birth of major pentecostal groups. This coincided with the explosion of charismatic fellowships in the country.

Today there are at least 18 pentecostal or pentecostal-like denominations or groups among 51 entries in the directory of the Philippine Council of Evangelical Churches (PCEC). Some of the major denominations are discussed below.

a. Assemblies of God. In Sept. 1926 Benjamin H. Caudle arrived in the Philippines as the first ►Assemblies of God (AG) missionary and began a work near Malate in Manila. His stay was short-lived, however, due to a health problem. Then a stream of Filipinos who had lived in America and experienced the pentecostal blessing returned home to share their experiences. Crispulo Garsulao arrived in 1928 and began a work in his hometown, Antique, Visayas. Pedro Collado returned in Mar. 1935 and preached to his folks in Nueva Ecija, and then in Antique and in Mindanao. Benito P. Acena returned in 1935 and began evangelism and training in the Ilocos region and later in Pangasinan. Rosendo Alcantara later joined Acena. Eugenio Suede pioneered the

first AG church in Iloilo and Pedro Castro in Ilocos Sur and Abra. Hermogenes Abrenica worked in Pangasinan, and the organizational convention of the AG took place in his church in Mar. 1940. Rodrigo C. Esperanza pioneered in Pangasinan and became the first Filipino leader (as district secretary and as general superintendent of the Philippine General Council of the AG in 1953). He was also involved in the establishment of Bethel Bible Institute, which opened in his church in Pangasinan. Servillano Obaldo also began his work in Pangasinan and later in Mindanao.

The Philippines District Council of the AG was formally organized in Pangasinan on Mar. 21–27, 1940, and Leland E. Johnson, an American missionary, was appointed superintendent by the AG–U.S. Rodrigo C. Esperanza was elected secretary. During the Japanese occupation, many American missionaries were incarcerated, and Bethel Bible Institute was transferred to Baguio City. The liberation of the country ushered in a period of enthusiastic missionary activities, such as evangelism, church planting, radio and literature ministry, revival meetings, and outdoor crusades. These included Elva Vanderbout in the Mountain Province; Edwin Brengle in Cebu (the establishment of Immanuel Bible College) and in Leyte; Paul Pipkin in Manila with other former missionaries from China; Warren Denton in Antique, Visayas; Gunder Olsen in Iloilo City; Calvin Zeissler in Bacolod City; Floyd Horst in Manila through the establishment of Evangel Printing Press; Glenn Dunn in Manila (Bethel Bible Institute) and in Mindanao (by establishing the AG Bible Institute of Mindanao); and Mayme Williams in evangelism. The contribution of visiting evangelists is also noted. Some of them are Mayme Williams, ►Harvey McAlister, ►A. C. Valdez, Clifton Erickson, ►Oral Roberts, Rudy Cerullo, ►T. L. Osborn, Hal Herman, and Ralph Byrd. The growth continued as the General Council was chartered in Apr. 1953, and many new churches were established during this period.

Efforts were made to expand the ministry through evangelism and church-planting programs, especially in cities and towns. By 1979 there were 1,195 ministers, 383 churches, 16 training schools, and two cross-cultural missionaries. The next 10 years, however, proved to be a turning point for the denomination. By the end of the 1980s the number of churches had more than tripled: 1,329 churches with 2,022 ministers, 20 training schools, and 4 overseas missionaries. This was a time of social and political unrest, and also a period of explosive growth, particularly among the pentecostal and charismatic segments of Philippine Christianity. According to statistics available in 1999, there were 2,357 local churches (almost twice the 1979 number) with close to 130,000 members, as well as 3,200 affiliated ministers/workers.

The Philippine AG also has 35 ministerial training schools (including one for the deaf) and has trained and sent 15 cross-cultural missionaries overseas.

b. Filipino Assemblies of God of the First Born. In order to distinguish themselves from the white pentecostal bodies, the Filipino Assemblies of God of the First Born (FAGFB) was formed among Filipino laborers in Hawaii and California who had experienced the pentecostal blessing. At almost the same time that Filipino pentecostals from the U.S. established the Philippine AG, Silvestre Tarerner, Clemente Balangui, and others returned to the Philippines in 1941 and spread the pentecostal message in Abra, La Union, and Ilocos Sur, all of which are in the northern part of the island of Luzon. Early believers had to endure severe persecution, especially from the Roman Catholic Church and other Christians. In 1943 the denomination was officially organized, and in the same year Messenger of the Cross Bible Institute was open in Ilocos Sur. The first general superintendent was Silvestre Tarerner. (In the 1980s Temple Bible College was opened in Manila, but it later closed down.)

In the 1960s the ministry was expanded to reach many other provinces in Luzon, and even Mindanao. Presently there are 240 churches all over the country, but the majority of them are in northern Luzon and hence Ilocano-speaking. Only recently, Ilocano was replaced by English and Tagalog as the common language for the general assemblies of this denomination.

c. Church of God (Cleveland, TN) World Missions of the Philippines. Although there were at least two previous, short visits by Church of God (CG) missionaries, the first long-term CG missionary from the U.S., Frank Porada, came to the Philippines in 1947 and began his ministry in the northwestern part of Luzon. By 1952 there were 14 ministers, 12 churches, and 551 members. Soon Fulgencio Cortez Sr., Teodorico Lastimosa, Manuel Gonzales Sr., and Florentino Cortez Sr. had emerged as national leaders. For the first 10 years the ministry was concentrated in the northeastern part of the country, and the first Bible school, Northeastern Evangel Bible College, was established in 1954 in Isabela Province, Luzon.

In 1957, after the first 10 years of ministry, mainly on Luzon, Florentino Cortez Sr. began ministries in Mindanao, the southern part of the nation. Immediately a Bible school was opened in Cotabato province, which was later transferred to Davao City and called Davao Bible College. The first work in Mindoro, located in the middle part of the country, began a few years later through the efforts of Ranulfo Navarette.

The year 1964 marks the beginning of CG urban ministries. Through the effort of Lovell Cary, a pioneer missionary, the Pasay City CG was established in the heart of Metro Manila among young college students. This was soon followed by the establishment of the CG Bible Academy in 1973 by Arthur W. Pettyjohn, a Canadian missionary. In 1982 the school was renamed Asian School of Christian Ministries, with Gerald Holloway as acting president. He was also overseer of the Central-Southern Luzon Region. Under the leadership of Miguel Alvarez, a Honduran missionary, the school obtained accreditation from the Philippine government as well as from the Asian Theological Association; it presently offers undergraduate and graduate courses and degrees, including the D.Min.

The 1980s proved to be a season of great harvest in the midst of social and political turmoil under martial law during the Marcos rule. More missionaries arrived, and ministries reached unprecedented levels. In 1981 there were 150,400 churches with more than 30,000 members served by 450 ministers. Holloway started a Bible study in Bel-Air, a wealthy barangay of Manila. The group grew rapidly and eventually evolved into the Word for the World Christian Fellowship. Under Glenn Maypa's leadership, there are presently 36 churches located throughout the country, with more than 7,000 members. Having its own missionaries who are mainly reaching overseas Filipinos, this fellowship has formed the most successful church group in their denomination. As the National Urban Region was created, more churches were established in urban centers as well as among Filipinos overseas in areas such as Dubai, Singapore, Hong Kong, and the U.S.

Presently CG World Missions includes six training schools, 631 local churches, and 803 affiliated ministers/workers, 60,888 members, and 11 training institutions. The CG maintains 60 overseas missionary units, while 29 foreign missionary units assist in the Philippines.

d. Foursquare Gospel. Even before the first American missionary set foot in the Philippines, several immigrant Filipinos who had had spiritual experiences at ▸Angelus Temple, Los Angeles, returned and planted churches in Iloilo City (Vicente De Fante Sr.), in Cavite (Gregorio Ilawan), and in Ilocos Norte (David Abrogena). By the time the first missionary, Everett Denison, began his church planting and day school ministry in Santa Mesa, Manila, in 1949, there were already five congregations in Luzon and Iloilo. Denison's main task, beside his own ministry in Manila, was to organize these churches, coordinate their work, and formally register the Church of the Foursquare Gospel in the Philippines (CFGP).

Unlike the AG, CG, or FAGFB, the CFGP established Calvary Foursquare Church in Manila to be a center for national coordination, a mother church for many daughter churches, and the home of a day school. When the first national convention took place in the early 1960s, there were already 80 churches nationwide. The 1960s proved to be a decade of rapid growth. The CFGP distinguished itself particularly in Mindanao and the Visayas, regions often neglected by other denominations due to transportation difficulties and the Muslim presence in the south. Progress was further augmented by the arrival of more missionaries. By 1972 there were more than 200 churches, 3 Bible colleges, and 2 Christian schools. This impressive achievement became widely known through the publication of *New Testament Fire in the Philippines* by J. Montgomery.

In 1973 the CFGP was registered as a religious body, and Ernesto B. Lagasca became the first national president. This provided a foundation for further growth and indigenization of the CFGP. Ten years later two more Bible colleges were established, the church had grown to 568 churches, and a new missionary movement emerged, resulting in the commission of six missionary units to Japan, Korea, and Papua New Guinea.

When the church celebrated its 50th anniversary in 1999, the denomination was actively engaged in an expansion program called Harvest Plan 2002. Under the leadership of Felipe S. Ferrez Sr., the CFGP has grown to 1,343 churches, 60,700 members, approximately 2,000 credentialed ministers in 41 cities and 60 provinces, 6 ministerial training schools, 3 academic schools, and 14 overseas missionary units in countries like Thailand, Hong Kong, Papua New Guinea, and Spain, in addition to establishing works among Muslims and tribal groups in the country.

e. Others. The ▸Holiness Pentecostal Church began its work in 1973 through the effort of Harold Edmund, a U.S. Air Force serviceman stationed at Clark Air Base in the northern Philippines, and working with Moises Angeles, a national leader. The first missionary, Willard Wager, arrived in that same year. Their first church was established in Tarlac a year later, and the Philippine Pentecostal Holiness Church was formally organized in 1975. Marianito Warisma was the first national superintendent. The work was concentrated primarily in Tarlac and northern Luzon, but in 1978 churches were established in Baguio and in Mindanao. Bible schools were also opened in Manila (Manila Bible Institute) with Edgar Banaga serving as the first director, and Baguio (Baguio Bible School), which existed from 1978 until 1987. In 1988 Baguio merged with Grace Bible College in Tarlac. A third school, Mindanao Bible Institute, was established in 1979 and closed in 1997. Presently there are 130 churches, close to 200 affiliated ministers/workers, 6,593 members, and 2 Bible schools. One missionary is working in Cambodia. Ministries include a children's feeding program. Ariel Munida is the first national superintendent to serve without a missionary counterpart (field superintendent), which he has done since 1997.

The Universal Pentecostal Church was established by Romeo Doming Corpuz in Oct. 1976. His life was greatly influenced by ▸A. A. Allen's preaching in 1965. The Corpuz family had been pentecostal believers through the FAGFB.

This indigenous pentecostal group began its work near Manila, using a Catholic chapel for six months, while the Catholic Mass was moved to Saturday. Today there are 113 local congregations with 100 ministers, 10 day-care centers, and one Christian school. The church is part of the Philippines for Jesus Movement (PJM).

There are many smaller groups with fewer than 100 local churches. Miracle Life Fellowship is a ministry department of Don Stewart Ministries Miracle Revivals, Inc. The genesis of this ministry traces to A. A. Allen's ministries in the Philippines in the mid 1960s. After Allen's death in 1970, Don Stewart continued the ministry's leadership and established Miracle Revivals in 1972. The comprehensive ministry includes a mail ministry, crusade and television evangelism, a feeding program, and church ministry. At present there are 83 churches with 160 pastors and Christian workers.

The Christ to the Philippines movement began as a result of a series of outdoor tent-revival meetings in 1969. Presently the ministry includes 80 churches, 152 affiliated workers, and 6,000 members with 7 training institutions. About 20 missionary families work together with the national ministers, while there are 6 overseas missionary units commissioned by Christ to the Philippines.

Triumphant Church Ministries was organized in 1988, with seven existing churches in the Manila area under the leadership of Vic Rabara and five associates. Presently there are 15 churches with 50 workers and 700 members.

All for Christ Church was started in 1982, mainly by young people. In 1987 the church was challenged to worship "in Spirit and truth," and this resulted in a turning point for the fellowship. Presently there are 4 churches with 12 workers and 350 members.

Although the ▸United Pentecostal Church maintains a ministry in the Philippines, it is difficult to obtain any information, as the church is not affiliated with either the PCEC or PJM.

Altar scene at the Manila Church of God in the Philippines during the 1970s.

Among PCEC members identified as pentecostal/charismatic by the present general secretary, Bishop Efraim Tendero, no detailed information is available for at least five groups. They are Corpus Christi Foundation (president: Paul Healy in Cebu City); First Christian Pentecostal Church (president: Saturnino Molina in Ilocos Norte), Lift Jesus Higher Fellowship (president: Ronnie G. Binas in Bacolod City), Pentecostal Christian Church (president: Felix Labang in Cagayan de Oro City), and Joint Heirs with the Lord (president: Bonifacio Masaoay in Davao del Norte). In addition, there are 21 independent churches identified by the PCEC as pentecostal/charismatic. By applying the available average number of churches of smaller pentecostal/charismatic groups, membership per church, and factoring in churches that are not accounted for, it is reasonable to conclude that this category may include around 450,000 believers.

The PCEC has been the main umbrella organization with which the majority of pentecostal denominations are affiliated. However, many smaller pentecostal groups, especially those who have regional bases outside metro Manila, are not accounted for by the PCEC. There are two pentecostal seminaries in the Philippines: Asia Pacific Theological Seminary (AG) and Asian Seminary of Christian Ministries (CG, Cleveland, TN). With the unlisted groups in mind, pentecostals in this category may number half a million or more.

2. Charismatic Fellowships.

Many house prayer groups mushroomed in the 1970s throughout metro Manila and major provincial cities. Among the dominant Catholic population (at least 80% of 70,000,000 Filipinos), enthusiastic seekers opened their homes, offices, factories, restaurants, and schools for Bible studies and prayer meetings. Unlike the classical pentecostals, who ministered among people in lower socioeconomic strata, these new seekers were businesspeople, educated professionals, corporate executives, government employees, teachers, and army officers, including many generals. They prayed regularly for healing and spiritual gifts. As small Bible studies grew rapidly, hotel ballrooms and big restaurants were rented for regular Sunday celebrations. These neutral locations were particularly attractive to Catholic believers who did not wish to be identified with "born-again" people. Likewise, groups did not call themselves "church" but "fellowship."

Often groups are centered around a gifted preacher or Bible teacher—not necessarily one with a traditional Bible school or seminary education—and many self-studied leaders have demonstrated creative leadership and active utilization of the laity in various ministries. Like-minded professionals often follow the leader's example and turn to ministry, and with in-house training (which is sometimes more effective than Bible school education), these dedicated laypersons become leaders of daughter churches. (However, this category has shown how fragile a fellowship built around a charismatic leader can be; the past decades have frequently witnessed how a successful ministry split and smaller "fellowships" began.)

With strong emphasis on Bible study and dedicated life, these fellowships attract many middle-class professionals and businesspeople to the gospel, and as a result, daughter churches are planted all over the country and sometimes among overseas Filipinos, such as those working as domestic helpers in Hong Kong, Singapore, Malaysia, and Taiwan; Filipino laborers in Korea and Japan; professionals in European countries; and immigrants in the U.S., Canada, and Australia. Eventually, many fellowships became more like denominations, training workers and ordaining them.

With this rather popular trend, similar fellowships sprang up among traditional pentecostal denominations, and some continue to maintain a strong denominational affiliation. For instance, Word for the World has maintained its affiliation, at least among ministers, with CG World Mission, while David Sobrepeña, pastor of the growing Word of Hope, was elected as head of the Philippine General Council of the AG, even though his church is not part of the denomination. In the same way, Eliezer Javier, former general superintendent of the Philippine AG, founded another charismatic group called Light of the World.

After two decades of consolidation, the independent charismatic fellowships

Tokyo bus and students of the Far East Advanced School of Theology (FEAST; now Asia Pacific Theological Seminary).

have influenced pentecostal worship and message. At the same time, the independent charismatic groups have become more like traditional "churches," with similar infrastructures. Even doctrinally, some charismatic fellowships are becoming more evangelical than pentecostal, at least in preaching. Here are several representatives of the charismatic group.

a. Jesus Is the Lord Fellowship. Bishop ▶Eddie C. Villanueva, a professor at Polytechnic University of the Philippines, began a small Bible study with about 15 students in July 1978. In the climate of sociopolitical unrest during the Marcos regime, college students often staged rallies and demonstrations. This small Bible study became the seedbed of what is the largest non-Catholic charismatic church in the Philippines, called Jesus Is the Lord Fellowship.

Although he has no formal biblical or theological training, Villanueva has led the church to be a change agent for society in moral, political, economic, and spiritual matters. The church is involved in a variety of ministries, such as jail ministry, schools, media evangelism, and others. Today there are 478 local congregations, (including 72 abroad), 937 workers, 2 regular Bible schools with 7 mobile schools, a college, and 21 Christian schools. Although the church claims to have 4 million constituents, regular members participating in local bodies may be numbered more realistically at about 150,000.

b. Love of Christ. This ministry was established by Mel Gabriel, a medical doctor, who had left Iglesia ni Cristo, a Filipino cultic group. He had held a national executive position in that powerful yet problematic group. In spite of many death threats, he started a home Bible study in his own clinic, and at the same time he started a campaign to expose the reality of the Iglesia ni Cristo. The ministry expanded steadily, as powerful worship and music became a trademark of the fellowship. Many testified to deliverance from cultic oppressions as well as from physical and mental problems. The church reached Mindanao and even Thailand. Presently there are 40 churches with 70 ministers.

c. Asian Christian Charismatic Fellowship. Founded by a U.S. AG missionary, Paul Klahr, in 1981, who pastored for seven years at Ali Mall, a thriving shopping center in the heart of Manila. The main congregation once reached 1,500, and by 1995, 20 satellite churches were planted throughout the country. The leadership was indigenized with Nilo Jaren Lapasaran, who succeeded Klahr; Nicky Boy C. Valdez is currently serving as national leader. At present, the church has established overseas congregations in at least four countries. Its unique Barangay Bible Study is often cited as a primary growth factor. Bible studies are held in homes, offices, and communities. Normally a lay leader leads the session; the Bible study program is held not only for adults but also for children. With active lay involvement, there are 22 pastoral staff members and 130 lay leaders.

d. Bread of Life. Established as an outgrowth of home Bible studies, Cesar Butch Conde held the first service in Nov. 1982 in the auditorium of Maryknoll College with 120 people. The main church moved its services to a former cinema in Manila as the congregation grew to 7,500, with 60 daughter churches planted all over the country. Conde continues in leadership, and 43 local churches maintain fellowship within the Bread of Life Fellowship. (At one point, the Bread of Life Fellowship had close to 100 congregations throughout the country.)

Special attention has been given to prayer as a result of Conde's intense search for spirituality. He and his deacons made many trips to prayer mountains in Korea. As a result, he opened what was probably the first prayer mountain in the Philippines, Touch of Glory. The monthly prayer meeting is attended by close to 1,000 people. Many fast as many as 40 days, and many have experienced miraculous healing, baptism in the Spirit, and other miracles through prayer.

e. Word for the World. In the mid 1980s, Gerald Holloway, a CG missionary, started a Bible study with several businessmen in his garage. With the surge of interest in Scripture, especially among middle-class urban professionals, his group grew quickly. Eventually they moved to the Intercontinental Hotel ballroom, which set a new trend among independent charismatic fellowships. Although the church has remained within the organizational structure of the CG, it clearly assumed the characteristics of an independent charismatic fellowship. Within the first 10 years, congregations were planted all over the Philippines and even overseas. After a recent split, Word for the World Fellowship has 41 local churches with 7,100 members. They also have sent three cross-cultural missionary families.

f. Jesus Reigns Ministries. This group broke away from the Jesus Is the Lord Church in 1986. Vincent Javier and 7 pastors established this ministry, and at present there are close to 300 local congregations with 8 international ministries, more than 100 full-time workers, and a total membership numbering around 20,000. There are more than 30 training institutions, reportedly in local churches, and one school foundation. Vincent Javier is the current chairman.

g. Jesus Christ Saves Global Outreach. This ministry began in 1980 as a Bible study group for couples. The focus of this ministry, therefore, is the family. Presently there are 140 local congregations, 8 overseas churches, close to 5,000 workers (including volunteer workers), and 25,000 members. There are 2 training schools, and 350 missionary units have been sent out from this group; many reportedly are tent-makers ministering among overseas Filipino workers.

h. Others. There are countless smaller, often regional, charismatic fellowships and independent churches. Thus, it was not possible to bring all of their data together. However, there are several significant groups in this category.

Ecumenical Ministries was founded by Jesse Candelaria. This ministry has concentrated its effort in Pampanga and Tarlac in central Luzon. There are 30 churches with 100 workers and one training center.

Victory Christian Fellowship began in 1984 with a team of evangelists that included Steve Murrell from the U.S. By the end of the 1980s there were 6 churches in metro Manila, with approximately 1,000 members. At present there are 10 churches in the metropolitan area, 25 churches in the rest of the country, and 9 churches overseas. Eighty-seven ministers serve 4,800 members, and 10 training institutions prepare workers. There are 20 long-term missionary units, and more than 700 short-term missionaries.

At this point it is difficult to estimate with accuracy the number of Christians in this category, as the Philippines for Jesus Movement (PJM), the umbrella organization for independent charismatic churches or fellowships, does not maintain updated statistics. One also needs to remember that there are still many independent churches, especially outside of Manila, that are not affiliated with PJM.

3. Catholic Charismatics.

The beginning of the Catholic charismatic movement is not easy to pinpoint. One account traces the Urdaneta Village prayer meeting in Manila in July 1969 as the beginning of the Roman Catholic charismatic movement in the country, with Brother Aquinas as the principal figure. Their first prayer meeting was held in La Salle Greenhills. In 1972 Mother Marie Angela of the Assumption Convent Sisters began prayer groups after her experience of the Holy Spirit in Paris. During her visit to the Philippines, she explicitly preached the baptism in the Holy Spirit for each participant. This ministry resulted in a regular prayer group in San Lorenzo Village in Makati, Manila. A dramatic turning point came during the World Missionary Assistance Plan (or World MAP) conference outside of Manila in Apr. 1973. Close to 2,000 pastors, priests, nuns, missionaries, and lay leaders registered, representing 20 different denominations and groups. The conference publicly displayed the ecumenical character of the charismatic movement. Henceforth, various Catholic and independent prayer and Bible study groups mushroomed all over the country but particularly in the metro Manila area.

Several characteristics of this movement have emerged. Participants are extremely diligent in studying Scripture. More educated Catholic believers had a strong desire to study the Word of God for themselves, for which ►Vatican II undoubtedly provided a strong encouragement. As a result of this study, they began to adopt several non-Catholic concepts, such as being "born-again," which, doctrinally, is a Protestant experience. They also sought distinctively pentecostal experiences,

such as the baptism in the Spirit, spiritual gifts—especially speaking in tongues—and physical healing. The emotional richness and the religiosity of the Filipinos found in these pentecostal phenomena a suitable form of expression for their spirituality. Hence, joyful singing and fervent prayer became a vital tradition of the Catholic charismatic movement.

All of these factors, however, created an uneasy tension between the traditional Catholic leadership and charismatic adherents as the "fellowships" outside the church began to replace attendance at the Mass; eventually there was a slow but steady exodus of many faithful members from the Roman Catholic Church. This prompted the Bishops Conference to deal with the issue. First, they acknowledged the presence of this powerful movement both within and without the Catholic Church. Second, they also provided room within the Catholic Church of the Philippines to form such groups and to celebrate the work of the Spirit. One needs to admit, however, that all these provisions were made rather reluctantly in response to the steady exodus of Catholic believers to independent charismatic fellowships and pentecostal ("born-again") churches. Some of the results are seen in the development of large Catholic charismatic groups.

a. El Shaddai. After a miraculous healing, Mariano "Mike" Velarde acquired radio station DWXI and began to broadcast an evangelistic program entitled *To God Be the Glory.* Reports poured in that people received healing and renewal through the radio program. With its tremendous popularity, the ministry developed into El Shaddai DWXI Prayer Partners Foundation in Aug. 1984. The aim was to bring revival in the church by bringing back to the parishes those who have neglected their Christian duties and have continually failed to attend the Mass. Unlike Couples for Christ (see below) and many other Catholic charismatic groups, El Shaddai holds its own Sunday meetings. Various ministries, such as a jail ministry and monetary support for disaster victims, have developed, and Bible studies and prayer meetings are also being conducted.

Soon overseas groups were formed, primarily among migrant Filipino workers, beginning as prayer meetings. Evangelism is a critical part of the El Shaddai ministry; magazines, newsletters, and audiotapes are distributed free of charge to friends and employers. Once a new group grows, an arrangement is made with the Makati office for affiliation. Today there are "chapters" in Hong Kong, Canada, Singapore, the U.S., Japan, Italy, Greece, and many other countries.

In addition to the highly publicized Sunday worship services, El Shaddai holds home meetings for Bible study and prayer as well as prayer rallies, and conducts ►Life in the Spirit Seminars. Today, about 300,000 registered members identify with the group, but a much larger number—estimated to be as high as 2 million—attend Sunday gatherings throughout the country and abroad.

b. Couples for Christ. Couples for Christ (CFC) was founded in 1981 by 16 Catholic married couples to study a Christian life program. With a firm commitment to the Roman Catholic Church, CFC has a strong emphasis on evangelism and renewal. The early leaders believed that a family could be renewed only through individual renewal, and the church, in turn, only through renewed families. With a focus on evangelism and renewal of married couples, they conduct weekly household meetings for worship, sharing, and fellowship under the guidance of a leader. Their meetings are often characterized by charismatic elements such as prophecy, speaking and singing in tongues, praying for healing, and spontaneous praise. The work of the Holy Spirit, however, will be seen ultimately in the transformation of lives.

In 1992 the ministry expanded to include the family in general. Presently the group is called Couples for Christ Family Ministries and includes ministries for children (CFC Kids for Christ), youth (CFC Youth for Christ), singles (CFC Singles for Christ), and others (such as CFC Handmaids of the Lord). Also, there are 10 specialized ministries, including jail and police ministries and ministries among immigrant workers and the poor.

Two things stand out: (1) CFC's strong commitment to the Roman Catholic Church. From its inception, this group set out to evangelize the unchurched and to renew nominal Catholic members. Thus, CFC does not hold a Sunday celebration, but every member is expected to attend Mass in a local parish church. By strengthening families, the church will be strengthened, according to CFC's belief. (2) A commitment to evangelism. This genuinely Filipino religious movement has become a powerful missionary force, establishing CFC ministries in 57 countries. Often a lay couple is sent as a missionary unit to another country, where they approach national Catholic leadership to begin their ministry. Today around 1.5 million, including children, are estimated to be regular members of CFC.

c. Others. New Catholic charismatic bodies are established constantly, and it will take an extensive study to follow up this amazing development. The Bukas Loob Sa Diyos (BLD) Covenant Community originated in the Philippines; the name roughly translates as "Open in the Spirit of God." This community, "Roman Catholic in essence, charismatic in practice," is headed by Bishop Angel N. Lagdameo. The popular Marriage Encounter provides not only spiritual renewal for the faithful, but also evangelistic opportunity for not yet committed spouses. The ▸Life in the Spirit Seminars include baptism in the Spirit as their main component. Today BLD is found throughout the Philippines as well as in Hong Kong, Canada, and the U.S.

Other charismatic groups include the Agnus Dei Catholic Charismatic Community, Rivers of Living Water Catholic Community, Shine Forth Catholic Charismatic Community, and Tanglaw Ng Espiritu Santo Outreach Ministry.

In 1978 about 30,000 were counted as Catholic charismatics. Today this category can easily reach 5 million believers, if not more. This group is growing like a wildfire, and more charismatic communities are constantly being established. With the effective Life in the Spirit Seminars, popularly conducted for newcomers needing orientation to the charismatic life, many nominal Catholics find that charismatic groups provide a radically renewed Christian experience.

■ **Bibliography:** "The Christian Centennial Almanac: Facts and Figures of Denominations, Missions Agencies and Service Organizations," *Evangelicals Today* 25 (4, 1998) ■ W. Cuarto, "History of the Church of God in the Philippines" (unpub. paper, 1999) ■ A. Francis, *Charismatic Renewal in the Philippines* (1980) ■ K. Kitano, "Spontaneous Ecumenicity between Catholics and Protestants in the Charismatic Movement: A Case Study" (diss., Centro Escolar U., Manila, 1981).   ■ W. Ma

PITCAIRN ISLAND

■ Pentecostals 0   ■ Charismatics 0   ■ Neocharismatics 0   ■ Total Renewal: 0

POLAND

■ Pentecostals 42,731 (2%)   ■ Charismatics 1,820,705 (90%)   ■ Neocharismatics 151,564 (8%)   ■ Total Renewal: 2,015,000

See Europe, Eastern.

PORTUGAL

■ Pentecostals 86,176 (13%)   ■ Charismatics 270,279 (42%)   ■ Neocharismatics 285,545 (44%)   ■ Total Renewal: 642,000

The roots of Portuguese pentecostalism go back to the Swedish pentecostal missionaries ▸Daniel Berg and ▸Gunnar Vingren, who arrived in Brazil in 1911. When they brought the pentecostal message of baptism in the Holy Spirit to Belém do Pará, Brazil, among the first converts was the family of José Plácido da Costa (1869–1965). In Apr. 1913 the Plácido family left Brazil to become evangelists in Portugal. They began work in Porto, where they served as interim pastors of a Baptist congregation before moving to the interior. They were followed by José de Mattos (1888–1958), who had been converted in 1913 in Brazil and returned to Portugal in 1921. There he developed a literature distribution ministry in the provinces of Beira Alta and Beira Litoral. He then settled in Algarve, where the first pentecostal congregation was established. He pastored this congregation until 1938, when he shifted his focus to founding congregations across the country. The church in Porto was finally organized in 1934 by Daniel Berg. The church in Lisbon was started by another Swedish pentecostal missionary, Jack Härdstedt. Other Swedish missionaries included Samuel Buström (Portugal 1936–38) and Tage and Ingrid Stählberg, who served as missionaries from 1938 until 1976.

The Portuguese pentecostal church was born of mission and began its own mission activities in 1931 by sending Manuel Sequiera to the Azores. This was followed by mission involvement in Mozambique, Madeira, Guinea-Bissau, Timor, Macau, and Angola, as well as Spain. Pentecostal clergy also accompanied or followed emigrants to South Africa, Canada, the U.S., Germany, France, Belgium, France, Luxembourg, Switzerland, and Australia. In each of these, congregations have been founded that serve the Portuguese emigrants but also undertake evangelism among the indigenous populations.

The Casa Publicadora das Assembleias de Deus was founded in 1943. It has produced a continuous flow of books and periodicals. The periodicals include: *Novas de Alegria, Revista Avivamento, Expositor Dominical* (biblical education), and *Boa Semente* (children). The national hymnbook is *Cantos de Alegria*, supplemented by the gospel songbook *Coros de Alegria*. A yearbook, *Prontuário das Assembleias de Deus*, is published with addresses and organizational information by the Casa Publicadora das Assembleias de Deus. The movement has produced a number of prolific scholars. Alfredo Rosendo Machado has written extensive biblical commentaries, including a volume on Galatians *(A Magna Carta da Liberdade: Epístola aos Galatas)* and on the 12 minor prophets *(Os Doze Profetas Imortais)* as well as volumes on spirituality, including *Como Jesus vê as Igrejas* (1975), *Vem Ofim, Ofim Vem* (1976), and *Entregues ao Espíritu* (1976). Among the many other contributions to pentecostal theology and scholarship are the books of Jorge Pinheiro on messianism *(O Messiaismo)* and the commentary on the Book of Tobit by António de Costa Barata *(O Apócrifo Tobias)*. In addition, there have been missiological studies, including *O Nosso Mundo Clama* by Maj-Lis Johanson (1983); a study of the life and ministry of the Holiness leader Sadhu Sundar Singh by Boanerges Ribeiro *(O Apóstolo dos Pés Sangrentos);* and novels such as Elvira Lopes's *Um Romance a Bordo* (1983).

Education has long been a central concern of the tradition. The initial paradigm was to encourage youth to profit from the public education system in Portugal and to supplement that with three- or four-week "Bible school" sessions on the Scandinavian model. In 1965, at the 17th Annual Convention of Workers, in Portimão, the development of a Bible Institute was approved, which opened in Lisbon in 1966. Among the faculty were Dr. Jorge Pinheiro and Dr. Fernando Martinez. The school was moved to Fanhões-Loures in 1975. The advantage of the project was that it was financially feasible for the Portuguese pentecostal churches, and it also encouraged the development of a cadre of educated pentecostal laity and clergy with degrees from Portuguese universities. In 1972 the Assemblies of God (AG-U.S.) convinced the Portuguese church to allow them to build a bigger educational institution on the North American Bible school model. With funds from the U.S., the school was built on a tract of land outside Lisbon called Monte Esperança. The faculty came predominantly from the U.S., and the curriculum and textbooks were built on the U.S. model.

Eleventh Annual Youth Congress, Lisbon, Portugal, in 1975.

In 1981 the Assembleias de Deus de Portugal reported 11,116 adult baptized members with another 15,000 adherents and Sunday school students in 12 congregations and 305 prayer houses/preaching points. Another 2,890 individuals were adult baptized members of churches in the Portuguese diaspora. By 1984 Paulo Branco reported 20,000 adult baptized members and 10,000 adherents with a Sunday school attendance of more than 7,500. In 1998 there were about 35,000 members and an equal growth in adherents. The Assembleias de Deus is the largest non-Catholic church in Portugal.

Portuguese pentecostalism has also been influenced by the "faith healing movement." Among the publications of the Casa Publicadora das Assembleias de Deus are several books by David Wilkerson, Gordon Lindsay, and Kathryn Kuhlman. More recently the Igreja Universal do Reino de Deus, founded in Brazil by ⟩Bishop E. Macedo, has developed a major presence in the country. In 1972 the United Pentecostal Church was founded in Portugal. It has (1999) two congregations with about 60 members. Among the other pentecostal churches in Portugal are the Church of God (Cleveland, TN), Church of God of Prophecy, and the Igreja Evangélica Pentecostal. There have also been missionaries from the Finnish Pentecostal Church, the Norwegian Pentecostal Church, and the ⟩AG in Great Britain and Ireland. These latter groups have worked to strengthen the Assembleias de Deus of Portugal.

Far more numerous than the classical Pentecostals are the Roman Catholic Charismatics, who number ca. 269,000 (out of a total of approximately 9 million Catholics in Portugal). By far the largest Neocharismatic group is the Mana Igreja Crista (Mana Christian Church), founded in 1980 as an outgrowth of a cell-based megachurch in Lisbon. It currently numbers about 75,000 members in Portugal, with a considerably larger following in twenty other countries (Europe, Africa, and South America). Mana leaders steadfastly refuse to be pulled into existing Pentecostal ecclesiastical structures.

■ **Bibliography:** L. K. Ahonen, *Suomen helluntaiheratyksen historia* (1994) ■ E. J. Anturi, "Helluntaiheratyksen toiminnen tarastelua," in Kai Anturi et al., *Helluntaiheratys tanaan* (1986) ■ A. C. Barata et al., *Linguas de Fogo: História da Assembleia de Deus em Lisboa* (Lisbon, 1999) ■ D. B. Barrett et al., *World Christian Encyclopedia* (1982) ■ Å. Boberg, *Svensk Pingstmission* (1990) ■ P. Branco, *Panorama Pentecostal das Assembleias de Deus em Portugal* (1981) ■ idem, *Pentecostes: Un Desafio al Mundo* (1984), 107–13 ■ D. L. Burk, *Foreign Mission Insight, 1999* (1999), 109 ■ A. Hämäläinen, ed., *Kaikkeen maailman 1929–1989: 60 vuotta helluntaiseurahuntien lähetystyöyä* (1989) ■ *Igreja Mana: Convensao de Fe* 92 (1992) ■ A. Ruuth, *Igreja Universal do Reino de Deus: Gudsrikets Universella Kyrka—en brasiliansk kyrkobildning. Resumen: Iglesia Universal del Reino de Dios* (1995) ■ E. Söderholm, *Den Svenska Pingstväckelsens spridning utom och inom Sverige* (1933), 181–88 ■ A. Sundstedt, *Pingstväckelsen*, 5 vols. (1967–73) ■ Materials provided by Adele Flower Dalton. In addition, numerous articles can be found in Portuguese, Norwegian, and especially Swedish pentecostal periodicals.
■ D. D. Bundy

PUERTO RICO

■ Pentecostals 239,572 (23%) ■ Charismatics 544,717 (53%) ■ Neocharismatics 240,711 (23%) ■ Total Renewal: 1,025,000

The earliest stages of pentecostalism in Puerto Rico are to be found in the stories of a Puerto Rican emigrant who returned to the island as a pentecostal evangelist. ⟩Juan Lugo and his friend Salomón Feliciano Quiñones, later a missionary to the Dominican Republic, experienced the pentecostal baptism of the Holy Spirit during a revival in Hawaii in June 1913. Both returned to Puerto Rico in 1916 via San Francisco and Los Angeles. The early days were difficult. There were no foreign-support funds, and it was difficult to find work. Lugo began preaching in Santurce without results. Later Lugo and Salomón Feliciano Quiñones went to Ponce, where together they established the first pentecostal church in Puerto Rico. From Ponce, evangelists went to other villages and cities. By 1920 there were at least eight pentecostal congregations. A U.S. missionary, ⟩Frank O. Finkenbinder, played an important role in the early evangelistic efforts. Laypersons were crucially involved in both the evangelism and in the leadership of the resultant congregations. Short-term theological education on the Scandinavian model became the predominant form of leadership development.

1. The Iglesia de Dios Pentecostal.

The mission became affiliated (1921) with the U.S. Assemblies of God (AG), but because the government would not recognize the name "Assemblies," the name Iglesia de Dios Pentecostal (Pentecostal Church of God) was chosen. Juan Lugo moved to the U.S. in 1929 to pastor a congregation in Brooklyn and to organize Puerto Rican congregations in the New York area. In 1956 the relationship with the AG–U.S. was terminated, and the Iglesia de Dios Pentecostal declared itself independent of all foreign intervention—an independence that had already become more or less a de facto reality before then. For example, in 1941 more than 91% of the denominational budget came from Puerto Rican congregations; this included the Istituto Bíblíco Mizpa established in 1937 for ministerial training.

By 1969 the Iglesia de Dios Pentecostal could claim 34 Bible school students, 25,000 members, and 200 congregations. In addition there were 16 missionaries in other countries, including the U.S., the Dominican Republic, Cuba, Haiti, Costa Rica, Panama, Colombia, Venezuela, Honduras, Mexico, Portugal, and Spain. This church continues to be the largest pentecostal church in Puerto Rico. In 1980 the church claimed 30,000 members and another 60,000 adherents in 207 congregations. Around 1990, there were about 470 congregations and 75,000 members. A split occurred in Iglesia de Dios Pentecostal in 1938, resulting in the Iglesia Pentecostal de Jesucristo (2,500 members by 1963; 4,400 by 1980).

2. The Iglesia de Dios.

Church of God (CG, Cleveland, TN) mission statesman ►J. H. Ingram visited Puerto Rico in July 1944 and convinced four pastors of three independent congregations totaling 147 members in San Juan and Santurce to join the denomination. A U.S. missionary, C. E. French, was appointed overseer. A year later French's interpreter, Antonio Collazo (son-in-law of Juan Lugo), brought his four independent congregations into the denomination. The next growth spurt occurred when Frank Hernández brought his Roca de Salvación denomination with 1,000 members and 26 preachers into the CG. The primary initial growth of the CG in Puerto Rico was through the early mergers.

From 1948 until 1958 Collazo served as overseer. In 1958, however, Collazo was transferred to the U.S. to organize Hispanic churches, and a U.S. missionary, W. D. Alton, was appointed to replace him. This change away from indigenous leadership, combined with other cultural insensitivities at a time of heightened nationalist awareness in Puerto Rico, caused the growth rate to decline to slightly more than 1% per year, far less than the birth rate. By 1980 the church claimed about 3,300 members, roughly half of whom lived in the San Juan metropolitan area.

3. Other Mission Churches.

Other North American mission churches include the Iglesia del Evangelio Quadrangular (Church of the Foursquare Gospel, 1934), the Iglesia de Dios de la Profecia (Church of God of Prophecy, 1938), the Open Bible Standard Churches (1958), and the Asambleas de Dios, which resulted from the union of a single congregation with the U.S. AG (1957). This brought AG missionaries back to the island. By 1987 the Asambleas de Dios claimed 179 congregations and 18,991 members. In 1964 (some sources say 1962) United Pentecostal Church missionary H. Glen Smith began work in Puerto Rico. This resulted in the Iglesia Pentecostal Unida, which claims 1,200 constituents in 22 congregations (1999). The Iglesia Evangélica El Buen Pastor is a "Oneness" church founded by missionaries from Mexico.

There are also a large number of independent pentecostal ministries in Puerto Rico, as well as ministries from the U.S., Canada, and Mexico.

4. The Influence of Francisco Olazábal in Puerto Rico.

►Francisco Olazábal (1886–1937) had a large influence in Puerto Rico. He had studied at the Methodist Seminary in San Potosi, Mexico, and immigrated to the U.S. In 1917, under the influence of ►Carrie Judd Montgomery, he experienced the pentecostal baptism in the Holy Spirit and affiliated with the AG. However, in 1923 he disaffiliated and established the Latin American Council of Christian Churches (LACCC). Olazábal demonstrated the efficacy and desirability of Hispanic leadership of indigenous Hispanic churches. He also proved himself an effective international evangelist and served as a model for many. He encouraged the development of ties between Puerto Rico and the Puerto Rican diaspora for spiritual and ecclesial communication and self-reliance. The churches established under his influence have always been self-supporting, self-governing, and self-propagating. After his death the LACCC split along Mexican/Puerto Rican lines. The Asamblea de Iglesias Cristianas was organized (1937) in New York. It began mission work in Puerto Rico in 1940. By 1999 this denomination claimed about 165 congregations with about 10,000 members in Puerto Rico.

Olazábal also influenced the formation of the Iglesia Defensores de la Fe. This church began in 1934 under the leadership of Juan Francisco Rodríguez Rivera, a onetime Christian and Missionary Alliance pastor, as an evangelistic effort with no intention of establishing a denomination. However, already by the end of 1934 congregations had been established. By 1950 there were 26 congregations and missionaries in the U.S. and the Dominican Republic. In 1963 membership had reached 3,834, and by 1980 there were more than 8,000 members with perhaps another 15,000 adherents. The church has remained totally indigenous.

The Iglesia de Cristo de las Antillas was started in 1934 as a result of the evangelistic work of Olazábal. In 1938 a majority of the denomination decided to rename itself the Iglesia de Cristo Misionera. A large group continued as the Iglesia de Cristo en las Antillas. The resulting two denominations have continued to grow. Ironically the Iglesia de Cristo en las Antillas later changed its name to Iglesia Universal de Jesucristo. The two denominations together have (1999) about 276 congregations and about 18,000 members.

5. The Other Pentecostal Churches.

There are other indigenous pentecostal denominations and congregations in Puerto Rico. The Iglesia pentecostal de Jesucristo was founded in Fajardo in 1938 and was led for decades by the renowned Benito Cintrón Santana. By 1966 there were about 3,250 members and about 7,000 by 1980. The Iglesia de Dios was founded in 1940 by a group of nine Puerto Rican pastors. A smaller denomination, the Samaria Iglesia Evangélica was founded in 1941 by Puerto Rican evangelist Julio Guzmán Silva. Other indigenous churches include the Asamblea Cristiana, Concilio de Dios Apostólica, Iglesia de Dios Primitiva, and Iglesia Evangélica del Avivamiento.

6. Charismatic Revival in the Iglesia Discipulos de Cristo.

Puerto Rico also witnessed a charismatic revival among the Puerto Rican clergy and members of the Christian Church (Disciples of Christ) (CCDC) beginning in 1933. The term *charismatic* is the term of preference in the Iglesia Discipulos de Cristo, although the documents of the 1930s exclusively use the term *pentecostal* to describe the phenomenon. The social and theological roots of this revival are quite complex. It began at the Iglesia de la Calle de Comerío at the end of Dec. 1932, under the leadership of the layperson Leonardo Castro. It spread throughout the church. The American mission of the CCDC made every effort to control and eradicate the revival. Funds were cut off and pastors, including Carmelo Álvarez-Pérez and Joaquin Vargas, were left with no salary. They became self-supporting and very influential pastors.

While the mission and missionaries of the CCDC were able to control the funds and the organization, they were unable to dampen the spirituality and the oral theology. The church has worked to maintain a balance between experience and theological reflection. One of the results of the revival was that the Discipulos de Cristo became the fastest-growing "mainline" denomination. C. Manley Morton, one of the missionaries involved in the repression, returned to Puerto Rico in 1972, just before his death, to apologize for his role in the earlier events and was reconciled to the Puerto Rican church. Members of this church, the Iglesia Discipulos de Cristo, have been very influential in ministry and ecumenism throughout Latin America, Asia, and Europe. This church has paved the way for the CCDC to be in "partnership" with pentecostal churches in Africa and Latin America. There has also been an influence on the charismatic movement in the Catholic and other Protestant churches.

■ **Bibliography:** Anon., *Constitución y reglamento de la Iglesia de Cristo Misionera* (rev. ed. 1962) ■ Anon., *Constitución y reglamento de la Iglesia de Dios Pentecostal* (rev. ed. 1954) ■ Anon., *Constitución y reglamento de la Mision de Iglesias de Cristo en las Antillas* (1963) ■ Anon., *Fire by Night and Cloud by Day: A History of Defenders of the Christian Faith* (1966) ■ P. S. Aponte, "Creación de Programa de Capellanía para Centro de Tratamiento Social (Hogar de Niñas) de Puerto Rico" (paper, Puerto Rico Extension, Church of God School of Theology, 1986) ■ D. L. Burk, ed., *Foreign Missions Insight: A Digest of Foreign Missions Faces, Facts, Fields and Figures* (1999), 86–87 ■ I. Caraballo, "Reflections of a Bible College Teacher" (paper, CG School of Theol., 1986) ■ C. W. Conn, *Like a Mighty Army: A History of the Church of God* (1955; rev. 1977) ■ idem, *Where the Saints Have Trod: A History of Church of God Missions* (1959) ■ P. Humphrey, *J. H. Ingram, Missionary Dean* (1966) ■ J. H. Ingram, *Around the World with Gospel Light* (1938) ■ A. L. Laruffa, "Culture Change and Pentecostalism in Puerto Rico," *Social and Economic Studies* 18 (1969) ■ idem, "Pentecostalism in a Puerto Rican Community" (diss., Columbia U., 1966; published as *San Cipolano: Life in a Puerto Rican Community* [1971]) ■ J. L. Lugo, *Pentecostés en Puerto Rico: Vida du un Missionero* (1951) ■ [H. McCracken], *History of Church of God Missions* (1943) ■ D. T. Moore, *Puerto Rico para Cristo: A History of the Progress of the Evangelical Missions on the Island of Puerto Rico* (1969) ■ S. W. Mintz, *Worker in the Cane: A Puerto Rican Life History* (1960; repr. 1974) ■ T. L. Osborn, *Revival Harvest with Miracles of Healing: Puerto Rico* (n.d.) ■ R. Perez-Torres, "The Pastor's Role in the Educational Ministry in the Pentecostal Church of God in Puerto Rico" (diss., School of Theol. at Claremont, 1979) ■ J. M. Rivera, "The Church in Puerto Rico: A Public Nuisance?" *Christian Century* 91 (Apr. 17, 1974) ■ A. Rodrigues de Navas, "La Educatión Ministerial a traves de los Centros de Extensión del Colegio Bíblico Pentecostal de P.R." (paper, Puerto Rico Extension, CG School of Theol., 1986) ■ R. E. Rodriguez and C. E. Álvarz, eds., *Visiones de Fe: Reflexiones Teológicos-Pastorales del Rev. Carmelo Álvarez-Pérez* (1984) ■ J. Vargas, *Los Discipulos de Cristo en Puerto Rico: albores, crecimiento y madurez de un peregrnar de fe, constancia y esperanze, 1899–1987* (1988) ■ A. Wilfredo Estrada, "The Reconciliation of Charismatic Pastors and Bible School Professors in the Service of Training for Future Ministry in the Pentecostal Bible College of the Church of God" (diss., Candler School of Theol., 1982).　　　　■ D. D. Bundy

QATAR

■ Pentecostals 0 (0%)　■ Charismatics 4,019 (28%)　■ Neocharismatics 10,381 (72%)　■ Total Renewal: 14,400

See AFRICA, NORTH, AND THE MIDDLE EAST.

RÉUNION

■ Pentecostals 23,624 (43%)　■ Charismatics 30,727 (56%)　■ Neocharismatics 649 (1%)　■ Total Renewal: 55,000

ROMANIA

■ Pentecostals 859,219 (64%)   ■ Charismatics 366,008 (27%)   ■ Neocharismatics 124,773 (9%)   ■ Total Renewal: 1,350,000

I. The Pentecostal Phenomenon in Romania after World War I (1917–31)

II. The REEM Period (1931–41)

III. Romanian Pentecostalism from World War II to 1989

IV. Romanian Pentecostalism from 1989 to the Present

I. THE PENTECOSTAL PHENOMENON IN ROMANIA AFTER WORLD WAR I (1917–31).

The Romanian pentecostal movement, with its rich heritage, experienced wide and rapid growth after the beginning of WWI with a sudden, spontaneous eruption in all the provinces of the country. As a result, it is difficult to ascertain the exact time and place of the movement's inception. Several sources, some more reliable than others, document these early days. A prime source links the northern part of Romania (Moldavia/Bukovina) with the birthplace of the pentecostal movement. As early as 1918, several villages of Bukovina received the pentecostal faith. Reliable records certify that WWI Romania veteran Nişu Constantin received the apostolic teachings from the Russian pentecostal believers with whom he had previous contacts during his army service in Russia (1914–18). When Nişu returned to his birthplace in Vicovul de Sus in 1918, he laid the foundation for a pentecostal community there. This nucleus of believers resembled the Russian pentecostal type of assembly Nişu had already encountered. In fact, Nişu's wife, Justina, had been noted as a recognized prophetess in Vicovul de Sus by 1920. Another source from the same geographical area attests the pentecostal ministry of Filaret Rotaru (1885–1959) from Udeşti. Rotaru received the apostolic faith in the U.S. sometime between 1911 and 1916, after his miraculous healing. As early as 1918, Rotaru spread the new teachings in northern Romania. Indeed, a distinct group of believers who exercised pentecostal manifestations had been established in Udeşti prior to 1922.

In contrast to the limited sources claiming Moldavia/Bukovina as the birthplace of Romanian pentecostalism, an impressive collection of data endorses the large ring-like region of Transylvania as the legitimate cradle of the movement. Two theories are noteworthy in this respect. The first is supported by Eugenie Bodor, an itinerant evangelist and teacher who has known the apostolic faith since 1929. Bodor wanted to collect "precise and reliable" historical facts, interviewing protagonists and eyewitnesses of the earliest known pentecostal manifestations in Romania. His research points specifically to the central area of Transylvania as the cradle of Romanian pentecostalism. According to Bodor, traveling circles of German Pietists spread the full-gospel message in the town of Mediaş, in the heart of the large Transylvanian Basin even before 1919. Their fiery messages triggered an awakening among the Transylvanian Saxons (Lutherans) of Mediaş and the surrounding area. Ardent prayers and tarrying for the Holy Spirit were reported among these groups of believers. Bodor states that the first evidences of Pentecost in Romania occurred during July 5–13, 1921, in the villages Dîrlos and Curei, within the central Carpathian plateau.

Several indigenous and nonindigenous sources corroborate Bodor's thesis. There are indications that the central area of Transylvania was visited in 1919 by a German-American sister called Konerth who preached the apostolic message in Dîrlos (district of Sibiu). This evidence suggests that a local congregation with pentecostal believers may have existed prior to 1919, since at least one indigenous woman had already experienced Spirit baptism.

Furthermore, an American missionary article, published in 1938, brings additional support. The report describes an episode that occurred either before or shortly after WWI. In this account, three German-speaking women from the central districts of Transylvania paid a short visit to Berlin, Germany, in order to received the water baptism after reading an article published in a German pentecostal magazine. Apparently they did not know any minister in Romania at that time who could perform this act. In Berlin the ladies met the pentecostal pastor who was, in fact, the editor of that publication. After baptizing the ladies in water, the pastor insisted that they tarry until they received the baptism with the Holy Spirit. Upon their return to Romania, one of these young women felt the call of God for evangelism and became "the first to carry Pentecost to [Romania], which resulted in a remarkable revival."

Another record consistent with Bodor's account indicates that the missionary work of Georg Stehn from Sweden in the central area of Transylvania is closely related to the earliest Romanian pentecostal roots. Unquestionably, his connections with the Transylvanian Saxons and his role in organizing their incipient apostolic assemblies make him one of the first pentecostal pioneers of Romania.

Other distinguished native chroniclers, such as Trandafir Sandru and Pavel Bochian, believe, in contrast to Bodor's theory, that the Romanian apostolic movement began on Sept. 10, 1922, on the western side of Transylvania, specifically at Pşuliş (district of Arad). From here then radiated the national pentecostal awakening. In this view, the Romanian apostolic faith appears as an indigenous experience without significant influences from any external sources. Nevertheless, the proponents of this position admit that the birth of Romanian pentecostalism was assisted by an indigenous "midwife"—the Romanian-American Assemblies of God (AG) evangelist Paul Budean.

Born in Romania and later emigrating to the U.S., Budean wrote tracts of his conversion and distributed them as evangelistic tools. As early as 1922, one of his brochures was sent overseas and impacted the life of George Bradin (1895–1962) from Pşuliş, who was to become one of the remarkable spiritual fathers of the Romanian apostolic faith. Later Bradin came to be depicted as the sole founder of the movement, according to Sandru and Bochian, who are both natives of the district of Arad and were involved in leading some of Bradin's later campaigns.

Several factors motivated Bradin to leave his Baptist congregation and embrace the new apostolic teachings. First, in 1921 he received reliable information from Romanian friends who emigrated to the U.S. about the manifestations of the Holy Spirit in the revival meetings of the renowned evangelist Aimee Semple McPherson. This news stirred Bradin's interest in divine healing and the baptism with the Holy Spirit. His wife, Persida, who was suffering from tuberculosis, experienced a miraculous healing after reading one of Budean's tracts. In addition, a booklet published by the Church of God (Cleveland, TN) reached Bradin and challenged him tremendously toward a life of holiness. Budean entered into an extensive correspondence with Bradin and in so doing nurtured the latter's pentecostal faith. Finally, Budean paid a visit to Romania and attempted to effect official recognition of the new movement. In 1924, when Budean met Bradin and his small group of followers, he witnessed severe persecution against born-again believers on the part of the political and religious supporters of the dominant Greek Orthodox Church. After he returned to the U.S., Budean designed a resolution in 1924 that, through the General Council of the AG–U.S., reached the United States government and requested that it petition the Romanian kingdom of Ferdinand I to grant religious freedom and spiritual tolerance to the pentecostals.

Under Bradin's leadership, the movement gradually penetrated Banat, Transylvania, and Moldavia. Bradin was a fervent advocate of "foot washing." This church practice became a main issue in the doctrinal agenda of his large, rapidly growing group. Later this main branch became known as the Apostolic Church of God. When the movement expanded, several groups of pentecostal believers dissociated themselves from Bradin's group. They disagreed with Bradin's inflexible interpretation of certain doctrinal matters, such as the biblical teaching of John 13. As a result, a new body of apostolic believers emerged in the Romanian pentecostal movement, known as the Christians Baptized with the Holy Spirit (CBHS) and led by John Bododea, which gained an influential role during the 1930s and 1940s. Thus, the Romanian pentecostal mainstream divided before the ▸Russian and Eastern European Mission (REEM) began to launch its missionary operations in the field.

II. THE REEM PERIOD (1931–41).

Romania entered the orbit of REEM's priorities at the beginning of 1931 through the efforts of Paul Budean and John Bododea. Before this, 130 pentecostal assemblies had already been established through indigenous efforts, with a total attendance of almost 2,000.

Throughout the 1920s, the full gospel message spread predominately by means of untrained ministers. Although this work proved to be extensive, it was also extremely disorganized. Budean reasoned that only a foreign mission could provide the necessary resources to assist and sustain the national spiritual harvest. His insistent plea to REEM to include Romania in its missionary agenda was successful in Jan. 1931. Two short prospective visits of C. W. Swanson and Paul S. Rahneff in Arad and Bucharest established the bridgehead of REEM for its future Romanian missionary endeavor.

Romanian pentecostal church leaders meeting in Bucharest in 1967. (Front row) A. Vamvu; D. Matache; André Nicholle, visiting French pentecostal leader; Pavel Bochian, president of the Apostolic Church of God; and Trandafir Sandru, director of the Pentecostal Theological Seminary.

Swanson's 1930 blueprint for the REEM pilot program indicates the starting of operations on the eastern side of the country through the already existing connections from Bulgaria, as well as the establishment of contacts in the western area through Hungarian agents. After the program was in place, it targeted the ethnic groups that existed in all the provinces.

During the 1930s, the fruitful activity of REEM in Romania materialized through a consistent training program of leaders and assemblies, financial support for renting public halls, and, in a limited form, supporting the expenses of a few of their representatives. Although only three full-time ministers were designated to receive a financial sponsorship in the initial phase, at least two others received and reported monetary benefits from the society by 1940.

REEM did not want to get involved in the controversial issues that had already divided the Romanian pentecostal mainstream. Despite its openness, the missionary agency was not welcomed by the pro-Bradin segment. The leader from Pşuliş resisted, probably afraid that the missionary "intruders" would launch a rival work that could jeopardize not only his own prestige but also the expansion of his group. In these circumstances, REEM decided to cooperate with indigenous workers who had manifested a sympathetic attitude toward its involvement in the field. Therefore, by the end of WWII, the CBHS became the major supporters of REEM's missionary projects in Romania. Beginning in 1931, John Bododea, the leader of the CBHS, represented the first recruited Romanian minister to develop and maintain a connection with REEM. His zealous disciples included Vasile Gaşpar (Banat and Wallachia), Alexandru Izbaşa (Banat and Severin), Ioachim Şunea (Banat), Pantelimon Cojocaru, Vasile Catargiu (northern Moldavia), and Eugenie Bodor (itinerant national evangelist). They were among the first pioneers to spread the pentecostal teachings. Starting in 1929, Bododea oversaw the editing of two pentecostal monthly papers, *The Word of Truth* (with a circulation of 1,400 copies) and *Sunday School Lessons* (800 copies). At Brşila he was involved in editing and printing the first Romanian pentecostal hymnbook, *A Harp of Christian Choir* (1931). He also authored a *Pilot Report, Baptism of the Holy Spirit, The Spiritual Gifts in the Light of the Scripture,* and a *Study in Revelation.* Eugenie Bodor was probably the most qualified pentecostal worker before and after WWII. In 1931 Bodor made contact with G. H. Schmidt and Gustav Kinderman. During 1932–34, Bodor edited and printed several works, including a Romanian songbook, *Constitution of Assemblies of God for the Pentecostal Fellowship, Principles of Faith of the Pentecostal Assemblies of Romania,* and *The Apostolic Faith.* Three thousand copies of the last booklet were printed. These resources reveal a constant care of the Spirit-filled assemblies to have a solid foundation in biblical truth. The amount of Christian literature in circulation among the apostolic congregations at that time

may also indicate the wide influence of, and deep interest in using, print media.

In Feb. 1931 ▸Joseph Wannenmacher sailed for Eastern Europe to preach and minister in music in Hungary and Romania. This faithful and dedicated violinist, who gave powerful testimonies in both countries, was probably one of the first missionaries of REEM sent to Romania.

From 1927 to 1934 the western Romanian provinces adjacent to Hungary (Banat and Transylvania) were evangelized through the industrious efforts of John Lerch. Based on successful experiences in the mission field of Gyonk, Hungary, this ambitious Hungarian-American evangelist proposed an effective strategy for church planting from his newly established Romanian pilot stations in Timişoara and Oradea. Indeed, Lerch made one of the earliest attempts of the society to establish official representation in Romania. He is credited with being the first foreign source to report to his officials in Danzig (Poland) about the necessity of trained ministers in Romania. Also, he was an eyewitness to the clashes between the two largest pentecostal groups on the much-disputed subject of foot washing. In 1934 Miss Vera Nitsch, the matron of REEM seminary from Danzig, spent two months among the German communities in Transylvania and Banat. Her reports deserve significant consideration. Nitsch was the first foreign visitor to recognize the widespread interest in Christian educational training among the Romanian pentecostals. She told about believers who would be willing to attend (Western) European seminaries in order to become more efficient ministers in their native land. Thus, a Romanian peasant-preacher from Siebenburgen (Transylvania) attended a Bible conference in Vienna (Austria) and returned and testified among his countrymen.

The charismatic authority of Paul Peterson and ▸Gustave H. Schmidt in leading Bible conferences is noteworthy. Several trips by Schmidt to Bucharest, Timişoara, Oradea, and Iassy occurred between 1931 and 1938. In 1935 Peterson and Gustav Kinderman led conferences primarily in the Moldavian sector of Romania. That same year, Bodor reports that Schmidt organized Bible studies in Transylvania among the Saxon assemblies. In reaction to the unstable and repressive political climate of Romania from 1932 to 1934, many of these conferences were organized secretly to preserve the lives of those in attendance.

It is significant to note that the REEM philosophy of missions was successfully applied in Romania. On Aug. 12, 1940, Paul Peterson informed ▸Noel Perkin that REEM had maintained "active workers" in Romania and other Eastern European countries. According to Peterson, REEM had succeeded in establishing "a self-governing group" in each land. The native workers had been trained for and initiated in new leadership responsibilities. The tenderly planted churches were also "self-propagating" (the technique of establishing "self-supporting" indigenous churches in Eastern Europe found a fervent advocate in the person of ▸Donald Gee).

III. ROMANIAN PENTECOSTALISM FROM WORLD WAR II TO 1989.

The expansion of the military conflict in WWII led to dramatic turning points in the missionary programs, such as the evacuation of the bulk of REEM's staff from East European countries. In reaction to either Nazi invasions or Communist persecutions, a significant segment of ministers of the apostolic faith, mostly from Poland, Russia, Bulgaria, and Hungary left their newly established congregations and emigrated to North and South America. In Romania, by contrast, the circle of ministers who had embraced pentecostal beliefs continued to remain in contact with their assemblies. In any case, these brave, Spirit-filled believers risked their lives by defying Communist threats, thus ensuring the continued existence and future growth of the apostolic church in Romania. Shortly after WWII, the national appeal of King Michael I for religious liberty and reconciliation triggered an enthusiastic reaction among the persecuted groups, including the pentecostals. As noted, even before 1941 Romanian pentecostals were divided into two camps. After the war both groups looked for legitimized status and applied for official approval. In response to their independent requests, the Ministry of Religious Denominations gave a provisory recognition to the Apostolic Church of God (1946) and to the Christians Baptized with the Holy Spirit (1947). (Shortly thereafter a third pentecostal faction known as the Disciples of the Lord, led by John Jiloveanu, also received official recognition. This small group was confined primarily to the area of Bucharest and did not play a significant role in the pentecostal movement.)

Sporadic efforts had been made since 1934 to bring the two main groups together, but these attempts failed to achieve lasting results. Animated by a common desire for fraternal unity, several delegates of these groups initiated intense, mutual contacts during 1946–50 and tried to negotiate terms of agreement. The mediating role of Pavel Bochian (Transylvania), Izbaşa Alexandru (Banat), Eugenie Bodor, and Irimiciuc Gheorghe (Bukovina) was decisive in completing the unifying process of all apostolic churches; a consensus was finally reached in early 1950. With regard to the contentious issue of foot washing, both groups agreed to preserve their own doctrinal distinctiveness. The agreement succeeded in uniting nearly all Spirit-filled believers despite their different interpretations of John 13. The subsequent inclusion of the small group of the Disciples of the Lord in 1948 established a trilateral

union known as the Pentecostal Apostolic Church of God (PACG). On Nov. 14, 1950, the newly formed bloc, encompassing almost 36,000 believers, received the official recognition of the procommunist government of Dr. Petru Groza. George Bradin became the first president of PACG in the summer of 1951. In the 1950s the pentecostal denomination was exposed to an extensive process of reorganization. Short-term seminar courses for the training of new ministers through an extension program were organized in various places in Romania (Arad, Rşdşupi, Timişoara, and Bucharest). Also, the *Bulletin of the Pentecostal Church* distinguished itself with its first issue in Sept. 1953 as a major information channel for Spirit-filled believers. The peaceful time did not last long for PACG, however. From the mid 1950s to the mid 1960s the totalitarian apparatus designed new methods to tighten control over born-again believers. The authorities put pentecostal leaders under systematic, rigid supervision and censorship. Far exceeding their brief and prerogatives, government officials attempted to manipulate or intimidate those PACG ministers who had manifested "malleability" during the communist "reform." Often the nonconformists were in danger of losing their ministerial credentials and jeopardizing the official standing of their churches. Also, it became virtually impossible to get the required permit to build a church. A bureaucratic tangle of red tape had been put in place to discourage any further efforts of the petitioners.

Throughout the tumultuous years of postwar reconstruction, profound economic and sociodemographic changes occurred in Romania. As the industrialization of the country expanded rapidly, a shift in population took place from rural, agrarian regions to the cities. As a result, beginning in the 1950s, the spreading of the apostolic faith in Romania shifted to the towns and cities. Then, with enormous risks and sac-

A congregation in Bucharest, Romania, in 1972.

rifices, numerous prayer houses were erected all over the country, predominantly from the 1960s to the 1980s.

The inauguration of president Nicolae Ceauşescu of Romania in Dec. 1967 inaugurated a type of Marxist communism that initially promised to be different than the Soviet pattern. During the first years of his leadership, Ceauşescu, initiated domestic reform favorable to all religious groups, including pentecostals. Foreign visitors were allowed to come to Romania without restrictions and to observe the "religious freedom."

As early as 1968, the leaders of PACG were allowed to participate in various world and European pentecostal conferences and to establish friendly connections with their counterparts from international pentecostal branches. Through PACG these external contacts became more informed about the spiritual needs of the Romanian people. They began to sustain the indigenous work, mainly through the church construction program, by supplying funds for denominational literature and in the founding of the Pentecostal Theological Seminary in Bucharest.

After George Bradin's death in 1962, Pavel Bochian became the newly elected leader of PACG. Respected in both religious and secular circles for his shrewd diplomacy, Bochian pursued a conciliatory policy during 1962–90. Although the evangelization of Romania after 1944 was essentially an indigenous undertaking, the country continued to remain in the focus of international regard.

Since the beginning of the 1960s, prominent officials from AG missionary centers in Western Europe and the U.S. agreed to include the countries behind the Iron Curtain in their agenda. In this matter J. Philip Hogan, the executive director of the AG Division of Foreign Missions, took note that Andre Nicolle, the general superintendent of AG–France, had been appointed by the European conference at Frankfurt to help pentecostal churches in Romania and to establish relationships with the local representatives. During the 1960s a British pentecostal agency represented by J. P. Wildrianne also included Romania in its missionary strategy by informing the European and American partners of the latest religious and sociopolitical aspects of Romanian life, noting possibilities for mutual collaboration and highlighting critical needs of the Romanian Spirit-filled believers.

The distinguished European leaders drew up several reports with data pertaining to the cardinal points of a successful missionary program in Romania. According to Nicolle, the "foursquare" agenda should include (1) building new churches, (2) discipleship and spiritual assistance, (3) sending Bibles and Christian literature, and (4) training indigenous ministers.

Apparently the most significant contribution of AG leaders from Europe and the U.S. during the 1960s and '70s was performed in the arena of social assistance. In 1967 and 1970 two disastrous floods affected large areas of the country. On July 28, 1970, Laurenşiu Fotescu, the head of the Romanian Red Cross, sent a letter of appreciation to the Division of Foreign Missions of the AG–U.S. He expressed appreciation for the humanitarian aid performed by Stephen Gulyas, a Hungarian-American AG minister who had donated $5,000 for medical relief for the flood's victims. On Mar. 4, 1977, a violent earthquake devastated Bucharest, the capital of Romania. More than 1,500 people died in the ruins and 10,000 were injured. In response, Robert Mackish, the American missionary representative of the AG for Eastern Europe solicited from Rev. C. E. Greenaway, secretary of DFM for Eurasia, $30,000 in financial assistance for the Romanian people ($15,000 for hospital reconstruction and $15,000 for rebuilding churches). As early as 1969, spiritual and material assistance was also furnished by representatives from the Church of God (CG, Cleveland, TN), with whom PACG had already established friendly contacts. Closer links have been pursued between these denominations since 1980. After the Romanian revolution, CG was fully involved in the sponsorship of the Pentecostal Theological Institute in Bucharest.

IV. ROMANIAN PENTECOSTALISM FROM 1989 TO THE PRESENT.

In Dec. 1989 the political revolution that had broken out in Timişoara ended the communist regime of Nicolae Ceauşescu and marked the beginning of a new chapter in the history of Romanian pentecostalism. The era of censorship and interdictions was over. A genuine "spiritual revolution" has emerged in almost all of the Romanian provinces since the beginning of 1990. Confronted with the multiple facets of democratic life, PACG engaged in an ambitious program of reforms. Its current leader, Pavel Riviş Tipei, formulated the vision of the movement for the 1990s. With about 500,000 apostolic believers, Romania presently has one of the highest numbers of Spirit-filled Christians in Europe. More than 20% of the Romanian pentecostals entered the denomination in 1995–98. Currently there are more than 2,153 apostolic churches in nine regions. Almost 1,900 ministers are involved in the spiritual work of 362 sections of the country. In the four years between 1994 and 1998, 238 new churches were built. Elim Church, led by Teodor Codreanu, is the largest pentecostal assembly in Romania and one of the most representative in Europe; it includes over 6,100 members and children. Elim has mothered 29 churches and is in the process of giving birth to 5 more fellowships.

For PACG, the launching of church-planting missions in the southern and southeastern parts of Romania (the province of Wallachia) is now of paramount importance. In fact, 90 home missionaries and church planters minister throughout the areas where the density of evangelical churches is low. Publishing efforts have developed significantly. There are actually 7 pentecostals periodicals (monthly or quarterly) with a combined circulation of 30,000.

The history of Romanian pentecostalism is still ongoing and being recorded. A new chapter of blessed opportunities and spiritual harvest is open at the beginning of this new millennium.

■ **Bibliography:** P. Bochian, *The Life of a Romanian Pastor* (1997) ▮ I. Bododea, "Foreword," *The Light of the Gospel* 2 (Feb.–Mar. 1946) ▮ idem, "Trying to Secure a Foothold," *The Gospel Call of Russia* 5 (June 1931) ▮ E. Bodor, *The Bible Study about the Spiritual Gifts* (1977) ▮ idem, "Overcoming Obstacles with God's Help," *The Gospel Call of Russia* 7 (Apr. 1933) ▮ G. Bradin, "The Pentecostal Movement in Romania," *The Herald of the Gospel* 3 (June 1947) ▮ P. Budean, Letter from Detroit (MI) to J. R. Flower (June 1, 1957) ▮ D. D. Bundy, "The Romanian Pentecostal Church in Recent Literature," *Pneuma* 7 (Spring 1985) ▮ G. Catargiu, "Deeply Grateful," *The Gospel Call* 10 (Feb. 1936) ▮ C. Cuciuc, *The Atlas of Religions and of Religious Historical Monuments in Romania* (1997) ▮ L. Fotescu, Letter from Bucharest, Romania, to DFM Officials, Springfield, MO (July 28, 1970) ▮ D. Gee, *Upon All Flesh: A Pentecostal World Tour* (1932) ▮ J. Lerch, "Romania Needs Teachers of the Word," *The Gospel Call of Russia* 5 (June 1931) ▮ A. Nicolle, Letter from Paris, France, to Philip Hogan, Springfield, MO (Oct. 23, 1967) ▮ N. Nikoloff, *Missionary Conference* [Mar. 16–18, 1943]: *Report on Europe-Confidential* (1943) ▮ P. Peterson, *History of the First Fifty Years (1927–1977) of Eastern European Mission* (1977) ▮ idem, "God's Quick Work in Russia," *The Gospel Call of Russia* (May 1927) ▮ idem, Letter from Chicago to Noel Perkins, Springfield, MO (Apr. 21, 1937) ▮ T. Sandru, *The Pentecostal Apostolic Church of God of the Socialist Republic of Romania* (1982) ▮ G. H. Schmidt, "Gospel Work in Romania," *The Gospel Call of Russia* 10 (Oct. 1933) ▮ P. R. Tipei, "The Report of the Church Council at the Sixth Congress of the Pentecostal Apostolic Churches from Romania," *The Word of Truth* 2 (Jan. 1999).   ■ M. Codreanu

RUSSIA

■ Pentecostals 140,319 (2%)   ■ Charismatics 1,001,265 (15%)   ■ Neocharismatics 5,333,416 (82%)   ■ Total Renewal: 6,475,000

[The history of Russia in the 20th century is dominated by the Union of Soviet Socialist Republics (USSR). The revolution of 1917 marked the end of the tsarist empire and the beginning of the Soviet Federative Socialist Republic of Russia. In 1922 Russia, Ukraine, Belorussia, and the Transcaucasian Federation (consisting of Armenia, Azerbaijan, and Georgia) formed the USSR. Later were added Uzbekistan (1924), Turkmenistan (1925), Tajikistan (1929), Kazakhstan and Kirgizia (1936), Estonia, Latvia, Lithuania, and Moldavia (1940). Since the dissolution of the USSR in 1991, these constituent republics have once again gained independence. For statistics, see entry for each of these countries.]

The official date of the beginning of Christianity in Russia is 988, when Vladimir became the first Christian ruler of the Rus, and the Russian Orthodox Church (ROC) began its tenure as the dominant church in Russia. The ROC traditionally viewed all Western forms of Christianity as part of the "Latin heresy"—including both Roman Catholicism and Protestantism (it was not until 1639 that the Russian Orthodox Church made any distinction at all between the doctrinal beliefs of the Protestants and Roman Catholics living in Russia).

However, when pentecostalism arrived in Russia shortly after the Revolution of 1917, it was the state rather than the ROC (which had had close ties with the tsars) that increasingly opposed and persecuted the church. In addition, Russia has had its share of sectarians who exhibited some form of speaking in tongues during their religious rituals.

For instance, at the close of the 17th century there was a sect of flagellants called *Khlysti*, who jumped, shrieked, and whipped themselves, and who were reported to prophesy and speak in other tongues. Their interpretations of tongues were collected in the *Book of the Dove*, which was given the place of highest authority, above that of the Bible.

In the 19th century the *Pryguni*, or jumpers, appeared in the Ukraine. They firmly believed that the Holy Spirit would fall upon them as they vigorously danced. Reports claimed that the *Pryguni* uttered "unintelligible words in various tongues" during their meetings.

Other glossolalists emerged in the 20th century, such as the *Smorodintsi* and the *Murashkovtsi*, each named after their leader. The *Smorodintsi* denied the doctrine of the Trinity. The *Murashkovtsi* championed the prophecies of Ivan Murashkov, the "Father of Zion," who warned of impending judgment. So convincing was he that his followers believed he would create a new "Zion," and 100 families sold their homes and offered the money for the purchase of land near Sarnom. But instead of remaining with his flock until the date prophesied, Murashkov and his wife absconded to Argentina with all the funds.

This sporadic emergence of fanatical Russian sects displaying some elements of glossolalia created suspicion toward anyone who claimed the supernatural gifts of the Holy Spirit. So it was that most of the Russian Baptists and evangelicals suspected and feared the man who introduced biblical pentecostalism on a large scale within the Soviet Union, ▸Ivan Voronaev, who founded hundreds of pentecostal churches during the 1920s.

Born in Russia in 1886, Voronaev served with the Cossacks in tsarist Russia. After his conversion in 1908 he ministered in Baptist churches in Irkutsk and Krasnoyarsk, Siberia. Experiencing a period of relentless persecution by the state church, the 25-year-old pastor left Russia in 1911 and, via Harbin, Manchuria, arrived in the U.S., where he initially pastored a Russian Baptist group in Seattle, WA, that met in an Assembly of God (AG) building. The American pastor ►Ernest Williams, who later became the general superintendent of the AG, introduced young Voronaev to the pentecostal beliefs. This seed was sown before Voronaev left for New York City to pastor the Russian Baptist church on Henry Street. While there he faced a spiritual crisis when his teenage daughter Vera accompanied a young neighbor on a visit to the pentecostal church on 33rd Street. At the close of an impressive afternoon service, Vera went forward to the altar and during prayer received the baptism in the Holy Spirit accompanied by speaking in other tongues.

Baptist pastor Voronaev, upset and embarrassed before his parishioners, nevertheless felt a deep desire to seek more of God, and one day while in private prayer received the pentecostal experience. He felt that, as a result, his leadership of the Russian Baptist church seemed untenable, so he resigned. Soon thereafter, on July 1, 1919, Voronaev founded the first Russian Pentecostal Church in New York City. Growth was immediate as Russians, Ukrainians, and Poles accepted Christ as Savior and were baptized in the Holy Spirit.

Amid joyous revival and significant growth, the congregation was not prepared for Voronaev's unexpected announcement that God called him to return to Soviet Russia. With his wife, Katherine, and their children, Voronaev left his beloved adoptive land to serve Christ in the land of his birth, which had gone through the Revolution (1917), a civil war (1918–20), and a famine that claimed 5 million lives (1921). The Voronaevs arrived in Odessa, a thriving seaport on the

Historic photo of the General Council of the Assemblies of God in Ukrena (Ukraine).

Black Sea. They received regular financial support from New York's Glad Tidings Assembly of God.

When Voronaev founded the pentecostal church in Odessa, fully half of his early congregation came from Baptists and evangelicals. Many Odessan Jews who attended accepted Christ as their Messiah. When his headquarters church in Odessa approached a membership of 1,000, Voronaev began to travel extensively, conducting evangelistic meetings and planting churches. On his trips, which often lasted as long as three months and took him as far north as St. Petersburg, Voronaev preached and prayed for the sick with signs following. Within six short years the labors of this pentecostal pioneer were rewarded with the birth of 350 AG churches and 17,000 members.

The leaders of the Baptists and the evangelical Christians did not write kindly of Voronaev's return to Russia. They saw him as a renegade Baptist who brought a new, harmful teaching from the U.S., causing many Russian Baptists to accept the pentecostal message. In 1924 Voronaev organized the Union of Christians of Evangelical Faith in the Odessa region, and by 1926 he extended it throughout the Ukraine. A pentecostal publication, *Evangelist*, published eight issues during its single year of existence in 1928.

Soviet persecution increased. The anti-religious law of Apr. 8, 1929, had a crushing effect on all Russian believers. It denied legal existence to all churches in the Soviet Union—including the ROC—and permitted no activity other than the performance of worship. That fateful year of 1929 alone saw 1,370 Orthodox churches shut down. Pentecostals continued to spread the good news of Jesus Christ in the slave labor camps and Siberian areas of exile. Voronaev did so to his dying day.

No evidence remains of pentecostal activities in the 1930s, but it is certain that many congregations built up by Voronaev's evangelistic fervor continued to exist. The pentecostal movement was strengthened in 1939, when a number of small but very active pentecostal groups of eastern Poland came under soviet rule.

After the terrible decade of the 1930s under Stalin, the great patriotic war saved the religious unions from total extinction. During the life-or-death struggle of the Russian nation against Nazi Germany, the state's need to obtain help from all its citizens was paramount. Stalin, shrewd and pragmatic, courted the religious leaders to rally behind "Mother Russia." He discontinued the atheist publications *Bezbozhniki* (Godless) and *Antireligioznik*. Stalin's new religious policy brought the demise of the league of militant godless, while concessions were granted to religious groups. The evangelicals were permitted to form a union, to publish an 80-page bimonthly periodical, *Bratskii Vestnik* (Fraternal Messenger), and to build prayer halls.

Thus, in 1944, the Baptists and the evangelical Christians were able to merge and form a single union, with headquarters in Moscow. It was impossible for the pentecostals to form an independent union, since the Soviet regime forbade it. The pentecostal believers thus were invited to join the official Union of Evangelical Christians and Baptists (UECB)—on condition that they would cease speaking in tongues in all public services. Despite this restriction, four recognized pentecostal leaders signed the document known as the August Agreement of 1945.

The pentecostals by and large ignored the prohibition on speaking in tongues in all public services. This caused Jacob Zhidkov, president of the UECB, to publish the following statement: "They say, 'The Spirit arouses us to prayer and you quench our spirits and thus destroy the word of God.' We do not quench the Spirit, but we strive to suppress noise and disorder."

Dissatisfaction continued after the August Agreement, and two of the four pentecostal leaders who had signed the agreement soon abandoned the UECB. A. I. Bidash, one of the leaders, chose to return to the nonregistered, illegal pentecostals rather than to continue denying his pentecostal heritage of liberty in exercising the gifts of the Spirit.

Problems in the UECB accelerated to the point that a drastic amendment was inserted in the August Agreement nine years after its adoption. Under the threat of excommunication, pentecostal members were forbidden to share personal testimonies with nonpentecostal members of the union. This resulted in the exodus of thousands of pentecostals who withdrew from the union, even though giving up their membership made them vulnerable to greater persecution as nonregistered pentecostals. The UECB considered them "extremists who, being fanatically trained in their views, do not have the desire to restrict themselves to the August Agreement."

In spite of these tensions, 10 years after the merger *Bratskti Vestnik* reported an increase in UECB membership of almost 200,000. However, slander, lies, and macabre accounts in the Soviet targeting of independent pentecostals helped to extend the denial of separate denominational status in the USSR.

Relatively little changed until shortly after the millennial celebration of the introduction of Christianity in Russia in 1988. One of the radical changes that took place in the USSR as it sped toward its 1991 dissolution was the legislation adopted by the Soviet parliament on Oct. 25, 1990, granting full freedom of conscience, to replace the restrictive 1929 law on religion. In a nearly unanimous vote (341–2), the passage of this new legislation granted freedom of religion to all—including the Russian pentecostals. They now are allowed to openly share their faith, teach children and young people about God, and hold Bible studies and prayer meetings. They can own property and engage in the printing and distribution of Christian literature.

Many pentecostal resident Bible schools have opened their doors to young people in the former USSR, including those in Moscow (Russia), Kiev (Ukraine), Minsk (Belarus), Irkutsk (Siberia), Jelgava (Latvia), and Vilnius (Lithuania). A historic gathering convened in Moscow on Mar. 12–15, 1991, with 815 delegates and guests in attendance. Today this pentecostal union, called—like the union Voronaev established in 1924—Christians of Evangelical Faith, has grown from 50 churches in 1991 to 1,348 Russian churches and exceeds 100,000 members. Another pentecostal union, led by bishop Ivan Fedotov (who was confined 19 years for his faith), has refused registration from its inception. This union also has more than 100,000 members.

■ **Select Bibliography:** *Bratskii Vestnik* (periodical, 1945–68) ■ A. Chalandeau, *The Theology of the Evangelical Christians-Baptists in the USSR* (1978) ■ S. Durasoff, *Bright Wind of the Spirit: Pentecostalism Today* (1972) ■ idem, *Pentecost behind the Iron Curtain* (1972) ■ idem, *The Russian Protestants* (1969) ■ F. I. Garkavenko, *What Religious Sectarianism Is* (Russian; 1961) ■ K. R. Hill, *The Puzzle of the Soviet Church* (1989) ■ W. Kolarz, *Religion in the Soviet Union* (1962) ■ G. M. Livshits, *Religion and the Church in the Past and Present* (Russian; 1961) ■ *Pentecost* (periodical [London] 1947–66) ■ W. Sawatsky, *Soviet Evangelicals since World War II* (1981).
■ S. Durasoff

RWANDA

■ Pentecostals 636,449 (51%) ■ Charismatics 502,657 (41%) ■ Neocharismatics 97,893 (8%) ■ Total Renewal: 1,236,999

For a general introduction to Central Africa and bibliography, see AFRICA, CENTRAL.

Rwanda was colonized by the Germans from 1899 until 1916, when it was mandated to Belgium until 1962. As in Burundi, there has been continual conflict between Tutsi and Hutu throughout its history. The latest and bloodiest resulted in the killing of more than three-quarters of a million Tutsi in 1994. This led to the installation of the present Tutsi-led government.

The first pentecostals to enter the country were those of the Swedish Free Churches' Mission. The first missionary was Alvar Lindskog, who had worked in Congo and entered Rwanda in 1940. He started out in the territory of Cyangugu. He did not know the local language of Kinyarwanda but spoke Swahili and used an interpreter. The problem was that his interpreter, Ludovigo Sagatwa, was not a Christian believer, and would often contradict what the missionary was saying. For three years there were no converts until the interpreter was himself converted. Mission stations were opened at Cyangugu (1950) and at Gisenyi (1955) from where evangelization of the rest of the country was launched. The autonomy of the Free Churches meant that each station was affiliated with the others but was at the same time completely independent. Those involved in the work started at Cyangugu, however, decided to form an organization called Eglises Unies de Pentecôte du Rwanda (The United Pentecostal Churches of Rwanda [not to be confused with the ▸Oneness pentecostal churches]). The churches founded from Gisenyi pressed ahead with the concept of autonomy but in 1970 formed a grouping called the Association des Eglises de Pentecôte (Association of Pentecostal Churches); this association included the churches from the Gisenyi and Ruhengeri areas. The churches from Gihinga (Kayove) called themselves Églises de Pentecôte de Gihinga (EPGI, The Pentecostal Churches of Gihinga) and those from Kigali and Kibungo, the Églises de Pentecôte de Kigali (EPKI, The Pentecostal Churches of Kigali). The confusion over the multiplicity of names, especially from the perspective of the governmental authorities, brought all the pentecostal churches together in conference at Kayove in 1982. At that time they decided to maintain their autonomy but call themselves l'Association des Églises de Pentecôte du Rwanda (ADEPR, Association of Pentecostal Churches of Rwanda). Pastor Joseph Nsanzurwimo has been responsible for organizing the ADEPR from 1983. Since the 1994 war, Jean Sibomana is the legal representative of the ADEPR. The largest churches are at Gihundwe, Gisenyi, Gihinga, Ruhengeri, and Gasave in the Kigali sector. In the 1980s a revival broke out among the young people through the work of Bible camps and the seminars organized through the organization of the Scripture Union. As a result, new churches were planted at Gakinjiro, Kimihurura, Gikongoro, Gitarama, Matyazo, and Nyanza. The young people have played a major role in the work of the churches, with large Christian groups gathering in schools around the country. The Bible Institute at Gisenyi and the Centre de Formation (Training Center) at Gitarama have both been of considerable significance in the training of pastors and leaders for all the pentecostal churches in Rwanda. One of the areas in which the ADEPR has not fallen behind is that of social involvement, which has been seen as a vital tool for evangelism. The ADEPR has 65 primary schools throughout Rwanda with more than 40,000 students. There is also an excellent health center at Mashesha near Cyangugu, a hospital at Bugesera, an agricultural project at Kayove, and a training center for those interested in woodworking at Gihundwe. Most of these projects have been built by funds coming from government aid from Sweden.

By the end of 1996 ADEPR counted more than 300,000 members over 12 years of age, 180 fully constituted churches, and more than 1,800 subchurches called *chapelles*. The ADEPR has more than 75,000 children in Sunday schools (1% of the more than 7.5 million population of the country).

There are two other charismatic groups: the Église Vivante (The Living Church) and the Restoration Church. The Finnish pentecostals are planning to become involved in Rwanda shortly. The Pentecostal Assemblies of Canada (PAOC) became involved in Rwanda in 1998, when they sent Elmer and Sherry Komant (former missionaries to Lusaka, Zambia, and Mombassa, Kenya) to do church planting in Kigali. Their strategy includes starting an English-speaking congregation among the many English-speaking refugees. Mbona Kolini, the archbishop of the Anglican Church in Rwanda estimates that as many as 60% of all Anglicans in Rwanda are charismatic. This is because many young people have been introduced to the work of the Spirit through Bible camps and Christian groups in the schools.

Elim–U.K. has supported ministry in Rwanda since 1995. This work was initiated in the refugee camp at Ngara Tanzania, where at one point 10,000 people were attending churches within the camp. This situation lasted until Dec. 1996, when the camp was disbanded and refugees were forcibly repatriated. When the refugees moved back to Rwanda they planted 45 churches, which have 3,000 members. Not all those who were attending the Elim churches in Ngara have been contacted since their return to Rwanda. Abeli Gashagari has undertaken to register the new denomination as the Église Pentecôtiste Elim du Rwanda (EPER, Elim Pentecostal Church of Rwanda). The government is favorably disposed toward the churches but insists that all meetings must be held in buildings and not outside under trees, as has been the custom in the past. All churches are also expected to be involved in the rehabilitation of the nation and in the building and running of clinics, orphanages, and other social services.

Despite the repatriation of the majority of the Hutu population that had fled to neighboring countries in 1994, there is much instability within Rwanda. Many of those returning found that their buildings and property had been confiscated by the state or taken over by other returning refugees. There is a great deal of mistrust, even between Christians in the same local churches, because many are suspected of having been responsible for the atrocities that took place. Even today it is not uncommon for individuals to disappear or fail to return home at the end of the working day. No one appears to be beyond suspicion, because during the massacres, many Anglican and Catholic pastors and even bishops were incriminated. The church has to prove itself and reveal the true nature of its message rather than merely proclaim a doctrinal position.   ■ D. J. Garrard

SAHARA

■ Pentecostals 0 (0%)   ■ Charismatics 0 (0%)   ■ Neocharismatics 370 (100%)   ■ Total Renewal: 370

SAINT HELENA

■ Pentecostals 0 (0%)   ■ Charismatics 765 (82%)   ■ Neocharismatics 165 (18%)   ■ Total Renewal: 930

SAINT KITTS AND NEVIS

■ Pentecostals 2,591 (36%)   ■ Charismatics 3,570 (50%)   ■ Neocharismatics 989 (14%)   ■ Total Renewal: 7,150

See CARIBBEAN ISLANDS.

SAINT LUCIA

■ Pentecostals 7,702 (60%)   ■ Charismatics 3,392 (27%)   ■ Neocharismatics 1,657 (13%)   ■ Total Renewal: 12,751

See CARIBBEAN ISLANDS.

SAINT PIERRE AND MIQUELON

■ Pentecostals 0 (0%)   ■ Charismatics 160 (100%)   ■ Neocharismatics 0 (0%)   ■ Total Renewal: 160

SAINT VINCENT

■ Pentecostals 8,551 (36%)   ■ Charismatics 4,485 (19%)   ■ Neocharismatics 10,964 (46%)   ■ Total Renewal: 24,000

See CARIBBEAN ISLANDS.

SAMOA (Western Samoa)

■ Pentecostals 18,962 (67%)   ■ Charismatics 7,849 (28%)   ■ Neocharismatics 1,489 (5%)   ■ Total Renewal: 28,300

For general introduction and bibliography, see PACIFIC ISLANDS.

Western Samoa consists of two large islands of recent volcanic origin—Upolu (425 mi² [1,100 km²]), and Savaii (655 mi² [1,700 km²])—and four small islands, three of which are populated. The total land area of 1,133 mi² (2,935 km²) is surrounded by a sea area of more than 46,000 mi² (120,000 km²).

Unlike most other countries in the South Pacific, the land area is not fragmented. Both main islands are mountainous, and the island of Savaii has active volcanic domes. Natural hazards like hurricanes, volcanic activities, and droughts are not unusual. The capital is Apia, with a population of about 40,000. The total population in 1995 was 178,000. In addition there is a large Samoan population of more than 50,000 living in New Zealand, and an unknown number of Western Samoans live in the U.S. and Australia. As in Tonga, the combination of a high fertility rate, relatively low mortality, and limited natural resources has made migration a kind of "population safety valve."

Pacific Area Conference in Suva, Fiji, in 1970. The man in the foreground wears traditional Samoan garb.

Since the 1850s the homogeneous Polynesian population has been modified to a comparatively small extent by the immigration of Europeans and later of Chinese, as well as of other, mainly Melanesian, Pacific Islanders, early in the 20th century.

The first two Assemblies of God (AG) missionaries came to Pago Pago in American Samoa in 1926. It was in 1952 that the work spread to Western Samoa. Because missionaries at that time were not permitted to reside in Western Samoa, they came for short evangelistic visits from American Samoa and the U.S.

In 1967 the Assemblies in American and Western Samoa formed separate districts with a combined council and general superintendent.

Today the AG is recognized as the fastest-growing church in the Samoas. In 1997 there were approximately 50 congregations in Western Samoa alone, with 70 ministers and 11,000 adherents. Financially the AG church is on the whole self-supporting. Money, material, and other kinds of support are usually granted from the international headquarters in the U.S. if needed and requested.

More than a thousand Samoan AG members are today living in other parts of the world. The World Samoan Convention brings these scattered believers together for fellowship once every year.

The First Samoan Full Gospel Church broke away from the AG. Today they have nine meeting points in Upolu, Savaii, and American Samoa.   ■ M. Ernst

SAN MARINO

■ Pentecostals 0 (0%) ■ Charismatics 485 (100%) ■ Neocharismatics 0 (0%) ■ Total Renewal: 485

SAO TOME AND PRINCIPE

■ Pentecostals 3,974 (19%) ■ Charismatics 3,222 (15%) ■ Neocharismatics 13,904 (66%) ■ Total Renewal: 21,100

SAUDI ARABIA

■ Pentecostals 0 (0%) ■ Charismatics 33,133 (28%) ■ Neocharismatics 83,367 (72%) ■ Total Renewal: 116,500

See AFRICA, NORTH, AND THE MIDDLE EAST.

SCANDINAVIA (Survey)

The character and organization of pentecostalism in Scandinavia owes much to the pioneering accomplishments of ▶Thomas Ball Barratt of Norway and ▶Lewi Pethrus of Sweden. The former brought the pentecostal movement to Scandinavia at the end of 1906; the latter became the champion of the local-church doctrine, which, to a large extent, characterizes pentecostal endeavors in the Nordic countries. Both men were outstanding spiritual leaders, gifted speakers, and composers of lasting hymns.

Most pentecostals in Scandinavia prefer the term "pentecostal revival" over the term "pentecostal movement." A cherished Scripture passage is found in the prophecy of Zechariah: "Look, those going toward the north country have given my Spirit rest in the land of the north" (Zech. 6:8).

The pentecostals of Scandinavia are well known for their extensive missionary outreach efforts, which include far-reaching radio and TV ministries. Most recently the pentecostal Christians have been engaged in social rehabilitation and development programs.

See individual articles on DENMARK, FINLAND, ICELAND, NORWAY, SWEDEN.   ■ L. Ahonen

SENEGAL

■ Pentecostals 3,281 (9%) ■ Charismatics 18,139 (52%) ■ Neocharismatics 13,580 (39%) ■ Total Renewal: 35,000

See AFRICA, WEST.

SEYCHELLES

■ Pentecostals 789 (19%)   ■ Charismatics 3,212 (79%)   ■ Neocharismatics 49 (1%)   ■ Total Renewal: 4,050

SIERRA LEONE

■ Pentecostals 25,234 (13%)   ■ Charismatics 23,666 (12%)   ■ Neocharismatics 151,100 (76%)   ■ Total Renewal: 200,000

See AFRICA, WEST.

SINGAPORE

■ Pentecostals 31,469 (22%)   ■ Charismatics 51,856 (36%)   ■ Neocharismatics 62,675 (43%)   ■ Total Renewal: 146,000

See also MALAYSIA.

1. Pentecostals.

On Easter Sunday 1928, Cecil and Edith Jackson, Assemblies of God (AG) missionaries, arrived in Singapore from Canton, China, because of the uprising against all foreigners led by the newly formed Red Army from Yunan province. They began pioneering a village mission for the Cantonese community, and a year later they started a school for the children in the Balestier Plain. Those who responded to the gospel at the school were channeled into the Sunday school of the church.

Further assistance in the work came from other AG missionaries, Carrie Anderson and Esther Johnson (both from Canton) in 1930, and Katherine Clause (1931) further strengthened the Cantonese mission and the school. Returning from furlough in late 1931 with a vision for an English work, Jackson started an English service at the home of an Indian couple in 1932. This work grew slowly, and they moved to larger premises in mid 1933.

By mid 1938 both the Cantonese church and the English church moved into the new building at 120 Balestier Road. The union was short-lived as Reverend Jackson had a fallout with the AG over the loan and debt of the church building. In mid 1939 the AG–U.S. instructed Lawrence O. McKinney, then copastoring the English congregation, to sever all ties with Jackson and to move out with those who desired to be affiliated with the AG–U.S. It is unknown who pastored the church at 120 Balestier Road between 1939 and 1947.

Jackson returned in Jan. 1947 under the name The Far East Missionary Society and assumed the pastorate of the church. In 1948 Russell and Willie Rothgeb joined Jackson in pastoring the Community Church at Balestier Road. In late 1949 Jackson sold off the church building to the Seventh-day Adventist Mission to pay off all debts and went back to the U.S. The Rothgebs, saddened by the sale of the building, returned to the U.S. in 1950. They carried a deep burden for the church members, however, and returned in Feb. 1953. Slowly they reestablished the church and named it Revival Centre Church, under the sponsorship of Revival Center Church in Long Beach, CA. A significant event occurred on Aug. 21, 1956, when they witnessed the outpouring of the Holy Spirit on 17 members. It was also around this period that other pentecostal churches experienced sim-

Malaysian kampong in rural Singapore.

ilar outpourings. Revival Centre Church remains independent to this day.

The members who left with McKinney formed the nucleus of Elim Church, AG, in the Serangoon area. This was the only AG church in Singapore until the Japanese invasion in 1942.

The pentecostal experience of speaking in tongues was rare. The earliest record of a national being baptized in the Holy Spirit was a Brother Lai in the early 1930s. He was the only early Chinese worker in the Cantonese mission church. Between 1932 and 1941 a number of the members received the baptism. There was no outburst of the pentecostal revival, and the church remained a small group. During the war (1942–45) all missionaries had to leave. Elim Church continued to have services conducted by lay leaders, and toward the close of the war its numbers dwindled to a faithful few.

The Ceylon Pentecostal Mission (CPM) started work in Singapore in 1936, primarily among the Tamil and Malayalee migrant workers from India and Ceylon (Sri Lanka). The movement was founded in Ceylon in 1927 by Rama Paul, a former AG worker from India. Registering their work as the Pentecostal Church of Malaya, works started initially in Singapore, Ipoh, and Kuala Lumpur in the 1930s. They did not maintain any membership records; only the pastor and workers knew who the members were. They preached a message of personal salvation and baptism of the Holy Spirit. They embraced stringent external membership standards (wearing of white and no jewelry) and adopted a type of monastic order for their workers.

After the war, the AG missionaries returned to Singapore and reestablished the pentecostal work. Between 1947 and 1960, five churches were started in addition to Elim Church. In Jan. 1958 seven pentecostal churches and one independent church jointly organized a salvation/healing crusade with evangelist ▸A. C. Valdez. The scheduled two weeks of meetings extended to three weeks when miracles and healings took place. In the third week almost 1,000 people packed the hall and vast crowds responded to the altar call. The converts were distributed among the participating churches, out of which two new churches were planted. This outburst of pentecostal fire spurred the churches forward, both in evangelism and in seeking for a manifestation of the Holy Spirit. An event that soon became a high point for AG members was the youth camp held for all AG churches in Singapore and Malaya. It was at these annual camps that many received the Holy Spirit baptism and the call to full-time ministry. In 1960 the AG established a Bible school, the Bible Institute of Malaya in Petaling Jaya, Malaysia. This national school trained many who were called to full-time ministry. Graduates from the school provided the impetus for the growth of the movement both in Singapore and Malaysia.

Singapore and Malaysia were separated in 1965. The AG of Singapore have a total of nine churches. When it proved difficult for Singaporeans to study at the Bible school in Malaysia, the Bible Institute of Singapore was established in 1976 to serve the national church. To date, the AG is the largest pentecostal group, with a total membership of 43 churches and 23,389 adherents (1999 General Council Report).

Another pentecostal group that came in after the war was the Finnish Free Foreign Mission of the Pentecostal Churches of Finland. Its foreign mission department was founded in 1927 by Nikolai Poysti, a missionary to Russia and Manchuria. Its philosophy is to establish national churches and then cooperate with them. These churches often become autonomous and independent. Their work in Singapore started in 1949 with the arrival of their missionaries who had been based in China but had to leave because of the communist takeover. They started a work in the Ganges Avenue area, which later became Zion Church (presently Zion Full Gospel Church).

In 1955 a young Finnish couple, Elias and Raakel Kossila, arrived in Singapore and found lodging with a William P. K. Lee, who saw the Kossilas as God's answer to his prayers. Lee had had a born-again experience in Mar. 1955. Led by the Spirit he turned on the radio, heard evangelist Oral Roberts preaching, and received a divine healing of his slipped disc. He then prayed that God would send someone to instruct him. That person would be the Kossilas. That year William Lee received the baptism of the Holy Spirit. He served as interpreter for the Kossilas in their mission work in the Redhill area for the next two years. In 1957 Elias Kossila and William Lee started a new work in the Hougang and Tampines region and named it Glad Tidings Church. The church was handed over to William Lee in Jan. 1960, when the Kossila felt led to go to Thailand. Through the leadership of William Lee, this work grew and became one of the strongest independent pentecostal churches. By the 1960s other Finnish missionaries who arrived in Singapore served in Zion Church. One of the couples, Joel and Pirkko Ikonen, later felt called to reach out to another area and started Salem Chapel in 1967. By the 1970s the Finnish mission group had founded four churches, each of which operates independently.

In 1963 the pentecostal witness reached the nonpentecostal churches when a converted Chinese film actress from Hong Kong, Kong Mui Yee, came to Singapore. Her popularity as an actress and eloquent testimony concerning her conversion attracted the Chinese-speaking people by the hundreds. Her meetings were filled with miracles of healing, and there were a great number of conversions even among a few gangsters. She spoke on the baptism of the Holy Spirit in her meetings, and a number of nonpentecostal Christians were baptized. A group of Christians from the Brethren background, not accepted back into their own churches, started the Church of Singapore. Madam Kong was a controversial figure in her later ministry, making extreme claims that embarrassed the sponsoring pentecostal churches so that they withdrew their invitation to her for further meetings in Singapore and Malaysia. Her ministry birthed 10 new independent pentecostal churches in Singapore and Malaysia. Her contribution has paved the way for the acceptance of the pentecostal message among the other traditional churches.

2. Charismatics.

Before the charismatic movement of the 1960s, John Sung, a revivalist from China, came to Singapore in 1935. In two weeks of evangelistic meetings he drew crowds of 2,000. Hundreds were saved, and it brought a spiritual revival into the churches. His message emphasized strongly the Word, holiness, and infilling with the Holy Spirit (without tongues). Open to the gifts of the Spirit, he usually ended his series of meetings with a healing service where miracles of healing took place. His ministry expanded to Malaya, and in 1935–37 he visited Singapore seven times. In 1935 alone, over 5,000 Chinese were converted to Christ in this region.

The first sign of the charismatic movement occurred in the early 1970s when there was an outburst of tongues among some students at the Anglo-Chinese School and two other schools. They met together weekly at the home of a pentecostal couple, Rev. and Mrs. David H. Baker, and started to call themselves Ambassadors for Christ. Some of the students were from Wesley Methodist Church. They prayed for their pastor, Richard Ong, who was ill with a kidney ailment. A few weeks later, Ong had a deep spiritual experience, and this encouraged them to share their charismatic experience with others.

In Dec. 1972 Bishop Chui Ban It of the Anglican Church attended an international conference in Bangkok and was given the book *Nine O'Clock in the Morning* by ►Dennis Bennett. Upon reading the book, a deep hunger arose in him. He asked God for the experience and received a divine visitation of the presence and infilling of the Holy Spirit. From then on, the pace of events quickened. In June and July 1973 the Anglican Church held a series of "Prayers for Healing Services," which packed the church halls. Healing, deliverance, and being slain in the Spirit were characteristics of these meetings. Beginning in 1974, weekly "Praise and Prayer" services were held at St. Andrew's Cathedral. A group of churchmen organized Spiritual Renewal Seminars to educate interested laypeople on the work of the Holy Spirit. These annual seminars ran for seven years, attracting hundreds of believers from a wide spectrum of churches. With Bishop Chui's endorsement of and blessing on the charismatic movement, soon most if not all the Anglican churches have experienced this renewal in their congregations.

In 1975 the Full Gospel Business Men's Fellowship (FGBMF) was organized, and soon hundreds were attending its monthly public meetings. Many professionals and businesspeople experienced fresh encounters with the Holy Spirit. Reports of conversions, healings, deliverance, and baptisms in the Holy Spirit at these meetings were common.

The charismatic renewal within the Anglican churches, the FGBMF, and the Spiritual Renewal Seminars impacted other traditional denominations both in spiritual renewal and membership growth. A number of people in the Methodist Church also experienced this renewal. In Wesley Methodist Church, a charismatic worship service was created to cater to those who prefered this form of worship, alongside the traditional worship service. Other churches soon included a charismatic service for those who had encountered the charismatic renewal.

The annual Spiritual Renewal Seminars provided a strong platform for the charismatic movement to grow by providing sound biblical teachings and careful instruction and motivation for a large number of renewed Christians across denominations. A number of independent charismatic churches were formed during this period when the renewed Christians could not reintegrate into their churches.

The charismatic renewal largely impacted the English-speaking churches. In the 1970s and '80s the charismatic churches (independent, pentecostal, and mainline churches) were the fastest-growing churches. The charismatic movement continues to play a significant part in the continued growth of the church in Singapore at the beginning of the 21st century.

■ **Bibliography:** F. and R. Abeysekera, *The History of the Assemblies of God of Singapore* (1992) ▓ K. Hinton, *Growing Churches Singapore Style* (1985) ▓ P. Ng, "Towards a New Frontier" (unpub. ms. on the history of Glad Tidings Church, 1999) ▓ B. E. K. Sng, *In His Good Time: The Story of the Church in Singapore 1819–1992* (1993) ▓ C. D. Thomas, *Diaspora Indians: Church Growth among Indians in West Malaysia* (1978) ▓ T. Tow, *The Asian Awakening: John Sung* (1988).   ■ D. Tan

SLOVAKIA

■ Pentecostals 5,262 (2%)   ■ Charismatics 236,722 (96%)   ■ Neocharismatics 4,016 (2%)   ■ Total Renewal: 246,000

See Europe, Eastern.

SLOVENIA

■ Pentecostals 973 (1%)   ■ Charismatics 36,117 (52%)   ■ Neocharismatics 32,409 (47%)   ■ Total Renewal: 69,499

See EUROPE, EASTERN.

SOLOMON ISLANDS

■ Pentecostals 4,626 (7%)   ■ Charismatics 37,230 (60%)   ■ Neocharismatics 20,145 (32%)   ■ Total Renewal: 62,001

For general introduction and bibliography, see PACIFIC ISLANDS.

The six major islands are Choiseul, New Georgia, Santa Isabel, Guadalcanal, Malaita, and San Cristobal. The Solomon Islands group stretches over 870 mi (1,400 km) from Bougainville southeast to Tikopia and Fataka. The total land area is 11,500 mi² (29,785 km²). The sea area (based on the 200-mile zone) is 51,740 mi² (1,340,000 km²). The capital Honiara is located on the biggest island, Guadalcanal.

The Solomon Islands have one of the fastest-growing populations in the world, with a growth rate of 3.5% between 1976 and 1986. Consequently, about 50% of the population is under 15 years old. About 94% of the population are of mainly Melanesian origin. About 4% are of mainly Polynesian origin, 15% of Micronesian origin, and the remaining 0.5% of European and Chinese origin. Based on the growth rates between 1976 and 1986, the total population of the Solomon Islands in 1995 was about 395,000 people. An estimated 15% of the population is living in the fast-growing urban areas.

1. Christian Outreach Centre (COC).

The ▸Christian Outreach Centre, established in 1989, is one of the most recent and obviously rapidly growing religious groups in the Solomon Islands. Affiliated with the headquarters in Brisbane, Australia, the COC claims to have about 2,800 adherents, organized in 28 so-called centers, mainly around the capital and Guadalcanal. The adherents are ministered to by 38 full-time pastors who get support from the adherents themselves. The COC also has its own local Bible college to train people for the ministry. Being a charismatic-fundamentalist group, the COC has close cooperation with the Rhema Church as well as with the Assemblies of God (AG) and Campus Crusade for Christ. The COC was one of the driving forces in the formation of a mission network operation among the charismatic, pentecostal, and evangelical churches for the Solomon Islands and the South Pacific Region.

2. Assemblies of God (AG).

The AG work in the Solomon Islands was started by a missionary from Fiji in 1971 after a revival in the South Sea Evangelical Church on Malaita in 1970. Since then the AG has spread to nearly all other major islands of the Solomons, but the majority of adherents is still found on the island of Guadalcanal and within greater Honiara, the capital. In 1997 two expatriate missionaries were active. At the same time the total number of ministers was 51, serving the 18 preaching points. The total number of adherents is about 2,000. A new Bible college was dedicated in 1992 on Malaita. As usual in the AG, each congregation tries to be as autonomous as possible, but bigger building projects are supported by the AG–U.S. headquarters.

3. Rhema Church.

The ▸Rhema Church grew out of the youth work of the Church of Melanesia (COM) in the early 1980s and was established as a separate group by Fr. Alfred Alufurai, an ex-minister of the COM, graduate of the Pacific Theological College, and son of the first local bishop of the COM. After internal rivalries in a struggle for leadership, and disagreement about the question of affiliation overseas, the founder separated from the Rhema Church in 1990 and established the Church of the Living Word. While the self-understanding of the Church of the Living Word is that of a local, independent charismatic church, the Rhema Church under its new leader became affiliated with the Rhema Church family in the U.S. and Australia. Both groups are of the charismatic-fundamentalist type, and in 1992 each had about 400 adherents in the Solomon Islands, the majority on Guadalcanal.

4. Evangelical-Fundamentalist Parachurch Organizations.

With World Vision, Campus Crusade for Christ, Every Home for Christ, Child Evangelism Fellowship, and Wycliffe Bible Translators International/Summer Institute of Linguistics, there are five evangelical-fundamentalist parachurch organizations active in the Solomon Islands. They have in common their U.S. background and the fact that they started quite recently in the 1970s and 1980s.   ■ M. Ernst

SOMALIA

■ Pentecostals 0 (0%)   ■ Charismatics 120 (2%)   ■ Neocharismatics 6,880 (98%)   ■ Total Renewal: 7,000

For general introduction to East Africa and bibliography, see AFRICA, EAST.

Because of the sensitive nature of the information concerning evangelization in Somalia, it is not possible to give details on all that is happening in this country. There are not any official missionaries working in Somali territories. However, there are pentecostal personnel working there with various relief and development organizations and other nongovernmental organizations. The actual Somali territories encompass Somalia proper, Somaliland, Djiboutie, East Ethiopia, and Northeastern Kenya. It is likely that there are

as few as 500 Somali believers worldwide. There are as many as 30 Western missionaries working with Somalis in these Somali territories, and there is a great deal of cooperation between all the pentecostal groups involved. It is reported that one fellowship that was started in Mogadishu resulted in most of the members being executed one by one over a three-year period. Where there are a few fellowships, pentecostal believers meet secretly in their homes. The main concern at present is to train Somalis and Ethiopians to evangelize the Somalis.   ■ D. J. Garrard

SOMALILAND

■ Pentecostals 0 (0%)   ■ Charismatics 59 (2%)   ■ Neocharismatics 3,621 (98%)   ■ Total Renewal: 3,680

SOUTH AFRICA

■ Pentecostals 1,772,371 (8%)   ■ Charismatics 2,331,365 (11%)   ■ Neocharismatics 17,096,264 (81%)
■ Total Renewal: 21,200,000

I. Pentecostal and Charismatic History
   A. The "Official" Histories of South African Pentecostalism
   B. Early African Charismatic Movements
   C. Missionary Influences: The Berlin Mission
   D. Missionary Influences: Henry Callaway
   E. African Independent/Indigenous Churches
   F. South Africa's Black African Charismatics
   G. Charismatic-type Movements among South African Indians
   H. So-Called "Coloured" Charismatics
   I. Multiracial Charismatic Initiatives
   J. New Charismatic Churches
   K. Charismatic Church Organizations

II. Charismatics and Their Critics in South Africa
   A. Methodological Problems in Faith for the Fearful?
   B. Statistical Validity
   C. Further Problems
   D. Evidence of Increased Racial Tolerance
   E. Other Academic Critics
   F. A Place to Feel at Home

The origins and growth of pentecostal and charismatic churches in South Africa is a complex story that cannot be separated from that of African independent/indigenous churches. Shocking as it may seem to many Christians,

prayers for healing, speaking in tongues, and similar phenomena were a part of many traditional African religions long before the arrival of European missionaries. In fact, when they observed traditional practices, many early missionaries thought that Southern African blacks were either a lost tribe of Israel or people whose ancestors had been Christians.

I. PENTECOSTAL AND CHARISMATIC HISTORY.

A. The "Official" Histories of South African Pentecostalism.

According to numerous semi-official accounts, such as the writings of ▸Gordon Lindsay, Bengt Sundkler (1948; 1975), ▸Walter Hollenweger (1972), Gerald Pillay, and even the *Dictionary of South African Biography*, pentecostalism entered South Africa in 1903 when Daniel Bryant was sent as an emissary of divine healing by ▸John Alexander Dowie (1847–1907). Initially, Bryant joined forces with two South Africans who had corresponded with Dowie, Petrus L. le Roux (1865–1943) and his coworker, a Swiss Pietist, Johannes Bücher. Later, in May 1908, four more American missionaries arrived in South Africa. This group was led by ▸John G. Lake (1870–1935) and ▸Thomas Hezmalhalch (1848–1934). They were inspired by Dowie, ▸Charles Parham (1873–1929), and the ▸Azusa Street revival of 1906, which they had visited. Subsequently, in cooperation with le Roux and Bücher, they worked with Lake to found the Apostolic Faith Mission of South Africa (AFMSA) on Oct. 14, 1913.

Earlier, the books and highly successful revival campaigns of Andrew Murray (1828–1917) had prepared the way for both the growth of holiness teachings and pentecostalism (Du Plessis, 1919). For example, le Roux was Murray's student and close confidant. He found Murray's teaching on holiness and healing, expressed in books such as *Absolute Surrender* (1895) and *Divine Healing* (1900), inspiring. After conflict with the Boers (South African whites) in his congregation, le Roux withdrew from the Dutch Reformed Church to found his own Zion Kerk (Zion Church). After joining forces with Lake he was elected president of the AFMSA, a post he held until his death in 1943.

Another influential member of the early pentecostal movement in South Africa was A. A. Cooper, an English sailor who was converted by Rodney "Gipsy" Smith's (1860–1947) mission to Cape Town in 1905. After his conversion he heard about the Azusa Street revival and began to receive the magazine *Apostolic Faith*. After Lake's arrival in South Africa, Cooper worked with him before becoming one of the founders of the Assemblies of God in South Africa (AGSA).

A Canadian pentecostal missionary, Charles William Chawner, arrived in South Africa in Mar. 1907. After church planting in Natal and the Transvaal, he eventually joined forces with Cooper and an American pentecostal missionary, R. M. Turney, who arrived in South Africa in 1908. Together this group formed the nucleus of the AGSA, which was founded around 1909, thus predating the AG–U.S., which was formed in 1914. After the creation of the American body, the Turneys applied to be recognized as ministers and formally registered the name of their mission as the Assemblies of God in South Africa. The affiliation between the American and South African AG lasted until 1925, when the South African church was recognized as an independent district. Finally, in 1932, the AGSA church became totally separate from the AG–U.S.

Another American, George Bowie, who arrived in South Africa in 1909, founded the Pentecost Mission in 1910. He was soon joined by Eleazer Jenkins, a product of the Welsh revival of 1904, who had immigrated as a missionary to South Africa in 1905. In 1910 Bowie and Jenkins joined with Cooper to found the Full Gospel Church of South Africa.

Thus South African pentecostalism is usually traced to a group of American missionaries and English preachers influenced by John Alexander Dowie, Charles Parham, the Azusa Street revival, and the quest for holiness and healing. Out of this mix the founding denominations of South African pentecostalism, the AGSA (1909/1914), Full Gospel Church of South Africa (1910), and the AFMSA (1913) were formed.

Although this history tells the story of white South African denominations, it fails to fully account for the rise of charismatic movements in South Africa and black pentecostalism. Nor does it allow for black African influences on

whites. Another unexplored area is the influence of black African Christians on their fellow blacks in North America.

In his pioneering *In Township Tonight*, David B. Coplan has demonstrated that American missionaries took black South African choirs and other converts to North America on a regular basis in the last quarter of the 19th century. These visits, Coplan convincingly argues, had a profound effect on both black South African music and music in America. Given this data, it is inconceivable that a similar exchange of religious ideas and experiences did not take place. It cannot be ruled out that black South Africans contributed to the growth of American pentecostalism before Azusa Street. It is therefore important to look at the growth of indigenous charismatic/prophetic movements in South Africa.

B. Early African Charismatic Movements.

The first recorded indigenous religious movement in South Africa was that of the Xhosa prophet Ntsikana (1780[?]–1821). Exactly what happened to cause Ntsikana to begin preaching a Christian message is unclear. What is certain is that he underwent a conversion experience at a time when he had no contact with whites, missionaries, or other Christians. This experience dramatically changed his life, and he began an itinerant preaching ministry that involved the giving of prophecies and composition of Christian hymns.

The traditional explanation for Ntsikana's behavior is that he received a message from God by direct revelation and that his teachings were entirely due to the Holy Spirit. In her study *Ntsikana's "Great Hymn,"* Janet Hodgson (1980) argues that this commonly held belief is wrong, because there are oral traditions that indicate that following his conversion Ntsikana initiated extended contact with missionaries. Although Hodgson makes a good case, her evidence is not conclusive, leaving open the possibility that the traditional account of his mission is correct.

What is certain is that Ntsikana developed a theistic theology that went well beyond the ancestor worship and traditional beliefs of his contemporaries. It is also clear that, while he made few lasting converts, many Xhosa flocked to hear his preaching, which prepared the way for later missionary activity. Therefore, although he did not work for any mission organization and never formed his own African independent church, there seems little doubt that his teachings predisposed many blacks to accept Christianity.

In 1857 the events known as the Xhosa Cattle Killing took place, leading to severe disruptions in many traditional societies. (A young girl prophesied that if the Xhosa killed all their cows and stopped growing maize, there would be a general resurrection of the ancestors, a renewal of the earth, and general prosperity.) From a religious viewpoint, the cattle killing episode appears to have gained legitimation from a synthesis between traditional beliefs and Christian preaching. Yet, as with Ntsikana's work, it left no lasting religious movement in African society.

C. Missionary Influences: The Berlin Mission.

A strong impetus for the development of African independent churches and charismatic religious movements was given by the arrival of missionaries from the Berlin Missionary Society, which established permanent stations in South Africa, beginning in 1834. Influenced by German Romanticism and the philosophy of Johann Gottfried von Herder (1744–1803) and Friedrich Julius Stahl (1802–61), the Berlin missionaries mastered African languages and encouraged the use of the vernacular in worship. Unlike many of their English counterparts, who tended to view African cultures as "primitive" and riddled with superstition, the Berlin missionaries respected African customs and spiritual experiences. Therefore, they did not question the reality of dreams and visions in African conversion and Christian living. On the contrary, they regarded such experiences as genuine expressions of the work of the Holy Spirit and encouraged their converts to report such things.

Berlin missionaries systematically taught Africans Christian stories about early church fathers, Christian reformers, and church formation. Africans were encouraged to accept these stories and make them their own. Consequently, they learned to draw analogies between their own experiences and those of the apostles and church fathers. In the process, they lived to create and tell stories about themselves as "fathers" of local congregations and churches. Not unexpectedly, some of these congregations grew into independent churches.

Wangemann, the director of the Berlin Mission Society from 1865 to 1894, was aware of this interweaving of local stories with the Christian historical tradition. For example, in his book *Maléo und Sekukúni* (1869), Wangemann drew an analogy between the experience of the apostle Paul in Greece and the experience of missionaries in Bapediland, and compared the violent persecution of African Christians in 1864 to the persecution of the early church by the Roman Empire.

When speaking about African converts, Wangemann and other Berlin missionaries saw them as akin to "Roman Catholic saints" and encouraged Africans to think of themselves in these terms. For example, following Jacob Mantladi's story of his brutal persecution ordered by Chief Sekukuni in 1864, Wangemann asked Mantladi, "And what was the state of your mind [following the violent beating when Mantladi nearly bled to death]?" Mantladi, who did not die of the beating, answered: "My body was in pain, but the pain was only that of the body! Then I remembered Polycarp, whom they wanted to burn, but who wouldn't burn right away!" (Wangemann, 1869, 160).

Thus, German missionaries taught African converts (1) the idea that Christianity could be followed in the distinct ethnic manner of their ancestors, and (2) the idea that their own life portraits were analogous to those of the founders of the early Christian church.

Consequently, these teachings gave some African Christians a clear sense of mission, namely, to create a genuinely African church in South Africa. In the process, traditional religious experiences, such as the importance of dreams, were given a Christian interpretation. Thus, when Jan Mafadi was about 26 years old in 1857 or 1858, he went to Uitenhage to earn money (Wangemann, 1871, 18). There he heard about "the Word of God." Soon he had three dreams that convinced him of the reality of God and foretold his impending death as a Christian martyr. Upon returning to his home, he and another convert started preaching.

In 1861 an awakening broke out (Wangemann, 1871, 21). On the morning of St. John's Day in 1862, Mafadi told his friend: "The Lord will call me today! Today I shall die!" It was during a battle between Sekukuni and the rebellious sub-chief Mokhoete that Mafadi was shot to death (ibid., 24–25). However, his spiritual power lived on because after his death many Africans claimed that Mafadi appeared to them in visions that led to their conversion.

D. Missionary Influences: Henry Callaway.

Another major influence on the growth of independent churches and charismatic experiences in South Africa was the Anglican missionary Henry Callaway, who was arguably the most remarkable missionary to work in Southern Africa during the 19th century. He was also one of the fathers of the modern charismatic movement, although until now the importance of his work has been completely overlooked by theologians and church historians.

Callaway was born in Lymington, Somerset, England, on Jan. 17, 1817, and died at Otterly St. Mary, Devonshire, England, on Mar. 26, 1890. In 1837 he joined the Society of Friends, but he converted to Anglicanism in 1853 and offered himself for missionary service with the Natal Mission headed by Bishop Colenso. He was ordained in 1856 and became a missionary to the Zulu at Springvale, near Richmond in Southern Natal. Later, in 1873, he was appointed the first missionary bishop of the Anglican Diocese of Kaffraria, which later became St. John's Diocese.

Callaway was the author of a number of important books and articles. He translated most of the Bible (1883) and the Anglican *Book of Common Prayer* (1882) into Zulu and published major collections of Zulu folk tales and history.

Like the Berlin missionaries, Callaway was strongly influenced by German Romanticism and the views of Herder. He believed that God works among all peoples, preparing them for the gospel through his Holy Spirit. Thus, because the Holy Spirit is an ever-present reality, Callaway was prepared to accept the validity of African religious experiences, such as dreams and visions, which were normally treated with scorn by other English missionaries. Like the Berlin missionaries,

Callaway also compared the experiences of his converts with those of early church fathers such as St. Antony, Hilarion, and other early saints (Callaway, 1970, 252).

From Callaway's writings it is clear that his approach to missionary work encouraged just those aspects of religious experience among the Zulu that contributed to the growth of the charismatic movement. Indeed, Callaway recorded aspects of the initiation of traditional diviners that sound very similar to speaking in tongues. These practices involved the composition of "songs," many of which were "without any meaning" (Callaway, 1970, 263, 273).

E. African Independent/Indigenous Churches.

Although there is considerable evidence that the first African independent churches were offshoots of the Berlin Mission, the first well documented African independent church is that of the Methodist preacher Nehemiah Tile, who founded his own church in 1883. Tile's movement, which was essentially a Thembu movement, combined Christian teachings with Thembu nationalism and indigenous African practices. Unfortunately, this brave experiment disintegrated soon after Tile's death in 1891.

From the 1890s on, many African independent churches developed, but most of these were small affairs that attracted few followers and soon failed. It was not until the turn of the century that African independent churches finally took root among blacks in South Africa with the establishment of Isaiah Shembe's amaNazaretha in 1913 and the Zion Christian Church of Ignatius Lekganyane in 1924 (Lukhaimane, 1980).

The growth of African independent churches (AICs) during this century is one of the truly amazing Christian stories of our time. Initially these churches reacted against both political and social discrimination. But they rapidly outgrew the negativity of protest to develop rich theologies that emphasize healing and the gifts of the Holy Spirit. As G. C. Ooshuisen has rightly pointed out, AICs today are rapidly becoming *the* church of South Africa.

In 1960 around 2 million Africans belonged to AICs. By 1990 the number had grown to a phenomenal 8 million, and their rapid growth shows no sign of abating. In other words, in 1960 around 18% of South African blacks belonged to AICs, but by 1990 the figure had grown to 35% of all blacks in South Africa. This makes the AICs larger than the largest "mainline" churches among black South Africans—the Roman Catholic Church and the Methodist Church.

In 1913 there were 32 recognized AICs; by 1949 this number had risen to 800. In 1960 over 2,000 were known, and by 1990 the number had grown to 6,000. The proliferation of "independent churches" or "denominations" is to be explained by the fact that this is essentially a House Church movement. Very few AIC congregations (Oosthuizen estimates about 5%) own or rent church buildings for worship.

He also claims that around 90% of AICs have between 25 and 60 members.

Because of their House-Church or cell structure, AICs create a strong sense of fellowship and belonging in a church community where mutual aid in terms of prayer, encouragement, and practical help are readily given. Through an emphasis on Christian love and the fellowship of the Holy Spirit, these small face-to-face communities meet the needs of members as no other institution in South Africa.

AICs blend aspects of the traditional African with the ever-changing secular culture of modern society (Welbourn; Daneel; Pretorius). Unlike many modern church movements, AICs do not draw primarily from members of established churches. Rather, the bulk of their members, in 1990 at least 5 million, are new converts from traditional African religions (Oosthuizen et al.).

One of the major influences and components of AICs is known as the Zionist movement, which was initiated through contact with *John Alexander Dowie's Christian Catholic Church in Zion, IL. Today around 80% of AICs belong to Zionist-type congregations. The Apostolic Faith Mission (AFMSA), which was founded in 1908 after the arrival of three missionaries from the U.S., was one of the main channels for the transmission of Dowie-inspired ideas to South Africa.

F. South Africa's Black African Charismatics.

The role of black, so-called coloured (mixed-race), and Indian charismatics in South Africa has been largely ignored in the academic literature. To make up for this inadequacy, Richard Shorten (1984) and Stephen Hayes (1990) researched and published accounts of the Iviyo loFakazi bakaKristu (Legion of Christ's Witnesses). Iviyo is a charismatic renewal movement within the (Anglican) church of the Province of Southern Africa (Hayes, 1990, ix). This movement started earlier than the American charismatic renewal and negates, for that reason alone, the claim of American domination that is made by some critics of the movements (see below).

The Legion of Christ's Witnesses is an African-initiated charismatic renewal movement that appeared in Natal and Zululand, South Africa, in the 1940s, some 20 years before a similar movement originated at Van Nuys, CA. Its name makes clear its evangelistic intent. Hayes and Shorten argue that the movement was ignored partly because it is preserved in oral history and partly because it was a semisecret organization that did not make itself fully public until the 1970s.

The reason for this secrecy is best illustrated by a story Bishop Bengt Sundkler told at the founding meeting of the South African Missiological Society in 1972. As a young missionary in Zululand, he observed that a particular woman always left the congregation shortly after he began to preach. Worried about this, he asked the woman if something he was saying upset her. Her reply surprised him and opened his eyes to the nature of African Christianity: "The Holy Spirit comes upon me and I have to shake." She then went on to say that she knew this was "wrong" and that missionaries did not allow shaking in church, so she always left at that point. Sundkler was moved by this explanation and assured her that in the future she was always welcome to shake and do anything else the Spirit of God led her to do in God's house.

Few missionaries were as open-minded as Sundkler, so most African converts lived a double life (Schutte, 1973). Officially, black congregations were Anglican, Methodist, Lutheran, Dutch Reformed, Reformed (Dopper), or belonged to some other mainline mission church. But unofficially, after the white missionaries returned to their homes or if they were not present, God's Spirit was allowed free reign. Thus, following the pattern of German Pietist conventicals, most African congregations held two Sunday services. The first, official service followed mission guidelines and was led by a white; the real worship began at a second, "African" service.

In the Anglican Church, Iviyo was founded to regularize this pattern, encourage spirituality, and prevent schism. Its founders, Alpheus Zulu (later bishop of Zululand) and Philip Mbatha, were concerned with "the lack of power in the life of the church" and with "the failure of the church to affect people's lives." Consequently, they "studied Scriptures and prayed together about this problem." The movement quickly spread beyond Zululand when they prayed together with a youth leader and her young charges in the early 1950s. Soon gifts of the Holy Spirit began to appear, especially the gifts of tongues, prophesying, and healing—the very gifts, it should be mentioned, that have always been part of African religion (Iliffe, 1987; Oosthuizen, 1988).

As inadequate as the data are, it is clear that this renewal movement among black South Africans, and similar movements in other mission churches, attracted people of all walks of life, including clergy, teachers, doctors and nurses, clerks, chiefs, government officials, politicians, and many others who did not fall into Western professions (Hayes, 1990).

Likewise, Iviyo soon forged links with similar groups in the Roman Catholic Church, the Christian Business Men's Fellowship, Derek Crumpton's Christian Interdenominational Fellowship (CIF), and the Scandinavian Baptist mission. Members of Iviyo also made contacts with an Argentinian pentecostal evangelist among other visitors to South Africa.

The absence of American influence at the inception of Iviyo is notable and significant, since academic critics of South African charismatics accuse the movement of being an American import. Since Derek Crumpton modeled the CIF after the ʾFountain Trust in Britain, his contact with the movement did not lead to any American influence either. Crumpton, furthermore, told Hayes that he witnessed white lay representatives from other parishes experience the baptism in the Holy Spirit under Iviyo preaching. In short, if there was any influence, it was from black to white, not the other way around, and certainly not from America (Hayes, 1990).

Another powerful influence on the growth of South African charismatic movements was the personality and success of the black evangelist ʾNicolas B. H. Bhengu (1909–86), who worked in the Transkei and Eastern Cape. Bhengu, an ordained minister in the Assemblies of God (AG), began his evangelistic work in 1945 with a "Back to God" crusade in East London. This led to the development of his mission church, the East London AG, and regular crusades throughout Africa and many other countries.

Bhengu's work inspired many other preachers, including ʾReinhard Bonnke, Paul Lutchmann, and Fred Roberts, the founder of the Durban Christian Centre. His work also had an important impact on the growth of the ʾFull Gospel Business Men's Fellowship International in South Africa, which in turn encouraged the growth of new charismatic churches.

Initially, the mainline pentecostal denominations in South Africa were racially integrated. Very soon after their founding, however, they became bastions of white exclusiveness. Nevertheless, they maintained a strong sense of mission and quickly established missions to black Africans. These missions in turn created separate black "daughter" denominations, in keeping with the dictates of apartheid.

It was not until the 1970s that a strong black leadership emerged that challenged the accommodation and passive racism of the white leadership. When this happened, and men like the Reverend Frank Chikane (1951–) spoke out, the white leadership of the AFMSA reacted with astonished outrage. The trials Chikane and others like him faced are recorded in his autobiography, *No Life of My Own* (1988). Today, however, Chikane and his fellow blacks who suffered for the truth are receiving the recognition they deserve and are playing an important reconciling role in the new South Africa.

G. Charismatic-type Movements among South African Indians.

Oosthuizen (1975) documents the growth of South Africa's largest pentecostal church among Indian people in the Durban area. This is an amazing story, which began through the work of a British immigrant from Bristol, John Alexander Rowlands (1878–1932), who with his son founded the United Pentecostal Mission in Pietermaritzburg in 1925. His remarkable son, ʾJohn F. Rowlands (1909–80), flaunted the racism and social conventions of white South Africans to devote himself fully to the service and evangelization of the Indian people of Natal, which led to the founding of a small chapel, Bethesda Hall, in Durban in 1931. Eventually this church became Bethesdaland, a major church movement that in 1990 boasted over 30,000 members and supported its own Bible school.

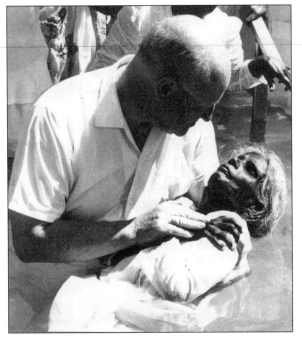

J. F. Rowlands baptizing an elderly convert in South Africa.

Gerald Pillay, an outstanding church historian who grew up in Bethesda, describes (1994) the origins of South African pentecostalism before discussing the central role of Bethesda and the spread of pentecostal religion among Indians throughout South Africa. The later multiplication of pentecostal groups and the growth of newer charismatic movements are well documented. Often inspired by the example of Bethesda, which had trained many of their evangelists, these newer movements often grew rapidly in the 1970s and 1980s.

The growth of integrated new charismatic churches under white leadership, such as the Durban Christian Centre, in the 1980s created a new situation. Former Bethesda evangelists such as Michael Abel and Timothy Rubin joined the new church, increasing its appeal to Indians. And for the first time in South African history, large numbers of Indians worshiped alongside whites, people of mixed race (so-called coloureds), and black Africans. Multiracial worship teams, Sunday schools, Bible studies, and eventually leadership groups developed. All of these in their own way began to break down the barriers of the divisions caused by apartheid.

Karla Poewe interviewed a so-called coloured woman, then in her 80s, who lived near Durban in 1987. This woman told the remarkable story of how her Indian father had been pronounced dead by a white doctor in the 1930s. Stricken with grief, her Zulu mother went to the morgue, where she prayed earnestly for God's help. After some time the "corpse" stirred and her father "returned to life" to live another 25 years. Of course, she added, "today people would say he was

in a coma. But we all believed he was dead." Following this man's remarkable recovery, many of his Hindu relatives converted to Christianity. Whatever really happened, this story is important because it demonstrates the complex interaction between different, and after 1948 officially separated, racial groups, and the spread of pentecostal beliefs from Africans to Indians.

H. So-Called "Coloured" Charismatics.

Under South Africa's apartheid laws, people of mixed race were designated a distinct racial category and known as "coloureds," a term many rejected in favor of "so-called coloured." The growth of pentecostal and charismatic movements and independent churches among the so-called coloured has not been well documented. Nevertheless, works like Donald R. Aeschliman's (1983) give some indication of the strength of these movements, many of which are highly charismatic. Today large pentecostal and charismatic church communities exist among so-called coloureds throughout South Africa.

One example shows the dedication of these Christians. Clive Dutlow, a leading medical researcher at the University of Cape Town, lived in the barren "coloured" township of Mitchell's Plain. He received many job offers in North America and Europe but refused to take the easy way out and emigrate. Instead, he helped found the thriving Mitchell's Plain Christian Fellowship and the Koinonia Foundation.

I. Multiracial Charismatic Initiatives.

The Koinonia Foundation was officially launched on Jan., 16, 1988, and seeks to encourage the growth of small businesses among Christians, regardless of race, thus making the poor productive. In addition, through a profit-tithing scheme, the businesses supported by the Koinonia Foundation in turn run feeding programs for poor children, help with educational initiatives, and carry out a host of other creative social programs.

Another example of interracial cooperation is Jesus for Africa, a charismatic evangelistic organization led by a South African Indian, Paul Lutchman, and Reinhard Bonnke's former African associate, Michael Kolisang. Such interracial cooperation, especially between East Indians and Africans, is rare in Africa and represents a real witness to the healing power of Christ.

In addition to holding tent meetings throughout South Africa's black townships, Jesus for Africa also seeks to encourage local churches to develop feeding programs and orphanages for needy children. Thus, charismatic Christian evangelism often grows into social action.

On a much smaller scale, movements such as the Joweto Project led by Bushy Venter, a white, and Paul Mbete, an African, illustrate the real concern that young people meet across racial barriers during the troubled 1980s. The Joweto Project ran a communal farm and a variety of church-related groups aimed at breaking down racial stereotypes and ministering to the needy through the encouragement of small businesses and the establishment of health centers and other social projects.

In addition to these practical projects, the highly visible charismatic music group Friends First made a significant impact on young South Africans during the troubled days of the 1980s. Originating in a 21-day fast by the Glenridge Fellowship in Durban in 1985, the group is now recognized by the secular press as one of South Africa's top music groups. It is a highly professional, multiracial band that has produced three records, including the prophetic *We See a New Africa* (1987).

Many of their songs were banned by the South African Broadcasting Company because they clearly rejected apartheid. At the same time more traditional pentecostal and charismatic churches were suspicious of them because of their perceived "political bias" and willingness to play to secular audiences. Yet, in fact, they were devout Christians who sought to take the message of reconciliation to all peoples.

Although not primarily a charismatic movement, South Africa's remarkable missionary organization Africa Enterprise deserves mention. Michael Cassidy, a young white South African, studied at Fuller Seminary in Pasadena, CA, where he was impressed by the healing services of ►Kathryn Kuhlman. Upon returning to South Africa in 1962 he founded Africa Enterprise on the model of the Billy Graham organization. From its inception, Africa Enterprise was multiracial and open to charismatic experiences.

Cassidy's concern for South Africa and his revulsion at the government's official policy of apartheid, which he rightly saw as anti-Christian and a hindrance to evangelism, led Cassidy to organize one of the first major multiracial Christian events in South Africa since the beginning of the apartheid era in 1948. This was the South African Christian Congress on Mission and Evangelism, held in Durban in Mar. 1973. For the first time in decades, black and white Christians such as Bishop Zulu, Desmond Tutu, David Bosch, and Beyers Naude shared a common platform. Following this remarkable achievement Cassidy went on to organize other conferences, such as the South African Christian Leaders Assembly in 1979, and he eventually founded the National Initiative for Reconciliation (NIR) in 1985. Highly respected throughout the whole of Africa, this organization is one of the success stories of African missions in this century.

Far more impressive in terms of attracting sheer numbers was the evangelistic work of Prussian evangelist ►Reinhard Bonnke (1940–), who arrived in South Africa in 1967 as a missionary for the German pentecostal mission Bund Freier Pfingstgemeinden (Association of Free Pentecostal Assemblies). In 1972 he founded the evangelistic organization Christ for All Nations. Following a highly successful healing crusade in Botswana in 1975, he purchased a tent capable of seating 10,000 people in 1977. His subsequent campaigns throughout Africa attracted huge crowds, sometimes in excess of 250,000. Although he never became involved in organizations like the NIR, Bonnke's South African crusades were always integrated, as was his evangelistic team.

Less well known, but important in South African history, was ►Youth With A Mission's Go Festival, held in Durban, June 25–July 3, 1987. It deserves mention because it was the first large conference during the apartheid era where young people shared accommodations regardless of race. Thus the Go Fest, which on at least two occasions concluded with joyful multiracial dancing, was a landmark in the destruction of apartheid.

J. New Charismatic Churches.

The remarkable rapid growth of new charismatic churches in South Africa during the 1980s was preceded by two extraordinary religious movements. The first was the healing crusades of Dr. van Zyl, a converted physician and the medical officer of health for the town of Stanger on Natal's north coast. According to his own testimony, these healing crusades began spontaneously in the 1970s, after a black African called at his free African clinic for the treatment of a serious eye condition. The condition was so serious that nothing could be done. Before he left the surgery the old African man who had come for treatment made a final request: "Please pray for me."

Although Dr. van Zyl was a good member of the Dutch Reformed Church, he did not really believe in healing prayer. Nevertheless, as an act of kindness he prayed over the old man. To his utter astonishment the man returned three weeks later completely healed. This was the beginning of a three-year healing ministry and the founding of a new charismatic congregation in Stanger. But, as Dr. van Zyl admits, after three years the amazing miracles that had accompanied his ministry suddenly became very infrequent. When asked how he understood this strange phenomena, he replied that "in the Scriptures the Lord seems to send miracles when revivals are needed. Then they grow less frequent."

Another forerunner of the new charismatic churches was Durban's Invisible Church. The remarkable movement was founded by Carl Cronje, formerly director of South Africa's Teen Challenge. After a messy divorce, Cronje dropped out of ministry and moved to Durban, where he found an "ordinary job." While in Durban he met members of the surfing subculture, which was the main drug culture among young whites. Over the next few years, Cronje witnessed to these people and gradually established a thriving congregation where he eventually became the minister. In the early 1980s Cronje told his congregation, which had over 2,000 members, that "the Lord had told him" to withdraw from ministry to prevent the creation of a personality cult. Abruptly he left the Invisible Church, which then split up into several thriving charismatic congregations, including the highly creative Glenridge Christian Fellowship.

From the late 1970s on, a series of similar events led to the rapid growth of numerous multiracial, independent churches that were soon labeled the "new charismatic churches" of South Africa. A typical example of this growth is the Durban Christian Centre, led by Fred and Nellie Roberts, which has around 2,000 members, 60% of whom are black. Like many other new charismatic churches, the Durban Christian Centre soon established a multiracial Bible school, with a woman, Ann Bellingham, as its principal.

In Pretoria Ed Roebert (1943–97) founded the 3,000-strong Hatfield Community Church (Michell, 1985). Although it was mainly white, due to its location, it managed to bridge the chasm between the traditionally hostile Afrikaners and English-speaking South Africans. Few visitors to South Africa realize the deep distrust that exists between the two white groups. Traditionally the Afrikaners hated the English; they accused them of genocide against Afrikaners during the Second Anglo-Boer War (1899–1902). For their part, the English looked down on Afrikaners and blamed them for creating apartheid.

In churches like Hatfield, the disappearance of Afrikaner-English tensions led people to question other old prejudices. Thus, one Hatfield pastor told how he grew up to "hate the English." Following his conversion, however, he realized that if he could love the English, he could also love blacks. As a result, the church as a body reached out to blacks.

Most spectacular of all is Ray Macaulay's (1949–) Rhema Church in Randburg with over 12,000 members. During the apartheid years, 25% of these were black. Black radicals scorned Rhema and claimed that only upwardly mobile blacks who see themselves as "middle class" attended (Steele, 1986a). But after the 1990 end to apartheid, and particularly after the election of President Mandela, Rhema was recognized as an important spiritual force in South Africa.

A different tradition is found in the New Covenant churches. Under apartheid the emphasis was more on community and direct political involvement. The New Covenant churches have produced some damning "prophecies," condemning apartheid as evil and calling for rapid social change. Although they appeared to be in the forefront of the struggle for a new society, many of their leaders and members received "a call from God" to leave South Africa in the early 1990s. Today many of these people live in Australia, where they have established flourishing charismatic churches.

Many other, smaller ministries, such as that of Derek Morphew's Tygerberg Christina Community, near Cape Town, and Tim Salmon's Christian Centre in Pietermaritzburg, deserve mentioning. Space does not permit a complete inventory of all these dynamic churches; suffice it to say that from 1980 on, South Africa saw revitalization movements that replicated the revival crusades of Andrew Murray in the 1880s.

K. Charismatic Church Organizations.

South African charismatic churches are loosely linked by various umbrella organizations that have proven to be remarkably unstable. The most informal group was the Fellowship of Christian Churches founded by Fred Roberts. Then there are the Relating Churches of the New Covenant community, which see Dudley Daniels, who now lives in Australia, in a prophetic or apostolic role. Finally, there is the large International Fellowship of Christian Churches, originally led by Ed Roebert, Ray Macaulay, Tim Salmon, and the Afrikaans evangelist Nikki van der Westhuizen.

It should also be observed that many South African founders, evangelists, and prophets cultivated links with ►Yonggi Cho of South Korea, Benson Idosa in Nigeria, and other non-Western charismatic leaders. Dudley Daniels, who headed New Covenant Ministries, and two other prominent founders of independent churches in his network now run Coastlands International Christian Centre and New Covenant Ministries in Australia. Their interest in the Far East in turn affects related churches in South Africa, just as their South African experiences affect churches in Australia and the Far East.

The best known South African with an international ministry was, of course, ►David du Plessis (1905–67), who originally belonged to the AFMSA. It was Du Plessis who spread the pentecostal experience to American Roman Catholics, thus beginning the charismatic renewal of the 1960s.

II. CHARISMATICS AND THEIR CRITICS IN SOUTH AFRICA.

During the mid 1980s a number of academics began to level serious charges against South African charismatics, accusing them of supporting apartheid, political reaction, racism, and various other heinous deeds. Because their writings appeared to be based on surveys and other forms of sociological research, rather than on theology, the criticisms received widespread attention and were generally believed to be true. As a result, some deep rifts were created between charismatic groups closely associated with mainline denominations, such as Africa Enterprise, and the newer charismatic churches that emerged from the renewal movement of the early 1980s. Thus, rather than helping rid the country of apartheid, the effect of these criticisms was to further divide Christians and weaken opposition to the regime by spreading distrust and ugly rumors.

More recently these vicious attacks on South African charismatics have reappeared in German literature, where they are used to lend credibility to similar attacks on evangelical and charismatic churches in Germany (Engel, 1993). They have also been incorporated into books like *Exporting the American Gospel: Global Christian Fundamentalism* (Bouwer, Gifford, Rose), which is a vicious attack on both evangelical and charismatic Christianity. Therefore, even though the claims made by the critics are dated and can be shown to be false, they deserve careful consideration because they fit into a pattern of anticharismatic propaganda worldwide.

The first major attack on South African charismatics was *Faith for the Fearful?* (Moran and Schlemmer, 1984), which soon became the benchmark against which all other studies of South African charismatics were measured.

Faith for the Fearful? had a big impact in South Africa during the mid 1980s by confirming the worst fears of mainline Christians about the charismatic movement. The force of the book's conclusions lay in the claim of its authors that they based their findings on sociological evidence, which, they claimed, showed people who joined new independent charismatic churches to be reactionary neurotics. These findings were widely reported in the press and generally accepted without criticism (Hunter and Hocken, 1993, 74–79; Poewe, 1994, 51–58).

Unlike earlier criticisms of new charismatic churches, this book did not look like the work of a disgruntled theologian or rival church leader concerned about the loss of members of his congregation to another church. Instead, the criticisms seemed to rest on scientifically validated sociological data and therefore could not be easily dismissed. But readers ought to have been alerted to potential problems by reading the opening statement in the book's preface: "This study of new churches was commissioned by Diakonia, . . . principally because the new churches appear to be discouraging their members from developing an interest in issues of social justice. . . . In addition the rapid growth of the new churches might to some extent reflect on the established churches' ability to address the needs of followers."

Whatever one may think about this statement, it is certainly not unbiased. Neither is the following one found at the beginning of the first chapter: "As a result of . . . their rapid growth, their controversial . . . teaching . . . and . . . effects on social change in South Africa, it was decided that an investigation into these churches in the greater Durban area would be interesting."

Quite clearly *Faith for the Fearful?* was not a disinterested academic study. From the start it was a polemic inspired by the challenge the new churches presented to established denominations, particularly the Roman Catholic Church. The authors also seem to have begun with the preconceived belief that these churches represented the forces of reaction. Anyone who doubts this judgment only has to read the conclusion: "Established church clergy can, and indeed should, without sensationalism or exaggeration, point out the dangers inherent in the new churches, and expose the hostility of the new churches to much that is correctly and essentially Christian . . . the doctrinal foundation of the new churches can be shown to be incorrect, if not heretical."

What made this strong language acceptable to readers was that it appeared to be validated by the sociological research the authors used to attack new charismatic churches by saying things like, "Survey results showed . . . There is therefore some suggestion that the new churches are appealing to people with problems or particular personality types, i.e., those who tend to be anxious, neurotic, or 'hysterical'" (1984, 170).

Not surprisingly, they also found that "most respondents in the sample perceive the world, and possibly South Africa particularly, as dangerous and threatening" (1984, 170). This led them to conclude that "the teachings of the new churches are enhancing the authoritarian tendencies or traits of their members" (1984, 171). Politically the implications of this was said to be that "new church charismatics are more politically conservative than their established church counterpart. . . . Their aversion to the social gospel is not neutral and amounts to support of the status quo" (1984, 179).

If these findings are correct, and if, as the authors claim, the teachings of charismatic churches encourage and actually increase such tendencies, then the case against the charismatics would be damning, not only in South Africa but worldwide.

On the other hand, if the author had made these and similar statements on the basis of theological arguments, or if they had invoked doctrines to justify their position, most people would have dismissed the book without further thought. Yet the "sociological" conclusions were in fact built on preconceived theological assumptions.

Not surprisingly, most readers, unfamiliar with the methods used in the social sciences, accepted the word of the authors on the authority of their claim to be presenting valid sociological evidence. The problem is, they were not. A close examination of the book shows that the entire study is fundamentally flawed—to the extent that its findings are almost totally invalid.

A. *Methodological Problems in* Faith for the Fearful?

The basic problem with *Faith for the Fearful?* is the book's lack of scholarly rigor. This becomes evident when it is realized that the entire study is based on a sample of 80 people and that the majority of these people belonged to what the authors call "established churches." Second, rather than being a study of South African charismatics, the book is actually a flawed study of one particular church in Durban. Thus, all of the authors' evidence about "new church charismatics" comes from a sample of 30 people belonging to one congregation, the Durban Christian Centre.

The other 50 people in the sample were drawn from an undisclosed number of congregations belonging to five different denominations. Twenty members of these established churches are identified as "charismatics." But they are "good" charismatics because they belong to mainline churches that are said to be socially concerned and politically active. The remaining members of the sample were traditionalists who had little sympathy for charismatic religion (1984, 47).

To be fair to the authors, they end the book by cautioning their readers that "because of the size and nature of the sample, the findings of this survey are necessarily tentative." But they immediately follow up this admission with the statement, "However, certain trends emerged fairly consistently and unambiguously through the survey and it is these trends which require consideration and comment" (1984, 169).

In the rest of the book, however, they repeatedly talk about "membership in the new churches," "new church charismatic respondents," "the new churches," and "new church charismatics" as though they were writing about charismatics throughout South Africa and not a mere 30 people selected from one church.

The confusion is increased by the fact that after explaining the nature of their sample in chapter 6, an entire chapter is devoted to discussing the history, organization, membership, and finances, etc., of six new charismatic churches in the Durban area (chapter 7). This information is totally unnecessary in terms of the sample itself. But it serves a propaganda purpose by creating the subconscious impression that the sociological data is based on a survey undertaken in all six churches. Thus, by associating "new church charismatics" with six different churches and never stating, except on page 47, that the survey centered on the Durban Christian Center, a totally misleading impression is created.

Further, the impression that the authors were working with a large sample is reinforced by the use of percentages in all their tables. It is, of course, normal to work with percentages, and the approach used would be acceptable if the sample were not a mere 30 people and if it were based on probability sampling. But it was not.

B. Statistical Validity.

Instead of telling their readers that this research has no statistical validity, the authors of *Faith for the Fearful?* misleadingly state, "We are fully aware that this study is not as rigorous in statistical and sampling terms as we would have liked it to be . . . it represents an exploratory piece of research and . . . was intended to provide insights into trends and tendencies rather than measurable differences between religious categories" (1984, 48).

The plain sense of this statement is that while the study is statistically valid, its margin of error is higher than the authors would like. In other words, the statement with its qualification about "measurable differences" strongly suggests high standards on the part of the authors who see limitations to their work but did their best on a limited budget. What the average layperson does not realize is that a study of this nature has *no statistical validity whatsoever* and cannot be used to extrapolate "trends and tendencies." Yet this is exactly what

the authors do, while suggesting that "certain trends emerged fairly consistently and unambiguously throughout the survey, and it is these trends which require consideration and comment" (1984, 169).

This is nonsense. A nonrandom sample of 30 is far too small to allow for statistically valid inferences. Yet instead of admitting this, the authors argue that because "the sampling could not be rigorous . . . the key focus group had to be sampled by means of a rough quota sample based on broad estimates of the social profiles of the new church group" (1984, 46).

Again, to the layperson the apparently technical terms and sociological jargon about "sampling," "focus group," "rough quota sample," and "broad estimates of the social profiles" sound competent and enhance the apparent value of the study. What most people do not realize is that whatever the authors thought they achieved with *Faith for the Fearful?* their work provides no data from which statistically valid generalizations can be drawn. They nevertheless throw caution to the wind and make numerous generalizations about South African charismatics that quickly became part of the received wisdom of mainline churches.

C. Further Problems.

Before the conclusions drawn in *Faith for the Fearful?* are accepted, several things need to be noted. First, even if the survey results were statistically valid, they would not allow for generalizations beyond membership of the Durban Christian Centre. Therefore, they cannot be applied to members of other new charismatic churches in Durban or in the rest of South Africa. The evidence presented, at best, applies to one specific church.

Second, when we examine the section of the book that deals specifically with political issues, things are not as clear as the authors claim. Compared with the respondents from the mainline churches used in the book, members of the Durban Christian Centre seem to support the government. But this finding is misleading, because it does not take into account ethnic background or the educational level of the people interviewed.

The Durban Christian Centre had a relatively large number of Afrikaners among its members. As a group, Afrikaners were more indoctrinated than English-speaking South Africans to believe in apartheid and to support the National Party, which was an Afrikaans political party.

Therefore, before anything can be said about the political attitude of members of the Durban Christian Centre, it is essential to compare their attitudes with those of people from a similar background belonging to other churches. One cannot simply compare a mixed group of people with English and Afrikaans backgrounds against members of "established," English-language churches whose membership is predominantly drawn from the English-speaking section of the South African population.

Equally important is the fact that in drawing conclusions from their data the authors did not take into account educational attainment when political attitudes were discussed. Thus, while 35% of the mainline church traditionalists held university degrees, only 3% of Durban Christian Centre members held one. Since education plays a large role in reducing prejudice, any comparison between two groups that does not factor in educational achievement is meaningless.

D. Evidence of Increased Racial Tolerance.

A very important but totally neglected finding of *Faith for the Fearful?* is the fact that "none of the sample groups was found to be particularly racist" and that membership of the Durban Christian Centre "apparently increased tolerance" of other races (1984, 82). These findings did not fit the authors' argument and were dismissed by saying, "These 'non-racist' findings are confusing in view if the fact that the majority of new church charismatics . . . vote Nationalist" (1984, 83). Yet according to a national poll published by Market and Opinion Surveys in 1984, only 58.5% of whites were prepared to accept blacks in their churches, while 87% of Durban Christian Centre members were prepared to accept blacks as personal friends (1984, 78).

What is more, members of the Durban Christian Centre as a whole backed up the answers they gave to survey questions by attending a church that even the authors of *Faith for the Fearful?* grudgingly admit was integrated. This admission points to another misrepresentation of the Durban Christian Centre found in the book: "The new churches have a predominantly white membership (80%)" (1984, 56). Yet in another place they clearly state that only 70% of the congregation at the Durban Christian Centre were white. The rest were black. The significance of this can be seen when it is realized that while the Anglican Church is theoretically integrated in South Africa, even today it is very difficult to find congregations attended by whites where there are more than a few token blacks. At the time of the study it was certainly difficult to find a South African Anglican church where more than 5% of its regular congregation were black. Seen in this light, the achievement of the Durban Christian Centre, where 30% of the members were black, looks positively amazing.

E. Other Academic Critics.

Three other academic writers, including Mary de Hass, Ove Gustafsson, and Paul Gifford, strongly attack charismatics in Southern Africa, using what they claim is evidence gathered through the use of social-scientific methods. In fact, when their work is carefully examined, all three fail to use acceptable empirical research methods.

Paul Gifford's *The Religious Right in Southern Africa* is a good example of the way charismatics have been condemned on the flimsiest of evidence. Gifford claims that the first three chapters of his book are "mainly historical and sociological." The biggest problem with this book is that although it has 118 pages, only 17 at most deal with Southern Africa. The rest contains an assortment of charges about the CIA and a right-wing American conspiracy to subvert Africa and the Third World.

Although Gifford provides extensive documentation to back up his claims, the works he cites in the first three chapters are essentially journalistic political and theological polemics. A careful examination of his footnotes show that out of 256 references in these chapters, only 10 are to writings by sociologists, 10 by historians, and 18 by theologians. In other words, a mere 38 out of 256 references are to serious academic works. The rest are to newspaper and magazine articles, journalistic books, and popular religious literature. Interesting as these references are, they are hardly the basis for a serious scholarly study of charismatics.

The only section of this book that appears to be based on empirical research is chapter 3, where Gifford uses material from six interviews and gives evidence of having visited a number of religious groups. Once again the problem here is the small number of interviews and the fact that they were all with individuals he considered significant. No attempt seems to have been made at a systematic study of charismatic organizations or at soliciting the views of their rank-and-file members. Further, no details are given of the method used in interviewing or of the way Gifford approached any of the groups he discusses when making his observations. The absence of any methodological specifics, combined with the scarcity of academically acceptable documentation in the rest of the book, leads to the highly probable conclusion that the interviews and observations are in fact unscientific reports that have no validity in generalizing about charismatic Christianity in Southern Africa.

Another feature shared by all the critics discussed here is their obsession with the danger of importing "American religion" into Africa. The problem is that these criticisms ignore the fact that the essential forms of American pentecostalism and charismatic religion share African roots. They also overlook the influence of Korean charismatics such as Paul Yonggi Cho and English and Australian charismatics, all of whom have had a great influence in South Africa. In fact, the growth of charismatic Christianity in South Africa is better seen as part of an international network representing a worldwide phenomena and not as the work of any particular national group.

After blaming the existence of new charismatic churches in South Africa on Americans, these critics link the theologies of charismatic churches to the so-called "prosperity gospel" found in the writings of Kenneth Hagin and his son-in-law, Kenneth Copeland. Once again the basic problem with these criticisms is that they single out one aspect of the preaching of some South African charismatics and in doing so fail to ask what these themes mean within the total theology of the people concerned.

The problem with these criticisms is that they do not explain why many black Africans are attracted to "prosperity" teachings. A better explanation of the popularity of prosperity preaching among black Africans is that these ideas tap a deep well of traditional concern among Africans. Fred Welbourn's now classic work *East African Rebels*, or Bishop Sundkler's equally important *Bantu Prophets in South Africa*, amply demonstrate that a concern for health, wealth, and material success was typical of many African charismatic and independent churches long before American-style prosperity teachings were introduced to Africa. Therefore, it can be argued that Africans did not need Western evangelists to "corrupt" them on this issue, and to suggest that they did is both to misunderstand traditional African religion and to insult the creativity of African Christians.

The truth is that the examples of the "prosperity gospel" used by the critics is almost entirely based on written sources, most of which come from America. Thus, they provide no evidence about what is actually taught by people in Southern Africa, nor do they examine the way Southern Africans, both black and white, accept, modify, or reject what they hear and read. Yet it is precisely this close analysis of what is happening in Africa that is needed before any meaningful discussion can take place about the impact of such preaching.

Nor do any of these criticisms take into account books like Derek Morphew's *South Africa: The Powers Behind* (1989), which offered a sharp critique of racism and related sins. Finally, the work of charismatic music groups like Friends First deserves a special mention. This courageous multiracial group sang out their criticisms of apartheid with inspiring music and powerfully worded songs written by people like Alan Paton's nephew Nicki Paton in defiance of the South African government and its unjust laws (see above).

F. A Place to Feel at Home.

In his classic studies of East African religion, Fred Welbourn suggested that the creation of a sense of community, or as he put it, "a place to feel at home," characterized the appeal of African independent churches. A similar point has been made much more recently by Inus Daneel in his *Quest for Belonging* (1987), and the evidence suggests that the same dynamic appears to be at work in new charismatic churches in South Africa, from which we should expect to see further developments in the future that will radically impact the rest of the world.

■ **Bibliography:** D. B. Aeschliman, "The Independent Churches of the Coloured People of the Cape Flats" (diss., U. of Cape Town, 1983) ▌ A. Anderson, *Bazalwane: African Pentecostals in South Africa* (1992) ▌ idem, *Moya: The Holy Spirit in an African Context* (1991) ▌ idem, with S. Otwang, *Tumelo: The Faith of African Pentecostals in South Africa* (1993) ▌ M. S. Benham, *Henry Callaway, M.D., D.D., First Bishop for Kaffraria: His Life–History and Work* (1896) ▌ C. J. Beyers, *Dictionary of South African Biography*, vol. 4 (1981) ▌ G. P. Brouwer and S. D. Rose, *Exporting the American Gospel: Global Christian Fundamentalism* (1996) ▌ H. Callaway, *The Religious System of the AmaZulu* (1970) ▌ M. Cassidy, *Prisoners of Hope: The Story of South African Christians at the Crossroads* (1974) ▌ idem, *Bursting the Wineskins* (1983) ▌ idem, *Chasing the Wind* (1985) ▌ F. Chikane, *No Life of My Own* (1988) ▌ D. B. Coplan, *In Township Tonight: South Africa's Black City Music and Theater* (1985) ▌ I. Daneel, *Quest for Belonging* (1987) ▌ D. du Plessis, *The Spirit Bade Me Go* (1970) ▌ J. du Plessis, *The Life of Andrew Murray of South Africa* (1919) ▌ A. A. Dubb, *Community of the Saved: An African Revivalist Church in the Eastern Cape* (1976) ▌ L. Engel, E. Kamphausen, and H. Linz, eds., *Fundamentalismus in Afrika und America* (1993) ▌ P. Gifford, *The Religious Right in Southern Africa* (1988) ▌ L. Hartwig, ed., *Religion and Oppression: The Misuse of Religion for Social, Political and Economic Subjugation* (1989) ▌ S. Hayes, *Black Charismatic Anglicans* (1990) ▌ J. Hodgson, *Ntsikana's 'Great Hymn': A Xhosa Expression of Christianity in the Early 19th-Century Eastern Cape* (1980) ▌ W. J. Hollenweger, *The Pentecostals* (1988; orig. ed. 1972) ▌ J. N. Horn, *From Rags to Riches: An Analysis of the Faith Movement and Its Relation to the Classical Pentecostal Movement* (1989) ▌ H. D. Hunter and P. D. Hocken, *All Together in One Place* (1993) ▌ G. Lindsay, *John Alexander Dowie: A Life Story of Trials, Tragedies and Triumphs* (1980) ▌ E. K. Lukhaimane, *The Zion Christian Church of Ignatius (Engenas) Lekganyane, 1924–1948: An African Experiment with Christianity* (thesis, U. of the North, 1980) ▌ J. Michell, *Church Ablaze: The Hatfield Story* (1985) ▌ S. E. Moran and L. Schlemmer, *Faith for the Fearful?* (1984) ▌ D. Morphew, *South Africa: The Powers Behind* (1989) ▌ A. Murray, *Absolute Surrender* (1895) ▌ idem, *Divine Healing* (1900) ▌ G. C. Oosthuizen, *The Healer-Prophet in Afro-Christian Churches* (1992) ▌ idem, *Moving the Waters: 50 Years of Pentecostal Revival in Bethesda* (1975) ▌ G. Pillay, ed., *Religion and the Future* (1992) ▌ idem, *Religion at the Limits: Pentecostalism among Indian South Africans* (1994) ▌ K. Poewe, ed., *Charismatic Christianity as a Global Culture* (1994) ▌ H. L. Pretorius, *Sound the Trumpet of Zion* (1985) ▌ G. Schutte, *Swart Doppers?* (1974) ▌ R. J. Shorten, *Iviyo Lofakazi Bakakristu (The Legion of Christ's Wittnesses): A Study of a Renewal Movement in the Church of the Province of Southern Africa's Diocese of Zululand* (thesis, U. of Cape Town, 1984) ▌ R. Steele, *Plundering Hell: The Reinhard Bonnke Story* (1984) ▌ idem, *Populating Heaven: The Ongoing Story of Reinhard Bonnke's Miracle Ministry* (1986a) ▌ idem, *Ray McCauley: A Biography* (1986b) ▌ B. Sundkler, *Bantu Prophets in South Africa* (1961) ▌ idem, *Zulu Zion and Some Swazi Zionists* (1975) ▌ U. van der Heyden and H. Liebau, eds., *Missionsgeschichte-Kirchengeschichte-Weltgeschichte* (1996) ▌ T. Wangemann, *Lebensbilder aus Südafrika* (1871) ▌ idem, *Maléo und Sekukúni: Ein Lebensbild aus Südafrika* (1869) ▌ F. B. Welbourn, *East African Rebels* (1961).

■ I. Hexham; K. Poewe-Hexham

SOUTH KOREA

■ Pentecostals 2,393,749 (32%)   ■ Charismatics 2,020,598 (27%)   ■ Neocharismatics 3,165,652 (42%)
■ Total Renewal: 7,579,999

  I. Revival Meetings as Pentecostalism
      A. *The Revival of 1903*
      B. *The Revival of 1905–6*
      C. *The Revival of 1907*

 II. The Prayer Mountain Movement
      A. *Yong Do Lee and Prayer in the Mountain*
      B. *The Yongmun Prayer Mountain Movement*

III. The Coming of the Pentecostal Denominations
      from Abroad
      A. *The Chosen Pentecostal Church (1928–45)*
      B. *The Korean Pentecostal Church (1945–52)*
      C. *The Korean Assemblies of God*
      D. *The Church of God in Korea*
      E. *The Church of God of Prophecy*
      F. *The Church of the Foursquare Gospel in
         Korea.*
      G. *The Korean Pentecostal Holiness Church*

 IV. Catholic Charismatics in Korea

Pentecostal missionaries did not land in Korea until 1928, when ʼMary Rumsey arrived as the first independent pentecostal missionary to Seoul. Under the blessing of the Lord, God poured out the Holy Spirit from the beginning stage of Korean missions. Pentecostal distinctives, such as healing, gifts of the Spirit, and supernatural miracles were manifested even before the arrival of the first pentecostal missionary. During her 118 years of church history, the Korean pentecostal church has grown enough to influence other churches. Not only the pentecostal churches, but mainline denominational churches also follow pentecostal theology and worship styles. They pray for the sick, encourage the congregation to speak in other tongues, lift up their hands when they worship the Lord, and pray for supernatural miracles. It would be better to describe the Korean church as "charismatic."

The pentecostal movement in Korea will be studied from four dimensions: the revival meetings in the early part of the 20th century, the prayer mountain movement of the 1950s, the coming of the pentecostal denominations from abroad after 1950, and the Catholic charismatic movement.

I. REVIVAL MEETINGS AS PENTECOSTALISM.

The beginning of the pentecostal movement in Korea is a little different from that which occurred in the United States at the beginning of this century. In Korea it began as a revival movement. Most Korean churches still hold revival meetings once or twice a year. Revivals have occurred in the Korean church, accompanied by what pentecostals describe as the baptism of the Holy Spirit, healing, gifts of the Holy Spirit,

and supernatural miracles. The revival movements in the early part of this century can be divided into three waves.

A. The Revival of 1903.

The first revival began at Wonsan in Aug. 1903. A group of seven Methodist missionaries met for a week of prayer and Bible study. Among the missionaries were R. A. Hardie, who had given up his medical practice in order to concentrate on evangelistic work, and three women: Mary C. White from Southern Methodist Mission in China and Josephine Hounshell from Seoul, who together had made a trip to Wonsan to visit their mutual friend Mary Knowles. The three women had a deep hunger for a new spiritual experience. The meeting took place under the leadership of the visiting missionary from China, Miss White; its theme was the Holy Spirit. Hardie, the senior missionary, was asked to prepare three messages on prayer. In the midst of preparing these messages, he was drawn again and again to the last portion of Luke 11:13: "How much more will your heavenly Father give the Holy Spirit to those who ask him!" Hardie began to desire this "more" of the Holy Spirit, and soon he experienced the fulfillment of the promise of the Holy Spirit. At the next Sunday morning service, he shared his pentecostal experience with the congregation.

This led several Christians to confess their sins and shortcomings. In subsequent Bible study meetings led by Frederick Franson, many Korean believers also confessed their sins. Confession of sins was an outstanding feature of the meeting. Even public confession of one's sins, although difficult and risky, took place by the power of the Holy Spirit. No matter what the cost might have been, restitution followed because of the genuine confession of sins.

The revival in Wonsan affected Christians and non-Christians alike in all major cities of Korea. The people in northern Chungchong Province responded warmly to the gospel. The people in Ulju county of northern Korea created an especially fruitful soil for missionary cultivation. One year later, in 1904, this same Wonsan Conference experience was repeated. Because of this revival, the number of Christians increased threefold in three years. But there was no report of speaking of tongues during the 1903 Wonsan Conference.

B. The Revival of 1905–6.

The pentecostal outpouring of the Holy Spirit swept Korea in 1905–6. Remarkable meetings were held in the city of Pyongyang. Both the Central and South Gate churches were crowded, and 700 converts enrolled during a two-week period. Deeper Life Conferences were held to allow for maximum participation at Wonsan, Pyongyang, and Seoul in 1906. A Bible study on the second coming of

Christ reinforced the need to face the question of human sin and the contrasting sinless nature of Christ.

In 1906 Howard A. Johnson of New York shared what he had witnessed of the working of the Holy Spirit in Wales and in India. Those who heard him felt a deep longing for a similar experience. Through the following months, daily noon prayer meetings were carried on. They were enthralled by the possibility that the same blessing might be poured out upon their beloved Korea of which they heard from those who had experienced the Welsh revival.

As soon as the harvest was finished, the church at Mokpo in the southwestern region of Korea held revival meetings in which J. L. Gerdine of the Southern Methodist Mission was invited as a speaker. Forty-two leaders from nearby churches took part in the meetings, which were held not only for evangelizing unbelievers but also to challenge believers to a deeper devotional life. After the revivals, the Korean church doubled in size. In December the Holy Spirit was manifested with great power during meetings held by W. L. Swallen in Chinmanpo, in which he spoke from 1 John. At every church in which the revivals were held, all seats were taken.

C. The Revival of 1907.

The revival that began in 1903 reached its climax in 1907, at the Pyongyang meeting. The missionaries held short-term Bible schools in January of every year. The meetings were scheduled to be held at the Jangdaehyun Church on Jan. 2–15. The revivals from the previous years had given people a hunger for the outpouring of the Holy Spirit. More than 1,500 people gathered every night (so women were excluded for lack of room). On the first night, Jan. 6, Rev. Sun Joo Kil preached on "Open Your Heart and Receive the Holy Spirit," emphasizing repentance. On the last night, Rev. Blair preached from 1 Cor. 12:27. The Spirit of God seemed to descend on the audience. Those who heard the sermon prayed fervently and repented of their sins. Missionaries and fellow Christians were all in tears. At the Edinburgh Conference in 1910 it was declared that "the Korean Revival ... has been a genuine Pentecost."

The outpouring of the Holy Spirit spread very rapidly to men, women, and students, and ultimately to the entire nation. But it did not end here. God raised up several key leaders, such as Sun Joo Kil, Ik Doo Kim, Yong Do Lee, Bong Suk Choi, and others. Even though speaking in tongues was not recorded in the revival meetings from 1903 till 1907, God performed many miracles, healings, the casting out of demons, and other supernatural miracles. Ik Doo Kim was even called "an apostle of divine healing." The Korean Presbyterian Church, where he was ordained, observed all of the supernatural miracles the Lord had done through him, but the church did not want to accept what was happening. But the Korean Presbyterian Church, which held to the doctrine of cessationism, had to change its bylaws,

specifically Article 1 of chapter 3 of the Presbyterian Bylaw, which stated, "The power of doing miracles has ceased at the present time." This was amended due to Ik Doo Kim's influence. The Presbyterian Church formed a group of four people to investigate all the signs and wonders that had been manifested through Ik Doo Kim's ministry. After examining all of the signs and miracles, they published a book called *Certificate of Miracles* in 1923.

The 1903–7 revival movements were the divine visitation of the Holy Spirit. As the Holy Spirit worked powerfully, people repented of their sins and the church grew miraculously. The Spirit-filled people of Korea would spread the gospel in spite of the persecutions during the Japanese occupation.

II. THE PRAYER MOUNTAIN MOVEMENT.

In studying Korean pentecostalism, the fervent prayer life of Korean Christians should not be ignored. Korean Christians have several different kinds of prayers, such as fasting, mountain, and decision prayers, the "Jooyeo Jooyeo Jooyeo" (Lord, Lord, Lord) prayer, among others. The prayer mountain movement is an indigenous Korean pentecostal movement.

A. Yong Do Lee and Prayer in the Mountain.

Yong Do Lee, a Methodist minister during the 1930s, was one of the leading pentecostal preachers of Korea. Although he ministered for only about five years (1928–33) and died from tuberculosis when he was only 33 years old, his influence was enormous. He received the pentecostal experience (perhaps including speaking in other tongues) and was totally changed.

After graduating from Bible college, Lee went to Kumkang Mountain and spent 10 days fasting and in prayer. He saw a vision and heard a voice from heaven calling him "to cast out the demons" at the beginning of his ministry. He became a mighty man of prayer. In 1930 he organized Pyongyang Prayer Group with his fellow ministers to spread the prayer movement to his generation. His preaching was anointed. Wherever Lee went to lead revival meetings, the Holy Spirit was poured out upon the congregation. People spoke in tongues, many people received healing, and supernatural signs followed his meetings. Due to his powerful ministry, he was banned by the Presbyterian Church in 1932 and even by the Methodist Church where he was ordained in 1933. However, in 1999, 60 years after his death, Lee was reinstated as an ordained minister by the Korean Methodist Church.

Like Lee, other early revival preachers spent time in the mountains praying and experiencing the pentecostal blessings. Even though there were many Buddhist temples in the mountains before the independence from Japan, there were no Christian prayer mountains in Korea.

B. The Yongmun Prayer Mountain Movement.

1. Elder Woon Mong Ra and Yongmun Prayer Mountain.

After the liberation from Japan in 1945, many prayer mountains developed throughout Korea. As a result, revivals were encouraged throughout the country. The manifestations of the pentecostal experiences, including speaking in tongues and healing, were more common than before. The revival movements of 1903–7 centered on ordained leaders and missionaries, but the prayer mountain movement was initiated by lay leaders. This also encouraged further participation of lay leaders in the future movement.

In 1940, when ᐧWoon Mong Ra was 26 years old, he entered Yongmun Mountain to meditate on the meaning of life. While he was fast asleep in a hut in a village of Yongmun Mountain, he was suddenly awakened by a loud voice from heaven that said, "Clean your heart and you will see me!" Later he came to realize that this was Jesus' statement, "Blessed are the pure in heart, for they shall see God" (Matt. 5:8). He read the Bible from that verse on and became aware of his sins. While Ra was in despair, Jesus' cross appeared, along with a voice saying, "I died for your sins." The Holy Spirit came down on him, and his entire body became hot. That was his conversion experience. Immediately he was called by God to preach the gospel. After experiencing all this on the mountain, he came down to the church nearby and

Korean prayer mountain with caves.

was asked to pray for the congregation. After seeing him pray in tears, the pastor thought that he was a longtime Christian and asked him to preach the following Sunday. At this time he had not even been baptized.

In 1942, while staying on the mountain, Ra spent time in prayer, fasting, and meditating on the Scriptures. His time alone on Yongmun Mountain allowed him to have a deeper relationship with God and to develop his personal faith. He experienced the presence of the Lord with power. Later that year he established Aehyangsook, which literally means "love-country-class"—in other words, a community for establishing a country of love. The spirit of Aehyangsook is expressed in five phrases: worship God absolutely, love other people as yourself, carry the truth, commune with the earth, and study in life. Since the Spirit of the Lord motivated him to preach, he could not just limit his preaching of the gospel to the nearby villages. He soon extended his ministry into the towns and cities.

In 1946 Ra was ordained as an elder at Soopo Bridge Methodist Church in Seoul, but the main center of his ministry remained at Yongmun Prayer Mountain. In 1947 he held a camp meeting for revival at Yongmun Prayer Mountain to commemorate the seventh anniversary of the visitation of the Holy Spirit to this mountain. Thousands of people gathered at this mountain from the four corners of the country to be blessed. This included solving life problems, healing the sick, casting out poverty, and so forth. Even though the country was being devastated by the Korean War, he traveled from village to village proclaiming the salvation of Christ and the baptism of the Holy Spirit, including healing. Ra faced many crisis opportunities, including being held by communist soldiers, but God saved him. He then returned to Yongmun Mountain to recover his spiritual power by fasting, praying, and meditating on the Scriptures. During this time he experienced the supernatural presence of the Lord and received the gift of tongues, the gift of prophecy, and other manifestations.

Seven years later, in 1954, following the end of the Korean War, an anniversary camp meeting for revival was held at Yongmun Mountain. It is reported that more than 10,000 people attended. This was when Ra decided to begin the prayer mountain movement by training the disciples. He established Yongmun Mountain Bible School in 1955. The next year he established the Gideon Theological Seminary and Yongmun Mountain Covenant. Yongmun Mountain Covenant was created for women who declared their celibacy for the Lord. More than half of the prayer mountains in Korea were established by the original graduates of these institutions.

2. The Spread of the Holy Spirit Movement.

Elder Ra's Yongmun prayer mountain movement was also called the Holy Spirit Movement. It began to have influence all over the country through three different channels: holding camp revival meetings at Yongmun Prayer Mountain, sending students to various parts of the country for evangelism and spiritual renewal, and through literature.

a. Camp Meetings. Regular camp meetings for revival are held at Yongmun Prayer Mountain. During the summer, the influential leaders from various denominations hold special revival meetings. In 1961 and 1969 the National Prayer Meeting and the National August Meeting for ministers were held at Yongmun Prayer Mountain. Important Korean leaders, such as ▸David (Paul) Yonggi Cho, senior pastor of Yoido Full Gospel Church; Chankook Kim, a professor at Yonsei University; Hyuk Huh, a church historian; and Yoontaik Suh were the guest speakers. By having these types of national meetings, Yongmun Prayer Mountain has contributed greatly to the spiritual awakening of Korean churches and spreading the Holy Spirit Movement.

b. Training and Sending of Students. Ra's training of the students at the training institutions was very rigorous. He not only taught the Scriptures to the students cognitively, but also trained them to pray fervently, fast up to 40 days, and preach the gospel with the power of the Holy Spirit. He taught them to obey the Lord. Those who were trained at the training institutions at Yongmun Prayer Mountain were different from those who were trained at the other seminaries and Bible schools. They were equipped not only with biblical knowledge but also with skills to preach and lead the revival meetings with power. Elder Ra sent them to villages and cities to preach the pentecostal messages with power. Under Ra's leadership, the students even tried to march to North Korea several times, without success. Even though they could not cross the DMZ, they crossed the Freedom Bridge near the DMZ.

c. Literature. Finally, Ra spreads the pentecostal movement through literature. He is a gifted writer. When he was young, he traveled all over Korea trying to find the meaning of life. In 1946 he started a monthly periodical, *Nongmin-sungbo (The Voice of the Farmer)* to awaken the farmers. He also published the Christian weekly newspaper *Kidok Gongbo* during the same year. He founded the monthly magazine *World of Faith* and the newspaper *The Gospel Times* in 1960. He also wrote more than 50 books on the doctrines of Christianity. When Elder Ra was young, he was trained in oriental thought and philosophy. He never received any formal, systematic theological training. Therefore, his writings came from his own thoughts, which were mixed with Confucianism, Buddhism, and Christianity. As he presented his theological conviction to Korean churches, he was opposed by many Korean theologians and church leaders. In his boldness he spread the pentecostal messages through all kinds of literature in spite of the criticism.

Several aspects of his teachings are different from those of the mainline churches. He approved Buddha and Confucius as Old Testament prophets. He also contends that when a person dies the spirit goes to the prison referred to 1 Peter 3:19, where one more opportunity for salvation is given. Therefore, he was banned by the Presbyterian Church in 1954 and 1955.

3. Elder Ra's Prayer Mountain Movement as the Pentecostal Movement.

In the early stage of the pentecostal movement, those who mentioned the Holy Spirit were treated as heretics. Elder Ra was a representative of this movement. Even though he was not well treated by the Korean churches, he stood on this position, which he based on the Scriptures and his Spirit-filled experience. The Holy Spirit Movement started with Elder Ra in 1952. In the spring of 1952 the Goshin Side of the Presbyterian Church had their meeting at Yongmun Prayer Mountain. After the denominational leaders finished their preaching that evening, Elder Ra was asked to preach the last session. Denominational leaders emphasized that the pentecostal experience in Acts 2 does not occur today. However, Elder Ra emphasized the baptism with the Holy Spirit by proclaiming, "The Holy Spirit comes even now on the

Entrance to cave on a prayer mountain.

persons who repent! Repent and be baptized with the Holy Spirit." He was preaching the pentecostal message. Suddenly a charismatic event happened among the audience. The people repented of their sins, and people spoke with other tongues. The place was filled with sounds of prayers, tongues, and crying.

Ra believes that we can see all gifts being exercised at the present time. Actually, at the Yongmun Prayer Mountain many people have been healed. Gifts in evidence there include miracles, foretelling, tongues, discernment of gifts, and others.

4. The Growth of the Prayer Mountain Movement.

Before the liberation from Japan in 1945, there were only two prayer mountains: Taehan Christian Prayer Monastery, established by Jaehun Yoo after Aug. 15, 1945, and Yongmun Prayer Mountain, established by Ra on Oct. 5, 1945. The number of prayer mountains increased to 207 in 1975, 239 in 1978, 462 in 1988, and 500 in 1994. There should be many more now. The prayer mountain movement contributed greatly to the expansion of pentecostalism in Korea. It is an indigenized Korean pentecostal movement. Elder Ra did not have any relationships with the pentecostal movements in the Western countries. Elder Ra's contribution in Korean pentecostalism should not be ignored; but due to the controversial theological statements he has made, Elder Ra and his ministries are not considered as significant by the Korean scholars.

Why has the prayer mountain movement in Korea grown so rapidly? There are several reasons. First, people can concentrate on prayer at prayer mountains. Christians can pray anywhere: in their closet, their home, and their church. But when they go to a prayer mountain, they can pray without any interference. As the country became increasingly urbanized, more prayer mountains were established in urban areas. More prayer mountains were established during the 1980s than in any other period, and more than half were established near Seoul. Christians in urban areas look for a solitary place where they can be with God personally.

Second, Christians who long for spiritual experiences visit prayer mountains. Prayer mountains are visited especially by those whose pastors do not emphasize the pentecostal experiences. Most of the prayer mountains emphasize the experiential dimension of Christian life. They not only preach the message of the gifts of the Holy Spirit but also help people to receive the baptism of the Holy Spirit.

Third, Christians visit the prayer mountains to solve their life problems. In a recent study, 26% answered that they visited the prayer mountains to solve their problems regarding business, family, personal struggles, and to receive physical and spiritual healings.

Fourth, recently many families have spent their vacations at the prayer mountains. Christians would rather spend time with their families praying, listening to sermons, and having private time on the mountain than at a beach or resort area.

The prayer mountains have met the spiritual and physical needs of Korean Christians. As long as the prayer mountains meet their needs, more and more of them will be established in the 21st century. Since prayer mountains are not common in other countries, it would not be an overstatement to say that the prayer mountain movement is an indigenous pentecostal movement in Korea.

III. THE COMING OF THE PENTECOSTAL DENOMINATIONS FROM ABROAD.

A. The Chosen Pentecostal Church (1928–45).

Mary Rumsey, who experienced the baptism of the Holy Spirit at the ►Azusa Street revival in 1906, felt the calling to be a missionary to Korea. She tried to come to Korea in various ways without success. Finally, in 1928 she was able to come as an independent pentecostal missionary by way of Japan. As she was not sent by any pentecostal denomination, she came without any support.

In 1931 Rumsey visited the Salvation Army headquarters in Seoul. She met with Heung Huh, who was working as a secretary at the Salvation Army. When Rumsey asked him to help her missionary work, he decided to help her because he felt her request was God's will. While Huh helped with Miss Rumsey's preaching, he became baptized with the Holy Spirit.

Rumsey preached the pentecostal message, which emphasized the baptism of the Holy Spirit, speaking in other tongues, and healing the sick by prayer. In Apr. 1932, with the help of Huh, she was finally able to plant the first pentecostal church in Korea, called Sukbinggo Pentecostal Church at Yongsanku. T. M. Parsons, who belonged to the American pentecostal church, arrived in Seoul, coming as an independent missionary and also without any support from his church. In 1933 E. H. Meredith and L. Vessey came to Korea as independent missionaries, even though they belonged to the British pentecostal church. Parsons planted the second pentecostal church, called Soochang-Dong Church, with the help of Boo Keun Pae, who graduated from Japan Bible School. Mary Rumsey and three other missionaries emphasized church planting. Therefore, by the time she left Korea in Feb. 1937, after receiving orders for forced deportation, there were 6 pentecostal churches with 10 ministers and 173 members.

The first ordination service of the Chosen Pentecostal Church was held on Oct. 5, 1938. The ordination service was led by the Rev. Carter, a bishop at the British Pentecostal Church. Three church leaders—Heung Huh, Sung-San Park, and Boo-Keun Pae—received ordination; the last two were trained in Japan. The persecution of Christianity on the part of the Japanese colonial government continued to worsen. In Dec. 1940 the other two missionaries were banished from Korea by the government. Having lost their leaders, the Chosen Pentecostal Churches had not grown enough to overcome the trials. Churches had to close their doors, and the members scattered. By 1941 only four pentecostal churches with four ministers and 80 members were left.

B. The Korean Pentecostal Church (1945–52).

Under the Japanese colonial government, several leaders preached the pentecostal gospel. Most of them were trained in Japan and China. Their work, however, was weak. After WWII Bokduk Lee and Gwieim Park organized the pentecostal church at Sunchon in the southern region of Korea in 1949 and named it Korean Christ Sunchon Pentecostal Church. About 300 people attended.

Pentecostal ministers such as Sung San Park, Heung Huh, and Boo-Keun Pae also tried to revive the pentecostal church. The first general assembly of the Korean Pentecostal Church was held in Soonchun, Jeonra-Namdo, on Apr. 9, 1950, just before the Korean War. Approximately 200 pentecostal believers attended. The meeting was more a revival campaign than a formal meeting.

C. The Korean Assemblies of God.

Two months after the first general assembly of the Korean Pentecostal Church, the Korean War broke out. Rev. Ellowed of the U.S. Salvation Army came to Korea as an Army chaplain. He met with Rev. Heong Huh and was introduced to the Korean Pentecostal Church. When he returned to the U.S. in 1951, he promised that he would introduce the U.S. Assemblies of God (AG) to him. As promised, Rev. Osgood, head of the Asian Mission for the AG–U.S., visited Korea in 1952. Rev. Arthur B. Chesnut, who worked as a missionary in China, was officially sent to Korea on Dec. 15, 1951, as the first AG missionary. He began to work together with the leaders in Korea, including Heong Huh, Sung San Park, and Boo Keun Pae. They began to gather the members who had scattered around the country. Finally, on Apr. 8, 1953, the opening service of the Korean Assemblies of God (KAG) was held at Namboo Church, located at Hangang-Ro, Yongsan-Ku, Seoul, where Heong Huh was pastoring. When Rev. Bong Jeo Kwak and Rev. Sung Duk Yoon, who studied in Japan, also joined, the Korean Assemblies of God became the unique pentecostal church in Korea. In May 1953 the Full Gospel Bible School was established at Namboo AG Church and began to train AG ministers.

In 1956 a student strike took place at the Full Gospel Bible School, which led to its closing. In Nov. 1957 Heong Huh was appointed as the second chairman of the KAG, while Bong Jeo Kwak and Sungn Duk Yoon joined the Far East Apostolic Mission.

The KAG grew by leaps and bounds until 1980. In 1981, however, due to doctrinal problems, the KAG divided into

two groups: the KAG (Original) and the KAG (Banpo). In Jan. 1985 the KAG (Banpo) divided into Jesus KAG (Yoido) and Christ KAG (Full Gospel). Thus, there were three KAG groups by 1985. All the leaders and members of the KAG desired to be unified. In May 1991 those who wanted to be unified left their respective denominations and organized a fourth AG. In 1998 the leaders from the four KAG denominations began to work for the unification of the KAG.

D. The Church of God in Korea.

In Apr. 1963 the Church of God (CG, Cleveland, TN) was introduced to Korea through Richard A. Jackson, who came to Korea as a U.S. military serviceman. He and Rev. Young Chul Han had the first opening worship service at Han's home at Mullae-Dong, Youngdungpo-Ku, Seoul. In Oct. 1963 a tent church was established as the first CG Church in Korea at 79 Gonghang Dong, Seoul. In Nov. 1965 the Church of God in Korea (CGK) built a church on the same location and named it Seoul Central Church of God. In 1969 Korean missions began to accelerate through the visit of James A. Slay, the executive secretary of world missions, along with Lovell R. Cary, the superintendent for the Far East. They appointed Young Chul Han as the overseer for the CGK. Under his leadership the CGK began to emphasize the training of leaders and planting churches in the four corners of Korea.

The CGK did not have any training institutions until Mar. 1970, when the CG Bible School was established by Youngchul Han at Seoul Central Church of God. It was initially called the Christ Pentecostal CGK but in 1972 changed its name to the Christ CGK after merging with Jesus Methodist CGK. Since there was initially no training program, potential leaders were sent to Lee College in the U.S. during the summer sessions. Through this program approximately 20 leaders finished the training as ministers of the

Pastor David Yonggi Cho of the Full Gospel Central Church in Seoul, South Korea, speaking to a massive audience.

CGK. Most of the present leaders were trained through this program.

Although the CG Bible College was established in 1970 as a training program for ministers, it was not until 1981 that the Bible College became fully accredited and changed its name to Hanyoung Theological University. Presently, the university has three majors at the undergraduate level and an unaccredited graduate program.

E. The Church of God of Prophecy.

Doowhan Kim worked together with Young Chul Han when the CG came to Korea. However, when Daniel J. Corbett was sent as a missionary by the Church of God of Prophecy (CGP) in the U.S. on Jan. 23, 1968, he left the CG and worked with the missionary in establishing the CGP in Korea. In July of 1976 he was appointed as a bishop in Korea and the church was officially called the Church of God of Prophecy in Korea. In 1993 Chul-Jea Rhee was appointed as a bishop in Korea after Reverend Kim.

F. The Church of the Foursquare Gospel in Korea.

In May 1969 the International Church of the Foursquare Gospel (ICFG) decided to send missionaries to Korea at the request of Kee Seuk and ‣Seen Ok Ahn, the director and founder of the Daesung Christian School Foundation.

The Ahns established the Daesung Christian High School with 45 refugee children in Taejon in 1952. By 1966 this small high school had grown to three junior high schools and three senior high schools with 5,700 students. The Ahns

were eager for the students in these schools to be evangelized. At that time, feeling the definite guidance of the Holy Spirit, Seen Ok Ahn went to the U.S. to study at age 45. One night she saw a person whom she had never met in a dream. He gave her a certificate of preaching. One year later, in 1969, she met the man from her dream personally at the ICFG headquarters building in Los Angeles, CA. He was ‣Rolf K. McPherson, the president of ICFG.

Arthur and Evelyn Thompson, who had ministered in the Philippines for 15 years, moved to Korea in 1969, arriving on Sept. 2. They first began the Student Church by using the facilities of Daedong Presbyterian Church, which was nearby. In two years attendance at the Student Church increased to over 900 students. One of the reasons for the rapid growth of the Student Church was Evelyn's evangelistic gift. In 1972 the Church of the Foursquare Gospel in Korea (CFGK) officially registered with the government.

Even after the Thompsons returned to the United States in 1972, the CFGK remained as one of the mission fields of the U.S. Foursquare Church until May 28, 1984, when the CFGK became independent and held its first national convention. During that time, the Harold Muetzels and Ron Meyers served the church as supervisors.

Seen Ok Ahn, who received theological training at ‣L.I.F.E. Bible College, emphasizes leadership training and church planting. Since she was the director of seven high schools at that time, she immediately began the Bible training program in 1972 and produced ministers. She felt the necessity of multilevel leaders for further growth and sent 27 potential leaders to various foreign countries for better training. In 1996 Gospel Theological Seminary was officially accredited by the Korean government.

G. The Korean Pentecostal Holiness Church.

Through the Yongmun Prayer Mountain Movement, Woon Mong Ra became known among the Korean people. Even though he was ordained as a Methodist elder, he worked as an interdenominational leader by leading the Yongmun Prayer Mountain movement, emphasizing "one church at every village" and a revival campaign. He then decided to established his own denomination.

In 1979 he went to Oklahoma City, OK, where he met Reverend Williams, bishop of the ‣Pentecostal Holiness Church in the U.S., and discussed the possibility of establishing the Pentecostal Holiness Church in Korea. They agreed and ordained Rev. Woon Mong Ra as their minister and appointed him as a bishop in Korea. On Mar. 29, 1979, the Pentecostal

The Full Gospel Central Church in Seoul, South Korea, the largest church in the world. (Right) The ten-story World Missions Center, which includes offices, hotels, dormitories, and classrooms for Church Growth International; (left) a new auditorium that seats 3,000 and serves as an overflow auditorium with closed-circuit TV.

Holiness Church in Korea (PHCK) was officially established. At that time there were 311 churches, 371 ministers, and 86,414 members. The PHCK grew continually under Bishop Ra's leadership.

When the denomination held its fourth national convention in Oct. 1982, Rev. Underwood, the director of foreign missions in the U.S., John Parker, the Asian coordinator working in Hong Kong, and James Campbell, missionary in Korea, attended the meeting. On the last day of the convention, the denomination was divided into two: the missionary side and Bishop Ra's side. Missionary Campbell studied Bishop Ra's theology and style from several different perspectives. He raised questions in four areas: theology, administration, attitude, and reputation, and reported them to the international headquarters. The report especially raised questions regarding Ra's theology: Ra approved of Buddha and Confucius as Old Testament prophets, and he claimed that the dead spirits have an opportunity to be saved before they go to either heaven or hell, based on 1 Peter 3:19. On the basis of the report, Bishop Stewart at international headquarters banned Ra from his office as bishop and stripped him of his ordination on Oct. 6, 1982.

Bishop Ra and his followers decided to banish missionary Campbell from Korea. Later there was a reconciliation between the International Pentecostal Holiness Church and Rev. Ra, but the PHCK is still inactive.

IV. CATHOLIC CHARISMATICS IN KOREA.

Miriam Knutas, who was a member of the Pentecostal Church in Sweden, was a nurse. While she was praying she received a word from the Lord to go to Korea and preach the pentecostal gospel to the Catholic members. Since she was brought up in the Protestant church, her feeling toward the Catholic Church was not positive. Also, she did not know much about Korea, nor was she interested in foreign missions. Therefore, she doubted the word from the Lord. However, the Lord continued to send her the same word whenever she prayed. In the end she asked God for a sign like Gideon's fleece, and she received an answer that convinced her that this was indeed her calling.

After she came to Korea she worked as a nurse and led the Bible class at the U.S. 8th Army camp. Tim Clark, who was very shy and quiet, experienced the baptism of the Holy Spirit in her Bible class. He witnessed of his experience to Erna Schmid, who worked at John Bosco Technical Institute as a lay missionary and encouraged him to attend the meeting. On Jan. 9, 1971, when Schmid and several of his friends met Miriam Knutas, they all experienced the baptism in the Spirit during that meeting.

At the end of May 1971, 13 foreign priests, friars, and laymen attended the conference led by Archer Torrey, a director at Jesus Abbey. In July 1971 Fr. Gerald Farrell, who returned after participating in the Catholic charismatic movement in the U.S., joined the newly born Catholic charismatic movement. Until that time the meeting was interdenominational, and most of the members were foreigners, ministers, and religious. However, as Fr. Gerald Farrell became deeply involved, the meeting became more Catholic centered.

In 1973 Farrell opened two Holy Spirit seminars in English at the U.S. 8th Army by using the materials developed by the U.S. Catholic charismatic renewal. In the fall of 1973 he opened the seminar at the Catholic Bible College, where 10 Korean students were blessed. On Jan. 15, 1974, he opened the seminar to Korean laypeople for the first time. As more and more Catholic priests experienced the Spirit baptism, they began to open the seminar to Korean believers. Presently, there are more than 700,000 Catholic pentecostal followers.

■ **Bibliography:** Chong Ho Byun, *History of Korean Pentecostal Movement* (1972) ■ Young Bae Cha, "The Korean Church and the Works of the Holy Spirit," *Ministry and Theology* (Sept. 1990) ■ A. D. Clark, *A History of the Church in Korea* (1971) ■ G. T. Davis, *Korea for Christ* (1910) ■ Yeol Soo Eim, "The History of Korean Foursquare Church" (unpub. ms., 1994) ■ idem, "Worldwide Expansion of Foursquare Gospel" (diss., School of World Missions, Fuller, 1986) ■ Han Young Theological University, *Teaching and Government of Church of God in Korea* (1996) ■ Yung-Chul Han, ed., *The Acts of Pentecost: Pentecost in the 21st Century* (1998) ■ Young Jae Han, ed., *The Christian Encyclopedia* (1996) ■ International Theological Institute, *History of Korea Assemblies of God* (1998) ■ idem, *The Works of the Holy Spirit in Church History* (1996) ■ Bum Joo Lee, *Study on the Strange Language from Theological and Practical Perspective* (1995) ■ Graham Lee, "How the Spirit Came to Pyengyang" ■ Yohan Lee, "The Analysis of the Christian Prayer Mountain Phenomenon in Korea" (diss., School of World Missions, Fuller, 1985) ■ Kyung Bae Min, *The History of the Korean Church* (1982) ■ E. J. Orr, *Evangelical Awakenings in Eastern Asia* (1975) ■ Choong Woon Park, "Why Do the People Visit Prayer Mountain?" *The Pastoral Monthly* 215 (July 1994) ■ Suh Young Ra, "The Church in Korea and Hospitable Exclusivism in Light of Bishop Woon Mong Ra" (diss., Union Theol. Sem., Dayton, OH, 1997) ■ Woon Mong Ra, *The Holy Spirit I Have Experienced and a Half Century of Its Movement* (1990) ■ idem, *I Would Have Liked to Live Nor to Die* (1986) ■ *The Twenty-Second General Assembly Records of the Presbyterian Church* (1991) ■ Unification Council of the Korea Assemblies of God, *The Agenda for the 2nd General Assembly and Its Report* (1993).

■ Yeol Soo Eim

SPAIN

■ Pentecostals 18,048 (2%)   ■ Charismatics 752,763 (69%)   ■ Neocharismatics 314,189 (29%)   ■ Total Renewal: 1,085,000

The first pentecostal mission in Spain was undertaken by Swedish missionaries, Jilia and Martin Wahlsten, in 1923 in the city of Gijón, Asturias. There they led a small Baptist congregation into the pentecostal movement. In Oct. 1927 another Swedish pentecostal missionary, Sven Johansson, began work in Madrid. Two years later the congregation received a major boost when Samuel Nyström held meetings at the church on his way from Brazil to Sweden. Tage and Ingrid Stählberg also served as missionaries in Sweden from 1931 until 1938, when they transferred to Portugal. The social unrest and civil war in Spain, along with severe persecution from the Catholic Church, made evangelistic work slow and dangerous. Especially effective, however, were the Spanish-language programs broadcast from Tangiers, Morocco, through IBRA Radio, an international ministry of the Swedish Pentecostal Church. The resulting Iglesia Evangélica Pentecostal de España today (1999) has about 25 congregations/preaching points, 2,500 members, and about an additional 3,000 adherents.

The U.S. ˒Assemblies of God (AG) began work in Spain in 1930 but were forced to withdraw until 1947, when the Cuban pastor Ramán Perruc and his wife, Carmita, arrived to work in Coruña, her home city. These were followed by American missionaries who, since the 1950s, established, among other things, a Bible school, initially at Coruña and later at Madrid. The AG claims (1999) about 2,000 members in 35 congregations, with about 60 clergy/workers. The Assambleas de Dios publishes the widely circulated periodical *Fiel*.

The largest pentecostal denomination is the Iglesia Evangélica Filadelfia, which claims about 200 congregations/preaching points, 20,000 baptized members, and more than 800 pastors and church workers. There are at least another 25,000 adherents. This church was begun in France in 1950 through the ministry of Clement le Cossec, French missionary to the ˒Gypsies. The church, started in Spain in 1964, works primarily with the Gypsies in Spain. The denomination publishes the periodical *Luz del Mundo*.

Other pentecostal denominations in Spain include the Assambleas Pentecostal de España (7 congregations, 700 adults), Iglesia Cristiana Evangélica de Pentecostés (2 congregations, 300 members), the Iglesia de Dios de España (4 congregations, 400 members), Iglesia de Dios Pentecostal (founded by missionaries from Puerto Rico; 15 congregations, 300 members, 3,000 adherents), Iglesia El Buen Pastor (founded by missionaries from Mexico; 3 congregations, 180 members), Iglesia de la Biblia Abierta (˒Open Bible Standard Church, U.S.; in 1995, 15 congregations, 1,140 members, 32 clergy), Iglesia Evangélica Pentecostal de Madrid, Iglesia Evangélica Pentecostal Salem (founded by Finnish pentecostal missionaries), and the Iglesia Pentecostal Unida (˒United Pentecostal Church; 4 congregations, 69 members). In addition there are a large number of local independent pentecostal congregations.

Parachurch organizations, such as ˒Full Gospel Business Men's Fellowship International, ˒Teen Challenge, and ˒Youth With A Mission (YWAM), have had a significant impact in Spain. Related to these—but more important—is the charismatic renewal in the Catholic Church in Spain. While official groups number about 100, there are probably others. There may be as many as 10,000 participants.

The history of the pentecostal movements in Spain is documented primarily in the periodicals as well as in the histories of mission of the missionary-sending countries. Thus, there are numerous articles about Spain in Spanish, Norwegian, Finnish, and Swedish pentecostal periodicals.

■ **Bibliography:** L. K. Ahonen, *Suomen helluntaiherätyksen historia* (1994) ▥ E. J. Anturi, "Helluntaiherätyksen toiminnen tarastelua," in K. Anturi et al., *Helluntaiherätys tänään* (1986) ▥ D. B. Barrett, *World Christian Encyclopedia* (1982) ▥ Å. Boberg, *Svensk Pingstmission* (1990) ▥ P. Branco, *Pentecostes: Un Desafío al Mundo* (1984), 70–74 ▥ R. Bryant and L. M. Mitchell, *Heritage and Harvests: The History of the International Ministries of Open Bible Standard Churches* (1995) ▥ D. L. Burk, *Foreign Mission Insight, 1999* ([United Pentecostal Church], 1999), 109 ▥ A. Hämäläinen, ed., *Kaikkeen maailman 1929–1989: 60 vuotta helluntaiseurahuntien lähetystyöyä* (1989) ▥ O. Nilsen, *Ut i all verden: Pinsevennenes ytre misjon i 75 år* (1984) ▥ A. Ruuth, *Igreja Universal do Reino de Deus: Gudsrikets Universella Kyrka—en brasiliansk kyrkobildning. Resumen: Iglesia Universal del Reino de Dios* (1995) ▥ E. Söderholm, *Den Svenska Pingstväckelsens spridning utom och inom Sverige* (1933), 181–88 ▥ A. Sundstedt, *Pingstväckelsen*, 5 vols. (1967–73) ▥ Materials provided by Adele Flower Dalton.

■ D. D. Bundy

SPANISH NORTH AFRICA

■ Pentecostals 66 (2%)   ■ Charismatics 2,167 (72%)   ■ Neocharismatics 767 (26%)   ■ Total Renewal: 3,000

SRI LANKA

■ Pentecostals 53,731 (13%)   ■ Charismatics 35,836 (9%)   ■ Neocharismatics 310,432 (78%)   ■ Total Renewal: 399,999

I.   Early Years (1907–23): Itinerant Evangelists and Indigenous Efforts

II. Arrival of Pentecostal Missionaries

III. Middle Years (1924–43): Formal Establishment of Churches
     A. Ceylon Pentecostal Mission
     B. The Assemblies of God

IV. Organizational Development: Structures and Strictures
     A. Assemblies of God
     B. Ceylon Pentecostal Mission

V.   Influence and Contributions of Missionaries
     A. Assemblies of God
     B. Foursquare Church
     C. Margaya Fellowship
     D. Other Groups

VI. Charismatics in Sri Lanka

VII. Persecution and Pulling Together

VIII. Present Status of the Movement

I. EARLY YEARS (1907–23): ITINERANT EVANGELISTS AND INDIGENOUS EFFORTS.

Although this period is poorly documented, the earliest evidence of pentecostal activity on the island of Ceylon is the arrival of ▸Alfred Goodrich Garr in 1907. His ministry attracted D. E. Dias Wanigasekera, who left his post at the Church Missionary Society and began itinerant preaching and distribution of literature in Ceylon. In regular letters to *The Christian Evangel* (from whom he also received financial support), Wanigasekera describes house meetings, healings, and glossolalia among those he evangelized. He also reports being baptized in the Holy Spirit in Fyzabad, India, in Oct. 1910. In 1910, a "Brother B. Dean from Ohio" arrived to assist Wanigasekera in his efforts.

During the ensuing journey, Dean and Wanigasekera preached to groups of Buddhists, Muslims, Hindus, Roman Catholics, and professing Christians and sold them portions of Scripture. Although a letter to *The Christian Evangel* in 1914 states his intention to become an Assemblies of God (AG) missionary, there is no documentation of this or of his subsequent activities.

Around this time J. J. B. de Silva (Baptist Mission) was also seeking the baptism in the Holy Spirit in Fyzabad. He would go on to found a pentecostal church in Galle. In 1918, Sadhu Sundar Singh arrived in Ceylon. Although not a classical pentecostal, his ministry of gospel preaching and praying for the sick made a strong impression on all Protestant denominations on the Island. Especially impressed and motivated by his example were Pastors Alwin de Alwis and Ram Paul. Both were part of the Baptist Mission at the time of Singh's visit. De Alwis and Paul would leave the Baptist Mission and found the Ceylon Pentecostal Mission (CPM) in 1923.

II. ARRIVAL OF PENTECOSTAL MISSIONARIES.

W. D. Grier arrived in Ceylon on Oct. 18, 1913, as the first full-time U.S. pentecostal missionary. He remained until 1917, when lack of finances forced him to leave. During his four-year stay, Grier lived in several towns and held cottage meetings.

Although Grier never adapted to the local culture, he was able make some converts and start congregations wherever he went. Before he left, he was able to find some individuals to take over the ministries he had begun. Alwin de Alwis took charge of Grier's work in Peradeniya.

Grier was succeeded by George Doyal, who probably only stayed a short while. Minnie Houck had arrived on the Island in 1909 to serve as principal of a school and orphanage in Nuwara Eliya. Although she arrived as a pentecostal missionary, the demands of the school did not allow full-time evangelistic activities. She was able to assist Anna Lewini (whom she first met in Bombay in 1922) when Lewini first arrived in Colombo. Houck remained in Ceylon until 1924.

Anna Lewini, after being converted to the pentecostal faith in Copenhagen in 1909, had received the baptism in the Holy Spirit on May 13, 1909. In 1922, during a world-encompassing evangelistic tour, she arrived in Colombo. Here she would remain until her death in the late 1940s. Somaratna considers her to be "the real founder of pentecostalism in Sri Lanka":

> Her mission had a lasting impact on the country at large. She was generous and humble enough to accept a role in the background when Clifford arrived by giving him the main stage of the ministry. . . . Thereafter she continued to be a partner in the mission by offering to be a minister in the fields of counselling and praying. . . . She did not consider the ministry as her personal property. (Somaratna, 1997)

When Lewini arrived in Sri Lanka, she was ably assisted by John Samuel Wickramaratna and J. J. B. de Silva. They held revival meeting in several places in Colombo but principally in the Tower Hall in Maradana. Eventually a more permanent location was found in Wellawatta and named Glad Tidings Hall (later renamed Colombo Gospel Tabernacle). This was the first formal pentecostal church in Sri Lanka.

Up to this time most of the pentecostal work done in Sri Lanka was the work of people drawn from the local denominations and independent pentecostal missionaries: Ram Paul (Anglican), de Silva, de Alwis, and Wickramaratna (Baptist Union). Lewini was a Danish pentecostal, and Wanigasekera was from the Christian Missionary Society.

III. MIDDLE YEARS (1924–43): FORMAL ESTABLISHMENT OF CHURCHES.

A. Ceylon Pentecostal Mission.

The CPM was founded in 1923 as a breakaway group from the Glad Tidings Hall and the ministry of Walter Clifford. The founders were Alwin de Alwis and Ram Paul. The first Faith Hall was in Galle. There is some evidence that when Clifford took over Lewini's Glad Tiding's Hall in 1925, a further group left and joined the CPM. The reason for the division was the emphasis by Paul and de Alwis on less organizational structure and a more ascetic approach to Christian life, including celibacy for those involved in ministry. The growing formalism of the AG mission did not coincide with Alwis and Paul's views about pentecostal missions. The CPM founders were determined to practice a New Testament ministry as described in Acts 2:44.

Within five years of the founding, Faith Homes had been established in major cities and towns of Sri Lanka. These Faith Homes served as a community home for the CPM members. They also served as healing centers where patients were brought for prayer, laying on of hands, anointing with oil, and drinking of blessed water. Alwin de Alwis remained the head of the CPM until 1962, when a "rift" in the movement forced him to leave.

Unlike the AG movement in Sri Lanka, the CPM was a totally indigenous work with no foreign missionaries influencing or contributing to its development. Its reluctance to document its own activities and personalities makes research difficult. Other than Ram Paul and de Alwis, there do not seem to be any major figures in the period 1924–62.

B. The Assemblies of God.

In 1924 Walter H. Clifford arrived in Colombo. He met Ana Lewini and conducted meetings in Sri Lanka. In 1925 Clifford arrived in Colombo on a permanent basis as an AG missionary. With the agreement of Lewini, he took charge of the Glad Tidings Hall, and Lewini ended her preaching ministry. This was an amicable handover; Lewini had been looking for a male to take over the work she had founded. Thus began the AG Mission that would become the AG of Ceylon.

A cooperative effort between local nationals and a succession of foreign missionaries lasted well into the 1980s.

This resulted in the establishment of AG churches and mission stations in major population centers (Colombo, Kandy, Galle, Jaffna) and some smaller towns. By 1940 there were 3 tabernacles, 8 outstation churches, 6 missionaries, 12 full-time workers, and about 1,500 members and believers.

In 1947 the AG of Ceylon was incorporated and became an independent entity recognized by the Sri Lankan government. Between 1963 and 1965 all missionaries left Sri Lanka. Some returned in the early 1970s. In 1980 there were 4 missionaries, 50 Sri Lankan ministers, 22 assemblies, 18 outstation churches, approximately 3,000 believers and members, and a Bible school with 14 enrolled. A 1991 AG publication claims 15,000 members, 151 churches and outstations, 166 pastors and lay leaders, 35 Bible school students, and one missionary functioning in an advisory capacity. In 1999 David Beling estimated that there were 20,000 "worshipers" in the AG of Ceylon.

Colton Wickramaratna is the pastor of the headquarters church (People's Church) in Colombo and is superintendent of the AG of Ceylon as of 1999. The AG of Ceylon is a member of the Evangelical Alliance of Sri Lanka.

IV. ORGANIZATIONAL DEVELOPMENT: STRUCTURES AND STRICTURES.

The first formal organization of any kind appeared in the pentecostal movement in Sri Lanka in 1923 with the founding of the CPM's first Faith Home in Magalle, which was Galle and Ana Lewini's Glad Tidings Hall in Colombo.

A. Assemblies of God.

With the handover of Glad Tidings Hall to AG missionary Walter Clifford, the informal organization of cooperative, but still independent, individuals and groups came under the umbrella of the worldwide AG missionary arm as part of the South India and Ceylon District of the AG.

The main themes of the AG constitution were applied to the previously ad hoc arrangements. What began as a casual arrangement became normative. (This was not to the taste of some and partially responsible for the split and formation of the CPM.) This was a "governing" structure with a district chairman and an assistant superintendent. This management group, composed of missionaries from India and Sri Lanka, was responsible for resolution of organizational and doctrinal issues.

At the field level in Sri Lanka, Clifford seems to have run a fairly "flat" organization. He was more concerned with getting things done than with building a complex administrative structure on the Island. Thus, there was room for local initiatives and the emergence of indigenous leaders (such as J. S. Wickramaratne) in the Sri Lankan AG movement.

There seems to have been very little stratification of duties among the foreign missionaries. Despite his role as head of the work in Sri Lanka, Clifford was directly involved in all manner of ministry: one-to-one evangelism, street meetings, and personally opening new works in the smaller towns in Sri Lanka. Accounts from Reinecker and Van der Wert (née Long) indicate that, in addition to their advisory and administrative roles, they worked hand-in-hand with "native workers" in the villages of Sri Lanka. Many ministry roles were recognized, including those of missionary, pastor, elder, native worker, evangelist, teacher, and preacher. Within the AG there was an opportunity for the laity to participate in many of these, and the philosophy of indigenization was practiced from the beginning of the work in Sri Lanka.

The role of women in ministry surfaced as an issue in the middle years of the work in Sri Lanka (1940s). This seems to have been resolved by suggesting that women's ministries always be under the authority of a male elder or pastor. Thus, Carl Graves proposed that "lady workers" in the Sri Lankan AG of this time would be allowed to preach, teach, and engage in "other helpful ministries." (To his credit, Graves acknowledges the great debt owed to women by the pentecostal movement and shows a broad understanding of 1 Cor. 14:34–35 and 1 Tim. 2:11.) Given the immense contribution by women missionaries to the AG in Sri Lanka, one would hope for this kind of response to this issue.

The AG organization of Walter Clifford managed most of its financial affairs without outside help. This was the result of the emphasis on tithing and offerings. Matters of theology and doctrine were informed by a literalist approach to the authority of Scripture and the Fundamental Statements of Faith as stipulated by the AG–U.S. Despite the heavy emphasis on the ministry of the Holy Spirit, Clifford's doctrine of the Trinity was in line with the mainline Protestant denominations of the Island and not a source of discord between them.

The present-day structure of the AG of Ceylon has preserved and incorporated the structures put in place by the missionaries and founding fathers and mothers. AG churches are recognized as self-governing and self-sustaining by the umbrella organization, which is led by a general superintendent. A pastor or senior pastor presides over a board of elders and a board of deacons. The historical emphasis on evangelism and church building has continued. The present organization supports social welfare programs as well, including feeding programs for children and medical assistance to victims of the Tamil and Singhalese ethnic conflict. They are members of the Evangelical Alliance of Sri Lanka.

B. Ceylon Pentecostal Mission.

The Ceylon Pentecostal Mission was structured along more simple lines. This consisted of Faith Homes, in which the community of believers/workers lived with 5 to 10 ministers. Men and women had separate quarters within the facility. Ministers were expected to remain celibate. Within the organization there were categories of believer, worker,

pastor, chief pastor, and senior pastor. Workers were expected to obey the chief pastor. Each pastor could start a new Faith Home. Somaratna writes that de Alwis believed that CPM ministers should sell all possessions and hold all things in common. Private possessions were not allowed in Faith Homes. There was a clear and functional distinction between believers and workers.

Although full-time women workers outnumbered the men, the position of authority in a Faith Home was always male. This was the result of a rigid interpretation of 1 Tim. 2:11. By excluding women from roles of organizational power or public authority, the CPM effectively confined the ministry of women to prayer and counseling. Women were allowed to prophesy and were required to cover their heads while in ministry. Wijesinghe of the Ceylon Bible Society says that women can be elders and have been "known to preach," but the role of pastor has been reserved for men. There is also a category of "senior sister." P. Joyfitch of the CPM says that women have been allowed to preach and teach but cannot perform baptisms, weddings, or administer communion.

The centrality of divine healing ministry was a major tenet, to the point of rejecting medicines and medical care. Prayer and fasting were the means to overcome all obstacles—including hunger! The CPM rejected theological education for their ministers in favor of intensive Bible study and prayer. Would-be ministers were also subjected to "humbling" experiences for a two-year period. According to Somaratna, "the central teaching of the CPM was the preparation of the believers to be the 'bride of Christ.' It was to this end that all their attention was devoted." The second coming of Christ therefore held a singularly important place in their teaching. This introspective emphasis on the quality of faith rather than on the Great Commission impeded the evangelistic aspects of the CPM. The intensive focus on study of the Bible limited the CPM's appeal to those who were literate, a minority of the population at the time.

The CPM has no association or support from any foreign church or missionary organization, but Somaratna thinks that the Faith Home/healing center concept was borrowed from the Holiness/healing movement in the U.S. The CPM has always been indigenously financed and governed.

The central authority seems to have been only the original leader and founder, Alwin de Alwis. He led the group until 1962, when a dispute over his plans for the CPM led to his ouster from the movement. The CPM has active foreign missions programs that were started in the 1920s and '30s, which enabled them to introduce Faith Homes in South India and Malaysia. An outreach to expatriate Sri Lankans, started in the 1940s, resulted in established congregations in Jamaica, the U.K., France, Switzerland, Canada, and the U.S.

The CPM has an Island-wide group of elders who serve as a quasi-administrative body. At this writing, there are five to six pastors on the Island; the current president of the CPM is Pastor Joyfitch.

Although the CPM is "antidocumentation," Wijesinghe estimates that there are 80 to 90 Faith Home churches on the Island and approximately 18,000 members; Joyfitch estimates 30,000 to 35,000. The CPM is not a member of Evangelical Alliance of Sri Lanka. The English-language version of their organizational publication is called *Divine Power*.

There is no indication that through the 1950s the pentecostal movements were part of any other Protestant/Christian associations or fellowships on the Island. There are reports that the mainline churches shunned them and that the animosity was often reciprocated. After the initial "honeymoon" period in the 1920s, the mainline organizations came to see the "sheep-stealing fundamentalists" as a threat to their own congregations. And most evidence suggests that growth in the AG and CPM came from individuals leaving the mainline Christian churches on the Island rather than from Buddhist or Hindu populations.

Thus, the AG and the CPM developed in relative isolation from the other churches—and often from each other as well. Except for some schools and an orphanage, there is little to indicate that any "social gospel" was practiced. Aside from the fact that the CPM would take in and care for some indigents, the emphasis of both groups focused on the eschatological rather than on improving the quality of life on earth for their converts. A more mature and indigenous organization of the 1980s and onward would assume these ministries.

V. INFLUENCE AND CONTRIBUTIONS OF MISSIONARIES.

A. Assemblies of God.

After Glad Tidings Hall was established, it served as the base for AG missionary operations in Colombo with outreaches to Galle, Jaffna, and Kandy. In Galle, Carl Graves built the Berean Gospel Tabernacle and dedicated it in 1939. As he was the first AG missionary to Ceylon with a Bible school education, he also began a Bible school in 1934. A work was started in Kandy among the Tamils in 1926. In Jaffna, where a group of believers existed since 1923, the effort was continuously supported by Clifford, who sent evangelists to help J. J. B. de Silva, who founded an AG church in Jaffna in 1927. ᐞSmith Wigglesworth held evangelistic campaigns in Galle and Colombo in 1922. In 1926 he visited again and participated in a campaign organized by Walter Clifford. His 1927 visit was especially important because of the impact it had on some of the prominent pentecostal leaders in Sri Lanka: J. G. Beling, C. F. Loos, and J. S. Wickramaratne.

In 1936–37 the Colombo Gospel Tabernacle was built on land donated by a prominent lawyer who had been converted under Clifford's ministry. This building could seat about 300.

In 1937 Kathryn Long and Rosa Reineker arrived and were assigned to Galle. Reineker moved to Jaffna to assume duties there when de Silva retired from the pastorate of the Jaffna church. Long developed a mission to the tea estate workers (mostly Hindu). Reineker was active in the promotion and development of local Sunday schools and in a long-term literature campaign as well as establishing the International Correspondence Institute in Sri Lanka. Reineker served until the mid 1960s, when political changes in Sri Lanka necessitated the departure of all foreign missionaries. She returned in 1971 and helped reopen the Ceylon Bible Institute.

When the AG of Ceylon was formed in 1947, Clifford served as the first general superintendent. He left Sri Lanka in 1948 and was succeeded as superintendent by Carl Graves. Aside from the late 1960s when all missionaries left the Island, foreign missionaries and evangelists continued to contribute to the work. ᐞDaniel M. Buntain, ᐞWilliam Branham, and ᐞA. C. Valdez conducted open-air healing crusades in the 1950s, as did Hoskins and McPherson in the 1960s and William Caldwell in 1973 and 1979. These were well-organized, well-publicized events with as many as 12,000 persons reported to have attended a single service.

In 1951 an English-language radio outreach program was organized by Derrick Hillary. The first broadcast over Radio Ceylon was on Dec. 3, 1951. This was a 30-minute broadcast known as *Introduction to Life*, with a monthly budget of $400. When Hillary left on furlough, Harold Kohl became director in 1953. There is also some evidence that Scandinavian pentecostal missionaries, expelled from Communist China in the early 1950s, came to Sri Lanka and associated themselves with the AG of Ceylon, since they now saw it as no longer an American organization.

In the 1970s and '80s there were ever fewer permanent AG missionaries. Although there are close ties to the AG–U.S., the AG of Ceylon today operates without the influence of on-site missionaries.

B. Foursquare Church.

According to Leslie Keegel, the Foursquare movement was introduced to Sri Lanka in Trincomalee in 1979 by U.S. missionary Richard Kaiser. When he left in 1983, there were 3 churches and 65 members. The present-day organization claims 422 churches, 12 of which meet in actual church buildings; the rest are home or cottage churches.

Keegel maintains the home church is the secret of their grassroots success since 1983. Although there have been some incidents, he thinks that the low profile of the home-church strategy has helped them avoid much of the persecution others have faced. There are also two churches in Australia and one in the U.K.

The Living Way Church in Colombo is the headquarters and serves about 800 members. Keegel estimates membership in Sri Lanka at 8,200 (60% Tamils, 25% Singhalese, the rest Burghers and Muslims). There are no restrictions on women in the ministry; they can play public roles and hold positions of authority such as elder or pastor. The Living Way Church is a member of the Evangelical Alliance of Sri Lanka.

C. Margaya Fellowship.

The Margaya Fellowship started as a home ministry to Buddhist families. After some abortive attempts to establish this ministry within the Anglican Church, the Margaya Missionary Society/Fellowship was founded in 1981. This was an interdenominational organization focusing on Buddhist ministries.

Although they initially tried to steer new converts to the established churches, their own ministry of "shepherding" and counseling grew until they decided to form an official church. Thus, the Margaya Fellowship of Sri Lanka was incorporated by an Act of Parliament in 1992. Margaya is Singhalese for "The Way." As of 1999 they have 18 churches in 13 of the 25 districts of Sri Lanka.

The chairman and founder, Rohan Ekanayaka, estimates that there are 1,475 adult adherents. He says that 80% of this group are first-generation converts from Buddhist and Hindu populations in the rural areas. The Margaya Fellowship is careful not to proselytize among the established churches.

D. Other Groups.

There are many other smaller groups with pentecostal affiliations. These include the Fellowship of Free Churches (100 churches) and the Church of South India (32 churches). Kithu Sevana (Youth for Christ) was established as a Sri Lankan church in 1993. Lanka Hope Mission International, Youth With A Mission, Campus Crusade for Christ, and the Church of God are also represented on the Island. Calvary Church in Colombo is an independent pentecostal church associated with the Swedish Free Churches and pastored by Tissa Weerasinghe.

VI. CHARISMATICS IN SRI LANKA.

A large charismatic group in the Catholic Church, Pubu Duwa, was started in 1970–71. Although Fr. Oscar Abhayaratna did not start the group, he provided the first leadership. He developed a training program consisting of eight initial talks followed by a meditation service and then a commitment service. A leader within the group, B. Kundalawa, says there are now 30,000 people participating in Pubu Duwa. The movement is represented in all the dioceses of Sri Lanka, including Colombo, Kandy, and Galle. In most of the villages there are groups that have prayer services and ministry within the "social dimension" to Buddhists, Hindus, and Muslims. Out of respect for their beliefs, there is no direct evangelism or proselytizing of these groups. They do try to provide spiritual guidance and often marital counseling.

Kundalawa says that there is no direct contact with the radical pentecostal groups on the Island. There is a relationship with the Anglican and Methodist groups such that occasionally the Pubu Duwa is invited to speak or hold youth rallies. The group is now organized and administered by the laity. Fr. Abhayaratna continues to serve as spiritual advisor.

The Anglican Church has only a small number of charismatics. Two such groups are the Anglican Inland Mission Society and the Anglican Evangelical Fellowship; the latter is estimated to have about 100 members. The bishop, Kenneth Fernando, is the patron of both groups.

VII. PERSECUTION AND PULLING TOGETHER.

The recent success of the evangelicals in winning large numbers of converts from the Buddhist populations has led to opposition, harassment, destruction of church properties, injuries, and deaths. Although the Sri Lankan constitution provides for freedom of worship, local politics seem to have dictated an aggressive attitude on the part of Buddhist authorities and a passive attitude on the part of local law enforcement.

An Internet site sponsored by the Evangelical Alliance of Sri Lanka has documented many such incidents over the past 10 years. An AG publication has also reported church burnings and harassment of some Christian workers as well as the death of an AG pastor.

In 1998 legislation was introduced to change the Sri Lankan constitution in ways that, according to the evangelical groups, would be detrimental to their religious freedom and evangelism efforts. A very vocal and organized protest resulted in this particular legislation being deferred. Inferring from some letters to the editor of a Sri Lankan daily newspaper, there is rising concern among Buddhists about the number of "unethical conversions" to Christianity. Joyfitch of the CPM points to the fact that most of the pentecostal groups on the Island have foreign affiliations and thus foreign money, which some Buddhists suspect is being used to buy converts—hence the term "unethical conversions." The CPM has faced far less persecution than the others, because it is completely indigenous and therefore not vulnerable to that accusation, says Joyfitch.

Keegel thinks that the Buddhist faith has little or no concept of "spirit" and thus has much difficulty understanding how or why "ethical" conversions to Christianity can take place. He feels, as does Beling, that the anti-Christian atmosphere and persecution has led to increased cooperation among the pentecostal groups.

VIII. PRESENT STATUS OF THE MOVEMENT.

After many years of slow or no growth, the entire movement has received an infusion of vitality and growth since the 1970s because of the worldwide interest in the charismatic movement and because of the maturation of the indigenous pentecostal movements.

The long-established pentecostal groups on the Island are reporting dynamic growth among Tamil and Singhala populations. This is in contrast to their historical strength, which was found only in the already Christian population on the Island.

With the exception of the CPM, most of the major pentecostal groups have established Bible schools, training institutes, discipleship institutes, and correspondence schools to provide their adherents with some formal training in evangelism and church building. The CPM is unique in that it has well-established branches in Canada, the U.S., and the U.K. that serve expatriate (mostly Tamil) Sri Lankans. The

AG of Ceylon, the CPM, and most of the other groups are self-governing and financially self-sufficient.

■ **Bibliography:** *Bridegroom's Messenger,* 1910–11 ■ *The Christian Evangel,* 1914–15 ■ International Congress on World Evangelization (1994) ■ *Latterday Evangel,* 1911 ■ *PE,* 1923–91 ■ G. P. V. Somaratna, *Origins of the Pentecostal Mission in Sri Lanka* (1996) ■ idem, *Walter Clifford: Apostle of Pentecostalism in Sri Lanka* (1997) ■ UCAN Report: SR91011.0959. Sri Lankan Church's Response to the Synod (1997) ■ *Weekly Evangel,* 1915–17 ■ Personal files (AG Archives): W. Clifford, C. Graves, R. Reineker ■ Personal interviews: D. Beling (Feb. 1999), R. Ekanayaka (Feb. 1999), P. Joyfitch (Feb.–Mar. 1999), L. Keegel (Feb. 1999), B. Kundalawa (Mar. 1999), E. Wijesinghe (Mar. 1999).

■ E. Leembruggen-Kallberg

SUDAN

■ Pentecostals 7,282 (1%) ■ Charismatics 511,678 (79%) ■ Neocharismatics 130,039 (20%) ■ Total Renewal: 648,999

See Africa, North, and the Middle East.

SURINAME

■ Pentecostals 1,413 (13%) ■ Charismatics 7,129 (64%) ■ Neocharismatics 2,558 (23%) ■ Total Renewal: 11,100

Formerly Dutch Guiana, Suriname occupies an area slightly larger than the state of Georgia (163,000 sq km) on the north coast of South America, bounded by Brazil, French Guiana, and Guyana. Since independence from the Netherlands in 1975, the country has witnessed some violent political conflicts, including military coups (in 1980 and in 1990), culminating in 1991 with the establishment of a very unsteady, democratically elected government. Governmental instability and corruption, racial divisiveness that is reflected even in the structure of its political parties, and the lack of foreign investment have brought the nation to the brink of economic ruin on several occasions, and Suriname remains one of the poorest countries in the Western Hemisphere, with an annual per capita income estimated to be less than $2,000 (US).

Ethnically, Suriname is more a stew than a melting pot. Native Amerindians and Europeans compose a small minority, while the majority is split between black, Chinese, East Indian, and Javanese. Wycliffe ethnologists catalog 16 distinct languages for Suriname (Dutch and native Sranan predominate), but due to a heavy influx of Amerindians from Brazil in recent years, the number of languages is probably slightly higher. Ninety percent of the population lives on Suriname's coastal plain, two-thirds of those in Paramaribo, the capital. The racial diversity is most arresting in Suriname's urban environment. In the center of the city, for example, visitors are struck by a modern mosque standing next to one of the oldest synagogues in the hemisphere.

The peaceful image represented by those two buildings does not, however, reflect a harmony among Suriname's religious communities. Islam and Hinduism are relatively recent imports, dating from the time of slavery and indentured servitude in the late 19th century. Emancipated Hindus rose to levels of financial dominance by the 1960s, and Javanese Muslims experienced great population growth. Competition for goods and services in impoverished Suriname has led to social and political conflict based on these two factors, and in the mid 1990s rioting and civil disturbance were aimed at Hindu store owners. At the same time, pandering to an increasingly Muslim population (and in a move widely seen as solicitous of funding from Libya and Iran), the government of Suriname officially declared the country an Islamic republic in 1998.

The Moravians first sent missionaries to the Afro-Caribbean and Amerindian populations in 1735, establishing churches alongside the Reformed churches founded primarily to minister to the colonial Dutch. As the demographic picture changed in the 18th and 19th centuries, the Moravians established missions to the newcomers, and by the middle of the 20th century, joined by Baptists and Lutherans, the older, traditional denominations had built schools, hospitals, and orphanages, as well as churches throughout the country. Theologically conservative to begin with, the major denominations in Suriname sought to protect their institutional identities—and thereby their links to external sources of funds—

through rigid adherence to church polity and liturgical religious expression. While encapsulating spirituality within liturgies can help maintain denominational identity and protect doctrinal purity, insulating people from change also results in making them unable to cope with its inevitability.

The pentecostal influence was first felt in Suriname during a time of great social and political change. In the late 1950s, during the era of postwar reconstruction when ties to colonial Europe were growing tenuous and popular sentiment for independence grew, John Stubbs from the U.S. found the country ripe for the establishment of a new church. In 1959 he and several Surinamese nationals founded the first Assemblies of God (AG) congregation in the Stubbs home in Paramaribo. The fledgling congregation did not grow but struggled to maintain itself.

In an attempt to broaden and deepen his congregation's life, Stubbs invited Karel Hoekendijk from Utrecht, Netherlands, to lead a series of evangelistic rallies in Suriname. Representing an interdenominational group called Stromen van Kracht (Streams of Power, later to become Volle Evangelie Gemeenten in Nederland [Full Gospel Churches in the Netherlands]), Hoekendijk arrived in 1961 with his team to begin a campaign in Suriname. Hoekendijk's boyhood friendship with Rev. G. Polanen, at that time the director of the Moravians' City Mission, led to an invitation to hold the rallies in the mission's large hall.

Many people, mostly Moravians but also some Roman Catholics, came to a knowledge of Christ during these rallies and joined the ensuing Bible studies. From the outset, leaders of the traditional denominations voiced hope that these rallies would infuse life into their own churches. But when many people were baptized later at large services held in the city's Thalia Theater, denominational officials charged Hoekendijk with "sheep stealing"; John Stubbs also expressed disappointment because most of those responding to Hoekendijk's campaign did not affiliate with the AG either. Instead, several small independent pentecostal fellowships were established: Stromen van Kracht, Gods Bazuin (God's Trumpet), Logos, Pinskterzending Suriname (Pentecostal Mission Suriname), and the Evangelisch Centrum (Evangelical Center). In the late 1980s these splinter groups associated themselves in a loose confederation called the Federation of Full Gospel Churches of Suriname. The AG has never joined the Federation and remains represented in Suriname by one small congregation in Paramaribo.

The Roman Catholic Church began its own charismatic explorations in the mid 1980s, when Fr. J. van Nimwigen established a charismatic fellowship among Paramaribo's Catholics. Among Moravians, many of the youth received the baptism of the Holy Spirit in the late 1970s; that charismatic "revolution" gained strength in the mid 1980s when two Moravian pastors from the U.S. held evangelistic rallies in Moravian churches throughout the nation.

Pentecostal growth in Suriname has been slow but steady; in 1990 there were reported to be only 900 pentecostals in the country, but in early 1999 reports indicated the presence of slightly more than 100 churches with a total Sunday attendance between 9,000 and 11,000.

A stunning development in Nov. 1994 has led to the possibility of more growth and charismatic/pentecostal unity in Suriname. The city of Nieuw Nickerie on Suriname's western border with Guyana had been 94% Hindu. A century and a half of Christian mission enterprise in the area had produced little fruit: a few churches, pentecostal and mainline, each boasted a handful of members. Most of those Christians were black-Creole; East Indian Christians had been almost nonexistent. Attempts to cross the line and win Hindus had proved unsuccessful, and over the years all efforts had stopped. But in Nov. 1994 Christian pastors in Nieuw Nickerie gathered together for two days of prayer and a Cornerstone Ministries, International, seminar on revival. When they came forward at the invitation to pray, the Holy Spirit fell on them and drove them to the floor. In tears, they hugged each other and asked for forgiveness for the years of gossiping, backbiting, fear, and distrust. Moravian, pentecostal, and even Salvation Army pastors rose from that floor about six hours later on fire with a desire to take the city out of the hands of Kali-mai, the Hindu goddess to whom it had been dedicated, and place it in the kingdom. Without common doctrines or methods (or even language—there were Javanese, Dutch, and Sranan speakers there), but with a common objective to take the city, these pastors and some of their lay members stormed out of the building just before nightfall. They fanned out across the city, talking to whomever about Jesus and inviting those they spoke with to come along. Several hours later they reconvened at a central gathering place, they and several hundred Hindus: More Hindus came to Christ in that one night than in the previous 140 years of mission work. Since that time, attendance in older churches in the region has swelled, and new churches have been established.

Church leaders throughout Suriname have taken note of the Nickerie experience and are excited by the possibilities of creating more effective ministries by coming together, transparently, to be Christ's body in the nation. In May and Nov. 1998, pastors and lay leaders of nearly every denomination in eastern Suriname's city of Moengo pledged themselves to removing barriers to unity and have begun ministering together, reporting "signs and wonders" and church growth. And in May 1998 there was a historic meeting with strong emphasis on reconciliation between Suriname's Council of Churches (consisting of six major denominations, including Roman Catholic) and the Federation of Full Gospel Churches.

Buoyed by the experiences of Nickerie and Moengo, and by a growing charismatic presence within all churches, pentecostals in Suriname feel themselves on the verge of a great *opwekking* (awakening).

■ **Bibliography:** E. Deira, "1998 Annual Report (Preliminary)" (Suriname Bible Society, 1999) ■ *Encyclopedie van Suriname* (1977) ■ B. F. Grimes, ed., *Ethnologue: 13th ed.* (1996) ■ P. Johnstone, *Operation World* (1993) ■ *Zendtijd voor Kerken* (web site, 1999).

■ D. P. Norwood

SVALBARD AND JAN MAYEN

■ Pentecostals 0　■ Charismatics 0　■ Neocharismatics 0　■ Total Renewal: 0

SWAZILAND

■ Pentecostals 53,612 (10%)　■ Charismatics 16,100 (3%)　■ Neocharismatics 455,288 (87%)　■ Total Renewal: 525,000

SWEDEN

■ Pentecostals 182,053 (29%)　■ Charismatics 382,949 (61%)　■ Neocharismatics 57,999 (9%)　■ Total Renewal: 623,001

At the turn of the century, Sweden experienced a thorough revival with some pentecostal characteristics. In 1907 the message of Pentecost reached Sweden again from Norway and the U.S. One of the most active initiators was pastor ▶Lewi Pethrus, who later became the foremost leader of the Swedish pentecostal movement.

The first pentecostal church was formed in 1913. At present (1998) there are 492 churches with a total of 90,850 members. This makes the pentecostal movement the largest Protestant Free Church movement in Sweden.

Pentecostal churches in Sweden are usually called Filadelfia or Pingstkyrkan (Pentecostal Church). Each local church is independent. The pentecostal movement of Sweden is not a denomination, but shared beliefs and experiences engender a strong sense of unity, which is also promoted and maintained by many joint activities.

Lewi Pethrus, who became the leader of Swedish pentecostalism.

The pentecostals of Sweden have no elected leaders, but this has not prevented several strong Christian personalities from leaving their mark on the movement. Lewi Pethrus, the leader of the Filadelfia Church in Stockholm, is notable in this respect. He saw the membership of his church grow to more than 6,000. He was also the founder of the majority of pentecostal foundations and associations and was an active leader until his death in 1974.

Each local pentecostal church is led by a group of elders, usually presided over by the pastor of the church. The latter is appointed by the church at a congregational meeting. Decisions concerning other church matters are also made at congregational meetings. Each member has the right to vote. One becomes a member through believer's baptism by immersion.

The pastors meet at regional and general conferences to discuss matters of common interest. Many elders and other church members take part in the larger conferences for edification and conversation. Some 10,000 people gather every June for Nyhem Week in southern Sweden, and around 7,000 pentecostals meet during Lappland Week in the north.

These conferences play an important role in unifying the movement. Here pastors, elders, and others study, comment, and discuss the biblical foundation they hold in common; meetings are held concerning the missionary work of the churches and joint bodies; and ordinary members meet and share spiritual experiences and practical advice on congregational work.

From the very start the pentecostal churches have been engaged in missionary work in other countries. The work in Latin America, Africa, and Asia has been very successful. More than 3,000 missionaries have served in foreign fields since 1916, when Samuel and Lina Nyström were sent to Brazil by the Stockholm Filadelfia Church. Even before that, Swedish missionaries began serving in China (1907) and Brazil (1910), although they left from the U.S. At present (1998) there are around 400 active missionaries in 52 countries, engaged in the building up of congregations, Bible schools, and various kinds of social work, which include 4 hospitals, 45 dispensaries, 18 maternity clinics, and school programs for several tens of thousands of pupils. The missionary enterprises are led by the local churches, and each missionary is supported by one or several local congregations in a spirit of voluntary cooperation. The amount of money appropriated for the Swedish Pentecostal Mission totaled some $25 million (US) in 1998.

Despite—or perhaps thanks to—the fact that the pentecostal movement of Sweden is not an organization, many joint spheres of activity have developed. The organizational structures of these working bodies vary somewhat, but all foundations and corporations are jointly owned by the pentecostal churches and are service bodies whose task it is to serve in the joint effort of spreading the Word of God.

Sten-Gunnar Hedin, pastor of the Filadelfia church in Stockholm.

Dagen (The Day) is the only daily Christian newspaper in Sweden. It is an important factor in maintaining the unity of the pentecostal movement and contacts with other evangelical denominations. The newspaper has a daily circulation of 23,000 and is thus a powerful force against the secularization of Sweden. The earlier *Evangelii Härold (Herald of the Gospel),* founded in 1916, was replaced in 1993 by *Petrus,* a joint ecumenical venture with three denominations close to the pentecostal churches. Special issues of *Dagen* and *Evangelii Härold* sometimes reach half a million copies when the local churches use them as an important part of their evangelism.

IBRA Radio (International Broadcasting Association) began transmissions from Radio Africa, Tangier, in 1955. Today the broadcasts reach 100 countries on all continents. IBRA broadcasts from about 80 stations and in 60 languages, with a daily broadcasting time of about 100 hours. There is also TV-Inter, television ministry.

PIL (International Literature Center of the Pentecostal Mission) is a support organization whose goal is the spread of Christian literature, and especially of the Bible, all over the world. PIL was founded in 1970 and has as its motto "Coins for Evangelical Literature." The idea of giving one's small change to PIL was an immediate success, and donations have increased ever since.

PMU Interlife is a relief and development agency owned by the pentecostal churches of Sweden. It was founded in 1965 to meet the increasing costs of the social work carried out by Swedish missionaries. PMU coordinates larger projects and serves as liaison between the Swedish government and the pentecostal movement. In 1998 alone the Swedish authorities have shown their respect for pentecostal missionary work by channeling more than $20 million (US) into educational projects, health care, well drilling, and other social projects of the mission. As a coordinating agency, PMU unites the efforts of local congregations, individuals, and other relief organizations. Thus, projects can be carried out even when these would be economically impossible for the supporting local church alone. Examples of such joint efforts are aid to refugees, disaster aid, building of churches, and student scholarships. In 1986 PMU Interlife decided to form an institute engaged in mission research. It was named MissionsInstitutet—PMU (MI). Since its start, the institute has produced several in-depth research studies of the work overseas. These evaluations help the churches and PMU Interlife to plan projects effectively. Some material used in the education of missionaries has also been published by the MI Institute.

Education The pentecostal movement of Sweden now owns four folk high schools (equivalent to high school plus approximately two years of college in the U.S.) where 1,000 students annually receive the education of their choice. The oldest is Kaggeholm, just outside the capital. Its branch,

Inside the largest Pentecostal church in Sweden: the Filadelfia church in Stockholm, which in 1997 had about 7,000 members. It became a "free and independent" church in 1913 after leaving the Baptist Union under the pastor, Lewi Pethrus.

Karl Erik Heinerborg and Lewi Pethrus (center), hosting two American penetcostal leaders in this a 1972 meeting in Stockholm. (Left) David J. du Plessis; (right) Joseph Mattson-Boze.

Brommaskolan, is located in central Stockholm. Dalkarlså is situated in the north, and Mariannelund and Viebäck in the south. The folk high schools offer general education as a preparation for a profession or for university studies. But of more interest are the special courses, such as the two-year Bible course for pastors and courses for missionaries. Besides these there are shorter Bible courses, language training, and a variety of special courses.

LP–verksamhetens idella riksförening. When pastor Lewi Pethrus celebrated his 70th birthday, he received gifts from people all over Sweden. These he used as initial contributions toward a foundation that was later called Lewi Pethrus Stiftelse (Lewi Pethrus Foundation). During the three decades since, the foundation has grown significantly. A lack of government funding and other causes led to a reconstruction of the foundation in 1998; it was renamed LP–verksamhetens idella riksförening.

Samspar. Difficulties in obtaining loans for the construction of churches led to the foundation of the pentecostal banking enterprise Samspar in the 1960s. Through the sav-ings of pentecostals and others, the bank has grown and Samspar has been able to help finance many churches as well as invest in joint ventures of the movement. Samspar has linked up with one of the biggest banking enterprises in Sweden, thus opening up a Samspar in every Swedish town. A relief fund that includes insurance for pastors and missionaries and a pension fund has also been organized, which supports pastors, evangelists, or their widows or widowers in need. To many ministers of the Word of God it ensures a safer retirement.

PingstRörelsens Informationscentrum (PRI, Pentecostal Movement Information Center) is situated at the Kaggeholms school just outside Stockholm. The center was established in 1983 and is currently engaged in building up a database concerning the Swedish pentecostal movement. It is also engaged in informing schools, researchers, and others about the movement. PRI is involved in a major "documentation of mission" project, interviewing hundreds of missionaries, and writing a mission history for each country. PRI holds the archives and library of Lewi Pethrus, which are open to churches, schools, and researchers. PRI also publishes *The Yearbook of the Pentecostal Movement*, which contains addresses, statistics, and other information.

See also BIBLIOGRAPHY AND HISTORIOGRAPHY OUTSIDE NORTH AMERICA; SCANDINAVIAN MISSIONS TO LATIN AMERICA.

■ **Bibliography:** N. Bloch-Hoell, *The Pentecostal Movement* (1964) ■ Å. Boberg, *Kaggeholm–Lemera* (1992) ■ E. Briem, *Den moderna pingströrelsen* (1924) ■ B. Carlsson, *Organisationer och beslutsprocesser inom Pingströrelsen* (1974) ■ J.-E. Johannesson, *Dokumentation av Svensk Pingstmission i Kina* (1992) ■ A. Lindberg, *Förkunnarna och deras utbildning* (1991) ■ idem, *Väckelse. Frikyrklighet. Pingströrelse.* (1985) ■ P. Pétursson, *Från väckelse till samfund* (1990) ■ C.-E. Sahlberg, *Pingströrelsen och tidningen Dagen* (1977) ■ G. E. Söderholm, *Den svenska pingstväckelsens historia 1907–1928* (1928) ■ M. Söderlund, *Pingstmission i Kongo* (1995) ■ A. Sundstedt, *Pingstväckelsen,* 5 vols. (1973) ■ I. Vingren, *Det började i Pará* (1994).

■ L. Ahonen with J.-E. Johannesson

SWITZERLAND

■ Pentecostals 40,562 (9%)　■ Charismatics 313,236 (66%)　■ Neocharismatics 118,702 (25%)　■ Total Renewal: 472,500

The Swiss pentecostal movement is very small. However, it is one of the oldest pentecostal movements. Its roots go back to the Holiness conferences in Oxford (1874) and Brighton (1875). Robert Pearsall Smith preached in Switzerland. His *Christian Pathway of Power* and many books of the American Holiness evangelists were translated into German and French, although they were "cleansed" from all social and political implications of holiness. That is why holiness was understood in purely religious and individualistic terms. All Swiss churches were influenced by this literature. And during the revival in Wales (1905), one could hardly open a religious (or even secular) periodical without reading about this revival.

In addition, 'John Alexander Dowie founded his European Catholic Apostolic headquarters in Zurich. When Dowie's empire in Zion City, IL, collapsed, his Swiss followers looked for another spiritual home and found it in the emerging pentecostal movement, together with members from the Methodist, Baptist, Reformed, and other churches.

Many foreigners worked in the Swiss pentecostal movement, such as ˈAlexander A. Boddy, ˈGeritt R. Polman, ˈSmith Wigglesworth, Arthur Booth-Clibborn (who had married the daughter of the founder of the Salvation Army), ˈThomas B. Barratt, ˈJonathan Paul, and C. E. D. Delabilière, who previously had worked in the American Church in Geneva. The Swiss periodical *Die Verheissung des Vaters*, founded in 1909 and later merged with *Wort und Geist*, is not only an excellent source of early Swiss pentecostalism but, because of its international reports, of the international pentecostal movement as well.

The first Swiss pentecostal pastors were the English aristocrat Anton D. Reuss (d. 1934) and P. Richard Ruff (1904–60), a former Methodist and high school teacher. Under Ruff's ministry, Swiss pentecostalism experienced an impressive expansion. When Ruff was forced to retire, Karl Schneider (1896–1967) took over.

Among the many Swiss pentecostal organizations, the oldest is the Schweizerische Pfingstmission (Swiss Pentecostal Mission [SPM]). In spite of an impressive building program (chapels in many places, an excellent luxury hotel in Emmeten, and a $6 million church building in Zurich), there has been no notable growth in the last 30 years.

A younger organization is the Gemeinde für Urchristentum (French name: Eglise Apostolique), in which a number of former Reformed pastors played a significant role (Christian Glardon, Robert Willenegger, Fritz de Rougemont). This organization experienced its most important growth period in the 1940s and '50s. It is slightly more ecumenical

than the SPM and does not oppose theological university education in principle.

In French Switzerland a number of English pentecostals (the brothers ˈJeffreys, ˈDouglas Scott, and ˈDonald Gee) have helped to found the Eglise Evangélique du Réveil.

For a long time, Swiss pentecostalism was reluctant to follow the American theological line. For instance, Leonhard Steiner, secretary of the SPM for many years, questioned already in 1939 the doctrine of ˈinitial evidence. There were a number of highly respected pastors (including Reuss) who were incurably ill, which led Leonhard Steiner and others to question the doctrine that healing follows automatically the prayer of faith.

A specialty of the Swiss pentecostal movement is the fact that it has exported many of its academically trained theologians, either to the Swiss Reformed Church (Jean-Daniel Plüss, Daniel Brandt-Bessire) or to overseas educational bodies (Siegfried Schatzmann, ˈW. J. Hollenweger). This is also mirrored by a solidifying of its relationship with the Catholic and the Swiss Reformed Churches.

Most of the pentecostal denominations and independent congregations are organized in a loose federation (Bund pfingstlicher Freikirchen der Schweiz). Zurich hosted the first World Pentecostal Conference (1947), and Swiss pentecostals played a leading role in this body.

Sociologically, Swiss pentecostalism was originally a working-class movement that in the first generation was led by well-educated men. Due to its cultural and ecclesiastical isolation, the later generations of pastors were recruited from its membership, which means that the present pastorate is composed mainly of self-taught preachers from the lower-middle class. This sector of society is, however, also the mission field of the other churches in Switzerland. Few churches evangelize the upper class, the artists, and the leading bankers (except some Swiss Reformed congregations).

The working class—which at present consists mainly of foreigners—is evangelized by neither the mainline churches nor the pentecostals. There are a number of South American, Asian, African, and other foreign pentecostal congregations, with which the native pentecostals have practically no contact, in spite of the fact that the native pentecostals are heavily engaged in mission work in the Third World. As of late there are a number of independent neo-pentecostal congregations, of which the Wimberite Basileia in Bern is the best-known example. It is the official center of the

Switzerland, a nation with one of the oldest pentecostal movements, influenced by people such as John Alexander Dowie, A. A. Boddy, Smith Wigglesworth, and Thomas Ball Barratt.

European ▸Vineyard Churches. This does not keep Basileia from remaining formally a part of the Swiss Reformed Church of Bern. The charismatic movement in Reformed and Catholic churches is modest. The French-speaking charismatics publish an academic theological review, *Hokhma*.

■ **Bibliography:** Very detailed sources and analysis in W. J. Hollenweger, *Handbuch der Pfingstbewegung* (1965–67; available from Yale Divinity School, no. 05.28, pp. 2031–2324; abridged in *Enthusiastisches Christentum: Die Pfingstbewegung in Geschichte und Gegenwart* [1969], 252–83) ■ D. Brandt-Bessire, *Aux sources de la spiritualité pentecôtiste* (1986) ■ C. Glardon, "Les dons spirituels dans la première épître aux Corinthiens" (diss., U. of Lausanne, 1966) ■ P. Helfenberger, ed., *Kalender der evangelischen Kirchen der Schweiz* (published annually; contains an almost complete list of pentecostal institutions and pastors [French-, German-, and Italian-speaking]) ■ J. D. Plüss, *Therapeutic and Prophetic Narratives in Worship: A Hermeneutic Study of Testimonies and Visions: Their Potential Significance for Christian Worship and Secular Society* (1988) ■ M. Schicker et al., *Begeistert von Gott! Jubiläumsschrift der Gemeinde für Urchristentum: Von den Anfängen bis in die Gegenwart* (1997) ■ L. Steiner, "Ist es richtig, unsere Auffassung von der Geistestaufe auf die Apostelgeschichte und die Erfahrung der zwölf Jünger aufzubauen? Kann dieselbe auch aus den apostolischen Briefen hergeleitet werden?" *Verheissung des Vaters* 31 (2, Feb. 1940) ■ idem, "Glaube und Heilung," *Verheissung des Vaters* 50 (4, Apr. 1957), and 50 (5, May 1957), English translation in D. Gee, ed., *Fifth World Pentecostal Conference, Toronto* (1958) (the decisive critical statements on the "healing evangelists" were left out in the English version) ■ M. Wenk, "The Holy Spirit and the Ethical Life of the People of God in Luke/Acts" (diss., London, 1998) ■ J. Zopfi, "Deutschland und die Schweiz," in W. J. Hollenweger, ed., *Die Pfingstkirchen* (1971).   ■ W. J. Hollenweger

SYRIA

■ Pentecostals 343 (0%)   ■ Charismatics 17,346 (16%)   ■ Neocharismatics 92,311 (84%)   ■ Total Renewal: 110,000

See Africa, North, and the Middle East.

TAIWAN

■ Pentecostals 26,554 (7%)   ■ Charismatics 66,246 (18%)   ■ Neocharismatics 266,200 (74%)   ■ Total Renewal: 359,000

I. The Pentecostal/Charismatic Community on Modern Taiwan
    A. *Mission-Centered Churches*
    B. *The Middle of the Spectrum*
    C. *Indigenized Churches*

II. Congruence and Double Marginality

III. Conclusion

Pentecostal and charismatic Protestantism, a force in Latin America and Africa and a challenge to the older, more established, conciliar and evangelical churches in those areas, is also a spiritual force in East Asia. This powerful spiritual "last wave" has been experienced on Taiwan, and it is the Taiwanese community that will be examined in this section.

Over the course of the past 70 years, this island, first held by the Japanese and now dominated by the Guomindang, has witnessed the coming of powerful and expanding pentecostal and charismatic churches. Of the 300,000 citizens of Taiwan who are Protestant, almost a third define themselves as charismatics or pentecostals (Swanson, 1981, 1986). Furthermore, members of more mainline conciliar and evangelical churches, such as the Presbyterians and the Southern Baptists, have participated in and have experienced the power of a nondenominational charismatic renewal movement. Each of these, whether church member or participant in renewal, is a believer in a Holy Spirit–centered, experiential form of Christianity that has continued to grow and to demonstrate dynamism even as mainstream churches have faltered.

I. THE PENTECOSTAL/CHARISMATIC COMMUNITY ON MODERN TAIWAN.

One must first recognize that the pentecostal/charismatic community on Taiwan is a small one, as is the Taiwanese Protestant community of which it is a part. It is, however, a complex community. The churches within the charismatic community fit into a spectrum or continuum. At one end of this spectrum are churches very close to their Western roots that remain linked to the mission bodies that helped to establish them. In the middle of the spectrum are churches that owe their origins to Western theologians and missionaries and that maintain a careful relationship with these spiritual parent churches or missionary "fathers" but that exist at the same time as aggressively independent entities. At the other end of the spectrum are churches that are both independent and indigenous. Such churches were founded by Chinese and have evolved theologies that demonstrate both their doctrinal independence and their leaders' ability to create a Chinese context for the Christian message.

A. Mission-Centered Churches.

The Taiwan Assemblies of God (AG) is a Chinese pentecostal church that lies at the mission-centered end of the spectrum. This church was founded by and continues to have strong ties to the AG–U.S., the largest of the American pentecostal denominations (Yang, n.d.).

In 1948 the China-based missionaries of the AG, a church well established on the mainland, decided that these efforts were being threatened by the Civil War and took a tentative step to develop another Chinese field that would prove to be both a safe haven for its missionaries and a new starting point for its evangelism. Two families of missionaries from the AG were sent from Shanghai to Taiwan. But it was not until 1952 that the AG mission board fully committed its men and women to the island in hopes of establishing pentecostal churches in the militarily secure Republic of China. They have been there ever since. On Taiwan these missionaries and their Chinese coworkers have been able to develop a small but dedicated body of believers who are part of the worldwide AG network.

In Taibei, Taizhong, Tainan, and Gaoxiong, and in villages in the reservation areas of the island's rugged interior, there are AG churches made up of mainlanders, Taiwanese, and mountain people. There is a Bible school in Taizhong, run by the mission, and a large AG-run and-financed correspondence school, now operating in Taibei. Radio ministries operate as well and serve to attract Chinese to the church. The AG mission on Taiwan is one that is rather classic in its operating style (Rubinstein, 1991).

While some progress has been made in more than four decades, the AG missionaries have not been able to expand among the Taiwanese majority or make much progress among the Yuanjumin ("Original People" or mountain people). The AG missionaries knew of the work of the other churches when they began their own efforts but decided that there were unreached peoples in the mountain areas. They have been able to carve out a place for themselves, but it has not been easy, since there has been intense competition for the minds and hearts of the mountain people. Catholic priests, Presbyterian ministers, and True Jesus evangelists (see below) have all worked with the mountain people and have established strong church communities among the various tribal peoples (Martin, n.d.).

Neither have the missionaries been able to plant a truly independent or indigenous Chinese AG church. While there is a Taiwan Convention, many of the member churches are tied to AG–U.S. purse strings. This dependence has proven most disappointing to missionaries and to nationals, but the reality is that the AG community is just too small and too close to Western ways to be truly independent. AG worship serves as a very establishment-oriented, very middle-class, and very proper form of pentecostal experience for those who participate. There is warmth and camaraderie but no overt displays of religious spirituality. The content of the sermon and the prayers are pentecostal, but the services are not the overtly emotional experience of the services conducted by the indigenous churches; in the AG churches, this author observed that no one spoke in tongues or went into any trance-like state. (For the significance of this in the context of Taiwan, see below.)

One senses that, aside from certain older congregations, the AG in Taiwan is relatively weak and not growing. Today, then, the AG exists as a small church within the larger Protestant community. It holds fast to its Western roots and maintains close ties to its U.S. founders. The Taiwan AG can be seen as an example of middle American revivalist pentecostal Christianity transplanted into an East Asian cultural and social environment.

B. The Middle of the Spectrum.

In the middle of the pentecostal and charismatic spectrum are those organizations that serve as a bridge between Western Protestantism and truly indigenized and Sinicized churches. The best example of such a bridge is the Prayer Mountain Revival Movement (PMRM).

The PMRM is not a church in any formal sense but is, instead, a nondenominational body that works with and for other Protestant churches on the island. It creates a special religious environment for members of the various denominations—denominations that range from conciliar to evangelical to charismatic—and then leads these individuals through a complex process of spiritual renewal. While the movement's leaders and workers are open to the work of the Holy Spirit in the renewal process, and while these same individuals are clearly charismatic in style and in personal beliefs, they stress that they do not rigidly hold to any one form of Christian belief or practice. Daniel Dai, the Southern Baptist trained minister who heads the organization, stresses that he provides the setting for Christian renewal and the emotional and religious atmosphere in which the renewal can take place, but that he does not present any one form of belief to his captive audience.

The renewal movement began in 1982. Since then, thousands of Taiwanese, mainlanders, and mountain people—members of the various churches that make up the island's Protestant community—have come to the mountain center and have participated in the prayer weekends. For many, the weekend renewal experience has strengthened their faith. This did not mean that these people left their home churches, however. Rather, they returned, more secure in their faith. They had experienced firsthand some of the power of the man who led the movement, Daniel Dai. Dai was a well-trained and highly intelligent man who was also a very powerful speaker with an attractive and magnetic personality; he could get across his new vision with great force. Even in a formal interview, the power and the deep faith of the man come through (author interview, Miaoli, Taiwan, Dec. 15–16, 1986).

Not all who participated in a weekend retreat wished to return to the status quo. For these individuals their experience at the retreat pointed the way to a new, more dynamic religiosity that involved an emotional and Holy Spirit centered experience. Because of their new feelings and their sense that Christianity was more than what was preached in their home congregation, these returnees came home to threaten the stability of their congregations.

Allen Swanson, a cofounder of the movement and now its major Western advisor, felt that much good was coming from the PMRM. While he was fearful that the movement could slip into unscriptural—i.e., Christo-pagan—patterns of belief, he felt that he could serve as guide and as watchdog. Dai trusted him and used him as confidant and as resident expert. Swanson, when interviewed at Prayer Mountain, was convinced that this movement was of importance in breathing new life into the larger Protestant community (author interviews, Taipei and Miaoli, Taiwan, Dec. 1986). To an outside observer, the PMRM is an important new organization on the Taiwanese Christian scene: It is a body that stands as a bridge between Western and Chinese churches and that also serves to unite in spirit those separated by the formal walls of denomination.

C. Indigenized Churches.

On the indigenized wing of the spectrum lies the True Jesus Church (TJC). This church represents a truly indigenous Chinese pentecostalism in its history, its organizational structures, its doctrines, and its patterns of worship. The TJC has been able to take Western religious concepts and put them into forms that Chinese and mountain people can be comfortable with. The roots of the TJC go back to the early 1910s. Three men—Zhang Lingsheng, Paul Wei, and Barnabas Zhang—founded the TJC in Beijing in 1917–18. They had become Christians at an earlier point in their lives and were searching for a deeper, more evangelistic, Holy Spirit–centered, Christian experience. They found what they sought in pentecostalism and took pentecostal ideas, redefined them so that they fit better their given emotional and cultural environments, and then went out to find other Chinese Christians who would listen to the newly indigenized doctrine. (For the origins of TJC, see Bays [1983].) The church was planted on the island of Taiwan in the 1920s. It grew slowly under the Japanese but has expanded rapidly since the Guomindang retreated to the island in 1949.

The TJC evangelists work with the two segments of the population they had evangelized in the decades preceding the Nationalist retreat: the Taiwanese and the Yuanjumin. They use time-proven tactics; they hold evangelistic meetings, bear witness, plant new congregations, organize new churches, and as a result have been able to bring more Taiwanese and mountain people into their ranks.

Furthermore, the process of church growth has been carefully systematized; each church member does his or her part in carrying it out. To be a TJC member means to be a missionary for the church. In practical terms, employing such a tactic means that the church needs a smaller formal evangelistic staff. Thus, church leaders can devote less of their energy to the actual work of expansion and more to the more difficult task of creating an atmosphere to retain the new members (Swanson, 1970, 1981).

Central and local headquarters seem able to deal with the ever-expanding network of both rural and urban churches. This can be seen in the way the church has set up and maintained control over its scattered congregations. Orders come out of Taizhong and reflect the decisions of the general assembly. (In style and function the general assembly seems much the same as the legislative organ of its great rival, the Taiwanese Presbyterian Church, although the TJC claims apostolic precedent for its structure [see TJC, *Description; Jiao-huei*]). However, in each geographical area there is one main church that runs things on this local level. This church serves the needs of the community and is organized to take care of most aspects of congregational life.

The church's publishing efforts have also helped the church to grow. Tracts have been written and produced in great numbers, and these have been made readily available to each church member. The press has become more sophisticated in its presentation of tracts and scriptural materials and is better able to meet the needs of the expanding church. They are now able to target their audiences more clearly, writing different types of articles for different types of church audiences. A perusal of a typical monthly issue of *The Holy Spirit* demonstrates this point.

The church has also been able to broaden its class base. The TJC has been, since it first began, a church of the lower and lower-middle classes. In recent years, however, the church seems to be attracting individuals in the new managerial and technocratic subclasses as well.

Finally, the church offers a safe haven in a troubled and uncertain political and social environment. The TJC is determinedly nonpolitical. It is removed from the type of activism that has lead the Presbyterian Church and the New Testament Church, another Holy Spirit–centered church, into direct conflicts with the Guomindang rulers of the Republic of China. It demonstrates to one and all that an alternative form of Christianity is available to Taiwanese, a form that is concerned with community but that will not challenge the existing political structure.

These, then, are the churches and parachurches that represent the pentecostal and charismatic spectrum. But what is the appeal of those churches and movements that have grown the most rapidly? One answer lies in congruence.

II. CONGRUENCE AND DOUBLE MARGINALITY.

While other churches have declined, pentecostal and charismatic churches have been able to make homes for themselves on Taiwan and have continued to grow because of congruence. The existence of congruence is a necessary precondition to the indigenization process and goes far toward explaining the appeal that the pentecostal/charismatic churches have for increasing numbers of Taiwanese and mountain people.

Congruence may be defined as the existence of parallel structures and processes one finds in social and cultural environments—in this case parallels between the pentecostal/charismatic religious system and the indigenous popular religious system. There are, in some societies, belief systems, patterns of intellectual analysis, and patterns of sociocultural interaction that can also be found in other, seemingly quite different, societies. The task of cultural transmitters—be they representatives of the Agency for International Development, or Christian missionaries, or indigenous evangelists—is to adapt the cultural and religious patterns of one society to the needs of another. They can achieve this only if they can first find key parallel cultural patterns and structures. Once they have done this they can then show their target audience that, although the cultural and/or religious system they represent may at first seem quite alien from what their hosts are familiar with, there are numerous points of congruence—patterns in the new system that are very similar to specific patterns in the host system, though perhaps on a subtextual or deeper level. If they are successful in doing this, they have much of the battle won. Their host audience will now be ready to see why it is possible to accept the new belief system or religious pattern.

This theoretical framework provides an explanation for the way in which pentecostal/charismatic churches deal with the challenge of adapting Christianity to Chinese modes of religiosity. The TJC provides us with examples of congruence.

The first example is the use of the basic biblicism that is so much a part of the TJC belief system (as well as of the belief systems of the PMRM and the AG). The theologians of these churches believe in biblical inerrancy. They are careful to use Scripture as the basis for all statements and arguments they make about the way the supernatural and the natural realms have evolved, and they also use Scripture as the moral basis for all acts and behaviors of individuals in society. (The basic TJC work on this subject is John Yang's *Essential Doctrines of the Holy Bible*.)

On the surface there is nothing here that is different from what most evangelicals do. The difference lies in the *form* such biblical argumentation takes—in the very way the TJC writers present their arguments. There are two basic formats that can be found in TJC materials—tracts, paperback books, and hardcover volumes, as well as periodicals. In one format

Scripture is quoted first, followed by comments showing why such Scripture is relevant to a given situation or how it would provide guidance in helping one deal with one's problems.

In the second format the procedure is reversed. The writers first discuss a given theological issue or a life-related problem. Then they quote the passage in Scripture that illustrates their argument.

Such forms of argument are congruent with traditional Chinese approaches to textual or scholarly argument. When one examines the classics—Mencius is one example and Xunzi is another—one finds similar patterns of argument. Usually a point is made or a specific point is presented, and then reference is made to one or another of the pre-Confucian classics. In later works of scholarship and in the examinations for the civil service, Mencius or Confucius (the Lun Yu) is used in much the same way.

TJC evangelists make the existence of this pattern of congruence clear to those outside the Christian tradition in their many publications. By doing so, they try to make their audience more willing to read TJC tracts. In the very way they present their material, the TJC leaders demonstrate their Chinese roots and their familiarity with Chinese forms of philosophical and religious argument.

Congruence is also found in the theological concepts that the TJC holds as fundamental. TJC writers and theologians, true to their biblicistic orientation, accept the idea that Satan, demons, and angels exist and play a role in the natural as well as the supernatural realms. John Yang, a TJC theologian, outlines the TJC perception of these beings and suggests the way they influence human life (Yang, 1970, 54–64). If one examines the Chinese popular religious tradition, one finds a congruent structure—the existence of a formal supernatural bureaucracy with its higher gods, lesser gods, and demons, and with each being playing a specific role and each possessing the capability of affecting human existence in direct ways. Thus, in general terms, parallels can be found between the biblical pantheon described in Yang's work and that found in Chinese popular religious thought. But there is an important caveat: Within the Chinese tradition there does not seem to be the type of transcendent yet immanent being we find as the core figure in the Western (Judeo-Christian-Islamic) tradition. Neither is there the *avatar*—god becoming flesh—in any specific or formal sense; in China human beings become gods with some regularity, and thus the thought of only one such being is looked upon as strangely limiting.

If the TJC writers can convince their Chinese audience that there is sufficient evidence of congruence, then they take the next step. They can show that they have adapted their faith to Chinese realities. For example, by arguing for the existence of a hierarchy and by setting forth, as they do, a theology of powers, they are able to make subtle linkages between their own pentecostal theology and the mainstream Chinese folk theology. This emerges clearly in TJC literature, and these discussions demonstrate the degree to which they are able to show how indigenized their own variety of pentecostalism has become.

Congruence can also be seen in patterns of church practice as well as in doctrinal presentation and development. A key facet of True Jesus Christianity is the stress on the gift of the Holy Spirit. In TJC practice, believers pray for the gift of the Spirit and through such prayer open themselves up to possession by the Holy Spirit. This prayer takes place at a given point during the worship service. The atmosphere has been created through the singing of hymns as well as through the recitation of short prayers. At the moment when congregational prayer is called for, all individuals present—the men sitting on one side of the sanctuary and the women on the other—pull down their kneeling stools, bowing down on their knees in supplication, and begin to pray. They begin with simple words or verses. Then many begin to shake and sway. From their mouths come strange sounds; some of these resemble formalized chanting, while others are sharp glottal sounds—this is glossolalia in its classic form. Such speaking in tongues continues for 10 to 15 minutes, and after a bell is rung, the sound fades away. People then come out of their trance-like states and the service continues. A similar period of speaking in tongues takes place about 20 to 30 minutes later, after the sermon. Less formalized speaking in tongues is a common feature of American, Latin American, and African pentecostalism.

There is congruence with the Chinese pattern of religious practice, as well as the more obvious parallels with Western and Third World pentecostalism. Within Chinese folk religious life there is the important personage of *tong khi (qi tang)*. The *tong khi* serves as communicator with the gods. When a person is troubled, he or she often turns to the *tong khi* who, when in a trance-like state, allows the god to speak to his client. The *tong khi* is a person of some importance in rural and urban Taiwan.

There is congruence between the baptism and gifts of the Spirit and the possession or trance the *tong khi* undergoes. TJC members, and other indigenous pentecostals who undergo the baptism of the Spirit, appear to be possessed at those times during the service. They become a collectivity of *tong khi* at such times, and each shares the status and spiritual power that a *tong khi* possesses in his home village. When confronted by this apparent congruence, TJC theologians, as well as the theologians of the other churches, are quick to argue that *tong khi* are inhabited by evil or demonic spirits, while those individuals within their church who are given the gift of the Spirit are possessed by the true spirit, by the Holy Spirit himself. What is important about this explanation is that there is no denial of the *fact* of possession. The focus

instead is upon the nature of that spirit that takes over the believer. Thus, here too is congruence, an approach church leaders use either implicitly or explicitly as a means of making their form of Christianity more palatable to the average Taiwanese.

By finding areas of congruence and by then making the necessary adaptations based on the existence of such congruence, the TJC and the other indigenous pentecostal or charismatic churches have been able to make themselves more attractive to the mass of Taiwanese who are of a more traditional bent, as well as to the mountain people, whose own religion is animistic in nature.

By defining the Christian doctrines as they have and by demonstrating in various ways the degrees of congruence that exist between their forms of Christianity and the basic forms of Chinese religion, the indigenous churches have also been able to carve out a place for themselves within the pentecostal and charismatic community and within the larger Protestant community.

In spite of the strength of these churches, the institutions and their members exist in a state of tension with the other Protestant churches on Taiwan and with the larger Taiwanese society. They bear the stigma of "double marginality." The members of the various pentecostal and charismatic churches are seen as marginal in the eyes of two very different communities. In the eyes of the larger Taiwanese community, they belong to religious bodies that are perceived as marginal. At the same time, because of their Holy Spirit–centered Christianity, they are also seen as marginal by members of the larger Taiwanese Protestant community. Thus they bear the burden of "double marginality."

III. CONCLUSION.

Pentecostal/charismatic churches are paradoxes that reflect the basic dilemma of Protestantism on Taiwan. They are unique in the forms and varieties of Christian experience they convey, and because of this they are often treated as pariahs. At the same time they have come the furthest toward creating a Christianity that is congruent with basic patterns of Chinese religion. They are thus both the cutting edge of Christian progress and the outside fringe, the dwellers living on the edge.

See also CHINA.

■ **Bibliography:** AG Foreign Missions Department: clip file Taiwan ■ D. Bays, "Western Missionary Sectarianism and the Origins of Chinese Pentecostalism in the 20th Century" (paper, Association of Asian Studies, 1987) ■ F. and P. Martin, "Development of the National Church" (unpub. ms., AGFMD clip file, #531, n.d.), 20–23 ■ M. A. Rubinstein, *The Protestant Community on Modern Taiwan: Mission, Seminary, and Church* (1991) ■ Allen J. Swanson, *The Church in Taiwan: Profile, 1980* (1981) ■ idem, *Mending the Nets:*

Taiwan Church Growth and Loss in the 1980s (1986) ■ idem, *Taiwan: Mainline versus Independent Church Growth* (1970), 180–83 ■ True Jesus Church, *Description of the True Jesus Church*, 9–17 ■ idem, *History of the TJC: Thirtieth Anniversary Volume* (1956) ■ idem, "*Jiao-huei Zuzhi Yuan-li*" ("Reasons for the Organization of the Church"; tract, 1980) ■ J. Yang, "The Assemblies of God Missionary Effort in China: 1907–1952" (unpub. ms.), 1–30 ■ idem, *The Essential Doctrines of the Holy Bible* (1970).   ■ M. A. Rubinstein

TAJIKISTAN

■ Pentecostals 416 (13%)   ■ Charismatics 1,562 (49%)   ■ Neocharismatics 1,221 (38%)   ■ Total Renewal: 3,199

See RUSSIA.

TANZANIA

■ Pentecostals 1,464,786 (43%)   ■ Charismatics 1,328,831 (39%)   ■ Neocharismatics 631,383 (18%)
■ Total Renewal: 3,425,000

For general introduction to East Africa and bibliography, see AFRICA, EAST.

Tanzania was formerly known as German East Africa. Later it became Tanganyika, and then Tanzania, when Tanganyika and the island of Zanzibar were united. Tanzania was colonized by Germany but mandated to Britain after WWI. This is significant, because although it became a British colony, a number of German-speaking pentecostal missions (as well as nonpentecostal German Protestants) have been involved in evangelization in this country. This includes the Volksmission (People's Mission, or the equivalent of the German Assemblies of God) and the German branch of the Pentecostal Assemblies of Canada (PAOC). The capital of Tanzania has been moved from Dar-es-Salaam to Dodoma, although the president and most ministers still live in Dar-es-Salaam and commute to the sessions of parliament. Nyerere, the country's first president after independence, introduced socialist systems that were strongly adhered to for the first few years. Although the country's official ideology is still socialist, however, it is primarily based on a market economy.

1. Earliest Beginnings.

The first pentecostal missionaries in East Africa (E.A.) and, as far as can be ascertained, the first pentecostal missionaries of any description in Tanzania were Karl and Marian Wittick and Clarence Grothaus. They were independent pentecostal missionaries who had originally left North America with the intention of settling in Kenya in 1913. Because of the opposition to missions in Kenya, they were given permission by the governor of the area to settle at Utigi in Tanzania, near present-day Dodoma, where no other missions were present. The first days of missionary work were marked by tragedy and death. Within three months of their arrival, Clarence Grothaus and Karl Wittick were dead. Marian Wittick remained, although she was strongly advised to return home to Canada. This was also a testing time, because when WWI broke out, all links with Marian Wittick's support base in Canada were cut. She was incarcerated for one week by the German authorities and then released.

The next group of pentecostals to arrive in German East Africa was a party of four led by George Bowie from Bethel Pentecostal Assembly in Newark, NJ. Bowie had started an association that was registered in South Africa (S.A.) as the Pentecostal Mission of Central and South Africa. This mission had sent a reconnoitering party from S.A. by boat to E.A. in 1914, but while they were in what was then Tanganyika, WWI broke out and they had to make their way quickly to what was then the Belgian Congo. Their exact intentions are unknown, as are the contacts they made during this visit. The only survivor of the journey was Bowie, and he did not return to Tanzania.

In 1921 a party of Scandinavian missionaries, most of whom were headed to the Congo, arrived in Tanganyika. This group consisted of Swedish and Norwegian pentecostals: Axel Lindgren, Gunnerius Tollefsen, Oddbjörg Tollefsen, and Hanna Veum. They passed through Tanganyika and Kigoma on their way to Congo in June 1921; however, Kigoma did not become part of the Swedish mission field until much later.

2. The Swedish Free Mission and the Finnish Free Foreign Mission.

The Svenska Fria Missionen (SFM, Swedish Free Mission) first became involved in missionary work in Tanganyika in Feb. 1932, when it sent Erland and Ester Dahlqvist to the country. They were joined by Erik and Julia Wiklund in November of the same year. At first they went under the Africa Inland Mission and were located at Kolandoto, but after their language studies in Kinyamwezi, they started their own mission at Nzega in 1933. The king of the area gave them a place to settle that had previously been a place where offerings were made to evil spirits. The place was called Tazengwa, which ironically means "Where nothing will be built." From there the mission work began to grow. The first assembly of believers was made up of six converts who were baptized in May 1935. In a short time six mission stations were started with 10 missionaries receiving appointment in the western part of the country. Their initial work was in the central regions with the Wezi and the Sukuma peoples. Before WWII five missions stations were started, one of them near Lake Tanganyika. It was not until after WWII, when between 20 and 30 new Swedish missionaries were sent to supplement the work force, that missionaries from the SFM went to the coastal and other regions. At that time 22 stations were opened. This effort meant that the SFM had more personnel in Tanzania than in any of its other fields worldwide. Collaborating with the SFM and its work in Tanzania have been pentecostals from Norway and Denmark, as well as from both the Swedish- and Finnish-speaking areas of Finland (which are supported by separate missions).

During the first years of mission, there was no real move of the Spirit of God. As a result, much prayer went up for the new churches. This concern for a move of God resulted in urgent requests being sent to home assemblies in Scandinavia to pray for an outpouring of the Holy Spirit, and from 1938 there are many testimonies of a move of the Spirit of God in the SFM field. A new devotion and a longing for separation from many non-Christian customs were witnessed. Many sick were healed and others were called to be preachers and evangelists. At the same time, the burning of amulets and fetishes after conversion drew great interest from non-Christians, who were convinced that the wrath of the ancestral spirits would be sure to follow and were amazed when this did not happen. The fact that no harm came to the converts who had burned their fetishes had considerable impact on the success of the church planters.

The largest of the pentecostal missions in Finland is the Finnish Free Foreign Mission (FFFM, Suomen Vapaa Ulkolähetys). The first missionary of the FFFM went to Tanganyika in 1934 to work with the SFM and the national church in the country. She was Sylvi Mömmö, who settled at Nzega. In the past there have been as many as 50 FFFM missionaries in Tanzania at any one time, but by 1997 this number was reduced to 32. The FFFM planted a Bible college for the training of pastoral leadership at Nzega, as well as a hospital and a school for missionary children. Between the FFFM and the SFM, 14 clinics were opened throughout the country. Churches were also started in the former capital, Dar-es-Salaam. Pioneer work has been done among the Barabaikki people in Kateshi.

The work of the Swedish missionaries was registered at first under the name Swedish Free Mission. However, in 1964, when the national language became Swahili, the name was replaced by Chama cha Umoja wa Makanisa ya Pentekoste Tanzania (CUMPT, Pentecostal Churches Social Association Tanzania). In 1986 the word *Social* was dropped

from the name, making it Umoja wa Makanisa ya Pentekoste Katika Tanzania (UMPT, Pentecostal Churches Association in Tanzania). Because of the insistence of the Swedish pentecostal churches on the maintenance of local church autonomy, there is not always a lot of uniformity between the practices of the churches belonging to UMPT. There appears to be more regional than national cohesion between the member churches and more input from the national leaders at a regional level than at a national level. There have been efforts at uniting the churches, but these have only served to create further splits in recent years. By 1982 this entire work had 40,000 members, and by 1998 there were 270,000 adult members in 100 autonomous churches and 2,600 sub-churches. The national chairman of the UMPT is Daudi Batenzi; the secretary general is Jackson Kaluzi. Kaluzi followed Steven Lubele, who served as general secretary for 20 years, until his death in 1995. Missionaries in charge of the mother churches still have a considerable say in how the churches are run. There is still a very high ratio of missionaries to national pastors within the UMPT, with about 1,800 local pastors and 90 missionaries in 1998. The total number of Scandinavian missionaries who have served in Tanzania since the start of the UMPT is approximately 400.

"And old woman of the Masai tribe near Arusha, Tanzania. In her face is mirrored the hopelessness of Africa's darkness. I said to her, 'Do you know the Lord Jesus Christ?' She answered, 'Bwana, I have never been more than five miles from my house in my life. I have never met any white man'" (Paul Bruton).

The missions that cooperate with the UMPT are involved in leadership training through as many as 15 schools, including two theological colleges and other branch schools. The UMPT is also involved in regular broadcasting through Radio Habari Maalum (IBRA), which is responsible for the production of its own programs for both radio and TV. In addition there is a printing press and a press for literature in Braille. Social work has been emphasized through the help of Swedish and Finnish foreign aid programs. There are 2 hospitals, 7 health centers, 2 orphanages, 68 preschool groups, a secondary school, and 2 agricultural colleges, as well as a teachers' college for training preschool teachers and a school for missionary children. The missions are also involved in two tree-planting projects.

The Finnish missionaries were vitally involved with the 700,000 refugees located at Ngara after the 1994 genocide in Rwanda, before the camps were closed and the people repatriated in Dec. 1996. It is estimated that there were as many as 7,000 pentecostals and 40 pastors in the Burundi camps located in Tanzania. The Lähetyksen Kehitysapu (LKA), the Finnish aid program of the FFFM, has five development aid projects in Tanzania. The Home Craft Centre at Mwanza is now completely nationalized. Nursery school projects are seen as the projects of the future. One was opened at Tarime in 1987, which has been a great success and is much appreciated by the local population. On the coast, youth centers have been set up with the aim of reaching Muslim youth through instruction about the dangers of AIDS and drugs, as well as providing courses on the English language. The same programs are planned for Tanga and Zanzibar. By 1992 the missionaries of the SFM realized that they needed to yield more responsibility to the national church. By 1998 two-thirds of the departments and projects were managed by nationals. Missionaries are still involved in church planting with Tanzanian nationals in the coastal area of the country, where Muslim influence is the strongest.

Some former members of UMPT believe that the churches have lost their momentum and that they tend to be too legalistic, with emphasis on dress codes and rules about socializing with unbelievers, attending football (soccer) matches, and the like.

3. The Pentecostal Holiness Association Mission.

Planted about 1938 by members of the Pentecostal Holiness Church (PHC) from Zambia and Malawi who crossed the border and started churches in the southern highlands among the Nyakusa people, this group is mostly located between Mbeya and Iringa. Before 1945 their work was recognized by the PHC in the U.S. Their growth has been limited by the number of areas in which the church is involved; they claim 95 congregations and 66,300 adherents (outsiders would question the latter figure).

4. Kanisa La Elim Pentekoste Tanzania.

The Kanisa La Elim Pentekoste Tanzania (KEPT, Elim Pentecostal Church Tanzania) was planted by Elim–U.K. The A. E. Tates went to Tanzania in 1946 and were joined in 1949 by the A. D. Bulls. Mission stations were opened at Morogoro, Kikilo, Kinonko, Tanga, and Arusha, where primary schooling, health clinics, and church planting became the priority in the early days. The schools were taken over by the government in 1964, and the work of the clinics was mostly discontinued. The KEPT is mostly in the area west and north of Dar-es-Salaam, from the main Tanzania/Zambia highway in the south to Arusha, not far from the border with Kenya, in the north. By 1995 it had more than 188 congregations, 4,849 adult members, and 12,000 adherents. A Bible school at Tanga serves most of the Elim work, including the newer outreach in Burundi. By 1992 the Elim churches had spread to the Muslim enclave on the island of Zanzibar, where Paulo Kairo, a carpenter on the island, began informal meetings. There is great and continued Muslim opposition to all efforts at Christian outreach on Zanzibar; nevertheless, KEPT has one central church and three house groups on the island. In 1992 the need to develop churches in Dar-es-Salaam was also recognized. KEPT is presently active in 21 of the 23 regions of the country. This national church is governed by an executive council whose members are elected at the biennial conference. The day-to-day administration is carried out by an elected chairman with executive authority. Ayubu Mgweno has been chairman of the KEPT churches since 1986. He was reelected in 1998. The secretary general is H. Ngagassi.

5. The Pentecostal Assemblies of God.

The Pentecostal Assemblies of God (PAG) work in Tanzania was started when Kenyan pentecostal believers moved to Tanzania (then Tanganyika) in search of land. Renata Siemans, who lived at Nyang'ori, Kenya, not far from the Tanzanian border, made frequent trips to Tanzania to hold services among the Kenyan immigrants in the 1940s. In 1948 Jack Lynn and Vernon Morrison, PAOC field director for East Africa, went to Tanzania from Kenya to help organize the churches. The first pentecostal churches were in the Mara region, in the villages of Murenyigo, Gruma, Bugwema, and Suguti. In 1956 Gus and Doris Wentland, from the German branch of the PAOC in Alberta, felt called to start church planting in Tanzania. They moved to this area around Lake Victoria, where there were already a few small churches. The national church was registered as The Pentecostal Assemblies of God–Tanzania, but it is generally known as the Pentecostal Assemblies of God, or merely as PAG.

In 1966 I. Mueller went to Mwanza to begin church planting among the Sukuma people. Although the PAG is predominantly in the northwest, around Lake Victoria, there are assemblies at Dodoma, Tanga, Dar-es-Salaam, Mwanza, and their surrounding districts. The Volksmission from Germany (see also article on Kenya) cooperates with the PAOC in Tanzania and sent Heinz and Edelgard Battermann to teach at the Mwanza Bible College of the PAG in the 1990s. By 1955 there were 15,000 adherents in the PAG; by 1986 there were 21,000 members. Between 1967 and 1975 the number of assemblies increased from 60 to 160, even though 55 congregations disappeared when Kenyan immigrants were repatriated to Kenya. In 1998 there were an estimated 750 assemblies and more than 44,800 adherents in the PAG. The PAG Bible school at Mwanza had a four-year program where students attended for three months every year. After 1988, however, the program was changed so that students attend the school for nine months each year for three years. Those who complete three years are awarded a diploma. In addition, there is an intensive two-month course in the place of a fourth year, which leads to a certificate in theology. Since Swahili is the national language, all subjects used to be taught in Swahili; however, within the last few years, courses in the central college are all taught in English. Because the Bible school is unable to meet all the needs within the country, regional Bible schools have been established in each of the regions where the PAG is present (now 10 regions). In these schools, eight-week courses for pastors are taught; enrollment for 1998 is 213. Most of the regional schools are led by graduates from the English-diploma course at Mwanza and are totally financed by their own regions.

The PAG is organized so that it has a general executive committee composed of general superintendent Francis Rwechungura, general secretary-treasurer Daniel Awet, and executive members from the regions. There is a general conference every four years. The missionary involvement within the PAG has been totally backed by the German branch of the PAOC; even today Tanzania is regarded as its particular field of responsibility within the PAOC. Numbers of missionaries, including the Ron Poseins, who presently teach in the Bible school at Mwanza, the Len Ruttens, the R. Middlestaeds, and others have served in this field. Because the ratio of missionaries to pastors is very low, responsibilities for leadership were passed to Tanzanians at a very early stage. The PAG churches have learned to carry the burden for their work and have been encouraged to follow the pattern of tithes and offerings. The PAOC, which has maintained a separate registration from the PAG in the country, is responsible for a primary school in Dar-es-Salaam and an orphanage at Mwanza. The PAG, unlike many other pentecostal denominations within the country, has never experienced a split in its ranks.

6. The Tanzanian Assemblies of God.

In the 1930s, independent American pentecostal missionaries Paul and Evelyn Derr went to Tanzania. They experienced an outpouring of the Holy Spirit on their ministry that resulted in many healings and other miracles. This move of God resulted in the salvation of many Tanzanians. In 1940 the Derrs joined the AG–U.S.; this resulted in Joseph and Ebba Nilson, who had previously been AG missionaries in what was then the Belgian Congo (Zaire/Democratic Republic of Congo), being sent to help the AG work in Tanzania. They stayed for only seven years; by 1948 there were no AG missionaries in the country. In 1952 three AG pastors from Tanzania, Yohanni Mpayo, Moses Kameta, and Ramsey Mwambipile, walked 120 miles to the AG mission in neighboring Malawi to request help and especially to request that an AG–U.S. missionary in that country be sent to give leadership to the new church. It was at this point that the Wesley R. Hursts responded; they went to Mbeya in 1953 to establish a station and a Bible school. At first the AG field was primarily in the Arusha, Moshi, and Mbeya areas. With the passage of time it has spread across the entire country. Dar-es-Salaam, the largest city in the country, has approximately 100 assemblies today. Bible schools are located at Mbeya, Arusha, and Dodoma, with a total of 407 students. The International Correspondence Institute (ICI) of the AG–U.S. has courses that are being studied by many Christians of all denominations throughout the country. Courses have been translated into Swahili to enable non–English-speaking students to benefit from the materials. The Tanzanian Assemblies of God (TAG), in cooperation with the AG–U.S., is involved in benevolent ministries such as famine relief and a program of education within the schools that is especially aimed at combating the AIDS epidemic. There are 12 AG–U.S. missionaries presently in Tanzania. In Dec. 1997 TAG reported 870 credential holders, 980 assemblies, 250,000 baptized adult members, and an aggregate attendance of 400,000. If these figures are correct, this would make TAG the largest pentecostal denomination in the country.

In the early 1980s the TAG churches suffered a number of splits that resulted in the formation of new groups: the Evangelical Assemblies of God and the Revival Assemblies of God. These splits were one of the reasons why the wrath of the government was directed against independent and unregistered church groups throughout the country.

A significant factor in the growth of this denomination has been the emphasis on the supernatural and the evidence of miracles and deliverance. Two national evangelists in the TAG have played an important role in the growth of the church. Emmanuel Lazaro has been used in a miraculous healing ministry, especially evident during the 1980s. Many crippled, deaf and mute, and blind people have been healed during his crusades. His colleague, Moses Kilola, is best known for his deliverance ministry. Many have been set free from demonic powers as a result of his prayers. Kilola and Lazaro have also been involved in church planting throughout Tanzania.

7. The Church of God.

The Church of God (CG, Cleveland, TN) World Mission began evangelizing in Tanzania in 1951, when immigrants from Zambia and Malawi, in the south of the country, were involved in planting churches. The church grew slowly and had 600 adherents by 1982; by 1995 it had 40 congregations and 11,125 adherents. Stan Hoffman planted a Bible college at Babati (c. 1960), but most of the missionary advisory work of the CG is now carried out from Kenya. The national leader is Lazaro Mayala.

8. The Pentecostal Evangelical Fellowship of Africa.

The Pentecostal Evangelical Fellowship of Africa (PEFA) is the fruit of the Elim Fellowship of Lima, NY (not to be confused with Elim–U.K.), and specifically of the ministry of Bud Sickler of Mombasa, Kenya (see article on Kenya). Initially, because of the Kenyan contact and influence, most of the PEFA churches were located in the western part of Tanzania around Musoma, Bukoba, Tarime, and Arusha. They have a Bible school at Mwanza and Moshi. In 1995 PEFA had 190 churches, 4,560 members, and 9,220 adherents. Until recently, World Missionary Assistance Plan, Ralph Mahoney's organization in California, had a missionary couple working with PEFA in their Bible schools. It appears that the PEFA administration tends to be legalistic; missionaries working under its umbrella have not always found it easy to coexist with what they see as rigid rules and regulations.

9. The Full Gospel Bible Fellowship.

The Full Gospel Bible Fellowship (FGBF) was originally started in Nigeria by Rev. Kumuyi. FGBF was introduced to Tanzania from Nigeria in the late 1980s. It is headed by Bishop Zacharia Kakobe, who is the pastor of what is likely the fastest-growing church in all of Tanzania, at Dar-es-Salaam: the assembly numbers some 12,000 regular attenders. One of the reasons for the present rate of growth is the fact that Kakobe has used the cell-church principle: all members are expected to win others to Christ and to care for their growth and maturity. In addition to this, the church has a day set aside each week for prayer and ministry directed at particular personal problems. This day is called "The Day of Great Works of God." Members are encouraged to bring unbelieving friends who may need healing or who have other problems. Many are healed and, after experiencing the power of God, turn to Christ. Kakobe believes that by making every member active, revival will be the normal result. This movement is beginning to spread to other parts of the country.

10. Other Groups.

Other international groups in Tanzania include The Church of God of Prophecy, with 1,450 adherents in 17 congregations, and the Church of the Foursquare Gospel, with 330 adherents in 12 congregations. The Yoido Full Gospel Church of Seoul, Korea, has a small work in Moshi.

Reinhard Bonnke held crusades at Tanga in June 1993, at which attendance reached 35,000. He also held crusades at Mbeya and Arusha in 1996. His crusade at Dar-es-Salaam was canceled by the authorities due to Muslim opposition and the fear of civil unrest. Aril Edvardsen, a Norwegian evangelist, has also held campaigns in recent years.

The *World Churches Handbook* (ed. P. Brierly, 1997) estimates that there were approximately 374,000 adherents of pentecostal churches throughout Tanzania in 1995. However, the AG alone estimates that it has 400,000 adherents, and the churches founded by the Swedish and Finnish pentecostals have approximately the same number. If these figures are reliable, then the total figure for all pentecostals is estimated at about one million.

11. Observations.

When the government of Julius Nyerere came to power, a clear anti-God attitude was evident in the attempt to limit the number of church groups in the country. Only churches that had their own building and were registered with the authorities were permitted to function legally. With the increase in the number of splits and the corrupt practices of government officials, some groups that had broken away from recognized pentecostal groups, as well as others that had sprung up independently, managed to obtain recognition. This gave hope to others to attempt to gain recognition as the administration grew more lax in the enforcement of its own legislation. As a result, many pentecostal groups and "ministries" sprang up throughout Tanzania from the mid 1980s. This has meant that there are now many denominations throughout the country that may represent anything from one local church to a much greater number. Most of the denominations and groups have little, if any, fellowship with other pentecostals, and most see themselves as the only true representatives of the Christian faith. Doctrines and practices vary greatly. Many include what traditional pentecostals would consider dubious doctrines that emphasize power and the manipulation of the members by the leaders. Not a few of those who have separated from their previous churches have started private ministries, which they register under titles such as "International" or "Global," even when they have a handful of members and their office is nothing more than a briefcase.

An attempt was made in 1994 to form a united fellowship of all pentecostals in the country to help coordinate efforts and show outsiders that all pentecostals were headed in the same direction. The Pentecostal Council of Tanzania (PCT) was registered with the government under the leadership of Sylvester Gamanywa in Dar-es-Salaam, but it has not been taken seriously by the majority of pentecostals. It would appear that there is much infighting, sheep stealing, and generally questionable ethical behavior among pentecostal denominations. This is evident in the number of lawsuits that are pending in the courts of the country in which members, or former members, are contending over representative authority and title deeds to land and property. Some missions have been accused of offering bicycles to national evangelists who are members of other pentecostal groups, in the hope that they will be drawn into their own teams and swell the denominational numbers. Such behavior is clearly far from ethical. Until such pettiness ceases, it is doubtful that the witness of the pentecostal churches is going to have the positive impact on the non-Christian community that is vital to the fulfillment of the divine imperative.

One of the biggest challenges in Tanzania, especially along the coastal strip and in Zanzibar, is the vast Muslim population that is estimated to be between 50% and 80% in those regions. Financial help for the construction of mosques is being provided by the Arab countries, as is true in the whole of Africa. Pentecostals need to recognize the urgency of the hour, especially in the evangelism of the predominantly Muslim areas. They have tended to concentrate on other areas and peoples, despite their claims to power in evangelism.

One mission organization has voiced the complaint that Tanzania has never experienced a real move of the Holy Spirit other than in the area around Kigoma on lake Tanganyika, where the pentecostals have a strong influence and have grown at a significant pace.

In spite of the number of years that this country has known the gospel message, there are still unreached people groups in the south and central parts of the nation. Greater participation in various projects is needed so that there will not be as much duplication of effort, especially in the training of leadership. Unlike those countries where missions have kept to set areas, there appears to be much competition between national churches and missions in Tanzania.

■ D. J. Garrard

THAILAND

■ Pentecostals 33,905 (4%)   ■ Charismatics 52,065 (6%)   ■ Neocharismatics 742,930 (90%)   ■ Total Renewal: 828,900

The Pentecostal movement in Thailand grew out of the Holiness revivals (1938, 1939), led by John Sung during WWII. John Sung was converted in China through contact with Wesleyan/Holiness Methodist missionaries. He came to the U.S. and received a Ph.D. in chemistry from Ohio State University. He went to Union Theological Seminary, New York, where he was "reclaimed" in a Baptist church. In a Holiness meeting he experienced entire sanctification and was committed by the president of Union Theological Seminary, William Sloane Coffin, to an insane asylum. After stays in Ohio and Wilmore, he returned to Asia, where he ministered initially in cooperation with the Bethel Bands of Andrew Gih, which were modeled on the Free Methodist "Pentecost Bands." His revivalist efforts had both immediate and mythic impacts and provided cultural warrants for the later arrival of revivalistic pentecostal missionaries.

Missionaries of the Finnish Free Foreign Mission arrived in 1946, and the first pentecostal churches were formed in Thailand by the efforts of Hanna and Verner Raassina. The Full Gospel Bible Training Center was established in 1965 and has trained clergy who have become leaders in the Thai Full Gospel Church as well as in other denominations, including indigenous churches. This center and the Finnish missionaries did much to gain acceptance of pentecostalism in Thailand. The *Encyclopedia of World Christianity* (ed. D. B. Barrett, 1982) reported a community of about 30 congregations and 3,000 adherents in the Thai Full Gospel Church by about 1980; in 1997 there were about 5,000 adherents in 50 congregations. By 1989 there were over 45 Finnish Free Foreign Mission missionaries in Thailand, involved in both traditional evangelistic activities and social ministries.

Assisting the Finnish Free Foreign Mission were missionaries from other pentecostal churches who chose to cooperate rather than compete. These include the Swedish Free

The first group of Christians to be baptized in the Assemblies of God work in Thailand in 1969 by the Rev. Wirachoi Kowae (at right).

Mission, which has maintained a presence in Thailand since 1951, and the Pentecostal Assemblies of Canada, who have had missionaries in Thailand since 1968. The Assemblies of God (U.S.) has established itself as a competitor but focuses especially on the U.S. military and expatriate communities and Thai people in their employ.

The story of these developments has finally been told. Numerous missionary biographies have been written in Finnish, as well as numerous articles in mission periodicals and archival materials. There are also histories of local ministries, many congregational histories, and other documents in Thai. The first effort to bring this data together into a narrative, and to enlarge the historical data base through interviews and examination of archival materials in Finland and Thailand, has been made by Hannu Kettunen, *Tungruangtong: History of the Finnish Free Foreign Mission in Thailand, 1946–1996* (in Thai, 1996). This volume focuses on the role of missionaries during the half century under consideration. A more extensive analysis was provided by Robert Nishimoto, *History of Pentecostalism in Thailand, 1946–1996* (in Thai, 1996). This monumental volume attempts to describe the development of the various aspects of the pentecostal movement as it has evolved in Thailand. Unfortunately, there was limited access to Finnish sources as well as to relevant English, Korean, and Chinese sources. On the other hand, Nishimoto conducted interviews with many leaders, members, and missionaries of the FFFM–related churches. The resulting story is carefully placed in its global context.

The second mission group to arrive in Thailand was the United Pentecostal Church (UPC). Elly Hansen, a Danish missionary, was converted in the pentecostal Free Gospel Evangelistic Church in Rungsted, Denmark, in 1938. After WWII she went as a missionary to Thailand (from 1950) with the Danish Missionary Society, a group associated with the China Inland Mission. In 1952 she experienced the baptism in the Holy Spirit. One of the leaders of the Thai Presbyterian congregation with which she was associated, Boon Mak, was converted to ʼOneness pentecostalism under the tutelage of UPC evangelist Billy Cole during a visit to the U.S. about 1960 and united with the UPC mission program in 1962. Elly Hansen attended a camp owned by Boon Mak in 1965 and was baptized "in Jesus' name." Soon thereafter evangelistic work was begun throughout Thailand. The UPC of Thailand has at least 10,000 members and another 10,000 adherents.

Another ʼOneness church, the True Jesus Church (from Taiwan) has made a vital contribution to the spread of pentecostalism in Thailand since its arrival in 1956. Although only 200 members were reported by the late 1970s, the church has experienced rapid growth during the last two decades. This primarily Chinese church has had a significant impact in Thailand and throughout the Chinese diaspora.

The Hope of Bangkok Church, under the leadership of Joseph ʼWongsak, has become an important mission church with congregations scattered throughout the world. It has (1997) about 800 congregations and/or preaching points. Estimates vary as to membership in this indigenous Thai church but may range as high as 50,000 members.

More recently arrived among the pentecostal mission agencies active in Thailand are South Korean pentecostal missionaries who work throughout the country. Another Asian church has had an active mission presence for a number of years, but authoritative information is difficult to find: the Sri Lankan (formerly Ceylon) Pentecostal Mission. There are a number of congregations and extensive evangelistic work, primarily in the larger metropolitan areas. Also worthy of additional research, analysis, and ecumenical attention are the numerous indigenous denominations that have spun off from the mission-influenced traditions. There is no accurate listing of these organizations outside Bangkok. Often these smaller indigenous churches stand in an ambiguous relationship to Thai laws on religious groups. Finally, there is a significant charismatic renewal in progress within the Church of Christ of Thailand, a church created by the merger of Christian Church (Disciples of Christ), Presbyterians, and Methodists.

Pentecostalism in Thailand is certainly diverse, both because of Thai regional cultures and because of the different mission agencies and cultures that have brought pentecostal ideas to Thailand. No single perspective dominates the definition of what it means to be pentecostal in Thailand. Sources are difficult to obtain and are preserved in numerous countries in at least six languages: Thai, Chinese, Korean, Finnish, Swedish, and English.

■ **Bibliography:** A. Hämäläinen, *Kaikkeen maailman 1929–1989: 60 vuotta helluntaiseurahuntien lähetystyöyä* (1989) ■ E. Hansen and M. Wallace, *Following Jesus All the Way: Elly* (1987) ■ J. Heinikainen, *Sitä Sanaa Varo* (1986) ■ H. Kettunen, ed., *Thaimaan Täyden Evankeliumin Raamattukoulu* (1985) ■ U. Kunnas, *Valkoisen Elefantin Maa* (1973) ■ L. Y. Lyall, *Flame for God: John Sung and Revival in the Far East* (1954) ■ J. Mäkelä, "Krischak Issara: The Independent Churches in the Bangkok Metropolitan Area, Thailand: Their Historical Background, Contextual Setting, and Theological Thinking" (thesis, U. of Åbo, Finland, 1993) ■ L.-R. Minalainen, "The Work of the FFFM and the Development of Thailand During 1965–1991" (thesis, Grand Rapids Baptist Seminary, 1992) ■ E. Pehkonen, *Hymyn Maa* (1967) ■ J. Rouhomäki, "The Finnish Free Foreign Mission in Thailand, 1946–1985" (thesis, Grand Rapids Baptist Seminary, 1988) ■ A. Salmenkivi, "The Development of the Curriculum of the Full Gospel Bible Training Center" (thesis, Grand Rapids Baptist Seminary, 1991) ■ R. Vaurula and V. Ontermaa, *V.O. Raassina—Lähetyspioneeri* (1988).

■ D. D. Bundy; D. W. Dayton

TIMOR

■ Pentecostals 3,783 (8%) ■ Charismatics 42,417 (92%) 0 ■ Neocharismatics 0 (0%) ■ Total Renewal: 46,200

TOGO

■ Pentecostals 87,526 (23%) ■ Charismatics 177,221 (47%) ■ Neocharismatics 110,253 (29%) ■ Total Renewal: 375,000

TOKELAU ISLANDS

■ Pentecostals 0 ■ Charismatics 0 ■ Neocharismatics 0 ■ Total Renewal: 0

TONGA

■ Pentecostals 1,306 (11%) ■ Charismatics 3,695 (30%) ■ Neocharismatics 7,300 (59%) ■ Total Renewal: 12,301

For general introduction and bibliography, see PACIFIC ISLANDS.

The kingdom of Tonga consists of about 150 islands, 36 of which are inhabited. These islands are arranged in four main groups, Tongatapu and Eua, Ha'apai, Vava'u, and the Niuas; they are spread in a north-south alignment over about 560 mi (900 km). The total land area is about 270 mi^2 (699 km^2) in a sea area of about 27,000 mi^2 (700,000 km^2). Most of the islands are of raised coral, with fertile soil developed from volcanic ash. The biggest island is Tongatapu (100 mi^2 [260 km^2]). The capital is Nuku'alofa, located on Tongatapu, with about 35,000 inhabitants. The total population in 1995 was just 98,000. With an estimated 97% Tongans, a very low level of immigration, and the absence of real minority linguistic or cultural groups, the population of Tonga is one of the most homogenous in the South Pacific region and probably in the world.

The emigration overseas, mainly to Australia, New Zealand, and the U.S. (an estimated 30,000 to 50,000 Ton-gans are today living overseas) can be seen as a kind of safety valve to avoid overpopulation of the limited land area. The remittances of the Tongans living overseas are also very important for the economy. The basic causes of this pattern of migration and emigration have been land shortages and limited opportunities for earning money in some areas, the availability of land elsewhere, employment and money-making opportunities, the desire for better education, and the amenities and attractions of urban areas.

1. Assemblies of God (AG).

The AG work first started in Tonga in Sept. 1966, when a group of missionaries arrived, led by an American and including Fijians, Indians, and one New Zealander, and immediately started a well planned evangelistic outreach program.

When most of the members of this first group went back after nine months, two missionary couples stayed behind and looked after the work. With an average annual growth rate of 20% since 1976, the AG is the fastest-growing religious group in Tonga. In 1997 there were 21 churches, most of them located on Tongatapu and around Nuku'alofa, where the work started. But smaller AG communities are also found in the Ha'apai and Vava'u group. There were 24 full-time pastors, led by a local superintendent, in 1997.

According to the president of the AG, most of the new converts come from the Free Wesleyan Church and a few from the Mormons, Free Church of Tonga, and the Roman Catholic Church. The AG is a member of an interdenominational committee of pentecostals and charismatics, which includes members of the Free Wesleyan Church, Church of Tonga, Free Church of Tonga, Seventh-day Adventists, Tokaikolo Christian Fellowship, Anglican Church, and Brethren; because of its composition this committee has a far wider range than the ecumenical National Council of

Baptismal service in Tonga, conducted by the Rev. Peni Naituku.

Churches. This proves that cooperation beyond denominational borders is possible in certain areas of common interest.

2. Tokaikolo Christian Fellowship (TCF).

The TCF broke away from the Free Wesleyan Church of Tonga in 1978 and was officially registered with the Tongan government in Oct. 1979. However, the official registration marked just the climax of a development that started much earlier. As in many similar cases, the prehistory of the TCF is tightly linked with a "charismatic" leader, in this case, Rev. Senituli Koloi (1926–80).

An office in Nuku'alofa functions as the TCF headquarters, with a general secretary and some assisting staff for administrative purposes. The new leader of the church, Liufau Vailea, is also the principal of Lavengamalie College. An executive committee makes the decisions; there is no annual conference and no proper structure of representation. At the end of 1992 Liufau Vailea announced the passing of a new constitution, which is supposed to be clearer about representation of the members. According to information from TCF headquarters, there were 20 ordained ministers and about 60 deacons active in the church (including groups overseas) in 1992. Today the TCF covers almost all islands of Tonga. Overseas groups exist in Australia, New Zealand, and the U.S. The TCF has its own Bible school in Nuku'alofa (the Bible School in Auckland was closed some years ago). In the primary school of the TCF at Lavengamalie College, 400 students were enrolled in 1992, and 800 students were enrolled in the Tokaikolo Christian Fellowship High School (Finau, 1992).

■ M. Ernst

TRINIDAD AND TOBAGO

■ Pentecostals 53,935 (39%)   ■ Charismatics 47,560 (35%)   ■ Neocharismatics 35,505 (26%)   ■ Total Renewal: 137,000

Robert and Elizabeth Jamieson, independent Canadian missionaries, began conducting pentecostal evangelistic services in Trinidad in 1923. The riots this provoked nearly caused Robert Jamieson's death. By 1926 there were enough converts throughout Trinidad to warrant affiliation with the ‣Pentecostal Assemblies of Canada. Harry and Marguerite Eggleton arrived in 1928 from British Colombia, where they had been influenced by the healing traditions of ‣Charles S. Price. Healing thus became a prominent feature of pentecostal ministry in Trinidad. The Eggletons started the Trinidad Bible School in 1935. This became a center for missions to Montserrat, Barbados, and Martinique. It was a precursor to the West Indies School of Theology, founded in 1947 through the efforts of Abe and Verna Jacobson.

The ‣Church of God (CG, Cleveland, TN) began to make contacts in Trinidad about 1940, but all of the early mission efforts collapsed. In 1955 Edward D. Hasmatali, founder of the Christian General Assembly (1950), sought affiliation with the CG. In July 1956 8 congregations, 8 missions, 15 clergy, and 350 members united with the CG. Hasmatali was a Trinidadian of East Indian descent, as were the majority of the congregations. From Trinidad, Hasmatali did evangelistic work in Grenada (1958) and Aruba. The resultant New Testament Church of God claimed 1,231 members and about 3,000 adherents in 1980.

From the 1950s, the Pinsevennenes Ytre Misjon of the Norwegian Pentecostal Filadelfia churches has maintained a presence in Trinidad. Their efforts served as the basis for the ministry of the ‣Open Bible Standard Church on the island. Norwegian missionaries Kaare and Jean Wilhelmsen built several churches and a school in San Fernando during their years in Trinidad. In 1960 they reported congregations in 25 towns. Andrew and Jennie Mitchell, Donald and Ruth Bryan, Dora Turner, Margaret Crandahl, and Minnie Bruns of the Open Bible Mission arrived in Trinidad during 1955. The Trinidad church became independent at a ceremony on Apr. 23, 1972. Keith Armoogan became the new leader of the denomination. By 1995 the church could claim 64 congregations, 91 ministers, 5,000 members, and two Bible schools. There are probably another 10,000 adherents; it is arguably the largest pentecostal denomination on Trinidad.

Among the other denominations in Trinidad and Tobago are the ‣Assemblies of God, ‣Church of God in Christ, Mt. Horeb Pentecostal Church, ‣International Church of the Foursquare Gospel, ‣Pentecostal Assemblies of the World, and the Pentecostal Church of God in Trinidad. There are a large number of independent missions as well as small local and regional denominations. The Church of the Lord (Aladura) from Nigeria also has a presence. An important part of Trinidad's pentecostal history is the connection of these churches, especially the predominantly Indian and African ethnic churches, with the emigrant churches in Great Britain.

■ **Selected Bibliography:** J. L. Arnold, "The Role of the Pastor in the Life of the Ministry in Trinidad and Tobago" (paper, CG School of Theol., 1992) ■ D. B. Barrett, *World Christian Encyclopedia* (1982), 674–77 ■ C. W. Conn, *Where the Saints Have Trod: A History of Church of God Missions* (1959) ■ D. L. Burk, ed., *Foreign Missions Insight: A Digest of Foreign Missions Faces, Facts, Fields and Figures* (1999), 80 ■ S. D. Glazier, "Pentecostal Exorcism and Modernization in Trinidad, West Indies," in *Perspectives on Pentecostalism,* ed. S. D. Glazier (1980) ■ S. M. Hodges, *Look on the Fields: A Survey of the Assemblies of God in Foreign Lands* (1956), 186–88 ■ W. J. Hollenweger, *Handbuch der Pfingstbewegung* (diss., Zurich,

1967), 1027–39 (para. 02b.13) ■ K. Juul, "Trinidad," *Til Jordens Ender: Norsk pinsemisjon gjennom 50 år* (1960) ■ T. W. Miller, *Canadian Pentecostals: A History of the Pentecostal Assemblies of Canada*, ed. W. A. Griffin (1994) ■ R. B. Mitchell and L. M. Mitchell, *Heritage and Harvest: The History of the International Ministries of the Open Bible Standard Churches* (1995) ■ O. Nilson, *Ut i all verden: Pinsevennenes ytre misjon i 75 år* (1984) ■ C. H. Walker, "Caribbean Charismatics: The Pentecostal Church as Community on the Island of Tobago" (diss., U. of North Carolina–Chapel Hill, 1987) ■ C. Ward and M. H. Beaubrun, "Spirit Possession and Neuroticism in a West Indian Pentecostal Community," *British Journal of Clinical Psychology* 20 (1981) ■ I. A. White, "Developing a Pentecostal Missiology in the Canadian Context (1867–1944): The Pentecostal Assemblies of Canada" (diss., Fuller, 1994).

■ D. D. Bundy

TUNISIA

■ Pentecostals 5 (0%)   ■ Charismatics 659 (4%)   ■ Neocharismatics 15,636 (96%)   ■ Total Renewal: 16,300

See AFRICA, NORTH, AND THE MIDDLE EAST.

TURKEY

■ Pentecostals 0 (0%)   ■ Charismatics 8,959 (14%)   ■ Neocharismatics 56,041 (86%)   ■ Total Renewal: 65,000

See AFRICA, NORTH, AND THE MIDDLE EAST.

TURKMENISTAN

■ Pentecostals 0 (0%)   ■ Charismatics 739 (7%)   ■ Neocharismatics 10,011 (93%)   ■ Total Renewal: 10,750

See RUSSIA.

TURKS AND CAICOS ISLANDS

■ Pentecostals 1,141 (27%)   ■ Charismatics 1,234 (29%)   ■ Neocharismatics 1,924 (45%)   ■ Total Renewal: 4,299

TUVALU

■ Pentecostals 0 (0%)   ■ Charismatics 1,836 (87%)   ■ Neocharismatics 264 (13%)   ■ Total Renewal: 2,100

UGANDA

■ Pentecostals 371,193 (7%)   ■ Charismatics 3,879,073 (77%)   ■ Neocharismatics 759,734 (15%)   ■ Total Renewal: 5,010,000

For general introduction to East Africa and bibliography, see AFRICA, EAST.

It is not possible to think of Protestantism in Uganda without considering the role played by the Anglican Church, the first Protestant denomination to evangelize the Buganda people. The East African revival, as it is called, had its roots in the Anglican Church and has also given place to an acceptance of the charismatic movement in the Anglican Church of Uganda even when what is called "charismatic" is understood variously by its members. Uganda, like a number of countries in the Central African region, has not been spared its traumas. Especially during the administration of President Amin Dada, who was a practicing Muslim and saw himself as the instrument of Allah, the Protestant church came under extreme and prolonged persecution. In June 1973 Amin banned 28 denominations in an effort to curb Protestant evangelism. Some of these decided to come under the umbrella of the Anglican Church, but others went underground. In 1977 there was a charismatic revival among youth, especially in the north of the country, that spanned all the denominations. Amin's successor, Milton Obote, was little better and continued the reign of terror in Uganda until Yoweri Museveni took over in 1986 and introduced gradual change. The AIDS outbreak in Uganda has had a drastic effect on the stability of the country, as has the prolonged civil war. These factors have been part of the reason for the drain on finances resulting in extreme poverty within the nation.

1. Pentecostal Assemblies of God–Uganda.

What is today regarded as the fruit of the Pentecostal Assemblies of Canada (PAOC) mission in Uganda began when a Bugishu man from Uganda visited some Christian Maragoli friends in Kenya, who led him to Christ. At the same time he was baptized in the Holy Spirit. When he returned to Uganda he began to share the pentecostal message and planted four churches. Later several other visitors from Uganda to Kenya were also filled with the Holy Spirit and returned to Uganda. For many years all these groups worked entirely on their own. In 1944 Vernon Morrison, who was at that time the PAOC field director for East Africa, was the first missionary to visit these churches on the slopes of Mt. Elgon; he encouraged their organization and growth. In 1956 William and Viola Brown (PAOC) negotiated with the colonial authorities to erect a mission headquarters at Mbale. In the 1960s Arn and Elsie Bowler went to Uganda and planted many churches throughout the eastern region. They were joined by the Alex Strongs in 1970, whose task was to plant churches and to be involved in regional teaching with the leadership of the new assemblies.

The church founded in Uganda was originally part of the greater Pentecostal Assemblies of East Africa. However, Pentecostal Assemblies of God (PAG) Uganda obtained its own registration in 1968 through the efforts of Robert Eames (PAOC), who was also the one to build the first Bible School at Mbale. Prior to this time the Ugandan pastors from PAG all trained at Nyang'ori in Kenya. During the upheaval in Uganda during the Amin years, all PAOC missionaries were forced to leave the country. It was not until 1980–81 that the Bowlers, together with Bill Bond, began trips to Uganda to reopen the work. The German Volksmission, which participates closely with the PAOC/PAG (see also article on Kenya) had sent Herbert and Christiane Ros to Kenya in 1965. They transferred to Uganda, where they began to work among the Iteso, Lango, and Karamojong peoples of the northern and northeastern section of the country. From 1989 until his retirement from the field in 1994, H. Ros was field leader in Uganda. Miracles played an important role in the opening of this area, which experienced considerable revival as many were added to the church. Since 1993 Siegmar and Priscilla Göhner (Volksmission), located at Lira, have been planting churches and holding teaching seminars among leaders in the northern area of Uganda. This is where special effort has been made to plant churches among the Labwor, Karamojong, Madi, Lugbara, Alur, Jonam, and peoples of the Masindi area. Priscilla Göhner (née Ros) is a medical doctor and runs a hospital in Lira.

From the very earliest days the pentecostal believers have had to stand on their own feet and be responsible for the running of their churches without the presence of missionaries. They have had strong national leaders. The first general superintendent of the PAG in Uganda was Gideon Okakaali, who was murdered by Amin's retreating army. He was followed by John Ekanyu and John Omara, who gave strong leadership and retired in 1996. Since then Simon Peter Emiau, who is a graduate of Pan African Christian College (PAAC is the PAOC/PAG college in Nairobi) and the director of the Pentecostal Bible Training Centre at Mbale, has been elected general superintendent.

Gary and Marilyn Skinner have been working in Uganda since 1983, when they pioneered the Kampala Pentecostal Church (KPC). Skinner, whose parents and grandparents were also PAOC missionaries in East and Central Africa, is presently the pastor of KPC. There have been remarkable visitations of the Holy Spirit in Kampala. On one occasion in 1989 nearly 300 were baptized at one time in the Holy Spirit. It is now common to see 7,500 people meet in the assembly during the multiple services held on Sundays. KPC operates on the cell principle and includes youth, university students, professional people, and civil servants among its members. Watoto Childcare Ministries operates out of KPC and presently cares for 1,200 children, 200 of whom are living in homes built at Buloba by the program. In Canada this program is called Child Care Plus. The children are primarily those left as orphans as a result of the AIDS epidemic in Uganda. Because KPC was the first large pentecostal church to use English and not Luganda (the main language of Uganda), it has had a great influence on educated English speakers in the business and professional community in this nation. As a result, the mainline denominations that were previously considered the spokespersons for Christianity (both Protestants and Catholics) have lost their influence to a considerable degree.

During the Amin regime, a number of pentecostal pastors among the Acholi and Lange peoples were killed by Amin's death squads. However, there are reports of supernatural intervention and the protection of many pastors and believers during the same period. Even some of those who were in the army became preachers as a result of what they experienced. In 1973, when Amin banned the majority of Protestant churches, there were 250 local churches in the PAG. All missionaries were forced to leave. Yet by the time Amin's regime was overthrown, there were 500 churches. Today it is estimated that there are more than 2,000 PAG churches in Uganda with over 60,000 adult members and 154,000 adherents. In *Weiszer Mann, geh heim!* Herbert Ros records how signs and wonders, together with deliverance from demon possession, frequently accompanied the preaching of the Word during the earliest days of the PAG work in Uganda. He admits that he does not see as much in the way of the supernatural nowadays.

2. The Elim Pentecostal Fellowship Uganda.

The Elim Pentecostal Fellowship Uganda (Elim–NY) began working in Uganda in 1962. This is the church that was started by Bud Sickler of Mombassa (see PEFA under Kenya and Tanzania). ⸕T. L. Osborn was involved in supporting this movement in its earliest days. In the 1960s this church was led by Pastor Clarke, but it is now under the leadership of nationals and led by Tom Okello of Lira. In 1982 Elim had 30,000 adherents, but by 1995 there were 98,000 in 1,110 congregations.

3. The Pentecostal Churches of Uganda.

The Norwegian and Finnish pentecostals who had previously worked together in Kenya had made visits with Kenyan believers to Uganda since its independence in 1963. From the initial visits came groups of small churches. In 1982 the group called the Pentecostal Churches of Uganda (PCU) was registered with the government. The pioneers in ministry were Åke and Pirkko Söderlund from Finland, who settled in Kampala. They were followed by Trygve and Karin Korneliussen from Norway (Pinsevennes Ytre Misjon) in 1986. In 1991 a Bible school was established at Mbuya, where three courses, each taught over a period of four months, are presented every year. The Lähetyksen Kehitysapu (LKA), which is the Finnish international relief and development aid department of the FFFM, started working in Uganda in 1986. Its first project was the Mpigi Health Care Program, which ran 1990–96. It is also involved in the Rural Development Program and the AIDS project. By 1997 the PCU had a total of 355 congregations and an estimated 18,000 believers. The chairman of the movement is Peter Wanyama. The Finnish mission recognizes the need to let the national leaders have greater control of this work and wants to develop Bible education as well as become more involved in the evangelism of unreached areas in the country.

4. Elim Foursquare Gospel Alliance of Uganda.

Because Elim–NY had already been registered in Uganda as Elim Pentecostal Fellowship Uganda, this denomination has been registered as Elim Foursquare Gospel Alliance of Uganda (EFGA). It was started in 1996. Don Hemmingway of Elim–New Zealand pioneered in Uganda as a result of having trained Joseph Omese at a Bible college in Zambia. EFGA has 49 churches and 3,500 adult members. The chairman is J. Omese. Joseph Serwadda of Victory Christian Centre, Kampala, approached EFGA in 1994 requesting affiliation; he has a loose affiliation with EFGA, as does a group of churches started by Jim Patterson, a former credential holder with Elim–U.K. EFGA still is waiting to see how committed Serwadda and his churches will be to this denomination. EFGA has most of its churches in the eastern region around Soroti, where their Bible school and a training center are based. There is an EFGA secondary school near Lira.

5. Other Churches.

The Full Gospel Churches of Uganda were started in 1959 and had 6,000 members by 1982. They were founded in Uganda by Hugh Lazelle and are supported by Glad Tidings Mission Society of Vancouver, Canada.

The AG–U.S. became involved in Uganda about 1980. By 1995 they had 35 congregations with 2,000 adult members and 3,250 adherents. They no longer have any missionary personnel in Uganda. AG–U.K. support Graham and Debbie Rees, who plan to be involved in evangelism and the training of pastors.

The Church of God (Cleveland, TN) started in Uganda about the same time as the AG–U.S. They now have 17 congregations with over 1,000 adult members and 3,440 adherents. The national leader is Joseph Kagarama.

Other pentecostal groups that have grown considerably include The Church of the Redeemed (410 congregations, 41,000 members, and 82,600 adherents [1995]); the Open Bible Standard Church (73 congregations and 8,250 adherents [1995]); and the United Pentecostal Church (an estimated 80 congregations and 7,850 adherents).

Smaller groups in Uganda include the Church of God of Prophecy (32 congregations and 2,610 adherents); the Deeper Life Christian Church (1 congregation with 225 adherents); and the Pentecostal Holiness Church (5 congregations and 1,120 adherents).

Some pentecostals are recent arrivals in Uganda. Victory Christian Church (AG–New Zealand) sent Jacky Tumusiime (née Legg) to Uganda in Oct. 1990. She was followed by a team of six others. They planted four churches with about 250 members. The group is called the New Life Church of Uganda and has Paddy Luzige as the national overseer. There is a Bible school in Kampala and another at Mbarara. These schools operate for one week of each month; this allows the two missionary teachers to rotate between both centers. Calvary Churches, which are based in Asia, are also now involved in church planting. Joe Kayo has found a ministry called Deliverance Church, which is present in most of East Africa as well as beyond its borders. It is connected to Deeper Life Christian Church with contacts in England. Its teaching and practices appear to be orthodox; however, it does place added emphasis on the importance of submission of women in the church. The leader of the Deliverance Church in Kampala is Pastor Waifola. The Yoido Full Gospel Church of Seoul, Korea, also became involved in Uganda during the late 1990s.

Pentecostal evangelists to visit this nation include T. L. Osborn, ⸕Richard Roberts, and ⸕Reinhard Bonnke.

6. Observations.

In spite of (perhaps because of) the horrors that took place under Amin, many were brought to Christ during that era. Even army officers and soldiers on both sides, including

Muslims, were converted. In many cases, while the Word of God was being proclaimed, people were immediately set free from their habits and evil practices. Phenomenal outpourings of the Holy Spirit in Uganda have undoubtedly served to strengthen the church as a whole and contribute to the growth of the pentecostal church in particular.

Uganda is one of the poorest countries in the world, and to add to the misery it has been struck with an epidemic of AIDS. At least 25% of the urban population are HIV carriers. In 1998 there were over 1.7 million orphans due to AIDS—and the number is increasing dramatically. The majority of the larger pentecostal denominations are involved in some form of relief that targets this segment of the population. Many missionaries and mission agencies are involved in relief alone.

The pentecostal community throughout Uganda is growing rapidly. However, the tendency to schism among the larger pentecostal denominations has resulted in numerous offshoots. There is no overall pentecostal fellowship in the country, and the newer churches have little to do with the established denominations, so that there is no overall unity among pentecostal/charismatic groups.

The need is great among newer pentecostal groups for teaching and training of pastors and leaders, because many have never had any formal Bible instruction and tend to get carried away by the "latest" teachings. Many younger pastors, between 20 and 40 years of age, have no training at all but have gravitated to leadership in the newer churches. In the newer groups there is emphasis on the pastor as "the man of God" who needs to be looked after with the greatest of care if the blessing of God is to be experienced by the members. Thus there is much manipulation for personal gain in these groups. In the newer churches it is not uncommon to have pastors demand thank offerings from their members if they have experienced success in any financial ventures.

Most of the largest churches and denominations have grown because of the miracles and healings at the start of their work, but some of the better-established ones are accused of having "settled down," because they do not appear to promote the power of God and the place of healing as much as they once did. Many among the traditional pentecostal groups agree that, especially in rural areas, the impetus that was gained at the time of the East African revival has lost its impact, and that many who attend pentecostal meetings are nominal in their practice of the Christian faith. Large numbers still attend meetings, but there is often a very shallow understanding on the part of adherents of what is involved in Christian living.

Within the last year Uganda has opened its first Christian TV station. This has brought a very American-style message to Uganda with Word of Faith and the prosperity gospel. This station broadcasts mostly TBN material, 24 hours a day, to Kampala and its surrounding area. The result is that in many of the newer churches there is an emphasis on a form of instant gospel, which sees no need for Bible training nor study of any kind in preparation for ministry. The manipulation of power and of God is at the center of this message, even if it is not put in those terms. It portrays to a hurting and needy society the pentecostal/charismatic message as holding the secrets to instant success and release from all trial and tribulation. Many evangelicals, as well as a good number of the older pentecostals, are very worried about the hopes this message gives to Ugandans and read into it an attempt at escapism from the severe problems that exist in this country. In addition to television, there are also three Christian radio FM stations.

The greatest danger for the church in East Africa and particularly in Uganda is that of materialism, legalism, and ritualism. The corruption of the nation has had a great influence on the lifestyle and thinking of the Christians so that there has been a lowering of moral standards among many believers. Inevitably, Western church trends have been felt in Uganda. A lot of free material in the form of glossy literature, tapes, and videos, has found its way into the country and has not always produced positive results, because it conveys the thought that what is Western is necessarily best and also that other programs that do not produce the same sort of materials cannot be valid.

By refusing to collaborate with pentecostal churches and missions already working in a given country or region, Western pentecostal missions have sometimes failed to set a good example. This is especially true in Uganda. The introduction of numerous pentecostal groups that hold almost identical doctrine and practice encourages dissenters and those who are under discipline for immoral conduct to join the newer groups, which are "desperate" for members. Church growth then becomes a matter of how many members one is able to win by transfer, not how many any group is able to evangelize.

There is a danger that the North American style of gospel with all its glitz will be considered to be the desirable norm. The presentation of this material is not contextualized, and in a nation that is struggling to make ends meet, the last thing Uganda needs is an artificial Western brand of Christianity.

■ D. J. Garrard

UKRAINE

■ Pentecostals 399,462 (10%)   ■ Charismatics 589,113 (15%)   ■ Neocharismatics 3,046,426 (76%)
■ Total Renewal: 4,035,001

See RUSSIA.

UNITED ARAB EMIRATES

■ Pentecostals 0 (0%)   ■ Charismatics 8,696 (16%)   ■ Neocharismatics 45,304 (84%)   ■ Total Renewal: 54,000

See AFRICA, NORTH, AND THE MIDDLE EAST.

UNITED KINGDOM

See BRITAIN.

UNITED STATES OF AMERICA

■ Pentecostals 4,946,390 (7%)   ■ Charismatics 19,473,158 (26%)   ■ Neocharismatics 50,736,451 (68%)
■ Total Renewal: 75,155,999

See, among others, BIBLIOGRAPHY AND HISTORIOGRAPHY OF PENTECOSTALISM; BLACK HOLINESS-PENTECOSTALISM; CATHOLIC CHARISMATIC RENEWAL; CHARISMATIC MOVEMENTS; CLASSICAL PENTECOSTALISM; GYPSIES; HISPANIC PENTECOSTALISM; NATIVE AMERICAN PENTECOSTALS; NONDENOMINATIONAL PENTECOSTAL AND CHARISMATIC CHURCHES.

URUGUAY

■ Pentecostals 38,878 (13%)   ■ Charismatics 215,453 (71%)   ■ Neocharismatics 49,669 (16%)   ■ Total Renewal: 304,000

The number of converts to pentecostalism in Uruguay does not rival that of neighboring countries, even though in 1994 more than 50% of all Protestant congregations in Montevideo were pentecostal. The same appears to be true for the rest of the country. The identity of pentecostalism in Uruguay is complicated by the various immigrant ethnic churches and the large number of pentecostal mission organizations from Finland, Sweden, the U.S., Argentina, Brazil, Chile, and Germany, as well as individual missionaries from other areas in Latin America and Europe. The story of pentecostalism in Uruguay remains the somewhat disjointed story of small denominations and independent congregations that have minimal contact with one another.

Pentecostal missionaries of the Finnish Free Foreign Mission, Anni and Victor Nievas, arrived in Montevideo, Uruguay, in 1943. The number of missionaries grew until in 1989 there were 14 Finnish pentecostal missionaries in Uruguay. The Asamblea de Dios Misión Finlandesa claims (1989) about 4,000 members with 14 congregations in Montevideo. These missionaries have often cooperated with the missionaries of the Svensk Fria Mission, whose efforts led to the establishment of the Iglesia Pentecostal Filadelfia (five congregations in Montevideo, 1993).

The earliest congregations of the ►Assemblies of God (AG) began as independent congregations of Russian immigrants in 1928 and 1929 that later affiliated with the U.S. denomination. The first AG (U.S.) missionaries, Raymond and Dorothy DeVito, arrived in Montevideo in 1946. Another missionary couple, Paul and Neva Pugh, who served in Uruguay in 1949–64, started a congregation in Paysandú. Among the early Uruguayan leaders were Juan and Elidia Buchtik, who pastored an independent Russian congregation in Progresso before affiliating with the AG and then pastoring in San José and Young. Important early roles were also played by, among others, Adolfo Píriz, the Lithuanian Jorge Dagys, Pedro and Ramona Solís, and María Benítez de Hernández. An innovative ministerial training program was developed in Montevideo in 1980 that was organized to allow persons to continue in ministry or other work during their education. At the end of the decade this was discontinued and a residential campus built in the outlying suburbs of Montevideo. The Asambleas de Dios (U.S.) claims 7,222 baptized members and another 8,700 adherents (1999).

The Iglesia Pentecostal Unida (►United Pentecostal Church) began in Uruguay during the early 1930s through the work of L. B. Sly. Other well-known missionaries were the Samuel Bakers and Fred K. Scott. The church has grown to claim 30 congregations, 14 ministers, and 840 constituents (1999). The Instituto Bíblico Apostolico de Uruguay is located in Montevideo.

The Iglesia de Dios (*Church of God [Cleveland, TN]) began through the work of Marcos Mazzucco of Buenos Aires, Argentina, who initiated together with Justo Videla a house church in the mid 1940s. By 1949 there were two congregations and 105 members. By 1959 there were 25 congregations with 1,204 members. Barrett reported 34 congregations with about 6,500 adherents (1982). More recent statistics have not been provided. The *Church of God of Prophecy began work in 1957 but has remained small. More recently from Argentina has come the "third wave" (*neocharismatic) pentecostal church, Ondas de Amor y Paz.

The Iglesia del Evangelio Cuadrangular was begun by Brazilian missionaries related to the Brazilian *International Church of the Foursquare Gospel in 1983. There are 17 congregations with 1,431 members and about 4,000 additional adherents (1999). Also founded by Brazilian pentecostal missionaries was the Iglesia de Cristo Pentecostal Internacional (Uruguay), which was established by the Evangelism Department of the Pentecostal Church of Christ of Brazil. The International Pentecostal Church of Christ of Uruguay was officially established Dec. 24, 1990, by Brazilian general superintendent Pedro Messias with Ruben Daniel Cabrera (Paysandú, Uruguay) as the general superintendent. Congregations are located in Montevideo, Artigas, and Paysandú. EBEN, a Bible training school, is located in Artigas. Iglesia de Cristo Pentecostal Internacional is an "adopted national church" of the *International Pentecostal Church of Christ (U.S.). Also from Brazil came the Asamblea de Dios Mission Brasilera del Uruguay and the Church of the Universal Reign of God.

The Iglesia de la Biblia Apierta of Uruguay (*Open Bible Standard Church, OBSC) was started by the Chilean missionary Hugo Castro in Aug. 1984. During 1986 and 1987,

open-air crusades were held in Montevideo by Julio González. On the basis of this crusade, a new effort was made in Montevideo by Juan Moreno. Another congregation was started at Salto, Uruguay. In 1995 the OBSC claimed 215 members in five congregations. Also from Chile came the Iglesia Metodista Pentecostal, Misión Evangélica Pentecostal, and the Iglesia Evangélica Pentecostal.

Among the other pentecostal churches in Uruguay are the Asamblea de Dios Misionera Siloe, La Iglesia Evangélica Asamblea de Dios, Asociación Cristo ha Resucitado, Iglesia Renovada de los Milagros de Jésus, Iglesia Cristo es la Esperanza, Iglesia Evangélica Alianza de Cristo, Iglesia Evangélica Cristiana Saron, Iglesia Evangélica El Shadai, Iglesia Jésus La Unica Esperanza, Iglesia Dios Viviente, Iglesia Misión Unida, Iglesia Pentecostal Naciente (13 congregations in Montevideo, 1993), Misión Cristiana Pentecostal, and Movimiento Misionero Mundial.

■ **Bibliography:** L. K. Ahonen, *Suomen Helluntaiherätyksen Historia* (1994) ■ Anon., *Uruguay* (Springfield, MO, c. 1960) ■ D. B. Barrett, *World Christian Encyclopedia* (1982), 773–75 ■ D. L. Burk, ed., *Foreign Missions Insight: A Digest of Foreign Missions Faces, Facts, Fields and Figures* (1999), 131–32 ■ C. W. Conn, *Like a Mighty Army: A History of the Church of God* (1955; rev. 1977, 1995) ■ idem, *Where the Saints Have Trod: A History of Church of God Missions* (1959) ■ *Directorio de Iglesias Evangélicas, Montevideo, 1993* (1993) ■ A. Hämäläinen, *Kaikkeen Maailmaan, 1929–1989. 60 vuotta helluntaiseurakuntien lähetystyötä* (1989), 35–36 ■ S. M. Hodges, *Look on the Fields: A Survey of the Assemblies of God in Foreign Lands* (1956), 139–40 ■ W. J. Hollenweger, "Handbuch der Pfingstbewegung" (diss., Zurich, 1967), 1112–14 (para. 02b.29) ■ L. Jeter de Walker, *Siembre y cosecha*, vol. 2 (1992) ■ O. Nilsen, *Ut i all Verden: Pinsevennenes ytre misjon i 75 år* (1984) ■ G. L. Pettersen, *Pinse over grensene* (1989) ■ F. K. Scott, "Fred Scott," in *Profiles of Pentecostal Missionaries* (1986) ■ A. Sundstedt, *Pingstväckelsen*, 5 vols. (1969–73).
■ D. D. Bundy

UZBEKISTAN

■ Pentecostals 0 (0%) ■ Charismatics 13,669 (9%) ■ Neocharismatics 136,331 (91%) ■ Total Renewal: 150,000

See RUSSIA.

VANUATU

■ Pentecostals 27,708 (59%)   ■ Charismatics 15,111 (32%)   ■ Neocharismatics 4,381 (9%)   ■ Total Renewal: 47,200

For general introduction and bibliography, see PACIFIC ISLANDS.

Vanuatu, known as the New Hebrides until it became independent on July 30, 1980, is a double chain of about 80 islands spread in the shape of a Y, extending about 500 mi (800 km) from north to south and 40 mi (65 km) from east to west. The main island, Efate, with the administrative center Port Vila, is about 1,400 mi (2,250 km) northeast of Sydney, Australia. Over 80% of the population is still involved in subsistence agriculture. Copra (dried coconut meat), fish, and beef are the main exports of Vanuatu.

The indigenous people (91.8%) are of Melanesian stock, speaking more than 100 languages. Bislama (Pidgin English) is the lingua franca; English and French are the other official languages. The indigenous people are also known as Ni-Vanuatu. Of the estimated population of 191,000 in 1995, approximately 20,000 lived in the capital, Port Vila.

Vanuatu has three mainline churches, the Presbyterian Church leading in terms of numbers before the Anglican Church and the Roman Catholic Church. Although officially only 2.4% of the population are adherents to pre-Christian religions, there is still a strong, underlying current of pre-Christian traditions across all Christian denominations, especially on the islands of Tanna, Aniwa, and Santo. The main pentecostal/charismatic denominations are the Apostolic Church, with about 1,700 adherents, and the Assemblies of God (AG). The AG began its mission officially in Oct. 1968, with the arrival of U.S. missionary Lawrence Larson and James Charles Williams, a missionary from Fiji. From that time on there has been a resident ministry in Vanuatu for the AG. While the beginnings were very humble, the AG experienced fast growth from the 1980s until now. By the end of 1997 there were still four expatriate missionaries sent by the AG–U.S. In 1998 there were already 10,000 baptized members and an estimated total of 21,000 adherents. At present there are about 110 ministers with credentials and 50 lay ministers for the 65 churches and 200 preaching points. In 1998, 45 students were enrolled in the local AG Bible school. All these figures point to an explosive growth of the AG in Vanuatu, especially over the past 10 years.   ■ M. Ernst

VENEZUELA

■ Pentecostals 157,275 (4%)   ■ Charismatics 3,212,900 (88%)   ■ Neocharismatics 299,825 (8%)   ■ Total Renewal: 3,670,000

1. The Beginnings of Pentecostalism in Venezuela.

The history of pentecostalism goes back to the activity of independent missionaries and others who served under the Christian and Missionary Alliance (CMA). Most notable were Gerard A. Bially and Alice Wood. Wood, after her conversion to pentecostalism, went on to serve in Argentina. Bially, who for a time served as the head of the CMA in Venezuela, continued to serve in Venezuela throughout his life. It was, however, a German immigrant to the U.S., Gottfried Frederick Bender, who would become the undisputed leader of the pentecostal revival in Venezuela during the first half of the 20th century. Bially and Bender would be credited with founding Venezuelan denominations; Wood would found the Assemblies of God (AG) mission in Argentina and be involved in the founding of the Unión Nacional de las Asambleas de Dios en Argentina.

2. G. F. and Christina Bender and the Early Converts.

Bender (1877–1961) was born in Oberstadt, Baden, Germany. When he was a child his family moved to Toledo, OH, where they became involved in a Holiness congregation of the Evangelical United Brethren Church. He was converted in 1902 and experienced the pentecostal baptism of the Holy Spirit in a CMA prayer meeting in Sept. 1907. Among his friends was ►Hans Waldvogel, a Brooklyn pastor of the Independent AG whose congregation would later play a crucial role in support of the work in Venezuela, and Fred Bullen, who would serve as an agent of the American Bible Society in Venezuela.

Bender arrived in Venezuela in early 1914. He worked initially at the CMA Bible school, Instituto Biblico "Hébron" near Lo Teques. After the death of Bullen, Bender returned to the U.S. on furlough and married on Mar. 21, 1918, Christina Schwager Kopittke (1875–1968). The wedding, in Riverside, CA, was officiated by Gerard Bially. Six months later they returned to Venezuela, where they undertook mission work in Barquisimeto, Lara, against the strong advice of Bially. The dispute over the site of ministry led to deteriorating relations with the CMA and the pentecostal denomination founded by Bially. Bethel Chapel was dedicated on Sept. 21, 1922. The opening of the chapel provoked severe persecution by the Catholic Church, and Bishop Alvarado threatened excommunication for anyone having contact with the pentecostal services.

Despite the opposition, conversions continued. The first converts to experience the pentecostal baptism of the Holy

Spirit were Felipe Vázquez and Alfonso Gravina G. The former became the first Venezuelan pentecostal pastor. In 1924 the Benders opened a school called the Instituto Evangélica and directed by Ada Winger. Winger was an effective missionary who, after her marriage to Mr. Wegner, went to Colombia as a missionary in 1932. One of the teachers at the school was John Christiansen, a missionary of the Swedish Pentecostal Church.

Revival broke out in Barquisimeto in 1925. This brought rapid growth to the congregations and opened numerous opportunities for ministry. From 1927 until 1931 Winger began a ministry to underprivileged girls, which evolved into a girls' residential school, Hogar de Paz. During this period, because of the intense organized persecution, it was necessary to win the trust of neighbors and to evangelize discretely. Nevertheless, the congregation grew, and additional congregations were established in nearby cities.

The congregations in the other parts of Venezuela had differing degrees of relations with the congregations in the state of Lara. In Caracas the pentecostal work was begun by independent Hispanic missionaries from a Hispanic congregation in New York. The Medina and Vidal families began work in Caracas in 1936. This work was taken over (c. 1940) by Irving Olson, a Swedish Baptist who had converted to the AG–U.S. Olson worked to establish additional preaching points.

A few years later Petra Vidal moved from Caracas to the city of La Victoria, Aragua. There she assisted in the church founded by David Finstrom, a missionary of the Swedish American Assemblies of God. Through her influence many were baptized in the Holy Spirit. The movement spread to Maracay and into the other evangelical churches of the city. Those experiencing the pentecostal baptism of the Holy Spirit were expelled from their churches and organized pentecostal congregations.

In Zulia and Falcon the pentecostal revival began among churches of the Svensk Missionsförbundet (SMF), reflecting the influence of the Örebro Mission. The SMF pastor, Sacramento Cobos, experienced a pentecostal conversion about 1929. A separate congregation was established, of which the pastor was Pedro Savedra. The first church in Falcon was established in 1931 by the German pentecostal missionaries Else and Rudolf Blattner, who had loose ties to the SMF.

3. Union with the AG–U.S. and the Founding of the UEPV.

From his arrival in Venezuela, Irving Olson worked to establish a credible AG presence. He was successful primarily in the Caracas area, where there was less contact with indigenous traditions. During the 1940s, Bender worked to develop the identity of all of the pentecostal churches that would relate to the work in Barquisimeto. He represented them in ecumenical encounters with various denominations. He worked to bring them into ways of working together. The

process he established was democratic and egalitarian. In 1937 Gottfried and Christina Bender applied for membership in the AG–U.S. and were accepted as AG missionaries. In 1947 the Benders retired to Toledo, OH, and, at his urging, the churches in Venezuela affiliated with the AG–U.S., which quickly took over direction of the church.

In 1948 the Istituto Biblico Central was established in Barquisimeto. This resulted in an influx of North American missionaries. The Venezuelan pastors were suddenly no longer involved in any significant way in the decisions about the pentecostal church in Venezuela. Most of the major decisions were made in Springfield, MO, or in the meetings of missionaries in Venezuela. This alienation led to confrontation between the missionaries and the national leaders at a convention in the church La Hermosa at Punto Fijo in 1956. When the missionaries refused to cede any power or open up the decision-making processes, the crisis escalated. Those Venezuelan pastors who valued an independent ministry more than the financial security provided by the AG–U.S. withdrew from the AG to form the Unión Evangélica Pentecostal Venezolana (UEPV) at a meeting on Jan. 12–13, 1957, in Barquisimeto.

The leader of the UEPV was Exeario Sosa, who had been trained in his ministry by G. F. Bender. The intent of the UEPV was to retain the radical social, ecumenical, and evangelistic traditions of Bender. The UEPV adopted an episcopal structure but retained the missiological and ecclesiological tradition of ►T. B. Barratt and ►Lewi Pethrus that they had experienced through contacts with the Independent Assemblies of God and the Swedish American Assemblies of God. In 1980 the UEPV reported about 10,000 adherents. The UEPV has provided crucial pentecostal ecumenical leadership, both among pentecostals (CEPLA), the Latin American Council of Churches (CLAI), and the WCC. Those who remained as part of the Asambleas de Dios en Venezuela have seen their church become more indigenous. It has grown to report 25,000 adherents in 1980.

4. The Other Pentecostal Traditions.

In addition to these churches are the Iglesia Apostólica Venezolana y Misionera founded by Gerard Bially. There is also a significant Iglesia del Evangélio Cuadrangular, which began in San Cristobal, Tachira. Lewis Morely founded the ►Oneness pentecostal church, Iglesia Pentecostal Unida, which began in Valera, Trujillo, in 1956. In 1999 it reported to have grown to about 60,000 members with 386 ministers and 603 congregations and preaching points (up from a reported 10,000 adherents in 1980). Other pentecostal denominations include Associación de Iglesias Pentecostales Peniel, Associación de Iglesias Pentecostales Peniel Libre, Associación Evangelistica Peniel "El Que Vive," Centro Evangélico Pentecostal, Iglesia de Dios Pentecostal, Iglesia Evangélica Emmanuel, Iglesia Evangélica Pentecostal de Las

Acacias, Iglesias Pentecostales El Buen Samaritano, Iglesias Pentecostales Emmaus, Iglesias Pentecostales Juan 3:16, as well as about a dozen smaller groups. There are large numbers of Catholic charismatics in Venezuela, generally among the middle and upper classes. Venezuela has also been the Latin American center of the ▸Cursillo Movement in the Catholic Church.

■ **Bibliography:** D. B. Barrett, *World Christian Encyclopedia* (1982), 738–42 ▌ C. Bender, "Gospel Trailblazer: The Story of G. F. Bender, Pioneer Missionary in Venezuela," *Bread of Life* (Jan.–June 1967; continued by G. P. Gardner, July 1967–Mar. 1968) ▌ G. F. Bender, "Carrying God's Own Word to the People," *PE* (Apr. 5, 1944) ▌ idem, "Dedication of the Chapel in Barquisimeto: Calm Amid Persecution," *Full Gospel Missionary Herald* (Oct. 1922) ▌ idem, "Faithful Sowing," *Full Gospel Missionary Herald* (Oct. 1924) ▌ idem, "How Pentecost Came to Barquisimeto," *PE* (Jan. 2, 1926) ▌ idem, "Instances of His Power in Barquisimeto," *Full Gospel Missionary Herald* (Mar.–Apr. 1927) ▌ idem, "The Pentecostal Work in Venezuela," *PE* (Feb. 16, 1918) ▌ idem, "'That the Word of God May Have Free Course': An Appeal for Prayer for Unopened Lands," *LRE* (Apr. 1934) ▌ idem, "When the Fire Fell," *Full Gospel Missionary Herald* (Jan. 1925) ▌ idem, "Why the Chapel Could Not Be Completed: Persecutions Abating," *Full Gospel Missionary Herald* (Apr. 1922) ▌ D. L. Burk, ed., *Foreign Missions Insight: A Digest of Foreign Missions Faces, Facts, Fields and Figures* (1999) ▌ R. Domínguez, *Pioneros de Pentecostés en el mundo de habla Hispana*, vol. 3: *Venezuela y Columbia* (1990) ▌ S. H. Frodsham, *With Signs Following: The Story of the Pentecostal Revival in the Twentieth Century* (rev. ed., 1941), 189–99 ▌ W. J. Hollenweger, *Handbuch der Pfingstbewegung* (diss., Zurich, 1967), 1115–16 (para. 02b.30) ▌ *Jubileo. La Fiesta del Espiritu. Identidad y misión del Pentecostalismo Latinamericano* (1999) ▌ G. L. Morales, "La UEPV: Identidad, compromiso y misión," *Presencia Pentecostal en Venezuela: Identidad, compromiso y misión de la UEPV, 1957–1997*, ed. G. Lugo M. (1997), 49–58 ▌ J. M. Rivera, "An Experiment in Sharing Personnel: From Historical Church to Pentecostal Movement," *International Review of Mission* 62 (1973) ▌ R. C. Rodríguez, "Breve reseña histórica de la Unión Evangélica Pentecostal Venezolana," in *Presencia Pentecostal en Venezuela: Identidad, compromiso y misión de la UEPV, 1957–1997*, ed. G. Lugo M. (1997) ▌ L. Sumrall, *Through Blood and Fire in Latin America* (1944), 44–49, 161–66.   ■ D. D. Bundy

VIET NAM

■ Pentecostals 52,101 (7%) ■ Charismatics 157,802 (20%) ■ Neocharismatics 588,097 (74%) ■ Total Renewal: 798,000

VIRGIN ISLANDS OF THE U.S.

■ Pentecostals 7,149 (32%) ■ Charismatics 7,290 (33%) ■ Neocharismatics 7,911 (35%) ■ Total Renewal: 22,350

See Caribbean Islands.

WALLIS AND FUTUNA ISLANDS

■ Pentecostals 8 (2%) ■ Charismatics 322 (98%) ■ Neocharismatics 0 (0%) ■ Total Renewal: 330

WESTERN SAMOA

See Samoa.

YEMEN

■ Pentecostals 0 (0%) ■ Charismatics 1,388 (16%) ■ Neocharismatics 7,112 (84%) ■ Total Renewal: 8,500

See Africa, North, and the Middle East.

YUGOSLAVIA

■ Pentecostals 11,078 (4%) ■ Charismatics 77,840 (31%) ■ Neocharismatics 161,082 (64%) ■ Total Renewal: 250,000

See Europe, Eastern.

ZAMBIA

■ Pentecostals 311,113 (15%)   ■ Charismatics 427,400 (21%)   ■ Neocharismatics 1,278,487 (63%)
■ Total Renewal: 2,017,000

ZIMBABWE

■ Pentecostals 164,858 (3%)   ■ Charismatics 241,644 (5%)   ■ Neocharismatics 4,523,498 (92%)   ■ Total Renewal: 4,930,000

PART II

Global Statistics

GLOBAL STATISTICS The past, present, and possible future of the Pentecostal/Charismatic/Neocharismatic renewal in the Holy Spirit is described here by a summary text followed by two large tables, a mass of explanatory footnotes, a global map, and a short selective bibliography. First, the overall summary description is given.

Renewal Arises in Three Waves

The two tables that follow trace the expansion of this renewal across 10 decades and two centuries, and also across seven continents and the entire world. Historically, the Renewal can be seen to have arrived in three massive surges or waves, whose origins are traced in table 1 to the years 1886, 1907, and 1656 respectively. The first wave is known today as Pentecostalism or the Pentecostal Renewal (line 4), the second wave as the Charismatic movement or the Charismatic Renewal (line 12), followed by a third wave of non-pentecostal, noncharismatic, but neocharismatic renewal (line 21). (References are to numbered lines in the tables plus their related numbered footnotes.)

The Pentecostals, Charismatics, and Neocharismatics who make up this Renewal today number 27.7% of organized global Christianity. They are here classified under 59 different categories (7 relating to Pentecostals, 8 to Charismatics, 44 to Neocharismatics).

Even with these three waves and 59 categories, an underlying unity pervades the movement. This survey views the Renewal in the Holy Spirit as one single, cohesive movement into which a vast proliferation of all kinds of individuals and communities and cultures and languages have been drawn under a whole range of different circumstances. This explains the massive babel of diversity evident today.

Participants in the Renewal are found in 740 Pentecostal denominations; 6,530 non-pentecostal, mainline denominations with large organized internal Charismatic movements; and 18,810 independent, Neocharismatic denominations and networks. Charismatics are now found across the entire spectrum of Christianity, within all 150 traditional non-pentecostal ecclesiastical confessions, families, and traditions. Pentecostals/Charismatics (the shorthand generic term preferred here for the whole three-wave phenomenon) are found in 9,000 ethnolinguistic cultures, speaking 8,000 languages, covering 95% of the world's total population.

A Massive Worldwide Phenomenon

The sheer magnitude and diversity of the numbers involved beggar the imagination. Table 1 and its footnotes document an A.D. 2000 total of 523 million affiliated church members (line 66). Of these, 65 million are Pentecostals, 175 million are Charismatics, and 295 million are Third-Wavers or Neocharismatics. Some 29% of all members worldwide are white, 71% nonwhite.

More members are urban than rural, more female than male, more children (under 18) than adults, more Third World (66%) than Western world (32%), more living in poverty (87%) than affluence (13%), more family-related than individualist.

These totals of believers today are not, however, the whole story. They do not include believers who died yesterday, last month, last year, or earlier in the 20th century. A complete tally of all Renewal believers throughout the century must therefore include the 175 million who are no longer alive. The total of all Renewal believers since A.D. 1900 can thus now be seen to amount to 795 million (see lines 81 and 82 in tables 1 and 2, and their footnotes).

Persecution and Diversity

Pentecostals/charismatics are more harassed, persecuted, suffering, and martyred than perhaps any other Christian tradition in recent history. They have been protected to some extent by the fact that their multiple cultures and vast diversity have made it virtually impossible for dictators, tyrants, archenemies, and totalitarian regimes to track them down and suppress them. Their incredible variety and diversity can be seen from the fact that to do justice to this diversity we have had to create a whole variety of neologisms and new statistical categories. Those described in the tables include pre-pentecostals, quasi-pentecostals, indigenous pentecostals, ethnic pentecostals, isolated radio pentecostals, postpentecostals, non-Christian believers in Christ, postdenominationalists, neo-apostolics, ‣Oneness apostolics, indigenous charismatics, grassroots neocharismatics, postcharismatics, crypto-charismatics, radio/TV charismatics, and independent charismatics. Of these 16 categories, only the last 2 have been universally recognized up to now as genuine pentecostals/charismatics. In this survey we are taking the position that all of these categories need to be recognized and enumerated as part of the Renewal.

Global Expansion Continues

All three waves are still continuing to surge in. Massive expansion and growth continue at a current rate of 9 million new members a year—over 25,000 a day. One-third of this expansion is purely demographic (births minus deaths in the pentecostal/charismatic community); two-thirds are converts and other new members.

In the early days of all three waves, annual rates of growth were enormous; now they have declined gradually to 2.7% per year for Pentecostals, 2.4% for Charismatics, 3.0% per year for Neocharismatics, and 3.2% per year for the Renewal as a whole (line 82). These overall figures hide a number of situations of saturation, some spheres of decline, and many situations of explosive, uncontrollable growth.

Charismatics greatly outnumber Pentecostals in numbers and in annual converts worldwide. They do, however, have a growing dilemma in that Charismatics in the non-pentecostal mainline Protestant and Catholic churches experience an average intense involvement of only two or three years—after this period as active weekly attenders at prayer meetings, they become irregular or nonattending, hence our term postcharismatics (line 15). This "revolving-door syndrome" results in an enormous annual turnover, a serious problem that has not yet begun to be adequately recognized or investigated.

Each Wave Augments the Others

Lines 67–75 in table 1 show the geographical spread of the Renewal today. Large numbers exist on every continent and in 236 countries. This table suggests the reason why Europe has always had the lowest response to Pentecostalism of any continent (less than 1%). Europeans rejected the First Wave because they were not prepared to leave the great state churches to become Pentecostals; since 1970, however, they have responded enormously as Charismatics *within* those churches. With 21 million Charismatics and 13 million Neocharismatics, Europe now has the highest ratio (6.6) of Charismatics to Pentecostals of all continents across the world.

At the other end of the spectrum from rejection to acceptance is Asia, whose Christians have become massively pentecostalized (line 70). This is due mainly to the phenomenal spread of the Renewal in Korea, India, the Philippines, Indonesia, and mainland China.

Permeating the Institutions

All state churches and national denominations, with their myriad agencies and institutions, are now rapidly becoming permeated with Charismatics. In addition, roughly 14% of Charismatics in these mainline churches have seceded or have become independent each year since 1970, forming over 100,000 white-led independent charismatic churches across the world, loosely organized into 830 or so major networks (line 49).

The enormous force of the Renewal can be observed in many ways. One is that a majority of the 50 or so megachurches—the world's largest single congregations, each with over 50,000 members—are Pentecostal/Charismatic/Neocharismatic.

Another indication of its dynamic is the disproportionately high pentecostal/charismatic penetration of the media (see footnote to line 92). Charismatics in particular have seized the global initiative in radio, television, movies, audio, video, publishing, literature, magazines, citywide evangelistic campaigns (800 each year), and so on. Virtually all varieties of ministries engaged in by institutionalized Christianity worldwide have now been penetrated by stalwarts of the Renewal.

Massive Resources Are Generated

Finance, stewardship, and giving also have risen well above the global Christian average (lines 89–90). Personal annual income of church members in the Renewal has grown from $157 billion in 1970 to $1,550 billion by A.D. 2000 (line 89).

Of this, $30 billion is donated to Christian causes (line 90). This means that the rank-and-file of the Renewal do not need to be further exhorted regarding stewardship. Its lay members are doing all they should, and more. There is, however, an almost universal failure by leaders of the Renewal to garner and organize these vast sums coherently for mission and ministry at the world level.

In consequence, giving to global foreign missions per member is stuck at the paltry figure of 15 cents per week (US $7.80 per year).

A further illustration of the permeation of global Christianity lies in the huge numbers of ordained pastors, priests, ministers, bishops, and other church leaders involved (lines 93–95). Over one-third of the world's full-time Christian workers (38%) are Pentecostals/Charismatics/Neocharismatics.

Evangelizing the World

Throughout the history of the Renewal, leaders have summoned members to the task of world evangelization. A favorite theme has been the saying of Jesus: "The fields are white unto harvest." The unharvested or unreached harvest field today consists of 1.6 billion unevangelized persons who have never heard of Jesus Christ (line 101), in 3,000 unevangelized population segments (cities, peoples, countries).

It includes 2,000 unreached ethnolinguistic peoples, 175 unreached megapeoples (of over 1 million population each), 140 unevangelized megacities, and 300 unevangelized Islamic metropolises. The harvest force, or harvesters committed to harvesting, consists of 5.5 million full-time Christian workers; of these, 2.1 million are Pentecostals/Charismatics/Neocharismatics (38%; line 93).

Another indicator concerns global plans to evangelize the world (line 102). Of the world's 1,500 such plans since A.D. 30, some 12% have been definitively Pentecostal/Charismatic. Probably 20% altogether—300 plans—have had significant Charismatic participation.

In the last 20 years, this percentage has risen markedly. Sixteen of the world's 24 current megaplans launched since 1960, or 67%, are Pentecostal/Charismatic. So are 9 (64%) of the 14 current giga-plans (global plans to evangelize the world, each spending over US $1 billion) launched since 1960.

New bodies are continually emerging. Over 100 new Charismatic mission agencies have recently been formed in the Western world and over 300 more in the Third World. Many are taking on the challenge of unevangelized population segments in restricted-access countries by appointing nonresidential missionaries.

With Pentecostals/Charismatics/Neocharismatics now active in 80% of the world's 3,300 large metropolises, all in process of actively implementing networking and cooperation with Great Commission Christians of all confessions, a new era in world missions clearly appears to be under way.

Table 1. The global expansion of the Pentecostal/Charismatic/Neocharismatic Renewal in the Holy Spirit, AD 1900–2025.

Ref	Category	Begun	Totals in AD 2000: Countries	Denoms	Participants in: 1900	1970	1995	2000	2025
1	2	3	4	5	6	7	8	9	10
1.	**PERIPHERAL QUASI-PENTECOSTALS**								
2.	Prepentecostals	1739	100	2,600	2,500,000	3,824,000	5,000,000	7,300,000	18,800,000
3.	Postpentecostals	1950	80	509	0	1,000,000	6,000,000	10,500,000	33,000,000
4.	**FIRST WAVE: PENTECOSTAL RENEWAL**								
5.	**Pentecostals**	1886	225	740	20,000	15,382,330	57,424,520	65,832,970	97,876,000
6.	Denominational Pentecostals	1910	225	740	20,000	15,382,330	57,424,520	65,832,970	97,876,000
7.	Classical Pentecostals	1906	220	660	20,000	14,443,480	54,961,090	63,064,620	93,583,000
8.	Holiness Pentecostals	1886	170	240	15,000	2,322,430	5,650,230	6,315,790	9,644,000
9.	Baptistic Pentecostals	1906	210	390	5,000	11,415,390	47,713,650	54,973,310	81,272,000
10.	Apostolic Pentecostals	1904	29	30	0	705,660	1,597,210	1,775,520	2,667,000
11.	Oneness Pentecostals	1914	130	80	0	938,850	2,463,430	2,768,350	4,293,000
12.	**SECOND WAVE: CHARISMATIC RENEWAL**								
13.	**Charismatics**	1907	235	6,530	12,000	3,349,400	156,041,320	175,856,690	274,934,000
14.	Mainline active Charismatics	1960	225	6,990	12,000	3,349,400	100,841,320	114,029,250	179,969,000
15.	Mainline Postcharismatics	1973	150	3,540	0	0	55,200,000	61,827,440	94,965,000
16.	Anglican Charismatics	1907	163	130	1,000	509,900	15,980,520	17,562,110	25,470,000
17.	Catholic Charismatics	1967	234	236	10,000	2,000,000	104,900,000	119,912,200	194,973,000
18.	Protestant Charismatics	1959	231	6,460	1,000	824,100	32,208,900	35,200,000	50,156,000
19.	Orthodox Charismatics	1970	25	140	0	15,200	2,941,900	3,167,380	4,295,000
20.	Marginal Charismatics	1980	15	130	0	200	10,000	15,000	40,000
21.	**THIRD WAVE: NEOCHARISMATIC RENEWAL**								
22.	**Neocharismatics** (Independents, Postdenominationalists)	1549	225	18,810	949,400	53,490,560	254,726,840	295,405,240	460,798,000
23.	(a) In 2 kinds of wholly Third Wave networks	1656	220	17,125	949,300	36,854,370	217,689,150	253,936,540	401,173,000
24.	Non-White indigenous Neocharismatics	1783	210	13,425	919,300	29,379,360	174,221,530	203,270,400	327,515,000
25.	African indigenous pentecostals/charismatics	1864	60	9,300	890,000	12,569,300	56,520,100	65,310,530	99,263,000
26.	Afro-Caribbean pentecostals/charismatics.	1783	38	420	10,000	217,610	649,670	736,080	1,168,000
27.	Arab/Assyrian/Semitic neocharismatics	1909	40	130	0	140,760	1,076,730	1,263,930	2,200,000
28.	Black American independent charismatics.	1955	4	10	0	62,500	1,236,800	1,471,660	2,646,000
29.	Black American indigenous pentecostals	1889	20	90	15,000	2,820,540	6,832,460	7,634,850	11,647,000
30.	Black American Oneness Apostolics	1886	10	150	0	559,120	2,560,600	2,960,900	4,962,000
31.	Brazilian/Portuguese grassroots neocharismatics	1656	20	460	0	2,512,200	19,604,340	23,022,770	39,115,000
32.	Colored/Mixed-race indigenous charismatics	1931	4	70	0	71,000	207,500	234,800	371,000
33.	Ethnic (Monoethnic) pentecostal churches.	1890	20	20	0	162,930	1,307,220	1,536,080	2,680,000
34.	Filipino indigenous pentecostals/charismatics	1913	25	380	0	1,818,020	5,950,340	6,776,800	10,909,000
35.	Han Chinese indigenous pentecostals/charismatics	1905	58	180	2,000	310,240	41,509,370	49,749,200	82,948,000
36.	Indian indigenous pentecostals/charismatics	1911	25	580	1,000	1,421,310	14,081,380	16,613,400	29,274,000
37.	Indonesian indigenous pentecostals	1920	5	170	0	2,649,780	6,076,000	6,761,240	10,187,000
38.	Japanese indigenous pentecostals	1930	15	50	0	298,650	1,016,140	1,159,640	1,877,000
39.	Korean indigenous pentecostals/charismatics	1910	30	170	500	100,700	2,799,030	3,338,700	6,037,000
40.	Latino-Hispanic grassroots believers	1909	24	990	0	2,988,090	10,427,650	11,915.560	17,355,000
41.	Messianic Hindu believers in Christ	1875	2	5	500	109,500	154,300	163,200	208,000
42.	Messianic Jewish believers in Christ	1894	14	20	100	13,000	136,000	160,600	284,000
43.	Messianic Muslim believers in Christ	1981	2	3	0	0	105,000	126,000	231,000
44.	Pacific/Oceanic indigenous charismatics	1917	20	70	0	25,730	183,100	214,570	372,000
45.	Red Indian/Amerindian neopentecostals	1870	3	4	0	361,000	506,300	535,360	681,000
46.	Vietnamese indigenous neocharismatics	1952	2	3	0	12,600	195,000	231,480	414,000
47.	Other Asian indigenous neocharismatics	1948	40	130	100	153,780	986,500	1,153,050	1,986,000
48.	Other Messianic non-Christian believers in Christ	1950	15	20	100	1,000	100,000	200,000	700,000
49.	White-led Independent Postdenominationalists	1805	210	3,700	30,000	7,475,010	43,467,620	50,666,140	73,658,000
50.	European/American White-led Neo-Apostolics	1805	200	3,510	10,000	5,760,760	35,174,210	41,056,900	60,470,000
51.	European White-led New Apostolics	1832	180	190	20,000	1,714,250	8,293,410	9,609,240	13,188,000

Ref 1	Category 2	Begun 3	Totals in AD 2000: Countries 4	Denoms 5	Participants in: 1900 6	1970 7	1995 8	2000 9	2025 10
52.	(b) as % of 7 kinds of non-Third-Wave denominations.....	1549	200	925	100	16,636,190	37,037,690	41,468,700	59,625,000
53.	Independent Anglican neocharismatics	1925	80	30	0	10,000	1,595,000	1,716,000	2,321,000
54.	Independent Protestant neocharismatics.	1920	180	450	0	11,832,690	18,642,360	20,489,290	25,724,000
55.	Independent Catholic neocharismatics	1724	30	60	0	700,000	1,187,260	1,314,800	1,953,000
56.	Independent Orthodox neocharismatics	1666	20	10	0	1,000	538,310	584,200	814,000
57.	Nonhistorical Independent neocharismatics	1549	100	90	0	1,000,000	3,200,000	3,500,000	5,000,000
58.	Isolated radio/TV neocharismatics	1930	30	5	0	30,000	159,100	188,100	333,000
59.	Hidden non-Christian believers in Christ.....................	1800	70	280	100	3,062,500	11,715,660	13,676,310	23,480,000
60.	Hidden Hindu neocharismatics	1800	4	10	0	3,000,000	8,637,500	9,715,000	15,103,000
61.	Hidden Muslim neocharismatics	1930	15	10	0	2,000	348,560	417,790	764,000
62.	Hidden Buddhist neocharismatics	1950	17	10	0	10,000	1,829,600	2,193,520	4,013,000
63.	Hidden Jewish neocharismatics	1896	15	50	100	50,000	200,000	250,000	500,000
64.	Hidden other-religionist neocharismatics.................	1980	50	200	0	500	700,000	1,100,000	3,100,000
65.	Doubly-counted First/Second/Third Wavers (see footnote 65)								
66.	**Global affiliated Pentecostals/Charismatics/ Neocharismatics**		**236**	**21,080**	**981,400**	**72,223,000**	**477,378,000**	**523,767,390**	**811,551,600**
67.	**RENEWAL MEMBERS ON 7 CONTINENTS**								
68.	Renewal members in Africa	1830	60	9,990	901,000	17,049,020	110,409,270	126,010,200	227,819,720
69.	Renewal members in Antarctica	1980	1	0	2	0	300	400	600
70.	Renewal members in Asia	1870	50	2,690	4,300	10,144,120	122,691,990	134,889,530	217,550,600
71.	Renewal members in Europe....................................	1805	48	1,870	20,000	8,018,180	36,097,050	37,568,700	47,179,500
72.	Renewal members in Latin America	1783	46	2,680	10,000	12,621,450	130,147,480	141,432,880	202,277,880
73.	Renewal members in Northern America	1889	5	3,520	46,100	24,151,910	73,997,060	79,600,160	110,204,580
74.	Renewal members in Oceania	1917	28	330	0	238,240	3,928,850	4,265,520	6,519,300
75.	Renewal members as % global church members	–	238		–0.2	6.4	26.9	27.7	32.5
76.	**PERIPHERAL CONSTITUENTS**								
77.	Quasi-Pentecostals (Prepentecostals, Postpentecostals) ...	1739	110	2,700	2,500,000	4,824,000	11,000,000	17,800,000	51,800,000
78.	Unaffiliated believers professing Renewal.....................	1950	230	2,000	210,000	5,300,000	52,000,000	78,327,510	120,000,000
79.	**WIDER GLOBAL TOTALS OF RENEWAL**								
80.	Total all Renewal believers alive at mid-year.....		236	26,565	3,691,400	82,346,270	529,597,680	619,894,900	961,000,000
81.	Renewal believers dying since AD 1900		236	11,565	–	34,657,900	146,743,000	175,728,800	270,000,000
82.	Total all Renewal believers ever, since AD 1900		236	29,500	3,691,400	117,004,170	676,340,680	795,623,700	1,231,000,000
83.	**CHURCHES, FINANCE, AGENCIES, WORKERS**								
84.	Pentecostal churches, congregations (1st Wave)		225	740	10	94,200	360,000	480,000	1,080,000
85.	Mainline Charismatic prayer groups (2nd Wave).		235	4,450	0	35,000	370,000	550,000	1,450,000
86.	Catholic Charismatic weekly prayer groups		234	239	0	2,185	143,000	160,000	245,000
87.	Anglican & Protestant Charismatic groups		231	3,700	0	32,815	200,000	250,000	500,000
88.	Independent congregations, house churches (3rd Wave)..........		—	—	15,000	138,970	450,000	591,000	1,296,000
89.	Personal income of all Renewal members, $ p.a.......		—	—	250 million	157 billion	1,280 billion	1,550 billion	2,400 billion
90.	Renewal members' giving to all Christian causes, $ p.a.		—	—	7 million	3 billion	25 billion	30billion	46 billion
91.	Renewal service agencies....................................		—	—	20	600	3,400	4,000	7,000
92.	Renewal institutions		—	—	100	1,300	13,000	14,000	19,000
93.	All pentecostal/charismatic full-time workers.........		—	—	2,010	240,790	1,200,000	2,100,000	4,300,000
94.	Nationals: pastors, clergy, evangelists, et alii		—	—	2,000	237,000	1,060,000	1,933,000	3,900,000
95.	Aliens: foreign missionaries		—	—	100	3,790	140,000	167,000	400,000
96.	**THE CONTEXT OF WORLD EVANGELIZATION**								
97.	Global population		238	—	1,619,626,000	3,696,148,000	5,666,360,000	6,055,049,000	7,823,703,000
98.	Christians (all varieties)		238	33,800	558,132,000	1,236,374,000	1,877,426,000	1,999,564,000	2,616,670,000
99.	Affiliated church members (baptized).......................		238	33,800	521,576,500	1,130,106,000	1,796,918,000	1,888,439,000	2,490,958,000
100.	Non-Christians		238	—	1,061,494,000	2,459,774,000	3,788,934,000	4,055,485,000	5,207,033,000
101.	Unevangelized persons...		230	—	879,672,000	1,641,245,000	1,678,205,000	1,629,375,000	1,845,406,000
102.	World evangelization global plans since AD 30		160	—	250	510	1,145	1,500	3,000

Table 2. Codes and characteristics of each of the 95 generic categories and ministries of Pentecostals/Charismatics/Neocharismatics.

Ref Column 1	Category 2	Definitions, characteristics, examples of major significant bodies 3
1.	**PERIPHERAL QUASI-PENTECOSTALS:**	Tables 5-6 and 5-7 divide all members into the 66 ecclesiastico-cultural categories below
2.	Prepentecostals	Charismatic denominations not officially in Renewal: Salvationists, Holiness, Wesleyans
3.	Postpentecostals	Former Denominational Pentecostals who have left to join nonpentecostal churches
4.	**FIRST WAVE: PENTECOSTAL RENEWAL.**	Oldest part of Renewal, claiming name, history, experiences, and theology of Pentecostalism
5.	Pentecostals	Churches of White origin (now 70% Non-White) requiring initial evidence of tongues-speaking
6.	Denominational Pentecostals	Members in the older, larger, more traditional Pentecostal denominations
7.	Classical Pentecostals	Self-designation of older White denominations, usually excluding Black Pentecostals
8.	Holiness Pentecostals	Those holding 3-fold Wesleyan experience of conversion, sanctification, infilling: IPHC
9.	Baptistic Pentecostals	Emphasizing 2-fold Pentecostal experience of conversion, Spirit-baptism: AG, CG, ICFG
10.	Apostolic Pentecostals	Denominations emphasizing Pentecostal church government by living apostles: ACG
11.	Oneness Pentecostals	Denominations emphasizing baptism in name of "Jesus Only"; anti-trinitarian: UPCI
12.	**SECOND WAVE: CHARISMATIC RENEWAL.**	Formula Members of nonpentecostal mainline churches who experience Pentecostal phenomena
13.	Charismatics	All who have experienced Spirit-baptism but remain within nonpentecostal mainline churches
14.	Mainline active charismatics	All in nonpentecostal churches regularly attending Renewal activities
15.	Mainline postcharismatics	Charismatics who no longer attend Renewal activities but still regard themselves as Charismatics
16.	Anglican Charismatics	Total Anglicans in Renewal, past and present, including children and infants
17.	Catholic Charismatics	Total baptized RCs in CCR, past and present, including children and infants
18.	Protestant Charismatics	Total Protestants in Renewal, past and present, including children and infants
19.	Orthodox Charismatics	Total Orthodox in Renewal, past and present, including children and infants
20.	Marginal Charismatics	Total marginal Christians in Renewal, past and present, including children and infants
21.	**THIRD WAVE: NEOCHARISMATIC RENEWAL**	Spirit-led Independents rejecting White Pentecostal/Charismatic denominationalism
22.	Neocharismatics (Independents, Postdenominationalists).	All baptized in the Holy Spirit in new churches independent of historic Christianity
23.	(a) In 2 kinds of wholly Third-Wave networks	Non-White and (2) White-led Neocharismatics in wholly Third-Wave networks/churches
24.	Non-White indigenous Neocharismatics	Spirit-baptized Non-Whites in 26 varieties of indigenous, independent, apostolic churches
25.	African indigenous pentecostals/charismatics	Most AICs are Zionist, Apostolic, Spiritual: ZCC, CCC, AICN, DLBC, AACJM, EJCSK
26.	Afro-Caribbean pentecostals/charismatics	West Indies churches of African origin: Spiritual Baptists/Shouters, Revival Zion, NESBC
27.	Arab/Assyrian/Semitic neocharismatics	Arabic/Aramaean/Assyrian/Berber/Semitic charismatic churches: Tree of Life Chs, GPC
28.	Black American independent charismatics	African American independent charismatic bodies: Full Gospel Baptist Chs Fellowship
29.	Black American indigenous pentecostals	Black Pentecostalism: Church of God in Christ, UHCA, Full Gospel Catholic Ch
30.	Black American Oneness Apostolics	PAOW, AWCF, Bible Way Churches of Our Lord Jesus Christ WW, COLJCAF
31.	Brazilian/Portuguese grassroots neocharismatics	OBPC (Brazil for Christ Ev Ch), IURD/UCKG, CCB, IPF, IPDA
32.	Colored/Mixed-race indigenous charismatics	Colored, Métis, mixed-race charismatics: Members in Christ Ch, Christen Gemeente
33.	Ethnic (Monoethnic) pentecostal churches	Yi Churches, Miao Churches, Nagaland Christian Revival Churches, Gypsy Ev Movement
34.	Filipino indigenous pentecostals/charismatics	Jesus is Lord Fellowship, CDCC, March of Faith, Ecclesiae Dei
35.	Han Chinese indigenous pentecostals/charismatics	True Jesus Church, NBM/BAM, AHC(Little Flock), Han Chinese house churches
36.	Indian indigenous pentecostals/charismatics	Indian Pentecostal Church of God, Believers' Chs of India, Christ Groups, IPA, MFGCM
37.	Indonesian indigenous pentecostals	Indonesia Pentecostal Church (GPI), GBI, GBIS, GPPS, GBT, GUP
38.	Japanese indigenous pentecostals	Spirit of Jesus Church, Primitive Gospel Ch, Holy Ecclesia of Jesus, JJCC
39.	Korean indigenous pentecostals/charismatics	Yoido FGC, Grace & Truth Ch, FGIGM, Korea Full Gospel Chs of America
40.	Latino-Hispanic grassroots believers	Autochthonous grassroots (GR) churches, IMPC, IPP, IOAP, IEMP, IEPC
41.	Messianic Hindu believers in Christ	Messianic temples, organized Hindu-Christian chs: Hindu Ch of the Lord Jesus, SRM
42.	Messianic Jewish believers in Christ	Messianic Jewish synagogues, Fellowship of Messianic Congregations, UMJC, IAMCS, JFJ
43.	Messianic Muslim believers in Christ	Messianic Muslim mosques: Jesus Mosques, Jamaat
44.	Pacific/Oceanic indigenous charismatics	Pacific indigenous churches: Christian Fellowship Ch, AGCFI, Samoan FGC
45.	Red Indian/Amerindian neopentecostals	Amerindian neopentecostals: UIEI, Halleluja Church
46.	Vietnamese indigenous neocharismatics	Vietnamese churches: Good News House Church Movement
47.	Other Asian indigenous neocharismatics	Other Asian churches: Hope of God Churches of Thailand, Latter Rain Ch of Malaysia
48.	Other Messianic non-Christian believers in Christ	Organized believers staying in Buddhism, Baha'i, Sikhism, &c
49.	White-led independent postdenominationalists	Spirit-baptized Whites in non-Pentecostal/Charismatic apostolic networks

50.	European/American White-led Neo-Apostolics	AIGA, AVC, CEEC, COTRI, FCFI, IAOGI, ICCC, ICCEC, ICFCM, RBC-RMAI, UEC, VFM, &c
51.	European White-led New Apostolics	Neuapostolische Kirche (NAK), begun as Universal Catholic Ch, and 30 schismatic bodies
52.	(b) as % of 6 kinds of non-Renewal denominations	Neocharismatics in non-pentecostal/charismatic (even anti-Renewal) denominations
53.	Independent Anglican neocharismatics	Neocharismatics within non-pentecostal/charismatic Independent Anglican bodies
54.	Independent Protestant neocharismatics	Neocharismatics within non-pentecostal/charismatic Independent Protestant bodies
55.	Independent Catholic neocharismatics	Neocharismatics within non-pentecostal/charismatic Independent Catholic bodies
56.	Independent Orthodox neocharismatics	Neocharismatics within non-pentecostal/charismatic Independent Orthodox bodies
57.	Nonhistorical independent neocharismatics	Neocharismatics in other nonpentecostal Independent chs: PIC/IFI, NBCA
58.	Isolated radio/TV neocharismatics	Neocharismatics among non-pentecostal/charismatic Independent radio believers
59.	Hidden non-Christian believers in Christ	Hindu, Muslim, Buddhist, Jewish, Sikh, Baha'i, New Religionist converts who stay hidden
60.	Hidden Hindu neocharismatics	Hindu believers in Christ (NBBCs) who have pentecostal/charismatic gifts
61.	Hidden Muslim neocharismatics	Muslim believers in Christ (NBBCs) who have pentecostal/charismatic gifts
62.	Hidden Buddhist neocharismatics	Buddhist believers in Christ (NBBCs) who have pentecostal/charismatic gifts
63.	Hidden Jewish neocharismatics	Jewish believers in Christ who have pentecostal/charismatic gifts
64.	Hidden other-religionist neocharismatics	Other religionist hidden believers in Christ who have pentecostal/charismatic gifts
65.	Doubly-counted First/Second/Third Wavers	Neocharismatics who join Pentecostal bodies; Charismatics who become Neocharismatics
66.	Global Pentecostals/Charismatics/Neocharismatics	Total all church members in the Pentecostal/Charismatic/Neocharismatic Renewal
67.	**RENEWAL MEMBERS ON 7 CONTINENTS**	Renewal (which is 28% of globe) is: 12% Pentecostals, 33% Charismatics, 55% Neocharismatics
68.	Renewal members in Africa	12% Pentecostals, 25% Charismatics, 63% Neocharismatics
69.	Renewal members in Antarctica	1% Pentecostals, 95% Charismatics, 4% Neocharismatics
70.	Renewal members in Asia	5% Pentecostals, 16% Charismatics, 79% Neocharismatics
71.	Renewal members in Europe	8% Pentecostals, 56% Charismatics, 36% Neocharismatics
72.	Renewal members in Latin America	23% Pentecostals, 52% Charismatics, 24% Neocharismatics
73.	Renewal members in Northern America	7% Pentecostals, 28% Charismatics, 65% Neocharismatics
74.	Renewal members in Oceania	14% Pentecostals, 63% Charismatics, 24% Neocharismatics
75.	Renewal members as % global church members	Rising rapidly at first to 6% by 1970 and to 28% by AD 2000
76.	**PERIPHERAL CONSTITUENTS**	
77.	Quasi-Pentecostals (Prepentecostals, Postpentecostals)	Defined above for lines 2 and 3, not counted here as Renewal members but as Renewal believers
78.	Unaffiliated believers professing Renewal	Individual believers experiencing Holy Spirit gifts but remaining unrelated to Renewal bodies
79.	**WIDER GLOBAL TOTALS OF RENEWAL**	
80.	Total all Renewal believers alive at mid-year	Total of lines 66, 77, and 78
81.	Renewal believers dying since AD 1900	Former members of Renewal who have died by the year indicated
82.	Total all Renewal believers ever, since AD 1900	Total of lines 80 and 81
83.	**CHURCHES, FINANCE, AGENCIES, WORKERS**	
84.	Pentecostal churches, congregations (1st Wave)	Mainly Assemblies of God buildings and properties
85.	Mainline Charismatic prayer groups (2nd Wave)	These groups' regular weekly attenders are known as the "shock troops" of the Renewal
86.	Catholic Charismatic weekly prayer groups	Massive growth since origin in 1967, to 2,185 groups (1970), 12,000 (1980), 90,000 (1990), 160,000 (2000)
87.	Anglican & Protestant Charismatic groups	Large-scale lay and clerical leadership from 1960 onwards
88.	Independent congregations, house churches (3rd Wave)	A huge number of smaller house groups, over half a billion
89.	Personal income of all Renewal members, $ p.a.	Enormous wealth but no organized finance or central bank accounts
90.	Renewal members' giving to all Christian causes, $ p.a.	Low at 2% of personal income given to Christian causes but higher than global Christian rates
91.	Renewal service agencies	A huge and variegated number of agencies (listed here in footnote)
92.	Renewal institutions	Vast variety (listed here in footnote)
93.	All pentecostal/charismatic full-time workers	Full-time church workers of all kinds: total of next 2 lines, 94 and 95
94.	Nationals: pastors, clergy, evangelists, et alii	Mostly well-documented by the major denominations and networks
95.	Aliens: foreign missionaries	Large and rapidly growing numbers serving abroad for shorter or longer terms
96.	**THE CONTEXT OF WORLD EVANGELIZATION**	
97.	Global population	Populations are shown at mid-year (30 June) for the years 1970, 1995, 2000, 2025.
98.	Christians (all varieties)	Professing plus crypto-Christians; affiliated plus unaffiliated; Great Commission plus latent Christians.
99.	Affiliated church members (baptized)	Baptized or other members of all the churches.
100.	Non-Christians	Now over 4 billion and growing rapidly.
101.	Unevangelized persons	All persons unaware of Christianity, Christ, and/or the gospel.
102.	World evangelization global plans since AD 30	Distinct plans and proposals for completing world evangelization.

METHODOLOGICAL NOTES ON TABLES 1 AND 2

Tables 1 and 2 present a descriptive survey of the phenomenon usually known as the Pentecostal/Charismatic Renewal, or, by participants, as the Renewal in the Holy Spirit. It takes in the somewhat expanded boundaries of the movement that most leaders now understand it as inhabiting. At the same time, the Renewal recognizes the existence and reality of large numbers of other branches or segments of global Christianity, to which it is related in varying degrees of closeness. This means that these tables do not claim to be describing a tradition of Christianity distinct and separate from all other traditions, but a contemporary movement that overlaps with the rest of the Christian world to a large degree (6% in 1970, rising to 27% by A.D. 2000). By 1985, in fact, the Renewal had penetrated, and had secured committed representation in, every one of the Christian world's 156 distinct ecclesiastical confessions, traditions, and families. By A.D. 2000 this had risen to all 250 traditions. The tables enumerate the progress of all branches of the Renewal across the century, with projections from A.D. 2000 to A.D. 2025 based on current long-term trends. A general overview of the Renewal will help clarify the categories used in these tables.

I. GENERAL OVERVIEW OF THE RENEWAL

A. The Renewal as a Single Movement.

Tables 1 and 2 view the 20th-century Renewal in the Holy Spirit as one single cohesive movement into which a vast proliferation of all kinds of individuals and communities have been drawn in a whole range of different circumstances over a period of 450 years. Whether termed pentecostals, charismatics, or third-wavers, they share a single basic experience. Their contribution to Christianity is a new awareness of spiritual gifts as a ministry to the life of the church. The case for this thesis could be made by listing historical, missiological, theological, sociological, and other data. It could also be made by drawing attention to the fact that news of the 1900, 1904, and 1906 revivals traveled throughout the globe (by rail, by ship, by telegraph) in a few days and weeks; while today, news of such happenings—conversions, blessings, healings, movements—travels worldwide within a few seconds by telephone, radio, television, electronic mail, and the Internet. Such rapid communication across time, space, and all varieties of the Renewal reinforces its underlying unity.

The case for the statistical presentation of the Renewal as a single interconnected movement can, however, best be made by considering how the movement starts off and spreads in any given area, from the days of the earliest pentecostals to those of current charismatics and third-wavers (neocharismatics). The start of the movement anywhere has always been an unexpected or unpredictable happening rather than the result of human planning or organization. First, individuals (at random across the existing churches), then groups, then large numbers in organized movements become filled with the Spirit and embark on the common charismatic experience. All of them, originally, can collectively and correctly be termed charismatics. All these charismatics find themselves living initially within existing mainline, non-pentecostal churches and denominations, where over the last 200 years they have been called or labeled charismatics, revivalists, enthusiasts, spirituals, or pentecostals, and where they often have been dismissed as cranks, fanatics, sectarians, heretics, schismatics, or worse. However, all of them initially attempt to stay within, and work within, those churches. But before long, evictions begin; and ejections, withdrawals, and secessions occur in varying degrees. First, individuals, then groups, then whole movements opt for (or are forced into) schism and so begin separate ecclesiastical structures and new denominations.

From its beginnings in this way, the Renewal has subsequently expanded in three massive surges or waves. We can further divide these waves into a typology of nine stages, explained and described in Table 2. These stages and categories are approximate and descriptive, not watertight or exclusive. For instance, as a result of the global influenza pandemic of 1918, large numbers of Blacks in Anglican churches in Africa (Nigeria, Kenya, Uganda, South Africa) became charismatics and formed charismatic prayer groups within Anglican parishes. The majority, however, were soon evicted (and so are enumerated in Tables 1 and 2 on lines 24, 25, 28, 29, 30, etc., becoming what we now refer to as Black pentecostals; only a minority (10%) remained within Anglicanism as charismatics in what later became known as the Anglican Charismatic Renewal.

B. The Three Waves of 20th-Century Renewal.

Having described the Renewal as a single movement, we shall next describe its component elements. The tables classify the various movements and types under the following three consecutive waves of the Renewal in the Holy Spirit, defining its three key terms as follows.

1. Pentecostals.

These are defined as Christians who are members of the major, explicitly Pentecostal denominations in Pentecostalism or the Pentecostal Movement or the Pentecostal Renewal, whose major characteristic is a rediscovery and new experience of the supernatural, with a powerful and energizing ministry of the Holy Spirit in the realm of the miraculous that most other Christians have considered to be highly unusual. This is interpreted as a rediscovery of the spiritual gifts of NT times and their restoration to ordinary Christian life and ministry.

Pentecostalism is usually held to have begun in the U.S. in 1901 (although the present survey shows the year of origin as 1886). For a brief period it was a charismatic revival that expected to remain an interdenominational movement within the existing churches, without beginning a new denomination. But from 1909 onward its members were increasingly ejected from all mainline bodies and so were forced to begin new organized denominations. Pentecostal denominations hold the distinctive teaching that all Christians should seek a postconversion religious experience called baptism in the Holy Spirit, and that a Spirit-baptized believer may receive one or more of the supernatural gifts that were known in the early church, which may include instantaneous sanctification, the ability to prophesy, to practice divine healing through prayer, to speak in tongues or to interpret tongues, singing in tongues, singing in the Spirit, dancing in the Spirit, dreams, visions, discernment of spirits, words of wisdom, words of knowledge, miracles, power encounters, exorcisms (casting out demons), resuscitations, deliverances, signs and wonders.

From 1906 onward, the hallmark of explicitly Pentecostal denominations, by comparison with Holiness/Perfectionist denominations, has been the single addition of speaking with other tongues as the "initial evidence" of one's having received the baptism of the Holy Ghost (or Holy Spirit), whether or not one subsequently regularly experiences the gift of tongues. Most Pentecostal denominations teach that tongues-speaking is mandatory for all members, but in practice today only between 5% and 35% of all members have practiced this gift, either initially or as an ongoing experience.

Pentecostal denominations proclaim a "full" or "fourfold" or "fivefold" gospel of Christ as Savior, Sanctifier, Baptizer with the Holy Spirit, Healer, and Returning King. Collectively, all these denominations are sometimes referred to as the "First Wave" of the 20th-century movement of Holy Spirit–centered renewal. In the U.S., Pentecostals usually refer to the entire body of these denominations founded before 1940 by the blanket term *Classical Pentecostals,* to distinguish them from the subsequent "Neo-pentecostals" or "Charismatics" in the non-pentecostal denominations.

2. Charismatics.

These are defined as Christians affiliated with non-Pentecostal denominations (Anglican, Protestant, Catholic, Orthodox), who receive the experiences above in what became known as the Charismatic Movement, whose roots go back to 1907 and 1918 but whose rapid expansion has been mainly since 1950 (later called the Charismatic Renewal). Charismatics usually describe themselves as having been renewed in the Spirit and experiencing the Spirit's supernatural, miraculous, and energizing power, but they remain within—and form organized renewal groups within—their older mainline, non-pentecostal denominations rather than leaving to join Pentecostal denominations. They demonstrate any or all of the NT gifts of the Spirit, including signs and wonders (though glossolalia is regarded as optional). The whole movement is sometimes referred to as the "Second Wave" of the 20th-century Renewal.

3. Neocharismatics (or Third-Wavers).

Since 1945 thousands of schismatic or other independent charismatic churches have come out of the Charismatic Movement; these independents have throughout the 20th century, from 1900 to the present, numbered more than the first two waves combined. They consist of evangelicals and other Christians who, unrelated to, or no longer related to, the Pentecostal or Charismatic Renewals, have become filled with the Spirit or have been empowered or energized by the Spirit and experience the Spirit's supernatural and miraculous ministry (though usually without recognizing a baptism in the Spirit as separate from conversion). They exercise gifts of the Spirit (with much less emphasis on tongues, which are considered optional or even unnecessary), and emphasize signs and wonders, supernatural miracles, and power encounters. These Neocharismatics leave their mainline, non-pentecostal denominations yet do not identify themselves as either pentecostals or charismatics. In a number of countries, they exhibit pentecostal and charismatic phenomena but combine this with a rejection of pentecostal terminology. These believers are increasingly being identified by their leadership as Independent, Postdenominationalist, Restorationist, Radical, Neo-Apostolic, or the "Third Wave" of the 20th-century Renewal. (The terms *Third Wave* and *third-wavers* were coined by a participant, C. Peter Wagner, in 1983.) Because they constitute a major new revitalizing force, we also call the movement the Neocharismatic Renewal in this table.

II. THE COLUMNS IN TABLES 1 AND 2.

A. Columns 1–10 in Table 1.
1. Reference number of line (same as in Table 2)
2. Usual current terminology for all major components and categories of the Renewal
3. Year when first manifestations began
4. Number of countries where category is in evidence in A.D. 2000
5. Number of distinct denominations (including networks, paradenominations, quasi-denominations) involved in A.D. 2000
6–10. Number of participants (total community or affiliated) at 1900, 1970, 1995, 2000, with projections to A.D. 2025 based on current trends

B. Columns 1–3 in Table 2.
1. Reference number of line (same as in Table 1)
2. Usual current terminology for all major components and categories of the Renewal (identical to listing in Table 1)
3. Definitions, characteristics, examples of major significant bodies within each category

III. LINE-BY-LINE EXPLANATIONS

The numbers of the explanatory notes below correspond to the numbered lines in Tables 1 and 2.

1. Peripheral Quasi-Pentecostals.

Lines 1, 2, 3, 77, with key years of origin or watersheds added.

2. Prepentecostals.

Scattered individual quasi-pentecostals have long been observed in mainline, non-pentecostal denominations. There have always been sizable numbers of such individuals who have experienced or demonstrated pentecostal phenomena in their own lives or ministries, although they do not call themselves, nor are regarded by others as, Pentecostals. For some it is a stage in a process that ends with them becoming members of Pentecostal bodies; most, however, do not reach that point. Those in the last 200 years who may reasonably be regarded as antecedents of the 20th-century Renewal fall into four main categories:

(1) Several thousands of individual monks, priests, brothers and sisters in Catholic, Orthodox, Anglican, and other monastic and religious orders who have been allowed unhindered to exercise personal gifts of the Spirit, including glossolalia, faith healing, etc. Many of these were indirectly responsible for the encyclical letter *On the Holy Spirit*, issued in 1897 by Pope Leo XIII, that directed attention to the sevenfold gifts of the Spirit (Isa. 11) and promoted a universal novena (nine-day cycle of prayer) to the Holy Spirit before Pentecost Sunday each year, which influenced millions of Roman Catholics.

(2) Numerous Mormons (Latter-Day Saints), including founder Joseph Smith and organizer Brigham Young, have practiced glossolalia (though they are not included here in the statistics for prepentecostals).

(3) Charismatic groupings in new movements of the 19th century, which have now become denominations that define themselves as part of the Renewal. Thus, the Salvation Army (London) states: "The history of the Salvation Army (beginning in 1865) is only intelligible as a work of the Holy Spirit. For this reason, the Salvation Army could itself be called a charismatic movement and its early meetings resembled charismatic meetings of today" (A. Bittlinger, ed., *The Church Is Charismatic* [1981], 42).

(4) Sanctified/perfectionist Anglicans and Protestants in Holiness movements within the churches. Especially in the years 1855–1900, which saw the rise in the U.S. of the doctrine of the baptism in the Holy Spirit, the term *prepentecostals* describes individuals with a perfectionist or "second-blessing" experience *plus* related pentecostal phenomena who are nevertheless members of antipentecostal, non-pentecostal, or prepentecostal denominations. These include particularly Holiness/Perfectionist bodies, popular American revivalism, and other denominations opposed to pentecostal phenomena (especially glossolalia), which claim that conversion and sanctification (often termed "infilling with the Spirit") are the only two necessary and complete experiences promised to believers. On the eve of the year 1900, this category included (a) in the U.S., several thousand scattered glossolalists, 100,000 "come-outers" (adults in Holiness split-offs and higher-life movements), and over 1,000,000 White (with some Black) "loyalists" with the sanctification/infilling experience, belonging to Holiness, Wesleyan, and Methodist denominations; and (b) abroad, similar numbers in Holiness/Wesleyan/Methodist denominations and movements and missions in Europe, South Africa, India, Chile, etc. (For the relation between the Holiness and Pentecostal movements, see H. V. Synan, *The Holiness-Pentecostal Tradition*, 1997.)

Historically, the prototype prepentecostal is considered to have been the Anglican revivalist priest John Wesley (1703–91). The best-known prepentecostal preacher before 1900 was the evangelist Dwight L. Moody, whose preaching from 1875 onward sometimes resulted in glossolalia. Before 1900 there were many such cases; tongues, according to some scholars, were a significant feature of the Camp Creek holiness revival in North Carolina in 1896 (other scholars produce contrary evidence).

For the years 1970–2000 on line 2, the statistics refer mainly to similar "sanctified Methodists" and other phenomenological pentecostals and quasipentecostals in these non-pentecostal denominations (especially in the Church of the Nazarene, Wesleyan Church, Free Methodist Church, Salvation Army), most of which differ from pentecostalism only in the absence of tongues-speaking or in the absence of a doctrine that tongues-speaking is the essential evidence of baptism in the Holy Spirit. Most of these prepentecostals are unrelated to, and are uninvolved with, either Pentecostalism or the Charismatic Movement or the Third Wave of the 1980s; they do not identify themselves as "pentecostals," "charismatics," or "third-wavers." However, a new complication is that a number of these denominations' largest congregations in the Third World have independently become Third-Wave; these are not enumerated on line 2 but later in the tables.

3. Postpentecostals.

Former members of Pentecostal denominations who have left to join non-pentecostal denominations (due to marriage, family moves, job transfers, upward mobility, new interests in liturgy and theology, etc.), but who have not renounced their pentecostal experience and who still identify themselves as pentecostal. Thus, for example, active postpentecostals who were formerly members of the International Pentecostal Holiness Church are currently estimated at 450,000 in the U.S.—which is three times IPHC's present membership of 150,000.

IV. NOTE ON LINES 4–64.

These lines reflect the total Christian community affiliated with (on the membership rolls of) denominations, churches, or groups, *including* baptized members, their children and infants, catechumens, inquirers, attenders, but *excluding* interested non-Christian attenders, casual attenders, visitors, etc.

Many Pentecostal denominations enumerate their children and infants, and a number are pedobaptists. Most, however, do not include children in their statistics, which has led to serious undernumeration of the spread of the Renewal. Whenever statistics of church membership are compared to total population figures (which almost always include children and infants), such membership figures must also include its children and infants.

4. First Wave: Pentecostal Renewal.

Pentecostals are defined here as all those associated with explicitly Pentecostal denominations that identify themselves in explicitly Pentecostal terms (see definition of "Pentecostals" above), or with other denominations that as a whole are phenomenologically pentecostal in teaching and practice. Current practice in the U.S. is to analyze the phenomenon as basically an American one, and as distinct from Neo-pentecostalism (the Charismatic Movement), and so to label the whole of denominational Pentecostalism worldwide by the parallel or synonymous term "Classical Pentecostalism." In the present table, however, we are concerned more to see the entire phenomenon as a global one, requiring a different set of descriptive terms. We therefore divide the movement into two major streams, as shown by two different spellings: the term *Pentecostal* (with a capital P) denotes what we call Classical Pentecostalism (which is mainly White-originated), whereas the term *pentecostal* (with a lowercase p) refers to the huge phenomenon of Black/non-White/Third-World indigenous pentecostalism unrelated to Western Classical Pentecostalism (see notes below on lines 6–12). To avoid excessive repetition of the comprehensive adjective "Pentecostal/pentecostal," the adjective "pentecostal" is often used below to denote the whole.

Historically, the First Wave developed out of Black slavery in the U.S., the Evangelical (Wesleyan) Revival from 1738 in Britain, and the Holiness (Perfectionist) movement in Britain, the U.S., and its worldwide missions in the 19th century.

Although many Pentecostal/pentecostal denominations had antecedents going back to the 18th century, the year 1901 (the Topeka, KS, revival) or the year 1906 (the Azusa Street revival) is usually quoted as the year of origin of Pentecostalism, because that is when the movement took off on a massive, universal scale, with widespread tongues and other pentecostal phenomena.

5. Pentecostals.

The numbers on this line are the sum of lines 7 and 11. These totals of all those associated with explicitly Pentecostal denominations, as elaborated above, are derived from the *World Christian Encyclopedia* (2001), Country Tables 2.

6. Denominational Pentecostals.

Pentecostals in 740 major recognized, clear-cut, wholly Pentecostal denominations of Pentecostal theology or practice or stance, committed as denominations to Pentecostal distinctives; these include many minor or very small denominations in 225 different countries. (This line is the same as line 5.)

7. Classical Pentecostals.

As explained above, in this global classification we use *Classical Pentecostals* as a blanket term for those in 660 traditional, Western-related denominations that identify themselves as explicitly Pentecostal. Almost all of these are of White, U.S. origin, but are now worldwide, with adherents among all races. They are found in 220 countries (sum of lines 8–10).

Pentecostal spokespersons in the U.S. use a somewhat wider definition of "Classical Pentecostals" (a term that dates from 1970). They include *all* denominational Pentecostals (in contrast to Neo-pentecostals [Charismatics]), not only the White-originated denominations but also the major early Black pentecostal denominations in the U.S., notably the Church of God in Christ with 6 million members today (which, however, we classify under line 29, "Black American indigenous pentecostals").

There has been a certain amount of blurred boundaries and movement between Pentecostalism and the Charismatic Movement. Thus, in 1948 the Latter Rain Revival (New Order of the Latter Rain) erupted among classical Pentecostals in Saskatchewan, Canada, and spread rapidly to Europe, the U.S., and across the world. It emphasized laying on of hands with prophecy and government by an order of living apostles, but from 1965 it merged into the Charismatic Movement.

8. Holiness Pentecostals.

Also known as Wesleyan Pentecostals, or Methodistic Pentecostals, this was the universal Pentecostal position until the 1910 northern U.S. change (see note 9 below), and it remains the major southern U.S. position. It is found today in 240 denominations worldwide, teaching a three-crisis experience (conversion, sanctification, baptism in the Spirit). First claimed glossolalia manifestations: 1897, Fire-Baptized Holiness Church; 1896, Church of God (Cleveland, TN); 1906, Pentecostal Holiness Church. Total countries involved: 170.

9. Baptistic Pentecostals.

Mainline Classical Pentecostals teaching "finished work" or two-crisis experience (conversion, baptism in the Spirit), found in 390 denominations in 210 countries. Scores of Pentecostal denominations trace their origin to the 1906–9 Azusa Street Revival in Los Angeles, under Bishop W. J.

Seymour and others, at which thousands first spoke in tongues; but the "finished work" teaching (combining conversion with sanctification or "second blessing") of W. H. Durham in 1910 shifted many northern U.S. Pentecostals out of the Wesleyan three-crisis teaching (see note 8 above) into the two-crisis position now known as Baptistic Pentecostalism. The first new denomination to hold this position was the Assemblies of God, founded in 1914, which with its foreign mission work now in 118 countries is by far the largest Pentecostal worldwide denomination. Its meticulously kept annual statistics for each country form Pentecostalism's most solid body of statistical data and hence the main documentation for the Renewal's phenomenal growth.

10. Apostolic Pentecostals.

The 1904 Welsh revival under Evan Roberts, which is often regarded by European writers as the origin of the worldwide Pentecostal movement, prepared the way for British Pentecostalism, especially Apostolic-type teaching that resulted in 1908 in the Apostolic Faith Church (Bournemouth), from which a schism in 1916 formed the Apostolic Church (headquartered in Wales). Apostolics are now found worldwide in 30 denominations, stressing a complex hierarchy of living apostles, prophets, and other charismatic officials. Total countries involved: 29.

11. Oneness Pentecostals.

'Oneness Pentecostals or Jesus' Name Pentecostals (called Unitarian Pentecostals or "Jesus Only" Pentecostals by outsiders) accept baptism in the name of Jesus only. They are widely accepted ecclesiastically as Evangelicals but are theologically modal monarchians; since 1920 they have comprised 25% of all Pentecostals in the U.S. and are found in 80 denominations in 130 countries. The major denomination is the United Pentecostal Church, a 1945 union of the Pentecostal Assemblies of Jesus Christ (1913) and the Pentecostal Church (1916). In contrast to this emphasis within denominational Pentecostalism, the Charismatic Movement has remained explicitly Trinitarian throughout. Many Third-Wave denominations (True Jesus Church, etc.) also hold Oneness theologies; they are listed not here but under lines 25–48 as they occur.

12. Second Wave: Charismatic Renewal.

Charismatics (or, until recently, Neo-pentecostals) are usually defined as those baptized or renewed in the Spirit within the mainline, non-pentecostal denominations, from the first mass stirrings in 1918 in Africa on to the large-scale rise from 1950 onward of the Charismatic Movement (initially also called Neo-pentecostalism to distinguish it from Classical Pentecostalism), who remain within their mainline non-pentecostal denominations. The Movement was later called the Charismatic Renewal. The exact definition used here is given above near the beginning of these footnotes.

Note that many individuals and groups in the mainline churches had already received the baptism in the Spirit without publicity for many years before the usually quoted beginning dates of 1900, 1907, 1924, 1950, 1959, 1962, 1967, etc. Note also that column 5 ("Denominations") for the Charismatic Renewal means totals of non-pentecostal, non-charismatic bodies with organized Renewal agencies within them: the total is 6,530 denominations in 235 countries.

13. Charismatics.

This line's statistics of members are computed as the sum of lines 14–15 or of lines 16–20 (the two are identical). These totals of all those associated explicitly with the Charismatic Renewal in the mainline, non-pentecostal denominations are derived from detailed surveys summarized in Country Tables 1 and 2 in *World Christian Encyclopedia* (2001) and given in full in the *World Christian Database*.

14. Mainline Active Charismatics.

Active members regularly (weekly, monthly, annually, including members' children) involved in prayer groups within the Charismatic Renewal in the older mainline denominations. During the period 1906–50, many thousands of mainline clergy and hundreds of thousands of laity received the pentecostal experience and spoke in tongues, but many were ejected and later joined the Pentecostal denominations. By 2000 the Renewal had penetrated every one of the Christian world's 250 distinct ecclesiastical confessions, traditions, and families, with Charismatics within every tradition, and in the 6,530 denominations.

15. Mainline Postcharismatics.

Self-identified charismatics within mainline non-pentecostal denominations who are no longer regularly active in the Charismatic Renewal but have moved into other spheres of witness and service in their churches. There are three major categories here.

(a) Protestant Postcharismatics are Charismatics formerly active in Renewal, now inactive but in wider ministries. These inactive persons are far fewer in number than inactive Catholics because of the more developed teaching, pastoral care, and ministry opportunities offered by the 20 or so organized denominational renewal fellowships in the U.S. and their counterparts in Europe. An indication of the rapid turnover in membership is the fact that 25% of the 12,000 attenders at the Lutheran ILCOHS annual charismatic conferences in Minneapolis (U.S.) are first-timers, which implies an average four-year turnover.

(b) Catholic Postcharismatics are Charismatics formerly active in the Catholic Charismatic Renewal (the average turnover period of active involvement in officially recognized Catholic Charismatic prayer groups is two to three years), now in wider ministries; inaccurately called "graduates" or

"alumni" of Renewal. In the U.S., these consist of 4.6 million inactive in addition to active Catholic charismatics, including children. Added to active persons this means that in 1985 Catholic Charismatics worldwide numbered 63.5 million (7.3% of the entire Roman Catholic Church), rising to 11.3% by A.D. 2000. A number of Catholic theologians hold that Spirit baptism is as irreversible as water baptism.

(c) Anglican Postcharismatics likewise are Charismatics formerly active in the Anglican Charismatic Renewal, often as far back as 1953, who now are not actively involved, though usually involved in foreign mission or other ministries.

16. Anglican Charismatics.

Anglican pentecostals began in 1907 with the ministry of clergyman A. A. Boddy (Sunderland, England). Then, from 1918 on, due to the global influenza pandemic, numerous prayer and healing groups sprang up in the Anglican churches of Nigeria and Kenya and other places. From 1925 on, there was the Spirit Movement (Aladura), which was expelled and seceded to become today's African Indigenous Churches (with a total membership of 50 million, here enumerated in line 25). This was followed by numerous isolated clergy and groups in several countries, up to the healing ministry of Agnes Sanford, a U.S. Episcopalian (from 1953); the ministries of priests R. Winkler (1956) and D. Bennett (1959); the Blessed Trinity Society (1961); and Church of England clergyman M. C. Harper (1962), who founded the Fountain Trust (1964). The Anglican Renewal had spread to 18 countries by 1978, expanding to 95 countries by 1987 (with 850,000 active adherents in the U.K. served by Anglican Renewal Ministries [ARM]; 520,000 [18% of all Episcopalians] in the U.S. served by Episcopal Renewal Ministries; and with branches of ARM in other countries as well). By A.D. 2000 there had been a rapid increase to 17.5 million in 130 denominations in 163 countries. Much of this expansion has been due to a unique structured international Charismatic ministry body, SOMA (Sharing of Ministries Abroad), begun 1979, which now covers 27 of the 37 Anglican Provinces worldwide and partially covers more, working by 1987 in 70 countries.

17. Catholic Charismatics.

Known at first as Catholic pentecostals or neo-pentecostals, then as the Catholic Charismatic Renewal (CCR). The CCR began with early stirrings in Third-World countries (Africa, Latin America), and then definitively in 1967 in the U.S.; in 1985 there were 60,000 prayer groups in 140 countries worldwide (in the U.S.: 10,500 English, Vietnamese, Korean, Filipino, Haitian, Hispanic, and several other language groups), rising to 143,000 by 1995. Since 1978 there have been National Service Committees in over 120 countries uniting Catholic Charismatics. There are streams with different emphases in the U.S. and several other

countries: (a) that centered on the Word of God Community (Servant Ministries, University Christian Outreach, *New Covenant* magazine, in Ann Arbor, MI, with overseas communities and work in Belgium, Honduras, Hong Kong, India, Indonesia, Lebanon, Nicaragua, Northern Ireland, Philippines, South Africa, Sri Lanka), with cohesive, authoritarian leadership, which originated ICCRO in Brussels, Belgium; and (b) that centered on the People of Praise Community (South Bend, IN), ICCRO after its relocation in Vatican City in 1987, and a wide international network of covenant communities, with a less authoritarian structure and leadership style. Since 1974 some 4% of U.S. priests have been active in the Renewal, including 2% who are now Postcharismatics. Priests worldwide (now 9,470) are proportionally less involved than bishops (now 450); foreign missionaries are more involved than home clergy. (For a more detailed survey and statistical data, see the article "Catholic Charismatic Renewal" in this volume.)

18. Protestant Charismatics.

Origins: 1909 Lutheran prayer groups in state churches (Germany); 1918 charismatics in African countries secede to form AICs (African Indigenous Churches); 1931 Reformed groups related to 1946 Union de Prière (southern France); 1932 charismatic revival in Methodist Church (Southern Rhodesia) leading to massive AACJM schism; 1945 Darmstadt Sisters of Mary (Germany); 1950 Dutch Reformed Church (the Netherlands); 1950 origins of Protestant neo-pentecostals in U.S.; 1958 large-scale neo-pentecostal movements in Brazil's Protestant churches (Renovação); by 1978 in 38 countries; by 1987 in 130 countries; and by A.D. 2000 in 6,460 denominations in 231 countries.

19. Orthodox Charismatics.

Contemporary successors of scores of charismatic movements within the Russian Orthodox Church dating from Spiritual Christians (A.D. 1650); also charismatics in the Greek Orthodox Church in Greece, and Eastern and Oriental Orthodox churches in the U.S. (1967, Fr. A. Emmert, who by 1987 had become a Melkite Catholic convert), Canada, Australia, Lebanon, Uganda, Kenya, Tanzania, Egypt, and some 30 other countries. Agency: Service Committee for Orthodox Spiritual Renewal (SCOSR). A recent significant development is the rapid spread of the Brotherhood of Lovers of the Church, a charismatic renewal within the Armenian Apostolic church in the USSR. Despite these stirrings, Orthodox authorities have generally harassed charismatics relentlessly; this hostility is due to the Orthodox assertion that they never lost the Spirit or the charismata.

20. Marginal Charismatics.

There has always been a small nucleus of practicing Charismatics within the various heterodox organizations in the marginal Christian megabloc.

21. Third Wave: Neocharismatic Renewal.

These terms describe a new wave of the 20th-century Renewal in the Holy Spirit that gathered momentum in the 1980s and 1990s with no direct affiliation with either Pentecostalism or the Charismatic Renewal. Note that large numbers of phenomenological charismatics (in Korea, East Germany, Poland, and elsewhere) do not identify themselves as either pentecostal or charismatic and exhibit a marked rejection of pentecostal terminology.

22. Neocharismatics (Third-Wavers, Independents, Postdenominationalists, Neo-Apostolics).

Persons in mainline non-pentecostal denominations, recently filled with or empowered by the Spirit but usually nonglossolalic, who do not identify themselves with the terms *pentecostal* or *charismatic*. Because they demonstrate the charismata and the phenomena of pentecostalism, they are also being labeled (by outside observers) "quasicharismatics." Totals in A.D. 2000: 295,405,240 members in 18,810 denominations or networks, in 225 countries. Neocharismatics can be divided into 2 categories: (a) those in 100% Neocharismatic networks (see line 23); and (b) Neocharismatic individuals in non-pentecostal/charismatic denominations (see line 52).

23. (a) In 2 Kinds of Wholly Third-Wave Networks.

These 100% Neocharismatic bodies have 253,936,000 members in 17,125 denominations/networks in 220 countries.

24. Non-White Indigenous Neocharismatics.

Apparent/seemingly/largely pentecostal or semipentecostal members of this 250-year-old movement of churches indigenous to Christians in non-White races across the world, and begun without reference to Western Christianity. Estimated in 1970 as 60% (rising by 1985 to 75%) of all members of the over 1,000 non-White/Third World indigenous denominations, which, though not all explicitly pentecostal, nevertheless have the main phenomenological hallmarks of pentecostalism (charismatic spirituality, oral liturgy, narrative witness/theology, dreams and visions, emphasis on filling with the Holy Spirit, healing by prayer, atmospheric communication [simultaneous audible prayer], emotive fellowship, etc.). These denominations are found in A.D. 2000 in 13,425 denominations in 210 different countries on all continents, with a total membership of 203,270,000. The case for enumerating adherents of these movements as pentecostals has been fully made by W. J. Hollenweger (most recently in "After Twenty Years' Research on Pentecostalism," *International Review of Mission* [Apr. 1986] and *Pentecostalism* [1997]). Note that the term *indigenous* as used here refers to the auto-origination of these movements, begun among non-White races without Western or White missionary support.

This whole category can be divided into various subcategories.

Indigenous Holiness-pentecostals, teaching three-crisis experience (conversion, sanctification, baptism in the Spirit), are found in some 60 denominations in 35 different countries. **Indigenous baptistic-pentecostals**, teaching two-crisis experience (conversion, baptism in the Spirit), exist in 70 denominations in 45 countries. **Indigenous Oneness-pentecostals**, practicing baptism in the name of Jesus only, are widespread in 60 denominations; the major such body with missions worldwide is the True Jesus Church (begun in China, 1917). The first such new denomination, a schism from the (mainly White) Assemblies of God (U.S.), was the Pentecostal Assemblies of the World (1916). These bodies are found in 38 countries today. **Indigenous pentecostal-apostolics**, who stress a complex hierarchy of living apostles, prophets, and other charismatic officials, have over 60 denominations in 18 countries. **Indigenous radical-pentecostals** are found in over 100 deliverance-pentecostal denominations in at least 40 countries and are expanding rapidly. Most of the mushrooming new youth churches, hotel churches, theater churches, cinema churches, store churches, and open-air churches are in this category. This category is also known as perfectionist-pentecostals, free pentecostals, deliverance-pentecostals, revivalist-pentecostals, teaching four-crisis experience including, variably, deliverance, ecstatic-confession, ascension, perfectionism, prophecy. They are found in over 40 denominations in more than 30 countries and are rapidly expanding.

25. African Indigenous Pentecostals/Charismatics.

Found in 60 countries and 9,300 denominations with 65 million members, 92 national councils of AICs, and the continent-wide Organization of African Instituted (formerly Independent) Churches, based in Nairobi, Kenya. Origins: 1864. An important historical note must be added here. In the year 1900 the mainline mission bodies in Africa (Catholic, Anglican, Protestant) regarded these believers as, at best, "nominal" Christians or "unaffiliated" Christians, and this is how they appear in this dictionary's Table 1 (for Nigeria, South Africa, etc.). Today they are classified (as they are here) as independent Neocharismatics.

26. Afro-Caribbean Pentecostals/Charismatics.

Begun in 1783 in Jamaica (Native Baptists, Revival Zionists, Shouters, Shakers, etc.), in 1860 in Trinidad and Tobago (West Indies Spiritual Baptist Churches, National Evangelical Spiritual Baptist Church, National Spiritual Baptist Council of Churches). Now in 420 denominations in 38 countries across the world.

27. Arab/Assyrian/Semitic Neocharismatics.

Only 130 denominations in 40 countries. Membership stands at 1.2 million.

28. Black American Independent Charismatics.

Only recently begun, with one large body: Full Gospel Baptist Churches Fellowship (New Orleans, U.S.); 10 denominations, 1.4 million members.

29. Black American Indigenous Pentecostals.

Black Christians in explicitly pentecostal denominations in 20 countries, indigenous to non-White races in that they were begun without outside Western or White missionary assistance or support. The largest is the Church of God in Christ (begun 1895). Most Pentecostal spokespersons in the U.S. view this group as an integral part of Classical Pentecostalism, although in this table we give this term a more restricted definition (see note on line 7). Our reasoning is that, seen in the total global perspective, this variety is far more accurately located as the archetype of global non-White pentecostalism. Furthermore, many Black pentecostals regard the terms *Pentecostal* and *Charismatic* as largely White in origin, and have traditionally preferred the term *sanctified*. Ninety denominations with 7.6 million members.

30. Black American Oneness Apostolics.

Some 150 denominations in 10 countries with 3 million members. Most belong to the Apostolic World Christian Fellowship (150 denominations).

31. Brazilian/Portuguese Grassroots Neocharismatics.

There were numerous early movements in Portuguese Africa (Angola): two prophetic movements, Nkimba and Kimpasi, had broken from Jesuit missions by 1656; later came the prophetess Fumaria and Donna Beatrice's attempt to found an independent Catholic church, for which King Pedro IV had her burned alive in 1706; Kiyoka (1872); Epikilipikili (1904); and others. By A.D. 2000 independent pentecostal bodies in Portuguese-speaking countries on five continents numbered 460 denominations with 23 million members in 20 countries.

32. Colored/Mixed-Race Indigenous Charismatics.

In four countries of Southern Africa, 70 denominations for Coloreds (*Christen Gemeente* and others).

33. Ethnic (Monoethnic) Pentecostal Churches.

In 20 denominations with 1.5 million members in 20 countries.

34. Filipino Indigenous Pentecostals/Charismatics.

Found in 380 denominations in 25 countries, with 6.7 million members; the earliest began in 1913.

35. Han Chinese Indigenous Pentecostals/Charismatics.

A strong tradition beginning in 1905, widespread by 1955, expanding rapidly throughout mainland China by 1982; by 1985, almost 25% of all Protestants were tongues-speakers. Estimates of the proportion of all Chinese Christians who are phenomenologically pentecostals/charismatics range from 50% to 85%, in large numbers and networks of de-facto independent pentecostal or charismatic churches. Total: 49 million members in 180 denominations in 58 countries.

36. Indian Indigenous Pentecostals/Charismatics.

With 16.6 million members in 580 denominations in 25 countries, including Europe and the U.S.

37. Indonesian Indigenous Pentecostals.

Over 6.7 million members in 170 major denominations in five countries.

38. Japanese Indigenous Pentecostals.

There are 50 denominations with 1.1 million adherents in 15 countries.

39. Korean Indigenous Pentecostals/Charismatics.

Begun 1910, there are now 170 denominations with 3.3 million members in 30 countries worldwide.

40. Latino-Hispanic Grassroots Believers.

There are 11.9 million believers in 990 denominations or networks in 24 countries. "Grassroots" churches is the name given in preference to Western terminology.

41. Messianic Hindu Believers in Christ.

Since 1921 five denominations or networks have arisen, now with 163,000 members.

42. Messianic Jewish Believers in Christ.

Some 2% of all Jews (350,000) are believers in Jesus Christ (Yeshua the Mashiach/Messiah), also known as Jewish Christians, Christian Jews, Hebrew Christians, or Messianic Jews (the latter being those who emphasize Jewish roots and rituals). Of the 150,000 Messianic Jews, 75% (110,000) identify themselves as charismatic, particularly in the 53 churches of the Union of Messianic Jewish Congregations (U.S.); other charismatics are found in Britain (London Messianic Fellowship), France (Paris), Italy, USSR (aided by Finnish Lutheran Jewish missions broadcasts), Argentina, and Israel (3,000, including Beth Emmanuel, Tel Aviv).

A smaller number of other Jewish charismatics are found in Pentecostal denominations (Assemblies of God with 37 centers in the U.S., International Church of the Foursquare Gospel, etc.), or in Anglican/Catholic/Protestant charismatic groupings and so are classified here under lines 16–18.

43. Messianic Muslim Believers in Christ.

The 126,000 believers in "Jesus mosques" are in two countries, but many more are incipient movements elsewhere.

44. Pacific/Oceanic Indigenous Charismatics.

Some 214,000 members in 70 denominations in 20 countries.

45. Red Indian/Amerindian Neo-pentecostals.

Over 530,000 members in three countries in four bodies, but not much growth or spreading elsewhere.

46. Vietnamese Indigenous Neocharismatics.

There are at least 230,000 believers in the Good News House Church Movement; they are faced with much opposition and persecution.

47. Other Asian Indigenous Neocharismatics.

Some 1.1 million believers in 130 denominations in 40 countries (Thailand, Malaysia, etc.).

48. Other Messianic Non-Christian Believers in Christ.

Some 200,000 believers in 20 denominations in 15 countries not covered by the above categories; most are hidden believers.

49. White-led Independent Postdenominationalists.

Independent charismatic and neocharismatic churches that either have separated from the Charismatic Renewal in parent mainline denominations (thus 50% of all Presbyterian charismatics in U.S. are known to have left to join these new churches) or have recently been founded independently (though from out of the same milieus), all being either independent congregations or in loose networks, and all being mainly or predominantly of White membership (Europeans, North Americans) or under overall White leadership or initiative. Total: 50 million members in 3,700 denominations in 210 countries.

50. European/American White-led Neo-Apostolics.

These number 41 million in 3,510 denominations or networks in 200 countries. Examples: House Church Movements in England (Restoration and five other major groupings), Scotland, Norway, Sweden (many, including Rhema Fellowship), Denmark, Hungary, Poland, France (several communities), Switzerland, Spain (Witnessing), the Netherlands (many), New Zealand, South Africa (many, including International Fellowship of Charismatic Churches, with 300 churches, Hatfield Christian Centre [162 churches], etc.), former Soviet Union/USSR (in Central Russia, Northern Russia, Ukraine, Baltic, Georgia, and others), and the U.S. (60,000 recently formed churches in several major groupings or networks, with some overlap: International Fellowship of Faith Ministries [2,000 churches], International Convention of Faith Churches and Ministries [495 churches; in Tulsa], Faith Christian Fellowship International [1,000 ordained ministers], Melodyland Christian Center, People of Destiny, International Communion of Charismatic Churches [former classical Pentecostals, very large, fastest-growing network in 1988], Network of Christian Ministries [Latter Rain emphasis], Fellowship of Christian Assemblies [101 churches], Maranatha Christian Churches [57 churches], Fellowship of Covenant Ministers and Churches [250 churches], Association of Vineyard Churches [200 churches, founder John Wimber; note that he and the churches have regarded themselves as Third-Wavers rather than Charismatics, though most observers hold the reverse is truer], National Leadership Conference, Charismatic Bible Ministries [1,500 ministers], Word Churches [Word of Faith Movement], Calvary Ministries International [200 churches], Local Covenant Churches [Shepherding], Rhema Ministerial Association [525 churches], International Ministers Forum [500 churches], Full Gospel Chaplaincy [3 million independent charismatics], Christ for the Nations [600 churches], Abundant Life Community Churches [25 churches], and others). This category also includes quasi-denominational networks, such as Full Gospel Fellowship of Churches and Ministers International (begun 1962; 425 churches). There are thus similar movements, related and unrelated, in 84% of all the countries of the world.

51. European White-led New Apostolics.

Origins: 1832 schism (Irvingites) in London ex-Church of Scotland (Presbyterian), stressing Catholic features, hierarchy of living apostles, glossolalia, and claiming that all the New Testament charismata have now been restored; Old Apostolics; 1863 formation of Universal Catholic Church (Germany), later renamed New Apostolic Church, emphasizing the gifts of the Holy Spirit including prophecy, tongues, interpretation of tongues, miraculous healing, sacraments, hierarchy of 48 living apostles (1970: 1,700,000 members worldwide; A.D. 2000: 9,600,000). Total countries involved: 48 in 1980, increasing to 180 by A.D. 2000.

52. (b) As % of 7 Kinds of Non-Third-Wave Denominations.

This category summarizes Neocharismatic individuals who are members of independent denominations or networks that are non-pentecostal/noncharismatic or even antipentecostal/anticharismatic. As shown in the *World Christian Database*, each such body is assigned a percentage estimating the size of its Neocharismatic members. Total in A.D. 2000: 41,468,700 in 925 denominations in 200 countries.

53. Independent Anglican Neocharismatics.

Some 1.7 million in 30 denominations claiming to be true Anglicans; in 80 countries since 1925.

54. Independent Protestant Neocharismatics.

Some 20.5 million in 450 denominations of Protestant origin, background, or ethos, in 180 countries since 1920.

55. Independent Catholic Neocharismatics.

Mainly within Old Catholic Churches in the Netherlands, U.S., and 10 other countries. At its origin in the Netherlands in 1723 at the Schism of Utrecht, the Jansenist

Church (later Old Catholic Church) specifically embraced "signs and wonders" (miracles, healings, supernatural signs, spiritual gifts).

56. Independent Orthodox Neocharismatics.
Some 580,000 since the 1666 origin in Russia of Old Believers; 10 denominations in 20 countries.

57. Nonhistorical Independent Neocharismatics.
Earliest manifestation: 1549 the underground movement in Japan, *Kakure Kirishitan* (Hidden Christians). 1995: 3.5 million Black neo-pentecostals within Black Baptist, Methodist, and other denominations in the independent megabloc in about 100 countries.

58. Isolated Radio/TV Neocharismatics.
Those in isolated regions with no denominations or churches, whose ongoing corporate Christian life derives only from foreign radio broadcasts: 188,000 in over 30 countries.

59. Hidden Non-Christian Believers in Christ.
Often termed NBBCs (non-baptized believers in Christ), these number over 13 million since 1800, in 280 networks.

60. Hidden Hindu Neocharismatics.
Some 9.7 million NBBCs mainly in India and three other countries.

61. Hidden Muslim Neocharismatics.
About 417,000 believers in 15 countries.

62. Hidden Buddhist Neocharismatics.
Some 2.1 million believers in 17 countries.

63. Hidden Jewish Neocharismatics.
Members are thought to number 250,000 in 50 groupings in 15 countries.

64. Hidden Other-Religionist Neocharismatics.
Some 1.1 million believers in 200 networks in 50 countries.

65. Doubly-Counted First/Second/Third Wavers.
This category, numbering several million persons, is difficult to assess because of differences in definition and enumeration procedures. An estimate may be obtained as the totals of lines 4–64 minus line 66. The category enumerates the growing number of believers and congregations who are enumerated as either Pentecostals (within the First Wave) or Charismatics (within the Second Wave), but who also are in addition regarded—or regard themselves—as Neocharismatics within the Third Wave. Many Methodist, Baptist, AG, and other congregations are in this position and thus are counted twice in our enumeration. The grand total on line 65 is therefore shown as a negative quantity in order to arrive at accurate overall totals. This category includes many African, Asian, and Latin American believers and many large, widely known or outstanding Third-World churches

and congregations belonging to non-pentecostal denominations founded by non-pentecostal or even antipentecostal mission boards from Europe and North America. Among the most prominent of such congregations are four from Korea: Sung Rak Baptist Church, Seoul (at 25,000 members the largest Southern Baptist–related congregation in the world until its secession in Sept. 1987); Central Evangelical Holiness Church, Seoul (at 6,000 members the largest Holiness congregation in the world); and the world's two largest Methodist congregations, in Inchon and Seoul (25,000 members each). All of these congregations exhibit charismatic and pentecostal phenomena.

66. Global Affiliated Pentecostals/Charismatics/Neocharismatics.
Sum of lines 5, 13, 22, minus line 65 (the Three Waves of Renewal).

67. Renewal Members on 7 Continents.
Ranked by size: (1) Latin America, (2) Asia, (3) Africa, (4) Northern America, (5) Europe, (6) Oceania, (7) Antarctica.

68. Renewal Members in Africa.
Total: 126,000,000 (12% Pentecostals, 25% Charismatics, 63% Neocharismatics).

69. Renewal Members in Antarctica.
Total: 400 (50% Catholics, 30% Protestants).

70. Renewal Members in Asia.
Total: 134,890,000 (5% Pentecostals, 16% Charismatics, 79% Neocharismatics).

71. Renewal Members in Europe.
Total: 37,569,000 (8% Pentecostals, 56% Charismatics, 36% Neocharismatics).

72. Renewal Members in Latin America.
Total: 141,433,000 (23% Pentecostals, 52% Charismatics, 24% Neocharismatics).

73. Renewal Members in Northern America.
Total: 79,600,000 (7% Pentecostals, 28% Charismatics, 65% Neocharismatics).

74. Renewal Members in Oceania.
Total: 4,266,000 (14% Pentecostals, 63% Charismatics, 24% Neocharismatics).

75. Renewal Members as % of Global Church Members.
Computed as line 66 divided by line 99, times 100.

76. Peripheral Constituents.
Not counted as Renewal members, but clearly related to or close to the Renewal are two more categories.

77. Quasi-Pentecostals.

This first category consists of Prepentecostals (of whom John Wesley is the archetype), and Postpentecostals (former members of Pentecostal denominations who have left to join such non-pentecostal mainline bodies as Anglicanism, Catholicism, Lutheranism, etc.).

78. Unaffiliated Believers Professing Renewal.

This use of the term *believers* refers to persons with pentecostal gifts or experience who are professing pentecostals/charismatics but who do not, or do not yet, belong to pentecostal or charismatic or third-wave organized churches or groups or communities or denominations. Large numbers become pentecostals/charismatics in personal experience several weeks, months, or even years before they find a church or group and get enrolled and are therefore enumerated. They can be estimated, as here, by careful comparison of polls of those professing with those affiliated (enrolled).

79. Wider Global Totals of Renewal.

Living persons associated with Renewal consisting of lines 66, 77, and 78.

80. Total All Renewal Believers Alive at Mid-Year.

It is important to remember that virtually all Pentecostal or Charismatic or Neocharismatic statistics collected, published, or quoted by members or observers are of living believers only and do not include believers who have just died or just been martyred. To balance this bias, line number 81 has been added here.

81. Renewal Believers Dying Since A.D. 1900.

These figures give a much truer picture of the size of the Renewal if one is speaking about the whole of the 20th century. The numbers on line 81 are arrived at by means of the following formula: $\{$death rate$/100$ x $(P_2 - P_1)\} / \{(P_2 / P_1)$ x $1 / (t_2 - t_1)\} - 1$, in which P_1 is the total of living believers initially at year t_1; P_2 is the total of living believers at end of year t_2; and the death rate is assumed to average 1% per year.

82. Total of All Renewal Believers Ever, Since A.D. 1900.

Calculated as lines 80 plus 81. By mid A.D. 2000 this total had passed 795 million.

83. Churches, Finance, Agencies, Workers.

All distinct organized local congregations, worship centers, parishes, fellowships, or groupings of all kinds, which are explicitly identified with or attached to the Renewal. *Megachurches:* A majority of the 150 or so largest megachurches (the world's largest single congregations, each with over 50,000 members) are pentecostal/charismatic. The largest Protestant church is Full Gospel Central Church, Seoul, Korea, with 600,000 members by 1988, and 800,000 by 1998.

84. Pentecostal Churches, Congregations (1st Wave).

Largest grouping: Assemblies of God (U.S. and overseas); churches excluding outstations numbered 77,976 in 1985, 92,355 in 1986 (a 15.6% per year increase). All denominations: 480,000 congregations.

85. Mainline Charismatic Prayer Groups (2nd Wave).

Growth of weekly groups: 10,000 in 1960, rising to 550,000 in A.D. 2000.

86. Catholic Charismatic Weekly Prayer Groups.

Growth of weekly groups: 2,185 (1970); 12,000 (1980); 90,000 (1990); 160,000 (2000).

87. Anglican and Protestant Charismatic Groups.

Some 250,000 regular prayer groups were meeting by A.D. 2000.

88. Independent Congregations, House Churches (3rd Wave).

Around 591,000 by A.D. 2000.

89. Personal Income of All Renewal Members, $ Per Year.

Defined as in the article "Silver and Gold Have I None," in *International Bulletin of Missionary Research* (Oct. 1983): 150. By A.D. 2000, personal income of all Renewal members was US $1,550 billion per year.

90. Renewal Members' Giving to All Christian Causes, $ Per Year.

By A.D. 2000 this amounted to at least US $30 billion per year.

91. Renewal Service Agencies.

National, countrywide, regional, or international bodies, parachurch organizations and agencies that assist or serve the churches but are not themselves denominations or church-planting mission bodies. Among the most significant categories are (a) Pentecostal agencies (missions, evangelism, publishing, etc.); (b) denominational charismatic agencies: Anglican Renewal Ministries (U.K.), Episcopal Renewal Ministries (U.S.), International Catholic Charismatic Renewal Services (Vatican City), National Service Committees for the Catholic Charismatic Renewal (in over 120 countries), and 100 more such bodies; (c) global mission agencies: SOMA, Advance, AIMS, and other missionary bodies serving the Charismatic Renewal; and (d) Third-World mission agencies: more than 500 locally organized and supported charismatic sending bodies. One of the fastest-growing varieties of renewal agency is TV production organizations, numbering over 500 in 1987 and 1,000 by A.D. 2000. Grand total by A.D. 2000: 4,000 agencies.

92. Renewal Institutions.

Major pentecostal/charismatic church-operated or -related institutions of all kinds, i.e., fixed centers with premises, plant, and permanent staff; excluding church buildings, worship centers, church headquarters or offices; including high schools, colleges, universities, medical centers, hospitals, clinics, presses, bookshops, libraries, radio/TV stations and studios, conference centers, study centers, research centers, seminaries, religious communities (monasteries, abbeys, convents, houses), etc. Many of these have been originated by Pentecostal bodies and a growing number by mainline Charismatics, and a vast mushrooming of new institutions has begun by Third-Wave networks and churches. But in countries where new initiatives have been prohibited or repressed (e.g., before 1989 in East Germany, Poland), thousands of traditionally Christian institutions have been infiltrated and virtually taken over by charismatics. *Charismatic covenant communities:* Since 1958 (Community of Jesus, Cape Cod, MA, now with 900 members) and 1965 (Episcopal Church of the Redeemer, Houston, TX), residential communities committed to intentional corporate charismatic life, service, and mission, mainly ecumenical or interdenominational, with married couples and families as well as celibates, have arisen in 50 countries across the world. Size varies from fewer than 20 persons each to 4,000 (Emmanuel Community, Paris, France, begun 1972). Total communities in 1987: 2,000 with over a quarter million members; rising to treble that number by 1998.

(For a very detailed survey, see P. Hocken, "The Significance of Charismatic Communities," in *Charismatic Renewal in the Churches,* ed. P. Elbert [1990]). Grand total by A.D. 2000: 14,000.

93. All Pentecostal/Charismatic Full-Time Workers.

Full-time church workers, pastors, clergy, ministers, evangelists, missionaries, executives, administrators, bishops, moderators, church leaders, etc. This line is the sum of lines 94 and 95. Grand total by A.D. 2000: 2,100,000.

94. Nationals: Pastors, Clergy, Evangelists, Etc.

Many ecumenical and evangelical parachurch agencies have 20% to 60% charismatics on staff. In the 2,000 or so Pentecostal agencies, virtually all staff are Pentecostal. Grand total by A.D. 2000: 1,933,000.

95. Aliens: Foreign Missionaries.

These include Pentecostals and the following varieties of Charismatics and Neocharismatics (renewed in the Spirit) in 1985: 25% of all Anglican foreign missionaries, 20% of all RCs, 40% of all Protestants (60% of WEC, 42% of ABCIM, etc.). By A.D. 2000 these figures are likely to have increased at least to 50% of Anglicans, 25% of RCs, 50% of Protestants, and 90% of Third-World missionaries. Grand total by A.D. 2000: 167,000.

96. The Context of World Evangelization.

This last section is added to illustrate what has always been the focus and goal of the Renewal as a whole.

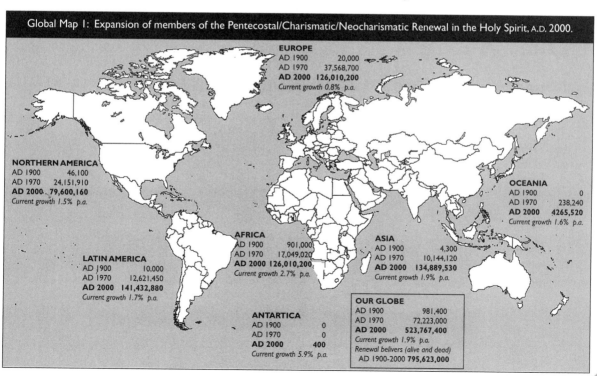

Global Map 1: Expansion of members of the Pentecostal/Charismatic/Neocharismatic Renewal in the Holy Spirit, A.D. 2000.

EUROPE
AD 1900   20,000
AD 1970   37,568,700
AD 2000 126,010,200
Current growth 0.8% p.a.

NORTHERN AMERICA
AD 1900   46,100
AD 1970   24,151,910
AD 2000 79,600,160
Current growth 1.5% p.a.

OCEANIA
AD 1900   0
AD 1970   238,240
AD 2000 4265,520
Current growth 1.6% p.a.

AFRICA
AD 1900   901,000
AD 1970   17,049,020
AD 2000 126,010,200
Current growth 2.7% p.a.

ASIA
AD 1900   4,300
AD 1970   10,144,120
AD 2000 134,889,530
Current growth 1.9% p.a.

LATIN AMERICA
AD 1900   10,000
AD 1970   12,621,450
AD 2000 141,432,880
Current growth 1.7% p.a.

ANTARTICA
AD 1900   0
AD 1970   0
AD 2000   400
Current growth 5.9% p.a.

OUR GLOBE
AD 1900   981,400
AD 1970   72,223,000
AD 2000   523,767,400
Current growth 1.9% p.a.
Renewal belivers (alive and dead)
AD 1900-2000 **795,623,000**

97. Global Population.

In mid 2000: 6,055,049,000.

98. Christians (All Varieties).

In mid 2000: 1,999,564,000.

99. Affiliated Church Members (Baptized).

Persons (adults and children) on the rolls of the churches and so of organized Christianity. In mid 2000: 1,888,439,000.

100. Non-Christians.

In mid 2000: 4,055,485,000.

101. Unevangelized Persons.

Total persons in the world who have never heard the name of Jesus Christ and remain unaware of Christianity, Christ, and the gospel. Total in mid 2000: 1,629,375,000.

102. World Evangelization Global Plans Since A.D. 30.

Grand total of all distinct plans and proposals for accomplishing world evangelization made by Christians since A.D. 30. (Most of these are described in *World Christian Encyclopedia* [2001], Part 24, "GeoStrategies," with their historical context in Part 2, "CosmoChronology." All global plans [770 by 1987, rising to 1,500 by A.D. 2000] are listed, enumerated, described, analyzed, and interpreted in Part 24 also.)

■ **Bibliography:** A. O. Atiemo, *The Rise of the Charismatic Movement in the Mainline Churches in Ghana* (1993) ▪ D. B. Barrett, "A Survey of the 20th-Century Pentecostal/Charismatic Renewal in the Holy Spirit, with Its Goal of World Evangelization," *International Bulletin of Missionary Research* 12 (3, July 1988) ▪ M. Berg and P. Pretiz, *Spontaneous Combustion: Grass-roots Christianity, Latin American Style* (1996) ▪ R. J. Bord and J. E. Faulkner, *The Catholic Charismatics: The Anatomy of a Modern Religious Movement* (1983) ▪ S. M. Burgess and G. B. McGee, eds., *Dictionary of Pentecostal and Charismatic Movements* (1988) ▪ E. Cantú and J. A. Ortega, eds., *Historia de la Asamblea Apostólica de la Fe en Cristo Jesus* (1966)
■ N. H. Cliff, *The Life and Theology of Watchman Nee, Including a Study of the Little Flock Movement* (1994) ▪ H. Cox, *Fire from Heaven: The Rise of Pentecostal Spirituality and the Reshaping of Religion in the Twenty-First Century* (1995) ▪ R. Dominguez, *Pioneros de Pentecostés*, 3 vols. (1990) ▪ P. Elbert, ed., *Faces of Renewal: Studies in Honor of Stanley M. Horton* (1988) ▪ C. L. d'Epinay, *Haven of the Masses: A Study of the Pentecostal Movement in Chile* (1969) ▪ M. Gaxiola-Gaxiola, *The Serpent and the Dove: The History of the Apostolic Church of the Faith in Christ Jesus in Mexico, 1914–1968* (1969) ▪ M. Guillen, *Historia del Concilio Latino Americano de Iglesias Cristianas* (1982) ▪ W. J. Hollenweger, *Pentecostalism: Origins and Development Worldwide* (1997) ▪ C. E. Jones, *The Charismatic Movement: A Guide to the Study of Neo-Pentecostalism with Emphasis on Anglo-American Sources*, 2 vols. (1995) ▪ idem, *A Guide to the Study of the Pentecostal Movement*, 2 vols. (1983) ▪ J. A. B. Jongeneel et al., eds., *Pentecost, Mission and Ecumenism: Essays on Intercultural Theology* (1992) ▪ P. F. Loret de Mola, "Origins, Development and Perspectives of La Luz del Mundo," *Religion* 25 (1995) ▪ L. G. McClung, "Readings in the Church Growth Dynamics of the Missionary Expansion of the Pentecostal Movement" (thesis, Fuller, 1984) ▪ K. McDonnell, *Presence, Power, Praise: Documents on the Charismatic Renewal*, 3 vols. (1980) ▪ P. G. Mansfield, *As by a New Pentecost: The Dramatic Beginnings of the Catholic Charismatic Renewal* (1992) ▪ D. Martin, *Tongues of Fire: The Explosion of Protestantism in Latin America* (1990) ▪ J. Napier, *Charismatic Challenge: Four Key Questions* (1995) ▪ R. Nauta, "Pentecostal Churches and Nicaraguan Politics," *Exchange* (Apr. 1994) ▪ J. E. Orr, *The Flaming Tongue: The Impact of 20th Century Revivals* (1973) ▪ K. Poewe, ed., *Charismatic Christianity as a Global Culture* (1994) ▪ C. M. Robeck Jr., ed., *Charismatic Experiences in History* (1985) ▪ R. P. Spittler, ed., *Perspectives on the New Pentecostalism* (1976) ▪ H. V. Synan, *The Holiness-Pentecostal Tradition: Charismatic Movements in the Twentieth Century* (1997) ▪ T. I. J. Urresti, *Carisma e institución en la renovación carismática* (1979) ▪ C. P. Wagner, *The Third Wave of the Holy Spirit: Encountering the Power of Signs and Wonders Today* (1988) ▪ A. Walker, *Restoring the Kingdom: The Radical Christianity of the House Church Movement* (1988).

■ D. B. Barrett; T. M. Johnson

PART III
Dictionary

CHURCH OF GOD IN CHRIST

THANK GOD
FOR
PROGRESSIVE LEADERSHIP
WITH VISION / PURPOSE

BISHOP C. H. MASON,
FOUNDER
September 8, 1866-1961

BISHOP CHANDLER D. OWENS
1st Asst. Presiding Bishop

BISHOP C. L. ANDERSON
2nd Asst. Presiding Bishop

BISHOP LOUIS HENRY FORD
Presiding Bishop

Bishop	Bishop	Bishop	Bishop	Bishop	Bishop	Bishop	Bishop	Bishop
J. Neaul Haynes	P. A. Brooks	O. T. Jones	Roy L. Winbush	Leroy Anderson	Charles Blake	L. E. Willis	Ithiel Clemmon	G. E. Patterson

BISHOP W. W. HAMILTON
GENERAL SECRETARY

BISHOP FRANK ELLIS
CHAIRMAN, GENERAL ASSEMBLY

BISHOP J. H. SHERMAN
CHAIRMAN, BOARD OF BISHOPS

SOLOMON WILLIAMS
CHAIRMAN, ELDERS COUNCIL

ELDER A. Z. HALL
SECRETARY TO THE PRESIDING BISHOP

BISHOP W. L. PORTER
COORDINATOR/DIRECTOR-SPECIAL ASSISTANT TO THE PRESIDING BISHOP

A page from the brochure for the 87th International Holy Convocation of the Church of God in Christ (1994).

A

ABRAHAM, K. E. (1899–1974). Leader of India Pentecostal Church (IPC). K. E. Abraham was born in Puthenkavu, Kerala, India, on Mar. 1, 1899. His parents were members of the Jacobite (Eastern Orthodox) church. He accepted Jesus Christ as his Savior at the age of seven in a Sunday school class at a Mar Thoma church. (Mar Thoma churches in India were allegedly founded by Mar [Bishop] Thomas, who is believed to have brought Christianity to India and to have been martyred in Madras in the 1st cent. A.D.) Abraham started his career as a school teacher but was called into the ministry. On Apr. 20, 1923, he received the baptism of the Holy Spirit and began a Full Gospel ministry. Several churches were born through his sacrificial work. In 1924 the group of churches Abraham founded took on the name South India Pentecostal Church. For a time Abraham worked in cooperation with the Assemblies of God and Church of God missionaries, but in 1930 he decided to keep his work indigenous.

Although Abraham had been working as a Christian minister since 1923, he was not ordained until Mar. 6, 1930, by the leader of the Ceylon pentecostal movement, Pastor Paul, on a visit to Kerala.

As the number of churches increased all over India, the South India Pentecostal Church was renamed the India Pentecostal Church and was registered with the Indian government under that name in 1935.

Pastor Abraham started the Hebron Bible School in 1930; *Zion Trumpet,* a monthly magazine in the Malayalam language, in 1936; and a free English language school in 1939. The Bible school and the magazine still function.

Abraham wrote several books, among them *The Tabernacle* (in Swedish), *The Baptism in the Spirit, Seven Paradises, IPC's Early Years,* and *Babylon the Great* (all in Malayalam). His autobiography is one of the best primary sources of pentecostal history in India.

K. E. Abraham passed away on Dec. 9, 1974, and is buried near the IPC headquarters in Kumband, Kerala. His elder son, T. S. Abraham, is currently the general secretary of the IPC. His second son, the late Oommen Abraham, migrated to America, where he pastored several immigrant churches. He is credited with founding the largest Asian pentecostal conference in North America, the ▸Pentecostal Conference of North American Keralites.

■ **Bibliography:** K. E. Abraham, *A Humble Servant of Jesus Christ: Pastor K. E. Abraham's Autobiography* (1965) ■ H. G. Varghese, *K. E. Abraham: An Apostle from Modern India* (1974).

■ T. K. Matthew

ABRAMS, MINNIE F. (1859–1912). Missionary to India, early pentecostal missiologist. Born in Wisconsin in 1859 to Franklin and Julia Abrams, Minnie Abrams was reared on a farm near Mapleton, MN. She graduated from Mankato Normal School and became a school teacher. She attended the University of Minnesota an additional two years before heeding the call to the mission field. In 1885 Abrams enrolled in the first class of the Chicago Training School for City, Home, and Foreign Missions, founded by Lucy Rider Meyer, a leader in the emerging Methodist deaconess movement. Abrams, inspired by J. Hudson Taylor, determined to be a "faith missionary," trusting God for her needs. Upon graduation, the Woman's Foreign Missionary Society commissioned her as a Methodist "deaconess-missionary." Abrams set sail for Bombay, India, in 1887, where she helped establish and supervise a boarding school for daughters of church members. Yearning to minister beyond the walls of the mission compound, Abrams studied the Marathi language to be able to engage in direct evangelism. After 10 years of waiting, she received permission to become a full-time evangelist.

In 1898 Abrams joined ▸Pandita Ramabai at the Mukti Mission, a school and home for widows and famine victims. Abrams, influenced by Wesleyan and Higher Life teachings, sought restoration of apostolic power. Her faith was bolstered by reports of revivals in Australia in 1903 and in Wales in 1904–5. By June 1905 news of revivals with unusual spiritual phenomena in Welsh Presbyterian missions in India sparked revival at the Mukti Mission. A dormitory matron who believed she saw flames nearly doused a Mukti resident who had been Spirit baptized with "fire," and the mission became a center for repentance and revival. Abrams authored *The Baptism of the Holy Ghost and Fire* in the spring of 1906, describing the revival and its theological underpinnings. This first edition encouraged believers to seek the Spirit baptism for purity of life and power to evangelize. Several months into the Indian revival, instances of speaking in tongues were reported at Manmad in June 1906, in Bombay in July 1906, and at the Mukti Mission by Dec. 1906. Abrams taught that the gift of prophecy, not tongues, was for preaching, and that the former was the more valuable gift. In the second edition of her book, published in Dec. 1906, Abrams included the restoration of tongues. She sent a copy of her book to Maria Hoover (Mrs. ▸Willis C. Hoover) in Valparaiso, Chile, a classmate at the Chicago Training School. Reports of the Mukti revival helped fuel the growth of "pentecostal Methodism" in that country.

▸A. G. Garr, a missionary visiting India in Jan. 1907 who had been to ▸Azusa Street, taught that the uniform "Bible evidence" of Spirit baptism is tongues speech. In a 1908 letter published in *Confidence* (England), Abrams registered her disagreement with Garr's formula, noting that "while others of us feel that … all may and should receive this sign, yet we dare not say that no one is Spirit-baptized who has not received this sign." Furthermore, she believed theological diversity on this issue should not bar fellowship: "We see the same gifts and graces and power for service in those who hold different beliefs, and, so far as I know, we are as yet working in love and unity for the spread of this mighty work of the Holy Spirit."

Abrams left India in 1908 for a promotional tour in America. She preached at Carrie Judd Montgomery's Home of Peace in Oakland, CA; Upper Room Mission in Los Angeles; Stone Church in Chicago; the regional camp meeting at Homestead, PA; and the headquarters of the Christian Worker's Union in Massachusetts. Desiring to push further into unreached northern India, Abrams formed the Bezaleel Evangelistic Mission, the only known pentecostal women's missionary society. She recruited six Spirit-baptized single women to accompany her on the return trip. Prior to returning to India, Abrams had a premonition that her missionary work would be ended within two years. Northern India's poor roads, heat, and resistance to the gospel caused Abrams to succumb to blackwater fever. She died on Dec. 2, 1912, two years to the day she had disembarked in Bombay on her return voyage.

A rare photograph of Minnie Abrams with Pandita Ramabai.

■ **Bibliography:** M. F. Abrams, "Battles of a Faith Missionary," *LRE* (Mar. 1910) ■ idem, "Brief History of the Latter Rain Revival of 1910," *Word and Work* (May 1910) ■ G. B. McGee, "Baptism of the Holy Ghost and Fire! The Revival Legacy of Minnie F. Abrams of India," *Enrichment* (Summer 1998) ■ idem, "'Latter Rain' Falling in the East: Early 20th-Century Pentecostalism in India and the Debate over Speaking in Tongues," *Church History* 68 (Sept. 1999) ■ "Minnie F. Abrams, of India," *Missionary Review of the World* (Feb. 1913).   ■ G. B. McGee; D. J. Rodgers

ACTS 29 MINISTRIES Acts 29 Ministries grew out of what was once known as the Episcopal Charismatic Fellowship (ECF). The ministry saw its genesis at a gathering of more than 300 Episcopal clergy at St. Matthew's Cathedral in Dallas, TX, in Feb. 1973. The meeting, the brainchild of ▸Dennis Bennett and Wesley (Ted) Nelson, called together all Episcopal clergy interested in the charismatic renewal and enabled them to share the excitement produced by their common experience of the baptism of the Holy Spirit. Until that conference the extent of the outpouring of the Spirit in the Episcopal Church was largely unknown.

Speakers at the Dallas event included William C. Frey, Robert B. Hall, and George W. Stockhowe Jr. Most of the clergy attending were surprised and elated to find that they were not alone in their Spirit-filled experiences; the conference statement reflected this joy: "We were drawn together by a shared awareness … and the power and love of the Risen Christ … and the power and love of the Holy Spirit." It was during this conference that the ECF was established as the unofficial renewal agency of the Episcopal Church; Fr. Nelson was appointed president of the board of directors, and Robert H. Hawn Sr. was made executive secretary.

The Dallas conference also birthed something that would help define the ministry in the years to come—*Acts 29* magazine. The conference report was issued in booklet form under the *Acts 29* name. For the next decade, *Acts 29* was printed as a newsletter. It served as the basic communication device for those who identified themselves as charismatics and members of the ECF nationwide. An effort at regionalized ECF activities languished for lack of clergy involvement.

The ECF was headquartered for three years in Denver, CO, and for two years after that in Winter Park, FL. During this time it launched a series of charismatic conferences around the country and became one of the sponsors for the large ecumenical conference held in Kansas City, MO, in 1977. This conference and others focused mainly on conversion to Jesus Christ, the gifts of the Holy Spirit, and daily life in the Spirit. They also served as an avenue for the clergy and laity who attended them to experience the baptism of the Holy Spirit.

In 1974 Tod W. Ewald was elected president of the executive board. At that time the ECF changed its thrust from leadership to servanthood. The decision was based on a belief that the ECF should not direct but rather assist the Episcopal Church in renewal. This, they believed, would prevent them from being perceived as an elitist organization. During its formative years, however, a commonly accepted vision for the ECF never emerged.

A new direction did emerge in 1977. At this time the ECF executive board ratified the vision that they should be dedicated to fostering parish renewal, believing that if charismatic renewal was ever to be useful to the church, it should be the catalyst for the renewal of individual parishes. This move from personal renewal to corporate renewal bore fruit in subsequent years. Thus, the role began to shift toward a leadership more proactive in the process of renewal; in 1977 ›Everett L. (Terry) Fullam, who had been present at the Dallas meeting, was elected president of the executive board.

In 1978 two other changes took place. First, ECF's name was changed to Episcopal Renewal Ministries (ERM) to reflect the actual ministry in which the organization was engaged and to avoid the misunderstandings and multiple meanings of the word *charismatic.* Second, when Fr. Hawn resigned to become part of a religious community, the ERM executive board appointed Charles M. Irish to succeed Hawn as the ministry's national coordinator. He assumed this work while continuing to serve as rector of St. Luke's Episcopal Church in Bath, OH.

In 1979, 14 conferences on parish renewal were conducted throughout the U.S. Scores of similar conferences were conducted in subsequent years. This not only launched ERM into the parish renewal ministry but also established a model that spread throughout a number of denominations both in the U.S. and abroad.

As part of its emerging role, ERM changed from serving a constituency of like-minded people to serving the entire Episcopal Church. Its motto became: "Dedicated to the renewal of people and parishes through Apostolic teaching, biblical preaching, historic worship and charismatic experience."

By 1977 only a handful of Episcopal parishes had been fully affected by the charismatic renewal—these were so-called lighthouse churches. Many Episcopalians, converted and filled with the Holy Spirit, found that they were unwelcome in their own parishes and thus discovered new homes in pentecostal and charismatic churches.

The efforts of ERM toward parish renewal helped change this, and by 1988 more than 400 of the 7,800 parishes in the Episcopal Church were fully involved in renewal. In addition, another 800 were beginning to change. Laity involved in renewal were estimated to number more than 300,000.

In 1986 Fr. Irish resigned from St. Luke's Church to become the first full-time national coordinator for ERM. It was at this time and through the encouragement of Truro Episcopal Church in Fairfax, VA, that the ministry moved its national headquarters to Fairfax. By this time ERM's work expanded to include clergy placement, conference planning, networking of clergy, parish renewal, and distribution of books and tapes. ERM also helped sponsor the second ›North American Congress on the Holy Spirit and World Evangelization, held in New Orleans, LA, in 1987.

In 1990, seeking a more permanent home, ERM purchased the Evergreen Conference Center in Evergreen, CO, which enabled the ministry to host conferences in a retreat environment in the Rocky Mountains. The center also served as the administrative headquarters of the ministry.

Fr. Irish retired as national coordinator in 1992. Charles B. Fulton Jr., then rector of St. Peter's Church in Jacksonville, FL, was chosen to succeed Fr. Irish. One of his first decisions was to relocate the ministry one last time, to Atlanta, GA, since most Episcopalians live east of the Mississippi River. The Atlanta location also placed the ministry in a thriving metropolitan setting with a transportation hub. This would become increasingly important in the coming years as ERM became strategically identified as a conference-based ministry.

In 1994 the ministry called Fred L. Goodwin to the staff as rector of national ministries. His primary function was to oversee the development of new curriculum, as well as to

Episcopalians gathered at the first meeting of the Episcopal Renewal Ministries, St. Matthew's Episcopal Cathedral, Dallas, in 1973.

increase the reach of the ministry through its conferences. That year also saw a notable change in *Acts 29*, as the magazine became a full-color publication.

The year 1997 saw two key changes. First, the ministry changed its name to Acts 29 Ministries. At the same time the board adopted a new vision statement: "A premier Christian resource force for evangelism, discipleship and ministry in the power of the Holy Spirit." Thus, the ministry no longer saw itself simply as a *factor* for renewal in the Episcopal Church; rather, it took on the challenge to become a *force* for the work of Jesus Christ through the power of the Spirit even beyond the bounds of the Episcopal community. In 1997 the ministry planned and executed more than 140 events that ministered to more than 20,000 people.

The 1990s also saw Acts 29 Ministries develop another key thrust—youth ministry. The first events were held near the former headquarters in Fairfax, VA. Subsequent conferences were held at the Ridgecrest and Lake Junaluska conference centers in the Smoky Mountains of North Carolina. In 1998 YouthQuake Ministries was formed as the official youth outreach arm of Acts 29 Ministries.

■ C. M. Irish; C. B. Fulton Jr.

ADAMS, JOHN A. D. (1844–1936).

John Adams emigrated from Scotland with his parents to New Zealand as part of the first wave of settlers in the new Otago settlement. After working at a number of different occupations, he entered the legal profession and gained admission to the bar in 1874. Although Adams was a member of the prominent Hanover Street Baptist Church in his early years, he later left to join the Methodist Church. The visit to N.Z. of ▸John Alexander Dowie, who stayed in Adams's home while in Dunedin in 1888, appears to have influenced him. The issue of divine healing eventually led to Adams's secession from the Methodist Church in 1900. Adams then opened his large home for prayer meetings, and he and others bought a block of land later that year for the building of the Roslyn City Road Mission. This early pentecostal assembly, which opened in 1903, modeled itself after the Plymouth Brethren, with the difference that there was "perfect liberty for the exercise of spiritual gifts."

Adams was a clear and articulate writer and wrote numerous books, pamphlets, and articles dealing with evangelical and pentecostal theology. He was also a prolific letter writer to the public newspapers, vigorously defending the pentecostal movement in the controversies that accompanied its arrival in N.Z. Adams ultimately became an elder of the Pentecostal Church of New Zealand upon its formation after the campaigns of ▸Smith Wigglesworth in 1922–23 and 1923–24. He made several overseas journeys for religious work and gave considerable time to the development of pentecostal work throughout N.Z.

■ **Bibliography:** J. E. Worsfold, *A History of the Charismatic Movements in New Zealand* (1974). ■ B. Knowles

ADINI-ABALA, ALEXANDER (c. 1927–97).

Born at Aru, in what is now the northeastern part of the Democratic Republic of Congo, near the border with Uganda. In the late 1950s Adini-Abala, who was in the Congo at the time, came across some literature advertising T. L. Osborn crusades in Kenya. Because he believed that this white man was spreading religious deception, he persuaded others of his youth gang to travel with him to Kenya to teach the white man a lesson. They took with them the grandmother of one of the gang, a woman who had been blind for many years.

The plan was to attack the preacher when he prayed for the blind woman, because they supposed that nothing would happen. As T. L. Osborn prayed, the woman was immediately healed and began to scream with excitement. Alexander believed that God was going to strike him down and ran from the meeting to hide. The next day he went to the crusade and gave his life to Christ.

After a very short time of Bible instruction, Adini-Abala began to preach. He started in Mombasa and set out on a preaching tour that led him inland throughout the towns of Kenya, Uganda, Rwanda, Burundi, and Tanzania. As he went, many were healed, delivered, and converted. When he attempted to return to Congo, he was arrested and deported. He struck up a close friendship with missionaries Bud Sickler and Art Dodzweit of the ▸Elim Fellowship (Lima, NY), who encouraged him and gave him advice.

In 1967 Adini-Abala flew with Art Dodzweit to Kinshasa and after reestablishing residency began to minister. He began by preaching from the traffic circles, where he was ridiculed; but two of the city's best-known street people, both of whom were demon possessed, were delivered and converted. Subsequently, Adini-Abala preached while the two new converts gave their testimonies. Within a short time others were being healed and saved.

T. L. Osborn held a crusade in Kinshasa in 1969, at which Adini-Abala, with ▸Jacques Vernaud (AG–France now AG–U.S.), was deeply involved as an interpreter. Osborn's rallying cry during the crusade was "God is good." This slogan translated into Lingala, the lingua franca of the Kinshasa area, was *"Nzambe malamu."* This became the name of the new churches that were started by Adini-Abala. The official name of this group is *Fraternité Evangélique de Pentecôte en Afrique: Congo* (FEPACO; The Pentecostal Evangelical Fellowship in Africa: Congo).

A bad automobile accident left Adini-Abala severely crippled, so that for eight years he walked with the help of crutches. He became depressed, resigned from the leadership of the church, and was ready to give up and return to his home village when the Lord appeared to him in a dream saying, "I have many people in this city. Forget about your leg and have a healing crusade. The willing and obedient shall eat the good of the land!" In the face of ridicule from the elders, Alexander went ahead and planned a crusade. During the first meeting, while he was praying for the sick, he himself was healed. This gave him great encouragement and purpose to evangelize throughout Congo and elsewhere.

Nzambe Malamu churches have been planted throughout Congo/Kinshasa, in neighboring Congo/Brazzaville, the Central African Republic, as well as in other, non-African countries by members from Africa. There are an estimated 350 churches in Kinshasa and 4,000 others in the Democratic Republic of Congo, with more than 500,000 adherents. Adini-Abala died in 1997 at age 70, after a ministry that was not without controversy. The mantle of leadership of the movement has been passed to his son, Pefa Adini-Abala.

■ **Bibliography:** B. Dodzweit, e-mails to D. J. Garrard, Apr. 1 and 5, 1998 ■ D. J. Garrard, unpub. private papers ■ R. Steele, *Plundering Hell* (1984).   ■ D. J. Garrard

AFRICAN INDEPENDENT CHURCHES See AFRICAN INITIATED CHURCHES.

AFRICAN INITIATED CHURCHES (AICS) IN DIASPORA—EUROPE

AICs is a collective name designating churches founded and led by Africans on and outside the African continent. These churches include prophetic-charismatic churches, such as Aladura and Zionist churches, and pentecostal churches, such as Deeper Life Christian Ministry and Church of Pentecost, all of which were founded through the initiatives of African charismatic figures.

The AICs represent a variety of religious experience that made inroads into the European religious scene in the wake of the increasing influx of legal and illegal African immigrants from the post–WWII era. Owing to deteriorating economic conditions, political instability, and a preference for further studies abroad, most migrants left their homes in a quest for the "golden fleece" or to make new homes. Most of these migrants, especially those from West Africa (Nigeria, Ghana, etc.), took their religion with them to Europe. These groups are especially noticeable in countries such as Great Britain, the Netherlands, France, Germany, Austria, and Italy.

The emergence and proliferation of the AICs is the result of rejection of, and even hostility toward, Christian African migrants on the part of the host communities—including dissatisfaction with European churches and their failure to meet the socioreligious needs of Africans, social deprivation, racism, and the urge to repackage and transmit Christianity to what hitherto was the home of missionary Christianity.

There are two kinds of AICs: those that have an affiliation with, or are daughter churches of, a mother church with origins and headquarters in Africa, and those that owe their existence solely to the African diaspora in Europe. The latter remain autonomous, localized, without branches elsewhere, self-reliant, and with little or no access to any wider network.

Most AICs started as house meetings of students and grew into larger religious communities. The religious life of most African Christian immigrants lacks a public character, especially in the earlier years of an AIC, due to the absence of a traditional church building. Membership increase is usually followed by a change from house fellowship to renting or leasing a hall or abandoned church building for worship. Financially strong AICs have either leased or purchased property to establish a permanent venue. Membership is largely African but with a sprinkling of non-Africans. Due to this mixed composition, services are usually multilingual. Problems encountered vary from lack of accommodations, a negative attitude of neighbors toward the style and mode of worship, racism, unemployment, language barriers, and a general feeling of insecurity on the part of members in a racially and culturally hostile environment.

The core of these Christians' spirituality lies in the emphasis on prayer, healing, prophecy, and other charismatic manifestations as a means to solve all existential problems. The diaspora experience is germane to the belief of African Christians in Europe and provides the context of their religious experiences. They are involved in social services, such as establishing day-care centers for children; caring for the sick, needy, and homeless; and educating young people. Thus, they establish a supportive socioreligious network for the benefit of members as well as for the overall well-being of society.

The role of community is emphasized in their organizational structure, beliefs, and praxis. Thus, AICs are "a place to feel at home" or "a home away from home" for their members. There is growing interest in building extensive ecumenical networks in Europe and beyond, reflecting an increasing internationalization.

■ **Bibliography:** C. Hill, *Black Churches: West Indian and African Sects in Britain* (1971) ■ R. Kerridge, *The Storm Is Passing Over: A Look at Black Churches in Britain* (1995) ■ H. Meldgaard and J. Aagaard, eds., *New Religious Movements in Europe* (1997) ■ G. Ter Haar, *Halfway to Paradise: African Christians in Europe* (1997) ■ T. J. Thompson, "African Independent Churches in Britain: An Introductory Survey," in R. Towler, ed., *New Religions and the New Europe* (1995).   ■ A. U. Adogame

AHN, SEEN OK (KIM)

(1924–). Influential pastor, educator, administrator, conference speaker, founder of private schools and a seminary, mission strategist, pentecostal preacher. She was born in North Korea and worked as an independent leader from Japan with her husband, Dr. Kee Seuk Ahn. After moving to South Korea during the Korean War in 1950, she and her husband founded an orphanage for war orphans, which developed into a public school after the war. She founded Daesung Christian School Foundation, which began with one junior high school and has now grown to six schools (three junior high schools and three senior high schools) in Korea. Currently (1999) there are more than 400 teachers and 8,000 students.

In 1966, at the age of 42, Seen Ok Ahn went to the U.S. to be trained as a full-time minister, leaving her husband, five children, and the school in Korea behind. She studied at ʼL.I.F.E. Bible College and met ʼRolf McPherson, president of the ʼInternational Church of the Foursquare Gospel and brought the Foursquare Church to Korea. She founded Taejon Foursquare Gospel Church in 1970, which grew to over 3,000 members, the largest church pastored by a woman in Korea.

Seen Ok Ahn worked in prison ministry for more than 20 years. She majored in economics in college and mostly ministered to the leftists in the prisons. Hundreds have been converted through her prison ministry. To preach the gospel to a socialistic country, she founded Shinkwang Agricultural Junior College on Sahkarin Island, Russia, in 1988. Bible and theology are taught in addition to agricultural techniques. More than 400 students have graduated from this college. She has also sent missionaries to the Philippines.

In 1990 Seen Ok Ahn founded the Youth Mission Training Institute (YMTI) to train young men and women with the love of Christ. It is an intensive training course that lasts for four days and three nights. More than 15,000 people had been trained by 1999. Many of the trainees have dedicated their lives to the Lord's work. Ahn sent 25 leaders abroad for leadership training, and when they returned to Korea, she founded the Gospel Theological Seminary in 1996.

Seen Ok Ahn is a woman of prayer and fasting, and she emphasizes prayer to her congregation. Since her ordination in 1970, she has never had supper. In 1984, at the age of 60, she did a 40-day fasting prayer. In addition, she normally fasts 10 days a month. She founded Taesung Prayer Mountain on 333 acres of land in 1975 to teach believers about the life of prayer. She used to lead revival meetings several times a year, and God has performed many miracles throughout her ministry.

■ **Bibliography:** Wan Suk Do, *The Way God Trains the Young People* (1997) ■ Yeol Soo Eim, *The Life and Ministry of Rev. Seen Ok Ahn* (1995) ■ idem, "The Worldwide Expansion of Foursquare Gospel" (diss., Fuller Sem., 1986).   ■ Y. S. Eim

ALAMO, TONY (1934–) and **SUSAN** (192?–82). Tony Alamo was born Bernie Lazar and raised a Jew. He moved from career to career, spending time as a singer, a health-studio operator, and a music promoter. He claims that one day in 1964 in an attorney's office, as he was about to close a big deal, he heard the voice of God telling him to proclaim to all those present that Jesus was coming back soon. Not long after that, he felt he was filled with the Holy Spirit and called to apostleship in the same way the original Twelve had been.

In the mid–1960s Alamo married Susan, who was already preaching in a variety of churches. The Alamos claim to have started the Jesus Movement when they began evangelizing street kids on Sunset and Hollywood Boulevards in Los Angeles. There they founded, in 1969, the Tony and Susan Alamo Christian Foundation Church and Seminary, which specialized in outreach to the down-and-out. During this time Alamo claims to have received other visions of Jesus in which he was told to teach the word incessantly. On the outskirts of Saugus, CA, the Alamos created a community of which they were the undisputed heads. New converts were moved right in without so much as a visit home, creating much anxiety for worried parents,

In the late 1970s the ministry expanded to Georgia Ridge, AR. Other outposts were established in Tennessee, Arizona, Florida, Oklahoma, and New York. The Alamos expanded their communities and opened a grocery store, a restaurant, a service station, a hog farm, and a trucking firm. They also created a line of glitzy western wear that they manufactured and sold. Followers who chose to join the communities contributed all their earnings to the church, which in turn provided for all the individuals' needs.

The Alamos also founded the Holy Alamo Christian Church, Consecrated (HACCC), and Tony Alamo identifies himself with the title "World Pastor." These groups use only the KJV, announce that they offer the only true means of salvation, and thus claim that they have won more souls to Christ than all the other churches in the world combined. Church services are held daily, with two on Sunday; each evening service is followed by a free meal. The HACCC stresses the baptism of the Holy Spirit in all of its printed material and its services. Alamo equates the Roman Catholic Church with the "Great Whore of Babylon" of the book of Revelation and proclaims that the government of the U.S. is a puppet of Catholicism, along with neo-Nazis, witches, and the Hare Krishnas, portending the one world government to come. The HACCC claims millions of members worldwide and defends polygamy as God's holy pattern. Susan Alamo died on April 8, 1982; for some days, Tony and the church prayed that she would be raised from the dead. Relatives of Susan allege that Alamo stole her body and hid it.

From 1976 until 1994 federal agencies from the IRS to the Labor Department filed a wide variety of suits against the Alamos. In 1976 the Tom and Susan Alamo Foundation was taken to court as being in violation of the Fair Labor Standards Act, since none of the church members received pay for their work in church-run workshops. In 1988 child-abuse charges were filed against Alamo, though the case was eventually dropped. In 1991 the IRS confiscated goods and properties that, Alamo claims, were worth more than $100 million. In 1994 Alamo was convicted of tax evasion and sentenced to six years in federal prison.

Throughout the years Alamo has been accused of living luxuriously while his followers have had their basic needs neglected—a charge Alamo vehemently denies. The Cult Awareness Network (CAN) and other cult-watching groups have paid great attention to the church, and Alamo has fought back with vigor, blaming his conviction and denials of parole specifically on CAN.

Currently the church has its headquarters in Alma, AR, and claims at least six other congregations, including the Music Square Church in Nashville, TN. It refuses to give membership details, claiming that this would involve the group in the same kind of sin of numbering of which King David was guilty (2 Sam. 24:1–17). The church produces radio and television programs that are broadcast throughout the world. Tony Alamo claims that his literature circulation is more than *USA Today,* the *New York Times,* the *L. A. Times,* and many other national publications combined.

■ **Bibliography:** T. Alamo, "Duped," "Genocide Treaty, EBT and the Neo-Nazis," "Leave Us Alone," "The Looking Glass," and other pamphlets ▌ R. Enroth, *Youth, Brainwashing, and the Extremist Cults* (1977) ▌ N. Ross, "The Tony Alamo Story."   ■ D. Embree

ALLEN, ASA ALONSO (1911–70). Healing evangelist.

A. A. Allen, born in Sulphur Rock, AR, grew up in poverty with an alcoholic father and an unfaithful mother. By age 21 Allen also had become an alcoholic. A turnaround came in 1934 when he was converted to Christ. His wife, Lexie, had a strong influence on his spiritual life and ministry.

Licensed by the Assemblies of God (AG) in 1936, Allen's reputation as an evangelist grew slowly and even included a two-year pastorate because of financial hard times. The *Voice of Healing* magazine reported Allen's success as an evangelist in 1950, however. The next year he bought a tent and soon established headquarters in Dallas, TX. He began broadcasting a radio program, *The Allen Revival Hour,* in 1953. His periodical, *Miracle Magazine,* began in 1954 (1969 circulation: 340,000).

"After Jack Coe died, [Allen] had no rival as the boldest of the bold" (Harrell, 68). Where others avoided the hard cases, Allen thrived on them. Of all the evangelists during his time, Harrell credits Allen with being "the leading specialist at driving out demons" (Harrell, 88). His services drew all types of people, but he identified especially with the poor and with blacks.

Allen ran into trouble with the AG in the mid 1950s due to his extravagant claims. Many of the miracles were considered questionable or at least exaggerated. However, the claimed miracles, along with Allen's preaching, continued to stir people.

A strong shadow was cast over Allen's ministry by his arrest for drunken driving during a Knoxville, TN, revival in 1955. In response to pressure, he resigned from the Voice of Healing organization. Also as a result of this incident, the AG suggested that Allen withdraw from public ministry until the matter was settled. Fearful that it would ruin his ministry, Allen claimed innocence but surrendered his credentials. Thereafter the arrest and the surrendered credentials made it difficult for Allen to work within AG churches.

In 1956 Allen started the Miracle Revival Fellowship (1956–70) while still headquartered in Dallas. Its Articles of Incorporation state that its purpose

> shall be to encourage the establishing and the maintenance of independent local sovereign, indigenous, autonomous churches, home and foreign missionary activities; to establish schools . . . to engage in other related ministries . . . by means of sermons, radio, television, publication, and any means whatsoever. To work in cooperation with all believers . . . to minimize nonessential doctrinal differences which divide the flock of God. (*Miracle Magazine* [Oct. 1956], 2)

To become a member, one had to be a "sincere born-again Christian" and uphold biblical standards of holiness. The articles provided for the licensing and ordaining of ministers. It claimed 500 affiliated churches and approximately 10,000 members in 1983.

At a Jan. 1958 revival in Phoenix, AZ, Allen expressed a dream to establish a training center for preachers. A man came to the platform and presented Allen with a gift of approximately 1,200 acres in the San Pedro Valley in southeastern Arizona. Allen claimed that four years earlier God had inspired the donor to give this gift. With additional gifts, Allen purchased another 1,200 acres. In Feb. 1958 Allen began readying his new headquarters in a community he would name Miracle Valley. Miracle Revival Training Center opened that October, and Allen began his stay there with a "Miracle Week" in Jan. 1959. Allen viewed Miracle Valley as a "totally spiritual community" consisting of 2,500 acres, a 4,000-seat church, private homes, a training school, headquarters, and a radio and television outreach.

Allen survived the pressures of media, isolation, and declining interest in the healing revival. His fund-raising ability, innovation, and daring contributed to his success. He was one of the first to appeal for support by using the theme of financial blessing for the giver. He introduced gospel rock music into his services and employed skilled entertainers.

Allen authored several books, including *The Curse of Madness* (n.d.); *God's Guarantee to Heal You* (1950); *Receive Ye the Holy Ghost* (1950); *Power to Get Wealth* (1963); *The Burning Demon of Lust* (1963); and *God's Guarantee to Bless and Prosper You Financially* (1968).

The commitment to old-time faith-healing campaigns was retained by Allen even though they were dying in the late 1950s and the 1960s. As late as 1970 he announced his plans to conduct his services in the world's largest tent.

Allen's divorce in 1967 caused unrest in his organization. He died three years later in San Francisco from sclerosis of the liver while his team conducted a revival in West Virginia. The ministry fell to Don Stewart, Allen's associate since 1958, who renamed it the Don Stewart Evangelistic Association.

■ **Bibliography:** A. A. Allen, *My Cross* (1957) ■ A. A. Allen and W. Wagner, *Born to Lose, Bound to Win* (1970) ■ D. E. Harrell, *All Things Are Possible* (1975) ■ C. E. Jones, *A Guide to the Study of the Pentecostal Movement* (1983) ■ J. Randi, *Faith Healers* (1987) ■ "About Revival Fellowship," *Miracle Magazine* (Oct. 1956) ■ "Miracle Week at Miracle Valley," *Miracle Magazine* (Mar. 1959) ■ "The San Pedro Valley Is Canaan" *Miracle Magazine* (Sept. 1958).
■ S. Shemeth

ALLIANCE OF CHRISTIAN CHURCHES

The Alliance of Christian Churches (ACC) is an international Christian fellowship of churches originally founded by homosexuals for evangelism in the gay community. Officially chartered in 1996 with 27 member churches, the ACC had previously been an annual conference and informal networking of churches and ministries under the umbrella of ADVANCE Christian Ministries, Dallas, TX, which was founded by Thomas Hirsch in 1985. Hirsch, along with six pastoral advisors, served as founder of the ACC and continues to serve as director of church ministries and as a permanent member of the executive committee. Each affiliate congregation is represented in the business of the annual conference by three elected delegates. The direction of the ACC is vested in its delegates, and the ministry of the ACC is carried out by its 10 standing committees.

As of Oct. 1999, membership of the ACC included (from both the gay and the heterosexual Christian community) 50 affiliate congregations and 10 parachurch ministries, such as gospel musicians, evangelists, and ministers. Affiliates are located in the U.S., Puerto Rico, and Colombia. The greater majority of congregations are full-gospel or Spirit-filled, and all are evangelical. The purpose of the ACC is to promote Christian fellowship, biblical education, evangelism, and missions. The national headquarters are in Dallas, TX. The annual conference known as the Fall ADVANCE as well as six regional spring weekends known as A.C.C.T.S. Weekends

are hosted in various locations around the U.S. An annual ADVANCE is also held in Colombia, South America.

■ **Bibliography:** T. Hirsch, e-mail to G. W. Gohr, Nov. 15, 1999 ■ The Alliance of Christian Churches web page (Nov. 1999).
■ G. W. Gohr

ALPHA COURSE

An evangelistic course with worldwide impact that originated in an Anglican parish, Holy Trinity, Brompton, in London, England (HTB).

Alpha was first devised in 1977 by Charles Marnham, a curate at HTB, as a course presenting new Christians with the basic principles of the Christian faith. Nicky Gumbel took over Alpha in 1990, reshaping the course to reach the unchurched in an attractive way. With the publication of Gumbel's *Questions of Life* in 1993 and the availability of the Alpha talks on video in 1994, the Alpha course quickly spread through Britain and then to other countries.

Alpha is based on six principles: (1) evangelism is most effective through the local church; (2) evangelism is a process; (3) evangelism involves the whole person; (4) models of evangelism in the NT include classical, holistic, and power evangelism; (5) evangelism in the power of the Holy Spirit is both dynamic and effective; (6) effective evangelism requires the filling and refilling of the Spirit.

The Alpha course runs for 10 weeks and contains 15 talks. Participants receive an *Alpha Manual,* and leaders and helpers prepare with the *Alpha Training Manual.* A journal, *Alpha News,* is published by HTB.

Gumbel has written several books related to Alpha: *Why Jesus?* (1991); *Searching Issues* (1994); *Telling Others* (1994); *A Life Worth Living* (1994); *Challenging Lifestyle* (1996); and *The Heart of Revival* (1997). Alpha offices have been opened in many countries; the U.S. office is in New York City. Alpha is being used across most of the denominational spectrum and in new charismatic churches. A Catholic Alpha office was opened in England in 1996 and one in the U.S. in 1997. An estimated 500,000 people participated in the Alpha course in 1997.
■ P. D. Hocken

AMERICAN BAPTIST CHARISMATIC RENEWAL

In the early 1960s the Holy Spirit brought renewal to a number of American Baptist (AB) Churches across the United States. A national fellowship of renewed American Baptists began meeting occasionally in the 1960s and annually in 1974 at the AB National Assembly in Green Lake, WI.

In 1981 the AB renewal group elected Gary Clark as president and national leader. At the time, Clark was pastor of First Baptist Church in Salem, NH, which had become a fully charismatic AB church during his tenure. Its membership had tripled in a decade, with 75% of the growth resulting from personal conversions and believer's baptism. Clark incorporated the movement into the Holy Spirit Renewal Ministries in American Baptist Churches (HSRM) in 1982.

More than 500 pastors have identified themselves with the charismatic renewal. HSRM has 1,300 members with many more thousands who participate in the national and regional conferences.

HSRM has enjoyed acceptance and participation in many areas of the denomination, including exhibits and workshops at the national biennials, regional renewal conferences, seminars and lectures at AB seminaries, and renewal teaching missions in other countries at the invitation of AB missionaries.

Another manifestation of the renewal is a commitment to pursue ecumenical relationships with other denominational churches and with independent and Roman Catholic fellowships who are also seeking the life in the Spirit. The HSRM is a founding member of the ▸North American Renewal Service Committee, which includes most mainline denominational renewal movements as well as independent charismatics, classical pentecostals, and Roman Catholic charismatics. ■ P. D. Hocken

AMERICAN EVANGELISTIC ASSOCIATION The purpose of the American Evangelistic Association (AEA) is to set professional standards and to license and ordain clergy and to coordinate independent missionary, educational, and charitable efforts in foreign countries. Established in 1954 by John Elwood Douglas Sr., former Methodist and convert of ▸A. A. Allen, and 17 other independent ministers, the AEA grew rapidly. The Baltimore headquarters reported 2,057 members in 1968 and also claimed a combined membership of more than 100,000 in self-governing congregations served by member clergy. In 1979 its overseas arm, Dallas-based World Missionary Evangelism, reported work in 12 countries. At that time it was sponsoring more than 30,000 children overseas.

■ **Bibliography:** D. E. Harrell, *All Things Are Possible* (1975) ■ C. E. Jones, *The Charismatic Movement: A Guide to the Study of Neo-Pentecostalism with an Emphasis on Anglo-American Sources* (1995) ■ idem, *Guide to the Study of the Pentecostal Movement* (1982) ■ idem, *Mission Handbook* (1979) ■ A. C. Piepkorn, *Profiles in Belief,* vol. 3 (1979). ■ C. E. Jones

ANDERSON, PAUL R. (1944–). Leader of the international Lutheran renewal movement (▸Lutheran Charismatics). The son of a Lutheran pastor, Anderson graduated from UCLA with a major in English literature and a minor in music. In 1970 he graduated from Luther Theological Seminary. The following year he studied in Israel. For 25 years Anderson pastored Trinity Lutheran Church in San Pedro, CA, before moving to St. Paul, MN, to become director of International Lutheran Renewal.

Anderson is the author of *Building Christian Character* (1980), a study of 34 Christian character traits. He also has coauthored *Mastering Pastoral Care* (1990) and writes regularly for a variety of periodicals. He is well known for his teaching on renewal and his training of the next generation to disciple the nations. He and his wife, Karen, have six children. ■ S. M. Burgess

ANDERSON, ROBERT MAPES (1929–). Social historian specializing in American pentecostalism. Anderson's interest was stimulated in his youth by acquaintance with a neighborhood storefront church in New York City, and this led to his Ph.D. dissertation on American pentecostal origins at Columbia University (1969). Published in 1979 under the title *Vision of the Disinherited*, Anderson's study was rapidly acclaimed as authoritative. Anderson has an unusual empathy for the world of early pentecostalism, enabling him as a social historian to paint a fuller picture of the life situations from which the pentecostal pioneers came. Skilled at distinguishing fact from legend and subsequent interpretation, Anderson sees the millennial expectation that "Jesus is coming soon" as primary among initial pentecostal convictions. He is currently professor of history at Wagner College, Staten Island, NY. ■ P. D. Hocken

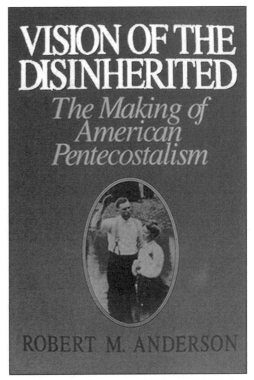

Robert Mapes Anderson's book *Vision of the Disinherited,* an early classic in pentecostal studies.

ANDERSSON, AXEL (c. 1891–1981). Pioneer Swedish pentecostal missionary to Mexico. Born and raised in Sweden, Axel Andersson was converted to Christianity by Swedish Baptists in 1905 at the age of 14. In Feb. 1910 he was baptized in the Holy Spirit under a Baptist pentecostal named John Ongman. After working as an evangelist in southern and central Sweden (1911–15), he allegedly had a vision from God in 1915 that instructed him to go to Mexico as a missionary. In preparation for his future ministry, he attended the pentecostal Bible school at Örebrö, Sweden, for two years. While at the Bible school, he met his wife and future coworker, Ester Svanstedt. They left for Mexico via New York City in Aug. 1919. They worked briefly as evangelists in a Swedish pentecostal church in New York City.

A short time later the Anderssons left New York for Mexico. They were supported by the famous Swedish Filadelfia Pentecostal Church and the Swedish pentecostal congregation they had attended in New York. The Anderssons were not the first Swedish missionaries in Mexico (in 1911 H. A. Johnson ministered briefly in Mexico). The Anderssons' ministry, however, was the first major Swedish work in Mexico. They ministered in San Luis Potosí and Mexico City, organized an extensive tract ministry, and planted new churches throughout the country. The need for ministerial instruction prompted the Anderssons and their Mexican coworkers to organize a Bible school in the 1920s. In 1926 they began publishing a small periodical, *Luz y Restauracion* (Light and Restoration). The Anderssons were later joined by other Swedish pentecostal missionaries, such as A. P. Franklin and Elsa Gustafsson. By 1937 there were 9 churches, 47 outposts, 8 pastors, 45 evangelists, and more than 4,000 adherents in Mexico. In 1936 alone, the Swedish and Mexican pentecostals built 12 chapels, four of which seated more than 400 people. That same year they printed more than 2,000 copies of *Luz y Restauracion*. They also published a songbook, which by 1937 had already sold 8,000 copies. The work the Anderssons founded eventually developed into two denominations: La Fraternidad Pentecostal Independiente and La Iglesia Cristiana Independiente Pentecostés. The former denomination has an estimated 1,500 congregations and 350,000 adherents; the latter reportedly has thousands of preaching points throughout Mexico. The Anderssons' missionary work shows the European roots of Mexican and Latin American pentecostalism.

■ **Bibliography:** D. D. Bundy, "Swedish Pentecostal Missions: The Case of Axel Andersson in Mexico" (unpub., 1993).

■ G. Espinosa

ANGELUS TEMPLE Located at 1100 Glendale Boulevard in Los Angeles, CA, the temple housed the headquarters congregation of the ▸International Church of the Foursquare Gospel. On Jan. 1, 1923, it was dedicated by ▸Aimee Semple McPherson, who served as its pastor until her untimely death in 1944. As she traversed the continent, holding meetings of up to 16,000 people in cities such as Denver, St. Louis, Dayton, Washington, DC, and Montreal, she shared the vision of the completed temple project, much of which she designed herself. When it was opened, it was debt free, and people from a wide number of historical denominations had helped to make it so.

Constructed largely of steel-reinforced concrete, the temple, semicircular in shape, seated 5,300 people. Its cornerstone proclaimed its dedication to the cause of interdenominational and worldwide evangelization. At that time it boasted the largest unsupported dome in the U.S. Situated at the intersection of major streetcar lines, the temple was easily accessible to commuters. Nationally renowned artist George W. Haskins was commissioned to design and construct eight stained-glass windows in the sanctuary at a cost of $15,000. A prayer tower, originally called the Watch Tower, went into operation in Feb. 1923, with volunteers praying around the clock in two-hour shifts. Services were carried on the temple's own radio station, KFSG (Kall Four Square Gospel) beginning Feb. 6, 1924.

From 1923 to 1926 "Sister" preached each evening and three times each Sunday. She drew standing-room-only crowds—some 25,000 worshipers weekly, who came to hear her vividly illustrated sermons, fully costumed operas, and cantatas. There was a 100-voice choir, a large Kimball organ, and a "Silver Band." While Sundays featured a communion service as well as inspirational and revivalistic services, each Monday the emphasis was on deeper life; Tuesday the focus

An early postcard of Angelus Temple with antenna tower of radio station KFSG (Kall Four Square Gospel).

was on evangelism; Wednesday was dedicated to prayer and Bible study; Thursday evening was reserved for baptismal services; Friday was set apart for the young people; and Tuesday afternoon and Saturday evening were given over to divine healing services.

The temple was active in both civic and social ministry in the community as well. "Sister" was a member of the Los Angeles Chamber of Commerce. She campaigned actively for higher pay for Los Angeles police and fire department employees. The temple entered floats in the famed Tournament of Roses Parade in Pasadena each year from 1923 through 1926, winning the coveted Sweepstakes trophy in 1925. When an earthquake occurred in Santa Barbara in 1925, she used the radio station to make a plea for food, clothing, and other supplies, and for trucks to carry them. The caravan arrived in the town before governmental agencies were on the scene.

In the late 1920s and early 1930s the temple's commissary ran at full speed. Taking care of indigents and the unemployed, some of whom were referred by Los Angeles County, was a major concern. From Aug. 1927 to May 1936, 99,520 families and 355,158 persons were fed, while 257,686 articles of clothing and over 3,000 quilts were distributed. By July 1942 the commissary was said to have fed and clothed over a million persons. The temple's employment agency was also at work. In the nine months from Sept. 1935 through May 1936, for instance, it supplied 4,850 jobs, 75% of which were permanent positions. An outgrowth of the temple's ministry also included the establishment of L.I.F.E. (Lighthouse of International Foursquare Evangelism) Bible College in Mar. 1923. A bookstore was opened in 1927.

The temple is little changed from its beginning. Earlier internal remodeling has set the current seating capacity at 3,300. The 1994 Northridge earthquake dealt a devastating blow to the main sanctuary, and some structural changes had to be made to the building, which is now listed on the National Historic Register.

The Anglo congregation regularly numbers about 700, while the Hispanic congregation has ballooned to 2,000. In addition, the temple hosts other Foursquare services for Filipino, Russian, Indonesian, Korean, Bulgarian, and Armenian congregations. The college has relocated to San Dimas, CA, but the bookstore, prayer tower, and radio station KFSG-FM continue to run as they were originally envisioned.

■ **Bibliography:** A. S. McPherson, *In the Service of the King* (1927) ■ idem, *The Story of My Life* (1951) ■ "The Opening of the Angelus Temple," *Triumphs of Faith* 43 (Jan. 1, 1923).

■ C. M. Robeck Jr.

ANGLICAN RENEWAL MINISTRIES (ARM). An organization founded in 1981 to establish an Anglican charismatic

service committee in the U.K. Its primary inspiration came from the Canterbury Conference of 1978. Spurred by the closure of ᐧFountain Trust, an ecumenical renewal organization, 70 clergy meeting at Scargill voted unanimously to begin the organization. Lawrence Hoyle became its first coordinator, followed by Michael Mitten, and John Leach, the present director. Other primary leaders were Thomas R. Hare and John Gunstone.

Among its activities ARM publishes a newsletter, *Anglicans for Renewal.* Their main ministry focuses on annual national renewal conferences for clergy and leaders, regional conferences about personal and parish renewal, and the distribution of teaching and resource materials called *Saints Alive* for clergy and lay leaders. ARM (U.K.) has been joined by similar organizations in Scotland, Ireland, Canada, Australia, New Zealand, and many other places in the Anglican Communion.   ■ C. M. Irish

ANIMISM AND PENTECOSTALISM: A CASE STUDY

A century of pentecostal mission shows pentecostals to have been uniquely effective among animists, a fact that has drawn much attention from missiologists and anthropologists. This article looks at animism and pentecostalism through the prism of the Igorot tribe of the Philippines.

It should be noted that "animism" is a term that has fallen out of favor with many scholars of religion, since it has been used to imply that nonliterate religious systems are simplistic, failing to recognize the often highly complex nature of these systems. However, missiologists have retained the term as useful in studying the interaction between nonliterate religious systems and Christianity.

1. Animism.

Animism is a belief in the existence of various spiritual beings who generate infinite power that can meet the diverse needs of human beings. They believe that all creatures, and sometimes material objects, such as trees and rocks, have spirits. Special attention is given to human spirits, which unite with other spirits, particularly those of their ancestors, and gods after death. These spirits closely interact with people, with whose lives they are fully familiar. Animists generally hold to the following beliefs.

a. Spirit Beings. The spirits that animists are most concerned with are the spirits of deceased humans. These spirits are perceived as actively assisting humans and generating power to help them. The spirits have different ranks, and each of these has its own functions. Among the Igorot tribes of the northern Philippine mountains, the following spirits are believed to exist.

Adika-ila: The highest spirit who created the sun, stars, moon, earth, and all creatures. All other spirits, including human spirits, are under the authority of *Adika-ila.* He has supreme wisdom and knowledge for fair judgment, which includes making decisions for public affairs in the interest of the tribe.

Kabunyan: There are 24 gods and goddesses with supernatural power in this category; they are next in rank to *Adika-ila.* These spirits dwell in the skyworld and were to a limited extent involved in the creation of the universe.

Ap-apo: The spirits of human beings who have long been dead. They travel from the skyworld to the earth, to the underworld and back. *Ap-apo,* while up in the sky, are smoothly awakened by the tempting sweet flavor of *tapey* (homemade rice wine) and the sound of gongs indicating the performance of a ritual.

Kak-kading: Spirits of humans who have recently died but still abide on the earth (low rank). During rituals a host family makes an offering and pours a few drops of wine to indicate admission of their presence in the ritual.

Anito: Spirits of the underworld are ranked lowest. They dwell in places such as big rocks, ravines, caves, abandoned buildings, bushy trees, waterfalls, creeks, springs, lakes, rivers, oceans, the ground, and various other places. These spirits are easily exasperated when people trespass, overlook sacrificial offerings, and commit other acts of delinquency. Provoked spirits may cause illness, death, and misfortune. Those who violate a taboo are obligated to offer a ritual to calm the anger of spirits. Health, for instance, will be restored as the spirits are appeased.

To the animists, there is no "luck" in the Western sense—all is the work of the spirits. There are many benevolent spirits that bring good luck and bless with material prosperity, long life, and that thus protect, comfort, and heal. People offer sacrifice to induce their blessing or help.

But in most animistic belief systems there are also malevolent spirits that cause bad luck. These spirits are easily hurt when people neglect their duty toward them. They then take revenge on humans by causing evil: misfortune, bad luck, and illness. In some cases, even benevolent spirits can cause evil when offended.

Learning to understand the characteristics of each kind of spirit allows a close relationship with them. Rituals are conducted based on such empirical knowledge and relationship.

In addition to their capability to bless or curse, spirits also help humans to decide daily affairs. In a dispute between two families over a stolen object, for instance, a community priest may convene a conference with the victim and the suspect to decide if the suspect is actually a thief. Spirits are invited by slaughtering a chicken. Then victim and suspect both dip their hands into boiling water. The spirits are believed to save the innocent while bringing harm to the offender.

b. Communication. The dream is a common means for spirits to communicate with people. In a dream the spirit often expresses its wish. The dreadful appearance of the spirit would cause physical sickness. A priest determines the cause of sickness and prescribes a suitable ritual to appeal to the spirit beings. The oracle conveys the words from the spirits through the priest, who mediates the communication between divinity and humanity. Divination often involves observing the entrails, such as liver and gall bladder, of a sacrificial animal or observing other natural phenomena. The priest carefully examines objects to detect any divine sign or indication, especially for the host family of the sacrifice. If the sign is not favorable, the host has to slaughter another animal until a favorable sign is found.

c. Priest. The priest is a man or woman who enacts the various roles of the spirits in human affairs. Priests gain power from an intimate relationship with spirit beings. They are considered to be the leaders of the community, thus often they handle disputes and help people by obtaining wisdom from the spirit beings. They act individually and collectively as ritual advisors, and they administer rituals. Their responsibility as mediators between spirits and people is critically important in the community. Priests interpret signs and omens, counsel as to which rituals are necessary, give authoritative words, and keep a sharp memory of ritual procedures and oral, chanted genealogies.

In some societies there is more than one kind of priest. Among the Igorot tribes, there are three priestly categories. A *manbunong* (shaman) performs a ritual for healing and thanksgiving. The priest offers prayer to the spirits to alleviate the illness from the afflicted member of the host family. A *mansib-ok* gives advice and determines the cause(s) of misfortune and sickness. A *mankotom* is recognized as a wise man, interpreting omens, signs, and dreams; the *mankotom* often resolves problems in interpersonal relationships.

d. Rituals. Ritual is a meaningful activity that appeases malevolent spirits and also induces favorable help from benevolent spirits. Rituals are performed for various occasions: conception, childbirth, marriage, agricultural rites, healing, and thanksgiving.

Thanksgiving rituals are practiced in connection with various events and situations that call for gratitude, such as weddings or good fortune. Among the Igorots, the ritual *dasadas* is usually performed after finishing a new house. The *manbunong* grips a mother hen and a cup of rice wine. He makes unique motions looking up to the eastern sky, facing the sun, to call for the living spirits of the owners of the house to come and take up the new home. Then pigs are offered to the spirits. The priest offers a *bunong* (prayer) of material blessing so that the owner will be able to render even greater rituals in the future. Then a pig is killed and the entrails of the pig are inspected as a course of ritual performance.

Rites are prepared for each stage of rice farming: the arrangement of the seedbeds through the sowing of the seeds, the transplanting of seedlings, protection from worms and drought, the harvest, and storing the yields in the granary. The spirits are believed to have influence over rain, planting, seed time, firstfruits, and other matters.

Healing rituals are perhaps the most common. Animists believe that one gets ill from being fatigued, from neglecting to offer sacrifices to the spirits, and from having a dreadful dream in which the spirit of a deceased ancestor appeared fearsome.

2. Comparison Between Animistic and Pentecostal Beliefs.

A comparison of several key categories in the two belief systems reveals some similarities that may explain the success of pentecostal mission among animists.

a. Spiritual World. The animistic belief in the spiritual world has been noted above. Pentecostals, somewhat unlike mainstream evangelicals, have a very keen awareness of the spiritual world. The activities of the Holy Spirit, angels, Satan, and demons are real to them. They are clearly aware that human problems often have spiritual roots and that the cause of illness is often spiritual. Thus, for example, pentecostals pray to cast out demons they perceive to be active. In the same way, they regularly seek the presence, power, and help of the Holy Sprit and angels.

b. Blessings. For animists, all blessings are manifestations of the divine power of the spirits on their descendants. Rituals are performed to receive divine blessing, material or otherwise, and the rituals are complete with the invocation of the spirits to answer petitions and bring blessings. The ritual provides a significant avenue by which animists' felt needs are met. According to this belief, the spirits have power to grow crops, raise animals, and provide protection and guidance. Rituals during the planting and harvesting seasons are thus a dominant part of celebrations. Diverse smaller rituals are likewise offered for occasions such as mending irrigation channels, hunting, mining, and so on. The spirits have control over natural resources.

Similarly, for pentecostals, blessing is the exhibition of God's care and provision for his people. Unlike their evangelical counterparts, pentecostals understand blessing to include the physical and material aspects of human life, and they strongly desire abundant blessings from the Lord. Pentecostals frequently confess God's faithfulness and mercy. Hence, faith and prayer are emphasized to appropriate God's blessing to his people.

c. Healing. In the animists' perception, sickness is caused by spiritual forces, so healing is also an act of a deity. The first step toward healing is to identify the cause of the sickness. A specific spirit is singled out, often through a ritual. Sickness is brought either through the violation of a taboo or by a demand made by a spirit. Items the spirit demands vary from food to a new burial blanket and are made known through dreams and sickness. When the demand is met or the offended spirit is appeased through a ritual, a patient recovers. The center of animistic belief is power, while healing is a dramatic manifestation of this belief. This power is discharged to the living through rituals.

According to pentecostal belief, healing is a demonstration of the power of the Holy Spirit. Often a dramatic healing triggers a group conversion, either of families or of an entire people group. Pentecostals take seriously and literally what Jesus commanded the Seventy: to heal and cast out demons (Luke 10:9). The healing account recorded in Acts 3 is interpreted by pentecostals as a direct result of the baptism in the Spirit in Acts 2. Accounts of healing are a significant factor in the growth of the pentecostal churches in the mountains of the northern Philippines. These healings through the power of the Holy Spirit became the most common and distinguishing characteristic of evangelistic beginnings. Since animists are often found among tribal groups, and because medical services are often inadequate, healings are a significant key in tribal conversions.

d. Revelation. "Revelation" often takes place among animists through two types of divine communication to humans: intentional and unintentional. In *intentional* communication a message from the divinity is disclosed to humans by various means; the most common modes are dreams and visions as well as the observation of omens and signs. Thus, intentional communication may involve strange dreams, the appearance of rare animals, a darkening of the moon, or unusual noises made by domestic animals. The divine message often reveals a significant event that will occur in the near future. In *unintentional* communication, on the other hand, humans must employ various means, such as ritual, to obtain a message from spirit beings by inducing them to "speak."

In many ways, pentecostals maintain a similar belief concept. Although the written Word is the fundamental revelation, this does not preclude God's direct communication through other means, such as visions, audible voices, dreams, strong impressions, prophecies in intelligible language or in tongues with interpretation, and others. Scriptural accounts, such as Peter's prediction of the deaths of Ananias and Sapphira (Acts 5:1–10), are taken at face value by pentecostals. For this reason, pentecostals are often accused of claiming extrabiblical revelation.

3. Conclusion.

A comparison of the two worldviews shows striking similarities and even commonalities between them. Categories such as the spiritual world, blessings, healing, and revelation—categories that have been relatively ignored by the majority of Christians—are viewed as significant both by animists and by pentecostals. This may provide a clue as to why pentecostals have been, and continue to be, successful in communicating the gospel to animistic societies. Thus, pentecostals have unique distinctives in the area of missions. Considering that the larger part of the world is still animistic in spite of rapid urbanization and development, pentecostal missiologists need to further develop their theological foundations, and pentecostal missionaries should take full advantage of their unusual preparation by the Spirit.

■ **Bibliography:** M. A. Dempster, B. D. Klaus, and D. Petersen, eds., *Called and Empowered: Global Mission in Pentecostal Perspective* (1991) ■ A. C. Lehmann and J. E. Myers, eds., *Magic, Witchcraft, and Religion: An Anthropological Study of the Supernatural* (1989) ■ E. A. Nida and W. A. Smalley, *Introducing Animism* (1959) ■ W. D. Sacla, *Treasury of Beliefs and Home Rituals of Benguet* (1988) ■ G. Van Rheenen, *Communicating Christ in Animistic Contexts* (1991).

■ J. C. Ma

ANOINTING WITH OIL Anointing with oil is used in the modern church predominantly in conjunction with prayer for physical healing. For centuries the Roman Catholic Church practiced the sacrament of extreme unction, known since Vatican II as the anointing of the sick. During the Middle Ages, kings and bishops began to be anointed with holy oil. From the 3d century on, a postbaptismal anointing and laying on of hands was practiced by the church to confer the gifts of the Holy Spirit.

Anointing with oil was used from early times throughout the East for cosmetic, preservative, and medicinal purposes. The OT regularly employs the root *sûk* and *ṭûaḥ* for this process (Ruth 3:3; 2 Chron. 28:15), words rendered in the Septuagint (LXX) predominantly by *aleiphō*. *Aleiphō* is found eight times in the NT, referring to the physical act of anointing people for personal hygiene (Matt. 6:17) or for healing (Mark 6:13; James 5:14), and as a sign of honor (Mark 16:1; Luke 7:38, 46). Mark 6:13 and James 5:14 suggest medicinal properties for the oil, but the practice of exorcism may also serve as background, the casting out of demons being symbolized in the anointing with oil.

Anointing with oil also carried sacred or symbolic significance, indicated in the OT by the term *mašaḥ*. Objects were anointed and consecrated to divine service (Exod. 30:26–29). Anointed persons received an infusion of divine presence and power, actualized for the Israelite by an endowment of the Spirit of Yahweh (1 Sam. 16:13). Kings were inducted into office by the pouring of oil over the head (1 Sam. 10:1). "Yahweh's anointed" is a synonym for Israel's king (1 Sam. 12:3). Priests were set apart and ordained for their office by anointing (Exod. 28:41). Elijah was commissioned to anoint Elisha as his successor in the prophetic office (1 Kings 19:16). "To anoint" is used metaphorically for the bestowal of divine favor in such passages as Pss. 23:5; 92:10.

The LXX regularly renders *mašaḥ* by *chriō*, a verb used five times in the NT. Three occurrences of the related noun *chrisma* appear in 1 John. Both terms are used only in a figurative sense. Anointing is a metaphor for the bestowal of the Holy Spirit, special favor, or divine commission. At his baptism, Jesus was confirmed in his royal and priestly roles by the anointing of the Holy Spirit, an anointing that confirmed him as *Christos,* the Messiah (a direct transliteration of the Hebrew word for *anointed*). Heb. 1:9 connects anointing with Christ's elevation and enthronement as eschatological ruler and high priest. In 1 John, *chrisma* involves the reception of the Holy Spirit (2:18, 27–28), the believer's Teacher and Guide, the one who enables the Christian to discern spirits (1 John 4:1–7). The reception of the Holy Spirit allows the believer to share in the messianic anointing of Jesus. The designation "Christian" connotes a member of the community of the "Anointed One."

■ **Bibliography:** M. DeJonge, "The Use of the Word 'Anoint' in the Time of Jesus," *VetTest* 8 (1966), 132–48 ■ D. Engelhard, "Anoint Anointing," *ISBE*, rev. ed (1979) ■ W. Grundmann et al., "*Chrio ktl.,*" *TDNT* (1974) ■ D. Muller, "Anoint," *NIDNTT* (1975) ■ J. N. Oswalt, "*mšh* *NIDOTTE* (1997) ■ H. Schlier, "*Aleiphō,*" *TDNT* (1964) ■ S. Szikazai, "Anoint," *IDB* (1962).

■ T. Powell

APOSTLE, OFFICE OF

1. Apostle: The Gospels and Acts.

Jesus chose from his disciples 12 "whom he also designated 'apostles'" (Luke 6:13; cf. Acts 1:2, 13). Mark 3:14 (see Metzger, 80, on the textual support of the reading "whom also he designated apostles") and Matt. 10:2 (no other Matthean references to "apostle" occur) have the same witness. "The Twelve" or "the twelve disciples" are also "the apostles." ("A disciple" may not be "an apostle," but "the disciples" or "the twelve disciples" are "the apostles"; cf. Rev. 21:14.)

Jesus gave to this innermost company "power and authority to drive out all demons and to cure diseases, and he sent them out to preach the kingdom of God and to heal the sick" (Luke 9:1–2; cf. Matt. 10:1; Mark 3:14–15). (Note the "sent" motif in John 13:16b ["neither is an apostle {*apostolos;* NIV: 'messenger'} greater than the one who sent him"].) Though sent away bearing the authority of the sender, the apostles were expected to return (Mark 6:30; Luke 9:10). Jesus did not establish them as agents of the kingdom of God apart from their relationship to himself as disciples (Matt. 16:24–25/Mark 8:34–35/Luke 9:23–24). We may deduce five aspects of being a member of the first apostolic group: call, authorization, dispatch, going and acting in obedience, and return.

Although the apostles had intimate contact with Jesus and personal, private teaching from him, they did not adequately comprehend either his person (cf. Luke 9:20, 45) or their role as his apostles (Luke 9:46–48). Their faith was lacking both before and after the resurrection of Jesus (Luke 17:5; 24:11). They did not have unalloyed commitment to him (cf. Luke 22:54–62 and parallels; Mark 14:50). Even Jesus' betrayer, Judas, was one of "the apostles" who ate Jesus' last meal with him (Luke 22:2–3, 14, 21).

Two considerations in particular suggest that Jesus did not establish an exclusive apostolate. (1) Jesus allowed nonfollowers to cast out demons "in Jesus' name," and he rebuked John for having thought otherwise (Mark 9:38–41; Luke 9:49–50). (2) The 12 designated as "apostles" (Luke 9:1–2, 10) and the Seventy, who were not so designated (Luke 10:1–12), had the same authority, abilities, and commission given to them. Jesus' intention was that selected persons—whether called "apostles" or not—were to be empowered and sent forth to preach the nearness and/or presence of the kingdom of God. Healing the sick and casting out demons were integral to the activity of those sent forth.

In the postresurrection community the apostolic tasks changed even as the relationship to Jesus did. Their tasks were preaching the Word of God (cf. Acts 2:14, 37; 4:1–2, 33; 6:2; 10:36–43), accompanied by signs and wonders (e.g., 3:6–7; 4:29–31); teaching (2:42; 2 Peter 3:2; Jude 17); praying (6:4); and fairly distributing goods so that all the company of believers might be without need (4:34–5:11).

Central to the content of the apostles' preaching was that they be witnesses to Jesus' resurrection (Acts 1:22). Hence, at the outset, there were two criteria for Judas's replacement: (1) the man must have been a traveling companion in all the active historical ministry of Jesus so that he could witness with them to the resurrection of Jesus in the light of those historical experiences (vv. 21–22). (2) The heart of the man had to be acceptable before the Lord, who was to make the final choice (v. 24). The selection process involved the apostles' submission to the Lord, even as in the pre-Passion context. Through prayer (v. 24) and the casting of lots (v. 26), they sought divine designation of the one whom the Lord himself had chosen (1:24, 26).

No one person was designated as leader of the apostolic band, though in the early chapters of Acts, Peter is quite clearly the vocal and forthright one. As one of the apostles, he became a dynamic, bold, tenacious witness for the risen Lord, but he worked under an authority from God that was confirmed by the Jerusalem apostles (8:14, 25; 15:7). In his dialogues with them he demonstrated an accountability toward them that was balanced with his own authority to challenge and silence the group (11:2–18; 15:7–11).

Until the dispersion of the saints into other areas (8:1), the apostles were the reconstituted Twelve, centered in Jerusalem, an exclusive, nontraveling band. After the scattering, a change in the constituency of the apostles may be detected. In Acts 8:14 one reads, "Now when the in-Jerusalem apostles heard . . ." (author's translation). Luke just said the apostles remained in Jerusalem (v. 1); by his word order he draws attention to *which* apostles: those in Jerusalem. Acts 16:4 ("the apostles and elders, the ones in Jerusalem") is another example of such emphasis, strongly intimating that "apostle" per se has come to mean more than the original Twelve or the Eleven plus Matthias. Had there been only the apostles in Jerusalem, Luke's added "in Jerusalem" and "the ones in Jerusalem" would be superfluous. The existence of apostles other than those in Jerusalem is confirmed with the naming of "apostles Barnabas and Paul" in Acts 14:4, 14.

In the course of time the Jerusalem apostolic group became less significant. Peter and John went to Samaria at their behest to confirm Philip's preaching (8:4–24). The Jerusalem apostles, and in particular the "circumcision party," objected to Peter's mission "here and there" in Lydda, Sharon, Joppa, and among the Gentiles of Caesarea (9:32–11:18). They had to yield, however, recognizing that God made the choice that Peter evangelize among the Gentiles (cf. 15:7). The Spirit had told him to go (11:12), and Peter had chosen not to resist God (11:17–18). The authority of the group had to be subordinated to the will of God, Jesus, or his Spirit.

When Greeks in Antioch received the word of the Lord through converts from Cyprus and Cyrene (11:20–21; not from the apostles in Jerusalem), "the church in Jerusalem"—not "the apostles"—sent Barnabas, who was not one of the original apostolic group, as their envoy (v. 22).

When the apostles of Jerusalem and the elders and prophets, together with the whole church (15:6, 22, 32), determined to convene and declare a position concerning the issue of Gentile conversions and the keeping of the Mosaic law, they sent no command to Antioch (15:23–29). Instead, they gave an exhortation as to how "you will do well" (v. 29).

Furthermore, this last recorded Lucan reference to the apostles in Jerusalem depicts neither Peter (15:7–11) nor James (vv. 13–21) nor any other individual as being in control of the group. Both Peter and James spoke. Each made suggestions. But the letter to Antioch was from "the apostles and elders" (vv. 22, 23; 16:4); the final position was that which "seemed good to the Holy Spirit and to us" (v. 28). Control of the group did not rest with any one person or clique. Equality, collegiality, and mutual submission under the leadership of the Holy Spirit appear to have ruled among the brethren during their deliberations and their hearing of the report by Barnabas and Paul "about the miraculous signs and wonders God had done among the Gentiles through them" (15:12). After these deliberations at Jerusalem, Luke does not again mention the apostles, their work, or their persons.

2. Apostle: A Period of Transition.

Philip was one of the seven chosen to handle the daily distribution (Acts 6:5) to the widows. He was a man full of the

Spirit and wisdom. When next met, he is not serving tables; instead, he is in Samaria, preaching Christ, casting out unclean spirits, and healing many paralyzed and lame persons (8:5–13)—all activities of the apostles.

When Saul of Tarsus was blinded, the Lord called a disciple of Damascus, Ananias, and sent him to Saul so that the latter might regain his sight and be filled with the Holy Spirit (9:17)—an appropriate activity for an apostle.

Prophets and teachers of the church in Antioch, under instructions from the Holy Spirit (13:1, 4), set apart Barnabas and Saul for evangelistic work. Their ministry was a proclamation of the "word of the Lord," accompanied by signs and wonders (13:7–12, 16–49; 14:3, 11) and persecutions from certain Jews and Gentiles of the region (13:50–52; 14:5; cf. 2 Tim. 1:11–12)—all activities and circumstances common to apostles. There are three new elements here: (1) Barnabas and Saul are chosen and sent by the Holy Spirit. The Holy Spirit, not the Lord Jesus, is now the one who calls, commissions, and certifies the activities of God's agents. (2) The apostles of Jerusalem are now joined by others—the prophets and teachers of the church at Antioch—whom God uses as agents of commissioning and sending forth. (3) These sent-forth ones function in essentially the same capacity, with like results and under the same circumstances of persecution, as the original postresurrection apostles, though for a while without the title "apostle."

3. Apostle: The Pauline Perspective.

a. Paul's Personal Apostleship. In his earliest letter Paul unhesitatingly introduces himself as "apostle—sent not from men nor by man, but by Jesus Christ and God the Father" (Gal. 1:1; cf. 2 Tim. 1:1, 11). Consistent with the witness of Acts, Paul insists that he is an apostle because of a direct, divine calling, rather than any human selection process (Gal. 1:17–19). Later he also rejects the notion of being an apostle because of any personal qualifications (1 Cor. 15:9; 2 Cor. 12:5–11).

Undergirding Paul's apostleship is the fact that, like the original apostles of Jerusalem, he had seen Jesus the Lord (1 Cor. 9:1; 15:5–9; Gal. 1:16). Seeing the Lord, however, whether in the flesh or as the Risen One, does not thereby automatically qualify any person as an apostle. Neither is such an encounter introduced as a necessity for someone to be an apostle. In 1 Cor. 15:6 there is no suggestion that the 500 brethren are apostles. In Paul's case his vision of the Lord is coupled with the fact that he was "called to be an apostle of Christ Jesus" (1 Cor. 1:1), set apart and called before he was ever born (Gal. 1:15). To this should be added that the indicators of an apostle—namely, (1) effective proclamation of the gospel and (2) signs, wonders, and mighty works—accompanied Paul's ministry, thereby verifying his apostolic service (1 Cor. 9:2; 2 Cor. 12:11–12; cf. Rom. 15:18–19).

Still, more must be said. Signs, wonders, and mighty works may verify an apostolic ministry, but they do not guarantee that a ministry is apostolic. Paul struggled against false apostles who were disguised as apostles of Christ and servants of righteousness but who in actuality were agents of Satan, who disguises himself as an angel of light (2 Cor. 11:12–15; cf. Matt. 7:22–23).

After Matthias was chosen (Acts 1:23–26), we find no indication that personal vision of the earthly Jesus or the risen Lord is a requisite for other persons being an apostle. The initial insistence by the 12 apostles was that the only person who could be enrolled as an apostle was someone who had seen the risen Lord and had been a personal companion of Jesus during his earthly ministry (Acts 1:21–22). This precludes Paul himself regardless of his Damascus Road experience. Having seen and accompanied the Lord was required prior to Pentecost and the outpouring of the Spirit because it was only as one related to Jesus that one was in the kingdom. After the outpouring of the Spirit at Pentecost one could know—by the Spirit—both the reality of the resurrection and the power of the risen Lord in one's life whether or not one had seen Jesus in flesh and blood (consider Paul's entire Gentile mission).

Being an apostle in the post-Pentecost church of God in Christ Jesus depends on the calling of the Lord and on his enabling grace for apostleship. In 1 Cor. 12:27–31 Paul affirms that God established apostles in the church—not just in the local congregation of Corinth, but in the "body of Christ" (v. 27). God himself graciously gave functional gifts to those called to be his one body (Eph. 4:1–6), whether apostles, prophets, evangelists, or pastors-teachers.

Neither 1 Cor. 12 nor Eph. 4 is expressed as a temporal matter. Paul simply says that in the church or in "'one body' God has placed or given...." (Note well that God has given these gifts "in," not "over" the church.) It follows that these gifts are available wherever persons are open to receive the proffered gifts for their intended purpose: that we, the body of Christ, "grow up into him who is the Head [of the body], that is, Christ" (Eph. 4:15).

b. Nondominical Apostles. Epaphroditus (Phil. 2:25) exemplifies an apostle as a congregation's commissioned representative rather than God's. Persons whom Paul sent to Corinth are apostles (2 Cor. 8:23); their job was to assist Paul in taking up a collection among the Gentiles for the poor in Jerusalem. When Paul described these, he called them "an honor to Christ," just as he, speaking of his own ministry, said he conducted a work "to honor the Lord himself" (v. 19). Whereas these apostles are sent with authority to act, they are not free, independent agents. Apostles have externally assigned responsibilities and people to whom they must render accountability—whether to the churches in Philippi or Jerusalem or to the Lord Christ.

See also GIFTS OF THE SPIRIT.

■ **Bibliography:** J. B. Lightfoot, *Galatians* (1866), 92–101 ■ B. M. Metzger, *A Textual Commentary on the Greek New Testament* (1971) ■ R. E. Nixon, "Apostle," *ZPEB* (1975) ■ K. H. Rengstorf, "Apostolos," *TDNT* (1964) ■ W. C. Robinson, "Apostle," *ISBE* (1979) ■ M. H. Shepherd Jr., "Apostle," *IDB* (1962).   ■ J. A. Hewett

APOSTOLIC ASSEMBLY OF FAITH IN JESUS CHRIST, INC.

(Asamblea Apostólica de la Fe en Cristo Jesús, Inc.). The largest and oldest Spanish-speaking Oneness pentecostal denomination in the U.S. It traces its roots back to Luis López and Juan Navarro, who, shortly after participating in the Azusa Street revival in 1909, began to teach that people baptized in the Trinitarian formula had to be rebaptized in the name of Jesus only. In 1912 Navarro baptized Francisco Llorente, who had recently arrived in the U.S. from Acapulco, Mexico. A year later, Llorente was ordained and began preaching among Mexican migrant workers throughout Southern California. His evangelistic preaching met with success, and in 1914 he converted and baptized Marcial de la Cruz. Together they preached to Mexican migrant farm workers throughout Southern California and planted a number of small congregations in Colton, San Bernardino, Riverside, Los Angeles, and Watts. In 1916 Marcial de la Cruz converted Antonio C. Nava in Los Angeles. De la Cruz and Nava conducted evangelistic meetings throughout California in 1918–19. In 1920 Nava established the first permanent Apostolic mission in the Imperial Valley. Nava continued to pastor that church until 1928 when, after Llorente's untimely death, he was asked to serve as the second "presiding bishop" of the Apostolic Assembly (AAFCJ).

The AAFCJ organized its first general convention in 1925. At the convention in San Bernardino, CA, the 27 pastors developed their doctrinal statement, uniform ordination qualifications, and church government. That year an estimated 700 members were attending 23 congregations in California, Arizona, New Mexico, and Baja California, Mexico. Only seven of these congregations met in regular church buildings, the rest in private homes. A schism in 1926 resulted in some disgruntled Apostolics leaving the AAFCJ to form their own organization in 1927. Despite the schism, the AAFCJ saw continued growth throughout the late 1920s. Antonio Nava led the AAFCJ to incorporate and sever its loose affiliation (for ordination purposes) with the black Oneness denomination called the ▸Pentecostal Assemblies of the World (PAW) in 1930.

Despite a second schism in the 1930s, the AAFCJ pressed ahead and organized its first youth crusade in 1934. The outbreak of WWII prompted the AAFCJ to create a policy that insisted that their members serve only in noncombat roles. Throughout the early 1940s the AAFCJ in the U.S. and the Apostolic Church of Faith in Christ Jesus in Mexico had been in dialogue about their fraternal relationship. In 1944 they jointly produced the Treaty of Unification, whereby they agreed to work together in promoting the Oneness message on both sides of the U.S.-Mexican border. In 1946 the AAFCJ opened up dialogue with the largest Anglo-American Oneness church, the ▸United Pentecostal Church. This resulted in a fraternal alliance in 1947 between the two denominations and joint missionary endeavors in Central America. In 1949 the AAFCJ department of education opened up Apostolic Bible Training School in Hayward, CA. Extension campuses in California, Texas, and Florida have been added, and in 1996 more than 580 students were enrolled in their Bible schools.

Throughout the '50s and '60s the AAFCJ saw tremendous growth. During that time, 42 new congregations were planted in California, Arizona, New Mexico, Texas, Colorado, Illinois, Washington, Oregon, Iowa, Pennsylvania, and Florida. They also sent missionaries to Costa Rica, Italy, and Honduras during this period. By 1968 there were 152 churches, 349 ordained or licensed ministers, and 8,000 communicant members in 12 states.

Since the 1960s the AAFCJ has witnessed phenomenal growth. In 1996 there were over 450 churches and missions, 2,100 ordained and licensed ministers, and 55,000 to 65,000 members in the U.S. In addition to this, there were over 345 churches, 635 ordained and licensed ministers, and 18,000 Apostolics in 15 countries around the world.

Until the 1950s the Apostolic Assembly was a largely Southwestern, Mexican-American, and Mexican immigrant denomination. Since the 1950s it has begun work in Chicago (1957), Italy (c. 1968), Florida (1969), New York (1970), Puerto Rico (1972), Canada (1992), and throughout Latin America. Because of its growing international constituency, it sees itself as a largely Hispanic denomination today.

Doctrinally, the Apostolic Assembly is part of the larger Oneness pentecostal movement in the U.S. and Mexico. It rejects the doctrine of the Trinity as unbiblical and affirms the Oneness position on the Godhead that Jesus revealed himself in three different manifestations—Father, Son, and Holy Spirit. They teach that Jesus is the name of the Father, Son, and Holy Spirit, and that water baptism by immersion is essential for salvation. People are to be baptized "in the name of Jesus," not of the Father, Son, and Holy Spirit (Matt. 28:19–20; Acts 2:38; 8:16). Those baptized in the Trinitarian formula must be rebaptized. They also teach that a person must be baptized in the Holy Spirit and that tongues is the initial physical evidence of baptism in the Holy Spirit and is a necessary sign of salvation (Mark 16:17; Acts 2:4). Only those who are baptized "in Jesus' name" will go to heaven (Acts 2:21; 3:38). They place a heavy emphasis on loud, enthusiastic singing, doctrinal standards, and the spiritual gifts of tongues, healing, miracles, discernment of evil spirits, words of knowledge, and evangelism. Like other pentecostals, they are millennialists who believe that Jesus Christ will return to earth to set up a millennial (1,000-year) kingdom. Their end-time focus and great emphasis on holiness have shaped their attitude toward dress codes and women's roles. They require women to wear a head covering in worship services, and they frown on women cutting their hair and wearing cosmetics or jewelry. Like their brethren in Mexico, they do not ordain women to the ministry. The AAFCJ organizational style is episcopal, with bishops and superintendents much like the Methodists. President Bishop Baldemar Rodríguez stated that in the future the AAFCJ plans to continue evangelistic crusades among the Spanish-speaking, send out more foreign missionaries, open Spanish-speaking bookstores, and produce radio and television programs.

■ **Bibliography:** B. Cantú, *Historia de la Asamblea Apostólica de la Fe en Cristo Jesús, 1916–1966* (1966) ■ M. J. Gaxiola y Gaxiola, *La Serpiente y La Paloma* (1970) ■ C. Holland, *The Religious Dimension in Hispanic Los Angeles* (1974) ■ D. Jauhall, *Why We Believe What We Believe* (1995) ■ B. Rodríguez, *Denominational Statistical Information Form for the Apostolic Assembly of Faith in Christ Jesus, Inc.* (1996).

■ G. Espinosa

APOSTOLIC CHRISTIAN ASSEMBLY (INDIA)

Theologians are reluctant to engage the beliefs and practices of ordinary Hindus (Caplan), but the popular Christianity that is prevalent today in a large number of pentecostal and other South Indian independent churches does address the Hindu folk religion. An outstanding example is the Apostolic Christian Assembly (ACA), one of the prominent indigenous church bodies of Madras.

Founded as an autonomous pentecostal church in Madras City by the late Pastor G. Sundram, who had left the exclusivist Ceylon Pentecostal Mission, the ACA has a strong appeal for Hindus. Many well-educated Hindu observers participate in the worship, and a large number are publicly baptized in weekly baptismal services. Worship is bilingual (Tamil and English) but combines a number of features familiar to Hindus and in harmony with Tamil religious tradition. Much of the worship is devoted to congregational singing, and Hindu converts have compared this to Saivite devotional hymn-singing of their past. A second similarity is an intense personal experience of the grace of God, testimonies of which reflect the pattern of the Saivite saints. Third is the attraction of the saintly Pastor G. Sundram as a religious guru. "Pastor Sundram has little churchly authority in a form familiar to Western Christians, but the fascination of the congregation with his saintliness and their willingness to accord him authority over their daily lives is a pattern that has a strong tradition in Tamil religious history" (Younger). Today ACA is led by Senior Pastor M. K. Sam Sundaram. In mid 1993 the main church at Purasawalkam reported a membership of 5,500, which had increased to 8,000 by the end of 1995. During these two years the number of branch churches increased from 57 to 102, and in 1996, 14 more churches were being planted. By 1997 there were 144 branch churches with a total of 20–25,000 members. In 1997 the main church had some 12,000 members and conducted two Sunday services with 7,500 to 8,000 worshipers at the 7:00 A.M. service and 2,500 at the 10:00 A.M. service.

The ACA represents a broad cross-section of society, rich as well as poor, educated as well as illiterate. The church engages in a wide range of activities including relief and welfare ministries, developmental projects, church planting, evangelistic outreach, and conventions. It maintains several schools and four children's homes. They have published a number of books, including Bible studies, testimonies, training manuals, and hymnals, as well as the *Herald of Deliverance* magazine. Audio, video, and music cassettes are also produced.

The pastor encourages the youth, who are a major key to growth, to go and contact new people, bringing them to conversion. Another important growth factor is the formation of small groups, which result in 20 to 30 baptisms every Sunday.

ACA missionaries are sent into North India. At least 10 churches have been started in Calcutta, Chandigarh, Delhi, Jabalpur and also in the states of Gujarat, Haryana, and Bihar. The ACA is a vibrant model of a South Indian indigenous church.

■ **Bibliography:** Apostolic Christian Assembly, Annual Report 1996–1997 ■ L. Caplan, *Religion and Power: Essays on the Christian Community in Madras* (1989) ■ idem, "Popular Christianity in Urban South India," *Religion and Society* 30 (2 June 1983) ■ R. E. Hedlund, "Church Planting in Selected Indian Cities," in *Evangelization and Church Growth Issues from the Asian Context* (1992) ■ S. S. Pillai, *Strategy to Reach Greater Madras* (1996) ■ P. Younger, "Hindu-Christian Worship Settings in South India" in Harold Coward, ed., *Hindu-Christian Dialogue: Perspectives and Encounters* (1990).

■ R. E. Hedlund

APOSTOLIC CHURCH

The Apostolic Church (AC) is the smallest of the mainline pentecostal groups in Britain, with 116 churches and 5,500 attendees (1995). Established in 1916, the founders were the brothers Daniel Powell Williams (1882–1947) and William Jones Williams (1891–1945). Both were converted in the 1904–5 ▸Welsh Revival, the former under the ministry of Evan Roberts. Early association was with the Apostolic Faith Church (AFC) founded by W. O. Hutchinson (1864–1928) in Bournemouth in 1908. D. P. Williams entered full-time ministry in 1911 and was called to be an apostle in a convention in London in 1913. Following disagreement with the Bournemouth parent body about church government, property, and accountability, the majority of the Welsh assemblies formally severed their relationship on January 8, 1916, to form the nucleus of the Apostolic Church. The first issue of the AC magazine, *Riches of Grace,* listed 19 assemblies in Wales. In August of that year the first annual convention at Penygroes, Carmarthenshire, Wales, was held. The convention, which is still held, has since become a key feature in the church's life.

In 1917 a further eight assemblies were added to the AC. In 1919 the Burning Bush Assembly of Glasgow, led by Andrew Turnbull (1872–1937), and the Apostolic Church, Hereford, led by Edgar Frank Hodges (1872–1949), joined the AC. Turnbull was recognized as an apostle in 1920; Hodges, in 1922.

In 1916 a group of people under Herbert V. Chanter (1890–1966; recognized as an apostle in 1919), R. A. Jardine (1878–1950; recognized as an apostle in 1916), and E. C. W. Boulton (1884–1959; recognized as a prophet before 1919) left the mission in Bradford associated with ›Smith Wigglesworth.

In 1920 the eleven tenets of the AC were published in English (previously they had been in Welsh). In addition to evangelical belief in the inspiration and authority of Scripture, the Trinity, and the atonement, the tenets affirmed "church government by apostles, prophets, evangelists, pastors, teachers, elders and deacons"; belief in the baptism and gifts of the Holy Spirit; the possibility of falling from grace; and the obligatory nature of tithes and offerings.

The group led by Chanter held an Easter convention in Bradford in 1922, and representatives from the AC in Scotland, Wales, and the midlands of England attended. It was agreed that the Apostolic Missionary Movement should be formed and that this would function as a visible unity in four sections (centered around Glasgow, Bradford, Hereford, and Penygroes). The missionary headquarters would be in Bradford. D. P. Williams was appointed president of the missionary council. By 1934 these four sections had become seven, and in 1937, at a meeting in Bradford, a new constitution was adopted that brought the churches into one framework under a general council of apostles and prophets who should meet twice a year. Within the U.K. the church was divided into 12 areas, and an overseas constitution was included for the benefit of the expanding AC abroad. To accommodate the August convention, the Apostolic Temple, Penygroes—the only building to commemorate the Welsh Revival—was opened in 1933, and the much larger Convention Hall was opened in 1962. The Bible College at Penygroes was started in 1933. Yet, once the 1937 constitution had been agreed on, committees and procedures tended to multiply, and spiritual and numerical growth slowed down. When the ›Latter Rain revival broke out in Canada in 1948, its effects were felt in the U.K. The revivalists emphasized decentralization of finance and property and insisted on the autonomy of each local assembly. Though the AC leadership in the U.K. reaffirmed its acceptance of Apostolic beliefs and principles, var-

ious ministers left to join the new movement. Subsequently, the constitution was revised by simplification in 1961, and again in 1985 and 1987, and the administrative offices were combined and moved to Swansea.

As a result of missionary and pioneering work, AC assemblies have been established on every continent; these are autonomous in Australia, Cameroon, Canada, Denmark, France, Germany, Ghana, Hungary, Italy, Jamaica, New Zealand, Nigeria, Papua New Guinea, Portugal, Switzerland, U.S., and Vanuatu. Assemblies have been opened in 43 countries, and their representatives meet at the World Apostolic Conference, which is held every four years in various centers.

AC leaders joined the Pentecostal Unity Conferences in London in 1939 and 1940 and took part in the formation of the British Pentecostal Fellowship. AC representatives have always been part of the Hymnal Committee that produced the two editions of *Redemption Hymnal,* until recently the most widely used pentecostal songbook in Britain. Pentecostal preachers have addressed many AC conventions (e.g., Donald Gee at Penygroes in 1939), while AC ministers have successfully conducted evangelistic campaigns and crusades throughout the world.

■ **Bibliography:** *The Apostolic Church World Wide Directory* (1995) ■ M. R. Hathaway, "The Role of William Oliver Hutchinson and the Apostolic Faith Church in the Formation of British Pentecostal Churches" (SPS, July 10–14, 1995) ■ H. B. Llewellyn, "A Study of the History and Thought of the Apostolic Church in Wales in the Context of Pentecostalism" (diss., U. of Wales–Cardiff, 1998) ■ W. A. C. Rowe, *One Lord One Faith* (1988) ■ T. N. Turnbull, *What God Hath Wrought* (1959) ■ idem, *Brother in Arms* (1963) ■ J. E. Worsfold, *The Origins of the Apostolic Church in Great Britain* (1991). ■ W. K. Kay

APOSTOLIC CHURCH OF FAITH IN JESUS CHRIST

(Iglesia Apostólica de la Fe en Cristo Jesús). First indigenous Oneness pentecostal denomination in Mexico. The Apostolic Church was founded in Villa Aldama, Chihuahua, Mexico, in Nov. 1914, by a remarkable woman named ›Romanita Carbajal de Valenzuela. After being converted to pentecostalism in Los Angeles in 1912, she decided to take the pentecostal message back to her family and homeland in 1914. The small church she founded in Villa Aldama quickly spread the Oneness message throughout Mexico. By 1932 there were 26 congregations and 800 members in Mexico. The greatest growth took place after WWII, when the church grew from 111 churches and 5,000 members in 1946 to almost 330 churches and 13,000 members by 1956. Forty years later, in 1986, there were an estimated 500 churches and 100,000 adherents throughout Mexico. Since the 1950s they have sent missionaries to work in Guatemala, El Salvador, Nicaragua, Honduras, Costa Rica, Colombia, Argentina,

Brazil, and most recently the U.S., which has caused some friction between them and the Apostolic Assembly of Faith in Jesus Christ in the U.S., although it has not hindered fellowship between the two Oneness denominations. Like other Mexican pentecostal denominations, it has gone through a number of major schisms (1930, 1965, 1974). Its organizational style is episcopal, with bishops and superintendents much like the Methodists. They operate at least two Bible schools, one in Mexico City, the other in Torreón. Doctrinally they are very similar to the ➤Apostolic Assembly of Faith in Jesus Christ, Inc., in the U.S. They reject the doctrine of the Trinity as unbiblical and affirm the Oneness position of the Godhead—that Jesus has revealed himself in three different manifestations—Father, Son, and Holy Spirit. They also believe that tongues is a necessary sign of salvation, that Jesus was himself the Father and the Son, and that people who are not baptized "in Jesus' name" (not the Trinitarian formula) are not saved. They place a heavy emphasis on loud enthusiastic worship, doctrinal standards, and the spiritual gifts of tongues, healing, miracles, discernment of evil spirits, words of knowledge, and evangelism. Like other pentecostals, they are millennialists, believing that Jesus Christ will return to earth to set up a millennial (1,000-year) kingdom. Their end-time focus and great emphasis on holiness have shaped their attitude toward women's roles. They require women to wear a head covering in worship services, and they frown on women cutting their hair and wearing cosmetics and jewelry. Like their brethren in the U.S., they do not ordain women to the ministry.

The Apostolic Church of Faith in Jesus Christ has given birth to a number of other Oneness movements in Mexico, most notably the ➤Light of the World Church (La Iglesia La Luz del Mundo). The Apostolic Church is the oldest and one of the largest Oneness pentecostal denominations in Mexico and Latin America today.

■ **Bibliography:** E. L. Cortés, *Pentecostalismo y milenarismo: La Iglesia Apostólica de la Fe en Cristo Jesús* (1990) ■ M. J. Gaxiola y Gaxiola, *La Serpiente y La Paloma* (1970) ■ W. R. Read et al., *Latin American Church Growth* (1969), 164–68.   ■ G. Espinosa

APOSTOLIC CHURCH OF GOD OF ROMANIA, THE

With a membership of about 400,000, the Apostolic Church of God of Romania (ACG) is the largest pentecostal group of Europe. Because of its tremendous growth in the last four decades, Romania has become known among missiologists as "the Korea of Europe."

History.

The history of the pentecostal movement of Romania goes back to Sept. 10, 1922, when the first Romanian pentecostal church was organized in Paulis, in the district of Arad. Two events had a significant impact on the beginning of

pentecostalism in Romania. The first was the miraculous healing of Persida Bradin, who suffered from tuberculosis; the second, the correspondence between George Bradin and the Church of God Publishing House in Cleveland, TN. Bradin asked for more information about the pentecostal faith, and the answer came in the Romanian language from Pavel Budeanu, a Romanian immigrant to the U.S. Between 1922 and 1929 the pentecostal churches were united under the leadership of Bradin, and on Feb. 22, 1929, they adopted the name the Apostolic Church of God.

Although the Romanian Constitution of 1923 stipulated full religious freedom, the Orthodox Church and the Romanian government opposed the new movement and persecuted the few pentecostal churches. During the next 20 years, seven decisions against the pentecostals were issued by the Ministry of Arts and Religion. The persecutions reached a climax in 1942, when the prime minister issued a decree that authorized the martial courts to jail pentecostals or send them to the battlefield. Most of the pentecostals remained firm in their faith during these persecutions.

But the steadfastness of the early Romanian pentecostals in face of persecution was not matched by their unity. In 1929, under the influence of an Assemblies of God (AG) school in Danzig (Gdansk), Poland, a missionary came to Timisoara, which led to a split on doctrinal grounds. Unlike the first pentecostal churches, the new pentecostal group, The Christians Baptized with the Holy Ghost, led by Alexandru Isbasa, did not practice footwashing and permitted the use of alcoholic beverages. A second split occurred in 1931, when Ioan Bododea of Braila and a few churches faithful to him separated from the ACG to form the group known as The Disciples of the Lord. In 1934 the three groups agreed to reunite, but the unity lasted only a short time.

Immediately after WWII, pentecostal churches convened to reorganize. On May 20 the leadership of the ACG was elected. On Dec. 23, 1946, the ACG received its first temporary government approval. Between 1946 and 1948 all pentecostal factions joined the ACG, mainly through the efforts of ➤Pavel Bochian, except for the Bucharest district offices of the Christians Baptized with the Holy Ghost and the Disciples of the Lord. These two groups joined the ACG in Feb. and Mar. of 1950 respectively. Full and final recognition of the ACG was received from the parliament on Nov. 14, 1950. The first congress of the newly recognized denomination convened in July 1951. A second congress convened in 1956, a year that marked the beginning of more than 30 years of Communist persecution.

During the Communist regime (1944–89), the pentecostal emphasis on the supernatural work of the Holy Spirit, both in theory and practice, made the ACG a special target of the Department of Cults. Through this agency, the government tightly controlled the activity of the ACG, but the Communist persecutions of Romanian pentecostals were not as harsh as those exerted by the Orthodox Church between the two World Wars. The Communist persecution included: (1) Interference in the internal affairs of the church. The government approved preachers, candidates to be baptized, visiting officials, etc. It also limited the number of authorized churches and ordained ministers. (2) Recruiting of collaborationists from among the pastors. These were required to regularly present reports of activity to the Department of Cults, especially any activities involving relationships with churches and church officials from Western countries. The pentecostals were constantly suspected to be spies for the capitalist world. (3) Severe restrictions on religious publications and distribution of religious materials. (4) Barring of pentecostals from professional jobs in some areas, such as management, education, media, etc.

Despite the tight controls, the ACG grew significantly during the Communist period to 800 churches in 1989, with a total membership of over 200,000. The ACG experienced unprecedented growth after the fall of Communism in Dec. 1989. In the first eight years of democracy, the number of churches grew from 800 to more than 2,100, and the membership from over 200,000 to almost 400,000. When the Romanian pentecostals celebrated the 75th anniversary of the ACG in Oct. 1997, there were 354 ordained ministers (1 for every 6 churches), 540 licensed ministers, 800 deacons, and 70 home missionaries who held credentials with the ACG.

Education.

Most ACG ministers have little or no theological education. One of the greatest achievements of the ACG during the Communist period was the college-level Seminarul Teologic Penticostal (STP), founded in 1976 by ˃Trandafir Sandru. The number of students enrolled was restricted by the Communist government: 15 in 1976, 5 in 1980, and 10 in 1984. From 1985 until 1989 three students were approved each year. In 1992 the STP was upgraded to a university-level institution and changed its name to Institutul Teologic Penticostal–Bucuresti (ITPB). The current enrollment at the ITPB is 63 full-time students and 310 correspondence students. The double-major degree ITPB offers adequately prepares the students to serve as pastors and as teachers of religion in public schools. A two-year training program is offered by each of the seven ACG district offices for Sunday school teachers and youth workers.

Publications.

The official publication of the ACG is the monthly periodical *Cuvantul Adevarului*, with a 1999 circulation of almost 20,000 copies in 15 countries. At least three other pentecostal magazines are published by district offices and local churches.

Mission.

Priority is given to church planting in the south and southeast of the country, regions poor in evangelical churches. About 40 home missionaries and church planters work in these areas.

Other Pentecostal and Charismatic Groups in Romania.

After the fall of the Communist regime in Dec. 1989, Romania became an open mission field for many Christian denominations and organizations from the West. Missions can function legally in Romania, but due to pressure exercised by the dominant Orthodox Church, they receive the status of "religious associations" rather than denominations. Many of the newly planted churches choose, however, to integrate into the ACG, the only pentecostal group with denominational status. The most significant pentecostal group registered as a religious association is the Assemblies of God Association (AGA), established in 1996. With fewer than 20 affiliated churches, this pentecostal group is best known for its theological school, Institutul Biblic Roman (IBR), founded in 1990 by Dr. Ioan Ceuta. The charismatic churches cannot be easily identified; there are about 15 churches, each registered individually as a religious association, with not much cooperation between them.

■ **Bibliography:** Archives of the Apostolic Church of God (Bucharest) I. Ceuta, "The History of the Pentecostal Apostolic Church of Romania" (diss., Columbia [SC] Biblical Seminary, 1990) ■ T. Sandru, *The Pentecostal Apostolic Church of God of Romania* (1982) ■ idem, *Trezirea Spirituala Penticostala din Romania* (1997). ■ J. F. Tipei

APOSTOLIC CHURCH OF PENTECOST OF CANADA

In 1921 Franklin Small (1873–1961) and 10 others affiliated with the infant Pentecostal Assemblies of Canada withdrew in protest against the reception that year of congregations in the four western provinces that had previously been affiliated with the General Council of the Assemblies of God (U.S.). At issue was the Small faction's belief in the ˃oneness of the Godhead. On Oct. 25, 1921, they obtained a Dominion charter as the Apostolic Church of Pentecost of Canada, with Oneness as the central tenet. Union in 1953 with the Evangelical Churches of Pentecost, which included many who held to the triunity of the Godhead, resulted in tolerance of both points of view. Baptism in the name of Jesus and the eternal security of the believer then became principal emphases.

The home constituency is concentrated in the prairie provinces. In 1996 the church reported 160 churches and 13,500 members.

■ **Bibliography:** C. E. Jones, *Guide to the Study of the Pentecostal Movement* (1982) ■ R. A. Larder, *Our Apostolic Heritage* (1971) ■

Mission Handbook (1979) ■ A. C. Piepkorn, *Profiles in Belief*, vol. 3 (1979). ■ C. E. Jones

APOSTOLIC FAITH (BAXTER SPRINGS, KS)

The Apostolic Faith (AF) became the earliest organized pentecostal sect when Charles F. Parham initiated a loose program for his followers in the spring of 1906. Proclaiming himself "projector," Parham established three state directors over the areas most affected by his new doctrine—Texas, Kansas, and Missouri—and ordained local elders to serve individual assemblies of AF workers. The local assemblies met weekly for a period of prayer and devotion. Late in 1906, however, Parham's attempt at organization and personal leadership met an abrupt end. He was personally rejected by the ▸Azusa Street AF Mission in Los Angeles, and amid rumors questioning his personal morality, much of his midwestern alliance defected under the leadership of W. Faye Carothers and ▸Howard Goss. Parham succeeded, however, in retaining several thousand followers and in 1909 established Baxter Springs, KS, as his home and informal headquarters of his small wing of the pentecostal movement.

Parham never formulated another plan for organized fellowship. During the last two decades of his life he led the collection of AF churches through the force of his own charismatic personality and the influence of his journal, *Apostolic Faith*. Parham retained a small national constituency for his ministry and held campaigns throughout the country. Still, the bulk of his followers lived in the midwestern states of Kansas, Missouri, Texas, Arkansas, and Oklahoma. At his death in 1929, Parham's journal registered 1,400 subscribers, and he had a regular following of 4,000 to 5,000.

After 1929 Sarah Parham assumed her husband's editorial work, and Robert Parham took the bulk of his father's preaching schedule. Upon Sarah Parham's death in 1937, Robert hoped to reorganize the fledgling band of churches gradually into a tighter organizational unit and to bring the group into closer fellowship

with other pentecostal denominations. He died prematurely in 1944, however, and the AF was left without a leader who could control the diverse assortment of locally run churches.

In 1951 the AF alliance, linked only by the *Apostolic Faith* and an annual Bible school held in Baxter Springs, split in half. Progressive-minded ministers considered it essential to form some cooperative organization to take advantage of

A group of Christian workers with Charles F. Parham (seated in center) at Bryan Hall, Houston, TX, 1905.

Ordination certificate of Howard A. Goss with the Apostolic Faith (Baxter Springs, KS), dated Aug. 26, 1906. It is signed by W. F. Carothers, field director, and Charles F. Parham, projector.

state and federal tax laws and to provide more efficient support of foreign missionaries. They also advocated increased contact with other pentecostal groups and allowed greater emotional displays in their worship services. Other ministers, conditioned by pentecostalism's rejection of Charles F. Parham decades earlier, feared the trappings of organization and considered much of the emotional display a "counterfeit" spawned by the popularity of pentecostal faith healers. In Spearman, TX, in 1951, the progressive faction withdrew from the fellowship and established the ▸Full Gospel Evangelistic Association (FGEA). This group created its own monthly periodical, *Full Gospel News,* and in 1960 organized Midwest Bible Institute in Webb City, MO. In 1971 the Bible school was relocated to a campus in Houston, TX, where it remained until its closing in 1995.

Permanent headquarters were established in Houston in 1976. Today FGEA claims 120 active ministers, 75 U.S. churches, and a little under 3,000 church members. The organization has missionary-affiliated congregations in Mexico, Honduras, and Nicaragua that more than double its U.S. size.

The older AF fellowship remains a loose band of churches centered around the monthly periodical—now the *Apostolic Faith Report*—and the Bible college in Baxter Springs. In addition, followers meet annually in a camp meeting that rotates between Baxter Springs and Laverne, OK. Recent totals are estimated at 100 ministers and 50 churches with a combined membership of 3,000. Unlike the FGEA, the AF affiliation continues to promote Parham's unique theological stand on "conditional immortality" and "destruction of the wicked."

See also APOSTOLIC FAITH MOVEMENT, ORIGINS.

■ **Bibliography:** J. Goff, *Fields White unto Harvest* (1988) ■ A. Nehrbass, *This Is Full Gospel Evangelistic Association* (1980).

■ J. R. Goff Jr.

APOSTOLIC FAITH MISSION (PORTLAND, OR) The

Apostolic Faith Mission (AFM) emerged directly out of the ▸Apostolic Faith (AF) movement supervised by ▸William J. Seymour in Los Angeles. Its founder, ▸Florence Louise Crawford, was a Holiness worker who embraced pentecostal views at ▸Azusa Street. In late 1906 she left Southern California for Oregon. Arriving in Portland on Christmas Day, 1906, she immediately began conducting mission services, out of which her organization developed.

During 1907 Crawford traveled to Seattle, Minneapolis, and Winnipeg, trying to determine where she should locate permanently. She decided to settle in Portland. In 1908 she acquired downtown property and began a faith publishing venture. Like Seymour (whose mailing list she took from Azusa Street), she called her paper *The Apostolic Faith.*

Crawford was critical of many aspects of pentecostal practice. An ardent ▸restorationist, she also subscribed wholeheartedly to Holiness teaching, divine healing, premillennialism, and faith living. She deplored centralized organization and minced no words in denouncing advocates of the ▸finished work, those whose separation from worldliness she deemed inadequate, and the organization of pentecostal denominations. Over the years, Crawford kept her group out of association with other pentecostals and evangelicals.

Crawford's Portland mission soon spawned related efforts, most of which were on the West Coast. Together these constituted her AF movement. Although membership never reached much over five thousand, the movement's publishing efforts have been extensive. Those who affiliated with her were required to take "an uncompromising stand" for official doctrines and to hold to strictly enforced moral codes.

Crawford's movement espoused a three-stage pentecostalism: first, justification by faith; then, entire sanctification; and finally, the baptism of the Holy Spirit. She demanded that her missions accept a "faith" stance: ministers could neither solicit funds nor receive regular offerings. An offering box near the church entrance sufficed. Her members not only relinquished dancing, card playing, theater attendance, smoking, and drinking, they also distanced themselves from those who practiced such activities. Proscribing all makeup and short hair for women, Crawford enjoined modest apparel and insisted that slacks, shorts, and short sleeves were inappropriate for women.

Unlike many pentecostal groups, the Portland-based AF movement sponsors no Bible training school. The headquarters make available various Bible studies as well as Crawford's sermons. It encourages the use of the KJV.

Florence Crawford died on June 20, 1936. Her son, Raymond Robert Crawford, who had served as assistant overseer under his mother, assumed leadership and served until his death on June 8, 1965. He was succeeded by Loyce Carver. Since 1993, leadership rests with Dwight Baltzell.

See also APOSTOLIC FAITH MOVEMENT, ORIGINS.

■ **Bibliography:** *The Apostolic Faith* (1965).

■ E. L. Blumhofer

APOSTOLIC FAITH MOVEMENT, ORIGINS The Apos-

tolic Faith Movement grew out of the ▸restorationist dreams of a young Kansas evangelist, ▸Charles F. Parham (1873–1929). Influenced during his childhood in Cheney, KS, especially by Methodism and the Winebrenner Church of God (a Methodist-like German body), Parham dedicated his life to the ministry. From his teens he demonstrated a proclivity for intense spiritual experiences as well as impatience with structure and authority. Parham briefly attended the academy and normal school associated with Southwestern Kansas College, a Methodist institution. In mid 1893 he accepted an assignment as a lay preacher in the Methodist Episcopal Church in Eudora, KS, where he served until 1895. By then he had determined to preach what he understood to be NT Christianity. Essentially self-taught, Parham read the Bible to find its meaning for himself. This approach to Scripture had already led him to some nontraditional conclusions. He espoused conditional immortality, taught an experience of Spirit baptism that "sealed" Christ's bride for the rapture, enthusiastically supported Zionism, and preached divine healing. He also lived "by faith." He traveled within Kansas, preaching in homes, schoolhouses, and churches as invited, living wherever he was offered shelter, proclaiming his message.

By 1898 Parham (now married and the father of a growing family) established a base of operations in Topeka, where he opened a faith home, a mission, and a small publishing enterprise. Probably the central practice of his outreach was prayer for the sick. While in Topeka, he began to call his message of "living Christianity" the "apostolic faith." He began to issue a biweekly magazine, *Apostolic Faith,* and to recognize his identity with a larger restorationist millenarian subculture.

Committed to recapturing fully the essence of primitive Christianity, Parham visited ministries that shared his hopes. His most important trip took him to Shiloh, ME, in mid 1900. There the efforts of ▸Frank Sandford deeply influenced him. Returning to Topeka in late summer, Parham determined to open a Bible school patterned after Sandford's Holy Ghost and Us Bible School in Shiloh. Other evangelists had already taken over most of his congregation and his facilities, so he was free to embark on a venture to promulgate and further develop his views. In Oct. 1900 he opened Bethel Bible School with some 40 people (including dependents).

Bethel Bible School was unusual in several ways. It had one text, the Bible, and one teacher, the Holy Spirit—who presumably channeled his message through Parham. Students studied biblical passages together and endeavored to "pray in" the lessons of each passage. Long hours of prayer, services of indefinite duration, and hours of visitation and evangelism filled each day. Parham stressed the NT views that he considered had constituted the apostolic faith. Toward the end of the year he turned the students' attention to a NT experience as yet unrealized among them—tongues speech. Basing his assertion primarily on Acts 2, he affirmed that speaking in tongues was the biblical evidence for an experience of Spirit baptism. Many of his contemporaries shared his emphasis on the baptism with the Holy Spirit; none, however, had posited a uniform biblical evidence for the experience.

As a result, in Jan. 1901, Parham's students and other followers began to speak in tongues. The school disbanded in the wake of enthusiasm to spread the message that yet another dimension of the apostolic faith had been restored. Enthusiasm waned rapidly in the face of considerable ridicule and opposition, however. For two years, Parham struggled to establish a setting in which he could preach and practice his variety of the NT faith.

The tide turned in 1903 when Parham, frustrated in his efforts to convince people of the validity of tongues speech as the evidence of Spirit baptism, focused again on healing. He distributed tracts at a popular southwestern Missouri health resort, El Dorado Springs, and conducted meetings in his rented rooms. The healing of Mary Arthur, a chronically ill resident of nearby Galena, KS, resulted in an invitation for Parham to visit Galena. There his efforts immediately evoked response. Daily services continued for months, with converts numbering near a thousand and nearly as many healings. Parham recruited dedicated young helpers in Galena who proved willing to share his itinerant "faith" life. He located his family in Baxter Springs, KS, and conducted services under the banner of the Apostolic Faith (AF) movement in surrounding towns.

The movement spread rapidly in the contiguous area of Kansas, Missouri, and Oklahoma. By 1905 Parham was in southern Texas, where he was to have some of his most dramatic success. He associated in the Houston area with a capable young lawyer who was also a licensed Methodist preacher, Warren Fay Carothers. In late 1905 the two opened a faith Bible school in which several who later became prominent pentecostals participated. Probably Parham's best-known Houston portage was ▸William Seymour, who responded (against Parham's wishes) to an invitation to carry the movement's message to Los Angeles. He took not only Parham's message but also the name of the movement and called his message and his paper *The Apostolic Faith.*

The AF movement, according to Parham, had a twofold purpose: the restoration of "the faith once delivered to the saints" (Parham yearned for "the old-time religion") and the promotion of Christian unity. In addition to evidential tongues (which Parham believed should be authentic human languages), the movement affirmed the necessity of crisis sanctification, proclaimed divine healing, espoused premillennialism, urged "faith" living for Christian workers, and valued the manifestation of spiritual gifts.

Once Seymour reached Azusa Street, leadership eluded Parham, except in the southern Midwest. AF missions sprang up in many places, as people who embraced Parham's essential message carried it elsewhere. Usually leaders of such missions shared Parham's distaste for organization and did not acknowledge his authority.

Parham's influence remained strong in Texas through mid 1907, even after he was arrested on a charge of sodomy. Some of his followers regrouped, keeping the name AF but disassociating from Parham. Parham, meanwhile, retained a loyal following and also used the name, claiming that his efforts alone represented the true vision of his original AF. Gradually, adherents of AF missions in the Midwest who had disassociated from Parham replaced the designation "Apostolic Faith" with the less troublesome term "pentecostal." Seymour's efforts in Los Angeles retained the name. Florence Crawford, who left Azusa Street for Portland, OR, introduced her efforts under the name Apostolic Faith. The group she founded continues to use the name today, as does the remnant of Parham's followers in Baxter Springs, KS.

In one sense, then, the AF movement can be regarded as an early synonym for "pentecostal." It quickly came to have a more specific usage, however, describing participants in several pentecostal ministries that operated independently of one another.

See also APOSTOLIC FAITH (BAXTER SPRINGS, KS); APOSTOLIC FAITH MISSION (PORTLAND, OR).

■ **Bibliography:** R. M. Anderson, *Vision of the Disinherited* (1979) ▌ J. Goff, "Fields White unto Harvest: Charles F. Parham and the Missionary Origins of the Pentecostal Movement" (diss., Arkansas, 1987).   ■ E. L. Blumhofer

APOSTOLIC OVERCOMING HOLY CHURCH OF GOD

A black Oneness pentecostal organization founded in Mobile, AL, in 1917 by William T. Phillips (1893–1974). A Holiness minister since 1913 who became an evangelist in 1916, Phillips embraced the Oneness doctrine. His own congregation, the Greater Adams Holiness Church, was incorporated in 1920 as the Ethiopian Overcoming Holy Church of God, with "Ethiopian" being changed to "Apostolic" in 1927. Due to Phillips's influence, the organization is the only Oneness body to hold the Holiness doctrine of sanctification. Wine is required in communion, and footwashing is an ordinance. The episcopally governed body ordains women. The Apostolic Overcoming Holy Church of God Publishing House distributes literature and its periodical, *The People's Mouthpiece.* Headquarters are in Birmingham, AL, which in 1987 recorded its membership as 13,000 in 197 churches. The church has foreign works in Haiti and West Africa.

■ **Bibliography:** C. E. Jones, *Black Holiness: A Guide to the Study of Black Participation in Wesleyan Perfectionist and Glossolalic Pentecostal Movements* (1987) ▌ idem, *Guide to the Study of the Pentecostal Movement* (1983) ▌ W. T. Phillips, *Excerpts from the Life of Rt. Rev. W. T. Phillips and Fundamentals of the Apostolic Overcoming Holy Church of God, Inc.* (1967) ▌ A. C. Piepkorn, *Profiles in Belief,* vol. 3 (1979).   ■ D. A. Reed

ARCHIVAL RESOURCES

Until recent years researchers interested in the pentecostal and charismatic movements generally had to discover a private collection, interview eye-witnesses to the revivals, or confer with a denominational official for archival resources. This is still true for certain resources, but since the late 1970s several denominations have organized repositories, and other nonpentecostal libraries and archives have added pentecostal and charismatic resources to their holdings. The 1990s saw archives developing digital libraries and serving researchers on the Internet, thus making their holdings accessible worldwide. And in 1999 the Assemblies of God Archives, U.S., changed its name to the Flower Pentecostal Heritage Center and added an interactive museum.

Documenting the early years of the pentecostal movement is difficult for at least two reasons. First, the movement was unorganized and few pentecostals showed interest in organizing, wishing rather to remain independent. Second, across the movement it was believed that Christ's coming was imminent. With this belief firmly settled in their minds, there was little reason to keep records for historians to ponder.

Fortunately, as the movement developed, some early pentecostals began to preserve diaries, periodicals, correspondence, photographs, and other documents. The items that have survived help tell the story of the movement's early years.

Likewise, documenting the charismatic movement has its difficulties, for it too has had little formal organization. Many who were baptized in the Spirit remained in their denominations while others formed independent congregations. More documentation is available for the recent charismatic movement, however, than for the early pentecostal movement simply because there has been more interest in documenting religious history in the latter half of the 20th century than there was in the first half of the century.

I. RESOURCE CENTERS.

Several archival repositories that have developed in recent years are open to researchers. Each center has established certain collecting and research policies. Persons interested in

Glenn Gohr, assistant archivist, with a portion of the holdings of the Flower Pentecostal Heritage Center.

researching a given repository are advised to check in advance with the center regarding the type of materials available and the hours the center is open. Often archival personnel can direct a researcher to other archives if their own does not have the desired documents.

- Archives of the Billy Graham Center, Wheaton College, Wheaton, IL 60187. An archives for nondenominational Protestant missions and evangelism. Collections include resources of groups and individuals having connections with the pentecostal and charismatic movements, such as the National Religious Broadcasters and the National Association of Evangelicals. Also included in the collections are papers and recordings of William Branham, Kathryn Kuhlman, Aimee Semple McPherson, and Corrie ten Boom.
- Archives of the David J. du Plessis Center for Christian Spirituality, Fuller Theological Seminary, 135 N. Oakland, Pasadena, CA 91182. Collects documentation on the pentecostal, charismatic, and ecumenical movements. Includes papers of David J. du Plessis and his collection of pentecostal and charismatic ephemera. Other papers include the history of early pentecostalism and its ethnic origins as well as records of interdenominational pentecostal leaders.
- Asbury Theological Seminary, 204 N. Lexington Ave., Wilmore, KY 40390. The Wesleyan Holiness Studies Center includes the John W. Carver Healing Collection, which includes 20,000 tapes, films, books, periodicals, broadsides, and more, documenting the salvation-healing movement of the 1950s.
- Charles F. Parham Center for Pentecostal-Charismatic Research, South Texas Bible Institute, 9234 FM–1960 West, Houston, TX 77070. The center focuses on Charles F. Parham, leader of the 1901 pentecostal outpouring in Topeka, KS.
- Donald Gee Centre for Pentecostal and Charismatic Research, Mattersey Hall, Mattersey, Doncaster, DN 10 5, HD, United Kingdom. Collections focus on Europe.
- Flower Pentecostal Heritage Center (Assemblies of God Archives), 1445 Boonville, Springfield, MO 65802. Collects materials relating to the denomination, the early pentecostal movement, charismatic movement, pentecostal and charismatic churches of North America, Pentecostal Fellowship of North America, Pentecostal World Conference, and collections on individuals such as Lillian Trasher, Smith Wigglesworth, and Maria B. Woodworth-Etter; also has audio and video interviews and radio and television programs from the salvation-healing movement of the 1950s.

- Hal Bernard Dixon Jr., Pentecostal Research Center (Church of God), P.O. Box 3448, Cleveland, TN 37320. This center's goal is to collect materials on the pentecostal-charismatic movements worldwide. On their own denomination they have records, journals, correspondence, periodicals, minutes, early books, tapes of radio programs and church services, and other materials.
- Holy Spirit Research Center, Oral Roberts University, 7777 S. Lewis, Tulsa, OK 74171. A collection of materials pertaining to the pentecostal-charismatic movement with emphasis on groups and individuals after 1950. Collection includes books, periodicals, sermon tapes, recorded interviews, and other materials. The Oral Roberts Evangelistic Association also maintains an archives for the association and the university.
- International Pentecostal Holiness Church Archives and Research Center, P.O. Box 12609, Oklahoma City, OK 73157. Denominational and interdenominational records that include taped interviews, missionary records, photographs, videos, memoirs, books, periodicals, newspaper and magazine clippings, and individual church histories.
- Pentecostal Historical Center (United Pentecostal Church), 8855 Dunn Rd., Hazelwood, MO 63042 (St. Louis area). This center is a part of the denomination's church division. The church division maintains denominational records. The center has several early periodicals published by Oneness groups that merged to form the United Pentecostal Church: diaries, photographs, recordings, radio programs, and various artifacts on display.

II. OTHER SOURCES.

In addition to the above repositories, researchers will find resources in pentecostal denominational headquarters that do not have organized archives. Other pentecostal resources can be found in the following:

Apostolic Faith Bible College, Box 653, Baxter Springs, KS 66713; Apostolic Faith Mission, 89197 Lynhurst, 2106 Johannesburg, South Africa; Church of God of Prophecy Archives, P.O. Box 2910, Cleveland, TN 37320-2910; Elim Library, Regent University School of Divinity, Virginia Beach, VA 23465; International Church of the Foursquare Gospel Heritage Ministries, 1910 W. Sunset Blvd., P.O. Box 26902, Los Angeles, CA 90028; Lewi Pethrus Library, Kaggeholm School, Stockholm, Sweden; Lewis Wilson Institute, Vanguard University (formerly Southern California College), 55 Fair Dr., Costa Mesa, CA 92626; Pentecostal Assemblies of Canada Archives, 6745 Century Ave., Mississauga, Ont. L5N 6P7 Canada; Pentecostal Assemblies of the World, Inc., 3939 Meadows Dr., P.O. Box 18525, Indianapolis, IN 46218-0525;

Pentecostal Church of God, P.O. Box 850, Joplin, MO 64802; Schomburg Center for Research in Black Culture, 515 Malcolm X Blvd., New York, NY 10037-1801.

Resources on nonpentecostal groups, such as the Holiness movement, are cataloged in denominational and college libraries and archives. The latter includes the Nazarene Archives, Kansas City, MO; Church of God Archives, Anderson, IN; The Alliance Archives, Colorado Springs, CO. The library at Regent University School of Divinity, Virginia Beach, VA, also has pentecostal/charismatic resources.

Local and state historical societies, local libraries, university libraries, newspaper files, court records, and other sources often turn up information on pentecostal-charismatic research projects.

An abundance of sources can be found on the Internet under pentecostal, charismatic, healing, miracles, speaking in tongues, Holy Spirit, etc., and under names of well-known individuals such as ˒Aimee Semple McPherson, ˒Kathryn Kuhlman, ˒Charles F. Parham, ˒Oral Roberts, ˒William Seymour, and ˒Smith Wigglesworth.

■ **Bibliography:** C. Jones, *A Guide to the Study of the Pentecostal Movement* (1983) ▪ E. W. Linder, *Yearbook of American and Canadian Churches* (annual).   ■ W. E. Warner

ARGUE, ANDREW HARVEY (1868–1959). Pastor and evangelist. A pioneering figure in the ˒Pentecostal Assemblies of Canada (PAOC), A. H. Argue founded Calvary Temple, Winnipeg, which was for decades one of Canada's largest pen-

A. H. Argue, who received the baptism of the Spirit in 1906 and became a pioneer in the Pentecostal Assemblies of Canada.

tecostal churches. Upon hearing of the pentecostal outpouring in 1906, he traveled to Chicago, where he experienced the baptism in the Holy Spirit himself. Leaving a profitable business and his Winnipeg pastorate, he traveled extensively in the U.S. and Canada, for a time in the 1920s in campaigns with his daughter ˒Zelma and son ˒Watson. His meetings brought him into association with ˒Maria B. Woodworth-Etter and ˒Charles S. Price, and led to the establishment of several churches, including Evangel Temple, Toronto, in 1927.

■ **Bibliography:** Z. Argue, *Contending for the Faith* (1923) ▪ C. Brumback, *Suddenly … from Heaven* (1961) ▪ G. G. Kulbeck, *What God Hath Wrought* (1958) ▪ W. E. McAlister, "A. H. Argue with the Lord," *Pentecostal Testimony* 40 (3, 1959).   ■ E. A. Wilson

ARGUE, WATSON (1904–85). Pastor and evangelist. Son of ˒A. H. Argue, Watson Argue distinguished himself as a competitive swimmer, speaker, and gospel musician by age 20. He held meetings in the U.K. in 1923 and in ˒Angelus Temple upon the disappearance of ˒Aimee Semple McPherson in 1926. He pastored Calvary Temple, Winnipeg (1937–48), and Calvary Temple, Seattle (1948–56). He was noted for his effective invitations at the close of an evangelistic message. His later ministry was devoted largely to overseas evangelistic crusades.

■ **Bibliography:** Z. Argue, *Contending for the Faith* (1923) ▪ C. Brumback, *Suddenly … from Heaven* (1961) ▪ G. G. Kulbeck, *What God Hath Wrought* (1958) ▪ W. Menzies, *Anointed to Serve* (1971).
                                                   ■ E. A. Wilson

ARGUE, ZELMA (1900–1980). Well-known pentecostal evangelist and teacher. Born in Winnipeg, Canada, Zelma, the eldest daughter of ˒A. H. and Eva Argue, was brought up in a strong pentecostal home and became a zealous witness for Christ. She was ordained as an evangelist in the ˒Assemblies of God in Mar. 1920. She regularly accompanied her father, ministering with him on his evangelistic travels in the 1920s and 1930s. She realized the power of the printed word and became a prolific writer, contributing more than 200 articles to the *Pentecostal Evangel*. She wrote *What Meaneth This?* (1923, reprinted as *Contending for the Faith* [1928]); *Garments of Strength* (1935); *Practical Christian Living* (1937); and *The Vision and Vow of a Canadian Maiden,* a book about her mother (1940). With a reputation of being otherworldly, she was known as a powerful intercessor. She pastored in Los Angeles in the 1950s and spent her last years in California.   ■ P. D. Hocken

ARGUINZONI, SONNY (1938–). Founder of Victory Outreach International. Born in New York to Puerto Rican parents, Arguinzoni joined a gang at the age of 12. A short while later he began experimenting with pills and marijuana and by the age of 15 was hooked on heroin. He stayed hooked on heroin for the next six years, during which time he found himself in and out of jail, including a stint at Rikers Island Penitentiary. After he was released from prison, he came into contact with ex-gang member Nicky Cruz and pentecostal street preacher David Wilkerson. Through their evangelistic efforts Arguinzoni was converted.

Wilkerson sent Arguinzoni to South California to prepare for the ministry. After studying at the Latin American Bible Institute (LABI) of the Assemblies of God in La Puente, CA, he began preaching to ex-drug addicts, gang members, and other social outcasts in Los Angeles about hope in Jesus Christ. While at LABI he began working with troubled youth in the barrio of Los Angeles as an evangelist for Teen Challenge, a ministry founded by David Wilkerson. In his second year at LABI, Arguinzoni met and married fellow LABI student Julie Rivera.

After completing their studies at LABI, the Arguinzoni's moved into the crime-infested Maravilla district in East Los Angeles. He named his ministry Victory Outreach (VO). A short while later, in 1967, the Arguinzonis and their growing number of followers purchased a small run-down church in the Boyle Heights section of East L.A. This single church has grown into more than 210 churches and 350 rehabilitation homes throughout the U.S., Latin America, Africa, Europe, and Asia. The growing number of people attending Sonny's church in East L.A. prompted him to move to a 15-acre site in La Puente, where he not only constructed a new church to accommodate the 4,000-plus members of his own congregation but also the VO International headquarters. In addition to leading VO International, Sonny has written an autobiography, an anecdotal history of the denomination, and his philosophy and vision of ministry. VO is unique in that it is one of the first Protestant denominations created to specifically target the inner city, drug addicts, gang members, prostitutes, homosexuals, alcoholics, ex-prisoners, and other social outcasts.

■ **Bibliography:** S. Arguinzoni, *Sonny* (1987) ■ idem, *Internalizing the Vision* (1995) ■ idem, *Treasures out of Darkness* (1991).
                                                           ■ G. Espinosa

ARNOLD, R. LOUIS (1889–1972). Louis Arnold was one of the early leaders of the Apostolic Church in New Zealand. He came from rugged pioneer stock and was originally a member of the Salvation Army. After joining the Apostolic Church shortly after its formation in 1934, Arnold became the full-time pastor of its Nelson congregation in 1936 and of the Christ church assembly in 1938. The following year he was appointed to Waitangi Pa, near Te Puke in the Bay of Plenty, to take on the oversight of the Apostolic Church's

Maori work, originally established by two Brethren women. Although the Waitangi Pa mission eventually closed down in the 1970s, it was the early base for Arnold's vigorous leadership as superintendent of the Apostolic Church's work among the Maori. Arnold was ably assisted in this work by his wife, herself of part-Maori *(Ngai Tahu)* descent. Although the Arnolds met with much spiritual opposition, including the placing of *makutu* (evil spells) upon them, their ministry saw some remarkable results, including the raising of a baby from the dead. After several changes of location, Arnold relocated in Rotorua, which later became the hub of the Maori work. He retired from the superintendency in 1952. After his retirement, Arnold opened an Apostolic church in Gisborne and pastored and built worship centers in New Plymouth and Thames. He finally moved back to Gisborne, where he died, still in active ministry, in 1972.

■ **Bibliography:** J. E. Worsfold, *A History of the Charismatic Movements in New Zealand* (1974).   ■ B. Knowles

ARNOTT, JOHN (1940–). Prominent figure of the "Toronto Blessing" and pastor of Toronto Airport Christian Fellowship in Toronto, Ont., Canada. Converted to Christ in 1955 at a Billy Graham crusade in Toronto, he left Ontario Bible College in 1968 shortly before graduation due to school rules restricting student work schedules. After a marriage contracted in 1962 began to disintegrate in the mid 1970s, he abandoned his hopes for ministry, but after meeting and marrying Carol in 1979, he went with her to Indonesia and Irian Jaya for short mission trips. Their success encouraged them to begin a church plant, Jubilee Christian Ministries in Stratford, Ont., in 1981, which later became affiliated with the Vineyard Christian Fellowship. In 1987 they started a small group in Toronto that became a church in May 1988. On Jan. 20, 1994, while Randy Clark of St. Louis, MO, was ministering at the Toronto church, there was an unusual outpouring of the Spirit of God. "Four days of meetings turned into . . . months of almost nightly meetings in numerous locations in Ontario. It has since poured out . . . into similar renewal meetings all over the United States, Canada, the United Kingdom, and even Europe" (Wimber, 1994, 3). Five thousand people yearly have since made decisions for Christ at the church, which has been attended by well over two million visitors.

■ **Bibliography:** J. Arnott, *The Father's Blessing* (1995) ■ R. Clark, *Lighting Fires* (1998) ■ J. Wimber, *Vineyard Reflections* (May–June 1994).   ■ R. M. Riss

ASCHOFF, FRIEDRICH (1940–). Major leader in Lutheran renewal in Germany. After theological studies in Münster, Heidelberg, and Erlangen, Aschoff became an assistant pastor in Fürth in Bavaria (1968–71) and then pastor in Kaufering (1971–97). Aschoff became both involved in charismatic renewal in Kaufering and a respected leader in the Evangelical (Lutheran) Church of Germany (Evangelische Kirche Deutschland—EKD). When Wolfram Kopfermann left the Lutheran Church in 1988, Aschoff was chosen to take his place as chair of the Geistliche Gemeinde Erneuerung (Spiritual Parish Renewal) in the EKD. Aschoff shepherded Lutheran renewal in Germany through the upheaval caused by Kopfermann's departure and presided over the integration of the renewal movements in East and West Germany. He has been prominent in work toward reconciliation and was the initiator in 1995 of a reconciliation walk to mark the 50th anniversary of the end of World War II.   ■ P. D. Hocken

ASSEMBLEA CRISTIANA (The Christian Assembly).

One of the more prominent ethnic churches that became part of the pentecostal movement. The first Italian-Pentecostal Church in the U.S., the Assemblea Cristiana was established in Chicago in 1907. Its beginning is a story of the struggles of a group of Italian emigrants from Tuscany who entered into the life of one of the Italian ghettos located on the city's Near North Side. During the latter part of 1907, many of its initial members became pentecostals after attending the meetings conducted by ▸William H. Durham at the North Avenue Mission. Shortly afterward these people established their own church at 256 W. Grand Avenue under the leadership of ▸Peter Ottolini and ▸Luigi Francescon. A few years later church members elected their first pastor, Peter Menconi, who remained as pastor until his accidental death in 1936. Beginning shortly after its inception, members of the Assemblea Cristiana traveled for the next 30 years to other Italian communities, particularly in the U.S., Italy, and South America, and established hundreds of Italian-Pentecostal churches and converted thousands of Italians to pentecostalism. Presently, many of the churches in the U.S. are organized under the Christian Church of North America.

■ **Bibliography:** R. Bracco, *Il Risveglio Pentecostale in Italia* (n.d.) ■ L. DeCaro, *Our Heritage: The Christian Church of North America* (1977) ■ idem, *Fiftieth Anniversary: Christian Church of North America* (1977).   ■ J. Colletti

ASSEMBLIES OF GOD

I. Formative Years: 1914–18
   A. Roots
   B. Doctrinal Issues
II. 1918–1930
   A. Missions
   B. Education
   C. Women in Ministry
III. 1930–50
   A. Cooperation
   B. "Latter Rain"
   C. Healing Revivalism
IV. 1950–85
   A. Charismatic Movement
   B. Outreach and Education
V. 1985–Present
   A. Growth
   B. Numerical vs. Spiritual Growth
   C. Education
   D. Doctrine
   E. Racial Reconciliation
VI. Conclusion

I. FORMATIVE YEARS: 1914–18.

A. Roots.

The largest, strongest, and most affluent white pentecostal denomination, the Assemblies of God (AG), was formed in 1914 to give coherence to broadly based pentecostal efforts. It organized in Hot Springs, AR, as a fellowship of pentecostal ministers who believed that cooperative action would enable them to fulfill their shared objectives expeditiously. In spite of the preponderance of southerners among its early members, the AG emerged specifically to meet the needs of a nationwide constituency. As opposed to other pentecostal organizations (most of which had existed prior to their embracing pentecostalism), the AG was neither locally defined nor organized around a Wesleyan view of holiness.

Those whose efforts shaped the AG had encountered pentecostal teaching—with its stress on ▸restorationist goals—in various places. Many had roots in ▸Charles Parham's Texas-based ▸Apostolic Faith (AF) movement; others had been influenced by the Rochester, NY, ministries known as ▸Elim; some brought experience and convictions molded by association with the ▸Christian and Missionary Alliance (CMA); many had ties, direct or indirect, to ▸John Alexander Dowie's Zion City or to other Chicago-area independent missions. These centers especially influenced those who led the denomination in its formative years.

The formation of the AG was the result of efforts initiated in 1913 by ▸Eudorus N. Bell, ▸Howard Goss, ▸Daniel C. O. Opperman, Archibald P. Collins, and ▸Mack M. Pinson. These men sought both to accomplish specific objectives and to repudiate unacceptable doctrines and practices. They issued a call to a general council through *Word and Witness*, a periodical edited by Bell in Malvern, AR. The announcement was publicized in other periodicals as well.

The announcement elicited varied response. Pentecostals tended to distrust organization, claiming that the NT offered no precedent for anything beyond local church order. Most pentecostals had distanced themselves from the denominations before embracing pentecostal teaching; some had been forced to break denominational ties when they had begun espousing glossolalia and divine healing. Most were convinced that organization stifled the Holy Spirit.

Such hesitations resulted in the formation at Hot Springs of a loosely conceived agency that adopted neither a constitution nor a doctrinal statement. The denomination established its headquarters at a small Bible school in Findlay, OH (˄Leonard, Thomas K.). In 1915 it moved its base of operations to St. Louis.

B. Doctrinal Issues.

Even as the organization took shape, however, some of its promoters accepted divergent views about the Trinity and began espousing more radically restorationist sentiments than most pentecostals could accept. In 1915 the third general council endeavored to promote harmony. A showdown in the 1916 general council in St. Louis, however, resulted in the expulsion of advocates of the "New Issue" (˄Oneness Theology) and assured the Trinitarian orthodoxy of the AG. The same general council adopted a Statement of Fundamental Truths, identifying acceptable doctrines. The original statement was not conceived as a full theological affirmation (e.g., it contained no reference to the Virgin Birth). Rather, it sought to help participants understand their pentecostal emphasis. Further clarification came later.

Before the AG had organized, another disagreement had agitated independent pentecostals. Early pentecostals had tended to regard sanctification as a second, instantaneous spiritual crisis. The leader of a Chicago mission, ˄William Durham, had challenged that view after 1908 and had advocated, rather, "the finished work of Calvary." Responding to the extreme teachings some contemporary Holiness advocates urged, Durham insisted that penitent sinners received both Christ's pardon and cleansing at conversion. Their further responsibility was not to pursue crisis cleansing but to live an "overcoming" life.

Durham's views circulated widely through his periodical, *The Pentecostal Testimony,* and through his travels. E. N. Bell, a Southern Baptist pastor who became the first chairman of the AG, had embraced pentecostalism in Durham's Chicago mission. Bell most likely encouraged his associates in the AF movement in Texas and Arkansas to accept Durham's views. Durham attended their camp meeting and convinced the majority of the leaders.

Durham's teaching coincided with the predilections of those who embraced pentecostalism within the CMA and of those with roots in Zion, IL. They sparked intense controversy, especially with Charles F. Parham and ˄Florence L. Crawford.

Since the AG did not seek to enforce doctrinal unity, it embraced people who held various views on sanctification. Participants at the first general council heard Mack M. Pinson advocate Durham's position. Early versions of the Statement of Fundamental Truths attempted to satisfy those with Holiness sympathies while identifying with Durham's essential approach. As time passed, it became increasingly evident that the AG supported Durham's understanding. The denomination's early leaders, accused by Holiness advocates of minimizing holiness, found it necessary to assert frequently that they believed in sanctification.

A third doctrinal issue, in addition to the Trinity and sanctification, that helped mold the AG emerged in 1918 when a popular evangelist, pastor, and former executive presbyter, ˄F. F. Bosworth, resigned from the denomination in a disagreement about evidential tongues speech. Bosworth published his critique of the movement's espousal of tongues as uniform initial evidence of Spirit baptism in a pamphlet entitled "Do All Speak with Tongues?" His actions prompted a thorough discussion of evidential tongues and marked the culmination in the AG of an evolution toward rigid promotion of evidential tongues. Early pentecostals had not all accepted evidential tongues without qualification, but increasingly the movement had tended to do so. It became evident in 1918 how strongly the leadership of the AG was committed to that position. The denomination was saved from a showdown by Bosworth's magnanimous spirit. Only he and his brother resigned over the issue.

II. 1918–1930.

Under the leadership of its first chairman, Eudorus N. Bell, the AG issued a weekly paper that in 1918 took the name *Pentecostal Evangel.* Its current circulation exceeds 265,000, making it one of the larger Protestant denominational weeklies in the U.S. A recently launched quarterly Spanish edition has a circulation of 20,000. During the first several years, much of the actual editorial work was done by ˄J. Roswell Flower, who had initially conceived the idea of a weekly publication. After several changes in editorial staff, ˄Stanley H. Frodsham, an Englishman, became editor of the *Evangel* as well as editor-in-chief of publications for the growing AG publishing effort known as ˄Gospel Publishing House. Frodsham served until 1949, when his longtime associate, Robert Cunningham, accepted editorial responsibility. On Cunningham's retirement in 1984, his assistant, Richard Champion, became editor.

Bell resigned from the chairmanship late in 1914 and was replaced by a fellow Texan and former Southern Baptist, Archibald P. Collins. In the ˄Oneness turmoil in the fall of 1915, ˄John W. Welch assumed the chairmanship, a post he held until Bell was returned to office in 1920. On Bell's unexpected death in 1923, Welch resumed office. W. T. Gaston succeeded Welch in 1925 and served until 1929. During his tenure, the AG adopted its constitution and bylaws. Under the new constitution, the chairman became the general superintendent. In 1929 ▸Ernest Swing Williams was elected the first general superintendent, a post he held until his retirement in 1949.

A. Missions.

Among the several purposes for establishing the AG was the support of foreign missions. J. R. Flower, the denomination's first missionary secretary, began the process of systematizing a missions program. The process was expedited when the 1927 general council ratified the selection of ▸Noel Perkin as missionary secretary. Perkin, an Englishman by birth and a former independent pentecostal missionary to Argentina, supervised an expanding missionary program until his retirement in 1959.

B. Education.

Another troublesome concern early in AG history was the provision of training for ministry. Pentecostals regarded Spirit baptism as "enduement with power for service," and, at least in the first several decades, the experience seemed to compel many to dedicate their lives to preaching and teaching ministries at home and abroad. The profusion of committed but untrained workers caused considerable difficulty in some places. Lacking both finances and the inclination to commit the new denomination to a single institution, the early leaders endorsed various existing "full gospel" schools. These tended to be short-term. D. C. O. Opperman conducted numerous such training institutes in various places. Several small schools—such as Bethel Bible Training School in Newark, NJ—established themselves more permanently.

In 1920 the executives decided to cooperate with several AG districts in organizing a permanent school in Auburn, NE. S. A. Jamieson, a former Presbyterian pastor, served as principal of this effort, known as Midwest Bible School. In spite of its dedicated staff, however, the school could not overcome financial and social problems. It closed in the spring of 1921.

That fall, AG leaders tried again, this time in Springfield, MO (where the denomination's headquarters had moved in 1918). Central Bible Institute began under the direction of ▸Daniel W. Kerr, an elderly pastor who had spent most of his ministry in the CMA. Kerr had already assisted in the formation of the two West Coast Bible colleges. During the 1920s, various men who would make lasting contributions to Central Bible Institute joined its faculty: ▸Frank M. Boyd, ▸Myer Pearlman, ▸William I. Evans, and ▸Ralph M. Riggs. As the only general council school, Central Bible Institute set the standard against which other locally sponsored AG institutions were evaluated.

The establishment of a council-sponsored school did not indicate unanimity about education, however. Strong senti-

ment against school-based training persisted for many years. Some were convinced that education hindered the Spirit; others, true to their restorationist origins, insisted that the NT offered no precedent for training beyond a form of apprenticeship with an experienced worker. The conviction of the imminence of the end also assured the persistence of the view that would-be workers had no time for specialized training.

C. Women in Ministry.

During these years, the AG addressed questions relating to the place of women in the ministry. The first general council limited voting to males. It noted that women were to be subject to male leaders but acknowledged their right to be evangelists and missionaries. The key issue was authority: males refused to admit women to positions that granted them authority over men. They dismissed Gal. 3:28 ("There is neither male nor female: for ye are all one in Christ Jesus," KJV) as a basis for equality, alleging that the text meant only that "in the matter of salvation the lines of sex [were] blotted out."

Membership in the general council was limited to ministers. Numerous pentecostal women had engaged in ministries before they had embraced pentecostalism. Some had been ordained (though usually in nontraditional and highly irregular settings). Although their ordination was recognized by the AG, such women could not vote at general councils until 1920. Full ordination of women by the AG was not granted until 1935. Even then the proviso "when such acts are necessary" was appended to women's permission to administer the ordinances.

Meanwhile, however, the *Pentecostal Evangel* had repeatedly informed women of their actual restrictions. In particular, E. N. Bell strongly opposed women pastors. He grudgingly accorded them temporary rights but urged the propriety of "pushing men" as soon as potential male leadership emerged in a female-led congregation. He considered that women ministers were God's second best—useful for instances in which men "failed God." He fully concurred with widespread early pentecostal restrictions on their appropriate roles. Ernest S. Williams shared Bell's views. "God," he noted (even as women gained ordination during his administration), had "placed headship" in the males. According to Williams, even the much-cited daughters of Philip (Acts 21:8) had prophesied under the authority of their father. Males, then, properly controlled the environments in which women ministered. With such assumptions prevalent, it is hardly surprising that relatively few women sought ordination. None ever achieved national office. The masculine language of the constitution and by-laws continues to make mockery of claims that the denomination as a whole fully supports ministering women.

III. 1930–50.

A. Cooperation.

Through the 1930s the AG developed in relative isolation from other religious groups. Awareness of circumstances in other pentecostal denominations was fostered by occasional visits by Europeans and others, but no formal channels existed to express shared concerns. In 1942, however, this changed when pentecostal participation in an evangelical gathering in St. Louis was solicited. Ernest S. Williams, J. Roswell Flower, and Noel Perkin represented the AG at the meeting, out of which the ›National Association of Evangelicals (NAE) emerged. Although some AG pastors expressed serious reservations about cooperation with evangelicals who privately opposed pentecostal teaching, most favored identifying their movement with the NAE. Closely related to the NAE was the National Religious Broadcasters, with which the AG has been deeply involved from the beginning.

Two other cooperative agencies emerged in the 1940s to foster pentecostals' awareness of their participation in a broader movement. In 1947 the ›Pentecostal World Conference was formed in Zurich. The gathering was similar to some that had convened before WWII, except that North American participation was added. Despite the fears of some that regular meetings would result in international organization, the conferences have continued with substantial support from AG leaders.

The ›Pentecostal Fellowship of North America (PFNA) emerged in 1948 to provide regular opportunities for contact among North American pentecostal denominations. While this agency has never won support from major segments of the movement (Oneness pentecostals are excluded by its doctrinal statement; black pentecostals have chosen not to affiliate), the AG has played a significant leadership role.

B. "Latter Rain."

In the late 1940s AG leaders began responding to the emergence of ›"Latter Rain" teaching in independent pentecostalism. The rhetoric of Latter Rain advocates closely resembled that of early pentecostals: they coveted a restoration of apostolic Christianity. They considered pentecostalism a step in the direction of restoration but indicted the movement for organizing and "quenching the Spirit." To effect a restoration, they promoted an emphasis on prophecy, spiritual gifts, the restoration of the offices of NT Christianity, and biblical organization. Emanating from Saskatchewan, they soon found response in some AG congregations.

While the teaching did not result in denominational division, it did prompt several resignations from the general council. More importantly, it was related to two other emerging issues that demanded assessment—healing revivalism and charismatic renewal.

C. Healing Revivalism.

Healing had historically been central to pentecostalism. Adherents believed that miraculous results would follow fervent prayer. Wherever pentecostal teaching spread, healing evangelism followed. Late in the 1940s, as Latter Rain advocates called pentecostal denominations to task for betraying their heritage in numerous ways, healing became the central focus of several emerging ministries. ›William Branham, ›Oral Roberts, ›A. A. Allen, and ›Jack Coe were among the best known of hundreds of tent-toting prophets of the miraculous. Their efforts, coordinated for a time by AG minister ›Gordon Lindsay through an organization he called the ›Voice of Healing, gave the teaching more visibility than it had ever achieved.

The trouble was that some of the major revivalists—especially Allen and Coe—found it impossible to advocate healing without criticizing those who objected to their style. The AG became a principal target as it urged adherents to consider carefully the spiritual and financial issues raised by forceful independent leaders. For some, the promise of miracles seemed far more attractive than advice to read the Bible, pray, and support the local congregation. During the 1950s, most healing evangelists opted for independence, even from the guidelines Lindsay had advocated. As their claims became increasingly radical, and as some fell into disrepute, their direct influence within the AG dissipated. They touched sensitive chords, however, and left a permanent legacy.

IV. 1950–85.

Early in the 1950s AG pastor ›David J. du Plessis had visited the office of the National Council of Churches of Christ in America to share his pentecostal testimony. To his surprise, the leaders welcomed him and solicited his involvement in a growing network of gatherings. Du Plessis ultimately gained acceptance among Protestants and Catholics who differed sharply with the fundamentalist assumptions of most AG adherents. His relationship with the AG became increasingly uneasy. Du Plessis found himself unable to adhere to restrictions advised by denominational leaders and, under pressure, submitted his resignation as an AG minister in 1962. His influence in the broadening charismatic movement continued to expand.

A. Charismatic Movement.

The ›charismatic movement posed numerous problems for pentecostals who had long assumed that their theological persuasions were absolutely requisite for valid Spirit baptism. AG leaders offered no firm response, simply saying that their intention was to be identified with what "God was doing in the world." Many AG churches were influenced by the charismatic worship style and attempted to recover some of their own heritage by identifying with its exuberance and simplicity. Changing grassroots attitudes became apparent in a tendency to welcome Du Plessis in AG churches. In 1980 Du Plessis again became a credentialed AG minister.

B. Outreach and Education.

After the long, stable administration of Ernest S. Williams, a succession of men served as general superintendents in the 1950s. ▸Wesley L. Steelberg, ▸Gayle F. Lewis, and ▸Ralph M. Riggs supervised the creation of new departments, a growing radio outreach, and the formation of Evangel College, a liberal arts institution that was created—in spite of lingering doubts about its mission—in 1955. Berean School of the Bible, a correspondence institute that had been created in 1947, serviced a growing lay constituency. In 1985 it became Berean College of the AG. After it made a fourth and fifth year of work available in 1947, Central Bible Institute gained accreditation through the Accrediting Association of Bible Colleges.

The general council meeting in San Antonio in 1959 marked an important leadership transition. J. R. Flower and Noel Perkin, men whose careers had shaped the AG, resigned. ▸J. Philip Hogan assumed direction of the growing missionary program. General superintendent Ralph Riggs was replaced by ▸Thomas F. Zimmerman.

Zimmerman's administration began during an era of disappointingly slow growth. A strong leader, Zimmerman sought the reasons for this, developed programs to foster growth, and determined to exploit AG participation in the NAE to bolster adherents' identity as evangelicals. Over the years, Zimmerman became a familiar figure on the boards of various evangelical agencies. By 1982 his emphasis on church growth had won the AG recognition as one of America's fastest-growing denominations. Subtle changes were at work, however: a denomination that had once savored rejection by "the world" basked in growing popularity. Adherents accommodated increasingly to a middle-American lifestyle.

By then growth had slowed again: at best, it was unevenly concentrated in Spanish and newly formed Korean districts. By any standard, however, the emergence and development of the AG is an impressive story. From humble beginnings, the denomination has grown so much that its membership exceeds that of numerous long-established denominations. America's largest church buildings and several of its prominent televangelists have ties to the AG. Per capita giving to foreign missions exceeds that of any mainline denomination.

V. 1985–PRESENT.

The year 1985 marked the end of another era. The general council, meeting again in San Antonio, turned from Zimmerman to ▸G. Raymond Carlson for leadership.

A. Growth.

Its stunning growth since 1960—particularly in the 1970s—made the AG (U.S.) the poster denomination for evangelical growth (usually used to contrast with mainline decline) through the mid 1980s. However, aside from the question of whether the AG (U.S.) wishes to be seen as "evangelical" (see below), it began a few years into the 1980s to face its own plateau, if not decline. AG membership growth in the U.S. went from 12.5% in 1960–65, to a spectacular 31.7% in 1970–75, to a middling 16% in 1980–85, and finally to a troubling 6% plateau in 1990–95. The demographic fact of slowing growth has loomed large in the denomination's collective consciousness since the 1989 inception of its "Decade of Harvest" church-growth program.

One must be careful not to generalize this plateau effect to include foreign missions, which have continued to explode. In some mission fields, growth through the mid 1990s has catapulted to four times the denomination's goals, as AG giving to world ministries nearly doubled between 1985 (over $122 million) and 1996 (over $235 million). Indeed, the AG's division of home missions has taken this foreign growth as a challenge, aggressively encouraging such new endeavors as special urban schools for training church planters. The national assembly, perceiving little domestic growth after the opening years of the Decade of Harvest, pitched in with ministerial-enrichment programs, spiritual-counsel hotlines for ministers, a national prayer center in Springfield, and numerous conferences and "sacred assemblies."

In the midst of this snowstorm of denominational initiatives, some observers perceived AG pastors as manifesting an increasing spiritual hunger—suggesting the beginnings of a return to historic pentecostal spirituality. Commensurably, recent statistics show some renewal in conversions and numerical growth, although it is too early to tell whether this amounts to a new upward slope. Inevitably, the figures have raised questions over whether these signs of increase have resulted more from top-down denominational initiatives or from high-profile but grassroots revivals—in particular, the revival at the ▸Brownsville Assembly of God in Pensacola, FL, which attracted a steady flow of visitors and "satellite revivals" for years after its June 1995 inception.

B. Numerical vs. Spiritual Growth.

Despite recent indications of renewed numerical growth, concern continues over the issue of spiritual growth. When AG adherents in the U.S. are compared, for example, to adherents in Latin America, where Christian commitment is perceived as leading directly to evangelism and activism, in the U.S. complacency, evangelical religion's old nemesis, seems (to some leaders) to settle over new converts all too quickly. Such differences in spiritual "tone" are of course notoriously difficult to measure, but for many longtime AG adherents, lively commitment to evangelism represents a key part of the denomination's spiritual character—a heritage without which the very identity of the AG comes into question. One place where this question of commitment comes to the fore is in the discrepancy between the recorded number of new converts (e.g., more than 500,000 in 1996), and the numbers of new adherents (79,606 in 1996) and new members (30,621 in 1996). Even allowing for skewed reporting and duplication in counting decisions to convert, these North American numbers seem to point to a certain flaccidity compared with the decidedly growth-oriented, "fiery" Latin American pentecostals.

Perhaps the most promising locus of spiritual growth on the home front has been revivals such as the one at Pensacola. While such revivals (including not only the Brownsville-Pensacola revival but for some AG adherents also the earlier Vineyard-sponsored Toronto Airport revival [▸Toronto Blessing]) have seemed to promise a renewal of spiritual commitment within the AG as well as among other evangelicals, they have brought a mixed response from the denomination. Districts have lined up pro- and anti-Brownsville. The sticking point has typically been the bodily and emotional "manifestations" that once characterized the camp-meeting Holiness heritage out of which pentecostalism arose but that have become unwanted intrusions in many AG churches. Such deep responses as trembling, crying out, and being ▸"slain in the Spirit" (not to mention the more extreme but rarer manifestations of animal noises, ecstatic dancing, and the host of apparently uncontrolled automatic behaviors long characteristic of heated revivals) have become unwelcome in the comfortable middle-class sanctuaries of the modern AG. In what some see as the age-old tension between charisma and institution, AG pastors and denominational leaders have often been reticent to endorse such "immature" or "extreme" emotional responses, seeing them as threats to the order enjoined by Paul in 1 Cor. 14—not to mention the order represented by denominational bureaucracies, hierarchies, and district offices housed in multimillion-dollar facilities.

C. Education.

The tension between institutional and grassroots approaches can also be seen in developments in denominational education. The larger, regional schools have begun seeking increased recognition and emphasis within the denomination, often taking on the name "university" in the bargain. Meanwhile, at the grassroots level, several hundred AG churches have started unaccredited, nonstandardized, church-based Bible institutes, intended to allow people to prepare for ministry within a local church without having to move their families.

Whether recent indications of increasing membership indicate a new spurt of growth in the U.S. or merely a passing season of revival, the larger question remains—what does it mean to belong to the AG? As the decade has progressed, particularly under the leadership (since 1993) of general superintendent ▸Thomas Trask, rhetoric at the national and district levels has turned to questions of spiritual as well as numerical growth. Increasing attention has been paid to the number of Spirit baptisms recorded across the country (which leveled off between 1986 and 1995 but showed signs of increase in 1996) and to signs that AG churches are in danger of becoming barely distinguishable from other evangelical churches in the nation.

Trask, representing a firm, third-generation national leadership, has not been hesitant to call for revival as the key both to church growth and to the strengthening of denominational identity. But in so doing, he and the denomination have continued to wrestle with their place on the continuum between the biblical rationalism, respectable reserve, and powerful denominational machines of the older evangelicals on the one hand and the freedom of worship, tolerance for emotional and physical manifestations, and loose, prophetic organization of many independent charismatic groups on the other. Far more than at their contested induction into the National Association of Evangelicals (NAE) in the 1940s, AG leaders in the 1990s have found themselves naturally taking on the "evangelical identities" of the interdenominational evangelicalism at whose seminaries many of them have trained (e.g., Fuller Seminary in California and Gordon-Conwell in Massachusetts). Today the AG, holding a comfortable and influential plurality within the NAE, has at last begun to look over its shoulder and wonder whether it has lost as much by the alliance as it has gained.

One controversial criticism of this "evangelicalization of the AG" was *Back to the Altar: A Call to Spiritual Awakening*, written in 1994 by Trask himself (with David A. Womack). Trask's message here and in person has been that AG adherents are more than evangelicals and are called to understand better the dynamics of pentecostal spirituality. One should not walk into an AG church, in other words, and find its liturgy indistinguishable from that of any other evangelical church. Facing statistics that suggested nearly half of AG members had not received Spirit baptism, Trask stated after his election as general superintendent, "we may be Pentecostal in doctrine, but not in experience."

Alongside the equivocal statistics on Spirit baptism, ambivalence and struggle have manifested themselves in the discomfort of many leaders and congregants with "slaying in the spirit" and other such demonstrative manifestations (see above). This hesitancy to endorse manifestations may in fact constitute an exercise in boundary drawing that serves to distinguish the AG from the more permissive independent charismatic churches with which it continues to trade members on a large scale (as it has throughout the 1970s and 80s). However, the trend may already have turned the corner, back toward reclaiming historic pentecostal experience and practice, as pastors renewed in old-fashioned revivals such as Brownsville have returned to their congregations with a revitalized pentecostal emphasis on Spirit baptism and spiritual gifts.

D. Doctrine.

On the doctrinal front, perhaps the most obvious skirmish in the battle for distinctiveness has arisen out of the proclivity of young AG ministerial hopefuls for training at interdenominational evangelical seminaries. As some students have studied with professors operating out of the Reformed tradition, they have come to question the entire theological category of "subsequent experiences" as either sharply separated from or even necessary to the key Protestant journey of conversion and growth in grace. Even some who have retained the traditional pentecostal understanding of Spirit baptism as a crisis experience subsequent to conversion have emerged from evangelical seminaries hesitant to sign the AG's doctrinal statement, which affirms speaking in tongues as the initial evidence of that baptism.

In a denomination that illustrates the cover of its glossy pamphlet *Our 16 Doctrines* with a hammer, a chisel, and chips of stone, such equivocation has met with swift rebuff. Owing not entirely to this issue, but also to the spectacular fall of Jimmy Swaggart, the denomination has shifted its credentialing policies to help address cases of doctrinal deviance. Although at one time (before the Swaggart scandal) credentialing occurred wholly at the district level, now the candidate's case is taken to the executive presbytery for decision if doctrinal questions arise at the district level. As a result of this process, some newly minted M.Div.'s of AG heritage have either joined other evangelical denominations or gone the independent route.

In short, the AG has found itself in a paradoxical situation. The denomination has been forced to admit that far from breaking down all traditions, as its historically restorationist convictions would dictate, it needs now to rediscover and draw upon its own acknowledged traditions if it is not to lose all distinctiveness in America's diverse, voluntarist religious marketplace. Between the modern independent charismatic megachurches and the older evangelical traditions (e.g., certain Baptist and Presbyterian groups), the AG must define its theological and spiritual "borders" and rehearse its history if it is to thrive.

E. Racial Reconciliation.

At the same time, the AG has in the 1990s finally tackled another identity issue—that of the historical division between white and black pentecostals. Although the AG began as an interracial movement traceable to both an African-American leader and a white leader, U.S. pentecostalism had fragmented along racial lines within 20 years of its birth. In the ensuing decades, while white pentecostals pursued (among other things) upward mobility and social and theological respectability in the American evangelical family, African-American pentecostals plotted their own course and formed their own organizations, usually operating in entirely separate spheres.

This racial division continued uninterrupted until a historic 1994 meeting in Memphis, TN. At this meeting, the ▸Pentecostal Fellowship of North America, an exclusively white umbrella organization that included among its members the AG, dissolved itself amid official statements of regret for a history of racism. At the same meeting, a new interracial group was formed, the ▸Pentecostal/Charismatic Churches of North America (PCCNA). Bishop ▸Ithiel Clemmons of the ▸Church of God in Christ was elected the group's first chairperson.

Some, particularly among black pentecostals, have found this "Memphis miracle" to be little more than a very belated and possibly hollow apology—which may or may not be followed by significant action for reconciliation. But others have seen it as an encouraging sign. At this point, African-American constituents of the new organization have combined a guarded optimism, or realism, with exhortations to go beyond

The historic "Memphis Miracle," which took place in 1994 in Memphis, TN.

spiritual gatherings to deep, programmatic change. As one leader has said, black pentecostals are reminded that the road to a truly color-blind pentecostalism is still a long one when they remember that the white pentecostals with whom they are now organizationally linked would by and large show little hesitation in voting against affirmative action.

VI. CONCLUSION.

Issues of growth, spiritual and doctrinal identity, and racial reconciliation have loomed for the AG in a decade that also featured exciting growth abroad and outbreaks of revival at home. Through such extradenominational organizations as the newly formed PCCNA and the scholarly Society for Pentecostal Studies, as well as denominational church-growth programs and grassroots revivals, AG hierarchs and teachers have increasingly found themselves returning with their people to the wells of pentecostal tradition and pentecostal experience as they take their denomination through the 21st century. Though this return to tradition is far from uncontested, particularly in the uncomfortable realm of emotional and physical manifestations, even this agitation may yet turn out to be the moving of the Spirit.

■ **Bibliography:** E. L. Blumhofer, *The Assemblies of God,* 2 vols. (1989) ▌ W. W. Menzies, *Anointed to Serve* (1971).

■ E. L. Blumhofer; C. R. Armstrong

ASSEMBLIES OF GOD IN GREAT BRITAIN AND IRELAND

The Assemblies of God in Great Britain and Ireland (AGGBI) was founded in 1924 from independent pentecostal congregations in the U.K. On his first furlough from Congo in 1922, ▸W. F. P. Burton attempted to bring together many of the scattered assemblies into a loose federation, in part for the purpose of providing support for missionaries. This gave rise to the Sheffield Conference and the setting up of a Provision Council "for the advice and assistance" of congregations in the U.K. and Ireland. In 1923 Archibald Cooper of South Africa, with the support of ▸John Nelson Parr of Manchester, went a step further. Parr sent out a circular letter on Nov. 23, 1923, inviting leaders to "establish a union of Assemblies" and giving his reasons for association. These were to (1) preserve the testimony to the full gospel, including the baptism of the Spirit and to save the work from false teaching; (2) strengthen bonds and create a fuller degree of cooperation; (3) cooperate in evangelistic and missionary work; (4) present a united witness to outsiders; (5) exercise discipline over the disorderly; (6) save the assemblies from falling into unscriptural organizations. Parr also knew that some pentecostal ministers had suffered imprisonment in WWI for conscientious objection and so, by writing pacifism into the constitution of the new body, Parr was able to articulate the predominant pentecostal attitude toward war and, at the same time, to lay the groundwork for exemption from

military service for participant ministers in any future conflict (Parr, 26–27).

A gathering was arranged at Aston, Birmingham, in Feb. 1924. Fourteen people met, while several others, including ▸Lewi Pethrus, who was visiting Britain at the time, were unable to be present owing to a railway strike. Parr was elected chairman that day and assured those present that "the autonomy of the local assembly would be strictly observed." He had in mind a British fellowship based on the pattern of the American Assemblies of God. The union of assemblies that was envisioned would operate at three levels. First, the assemblies would adhere to the same "fundamental truths." Second, the assemblies should maintain fellowship through district presbyteries. Third, a general presbytery would be set up, composed of local pastors and elders.

The fundamental truths subsequently agreed on declared that speaking in tongues is the initial evidence of the baptism of the Holy Spirit, the return of Christ is premillennial, and those whose names are not in the Book of Life are to be everlastingly punished. Baptism should be by total immersion, and deliverance from sickness is provided for in the atonement.

A second meeting was held in Highbury, London, in May 1924 with 80 people present. During the first day a letter was received from the ▸Elim leaders who had already organized themselves along more centralized lines than the AGGBI leaders had in mind and who were therefore excluded from the Highbury invitation. When they arrived on the second day, E. J. Phillips suggested that those represented at the meeting should work together and that Elim, whose crusading success under ▸George Jeffreys was already evident, should provide the evangelistic arm of the combined work. The idea was too bold for the time; the view was expressed that the survival of pentecostalism would be better safeguarded by two independent works than by one slightly larger one. Among the leaders at this London meeting were ▸Donald Gee (who joined later after consulting his Leith Assembly), ▸John Carter, ▸Howard Carter, and ▸Nelson Parr. Thirty-seven assemblies in England and one in Belfast joined immediately, and 38 from Wales and Monmouth joined in August, accepting the pattern that had been worked out at the Aston meeting. The AGGBI was established, and the Elim workers continued on their own.

At the end of 1925 several senior members of the ▸Pentecostal Missionary Union (PMU) resigned. The remaining members, who were by now representatives of the AGGBI, took responsibility for whole enterprise, and the two bodies merged. This provided AGGBI with a ready-made missionary work. Howard Carter (1891–1971), who had been in charge of the PMU Bible School at Hampstead, London, since Feb. 1921 was joined there by his brother John, C. L. Parker (sometime Fellow of University College, Oxford), T. J. Jones, and ▸Harold Horton. Though the school maintained its independence, it served the assemblies and taught the distinctive doctrines of AGGBI. When the building was destroyed in 1940–41, new premises were found in Kenley, Surrey. The school then became the official AGGBI college (owned by the denomination), and Donald Gee became its first principal. In 1973 the school transferred to Mattersey in Nottinghamshire, became known as Mattersey Hall, and classified itself as a Bible college (the change in name indicating greater academic emphasis). David Petts became principal in 1977, educational offerings expanded steadily, and student numbers gradually climbed.

The minimal administration of AGGBI was carried on through general offices in Lewisham, London, until 1940, when they transferred to Luton, Bedfordshire, before returning to London in 1953. Eighteen years later they moved to Nottingham, where they remain.

The number of assemblies increased steadily: 140 in 1927; 200 in 1929; 250 in 1933; 350 in 1939; 403 in 1946; 506 in 1957; and over 670 today (2000). The period of fastest growth occurred in the period 1926–28 as a result of the ministry of ᐅStephen Jeffrey.

The 1930s and 1950s were periods of steady growth. The war years put a stop to campaigning, but they were a period of a more than usual sense of unity among ministers. By the 1960s, when the charismatic movement burst on the scene, AGGBI was in need of "another springtime" (the title of a sermon preached at the general conference by Donald Gee in 1960), and many attempts were made to secure this, mainly by reforming the intricate and increasingly complex constitution.

Tensions between reformers and conservatives in the 1970s ultimately led, at the end of the 1980s, to a simplified constitution, which also appeared to encroach on local church autonomy, since it gave authority to regional and national superintendents. A policy of regionalization grouped congregations together into larger blocks and also allowed for the delegation of business matters to smaller subgroups of ministers. When it worked, this had the effect of replacing tiresome business with fellowship and ministry; when it did not work, it had the effect of forcing ministers to travel larger distances to keep in denominational contact. During this time several large assemblies left the denomination and identified themselves with the new churches in the charismatic movement.

Efforts to combine reforms with an emphasis on church planting were partly successful, but it was difficult to accelerate growth at home while maintaining overseas efforts. Shortages of money were both a symptom and a cause of these strains, especially as, for several years after the mid 1980s, AGGBI was troubled by financial losses as a result of the purchase of a building in Paderborn, Germany.

In the late 1990s attempts were made to ensure that efforts and departmental structures, particularly in education, training, and church planting, were coordinated, and ambitious targets for growth were set. At the same time expansion of facilities permitted a full range of degree courses to be offered at Mattersey Hall. The general superintendence (in the hands of Paul Weaver), combined with a national leadership team, a body comprising regional superintendents and heads of departments, has the potential to provide both spiritual and practical leadership while allowing individual ministries to operate productively at the local level.

■ **Bibliography:** D. Allen, "Signs and Wonders: The Origins, Growth, Development and Significance of Assemblies of God in Great Britain and Ireland 1900–1980" (diss., U. of London, 1990) ▮ D. Gee, *Wind and Flame* (1967) ▮ P. K. Kay, "The Four-fold Gospel in the Formation, Policy, and Practice of the Pentecostal Missionary Union" (thesis, Cheltenham and Gloucester College of Higher Education, 1995) ▮ W. K. Kay, "A History of British Assemblies of God" (diss., U. of Nottingham, 1989; published in abbreviated form as *Inside Story* [1990]) ▮ R. Massey, "A Sound and Scriptural Union: An Examination of the Origins of the Assemblies of God in Great Britain and Ireland 1920–25" (diss., U. of Birmingham, 1987) ▮ A. Missen, *Sound of a Going: The Story of the Assemblies of God* (1973) ▮ J. N. Parr, *Incredible: The Autobiography of John Nelson Parr* (1972).   ■ W. K. Kay

ASSEMBLIES OF GOD IN MEXICO (Asambleas de Dios en México). The Assemblies of God (AG) in Mexico traces its main origins back to the work of ᐅHenry C. Ball in South Texas in 1915, although work in Mexico did not begin in earnest until 1917. That year ᐅAlice E. Luce and Sunshine Marshall (who later married H. C. Ball) went to Monterrey, Mexico, as AG missionaries. After three months of door-to-door proselytizing, preaching in prisons, and holding services in their home, the Mexican Revolution forced them to return to the U.S. Upon their return to South Texas, they began helping H. C. Ball, who by then had converted and sent out a number of Mexican nationals to Mexico as evangelists.

Key pioneers of the Mexican work include H. C. Ball, ᐅMiguel Guillén, ᐅAnna Sanders, George and ᐅFrancisca Blaisdell, ᐅRodolfo Orozco, ᐅDavid Ruesga, ᐅCesáreo Buciaga, ᐅModesto Escobedo, Ruben Arevalo, Manuel Bustamante, and Juan Orozco. David and Raquel Ruesga and Anna Sanders pioneered the work in Mexico City in 1921. A year later, Rodolfo C. Orozco traveled to Monterrey, Mexico, where he set up one of the first permanent (AG) churches in that country.

The AG in Mexico held its first national convention in 1926. In order to prepare native Mexican evangelists, pastors, and teachers, the AG opened a Bible institute in Mexico City in 1928. A few years later, in 1933, the AG in Mexico began printing the periodical *Gavillas Doradas* (Golden Sheaves). The Mexican work, which was under the supervision of the

Latin District Council of the AG in the U.S., severed its formal ties with the U.S. church in 1929. Shortly after the Mexican work became autonomous, it experienced a schism led by David Ruesga, who founded the ʾChurch of God in the Republic of Mexico (Iglesia de Dios en la República Mexicana) in 1931. Despite this early schism, the AG in Mexico witnessed rapid growth. By 1935 there were approximately 31 congregations and 2,800 adherents in Mexico. During the 1950s, the AG in Mexico held large evangelistic campaigns throughout the country. By 1963 there were 5 Bible institutes, 647 ministers, 11 foreign missionaries, and approximately 13,500 adherents. In 1972 Gordon and Marilyn Marker opened the national office of the International Correspondence Institute (ICI) in Mexico City. By 1990 over a million people throughout Latin America had studied with ICI. Throughout the 20th century the AG in Mexico has worked closely with AG missionaries from the U.S. Their cooperation is partly responsible for the rapid growth of the AG in Mexico in the latter half of the century.

By 1990 the work in Mexico had blossomed to an estimated 3,100 congregations and more than 570,000 adherents. They were served by 3,280 ministers and lay leaders. In the early 1990s more than 1,400 students were enrolled in the more than 30 Bible institutes throughout Mexico. The AG in Mexico is one of the largest and most efficiently organized indigenous pentecostal denominations in Mexico today.

■ **Bibliography:** L. J. de Walker, *Siembra y Cosecha: Reseña histórica de Las Asambleas de Dios de México y Centroamérica,* vol. 1 (1990) ■ C. Holland, *The Religious Dimension of Hispanic Los Angeles* (1974) ■ Patrick Johnstone, *Operation World* (1993).   ■ G. Espinosa

ASSEMBLIES OF THE LORD JESUS CHRIST

A Oneness pentecostal organization founded in 1952 as a merger of the Assemblies of Jesus Christ, the Church of the Lord Jesus Christ, and the Jesus Only Apostolic Church of God. The racially integrated body is congregational in polity and calls its leader the general chairman.

Doctrinally the Assemblies of the Lord Jesus Christ allow the use of either grape juice or wine at communion, practice footwashing, teach that women should not cut their hair, and disapprove of divorce and remarriage.

Headquarters, publishing house, and offices of the organization's periodical, *Apostolic Witness,* are in Memphis, TN. Its two Bible schools are in Memphis and Parkersburg, WV. In 1997 there were 40,000 members in 339 churches in the United States, with an additional 8,500 members and 87 churches in foreign countries.

■ **Bibliography:** T. French, "Oneness Pentecostalism in Global Perspective" (thesis, Wheaton College, 1998) ■ C. E. Jones, *Guide*

to the Study of the Pentecostal Movement, vol. 1 (1983) ■ A. C. Piepkorn, *Profiles in Belief,* vol. 3 (1979).   ■ D. A. Reed

ASSEMBLY OF CHRISTIAN CHURCHES

(est. 1938). A pentecostal group with churches in New York and Puerto Rico. The Assembly of Christian Churches (ACC) was organized from the Puerto Rican congregations that had come into being under the influence of ʾFrancisco Olazábal, the leading Hispanic evangelist during the 1920s and 1930s. Upon his death, the Atlantic coast churches were left with tenuous ties to the predominantly Mexican branch of Olazábal's ʾConcilio Latino-Americano de Iglesias Christianas, with headquarters in Texas. The first elected president of the newly formed ACC was ʾCarlos Supúlveda Medina, a former Presbyterian minister who had studied at the University of Puerto Rico and the Evangelical Seminary. The ACC has 250 churches with a membership of 14,000, more than half of whom are in Puerto Rico.

■ **Bibliography:** D. Barrett, *World Christian Encyclopedia* (1982) ■ R. Domínguez, *Pioneros de Pentecostes* (1971), 1:15–51, 167–73 ■ F. Whitam, "New York's Spanish Protestants," *Christian Century* 79 (1962) ■ idem, "A Report on the Protestant Spanish Community in New York City," in C. Cortés, ed., *Protestantism and Latinos in the United States* (1980).   ■ E. A. Wilson

ASSOCIATION OF FAITH CHURCHES AND MINISTRIES

(AFCM). Founded by ʾJim Kaseman in 1981 as the Upper Midwest Faith Churches and Ministries, Inc. The association issues ministerial credentials and provides teaching on current issues to its members. The main purpose, however, is to provide fellowship to those who are ministering in the "faith movement" (ʾPositive Confession). In order to fulfill this goal, AFCM holds regular meetings and annual conventions. In recent years the AFCM has also established offices in Australia and Canada.   ■ J. R. Zeigler

ASSOCIATION OF INTERNATIONAL MISSION SERVICES

The Association of International Mission Services (AIMS), founded on Mar. 21, 1985, in Dallas, TX, is a transdenominational organization that promotes the work of foreign missions among independent pentecostal and charismatic churches. Its primary aim is "to challenge and mobilize the church for World Missions and to expand its capabilities and opportunities to fulfill the Great Commission. AIMS will provide a framework for unity and fellowship among churches, mission agencies, and training institutions in cooperative efforts for world evangelization" (AIMS, 1987, 2).

Since the charismatic renewal had not yet produced a structure for fostering unity between individual churches and mission agencies to further promote overseas evangelism,

AIMS was formed with the following objectives: (1) to develop a consortium of participating churches and agencies; (2) to provide services to local churches for missions mobilization; (3) to provide services to mission agencies; (4) to provide services to training institutions involved in preparing missionaries; (5) to appoint regional coordinators and area representatives for promoting AIMS activities; (6) to foster relationships with other evangelical organizations in the U.S. and abroad; and (7) to determine overseas needs and develop sister organizations abroad. Since AIMS does not send or train missionaries under its own auspices, it focuses on improving the capabilities of those organizations that do.

The main office is in Virginia Beach, VA. Howard Foltz, a professor at CBN University and former missionary who directed Eurasia Teen Challenge, serves as the president.

See also MISSIONS, OVERSEAS.

■ **Bibliography:** Association of International Mission Services, "Background Paper" (Feb. 1987).   ■ G. B. McGee

ATKINSON, MARIA W. (1879–1963). Pioneer of the ‣Church of God (CG, Cleveland, TN) in northern Mexico. Born in Sonora, Mexico, Maria was a deeply religious young woman. In 1905 she and her husband moved to Douglas, AZ, where he died soon afterward. In 1920 she married an American, M. W. Atkinson. She was healed of cancer and baptized in the Holy Spirit in 1924. Immediately she began to preach and pray for the sick in Arizona and Mexico.

In Aug. 1931 Atkinson met ‣J. H. Ingram and joined the CG. Her missions in Obregon and Hermosillo became the foundation of the CG in Mexico. The work has enjoyed great growth throughout northwest Mexico, where Atkinson became known as "La Madre de Mexico." She continued her ministry in Mexico until her death at age 84 in 1963.

■ **Bibliography:** C. W. Conn, *Where the Saints Have Trod* (1959) ▮ P. Humphrey, *Maria Atkinson: La Madre de Mexico* (1967).
                                                                                    ■ C. W. Conn

AWAKENED The Lutheran revivalistic movement in Finland called "Awakened" *(heränneet)* started at the end of the 18th century as the result of a sudden outpouring of the Holy Spirit accompanied by such observable signs as visions and glossolalia. In 1837 the leader of the Awakened, Paavo Ruotsalainen (1777–1852), gave the following account of that occurrence:

In the year 1796 happened a wonderful manifestation of God's love and mercy for the awakening of the people in the province of Savo, in the district of Kuopio, in the county of Idensalmi, in the village of Savojärvi. It began in this manner: the people of two households were haying in the fields; then one day the Holy Spirit fell upon them so

mightily that they fell to the ground as if they were dead, and they saw wonderful heavenly visions and spoke in various tongues which were thought to them by the Spirit, just as in the days of the apostles. And little by little [the revival] spread to the other villages, and in Dec. [1796] their number was quite large. And then they were having joyous celebration just like those 3,000 souls who were awakened through the sermon of [the apostle] Peter. (Niskanen, 1837, 3–5)

Another charismatic revival broke out among the Awakened of Pielisjärvi (east of Savojärvi) in 1817:

Right after the first revival, when they had gathered to hear the Word in a meeting place, the Holy Spirit fell on them just like upon the apostles on the Day of Pentecost, so that over 30 persons from the younger folks spoke in strange tongues and prophesied; and there were some who interpreted those messages to our language, although they could not elucidate everything." (Rosendal, 1902, 82)

At that time, there was not much theological instruction regarding the gifts of the Spirit, and within two years of its inception, the revival in Pielisjärvi showed signs of arrogance, ecstasy, and disorderly conduct. Consequently, the leader of the Awakened, Paavo Ruotsalainen, was invited to settle the confusion.

During the 19th century, the charismatic gifts were widely accepted among the Awakened. The church historians of the Awakened mention by name a number of people who spoke in tongues. Paavo Ruotsalainen was rather permissive of glossolalia; for example, his daughter Eva spoke in tongues. He disciplined his flock, however, when the use of spiritual gifts disturbed meetings. Sometimes Ruotsalainen himself listened with wonder at their extraordinary utterance. Some who were in that condition prophesied, others spoke words of encouragement, still others prayed for themselves or for others, tenderly and in a very cultivated manner. Of those who prayed in this manner, Katarina Pakarinen (d. 1868) was the best known. In the church records of Suonenjoki there is written beside her name, "tongues speaker" (Rosendal, 1905, 438–39).

Occurrences of glossolalia continued among the Awakened until the 20th century. Major concentrations of people speaking in tongues were located in Pielisjärvi, Nurmes, and Suonenjoki.

■ **Bibliography:** J. Kauppala, *Helluntai-ilmiöitä Suomen Siionissa entisaikana* (1932) ▮ J. Kuurne, *Hengen tuulta Karjalassa* (1944) ▮ L. J. Niskanen, *Hengellisten asian muistokirja* (1837; Helsinki: The Finnish National Archives [SKHASA B 62]) ▮ M. Rosendal, *Suomen herännäisyyden historia XIX:llä vuosisadalla I* (1902) ▮ idem, *Suomen herännäisyyden historia XIX:llä vuosisadalla II* (1905) ▮ A. Saarisalo, *Erämaan vaeltaja: Paavo Ruotsalainen* (1969).
                                                                                    ■ L. Ahonen

AWREY, DANIEL P. (1869–1913). Evangelist, missionary, and Bible teacher. Daniel Awrey was born Feb. 10, 1869, in Mimosa, Ont. In 1887 his family moved to Hawley, MN, where Daniel apprenticed for three years as a miller. After accepting salvation in 1890, Awrey attended college in the holiness hotbed of Delaware, OH. He began to hunger for a deeper spiritual experience while reading J. A. Wood's *Perfect Love*. On New Year's Eve, Awrey felt the "old man" being rooted out of his heart, and during a prayer meeting the following evening he suddenly starting speaking in tongues after seeing a flame shoot toward his head.

Awrey married Norwegian immigrant Ella Braseth in 1893 and moved to eastern Tennessee, where he evangelized as an elder of the Congregational Methodist Church. In 1895 Awrey claimed to receive the gift of prophecy, which he understood as both a special preaching unction and the ability to predict future events. Always sensitive to divine direction, Awrey shortly thereafter heard God instruct him to walk more than 1,000 miles to preach holiness in Texas. Over the next three years he also began to proclaim divine healing and "the baptism in the Holy Spirit in addition to sanctification" (although without identifying glossolalia as its initial evidence). Awrey moved back to Tennessee in 1898 and became a leader in B. H. Irwin's new Fire-Baptized Holiness Association. The following year he preached "fire and dynamite" across 13 states and Canada before returning to Tennessee to teach in the short-lived Beniah School of the Prophets.

After Irwin's moral failure in 1900, Awrey traveled widely as an independent evangelist. In 1906 he was conducting a "little Bible School" in Dudleyville, AZ, when he read of the Asuza revival and headed immediately for California. Over the next year Awrey developed a reputation in Los Angeles as an outstanding Bible teacher. For example, when the enthusiastic crowd at the 1907 Apostolic Faith Camp Meeting agitated to dismiss the leaders so they could hear directly from the Spirit, Awrey turned the tide with his impromptu expositions on biblical order. He left California convinced that God had called him to travel as broadly as possible and teach on the proper use—and potential abuse—of spiritual gifts. In particular, Awrey began to emphasize the need to seek the full restoration of the "fivefold ministry offices" (Eph. 4:11) in order to prevent Spirit-baptized believers from initiating manifestations and prophetic speech out of their own "human spirits."

Daniel P. Awrey, evangelist, missionary, and Bible teacher, who claimed pentecostal experiences (including glossolalia) in the last decade of the 19th century.

Awrey next moved to Beulah Colony, a new holiness-pentecostal community near Doxey, OK, where he taught at Emmanuel Bible School for about 18 months. By early 1909 Awrey felt God leading him to take his message to pentecostal outposts around the world. While relocating his family to China, Pennsylvania, and finally California over the next five years, Awrey circled the globe several times speaking at conventions and conducting short-term schools. On Dec. 4, 1913, Awrey died of fever while ministering in Liberia.

■ **Bibliography:** "A Few Nuggets," Houston *AF* (Oct. 1908), 3 ■ D. Awrey, "Letter," *Live Coals of Fire* (Dec. 1, 1899), 5 ■ idem, "Life Sketches," *LRE* (in three parts, Mar.–May 1910) ■ idem, *Telling the Lord's Secrets* (n.d. [c. 1910]) ■ A. Boddy, "Editor's Report," *Confidence* (Aug. 1909), 177–79 ■ H. Hunter, "Beniah at the Apostolic Crossroads," *Cyberjournal for Pentecostal-Charismatic Research* (Jan. 1997).   ■ D. Woods

AZUSA STREET REVIVAL The term given to events that ran from 1906 to 1913 in and around the Apostolic Faith Mission (AFM), located at 312 Azusa Street in Los Angeles, CA. The mission, an outgrowth of cottage prayer meetings held at the Richard and Ruth Asberry home at 214 N. ▸Bonnie Brae Street in the winter and early spring of that year, was established Apr. 14, 1906, under the leadership of Elder William J. Seymour. While it is more or less possible to date the beginning of this revival with the founding of the mission, the end of the revival is more elusive. The culmination of the second international camp meeting sponsored by the AFM in the Arroyo Seco between Los Angeles and Pasadena in Apr.–May 1913, however, seems to provide an adequate terminus.

The significance of what occurred in the former Stevens AME Church building that housed the mission on Azusa Street must be seen within a larger context. Several theological threads emerged in American religious life during the 19th century that eventually were woven into the tapestry of Azusa. ▸Restorationism, for one, spawned several new religious movements that viewed the church as returning to its NT glory. In some cases it brought an expectation of a "latter rain" outpouring of the Holy Spirit with an accompanying revival. Appeal was also made to the "apostolic faith," "once for all delivered to the saints" (Jude 3) to demonstrate the relationship between the contemporary faith and that of the first apostles. Frontier revivalism contributed anxious benches, brush-arbor and protracted meetings, tarrying sessions, and altar calls for personal salvation and holiness of life from evangelists such as Charles G. Finney. F. B. Meyer helped popularize the "overcoming life" doctrine taught at Keswick, which became very influential in many American churches. Personal holiness and sanctification as a "pentecostal" experience of the "full gospel" were given a theological framework in Asa Mahan's work *The Baptism of the Holy Ghost* (1870). The Holiness movement also brought an understanding of the atonement of Christ as providing a "double cure for a double curse" that ultimately led to an emphasis on divine healing. Finally, concern for the Second Coming and prophetic events, originating in Britain with J. N. Darby and the Plymouth Brethren, came to the American context through a host of Bible prophecy conferences and the widespread usage of the *Scofield Reference Bible*, which provided annotated notes on Darby's scheme. By 1900 these threads were all present in the religious life of the Los Angeles area.

In 1904–5 reports came to Los Angeles of the ▸Welsh Revival, a substantial revival that was taking place in Wales, largely associated with the work of the young evangelist Evan Roberts. In Chicago, Holiness publisher S. B. Shaw wrote *The Great Revival in Wales* (1905), which was widely read in the Los Angeles area in 1905 and 1906. People who read the book began to establish cottage prayer meetings where they sought God for a similar revival among the churches of Los Angeles.

Prayer for revival was frequently offered in the Free Methodist colony at Herman, CA, a suburb lying northeast of the downtown area. It was heard in the Holiness Church of Southern California, the Peniel Mission, the Holiness group known as the Burning Bush, and in a local tent meeting of the Household of God led by W. F. Manley as well. But it was a preeminent concern of ▸Joseph Smale, pastor of First Baptist Church in Los Angeles.

So taken by reports of the Welsh revival was Smale, an immigrant from England, that in 1905 he made a trip home to meet with Evan Roberts and to observe firsthand the factors that made revival possible. Upon his return to Los Angeles, he began to preach a message that encouraged people to be open to the work of the Holy Spirit to convict of sin and to restore some of the more spectacular charisms. He organized his church into smaller home prayer groups and began a series of meetings that lasted for 15 weeks.

Not everyone at First Baptist Church was satisfied with this approach. The board confronted Smale with the fact that they thought he had become too fanatical. He resisted them but soon resigned his pastorate, taking with him those who believed in what he was doing. With this core of followers, he

founded the First New Testament Church. Because Smale had been the pastor of a prominent church in Los Angeles, the local press featured the novelty of his new congregation more than once. Yet Smale continued his search for revival.

In the spring of 1905 Second Baptist Church in Los Angeles was struck by division when several of its members embraced the "second work" teaching of the Holiness movement and attempted to teach it there. Julia W. Hutchins and several families were expelled from membership, and for a time they met with W. F. Manley's Household of God tent meeting at First and Bonnie Brae streets. Soon they ventured to establish a small storefront mission at Ninth and Santa Fe avenues, where they could teach their Holiness doctrine freely. Their quest for a pastor led them to summon from Houston, TX, a Holiness preacher with a pentecostal message, Elder W. J. Seymour, who had been recommended to them by one of their members, Neely Terry.

Seymour arrived in Los Angeles on Feb. 22, 1906, and began to hold meetings at the mission on Santa Fe two days later. Seymour's recent training had come from Charles Parham, founder of the Apostolic Faith Movement (Baxter Springs, KS), a group that claimed as many as 13,000 members in the south-central region of the U.S. A distinctive of the AFM involved speaking in tongues (unlearned foreign languages), which was thought to have an evidential relationship to baptism in the Spirit. When Seymour broached the subject of speaking in tongues to his new congregation, Hutchins, who disagreed with him, locked him out. He had to resort to holding meetings first in the home of Edward S. Lee, with whom he was staying, then for several weeks at the home of the Asberrys on Bonnie Brae.

The Asberry home was small, but a number of people from Hutchins's mission, others from First New Testament Church, and still others from a variety of Holiness churches moved in and out of the prayer meeting and Bible study led by Seymour. Blacks and whites mingled freely, and high on their agenda was prayer for revival and an expectation that God was about to move in their midst.

On Monday, Apr. 9, 1906, before Seymour left Edward Lee to go to the Asberry home for the evening meeting, Lee told him of a vision that he had had in which the apostles showed him how to speak in tongues. The two men prayed together, and in moments Lee was speaking in tongues. Seymour carried the news to his meeting on Bonnie Brae, where ▸Jennie Evans Moore and several others also broke into tongues. News spread rapidly, and people came to Bonnie Brae to see and hear for themselves. Within a week the group had rented 312 Azusa Street, and the mission had begun.

That this was a revival, however, was something that was not immediately apparent. By year's end critics still proclaimed that what was happening at Azusa was "of small moment." Even such a sympathetic observer as ▸Carrie Judd

Montgomery, whose husband George had visited Azusa in Dec. 1906 and had come away with glowing reports of what God was doing there, wrote the following month, "There is no real revival as a whole in Los Angeles, but only here and there a little company who are trusting God fully and receiving a rich experience of His grace."

For the most part these reports were accurate. Yet the opening of the Azusa Street Mission was something that did not escape the notice of many, including members of the secular press. The *Los Angeles Times* sent a reporter to an evening meeting during the first week of its existence. The ensuing article served as free publicity in spite of its patently derogatory tone. Jennie Evans Moore, who was a member of First New Testament Church, spoke in tongues at the conclusion of the Easter morning (Apr. 15) service at that church, causing quite a stir. She moved quickly to attach herself to Azusa Street on a permanent basis, and others soon followed.

At Azusa, services were long, and on the whole they were spontaneous. In its early days music was a cappella, although one or two instruments were included at times. Services included singing, testimonies given by visitors or read from those who wrote in, prayer, altar calls for salvation or sanctification or for baptism in the Holy Spirit, and, of course, preaching. Sermons generally were not prepared in advance but were typically spontaneous. W. J. Seymour was clearly in charge, but much freedom was given to visiting preachers. Prayer for the sick was also a regular part of services. Many shouted. Others were "slain in the Spirit" or "fell under the power." Sometimes there were periods of extended silence or of singing in tongues. No offerings were collected, but there was a receptacle near the door for gifts.

The upstairs at Azusa doubled as an office for the mission and as a rooming house for several residents, including Seymour and later his wife, but it was also sufficiently large to handle the overflow at the altar or to accommodate those who were tarrying for one or another experience with God. High on the agenda of most of those who tarried was a pentecostal baptism in the Spirit and the ability to speak in tongues.

Arthur Osterberg, who later reminisced about the first service at Azusa, claimed that some 100 people were present. The *Los Angeles Times* reported a "crowd" that included a majority of blacks with "a sprinkling of whites" when a reporter visited the mission on Apr. 17. Frank Bartleman, who attended first on Thursday, Apr. 19, said that it was somewhat smaller—"about a dozen saints," some black, some white. Weekend crowds were larger than those on weekdays.

Growth was quick and substantial. Most sources indicate the presence of about 300 to 350 worshipers inside the 40-by-60-foot whitewashed, wood-frame structure, with others mingling outside before the end of summer, including seekers, hecklers, and children. At times it may have been double that.

W. F. Manley reported in Sept. 1906 that there were 25 blacks and 300 whites at the meetings he attended. But what had occurred at Azusa began to spread quickly to other churches.

Smale opened the doors of First New Testament Church, if somewhat cautiously, to those who had received the pentecostal experience, offering room for the free expression of their newly discovered gifts of the Spirit, including tongues. A. H. Post, a Baptist pastor who had joined forces with Manley's Household of God, attempted to establish a pentecostal work in Pasadena in July, but he met stiff resistance from some local residents. Frank Bartleman established a congregation at the corner of Eighth and Maple in Los Angeles in August. Seymour, the Lemons, and others from the mission held meetings in Whittier in August, September, and October of that year. Another group held pentecostal meetings in the Holiness Church at Monrovia. Edward McCauley went to Long Beach, while Thomas Junk, Ophelia Wiley, and others went north to Oakland, Salem, Spokane, and Seattle. Still others, like Abundio and Rosa de Lopez, moved southward to San Diego.

Seymour believed greatly in what was happening at the mission. He knew that it was something important and new, but he sought first to acknowledge its relationship with the work of Charles Parham. In July 1906 he wrote to W. F. Carothers, field secretary to the AFM, asking for promised ministerial credentials from Parham. Carothers sent the note on to Parham, remarking that he had filled the request.

Five early pentecostal leaders pictured at the the Azusa Street Mission. (Front) William J. Seymour, the mission pastor, and John G. Lake; (standing) Brother Adams, F. F. Bosworth, and Tom Hezmalhalch.

In Sept. 1906 Seymour published a letter in Azusa's newspaper, *The Apostolic Faith (AF)*, in which Charles Parham told of his plans to visit the mission. The following month Seymour acknowledged that the message of Pentecost had been preached ever since Agnes Ozman's experiences in Parham's Topeka, KS, Bible school in 1901. Now, however, it had "burst out in great power" and was being carried worldwide from the Pacific Coast.

When Parham visited Azusa in Oct. 1906, he did not approve of what he found but rather repudiated it. Theological, racial, and power issues all entered into his assessment and the resulting rupture. Seymour and the mission were left to an independent existence. This did not dampen the movement in Los Angeles but served to provide it with greater independence and freedom as it became the center of the Pacific Apostolic Faith Movement. Parham's reputation was irreparably damaged among pentecostals in 1907, when he was arrested on charges of committing "an unnatural offense" in San Antonio, TX. Seymour and his mission, however, gained increasing respect as well as notoriety, spread in part through firsthand testimonies and also through *AF*, which was published between Sept. 1906 and May 1908 by members of the mission staff.

It appears that the core of the mission's membership ran to no more than 50 or 60 people. The official membership was racially integrated, although predominantly black, but a disproportionate number of whites served in leadership positions. Seymour, the pastor, was black, as were trustees Richard Asberry and James Alexander. But whites Louis Osterberg (trustee), George E. Berg (secretary), Glenn Cook (business manager), and R. J. Scott (camp meeting organizer) also held responsible positions. Highly gifted black women, such as Jennie Evans Moore, ▸Lucy Farrow, and Ophelia Wiley were joined by white women ▸Clara E. Lum and ▸Florence Crawford in public leadership roles. They led in singing, read written testimonies, aided in the publication of the mission's newspaper and in visitation and outreach evangelism, and sometimes they "exhorted" the congregation. Indeed, Seymour served as pastor of an anomalous congregation in Los Angeles, a fully integrated work with leadership drawn from blacks and whites, with Hispanics and other ethnic minorities comfortably present in most of its services.

There appear to have been two periods in which the number of people worshiping at Azusa was much larger than the core membership. In each case, several hundred people were involved. The initial surge was in 1906–8, and the second one was in 1911. Attendance peaked at these times, with a major attendance dip between 1909 and 1911. Only days before the second big surge, it was reported that there were as few as a dozen blacks and no whites in attendance. While the second rise was short-lived, it was sufficient to cause Bartleman to describe it as "the second shower of the Latter Rain." In 1912

Anglican pastor and publisher of *Confidence,* ▸A. A. Boddy, came from England and found a "good-sized" crowd though greatly reduced from that of the previous year.

In spite of the fact that Azusa was often described as a "colored" mission, the large crowds it attracted proved to be dominated by whites who were both volatile and extremely mobile. Evangelists, such as ▸Gaston B. Cashwell, ▸Frank Bartleman, and ▸"Mother" Elizabeth Wheaton came. Pastors ▸Elmer Fisher, ▸William Pendleton, ▸William H. Durham, and ▸Joseph Smale attended. Publishers, such as ▸Carrie Judd Montgomery *(Triumphs of Faith),* ▸M. L. Ryan *(Apostolic Light),* and ▸A. S. Worrell *(Gospel Witness)* passed through and quickly spread the news. Veteran missionaries, such as Samuel and ▸Ardelle Mead, and Mae F. Mayo were there, while church executives, such as ▸Charles H. Mason, from the Church of God in Christ, and Christian and Missionary Alliance district superintendent ▸George Eldridge attended. Some of them came for extended periods of time.

Most, but not all, seem to have come out of curiosity, though many came with the hope that they would receive something they could take elsewhere—a new teaching, a renewed commitment, a new experience, or added power for their already existing ministries. Many who came were spiritually hungry, but there were also those who sought to establish a name for themselves, would-be preachers, and those who would occupy the fringe of the movement because of their fanatical antics. Charges of fanaticism, of "whipping up the saints," and of "wild-fire" were reported on occasion, and even Seymour wrote of his frustration with the whites who imported certain excesses into the mission. On the whole, though, Seymour provided the necessary leadership to ensure the success of the revival.

As for its local revival impact, by 1912 Azusa Street could be credited directly with contributing to the establishment of such congregations as Elmer Fisher's Upper Room Mission; Bartleman and Pendleton's Eighth and Maple Mission; ▸William Durham's Seventh Street Mission; ▸W. L. Sargent's Florence Avenue Pentecostal Mission; A. G. Osterberg's Full Gospel Assembly; ▸John Perron's Italian Pentecostal Mission; ▸James Alexander's Apostolic Faith Mission on 51st Street (Alexander was one of Seymour's original trustees) as well as one other Apostolic Faith Mission, at Seventh and Sentous; W. F. Manley's Pentecostal Assembly; G. Valenzuella's Spanish Apostolic Faith Mission; William Saxby's Carr Street Pentecostal Mission; and an Apostolic Faith Rescue Mission on First Street.

Azusa's effect on the local religious establishment provoked the conservative churches of Los Angeles to work with the police commissioner so that they could hold "approved" street meetings. They added "prayer meetings" to their lists of services and bound their participants to agree that they would engage in substantial acts of "secret prayer, at certain intervals." All of this moved toward a culmination in Mar. 1907, when these churches sponsored a citywide evangelistic campaign with special speakers from around the country.

The revival spread nationally with the establishment of new congregations and the transformation of existing ones. William Hamner Piper's Stone Church in Chicago joined the Full Gospel Assembly, or North Avenue Mission, begun initially by William Durham as a new and significant pentecostal voice, complete with a major periodical *(Latter Rain Evangel)* and a publishing house (Evangel Press). In New York City the Glad Tidings Tabernacle, pastored by ›Marie Burgess Brown and her husband Robert Brown, joined the pentecostal ranks. Throughout the South and Midwest many missions and churches were planted.

Internationally the message spread rapidly as people who believed themselves to have been freshly touched by the Spirit and, in many cases, to have been given a gift of languages (tongues) for purposes of missionary work, went abroad. Lucy Leatherman made a trip around the world, while Frank Bartleman circled the globe once and made a second two-year evangelistic tour to Europe. Thomas Junk, as well as Bernt and Magna Bernsten, went from Azusa to China. M. L. Ryan led a number of young people to missions in the Philippines, Japan, and Hong Kong. The George E. Bergs and the ›A. G. Garrs went to India, while ›Tom Hezmal-

halch and ›John G. Lake went to South Africa. Pastor ›A. H. Post became a long-term missionary to Egypt, and a host of people, mostly black, including Edward and Mollie McCauley, G. W. and Daisy Batman, and Julia W. Hutchins took the pentecostal message to Liberia. In Toronto the ›Hebden Mission was established.

Sometimes existing denominations were split, while others were totally transformed into pentecostal vehicles. Among these were the Church of God in Christ, the Church of God (Cleveland, TN), and the Pentecostal Holiness Church. A portion of the Free Will Baptist Church also fell into this category, becoming the Pentecostal Free Will Baptists. But new groups were formed as well. The Apostolic Faith (Portland, OR), the Pentecostal Assemblies of the World (Los Angeles), and in 1914 the Assemblies of God, fell into this category. Indeed, nearly every pentecostal denomination in the U.S. traces its roots in some way or other to the Apostolic Faith Mission at 312 Azusa Street. The Apostolic Faith Church of God (Franklin, VA), whose founder, Charles W. Lowe, was appointed bishop of that group by William J. Seymour, is the most clearly identifiable denominational descendant of the Azusa Street Mission.

In order to assess the significance of the Azusa Street revival, one cannot look merely at what was initially perceived to be a ministry of W. J. Seymour to "the colored people of

The building at 312 Azusa Street in Los Angeles that became world famous in 1906 as the Azusa Street Mission, from which the pentecostal message spread throughout North America and the world.

the City of Los Angeles." Its significance will also be lost if one concentrates on the growth in the number of people who attended Azusa Street in any ongoing way. By 1915 the congregation numbered but a handful, and the mission had been permanently lost to any further leadership role in a now burgeoning movement. W. J. Seymour died on Sept. 28, 1922, and his wife continued to lead the congregation until her health broke. The building was demolished in 1931 and the land lost in foreclosure in 1938. Thus, one must look at the impact of what took place outside the walls of the mission to grasp the full impact of the revival that was sparked there.

To look elsewhere for primary evidence of the revival's extent, however, should in no way detract from the fact that something very significant did take place at Azusa Street. It attracted many people—skeptics, seekers, and church leaders alike from around the world, people of all colors and from all stations in life. They came, and in many cases stayed there for an extended period of time. Unlike most churches of its day, Azusa was very much freely integrated in a day of racial segregation and Jim Crow laws. It is not an insignificant fact that a black man, W. J. Seymour, provided its leadership and that everyone sensed a form of equality as sisters and brothers seeking God together.

Azusa was typically described by the press as a "colored" congregation that met in a "tumble-down shack" and made the night "hideous" through the "howlings of the worshipers," yet it was a church where whites, blacks, Hispanics, Asians, and others met together regularly and where from their own perspective the color line was virtually nonexistent. Clearly, Seymour may be credited with providing the vision of a truly color-blind congregation. His was a radical experiment that ultimately failed because of the inability of whites to allow for a sustained role for black leadership.

The significance of the revival is equally related to its teaching about baptism in the Spirit and in the gift of tongues. Unlike later pentecostals, and clearly in opposition to the pentecostal message of the Upper Room Mission a few blocks away, Seymour moved away from a theology of tongues as the initial physical evidence of baptism in the Spirit. In fact, Seymour ultimately repudiated the "initial evidence" teaching as providing "an open door for witches and spiritualists and free loveism." From the beginning he taught that "baptism in the Holy Ghost and fire means to be flooded with the love of God and Power for Service." The gift of tongues, however, was viewed as a sign that would follow this baptism.

While speaking in tongues played a significant role in the life of Azusa, it was the emphasis on power for ministry that most frequently sent people to the evangelistic or mission field. In some cases the gift of tongues was viewed as a form of supernatural endowment that equipped its recipients with the necessary ability to communicate the gospel to the lost of another culture. The experience of an immanent God in a day in which transcendence was the dominant theme set the mission apart from many churches, and the experiences of tongues, healings, and other "spectacular" gifts tended to underscore the immanence of God.

The significance of Azusa lies also in the testimonies of those whose lives were transformed by an experience of an immanent God, through the Holy Spirit. Many found their intellectual orientation transformed. Their own ministries suddenly gained new direction or power, their personal spirituality was enriched, and their vision of the church's task immeasurably broadened. Thus, the significance of Azusa was centrifugal—those who were touched by it took their experiences elsewhere and touched the lives of others. Coupled with the theological threads of personal salvation, holiness, divine healing, baptism in the Spirit with power for ministry, and an anticipation of the imminent return of Jesus Christ, ample motivation was provided to assure the revival a long-term impact.

Today the site of the Azusa Street Mission is dominated by the Japanese-American Cultural and Community Center. Since 1997 a group known as the Azusa Street Memorial Committee, composed of church and civic leaders, has sought to mark and commemorate this site. In Feb. 1999 the committee laid a plaque in Naguchi Plaza that reads,

> Azusa Street Mission. This plaque commemorates the site of the Azusa Street Mission, which was located at 312 Azusa Street. Formally known as the Apostolic Faith Mission, it served as a fountainhead for the international Pentecostal Movement from 1906–1931. Pastor William J. Seymour oversaw the "Azusa Street Revival." He preached a message of salvation, holiness, and power, welcomed visitors from around the world, transformed the congregation into a multicultural center of worship, and commissioned pastors, evangelists, and missionaries to take the message of "Pentecost" (Acts 2:1–41) to the world. Today, members of the Pentecostal/Charismatic Movement number half a billion worldwide.

The committee is continuing to work on a larger commemorative project that will ultimately provide the history of this piece of property.

■ **Bibliography:** "Azusa to Portland: A Moment in History Revisited," *Higher Way* 89:6 (Nov.–Dec. 1996) ■ "Baba Bharati Says Not a Language," *Los Angeles Daily Times* (Sept. 19, 1906), pt. 2, 1 ■ F. Bartleman, *How Pentecost Came to Los Angeles* (1925; repr. as *Azusa Street* [1980]) ■ idem, "The Pentecostal Work," *Word and Work* 39 (1, Jan. 1908) ■ idem, "Praying Bands for Churches," *Los Angeles Express* (July 25, 1906) ■ idem, *Witness to Pentecost: The Life of Frank Bartleman* (1985) ■ idem, "Work in Los Angeles," *Word and Work* 33 (6, June 1911) ■ F. Corum, *Like as of Fire* (1981) ■ D. Dayton, *Theological Roots of Pentecostalism* (1987) ■ S. H.

Frodsham, *"With Signs Following"* (1926, 1941) ■ H. A. Ironside, "Apostolic Faith Missions and the So-Called Second Pentecost" (pamphlet, n.d.) ■ idem, "The Gift of Tongues," *Nazarene Messenger* 11 (24, Dec. 13, 1906) ■ C. J. Montgomery, "The Work in Los Angeles," *Triumphs of Faith* 27 (2, Jan. 1907): 14 ■ D. J. Nelson, "For Such a Time as This" (Ph.D. diss., U. of Birmingham, 1981) ■ A. M. Otis, "Apostolic Faith Movement," *Word and Work* 39 (2, Feb. 1907) ■ Robert R. Owens, *Speak to the Rock: The Azusa Street Revival: Its Roots and Its Message* (1998) ■ "Queer 'Gift' Given Many," *Los Angeles Daily Times* (July 23, 1906), pt. 2, 7 ■ Cecilia Rasmussen, "Vision of a Colorblind Faith Gave Birth to Pentecostalism," *Los Angeles Times* (June 14, 1998), B–3 ■ C. M. Robeck Jr., "The Earliest Pentecostal Missions in Los Angeles," *AGH* 3 (3, Fall 1983) ■ "Rolling on Floor in Smale's Church," *Los Angeles Daily Times* (July 13, 1906), 1 ■ W. J. Seymour, *The Doctrines and Discipline of the Azusa Street Apostolic Faith Mission* (1915) ■ J. H. Sparks, "Azusa Street Mission," *Word and Work* 33 (4, Apr. 1911) ■ idem, "Convention in Los Angeles," *Word and Work* 30 (5, May 1908) ■ George B. Studd, "My Convictions as to the Pentecostal Movement Irreverently Called 'The Tongues'" (pamphlet, n.d.) ■ A. C. Valdez with James F. Scheer, *Fire on Azusa Street* (1980) ■ "Weird Babel of Tongues," *Los Angeles Daily Times* (Apr. 18, 1906), pt. 2, 1 ■ "Weird Fanaticism Fools Young Girl," *Los Angeles Daily Times* (July 12, 1906), 1 ■ A. S. Worrell, "At Los Angeles," *Confidence* 5 (10, Oct. 1912) ■ idem, "Azusa's First Camp-Meeting," *Word and Work* 58 (1, Jan. 1936) ■ idem, "Letter from Los Angeles," *Triumphs of Faith* 26 (12, Dec. 1906) ■ idem, "A Meeting at the Azusa Street Mission, Los Angeles," *Confidence* 5 (11, Nov. 1912) ■ idem, "The Movements in Los Angeles, California," *Triumphs of Faith* 26 (12, Dec. 1906).

■ C. M. Robeck Jr.

B

BADA, ALEXANDER ADEBAYO ABIODUN (1930–2000). Bada was the second pastor and supreme head of the ▸Celestial Church of Christ (CCC) Worldwide. He was successor to pastor-founder ▸Samuel Oschoffa. He was born in Lagos, Nigeria, on Dec. 4, 1930, to a Yoruba family from Ogun State. He received his elementary and secondary education at Ilesha, Western Nigeria, and later worked with Nigerian Breweries, Ltd., until 1952, when he joined the nucleus of the CCC in Nigeria—then located in Makoko-Lagos—as one of their earliest converts.

In 1955 Bada was anointed the first Nigerian leader of the CCC by the pastor-founder. He held several positions until he was appointed the only "supreme evangelist," a rank he held until the death of Oschoffa in 1985. He was formally installed and enthroned as pastor on Dec. 24, 1987. The routinization process started by Oschoffa continued after his death under Bada, whom members saw as one who had the charismatic initiative to ensure continuity within the fold. Bada combined his power of miraculous healings with organizational and training skills, which he used to introduce institutional adjustments that put CCC on the road toward modernization and globalization.

He held several other positions, such as founding member and vice president of the Organization of African Instituted Churches (OAIC). He was the grand patron of the Youth Wing of Christian Association of Nigeria (YOWICAN). Bada was appointed by the Nigerian government to serve on its Advisory Committee on Religious Affairs (ACRA). He also served as a trustee of the Ogun State University Endowment Fund and received several honorary titles, such as "Citizen of Buake, Ivory Coast."

Bada died on Sept. 8, 2000, in Greenwich Hospital in London, U.K.

■ **Bibliography:** A. U. Adogame, "Celestial Church of Christ: The Politics of Cultural Identity in a West African Prophetic-Charismatic Movement" (diss., Bayreuth, Germany, 1997) ■ idem, *Celestial Eye: A Decade of Pastoral Leadership* (1995) ■ personal interview with A. A. Bada at CCC International Headquarters, Ketu-Lagos, Nov. 23, 1995. ■ A. U. Adogame

BAKER, ELIZABETH V. (c. 1849–1915). Faith healer and educator. An important center of early pentecostalism, established in Rochester, NY, was a result of the efforts of Elizabeth V. Baker, the eldest daughter of Methodist pastor James Duncan, and her sisters—Mary E. Work, Nellie A. Fell, ▸Susan A. Duncan, and Harriet "Hattie" M. Duncan. From their ministry activities, spearheaded by Baker, came the Elim Faith Home (▸Faith Homes), Elim Publishing House, Elim Tabernacle, and the Rochester Bible Training School.

Baker's early life indicates a great deal of personal grief. Her first marriage, entered into before she was 20 years old, ended in divorce due to abuse by her husband. Some time after this she attended a lecture on the Ohio "Women's Crusade," a forerunner of the Woman's Christian Temperance Union. She felt little interest until the speaker referred to the women who in the power of Christ courageously entered saloons to protest the sale of alcoholic beverages and knelt in the sawdust on the sidewalks to pray. More than the temperance issue, Baker was confronted by the living Christ.

Several years later (c. 1881), a severe throat condition threatened Baker's health. Her second husband, a medical doctor, called in specialists to treat her, but her condition worsened. Finally, she was anointed and prayed for by C. W. Winchester, pastor of the local Asbury Methodist Episcopal Church, who had come to believe in faith healing. Immediately after his prayer she was able to swallow and her illness ended.

Baker and her husband eventually separated. This resulted in part from her embracing the doctrine of faith healing and her subsequent activities in that ministry.

By the time Baker and her sisters opened a mission and the Elim Faith Home in 1895, she had been influenced by the advocates of faith healing; the writings of George Müller, which depicted his life of faith; and the premillennial teachings of Adoniram J. Gordon. The faith home opened to meet the needs of those who sought physical healing and to provide a place "where tired missionaries and Christian workers could for a time find rest for soul and body" (Baker, 51).

Feeling directed by the Holy Spirit to visit India, Baker traveled there in 1898 and met the famous ▸Pandita Ramabai, director of the Mukti Mission. This trip heightened the missionary vision of the sisters and their followers in Rochester. By 1915, $75,000 had been contributed to foreign missions—a considerable sum for that time.

Other activities followed. In 1902 the sisters began to publish *Trust,* a periodical edited by Susan A. Duncan and devoted to teaching the doctrines of salvation, faith healing, the Holy Spirit, premillennialism, and world evangelization. Several years later the Elim Tabernacle was constructed, and in 1906 the Rochester Bible Training School opened "for the training of those who felt His call to some special work but lacked the educational fitness."

The news of the Welsh revival in 1904–5 had impressed Baker and her sisters of the need for a similar occurrence in

Rochester. When word of the ⸬Azusa Street revival reached them, they pondered for a year the pentecostal baptism accompanied by speaking in tongues. Through study and prayer, they concluded that it was valid. At their summer convention in 1907, the participants sought for this experience, and a pentecostal revival followed.

The Duncan sisters were sensitive to the criticisms made by many about the legitimacy of women preachers. Baker justified her ministry because of a direct calling from the Holy Spirit. With the construction of the Elim Tabernacle, they prayed that God would send the right man as pastor. When no one suitable appeared, however, their leadership continued. Nevertheless, they refused ordination because they were women.

After Elizabeth V. Baker died at age 66 on Jan. 18, 1915, her two sisters, Susan A. Duncan and Harriet "Hattie" M. Duncan, directed the ministries until they were too advanced in age to continue. The legacy of Baker and her sisters lived on through the students who attended their school. By 1916, 17 of the students had traveled overseas as missionaries. Two of them, Beatrice Morrison and Karl Wittick, had died in Africa by this time. Other noteworthy pentecostals attended, including Alfred Blakeney, ⸬John H. Burgess, Marguerite Flint, ⸬Ivan Q. Spencer, ⸬Ralph Riggs, Grace Walther, Charles W. H. Scott, and Anna Ziese.

■ **Bibliography:** E. V. Baker et al., *Chronicles of a Faith Life* (2d ed., c. 1926) ▪ G. B. McGee, "Three Notable Women in Pentecostal Ministry," *AGH* 1 (1986).   ■ G. B. McGee

BAKER, H. A. (1881–1971). Early pentecostal missionary to Tibet, China, and Taiwan. At 13 or 14 years of age, Baker was baptized in the Christian Church but professed that a real experience of conversion did not come until five years later. He entered Hiram College to prepare for ministry and while there served as president of the local chapter of the Student Volunteer Movement for Foreign Missions. After graduation in 1909 he married Josephine Witherstay and pastored in Buffalo, NY. In 1912 the couple went to Tibet as missionaries under the auspices of the Christian Church.

After five years of work on the Tibetan border, the Bakers returned to the U.S. While on furlough they received the baptism in the Holy Spirit, having been influenced by Allan A. Swift, another missionary to China. They returned to China as independent pentecostal missionaries to work in Yunnan Province, where they opened an orphanage and eventually witnessed an outpouring of the Spirit among the tribal people. In his book *Visions Beyond the Veil* (c. 1938), Baker described the experiences these children had when they received visions of heaven and hell; this proved to be his most popular book and was eventually printed in 13 languages. He also wrote *Through Tribulation* (n.d.) and *Tribulation to Glory*

(c. 1951), in which he argued for a posttribulational rapture of the church, somewhat of a doctrinal novelty among American pentecostal missionaries. His other publications included *God in Ka Do Land* (1937), *The Three Worlds* (1937), *Seeking and Saving* (1940), *Devils and Dupes* (n.d.), *Heaven and the Angels* (n.d.), *Plains of Glory and Gloom* (n.d.), and *The Adullam News* (booklets that described and promoted his ministry); his autobiography is entitled *Under His Wings* (n.d.).

Although Baker remained an independent missionary, he had strong links to the Assemblies of God. The Bakers remained in China until a year after the Communist takeover. Returning to the U.S., they ministered among the Navajo Indians in New Mexico. For the last 16 years of Baker's life he ministered among the Hakka people of Taiwan until his death at the age of 90 (his wife preceded him in death by several months). The Bakers' one son, James, and his wife, Marjorie, minister with Asian Outreach in Hong Kong.

■ **Bibliography:** H. A. Baker, "The Lord Opened the Way to China," *FGMH* (Apr. 1924), 12–13 ▪ idem, *Under His Wings* (n.d.) ▪ "Pentecostal Pioneer Dies in Taiwan," *PE* (Feb. 6, 1972), 14.
■ G. B. McGee

BAKKER, JAMES ORSEN ("JIM") (1940–). Television evangelist and founder of the PTL Network. Jim Bakker was born to Raleigh and Ferne Bakker of Muskegon Heights, MI. In his autobiography, *Move That Mountain* (with R. P. Lamb, 1976), Bakker relates his modest origins, including his embarrassment over an unsightly house, his small and frail body, and his mediocre performance in school. He surrendered his life to God as the result of a crisis experience in which he ran over a child with his father's automobile.

Following graduation from high school in 1959, Bakker attended North Central Bible College of the Assemblies of God (AG), where he met Tammy Faye La Valley. Several months after meeting, and in the middle of a school term, Jim and Tammy decided to marry (1961). This resulted in

THE PTL CLUB SYMBOL

"P" represents the Fish symbol used by first century Christians to identify one another.

"T" symbolizes the cross of Christ, our only means of salvation.

"L" is the Fishhook, a reminder of Christ's call for us to be "Fishers of Men."

The Circular design means that in Christ there is completeness.

PRAISE THE LORD!

PTL Television Network, Charlotte, NC 28279

their expulsion from NCBC and marked the end of their formal education. For the next five years they lived as itinerant preachers, specializing in children's ministry, including the use of puppets. In 1964 Jim was ordained by the AG. In 1965 he was hired by *Marion G. (Pat) Robertson (CBN) for a children's radio/TV show *(The Jim and Tammy Show)* and as host of the new *700 Club*. In 1973 Jim became cofounder of the California-based Trinity Broadcasting Network. The following year he inaugurated another Christian talk show, the *PTL Club* (originally meaning "Praise the Lord," later "People That Love") in Charlotte, NC.

In this new venture, the Bakkers were phenomenally successful, as the *PTL Club* grew into the PTL Television Network with a worldwide outreach. By early 1987 they had developed a $172 million religious empire, including state-of-the-art TV production studios and Heritage Village (with the Grand Hotel, condominiums for those who wished to live in a Christian environment, a water amusement park, and a home for handicapped children). This Christian entertainment complex drew visitors at a rate third only to Disneyland and Disney World.

While it was quite apparent to the average viewer that the Bakkers had experienced difficulties in their marriage and crises in their ministry, the events of early 1987 came as a shock. Tammy was admitted into a California clinic, suffering from drug dependency. Then on Mar. 19, 1987, Jim Bakker announced that he had resigned as chairman of PTL ministries and from ministry in the AG. He claimed that a "hostile force" (later identified as fellow evangelist *Jimmy Swaggart) was plotting to take over his religious empire and that he was being blackmailed by former friends over a 1980 sexual encounter with church secretary Jessica Hahn. He explained that the tryst with Hahn had been an attempt to make his wife jealous at a time when their marriage was in trouble. Bakker then turned his empire over to another televangelist, Jerry Falwell. Meanwhile, the public became aware that Richard Dortch, Bakker's assistant at PTL, had paid hush money to Jessica Hahn for "the sake of the ministry."

These revelations—called "Pearlygate" by the media—were followed by a "holy war" between televangelists Bakker, Falwell, and Swaggart. For several weeks Bakker and his accusers dominated the news, including such TV shows as *Good Morning America* and *Nightline*, with charges and counter-charges. Swaggart declared that Bakker was a "cancer" that needed to be excised from the body of Christ. Falwell contended that Bakker was the greatest scab and cancer on the face of Christianity in 2,000 years. John Ankerberg, a Baptist television personality, accused Bakker of bisexuality. Bakker countered by denying additional sins of the flesh and by demanding the return of his empire from Falwell, which he said the fundamental Baptist evangelist had promised. When Falwell refused, Bakker accused him of theft.

Jim and Tammy Bakker's early puppet ministry.

It soon became apparent that Bakker's early confessions only addressed the tip of a scandalous iceberg. Auditors discovered that the Bakker's salary and bonuses for 1986–87 totaled $1.6 million (Bakker frequently had presented a "prosperity theology," arguing that God wanted his people to live first class). At the same time, it was revealed that the PTL ministry had piled up a $70 million debt. Shortly after the scandal broke, PTL lawyers petitioned for bankruptcy. An Internal Revenue Service investigation into the finances of PTL followed.

The PTL enterprises survived the demise of the Bakkers until mid 1988. First Jerry Falwell and then David Clark guided the empire through the stormy period following the Bakkers' exit. In 1989 Jim Bakker was convicted on 24 counts of defrauding the public by overselling lifetime "partnerships" and promising lifetime lodging rights at the Heritage USA theme park. At age 48, he was handed a 45-year sentence. A federal appeals court in 1991 ruled the punishment excessive and reduced the sentence. After serving almost five years, Bakker was paroled in 1994. Tammy Faye divorced Jim in 1992, claiming she could no longer bear the separation. A year later she married Roe Messner, a developer who had built much of the Heritage USA resort. Shortly thereafter Messner was convicted of bankruptcy fraud.

While in prison, Jim Bakker rethought his prosperity theology, coming to the conclusion that he had twisted Scripture to serve his own desires. In 1996 his book *I Was Wrong* was released. Bakker confessed that he was mistaken in preaching the so-called health-and-wealth doctrine. In Sept. 1998 Jim Bakker married Lori Graham (1957–) of Phoenix, AZ. Shortly thereafter they went on back-to-back ministry trips to England and Australia.

In addition to *Move That Mountain* and *I Was Wrong,* Bakker has written *Eight Keys to Success* (1980); *Survival* (1981); *You Can Make It* (1983).

■ **Bibliography:** B. Bruce, "Jim Bakker Rejects 'Prosperity Gospel,'" *Charisma* (Sept. 1996) ■ "Fresh Out of Miracles," *Newsweek* (May 11, 1987) ■ "Heaven Can Wait," *Newsweek* (June 8, 1987) ■ C. C. Stertzer, "Jim, Lori Bakker to Minister Together," *Charisma* (Jan. 1999) ■ *Who's Who in America* (43d ed., 1984–85), 148.

■ S. M. Burgess

BALL, HENRY CLEOPHAS (1896–1989). Indigenous-church pioneer and missionary. Henry Cleophas Ball was born in Brooklyn, IA, and was reared in Ricardo, TX, by his widowed mother. Converted to Christ under the preaching of a Baptist minister, he nevertheless followed the lead of his mother and joined the Methodist church in Kingsville, TX, in 1910. Inspired by the message of a missionary from Venezuela, Ball became burdened to minister to the Mexicans living in Ricardo.

Ball's inability to speak Spanish did not deter his missionary impulse. Through inviting people to his services and relating his testimony in Spanish, Ball slowly began to master the language. Eventually he was able to preach in Spanish and give invitations at the end of the services for people to accept Christ. Such was the beginning of a lifelong ministry to Hispanics that would take him from Texas to Central and South America and the West Indies.

When Felix A. Hale, an Assemblies of God (AG) evangelist, preached in Kingsville, Ball was baptized in the Holy Spirit. This signaled an end to his Methodist affiliation. In 1915 Arch P. Collins, E. N. Richey, and Hale ordained him as a minister of the AG. His increasing activities in Hispanic evangelism led to his selection as the first superintendent of the Latin American Conference in 1918 (District 1925), a post he occupied until 1939. Ball was deeply committed to establishing indigenous churches, partially reflecting the influence of his friend ▸Alice E. Luce. He promoted annual conventions for the Mexican converts to provide fellowship and instruction. In 1916, while pastoring in Kingsville, he began the publication of the *Apostolic Light*. It later became the official publication of the Latin American District Council of the AG. This monthly magazine, designed as a tool for evangelism, had an enormous impact. Ball became a prolific writer, and his many publications gave positive direction to the growth of Hispanic pentecostalism. He published a songbook in Spanish called *Hymns of Glory*, which was printed without musical notation. Financed with money from his father's estate, Ball published a new edition with the music included in 1921. Both editions sold hundreds of thousands of copies. Other songbooks followed.

Another milestone passed with Ball's establishment of the Latin American Bible Institute in San Antonio, TX, in 1926. The graduates of this institute preached the gospel in various parts of the U.S., Mexico, Spain, Nicaragua, Puerto Rico, and Cuba. Thus, the impact of Ball's school in San Antonio reached beyond the borders of the U.S. to Latin America and Europe.

Faced with a lack of curricular materials, Ball wrote extensively to provide class notes for his students. These notes in turn were used in other Bible institutes in Latin America and are still highly valued.

Ball's activities eventually transcended educational, editorial, and district responsibilities to include a two-year period of missionary work in Chile (1941–43). In 1943 the AG Department of Foreign Missions appointed him to serve as the first overseas field secretary for Latin America and the West Indies. He continued in this capacity until 1953.

Ball's departure from this position afforded him the opportunity to devote his full attention to Spanish literature production. He had begun an agency for this purpose in 1946. It is currently known as Life Publishers International. His labors in evangelism, administration, Bible institute training, and Spanish literature production gained him widespread respect. In many areas he proved to be one of the most farsighted and creative missionary strategists the pentecostal movement, and the AG in particular, has produced.

■ **Bibliography:** V. De León, *The Silent Pentecostals* (1979) ■ G. B. McGee, "Pioneers of Pentecost: Alice E. Luce and H. C. Ball," *AGH* 2 (1985) ■ I. Spence, *Henry C. Ball: Man of Action* (n.d.).

■ G. B. McGee

BAPTISM IN THE HOLY SPIRIT

1. Baptism in the Holy Spirit and Other Terminology

2. Baptism in the Holy Spirit and Salvation

3. Baptism in the Holy Spirit and Sanctification

4. Baptism in the Holy Spirit and Speaking in Tongues

5. The Purpose of Baptism in the Holy Spirit

6. Baptism in the Holy Spirit and Water Baptism

7. The Reception of the Holy Spirit

In the pentecostal and charismatic traditions the doctrine of baptism in (or with) the Holy Spirit occupies a place of critical importance. The Pentecostal and Charismatic Churches of North America (PCCNA) affirm, "We believe that the full gospel includes holiness of heart and life, healing for the body, and baptism in the Holy Spirit with the evidence of speaking in other tongues as the Spirit gives the utterance." M. P. Hamilton's book on the charismatic movement offers the following prefatory statement: "The term *charismatic* applies to those who have experienced a 'baptism of the Holy Spirit' that involves receiving certain spiritual gifts" (Hamilton, 1975, 7). This article gives primary attention to pentecostal understanding of baptism in the Spirit, although some reference to charismatic thinking also is made.

Baptism in the Holy Spirit is viewed as a distinctive Christian experience. For pentecostals Spirit baptism refers to an experience whose basis is believed to be found in the Jerusalem event of Pentecost as recorded in Acts 2:1–4. At the beginning of Jesus' ministry, John the Baptist preached "baptism of repentance for the forgiveness of sins" (Mark 1:4) so that many confessed their sins and were baptized in water. He also declared about Jesus, "I baptize you with water, but he will baptize you with the Holy Spirit" (Mark 1:8). Some three years later, shortly before Pentecost, Jesus talked with his apostles about a gift promised by the Father, and he then commanded: "Do not leave Jerusalem, but wait for the gift my Father promised, which you have heard me speak about. For John baptized with water, but in a few days you will be baptized with the Holy Spirit" (Acts 1:4–5). Hence the gift the Father promised would be the Holy Spirit, who would come from Jesus (as John the Baptist had said), and the reception of that gift would be baptism in the Holy Spirit. On the Day of Pentecost the promise was fulfilled—"all of them were filled with the Holy Spirit" (2:4). Thereafter the same gift was offered to the thousands who assembled: "Repent and be baptized, every one of you, in the name of Jesus Christ for the forgiveness of your sins. And you will receive the gift of the Holy Spirit. The promise is for you and your children and for all who are far off—for all whom the Lord our God will call" (vv. 38–39). Viewing this promise extended to all generations and peoples as the gift of the Holy Spirit, pentecostals claim that they also have received this gift. They too have been baptized, or filled, with the Holy Spirit as a distinctive Christian experience.

1. Baptism in the Holy Spirit and Other Terminology.

The expression "Baptism in [with] the Holy Spirit"—or, more precisely, "baptized in the Holy Spirit"—occurs twice in the book of Acts. Its first use by Jesus has been noted; the other is found in Acts 11:16. Here Peter declared, "Then I remembered what the Lord had said: 'John baptized with water, but you will be baptized with the Holy Spirit.'" Peter was recalling the Caesareans—the Roman centurion Cornelius, his relatives, and close friends—who previously had been baptized in the Holy Spirit (10:44–46). Pentecostals view the Caesarean narrative as further evidence that Spirit baptism is not limited to the event of Pentecost but continues through the years.

Outside the book of Acts there is one possible reference to Spirit baptism. According to Paul, "we were all baptized by one Spirit into one body" (1 Cor. 12:13). However, pentecostals generally do not identify this baptism with baptism in the Spirit. Taking the usual reading "*by* one Spirit" as the proper translation, they view the agent of baptism as the Holy Spirit: the Spirit baptizes us into the one body of Christ. On the other hand, when we are baptized in the Holy Spirit, Christ is the agent who baptizes us in the Holy Spirit. Hence, from the pentecostal viewpoint, we must look to Acts for an adequate understanding of baptism in the Spirit.

Since the essential meaning of baptism is immersion, pentecostals often emphasize that to be baptized in the Holy Spirit is to be immersed in the Holy Spirit. This signifies a total submergence within the reality of the Holy Spirit so that whoever is so baptized has a vivid sense of the Spirit's presence and power. According to one pentecostal testimony: "Talking about a baptism, it was just like I was being plunged down into a great sea of water, only the water was God, the water was the Holy Spirit" (K. Ranaghan and D. Ranaghan, 1969, 16). Immersion, similar to that in water but in the reality of the Spirit, is a central emphasis in pentecostalism.

Other terminology in Acts relevant to baptism in the Spirit is much used by pentecostals. First, there is the language of *filling*. The text says that on the Day of Pentecost "all of them were filled with the Holy Spirit." Jesus had promised they would be baptized in the Spirit, but when the event actually occurred they were said to be filled. If the word "baptized" suggests a submergence within the Holy Spirit, "filling" points to an inner penetration or pervasion. Both are words expressing totality, without and within. In Acts 9:17 Saul (Paul) is ministered to by Ananias that he might be "filled with the Holy Spirit." Since "baptized" and "filled" in Acts 1 and 2 refer to the same event, Paul's resulting experience may also be viewed as a baptism in the Holy Spirit.

Pentecostals sometimes speak of this as the "infilling" of the Holy Spirit. Though the word "infilling" is not directly biblical, the reason for its usage is to differentiate this experience from the "indwelling" of the Spirit. Pentecostals generally acknowledge that all believers have the Spirit within them (Rom. 8:9–11; 1 Cor. 6:19); hence "filling" must refer to the full penetration of the indwelling Spirit. Some pentecostals, especially charismatics, refer to this as the "release" of the Spirit: the Spirit within is released for a total inward occupancy.

Another term used in Acts is the "outpouring," or "pouring out," of the Holy Spirit. After the disciples on the Day of Pentecost were filled with the Holy Spirit, Peter declared that this was in fulfillment of the prophecy by Joel: "In the last days, God says, I will pour out my Spirit on all people. . . . Even on my servants, both men and women, I will pour out my Spirit in those days, and they will prophesy" (Acts 2:17–18, referring to Joel 2:28–29). Later Peter said that this happened through Jesus: "Exalted to the right hand of God, he has received from the Father the promised Holy Spirit and has poured out what you now see and hear" (Acts 2:33). The imagery of outpouring is also used many years thereafter to describe the Caesarean's experience: "The gift of the Holy Spirit has been poured out even [or "also," KJV] on the Gentiles" (Acts 10:45).

The language of "outpouring," like "baptizing" or "filling," suggests totality, but it also points to abundance. God does not give sparingly: "God gives the Spirit without limit" (John 3:34). It is not as if a person may have a partial measure of the Holy Spirit at one time and more later; the Spirit is given without measure. Pentecostals usually emphasize that such language as "outpouring" and "infilling" does not mean that one has more of the Spirit. Rather, the Spirit who is totally present now totally claims the person. In popular pentecostal language, "You may have the Spirit, but now the Spirit has you!" When the Spirit is poured out, there is abundance.

Another expression used in Acts is the "falling" of the Holy Spirit. In the account of the Samaritans, Peter and John come from Jerusalem to minister to them the Holy Spirit, for the Spirit "had not yet fallen upon any of them" (Acts 8:16 NASB). In Caesarea, just before reference is made to the Spirit being poured out, the text reads, "The Holy Spirit fell upon all those who were listening to the message" (10:44 NASB). The word "falling" suggests suddenness, forcefulness—as in the account at Pentecost when "suddenly a sound like the blowing of a violent wind came from heaven and filled the whole house" (2:2). The word "fall" has had much usage in pentecostal circles where testimonies abound as to a certain occasion when the Holy Spirit fell. Agnes Ozman, whose experience is often viewed as the beginning of 20th-century pentecostalism, testified that "the Holy Spirit fell upon me and I began to speak in tongues, glorifying God" (Kendrick, 1961, 52).

One further term in Acts is "come on." In the earliest Acts account when Jesus spoke of the apostles' future baptism in the Spirit, he added the words, "You will receive power when the Holy Spirit comes on you" (Acts 1:8). Thus, their later experience in Acts 2:4 of being filled was both a coming on and a baptism. Much later, when Paul ministered the Holy Spirit to the Ephesians, "the Holy Spirit came on them" (19:6). Hence the Ephesians likewise were baptized in the Holy Spirit. The language of "coming on," incidentally, may be related to another expression used in Luke 24:49, namely, "clothed with": "stay in the city until you are clothed with power from on high." Both terms, "coming on" and "clothed with," express an active, continuing endowment of the Spirit wherein there is both possession by and investiture with the Holy Spirit.

For many pentecostals the imagery of coming on, or upon, is particularly significant. "The Holy Spirit may be *in* you, but is he also *on* you?" This kind of question is more than semantical, because the latter is viewed as an additional operation of the Holy Spirit in relation to the believer. The pentecostal "filling," accordingly, is not only an internal moving but also an external coming of the Holy Spirit. As a result, one is both Spirit-filled and Spirit-endowed.

All of this terminology—baptizing, filling, outpouring, falling, coming on—suggests a total experience of the presence of the Holy Spirit. In one sense it is an immersion, a submergence within (baptized); in still another it is an invasion from without (outpouring, falling upon, coming on). Such terminology is variously used by pentecostals to describe their own experience.

Baptism in the Holy Spirit therefore is one of many expressions that relates to the gift of the Holy Spirit. However, both because it is language used by Jesus himself and also because it expresses a profound experience of the reality of God's presence, this phrase is used most often in the pentecostal and charismatic traditions.

2. Baptism in the Holy Spirit and Salvation.

Pentecostals view baptism in the Holy Spirit as an experience that presupposes conversion. Preparatory to the event of Acts 2:1–4 Jesus had said to his apostles, "Do not leave Jerusalem, but wait for the gift my Father promised. For John baptized with water, but in a few days you will be baptized with the Holy Spirit" (Acts 1:4–5). Pentecostals hold that the apostles had already been converted. Many point to such Scriptures as Luke 10:20 ("Rejoice that your names are written in heaven"), John 15:3 ("You are already clean"), and John 17:14 ("They are not of the world") as signifying their conversion. Also attention is frequently called to the Resurrection Day scene in the Gospel of John where Jesus "breathed on them and said, 'Receive the Holy Spirit'" (20:22). This is often interpreted to refer to regeneration whereby the Holy Spirit comes to dwell within. Whether conversion/regeneration occurred during Jesus' ministry or on the day of his resurrection, the importance for pentecostals is that it occurred prior to Pentecost. Hence it is assumed that the apostles and their company were already believers when they were baptized in the Holy Spirit. Salvation came first, then baptism in the Holy Spirit. Reinforcement for this view is pointed to in Acts 11:17, where Peter, speaking in relation to the gift of the Holy Spirit to the Caesareans, declares: "God gave them the same gift as he gave to us, who believed [or "after believing," NASB] in the Lord Jesus Christ." Peter and those with him at Pentecost accordingly were already believing when they were baptized in the Holy Spirit.

Sometimes an objection is raised against pentecostals that the faith experience of this first apostolic group prior to Pentecost should not be used in relation to any event thereafter, since that was a unique situation. Against this objection pentecostals point to other accounts in Acts in which they see a similar distinction between conversion and baptism in the

Spirit. According to Acts 8, before Peter and John arrived to minister the Holy Spirit, the Samaritans had already come to faith and been water baptized: "They believed Philip ... [and] were baptized, both men and women" (v. 12). Sometime later, through the ministry of the two apostles, the Samaritans "received the Holy Spirit" (v. 17). There can be little doubt that their conversion preceded their reception of the gift of the Holy Spirit. The occasion of Paul's being filled with the Spirit (9:17) occurred three days (v. 9) after his initial encounter with the risen Christ (vv. 4–6). Viewing this as Paul's conversion, pentecostals see further biblical evidence of Spirit baptism as following conversion. In the narrative of Acts 19 the Holy Spirit comes upon the Ephesians after they have believed and been baptized. "On hearing this [the call to faith in Christ], they were baptized into the name of the Lord Jesus. When Paul placed his hands on them, the Holy Spirit came on them" (vv. 5–6). Based on these accounts, pentecostals hold that there is good biblical evidence for baptism in the Holy Spirit subsequent to conversion.

Pentecostals often speak of baptism in the Spirit as being both distinct from and subsequent to salvation. According to the Assemblies of God (AG), "This wonderful experience is distinct from and subsequent to the experience of the new birth." To pentecostals this does not necessarily mean a chronologically separate experience, for they point out that in another account, namely, that of the Caesareans (Acts 10), there is no reference to a later experience of receiving the gift of the Holy Spirit. After Peter calls for faith in Christ—"everyone who believes in him receives forgiveness of sins through his name" (v. 43)—the next words are: "While Peter was still speaking these words, the Holy Spirit fell ..." (10:44 NASB). Priority is still given to the Caesareans' believing before the falling of the Holy Spirit, even if the latter follows immediately upon the other. The important matter for the pentecostal is not chronological but logical subsequence, namely, that even if salvation and baptism in the Spirit are at the same moment, salvation (conversion, regeneration) precedes Spirit baptism. Moreover, pentecostals hold that there

Holy Ghost receiving service, Myiba, Tanzania.

is nonidentity of the two, for the Caesareans' Spirit baptism is later attested to be a confirmation of their salvation. According to Acts 11, when Peter seeks to convince the church in Jerusalem that the Gentiles in Caesarea had come to salvation, he says to the apostles and brethren: "As I began to speak, the Holy Spirit fell upon them, just as He did upon us at the beginning" (11:15 NASB). This fact was unmistakable evidence to the church in Jerusalem of the Gentiles' salvation, for the Scripture later reads, "When they heard this, they had no further objections and praised God, saying, 'So then, God has granted even the Gentiles repentance unto life'" (11:18). The Caesareans' Spirit baptism, while not chronologically subsequent to their faith in Christ, was by no means identical with it. The falling of the Spirit was rather the certain sign of their conversion—their repentance unto life.

It is a pentecostal distinctive, therefore, to affirm that salvation precedes baptism in the Spirit or, to put it a bit differently, that one may truly believe in Christ and not yet have received the gift of the Holy Spirit. In the account of the Ephesians in Acts 19, before Paul proceeds to water baptism and the laying on of hands, he asks them, "Did you receive the Holy Spirit when [or "after," NIV mg.] you believed?" (v. 2). The very question implies the possibility of believing in Christ without an accompanying reception of the Holy Spirit. The Ephesians had not yet come to a full faith in Christ, so Paul ministers Christian baptism and laying on of hands (vv. 3–6). Still the question itself remains with its clear implication. Whether the question is "when" or "after" (or "since," KJV) "you believed," baptism in the Spirit may not yet have followed upon faith in Christ. Hence, pentecostals emphasize that one of the most pressing questions to be asked today of believers is that of Paul: "Did you receive the Holy Spirit when you believed?"

Pentecostals are quick to affirm that this question has nothing essentially to do with salvation. They do not mean to suggest that people may be only partially saved and that by Spirit baptism they may receive the rest. Rather, even as the word about salvation relates to sinners, so the word about baptism in the Holy Spirit relates to saints. The former is the call to believe; the latter is the call to receive.

It should be added that in the charismatic movement there has been a wide range of views concerning salvation and Spirit baptism. While many have adopted the basic pentecostal pattern as described, there are those who hold that there is no "second stage" beyond salvation. Larry Christenson, a Lutheran charismatic leader, speaks rather of an "organic view" of the Spirit's work that sees "the gift of the Holy Spirit ... as being given to all Christians" (1976, 38). This means that the gift of the Holy Spirit (or being baptized in the Spirit) occurs with the experience of salvation. From this perspective, what pentecostals really have been talking about is an experience of spiritual renewal, not a separate Spirit baptism. Brick

Bradford, longtime general secretary of the Presbyterian Charismatic Communion (now known as Presbyterian and Reformed Renewal Ministries), writes that "we were 'baptized with the Holy Spirit' when we became Christians, but we find ourselves wanting to more fully experience the release of the power of the Holy Spirit in our lives in order to become more effectual Christians" (1983, 23). It seems to this writer that such views, while congenial to Lutheran and Reformed traditions, have difficulty with the record in the book of Acts. The traditional pentecostal viewpoint would appear to be a more adequate interpretation.

3. Baptism in the Holy Spirit and Sanctification.

Pentecostals in general affirm the importance of holiness in the Christian life. The PCCNA (as earlier quoted) affirms "holiness of heart and life" as belonging to "the full gospel." Early pentecostalism had its roots largely in the Wesleyan Holiness tradition with its strong emphasis on sanctification. As a result, sanctification was held to be a "second work of grace" to be received prior to Spirit baptism. Sanctification was therein understood to be an instantaneous operation of heart purification following regeneration but preceding Spirit baptism. Many branches of pentecostalism continue to affirm this viewpoint. The Church of God (CG, Cleveland, TN) declares that "we believe ... in sanctification subsequent to the new birth ... and in the baptism of the Holy Ghost subsequent to a clean heart." This three-stage pattern is affirmed by other such major pentecostal bodies as the Pentecostal Holiness Church and the Church of God in Christ.

Other pentecostal churches, with non-Wesleyan origins, such as the AG, the Elim Pentecostal Church, and the International Church of the Foursquare Gospel, view sanctification as both given in salvation and progressive throughout the Christian life. Sanctification, therefore, is understood not to be a second work of grace prior to baptism in the Holy Spirit. Rather, from this perspective, the heart has been made essentially clean in regeneration; hence there is no need for heart purification before Spirit baptism may occur.

The charismatic tradition has generally held this latter viewpoint. With its adherents largely in such non-Wesleyan denominations as Episcopal, Lutheran, and Presbyterian, there has been little, if any, recognition of an intervening stage between regeneration and the gift of the Holy Spirit. Sanctification is by no means denied, but such is not viewed as a second stage the believer must pass through before being eligible for baptism in the Holy Spirit.

It is difficult to deduce from the book of Acts a second stage of sanctification between salvation and the gift of the Holy Spirit. There are two references to sanctification in Acts. In the first of these, Paul, speaking to the Ephesian elders, says, "Now I commit you to God and to the word of his grace, which can build you up and give you an inheritance among all those who are sanctified" (20:32). In the other, Paul

quotes Jesus as saying to him that he was being sent to both Jews and Gentiles that "they may receive forgiveness of sins and a place among those who are sanctified by faith in me" (26:18). Sanctification in both cases would appear to be a given fact of the Christian life. In the latter instance, since forgiveness of sins and sanctification are juxtaposed, they would seem to refer to two aspects of the same experience.

4. Baptism in the Holy Spirit and Speaking in Tongues.

The pentecostal and charismatic traditions are often identified with speaking in tongues. Pentecostals have laid particular stress on speaking in tongues as "initial evidence" of baptism in the Spirit (as the PCCNA statement attests). The word "initial" is emphasized since other evidence may be spoken of; however, the immediate evidence of Spirit baptism is viewed as speaking in tongues. Sometimes speaking in tongues (or glossolalia) is described as the "initial physical sign" (the Apostolic Faith Movement) of baptism in the Holy Spirit. Whether evidence or sign, the point made is that the distinctive event of Spirit baptism is primarily exhibited through speaking in tongues.

Scriptural basis for the pentecostal doctrine is again drawn from several Acts passages. In regard to the Day of Pentecost, the first thing said about those who were filled with the Holy Spirit was that they "began to speak in other tongues as the Spirit enabled them" (Acts 2:4). At Caesarea the text reads that "the circumcised believers who had come with Peter were astonished that the gift of the Holy Spirit had been poured out even on the Gentiles. For they heard them speaking in tongues and praising God" (10:45–46). Speaking in tongues was unmistakable evidence to the Jewish believers that the Caesareans had experienced Spirit baptism. When Paul laid his hands on the Ephesians, "the Holy Spirit came on them, and they spoke in tongues and prophesied" (Acts 19:6). The coming of the Spirit is immediately followed by tongues and prophecy. However, the initial activity after the Ephesians' Spirit baptism is speaking in tongues.

Pentecostals further observed that in the account of the Samaritans' reception of the Spirit (Acts 8:17), speaking in tongues is implied. For "when Simon [the magician] saw" (8:18) that the Samaritans had received the Spirit through the laying on of hands, he offered money to the apostles, seeking to buy the power to bestow the same gift on others. What Simon saw, it may be assumed—and for which he was willing to pay—was the spectacle of the Samaritans' speaking in tongues. In regard to the account of Paul's being filled with the Holy Spirit (9:17), nothing is said about his speaking in tongues at that time. However, since Paul in one of his letters later attests to his own speaking in tongues—"I thank God that I speak in tongues more than all of you" (1 Cor. 14:18)—pentecostals surmise that it could well have begun (as with the other apostles in Acts 2:4) when he was Spirit baptized.

On the basis of these five passages pentecostals affirm that they have an adequate scriptural basis for their view of initial evidence. Further, they see in glossolalia an extraordinary sign of an extraordinary event—the gift of the Holy Spirit. Since the coming of the Spirit, however often repeated, is a supernatural happening, the supernatural occurrence of tongues is its peculiar immediate expression. For pentecostals the dynamic connection seen between speaking in tongues and Spirit baptism again confirms their view that tongues occurred in all five of the narratives in Acts.

Further, when the nature of glossolalia is properly understood, pentecostals claim, its connection with Spirit baptism is all the more apparent, for speaking in tongues is basically the language of praise. In the narrative of Pentecost the crowd, upon hearing the tongues, said in amazement, "We hear them declaring the wonders of God in our own tongues" (Acts 2:11). At Caesarea the close connection between tongues and praise is shown in the words, "They heard them speaking in tongues and praising God" (10:46). Accordingly, speaking in tongues may be understood as the way of praising God that goes beyond ordinary speech: it is transcendent praise. If such is the case, then the connection between Spirit baptism and glossolalia is readily seen: the dynamic experience of the presence of God in the Holy Spirit overflows in self-transcending speech glorifying God.

Pentecostals also frequently call attention to Paul's words in Ephesians 5:18–19: "Do not get drunk with wine ... but be filled with the Spirit, speaking to one another in psalms and hymns and spiritual songs" (NASB). The intimate connection between being Spirit-filled and manifold praise (including "spiritual songs," i.e., songs inspired by the Holy Spirit) is apparent. Fullness of the Spirit leads to fullness of praise. Thus do Spirit baptism, praise, and tongues fit naturally together.

In sum, from the pentecostal perspective, speaking in tongues as the speaking forth of praise is due to the dynamic presence of God in the Holy Spirit. It is hardly strange that the immediate response to such a holy presence may well be transcendent praise to God.

A word should be added about the charismatic movement and tongues. Though speaking in tongues is a common practice, there is less emphasis on tongues being *the* initial evidence. First, many charismatics do not find the evidence in Acts of glossolalia to be conclusive; second, because of the variety of gifts of the Holy Spirit (see esp. 1 Cor. 12:8–10), they often prefer to speak of spiritual gifts—any of which may signify the Spirit's coming. One Roman Catholic theologian, Edward O'Connor, reporting on the early movement among Catholics, wrote, "Some people begin speaking in tongues at the moment of the [Spirit] baptism. Others do not begin until hours, days, or even weeks later, and some never do" (1971, 134). However, there are many charismatics that do affirm the close connection between the Spirit

baptism and tongues. Dennis Bennett, early Episcopal charismatic leader, states about speaking in tongues: "It comes with the package! Speaking in tongues is not the baptism in the Holy Spirit, but it is what happens when and as you are baptized in the Spirit" (1971, 64). This statement seems better to accord with the evidence in Acts and more closely approximates the pentecostal view.

5. The Purpose of Baptism in the Holy Spirit.

The primary purpose of Spirit baptism, according to the book of Acts, is *power*. The biblical term is *dunamis*—power, strength, force—and represents an endowment of spiritual power. Jesus promised his disciples that upon being baptized in the Holy Spirit, "you will receive power when the Holy Spirit comes on you" (Acts 1:8). The command of Jesus in Luke 24:49 makes the same point: "Stay in the city until you have been clothed with power from on high." The power of God—transcendent power—is the purpose of the gift of the Holy Spirit.

At the beginning of Jesus' own ministry the Holy Spirit had already "descended on him" (Luke 3:22, also see other Gospel parallels). As a result, Jesus was "full of the Holy Spirit" (Luke 4:1) and, after his temptations, "returned to Galilee in the power of the Spirit" (v. 14). Therefore, Jesus intended that the same Spirit of power that rested upon him should rest upon his disciples. Further, since what Jesus received was power for ministry, it would be the same for his disciples. They would likewise be able to move in the power of the Spirit for the ministry that lay ahead. Hence, though the immediate response of the disciples to the gift of the Spirit will be the praise of God directed upward, the purpose of that gift will be the service of humanity and therefore directed outward.

Primarily, Spirit baptism will be a *power for witness*. Following Jesus' promise of power, he declared, "You will be my witnesses in Jerusalem, and in all Judea and Samaria, and to the ends of the earth" (Acts 1:8; cf. Luke 24:48—"You are witnesses of these things" prior to "stay in the city"). After the 120 spoke in tongues on the Day of Pentecost, Peter first explained the phenomenon and then bore witness to the gospel, saying, "Men of Israel, listen to this" (Acts 2:22). It was his powerful witness that brought about conviction of sin (v. 37), repentance, and forgiveness (v. 38), and thereby the salvation of some 3,000 persons (v. 41). That Spirit baptism is directly related to witness is also demonstrated in the account of Paul's being filled with the Spirit. Before Ananias laid hands on Paul, he was told by the Lord, "Go! This man [Paul] is my chosen instrument to carry my name before the Gentiles and their kings and before the people of Israel" (9:15).

This power for witness in Acts is by no means limited to such apostles as Peter and Paul but also belongs to the whole community of Christians. On one occasion when the believers corporately prayed for greater boldness in witness, the result was that "they were all filled with the Holy Spirit and spoke the word of God boldly" (4:31). Hence, being Spirit-filled produces a powerful witness among believers in general.

Baptism in the Holy Spirit also enables the performance of *mighty works*. After Jesus returned in the power of the Spirit, he went throughout Galilee not only teaching and preaching but also "healing every disease and sickness among the people" (Matt. 4:23). According to Luke, "the power of the Lord was present for him to heal the sick" (5:17). Moreover, he cast out demons "by the Spirit of God" (Matt. 12:28) and wrought many miracles. Likewise, he said to his disciples, "I tell you the truth, anyone who has faith in me will do what I have been doing. He will do even greater things than these, because I am going to the Father" (John 14:12). After his ascension, Jesus would send believers the Holy Spirit to equip them to do these works. Thus, shortly after the event of Pentecost, Jesus' apostles began to perform numerous mighty works: "Many wonders and miraculous signs were done by the apostles" (Acts 2:43). So great was the anointing of the Spirit on Peter that his shadow alone was sufficient to bring healing (5:15). Handkerchiefs and aprons touched by Paul brought healing to the sick and deliverance from evil spirits (19:12).

However, it was not only apostles who did these works but deacons also. Stephen, "a man full of faith and of the Holy Spirit . . . did great wonders and miraculous signs among the people" (Acts 6:5, 8). Philip, also "full of the Spirit" (v. 5), did many "miraculous signs . . . evil spirits came out of many, and many paralytics and cripples were healed" (8:6–7). Spirit-anointed men of God were performing mighty deeds.

Nowhere in the Scripture is there any suggestion that either the powerful witness or the mighty works would end with the NT period. According to Mark 16:17–18, "these signs will accompany those who believe," and among the signs listed are driving out demons, speaking in new tongues, and healing the sick. Jesus' mighty works will thereby be continued over the years through his people.

Pentecostals have no hesitation in affirming this continuity in the *dunamis* of the Holy Spirit down to the present day. They lay much emphasis on the power of the Spirit as essential for anointed witness and believe that mighty works such as miracles of healing and deliverance are vital components of a full ministry. On this latter point pentecostals differ with many evangelical Christians who claim that miracles ceased with the apostolic times. Pentecostals view both a fully anointed witness and the working of miracles as inseparable: if the witness continues, so do miracles. Moreover, they maintain that both become truly effective through baptism in the Holy Spirit.

Here then is a critical point in the pentecostal outlook. Pentecostals declare that what many Christians today need is precisely this baptism of power. In addition to being born of the Spirit wherein new life begins, there is also the need for being baptized, or filled, with the Spirit for the outflow of the life in ministry to others.

Pentecostals frequently draw a parallel between Jesus and believers by pointing out that he was first conceived by the Holy Spirit (Luke 1:31–35) and then 30 years later was filled with the Holy Spirit (3:21–22; 4:1). Though he was born as the Son of God, he still needed the empowering for ministry that occurred when the Holy Spirit came upon him. So it is with believers who have been reborn by the Spirit as sons of God. They need—surely far more than Jesus did—Spirit baptism to fulfill the ministry Christ gives them. It is the same Holy Spirit but in two distinct operations: one in birth (or rebirth) and the other in empowering for service. Pentecostals sometimes depict this by speaking of Jesus as fulfilling both the roles of Savior and Baptizer. According to the Fourth Gospel, John the Baptist on one occasion acclaimed Jesus as "the Lamb of God, who takes away the sin of the world" (John 1:29), hence the Savior. Shortly thereafter John spoke of the Spirit-anointed Jesus ("the man on whom you see the Spirit come down") as "he who will baptize with the Holy Spirit" (v. 33). There is need, accordingly, for Jesus as Savior to take away sins and as Baptizer to equip for participation in his ministry.

Returning to the matter of power as the purpose of Spirit baptism: pentecostals emphasize that this is a special anointing of power. Whatever power there may be resident in a believer—and this is surely greatly due to the Holy Spirit within—Spirit baptism is an amplification of that power. Pentecostals do not intend to say that only the Spirit-baptized have experienced power, for the gospel itself "is the power of God unto salvation" (Rom. 1:16 KJV). However, they do urge that in addition—and for an entirely different reason than salvation—there is another action of the Holy Spirit that equips the believer for further service. This is not salvation but implementation; it is not transformation into a new creature but his commissioning for the sake of Christ and the gospel.

6. Baptism in the Holy Spirit and Water Baptism.

Pentecostals in general view water baptism as important but not essential to baptism in the Holy Spirit. With the book of Acts again as basic guide, pentecostals speak of water baptism as either preceding or following Spirit baptism but as having no necessary connection with it.

In the case of the Samaritans Philip preached the gospel, and many were baptized (Acts 8:12). However, it was only after Peter and John had come down from Jerusalem that the Samaritans were Spirit baptized. Prior to this "they had simply been baptized into the name of the Lord Jesus"; now when "Peter and John placed hands on them . . . they received the Holy Spirit" (vv. 16–17). The same thing was true with the Ephesians. Paul baptized the Ephesians in the name of Christ and thereafter laid hands on them for the reception of the Spirit (19:5–6). Water baptism, in both instances, preceded baptism in the Spirit.

In two other cases water baptism followed Spirit baptism. While Peter was proclaiming the gospel to the Caesareans, the Holy Spirit fell upon his hearers (Acts 10:44). After this Peter said, "Can anyone keep these people from being baptized with water? They have received the Holy Spirit just as we have" (v. 47). Then the apostle proceeded with water baptism. In the other instance, Paul first had hands laid on him by Ananias for Spirit baptism (9:17); then he was baptized in water (v. 18). Water baptism in both cases followed baptism in the Spirit.

It is also apparent from these accounts in Acts that water baptism was neither a precondition nor a channel for baptism in the Holy Spirit. On the matter of precondition, Peter's words on the Day of Pentecost might suggest such: "Repent and be baptized. . . . And you will receive the gift of the Holy Spirit" (Acts 2:38). However, since at Caesarea Peter baptized subsequent to the reception of the Spirit, there was clearly no precondition of water baptism. Moreover, in none of the Acts narrations is there any suggestion of water baptism conveying the gift of the Holy Spirit.

Pentecostals thus see no essential connection between water baptism and baptism in the Holy Spirit. This does not mean that for them water baptism is unimportant, but the importance lies at another point, namely, in relation to forgiveness and salvation. As Peter said at Pentecost, "Repent and be baptized, every one of you, in the name of Jesus Christ for the forgiveness of your sins" (Acts 2:38). Water baptism is connected with forgiveness of sins, not the gift of the Spirit that is thereupon promised. Pentecostals, however, do not view water baptism as essential to forgiveness (salvation), though water baptism is seen to be important as a sign or symbol of salvation.

With regard to the laying on of hands, pentecostals view this to be more directly connected with baptism in the Spirit than is water baptism. Even as water baptism relates to salvation, so does laying on of hands relate to the gifts of the Holy Spirit.

The relation of water baptism to baptism in the Holy Spirit is variously understood in the charismatic movement. For those whose traditions are less sacramental (e.g., Baptists, Methodists, Presbyterians), water baptism is not viewed as necessary for Spirit baptism. For charismatics whose traditions are more sacramental (e.g., Roman Catholics, Greek Orthodox, Lutherans), baptism in the Spirit is usually viewed as essentially connected with the sacrament of water baptism. From their perspective the Holy Spirit is often said to be given objectively in the sacrament of baptism. Accordingly, what these charismatics are really talking about in reference to Spirit baptism is an actualization or appropriation of what presumably they have already sacramentally received.

Kilian McDonnell, a Roman Catholic theologian in the Catholic renewal, writes that "baptism, in its New Testament context, is always a baptism of the Spirit" (1975, 73). However, the occasion may come, McDonnell adds, when "the Spirit already present becomes a fact of conscious experience" (ibid., 82). This actualization or coming to consciousness may then be called Spirit baptism in a subjective and experiential sense. The problem with such a sacramental understanding is twofold: first, there is difficulty in harmonizing this view of the Spirit with the record in Acts (e.g., water baptism is in no place depicted as a rite in which the Holy Spirit is given); second, it reduces what charismatics have experienced to an actualization or appropriation of a prior sacramental action. It is apparent, however, both in Acts and today, that far more happens to people subjectively and experientially than the sacramental viewpoint can contain.

7. The Reception of the Holy Spirit.

Pentecostals hold that the basic requirement for receiving the Holy Spirit is faith. Even as salvation is received by faith, so is the Holy Spirit. Baptism in the Holy Spirit happens only to those who believe in Jesus Christ.

In all the Acts narratives the necessity of faith is apparent. Regarding the first pentecostal reception of the Spirit, Peter later speaks of this as the "gift . . . he gave us, who

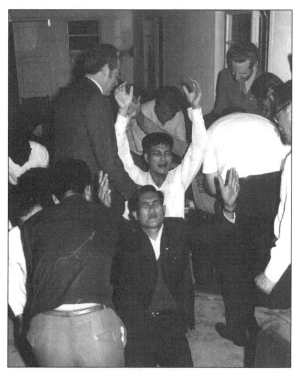

Prayer after evening service, Ta Tan, Taiwan.

believed in the Lord Jesus Christ" (Acts 11:17). So it was with the Samaritans who believed (8:12) and thereafter received (v. 17). Paul acknowledged Jesus as "Lord" (9:10) and later was "filled" (v. 17). The Caesareans heard Peter's proclamation, "Everyone who believes in him receives forgiveness of sins through his name" (10:43), and immediately the Holy Spirit fell upon them (v. 44). And the Ephesians were exhorted by Paul to believe in Christ (19:4) and shortly thereafter received the Holy Spirit (v. 6). The reception of the Holy Spirit was and is by faith.

Reference may be made also to two Pauline statements outside Acts. In Ephesians 1:13 Paul declares that "having believed, you were marked in him with a seal, the promised Holy Spirit" (cf. the "promise of the Spirit" in Acts 1 and 2). In Gal. 3:2 Paul asks, "Did you receive the Spirit by observing the law or by believing what you heard?" Faith is essential to the reception of the Spirit.

Pentecostals, while recognizing the necessity of faith, also hold that baptism in the Holy Spirit does not always occur at faith's inception. They point again to Acts, which shows the Spirit being received *after* faith has begun (e.g., the Samaritans and Paul, whose faith is presupposed). The pentecostals particularly view Paul's question to the Ephesians, "Did you receive the Holy Spirit when ["after," NIV mg.] you believed?" (Acts 19:2) as undoubtedly implying a possible reception of the Spirit after the initiation of faith.

On the basis of a possible temporal separation between the beginning of faith and Spirit baptism, the pentecostal tradition has commonly spoken of certain conditions. Whereas faith remains fundamental, additional factors are emphasized. Attention is often focused on such matters as prayer, obedience, and yielding.

In the matter of *prayer*, pentecostals call attention to the company of disciples before Pentecost who "all joined together constantly in prayer" (Acts 1:14). Jesus had earlier said, "Tarry ye in the city of Jerusalem, until ye be endued with power from on high" (Luke 24:49 KJV). "Tarrying" meetings—often over long periods of time—were commonplace in early pentecostal circles. Constancy in prayer, awaiting the coming of the Holy Spirit, continues to be emphasized. Pentecostals call attention not only to the upper room account of prayer prior to Pentecost but also to the preparatory nature of prayer in other accounts. In the Gospel of Luke Jesus himself is shown to be praying when the Holy Spirit first descended: "As he was praying, heaven was opened and the Holy Spirit descended on him" (3:21–22). Later he taught his disciples the importance of persistence in prayer—asking, seeking, knocking—and added: "Your Father in heaven [will] give the Holy Spirit to those who ask him" (11:13). In Acts several further accounts describe an atmosphere of prayer. Regarding the Samaritans, Peter and John "prayed for them that they might receive the Holy Spirit" (8:15); only after that did the apostles lay hands on others. Paul fasted and

prayed for three days (9:9, 11) prior to his being filled with the Spirit (v. 17). The centurion at Caesarea was a "devout man who ... feared God with all his household ... and prayed constantly to God" (10:2 RSV). To these devout and prayerful people Peter preached, and upon them the Holy Spirit fell. Prayer was the background and context in which Spirit baptism occurred. Pentecostals, taking such things as their lead, emphasize the need for earnest prayer in preparing for the reception of the Holy Spirit.

Pentecostals also stress the importance of *obedience*. Peter on one occasion speaks of the Holy Spirit "whom God has given to those who obey him" (Acts 5:32). Obedience is usually understood in two ways. First, the believers in the upper room obeyed Christ's injunction to wait in prayer for the Holy Spirit to be given (1:14). Many people are unwilling to take the time to wait upon the Lord and thereby fail to receive his blessing. Second, obedience is also viewed in the larger context as obedience to Christ's commands. Jesus had earlier declared, "If you love me, you will keep my commandments. And I will pray the Father, and he will give you another Counselor ... even the Spirit of truth" (John 14:15–17 RSV). The Holy Spirit will be given to those who obey Christ's commands. One who seeks to walk the way of righteousness is better prepared to receive Spirit baptism. The centurion of Caesarea and his family were already "devout and God-fearing" (Acts 10:2); they were among those who "do what is right" (10:34) even before they come to salvation. Their faith and obedience was honored by the outpouring of the Holy Spirit as Peter preached the gospel to them.

A third factor frequently mentioned by pentecostals in relation to Spirit baptism is *yielding* or *surrender*. A parallel is often drawn between water baptism and Spirit baptism. In believer's baptism one must totally yield oneself to immersion by another in water; likewise, one must totally yield oneself to be baptized by Christ in the Holy Spirit. Yieldedness in relation to speaking in tongues is particularly significant since the tongue is described as an "unruly evil" (James 3:8 KJV). It must also be surrendered to become ruled by the Holy Spirit and thereby speak a new language inspired by the Spirit. In any event, what is important is a total surrender to the lordship of Jesus Christ. Donald Gelpi, a Roman Catholic theologian, speaks of the need for "full docility to the Spirit of Christ" (1971, 183). Yielding, surrender, full docility—however expressed—is the attitude of one who is to receive the Holy Spirit.

The conditions just mentioned are best understood not as requirements in addition to faith but as expressions of faith. F. Dale Brunner, in his book *A Theology of the Holy Spirit: The Pentecostal Experience and the New Testament Witness* (1970, 111), criticizes pentecostalism for its various conditions as representing a call to "superhuman effort," hence going beyond "ordinary faith." Doubtless there is some merit in his criticism, for pentecostals have at times so stressed conditions as to seem to leave faith behind. The basic concern of pentecostals, however, is with active faith: praying in faith, the obedience of faith, faith as yielding. The Holy Spirit is still a gift of God's grace; there is no way of earning or achieving him. God delights to give to those who are eager to receive.

See also GIFTS OF THE SPIRIT; GLOSSOLALIA; INITIAL EVIDENCE.

■ **Bibliography:** D. and R. Bennett, *The Holy Spirit and You* (1971) ■ B. Bradford, *Releasing the Power of the Holy Spirit* (1983) ■ L. Christenson, *The Charismatic Renewal among Lutherans* (1976) ■ S. Clark, *Baptized in the Spirit and Spiritual Gifts* (1976) ■ H. Cox, *Fire from Heaven* (1995) ■ H. M. Ervin, *These Are Not Drunken, As Ye Suppose* (1976) ■ R. M. Frost, *Set My Spirit Free* (1973) ■ D. Gelpi, *Pentecostalism: A Theological Viewpoint* (1971) ■ M. P. Hamilton, ed., *The Charismatic Movement* (1975) ■ S. M. Horton, *What the Bible Says about the Holy Spirit* (1976) ■ H. D. Hunter, *Spirit-Baptism* (1983) ■ K. Kendrick, *The Promise Fulfilled* (1961) ■ F. Martin, *The Baptism in the Holy Spirit: A Scriptural Foundation* (1986) ■ K. McDonnell, *The Holy Spirit and Power: The Catholic Charismatic Renewal* (1975) ■ R. P. Menzies, *The Spirit in Luke-Acts* (1994) ■ E. O'Connor, *The Pentecostal Movement in the Catholic Church* (1971) ■ K. and D. Ranaghan, *Catholic Pentecostals* (1969) ■ R. M. Riggs, *The Spirit Himself* (1949) ■ J. S. Schep, *Spirit Baptism and Tongue Speaking* (1970) ■ J. R. Williams, *Renewal Theology* (1996) ■ idem, *The Gift of the Holy Spirit Today* (1980).　　　■ J. R. Williams

BAPTIST PENTECOSTALS AND CHARISMATICS

1. Baptist Pentecostals.

A. C. Piepkorn lists two Baptist Pentecostal denominations: the Pentecostal Free-Will Baptist Church, Inc. (PFWBC), and the Free-Will Baptist Church of the Pentecostal Faith (FWBPF). The PFWBC traces its Baptist roots to the 18th-century Baptist preacher Benjamin Randall. It organized in Dunn, NC, in 1908 as a pentecostal church after ⸰G. B. Cashwell, who had himself experienced the ⸰Azusa Street revival, led many Free-Will Baptists into a pentecostal experience. Today the PFWBC has some 13,000 members in 150 churches.

The FWBPF is a group of South Carolina Baptists who share basically the same beliefs as the PFWBC. From 1943 to 1958 the two were one church. The South Carolina group, considering itself more conservative, withdrew to form its own denomination in 1959.

2. Baptist Charismatics.

Within the mainline Baptist churches the charismatic renewal has met with mixed responses, from warm embrace to outright rejection and hostility. A support group for charismatics is the American Baptist Charismatic Fellowship in Pasadena, CA. Since 1975, annual summer conferences are held at the denomination's campground in Green Lake, WI.

Howard Ervin, an American Baptist minister and professor at Oral Roberts University, is one of their principal speakers and a leading advocate of neo-pentecostalism.

The Southern Baptist Convention (SBC), Protestantism's largest denomination in the U.S., has grown increasingly negative in its official public stance toward Baptist charismatics. Among Baptists nationally, it is reckoned that fully 20% consider themselves pentecostal or charismatic. That, however, is a minority, and the majority has unequivocally rejected charismatic practices, especially glossolalia. The SBC Home Mission Board, in July 1987, voted to forbid even the private practice of glossolalia among its missionaries. This is but a further intensification of the position set forth in "The Baptist Faith and Message" (1963), in which the SBC repudiated public glossolalia and public faith-healing services where people are declared healed.

Prior to this 1987 decision many Southern Baptist pastors and laypersons had sought to maintain their affiliation with the SBC and their identification as an SBC church. At that time there were more than 100 "Fulness" pastors and churches (as the SBC charismatic community is sometimes named). Some observers, including C. P. Wagner, professor of church growth at Fuller Theological Seminary, estimated the number to be between 200 and 300 charismatic SBC congregations (Synan, 57).

Baptists who have personally participated in some aspect of the charismatic or pentecostal experience have often not been welcome to remain within the SBC. ⸰C. H. Mason withdrew to found the Church of God in Christ. ⸰E. N. Bell was the first general superintendent of the Assemblies of God. ⸰William Branham and ⸰Tommy Hicks were Baptists who, after pentecostal experiences, became leaders of the pentecostal and healing revival of the late 1940s and 1950s. ⸰M. G. "Pat" Robertson, ⸰Jamie Buckingham, ⸰Ken Sumrall, ⸰Charles Simpson, ⸰John Osteen, ⸰Larry Lea, and ⸰James Robison represent but a few of the contemporary

Southern Baptist charismatic church, Marshfield, MO.

charismatic ministers or leaders who have come out of Baptist backgrounds. At the level of the laity, "the Pentecostal churches have probably seen more adherents from among Baptists than from any other Protestant group in the United States" (Synan, 54).

Fulness magazine seeks to be an agency that fosters ministry without divisiveness among its SBC charismatic constituency, rather than highlighting any particular spiritual gift. The magazine, together with Fulness Ministries, seeks to foster "growth into the fulness of Christ." Fulness Conferences are held periodically throughout the nation.

In the 11 years since the first edition of *DPCM* there has been little official softening of the SBC's stance toward Christianity with a charismatic touch. In 1999 *Charisma and Christian Life* featured an eight-page study of charismatic renewal within the SBC. Ministers and churches all across the denomination are embracing manifestations of the Spirit, such as anointing with oil and praying for the sick, speaking in tongues, raising hands in worship, and falling under the power of the Spirit before congregation and God.

Speaking in tongues is not emphasized. Rather, the person of the Holy Spirit is being celebrated however the Spirit chooses to manifest his presence and power. Miracles are occurring and being affirmed. God is not being kept in a box labeled "traditional Southern Baptist."

Two phenomena that touched the denomination may be central to the Spirit's moving. One is the widespread reception of Henry Blackaby and Claude V. King's Bible study workbook, *Experiencing God* (LifeWay Press, 1990). This study emphasizes that God is at work in the individual through the person of the Holy Spirit to accomplish God's work. It has brought an openness to the person and work of the Spirit among countless thousands in the SBC and other denominations.

Second, conservative evangelicals within the SBC have gained control of the denomination's leadership. Many see this as a critical step toward opening the door for God to work through God's Spirit.

The estimated number of Baptists who may consider themselves charismatic continues to be some 15 to 20% (Walker, 71). The persistent rejection known as "disfellowshiping" of congregations who practice "neo-pentecostalism" is likely to keep their numbers from becoming larger.

See also CHARISMATIC MOVEMENT.

■ **Bibliography:** C. L. Howe, "The Charismatic Movement in Southern Baptist Life," *Baptist History and Heritage* 13 (3, 1978): 20–27, 65 ■ J. Moody, "A Baptist Pastor Looks at the Charismatics," *Fulness* 10 (6, 1987): 26–29 ■ Pentecostal Research Center, Oral Roberts U., Tulsa, OK, letter by D. LeMaster, including, "Directory of Fulness Pastors and Churches, January 1988" ■ A. C. Piepkorn, *Profiles in Belief*, 3 vols. (1979) ■ "Southern Baptists Disagree over Tongues," *Charisma and Christian Life* 13 (7, 1988): 22 ■ V. Synan, "Baptists Ride the Third Wave," *Charisma and Christian Life* 12 (5, 1986) ■ K. Walker, "Shaking Southern Baptist Tradition," *Charisma and Christian Life* 24 (8, 1999). ■ J. A. Hewett

BARNES, LEANORE O. ("MOTHER") (1854–1939). An early pentecostal evangelist in the Midwest. She was born Leonore O. Chesley and married Victor A. Barnes, a railroad engineer. Although biographical data on Barnes are sketchy, she apparently gained initial notoriety in a revival meeting she helped conduct in Thayer, MO, in 1909. Despite hoodlums threatening to kill the evangelists, a six-week meeting netted more than 100 converts and at least 50 baptized in the Spirit. She was associated with the pentecostal social worker "Mother" ˃Mary Moise in St. Louis, beginning in about 1909. She became a charter member of the ˃Assemblies of God in 1914 but later went into the ˃Oneness movement. She taught at the Oneness Bible school in Eureka Springs, AR, and was associated with a St. Louis church for many years. One of her daughters married an early pentecostal preacher and writer, ˃Bennett F. Lawrence.

■ **Bibliography:** "'Mother' Barnes, Evangelist Here Many Years, Dies," *St. Louis Post-Dispatch* (May 9, 1939) ■ W. Warner, "Mother Mary Moise of St. Louis," *AGH* (Spring 1986). ■ W. E. Warner

BARR, EDMOND S. and **REBECCA** (early 20th century). Natives of the Bahama Islands, Edmond S. Barr and his wife, Rebecca, migrated to Florida near the turn of the 20th century. In 1909 they were saved during the Pleasant Grove Camp Meeting in Durant, FL, and thereafter received the baptism of the Holy Ghost.

Accepting God's call into the ministry, the Barrs were licensed as evangelists in the Church of God in 1909, becoming the earliest black ministers in the denomination. By Nov. 1909 the Barrs had returned to their native land, becoming the first Church of God ministers to introduce the pentecostal faith outside the continental U.S.

The Barrs returned to Florida in 1911, and Edmond was elevated to the office of bishop in 1912. He served as the first overseer for the black congregations in Florida from 1915 to 1917, pastored the black congregation in Miami during this time, and also served as a church planter. In 1917 the black and white congregations in Florida were reunited for a short time, and Bishop Barr ceased to serve as an overseer. Edmond and Rebecca Barr's ministry ended in the Church of God in 1917.

■ **Bibliography:** C. W. Conn, *Like a Mighty Army: A History of the Church of God* (1996) ■ idem, *Where the Saints Have Trod* (1955) ■

J. E. Jackson, *Reclaiming Our Heritage: The Search for Black History in the Church of God* (1993) ▪ C. Moree, ed., "Until All Have Heard: A History of Church of God World Missions" (unpub.).

▪ L. F. Morgan

BARRATT, THOMAS BALL (1862–1940). Norwegian pentecostal leader. Thomas Ball Barratt was born in Albaston, Cornwall, England. Barratt's father, a miner, emigrated to Norway in 1867. Barratt attended school in England (ages 11–16) and, in Norway, studied art with O. Dahl and music with E. Grieg. At age 17 he began preaching. He was ordained deacon (1889) and elder (1891) in the Methodist Episcopal Church of Norway and pastored several churches. In 1902 he founded the Oslo City Mission and in 1904 became editor of its paper, *Byposten*. During a visit to the U.S. (1906), he came into contact with the pentecostal movement and returned to Norway an ardent proponent, becoming the founder of the Norwegian movement and a key figure in the establishment of indigenous pentecostal churches throughout Europe and the Third World. His periodical, *Korsets Seier*, was published in Swedish, Finnish, German, Russian, and Spanish as well as Norwegian.

After Barratt's conversion to pentecostalism, he worked with the City Mission and continued to edit *Byposten*. He hosted people from all over the world who came to witness the Oslo revival firsthand. Barratt made trips to England, India, Sweden, Finland, Poland, Estonia, Iceland, and Denmark to encourage the new churches. In 1909 his membership in the clergy of the Methodist Episcopal Church was terminated. He was an initiator of the ▸Pentecostal Missionary Union and the International Pentecostal Conferences. As a mission theorist, influenced by ▸William Taylor, he established the framework from within which Scandinavian mission flourished. Barratt was a prolific author. He wrote more than 300 books, pamphlets, and major articles. He founded and pastored the Filadelfia Church in Oslo until his death.

■ **Bibliography:** T. B. Barratt, *The Gift of Prophecy* (1909; repr. 1974) ▪ idem, *In the Days of the Latter Rain* (1909; rev. ed., 1928) ▪ idem, *Kvinnens stilling i menigheten* (1933) ▪ idem, *To Seekers After "The Promise of the Father"* (1911) ▪ idem, *When the Fire Fell, and an Outline of My Life* (1929), reprinted in *The Work of T. B. Barratt*, ed. D. W. Dayton (1985) ▪ N. Bloch-Hoell, *Pinsebevegelsen, en underso/okelse av pinsebevegelsens tilblivelse . . .* (1956; partial English trans., *The Pentecostal Movement* [1964]) ▪ D. D. Bundy, "Spiritual Advice to a Seeker: Letters to T. B. Barratt from Azusa Street, 1906," *Pneuma* 14 (1992) ▪ idem, "Swedish Pentecostal Mission Theory and Practice to 1930: Foundational Values in Discussion," *Mission Studies* 14 (1997) ▪ idem, "T. B. Barratt's Christiania (Oslo) City Mission: A Study in the Intercultural Adaptation of American and British Voluntary Association Structures," in *Crossing Borders*, ed. J. D. Plüss (1991), 1–15 ▪ idem, "Thomas B. Barratt and *Byposten*: An Early European Pentecostal Leader and His Periodical," in *Pentecost, Mission and Ecumenism: Essays on Intercultural Theology. Festschrift in Honor of Professor Walter J. Hollenweger* (1992), 115–21 ▪ idem, "Thomas Ball Barratt: From Methodist to Pentecostal," *EPTA Bulletin* 13 (1994) ▪ W. J. Hollenweger, *Handbuch der Pfingstbewegung*, 10 vols. (diss., Zurich, 1966) ▪ C. van der

Scandinavian pentecostal leaders discussing Bible doctrines: (left to right) Lewi Pethrus (Sweden), Mrs. Barratt and T. B. Barratt (Norway), Anna Larssen Bjorner and her husband, Sigurd (Denmark).

Laan, "The Proceedings of the Leader's Meetings (1908–1911) and of the International Pentecostal Council (1912–1914)," *EPTA Bulletin* 6 (1987).   ■ D. D. Bundy

BARTLEMAN, FRANK (1871–1936). Early pentecostal evangelist, critic, and the primary chronicler of pentecostal origins in Los Angeles. The third of five sons, he was born on a farm near Carversville, PA, to Frank Bartleman, a stern Roman Catholic who immigrated to the U.S. from Wurttemberg, Germany, and Margaret (Hellyer) Bartleman, an American-born Quaker of English and Welsh descent. A relatively sickly youngster, he attended school and worked on his father's farm until he left home at age 17.

Moving to Philadelphia, the younger Bartleman worked a number of odd jobs and attended Grace Baptist Church, pastored by Russell H. Conwell. On Oct. 15, 1893, he was converted. The following summer he received his call into full-time ministry and began formal preparation by attending Temple College. He also studied briefly at Moody Bible Institute. In succeeding years Bartleman ministered with the Salvation Army, the Wesleyan Methodists, Pillar of Fire, and the Peniel Missions, while working at a number of tent-making jobs.

On May 2, 1900, Bartleman married Anna Ladd, a Bulgarian-born woman who had been adopted and reared by American Methodist missionaries to Bulgaria. The Bartlemans had four children; the first, Esther, was born Apr. 30, 1901, and died shortly after the family's arrival in Los Angeles in Dec. 1904. This tragedy affected Frank profoundly, and he reiterated his commitment to the ministry as a result.

From 1906 to 1908 Bartleman attended a few prayer meetings led by ►W. J. Seymour prior to the Azusa Street revival. For a time he supported ►Joseph Smale in the First New Testament Church, attended the ►Azusa Street Mission, and established another mission at Eighth and Maple Streets in Los Angeles, then turned it over to ►W. H. Pendleton. But he seldom remained at one address or in one church for very long.

Bartleman preached as an itinerant evangelist for 43 years. He crisscrossed the U.S. on several occasions, preached his way around the world while leaving his family in Los Angeles (1910–11), and made a second extended evangelistic tour through Europe (1912–14), this time with his family.

Frank Bartleman, an important figure in the early years of the pentecostal movement who was involved in the Azusa Street Mission meetings.

Bartleman's most obvious contribution came in more than 550 articles, 100 tracts, and 6 books he authored during his ministry. His writings appeared in popular religious journals of both the Holiness and pentecostal movements in the U.S. and England. He was a frequent contributor to the *Way of Faith* (Columbia, SC), *Word and Work* (Framingham, MA), and *Confidence* (Sunderland, U.K.). His first book, *My Story: "The Latter Rain,"* published in 1909 by J. M. Pike, was superseded by Bartleman's own publication *From Plow to Pulpit* (1924), which described his life from his birth through 1904. *How Pentecost Came to Los Angeles* (1925) chronicled events in which he participated in Los Angeles from 1905 through 1911. These works were followed by *Around the World by Faith* (1925) and *Two Years' Mission Work in Europe Just Before the World War: 1912–1914* (1924).

Theologically, Bartleman was always looking for the latest work of God. He wished for more unity among pentecostals, and he wrote *The Deity of Christ* (1926), arguing for liberty of conscience in the "Jesus Name" baptismal formula controversy. Always his own person, Bartleman was quick to write and speak his opinion on a wide range of topics. He criticized church leadership and denominational organization, and he argued strongly for separation in church-state relations, condemning the presence of national flags in church buildings. He harangued on the economic evils of communism and capitalism, the pitfalls of political involvement by Christians, and the nature of the controlled "free" press. He vehemently opposed all forms of militarism, including the purchase of War Bonds and the existence of Boy Scouts, and he argued passionately for a neutral pacifism in World War I.

Frank Bartleman died on the afternoon of Aug. 23, 1936. He is buried at Valhalla Memorial Park in Burbank, CA.

■ **Bibliography:** A. Cerillo Jr., "The Azusa Street Revival according to Frank Bartleman," *Toward Healing Our Divisions* (Papers, 28th Annual SPS Meeting, 1999) ■ C. M. Robeck Jr., "The Writings and Thought of Frank Bartleman," in *Witness to Pentecost: The Life of Frank Bartleman* (1985), vii–xxviii (*Witness* is a reprint of four of Bartleman's autobiographical works) ■ V. Synan, "Frank Bartleman and Azusa Street," in Frank Bartleman, *Azusa Street* (1980), ix–xxv.   ■ C. M. Robeck Jr.

BASHAM, DON WILSON (1926–89). Journalist, author, Bible teacher. Basham was born Sept. 17, 1926, in Wichita Falls, TX, and spent his childhood and school years there, meeting his wife, Alice, in a Disciples of Christ church. He left a promising career in commercial art in 1952 to pursue Christian ministry. Basham received his B.A. and B.D. degrees from Phillips University and its graduate seminary in Enid, OK.

In the summer of 1953, while on a break from college, Basham was baptized in the Holy Spirit. He later pastored Disciples of Christ churches in Washington, DC; Toronto, Canada; and Sharon, PA. With the blossoming of the charismatic renewal in the 1960s, Basham traveled extensively, ministering in charismatic meetings, particularly in the ⊳Full Gospel Business Men's Fellowship International. In the fall of 1967 Basham decided to leave the pastorate and begin a full-time teaching and writing ministry. He moved to Ft. Lauderdale, FL, in Jan. 1968.

While in Ft. Lauderdale, Basham became associated with charismatic Bible teachers ⊳Bernard (Bob) Mumford, ⊳Derek Prince, and ⊳Charles Simpson through involvement with the ⊳Holy Spirit Teaching Mission and its publication, *New Wine* magazine. From this association the controversial ⊳shepherding movement emerged, of which Basham became a principal leader. *New Wine* became the primary voice of the movement. Basham was the shaping force behind the magazine, serving as editor and as chief editorial consultant until it ceased publication in Dec. 1986.

Basham was a talented and prolific author whose books were widely distributed. His ministry emphasized Spirit baptism, the gifts of the Holy Spirit, and deliverance from demonic power. His belief that Christians could be demonized was a point of controversy for many charismatics.

After the shepherding movement's dissolution at the end of 1986, Basham moved to Ohio, where he continued his writing and teaching ministry. He died of a heart attack on Mar. 27, 1989.

■ **Bibliography:** D. Basham, *Face Up with a Miracle* (1967) ▌ idem, *Deliver Us from Evil* (1972) ▌ idem, *The Way I See It* (1986).
■ S.D. Moore

BAUMERT, NORBERT (1932–). Priest-scholar active in leadership of ⊳Catholic Charismatic Renewal (CCR) in Germany. Born in Silesia, Baumert entered the Jesuit order and was ordained priest in 1961. A NT scholar whose doctoral dissertation was published as *Täglich sterben und auferstehen* (Dying and Rising Daily, 1973), Baumert has taught at Sankt Georgen, Frankfurt am Main, since 1982.

Active in CCR since 1972, Baumert has played a major role as pastoral leader and as scholar-theologian. Defending CCR as a worldwide movement of the Spirit against strong theological criticism, he chaired the Theological Commission of the Charismatische Gemeinde Erneuerung (Charismatic Church Renewal) from 1985 on; he made major contributions to their reports *It Is the Spirit That Gives Life* (1987, Eng. 1989) and *Extraordinary Bodily Phenomena* (1995). Baumert has particularly focused on the charisms of the Spirit, studied in *Gaben des Geistes Jesu: Das Charismatische in der Kirche* (Gifts of the Spirit of Jesus: The Charismatic Element in the Church, 1986) and numerous articles. His other books include *Dem Geist Jesu folgen* (Following the Spirit of Jesus, 1988); *Woman and Man in Paul* (1992; Eng. 1996); and *Endzeitfieber?* (End-Time Fever? 1997). Baumert has been active in the ⊳European Charismatic Consultation, and he was a participant in the Roman Catholic–Pentecostal ⊳Dialogue (1993–97). ■ P. D. Hocken

BAXTER, W. J. E. ("ERN") (1914–93). Canadian pastor, preacher, Bible teacher. William John Ernest Baxter was born June 22, 1914, in Saskatoon, Sask., Canada. Baxter's parents were converted in a Holiness church and later became pentecostals. As a teenager Baxter rebelled against what he saw as legalism and emotionalism in his childhood faith. In 1932, after a serious illness, he recommitted his life to Christ. Baxter, a gifted musician, soon began to travel as the pianist for an evangelist, and on July 2, 1932, he received the pentecostal experience of Spirit baptism.

Baxter later received an invitation to pastor Evangelistic Tabernacle in Vancouver, B.C. Under his leadership the church grew rapidly and was at one time the largest church in Vancouver. In 1949, while continuing to pastor, Baxter became the campaign manager and Bible teacher for healing evangelist ⊳William Branham, with whom he traveled extensively for seven years. Pastoring and traveling left Baxter severely fatigued. He left Branham's ministry and soon resigned from his church. After a period of rest Baxter started a small storefront church in Vancouver, the Open Bible Chapel, which grew to several hundred members.

Baxter's first wife, Margaret, died in 1961. In Feb. 1964 Baxter married his second wife, Ruth, and for the next six years he served as a Bible teacher in several churches in the U.S. while continuing to travel in ministry. Moving back to Canada in 1970, he continued to travel and preach worldwide in pentecostal-charismatic churches and conferences.

At the Montreat, NC, Shepherds Conference in June 1974, Baxter became formally associated with the leaders of the ⊳shepherding movement: ⊳Don Basham, ⊳Bob Mumford, ⊳Derek Prince, and ⊳Charles Simpson. He moved to Ft. Lauderdale, FL, in early 1975. While associated with the shepherding movement, Baxter continued his teaching ministry among charismatics and in 1980 moved to Mobile, AL, after a short stay in Southern California. He returned to the San Diego, CA, area in 1984. After the shepherding movement's dissolution at the end of 1986, Baxter continued his ministry from California until his death on July 9, 1993.

Baxter was known as a great preacher. Though without formal theological training, he became a self-taught theologian and avid Bible student. Baxter's Reformed theological orientation, along with his classical-pentecostal background, created a unique blend. Baxter participated directly or indirectly in classical pentecostalism, the healing revival, the Latter Rain movement, and the charismatic renewal.

■ **Bibliography:** W. J. E. Baxter, *The Chief Shepherd and His Sheep* (1987) ■ idem, *I Almost Died!* (1983).   ■ D. Moore

BAZÁN, DEMETRIO (1900–1976). Pioneer pentecostal pastor, evangelist, and second president of the Latin American District Council of the Assemblies of God (AG) in the U.S. Demetrio Bazán was born in La Pesca, Tampaulipas, Mexico, on Dec. 22, 1900. He was converted to pentecostalism in Kingsville, TX, in 1917, and ordained pastor in 1920. From 1920 to 1939 he conducted pioneer evangelistic work in Texas, New Mexico, and Colorado with his wife, Nellie. In 1939 he was elected to take H. C. Ball's place as president of the Latin American District Council of the AG in the U.S. and served in this capacity from 1939 to 1958. He founded six churches, including churches in Houston, Dallas, San Antonio, and Denver. He served as a pastor for 19 years, as superintendent for 19 years, and as an AG evangelist for 19 years, traveling throughout the U.S., Mexico, and Latin America. Bazán wrote a number of manuals for Sunday school teachers and sermon outlines for pastors. Under his creative and energetic leadership the council grew rapidly from 80 churches with 4,500 members in 1935 to more than 296 churches and 19,790 members in 1958, the year he became an AG evangelist.

■ **Bibliography:** N. Bazán with E. and D. Martinet Jr., *Enviados De Dios: Demetrio y Nellie Bazán* (1987) ■ G. Espinosa, interview with Alex and Anita Bazán, 1996.   ■ G. Espinosa

BÁZAN, MANUELITA (NELLIE) TREVIÑO (1898–1995). Pioneer Mexican-American pentecostal evangelist, pastor, woman's leader, and writer. Nellie was born in Helotes, TX, and converted by M. M. Pinson and R. D. Baker in pentecostal tent meetings in 1914. Six years later she married Demetrio Bazán; that same year they were ordained pentecostal evangelists to the Mexican population by the Latin American District Council of the Assemblies of God (AG). Together they conducted pioneer evangelistic work among Mexican Americans and Mexican immigrants in Texas, New Mexico, and Colorado. Although Nellie never served as a senior pastor, she did serve as copastor and regularly preached from the pulpit of her husband's churches when he was on the road conducting evangelistic crusades. In addition to working alongside her husband and raising 10 children, she found time to conduct door-to-door evangelistic work with her children and plant three new Spanish-speaking churches on her own in Texas and New Mexico. She also served as vice president of the Women's Missionary Council. Although she only finished the seventh grade, Nellie was nonetheless a talented writer. She wrote poetry, regular articles for the denominational magazine *La Luz Apostólica*, and even her autobiography, *Enviados De Dios: Demetrio y Nellie Bazán* (1987).

■ **Bibliography:** N. Bazán with E. and D. Martinet Jr., *Enviados De Dios: Demetrio y Nellie Bazán* (1987) ■ G. Espinosa, interview with Alex and Anita Bazán, 1996 ■ idem, "'Your Daughters Shall Prophesy': A Comparative Study of Women's Roles in the Latino Assemblies of God and the Apostolic Assembly," in *Women and Twentieth-Century Protestantism*, ed. M. L. Bendroth and V. L. Brereton (1998).   ■ G. Espinosa

BEALL, JAMES LEE (1925–). Prominent figure in the charismatic renewal and pastor of Bethesda Missionary Temple in Detroit, MI. Son of Myrtle D. Beall, he was ordained in the late 1940s and became senior pastor of his mother's church of more than 3,000 members in the late 1970s. Known for his nationwide radio broadcast *America to Your Knees*, Beall has contributed frequently to *Logos Journal* and to many other charismatic periodicals and has been in continual demand at charismatic conferences and workshops. His most recent publication is *Your Pastor, Your Shepherd* (1997).

■ **Bibliography:** "James Beall—An Interview," *Pathfinders* 1 (Mar.–Apr. 1983).   ■ R. M. Riss

Myrtle D. Beall, pastor of the Bethesda Missionary temple, Detroit, who became a leader in the New Order of the Latter Rain Movement in 1948.

BEALL, MYRTLE D. (1896–1979). Founder and pastor of Bethesda Missionary Temple in Detroit, MI. Born in Hubbell, MI, as Myrtle Monville, she was reared in a devout Roman Catholic home. After success in preaching among Methodists, she felt a call to preach independently in the early 1930s, at which time she began a Sunday school for children. As more people became interested in her ministry, a church developed, which eventually became associated with the Assemblies of God (AG). In 1947 she began construction of a 3,000-seat "armory." It was dedicated in 1949. Her church became a center for the 1948 ˒Latter Rain movement, resulting in her withdrawal from the AG in 1949. It attracted thousands of visitors seeking a fresh anointing from God. Churches in many parts of North America look to Bethesda for guidance and direction, many of them using for catechetical instruction *Understanding God* (1962) by Mrs. Beall's daughter, Patricia D. Gruits.

■ **Bibliography:** M. D. Beall, "A Hand on My Shoulder" (serial article), *LRE* (Detroit) (July 1951–Jan. 1955).

■ R. M. Riss

BELL, EUDORUS N. (1866–1923). Former Baptist pastor and first general chairman (title later changed to general superintendent) of the General Council of the ˒Assemblies of God (AG) (1914; 1920–23). Bell was a twin (his brother was Endorus) and was born at Lake Butler, FL. Their father died when the boys were only two years old. E. N., as he preferred over Eudorus, was converted at an early age and felt a call to the ministry.

Bell was one of the better-educated pentecostals during the period. He received higher education at Stetson University in the 1890s, Southern Baptist Theological Seminary

E. N. Bell, a Southern Baptist pastor baptized in the Spirit who became the first chairman of the Assemblies of God.

(1900–1902), and the University of Chicago (B.A., 1903). He pastored Baptist churches for 17 years.

After hearing about the pentecostal outpouring in ˒William Durham's North Avenue Mission, Chicago, in 1907, Bell took a leave of absence from his church in north Fort Worth. For 11 months he sought the pentecostal experience and then received it on July 18, 1908. He returned to Texas and offered his resignation, but the church asked him to stay, which he did for another year.

Bell's first pentecostal pastorate was in Malvern, AR, where he published a monthly paper, the *Word and Witness*. In Dec. 1913 this paper published the "call" to Hot Springs that resulted in the organization of the AG. Characteristic of his generosity, he gave the *Word and Witness* to the newly formed AG. As editor and general chairman, he helped move the publishing interests to Findlay, OH, and then pastored again for two years. From 1917 to 1919 he edited the *Pentecostal Evangel* (also known as *Christian Evangel* and *Weekly Evangel*) and then was elected secretary of the AG in 1919, a position he filled until 1920, when he was once again named general chairman.

˒J. Roswell Flower, another early leader of the AG, described Bell, whom he met in 1912, as the "sweetest, safest, and sanest" man he had met in the pentecostal movement.

Bell's influence in the pentecostal movement was far-reaching. When he was rebaptized during the early years of the ˒Oneness controversy, it both shocked and pleased pentecostals who were divided over the issue. Trinitarians, however, were relieved when he returned to their camp.

Selections from the answer column in the *Pentecostal Evangel* were compiled for a book, *Questions and Answers* (1923), which ˒Gospel Publishing House published after Bell's death. He supported the creation of a Bible school in Springfield, MO, and hoped to teach there after completing his duties as general chairman, but he never lived to fulfill that wish, for he died in office in June 1923.

■ **Bibliography:** C. Brumback, *Suddenly . . . from Heaven* (1961) ■ S. Frodsham, biographical sketch in E. Bell's *Questions and Answers* (1923) ■ R. Lewis, "E. N. Bell: An Early Pentecostal Spokesman" (unpub. paper, 1985) ■ W. Menzies, *Anointed to Serve* (1971).

■ W. E. Warner

BENNETT, DENNIS JOSEPH (1917–91), and **RITA** (1934–). Dennis Bennett was an Episcopal clergyman prominently identified with the charismatic renewal from the beginning. The movement is usually dated from the Sunday morning in 1959 when Bennett announced to his congregation in Van Nuys, CA, that he had been baptized with the Holy Spirit and had spoken in tongues.

Bennett was born in England, the son of a Congregational minister. The family moved to the U.S. in 1927. He was ordained into the ministry of the Congregational Church in 1949 and served congregations in San Diego, CA, from 1949 to 1950.

In 1951 Bennett was appointed lay vicar of St. Paul's Episcopal Church in Lancaster, CA. He was ordained a deacon in the Episcopal Church in Feb. 1952 and a priest in Oct. 1952. He was called to be rector of St. Mark's Episcopal Church in Van Nuys, CA, in 1953.

In 1959, along with many members of his congregation, Bennett received the baptism with the Holy Spirit. A small opposition group in the congregation challenged him to cease and desist from what later came to be called charismatic experiences. He voluntarily resigned his pastorate, feeling that he did not have adequate understanding to defend his position.

Bennett conferred with the presiding bishop of the Episcopal Church and with the other bishops on the West Coast. He was offered churches in both Oregon and Washington. In 1960 he accepted an invitation to become vicar of St. Luke's Episcopal Church in Seattle, WA, a church that was ready to be closed for the third time.

Within 6 years the little mission church had become a strong parish and in 12 years one of the strongest churches in the Northwest. For a decade it was the major center from which word of baptism with the Holy Spirit spread worldwide, especially in the mainline denominations. Thousands of people experienced the baptism with the Holy Spirit as a result of hearing Bennett's testimony. He ministered throughout the U.S. and in many foreign countries, he lectured in major universities and theological schools worldwide, and he was one of the founders of the Episcopal Charismatic Fellowship, later called ▸Episcopal Renewal Ministries. In 1981 he was designated a canon of honor of the Diocese of Olympia by Bishop Robert H. Cochrane, in recognition of his work in the charismatic renewal.

Bennett's first wife, Elberta, died in 1963. He married Rita Marie Reed of Tampa, FL, in 1966. In 1981 he resigned as rector of St. Luke's to pursue a ministry of writing, traveling, speaking, and conducting seminars and conferences with his wife.

Bennett has authored several books, some with his wife, Rita, that set forth the significance of charismatic experience both for the individual and for the church as a whole. Together with her husband, Rita Bennett has been a leading spokesperson for charismatic renewal, particularly in the Anglican communion. She was

Dennis and Rita Bennett, two of the best-known Episcopalians in the charismatic renewal. They conducted charismatic seminars and authored several books, individually and together.

born in Michigan, but her family moved to Florida in 1936, where she grew up and received her formal education.

Rita worked in the Florida State Department of Education in child welfare. She placed children in foster care, worked with juvenile court cases, and did adoption studies. She assisted her brother, Dr. William Standish Reed, in forming the Christian Medical Foundation. In 1963–64 she served as assistant editor of *Trinity* magazine, an influential publication in the early years of the charismatic movement.

Two years after their marriage, Rita and Dennis Bennett formed Christian Renewal Association to minister worldwide and transdenominationally in evangelization, healing, and church renewal. Rita made her mark as a writer with the best-seller *The Holy Spirit and You* (1971), which she co-authored with her husband. By 1987 she had authored seven books, three with her husband.

Rita Bennett was in frequent demand as a speaker and Bible study leader for retreats, seminars, and churches in many denominations both in the U.S. and overseas. Since Dennis's death in 1991, Rita Bennett has continued to write, especially on inner healing and emotional freedom; her platform is Christian Renewal Associates, Inc.

■ **Bibliography:** D. Bennett, *Nine O'Clock in the Morning* (1970) ■ idem, *The Trinity of Man* (1979) ■ D. Bennett and R. Bennett, *The Holy Spirit and You* (1971) ■ idem, *The Holy Spirit and You Study Supplement* (1973) ■ idem, *How to Pray for Inner Healing for Yourself and Others* (1984) ■ idem, *How to Pray for the Release of the Holy Spirit* (1985) ■ idem, *Moving Right Along in the Spirit* (1983) ■ R. Bennett, *Emotionally Free* (1982) ■ idem, *I'm Glad You Asked That* (1980) ■ idem, *Making Peace with Your Inner Child* (1987) ■ idem, *You Can Be ... Emotionally Free* (1998).

■ L. Christenson

BERG, DANIEL (1884–1963). Swedish pentecostal missionary. Daniel Berg was born Apr. 19, 1884, in the city of Vargon, Sweden. His parents were members of the Swedish Baptist movement, and through their influence Berg converted to the movement and was water baptized in 1899. Because of an economic depression, he left Sweden for Boston in 1902. Berg was introduced to the pentecostal movement through a friend while visiting Sweden in 1909. Upon his return to America, he met ▸Adolf Gunnar Vingren during a pentecostal conference sponsored by the First Swedish Baptist Church in Chicago and later attended several independent pentecostal churches in the Chicago area, including ⸌William H. Durham's North Avenue Mission and the Svenska Pingst Forsamlingen. When Vingren accepted the pastorate of a Swedish Baptist church in South Bend, IN, Berg remained in Chicago and worked in a fruit shop. A year later he joined Vingren in South Bend and received the same prophecy from Adolf Uldine, to go as a missionary to Para (Belém), Brazil. Berg and Vingren were both dedicated as pentecostal missionaries in Chicago by William H. Durham.

Shortly afterward they left America and arrived in Brazil on Nov. 19, 1910. During the rest of the decade both men dedicated themselves to establishing the country's first pentecostal church. As they struggled to organize a church, Berg began working for a shipping company and used part of his income to pay for Vingren's Portuguese lessons. On June 11, 1918, they officially registered their congregation as a church under the name Assembly of God. From this church grew Brazil's largest Protestant body, the Assemblies of God (AG). After Vingren died in 1932, Berg continued to support pentecostalism in Brazil. Just two years before his death Berg attended the 15th anniversary celebration of the Brazilian AG.

■ **Bibliography:** W. J. Hollenweger, *The Pentecostals* (1972) ▪ I. Vingren, *Pionjarens dagbok dagboksanteckingar* (1968).

▪ J. Colletti

BERLIN DECLARATION *(Die Berliner Erklärung).* A statement strongly opposing the new pentecostal movement, issued in Sept. 1909 by 56 leaders in the Gnadau Alliance, a body representing the Pietist-Holiness current *(Gemeinschaftsbewegung)* in German evangelical Protestantism. The declaration began with the frequently quoted statement that the pentecostal movement was *"nicht von oben, sondern von unten"* (not from on high, but from below): evil spirits from Satan were at work to lead souls astray through cunning and deception.

Reasons given for this rejection included a list of disturbing manifestations alleged to characterize the movement; the practice of prophecy replacing obedience to the Word of God by enslavement to "messages"; and the "clean heart" doctrine associated with ⸌Jonathan Paul, who was accused of teaching the possibility of a condition of *Sündlosigkeit* (sinlessness). The German pentecostals responded the following month with the Mühlheim Declaration, which, however, never gained the publicity of the Berlin original.

German evangelicals became divided into a smaller party of "neutrals," who, while not accepting the pentecostal movement, were open to dialogue and fellowship, and a larger party of *Gegner* (opponents), who refused all association with pentecostals and stuck by the original declaration. The opposition to pentecostalism was both fiercer and more theologically sustained in Germany than in any other country, and the shadow of the Berlin Declaration still hovered over German evangelicalism when the charismatic movement arrived in the 1960s.

In 1995, however, representatives of the Pietists and evangelicals on one side and of the pentecostals and charismatics on the other side made a *Bussbekenntnis versöhnungswilliger Christen* (confession of repentance by Christians open to reconciliation), recognizing that the Berlin Declaration has no further contemporary relevance.

■ **Bibliography:** E. Edel, *Der Kampf um die Pfingstbewegung* (1949) ▪ L. Eisenlöffel, *... bis alle eins werden* (1979) ▪ P. Fleisch, *Die Pfingstbewegung in Deutschland* (1957) ▪ E. Giese, *Und flicken die Netze* (1976) ▪ H. Masuch, *Pflüget ein Neues!* (1997), 145–209 ▪ *Charisma* [German] 94 (Oct.–Dec. 1995): 14–15.

▪ P. D. Hocken

BERTOLUCCI, JOHN (1937–). Catholic charismatic evangelist-preacher. Ordained priest for the diocese of Albany, NY, in 1965, Bertolucci spent much of his first six years as priest teaching in Catholic schools. In Feb. 1969 he was baptized in the Spirit at a nearby charismatic prayer meeting. From 1971 until 1976 Bertolucci served as vice chancellor of the Albany diocese, then became pastor in Little Falls, NY (1976–80). During the early 1970s, Bertolucci's gift for popular evangelism became evident and was recognized by his bishop. By 1980 he sensed the need for a sabbatical and moved to Steubenville, OH, joining the faculty of the University of Steubenville as an assistant professor of theology. In 1981 Bertolucci established the St. Francis Association for Catholic Evangelism (FACE), which supports his preaching and his radio and television ministry. His weekly television series, *The Glory of God*, begun in 1981, was aired by many networks, cable systems, and television stations in the U.S., Canada, and the Caribbean. Bertolucci began a daily radio ministry in 1984 as host of the program *Let Me Sow Love*. His media ministry was terminated in 1987 due to financial and personal stresses.

In 1983 Bertolucci became part of the F.I.R.E. team (⸌Michael Scanlan). His personal story is told in *On Fire with the Spirit* (1984), and his other books include *The Disciplines of a Disciple* (1985); *Straight from the Heart* (1986); and *Healing: God's Work among Us* (1987). He is currently associate pastor at St. Ambrose Church, Latham, NY.

■ **Bibliography:** F. Lilly, "At the Heart of the Renewal," *Charisma* 12 (8, 1987).   ▪ P. D. Hocken

BETTEX, PAUL (1864–1916). Missionary. Bettex was born in Switzerland to Huguenot parents. His father, Jean Fred-eric Bettex, was a distinguished Christian apologist whose books were later published in English by Moody Bible Institute. The younger Bettex studied at the University of Geneva, various Italian schools, and the Sorbonne, with the intention of entering the French diplomatic corps.

Bettex was converted to Christ through the ministry of the Salvation Army in Paris. In 1886 he traveled to Ireland and then, in 1889, to Santiago, Chile, to teach at an American Presbyterian mission. On the advice of a colleague, he enrolled at Princeton Theological Seminary in 1890. One biographer, Stanley H. Frodsham, claims that Bettex received the baptism in the Holy Spirit and spoke in tongues during a revival on campus. After pastoring rural churches near Detroit and Pittsburgh, Bettex traveled to Uruguay, Argentina, and Brazil for missionary service. Stories about his dedication and the hardships that he faced circulated back to the U.S., and he became a missionary hero in some circles.

Returning to the U.S. in 1903, Bettex taught at Central Holiness University in Oskaloosa, IA, during the winter of 1906. The trustees of the institution later dismissed him for what they considered to be fanatical behavior. He eventually attended meetings at the ᐧAzusa Street revival in Los Angeles, CA, and quickly joined the ranks of the pentecostal movement. A burden for evangelism in China prompted him to travel there in 1910. While there he met and married Nellie Clark, a missionary with the London Missionary Society.

Although the circumstances surrounding the death of Nellie Clark Bettex in 1912 are contradictory, her passing aided in convincing some independent pentecostals that the problem of missionary support needed to be addressed. Paul Bettex was murdered in China in 1916, and the events surrounding his death remain uncertain. He was buried in Canton, where a memorial chapel was erected. Although his methods were often unorthodox, his concern for world evangelization inspired others for the cause of foreign missions.

■ **Bibliography:** S. H. Frodsham, *Wholly for God* (n.d.) ■ E. Gordon, *A Book of Protestant Saints* (1940) ■ G. B. McGee, *This Gospel Shall Be Preached* (1986). ■ G. B. McGee

BHENGU, NICHOLAS BHEKINKOSI HEPWORTH

(1909–86). Church leader and evangelist known throughout Africa as "the black Billy Graham." Nicholas Bhengu was born in Zululand, the grandson of a Zulu chief. His father was an evangelist at the Norwegian Lutheran mission church at Eshowe, Zululand, where Nicholas attended school. Later he enrolled at the Roman Catholic Institute there for his secondary education. As a youth he was attracted to Marxism but returned to Christianity by the time he was 20. He later studied at the South Africa General Mission Bible Training School in Dumisa, Natal, Republic of South Africa. After graduating in 1937 he began work as a court interpreter

because of his proficiency in several languages. Feeling called to the ministry, he resigned to enter full-time evangelism in 1938. He began to conduct "Back to God Crusades," having been inspired by a dream in which he heard the words "Africa must get back to God." Eventually he became affiliated with the South African Assemblies of God (SAAG).

Bhengu traveled extensively in evangelistic work and financed his Africa crusades with funds he raised on preaching tours in the U.S. (1954, 1958), Canada, England, Scotland, and Norway. By 1959 he had established, directly or indirectly, more than 50 churches, with an approximate membership of 15,000. At the time of his death, there were 1,700 assemblies, 450 ministers, and 250,000 members.

Bhengu's preaching had a profound effect on the spiritual and moral values of South Africans. In some areas where he ministered, the crime rate dropped by as much as one-third. It was not unusual for people to respond to his messages by leaving their weapons (knives, blackjacks, brass knuckles) and stolen goods in piles at his feet. At one time Bhengu set as his goal the reduction of crime in Johannesburg by 25%.

The SAAG eventually came to be closely governed by "apostles" who also spearheaded evangelism and church planting; Bhengu was considered one of the apostles and strongly defended this system of church government.

In 1974 Bhengu served as a Fellow at Selly Oak Colleges in England, teaching in the field of evangelism. Eleven years later he became ill with cancer. His memorial service was held in the Methodist Central Hall in Durban. Crowds upward of 20,000 attended the interment at Pietermaritzburg, Natal.

■ **Bibliography:** N. B. H. Bhengu, *Revival Fire in South Africa* (1949) ■ "The Black Billy Graham," *Time* (Nov. 23, 1959) ■ "The Growth and Expansion of Brother Bhengu's Work from 1945 to Date," "Homecall of 'The Black Apostle,'" "Nicholas Bhengu Was a Man with a Mission," *World Pentecost* (July 1986) ■ W. J. Hollenweger, *Pentecostalism* (1997) ■ idem, "Farewell Message to the Church," *World Pentecost* (July 1986) ■ idem, "The Soul of South Africa," *Decision* (Oct. and Nov. 1974) ■ P. Watt, *From Africa's Soil: The Story of the Assemblies of God in Southern Africa* (1992). ■ G. B. McGee

BIBLE INSTITUTES, COLLEGES, UNIVERSITIES

1. Philosophy.

Pentecostals have generally been ambivalent about higher education, many regarding it with open suspicion. Although from the beginning some groups recognized the need to provide at least basic theological training for their ministers, it was generally agreed that the historic denominations had lost their spirituality in direct relationship to their emphasis on education. In fact, higher education was thought to be so threatening to one's spiritual welfare that for decades few pentecostals chose to enroll in any but pentecostal schools.

Pentecostals claimed that it was not education they opposed but an education that destroyed faith or reduced dependence on the Holy Spirit. The lack of pentecostal liberal arts colleges, universities, and seminaries thus effectively limited most adherents to a modest Bible school education. As late as 1949, the General Council of the ⟩Assemblies of God (AG), the pentecostal denomination with the largest number of schools, refused to authorize the creation of a liberal arts college and took action to ensure that an academic degree could never be required for ministerial ordination. The pentecostal experience rather than formal education had become the essential requirement for pentecostal ministry. A residual belief that spirituality and higher education are basically incompatible has limited the support of pentecostals for higher education throughout their movement's history.

The development of pentecostal schools has also been affected by the movement's deep commitment to the doctrine of the imminent return of Christ. Because the pentecostal revival was regarded as the fulfillment of Joel's prophecy of a latter rain that would prepare for the Second Coming (Joel 2:23), it followed that the limited time before that climactic event should be used for matters more urgent than building or even attending schools. This sense of urgency prompted more than one early pentecostal to leave college to begin preaching, and it partially explains the great evangelistic and missionary emphasis of the movement. It also explains why pentecostals have generously supported foreign missions and overseas Bible schools but, paradoxically, have been reluctant to adequately support the domestic colleges that prepare their missionaries.

Support for strong pentecostal colleges and universities has also been compromised by the belief that, whatever its value, formal education is unnecessary. From the earliest days, pentecostal ministers and laypersons alike seemed to do quite well without formal education. Many felt that as Christ had used untutored fishermen to begin his church, he could use "unlearned men" to complete it (Acts 4:13 KJV). Although of the 27 early pentecostal leaders identified in one study, 78% had received some postadolescent education—well above the national average for the time (Anderson, 102)—many pentecostal pioneers lacked any formal theological training, and a few were barely literate. One of the most admired of the early pentecostals, ⟩Smith Wigglesworth, had been a semi-

BETHEL BIBLE SCHOOL, PUNALUR, U. S. T. C. 1949.

Bottom:— (Left to Right) M/s. K. C. John,   C. K. Mathai,   P. K. Varkey,   A. Gabriel,   P. N. Zachariah.
Faculty:—   „   M/s. Pastor C. Kunjummen,   Rev. J. H. Burgess,   Miss M. C. Ginn,   Miss L. H. Graner.
3rd Row:—   „   M/s. P. D. Thomas   M. Idichandy,   T. C. Paulose,   K. J. David,   T. Jesudasan Regulus,   M. K. Samuel,   A. V. George.   K. J. John,   C. G. Varughese,
          T. Varughese Regulus,   K. B. Lazar
4th Row:—   „   M/s. A. Joshua,   M. P. Varughese   K. Lazar,   K. G. Yohannan,   D. Israel,   D. Chellaiyan,   M. C. Jacob,   M. Johnson,   A. Bernabas,   J. David,   G. Philipose.

Photo by Sundaram Studio, Quilon.

Students and faculty of the Bethel Bible School, Punalur, India.

literate plumber before his pentecostal experience propelled him into worldwide evangelism. His proud boast was that he had never read a book other than the Bible (Frodsham, 109). Almost any pentecostal who wished to could find a place to preach without benefit of formal education, and as late as the mid 1950s a significant number of pentecostal ministers lacked formal theological training (Hollenweger, 40).

Few in the lower-middle-class constituency that comprised the membership of most of the classical pentecostal churches in their formative decades had attended college. Not surprisingly, disciplined, hardworking pentecostals who had succeeded as businessmen or farmers with little or no formal education tended to discount its value. Their bias was reinforced by the subtle or even overt criticism of higher education often heard in their churches. Some smaller pentecostal groups have opposed all formal training for their ministers, adopting a policy of providing any needed preparation through the local church. Pentecostal ministers with limited educational credentials have continued to enjoy places of prominence, which seemingly proves that formal education is unnecessary or even harmful.

Even if pentecostals had been more sympathetic to higher education, the practical problems of building and supporting colleges would have limited the enterprise. The early fragmentation of the pentecostal movement into struggling and even competitive denominations worked against the establishing of large schools, and the limited financial resources of

most modest pentecostal congregations made it difficult to obtain the fiscal support required to create quality schools. The struggle to maintain even modest Bible institutes made the development of more comprehensive and expensive accredited colleges seem virtually impossible.

But in spite of this resistance to higher education, pentecostals have always recognized that schools afford an effective means to train workers, perpetuate their distinctive doctrines and experiences, and deepen the devotion and commitment of their youth. Consequently, in their 100-year history, pentecostals have established more than 100 Bible institutes and colleges in the U.S. and well over 300 in the rest of the world. The major pentecostal denominations, strong local churches, and prominent pentecostal personalities, from ▸Aimee Semple McPherson to ▸Jimmy Swaggart, founded schools to share and perpetuate their visions. Over the decades, probably a majority of the pentecostal clergy have attended some type of Bible institute or college. Most recognize the important role played by such institutions, remain loyal to their own schools, and give at least moral support to pentecostal higher education.

Growth and prosperity among classical pentecostals and the impact of the charismatic movement have brought some changes. More pentecostal youth attend college, and a growing number of pentecostal colleges have been accredited. Graduate programs and even charismatic universities have been established, and some former Bible schools have achieved university status. However, the programs and schools, though promising, have yet to earn academic distinction. In striking contrast to their achievements in church building, foreign missions, Sunday schools, and the electronic media, pentecostals, through most of their history, have been content with small, modestly funded, minimally staffed, and often unaccredited Bible institutes and colleges.

2. History.

In the first two decades of their movement, the pentecostals who wished formal study utilized two types of schools. Short-term Bible schools, such as ▸Charles F. Parham's Bethel Bible School in Topeka, KS, where the 20th-century pentecostal movement may have begun, provided one option. Bethel opened in 1900 in a rented three-story residence, with Parham as the only teacher. Though he had attended

An important early center of pentecostal ministry in the eastern part of the U.S., Bethel Pentecostal Assembly (on the right) and Bethel Bible Training School (left) in Newark, NJ.

college briefly, he lacked a degree and teaching and administrative experience. Students were attracted to the school by announcements in his bimonthly paper, *Apostolic Faith*. No charge was made for tuition or living expenses. Students contributed whatever they could—which included a cow that was pastured in the backyard. Approximately 35 students enrolled, 12 of whom already held ministerial credentials with the Methodists, Friends, Holiness, or other churches. The Bible was the only textbook. A subject such as repentance, conversion, or healing was selected. References on the subject were located and Bible passages memorized for presentation to the class. Parham also gave lectures and ended the unit with an examination. Bethel was not intended to be a permanent school, and, in fact, lasted less than a year (Parham, 51–67).

Dozens of similar schools were conducted in the midwestern and southern states in the next two decades, including another that Parham opened in Houston, TX, in 1905. Lacking textbooks, developed curricula, and permanent facilities, the schools had little more to offer than the skills and zeal of their teachers, which, in some cases at least, were substantial. ⸢D. W. Myland, who directed a short-term school at Plainfield, IN, was described by a knowledgeable student as "a prince among Bible teachers" (Brumback, 227). ⸢D. C. O. Opperman, who had headed ⸢John Alexander Dowie's educational system in ⸢Zion, IL, conducted scores of six-week Bible schools in midwestern states before becoming a highly respected leader in the AG.

Although the limitations of such schools were obvious, they did provide basic training in pentecostal beliefs and experience. The stated purpose of Opperman's schools was to learn "how to pray, how to study the Word, how to know God and walk with Him" (*Word and Witness*, Dec. 20, 1913). Classes were sometimes interrupted by spontaneous prayer, praise, and the exercise of spiritual gifts. Some of the distinctive aspects of pentecostal worship apparently developed in these classes. Certainly some of the future pentecostal pastors and leaders received their training at such schools. Opperman alone is credited with the training of hundreds of pentecostal ministers. The mobility of these schools allowed them to take their teaching to the people who could not attend a conventional school. However, none of them had more than a few dozen students, and thus their effectiveness and contribution were limited.

The early pentecostal movement was also served by more permanent faith Bible or missionary training schools, such as Rochester Bible Training School in Rochester, NY. ⸢Elizabeth V. Baker and her four sisters founded the school in 1906 in conjunction with their Elim Missionary Home and Tabernacle just prior to their acceptance of the pentecostal experience. Housed in a three-story brick building adjacent to the tabernacle, the school opened with 20 students and 5 teachers. The two-year course was described as "strictly Biblical having the Bible as our chief text-book" (Baker, 132). In addition to book-by-book surveys of the Bible, courses in theology, evangelism, homiletics, exegesis, ⸢dispensational truth, tabernacle studies, and missionary work were offered. The school operated on faith, and students who could contribute little or nothing were encouraged to learn to trust God by praying in their fees. A strong missionary emphasis led many of the students to leave for the mission field immediately after graduation. When the school closed after 18 years of operation, it had trained 400 graduates, including 50 foreign missionaries.

When a small group of southern Holiness churches accepted the pentecostal experience in 1907, they continued to be served by Holmes Theological Seminary, a small but established Bible school in Greenville, SC, that had been founded in 1898. The Gospel School in Finley, OH, which opened in 1908 and operated for a decade before moving to Chicago; Beulah Heights Bible and Missionary Training School (1912), which operated in North Bergen, NJ, for 30 years; and Bethel Bible Training Institute in Newark, NJ (1916), also provided a modest education for early pentecostals.

These institutions rarely had more than 40 students and emphasized practical training and personal piety more than academic excellence. They did provide a two-year course, a more extensive curriculum, and better facilities than the short-term schools. These modest institutions turned out an impressive number of pastors and future pentecostal leaders who would shape and direct their infant churches. Several of their teachers were to have long and illustrious careers in pentecostal education, thereby influencing the more permanent pentecostal schools that were to follow.

By 1920 it was apparent that the pentecostals had been isolated from the established churches, and in spite of their opposition to man-made organizations, had in effect established new pentecostal denominations that required more

Rowhouses on the Scheringseweg in The Hague, the Netherlands, one of which houses the Assemblies of God Bible school (1970).

permanent and structured schools for their workers. By that time the Bible institute, pioneered by ᐧA. B. Simpson, D. L. Moody, and A. J. Gordon in the 1880s, had been widely adopted as the appropriate means of training fundamentalist/evangelical youth. Many pentecostals, including ᐧD. W. Myland and each of the principals at Bethel in Newark, had attended such schools and recognized them to be particularly applicable to the needs of the pentecostal movement.

Bible schools required neither a college degree nor even a high school diploma for admission. Academic standards were of less importance than spiritual commitment. Low tuition allowed many to attend who would not have been able to attend a conventional college. At a time when few seminaries accepted women, Bible institutes were open to both sexes. Courses were designed to encourage faith in the power of the Bible as opposed to its critical analysis. Terms were short, and the entire course of study was rarely more than two years. The brief time in school was sufficient to inspire students with a vision for service while pushing them into ministry before the vision was lost. Every effort was made to maintain a spiritually charged environment that would encourage personal piety and prepare gospel workers without using the limited time available in theological speculation or unnecessarily subjecting students to controversial issues. Consequently, to avoid compromise and assure the propagation of the full gospel, a greater emphasis was placed on indoctrination than intellectual development. And so the Bible institute became the pentecostal answer to the challenge of providing ministerial training while protecting students from the perceived threats of higher education.

But even a simple Bible institute required greater resources than the embryonic pentecostal denominations could muster, and the early pentecostal schools proved to be only modest versions of the established and better-known Bible institutes. Although the Church of God (CG) at Cleveland, TN, recognized the need for a school and formed a committee in 1911 to find a location and erect buildings, its first Bible institute did not open until 1918, when 12 students and their teacher met in a room over the denominational print shop (Conn, 148). It took the AG six years to open its first school, the Midwest Bible School in Auburn, NE, and it lasted only nine months because of lack of support (Moore, 105).

Eventually, denominational schools were established. In addition to the school begun by the CG in 1918, the ᐧPentecostal Holiness Church, though served by Holmes Theological Seminary, opened a second school in Franklin Springs, GA, in 1919; the AG began Central Bible Institute in Springfield, MO, in 1922; ᐧAimee Semple McPherson began the Lighthouse of International Foursquare Evangelism (L.I.F.E.) in 1923; and Bible Standard, Inc., established its school in Eugene, OR, early in 1925. Over the next two decades 40 other pentecostal Bible institutes were established

across the nation. Many were founded, owned, and operated by individuals or strong local churches, though they sought to serve the wider pentecostal community. After a slow start, the ᐧOneness pentecostals began their first school in St. Paul, MN, in 1937, followed by nine other endorsed schools in America. Black pentecostals were unsuccessful in their early attempt to start a Bible institute in Dallas, TX, but did begin one in Goldsboro, NC, in 1944.

Though each of these schools was unique, they shared certain characteristics. For example, they were small. Until the late 1940s their enrollments ranged from fewer than 50 to more than 500 students, but few exceeded 200. Over a 20-year period, one of the stronger schools averaged 17 in its graduating classes. Although this allowed a personal concern and intimacy that a larger school could not match, it also resulted in a high mortality rate. At least 15 Bible institutes in the AG alone closed by 1941 (Menzies, 355). Those that survived into the 1950s tended to be older and larger, with some student bodies exceeding 500. However, in 1970 the seven remaining Oneness pentecostal schools averaged 144 students.

These schools were located in a variety of facilities, from converted mansions to a former nightclub. They often met in or adjacent to a sponsoring church. On occasion new facilities were constructed. An imposing six-story reinforced concrete building to house students and classrooms was erected in San Francisco for Glad Tidings Bible Institute (GTBI) in 1924. Although that metropolitan school lacked a campus, Central Bible Institute (CBI) in Springfield, MO, was housed in a new brick building on what would become a 50-acre site. Elim Bible Institute near Rochester, NY, founded in

The Chateau Bible Institute in Andremont, Belgium.

1924, eventually moved to a historic 85-acre campus that had housed colleges for 140 years.

A study of the English Bible was the heart of the curriculum, but classes in such subjects as English, biblical languages, music, and applied classes in soul winning, missions, and apologetics were gradually added. What passed for a library was usually little more than a few hundred, largely donated, volumes on religious subjects, shelved in a small room. Emphasis was placed on the mastering of doctrinal positions and the memorization of Scripture rather than on critical thought or scholarly research. Study time was limited for students who were working their way through school and spending considerable time in applied ministry.

Teachers were not required to have degrees, and few did. As late as 1943 their average post–high school education was less than four years (Menzies, 355). Graduate degrees were even rarer. Experience, teaching gifts, or willingness to serve were the primary qualifications. Although some of the teachers were well trained and their classes became legendary, they were the exception. At times the wives of teachers were also given classes for which they had few apparent qualifications. No accreditation body existed to recognize or evaluate these schools, and acceptance of transfer credit by accredited colleges was rarely expected or granted. Admission was open to virtually anyone who professed conversion and a desire to study the Bible. Few academic records were maintained, and graduation was achieved by remaining in the school for the full course. Although the early Bible institutes initially offered only two years of study, a third was eventually added by most.

Especially in their early days, the Bible institutes tended to be dominated by a strong leader. GTBI, which had opened in San Francisco in 1919, was led and controlled by its founders, Robert and Mary Craig. Craig, a former Methodist minister, became a veritable spiritual father, shaping the lives and ministries of his students through his daily early morning chapel sessions. The Craigs' influence was enormous, extending even to such personal matters as the choice of a marriage partner. Students who failed to fulfill the ministry expected of them were reluctant to return and meet the Craigs' disapproval, while the more successful were proud to report any achievements. ⬧Ivan Q. Spencer at Elim in Rochester, ⬧P. C. Nelson at Southwestern Bible School in Enid, OK, and ⬧W. I. Evans at CBI in Springfield, MO, were only a few of the other strong personalities who dominated their respective schools.

This education was designed to prepare students for the pentecostal ministry, and consequently formal classes were only a part of the program. Spiritual development and applied ministry were of major importance. Students were expected to participate in such activities as mission services, street meetings, and jail ministry. The schools that were related to churches also required choir, orchestra, and prayer participa-

tion in regular services, in some cases on a nightly basis. Although a majority of the graduates at least attempted to enter full-time ministry as pastors, evangelists, or missionaries, the attrition rates for these ministries was high. As a result, the majority of students were educated for work they failed to pursue.

For this education students paid a tuition of only a few dollars a month—when it was collected. In some cases, none was charged, and the schools operated by faith. This was made possible, in part, by employing teachers and staff who were willing to work for little more than a subsistence wage. The schools lacked endowment but depended on the gifts of friends. One founder's $80,000 inheritance made a new building possible (Brumback, 234). Because pentecostals made little provision for the support of their schools, the normal procedure was for them to appeal to their constituencies for emergency offerings to keep the doors open in the frequent times of financial exigency.

Little social activity was provided and fewer recreational facilities. With rare exception, there were no organized intramural or intercollegiate athletic programs. Through the 1940s, most schools required their women students to wear uniforms and men to wear ties and jackets. Strict regulations attempted to prevent romantic contact between the sexes, and marriage during the school year was a cause for immediate dismissal. In spite of this, many couples who were inspired with the same ministry ideals married soon after graduation.

Whatever their strengths or limitations, these schools shaped the pentecostal churches. Their graduates became the pioneers of the majority of pentecostal churches in the U.S. and the missionaries responsible for planting them around the world. The doctrines and practices they had learned provided the accepted norms for church administration, doctrine, and personal piety. Equipped with but two or three

Ambon Bible School on the island of Ambon, one of the Moluccas (or Spice Islands) in Indonesia.

years of training, graduates often began ministry in their early twenties. Their modest education had given them few illusions about their professional standing, and because little or no financial support was available from their developing denominations, the Bible-institute graduates were ready to make sacrifices, live modestly, and even work with their hands to support their families and build churches.

There were, however, less happy consequences. The meager quality of their education hardly prepared these committed souls for certain aspects of the ministry. Poorly trained ministers often remained at a given charge for only months before moving on, leaving an infant congregation behind. As a direct consequence of these rapid changes by eager but inexperienced pastors, pentecostal churches in many communities failed to grow for many decades.

Those who did identify with the pentecostals were more often from the working class with limited education themselves. Educated professionals who were already biased against the supernatural and emotional aspects of pentecostalism found little in these poorly trained ministers to attract them. The result was the creation of churches virtually without professionals, such as doctors, lawyers, and teachers and without the financial and leadership resources they could provide. With limited contact with the intellectual community, pentecostals became increasingly anti-intellectual, glorying in being the Lord's despised few. One result of this alienation was the development of something of a pentecostal subculture. In spite of the impressive numerical gains of the pentecostals, the movement appeared limited to a lower-middle-class constituency.

By the outbreak of WWII, there were signs that this trend was changing. Experience had demonstrated that for those students who had not entered, or at least remained, in the ministry, their Bible-institute education had not prepared them for the marketplace. Recognizing this, several schools added business courses. Key pentecostal denominations had considered the need for liberal arts colleges as early as 1935, though no apparent progress had been made in implementation. Progress in the development of junior colleges came first. Black pentecostals began a small junior college in Lexington, MI, in 1918. The Bible Training School (later Lee College), operated by the Church of God, added a junior college division in 1941. Southwestern Bible Institute (AG) followed with a similar program in 1944.

In 1939, believing that a broader education was required to meet the needs of the fast-growing pentecostal movement, Southern California Bible College (SCBC) in Pasadena added a fourth year and was recognized by the state as a degree-granting institution. During the war this allowed SCBC to train military chaplains, a fact not unnoticed by other pentecostal schools. After the war, thousands of pentecostal servicemen returned, ready for further educa-

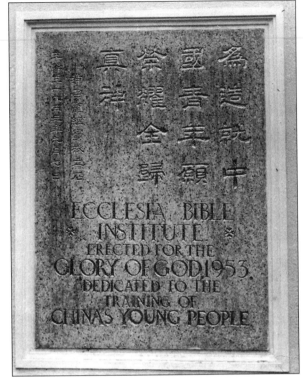

The Ecclesia Bible Institute in Hong Kong (1953).

tion at government expense. To qualify to train these veterans, schools were required to meet certain standards. Nonetheless, mature servicemen recognized some of the deficiencies in the quality of the pentecostal schools that were available to them and, in some cases, worked for their improvement.

The war had also brought new affluence to many first- and second-generation pentecostal parents who wanted a better education for their offspring than they had enjoyed. A new educational discrimination became apparent as some parents began sending their pentecostal children to better developed evangelical or even secular colleges and universities. The fact that those who went off to nonpentecostal schools were often lost to the movement contributed to a growing sentiment for better pentecostal schools.

In 1947 the new *National Association of Evangelicals was instrumental in forming the first Bible institute accrediting association, which would become the American Association of Bible Colleges (AABC). Pentecostals sat on its founding board, and a number of pentecostal Bible institutes and colleges immediately applied for accreditation. To gain recognition with the new body, Bible schools were forced to meet higher library, record-keeping, and faculty educational standards. Eventually, more than 20 schools, affiliated with five pentecostal denominations, became members of this body, substantially improving their educational offerings. After rejecting outside accreditation for many years, L.I.F.E. Bible College, the Foursquare school in Los Angeles, was accredited by the AABC in 1980.

Once begun, the movement toward accreditation proved hard to resist. Following the lead of many evangelical Bible institutes that had determined that the needs of their youth could be better served through regionally accredited liberal arts colleges, some pentecostal educators began promoting and working for regionally accredited liberal arts colleges that would provide the education required for most graduate programs, teacher certification, and entrance into virtually all professions.

In 1962 SCBC, which in 1950 had moved from Pasadena to Costa Mesa, CA, dropped Bible from its name, withdrew from the AABC, and two years later was accredited by the Western Association of Schools and Colleges as a four-year liberal arts college. It did so at the cost of at least temporarily alienating some of its constituency, who feared the school was following the path of the many church-related colleges that had lost their evangelical fervor and even their Christian commitment. In 1955 the AG opened Evangel College on 59 acres in Springfield, MO, as a denominationally sponsored liberal arts college (Menzies, 362–63). Lee College of the CG, which had added a four-star liberal arts curriculum, received regional accreditation in 1969.

Accreditation required higher salaries, a more complex curriculum, science laboratories, a more extensive library, and other requirements that made liberal arts schools much more expensive than Bible colleges. Because pentecostals had never learned to support higher education, and their middle-class young people could not pay high tuition, maintaining the liberal arts colleges proved difficult. The alumni funds that assisted many schools were unavailable because many graduates served as low-paid ministers or missionaries. A qualified faculty presented another problem. By its failure to emphasize higher education, the pentecostal movement lacked the required supply of accredited doctorates in many academic disciplines.

Nonetheless, one by one Bible colleges saw the need for and advantages of regional accreditation. To avoid alienating conservative supporters, the name "Bible" was sometimes retained and a substantial Bible requirement placed on all students. In a number of cases, the U.S. government contributed to the move toward accredited education by providing financial assistance through student loans, veterans' benefits, and state scholarships. Govern-

ment programs to encourage the expansion of colleges in the postwar era even made possible the building of new buildings. Several major grants of surplus property assisted in the development of new college campuses (Nelson, 417–46). Though many pentecostal schools have remained Bible colleges, well over a dozen regionally accredited pentecostal colleges now exist.

Nationally known evangelist ▸Oral Roberts had experienced the frustration of seeking an education within pentecostal ranks, and believing that thousands of young people were being lost to the full gospel movement for want of a quality pentecostal university, Roberts determined to provide a university to serve traditional pentecostals as well as the growing number of charismatics. Oral Roberts University opened in 1964 on 180 acres in Tulsa, OK. Its futuristic architecture and educational innovation won it immediate recognition, and in an unusually short six years it was granted accreditation by the North Central Association of Colleges and Schools. By recruiting outstanding athletic talent, ORU was soon competing with the nation's best-known universities and earning national recognition. The fund-raising ability of its founder allowed the continued development of the $60 million campus, including a $2 million aerobic center, a 10,000-seat special events center, and a 200-foot-high prayer tower. Subsidized tuition further assisted the rapid growth of the university so that by 1986 it had a student body of nearly 5,000, more than twice the size of any other pentecostal college. Professional schools were added in dentistry, law, medicine, nursing, social work, theology, and music. Accreditation for these programs led to prolonged, bitter, but eventually successful fights with the American Bar Association and the medical community (Harrell, 223).

Part of the campus of the Assemblies of God Bible school in Tokyo, Japan.

Unlike the earlier pentecostals, the new charismatics expected their youth to be educated, and many flocked to the beautiful new ORU campus. By 1975 only half of the student body was associated with classical pentecostal denominations even though its pentecostal commitment remained strong.

In 1975 ˒Pat Robertson, founder of the Christian Broadcasting Network (CBN), believed he was directed to buy 200 acres of land in Virginia Beach, VA, to house a new headquarters and university. Over the next three years the vision developed so that in 1978 CBN University opened its doors with 79 graduate students in communication. It was determined that the university would offer only graduate education and soon was drawing students from scores of secular and religious schools. Within six years it had won regional accreditation and had begun offering degrees in education, business administration, biblical studies, public policy, and journalism. In 1986 the law school that had been located at ORU was transferred to CBN. Enrollment exceeded 900 students coming from all 50 states and many foreign countries. Though the leadership of CBN is charismatic, only one-third of the students indicating a church membership came from classical pentecostal churches.

In the early 1980s, ˒Youth With A Mission, a charismatic missionary-evangelistic ministry operating in many countries, founded Pacific and Asia Christian University in Hawaii. A nontraditional school, it alternates terms of study with extended periods of ministry in an attempt to join the theoretical with the practical. Its lack of a paid faculty, meager library, and limited curriculum indicate that regional accreditation may be difficult to obtain.

Southern California College also joined the move toward graduate education in 1984. With the collapse of Melodyland School of Theology in Anaheim, CA, the college recognized that no regionally accredited programs with a pentecostal emphasis existed in the western U.S. and began an M.A. program in biblical studies and church administration.

3. Present.

This movement toward accredited education produced a reaction among many pentecostals who believed the early unaccredited Bible institutes had better served the needs of pentecostals. Some of the existing schools refused to move toward accreditation and continued to offer a traditional Bible-college education. ˒Gordon Lindsay, who had been a leader in the healing movement of the 1950s, founded Christ for the Nations in Dallas, TX, in 1972, shortly before his death. Though its 75-acre campus was impressive, its curriculum and emphasis were a return to the earlier Bible and missionary training schools. It grew rapidly to over 1,000 students who could earn an Associate of Practical Theology degree in two years. It has never sought accreditation.

In the 1970s and '80s numerous Bible institutes were founded across the nation that were designed to promote personal spiritual growth and service with no expectation of accreditation. Genesis, which began in Santa Rosa, CA, and ˒Rhema Bible Training Center in Tulsa, OK, were two of the earlier of such institutions. Many of them were sponsored by local churches with classes offered exclusively at night. Housed in local churches without extensive libraries and expensive faculties, these schools were able to operate economically at a time when accredited Bible colleges were raising their tuition beyond the means of many.

In 1982 evangelist Jimmy Swaggart opened a Bible school in Baton Rouge, LA. Although his name and resources enabled him to construct a handsome campus and attract more than 1,500 students within five years, his much publicized moral failure soon led to its collapse.

Currently pentecostal higher education is offered in a wide range of options from modest local Bible institutes to accredited universities. Although this variety makes pentecostal education widely available, it has also fragmented resources. Though pentecostal attitudes toward higher education have been changing, if stronger colleges and universities that might better serve the pentecostal movement are to develop, pentecostals will have to recognize the need for such schools and make a commitment to support them.

■ **Bibliography:** R. Anderson, *Vision of the Disinherited* (1979) ■ E. Baker, *Chronicles of a Faith Life* (1984) ■ V. Brereton, *Protestant Fundamentalist Bible Schools 1882–1940* (diss., Columbia U., 1981) ■ C. Brumback, *Suddenly . . . from Heaven* (1961) ■ R. Chandler, "Melodyland School: The Spirit's Time," *Christianity Today* 17 (July 20, 1973) ■ C. Conn, *Like a Mighty Army: A History of the Church of God* (1955) ■ A. Flower, *Grace for Grace* (privately printed, n.d., 1961) ■ S. Frodsham, *Smith Wigglesworth, Apostle of Faith* (1951) ■ D. Harrell Jr., *Oral Roberts* (1985) ■ W. Hollenweger, *Pentecostalism* (1997) ■ idem, *The Pentecostals* (1977) ■ C. Jones, *A Guide to the Study of the Pentecostal Movement* (1983) ■ W. Menzies, *Anointed to Serve* (1971) ■ R. Mitchell, *Heritage and Horizons: The History of Open Bible Standard Churches* (1982) ■ E. Moore, "Handbook of Pentecostal Denominations in the United States" (thesis, Pasadena College, 1954) ■ L. Nelson, "The Demise of O'Reilly Hospital and the Beginning of Evangel College," *Missouri Historical Review* (1987) ■ J. Nichol, *Pentecostalism* (1966) ■ S. Parham, *The Life of Charles F. Parham* (1930) ■ *Word and Witness* 9 (Dec. 20, 1913). ■ L. F. Wilson

BIBLE INSTITUTES, SPANISH-SPEAKING.

Bible institutes and Bible schools have long been an important part of the Latino pentecostal movement in the U.S., Mexico, and Puerto Rico. They are an important legacy of the fundamentalist-modernist controversy that prompted conservative Protestant Christians to form their own educational institutions to train their clergy and lay leaders. Just about every major Latino pentecostal denomination in the U.S. sponsors some kind of Bible school. Most of the first Spanish-speaking Bible institutes in the U.S. were founded by Anglo-Americans ministering to Spanish-speaking people. The Assemblies of God (AG) missionary-evangelist ▸Alice E. Luce is credited with founding one of the first Spanish-language pentecostal Bible institutes in the U.S. In 1926 she founded Berean Bible Institute in San Diego, CA, which later changed its name and location to the Latin American Bible Institute (LABI) in La Puente, CA. Her coworker ▸H. C. Ball founded a second LABI in San Antonio, TX, that same year.

Because Alice E. Luce was better educated than H. C. Ball, she wrote most of the early textbooks and curriculum for the LABIs. The course offerings were identical in the two schools. After completing a two-year course of study, students were awarded a diploma. In the first year of study, they took courses in preliminary studies, personal evangelism, Christian doctrine, prophecy, types of Christ, music, rhetoric, Bible geography, and synthetic studies in both the OT and NT. In the second year of study, they were required to take more advanced courses in the same subjects, as well as courses on divine healing, types of the Holy Spirit, Christian evidences (apologetics), preaching (homiletics), and pastoral theology.

Today the LABIs offer diplomas as well as B.A. degrees. In addition to the courses offered at La Puente and San Antonio, students can also take courses by correspondence. It is worth noting that both schools have always had an interracial faculty and a very high percentage of female faculty and students.

The concept of the LABIs spread to Mexico and Puerto Rico. The AG opened their first Bible school in Mexico City in 1928. In 1940 ▸Rodolfo Orozco founded Alba Institute, one of the first all-women pentecostal Bible institutes in Mexico. By 1990 over 1,400 students attended one of the 30 Bible institutes scattered throughout Mexico. One of the first Spanish-speaking pentecostal Bible schools among Puerto Ricans was the Hispanic Bible Institute of the AG (Institute Bíblico Hispano del Este Asambleas de Dios), founded in New York City by Edmundo Jordan in 1936. A year later Juan L. Lugo founded Mizpa Bible Institute (known today as the Colegio Pentecostal Mizpa) in Puerto Rico. Mizpa claims to have trained approximately 15,000 people since 1937. Today Mizpa belongs to the Pentecostal Church of God (M.I.) and offers the B.A., A.A., and certificates in pastoral theology and Christian education. The Pentecostal Church of God (M.I.) has spawned at least 19 additional Mizpa Bible Institutes in as many countries throughout Latin America and the world. The Church of God (Cleveland, TN) opened its first Bible school in Mexico in 1940, in Mexico City, and in 1956 founded the Pentecostal Bible College of Puerto Rico (Colegio Bíblico Pentecostal de Puerto Rico). ▸Miguel Guillén and the Latin American Council of Christian Churches (CLADIC) opened a seminary in 1954 in Los Angeles.

Oneness denominations also founded their own Bible schools. The Apostolic Assembly of Faith in Jesus Christ, Inc., opened the Apostolic Bible Training School in Hayward, CA, in 1949 and has since opened other schools in Texas and Florida. In 1996 more than 580 students were enrolled in Apostolic Assembly Bible schools. Their sister denomination, the Apostolic Church of Faith in Jesus Christ, located in Mexico, operates two Bible schools, one in Mexico City and one in Torreón.

Since the 1930s, the number of Spanish-language Bible schools and correspondence programs has continued to increase throughout the U.S., Mexico, and Puerto Rico. These Bible schools show that Latino pentecostals have been more interested in education than many originally believed; they have enabled Latinos with limited schooling the opportunity to further their education and train for the ministry, an opportunity they would have been denied in most other forms of Christianity. In addition, these schools have afforded women the opportunity to train for the ordained and lay ministry.

■ **Bibliography:** V. De León, *The Silent Pentecostals* (1979) ■ J. L. Gonzáles, *The Theological Education of Hispanics* (1988) ■ B. Rodríguez, *Denominational Statistical Information Form for the Apostolic Assembly of Faith in Christ Jesus, Inc.* (1996) ■ *50 Aniversario: Institute Biblico Hispano del Este Asamblea de Dios* (1986).

■ G. Espinosa

BIBLE QUIZZING Teen Bible Quizzing in pentecostal churches traces back to the late 1950s. Many pentecostal denominations and fellowships have their own programs; others participate in multidenominational quiz tournaments such as World Bible Quiz. The Assemblies of God (AG) and the Church of the Nazarene are, as of 2000, considered to have the largest teen quiz programs, each involving 8,000 or more youth in the structured study of a book, or books, of the Bible. Junior Bible Quiz (JBQ), for elementary children, was introduced in 1975 and involves twice as many teams as teen quiz.

Most denominational teen quiz programs copied the Youth for Christ quizzing of the 1950s. Many pentecostal groups have very similar rules and frequently quiz in each others' leagues and tournaments. Each group has its own national championship each year, often in conjunction with a larger convention of the denomination or fellowship.

Quizzing provides an incentive for the memorization and study of God's Word through lively and friendly competition. Matches consist of 20 questions. The first quizzer who responds, as indicated by electronic equipment, is permitted to answer. Questions may range from very simple ("What was Luke's occupation?") to very demanding ("Quote the three verses of John's Gospel in which Jesus prophesied he would be 'lifted up'"). Quotations must be absolutely accurate to be ruled correct.

Junior Bible quizzers in competition.

The in-depth study of God's Word produces lasting effects. Missionaries and ministers testify that the Scripture they memorized for quiz remain a powerful influence in their lives and ministries. Those who have chosen other careers mention the benefits they gained through learning to memorize, associate, and categorize the Bible text, as well as the spiritual impact on their personal development.

The roots of quizzing come from the catechisms of many mainline denominations—a question-and-answer approach to learning valuable biblical facts and doctrinal understanding. The Bible Fact-Pak, 576 questions covering highlights from and about the Bible plus questions of basic doctrine (such as, "What do we mean when we say God is omnipotent?"), serves as a catechism for elementary children. Developed by the AG, it has been used by many pentecostal groups and adapted for use by other evangelical churches. The Fact-Pak has also been translated into at least eight languages, including Chinese and Swahili. Latin America has a strong JBQ program.

Sponsored by a grassroots committee, JBQ (using the Bible Fact-Pak questions) culminates in an annual JBQ Festival involving 60 or more teams. Although predominantly AG, teams from other denominations frequently participate in district tournaments and advance to the national festival.

■ G. Edgerly

BIBLE WAY CHURCHES OF OUR LORD JESUS CHRIST WORLD WIDE

Charges of misgovernment in the ʼChurch of Our Lord Jesus Christ of the Apostolic Faith led to the calling of the 1957 ministers' conference in Washington, DC, which established the Bible Way Churches of Our Lord Jesus Christ World Wide. Approximately 70 congregations followed elders Smallwood E. Williams (b. 1907), John S. Beane, McKinley Williams (b. 1901), Winfield Showall, and Joseph Moore into the new church. The Oneness teachings of the new body are identical to those of the parent. Members are required to tithe, to be present each time Holy Communion is observed, and to attend all business meetings. Bible Way churches forbid the use of tobacco and alcohol and the remarriage of divorced persons as long as their original partners live. They label as fanatical those who preach against the straightening and shampooing of hair and the wearing of neckties or of shoes without toes or heels. The denomination is centered in Bishop Smallwood Williams's church in Washington. By 1993 it claimed 350 congregations and 300,000 members in the U.S. and 16 congregations and 1,000 members in the U.K. It sponsors missions in Jamaica, Trinidad and Tobago, Liberia, and Nigeria.

■ **Bibliography:** C. E. Jones, *Black Holiness* (1987) ■ A. C. Piepkorn, *Profiles in Belief,* vol. 3 (1979). ■ C. E. Jones

BIBLIOGRAPHY AND HISTORIOGRAPHY OF PENTECOSTALISM IN THE UNITED STATES

I. Bibliography

II. Historiography
    A. The Early Historians
       1. The Governance of History
       2. The Direction of History
       3. Supernatural vs. Natural Causation in History
       4. The Definition of the Movement
       5. Geographical and Social Origins of Pentecostalism
       6. The Movement's Place in History
    B. Recent Historians
       1. The Providential Approach
       2. The Genetic Approach
       3. The Multicultural Approach
       4. The Functional Approach

III. Conclusion

I. BIBLIOGRAPHY.

After years of benign neglect, scholarly resources for the study of American pentecostalism are beginning to tumble off the presses at an astonishing rate. The literature on the subject has become so extensive that bibliographic guides are virtually indispensable. For serious researchers, Charles Edwin Jones, *A Guide to the Study of the Pentecostal Movement* (2 vols., 1983), looms as the most comprehensive listing of primary and secondary materials available in English. Most of its 7,000 entries refer to primary texts. The majority are doctrinal or devotional in nature, yet scores of dissertations and hundreds of historical and social-scientific items also are noted. Perhaps the most valuable are the numerous listings for tunebooks, pamphlets, and tracts, as well as articles in obscure or long-extinct popular magazines. The focus falls on North American English-language materials, but the growth of pentecostalism in other parts of the world is not ignored.

Additional bibliographies of varying comprehensiveness and emphasis are worth noting. Watson E. Mills, *Charismatic Religion in Modern Research: A Bibliography* (1985), contains 2,100 entries, primarily limited to more scholarly books and articles. Another helpful resource is the note section of Arthur Carl Piepkorn, *Profiles in Belief*, vol. 3, *Holiness and Pentecostal* (1979). David W. Faupel, *The American Pentecostal Movement* (1972), offers a much slimmer survey of the literature than the ones noted above, but for routine reference needs it is quite adequate and handily organized. Still more compact, but more up to date and broad-ranging, are Cecil M. Robeck Jr., "The Pentecostal Movements in the U.S.: Recent Historical Bibliography," in *Evangelical Studies Bulletin* 3 (Mar. 1986); and Russell P. Spittler, "Suggested Areas for Further Research in Pentecostal Studies," *Pneuma: Journal of the Society for Pentecostal Studies* [hereafter *Pneuma*], 5 (1983). For bibliography on Hispanic pentecostals, see Arlene Sanchez Walsh, "Latino Pentecostalism—A Bibliographic Introduction," *Evangelical Studies Bulletin* (Spring 1998). The semiannual *Newsletter* of the Society for Pentecostal Studies (SPS), which lists recent dissertations and publications, also registers bibliographic trends in the field. (For African Americans, see resources noted below.)

A still serviceable one-volume history of the rise of pentecostalism around the world is John Thomas Nichol's *The Pentecostals* (1971; originally published as *Pentecostalism* in 1966). Nichol includes chapters on regional, ethnic, and small pentecostal groups. For the casual reader, *In the Latter Days: The Outpouring of the Holy Spirit in the Twentieth Century* (1984) by Vinson Synan, offers a brief and sprightly overview of worldwide trends, emphasizing recent developments in Third World countries. Synan sculpts a clear and therefore valuable typology of the various forms of pentecostal piety in North America and elsewhere in "Pentecostalism: Varieties and Contributions," *Pneuma* 9 (1987). More recently, Harvard University's Harvey Cox, in *Fire from Heaven: The Rise of Pentecostal Spirituality and the Reshaping of Religion in the Twenty-First Century* (1995), provides a perceptive assessment of the origins, meaning, and significance of pentecostal spirituality in a global context.

The most authoritative study of pentecostal origins in the United States is Robert Mapes Anderson, *Vision of the Disinherited: The Making of American Pentecostalism* (1979). Anderson approaches the subject from a forthrightly naturalistic perspective, but his research is exhaustive, accurate, and methodologically sophisticated. Another useful survey is Vinson Synan, *The Holiness-Pentecostal Movement in the United States* (1971; reissued and expanded as *The Holiness-Pentecostal Tradition: Charismatic Movements in the Twentieth Century* [1997]). In this volume he argues—a bit too insistently, perhaps—that the Wesleyan Holiness tradition served as the theological wellspring of the movement as a whole. For

accounts that include material on the non-Wesleyan roots of pentecostalism, see Edith Blumhofer, *Restoring the Faith: The Assemblies of God, Pentecostalism, and American Culture* (1993); and Grant Wacker, "Pentecostalism," in *Encyclopedia of the American Religious Experience*, ed. Charles H. Lippy and Peter W. Williams, vol. 2 (1987). Wacker's essay offers a chapter-length summary of the history of the movement, with particular attention to the early years. Wacker expands this study in a book-length examination of first-generation converts' everyday life in *Heaven Below: Early Pentecostals and American Culture* (2001).

Differing interpretations of pentecostal origins have been treated in several sources. These include Cecil M. Robeck Jr., "Pentecostal Origins from a Global Perspective," in *All Together in One Place: Theological Papers from the Brighton Conference on World Evangelization*, ed. Harold Hunter and Peter D. Hocken (1993); Augustus Cerillo Jr.'s two recent articles, "Interpretative Approaches to the History of American Pentecostal Origins," *Pneuma* 19 (Spring 1997); and "The Beginnings of American Pentecostalism: An Historiographical Overview," in *Pentecostal Currents in American Protestantism*, ed. Edith L. Blumhofer, Russell P. Spittler, and Grant A. Wacker (1999).

In the mid 1950s many of the ideas and practices of old-line pentecostalism started to erupt in the Roman Catholic Church and in some of the mainline Protestant bodies, and by the 1970s in evangelical and independent churches. The literature on this phenomenon, which is commonly known as the neo-pentecostal or charismatic movement, already is extensive. Charles Edwin Jones's, *The Charismatic Movement: A Guide to the Study of Neo-Pentecostalism, with Emphasis on Anglo-American Sources* (2 vols., 1995), consists of nearly 11,000 entries of both a positive and critical nature regarding the beliefs and practices of the charismatic movement. Two early autobiographical accounts are Dennis J. Bennett, *Nine O'Clock in the Morning* (1970); and Kevin and Dorothy Ranaghan, *Catholic Pentecostals* (1969); and a revised edition, *Catholic Pentecostals Today* (1983). Another influential account by a journalist and participant is John Sherrill, *They Speak with Other Tongues* (1964). These accounts, along with David du Plessis's *The Spirit Bade Me Go* (1970) and *A Man Called Mr. Pentecost: David Du Plessis as Told to Bob Slosser* (1977), which chronicle Du Plessis's pioneering efforts to bring the pentecostal message to the mainline Protestant and Roman Catholic leadership, show the influence of classical pentecostals on the charismatic movement.

Historians and other scholars have sketched the contours of the history of the charismatic movement. In 1972 Steve Durasoff, then a professor at Oral Roberts University, published a popular history of pentecostalism, *Bright Wind of the Spirit*, which includes chapters on the still relatively new Protestant and Roman Catholic charismatic movements. He placed these religious renewal movements on a continuum with classical pentecostalism and earlier "spirit movements" in church history. Four years later Richard Quebedeaux published *The New Charismatics* (1976; reissued as *The New Charismatics II* [1983]), in which he traced the spread of pentecostal piety among traditionally nonpentecostal groups. Vinson Synan's *In the Latter Days: The Outpouring of the Holy Spirit in the Twentieth Century* (1984), cited earlier, contains several chapters sketching pentecostalism's emergence among mainline Protestants, Roman Catholics, and evangelicals (sometimes labeled the third wave or neocharismatic movement). This 1984 book was followed by *The Twentieth-Century Pentecostal Explosion* (1987), which traces the growth of pentecostal stirrings within particular—and seemingly unlikely—denominational families, such as Lutherans, Mennonites, and Orthodox Catholics. Synan's *The Holiness Pentecostal Tradition: Charismatic Movements in the Twentieth Century* (2d ed., 1997), cited earlier, also contains new chapters on the history of the charismatic movement from the 1960s to the 1990s. His *Under His Banner* (1992), a brief popular history of the Full Gospel Business Men's Fellowship International, documents that organization's role in fostering the pentecostal renewal in the mainline churches. Peter Hocken, British Roman Catholic theologian and, until his retirement, longtime secretary-treasurer of the SPS, has published several comprehensive essays that detail the history of the charismatic movement. He updated his survey published in the first edition of this *Dictionary* (1988), 130–60, with "The Charismatic Movement in the United States," *Pneuma* 16 (Fall 1994); "Youth With A Mission," *Pneuma* 16 (Fall 1994); and "A Survey of Independent Charismatic Churches," *Pneuma* 18 (Spring 1996). (See also ▶Charismatic Movements.)

Theological assessments of the charismatic movement include J. Rodman Williams, *The Pentecostal Reality* (1972); Edward D. O'Connor, C.S.C., *The Pentecostal Movement in the Catholic Church* (1971); Kilian McDonnell, O.S.B., ed., *The Holy Spirit and the Power: The Catholic Charismatic Renewal* (1975), and his earlier *Catholic Pentecostalism: Problems in Evaluation* (1971); Ralph Martin, ed., *The Spirit and the Church* (1976); James C. Connelly, C.S.C., "Neo-Pentecostalism: The Charismatic Renewal in the Mainline Protestant and Roman Catholic Churches of the United States, 1960–1971" (diss., U. of Chicago, 1977); Peter Hocken, "The Significance and Potential of Pentecostalism," in *New Heaven? New Earth? An Encounter with Pentecostalism*, ed. Simon Tuckwell et al. (1977); and Francis A. Sullivan, *Charisms and Charismatic Renewal: A Biblical and Theological Study* (1982). For a multidenominational view, see the pioneering *Perspectives on the New Pentecostalism* (1976), ed. Russell P. Spittler. On charismatic communities, see Theophane Rush, "Covenant Communities in the United States," *Pneuma*

16 (Fall 1994). The theological influence of the charismatic movement on classical pentecostalism is explored in Frank D. Macchia, "God Present in a Confused Situation: The Mixed Influence of the Charismatic Movement on Classical Pentecostalism in the United States," *Pneuma* 18 (Spring 1996).

The most noted sociological critique of Catholic pentecostalism is Meredith B. McGuire, *Pentecostal Catholics: Power, Charisma, and Order in a Religious Movement* (1982). Sociologist Margaret Poloma contributed *The Charismatic Movement: Is There a New Pentecost?* (1982), a volume in Twayne's Social Movements Past and Present series. Using insights from the sociology of religion, Poloma analyzes the internal strengths and weakness and the larger impact of the charismatic movement in the U.S. More recently, Poloma scrutinizes the Toronto Airport Christian Fellowship in "Inspecting the Fruit of the 'Toronto Blessing': A Sociological Perspective," *Pneuma* 20 (Spring 1998). Donald E. Miller examines the history, ideology, and practices of Calvary Chapel, the Vineyard, and Hope Chapel, three contemporary movements he calls new paradigm churches, in *Reinventing American Protestantism: Christianity in the New Millennium* (1997).

Statistical and poll data on the beliefs and practices of both old-line pentecostals and the newer charismatics can be found in Kenneth S. Kantzer, "The Charismatics among Us," *Christianity Today* (Feb. 22, 1980); and in David Barrett, *World Christian Encyclopedia* (1982; rev. ed., 2000). Barrett updates pentecostal statistics yearly in the January issue of the *International Bulletin of Missionary Research*. For a fine-grained statistical analysis of pentecostal beliefs, behavior patterns, and demographic profiles see Corwin E. Smidt et al., "The Spirit-Filled Movements in Contemporary America: A Survey Perspective," in *Pentecostal Currents in American Protestantism*, ed. Edith Blumhofer et al. (1999).

All of the major and several of the minor old-line pentecostal bodies are examined in book-length monographs. A pioneering attempt to sketch in one volume the history of the major Wesleyan and Reformed pentecostal denominations is pentecostal historian Klaude Kendrick's *The Promise Fulfilled: A History of the Modern Pentecostal Movement* (1961).

Not surprisingly, the Assemblies of God (AG), largest and strongest of such groups, is treated most extensively and with most sophistication. One of the first works on the AG produced by an academic was William Menzies's *Anointed to Serve: The Story of the Assemblies of God* (1971). Menzies provides a wealth of carefully researched information about the history and the organizational and doctrinal development of the denomination, including its identification with post–WWII evangelicalism. By far the best is Edith L. Blumhofer, *Restoring the Faith: The Assemblies of God, Pentecostalism, and American Culture* (1993), a revised edition of her *The Assemblies of God*, 2 vols. (1989). Blumhofer meticulously explores the turn-of-the-century social and cultural context in which the AG was born and breaks new ground by demonstrating how strongly restorationist impulses influenced the thinking of first-generation leaders. More generally, Blumhofer's book, in her own words, "is at once a denominational history, an overview of the ideas that describe this constituency's beliefs, and a look at how Pentecostal people have related to American culture." Margaret M. Poloma, *The Assemblies of God at the Crossroads: Charisma and Institutional Dilemmas* (1989), offers a sympathetic study of the AG's structure and ethos, with emphasis on the determinative role the clergy has played in shaping the daily lives of its people. Particular aspects of the AG's development are explored in various dissertations and monographs. The most valuable include Howard N. Kenyon, "An Analysis of Ethical Issues in the History of the Assemblies of God" (diss., Baylor U., 1988), which focuses on the issues of race, women, and war; Gary B. McGee, *This Gospel Shall Be Preached: A History and Theology of Assemblies of God Foreign Missions,* 2 vols. (1986, 1989); and Everett A. Wilson, *Strategy of the Spirit: J. Philip Hogan and the Growth of the Assemblies of God Worldwide, 1960–1990* (1997).

The smaller, long-established pentecostal groups receive careful study in Vinson Synan, *The Old-Time Power: A History of the Pentecostal Holiness Church* (1973; rev. 1986); Charles W. Conn, *Like a Mighty Army: A History of the Church of God* (1955; rev. 1977); Mickey Crews, *The Church of God: A Social History* (1993); James Stone, *The Church of God of Prophecy: History and Polity* (1977); Robert Bryant Mitchell, *Heritage and Horizons: The History of Open Bible Standard Churches* (1982); Deborah V. McCauley, *Appalachian Mountain Religion: A History* (1995), ch. 13, in which she stresses the radically independent, mountain primitivist, vaguely baptist, non-Wesleyan origins of the Church of God tradition; and Donald N. Bowdle, "Holiness in the Highlands," in *Christianity in Appalachia: Profiles in Regional Pluralism,* ed. Bill J. Leonard (1999). The story of the largest Oneness denomination, the United Pentecostal Church, is outlined in Arthur L. Clanton and Charles Clanton, *United We Stand* (Jubilee ed., 1995; originally published by A. L. Clanton in 1970). Joseph H. Howell, "The People of the Name: Oneness Pentecostalism in the United States" (Ph.D. diss., Florida State U., 1985), offers an astute analysis of the religious and cultural dynamics that have animated the Oneness tradition since its inception. Thomas William Miller traces the history of Canada's largest pentecostal groups in *Canadian Pentecostals: A History of the Pentecostal Assemblies of Canada* (1994).

The literature of black pentecostalism is described in Charles Edwin Jones, *Black Holiness: A Guide to the Study of Black Participants in Wesleyan Perfectionist and Glossolalic Pentecostal Movements* (1987). Also valuable is James S. Tinney, *Black Pentecostalism: An Annotated Bibliography*. This special issue of *Spirit: A Journal of Issues Incident to Black Pentecostalism,* 3 (1, 1979), includes a listing of dissertations, books, journal and magazine articles, newspaper articles, relevant book chapters, lists of denominational records, pentecostal periodicals, and some unpublished material. The most recent bibliography is Sherry Sherrod Dupree's *African-American Holiness Pentecostal Movement: An Annotated Bibliography* (1996). In 650 pages it contains over 3,000 entries, including items on religious plays, gospel records, videotapes, newspaper articles, and WPA and FBI reports.

No comprehensive treatment of black pentecostalism in the United States exists, although the Synan (1971), Anderson, and Howell works noted above contain useful chapters, and several Ph.D. dissertations, essays, book chapters, and monographs probe aspects of the black pentecostal experience. For a valuable overview of black Holiness-pentecostal denominations, see David D. Daniels, "Pentecostalism," in *Encyclopedia of African American Religions,* ed. Larry G. Murphy, J. Gordon Melton, and Gary L. Ward (1993). Paul Thigpen provides a brief but useful survey of newer independent black charismatic churches in "The New Black Charismatics," *Charisma and Christian Life* (Nov. 1990). Historical accounts that strongly emphasize the African and African-American origins of pentecostalism include Iain MacRobert, *The Black Roots and White Racism of Early Pentecostalism in the USA* (1988); and Leonard Lovett, "Black Origins of the Pentecostal Movement," in *Aspects of Pentecostal/Charismatic Origins,* ed. Vinson Synan (1975). For denominational histories, see Bishop Ithiel C. Clemmons, *Bishop C. H. Mason and the Roots of the Church of God in Christ* (1996): a helpful addition to the book is an appendix listing 100 old-time songs and choruses favored by the denomination's pioneering generation; Morris E. Golder, *History of the Pentecostal Assemblies of the World* (1973); James L. Tyson, *The Early Pentecostal Revival: History of Twentieth-Century Pentecostals and the Pentecostal Assemblies of the World, 1901–1930* (1992); James C. Richardson, *With Water and Spirit: A History of Black Apostolic Denominations in the U.S.* (1980); William Clair Turner, "The United Holy Church of America: A Study in Black Holiness-Pentecostalism" (Ph.D. diss., Duke, 1984); and Lucille J. Cornelius et al., *The Pioneer: History of the Church of God in Christ* (1975). Cornelius is particularly attentive to the much-neglected role of women in black pentecostalism. The appropriate chapters in George Eaton Simpson, *Black Religions in the New World* (1978); C. Eric Lincoln and Lawrence Mamiya, *The Black Church in the African American Experience* (1990); Hans Baer Singer and Merrill Singer, *African-American Religion in the Twentieth Century: Varieties of Protest and Accommodation* (1992); and Walter J. Hollenweger, *The Pentecostals* (1972) and *Pentecostalism: Origins and Developments Worldwide* (1997) are also helpful.

For historical, anthropological, and sociological case studies, one should consult Cheryl J. Sanders, *Saints in Exile: The*

Holiness–Pentecostal Experience in African American Religion and Culture (1996), which views black Holiness and pentecostal churches as countercultural centers of African-American self-expression and social action; Clarence Taylor, *The Black Churches of Brooklyn* (1994), which demonstrates how these city churches "operated as both accommodating and protest institutions"; Melvin D. Williams, *Community in a Black Pentecostal Church* (1974); and Arthur E. Paris, *Black Pentecostalism: Southern Religion in an Urban World* (1982). The last, an examination of three "storefront" black congregations, seeks to normalize that form of pentecostal expression by showing how it serves enduring social, cultural, and religious needs. For a convenient introduction to black pentecostal leaders, see Sherry Sherrod DuPree, *Biographical Dictionary of African-American Holiness-Pentecostals, 1880–1990* (1989), a collection of more than 1,000 biographical sketches and approximately 300 interviews. On black pentecostal music, consult the two relevant chapters in Jon Michael Spencer, *Protest and Praise: Sacred Music of Black Religion* (1990).

Scholarly resources for the study of socially or culturally marginal pentecostals are sparse for some groups, ample for others. Although non-English-speaking bodies generally have been overlooked, a beginning has been made by Joseph Colletti, who sketches the early history of Chicago's Italian and Scandinavian pentecostals in "Ethnic Pentecostalism in Chicago: 1890–1950" (diss., U. of Birmingham, 1989). Louis De Caro surveys the Italian-American Christian Church of North America in *Our Heritage* (1977); Victor De León writes of the Latin American Assemblies of God in *The Silent Pentecostals* (1979); and Fred Smolchuck provides a brief history of pentecostalism among Slavic immigrants in *From Azusa Street to the U.S.S.R.* (1992). Snake-handling believers in the Southern Appalachians, on the other hand, have been, if anything, overstudied. The best known of such works is Weston LaBarre, *They Shall Take Up Serpents: Psychology of the Southern Snake-Handling Cult* (1962; rev. 1969). See also Dennis Covington, *Salvation on Sand Mountain: Snake Handling and Redemption in Southern Appalachia* (1995); and Mary Lee Daughtery, "Serpent Handlers: When the Sacrament Comes Alive," in *Christianity in Appalachia* (cited earlier). A classic and widely viewed one-hour documentary film, *Holy Ghost People*, graphically depicts the ritual practices of the snake-handling sects. The relation between chronic poverty and pentecostal religion in the southern highlands region is sensitively explored in Troy D. Abell, *Better Felt Than Said: The Holiness-Pentecostal Experience in Southern Appalachia* (1982). For a brilliant portrayal of a slice of Southern Holiness—and indirectly pentecostal—religious behavior, see actor Robert Duvall in the movie *The Apostle*.

A number of pentecostal leaders have attracted the attention of professional historians. Oral Roberts is the subject of a magnificent and scrupulously objective biography by David Edwin Harrell Jr., *Oral Roberts: An American Life* (1985). Aimee Semple McPherson's importance rivals Roberts's. She is the subject of a scholarly biography by Edith Blumhofer, *Aimee Semple McPherson: Everybody's Sister* (1993), which places the evangelist's life and ministry within the nation's larger social and cultural history. Poet and playwright Daniel Mark Epstein has written a sympathetic account, *Sister Aimee: The Life of Aimee Semple Pherson* (1993). For an older account, see Lately Thomas, *Storming Heaven: The Lives and Turmoils of Minnie Kennedy and Aimee Semple McPherson* (1970), which covers the first half of her career in a study that is lively, painfully funny, yet hardly objective. William G. McLoughlin's essay in *Notable American Women*, vol. 2 (1971), provides a competent, brief survey of McPherson's career. Maria B. Woodworth-Etter never attracted wide recognition outside of pentecostal circles, but her influence within them actually may have been greater than Roberts's or McPherson's. Her ministry is traced in an exhaustively researched study by Wayne E. Warner, *The Woman Evangelist: The Life and Times of Charismatic Evangelist Maria B. Woodworth-Etter* (1986). Warner also authored *Kathryn Kuhlman: The Woman behind the Miracles* (1993), a clearly written and even-handed assessment of the life and ministry of one of this century's most influential and flamboyant healing evangelists.

Virtually all historians of American pentecostalism agree that Charles Fox Parham and William J. Seymour rank among the most important of the first generation leaders. Parham is the subject of a first-rate study by James R. Goff Jr., *Fields White unto Harvest: Charles F. Parham and the Missionary Origins of Pentecostalism* (1988), based on his University of Arkansas Ph.D. dissertation. Goff previewed his work in "Charles F. Parham and His Role in the Development of the Pentecostal Movement: A Reevaluation," *Kansas History*, 7 (1984). Goff places Parham, theological founder of the pentecostal movement, within the context both of the 19th-century Holiness movement and the culture and ideology of American Populism. Blumhofer's history of the Assemblies of God (noted above) also contains a revealing chapter on Parham and the early history of Parham's Apostolic Faith Movement. For Seymour, the best resource is Douglas J. Nelson, "For Such a Time as This: The Story of Bishop William J. Seymour and the Azusa Street Revival: A Search for Pentecostal/Charismatic Roots" (diss., U. of Birmingham, 1981). Overstatement weakens Nelson's work. Even so, he unearths a remarkable amount of evidence about Seymour as well as the Azusa Street revival. For brief sketches of pioneer pentecostal evangelist, social critic, and journalist Frank Bartleman's life and ministry, see Vinson Synan, "Introduction: Frank Bartleman and Azusa Street," in Frank Bartleman, *Azusa Street*, ed. Vinson Synan (1980), ix–xxv; Cecil M.

Robeck Jr., "Introduction: The Writings and Thought of Frank Bartleman," in *Witness to Pentecost: The Life of Frank Bartleman*, ed. Donald Dayton (1985), vii–xxiii; and Augustus Cerillo Jr., "The Azusa Street Revival according to Frank Bartleman," an essay included in the papers of the 28th annual meeting of the SPS (1999). Insight into the career of one of the Church of God in Christ's leading female educators can be found in Dovie Marie Simmons and Olivia L. Martin, *Down behind the Sun: The Story of Arenia Cornelia Mallory* (1983). The career of A. J. Tomlinson, who loomed as one of the most influential and colorful figures in early pentecostal history, is brilliantly charted in Roger G. Robins, "Plainfolk Modernist: The Radical Holiness World of A. J. Tomlinson" (Ph.D. diss., Duke, 1999). Finally, *Portraits of a Generation: Early Pentecostal Leaders*, edited by James R. Goff Jr. and Grant Wacker (forthcoming, 2001) contains biographical essays that interpret the lives and influence of more than a dozen pentecostal or quasi-pentecostal pioneers, including Minnie Abrams, Frank Bartleman, Florence Crawford, John Alexander Dowie, William H. Durham, Thomas Gourley, G. T. Haywood, Alice Luce, C. H. Mason, Carrie Judd Montgomery, Antonio Nava, Francisco Olazabal, Ida Robinson, Frank Sandford, George Floyd Taylor, A. J. Tomlinson, Kent White, and Maria Woodworth-Etter.

The theological origins of pentecostalism in the sprawling evangelical subculture of Great Britain and the United States in the late 19th century are traced in Donald W. Dayton, *Theological Roots of Pentecostalism* (1987). Although Dayton stresses the Wesleyan contribution more than most historians, his work stands as the most learned and careful treatment of the theological tributaries to the pentecostalism stream. Another study, which focuses almost exclusively on Reformed and Keswick (as opposed to Wesleyan) influences, is Edith L. Waldvogel [Blumhofer], "The 'Overcoming Life': A Study in the Reformed Evangelical Origins of Pentecostalism" (diss., Harvard, 1977). In her essay "Transatlantic Currents in North Atlantic Pentecostalism," in *Evangelicalism: Comparative Studies of Popular Protestantism in North America, the British Isles, and Beyond, 1700–1990*, ed. Mark A. Noll, David W. Bebbington, and George A. Rawlyk (1994), Blumhofer shows how influences on both sides of the Atlantic mingled to form the early pentecostal movement. Charles W. Nienkirchen focuses on the contributions of Albert Benjamin Simpson's theology and his Christian and Missionary Alliance to later pentecostal—especially Assemblies of God—theological, spiritual, and organizational development in *A. B. Simpson and the Pentecostal Movement* (1992), while D. William Faupel, in *The Everlasting Gospel: The Significance of Eschatology in the Development of Pentecostal Thought* (1996), views American pentecostalism as a millenarian belief system emerging out of 19th-century Perfectionism. The works cited previously by Anderson, Blumhofer

(1989, 1993), Goff, Kendrick, Menzies, Synan, and Wacker also include descriptions of the pre-1900 religious roots of pentecostalism. In "Knowing the Doctrines of Pentecostals: The Scholastic Theology of the Assemblies of God, 1930–1955," in *Pentecostal Currents in American Protestantism*, ed. Edith Blumhofer et al. (1999), Douglas Jacobsen argues for the enduringly normative influence of second-generation pentecostal theologians. The theological heritage of the large minority of pentecostals who adhere to the Oneness position is explored in David A. Reed, "Origins and Development of the Theology of Oneness Pentecostalism in the United States" (diss., Boston U., 1978). Reed provides a brief introduction to Oneness thought in "Aspects of the Origins of Oneness Pentecostalism," in *Aspects of Pentecostal/Charismatic Origins*, ed. Vinson Synan (1975). David K. Bernard offers the most recent treatment of Oneness beliefs in *A History of Christian Doctrine*, vol. 3: *The Twentieth Century* (1999).

Particular aspects of the pentecostal tradition—beyond those that already have been noted—have been closely studied and are worth mentioning here. James R. Goff has explored the connection between pentecostalism and southern gospel music in "The Rise of Southern Gospel Music," *Church History: Studies in Christianity and Culture* 67 (Dec. 1998). Factors that sustained the movement when the glow of the revival began to dim are suggested in several essays by Grant Wacker: "The Functions of Faith in Primitive Pentecostalism," *Harvard Theological Review* 77 (1984); "Playing for Keeps: The Primitivist Impulse in Early Pentecostalism," in *The American Quest for the Primitive Church*, ed. Richard T. Hughes (1988); and "Searching for Eden with a Satellite Dish: Primitivism, Pragmatism, and the Pentecostal Character," in *The Primitive Church in the Modern World*, ed. Richard T. Hughes (1995). Richard M. Riss, *Latter Rain* (1987), describes a significant yet curiously understudied rigorist movement that rocked many pentecostal churches in the middle decades of the century.

There is still a paucity of scholarly work on women in the pentecostal and charismatic movements. In addition to the books by Blumhofer and Warner cited above, see Elaine J. Lawless, "Rescripting Their Lives and Narratives: Spiritual Life Stories of Pentecostal Women Preachers," *Journal of Feminist Studies in Religion* 7 (Spring 1991): 53–71; Mary Elizabeth Jones Jackson, "The Role of Women in Ministry in the Assemblies of God" (diss., U. of Texas, 1997); David G. Roebuck, "Limiting Liberty: The Church of God and Women Ministers, 1886–1996" (diss., Vanderbilt, 1997); the essays by Edith Blumhofer, David Roebuck, Deborah M. Gill, Kurt O. Berends, and Wayne Warner in a special issue devoted to "Women and Pentecostalism" in *Pneuma* 17 (Spring 1995); and R. Marie Griffith, "A 'Network of Praying Women': Women's Aglow Fellowship and Mainline American Protestantism," in *Pentecostal Currents in American*

Protestantism, ed. Edith Blumhofer et al. (1999), and *God's Daughters: Evangelical Women and the Power of Submission* (1997).

Other themes have won scholarly attention. The tradition's distinctive approach to biblical scholarship is analyzed in Russell P. Spittler, "Scripture and the Theological Enterprise," in *The Use of the Bible in Theology: Evangelical Options,* ed. Robert K. Johnston (1985). Spittler also analyzes the ethos of pentecostal worship in "Corinthian Spirituality: How a Flawed Anthropology Imperils Authentic Christian Existence," in *Pentecostal Currents in American Protestantism,* ed. Edith Blumhofer et al. (1999).

Attitudes toward ecumenism are probed in several essays by Cecil M. Robeck Jr.: "A Pentecostal Looks at the World Council of Churches," *The Ecumenical Review* 47 (1995); "The Assemblies of God and Ecumenical Cooperation: 1920–1965," in *Pentecostalism in Context: Essays in Honor of William W. Menzies,* ed. Wonsuk Ma and Robert P. Menzies (1997); "Evangelicals and Catholics Together," *One in Christ* 33 (1997); and "A Pentecostal Assessment of 'Towards a Common Understanding and Vision' of the WCC," *Mid-Stream: The Ecumenical Movement Today* 37 (Jan. 1998). See also the essays by Kilian McDonnell and Jeffrey Gros in *Pneuma* 17 (Fall 1995), a special issue of the journal that focuses on the theme of "Pentecostals in Dialogue." For convenient reprints of the Final Reports of the International Roman Catholic/Pentecostal Dialogues, 1972–1976 and 1985–1989, and commentary, see *Pneuma* 12 (Fall 1990), and for the dialogues, 1990–1998, see *Pneuma* 21 (Spring 1999).

Pentecostals' relation to political culture in general, and to the state in particular, has received extensive examination. Dwight Wilson, *Armageddon Now! The Premillenarian Response to Russia and Israel Since 1917* (1977), describes the movement's political views in general and its enduring fascination with Israel in particular. This book should be placed in the broader cultural context described in Paul Boyer, *When Time Shall Be No More: Prophecy Belief in Modern American Culture* (1992). The pentecostal revival's recent affinity for right-wing politics is highlighted in David Edwin Harrell Jr., *Pat Robertson: A Personal, Political and Religious Portrait* (1987). Journalist Dan Morgan's *Rising in the West: The True Story of an "Okie" Family from the Great Depression through the Reagan Years* (1992) recounts the history of four generations of the pentecostal Tatham family, a real-life counterpart of John Steinbeck's fictional Joad family in *Grapes of Wrath.* Following the former's trek from Oklahoma to California in the 1930s, Morgan shows how they achieved economic and social mobility as well as an affinity for conservative politics. In his 1997 presidential address to the SPS, Grant Wacker reveals the ambivalent relationship of early pentecostals to the civic realm: "Early Pentecostals and the Almost Chosen People," *Pneuma* 19 (Fall 1997). However, all of these works

should be read in conjunction with Everett A. Wilson, "Sanguine Saints: Pentecostalism in El Salvador," *Church History* 52 (1983); Murray W. Dempster, "Pacifism in Pentecostalism: The Case of the Assemblies of God," in *Proclaim Peace: Voices of Christian Pacifism from Unexpected Sources,* ed. Theron F. Schlabach and Richard T. Hughes (1997); "Christian Social Concern in Pentecostal Perspective: Reformulating Pentecostal Eschatology," *Journal of Pentecostal Theology* 2 (Apr. 1993); "Evangelism, Social Concern, and the Kingdom of God," in *Called and Empowered: Global Mission in Pentecostal Perspective,* ed. Murray Dempster, Byron Klaus, and Douglas Peterson (1991); "Pentecostal Social Concern and the Biblical Mandate of Social Justice," *Pneuma* 9 (Fall 1987); Jay Beaman, *Pentecostal Pacifism: The Origin, Development, and Rejection of Pacific Belief among Pentecostals* (1989); Cecil M. Robeck Jr., "The Social Concern of Early American Pentecostalism," in *Pentecost, Mission and Ecumenism: Essays on Intercultural Theology,* ed. Jan A. B. Jongeneel (1992); and Augustus Cerillo Jr., "Pentecostals and the City," in *Called and Empowered: Global Mission in Pentecostal Perspective,* ed. Murray Dempster et al. (1991). These texts show that social and political conservatism have not always been as uniform in the pentecostal tradition as the contemporary North American scene might lead one to suppose.

Although there is no comprehensive treatment of the pentecostal view of healing, its origins are sketched in Dayton (noted above); Grant Wacker, "Marching toward Zion," *Church History* 54 (1985); and in Raymond J. Cunningham, "From Holiness to Healing," *Church History* 43 (1974). The broader cultural context of healing claims receives analysis in Robert Bruce Mullin, *Miracles and the Modern Religious Imagination* (1996). Pentecostal attitudes toward human well-being in general and the post-WWII surge of interest in physical health and financial prosperity in particular are discussed in Grant Wacker, "The Pentecostal Tradition," in *Caring and Curing: Health and Medicine in the Western Religious Traditions,* ed. Ronald L. Numbers and Darrel W. Amundsen (1986; repr. 1998). For a recent sociological assessment of views of healing in one pentecostal denomination, see Margaret M. Poloma, "An Empirical Study of Perceptions of Healing among Assemblies of God Members," *Pneuma* 7 (Spring 1985). The rise and partial demise of independent deliverance ministries in the mid 20th century are traced in David Edwin Harrell Jr., *All Things Are Possible: The Healing and Charismatic Revivals in Modern America* (1975). Two of this book's virtues are its photographs and its extensive bibliographic essay on hard-to-find primary materials. Gordon Lindsay, *John Alexander Dowie: A Life Story of Trials, Tragedies and Triumphs* (1980), stands out as a wide-eyed yet informative biography of the father of modern healing evangelism. C. Douglas Weaver, *The Healer-Prophet: William Marrion Branham: A Study of the Prophetic in American Pentecostalism* (1987), considers the career of this uncannily gifted figure who nearly displaced Oral Roberts as the leader of deliverance evangelism in the 1950s and 1960s.

The following essays, published in Edith Blumhofer et al., *Pentecostal Currents in American Protestantism,* cited above, all deal with adversarial relationships between pentecostalism and other traditions: Grant A. Wacker, "Travail of a Broken Family: Radical Evangelical Responses to the Emergence of Pentecostalism in America, 1906–16"; Daniel Bays, "The Protestant Missionary Establishment and the Pentecostal Movement"; Kurt O. Berends, "Social Variables and Community Response"; Nancy L. Eiseland, "Irreconcilable Differences: Conflict, Schism, and Religious Restructuring in a United Methodist Church"; and Frederick W. Jordan, "At Arms Length: The First Presbyterian Church, Pittsburgh, and Kathryn Kuhlman."

Predictably, pentecostalism has sparked the interest of many social scientists. Much of this literature is described in Kilian McDonnell, *Charismatic Renewal and the Churches* (1976). For a thought-provoking and surprisingly sympathetic study of the social and cultural fabric of the movement, one should see Luther P. Gerlach and Virginia H. Hine, *People, Power, Change: Movements of Social Transformation* (1970). Linguistic analyses of glossolalia and related behavior are summarized in William J. Samarin, *Tongues of Men and Angels: The Religious Language of Pentecostalism* (1972); and in H. Newton Malony and A. Adams Lovekin, *Glossolalia: Behavioral Science Perspectives on Speaking in Tongues* (1985).

Several anthologies that bring together scholarly assessments by historians, theologians, and social scientists have been published in recent years. Some of the better ones include Vinson Synan, ed., *Aspects of Pentecostal/Charismatic Origins* (1975); Russell P. Spittler, ed., *Perspectives on the New Pentecostalism* (1976); Gary B. McGee, ed., *Initial Evidence: Historical and Biblical Perspectives on the Pentecostal Doctrine of Spirit Baptism* (1991); Watson E. Mills, ed., *Speaking in Tongues: A Guide to Research on Glossolalia* (1986); and Edith Blumhofer et al., *Pentecostal Currents in American Protestantism* (1999).

Until recently primary sources, especially from the crucially important pre-WWI years, have proved hard to come by. But growing historical consciousness, especially within the major denominations, has prompted a systematic effort to identify and collect textual and, to a lesser extent, material artifacts of pentecostal culture. A one-volume anthology of documentary materials representing the various periods and aspects of the movement's history does not yet exist, but a 48-volume set does. The latter has been edited by Donald W. Dayton et al. as *"The Higher Christian Life": Sources for the Study of the Holiness, Pentecostal and Keswick Movements* (1984–85). This series contains photographic reproductions

of works by early leaders, such as Elizabeth V. Baker, Frank Bartleman, Andrew Urshan, G. T. Haywood, Frank Ewart, D. Wesley Myland, G. F. Taylor, B. F. Lawrence, Agnes [Ozman] LaBerge, Aimee Semple McPherson, Carrie Judd Montgomery, Charles Fox Parham, and A. J. Tomlinson. Most are taken from original or very early editions. All are relatively rare, some extremely so.

Other primary resources also have become available in recent years. The first 13 issues of the Azusa Mission's newspaper, which ran from Sept. 1906 through May 1908, have been photographically reproduced by Fred T. Corum under the title *Like as of Fire: A Reprint of the Azusa Street Documents* (1981) and reissued as *Azusa Street Papers,* ed. Wayne Warner (1997). These papers are also available on the Internet. Wayne E. Warner, ed., *Touched by the Fire: Patriarchs of Pentecost* (1978; reissued as *Revival! Touched by Pentecostal Fire* [1982]), offers a standard set of first-generation autobiographical accounts. Frank Bartleman's eyewitness report of the Azusa Street revival, published in 1925 as *How "Pentecost" Came to Los Angeles—How It Was in the Beginning,* may well be the most important primary document of all. This volume was edited by Vinson Synan and reissued in unabridged form in 1980 as *Azusa Street.* Edith Blumhofer, in *"Pentecost in My Soul": Explorations in the Meaning of Pentecostal Experience in the Early Assemblies of God* (1989), provides a representative sample of the writings of early AG leaders. Larry Martin has published a user-friendly collection of primary sources on the Topeka revival of 1901 and Azusa Street in a series of small paperbacks, including *In the Beginning: Readings on the Origins of the 20th Century Pentecostal Revival and the Birth of the Pentecostal Church of God* (1994); *The Topeka Outpouring of 1901* (1997); *Holy Ghost Revival on Azusa Street: The True Believers* (1998); and *Azusa Street Sermons by William J. Seymour* (1999). Primary works that defended the distinctive features of pentecostal theology and enjoyed wide support at one time or another include George Floyd Taylor, *The Spirit and the Bride* (1907); D. Wesley Myland, *The Latter Rain Pentecost* (1910); Lilian B. Yeomans, M.D., *Healing from Heaven* (1926); Ralph M. Riggs, *The Spirit Himself* (1949); Charles W. Conn, *Pillars of Pentecost* (1956); and Stanley M. Horton, *What the Bible Says about the Holy Spirit* (1976). From the 1920s to the 1960s no pentecostal theologian exercised greater influence in the United States than the Englishman Donald Gee. Among his many books, *Concerning Spiritual Gifts* (1928; rev. 1937) remains the most influential. Important primary sources bearing on the charismatic movement and its relation to other Christian groups are collected in Kilian McDonnell, ed., *Presence, Power, Praise: Documents on the Charismatic Renewal,* 3 vols. (1980).

Many of the founding figures wrote autobiographies or left autobiographical reminiscences in one form or another.

Some provide a rare glimpse into the inner world of early pentecostalism. Two of the most important include *The Life of Charles F. Parham, Founder of the Apostolic Faith Movement* (privately printed, 1930; repr. 1977), comp. Sarah E. Parham; and *Diary of A. J. Tomlinson*, 3 vols. (1949–1955), ed. Homer A. Tomlinson. The original typescript version of the latter also is available from the Library of Congress. Other autobiographical works, both early and recent, that are particularly worth noting include Elizabeth V. Baker, *Chronicles of a Faith Life* (n.d.; repr. 1984); Mrs. M. B. Woodworth-Etter, *Signs and Wonders* (1916; repr. 1980); Thomas Ball Barratt, *When the Fire Fell and An Outline of My Life* (1927; repr. 1985); Aimee Semple McPherson, *This Is That: Personal Experiences, Sermons and Writings* (1919; rev. 1921, 1923; repr. 1985); J. H. and Blanche L. King, *Yet Speaketh: Memoirs of the Late Bishop Joseph H. King* (1949); Oral Roberts, *The Call: Oral Roberts' Autobiography* (1971); and Pat Robertson, *Shout It from the Housetops* (1972).

Since 1979 the SPS has published *Pneuma*, a journal that deals with a variety of historical, biblical, theological, and occasionally sociological subjects. The same is true of the papers given and made available in bound form each year at the SPS annual meeting, currently held in March. Both strive, not always successfully, to transcend the sectarian defensiveness that still limits the scholarly usefulness of most pentecostal publications. And both offer a continual river of data, insights, and bibliographic tips for serious students of the subject. Another, more recent journal that focuses on pentecostal theological issues but in fact covers much more is the *Journal of Pentecostal Theology*. The AG's *Heritage*, the Church of God's *History & Heritage*, and the International Pentecostal Holiness Church's *Legacy*, all published by these denominations' archival and research centers, offer valuable sources of pentecostal essays, pictures, reminiscences, book reviews, documents, and much more.

Finally, issue number 58 of *Christian History* magazine (Spring 1998) is devoted entirely to the "Rise of Pentecostalism." This sprightly special edition features articles written for a popular audience and an array of rare photos from the early days.

II. HISTORIOGRAPHY.

History and historiography are similar but not identical concepts, more like kissing cousins than twins. The former is the study of past events themselves. The latter is the study of the books and articles that scholars write about past events. In practice this distinction is difficult to maintain, for it is virtually impossible to know the former except as it has been mediated through the latter. Nonetheless, in principle, the difference is clear. History deals with the past, taken by itself, while historiography deals with scholarship *about* the past, and especially the way in which successive generations of historians presuppose and build upon each other's insights. This article deals only with historiography, the way in which historians have interpreted the origins and historical significance of the early pentecostal movement.

A. The Early Historians.

The historiography of modern Western religious movements—which is to say, movements that emerged within Euro-American Christianity during the 19th or 20th centuries—follows a predictable pattern. The first stage of that pattern is widespread lack of interest. This is true of both outsiders and insiders. If a new movement is small, outsiders are bemused; if it is large, they are frightened. Either way, they have better things to do than to worry about why it came into existence. Insiders too are slow to tell the story. Preoccupied with the task of proclaiming their message, they rarely take time to think, much less write, about their origins. And when they do, they instinctively assume that their beginnings were supernatural, directly launched by God outside the channels of ordinary human history. In time, however, movement leaders begin to grow self-conscious about who they are and where they fit on the religious landscape. At that point they also become curious about their roots. First one, then another, and then another sets down recollections about the way it "really was" in the beginning. Eventually someone with a measure of formal education gathers these firsthand accounts into a coherent narrative that identifies the "relevant" influences, establishes the "proper" sequence of events, and orders the "true" hierarchy of importance among leaders.

The books that partisans initially write about themselves almost always come across as self-serving and triumphalist, more like parodies than serious works of history. Even so, they usually merit careful attention. Their musty pages bend under the weight of factual details not available anywhere else and, to the discerning eye, such details illumine the moods and motivations that sustained the revival during its formative years. Further, the first histories of a movement inevitably cast a long shadow over all subsequent efforts to tell the story. They set the terms of the discussion, not only because of the things they do say but also, and perhaps more important, because of the things they do not say. Every effort to include the factors that are deemed relevant to a movement's beginnings is at the same time an effort to exclude the factors that are deemed irrelevant. Later historians may tell the story and construe its significance in radically different ways, but they cannot ignore the interpretations set forth by the pioneer writers.

The work of the earliest historians of the pentecostal movement fits the pattern sketched above. It was fiercely apologetic, but it was packed with information gleaned from firsthand observations, and it offered priceless insights into the social structure and cultural texture of the early days. Later scholars necessarily built on the primitive authors' labor, presupposing their research and borrowing their ideas more often than they realized. For this reason alone it is important to know who the original writers were and what the corpus of their work is like.

The initial historians of the pentecostal movement can be divided into two broad groups. The first consisted of authors who explicitly understood themselves to be writing a comprehensive account of the revival's beginnings. Significantly, no one attempted a work of this sort for more than 15 years, but in 1916 B. F. Lawrence published *The Apostolic Faith Restored*. Although this slender volume purported to offer a general survey of pentecostal origins, it focused almost entirely on events in the lower Midwest, especially in Texas. About a third consisted of Lawrence's personal recollections, while the remainder presented extracts from periodicals and letters from various leaders. More a compilation than a composition, the book proved, nonetheless, singularly valuable, for it was the first sustained effort by a pentecostal writer to survey the movement's beginnings. (As things turned out, the book also proved valuable because it preserved meaty quotations from documents later lost.) In 1925 Frank Bartleman published *How "Pentecost" Came to Los Angeles—How It Was in the Beginning*. Bartleman structured this work as an autobiography, but it was much more than that, since he happened to be one of the leading actors in the unfolding drama in California as well as in other parts of the country. Like most of the early writers, Bartleman was a heavenly minded man. Yet he possessed shrewd historical instincts, a fine eye for significant details, and a colorful writing style filled with memorable one-liners (when Pentecost came to town, he deadpanned, an opposition sect called the Pillar of Fire went "up in smoke"). The following year (1926) Stanley Frodsham published *"With Signs Following": The Story of the Latter-Day Pentecostal Revival* (rev. 1928; rev. and enlarged 1946). Perhaps four-fifths of this work consisted of extracts from periodicals and letters from converts in all parts of the world. Although Frodsham too was principally a compiler, he seemed the first to grasp fully the international dimensions of the revival. Precisely for this reason, perhaps, he drew on a wider range of sources, both in type and in geographical provenance, than either Lawrence or Bartleman.

Two additional attempts to forge a comprehensive account of pentecostal origins did not come out until after WWII, but they should be mentioned here because they were based on notes taken during the initial flowering of the revival. One was *The Phenomenon of Pentecost: A History of "The Latter Rain,"* published by Frank J. Ewart in 1947. Ewart was on hand nearly from the beginning (taking over William H. Durham's mission in Los Angeles in 1912), and he seems to have relied on his own carefully recorded diary entries. Ewart's work highlighted developments on the West Coast and in Asia. In 1958 Ethel E. Goss, the second wife of Howard A. Goss, released *The Winds of God: The Story of the*

Early Pentecostal Days (1901–1914) in the Life of Howard A. Goss, as Told by Ethel E. Goss. This volume claimed to be a slightly edited version of her husband's personal diary, but since the latter is not publicly available, it is difficult to know exactly how much the published version differs from the original. However that may be, H. A. Goss loomed as a key figure in the growth of the movement in the lower Midwest, and he played a pivotal role in the organization of the Assemblies of God. Thus, his autobiography, like Bartleman's, bears a wider significance than the title suggests.

These systematic, book-length efforts by Lawrence, Bartleman, Frodsham, Ewart, and Goss to describe the origins of the movement paralleled another broad category of retrospective writings that might be called "incidental" observations. The latter included essays by authors like Henry G. Tuthill, Minnie F. Abrams, and Mother Emma Cotton, who tried to tell the story in a self-consciously historical fashion but devoted only a brief article or two to the task, usually in now-extinct periodicals, such as *Faithful Standard*, *Word and Work*, or *Message of the "Apostolic Faith."* This category also included theological and polemical expositions by well-known figures, such as Charles Fox Parham, William J. Seymour, and A. J. Tomlinson, and by some not-so-well-known figures, such as Elizabeth V. Baker, A. A. Boddy, and J. G. Campbell. Such expositions were relevant to the growth of pentecostal historiography when they contained, as they often did, recollections about the sequence of events or state of affairs in the early years. Still another source appropriately included under the "incidental" rubric were observations by outsiders. Some, such as Alma White's five-volume autobiography, *The Story of My Life and Pillar of Fire* (1935), remained unremittingly hostile. Others, such as Charles W. Shumway's University of Southern California A.B. thesis, "A Study of the 'Gift of Tongues'" (1914), made no pretense of impartiality but did maintain a measure of objectivity. Documents of this sort are useful because they show how pentecostals were perceived by others, or because they contain data preserved nowhere else, or because they tell a seamy side of the story that insiders overlooked.

What continuities of outlook and interpretation bound these men and women together? The answer is not pure guesswork, but rather a matter of inference, since the original writers did not take time to talk about, much less analyze, the principles that informed their thinking. In order to understand these authors, in other words, we need to ask questions of them that they did not ask of themselves, at least not explicitly.

Our six queries can be divided into two sets. The first set is: (1) In their minds, how was history governed? (2) Where was history headed? (3) How did supernatural causation interact with natural causation? The second set of three is: (4) How was pentecostalism to be defined? (5) How did it get started? (6) Where did the revival fit in the overall pattern of human history? It should be evident that the first three questions, which are general in scope, deal with the early writers' overarching philosophy of history, while the next three, which are quite specific, probe their understanding of the origins and historical significance of the pentecostal movement itself. It is only by combining these two perspectives, the general and the specific, that we can gain an adequately nuanced perspective on the assumptions and arguments that the primitive historians brought to the their work.

1. The Governance of History.

Let us begin, then, with the first question. How did the initial historians conceive the governance of history? Simply stated, who, in their minds, was in charge of human affairs— God or human beings? For most of the early writers the answer was more complicated than we might suppose.

To begin with, pentecostals, like most Christians, assumed that history was providential, which meant that it moved by supernatural guidance from creation to final judgment, whether humans cooperated or not. But unlike most Christians, or at least most modern Christians, pentecostals also believed that God's governance of history was intimately tied up with human responses. Simply stated, God was both sovereign and subject, both changeless and changeable. This state of affairs posed a logical contradiction, of course, but pentecostals did not worry about it very much. They were content to assert on one hand that God stood wholly above and outside of history, and on the other hand also to say that human repentance and obedience—or the lack of them— powerfully affected the timing and the placement of God's actions within history. To take a case in point, pentecostals remained certain that God himself had determined to bring about a worldwide revival to prepare men and women for the Lord's coming. Yet they were equally certain that the exact time and place of the revival depended on human responses. The terrible San Francisco earthquake of 1906 illustrated the paradox. Frank Bartleman argued that God had sent that calamity to San Francisco to alert the city to its spiritual peril, but he also insisted that God had been dissuaded by the prayers of the saints in Los Angeles from sending a similar disaster to the Southern California area. No one knew why the prayers rising from Los Angeles had been more effective than the ones rising from San Francisco. All that they knew was that God assuredly had acted according to his own calculus, and yet human beings had been permitted to stipulate the numbers.

Another way to describe the pentecostal view of history is to say that it resembled a great black line drawn across a page, running from a divinely determined starting point at one end to a divinely determined ending point at the other. Although from a distance the line appeared straight, close up one could see that it contained internal striations running in all directions. The overall pattern, in short, was fixed, but the details were not, for humans were free to obey or disobey God's laws as they wished—and God, in turn, was free to stray from his own predetermined line of behavior as freely or as often as he wished.

2. The Direction of History.

If the governance of history was simultaneously divine and human, so too the direction of history was simultaneously linear and cyclical. Differently stated, history was linear insofar as God exercised control, cyclical insofar as God permitted humans to use and misuse their freedom. Human freedom took a disturbingly repetitive form. Over time vibrant churches would become respectable churches, and respectable churches would become, almost by definition, spiritually cold and lifeless. Sooner or later a small body of saints, humble and repentant, would break away to set up their own fellowship. God would bless them and for a while they too would prosper, but prosperity would lead to pride and pride would lead once again to spiritual death. Throughout the history of Christianity this pattern repeated itself countless times. One gains an image of a single line (providential history) repeatedly looping back on itself (human vicissitudes). (See chart on next page.)

Pentecostals were certain, of course, that their own revival constituted the final cycle of renewal within the timeline of history. Bartleman and perhaps others feared that they too might backslide into apostasy and that another cycle might replace them, but most early writers seem never to have considered that possibility, much less worried about it. Their smugness stemmed from two assumptions. First, they expected the Lord's return momentarily, and thus they could not imagine that there would be time for a relapse. The other and more important assumption was that the historical timeline was, in a sense, curving back to the beginning. The present revival promised to replicate both the form and the power of the apostolic revivals. Thus, the 20th-century revival constituted not merely another round of decay and renewal, but also, and more fundamentally, it was the final cycle that would bring history full circle. When this process was complete, when the present had become a mirror of the beginning, history itself would come to an end.

First-generation pentecostals sometimes talked about these matters in the terms we have been using—cycles of renewal, the full circle of history, and so forth—but ordinarily they used a quite different vocabulary. They called it the promise of the Latter Rain. To unravel the intricacies of Latter Rain theology would require a major essay in itself. Here it is sufficient to say that in their minds the signs and wonders of the apostolic age—including, most notably, speaking in tongues—were destined to reappear at the end of history. When the miracles of the NT church came back after centuries of apostasy and disuse, Christians would know that the

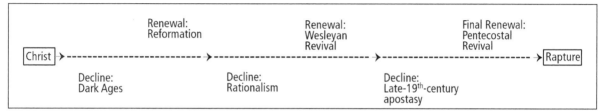

Lord's return was at hand and that history itself was finally drawing to a close.

The early writers' conviction that their revival uniquely replicated the beliefs and practices of the apostolic church partly accounts for their studied *dis*interest (as opposed to simple lack of interest) in the centuries of Christian tradition stretching from the 2d to the 20th centuries. The older denominations, B. F. Lawrence judged, had existed long enough to "establish precedent, create habit, formulate custom." But the pentecostal movement possessed no such history. Rather it leaped the intervening years, crying "BACK TO PENTECOST!" Admittedly, this deliberate disinterest in the Christian tradition sometimes was more apparent than real. From time to time pentecostal historians compared their leaders with Martin Luther, George Fox, and John Wesley, or portrayed their revival as the direct successor to the Irvingite and Holiness revivals of the previous century. Their reasons for doing this are easy to see. Fear of being depicted as schismatics or heretics prompted them to claim at least some measure of continuity with the main body of Christians. Nonetheless, the movement's fundamental impulse was to deny its rootedness in Christian tradition and to insist that it represented the final renewal that would complete history by bringing it full circle.

3. Supernatural vs. Natural Causation in History.

A third prominent feature of the early pentecostal writers' philosophy of history was their eagerness to use supernaturalistic principles of explanation whenever they wished to account for their own beginnings and successes. The opposite side of this trait—and another way of describing it—is to say that they resisted historicist assumptions. The latter might be defined as the supposition, which was virtually universal among professional historians even then, that all social and cultural patterns were products of—and therefore explainable in terms of—antecedent social and cultural patterns. Admittedly, pentecostals used historicist principles adroitly enough whenever they wanted to explain (or more precisely, explain away) their opponents' motivations. But when they considered their own origins, they instinctively dropped historicist principles in favor of supernatural ones. Illustrations are countless. Frank Bartleman was certain that the devil had tried to keep him from attending a revival service by electrocuting the motorman on the streetcar he was riding. Or when Charles F. Parham got into a fight with William H. Durham,

another early leader, over the timing of sanctification, Parham publicly prayed that God would smite dead whoever was wrong—and crowed about the results when Durham died six months later.

This habit of mixing supernatural and natural principles of explanation helps explain the early writers' repeated assertions that God himself had directly produced the movement, with little or no involvement of secondary causes or agencies. One pioneer made this point with memorable simplicity: "The source is from the skies." The denial or at best severe minimalization of human agency helps account for the movement's lack of curiosity about its beginnings. If the source was from the skies, and if human instruments were irrelevant, there really was not much to write about. It is significant that the first major effort by a pentecostal historian to reconstruct the story of the Assemblies of God was Carl Brumback's *Suddenly . . . from Heaven* (1961). Although this work reflected careful research in primary materials, its title hardly could have been more nonhistorical, if not antihistorical, in implication, if not in intent.

The idea that the pentecostal revival had tumbled from the skies like a sacred meteor took another form too. This was the assertion that the fire had fallen more or less simultaneously in all parts of the world, which meant that the revivals on the various continents had been ignited not by sparks of influence from other revivals, but by God himself. One historian typically insisted that the pentecostal stirring had flared up in mission schools in India long before news from the United States could have reached them, and from there it swept around the world, "even though no one had brought the message. It was the Lord's doing." Granted, the early authors occasionally sketched the lines of communication that seemed to link one leader or group with another. Almost everyone noted, for example, that the North Carolina evangelist G. B. Cashwell had been instrumental in carrying the message from Azusa back to the camp meetings of the Southeast. Yet they traced those connections haphazardly. Figuring out who had talked to whom, or who had converted whom, served as interesting sidelights to the story perhaps, but only sidelights. Everyone knew that such connections had little to do with the real reasons the movement had emerged.

4. The Definition of the Movement.

These broad assumptions about the governance, direction, and causal mechanisms that turned the wheels of history informed the early historians' interpretation of how the movement actually began. Before they could explain how it began, however, they first had to decide what pentecostalism was. Differently stated, it was necessary to settle the definitional question—who belonged and who did not—before they could determine where it had started and what kind of people the Lord had used to get it going.

Modern pentecostals commonly think that the practice of speaking in tongues, coupled with the doctrine that tongues is the sole initial physical evidence of the baptism of the Holy Spirit, is and always has been the definitional hallmark of the movement. There can be little doubt that this norm became the litmus test of orthodoxy among pentecostals, especially white ones, after WWI. But the first 10 or 15 years of the movement's life witnessed occasional yet real debate about other definitional features. Howard Goss, for example, highlighted "fast music" as the distinguishing feature of the movement. J. G. Campbell, editor of *The Apostolic Faith* in Goose Creek, TX, believed that the most notable aspect of Parham's Bible school in Topeka (both before and after 1901) was that all property was held in common and that no one held outside jobs. Parham himself at one point even asserted that conditional immortality (that is, the annihilation of the wicked) stood out as the "most important doctrine in the world today." An unnamed Church of God historian writing in the *Faithful Standard* designated baptism by immersion, speaking in tongues, and divine healing as coequal and cardinal doctrines of the movement. Indeed, Elizabeth V. Baker, a prominent evangelist and a founder of the Rochester Bible and Missionary Training Institute, at first debunked the idea that tongues formed the only valid evidence of baptism in the Holy Spirit. To say that stalwarts like Huss and Wesley did not have the baptism, she urged, was the "same as to say that one can live the most Christ-like life, bringing forth all the fruits of the Spirit, *without the Holy Spirit.*" Although Baker soon changed her mind and fell into step, her initial resistance to the necessity of tongues remains noteworthy.

We must be careful, on the other hand, not to overstate the case. For the early historians the outer boundaries of the movement may have been fuzzy, but the inner core was not. Frank Sandford's Shiloh Bible School near Brunswick, ME, presents a case in point. That institution was almost never mentioned in the early historical literature. Why? Throughout the 1890s and the first decade of the 20th century, all of the characteristic beliefs and practices of pentecostalism, including resurrections from the dead, took place at Shiloh. All, that is, except regular speaking in tongues. Although first-generation pentecostals wrangled endlessly about the theological significance of tongues, none doubted that it was a highly coveted part of Christian experience. As a result, the effective absence of tongues at Shiloh precluded it from serious consideration as one of the fountains of the pentecostal revival. In sum, the range of beliefs and behavior patterns that the early writers considered authentically pentecostal proved relatively elastic at the edges but remained firm at the center.

5. Geographical and Social Origins of Pentecostalism.

Keeping these qualifications in mind, then, the early historians' flexibility about the precise boundaries of the revival naturally led to disagreement about where it had started. Some writers, manifestly trying to be generous, suggested that the movement did not have a single historical origin but grew from several sources. Thus, Lawrence and Goss traced the movement's beginnings in about equal measure to the Houston and Los Angeles stirrings of 1905 and 1906, while Frodsham tossed in the Zion City revival of 1904 as another equally important wellspring.

Often, however, the question of origins provoked hot dispute. Not surprisingly, Henry G. Tuthill, a Church of God historian, insisted that the first sprinkle of the Latter Rain had fallen not in Houston, Los Angeles, or Zion City, but in the heart of Church of God country, in Cherokee County, NC, way back in the 1890s. Bartleman blew up when pentecostal newspapers in the Midwest asserted that the California revival had sprung from tributaries in other parts of the country. "We ... prayed down our own revival," he shot back. "The revival in California was unique and separate as to origin." The Los Angeles edition of *The Apostolic Faith* traced the beginning of the "world wide revival" to the Azusa Mission, barely acknowledging its connection, much less provenance, in other streams. Parham was even more adamant about getting the story straight. Seymour, he charged, "drunken with power and flattery," was using all his abilities to prove that "Azuza was the original 'crib' of this Movement." But the plain truth was that the apostolic faith had started in Parham's school in Topeka, KS, Jan. l, 1901, and "all who now accept ... the wildfire, fanatical, wind-sucking, chattering, jabbering, trance, bodyshaking originating in Azuza ... will fall." All in all, Tomlinson took the prize for historical ingenuity by insisting that his group, the Church of God, had only uncovered or made explicit the one true tradition that had been continuously present since the days of the apostles. Thus, the revival had no American beginning at all; it had been passed down directly to the Church of God from the hands of Christ himself.

Just as there was measured disagreement about where the revival had begun, so too there was measured disagreement about who the first pentecostals were. The early historians sometimes debated whether the Wesleyan or the Reformed traditions had fathered the movement, and sometimes they argued about which denominations and sects the initial converts had come from, but in general none of them seem to have been deeply interested in either of these questions. From time to time the racial and ethnic makeup of the movement was discussed. Bartleman, for instance, noted that on the West Coast the revival was led primarily by whites, while Seymour and Mother Cotton emphasized its black origins. Yet by and large the early writers do not seem to have been strongly interested in the racial question either. What all of the first-generation authors were interested in, however, was the movement's social composition.

Two tendencies prevailed. One was to stress its lower-class character. Many proudly pointed out that the revival had started among poor people. If God had waited for middle-class people in the established churches to open their hearts to the Spirit, it never would have happened. That outlook predominated, but there was another—and seemingly opposite—tendency among the early writers to stress the movement's middle- or even upper-middle-class origins. Goss, for example, boasted that some of the "best people" in Texas attended his services. A. W. Orwig remembered that the Azusa Mission attracted all types of people, "not a few of them educated and refined." Pentecostals rarely missed a chance to excoriate secular entertainment, but they also gloated about converts from that world. "One of the results of the revival [in Copenhagen]," Frodsham wrote, "was the salvation of a great Danish actress, Anna Larsen.... Another Danish actress, Anna Lewini, was also saved and filled." Such remarks probably reveal more about the status hunger of the writers than the actual social position of the converts, but they do suggest that the movement was not, in its own historical perception at least, uniformly drawn from the most destitute ranks of society.

6. The Movement's Place in History.

If the early writers evinced healthy debate about the theological, geographical, and social provenance of the movement, they displayed remarkable unanimity when they assessed its significance in the history of Christianity. Simply stated, they all believed, without exception, that the eyes of the world were fixed squarely upon them. Nine months after the Azusa Mission opened, *The Apostolic Faith* headlined a brief survey of its development with the words: "Beginning Of World Wide Revival." Eleven months later Bartleman exuberantly claimed that the California work was "spreading worldwide." Parham and Tomlinson insisted that the events taking place in northeastern Kansas and in western North Carolina served as the pivot of a global revival. By 1922 the *Faithful Standard* was prepared to assure its readers that this was, quite simply, the "greatest revival the world has ever known." However parochial these spokesmen may have been, they also—paradoxically—reflected a global consciousness that was grandly imperial in scope.

The image, here, of a revival focal point radiating outward around the earth effectively contradicted the other image, which pentecostals also cherished, of causally unconnected stirrings simultaneously springing up all around the world. But that contradiction did not bother anyone, because the issue was not causation but consummation; not "Where did it all come from?" but rather "What did it all mean?" In their minds the pentecostal revival loomed as the fulfillment of history, the end toward which everything was moving. As noted before, the early historians remained certain that the present revival signaled the beginning of the Latter Rain, the apocalyptic events of the last days. Differently stated, the "signs and wonders" of the present revival constituted dispensational occurrences, designed, as evangelist Elizabeth Baker put it, to "ripen the grain before the Husbandman gathers it." In Tomlinson's words, the purpose of the outpouring was to bring about the "evangelization of the world, [the] gathering of Israel, [the] new order of things at the close of the Gentile age." No one captured the universal and radically primitivist sweep of their vision better than Ewart: "By one great revolutionary wrench," he exclaimed, God "is lifting His church back over the head of every sect, every creed, every organized system of theology, and [putting] it back where it was in power, doctrine and glory, on and after the Day of Pentecost."

The nonpentecostal historian Robert Anderson has argued that "fratricidal brawling" marked early pentecostal life. He is right, yet it is important to see that most of those brawls were not personal controversies but ideological disputes about one's position in history. Jostling for pride of place provoked endless arguments over which branch of the movement was going to win in the long run. Ewart, for example, who stood on the Reformed side of the tradition, wrote off his Wesleyan rivals as "inconsequential ... die-hards." Parham dismissed those who were attempting to organize the Assemblies of God as a "bunch of imitating, chattering, wind-sucking, holy-roller preachers." On and on it went. The one thing they all could agree upon was that the Holiness churches, who had rejected the pentecostal message, were all but washed up; the tide of history had passed them by. Most Holiness people, charged the *Faithful Standard*, were now back into "formal churches, or out all together.... It is difficult to find a little group of Holiness people anywhere." Pentecostals were convinced beyond question that they, and they alone, were riding the crest of history. When Frodsham drew an analogy between the apostle John's effort to write a narrative of the "things which Jesus did" and his own effort to describe "how the Holy Spirit fell in ... this twentieth century," he may have revealed more about his assumptions than he intended.

This survey of the early historians' general philosophy of history, variegated view of the theological, geographical, and social origins of the movement, and their unanimous conviction of its pivotal place in world history brings us finally to the question of reliability. Bluntly stated, is their work trustworthy? Are the golden oldies of pentecostal historiography still worth playing?

The initial answer is no—not if we expect their books and articles to serve as reliable representations of what "really happened." All historical works are of course interpretive. None offers a God's-eye view of anything. But some come closer than others. And by the standards of modern, professional scholarship, the writings of self-ascribed historians, such as Bartleman and Frodsham, not to mention the historical recollections of popular leaders like Parham and Tomlinson, were far from reliable. Yet here we need to be as precise as possible. While simple factual errors of name, date, place, and sequence marred the works of all of the early writers, such mistakes probably were no more numerous than in any good newspaper. The real problems, rather, were defensiveness and lack of critical standards.

Defensiveness showed up as a determination to omit anything that might reflect poorly on the pentecostal message. A few writers, such as Bartleman, let the chips fall where they might, but most steered clear of controversy. The long-standing eclipse of Parham offers a case in point. According to contemporary newspaper reports, in the summer of 1907 Parham was arrested in Houston and charged with committing an "unnatural" act. Although the charge was never proved, from that point forward pentecostal historians went out of their way to minimize his contribution. Some, such as Lawrence, mentioned his name two or three times but no more than absolutely necessary in order tell the story. Others, such as Frodsham, pretended that Parham had never existed. (Indeed, by consistently using the passive mood—"a school was built," "a revival was held"—Frodsham managed to write two entire chapters about Parham's schools and revivals without once mentioning his name.) Unfortunately, Frodsham set the tone for the next half-century. Not until 1961, when Klaude Kendrick published his University of Texas Ph.D. dissertation as *The Promise Fulfilled: A History of the Modern Pentecostal Movement*, was Parham's crucial role in the articulation and propagation of the pentecostal message finally brought to light.

Frodsham's defensiveness proved typical of the first-generation writers. If they had had their way, the contribution of any leader who did not fully toe the line would have been forever buried in the mists of the passive mood. The sentiment was laudable, but the result was not, for in their zeal to protect the movement they omitted many deserving figures whom they disliked or considered unsound. Besides being unfair, such edginess proved counterproductive. Sanitizing the story rendered it less than believable and thus guaranteed that unsympathetic outsiders would step in to fill the lacuna with exaggerated tales of sexual and financial misconduct.

A more serious deficiency in the work of the early historians was their lack of critical standards. They were unable or unwilling to see that sound historical writing consisted of the presentation of publicly available facts and the interpretation of those facts in terms of publicly available theories of human motivation and social change. Simply stated, they failed to recognize that history was not theology. Figuring out what God had or had not done in human history should have been the business of the theologian, not the historian. But pentecostal writers almost never understood this. They rarely realized that when they forthrightly made God the central actor in their stories, they made their works unpersuasive to outsiders, not because outsiders were necessarily irreligious, or even unsympathetic, but because theological assertions smuggled in as historical "facts" violated the rules by which the game was played.

This was not the end of the matter, however. If the golden oldies were unreliable as conventional historical works, they were, nonetheless, useful as "ritualizations" of pentecostal history. They presented a version of the past that was congruent with the theological and institutional needs of the movement at the time that they were written. Hence the data were filtered and the interpretations of the data were simplified and dramatized to make them serve the larger purposes of the movement. Davis Bitton's assessment of early Mormon history writing is equally applicable to that of the early pentecostals. Ritualized history, he pointed out, "was not invention." Rather, it was history cast in the form of a morality play.

> Seized upon as a useful symbol of the struggle of darkness against light, of the triumph of the latter, and of God's providential care over his Saints, the incident was simplified, dramatized and commemorated. . . . New converts, as part of their assimilation into the body of the faithful, could easily master the simplified history and accept it as their own. ("The Ritualization of Mormon History," *Utah Historical Quarterly* 43 [1975])

Examples of the ritualization of pentecostal history abound. One of the more egregious was white racial bias. The problem here was not that the presence of blacks was denied, but that the influence of black leaders received little attention. A more serious distortion was male bias. The pivotal role of women pastors and evangelists, such as Aimee McPherson, Emma Cotton, Julia Delk, Maria Woodworth-Etter, Carrie Judd Montgomery, Elizabeth V. Baker, and Susan Duncan, was systematically eclipsed in the historical literature. Or again, the primary evidence contained hints that Lucy Farrow may have been as instrumental as William Seymour in bringing about the Azusa Street revival, yet male historians—both black and white—consistently overlooked that data.

The most persistent form of distortion was, however, theological. Time and again the early historians allowed their theological desires to shape, if not create, their facts, rather than the reverse. One especially clear example of this tendency was the way in which the events that took place in

Parham's Bible school in Topeka, KS, in the fall and winter of 1900 was reported. As the conventional story went, the students in the school *first* read the account of the Day of Pentecost in the book of Acts, *then* sought the baptism of the Holy Spirit with the evidence of speaking in tongues. However, from the beginning there was substantial evidence that the events in the Topeka Bible School followed the reverse sequence. As Robert Anderson and other professional historians recently have shown, after sustained prayer and fasting, the students first started to speak in tongues and, then, in an effort to figure out what it might mean, started to search the NT for similar occurrences in apostolic times.

Why did the early writers insist on telling the story the other way around? The answer is clear: the "ritualized" version suggests that the normativeness of speaking in tongues was, or at least ought to have been, self-evident to anyone who read Acts 2 with an open mind and honest heart. As J. Roswell Flower put it in 1950 in a typescript history of the Assemblies of God, "These students had *deduced* from God's Word that in apostolic times, the speaking in tongues was considered to be the initial physical evidence of a person's having received the baptism in the Holy Spirit.... It was this decision which has made the Pentecostal Movement of the Twentieth Century" (italics added). Flower's last sentence is particularly revealing. From the beginning, the traditional pentecostal denominations have distinguished themselves from other evangelicals, especially from their Holiness rivals, by their insistence on the necessity of tongues. Yet that doctrine has been perennially disputed, not only by outsiders, but also by a vocal minority within the movement. Thus, institutional needs have determined that a particular version—a ritualization—of the events that took place in Topeka in 1901 would prevail.

In sum, the works of the primitive historians are not satisfactory for all purposes. They are simplified, designed to celebrate that which they thought should be celebrated. "Those who probe more deeply," Bitton has written, "are bound to discover that men of the past were not one-dimensional and, more essentially, that the past was not that simple. Historians have a duty to criticize and correct inaccurate, inadequate, or oversimplified versions of the past." Yet it is equally important to remember that arguments about one's true history are usually struggles between forms of legitimacy, not between legitimacy and illegitimacy. Students of pentecostal history need to learn, in short, how to take the early histories in stride, respect them for what they are worth, and remember that we all see through a glass darkly.

B. Recent Historians.

Building on the work of these early historians, contemporary scholars since the 1950s have continued to probe the question of pentecostal origins. They have taken at least four interpretive approaches—the providential, the genetic, the

multicultural, and the functional—to conceptualizing and understanding how, why, and where the pentecostal movement emerged and survived during the first two decades of the 20th century. Few historians use only one approach in their interpretative accounts of pentecostalism's beginnings; they often combine any number of the four or even employ different approaches in separate publications. For example, several have combined a providential approach, which they share with pentecostalism's earliest chroniclers, with a multicultural approach, arguing that God, in pouring out a new Pentecost at the turn of the 20th century chose to use black Americans as his instruments to bring revival and a new Christian community into being. Other historians have combined a genetic approach with a functional approach, arguing that the 19th-century religious currents that ultimately fed into and shaped a new 20th-century pentecostalism were not a string of disembodied ideological forces that in some predetermined fashion came together in a new religious movement, but rather a collection of religious ideas and behaviors that flourished in pre-WWI America because they met the religious, emotional, status, and economic needs of a group of Americans who became pentecostal adherents. The balance of this essay will briefly describe these four modern approaches to pentecostal origins by citing the literature pertinent to each. The works of several scholars will be discussed in more than one category.

1. The Providential Approach.

The providential interpretation of pentecostal origins, which, as discussed above, dominated accounts of pentecostal beginnings by participants in the revival, has continued to inform the histories written by pentecostal ministers or church officers and a few modern scholars.

For example, Charles Conn of the Church of God, Cleveland, TN, and Carl Brumback of the Assemblies of God, both authors of popular histories of their respective denominations, attributed pentecostalism's eruption to God (Brumback, *Suddenly ... from Heaven: A History of the Assemblies of God* [1961]; Conn, *Like a Mighty Army: A History of the Church of God, 1886–1976,* [rev. ed., 1977]). "We Pentecostals regard the absence of a progenitor of our own Movement as an indication that this mighty revival was begotten directly by an extraordinary outpouring of the Holy Spirit," Brumback triumphantly wrote. "We believe that the facts warrant an affirmative answer to the slightly paraphrased question, 'Hath not the Latter Rain been our father?'" Pentecostals have "no earthly 'father'"; the movement is "in a definite sense, a 'child of the Holy Ghost,'" he further boasted. Conn knowingly asserted that the pentecostal awakening, unlike other revivals, was "not the work of any one man or group of men. Distinctively, it appeared spontaneously and simultaneously in many far flung regions of the world."

Despite their common stress on the providential nature of pentecostal origins, Brumback and Conn differed significantly in the emphases they placed on specific events and personalities that they claimed the Almighty used to construct the internal history of early pentecostalism and their respective denominations. Brumback acknowledged that "charismatic aspects of New Testament life," including speaking in tongues, had surfaced in diverse settings among late-19th-century believers seeking revival; that the 20th-century "pentecostal outpouring" began at Parham's Bethel Bible College but "received its greatest impetus" and became "a movement with a world-wide mission" only at Azusa Street under William J. Seymour's wise leadership. Conn, seeking to place the early history of the Church of God at the center of pentecostal beginnings, ignored Parham and Topeka altogether, acknowledged Seymour and Azusa Street only in a footnote, and, not very convincingly, sought to establish a direct line of continuity running from the post-1900 pentecostal movement back to the Holiness revival at Camp Creek, NC, in 1896, and more dubiously even further back to the creation of the Christian Union by R. G. Spurling 10 years earlier in Monroe County, TN.

The volumes by Conn and Brumback, still in print and widely read by pentecostals, have kept alive what might be termed the "classical" providential interpretation of pentecostal beginnings sketched by the initial historians of the movement. Conn's and Brumback's writings, therefore, represent a link between the "golden oldies" previously discussed and a more recent attempt by a few pentecostal scholars to reassert the primacy of the providential view of pentecostal origins. These writers challenged what they consider the reductionist tendencies of secular authors to dismiss arbitrarily the reality of the supernatural in human affairs.

The publications of social ethicist Leonard Lovett ("Black Origins of the Pentecostal Movement," in Vinson Synan, ed., *Aspects of Pentecostal-Charismatic Origins* [1975]), historian Vinson Synan (*In the Latter Days: The Outpouring of the Holy Spirit in the Twentieth Century* [1984]), and missiologist Paul A. Pomerville (*The Third Force in Missions* [1985]) illustrated the modern providentialist stream in the historiography of pentecostal origins. In the early 1970s Lovett used the Latter Rain theory popularized by the pioneer generation of pentecostal historians to provide the overarching interpretive framework for his view of the origins of pentecostalism. "Belief in the Latter Rain theory presupposes a 'faith' stance," he wrote. "I share and embrace such a stance unashamedly." On the basis of such a theory Lovett dogmatically asserted that at Azusa Street "the Latter Rain poured"; earlier manifestations of the Spirit, including what took place under Charles F. Parham at Topeka, KS, in 1901, were only "early raindrops of the Latter Rain."

Interpreting pentecostalism more broadly, historian Synan recently has viewed the development of classical pentecostalism, the Protestant and Roman Catholic renewal movements, and the so-called third wave or evangelical practitioners of signs and wonders, as phases of a singular pentecostal movement, "variations on one Holy Spirit movement with one common factor of Spirit Baptism accompanied by glossolalia and/or other gifts of the Spirit." Much like early pentecostal writers, he viewed this century's pentecostal explosion as the biblically implied "latter rain" outpouring of God's Spirit promised in Scripture to precede the Lord's return. Moreover, he labeled pentecostals and charismatics "The Latter-Rain People," and throughout *In the Latter Days* employs "rain" terminology to entitle his chapters. "The Rain Falls in America" sketched the rise of the pentecostal movement; "The Rain Falls around the World" treated pentecostalism's early global expansion; "The Rain Rejected" discussed opposition to pentecostalism; three chapters, "The Rain Reconsidered," "The Rain Falls on Roman Catholics," and "The Cloudburst" traced the story of pentecostalism's emergence among first mainline Protestants, then Roman Catholics, and finally evangelicals and others. Unlike his classical pentecostal predecessors, Synan is a professionally trained historian and author of a very significant book that stressed the roots of the pentecostal movement in 19th-century Holiness and Methodist religious developments. Thus, he also paid serious attention to the historical antecedents and worldly influences that shaped the rise of pentecostalism.

Missiologist Pomerville recognized, much as did historian Synan, the significance of what he called the horizontal "historical-causal" factors that operated to produce the modern pentecostal revival, but he additionally argued that any theory of pentecostal origins must give "a priority role to the divine dimension of the Movement." The pentecostal movement, he asserted, "is a renewal of the Holy Spirit first and foremost. Only secondly is it an effort of men to reinstitute a neglected apostolic orientation to the contemporary church." Unlike Synan and Lovett, however, who located pentecostalism's beginnings in the U.S., Pomerville asserted that pentecostalism was birthed by a series of roughly spontaneous global outpourings of the Holy Spirit. This missiologist not only widened the geographic scope of pentecostal beginnings, but also lengthened the birthing time of the movement, reaching back into the 19th century to include Edward Irving's Catholic Apostolic Church, the Welsh revival of 1904–5, revivals in Russia in 1862, Armenia in 1880, and other "early Pentecostal outpourings of the Spirit in Northern Europe and Asia at the turn of the century." Thus, for Pomerville, "the universal and spontaneous origins of the Movement point to the divine dimension of the Movement as the crucial dimension in understanding causation."

The contemporary providential approach opens for consideration the role of God in human history by insisting on the reality of spiritual forces working both in the human agents who make history and in the broader structures of society and culture. But there are limitations to the providential approach to history, including pentecostal history. In *A Christian View of History?* ed. George M. Marsden and Frank Roberts (1975), historian Marsden makes the point that Christian historians certainly can assert that God works in history as well as in the human heart, but he went on to state that "outside of biblical revelation we do not know clearly his precise purposes in permitting particular historical developments." He further suggested that it is extremely difficult to judge the genuineness of a conversion or to be sure of the relative importance of spiritual as against other factors that motivate human behavior. Marsden's contentions, if accepted, severely limit the persuasiveness of the providential approach to pentecostal origins even for pentecostal historians. Furthermore, because the providential interpretation of pentecostal origins cannot be verified by research and interpretive methods commonly accepted within the historical profession, it will not gain a place in mainstream religious historiography.

2. The Genetic Approach.

Currently the genetic approach to pentecostal origins is used by a majority of historians. It stems from the recognition by scholars that early American pentecostalism shared many of its doctrinal beliefs, leadership and organizational polities, behavioral practices, and social thought with prior 19th-century Holiness and evangelical movements. This approach, therefore, tends to stress the continuity of 20th-century pentecostalism with 19th-century religious and social developments: the pentecostal revival is seen as part of a continuous flow of revivalistic religion that spanned both sides of the turn of the century. Because of the diverse nature of pentecostalism and its two-decades-long formative period, historians focusing on the 19th-century roots of the movement have divided over which and how many of the theological, social, and behavioral strands that comprised Gilded Age evangelicalism carry the most explanatory power for an adequate understanding of pentecostal origins and institutional development. Initially they divided into two schools of thought, one stressing the Wesleyan Holiness contributions and the other, the non-Wesleyan or Reformed Evangelical sources. More recently scholars have incorporated these and other strands of the Gilded Age evangelical subculture into more multivariate analyses of the pre-1900 religious contributions to pentecostalism.

Pioneer pentecostal historian Klaude Kendrick, in his book *The Promise Fulfilled*, and Vinson Synan, in his first scholarly book on pentecostal history, sketched out the contours of the Wesleyan roots of pentecostalism. Missing from their accounts, both revised doctoral dissertations, were overt statements about the role of providence in pentecostalism's arrival. There was no latter rain, or for that matter any other theories of causation, employed as overarching interpretive frameworks for their narratives. Their published research, taken as a whole, convincingly demonstrated, in the words of Assemblies of God historian Kendrick, that the 19th-century Holiness movement "prepared fertile ground from which modern Pentecost could ultimately spring." In his *The Holiness-Pentecostal Movement,* Synan nicely summarizes the case for the link between Wesleyan Methodism and pentecostalism:

> The pentecostal movement arose as a split in the Holiness movement and can be viewed as the logical outcome of the Holiness crusade which had vexed American Protestantism for 40 years, and in particular the Methodist Church. The repeated calls of the Holiness leadership after 1894 for a "new Pentecost" inevitably produced the frame of mind and the intellectual foundations for just such a "Pentecost" to occur. In historical perspective the pentecostal movement was the child of the Holiness movement, which in turn was a child of Methodism. Practically all the early Pentecostal leaders were firm advocates of sanctification as a "second work of grace" and simply added the "Pentecostal baptism" with the evidence of speaking in tongues as a "third blessing" superimposed on the other two. Both Parham and Seymour maintained fully the Wesleyan view of sanctification throughout their lives.

The historical studies of Kendrick, Synan, and others that demonstrated the Wesleyan Holiness contributions to pentecostalism were significantly supplemented and supported by the scholarship of historical theologian Donald Dayton. In his *Theological Roots of Pentecostalism,* Dayton identified four core theological tenets of pentecostalism—the doctrines of salvation, healing, baptism in the Holy Spirit, and the second coming of Jesus Christ—and in several closely reasoned chapters provided a convincing intellectual history of the genesis, development, and changing meanings of these doctrinal strands as they evolved in Holiness circles over the 19th century, ultimately to coalesce within pentecostalism. Although he stressed the Wesleyan Holiness contribution to the distinctive pentecostal theological gestalt, he also noted the contributions to a later pentecostalism of more Reformed, evangelical, and higher-life advocates of holiness who emphasized the very important notion of a baptism of the Spirit as an enduement of power. Dayton therefore, as Douglas Sweeney noted in "The 'Strange Schizophrenia' of Neo-Evangelicalism: A Bibliography" (*Evangelical Studies Bulletin* 8 [Spring 1991]), pointed the way from the Holiness side of pentecostal historiography toward a synthesis of Wesleyan and Reformed contributions to pentecostal thought.

Dayton's important study, then, clearly established that "nearly every wing of late nineteenth-century revivalism was teaching in one form or another all the basic themes of pentecostalism except for the experience of glossolalia, or 'speaking in tongues.'" This being the case, he wrote, "the whole network of popular 'higher Christian life' institutions and movements constituted at the turn of the century a sort of pre-pentecostal tinderbox awaiting the spark that would set it off." Accordingly, it was "no accident that Pentecostalism emerged when it did"; or as Dayton unhesitatingly stated in an earlier essay, the emergence of pentecostalism "may be seen as a natural development of forces that had been set in motion much earlier" ("From 'Christian Perfection' to the 'Baptism of the Holy Ghost,'" in Synan, ed., *Aspects of Pentecostal-Charismatic Origins* [1975]).

If Dayton's book showed the ideological connections between 19th-century Holiness doctrinal currents and pentecostalism, a year later historian James R. Goff Jr., in *Fields White unto Harvest: Charles F. Parham and the Missionary Origins of Pentecostalism* (1988), provided a detailed, sharply focused account of how the diverse religious strands that fed into pentecostalism and the social strains experienced by Holiness people came together in one individual, the Holiness preacher Charles F. Parham, who responded by formulating the theological tenet—tongues as the Bible evidence of Holy Spirit baptism—that produced a pentecostalism distinct from the Holiness and evangelical movements out of which it emerged. More clearly than anyone before him, Goff showed how Parham, during the turbulent decade of the 1890s, drew from a variety of personal, family, and Holiness religious sources, including the teachings of radical Holiness leaders Benjamin Hardin Irwin and Frank Sandford, the theological building blocks on which he constructed his historically significant pentecostal doctrine. Goff explained how Parham had come to his concept of "missionary tongues"— Parham believed that tongues were actual existing languages given to Holy Spirit baptized believers to expedite world evangelization in the last days before the second coming of Christ—as early as 1899. That year he received a report published in a Holiness periodical indicating that a young woman named Jennie Glassey, associated with Sanford's Shiloh community, had spoken in an African dialect after receiving a missionary call to Africa. Such missionary tongues, Parham informed his followers, duplicated the apostles' experience recorded in Acts 2. (See also Goff's "Initial Tongues in the Theology of Charles Fox Parham," in Gary B. McGee, ed., *Initial Evidence* [1991].)

Goff's biography significantly added historiographical clout to the view that the initial-evidence doctrine, first formulated by Parham, fundamentally defined pentecostalism and "in effect, created the Pentecostal movement." His book's "dual thesis," Goff summarized, "is that Charles Parham founded the pentecostal movement in Topeka, Kansas, early

in 1901 and that the essential character of this new faith revolved around an intense millenarian-missions emphasis." Kendrick, Synan, Dayton, and Goff effectively outlined the Wesleyan side of the Gilded Age Holiness beliefs that fed into a later pentecostalism. Concurrently, other historians argued that non-Wesleyan Reformed and evangelical higher-life currents more adequately accounted for the theological and political contours of contemporary non-Wesleyan pentecostal denominations. For example, Edith Blumhofer (née Waldvogel) devoted four out of the six chapters comprising her 1977 doctoral dissertation at Harvard University, "The 'Overcoming Life': A Study in the Reformed Evangelical Origins of Pentecostalism," to an extended discussion of the theological contributions of non-Wesleyan evangelicals, such as Reuben A. Torrey, Albert B. Simpson, Dwight L. Moody, and various British Keswick leaders, to what she called "Reformed Pentecostal theology": insistence on the need for a Holy Spirit baptism separate from conversion, belief in sanctification as a progressive overcoming of sin and not as an instantaneous eradication of the sinful nature, advocacy of the premillennial return of the Lord, and healing in the atonement. Historian Robert Anderson's general interpretative approach to pentecostal origins will be discussed later in this essay, but in his *Vision of the Disinherited: The Making of American Pentecostalism* (1979) he weighed in emphatically on the issue of the Reformed versus Wesleyan theological sources of pentecostalism:

> The Keswick movement . . . was absolutely crucial to the development of Pentecostalism. Thus, I find it necessary to reject the central thesis of Synan that "the historical and doctrinal lineage of American Pentecostalism is to be found in the Wesleyan tradition." To the contrary, that wing of Pentecostal movement which had earlier connections with Wesleyanism became Pentecostal by accepting Keswick (i.e., Calvinist) teachings on dispensationalism, premillennialism and the Baptism of the Holy Spirit. . . . In short, the Pentecostal movement was as much a departure from the Wesleyan tradition as a development from it.

Inevitably historians stressing the genetic approach combined into a holistic narrative of pentecostal origins the multiple strands of late-19th-century evangelical and Wesleyan Holiness religious thoughts and practices. Although this synthetic path had been plowed earlier by historians cited previously in this essay—John Thomas Nichol, William Menzies, Donald Dayton—and had been most fully developed by Blumhofer in her previously cited history of the Assemblies of God, historian Grant Wacker, in an essay on pentecostalism in Charles H. Lippy and Peter W. Williams, eds., *Encyclopedia of American Religious Experience,* vol. 2 (1988), comprehensively weaved together in his analysis of pentecostal roots the major 19th-century Holiness strands that fed into an emerging pentecostal movement at the turn of the

20th century. He wrote that "Pentecostalism was the product of clashing forces within the vast and amorphous Holiness movement that had swept across evangelical Protestantism in the last third of the nineteenth century." More specifically he described pentecostal antecedents in terms of the "fusion" or "confluence" of the Wesleyan doctrine of entire sanctification, the Reformed idea of a baptism of power for Christian service, the Plymouth Brethren notion of dispensational premillennialism, and the evolving evangelical theology and practice of faith healing. At the same time, he resisted both a crude determinism and an oversimplification of what was a dynamic and complex interplay of religious ideas and practices: "As the century drew to a close," he wrote, "these various traditions collided, broke apart, and reassembled in unpredictable ways." Nevertheless, he pointed out, the common element in all of these facets of the Holiness movement was a commitment "to the doctrine and experience of baptism in the Holy Spirit."

In contrast to the providential view, the genetic approach to pentecostal origins fits centrally within the traditional concern of historians with issues of historical change and continuity. As it applies to pentecostal history, the search for the 19th-century roots or sources of pentecostal religious beliefs and practices has unearthed, and is still unearthing, a wealth of information and new insights into Gilded Age black and white Holiness and evangelical religion. Just as we now know that significant aspects of Progressive Era reform had antecedents in late-19th-century reform thought and movements, so too do we now know that the pre-WWI pentecostal revival shared much with revivalistic religion that flourished before the turn of the 20th century.

The stress on continuity, however, can blur what was in fact new, or at least different, about the modern pentecostal movement: its insistence that glossolalia was the biblical evidence of the baptism of the Holy Spirit, differences of opinion about the meaning and purpose of the baptism notwithstanding. Even Donald Dayton, for all his stress on the continuity of pentecostalism with 19th-century Holiness thought, also rightly warned against overemphasizing the old over against what was new in pentecostalism. "The search for 'antecedents' and 'roots' may uncover parallels and continuities to the overshadowing of novelty and discontinuity," he wrote in the previously discussed *Theological Roots of Pentecostalism.* What was theologically new in pentecostalism, that "spark" as he called it, was the teaching that glossolalia was the biblical evidence of the baptism of the Holy Spirit. That belief, he admitted in his 1987 book, was "not a natural part of the currents" that he had described in his study and therefore constituted "a significant novum for the most part that truly does set Pentecostalism apart from the other 'higher Christian life' movements." Dayton thus left open the door to a consideration of what in early pentecostalism may have been unique and thus discontinuous with 19th-century evan-

gelicalism. This then raises anew the question of the sources of that "hairsbreadth of difference," to borrow Dayton's language, and what an answer might imply for an analysis of pentecostal origins. It also opens up for consideration redefinitions of pentecostalism that would require historians to consider additional causative events and ideas operating on both sides of 1900.

3. The Multicultural Approach.

A third interpretative approach offers an entry into pentecostal beginnings via the role of ethnic and racial minorities, especially Latinos and African Americans. (Though not free of complications, we use *ethnic* and *racial* in a historical sense to refer to the differing social experiences of culturally Anglo and non-Anglo pentecostals and of white and black pentecostals.) This approach, explains pentecostal historian David Daniels, seeks to redefine pentecostalism "as a multicultural phenomenon rather than deeming white Pentecostalism as normative" ("Dialogue between Black and Hispanic Pentecostal Scholars: A Report and Some Personal Reflections," *Pneuma* 17 [Fall 1995]). Daniels echoed the earlier sentiments of Church of God in Christ scholar and churchman Bishop Ithiel Clemmons. In his 1981 presidential address to the mostly white Society for Pentecostal Studies, Clemmons blamed the racial blindness of white theologians and historians for what he called the shameful neglect of the contributions of "people of color" to the story of pentecostal origins. ("True Koinonia: Pentecostal Hopes and Historical Studies," *Pneuma* 4 [Spring 1982]). A multicultural perspective, utilizing ethnic and racial as well as white primary and secondary sources, Daniels stated, would help "us in recognizing the various streams of nineteenth-century Protestantism which shaped early Pentecostalism." It would also, he suggested, clarify the social, theological, and political diversity that exists within the various white, black, and ethnic pentecostal groups.

Thus far little scholarly work has been done on the roles played by Latino and other ethnic groups in pentecostal history, but that is changing. Important recent contributions include Gaston Espinosa, "Borderland Religion: Los Angeles and the Origins of the Latino Pentecostal Movement in the U.S., Mexico, and Puerto Rico, 1900–1945" (Ph.D. diss., U. of Calif.–Santa Barbara, 1998), and the articles by Gaston Espinosa, Daniel Ramirez, and Manuel A. Vasquez in the "Latino Religion" theme issue of the *Journal of the American Academy of Religion* 67 (Sept. 1999).

In the 1970s a growing body of literature started seriously to explore the history and experience of African-American pentecostals. Most intriguing and controversial was a revisionist thesis that asserted the black origins of pentecostalism. The first part of the thesis argued that American pentecostalism flowed out of the black-led Azusa Street revival of 1906. The Azusa revival exhibited a form of spirituality, including the ring shout, spirit possession, and sacred dance, that partly derived from black slave and postbellum religious beliefs and practices, some of which had their origin in West African folk religion. The second part of the thesis held that William J. Seymour and other black pentecostals preached the revolutionary message that the 20th-century outpouring of the Holy Spirit was God's way of creating a new egalitarian community where divisions based on race, gender, and class would disappear.

The "black origins" interpretation of American pentecostalism has been argued by both black and white pentecostal scholars, including Leonard Lovett, "Perspective on the Black Origins of the Contemporary Pentecostal Movement," *The Journal of the Interdenominational Theological Center* 1 (1973); idem, "Black Origins of the Pentecostal Movement," in Vinson Synan, ed., *Aspects* (1975); idem, "Black Holiness-Pentecostalism: Implications for Ethics and Transformation" (diss., Emory, 1978); James S. Tinney, "William J. Seymour: Father of Modern-Day Pentecostalism," *The Journal of the Interdenominational Theological Society*, 4 (Fall 1977); idem, "Exclusivity in Pentecostal Self-Definition," *Journal of Religious Thought* (Spring 1980); Douglas J. Nelson, "For Such a Time as This: The Story of Bishop William J. Seymour and the Azusa Street Revival" (diss., Birmingham, U.K., 1981); Iain MacRobert, *The Black Roots and White Racism of Early Pentecostalism in the USA* (1988); Walter J. Hollenweger, "A Black Pentecostal Concept," *Concept* 30 (June 1970); idem, "After Twenty Years' Research on Pentecostalism," *International Review of Mission* 75 (Jan. 1986); idem, *Pentecostalism: Origins and Developments Worldwide* (1997); and Bishop Ithiel Clemmons, "True Koinonia: Pentecostal Hopes and Historical Studies," *Pneuma* 4 (Spring 1982); idem, *Bishop C. H. Mason and the Roots of the Church of God in Christ* (1996).

The following summary of this interpretation is drawn from the works cited above. At the outset it is important to note that historians who argued the black origins thesis did not agree on all the particulars of that approach (e.g., Douglas Nelson disassociated himself from the African-influence thesis regarding Seymour). That said, Leonard Lovett, one of the pioneer black pentecostal scholars, asserted that pentecostalism "originated from the womb of the Black religious experience," although he attached this black-roots analysis to a providential Latter Rain conceptual framework. Political scientist James Tinney and European theologian Walter Hollenweger likewise viewed the Azusa Street revival under Seymour as the single most important founding event of the pentecostal movement and relegated the white Parham to a lesser role. Tinney, who rejected the providential framework employed by Lovett, also dismissed as fiction historian Vinson Synan's interracial theory of origins. He countered that the Azusa Mission was a mostly black event and that, in fact, right from the beginning the rest of the pentecostal ranks

were divided along racial lines. "Pentecostalism," he wrote, "originated as a Black religious development . . . springing from African and Afro-American impulses in the most immediate sense." Hollenweger supported the contention that the black community in the U.S. contributed to the "universal church" not only the spiritual, but also "Pentecostal spirituality," which, he wrote, began "in a humble Black church in Los Angeles in 1906." Hollenweger credited Parham for converting Seymour to pentecostalism yet still insisted that "the Pentecostal Revival was a contribution from the Black community to the white one." In his *Pentecostalism* (1997), Hollenweger suggested that Seymour was the theological founder of the global pentecostal movement.

In the 1980s and 1990s Douglas J. Nelson and Iain MacRobert (both students of Hollenweger), and Ithiel Clemmons and Cheryl J. Sanders picked up on the previous decades' work by Lovett, Tinney, and Hollenweger. They too argued for the importance of African-American religion for the origins of modern American pentecostalism. They described Seymour's brand of pentecostalism, especially its teaching on Holy Spirit baptism, as a revolutionay religious experience that allowed participants to overcome racial, ethnic, gender, and class differences and create a genuinely egalitarian community. In their interpretation pentecostal religion radically challenged the racist and unjust social structures of Progressive Era America. For Seymour, Nelson wrote, glossolalia was "the means to a restored community." MacRobert later added that for the black founder of pentecostalism, "the baptism of the Holy Ghost was much more than a glossolalic experience; it was the fulfillment of Joel's prophecy that once again the barriers between the races would be broken down by the coming of the Spirit as on Pentecost." "Faith" for the Azusa Street participants, stated Clemmons, "became an event that transcended, challenged and transformed the social context."

Nelson and MacRobert did acknowledge Parham's doctrinal contribution to pentecostalism, Nelson even going so far as to join Synan and admitting to the interracial origins of the movement, but they insisted that what emerged at Azusa Street in 1906 was something brand-new in history: it was radically discontinuous with the past. At the same time they urged that Seymour's message also was profoundly old: the Azusa Street vision, Nelson stated, "was the spirit of that first Pentecost born again under Seymour 1,900 years later." Nelson and MacRobert thus attached a restoration theme to an essentially African-American interpretation of pentecostal origins.

MacRobert also developed Lovett's suggestion that the crucial source of Seymour's revolutionary new message and many pentecostal worship practices was black American Christianity, a synthesis of American Protestantism and West African folk religion. "To West African concepts of community, spiritual power, spirit possession and the integration of the natural and supernatural," MacRobert wrote, "were added freedom, equality, black personhood and dignity, and the desire for revolution—the Second Advent, divine intervention or at least divine aid." In MacRobert's interpretation a direct line of continuity ran from pentecostalism back to black Christianity to West African folk religion.

Bishop Clemmons, on the basis of his own research on the history of the Church of God in Christ and especially of the role of Charles Harrison Mason, affirmed the revisionist view, which located pentecostal origins in African-American spirituality mediated through the Azusa Street revival under the leadership of William J. Seymour. Most significantly for pentecostal historiography, Clemmons noted the pre– and post–Azusa Street advisory relationship and friendship between Seymour and Mason; the shared vision of the two ministers for an egalitarian "transformation of society through the experience of the Holy Spirit"; and Mason's success in institutionalizing the interracial vision of the Azusa Street revival. Mason must therefore, Clemmons argued, be viewed as a partner with Seymour in bringing to the pentecostal revival "three interdependent dynamics of African-Christian consciousness—holiness, spiritual encounter/empowerment, and prophetic social consciousness, rooted in Slave Religion and preserved in black Holiness-pentecostalism." In Clemmons's view, then, the "Seymour-Mason partnership" was the single most significant event for understanding the theology, social vision, and endurance of the 20th-century pentecostal movement. Seymour "pointed the way to the beloved community and died," and "Mason gave the fragmented community enduring significance," Clemmons wrote in "True Koinonia: Pentecostal Hopes and Historical Studies."

The work of scholars pursuing a multicultural approach to pentecostal history certainly opens up some new ways for historians to think about the meaning and origins of pentecostalism, especially early pentecostalism's diverse ideological and institutional roots and rudimentary structure. But to date a convincing black interpretation of pentecostal origins awaits further research and must successfully answer historian Edith Blumhofer's charge that it derives not from the primary sources but from the presentist-driven creation of "the myth of Azusa Street." In "For Pentecostals, a Move toward Racial Reconciliation," *Christian Century* (Apr. 27, 1994), Blumhofer pointed out the paucity of historical evidence informing our understanding of what actually went on at Azusa Street; questioned the representativeness of what took place at the mission; denied that there was anything "intrinsic to early Pentecostalism that fostered racial (or for that matter, gender) inclusivism," and noted that "Azusa Street could not hold the allegiance of its own enthusiasts, who broke away to form numerous rival congregations nearby, none of which was known to replicate the racial mix

of the mother congregation." Blumhofer's cautionary words are reinforced in Joe Creech, "Visions of Glory: The Place of the Azusa Street Revival in Pentecostal History," *Church History* 65 (Sept. 1996). Additionally, the black-origins view thus far assumes rather than proves the centrality of the Azusa Street Mission to the emergence of a national pentecostalism. The racial interpretation also must satisfactorily answer the questions, Would Azusa Street have happened without Topeka? or Would a pentecostal movement have emerged without the white Parham's new doctrine of initial evidence?

4. The Functional Approach.

A fourth interpretative approach to understanding why and how pentecostalism arose and lasted despite intense opposition from mainline Protestant, Holiness, and evangelical elements focuses on the "functional" nature of pentecostal religion. By seeking to connect pentecostalism to its cultural setting and pentecostal adherents to their place in the nation's social and economic structure, the functional view attempts to understand pentecostal thought and practice in order to learn why and how it appealed to those who joined the movement.

Those who look to the functions of pentecostalism to provide the primary explanation for the rise, and especially the persistence, of the pentecostal movement divide into two groups. One group of scholars, largely drawing on theories of social disorganization, economic and social deprivation, and psychological maladjustment, focuses on the socially dysfunctional aspects of pentecostal religion. Kilian McDonnell, in *Charismatic Renewal and the Churches* (1976), cited above, explained and critiqued much of the social-science literature that views pentecostalism in this negative way. The most important book by a historian stressing the dysfunctional nature of pentecostal religion is Robert Anderson's immensely important *Vision of the Disinherited* (1979). Taking a naturalistic approach to religious experience, Anderson explained pentecostalism's arrival as the psychologically unhealthy and socially dysfunctional religious response of marginalized poor farmers, working and lower-class city dwellers, new immigrants, and black Americans to a rapidly industrializing and urbanizing America. These disinherited Americans who turned pentecostal, Anderson critically explained, spoke in tongues and longed for the imminent second coming of Jesus as a way to escape from their terrible life in the here and now.

More recently historian Grant Wacker, who noted the positive functions of pentecostal religion, nevertheless also suggested that pentecostal ideology, opposing much that was modern in early-20th-century American life, contained within it regressive and socially dysfunctional cultural attitudes that reflected the pentecostal's marginal and outsider status in American society. As part of its attempt to withdraw from modern society and create its own social and religious space, Wacker wrote, the pentecostal movement "harbored a regressive strain that was, by any reasonable measure of such things, socially disruptive. Its defiance of social conventions, its bellicosity and zealotry, its ecstatic excess and deliberate scrambling of human language, surely reflected a darkly primitivist urge toward disorder" ("Playing for Keeps: The Primitivist Impulse in Early Pentecostalism," in Richard T. Hughes, ed., *The American Quest for the Primitive Church* [1988]).

The contemporary explosive growth of pentecostalism worldwide, especially among the nation's poor, has forced scholars seeking to understand the origins and appeal of primitive pentecostalism at the turn of the 20th century to recognize the socially positive functions pentecostalism served for a variety of constituents and to see how pentecostalism was sensitive to its largely poor and powerless adherents. By seeking to connect pentecostalism in a positive way to its economic and cultural setting, the socially functional view avoids the crude determinism, religious and psychological reductionism, and wholly negative assessment of the consequences of pentecostal religion for its followers characteristic of the socially dysfunctional approach. Instead, it shares with the multicultural interpretation a more positive and optimistic evaluation of pentecostalism's power to liberate and empower the disinherited—farmers, workers, and minorities—in Progressive Era America.

As with several interpretative issues, historian John Nichol pointed the way early on. In *The Pentecostals* (1971) he outlined several sociological and psychological factors that he thought explained how pentecostalism as a doctrine and experience became a movement with staying power. Pentecostal preaching's stress on the eschatological hope of a better future for the Christian in God's coming kingdom, he noted, served as a compensatory antidote to the pentecostals' low economic and social status in the present world. As participants in the nation's pre-WWI popular democratic culture, pentecostals effectively utilized the culture's methods—mass rallies, street meetings, door-to-door recruitment, cheap or even free magazines and newspapers, low-brow but popular religious tunes and songs—to reach out to the nation's lower and working classes. He further suggested that a structurally decentralized pentecostalism, which encouraged lay participation in all phases of worship and church life, embodied a democratic ethos that potentially was more egalitarian than many other early-20th-century societal institutions with respect to class, gender, and ethnicity. Nichol also briefly noted the psychologically transforming nature of Spirit baptism. Spirit baptism often seemed able to transform people of little means or abilities into individuals of great boldness, poise, and confidence and people buffeted by circumstances into individuals ready to face any adversity.

Picking up on the more positive dimensions of the social functions of primitive pentecostalism in the lives of the movement's adherents, biographer James Goff, in his book cited previously, showed how Charles F. Parham's pentecostal full gospel message of salvation, sanctification, Holy Spirit baptism, divine healing, and the premillennial rapture of the saints collectively met the social and spiritual needs of struggling farmers and urban workers. Indeed, Parham was the father of "a revolution of socioreligious significance."

In several essays historian Grant Wacker has sketched out the positive functions primitive pentecostalism served in the lives of its recruits. Such functions, he asserted, explain not only the movement's appeal to plain folk, but also its durability. Pentecostal ideology, including its teachings about salvation, tongues speaking, divine healing, the soon-to-take-place second coming of Jesus Christ, the role of the supernatural in everyday life, and the evils of modern social and intellectual trends, had broad appeal, Wacker claimed, and met people's needs by offering them "certitude that the supernatural claims of the gospel were really true." Moreover, pentecostalism's pragmatic outlook functioned in ways that allowed the movement's members to find creative ways to spread its message. Pentecostal churches, Wacker further pointed out, functioned as small communities wherein members found refuge from modern culture, nourishment for the spirit, an extended familylike social support network, and affirmation of the movement's core beliefs. The pentecostal belief system, Wacker wrote, offered members "an island of traditionalism in a sea of modernity," and as such, "met the needs of ordinary people with a faith that was largely impervious to historical, rational, or empirical criticism" (Grant Wacker, "The Functions of Faith in Primitive Pentecostalism," *Harvard Theological Review* 77 [1984]; "Pentecostalism," in Charles H. Lippy and Peter W. Williams, eds., *Encyclopedia of American Religious Experience*, vol. 2 [1988]; "Playing for Keeps: The Primitivist Impulse in Early Pentecostalism," in Richard T. Hughes, ed., *The American Quest for the Primitive Church* [1988]; "Character and the Modernization of North American Pentecostalism" [paper, SPS, 1991; a revised version has been published as "Searching for Eden with a Satellite Dish: Primitivism, Pragmatism, and the Pentecostal Character," in Richard T. Hughes, ed., *The Primitive Church in the Modern World* [1995]).

Historian Edith Blumhofer likewise sought to connect the early pentecostals with the broader economic and social milieu of Progressive Era America. In her story of the rise and development of the Assemblies of God (*Restoring the Faith* [1993]), which included a detailed account of pentecostalism's roots in the 19th century, she summarized her view of the intersection between pentecostalism and early-20th-century American society:

Pentecostalism extended among people already distanced—either by choice or by chance—from the cultural mainstream. Those who embraced pentecostalism routinely explained their choice in theological terms: they saw it as restoration, as full gospel. That does not diminish its role in giving individuals identity and purpose by focusing their understanding of society and world events around nostalgia for the "good old days" when America was Protestant and evangelical with pride in national mission and destiny and when the home was the center of everyday life. It also legitimated their reluctance and inability to address the overwhelming social evils of their own day by offering a simple explanation for the social predicament. And it helped root migrant people—immigrants from other nations as well as those dislocated from families by moves from rural to urban America. But, at face value, its primary significance lay in its ability to overwhelm human emotions, replacing despair with hope and uncertainty with assurance and an inner sense of peace.

Commenting specifically on the famed Azusa Street Mission, Blumhofer noted how the restorationist view of history allowed these poor and maginalized pentecostals to place themselves "at the center of God's end-time dealings with humanity"; "they reconsidered who they were from the perspective of participation in God's divine plan, and in so doing, they discovered a new sense of purpose, importance, and identity." What Blumhofer claimed about the Azusa Street participants' view of their place in history, she argued, was shared by all pentecostals. Intrinsic to the pentecostals' self-understanding was their belief that the pentecostal movement "was both part of an extensive end-times revival and the promised latter rain" (Blumhofer, *The Assemblies of God*, vol. 1 [1989]). The countercultural communities they created, she wrote, "functioned as exclusive total worlds, redefining reality, priorities, vocation, and relationships" (*Restoring the Faith* [1993]). At the grassroots level, pentecostal assemblies functioned as enclaves that provided pentecostals a secure place in which to worship as they pleased and offer each other mutual support in a world assumed to be hostile. This building of a restorationist-infused culture of pentecostalism, Blumhofer seemed to suggest, was the source of the staying power of the pentecostal movement.

The functional approach, at least in its socially positive form, opens up fresh lines of inquiry that start not with the pre-1900 antecedents of pentecostalism, but with the fact of the movement's existence and durability. With its focus on pentecostalism's core values and beliefs and its organizational structures and programs, the functional approach is attuned to the institutional side of the creation of the pentecostal movement. It demonstrates how even relatively poor and for the most part minimally educated American pentecostals actively participated in the building of a pentecostal subcul-

ture that both ideologically and institutionally found a permanent place in an increasingly pluralistic American religious and social structure. Ironically, much like the providential view of origins, the functional or sociological approach implies that pentecostalism, with its emphasis on Holy Spirit baptism, in some fundamental ways was discontinuous with earlier religious revivals and movements: pentecostalism owed its existence not primarily to antecedent religious developments, as the historical-roots view might argue, but to the historically particular combination of an innovative theological formulation and religious experience, the social and economic location of pentecostal recruits, and the setting of an America in social and economic transition around the turn of the century. In the hands of historians who view religious belief and experience in naturalistic terms, and in the main as a socially dysfunctional form of behavior, the functional approach can lead to a patronizing dismissal of pentecostalism as a religion without redeeming social or economic value. Even in the hands of scholars appreciative of the reality of the spiritual dimension of human existence, and the religious and social usefulness of Christian experience, the functional or social-analysis approach to pentecostal beginnings tends toward a present downplaying of the long-in-the-making historical religious and social forces that came together in pentecostalism. In other words, the functional orientation to pentecostalism slights the continuity of 20th-century pentecostalism with 19th-century religious and social developments.

III. CONCLUSION.

Each of the four contemporary interpretive approaches—providential, genetic, multicultural, and functional—to understanding American pentecostal origins answers a slightly different set of questions and analytic concerns; each provides a slightly different angle of vision from which to view pentecostalism's beginnings. Each, as has been pointed out, has its strengths and weaknesses. Each of the four approaches helps illumine the broader contours that shaped the new pentecostal movement. Taken together they promise a way toward a more comprehensive and historically satisfying synthesis of the story of the emergence of the American pentecostal religious tradition.

■ A. Cerillo Jr.; G. Wacker

BIBLIOGRAPHY AND HISTORIOGRAPHY OF PENTECOSTALISM OUTSIDE NORTH AMERICA

I. Early Sources and Interpretations

II. Bibliographies of Global Significance

III. Interpretations of Pentecostalism as a Global Phenomenon

IV. Hollenweger and His Students

V. Scandinavian Mission History and the History of Global Pentecostalism
  A. *Sweden*
  B. *Norway*
  C. *Finland*
  D. *Influence of the Scandinavian Approach*

VI. Latin America: Battleground for Competing Theories
  A. *Latin American Pentecostalism as Response to Social Alienation*
  B. *Sect Theory*
  C. *Deprivation Theory*
  D. *Latin American Pentecostalism as Subject for Sociological and Anthropological Analysis*
  E. *Latin American Pentecostalism as "Popular Religion"*
  F. *Latin American Pentecostalism as Exported North American Fundamentalism/Evangelicalism and Rightist Politics*

VII. Asia: The Example of Thailand

VIII. Africa: Pentecostalism and the African Independent Churches

IX. Conclusion

I. EARLY SOURCES AND INTERPRETATIONS.

Pentecostalism perceived itself from the beginning as a global movement. Indeed, the fact of its rapidly developed global presence, with revivals in North America, Europe, Asia, and Latin America, was interpreted as a confirmation of the divine origins of the movement. The early pentecostal periodicals printed news and testimonies from around the world and attributed equal value to all. To read the early pages of the *Apostolic Faith* (Los Angeles), *Pentecost* (Indianapolis), *Upper Room* (Los Angeles), *Die Verheissung des Vaters* (Switzerland), *Pfingstgrüsse* (Germany), *Korsets Seier* (Norway), *Esprit et vie* (Belgium and France), *Korsets Seger* and *Evangelii Härold* (Sweden), *Chile Evanjélico* and *Chile Pentecostal* (Chile), and *Confidence* (Great Britain) is to be introduced to early pentecostalism around the world. ▸G. T. Haywood continued this tradition in the primarily African-American Oneness periodical, *Voice in the Wilderness* (Indianapolis). These periodicals, and hundreds of lesser lights around the world, are the most basic bibliography for the study of global pentecostalism. Early pentecostal leaders believed that their spiritual vision transcended all human boundaries, including class, national origin, gender, race, and religious affiliation. It was ▸T. B. Barratt who seems to have realized, based on his travel in the U.S. in 1906, in Europe, and in India from 1907 to 1908, that there were organizational, theological, and historiographical implications embedded in the spirituality. From this came his vision for

the International Pentecostal Conferences (1908 and after) and the ▸Pentecostal Missionary Union (1908).

There were several early interpretations of pentecostalism as a global phenomenon. Early pentecostal traveling clergy, such as Barratt (articles in *Byposten* and *Korsets Seier* with summaries of these in T. B. Barratt, *When the Fire Fell and An Outline of My Life* [1927], reprinted in *The Work of T. B. Barratt*, ed. ▸D. W. Dayton [1985]); T. B, Barratt, *Erindringer*, ed. S. Barratt Lange (1941); ▸Frank Bartleman, *Around the World by Faith* (n.d.) and *Two Years Mission Work in Europe, Just Before the World War, 1912–1914* (n.d.); ▸Andrew Urshan, *Life Story of Andrew bar David Urshan* (1967; serialized earlier); and G. T. Haywood (reports in *Voice in the Wilderness*) reinforced this identity through their widely circulated reports. This approach was first systematized by the Swedish scholar Efraim Briem in 1924 (see below, section V.A). The first European/American to develop the theory in detail was ▸S. H. Frodsham, *With Signs Following* (1926). It was also occasionally thus understood by detractors of the tradition, such as J. C. Vanzandt, *Speaking in Tongues: A Discussion of Speaking in Tongues, Pentecost, Latter Rain, Evidence of Holy Spirit Baptism and a Short History of the Tongues Movement in America and Several Countries* (1926).

Three phenomena led to the breakdown of this perspective between 1914 and 1947: (1) the rise of pentecostal denominations, each of which was most interested in its own projects and its own survival; (2) the replacement of the initial leaders with persons less educated, less global in orientation, and less committed to transcending racial and cultural barriers; and (3) the two world wars, which separated people, interrupted correspondence, increased regionalization, and eventually led to the political division of the world. The exceptions to these generalizations were to be found primarily among the mission historians of Scandinavia (see below, section V). The ▸World Pentecostal Conferences of 1947 and later were efforts to reverse this trend. Although these produced little literature, they significantly influenced pentecostal historians.

II. BIBLIOGRAPHIES OF GLOBAL SIGNIFICANCE.

The essential bibliographic source for global pentecostalism remains Walter Hollenweger, *Handbuch der Pfingstbewegung* (10 vols., diss., Zurich, 1966; microfilm 1967). Unfortunately, this magnificent work is rarely cited, and because of the collecting habits of libraries, much of the material cited or discussed is difficult to find. This dissertation had an initial interpretative volume and then provided, for each country in alphabetical order, a brief history, prosopography, and bibliography for each "denomination" found in each country. Already during the decade 1955–65 when Hollenweger compiled this material, it was impossible to exhaustively identify and catalog this ephemeral literature. However, the care with which the work was done provided a quite accurate and essential basic bibliographic and historical introduction to global pentecostalism.

Also useful are two of the bibliographies by Charles E. Jones: *Guide to the Study of the Pentecostal Movement* (2 vols., 1983) and *The Charismatic Movement: A Guide to the Study of Neo-Pentecostalism with Emphasis on Anglo-American Sources* (2 vols., 1995). Jones provides a meticulously accurate guide to many materials in North American libraries, but with resources for a more global understanding. These provide an important supplement to and updating of Hollenweger's *Handbuch der Pfingstbewegung*.

Additional bibliographic resources can be found by searching two computer networks: WorldCat (OCLC) and RLIN (Research Libraries Information Network). National libraries in Britain, Germany, Norway, and Sweden (other nations will follow this example) are establishing national on-line automated catalogs that are very useful for pentecostal research. Projects such as that of the Ricci Institute at the University of San Francisco, which attempts to document all Chinese involvement with Christianity, will be important contributions. Unfortunately, most resources available for documenting pentecostal life and spirituality (printed matter, videos, audiotapes, dances, music, liturgies) are still not being collected by either deposit or research libraries. For the ▸African Initiated Churches and other indigenous religious movements around the world, many of which were directly or indirectly influenced by pentecostalism, the collection and bibliography collected by Harold Turner is an essential base line. Turner's *Bibliography on New Religious Movements in Primal Societies* (6 vols., 1977–92) has no competitors. The Harold Turner Collection on New Religious Movements is maintained by the Centre for New Religious Movements (CENERM), Selly Oak Colleges, Birmingham, England, and is owned and housed by the Central Library, Selly Oak Colleges. A computer-generated catalog is in preparation. For a discussion of this collection, see Ralph Woodhall, "The Harold W. Turner Collection in Selly Oak Colleges Library," *Bulletin of the Association of British Theological and Philosophical Libraries* 4 (1, Mar. 1997).

Major institutional repositories in the U.S. of material related to pentecostalism outside North America are the libraries and/or archives at Oral Roberts University, Tulsa, OK; Flower Pentecostal Heritage Center, Assemblies of God Headquarters, Springfield, MO; Pentecostal Research Center, Lee University and Church of God Theological Seminary, Cleveland, TN; Archives of the Pentecostal Holiness Church, Oklahoma City, OK; Asbury Theological Seminary, Wilmore, KY; Methodist Center, Drew University, Madison, NJ; Billy Graham Center Library, Wheaton College, Wheaton, IL; Heritage Center, United Pentecostal Church Headquarters, Hazelwood, MO; and the ▸David du Plessis Center at Fuller Theological Seminary, Pasadena, CA.

Outside North America, major repositories include the Donald Gee Center, Mattersey Hall, Mattersey, England; Pentecostal Information Center, Kaggeholm, Ekerö, Sweden; National Archives and National Library, Stockholm, Sweden; School for Oriental and African Studies, University of London; Protestant Research Library, Paris; as well as denominational centers throughout the world, most of which are minimally organized and endangered because of environmental and political preservation issues. National libraries in most countries contain important resources.

Another valuable resource is *The World Christian Encyclopedia,* ed. David B. Barrett et al. (1982). This tool provides a country-by-country analysis of Christianity, listing as many pentecostal denominations as were identified by the editors at that time. It is the most up-to-date list available of pentecostal denominations, with statistics and occasional clarification of historiographical issues. (A new edition that promises to be more complete is in preparation.)

III. INTERPRETATIONS OF PENTECOSTALISM AS A GLOBAL PHENOMENON.

The first author to respond to the new reality of pentecostalism after WWII, fostered by ▸Donald Gee, ▸David du Plessis, and ▸Lewi Pethrus, was the Swiss scholar and theologian ▸Leonhard Steiner, *Mit folgenden Zeichen: Eine Darstellung der Pfingstbewegung* (1954; Swedish translation, *Med Åtföljande Teken: En översikt av den internationelle pingstväckelsen,* 1955). Steiner began with an analysis of the American origins of the tradition but noted that it had become indigenous throughout the world, often with minimal influence from missionaries. It is clear, both in the historiographical and theological sections of the work, that Steiner gave no priority to the American experience of pentecostalism but was working toward a more global perspective. He tended to universalize the analysis of the Wesleyan historical and theological roots of pentecostalism pioneered by Paul Fleisch in *Die moderne Gemeinschaftsbewegung in Deutschland* (3d ed., 1912; repr. 1985). Steiner's coverage was generally limited to groups recognized for membership in the World Pentecostal Conference, but the work was more comprehensively "ecumenical" than any volume to that time. This book has had minimal influence on pentecostal historiography outside Europe.

Two volumes were heavily influenced by Steiner's work. Norwegian missiologist ▸Nils Bloch-Hoell contributed *Pinsebevegelsen: En ondersøkelse av pinsebevegelsens tilblivelse, utvikling og saerpreg med saerlig henblikk på bevegelsens utformning i Norge* (1956), with a partial translation into English, *The Pentecostal Movement: Its Origin, Development and Distinctive Character* (1964). Bloch-Hoell was keenly aware of the transatlantic nexus of pentecostalism and the development of pentecostalism in Latin America, Asia, and Africa, although his focus was on the experience in Scandinavia and the U.S. Another author influenced by Steiner was John Thomas Nichol, *Pentecostalism* (New York, 1966), second edition, *The Pentecostals* (Plainfield, NJ, 1971). He was the first American author after WWII to attempt to understand pentecostalism as a global phenomenon. Given the resources available while he was working on the dissertation at Boston University, the work is remarkably comprehensive in its description of the movements around the world.

The work of Walter Hollenweger began a new era in the historiography of global pentecostalism. The first volume of his *Handbuch der Pfingstbewegung* was published in three different versions: *Enthusiastisches Christentum: Die Pfingstbewegung in Geschichte und Gegenwart* (1969); *The Pentecostals: The Charismatic Movement in the Churches* (1972); and *El Pentecostalismo, historia y doctrina* (1976). Based on his readings of large quantities of primary sources and travels to collect the documentation, Hollenweger's project was massive and erudite. He interpreted the tradition as both a social and a theological tradition, with an eye already to the complex problem of origins. These issues would continue to preoccupy him and his students for decades. As he looked at pentecostalism, he saw much that could not be explained by the Fleisch paradigm, although he recognized the validity of some of Fleisch's argument. He saw traditions that were not invited to participate in the World Pentecostal Conferences. He saw much that could not be easily explained by recourse to North American realities and models. Nowhere was this more clear than in his treatments of pentecostalism in Italy, Brazil, the U.S.S.R., and Zaire/Congo. Hollenweger's volume has been criticized as having no uniform interpretative thesis, but Hollenweger had discovered that the state of research and the complexity of the interpretative problems involved defied the imposition of a single interpretative framework from Zurich!

Three other approaches to global pentecostalism require mention:

1. Edith L. Blumhofer (then Edith L. Waldvogel) wrote her dissertation "The 'Overcoming Life': A Study in the Reformed Evangelical Origins of Pentecostalism" (diss., Harvard, 1977); she later generalized her findings to interpret American Assemblies of God experience in her *Restoring the Faith* (1993), and the broader pentecostal experience in "Transatlantic Currents in North Atlantic Pentecostalism," in *Evangelicalism: Comparative Studies of Popular Protestantism in North America, the British Isles, and Beyond, 1700–1990*, ed. Mark A. Noll et al. (1994). While many would argue against describing people like R. A. Torrey, A. T. Pierson, A. J. Gordon, and others analyzed by Blumhofer as "Reformed" in any classical sense of that term, it is certainly true that their works were used throughout the pentecostal world and translated, either in whole or in part, into most European and so-called Third World languages.

2. Karla Poewe, in the introduction to her edited volume *Charismatic Christianity as a Global Culture* (1994), traced the theoretical framework back to Continental Pietism, with minimal attention to the American, African, or European roots of the tradition. In her analysis, pentecostalism sits firmly in that branch of the Protestant Reformation tradition.

3. Steve Brouwer, Paul Gifford, and Susan D. Rose, *Exporting the American Gospel: Global Christian Fundamentalism* (London and New York, 1996), argued that all revivalistic Christianity outside North America is to be understood as exported American fundamentalism. No distinctions were made between denominations, faith traditions, or origins. This latter approach is very popular with North American scholars but is based on an analysis unrelated to the literature and/or observation of the traditions outside North America. (More of this approach can be seen below in the discussion of Latin America.)

IV. HOLLENWEGER AND HIS STUDENTS.

Walter Hollenweger became professor of mission at the University of Birmingham and Selly Oak Colleges in 1971. Building on his earlier work, Hollenweger developed a way of understanding his research as "intercultural theology." Volumes began to appear that explored this understanding: *New Wine in Old Wineskins: Protestant and Catholic Neo-Pentecostals* (1973); *Evangelization Gestern und Heute* (1973), English translation, *Evangelism Today: Good News or Bone of Contention?* (1976); *Marxist and Kimbanguist Mission: A Comparison* (1974), with partial translations in Spanish, French, and Dutch (*De Geest spreekt alle talen: Een analyse van de Pinksterbeweging*, 1976), among many others.

Perhaps most important for future research were *Christen ohne Schriften: Fünf Fallstudien zur Sozialethik mündlicher Religion* (1977), in which Hollenweger explored on the basis of carefully defined case studies the development of theology and social ethics in oral cultures; and the closely related *Pentecost between Black and White: Five Case Studies on Pentecost and Politics* (1974), from which many readers were first tantalized with hints of his understanding of the African-American roots of pentecostalism.

These works and Hollenweger's reputation as a demanding but gracious mentor brought people from all over the world to study with him. Intrigued by his theories and analyses, they worked to nuance or transform these from within their contexts. Among the students who worked on issues related to pentecostalism outside North America were Arnold Bittlinger, *Papst und Pfingstler: Der römisch katholische/pfingstliche Dialog und seiner ökumenische Relevanz* (1978); Manuel J. Gaxiola-Gaxiola, *La Serpiente y la Paloma: Historia, Teología y Análisis de la Iglesia Apostólica de la Fe en Cristo Jesús* (2d ed., 1994; this was not Gaxiola's dissertation but closely related it); Roswith Gerloff, *A Plea for British Black*

Theologies: The Black Church Movement in Britain in Its Transatlantic Cultural and Theological Interaction with Special Reference to the Pentecostal Oneness (Apostolic) and Sabbatarian Movements (2 vols., 1992); Ken Gill, Toward a Contextualized Theology of the Third World: The Emergence and Development of Jesus' Name Pentecostalism in Mexico (1994); Cornelis van der Laan, Gerrit Roelof Polman: Sectarian against His Will. The Birth of Pentecostalism in the Netherlands (1991); and Boo-Wong Yoo, Korean Pentecostalism: Its History and Theology (1988). In addition there were hundreds of scholars around the world inspired, assisted, or angered by Hollenweger to continue research on "global" pentecostalism.

Many of these and other colleagues contributed to a Festschrift for Hollenweger: Pentecost, Mission and Ecumenism: Essays on Intercultural Theology: Festschrift in Honour of Professor Walter J. Hollenweger, ed. J. A. B. Jongeneel (1992). The volume contains a complete bibliography of Hollenweger's publications to 1991 as well as biographical material and analyses of Hollenweger's contributions to the discipline.

Hollenweger returned the favor in his Pentecostalism: Origins and Developments Worldwide (1997). In this volume he summarized the historical development of pentecostalism and proposed a multifaceted theory of pentecostal origins that included Wesleyan, African-American, Catholic, and Protestant Enlightenment roots. Drawing from research done during the decades since the publication of three versions of the first volume of his dissertation (see above), he has established a new historiographical benchmark from which others will build.

V. SCANDINAVIAN MISSION HISTORY AND THE HISTORY OF GLOBAL PENTECOSTALISM.

Quite apart from what was going on in the rest of the pentecostal world, and generally unread outside that area because of language barriers, a school of pentecostal historiography developed in Scandinavia that understood pentecostal history as both local and mission history. This began with the two periodicals edited by Thomas Ball Barratt, Byposten (which became Korsets Seier) and Korsets Seger, which were published in Stockholm and circulated in Sweden and Finland. They were followed by Evangelii Härold, edited by Lewi Pethrus for Sweden and Ristin Voitto in Finland. These all reported on pentecostal developments around the world (see D. D. Bundy, "Thomas B. Barratt and Byposten: An Early European Pentecostal Leader and His Periodical," Pentecost, Mission and Ecumenism: Essays on Intercultural Theology: Festschrift in Honour of Professor Walter J. Hollenweger [1992], 115–21).

In addition, because of the experience with the Methodist Episcopal Mission Board (see D. D. Bundy, "T. B. Barratt: From Methodist to Pentecostal," EPTA Bulletin 13 [1994]), Barratt and the Scandinavian churches were attracted to con-

gregational polity and the theory of mission promulgated by the life and writings of William Taylor (see D. D. Bundy, "Bishop William Taylor and Methodist Mission: A Study in Nineteenth-Century Social History," Methodist History 27 [4, July 1989] and 28 [1, Oct. 1989], and G. A. Gustafson, En Apostlagestalt på missionsfält . . . eller Biskop William Taylors lif och värksamhet [1898]). This resulted in an approach to mission that respected other pentecostal churches and did not only allow but insisted on indigeneity (see D. D. Bundy, "Swedish Pentecostal Mission Theory and Practice to 1930: Foundational Values in Discussion," Mission Studies 14 [1997]).

This was reinforced by the tradition of the Swedish ˒Örebro Mission and the Örebro Missionsskola (charismatic Baptist/Holiness/pentecostal), both founded by John Ongman. Many Scandinavian pentecostal missionaries received education at Örebro. Pentecostal missiologists and mission executives Carl Andin, Rikard Fris, and Paul Ongman taught at the Örebro Mission School. (See Paul Ongman and Carl Andin, I den elfte timmen: Överblick av Örebro Missionsförenings evangelistversamhet [1917]; the anonymous Skördemän och Skördefält: Några uppgifter om Örebro Missionsförenings historia och arbete [1925]; John Magnusson, John Ongman: En Levnadsteckning [1932]; Örebro Missionsskola, 1908–1933 [1933]; and case studies of pentecostal missionaries who were students there by D. D. Bundy, "Pentecostal Missions to Brazil: The Case of the Norwegian G. L. Pettersen," Norsk tidsskrift for misjon 47 [1993], 171–79; idem, "Swedish Pentecostal Missions: The Case of Axel Andersson in Mexico," in To the Ends of the Earth (23d Annual Meeting of the SPS, 1993), with Spanish version, "Las Misiones Pentecostales Suecas: El caso de Axel Andersson en Mexico.")

General information, normally written by nonpentecostals, can be found in the surveys of Scandinavian mission history. The most important of these remains that by Knut B. Westman et al., Nordisk Missionshistorie (1950). The bibliographic index edited by C. Hallencreutz entitled Missio Nordica has been collecting bibliographies since 1990. For each of the countries discussed, extensive historical and biographical material as well as archival resources exist. Reference is made here only to published resources that have implications for pentecostalism beyond the borders of the particular country. The method here is to begin with Sweden before discussing Norway and Finland.

A. Sweden.

These and subsequent developments need to be understood in light of the work of three scholars published in the 1920s. Efraim Briem, Den Moderna Pingströrelsen (1924) interpreted pentecostalism as a global and missionary tradition that emphasized glossolalia, prophecy, and healing. Because of this book, pentecostalism came to be understood in the culture in light of its mission history. Emanuel Linderholm, *Pingströrelsen i Sverige: Ekstas, under och apokalyptik i nutige Svensk folkreligiositet* (1925), interpreted the early development of the tradition in Sweden, building on the work of Briem, as a development of popular religious culture with emphases on personal experience of the divine and apocalyptic theology. The Danish scholar J. P. Bang, with the encouragement of Briem, contributed *De Stora Väckelserörelserna: En historisk och psykologisk framsällning*, tr. Gösta Olai (1926). While these books could not be understood as pro-pentecostal, they were evenhanded, serious scholarly works that sought to provide an interpretation of the movements based on phenomena observed. Most importantly, they gave a larger cultural warrant for pentecostal self-understanding.

Historian G. E. Söderholm, *Den Svenska Pingstväckelsens Historia, 1907–1927* (2 vols., 1929), interpreted the origins of the Swedish pentecostal movement as part of a global revival with complex roots in Methodism, Pietism, the ▸Welsh revival, and the tradition of ▸Pandita Ramabai, among others. This was followed by his *Den Svenska Pingstväckelsens spridning utom och inom Sverige* (1933). In this volume, Söderholm carefully documents the role of Swedish pentecostal missionaries around the world, but he makes it clear that the polity and ecclesiology make the churches founded outside Sweden equal with and independent from Swedish pentecostal churches and mission organizations. Therefore, it provides a history of the origins of many pentecostal denominations around the world. This ecclesial vision was the background for the formation of the Pentecostal European Conferences that began at Stockholm in 1939: *Europeiska Pingstkonferensen I Stockholm, den 5–12 Juni 1939* (1939). The first, hosted by Lewi Pethrus, drew 48 speakers from 19 countries. Each reported from their own work as part of a larger movement. It was a conference of equals that spanned national and cultural differences on the eve of WWII.

This tradition was continued by Arthur Sundstedt's massive, carefully documented, scholarly five-volume history of pentecostalism in Sweden and around the world: *Pingstväckelsen—dess uppkomst och första utvecklingsskede* (1967); *Pingstväckelsen—och dess vidare utveckling* (1971); *Pingstväckelsen och dess genombrott* (1971); *Pingstväckelsen och dess utbredning* (1972); and *Pingstväckelsen: En världväckelse* (1973). Sundstedt also focused mostly on the role of Swedish missionaries and churches but, once again, because of the mission theory of Swedish pentecostalism, the histories are central to pentecostal traditions around the world.

The Missions Institutet-PMU and Swedish Pentecostal Information Center at Kaggeholm, Sweden, have made a concerted effort to document the development of churches around the world that are or have been related to, or influenced by, Swedish pentecostalism. This effort is led by Jan-Endy Johannesson, scholar of Chinese history and former missionary to Taiwan, and Jan-Åke Alvarsson, cultural anthropologist at the University of Uppsala. This project, which publishes *Forskningsrapporter i missionsvetenskap, missionshistoria och missionsantropologi* (Research Reports in Missiology, Mission History and Missionary Anthropology), has several facets. The first group of publications are a series on pentecostal mission history, including Åke Boberg, *Svensk Pingstmission* (1990); Jan-Endy Johannesson, *Documentation av Svensk Pingstmission i Kina, 1907–1951* (2d ed., 1992); Barbro och Eric Andréasson, *Documentation av Svensk Pingstmission i Indien, 1922–1962* (1989); and, Jan-Endy Johannesson, *Missionsdokumentation: En kortfattad handledning* (1990).

Other volumes describe and evaluate mission projects around the world, including Jan-Åke Alvarsson, *Socio-Cultural Effects of a Rural Development Project among Pastoralists in the Lower Omo, Ethiopia* (1989); idem, *Skola för de allra fattigaste? Utvärdering av gymnasieskolan Buenas Nuevas i Cochabamba, Bolivia* (1989); Björn Larsson, *Kess Bekess . . . : En bertraktelse av Swedish Philadelphia Church Missions project och personalorganisation i Ethiopien, April 1989* (1989); Anders Kammensjö and Md. Mukhlesur Rahman, *Evaluation of the Swedish Free Mission's Disaster Aid & Rehabilitation Programme after the 1991 Cyclone in Bangladesh* (1994); as well as Margareta Mobergh and Francisco Pereyra, *Utvärdering av Barnhemsprojektet i Ituzaingó, Argentina* (1994). The philosophy of and approach to evaluation of mission work was developed by Karl-Erik Lundgren, *Utvärdering: Gissel eller möglighet?* (1991), in which it is argued that evaluation should be done cooperatively between the givers and recipients. The research and mission projects in Tanzania have been evaluated by Elias Shija, "Information Flow: A Critical Look at the Pentecostal Churches Association in Tanzania and Philadelphia Church in Stockholm, Sweden" (diploma thesis, Tanzania School of Journalism, Dar es Salaam, 1992). The history and development of Swedish pentecostal developmental mission work was discussed by Åke Boberg et al. in *Från vision till verklighet: 15 år med Pingstmissionens U-landshjälp* (n.d.).

A third facet of the project endeavors to promote the Swedish pentecostal worldview, mission history, and theory among the congregations in Scandinavia. These publications include Gunnar Swahn, *Vi lär oss om vår mission* (1991); Jan-Åke Alvarsson, *Mission och Missionärsutbildning* (1990); Jan-Endy Johannesson, *Sådd i Mittens Rike* (1988); and Barbro and Eric Andréasson, *Pingst i Indien* (1989). The approach of the entire project is phenomenological and written for audiences beyond the pentecostal movements, including government agencies. Jan-Åke Alvarsson has also contributed an important volume on intercultural evangelism and theology, *Dela som syskon: Att förmedla evangeliet över kulturgränserna* (1992). The Missions Institutet-PMU circulates films and videos that describe the mission work.

B. Norway.

Norwegian pentecostal mission theory, like that of the Swedish pentecostals, comes from T. B. Barratt, William Taylor, and John Ongman. Being congregational, with the expectation that the results of mission will be autonomous churches with no supervision from Norway, there is no effort to control the results of mission, and so, as in the case of Sweden, Norwegian pentecostal mission history is also the history of denominations around the world. The Norwegian and Swedish pentecostals also share, thanks to Barratt, a vision of themselves as a missionary movement and part of a global reality. There were two major efforts to describe this history. The first was by Martin Ski, *Fram til Urkristendommen: Pinsevekkelsen gjennom 50 år* (3 vols., 1956–59). A volume edited by Kåre Juul, *Til Jordens ender: Norsk pinsemisjon gjennom 50 år* (1960), brought together essays by 27 authors to describe and reflect on the history and theory of Norwegian pentecostal missions. This history was rewritten and updated in Oddvar Nilsen, *. . . og Herren virket med: Pinsebevegelsen gjennom 75 år* (1981), which did not attempt a narrative history but chose to collect previously published materials and photos, some of which have to do with missions. Mission was the focus of the very interesting volume by Oddvar Nilsen, *Ut i all verden: Pinsevennenes ytre misjon i 75 år* (1984). Drawing on published and unpublished materials, it provided for the first time a coherent history as well as a statement of the mission theory of Barratt and the Norwegian pentecostal mission. The mission theory supportive of this tradition was most recently discussed by Reinert O. Innvaer, *Sennepsfrøet: En bok om misjon* (1993).

C. Finland.

The first major history of pentecostalism in Finland was that of Wolfgang Schmidt, *Die Pfingstbewegung in Finnland* (1935), which was followed by his more comprehensive study, *Finlands kyrka genom tiderna, en översikt* (1940). Schmidt continued the interpretative traditions established by Briem and Fleisch mentioned above. There are two separate primary pentecostal traditions in Finland, the one Finnish-speaking, the other Swedish-speaking. Each has its own history and its own mission traditions, although relations between the two are cordial.

First, some comments about the bibliography and historiography of the larger Finnish-language movement. During the decade of the 1990s, there has been a flurry of publications on Finnish pentecostalism that provides access to aspects of the history of global pentecostalism. At the beginning of the period, an important contribution was made by the work of Juhani Kuosmanen, *Herätyksen Historia* (1989). In this "history of revival," Kuosmanen used a traditional and popular pentecostal historiography, generally eschewed in Scandinavia, which may be described as identifying pentecostalism as a continuation of a long sequence of revival movements misjudged by the established churches as "heresies." The difference is that he also understands pentecostalism as a global movement in which there are many players and local traditions that need to be respected. No particular pride of place is given to Finland or Scandinavia, although this area serves as the primary information base.

A completely different approach was taken by Lauri K. Ahonen, *Suomen helluntaiherätyksen historia* (1994). Ahonen provides a modern phenomenological, scholarly history of Finnish pentecostalism. He continues the Scandinavian approach to pentecostal history described above, that is, congregational, focused on indigeneity, socially concerned, as well as part of and contributing to the larger global development of pentecostalism. Although the volume is about Finnish pentecostal history, there is much with implications for pentecostalism beyond those borders. This is not surprising, since his first scholarly work, based on his M.A. thesis at Fuller Theological Seminary, was entitled "Missions Growth: A Case Study on Finnish Free Mission" (1984). The book, using the traditional "church growth" categories, described the origins, mission theory, and expansion of Finnish pentecostal missions. Ahonen also wrote a biography of the mission theorist and theologian Eino O. Ahonen (=Ahosen), *Kohti Päämäärää: Päätoimitta ja Eino O. Ahosen elämäkerta* (1993). This scholarly volume provides a careful analysis of the theory and values of Finnish pentecostal mission. Because Ahonen, who also wrote at least 10 books and uncounted articles, was at the center of Finnish mission for so long, it also gives access to data for an eventual analysis of the diachronic and global structures of Finnish mission praxis throughout the world.

This was followed by an essay by Eero J. Anturi, "Helluntaiherätyksen toiminnen tarastelua," in Kai Anturi et al., *Helluntaiherätys tänään* (1986), 64–74, which vouchsafed the centrality of mission to Finnish pentecostal self-understanding. Then came the volume edited by Arto Hämäläinen, *Kaikkeen maailmaan 1929–1989: 60 vuotta helluntaiseurahuntien lähetystyöyä* (1989). This book brought together 11 chapters by 10 authors, all recognized historians, missiologists, or church leaders of the Finnish pentecostal church, to reflect on the history, mission theory, and future of the mission. Contributors include Juhani Kuosmanen, Veikko Manninen, Lauri Ahonen, K. Tapani, E. Roisko, V. Kivikangas, and Arto Hämäläinen. Arto Hämäläinen also contributed *Etei ytsikään hukkuisi: Sinun paikkasi lähetystyössä* (1992), which explored the theological and praxis issues related to social ministry in mission and discussed the historical precedents in various countries.

Finnish pentecostal missionaries have been numerous and tenacious. They have had a major presence almost anywhere outside of North America. They have also written of their experiences and the development of the churches where they have served. Exemplary of these books are Annikki Raatikainen, *Vastasin Bangladeshin kutsuun* (1978); idem, *Ilon ja itkun Bangladesh* (1988) (Bangladesh); Elhi Aho, *Anna ja Mao Tse-Tungin miehet* (1981) (China); Helvi Taponen, *Kiinalainen matka* (1978) (China); Eino Ahonen, *Ja Ganges soitteli univirttä* (1962) (India); E. Walter Eerola, *Säihkyvä loimu: Lähetysveteraanin muistelmia Filippineitä* (1990) (The Philippines); Reijo Vaurula and Veikko Ontermaa, *V. O. Raassina: Lähetyspioneeri* (1988) (Thailand; see also below, section VII); Unto Kunnas, *Kaarlo Syvanto—Pioneer: Forty Years in Israel* (1993); and T. Vatanen, *Ilosanoman Julistajana Birmassa* (1945) (Burma), to mention but a few.

Swedish-language Finnish pentecostals support a missionary for every 100 church members (1997), so although the tradition is small, it has maintained a presence throughout the world. The efforts were briefly discussed in Arthur Sundstedt (*Pingstväckelsen: En världsväckelse* [1973], 53–64), but there is also the more detailed volume of Arne Herberts, *I Kärlekens tjänst: Finlands Svenska Pingstmission under 70 år* (1994). The larger context was discussed in the volume edited by Robert Kanto, *Pingströrelsen i Svenskfinland ... en liten presentation* (1994). Once again mission history becomes global pentecostal history in these volumes, especially in the work of Herberts, which provides access to reports about missionaries and churches outside Finland published in the periodical *Korsets Budskap*.

D. Influence of the Scandinavian Approach.

The tradition of writing about pentecostalism fostered in Scandinavia that is phenomenological and focused on both the local and global has influenced the historiography in other areas of the world. For example, in Brazil there is now a multigenerational historiographical tradition that began with Emelio Conde, *Historia das Assembleias de Deus no Brasil* (1960) followed by the collaborative work edited by Abraão de Almeida, *Historia das Assembleias de Deus no Brasil* (1982). There are also numerous biographical volumes, including Eliézer Cohen, *Simon Lundgren e a Obra Missionária no Brasil* (1986), and Ivar Vingren, *Det började I Pará: Svensk Pingstmission I Brasilien* (1994). Not unrelated in its approach is the work of Anders Ruuth, *Igreja Universal do Reino de Deus: Gudsrikets Universella Kyrka—en brasiliansk kyrkobildning. Resumen: Iglesia Universal del Reino de Dios* (1995), which provides a thorough analysis of the Church of the Universal Reign of God.

Closer to Sweden, one finds a continuation of this approach in quite a different context, and with quite a different thesis, in the examination of the development of pentecostalism in the islands of the North Atlantic by Pétur

Pétursson, *Fran väckelse till samfund: Svensk pingstmission på oarna i Nordatlanten* (1990), and in the history of pentecostalism in Estonia by Evald Kill, *Issandast kutsutud viinamäe Tööle* (1993). With regard to Asia, the example of Thailand will be discussed below.

VI. LATIN AMERICA: BATTLEGROUND FOR COMPETING THEORIES.

There was, up through the 1960s, a slow, steady production of materials related to the history and theology of pentecostalism in Latin America. Since that time, due the numerical success of pentecostalism and the failure of the rest of the churches (both Protestant and Catholic) to marginalize the newer tradition in Latin American culture, various efforts have been made to interpret pentecostalism in Latin America. This process has been complicated by the difficulties in admission and in gaining privileges of research in the university and/or seminary cultures. Therefore, most of the research has been undertaken outside the university contexts or in the departments of sociology of religion or anthropology, where the methods have been different from those applied to the phenomenon of pentecostalism in other parts of the world. However, since the late 1960s there have been a large number of studies that take specific cases as illustrative of the whole or synthetic efforts that attempt to describe the whole. All of these cannot be mentioned in this essay, but an effort is made to identify important expositions from different perspectives. Most of these have been written by persons outside the pentecostal tradition.

Beginning with *Handbuch der Pfingstbewegung* by Hollenweger in 1967, there has been a steady stream of materials from a variety of ecclesial and scholarly perspectives. Hollenweger's approach was generally phenomenological and dealt with pentecostalism throughout the world. His introductory and interpretative volume contained short chapters on pentecostalism in Brazil that discussed the Assembléias de Deus and the Congregação Christã do Brasil in terms of social and ecumenical issues. There was little attention to the Spanish-language churches on the Continent. However, when the Spanish version was published later, it included a chapter on Mexico: *El Pentecostalismo: Historia y doctrinas* (1976).

A careful historical and social analysis that reflects a phenomenological approach to pentecostalism was published by J. A. B. Kessler, *A Study of the Older Protestant Missions and Churches in Peru and Chile, with Special Reference to the Problems of Division, Nationalism and Native Ministry* (1967). Kessler treated the development of pentecostalism in those two countries in the context of the Protestant experience. He had sympathy for the integrity of the pentecostal believers and an extensive awareness of the historical and cultural structures that impinged on the beginnings of pentecostalism in Chile and Peru, as well as the larger Protestant mission efforts. His work remains the best historical and social macro-scale analysis of the phenomena. There are other important histories that share this phenomenological approach, including Santiago Aquilino Huamán P., *Historia del Movimiento Pentecostal en el Peru* (1982); Rubén Zavala Hidalgo, *Historia de las Asambleas de Dios del Peru* (1989); Reinerio Arce et al., eds., *Carismatismo en Cuba* (1997); as well as material mentioned above in the context of the impact of Scandinavian historiography.

A. Latin American Pentecostalism as Response to Social Alienation.

Beginning with the work of Emile Willems, *Followers of the New Faith* (1967), the alienation theory became a widely accepted heuristic device for understanding pentecostalism in Latin America. Pentecostalism, he argued, is a response to social alienation and provides an "opiate" or refuge for those attempting to escape present cruel realities through millenarian escapism. This Marxist-style analysis was further developed by Christian Lalive d'Epinay in *El Refugio de las masas* (1968) and *Réligion, dynamique social et dépendence: Les mouvements protestantes en Argentine et au Chile* (1975). Lalive d'Epinay argued that the "symbols of salvation" of pentecostalism responded well to the social needs of the poor and oppressed. From this interaction between ideology and social conditions was born "the religion of the masses," a populist, isolationist, nationalist tradition with few significant intellectual and religious structures. It is a "poor religion for the poor" that enables the lower classes to deal with the present. Since it is by definition unsophisticated and lower-class in orientation and rationalization, it could not be considered transformative. Indeed, it is seen as deadening the desire of the masses to transcend their present. It is clearly perceived to be lower on the evolutionary scale than the older European-originated Christian theological and social systems.

Within these parameters, the volumes of Lalive d'Epinay and Willems are careful descriptions and analyses of the pentecostals and their churches and are built on careful social research. These works provided access to groundbreaking socioreligious research, which generally has not been completely superseded by the efforts of later scholars. These established the tone for much subsequent research.

B. Sect Theory.

Lalive and Willems, and Bryan R. Wilson, the British interpreter of the theoretical structures and analysis of the British Elim Pentecostal Churches (*Religion in Secular Society* [1961]; *Religious Sects: A Sociological Study* [1970]; and, ed., *Patterns of Sectarianism* [1967]) provided a legitimacy to the sect analysis that was promulgated within Protestant and, especially, Roman Catholic religious circles. Sect analysis depends on both the "church/sect" distinction as well as the evolutionary thesis about the lower value of the less completely evolved newer churches. The Roman Catholic sect analysis has been and continues to be a primary form of apologetic effort, especially in Latin America. These are but a few of the more widely circulated titles: José A. Gilles Marchand, *Hablar de sectas en la Argentina y en América Latina* (1989); Pietro Canova, *Las Sectas: Un volcan en erupcion* (1991); Juan Miguel Ganuza, S.J., *Las Sectas nos Invaden* (1987); Felipe Navarrette, S.J., *La Iglesia en su hora más dramática (El desafío de las sectas)* (1992); Oscar A. Gerometta, *Aproximaciones . . . al fenómeno de las Sectas: Una reflexión en torno a la atomización de la experiencia religiosa contemporánea* (1995); Abelino Martinez, *Las Sectas en Nicaragua: Oferta y demanda de salvación* (1989); Osvaldo D. Santagada et al., *Las sectas en America Latina* (9th ed., 1993); and the anonymous *Sectas: Un Desafío a la Nueva Evangelización. Material de Estudio y Reflexión para los Católicos* (1993). The last item is a "comic book" that caricatures pentecostalism and argues for traditional Catholic loyalties and theology as well as obedience to the pope as essentials for being in conformity to the gospel. The official Vatican approach is somewhat more nuanced, due perhaps to nearly three decades of Roman Catholic–Pentecostal dialogue. (See "Documento del Vaticano sobre las sectas y nuevos movimientos religiosos," *Cristianismo y sociedad* 24 [88, 1986], 113–30.)

C. Deprivation Theory.

Another approach to Latin American pentecostalism, not unrelated to the above, is the "deprivation theory": pentecostalism is the religion of the "disinherited," modeled by Robert Mapes Anderson in *The Vision of the Disinherited* (1978). Among those who have sought to understand the Latin American tradition in this way is the Brazilian scholar Francisco Cartaxo Rolim, *Pentecostais no Brasil: Uma interpretação sócio-religiosa* (1985). Following the social theorist Max Weber, Rolim insists that it is not the theology of pentecostalism that is attractive or important but the social conditions of relative deprivation. The movement serves to provide a buffer between the oppressor of the capitalist system and those exploited by that system. It is, he argues, a function of class structures in which the reciprocal relations within the social system are defined as a binary opposition of dominators and dominated.

D. Latin American Pentecostalism as Subject for Sociological and Anthropological Analysis.

The process of social analysis is an important aspect of the analysis of religious aspects of global culture. One could take issue with many of the scholars of Latin America, not so much with regard to the methods used as to the assumptions with regard to the value and significance of the theoretical structures of pentecostalism. Others have used these tools in a more phenomenological way, including the research team of A. Frigerio in Argentina. From this group have come Alejandro Frigerio, ed., *Nuevos movimientos religiosos y ciencias sociales* (2 vols., 1993); idem, *Ciencias sociales y religión en el Cono Sur* (1993); idem, *El Pentecostalismo en la Argentina* (1994); Eduardo Basombrio, *El encuentro episcopal latinoamericano y la renovacion carismatica catolica* (1991); Maria Isabel Tort, *El pentecostalismo en la Argentina: Un estudio de caso* (1993). See the analysis in D. D. Bundy, "Pentecostalism in Argentina," *Pneuma* 20 (1998).

The anthropological research team of A. Droogers of the Free University of Amsterdam has produced A. Droogers, G. Huizer, and H. Siebers, eds., *Popular Power in Latin American Religions* (1991), and also Frans Kamsteeg, "Prophetic Pentecostalism in Chile: A Case Study on Religion and Development Policy" (diss., Vrije Universiteit, Amsterdam, 1995). A similar approach has been used by the Chilean scholars Arturo Fontaine T. and Harald Beyer, "Retrato del movimiento evangélico a la luz de las encuestas de opinión pública," *Estudios Publicos* 44 (Spring 1991), 63–124.

Droogers and his colleagues argue that popular religion cannot be understood apart from the power relations within the larger culture. The use of religious metaphors and concepts for faith and community organization are not seen as opiates. Instead, after careful anthropological analysis in Latin America, they argued that the appropriation of religious tools by the pentecostal communities functioned in quite a different way. Pentecostalism, they insisted, provides effective tools for dealing with modernity, not by escaping from it but by transforming the relationship of the individual and the community to the past, present, and future realities of life (B. Boudenwijse, A. Droogers, and F. Kamsteeg, *Algo más que opio: Una lectura antropológica del pentecostalismo latinoamericano y caribeno* [1991]).

E. Latin American Pentecostalism as "Popular Religion."

From the interaction between ideology (pentecostal ideas) and social conditions, it is argued, was born "popular religion," which, while insignificant in its intellectual and religious structures, did the lower classes a service by enabling them to deal with the present. While the literature is generally quite sympathetic toward the social goals, it is generally clear that popular religion is considered to be lower on the evolutionary intellectual scale than other forms of Christian theological and social reflection. This is the analysis often given in the literature that compares pentecostal churches and "base communities" in Latin America, as, for example, Orlando Mella and Patricio Frías, eds., *Religiosidad popular, trabajo y communidades de base* (1994), and the quite excellent volumes of Manuel Ossa, *Lo Ajeno y lo propio: Identidad Pentecostal y trabajo* (1991), and *Espiritualidad popular y accion politica: El Pastor Victor Morra y la Misión Wesleyana Nacional: 40 años de historia religiosa y social (1928–1969)* (1990). This approach has also been used by pentecostal scholar Juan Sepúlveda,

"Pentecostalism as Popular Religion," *International Review of Mission* (1989); idem, "Reflexiones sobre el aporte pentecostal a la misión de la Iglesia en Chile," in *Pentecostalismo, Sectas y Pastoral,* ed. F. Sampedro (1989), 43–48; and idem, *The Andean Highlands: An Encounter with Two Forms of Christianity* (1997), which deals with cultural issues raised by the conversion of significant numbers of the Aymara tribe of Chile to pentecostalism.

F. Latin American Pentecostalism as Exported North American Fundamentalism/ Evangelicalism and Rightist Politics.

In North America a major trend has been to interpret Latin American pentecostalism as an export of American fundamentalism. Volumes on "global" Christianity have demonstrated the interest of those newer traditions for the task of reflecting about developments in religion in the 20th century. However, North American scholars have often lumped pentecostalism with Protestant fundamentalism and other "conservative" movements (Holiness, evangelical, dispensationalist, Keswick) without an understanding of the significant theological, philosophical, and sociopolitical differences between most representatives of these traditions. Furthermore, there appears to be an assumption that the representatives of these traditions in Europe, Africa, Asia, and Latin America are clones of a stereotypical, simplistic, North American phenomenon. When treated simplistically as American prepackaged exports, the influence of context, culture, and social location on the expression of ideas is either ignored or viewed as unimportant.

This is the case in the volume by Steve Brouwer, Paul Gifford, and Susan D. Rose, *Exporting the American Gospel: Global Christian Fundamentalism* (1996), in which the newer churches (pentecostal, Holiness, evangelical, Keswick, and fundamentalist) are treated as basically monolithic "global Christian fundamentalism." In addition to homogenizing the different traditions, it is assumed by these authors (and many others) that the simplistic analyses of social, political, and intellectual life expounded by American television evangelists are taken over by believers in Latin America and other places with minimal nuancing of the arguments. Often, as in this volume, the analysis is based almost exclusively on North American sources; the analysis of "global Christian fundamentalism" cites only six non-English sources, and it would appear that none of these was produced by the groups analyzed.

A similar approach and similar database were used, with about the same results, by David Stoll and David Martin in their studies of Protestantism in Latin America: David Stoll, *Is Latin America Turning Protestant? The Politics of Evangelical Growth* (1990); David Martin, *Tongues of Fire: The Explosion of Protestantism in Latin America* (1990). Again there is the assumption that all of these groups are "fundamentalists" and that they and related groups are always attached to the political right. It is significant that when precise, phenomenological, nonideological studies of congregations were made by scholars of the Free University of Amsterdam the results were quite different (see Boudenwijse et al., *Algo más que opio*, discussed above).

VII. ASIA: THE EXAMPLE OF THAILAND.

The writing of the history of pentecostalism in Asia is generally in its initial stages. One could discuss the examples of Korea, Japan, India, China, Indonesia, Singapore, and the Philippines. In each country there have been serious efforts and many publications, both in the context of educational institutions and in the context of the denominations. However, due to the recent publication of two important volumes in Thai that discuss the history of pentecostalism in Thailand, this country has been chosen as an example. The goal is to indicate both the complexity of the historiographical problems and the connections to global pentecostal historical writing.

The pentecostal movement in Thailand grew out of the Holiness revivals (1938, 1939) led by John Sung during WWII (Leslie Y. Lyall, *Flame for God: John Sung and Revival in the Far East* [1954]). Missionaries of the Finnish Free Foreign Mission arrived in 1946, and the first pentecostal churches were formed (see the discussion of Finnish historical writings above). There is an extensive bibliography about the work of this mission in Thailand, in Finnish and English, as well as in Thai. Among the English materials are three unpublished MRE theses submitted at Grand Rapids Baptist Seminary: Jouko Rouhomäki, "The Finnish Free Foreign Mission in Thailand, 1946–1985" (1988); Aarno Salmenkivi, "The Development of the Curriculum of the Full Gospel Bible Training Center" (1991); and Lea-Raija Minalainen, "The Work of the FFFM and the Development of Thailand during 1965–1991" (1992). In addition, there is an unpublished licentiate thesis at the University of Åbo, Finland: Jaako Mäkelä, "Krischak Issara: The Independent Churches in the Bangkok Metropolitan Area, Thailand: Their Historical Background, Contextual Setting, and Theological Thinking" (1993). There are numerous missionary biographies in Finnish and many local congregational histories and other documents in Thai. The first effort to bring this material together into a narrative and to enlarge the historical database through interviews and examination of archival materials in Finland and Thailand has been made by Hannu Kettunen, *Tungruangtong: History of the Finnish Free Foreign Mission in Thailand, 1946–1996* (in Thai) (1996). This well-crafted volume follows the Scandinavian historical method described above.

The same is true of the work of Robert Nishimoto, *History of Pentecostalism in Thailand, 1946–1996* (in Thai) (1996). This monumental volume attempts to describe the development of the various aspects of the pentecostal movement as it has evolved in Thailand. Unfortunately, access to Finnish sources as well as to relevant English, Korean, and Chinese sources was limited. On the other hand, Nishimoto conducted interviews with many leaders, members, and missionaries of the FFFM-related churches. The resulting story is carefully placed in its global context.

Five important branches of pentecostalism in Thailand are minimally discussed in these works. Through these the reality of pentecostalism is seen to be even more complex. First is the United Pentecostal Church. Elly Hansen, a Danish pentecostal missionary to Thailand (from 1950), was converted in 1960 to the Oneness view under the influence of a Thai Christian, Boon Mak (Elly Hansen and Mary Wallace, *Following Jesus All the Way: Elly* [1987]). They eventually united (1962) with the mission program of the (U.S.) United Pentecostal Church. The denomination has more than 10,000 members.

The second denomination is the True Jesus Church, also a Oneness group. This primarily Chinese church has had a significant impact in Thailand and throughout the Chinese diaspora. Third are the churches created by the efforts of South Korean missionaries that are scattered throughout the country. The fourth denomination is the rapidly growing Hope of Bangkok Church. This church has generated a significant literature and is becoming global in its mission programs and affiliations (Joseph A. Wonsak, "Hope of Bangkok Church," in *The New Apostolic Churches*, ed. C. Peter Wagner [1998]). In addition to these there are, fifth, a number of smaller denominations that have come into existence through various mission efforts (especially important were the pentecostal missionaries from Sweden, Norway, and Finland and the Pentecostal Assemblies of Canada) and personal disaffection. Finally, there is a significant charismatic renewal in progress within the Church of Christ of Thailand, a church created by the merger of Christian Church (Disciples of Christ), Presbyterians, and Methodists.

This case study demonstrates the difficulty of historical research on pentecostalism in Asia. If one is to adequately understand the phenomena in Thailand, for example, one must be conversant with a diversity of traditions (both in their original and in their Thai versions!) and able to work with literature in at least six languages (Thai, Chinese, Korean, Finnish, Swedish, and English). Similar problems with source materials, bibliography, and language are posed by every area of Asia.

VIII. AFRICA: PENTECOSTALISM AND THE AFRICAN INDEPENDENT CHURCHES.

The bibliography and historiography of pentecostalism in Africa is complicated by the existence of pentecostal churches related in some direct way to North American or European churches, and the ›African Independent (Initiated) Churches (AIC). The AIC have been the beneficiaries of major bibliographic efforts, especially H. W. Turner and R. C. Mitchell, *A Bibliography of Modern African Religious Movements* (1966), and studies such as those of Bert Sundkler, *Bantu Prophets in South Africa* (2d ed., 1961), and of David Barrett, *Schism and Renewal in Africa: An Analysis of Six Thousand Contemporary Religious Movements* (1968). Among the more influential scholars of these movements are G. C. Oosthuizen and M. L. Daneel. Scholarly articles on the AICs are regular features of scholarly journals devoted to Africa, and a significant bibliography is produced each year; the study of AICs is solidly part of the university culture and the scholarly interpretation of African history and identity.

The project of writing the history of the more traditional pentecostal churches of Africa, on the other hand, is in its infancy. The lists of denominations provided in Hollenweger, *Handbuch der Pfingstbewegung* (1965), and D. Barrett et al., *World Christian Encyclopedia* (1982), are quite incomplete, although they are the most complete published. Hollenweger's bibliographies, and those of Charles Jones mentioned above, remain important. Archival and published materials are scattered throughout the world, as noted above. Many larger congregations in Africa have small archives or files; most include individuals who have committed the story of the congregation to memory. Raw material is not as plentiful as in many areas of the world, but most of that which is available has not been exploited. In every case there are resources in a number of European and/or American mission-sending countries as well as in the African context.

Most of the research and writing that has been done and is continuing is in South Africa. F. P. Poggenpoel, *'N Sosiologiese studie van die Barmhartigheidsdiens van die Apostoliese Geloof Sending (UNISA)* (1960), and F. P. Möller, *Die Diskussie oor die Charismata soos wat dit in die Pinksterbeweging geleer en beoefen word. Hoofsaaklik met betrekking tot die Pinksterbeweging in die Verenigde State van Amerika, die Verenigde Koninkryk en die Republiek van Suid-Afrika, tot die begin van die Neo-Pentecostalisme* (1975), were important contributions that examined South African practice in light of the larger pentecostal world. More recent are the works of A. A. Dubb, *Community of the Saved* (1976), and Peter Watt, *From Africa's Soil: The Story of the Assemblies of God in Southern Africa* (1992). Watt's volume documents Assemblies of God theology and practice and discusses the racial, missionary, and gender tensions faced by the denomination. Many of the South African pentecostal denominations support financially the UNISA project on pentecostalism, and eventually this will result in numerous publications.

The Christ Apostolic Church (CAC) of Nigeria provides another case study. A history by Alokan J. Adewale, *The Christ Apostolic Church, 1928–1988* (1991), complements the older volume by D. O. Babajide, *Iwe Itan* (Historic Book) (1987). There are biographies (e.g., John O. Ojo, *The Life and Ministry of Apostle Joseph Ayodele Babalola (1904–1950)* [1988]) and literature about internal dissent and discussion (such as Ekan Etim, *The C.A.C. Crisis in Home Mission and in Section F Issues Involved* [1995]). A variety of studies and polemical documents discuss the role of the CAC in Nigeria (e.g., J. L. Akeredolu, *The Church and Its Denominations in Nigeria* [1986]). In addition, a number of theses have been written in the seminaries and universities of Nigeria, including, e.g., Joshua Owolola Balogun, "Power Tussle in Christ Apostolic Church (C.A.C.) in the Light of Biblical Servant-Leadership Model" (M.A.B.S. thesis, Ecwa Theol. Sem., Igbaja; 1997). There are unused archival materials in New Zealand, Wales, and Denmark. To this point the literature is so consumed with the internal strife within the denomination over leadership and finances that the historical research has been devoted to these issues rather than an effort to interpret the denomination or Nigerian pentecostalism within the context of global pentecostalism.

The example of the CAC is illustrative of the situation of many denominations across Africa. When there are closer missionary ties, there are also the biographies of missionaries, references in denominational histories in the U.S. or Europe, archival resources, and, on occasion, periodicals. This process of African pentecostal documentation must, for Portuguese-speaking countries, also include Brazil. The Igreja Universal do Reino de Deus (Church of the Universal Reign of God) has mission efforts that are attracting numerous converts in Angola and Mozambique as well as in several other countries.

Still relatively unexamined, and of enormous significance for the future of global Christianity, are the historical, theological, liturgical, and political relationships between the AICs and the Africa pentecostal churches with more clear relationships to either European or American churches. There are tantalizing hints in the literature about the importance of the Keswick Holiness revivals in Central Africa under the auspices of the SCM, Universities Mission to Central Africa, and the London Missionary Society. Mills suggested a relationship between the Wesleyan/Holiness missions and Black African religions/political nationalism (W. G. Mills, "The Taylor Revivals of 1866 and the Roots of African Nationalism," *Journal of Religion in Africa* 8 [1976]). These suggestions remain unexplored.

The same is true of suggestions about the roles of South African Assemblies of God (the tradition of ›Nicholas Bhengu, not the American-dominated church) and the earlier Zionist revivalist movements in South Africa (1908 and after) on the evolution of the AICs. Also unexamined are the relationships between Belgian Gospel Mission evangelists (led by W. F. P. Burton) on the theological structures of Kimbanguism. The first person to suggest the complexity of these relationships was Walter Hollenweger in his *Handbuch der Pfingstbewegung* and in the published introductory volumes.

IX. CONCLUSION.

The process of writing the history of the pentecostal and charismatic movements around the world is still in its initial stages. The diversity and complexity of the traditions stand out clearly. No one has developed a successful meta-theory of pentecostalism. Certainly no theory that makes the American experience paradigmatic can explain the global realities of pentecostalism. Thousands of precisely defined case studies from a variety of points of view and methods, based on careful historical, sociological, and anthropological research, are needed. In early 1906 there were no persons identified as "pentecostal" or "charismatic" as those terms are currently understood. It has been suggested that there are (1998) at least 461 million pentecostals and charismatic believers as well as millions of members of AICs (David B. Barrett and Todd M. Johnson, "Annual Statistical Table on Global Mission: 1998," *International Bulletin of Missionary Research 22* [1998]). Much more research is needed to preserve and clarify the identity and heritage of these movements.

■ D. D. Bundy

BICKLE, MIKE (1955–). Pastor of Metro Christian Fellowship (MCF) of Kansas City. Born again in 1971 at a Fellowship of Christian Athletes summer camp in Estes Park, CO, Billy Graham's preaching at Campus Crusade's Expo '72 in Dallas, TX, had a powerful impact on him. In 1973 he went to St. Louis to attend Washington University, but within a month he left to care for his brother, Pat, who had broken his neck in a football accident. In 1974, after the death of his father, who was a lightweight boxing champion from Kansas City, he attended the University of Missouri for a year. In 1982, after seven years of church planting and pastoring in St. Louis, he moved to Kansas City to plant Kansas City Fel-

Mike Bickle, pastor of Metro Christian Fellowship in Kansas City, and his wife, Diane.

lowship (KCF). In 1985 he began refocusing on prayer and intercession, which continues as a main emphasis. In 1990 a leadership training program, Grace Training Center, was founded, and in the same year, KCF became a part of the ⸎Vineyard (Metro Vineyard Fellowship) until 1996. Attendance reached 7,000 by early 1991, and by 1993, six additional congregations had been planted in Kansas City. MCF's ⸎Kansas City Prophets have been controversial, especially since 1988, when ⸎John Wimber became closely associated with one of them, Paul Cain. Mike Bickle and his church became prominent in the ⸎"Toronto Blessing," beginning with its outbreak in early 1994.

■ **Bibliography:** M. Bickle, *Growing in the Prophetic* (1995) ■ idem, *Passion for Jesus* (1993) ■ D. Pytches, *Some Said It Thundered* (1991). ■ R. M. Riss

BILBY, IAN (1945–). Ian Bilby represents a fourth generation of New Zealand pentecostalism. His maternal great-grandfather and grandfather (⸎Henry Roberts and ⸎Harry Roberts) were both leaders in the Pentecostal Church of N.Z. His father, Charles ("Chas") Bilby was a pastor in the Elim Church of N.Z., the successor to the Pentecostal Church of N.Z. Ian Bilby was formerly a high school science teacher; he moved to Blenheim in 1972 to pastor the small Elim church there. The church had been closed for six months, and the congregation consisted of only four elderly people who gathered for house meetings. Under Bilby's leadership the church reopened, and the congregation grew to 500 people over the next 10 years. By 1982 it had become one of the most significant churches in N.Z. It planted a daughter church in Picton, inspired growth in other Elim churches, and sent a number of congregational members out to pastor new Elim churches.

In the mid 1980s Bilby moved to Auckland to establish the Auckland City Elim Church. This church soon became the flagship of the Elim movement and grew to more than 1,000 people by 1991. Bilby also held the presidency of the Elim Church of N.Z. for 18 years, and the growth of the churches he led reflected that of the movement as a whole during this period.

■ **Bibliography:** Y. Dasler, "Then They Came to Elim ..." *New Zealand Listener* 24 (Apr. 1982). ■ B. Knowles

BIOLLEY, HÉLÈNE (c. 1854–c. 1947). An important background figure in the origins of French pentecostalism. Born in Switzerland, Biolley came to Le Havre, France, in 1896, where she opened a temperance hotel and restaurant, the Ruban Bleu, combined with a gospel outreach and prayer meetings. Following a visit by ⸎Alexander Boddy in 1909, she regularly invited pentecostal evangelists to visit and speak, e.g., ›Smith Wigglesworth (1920, 1921) and ›Douglas Scott (1927, 1930). Biolley's greatest contributions to French pentecostalism were, however, her persuading Scott, who became the nation's foremost pentecostal evangelist, to spend time in France before going to Africa, and her formative influence on three young men—Felix Gallice (France), Cristo Domoutchief (Romania), and Ove Falg (Denmark)—who became major figures in the French movement. Biolley translated into French ›Maria B. Woodworth-Etter's *Signs and Wonders* (1919), which ran to at least five editions.

■ **Bibliography:** G. R. Stotts, *Le Pentecôtisme au pays de Voltaire* (1981).   ■ P. D. Hocken

BITTLINGER, ARNOLD (1928–). European charismatic leader and scholar. Bittlinger, then evangelism director in the Protestant state church (Landeskirche) in Germany, first encountered charismatic renewal (CR) in the U.S. in late 1962. He arranged a German conference with ›Larry Christenson the following summer. Bittlinger then became the main Lutheran leader of West German CR, which he promoted ecumenically; in 1968 he helped to establish an ecumenical center at Schloss Craheim. With ›J. Rodman Williams he initiated the European Charismatic Leaders Conference in 1972. Bittlinger, a biblical scholar, was one of the earliest charismatic exegetes to use the methods of biblical criticism. Of his many works, only *Gifts and Graces* (1967), *Gifts and Ministries* (1973), and *Letter of Joy* (1975) are available in English.

During a year's residence as fellow of the Institute for Ecumenical and Cultural Research at Collegeville, MN, Bittlinger coauthored *The Baptism in the Holy Spirit as an Ecumenical Problem* with K. McDonnell (1972). As a charismatic scholar, he participated in the first five years of the ›dialogue between Catholics and classical pentecostals (1972–76). His doctoral dissertation on the dialogue was published under the title *Papst und Pfingstler* (Pope and Pentecostals) (1978).

Bittlinger was chairman of the committee that produced theological guidelines for the charismatic parish renewal in the West German Evangelical Church (1976). In 1978 he became part-time consultant to the World Council of Churches (WCC) on CR and part-time pastor in Oberhallau, Switzerland; he convened the WCC consultation on charismatic movements held at Bossey, Switzerland, in Mar. 1980 and edited its papers, published as *The Church Is Charismatic* (1981). Bittlinger arranged a further WCC consultation on CR in Zaire at the end of 1981, but his work in the next few years was channeled into a study project for the WCC Commission on World Mission and Evangelism.

■ **Bibliography:** U. Birnstein, *Neuer Geist in alter Kirche?* (1987).   ■ P. D. Hocken

BJÖRK, OLOV LEONARD (1873–1950). Editor, pastor, mission leader, mission theorist, educator. O. L. Björk, a Baptist pastor in Stora Mellösa near Örebro, Sweden, where he served from 1903 until 1913, was perhaps the first Swedish clergyman to experience the pentecostal baptism of the Holy Spirit, which he did on Feb. 5, 1907.

Born in Ljusne, Hälsingland, on Mar. 12, 1879, Björk studied at the (Baptist) Betelseminariet in Stockholm (1899–1903). He had been active in the Swedish Holiness revival since 1903 and monitored carefully the waxing and waning of the Welsh revival. In early 1907 he received information about the revival in Kristiania (Oslo), Norway, led by ›T. B. Barratt. A few months later he also had contact with Andrew J. Johnson (who later changed his name to Andrew Ek), a Swedish seaman who had been a participant in the Azusa Street Mission. Björk became an effective proponent of the new tradition, and his congregation became the mother church of pentecostalism in Sweden. Unlike most other Swedish pentecostals, he accepted the doctrine of ›"initial evidence."

In Feb. 1911 he began to publish *Brudgommens röst* (1911–22), a periodical through which Björk promoted pentecostal mission around the world, in cooperation with ›Paul Ongman and others. However, Björk was the primary contact with the missionaries and raised monies to support their efforts. Among the pentecostal missionaries first supported by Björk were ›Daniel Berg and ›Gunnar Vingren in Brazil and ›Axel Andersson in Mexico. His approach to mission was influenced by T. B. Barratt and ›William Taylor as well as by his Baptist experience.

From 1913 until 1918 Björk served as pastor of Fifth Baptist Church in Stockholm, a church that had become pentecostal/Baptist in 1907 under the influence of Barratt. Unlike ›Lewi Pethrus, Björk was able to maintain good relations with the Swedish Baptist denomination while remaining thoroughly pentecostal. In 1918 Björk succeeded ›John Ongman as pastor of the Filadelfia Church in Örebro, where he served until 1928. Thereafter he traveled throughout the world, but especially in Sweden, preaching and teaching. He also wrote for the Örebro Mission periodical *Missions Banaret*. From 1918 onward, he taught regularly at the Örebro Mission School, a primary center for educating pentecostal clergy and missionaries. He died on Aug. 31, 1950.

■ **Bibliography:** Books by Björk. *Rätt väg och sidostig. Några tanker i fråga om äktenskapet* (1915) ■ *Min erfarenhet av andedopet* (1920) ■ *De andliga gåvorna* (1922; 1928) ■ *Vem har skrivit Jesaja bok? Anteckningar efter olika källor* (1934) ■ *Guds församling framstäld i bilder. Sju predikningar* (1927; 2d ed. 1945) ■ *Genom bibeln på ett år. Plan för daglig bibelläsning* (1931; repr. 1944.) ■ *Bibelns bildersprak* (1934) ■ *Äktenskap och Skilsmässa* (1938; 2d ed. 1944) ■ *555 frågor besvarade* (1943) ■ *Rätt väg och sidostig. Några tanker i fråga* (n.d.) ■

Det härliga landet. Skildringar från en resa till Palastina våren 1930 (1931) ■ *På tusenmilfärd. Minnen och intryck från en resa genom Förenta Staterna, 1926–1927* (1928) ■ Samuel Rutherford, *Märkliga brev. Djupa sanningar om det andliga levet,* ed. James Stephen, tr. O. L. Björk (1945).

Books on Björk. *O. L. Björk, En minnesbok* (1953) ■ Fredrik Hedvall, *Betel Seminarister, 1866–1966. Biografiska, uppgifter om lärere och elever* (1966), 69 ■ Willy Svahn and Gustav Olsson, *En öppen dörr* (1981) ■ *100 år i ord och bild. Örebromissionen, 1892–1992* (1992).   ■ D. D. Bundy

BJORNER, ANNA LARSSEN (1875–1955). Pioneer figure in the pentecostal movement in Denmark. A well-known actress in Copenhagen, Anna Larssen was converted through the preaching of H. J. Mygind. She was baptized in the Spirit during a visit of ʼT. B. Barratt in Dec. 1908. She held pentecostal meetings in her large house, attracting many colleagues from the stage, though she gave up her acting career in 1909. In 1912 she married Sigurd Bjorner, then general secretary of the Danish YMCA.

The Bjorners held pentecostal meetings all over Denmark. In 1919 they were both baptized in water in Sweden, an act that finally excluded them from the Danish state church. Following a visit to Wales in 1923, the Bjorners' fellowship joined the ʼApostolic Church. This relationship was broken in 1936, when their assembly objected to the Apostolic Church in Denmark being under British control. Anna Bjorner died in 1955, two years after her husband.

■ **Bibliography:** N. Bloch-Hoell, *The Pentecostal Movement* (1964) ■ T. N. Turnbull, *What God Hath Wrought* (1959).
                                                                    ■ P. D. Hocken

BLACK HOLINESS PENTECOSTALISM

I. Introduction

II. Beginnings
   A. Slaves' Religious Beliefs
   B. Holy Spirit Controversy

III. Growth
   A. The Rise of Black Independent Churches
     1. Segregation
     2. Holiness Message
   B. Baptism in the Holy Spirit
     1. Azusa Street Revival Confirmation
     2. Churches Emerged
   C. Persecution
   D. Issues
   E. 1920s and 1930s
     1. Rifts in BHP Churches
     2. Women's Participation
   F. 1940s and 1950s
     1. Spread throughout the World
     2. Education
   G. 1960s and 1970s
     1. Further Institutionalization
     2. Polity Rifts
   H. Final Decade of the Twentieth Century

IV. Conclusion
   A. Contributions
   B. Active Discipleship to Be Witnesses

I. INTRODUCTION.

Black Holiness pentecostalism (BHP) is not a denomination but rather a movement encompassing several denominations professing belief in Spirit baptism accompanied by various signs, including speaking in tongues, with historic roots embracing, but not always restricted to, both a Wesleyan-Arminian and finished-work-of-Calvary orientation. Participants believe that the baptism in the Holy Spirit is a normative postconversion experience available to all Christians for the purpose of becoming more effective witnesses in carrying out the Great Commission (Matt. 28:19).

Perhaps more than any other 20th-century religious movement in the West, BHP is regarded by many as a highly significant catalyst and spawning ground for scores of denominations as well as the charismatic renewal, all emphasizing the centrality of the Holy Spirit. So little attention had been given to BHP by historians that Dietrich Bonhoeffer, while visiting the U.S. from Germany, referred to its participants as the "step-children of modern church history." The early BHP pioneers, while often sequestered from the view of even major American church historians, have nevertheless spoken to our times and deserve their rightful place in history.

II. BEGINNINGS.

BHP was born amid the fleeting shadows of slavery in America. The movement encompasses those black religious groups whose leadership for the most part developed primarily from established mainline black Protestant denominations between 1885 and 1916. The genesis of BHP occurred approximately 25 years after the signing of the Emancipation Proclamation, some 15 years before the formation of the National Association for the Advancement of Colored People and parallel to the ascendancy of the noted black educator Booker T. Washington.

A. Slaves' Religious Beliefs.

While the significance of African survivals within black religion in the New World have been the subject of much debate among anthropologists, sociologists, and historians, it appears from the evidence that BHP shares the legacy of black slave religion, whose historic roots are anchored deep in

African and Afro-Caribbean religion. It was not coinciden-
tal that Philip the evangelist in the NT baptized the high-
born African treasurer of the queen of Ethiopia, a ceremony
that was symbolic of African involvement in the further
spread of the Christian faith.

It should be stated at the outset that it is primarily in worship form, religious expression, and lifestyle, rather than in a
codified belief system that BHP shares in the rich tradition
and legacy of black slave religion. Since most of the first slaves
to be brought to the American colonies came from the Antil-
lean region, it is quite possible that some of them had already
made a partial transition from their native religions to Christianity prior to any systematic evangelization on the mainland. It was from slave religion that a "black style" of worship
developed in an unstructured way as black slaves encountered
the almighty God of their fathers.

The degree to which these Christianizing influences
modified slave religion is a matter still under debate and
requires a far more detailed treatment. While slaves were not
well educated by Western standards and cultural ethos, their
ancestral religions and the religious consciousness engendered
were highly complex. Specific religious beliefs salvaged from
Africa often came under vigorous assault by Protestant missionaries. It was the slaves' adaptation to Christianity without being completely divested of their native religious
worship style that later proved to be significant in its impact
on black religious lifestyle.

Carter E. Woodson, a prominent black historian,
reminded us several decades ago of the affinity of African
religion with the Hebraic background of Christianity pointing to the fact that the African stories of creation and belief
in the unity of God paralleled Christian theology. He contended that there was so much affinity between the two traditions that about the only changes the black slave made was
to label as Christian what he practiced in Africa. The resolution of the issue with regard to the survival of African cultural ethos is decisive for black pentecostalism.

The issue of the survival of African influence was debated
by E. Franklin Frazier, a prominent black sociologist who
contended for a sharp break with the African past. He argued
that due to the emasculating process of chattel slavery, blacks
brought to America were completely stripped of all vestiges
of the African past. Frazier focused on two basic institutions
of the black community: the family and the church. He
observed that "of the habits and customs as well as the hopes
and fears that characterized the life of their forebears in
Africa, nothing remains." However, once the black family was
destroyed, Frazier claimed, it was the Christian faith rather
than any vestiges of African culture or religious experience
that provided a new basis of social cohesion for slaves.

Frazier's view was countered by Melville J. Herskovits,
the renowned cultural anthropologist who argued a case for

the slaves' continuity with the African past. In his study of
human behavior among large groups of persons undergoing
acculturative change, it was difficult to distinguish between
form and meaning. He observed that as persons moved from
one culture to a new one, there was a tendency to adopt new
forms more readily than new meanings. However, under
acculturation, form changes more readily than meaning.
Herskovits concluded that during this process, persons characteristically assign old meanings to new forms, thereby
maintaining their preexisting systems of values and, as far as
their cognitive responses are concerned, making the break
with established custom minimal. On the emotional level
persons tend to retain the satisfaction derived from earlier
ways while adopting new forms that seem advantageous to
them. Both viewpoints have their own value, and both serve
to enrich each other and to foster the continuing discussion
relative to the issue of African survival in the New World.

It is generally known that the Cavaliers and Huguenots
controlled the Southern colonies at the points where slaves
were traded and were said to be far more tolerant with regard
to their religious views than the Puritans in the Northeast.
Their high degree of tolerance proved to be the proper setting for black slaves under acculturation who could very easily assign old meanings to new forms and in the very process
maintain their preexisting system of religious values. At the
emotional level they could readily cling to those values that
had substance as they adopted new forms that symbolized
survival. Under the influence of the Cavaliers and Huguenots,
black slaves throughout the South revised where necessary
and reinterpreted their religious practices. While the slaves
were physically "in" enough to "feel" the spirit of their slave
master's religion, their African cultural background to a large
extent kept them intellectually "out."

Only as black slaves were able to co-opt the outward
observable acts of their masters and interpret them in terms
of their African culture did they discover genuine spiritual
meaning and religious vitality. During the long trek of slavery, the freedom to worship provided slaves with the best
avenue of articulation and meaningful expression when other
ways were closed. Under such conditions slaves developed a
strong, simple faith permeated with ample superstition from
their African past. Such conditions also provided fertile soil
for the birth, growth, and development of a much later phenomenon known as Black Holiness sects.

It has been cogently argued that where European practices were relatively weak, the opportunities for the maintenance of African practices were correspondingly
strengthened. The South was a natural habitat for the birth
and development of BHP. By 1836 several thousand slaves
were taken into Texas annually. Bay Island in the Gulf of
Mexico was a depot where at times as many as 16,000
Africans were on hand to be shipped to Florida, Texas,

Louisiana, Mississippi, and other markets. Cities such as Vicksburg, MS, and Memphis, TN, received large contingents of imported slaves during this period. The presence of hostile white power and the early closing of the slave trade did much to crush the specific African religious memory but did not annihilate it.

B. Holy Spirit Controversy.

Long before the pentecostal revival at Azusa Street, Charles G. Finney in his "Letters to Ministers of the Gospel" had acknowledged that his instructions to converts had in former times "been very defective, for he had not clearly seen that the baptism of the Holy Ghost is a thing universally promised to Christians under this dispensation and that blessing is to be sought and received after conversion." Finney's revival methodology had a pronounced influence on the Methodism of his day and proved to be decisive in its impact on the Holiness movement as it attempted to embrace primitive Wesleyanism, with its emphasis on sanctification. American revivalism planted the seeds for the much later pentecostal movement.

The literature published in connection with the gradual development of the Holiness movement proved to be invaluable as well as decisive as a formative influence. William E. Boardman's *The Higher Christian Life* (1859) was said to have been the single most influential book in the literature of the Holiness movement. John P. Brook's *The Divine Church* (1891) became the bible for radical fringe groups labeled by older denominations as "come-outers." Also considered were Asa Mahan's *The Baptism of the Holy Ghost* (1870) and Finney's *Memoirs* (1876), in which he relates his Spirit baptism. Finally, R. A. Torrey's important work *Baptism with the Holy Spirit* (1895) found its way into the hearts of many Holiness leaders who later became prominent in the development of the pentecostal movement.

With a new interest in the Holy Spirit came controversy over Wesley's doctrine of sanctification, which resulted in a division within the Methodist church between 1880 and 1900. This was generated by Holiness advocates who stressed complete perfection characterized by "perfect love" or, better yet, entire sanctification, while those of pentecostal persuasion stressed baptism in the Holy Spirit as an experience subsequent to, and distinct from, conversion.

III. GROWTH.

A. The Rise of Black Independent Churches.

The spirit of religious individualism soon found its true expression in the emergence and development of black independent Protestant churches. This trend had begun in the 18th century with such notable ecclesiastical leaders as Richard Allen, James Varick, Peter Williams, George Collins, and Christopher Rush. The precedent was set in the case of Richard Allen in the formation of the African Methodist Episcopal Church (AME) in 1816, and Absalom Jones in founding the St. Thomas Protestant Episcopal Church in 1794 in protest against white racism and discrimination in the body of Christ.

1. Segregation.

The first few decades of the 19th century experienced a great deal of spiritual upheaval. New black churches were formed as black leaders sought to exercise their powers of leadership and to control their own affairs and destiny. By 1800 Peter Williams, James Varick, George Collins, and Christopher Rush had constituted a church they called "Lion" as a direct consequence of racial segregation. The Reverend Thomas Paul founded the first African Baptist Church in Boston by 1805 and later assisted in organizing a congregation in New York that became the Abyssinian Baptist Church. The First African Baptist Church in Philadelphia was founded in 1809 as a direct result of 13 blacks who had been dismissed from a white Baptist church. The Lombard Street Presbyterian Church in Philadelphia was also founded as a direct result of racial separation. The Dixwell Avenue Congregational Church was founded by blacks in New Haven, CT, by 1829.

These native and original black churches emerged for several reasons. Some were initiated because blacks were encouraged to form separate congregations, often under white supervision, due to the vast size of the mixed congregations. Several congregations were founded as a direct result of missionary activity. Frequent cases of blatant discrimination and the desire of black Christians for equal privileges within mixed congregations also became the basis for separation. The disapproval by whites of black worship and lifestyle played a major role in the separation of blacks from mixed fellowships and in the founding of independent black churches.

2. Holiness Message.

It was into this historical context that those persons were born who were destined to give leadership to what was to become the BHP movement. ►William Edward Fuller, born Jan. 29, 1875, in Mountville, SC, was destined to lead the ►Fire-Baptized Holiness Church of God of the Americas. ►Charles Harrison Mason was born Sept. 8, 1866, on a plantation known as the Prior Farm near Memphis, TN, to Jerry and Eliza Mason, who had been converted to the Christian faith; he later founded the ►Church of God in Christ (COGIC). Charles Price Jones, who later established the Church of Christ Holiness U.S.A., was born Dec. 9, 1865, near Rome, GA, and grew up in the brokenness of post–Civil War black existence. These BHP leaders were the sons of devoutly religious slaves whose African roots were deep within the black religious tradition where freedom of worship and varied lifestyle were dominant motifs.

In 1892 Elijah Lowney, a former Methodist minister from Cleveland, OH, held a revival at Wilmington, NC, where he preached the message of Holiness. Among the persons from various races and denominations gathered to hear this black scholarly Holiness advocate preach with unusual power and unction was Henry Lee Fisher, who was instrumental in the formation of the United Holy Church in 1894 at Durham, NC.

The emergence of BHP from established black independent churches became more pronounced as in the case of Robert H. White, who had been a local preacher in the St. Stephens AME Church. When some accepted the Holiness message, he volunteered to provide leadership to the new converts who needed a place to worship and express their newfound experience. W. H. Fulford, a former member of the AME Zion Church, had earlier embraced Holiness, having preached to integrated audiences; he later organized a congregation under the name New Covenant Church.

As a Holiness body, the ▸United Holy Church of America (UHCA) traces its genesis to a revival meeting held at Method, NC, in 1885–86, parallel to that which started the ▸Church of God (Cleveland, TN). Several personalities are associated with its beginnings: Isaac Cheshier, L. M. Mason, G. A. Mials, H. C. Snipes, W. H. Fulford, and H. L. Fisher, who later became president of the movement. The United Holy Church originated as a typical Holiness group and later was among the first Holiness bodies on record to become pentecostal. The first convocation convened at Durham, NC, in 1894, resulting in the establishment of its headquarters in that city.

A division occurred during the early developmental period of the United Holy Church over belief in the necessity of the Lord's Supper for salvation, but this schism was resolved in 1907. When the Holiness message began to spread rapidly to other cities, some groups severed denominational ties while others retained them. Two organizations were formed, the United Holiness Convention and the Big Kahara Holiness Association. Those groups retaining denominational ties became known as the "in church people" and joined the Big Kahara Holiness Association. Those who severed their ties were known as the "come-outers" and later became members of the United Holiness Convention. Severe criticism of the "in-church people" by their denomination gradually forced the two groups into a merger. In 1900 the groups merged and consented to use the name Holy Church of North Carolina. "Virginia" was later added as the movement spread northward, and in 1916 at Oxford, NC, the name was changed to the UHCA.

The example of the UHCA significantly illustrates that the same trend that occurred among advocates of white Holiness bodies in their genesis also occurred within black fellowships. Unlike the United Holy Church, the ▸Pentecostal Assemblies of the World and the ▸Fire-Baptized Holiness Church of God of the Americas grew out of white Holiness-pentecostal bodies.

The genesis of the Church of Christ Holiness U.S.A., occurred between 1894–96 under the leadership of Charles Price Jones (1865–1949), a black missionary Baptist preacher in Jackson, MS. While pastor of Tabernacle Baptist Church, Selma, AL, Jones became dissatisfied with his personal religious experience. After acceptance of the Holiness principle of entire sanctification, Jones attempted to remain pastor of the Mt. Helm Baptist Church in Jackson, MS. He held a series of annual Holiness convocations and met objections by his Baptist brethren, later resulting in his expulsion. In 1900 Jones formed Christ's Association of Mississippi of Baptized Believers and developed an antidenominational stance.

Jones, Mason, and other prominent BHP leaders participated in what was known as "the movement," which primarily consisted of persons who embraced the "new doctrine of entire sanctification." From "the movement" emerged a federation of loosely organized congregations bearing such titles as "Churches of God" and "Churches of Christ." They held dual membership in their own denominations and in the emerging new federations stressing sanctification. This emphasis could be traced to the leadership efforts of Phoebe Palmer, who used the National Association for the Promotion of Holiness as a vehicle to promulgate the message of Wesleyan perfectionism in the South.

B. Baptism in the Holy Spirit.

1. Azusa Street Revival Confirmation.

These perfectionist teachings were heard by other prominent leaders, such as Amanda Berry Smith, a convert of John S. Inskip; John and William Christian; and John Jeter, a companion to C. P. Jones. It was Jones who sent Mason, D. J. Young, and J. A. Jeter to Los Angeles in 1906 to scrutinize the revival being held at Azusa Street under the leadership of William J. Seymour. When Mason returned, laying claim to a third crisis experience, the baptism in the Holy Spirit, he was disfellowshiped by Jones and Jeter. There is now historical evidence to suggest that the Azusa Street revival was no more than a confirmation of a phenomenon that had already begun among BHPs. (One year prior to Mason's claim to sanctification in Preston, AR, a black woman, Lucy Smith, testified to having received Spirit baptism in Aug. 1892.)

2. Churches Emerged.

After his expulsion Mason reorganized the loosely federated band of churches in 1907 into the ▸Church of God in Christ (COGIC), the name divinely revealed to him according to Scripture (Gal. 1:22; 1 Thess. 2:14; 2 Thess. 1:1) as he walked along a street in Little Rock, AR, in 1897. Perhaps the greatest impetus in the founding of the COGIC was a successful revival in 1896 at Jackson, MS, conducted jointly by Mason, Jones, Jeter, and W. S. Pleasant. The response was so overwhelming that opponents came from every direction and many persons were dramatically and miraculously healed by the power of faith. By 1897 the revival had made its way to Lexington, MS, which was 60 miles north of Jackson. Elder John Lee gave Mason permission to use his living room, which was of no value within hours because of the throngs of persons. A Mr. Watson generously donated an abandoned gin house located on the bank of a little creek and gave Mason permission to use it for revival. Opposition increased to the point that gunshots were fired into the services, but none were fatal. The emerging movement chose C. P. Jones as general overseer and appointed Mason over Tennessee and Jeter over Arkansas. While a general assembly was in session at Jackson, MS, in 1907, voting to sever the fellowship with Mason and his followers, a similar meeting was being held by Mason in Memphis. It was the latter meeting convened by Elder C. H. Mason that constituted the first general assembly of the COGIC. During this meeting he was unanimously chosen as chief apostle, a position held until his death on Nov. 17, 1961.

Between 1890 and 1898 a small group originally formed as an "association" after separating from the Pentecostal Fire-Baptized Holiness Church with roots in Georgia. Under the leadership of its founder, Benjamin Hardin Irwin, the first general council of the ⏵Fire-Baptized Holiness Church convened at Anderson, SC, on Aug. 1, 1898. W. E. Fuller was the only black among the 140 founding members. By 1911 the problem of a biracial constituency proved too difficult for the times. One-third of the constituency was released by the Pentecostal Holiness church, the parent body, to follow W. E. Fuller. From 1910 to 1922 the group was known as the Colored Fire-Baptized Holiness Church of God, with "of the Americas" added four years later. The headquarters are currently in Atlanta.

The ⏵Pentecostal Assemblies of the World emerged as a ⏵Oneness pentecostal body between 1906 and 1914. Its first general assembly was held Mar. 12, 1912, in Los Angeles, where J. J. Frazee of Portland, OR, was selected as its first general superintendent. This group merged with the all-white general assembly of Apostolic Assemblies at St. Louis in 1918. With ⏵Garfield T. Haywood as one of its first bishops, the body moved to Indianapolis, IN, where it began to thrive. It originally began as an interracial body, and by 1924 whites had formed the Pentecostal Church, Inc., a constituent body of the United Pentecostal Church that formed largely by merger in 1945. The Pentecostal Assemblies of the World is parent to the black Oneness fellowships that trace their spiritual genesis to G. T. Haywood.

C. Persecution.

In a letter to the Apostolic Faith just two years after the beginning of the Azusa Street revival, C. H. Mason wrote: "The fight has been great. I was put out, because I believed that God did baptize me with the Holy Ghost among you all. Well, He did it and it just suits me.... His banner over me is love." Religious and civil persecution began to plague BHP adherents. It was in the providence of God that William Joseph Seymour, a Baptist preacher with Holiness affiliation, born in Louisiana around 1855, would be used as a catalyst to usher in 20th-century pentecostalism. The converted livery stable in the ghetto of Los Angeles, a former AME church, became in God's providence a beacon light to the world as well as a spawning ground from which virtually all pentecostals trace their lineage; at least 26 church bodies trace their pentecostal doctrine to Azusa Street. No revival prior to this outpouring bore such interracial and ecumenical fruits. Not only did persons of various races in America participate, but adherents from 35 nations responded to the mighty call of the Holy Spirit.

A few years after this three-year revival, however, BHPs found themselves facing suffering from within and without their enclaves. It was not long before they found themselves in a condition of triple jeopardy—black, poor, and pentecostal. The harsh invectives imposed on these pioneers caused them to develop a worldview much closer to the reality of the world than that of the privileged few. Unearned suffering imposed on BHP adherents gave them special insight into the working of the Spirit in the world. Their suffering forced them to reject the abstract god of the philosophers for a more concrete God who could be encountered and known at a deeply personal level.

Lynchings and Klan activity were not the only plagues on the South and other parts of the nation at the turn of the century; another problem was paranoia among governmental officials that eventually brought pressure to bear on anyone who was openly opposed to warfare. C. H. Mason directed W. B. Holt (a white) and E. R. Driver, the COGIC West Coast representative, who had a legal background, to draft a statement reflecting the church's stance on war. The statement, "We are opposed to war in all its various forms and believe the shedding of blood and the taking of human life to be contrary to the teachings of our Lord Jesus Christ," remains to this day the COGIC stance. The drafted document affirmed loyalty to the president, the Constitution, civil laws, the flag, magistrates, and all God-given institutions; but on the other hand, it forbade members to bear arms or shed blood.

The COGIC conscientious-objector stance set the stage for other newly formed Holiness-pentecostal groups to follow. The strains of WWI brought greater pressure on churches that openly encouraged others to disobey the draft law. The *Memphis Commercial Appeal* carried an article (Apr. 1918) about elder Jessie Payne, a COGIC pastor in Blytheville, AR, who was tarred and feathered as a result of "seditious remarks concerning the president, the war, and a white man's war." Mason had presented a clear message on "The Kaiser in the Light of the Scriptures," in which he condemned German militarism, but he was misinterpreted when under the power of the Spirit he admonished listeners not to trust in the power of the U.S., England, France, or Germany, but to trust in God: "The enemy [the devil] tried to hinder me from preaching the unadulterated word of God. He plotted against me and had the white people arrest me and put me in jail for several days. I thank my God for the persecution. 'For all that live godly must suffer persecution'" (2 Tim. 2:12).

The impact of Mason's stance was so great on persons entering the military that the government tried in vain to build its own case against Mason for fraud and conspiracy. With other followers, he was subjected to a thorough and ongoing investigation by the FBI but all to no avail. When agents confiscated Mason's briefcase for what they knew would be incriminating evidence, they found only a bottle of anointing oil and a handkerchief with his Bible. The U.S. district court in Jackson, MS, failed to render a federal grand jury indictment against Mason and his followers. The kangaroo court in Paris, TX, in 1918 dropped its case when the presiding judge looked at Mason, laid down his books, and said, "You all may try him; I will not have anything to do with him."

No courtroom, no government, no amount of persecution or prosecution could withstand the powerful witness of those pioneers whose lips had been touched by divine fire. Throughout the Deep South and throughout the U.S., the message of pentecostalism spread. It was C. H. Mason who responded to the call of ▸E. N. Bell and ▸H. A. Goss, who convened a general council of "all the churches of God in Christ" and "Pentecostal or Apostolic Faith Assemblies" to meet at Hot Springs, AR, in Apr. 1914, the meeting at which the Assemblies of God (AG) came into being. Significantly, many white ministers from the AG had been ordained by Mason for purely practical reasons because his organization had been officially chartered by the state of Tennessee.

D. Issues.

Between 1909 and 1915 the "finished work" controversy raised objections about sanctification as a definite second work of grace; opponents proposed a progressive view of sanctification. The challenge was raised by ▸W. H. Durham, pastor of the North Avenue Mission in Chicago, IL. This issue wrought havoc among several pentecostal denominations that were organized after 1911 but did not affect BHP denominations.

The most notable controversy to affect all pentecostal denominations after 1914 was the "New Issue" (Jesus Only) controversy espoused initially by ▸R. E. McAlister and ▸Frank J. Ewart. Ewart converted ▸Glenn A. Cook, who later traveled to the Midwest and influenced G. T. Haywood. E. N. Bell, the general chairman of the AG, initially opposed this new doctrine but later accepted it.

Between 1916 and 1922 several ▸Oneness pentecostal denominations were formed. W. T. Phillips, a former black Methodist preacher, founded the Apostolic Overcoming Holy Church of God at Mobile, AL. Robert Clarence Lawson founded in 1919 the Refuge Churches of Christ in Columbus, OH, and moved the headquarters to Harlem in New York City. The unity continued until 1930, when Sherrod C. Johnson, a native of Edgecombe County, NC, withdrew and established the Church of Our Lord Jesus Christ of the Apostolic Faith. Johnson, who succumbed in 1961, remained highly controversial until his death. His successor, S. McDowell Shelton, presides from the Philadelphia headquarters. The second division of Lawson's church came in 1957 when Smallwood E. Williams of Washington, DC, founded the ▸Bible Way Church of Our Lord Jesus Christ World–Wide due largely to the rigid authoritarianism of K. C. Lawson.

E. 1920s and 1930s.

1. Rifts in BHP Churches.

In 1917 Lightfoot Solomon Michaux became licensed in the Church of Christ Holiness at Newport News, VA. The "Happy Am I" evangelist refused to leave his independently established Everybody's Mission to accept reassignment by his bishop and incorporated his work as the Gospel Spreading Association. Known for his flamboyance, Michaux attracted widespread attention by sensational stunts, all preceded by a buildup in the mass media. With his death in 1968, the Church of God (Gospel Spreading) declined.

King Hezekiah Burruss also left the Church of Christ Holiness U.S.A. and formed the Church of God Holiness in 1920. Burruss and C. P. Jones had a personality clash rather than doctrinal differences. The church remained small until Burruss's death in 1963. The rigid authoritarian leadership was passed on to Burruss's son, Titus Paul Burruss, with its headquarters in Atlanta, GA.

William Christian, an associate of C. H. Mason, founded the Church of the Living God, Christian Fellowship Workers, and later changed the latter part of the name to Christian Workers for Fellowship. Christian's movement contended that many biblical personalities were black and consequently affirmed his own racial pride. Finally, three groups formed from Christian's church. They are the Church of the Living God, General Assembly, founded by Charles W. Harris; the Church of the Living God, the Pillar and Ground of the Truth, incorporated initially under the leadership of Arthur Joseph Hawthorne in 1918; and a related movement affirming black people as the true Israel, founded by Frank S. Cherry around 1920: the Original Church of the Living God, the Pillar and Ground of the Truth.

Many BHP churches came into existence during the 1920s and 1930s over issues ranging from baptism to dress. The exception was Elias Dempsey Smith, who claimed that God revealed to him through special revelation in 1897 (the same year C. H. Mason received the name COGIC at Little Rock, AR) the name Triumph the Church and Kingdom of God in Christ at Issaquena County, MS. Smith led his new church for approximately 20 years and left for Ethiopia, never to return. This organization taught a highly controversial doctrine relative to the finality of life. It taught that sickness and death were signs that believers had lost the faith. It was this that C. H. Mason had in mind when he wrote a brief apologetic treatise addressing what he called the "no dying" issue. As a result, the issue was forthrightly opposed and did not create the expected rift in existing Black Holiness pentecostal churches. The Triumph church remained relatively small and thrived mainly in a few Southern states.

Rifts within newly established BHP churches resulted in the formation of several new organizations that later achieved denominational status. Such was the case of Bromfield Johnson in 1929, who formed the UHCA, accompanied by some two hundred followers. Johnson founded the Mount Calvary Holy Church of America, establishing its headquarters in Boston, MA. Some 80 churches in 13 states represented the fruits of Johnson's labors at the time of his demise in 1972.

2. Women's Participation.

Throughout the genesis and historical development of BHP, women often have participated, but usually in minor supportive roles. One has to recall the arduous evangelistic efforts of ▸M. L. Esther Tate as the exception. Known affectionately among her followers as "Saint Mary Magdalene Tate," she, with her sons, F. E. Lewis and W. C. Lewis, founded the Church of the Living God, the Pillar and Ground of the Truth in 1903. After its first general assembly, which convened at Greenville, AL, the organization splintered with dissension and schism upon the founder's demise in 1930.

A young, deeply spiritual visionary, ▸Ida Robinson, became disenchanted with the UHCA after a series of dreams and a 10-day fast. In 1924, after envisioning herself as a spiritual advisor to persons from many directions (a calling Ida attributed to the leading of the Holy Spirit), she founded the Mt. Sinai Holy Church of America. Not only did her group adopt a strict code of personal ethics, but it also gave women prominent roles in its hierarchy.

F. 1940s and 1950s.

1. Spread throughout the World.

The 1940s and 1950s witnessed the spread and development of BHP throughout the U.S. and the world. Mass migration of blacks from the rural South to the midwestern and northern states during and after the war years proved to be a major social factor that impacted the movement's growth

Water baptismal service in a river near Erastus, FL, in the early decades of the 20th century.

and expansion. The impact of cultural shock on these newly arrived settlers from the South often brought them face to face with the search for primary contacts and relationships that were often missing at the gatherings of established mainline black churches in the cities. This period sparked the heyday of several sociocultural messiahs, where the masses flocked. M. J. Divine, known as "Father Divine," established his earthly kingdom in Philadelphia, while "Daddy Grace" reigned in Detroit, MI. Gone were the embers and fires of Azusa with its dream of restoring pentecostal spirituality to Western Christianity by way of the "Black face of church renewal."

However, this was the time when Riley F. Williams, an eminent COGIC preacher without peer, would capture audiences with his preaching throughout the U.S. In 1933 he became one of the first five COGIC bishops appointed by Bishop Mason. Williams was instrumental in the planning, designing, and building of the Mason Temple in Memphis, TN, the COGIC headquarters.

2. Education.

With growth came the need for education—the foundation for institutionalization within denominations. BHP had indeed returned to the very same set of values that brought it into existence, the indictment of C. P. Jones that "denominationalism is slavery." The return to denominationalism found BHPs with a different agenda, namely, how they could most effectively impact the larger society and at the same time overcome the stereotypes that had been imposed on them since their inception.

Contrary to the common notion held by the larger society regarding education, BHP leadership maintained from the movement's early stages of development a vital concern about education in the lives of its constituents. As early as 1897 the Church of Christ Holiness U.S.A., under the visionary leadership of C. P. Jones, had founded the Christ Missionary and Industrial College in Jackson, MS.

Likewise, Bishop C. H. Mason, who had earlier heard God admonishing him that "salvation was not to be found in schools," used Miss Pinkie Duncan to establish Saints Industrial and Literary School at Lexington, MS, in 1918. Mason further stated that the Lord spoke to him in special revelation and said, "If you will leave Arkansas Baptist College, I will give you a mouth of wisdom that your enemies cannot resist or gainsay." Even though Mason left that institution in 1926, he sent the youthful ▸Arenia Cornelia Mallory, a protégé of Mary McCleod Bethune, to develop the work initiated by professor James Courts, who died one month after she arrived on campus. She became the foremost educator in the COGIC.

In 1912 the Fire-Baptized Holiness Church of God of the Americas established the Fuller Normal and Industrial Institute, named in honor of its founder. The UHCA founded as a Bible training institute the United Christian College in 1944. The Bible Way Training School, established in 1945, served the (Oneness) Bible Way Church of Our Lord Jesus Christ World-Wide, led by Bishop Smallwood Williams in Washington, DC. The Aenon Bible College, established in 1941, met the educational needs of the constituents of the Pentecostal Assemblies of the World.

Enamored by educational opportunities afforded Black Holiness pentecostals, the COGIC paved the way for education for pentecostals of all races with its establishment of the first fully accredited pentecostal seminary in North America. In 1970 Bishop ▸J. O. Patterson, presiding prelate of the denomination, sent Leonard Lovett, who at that time was a young Pennsylvania preacher engaged in ministry at his first pastorate, to pioneer the C. H. Mason Theological Seminary and its system of extension schools in Atlanta, GA. Students from several BHP constituencies have received graduate theological education at this institution.

G. 1960s and 1970s.

1. Further Institutionalization.

The 1960s and 1970s saw further institutionalization among Black Holiness pentecostal churches in various ways. Major organizations, such as the COGIC and UHCA, witnessed rifts within its leadership hierarchy that threatened the future existence and unity of both denominations to some degree. The civil rights thrust, which set the stage for social ferment throughout the larger society, also spilled over into BHP churches.

2. Polity Rifts.

As far back as 1932, Elder Justus Bowe, a pioneering comrade of Bishop C. H. Mason, left the COGIC over a dispute concerning its polity. He argued that the structure of the church was congregational, not episcopal. He founded the Church of God in Christ Congregational but later returned to the denomination in 1945. Upon the demise of Bishop Mason in 1961, the issue of leadership succession erupted into a major debate. At the annual convocation held in Nov. 1962, Bishop ▸Ozro Thurston Jones Sr. was elected successor by acclamation, an action that was later disregarded and repudiated by the church and led to several years of litigations. The extended dispute led to the departure in 1969 of 14 bishops who met in Kansas City, MO, to form the Church of God in Christ International, which proved to be short-lived. The year 1968 witnessed the formation of a new leadership structure for the COGIC, a 12-man presidium, which recognizes one person as the presiding bishop, an honor accorded to ▸James Oglethorpe Patterson, son-in-law and successor to the founder.

As recently as June 29, 1977, some within the UHCA organized at Raleigh, NC, to form the Original United Holy Church International. The rift developed around a dispute over polity between Bishop W. N. Strobhar, denominational president, and Bishop J. A. Forbes, president of the Southern District Convocation.

H. Final Decade of the Twentieth Century.

BHP today consists of many diverse strands. Traditional BHP has experienced explosive growth in urban areas in the last decade. Such diversity has been leveraged by the influx of independent fellowships under the banner of "Word of Faith" and "deliverance" movements. Televangelist ʼKenneth Hagin Sr. and ʼKenneth Copeland have equally contributed to the spanning of these movements. They have benefited from the perceived weakness of and dissatisfaction with traditional classical pentecostals and mainline Protestant and Catholic churches. With an emphasis on ʼpositive confession and material prosperity, they have attracted many young upwardly mobile adherents.

The presence of charismatic renewal in traditional mainline African-American churches has generated new trends. When Paul Morton, a former COGIC minister, broke with the National Baptist Church during the early 1990s while senior pastor of a Baptist church in New Orleans and formed the Full Gospel Baptist Church, a new trend was born. His well-over-20,000-member church in three locations attests to the popularity of this new wave of religious enthusiasm. The making of bishops by Morton was welcomed by some but flew in the face of historic Baptist autonomy. Several mainline traditional Baptist and Methodist churches have embraced charismatic renewal without leaving the denomination. However, this is not always the norm. Recently John Cherry of the Full Gospel AMEZ Church of Temple Hills, MD, broke with the African Methodist Episcopal Zion denomination and formed Heart to Heart Ministries.

BHP denominations continue to struggle to maintain their identity in the urban context with the new influx of African churches. A stream of African pastors and evangelists, particularly from West Africa, have formed new congregations throughout North America, Canada, and Europe to accommodate the influx of newly arrived Africans seeking economic parity. Pastors Duncan William and Mensa Otabil from Accra, Ghana, are indicative of this trend. Several churches modeling Otabil's International Central Gospel Church have sprung up from coast to coast. Africa has begun to evangelize North America and the world.

The COGIC, among the largest pentecostal bodies in North America, has sought to maintain its identity after the demise of two presiding bishops within a five-year period. COGIC faces the challenge of coping with growth and change in a challenging urban environment. It has maintained a presence in the urban environment, ranging from storefronts to an 18,000-member West Angeles COGIC led by Bishop Charles Blake. Effectively evangelizing the urban arena and revising its ministry and leadership paradigm for the new millennium appear to be the denomination's greatest challenges. The Apostolic movement, which consists of several denominations, has multiplied in significant numbers throughout North America but has suffered from leadership fragmentation. Less emphasis on controversial doctrinal issues and avoidance of further schisms appear to be its greatest challenges. The Apostolic movement has the potential for explosive growth. The UHCA has maintained a strong Southern base, particularly in the Carolinas, but has experienced serious leadership challenges during this decade. Its greatest challenge is the need to attract new adherents within a changing urban environment. The Church of Christ Holiness, U.S.A. and Fire-Baptized Holiness Church of America have not shown significant growth during this decade. While low-key, both continue to hold their own in the southern and western portions of the United States.

The social involvement of BHP during this final decade reveals much about its changing focus. They were present and involved in what was labeled the "Memphis Miracle" dialogue on racial reconciliation and have exerted political influence in the White House. The same Spirit that descended upon believers on a Jewish feast day of celebration called Pentecost has empowered BHP to live on the cutting edge of God's new future for the church.

IV. CONCLUSION.

A. Contributions.

Throughout its history, BHP spiritual contributions have arisen from serious allegiance to God in Jesus Christ, through the power of the Holy Spirit, disregarding the divisive allegiances of the gods of this world. Allegiance to God's dominion called BHP leadership to a double discernment. In their early history they discovered how to say no to loyalties that divide and yes to the moving Spirit that heals and restores persons and institutions torn asunder by idolatrous loyalties.

B. Active Discipleship to Be Witnesses.

Throughout their brief history on the continent of North America, BHPs have rejected the abstract god of the philosophers and creeds and have opted for a more concrete God who could be encountered at a deeply personal level of existence. BHPs perceive the baptism in the Holy Spirit to be an empowering symbol of active discipleship to be witnesses and servants of Christ, whose kingdom knows no caste or divisions.

The history of BHP is exciting as well as embarrassing, full of triumphs as well as tragedies, full of promise and riddled with failures. It is the saga of people who heard the liberating call of Jesus Christ and took his call seriously. Through them the "first love" of the kingdom broke through the boundaries of creeds, denominations, race, and class to demonstrate that

God has once again, in his "saving moment," "chosen the foolish things of this world to confound the wise;... the things which are despised, to bring to nought things that are, that no flesh should glory in his presence."

See also BLACK THEOLOGY.

■ **Bibliography:** M. K. Asante, *Afrocentricity* (1988) ■ R. Bastide, *African Civilization in the New World* (1971) ■ B. Brawley, *A Social History of the American Negro* (1921) ■ O. B. Cobbins, *History of Church of Christ Holiness U.S.A.* (1966) ■ M. W. Costen, *African American Christian Worship* (1993) ■ H. Courlander, *Negro Folk Music U.S.A.* (n.d.) ■ D. D. Daniels III, "The Cultural Renewal of Slave Religion: Charles Price Jones and the Emergence of the Holiness Movement in Mississippi" (diss., Union Theol. Sem., 1992) ■ W. E. B. Dubois, *The Negro Church* (1903) ■ P. D. Dugas, ed., *The Life and Writings of Elder G. T. Haywood* (1968) ■ J. H. Franklin, *From Slavery to Freedom* (1947) ■ E. F. Frazier, *The Negro Church in America* (1963) ■ E. D. Genovese, *Roll Jordan Roll: The World the Slaves Made* (1972) ■ C. T. Gilkes, "The Role of Women in the Sanctified Church," *Journal of Religious Thought* 43 (1, 1986) ■ idem, "Together and in Harness: Women's Traditions in the Sanctified Church," *Signs* 10 (4, 1985) ■ M. E. Golder, *History of the Pentecostal Assemblies of the World* (1973) ■ idem, *The Principles of Our Doctrines* (n.d.) ■ M. J. Herskovits, *Cultural Relativism* (1972) ■ idem, *The Myth of the Negro Past* (1941) ■ idem, *New World Negro* (1966) ■ W. J. Hollenweger, *The Pentecostals* (1972) ■ D. Hopkins and G. Cummings, eds., *Cut Loose Your Stammering Tongue: Black Theology in the Slave Narratives* (1990) ■ J. E. Holloway, ed., *Africanisms in American Culture* (1990) ■ Z. N. Hurston, *The Sanctified Church* (1981) ■ C. E. Jones, *Black Holiness: A Guide to the Study of Black Participation in Wesleyan Perfectionist and Glossalalic Pentecostal Movements* (1987) ■ idem, *Perfectionist Persuasion: A Guide to the Study of the Holiness Movement* (1974) ■ L. Lovett, "Aspects of the Spiritual Legacy of the Church of God in Christ: Ecumenical Implications," in *Black Witness to the Apostolic Faith* (1985) ■ idem, "Perspective on the Black Origins of the Contemporary Pentecostal Movement," *Journal of the ITC* 1 (1, 1973) ■ idem, "BHP: Implications for Ethics and Social Transformation" (diss., Emory U., 1978) ■ W. G. McLoughlin, *Modern Revivalism* (1959) ■ H. Mitchell, *Black Preaching* (1970) ■ D. J. Nelson, *The Black Face of Church Renewal* (1984) ■ idem, "For Such a Time as This: The Story of Bishop William J. Seymour and the Azusa Street Revival" (diss., Birmingham, 1981) ■ J. T. Nichols, *Pentecostalism* (1966) ■ P. J. Paris, *Black Pentecostalism: Southern Religion in an Urban World* (1982) ■ idem, *The Social Teaching of the Black Churches* (1985) ■ C. M. Robeck Jr., ed., *Witness to Pentecost: The Life of Frank J. Bartleman* (1985) ■ G. Ross, *History and Formative Years of the Church of God in Christ* (1969) ■ M. R. Sawyer, *Black Ecumenism: Implementing the Demands of Justice* (1994) ■ L. B. Scherer, *Slavery and the Churches in Early America 1619–1819* (1975) ■ W. J. Seymour, *Doctrine and Discipline of the Azusa Street Apostolic Faith Mission of Los Angeles* (1915) ■ J. M. Shropshire, "A Socio-Historical Characterization of the Black Pentecostal Movement in America" (diss., Northwestern U., 1975) ■ T. Smith, *Called unto Holiness* (1962) ■ idem, "Freedom through the Sanctifying Spirit: A Forgotten Chapter in America's Theological History" (unpub. draft, Aug. 1977) ■ idem, *Revivalism and Social Reform in Mid-Nineteenth-Century America* (1957) ■ Th. H. Smith, *Conjuring Culture: Biblical Formations of Black America* (1994) ■ V. Synan, ed., *Aspects of Pentecostal-Charismatic Origins* (1975) ■ idem, *The Holiness-Pentecostal Movement in the U.S.* (1971) ■ J. S. Tinney, "The Blackness of Pentecostalism," *Spirit* (2, 1979) ■ idem, "A Theoretical and Historical Comparison of Black Political and Religious Movements" (diss., Howard U., 1978) ■ D. M. Tucker, *Black Pastors and Leaders, 1919–1972* (1975) ■ L. Turner, *Africanisms in the Gullah Dialect* (1949) ■ W. C. Turner, "The United Holy Church of America: A Study in BHP," (diss., Duke, 1984) ■ G. S. Wilmore, *Black Religion and Black Radicalism* (1972).   ■ L. Lovett

BLACK THEOLOGY There is consensus among most black American theologians and religious specialists that black theology is critical reflection about God through the prism of oppression and African cultural adaptation in North America. Black theology's roots are traceable to the 18th century within the corpus of the first black American "independent churches." In the words of its contemporary seminal thinker, James Cone, black theology is said to be "Black God Talk" and is situational and contextual. In unequivocal terms, black theology insists on biblical grounds that the liberation of the poor and oppressed is at the very core of the Christian faith.

Black theology in its contemporary expression developed as a response to the continuing debate among black religionists on the issue of racial integration or separation within the vortex of American society. Such racial dualism was represented by majority voices within the black churches and the civil rights movement. The late Dr. Martin Luther King Jr. supported integration, while nationalists—from Bishop McNeal Turner of the African Methodist Episcopal (AME) Church to Malcolm X—advocated separation. The first half of the 1960s was virtually dominated by the integrationist posture of King with a positive stress on love and nonviolence within the black religious community. After the assassination of Malcolm X in 1965, Stokely Carmichael, a black nationalist, came to the fore, espousing the notion of "Black Power." After the tragic demise of King in 1968, Black Power, with its emphasis on self-determination and political liberation by "any means necessary," became more attractive even among black churchmen as a possible viable alternative to nonviolence. The attempt to resolve the continuing dilemma of how to reconcile Christian faith and Black Power became pronounced when an ad hoc committee of black churchmen published a position statement in the *New York Times* in July 1966. In the ensuing debate, National Council of Black Churchmen (NCBC) clergymen endorsed the positive features of Black Power, and in the process a view of the Christian faith emerged that was radically different than traditional Western Christian theology. It was in such a context that black theology in its contemporary expression was born. From their interpretation of the gospel emerged a view of theology that embraced justice, hope, suffering, and liberation in terms of strong political implications, thereby maintaining solidarity with their suffering brothers and sisters in the urban ghettos of America.

1. The 1960s.

Just two years before the NCBC statement, a young, articulate black interpreter of the black religious experience, J. Washington, published a book entitled *Black Religion* (1964), taking to task the exponents of the traditional view of black religion and stressing its unique relationship to its African heritage. Washington came under severe attacks by other black religionists, thus triggering a string of writings in black theology and lifting up racism as being heretical to the cause of the gospel. In 1968 Albert Cleage wrote *The Black Messiah*, while serving as pastor of the Shrine of the Black Madonna, in Detroit. Later, in *Black Christian Nationalism*, Cleage pleaded with the masses to abandon whiteness totally and to reinstate blackness, beginning with the belief that Jesus, the black Messiah, was a revolutionary leader sent by God to rebuild the black nation Israel and to liberate black people from the oppressive brutality and exploitation of the white Gentile world. Espousing a black nationalist posture, he contended that Jesus Christ was literally black and attempted to carve a theological position known as "Black Christian Nationalism." In 1969 a young scholar, James H. Cone, wrote the first book on black theology, *Black Theology and Black Power*. This work was preceded by an article entitled "Christianity and Black Power," Cone's first published essay, which served as the basis for his first book. Cone argued that Black Power was not peripheral to Christian faith but is an authentic embodiment of the Christian faith in our time. The point of departure for black theology is the liberation of the oppressed. In this seminal work, the task of black theology is to analyze "black people's condition in the light of God's revelation in Jesus Christ with the purpose of creating a new understanding of black dignity among black people and providing the necessary soul in that people to destroy white racism." For Cone, self-determination, self-identity, emancipation from white oppression "by whatever means necessary," all of which are goals of the Black Power movement, are synonymous with his view of what God is doing in history in his task of liberation.

That black theology developed out of the corpus of the black experience can be seen in the social tensions of the times in which it emerged. The black insurrections in Watts, Detroit, Newark, and other parts of America impacted James H. Cone to search for a new way of viewing theology that would emerge out of the dialectic of black history and culture.

Cone's quest led him to the Scriptures as the primary source for the new approach. He determined to find out what the biblical message had to do with the Black Power revolution. His first response came in *Black Theology and Black Power* (1969). The same problem emerged in a second work, *A Black Theology of Liberation* (1970), in which it was probed in the light of the classical structures of theology. Those primary works left Cone dissatisfied, particularly after his earlier insistence that black theology has to emerge out of an oppressed community. The result was the publication of *The Spirituals and the Blues* (1972), which was an inquiry about the theological significance of the black experience as reflected in such sources as sermons, sayings, songs, and stories. Cone had laid the foundations for further inquiry by insisting that Christianity, as espoused biblically, is essentially a movement of liberation and that the starting point for theology must be the liberation of the oppressed. Consequently, several subsequent debates among black theologians revolved around three categories of issues set forth initially by Cone: (1) black theology and black suffering; (2) black religion and black theology; and (3) liberation, reconciliation, and violence.

2. The 1970s.

One of the first serious counterresponses to Cone came from J. Deotis Roberts, who readily established himself as a major interpreter of black theological thought for this era. In contrast to Cone, Roberts proceeded to argue that we must not only lead the oppressed to liberation, but that the demands of the gospel obligate us to reconcile with the oppressor. It was that argument that sparked the title of his primary work, *Liberation and Reconciliation: A Black Theology* (1971). Roberts proposed a theology that sought to retain a universal vision. By struggling with the tensions between the particular and universal categories, Roberts presents us with a universal Christ who will embrace the entire community of faith and at the same time participate in the task of liberation. In his less controversial and more balanced theological program, Roberts sought to bridge the gap between blacks and whites. He contended that intercommunication was a necessary task of black theology if reconciliation was to be achieved. For Roberts, liberation is personal and social, particular and universal. He refused to accept the view of many colleagues that black liberation versus white oppression was indeed an adequate formula to overcome the human condition of estrangement. He was not hesitant to suggest liberation between blacks and blacks as well as between blacks and whites in anticipation of the possibility that the oppressed would become the liberated. But what would happen to our theology? In reaction to Stokely Carmichael's Pan-Africanism, Roberts insisted that we must find a way to interracial togetherness in this country. This concern came to fruition in Roberts's second discussion, *A Black Political Theology* (1974), in which he insisted that the only Christian way in race relations is a liberation experience of reconciliation for the white oppressor as well as for the black oppressed. Roberts attempted to resolve the theological tension in his system by insisting that reconciliation includes cross bearing for whites as well as for blacks. Whites who are aware of the widespread and all-embracing effects of white racism have the responsibility to awaken and activate other whites to the end that racism may be eliminated, root and branch. He was primarily concerned about the relationship of church and family in the black tradition as a basis for theological construction. Jones contributed to the dialogue in his *Black Awareness: A Theology of Hope* (1971), under the influence of Jürgen Moltmann, Ernest Bloch, Wolfhart Pannenberg, and others; he insisted that a new direction for black theology was needed. The new direction was identified as the infusion of a Christian theology of hope into the black-awareness movement, while at the same time moving toward the goal of a radically new community beyond racism.

The issue of the legitimacy of black theology and its relationship to black religion came to the fore of black theological debate. William R. Jones, in his principal work, *Is God a White Racist?* (1973), influenced by Camus and Sartre, structures his theology upon the question of racism in light of the historic suffering of black people in their horizontal relationship with white people. For Jones theodicy is the point of departure for black theology. He radically questions Cone and challenges him to prove the assertion that God is the God of oppressed blacks, liberating them from bondage in the absence of an exaltation-liberation event. In *God of the Oppressed* (1975), Cone not only identifies primary sources for doing black theology, such as songs, sermons, testimonies, and slave narratives of the black religious tradition, he also lifts up the Christ-event as the exaltation-liberation event to which Christians turn in order to resolve the theodicy issue posed by Jones. Charles Long, a renowned black scholar in the field of history of religion, in two key articles, "Perspectives for a Study of Afro-American Religion in the United States" and "Structural Similarities and Dissimilarities in Black and African Theologies," first raised the issue about the legitimacy of black theology to new levels of concern. Long's theoretical analysis questions the legitimacy of black theology during its infancy because of its reliance on Western theological constructs that have viewed the whole of religious reality through the bifocals of Immanuel Kant. As a provocative debater, Long persuades us to examine what he views as "a characteristic mode of orienting and perceiving reality"— an African rather than a European mode. Long identifies the process as the "historical and present experience of opacity, the meaning of which is not altogether clear, but definitely related to the otherness of Blackness."

Cecil Cone, brother of James Cone, in his *The Identity Crisis in Black Theology* (1975), and Gayraud Wilmore, in his *Black Religion and Black Radicalism* (1973), set forth analyses of religion similar to Long's, but neither rejects theology. Cecil Cone argues that the lack of a correct point of departure for black theology, namely, black religion, and the tools derived from white seminaries are inadequate and that both are responsible for producing an identity crisis in black theology. Cone relies heavily on the vertical encounter with God in black slave religion as a viable option for empowering persons to transcend and transform negative oppressive situations into an oasis of hope. Wilmore sought to make black theology palatable to non-Christian blacks by lifting up its sources—the traditional religions of Africa; black folk religion; and the writings, sermons, and addresses of black preachers and public men of the past. C. Eric Lincoln, a distinguished black interpreter of religion, has cogently argued on behalf of the sustaining power of black religion and its peculiar genius for having made oppression less onerous in the lives of black people.

3. The 1980s.

James Cone and several black theologians have shifted their focus to ecclesiology. Cone engages in what may be labeled an internal critique of the black church in his recent work *My Soul Looks Back* (1982). Cone critically assesses the past and present development of black theology as a servant to and for the black church. He helps us to understand that the identities of our theologies—whether they be black, African, Hispanic-American, Asian, Native American, Latin American, Minjung, black feminist, or whatever—are determined by the human and divine dimensions of reality to which we are attempting to bear witness. In *Speaking the Truth* (1986), Cone not only engages the issue of ecumenism, but links our struggle to South African apartheid and urges us to bear witness now to God's coming liberation by refusing to obey the agents of death.

A similar concern comes to the fore in J. Deotis Roberts's *Black Theology in Dialogue* (1987). Using the contextual approach, he proposes a theology concerned with specific and concrete situations while retaining a universal vision that relates black theology to African, feminist, Asian, Euro-American, and liberation theologies. Roberts's contextual approach takes seriously the unique contribution of black church theology to the doctrine of the Holy Spirit in a chapter on the Holy Spirit and liberation. He uses the internal critique of Bennie Goodwin, James Tinney, James Forbes, and Leonard Lovett to call into question the manifestation of racism within pentecostal ranks. He concludes by reminding us that in the black church tradition, the Spirit is not merely a dove but wind and fire also. The Comforter is also the Strengthener. Justice in the social order for the black church, no less than joy and peace in the hearts of believers, is evidence of the Spirit's presence and power. Authentic pentecostal encounter cannot occur unless liberation becomes the consequence.

4. The Final Decade of the Twentieth Century.

Black theology has survived to see the fruits of seeds sown in previous decades in social ferment within the global village. African-American theologians linked up with African theologians in paving the way for the demise of apartheid in South Africa. South African black theologians embraced radical ideas embedded within black theological trends in North America, thus enabling them to develop their indigenous theology. Black theologians James Cone, Gayraud Wilmore, and Cornel West were in dialogue with John Mbiti, David J. Bosch, and Bishop Desmond M. Tutu. South African theologians were politically astute and avoided running afoul of the law by calling for violent revolution in their struggle against frightening oppression. They did, however, call upon black people to throw off the shackles of their own internal enslavement as a precursor to defying external bondage. The brutal death of Steve Biko became a rallying point for critics of the government. Voices such as Manas Buthelezi, Desmond Tutu, Allan Boesak, John W. de Gruchy, Mmutlanyane S. Mogoba, and Basil Moore rose in concert to challenge the last vestiges of apartheid in South Africa.

While earlier black theologians were preoccupied with consciousness-raising issues and questions from the 1960s through 80s that focused on identity, second-generation theologians shifted their emphasis. Initially the defining issue was "What does it mean to be black in a world that defines whites as human and blacks as less than human?" "What does it mean to be a Christian, a follower of Jesus, in a world that portrays Jesus as a white man and Christianity as a European religion?" James Cone, at Union Theological Seminary, urged black theologians to "constructively and critically engage each other and the world in which we live" as we approach the 21st century. This challenge set the stage for black theologians, biblical scholars, and black female theologians to talk to each other in a "critical and constructive way."

Black theologians formed new alliances with womanist theologians in their struggle against supporters of sexism, racism, and classism in the black church and the larger society. Black novelist Alice Walker's definition of womanism ("a woman who loves other women, sexually and/or nonsexually; appreciates and prefers women's culture, women's emotional flexibility, and women's strength; a womanist is a woman who loves other women but is committed to the survival and wholeness of entire people") was the lynchpin for new Christian womanist theologians. They sought to close the gap between black male liberation theology and white feminist theology. Kelly Delaine Brown, Katie Geneva Cannon, M. Shawn Copeland, Toinette M. Eugene, Cheryl Townsend Gilkes, Jacquelyn Grant, Diana L. Hayes, Renee Hill, Joan Martin, Imani Sheila Newsome, Marcia Riggs, Cheryl J. Sanders, Joan Speaks, Emily Townes, Renita J. Weems, and Delores S. Williams represent key voices in womanist thought in theology, ethics, biblical studies, sociology of religion, and ministry. Black African-American female theologians have been hailed as the most creative group of scholars among blacks in religion.

A black biblical revolution has taken place in seminaries and churches. When Cain Hope Felder, professor of New Testament at Howard University School of Divinity published his *Troubling Biblical Waters* (1989), a new era for black biblical scholars had emerged. At the Kansas City meeting of the American Academy of Religion in 1991, white scholars gave a measure of attention to black biblical scholarship after two books by Felder were critically reviewed. Clarice J. Martin, Renita J. Weems, Thomas Hoyt Jr., Vincent Wimbush, and Itumeleng J. Mosala have made significant contributions to this new conversation. Black theologians are linking their biblical faith to the eradication of racism, gender discrimination, and other forms of oppression as we enter the new millennium.

See also BLACK HOLINESS PENTECOSTALISM.

■ **Bibliography:** H. Adam and H. Gillomee, *The Rise and Crisis of the Afrikaner Power* (1979) ■ R. Aronson, *The Dialectics of Disaster: A Preface to Hope* (1983) ■ A. A. Boesak, *Black and Reformed: Apartheid, Liberation, and the Calvinist Tradition* (1984) ■ K. G. Cannon, *Black Womanist Ethics* (1988) ■ A. Cleage, *Black Christian Nationalism* (1972) ■ idem, *Black Messiah* (1969) ■ C. Cone, *The Identity Crisis in Black Theology* (1975) ■ J. Cone, *Black Theology and Black Power* (1969) ■ idem, *A Black Theology of Liberation* (1970) ■ idem, *For My People* (1984) ■ idem, *God of the Oppressed* (1975) ■ idem, *Martin and Malcolm and America: A Dream or a Nightmare?* (1991) ■ idem, *My Soul Looks Back* (1982) ■ idem, *Speaking the Truth* (1986) ■ idem, *The Spirituals and the Blues* (1972) ■ idem, "Christianity and Black Power," in *Is Anybody Listening to Black America?* ed. C. E. Lincoln (1968) ■ idem, "The Content and Method of Black Theology," *JRT* 33 (Fall/Winter 1975) ■ idem, "Sanctification, Liberation and Black Worship," *Theology Today* (July 1978) ■ J. H. Evans Jr., *Black Theology: A Critical Assessment* (1987) ■ C. H. Felder, *Stony the Road We Trod: African-American Biblical Interpretation* (1991) ■ idem, *Troubling Biblical Waters: Race, Class and Family* (1989) ■ R. M. Franklin, *Another Day's Journey* (1997) ■ idem, *Liberating Visions: Human Fulfillment and Social Justice in African-American Thought* (1990) ■ J. Grant, *White Women's Christ and Black Women's Jesus: Feminist Christology and Womanist Response* (1989) ■ D. N. Hopkins, *Black Theology USA and South Africa: Politics, Culture and Liberation* (1989) ■ M. J. Jones, *Black Awareness* (1971) ■ idem, *Christian Ethics for Black Theology* (1974) ■ idem, *The Color of God: The Concept of God in Afro-American Thought* (1987) ■ W. Jones, *Is God a White Racist?* (1973) ■ idem, "Theodicy: The Controlling Category for Black Theology," *JRT* 30 (1, 1973) ■ M. L. King Jr., *Where Do We Go from Here: Chaos or Community?* (1967) ■ C. E. Lincoln, *The Black Church Since Frazier* (1974) ■ C. E. Lincoln, ed., *The*

Black Experience in Religion (1974) ■ idem, *Race, Religion and the Continuing American Dilemma* (1984) ■ C. H. Long, *Significations: Signs, Symbols, and Images in the Interpretation of Religion* (1986) ■ idem, "Perspectives for a Study of Afro-American Religion in the U.S.," *History of Religions* 2 (Aug. 1971) ■ idem, "Structural Similarities and Dissimilarities in Black and African Theologies," *JRT* 33 (Fall/Winter 1975) ■ L. Lovett, "Color Lines and the Religion of Racism," in *Ending Racism in the Church,* ed. S. E. Davies and P. T. Hennesee (1998) ■ idem, "Conditional Liberation: An Emergent Pentecostal Perspective," *Spirit* 1 (2, 1977) ■ idem, "Liberation: A Dual Edged Sword" in *Pneuma* 9 (2, Fall 1987) ■ B. Moore, ed., *The Challenge of Black Theology in South Africa* (1973) ■ E. H. Oglesby, *Racism and Christian Ethics* (1998) ■ J. D. Roberts, *A Black Political Theology* (1974) ■ idem, *Black Theology in Dialogue* (1987) ■ idem, *Black Theology Today* (1983) ■ idem, *Liberation and Reconciliation: A Black Theology* (1971) ■ idem, *Roots of a Black Future* (1980) ■ idem, "Black Theology and the Theological Revolution," *JRT* 28 (1, 1971): 5–20 ■ idem, "Black Theology in the Making," *Review and Expositor* 70 (Summer 1973): 321–30 ■ H. Thurman, *Jesus and the Disinherited* (1949) ■ B. Tlhagale and I. Mosala, eds., *Hammering Swords into Ploughshares* (1986) ■ idem, *The Unquestionable Right to Be Free: Black Theology from South Africa* (1989) ■ T. Walker Jr., *Empower the People: Social Ethics for the African-American Church* (1991) ■ J. Washington, *Black Religion* (1964) ■ idem, *Black Sects and Cults* (1972) ■ idem, "The Roots and Fruits of Black Theology," *Theology Today* 30 (July 1973) ■ C. West, *Prophesy Deliverance* (1982) ■ idem, *Race Matters* (1994) ■ D. S. Williams, *Sisters in the Wilderness* (1993) ■ G. Wilmore, *Black Religion and Black Radicalism* (1973) ■ idem, *Last Things First* (1982) ■ "Black Messiah: Revising the Color Symbolism of Western Christology," *Journal of the Interdenominational Theological Center* 2 (Fall 1974) ■ G. S. Wilmore and J. H. Cone, *Black Theology: A Documentary History, 1966–1979* (1979) ■ idem, *Black Theology: A Documentary History. Volume Two: 1980–1992* (1993) ■ T. Witvliet, *The Way of the Black Messiah* (1987) ■ H. J. Young, *Hope in Process: A Theology of Social Pluralism* (1990) ■ J. U. Young III, *Black and African Theologies: Siblings or Distant Cousins* (1986) ■ idem, *A Pan-African Theology: Providence and the Legacies of the Ancestors* (1992). ■ L. Lovett

BLAISDELL, FRANCISCA D. (c. 1885–1941).

Pioneer Assemblies of God (AG) woman evangelist, missionary, and pastor in the U.S. and Mexico. Francisca was a Mexican immigrant from Sonora, Mexico. She began lay preaching in 1916 and was ordained by ›H. C. Ball and ›Juan L. Lugo as an evangelist to the Mexicans by the Latin District Council of the AG in 1923. She, along with her Anglo husband, George Blaisdell, conducted evangelistic work along the Arizona-Mexico border in Douglas, AZ, and Nacozari, Sonora, Mexico. Around 1922 Francisca helped organize the first women's group, called Dorcas (Acts 9), in Agua Prieta, Sonora, Mexico. She organized another women's group in

Gallina, NM, a few years later. She was one of the first Latinas to pioneer pentecostal work along the border, and she also pastored her own churches in Douglas, AZ, and Agua Prieta, Sonora, Mexico (1932–33, 1938–39), and El Paso, TX (1933–35). In these churches, she preached two or three times a week to 40 to 60 Mexican parishioners, including every Sunday morning and evening. Along with her regular work in Arizona and Mexico, she went on annual evangelistic tours throughout the state of Sonora, Mexico, and the U.S. Southwest from Arizona to El Paso, TX.

■ **Bibliography:** G. Espinosa, "'Your Daughters Shall Prophesy': A Comparative Study of Women's Roles in the Latino Assemblies of God and the Apostolic Assembly," in *Women and Twentieth-Century Protestantism,* ed. M. L. Bendroth and V. L. Brereton (1998). ■ G. Espinosa

BLASPHEMY AGAINST THE HOLY SPIRIT

Blasphemy against the Holy Spirit is the sin for which there is no forgiveness, the "unpardonable sin." It particularly denotes a saying of Jesus in three texts—Matt. 12:32; Mark 3:29; Luke 12:10—and while some may wish to interpret the "sin unto death" in 1 John 5:16 as equal to the "unpardonable sin," there is no justification for such an equation except in the broadest of terms, because, as will be shown, even "blasphemy against the Spirit" is not understood in any monolithic sense in Scripture. Similarly, Heb. 10:29, a reference to "insulting *[enybrisas]* the Spirit of grace," may have the same general implications, but it is not parallel to the Jesus saying in the strict sense. A textual variant at 1 Peter 4:14 also contains a reference to blasphemy of the Spirit, which is an act attributed to those who revile believers. Some commentators think this text is original (Michaels, 1988).

"To blaspheme" (Gk. *blasphemeom;* cf. the noun, *blasphemia,* and the adjective, *blasphemos*) is an especially strong word conveying insult, derision, abusive speech, or ridicule (Beyer, 621). It particularly denotes religious profanation in the Scriptures, although this is not ordinarily the case in secular literature *(LSJ).*

The word family is relatively rare in the Septuagint (LXX), with the verb appearing 8 times; the noun *blasphemy,* 6; and the adjective/substantive *blasphemous/blasphemous one,* 6 times. All of these 20 occurrences refer to religious blasphemy of God. Usually blasphemy is a verbal act (e.g., 2 Kings 19:4, 6, 22; Isa. 52:5; Ezek. 35:12; 2 Macc. 10:34), but it can denote an action directed against God (e.g., 1 Macc. 2:6; 2 Macc. 8:4; Sir. 3:16). Israel's enemies are typically "blasphemers" (e.g., Isa. 52:5; 1 Macc. 8:4; 10:34–36).

Blasphemeom surprisingly occurs 34 times in the NT, appearing in 15 books by 11 writers. The cognates *blasphemia* and *blasphemos* occur 18 and 4 times respectively. Like the LXX, the NT conception of blasphemy is almost exclusively regarded as directed against God (Acts 6:11; Rev. 13:6), his name (Rom. 2:24; cf. Isa. 52:5), his Word (Titus 2:5), or indirectly against him (e.g., of "the way of truth," 2 Peter 2:2; but cf. Acts 13:45; 18:6; Paul is the object of Jewish "insults").

Blasphemy is also a charge frequently leveled against Jesus by his antagonists (e.g., Matt. 9:3; 25:65; cf. Mark 2:7; John 10:36). At the crux of the Jewish charge of blasphemy against Jesus lies the assumption that Jesus claimed equality with God (John 10:33–36; cf. Mark 2:7 and parallels). As a result of asserting his messiahship (Mark 14:61–62), Jesus is condemned to death for committing blasphemy (Mark 14:64). Ironically—and probably reflecting consummate literary design—his opponents "blaspheme" him (Matt. 27:39; Mark 15:29; Luke 22:65; 23:39).

It is within such literary settings that one must interpret what each Gospel writer has to say concerning blaspheming the Spirit. The issue of religious blasphemy is not unique to NT theology; the Jewish experts in the law were "thoroughly familiar with this concept under the rubric 'the profanation of the Name'" (Lane, 145). "The Holy One, blessed be he, pardons everything else, but on profanation of the Name [i.e., blasphemy] he takes vengeance immediately" (Lane, ibid., citing Sifré on Deut. 32:38). Profanation of the Name *(h.illul ha-Shem)*, however, "includes every act or word of a Jew which disgraces his religion and so reflects dishonor upon God" (Moore, 2:108). Thus, in Jewish casuistry there were several "unpardonable sins," including "murder, unchastity, apostasy, contempt for the Law, etc." (Jeremias, 149–50).

The saying about blaspheming the Holy Spirit occurs in three locations in the NT: Matt. 12:31–32; Mark 3:28–30; and Luke 12:10. (The Gospel of Thomas [logion 44] also records an interesting Trinitarian version in which the Father and Son cannot be blasphemed—only the Holy Spirit.) Apparently the saying circulated in two forms; one form occurs in the double-tradition material (Q), while Mark has the other, more original (e.g., Bultmann, 131; Manson, 110; but cf. Boring, who argues that the Q form was older). Dunn's assertion that both forms were probably derived from an Aramaic original seems logical, especially if one accepts this as an authentic saying of Jesus (cf. Boring, who is reluctant to originate the saying with Jesus). Matthew's version reflects a union between Q and Mark, while Luke probably reflects the Q version.

Both Matthew and Mark associate the saying with the Beelzebub controversy (cf. Luke 11:14–16), while Luke makes no such connection, preferring instead to link it to a confession/denial lesson (Luke 12:8–11). Each evangelist shapes the saying's import, but Luke's repositioning of the text affects it most radically. Therefore, any blanket interpretation of what constitutes "blasphemy against the Spirit" ignores how each evangelist uses the saying. The context of each appearance will be analyzed below to determine differences, emphases, and similarities. Following that the implications of the gospel teachings will be offered.

1. Mark 3:28–30.

Jesus' mission in the Gospel of Mark is carried out under the power of the Spirit received at his baptism by John. Empowered by the Spirit, Jesus is portrayed in the earliest chapters of Mark as an exorcist par excellence (Mark 1:23, 27, 32, 34; 3:11), and the passage in which the saying about blaspheming the Spirit occurs is precisely such an exorcism story (Dunn suggests that "Mark or the pre-Markan tradition was right to link [the blasphemy saying] into the exorcism context" [1975]).

The Markan understanding of blasphemy against the Spirit is revealed in Mark 3:30, where the narrator interrupts the story with an explanation as to why Jesus uttered this warning: "for *[hoti]* they were saying he had an unclean spirit *[pneuma akatharton]*." Of the evangelists, only Mark reads this. It is important both for Mark's perspective of who Jesus is and for what Mark's community is experiencing. While Mansfield's main thesis is perhaps exaggerated, he rightly sees Mark's editorializing here as one of the key signs that the Spirit continues to guide the Markan church in its understanding of "Gospel" (Mansfield, 5–7, 17–19, 61, 65–70). Those in the community who would wrongly appeal to Satan as the source for power wielded by either Jesus or his disciples—who are authenticated in terms of cross bearing and self-denial and who have been granted "authority" *(exousia)* to drive out demons (3:15)—are in danger of blasphemy. The question is not whether Jesus and his disciples drive out demons, but how they do it. The answer is—as the reader knows—Jesus does this by the power of the Spirit, not by Satan, who resists Jesus at every turn.

Mark underscores this both with the intercalated parable of the strong man and with his portrayal of Jesus' family and the scribes. The "they" of "they were saying" (v. 30) need not be limited to the scribes alone. The observant reader will note that Jesus' family, who first appears in v. 21, reappears in v. 31, thereby bracketing the parable of the strong man and the saying against blasphemy. Their attitude parallels that of the teachers of the law from Jerusalem. His family thinks he is "mad" *(exestem,* i.e., "crazy," or possibly "in a state of ecstasy," v. 21), while the scribes say he is "possessed" (lit., "he has Beelzebub"; *Beelzeboul echei,* v. 22). Not insignificantly, it is his family who "stands outside" *(exom stekontes,* 3:31–32) and who is among those "on the outside *[exom]* to whom everything is given in parables" (4:11). Jesus' rejection in his own hometown of Nazareth further implies his family's rejection of him (Mark 6:1–6). Similarly, the scribes risk blasphemy by asserting that Jesus' power comes from Satan rather than from God. Ironically, it is they who are under the control of Satan, not Jesus or his disciples.

The Markan saying on blasphemy thus points up a problem in the Markan community. It is not necessary to go to the extent that Mansfield (following T. Weeden) does in trying to link the actions of Jesus' family as in some way representative of "pneumatic prophets who misunderstood and opposed (unknowingly?) the true Gospel of Jesus" (Mansfield, 65; cf. Alexander, 1985). If anything, Jesus' family represents the anticharismatic, more institutionally oriented element in Mark's community. Mark endeavors to salvage the charismatic ministry of the church; at the same time he wishes to safeguard against imitation. The genuine "charismatic" disciple not only does the "works" of Jesus, he or she lives the life of Jesus as well. The disciple denies self and takes up the cross, following the footsteps of the Lord.

A coinciding relationship between blasphemy and charismatic manifestations is also related in the *Didache*, an early Christian document. There it is blasphemous to "test" *(peirazom)* or "judge" *(diakrinom)* a prophet speaking by *(en)* the Spirit *(Did.* 11:7).

2. Matthew 12:31–32.

Matthew's interpretation of the saying concerning blaspheming the Spirit is intelligible only in light of its immediate context. While Matthew apparently knows Mark (and Q), his application of the saying is quite different from Mark's. He does not incorporate Mark's explanatory comment in 3:30 that "he [Jesus] said this because they [the Pharisees] were saying, 'He has an evil spirit.'" Instead, Matthew reads the controversy as a question over the source of Jesus' power to drive out demons (Matt. 12:28). He further subordinates that issue to a larger one: the issue of Jesus' messiahship.

O. L. Cope has shown on the basis of the Targumic translation of the opening verse of Isa. 42 (servant = "servant Messiah") as well as on the basis of redactional elements (the inclusion of *agapemtos,* which is not in the LXX but points back to Jesus' baptism in Matt. 3:17) that Isa. 42:1–4 is understood by Matthew to be a messianic text (Cope, 36). Further evidence pointing to this is implicit in the response of the crowd to Jesus' healing the demon-possessed man who was blind and mute. They exclaim, "Could this be the Son of David?" i.e., the Messiah? Only Matthew has this comment from the crowd. To counter the conclusions of the crowd, the Pharisees argue that Jesus exorcises demons by the power of Beelzebub. Jesus retorts with the parable of the strong man and with his own question, "And if I drive out demons by Beelzebub, by whom do your people drive them out?"

Jesus clarifies himself further by asserting that he casts out demons by "the Spirit of God." This forms a crucial link to the messianic interpretation of Isa. 42:1–4, which confirms that God's servant will have God's Spirit upon him (cf. Isa. 42:1 with Matt. 13:18). The saying against blasphemy, accordingly, is affixed in this messianic frame. The question is not whether Jesus was exorcising demons—even the Pharisees had their "exorcists" (Matt. 12:27; cf. on this as a Jewish practice, Acts 19:13–16; Josephus, *Antiq.* 8.44–49); rather, the question is whether Jesus is doing this as God's Messiah, as the crowd believes. "To blaspheme" is to speak against the power by which God's servant the Messiah announces the arrival of the kingdom, since Jesus is indeed casting out demons "by the Spirit of God" (cf. 12:18, 28). For Matthew, "to blaspheme the Spirit" is to reject God and his purpose in Jesus as Messiah.

3. Luke 12:10.

Unlike Matthew, Luke departs totally from the Markan sequence and wording. As a result, his understanding of blaspheming the Spirit is utterly different. The saying does not occur in the Beelzebub controversy as it does in Mark and Matthew (cf. Luke 11:14–28); instead, it surfaces in conjunction with an admonition about remaining faithful during the trials the disciple of Jesus will inevitably face. The context is that of confession (*homologeom;* Luke 12:8) and denial (*arneomai;* Luke 12:9). Luke 12:11 envisions conditions of persecution and trial for the believer: "when you are brought before synagogues, rulers and authorities." Under such circumstances the Holy Spirit will instruct the disciple in what to say (cf. John 16:8–11).

It is not surprising that Luke should have Jesus provide such a postresurrectional glimpse of the fate of the disciples. Clearly this relates to Luke's own readers, who are enduring hardship for the sake of the gospel and who have been promised "power" *(dynamis)* specifically to bear witness (e.g., Luke 24:48–49; Acts 1:8). Thus, for Luke, to reject the Spirit's help at this critical juncture—and as a consequence to deny Jesus—is tantamount to blaspheming the Holy Spirit.

4. Implications.

The teaching from Scripture concerning blaspheming the Spirit depends on whose version one reads, yet each evangelist can speak to the church today. A central scriptural lesson can be blended from this saying of Jesus in its various contexts. First, contrary to some thinking, God's grace is not irresistible; it can be spurned, rejected, and ignored. Moreover, persistent denial of God's revealing himself in Jesus through the power of the Spirit can have eternal consequences. God's revelation of himself is not limited to, but certainly includes, manifesting his grace through the gifts of the Spirit. Any refusal of grace (i.e., salvation) is in a sense "unforgivable," because grace that is "given" must be "received." Second, blaspheming the Spirit concerns a willful rejection of God's grace and power. This especially includes attributing God's working through the power of the Spirit—whether in Jesus or his disciples—to Satan. To blaspheme the Spirit is also to reject both the offer of grace and the power to remain faithful to God. Thus, the one blaspheming the Spirit rejects the very power through which grace is manifest and made available. Therefore, have those who have denounced pentecostalism and the charismatic movements been guilty in any sense of blaspheming the Spirit because they deny the validity of such manifestations? Certainly not if they have accepted the greater gift of salvation through Jesus Christ, the ultimate manifestation of God's power and grace.

As Jeremias astutely points out, appreciating the uniqueness of blaspheming the Spirit lies in understanding that for Jesus' hearers the Spirit's activity had largely ceased. Jesus, though, knows the Spirit is active through his ministry and is himself revealing that presence. "In other words, Mark 3:28 speaks of sin against the God who is still hidden, v. 29 of sin against the God who is revealing himself. The former can be forgiven, the latter is unforgivable" (Jeremias, 150). Thus, he rightly continues, "the unforgivable sin is not a particular moral transgression, as it is in the sphere of Rabbinic casuistry ...; rather, it is the sin that arises in connection with revelation" (ibid.).

■ **Bibliography:** P. H. Alexander "A Critique of Theodore Weeden's Traditions in Conflict," unpub. paper, Central States Regional SBL, 1985 ■ idem, "The Literary Function of Mark 6:6b–13 and Its Message to Mark's Church," *Debarim* (1982–83) ■ H. W. Beyer in *TDNT* (1964), 1:621–25 ■ M. E. Boring, "The Unforgivable Sin Logion Mark III 28–29/Matt XII 28–32/Luke XII 10: Formal Analysis and History of the Tradition," *NovT* 18 (1976) ■ R. Bultmann, *History of the Synoptic Tradition* (1963) ■ O. L. Cope, *Matthew: A Scribe Trained for the Kingdom* (1976) ■ F. Danker, *Jesus and the New Age* (1972) ■ J. D. G. Dunn, *Jesus and the Spirit* (1975) ■ J. A. Fitzmyer, *The Gospel according to Luke,* 2 vols. (1983, 1985) ■ H. Gloer, ed., *Eschatology: Essays in Honor of George Raymond Beasley-Murray* (1988) ■ J. Jeremias, *New Testament Theology: The Proclamation of Jesus* (1971) ■ W. L. Lane, *The Gospel of Mark* (1974) ■ *LSJ* (1968) ■ M. R. Mansfield, *Spirit and Gospel in Mark* (1987) ■ T. W. Manson, *The Sayings of Jesus* (1957) ■ I. H. Marshall, *The Gospel of Luke* (1978) ■ J. R. Michaels, *1 Peter* (1988) ■ G. F. Moore, *Judaism in the First Centuries of the Christian Era: The Age of the Tannaim,* 2 vols. (1932).   ■ P. H. Alexander

BLESSED TRINITY SOCIETY An organization founded in 1960 to publicize and support charismatic renewal in mainline Protestant churches. The founder, ▸Jean Stone Wilans, was active in St. Mark's Episcopal Church in Van Nuys, CA, when ▸Dennis Bennett, the rector of the parish, received the baptism of the Holy Spirit. After her own Pentecost experience, Mrs. Wilans began the society, which later claimed about 7,000 members.

The society first distributed booklets and tracts and supplied speakers to groups who wished to learn more about spiritual gifts. In 1961 the society's chief publication, *Trinity* magazine, began appearing quarterly. It was the first nonpentecostal publication dedicated to promoting the pentecostal experience. As interest grew, the society sponsored meetings in various cities to teach about, and lead people to experience, the outpouring of the Holy Spirit. When dissent among congregations over the role and influence of the Spirit occasionally led to division and resignations, the society provided assistance for some ministers until they could find new posts.

Debate and controversy chiefly centered around speaking in tongues. In 1963 the society's board of directors stated its position, which included the belief that tongues should be used primarily for private devotions; that in public, tongues should always be interpreted; and that when a Christian receives the baptism of the Holy Spirit promised by Jesus (Acts 1:5, 8), the consequence is the ability to speak in low tongues.

The society ceased operations several decades ago.

■ C. M. Irish

BLOCH-HOELL, NILS EGEDE (1915–). Historian. The Norwegian historian Nils Bloch-Hoell, a Lutheran, was the first scholarly commentator to address the Anglo-American pentecostal audience from a Scandinavian standpoint and from outside the movement's subjective confines. Sometime lecturer at the University of Oslo and the Teologiske Menighetafakutet and editor of *Tidsskrift for Teologi og Kirke,* Bloch-Hoell wrote *Pinsebevelgelsen* (1956), revised and translated into English as *The Pentecostal Movement* (1964). The main difference between the Norwegian and English-language versions was the reduction of pages devoted to Norway (from 150 to 12) and expanded coverage of the American and British movements. Although giving close attention to North American origins, Bloch-Hoell highlights European developments, giving special attention to Norway and the other Scandinavian countries. The stress on Norway in the original book was in fact its unique feature. To pentecostal readers who at the time of publication were not used to objective and critical scrutiny, the sociological and phenomenological analysis of their institutions, beliefs, and worship was at first unsettling. Taken together with the later work of ▸W. J. Hollenweger, Bloch-Hoell's work proved to be a useful corrective to the earlier narrow-gauge, apologetic works of American and British insiders.

See also BIBLIOGRAPHY AND HISTORIOGRAPHY OF PENTECOSTALISM OUTSIDE NORTH AMERICA.

■ **Bibliography:** N. Bloch-Hoell, *The Pentecostal Movement* (1964) ■ R. Quebedeaux, *The New Charismatics II* (1983).

■ C. E. Jones

BLOOMFIELD, RAY (1924?–) Ray Bloomfield's evangelistic ministry had a significant impact on the later development of the New Zealand Assemblies of God (AG). This was due both to his powerful faith ministry and irrepressible personality and to the influence he had on his protégé, ›Frank Houston, who later became the superintendent of the AG. Bloomfield started a small pentecostal mission in Auckland in the mid 1950s—the Ellerslie-Tamaki Faith Mission—and later enlisted Houston as his assistant. Houston learned much from Bloomfield, and their joint ministry saw a level of supernatural power uncommon in N.Z. at the time and attracted people from all over Auckland.

Bloomfield later began healing meetings among rural Maori in the Waiomio Valley near Kawa Kawa, 250 km. (155 mi.) north of Auckland, in 1956. These meetings escalated into revival, and Bloomfield and Houston continued to travel between Waiomio and Ellerslie for some months, preaching and following up the converts. Bloomfield later relocated to Canada, and Frank Houston took over the leadership of this revival until he became pastor of the Lower Hutt AG in late 1959.

■ **Bibliography:** Hazel Houston, *Being Frank: The Frank Houston Story* (1989), 70–112. ■ B. Knowles

BLUMHOFER, EDITH (1950–). Historian of American pentecostalism. Born in Brooklyn, NY, and a graduate of Hunter College of the City University of New York and Harvard University, she has held full-time appointments at Southwest Missouri State University, Evangel College, and Wheaton College. She moved to Wheaton, IL, in 1987 as project director for the Institute for the Study of American Evangelicals. From 1995 to 1996 she was a religion program officer at the Pew Charitable Trusts in Philadelphia. From 1996 to 1999 she was associate director of the Public Religion Project at the University of Chicago Divinity School. In 1999 she returned to Wheaton College as professor of history and director of the Institute for the Study of American Evangelicals.

A past president of the Society for Pentecostal Studies, she has published articles and chapters on pentecostalism in various journals and books. Her books include *Aimee Semple McPherson: Everybody's Sister* and *Restoring the Faith: The Assemblies of God, Pentecostalism and American Culture*. She is a member of Gary Memorial United Methodist Church in Wheaton, IL. ■ G. A. Wacker

BOCHIAN, PAVEL (1918–96). President of the Apostolic Church of God in Romania. The first pentecostal church in Romania was established in 1922. As pentecostalism grew, its adherents experienced considerable persecution from ecclesiastical (Romanian Orthodox) and governmental officials. Bochian, as a young pentecostal minister, experienced many difficulties, particularly in the 1930s and 1940s. Full government recognition of the pentecostal churches came in

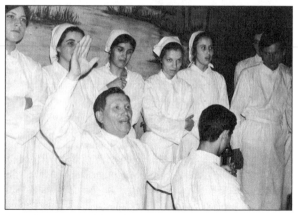

Pavel Bochian, president of the Apostolic Church of God in Romania, baptizing converts in Bucharest in 1972.

1950. From 1962 to 1990 he served as president of the Apostolic Church of God, later known as the Pentecostal Union of Romania. After his retirement, Bochian continued to pastor Emanuel Pentecostal Church in Bucharest.

During his years in office the church experienced intense pressures, witnessed remarkable growth, established a theological seminary (1976), and established fraternal links to the Church of God (Cleveland, TN, 1980).

Bochian was a member of the Pentecostal European Fellowship (PEF) committee and attended the Ninth Pentecostal World Conference in Dallas, TX, in 1970.

■ **Bibliography:** P. Bochian, "The Pentecostal Church in Romania," *World Pentecost* (1, 1972) ■ Church of God (Cleveland, TN) press release, Sept. 8, 1980 ■ C. Roske, "Pavel Bochian (1918–1996)," *World Pentecost* (Winter 1996).
■ G. B. McGee; B. A. Pavia

BODDY, ALEXANDER ALFRED (1854–1930). Early pentecostal leader in Great Britain. Son of an Anglican rector, Boddy was heavily influenced by ›Keswick and studied theology at Durham. He was ordained by Bishop J. B. Lightfoot and began ministry at Elwick before being appointed to Sunderland (1884–1922) and Pittington (1922–30). Boddy traveled widely, exploring western Canada, Egypt, North Africa, Palestine, and Russia. Books describing these trips won him membership in the Royal Geographical Society (England) and the Imperial Geographical Society (Russia). Concerned about the spiritual life of his parish, he investigated the Welsh revival and in 1907 went to Oslo to study the pentecostal revival. T. B. Barratt visited Sunderland (Sept. 1907), and under his leadership several experienced the baptism of the Holy Spirit. Boddy became active in the pentecostal revival in England. He hosted the Annual Whitsuntide (Pentecost) Pentecostal Conventions at Sunderland (1908–

14). Participants included G. Polman from the Netherlands and J. Paul from Germany. Boddy also edited and published the pentecostal periodical *Confidence* (1908–26).

■ **Bibliography:** A. A. Boddy, *By Ocean, Prairie, and Peak* (1896) ■ idem, *Christ in His Holy Land: A Life of Our Lord* (1897) ■ idem, *Days in Galilee and Scenes in Judea* (1900) ■ idem, *From the Egyptian Ramleh* (1900) ■ idem, *The Laying on of Hands, a Bible Ordinance* (1895) ■ idem, *To Kairwan the Holy* (1884) ■ idem, *With Russian Pilgrims* (1893) ■ J. V. Boddy (Mother Joanna Mary), "Alexander Alfred Boddy, 1854–1930" (unpub. typescript, c. 1970) ■ E. Blumhofer, "Alexander Boddy and the Rise of Pentecostalism in Britain," *Pneuma* 8 (1986) ■ D. Gee, *Wind and Flame* (1967) ■ idem, *These Men I Knew* (1980) ■ W. K. Kay, *Inside Story: A History of the British Assemblies of God* (1990) ■ idem, "Alexander Boddy and the Outpouring of the Holy Spirit in Sunderland," *EPTA Bulletin* 5 (1986) ■ A. Missen, *Sound of a Going: The Story of the Assemblies of God* (1973) ■ C. van der Laan, "The Proceedings of the Leader's Meetings (1908–1911) and of the International Pentecostal Council (1912–1914)," *EPTA Bulletin* 6 (1987).   ■ D. D. Bundy

BODDY, MARY (d. 1928). Wife of the Reverend ▸Alexander A. Boddy, vicar of All Saints', Monkwearmouth, Sunderland, England. Daughter of an Anglican minister, she assisted Boddy during revival services in 1890. They were married in 1891. Mary was healed of asthma in 1899 and exercised a healing ministry before and after her pentecostal experience, which occurred on Sept. 11, 1907. Their two daughters, Mary and Jane, also spoke in tongues. Mrs. Boddy possessed musical ability and teaching skills, which were coupled with her healing ministry. She also had a special gift for helping seekers into the experience of the baptism of the Spirit. Among the number who received the baptism when she laid hands on them were the Bradford plumber ▸Smith Wigglesworth and ▸G. R. Polman from Holland. For the last 16 years of her life she was an invalid, but she still ministered healing to others, both in Sunderland and at Pittington, Durham, where the Boddys retired in 1922.

■ **Bibliography:** Mary Boddy, *"Pentecost" at Sunderland: The Testimony of a Vicar's Wife* (n.d.).   ■ D. W. Cartwright

BONNIE BRAE STREET COTTAGE During the winter–spring months of 1906, a group of black Los Angeles Christians gathered at 214 (now 216) North Bonnie Brae Street, the home of a janitor and his wife, Richard D. and Ruth Asberry, for prayer and Bible study. Included among them was Mrs. Julia W. Hutchins, who, with eight other families, had been expelled from the Second Baptist Church in Los Angeles for embracing "Holiness" teaching. When the group proved to be too large for the Asberry home, Hutchins opened a storefront mission on Santa Fe Street.

William J. Seymour was called to serve as the pastor of this new congregation. He arrived by train on Feb. 22, 1906, and commenced his ministry on Feb. 24. At first all went well, but when Seymour argued that the ability to speak in tongues was a sign that would follow the baptism in the Holy Spirit, Hutchins had him locked out of the church.

Seymour had been staying in the home of Mr. and Mrs. Edward S. Lee on South Union Avenue, near First Street. They opened their small home so that those from the church who were interested could pursue their Bible study with Seymour. When the group grew to the size when it could no longer meet at the Lee's home, they moved back to the Asberry home.

At 6:00 on the evening of Apr. 9, 1906, Edward Lee called Seymour and asked for prayer that he would at that time be given the gift of tongues. Seymour prayed, and Lee spoke in tongues. Seymour went immediately to the Asberry home for the 7:30 P.M. meeting. Following the singing of a

A. A. Boddy, his wife, Mary, and their daughters. Boddy was an Anglican rector in Sunderland, U.K., who was baptized in the Spirit in 1907.

song, a time of prayer, and a few testimonies, Seymour began to speak on Acts 2:4, sharing the news of Edward Lee's experience less than two hours earlier. He never finished his study. Someone began to speak in tongues. That person was joined by others, among them ▸Jennie Moore, who improvised a melody on the piano to accompany her gift of tongues. The meeting concluded about 10 P.M., and word traveled fast within the black community and into the white community. For the next several nights crowds gathered at the Bonnie Brae home, so that the services moved to the ready-made pulpit of the front porch and the street below. On Apr. 12, 1906, the front porch collapsed from the weight of the worshipers. Meetings were moved to 312 Azusa Street after a lease was negotiated with the Stevens AME Church, where several of the crowd had formerly been members.

The cottage remained in the Asberry family until 1985, when it was purchased by Pentecostal Heritage, Inc., a nonprofit entity under the leadership of Art E. Glass. In 1997 Pentecostal Heritage entrusted the property to the First Jurisdiction, Southern California, of COGIC. Under the leadership of Bishop Charles E. Blake, the jurisdiction has purchased adjacent properties and refurbished the house. It is currently open to the public by appointment. Further plans call for the addition of adequate parking and the construction of a museum to showcase the Azusa Street revival.

See also AZUSA STREET REVIVAL.

■ **Bibliography:** A. M. Cotton, "Inside Story of the Outpouring of the Holy Spirit, Azusa Street, Apr. 1906," *Message of the "Apostolic Faith"* 1 (1, 1939): 1–3 ■ R. L. Fidler, "Historical Review of the Pentecostal Outpouring," *International Outlook* (Jan.–Mar. 1963) ■ C. W. Shumway, "A Study of 'The Gift of Tongues'" (thesis, U. of S. Calif., 1914). ■ C. M. Robeck Jr.

BONNKE, REINHARD WILLI GOTTFRIED (1940–). International evangelist. Reinhard Willi Gottfried Bonnke was born in Königsberg, Germany, on Apr. 19, 1940, the son of a pentecostal pastor belonging to the Federation of Free Pentecostal Churches (*Bund Freier Pfingstmeinden* [BFP]). Educated in Wales, he met George Jeffreys (1889–1962) as a youth. From his earliest days he felt called to be a missionary to Africa. His marriage to Anna Sulzle in 1964 produced three children: Kai-uwe (1966), Gabriele (1967), and Susanne (1969). After several years as a pastor and evangelist in Germany, he arrived in Africa in May 1967.

From 1967 to 1974, Bonnke labored with meager results as a traditional missionary for the BFP in Lesotho, Africa. In 1974 he received a call to minister "to the whole of Africa" with the assurance that "Africa shall be saved." His first mass healing crusade took place in Gaberones, Botswana, in Apr. 1975, which began with only 100 persons in attendance and ended in a packed stadium with over 10,000 present.

In 1977 he purchased a 10,000-seat tent, which often was inadequate when as many as 40,000 attempted to enter. A blond-haired, blue-eyed German, Bonnke was at a loss to explain his popularity among the blacks with whom he identified. Everywhere he ministered, even in South Africa, Bonnke refused to practice racial segregation in his services.

A major attraction in Bonnke's meetings were the signs and wonders that accompanied his preaching, with thousands testifying to miracles of physical healing and exorcisms in his crusades. Also featured in many meetings were bonfires that were set as converts burned their magic amulets and charms associated with witchcraft. Everywhere Bonnke encouraged his converts to receive the baptism in the Holy Spirit with the evidence of speaking in tongues. Also, at times, thousands would be "slain in the Spirit" as he preached.

During the early 1980s, Bonnke's crusades attracted some of the largest crowds in the history of mass evangel-

The house on North Bonnie Brae Street (which is still standing), where the pentecostal revival in Los Angeles began in 1906. Because of the crowds, the meetings were moved to what became known as the Azusa Street Mission.

ism. One crusade in Nigeria in 1986 attracted as many as 250,000 to one service. His crusades in Soweto attracted thousands of blacks and whites despite the official government policy of apartheid.

In 1983 Bonnke purchased the largest gospel tent ever built, one that would hold some 34,000 persons. Although it was torn apart in a severe storm in Capetown in 1984, it was rebuilt and put back into use by 1986. In that year, Bonnke's team reported 1,500,000 responses to the call for salvation, including many thousands of Muslims.

By the mid 1980s Bonnke also began conducting leadership conferences in Africa and Europe. His "Fire Conference" in Zimbabwe in 1986 drew thousands of African pastors and evangelists, while his "Eurofire" conferences in Frankfurt in 1987 and Birmingham in 1988 brought his ministry to the attention of Europeans. His ministry in the U.S. increased after speaking in the New Orleans Superdome in 1987 to the Congress on the Holy Spirit and World Evangelization.

In 1987 Bonnke moved his family from Johannesburg, where he had lived for many years, to Frankfurt, Germany, where he set up headquarters for his organization, which, since its legal beginning in 1972, has been known as Christ for All Nations (CFAN). In the 1990s Bonnke's major evangelistic thrust was an attempt at mailing a gospel booklet, *From Minus to Plus,* to every postal address in the world.

■ **Bibliography:** R. Bonnke, *Mighty Manifestations* (1994) ▌ R. Steele, *Plundering Hell to Populate Heaven* (1987).

■ H. V. Synan

BOSWORTH, FRED FRANCIS (1877–1958). Early pentecostal pioneer, pastor, and healing evangelist. When Bosworth was young, his family moved to Chicago to be a part of ▸John Alexander Dowie's church. He later became director of Dowie's Zion City, IL, band. When Charles F. Parham brought the pentecostal message to Zion City in Sept. 1906, Bosworth and Marie Burgess were baptized in the Holy Spirit on the same evening.

Persecuted for his pentecostal beliefs, Bosworth went to Dallas, TX, where in 1910 he pioneered a church that rose to prominence as a center of great revival. In 1912 ▸Maria B. Woodworth-Etter held tent meetings at his church every night for several months. Many were healed of serious medical problems, and this attracted people from all parts of the U.S. While pastor of this church, Bosworth suffered a great deal of persecution for befriending blacks and for holding racially integrated meetings.

Bosworth was a delegate to the first general council of the Assemblies of God (AG) at Hot Springs, AR, in 1914, and later became one of the 16 members of its executive presbytery. However, Bosworth began to express his belief that the gift of tongues was only one of many possible indications that

F. F. Bosworth, an early pentecostal with roots in John Alexander Dowie's Zion City, IL.

a person was baptized in the Holy Spirit. As a result of the ensuing ▸"initial evidence" controversy, he resigned from the AG in 1918. He was permitted to attend a meeting of the general council later that year, which, after a period of discussion, reaffirmed its commitment to the gift of tongues as the only initial sign of baptism in the Spirit.

As members of the Christian and Missionary Alliance, F. F. Bosworth, his brother B. B. Bosworth, and their wives, held healing campaigns in many major cities. At meetings in Pittsburgh in 1919, 4,800 conversions were reported. There were many dramatic healings; at a Jan. 1921 meeting in Detroit a woman was healed of blindness. In 1922 and 1923 the Bosworth team held meetings in Toronto with Oswald J. Smith, Paul Rader, and the "Cleveland Coloured Gospel Quintette." Campaigns were held in many other cities, including Chicago, Ottawa (where more than 12,000 people attended nightly), and Washington, DC. During these years, Bosworth became a pioneer in radio evangelism and established the National Radio Revival Missionary Crusaders, broadcasting over WJJD in Chicago.

During 1948–50, soon after ▸William Branham began his healing ministry, Bosworth came out of semiretirement to join him in campaigns in Pensacola, Seattle, Miami, Zion, and Houston. Bosworth was an important influence on the healing evangelists of the post-WWII era. Bosworth, in turn, had been influenced by ▸E. W. Kenyon. He gave the last six years of his life to the work of missions in Africa.

■ **Bibliography:** F. F. Bosworth, *Christ the Healer* (1924, 1948) ■ C. Brumback, *Suddenly . . . from Heaven* (1961) ■ D. E. Harrell Jr., *All Things Are Possible* (1975) ■ E. M. Perkins, *Fred Francis Bosworth: His Life Story* (1927) ■ "Rev. and Mrs. F. F. Bosworth Work with Branham Party," *Voice of Healing* (May 1948) ■ R. L. Niklaus, J. S. Sawin, and S. J. Stoesz, *All for Jesus* (1986) ■ M. B. Woodworth-Etter, *Signs and Wonders* (1916).   ■ R. M. Riss

BRADFORD, GEORGE CRAIN ("BRICK") (1923–). Pastor and Presbyterian charismatic leader. Brick Bradford was born in Mercedes, TX. He attended the University of Texas at Austin and earned a B.B.A. (1949) and J.D. (1952). In 1955 Brick married Marjorie Jane Lloyd. They have four children. Receiving a diploma from Austin Presbyterian Theological Seminary in 1957, he was ordained into the ministry of the present-day Presbyterian Church U.S.A.

Bradford pastored Faith Presbyterian Church at Pasadena, TX (1957–62), and First Presbyterian Church at El Reno, OK (1962–67). He was baptized in the Holy Spirit in 1966 at a CFO ("Camp Farthest Out") meeting in Ardmore, OK. This "revolutionized" his ministry, but when the presbytery heard that Bradford was speaking in tongues, they removed him from his pastorate in 1967.

In May 1966 Bradford and five other ministers founded the Charismatic Communion of Presbyterian Ministers in Oklahoma City, later renamed the Presbyterian and Reformed Renewal Ministries International. Bradford was chosen as general secretary and editor for this group and served in that capacity until 1989. He also became a trustee for Literacy and Evangelism, Inc. (1973), and was a regent for Melodyland School of Theology. He has written several articles and booklets on the Presbyterian charismatic renewal, including *Releasing the Power of the Holy Spirit* (1983).

■ **Bibliography:** V. Synan, *The Twentieth-Century Pentecostal Explosion* (1987), 165–71 ■ *Who's Who in Religion* (2d ed., 1977).
■ G. W. Gohr

BRANDING, HARRY W. (1891–1969). Pastor and church official. Born near Granite City, IL, Branding received the baptism in the Holy Spirit in 1929 through the ministry of ▸Benjamin H. Hite. Shortly after that experience, he began pastoring, and for 34 years he served the Apostolic Pentecostal Church in St. Louis, MO. Under his ministry it became one of the largest congregations in the ▸United Pentecostal Church, International (UPCI).

Branding's denominational responsibilities included serving as general secretary of the Pentecostal Church, Inc., a

forerunner of the UPCI (1943); district superintendent of the Missouri District (1948–69); and member of a number of UPCI boards: executive board, foreign missionary, Christian education, publication, and Tupelo Children's Mansion. He also served as chairman of the board of directors of Gateway College of Evangelism in St. Louis, which he helped found in 1968.

■ **Bibliography:** A. L. Clanton, *United We Stand* (1995).
■ G. B. McGee; E. J. Gitre

BRANHAM, WILLIAM MARRION (1909–65). Initiator of the post-WWII healing revival. Born in a dirt-floor log cabin in the hills of Kentucky, Branham carried his prophetic message of healing and deliverance to the far corners of the earth. A mystic from his youth, he reported divine visitations

William Marrion Branham, one of the faith healers prominent in the post-WWII salvation-healing movement.

at ages three and seven. After a personal healing, he felt called to preach and became an independent Baptist. In 1933 he preached to 3,000 people in a tent revival in Jeffersonville, IN, and later built Branham Tabernacle there. He attributed the death of his wife and baby in 1937 to his failure to heed the call to conduct revivals in ▸Oneness pentecostal churches.

Branham reported that throughout his life he was guided by an angel who first appeared to him in a secret cave in 1946. He was given the power to discern people's illnesses and thoughts. David Harrell reports of his popularity: "The power of a Branham service . . . remains a legend unparalleled in the history of the charismatic movement" (Harrell, 162). Branham's accuracy is attested by Walter J. Hollenweger, who interpreted for him in Zurich and "is not aware of any case in which he was mistaken in the often detailed statements he made" (Hollenweger, 354). But he further reports that although many healings were well attested, there were not as many as were claimed. Branham filled the world's largest auditoriums and stadiums. In contrast to the caricature of the image-minded evangelist, he lived moderately, dressed modestly, and boasted of his youthful poverty. This endeared him to the throngs who idolized him. He was self-conscious about his lack of education, but the simplicity of his messages had worldwide appeal.

By emphasizing healing and prosperity and neglecting his Oneness theology, Branham was able to minister in Trinitarian pentecostal circles as well. In 1947 he acquired as his manager ▸Gordon Lindsay, who edited the *Voice of Healing* magazine, which served as an advertising vehicle for the rapidly multiplying healing evangelists. He was also highly touted by the ▸Full Gospel Business Men's Fellowship International, but support declined as he became more controversial in the 1960s.

Branham's insistence that believers baptized by a Trinitarian formula must be rebaptized in the name of "Jesus only" was a view shared by a number of pentecostals. But other teachings placed him on the fringes of orthodoxy. His doctrine of the "serpent's seed" taught that Eve's sin involved sexual relations with the serpent. Some humans are descended from the serpent's seed and are destined for hell, which is not eternal, however. The seed of God, i.e., those who receive Branham's teaching, are predestined to become the bride of Christ. There are still others who possess free will and who may be saved out of the denominational churches, but they must suffer through the great tribulation. He considered denominationalism a mark of the beast (Rev. 13:17).

Branham proclaimed himself the angel of Rev. 3:14 and 10:7 and prophesied that by 1977 all denominations would be consumed by the World Council of Churches under the control of the Roman Catholics, that the rapture would take place, and that the world would be destroyed. He died in 1965, but many of his followers expected him to be resurrected, some believing him to be God, others believing him to be virgin-born.

Branham's influence has continued in many churches where his prophecies are considered to be divinely inspired. His teaching on the power of the spoken word has been a characteristic of later revivalists. Kenneth Hagin identifies Branham as a prophet.

■ **Bibliography:** W. M. Branham, *Footprints on the Sands of Time* (1975) ■ C. Dyck, *William Branham: The Man and His Message* (1984) ■ D. E. Harrell Jr., *All Things Are Possible: The Healing and Charismatic Revivals in Modern America* (1975) ■ W. J. Hollenweger, *The Pentecostals* (1977) ■ G. Lindsay, *William Branham: A Man Sent from God* (1950) ■ E. Pement, "An Annotated Bibliography of Material by and about William Marion Branham," *Cornerstone* (1986) ■ idem, "William Branham: An American Legend," *Cornerstone* 15 (81).   ■ D. J. Wilson

BRAXTON, S. LEE (1905–82). The first vice president of ▸Full Gospel Business Men's Fellowship International and a staunch worker with ▸Demos Shakarian in its development. Braxton was a successful businessman and civic leader in North Carolina: mayor of Whiteville; organizer and for 13 years chairman of the board of First National Bank of Whiteville; president of Braxton Enterprises; member of the local Rotary; president, vice president, chairman, or director of numerous auto-related companies and civic groups; national director of ▸Oral Roberts's *Coast-to-Coast* radio broadcast; director of Whiteville Merchants Association and Chamber of Commerce; and director of North Carolina Merchants Association.

In 1949 Braxton, who was by that time a millionaire considering retirement, began providing business counsel to Oral Roberts. For 16 years he was chairman of the board of regents of Oral Roberts University and personal consultant to Roberts.

■ **Bibliography:** L. Braxton, "A Better Way," *Full Gospel Business Men's Voice* 20 (4, 1972) ■ idem, "A Dream Come True," *Full Gospel Business Men's Voice* 1 (1, 1953) ■ O. Roberts, "One of the Greatest Laymen of This Century," *Abundant Life* 37 (2, 1983).
                                                        ■ J. A. Hewett

BREDESEN, HARALD (1918–). Pastor and conference speaker and an important figure in the origins of the ▸charismatic movement. Ordained a Lutheran minister in 1944, Bredesen was baptized in the Spirit at a pentecostal summer camp in 1946. His proffered resignation was refused by the Lutheran authorities, which Bredesen took as a sign to remain within his church. Holding various nonpastoral church appointments, Bredesen witnessed to the baptism in the Spirit. He was encouraged during these "years in the wilderness" by David du Plessis and later by the Full Gospel Business Men's Fellowship International (FGBMFI). In 1957 he became pastor of Mount Vernon Dutch Reformed Church in New York City and soon began a charismatic prayer meeting. Bredesen had a remarkable flair for showing up in unexpected places, and many prominent figures speak of his role in their Spirit baptism, e.g., P. Boone, J. Sherrill, B. Slosser, and M. G. (Pat) Robertson, who was his student assistant (1958–59).

Harald Bredesen, Lutheran minister who played an important role in the origins of the charismatic movement. He coined (with Jean Stone) the term *charismatic renewal.*

When Jean Stone (see Willans, Jean Stone) formed the Blessed Trinity Society (BTS) in 1960, Bredesen became chairman of the board. Together with Stone, he spoke at numerous "Christian Advances" sponsored by BTS. In 1963 Bredesen's mission on the Yale campus attracted national publicity. He and Stone coined the designation "charismatic renewal" in 1963, in contrast to "Neo-Pentecostalism," which had been used in an *Eternity* editorial. In these years Bredesen was featured in all the major media presentations of the movement, including Walter Cronkite's mini-documentary on *World News Tonight* (1963). Bredesen has traveled widely, often financed by the FGBMFI. After the beginnings of Catholic charismatic renewal, he played a part in its early stages in Colombia and Yugoslavia. Bredesen's ministry has also been marked by an ability to reach political leaders, including various heads of state.

Bredesen resigned from Mount Vernon in 1970, and after a break he pastored Trinity Christian Center in Victoria, B.C., from 1971 until 1980, when he retired to Escondido, CA, where he carries on his distinctive charismatic ministry, including the Prince of Peace Foundation. His earlier story is told in *Yes, Lord* (1972).

■ **Bibliography:** J. T. Connelly, "Neo-Pentecostalism: The Charismatic Revival in the Mainline Protestant and Roman Catholic Churches of the United States, 1960–1971" (Ph.D. diss., U. of Chicago, 1977) ■ J. Sherrill, *They Speak with Other Tongues* (1964) ■ V. Synan, *The Twentieth-Century Pentecostal Explosion* (1987).
■ P. D. Hocken

BREWSTER, PERCY STANLEY (1908–80). British pentecostal leader, pastor, and evangelist. Born in London, he was converted under the ministry of ▸George Jeffreys. He was made youth leader at East Ham and was asked to assist in the follow-up after George Jeffreys's most successful crusade in Birmingham in 1930. He spent a short time at the Elim Bible College, London, before being sent to a joint charge.

Brewster's developing gifts found expression in evangelistic outreach. Following a vision in which he saw a hall packed with people, he lead a crusade in Neath, Wales. The hall they booked was the one seen in the vision. It was a great success, the first crusade of more than 40 that established new churches. This was a time when Elim's founder (George Jeffreys) was at the close of his major success. In 1939 Brewster became minister of Cardiff City Temple. He remained as minister until 1974. During this period he left Cardiff twice a

Percy S. Brewster, a prominent Elim minister in Wales and an active participant in the Pentecostal World Conference.

year to conduct crusades and establish churches all over Britain. At the close of the war he took a leading part in the new evangelistic thrust in Elim, beginning in Wigan, Lancashire. He was superintendent in Wales, where in spite of his other duties he continued to pioneer new churches.

A man of vision and boundless energy, Brewster was a gifted evangelist with a particular skill for gathering in converts; he combined this with a caring pastoral ministry. He was elected to the executive council of the Elim Foursquare Gospel Alliance in 1952 and served as president twice, becoming secretary-general in 1974–77. From 1964 he served on the advisory committee of the Pentecostal World Conference (secretary, 1970) and editor of *World Pentecost*. Known affectionately as "P.S." by his friends, "Mr. Brewster," by his younger ministers, he was "Pastor Brewster" to his loving congregation. He also traveled extensively in the interests of the worldwide pentecostal movement, visiting New Zealand, Europe, the U.S., and Korea. He died in London in July 1980 after suffering with a brain tumor. He was buried in Cardiff, Wales, the land of his adoption.

■ D. W. Cartwright

BRITTAIN, BLANCHE ELIZABETH (1890–1952). Evangelist, church planter, pastor. Born Blanche Elizabeth Florum on Dec. 6, 1890, near Stockville, NE. An orphan, she was reared in an adoptive family's Methodist home. She completed the eighth grade and attended business school but had no formal theological training. A brief marriage to Bryan Brittain produced no children. They separated due to his disapproval of her faith and ministry. Licensed as a missionary evangelist by the Assemblies of God (AG) on Aug. 13, 1915, she held meetings in Nebraska, Iowa, Minnesota, Montana, North and South Dakota, and Canada. She moved to North Dakota in 1918, where she spent much of her ministry. Known as the "sod buster," Blanche planted more than 40 churches. A powerful and animated speaker, she drew large crowds and was synonymous with the AG in the northern Great Plains. Herself an alto, she usually traveled with female coworkers with musical abilities. Mildred Westerlund, pianist and soprano, accompanied her from 1929 to 1939. Blanche was a supporter of gender equality in the ministry. After Bryan Brittain died, she married Osmund Urdahl, a farmer from Goodridge, MN, on Apr. 21, 1945. She continued on the evangelistic circuit, assisted by her husband, until her death on Jan. 30, 1952.

■ **Bibliography:** "Evangelist Blanche Urdahl Summoned," *North Dakota District Echoes and Ambassador* (Mar. 1952).
                                                            ■ D. J. Rodgers

BRITTON, BILL

BRITTON, BILL (1918–85). Founder and pastor of the House of Prayer in Springfield, MO, and proponent of the "sonship" message. He was highly regarded by many in the charismatic movement as an individual who moved in the realm of prophetic ministry. At the 1949 annual Sunday school convention of the Assemblies of God in Springfield, MO, he heard about the ▸Latter Rain revival and became involved in it. He became a prolific writer of books and pamphlets on some of the "deeper truths" of the Christian faith, which he mailed free of charge on request. While his major emphasis was on growth to Christian maturity, some of his teachings became controversial, especially as others took some of his teachings and pushed them to extremes. As a result of the demand for his preaching, he traveled frequently and had an extensive influence both in the U.S. and in many foreign countries.

■ **Bibliography:** B. Britton, *Prophet on Wheels* (1979).
                                                            ■ R. M. Riss

BRITTON, FRANCIS MARION

BRITTON, FRANCIS MARION (1870–1937). A pioneer evangelist and leader of the ▸Fire-Baptized Holiness Church (FBHC) in North Carolina. Britton was converted in 1888 at age 18 and joined the Union Methodist Church. Early in 1907 he received the Holy Spirit baptism and immediately began a vigorous pentecostal ministry. He introduced Pentecost to the South Florida Holiness camp meeting in 1907, and in 1908 he established a FBHC in Florida. Also in 1908 he introduced Pentecost to the Beulah Holiness Bible School in Oklahoma.

As assistant general overseer of the FBHC, Britton helped to form its merger with the Pentecostal Holiness Church in 1911 He died in 1937.

See also INTERNATIONAL PENTECOSTAL HOLINESS CHURCH.

■ **Bibliography:** F. M. Britton, *Pentecostal Truth* (1919) ■ *The Pentecostal Holiness Advocate* (Feb. 14, 1970).   ■ C. W. Conn

BROTHERHOOD OF THE CROSS AND STAR

BROTHERHOOD OF THE CROSS AND STAR The Brotherhood of the Cross and Star (BCS) was founded in Calabar in southeastern Nigeria in the late 1950s through the charismatic personality of Olumba Olumba Obu (or "OOO"), its current leader and sole spiritual head. Obu was born in 1918 in Biakpan village, near Calabar, and he is believed to have had little or no formal education. Members believe that BCS is eternal in nature (it has no origin or beginning), even though it came into physical existence in 1956, when it was officially registered under the Land (Perpetual Succession) Act of the Federal Republic of Nigeria (the certificate of incorporation was granted in 1964). Members also refer to their movement as Christ's Universal Spiritual School of Practical Christianity. By using both names, they stress that their movement, far from being a "church," rather represents a "Christian movement," a "brotherhood," or a "spiritual school" for the learning and praxis of Christianity.

BCS started as a prayer/Bible study group as well as a "spiritual" healing home; its core membership consisted mainly of women and children. It is today witnessing increasing international expansion and is attracting people from all levels of society. BCS sees the whole world as its mission field; the "brotherhood" in its name signifies its claim to universality. Branches are now found in other parts of Nigeria as well as in the U.S., Europe, Australia, and other parts of the world. Its current worldwide membership is estimated at about 2 million. BCS owns prayer/healing centers called "Bethels." The initials "OOO" are seen by members as a symbol of protection and are thus inscribed on homes, cars, or other property.

BCS maintains its religious identity as a Christian movement (not a church), but some of their beliefs have generated much controversy among nonmembers, especially among Christian churches. Examples are the "deity" of its founder and leader, whom followers believe to be the eighth and final incarnation of Jesus Christ, as well as the very embodiment of the Holy Trinity; the bisexual nature of God; the relative goodness and evilness of God; the relative perfection of Jesus Christ; and the obsolescence of some portions of the Bible, especially the OT.

BCS's eschatology includes the claim that the movement will take over the affairs of the world in the foreseeable future. Obu claims that BCS is the "new Kingdom of God" (the reign of the Holy Spirit) and that the spiritual rule of BCS will be the new ideology governing the world. Obu is critical of the "foreign" religious domination that characterizes the African religious scene. He advocates for what he calls religious or spiritual liberation from foreign missionary religions. BCS expresses the desire for an African ideology, that is, "the worship of the True God which is the God of Love, Truth, and Brotherhood." It recommends strict vegetarianism and monogamy for its members. BCS disseminates its objectives and programs through books and pamphlets published by its own press.

■ **Bibliography:** R. I. J. Hackett, *Religion in Calabar: The Religious Life and History of a Nigerian Town* (1989) ■ F. M. Mbon, *Brotherhood of the Cross and Star: A New Religious Movement in Nigeria* (1992) ■ idem, "Nationalistic Motifs in a Nigerian New Religious Movement" in G. Ludwar-Ene, *New Religious Movements and Society in Nigeria* (1991).   ■ A. U. Adogame

BROWN, JAMES H. (1912–87). Presbyterian charismatic leader. Brown was born in Pittsburgh, PA, on Mar. 27, 1912. He graduated from Grove City College, PA, in 1935 and from Princeton Theological Seminary in 1939. From 1939 to 1977 Brown pastored the Upper Octorara Presbyterian Church, Parkesburg, PA. During his pastorate he served for 12 years (1946–58) as assistant professor of theology and ethics at Lincoln Theological Seminary.

In the early 1950s Brown had a decisive conversion experience through the witness of a pentecostal meeting and Bible study. Toward the end of the 1950s he was baptized in the Holy Spirit. Soon thereafter the Upper Octorara Church became famed for its charismatic life, and people came literally from around the world especially to attend the Saturday night prayer and praise service.

James H. Brown, a Presbyterian leader early in the charismatic renewal, who turned his Parkesburg, PA, church into a popular charismatic center.

Brown served as an early president of the Presbyterian Charismatic Communion (now Presbyterian and Reformed Renewal Ministries). His ministry carried him to many denominations across America, also to Europe, the Middle East, and Far East.

See also PRESBYTERIAN AND REFORMED CHARISMATICS.
■ J. R. Williams

BROWN, ROBERT (1872–1948), and **MARIE** (1880–1971). Founders and pastors of ⏵Glad Tidings Tabernacle in New York City. Robert was born in Enniskillen, Northern Ireland, seventh of Christopher and Alice Reed Brown's 12 children. After brief service on London's police force, Robert was converted under Methodist influences and dedicated his life to the Wesleyan Methodist ministry. He migrated to New York in 1898, where he found daytime employment to support his evening and weekend evangelistic efforts. In 1907 he met Marie Burgess, who conducted a pentecostal storefront mission in midtown Manhattan. Burgess had been sent to New York by ⏵Charles F. Parham as a pioneer pentecostal evangelist. Reared an Episcopalian in Eau Claire, WI, Burgess and her family had moved to healing evangelist ⏵John A. Dowie's religious community, Zion City, IL, after embracing divine-healing teaching. In Zion in 1906 she encountered the ministry of pentecostal pioneer Charles F. Parham, whose message she promptly accepted. In Jan. 1907 she followed Parham's advice and embarked on full-time ministry.

In Jan. 1908 Robert accepted pentecostalism. On Oct. 14, 1909, he and Marie Burgess were married in her parents' home in Zion City by prominent pentecostal pastor ⏵William

H. Piper. Their midwestern contacts led them into association with the loosely structured white Churches of God in Christ in 1912 and 1913. By 1916 they had affiliated with the Assemblies of God (AG).

Robert and Marie Brown's combined efforts in New York were fruitful: the congregation moved to larger quarters and extended them; then in 1921 they purchased a large former Baptist church, which they named Glad Tidings Tabernacle. At least until WWII, Glad Tidings was a hub for northeastern pentecostals. It supported a weekly radio broadcast, was the site of huge evangelistic rallies, and sent its young people to missions efforts around the world. From the 1920s through the 1940s, it typically led AG congregations in missionary giving.

Robert served the AG as a general presbyter (1918–25) and played a prominent role in the 1918 general council debate on the pentecostal distinctive of evidential tongues. After her husband's death Marie continued to serve the congregation as pastor until her death in 1971.

■ **Bibliography:** "A Man Greatly Beloved," *Glad Tidings Herald* (May 1948) ▮ E. L. Blumhofer, "Marie Burgess Brown," *Paraclete* (Summer 1987).   ■ E. L. Blumhofer

Robert and Marie Brown, who pastored Glad Tidings Tabernacle in New York, which for years was the leader in foreign-missions giving among churches in the Assemblies of God.

BROWN, VIN R. (20th century) Vin Brown was originally a member of the Baptist Church, where he achieved some early recognition as a lay preacher, winning the Baptist Union Spurgeon Cup for lay preachers in 1922 and 1923. He later became honorary minister of the Lower Hutt Church of Christ (Associated) in the 1930s.

Although Brown's brothers were longtime leaders in the Pentecostal Church of New Zealand, he himself did not receive the baptism of the Spirit until early 1939. After this pentecostal experience, he associated with the Commonwealth Covenant Church, a group with British Israel associations, where he lectured on prophetic subjects. He later seceded from this movement and founded the New Covenant Assembly in Wellington, which he continued to pastor until the 1970s.

This independent pentecostal church and its British Israel associates later formed links with the Australian Christian Revival Crusade as a result of Pastor ▸Leo Harris's visit to N.Z. in 1941. This led to the adoption of the name National Revival Crusade for the movement, although this title has now been relinquished in favor of Christian Revival Crusade. The British Israel emphasis of these churches is now less prominent than in the past. The Christian Revival Crusade remains one of the smaller pentecostal groups in N.Z., with only 11 churches in the movement in 1997.

■ **Bibliography:** James E. Worsfold, *A History of the Charismatic Movements in New Zealand* (1974).   ■ B. Knowles

BROWNSVILLE REVIVAL Also known as the "Pensacola Outpouring" or "Pensacola Revival" (the Brownsville church and community are part of the city of Pensacola, FL), this revival broke out on Father's Day 1995 (Sunday, June 18) and has been continuing for more than five years (as of mid 2000). Centered in the Brownsville Assembly of God (AG), the revival has also led to the founding of the Brownsville Revival School of Ministry as well as the establishment of Awake America crusades, held in various American cities by the revival team (nine U.S. and eight overseas crusades in 2000), and robust sales of books, videotapes, and music CDs.

The starting date of the Brownsville revival has traditionally been reckoned as when, in the words of the senior pastor of the church, Rev. John Kilpatrick, "Suddenly I felt a wind blow through my legs, just like in the second chapter of the book of Acts. A strong breeze went through my legs and suddenly both my ankles flipped over so that I could hardly stand. I thought, *That's weird!* 'O God,' I prayed, 'What in the world is happening?' I stood on the side of my ankles, unable to get my footing. I literally could not straighten up my feet. . . . Finally, I had to ask a friend . . . to come over and help me. He lifted my legs by pulling on my pants and helped me walk back up the platform, step by step.

I took the microphone and shouted, 'Folks, this is it. The Lord is here. Get in, get in!'

"I realized God had indeed come, that he had answered our prayers for revival. The *feast of fire* had begun! [Visiting evangelist] Steve [Hill] walked by me at that point, waved his hand in my direction, and said simply, 'More, Lord.' I hit that marble floor like a ton of bricks.

"Now, I'm as critical as the next person when it comes to things like this. I have seen it all and just don't think I can be fooled. So when I hit that floor and it felt like I weighed 10,000 pounds, I knew something supernatural was happening. God was visiting us. In fact, I lay on that floor from 12:30 through 4 P.M. until some men finally were able to get me up. . . .

"Many families never did make it to celebrate Father's Day dinners with their earthly fathers that afternoon. We had a different kind of Father's Day celebration that lasted throughout the day and then picked up again that evening. It has been going every night since" (Kilpatrick, 76–77; emphasis in original).

Services began to be held seven nights a week (later no meetings were scheduled for Monday nights), often lasting well past midnight. A few months later, Tuesday and Saturday nights were set apart for prayer and rest. Still, Kilpatrick felt led to schedule revival services some six times a week "until the people stopped coming." Steve Hill, the evangelist who preached the Father's Day message that marked the beginning of the revival, postponed indefinitely his planned trip to Russia during that summer.

For the past several years, the Brownsville revival services have settled into the following pattern: meetings virtually every Wednesday, Thursday, Friday, and Saturday evening, typically lasting four or five hours, sometimes longer, with an hour or more of worship led by music director Lindell Cooley, often followed by testimonies; then preaching by Steve Hill, leading to the altar call; and finally prayer time, where the prayer team circulates throughout the sanctuary, praying one-on-one for anyone who desires "a fresh touch of God." Youth services meet concurrently on Thursdays in the youth chapel across the street, and baptisms are scheduled on Fridays in the main sanctuary. This schedule has not changed significantly in the first five years.

Sunday morning services (geared more for Brownsville church members, who have special passes to get into the sanctuary), prayer meetings on Tuesday evenings (as well as throughout the week, especially before and during the revival services), and midday teaching sessions on Thursdays, Fridays, and Saturdays also take place (there is no Sunday evening service). Several times a year, four-day seminars are also scheduled (e.g., for pastors and church leaders or for women). For five years now (mid 2000) this ambitious revival schedule has continued unabated except for a few scheduled "mini-breaks" throughout the year, plus a lengthier Christmas break in December.

John Kilpatrick has served as the senior pastor of the Brownsville AG since Feb. 1982. For several years before Father's Day 1995 he had felt that it was God's will for him to direct his congregation to spend Sunday evenings in prayer—no sermon, no altar call, only an hour or so of prayer, and then a communion service. Not long after the inauguration of those Sunday evening prayer meetings, he and his congregation felt a particular emphasis to pray for revival—so the divine outpouring in June 1995 was not entirely unexpected.

Evangelist Steve Hill preached nearly all of the revival services until Father's Day 2000, when he felt led to move his ministry to the Dallas, TX, area to pursue a national TV ministry and national and international crusades. Other leaders of the revival include Associate Pastor Carey Robertson and Dr. Michael Brown, president of the Revival School of Ministry. Despite their extensive travel and ministry opportunities, these leaders have made a concerted effort to attend nearly every revival service at Brownsville over the past several years. A common refrain heard at Brownsville is that "the first thing to go when revival comes is the schedule." Or as the noted revivalist Leonard Ravenhill (under whom both Steve Hill and Michael Brown studied) put it, "The opportunity of a lifetime must be seized during the lifetime of the opportunity" (this quote is featured prominently in Brownsville publicity literature).

A memorable image of the Brownsville revival is people of all ages and backgrounds waiting patiently in line on a bare parking lot sidewalk up to 14 hours or more simply to be able to gain entrance into an evening service in a North American church; even the secular news media have been quick to focus on this remarkable phenomenon.

Another memorable image (which is disturbing to a number of sincere believers) is the "manifestations," some of which can be quite unsettling for the uninitiated. People twitch and jerk uncontrollably, even while casually walking about or carrying on otherwise normal conversations. Not surprisingly, critics of the revival have focused particularly on this latter phenomenon (even though analogous manifestations are said to have accompanied the great revivals of Wesley and Whitefield, not to mention the historical origins of the terms *Quakers, Shakers, Holy Rollers,* etc.)

Criticisms of the revival include alleged financial improprieties, whether nonpayment of state taxes on merchandise sold at the church and in the various outreaches, or lavish salaries and perquisites for the leadership, or excessive pressure on the congregation to give large donations to the church and/or the independent ministries (e.g., Friday offerings are dedicated to Rev. Steve Hill's "Together in the Harvest" ministry). The local newspaper, *The Pensacola News Journal,* has printed a series of articles documenting such financial excesses, although a number of the claims, at best, bordered on the trivial in the opinion of many.

A serious controversy erupted in the spring of 1997, when noted revival critic Hank Hanegraaff, president of the Christian Research Institute, appeared on CNN's *Larry King Live* program and likened the Pensacola revival to the recent mass suicide of the Heaven's Gate cult members. The next Sunday, Pastor Kilpatrick strongly denounced Hanegraaff's comparison, and he went on to predict that unless Hanegraaff "backed off" criticizing the revival, his ministry would be brought down within 90 days by the Holy Spirit. But by June 18th Kilpatrick had himself backed off considerably from those harsh words, issuing a public apology and recanting his 90-day doomsday prediction. By the fall of that year, revival apologist Michael Brown and Hanegraaff, after a number of sharp disagreements both verbally and in print, were able to meet in person in October, and by the end of the year Hanegraaff finally made a personal visit to the Brownsville church and the Revival School. At last report, relationships were reasonably cordial among all parties.

It is still too early to determine with precision the historical impact of the Brownsville revival. Noted pentecostal historian ▸Vinson Synan has said that "this is probably the most important revival to come out of a local church since ▸Azusa Street" (*CT* [Feb. 9, 1998]). AG general superintendent ▸Thomas Trask is only marginally more reticent: "The impact [of Brownsville] has been powerful. Many, many of our pastors have gone [there] searching, looking, and believing, and they have witnessed the power of God. It has done something for their own hearts and lives" (*CT* [Feb. 9, 1998]). Fuller Seminary religious historian ▸Cecil Robeck Jr. is quoted as saying, "There is no question in my mind that the Brownsville revival is significant" both in terms of its length as well as the depth to which it has touched people's lives. He also went on to speak of Brownsville in terms of Azusa Street, which he characterized as being the last major revival producing significant cultural change in the church. Robeck further noted that research has shown that Azusa Street had a formative effect on the spiritual development of some 500 million people. Only time will tell whether future generations in the church will look back on the mighty move of God at Brownsville in the final years of the 20th century and see it as comparable to the Azusa Street revival at its first decade.

■ **Bibliography:** M. Brown, *From Holy Laughter to Holy Fire* (1996) ■ idem, *Let No One Deceive You: Confronting the Critics of Revival* (1997) ■ J. Grady, "Newspaper Blasts Pensacola Revival," *Charisma* (Jan. 1998) ■ J. Kilpatrick, *Feast of Fire* (1995) ■ S. Rabey, "Brownsville Revival Rolls Onward," *Christianity Today* (Feb. 9,

1998) ■ G. Volgenau, "God in Florida," *Detroit Free Press* (Oct. 11, 1997) ■ various articles in the *Pensacola News Journal* (Nov. 16–20, Dec. 21, 1997; Mar. 5, Apr. 5, June 21–24, 1998).

■ W. H. Barnes

BRUMBACK, CARL (1917–87). Pastor and historian of the pentecostal movement. Brumback was converted and received the baptism of the Holy Spirit at age 14 in Washington, DC. He attended Central Bible Institute, Springfield, MO, and served pastorates in Sperryville, VA; Tampa, FL; Bedford, OH; and Silver Spring, MD. A series of 12 radio sermons Brumback preached in Florida from 1942 to 1944 were expanded into his significant defense of pentecostalism, *"What Meaneth This?"* (1947).

Brumback's *God in Three Persons* (1959) was a major contribution to the Trinitarian debate with the ►Oneness movement. He wrote the first official history of the ►Assemblies of God, *Suddenly ... from Heaven* (1961). His writings brought him into full-time demand on the lecture and evangelistic circuit.

■ **Bibliography:** C. Brumback, *God in Three Persons* (1959) ■ idem, *Suddenly ... from Heaven* (1961) ■ idem, *"What Meaneth This?": A Pentecostal Answer to a Pentecostal Question* (1947).

■ D. J. Wilson

BRUNER, FREDERICK DALE (1932–). Missionary, NT scholar, and author. Currently professor of religion at Whitworth College in Spokane, WA, Bruner studied at Princeton Theological Seminary and completed a Th.D. in 1963 at the University of Hamburg, Germany. His dissertation was revised for publication as *A Theology of the Holy Spirit: The Pentecostal Experience and the New Testament Witness* (1970), an important resource in pentecostal studies. A Presbyterian, Bruner was influenced as a young man by Henrietta Mears of First Presbyterian Church of Hollywood, CA (Bruner, 1970, 8). As a theological student, he came to a deep appreciation of Martin Luther in a quest for answers to questions raised by pentecostalism. Although not a pentecostal himself, he has done extensive research on pentecostal doctrine and history. While he upholds the importance of new infillings of the Holy Spirit (for him, equivalent to new drafts of faith in Christ), he disagrees with the idea of a second crisis encounter with God as necessary for the fullness of the Spirit. He argues that the Scriptures teach that the baptism with the Holy Spirit and water baptism belong together to form the "one baptism" of the church.

■ **Bibliography:** F. D. Bruner, *The Christbook* (1987) ■ idem, *The Churchbook* (1988) ■ idem, *A Theology of the Holy Spirit* (1970) ■ F. D. Bruner and W. Hordern, *The Holy Spirit: Shy Member of the Trinity* (1984) ■ J. D. G. Dunn, *Baptism in the Holy Spirit* (1970) ■ H. M.

Ervin, *Conversion-Initiation and the Baptism in the Holy Spirit* (1984) ■ H. D. Hunter, *Spirit-Baptism: A Pentecostal Alternative* (1983) ■ R. Stronstad, *The Charismatic Theology of St. Luke* (1984).

■ R. M. Riss

BRYANT, JOHN (1948–). Bishop, evangelist. Born in Baltimore, MD, son of an African Methodist Episcopal (AME) bishop, John Bryant returned there in 1975 as pastor of Bethel AME Church, one of the oldest (c. 1785) black congregations in the country. While serving in Africa with the Peace Corps, Bryant (D.Min., Colgate-Rochester) became "aware of a realm of the spirit" that he "could not explain away." Returning to the States, he experienced the power of the Holy Spirit, and his ministry took on new directions. Membership at Bethel grew to more than 7,000, placing it among the largest charismatic congregations among mainline black denominations. Bryant locates Bethel's ministry squarely within the "full gospel" tradition of the black church, teaching the baptism of the Holy Spirit (with the fruit of the Spirit as evidence, though glossolalia and other gifts are present in the church). There is also an emphasis on a social outreach program that meets needs for food, shelter, employment, and education. Notable among these programs is Bethel Bible Institute, offering an accredited associate of arts degree. Bryant was elected a bishop of the AME Church in 1988.

■ **Bibliography:** J. Bryant, "Worship in the A.M.E. Context," in L. Campion, ed., *A Pastor's Manual for the A.M.E. Church* (1985) ■ L. Creque, "St. Paul's A.M.E. Church," *Black Church* 2 (4, 1974) ■ C. E. Lincoln and L. Mumiya, *The Black Church in the African American Experience* (1990) ■ "Shepherds in the Pulpit," *The Black Church Magazine* (May 1987) ■ "Silent the Giants Have Grown," *The Black Church Magazine* (May 1987) ■ G. Singleton, *The Romance of African Methodism* (1952).

■ H. D. Trulear

BUCHANAN, WILLIAM ALEXANDER (ALEX) (1893–1964). Australian pentecostal pioneer, pastor, and publisher. Buchanan, a farmer's son in Gippsland, Victoria, was baptized in the Spirit in 1912 through the ministry of Good News Hall, Australia's first pentecostal church. His five sisters and one brother also received the Spirit. He soon began meetings in his parents' farmhouse, and in 1915 he left home to engage in evangelism. One year later to the day, he married Leila Mary Lancaster (1895–1966), daughter of ►Sarah Jane Lancaster. He was fluent in the Scriptures and regularly preached without notes. For a time he took over the printing of *Good News* magazine in Melbourne and also printed tens of thousands of tracts, but he returned to itinerant work in Queensland in 1921. Shortly after he traveled with ►Smith Wigglesworth, for whom Leila acted as amanuensis, taking down his sermons in shorthand—later published as Wigglesworth's *Ever Increasing Faith*.

For a time Buchanan accompanied ▸F. B. Van Eyk in campaigns all over the country with the Apostolic Faith Mission. After a brief stay in Victoria, the Buchanans returned to Queensland in 1931, and most of their subsequent ministry took place there. Leila Buchanan was baptized in the Spirit at the age of 13. She gave herself to ministry to the outcasts of society, especially neglected children. Initially, "through fear of man," she hesitated to preach, but one night she had a vision that she took as a divine commission to preach the gospel in the light of the urgency of the hour and was later fully ordained as an Assemblies of God (AG) minister. She was recognized as an accomplished preacher. In 1931–32, both Alex and Leila preached in William Booth-Clibborn's Canvas Cathedral in Brisbane. Meanwhile, they also ministered in Cooroy (north of Brisbane) on the Sunshine Coast, where there was a steady flow of converts and "a whole crowd of hungry believers." They visited a dozen other places in the vicinity, Alex and Leila ministering independently. Buchanan reported 24 conversions and 23 baptized in water during November in Cooroy—a total of 105 commitments and 87 baptisms since he began the work. Later the Buchanans settled in Gympie (north of Brisbane) where, with the help of others, they were soon conducting 24 meetings a week. He pastored various churches in Queensland and ultimately joined the AG. In 1946 he opened a Christian book ministry that still bears his name today. Both Alex and Leila Buchanan had more than a little to do with shaping the Australian pentecostal movement. Alex held various executive positions in both the Apostolic Faith Mission and the AG, and Leila was the editor of *The Australian Evangel* for an extended period. "There is much that could be said concerning the good hand of God upon us," wrote Alex the year before he died, "but at best we are unprofitable servants—graciously His for Time and Eternity."

■ **Bibliography:** W. A. Buchanan, "Know Your Ministers," *Australian Evangel* (Dec. 1983) ■ B. Chant, *Heart of Fire* (1984).
■ B. Chant

BUCKINGHAM, JAMES WILLIAM II ("JAMIE") (1932–

92). Pastor, columnist, and author. Buckingham was born in Vero Beach, FL, and educated at Mercer University (A.B.) and Southwestern Baptist Theological Seminary (B.D. and M.R.E.). He was pastor of South Main Street Baptist Church in Greenwood, SC, for eight years and then pastored Harbor City Baptist Church, Melbourne, FL, for 15 months. Buckingham said, "After being fired from two churches because of my emptiness and pride and penchant to sexual immorality, I attended a Full Gospel Business Men's convention in Washington, DC, while researching my first book, *Run, Baby, Run.* While there I responded to an invitation and was filled with the Holy Spirit."

In 1967 Buckingham formed Tabernacle Church (now nondenominational) in Melbourne, FL. The church grew to a membership of 4,000 under his pastorate.

Buckingham wrote an award-winning column for *Charisma* and was the editor-in-chief of *Ministries Today.* He also wrote 48 books, including *Power for Living, Daughter of Destiny,* and *A Way through the Wilderness.* His video Bible series taped in the Holy Land continues to be distributed throughout prisons in the United States. At his death, his legacy was summed up by the words of Bible teacher Bob Mumford: "He was a prophet with a pen."

■ **Bibliography:** J. Buckingham, *Where Eagles Soar* (1980).
■ S. Strang

BUFFUM, HERBERT (1879–1939). A Holiness-pentecostal

evangelist and prolific songwriter with some 10,000 songs to his credit. Although a talented musician, he received no musical training. Most of his songs were sold for five dollars or less.

Born in Illinois, Buffum later moved to California with his family. There he felt a call to the ministry after his conversion at age 18. He held credentials with the Church of the Nazarene. He also began to write songs, many of which were inspired by personal experiences. Some of these were, "My Sheep Know My Voice," "I'm Going Through," "The Old Fashioned Meeting," "I'm Going Higher Some Day," "When I Take My Vacation in Heaven," and "In the City Where the Lamb Is the Light."

When Buffum died in 1939 the *Los Angeles Times* called him "The King of Gospel Song Writers."

■ **Bibliography:** W. Warner, "Herbert Buffum," *AGH* 6 (Fall 1986).
■ W. E. Warner

BUNDY, DAVID DALE (1948–). Scholar in American reli-

gious history, pentecostalism (primarily outside North America), Pietism, and the Wesleyan/Holiness traditions, and Middle Eastern Christian studies (Syriac, Armenian, and Arabic sources). Born in Longview, WA, Bundy graduated from Seattle Pacific University (B.A., 1969), Asbury Theological Seminary (M.Div., 1972, Th.M., 1973), and the Université Catholique de Louvain, Institut Orientaliste (Licence en Philologie et Histoire Orientale, 1978; Cand. Doctorate en Philologie et Histoire Orientale). At present he also is a candidate for the doctorate in church history, University of Uppsala. He has served on the faculties of Asbury Theological Seminary (1973–1990), the Université Catholique de Louvain (1978–1986), and Christian Theological Seminary in Indianapolis, IN (since 1991), where he is currently associate professor of church history and librarian.

A prolific writer, Bundy is coeditor of the scholarly monograph series *Pietist and Wesleyan Studies* (now 11 vols.). He

David Bundy, a leading scholar of world pentecostalism.

has contributed hundreds of articles to such journals as *EPTA Bulletin*, *Pneuma*, *AG Heritage*, *Church History*, *Methodist History*, *International Review of Mission*, *Wesleyan Theological Journal*, *Missiology*, *The Second Century: A Journal for Early Christian Studies*, *Catholic Biblical Quarterly*, *Le Muséon*, *Studia Patristica*, and *Religious Studies Review*. He also has written extensively for the *Dictionary of Pentecostal and Charismatic Movements*, the *Dictionary of Religion in America*, *The Encyclopedia of Early Christianity*, *The Anchor Bible Dictionary*, *Blackwell's Dictionary of Evangelical Biography*, and the present volume.   ■ S. M. Burgess

BUNTAIN, DANIEL MARK (1923–89). Missionary to India. Mark Buntain was born in Winnipeg, Man., the son of a Pentecostal minister, ▸Daniel Newton Buntain. He left his work as a successful radio broadcaster and, after marrying Huldah Monroe in 1944, began pastoring churches in Saskatchewan. Before going to India as a missionary, he ministered as an evangelist in Canada, the U.S., Taiwan, the Philippines, Sri Lanka, Hong Kong, and Japan.

Buntain went to India in 1953 with a reluctant wife and a four-month-old baby. They started the Calcutta Mission of Mercy as a response to the cry he heard as he preached: "Don't try to give us food for our souls until you give us food for our stomachs."

For many years the Buntains pastored the Assembly of God (AG) in Calcutta, which has more than 1,500 people in Sunday school each week and 4,000 parishioners representing six languages. He was the assistant superintendent of the AG in North India and aired a radio broadcast three times a week to a potential audience of 145 million listeners. The mission feeds 22,000 people each day. It is run by nearly 1,000 Indian nationals, and the operation contains a hospital, a school of nursing, six village clinics, a hostel for destitute youth, a drug prevention program, and 12 schools that provide instruction

Mark Buntain, missionary to India, who started the Calcutta Mission of Mercy, which feeds 22,000 people each day.

for 6,000 children. As a result of his ministry, more than 250,000 have been saved from hunger, more than 100,000 have had the chance to go to school, and tens of thousands have been treated at the hospital. Huldah Buntain vigorously continued Mark's ministry following his death in 1989.

■ **Bibliography:** D. M. Buntain, "God Broke My Heart for India," *Mountain Movers* (Apr. 1979) ■ R. Hembree, *Mark* (1979) ■ D. Wead, *The Compassionate Touch* (1977).   ■ S. Shemeth

BUNTAIN, DANIEL NEWTON (1888–1955). Canadian churchman and executive. Buntain began his ministry among the Methodists; he was ordained in Saskatchewan in 1918. The following year he moved to Winnipeg, Man., to pastor a Methodist church and to attend Wesley College.

Buntain had come into contact with pentecostalism in 1916, and in 1925 his interest deepened as a result of the ministry of ▸Charles Price. That same year the Methodist Conference, in response, gave him the option of being left without a charge or being assigned to a rural parish. Buntain chose the former. Shortly thereafter he was baptized in the Holy Spirit, and three days later he became the pastor of Wesley Church, the largest ▸Pentecostal Assemblies of Canada (PAOC) congregation.

Buntain quickly moved into leadership among the pentecostals, becoming the first superintendent of the Manitoba District of the PAOC in 1928, a position he held until 1936, when he rose to national leadership through being elected general superintendent. He served in that office until 1944. The remainder of his life was spent in Edmonton, Alb., where he was pastor of Central Pentecostal Tabernacle and president of Northwest Bible College, which he founded in 1947.

Buntain had a very significant impact on the PAOC. A man of intense spirituality, he was driven by a burden for missions, evangelism, revival, and prayer. At the same time, he was convinced that the church had to be organized in order to function efficiently. It was in this area that he made his most unique contribution. Under his leadership the PAOC endorsed the implementation of indigenous church principles on its mission fields, began to receive annual reports from its superintendent, and created national Sunday school and women's departments. Buntain also led the PAOC into the Canadian Association of Evangelicals, demonstrating the increasing self-confidence and self-awareness the denomination felt.

■ **Bibliography:** D. M. Buntain, *Why He Is a Pentecostal Preacher* (1944) ▪ D. N. Buntain, "He Leadeth Me!" *Pentecostal Testimony* 17 (13, 1937) ▪ G. G. Kulbeck, *What God Hath Wrought: A History of the Pentecostal Assemblies of Canada* (1958) ▪ R. A. N. Kydd, "The Contribution of Denominationally Trained Clergymen to the Emerging Pentecostal Movement in Canada," *Pneuma* 5 (1983).

■ R. A. N. Kydd

BURCIAGA, CESÁREO (c. 1898–1960s). Pioneer Mexican Assemblies of God (AG) evangelist, pastor, and national church leader in Mexico. While working as a laborer in Texas, he met and was converted by ▸Rodolfo Orozco in 1918. In 1921 he returned to Mexico, where he worked in the mines by day and in the church by night as pastor. In 1922 he and his small group of believers purchased land and built what many believe was the first AG church building in Mexico. Burciaga was ordained by the Latin American District Council of the AG in 1925 to serve as an evangelist and then as pastor in Múzquiz, Coahuila, Mexico. From 1925 to 1961 he pastored churches on both sides of the U.S.-Mexican border in Coahuila, Mexico, and in Texas. He provided leadership for the AG movement in Mexico after it nationalized and broke off its paternalistic relationship with the U.S. church in 1929.

■ **Bibliography:** L. J. de Walker, *Siembra y Cosecha: Reseña Histórica de Las Asambleas de Dios de México y Centroamérica*, vol. 1 (1990).

■ G. Espinosa

BURGESS, JOHN HARRY (1903–2001). Missionary, educator, and pastor. John H. Burgess was born in Muskegon,

MI, to Harry and Winnie (Bakker) Burgess. He attended Rochester (NY) Bible Training School (1924–25) and Bethel Bible Training School, Newark, NJ (1925–26). He later earned degrees in history (B.A., 1958; M.A., 1963) at the University of Michigan.

John H. Burgess, missionary to India and founder of the oldest still-functioning Assemblies of God ministerial training institution in the world, Bethel Bible School (now Bethel Bible College) in Punalur, India. (Photo c. 1921.)

While a student at Rochester, Burgess met Bernice Frances Andrews (1901–1990), a student at Beulah Heights Bible and Missionary Training School in North Bergen, NJ. They were married in India in 1927; one son was born to their union, Stanley Milton Burgess (1937–).

In 1925 Burgess became pastor of the Assemblies of God (AG) church in White Plains, NY. Ordained in 1926, he left for India in the same year. He ministered for the next 25 years in the state of Travancore (now Kerala) on the Malabar coast, in such towns as Chenganur, Quilon, Mavelikara, and Punalur. Aware that missionaries alone were unable to convert the Indian masses to Christ, Burgess founded the Bethel Bible School (later College) at Mavelikara in 1927. The school was relocated to Punalur in 1949. Outside the United States, Bethel Bible College is the oldest AG institution for ministerial training in the world.

Burgess served as superintendent of the South India District Council of the AG and chairman of the South Indian Missionary Fellowship for many years. One of his primary objectives was to develop native leadership in the Indian church. This dream was realized; the church in Kerala now functions without missionaries, governed exclusively by Indian leaders.

In 1950 the Burgesses returned to the United States because of Bernice Burgess's poor health. They pastored Trinity AG in Flint, MI, from 1951 to 1965, when John Burgess left to join the faculty of Central Bible College in Springfield, MO. He retired in 1972.

■ **Bibliography:** J. Burgess, *Opportunities in South India and Ceylon* (c. 1934) ▪ interview with J. Burgess, June 1987.

■ G. B. McGee

BURNETT, BILL (1917–94). Prominent Anglican charismatic leader. Born in South Africa, Burnett was captured at

Tobruk, Libya, in 1942. He escaped from a prisoner-of-war camp and was on the run in the Italian mountains for a year. Married in 1945, he was ordained an Anglican priest in 1947 and became bishop of Bloemfontein in 1957.

Burnett was general secretary of the South African Council of Churches (1967–70) when the council produced *The Message to the People of South Africa*, a theological refutation of apartheid. In 1970 he became bishop of Grahamstown, and in 1972 he was baptized in the Spirit. In 1974 Burnett was elected archbishop of Cape Town and metropolitan of the Anglican province of South Africa, the first native-born South African to hold these positions.

Burnett's ministry as bishop and archbishop was deeply changed through his baptism in the Spirit. The difference it made in his opposition to racial injustice in South Africa is described in "The Spirit and Social Action" (in *Bishops' Move*, ed. M. Harper, 1978). He was a strong influence for renewal in South Africa; several Anglican bishops there were baptized in the Spirit. He chaired the Spiritual Renewal Conference in Canterbury before the Lambeth Conference of 1978 and participated in the World Council of Churches Consultation on Charismatic Movements at Bossey, Switzerland, in 1980.

After his retirement in 1981, Burnett founded Support Ministries to undergird his ministry of teaching and reconciliation, particularly in South Africa. His teaching was characterized by an emphasis on the cross of Jesus triumphing over the forces of evil and leading to holiness of life and the transformation of society. Burnett was active in Sharing of Ministries Abroad (SOMA), the Anglican international renewal organization from its foundation in 1981, and became chairman of its international council. He wrote an autobiography, *The Rock That Is Higher Than I,* published posthumously in 1997.   ■ P. D. Hocken

BURNING BUSH MOVEMENT See Metropolitan Church Association.

BURTON, WILLIAM FREDERICK PADWICK (1886–1971).
British pioneer missionary and author. Born in Liverpool, son of a sea captain, he was trained as an engineer. Converted in 1905, he attended the ▸Pentecostal Missionary Union (PMU) Bible School at Preston and pastored Henry Mogridge's Elim Mission, Lytham, Lancashire (1911–14). He was to have sailed for Africa with James McNiell but came into conflict with the leaders of the PMU and sought an opening with other societies without success.

Burton left Britain in May 1914 to be joined in June 1915 by ▸James Salter. With one other missionary, they arrived in Mwanza, Congo, in September. They joined the Pentecostal Mission in South and Central Africa, Burton being their legal representative. In 1917 he visited Dan Crawford's work

in Luanza, and the lessons he learned there were put into practice at Mwanza. Because he was serving in an area where there were 250,000 people within a radius of 40 miles, he had to go to South Africa to recruit new workers. He returned with four, including Hettie Trollip, whom he married in May 1918. Other workers came from the U.S., but the burden fell on Burton. He possessed great gifts as an artist, builder, engineer, and teacher. The impetuous youth became a wise counselor to officials and missionaries. He wrote 28 books, including a standard work on the Lubu religion. Honors were given to him, but he was content to be known as "the tramp preacher." He was named "Kapamu," the "rusher-forth." He became field director of the Congo Evangelistic Mission (later called the Zaire Evangelistic Mission) on its foundation in 1919 and served until 1954. When he left the Congo in 1960 there were 65 European missionaries out of a staff of 80 in 13 stations. He died in South Africa in June 1971.

■ **Bibliography:** M. W. Moorhead, *Missionary Pioneering in the Congo Forests* (1922) ■ C. C. Whittaker, *Seven Pentecostal Pioneers* (1983) ■ H. Womersley, *Wm. F. P. Burton* (1973).

                                                                ■ D. W. Cartwright

BYRD, VERNON (1931–). Bishop (105th) of the African Methodist Episcopal Church. Born in Clinton, SC, he began preaching at age 13 and was ordained at age 17. Educated at Richard Allen and Boston Universities, he later served

William F. P. Burton, who founded, with James Salter, the Zaire Evangelistic Mission.

churches in South Carolina, Delaware, New Jersey, Pennsylvania, and Bermuda. He was elected to the episcopate in 1984 and assigned to West Africa. While in the pastorate he received the baptism of the Holy Spirit at a service sponsored by ʾKathryn Kuhlman. He returned to his church with a new "inner security" and "sense of fulfillment" in the ministry.

Drawing on the resources of black folk theology concerning the Holy Spirit, he began a crusade ministry that has taken him across the U.S. and abroad, emphasizing conversion, healing, and the laying on of hands for power. He has been one of the leading figures in the charismatic revival among black mainline denominations.

■ **Bibliography:** V. Byrd, *Book of Discipline of the A.M.E. Church* (1984) ▌ C. E. Lincoln and L. Mumiya, *The Black Church in the African American Experience* (1990). ■ H. D. Trulear

C

CALVARY CHAPEL A congregation in Costa Mesa, CA, that reached national prominence as a primary place of outreach during the "Jesus People" revival of the early 1970s. ▸Chuck Smith was called to lead what was originally a struggling congregation of 25 members, first as an associate pastor in 1965, then as its pastor. It began to grow as a result of Chuck's openness to a variety of young people in the counterculture of Southern California.

Through a series of Bible studies, disciplined prayer, and a genuine concern for hippies, drug addicts, and societal dropouts, the congregation soon became a vibrant center for worship and of caring for culture and counterculture alike. It included Christian rock concerts with Maranatha Singers, Love Song, and Children of the Day. More staid congregations labeled it as "unorthodox" and "faddish" and accused it of soft-pedaling the gospel. To be sure, it was unconventional, but it managed to grab the attention of thousands of young people who had written off other forms of gospel proclamation.

In 1971, following a series of moves, Calvary Chapel purchased a 10-acre campus, where it is presently located. The auditorium was fitted with 2,500 seats and equipped with moveable furnishings designed for flexible use. Closed-circuit televisions are used in the fellowship hall and another auditorium that act as overflow areas.

Early in its ministry to hippies and former addicts Calvary Chapel demonstrated the strength of community living for the new convert. By the mid 1970s, the church registered 900 conversions a month with 8,000 baptisms performed in a two-year period. It established a series of Christian communes, first in Costa Mesa, then in the San Bernardino/Riverside area, then at a number of other sites in the western U.S.

New converts were encouraged to share their experience with others. At the same time, they were put into relationship with more mature Christians and were led through a range of Bible studies. As these converts matured, they were encouraged to launch out in ministry. The result is that Calvary Chapel has grown to 35,000 members, making it the 18th largest congregation in the world. Since its facilities cannot handle its total membership adequately, multiple services are held, and twice each month Calvary Chapel meets for back-to-back services in the Anaheim Convention Center, enabling the majority of the members to enjoy fellowship with many who typically attend other services. Calvary Chapel has also spawned more than 300 other Calvary Chapels throughout the U.S., and it has become the home of Calvary Chapel Ministries, which include an extensive tape ministry, some publications, and a weekly radio broadcast, *Word for Today,* featuring Pastor Chuck Smith.

About 1983 a small group of Calvary Chapels that had come under the influence of ▸John Wimber, then pastor of the Calvary Chapel in Yorba Linda, left Calvary Chapel ministries and gathered with a half-dozen ▸Vineyards started by Ken Gullichson. Wimber's "Calvary Chapel" was renamed a "Vineyard," and Wimber was soon asked to head the new fellowship of congregations. Under the leadership of Wimber, the Vineyard Christian Fellowship has grown to more than 200 congregations. While Smith and Wimber have worked hard at maintaining a cordial relationship, their reasons for the separation involved the fact that both men were very strong leaders and that they took different positions with respect to their emphasis on the use of certain spiritual gifts. Chuck Smith's concerns have been expressed in his book *Charisma vs. Charismania* (1983), while Wimber's views have been popularized in *Power Evangelism* (1986) and *Power Healing* (1987).

In keeping with Smith's low-profile approach to the "charismatic," Calvary Chapel is supportive of a range of more standard evangelical organizations. Until it developed its own Bible-study program, it enrolled its new converts in the respected Navigators program. It supports Wycliffe Bible Translators, whose headquarters are nearby; Campus Crusade for Christ; Missionary Aviation Fellowship; and a variety of mission endeavors in Latin America.

■ **Bibliography:** R. Balmer and J. T. Todd Jr., "Calvary Chapel, Costa Mesa, California," in J. P. Wind and J. W. Lewis, eds., *American Congregations* (1994) ■ R. Enroth et al., *The Jesus People* (1972) ■ D. E. Miller, *Reinventing American Protestantism: Christianity in the New Millennium* (1997) ■ L. Parrott III and R. D. Perrin, "The New Denominations," *Christianity Today* 35 (3, Mar. 11, 1991) ■ C. Smith with T. Brooke, *Harvest* (1987) ■ C. Smith with H. Steven, *The Reproducers: New Life for Thousands* (1972) ■ J. Vaughan, *The World's Twenty Largest Churches* (1984). ■ C. M. Robeck Jr.

CALVER, CLIVE (1949–). Dynamic Christian leader from Britain. Brought up first in East Anglia and then in the East End of London, Calver was converted in the late 1960s and studied at London Bible College, where he earned a B.D. (1971). In 1971–76 he was engaged in evangelistic work, becoming national director of British Youth for Christ (1976–82). With Pete Meadows, Calver was the founder of Spring Harvest, since 1979 one of the world's largest teaching and worship weeks. In 1982–83 he was program director of Billy Graham's Mission England and leader of Milton

Keynes Free Church. Calver was director general of the Evangelical Alliance in Britain (1983–97); during this period membership grew by 500%. In 1997 he was appointed president of the World Relief Corporation, the assistance arm of the National Association of Evangelicals, and moved to the U.S.

Calver has demonstrated strong communications skills and is in regular demand for radio and TV interviews. His charismatic experience and his personal qualities were a major influence in the opening up of British evangelicalism to charismatic emphases. Clive and his wife, Ruth, have four children. Calver has authored several books, including *With a Church Like This Who Needs Satan?* (1981); *Holy Spirit* (1984); *Growing Together* (with his wife; 1986); *Thinking Clearly about Truth* (1995); *Together We Stand* (with Rob Warner; 1996); and *For Such a Time as This: The Rise and Fall of the Evangelical Alliance: 1835–1905* (1996).

■ P. D. Hocken

CAMPBELL, IVEY GLENSHAW (1874–1918). Early pentecostal evangelist. Campbell was born in Service (Beaver County), PA, and reared in East Liverpool, OH, by United Presbyterian parents who practiced strict religious discipline in their home. Ivey (nicknamed "Iva") had two sisters: Sarah Agnes Campbell (1867–1948) and Alice Mary Campbell Kennedy (1872–1955). Ivey Campbell was a seamstress by profession. Although she faithfully supported her Presbyterian church, she later claimed to have received an experience of sanctification (c. 1901) during services held by a visiting evangelist; this prompted her pastor to condemn Holiness theology. Subsequently, she joined a group of local men and women who opened the Broadway Mission (c. 1902) in East Liverpool. She became a prominent leader in this ministry and remained in it for four years.

In 1906 Campbell traveled to Los Angeles to visit relatives. While there she attended services at the ▸Azusa Street Mission and received the baptism in the Holy Spirit. Having written to ▸Claude A. McKinney, pastor of the Union Gospel Mission in Akron, OH, to share the news of revival with him, she returned to Ohio and, after visiting her home, began holding services at his church on Dec. 5, 1906. Early pentecostal leaders reported that she was the first person to bring the pentecostal message from Azusa Street to Ohio. Other revivals took her to Cleveland, OH, as well as to Pittsburgh and Springboro, PA. In June 1907 Campbell collaborated with McKinney and ▸Levi R. Lupton to lead the pentecostal camp meeting in Alliance, OH, that had a major impact on the spread of pentecostalism in the northeastern U.S.

Campbell's later activities are currently obscure. ▸A. A. Boddy, reporting on his visit to Los Angeles in 1912, indicated that he had met her but observed that she was in poor health. Her last years were spent in California, where she died.

■ **Bibliography:** A. A. Boddy, "Some Los Angeles Friends," *Confidence* (Nov. 1912) ■ P. Bowen, "Akron Visited with Pentecost," *AF* (Jan. 1907) ■ I. Campbell, "Report from Ohio and Pennsylvania," *AF* (Feb.–Mar. 1907) ■ "Converts Claim Strange Powers," *The Evening Review* (East Liverpool, OH) (Jan. 7, 1907).

■ G. B. McGee

CANTALAMESSA, RANIERO (1934–). Perhaps the best-known preacher-teacher in the ▸Catholic charismatic renewal. Ordained priest in the Franciscan Capuchin order in 1958, Fr. Raniero was professor of the history of ancient Christianity at the Catholic University of Milan until he felt called in 1979 to leave his teaching position to become a full-time preacher of the gospel.

He was a member of the International Theological Commission appointed by the Vatican (1975–81). In 1980 Pope John Paul II appointed Fr. Raniero preacher to the papal household, in which capacity he still serves, preaching weekly during Advent and Lent to the pope and the cardinals, bishops, and prelates of the Roman Curia and the general superiors of religious orders.

Fr. Cantalamessa is a frequent speaker at international and interchurch conferences and rallies. He spoke at Brighton (1991) and Orlando (1995) on unity and common evangelization. He frequently preaches at national retreats to priests in many countries, and preached at a retreat in Sweden to 70 Lutheran pastors. Among Cantalamessa's many books translated into English are *The Mystery of Christmas* (1988); *Obedience* (1989); *Life in the Lordship of Christ* (1990); *Jesus Christ, the Holy One of God* (1992); *Mary, Mirror of the Church* (1992); *The Mystery of Easter* (1993); *Ascent to Mount Sinai* (1996); and *The Power of the Cross* (1996). ■ P. D. Hocken

CANTEL, MARGARET (1878–1926). Early British pentecostal. Born in America, Margaret L. Fielden was the daughter of one of ▸J. A. Dowie's elders at Zion City, IL. In 1907 she married Harry Eugene Cantel, who was overseer of Dowie's work in Britain from 1900 on. After their marriage they returned to London, where they introduced the pentecostal message to their assembly in Islington. Renting a shop in Upper Street, Islington, they turned it into an assembly hall with pentecostal gospel meetings four days a week. In 1909 the Cantels published a magazine, *The Overcoming Life* (Feb. 1909–Aug. 1910). Harry Cantel was a very successful evangelist with a healing ministry, but he died of peritonitis in Aug. 1910. The Cantels had opened a guest house called Maranatha in Highbury. This was moved to 73 Highbury New Park and opened in Oct. 1912 as a missionary guest house. Mrs. Cantel managed this home, and many pentecostal missionaries stayed there. The guest list is a veritable "Who's Who." Donald Gee experienced Spirit baptism there. Margaret Cantel died in Mar. 1926.

■ **Bibliography:** G. Gardiner, "Out of Zion ... into All the World," *Bread of Life* 31 (July 2, 1982) ■ D. Gee, *These Men I Knew* (1980). ■ D. W. Cartwright

CANTÚ, BENJAMÍN (1913–). Key founder and presiding bishop of the ⸀Apostolic Assembly of Faith in Jesus Christ, Inc. Born in Mission, TX, in 1913, he was baptized by José Guerra and later ordained by Bishop Felipe Rivas in 1932. He ministered both in Mission, TX, and in Torreón, Mexico, for the ⸀Apostolic Church of Faith in Jesus Christ. In 1937, after an agreement that handed over the Apostolic Church's work in Texas to the Apostolic Assembly, Cantú began working for the Assembly.

After working in Mission, Weslaco, and El Paso, TX, from 1932 until 1948, Cantú transferred to California to work as general secretary of the Apostolic Assembly under Bernardo Hernández. At the 19th general convention of the Apostolic Assembly in Phoenix, AZ, he was elected bishop president of the Assembly, replacing Antonio C. Nava. He served in this capacity from 1950 until 1963. An exceptionally strong and charismatic leader, it would be difficult to overestimate the influence Cantú's leadership, authority, preaching, and teaching have had on the Apostolic Assembly throughout the second half of the 20th century.

■ **Bibliography:** B. Cantú, *Historia de la Asamblea Apostólica de la Fe en Cristo Jesús, 1916–1966* (1966). ■ G. Espinosa

CAPPS, CHARLES EMMITT (1934–). Leader in the Word of Faith movement (⸀Positive Confession movement). Born in Brummett, AR, to a family of farmers who joined the ⸀Assemblies of God in his youth. His marriage to Peggy Walls in 1951 produced two children: Annette (b. 1954) and Beverly (b. 1957). Converted at age 13, Capps became a lay minister in 1962. After hearing, in 1969, the faith message as taught by ⸀Kenneth Hagin, he began in 1973 an itinerant ministry emphasizing the power of the spoken word for victorious Christian living.

Capps teaches that God's words "are the most powerful things in the universe," which, when spoken in faith, become "the creative power that releases God's ability within you." These teachings were promoted in his first and most important book, *The Tongue, a Creative Force*, published in 1976, and in his popular booklet *God's Creative Power*. These books had sold more than 1.5 million copies by 1988.

In 1977 Capps began a national radio broadcast titled *Concepts of Faith*. By 1979 he had forsaken farming to carry the faith message nationwide. In 1980 Capps was ordained by Kenneth Copeland and became a minister in the International Convention of Faith Churches.

■ **Bibliography:** C. Capps, *The Tongue, a Creative Force* (1976). ■ H. V. Synan

CARLSON, GLEN (1937–). Leader of Lutheran renewal in Canada (⸀Lutheran Charismatics). In 1965 Glen Carlson was called from seminary in Saskatoon, Sask., to serve a three-point parish in Stony Plain, Alb. The Immanuel congregation of Rosenthal was very small, and the church was scheduled by the bishop to be closed. Carlson knew that this was not the congregation's desire. Not only did the church not close, but shortly thereafter it flourished with a strong charismatic renewal, beginning in 1977 when Carlson received a renewal experience. He especially emphasized the fruit of the Spirit, to be followed by spiritual giftings.

The Immanuel congregation grew dramatically, with charismatic worship and music, together with a strong emphasis on prayer ministry and healing, a love for the Bible, and a change in administrative structure. As dean of the North Conference and chairperson of the Synod of Alberta and the Territories, Carlson influenced many pastors and their congregations in the direction of renewal. He began the Holy Spirit Seminar at the Immanuel congregation in 1983, followed by the Alberta Lutheran Renewal Retreat for pastors and their spouses. He has been the dean of Family Renewal camp for many years. The Immanuel congregation has now become the headquarters for Lutheran Renewal Canada, with Pastor Carlson as director. He is also a member of the board of the International Renewal Center.

■ P. Anderson

CARLSON, GUY RAYMOND (1918–99). Author, college president, and denominational executive. Carlson was born in Crosby, ND, to Ragna and George Carlson. Both he and his father were converted in a small storefront mission in 1925 under the preaching of evangelist Blanche Britton. He was baptized in the Holy Spirit as a youth and called into ministry as a 15-year-old at a Bible camp. That same year he began preaching in churches, outstations, and jails. In the fall of 1934 he attended Western Bible College in Winnipeg, Man., where he studied for one year. He moved back to Crosby and married Mae Steffler in 1938; they had three children: Gary, Sharon (Bontrager), and Paul (d. 1994).

Carlson's pastoral ministry began in Thief River Falls, MN; ordination with the Assemblies of God (AG) followed in 1941. In 1944 he was elected as a district presbyter of the North Central (later Minnesota) District of the AG and also served as its Sunday school superintendent. Four years later he became the district superintendent—the youngest man to serve any district in this capacity. During his appointment, the Latter Rain movement advanced into the Upper Midwest, threatening stability within the district. That threat, however, was minimized under his levelheaded leadership. Such diplomacy would serve him well in his later years.

Along with Carlson's many responsibilities as district superintendent, he taught classes at North Central University when it was a fledgling Bible institute sharing office space with the Minnesota District Council. When North Central President and founder Frank J. Lindquist retired, he recommended Carlson for the office. In 1961 Carlson accepted and relinquished his superintendency. When he left that position in 1969, the college conferred an honorary D.D. degree on him for services rendered to the institution, the district, and the AG.

From 1969 to his retirement in 1993, Carlson served as an elected official of the AG in its national headquarters. In 1969 he was elected as one of five assistant general superintendents. The AG reorganized its leadership structure in 1971, and he became the sole assistant superintendent. He later succeeded ➤Thomas F. Zimmerman as the general superintendent in 1986, a position he held until his retirement.

During Carlson's years in national leadership, he was involved in various projects and served on the boards of directors of the Ministers Benefit Association, Central Bible College, Evangel University, the Assemblies of God Theological Seminary (AGTS), and the executive committee of the ➤National Association of Evangelicals. He served as chairman of the ➤Pentecostal Fellowship of North America, as a member of the advisory committee of the ➤Pentecostal World Conference, on the executive committee of the World Assemblies of God Fellowship, and on the executive committee for the Religious Alliance Against Pornography. He preached across the U.S., Canada, and in many foreign countries, particularly those in Eastern Europe after the fall of communism.

Carlson not only served the AG's national headquarters, but also his community. In Springfield he served on the boards of Cox Medical Center and the United Way. He likewise involved himself in the activities of the American Red Cross and the Salvation Army.

Carlson wrote extensively for church publications, including 15 books and numerous articles. His books include *Preparing to Teach God's Word* (1975); *Spiritual Dynamics* (1976); *Our Faith and Fellowship* (1977); *The Acts Story* (1978); *Prayer and the Christian's Devotional Life* (1980); *Christ's Gifts to His Church* (1990); and *The Assemblies of God in Mission* (with D. V. Hurst and Cyril E. Homer; 1970).

Under Carlson's leadership the AG instituted the "Decade of Harvest," an ambitious evangelistic program. The Michael Cardone Media Center was created, as was the Assemblies of God Financial Services Group. A long-time proponent of education in the denomination, Carlson oversaw the appointment of AGTS's first full-time president, the restructuring of the Division of Christian Education, and the formation of the Division of Christian Higher Education.

During Carlson's tenure as general superintendent, he saw the denomination through its most turbulent period as it faced the fallout from the ➤Jim Bakker and ➤Jimmy Swaggart

scandals. His diplomacy, sincerity, personal integrity, and call for spiritual renewal and holiness brought comfort and assurance to the AG constituency during that stormy period.

■ **Bibliography:** "G. Raymond Carlson with Christ," *Enrichment* (Summer 1999) ■ F. M. Hall, "G. Raymond Carlson: The Early Years in the Upper Midwest," *AGH* (Summer 1993) ■ idem, "G. Raymond Carlson: The Executive Years in Springfield, 1969–93," *AGH* (Fall 1993). ■ G. B. McGee; E. J. Gitre

CARTER, ALFRED HOWARD (1891–1971). British pentecostal leader and educator. After several visits to Sunderland, England, where ➤A. A. Boddy ministered, Carter became a pentecostal (1915). He pastored briefly at Saltley, Birmingham, but was imprisoned as a conscientious objector during WWI. From 1921 to 1948 he was principal of Hampstead Bible School (London). He also developed a program of correspondence study. A founding member of the Assemblies of God in Great Britain and Ireland, he served as vice chairman (1929–34) and chairman (1934–45). Carter traveled widely as a preacher and conference speaker.

■ **Bibliography:** A. H. Carter, *Cyril J. Duxbury as I Knew Him* (n.d.) ■ idem, *The Gifts of the Holy Spirit* (1946) ■ idem, *Questions and Answers on the Gifts of the Spirit* (1946) ■ idem, *Spiritual Gifts and Their Operation: Anecdotal Lectures* (1968) ■ idem, *When the Time Flew By* (1957) ■ J. Carter, *Howard Carter, Man of the Spirit* (1971) ■ D. Gee, *Wind and Flame* (1967) ■ W. K. Kay, *Inside Story: A History of the British Assemblies of God* (1990) ■ idem, "The British Assemblies of God in the 1930s," *EPTA Bulletin* 7 (1988) ■ R. D. Massey, "'Sound and Scriptural Union': An Examination of the Origins of the Assemblies of God in Great Britain and Ireland during the Years 1920–1925" (Ph.D. diss., U. of Birmingham, 1988) ■ A. Missen, *The Sound of a Going: The Story of the Assemblies of God* (1973) ■ L. F. Sumrall, *Adventuring with Christ* (1939) ■ C. Whittaker, *Seven Pentecostal Pioneers* (1983). ■ D. D. Bundy

CARTER, JOHN H. (1893–1981). British Assemblies of God leader. Carter was born in Birmingham and saved in the Churches of Christ. He was introduced to the pentecostal movement and attended the Sunderland Convention in 1913. After engaging in pastoral ministry in Birmingham, he joined the Elim Evangelistic Band in Belfast in 1919. He left in 1921, joining his brother Howard to pastor the Lee Assembly, London. As tutor at Hampstead (1923–28), he engaged in evangelistic ministry (1928–34). A founding member of the Assemblies of God in Great Britain and Ireland (AGGBI) in 1924, he served as general secretary (1936–63), editor of *Redemption Tidings* (1934–49), tutor at Kenley Bible College (1955–63), and principal at Kenley (1966–70). Carter also served as a member of the advisory committee of the ➤Pentecostal World Conference (1955–61) and chairman of AGGBI conferences in 1952 and 1964. Carter was gracious, efficient, and hardworking. He died at Mattersey, Doncaster, in Apr. 1981.

■ **Bibliography:** J. H. Carter, *A Full Life* (1979) ▌ A. Missen, *The Sound of a Going: The Story of the Assemblies of God* (1973).

　　　　　　　　　　　　　　　　　■ D. W. Cartwright

CASHWELL, GASTON BARNABAS (1862–1916). The

apostle of Pentecost in the South. Gaston Barnabas Cashwell was born in Sampson County, NC, near the city of Dunn. As a young man he became a minister in the North Carolina Conference of the Methodist Episcopal Church, South. In 1903, under the influence of ˒A. B. Crumpler (1862–1952), he left the Methodist Church to join the newly formed Pentecostal Holiness Church (PHC), then known as the Holiness Church of North Carolina (HCNC).

Cashwell made a name in the ˒Holiness movement as an evangelist, ministering to both blacks and whites in tent meetings and local Holiness churches. Although his relationship with Crumpler and the leadership of the church was often stormy, Cashwell became a leading minister in the church.

Upon hearing of the ˒Azusa Street meeting in California, Cashwell was overcome with a desire to receive the baptism in the Holy Spirit with the evidence of speaking in tongues as taught by ˒William J. Seymour, the pastor of the Azusa Street Mission. His knowledge of the California Pentecost came

G. B. Cashwell, a Holiness evangelist who received the baptism of the Spirit at Azusa Street in 1906 and held meetings in Dunn, NC, that were an East Coast counterpart to the Azusa Street meetings.

from reports by ˒Frank Bartleman in the *Way of Faith* magazine published by ˒J. M. Pike in Columbia, SC.

In Nov. 1906 Cashwell borrowed money to travel by rail to Los Angeles. His letter to the annual conference in Lumberton, NC, explained his absence and asked forgiveness for wrongs done to anyone he had offended. In his first service at Azusa Street he was taken back by some practices that to him seemed "fanatical," but overall he felt that "God was in it." On first seeking for the baptism in the Holy Spirit, he was antagonized by his aversion to being prayed for by blacks. He went to his hotel room, where he "suffered a crucifixion" and "died to many things," including his racial prejudice. He went the next night requesting that Seymour and other blacks lay hands on him. He promptly received the pentecostal experience and, according to his own account, spoke in "English, German, and French."

After an offering in which the Azusa Street congregation bought him a new suit and a train ticket back home, Cashwell returned to Dunn, NC, where he brought the pentecostal message to the local Holiness church on Dec. 31, 1906. Invitations were sent to the ministers of the Holiness churches of the region to attend pentecostal services in January in Dunn. Due to the intense interest in the meeting, Cashwell rented a three-story tobacco warehouse by the railroad tracks to hold the crowds.

The Dunn meetings lasted through Jan. 1907 and became an East Coast counterpart to the Azusa Street meetings. Most of the ministers of the Holiness churches in the area came to Dunn and received the tongues experience, including ˒G. F. Taylor, H. H. Goff, and ˒F. M. Britton. Through the Dunn meetings, the PHC, the ˒Fire-Baptized Holiness Church (FBHC), and the Pentecostal Free-Will Baptist Church entered the pentecostal movement.

In Feb. 1907 Cashwell visited ˒J. H. King (1869–1946), general overseer of the FBHC in Toccoa, GA, where King received the pentecostal experience. Also through a whirlwind series of tent meetings in South Carolina, N. J. Holmes and the Holmes Bible and Missionary Institute in Greenville, SC, was swept into the pentecostal movement. In the summer of 1907 Cashwell visited Birmingham, AL, where O. N. Todd Sr. and future founders of the Assemblies of God, ˒M. M. Pinson and H. G. Rodgers, were baptized in the Holy Spirit.

In Jan. 1908 Cashwell was invited by ˒A. J. Tomlinson to speak in Cleveland, TN, to leaders of the Church of God (CG). While Cashwell was preaching, Tomlinson fell to the floor speaking in tongues. Thereafter, the CG with its subsequent branches became part of the pentecostal movement.

In order to promote pentecostalism in the South, Cashwell began publication in 1907 of the *Bridegroom's Messenger,* a paper that carried news of the spreading pentecostal revival. In the space of six months he had established himself as the apostle of Pentecost in the South.

The major obstacle to the sweep of Cashwell's ministry was the leader of his own church, A. B. Crumpler, who began a campaign to stop the spread of pentecostalism in his HCNC. While Cashwell and G. F. Taylor led the pentecostal faction, Crumpler attacked the initial evidence theory in the church periodical the *Holiness Advocate.* At the Annual

Conference of 1908 the issue was settled in favor of the pentecostals, after which Crumpler left the church permanently. Cashwell and the victorious pentecostal party then redrafted the articles of faith to include the initial-evidence theory.

By 1909 Cashwell himself left the PHC, evidently over disappointment at not being elected to head the church after successfully leading the pentecostal revolution. Until his death in 1916 he conducted revivals in independent churches in the South, but his reputation as a pentecostal pioneer was firmly established by his barnstorming ministry in 1907, which forever altered the religious landscape of the South.

■ **Bibliography:** V. Synan, *The Old-Time Power: A History of the Pentecostal Holiness Church* (rev. ed., 1998).   ■ H. V. Synan

CATHCART, WILLIAM (1893–1989). Founder of the Apostolic Church in Australia. Cathcart was tall, commanding in presence, and an accomplished Bible teacher. Born of Scottish parents in Northern Ireland, he was converted at the age of 16. He fought in France in WWI, from where he was repatriated to a convalescent home. While attending a Brethren assembly, he came in touch with an Apostolic church and was healed. At the 1929 Apostolic Church convention in Penygroes, Wales, the church council unanimously decided to send him to Western Australia.

On Feb. 1, 1930, together with his wife and small son, Cathcart sailed for Perth. To survive in Depression times, he and two others made their own mixture of tea and sold it door to door. They conducted street meetings and gave food to the poor. Cathcart taught the "Apostolic vision." Before long, two small groups of believers combined under his leadership. The Apostolic Church appealed to some because it was centralized and tightly organized. Also, Cathcart's reserved and nondemonstrative approach won the confidence of those who were uneasy with the more flamboyant stance of some pentecostals. There was emphasis on the roles of apostles and prophets—apostles exercised a governmental role, while prophets provided guidance and direction.

With a love gift of £10 from the Perth church in his pocket, Cathcart moved to Adelaide in Jan. 1932. Only eight people attended the first meeting, but numbers grew quickly. A series of six crowded Sunday night services in the Adelaide town hall resulted in a new church being born. People from the two existing pentecostal congregations joined the Apostolic church—as many as 70 from one of them.

In the meantime, the British Missionary Council appointed Joshua McCabe (b. 1903) of Edinburgh, to go to Perth, where he arrived on Jan. 8, 1932, to take Cathcart's place. Soon 200 people were attending regularly. Before long, new assemblies were opened in Perth: Victoria Park, Claremont, and Fremantle. In Adelaide, Zion Temple was opened on Oct. 30, 1932.

Cathcart's teaching in Adelaide continued to attract people hungry for the Word of God. People who were materially poor were "rich in spiritual goods," wrote Cathcart. Local assemblies were established in suburban and rural areas. Bearing in mind a prophecy that Melbourne, Victoria, would be the headquarters of the Apostolic Church, Cathcart left Adelaide for that city, while McCabe moved to Adelaide and A. S. Dickson, an apostle from England, took over the work in Perth.

Cathcart's strategy bore the marks of a military campaign. An advance was made and ground taken; reinforcements brought in and the ground secured; then another advance, and so on. To the Apostolic Church it was the result of a plan "prophetically revealed" to McCabe and Cathcart.

Cathcart arrived in Melbourne knowing only one person. "I spent long hours in prayer," he recalled later. Around 100 began to attend on weeknights and up to 300 on Sundays. Finally, on Easter Sunday 1933, the first Communion service was held in Melbourne with 160 in attendance. Cathcart generally focused on two themes—church government and the second coming of Christ. He prepared a huge chart, nearly 12 m. (40 ft.) long and 2.5 m. (more than 8 ft.) high, that outlined in graphic form the destiny of humankind from creation to culmination.

In May 1933, together with John Hewitt of Wales, Cathcart began an evangelistic campaign. More than 1,000 people attended the first meeting. On the opening night, 25 people responded to Hewitt's invitation to confess Christ, and about 100 sought laying on of hands for healing. Within six weeks there were no empty seats. Dozens of handkerchiefs were prayed over and sent to the absent suffering. As the campaign continued, there were many testimonies of healing. One outstanding case was that of Ensign H. Jenkins of the Salvation Army, who for nine years had used a walking stick, crutches, or a wheelchair but was instantaneously healed. A week later she gave a public testimony and walked around the platform to enthusiastic applause from the people.

Cathcart now visited Wellington, N.Z., where he had "phenomenal success" and where he was later assisted by both Isaac and John Hewitt. By the end of 1934 there were churches in every state of Australia and in New Zealand. All in all, some 40 congregations were established in Australia. In 1935 Cathcart moved to South Africa, returning to Australia in the 1940s. At the end of WWII Cathcart left the Apostolic Church to join ▸Leo Harris in his newly formed National Revival Crusade. He finally moved to the U.S., where he spent the remaining years of his life.

■ **Bibliography:** W. Cathcart, *To Glory from Gloom* (1976) ■ B. Chant, *Heart of Fire* (1984) ▐ T. N. Turnbull, *What God Hath Wrought* (1959).   ■ B. Chant

CATHOLIC APOSTOLIC CHURCH The Catholic Apostolic Church (CAC) began as a dissenting church movement in England in the 1830s and developed into an international denomination based on apostolic church government. The CAC was armed with a mission to call Christendom into a restoration of the fourfold gift ministries of Ephesians 4:11—apostle, prophet, evangelist, and pastor-teacher—organized under apostolic authority. They were also known for recognizing the expression of the NT charismata of 1 Cor. 12:8–10 in the modern era, although the use of spiritual gifts in their churches was restricted within a carefully structured liturgical worship format. Today only a few members of the CAC survive. Since their last apostle died in 1901, the 20th century has witnessed the near extinction of this once vibrant organization.

The CAC is often called the Irvingite church, but the church never has accepted this title. They seek to minimize the role of Edward Irving in their founding, even though the roots of the CAC can be found in London's Newman Street Church, an independent church organized in 1832 under the leadership of pastor Edward Irving (1792–1834). This minister of the Church of Scotland had been barred from his 2,000-member church in Regent Square, London, for allowing the expression of spiritual gifts in the regular services of his church. Hundreds left Regent Square with Irving. The Newman Street Church became a haven for laity and clergy who (1) acknowledged that Spirit baptism was an experience of empowerment distinct from conversion; (2) supported the expression of spiritual gifts in worship; and (3) accepted the restoration of apostolic authority in the modern church. Initially, six churches affiliated with the Newman Street Church forming the London Council. Although Irving did not aspire to apostleship, he assumed the presidency of the London Council. A commanding and inspirational leader, Irving found it difficult to step aside and allow the apostles, the first of whom were appointed in 1832, to assume their designated authority. Irving's untimely death in 1834 allowed the apostles to function freely.

In Nov. 1832 the first apostle to take office at Newman Street was lawyer John Cardale (1802–79). In Jan. 1833 Henry Drummond (1786–1860) was appointed as the church's second apostle. Drummond, a wealthy banker and politician, had made his presence known as early as 1826. He hosted a prophecy conference at Albury Park, his country estate some 30 miles south of London, which drew leaders such as Edward Irving and James Haldane Stewart. The conference became an annual event through 1830. In addition, Drummond offered spiritual direction to a group of believers at his Albury mansion. When in London, he attended Irving's church. Cardale and Drummond became the primary figures in organizing and shaping the CAC. By 1835, 12 apostles had been called out to lead a new ecclesiastical movement. The name Catholic Apostolic Church stuck as the "apostolic college," and a core of seven prophets retired to Apostle Drummond's Albury estate for a year of prayerful seclusion to forge the details of a new church. One of their conclusions was to apportion Christendom into 12 territories, with each apostle assuming responsibility for one portion. The apostles agreed to live in their territory for three and a half years, learning about its culture and religious traditions and bearing witness of their vision of a unified Christendom under apostolic authority.

As the apostles returned to England from their journeys and shared their findings with one another, a new church structure emerged with a common standard of worship and government. An elaborate liturgy combining aspects of Latin, Eastern, and Protestant forms of worship became the norm for the CAC. Other aspects of their "high church" approach included a formal prayer book, vestments for all clergy, and the use of candles and incense in worship.

The peaceful serenity of Albury proved to be an ideal permanent home for the apostolic college, especially as Drummond in 1840 built a beautiful Apostle's Chapel on his estate, serving as headquarters for a developing international movement. In the 1840s and '50s, under the leadership of Apostle Thomas Carlyle (1803–55), the German people were the most receptive of the 12 CAC regions to the church's vision. The growth continued even after Carlyle's death in 1855. Local German leadership felt the need for apostles to be functioning on their home front. But the CAC's eschatology predicted Christ's second advent during the lifetime of their apostles, so no provision was made for additional apostles, not even to replace those who died. The CAC saw no biblical warrant for altering their original policy and allowing apostles to be appointed in the German church. This led to the official severing of the relationship between the CAC and the New Order, as the German organization was initially called (it later became the ▸New Apostolic Church [NAC]).

By 1879 Francis Woodhouse was the lone surviving apostle of the CAC. When he died in 1901 no provision remained for the organization to ordain future priests for their congregations. Gradually, a shortage of priests led to the disbanding of churches. Little by little, the 20th century has witnessed the dying out of what was once a unique experiment in restored apostleship. Remaining members have embraced an official "time of silence," a state of inactivity and mourning until the return of Christ.

■ **Bibliography:** C. W. Boase, *Supplementary Narrative to the Elijah Ministry* (1870) ■ J. B. Cardale, *The Character of Our Present Testimony and Work* (1865) ■ Thomas Carlyle (apostle), *A Short History of the Apostolic Work* (1851) ■ R. Davenport, *Albury Apostles* (1970) ■ J. Dix, *The New Apostles, or Irvingism* (1861) ■ D. W. Dorries,

"Edward Irving and the 'Standing Sign' of Spirit Baptism," in G. B. McGee, ed., *Initial Evidence* (1991) ▪ T. Dowglass, *A Chronicle of Certain Events* (1852) ▪ H. Drummond, *A Brief Account of the Commencement of the Lord's Work to Restore His Church* (1851) ▪ idem, *Narrative of the Circumstances Which Led to the Setting Up of the Church of Christ at Albury* (1834) ▪ C. G. Flegg, *Gathered under Apostles* (1992) ▪ S. Newman-Norton, ed., *The Hamburg Schism* (1974) ▪ idem, ed., *The Time of Silence* (n.d.) ▪ R. Norton, *Neglected and Controverted Scripture Truths* (1839) ▪ idem, *The Restoration of Apostles and Prophets in the Catholic Apostolic Church* (1861) ▪ M. O. W. Oliphant, *The Life of Edward Irving* (1862) ▪ P. E. Shaw, *The Catholic Apostolic Church, Sometimes Called Irvingite* (1912) ▪ G. L. Standring, *Albury and the Catholic Apostolic Church* (1985) ▪ Apostle Weinmann, *History of the Kingdom of God* (1971) ▪ F. W. Woodhouse, *A Narrative of Events Affecting the Position and Prospects of the Whole Christian Church* (1847). See also article on Edward Irving, bibliography. ▪ D. W. Dorries

CATHOLIC CHARISMATIC RENEWAL

1. Origins
2. Expansion
3. Organization
4. Relations with the Catholic Church Hierarchy
5. Distinctives of Catholic Charismatic Theology and Practice
6. A Mixed Reception
7. Statistics

1. Origins.

Pope John XIII prayed that the Second Vatican Council might be a "New Pentecost," and Catholic charismatics have typically viewed themselves as an answer to that prayer. The council did in fact prepare the ground for the pentecostal movement that was to spring up in the Catholic Church soon after.

Several themes that emerged at Vatican II were of special significance in this regard. The opening message emphasized self-renewal under the guidance of the Holy Spirit, and references to the renewing power of the Spirit are scattered throughout the council's pronouncements. The documents of the council placed considerable stress on the role of the laity in the life of the church, and they also recognized the importance of charismatic gifts—a stress that was championed in council sessions by the Belgian Cardinal ▸Léon-Joseph Suenens, who was later to provide critical support for the charismatic movement. Finally, the council's opening up to ecumenical activity and recognition that the Spirit could bestow graces among the "separated brethren" allowed for the possibility that Protestant pente-

costals might be able to contribute to the renewal of the Catholic Church.

Despite these new emphases, even Suenens could hardly have anticipated the series of events in the early months of 1967 that gave birth to a movement of now global proportions within the church. Ralph Keifer, Patrick Bourgeois, and a few other lay faculty at Duquesne University had been praying intently for a return to the kind of vibrant Christian community they believed had characterized the first Christians. During this time they read two books that introduced them to pentecostal faith and practice: David Wilkerson's *The Cross and the Switchblade* (1963) and John Sherrill's *They Speak with Other Tongues* (1964).

Fired by a desire to experience the "baptism of the Holy Spirit" they had read about, these men sought out a prayer group in the area that was attended by mainline Protestant charismatics. During their second meeting, they received the typical pentecostal experience, including speaking in tongues. In the days following they told two close friends about their experience and laid hands on them to receive the "baptism" as well. Soon after, the four faculty members met with about 30 students on a religious retreat at Duquesne. The students had also read Wilkerson's book and had come together to meditate on the first few chapters of Acts and to seek God's will for their lives. In the course of the Duquesne Weekend, as it came to be known, each of the young people on the retreat experienced a baptism of the Holy Spirit at various times and in various ways. In this way the first prayer group came into existence, the "official" beginning of the Catholic Charismatic Renewal (CCR).

A charismatic network soon developed through connections between Catholic university campuses. In early March of that year (1967) a visitor from Duquesne to Notre Dame brought news of the nascent movement; two recent graduates of Notre Dame, ▸Ralph Martin and ▸Stephen Clark,

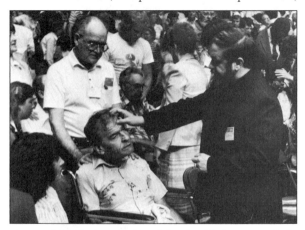

The practice of laying on of hands for the sick during a Catholic charismatic conference.

went to Dusquesne to check things out. Martin and Clark were baptized in the Spirit during their visit and then began a prayer group at Michigan State University. Before long the movement had spread to Iowa State University and other Midwestern campuses, from where it spread throughout the rest of the U.S.

The press first took note of the new charismatics in Apr. 1967, when about 100 students and a number of faculty members from several universities gathered on the Notre Dame campus for a weekend of prayer and reflection on their recent experiences. Along with several student publications, two widely read periodicals—the *National Catholic Reporter* (Apr. 19, 1967) and *Our Sunday Visitor* (May 14, 1967)—reported on the meeting and brought the Catholic pentecostal phenomenon to the attention of a national audience. The news was also spread by students as they scattered across the country for summer vacation.

At the end of the summer, a second Notre Dame gathering brought together those who were discovering Spirit baptism. In September Martin and Clark joined the staff of the Catholic campus ministry at the University of Michigan at Ann Arbor, where they initiated a prayer meeting. Since then, charismatic Catholic communities in South Bend and Ann Arbor have continued to play prominent roles in the leadership, expansion, and consolidation of the CCR (see ▸Charismatic Communities).

2. Expansion.

The movement, at least in its early years, spread largely through social networks of families and friends, creating small local prayer groups. Yet frequent large conferences have helped to provide the CCR with visibility, unity, and a sense of identity. Attendance at annual gatherings at Notre Dame in the late 1960s and '70s reflected rapid growth. The second conference, in Mar. 1968, had about 150 participants, most from the Midwest. The third, in Apr. 1969, brought together more than 450 from most of the states and several Canadian provinces. The June 1970 meeting attracted more than 1,300; the 1971 gathering, rightly labeled "international," included representatives from 11 countries among its nearly 5,000 participants. In 1972 more than 11,000 came together from 16 countries; in 1973 more than 20,000 had to assemble in the football stadium to accommodate the large crowds. By this time the CCR not only had become firmly rooted in the U.S. but had also extended—often through conferences—into Latin America, Europe, and Asia. By the end of 1975 the recently established charismatic Catholic magazine *New Covenant* boasted a list of 60,000 subscribers in more than 100 countries.

After 1976, when the Notre Dame meeting reached 30,000, conference leaders decided to promote regional conferences instead and to limit registration at Notre Dame to

Mural of the Day of Pentecost at the Divine Retreat Centre, Muringoor, India, showing Mary surrounded by the eleven apostles.

about 12,000, allowing plenary sessions to be held outdoors. Subsequently, while attendance at Notre Dame dropped well below 10,000, total attendance at all the regional conferences soared; the 1977 conference in Atlantic City alone gathered more than 37,000.

Nevertheless, the number of active Catholic charismatics and the dynamism of the movement as a whole in the U.S. began a decline in the 1980s, with many charismatics exiting the Catholic Church altogether to join Protestant groups and others coming to see themselves as "ex-charismatics." This latter category included some who came to question the validity of the pentecostal experience; some who came to see that experience as simply one facet of a much richer and more complex Catholic spirituality (and therefore not grounds for a special identity); and some whose attention came to be preoccupied with other concerns, such as the growing Marian movement. (Interest in the supernatural aspects of the charismata often shows some continuity with interest in the supernatural aspects of Marian apparitions, and the end-time themes commonly emphasized among Protestant pentecostals easily find a parallel in the apocalyptic warnings of Marian visionaries.)

By 1982 Stephen Clark was asking publicly, "Has the charismatic renewal peaked?" and CCR leaders were calling for a "back to basics" strategy for the CCR—a tacit admission that redirection was needed. By 1986, in part in response to ▸Pope John Paul II's stress on the "New Evangelization," evangelism was coming into focus as a primary task for the movement. This new focus was clear in the New Orleans conferences on evangelization of 1986 and 1987 organized by the ▸North American Renewal Services Committee and including a number of Catholics among its organizers and participants. Evangelism also came to figure prominently in the mission statement of a number of CCR organizations, while charismatic priest ▸Tom Forrest, as director of the church-wide effort called Evangelization 2000, led that organization's emphasis on the role of the Holy Spirit in mission efforts.

Through the 1990s CCR evangelistic energies worldwide crystallized into a network of schools of evangelization designed to train laypeople for the task. By 1995 an estimated 1,100 such schools were operating around the globe, with 100 in 54 African nations alone. Some are geared to youth and run by CCR communities, offering residential programs that last four months to a year. Others focus more on training for laypeople with full-time jobs, providing courses in the evenings or on weekends, and are sponsored by parish or diocesan officials.

One of the most successful of these schools, the International Catholic Programme of Evangelization, is based in Malta. Within its first decade, this group—modeled on similar programs of the charismatic nondenominational ministry ▸Youth With A Mission—had trained an estimated 50,000 workers in Europe, Africa, and New Zealand in methods of street evangelism, preaching, and outreach through dance and drama.

In the international setting, social justice and service issues have often become a priority in the CCR communities, especially in the developing nations. In 1994, for example, when a severe earthquake devastated Colombia, the Colombian Conference of Bishops appointed Fr. Camilo Bemal of the ICCRS and the charismatic community Minuto de Dios to coordinate the action of the Catholic Church in the disaster zone. In 1995 the Argentine national team for CCR sponsored the First National Meeting of Social Promoters, meant for those working in politics, trade unions, economics, and social promotion. CCR communities in central African nations have held public rallies praying for peace.

Estimates of the number of charismatic Catholics worldwide in the late '90s range as high as 72 million in more than 120 nations according to ICCRS in Rome. (See also ▸Catholic Charismatic Renewal: Statistics.) While numbers may have declined in the U.S., growth continues in many areas of the world. The Pentecost pilgrimage to Our Lady of Czestochowa, organized by the Polish charismatic community, grew from 20,000 participants in 1992 to more than 150,000 in 1995. Charismatic gatherings in the late 1990s in places such as Italy and Brazil have attracted crowds that range from 20,000 to 160,000. CCR leaders in Korea, Pakistan, Malaysia, sub-Saharan Africa, and even Papua New Guinea have continued to report steady growth in the numbers of charismatic Catholics.

3. Organization.

The CCR's losses in the U.S. may simply reflect the historical pattern of growth and decline common to religious

Catholic charismatics celebrating the Eucharist.

movements such as this. But other factors may have contributed, in particular the controversies surrounding the "covenant communities," groups that have figured significantly in the organizational structure of the movement.

The primary form the CCR has assumed is the small prayer group. Like the first such group at Duquesne, often lay-initiated and lay-led, these cells have multiplied wherever the movement has grown. In 1986 an estimated 6,000 prayer groups or more were thriving in the U.S., though their numbers have fallen since that time. The decline resulted in part from the reasons noted above, but it also reflects the frequent merging of smaller groups into larger ones—a strategy that provides some relief for the common problem of too few group leaders and teachers.

At the other end of the scale, national and international structures were gradually set in place to consolidate the fruit of the movement. In 1970 the ▸National Service Committee (NSC) was created to coordinate services such as the national conferences, a communications center (now the CharisCenter USA) had been established the year before, as well as the newly created *New Covenant* magazine. In 1972 leaders in the U.S. founded an International Communications Office (ICO) in Ann Arbor, MI, with Ralph Martin as director.

The next year leaders from eight Latin American countries met in Bogota, Colombia, and decided to establish a communication center, the Encuentro Carismatico Catolico Latin-Americano (ECCLA). In 1976 the ICO moved to Brussels, and in 1981 to Rome, when it changed its name to the International Catholic Charismatic Renewal Office (now the International Catholic Charismatic Renewal Services, or ICCRS). This organization, officially recognized by the Vatican, has sponsored numerous international conferences and offered other kinds of support for the extension and maintenance of the movement worldwide.

Lying between these two organizational structures, and for a number of years providing leadership and energy to both, have been the covenant communities. The covenant community is typically an intentional community with explicit forms of commitment beyond those of regular church membership. Though not exclusively Catholic, the Catholic covenant communities have been among the most influential and controversial within the wider charismatic movement and have often seen themselves in some kind of continuity with more traditional communities such as the Catholic religious orders. The first of the major Catholic communities was the Word of God community, founded in Ann Arbor in 1967 by Ralph Martin, Stephen Clark, and others not long after their initial pentecostal experience. Though primarily Catholic in leadership, this group soon developed an ecumenical membership and identity.

Two more covenant communities were founded at South Bend, IN: True House, which did not survive long, and People of Praise, led by ►Kevin Ranaghan and Paul DeCelles. Other major communities have been Mother of God, in Gaithersburg, MD; Alleluia Community, in Augusta, GA; and the covenant community of St. Patrick's parish in Providence, RI. A few charismatic communities of similar structure have flourished in Europe and other continents, especially in France.

The "covenant" aspect of the covenant communities has typically involved a commitment to at least some degree of sharing financial resources, regular participation in community gatherings, and submission to the direction of the group's designated authorities. The larger communities are often divided into "households," composed of those who live in the same house or close enough to one another to allow for some sharing of meals, prayer times, and other activities. One or two families form the heart of most households, but others may be made up of single men or women. Each household usually recognizes one "head," who is normally the father of the family the household is structured around; households of singles will have one member appointed as head. Other levels of authority may be layered above the household heads, designated as "coordinators" or by some other title.

In its early years the CCR was led primarily from the covenant communities at Ann Arbor and South Bend. Stephen Clark, Ralph Martin, and Kevin Ranaghan in particular helped to establish the framework of institutions upon which the movement was built: a national office, the National Service Committee, a communications center, *New Covenant* magazine, national conferences, ►"Life in the Spirit" seminars to prepare people for Spirit baptism, and "Foundations" courses as follow-up for those who had been Spirit-baptized. Through these tools the covenant communities profoundly shaped the vision of Catholic charismatic renewal throughout the U.S. and abroad.

In 1975 the Association of Communities was formed by Word of God, People of Praise, and several other major covenant groups, but it dissolved after four years because of disagreements between Ann Arbor and South Bend. The communications media of the group were divided up between these two; *New Covenant* stayed with the Word of God community, and the National Communications Office retained its staff from the People of Praise. This fissure inevitably eroded the influence and credibility of the covenant-community leadership within the larger movement.

Meanwhile, some CCR participants challenged the dominance of the covenant communities. Many priests and religious leaders especially cautioned that these groups were often led by laypeople who were theologically untrained. Perhaps most common were complaints of authoritarianism and the exclusively male "headship" model of leadership.

In the mid 1970s, individual charismatic leaders not affiliated with the covenant communities began to voice their criticisms publicly, both in publications and in the eastern regional conferences in Atlantic City, NJ, which rivaled the Notre Dame conferences in attendance. Alternative visions of charismatic renewal were offered by writers and speakers, such as ►Josephine Massyngbaerde Ford, a professor at Notre Dame; Fr. John Haughey, a Jesuit theologian; Fr. Joseph Lange, the managing editor of *Catholic Charismatic*, a rival to

The Mother of God community choir singing at the Eastern General Conference of the Catholic Charismatic Renewal, Atlantic City, NJ, in 1978.

New Covenant; and Fr. Ralph Tichenor, SJ, who helped to establish Southern California Renewal Communities. These and other leaders stressed a stronger identification with Catholic distinctives, promoted parish renewal through parochial prayer groups (a model perhaps best exemplified by St. Patrick's parish in Providence), and challenged authoritarian practices and the exclusion of women from community leadership roles.

With the decline of covenant-community influence, the National Service Committee attempted to become more representative in its makeup and focus. Beginning with a restructuring in 1984, this group sought to connect with institutions and ministries that had been alienated from the covenant groups, and *New Covenant* broadened its scope as well. The NSC has also cultivated its relationship with the Association of Diocesan Liaisons to the CCR (see below), a network that has become more prominent in the movement's leadership in recent years.

Even though they have lost their central place of influence in the movement, the covenant communities have continued to make significant contributions. Rallies to encourage renewal have been held by the FIRE (Faith, Intercession, Repentance, Evangelization) Teams (organized 1983) from Ann Arbor, MI, and Steubenville, OH—where Franciscan University has become an enduring promoter of charismatic Catholic spirituality, despite some difficulties in the early 1990s that led to a less close association between the campus and the Steubenville Covenant Community. Conferences, publications, and television broadcasts (mostly on the Eternal Word Television Network, founded by charismatic Franciscan sister Mother Angelica) also continue to emanate from these sources. New associations of covenant communities have emerged, such as the Sword of the Spirit, Christ the King Association, and the International Catholic Fraternity of Charismatic Covenant Communities, which was officially recognized in 1990 by the Pontifical Council for the Laity and received full canonical status in 1995.

4. Relations with the Catholic Church Hierarchy.

Relations between the CCR and Catholic church officials have not always been warm, for perhaps obvious reasons. Bishops and priests are well aware of the antinomian potential in a movement that claims that immediate divine revelations are common among its members. In addition, charismatic spontaneity and exuberance represent a model of worship not easily integrated with the traditional formality and solemnity of Catholic worship, particularly the Mass. Finally, CCR leaders have from the beginning been drawn largely from among the laity and have often been criticized for a lack of theological and pastoral preparation.

The United States Conference of Catholic Bishops (USCCB) issued its first statement on the movement at its annual meeting in 1969. The Bishops' Committee on Doctrine presented a report expressing a positive judgment on the CCR but cautioned that the movement needed careful pastoral guidance. In 1973 the episcopal conference established an ad hoc committee to nurture closer ties with movement leaders. Bishop Joseph McKinney, a member of this committee, was himself an active participant in the CCR and served as episcopal advisor to the NSC.

This Bishops' Committee issued a second report on the movement in 1975, "Guidelines for the Catholic Charismatic Renewal." This statement was generally positive but focused on areas in which pastoral guidance was necessary to avoid errors and excesses. A decade later (1984) the Bishops' Committee prepared for the episcopal conference a third report, "A Pastoral Statement of the Catholic Charismatic Renewal." This statement was much more generous in its praise of the movement, though it still offered pastoral advice. Soon after, the committee was renamed the Bishops' Liaison Committee with the Catholic Charismatic Renewal; McKinney was made its chairman. In a statement issued in 1997 by the episcopal conference, the bishops affirmed "the positive impact this move of the Spirit has had in the lives of millions of people and through them the life of the Church."

At the urging of McKinney in 1975, individual bishops had begun to appoint their own diocesan liaisons—mostly priests, but also some sisters and some laypeople—to serve as their representatives for the CCR in their dioceses. Throughout the next decade, a number of diocesan centers for charismatic renewal began to emerge under the leadership of these liaisons. In 1978 the liaisons created a national association, established a newsletter, and initiated two annual conferences—one for the liaisons and one as a theological symposium. Recent years have seen the appointment of association members to joint committees in conjunction with the NSC to cooperate on matters of mutual concern.

During this same period, the proportion of priests and religious participating in the movement has continued to grow, leading some to speak of a "clericalization" of the CCR. As especially more priests have become active in this regard, they have stressed the importance of the movement as a tool of parish renewal, promoting a model in which charismatics seek to be integrated into the life of the local Catholic congregation rather than separated into covenant (and often interdenominational) communities. This increase in clerical involvement is reflected in the greater number of priests in official leadership positions of groups such as the NSC as well as in the number of cleric-led prayer groups affiliated with the diocesan liaison offices.

Undoubtedly, the key figure in the CCR's relations with Rome for most of the movement's history was Léon Joseph Cardinal Suenens, archbishop of Malines-Brussels in Belgium. He had heard of the CCR by 1973 and decided to visit several charismatic communities in the U.S. Favorably impressed by what he found, he attended the Notre Dame conference that year. A few months later he took part in the first international leaders conference at Grottaferrata, when he arranged to introduce a group of the leaders to Pope Paul VI.

From this point on Suenens was publicly identified as a participant in the movement. He spoke at the Notre Dame conference in 1974 and published that same year his positive account of the CCR entitled *A New Pentecost?* The cardinal also hosted a conference at Malines that offered an evaluation of the movement and provided "Theological and Pastoral Guidelines on the Catholic Charismatic Renewal" (1974).

Helping to arrange for the movement's 1975 international congress in Rome, Suenens was at that time given a special mandate by Pope Paul VI to exercise pastoral oversight for the worldwide renewal. At the cardinal's invitation, Ralph Martin and Stephen Clark developed a CCR International Information Office in Brussels; in 1978 it was moved to Rome, when the new pope, John Paul II, confirmed Suenens's special pastoral mandate. Within that role, he became concerned about certain parachurch tendencies of the CCR, and he eventually decreed that in Belgium only priests could lead prayer groups. But the cardinal remained until his death in 1996 an enthusiastic proponent of charismatic spirituality as "an answer to the questions now facing the Church."

Pope John Paul II has been especially warm in his endorsement of the CCR, personally addressing a number of charismatic gatherings and "giving praise to God for the many fruits which it has borne in the life of the Church" (address to the ICCCR, 1992). At the same time, he has urged participants in the movement not to distance themselves from the church, but to maintain "fidelity to the ecclesial Magisterium, filial obedience to pastors and the spirit of service with regard to local churches and parishes" (address to the Italian NSC, 1998).

5. Distinctives of Catholic Charismatic Theology and Practice.

Given the Protestant pentecostal roots of the CCR, it is not surprising that "Spirit-baptized" Protestants and Catholics should hold much in common with regard to their expression of charismatic faith and practice. Charismatic Catholics, like others in the pentecostal movement, have come to share a basic experience: an encounter with the Holy Spirit with certain charisms that typically follow. These commonalities have made it possible for Catholics and Protestants to take part in charismatic meetings and even live together in covenant communities from the very beginning of the movement.

Nevertheless, charismatic spirituality has developed several distinctives within the Catholic tradition as it has sought to reconcile the experiences resulting from Spirit baptism with the traditional understandings of Catholic faith.

First, while Protestant pentecostals have often concluded that for most of its history the church has lacked the power of the Holy Spirit, charismatic Catholics are more likely to search the church's tradition for evidences of charisms manifested throughout the centuries, insisting on a degree of continuity in the Spirit's works since the Day of Pentecost. Kilian McDonnell and ›George T. Montague's *Christian Initiation and Baptism in the Holy Spirit: Evidence from the First Eight Centuries* (1991) was one such effort to establish historical connections.

Second, Catholics have attempted to fit Spirit baptism into the framework of traditional sacramental theology, especially to reconcile it with the teaching that the Holy Spirit is already given to the believer in baptism and confirmation. Some have preferred to speak of the "release of the Spirit" rather than the "baptism of the Spirit," to emphasize that the experience is a release or stirring up of gifts already given in the sacraments. Others teach that the Spirit can be sent many times to be pres-

The Catholic Charismatic Renewal, 1967–2000

Year	Prayer groups	PARTICIPANTS: Weekly	Monthly	Yearly	Involved	Familial	Community	Rate %Cath	% p.a.	Countries
1	2	3	4	5	6	7	8	9	10	11
1967	2	First Charismatic prayer groups formed in USA and Colombia						0.0	500.0	2
1970	2,185	238,500	500,000	1,000,000	1,600,000	2,000,000	2,000,000	0.3	100.0	25
1973	3,000	900,000	2,000,000	3,500,000	5,000,000	7,000,000	8,000,000	1.1	58.7	71
1975	4,000	1,995,730	3,000,000	6,000,000	9,000,000	11,000,000	15,000,000	2.7	36.9	93
1980	12,000	3,000,000	4,771,390	7,700,000	16,000,000	30,000,000	40,000,000	5.0	21.6	110
1985	60,000	4,200,000	7,547,050	12,000,000	22,000,000	40,100,000	63,500,000	7.3	9.7	140
1990	90,000	7,000,000	10,100,000	17,000,000	30,000,000	45,000,000	85,000,000	9.2	6.0	180
1995	143,000	11,000,000	14,000,000	20,000,000	34,000,000	60,000,000	104,900,000	10.4	4.3	210
2000	160,000	13,400,000	19,300,000	28,700,000	44,300,000	71,300,000	119,900,000	11.3	2.7	233

This statistical section is taken from D. B. Barrett and T. M. Johnson, *World Christian Encyclopedia*, © 2001 D. B. Barrett and T. M. Johnson. Used by permission.

ent in many ways and to bring many kinds of graces and that Spirit baptism, though it cannot take the place of any sacrament, can nonetheless represent a new sending of the Spirit to begin a decisively new work of grace in the believer's life.

Third, probably most charismatic Catholics do not accept the claim of many Protestant pentecostals that every genuine Spirit baptism must be evidenced initially by glossolalia; the Spirit chooses sovereignly, they insist, which believers are to receive which gifts. At the same time, the Catholic understanding of charisms, based on both Scripture and the church's long historical experience, allows for a much wider array of spiritual gifts than is found in the brief biblical lists often cited by their Protestant brothers and sisters. Catholics reading the lives of the saints find not only evidence of tongues, prophecy, healing, and the other charisms noted in the Pauline epistles; they read about gifts that most Protestant pentecostals have never even heard about: St. Thomas's levitation in prayer; St. Joseph Cupertino's flights to the treetops; Padre Pio's bilocations.

A fourth distinctive of CCR practice centers on the belief in a special divine presence in the Eucharist. Catholic charismatics often speak of charisms being received through reception of Holy Communion, physical and emotional healing in particular. In addition, while Protestant pentecostal services are typically dominated by singing and by expression of the Spirit's gifts, Catholic charismatics prefer to have separate gatherings for praise and prayer apart from the Mass (or sometimes just before or after the Mass) in order to preserve the centrality of the Eucharist in worship.

Finally, the blessed Virgin Mary, though typically not the focus of a Catholic charismatic meeting, is nevertheless expected to be present and is sometimes invoked in hymns or prayers. CCR participants who have found their way into the Marian movement, having grown accustomed to acting as channels of messages from heaven, may not hesitate to express prophecies they believe they have received from Mary or other saints through dreams, visions, or "inner locutions."

6. A Mixed Reception.

Though the closer relations between the CCR and the Catholic church hierarchy have muted some of the controversy that has surrounded the movement since its inception, many Catholics remain skeptical about its origins and its fruits. One international CCR leader complained in 1996 that "the passivity and even hostility of priests and religious leaders toward the charismatic renewal is still a major problem in some areas." The more extreme manifestations of Protestant pentecostalism, such as the "holy laughter" of the Toronto Blessing movement, have easily crossed over into some charismatic Catholic circles, making more traditional Catholics even more suspicious. In the wake of well-publicized mass suicides, terrorist attacks, and other disturbing behavior on the part of some new religious groups around the world in the late '90s, Western European governments in particular have begun surveillance of religious communities they consider cultic, with charismatic Catholics sometimes appearing on the official lists of organizations to be watched.

Such attitudes suggest that the CCR, despite the gains it has made over three decades in becoming a familiar part of the Catholic landscape, has yet to win universal recognition. Even so, the extensive network of diocesan CCR offices and liaisons, the durability of the covenant communities, the ICCRS office at the Vatican, and the large crowds at charismatic conferences in some parts of the globe are all signs that this still-young movement has achieved a remarkable degree of acceptance and permanence within the ancient borders of the Catholic Church.

7. Statistics

The table on page 465 summarizes the growth of the CCR from its origin. Columns 3–8 enumerate participation by means of the following sixfold statistical typology of participants.

With a mushrooming movement such as this, it is essential to understand the exact definition of each statistic that is generated, published, or quoted. As the pentecostal/charismatic renewal's best-documented membership data, Catholic statistics each refer to one of the following six types or categories, *each of which includes the previous category.* Columns 3–6 include only adults, grouped by their level of involvement. Columns 7–8 are demographic totals including children and infants. These last two are just as important, because the whole renewal is not a movement of isolated adults, but is largely a family movement in which the presence of children cannot be ignored.

Actively involved adults.

The first 3 categories (columns 3–5) refer to adults related to the mainline CCRs served by ICCRS.

a. Weekly-attender adult charismatics (column 3). These are defined as those adults actually attending (involved in/enrolled in/participating in) the renewal's officially recognized prayer meetings regularly every week. These have been called the "shock troops" of the movement. By 1995 their number had increased to 11 million adults; by 2000, to 13 million.

b. Monthly-attender adult charismatics (column 4). These are defined as adults attending the renewal's prayer meetings once a month or more, enumerated at 7 million worldwide in 1985; 14 million in 1995; and 19 million in 2000 (numbers include those in category [a] above).

c. Yearly-attender adult charismatics (column 5). This total covers all adults who attend less regularly, often only a large annual congress or rally (numbers include those in category [b] above).

d. Self-identifying involved adult charismatics (column 6). A somewhat larger number of adults identify themselves in public-opinion polls either as Catholic charismatics or as otherwise involved in the renewal (numbers include those in category [c] above). Also included at this point are the large number of Catholics in charismatic renewal movements not related to ICCRS.

Actively involved families.

To all of these statistics of adults must now be added their children and infants to arrive at demographic figures or family figures that can be directly and legitimately compared with secular population figures, and also with standard Catholic statistics of baptized Catholics, both of which always include children and infants.

e. Charismatic family members (column 7). This is defined as active or involved adults plus their children and infants enumerated in this table at 30 million in 1980 and 71 million by 2000. This category also includes those enumerated under categories (a), (b), (c), and (d) above.

Active and inactive charismatic community.

f. Active charismatic and postcharismatic community (column 8). This last category is defined as consisting of two distinct figures: (1) the active family of category (e) above plus (2) a large fringe of Catholic postcharismatics (formerly active charismatics who have become irregular, or less active, or inactive, or active elsewhere). Together these two constitute the total Catholic charismatic demographic community, amounting to 40 million in 1980, increasing to 63 million by 1985, to 104 million by 1995, and to 119 million by 2000.

■ **Bibliography:** R. J. Bord and J. E. Faulkner, *The Catholic Charismatics* (1983) ■ J. Fichter, *The Catholic Cult of the Paraclete* (1975) ■ J. M. Ford, *Which Way for Catholic Pentecostals?* (1976) ■ R. Laurentin, *Catholic Pentecostalism* (1977) ■ K. McDonnell and G. Montague, *Christian Initiation and Baptism in the Holy Spirit* (1991) ■ E. D. O'Connor, *The Pentecostal Movement in the Catholic Church* (1971) ■ idem, *Theological and Pastoral Orientations on the Catholic Charismatic Renewal* (1974) ■ K. Ranaghan and D. Ranaghan, *As the Spirit Leads Us* (1971) ■ idem, *Catholic Pentecostals* (1969) ■ L. J. Suenens, *A New Pentecost?* (1974) ■ United States Catholic Conference of Bishops, "Grace for the New Springtime" (1997) ■ K. Wojtyla (Pope John Paul II), "Address to the Italian National Service Committee" (1998).   ■ T. P. Thigpen

CATHOLIC FRATERNITY OF CHARISMATIC COVENANT COMMUNITIES AND FELLOWSHIPS See CHARISMATIC COMMUNITIES.

CELESTIAL CHURCH OF CHRIST
The Celestial Church of Christ (CCC) is an indigenous African Christian move-

ment concentrated in the Yoruba-speaking area of southwestern Nigeria. Founded in 1947, this group is one of the best-known examples of Aladura (lit. "people of prayer") Christianity and is by some estimates the most popular independent pentecostal church in West Africa. In 1995 the church supported approximately 1,900 branches around the world (including 36 in Europe and 28 in the U.S. and Canada) and could claim close to 1 million members.

The CCC ascribes its origin to a semiliterate carpenter named ▸Samuel Bilewu Joseph Oshoffa (1909–85), who, while born in Dahomey (now the Republic of Benin), can trace his ancestors to the Egbado Yoruba of Ogun State, Nigeria. Beginning in May 1947, Oshoffa received several visions while collecting wood in the forest, visions he later narrated in detail to his followers. He described seeing on one occasion "a winged being whose body was like fire" and who explained, "God wants to send you [Oshoffa] to the world on a mission of preaching and exhortation, but the world will not believe you. To assist you in your work so that men may listen and follow you, miraculous works of holy divine healing will be wrought by you in the name of Jesus Christ." Upon returning to Porto Novo, the capital, Oshoffa suddenly had the power, "by prayer alone," to heal people and reportedly to raise people from the dead. Oshoffa continued to have visions in which God commanded him to found a new, revitalized, purified Christian church based on a detailed and distinct liturgy, a complex organizational structure, and a code of rigorous ethical and doctrinal principles. As Oshoffa's reputation for miraculous healing expanded in the early 1950s, traders and fishers who regularly traveled between Dahomey and Lagos established a branch of this new church in Nigeria. Later, in 1951, Oshoffa visited Makoko-Lagos, where he declared the nascent CCC parish in that city to be the new Nigerian national headquarters of the church. Now based in the heart of Yorubaland, the CCC quickly expanded to establish parishes in most Yoruba towns and villages, and eventually in every major city around the world that is home to a concentration of Nigerians. Despite Oshoffa's death in 1985, the church has continued to expand under the leadership of the current pastor, ▸Alexander Abiodun Bada.

Oshoffa, in founding the CCC, was more than simply a "charismatic leader" capable of inspiring followers to grant him authority. He was also the architect of a complex organizational structure for the church. Nevertheless, like many other pentecostal groups, the CCC claims its organization was not invented by Oshoffa (a human being) but was revealed to him by God. Divided first by gender, the CCC recognizes a series of hierarchical ranks for it members. There are 26 ranks for men, organized further into four "lines" according to function: leaders, elders, prophets, and honored men. For women, the church defines 15 ranks divided into two categories: sisters and prophetesses. With the pastor at the top, these male and female ranks form the "spiritual hierarchy" of the church. Each rank wears a distinct uniform (known as a *sutana*) that begins with a stylized white robe (explaining why some have dubbed this group a "white-garment church"), but adds different colored belts, capes, and waist-length overcoats, according to rank. With members clad mostly in white, but with flashes of blue, yellow, green, pink, and purple, CCC worship services are extraordinarily colorful.

The church has further established a hierarchical governing structure. With the pastor at the top, the church's constitution assigns graded authority to several administrative bodies, including a board of trustees, dioceses, state councils, districts, regional zones, and local parishes. This bureaucratic division, however, is mostly an ideal, for in practice (again, like many pentecostal denominations) decision-making power is concentrated at the top in the religious office of the pastor and at the bottom of the hierarchy in the local leaders (called shepherds) of individual parishes.

At the center of CCC doctrine and belief is the notion of "sanctification." The church understands this ideal as that state of being (or sometimes the process that leads to such a state) characterized by unencumbered relations (communication, communion, and so forth) between the divine and human realms. For members of the church, sanctification is a state of spiritual cleanliness defined by the absence of impurities that may block the presence of the divine in the human world.

This presence, members claim, is manifest in the action of spiritual beings called angels. Instead of the Holy Spirit, as is the case for most Western pentecostal groups, the CCC views the activity of angels (the effects of their presence) as evidence of sanctification, divine favor, and spiritual significance. Known to possess individual characteristics and names, angels are God's associates in the material world. They are spiritual intermediaries between human beings and God who not only implement divine directives—e.g., bestowing "blessings" like health, fertility, and affluence—but also deliver divine messages in the form of prophecy. Carrying a message from God, angels draw certain men and women (deemed prophets and prophetesses) into a trance state in order to transmit that message to the worshiping community or to a specific individual. Here, too, angels and not, strictly speaking, the Holy Spirit are responsible for this spiritual gift.

There are two domains of reality, however, that disrupt the ideal of sanctification, two basic sources for human problems—one cosmological, the other ethical. For the CCC, human beings must work to overcome both realities to achieve the desired state of sanctification and the divine blessings (delivered by angels) it promises.

The CCC cosmology agrees substantially with the traditional religious worldview of the Yoruba. Most significantly, Celestians believe, as do many in West Africa, that the world is populated by a vast number of "evil spirits" (e.g., witches,

wizards, and so-called born-to-die children) that roam about looking for ways to cause human suffering. Church members often suspect evil spirits are behind problems such as physical and mental illness, childlessness, and poverty. As agents of Satan, the ultimate adversary of God, evil spirits do not ordinarily possess people, but instead strive to obstruct human-divine relations, to desanctify human life, and thereby to make the world a frustrating and dangerous place. Capricious and malicious, evil spirits represent, for this church, a constant threat to the happiness and success God intends for human beings.

In addition to thwarting evil spirits, sanctification for the CCC also requires adhering to specific ethical guidelines. The church accepts the biblical decalogue but adds further rules and regulations, further commandments that God revealed to Oshoffa early in his life as the prophet-founder of the group. These special rules serve, in many cases, to distinguish the CCC from other Christian groups. For example, members may not wear red or black clothing; may not eat traditional Yoruba sacrificial foods, such as snails, snakes, and cola nuts; may not wear shoes when dressed in their white prayer garments; and may not enter a parish worship space while menstruating. There are many of these commandments, but in general members of the church understand them as vital to attaining a sanctified Christian life. Those who ignore these rules, as do most other Christian denominations, risk alienating themselves from God and will, as a result, experience a variety of "problems."

The important point here is that, whether caused by an evil spirit or an ethical lapse, the CCC promises to "solve people's problems" by offering a clear path toward human sanctification. The church presents an entire way of life comprised of concrete modes of action that define positive relations with God. Put differently, the church aims to improve the quality of its members' lives by emphasizing ritual. For this religious group, ritual (including ethics as a subset) has the power to sanctify, to attract angels, to combat evil spirits, to ensure communication between people and God, and ultimately to solve the day-to-day problems of its members.

This emphasis on sanctification and on the understanding of ritual as sanctifying activity explains the central role of prayer in the CCC. Recognized as an "Aladura Church" (*adura* is a Yoruba word that means "prayer") by members and nonmembers alike, it is no exaggeration to claim that prayer is the most basic element of CCC worship. For this church, prayer is an act of speaking to God, a verbal means of communication with the divine, a way of making human concerns known in the spiritual realm. Believing angels are messengers who carry prayers to God and blessings to human beings, and believing they are closely associated with sanctified spaces (e.g., worship buildings) and persons (those who live ethically), Celestians trust that when performed under sanctified conditions, God answers all prayers. Ultimately, therefore, this religious movement emphasizes sanctification because it seeks answers to prayers. More specifically, it seeks the "good things in life" that flow from God.

Four main purposes dominate prayers in the CCC: most frequently, petition (a request for divine assistance, benefit, or favor), but also thanksgiving (a recognition of receiving divine blessing), praise (an expression of honor and adoration for the divine), and confession (an admission of fault, impurity, or offense against the divine). Most CCC worship services contain at least one prayer devoted to each of these purposes.

During their worship services, Celestians employ a number of ritual objects and substances. Each of these are thought to be sanctifying substances and are said, therefore, to attract heavenly angels and thus to improve the efficacy of prayer. Most important among these objects are simple white candles, which are involved in almost every aspect of Celestial worship. Always lit during services and often held by individuals praying, candles recall for Celestians "divine light and holiness." They serve as a concrete symbolic medium through which to pray. Similarly, parishes burn a special incense during their worship services, and they frequently sprinkle perfumes or perfumed water throughout the worship space. Celestians claim the pleasant smell of these substances attracts angels and is therefore conducive to effective prayer.

Another important substance in the CCC is water. While somewhat controversial, the church has many ritual uses for various types of naturally occurring water (e.g., rain, dew, river water, lake water, and so forth) and for different water solutions (e.g., soap and water, perfume and water, fruit juice and water, etc.). Celestians believe that these forms of water are "spiritually powerful," that each has distinct qualities and, accordingly, utilities. Most important, the church advocates using these spiritually charged forms of water for healing. When members seek relief from a specific problem, whether it be personal, physical, or financial, the church will consult a prophet or prophetess who, after entering a trance, will frequently prescribe sprinkling (perhaps in the patient's bedroom), ingesting, or bathing in a specific type of water. When combined with prayer, these healing techniques are often successful for members of this church.

Like these ritual substances, the CCC attributes special religious qualities to the music of its worship services. The church is well known for its music throughout Nigeria, for it combines Western and traditional African instrumentation (e.g., an organ and drums), harmonic patterns, and rhythmic styling. Beyond being simply popular, however, singing and performing music, particularly the unique hymns of the church, creates a festive and joyous atmosphere members believe is pleasing to angels and thereby favorable to successful prayer. Singing hymns moves one closer to God. Consequently, Celestial hymns almost always play an important role

in typical healing rituals the church conducts. Over the years the church has classified over 400 original hymns into thematic categories, such as praise, faith, God's work, forgiveness, and victory. Members insist that these hymns are spiritual revelations received through dreams and prophecies and are not "composed by men." They are musical forms of effective sanctification.

Beyond praying, lighting candles, sprinkling water, and singing hymns, CCC ritual also includes such activities as ringing a handbell, chanting certain words or biblical passages like "Hallelujah" or Psalm 51, reading from the OT and NT, accepting various financial and material offerings, preaching sermons, administering communion, and assuming different bodily postures like kneeling, bowing, and complete prostration. CCC worship is elaborate, complex, and lengthy. Members dress in their white prayer garments (barefooted) and spend several hours alternating through a series of prayers, hymns, Bible readings, offerings, and processions, all while elders fill the room with incense or asperse it with perfume. The atmosphere of CCC worship services varies from moments of calm, serious prayer and focused attention (perhaps on lighted candles) to extended periods of enthusiastic dancing and drumming when numerous participants may fall into a trance state (what members call "being in spirit" and which may or may not include glossolalia) and others may prophesy.

The CCC conducts six different weekly worship services: most important, a Sunday morning "full" service, a Wednesday evening "mercy" service, a Friday evening "power" service, a Wednesday morning service especially for "those seeking favor from God" (particularly barren women), a Friday noon service for prophets and prophetesses, and a Friday afternoon service for pregnant women. The church also holds a watch-night vigil service on the first Thursday evening of each month. In addition to the major annual Christian celebrations like Christmas and Holy Week, the church also holds a harvest thanksgiving service, and a foot-washing service. Every year for Christmas, Celestians from around the world convene for services in the Nigerian town of Imeko where Oshoffa is buried and where the church is building a massive cathedral. Finally, several special, unscheduled worship services are important to the church, for example, a naming ceremony for eight-day-old infants, an immersion-baptism ceremony for adults, marriages, funerals, a foundation-stone laying service performed for new buildings, and outdoor public revival services. Overall, the CCC conducts no fewer than 30 different kinds of worship services throughout its liturgical year.

Like most pentecostal and charismatic Christian groups, the CCC revolves around what it considers essential to living a life closely associated with the divine. Its beliefs and practices all reinforce the centrality of manifest sanctification, of experiencing God's presence and the practical benefits it

Children in Pentecostal/Charismatic Communities

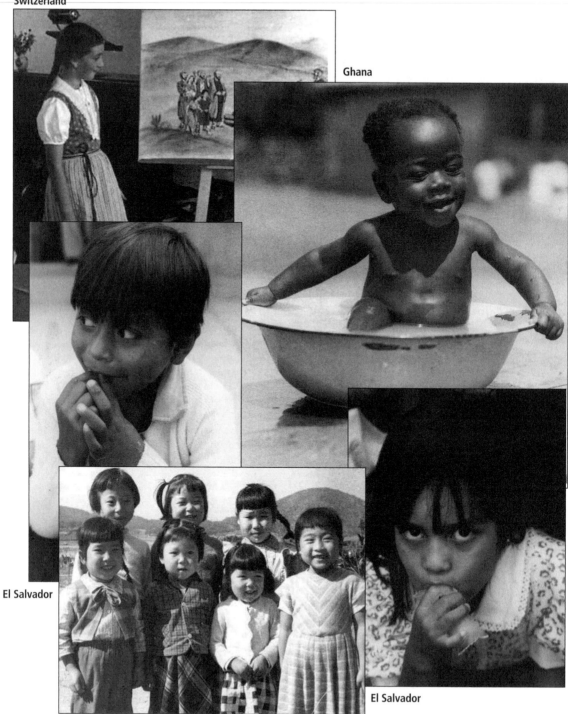

Switzerland

Ghana

El Salvador

El Salvador

Korea

Children in Pentecostal/Charismatic Communities

El Salvador

El Salvador

Korea

El Salvador

brings. Celestians believe that if they prepare themselves spiritually, if they conduct their rituals properly, God will solve their problems in this world.

■ **Bibliography:** A. A. Agbaje, "The Celestial Church of Christ" (diss., Obafemi Awolowu U., 1986) ■ J. D. Carter, "The Celestial Church of Christ: Syncretism, Ritual Practice and the Invention of Tradition in a New Religious Movement" (diss., U. of Chicago, 1997) ■ D. H. Crumbley, "Indigenous Institution Building in an Afro-Christian Movement: The Aladura as a Case Study" (diss., Northwestern U., 1989) ■ M. T. Fatoyinbo, "The Celestial Church of Christ: An Inquiry into the Place and Use of Spiritual Manifestations in the Life and Faith of an African Independent Church" (diss., Trinity College, Bristol, 1983) ■ J. W. Fernandez, "The Cultural Status of a West African Cult Group on the Creation of Culture," in S. Ottenberg, ed., *African Religious Groups and Beliefs* (1982) ■ R. I. J. Hackett, "Explanation, Production and Control—the Raison d'Etre of a West African Independent Church—the Celestial Church of Christ" (diss., King's College, U. of London, 1978) ■ D. O. Olayiwola, "The Celestial Aladura Christianity in Yoruba Religio-Cultural Matrix," in C. Steed, ed., *The Triple Religious Heritage of Nigeria* (1995) ■ J. K. Olupona, "The Celestial Church of Christ in Ondo: A Phenomenological Perspective," in R. I. J. Hackett, ed., *New Religious Movements in Nigeria* (1987) ■ B. C. Ray, "Aladura Christianity: A Yoruba Religion," *Journal of Religion in Africa* 23 (3, 1993). ■ J. D. Carter

CERULLO, MORRIS (1931–). Missionary, evangelist, and faith healer. Morris Cerullo was raised in an Orthodox Jewish orphanage in New Jersey. A Christian woman who worked at the orphanage talked to the young man and gave him a NT. This action lead to her dismissal. Cerullo left the orphanage at age 14 and was supernaturally led to the woman who had befriended him and who now took him into her home. He began attending a Full Gospel church and soon received the baptism of the Holy Spirit and a call to preach the gospel. Cerullo was ordained by the ˒Assemblies of God in the early 1950s, and in 1956 he began a healing ministry. He was active with the ˒Voice of Healing organization in his early ministry and has been quite closely associated with the ˒Full Gospel Business Men's Fellowship International. Cerullo's own organization is called World Evangelism and is based in San Diego, CA, where an annual school for the training of ministers is held.

■ **Bibliography:** M. Cerullo, "From Jewish Orphanage to the Christian Pulpit," *World-Wide Revival* (Sept. 1968) ■ D. E. Harrell Jr., *All Things Are Possible* (1975). ■ J. R. Zeigler

CHAMBERS, GEORGE AUGUSTUS (1879–1957). Prominent Canadian pentecostal leader. A native of Ontario, Chambers studied in Cincinnati, OH, and became a pastor with the New Mennonite Brethren. His first contact with the pentecostal movement was with the ˒Hebden mission in Toronto. Influenced by ˒A. G. Ward, he began preaching the baptism in the Spirit and opened a pentecostal mission, though he himself only received the baptism later at Elkland, PA. When the ˒Pentecostal Assemblies of Canada (PAOC) was organized in 1919, Chambers was elected general superintendent, a post he held until 1934. An indefatigable traveler, he played a major part in the steady expansion of PAOC. He served pastorates in Vineland, Ottawa, Amprior, Peterborough, and Kitchener. Near the end of his life he wrote an autobiography, *Fifty Years in the Service of the King: 1907–1957* (1960).

■ **Bibliography:** G. G. Kulbeck, *What God Hath Wrought* (1959) ■ T. W. Miller, *Canadian Pentecostals* (1994). ■ P. D. Hocken

CHAMBERS, STANLEY WARREN (1915–). General superintendent of the ˒United Pentecostal Church (UPC; 1968–78). Born and reared in Ohio, Chambers was converted in a pentecostal church in 1927 and received the Holy Spirit in 1930. In 1943 he was ordained and became pastor of a church in Hazelton, PA. Chambers became the first general secretary of the UPC in 1945, a position he held until he was elected general superintendent. In 1983 he was elected to the office of superintendent of the Missouri District of the UPC and served in this office and as president of Gateway College of Evangelism in St. Louis, MO, until 1993. He is also an honorary member of the UPC general board.

■ J. L. Hall

CHARISMA IN MISSIONS Roman Catholic charismatic missionary society founded by Marilynn Kramar in Los Angeles in 1972. A former Assemblies of God (AG) missionary-evangelist to Colombia from 1967 to 1972, Kramar converted to the Roman Catholic Church in 1972. That same year, at the urging of Cardinal Timothy Manning of Los Angeles, she founded Charisma in Missions (CM), a Catholic international lay-missionary evangelization society.

Although international in scope, the two primary goals of CM are to evangelize alienated Latino Catholics and to train evangelizers to work in the Spanish-speaking Roman Catholic community. In 1975 CM began holding the International Latin Encounter for Renewal and Evangelization, better known as the Latin Encounter (Encuentro Latino). The annual Encuentro Latino has grown in attendance from 600 in 1975 to 18,000 in 1997.

In addition to the Latin Encounter, CM also sponsors the Latin Encounter for Youth, an annual family convention, the Catholic Campaigns of Faith, one-day faith rallies, a Missionary Institute of Proclaimers (school of evangelism), spiritual growth seminars, children's ministry, and a drama ministry. In addition to the various programs and events, CM serves through CharisBooks, CharisTapes, CharisMedia, and CharisPublications.

The CM International headquarters is located at the Porciuncula Center in East Los Angeles. The center was founded in 1982 with the pastoral blessing of Cardinal Timothy Manning. Between 2,000 and 3,000 people attend services, programs, and workshops at the Porciuncula every week. Kramar estimates that by 1997 CM had ministered to over a million Latino Catholics in the U.S. and Latin America. CM has not only organized evangelistic ministries, it has also produced a television program called *¡Alabaré!* The role and importance of the spiritual gifts is evident throughout the organization, programs, services, and leadership. CM has almost single-handedly introduced the pentecostal movement into the Latino Roman Catholic community throughout the U.S., but especially in the Southwest.

■ **Bibliography:** CharisMedia, *Charisma in Missions* (video, n.d.) ▌ Marilynn Kramar, *Charisma in Missions: Catholic Missionary Evangelization Society* (n.d.) ▌ idem, with Robert C. Larson, *The Marilynn Kramar Story: Joy Comes in the Morning* (1990).

▌ G. Espinosa

CHARISMATIC COMMUNITIES From its earliest days, the charismatic movement sparked an interest in Christian community. Whereas the eyes of the first pentecostals had been more focused on the 20th-century "Pentecost" heralding the imminent return of the Lord, the focus of most charismatics was on church renewal, seeing the restored charismata as divine equipment for this purpose. Many local congregations touched by the Holy Spirit through the charismatic movement experienced new life in their corporate life and ministry and developed a vision for a revitalized body of Christ, either within the existing denominations (a vision of renewal) or in new assemblies and networks (a vision of restoration). Some charismatics, however, formed separate intentional communities with explicit forms of commitment over and above regular patterns of church initiation. It is these charismatic communities that are the subject of this article.

1. Origins and Early History.

The first impulse toward charismatic community with widespread repercussions was in the Episcopalian parish of Holy Redeemer, Houston, TX. From 1965, under the leadership of ˃W. Graham Pulkingham, a core of committed members lived for some years in households and developed a powerful corporate ministry. In the early to mid 1970s, the Houston community provided a model and inspiration for many people, particularly through ˃Michael Harper's book *A New Way of Living* (1973), which was translated into several languages. It did not, however, survive long enough to provide ongoing leadership, even though the Community of Celebration that issued from Houston continued on a small scale in a few places.

The first of the major charismatic communities to exercise a major leadership role and to shape the wider development of such communities was the Word of God community (WG) in Ann Arbor, MI, founded in 1967 by ˃Ralph Martin, ˃Stephen Clark, and others soon after their baptism in the Spirit. Though the founding leaders were all Catholics, WG soon had an ecumenical composition and identity.

WG first developed the patterns that characterized most of the new charismatic communities, especially in the English-speaking world. Their basic unit was the "household," a group of community members committed to a corporate lifestyle and living under the same roof. In the earliest days, many of these households consisted of young singles of the same sex. Others involved single members living with a family. Later the "nonresidential household" came to refer to small groups of people not living under the same roof who met frequently for shared meals, worship, and personal exchange. The community vision was expressed in the community covenant, to which the members corporately committed themselves each year. The community covenant expressed the obligations as well as the vision accepted by the members, including commitment to a discipline of personal prayer, participation in community meetings, and acceptance of the authority of pastoral leaders, generally called coordinators. The growing number of community members was soon organized into small fellowship groups with their leaders normally having immediate pastoral care of those in their groups.

Other communities sprang up in the next five years. Two covenant communities were formed at South Bend, IN: first True House, which encountered difficulties and did not survive, and later the People of Praise (PP), led by ˃Kevin Ranaghan and Paul DeCelles. Others included Servants of the Light (Minneapolis, MN); the Work of Christ (East Lansing, MI); the People of Hope (Newark, NJ); the Lamb of God (Baltimore, MD); Alleluia Community (Augusta, GA); Mother of God (Potomac, MD); and Emmanuel (Brisbane, Australia). Almost all had Protestant members, some in leadership roles, within a Catholic majority and embraced some form of ecumenical vision. All the main leaders at the outset were laypeople, unordained; all were men, except for the two foundresses of Mother of God.

The covenant communities, especially WG, provided a leadership for the ˃Catholic charismatic renewal (CCR) in its earliest years and a model for the rapidly multiplying prayer groups to follow. WG leaders were the first organizers of leadership training in CCR, and visitors came to Ann Arbor from many parts of the world. The writings of WG leaders, especially Clark, provided much guidance for aspiring communities. The influence of WG and PP on CCR was spread through *New Covenant* magazine (from 1971), through the service agency later known as ▸Charismatic Renewal Services (from 1969), and through their strong influence within the National Service Committee (from 1970). The vision of forming covenant community was in effect the only model to acquire any circulation and was given credibility by their rapid growth and by the zeal, commitment, and efficiency of their youthful leaders. Where the formation of a vibrant community was deemed impossible, prayer-group members were often encouraged to move to join an established community. Such moves increased the growth rate of the covenant communities throughout the 1970s.

The first opposition within CCR to the dominance of the covenant communities came from two sources: a few disaffected former members, in particular ▸Josephine Massyngberde Ford, in her book *Which Way for Catholic Pentecostals?* (1976), and some priests who urged alternative models to covenant community and were often concerned for parish renewal. Alternative visions and ideas were expressed for a while through the magazine *Catholic Charismatic*.

In Europe, France led the way in the formation of new forms of charismatic community. Most of the French communities trace their origins to the period 1972–74, soon after the appearance of CCR in Europe. Some had a strongly urban character: Emmanuel, founded in Paris in 1972, were Catholic pioneers in street evangelism; Chemin Neuf, founded in Lyon in 1973, had some Protestant members and a more ecumenical vision; the Communauté Chrétienne de Formation, founded at Poitiers in 1974, appealed to professional people. Others had a monastic character and located in more rural areas: Lion de Juda, founded at Cordes in 1974, later changed its name to Les Béatitudes; Théophanie, begun in Montpellier in 1972, evolved in a direction away from identification with CCR. Pain de Vie, dating from 1976, has had a strong focus on welcoming the poor. La Sainte-Croix, begun in Grenoble in 1974, was dissolved in 1984. The development of the French charismatic communities has been thoroughly documented and researched through the works of Monique Hébrard. The French communities have an ethos notably different from the American, with a greater interaction between inherited traditions of Catholic spirituality and community life and the new impulses coming from charismatic renewal. They have had closer links with the Catholic hierarchy, often including priests in important roles (e.g., Fr. Laurent Fabre, the founder of Chemin Neuf, and Fr. Albert de Monléon, a theologian active in Emmanuel until his nomination as bishop of Pamiers); this has led to more rapid acquisition of official church status and their being entrusted with pastoral tasks by local bishops. From an early stage, the French communities have developed their own patterns of organization and expansion. The American model of households from mobile suburbia fit European cities less well.

By the end of the 1970s the French communities were being offered unused or underused monastic and religious properties; this has mostly led to the communities having two patterns: *communautés de vie*, which include families living in common within large buildings, and *communautés de quartier*, which form neighborhood groupings of people living in their own homes. The French never followed the American pattern of consolidation at one major base but developed community branches in several places, initially within France and by the 1980s on other continents as well, especially in French-speaking Africa. This development has increased in extent and numbers through the 1990s; Emmanuel Community is now present in all French-speaking African countries, and Chemin Neuf and Pain de Vie are at work in several.

An official Catholic report from France giving 1997 data mentions 37 charismatic communities with 9,696 adults, a definite increase since 1994. Besides those already listed, the following communities are listed as forming significant bodies: Béthanie, Famille de Saint-Joseph, Puits de Jacob (Strasbourg), and Réjouis-toi (Coutances, Normandy).

The formation of charismatic communities was slower in other European countries than in France. Of communities with more than 100 members, only Maranatha Community in Brussels, Belgium, dates back to the mid 1970s. Since the 1980s there have been new charismatic communities growing up in Central and Eastern Europe, different in style from the first wave of the 1970s: many have a strong youth component, with some relating to RELAY, a service body formed out of the outreach of ▸Youth With A Mission to renewal groups in the Catholic Church. Outside North America and Europe, the charismatic community with the largest influence has been Emmanuel in Brisbane, Australia, formed in 1975 and led by Brian Smith, with an extensive outreach in Oceania and southeast Asia. The American model seemed to work better in Australia than in Europe, perhaps because it is another "new world" with greater mobility and fewer old buildings. With Emmanuel, Brisbane, leading the way, other communities soon developed: Hephzibah in Canberra; The Disciples of Jesus and the Servants of Jesus, both in Sydney; and Bethel in Perth.

2. Crisis and Challenge.

The period of most rapid growth in the North American covenant communities was the time of the most rapid growth in the Catholic charismatic renewal, namely, the 1970s. Through the 1980s there was generally slow growth or maintenance of numbers, but by the mid to late 1980s, there were the first signs of major problems. In 1985 two covenant communities had difficulties with their local bishops: Bread of Life (Akron, OH) and the People of Hope in NJ. The bishops were particularly concerned about the manner of exercise of authority and the role of women. At first these seemed to be just local difficulties, but by 1990 there were major upheavals in the communities in Steubenville, OH, and in the Word of God at Ann Arbor. As with the People of Hope, the local bishop ordered the Steubenville community to leave the Sword of the Spirit (see below). In Ann Arbor there was in effect a schism; some members stayed in Word of God under Ralph Martin, others went into a new local community, the Washtenaw Covenant Community, remaining in the Sword of the Spirit under Steve Clark and Bruce Yocum. Many simply left altogether. Martin represented a more radical criticism of the covenant communities, in effect renouncing shepherding practices and repenting for their authoritarian excesses, while Clark and Yocum remain committed to the vision of discipling covenant communities, with some modifications. The prominence of Word of God among the charismatic communities meant that assessment and reform were hard to avoid. Other communities went through painful times of reassessment and transition (Lamb of God, Baltimore, 1993; Mother of God, Gaithersburg, MD, 1994–95), with investigations within their dioceses, ending up with new leadership, more democratic structures, and a much reduced membership.

3. Other Forms of Charismatic Community.

There are several instances of new charismatic communities developing along lines different from the patterns described. Two obvious instances in the U.S. are the Reba Place Fellowship (RPF) at Evanston, IL, and the Community of Jesus (CJ) at Orleans, MA (on Cape Cod). Both are instances of the foundation of community preceding the arrival of charismatic renewal. RPF developed within the Anabaptist tradition, where communal ties have been more important than in mainline Protestantism; it has always had a strong Mennonite component and a call to inner-city ministry.

CJ's origins go back to the healing of one foundress, Cay Andersen, through the ministrations of the other, Judy Sorensen. From their association in healing ministry came the Rock Harbor Fellowship, which, after the leaders' baptism in the Spirit, became CJ in 1970. CJ is interdenominational, with strong Anglican associations and several resident clergy, mostly Presbyterian; it has 300 members at Cape Cod, including children, and a nonresident membership of 600. Another pattern in CCR has been the rise of some charismatic monasteries and convents, associated both with newly formed congregations (e.g., the Disciples of the Lord Jesus Christ in Channing, TX) and with older orders (e.g., the Pecos Benedictines in New Mexico). Another category is the ministry-oriented community, formed primarily for more effective service to the church. These are more common in Europe, often acquiring large properties to run as charismatic conference centers. Found equally among Catholics and Protestants, these communities generally have a less permanent membership. An important example in Northern Ireland has been the Christian Renewal Centre at Rostrevor founded by ʼCecil and Myrtle Kerr in 1974 to promote reconciliation between Catholic and Protestant. Another was the Communauté Chrétienne de la Réconciliation in Lille, France, with an impressive outreach to addicts and the homeless until the resignation of the founder, D. Berly, in 1995.

4. The Rise of Networks of Communities.

In 1975 an "association of communities" was formed by WG and PP, assisted by Servants of the Light (Minneapolis); the Work of Christ (East Lansing, MI); the Lamb of God (Baltimore); and Emmanuel (Brisbane, Australia). This association ended after four years, since the emphases and visions of the founding communities were too disparate. WG then formed a new network, the Sword of the Spirit (SS), to embody its ecumenical and prophetic convictions. SS has been established as one international community with member communities becoming branches of SS. In spring 1987, SS had 12 branches, 25 affiliated groups, and 6 associated communities. There were 7,600 committed adult members of whom 1,505 were in WG (two-thirds Catholic). Among the larger branches besides WG were the Joy of the Lord (Manila, Philippines); the City of God (Managua, Nicaragua); the Lamb of God (Baltimore); and the Community of the King (Belfast, Northern Ireland). With the crisis at Ann Arbor around 1990, SS went through a period of loss of communities and personnel (especially in North America) and subsequent regrouping. The Third World communities in SS were the least affected; the two largest SS communities now are Ang Ligaya in Pasig City, Philippines (1,300 members) and La Ciudad de Dios in Nicaragua (1,000 members). SS currently has about 10,000 committed members, divided among 55 communities (8 in Asia, 17 in North America, 15 in Latin America, 12 in Europe, 1 in the Middle East, 2 in the South Pacific).

People of Praise, less structured than SS, then integrated affiliated communities into its branches, including the greater part of the Minneapolis community, and organized the Fellowship of Communities, a loose coalition of kindred bodies. As of early 1987, PP consisted of some 3,000 people, including children, living in 18 locations.

In 1983 Emmanuel (Brisbane, Australia) and the Community of God's Delight (Dallas, TX) launched a new association known as International Brotherhood of Communities (IBOC) as a consultative fellowship body, including communities from Malaysia (the Light of Jesus Christ, Kota Kinabalu, Sabah; the Servants of Yahweh, Kuala Lumpur), Australia (Hephzibah, Canberra; Bethel, Perth), and New Zealand (Lamb of God, Christchurch). Established as an interdenominational body, IBOC meetings were soon accompanied by Catholic meetings for the wholly Catholic communities and the Catholic fellowships of the ecumenical communities. Soon the Catholic meetings became more important than those of IBOC, leading to the end of IBOC and the further development of this new Catholic body, which was inaugurated in 1990 as the Catholic Fraternity of Charismatic Covenant Communities and Fellowships (CFCCCF). In 1995 CFCCCF received final recognition from the Pontifical Council for the Laity.

In 1998 there were 24 member communities in CFCCCF (6 more communities have "under-way" status):

U.S.: The Christian Community of God's Delight (Dallas, TX); City of the Lord (Tempe, AZ); Glory to God (Topeka, KS); Alleluia (Augusta, GA); Comunidad Catolica A.M.A. (Brownsville, TX).

Latin America: Shalom (Fortaleza, Brazil); Neuva Alianza (San Luis Potosi, Mexico); Comunidad de Convivencias (Buenos Aires, Argentina); La Santisima Trinidad (Cordoba, Argentina).

Australia and New Zealand: Emmanuel (Brisbane); Bethel (Perth); Disciples of Jesus (Canberra); Bread of Life (formerly Servants of Jesus, Sydney); Lamb of God (Christchurch, N.Z.).

Asia: Servants of Yahweh (Kuala Lumpur, West Malaysia); Light of Jesus Christ (Kota Kinabalu, Sabah, Malaysia); Community of God's Little Children (Tacloban City, Philippines).

Europe: Emmanuel (Paris); Comunita di Gesu (Bari, Italy); Réjouis-Toi (Coutances, France); Family of God (Dundalk, Ireland); Glory of God (Oppenau, Germany); Koinonia Giovanni Battista (Rome, Italy); Magnificat (Foggia, Italy).

Two of the major French communities have "under-way" status: the Matitudes and Fondations du Monde Nouveau. CFCCCF has thus succeeded in bringing together in a new way the American, French, and Third World communities.

■ **Bibliography:** T. J. Chordas, *Language, Charisma, and Creativity* (1997) ■ S. Clark, *Building Christian Community* (1972) ■ S. Clark, ed., *Patterns of Christian Community* (1984) ■ M. Hébrard, *Les Nouveaux Disciples* (1979) ■ idem, *Les Nouveaux Disciples Dix Ans Après* (1987) ■ D. and N. Jackson, *Glimpses of Glory: The Story of Reba Place Fellowship* (1987) ■ F. Lenoir, *Les Communautés Nouvelles: Interviews des Fondateurs* (1988) ■ P. Pingault, *Renouveau de l'Eglise: Les Communautés Nouvelles* (1989) ■ R. Quebedeaux, *The New Charismatics II* (1983).   ■ P. D. Hocken

CHARISMATIC EPISCOPAL CHURCH (CEC).

The CEC was founded in 1992 as an expression of the ›Convergence movement, affirming the necessity of holding together the evangelical, charismatic, and liturgical-sacramental dimensions of church life. In the words of its first bishop, Randolph Adler, CEC began as "a journey by charismatics and evangelicals who longed to return to the Ancient Faith." Adler was originally a pastor in the Church of God (Cleve-

land, TN) but for many years pastored an independent charismatic congregation. Deeply involved in the pro-life cause, he had become concerned about the rootlessness, self-orientation, and lack of staying power in charismatic churches. When Adler was ordained bishop in June 1992, there were three congregations in the CEC: St. Michael's in San Clemente, CA (its first pro-cathedral [church serving as cathedral until a permanent cathedral is built] and organizational center); St. Andrew's near Sacramento, CA; and St. Luke's in Tucson, AZ.

"Not birthed in schism by disenchanted sacramentalists, the CEC began with people from a foreign land to whom God had spoken about signs and sacraments, liturgy and legacy" (Adler). Further impetus was given to this convergence vision by an influential article of Paul Thigpen, "Ancient Altars, Pentecostal Fire," in *Ministries Today* (Nov.-Dec. 1992).

While the CEC leaders expected growth primarily from the evangelical-charismatic sector, the CEC quickly began to attract Episcopal priests and their people who were disenchanted with the liberal direction of the Episcopal Church. These included Dale Howard, rector of an Episcopal church in Jacksonville, FL, with his congregation; Philip Zampino with the Life in Jesus Community near Frederick, MD; Mark Pearson of Plaistow, NH, well known for his teaching and healing ministry; and Philip Weeks of Barnabas Ministries. The house (college) of CEC bishops in the U.S. has been expanding year by year; the first group of five around Archbishop Adler in spring 1995 (R. Sly, D. Howard, M. Smith, D. Woodall, J. Moats) had expanded to 19 by early 1999. Adler was called patriarch, and Howard and Sly became archbishops.

CEC's expansion into other continents has been primarily through the affiliation of blocks of congregations. In Europe a network of independent charismatic churches for Filipino migrants, begun in 1984 by T. Hines (now CEC bishop for Southeast Asia) joined, as did several congregations in Estonia belonging to the Union of Evangelical Charismatic Churches of Estonia. The CEC has four dioceses in the Philippines, where Canon Weeks exercised a significant ministry for many years. CEC's growth in Africa has been strongest in Kenya, where the first grouping was received into the International Communion of the CEC in 1997. The 40-congregation Episcopal Church of Africa was received in May 1998, followed by the whole of the Anglican River Nzoia diocese and major parts of two other Anglican dioceses (Kajiado, Kitui), 200 congregations and 12,000 members in all. In Uganda, the first CEC bishop was consecrated in Sept. 1998. The CEC generally uses Episcopalian liturgical forms, particularly the Book of Common Prayer. It produces a news journal, *Sursum Corda*, from San Clemente, CA.   ■ P. D. Hocken

CHARISMATIC MOVEMENT

I. Development in North America
   A. *Earliest Stirrings (Before 1960)*
   B. *The Emergence of the Movement (1960–67)*
   C. *The Movement Takes Shape (1967–77)*
   D. *Consolidation (1977–87)*

II. Development in Europe
    A. *Origins*
    B. *Development and Expansion until 1987*
    C. *Developments at the Continental Level*

III. Development in Latin America
     A. *Protestant Beginnings*
     B. *The Ecumenical Period*
     C. *Separate Development*

IV. Globalization and Turning Outward (1988–98)
    A. *Global Trends*
    B. *Extent and Spread*

V. Analysis
   A. *Constant Characteristics*
   B. *A Comparison with the Pentecostal Movement*
   C. *Major Challenges*

The term *charismatic movement* (CM) is here understood in its most common usage to designate what ►Donald Gee in the late 1950s called "the new Pentecost," namely, the occurrence of distinctively pentecostal blessings and phenomena, experience of infilling/empowerment with the Holy Spirit (generally termed ►baptism in the Holy Spirit [BHS]) with the spiritual gifts of 1 Cor. 12:8–10, outside a denominational and/or confessional pentecostal framework. Although the designation CM was originally applied to this work of the Spirit within the historic church traditions, it came to be used in a wider sense to include nondenominational patterns of charismatic Christianity. That is to say, CM here refers to all manifestations of pentecostal-type Christianity that in some way differ from classical pentecostalism in affiliation and/or doctrine.

I. DEVELOPMENT IN NORTH AMERICA.

A. Earliest Stirrings (Before 1960).

The roots of CM in North America go back more than a decade before the 1960 event commonly seen as the birth of the movement, namely, ►Dennis Bennett's public announcement to his Episcopal congregation at St. Mark's, Van Nuys, CA, that he spoke in other tongues. Already in the late 1940s, healing evangelists, such as ►William Branham, ►Oral Roberts, ►Gordon Lindsay, and ►T. L. Osborn, were instrumental in spreading "Spirit-baptized" Christianity beyond explicitly pentecostal milieus. Although these evangelists were virtually all pentecostal in doctrine and some in church membership or close association, their independent ministries were not under denominational control. While in the popular view these men were "healers," most saw themselves as evangelists, saving souls for Jesus through healing signs and wonders. Their ministries produced a following of Spirit-baptized believers who could not all be classified as pentecostal. These believers did not constitute a readily identifiable category because of the itinerant and varied character of the healing ministries. In this way, many people belonging to mainline Protestant denominations received BHS in the 1940s and '50s.

This pentecostal outreach beyond explicit pentecostal boundaries received its first organized expression in the ►Full Gospel Business Men's Fellowship International (FGBMFI), formed by ►Demos Shakarian, a California millionaire dairy farmer of Armenian descent. From the start, FGBMFI was closely associated with the leading healing evangelists, and Oral Roberts was the guest speaker at its first meeting, which was held in Los Angeles in Oct. 1951. FGBMFI, which had its first national convention in 1953, was conceived as an organization of Spirit-filled businessmen to evangelize and witness to nonpentecostals. Its ministry was mainly accomplished through prayer breakfasts and larger conventions, regional and national, supplemented from 1953 by its monthly magazine *Voice,* edited by ►Thomas R. Nickel. Not only did FGBMFI extend beyond pentecostal circles with its outreach, its local chapters provided a forum for regular "charismatic" fellowship for nonpentecostal Christians. Most of the first printed witnesses to BHS by mainline Protestant Christians are to be found in the early issues of *Voice.* FGBMFI was successful in reaching many mainline Protestants with the pentecostal message because it did not attempt to make its "converts" become denominational pentecostals. As an early article in *Voice* stated, "God never intended that the Full Gospel or pentecostal groups should have a religious monopoly on the Baptism of the Holy Spirit" (Hoekstra, 1956, 23).

While the healing evangelists and FGBMFI helped to create and influence a clientele of Spirit-filled Christians outside pentecostal boundaries, both saw the filling with the Spirit as an individual work of spiritual blessing and empowerment. They did not have any vision of the Holy Spirit renewing the historic churches. This element, central to much of charismatic renewal (CR) as it later developed, first entered North American thinking through the vision and witness of ►David du Plessis.

Although Du Plessis's distinctive ministry of pentecostal truth to those within historic church traditions did not fully emerge until the early 1960s, the call and the preparation went back to a prophecy of ►Smith Wigglesworth in South

Africa in 1936. This prophecy spoke of a coming pentecostal revival in the churches, of which Du Plessis would be a part. The first steps toward its fulfillment came in 1949, when Du Plessis felt called to visit the New York City office of the World Council of Churches. Throughout the 1950s, Du Plessis's contacts with historic church leaders increased, a work that helped prepare the way for later church acceptance of CR. During these years, his pentecostal exclusiveness was being broken and replaced by a vision of the Holy Spirit renewing the churches through BHS. By 1960 Du Plessis was regularly reporting the thrilling news that God was pouring out his Spirit on Christians of the "denominational churches" in many lands.

From the early years of the pentecostal movement, ministers from the historic churches had occasionally received BHS, but they generally joined a pentecostal church or became independent. The first significant case of an American minister remaining within a historic church framework after BHS was ›Harald Bredesen, then a young Lutheran minister, who received BHS in 1946. Another was ›Tommy Tyson, pastor of a United Methodist church in North Carolina, who was baptized in the Spirit in 1951. Without any knowledge of spiritual gifts, Tyson was touched by the Lord following a congregational study of Acts 2.

A major influence in the spread of the pentecostal experience within the historic church traditions was ›Agnes Sanford. With several years' experience in healing ministry, she experienced the strong inner working of the Spirit around 1953–54 when two friends laid hands on her to receive the Holy Spirit and shortly afterward she received the gift of tongues. From this time on, Sanford spoke privately of BHS to those to whom she was ministering. The scope for such ministry expanded in 1955 when Sanford and her husband started the Schools of Pastoral Care, weeklong conferences for those involved in healing (ministers, doctors, and nurses). In these conferences they spoke of "the power of the Holy Spirit working in men and women to the healing of their physical, mental and social ills."

Sanford was also active in the Order of St. Luke (OSL), founded by John Gayner Banks and Ethel Tulloch Banks in 1947. Although it was interdenominational, OSL had a strong Episcopalian membership. It sought to promote the restoration of "the Apostolic practice of Healing as taught and demonstrated by Jesus Christ." Although OSL's official declarations did not speak of healing as one of the spiritual gifts of 1 Cor. 12:8–10, it was not surprising that when some OSL members rediscovered the power of the Lord in healing, they were led to experience other spiritual gifts, including tongues, even though the OSL leadership was unsympathetic and came out openly in 1963 against any practice of glossolalia under its auspices. One of the first priest members of OSL to receive BHS was ›Richard Winkler, rector of Trinity Episco-

pal Church, Wheaton, IL. Winkler, who received BHS in Apr. 1956 at a meeting of an Assemblies of God (AG) evangelist, was already holding meetings in his home but began a public prayer meeting after a healing mission by Sanford in the fall of 1956. Following the public meeting in church, there was a smaller meeting in a lounge with exercise of the spiritual gifts and charismatic ministry. This was the first pentecostal-type prayer meeting among Episcopalians.

Around 1956 a Presbyterian minister, ›James Brown, was baptized in the Spirit and began a prayer meeting with the exercise of the spiritual gifts in his church, Upper Octorara Presbyterian Church in Parkesburg, PA. The Parkesburg services had wide influence, aided by Brown's reputation and high standing among local Presbyterians. In 1957 Bredesen accepted the pastorate of Mount Vernon Dutch Reformed Church in New York, and this church soon became another center with pentecostal prayer meetings. It also became a point of referral for interested persons.

Another milieu in which many "mainline" Christians first heard of BHS was Camps Farthest Out (CFO), founded by Glenn Clark in 1930 to aid Christians to become "athletes of the Spirit." CFO conferences, like those of OSL, proved to be an environment receptive to the pentecostal message, even though the organizers eventually came out against any identification with CM. CFO gatherings, usually a week in length, gave much scope to the camp leaders, who over the years included Sanford, Tyson, Bredesen, Brown, ›Derek Prince, and many others who had been baptized in the Spirit. As a result, many people received BHS at CFOs, including ›Don Basham in the early 1950s.

Anglican clergymen participating in worship at the charismatic Conference for Spiritual Renewal, Canterbury Cathedral, July 1978.

A major instrument for alerting the evangelical public to the power of the Holy Spirit in BHS was the monthly *Christian Life*. Its editor, ►Robert Walker, was baptized in the Spirit around 1952. Without using explicitly pentecostal terminology, he soon began to publish items dealing with a fuller life in the Spirit. Myrrdin Lewis's 1953 article "Are We Missing Something?" elicited unusual interest. Beginning in 1959, *Christian Life* published articles on congregations experiencing awakening through a pentecostal-type outpouring of the Spirit.

By the end of the 1950s there was a considerable pentecostal stirring reaching beyond the pentecostal churches. Much of it was not congregationally based or congregationally organized, though there were the beginnings of pentecostal groups in mainline church traditions at Parkesburg, PA; Mount Vernon, NY; and the Lutheran Bethany Fellowship in Minneapolis, MN; as well as less openly at Wheaton, IL. As the only organ for this expansion was *Voice* magazine, the overall perspective was one of pentecostal expansion beyond pentecostal boundaries, with little sense of unity and cohesion among those in the historic churches who had been baptized in the Holy Spirit.

B. The Emergence of the Movement (1960–67).

The events that brought the nascent movement into public view and consciousness occurred among Episcopalians in California. In the spring of 1959 a young Episcopalian couple, John and Joan Baker received BHS with the sign of tongues in a pentecostal church. They heard the Lord telling them to go back to the Episcopal Church. They went to Holy Spirit Parish at Monterey Park, where a group of 10 parishioners soon experienced BHS and met for worship. The vicar, Frank Maguire, was troubled and sought counsel from a neighboring pastor, ►Dennis Bennett of St. Mark's, Van Nuys. In Nov. 1959 both Bennett and Maguire received BHS. Bennett was soon sending over interested people from St. Mark's, and by spring 1960 some 70 people from St. Mark's—including the leaders of most of the parish organizations—had received BHS and were meeting for prayer. Unknown to the people in Monterey Park and Van Nuys, a small group of Episcopalians in St. Luke's, Monrovia, another Los Angeles suburb, experienced tongues, interpretation, and prophecy in the fall of 1959.

After several months of widening pentecostal blessing and increasing rumors at Van Nuys, Bennett felt obliged to share his experience publicly. This he decided to do on Passion Sunday, Apr. 3, 1960. At all three morning services Bennett explained in a quiet, unemotional way how he had been led to receive the power and the fullness of the Holy Spirit, and how this had included "the gift of unknown tongues." After the second service, an associate priest resigned, and a church officer called for Bennett's resignation. Bennett announced his resignation at the third service. The bishop of Los Angeles then wrote a pastoral letter to the people of St. Mark's, temporarily forbidding any group to meet under parish auspices if "speaking in tongues is encouraged or actually engaged in." In fact, the pentecostal Episcopalians in the parish formed two different groups, one simply a private prayer group, the other with a more evangelistic vision, led by Jean Stone (later ►Jean Stone Willans).

These events would have had little effect beyond the Los Angeles area had Stone not been determined to make them known. She contacted *Newsweek* and *Time,* which respectively ran stories under the headlines "Rector and a Rumpus" (July 4) and "Speaking in Tongues" (Aug. 15). Only with these reports did the Van Nuys story, with a focus on glossolalia, reach the church press. It was this publicity that first generated the sense of a new movement of the Spirit, combining pentecostal blessing and historic church attachment.

These developments in Southern California and the ensuing publicity gave rise to two thrusts in CM. The first was in the life and ministry of Dennis Bennett. By the time of the national publicity Bennett had received a welcome from the bishop of Olympia (western Washington State) and was being installed as vicar of St. Luke's in Seattle, WA, a mission the bishop had thought of closing. Within a year, church attendance had quadrupled from 75 to 300. Two events that year triggered this expansion: one, a joint clergy conference of the Episcopal dioceses of Olympia and Oregon, at which many asked Bennett to share his experience; the other, a visit to St. Luke's from Richard Winkler, who directly asked the parishioners, "Does anyone here want to receive the baptism in the Holy Spirit?" It was paradoxical that Winkler, who had kept his pentecostal experience quiet for several years, should so prod Bennett, whose experience had reached the national media. From this point on, St. Luke's, Seattle, developed as a parish whose committed members were baptized in the Spirit and where seekers from elsewhere regularly came for this blessing. Bennett was now receiving invitations to speak to Christian groups of many traditions, to whom he bore clear witness to the compatibility of BHS and membership of the Episcopal Church.

The second thrust that developed from the Van Nuys events centered on the group led by Jean Stone. In 1961 this group became the ►Blessed Trinity Society (BTS), which produced a number of pamphlets and a quarterly magazine, *Trinity,* of which the first issue, dated "Trinitytide 1961," appeared in the fall of that year. Stone mailed copies of the first issue to every Episcopal priest in the country, just as she had done with the issue of *Voice* that featured Bennett's witness. The members of *Trinity*'s board of directors were all Episcopalians except for Du Plessis and Bredesen. Bredesen became for a time a close associate of Stone; together they traveled across the western states, presenting the pentecostal message at gatherings known as Christian Advances.

For the next five years *Trinity* and *Voice* were the two publications promoting this movement of the Spirit. Both magazines advocated BHS and spiritual gifts, both gave prominence to personal testimonies, both had lay editors, and both came from California. However, while *Voice* included both pentecostal and neo-pentecostal items, *Trinity* was more oriented to the mainline churches and did not ordinarily present merely pentecostal news. Though *Voice* had a vastly larger circulation, *Trinity* played a definite role in the growing consciousness of a new movement of pentecostal blessing appearing in the historic Protestant traditions.

The first publicity concerning CM in Canada occurred in Prince Rupert, a remote area of British Columbia, where a young Anglican priest returned from California in Sept. 1961 with news of the pentecostal outbreak among Episcopalians. Soon the dean of the Anglican cathedral, George Pattison, and some local clergy were baptized in the Spirit. Controversy broke out; the bishop forbade glossolalia in public, and the clergy involved felt constrained to leave the area. CR with greater longevity began in Ontario in 1962 under the leadership of Ron and June Armstrong, who both received BHS without contact with charismatics. Ron, an Anglican priest, soon began praise meetings in his parish, St. Elizabeth's, Etobicoke. Some other Anglicans received BHS following contacts made at the international Anglican Congress at Toronto in 1963.

By the early 1960s people in virtually every major Protestant tradition (Baptists, Lutherans, Mennonites, Methodists, and Presbyterians) were receiving BHS. By 1963 these developments had come to the attention of most Protestant leaders and editors, and a large number of church journals published items on glossolalia that year. The evangelical monthly *Eternity* had an article by its editor, Russell Hitt, entitled "The New Pentecostalism," which elicited a response in *Trinity* from Bredesen and Stone; they objected to the "neo-pentecostal" label, preferring "charismatic renewal," the first time this designation was used in a definitive manner. The term *neo-pentecostalism,* however, continued to be used in scientific studies of CM by outside observers.

One of the first denominational groups to come together on this issue were the American Baptists. The charismatic pastors attending the 1963 denominational convention in Detroit, MI, heard a presentation on "The Ministry of the Charismatic Church" by Harold Jackson of Arcata, CA. From that time on, American Baptist charismatics came together at each convention for a dinner and late-night worship.

The largest penetration was among the Episcopalians. It was influenced by Bennett, Sanford, and Stone and encouraged by a positive statement of the Episcopal bishops in 1962, "New Movements in the Church." Among other denominations, the early history of CR is less well-documented, except in the few cases where the first recipients later became major charismatic leaders.

One of these pioneer leaders was an American Lutheran pastor, ⸢Larry Christenson of San Pedro, CA. Christenson, who was baptized in the Spirit in Aug. 1961, had been active in OSL for some years but actually received BHS following contact with a pentecostal. Christenson made his experience public on Pentecost 1962. This caused some dissension, which he narrowly survived. Christenson's role as Lutheran leader was actually enhanced because, in a more theological tradition, he consciously sought to relate the pentecostal experience to the Lutheran tradition. His pamphlet "Speaking in Tongues . . . a Gift for the Body of Christ" had a wide influence and was translated into German.

Christenson's denomination, the American Lutheran Church (ALC), was the first to address the issue of the charismatic revival. (Earlier Episcopalian studies and statements had been conducted by individual diocesan bishops, not by the Protestant Episcopal Church as a whole.) The ALC's concern began in 1962 following complaints that an ALC evangelist, ⸢Herbert Mjorud, had been emphasizing glossolalia in his ministry. Mjorud had been baptized in the

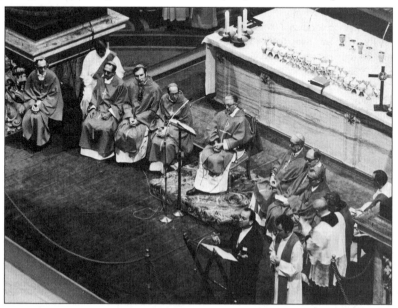

Leon-Joseph Cardinal Suenens presiding at concelebrated mass at the main altar of St. Peter's Basilica during a Rome conference in 1975.

Spirit following a visit to Bennett's parish in Seattle. A Committee on Spiritual Gifts was established to study and make recommendations concerning both glossolalia and "extra-medical" healing. The committee's report in 1963 was followed in 1964 by an official ALC statement rejecting any promotion of glossolalia and restricting its usage to private devotions.

A more aggressive opposition to CR on doctrinal grounds came from the Lutheran Church–Missouri Synod (LC–MS). The initial confrontation concerned Donald Pfotenhauer, a pastor in Minneapolis, MN, who was baptized in the Spirit at the end of 1964. In Mar. 1965, Pfotenhauer was suspended by his district president, beginning five years of church litigation that ended to Pfotenhauer's disadvantage in 1970. During the church trials, the main objection was not to glossolalia, but to prophecy, which was seen as detracting from the uniqueness of God's word in Scripture. Despite these discouragements, other LC–MS pastors continued to witness to BHS (including *Rodney Lensch, *Delbert Rossin, Don Matzat, and theologian *Theodore Jungkuntz).

The pentecostal experience also became a contentious issue among Presbyterians. Although J. Brown of Parkesburg, PA, never encountered difficulties with his Presbyterian authorities, others were not so fortunate. Robert Whitaker, a United Presbyterian pastor in Chandler, AZ, baptized in the Spirit in the fall of 1962, was removed from office in 1967 after several years of dispute. In 1966 the difficulties of Whitaker and other ministers led Brown and others to form the Charismatic Communion of Presbyterian Ministers, the first denominational charismatic body to be formed. Its full-time secretary was *George C. ("Brick") Bradford, a former attorney who had also been expelled from the ministry and who then helped Whitaker win his appeal against expulsion. Of major importance was a retreat Bradford organized in Austin, TX, in 1967. At this retreat the speakers were two theologians: *J. Rodman Williams, who was to make a valuable theological contribution from within CR, and John A. Mackay, a former president of Princeton and a respected international church leader. Mackay's advice and influence helped to end the harassment of charismatic Presbyterian pastors and contributed to CM being taken more seriously by the United Presbyterian Church, whose 1970 report "The Work of the Holy Spirit" remains one of the most comprehensive church studies of CM.

It is almost impossible to gauge the precise influence of particular leaders and publications in CR's accelerating spread. However, mention should be made of two men whose contributions may easily be undervalued: *David du Plessis and *Harald Bredesen. Du Plessis began his unique globe-trotting ecumenical witness in this period. His distinctive contribution was to emphasize that what the charismatics were receiving was indeed BHS, the same blessing that had characterized the pentecostal movement. Through his talks, his book *The Spirit Bade Me Go* (1961), and his quarterly personal newsletter, Du Plessis disseminated an ecumenical vision of CR as he testified to its worldwide scope. He was also responsible for the first meeting of leaders from many traditions, held near Columbus, OH, in Oct. 1962.

Harald Bredesen was instrumental in almost all CR impact on the mass media. He had a gift for reaching key people and telling them of BHS. He was featured in nationwide presentations on ABC's *World News Tonight* and on Walter Cronkite's *The World Tonight*. Bredesen had an indirect hand in the two books that contributed most to the spread of CR in the 1960s, for he introduced *John Sherrill to *David Wilkerson. Wilkerson's book *The Cross and the Switchblade* (1963) vividly describes the impact of the Holy Spirit on young drug addicts in New York City, while Sherrill's *They Speak with Other Tongues* (1964) is a journalist's personal investigation into glossolalia, which led to his own BHS.

C. The Movement Takes Shape (1967–77).

More than any other development, the spread of CR to the Roman Catholic Church decisively affected the shape of the wider movement. While individual Catholics had been baptized in the Spirit before 1967—such as Barbara Shlemon (now *Barbara Shlemon-Ryan) as well as some visitors to Bennett's parish in Seattle—the development of Catholic charismatic renewal (CCR) was determined by events at Duquesne University, Pittsburgh, PA, and the University of Notre Dame, South Bend, IN, in Feb. 1967, and their immediate aftermath. These events differed in significant ways from the origins of CR among Protestants: (1) They occurred in a university setting; the first Catholic charismatics were well educated, a factor ensuring that CCR would not begin with an anti-intellectual bias. (2) These pioneers, from whose ranks initial CCR leadership was drawn, were young lay Catholics; the first priest participants, such as *Fr. Edward O'Connor, acted more as theological and spiritual advisors, an important but complementary role. (3) These lay leaders had almost all worked and worshiped together on the Notre Dame campus over the preceding three to four years; this gave CCR a cohesion the movement had not achieved in other churches. (4) These Catholics had been strongly influenced by the debates, ethos, and decrees of the Second Vatican Council that had recently ended. They were "renewal-minded" and wanted to advance the renewal that Vatican II envisioned for the Catholic Church. As a result, they interpreted this outpouring of the Spirit in relation to Vatican II. They saw it as God's answer to Pope John's prayer that the council might be a new Pentecost for the church and immediately recognized that this outpouring must be for the sake of the whole church. Thus, from its inception, CCR had a sense of mission to the Catholic Church.

Church Tradition	First National Conference	Service Agency	Year Formed	Newsletter (First Issued)
Catholic	1970	National Service Committee	1970	*Pastoral Newsletter* (1968) *New Covenant* (1971)
Episcopalian	1973	Episcopal Charismatic Fellowship (Renamed Episcopal Renewal Ministries)	1973 1980	*Acts 29* (1973)
Lutheran	1972	Lutheran Charismatic Renewal Services	1974	*LCRS Newsletter* (1975)
Mennonite	1972	Mennonite Renewal Services	1975	*MRS Newsletter* (1976) *Empowered* (1983)
Methodist	1974	United Methodist Renewal Services Fellowship	1977	*Manna* (1977)
Orthodox	1973	Service Committee for Orthodox Spiritual Renewal	1977	*Logos* (1968) *Theosis* (1978)
Presbyterian	1972	Charismatic Communion of Presbyterian Ministers Presbyterian Charismatic Communion (Renamed Presbyterian and Reformed Renewal Ministries International) (Renamed Presbyterian and Reformed Ministries International)	1966 1973 1984 2000	*PCC Newsletter* (1966) (Renamed *Renewal News*) (1980)

Decisive in the development of CCR was the coming together of ›Stephen Clark, ›Ralph Martin, Gerry Rauch, and Jim Cavnar to form the basis of the Word of God Community in Ann Arbor, MI. Clark and Martin were working as staff members of the ›Cursillo movement, for which Clark had done much strategic thinking and training. These men were convinced that for the renewal to affect the whole church, it was essential to train leaders and give them a thorough formation. So from its early days, CCR was characterized by conferences with an emphasis on teaching and by the production of literature for wider diffusion. From 1967, Days of Renewal were held in Williamston, MI, as occasions for initiation and teaching, gathering members of the growing number of charismatic prayer groups together with people interested in this move of the Spirit. These became a model widely followed by CCR in many countries. Each year from 1969 on, CCR leaders were invited to a conference at Ann Arbor, at which Clark and others shared their vision and strategy for church renewal through CCR and BHS. ›Life in the Spirit seminars were developed within the Word of God community to prepare people for BHS, and these were soon made available for wider use. This prominence of the Word of God community ensured that covenant-community concept became a dominant model and an attractive option for many Catholic charismatic groups in these years.

While Clark was the strategist behind these formative initiatives, close links remained between the Ann Arbor leaders and those in South Bend, IN, where each spring an annual CCR conference was held. In 1969 a Center for Service and Communication was formed to serve CCR. Out of this center grew ›Charismatic Renewal Services as an agency to service CCR with literature, tapes, and prayer-group directories.

In 1970 a National Service Committee (NSC) for CCR was formed with nine members, all from the southern Michigan–northern Indiana area, combining the administrative experience of the South Bend leaders and the teaching gifts of Ann Arbor. Such structures, unthinkable in early pentecostalism, can be seen as a fusion of pentecostal elements with Catholic expertise in organized Christian formation. As a result, CCR acquired within four years a sense of identity with a coordinated leadership and the channels of communication needed for rapid expansion.

These Catholic patterns were soon to have a major impact on CR in other churches. The greater publicity given to "Catholic pentecostalism" and its rapid expansion challenged the charismatics in other churches. They were stimulated to relate their charismatic experience to their own tradition and to have a vision for church renewal through the Holy Spirit. As a result, charismatics in other traditions began to hold their own conferences and organize their own fellowships. Some were denominational (such as the Episcopalian), though more of them represented confessional families (such as the Lutheran, the Mennonite, and the Presbyterian). Although the Presbyterian Charismatic Communion was formed before CCR began, it was initially limited to ministers and only began its promotional role following the Catholic lead. The chart below illustrates the sequence of these developments in the wake of the organization and expansion of CCR.

Among these confessional or denominational groupings, the Episcopalians and the Lutherans were the strongest. This may reflect a greater sense of confessional identity in liturgical and sacramental traditions, though it also reflects factors intrinsic to the renewal movement. Among Episcopalians, the influence of Dennis Bennett and St. Luke's, Seattle, was further enhanced by his best-selling book *Nine O'Clock in the Morning* (1970). By the mid 1970s, more than 150 pastors from the Seattle area had been baptized in the Spirit through the ministry of Bennett's church, and a pastors' fellowship that sponsored several teaching conferences was formed. Another major Episcopalian influence antedating CCR was Holy Redeemer Parish, Houston, TX, under the leadership of ►W. Graham Pulkingham. Although the Holy Spirit's work of renewal began there in 1965, it was in the early 1970s that it received wide publicity and became a model, not only for the integration of the denominational and the charismatic, but also for the formation of church community with its potential for social transformation. Another characteristic of Episcopalian renewal favoring denominational integration was the connection with the movement in Britain, with ►Michael Harper and a strong Anglican presence in the ►Fountain Trust.

The emergence of a strong current of CR among Lutherans was fostered both by the emergence of Larry Christenson as foremost leader and by the geographical concentration of American Lutherans in the Upper Midwest. The annual Lutheran renewal conference in Minneapolis, MN, attracted an attendance second only to the Catholic conferences. Lutheran charismatics were also drawn together to defend their orthodoxy against the accusation that they fell under Luther's condemnation of 16th-century Spirit enthusiasts as *Schwärmer* (fanatics). The strong ecumenical thrust of the first years is shown in the invitation of Stephen B. Clark and the Word of God Community to host two national leaders' conferences for Lutherans in 1974 and 1975.

The early to mid 1970s saw a steady stream of official church reactions to CR in North America. Only a minority of denominations clearly opposed the movement: the Church of the Nazarene (1970) declared the incompatibility of glossolalia with their formularies, while the LC–MS came out with lengthy and consistently negative statements, whose regularity (church documents of 1972 and 1977 and a seminary statement of 1975) pointed to the extent of charismatic activity within LC–MS. The LC–MS regarded CR as both unscriptural and un-Lutheran (1975), though it did not deny authenticity to every aspect of charismatic experience. Although the denomination did not call for the expulsion of charismatics and called for charismatic pastors to be "allowed time to wrestle with their consciences" (1977), their seminary in Springfield, IL (later in Fort Wayne, IN) established procedures to exclude professed charismatics from ordination (1975).

The majority of denominations adopted positions of cautious openness, neither welcoming CR with enthusiasm nor rejecting it as inauthentic. They generally accepted in principle the validity of pentecostal experience and the availability of the charismata but rejected the pentecostal theology of a second baptism subsequent to conversion and the necessity

of glossolalia. Most, however, made a genuine effort to recognize the positive elements of new life brought to the churches by CR. This is in general the position of the United Presbyterian Church (1970); the Presbyterian Church in the U.S. (1971); ALC (1973); the Lutheran Church in America (1974); the Presbyterian Church in Canada (1974, 1975, 1976); the Reformed Church in America (1975); the Roman Catholic Church in the U.S. (1975); the Roman Catholic Church in Canada (1975); the United Methodist Church (1976); and the Mennonite Church (1977). The statements of the Lutheran and Reformed churches tend to be the most theological, while the thrust of the Catholic statements is predominantly pastoral.

CR frequently encountered strong resistance in the largest white Protestant denomination in the U.S., the Southern Baptist Convention (SBC), though no denominational statement was made at the national level. Some charismatic Baptist congregations were expelled by their state associations, such as the large Beverly Hills Baptist Church in Dallas, TX, pastored by ►Howard Conatser; this church, however, continued its membership in the national SBC until Conatser's death in 1978. Others simply withdrew in the face of assertions that charismatics had no place in SBC. Many others continued as charismatic congregations within SBC, keeping a low profile by not advertising their charismatic involvement.

Among the American (Northern) Baptists, CR encountered much less resistance, as the regular holding of popular workshops on CR within the American Baptist conventions showed. Throughout the 1970s, effective leadership for American Baptist charismatics came from the First Baptist Church, Chula Vista, CA, led by Ken Pagard. Their local church newsletter, *Our Life Together*, was expanded around 1972 to serve the denomination more widely. Pagard's church emphasized community life and developed an extensive system of residential households, rather similar to Holy Redeemer in Houston among Episcopalians. An important teaching role was played among American Baptist charismatics by ►Howard Ervin, professor of OT at Oral Roberts University in Tulsa, OK.

These years of denominational organization in CR did not inhibit or prevent cross-fertilization and interaction across church and national boundaries. While leaders in particular church traditions began to exercise greater influence within their own territories, the charismatic rank and file were generally eager to accept the teachings and inspiration of any Spirit-filled preacher. The early 1970s saw a torrent of charismatic literature, some from new pentecostal-charismatic publishing houses like Logos International, Plainfield, NJ, begun by ►Dan Malachuk in 1971, others from existing publishers, such as Fleming H. Revell and the Paulist Press, who saw the potential in the charismatic market. Several charismatic books became best-sellers, both by mainline-church authors, such as ‣Kevin and Dorothy Ranaghan (*Catholic Pentecostals* [1969]) and Dennis Bennett (*Nine O'Clock in the Morning* [1970]), and independent writers, such as Merlin Carothers (*Prison to Praise* [1970]), Pat Boone (*A New Song* [1970]), and ‣Don Basham (*Deliver Us from Evil* [1972]). Toward the mid 1970s a wave of new books on healing began, from authors such as ‣Francis MacNutt, Dennis and Matthew Linn, ‣Michael Scanlan, ‣Barbara Shlemon, and Ruth Carter Stapleton. All these books achieved sales crossing denominational boundaries and contributed to the wider spread of the movement.

The period that saw the organization and mushrooming of CR in the historic churches was also the time of the dramatic rise and growth of nondenominational Spirit-filled assemblies and networks and of the first signs of major charismatic use of the mass media. These years saw the rise of Melodyland Christian Center in Anaheim, CA (under ‣Ralph Wilkerson); the expansion into the media of the teaching ministry of ‣Kenneth Hagin in Tulsa, OK; the founding by ‣Pat Robertson of the Christian Broadcasting Network (CBN) in Virginia Beach, VA; and the spread across Canada of *Crossroads*, led by ‣David Mainse in Ontario; as well as the proliferation of many other ministries, such as those of Charles and Frances Hunter, ‣Kenneth and Gloria Copeland, ‣John Osteen, Roxanne Brant, ‣Gerald Derstine, and ‣Bob Weiner. With many of these independent ministries, the labels "charismatic" and "pentecostal" were sometimes used interchangeably. Even if independents whose ethos and doctrine are indistinguishable from those of classical pentecostal preachers are termed "independent pentecostals," and those whose patterns and teaching are influenced by nonpentecostal sources are called "charismatic," the independent pentecostals would still need mention in any history of CR. For the clientele of the independent pentecostals has been primarily outside the pentecostal churches, with vast numbers of hearers and viewers coming from mainline church membership.

Among the independent developments having a major impact on the American scene was the rise of Christian Growth Ministries (CGM) and the *New Wine* magazine in Fort Lauderdale, FL. CGM was originally known as the ‣Holy Spirit Teaching Mission (HSTM); it was begun by a committee of 40 who were mostly denominational charismatics in search of solid teaching. HSTM organized teaching conferences; the teachers included four men who later became the basic CGM team: ‣Derek Prince, a classics scholar with some years in pentecostal missions in Kenya; ‣Don Basham, a pastor originally from the Disciples of Christ; ‣Charles Simpson, a Southern Baptist pastor from Mobile, AL; and ‣Bob Mumford, a former pentecostal who had then trained at a Reformed Episcopal Seminary. In 1969

HSTM began the monthly magazine *New Wine* to promote solid teaching to help the vast members of new charismatics to mature in their faith. In 1970 Basham, Mumford, Prince, and Simpson were asked to become more involved in HSTM when a moral problem and financial difficulties threatened its future. These four men soon sensed a call to submit their lives to one another for mutual protection and direction. All four maintained their existing personal ministries, while submitting to each other the basic pattern of their lives and ministries. They were joined in 1974 by ‣Ern Baxter.

The initial thrust of CGM was to bring Spirit-baptized Christians to maturity and to teach church-building. In 1972 they terminated the regular teaching conferences at Fort Lauderdale, sensing a need to spread these across the nation. Even though the issues for which the CGM team became known in the mid 1970s—discipling and pastoring—were consciously pursued only from 1972 on, the leaders had already practiced discipling for a few years, preparing young men for ministry through the sharing of life on the model of Jesus' training of the Twelve. As they began to reflect more systematically on the patterns of biblical pastoral authority, they taught explicitly on such topics as authority, submission, discipleship (training of Christians for ministry), and pastoring-shepherding (pastoral care of practicing ministers). As a result, large numbers of charismatic pastors began to be shepherded by the CGM leaders, a development that went uncharted but not unnoticed. It was uncharted because these relationships were personal and not institutional, so there were never any published lists of pastors and congregations being shepherded by CGM leaders. It did not pass unnoticed because involvement with CGM changed local patterns of ministerial cooperation, and problem cases caused growing friction between the CGM teachers and other charismatic leaders, particularly heads of other independent ministries. In 1975 these difficulties erupted in public controversy. While many respected leaders were opposed to the CGM discipleship teaching (e.g., D. Bennett, D. du Plessis), matters came to a head when ‣Kathryn Kuhlman refused to speak at the Holy Spirit Conference in Jerusalem if Mumford was on the platform, Pat Robertson banned CGM speakers from CBN programs, and Demos Shakarian likewise excluded them from FGBMFI gatherings.

The key concepts in contention were authority, submission, shepherding, and discipleship. The CGM team saw these as scriptural principles, much needed to combat Protestant individualism and charismatic freelancing. In this, they found support from the Catholic leaders of the ecumenical Word of God community, Ann Arbor, MI, particularly S. Clark and R. Martin, with whom they had collaborated in holding Shepherds Conferences at Montreat, NC (1974), and Kansas City (1975). Their positions also found support in the book *Disciple* by the Argentinian ‣Juan

Carlos Ortiz, published in 1975. The opponents of CGM saw themselves as the defenders of the Reformation heritage of the priesthood of all believers threatened by new sources of authority and teaching over and above the Word of God. A series of meetings were held between the summer of 1975 and the spring of 1976 involving CGM teachers, some of their principal critics, and other respected CR leaders. These led to "a statement of concern and regret" by the CGM leaders, in which they affirmed the essential soundness of their teachings but asked forgiveness for the pastoral mistakes they had made. The discipleship debate received extensive coverage in charismatic journals, especially *Logos, New Wine,* and *New Covenant.*

Despite such headlines as "Deepening Rift in the Charismatic Movement" (*Christianity Today,* Oct. 10, 1975), this controversy probably contributed to the overall maturing of the movement. It led to a meeting of most of the disputants for prayer and discussion, with a common recognition of the need for reconciliation. This somewhat uncommon occurrence in ecclesiastical disputes made both sides face up more squarely to what all recognized to be important issues. Concretely, as a result, an annual meeting of charismatic leaders became more formally constituted as the Charismatic Concerns Committee, which has subsequently met each year, initially at Glencoe, MO. Furthermore, the more formal organization made possible the participation of persons from both sides of the dispute in the Kansas City, MO, conference of July 1977.

The 1977 Conference on CR in the Christian Churches at Kansas City concluded this formative period of American CR. In many ways Kansas City summed up the achievements and advances of the previous decade. It brought together in one demonstration more than 50,000 charismatic leaders and people from virtually all strands of the movement: denominational CR leaders, independent teachers, both discipling and antidiscipling, messianic Jews, and a few pentecostal leaders. Its format recognized both the distinctiveness of each grouping (the morning sessions were arranged according to church membership) and the overall unity of this work of the Spirit (all met together for plenary sessions each evening in Arrowhead Stadium). The conference reflected the confident forward surge of CR and provided many memorable vignettes of God's power to transcend human expectations— of ▸Cardinal Suenens of Belgium seated alongside ▸Thomas F. Zimmerman of the AG; of the first major impact on CR of the ▸messianic Jews, with their chant and the footwashing at their symposium; of the joint witness to reconciliation by ▸Bill Burnett, white archbishop from South Africa, and ▸James Forbes, black pentecostal preacher.

Participants in Kansas City (July 1977) experienced the conference as an outstanding ecumenical event. It strongly reinforced people's sense of CR as a remarkable work of God intentionally spanning all the churches and with an evident power to transcend inherited patterns of division. It gave signs of a new maturity and depth, as in the prophecies that summoned Christians, particularly church leaders and pastors, to repentance for attachment to their own priorities, and to "mourn ... weep ... for the broken body of my Son."

The conference by its organization and structure underlined the importance of the denominational renewal fellowships and indeed helped to ensure their formation in church traditions previously without any charismatic service agency, such as the United Methodists and the United Church of Christ. The decade from 1967 to 1977 thus ended with denominational CR firmly established with its own structures, yet with a recognition of CR's ecumenical character, plus a plethora of independent ministries of evangelism, healing, and teaching.

D. Consolidation (1977–87).

The heading "Consolidation" indicates agreement with the subtitle of ▸Richard Quebedeaux's *New Charismatics II,* "How a Christian Renewal Movement Became Part of the American Religious Mainstream." However, what was happening to CR besides more widespread recognition can be variously interpreted. Some saw the movement in America peaking in the early 1980s; the majority, however, saw CR as continuing to spread, but in a new and less sensational pattern of growth. Certainly, CR in the historic churches was no longer a novelty and attracted less attention than in the previous decade. Moreover, most would agree that the élan and promise of the Kansas City conference did not last.

Some of the Kansas City ecumenical enthusiasm was manifest in the Jesus rallies held on Pentecost Sunday for a number of years. The first rally, "Jesus '78," in Meadowlands, NJ, was the brainchild of pentecostal ▸Dan Malachuk, strongly supported by Catholic Fr. Jim Ferry. This rally drew 55,000 people. In the following years, Jesus rallies were held in many U.S. cities, reaching more than 100 in 1980. They were intended to be manifestations of Christian unity in praise and witness, animated by, but not restricted to, charismatic Christians. In many places, the Jesus rallies were the largest and most representative Christian gatherings ever held, and they did much to impart a sense of the grassroots ecumenical thrust of CR. Their momentum, however, did not continue far into the 1980s.

That things were never quite the same after Kansas City was more quickly evident in CCR. The era of the big conferences ended, partly because the leaders of some major covenant communities believed they had served their purpose and that the future thrust should be the formation of strong and lasting communities. Thus, no subsequent annual CCR conference at Notre Dame ever reached the numbers that attended prior to 1977. The year 1978 saw the last of the large East Coast CCR conventions, which did not survive a change of venue from Atlantic City, NJ, to New York City.

Business at Charismatic Renewal Services and other CCR agencies began to level out and then decline.

The impression of decline or peaking seems to have been a predominantly Catholic perception, reflecting the distinctive patterns within CCR. It is largely made up of charismatic prayer groups, only loosely associated with official church structures; such informal groups do not have a high survival rate in an eclectic and highly mobile society. The strength and continuity in CCR's first 20 years was most marked in the covenant communities (see ▸Charismatic Communities).

While in the mid 1970s the alternative to communities was sought in parish prayer groups, in the 1980s the thrust of CCR outside the covenant communities came increasingly from the diocesan liaisons. Since the mid 1970s, Catholic bishops in the U.S. had been appointing individuals (generally priests but occasionally religious sisters and laypeople) as liaisons between the bishop and CCR in each diocese. By the late 1970s the liaisons were organizing themselves nationally, with a national newsletter and annual conferences (from 1978) augmented by an annual theological symposium (from 1979). By the mid 1980s most liaisons had become full-time diocesan coordinators for CR. The number of diocesan pastoral centers for CR, or for spiritual renewal but staffed by CR people, soared to over 50 by 1986 and 80 by 1987; these provided new focal points for the movement locally. CCR conferences became regional, sometimes diocesan, organized by local service committees. Among the most successful was Southern California Renewal Communities (known as SCRC), led by Fr. Ralph Tichenor until his death in 1983.

The rapid diffusion of CR among Catholics has stimulated much greater Catholic interest in Bible reading and Bible study. This need was principally met by two monthly magazines—*God's Word Today* (begun in 1979 and edited by George Martin, originally of the Word of God Community, Ann Arbor, MI) and *The Word among Us* (begun in 1981 and associated until 1995 with the Mother of God community, Gaithersburg, MD).

In most of the historic Protestant denominations CR grew steadily during this decade, particularly in churches with denominational or confessional renewal fellowships. Their conferences, with the exception of the Lutherans, who are more geographically concentrated in the Upper Midwest, were relatively small in numbers and attracted less attention. However, the number of denominational renewal conferences multiplied during the 1980s, as did the staff of the denominational fellowships and the size and circulation of their newsletters (the Episcopalian *Acts 29* increased circulation from 20,000 to 40,000 between 1985 and 1987, and the Methodist *Manna* increased to 15,000). CR among American Baptists had been flagging in the late 1970s, in part because the community model and style of the Chula Vista church had become a contentious issue, but it took on new momentum in 1982. Gary Clark, formerly of Salem, NH, took over the leadership of the ▸American Baptist Charismatic Fellowship, changing it from an informal body into a legal organization and forming a national service committee in 1983.

In the Protestant churches in Canada, CR was much slower to develop national structures than in the U.S., as both geography and economics favored north-south communications (to and from the U.S.) rather than east-west. A Renewal Fellowship was established in the United Church as an association of evangelical Christians as early as 1965. Over the years more of its chapters have become charismatic in some sense, reaching 80% by 1987. Its magazine, *The Small Voice*, was changed to a larger format in 1986, becoming simply *Fellowship Magazine* in 1989. In the Anglican Church of Canada there are many parishes with small charismatic groups but as yet few in which rectors have been leading whole congregations into renewal. Anglican Renewal Ministries was formed as a national service agency for CR, publishing since 1986 a quarterly, *Tongues of Fire*, renamed *Anglicans for Renewal Canada* in 1991. In general, Protestant opposition to CR in Canada, unlike the U.S., came from traditionalist more than from liberal circles.

CR in the Protestant churches has concentrated more on congregational renewal, in contrast to CCR, where many parish prayer groups have been formed, but few charismatically renewed parishes have resulted. The main thrust of Protestant denominational renewal fellowships has been to foster and encourage strong renewed congregations. This concern led in 1981 to the establishment of the interdenominational Parish Renewal Council. The council did not lead to the results hoped for, and the organization did not long survive the first reassessment of its goals in 1984.

Whereas the earlier strength of CCR was in the covenant communities, the role models in Protestant CR throughout have been the renewed parishes, in which there has been an integration of denominational and charismatic elements over many years. For a list of local churches that were recognized in the 1980s as pioneering models of renewed congregational life, see the first edition (*Dictionary of Pentecostal and Charismatic Movements*, 1988, 140).

The decade since 1977 saw an increased emphasis on teaching among mainline Protestant charismatics. The only Protestant church grouping using the Word of God community ▸Life in the Spirit seminars to any appreciable extent was the Episcopal, though Episcopalian charismatics also use the Saints Alive program from Britain. From 1983 on, the Presbyterians developed their own initiation-teaching program known as Spirit Alive Missions. This is a three-year series, with the first year focusing on the lordship of Jesus Christ, the second on the healing ministry of the church, and the third on discovering and ministering one's gifts. There were several initiation programs among the Methodists, while among the Lutherans individual congregations formulated their own patterns of teaching.

Opposition to CR was fiercest and most sustained among the leaders of the Orthodox church, whose bishops and theologians viewed the movement as intrinsically Protestant. A small group led by Fr. Boris Zabrodsky continued to produce *Theosis* until 1988, but almost all the Orthodox priests renewed in the Spirit over the previous 20 years withdrew under pressure. ▸Fr. Eusebius Stephanou, formerly of Fort Wayne, IN, was canonically suspended for a number of years, and Fr. Athanasios Emmert, faced with a choice between CR and Orthodoxy, became a Melkite Catholic at the end of 1987.

While the opposition to charismatics was declining in many other denominations, opposition continued in LC–MS and SBC. CR continued to spread among Southern Baptists, however. Many Southern Baptists baptized in the Spirit used the term *fullness* rather than *charismatic* to describe Spirit-filled Christian life, avoiding explicitly pentecostal terminology and doctrine (e.g., tongues as initial evidence) and other emphases seen as extreme or narrow. There were approximately 400 Fullness churches in SBC in 1987. The bi-monthly *Fullness,* published from 1978 on in Fort Worth, TX, by Baptist layman Ras Robinson, sought to build bridges between Fullness people and traditional Southern Baptists. The ministry of James Robison, a Southern Baptist pastor in Euless, TX, increasingly had a charismatic dimension, with prayer for the sick and the exorcism of evil spirits. His bimonthly *Restoration* testified to "God's move to return His Church to the power, purity and majesty He intended it to have in preparation for the coming of Christ in glory."

This decade also saw a multiplication in the number of healing ministries. New developments included the emergence of Catholic healing ministries concentrated in parishes and dioceses, such as those of ▸Ralph DiOrio of Worcester, MA, and Edward McDonough of Boston, MA. Ministries focusing on inner healing saw major expansion: among Protestants, those of John Sanford, an Episcopal priest and son of Agnes Sanford, and of ▸Leanne Payne; among Catholics, the ministries of ▸Briege McKenna, the Linn brothers, ▸Barbara Shlemon, and others. Some noticeable differences have emerged among those ministries that have a stronger psychological base, often Jungian, and those with a greater spiritual emphasis on repentance for sin. While these healing ministries have been charismatic in experience and expression, though not all in origin, the people they reach are the sick, whether or not they are interested in CR. As with the healing evangelists of the 1950s and '60s, these divine healers of the '80s contributed to the spread of charismatic experience but not by the formation of explicitly charismatic groups.

This period was particularly characterized by an explosion of nondenominational charismatic assemblies, among whom a complete classification is virtually impossible. The majority of these assemblies, however, tend to acquire affiliation or connections with some network or association of charismatic assemblies and/or pastors. These cover a spectrum ranging from explicit acceptance of the transcongregational authority of a charismatic leader to occasional participation in leaders' fellowships that in no way restrict congregational autonomy.

The largest association in this period representing a particular bloc of convictions was the National Leadership Conference (NLC), formed in 1979 largely through the initiative of Ken Sumrall. NLC brought together leaders whose ministries already served networks of charismatic assemblies, in particular Sumrall of Liberty Church, Pensacola, FL (with some 350 to 400 local churches); ▸Gerald Derstine of Bradenton, FL (who followed Sumrall as president); Bill Ligon of Brunswick, GA; Russ Williamson of Hopewell Junction, NY; Ernest Gruen of Kansas City, MO; Bob Heil of Hillsboro, MO; and Bob Wright of Davidsonville, MD. The director of the NLC was Jim Jackson, of Montreat, NC. As this list indicates, the NLC constituency was almost entirely east of the Mississippi. NLC was clear that it was not a new denomination, but a fellowship of charismatic leaders with common convictions and a similarity of vision. Many new churches named "Community Church" or "Covenant Church" belonged to NLC, reflecting a conviction that they were bound together by regeneration in the one new covenant of Jesus Christ. This "covenant" usage is thus different from that of the covenant communities constituted by an explicit covenant commitment. It reflected rather a desire for unity in the body of Christ and a willingness to fellowship with all in whom they recognized the work of the Spirit. NLC churches practiced believers' baptism and regarded BHS as part of the normal Christian life. They expected to see the fivefold ministry of Eph. 4:11 operative in their churches without entitling leaders with particular ministries. The NLC committee was made up of leaders recognized to have an apostolic dimension to their ministry. Thus, groupings within NLC represented more-organized networks under an apostolic leader, but NLC remained a nondirective fellowship of like-minded leaders.

A similar pattern of "nondenominational" charismatic Christianity arose in the People of Destiny network. In 1977 Larry Tomczak and C. J. Mahaney founded a church in Wheaton, MD, which became Covenant Life Church in Gaithersburg, MD, pastored by Mahaney. In 1982 they founded People of Destiny International to provide pastoral care for other local churches and the training of leaders. By 1987 there were 16 churches in this network. These assemblies were similar in many ways to the churches linked to NLC, both in their style of worship and in their presbyterian patterns of church government. Their main distinction was a stronger emphasis on God's restoration of the NT church in the end times, a point on which they may have been influenced by the Bradford (Harvestime) network of the ▸House Church Movement in Britain. Their bimonthly magazine, *People of Destiny*, was similar to the Bradford bimonthly *Restoration*. This group also had close links with the Maranatha Christian churches that had their origin in the campus and youth ministry of Bob Weiner, based in Gainesville, FL.

Another stream is the Fellowship of Covenant Ministers and Conferences (FCMC) formed by ▸Charles Simpson in 1987. FCMC, with approximately 350 members, represented the sector of the discipling-shepherding ministry of CGM that survived the final dissolution of the old CGM team in 1985. The FCMC theology of covenant was similar to that of NLC, except that a functional commitment (not regarded as a covenant) was made between the pastoring pastor and the pastored pastor.

Alongside these independent charismatic assemblies was the controversial phenomenon of the "electronic church," the world of the television evangelists. Some of these were pentecostal in ministerial affiliation, as were ▸Jim Bakker (until 1987) and ▸Jimmy Swaggart (until 1988), whereas others were independent, like ▸Kenneth Copeland and ▸Kenneth Hagin. ▸Pat Robertson had Southern Baptist credentials until he resigned in 1987 in view of his presidential candidacy. These and other TV ministries became multimillion-dollar industries with enormous followings. Studies showed that members of historic denominations formed a large part of their clientele, including many Catholics. Concern about aspects of these ministries, such as their lack of accountability, found clearer expression following the scandals uncovered in the Bakkers' PTL ministry at Charlotte, NC, in 1987.

In Canada, where access to media time is more regulated, a different pattern emerged in charismatic media ministry. In 1977 David Mainse began daily Christian TV, known by the address of his Toronto studios: *100 Huntley Street*. Mainse, a PAOC minister, accepted denominational regulations regarding accountability, with PAOC representatives on his board. At the same time, Mainse made *100 Huntley Street* a vehicle for all Spirit-filled Christianity, inviting charismatic participation by having two priests on his staff, Al Reimers (Anglican) and Bob MacDougall (Roman Catholic). In many ways, *100 Huntley Street* has provided a distinctive Canadian charismatic focal point in a country where national organization has been slow to develop. In 1984, with support from Mainse, MacDougall started a separate Catholic charismatic ministry, *Food for Life*.

Besides the associations of "nondenominational" assemblies already mentioned, one grouping that is pentecostal in origin and confession evolved to become more like the NLC

assemblies than the old-line pentecostal denominations. This is the International Communion of Charismatic Churches, led in the U.S. in the 1980s by Bishops ▸John Meares of Evangel Temple, Washington, DC, and ▸Earl Paulk of Chapel Hill Harvester Church, Decatur, GA. Prior to any influence from CR, these pentecostals focused their ministry more on worship, teaching, and church formation than on dramatic preaching and healings. Other large city churches that followed the same path were those pastored by Charles Green in New Orleans, LA, and ▸James Beall of Detroit, MI. In addition, a number of pentecostal churches have been renewed through their contact with CR, one being the Calvary Assembly of God, Orlando, FL, out of which came the initiative for the monthly *Charisma*, edited by ▸Stephen Strang, which perhaps uniquely spans the pentecostal and charismatic public.

The International Convention of Faith Ministries (ICFM), headquartered in Tulsa, OK, was formed in 1974 as an "organization without denomination." ICFM (with Happy Caldwell as president and Terry Mize as secretary) held regular conventions at many levels and had a particular emphasis on leadership training. A looser fraternal fellowship entitled Charismatic Bible Ministries (CBM) was established by Oral Roberts in 1986 "for the advancement of the Unity of the Body of Christ through Love and Mighty Signs and Wonders." CBM brought together for mutual support both pentecostal and nondenominational ministers and in 1987 had 1,200 members across the U.S., many of whom were involved in closer forms of fellowship and association already noted. CBM's Statement of Beliefs mentioned the spiritual gifts, including tongues as "the prayer language of the Spirit," but without any mention of BHS.

Besides the nondenominational assemblies forming part of wider associations, there were independent charismatic churches without any such links. Many of these were former Southern Baptist churches, whose convictions about congregational autonomy discouraged them from participation in any national networks. There remained some independent teachers, such as Judson Cornwall, who remained unaffiliated and who opposed discipleship teaching.

One of the most dramatic new developments of the 1980s was the rise of the ▸"signs and wonders" praxis and teaching associated with ▸John Wimber and his ▸Vineyard Fellowship, based in Yorba Linda, CA. While the origins of the Vineyard go back to 1978, Wimber's distinctive ministry came to prominence in 1983 through publicity given to the Signs and Wonders course offered at Fuller Theological Seminary in Pasadena by ▸C. Peter Wagner, assisted by Wimber. Wagner was responsible for labeling the resulting movement "The Third Wave": he saw the "signs and wonders" teaching as a third phase in some continuity with, but distinct from, the pentecostal and charismatic movements. The proliferation of Vineyard Fellowships across the American continent (200 churches in 1987) gave rise to another grouping of nondenominational charismatic assemblies.

The "third wave" terminology was introduced because Wimber's teaching was welcomed in many evangelical circles previously closed to CR. Wimber's wider acceptability partly resulted from his emphasis on signs and wonders as a normal element in evangelism and church growth rather than any second-blessing experience. Ministers were reassured by his openness to evangelical scholarship, shown in his links with Fuller and by his homely style and lack of self-promotion in contrast to some more flamboyant ministries. Wimber's ministry undoubtedly gave CR a boost in the mid 1980s, as shown by the increased attendance at the events in which he participated. His "signs and wonders" teaching has been accepted in many charismatic milieus, as, for example, among the Episcopalians where ›Bishop David Pytches of England has formulated this emphasis in an Anglican framework.

The ecumenical dimension of CR received a new stimulus from the New Orleans conference of Oct. 1986 (leaders) and July 1987 (general public) organized by the ›North American Renewal Service Committee, with ›Vinson Synan as chairman. The committee established for this purpose represented a wider range of denominations and charismatic networks than that for Kansas City 10 years previously. The newcomers included pentecostal denominations such as the Pentecostal Holiness Church, the Church of God, the Church of God Pentecostal, and the International Church of the Foursquare Gospel, as well as groupings like Youth With A Mission (YWAM) and Maranatha Christian Churches. Both conferences linked the outpouring of the Spirit with world evangelization and were planned as part of a process leading to a world congress in 1990 followed by a decade of evangelism to win at least half the world for Christ by the year 2000.

Neither of the New Orleans conferences drew the crowd the organizers hoped for and initially predicted. The numbers at the general conference in July 1987 reached 35,000 and may have been reduced by the Bakker scandal and associated publicity. As at Kansas City, the Catholics constituted 50% of the attendance. New Orleans 1987 lacked something of the prophetic thrust and élan of Kansas City 1977, but any event that gathers so many in fellowship from such a wide range of backgrounds has many unforeseen effects.

The number of Americans claiming to be involved in CR varied according to sources and methods of computation. A *Christianity Today* poll in 1980 found that between 18% and 21% of adult American Baptists, Catholics, Lutherans, and Methodists considered themselves charismatic. The same poll, however, discovered that only a small fraction of the professed charismatics have ever spoken in tongues (17% of all pentecostals and charismatics, higher among pentecostals and lower among charismatics).

There is no reason to doubt the accuracy of the poll statistics; however, they tabulate how American Christians understand their own experience and do not provide evidence for active participation in charismatic groups. The statistics, however, do suggest that church people in general viewed CR positively and accepted it as part of the religious mainstream. CR leaders in the Lutheran and Presbyterian churches estimated that at least 10% of their ordained ministers are charismatic, a higher percentage than among the laity. American Catholics active in CR were calculated in the mid 1980s as 250,000 in some 6,000 groups.

Continued ascent or commencing decline? The overall evidence suggested that the number of Spirit-baptized Christians in North America continued to increase throughout the 1970s and '80s. But the increase was not equal in every sector. A Presbyterian leader estimated that 50% of Presbyterian charismatics were leaving to join independent charismatic or pentecostal churches. It seems likely that this percentage was similar to that in many mainline church traditions, though the figure would be lower among Catholics, except in Quebec. The membership of major pentecostal denominations, such as AG, soared during this period, and their leaders agreed in attributing their extraordinary growth rate to the accession of many charismatics who were unable to accommodate their new spiritual fervor within their previous churches. The fastest growth, however, was among nondenominational charismatics, with perhaps the most significant expansion among those who practice a corporate leadership.

II. DEVELOPMENT IN EUROPE.

A. Origins.

In Europe, more than in America, CR had some antecedents in the ecumenical elements in pentecostal origins. European CR had precursors in those pentecostal pioneers who never left their churches of origin: ›Alexander Boddy and ›Cecil Polhill in England; ›Jonathan Paul, Karl Ecke, and C. O. Voget in Germany; Morten Larsen in Norway; J. Ongman and the Örebro Baptists in Sweden; C. E. D. DeLabillière and later Jean and Fritz de Rougemont in Switzerland; Henri de Worm in Belgium. The only direct link between these "old church" pentecostals and the later charismatics, however, appears to be through ›Louis Dallière, with whom de Worm worked closely in the 1930s, and the ›Union de Prière (UP) in France.

Although the charismatic movement in Europe did not acquire a clear-cut identity or develop recognizable structures until the 1960s, there were, besides the Ardèche revival and UP, a number of other anticipatory strands of pentecostal blessing outside the pentecostal churches. In Germany there were from 1945 on manifestations of spiritual gifts with ›Basilea Schlink and the Mary Sisters in Darmstadt. In Britain various strands are traceable back to the 1950s: the largely ex-Brethren independent groups associated with David Lillie and ›Arthur Wallis; the incidence of glossolalia among those involved in healing ministries, such as the London Healing Mission and the Evangelical Divine Healing Fellowship; the Methodist lay preacher Edgar Trout; and the spiritual quest of men active in prayer fellowships for revival, such as W. B. Grant and Eric Houfe. In Holland the "New Pentecost" goes back to the early 1950s, when ›Wim Verhoef started the Vuur (Fire) group among students. In these preparatory strands, virtually none owed their beginnings to American influences, though several (Lillie; the London Healing Mission; Trout, Grant, Houfe; Vuur) stemmed from links with European pentecostals.

The emergence of a conscious movement of CR in the early 1960s was primarily the consequence of news from America of the outbreak among Episcopalians at Van Nuys, CA, under Dennis Bennett, publicized in *Newsweek* and *Time*. British awareness owed much to Philip E. Hughes's description of a visit to California in *The Churchman* of Sept. 1962. Some 39,000 copies of Hughes's editorial were circulated in leaflet form. Of great importance too were the visits of David du Plessis, spreading the news of "Pentecost outside Pentecost." He visited England, Holland, and Switzerland in the fall of 1963, while 1964 saw him in Britain for a month, in France (Alsace), in Holland, and in Switzerland.

The deliberate correlation of the pentecostal life with a received church tradition began in Holland with Verhoef's separation from the nondenominational Karel Hoekendijk and the launching in 1957 of *Vuur* magazine, the first charismatic journal in the world to affirm pentecostal experience with traditional denominational commitment. *Vuur* was described as an ecumenical monthly by 1961, with the editorial board composed of members of both Reformed churches and the Remonstrants, expanding to include a Baptist and a Catholic by 1964.

The explicit combining of pentecostal and historic church convictions was especially the work of ›Michael Harper in England and ›Arnold Bittlinger in West Germany. The English movement developed rather more quickly for several reasons: the wider number of preparatory strands, the ready availability of American literature, and Harper's resignation from parish work and his establishment of the ›Fountain Trust (FT) in 1964 as a service agency for CR. The West German origins followed Bittlinger's American visit in late 1962, which led to Larry Christenson addressing the Enkenbach conference in Aug. 1963. In East Germany the first charismatic manifestations occurred in the early 1960s in church centers associated with evangelism and revival, helped by links with some West German Protestant religious communities.

B. Development and Expansion until 1987.

The later origins in other European countries and the development of CR throughout the continent will be described country by country, in geographical blocs.

1. The British Isles.

a. Britain. The growth of CR in Britain was slow but steady during the years 1964–70. The main thrust of expansion came from the work of Michael Harper at FT. The FT residential conferences, begun in Jan. 1965, featured the best-known teachers in the British movement (›Cecil Cousen, Campbell McAlpine, Edgar Trout, ›Arthur Wallis), and its bimonthly magazine *Renewal* served CR nationally from Jan. 1966. In the first years there was some influence by pentecostal preachers, but this declined after the mid 1960s, as the two movements settled for largely friendly coexistence rather than close cooperation. The American literature, especially David Wilkerson's *The Cross and the Switchblade* (1963) and John Sherrill's *They Speak with Other Tongues* (1964), accelerated the spread of the movement, as did regular tours by David du Plessis and visits by ›Jean Stone (1964) and Dennis Bennett (1965, 1968).

The initial impact of the movement in Britain was strongest among evangelical Anglicans. At the time of his BHS, Harper was an assistant priest at the prominent Central London evangelical parish of All Souls', Langham Place, then under the leadership of John Stott. The first Anglican parish to become a focal point for CR (from 1963) was St. Mark's, Gillingham, Kent, under John Collins, a former assistant at All Souls'. Collins's two assistants, ›David Watson and David MacInnes, soon became major figures in the movement. Other parishes in which CR had a definite impact by the mid 1960s were St. Andrew's, Chorleywood (under John Perry), and then St. Cuthbert's, York (under David Watson). Stott's opposition to the movement from early 1964 on was supported by other evangelical leaders, creating an evangelical-charismatic tension that was only overcome with the joint statement "Gospel and Spirit" in 1977.

Some Anglo-Catholic and more "high church" clergy were involved from quite an early stage (of whom ›John Gunstone was to become a valued teacher), but the main impact in these circles came in the late 1970s. After the Anglicans, the Baptists were the most impacted in the early years, with the main leadership coming from ›David Pawson, Douglas McBain, Barney Coombs, Harold Owen, Edmund Heddle, and Jim Graham. Headway was slower among the Methodists, though the first denominational initiative in British CR was ›Charles Clarke's *Newsletter for Methodists Interested in Charismatic Renewal*, begun in 1968.

The first impetus to ›restorationist thinking in Britain among those baptized in the Spirit came from the Devon conferences convened by Lillie and Wallis between 1958 and 1962. Its subsequent development is treated under ›House Church Movement (HCM). A boost to charismatic revival among Free Church and independent circles was given by the Capel (Surrey) Bible Week, held annually from 1970 to 1976. This was initiated by Fred Pride, ex-Plymouth Brethren, who had organized the evangelical Abinger Convention for many years and now saw in the Capel Bible Week its charismatic successor. Capel brought together a wide spectrum of non-Anglican charismatics: later Restoration leaders like ⸲Bryn Jones, Wallis, and ⸲Gerald Coates; independent Baptists like Owen and Michael Pusey; teachers acceptable in all circles like Cousen and McAlpine.

The high point of FT's contribution to CR in Britain was from 1971 to 1976, the era of the major conferences: Guildford (1971), Nottingham (1973), and Westminster (1975). These conferences, though small by American standards, were nonetheless national gatherings, giving the movement a higher profile and a stronger sense of identity. They also drew wider European participation, which was significant for later international fellowship. During this period, Harper was first assisted and then succeeded by ⸲Thomas Smail, whose arrival strengthened theological reflection on the movement, particularly through the journal *Theological Renewal.*

This same period saw the rise of CCR in Britain. Its beginnings were less influenced by contacts with mainline Protestant charismatics than by circles associated with the young Dominican ⸲Simon Tugwell and by their contacts with British pentecostals; by some priests' contacts with American Catholics; and by the work of an American layman, Bob Balkam, whose work in Britain began with an ecumenical society concentrating on CR. The first Catholic prayer groups developed days of renewal in London around 1970, and a National Service Committee (NSC) was formed in 1973. NSC worked closely with FT until the latter's closure in 1980.

While CCR gave rise to many prayer groups, most of them with fewer than 50 members, CR among Anglicans during the 1970s caused some parishes to acquire a reputation as centers of renewal. Besides Watson's parish in York (since 1973 at St. Michael-le-Belfrey) and St. Andrew's, Chorleywood, Hertfordshire (under Bishop ⸲David Pytches, 1977–96), CR had a major impact on St. Hugh's, Luton, Bedfordshire (first under ⸲Colin Urquhart and later under David Gillett); in St. Philip and St. James, Bristol (under Malcolm Widdecombe); in St. John's, Harborne, Birmingham (under Tom Walker); and (from the late 1970s) at Hawkwell, Essex (under Tony Higton). St. Aldate's, Oxford, welcomed a charismatic dimension under Michael Green, a development confirmed by the appointment of David MacInnes as Green's successor in 1987. Centers such as Lamplugh House, Yorkshire (under Lawrence Hoyle), and Whatcombe House, Dorset (led by Reg East), had influence for a time.

With the voluntary closure of FT at the end of 1980, when the trustees were convinced it had completed its task, the thrust of the movement within the churches shifted to denominational groupings. CR among Anglicans received a boost from an international conference held at Canterbury in July 1978, immediately before the bishops' Lambeth confer-

ence. This led the more Anglo-Catholic London Committee for Renewal to launch in 1979 the newsletter *Anglicans for Renewal.* In 1981 the General Synod of the Church of England published their favorable report *The Charismatic Renewal in the Church of England,* and in the same year Anglican Renewal Ministries was established as a service agency, taking over *Anglicans for Renewal,* retitled *ARM-Link* in 1988. Many Anglican parishes use a nine-week course called *Saints Alive!* by John Finney and Felicity Lawson to prepare church members for BHS. An Anglican survey conducted in 1984 reported between 1% and 33% of parishes per diocese experiencing renewal through CR, with a national average of 7%.

The Methodists produced a charismatic magazine, *Dunamis* (1972–95), edited for some years by William Davies, Ross Peart, and Charles Clarke. With the growing denominationalization of the movement, the *Dunamis* editors took the initiative in forming the Dunamis Renewal Fellowship in 1983. Both the United Reformed GEAR (Group for Evangelism and Renewal), dating from 1974, and Mainstream (Baptists for Life and Growth), begun in 1978, are church renewal groups wider than CR, but both have had significant charismatic membership and influence. The movement among Catholics lost impetus in the late 1970s and early '80s but in the mid 1980s acquired new dynamism with the accession of ⸲Charles Whitehead as chairman of the NSC. This new lease of life was also shown by the doubling in size of the NSC's bimonthly *Goodnews.*

The main impact of CR on the Baptists came after 1980. In the 1970s some prominent Baptist charismatic churches had become independent, with Woking (Owen), Basingstoke (Coombs), and Farnborough (Pusey) in effect becoming new ⸲restorationist networks alongside the various strands of HCM. Baptist churches such as Streatham, London (under McBain), and Gold Hill, Bucks (under Graham), continued to promote CR within the Baptist Union. Several factors helped to stabilize and promote CR among Baptists: the formation of Mainstream; the closure of the Anglican-led FT; and the rise of the ⸲Spring Harvest Easter camps that weakened the pull of the HCM Bible weeks. Mainstream, which held together evangelical and charismatic emphases, has had a major influence on Baptist life in Britain. New Baptist leaders emerged, such as Nigel Wright and Steve Gaukroger.

The 1980s saw increasing friction between CR in the mainline church traditions and some sections of HCM, particularly those centered on Bradford in Yorkshire and the bimonthly *Restoration.* The points of contention included *Restoration's* antidenominational stance and accusations of "sheep-stealing." Many charismatics from mainline denominations and several local churches (among them some pentecostal assemblies) joined HCM networks, partly through frustration at the apparent slowness of CR in the older churches, partly by being persuaded that HCM networks offered a more fully biblical pattern of church life. Not all HCM leaders distanced themselves from CR in the historic churches, however, and John Noble of Romford played a major role in the All Saints Celebrations in London, bringing together Spirit-filled believers from many traditions.

b. Scotland. The movement's growth in Scotland and Northern Ireland was somewhat slower. After an initial flurry of charismatic life in the Motherwell area in Scotland (1962–64), conferences on the movement were held at Crieff (1966) and Dunblane (1967), but the death in 1974 of D. P. Thomson, the founder of St. Ninian's Lay Training Centre at Crieff, deprived the movement of a respected leader. Various ministers in the Church of Scotland and the Free churches were baptized in the Spirit, but the Scottish movement lacked a focus for many years. FT's activities in Scotland increased in the mid 1970s with more regular teaching conferences, while in 1974 their link-man, David Black, a Baptist minister, launched Scottish Churches Renewal, which he directed, editing its bulletin, until 1980. CCR in Scotland was slower developing, with a National Service Committee being formed in 1977, but the participation of Bishop Maurice Taylor of Galloway and the magazine *The Vine,* produced by the Risen Christ community in Glasgow from 1981 until 1987, provided a more solid base for the movement. The Scottish Episcopal Renewal Fellowship was formed in 1982 under the leadership of Duncan Sladden, producing a small magazine, *The Go-Between.*

c. Ireland. In Ireland, CR among Protestants was found at least by 1963, when a Presbyterian missionary in India, David McKee, was baptized in the Spirit while on furlough in Belfast. Some ▸Elim pentecostal pastors helped other ministers to receive BHS. Around 1968 CR became more visible among Northern Irish Protestants with the arrival of Tom Smail from Scotland as minister at Whiteabbey Presbyterian Church in Belfast. The Hollywood Fellowship (pentecostal) under Keith Gerner was much involved with the new charismatics.

CCR in Ireland began in Dublin in early 1972 at a meeting addressed by Smail and Fr. Joe McGeady, an Irish priest working in England. Several other Irish Catholics received BHS around this time through American contacts. In its origins, Irish CR was notably ecumenical, and in 1974 a national committee of four Catholics and two Protestants was formed, a unique instance in worldwide CR. In the strife-torn north of Ireland, CR aroused great hope in being the first grassroots movement to touch both sides of the religious divide. The CR New Year conference in Belfast was the only major ecumenical event in the province with popular participation. The Christian Renewal Centre at Rostrevor, County Down, founded by ▸Cecil Kerr in 1974, has been a center for reconciliation.

However, the rapid growth of CR among Catholics in the south led to the organization of national conferences in Dublin beginning in 1974. Although Protestant speakers were invited, these conferences were not organized by the national committee but by Catholics only, and in Eire the earlier ecumenical dimension became largely lost. The Light of Christ community in Dublin, initially led by Fr. Martin Tierney and Tom Flynn, helped to host the international CCR conference in Dublin in 1978 and to produce the CCR monthly *New Creation.* In a strongly Catholic country with less secularized media, the Dublin conference attracted national attention, but by the mid 1980s Irish CCR was in decline, with many prayer groups becoming "Medjugorje groups," centering on Marian devotions related to the messages received in Medjugorje.

2. West-Central Europe.

a. West Germany. Initial trends toward Holy Spirit revival in the German churches were particularly associated with new communities, such as the Mary Sisters in Darmstadt [under ▸Basilea Schlink], the Jesus Brüderschaft, and Julius Schniewindhaus near Magdeburg. Some openness to the spiritual gifts occurred among groups aware of the 19th-century healing ministry of J. C. Blumhardt. The influence of these renewal centers and the impact of the movement was stronger in East Germany than in the West. (For East Germany, see below under Eastern Europe.)

CR in West Germany (FRG [Federal Republic of Germany]) was marked from the start by a strongly theological interest. The first major gatherings from 1965 were the ecumenical Königstein conferences near Frankfurt on the theme "Church and Charisma." These conferences were as much theological explorations as pastoral or evangelistic expositions. In 1968 a residential community for Christian Unity was formed at Schloss Craheim by the leaders mainly responsible for the Königstein conferences—namely, Arnold Bittlinger and R. F. Edel (Lutheran), Wilhard Becker and Siegfried Grossman (Baptist), and Eugen Mederlet (Catholic). For the next decade Schloss Craheim was the focal point for CR in the FRG, with Bittlinger as main author and Edel as publisher.

CCR in the FRG came from two main sources: (1) a visit of Fr. Herb Schneider of Manila, Philippines, to Innsbruck, Austria, in 1971 and (2) the meeting of Fr. Hubertus Tommek of West Berlin with some American charismatics in Lyon, France, and his reception of BHS in Grenoble on Pentecost 1972. From the mid 1970s until the late 1980s there were two contrasting strands of the renewal movement among German Catholics. The larger strand was led by the Paderborn theologian ▸Heribert Mühlen, who was originally influenced by his participation in the Catholic-pentecostal dialogue. Mühlen promoted *Charismatische Gemeinde Erneuerung* (CGE), parish renewal led by the clergy and based on the renewal of the sacraments, expounded in the magazine *Erneuerung in Kirche und Gesellschaft* (Renewal in Church and Society), begun in 1977. Mühlen distinguished CGE from CCR, which he saw as theologically "neo-pentecostal." The lesser strand—led by Tommek, Otto Knoch, and ▸Norbert Baumert—identified with worldwide CCR and published *Rundbrief für Charismatische Erneuerung in der Katholischen Kirche* (Circular Letter for Charismatic Renewal in the Catholic Church) from 1976. By the mid 1980s, however, the contrast between CGE and CCR was less marked, a welcome change due to the rise of new leaders in CGE and the work of the theological commission for CGE established by the West German bishops.

CR among Protestants in the state churches of the FRG, notably stronger in Bavaria than in the northern provinces, was also influenced by the CGE model, with a leadership role being taken by Wolfram Kopfermann, whose church (St. Peter's, Hamburg) was a center of renewal from 1978. Other centers of parish renewal in the West German Evangelical Church were Bendorf am Rhein (under Peter Gleiss) and Herschweiler-Pettersheim (under Günter Moll). The CGE pattern was also followed in Austria and Switzerland. In German-speaking Switzerland, the Albanarbeit, a charismatic parish in the Reformed Church in Basel, under Johannes Cswalina, exercised a strong influence. Other Reformed CR centers were Calvin House in Biel (under Markus Jakob) and the Basileia Group in the Johanneskirche in Bern under Marcel Dietler, who was often the Swiss representative at European CR meetings. In Austria, the main CGE leader was Msgr. Johann Koller, a parish pastor in Vienna.

Independent centers exercising an important influence in the FRG have been Jesus-Haus in Düsseldorf, led by Gerhard Bially, which produces the magazine *Charisma,* and the organization Projektion J, founded by Günter Oppermann. Projektion J introduced ▸John Wimber and his ▸"signs and wonders" message into Germany.

b. France. In France, a charismatic movement within the French Reformed Church arose in the early 1930s in the Ardèche revival. It was associated with the preaching of the pentecostal missionary ▸Douglas Scott and the leadership of Louis Dallière. Although Dallière became disillusioned with pentecostal sectarianism, his ecumenical charismatic vision found expression in the Union de Prière, formed after WWII. Jules Thobois, a Baptist pastor in Paris, was baptized in the Spirit following an accident in 1947 and the influence of Scott; other Baptists followed, so that in 1952 the French Baptist Federation passed a resolution allowing pentecostal practices. The beginnings of CR as an identifiable movement in France, however, resulted when, from 1968 on, several Protestant pastors received BHS through contact with pentecostals, particularly Clément le Cossec and the evangelical center at Carhaix in Brittany. In 1971 a significant meeting

was held at Charleville in northeast France, where Protestant pastors from France and Belgium met with American Presbyterian J. Rodman Williams. Links between the UP and the new wave of CR were established especially through ▸Thomas Roberts, Arnold Brémond, and Jean-Daniel Fischer. In 1971 Roberts launched an annual charismatic conference at the Protestant center La Porte Ouverte near Chalon-sur-Saone, that became one of the few regular ecumenical teaching gatherings in Western Europe; it was later moved to Gagnières.

The beginnings of CR among French Catholics occurred through a visit to France of Jean-Paul Régimbal of Quebec and through French visitors to the U.S. Xavier le Pichon, a layman from Brest, and Albert de Monléon, a young Dominican theologian, both encountered CCR during visits to America. French CCR particularly dates from a meeting near Paris in Feb. 1972 attended by Pierre Goursat and Martine Lafitte, who became the founders of the Emmanuel community. CCR's rapid spread in the years 1972–75 was aided by the translation of American literature, especially the Ranaghans' book, *Catholic Pentecostals.* The French movement in those years was notably ecumenical, with two important meetings in 1973, a theological consultation at Montpellier, and a conference for leaders at Viviers organized by the UP, presided over by Roberts, and addressed by Du Plessis, Harper, Bittlinger, and the Catholic Val Gaudet. At the Viviers conference, the UP conviction about the centrality of Israel in God's purposes was manifest, and this emphasis has since influenced much of French CR.

The movement among Protestants has been strongest in Alsace, aided by the influence of J. D. Fischer of Mulhouse (d. 1983) and the current leadership of Kurt Maeder in Strasbourg. Among the Free churches, the main centers for CR were the Point du Jour Baptist Church in Paris, led by J. Thobois, and until 1995 the largely Baptist community of Reconciliation in Lille, led by David Berly. Although charismatics have not been enthusiastically welcomed by the major French Protestant denominations, a consultation organized in 1984 by the Protestant Federation of France on the place of CR in church life led to some reconciliation and more positive attitudes.

CCR has had more impact in France than in other European countries, with some 500,000 participants. Many communities have arisen (▸charismatic communities), and the urban communities have exercised a strong leadership in the national movement. The shrine at Paray-le-Monial in central France, long associated with devotion to the Sacred Heart of Jesus, has been rejuvenated through becoming a center of renewal under the direction of the Emmanuel community, with a succession of teaching conferences each summer. Another pilgrimage center at Ars has also had an increasing charismatic presence. The magazines *Il est Vivant! (He Lives!*; published by Emmanuel in Paris from 1975), *Tychique* (more scholarly, though not technical, published by Chemin Neuf from 1977), and *Feu et Lumière* (Fire and Light; published by the Lion de Juda/Beatitudes community since 1983) are of an impressive quality. The movement has been taken more seriously by more Catholic theologians in France than elsewhere, these theologians being both sympathetic observers (such as Yves Congar) and participants (such as ˈRené Laurentin, Jean-Claude Sagne, Albert de Monléon, and Juan-Miguel Garrigues). A positive report on CR was made to the Catholic bishops in 1982 by Msgr. Marcus, then bishop of Nantes, and many French bishops have entrusted significant pastoral responsibilities to CR groups, particularly to the major communities. This greater church acceptance has been accompanied by some loss in ecumenical expression, and some disappointment among Protestant charismatics who earlier were excited by the ecumenical beginnings. The ecumenical thrust in French CCR came mostly from the Chemin Neuf community centered in Lyon and the Puits de Jacob community in Strasbourg.

c. Holland. The charismatic movement in Holland was associated from an early date with the magazine *Vuur,* edited by ˈWim Verhoef and described as an "ecumenical monthly for revival." The 1958 Dutch campaign of the healing evangelist T. L. Osborn gave a further impetus to CR. Important for reaching ministers in the historic churches were the visits of ˈDavid du Plessis, who as an Afrikaans speaker was able to preach without an interpreter. Fr. Jos Biesbrouck, later prominent in CCR in the Low Countries, was baptized in the Spirit at a Du Plessis meeting in Utrecht in 1965.

In 1972, following the European leaders' meeting at Schloss Craheim, three organizations (Vuur, Oase, and the Near East Mission) joined forces to form the Charismatische Werkgemeenschap Nederland (Dutch charismatic work fellowship; CWN). The Near East Mission soon left but was replaced by the Dutch CCR. The role of CWN helped the Dutch movement to be more ecumenical than in many other countries, though some Catholic charismatics showed more ecumenical reticence in the 1980s.

In recent years CR has made the most impact on the Re-reformed church, the most Calvinist grouping, and their national organization has established a committee for official relationships with CWN. Besides Verhoef, the most prominent leader in CR among Protestants was Willem (Wim) van Dam of Geldrop. The parachurch movement ˈYouth With A Mission (YWAM) has also had considerable impact in Holland, especially through the ministry of Floyd McClung.

The movement in Holland was always rather theological (Verhoef being theologically qualified) and attracted the attention of a few theologians—e.g., Hendrik Berkhof (Reformed), J. Veenhof (Re-reformed), and Piet Schoonenberg (Catholic). Since 1978 the CWN theological commis-

sion has produced the quarterly *Bulletin voor Charismatische Theologie.*

d. Belgium. CR in French-speaking Belgium was primarily influenced from France. Belgian CCR has been marked with the involvement and influence of ˈCardinal Léon-Joseph Suenens, Catholic primate of Belgium (1961–79). Suenens, whose episcopal motto was *In Spiritu Sancto* (In the Holy Spirit), first encountered CCR in the U.S. in 1972. He sent Belgian priests to the U.S. to learn more about the movement and appointed ˈFr. Paul Lebeau his theological assistant for CCR. At Suenens's invitation, the International Catholic Charismatic Renewal Office (ICCRO) was established in Brussels, and a community was formed in Brussels under Ralph Martin and Stephen Clark from the Word of God community, Ann Arbor, MI. This association did not last; transatlantic differences proved too strong. CCR in Belgium has received the strong backing of Suenens's successor, Cardinal Godfried Danneels.

3. Eastern Europe.

CR in Eastern Europe existed in widely varied conditions of harassment and persecution until the collapse of Communism in 1989. Relatively greater freedom existed in East Germany (GDR [German Democratic Republic]), Poland, Hungary, and Yugoslavia, though state regulations prohibited all unofficial church gatherings. More information was available about these countries than for the other communist lands of Eastern Europe, in which all church life was tightly restricted and often forcibly suppressed. Especially for the latter it was more difficult to speak of a movement, for Christians baptized in the Spirit had little opportunity for fellowship and were often forced to live their faith in isolation.

a. East Germany. Around 1962–63 CR began in two parishes that were also retreat centers in the GDR: Grosshartmannsdorf (under Christoph Richter) and Braunsdorf (under Gerhard Küttner). These centers, together with Julius Schniewindhaus at Schönebeck (under Bernhard Jansa) and the parish center at Slate (under Ervin Pähl), became the focal points for CR in the GDR. It was estimated that 400 Protestant pastors were participants, about 10% of the clergy of the Protestant (Lutheran) churches.

The movement in the GDR, which followed the CGE pattern of parish renewal, gave rise to more thorough theological reflection than in any other country, especially through the work of Gottfried Rebner and Paul Toaspern. A series of theological studies on the movement in the GDR was issued in the late 1970s (part of one document is in McDonnell, *Presence, Power, Praise*).

The CGE model of renewed parish congregations without separate charismatic structures found acceptance in the GDR, Poland, and Yugoslavia. In the GDR there were many hundreds of prayer and Bible groups in private houses as steps to renewed parishes. Since 1976 many renewed Christians met at an annual interchurch Conference on Spiritual Renewal of the Church in East Berlin, which drew participants from several Eastern European nations. There were also annual pastors' conferences in several locations. International contacts and imported literature were much valued, due to state restrictions in the GDR, where only one book on CR was published (by the theological department of the evangelical churches).

b. Poland. In Poland the way was prepared by a visit of the American music group The Living Sound, who were welcomed by the then archbishop of Krakow, Cardinal Wojtyla. The first charismatic groups among Catholics date from 1975 (Poznan) and 1976 (Warsaw), started by people who had encountered the movement in America or Western Europe. CCR's spread in Poland was much aided by the Oasis renewal movement, known since 1976 as Light-Life. In 1977 the Catholic University of Lublin held its annual theological week on CR, the first occasion on which the future Pope John Paul II met active participants in CCR from the West. This visit was the occasion for the founder of Light-Life, Fr. Franciszek Blachnicki, who was already in touch with Campus Crusade and YWAM, to enlist help from CCR. As a result many Light-Life members took part in Life in the Spirit seminars and received BHS. CCR in Poland spread more rapidly as a result of its permeation of the Light-Life movement, which had 50,000 committed members and a high reputation in the country.

c. Hungary. In Hungary CR among Reformed Christians had begun by the early 1970s, and among Catholics in the mid 1970s. In both cases, Hungarian charismatics encountered opposition. Among Protestants there was initial conflict between "revival" evangelicals and charismatics and a hostile reception from church leaders. The Reformed Church tolerated but did not encourage CR. CR leaders met monthly. Among Catholics, CR found the greatest welcome among the Basic Communities led by Fr. Bulanyi, that were already in conflict with the hierarchy on other grounds, e.g., pacifism.

d. Czechoslovakia. In Czechoslovakia, church life was persistently repressed. CR was strongest in Prague; however, more and more prayer groups were formed all over the country among Lutherans, Reformed, and Catholics. And increasing contacts were made between CR in the FRG, Hungary, and Czechoslovakia. Among Catholics, there was some influence from Poland.

e. Soviet Russia. In Soviet Russia, charismatic faith was mostly represented by various types of pentecostal Christianity. Some Lutheran charismatics could be found in Latvia and Estonia, mostly influenced from Scandinavia. In the cen-

tral Soviet republics there was evidence of CR arising in some Protestant groups—e.g., Baptists—but any corporate expression of charismatic fellowship tended to lead to expulsion and the formation of independent churches.

4. Scandinavia.

CR in the Scandinavian countries has arisen and developed in ways particular to each country. In general, it arrived later than in West Central Europe, and the movement burgeoned in the 1970s rather than in the 1960s. Pentecostal influence on the movement has been stronger than in the rest of Europe.

a. Denmark. In Denmark CR began when Michael Harry, an English doctor working in Denmark, was baptized in the Spirit after attending the FGBMFI international convention in London in 1965. In the late 1960s and early '70s Harry organized visits to Denmark by ►Harper and ►Cousen; this helped to spread the movement. The first surge was in western areas of the country, but the movement lacked integration in the state church because of the absence of Lutheran pastors, and some leaders were rebaptized in pentecostal churches. From the early 1970s, some Lutheran pastors became involved, and by the late 1970s some 40 to 50 were active in the movement. For some years CR in the Copenhagen area was more ecumenical, but in 1981 charismatic leaders in Copenhagen and the rest of Zealand (Sjælland) formed the Spirit and Light group to focus CR in the state church.

b. Finland. This was one of the last European countries to be reached by CR. The beginnings go back to a 1971 conference with Harper and Harry, but the movement did not became fully established in Finland until 1977, when pentecostal preacher Niilo Yli-Vainio drew many Lutherans to his meetings and did nothing to undermine their church affiliation. In 1978 a coordination committee for the "spiritual renewal of the church" was formed. Since then, CR has grown faster and more evenly in Finland than in the rest of Scandinavia, with 173 state-church parishes reporting its presence by 1983. A prominent Lutheran leader has been Olli Valtonen, a pastor who became well-known on Finnish television and edited *Sana,* an evangelistic magazine that penetrated the secular market. The movement in the state church presents itself as in continuity with the distinctively Finnish revival movements, Lutheran and Pietist, and cooperates closely with evangelical and neopietistic organizations. It has not been at ease with the terminology of BHS, and like OASE in Norway (see below) the movement has spoken of the filling of the Spirit as a continuation and renewal of God's work in water baptism. Glossolalia has been less prominent than healing, with indications that one-tenth of Lutheran participants in Finland speak in tongues.

c. Norway. In Norway the emergence of CR is generally dated to a gathering of ministers held in Oslo in Feb. 1970, organized by ▸Herbert Mjorud and ▸Hans-Jakob Froen, a Norwegian Lutheran pastor, and the FGBMFI convention in Oslo in Oct. 1970. The way had already been prepared by the ministry of the pentecostal evangelist ▸Aril Edvardsen, who had been reaching many people within the majority state church, and by the writings of an early 20th-century theologian and revival preacher, Ole Hallesby, who taught the need for a postbaptismal "filling with the Spirit." In 1971 Froen formed an organization, Agape, to promote charismatic revival in Norway. The Agape society was somewhat influenced by the FT model in Britain, though Froen was not as committed to Lutheranism as Harper was to the Church of England. For some years, the main thrust of CR for Norwegian adults was provided by Froen through Agape and by Edvardsen through his center at Kvinesdal. In 1971–72, however, groups influenced by the Jesus movement were formed, reaching many young people: the Peace of God community in Oslo, YWAM, and Young Vision; however, none of these currents really penetrated the Lutheran state church, which itself has a tradition of revival outside the parish structures.

Moves toward a more integrated Lutheran renewal began among students at the Free Faculty of Theology at Oslo as they were influenced by Hallesby's theology of the Spirit. A conference convened by H. C. Lier and Jens-Petter Jorgensen in Feb. 1977 was a turning point, leading the 100 people who were present through a "Holy Spirit seminar." The success of the seminar led to further conferences and in 1980 to the formation of the OASE Foundation with Jorgensen as chairman to promote renewal in the Lutheran churches. OASE conferences were held in southern Norway each summer, with 5,000 to 7,000 participants. The OASE teaching did not use baptismal language of the initial charismatic experience; neither did it link this with glossolalia. Estimates show that there were about 50,000 charismatics in the Lutheran churches in 1987.

d. Sweden. In Sweden, CR in the state church owes much to the indigenous pentecostal groupings, such as the Baptist Örebro Mission with its annual conferences and to impulses from outside Sweden, such as the English evangelist Harry Greenwood. These early influences were later aided by the translation of many books from English originals. The movement received a major boost nationally from the ecumenical conference at Stockholm in Oct. 1972 under the leadership of Du Plessis, Harper, the Catholic George di Prizio, and the pentecostal pioneer ▸Lewi Pethrus. CR in Sweden particularly impacted the southwest of the country, where the leadership of Pastor Carl Gustaf Stenbäck was encouraged by the bishop of Gothenburg, Bertil Gartner. From the late 1970s the retired bishop Helge Fosseus, working from a significant conference center, gave further focus for CR in the state church.

In Iceland a particular impact was made in the Lutheran parish in Reykjavik. The movement was led by Halldor Grondal with help from YWAM.

5. The Latin Countries.

a. Italy. In Italy the beginnings of CCR occurred in late 1970, through American students in Rome and a Canadian priest, Val Gaudet, who had received BHS after a meeting with the Dutch Fr. Biesbrouck. During 1971, regular prayer meetings began at the Jesuit Gregorian University, led from 1971 to 1973 by the American ▸Francis Martin. Meeting in Rome, this English-language prayer group with its international membership rapidly became an instrument for diffusing CCR throughout the world. The American Jesuit theologian Francis Sullivan attended the meetings almost from the beginning, having been initially sent by church authorities who were concerned about the movement. Although the first Italian Catholic charismatic prayer group in Rome began in early 1972, CCR in Italy did not gather momentum until the late 1970s, following the International Conference in Rome on Pentecost Day in 1975 and the participation of respected priest-theologians such as ▸Robert Faricy and Domenico Grasso (who, like Sullivan, were professors at the Gregorian University) and the patristic scholar ▸Raniero Cantalamessa of Milan, who soon after was appointed special preacher at the Vatican.

The bimonthly *Alleluja* began publication in 1976 and prompted the formation of the Italian National Service Committee for CCR and the annual conferences held in Rimini since 1978. The Service Committee organized Italian CCR with regional councils and numerous delegates for specific tasks. Since 1985 it has produced its own monthly, *Rinnovamento nello Spirito Santo.* The magazine *Alleluja* continued as an independent venture until 1989, as did another magazine, *Risuscito,* produced since 1977 by Comunità Maria, a group founded by Alfredo and Jacqueline Ancellotti. *Risuscito* has from the beginning maintained its independence from *Alleluja* and later official CCR publications. Pope John Paul II has twice spoken in encouraging terms to large gatherings of Italian Catholic charismatics in St. Peters, Rome (1980, 1986). CCR in Italy numbered about 800 prayer groups, totaling some 70,000 to 80,000 participants. Before the 1990s, there was hardly any ecumenical dimension to CR in Italy, with Italian pentecostals mostly rejecting any possibility of authentic pentecostal life within the Roman Church.

b. Spain and Portugal. CCR in Spain appeared around 1973–74, when several prayer groups began to meet in Salamanca and Madrid. The first steps toward national coordination occurred in 1976, with a leaders' conference in Salamanca, the formation of a national service committee (led by Fr. Manuel Casanova, baptized in the Spirit in India in 1972), and the beginning of the bimonthly *Koinonia* (initially edited by Fr. Luis Martin of Barcelona). CCR in Spain has grown steadily since that time, with the beginnings of small communities in Madrid, Granollers (Barcelona), and Saragossa. In 1987 there were 275 CCR prayer groups in Spain, with some 20,000 participants.

The first CCR prayer meeting was held in Portugal in late 1974. As in Spain, national organization began in 1976 with the formation of a service committee and the launching of a bimonthly periodical, *Pneuma*, edited by Fr. José da Lapa of Lisbon.

C. Developments at the Continental Level.

The idea of gathering European leaders in CR seems to have come first to ▸J. Rodman Williams during the sabbatical year he spent at St. John's, Collegeville, MN, with ▸Larry Christenson and ▸Arnold Bittlinger in 1971–72. As a result, the first European Charismatic Leaders' Conference was held at Schloss Craheim, West Germany, in 1972, with 16 countries represented. These conferences were held regularly until 1988, generally at two-year intervals. At the third meeting in 1975, three theses were adopted on the theme "Charismatic Renewal and the Unity of the Church" (printed in McDonnell 2:14). Between 1976 and 1984, the meetings were organized and chaired jointly by ▸Smail and ▸Lebeau. The British churches, together with those from the Low Countries, France, West Germany, and Switzerland, were generally well represented, Scandinavia intermittently, and the Mediterranean countries rather poorly.

In 1978 Thomas Roberts had a vision of a European-wide gathering to celebrate jointly the work and power of the Holy Spirit. Pursued at the leaders' meeting in Strasbourg in 1980, this vision became reality in 1982, when 20,000 Christians from many different backgrounds, mostly charismatic, came together at Strasbourg to celebrate "Pentecost over Europe." This conference seems to have had an effect in Europe similar to that of the 1977 Kansas City conference in the U.S., deepening the sense of the ecumenical grace of CR and leading to a call for a common humbling before the Lord in repentance and mutual reconciliation.

A large ecumenical European charismatic conference called Acts 1986 was held at Birmingham, England, in July 1986, on the initiative of Michael Harper, who formed a European committee. Whereas Strasbourg 1982 was primarily made up of French and German speakers, Birmingham 1986 had a mostly English-speaking participation, though significant groups came from Hungary and Scandinavia, especially Finland.

In 1988 a larger European Charismatic Leaders' Conference was held in Berlin, Germany, bringing together the leaders from the older meetings begun in Schloss Craheim and the members of the Acts 1986 committee. The two committees decided to disband and together form the European Charismatic Consultation, which held its first conference at Disentis, Switzerland, in 1989.

III. DEVELOPMENT IN LATIN AMERICA.

CR has been less researched and analyzed in Latin America than in North America and Europe. It is easier to obtain information about CCR than about CR among Protestants, because CCR has developed national and continental structures that interact with the International Catholic Charismatic Renewal office (ICCRS) in Rome. The distinction between CR among Protestants and the pentecostal movement is more difficult to make in Latin America than elsewhere for reasons that will emerge in the following brief survey.

A. Protestant Beginnings.

1. Brazil.

Brazil was the first Latin American country to experience widespread outbreaks of pentecostal phenomena within historic church traditions (aside from the origins of the pentecostal movement in Chile; see below). There were stirrings in Brazil in the mid 1950s, as in North America and Europe, with small groups of praying Christians seeking a deeper spiritual life. Many found help and encouragement from a Southern Baptist missionary, Rosalee Appleby, who was increasingly burdened for world revival. Public preaching of BHS began in some Baptist circles in 1958, particularly in Belo Horizonte, under José de Nascimento, impacting Baptist pastors as well as laypersons. By the mid 1960s pentecostal outbreaks were also reported among Methodists, Presbyterians, Congregationalists, and Seventh-day Adventists. All these experiences of *renovacao* (renewal) attracted opposition within their denominations. The first to be expelled from the parent body were the charismatic Baptists, who formed themselves into the Igreja do Renovacao (Church of Renewal). Subsequent conflicts led to other new denominations—the Igreja Metodista Wesleyana (Wesleyan Methodist Church), the Igreja Crista Presbiteriana do Brasil (Presbyterian Christian Church of Brazil), and the Igreja Adventista da Promessa (Adventist Church of the Promise). These denominations prefer the language of renewal or of restoration to any pentecostal label. By 1987 these churches combined accounted for 140,000 or more committed Christians.

2. Colombia.

In Colombia a spontaneous movement began around 1960 in the north Colombian forest under the leadership of Victor Landero, with manifestation of spiritual gifts following intense spiritual seeking and reading of the book of Acts. Like many other such groups in Latin America, the assemblies linked with Landero call themselves *renovacion,* reject the label "pentecostal," and are affiliated with the Association of Evangelical Churches of the Caribbean, a nonpentecostal body.

3. Argentina.

In Argentina CR began among the Hermanos Libros (the Open Brethren) in a prayer meeting in the Buenos Aires home of business executive Alberto Darling in Feb. 1967, helped by the ministry of Keith Bentson. Soon after, a missionary with pentecostal experience, Orville Swindoll, conducted a mission in an independent church in Villa Soldati, pastored by Jorge Himitian. The success of this mission led to fusion of the Darling and Himitian meetings, which became a focus for pentecostal renewal. In the ensuing expansion, important teaching and guidance roles were played by Swindoll, Bentson, Ed Miller of the Peniel Bible Institute in La Plata, and ʼJuan Carlos Ortiz, pastor of Central Assembly of God Church in Buenos Aires. Swindoll's influence was increased by his magazine, *Vision Celestial*. The Baptists and the Mennonites soon saw pastors and congregations affected by this movement that was called Renovacion (Renewal). The Charismatic Brethren, who numbered 5,000 within three years, were forced out of their fellowship, and the movement was denounced as "spiritistic." Among the Brethren who received BHS was Daniel Somoza, who had edited the main Brethren magazine for many years. Opposition also arose among the Baptists, who expelled some pastors. One former Baptist prominent in CR was Alberto Motessi. As a result of this opposition, the development of CR among Argentinian Protestants was to be primarily in the independent sector, with the discipleship teaching of Ortiz playing an important part in the growth of many assemblies.

4. Chile.

An Anglican missionary to Chile with the South American Missionary Society, Kath Clarke, was baptized in the Spirit while on furlough in England in the mid 1960s, and on her return she was the instrument of charismatic blessing in the seminary where she taught. Asked to desist from pentecostal practices by the church authorities, Clarke complied, but the Spirit of Pentecost was already spreading and soon touched ʼDavid Pytches, first assistant bishop and then bishop of the Anglican diocese of Chile, Bolivia, and Peru. Also in Chile during this period, CR began among Methodists around the city of Tome.

B. The Ecumenical Period.

The beginnings of CCR in Latin America flowed from a visit paid to Colombia by Harald Bredesen and an ecumenical team of charismatics from North America. During this visit, Fr. Rafael Garcia-Herreros, who was well-known in Colombia for his TV program *El Minuto de Dios,* was baptized in the Spirit. In the early 1960s Fr. Garcia had launched the construction of a new estate to rehouse the homeless in an area then on the edge of Bogota. Fr. Garcia communicated his newfound enthusiasm for the Lord to a young priest, ʼDiego Jaramillo, who in 1970 rejoined him to work in the development that became known as El Minuto de Dios. Jaramillo later became a prominent leader in Latin American CCR and its main international spokesperson.

One of the first centers of CR in Central America was the Templo Biblico of the Evangelical Association of Bible Churches in San José, Costa Rica. The Christians here experienced pentecostal blessing through the ministry of Argentinian pastors Alberto Motessi and Juan Carlos Ortiz and the unexpected visits of the U.S. Catholics ʼFrancis MacNutt and ʼBarbara Shlemon. In Guatemala Timothy Rovenstine was instrumental in bringing Catholics and Protestants together in the beginnings of CR, aided by visiting members of FGBMFI and of the Word of God community, Ann Arbor, MI, as well as MacNutt.

In the early to mid 1970s this ecumenical character marked CR in the Latin American countries, especially in Central America. One successful pattern involved teams of charismatic Protestants and charismatic Catholics working together. Of particular importance was the teaming up of the Catholic Francis MacNutt with Joe Petree, a Methodist. In 1970 they visited Costa Rica, Peru, and Bolivia, along with another Methodist, ʼTommy Tyson. This unprecedented combination opened many doors and attracted great interest, MacNutt being invited to speak in an evangelical seminary and at Templo Biblico in San José, Costa Rica. Ecumenical teams with some of these men visited Ecuador, Peru, and Bolivia in early 1971 and Costa Rica later the same year. Another ecumenical team, with Catholic priests Jim Burke and George di Prizio, plus Petree and a Protestant businessman from North Carolina, conducted a retreat in Puerto Rico in Nov. 1971. At this retreat ʼFr. Tom Forrest, then working in Aguas Buenas, was baptized in the Spirit, an event that loosed a flood of charismatic blessing on the island. CCR also began with explosive power in the Dominican Republic, where the French Canadian missionary ʼFr. Emilien Tardif returned from sick leave in 1974, healed and baptized in the Spirit.

The First Latin American Renewal Congress was held in Buenos Aires in 1972, bringing together 80 leaders, mostly Protestant, at a Catholic retreat center; but within a year the second congress at Porto Alegre, Brazil, drew 2,000 participants. The beginnings of CCR in Brazil had come from the U.S. through two American Jesuit priests, Edward Dougherty and Harold Rahm. Dougherty was baptized in the Spirit during a visit to Canada in 1969, and he worked full time for CCR from the early 1970s. Rahm was the first to spread CCR in Brazil through a course called Experience of the Heart.

The first international CCR meeting occurred early in 1973 when 23 leaders representing eight Latin American countries—priests, sisters, and one Baptist—met in Bogota,

Colombia, and laid the foundations for ECCLA (Encuentro Carismatico Catolico Latino-Americano), a body that has since developed its own structures and holds regular congresses.

Latin American CR is characterized by a populist enthusiasm that has gathered huge crowds at football stadia and other public places. Such gatherings attract the masses of every religious background and those with none, whatever the denomination of the visiting speaker. TV evangelists from the U.S., such as Rex Humbard and Jimmy Swaggart, have held such campaigns. One remarkable instance of this populist character was the ministry of a young man of Catholic background, Julio Cesar Ruibal, who was initially converted at a ►Kathryn Kuhlman meeting in California. Returning to Latin America, he began preaching and praying for the sick, with remarkable results that attracted vast crowds. Between Dec. 1972 and Feb. 1973, over 200,000 people were touched by God during Ruibal's virtually unplanned three-day campaigns in La Paz, Santa Cruz, and Cochabamba, Bolivia. In Colombia he appeared on the Catholic TV program *El Minuto de Dios,* and when he spoke in Medellin, the soccer stadium was filled. Ruibal's ministry belongs to the ecumenical beginnings, for his campaigns initially received support from Catholics, especially those already in CCR, while inspiring Protestants by his gospel preaching.

Ruibal is but one more dramatic example of a leader in a process that has occurred throughout CCR—namely, that in this grassroots movement of the Holy Spirit, those first finding themselves in positions of ministry and leadership were not all priests but included many laypeople with little or no theological or spiritual formation. These lay leaders often found ecumenical contacts with Spirit-filled Christians in other churches easier to make than the priests and religious with their traditional Catholic formation. Filled with a desire to know the Scriptures after BHS, many lay leaders welcomed the help that many evangelical Protestants were keen to give them, particularly in Central America. In this situation were sown the seeds of future developments.

C. Separate Development.

While pentecostal-charismatic Christianity has continued to spread in Latin America, both among Catholics and Protestants, it has not preserved the ecumenical openness and hope of its beginnings. The reasons for this are not so much deliberate suppression by unsympathetic church authorities than the lack of interchurch relations when CR appeared. Unlike North America and Europe, where there had been growing patterns of ecumenical relationship over recent decades, accentuated by Vatican II, in Latin America Catholics and Protestants still viewed each other with suspicion if not outright hostility. Catholics tended to view evangelical Protestants as proselytizing interlopers, luring away their faithful with a simplistic creed, whereas evangelical

Protestants would regard Catholics as little better than pagans lost in a morass of superstition.

Faced with this unexpected grassroots ecumenical eruption, the Catholic hierarchy was concerned about the influence of Protestant teachers on lay Catholic leaders, a concern that saw its justification in the generally unecumenical stance of the evangelicals concerned and their evident antipathy toward the Catholic faith. On the other hand, many Latin American Catholic bishops, particularly in Colombia, Venezuela, and Mexico, were sympathetic to CCR, sensing its potential for spiritual rejuvenation of the Latin American church. The result was a more explicit promotion of CCR, with priests appointed to lead and teach. Especially from the late 1970s, the structuring of CCR throughout the continent proceeded at all levels with regular ECCLA meetings for leaders from all nations, with national and diocesan directors, conferences, and guidelines. Of particular importance was the leadership in Colombia, with Bishop Uribe Jaramillo of Sonson Rio Negro and Fr. Diego Jaramillo, then of Bogota. From 1977, annual charismatic retreats for priests from all of Latin America took place at La Ceja in Bishop Jaramillo's diocese, which later held a conference on CCR for Latin American bishops.

The ICCRO office in Rome estimated that in 1987 there were 2 million Catholic charismatics in 21 Latin American countries. The ECCLA VII meeting in Belo Horizonte, Brazil, in 1982 authorized the establishment of a CCR Latin American office in Bogota, Colombia, and decided to initiate meetings of theologians and CCR leaders to study problem topics such as healing and deliverance, as well as the relationship between CCR and social action. Father Diego Jaramillo, who was appointed director of ICCRO in 1987, stated at an earlier ICCRO meeting: "The distinguishing characteristic of the Renewal in Latin America is the special effort to incorporate the Renewal into Church structures, and to enter into serious dialogue with priests and bishops" (ICCRO, *International Newsletter* 8 [6, Nov.–Dec. 1982]: 1).

In this process of Catholic structuring, pioneer lay leaders were often unhappy with the clerical authority provided for them. As a result, numerous charismatic groups that were formed in the first wave of CCR did not continue within the Roman Catholic Church but became independent charismatic assemblies under their former lay leaders. Sometimes such groups exist in uneasy tension with both their Catholic past and their evangelical present. In Bolivia the Eklesia Mission stemming from Ruibal's campaigns became independent and is now under a new leader.

One ecumenical bridge in the late 1970s and early '80s was the John 17:21 Fellowship associated with David du Plessis. The John 17:21 Fellowship was established in Guatemala City after the major earthquake in 1976. A Latin American branch of John 17:21 coordinated by Robert Thomas of Los Altos, CA, worked closely with Fr. Alfonso

Navarro and the Catholic Missionaries of the Holy Spirit to form UCELAM, the Christian Union for Evangelizing Latin America, with annual conferences in Mexico City. UCELAM teams whose leaders included Bill Finke and ➤Juan Carlos Ortiz spoke in several Latin American countries in the early 1980s.

Among Latin American Protestants, it has been estimated that by 1987, 80–85% were pentecostal or charismatic. Of those who are not in pentecostal denominations, only a small percentage are in the historic Protestant denominations (Anglican, Baptist, Lutheran, Methodist, Reformed-Presbyterian, Mennonite). In most of these bodies, charismatic outbreaks have occurred, but where these have led to any coherent charismatic groupings, they have often encountered resistance from church authorities. In many cases, the results have been either expulsion or voluntary withdrawal under heavy pressure. Most of these groups formed new denominations, as in Brazil in the 1960s, while far more new indigenous churches of a pentecostal type grew from scratch.

In Latin America all evangelistic Protestant groups are called evangelical, including those that would be termed pentecostal or charismatic elsewhere. The groups and churches calling themselves Renovacion or Renovacao are generally more middle-class. Charismatic Protestant Christianity in Latin America outside the major pentecostal churches is overwhelmingly in the independent sector, unaffiliated with any of the major confessional families. A small percentage is found within the historic churches, particularly the Anglican Communion, in which some bishops endorse, some tolerate, and some oppose CR. In Ecuador the Anglican diocese, which in 1971 had only three congregations catering to expatriates and had grown to over a hundred congregations, saw a remarkable expansion from 1986 following the visits of SOMA (Sharing of Ministries Abroad) teams invited by bishop Adrian Caceres. A majority of the priests in the Ecuador diocese have received BHS, and the influx of converts includes many youth, with a resulting indigenous church of 220 congregations and 16,000 members by 1987.

In Brazil CR has developed since the late 1970s among a group of independent Lutheran churches in the area of Porto Alegre, sparked by the leadership of a former LC–MS pastor, Aloisio Hoffmann. In addition, the Brazilian Lutheran Church of German background (Igreja Evangelica da Confissao Luterana no Brasil) has seen since the early 1970s an extensive renewal movement known as Encontrao, characterized by evangelism, praise, and healing, though without the CR emphasis on the word gifts and glossolalia. These movements, like the new Renovacao denominations, are found more in middle-class Brazilian society than the pentecostal churches.

Among the many independent churches of a charismatic type that have sprung up are the Templo Biblico in San José, Costa Rica, and that in Caracas, Venezuela, pastored by Sam Olson. The church in Caracas is the largest Protestant church in the country. Some independent churches have become charismatic since their original establishment, such as the Union Church in San José, Costa Rica. In Argentina the fastest-growing currents outside the pentecostal churches are flowing from the independent charismatic ministries of evangelist Carlos Annacondia, of Omar Cabrera, and of Hector Gimenez. While these assemblies and currents are not called charismatic, they are the Latin American equivalent of North American nondenominational CR. That is to say, their differences from denominational pentecostals lie in their foreign contacts (independents rather than pentecostals) and, in many cases, in the espousal of teachings such as discipleship, which are generally suspect among the pentecostals.

These developments in Latin American CR suggest that the growth of a Catholic movement with little ecumenical contact, and of Protestant pentecostal-charismatic faith mostly outside the mainline denominations, is at least partly the result of the absence of ecumenical relationships. When CR arrived, neither side had sufficient recognition of the Lord's presence and activity through the others. In this situation, although the charismatic explosion has multiplied basic Christian evangelism, the challenge presented by the Holy Spirit's transcendence of inherited patterns seems to have been more than either side could handle.

IV. GLOBALIZATION AND TURNING OUTWARD (1988–98).

The last decade is characterized by the globalization of CM–CR, which is why it is covered here in a separate section rather than by extending the discussion of the individual countries in sections I–III. New trends are quickly impacting all nations and continents. Whereas in previous decades the expansion of CM–CR was more closely tied to North American initiatives, the major trends of the 1990s originated in many different places. The growth of charismatic Christianity in particular nations and places is closely related to the impact of the new global trends. This latest decade is thus treated first by a survey of the global trends, and then by the provision of more detailed information for each continent. (The sections on Africa, Asia, and Oceania provide some background from earlier decades, since they are not covered in the earlier sections.)

A. Global Trends.

1. Charismatic Assimilation and Penetration.

In the 1990s there was much less emphasis on CR as a distinct movement. Most agencies originally formed to promote CR dropped the term *charismatic* (a major exception is CCR, especially in the English-speaking world), as CR in the mainline churches sought to be a cooperative movement rather than to assert its distinctiveness.

In the 1980s evangelicalism worldwide became massively penetrated and permeated by distinctive features of CM in worship and in forms of ministry, but it was in the 1990s that the results became apparent. The opposition of evangelicals to spiritual gifts, expressive worship, and tactile ministry has largely evaporated, aside from a few bastions of fundamentalist orthodoxy, with the result that large numbers of churches worldwide now sing songs of charismatic origin, pray for healing, promote Spirit-empowered intercession, often without calling themselves charismatic, without regarding themselves as part of a movement, and without any doctrine of BHS.

Moreover, in the Third World—including the historic churches—dynamic instances of church planting and church growth with the manifestation of spiritual gifts and evident power of the Holy Spirit are being lived and seen as normal Christian life and not as the expression of a particular movement. However, these developments would seem to have become possible through the earlier phase of distinctive CR. This is different from the situation in much of the First World, where charismatic boundaries have been blurred by the large number of what David Barrett calls "postcharismatics," those once part of CR who no longer participate in specific CR gatherings but who have taken something of their CR experience into their ongoing Christian life. This contrast with the Third World suggests that there is an ambiguity in the loss of charismatic distinctiveness in First World CR, of which one element is the eclecticism of affluent Western Christians passing from one spirituality to another. In this situation, the seepage of charismatic elements into the bloodstream of the mainline churches may often be more assimilation than penetration, hardly comparable to the dynamic transformation now being seen in Third World churches living in situations of poverty, violence, and dire human need.

Much growth in the realm of the charismatic reported below reflects these patterns: growth, not necessarily of CR as it was understood in the 1970s, but of a Spirit-filled Christianity with clearly charismatic features that has developed largely out of CM–CR.

At the same time as many in CR were dropping the term *charismatic,* some new currents—including many "Faith churches" with a prosperity message—that were outside the historic churches and not aligned with traditional evangelicalism were taking it up and calling themselves "charismatic churches." All these factors have complicated the terminology, and as a result, many are less comfortable with the designations CM and CR. These same factors also make it far more difficult to provide statistics for the total number of "charismatic Christians." For the purpose of this article, however, what is surveyed is the whole spectrum of Christian life that is in continuity with, and a development of, the major emphases first described as CM and CR.

2. Evangelism and Evangelization.

Both terms are used here; *evangelism* is favored by Protestants, *evangelization* by Roman Catholics. (In Catholic parlance evangelization refers to the spread of the gospel and its influence at all stages, with the new terms *primary* or *initial proclamation* being the equivalent of evangelism in evangelical Protestant usage.) The approach of the new millennium sparked many plans and targets for worldwide evangelism/evangelization. The charismatic penetration of the evangelical world in the 1980s has led to most evangelistic initiatives of evangelicals having a charismatic dimension. Of these, DAWN (Disciple A Whole Nation), founded by Jim Montgomery in 1984, has focused evangelical strategy in many countries, applying church-growth theory in a practical way. DAWN, which is now in 40 countries, has recruited and trained national directors to raise an army of church planters to form witnessing congregations in every village or neighborhood. The Colorado-based AD 2000 and Beyond movement, established in 1989 and directed by Luis Bush, adopted the goal: "A church for every people, and the gospel for every person by the year 2000." AD 2000 and Beyond formed 10 networks to advance particular aspects of the common vision, including one for unreached peoples, one for the mobilization of new missionaries, and another for united prayer (see section 4 below). Bush has devoted attention to the lands in the 10/40 window (between 10° and 40° north of the Equator), where most of the least-evangelized peoples live, where the least-evangelized megacities are found, and where 80% of the poorest of the poor live.

Short-term mission teams, long a specialty of groups like YWAM, have been developed by CR groups in the mainline churches; e.g., in SOMA, the Anglican agency, which has national committees wherever Anglican CR is thriving, and in the Presbyterian-Reformed body, Presbyterian-Reformed Ministries International (PRMI, formerly PRRMI), which works primarily out of the U.S.

The 1990s were also the decade of the ▸Alpha course, developed by Nicky Gumbel within the Anglican parish ▸Holy Trinity Brompton, London, England, under the leadership of Sandy Millar. Alpha is directed at the unchurched and has been devised as an evangelistic tool for local congregations. Although Alpha is not overtly charismatic, it envisages a conscious reception of the Holy Spirit and an openness to spiritual gifts. Alpha's initial thrust in many places comes from charismatic-type congregations and groups, but it is being used by many congregations previously untouched by CR. By mid 1998, 5,000 churches in Britain were running Alpha courses, and the momentum was building in the U.S. and many other lands. Alpha has led to increasing interchurch cooperation, and in Britain it has produced closer relations between the New Churches, strong promoters of Alpha, and the congregations of the older churches open to Alpha.

The Roman Catholic Church endorsed ►Fr. Tom Forrest's vision of a Decade of Evangelization in the 1990s. This has led to the establishment of many schools for evangelists; to the spread of the International Catholic Programme of Evangelization (ICPE), originating in Malta and with centers now in Rome, Germany, and New Zealand; to the Kekako schools of evangelization, begun by the Mexican José Prado Flores (*Kekako* stands for *Kerygma, Karisma, Koinonia*); and to the popular formation courses produced by Koinonia Giovanni Battista, a charismatic community founded in Italy by Fr. Ricardo Argañaras from Argentina.

3. New Currents.

CR has continued to be a movement of new currents and occasional surprises. Several of these had a relationship to ►John Wimber and the ►Vineyard churches. In general, Wimber helped to focus attention on the role of ►signs and wonders in church life, particularly in evangelism, as well as democratizing the gifts with his encouragement to all charismatic believers to "go and do likewise." In the late 1980s a prophetic movement surfaced, particularly associated with the Metro Church of Kansas City, led by ►Mike Bickle. The "Kansas City prophets," as they were briefly known, in particular Paul Cain, John Paul Jackson, and Bob Jones, attracted attention by their use of words of knowledge and prophetic messages, particularly focused on revival. Although the excitement associated with the Kansas City prophets died down rather quickly, there was an enhanced emphasis on the prophetic in the 1990s. There is more talk of prophetic ministries, prophetic preaching, prophetic intercession, etc. This has been strongest in the New Church sector, as, e.g., in the ministry of ►Rick Joyner and *Morning Star Journal;* of Marc Dupont, based in Toronto until 1998; of ►Mahesh Chavda of Charlotte, NC; and of the prophetic schools established in Belfort, France.

Focus on revival and the prophetic was further stimulated by the outbreak of revivalist phenomena in Toronto in Jan. 1994, at the Toronto Airport Vineyard Christian Fellowship under the leadership of ►John Arnott. The airport church, which soon had to move to larger premises, rapidly became a place of charismatic pilgrimage, particularly from Northern Europe, Korea, and Indonesia. The ►Toronto Blessing, as it quickly came to be known, was primarily experienced as a revelation of the Father's love, as a concentrated form of inner healing, and as a spiritual refreshing of the jaded and weary. It had a considerable impact in Britain, particularly in Anglican and New Church circles; some local churches became centers of such blessing, including ►Holy Trinity Brompton, London (Anglican), an AG church in Sunderland, and St. Andrew's, Chorleywood, Hertfordshire. Other churches that became centers of diffusion were the Basileia Vineyard in Bern, Switzerland; Christian Life Centre Mount Annan, New South Wales, Australia; and Espace du Plein Evangile in Maçon, France.

Toronto was followed by a revivalistic outbreak at Pensacola, FL, from June 1995 in the ►Brownsville Assembly of God under John Kilpatrick. While Brownsville attracted more pentecostals than Toronto, it deserves mention here because of its considerable influence on CR. Brownsville has been characterized by an emphasis on repentance for sin; while Toronto seemed to refresh existing believers, including many pastors, Pensacola seems to have had more impact on the unchurched. The influence of Toronto has since decreased, partly because of the impact of Pensacola and partly due to Wimber's asking the Toronto Airport church to leave the Association of Vineyard Churches, which happened in Jan. 1996. Although discussion of the Toronto Blessing has virtually ceased, its characteristic emphases and blessings have become widely disseminated and continue to shape much of the contemporary CM.

4. The Cell Church.

The rapidity of the spread of pentecostal-charismatic Christianity in the 1990s is not only the result of spiritual gifts and manifestations, but also of the wide development of the cell-church strategy, first implemented on a large scale in Yonggi Cho's Yoido Full Gospel Church in Seoul, South Korea. Within the cell-church movement, the local cell becomes the primary point of church belonging and evangelistic outreach but always as an expression of the larger local church. The cell church has made possible the emergence of the megachurch without a loss in coherence and relatedness. Cell-church formation has often been accompanied by a teaching on the importance of three-level church expression: neighborhood cells (focusing on discipleship and fellowship), local church assemblies (focusing on worship and teaching), and city-/regionwide gatherings (focusing on celebration and wider vision).

Cell-church strategy has been taken up and taught by many leaders, not all marked by pentecostal-charismatic emphases, but CM has lent itself to cell-church thinking with its emphasis on the empowering and gifting of every believer. It is widely used among the new charismatic churches. Two of the most widely used handbooks on the cell-church concept are Ralph Neighbour Jr.'s *Where Do We Go from Here?* (1990) and William J. Beckham's *Reshaping the Church for the 21st Century* (1995).

CCR has also utilized the cell concept, particularly through the work of Fr. Michael Eivers, of St. Boniface parish, near Fort Lauderdale, FL, and Fr. PierGiorgio Perini of St. Eustorgio, Milan, Italy. This has been taken up for the French-speaking world by the Maranatha community in Brussels.

5. Prayer Movements and Spiritual Warfare.

During this last decade, there has been an intensification of prayer movements and important new initiatives in intercessory prayer. Earlier movements, such as the Prayer Summits initiated in the U.S. by Ray Bringham in 1983, have multiplied and diversified. Annual prayer summits were held near Washington, DC, to "repent of our sins of division, indifference and prayerlessness and to pray and believe God for a nationwide and worldwide spiritual awakening." Prayer summits for nations and politicians led to prayer summits for pastors and the needs of the church.

The rising tide of prayer has been accompanied by increasing attention to spiritual combat with the powers of evil and its necessity as a basis for successful evangelism and a stronger Christian presence in society. Much teaching and practice on spiritual warfare has been pioneered by leaders such as Omar Cabrera of Argentina; Ed Silvoso, an Argentinian now in the U.S.; and David (Paul) Yonggi Cho of Korea. This development no doubt reflects the sharper clash in the Third World between the pentecostal-charismatic power of the Spirit and more overt expressions of demonic power.

Strategic intercessory prayer was initially developed in the context of impact on modern cities. ›John Dawson's book *Taking Our Cities for God* (1989) emphasized love and commitment to the city and provided spiritual mapping instructions. Francis Frangipane, in *The House of the Lord* (1991), examined the city in terms of the "one church of the city" and the strategic importance of unity among city pastors.

Spiritual warfare teaching and practice is now widely seen as a necessary strategy for church growth and church planting, asserting the need to identify and overcome the spiritual forces controlling or influencing particular cities and regions. With this teaching, there has been a major focus on repentance and reconciliation, and the urging of identificational repentance for the sins of nations and peoples. ›John Dawson has done pioneer work here with his book *Healing America's Wounds* (1994), which along with works by ›Cindy Jacobs and Dutch Sheets, has been used in the many initiatives of the United Prayer Track of the AD 2000 movement, coordinated by ›C. Peter Wagner.

Repentance and reconciliation have been prominent motifs in the growing number of prayer walks and prayer journeys. The United Prayer Track designated 1996 the year of the land, which included prayer journeys addressing white American sins against the American Indians, racial divisions, and all the sins associated with the slave trade and the American Civil War. The Thirteen Colonies Prayer Journey in 1997, led by Rick Ridings, addressed the sinful elements in the colonial legacy. The Reconciliation Walk, organized by ›YWAM leader ›Lynn Green to retrace the steps of the armies of the first Crusade from western Europe to Jerusalem on its 900th anniversary, lasted from 1995 to 1999, repenting especially for the violence toward, and massacres of, Jews and Muslims. The ›March for Jesus, founded in Britain in 1987 and now a worldwide phenomenon, also has a strongly intercessory character and spiritual battle methodology.

6. Praise Explosion.

This decade has seen a flowering of the "praise movement" that began with David and Dale Garratt's Scripture in Song ministry in New Zealand in 1968. An important step was the first live praise recording made by Alabama-based Integrity Music in 1985. It was in the mid to late 1980s that the music of Graham Kendrick became popular, further spread by the ›March for Jesus. The ›Vineyard movement has contributed many worship leaders and writers of praise songs, including Eddie Espinosa, David Ruis, Kevin Prosch, Cindy Rethmeier, and Terry Butler. In Britain Dave Fellingham, Noel Richards, and Dave Bilbrough have been major contributors. The praise movement is closely allied to the prayer and spiritual warfare developments, with Robert Gay of the Network of Prophetic Ministries and Bob Fitts of YWAM leading Christians to discover the power of praise to defeat demonic powers. In the 1990s this praise music overflowed the boundaries of CM and was found in the worship of almost all denominations. Songs written in English were being translated into many languages, and there was a steady flow of new songs from charismatic churches and communities in other countries.

7. New Church Networks.

What has been called the nondenominational or the independent charismatic churches have been the fastest-growing sector in the 1990s. Many of the initiatives and new currents already noted have come from these new churches and their leaders. This decade has seen the expansion of existing networks and the multiplication of new networks in all parts of the world, some of them international in their range.

New church networks are a worldwide phenomenon. C. Peter Wagner speaks of them as "the new apostolic churches." Some of their characteristics are charismatic leadership based on proven ministry skills and anointing; vision rather than heritage driven; contemporary worship styles; new prayer forms; outreach and mission-oriented; openness to supernatural power (*The New Apostolic Churches*, 18–25). Most networks believe in the restoration of the fivefold ministries of Eph. 4:11.

In general, the network model has been chosen to maximize evangelistic and pastoral flexibility with a firm determination not to fall into denominational patterns. Dick Iverson lists the factors causing fellowships to become denominations as credentialing, ownership of buildings, and central mission boards, all of which the new networks want to avoid, focusing instead on relationships, integrity, and doctrinal compatibility (*The New Apostolic Churches*, 176–77). The networks are based on personal relationships and trust between the leaders, with a recognition both of the apostolic authority of the network leader(s) and of the autonomy of the local congregation. The first three statements in one network self-description read: "1. ___ is not a denomination but an association birthed out of Spirit-born relationships. 2. ___ will not own church property of those associate local churches. 3. ___ will not violate the autonomy of each local congregation and will abide by the constitution and bylaws of each local church." This pattern is common, especially in First World networks, where expansion often occurs through existing churches joining and not only through new church plants. With Third World networks, the percentage of new plants among member churches is generally higher.

Most networks begin to develop their own patterns of education and formation after a few years. Thus, Morning Star International, led by Rice Broocks of Brentwood, TN, has formed the Victory Leadership Institute, with headquarters in Manila, Philippines, and branches in three U.S. cities, Ukraine, Indonesia, and Costa Rica. The Antioch Churches and Ministries, led by John Kelly of Southlake, TX, have formed Antioch University International. Third World networks usually organize leadership-training programs wherever they spread, such as the Jesus Is Lord Church, founded and led by Eddie Villanueva, with its Leadership Enhancement and Advancement Program. Network patterns are also spreading within mainline churches, as in the New Wine grouping developing around David Pytches, St. Andrew's, Chorleywood, and the New Wine conferences in England.

8. Convergence Movement.

A quite different kind of new current is the so-called ›Convergence movement. The Convergence movement represents the coming together of three major streams of Christian teaching and practice: the charismatic, the evangelical, and the liturgical-sacramental. In practice its major characteristic is the discovery by Christians from evangelical, charismatic, and pentecostal backgrounds of the riches of liturgical worship, sacramental life, and the teaching of the church fathers, allied to a new concern for the unity of the whole visible body of Christ.

The Convergence movement has developed several forms of expression: (1) pentecostals and charismatics developing more liturgical forms where they are; (2) their joining historic liturgical churches; and (3) the formation of new charismatic denominations/communions with episcopal ministry claiming apostolic succession. The first and second categories are found primarily in North America, and the third category reflects North American initiatives. In the second category, many have joined the Episcopal Church (Robert Webber of Wheaton College [IL] has been a key influence by his teaching and his writings, e.g., *On the Canterbury Trail* [1985]), but the more notable development has been the number joining the Orthodox Church. The trend toward Orthodoxy began with some young evangelicals dissatisfied with their parachurch existence, who began a search in 1966 that led to what in 1979 they called the Evangelical

Orthodox Church. Most of them were received corporately into the Antiochian Orthodox Church in 1987 as the Antiochian Evangelical Orthodox Mission.

In the third category are the ›Charismatic Episcopal Church (CEC) and the ›Communion of Evangelical Episcopal Churches (CEEC). CEC was founded in 1992 by Randolph Adler of San Clemente, CA, now described as the patriarch. CEC has about 180 congregations in the U.S. and has received into fellowship clergy and congregations in Estonia, the Philippines, and Kenya. In the last four years it has drawn several former Episcopalian charismatic leaders, including Philip Zampino, founder of the Life in Jesus Community in Frederick, MD; Mark Pearson, prominent for his healing and teaching ministry; and Philip Weeks, well-known for his ministry in the Philippines. CEEC is based in Oklahoma, with the presiding bishop, Wayne Boosahda, in Tulsa and with four other bishops in Oklahoma City. CEEC describes itself as "a communion in The Holy Catholic Church whose identity and self-understanding is rooted in the Anglican Spiritual Tradition." Outside the U.S. (approx. 200 congregations) its member churches are mostly in the Philippines (3,000), the Ivory Coast (100), Kenya (100), and India (50).

9. Messianic Judaism.

Although the ›messianic Jewish movement dates back to the late 1960s as a new charismatic thrust of the Holy Spirit, it is the last decade that has seen its more marked growth and expansion. The number of messianic congregations in the U.S. approaches 300; there are over 50 in Israel, together with remarkable growth in several states of the former Soviet Union. The latter is partly a fruit of the Hear O Israel festivals led by Jonathan Bernis, who has emerged as a major messianic Jewish evangelist. In 1994 there was a reconciliation between two rival North American bodies, the Messianic Jewish Alliance of America (MJAA), led by Robert Cohen and David Chernoff, and the Union of Messianic Jewish Congregations (UMJC), in which ›Daniel Juster and Martin Waldman have been key figures.

Toward Jerusalem Council Two (TJC2), a new initiative for Jewish-Gentile reconciliation within the body of Christ, was formed in 1996 with a committee of 14 (seven Jews and seven Gentiles). The vision for TJC2, which had come to Waldman and Juster, was of a "second council of Jerusalem" that would be the inverse of the first council in Acts 15: whereas the first council was a gathering of Jews determining the conditions for Gentiles to enter the church, so the second would be a council of Gentile leaders acknowledging the freedom and the right of Jews to belong to the church as Jews. TJC2 has arranged visits to church leaders presenting the reality and the hopes of messianic Jews and prayer journeys to historic sites associated with anti-Jewish measures and outbreaks. TJC2 is a sign of a growing confidence among messianic Jews and a new desire to relate to Gentile Christians and their churches.

10. Unity and Cooperation.

As in its earlier decades, CR has had its share of tensions and divisions, and its stories of reconciliation and widened fellowship. In line with the ethos of networking, there has been increasing cooperation between different strands in CM during the 1990s.

The ICCOWE (International Charismatic Consultation of World Evangelism) conference held at Brighton, England, in July 1991 brought together leaders from most streams on all continents and unleashed a new dynamic for cooperation, particularly in France, where an important ecumenical rally at Charlety, Paris, gathered 12,000 in 1998. NARSC (North American Renewal Service Committee) has remained active in North America and planned a major pentecostal-charismatic conference for June 2000 in St. Louis, while ECC in Europe has lost some momentum, despite the Prague conference of 1997, with its theme "Building Bridges, Breaking Barriers" and its significant Orthodox presence.

Charismatic leaders meetings spanning the different streams continue to meet in the U.S. (the Charismatic Concerns Committee), Britain, France, and the Netherlands, while one has been resuscitated in France and others formed in Germany (1993) and Ireland (1997). Many of the New Church networks have a cooperative philosophy and work together in many of the new initiatives already mentioned: United Prayer Track, March for Jesus, and the Alpha course.

Particularly notable is the new level of Catholic-Evangelical collaboration in Vienna, Austria, initiated by Catholic Archbishop Schönborn's appointment of Johannes Fichtenbauer as his personal delegate to the Free churches. The relationships developing as a result have led to joint services of praise in St. Stephen's Cathedral in Vienna.

B. Extent and Spread.

The decade 1988–98 has seen continued growth in CM and its offspring on all continents, though particularly in the independent sector. The growth has been most rapid in Africa, parts of Asia, and Latin America.

1. North America.

CR within the historic churches has been uneven during this period. In spring 1992, a national survey of evangelicals registered 4.7% of the U. S. population as pentecostal, 6.6% as charismatic, with 0.8% using both terms, giving a total of 12.1%. However, the percentage who have spoken in tongues is lower: the survey found that 8.7% of the sample made this claim, of whom 2.5% were white pentecostal and 1.1% black pentecostal. A later survey by the Barna Research Group reported that 90% of all Americans "pray to God" and 12% pray "in charismatic tongues."

Using a wider range of markers than self-description and glossolalia, 22.9% of the American public were pentecostal/charismatic, of which the larger number, 25.8%, were charismatics within evangelical denominations, 22.1% Roman Catholics, and 15.5% pentecostals (white and black). This 1992 survey indicates that (1) charismatic experience has been steadily spreading in the general population of the United States, and (2) it is not a deeply anchored phenomenon in the life of the mainline churches.

Numbers actively involved in charismatic groups have declined in the Roman Catholic Church; and after periods of decline, Holy Spirit renewal seems to be increasing among Lutherans, Presbyterians, and United Methodists. Some of the general trends mentioned may be responsible for recent growth, especially the prayer movement and Promise Keepers.

The charismatics in the mainline Protestant churches are often involved in the struggle to maintain traditional positions on doctrine and morality. Widespread liberal policies have contributed to an undoubted leakage from mainline Protestant CR to new charismatic churches and to new bodies in the ▸Convergence movement. While renewed congregations generally grow in membership, the loyalty of the new members is often more to the pastor, the charismatic teaching and ministry, than to the denomination.

a. Episcopal. By the late 1980s, CR in the Episcopal Church was largely made up of (1) small groups of charismatics scattered across the United States without ready access to any renewed parish; (2) parishes that incorporated many elements from CR into their corporate life—emphasis on personal experience of the Spirit, every member ministry, styles of praise and music in worship, ministries of healing—without describing themselves as charismatic; and (3) overtly charismatic parishes with the regular manifestation of spiritual gifts in their Sunday liturgy. Besides these people and parishes, there are numerous "postcharismatics," many of whom see their charismatic experience as a significant phase on the way to a richer spirituality, a feature found in other mainline churches.

An important center for Episcopalian Renewal has been Trinity Episcopal School for Ministry (TESM) in Ambridge, PA, founded in 1976. Arising from evangelical currents within the Episcopal Church, but not founded as a charismatic institution, TESM has had an increasing charismatic presence and influence, enhanced by ▸Bishop William Frey, dean-president of TESM (1990–96).

From the early 1990s the struggle to maintain traditional Christian orthodoxy in faith and morals within the Episcopal Church became more acute. Committed Episcopalians began to ask, "Will there be a future for renewal within the Episcopal Church?" Many Episcopal charismatics became convinced that it is not sufficient to evangelize and provide formation; there is also a battle to be fought against unbelief within the church. Until now, Episcopal Renewal Ministries

(ERM) has not played an apologetic role, largely because a 1986 meeting of Evangelicals, Anglo-Catholics, and charismatics in the Episcopal Church had formed an organization for this purpose, Episcopalians United for Revelation, Renewal and Reformation.

There has been a widespread Episcopal tendency to play down a distinctive charismatic movement and to understand instead charismatic renewal as one dimension of a wider renewal. In the 1990s there was a stronger affirmation of basic evangelical-catholic identity among renewed Episcopalians, though the assertion of charismatic identity remains more problematic.

b. Lutheran. Renewal among Lutherans seems to have changed less than CR in other traditions. One reason is the strongly confessional character of Lutheranism; another is that its service agency remained under the leadership of Larry Christenson from 1974 until 1995. LCRS, replaced by the International Lutheran Renewal Center (ILRC) in 1982, serves all Lutheran denominations and includes on its board representatives from the different churches (the Evangelical Lutheran Church of America [ELCA] is now by far the largest numerically). Because the Lutheran Church-Missouri Synod (LC–MS) did not allow fellowship with other Christians, LC–MS charismatics formed their own renewal service organization under ▸Delbert Rossin, Renewal in Missouri (RIM), in 1987, after opposition to renewal had decreased. A series of meetings was held in 1990 and 1992 between representatives of the LC–MS and RIM to resolve the remaining difficulties. A significant advance in understanding occurred, and a statement was drawn up with a series of common affirmations and rejections.

After some decline in the late 1980s and early 1990s, renewal among Lutherans has been picking up momentum. The annual Holy Spirit conferences are growing, and more young people are attending. There is new interest in ELCA, and RIM continues to grow. Lutheran renewal in Canada is growing but at a slower pace.

c. Presbyterian and Reformed. CR among Presbyterians and Reformed had been in decline in the 1980s, with much loss of charismatic members to pentecostal and new charismatic churches. A revitalization began in 1990 when Brad Long took over as executive director of PRMI. Long, a missionary since 1980, brought the dynamism of Taiwan into Presbyterian-Reformed renewal. In addition to the Spirit Alive campaign introduced in 1983, PRMI introduced the Dunamis Project (1991), a retreat program aimed at leadership development, as well as promoting prayer mountains (an idea brought from Korea) and overseas mission outreach, especially in Taiwan and Brazil. A new PRMI Mission Statement (1993) added these further emphases to congregational renewal.

PRMI's emphasis on prayer has led to regular teaching on spiritual warfare and since 1991 to the holding of prayer vigils during the annual general assembly of the Presbyterian Church (U.S.A.). During this period PRMI has played an increasing role as a defender and advocate of traditional biblical orthodoxy in faith and morals.

d. Methodist. CR within the Methodist tradition was not strong in the 1980s, but here too there has been a new wind blowing in the 1990s. There has been a growing grassroots desire among many Methodists to recapture the revival fire of John Wesley and the first Methodists. Renewed congregations have been active in resisting liberal tendencies in the United Methodist Church, often through evangelical Methodist groupings like *Good News* magazine (Wilmore, KY) and a group called Transforming Congregations. Besides the work of the Aldersgate Renewal Fellowship within the United Methodist Church, there is what some call "Third-Wave Methodism," influenced from Toronto and Pensacola, represented by Washington Crossing UM Church near Philadelphia; Pine Forest UM Church in Pensacola, FL; and Upton UM Church in Toledo, OH. A black congregation strongly into renewal is Gibbons UM Church in Brandywine, MD.

e. American Baptist. Among American Baptists, there has been growth in CR under the continued leadership of Gary Clark. Holy Spirit Renewal Ministries in American Baptist Churches (HSRMABC) began the newsletter *Refreshing Times* in 1990. HSRMABC, which has 1,300 members, holds an annual conference at Green Lake, WI, as well as organizing regional conferences and renewal teaching missions and promoting lectures in American Baptist seminaries.

f. Southern Baptist. Among Southern Baptists, a suspicion of CR has remained, and local churches are occasionally expelled from state Baptist associations for charismatic practices. Constant tension exists between a dominant SBC instinct that CR is inherently un-Baptist and the SBC emphasis on congregational autonomy. Only a minority of charismatic pastors and churches within the SBC have managed to maintain their church position and charismatic witness over a long period. Ras Robinson, who led the Fulness group for many years, formed his own Fulness church in 1991. Yet SBC churches continue to be affected by forms of CR, including a Toronto-style current centered in Central Baptist Church in Chattanooga, TN, led by Ron Phillips.

g. African-American. During the 1990s, there was an increasing neo-pentecostal revival among the African-American churches in the U.S. Among the black Baptists, there was a pentecostal outpouring that led to the formation by Paul Morton of the Full Gospel Baptist Church Fellowship (FGBCF) in 1993, which broke away from the National Baptist Convention in 1995. About 5,000 churches affiliated with FGBCF. In the AME Zion Church, a flagship renewed church is Full Gospel AME Zion in Temple Hills, MD, under John Cherry.

h. Anabaptist. In 1989 Empowered Ministries (EM) was formed to foster "Renewal, Unity and Mission in the Anabaptist Stream." It was estimated that 50 to 55% of those who associated with EM were Mennonites, 25 to 30% were Brethren, and 20% were from related renewal congregations. EM focused on renewal of congregational life, with many renewed congregations within EM adopting a cell-growth strategy. EM, however, disbanded in 1995.

CR in the Anabaptist streams has probably had more impact on general church life than in other church traditions. At the 1990 Mennonite World Conference in Winnipeg, many attributed the growth rate of over 50% in Mennonite membership worldwide since 1974 to Spirit-led renewal. The renewal has been taken seriously in the Anabaptist churches with regular meetings between denominational officials and renewal leaders.

i. Roman Catholic. The situation in the Roman Catholic Church in the U.S. and Canada has been rather different from that in the mainline Protestant traditions. CCR has overall declined in numbers, except among the ethnic minorities (Hispanic CCR has flourished as has CCR among the Filipino and Korean communities). While many Catholic charismatics read *Charisma,* watch Protestant TV ministries, and visit Toronto and Pensacola, CCR leadership has not been as influenced by these trends as their Protestant counterparts. There are some notable exceptions; e.g., Henri Lemay of Quebec, a member of ICCRS, has been a major promoter of "the Father's blessing" in the Catholic Church, as has Msgr. Vincent Walsh of Philadelphia, a veteran leader in CCR.

In its first decade CCR in North America was strongly shaped by the covenant communities; in its second decade this influence was decreasing, and by its third decade it was minimal (though the ministry of Ralph Martin has continued to be important nationally and internationally). The efforts of the NSC to fill the void resulting from the relative marginalization of the covenant communities eventually crystallized around the concept of bringing "the Renewal to the heart of the [Catholic] Church." An NSC-sponsored consultation of leaders and theologians produced the booklet *Fanning the Flame,* which is in many ways a manifesto for the pastoral application of the key concepts in *Christian Initiation and Baptism in the Holy Spirit* by K. McDonnell and G. Montague (1991).

j. New Churches. New churches and new church networks have seen the greatest expansion in this decade, with the for-

mation of networks often crossing national boundaries, and a wave of new missionaries from this sector, which comprises some 2.5 million members in all, according to *Operation World* (1993). This sector tends to experience rapid change, and the patterns of one decade often differ from those of the previous decade. Other major networks in the U.S. (besides those listed in IV.A.7 above) are the ▸Vineyard churches, founded by ▸John Wimber, which have grown steadily, reaching some 500 in the U.S. and 60 in Canada by 1998. The Vineyard churches are noted for their vibrant worship and musical creativity, with several major songwriters belonging to the Vineyard movement. People of Destiny International now has 38 team-related churches (34 in the U.S., 3 in Mexico, and 1 in the Philippines). CM, especially in the U.S., tends to produce its own stars: new names and faces that have become prominent in this decade include ▸Rick Joyner of Morning Star Ministries (producing *Morning Star Journal*) and ▸Mahesh Chavda, both of Charlotte, NC; ▸Francis Frangipane of Iowa; ▸Mahesh Chavda; and ▸Mike Bickle of Metro Fellowship, Kansas City.

Many new church networks that had been developing in the U.S. saw rapid expansion in the 1990s. Wagner includes the following networks in *The New Apostolic Churches:* Antioch Churches and Ministries, led by John P. Kelly, with more than 100 churches in the U.S. and presently working in many other nations; Crusaders Ministries, led by John Eckhardt of Chicago; Grace Presbytery, led by Michael P. Fletcher of Fayetteville, NC; Dove Christian Fellowship, led by Larry Kreider of Ephrata, PA; Morning Star, led by Rice Broocks of Brentwood, TN (the original nucleus of leaders coming from Bob Weiner's Maranatha Campus Ministries, disbanded in 1989); Ministers Fellowship, led by Dick Iverson of Portland, OR; Grace Korean Church, led by David Kim of Anaheim, CA. Other networks based in the U.S. include Liberty Fellowship, led by Ken Sumrall of Pensacola, FL; Calvary Ministries, led by Paul Paino of Fort Wayne, IN; Harvest International Ministries (HIM), led by Che Ahn of Pasadena, CA; People of Destiny, led by C. J. Mahaney of Gaithersburg, MD (34 churches in U.S., 4 outside); and the newly formed Morning Star Fellowship, led by Rick Joyner. The Network of Christian Ministries, now led by Paul Paino, holds an annual conference for network and ministry leaders.

k. Canada. In Canada, patterns of renewal in the mainline churches are generally similar to those in the U.S., except that the United Church of Canada (UCC) plays a bigger role than any U.S. denomination and has been the scene of the fiercest liberal-conservative battles. The 1988 General Council stance on homosexuality led many CR leaders and congregations to leave the UCC. Many joined the Congregational Christian Church, then only present in Ontario, leading to the formation in 1990 of the Congregational Christian Churches of Canada, with John Tweedie elected as first national president, while others joined the Reformed Church of Canada. The Renewal Fellowship in the UCC continues, but its membership in the mid 1990s was only a quarter of the 1988 figure. It has collaborated with other renewal groups within the UCC—Church Alive, the Community of Concern, and the National Alliance of Covenanting Congregations—to uphold traditional biblical standards. Similarly, the Anglican Renewal Ministries of Canada has joined with Barnabas Anglican Ministries (Evangelical) and the Prayer Book Society of Canada to form the Anglican Essentials Coalition to defend traditional Anglican essentials.

2. Europe.

The decade 1988–98 has been marked in Europe by the collapse of Communism and the opening up of Eastern Europe. As a result, the CM in Eastern Europe has been developing steadily but more strongly among new charismatic churches and in CCR. There has been a great influx of Western personnel and resources, both from Western Europe and from North America. Charismatic groups have been among those flooding into the former Soviet Union and arousing the opposition and ire of the Orthodox Church. In CCR, Emmanuel community from France was asked by Bishop Cordes of the Vatican to form new communities in Eastern Europe (which they have done in Hungary and in the Czech Republic), while evangelistic and formation work has also been done by Daniel-Ange of France; Ralph Martin's Renewal Ministries of Ann Arbor, MI; and Dave Nodar's Christlife of Baltimore, MD.

As on other continents, the growth of new churches and new church networks in Europe has accelerated in this decade. Charismatic churches have been springing up in countries such as Austria, France, and Germany, where evangelical Free churches had in the past always been small and marginal.

a. Britain. In Britain, CR among Anglicans has increased during the period, helped by the evangelical-charismatic rapprochement, an increasing openness to healing, the influence of John Wimber, the Toronto Blessing (which some would consider a mixed blessing), and most recently by the Alpha course. ⃗Holy Trinity Brompton, the home of ⃗Alpha, and St. Andrew's, Chorleywood, have become major centers of renewal, with their own outreach, programs, and church links. As a result, Anglican Renewal Ministries (under ⃗Michael Mitton from 1989 to 1997 and John Leach since 1997) has become mostly a service agency for renewal in smaller parishes, especially in rural areas. The movement is taken more seriously by church authorities, as is evidenced by "The Way of Renewal" (1998), an official report by the Board of Mission of the General Synod of the Church of England, edited by M. Mitton. There has been some increase among Baptists, with leading roles being played by Steve Gaukroger, Graham's successor at Gold Hill, and Steve Chalke, well-known on national television. Among Methodists, renewal has been spurred since the late 1980s by Headway, a combination of evangelicals and charismatics committed to evangelism and prayer for revival, and the annual Easter People gatherings pioneered by Rob Frost, now drawing about 12,000 people.

Britain has seen steady growth in new church networks, formerly called the ⃗House Church Movement, with an increasing outreach and influence on other countries, particularly in continental Europe and the Commonwealth. The largest is New Frontiers, led by ⃗Terry Virgo of Brighton (with outreach especially in South Africa and in India), followed by Pioneer, led by ⃗Gerald Coates of Cobham. The characteristic features of the new charismatic churches have been well illustrated in the ⃗March for Jesus, founded in 1987 by G. Coates, R. Forster, L. Green, and G. Kendrick: evangelistic thrust, an emphasis on spiritual warfare, musical creativity, and confidence for revival and spiritual advance.

b. Ireland. In Ireland, CCR declined sharply in the 1980s after peaking at the time of the Dublin conference in 1978. The mid 1990s saw the reconciliation within CCR of the Irish NSC and the mostly lay group known as the Evangelical Catholic Initiative, making possible in 1997 the formation of a representative Irish Charismatic Leaders Conference. The statement "Evangelicals and Catholics Together in Ireland" (1998), modeled on the U.S. statement of 1994, was a pastoral charismatic initiative, a factor reflected in the Irish statement's additional sections "We Repent Together" and "We Pray Together." In Northern Ireland, CR remains one of the few places where Protestants and Catholics pray together. Paul Reid of Belfast leads a new church network called Lifelink.

c. Italy. In France and Italy, CCR has continued to grow. The major expression of CCR in Italy is called Rinnovamento nello Spirito (RnS), whose conference attracts 40,000 to Rimini each spring. RnS grew from 1,202 groups in 1994 to 1,385 in 1998, with 205 groups in Sicily, 153 in Piedmont, and 143 in Lombardy. In 1996, the Casa del Padre community in Sanremo, led by Gabriele de Andreis, launched the Iniziativa di Comunione nel Rinnovamento Carismatico Cattolico (ICRCC), gathering many Italian CCR communities into closer relationship. ICRCC has been advocating an important principle, namely, the right to form their own expression of CCR within the Roman Catholic Church, arguing that CR is a spiritual current that cannot be restricted to any one church organization. These initiatives have led to reconciliation within Catholic renewal in Italy, including Comunità Maria, the first Italian CCR community belonging neither to RnS nor to ICRCC. RnS publishes a monthly, *Rinnovamento nello Spirito Santo*, while the Casa del Padre and ICRCC produce *La Forza della Verità* three times a year. In Italy an important witness to reconciliation has been given by Matteo Calisi (Catholic) and Giovanni Traettino (pentecostal), who organize an annual Catholic-pentecostal conference.

d. France. In France the major charismatic communities (Emmanuel, Chemin Neuf, Béatitudes, Pain de Vie) have continued to expand, forming more houses or centers in France and increasing their presence in other parts of the world, especially in French-speaking Africa and Eastern Europe. Their magazines remain the most influential publications in CCR. The CCR prayer groups in France have asserted their own role and identity in occasional major rallies in Paris that have attracted 20,000. CCR continues to have a significant impact in Malta, where it is generally welcomed by the Catholic Church.

e. Portugal. In Portugal there are approximately 250 CCR groups involving some 12,000 people. Manna Christian Church, founded in the mid 1980s by Jorge Tadeu in Lisbon, is a charismatic network of Faith churches not in relation to other charismatic and pentecostal expressions.

f. Germany. In Germany, CR in the Evangelical Church (mostly Lutheran) has recovered since the loss of W. Kopfermann in 1988, benefiting from the integration of the East German leadership in 1991. The leadership of ▸Friedrich Aschoff from Bavaria was firm but open, followed by a leader from the East, W. Breithaupt. About 500 pastors are involved, and their magazine *Gemeinde Erneuerung* has a circulation of about 9,000. Within the Free churches, CM had the biggest impact on the Association of Evangelical Free Church Congregations (Bund Evangelisch-Freikirchler Gemeinden), in which at least a third are charismatic in expression. After the withdrawal of ▸H. Mühlen, CCR in Germany was no longer divided into two camps, though new tensions arose between more Marian and more ecumenical emphases. The interconfessional conference held each year in East Berlin continues to draw participants from Eastern European countries. There has been a marked growth in new charismatic churches, of which the largest are the Christian Centers (Christliche Zentren) in several major cities.

g. Scandinavia. In the Scandinavian countries, renewal groupings continue to exert an influence within the state Lutheran churches, though streams have been developing outside the historic churches. Norway and Finland, which are less secularized than Denmark and Sweden, have stronger renewal currents. The movements within the Lutheran state churches are all now known as OASE, with Denmark, Finland, and Sweden following Norway's lead. The OASE leaders from these four countries have been

meeting every three years, though the emphases, strengths, and weaknesses vary from one country to another.

In Denmark Dansk OASE was founded in 1989. It hosts annual conferences for leaders (attended by 100 to 150) and for all (about 500 to 600 people). Over its first 10 years, OASE has placed an increasing emphasis on training cell leaders and building up the local church; since 1995 Morten Munch is in full-time leadership. Another grouping founded in 1989, Forum for a Free People's Church (Folkekirke), led by Ole Madsen, pastor of the Bethlehemskirken in Copenhagen, has planted Lutheran congregations outside the state church and includes churches within who want to be freer from state influence. The Forum has 13 congregations and two mercy organizations; it cooperates with OASE.

In Norway, the OASE movement, now led by Kari Foss, whose summer conference draws about 5,000 people, has also moved more toward equipping the people and being a servant movement within the state church. Closer relationships than previously now exist between OASE and charismatic groupings outside the state church. The English-based Covenant Ministries network has six churches in Norway, the largest in Bergen, while the Vineyard has four, with about 500 members. The charismatics in the nonpentecostal Free churches do not have their own official groups, a stance made easier by the recognition of some charismatic expressions within these churches.

In Sweden, CR in the Lutheran state church is expressed through OASE-Sweden. A major charismatic center in Sweden is the Livets Ord (Word of Life) church in Uppsala, a Faith church pastored by Ulf Ekman, with its own schools and university.

In Finland, data from 1995 indicate that CR has influenced 49% of Lutheran parishes, with the highest figures in Mikkeli, East Finland (67%) and Helsinki (62%), with 13% regular and 36% occasional charismatic activities. The Lutheran CR magazine *Kädenojennus* has a circulation of 3,000. The number of new nondenominational charismatic churches is growing fast, totaling some 90 congregations. Many are DAWN-related, and many practice the "new wine blessing" (what the Toronto Airport Christian Fellowship calls the Father's blessing). This has been strongly opposed within the Finnish pentecostal church, and the members of the "new wine" churches are ex-Lutherans and ex-pentecostals. The new churches see the pentecostals becoming a traditional church in a negative sense, while the conservative evangelical wing of the Lutheran church is showing new respect for the pentecostals due to their similar response to the phenomena associated with the "new wine." Interdenominational pastors' prayer meetings are held in 20 towns, arising from March for Jesus 1993.

e. Eastern Europe. The years since the collapse of Communism in Eastern Europe have been years of growth for

CR in most Eastern European churches, except in Poland, where the movement was generally small and undeveloped prior to 1989. In Lithuania and Slovakia, CCR has perhaps received the most help with the encouragement of the local bishops. In Lithuania the first CCR group was formed in 1986.

In Poland, CCR is the largest in Eastern Europe due to the more successful resistance of the church under Communism and the influence of the Light-Life (Oasis) movement. The annual CCR pilgrimage to the Marian shrine of Czestochowa increased from 20,000 in 1992 to 150,000 by 1995. Official CCR in Poland is primarily ordered toward the 300 prayer groups, and new communities of young people have not been well integrated. The Catholic hierarchy has had difficulty in accepting lay leadership, especially in new communities. A community of 500 in Kalisz left the Catholic Church in 1997, while earlier the Nowe Zycie (New Life) community in Krakow largely disintegrated after the lay founder was replaced by a priest. The first national meeting of leaders in CCR in the spring of 1998 gathered 300 leaders, half priests, half laity, to address the issue of hierarchy-laity relations.

CCR has been growing in Hungary, but in an uncoordinated way until the formation of an NSC in 1995. In early 1999, 120 prayer groups were registered with the NSC, though the estimated number involved in some way in CCR is 20,000. About 10,000 people attend their annual conference. CR exists in the Hungarian Reformed Church but has not received much encouragement. Ecumenical contacts have been facilitated by the youthful New Jerusalem Community in Budapest and a pentecostal pastor, L. Simonfalvi, though the largest charismatic church in Budapest, the independent Faith Church of Sandor Nemeth, is strongly separatist. CCR is stronger in Slovakia, with its center in Zvolen, than in the Czech Republic, which has not much over 1,000 regular participants, though with communities in Brno and Plzen.

Tensions have been growing in Russia between new Free church groupings and the Russian authorities, both church and state. Efforts such as the Mission Volga (1992) and Mission Urals (1994–95), led by Kalevi Lehtinen of Finland, which sought to work in association with the Orthodox Church, had only limited success. Among the national bodies are the Russian Union of Christians of the Evangelical Faith, which incorporates about 1,000 churches previously independent or led by foreigners, and the Charismatic Association of Christian Churches of Russia. Calvary International of Jacksonville, FL, had planted 125 churches in the former Soviet Union.

3. Africa.

CM has grown steadily throughout Africa, except in the almost totally Islamic nations of the north. The new wave of charismatic-type churches that have sprung up in Africa since the 1970s often call themselves pentecostal, but many have no particular relationship with the pentecostal movement and are in effect an African version of new charismatic churches. These new churches are different in theology, emphases, and style from the African Independent Churches (AICs, now often called African Instituted Churches or African Initiated Churches), more evangelical in their theology and less liturgical, and hostile to the perceived syncretism of many AICs. Their similarities to Western pentecostal-charismatic patterns can lead to an overlooking of their more African features. The new African charismatic churches give a major place to ministries of healing and deliverance, taking seriously the power of witch doctors and spiritism in a way that the missionary churches have not. Their new members are often recruited from the ranks of the mainline churches amid accusations of "sheep-stealing."

Among the many huge African churches of a charismatic type are Yopogon Baptist Church in Abidjan, Ivory Coast; Victory Christian Church in Lagos, Nigeria (10,000); the Redeemed Evangelical Mission of Lagos, led by Bishop M. Okonkwo; Calvary Baptist Church in Accra, Ghana; Lighthouse Cathedral, Accra, led by Bishop Dag Heward-Mills; Bethel World Outreach Centre and the Faith church in Monrovia, Liberia; Living Water Church in Blantyre, Malawi, led by Stanley Ndovi; Rhema Bible Church in Harare, Zimbabwe; All Nations Christian Church in Windhoek, Namibia; and Prayer Palace Church in Kampala, Uganda, led by Bishop Grivas Musisi.

CR in the missionary churches, Catholic and Protestant, has flourished in many countries, though more in East Africa (Kenya, Uganda, Rwanda) and West Africa (Nigeria, Ghana, Burkina Faso, Ivory Coast) than in much of Central Africa (Zimbabwe, Zambia, Malawi).

Both Nigeria and Ghana have been strongly impacted by CM. In both countries, a major thrust for renewal in the Protestant churches came through student groups holding interdenominational prayer meetings, and through the influence of FGBMFI and Women's Aglow. In Nigeria a charismatic group at the University of Ibadan formed World Action Team for Christ in 1970, which had reached all six Nigerian universities by 1975. Although the Deeper Life Church of William Kumuyi in Lagos dates back to 1973, in the early 1980s, several flourishing student bodies in Nigeria became new charismatic churches, a process often begun when they decided to meet on Sunday mornings. The rapid spread of new charismatic churches in Nigeria and Ghana has caused the mainline churches to become more open to CR in the hope that this will stem the drift of young people to the new churches. CR is strong in Ghana, except in the Anglican Church, with renewal groups including the Methodist Prayer and Renewal Programme and the Bible Study and Prayer Group movement in the Presbyterian Church.

In Nigeria below the Islamic north, all the denominations are experiencing renewal. Prayer and fasting and signs and wonders of healing and deliverance are common. Anglican CR has multiplied, supported by regular SOMA missions. Presbyterian pastor James Ukaegbu had a profound experience of the Holy Spirit in 1979, and he immediately had an impact on fellow Nigerian pastors. Ukaegbu was investigated by the general assembly of his church, but several years later, in 1989, he was elected moderator for three years and was then appointed full-time director of evangelism.

Anglican renewal has flourished in East Africa, often battling against corruption in society. There are many renewed clergy in Kenya, but CR is strongest in Uganda, especially in the southwest closest to the Rwanda conflict. However, many Anglican charismatics have defected to the newly formed Charismatic Episcopal Church (CEC). A Ugandan Presbyterian, Peterson Sozi, formed the Back to God Evangelistic Association in 1983 and led thousands to Christ through mass crusades. In 1990 Sozi founded the Reformed Presbyterian Church in Uganda, which has recently been joined by 70 formerly pentecostal congregations. CR has also flourished in Ethiopia, particularly in the Evangelical Mekane Yesu Church (Lutheran) and in the Meserete Kristos Church (Mennonite). Lutheran renewal has also been strong in Tanzania.

New charismatic churches and networks in South Africa have multiplied. The largest church is Rhema Bible Church in Randburg, founded and led by ▸Ray McCauley, with 16,000 members. In 1989 Ed Roebert (1940–97), founding pastor of Hatfield Christian Church in Pretoria, formed the International Fellowship of Christian Churches (IFCC). Since Roebert's death, Hatfield Christian Church, led by François van Niekerk, has left IFCC and formed its own Harvest Network. IFCC, which has a Faith emphasis, is now led by McCauley and has some 270 churches in association. Another grouping, the Network of Christian Ministries of Southern Africa, which coordinated more restoration-oriented churches, was dissolved due to the constant fluidity of leaders and networks. The former Network leaders lead their own groupings: New Covenant International (Dudley Daniel), Agape Ministries International (Johan Filmalter), and Foundation Ministries (Derek Crumpton). Derek Morphew, who had led Associated Christian Ministries, joined the Vineyard. Bishop Joseph Kobo leads the Anointed Voice of Africa Ministries from Umtata in the Transkei. His People Christian Ministries, led by Paul Daniel, has growing campus-centered churches in seven South African cities, as well as one each in Namibia and Zambia.

The charismatic impulses in the Anglican Church of South Africa are still present, particularly in Port Elizabeth (Bishop Eric Pike). A strong leader has emerged in northern Mozambique in the person of Anglican bishop Dinis Sengulane, who has developed a five-stage reconciliation program for his country.

In many African countries, CCR dates from the early to mid 1970s, often through missionaries encountering CR on furlough in Europe. The growth in the French-speaking countries has been stronger than in the English-speaking ones, due to big evangelistic healing meetings held by Fr. Tardif and, in the last decade, to the French communities, who generally began their presence with charitable work and later opened up into evangelization. The African foundations of Emmanuel community, begun in Zaire (now Congo-Kinshasa) in 1989, now extend to 10 francophone countries. Prayer groups are much bigger than in the U.S. and Europe. In Benin there were 72 prayer meetings with 18,000 regular participants in 1996. In Cameroun, there are over 300 prayer groups falling into three main families, Ephphata, Cana, and Colonne de Feu. Before the recent political disturbances in Zaire, there were 113 CCR groups in Kinshasa. The archdiocese of Lubumbashi has an association LEMED for the ministry of evangelization and deliverance. In Zaire there is a civilly registered association of interconfessional charismatic prayer groups that numbered 135 before the civil war. Reports indicate that charismatic worship and ministry are flourishing in countries devastated by war and famine such as Congo (former Zaire) and Brazzaville-Congo.

In CCR, in anglophone Africa, the countries with leaders working full-time for CCR (Fr. E. Sievers in Uganda; Bro. D. Muller in Tanzania; T. Assibey in Ghana) are leading the way, with full programs, community centers, and schools of evangelization.

In Uganda there have been signs of revival since 1995, with some prayer meetings attracting thousands of people. In Ghana, formation programs are more developed, with 10 indigenous formation programs for leaders in 1998. In Nigeria, CCR is represented in almost all dioceses, with the greatest strength being in the Onitsha province in the Southeast.

4. Asia.

While Asia as a whole remains a continent where Christians are a minority, some Asian countries have been seeing an increasing wave of revival/renewal, in particular South Korea and the Philippines, with significant impact also in areas of India, Indonesia, Malaysia, as well as in Singapore. These countries are now sending an impressive number of missionaries to other nations and continents.

Several of the world's megachurches are found in Korea; these churches are pentecostal-charismatic or open to charismatic-type worship and ministry. From the 1970s, many denominations joined together in large-scale revival meetings with an emphasis on the Holy Spirit, contributing to rapid church growth, although not as rapidly as Korean pentecostalism. Presbyterianism has grown faster than other mainline denominations, aided—some would say—by many divisions. Among the many Presbyterian churches impacted by CR is the 55,000 member Ju An Church in Inchon, led by

Na Kyum-il. Older Presbyterian churches such as Young Nak Church in Seoul now manifest a great freedom in worship and emphasize hearing God in dreams and visions. Similar patterns are found in Kwang Lim, one of the largest Methodist churches in the world, led by Kim Sun Do. Sung Rak Church in Seoul, which is independent Baptist, led by Ki Dong Kim, has seen explosive growth, forming Berea Academy and developing outreach in Ghana. In the 1990s the Korean churches are devoting more attention to growth in depth as well as numerical increase.

In the Philippines, the Jesus Is Lord Fellowship, founded and led by Eddie Villanueva, has 300,000 members in Metro Manila and 1 million elsewhere in the Philippines. Also centered in Metro Manila is the Power of Faith Christian Fellowship, a network begun by Nelio Liga. The Philippines have also seen many churches joining the new Convergence bodies, the charismatic Episcopal Church and the Communion of Evangelical Episcopal Churches (3,000 congregations).

Singapore has been a vibrant center for CR. In the Anglican Church, first under Bishop Chui Ban It, who was baptized in the Spirit in 1973, and then from 1982 under Bishop Moses Tay, assisted by Canon James Wong. In 1990, 800 Anglicans from 40 nations gathered in Singapore dedicated the 1990s to be a Decade of Evangelism. Other influential churches in Singapore are Faith Community Baptist, led by Lawrence Khong, with 5,000 members following a cell-group strategy, and Calvary Charismatic Centre, which has an active missionary program to Africa.

In China the House Church Movement has continued to spread at an astonishing rate; estimates for numbers attending run as high as 60 million. Besides stressing a personal relationship with Jesus Christ and the Bible as the Word of God, the major emphases in this charismatic-type revival in China are recognition of signs and wonders, an entry into Christ's

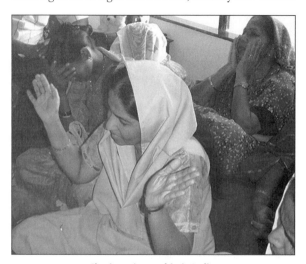

Charismatic worship in India.

sufferings, the power of prayer, belief in the church as a spiritual structure, and a strong sense of mission. Within CCR, the Catholic Charismatic Council for Asia-Pacific (CCCAP) was formed in 1994 with an office in Tacloban, Philippines. Covenant communities have been formed in the Philippines, Malaysia, Indonesia, and Sri Lanka. Healing and deliverance ministries have played an important role in its spread.

In the Philippines, the Second National Congress on the Holy Spirit, organized jointly by CCR and the Archdiocese of Manila in Jan. 1998, involved 40 bishops and nearly 4,000 lay leaders; it was followed by an all-night vigil attended by 300,000. The communities include the Community of God's Little Children in Tacloban City, led by Fr. Bart Pastor; the Bukas Loob Sa Diyos (Open to the Spirit of God) Community in Makati City, led by Antonio de Los Reyes; and Ang Ligaya ng Panginoon Community, in Pasig City, led by Fr. Herb Schneider. The Couples for Christ movement, based on a covenant commitment, arose out of Ang Ligaya in 1981, produces the magazine *Ugnayan*, involves half a million people in the Philippines, and had spread to 44 other countries by 1997.

In India, CCR has flourished under the leadership of Fr. Rufus Pereira with 25,000 at the 1997 national convention, though the most astonishing impact has been at Chalakudy in Muringoor, Kerala, where 15,000 attend healing and evangelistic crusades each week led by ˈFr. Mathew Naikomparambil and his team, and up to 200,000 participate in the occasional conferences. In general the emergence of indigenous leadership in the Indian church has favored an openness to the Holy Spirit, and in many places church leaders are actively fostering renewal. In the Church of South India (CSI), CM in the wide sense has been growing, with the leadership of Bishop K. J. Samuel of East Kerala, who, inspired by the Brighton Conference of 1991, launched a successful program of church planting. In 1997 a SOMA team was invited by the CSI Council for Mission and Evangelism to teach at an official conference.

5. Latin America.

Argentina has had a major influence on CM in the 1990s, even beyond Latin America, through several pentecostal leaders, such as Carlos Annacondia, Omar Cabrera, Hector Giminez, and Claudio Friedzon. The major emphases coming from Argentina have been prayer, repentance, holiness, and unity. Many Baptist churches in Argentina are charismatic, such as Central Baptist in Buenos Aires (Carlos Mraida and Pablo Bottari) and Nuevo Pueblo Baptist Church in Berisso (3,000 people plus 15 annex churches in the La Plata area). After years of tension between the Móron Mennonite Church in Buenos Aires with their denomination, relations are much easier in the climate of reconciliation pervading the recent revival, and there are now many renewed Mennonite congregations.

Throughout Latin America, there has been a "pentecostalization" of evangelical Protestant churches in the last 10 years. Among the larger charismatic churches are the International Charismatic Mission in Bogota, Colombia, led by Cesar and Claudia Castellanos, with 30,000 members in 19 congregations; Ekklesia Centro Cristiano Colombiano in Cali, founded by Julio Ruibal (1953–95); Los Pinos Christian Center in Cucuta, Colombia, begun by José Satirio; Las Acacias Evangelical Church in Caracas, Venezuela, led by S. Olson; Igreja Evangélica Renascer em Cristo (Evangelical Church of the Rebirth in Christ), in Sao Paolo, Brazil, which had 50,000 members in 1995; Ekklesia Church in La Paz, Bolivia, founded by Ruibal, with 11,000 members; El Shaddai Church in Guatemala City, led by Harold Caballeros, with 8,000 members; Center of Faith Church in Mexico City; Calacoaya Christian Center in Mexico City, founded by Gonzalo Vega (6,000 members plus 27 affiliated Christian Centers throughout Mexico); Centros de Fe, Esperanza y Amor (Centers of Faith, Hope, and Love), begun in the Monterrey area of Mexico. The Sana Nossa Terra (Heal Our Land) movement of 200 charismatic churches, centered in Brasilia and focused on combating spiritism and the occult to open Brazil for Christ.

Among the historic Protestant churches in Latin America there has been an opening to the renewing work of the Holy Spirit, even in some churches traditionally opposed to gifts of the Spirit, such as the Presbyterian Church in Brazil. Both there and in the more liberal Independent Presbyterian Church, where more congregations have been impacted by CR, there is an increasing desire to integrate the experience of the Holy Spirit with a Reformed theological understanding.

In Cuba the Methodist Church has become predominantly charismatic with Emilio Gonzales as the major leader. There is also a strong charismatic presence among Cuban Baptists. Anglican CR has continued to grow, including the formation of ARM-Brazil. Also, the Brazilian Evangelical Association (AEVB) was formed in 1991 under the leadership of Caio Fábio D'Araújo Filho, a Presbyterian pastor influenced by CR. AEVB is an attempt to provide a united voice for Brazilian evangelicals (pentecostal, charismatic, and other) and to promote a more holistic view of mission.

In CCR the meetings of ECCLA have been supplemented by CONCCLAT (Consejo Carismático Católico Latinoamericano), founded in 1995 and made up of national coordinators and advisors from every country in Latin America. This development reflects the fuller structuring of CCR and the growth of the movement in every Latin American country. For many years, CCR was accepted within the Roman Catholic Church but not strongly supported by the bishops. In the 1990s the widespread advance of pentecostal and charismatic churches in Latin America persuaded many bishops that the only effective Catholic response is spiritual renewal and encouragement of CCR.

In Brazil, CCR has seen an immense growth from an estimated 2 million charismatic Catholics in 1989, and 4 million in 1994, to an estimated 8 million in 1998, belonging to 60,000 groups. The biggest Catholic gatherings in Latin America are the CCR rallies often held at Pentecost in football stadiums. The rally in Sao Paolo, Brazil, gathers as many as 170,000. The Comunidade Emanuel in Rio de Janeiro produces the magazine *Jesus vive é o Senhor* with about 14,000 subscribers. In Argentina there are 3,000 groups varying between 20 and 300 persons. The Comunidad de Convivencia with 800 members promotes weeklong charismatic retreats called Convivencias con Dios (Living with God). The NSC in Argentina has held meetings for those working in politics, trade unions, and for the promotion of social justice. In Colombia, the El Minuto de Dios Community in Bogota, led by Frs. Diego Jaramillo and Camillo Bernal, continues to exercise an important role, with its radio station (begun in 1987), its university, and its work for the poor. Mexico is another country with a major CCR presence; its National Youth Gathering drew over 14,000 young people in 1998, while a similar gathering in Panama drew 6,000. A major influence in Mexico is Fr. Alfonso Navarro, pastor of Resurrection parish in the south of Mexico City, where a Center of Evangelization trains evangelists and forms leaders. Haiti's national conference for CCR drew 30,000 people in 1997; the Ecuador conference drew 8,000.

6. Oceania.

In Australia, CR in the mainline Protestant churches has generally weakened, with many charismatic congregations leaving in the second half of the 1990s, especially from the Uniting Church, to join new charismatic networks or denominations. The Christian Outreach Centre, begun at Mansfield, Brisbane, in 1974, has been aggressively evangelistic, growing to 180 churches in Australia and more than 400 in other nations, and forming the South Pacific School of Ministries in the Solomon Islands. Australian renewal has been much impacted by the Toronto Blessing, with details chronicled in *Renewal Journal,* edited by Geoff Waugh of Brisbane. Crosslink Christian Network was formed about 1995 to link new wave churches. "Share the Holy Spirit" conferences, convened by Joseph Chircop of Sydney, were held annually from 1995 to culminate at the time of the Sydney Olympics in 2000. By 1995, 11 Australian churches were accepted into Vineyard, and 10 in New Zealand. The pentecostal-charismatic monthly *New Day* ceased publication in July 1997.

In New Zealand, CR in the mainline churches has survived more strongly than in Australia, especially among Anglicans and Presbyterians, though, as in the U.S., there has been an increasing struggle to maintain biblical moral standards. Anglican Renewal Ministries New Zealand, for many years under the leadership of Don Battley, has been expanding its activities, with the promotion of the Summer Wine camps, along the lines of the British New Wine meetings, and with the appointment of a coordinator for the South Island as well as the North. Renewal Ministries–New Zealand, formerly Presbyterian Renewal Ministries New Zealand, under the leadership of Margaret Waite and Ian Woods, has had a major impact, influencing about one-half of the Presbyterian churches. Unusual is the Te Atatu Church in Auckland, led by Brian Hathaway, a Brethren church that has opened to CR, seeking to bring together the evangelical, charismatic, and social justice streams of Christian life.

Charismatic expressions have been spreading steadily in the Pacific Islands, with numerous theophanies of the Spirit, particularly in the Solomon Islands and in Papua New Guinea, as for example at the Lutheran Training Centre for Evangelists in the Eastern Highlands of P.N.G. in 1988–89, although some charismatic Lutherans there have been disciplined or expelled.

V. ANALYSIS.

As the earlier sections (I.A and II.A) indicate, CM dates from the first stirrings in the 1950s and the beginnings of organized forms and the first consciousness of a distinctive movement in the early 1960s. In the first phase, the new movement was distinguished from the pentecostal movement primarily by the formation of groupings affirming pentecostal experience and gifts *within* historic denominations. At the outset, there were also nondenominational groupings witnessing to baptism in the Spirit and the spiritual gifts, but the facet attracting greater attention was the combination of pentecostal grace and historic church affiliation.

The 1970s saw major expansion in CR in the historic churches of North America, slower growth in the historic churches of Western Europe and Australasia, and the first beginnings in many countries of Africa, Asia, and Latin America. The same period saw the expansion of CM *outside* the historic churches, in the nondenominational sector: this was primarily in North America and Great Britain.

The 1980s saw very uneven patterns in CR within the historic churches. Countries like the United States, Canada, and Ireland witnessed a real decline in most churches, while most non-Islamic countries in the Third World experienced increased growth. However, this was the decade in which the explosion of new charismatic churches began on virtually all continents. These new churches and networks multiplied in countries such as the U.S. and Britain, where they were already a significant presence within the CM, and impacted many countries in Africa and Asia, as well as penetrating some European countries historically resistant to Free church patterns. As a result, by the end of the 1980s, there were more charismatic Christians outside the historic churches than within them.

However, as noted in section IV.A, the 1980s also saw the widespread penetration of the evangelical world by distinctively charismatic features in worship and ministry. The "third wave" terminology, coined by Wagner, has often been used to describe this new Spirit-empowered evangelicalism that accepts spiritual gifts and demonstrative praise, but eschews the charismatic label and any theology of baptism in the Spirit. The "third wave" language, however, suggests too great a distinction between the charismatics and the "third wavers" and does not pay enough attention to the evolution occurring within what had been known as CM or CR. For, some exceptions aside, most notably in CCR, CR had been redefining itself from at least the early 1980s, often moving away from the language of CR to simply "renewal" and placing more emphasis on cooperation with other currents of spiritual renewal in their churches. Charismatic distinctives continue to exist but have generally been downplayed. As a result, much of what has been explicitly charismatic has moved in the direction of Spirit-empowered evangelicalism, while much of evangelicalism has been opening up to this Spirit empowerment. There is not a clear-cut division between "second wavers" (charismatic) and "third wavers" (noncharismatic).

These developments have also been accompanied by a maturing in much of the old CR and a less abrasive and arrogant stance toward other Christians. The charismatic or Spirit-filled current has become more user-friendly and more cooperative with other believers (witness the appeal and the style of March for Jesus and the Alpha course). In the 1990s Holy Spirit renewal was still spreading, though fastest in the new-church sector.

A. Constant Characteristics.

Despite the ongoing evolution of the movement, there are constant characteristics that can be found at each stage and in all its different manifestations. The nine essential elements in CR, described in the first edition of this work (1988), are still the constant characteristics, though some of the changing emphases will be noted.

1. Focus on Jesus.

Renewal in the Spirit is everywhere marked by a focus on Jesus Christ. Testimonies constantly refer to an encounter with Jesus, a deeper yielding to Jesus, and a fuller acceptance of Jesus as Lord. All the distinctive elements of the movement subsequently listed are in fact manifestations of the exercise of Jesus' lordship. Thus, Jesus is known as the living Lord at the heart of Christian worship, the Lord who speaks in the present, who speaks through the Word, who delivers from evil, who heals now, etc.

2. Praise.

Being filled with the Holy Spirit always issues in the praise of God and of his Son Jesus Christ. The first result of the coming of the Holy Spirit is a flow of praise from within the believer, a verification of John 7:38. The believer has a new capacity to give glory to God, evident in the spontaneity of charismatic praise and symbolized in the gift of tongues. Together with this flow of praise has come a great explosion of new songs of praise, possibly unparalleled in Christian history.

3. Love of the Bible.

Despite some evangelical fears that the charismatic emphasis on experience and on spiritual gifts devalues the Scriptures, CR has been consistently marked by a great love and thirst for the Scriptures. Charismatics are typically Bible carriers.

4. God Speaks Today.

Renewal is characterized by the conviction that God speaks to his people, corporately and personally, as directly and as regularly as in the first Christian century. People filled with the Spirit hear the Lord. They experience a directness of communication and guidance from the Lord in a way that shocks or puzzles, attracts or repels other Christians. This experience of God speaking is experienced as intrinsic to knowing God as a loving Father who converses with his children and opens up his inheritance to them. Although personal messages from the Lord to believers often attract attention, experience in CR in general confirms John 16:13–15, that is, that what God most wants to reveal through the Holy Spirit is his Son and his saving plan for creation centered in Jesus.

5. Evangelism.

Holy Spirit renewal regularly brings a heightened urgency for evangelism. This was more evident in the 1990s than in the 1970s. For some, this is an evangelism with a new effectiveness; for others, an inner impulse to evangelize for the first time. Just as Christians filled with the Spirit have a new capacity to speak freely to God in praise, so they have a new capacity and freedom to speak to others about the Lord.

6. Awareness of Evil.

Conscious awareness of the Holy Spirit is typically followed by a new awareness of the reality of Satan and the powers of evil. The spread and development of the movement has led to an increased practice of deliverance and exorcism.

7. Spiritual Gifts.

The spiritual gifts listed in 1 Cor. 12:8–10 were seen from the start as characteristic features of CR. While glossolalia attracted most attention in the early years, the gifts that have come most to the fore in the last decade have been prophecy and healing. Holy Spirit renewal urges the availability of the gifts and their place as an intrinsic part of God's equipment of each local church for its mission. In the 1990s there is much greater experience than in the early years of local churches using the gifts in their ordinary worship and ministry.

8. Eschatological Expectation.

The coming of the Spirit is generally accompanied by an increased expectancy and longing for the return of Jesus. While many charismatics think the end of the world will occur in the near future, the most widespread conviction is of the imminence of Christ's return in the sense that the outpouring of the Holy Spirit in our day represents history moving toward its climax, with Christians ardently longing for the completion of all things as they pray, "Come, Lord Jesus."

9. Spiritual Power.

Holy Spirit renewal is everywhere concerned with spiritual impact and a concern to transform the condition of a powerless church. Being filled with the Holy Spirit is an essential prerequisite for the capacity to praise, for the ability to evangelize, for all ministries of deliverance and the overcoming of evil, and for the exercise of the spiritual gifts. This power of the Spirit is experienced as a gift of the risen Lord Jesus, flowing from obedience to God's Word and manifested in every form of Christian ministry and service, in Word and in sacrament, in ministries within the body of Christ, and in service to those outside.

B. A Comparison with the Pentecostal Movement.

A comparison of CM with the pentecostal movement shows that these nine elements characterize both movements. The differences concern the framework, both ecclesiastical and theological, in which they occur and the social milieu that is most penetrated. It is undeniable that CM and its progeny, at least in the First World, have made most progress in the white middle-class sectors of society, whereas the pentecostal movement in its beginnings was largely a proletarian phenomenon among poor people of all colors. However, CM has from the late 1970s made great progress among the churches of the Third World, most dramatically perhaps in Asia, where it is clearly not the preserve of the middle classes. One conclusion is that the social strata penetrated by CM are those where the historic churches have their strongest membership.

A comparison of the origins of CM and of the pentecostal movement shows that the charismatic origins were more diverse than the pentecostal. There has never been any charismatic equivalent of Azusa Street. In the origins of CM there were many paths by which believers were led to BHS: direct contact with pentecostals or charismatics already baptized in the Spirit, growing experience of spiritual gifts following rediscovery of the power of God in divine healing, outbreaks of glossolalia in circles praying for revival (more so in Europe than in America), Bible studies (especially on the book of Acts), and sovereign interventions of God among people who knew nothing of the pentecostal blessing. While there are instances of these latter sources in pentecostal beginnings, they seem to have been more widespread and decisive in the origins of CM.

CM in the mainline denominations did not immediately unleash the missionary drive that characterized Azusa Street and the beginnings of pentecostalism. In CM's early stages, the main evangelistic thrust was toward fellow church members, to bring them to BHS, rather than toward the unchurched. The strongest consistent missionary thrust among charismatics has come from restorationist, nondenominational circles and from parachurch groups with a strong charismatic membership, such as Operation Mobilisation and the pentecostal-originated YWAM, though in the 1980s some charismatic communities with a sizable Catholic membership have developed a strong missionary outreach. With the 1990s being named a decade of evangelization, CM's evangelistic thrust has increased, though it remains strongest in the new church sector.

Holiness of life was a much more dominant concern among first-generation pentecostals than among first-generation charismatics. This aspect reflects the Holiness background of many pioneer pentecostals, whereas the charismatics have come from a wide variety of church and confessional backgrounds. This difference helps to explain a constant source of pentecostal suspicion about charismatic authenticity, namely, depth of conversion and moral transformation. This concern also reflects a difference between the original pentecostal pattern of "tarrying for the baptism" with much soul-searching and intensity and the widespread charismatic practice of immediate "praying over" people for BHS. Many charismatics, particularly Catholics, have dealt with this problem by preparing candidates for BHS by teaching and formation courses, often known as ▸Life in the Spirit seminars. The ▸Alpha course represents the latest form of preparation for receiving the Holy Spirit.

CM has had more sense of the corporate work of the Holy Spirit than has classical pentecostalism. The widespread conviction that CM is for the renewal of the church as a whole recognizes that the coming of the Holy Spirit creates *koinonia* in the body of Christ. This conviction appears to have been strongest among charismatics in the sacramental-liturgical traditions, among the independents of restorationist tendencies who have rediscovered covenant relationships, and among groups like the Mennonites, who have always had a more corporate sense than mainline evangelicalism. CM in these groupings has a stronger sense of the close link in the Pauline epistles between the spiritual gifts and the corporate life of the body of Christ.

The power to form *koinonia* across confessional boundaries has been more evident in CM than in the pentecostal movement. Thus CM abounds in examples of spiritual fellowship and bonds arising between Christians traditionally seen as most incompatible. The rise of ecumenical communities is one sign of the power of the Spirit to overcome historic barriers. Nonetheless, CM, like the pentecostal movement, has its history of division, with doctrinal disputes on discipleship and on modes of baptism, with unresolved conflicts among leaders, with unseemly rivalry and competition. The evidence suggests that the immediate fruit of BHS is reconciliation but that its maintenance is a harder task, requiring the crucifixion of the desires of the sinful nature (Gal. 5:24). Where this depth is achieved, the fruit is impressive; where it is not, the promise can give way to scandal.

Both movements have had their share of scandals, magnified in recent times, particularly in America, by enormous budgets and media publicity. The most vulnerable seem to be independent entrepreneurs, because of their independence from church tradition and pastoral supervision. The stronger sense of *koinonia* in some sectors of CM is an important protection against the dangers of moral and doctrinal aberration to which independent and successful Christian ministries are more subject.

Some sectors of CM have seen a close link between the contemporary outpouring of the Holy Spirit and the fulfillment of God's purposes for Israel, a development significantly different from the origins of the pentecostal movement. This concern was linked with charismatic experience in the French pastor Louis Dallière and the Union de Prière he founded, which influenced other French Christians, both Catholic (as the Lion de Juda community) and Protestant (especially Thomas Roberts). This burden for Israel has also marked the Evangelical Sisterhood of Mary in Darmstadt, West Germany. A similar concern has arisen among some Protestant charismatics in the Anglo-Saxon world, such as Tom Hess from the U.S., who has convened the All Nations Convocations (1994, 1996, 1998) on the Feast of Tabernacles in Jerusalem; the groups associated with the International Christian Embassy Jerusalem; and David Pawson in England, but it has evoked few echoes among English-speaking Catholics. This development has been connected in the last 20 years with the growth of ▸messianic Judaism, with the formation of synagogues of Jews who have accepted Jesus as the Messiah.

The nondenominational sector of CM has from an early stage had a restorationist emphasis, urging not simply the restoration of the spiritual gifts of 1 Cor. 12:8–10 but also the fivefold ministries of Eph. 4:11. Although there have been a few pentecostal groupings, such as the Apostolic Church, that have instituted the fivefold ministries, the major pentecostal denominations have generally viewed the restorationist emphasis as dangerous and deviant. The increasing percentage of nondenominational or new-church groupings in CM has led to a much more widespread exercise of the fivefold ministries, particularly those of apostle and prophet. However, the new-church networks generally have a pragmatic and nondoctrinaire character, which means that the emphasis is more on apostolic and prophetic ministry than on the attribution and conferral of titles. As a result, this issue is becoming less contentious among many pentecostals.

While the pentecostal movement generally accepted the dispensationalist teaching popularized in the Scofield Bible and incorporated premillennial teachings in their declarations of faith, charismatic milieus have not endorsed premillennialism to the same degree. CR in the historic churches tended to produce a heightened "end times" consciousness within the faith framework of each tradition. Among evangelical charismatics, this would often be premillennial; in CCR and other liturgical traditions amillennial. Most of the new-church networks have rejected the pessimism of premillennialism and anticipate a restored church ushering in the kingdom.

Healing has become as prominent a ministry among charismatics as among pentecostals, although the patterns of healing ministry show obvious contrasts. Whereas physical healing with demonstrative styles of ministry has been more emphasized among pentecostals, inner healing with a focus on the healing of emotions has characterized many charismatic ministries. This contrast reflects differences in social background and theology. Awareness of mental states is more characteristic of a middle-class milieu than of working-class people, and the theology of many charismatics is more sympathetic to psychology than that of many pentecostals.

The area of theology manifests another obvious contrast between pentecostals and charismatics, especially those from Christian traditions with a rich theological inheritance, whether Catholic, Orthodox, Lutheran, or Reformed. Charismatics from these traditions, especially priests and ministers, have attached more importance to a coherent theological basis for the pentecostal experience than do pentecostals and independent charismatics. The spread of CR to the Roman Catholic Church led to a rapid rise in theological output on topics of BHS and the charismata, and the NSC sponsored a theological symposium in Chicago in 1976 (papers published in *Theological Reflections on the Charismatic Renewal,* ed. John D. Haughey, 1978). The major theological contribution from CCR in the last decade has been the work of K. McDonnell and G. Montague, *Christian Initiation and Baptism in the Holy Spirit* (1990), which has led to a much wider theological debate on BHS. Other important works of the 1990s have been ⌐Miroslav Volf's *After Our Likeness* (1998), a pentecostal-charismatic Trinitarian ecclesiology, and Clark Pinnock's work *Flame of Love* (1996) on the Holy Spirit. The theological task imposed by CR has been perhaps most recognized by Lutheran leaders, as shown in the book *Welcome, Holy Spirit,* ed. Larry Christenson (1987), produced by an international team of Lutheran scholars and pastors.

Generally speaking, there has been a strong correlation between use of the term *charismatic* and reference to BHS,

though in the assimilation process of the last decade there has been a decrease in the use of this *terminology* but ongoing affirmation of this *experience* of the Spirit. Like the pentecostals, charismatics regularly associated this spiritual event with the gift of tongues, though few charismatics accepted the AG and majority pentecostal position "No tongues, no baptism." Many charismatic teachers in liturgical-sacramental traditions had reservations about the term BHS on the grounds that it makes BHS appear to be another sacrament and because there is only "one baptism" (Eph. 4:5). Although these reservations led many continental European Catholics, for example, to use alternative terminology, such as *Effusion de l'Esprit* (outpouring of the Spirit), *Tauferneuerung* (baptismal renewal), and *Geisterfahrung* (experience of the Spirit), in the English-speaking world, BHS remained the common designation, even within Catholic circles. There was a widespread sense that the baptismal language was important, even if it posed some theological questions that are not easily resolved.

The grounds of opposition to the pentecostal movement and to CR have varied very little, thus confirming the basic spiritual unity and identity of the two currents. Many evangelicals objected to the belief in one postconversion reception of the Spirit and to an alleged devaluation of the Word by belief in contemporary revelation in the Spirit, but outright evangelical opposition is now found only in small circles of fundamentalist and dispensationalist Christians.

C. Major Challenges.

CM–CR as a current of revival and renewal faces as well as presents many challenges. We will look at a number of areas of challenge, all of which involve both challenges to those in CM–CR and challenges presented by CM–CR to the wider Christian world.

1. Faith and Theology.

As an experiential movement, CM–CR has always been strong on faith-affirmation and short on critical reflection. Charismatic faith strongly upholds divine intervention in miraculous occurrences, supernatural guidance, and prophetic messages. But while the need for discernment is widely recognized, charismatic discernment is mostly intuitive and generally lacks an adequate underlying theology, particularly of the relationship between the working of the Holy Spirit and the functioning of the various layers of the human spirit. On the one hand, charismatic faith strongly challenges all forms of skepticism and unbelief in the supernatural; on the other hand, intelligent faith challenges naiveté and simplistic identifications of unusual phenomena with the divine or the demonic.

Linked to the faith-theology issue is the relationship between activity and reflection. CM–CR has been very activist, seeking to see immediate results in the spiritual realm, with leaders easily becoming overworked and in danger of burnout. It is not that charismatic leaders never reflect but that their reflection is mostly on programs and methodology, and less on theology, history, and scholarly exegesis. There have been a few scholars active in CM–CR, but it is their popular books rather than their scholarly works that are widely read.

On the other hand, the challenge of CM–CR to mainline church theology has rarely been recognized. This challenge comes at two levels: the particular level of issues raised directly by charismatic experience, and the general level of the role of faith experience in theology. Thus, one will find very little examination in university or seminary theology of such issues as the spiritual gifts of prophecy and healing, inner healing of emotions and physical healing, deliverance and exorcism, the relationship between the Holy Spirit and physical manifestations, and the nature of leadership in the church. The role of faith in theology relates closely to patterns of Christian formation, in which CM–CR has been pioneering many forms of training that link theory with practice, whether in the Discipleship Training Schools of YWAM, the work of ICPE and the Schools of Evangelization in CCR, or the new colleges being established by many of the new church networks.

2. Success, the Cross, and Mystery.

Within CM–CR, leaders are looking for results: conversions; people baptized in the Spirit, healed, hearing from the Lord, receiving gifts, ministries and callings; churches and groups growing, planting new ones, impacting their city. CM–CR is a movement that hails success and easily interprets lack of immediate growth as a sign of the Spirit's absence. CM–CR easily focuses on the visible and can pay insufficient attention to the hidden and invisible. These tendencies, which are easy to understand, can fail to grasp the centrality and the meaning of the Cross for the life of the church, and fail to penetrate the mystery of Christ. The ministry of Jesus himself that had a strong charismatic dimension was not exactly a success in human terms. While the message of the risen Lord was confirmed by signs and wonders, the messengers shared in the death-resurrection pattern of their Lord.

CM–CR challenges all cessationist doctrines that limit signs and wonders to the apostolic age. It also challenges every assumption that charismata are optional extras for the church, crutches for the less mature, mere phases on the way to discovering the mystery of the Cross. CM–CR challenges every form of resignation to inevitable decline in churches, with dwindling attendance and ministerial recruitment. Yet CM–CR is itself challenged by the message of resurrection only through the Cross, questioning all charismatic idolizing of outward success and exposing every evocation of Pentecost that bypasses Calvary. The key to authentic renewal in depth lies in the relationship of Cross and Resurrection in

Christian faith, which is itself closely linked to the church's life being "hidden with Christ in God" (Col. 3:3).

3. New-Church Explosion and Old-Church Renewal.

Since the 1970s, CM–CR has had two major contrasting expressions: on the one hand, the new charismatic churches and networks, and on the other hand renewal within the historic churches. The 1990s have seen the new churches and networks expand on a massive scale, not widely paralleled by CR within the historic churches. To some, like R. Hempelmann of Germany, it can seem that the new churches have hijacked CM.

This double aspect of CM poses major challenges to both groupings. Can God's purpose for the kingdom of God be fulfilled by one sector of the Christian world alone? And are they both spheres of working of the Holy Spirit? The characteristics listed in section V.A above point to the presence of the same Spirit of God, whatever the shortcomings.

In this way, the new charismatic churches pose major challenges to the historic churches, suggesting such questions as: Is such a development outside the historic churches a judgment on their spiritual complacency and their pastoral inflexibility? To what extent do the new churches represent a Christian adaptation to the hi-tech networking world of the late 20th century and to what extent do they represent a capitulation to spiritual consumerism? What do the historic churches need to learn from the greater variety of ministries emerging in the new churches, and how do historic forms of ordained ministry relate to the fivefold pattern of Eph. 4: 11, especially the prophetic ministry?

However, the historic churches also pose important challenges to the new churches. Are the new churches self-sufficient? Do they really represent God's future on their own? Or do the new churches also need the older churches and their authentic witness? Do not the historic churches, and particularly renewal streams within them, witness in a particular way to "the treasure in earthen vessels"? Does renewal within the historic churches that is forced to grapple with the received patterns of worship, doctrine, and church government, with the frustration and suffering this encounter involves, contain the antidote to the dangers already mentioned, of anti-intellectualism, theological naiveté, and the ideology of success?

A perspective that recognizes the work of the Holy Spirit in both spheres will not only be truer to the evidence, but it will be humbler. A recognition of the need of both for each other would acknowledge that the historic churches need the challenge of the new churches to face their own limitations, and the new churches need the long experience of struggle for renewal to be real and incarnate. A more humble stance will also be more open to recognize the work of the Holy Spirit beyond CM–CR and the pentecostal movement. In his book *Streams of Living Water*, Richard Foster sees signs of a "new gathering of the people of God in our day," a flowing together of "the streams of faith ... contemplative, holiness, charismatic, social justice, evangelical, incarnational ... into a mighty movement of the Spirit."

4. The Challenge to the Churches.

CM–CR is a worldwide phenomenon affecting millions of believers from an extraordinary range of Christian churches and streams. The evidence of its characteristic features indicate that it cannot be regarded simply as a prayer movement, an evangelistic movement, or a healing movement. It is all of these and more; it is a movement in which the power of the Holy Spirit is experienced in the revitalization of essential areas of Christian life and mission.

It can be questioned whether any church or denomination has really acknowledged the significance, the importance, and the extent of CM. The church opposition and suspicion of the 1960s and '70s has generally disappeared—with a few exceptions such as the Southern Baptists, the Church of the Nazarene, and to some degree LC–MS—and has been replaced by an acceptance of charismatic legitimacy and the recognition that CR has a place within the life of the church. The impact of CR in the Anglican communion was demonstrated at Lambeth 1988, with the acceptance of the 1990s as a Decade of Evangelism, and even more at Lambeth 1998, where the evangelical and charismatic bishops of the Third World significantly influenced the massive vote for traditional sexual morality. In the Church of England, charismatics are playing a much bigger role in church life and contribute significantly to the theological colleges among administrators, faculty, and students. The Roman Catholic Church accepted CCR from an early date and gave it space. The Pentecost 1998 gathering in Rome of new movements and new communities in the Catholic Church manifested the major impact of CCR, and the pope's address underscored the importance of the charismatic dimension that had been restored to the church through Vatican II. As Lambeth 1998 indicated, it is in the Third World that the significance of CM–CR has been the most recognized, a development already foreshadowed by the many Filipino bishops at the Vatican charismatic retreat of 1984 and the participation of African and Asian bishops (both Anglican and Roman Catholic) at the Brighton conference in 1991.

Despite this progress, it remains true that much church life continues as though CM–CR had never happened. The WCC assembly in Canberra (1991) with the theme "Come, Holy Spirit" virtually ignored CM–CR in the program planning, and the Ecumenical Directory from the Vatican (1993) with guidelines for Catholic participation in ecumenical activities and worship does not call attention to the widespread rise of charismatic groups. Even Pope John Paul II's encyclical on ecumenism, *Ut Unum Sint* (1995), which is strongly aware of the role of the Holy Spirit and the centrality of prayer and repentance, makes no reference to CR.

A major challenge here is to examine the ways in which CM–CR is different from other movements and streams of renewal within the churches. Essential to the challenge of CM–CR is the evidence of divine initiatives and activity, a witness to the living lordship of Jesus Christ over the church and the world in our day. In this respect, the absence of any one human founder for CM–CR is an integral element in its distinctiveness and its ecumenical range. In this sovereign, catholic, and unexpected character lies both its significance and its fragility.

Just as the renewing work of the Holy Spirit reveals the active lordship of Jesus the Messiah, so it also restores a sense of divine purpose to the church. Charismatic hubris can easily exaggerate our human understanding of God's unfolding purpose and have too narrow a view of the work of the Holy Spirit. But the renewed sense that God is moving history and the church toward the climax of the Lord's return and his kingdom is surely central to God's purpose in CM–CR and beyond it.

■ **Bibliography:** A. Bittlinger, ed., *The Church Is Charismatic* (1981) ▪ L. Christenson, ed., *Welcome, Holy Spirit* (1987) ▪ O. Föller, *Charisma und Unterscheidung* (1994) ▪ D. E. Harrell, *All Things Are Possible* (1975) ▪ M. Hébrard, *Les Nouveaux Disciples Dix Ans Après* (1987) ▪ R. Hempelmann, *Licht und Schatten* (1998) ▪ P. Hocken, *The Glory and the Shame* (1994) ▪ idem, *The Strategy of the Spirit?* (1996) ▪ idem, *Streams of Renewal* (1986, 1997) ▪ R. G. Hoekstra, "God Is Breaking through All Barriers!" *Voice* 4 (1, 1956) ▪ C. Hummel, *Fire in the Fireplace* (1993) ▪ D. McBain, *Fire over the Waters* (1997) ▪ K. McDonnell, ed., *Presence, Power, Praise*, 3 vols. (1980) ▪ R. Quebedeaux, *The New Charismatics II* (1983) ▪ D. A. Rausch, *Messianic Judaism* (1982) ▪ A. Reimers, *God's Country* (1979) ▪ J. Sherrill, *They Speak with Other Tongues* (1964) ▪ V. Synan, *The Twentieth-Century Pentecostal Explosion* (1987) ▪ C. van der Laan and P. van der Laan, *Pinksteren in Beweging* (1982) ▪ C. P. Wagner, ed., *The New Apostolic Churches* (1998) ▪ J. Williams, *The Gift of the Holy Spirit Today* (1980). See also bibliography for CATHOLIC CHARISMATIC RENEWAL.   ■ P. D. Hocken

CHARISMATIC RENEWAL SERVICES (CRS). Service agency for Catholic Charismatic Renewal (CCR) in the U.S. Charismatic Renewal Services (CRS) was formally incorporated in South Bend, IN, in 1971 by the newly formed Catholic Charismatic Renewal Service Committee—later known as the National Service Committee for CCR (NSC)—to develop and continue services begun by the Communications Center at Notre Dame. These services included the organization of the annual CCR conferences at Notre Dame, the compilation of a national prayer-group directory, publication of the CCR monthly *New Covenant*, the retailing of charismatic literature and cassettes, and the publication of a few books.

In 1975, due to accelerating expansion, CRS incorporated Catholic Charismatic Renewal Services (CCRS) and the NSC separately. In 1975–79 CCRS was serviced by the People of Praise Community in South Bend and the Word of God Community in Ann Arbor, MI. The Ann Arbor operations, including *New Covenant,* were then withdrawn from CCRS and incorporated as Servant Publications. CCRS has continued as a book and audio service, while CRS stills exists as an administrative service to CCR in the U.S. Their offices were moved from South Bend to Locust Grove, VA, in 1991.

■ P. D. Hocken

CHARISMS See Gifts of the Spirit.

CHAVDA, MAHESH (1946–). Evangelist and pastor of All Nations Church, Charlotte, NC. Raised a devout Hindu in Kenya by parents from India, he began studying a NT given him at age 13 by a Baptist missionary and came to Christ three years later when Jesus appeared to him. In 1964 he left Kenya to attend Wayland Baptist College in Plainview, TX. Baptized in the Holy Spirit in 1972 while doing graduate work in English literature at Texas Tech University, he began working at Lubbock State School for Retarded Children, where there were several healings. In 1974 a prayer group in Levelland, TX, asked him to become their pastor. Three years later he and his new wife, Bonnie, accepted an invitation to help launch Good News Fellowship Church in Ft. Lauderdale, FL, in association with Jim Croft and ►Derek Prince. His ministry soon became worldwide, and there were reports of many miracles, including the raising from the dead in 1985 of Katshinyi Manikai in Zaire. By 1998 he had itinerated in Zambia, Cameroon, Ivory Coast, South Africa, Nigeria, Israel, China, Hong Kong, Finland, Russia, Mexico, Central America, Eastern Europe, the Caribbean, and the U.S. Over 700,000 people have received salvation through his ministry, and more than 450 churches have joined his all-night prayer movement, "The Watch of the Lord," begun in early 1996. He became prominent in the ►Toronto Blessing after embracing it in 1994.

■ **Bibliography:** M. Chavda, *Only Love Can Make a Miracle* (1991).

■ R. M. Riss

CHAWNER, C. AUSTIN (1903–64). Missionary to Africa, author, composer, publisher, and linguist. Chawner, Canadian born, moved to South Africa in 1909, when he was six years old, with his father, Charles Chawner, who was the first ►Pentecostal Assemblies of Canada (PAOC) missionary to South Africa. He graduated from Bethel Bible Training School in Newark, NJ, where he received the baptism in

the Holy Spirit in 1923. Upon being ordained in London, Ont., in 1925 and returning to South Africa as a PAOC missionary in the same year, Chawner took the gospel message to many areas where it had never been heard. Chawner and Ingrid Lokken, who was affiliated with the Norwegian Pentecostal Assemblies and later became his wife (c. 1935), were the first PAOC missionaries in Mozambique (c. 1929) and Rhodesia (c. 1942).

Chawner's evangelistic methodology emphasized education and publishing. He started the first pentecostal Bible schools in South Africa (1930) and Mozambique (c. 1935) in order to train national leaders for an indigenous church. Chawner wrote, translated, and published gospel tracts, Bibles, hymnals, free correspondence Bible courses, and gospel literature in 44 different languages at Emmanuel Press. More than 24.5 million pieces of literature were distributed by this press in 1959 alone. When the Mozambique government prohibited further Protestant missionary work (c. 1950), the 200 churches Chawner had established in the country were ready to survive under the leadership of national ministers with the support of literature produced by Emmanuel Press in Nelspruit, South Africa, near the border of Mozambique.

Part of Chawner's success in establishing churches was due to his achievements in six languages. He helped to develop written Tsonga and wrote a Tsonga grammar (1938), Bible studies, and hymns. Chawner held many important positions: managing director of Emmanuel Press, member of the Orthography Committee of the Tsonga language, member of the Translation Committee of the British and Foreign Bible Society, field secretary for the PAOC in Africa, and general secretary of the South African Assemblies of God.

■ **Bibliography:** F. Burke, "Austin Chawner—South Africa" (typed report, 1979) ■ C. A. Chawner, *Step by Step in Thonga* (1938) ■ idem, "Trip Through N. E. Transvaal," *PE* (Nov. 12, 1927) ■ W. J. Hollenweger, *The Pentecostals* (1972) ■ G. G. Kulbeck, *What God Hath Wrought* (1958) ■ E. A. Peters, *The Contribution to Education by the Pentecostal Assemblies of Canada* (1970).

■ E. B. Robinson

CHERNOFF, DAVID L. (1951–). International leader in messianic Jewish movement. The son of messianic Jewish pioneers Martin and Yohanna Chernoff, David had a Pentecost experience in Cincinnati, OH, in 1970, leading him into youth ministry in the fledgling messianic Jewish movement. In 1974 David with others formed the Messianic Jewish Movement Outreach, a college-campus ministry. In 1975 the Chernoff family moved to Philadelphia, PA, where Martin Chernoff became rabbi of Beth Yeshua congregation, with David first as assistant and, after his father's death in 1985, as rabbi. David

Chernoff was president of the Young Messianic Jewish Alliance of America (1975–79), its executive director (1979–83), and president of the Messianic Jewish Alliance of America (MJAA; 1983–87). He was a founder of the International Alliance of Messianic Congregations and Synagogues in 1984 and the first chair of its steering committee. In 1994 David was involved in the reconciliation between the MJAA and the Union of Messianic Jewish Congregations. He has an active role in international outreach, especially in Europe. David is the author of *Yeshua the Messiah* (1983). David married Debra Gershman in 1983; they have two children.

■ **Bibliography:** Y. Chernoff, *Born a Jew ... Die a Jew* (1996) ■ R. L. Winer, *The Calling* (1990). ■ P. D. Hocken

CHEROKEE COUNTY (NC) REVIVAL

One of the earliest known outpourings of the Holy Spirit in America. The Cherokee County revival occurred in 1896 in the Unicoi Mountains along the North Carolina–Tennessee border. Ten years before the outpouring, R. G. Spurling and his Baptist followers organized a Christian Union (which is now the ▸Church of God, Cleveland, TN) on the Tennessee side of the mountain region. In 1892 a kindred fellowship was organized by W. F. Bryant on the North Carolina side. The two congregations were virtually the same, with only the state line between them. In the summer of 1896 three lay evangelists conducted revival services in the Shearer schoolhouse that served as a meeting place for the area. William Martin, a Methodist, and Joe M. Tipton and Milton McNabb, both Baptists, were the evangelists. The Wesleyan emphasis on sanctification was their insistent theme. It was a time of spiritual renewal and religious fervor, with numerous conversions of sinners.

The meetings closed at the schoolhouse and were continued in the Bryant home, where a new thing happened. Numerous men, women, and children began to speak in tongues and otherwise manifest the presence of the Holy Spirit. At first the people were puzzled by these occurrences, but a search of the Scriptures revealed that they were experiencing an outpouring of the Holy Spirit such as that in Acts 2:4; 10:46; and 19:6. The revival continued all summer (1896), and about 130 were filled with the Spirit and spoke in tongues. Hundreds of others were converted and numerous sick persons were healed.

The people did not immediately become evangelistic about their experience and formulated no doctrine about it. They simply thanked God for "the blessing" and wished that all people had it. That universal outpouring would begin 10 years later, in 1906, in faraway California.

■ **Bibliography:** C. W. Conn, *Like a Mighty Army: A History of the Church of God* (rev. ed., 1977) ■ H. Hunter, "Spirit-Baptism and the

1896 Revival in Cherokee County, North Carolina," *Pneuma* 5 (2, 1983). ■ C. W. Conn

CHESSER, H. L. (1898–1987). Sixth general overseer of the Church of God (CG, Cleveland, TN), from 1948 until 1952. After attending Bible training school (1923–26), he served as pastor in Florida in the 1930s and 1940s. Chesser was an effective counselor and state overseer; in 1948 he was elected general overseer, a post he filled for four years. Also in 1948 he was a member of the ▸Pentecostal Fellowship of North America constitution committee and the ▸National Association of Evangelicals executive committee. During his tenure as general overseer he led the CG in its amalgamation with the Full Gospel Church of South Africa (1951). In 1954 Chesser returned to a local ministry in his native Florida.

■ **Bibliography:** Archives of the Church of God (Cleveland, TN) ■ C. W. Conn, *Like a Mighty Army: A History of the Church of God* (rev. ed., 1977). ■ C. W. Conn

CHI ALPHA Assemblies of God (AG) national campus ministry program. The letters stand for the Greek words *Christou Apostoloi*, Christ's Sent Ones or Ambassadors. Founded by the AG in the fall of 1953, Chi Alpha is the national society for Christian witness on non-Christian campuses in recognition of the fact that the university has always been the center of changing ideas and religious awakenings. The first chapter was formed in Springfield, MO, by J. Calvin Holsinger on the campus of Southwest Missouri State College. Its purpose was to minister to students in secular colleges with a four-pronged program—worship, Bible study, social life, and community outreach. Other chapters were established on college and university campuses in the U.S., providing a pentecostal ministry. In 2000 some 300 full-time campus ministers served on 206 secular campuses.

■ **Bibliography:** J. C. Holsinger, "Epiphany Day 1984," Assemblies of God Archives, Springfield, MO. ■ F. Bixler

CHO, DAVID (PAUL) YONGGI (YONG-GI) (1936–). Positive-thinking Korean prophet who is pastor of Yoido Full Gospel Church in Seoul, the world's largest congregation, with about 700,000 members. Raised as a Buddhist, Cho rejected his religion as he was dying of tuberculosis but was converted to Christianity. He recovered and aspired to become a medical doctor, but Jesus later appeared to him in the middle of the night dressed as a fireman, called him to preach, and filled him with the Holy Spirit.

After graduation from an ▸Assemblies of God (AG) Bible school, Cho started a tent church in Seoul in 1958. By 1962 he was able to build a 1,500-seat downtown "revival center," soon changing the name to Full Gospel Central Church.

Yonggi Cho, pastor of the world's largest church, the Yoido Full Gospel Church in Seoul, Korea.

Divine healings at the dedication stimulated growth to a membership of 2,000 by 1964.

Cho suffered a nervous breakdown but was divinely guided to delegate responsibility. In 1966 he became general superintendent of the Korean AG. He found time to complete a degree in law at the National College of Korea in 1968 and was awarded an honorary D.D. degree from Bethany College, Santa Cruz, CA, the same year.

A 10,000-seat auditorium was dedicated in 1973 by Billy Graham. By 1974 there were 23,000 members; by the end of 1979, 100,000; and by 1987, more than half a million. There were hundreds of assistant pastors and thousands of home cell group leaders, the majority of both groups being women—a breakthrough in Korean culture.

Pastor Cho's success formula is a combination of positive thinking and positive confession: "Think it. See it. Name it. Speak it—in boldness" (Kennedy, 202). He teaches that through the power of the spoken word the Spirit-led believer can "create and release the presence of Jesus Christ" (Cho, 81). He emphasizes being specific in prayer: one must visualize and specify exactly what is needed. This implies financial prosperity, but it is not an instant cure-all. Answers to prayer may take weeks or months.

As president of Church Growth International, Cho has stressed massive prayer as the key to church growth. He recommends that ministers in his church spend three hours daily in prayer.

Coming out of the oriental tradition, Cho has emphasized the mystical, including the power of satanic forces. But at the same time he has elevated the believer even more—to the "class of gods" as children of God who have power over the angelic class (including Satan). This is the language of the mystic, not the lawyer-theologian, and must be interpreted as such. He has been criticized for mind-power statements, such as, "Through visualizing and dreaming you can incubate your future and hatch the results." But these must be interpreted in their context: "The subconscious has certain influence, but it is quite limited, and cannot create like our Almighty God can" (Cho, 42, 44). Cho teaches that only the Holy Spirit can bring the true understanding of Scripture.

Such traditional subjectivism among Pentecostals has always had the potential for abuse.

■ **Bibliography:** J. Buckingham, "The World's Largest Pastorate," *Charisma* (June 1982), 20–23 ■ P. Y. Cho, *The Fourth Dimension* (1979) ■ N. L. Kennedy, *Dream Your Way to Success* (1980).
                                                          ■ D. J. Wilson

CHOI, JA-SIL (1915–89). Early Korean pentecostal evangelist. She was born on Aug. 25, 1915, in Hwanghae province in North Korea. She graduated from Pyung-Ahn nurses' training school established by the province. After consecutive failures in business, she had determined to commit suicide, but at that very time God called her to become a great woman evangelist. She had a marvelous encounter with God and decided to enter seminary. At the Full Gospel Seminary she met classmate ˒Paul Yonggi Cho, who later became her son-in-law. The two graduated from the seminary in 1958. Yonggi Cho started a tent church in the same year, and Ja-Sil Choi became his associate pastor. The tent church started with only five persons: Yonggi Cho, Ja-Sil Choi, and her three children. Choi's ministry was visitation of slum-dwellers, the sick, alcoholics, demoniacs, and so forth. She prayed to God for the these forlorn people, preaching the good news of hope, which consists not only of spiritual blessing but also of material and mundane blessings. Many miracles and divine healings followed her co-ministry with Pastor Yonggi Cho, which lasted for about 30 years. Her ministry emphasized Spirit baptism and the subsequent sign of tongues speaking. She also stressed especially the importance and merit of "fasting prayer" and wrote several books on this subject. She was a great pentecostal woman evangelist in the history of the Korean church. She died of a heart attack on Nov. 8, 1989, during a stay in Los Angeles for revival meetings. In memory of her pentecostal achievements, Yoido Full Gospel Church, whose senior pastor is Yonggi Cho, named its local facilities for prayer Osanri Fasting Prayer Mountain Commemorative of Ja-Sil Choi.

■ **Bibliography:** J. Choi, *I Was Hallelujah Woman* (1978) ■ idem, *The Power of Fasting Prayer* (1977) ■ idem, *The Fruits of Fasting Prayer* (1981).   ■ Y.-H. Lee

CHRISTENSON, LAURENCE DONALD ("LARRY") (1928–). Lutheran charismatic and author. Christenson was born in Northfield, MN, to a Norwegian Lutheran family. His father served at the time as the football coach at St. Olaf College in Northfield. Christenson was married to Nordis Evenson in 1951, who bore their four children.

After graduating from high school in 1946, Christenson served as a parachutist in the Army Airborne. Before graduating from St. Olaf in 1952 he entertained hopes of being a playwright but decided to enter the ministry in 1955. Graduating from Luther Theological Seminary in St. Paul, MN, in 1959, he was called to serve as pastor of Trinity Lutheran Church (ALC) in San Pedro, CA, in 1960.

Through reading the works of Agnes Sanford, Christenson became interested in pentecostalism. In 1961 he was baptized in the Holy Spirit and spoke in tongues in a Foursquare Gospel church. Leading his church into a pentecostal revival, he immediately became a national leader in the Lutheran charismatic renewal movement.

Author of *The Christian Family* (1970) and *The Renewed Mind* (1974), Christenson soon gained influence as an ecumenical leader in the international charismatic movement. In 1974 he was instrumental in organizing a renewal organization known as Lutheran Charismatic Renewal Services. After retiring from the pastorate in San Pedro in 1983, he became director of the International Lutheran Renewal Center in St. Paul.

See also LUTHERAN CHARISMATICS.

"Larry" Christenson, one of the early leaders in the Lutheran charismatic movement.

■ **Bibliography:** L. D. Christenson, *The Charismatic Renewal Among Lutherans* (1976). ■ H. V. Synan

CHRIST FOR THE NATIONS INSTITUTE (CFNI).

Two-year educational institution in Dallas, TX, serving the charismatic and pentecostal traditions. Founded in 1970 by ▶Gordon and Freda Lindsay, longtime leaders of the healing movement. This was not the Lindsays' first involvement in education. In 1959 they had established the World Correspondence Course, which by the late 1960s had more than 11,000 students enrolled. The library established to provide research resources for writing the courses provided the core of the CFNI library.

To supplement the educational background of regional evangelists and teachers, a series of seminars dealing with theological, missiological, and ministry concerns was conducted at the Dallas Christian Center where Lindsay was pastor and director of the center's various publishing, mission, and educational efforts. This proved popular, and the Lindsays were encouraged to develop a Bible school to train pastors, evangelists, and lay workers.

CFNI opened in 1970 with one full-time teacher in addition to Lindsay, 45 students, and few resources. Gordon Lindsay was president. By the time of his death in 1973, the school had grown to about 250 students. Freda Lindsay was elected president, a position she held from 1973 to 1985. Her son, Dennis Lindsay, succeeded her as

president. Freda Lindsay remained CEO and chairperson of the board of trustees.

Enrollment peaked at 1,500 during the mid 1980s and had declined to about 900 in 1988 because of a daring educational experiment. Concerned that many foreign students, as well as students from areas lacking strong charismatic churches, were being taken from their environment never to return, CFNI has been instrumental in establishing Bible schools in Bad Gandersheim (West Germany), Montego Bay (Jamaica), and New York City (Long Island). CFNI alumni have established schools modeled after CFNI in Argentina, Finland, Mexico, Malaysia, Spain, and Thailand. These events and the life of CFNI have been reported in *Christ for the Nations* (until 1967 called ▶*Voice of Healing*). A yearbook (variously titled) published by the student association reports annual events and records the student population. To date, more than 27,000 students have studied at CFNI.

■ **Bibliography:** F. Lindsay, *Freda* (1987) ■ idem, *My Diary's Secrets* (1976) ■ G. Lindsay, *The House the Lord Built* (1972).

■ D. D. Bundy

CHRISTIAN AND MISSIONARY ALLIANCE (CMA).

Incorporated in 1897, the Christian and Missionary Alliance (CMA) was the product of an amalgamation of two organizations, the Christian Alliance and the Evangelical Missionary Alliance (later renamed the International Missionary Alliance), founded in 1887 at Old Orchard, ME, by the Canadian-born ▶Albert Benjamin Simpson. Since its inception, the CMA has evolved into a missionary denomination composed of churches in 51 nations with over 2 million adherents. Its international headquarters are located in Nyack, NY.

Reflecting its roots in the American Holiness movement of the later 19th century, the CMA has historically highlighted the doctrines of the Spirit-filled life and healing in the atonement. Articles 7 and 8 of the CMA Statement of Faith (1965) read as follows:

7. It is the will of God that each believer should be filled with the Holy Spirit and be sanctified wholly, being separated from sin and the world and fully dedicated to the will of God, thereby receiving power for holy living and effective service. This is both a crisis and a progressive experience wrought in the life of the believer subsequent to conversion.

8. Provision is made in the redemptive work of the Lord Jesus Christ for the healing of the mortal body.

Prayer for the sick and anointing with oil are taught in the Scriptures and are privileges for the church in this present age.

Various pioneers of the pentecostal movement acknowledged their connection with A. B. Simpson and the CMA. In 1900 ▸Charles Parham visited "Dr. Simpson's work in Nyack," where spiritual truths were being "restored." ▸Agnes Ozman warmly recalled the time she spent at the Missionary Training Institute (MTI) at Nyack, where she was exposed to the teachings of A. B. Simpson and his colleagues. ▸Thomas Barratt recounted his seeking of the baptism of the Holy Spirit in 1906 while staying in the Alliance guest house in New York City. ▸Alexander Dowie derived inspiration from Simpson's healing ministry and once invited the CMA founder to accompany him across the U.S. on a healing tour. Other prominent pentecostal personalities who were influenced by the CMA include ▸Alice Belle Garrigus, founder of the ▸Pentecostal Assemblies of Newfoundland, and ▸D. Wesley Myland, founder of the Gibeah Bible School near Indianapolis, IN.

John Salmon, an early leader of the Christian and Missionary Alliance in Canada, who was baptized in the Spirit but remained in the Alliance.

Out of Simpson's MTI came pentecostal pastors, administrators, and missionaries. ▸William I. Evans and ▸Frank M. Boyd became deans of Bethel Bible Training School in Newark, NJ, and Central Bible Institute in Springfield, MO. On the Canadian scene, R. E. Sternall, the first pastor of the influential pentecostal assembly in Kitchener, Ont., received the pentecostal baptism at Nyack in 1911. The three-year Bible institute model perfected by A. B. Simpson and D. L. Moody, in which the atmosphere of the school was geared more to spiritual development than to academic performance, became the dominant strategy for the preparation of pentecostal leadership.

According to ▸Assemblies of God (AG) historian Carl Brumback (1977, 92), the pentecostal movement owes the CMA a sevenfold debt: (1) doctrines borrowed from the CMA; (2) the hymns of Simpson; (3) the books of Simpson, Pardington, Tozer, and others; (4) the term *Gospel Tabernacle*, which, when supplemented with *full*, became a popular name for churches among pentecostals; (5) the polity of the early Alliance Society, after which the AG was styled; (6) a worldwide missionary vision; and (7) numerous leaders converted and trained in Alliance circles. ▸Aimee Semple McPherson's "Foursquare Gospel," which she claimed was given directly to her by divine revelation, was noticeably similar to A. B. Simpson's "fourfold Gospel." The emblem of the Foursquare movement, a cross, a laver (representing healing), a dove, and a crown, bore a marked resemblance to the already existing Alliance symbol, which included a cross, laver (representing sanctification), a pitcher of oil, and a crown.

The incursion of pentecostalism into the ranks of the CMA during the first two decades of the 20th century constituted the most severe crisis faced by the CMA during its entire history. The years 1908–12 were particularly stressful as attitudes toward pentecostalism within the CMA polarized. Many of those CMA persons who had received the pentecostal baptism felt constrained to leave and identify themselves with the burgeoning pentecostal movement, in which they quickly emerged as leaders. Significantly, there were notable persons such as Robert Jaffray and John Salmon, who received the gift of tongues and chose to remain within the CMA. Losses to the CMA were substantial among branch members, official workers, and missionaries. In 1912, in order to protect itself, the CMA adopted as part of its new constitution the controversial "reversion clause," which ensured that the property of local branches, schools, and undenominational churches would "revert to and become the property of the CMA as incorporated under the laws of the State of New York."

Throughout the pentecostal controversy, A. B. Simpson affirmed the orderly expression of supernatural gifts within the Alliance. During the post-Simpson period, however, the CMA has increasingly distanced itself from the pentecostal and charismatic movements. In 1963, responding to the spread of the charismatic movement within established Protestant churches, the Alliance board of managers issued an official statement regarding the charismatic movement that reiterated Simpson's earlier assessment of pentecostalism made in 1908:

> Certainly some persons of impeccable Christian character are associated with the present charismatic movement. But the gift of tongues belongs in the category of things earlier imitated and by the very nature of it is capable of abuse and wild excesses....
>
> ... We do not believe that there is any scriptural evidence for the teaching that speaking in tongues is the sign of having been filled with the Holy Spirit, nor do we believe

A photograph taken at the 1906 Old Orchard Convention in Maine that reflects the early link between the Christian and Missionary Alliance and the emergence of pentecostalism. (1) Henry Wilson, who investigated pentecostalism within the Alliance; (2) Mrs. A. B. Simpson; (3) A. B. Simpson; (4) W. C. Stevens, principal of the Missionary Training Institute; and (5) Minnie T. Draper, prominent Alliance official and speaker who later helped in the founding of the Bethel Pentecostals Assembly in Newark, NJ, and the Pentecostal Mission in South and Central Africa.

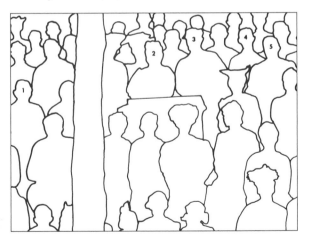

An outline sketch of the above photo of the 1906 Old Orchard Convention in Maine.

that it is the plan of God that all Christians should possess the gift of tongues.

Under the influence of A. W. Tozer, the board of managers proposed the phrase "Seek not, forbid not" as embodying the "wisdom for this hour" regarding the gift of tongues. (The widespread notion that this expression originated with A. B. Simpson is erroneous.)

An unofficial report entitled "Dealing with the Charismatic in Today's Church" was distributed to all North American Alliance workers in 1977, with the recommendation that it be received as "scriptural and consistent with the Alliance position." While insisting that the CMA had never endorsed a cessationist view of the gifts of the Holy Spirit, the study nonetheless proscribed neo-pentecostalism as "the most devastating and dangerous of all the other charismatic movements in the twentieth century." It further advised that tongues speaking, though legitimate, nevertheless should be prohibited in "certain services of the church."

As a result of its unpleasant encounter with the pentecostal movement during the early years of the 20th century, the CMA has tended to diminish its working relationships with groups of Holiness, pentecostal, or charismatic persuasion. It has sought instead to maintain fidelity to its traditional emphasis on the "deeper life" while aligning itself more closely with nonpentecostal, evangelical Protestant bodies.

■ **Bibliography:** W. B. Bedford, "A Larger Christian Life: A. B. Simpson and the Early Years of the Christian and Missionary Alliance" (diss., U. of Virginia, 1992) ■ C. Brumback, *A Sound from Heaven* (1977) ■ R. Niklaus, J. Sawin, S. Stoesz, *All for Jesus* (1986) ■ L. Reynolds, *Footprints: The Beginning of the Christian and Missionary Alliance in Canada* (1981) ■ S. Stoesz, *Understanding My Church* (1983) ■ A. E. Thompson, *A. B. Simpson* (1960).
■ C. Nienkirchen

CHRISTIAN CHURCH OF NORTH AMERICA The Christian Church of North America (CCNA), a pentecostal denomination, is a cooperative fellowship that has a congregational form of government governed by overseers and presbyters. Their doctrine and emphasis on missions is very similar to the Assemblies of God (AG). The CCNA is affiliated with Assemblee di Dio in Italia (ADI), Iglesia Cristiana Pentecostal De Argentina, the Italian Christian Churches of North Europe, the Igreja Evangelica Pentecostal of Brazil, the Councilio Iglesia Cristiana de Colombia, the Christian Churches of Barbados, the Christian Church of Australia, the Christian Church of the Philippines, the Iglesia Evangelica Cristiana in Uruguay, the Manna Full Gospel Mission in India, the India Evangelistic Crusade in India, and the Emmanuel Full Gospel Mission in India. It has close affinity with the Association of Italian Pentecostal Churches in Canada and has membership in the ►Pentecostal Fellowship of North America, National Religious Broadcasters, and the ►National Association of Evangelicals. The international headquarters for CCNA is located in Transfer, PA. CCNA has two official organs, *Il Faro* (Italian) and *Vista* (English). The General Council of CCNA is affiliated with the Rochester Bible College in Rochester, NY. CCNA has been influenced by Roman Catholic converts and its religious heritage.

The religious heritage of CCNA includes the pentecostal revival that started in Topeka, KS (1901), and a group of Italian evangelicals living in a Chicago Near North Side ghetto. ►W. H. Durham received the baptism in the Holy Spirit at ►Azusa Street (1907) and carried the pentecostal message back to Chicago. ►Luigi Francescon and ►Pietro Ottolini, mosaic artisans, who had already left the Italian Presbyterian Church in Chicago, heard Durham preach at the North Avenue Mission. Francescon and two members of his group received the baptism in the Spirit (Aug. 25, 1907, and July and Aug. 1907, respectively). On Sept. 15, 1907, the Sunday after Ottolini received the baptism in the Spirit, the power of God was manifested at Grand Avenue Mission, ►Assemblea Cristiana; and many people in Ottolini's Italian evangelical group received the baptism in the Spirit. This marked the beginning of the Italian pentecostal movement (IPM). The power of the Spirit continued to be manifested at the mission—now under the charge of Francescon and Ottolini—with healings and additional baptisms in the Spirit. The membership expanded and became missionaries to other Italian populations in the U.S. and the world. Their efforts produced churches in 13 states and several foreign lands. This growth was without the benefit of organization; however, dissension in 1927 indicated that structure was needed.

The structure for the movement developed as a result of three needs: (1) to resolve dissension, (2) to facilitate foreign missions, and (3) to balance foreign missions with evangelization of the U.S. The first need, to resolve dissension over the interpretation of Acts 15:13–29—should Christians drain all blood from meat before they eat it or not?—resulted in Luigi Francescon, Maximilian Tosetto, and Joseph Petrelli combining their efforts to solve the problem during the first general convention of the movement at Niagra Falls, NY. Francescon was the first Italian charismatic leader and disliked formal organization. Petrelli, an attorney and a newsman, also

disapproved of formal organization and provided written expression of the early theology. Tosetto, founder and pastor of the host church, was the organizer. The result of this convention was (1) the adoption of 12 articles of faith, (2) publication of a hymnal, (3) the formation of the general council, (4) the adoption of the name Unorganized Italian Christian Churches of the United States, (5) the call for an annual conference, and (6) the historical beginning of CCNA (1927).

The need to facilitate missions was accomplished by (1) forming a missions fund (1929), (2) electing a missions committee to administer the fund (1929), (3) creating the office of missionary secretary-treasurer (1943), (4) incorporating as the Missionary Society of the CCNA (June 1948), and (5) making the director of missions the first permanently, fully supported office of CCNA (1953). This emphasis on foreign missions initially established works in 19 countries but neglected the growth of CCNA at home.

Subsequently, CCNA drew up an eight-point program to correct the imbalance in growth (1961); restructured their organization; incorporated as a legal religious denomination under the name General Council of the CCNA (1963); expanded the home missions organization; regionalized their world mission fields; and made the general overseer's office a permanent, fully supported position (1965). This structure has enabled the directors of missions and the general overseers (Carmelo Paglia [1952–54], Frank P. Fortunato [1954–75], Carmine Saginario [1975–84], Guy BonGiovanni [1984–89], David Farina [1989–93], and John DelTurco [1993–]) to develop affiliated missions in 40 nations and the church at home. Currently, CCNA has a national executive board consisting of 12 overseers and presbyters who use management by objective, five U.S. districts being governed by district presbyteries, 150 churches in 12 U.S. states, and 500 credentialed workers. One annual goal is to establish two new churches in each district.

Initially, CCNA's purpose was to evangelize all Italian people; however, their mission is now multiethnic. During WWII they dropped the Italian identity from the denomination name, and in 1961 they began to expand their missionary outreach beyond their ethnic group. Today, approximately 20 to 25% of the U.S. ministers and 75 to 85% of the U.S. members are non-Italian as a result of CCNA members being assimilated into the American culture and making an effort to evangelize Korean, Hispanic, black, Vietnamese, Haitian, and Portuguese Americans.

Even though CCNA and AG developed out of the same pentecostal revival in 1901, there was almost a half century difference in their dates of incorporation as denominations (1963 and 1914, respectively). This was undoubtedly due to the founders of the CCNA being even more leery of organizational structure than the early leaders of the AG. Evidences of the CCNA's distaste for structure were the founders of the

CCNA leaving the Presbyterian Church because they did not like the organizational requirement of membership (1903); the use of the word "Unorganized" in the name of the CCNA's first general council (1927); and 1941 being the date for the first certificate of ordination by CCNA.

The IPM felt the consequences of not being incorporated in Italy and the U.S. During the early years, the movement splintered into many independent, unincorporated groups in the U.S., including the CCNA (Francescon's group, because of displeasure with organization), the Evangelical Christian Pentecostal Churches (ECPC), Ottolini's group (because of doctrinal differences about the baptism in the Spirit as a requirement for salvation), and Petrelli's group (because of "the issue of the blood"). An attempt was made to merge these groups in Chicago (1945), but the attempt failed. This was followed by the merger of ECPC into the AG as the Italian Branch of the AG (Jan. 1948), today called the Italian District of AG (IDAG). IDAG at a New York City banquet brought together the leadership of its group and of the CCNA to explore a merger with the CCNA (1959). This merger attempt also failed; however, about 25% of CCNA did join IDAG. Today most of the churches that developed out of the IPM have merged into the CCNA or IDAG, and some members attend the conventions for both groups. There are still a few independent IPM churches in the US.

The IPM groups sent many laymen and established many churches in Italy, starting with Giacomo Lombardi in 1908. The Saginarios, Bellisarios, DiSantises, DiBiases, Palmas, Fiorentino, and others provided extended missionary service in those early days under direct sponsorship of the CCNA. As a result of the churches established by these men and the other IPM groups having experienced persecution before, during, and after WWII under Benito Mussolini, the American AG offered to help them at the first ⁕Pentecostal World Conference in 1947. Later that year, many of these churches took the name ADI, and an agreement of association was signed between ADI and the American AG (Dec. 1947). The first AG missionaries from IDAG were sent to Italy in 1949. There were still many independent IPM churches in Italy. The Italian government stated that these churches should affiliate with a legal church in the U.S. if they wanted religious freedom instead of persecution. The CCNA encouraged them to merge their work with ADI since CCNA was incorporated only as a missionary society. Following this there were several cooperative efforts between CCNA and IDAG in establishing 100 Sunday schools by the "Sunday School Squad" (1953–1954) and the Italian Bible Institute (1954). ADI became incorporated in Italy (1959). CCNA and ADI signed an agreement of association (1977), but this important work of CCNA remained ADI, Assemblies of God in Italy. Thus, ADI has formalized association with AG and CCNA while retaining a strict autonomy. In 1999 ADI,

which has received substantial support from the American AG and CCNA, had 1,500 churches and outstations and more than 1,500 ministers. There are still some independent IPM churches in Italy.

CCNA's largest work is in India. This was begun with missionary work c. 1969. Today the work consists of 1,500 churches, a leper colony, a college, a hospital, Christian academies, and trade schools.

■ **Bibliography:** G. BonGiovanni, *CCNA 60th Anniversary Ricordo* (1987) ■ idem, *The Ministry of Reconciliation in the Christian Church of North America* (1983) ■ idem, "The Christian Church of North America" (pamphlet, 1987) ■ J. Colletti, "A Sociological Study of Italian Pentecostals in Chicago: 1900–1930" (paper, SPS, 1986) ■ A. F. Dalton. "Field Focus: Italy," *AG Foreign Missions Report* (1988) ■ L. DeCaro, *Our Heritage: The Christian Church of North America* (1977) ■ J. DelTurco, telephone interview by author (Aug. 20, 1999) ■ A. Erutti, *The Life and Early Ministry of Leonard Erutti* (c. 1982) ■ S. H. Frodsham, *With Signs Following* (1946) ■ S. Galvano, ed., *The Fiftieth Anniversary of the Christian Church of North America, 1927–1977* (1977) ■ W. J. Hollenweger, *The Pentecostals: The Charismatic Movement in the Churches* (1972) ■ C. E. Jones, *A Guide to the Study of the Pentecostal Movement*, vol. 1 (1983) ■ G. B. McGee, *This Gospel Shall Be Preached* (1986) ■ R. T. McGlasson, "Observations on the Work of the Assemblies of God in Italy" (unpub. report, Mar. 10, 1952) ■ D. Martino, *The Emergence and Historical-Theological Development of the Christian Church of North America* (thesis, Ashland Theol. Sem., 1988) ■ "Meet Our Ministries," CCNA web site (June 1999) ■ W. W. Menzies, *Anointed to Serve* (1971) ■ P. Ottolini, *The Life and Mission of Peter Ottolini* (c. 1962) ■ A. Palma, *The Articles of Faith* (1987) ■ N. Perkin, "Persecution Continues in Italy," *PE* (Mar. 22, 1953) ■ A. Piraino, "Minutes of Convention of Italian Brethren Held in Grace Tabernacle Syracuse, N.Y., on Jan. 15, 16, 17, 1948, for the Purpose of Forming, If Feasible and Expedient, an Italian Branch of the Assemblies of God" (1948) ■ R. Tedesco, ed., *General Council of Christian Church of North America Annual Report Book—1977* (1977) ■ "What's Available to You," CCNA web site (June 1999) ■ E. S. Williams, J. R. Flower, N. Perkin, U. N. Gorietti, R. Bracco, P. A. di Domentio, "Agreement for Association between the General Council of the Assemblies of God with Headquarters in Springfield, Missouri, U.S.A. and the Assemblies of God of Italy with Headquarters in Rome, Italy" (unpub., 1947).

■ E. B. Robinson

CHRISTIAN CITY CHURCHES INTERNATIONAL

Emerging out of the counterculture in Christchurch, New Zealand, Phil and Chris Pringle came to Sydney, Australia, in 1979 after conversion in the Assemblies of God (AG) church of Dennis Barton. Together with a small group who followed them from N.Z. (some of whom had been influenced by ⁕Christian Outreach Centre founder Clark Taylor), the

Pringles met first in Roseville and then took over the small church being run by a prominent independent pentecostal minister, Paul Collins, in the Dee Why Surf Club.

With free, energetic worship based on contemporary music, and a ministry adapted from classical revivalist pentecostalism (emphasizing preaching, the altar call, conversion, baptism in the Spirit, healing and prophecy/vision), the Pringles energized the small group through a common vision of church growth. Many people were converted from the prominent drug and surf cultures of the northern beaches, while others, influenced by the charismatic movement in the mainline churches and finding themselves unwelcome there, transferred their membership to the lively young church.

As the church grew and moved from Dee Why to Brookvale, the original group formed the leadership, articulating an increasing number of ministries into various areas, including recording, youth, evangelism, television, ministry training, creative arts, and others. Influenced by ministers such as ▶Yonggi Cho, the church by the mid 1980s had developed into the leading independent charismatic megachurch in Sydney and was spawning off-shoots in other suburbs and cities. By 1997 the movement was one of the more significant pentecostal groupings in Australia, with an average weekly attendance of approximately 7,850 in 31 churches, not including churches planted internationally in such places as New York, London, and Sri Lanka.

A movement of common worship and experience rather than theology, its branches range both in size and method, including people from all denominational backgrounds and from none. Its influence on Christian music in the Pacific region continues to be profound, and the original church continues to act as a mediator of key revivalist influences.

■ **Bibliography:** J. Barclay, *Arise: The Story of Christian City Church* (1987) ▪ B. Chant, *Heart of Fire* (1984). ▪ M. Hutchinson

CHRISTIAN GROWTH MINISTRIES See HOLY SPIRIT TEACHING MISSION.

CHRISTIAN OUTREACH CENTRES A charismatic church movement, the Christian Outreach Centres were begun in 1974 by former stockman and Methodist minister Clark Taylor, with relatively small meetings in his Brisbane home. Coming out of a revival in their local church, the movement grew exponentially, such that by 1983 there were some 2,500 people in regular attendance at the main Mansfield church, and 31 other churches had been planted, mostly throughout Queensland and northern New South Wales, with a total membership around 10,000. Emerging from the charismatic movement of the 1970s, the movement strongly emphasizes faith, evangelism, and church planting, with a prophetic slant directed at the conquest of Australia for Christ. The churches have a strong emphasis on contemporary music and worship. By 1986, with 3,500 members, the Mansfield Church was the largest congregation of any type in Australia and, in addition to its Bible school and K–12 school, responded to the growing need for teachers for the Christian schooling movement by founding Christian Heritage College, Australia's first Christian liberal arts college. Founded with a threefold purpose, "to meet the needs of Christian schools for Christian teachers, to provide Christian young people with higher education opportunities in a Christian setting, and to establish a Christian presence in the realm of intellectual life generally," the college has been virtually unique in Australian pentecostal/charismatic circles. With the departure of its founder under a cloud in the late 1980s, the movement went through a time of reorganization and reassessment but has continued to grow and spread internationally under the leadership of Neil Myers. At the time of writing the movement has some 25,000 members in Australia and has spread to some 25 other nations throughout the world. The church remains strongest in Queensland and northern New South Wales and weakest south of Sydney.

■ **Bibliography:** B. Chant, *Heart of Fire* (1984) ▪ R. Humphreys and R. Ward, *Religious Bodies in Australia* (2d ed., 1988) ▪ C. Taylor, interview, CSAC Archives. ▪ M. Hutchinson

CHRISTIAN WORKER'S UNION The Christian Worker's Union (CWU) was established by Holiness evangelist S. G. Otis in Springfield, MA, in the 1870s. Among the ministries sponsored by the Union were a periodical, *Word and Work,* a camp meeting, and mission work in Eastern Europe. Increasingly frustrated with the conservatism of the National Holiness Association, Otis invited E. L. Harvey and a team of ▶Metropolitan Church Association evangelists to conduct meetings in Springfield in the fall of 1902. In the wake of the Azusa Street revival, Otis and the CWU became an important regional center for pentecostalism in New England. Otis and William Plummer, his successor as editor of *Word and Work,* embraced the ▶finished work teaching of ▶William Durham. Continuing to operate as an important regional pentecostal center for the first three decades of the 20th century, the CWU hosted such prominent pentecostal figures as ▶Stanley H. Frodsham and ▶Aimee Semple McPherson. In 1935 the CWU disbanded and *Word and Work* ceased publication; Fred Corson was its final editor
. ▪ W. Kostlevy

CHRIST'S CHURCH FELLOWSHIP Christ's Church Fellowship (CCF) is a ▶neocharismatic renewal group founded in 1989 by a group of leaders who had been part of the renewal movement associated with churches of the "Restoration Movement," which are traditionally noncharismatic churches (Christian Churches, Churches of Christ, and Disciples of Christ). In addition to affirming and practicing all the foundational gifts of Eph. 4:11 (CCF feels that apostleship and prophecy have been most neglected), CCF desires to provide support and accountability relationships for member pastors and to provide a network through which like-minded Christians can work together.

CCF International is based in Cincinnati, OH, and is overseen by a seven-member leadership presbytery. Tom Smith was the founding president of what CCF calls a "covenant fellowship of churches." Jeff Crabtree assumed that position in 1995. The church emphasizes five key ministries: evangelizing the lost, training and equipping believers through conferences, planting new churches, pastoring and assisting local church pastors, and developing significant teaching and equipping materials. The churches join together in annual "kinship conferences," men's and women's retreats, and pastors' conferences held at various locations around the United States. CCF publishes a quarterly newsletter called *CCF Viewpoints,* which is distributed among the CCF churches.

At its inception, the CCF consisted of a small cluster of five churches anchored by Fellowship Christian Church in Cincinnati, OH. By the mid 1990s, 24 congregations in 13 U.S. states and 50 congregations in 5 foreign countries (Russia, Nigeria, Zimbabwe, India, and Ethiopia) were affiliated with or had been started by CCF. CCF estimates total involvement at nearly 10,000 members. In addition, the fellowship operates an orphanage, a hospital, a Christian school, various humanitarian outreaches, and Bible training centers.

■ **Bibliography:** *CCF Viewpoints* (Apr. 1989–Summer 1993) ▮ J. Crabtree, personal correspondence, Feb. 12, 1996 ▮ S. J. Dahlman, "New Denomination Formed," *The Christian Standard* (Mar. 26, 1989) ▮ S. Rabey, "New Church Body Formed," *Christianity Today* (Apr. 7, 1989) ▮ T. Smith, informational letters (Dec. 1988–Dec. 1992) ▮ idem, personal correspondence, Dec. 3, 1993.
■ D. Embree

CHURCH MEMBERSHIP Membership in the local pentecostal church today differs little from that in other evangelical groups. Most churches do not equate the body of Christ only with those baptized in the Spirit; therefore, a pentecostal experience is not required of members. Church discipline of members tends to reflect the Holiness traditions and manifests the same taboos.

1. Historical Developments.

Early pentecostals did not attach great significance to the formal matter of church membership. They equated the mainline church with apostate Babylon or Antichrist and emphasized that church membership did not equate with salvation as a part of the true body of Christ. Participation in fellowship and worship was the bonding element rather than the institutional legalism of membership. As a result, open rather than closed communion is the general practice. Some had been ejected from their former church denominations and were so suspicious of ecclesiastical structures that they even rejected the whole idea of a membership list. They were one in the unity of the Spirit.

With the development of church polity, however, institutional structures became standard. Particularly important was the power of a voting membership in a congregational decision such as who the pastor would be. Membership, though, does not bestow power in all groups; only male members of the ▸Church of God (Cleveland, TN) have votes in the local conference.

In some of the modern charismatic fellowships, membership is not exclusive. Members may hold dual memberships in the local fellowship as well as in a historical Catholic, Orthodox, Anglican, or Protestant church.

2. Requirement for Membership.

All pentecostal churches require testimony of a conversion experience for admission to membership. Most do not emphasize water baptism as a prerequisite to joining, but all are expected to be baptized. It is required in some ▸Assemblies of God churches and in all ▸United Pentecostal churches. In ▸Pentecostal Holiness churches parents may follow the Wesleyan pattern and have their infants baptized or merely dedicated if they prefer. Of particular interest is the fact that only in a few instances, such as in the United Pentecostal Church, is the uniquely pentecostal experience of the baptism in the Holy Spirit required for membership. Many second-generation pentecostals either have not been baptized in the Spirit or do not continue the practice of speaking in tongues after a childhood or adolescent experience. Those who do not claim Spirit baptism may, however, become somewhat second-class saints, as they are barred from positions of church leadership or kept from advancing to the clergy.

Financial support of the church may be either an explicit or implicit obligation. Tithing may be required, as in the ▸Pentecostal Church of God, or a commitment to support may be demanded, as in the ▸International Church of the Foursquare Gospel, but enforcement may not be consistent. Members who do not attend worship for extended periods of time, from one to six months, may be dropped to an inactive status on the rolls. This is not so much a disciplinary matter as it is a means of keeping rosters current to be able to meet legal quorum requirements when conducting church business.

Loyalty and cooperation are required by all groups, but toleration of dissent may vary widely. In many independent charismatic fellowships that developed in the 1960s, membership meant submission to authority figures in the details of life that most Christians consider private.

3. Standards of Conduct.

Church members represent the body to the public and, therefore, standards of ethical conduct are imposed. The early pentecostals emphasized the Bible as the authoritative rule of faith and practice, but the deemphasis on creeds left the practices as the focus of tensions. The issues were the taboos of the Holiness and revivalistic traditions. Urbanization and affluence have eroded these standards over the years, but they still remain points of contention in many fellowships. Alcohol, tobacco, and dancing are still generally not permitted, but television has eroded the opposition to theater attendance. A few groups do not even allow television, and some do not permit women to cut their hair or wear makeup. The modern charismatic movement, however, has not been characterized by these traditional Holiness taboos.

See also CHURCH, THEOLOGY OF THE.

■ **Bibliography:** W. J. Hollenweger, *The Pentecostals* (1972) ■ J. T. Nichol, *Pentecostalism* (1966) ■ R. Quebedeaux, *The New Charismatics: The Origins, Development, and Significance of Neo-Pentecostalism* (1976) ■ K. M. Ranaghan, "Conversion and Baptism: Personal Experience and Ritual Celebration in Pentecostal Churches," *Studia Liturgica* 10 (1974).   ■ D. J. Wilson

CHURCH OF GOD (CLEVELAND, TN)

I. History
    A. Beginnings
    B. Early Expansion

II. Ministries
    A. The Church of God and Race Relations
    B. The Missions Cause
    C. Education

III. Special Ministries
    A. Ministries to the Military
    B. Ministries of Restoration
    C. Beyond the Walls

The Church of God (CG), with headquarters in Cleveland, TN, is one of the oldest and largest pentecostal bodies in America and very likely in the world. It has local congregations in all 50 states and mission outposts in 107 countries. In 1986 the 1,650,000-member denomination celebrated its centennial under the theme "A Century of Pentecostal Witness," which signified that its earliest years of searching and preaching resulted in a pentecostal outpouring and that its subsequent ministry has been a multifaceted witness to pentecostal truth and experience.

I. HISTORY.

The CG was instituted under the name Christian Union on Aug. 19, 1886, in Monroe County, TN. R. G. Spurling, a Missionary Baptist preacher who led in the organization, was joined by only eight others, one of whom was his son, Richard G. Spurling Jr., also a Missionary Baptist preacher. The original compact of this small group was "to take the New Testament, or law of Christ, for your own rule of faith and practice, giving each other equal rights and privilege to read and interpret for yourselves as your conscience may dictate, and . . . sit together as the Church of God to transact business as the same. . . ." Their stated intention was "to restore primitive Christianity and bring about the union of all denominations." They chose the name Christian Union because it expressed the simple agreement that bound the original members together.

A. Beginnings.

The elder Spurling died soon afterward, and his son carried on alone. In 1892 a second fellowship was formed, 12 miles away in Cherokee County, NC, in the home of W. F. Bryant, a Baptist lay preacher. Spurling and Bryant ministered in the isolated Unicoi Mountain region for four years before seeing any significant response to their efforts. Then in the summer of 1896 a revival was conducted in the Shearer Schoolhouse in ▸Cherokee County, which resulted in a strange and wonderful occurrence—men and women became enraptured by the Holy Spirit and spoke in unknown tongues. During the outpouring about 130 persons received the experience, which was identified in the Scriptures as the baptism of the Holy Spirit. It was also recorded that numerous sick people were healed. Such things had never been seen or even heard of in the mountains. Few knew what to make of it, so much opposition followed. The opposition turned hateful, and a period of violent persecution swept across the mountains and tested the faith and courage of the believers. Churches and homes were burned; the people were flogged, shot at, stoned, and otherwise tormented for almost a decade. They were opposed in more subtle ways for many years thereafter.

On May 15, 1902, the church added guidelines and regulations to its policy and changed its name to the Holiness Church. On June 13, 1903, a new minister, ▸A. J. Tomlinson, who had recently come to the mountains from Indiana, joined the church and was chosen as pastor. Soon thereafter another preacher and newcomer to the mountains, M. S. Lemons, joined the growing body.

By 1905 there were four congregations in three contiguous states: Tennessee, North Carolina, and Georgia. On Jan. 26–27, 1906, these four came together for a "general assembly" in Cherokee County, NC. Thereafter, an annual or biennial general assembly would be a prominent feature of the CG.

As early as 1904 the center of activities began to shift westward from the mountains to the town of Cleveland, TN. By 1907 the move was complete and permanent. On Jan. 11, 1907, the church officially adopted the name

Church of God, the name that had been used in the original compact in 1886.

From 1906 on the CG became more aggressive in preaching the baptism of the Holy Spirit. Although many of the members had received the experience as early as 1896, they seem to have thought of it as a phenomenon that had happened only to them; they testified to the experience and wished that others would share "the blessing," but they did not aggressively preach it to others. From 1906, when their experience was affirmed with news of similar outpourings in other places, particularly California, the people of the CG became more evangelistic in proclaiming the Holy Spirit baptism as a doctrine and spiritual experience for all believers.

B. Early Expansion.

In 1909 the CG created its first administrative office, that of general overseer, for full-time supervision of the affairs of the church. A. J. Tomlinson was elected to the post and proved effective in pressing the pentecostal message across the southeastern U.S. Congregations were established in Tennessee, North Carolina, Georgia, Alabama, Florida, Kentucky, and Virginia. This led the church to the most creative year of its early history: 1910. In January of that year the first CG missionaries went to a foreign country, the Bahama Islands; in Mar. 1910 the church began publication of a denominational journal, the *Church of God Evangel;* in Aug. 1910 the teachings of the CG were formally codified for the first time; and the evangelists were so effective that the church almost doubled in size during the year, from 1,005 to 1,885 members. With the surge of growth, overseers were appointed in 1911 to supervise the work and lead the evangelistic effort in the separate states.

From these early days the CG endeavored to use scriptural designations and terms for its operation. This was seen in its use of names, such as "Church of God," *"Evangel,"* and "overseers." This practice was particularly evident in the adoption of the tithing plan of finances. The plan had been encouraged from the formative days, but it was officially adopted and developed in 1914–17. In 1917 the CG agreed that each congregation would retain 80% of the tithes paid by its members and send 10% each to the state headquarters and general headquarters. The result was a dramatic increase of funds for such purposes as evangelism, missions, publishing, and general expansion. The individual states and the CG in general were soon able to expand their ministries into new fields and services.

The assembly of 1916 created the most powerful body of the CG—a council of 12 men to care for the affairs of the church between its general assemblies. Following the pattern of Scripture, it was called "Council of Twelve" or "Elders Council." This influential body presently meets with the full-

The upper room in the headquarters building of the Church of God in 1917. A. J. Tomlinson and secretary Blanche Koon are seated; the first Council of Elders is standing with opened Bibles. This room was also the first location for Bible Training School classes.

time executive committee as an executive council. (In 1986 the body was made international and enlarged by six seats to a "Council of Eighteen.")

With growing resources and leadership, the CG moved ahead boldly into new areas of ministry. It began its own publishing plant in 1917 for printing its expanding Sunday school literature and church journals. This plant grew and is today a productive arm of the church, ▸Pathway Press.

In 1917 the CG instituted a Bible Training School, a dream that had occupied the church since 1911. The first class began on Jan. 1, 1918, in the midst of WWI and the influenza epidemic of 1918. Despite the difficulties, the school survived and grew under the leadership of such teachers as Nora Chambers, ▸Flavius J. Lee, and J. B. Ellis. Today it is Lee University, a four-year, fully accredited liberal arts college of 1,400 students.

Another long-cherished dream of the CG, an orphanage or home for children, was realized in 1920 when a home was opened in Cleveland, TN. Lillian Kinsey was the first matron. Almost immediately new homes were built to accommodate the critical need.

1. Transition.

The CG suffered a painful disappointment in 1923 when A. J. Tomlinson, upon being replaced as general overseer, withdrew from the denomination and organized a separate group. The break occurred when leaders of the CG, especially members of the Council of Twelve, became unhappy with Tomlinson's autocratic style of leadership and sought a change of administration. Tomlinson took the position that the council could not remove him, for he had been elected "for life" in 1914. The impasse was not resolved, and the unfortunate break occurred in June 1923.

Flavius J. Lee, a singularly pious man and effective teacher, was elected to replace Tomlinson. Under Lee's leadership the CG regained its unity and sense of direction. This was due in large part to the high character and spiritual depth of the new leader. The CG enjoyed considerable growth and expansion and by 1926 had 25,000 members in 31 states. It maintained foreign missions in the Bahama Islands and Jamaica.

When Lee died in 1928, S. W. Latimer succeeded him as general overseer. The Great Depression shortly thereafter had an adverse effect on the CG in some ways, particularly in the area of finances, but it did not dampen the spiritual ardor or evangelistic zeal of the church. In many respects the Depression period can be called a "golden era." Camp meetings, which had been a part of each state's annual calendar since 1909, became even more important times of fellowship, evangelism, and devotion. Outstanding preachers arose in most parts of the CG, and numerous new programs were begun. In 1929 a few local youth organizations resulted in a national organization called Young People's Endeavor (YPE). The

YPE fueled such enthusiasm among the youth that they became a dynamic new force in the CG. A national youth magazine, *The Lighted Pathway*, was begun in 1929 by ▸Alda B. Harrison at her own expense. After a year the denomination assumed responsibility for the journal and made it its official youth magazine.

2. Missions Outreach.

The decade of the 1930s saw the opening of new missions in several lands in the Western Hemisphere: Mexico (1932), Turks Islands (1932), Haiti (1933), Guatemala (1934), Costa Rica (1935), and Panama (1935). The principal missionary force of the period was ▸J. H. Ingram, who became a factor in world outreach for more than three decades.

When the CG emerged from the Depression in 1936, it was 50 years old and had 64,000 members. Behind the vigorous leadership of ▸J. H. Walker, general overseer, and J. H. Ingram, missions field representative, the membership was in an expansive mood. The CG used its 50th anniversary to quicken an awareness of the world's need of the gospel. During a "Golden Jubilee World Tour" in 1936, Ingram brought the South India mission work of R. F. Cook into the fellowship of the CG and opened missions in several other lands. Also in 1936 ▸Herman Lauster returned to his native Germany and began a vigorous work in the face of Nazi tyranny. Within the North American continent, congregations were established in virtually every state and in Saskatchewan, Canada.

a. The Modern Era. In 1942–43 the CG was one of the founding organizations of the ▸National Association of Evangelicals (NAE). It was a significant move for pentecostal churches to develop strong bonds with some of the very churches from which they had withdrawn only a few years earlier. This was followed in 1947 by the formation of the ▸Pentecostal World Conference (PWC) and in 1948 by the ▸Pentecostal Fellowship of North America (PFNA). These moves indicated that the CG, along with the entire pentecostal movement, had come of age.

The CG set limits in 1946 on the time its leaders could serve in executive offices. This plan of limited tenures proved to be popular with the ministers, and the church has been treated to a notable succession of administrators at both general and state levels.

b. Amalgamations. Twice in the modern era the CG has formed an amalgamation with a kindred body outside America. The first was in 1951, when the church formed a union with the ▸Full Gospel Church of South Africa. The 30,000-member South African church changed its name to Full Gospel Church of God. The immediate result was a remarkable growth in South Africa and increased opportunities for evangelism on the African continent.

The second amalgamation came about in 1967 between the CG and the 70,000-member ▸Gereja Bethel Indonesia (Bethel Full Gospel Church of Indonesia). The Indonesian leader, Ho L. Senduk, was a member of the CG, but his work was not a part of the denomination's missionary program. The union of the Gereja Bethel Indonesia and the CG resulted in an international Bethel Church of God, with congregations in all of the 27 provinces of Indonesia and in Holland.

II. MINISTRIES.

The modern ministry of the CG consists of a full range of Christian activities and endeavors. These include such departments as evangelism and home missions, world missions, publications, higher education, youth and Christian education, benevolences, radio and television, women's ministries, lay ministries, stewardship, and other special ministries.

A. The Church of God and Race Relations.

Since 1909 the CG has had a considerable number of black ministers and congregations. Despite the fact that its roots were in the South, where racial discrimination was strong, the denomination made no official distinction between black and white churches or ministers until well after 1920.

Edmond S. Barr, a Bahamian, was licensed in 1909 and ordained on June 3, 1912. The first official register of ministers in Jan. 1913 included 11 black ministers (three with full ordination) without any reference to race or color. Five others were added to the ranks before the end of 1913. Most of the black constituency of that period was in Florida, although there were black congregations in Tennessee. There is no record of the number of black members in predominantly white congregations, although there were many.

There was a dubious separation of the black and white congregations in 1926. Even though it came at the request of the black ministers, the unfortunate division was probably a consequence of prevailing social attitudes of the period. For 40 years the separation existed but with close harmony and fellowship between the two entities. The CG struck down all official barriers in 1966 and returned to the racial idealism that prevailed in the earliest years of the church.

In 1986 there were about 800 black CG ministers and 400 congregations in the U.S. that were totally or predominately black. Yet there are no official barriers to whites or blacks in their choices of local congregations, congregational or denominational schools, or any other church participation. It was mandated in 1986 that the Council of Eighteen always have black membership. Much earlier, in 1932–38, a black minister, J. H. Curry, served on that important body, and several others later served as ex officio members.

B. The Missions Cause.

In 1909 the earliest CG missionaries went beyond the U.S. when R. M. Evans and his wife, of Florida, went to the Bahama Islands. The couple arrived in Nassau on Jan. 4, 1910, and worked with Bahamians ▸Edmond S. and Rebecca Barr. At the same time, ▸Lillian Trasher, a young woman of North Carolina associated with the Dahlonega, GA, church went to Assiout, Egypt, and established a mission and orphanage. Both Evans and Trasher went at their own expense, since there was no mission fund in 1910 to support pentecostal missionaries. The *Church of God Evangel* constantly appealed to its readers to support the missionaries. The support was so inadequate that R. M. Evans had to return home, and Lillian Trasher ultimately found other sponsorship for her Egyptian mission.

Although the CG continued its Bahamian work without a break, it was not until 1918 that another successful missionary ministry was begun, in Jamaica. A missions board was appointed in 1926 to promote the missions cause, examine applicants, and raise funds for missions. After this rather tardy step, the missions cause took on new vigor. From its beginning the CG had a vision of reaching the world but no clear understanding of how it was to be done, a circumstance true of most other denominational efforts in world ministry. It is therefore understandable that many of the most vigorous foreign undertakings were independent or nondenominational.

In the 1930s the CG missionary program finally came into its own, with consistent financial support from the homeland but with the use of native converts as ministers wherever that was possible. Each new field was opened with the aim of making it indigenous as soon as possible. This was effected as schools were established in the various countries for the purpose of training workers. In 1966 the foreign membership of the CG surpassed that in the U.S., a trend that has continued. The U.S. and Canadian membership was 547,000, of a worldwide membership of 1,652,000. Local congregations and missions have been established in 107 countries and territories on every continent. American missionaries presently serve in many, but not all, of the 107 countries. Non-American missionaries, especially from European and Latin American countries, also go from their homelands to other parts of the world.

Several programs of internationalization were begun by the CG in 1973. This has included bilingual general assemblies (plus interpreters for many languages); international congresses in Mexico (1973) and Puerto Rico (1977, 1985); and in 1986, the requirement that no less than two members of the Council of Eighteen come from outside the U.S. In 1986 members were elected to the council from Mexico, Bermuda, and Korea.

C. Education.

After founding Lee College in 1918, the CG established numerous other colleges and schools, mostly Bible colleges. In 1935 Northwest Bible College was established first at Lemmon, SD, and later at Minot, ND; in 1936 International

Bible College was established in Saskatchewan, Canada; in 1949 West Coast Christian College was instituted in Fresno, CA; and in 1976 East Coast Bible College was established in Charlotte, NC.

The Church of God School of Theology was instituted in Cleveland, TN, in 1975, and, like Lee University, is fully accredited by the Southern Association of Colleges and Schools. The seminary campus adjoins that of Lee University; the two institutions share a Pentecostal Resource Center, which houses a library of 116,000 volumes and a modern media resource center. The resource complex features the Pentecostal Research Center, a comprehensive collection of pentecostal literature, materials, and memorabilia from the worldwide pentecostal movement.

Other college-level educational institutions are operated by the CG in South Africa (two colleges), Indonesia, Korea, Puerto Rico, Germany, Panama, Mexico, Argentina, and the Philippines. Schools of institute level also are operated in 52 countries.

III. SPECIAL MINISTRIES.

In addition to its traditional ministries, the CG also operates several specialized, nontraditional agencies that serve contemporary societal needs.

A. Ministries to the Military.

Following WWII the CG responded to the needs of its servicemen with a worldwide program of servicemen's centers and fellowships. Begun in Germany and Japan in 1961, the ministry maintains centers in all parts of the world and conducts a regular program of servicemen's retreats that minister to military personnel of all denominations. There are also 23 CG chaplains in the U.S. Armed Forces.

B. Ministries of Restoration.

The CG has long operated a wide range of special ministries, such as prison evangelism, ethnic ministries, and homes for children, to which have now been added new ministries that are restorative in purpose. These are in response to contemporary societal problems, such as child abuse, drug abuse, and unwed motherhood. It sponsors the Peniel Ministry (for drug rehabilitation) in Harrisburg, PA; Jireh House (for unmarried mothers) in Portland, OR; and the Raymond E. Crowley Center (for abused children) in Sevierville, TN. These and other CG ministries in response to the ills of humankind reflect a consciousness of the diverse responsibilities that come with age and experience.

C. Beyond the Walls.

The CG launched its second century with a growing emphasis on reaching beyond its walls to help those who are not a part of the denomination. This reflected the 1886 compact of the church, when it was called Christian Union, and revealed a continuing awareness that Christians should "by love serve one another" (Gal. 5:13). Several ministries of the CG were designed to help those in need for the simple reason that they were in need, when there could be no reasonable expectation of returns to the denomination. Most obvious among those extramural efforts were the restorative ministries already mentioned. This maturity is deemed to be natural—a coming to that place God intends his people to reach. In addition to its outreach to servicemen, to the unfortunate, the disenfranchised, and the abused of the world, the CG involved itself in ministries that strengthen the whole brotherhood of Christ rather than only the CG itself.

In the last decade of the 1900s the CG ministered in about 120 countries and grew to 4 million members worldwide. That growth has come from many forms of service and has involved numerous strategies in lands where overt evangelism is impossible. Educators, doctors, nurses, technicians, and others have had to replace traditional missionaries in order to go into all the world and preach the gospel to every creature.

Education also played a great part in preaching Christ to the world. Han University in Korea became a striking example of Christian service. It was the first university-level CG institution outside the U.S.

In the same decade, Lee College became Lee University, with full academic accreditation, more than 3,000 students, and a greatly expanded campus. In 1984 the school began vigorous exchange programs for students and faculty with such institutions as Henan University in China, Poltava University in the Ukraine, and others. *The Chronicle of Higher Education* listed Lee as among the top 20 baccalaureate institutions with studies abroad.

■ **Bibliography:** Archives of the Pentecostal Research Center (Cleveland, TN) ■ C. W. Conn, *Like a Mighty Army: A History of the Church of God* (definitive ed., 1996) ■ M. Crews, *The Church of God: A Social History* (1990) ■ L. H. Juillerat, ed., *Book of Minutes* (1922) ■ E. L. Simmons, *History of the Church of God* (1938).
                                                              ■ C. W. Conn

CHURCH OF GOD (CLEVELAND, TN) IN CANADA

The Church of God (CG, Cleveland, TN) was organized in Canada in 1920. The small congregation in the rural town of Scotland Farm, Man., was at first regarded as part of the foreign-missions work, and offerings were given for its support. With the earnest evangelization of Saskatchewan and Ontario in the 1930s, however, the Canadian work was regarded as one with the U.S. In 1936 a Bible school was established in Consul, Sask., which continues today as International Bible College in Moose Jaw.

From 1939 to 1962 the Canadian work was administered mainly from the U.S., with most of its activities correlated with the U.S. churches. It is now under the direction of a superintendent of Canada. The Canadian churches have provided the CG with many of its most effective ministers, missionaries, and teachers.

■ **Bibliography:** C. W. Conn, *Like a Mighty Army: A History of the Church of God* (1996).   ■ C. W. Conn

CHURCH OF GOD (HUNTSVILLE, AL) See TOMLINSON, HOMER A.

CHURCH OF GOD (ORIGINAL) In 1919 J. L. Scott withdrew from the ▸Church of God (CG, Cleveland, TN) and founded the (Original) Church of God (OCG) in Chattanooga, TN. He opposed the CG's emphasis on tithing and ▸A. J. Tomlinson's autocratic leadership.

Scott and his followers claimed to follow the "teachings of the CG as originally set up in 1886." The OCG followed the structure and doctrine of the CG, with an annual general assembly and general overseer. There are about 50 congregations and 2,500 members in six states other than Tennessee. The OCG operates a publishing house in Chattanooga and works with the ▸Church of God of the Mountain Assembly, though the two are not related.

■ **Bibliography:** *Manual of Discipline of the (Original) Church of God* (1966).   ■ C. W. Conn

CHURCH OF GOD (QUEENS, NY) See TOMLINSON, HOMER A.

CHURCH OF GOD BY FAITH Founded in 1919 and chartered in 1923, the Church of God by Faith (CGF) has its headquarters in Jacksonville, FL. Elder John Bright was its founder and first moderator. Its doctrine and teachings are centered in the principles of Holiness and Pentecost, with strong emphasis on "sanctification and clean living."

The predominantly black church reports 5,000 members and 100 churches, mostly in Florida, Georgia, Alabama, and South Carolina. There are a few churches in other states, plus foreign mission works in Nigeria.

The CGF is led by a bishop, an executive secretary, and three ruling elders. Its official journal is *Spiritual Guide*.

■ **Bibliography:** Church of God by Faith, *Handbook for the Laymen* (n.d.) ■ idem, *Ritual of the Church of God by Faith, Inc.* (1984).   ■ C. W. Conn

CHURCH OF GOD IN CHRIST The Church of God in Christ (COGIC) is the largest African-American Holiness pentecostal church in North America, with more than 5.5 million members, as reported in the 1977 *Yearbook of American and Canadian Churches*.

The church was founded in 1896 by Charles Price Jones (1865–1949) and ▸Charles Harrison Mason (1866–1961).

These two Baptist ministers met in 1895 in Jackson, MS, and were rejected by their Baptist church in 1896 for insisting on the deeper spiritual experience of entire sanctification as a second work of grace (the basic experience of the Holiness people). That same year, Jones and Mason conducted a successful Holiness revival in Lexington, MS, and formed the Church of God. In Mar. 1897, Mason was walking the streets of Little Rock, AK, when the Lord revealed to him the name "The Church of God in Christ" (through 1 Thess. 1:1 and 2:14). That same year the name Church of God in Christ was chartered and the church headquarters moved to Memphis, TN.

In Mar. 1907, C. H. Mason, J. D. Young, and J. A. Jeter traveled to Los Angeles to attend the ▸Azusa Street revival, of which ▸William J. Seymour (1870–1922) was the leading figure. Mason and Young received the baptism of the Holy Spirit with the evidence of speaking in other tongues. Jeter did not receive the baptism. The three ministers returned to Memphis, but when they returned, the church was already divided over the doctrine of the baptism in the Spirit.

In Aug. 1907 the general assembly of the church met in Jackson, MS. The discussion of the future of the church lasted for three days and nights, after which the assembly withdrew the right hand of fellowship from Mason and all who promulgated the pentecostal doctrine of speaking in tongues. Mason left the assembly with about half of the ministers and members, and reorganized as the First General Assembly of the Pentecostal Church of God in Christ. For two years, Jones and Mason were in lawsuits over the name of the church and control of properties.

In 1909 the courts allowed Mason and his followers to keep the charter and the name COGIC. The date of the church's founding became 1907, and the articles were changed to include the belief in the Holy Spirit, who proceeds from the Father and the Son and is equal with them in

In Liberia, missionary Paul Davis welcoming President Tubman to ceremonies in 1971. (Center) Bishop Simmons of the Church of God in Christ.

deity and unity. The other articles were already in place, which included the belief that Christ is head of the church, belief in divine healing and anointing the sick with oil, and belief in the second coming of Christ. (In 1910 Jones and his followers became the Church of Christ Holiness U.S.A. and continued as a Holiness church with an episcopal structure.)

At first the church was held together by Mason's charisma, an annual convocation in Memphis, and a periodical *(The Whole Truth)*. By 1934 the COGIC claimed 345 churches in 21 states and the District of Columbia. Membership totaled more than 25,000. Five bishops (I. S. Stafford of Detroit, E. M. Page of Dallas, W. M. Roberts of Chicago, O. T. Jones of Philadelphia, and R. F. Williams of Cleveland), whom Mason had consecrated the year before, and 10 other state overseers were put in charge. Under this plan, growth was phenomenal. Membership increased tenfold during the next three decades. In 1962 (a year after the founder's death), it totaled 382,679.

The founder designated O. T. Jones (1890–1972), one of the first bishops, as his successor. After Mason's death this appointment resulted not only in a prolonged constitutional crisis and the seating of Mason's son-in-law, J. O. Patterson (b. 1912), rather than Jones as presiding bishop, but in the blurring of doctrinal and disciplinary distinctives as well. Although in 1969 a major split rent the body, dynamic leadership and quiet rapprochement resulted in spectacular growth. With a reported 3,709,661 members in 1982, the COGIC was nearly 10 times as large as it had been 20 years earlier. Part of the increase may be attributed to the friendship its leaders have extended to the charismatic movement, a stance unique among black denominations. By the end of the century, the COGIC had grown by another 50%, to more than 5.5 million.

The COGIC has a number of strong departments. In 1911 Mother Lizzie Woods Roberson (1860–1945) was appointed by Mason as the leader of the women's department, in accordance with Jeremiah 9:17–20. (The honorific "Mother" is used for those in authority in the women's ranks.) Roberson established the Prayer and Bible bands, the Sunshine Bands for children, and the Sewing Circle. The women developed the missionary departments in the churches. In 1925 home and foreign missions were funded by the Women's Department with missions in Haiti, Africa, India, and Germany.

Following Mother Roberson was Mother Lillian B. Coffey (1896–1964); Mother Annie L. Bailey, Detroit (1964–76); Mother Mattie Carter McGlothen, Richmond, CA (1976–95); and Mother Emma Crouch, Dallas (1995–97). The present leader is Mother Millie Mae Rivers of Goose Creek, SC, a suburb of Charleston. The Women's Convention is held in various cities in May of each year.

The International Sunday School Department, founded in 1916, is the largest activity in the church. The founder was Elder F. C. Christmas (1865–1955), followed by Bishop L. C. Patrick, who served from 1938 to 1955, followed by Bishop C. W. Williams. The present leader is Elder Jerry Macklin.

In 1914 the National Youth Department was established under Elder O. T. Jones Sr., a position he held until 1962. The present leader is Elder J. Drew Sheard (1959–). The Music Department's president is Evangelist LuVonia Whittley. Many gospel-singing families got their start in this department: the Crouches, Winanses, Clarks, Hawkinses, and Paces, to name a few. The Sunday School, Music, and Youth Departments have a combined annual summer convention called Auxiliaries in Ministry (AIM). Each summer the AIM convention has activities for all ages, including spelling bees, marching drill teams, and talent shows.

COGIC established a school in 1918. Sister Pinkie Duncan and Professor James Courts initiated the Saints Industrial School and Academy in Lexington, MS. The next leader was Dr. Arenia C. Mallory (1905–77). Today the school has grades K–12. The church has established C. H.

A communion service during a National Convocation of the Church of God in Christ.

Mason Bible Colleges in all jurisdictions to enhance the church's teachings. The C. H. Mason Seminary, founded in 1970, is part of the International Theological College (ITC) in Atlanta. The president of ITC is Dr. Robert Franklin, a COGIC elder.

The leaders following Bishop C. H. Mason were Bishop O. T. Jones Sr. (Philadelphia; 1891–1972), who led the church from 1962 to 1968; Bishop J. O. Patterson Sr. (Memphis; 1912–89), from 1968 to 1989; Bishop L. H. Ford, (Chicago; 1911–95), from 1989 to 1995. The present leader is Bishop Chandler Owens of Atlanta.

On Apr. 3, 1968, Rev. Martin Luther King Jr. gave his last speech at the Mason Temple, the church's headquarters, which was completed in 1945. His sermon was entitled "I Have Been to the Mountaintop." The Annual Holy Convocation is held in Memphis in November. The church's publication is *The Whole Truth*. The church has its own publishing house.

■ **Bibliography:** S. S. DuPree, *African-American Holiness Pentecostal Movement: An Annotated Bibliography* (1996) 4:650 ■ C. E. Jones, "Church of God in Christ," in *DPCM* (1988) ■ L. Lovett, "Aspects of the Spiritual Legacy of the Church of God in Christ," *Mid-Stream* 24 (Oct. 1985): 389–97 ■ J. O. Patterson, *History and Formative Years of the Church of God in Christ* (1969) ■ V. Synan, *The Twentieth-Century Pentecostal Explosion* (1987).
■ S. S. DuPree

CHURCH OF GOD IN CHRIST (WHITE)

An association of pentecostal ministers operating primarily in the South and Southwest between 1910 and 1914. ʼHoward A. Goss, who had been associated with ʼCharles F. Parham since 1903, received permission from ʼCharles H. Mason, bishop of the black ʼChurch of God in Christ, to use his organization's name to ordain some white ministers. The new group issued credentials and was able to obtain clergy railroad discounts under the borrowed name. Since there are apparently no minutes extant of meetings conducted by this group, there is a certain amount of confusion as to when they actually started, where they met, whom they ordained, and other details. Existing ministerial credentials give the organization's name as "The Church of God in Christ and in Unity with the Apostolic Faith Movement." This only adds to the confusion, because several founding ministers of the group left what was known as the ʼApostolic Faith Movement, directed by Charles F. Parham.

Another ministerial association, one of the many groups to use the name Church of God, apparently merged with the Church of God in Christ (white) in 1913. This Church of God was formed as a loose fellowship of pentecostal ministers at Dothan, AL, in 1909. Four of the leaders were H. G. Rodgers, ʼM. M. Pinson, D. J. Dubose, and J. W. Ledbetter.

By the end of 1913 a published list of ministers of merged groups numbered 352. Five of the men on the list—M. M. Pinson, A. P. Collins, H. A. Goss, ʼD. C. O. Opperman, and ʼE. N. Bell—prepared and published "the call" to what became the organizational meeting of the ʼAssemblies of God (AG). Apparently, with the forming of the AG, the Church of God in Christ (white) ceased to exist. Its importance was to bring pentecostal ministers together in an association and prepare the way for the formation of the AG.

■ **Bibliography:** C. Brumback, *Suddenly . . . from Heaven* (1961) ■ J. Flower, *History of the Assemblies of God* (1949) ■ W. Menzies, *Anointed to Serve* (1971) ■ V. Synan, *The Holiness-Pentecostal Movement in the United States* (1971).   ■ W. E. Warner

CHURCH OF GOD IN THE REPUBLIC OF MEXICO

(IGLESIA DE DIOS EN LA REPÚBLICA MEXICANA). Founded by ʼDavid Ruesga as a schism from the Assemblies of God (AG) in Mexico. Ruesga was named the first leader of the AG in Mexico in 1929. He served in that capacity until 1931, when after several years of quietly suppressing his negative feelings toward the influence of Anglo AG leaders in Mexico, he and a number of disgruntled followers left the AG and formed the Church of God in the Republic of Mexico (CGRM). They took a significant number of followers and churches with them. Ruesga's decision to leave the AG in Mexico split up the work in that country and greatly weakened it for a few years. Ruesga's actions led ʼRodolfo Orozco and ʼModesto Escobedo to suspend his ordination credentials.

The schism led not only to the formation of Ruesga's own denomination, but also to the creation of a number of other pentecostal denominations in Mexico, such as the Iglesia Cristiana Interdenominacional in the Portales neighborhood, the Independent Sarón Church, and the Movimiento de Iglesias Evangélicas Pentecostés Independientes (MIEPI).

In 1940 Ruesga established formal ties with the U.S.–based Church of God (CG, Cleveland, TN). In 1946 still another split took place, resulting in the creation of the Iglesia de Dios Evangelio Completo, which has kept formal ties with the CG. After Ruesga's death in 1960, the CGRM selected Gregorio Muhoz to be the new ruling bishop; he served until his death in 1985.

The CGRM has an episcopal form of government with bishops who exercise great control over the denomination. They operate their own seminary in Mexico City, where they train their pastors and Christian workers. The church is officially apolitical, although it tends to be politically and socially conservative on most issues. Theologically, they have been heavily influenced by dispensationalist, premillennial theology. They also place a heavy emphasis on divine healing and encourage dancing in the Spirit. As for women's roles, they admonish women to wear head coverings in worship services and not to wear jewelry, cosmetics, or pants. They strongly oppose the drinking of alcoholic beverages, smoking, dancing, movies, and extramarital sex. The CGRM has experienced rapid growth, going from 17,000 adherents in 1961 to 80,000 adherents in 1970. By 1993 there were an estimated 625 congregations and 150,000 adherents throughout Mexico.

■ **Bibliography:** D. Barrett, *World Christian Encyclopedia* (1982) ■ G. Espinosa, "Borderland Religion: Los Angeles and the Origins of the Latino Pentecostal Movement in the U.S., Mexico, and Puerto Rico, 1906–1946" (Ph.D. diss., U. of Calif.–Santa Barbara, 1998) ■ P. Johnstone, *Operation World* (1993) ■ M. J. Penton, "Mexico's Reformation: A History of Mexican Protestantism" (diss., U. of Iowa, 1965) ■ L. Scott, *Salt of the Earth: A Socio-Political History of Mexico City Evangelical Protestants (1964–1991)* (1991).

■ G. Espinosa

CHURCH OF GOD, JERUSALEM ACRES The Church of God, Jerusalem Acres (Cleveland, TN), considers itself to be the NT church. Its version of church history traces the true early church up to the Council of Nicea in A.D. 325. After that it is swallowed up, not to reemerge until June 13, 1903, when the church was rediscovered. It is said that ▸A. J. Tomlinson provided the true lineage through the 1922–23 controversy, as did Grady R. Kent facing similar circumstances in 1957.

Grady R. Kent, born in 1909 in Rosebud, GA, was converted at age 21 in a Congregational Holiness church. His Spirit baptism soon followed in the ▸Church of God (CG, Cleveland, TN). Church officials insisted that because of Kent's speech impediment and literary crudeness, he should attend Bible school if he wanted a ministerial license. By 1931 he had joined the ▸Church of God of Prophecy (CGP), and he received a ministerial license in 1932. From 1934 to 1936 he served as state overseer of Minnesota and then spent the next two years in the same capacity in Nebraska. In 1938 he went to Egan, GA, as pastor. He received considerable attention in the following year as a result of his part in a highly publicized trial of members of the Ku Klux Klan who had severely beaten him. The governor of Georgia, Gene Talmadge, attended the court proceedings, as did A. J. Tomlinson, who, after remaining through the completion of the trial, brought Kent to Cleveland to pastor the local church that met in the Tabernacle House of Blessings. On Sept. 1, 1940, Kent's sermon focused on Mic. 4:1 and Ps. 132:4–6. He and Tomlinson had previously discussed biblical prophecy, and as a result of their conversation that afternoon, Tomlinson purchased a place he named ▸Fields of the Wood and started a new auxiliary, Church of Prophecy Marker Association, over which Kent was placed as world supervisor in 1943. Kent was

a stirring speaker, although crude in speech, who could hold audiences for two to three hours. His continued influence was evident in various projects, such as the "white angel fleet" (i.e., airplanes), which he called Ezekiel's cherubim.

Confronting a problem previously encountered by groups and individuals such as the Zwickau prophets, Spiritual Franciscans, Jansenists, Seekers, ▸John Alexander Dowie, and ▸Frank Sandford, the 1956 general assembly of the CGP passed the following resolution: "The Church does not endorse attempts by its ministers to identify themselves or other ministers as the Two Witnesses mentioned in Rev. 11. Neither does it approve of anyone indicating that he is John the Revelator." This action was clearly directed at Kent, later called St. John II. The following January he printed and began to circulate his view that he was in the spirit and power of John the Revelator. ▸M. A. Tomlinson, general overseer, called on Kent to recant or resign, and he did the latter on Feb. 13, 1957.

Kent saw the above as the next great reformation of the Bible church, because, in his view, M. A. Tomlinson had in 1948 wrongly given the general assembly priority over the general overseer, thus failing true theocracy. On Feb. 17, 1957, Kent formed his group of 300 as the Church of God of All Nations. Kent declared himself the chief bishop, formed seven auxiliaries, restored the offices of 12 apostles (with names changed to Apostle Emerald, Apostle Chrysopraus, etc.), seven Spirits of God (or Seven Men of Wisdom), female prophets (ministers), and the Seventy (this group, also known as the elders, was never full). He grew a beard as a constant reminder of the revolution, and many male members did likewise. The official publication, *The Vision Speaks,* was first issued in April, and the next year a church flag, modified from that of the CGP, was released. On Aug. 1, 1958, he bought a seven-acre tract of land in Cleveland to be called Jerusalem Acres, which he intended to be a more complete fulfillment of John's Revelation than Fields of the Wood. On Aug. 20, 1958, the name "The Church of God" was adopted.

By 1962 Kent was preoccupied with the Jewish people. The resultant approach was called NT Judaism. Some evidences of this were the forbidding of certain meats, worshiping on Saturday rather than Sunday, using the Jewish calendar, surnaming, using staffs, observing various Jewish festivals (their general assembly is also the Feast of Pentecost). Kent retained his position for seven years, until his death on Mar. 31, 1964. Attention was drawn to the concurrent Passover celebration and the great earthquake in Alaska. Various steps, including an open grave, were taken to comply with the belief that soon Kent was to rise from the dead. In the meantime—although two of his sons, along with David Williams, thought themselves his successor—the council chose Marion W. Hall, apostle to the Gentiles, as the chief bishop. Hall retained this position until 1972, when he was replaced by Robert S. Somerville, who served until 1980. The church has increasingly come on hard times financially, since the membership base was never very large and has declined in recent years.

■ **Bibliography:** J. D. Garr, *The Lost Legacy* (1981) ■ G. R. Kent, *Basic Bible Teachings* (n.d.) ■ idem, *Manual of Apostles' Doctrine and Business Procedure* (n.d.) ■ idem, *Sixty Lashes at Midnight* (1942; repr. 1962) ■ idem, *Treatise of the 1957 Reformation* (n.d.) ■ idem, *The Vision Speaks* 18 (12, 1976). ■ H. D. Hunter

CHURCH OF GOD OF ALL NATIONS See CHURCH OF GOD, JERUSALEM ACRES.

CHURCH OF GOD OF PROPHECY

(CGP). The Church of God of Prophecy (CGP), as it is known since 1952, shared some of the early years of the ˃Church of God (CG, Cleveland, TN). ˃A. J. Tomlinson, a dynamic pentecostal pioneer, was the church's most prominent figure of the first half of this century. In this limited amount of space we cannot adequately treat the multiplex of events that resulted in Tomlinson's becoming the head of the CGP as a distinct organization in 1923. Suffice it to say that numerous sociological, theological, historical, and personal factors plus different views of church government and financial dilemmas were involved. Failure was not limited to any one category or group. [For one perspective on the events, see H. V. Synan, *The Holiness-Pentecostal Tradition* (1997), 197–98—Ed.]

Relations between the two groups were tense for several decades. The legal consequences included the small group being designated the Tomlinson Church of God by the chancery court of Cleveland, TN. By 1952 the court's judgment allowed the group to use the name Church of God of Prophecy in its "secular affairs." During that time and to this day the church refers to itself as the "Church of God" (with A. J. Tomlinson, and then ˃M. A. Tomlinson, as general overseer). The strained relationship between the CG and CGP has become more relaxed through the years, and since the late 1960s various regional, national, and educational concerns have been addressed jointly by the two churches.

The CGP has laid considerable emphasis on many events prior to 1923. One of the most tangible evidences of this line of thought is realized in that it counts among its binding polities those decisions of the general assemblies from 1906 onward, unless later clarified or reversed by the CGP. Also, the home that hosted the first general assembly of 1906 is owned by the CGP. An annual service is held by the church in the house to commemorate the first assembly and to honor the participants, activities, and resolutions.

The theme most often sounded about these early years is related to June 13, 1903, the date on which A. J. Tomlinson joined the Holiness Church at Camp Creek. A total of 5 joined that day, bringing the number to 20. Tomlinson was made pastor of the congregation and later general overseer of the fledgling church that grew to a membership of 21,076 by 1922. The local body had been formed in May 1902 and included persons from the now defunct Christian Union (1886) and the 1896 revival in ˃Cherokee County, NC, that was followed by a few temporarily speaking in tongues. Tomlinson had previous contact with some of these people and

19th Annual General Assembly of the Church of God of Prophecy, the first year the assembly was held in the newly built tabernacle on Central Avenue in Cleveland, TN.

had joined other groups, but when he joined them that day he meant for it to be a final decision. The CGP also owns the property that includes the site of the meeting place for the Camp Creek church. The site is now called ▸Fields of the Wood, situated near Murphy, NC. Following Tomlinson's death in 1943, his youngest son, Milton, was chosen his successor by the assembled state and national overseers, whose decision was greatly influenced by an interpreted message in tongues. This verdict was accepted and confirmed by the 1944 general assembly. M. A. Tomlinson continued in this position until 1990, making him perhaps the second (after ▸Charles H. Mason) in length of tenure as an international pentecostal church head.

A central focus of the CGP has been that worship services are considered an essential part of the Christian pilgrimage. Thus, members have often been engaged in at least four services a week and some specialized meetings that have lasted for a number of weeks. Some of these services have lasted for several hours, including some late into the night. Further, members have been generally engaged in prayer meetings, various forms of evangelism, and special times of fellowship.

Revival campaigns traditionally included services every night for at least a week and were known to continue for up to 10 weeks. The 1980s still recorded some revivals of eight-week duration. Often these services last for hours and center on invigorating music, stirring preaching, intense prayer for spiritual experiences, healings, and for reaching the unconverted in the U.S. and abroad. The preaching at these meetings has often been issue-oriented. Evangelists have been particularly concerned to confront the individual's relationship with God. The manner in which they have done this is of such a nature that it might be labeled "divine drama." Ministers would often engage in various forms of physical agitation when it was believed that this aided the cosmic battle between good and evil.

The time spent at the altar, a bench built to accommodate seekers of spiritual experiences, has always been a centerpiece in any worship service and especially in revival meetings. This was the place where one surrendered all to God, sought God, and received blessings ranging from salvation to physical healing and to specific directives ("calls") from the Lord. Prayers of many kinds have been encouraged as central to the believer's walk. Some have regularly prayed one hour a day and some have engaged in 12-hour prayer sessions along with short- or long-term fasting. In a public service, most members of the congregation kneel and pray while different ones pray for the seekers gathered at the altar. Some are "slain in the Spirit" on the floor, and others "shout" (i.e., physically demonstrate) their praises to God. It is not unusual for the flow of the service to be interrupted by those who want to pray for whatever need is at hand. These and similar things,

along with charismatic outbreaks, such as a "message in tongues," could result in the scheduled sermon being replaced by an extended prayer session. This kind of activity is not understood as minimizing the importance of Scripture but rather as undergirding it by obedience to the pertinent directives. It is also true that church events planned without sermons have been known to "erupt in pentecostal power" that included extemporaneous services.

CGP members have shared a distinct ethos with the majority of early pentecostals. Among the characteristics are intensity of faith, sincerity, devoutness, commitment, praxis, and humility. This translated into criteria such as "the anointing" and/or "the calling" as basic to judging the usefulness of members, and especially ministers. Every member was called to be passionate about his or her work for the church. The local church, in addition to state, national, and international leadership, has been routinely involved in implementing the guidelines. Pentecostals in general and the CGP in particular are not rightly understood by those outside the movement if doctrinal formulas and behavioral studies alone are given priority. Any comprehensive analysis must reckon with matters of ethos. Not surprisingly, the last generation has seen a gradual deterioration of emphasis on this ethos and a simultaneous preoccupation with various propositions.

In terms of officially determined doctrinal propositions, at the center stands an Arminian version of the *ordo salutis* that includes a special emphasis on sanctification. It culminates with a doctrine of Spirit baptism that regards tongues speech as the initial evidence. Other prominent teachings from the well-publicized list of 29 include an imminence-oriented eschatology that involves a premillennial return of the risen Jesus; a call for the sanctity of the nuclear family, which includes denial of remarriage under certain circumstances (involving fornication as defined in the teachings); practice of water baptism by immersion and rebaptism after "reconversion"; the Lord's Supper (with grape juice) and the washing of the saints' feet; total abstinence from intoxicating beverages and tobacco; a concern for modesty in all dimensions of life; and an emphasis on nine Holy Spirit charisms with special attention given to divine healing. For the most part, the result of the formulas has been to stabilize many of the adherents, but there have also been some aberrant results, such as the refusal to purchase life insurance, opposition to formal education, opposition to medicine to the extent that pain and death were accepted rather than formal medical treatment, and dissolution of existing marriages.

One of the results of the ▸restorationist impulse of the CGP has been an exclusive body ecclesiology. The restorationist impulse produced a view of history that said Jesus founded the church on Mount Hattin (Mark 3:13ff.). This body survived until A.D. 325, at which time it ceased to exist as before because it was layered over with much foreign matter. But layers began to be removed by Luther, then Wesley, etc., until the complete revelation was unveiled on June 13, 1903. This is the ancestry the CGP has claimed as its own. Although this ecclesiology was not originated by A. J. Tomlinson, he became its most forceful advocate, and it has been reinforced by M. A. Tomlinson. One result has been the ongoing, repeated exaltation of "the Church." Those outside the organization often view this as self-indulgence, while those inside thought they were glorying in Jesus Christ. A typical service can include someone lifting up "the Church" with the rejoinder that members are unworthy of such a thing and prove their humility by their various failures to fulfill Christian obligations. A person joins "the Church" by publicly covenanting his or her allegiance to the Scriptures as the final authority. Further, although the doctrine of salvation is predicated on a rugged individualism, this ecclesiology insists that no person seek celebrity recognition but be immersed in the group identity.

A noteworthy result of this teaching is that the CGP has not joined the ▸National Association of Evangelicals (NAE) or the ▸Pentecostal Fellowship of North America (PFNA). An interesting by-product of this and like prohibitions is that the church has not undergone "evangelicalization" or "charismatization" and has retained more of the original pentecostal agenda than other similar pentecostals—with the exception of ▸Oneness pentecostals. Thus, although the CGP does not ordain women, they have one of the highest percentages of female ministers who serve as pastors and state, national, and international leaders. In the late 1990s the parameters of authority were set by granting women ministers authority to administer ordinances while at the same time excluding them from the rank of presbyter. Previously women were not allowed to lead marriage ceremonies or administer ordinances, which showed the strength of oral tradition, since there was no general assembly ruling on record that limited women in this regard. Meanwhile, ordained males are licensed as bishops, a term that generates no little confusion outside the CGP.

The CGP may be the most racially integrated pentecostal church in the world, judged by the number of racially mixed congregations and the integrated state, national, and international leadership. African Americans, African Carribeans, and Latin Americans are charged with the leadership in states whose composition includes European Americans as the majority. The CGP may have been the first church to defy Jim Crow laws in their worship services, and they have long opposed the Ku Klux Klan. The church has also been generally unencumbered by the conservative battle plan with regard to a specific view of biblical inspiration and science versus Scripture.

The CGP has long called for a oneness in Christ that transcends human expectations and is truly organic. CGP is a founding member of the ▸Pentecostal-Charismatic Churches of North America (PCCNA), and its leaders serve on the boards of the ▸Pentecostal World Conference, the ▸North American Renewal Service Committee (NARSC), and the ▸International Charismatic Consultation of World Evangelization (ICCOWE). Starting with the third Quinquennium (1985–89) of the Roman Catholic and Classical Pentecostal ▸Dialogue, CGP was among the first pentecostal denominations to send an official representative. Various ministers attend functions organized by the NAE, while a few have engaged in the National Council of Churches and the World Council of Churches (WCC).

The term *theocracy* has been used throughout church history from the likes of John Calvin in Geneva to ▸John Alexander Dowie in Zion. Under the Tomlinsons, the term *theocracy* was employed to describe a government that proclaimed the annual general assembly to be the highest tribunal, while the entire ecclesiastical structure collapsed on the office of the general overseer. Prior to 1990, no resolution before the general assembly was accepted without a unanimous decision of the attending male members. Women remain excluded from the decision-making process, while no distinctions of clergy, laity, or nationality are made between the males. The impact of oral tradition is well illustrated by the fact that the practice of unanimous decision making did not become an official assembly ruling until Sept. 4, 1986. A "unanimous decision" often means that some who disagree simply have to defer to the prevailing view, but should they persist in supporting their view, that particular item fails to pass at that time. A form of episcopacy is used by the church as the general overseer (since 1911) appoints state and national overseers, who in turn appoint their staff and pastors, who in turn determine the local leaders. This practice has not been uniformly observed through its history, because into the 1950s the churches "called" pastors.

In the 1980s the 10,000-seat auditorium in Cleveland, TN, drew 20,000 registered attendees to a meeting that was principally a time of celebration and fellowship with church members from around the world. Various projects were promoted by the international departments, and there was much fervent preaching (some delivered in Spanish, and everything translated into Spanish and French) and praying, while the doctrinal and business concerns were held to a minimum. The greatest attendance at each such assembly was during the annual address by the general overseer, M. A. Tomlinson. Much time was devoted to state and national marches (started in 1925), which were swept along by the Bahama Brass Band. These marches, however, were discontinued in 1988. Many of these things also characterized the state and national annual conventions at the time.

The governmental system that evolved to insure the success of prioritized concerns centers on five departments. Each of these departments has a comprehensive network of international, state or national, district, and local directors. These are still commonly referred to as "auxiliaries," which in order of appearance are: Sunday School (1906); Assembly Band Movement (ABM; 1916, 1928); Women's Missionary Band (WMB; 1928); Victory Leaders' Band (VLB; 1928); and Church of Prophecy Marker Association (CPMA; 1941). Sunday schools exist as part of almost every congregation in the world and engage students of all ages in the study of Scripture. Long before cell groups gained prominence in many charismatic churches, the CGP first named this ministry "watchers over ten," and then, taking a term from John Wesley, called them "[prayer] bands."

A. J. Tomlinson opened an orphanage in Cleveland, TN, in 1919 and another one in 1928. A variety of similar homes and schools around the world are maintained by the church today. In 1932 the Emergency Fund (discontinued in 1992) was begun to assist members during financial crises. The general assembly of 1933 adopted a distinctive church flag. The colors and symbols were carefully chosen to represent important biblical themes like truth, purity, and the blood of Jesus. Some zealous adherents have at times—contrary to the official pronouncements of the assemblies—made an icon of the church flag. In 1939 a white field secretary was added to assist the general overseer. In 1941 a black field secretary joined the staff, and a Hispanic field secretary completed the group in 1953. This missions orientation of the church evidenced itself by not only insisting that members tithe their income and give in regular offerings but also give sacrificially to missions. A general secretary was appointed to head this work in 1938, followed in 1940 by a foreign-language department. A department focusing on the needs of retired and disabled ministers was established in 1941, along with a short-term school known as Bible Training Camp (BTC). BTC is now called Bible Training Institute in its fifty-plus sessions held around the world. In 1951 a radio and recording ministry was firmly established, and it led (1953) to the weekly program *Voice of Salvation* (broadcast in four languages). This was followed by a limited television ministry initiated in 1971 and revived in 1987 (the 1952 and 1957 assemblies ruled against members owning television receivers) and subsequent separate broadcasts in Spanish and English. In 1964 a public relations department was established, and a full-time music department followed the next year. The year 1966 saw the birth of Tomlinson College, a two-year accredited liberal arts college that has produced more than 1,300 graduates. The servicemen's department was founded in 1967 and the evangelism department in 1970.

The influence of the Holiness movement is quite apparent in several ways. One product of this influence is a list entitled "Advice to Members." This first appeared in the assembly minutes of 1919, was not revised from 1968 to 1988, and then underwent major changes in the 1990s. The document opened with exhortations to an obedient church life shown in things like manifesting fellowship, being courteous, and being cautious in conversation. Subsequent revisions focused on clothes and recreation. Specifically prohibited were wearing such things as shorts in public, rings and lipstick, and going to movie theaters and public swimming areas. The power of oral tradition is again evidenced in that, despite the lack of an assembly ruling, a person is not accepted for membership if he or she is wearing any jewelry, including a wedding band.

Billy D. Murray was chosen to fill the position of general overseer when M. A. Tomlinson resigned in 1990. The church experienced rapid changes, such as the closing of Tomlinson College, financial restructuring with an emphasis on local churches, plurality of the office of general overseer, and relaxing of previous taboos. An exodus of European Americans that started late in the 1980s gained momentum under Murray. An investment marked to generate funds for the ministers' pension program suffered a loss of $435,000, which doomed the entire program. Murray retired in July 2000 and Fred S. Fisher Sr. was chosen as his successor.

The official mouthpiece remains the monthly *White Wing Messenger*. The magazine is published in eight languages and has 6,500 subscribers. The CGP reported a membership of 75,027 in the U.S. with 1,882 churches, while 115 countries outside the U.S. had an aggregate membership of 520,133 with 7,250 churches. In the earlier decades the membership came almost exclusively from a low socioeconomic stratum. Yet the "working poor" have been increasingly replaced by the middle class in the industrialized West. Accompanying the social upward mobility of the membership has been a moderation of many of the sectarian idiosyncrasies and a concomitant lack of membership gains in the U.S. The organization at large continues its anti-intellectual tradition, while the official doctrinal formulas increasingly fade in significance for the emerging middle-class constituency.

■ **Bibliography:** *Book of Minutes: General Assemblies of the Churches of God* (1922) ■ *Cyclopedia Index of Assembly Minutes of the Church of God of Prophecy: 1906 to 1974* (1975) ■ C. T. Davidson, *Upon This Rock*, 3 vols. (1973–76) ■ B. M. Johnson, *Written in Heaven* (1972) ■ J. Stone, *Church of God of Prophecy: History and Polity* (1977) ■ A. J. Tomlinson, *Last Great Conflict* (1913; repr. 1984) ■ idem, *Historical Annual Addresses*, 3 vols. (1970–72) ■ H. A. Tomlinson, *The Great Vision of the Church of God* (1939) ■ Other publications: *Church of God Evangel, Faithful Standards, White Wing Messengers*, tracts, brochures, assembly minutes, court proceedings, etc.

■ H. D. Hunter

CHURCH OF GOD OF PROPHECY IN CANADA The Church of God of Prophecy in Canada (CGPC) traces its heritage to the ministry of ˄Ambrose Jessup Tomlinson. When a "disruption" affected the ranks of the ˄Church of God (Cleveland, TN) in 1923, the Tomlinson loyalists formed the Church of God (Tomlinson), considered by its membership to be the true successor of the original organization. The name was later changed to ˄Church of God of Prophecy. The denomination has churches in all 50 states of the U.S.

In 1937 the first CGPC congregation was organized in Swan River, Man. Fifty years later there were 88 ordained clergy and 38 congregations in British Columbia, Manitoba, Alberta, Saskatchewan, Ontario, and Quebec. Current total membership is 3,107, with 100 clergy. The national headquarters is located in Brampton, Ont. National and provincial meetings are held annually.

■ **Bibliography:** C. H. Jacquet Jr., *Yearbook of American and Canadian Churches* (1999).   ■ G. B. McGee; B. A. Pavia

CHURCH OF GOD OF THE MOUNTAIN ASSEMBLY

With headquarters in Jellico, TN, the Church of God of the Mountain Assembly (CGMA) has an extensive outreach in the mountains of Kentucky and Tennessee. It also has extended its ministry into the Midwest, the Southwest, and as far as California. In 1986 it reported a world membership of 6,911.

Like many of the churches that arose around the turn of the century, CGMA came about because of dissatisfaction with the existing churches in its region. In 1903 several ministers were turned out of the United Baptist Church of the South Union Association for preaching "a closer communion with God and the danger of apostasy." More specifically, they preached that it is possible for a person to be lost after regeneration. Five congregations withdrew from the Baptist fold to protest the harsh stand taken by the association.

On Aug. 24, 1906, ministers S. N. Bryant, J. H. Parks, Newt Parks, and Andrew Silcox and five congregations met in council at Jellico Creek, Whitley County, KY, and formed a new organization. (They first called themselves the Church of God, but in 1911 they learned of the Cleveland, TN, group with that name and added "Mountain Assembly" to their name.) Andrew Silcox was chosen as general moderator of the new church. The following year, 1907, S. N. Bryant succeeded Silcox and served as the denomination's leader until 1938.

Because the CGMA was strongly pentecostal and Holiness in its doctrine and practices, it was subject to fierce persecution in its formative years. It grew, however, to a membership of 966 in 1912, and 1,612 in 1914. This was remarkable in the face of the hostility that confronted the church all across the mountains.

In 1919 the church adopted the tithe plan as its financial base, which enabled it to do more evangelistic work following WWI. Also in 1919 the church instituted a board of 12 elders, who were responsible "to plan the program for the future course of the church." With the improved organization and financial system in place, the church grew to more than 2,000 members in 1922 and erected a new tabernacle for its permanent headquarters in Jellico, TN.

The CGMA experienced both advances and setbacks in the decades that followed. A new system of government was adopted in 1944, following a long static period, and a general overseer, A. J. Long, became the chief executive of the church. The present administrative structure consists of a general overseer, two assistants, and a general secretary-treasurer.

In 1968 the CGMA began a missions outreach in Brazil and in 1986 reported missionary works in Jamaica, Haiti, and India. Missions in Liberia, Nigeria, Malawi, and Zambia also were taken into the fellowship of the church in 1986. The church now has churches in 20 nations. A training school, the International Institute of Ministry, was opened in 1997.

■ **Bibliography:** L. Gibson, *History of the Church of God of the Mountain Assembly* (1954) ▮ Minutes of the Assemblies of the CGMA (1907, 1986).   ■ C. W. Conn

CHURCH OF OUR LORD JESUS CHRIST OF THE APOSTOLIC FAITH

The Church of Our Lord Jesus Christ of the Apostolic Faith was established by Robert Clarence Lawson in 1919 in Columbus, OH. From this church emerged the ˄Church of the Lord Jesus Christ of the Apostolic Faith in 1930 under Sherrod C. Johnson and the ˄Bible Way Church of Our Lord Jesus Christ in 1957 under Smallwood E. Williams.

CHURCH OF THE LIVING GOD, CHRISTIAN WORKERS FOR FELLOWSHIP

Organized at Wrightsville, AR, in 1889, the Church of the Living God, Christian Workers for Fellowship (CLGCWFF) resembles the ˄Church of God in Christ in several ways. The founder, William Christian (1856–1928), a former Baptist minister, was in fact an early associate of ˄C. H. Mason (1866–1961). The CLGCWFF differs, however, in permitting tongues speech in recognizable languages only, and it rejects the initial-evidence theory. It recognizes three biblical sacraments: baptism by immersion, the Lord's Supper (using unleavened bread and water), and the washing of the saints' feet. Each ordinance is administered only once. It holds that the Lord's Prayer is the only prayer "to be prayed by all Christians." It upholds the racial pride of its members by asserting that many biblical saints were black. Following its founder, who was a Mason, it approves the essentials of Freemasonry. Churches are called temples and are numbered consecutively by dates of organization. In 1996 the CLGCWFF reported 170 churches and

42,000 members. Headquarters moved from St. Louis to Cincinnati in 1984.

■ **Bibliography:** *Glorious Heritage: The Golden Book* (1967) ■ C. E. Jones, *Black Holiness* (1987) ■ A. C. Piepkorn, *Profiles in Belief*, vol. 4 (1979).   ■ C. E. Jones

CHURCH OF THE LORD JESUS CHRIST OF THE APOSTOLIC FAITH

A multiracial Oneness pentecostal organization founded in Philadelphia by Bishop Sherrod C. Johnson (1897–1961) in 1933. The organization came out of the ＞Church of Our Lord Jesus Christ of the Apostolic Faith.

The predominantly black body teaches the multiracial nature of the church. Other distinctive teachings by Johnson include a variant Oneness view that the Sonship of Jesus ceased with his death, the use of wine in communion, the practice of footwashing, and the rejection of all military service. Condemned are celebrations of Christmas and Easter, remarriage after divorce, and ordination of women. Women are to cover their heads when praying or prophesying, shun cosmetics, and wear plain, long dresses. Suffering only one schism in 1961, the organization has grown by 1997 to a membership of 17,000 members and 80 churches in the United States, and 8,000 adherents in 60 congregations in the Caribbean, Belize, West Africa, and United Kingdom. Its official publication is *The Whole Truth*.

■ **Bibliography:** T. French, "Oneness Pentecostalism in Global Perspective" (thesis, Wheaton College, 1998) ■ C. E. Jones, *A Guide to the Study of the Pentecostal Movement*, vol. 1 (1983) ■ L. McCoy, *A True History of the True Church* (rev. ed., 1977) ■ A. Piepkorn, *Profiles of Belief*, vol. 3 (1979).   ■ D. A. Reed

CHURCH, THEOLOGY OF THE

I. Pentecostal Theology of the Church
   A. Initial Presuppositions
   B. Factors Promoting Attention to the Church
     1. Concern for the Unity of the Movement
     2. The Denominationalization of the Movement
     3. Church Growth Theory
     4. The Catholic–Pentecostal Dialogue
   C. Pentecostal Presentations of the Church
   D. Distinctive Pentecostal Contributions
   E. The Free Church Ecclesiology of Miroslav Volf

II. Charismatic Theology of the Church
   A. Charismatics Committed to Historic Church Traditions
   B. Restorationists Rejecting Denominationalism
     1. United Kingdom
     2. United States

III. Overview

I. PENTECOSTAL THEOLOGY OF THE CHURCH.

Pentecostals commonly believe that the one church of Christ is composed of all who are regenerate in Jesus through repentance and faith. This conviction is explicitly stated in some denominational declarations of faith (＞Assemblies of God [AG]; AG of Spain; ＞Elim Pentecostal Church of Great Britain and Ireland; ＞International Church of the Foursquare Gospel [ICFG]; ＞Apostolic Faith [AF] of Baxter Springs, KS; Pentecostal Apostolic Church of Romania). Its absence from other denominational statements, however, reflects a lack of centrality in pentecostal faith rather than a different ecclesiology. Denominations that do not mention the church in their statements of faith include ＞AF of Portland, OR; ＞Church of God (CG, Cleveland, TN); AG of France; and AG of Italy. The ＞United Pentecostal Church (UPC) has one tangential reference. Some pentecostal declarations only mention the church in relation to patterns of church government (＞Apostolic Church and ＞AG of Great Britain and Ireland) and another only in relation to the spiritual gifts (＞Church of God of Prophecy [CGP]).

Almost all pentecostal denominations are pretribulational and premillennial, believing that this invisible church of all the saints will be raptured by Christ prior to the great tribulation, after which Christ will reign on earth with the saints for a thousand years. These convictions concerning the rapture and the millennium feature in the majority of denominational declarations of faith, whether or not the term *church* as such is used.

While pentecostals have nearly always affirmed the invisibility of the universal church, they have regularly used the term *assembly* for the visible local congregation. However (with some restorationist exceptions, see below), they do not correlate entire denominations with the theological concept of the church, typically seeing the church in spiritual rather than institutional terms. Thus, pentecostals often say that the church is an organism, not an organization—an emphasis that is reflected in the expressed faith of the Pentecostal Assemblies of Canada (PAOC) in "Christ's Lordship over the Church."

Though the pentecostal movement is characterized by belief in a postconversion ＞baptism in the Holy Spirit, this is virtually never regarded as necessary for salvation and only rarely as a criterion for membership in the church. However, for many pentecostals of earlier generations, only those baptized in the Spirit had the Holy Spirit, an attitude that was formed in times of expulsion and exclusion. Thus, for a time some pentecostals did not readily accept the Christian character of nonpentecostal denominations.

The concept of the church has not generally been central to pentecostal faith, though it has been more prominent among those churches formed and living in situations of hardship and oppression. Thus, the black pentecostal churches generally manifest a greater social consciousness *as church*, although their self-understanding as God's people together, delivered from bondage, is more distinctively black than pentecostal. The most articulate theological reflection among pentecostals has probably come from the Pentecostal Apostolic Church of God of Romania, where conditions of persecution deepened the bonds of church fellowship. In the movement at large, however, there are some signs in recent decades of increasing attention to ecclesiology. Past and present pentecostal understanding of the church can be illustrated from a summary of developing attitudes and convictions.

A. Initial Presuppositions.

The first-generation pentecostals brought with them the understanding of the church commonly found among revival-conscious evangelical Protestants. The exciting message of ▸Azusa Street that "Pentecost has come" was understood as individual blessing on a large scale. This personal focus, however, did not totally exclude church consciousness. Their understanding of the church reflected two distinct thrusts in early pentecostalism, the apocalyptic and the restorationist. The apocalyptic thrust, very vocal and emphasized in the study of ▸Robert Mapes Anderson, focused on the imminence of the parousia, seeing the outpouring of the Spirit in the "baptism" as empowerment for effective evangelism of the entire world before the end came. In this perspective the dominant image of the church was the bride awaiting the coming of the bridegroom and her consequent rapture. ▸Charles F. Parham's view, distinguishing the bride from the church, was a minority view.

The restorationist strand, perhaps owing something to Campbellite inspiration, saw the outpouring of the Spirit as given for the restoration of authentic NT Christianity. The pentecostal outpouring was heralded as the culmination of several divine interventions, given to restore authentic Spirit-filled Christianity: first, the restoration of the gospel of justification by faith at the Reformation; then the restoration of the Spirit's work of sanctification in the Wesleyan movement; and finally, the restoration of divine power with the baptism in the Holy Spirit and the full range of spiritual gifts in the pentecostal movement. Although the term *restoration* later came to have negative connotations for many mainline pentecostals (being associated with groups seen as deviant), this reading of church history is restorationist. While rarely focusing on the concept of the church, it clearly had ecclesiological implications.

These two strands in early pentecostalism came together in the Latter Rain concept. The ecclesiology of the first pentecostals is then best characterized as an implicit and largely unformulated Latter Rain theology. The Latter Rain idea, based on Joel 2:23 and James 5:7, contained both an apocalyptic "end times" message (this rain is the final downpour immediately preceding the end) and a restorationist empha-

sis (it restores NT intensity blessing). Virtually all first-generation pentecostals saw their movement in terms of the "Full Gospel" and not simply as the most powerful demonstration of the Spirit since the 1st century; however, for most pentecostal groups the church was not really part of the "Full Gospel" but would grow from its proclamation. The restoration of the "Full Gospel" was seen in a few circles as restoring the church according to the mind of God in the Scriptures. This restorationist strand was more explicit in the CG. First K. G. Spurling and then ▸A. J. Tomlinson saw the church in theocratic terms, with a focus on the government of God's people. The structures given to the people of Israel in the wilderness received as much attention as passages in the NT. As late as 1916 Tomlinson was saying, "We are diligently searching for the original system of Church government" (*Book of Minutes*, 1922, 216). However, this restorationist vision has faded in the CG, though it survives somewhat more in the CGP. A different form of church restorationism is found in the Apostolic Church (AC) in Great Britain. The restoration of the fivefold ministries of Eph. 4:11 was central in the formation of the AC; the church constitution of 1937 provided for the ordination of apostles, prophets, etc., and for the regulation of these ministries. D. P. Williams, one of the founding brothers, wrote, "We believe that the Apostolic Church, as at present working, gives the freest expression to the New Testament form of Church government, ministry, and relationships" (Williams, n.d., xxiv). This restorationist emphasis on the fivefold ministries of Eph. 4:11 was to reappear in the late 1940s in the ▸Latter Rain movement that broke out in Saskatchewan, Canada, and subsequently influenced centers such as Elim Bible Institute in Lima, NY, and Bethesda Missionary Temple in Detroit, MI.

B. Factors Promoting Attention to the Church.

1. Concern for the Unity of the Movement.

The Azusa Street revival in Los Angeles (1906–9), which triggered the worldwide pentecostal explosion, was a powerfully unifying event. Its astonishing interracial character and its unusual interdenominational makeup demonstrated that "Pentecost" was the outpouring of the Holy Spirit upon "all flesh." Thus, there was an awareness of a God-given spiritual unity among the Spirit-baptized. This unity occasioned frequent comment in the first years, as in, e.g., this statement in *Apostolic Faith* (Azusa Street): "This Pentecostal movement is too large to be confined in any denomination or sect. It works outside, drawing all together in one bond of love, one church, one body of Christ."

That this experience of Christian unity did not generate an explicit ecumenical vision was partly due to the movement's populist and largely proletarian character. Moreover, the subsequent racial segregation and the doctrinal divisions in the movement obscured the unifying power of the Spirit of Pentecost. Those leaders who saw the unity of the movement as a sign of its heavenly origin were deeply disturbed by emerging rivalries and divisions and became ardent advocates of pentecostal unity. These figures included ›Thomas Ball Barratt, ›Alexander Boddy, ›W. F. Carothers, ›William Hamner Piper, ›Gerrit R. Polman, and ›William J. Seymour. As early as Aug. 1908, Piper had preached a sermon, "The Prayer of Jesus Must Be Answered: His Body Must Be United: The Gifts and Offices of the Early Church Must Be Restored" (*LRE,* Oct. 1908). In 1911 Barratt's article "An Urgent Plea for Charity and Unity" argued, "We have to do with facts: that people, honestly professing to having received the Holy Ghost, do not agree in everything on doctrinal points.... What is there to be done? We must either find some form of union, or stand as separate bodies, and aim at some form of alliance between these" (*Confidence,* Feb. 1911, 31). Boddy emphasized pentecostal unity during his American tour of 1912, getting leaders to agree not to engage in mutual condemnation in relation to the ›"Finished Work" (*Confidence,* Nov. 1912, 246). In the mid 1920s Carothers held several "unity conferences," spreading his message through his magazine, *The Herald of the Church.* While none of these authors systematically studied the relationship between fellowship in the Spirit and understanding of the church, their concern for unity necessarily had an ecclesiological component.

The most common pentecostal position has seen the unity of the Spirit-baptized as a sovereign work of God based on the working of the Holy Spirit within each believer. "Within the Pentecostal Revival itself a profound, and indeed unique, unity of the Spirit has been given to us by Christ Jesus: it leaves nothing for us to 'make,' but much that we must zealously endeavor to 'keep'" (Gee, 1947, 2). This spiritual unity was thus seen as personal rather than as institutional.

2. The Denominationalization of the Movement.

Greater attention to the concept of church was thrust on pentecostals by the formation of new pentecostal denominations from the 1910s in America and the 1920s in Europe. In these years the local pentecostal congregations came to be known more as *assemblies* and less as *missions,* the original terminology. Somewhat paradoxically, the formation of new denominations initially hindered rather than promoted reflection on the nature of the church, diminishing the sense of the unity of the movement, at least until the launching of the ›Pentecostal World Conferences in 1947. The church issue was largely restricted to patterns of church government.

Apart from some lesser pentecostal denominations, which were like family businesses, and those that regarded themselves as the restored NT church, the new denominations were formed for pastoral and pragmatic rather than doctrinal reasons: the need to have ministerial credentials for protection against unknown itinerant preachers; the need for accreditation of missionaries and some central organization for dis-

bursement of mission funds; the need for some basic statements of pentecostal belief. In fact, pentecostal churches have adopted virtually every form of church government known to Christians. There are denominations with episcopal government (the Pentecostal Methodist Church of Chile); denominations with congregational patterns of church government (the Scandinavian churches; most of the Russian pentecostals); churches with a mixture of presbyterian and congregational polity (AG); churches with a centralized national organization (Elim Pentecostal Church); churches with a form of monarchical government by one charismatic leader (many smaller denominations, especially in their first generation). The process of denominationalization did not therefore produce any distinctively pentecostal view of the church, except for those bodies seeking to restore the fivefold ministry of Eph. 4:11.

The formation of pentecostal denominations inevitably hastened the tendency toward a full-time ordained ministry trained in pentecostal colleges. A full-time pastorate tends to raise interest in church questions, and the development of ministerial training produces more schematic studies that can hardly avoid the issue of church.

3. Church Growth Theory.

The church growth movement pioneered by Donald McGavran at the Fuller Seminary School of World Mission in Pasadena, CA, has since the mid 1960s contributed indirectly to greater pentecostal attention to the church. Because pentecostal churches have been among the fastest-growing in the world, McGavran's scientific study of what causes churches to grow has attracted the attention of pentecostals, particularly in North and Central America. This current has reinforced the trend fostered by ›Melvin Hodges (see below), leading pentecostals to think more precisely about the formation of churches and not just about the multiplication of converts.

4. The Catholic–Pentecostal ›Dialogue.

Although only a minority of classical pentecostals have supported this dialogue, its third series, which was begun in 1984, has necessitated more pentecostal attention to the church. In 1985 Miroslav Volf and ›Peter Kuzmič of Yugoslavia presented a paper entitled "Communio Sanctorum: Toward a Theology of the Church as a Fellowship of Persons," and in 1987 the Charismatic Baptist ›Howard Ervin made the presentation "Koinonia, Church and Sacraments," implying that pentecostalism should strengthen the vision of the church as corporate human participation in the inner life of the Trinity. The final report for the third series, "Perspectives on Koinonia," contains a fuller reflection on the church than any exclusively pentecostal document.

C. Pentecostal Presentations of the Church.

Explicit treatments of the theology of the church have not been common among pentecostal authors and publications.

Thus, ▸Ernest S. Williams's three-volume *Systematic Theology* (1953) has no treatment of the church. W. A. C. Rowe's *One Lord, One Faith* treats the church only in subsections under "Governmental," while the volume *Pentecostal Doctrine* (1976), edited by ▸Percy S. Brewster, has one item by Ramon Hunston, "The Church—the Body of Christ." ▸Russell P. Spittler's small book *The Church* (1977) is written for a popular readership. The volume *Systematic Theology: A Pentecostal Perspective*, edited by ▸Stanley Horton (1994), has two articles, "The New Testament Church" (M. L. Dusing) and the "Mission of the Church" (B. D. Klaus).

An interesting book on the church from a restorationist background by Hugh Dawson of the AC has the rather daunting title *Through Analogy to Reality* (1968). A characteristic pentecostal view of church history from a CGP perspective is provided by Daniel D. Preston in *The Church Triumphant* (1969). The work of an early pentecostal, Eugen Edel of Germany, was reprinted in 1971 under the title *Das Symbol der Stiftshütte und die Kirche Jesu Christi* (The Symbol of the Tabernacle and the Church of Jesus Christ). Possibly the most creative pentecostal work on the church is by Romanian leader ▸Pavel Bochian, who presents an ecclesiology grounded in the faith-life and worship of the community with an eschatological orientation (see review by D. D. Bundy in *EPTA Bulletin* 4 [2, 1985]). The textbook *Foundations of Pentecostal Theology* (1983) by ▸Guy P. Duffield and ▸Nathaniel M. Van Cleave (from ICFG), gives increased attention to church with one out of ten chapters. Duffield and Van Cleave illustrate a pentecostal tendency to treat the local church as a visible body of Christ but remain reluctant to speak of any visible embodiments of the universal church. This partly reflects a historic Protestant mistrust of church institutions and partly a concern not to make exclusive claims for one's own denomination. However, they make one interesting statement concerning the NT understanding of the church: "Every local church was considered to be the physical manifestation of the Universal Church in that community" (422).

D. Distinctive Pentecostal Contributions.

The most distinctive pentecostal contribution to ecclesiology might be made in the understanding of the local church. Here there are two distinct but complementary thrusts. The first sees the spiritual gifts as an intrinsic element in the life and equipment of the local church. Not unlike Orthodox and Catholics who see baptism and Eucharist as constitutive of church, so some pentecostals see these charismatic endowments of the Holy Spirit not just as evangelistic equipment but as forming and shaping the church. Thus, a pentecostal view of the church expects the full range of the spiritual gifts to be manifested in each local assembly, even though this is not actually verified in most American and European churches. However, this position is more implicit than spelled out in such well-known works as those of ▸Donald Gee and ▸Harold Horton on the spiritual gifts. W. G. Hathaway is more explicit. "While the gifts rest in individuals, they are only given through individuals to the Church" (Hathaway, 1963, 20–21). Hathaway is unusual in that he argues that every gift belongs to the whole church, not just to the local church assembly.

A pentecostal vision of the local church rooted in the power of the indwelling Spirit has been presented by Elim pastor John Lancaster in *The Spirit-Filled Church* (1973, rev. 1987) and by Dutch pastor Willem J. Lentink in *De Bijbelse Gemeente* (1980). These works are typical in being not theological treatises but pastoral teachings on congregational life ordered under the lordship of Jesus in the power of the Holy Spirit. They characteristically emphasize both worship and ministry. This perspective has also been prominent in the vision communicated by ▸Lewi Pethrus and the movement in Scandinavia.

The second thrust has come from reflection on pentecostal missionary experience. While many pentecostal assemblies initially experienced rapid growth through the Holy Spirit's endowment of all members, some missionary labors led to numerical expansion but not to the equipment of all believers. This led some missionaries to reflect on the purpose of mission and produced a greater focus on the nature of the church. The pioneer missiologist was ▸Melvin Hodges of the AG, whose book *The Indigenous Church* (1953) broke new ground. Hodges saw that initial conversion to Christ had to be followed by conscious building of the church. He argued that each NT church was self-propagating, self-governing, and self-supporting. While this and Hodges' later book, *Build My Church* (1957), were important correctives to colonial patterns of American pentecostal missions, his treatment seeks practical rather than theological principles from the Scriptures. He ends up pragmatically advocating an AG–type church polity, combining an independence of local congregations with some national structures and leadership.

A study of the pentecostal contribution to ecclesiology ought to take into account the writings of Donald Gee. Gee's editorials in *Pentecost* from 1947 to 1966 constitute the most penetrating and honest reflection of pentecostal life and convictions to date. Though such reflection is an essential element in ecclesiology, Gee's writings did not directly encourage the emergence of a distinctively pentecostal theology of the church. This was because he saw the pentecostal movement as a Holy Spirit revival weakened by denominationalization and also because he consistently argued that it was but a part, though the most vital part, of the worldwide body of Christ. Nonetheless, Gee pointed the way to a more constructive pentecostal theology by his defense of intelligence enlightened by supernatural faith and by his lack of fear in relating to the non-pentecostal Christian world.

E. The Free Church Ecclesiology of Miroslav Volf.

The appearance of Volf's *After Our Likeness: The Church as the Image of the Trinity* (1998) represents a major contribution to ecclesiology. It is included here under the pentecostal, rather than under the charismatic, heading for several reasons: Volf comes from a pentecostal background; it is the first major work on ecclesiology to take seriously the Holy Spirit's-empowerment of every believer; and it does not arise from a charismatic-renewal context. Volf is a theologian aware of the multiplication of evangelical and Spirit-filled assemblies: "The dynamic life and the orthodox faith of the many, quickly proliferating Free Churches make it difficult to deny them full ecclesiality" (133).

Volf's ecclesiological study is fashioned from the start in dialogue with the Catholic and Orthodox traditions, seeking an alternative that does justice to the centrality of the church in Christian life and history, to the directness of God's work in salvation, and to Free church convictions concerning the local church. He argues against all individualism that regards salvation as simply between "the lonely soul and its God" (172) and that reduces the church at best to a voluntary association. Faith is both a gift of God and mediated through the church. "The ecclesial mediation of faith serves to bring human beings into a direct (though not unmediated) relation to God; they must in faith accept salvation from God" (172).

Volf's pentecostal roots show most clearly in his conviction that the church is structured by the Holy Spirit, and particularly through the charismata. He deplores any juxtaposition of charism and office, arguing for an "interactional model of the bestowal of charismata" (233), which are distributed among all believers, including officeholders. This makes the church "fundamentally a polycentric community" (224).

Another strand in Volf's ecclesiology that takes the pentecostal witness seriously is his eschatological framework. "The Spirit unites the gathered congregation with the triune God and integrates it into a history extending from Christ, indeed, from the Old Testament saints, to the eschatological new creation" (129). Volf provides a theology of the church filled with the Holy Spirit that is pentecostal without being sectarian: "The catholicity of the entire people of God is the ecclesial dimension of the eschatological fullness of salvation for the entirety of created reality" (267).

II. CHARISMATIC THEOLOGY OF THE CHURCH.

Within the many streams constituting the worldwide charismatic-renewal (CR) movement, there are two contrasting attitudes toward the church: (1) the position of charismatics committed to the historic church traditions, both Catholic and Protestant, and (2) the restorationist position of those intentionally rejecting all forms of denominationalism.

A. Charismatics Committed to Historic Church Traditions.

The emergence of CR as a distinct movement of the Holy Spirit, or as a clearly new phase in an existing movement of the Spirit, occurred when leaders and teachers became committed both to the pentecostal experience of baptism in the Holy Spirit and to their own historic church traditions. Unlike the pentecostals, these charismatic Christians immediately saw this outbreak of the *charismata pneumatika* in relation to the church and its renewal. In 1964 ▸Michael Harper wrote: "It is the renewal of the Church that God is principly [sic] concerned about—not that of the gifts. The gifts are for the building up of the Church—in order that it may become once more a powerful and influential force in the world. It is the recovery of New Testament Church life which is our greatest need today" (Harper, 1964, 5).

This view became common among charismatics, but since charismatic teachers were pastors and not theologians, the initial presentations of CR and of the gifts of the Spirit as being for the renewal of the church are mostly in popular periodicals or more descriptive works, such as Harper's book *A New Way of Living* (1973), about Holy Redeemer Episcopal Church in Houston, TX.

More theological reflection on CR and the church began in Europe, first in Holland in the circles associated with the monthly *Vuur (Fire)*, edited by ▸W. W. Verhoef, who combined a dedication to serious theology with a regular association with pentecostals. More scholarly biblical studies came from ▸Arnold Bittlinger in West Germany (1967–68; English ed. 1973). Bittlinger brought to his exegesis a more systematic theological mind than was then found among the more pragmatic pentecostals. He writes of Jesus as being himself the internal order of his body. "Just as in him all the charismata are united, so he is also the prototype of all church ministries" (Bittlinger, 1973, 98).

Among Protestant charismatic theologians, ▸Thomas A. Smail, at one time director of the ▸Fountain Trust in Britain, has written on the church, particularly in *Theological Renewal* (*TR*). Smail's theological reflections on CR are strongly ecclesial, with the constant emphasis that church life reflects the patterns of the Trinity (see, e.g., "Towards the Trinitarian Renewal of the Church," *TR* 25 [Nov. 1983]). More recently, Jean-Jacques Suurmond of the Netherlands has contributed *Word and Spirit at Play: Towards a Charismatic Theology* (1995; Dutch ed. 1994), which presents the church as a charismatic community of celebration. "So the great prophecies are fulfilled in a community which is already living 'in the last days' because it has a share in the sabbath play of God's kingdom," in which "the last come first" and "no one is left out of the game" (53–54).

The Protestant charismatics interacting most seriously with their own theological and liturgical traditions have been the Lutherans, who brought a strong sense of confessional identity to their reflections, without, however, much explicit attention to the church. ⸗Theodore R. Jungkuntz of the Lutheran Church–Missouri Synod has explicitly repudiated the accusation that Lutheran charismatics made baptism in the Spirit, instead of Word and sacrament, the basis for church fellowship. An international group of Lutheran leaders and theologians under the leadership of ⸗Larry Christenson has produced a study of CR entitled *Welcome, Holy Spirit* (1987), of which a substantial portion is devoted to the church.

With the spread of CR to the Roman Catholic Church came a sharp increase in charismatic reflection on ecclesiological themes. Several Catholic theologians baptized in the Spirit were already specialists in ecclesiology (⸗Heribert Mühlen, ⸗Paul Lebeau, Francis Sullivan). Mühlen was in fact the author of one of the most original contributions to Catholic ecclesiology since the era of John XXIII and one that centered on the role of the Holy Spirit. In his book *Una mystica persona: Die Kirche als das Mysterium der Identität des Heiligen Geistes in Christus und den Christen* (One Mystical Person: The Church as the Mystery of the Identity of the Holy Spirit in Christ and the Christians, 1964), Mühlen presented the nature of the church as "one Person in many persons," that is to say, the person of the Holy Spirit in Christ and in Christians. A glimpse of Mühlen's position can be seen in his contributions to *The Holy Spirit and Power* (ed. ⸗Kilian McDonnell, 1975). Rejecting as ambiguous the widespread Catholic view of the church as the continuation of the incarnation, Mühlen saw the continuity in the mission of the Holy Spirit instead. Another Catholic theologian whose writings unconsciously prepared the way for the integration of CR into the Catholic Church was Karl Rahner (1904–84), who emphasized that the unpredictable charismatic work of the Holy Spirit belongs to the nature of the church, which cannot be reduced to merely institutional factors. Rahner's essay "The Charismatic Element in the Church" is published in *The Dynamic Element in the Church* (1964) and in *The Spirit in the Church* (1979). A similar study can be found in *Theological Investigations* (12:81–97).

Catholic reflections on CR all insist on seeing this grace of the Spirit in relation to the church. This innate Catholic tendency had been strengthened by the inclusion of a passage on charismata as both universal and contemporary in Vatican II's constitution on the church (para. 12). This passage owed much to a speech by ⸗Cardinal Suenens of Belgium, who a decade later was to encourage Catholic theological reflection on CR. While Catholic writers on CR gave most attention to the baptism in the Spirit, spiritual gifts, and the believers' relationships with the persons of the Trinity, these topics were all addressed in relation to the body of Christ.

More explicit reflection on ecclesiological issues focused on the following points: (1) *The church as constituted by the distinct divine missions of the Son and the Spirit* (J. H. Nicolas; A. de Monléon; ⸗E. O'Connor). Thus, the renewal of ecclesiology is dependent on a balance between Christology and pneumatology, a point recurring in the writings of Yves Congar, the major 20th-century Catholic theologian to devote attention to CR.

(2) The first point grounds the second: *the complementary nature of the institutional and the charismatic; both are integral to healthy church life* (J. Haughey; E. O'Connor). Charism and church office mutually belong, like the Spirit and the Son in the Trinity (⸗N. Baumert). Institutional ministries can themselves be seen as charisms (⸗P. Lebeau). The charisms are ways the Spirit structures the church from within (⸗R. Laurentin).

(3) *The work of the Spirit in conversion and baptism in the Spirit has an inner dynamic toward the formation of community and integration into ecclesial life* (⸗D. Gelpi; ⸗R. F. Martin; ⸗K. McDonnell).

(4) *Study of interchurch dynamics in CR has led to some reflection on essentials and inessentials in each tradition.* Kilian McDonnell has urged that attention be given to "theological ecclesial cultures," referring to the coherence in each tradition of belief, worship, piety, church government and law, theology, and ethos.

(5) *Received traditional patterns of theology and church life have influenced pentecostal and charismatic understanding of CR and baptism in the Holy Spirit* (F. Sullivan). Heribert Mühlen has insisted that CR is "the church in movement, not a movement in the church." ⸗Peter Hocken has maintained that CR's movement character is inherent in its ecumenical nature as a work of God across all the churches. At issue here are different models of what is meant by the integration of CR into the life of the churches, a goal endorsed by all who are committed to the historic church traditions.

B. Restorationists Rejecting Denominationalism.

1. United Kingdom.

A different kind of restorationist thinking appeared in CR's earliest days in Great Britain. While restorationist groups have gained many recruits from charismatics disenchanted with CR in the historic churches, the existence of this current cannot be attributed to such a reaction. The father of restorationist thinking about the church within CR is David Lillie of Exeter, U.K. Lillie brought with him from his Plymouth Brethren background clear convictions about the centrality of the church in God's plan, the unscriptural character of the historic denominations, the governmental independence of each local church, and the organic rather than organizational bonds between authentic local churches. Lillie, suspended by the Brethren for his pentecostal interests, was baptized in the Spirit in 1941. Helped by G. H. Lang, he came to see the baptism in the Spirit and the spiritual gifts as poured out for the sake of the restoration of the NT church.

Lillie's scope in spreading this "Pentecostal-Brethren" vision of the church expanded in the late 1950s through fellowship with ▸Arthur Wallis and the conferences to which they invited sympathetic pastors and preachers. Some men who later would be prominent in the ▸House Church Movement first met at these conferences (▸Bryn Jones, Graham Perrins, Barney Coombs). Lillie was the main teacher on the church; his audience included other former Plymouth Brethren already well disposed to this ecclesiology. Notwithstanding the role of ▸Cecil Cousen in these conferences, restorationist thinking in British CR did not arise from previous pentecostal restorationist currents (such as the ▸Apostolic Church or the ▸Latter Rain movement).

Characteristic of this Brethren ecclesiology were the priesthood of all believers, to which was added the charismatic equipment of church members with the gifts of the Spirit, and the rejection of "special ministry" (professional pastors and the one-man pastorate) and "special membership" (i.e., denominational exclusivity by which membership in one denomination excludes membership in another). Each local church is a full manifestation of the church, called to be self-sufficient, self-governing, self-supporting, and self-edifying. Communion between local churches is not a matter subject to external authority.

However, by the early 1970s, as the British House Church Movement was gathering momentum, the majority of leaders departed from Lillie's strict congregationalism by espousing the fivefold ministries of Eph. 4:11 (apostles, prophets, evangelists, pastors, teachers), with apostles having authority across a range of local churches.

This vision was first embodied in the Harvestime network centered in Bradford, Yorkshire, in which Bryn Jones was seen as a leading apostle, and in a somewhat lower key in the networks led by ▸Terry Virgo of Hove, Sussex, and Tony Morton of Southampton, Hampshire. Their convictions were expressed in numerous publications, such as the bimonthly *Restoration;* David Matthew's history *Church Adrift;* and Virgo's *Restoration in the Church.* Until the mid 1980s these British restorationists were perceived as advocating a "come-out" policy toward charismatics in the historic churches, provoking controversy over their goals and methods. Michael Harper's book *That We May Be One* (1983) addressed this troubled situation. More recently, restoration teaching has continued but in a less militant and more cooperative way.

2. United States.

Meanwhile, there were parallel developments in the U.S., although the American approach was generally more pragmatic and less dogmatic than the British. In the early 1960s, a magazine, *A Voice in the Wilderness,* edited by John Myers of Northridge, CA, presented restorationist views with positive reports on CR. In the early 1970s the leaders of Christian Growth Ministries in Fort Lauderdale, FL, focused on church formation through the tools of discipling and shepherding. However, they never favored the "come-outism" often stimulated by a restorationist view of the NT church.

Much American charismatic restorationism has been fueled by a growing sense of the covenantal nature of relationships in the body of Christ. This stronger sense of the corporate character of Christian ministry is widely represented among the new charismatic churches, often called covenant or community churches, often knit together in networks under leaders recognized as having apostolic authority, such as ▸Charles Simpson of Mobile, AL, and C. J. Mahaney of Gaithersburg, MD.

III. OVERVIEW.

This survey of pentecostal and charismatic understandings of the church suggests that, at least until the recent appearance of Volf's *After Our Likeness,* theologians and scholars have not done justice to the ecclesiological implications of Pentecost. For different reasons, the pentecostals and the charismatics (whether mainline or restorationist) have not elaborated a theology of the church that captures the distinctive thrust of this outpouring of the Spirit and that manifests the scope of its challenge to received ecclesiologies. The pentecostals have not done so—in part because their forte has been action, not reflective theology, in part, perhaps, through a Protestant fear that focus on the church diminishes the focus on Christ. The mainline charismatics, especially the Catholics, have given more attention to ecclesiological issues, but no theologian has attempted a major study on the church from a distinctively charismatic perspective. The fullest attempt has been ▸J. Rodman Williams's three-volume *Renewal Theology;* one half of volume 3 is devoted to the church. He seeks to hold together spiritual reality and social expression, but the largest amount of space is given to functions, ministries, and ordinances. The restorationists are the people who have focused most on the nature of the church and its significance in God's plan, but their interest has been practical rather than academic, and their works lack the theological weight of the best Brethren writers of the last century.

The importance of Volf's ecclesiology is that for the first time a theologian has manifested a breadth of theological scholarship, a commitment to the creative work of the Holy Spirit, and an ecumenical sensitivity that not does blur but enriches his distinctive convictions. Volf follows in the footsteps of the seminal study of Lesslie Newbigin, *The Household of God* (1953). Newbigin sensed the originality of the pentecostal eruption of the 20th century, since the pentecostals represented a third type of Christianity, distinct from the Catholic and the Protestant. In contrast to the Catholic, who stresses the continuation of Christ's saving mission, and the Protestant, who emphasizes the gospel message as the content of the apostolic witness, the pentecostal sees the church as the place where the Holy Spirit is recognizably present with power.

The distinctiveness of the pentecostal-charismatic understanding of the church is indicated by considering the inherited patterns of Christian worship. Whereas the pre-ecumenical Catholic pattern presented a hierarchically ordained priest, acting *in persona Christi,* offering the eucharistic sacrifice at the altar for the people, and the Protestant pattern presented an educated preacher expounding the Word of God from the pulpit, the pentecostal pattern is that of the upper room—an entire congregation filled with the Holy Spirit giving praise to Almighty God.

While Word and sacrament should have a major place in pentecostal-charismatic church life, this movement poses a radical challenge to the inherited clericalism of both Catholic altar and Protestant pulpit. A pentecostal-charismatic theology of church such as Volf develops can unpack the fuller implications for all aspects of ecclesiology (ordained ministry, Word and sacrament, differentiation of ministries, pastoral authority, marriage and family, evangelism, and nurture) on the basis of all members being indwelt, moved, and filled with the Holy Spirit. Pentecostalism thus takes up a concept dear to the Reformation heritage, the priesthood of all believers, but invests it with more existential content in terms of active deputation to worship and service in ministry. Pentecostal scholar Roger Stronstad has emphasized, particularly from the Lukan writings, the prophethood of all believers.

As Nigel Wright has written: "If it should seem right to expect the restoration to the church of New Testament gifts, why should we not also expect the restoration of New Testament ministries!" (*The Radical Kingdom,* 1986, 76). If this is correct, the restorationist resurrection of the Eph. 4:11 ministries may be in line with the movement's basic impulse, rather than a deviation. This would be the case where the fivefold pattern is presented as a distribution of ministries that in fact belong to the whole body, and where the apostolic, prophetic, evangelistic, and other activities are not restricted to church leaders. It would seem that the mainline pentecostal rejection of such restorationism owes more to negative pastoral experience than to theology or exegesis, as well as to the fear that contemporary apostles could easily become absolute monarchs, though Volf's theological emphasis on the local church does not provide a role for translocal ministries. These reflections point to the restorationist currents, apparently the fastest-growing sector of the movement, as being more important than has thus far been recognized by pentecostals and other charismatics.

Study, prayer, and dialogue are then needed concerning the relationship between historic patterns of Christian ministry and the patterns emerging in restorationist circles. Theologians in the sacramental-liturgical traditions will argue that the historic pattern of bishop-priest-deacon reflects a participatory understanding of Christian ministry as deputation to act *in persona Christi,* a role that none can take to themselves. The revival of other ministries, most explicitly in the restorationist currents but less officially throughout CR, questions the adequacy of "one pastor" ministries (whether more sacramental or more evangelical or even pentecostal) and raises the relationship between ordination as empowerment-deputation and ordination as recognition of graces already bestowed by the Lord. It poses the difficult question as to whether a higher synthesis is possible between traditional patterns of "one person" ministry, especially the historic threefold pattern, and patterns of complementary ministries forming teams within the body of Christ.

See also ORDINANCES, PENTECOSTAL; SACRAMENTS.

■ **Bibliography:** R. M. Anderson, *Vision of the Disinherited* (1979) ■ A. Bittlinger, *Gifts and Ministries* (1973) ■ *Book of Minutes,* Church of God, Cleveland, TN (1922) ■ L. Christenson, ed., *Welcome, Holy Spirit* (1987) ■ H. Dawson, *Through Analogy to Reality* (1968) ■ G. P. Duffield and N. M. Van Cleave, *Foundations of Pentecostal Theology* (1983) ■ D. Gee, "Editorial," *Pentecost* (1, 1947) ■ M. Harper, *Prophecy* (1964) ■ idem, *That We May Be One* (1983) ■ W. G. Hathaway, *The Gifts of the Spirit in the Church* (1963) ■ W. J. Hollenweger, *Pentecostalism* (1997) ■ idem, *The Pentecostals* (1972) ■ M. L. Hodges, *Build My Church* (1957) ■ idem, *The Indigenous Church* (1953, rev. 1976) ■ J. Lancaster, *The Spirit-Filled Church* (1987) ■ D. Lillie, *Beyond Charisma* (1981) ■ K. McDonnell, ed., *The Holy Spirit and Power* (1975) ■ L. Newbigin, *The Household of God* (1953) ■ C. F. Parham, *A Voice Crying in the Wilderness* (1944) ■ A. C. Piepkorn, ed., *Profiles in Belief,* vol. 3 (1979) ■ K. Rahner, *The Spirit in the Church* (1979) ■ R. P. Spittler, *The Church* (1977) ■ M. Volf, *After Our Likeness: The Church as the Image of the Trinity* (1998) ■ various authors, "Perspectives on Koinonia," *Pneuma* 12 (2, 1990) ■ D. Watson, *I Believe in the Church* (1978) ■ D. P. Williams, *Apostolic Church: Its Principles and Practices* (n.d) ■ J. Rodman Williams, *Renewal Theology,* vol. 3 (1992) ■ N. Wright, *The Radical Kingdom* (1986).

■ P. D. Hocken

CLARK, IAN GEORGE (1935–). After serving overseas with the New Zealand Ministry of Foreign Affairs in the late 1960s, Clark became an Assemblies of God (AG) pastor in Lower Hutt and general secretary of the AG between 1971 and 1981. He was also appointed the first secretary of the Associated Pentecostal Churches of N.Z. (APCNZ)—formed to facilitate united action from all the pentecostal churches on moral issues—on its formation in 1975.

Clark saw the role of the APCNZ as being more than this, however, and in 1979 he published a proposal to amalgamate all N.Z. pentecostal churches into a loosely united body. His proposal provoked considerable discussion but was eventually rejected, partly because of the perceived difficulty in merging the varied structural leadership styles of the pentecostal churches.

Clark's observation that failure to facilitate pentecostal unity would open the door to further division turned out to be a prophetic statement. At the beginning of the 1980s there were five major pentecostal groups (Apostolic Church, Assemblies of God, Christian Revival Crusade, Elim Church, and New Life Churches) in N.Z. Other pentecostal denominations started up in the 1980s, with the result that there were at least 11 different pentecostal groupings in the country by 1997. Clark went on to pastor the Rotorua AG and in 1986 became principal of the AG Bible College in Auckland.

■ **Bibliography:** B. Knowles, "Some Aspects of the History of the New Life Churches of New Zealand 1960–1990" (diss., U. of Otago, 1994).   ■ B. Knowles

CLARK, RANDY (1952–). Revivalist and instigator of the "Toronto Blessing." He heard a sermon at age seven that affected him profoundly, but he did not come to Christ until his 16th birthday. At 18 he was in a serious car accident after which he was miraculously healed. As a student at Oakland City College beginning in 1971, he frequently preached revivals at General Baptist churches in Kentucky, Indiana, Illinois, and Michigan. After graduation from Southern Baptist Theological Seminary in Louisville, KY, in 1978, he pastored an American Baptist church in Spillertown, IL, from which he resigned to found Vineyard churches in southern Illinois (1984) and in St. Louis, MO (1986). After experiencing a touch from God at a ►Rodney Howard-Browne conference in Tulsa, OK, in Aug. of 1993, he spoke at the Toronto Airport Vineyard at the invitation of ►John Arnott, beginning Jan. 20, 1994. "What began as a simple series of revival meetings developed into a mighty outpouring of God's Spirit, complete with such biblical manifestations as peace, healing, shaking, falling under the power of God, laughter, and diversities of tongues" (Clark, 87). On Jan. 1, 1995, he began two weeks of meetings in Melbourne, FL, where there were many healings. After his departure, powerful meetings continued there almost nightly until August. He has ignited the fires of revival in many other North American cities and several countries, including Guatemala, Russia, Norway, England, Ireland, Chile, Australia, South Africa, New Zealand, and Colombia.

■ **Bibliography:** R. Clark, *Lighting Fires* (1998).
        ■ R. M. Riss

CLARK, STEPHEN B. (1940–). Prominent teacher in the ►Catholic charismatic renewal and promoter of Christian communities. Educated at Yale, Freiburg (Germany), and Notre Dame, Clark worked for the ►Cursillo movement, authoring *The Work of the Cursillos* and *The Work of Renewal* (1967). With his friend and colleague ►Ralph Martin, he was baptized in the Spirit in the spring of 1967 and became a cofounder of the Word of God community in Ann Arbor, MI. In the charismatic renewal among Catholics, Clark became a valued teacher, a gift demonstrated in his books *Baptized in the Spirit* (1969), *Spiritual Gifts* (1970), *Growing in Faith* (1972), and *Knowing God's Will* (1974).

He was also the strategist, applying the concepts he had developed in Cursillo to the ecumenical situation that opened up in charismatic renewal. A member of the National Service Committee (1970–78), he sought ways to structure the renewal so as to promote lasting fruit within the churches.

Clark was primarily responsible for the ►Life in the Spirit Seminars, first developed in the Word of God community and then published for wider use. His strategic thinking was developed in *Building Christian Communities* (1972) and *Where Are We Headed?* (1973). Within the Word of God community, Clark was overall coordinator (1972–82) and led "the brotherhood" of men called to be "single for the Lord" as well as serving younger communities throughout the world.

With the formation of the Sword of the Spirit international community in 1982, in which he has served as assembly president, Clark cut back on general charismatic ministry to concentrate on building strong Christian communities as instruments for the shaping of a Christian culture. He authored the major studies *Unordained Elders and Renewal Communities* (1976) and *Man and Woman in Christ* (1980); he edited *Patterns of Christian Community* (1984). Following the Word of God's disengagement in 1990, Clark has continued to pursue his community vision with Bruce Yocum within a reduced Sword of the Spirit.

See also CHARISMATIC COMMUNITIES.

        ■ P. D. Hocken

CLARKE, CHARLES J. (1903–84). Pioneer figure among Methodist charismatics in Britain. As a young minister, Clarke was much influenced by Samuel Chadwick's *The Way to Pentecost*. A prolonged inner search, intensified by the death of his wife, culminated in his being baptized in the Spirit in early 1963. Clarke, then a minister in the English Midlands, developed his quarterly, *The Quest*, begun in 1961, into a vehicle for charismatic renewal. Long interested in revival, Clarke saw the renewal as the start of a new outpouring. After his retirement in 1967, Clarke, assisted by his second wife, Mary, concentrated on calling Christians to holiness and depth of prayer by making known the great Christians of the past, as in *Pioneers of Revival* (1971). A member of the ▸Fountain Trust's advisory council, Clarke merged *The Quest* into *Renewal* in 1966. Clarke's *Newsletter for Methodists Interested in Charismatic Renewal* (1968–72) was superseded by *Dunamis,* of which he became coeditor.

■ **Bibliography:** P. D. Hocken, *Streams of Renewal* (1986, 1997).
■ P. D. Hocken

CLASSICAL PENTECOSTALISM

The classical pentecostal churches, which had their origins in the U.S. at the beginning of this century, have since grown to be the largest family of Protestant Christians in the world. Known at first simply as "pentecostal" churches, they were given the added designation "classical" about 1960 to distinguish them from the neo-pentecostals in the mainline (nonpentecostal) churches and the Roman Catholic Church, which were soon called charismatics.

The roots of modern pentecostalism lie in the 19th-century Holiness and Higher Life (▸Keswick) movements in England and America that stressed "second blessing" sanctification and the baptism in the Holy Spirit as an endowment of power for service. From these earlier movements the pentecostals emphasized a postconversion experience known as "the baptism in the Holy Spirit." The unique teaching of the pentecostals, however, was that gifts of the Spirit (or charismata) should normally accompany this baptism experience and continue to be manifested in the life of the believer and in the church thereafter. The gifts most often singled out by pentecostals were speaking in tongues and divine healing.

Most histories date the beginning of the movement to Jan. 1, 1901, when ▸Agnes Ozman spoke in tongues at the Bethel Bible School in Topeka, KS, operated by former Methodist preacher ▸Charles F. Parham. It was Parham who subsequently formulated the "initial evidence" teaching that is central to the theology of most of the classical pentecostal churches of the world. This teaching holds that speaking in tongues (glossolalia) unknown to the speaker is the necessary first sign that one has received the pentecostal experience. This teaching was based on the fact that tongues appeared as the Spirit was poured out in the early church in Acts 2, 10, and 19, and were implicit in Acts 8 and 9.

The effect of this doctrine was to deny the "cessation of the charismata" teaching that had been the standard understanding of the Western churches since the days of Augustine. The cessation view held that the charismata had been withdrawn from the church at the end of the apostolic age. Classical pentecostalism thus forced the church to reexamine this position in the light of the many claims it made for current manifestations of the gifts. Along with the manifestation of tongues as evidence of the baptism in the Holy Spirit, the pentecostals also emphasized divine healing as "in the atonement" for modern believers.

Pentecostals also taught that all the other gifts of the Spirit had likewise been restored to the church. From the beginning the restoration of the charismata was seen as a sign of the imminent second coming of Christ. This "latter rain" outpouring of the Holy Spirit, the movement taught, was clear proof that the end of the age was near.

The new pentecostal movement received its greatest impetus from the ▸Azusa Street revival of 1906–9 led by William J. Seymour, a black Holiness preacher from Texas. This revival launched pentecostalism into a worldwide movement. Located at 312 Azusa Street in Los Angeles, the Azusa Street Mission became the international mecca for those seeking the pentecostal experience. From Azusa Street, the movement spread throughout the world through the mission's newspaper, *The Apostolic Faith,* and by pilgrims who flocked to Los Angeles to experience tongues.

The first persons to receive the experience were poor and disinherited people from the mainline churches, primarily those from the Methodistic and Holiness movements that flourished in the late 19th century. The first avowedly pentecostal churches were the ▸Pentecostal Holiness Church, led by ▸Joseph H. King; the Church of God (CG, Cleveland, TN), led by ▸A. J. Tomlinson; and the Church of God in Christ (COGIC), led by ▸C. H. Mason. These churches were formed as Holiness denominations before the advent of the pentecostal movement.

The pentecostal movement soon spread far beyond the ▸Holiness movement to practically every Protestant denomination in America. In time pentecostal converts without roots in the Holiness movement formed newer churches. Led by ▸E. N. Bell, the ▸Assemblies of God (AG) was

The E. M. Adams family at a camp meeting in Oklahoma in 1925.

formed in 1914 to serve those from a Baptistic background. Other churches of this type were the Pentecostal Church of God, founded in 1919 by ⸜John Sinclair; the ⸜International Church of the Foursquare Gospel founded by Aimee Semple McPherson in 1927; and the ⸜Open Bible Standard churches formed by an amalgamation of two smaller organizations in 1935. Doctrinal divisions concerning the "second work" and "finished work" views of sanctification continue to this day.

In 1916 the infant AG organization was torn by a division concerning the Godhead known at the time as the "New Issue." Adherents of the "Jesus' Name" pentecostal movement taught a modalistic view of the Godhead that denied the Trinity while ascribing to Jesus Christ the deity of the Father, the Son, and the Holy Spirit. Those who left formed ⸜"Oneness" denominations known today as the ⸜United Pentecostal Church and the ⸜Pentecostal Assemblies of the World, among others.

Because of their teachings and their noisy and expressive worship, all the early pentecostal groups were criticized and persecuted by the mainline churches. Ironically, the most bitter criticism came from the older Holiness and fundamentalist churches that were nearest to the pentecostals in theology and practice.

With little public acceptance, the growth of the movement in America was slow between 1901 and WWII. Yet seeds of future massive growth were planted around the world through the development of aggressive missionary programs, especially by the AG. By 1920 the movement was firmly planted in Europe, Latin America, Africa, and Asia.

Pentecostalism began to experience unprecedented growth in America and around the world immediately after WWII. Under the impetus of the divine healing and deliverance crusades of ⸜Oral Roberts, ⸜Tommy Hicks, and ⸜Jack Coe, masses of people flocked to pentecostal churches. By 1953 pentecostalism entered the living rooms of the nation through the pioneering television ministry of Roberts.

Countless others were led into the pentecostal experience by the ⸜Full Gospel Business Men's Fellowship International, which was founded by Los Angeles dairyman ⸜Demos Shakarian in 1952. The mass healing crusades of ⸜T. L. Osborn in Europe, Africa, Latin America, and East Asia led to burgeoning growth in the developing nations of the Third World.

The postwar period also saw the beginnings of pentecostal ecumenism. Although pentecostals had been disfellowshiped by organized fundamentalism in 1928, relations improved with the more moderate evangelicals, who began to distance themselves from the fundamentalists during WWII. By 1942 the pentecostals were admitted as charter members of the ⸜National Association of Evangelicals (NAE). This was done despite the strong objections of Carl McIntire and his fundamentalistic American Council of Christian Churches.

Relationships with mainstream evangelicals continued to improve in the decades after WWII. The most positive sign of this new atmosphere was the election of ⸜T. F. Zimmerman, general superintendent of the AG, to serve as president of the NAE in 1960. Another sign was the positive reception of pentecostal evangelist Oral Roberts at the 1966 Berlin World Congress on Evangelism sponsored by the Billy Graham organization.

In 1948, due to contacts made in the NAE, the American pentecostals formed the ⸜Pentecostal Fellowship of North America (PFNA), a fraternal body that included most of the major North American pentecostal denominations. Although blacks did not join and Oneness pentecostals were excluded, the PFNA represented the mainstream of classical pentecostalism in the U.S. In 1994 the PFNA was disbanded in favor of a new, racially integrated body known as the ⸜Pentecostal/Charismatic Churches of North America (PCCNA). Leading in this movement were Bishop B. E. Underwood (PHC) and ⸜Bishop Ithiel Clemmons (COGIC). The latter served as the first chairman.

Most of these American groups also cooperated with the ⸜Pentecostal World Conferences, which first convened in Zurich, Switzerland, in 1947. After the outbreak of the neo-pentecostal movement in the mainline Protestant churches in 1960 and the Catholic charismatic movement in 1967, the most

Wilton, ND, 1922.

important voice calling for fellowship and cooperation was ▸David J. du Plessis, a South African pentecostal minister who had immigrated to the U.S. after World War II.

By 1980 the classical pentecostals had grown to be the spearhead of the largest and fastest-growing family of Christians in the world. They also led the world in church growth, with the largest Protestant congregations in the world counted in the pentecostal camp. By A.D. 2000 David Barrett estimated the world constituency of the classical pentecostal churches at 66 million, and of the wider pentecostal renewal at 523 million.

■ **Bibliography:** D. Barrett, ed., *World Christian Encyclopedia* (2001) ■ W. J. Hollenweger, *The Pentecostals* (1972) ■ V. Synan, *The Holiness-Pentecostal Tradition* (1997).   ■ H. V. Synan

CLEMMONS, ITHIEL CONRAD (1921–99). Pastor, bishop, denominational executive, scholar, and churchman.

He was born in Washington, NC, to Frank and Pauline (Williams) Clemmons. His mother had been reared as a Baptist, and his father had been in an independent Holiness church since 1908. By the time of his birth they had joined the Church of God in Christ (COGIC). The third of seven children and the eldest to survive those early years, he lived in North Carolina until 1926, when the family moved to Brooklyn, NY, where his father became the pastor of the earliest COGIC there.

Clemmons received a B.A. from Long Island University (1948), an M.A. from College of the City of New York (1951), and the M.Div. from Union Theological Seminary (1956). In the mid 1960s he studied at the Urban Ministries Institute in Chicago and was one of the first pentecostals to participate in the College of Preachers at Washington Cathedral in Washington, DC. He was awarded the D.Min. from a joint program of Union Seminary and New York Theological Seminary. His dissertation was revised and published in 1996 as *Bishop C. H. Mason and the Roots of the Church of God in Christ*. It was the first comprehensive narrative published on Bishop Mason.

Reared in a pastor's home, Clemmons came to faith at a young age and entered the ministry. In 1955 he pastored Gethsemane Church of God in Christ in Clairton, PA. Twelve years later he moved to New York, where he copastored First Church of God in Christ in Brooklyn with his father before succeeding him as pastor. From 1975 he also served as copastor of Well's Memorial Church of God in Christ in Greensboro, NC.

Clemmons played a significant role in helping to map strategy for the civil rights work of Dr. Martin Luther King Jr. in New York in 1963. In 1964–65 he was heavily involved in Robert Kennedy's Bedford-Stuyvesent restoration project. He was also the founding president of the Foundation for Urban Ministries from 1967 to 1977, and he worked with Leon Sullivan to establish Opportunities Industrialization Centers in 1968–69.

In Apr. 1977 Clemmons was consecrated to the COGIC board of bishops and was also named commissioner for the Armed Forces and Institutional Chaplaincies. During that same year he served on the planning committee of the large and very significant charismatic conferences held in Kansas City, MO. He also served on the North American Renewal Services Committee.

Throughout the '70s, '80s, and '90s, Bishop Clemmons worked tirelessly to bring pentecostal leaders and scholars together in meaningful ways. A member of the Society for Pentecostal Studies since 1972, he was elected to serve as its president in 1981. His presidential address was later published in *Pneuma*.

Drawing on members of the pentecostal scholarly community, Bishop Clemmons allowed his ecclesiastical office and his acumen as a churchman to play a unique role in a bid for racial reconciliation between pentecostals. He challenged the Pentecostal Fellowship of North America (PFNA) to expand its horizons. His challenge led to the much-touted Pentecostal Partners conference in Memphis, TN, on Oct. 17–19, 1994—the so-called Memphis Miracle. Cochairing this conference with Pentecostal Holiness Bishop B. E. Underwood, Clemmons enlisted the aid of pentecostal scholars to address the history of racism in the pentecostal movement, then build a biblical, theological, and ethical case for racial reconciliation. The result was that the PFNA disbanded and a new organization, the Pentecostal/Charismatic Churches of North America (PCCNA) was founded.

At the initial meeting of the PCCNA, Clemmons sponsored a jointly authored "Racial Reconciliation Manifesto," which passed unanimously. He was elected to the executive committee and served as chair in 1996 and 1997. It was at his insistence that the PCCNA issued a magazine titled *Reconciliation* to address his continuing concern for pentecostal race relations.

Clemmons was married to the former Clara Agnes Cantrell. They had three daughters, (Mrs.) Pamela Rosborough, Constance, and Debra. He died on Jan. 9, 1999, after a bout with cancer.

■ **Bibliography:** V. G. Lowe, "Leading Pentecostal Bishop Dies," *Charisma* 24:8 (Mar. 1999), 44 ■ D. Manuel, *Like a Mighty River* (1977) ■ C. Taylor, *The Black Churches of Brooklyn* (1984), 35–65, 146 ■ "Clemmons, Ithiel," in S. S. DuPree, ed., *Biographical Dictionary of African-American, Holiness Pentecostals 1880–1990* (1989) ■ "True Koinonia: Pentecostal Hopes and Historical Realities," *Pneuma* 4 (1, 1982).   ■ C. M. Robeck Jr.

COADY, A. RON (1928–). Coady is Australian-born and a former Roman Catholic. After converting to pentecostalism, he attended Ray Jackson's Bible School in Sydney in 1952 (from which most of the early leaders of the New Zealand New Life Churches came). Coady moved to N.Z. in 1957 and copastored the Upper Room Fellowship in Tauranga with ˃Rob Wheeler. Coady and Wheeler set up a successful pentecostal evening Bible school in Tauranga, which produced pastors for the churches that resulted from the campaigns of Wheeler and other evangelists in the early 1960s.

In early 1960 Coady moved to Timaru on the South Island to assist American evangelist ˃A. S. Worley in his successful healing campaign there. This marked a new beginning for Coady, inspiring him to undertake his pioneer evangelistic campaigns throughout the South Island. Much of the growth of the New Life Churches on the South Island up to 1965 was a direct result of Coady's personal drive and energy and of his controversial, aggressive style of evangelism. Coady moved to the U.S. in 1970. He adopted a semi-Catholic orientation and accepted ordination with the Syro-Chaldean Church of South India two years later. Coady then became bishop of a church with Syro-Chaldean associations, the Catholic Apostolic Church–Glastonbury Rite in Davis, CA. He resigned his see in 1989 and has now returned to his first love, healing evangelism.

■ **Bibliography:** Bro. [A. R.] Coady, *I Shall Not Want* (n.d.) ■ B. Knowles, "For the Sake of the Name: A History of the 'New Life Churches' from 1942 to 1965" (thesis, U. of Otago, 1988) ■ idem, "Some Aspects of the History of the New Life Churches of New Zealand 1960–1990" (diss., U. of Otago, 1994) ■ *Revival News* (1962–66).   ■ B. Knowles

COATES, GERALD (1944–). Prominent leader and teacher in the ˃House Church Movement (now known as the New Church Movement) in Britain. As a young man, Coates spent six years with the Plymouth Brethren but had to leave when he spoke in tongues. He formed the Cobham Christian Fellowship in 1970, which became the center of an emerging network of new churches looking to Coates for apostolic leadership. This network changed its name to Pioneer People in 1991. He married Anona in 1966; they have three grown sons.

Coates is a dynamic and sometimes flamboyant figure, whose insistence on the gospel of grace has sometimes produced controversy, as can be seen from his autobiographical book, *An Intelligent Fire* (1990). He has been an energetic proponent of church planting and has shown an ability to reach influential people in politics, sports, and the media. One of the founders of the ˃March for Jesus (1987), Coates has had a burden for revival; he entered into the ˃Toronto Bless-

ing and began regular meetings for revival in central London (1997). Together with Dr. Patrick Dixon he has been responsible for ACET (AIDS Care Education and Training), the largest AIDS care and education service in the U.K. He has been a strong voice for reconciliation and cooperation, particularly in the various charismatic streams, collaborating closely with Kensington Temple (Elim Pentecostal) and Holy Trinity Brompton (Anglican), which originated the ˃Alpha course. His other books include *What on Earth Is This Kingdom?* (1984), *Gerald Quotes* (1984), *Divided We Stand* (1987), *Kingdom Now* (1990), and *The Vision: An Antidote to Post-Charismatic Depression* (1994).

■ **Bibliography:** B. Hewett, *Doing a New Thing?* (1995). ■ A. Walker, *Restoring the Kingdom* (1988).   ■ P. D. Hocken

COE, JACK (1918–56). Healing evangelist. Born in Oklahoma City, Coe was abandoned by his parents and reared in an orphanage. He left the orphanage at age 17 and became a heavy drinker. While in the army during WWII, he received a miraculous healing and decided to become a minister. He began conducting revival meetings while still in the service and was ordained by the Assemblies of God (AG) in 1944.

Coe had a dynamic personality and quickly won the allegiance of thousands as he conducted healing revivals all across the U.S. He became one of the leaders in the ˃Voice of Healing movement. In 1950 he began to publish the *Herald of Healing* magazine, which eventually had a circulation of 300,000. That same year he opened a children's home in Waxahachie, TX, near Dallas. Coe established a ministry in Dallas known as the Dallas Revival Center in 1952. He was expelled from the AG in 1953 when church leaders became increasingly frustrated and embarrassed by some of his methods and teachings. Coe's church became one of the largest churches in Dallas, and in 1954 he began a television series, but it was short-lived.

In Feb. 1956, at a healing crusade in Miami, FL, Coe was charged with practicing medicine without a license. A trial ensued, but eventually the judge dismissed the case. Then in December of that year, Coe became critically ill and was diagnosed with bulbar polio. He died within a matter of weeks.

After Coe's death, his widow, Juanita, continued to hold healing campaigns for a while and established the Coe Foundation in 1961 as a successor to Herald of Healing, Inc. The Coe Foundation published two periodicals, *Christian Challenge* and *Pentecostal Echoes,* as a means to continue the ministry of Jack Coe. She also directed her energies to the support of foreign missions and to what became known as the Jack Coe Memorial Children's Home in Waxahachie. Mrs. Coe, along with her second husband, Dan Hope, continued to pastor the Dallas Revival Center until the early

1970s. Mrs. Coe and her two sons are still active in ministry in the Dallas area.

■ **Bibliography:** J. Coe, *The Story of Jack Coe* (1951) ■ D. E. Harrell, *All Things Are Possible* (1975) ■ *Obituaries on File* (1979).
■ G. W. Gohr

COMMUNION OF EVANGELICAL EPISCOPAL CHURCHES

(CEEC). The CEEC is an expression of the ᐟConvergence movement, which seeks to hold together the charismatic, evangelical, and liturgical-sacramental aspects of the church. The CEEC represents a segment of the Convergence movement that has crystallized around the leadership of pastors from the Tulsa–Oklahoma City areas: Wayne Boosahda, now presiding bishop of CEEC and senior rector of the Church of the Epiphany in Tulsa; Mike Owen of the Church of the Holy Spirit and Robert Wise of the Church of the Redeemer, both in Oklahoma City.

Formed in Oct. 1995, the CEEC sees itself as "a communion in The Holy Catholic Church whose identity and self-understanding is rooted in the Anglican Spiritual Tradition." Its vision statement affirms: "(1) Make visible the Kingdom of God to the nations of the world; (2) bring the rich sacramental and liturgical life of the early church to searching evangelicals and charismatics; (3) carry the power of Pentecost to our brothers and sisters in the historic churches; (4) provide a home for all Christians who seek a catholic, evangelical, charismatic church and foundation for their lives and gifts of ministry."

CEEC affirms the autonomy of each member parish, and its dioceses are nonterritorial (four of their bishops reside in Oklahoma City). They accept the ordination of women. In Jan. 1999, CEEC had 35 churches in the U.S.; 121 in India; approximately 3,000 in the Philippines; 2 in Canada; 1 each in the U.K., Romania, and Guam; and 63 in the Caribbean. CEEC publishes a small magazine, *Treasures Old and New*, from its central office in Oklahoma City.
■ P. D. Hocken

CONATSER, HOWARD

(1926–78). Pastor and Baptist charismatic leader. A graduate of Southwestern Baptist Theological Seminary in Fort Worth, TX, Conatser was pastor, until his death, of the Beverly Hills Southern Baptist Church, Dallas, TX. At that time Beverly Hills Church was the denomination's most renowned charismatic congregation. Though W. A. Criswell, pastor of the First Baptist Church of Dallas, vigorously opposed Conatser and his charismatic ministry, the church grew to more than 5,000 members by the mid 1970s. Conatser was a leader of and speaker at the first National Southern Baptist Charismatic Conference, July 21–23, 1976.

■ **Bibliography:** "Excluding the Charismatics," *Christianity Today* (Nov. 7, 1975) ■ V. Synan, "Baptists Ride the Third Wave," *Charisma* 5 (12, 1986).
■ J. A. Hewett

CONCILIO LATINO-AMERICANO DE IGLESIAS CRISTIANAS

Formed in 1923, the Concilio Latino de Iglesias Cristianas (CLAIC) owes its existence to ᐟFrancisco Olazabal (1886–1937), a Mexican national who six years earlier had received the baptism of the Holy Spirit under the ministry of George and Carrie (Judd) Montgomery in California. Until that time a minister of the Methodist Episcopal Church, South, Olazabal at first worked with the Assemblies of God (AG) but withdrew with his followers because of the attitude of the leader the AG placed over the Spanish-speaking churches. A proposed union of the CLAIC and the (Tomlinson) Church of God failed to be consummated because of the founder's death in an automobile accident near Alice, TX, in 1937. ᐟMiguel Guillén of Brownsville, TX, who then assumed leadership, became president for life in 1956. Under his leadership the CLAIC Seminary opened in Los Angeles. By the mid 1970s, CLAIC claimed 105 churches and 4,200 members in nine states of the U.S., and 55 churches and 2,200 members in five states of Mexico. Half of the U.S. membership was in Texas.

■ **Bibliography:** M. Guillén, *La Historia del Concilio Latino-Americano de Iglesias Cristianas* (1982) ■ A. C. Piepkorn, *Profiles in Belief*, vol. 3 (1979).
■ C. E. Jones

CONCILIO LATINO-AMERICANO DE LA IGLESIA DE DIOS PENTECOSTAL DE NEW YORK

In 1956 work begun in the New York area five years earlier by the Iglesia de Dios Pentecostal de Puerto Rico became autonomous. Taking the name Concilio Latino-Americano de la Iglesia de Dios Pentecostal de New York, Incorporado, it established "affiliation" with the parent body and continued contributing to its support. By the mid 1970s the Manhattan-based Concilio Latino-Americano had about 75 churches and 8,000 members in the metropolitan area. It was sponsoring missionary work in the Netherlands Antilles and Central America. At that time Abelardo Berrios was president.

■ **Bibliography:** A. C. Piepkorn, *Profiles in Belief*, vol. 3 (1979).
■ C. E. Jones

CONGREGATIONAL HOLINESS CHURCH

The Congregational Holiness Church (CHC), with headquarters in Griffin, GA, resulted from a split in the Pentecostal Holiness Church (PHC) in 1920. Watson Sorrow, a minister of the Georgia Conference of the PHC, had sharp doctrinal disagreements with his denomination, particularly on the subject of divine healing. As was not uncommon in those early days, some influential PHC leaders took the position that it was sinful to resort to medicine or physicians in times of sickness. According to this view, healing was provided for in the atonement, and any reliance on human remedies was wrong.

Sorrow and a few others disagreed with this teaching and with some aspects of denominational polity. *F. M. Britton and *G. F. Taylor held to the episcopal form of government practiced by most Holiness groups, while Sorrow and Hugh Bowling believed in a congregational form of government. The conflict ended in Sorrow's and Bowling's expulsion from the PHC in 1920. On Jan. 29, 1921, Sorrow led a large part of the Georgia Conference in organizing the CHC. The name of the new group reflected its views on local church autonomy.

The CHC was chartered in 1925 and began publication of the *Gospel Messenger* to carry regular news of the young church. Under the leadership of Joe Sorrow, the first general moderator and brother of Watson, the CHC showed considerable vitality. Joe Sorrow was followed as moderator by such men as Watson Sorrow, B. L. Cox, Terry Crews, Cullen L. Hicks, and James Martin. At present, Chester M. Smith serves as bishop.

■ **Bibliography:** *Discipline of the Congregational Holiness Church* (1980) ■ W. Sorrow, *Some of My Experiences* (1954).
■ C. W. Conn

CONN, CHARLES WILLIAM (1920–). Author, editor, educator, and former general overseer of the Church of God (CG, Cleveland, TN). Born in Atlanta, GA, Conn married Edna Louise Minor in 1941 and was ordained by the CG in 1946. The Conns have 12 children. Conn was involved in pastoral work before serving as director of Sunday school and youth literature for the CG in 1948. That same year he became editor of *The Lighted Pathway.* Later he worked as editor-in-chief of publications and editor of the *Church of God Evangel* (1952–62). After serving as assistant general overseer (1962–66), Conn served as general overseer (1966–70) and president of Lee College (1970–82). He has also served on a number of boards and committees for the denomination.

Charles W. Conn, an educator and historian with the Church of God (Cleveland, TN). He is the author of *Like a Mighty Army*, the history of the denomination.

Since 1977 Conn has served as the official historian of the CG.

Conn is well-known in evangelical and pentecostal circles. He has been a member of the Society for Pentcostal Studies and served on the executive committee for the *Pentecostal Fellowship of North America (1962–70), the executive committee for the *Pentecostal World Conference (1966–70), and the board of directors for the *National Association of Evangelicals (1966–70).

A prolific writer, Conn has written for numerous publications and has contributed to several encyclopedias and reference works. He has traveled in more than 80 countries, lecturing and doing research for his writings. Some of his best-known books include *Like a Mighty Army: A History of the Church of God* (1955; rev. ed., 1977; definitive ed., 1996); *Pillars of Pentecost* (1956); *Where the Saints Have Trod* (1959); *The Bible: Book of Books* (1961); *Cradle of Pentecost* (1981); *Our First 100 Years, 1886–1986: A Retrospective* (1986); and *When Your Upright World Turns Upside Down* (1990). *The Promise and the Power*, ed. Donald N. Bowdle (1980), was published as a Festschrift dedicated to Charles Conn.

■ **Bibliography:** ■ *Contemporary Authors Online* (1999) ■ J. Melton, *Religious Leaders of America* (1991) ■ D. Roebuck to G. W. Gohr, Apr. 22, 1999 ■ *Who's Who in Religion* (2d ed., 1977).
■ G. W. Gohr

CONVERGENCE MOVEMENT A movement seeking the integration of the evangelical, charismatic, and sacramental streams within the church into the fullness of the historic body of Christ. The convergence concept developed independently in a number of settings, principally in North America, where the evangelical and charismatic streams are both widespread and apparently successful, but with evident weaknesses. The roots of the convergence movement (CoM) lie in the search of those from evangelical and charismatic backgrounds to remedy these defects and in their rediscovery of the riches and depth of liturgy and spirituality in historic traditions. Among the people and groups playing an important role in this quest and discovery have been Peter Gillquist and other ex-evangelicals now in the Antiochean Orthodox Church; Robert Webber of Wheaton College (IL); and the spirituality author Richard Foster.

In 1968 some senior staff resigned from Campus Crusade for Christ, concerned about the meager long-term fruit of their work and seeking a fuller NT expression of church life. Their search led during the 1970s to the formation of a committed fellowship that in 1979 found expression in the Evangelical Orthodox Church (EOC). Almost a decade later (1987), most of the EOC (67 priests, 84 deacons, and nearly 2,000 believers) were received corporately into the Antiochian Orthodox Church and established as the Antiochian Evangelical Orthodox Mission (AEOM). Their magazine, *Again,* begun in 1978, continues as the magazine of AEOM.

Robert Webber, a professor at Wheaton College, is an evangelical who discovered the power and the depth of liturgical worship. Webber, now an Episcopalian, has lectured and written for those evangelicals and charismatics who are thirsty for a depth in corporate worship rooted in the biblical symbolism of classical liturgy. Webber's books have had a major influence: *Common Roots: A Call to Evangelical Maturity* (1978); *Worship Old and New* (1982); *Evangelicals on the Canterbury Trail* (1985, 1988); *Signs of Wonder: The Phenomenon of Convergence in the Modern Liturgical and Charismatic Churches* (1992).

Richard Foster, who comes from a Quaker background, brought together elements from different traditions of Christian spirituality in *Celebration of Discipline* (1980). Foster convened a conference called "Renovare" in Wichita, KS, in 1988, which contributed significantly to the advancement of convergence thinking. Whereas most convergence advocates have focused on the coming together of the evangelical, charismatic, and liturgical-sacramental, Foster also adds the contemplative, holiness, and social justice traditions. A recent book on this subject by Foster is *Streams of Living Water* (1998).

Central to the journey of Gillquist and others has been the discovery of the early church, the writings of the Fathers, and the celebration of the sacred mysteries as the foundation for the unity of the church. The CoM can be seen as revivalist Christians finding their roots by rediscovering the church between the NT and the Reformation.

A catalytic event that drew attention to the emergence of CoM was the reception into the Episcopal Church of a former Assemblies of God pastor, Stan White, and his congregation in Valdosta, GA, with a report in *Christianity Today* (Sept. 1990). By this time, there was a growth in the numbers of evangelicals joining the Orthodox Church, a trend stimulated by Gillquist's book *Becoming Orthodox: A Journey to the Ancient Christian Faith* (1988). Another influential book much recommended in convergence circles has been *Evangelical Is Not Enough* (1984, 1989) by Thomas Howard, an evangelical scholar who joined the Roman Catholic Church.

Convergence thinking has found expression in a variety of contexts. First, there are those who have joined historic liturgical churches, bringing with them their evangelical and charismatic convictions. This has often involved discovering more evangelical and charismatic elements within the traditions they have joined. Second, there are those already belonging to churches with a revivalist background who have sought to develop or add liturgical-sacramental dimensions to their church life. Those articulating this kind of vision include United Methodist scholar Thomas Oden, Baptist

theologian Clark Pinnock, and Free Methodist pastor-author Howard Snyder.

A third context has been the emergence in the 1990s of groupings that are explicitly convergence-oriented, first the ▸Charismatic Episcopal Church (CEC) in 1992 and then the ▸Communion of Evangelical Episcopal Churches (CEEC) in 1995. The new convergence groupings are seeking to combine the evangelical, charismatic, and sacramental, allowing space within their liturgical celebrations for spontaneous worship and the exercise of the charisms. The CEC is more centralized than the CEEC (the CEC bishops take a vow of obedience to their patriarch and primate), while the CEEC emphasizes its character as a communion rather than a denomination.

There are also leaders and milieus in the historic liturgical churches who are urging the rediscovery of evangelical and charismatic elements for the renewal of church life. Among these are many Roman Catholics working for reconciliation with the evangelical revivalist streams, such as Matteo Calisi (Bari, Italy), Paddy Monaghan and the Evangelical Catholic Initiative (Dublin, Ireland), and Johannes Fichtenbauer (Vienna, Austria). These, however, tend to use the language of ecumenism rather than that of convergence.

One question posed by this recent history concerns the coherence of CoM as a movement. On the one hand, the evangelicals and charismatics joining the Orthodox Church do not tend to continue an active involvement in the charismatic movement but rather seek to persuade others to follow them—which is not a model of ecumenical convergence. On the other hand, those in the CEC and CEEC are often zealous recruiters for their new churches and can give an impression of convergence as a ready-made package that underestimates the lengthy interaction and travail needed for an authentic meeting-in-depth of long-separated traditions. These reflections raise the question as to whether the real meeting of the disparate streams in what Foster calls the "Mississippi of the Spirit" is primarily happening in these reconfigurations represented by EAOM, CEC, and CEEC, or whether it is happening—also or even more profoundly— in the largely hidden patterns of reconciliation stimulated by Foster's teaching and the commendation of *l'émulation spirituelle* (spiritual emulation) ecumenism, first articulated by the Abbé Paul Couturier in the 1930s.   ■ P. D. Hocken

COOK, GLENN A. (1867–1948). Early pentecostal evangelist and advocate of the ▸Oneness doctrine. Originally a Baptist from Indianapolis, he worked for a daily newspaper in Los Angeles. At the onset of the pentecostal revival in 1906, Cook resigned his position to work with ▸W. J. Seymour. During this time, Cook handled the finances and correspondence at the ▸Azusa Street Mission and began assisting in the publication of *The Apostolic Faith*. During early 1907,

Glenn A. Cook, who took the pentecostal message from the Azusa Street Mission to Indianapolis in 1907 and later united with the Oneness movement.

he brought the message of Pentecost to Indianapolis, which quickly became a center for the new movement, as well as to the Church of God in Christ. ᐧC. H. Mason, its coleader, who had just been baptized in the Spirit while at Azusa Street, returned to Memphis, TN, to find that many people in his organization had already received this experience through Cook's ministry. Cook also held highly successful campaigns in Oklahoma, Arkansas, and Missouri.

Beginning in 1914, Cook traveled throughout the Midwest and the South, proclaiming the "Jesus Only" message, after he and ᐧFrank J. Ewart had baptized one another in the name of Jesus in Belvedere, near Los Angeles. Others rebaptized by Cook included ᐧG. T. Haywood, who later became general secretary of the ᐧPentecostal Assemblies of the World, a Oneness organization, and L. V. Roberts, who later rebaptized ᐧE. N. Bell and H. G. Rodgers, although these three men later repudiated Oneness teachings. Cook later worked for many years with Ewart in the Los Angeles vicinity.

■ **Bibliography:** G. A. Cook, *The Azusa Street Meeting* (n.d.) ■ idem, "The Truth About E. N. Bell," *Herald of Trust* (Aug. 1947) ■ F. J. Ewart, *The Phenomenon of Pentecost* (rev. ed., 1975) ■ V. Synan, *The Holiness-Pentecostal Movement in the United States* (1971).

■ R. M. Riss

COOK, RALPH G. (1899–1981). Pastor and denominational official. Cook was born in Boston, MA, and reared in a Methodist church. He later attended services in the Nazarene Church, the Holiness Church, and the Salvation Army, but did not profess conversion until age 16 in a pentecostal church in Chelsea, MA. In 1917 he adopted ᐧOneness pentecostal theology. He was ordained to the ministry by N. Alexander in Boston, and he traveled to Indianapolis in

1919 to attend ᐧGarfield T. Haywood's church. From there he pastored various churches in Bloomington, IN; Carrollton, IL; a congregation in Louisiana; Hot Springs and Little Rock, AR; Foxboro, MA; and Lancaster, OH.

Cook served in several administrative capacities: as district elder of the ᐧPentecostal Assemblies of the World; member of the General Board of the ᐧPentecostal Assemblies of Jesus Christ (1938–45); district superintendent of the Ohio District of the United Pentecostal Church, International (UPCI; 1945–54); and member of the UPCI Foreign Missionary Board for about nine years. He was elected as assistant general superintendent of the UPCI in 1963 and served in this capacity until 1971. A biography of his life, *He Stands Tall* (1980), was written by Mary H. Wallace.

In 1917 Cook married Hattie Lowell, who died a year later during an influenza epidemic. Three years later he married Nellie Reppond, a young evangelist.

■ **Bibliography:** A. L. Clanton, *United We Stand* (1995).

■ G. B. McGee; E. J. Gitre

COOK, ROBERT F. (1880–1958). Pentecostal missionary to India. Cook was a Russian immigrant to the United States. He was converted at age 12 and called into the ministry by age 14. In 1908 he and his wife, Anna, attended the ᐧAzusa Street revival in Los Angeles, where they were introduced to pentecostalism. Following Anna's miraculous healing, Robert Cook received the baptism of the Holy Spirit and spoke in tongues while resting in bed one evening. In Oct. 1913 the Cooks moved to Bangalore, India, as independent missionaries. There they experienced apostolic ministry including casting out demons, instantaneous healings, and remarkable conversions. They also established orphanages and the first

YOUR BROTHER & SISTER, CO-LABOURERS WITH YOU UNTIL THE HARVEST ENDS
PASTOR & MRS. R. F. COOK AND FAMILY.

Robert F. Cook, who went to India as an independent pentecostal missionary but later affiliated with the Church of God (Cleveland, TN).

pentecostal Bible school in South India, the Mount Zion Cook Memorial Bible School.

Following the death of Anna, Cook married Bertha N. Fox in 1918. Briefly affiliated with the Assemblies of God, they united with the Church of God (Cleveland, TN) in 1936 while serving in Travancore State, South India. Robert and Bertha Cook retired in 1949 and settled in Cleveland, TN.

■ **Bibliography:** Cook, Robert F., *Half a Century of Divine Leading and 37 Years of Apostolic Achievements in South India* (1955).
■ L. F. Morgan

COOLEY, ROBERT EARL (1930–). Archaeologist, educator, seminary president. Born in Kalamazoo, MI, Cooley received his academic training at Central Bible College (three-year diploma, 1952), Wheaton College (B.A., 1955), Wheaton Graduate School (M.A., 1957), and New York University (Ph.D., 1968). In 1952 he married Eileen H. Carlson; they have two sons, Bob and Jerry. The Michigan District of the Assemblies of God (AG) ordained him in 1958.

Since 1960 Cooley has been involved with supervising archaeological expeditions in Israel (Dothan, Khirbet Haiyan, and Khirbet Raddana), Egypt (Tell Retaba), and numerous sites in North America. Guest lectureships have taken him to Belgium, Brazil, Israel, Korea, and Portugal. The W. F. Albright Institute for Archaeological Research in Israel appointed him annual professor for the spring term of 1980. He has conducted 60 student trips to Europe, Mediterranean countries, and the Middle East, and has also directed the Dothan Publication Project.

Cooley's extensive teaching and administrative experience has included serving at Central Bible College, New York University, Wheaton College, Dropsie University, Drury College, Evangel University, Southwest Missouri State University (where he directed the Center for Archaeological Research from 1973 to 1981), and Gordon-Conwell Theological Seminary.

In 1981 Cooley was appointed president and professor of biblical studies and archaeology at Gordon-Conwell Theological Seminary in South Hamilton, MA. Fuller Seminary provost Russell P. Spittler contends that that appointment "completed the evangelicalization of the Assemblies of

Robert Earl Cooley, former president of Gordon-Conwell Theological Seminary and an ordained minister in the Assemblies of God.

God." Under Cooley's leadership at Gordon-Conwell, the seminary saw marked growth in terms of enrollment, financial stability, and expansion of facilities, programs, and endowed chairs. Several branch campuses were added, as was Boston's Center for Urban Ministerial Education. Upon his retirement in 1997, the seminary appointed Cooley chancellor of the seminary; he was the first to fill this position.

Cooley has published articles in *The Journal of Educational Sociology, Bulletin of the American Schools of Oriental Research, The Bulletin of the Near East Archaeological Society,* and *Theological Education.* He has contributed and coauthored essays in other publications as well in *The Living and Active Word of God: Studies in Honor of Samuel J. Schultz* (contributor, 1980), *The New Encyclopedia of Archaeological Excavations in the Holy Land* (contributor and coauthor, 1993), *Scripture and Other Artifacts* (contributor and coauthor, 1994), and *The Oxford Encyclopedia of Archaeology in the Near East* (contributor, 1996). He served as the principal investigator for the Cultural Resource Management Studies (106 monographs published by the Center for Archaeological Research at Southwest Missouri State University). From 1990 to 1991 he was a senior editor of *Christianity Today.*

In addition to Cooley's responsibilities as a professor and administrator, he has participated in numerous ministerial, scholarly, and civic organizations. He has held offices with World Relief Corporation, ▸National Association of Evangelicals, *In Trust,* Association of Theological Schools, Evangelical Theological Society, National Association of Professors of Hebrew, Missouri Association of Professional Archaeologists, American Schools of Oriental Research, and Near East Archaeological Society.

■ **Bibliography:** "Chancellor and President Named at Gordon-Conwell," press release (Oct. 12, 1996) ■ Curriculum Vitae ■ R. P. Spittler, "The Cooley Inauguration: A Celebration of Sovereignty," *Agora* 5 (Summer 1981).   ■ G. B. McGee; E. J. Gitre

COOMBS, BARNABAS (BARNEY) (1937–). Pastor/apostle, founder of Salt and Light Ministries. Reared in a Plymouth Brethren family in England, he married Janette in 1958 and began to work in the Metropolitan police. Following baptism in the Spirit in 1966, he studied at Capernwray Bible School before becoming pastor of Basingstoke Baptist Church in 1967 and taking it through a restructuring process that identified it as one of the leading restoration fellowships in the U.K. He was influenced by the ministry of W. F. P. Burton, the missionary/apostle to the Congo, and by the writings of De Vern Fromke and Watchman Nee. In 1976 he became pastor of West Coast Christian Fellowship in Vancouver, Canada, while continuing to exercise apostolic care over a group of congregations in the U.K. He founded Salt and Light Ministries, which now has some 70 congregations in the U.K; King's Bible College (Scotland); and Church Relief International. Their impact reaches more than 20 nations. He wrote *No Other Way* (1971), *Echoes of Eden* (1985), *A Practical Guide to Pastoring* (1991), *Snakes and Ladders* (1995), and *Apostles Today: Christ's Love Gift to the Church* (1996).   ■ K. Kay

COPELAND, KENNETH (1937–). Televangelist, author, and leading proponent of the "Word of Faith" message (*Positive Confession). Copeland consecrated his life to God in 1962. Five years later he enrolled in Oral Roberts University (ORU), where he became a copilot on Oral Roberts' cross-country crusade flights.

While at ORU, Copeland attended Kenneth Hagin's Tulsa seminars. Unable to pay for Hagin's tapes, he offered the title to his car for them. Hagin's manager, Buddy Harrison, took one look at the car and said, "Just go ahead and take the tapes. Bring the money in when you can" (Hagin, 1985, 67).

In 1968 Copeland and his wife, Gloria, returned to Fort Worth, TX, where they founded an evangelistic association. Their meetings began as Bible studies in local homes but grew rapidly.

In 1973 the Copelands began publishing the *Believer's Voice of Victory*. Two years later, after an extended time of prayer, Copeland reported that the Lord had commanded him to "preach the Gospel on every available voice" (Copeland, 1981, 6). The following year the Copelands began radio broadcasts that quickly spread throughout North America. In 1979 they launched an equally successful television ministry that soon became international in scope. Copeland began to use special satellite communications in 1981, initiating a global religious broadcast the following year.

Copeland's ministry has been accompanied with many reports of healings, even for victims of cancer and of AIDS. *Jerry Savelle reported that at one meeting Copeland jumped off the platform, pointed to a man paralyzed from the neck down, grabbed him by the hand, and ran around the church with him.

Heavily influenced by *E. W. Kenyon, Copeland emphasizes that for those who do not love their own lives but submit themselves totally to God's purposes, there is great prosperity: a flourishing of spirit, soul, and body.

As of 1999, Copeland and his wife, Gloria, have written 58 books. Their teaching materials have been translated into 22 languages.

■ **Bibliography:** "Copeland Reaches Out to AIDS Victims," *Charisma and Christian Life* (Jan. 1988) ■ G. Copeland, "Love Not Your Life," *Believer's Voice of Victory* 13 (Apr. 1985) ■ K. Copeland, "And God Said," *Believer's Voice of Victory* 9 (Sept. 1981) ■ K. Hagin Jr., "Trend toward Faith Movement," *Charisma* (Aug. 1985) ■ J. Savelle, *If Satan Can't Steal Your Joy* (1982).   ■ R. M. Riss

CORRELL, NORMAN LEIGH (1926–). Missionary and administrator. Born in Bridgeport, NE, Correll attended North Central Bible College at Minneapolis, MN, and was ordained by the Assemblies of God (AG) in 1951. He married Norma Jane Shoff in 1946. They have two children.

After several years of pastoral and evangelistic work, Correll served as a missionary to Tanzania, East Africa (1958–1966). He became the first national field representative for the AG Mobilization and Placement Service (MAPS) in 1966. He was appointed secretary of Christ's Ambassadors (Youth Department) in 1968. From 1975 to 1979 Correll was dean of evangelism and Christian education at the International Correspondence Institute in Brussels, Belgium.

Correll served as secretary of missions support for the AG Division of Foreign Missions (DFM) (1979–82); administrative assistant (1982–92); and executive administrator of DFM (1992–93). Retiring from his position with DFM in 1993, he later served as director of international relations for the World Assemblies of God Congress in Seoul, Korea (1994).

■ **Bibliography:** Personal data sheet, AG Office of Public Relations (1980) ■ missionary file in AG Division of Foreign Missions.   ■ G. W. Gohr

CORTESE, AIMEE GARCÍA (1929–). Puerto Rican pentecostal pastor, evangelist, and prison chaplain. Born to Puerto Rican parents in New York City on May 26, 1929, she was named after Aimee Semple McPherson. Her parents were converted in a small Spanish-speaking pentecostal storefront church in the early 1940s. The daughter of a pentecostal minister, she decided to go into the ministry at the age of 15. She attended the Hispanic American Bible School of the Assemblies of God (AG) in New York City and then the Central Bible College (CBC) of the AG in 1951. She was licensed (1951) by the AG and then later ordained by the Wesleyan Methodist Church (1964) and finally the AG. She served as an evangelist and associate minister at Thessalonica Christian Church in the Bronx before she joined the Wesleyan Methodist Church (1962–64) in San Juan, Puerto Rico. She returned to the AG in 1965.

Cortese was a delegate to the First World Congress on Evangelism in West Berlin, Germany, in 1966. She later served as legislative aid (1969–72) to her brother, New York State Senator Robert García. Cortese became the first female chaplain (1973–83) in history of the New York State Department of Corrections. In 1983 she founded Crossroads Tabernacle Church of the AG in the South Bronx, a church that has grown from a few dozen people in 1983 to 1,500 members in the 1990s. Her church is one of the largest multicultural churches in New York City.

Cortese is a highly sought-after speaker and has preached throughout the U.S., Puerto Rico, Cuba, Mexico, Venezuela,

Guatemala, Colombia, and Bolivia. She was chosen to be a member of the New York State Governor's Task Force on Domestic Violence and Mayor Koch's Commission on Hispanic Affairs and Commission on Bias Affairs. She has also been invited to address the National Convention of the AG, the Hispanic Caucus of New York State, New York State Senate, U.S. House of Representatives, U.S. Hispanic Caucus in Washington, DC, National Hispanic Bar Association, and the Federation of Hispanic Women in America. Cortese is considered one of the most respected Hispanic Protestant women ministers in the U.S. and Puerto Rico.

■ **Bibliography:** G. Espinosa, "'Your Daughters Shall Prophesy': A History of Women's Roles in the Latino Pentecostal Movement in the United States," *Women and Twentieth-Century Protestantism,* ed. M. L. Bendroth and V. L. Brereton (forthcoming) ■ V. S. Korrol, "In Search of Unconventional Women: Histories of Puerto Rican Women in Religious Vocations Before Midcentury," in D. L. D. Heyck, *Barrios and Borderlands* (1994).   ■ G. Espinosa

CORVIN, RAYMOND OTHEL (1915–81). Pastor, church leader, and educator. Corvin was born on a farm near Ada, OK. He was a childhood friend of Oral Roberts, who was born in the same region. Converted in a rural congregation of the ▸Pentecostal Holiness Church (PHC) in 1932, Corvin immediately enrolled in Holmes Bible College in Greenville, SC. In 1939 he married Eula Kathleen Staton, a union that produced two daughters.

Ordained in the Upper South Carolina Conference of the PHC in 1935, Corvin served churches in South Carolina and Oklahoma before being elected general secretary of the denomination in 1945. He held this position until 1969 when he was elected vice chairman of the PHC.

During these years, Corvin earned two doctoral degrees and founded Southwestern Bible College in Oklahoma City. In 1962 he served as founding chancellor of Oral Roberts University (ORU) in Tulsa. He also served as the first dean of the ORU Graduate School of Theology. In his later years he pioneered in developing modular education programs for home ministerial training.

■ **Bibliography:** D. Harrell Jr., *Oral Roberts: An American Life* (1985) ■ H. V. Synan, *The Old-Time Power: A History of the Pentecostal Holiness Church* (rev. ed., 1998).   ■ H. V. Synan

COTTON, EMMA L. (1877–1952). Evangelist, church planter, pastor, and editor. Born in Louisiana of Creole descent, Emma Cotton first appeared at the ▸Azusa Street revival in 1906. She was attracted by word of "the great awakening of the Spirit." At Azusa she was healed of "weak lungs and cancer," the latter disease having attacked her nose. Emma was married to Henry C. Cotton (1879–1959), who

worked as a cook on a railway run between Los Angeles and San Antonio, TX. Henry's frequent trips left "Mother" Cotton free to engage in evangelistic work throughout California. In 1916, for instance, she held divine healing services at the Pentecostal Assembly in San Jose. By 1933 she had founded independent pentecostal churches in Bakersfield, Fresno, and Oakland. She was described as courageous, hardworking, and dedicated by those who knew her.

During the early 1930s, Mother Cotton enjoyed a friendship with ▸Aimee Semple McPherson. In 1935 Mother Cotton asked McPherson to host a 30th anniversary celebration of the Azusa Street revival's beginnings. Cotton was invited to address the crowds at Angelus Temple, where she reminded them that people had come to Azusa Street oblivious to any sectarian interests; she went on to exhort the temple to greater unity.

McPherson encouraged her to establish a church in Los Angeles. Known as Azusa Temple, it was located at 27th and Paloma. Together, Emma and Henry, who held credentials with the Church of God in Christ (COGIC), copastored this independent congregation. The church remained independent during Mother Cotton's lifetime, since the COGIC did not ordain women, and Mother Cotton did the bulk of the preaching. Today the church is known as Crouch Memorial Church and is an important congregation affiliated with the COGIC.

In Apr. 1939 Mother Cotton edited and published a four-page paper called the *Message of the "Apostolic Faith,"* intended to be the first volume of a regular series. She included her eyewitness account of events surrounding the 1906 outpouring of the Holy Spirit in Los Angeles in that volume. No other issues are known to exist. About 1950, after a reprieve of nearly half a century, her cancer reappeared. Mother Cotton died on Dec. 27, 1952. Emma and Henry Cotton are buried in Lincoln Memorial Park in Compton, CA.

■ **Bibliography:** "Divine Visitation at Temple Like at Old Azusa Mission," *The Foursquare Crusader* 2:45 (Apr. 29, 1936) ■ S. H. Frodsham, *With Signs Following* (1941) ■ *Los Angeles City Directory* (1910, 1920) ■ *Message of the "Apostolic Faith"* 1 (1, 1939) ■ A. S. McPherson, "Mother Cotton Sounds Bugle," *The Foursquare Crusader* 2:47 (May 13, 1936) ■ T. R. Nickel, *Azusa Street Outpouring* (1979, 1986) ■ *Triumphs of Faith* 36 (6, 1916) ■ "What the Old-Time Azusa Warriors Say," *The Foursquare Crusader* 2:46 (May 6, 1936).   ■ C. M. Robeck Jr.

COURTNEY, HOWARD PERRY (1911–2000). Pastor, teacher, author, denominational executive, and churchman. Howard Courtney was born in Frederick, OK, to Christopher Columbus and Dotty Lee (Whelchel) Courtney. Educated in public schools, Howard Courtney was reared in Santa Monica, CA. He attended L.I.F.E. Bible College, receiving his diploma in 1932. On Mar. 21, 1932, he married Vaneda Harper and entered the ministry. His first pastorate (1932–34) was in Racine, WI. While serving in Racine, he was ordained in 1933 by the ʼInternational Church of the Foursquare Gospel (ICFG). His ordination was followed by a short term in Terre Haute, IN (1934). In 1935 Courtney moved to Portland, OR, where he served as an assistant pastor and entered, for the first time, denominational administration. From 1935 to 1936, while he was in Portland, he served as the assistant supervisor of the Northwest District of the ICFG. The Courtneys moved to Riverside, CA, in 1936, where Howard served as pastor until 1939 while teaching as an adjunct at L.I.F.E. Bible College. Following another short pastorate in Urbana, IL (1939), Courtney was named district supervisor of the Great Lakes District in 1940, a position he held until 1944.

Before the death of ʼAimee Semple McPherson in Sept. 1944, leadership of the ICFG was already shifting toward ʼRolf McPherson. Howard Courtney was called to serve with him in national office and was one of the last appointments made by Aimee McPherson. He was named general supervisor and director of foreign missions for the denomination and was awarded an honorary D.D. from L.I.F.E. In 1950 he was named general supervisor and vice president of the ICFG, and for the next four years (1950–53) he also served as copastor of Angelus Temple.

During his years in national office with the ICFG (1944–1974), Courtney regularly offered classes on church administration on a part-time basis at L.I.F.E. Bible College. He authored several booklets, including "The Vocal Gifts of the Spirit" (1956) and "The Baptism in the Holy Spirit" (1963). He was instrumental in helping the ICFG move into the larger pentecostal world when he chaired the constitutional drafting committee for the ʼPentecostal Fellowship of North America (PFNA), and in 1948 he was elected vice chairman of the PFNA. He served as the chair of the PFNA in 1953, 1954, and again in 1965–66. Courtney also chaired the advisory committee to the 1958–61 triennium of the Pentecostal World Conference, chairing the 1961 conference in Jerusalem. Once the ICFG joined the National Association of Evangelicals (NAE) in 1952, Courtney was an active member of the board of that organization. In 1966 he preached a plenary address, "Christ and Modern Man," at its annual convention.

Since 1974, when Courtney resigned as general supervisor of the ICFG, he has participated in a variety of ministries. Notable among them was his participation in the planning committee of the 1977 Conference on the Charismatic Renewal in the Christian Churches held in ʼKansas City, MO. From 1977 to 1981 he served as pastor of Angelus Temple. He died on Oct. 29, 2000.

■ **Bibliography:** D. Manuel, *Like a Mighty River* (1977) ■ W. Menzies, *Anointed to Serve* (1971) ■ *United Evangelical Action* 25 (1, Mar. 1966): 6 ■ *Who's Who in America* (1976–77) ■ *Who's Who in Religion* (1977).   ■ C. M. Robeck Jr.

COUSEN, CECIL (1913–89). British pastor and teacher. Son of a founding member of the ʼApostolic Church who had been an associate of ʼSmith Wigglesworth at the Bowland Street Mission in Bradford, U.K., Cousen was baptized in the Spirit at the age of 10 and became one of the first pentecostals to go to university (Cambridge). After some years in the family business (1934–48), he became a pastor and was sent to Hamilton, Ont. (1944–51). Receiving new depth of active faith through the ʼLatter Rain movement, Cousen took some of its practices back to Britain, including imposition of hands for the baptism of the Holy Spirit. Expelled by the Apostolic Church in 1953, Cousen formed the Dean House Christian Fellowship in Bradford, which he pastored until 1968.

A gifted Bible teacher, Cousen taught at many British conferences from the mid 1950s on and later also in Denmark. He edited *A Voice of Faith* (1957–77). As the charismatic movement developed, Cousen became one of its most valued teachers. He was closely associated with the ʼFountain Trust and was a member of its advisory council from 1969 on. He authored *The Gifts of the Spirit* (1986) and *The Curse of the Law* (1988).

■ **Bibliography:** P. D. Hocken, *Streams of Renewal* (1986, 1997).   ■ P. D. Hocken

CRAWFORD, FLORENCE LOUISE (1872–1936). Founder of the ʼApostolic Faith evangelistic organization in Portland, OR, in 1907. The mother of two, Florence Crawford was

active in social work and women's organizations in spite of a childhood injury and spinal meningitis. Her parents were atheists, but she had had a conversion experience before attending the ʼAzusa Street Mission in 1906. After the experiences of sanctification and Spirit baptism, she was healed. She assumed an active role in the mission. She was soon parted from her building-contractor husband of 16 years, Frank Mortimer Crawford, who did not accept her faith until after

Florence Crawford, one of the first pentecostals at the Azusa Street Mission in 1906, who later founded the Apostolic Faith (Portland, OR).

her death. A series of evangelistic trips to the Northwest and Canada returned Crawford to her native Oregon. For the next 30 years "Mother" used her position as general overseer of the Apostolic Faith Church to maintain a strict Holiness standard of doctrine and practice. Crawford's relationship with ›W. J. Seymour was strained for two reasons: Seymour's 1908 marriage, of which Crawford disapproved, and Crawford's transfer of the *Apostolic Faith* paper and its mailing lists from Azusa Street to Portland despite Seymour's objections. Though the Apostolic Faith organization had fewer than 3,000 members at Crawford's death, branch churches extended its influence around the world.

■ **Bibliography:** *A Historical Account of the Apostolic Faith* (1965) ■ *The Light of Life Brought Triumph* (1936) ■ D. J. Nelson, "For Such a Time As This: The Story of Bishop William J. Seymour and the Azusa Street Revival" (diss., U. of Birmingham, 1981). ■ L. F. Wilson

CRAWFORD, RAYMOND ROBERT (1891–1965).

General overseer of the ›Apostolic Faith Church in Portland, OR, from 1936 to 1965. As a teenager Crawford joined his mother, ›Florence Crawford, the founder of the church, in Portland, where he was converted, received the experiences of sanctification and Spirit baptism, and began to preach. He attended a local business college and was an accomplished musician. In 1919 he was licensed to fly and purchased a plane for evangelistic efforts. He also captained a series of boats used in missionary endeavors along the Northwest Coast. Through evangelistic trips he assisted branch churches, and on his mother's death he succeeded her as general overseer. During his tenure, the church grew to nearly 5,000 members in 43 congregations while maintaining a commitment to its distinctive doctrines and standards of conduct.

■ **Bibliography:** *A Historical Account of the Apostolic Faith* (1965) ■ T. L. Miles, comp., *Saved to Serve* (1967). ■ L. F. Wilson

CROSS, MILO PARKS (1895–1983).

Church of God (CG, Cleveland, TN) pastor and administrator. Born in Sherman, TX, six weeks after his father's death, Cross was converted following a CG cottage prayer meeting in 1912. The evangelist was Lettie Hause, who later became his bride. Granted his ministerial license in 1916, Cross served as pastor of numerous churches, including the North Cleveland Church in Cleveland, TN, and as a state overseer for 25 years. Appointed a member of the first foreign missions board in 1926, he served on that board until 1942 and again from 1946 to 1952. Between 1942 and 1946, he was the first executive secretary (director) of the world missions department. Cross also served on the board of Lee University and of the orphanage, and on the editorial and publications boards as

well as the Council of Seventy and the executive council. A friend of youth, he was instrumental in initiating the CG's national youth organization, the Young People's Endeavor, in 1929, and he served as superintendent of the CG Orphanage. A promoter of fellowship with other Christian organizations, he was an official delegate to both the St. Louis exploratory meeting and the Chicago constitutional convention of the ›National Association for Evangelicals in 1942 and 1943.

■ **Bibliography:** C. W. Conn, *Like a Mighty Army: A History of the Church of God* (1996) ■ M. P. Cross, *In the Good (?) Ole Days* (n.d.) ■ M. P. Cross Collection, Dixon Pentecostal Research Center, Cleveland, TN. ■ D. G. Roebuck

CROUCH, ANDRAE (1940–).

Contemporary gospel singer, composer, and producer. The son of a Los Angeles street preacher and ›Church of God in Christ pastor, he became a Christian at age nine and two years later determined to use his musical gifts for the glory of God. He directed a ›Teen Challenge choir and performed with local groups before signing a record contract in 1971. His many albums present the gospel songs he learned as a child in a contemporary form. He has performed in the most prestigious concert halls in over 40 countries and has appeared on popular secular and Christian television programs. His songs have won numerous Grammy and Dove awards and have been recorded by secular and religious artists. He received an Oscar nomination for his music in the film *The Color Purple*. Since 1995 he has also pastored the Los Angeles church served by his father.

■ **Bibliography:** *Billboard* (Mar. 22, 1986) ■ *Cashbox* (Oct. 12, 1985). ■ L. F. Wilson

CROUCH, PAUL FRANKLIN (1934–).

Founder and president of the Trinity Broadcasting Network (TBN), which owns and operates a growing number of Christian television stations across the U.S. and the world. After graduating from Central Bible College in Springfield, MO, Crouch worked in radio and television for several years before moving to California in 1961 to direct film and TV production for the ›Assemblies of God. In 1973 he and his wife, Jan, together with ›Jim and Tammy Bakker, established TBN's flagship station in Santa Ana. Under Crouch's leadership the station prospered, and in the process he became known by millions. Within four years TBN acquired a station in Phoenix, AZ, and the following year the network was licensed to broadcast across the nation by satellite. Additional full-powered, low-powered, and cable stations have extended the ministry of TBN and the influence of its president across the nation and to many other countries. According to the network, TBN is on 536 radio and TV stations worldwide.

■ **Bibliography:** M. K. Evans, "Where Miracles Are a Way of Life," *Christian Life* (May 1983). ■ L. F. Wilson

CRUMPLER, AMBROSE BLACKMAN (1863–1952). ⸲Holiness evangelist, pastor, and church leader. Ambrose Blackman Crumpler was born near Clinton, NC, at the height of the Civil War. In the late 1880s he moved to Missouri, where he was converted and licensed as a local preacher in the Methodist Episcopal Church. In 1890, under the preaching of Beverly Carradine, he received an experience of entire sanctification as taught by the Holiness Association movement.

In 1896 Crumpler returned to North Carolina, determined to establish the Holiness message in his native state. Holding meetings both in Methodist churches and in gospel tents, he ignited Holiness revivals across eastern North Carolina. Everywhere he went, people shouted, danced before the Lord, and "fell under the power" when they received the second blessing. He was more noted, however, for his claim that he had not sinned since his sanctification experience in 1890. This claim led to much discussion and controversy wherever he preached.

In time Crumpler's ministry attracted enough Methodist support to form a regional component of the National Holiness Association movement for the state of North Carolina. Accordingly, on May 15, 1897, in the town of Magnolia, the North Carolina Holiness Association was formed with Crumpler as president. From this organizational base, he conducted further meetings throughout the state.

His attacks on religious coldness and worldliness soon included his own Methodist denomination, which since 1894 was moving to curtail the Holiness movement within its ranks. In the general conference of 1898, Southern Methodism passed a resolution known as Rule 301, which forbade evangelists to hold meetings in a local Methodist charge without permission of the pastor.

In the summer of 1898 Crumpler tested the rule by holding a tent meeting in Elizabeth City, NC, without the prior approval of the pastor. When he was criticized for this infraction, he left the Methodist Church in Nov. 1908 to form a new group in Goldsboro, NC, which he called the ⸲Pentecostal Holiness Church (PHC). This became the first continuing congregation of the new denomination to bear the PHC name.

The next year, Crumpler rejoined the Methodist Church, determined to overturn Rule 301. After holding a meeting near Stedman, NC, without pastoral approval, he was tried by an ecclesiastical court in Oct. 1899 for the "immorality" of violating Rule 301. Although acquitted in the trial, Crumpler once again left Methodism to lead in the formation of the new church.

In 1900 G. B. Cashwell conducted a convention in Fayetteville that resulted in the formation of the PHC as an ecclesiastical body modeled on the Methodist Church. A "Discipline" was adopted as well as a periodical edited by Crumpler known as the *Holiness Advocate*. Of the dozen or so churches associated with the movement, the one in Goldsboro grew to be the largest. By 1902, under Crumpler's pastoral leadership, it had grown to more than a thousand members and for a time was one of the largest Holiness congregations in America. In 1903 the group adopted the name Holiness Church of North Carolina.

In 1906 Crumpler's infant denomination was wracked by controversy, engendered by the introduction of pentecostalism by a minister in the church, ⸲G. B. Cashwell of Dunn, NC. In a historic meeting in Dunn in 1907, practically the entire ministerium of the church received the baptism in the Holy Spirit, evidenced by speaking in tongues. At first Crumpler cooperated with the new movement and published positive reports of Cashwell's meetings in the Holiness Advocate. But by 1908 Crumpler began to oppose those in the church who insisted on tongues as the only initial evidence of the baptism.

The controversy came to a head in the convention of the church that convened in Dunn in Nov. 1908. The pentecostal faction led by Cashwell and ⸲G. F. Taylor easily defeated Crumpler and the few anti-pentecostal delegates who were present. Despite his opposition to the pentecostal majority, Crumpler was reelected to head the church. The next day, however, he left the convention and the church he had founded. Thereafter, he returned to the Methodist Church, where he remained for the rest of his life.

In his later years, Crumpler accepted location (laicization) from the itinerant Methodist ministry and practiced law in Clinton. His occasional ministry in Methodist churches until his death in 1952 mainly involved his interest in the prohibition movement.

■ **Bibliography:** J. Campbell, *The Pentecostal Holiness Church, 1898–1948* (1951) ■ H.V. Synan, *The Old-Time Power: A History of the Pentecostal Holiness Church* (rev. ed., 1998). ■ H. V. Synan

CRUZ, NICKY (1938–). Youth evangelist. Nicky Cruz was born in Puerto Rico in 1938. He came to New York City at age 15 and shortly thereafter became involved with the Mau Mau street gang.

The story of Cruz's conversion has been detailed in *The Cross and the Switchblade* (1963) by David Wilkerson and *Run, Baby, Run* (1968) by Nicky Cruz. Since his conversion and training at Latin American Bible Institute, La Puente, CA (1958–61), he has been active in ministry with ⸲Teen Challenge and citywide crusades.

Cruz has traveled to many Latin American countries by invitation of churches and governments. In 1985 he was in Hungary for crusades. As a result of those meetings, the government granted permission for a Teen Challenge center in Budapest.

The conversion of Nicky Cruz was one of the keys to the breakup of the gangs of the 1950s in New York City. It also inspired many other ministries to youth on the streets in other metropolitan areas in the U.S. and overseas.

■ F. M. Reynolds

CULPEPPER, RICHARD WESTON (1921–). Evangelist R. W. Culpepper was converted while stationed in Havana, Cuba, during WWII as a staff sergeant in the U.S. Army. When Normandy was invaded, he was serving in England. He was baptized in the Holy Spirit while fellowshiping in a hollowed-out haystack with a group of pentecostal soldiers. Culpepper reported that after he quite reluctantly taught this group one night, God audibly told him, "I want you to preach the gospel" (Culpepper, 1960, 8–9).

For about two years after the war Culpepper traveled in the U.S. as an evangelist. Settling in the Los Angeles area, he held two pastorates until 1957, when he was called into foreign evangelism. Many articles in ʾ*The Voice of Healing,* of which he was chairman of conventions from 1959 to 1961, featured his international, evangelistic healing ministry around the world.

Culpepper, David Nunn, ʾMorris Cerullo, and W. V. Grant in 1958 formed the World Convention of Deliverance Evangelists. Culpepper was an active leader until the group ceased meetings in 1965.

Culpepper's own organization was a "missionary church," supporting missionaries "in East, West, and South Africa, India, the Philippine Islands and Jamaica and orphan children in India" (*WWRR* 2 [12, 1963]: 2). In 1968 Culpepper supported "more than 90 missionaries and native evangelists around the world" (*WWRR* 6 [4, 1968]: 4).

In 1970 Culpepper joined ʾA. C. Valdez Sr. as copastor of the Milwaukee Evangelistic Temple.

■ **Bibliography:** R. W. Culpepper, "God Works in Mysterious Ways His Wonders to Perform," *Voice of Healing* 13 (2, 1960) ▪ R. W. Culpepper, ed., *WWRR* (1961–70) ▪ *Full Gospel Business Men's Voice,* 1 (1, 1953) ▪ D. E. Harrell Jr., *All Things Are Possible* (1975) ▪ G. Lindsay, ed., *Voice of Healing* 11 (4, 5, 9) ▪ ibid., 12 (7) ▪ ibid., 13 (2, 3, 5, 6) ▪ ibid., 14 (3, 4, 6, 7).   ■ J. A. Hewett

CUMMINGS, ROBERT WALLACE (1892–1972). Missionary, educator, and mystic. Robert Cummings, an American citizen born in India, was the son of United Presbyterian (UP) missionaries and attended UP schools. While studying the Bible as a UP missionary (he was a third-generation missionary to India), he became convinced that he needed to receive the baptism in the Spirit in order to be effective. After two years of seeking, he received this experience in 1925.

Robert Wallace Cummings.

Cummings went to India as a missionary seven times (21 years total). The last two times he went as an Assemblies of God (AG) missionary, with whom he affiliated in 1944. He served as AG field secretary for Southern Asia (India and Ceylon) from 1946 to 1948. Cummings earned four degrees: B.A., Westminster College; B.Th. and M.Th., Pittsburgh-Xenia Theological Seminary; M.A., Kennedy School of Missions. He also served as a Central Bible College teacher in Springfield, MO. Cummings's gifted life was marred by two episodes of mental illness. He is remembered for his missionary work, his worship of God, and the idea that Christ can help each individual to be victorious over his or her own Gethsemane, which he wrote about in *Gethsemane* (1944).

■ **Bibliography:** M. Craig, *Prepared by God: Robert Cummings* (1962) ▪ R. W. Cummings, *Gethsemane* (1944) ▪ idem, *"Unto You Is the Promise"* (c. 1940).   ■ E. B. Robinson

CUNNINGHAM, LOREN See Youth With A Mission.

CURSILLO MOVEMENT A renewal movement within the Roman Catholic Church. The techniques of Cursillo have been adapted by other denominations, including the United Methodists (Emmaus Walk) and Episcopal Church (Episcopal Cursillo). Cursillo is crucial for understanding the Catholic charismatic renewal (CCR).

Cursillo, Spanish for "little course" (officially, Movimiento de Cursillos de Cristiandad), began in Spain in the 1940s as an effort by a Mallorca layman, Eduardo Bonnin, to make Catholic Action retreats to Santiago de Compostella more meaningful. This was supported by Bishop Juan Hervas, and a priest, Juan Capo Bosch. The bishop was disciplined by the church for his involvement and was transferred to Cuidad Royale, where he continued to defend the movement as a means of pastoral planning and priestly direction. The origins of Cursillo are debated within the movement, as official church documents indicate Hervas as founder or cofounder. Cursillo thus became an issue in the discussion of the role of laypersons within the Roman Catholic Church. Eventually,

Cursillo was accepted as a legitimate renewalist movement. A national secretariat was organized in Spain (1962–73), and the movement soon spread to most Spanish-speaking countries. It was first introduced to the U.S. in 1957 by Spanish pilots being trained in Texas.

It was not until 1966 that Pope Paul VI gave approbation to the efforts in his address published by Cursillo, *Christ, the Church, the Pope Are Counting on You* (1966). Since that time there have been a number of international leadership meetings; the proceedings of several have been published: *Corrientes nuevas en los Cursillos de Cristiandad* (1972); *Los Cursillos se Renuevan* (1973); *El M.C.C. Agente de Evangelizacion* (1976); and *Los Cursillos y Puebla* (1982).

An extensive literature has been produced by Cursillo, but little effort has been made to examine it beyond the brief bibliographic essay of Stephen Clark, *The Evolution of the Cursillo Literature* (1971), and the only history of the movement, Ivan Rohloff, *The Origins and Development of Cursillo* (1976). The basic perspectives of North American Cursillo are expounded by Stephen Clark, *Developing Christian Communities* (1972), and in a volume produced by the World Encounter, translated and revised as *Fundamental Ideas of the Cursillo Movement* (1974).

Cursillo endeavors to produce vital Christians who as a committed community will lead in the development of parish spirituality. The rationale of the method is described in E. Bonnin, *The How and the Why* (1966), and F. Forteza, *Ideario* (rev. ed., 1971). The basic formula of the Cursillo program has changed little since its inception in Spain. There are four elements to the structure: Pre-Cursillo, Cursillo, Closing, and Ultreya. Pre-Cursillo involves both recruitment of potential participants and establishing relationships between a sponsor and prospective participants. Cursillo is a three-day retreat with a carefully constructed set of activities and homilies. The Closing is the point at which the individual is encouraged to testify to the personal significance of the retreat before friends and family. Ultreya, or post-Cursillo, are regular meetings designed to encourage living as a renewed Christian. Detailed descriptions of the Cursillo program are available in W. Alcuin et al., *Cursillo Spiritual Director's Manual* (1976); *The Cursillo Movement's Leader's Manual* (1981); and *Our Fourth Day* (1985). *A General Commentary on the Lay Talks of the Cursillo Weekend* (1984) seeks to provide for continuity within the programs. Participatory observations of the life of a Cursillo community are found in M. Marcoux, *Cursillo: Anatomy of a Movement* (1982).

Several of the early leaders of the CCR were involved in the leadership of Cursillo in the U.S. but separated from the movement over the issue of spiritual gifts, especially glossolalia. Stephen Clark and Ralph Martin brought to the CCR the ambiguous attitudes toward episcopal authority and a pattern for renewal that has been adapted into the ›Life in the Spirit seminars (n.d.) and a number of support publications.

■ **Bibliography:** A. Augustinovich, *Lineas biblicas del movimiento de cursillos* (1970) ▮ E. Bonnin, *The Cursillo Movement: Explanation and Purpose* (n.d.) ▮ idem, *The Cursillo Movement: The Precursillo* (n.d.) ▮ idem, *Structure of Ideas* (1965) ▮ J. Capmany, *Presencia del cristiano en el mundo* (n.d.) ▮ J. Capo Bosch, *The Basic Concepts of the Cursillo Movement in the Light of Vatican II* (n.d.) ▮ idem, *The Cursillo, Yesterday and Today* (1974) ▮ idem, *The Group Reunion: Theory and Practice* (1969) ▮ idem, *Lower Your Nets* (n.d.) ▮ H. Castano, *New Men* (1967) ▮ S. Clark, *The Work of the Cursillos and the Work of Renewal* (1967) ▮ R. K. Crandall, "The Cursillo/Walk to Emmaus Movement: An Apostolic Model," *Journal of the Academy of Evangelism in Theological Education* 4 (1988–89) ▮ S. Dragastin, "All That Glistens Isn't: A Look at the Cursillo Exercise," *Una Sancta* 23 (1966) ▮ idem, "The Cursillo as a Social Movement," in W. Lieu, ed., *Catholics in the USA: Perspectives* (1970) ▮ J. M. Fernandez, *Los cursillos y el cambio del hombre* (1977) ▮ C. Gil, *Los cursillos y la evangelizacion* (1976) ▮ J. Hervas, *Cursillos in Christianity* (1965) ▮ idem, *The Priest and the Cursillos* (n.d.) ▮ idem, *Questions and Problems Concerning Cursillos in Christianity* (1966) ▮ E. Higuet, "O misticismo na experincia católica," in J. Maraschin, ed., *Religiosidade popular e misticismo no Brasil* (1994) ▮ G. Hughes, *The Postcursillo, Group Reunion and Ultreya* (n.d.) ▮ F. L. Keith, "A Critique of the Cursillo Program and a Manual for the Presbyterian Cursillo Program" (diss., Columbia Theol. Sem., 1990) ▮ D. Knight, *Cursillo Spiritual Direction Program* (1984) ▮ E. Seidl and A. Klose, eds, *Die Dynamik der Cursillobewegung* (1988) ▮ G. W. Short, "Religious Experience in the Cursillo Movement: Making the Extraordinary Ordinary" (diss., Andover Newton, 1993). ■ D. D. Bundy

D

DAKE, FINIS JENNINGS (1902–87). Author of the famous *Dake's Annotated Bible* (1961, 1963), teacher, and pastor. The 24-year-old Dake resided with his wife in Amarillo, TX, at the time of his ordination to the Texas–New Mexico District of the Assemblies of God (AG) in 1927, following two years of pastoral ministry there. In the mid 1920s Dake attended Central Bible Institute. He pastored in the Dallas area for approximately nine months before becoming an evangelist. During his stint as an evangelist (1928–31), he lived in Tulsa and Enid, OK.

Dake accepted the pastorate of the Christian Assembly in Zion, IL, in Oct. 1932. Shortly after arriving in Zion, Dake spoke with his church board about purchasing the home and carriage house of John Alexander Dowie for the purpose of establishing Shilo Bible Institute, which would later be renamed Great Lakes Bible Institute and would eventually merge with Central Bible Institute.

Dake's stay in Zion was not without controversy. On Feb. 9, 1937, Dake received a six-month jail sentence in the Milwaukee County Jail after pleading guilty to a charge of violating the federal Mann Act by transporting 16-year-old Emma Barcelli from Kenosha, WI, to East St. Louis, IL. Although pleading guilty, Dake insisted that he did not harm the girl. Despite the fervent loyalty of his wife and parishioners at Christian Assembly, as a consequence of this "unfortunate mistake," as Dake's lawyer called it, Dake's relationship with the AG ended in 1937. He later joined the Church of God (Cleveland, TN) and finally became an independent. He remained pentecostal nonetheless and did not allow this unfortunate event to ruin his life.

Dake was the author of numerous books, tracts, and pamphlets (e.g., *Revelation Expounded*, 2d ed. [1950]; *God's Plan for Man: Contained in Fifty-Two Lessons, One for Each Week of the Year* [1949]; *Foundation Studies of Scripture; or, Dispensational Truth* [1946]). Sales of these and other books crested 180,000 by 1988.

Dake is best known, however, for the notes in the strongly dispensationally oriented *Dake's Annotated Reference Bible*, published by the family-operated Dake Bible Sales, Inc., of Lawrenceville, GA. In 1961 the NT was published together with Psalms, Proverbs, and Daniel. Based strictly on the KJV, the OT and NT were published together in 1963. This Bible contained a "Complete Concordance and Cyclopedia Index" as well as maps of the Holy Land, charts of the "Ages and Dispensations," and Dake's prized marginal notes. Until the appearance of Dake's decidedly pentecostal brand of dispensationalism, the *Scofield Reference Bible* held sway. But the pentecostal ingredients of *Dake's* (as it was popularly known) soon made it a favorite among pentecostals. His impact on conservative pentecostalism cannot be overstated. His notes became the "bread and butter" of many prominent preachers and the staple of pentecostal congregations. Thus, Jimmy Swaggart, in a tribute to Dake, could say, "I owe my Bible education to this man." A 1988 article on *Dake's Annotated Reference Bible* was titled "The Pentecostal Study Bible."

Finis J. Dake died in 1987. Dake Bible Sales, Inc., continues to be family owned and operated. First, Dake's son, Finis J. Dake Jr., succeeded his father to lead the organization; currently Dake's grandson Derrick Germaine is the general manager. Products available from Dake Bible Sales, now with its own web site, range from *Dake's Annotated Reference Bible* and other books to tapes, Bible covers, "Plan of the Ages Charts," and an interactive *Dake Bible*.

■ **Bibliography:** AG Archives, "Finis J. Dake" ■ *Dake's Annotated Reference Bible* (1961, 1963) ■ C. E. Jones, *A Guide to the Study of the Pentecostal Movement* (1983) ■ H. V. Knight, *Ministry Aflame* (1972) ■ R. Love and J. B. Owen, "The Pentecostal Study Bible," *Charisma* (Jan. 1988) ■ "Petting Parson Sent to Jail," *Chicago Tribune* (Feb. 10, 1937), 1 ■ J. Swaggart, "In Memory. Finis Jennings Dake 1902–1987," *Evangelist* 9 (1987).

■ P. H. Alexander

A rare photo of Finis Dake, author of *Dake's Annotated Bible*, with daughter, Finette.

DALLIÈRE, LOUIS (1897–1976). Precursor of charismatic renewal in the French Reformed Church and founder of the Union de Prière (UP). Ordained as pastor of Charmes-sur-Rhône in 1925, Dallière initially combined his pastorate with creative theological and philosophical writing. Convicted by the preaching of ▸Douglas Scott, Dallière sought the Lord, receiving a fullness of the Spirit in 1930 and the gift of tongues two years later. In 1932 he wrote *D'aplomb sur la Parole de Dieu* (Squarely on the Word of God), a monograph on the pentecostal revival (reprinted by UP in 1996). From 1932 until 1939 he collaborated with

H. T. de Worm of Belgium on the monthly *Esprit et Vie (Spirit and Life),* to promote the revival.

Increasingly distressed by pentecostal sectarianism, Dallière withdrew to his pastorate, still nourishing his ecumenical vision of a charismatic revival within the churches, which found expression in the charter of the UP, formed in 1946. He urged and practiced baptismal immersion in view of the Lord's return, which he saw neither as "rebaptism" nor as denying previous water baptism.

■ **Bibliography:** A. and E. Brèmond, *Sur le Chemin du Renouveau* (1976) ■ D. D. Bundy, "Pentecostalism in Belgium," *Pneuma* 8 (1, 1986): 41–56 ■ "Louis Dallière: Apologist for Pentecostalism in France and Belgium, 1932–1939," *Pneuma* 10 (2, 1988): 85–115 ■ "Louis Dallière (1932–1939): The Development of a Pentecostal Apologetic," *EPTA Bulletin* 8 (1989): 60–93 ■ F. Lovsky, "La pensée théologique du Pasteur Louis Dallière," *Etudes théologiques et religieuses* 53 (1978): 171–90 ■ "The Making of a Pentecostal Theologian: The Writings of Louis Dallière, 1922–1932," *EPTA Bulletin* 7 (1988): 40–68.   ■ P. D. Hocken

DALLIMORE, A. H. (1867–1969). A. H. Dallimore was one of the more colorful characters in the history of New Zealand pentecostalism. As a child he had been close to death through typhoid fever but had been healed through his parents' prayers. He was originally a Baptist but later joined the Church of England before coming to N.Z. in 1886. While living in Opunake, Dallimore associated with the Methodist church, during which time he began to minister. He returned to England, married, and later settled in Canada, where he went into business and later suffered a nervous breakdown. He regained his health through attending divine healing services at St. Paul's Episcopal Church, Vancouver, B.C., and at a Baptist mission conducted by ‣Charles S. Price.

In 1920 Dallimore met veteran pentecostal missionary ‣John G. Lake at a British Israel conference in Vancouver, where Lake encouraged him to begin a healing ministry. Dallimore conducted independent healing meetings in Vancouver for some years, returning to N.Z. in 1927. He began independent healing services in Auckland, and although numbers were at first small, attendance increased, and by 1931 he was attracting over 1,000 people to his meetings in the Auckland town hall. Dallimore's flamboyant style gained wide public attention, and services received extensive publicity through the press and through broadcasts of his meetings over the radio. His use of "blessed handkerchiefs" for laying on the bodies of the sick and the healings of humans as well as birds and animals were widely reported.

Dallimore's Revival Fire Mission meetings faced opposition throughout 1932 from some of the mainstream religious leaders in Auckland, who promoted a joint clerical, medical, and professional committee of inquiry into his claims of heal-

ing. The findings of this committee were published in a pamphlet, the title of which gave some indication of its negative findings—*The Dallimore Campaign Exposed.* Dallimore's opponents eventually convened a public "mass indignation meeting" in the town hall to protest against his meetings in late 1932. As a result, the city council placed a ban on Dallimore's use of the town hall. This ban was later lifted after the presentation of a large public petition to the council protesting its decision. Following the waning of this controversy, the Revival Fire Mission continued for a number of years, although it remained centered on Dallimore himself and did not spread widely beyond Auckland. Nevertheless, Dallimore's campaigns had a lasting effect; they influenced a number of people who later became leaders in other pentecostal groups.

■ **Bibliography:** James E. Worsfold, *A History of the Charismatic Movements in New Zealand* (1974).   ■ B. Knowles

DAMASCUS CHRISTIAN CHURCHES, INC. The Damascus Christian Churches (Concilio de las Iglesias Cristianas) is a Hispanic church organization formed in 1939 by Francisco and ‣Leoncia Rosado. The church teaches a Wesleyan form of pentecostalism. Intended as an outreach to Spanish-speaking people in New York City, the group now ministers in New York, New Jersey, Florida, Ecuador, Mexico, the Dominican Republic, the Virgin Islands, Puerto Rico, and Nicaragua—with a total 103 churches in 1999. F. Vega directs the Christian Education Department with the main focus on missions, with both public services and correspondence courses. Since 1981 the organization has also included English-speaking churches.

The council is governed by an executive board of seven members. Enrique Melendez, former pastor and president, was succeeded as pastor of the Bronx mother church by Angel M. Rios in 1994. Rios was delivered from drug addiction and alcoholism through the efforts of the church. Headquarters for the council is in Bronx, NY.

■ **Bibliography:** *Constitution and Articles of Faith of the Council of the Damascus Christian Church and Missions* (1984) ■ *Damascus Christian Church Directory* (1986–87).   ■ W. E. Warner

DANCING IN THE SPIRIT Physical movement akin to dancing, presumably done while under the influence and control of the Holy Spirit. According to T. Burton Pierce, "Most older pentecostal believers who have participated in spiritual revivals over a period of years have witnessed what is known as 'dancing in the spirit'" (1986, 9). Pierce lists humility, gracefulness, and beauty as characteristics of a person engaged in this form of worship. He also suggests that these persons are usually "shy, ungainly," and not normally given to attracting attention to themselves.

Pentecostal believers in the revival occurring during the early 20th century eschewed dancing as a social activity in their zeal to become more Christ-like. Thus, it is a bit surprising that dancing in the Spirit became an acceptable mode of worship. However, another characteristic of early pentecostal movements was their flexibility in accepting new spiritual phenomena. Pierce's description matches oral reports by older pentecostals who have observed this phenomenon, though some are hesitant to fully endorse it. Many reservations grow out of the fear that encouraging people to dance in the Spirit opens the door to excesses ranging from the need to be noticed to the breaking of necessary decorum in the church service. Other reservations stem from a certain caution regarding the credibility of the act itself. Thus, while many older pentecostals refuse to eliminate dancing in the Spirit as a form of worship, many of them also express strong doubts that it is "Spirit-filled."

E. Louis Backman, a professor of pharmacology at the Royal University of Uppsala, observes that dancing has a "ritual significance" in all religions. He says, "The types of dance varied even in the earliest Church. Frequently there seems to have been a question of round dances, usually with stamping and hopping, but always with clapping of hands and a certain rhythm. Sometimes the dance was a solo dance, and in such cases it appears to have been a typical pirouette" (1952, 329).

Backman asserts that a close relationship between the urge to dance and the need for healing is nearly always apparent in church dances. The Dance of the Angels, practiced for centuries in the church, was often described as an attempt to mirror the ecstasy of the resurrection. Church dancing did degenerate into what Backman calls "dance epidemics" (1952, 331). People tried to find relief from pain or sickness through dancing. Backman now believes that the cramping and twitching experienced by the dancers can be traced to poor nutrition and ergot poisoning of grain and bread. Some of the dance epidemics took on characteristics of demon possession and were treated by the church as such. Especially during the Middle Ages, choreomaniacs presented a special problem for the church because of their irrational behavior (1952, 333).

In the 1980s similar dance epidemics occurred in some pentecostal and charismatic churches. These epidemics cannot be linked to malnutrition but may more closely coincide with a strong need on the part of a congregation for physical evidence of the presence of the Holy Spirit. Contrary to the spontaneous movement of earlier times, these dances appear structured, even loosely choreographed, giving rise to some doubt that the dancers are moving under the control of the Holy Spirit.

See also WORSHIP.

■ **Bibliography:** E. L. Backman, *Religious Dances in the Christian Church and Popular Medicine* (1952) ▌ T. B. Pierce, "The Dance and Corporate Worship," *PE* (Nov. 2, 1986).   ■ F. Bixler

DAUGHERTY, BILLY JOE (1952–). Prominent pastor, evangelist, and leader in the charismatic movement. Billy Joe Daugherty was born in Magnolia, AR, and grew up in the Methodist Church. As a student at Oral Roberts University he received the baptism of the Holy Spirit and sought understanding of how to minister healing and miracles. He graduated with bachelor's and master's degrees in practical theology. He also attended ˒Rhema Bible Training Center and ˒Christ for the Nations Training Institute.

Daugherty's ministry has come to be characterized by biblical preaching, divine healing, and foreign missions. He is considered a close associate of ˒Oral Roberts and ˒Kenneth Hagin and is said to be a key leader in the next generation of the Word of Faith movement (˒Positive Confession).

In 1981 Daugherty became the founding pastor of Victory Christian Center in Tulsa, OK, which has grown to more than 11,000 members with several affiliated ministries, including a large Christian school as well as Victory Bible Institute and Victory Fellowship of Ministries, an association of charismatic ministers that ordains pastors. The development of Daugherty's ministry has been closely associated with Oral Roberts University, where his church has held services at the Maybee Center for several years.

Daugherty sponsors major missions endeavors through Victory World Missions Training with programs in 22 coun-

Woman dancing in the Spirit during a service of the General Assembly of the Church of God of Prophecy, c. 1930.

tries in Europe, Africa, Asia, and Central and South America. In recent years he has done extensive work in assisting the evangelical church in Russia. He also serves as a regent for Oral Roberts University, board member for the ›Pentecostal Fellowship of North America, and chairman of the International Charismatic Bible Ministries Association.

Broadcasts of Daugherty's services are carried throughout the U.S. and several countries. He is the author of several books and numerous pamphlets.

■ **Bibliography:** B. Daugherty, *Led by the Spirit* (1994) ■ idem, *You Can Be Healed* (1991) ■ J. L. Grady, *Not Your Average Joe* (1997).

■ D. J. Hedges

Billy Joe Daugherty, pastor, evangelist, and a leader in the charismatic movement.

DAVID J. DU PLESSIS CENTER FOR CHRISTIAN SPIRITUALITY

Established in 1985 as an organizational unit of Fuller Theological Seminary, Pasadena, CA. As he neared his ninth decade, pentecostal ambassador-at-large ›David du Plessis naturally gave thought to the future of his personal papers and library—an extensive collection, acquired over nearly 60 years of ministry. Around 1983 Du Plessis shared a conference platform with David Allan Hubbard, president of Fuller Seminary. Their conversation planted an idea in the mind of Du Plessis: perhaps he could move to Pasadena, which would reduce the arduous travel that so long had characterized his itinerant ministry and allow him to give himself to writing and consulting. With the advice and support of a close circle of friends on making such a change, Anna and David du Plessis sold their home of 20 years in Oakland, CA, and moved to Pasadena. On Feb. 7, 1985, Du Plessis's 80th birthday, a formal academic convocation at Fuller Seminary marked the establishment of the Du Plessis Center.

Du Plessis was particularly attracted to Fuller by its commitment to ecumenical breadth coupled with its friendly openness to the pentecostal and charismatic sectors of the church. From 1985 until his death on Feb. 2, 1987, Du Plessis served as resident consultant for ecumenical affairs at the seminary, which was located a block from his new home.

The Du Plessis Center aims to facilitate the study and practice of Christian spirituality over a broad range of ecumenical diversity. It encourages research in the literature, practice, institutions, and movements of spirituality within the Christian church. By late 1987 the first major phase of the work of the Du Plessis Center was concluded—the completion in the seminary library of an archive for the Du Plessis papers and correspondence. The Du Plessis papers, which bear dates as early as the 1930s (a number are in his native language, Afrikaans) form an important resource for the development of three movements through the middle quarters of the 20th century: the pentecostal movement, the ecumenical movement, and the charismatic movement. Preserved records contain valued correspondence with such pentecostal leaders as ›Stanley Frodsham, ›Donald Gee, ›Kathryn Kuhlman, ›Joseph Mattsson-Boze, ›Lewi Pethrus, and ›Carlton Spencer. They include correspondence with ecumenical leaders such as Visser 't Hooft, John Mackay, and Henry P. van Dusen, as well as with Roman Catholic churchmen such as Augustin Cardinal Bea and Jan Cardinal Willebrands. Materials appear as well from the earlier years of the Roman Catholic/Pentecostal ›Dialogue (1972–). The center has been designated by the Society for Pentecostal Studies as the location of its official archives. The archive also holds letters exchanged with charismatic leaders, including ›Dennis Bennett, ›Larry Christenson, and ›Harald Bredesen. Among the resources in the Du Plessis archive are his personal collection of correspondence, published addresses and sermons, minutes, and conference papers related to the first 15 years of the ›Pentecostal World Conference (1947–62).

Gathered personal effects of Du Plessis include mementos of his personal friendship with three popes and numerous awards presented over his lengthy and distinguished ecumenical career. To the papers of Du Plessis, which by late 1987 had been sorted and positioned in permanent containers for access by scholars and researchers, have been added the papers of other pentecostal leaders. Notable among these are the extensive correspondence of Joseph Mattsson-Boze (who was born the same day as Du Plessis, Feb. 7, 1905), papers related to early-20th-century ethnic immigrant pentecostals (especially Italian and Swedish), and the effects of several minor pentecostal figures.

The Du Plessis archive participates in an informal network of evangelical, pentecostal, and fundamentalist archival efforts. Joseph Colletti serves as the first archival assistant, and he largely has been responsible for the refinement of the collection. The formation of the Du Plessis archive has had the able guidance of consultant Nicholas Olsberg, head archivist of the famed Getty Museum of Santa Monica, CA. Fuller faculty member and pentecostal minister ›Russell P. Spittler served as the founding director of the Du Plessis Center. In 1994–95, a federal grant in the amount of $53,000 allowed completion of the processing of the Du Plessis papers. The same funding brought Kate McGinn, the center's first professional archivist, to the staff.

As it grows, the Du Plessis Center projects sponsorship of seminars, conferences, and courses that will enhance and communicate the spiritual and ecumenical values characteristic of David du Plessis. In 1986 the center sponsored the first session of the International Roman Catholic/Pentecostal ►Dialogue to have been held outside the European continent. This venue was arranged particularly to honor Dr. Du Plessis.

During 1986 the Du Plessis Center sponsored the presence of visiting research scholars especially interested in religious ecstasy in antiquity. In 1987 it hosted an invitational conference of evangelical social activists and charismatics involved in socially ameliorative ministries.

It is an aim of the Du Plessis Center to deepen trust among diverse sectors of leadership in the church. With the pentecostal and charismatic movements combined now numbering in excess of 20% of the world's known Christians of any persuasion, the need and opportunity for a center combining ecumenical and pentecostal interests is apparent.

■ **Bibliography:** Cecil M. Robeck Jr., "David J. du Plessis Center Established," *Glad Tidings* (May 1985) ■ C. Woehr and S. Lawson, "Doors Open at Du Plessis Center," *Charisma* (Jan. 1987).
■ R. P. Spittler

DAWSON, JOHN (1952–). International leader in ►Youth With A Mission (YWAM) and reconciliation ministry. Dawson was born and brought up in New Zealand, the oldest child of Jim and Joy Dawson and the grandson of a Plymouth Brethren radio evangelist. Already sensitive to the Holy Spirit as a teenager, he went from high school to a YWAM training school in Switzerland. Strongly drawn to missionary service, Dawson heard a call to Southern California, where he and his wife, Julie, lived in a racially mixed area in Los Angeles for 20 years. This experience led Dawson into intercession for cities and the spiritual warfare required, resulting in his book *Taking Our Cities for God: How to Break Spiritual Strongholds* (1990). During this time, Dawson was international director of urban missions for YWAM, a post he held until 1997. As his urban ministry led him further into reconciliation work, Dawson founded the International Reconciliation Coalition, an organization dedicated to healing wounds between people groups; the principles of this ministry were set forth in *Healing America's Wounds* (1994). Dawson has served on many boards, but since the mid 1990s he has focused more on the ►Women's Aglow International Fellowship, March for Jesus International, YWAM International, Mission America 2000, and the AD 2000 and Beyond movement. He has been a frequent speaker for Promise Keepers, and his reconciliation ministry has found further expression through his role in Toward Jerusalem Council II, a messianic Jewish and Gentile initiative to heal this original wound in the body of Christ.

■ **Bibliography:** S. Lawson, "Defeating Territorial Spirits" *Charisma* (4, 1990) 47–55.
■ P. D. Hocken

DAYTON, DONALD WILBER (1942–). Educator, author, and specialist in the study of the Holiness movement as an antecedent to pentecostalism. As a student in the 1960s, Dayton left an evangelical college to become a civil rights advocate. He soon discovered, however, that the 19th-century evangelicals who founded such institutions had been social activists. This prompted him to study the American Holiness movement, for which he wrote an extensive bibliography in 1971. As a Ph.D. student at the University of Chicago, Dayton wrote an award-winning paper tracing the origin and development of the term *baptism of the Holy Ghost* within the Holiness movement (Synan, 1975, 39).

Dayton has done a great deal to preserve works valuable for the study of the milieu from which pentecostalism arose, reminding us of the emphasis on social justice in these works. He is editor of the 48-volume series The Higher Christian Life (1985), a collection of facsimile reprints of original sources for the study of the Holiness, pentecostal, and Keswick movements. He is also coediting a collection of secondary works on these topics, "Studies in Evangelicalism" (1980–). His most recent publications are two edited volumes, *The Prophecy Conference Movement* (1988) and *The Variety of American Evangelicalism* (with R. Johnston; 1991).

■ **Bibliography:** D. W. Dayton, *Discovering an Evangelical Heritage* (1976) ■ idem, *Theological Roots of Pentecostalism* (1987) ■ idem, "From 'Christian Perfection' to the 'Baptism of the Holy Ghost,'" in V. Synan, *Aspects of Pentecostal-Charismatic Origins* (1975) ■ idem, "The Rise of the Evangelical Healing Movement in Nineteenth-Century America," *Pneuma* 4 (Spring 1982). ■ R. M. Riss

DE LA CRUZ, MARCIAL (1875–1934). Pioneer Mexican Oneness pentecostal evangelist and hymn writer for the ►Apostolic Assembly of Faith in Jesus Christ, Inc. Born in the city of Torreón, Coahuila, Mexico, in 1875, De la Cruz emigrated to the U.S. in 1914, where he was converted in San Diego, CA. He began preaching in 1915 and was ordained evangelist by Francisco Llorente and the ►Pentecostal Assemblies of the World in 1917. From that year until 1924, he ministered as a traveling evangelist in San Diego, Riverside, San Bernardino, Los Angeles, Oxnard, and throughout the Imperial Valley in CA, and in Yuma, AZ. In 1925 he and Tereso Gamboa began pioneering the Apostolic Assembly work in Arizona. De la Cruz was the first great songwriter of the Apostolic Assembly. He is perhaps best remembered for the 25 original songs and hymns he composed. In both his preaching and hymnody he always stressed the work and necessity of the Holy Spirit in the everyday life of the believer.

■ **Bibliography:** B. Cantú, *Historia de la Asamblea Apostólica de la Fe en Cristo Jesús, 1916–1966* (1966). ■ G. Espinosa

DEEPER CHRISTIAN LIFE MISSION (INTERNATIONAL)

In Aug. 1973 the Deeper Christian Life Mission (DCLM) or Deeper Life Bible Church (DLBC), simply identified as "Deeper Life," was founded in Lagos, Nigeria, through the personal charisma of William F. Kumuyi, its current pastor and general superintendent. He was formerly a mathematics lecturer at the University of Lagos. He was a member of the Anglican Church, from where he joined the Apostolic Faith Church. His later withdrawal from the Apostolic Faith was linked to doctrinal controversies. He attributed his expulsion by the church to his nonconformity with what he described as the "conservative doctrines of the church." What started with only 15 members as a house fellowship in his official residence at the university staff quarters has developed into one of the largest pentecostal/charismatic movements in Africa.

Many DCLM branches have been established elsewhere in Africa and in many parts of the world. Its current total membership runs into several million. In 1983 Kumuyi officially resigned his university job to engage in full-time evangelism, though without any formal pastoral training. Prior to Nov. 14, 1982, when the movement took the name Deeper Christian Life Mission (International), it was referred to, first, as Deeper Life Fellowship and later as Deeper Christian Life Ministry.

The movement lays emphasis on strict adherence to biblical doctrines (they believe that the Christian faith is built on 22 pivotal doctrines), prayer, holiness or sanctification (removal of the Adamic nature or inbred sin), restitution, and spiritual rejuvenation (to be born again). The members' commitment to evangelism (distribution of tracts and personal witnessing) and Bible study, and their somewhat distinct modes of dressing and exclusivistic tendencies of "separation from the world" (i.e., radical views on marriage and home life) reveal much of their religious identity.

The establishment in the late 1970s of the Higher Institution Programme of Deeper Life (renamed Deeper Life Campus Fellowship) as a fertile ground for the recruitment of its leadership and workforce marked the beginning of remarkable growth for the church. Its headquarters are in the Gbagada area of Lagos. DCLM has also founded an International Bible Training Centre (IBTC) at its revival campground in Ayobo, near Lagos.

■ **Bibliography:** A. Isaacson, *Deeper Life* (1990) ■ M. A. Ojo, "Deeper Life Christian Ministry: A Case Study of the Charismatic Movements in Western Nigeria," *Journal of Religion in Africa* 18, (2, 1988) ■ idem, "The Growth of Campus Christianity and Charismatic Movements in Western Nigeria" (diss., U. of London, 1986) ■ B. Steward, *Historical Background of Churches in Nigeria* (n.d.).   ■ A. U. Adogame

DENNY, RICHARD (DICK) (1923–). Lay leader in the Lutheran charismatic movement. Together with his wife, Betty, Denny served as manager and coordinator of a variety of activities and ministries among Lutheran charismatics. He was one of the original sponsors of the International Lutheran Conference on the Holy Spirit (1972), which became the chief annual gathering of Lutheran charismatics.

Denny and his wife experienced marked conversions and the baptism with the Holy Spirit shortly after their oldest son was killed in Viet Nam in 1968. As a result, Denny sold a successful business and became a business manager for Lutheran Youth Encounter, a Minneapolis-based youth organization that ministered on college campuses and in local Lutheran congregations.

Later Denny served as lay assistant at North Heights Lutheran Church, St. Paul, MN. In 1975 he became executive secretary for Lutheran Charismatic Renewal Services, which subsequently became a part of a merger of Lutheran charismatic leadership to form the International Lutheran Renewal Center (ILRC; 1983). Denny became ILRC's coordinator of national ministries. He traveled widely, teaching and counseling congregations in regard to charismatic renewal. He and his wife became officially accredited lay ministers in the American Lutheran Church.

See also LUTHERAN CHARISMATICS.

■ **Bibliography:** L. Christenson, ed., *Welcome, Holy Spirit* (1987).   ■ L. Christenson

DERSTINE, GERALD (1928–). Evangelist and church leader. Born and reared a Pennsylvania Mennonite, Derstine was converted in a T. L. Osborne crusade (1949). Shortly thereafter Derstine was healed of chronic stuttering.

With his Mennonite wife, Beulah Hackman, Derstine established a mission and then a church among the Chippewa Indians of northern Minnesota (1953). After being ordained as pastor of the Strawberry Lake Mennonite Church, Ogema, MN, he was asked to leave in 1955 when he and members of his church experienced a week of pentecostal experiences like those of the 1st-century believers.

Derstine's subsequent evangelistic, healing revival efforts were first sponsored by Henry Brunk, a Mennonite and Florida building contractor who had earlier established "Gospel Crusade" (1953, a nondenominational missions organization).

Derstine is founder of the Christian Retreat Family Center (est. 1968) in Bradenton, FL. Retreat centers for the ministry are also located in Ogema, MN, and Hermon, NY. To further lay education and renewal, and to train persons for active ministry, Christian Retreat sponsors a 10-week, 250-class-hour Institute of Ministry at the Bradenton site three times a year.

Derstine serves as chairman of the board of Gospel Crusade, Inc., and Gospel Crusade Ministerial Fellowship. The latter is the credentialing arm of Gospel Crusade (more than 900 ministers have been certified to date; 67 churches and ministries are affiliated with Gospel Crusade). He also serves as a trustee of the International Bible Charismatic Ministries of Tulsa, OK.

Gospel Crusade, Inc., supports ministries in Haiti, Honduras, Trinidad, the Philippines, and Israel. Beginning in 1981, Derstine has ministered as an apostle in Israel, planting churches in many Jewish and Arab locations. Worldwide, Gospel Crusade has been involved in planting over 2,000 churches in some 20 countries.

■ **Bibliography:** G. Derstine, *Destined to Mature* (n.d.) ■ idem, *Fire over Israel* (n.d.) ■ idem, *Following the Fire* (1980) ■ idem, ed., *Harvest Time* 1 (1, 1958ff.) ■ idem, *Three Decades of World-wide Ministry* (1983).   ■ J. A. Hewett

DIALOGUE, REFORMED–PENTECOSTAL The pentecostal movement has just completed five years of dialogue with the World Alliance of Reformed Churches (WARC). Heralded in the ecumenical press as a "major breakthrough," this series of talks represents the first international dialogue between pentecostalism and a world family of Protestant churches (*WARC Update,* June 1996, 2). Though not including all churches of the Reformed tradition, WARC represents 200 member churches in 99 countries of the world, embracing Presbyterian, Reformed, Congregational, and United Churches. The churches of WARC emphasize the centrality of the Word of God, accept the historic church creeds, understand the church as the people of God, and pursue bilateral theological dialogue with Christians of different traditions.

The dialogue between WARC and pentecostalism was initiated in 1989 when WARC voted at its general council in Korea, at the suggestion of the Korean delegates, in favor of investigating the possibility of dialogue with the pentecostals. Contact was eventually made with the World Pentecostal Conference (WPC) in search of dialogue partners, but the WPC voted against any such ecumenical involvement. Informal meetings were then arranged by representatives of WARC, especially general secretary Milan Opocenski and theology secretary Henry Wilson, to explore the matter further with ˃Cecil M. Robeck Jr. of the ˃Assemblies of God, due to his extensive ecumenical involvement. Wilson and Robeck then convened a meeting in Mattersey, England, in July of 1995 to discuss the possibility of the dialogue.

At the preliminary meeting, the delegations reviewed the current state of Reformed/pentecostal relations around the world, taking note of the fact that regional discussions between members of both sides have taken place in the Netherlands, South Africa, and the U.S. The teams also explored the distinctive emphases of the different traditions. It was decided that a five-year series of talks would be feasible and beneficial. The purpose of the talks would be to increase mutual understanding and respect, identify areas of theological agreement, convergence, and disagreement, and explore possibilities for common witness.

Due to various difficulties on the Reformed side in maintaining continuity in team participants over the first few years of the talks, the dialogue did not gain significant momentum until the third year. The efforts of Cecil Robeck and Milan Opocenski kept the dialogue alive and productive. The final document is under preparation that covers the work done in the first four years of conversation. Below is a summary of the topics discussed in these talks.

The first round of talks convened in Torre Pellice, Italy, hosted by the Waldensian Church. The theme was "Spirituality in Today's World." Papers were offered on spirituality and Scripture, spirituality and justice, and spirituality and ecumenism. Several issues emerged from the papers and the discussions that followed. The issue of Spirit and Word naturally came to the forefront on several occasions. Both sides emphasized their historic devotion to the Word of God and Scripture but also to the role of the Spirit. Divergence tended to relate to the contexts in which the Word is received and interpreted, with the pentecostals stressing anointed preaching and the exercise of various spiritual gifts (especially discernment), while the Reformed side pointed to preaching, historic confession, and social context. The pentecostals also noted their increasing awareness worldwide of the importance of social context but added that responses to this awareness among pentecostals tended to take the form of pastoral care and home missions instead of engagement with existing social structures.

The topic of Word and Spirit was also the prominent issue of the second round of talks convened at McCormick Theological Seminary (Chicago), hosted by the pentecostal team. The theme was "The Role of the Holy Spirit in the Church." Papers were offered on the role of the Spirit in proclamation and the manifestation of gifts and signs of the Spirit. A paper was also given on the Holy Spirit and the Bible, with a focus on prophecy and the issue of *revelatio continua* (continuing revelation). Both sides affirmed the centrality of God's revelation in Jesus Christ and the Scriptures for the life and mission of the church. Also affirmed by both sides was the significance of prophecy in the ongoing understanding of God's Word in the church. But both sides struggled over the issue of ongoing or continuing "revelation" in the church. The issue remained open for further exploration and discussion.

The topic shifted to "Missions in Eschatological Perspective" in the third round of talks, which convened in Das Haus der Stille (Kappel, Switzerland) in May 1998. Papers were presented on this theme. While upholding the historic pentecostal focus on the evangelistic role of the church in the light of Christ's coming, the pentecostal side also affirmed the importance of the kingdom of God as a theme that implied a holistic missionary task that would also include social concern. The Reformed delegates recognized the lack of attention to eschatology and mission in classical Reformed theology but affirmed the recent theological shift that has occurred, which has placed eschatology at the beginning and the end of theological reflection. They affirmed a holistic missionary task for the church that stressed personal wholeness and social transformation. Both teams recognized the focus on the coming of Jesus as both Savior and Judge and the consequent sense of eschatological urgency for the evangelistic task of the church as emphases unique to pentecostals.

The next round of talks took place in South Korea in May 1999, with the theme "The Gifts of the Spirit and the Kingdom of God." The pentecostals upheld the importance of affirming the charismatic structure of the church, including the gifted ministries of the entire laity, in an effort to understand the church today as in service to the kingdom of God on earth in fulfillment of the original charismatic ministry of Jesus Christ. The pentecostals laid particular value on the extraordinary gifts of the Spirit discussed in 1 Cor. 12–14, wanting to know why the Reformed churches have neglected this most detailed and thoroughly discussed list of spiritual gifts in the NT. The pentecostals also wanted to know why those gifted with such extraordinary charismata tended to be marginalized in the lives of Reformed congregations. Pentecostals did recognize that a broader theology of spiritual gifts was needed that involved a variety of gifts, both natural and extraordinary, as channels of God's grace in the redemptive work of new creation.

While not wanting to dismiss the gifts mentioned in 1 Cor. 12–14, the Reformed team focused on other lists of gifts mentioned in the NT and resisted using any one list of spiritual gifts, such as 1 Cor. 12–14, as a template to place over the church, with the added refusal to see any one gift (e.g., speaking in tongues) as normative for all Christians. The Reformed team did recognize that they have tended to accent the role of the Spirit in illuminating the Word of God in a rationally understandable way and that they have sometimes been too casual in pursuing a broader variety of spiritual gifts in the church. Both teams confessed that they have tended to focus on certain favored gifts in the NT as a template for the church and that both can challenge each other in developing a more diverse understanding of the ministry of the entire church in service to the kingdom of God in the world.

During the fifth year, the teams met in São Paulo, Brazil, to complete work on a document that represents their findings during the previous years. It was given the title "Word and Spirit, Church and World" and released to the public in Sept. 2000. It has been published in the *Reformed World* and in *Pneuma: The Journal of the Society for Pentecostal Studies*.

■ F. D. Macchia

DIALOGUE, ROMAN CATHOLIC AND CLASSICAL PENTECOSTAL

The beginnings of the modern pentecostal movement were full of hope for the unity of the church. Intervening years brought disappointment and politically expedient realignments in the realities that marked pentecostalism's flirtation with evangelicalism. Earlier cooperative efforts were shelved as that flirtation developed into a full-fledged wedding. In spite of early pentecostal hopes that they would, in some way, play a significant role in bringing the churches together, few would have guessed how that might look at the end of their first century.

Today, pentecostalism constitutes the fastest growing Christian movement in the world. And it is involved in a vital dialogue with the world's largest church. Approximately 60 years after the formation of the first pentecostal denominations, the international dialogue between the Vatican Secretariat [now Pontifical Council] for Promoting Christian Unity and some members of the pentecostal churches began. Several significant things happened that made it possible for this theological discussion to take place. Among them were the Second Vatican Council (ᐟVatican II) and the emergence of the charismatic renewal.

1. Historical Background.

Initial contact between Roman Catholics and classical pentecostals came about through the ecumenical ministry of ᐟDavid J. du Plessis. In 1961 Du Plessis visited Rome and was received by Augustin Cardinal Bea, president of the Secretariat for Promoting Christian Unity (SPCU). As a result of this meeting, Cardinal Bea invited Du Plessis to be an observer at the third session of the Second Vatican Council (1964). Later, at the Fourth Assembly of the ᐟWorld Council of Churches (WCC) in Uppsala, Sweden (1968), Du Plessis became acquainted with Fr. ᐟKilian McDonnell, OSB, a Benedictine monk and theologian whose specialty was the theology of John Calvin. It was the friendship that developed between McDonnell and Du Plessis that made such a dialogue possible.

In 1969 the Reverend Ray Bringham, a charismatic Church of God (Anderson, IN) minister and personal friend of Du Plessis, visited Rome while on a trip to Europe. There he met John Cardinal Willebrands, president of the SPCU, and Fr. (now Bishop) Basil Meeking. They discussed the possibility of a dialogue between the SPCU and representatives of the pentecostal and charismatic movements. Bringham informed Du Plessis of the discussions, which the two had talked about prior to Bringham's trip.

In Nov. 1969 Cardinal Willebrands spoke at the annual plenary meeting of the Secretariat in Rome. In his speech, which was later published in the *Information Service* of the SPCU, Willebrands declared, "The problem of establishing an ecumenical contact with the Christians who do not belong to any of the Churches and ecclesial communities created by the Reformation of the 16th century remains an open one. I am thinking of those who are sometimes called 'conservative Evangelicals,' for example, pentecostals, the Seventh-day Adventists, and others. As a result of their fanaticism and their refusal of any form of institution, they often are considered as sects. They represent a large and growing group of Christians. In Latin America they constitute between 80 and 90% of the non-Catholic Christians. Even after the integration of the International Missionary Council into the World Council of Churches, the latter still does not include more than about one third of all Protestant missionary activities, largely because of the missions of these independent groups" (*Information Service,* no. 9 [1970]: 7).

David du Plessis read this article and, remembering the visits of Ray Bringham in Rome a few months earlier, wrote Cardinal Willebrands in June 1970 and requested that a dialogue be established. Willebrands responded favorably, suggesting that there be a "small, informal and private meeting in September to explore whether it is possible to have such a dialogue, and if so, what the method might be." The first preliminary discussion was held in Sept. 1970. After two days of meetings, they decided to hold further exploratory talks.

A second preliminary meeting, held in June 1971, led to several important decisions. All parties expressed a unanimous desire to enter into dialogue. They selected a steering committee to select topics for discussion and to administrate the deliberations. And they agreed to meet five times over the next three years with six to eight persons on each team.

The steering committee met in Rome in Oct. 1971 to work out details in a third and final preliminary discussion. They agreed that two cochairpersons would moderate the Dialogue, Kilian McDonnell for the Roman Catholics and David du Plessis for the pentecostals. They would hold five meetings in as many years (a quinquennium). The pentecostal team would include classical pentecostals and charismatics (ᐟneo-pentecostals) from the historic Protestant churches. Theologians on each side would present papers on topics selected by the members of the steering committee. Each side would bring nine persons to the Dialogue table. At the end of each week of dialogue, they would produce an "agreed account" and prepare a press release.

The steering committee also outlined the reasons for establishing such a dialogue. Their seven-page report reads in part,

> In an age of spiritual crisis a dialogue on spirituality seems much in place, especially since such a dialogue is concerned with the centrality of prayer. . . . It is therefore not inappropriate that prayer, spirituality and theological reflection be shared concerns at the international level in the form of a dialogue between the Secretariat for Promoting Christian Unity and pentecostal Churches and participants in the charismatic movement within the Protestant and Anglican Churches.

The report went on to explain that the Dialogue would "give special attention to the meaning for the Church to fullness of life in the Holy Spirit." The desire was to "share in the reality of the mystery of Christ and the Church, to build a united Christian testimony, to indicate in what manner the sharing of truth makes it possible for us Roman Catholics and Pentecostals to grow together." A significant objective was for the Dialogue to serve as an exchange of information "rather than action." The Dialogue was not to "concern itself with the problems of imminent structural union but with unity in prayer and common witness" (*New Covenant* [1972], 6–7).

2. First Quinquennium (1972–76).

The first series of discussions has been well documented in Arnold Bittlinger's *Papst und Pfingstler* (1978). The "agreed accounts" and final report can be found in *Presence, Power, Praise; Pneuma;* and *Deepening Communion.* Most of the theological papers from these years were published in *One in Christ,* a British Roman Catholic ecumenical journal.

The deliberations for the five years touched the concerns of the charismatic renewal, which was at its peak. In this first series, the Dialogue covered a range of topics including "the scriptural basis for fullness of life in the Spirit, the relation of baptism in the Holy Spirit to Christian initiation, the role of the gifts in the mystical tradition, the charismatic dimensions and structures of sacramental and of ecclesial life, psychological and sociological dimensions, prayer and worship, common witness, and evangelism" (McDonnell, 1980, 3:373).

At the end of the Quinquennium several topics were suggested for further discussion, most of which were presented in the second five-year series. The final report made it clear that the conclusions reached did not necessarily reflect the official teaching of the Roman Catholic Church or the classical pentecostal churches. The report bound neither side to the theological positions expressed. Rather, the reports were portrayed as "the result of serious study by responsible persons who submit[ted] the reports to the churches 'for suitable use and reaction'" (McDonnell, 1980, 3:376).

3. Second Quinquennium (1977–82).

John Cardinal Willebrands authorized a second series of discussions in Aug. 1976. While serving as a missionary of the ᐟAssemblies of God in Belgium, ᐟJerry L. Sandidge completed a Ph.D. dissertation on the work of the second Quinquennium (and parts of the third) at the University of Leuven. It was published as *The Roman Catholic–Pentecostal*

Dialogue (1977–1982): A Study in Developing Ecumenism (1987).

The first Quinquennium had included persons involved in the pentecostal movement as well as those in the charismatic renewal in the historic churches—Anglican, Baptist, Lutheran, Orthodox, Presbyterian, and others. After some discussion it was decided that for the second Quinquennium, only classical pentecostals would participate. There were at least three reasons for this change. First, Roman Catholics wanted specifically to engage members of the worldwide pentecostal movement. Second, a number of national or international dialogues already existed between Roman Catholics and the various non-Roman churches represented in the charismatic renewal. Third, the pentecostals wanted to involve a broader spectrum of pentecostal denominations in the Dialogue process.

During this Quinquennium, David du Plessis introduced the idea of "observers" to the Dialogue. His intention was to get word of the Dialogue more widely spread among pentecostals. The larger the number of people who saw the discussion firsthand, he argued, the more the process would find support. In order for the pentecostals not to dominate the discussion, up to six pentecostal observers, in addition to the nine participants, would be invited. They would not participate directly in the plenary conversations. They would be limited to "absorbing" the Dialogue process.

The Dialogue was scheduled to meet Oct. 16–20, 1978, but the death of Pope John Paul I on Sept. 28 led to its cancellation. Karol Cardinal Wojtyla was elected Pope ›John Paul II on Oct. 16, the day the Dialogue was to have begun. This break led to some changes in the way the first year of the Quinquennium was conducted and the process used during the remaining years of the Dialogue.

In 1979 Kilian McDonnell offered a change in methodology by introducing the use of "hard questions" designed to elicit the underlying theological issues. This procedure proved highly successful, moving subsequent discussions more effectively into the substantive issues raised in the theological presentations.

While the work of the second Quinquennium generally went well, it was clear that the Dialogue was somewhat scattered in its focus. Too many papers made it impossible to carry on deep discussions on any one theme. A total of 16 theological papers were represented during this Quinquennium. They covered topics ranging from speaking in tongues, faith and experience, hermeneutics, healing, tradition, the church as communion, and Mary, to the ministry. Several of these papers were published in *One in Christ* between 1983 and 1985.

This round of discussions was also hampered by the attempts of at least one dominant world pentecostal leader to blunt its effectiveness. The secular press did not help the Dialogue. They frequently reported the facts in a manner intended to shock and attract readers. Jerry L. Sandidge, a member of the Dialogue for several years, was given an ultimatum. Either he had to leave the Dialogue or lose his missionary appointment. In the end, he returned to the United States but remained on the Dialogue. Even so, the report for this series ended on a note of optimism:

> The members of the Dialogue have experienced mutual respect and acceptance, hoping that the major points of difference will provide an occasion for continuing dialogue to our mutual enrichment. It is the consensus of the participants that the Dialogue should continue in this same spirit. Every effort will be made to encourage opportunities for similar bilateral theological conversation at the local level. The Dialogue was to be affirmed as an ongoing instrument of communication. (*Information Service*, no. 55 [1984])

4. Third Quinquennium (1985–89).

At the close of the second series of discussions, the steering committee decided to take a brief break to assimilate and reflect on what had been accomplished by its work. The break would allow time for the various papers and reports to be published, and both teams could familiarize themselves with the documents.

Kilian McDonnell and David J. du Plessis had served as the chairpersons of the Dialogue for a decade, and the health of Du Plessis had begun to decline. At a 1983 steering committee meeting in Rome, both cochairs resigned but were encouraged to stay on the committee in an emeritus status. ›Justus T. du Plessis, the Ecumenical Liaison of the Apostolic Faith Mission (AFM) of South Africa, and a younger brother to David, succeeded his brother as the pentecostal chair. He had been part of the Dialogue since 1974 and had served on the steering committee. His leadership would guarantee continuity with the spirit that David du Plessis had brought to the task, but he would bring new gifts to the table as well. After considerable review, the Roman Catholic side returned to Kilian McDonnell and asked him to remain as cochair.

The steering committee held a second meeting in Rome in 1984 and decided to begin a new series of discussions in May 1985. More changes were made in the working style of the Dialogue. The steering committee decided that the topics would move from "Communion of Saints" (1985) to "The Holy Spirit and the New Testament Vision of Koinonia" (1986); "Koinonia Church and Sacrament" (1987); and "Koinonia and Baptism" (1988). The 1989 session was used to prepare the final report for the Quinquennium.

The Secretariat for Promoting Christian Unity took the opportunity to make changes in its team. With the naming of Justus du Plessis as cochair, the pentecostal side of the steering committee also made changes in how its team would be constructed. It invited a mix of participants, ranging from well-trained theologians to local pastors and denominational leaders.

Denominations were invited to send official delegates. During the third Quinquennium, the Dialogue succeeded in gaining official delegations from the Apostolic Church of the Faith in Jesus Christ (Mexico), Apostolic Faith Mission of South Africa, Church of God (Cleveland, TN), Church of God of Prophecy, Independent Assemblies of God International, the International Church of the Foursquare Gospel, and the International Evangelical Church. Pentecostal leaders from the British Isles, the Netherlands, and Sweden also attended with the approval of their churches, though not necessarily in an official capacity.

Previously, news of the work of the Dialogue had been consistently suppressed by large portions of the popular pentecostal press, but with the involvement of members of the pentecostal academic community in the discussion, news was circulated broadly in the pentecostal community. The full reports of the first three Quinquennia were collected and published for the first time in a pentecostal organ, *Pneuma: The Journal of the Society for Pentecostal Studies* 12:2 (1990).

A Jesuit priest, Paul D. Lee, made this round of the Dialogue the subject of his Ph.D. dissertation at the Pontifical University in Rome in 1994. It was published under the title *Pentecostal Ecclesiology in Roman Catholic–Pentecostal Dialogue: A Catholic Reading of the Third Quinquennium (1985–1989)*. His work was joined by the Ph.D. dissertation completed at the University of Helsinki by Veli-Matti Kärkkäinen, the Finnish pentecostal minister and principal of the Iso Kirja College in Keuruu, Finland. *Spiritus ubi vult spirat: Pneumatology in Roman Catholic–Pentecostal Dialogue (1972–1989)* assessed the first three Quinquennia of the Dialogue.

David J. du Plessis died in Feb. 1987, but the instrument he had set in place to carry on the Dialogue continued to function well after his death.

5. Fourth Round (1990–97).

Discussions in the third Quinquennium had concentrated on the nature of the church as *koinonia*. Among the points on which the participants agreed was the fact that while their basis for agreeing might be different, pentecostals and Roman Catholics already enjoyed a *real though imperfect koinonia*. This fact raised questions about how Roman Catholics and pentecostals treat one another.

As the discussion on *koinonia* came to a close, debate arose over a suitable topic for the fourth round of discussions. Jerry Sandidge made an impassioned plea for the topic of "Evangelization, Proselytism, and Common Witness." Despite the volatility of the topic and its potential to damage or destroy the Dialogue altogether, the teams agreed to pursue it. Participants agreed that if they shared a common *koinonia*, charges of persecution, oppression, proselytism, and the potential for common witness would have to be investigated. This would prove to be a difficult undertaking. Stakes were high.

The discussions had barely begun when in 1991 Justus du Plessis announced his retirement as pentecostal cochair. Cecil M. Robeck Jr., a member of the pentecostal steering committee since 1985, an AG minister, and a professor of church history and ecumenics at Fuller Theological Seminary, was asked to serve as the new pentecostal cochair. These years were difficult because of the untimely deaths of Jerry L. Sandidge, cosecretary for the pentecostals, and Fr. Heinz-Albert Raem, cosecretary for the Roman Catholics.

The discussion began with a study of the history of mission and evangelization in the two traditions (1990). It explored the biblical and systematic foundations for evangelization (1991), the relationship between evangelization and culture (1992), evangelization and social justice (1993), and proselytism and evangelization (1994). It ended by reflecting on the potential for common witness (1995). Because of the complexity of these issues and continuing concerns over poor Roman Catholic–pentecostal relationships in various parts of the world, the teams spent 1996 and 1997 writing and evaluating their work together. There were sessions in which tears flowed freely, stories were told with passion and pathos, tables were pounded, words were critiqued, honed, and carefully defined. Dialogue members were given an audience with Pope John Paul II in Rome on June 31, 1997. Acting as spokesperson for the Dialogue, Robeck commended their work on "Evangelization, Proselytism, and Common Witness" to "His Holiness", and the Dialogue celebrated its 25th Anniversary.

The Vatican released the report in July 1998 in English and French. In 1999 it was published in the *Asian Journal of Pentecostal Studies,* in a Portuguese edition in Brazil, and in *Pneuma.* Staff at the University of Salamanca have also completed a Spanish-language version of the report soon to be published. Veli-Matti Kärkkäinen made the work of this round of discussions the subject of his postdoctoral *Habilitation* at the University of Helsinki in 1998. It was titled "Ad ultimum terrae: Evangelization, Proselytism and Common Witness in the Roman Catholic–Pentecostal Dialogue 1990–1997" and was published in 1999.

6. Fifth Round (1998–2002).

The previous two reports raised further questions for the Dialogue. Even if it were possible for pentecostals and Roman Catholics to begin to work through issues related to persecution and proselytism, it appeared that they disagreed on when and how one became a Christian. Who is it legitimate to evangelize? How are the "unchurched" best defined? How are people best formed as Christians? What role does popular religion play in these discussions? Is it a useful tool, or does it merely confuse the issue?

In the early 1990s, Kilian McDonnell had coauthored a volume called *Christian Initiation and Baptism in the Holy Spirit: Evidence from the First Eight Centuries.* It had been written in response to questions raised by the pentecostals, and he asked that his response be assessed. As a result, in 1997 the steering committee decided that the Dialogue should give attention both to biblical and patristic sources. It chose as the general topic for the fifth round "Conversion and Christian Initiation in the Early Church."

The Dialogue began its work in 1998 on the topic "Christian Initiation and the Baptism in the Holy Spirit: Biblical and Patristic Perspectives." This was followed by a discussion on "Faith and Christian Initiation" (1999). The topics projected for future treatment in this round include "Conversion and Christian Initiation" (2000), "Christian Experience in Community" (2001), and "Catechesis and Formation in Community" (2002). The Dialogue teams were consulted and asked that the subject of charism/charismata be addressed at some point as well.

7. Evaluation.

In its first quarter century of existence, a number of important lessons have been learned. First, this Dialogue is unique in the history of modern ecumenical discussion. It is one of the oldest continuing dialogues in which the Roman Catholic Church has been involved. It is the only dialogue in which structural union is stated not to be the ultimate goal. It has provided a model for other dialogues as well (►Dialogue, Reformed-Pentecostal). But it is also a dialogue that is taking place between a movement of churches (the pentecostals) and a denomination (the Roman Catholics). This fact sets up the discussion in ways that are not always equal.

One of the ways this unevenness or inequality expresses itself results from the fact that the Roman Catholic Church has a well-developed and broadly documented theological tradition from which to draw, whereas the pentecostals do not. It has been easier for the Catholics to speak with one mind than it has for the pentecostals to do so—indeed, some pentecostals, notably the large block of ►Oneness pentecostals, are not currently represented in the Dialogue.

A second difference manifests itself in the methods that are employed. Pentecostals often approach theological issues from a personal witness or pastoral dimension. Testimony, oral theology, song, and narrative approaches are essential parts of pentecostalism. Roman Catholics on the other hand, are practiced in developing precise theological formulations and tend to be less comfortable with testimony and the sharing of personal thoughts and feelings. These differences have sometimes led to misunderstanding. The very fact that the Dialogue manifests itself in tightly argued theological papers and reports that reflect this way of thinking suggests that pentecostal participants are required to work more strenuously than their Catholic counterparts because the Dialogue is conducted using unfamiliar methodologies. More importantly, it may explain one rea-

son that so few pentecostals outside the Dialogue take the time to understand the discussions.

Third, the two sides sometimes employ different hermeneutical starting points. As a result, the ways in which they approach certain biblical texts differ. Roman Catholics are frequently trained in the historical-critical method of biblical exegesis while many pentecostals do not understand this approach or are skeptical of its ultimate usefulness. The result is that the two sides have not always understood each other very well when discussing biblical themes, and this has diminished the value of the exchange.

Finally, the two sides often desire to emphasize different things in the same walk of faith. Pentecostals generally emphasize spiritual experience, crisis moments of faith, and the power of the Holy Spirit. Roman Catholics speak more of the role of the sacraments, the life of the church, and the Trinitarian dimension of the Holy Spirit. The crisis paradigm of sanctification is followed largely by pentecostals, while the growth paradigm is the approach of Roman Catholics.

On the other hand, the very inequality that exists between the teams challenges the pentecostals to develop a more substantive theological tradition of their own. These discussions reveal the diversity of the movement. But they also reveal both the strengths and the lacunae that one can find when reading the various pentecostal theologies.

It also must be recognized that this Dialogue has always received official support and representation from the Roman Catholic Church. This is not the case among the pentecostals. A few pentecostal groups have embraced this Dialogue and its work. Some others have chosen to treat it with benign neglect. Still others have worked tirelessly to put an end to it by calling for the discipline of its participants or suppressing news of its work among their constituents. These facts have taken a personal toll on many of the participants, and they have led some pentecostals and Roman Catholics who have not had the opportunity to evaluate the fruit of the Dialogue themselves to question the value of the Dialogue.

If this is to change, it is essential that pentecostals approach dialogue with a thorough understanding of the Roman Catholic Church from a post–Vatican II perspective and not from the stereotypes of Rome that are rooted in the 16th century. The entry of the Roman Catholic Church into the modern world came substantially through this council, and the church deserves credit for the growth that it has made, particularly in matters such as justification by faith. It is equally the case that Roman Catholics need to reassess how they view pentecostals. Do they lump them into the larger phenomenon of fundamentalism and write them off as simply members of a "religious right"? Do they view them as fanatics with no theological ground to stand on? Or are they willing to explore the beliefs and practices that pentecostals hold dear?

Admittedly, there are many people alive today in different parts of the world who view the Roman Catholic Church as an oppressive body that is guilty of persecuting them. Their testimony must be heard and addressed. But it is also the case that many pentecostals have had nothing but good and positive relations with Roman Catholics through this century, and their testimony must not be drowned out. Both testimonies are of value, and both may be useful in bringing greater unity to the church.

On the other hand, many Roman Catholics look at pentecostals as interlopers and proselytizers in their land. Their presence is not welcome, and these Roman Catholics treat pentecostals as members of some "sect," with all the negative connotations that term carries. Other Roman Catholics, especially those who have entered into charismatic renewal, have many good things to say on behalf of pentecostals. But this disparity is part of the call for greater discussion between Christians of all kinds. The fact that pentecostals have not yet learned how to talk peacefully and publicly among themselves on such a topic is a sign that greater Christian love is needed on all sides.

Roman Catholics come to the Dialogue with more experience in theological and ecumenical dialogue. For pentecostals this is a new experience. The pool of participants needs to be drawn from where pentecostals live, and thus far only a few have learned to dialogue with skill. It is also the case that Roman Catholics come with far fewer fears than those embraced by prophecy-conscious pentecostals. This fact needs to be understood and a long-term commitment lived out that will guarantee the ultimate success of the Dialogue.

The fruit of this Dialogue must not be expected immediately in terms of the unity of the church. Great patience is needed. Each side is growing in acceptance, understanding, and respect for the other. In spite of this slow growth, recent events in which Roman Catholic leaders have intervened on behalf of pentecostals may be attributed, in part, to the foundation laid by this Dialogue. The Dialogue has aided the president of the Pontifical Council for Promoting Christian Unity to condemn the use of sectarian language when speaking about pentecostals. Pentecostals were even invited to participate in the services surrounding the opening of the great doors on the Roman basilicas in Jan. 2000, a privilege reserved only for members of churches and ecclesial communions. One thing is sure: the encounters provided by the Dialogue have been lessons in spiritual growth for participants on both sides, and the fruit of their labor is only just emerging as the church begins its third millennium.

■ **Bibliography:** *Asian Journal of Pentecostal Theology* 2:1 (1, 1999), 105–51 ■ A. Bittlinger, *Papst und Pfingstler: Der römisch katholisch-Pfingstliche Dialog und seine ökumenische Relevanz* (1978) ■ D. L. Cole, "Pentecostal Koinonia: An Emerging Ecumenical Ecclesiology among Pentecostals" (diss., Fuller Theol. Sem., 1998) ■ T. R. Crowe, *Pentecostal Unity: Recurring Frustration and Enduring Hopes* (1993) ■ J. Dart, "Theologians Call for Church Truce in Proselytizing," *Los Angeles Times* (July 15, 1998), B4–5 ■ *Diálogo Católico-Pentecostal: Evangelização, Proselitismo e Testemunho Comum* (1999) ■ D. du Plessis and B. Slosser, *A Man Called Mr. Pentecost* (1977) ■ P. Duprey, "L'Eglise catholique et le dialogue oecumenique," *Episkepsis*, 10, 212 (June 15, 1979) ■ N. Ehrenstrom and G. Gassman, *Confessions in Dialogue* (1975) ■ "Evangelization, Proselytism and Common Witness" *Information Service*, no. 97 (1998/I–II), 38–56 ■ M. Harper, *Three Sisters* (1979) ■ *Information Service*, no. 9 (1, 1970): 7 ■ ibid., no. 32 (3, 1976): 32–37 ■ ibid., no. 55 (2–3, 1984): 72–80 ■ P. D. Hocken, "Dialogue Extraordinary," *One in Christ* 24 (1988) ■ idem, "Ecumenical Dialogue: The Importance of Dialogue with Evangelicals and Pentecostals," *One in Christ* 30 (1994) ■ W. J. Hollenweger, *Pentecostalism: Origins and Developments Worldwide* (1997), 165–80 ■ *Service d'information*, no. 97 (1998/I–II), pp. 38–57 ■ V. M. Kärkkäinen, *Ad ultimum terrae: Evangelization, Proselytism and Common Witness in the Roman Catholic–Pentecostal Dialogue 1990–1997* (1999) ■ idem, *Spiritus ubi vult spirat: Pneumatology in Roman Catholic–Pentecostal Dialogue (1972–1989)* ■ P. D. Lee, *Pneumatological Ecclesiology in the Roman Catholic–Pentecostal Dialogue: A Catholic Reading of the Third Quinquennium (1985–1989)* (1994) ■ K. McDonnell, "After a Church Burning in Ecuador, Evangelicals and Catholics Reach Accord," *Pneuma* 20 (1998) ■ idem, "Can Classical Pentecostals and Roman Catholics Engage in Common Witness?" *Journal of Pentecostal Theology* 7 (1995) ■ idem, "Classical Pentecostal/Roman Catholic Dialogue: Hopes and Possibilities," in R. P. Spittler, ed., *Perspectives on the New Pentecostalism* (1976) ■ idem, "The Experiential and the Social: New Models from the Pentecostal/Roman Catholic Dialogue," *One in Christ* 9 (1973) ■ idem, "Five Defining Issues: The International Classical Pentecostal–Roman Catholic Dialogue," *Pneuma* 17 (1995) ■ idem, "Improbable Conversations: The International Classical Pentecostal/Roman Catholic Dialogue," *Pneuma* 17 (1995) ■ idem, "Pentecostals and Catholics on Evangelism and Sheep-Stealing," *America* 180 (3, 1999) ■ idem, ed., *Presence, Power, Praise: Documents on the Charismatic Renewal*, 3 vols. (1980) ■ H. Meyer and L. Vischer, eds., *Growth in Agreement* (1984) ■ "The Pentecostal/Catholic Dialogue," *Information Service*, no. 91 (1996/I–II), 42–44 ■ *Pneuma* 12:2 (Fall 1990) ■ ibid., 21:1 (Spring 1999) ■ J. F. Puglisi and S. J. Voicu, *A Bibliography of Interchurch and Interconfessional Theological Dialogues* (1984) ■ S. Rabey, "Conversation or Competition?" *Christianity Today* 42 (10, Sept. 7, 1998) ■ C. M. Robeck Jr., "David du Plessis and the Challenge of Dialogue," *Pneuma* 9 (1, Spring 1987) ■ idem, "Do 'Good Fences Make Good Neighbors'? Evangelization, Proselytism, and Common Witness," *Asian Journal of Pentecostal Studies* 2:1 (1, 1999) ■ idem, "Evangelicals and Catholics Together," *One in Christ* 33 (2, 1997) ■ idem, "Evangelization or Proselytism of Hispanics? A Pentecostal Perspective," *Journal of Hispanic/Latino Theology*

4 (4, 1997) ■ idem, "Introductory Note," in W. G. Rusch and J. Gros, eds., *Deepening Communion: International Ecumenical Documents with Roman Catholic Participation* (Washington, DC: United States Catholic Conference, 1998), 363–65 ■ idem, "The International Roman Catholic–Pentecostal Dialogue: A Status Report," *National Association of Diocesan Ecumenical Officers Newsletter* (Summer 1988) ■ idem, "Les pentecôtistes et l'unité visible de l'Eglise," *Unité des Chrétiens* 94 (4, 1994) ■ idem, "Mission and the Issue of Proselytism," *International Bulletin of Missionary Research* 20 (1, 1996) ■ idem, "Pentecostalism and Ecumenical Dialogue: A Potential Agenda," *Ecumenical Trends* 16:11 (12, 1987), 185–88 ■ idem, "Pentecostals and Visible Church Unity," *One World* 192 (1/2, 1994) ■ idem, "Specks and Logs, Catholics and Pentecostals," *Pneuma* 12 (2, Fall 1990) ■ idem, "Taking Stock," *One World* 210 (11, 1995) ■ idem, "What Catholics Should Know about Pentecostals," *The Catholic World* 238, no. 1428 (11/12, 1995) ■ idem, "Pentecostals and Ecumenism in a Pluralistic World," in D. Peterson, M. W. Dempster, and B. Klaus, eds., *The Globalization of Pentecostalism* (1999) ■ idem, "Taking Stock of Pentecostalism: The Personal Reflections of a Retiring Editor," *Pneuma* 15 (1, Spring 1993) ■ idem, "When Being a 'Martyr' Is Not Enough: Catholics and Pentecostals," *Pneuma* 21 (1, Spring 1999) ■ C. M. Robeck Jr. and J. L. Sandidge, "The Ecclesiology of Koinonia and Baptism: A Pentecostal Perspective," *Journal of Ecumenical Studies* 27 (3, Summer 1990) ■ W. G. Rusch and J. Gros, eds., *Deepening Communion: International Ecumenical Documents with Roman Catholic Participation* (1998), 367–422 ■ J. L. Sandidge, *Roman Catholic/Pentecostal Dialogue [1977–1982]: A Study in Developing Ecumenism* 2 vols. (1987) ■ idem, "Roman Catholic/Pentecostal Dialogue: A Contribution to Christian Unity," *Pneuma* 7 (Spring 1985) ■ *Documentation Catholique* (1972–83) ■ *Irenikon* (1972–1981) ■ *Service d'information* (1972–81) ■ *Unité de Chrétiens* (1978–83) ■ "Vatican Enters Dialogue on Pentecostalism," *New Covenant* 7 (1, 1972).
■ C. M. Robeck Jr.; J. L. Sandidge

DIORIO, RALPH A. (1930–). Catholic priest with full-time healing ministry. A second-generation Italian-American, DiOrio was ordained priest for the Scalabrini Fathers, a religious order of Italian origin. In 1968 he transferred to the diocese of Worcester, MA. DiOrio's first contacts with charismatic renewal were in 1976, when he attended healing services led by Fr. Edward McDonough. There he experienced God's power flowing through him for healing, a ministry that developed during two years in St. John's parish, Worcester. In 1979 DiOrio was authorized by his bishop to move his Apostolate of Prayer for Healing Evangelism to Leicester, MA. The name has since been changed to the Apostolate of Divine Mercy and Healing. DiOrio's main ministry outside his home base is in officially sponsored healing services, diocesan rallies and parish missions, as well as pilgrimages. His story is told in *The Man Beneath the Gift* (1980); his other works include *Called to Heal* (1984), *A Miracle to Proclaim* (1984), *The Healing Power of Affirmation* (1985), and *Healing Love* (1987).   ■ P. D. Hocken

DISCERNMENT OF SPIRITS, GIFT OF The expression "discernment of spirits" *(diakriseis pneumatōn)* occurs in the Scriptures only in 1 Cor. 12:10. Its meaning can be understood only if viewed in the context of discernment as a whole. This article will discuss, first, general biblical teaching regarding discernment; second, the gift of discernment of spirits; and third, the ways in which this gift has been considered throughout the centuries to today.

I. GENERAL CONSIDERATIONS.

A. The Old Testament.

1. The Requirements of Faith.

Discernment is required, basically, because God calls humankind to a goal beyond itself. The response to this call is faith, a trusting and obedient commitment of oneself to God based on his solemn word of promise. It is imperative that each person, and God's people as a whole, be able to discern God's voice directing him or her to this goal and to distinguish his voice from Satan's or from the illusory desires of the human heart.

2. Discerning Prophecy.

A prophet is someone called by God and entrusted with a message for God's people. Since this word reveals God's thoughts concerning his people (Amos 3:7), it is extremely important to be able to distinguish true from false prophecy. The criteria for this discernment were developed particularly in the Deuteronomic tradition and in Jeremiah (Guillet, 3:1225–26). (a) A prophet who prophesies woe may be believed, but one who prophesies peace must await the fulfillment of his prophecy (Deut. 18:21–22; Jer. 28:8–9). This criterion is modified in the new covenant because of the presence of the fulfillment of all God's promises (see Mark 1:14–15). (b) A true prophet works signs as part of his credentials (Jer. 28:16–17), but this must be accompanied by true doctrine (Deut. 13:1–3), an upright life (Jer. 23:13–15), and a pure intention to proclaim God's word (Mic. 3:5–7). (c) Finally, the criterion to which the prophets themselves make appeal is their personal experience of being called by God (Isa. 6; Jer. 1; Ezek. 1–3; Hos. 1–3; Amos 7:14–15).

3. Discerning the Human Heart.

Jeremiah declared the heart "deceitful above all things," "beyond cure," and known only to the Lord (Jer. 17:9–10). The Wisdom tradition applied itself to the work of discerning the ways of the heart and of teaching men how to walk in the light of the "secret purposes of God" (Wis. 2:22). Qumran, despite its dualistic tendency, perpetuated this practical approach in the light of prophetic teaching and was a factor in the Jewish matrix of Christianity that rendered the early Christians sensitive to the need to discern the movements of the heart in order to make a judgment. The Qumran Manual of Discipline (3:13–14) says that the leader must learn and teach others "the nature of all the children of men according to the kind of spirit they possess, the signs identifying their works," and the ultimate end of their actions. Not only at Qumran, but also elsewhere, we have indications that the Jewish people had been rendered sensitive to the need to look into the human heart to discern its dominant influence.

B. The New Testament.

1. The Synoptic Gospels and Acts.

We frequently read of Jesus' discernment in the synoptic Gospels. The better reading of Matt. 9:4 speaks of his "seeing the thoughts" of his adversaries, and several texts speak of his knowing their thoughts and interior debates (Mark 2:8/Luke 4:22; Matt. 22:18/Mark 10:21/Luke 20:23; et al.). He not only confronts evil spirits and drives them out, he is able to see behind their strategy of openly acknowledging him to be Son of God in order to discredit him (Mark 1:25/Luke 4:35; Mark 1:34/Luke 4:41).

On another level the very presence of Jesus and his activity of preaching and healing compel his contemporaries to discern: "If by the Spirit/finger of God I cast out demons, then the kingdom of God has come upon you" (Matt. 12:28/Luke 11:20).

Luke portrays the disciples as continuing the above two aspects of Jesus' ministry. Both Peter and Paul are endowed with the capacity to discern what is in the heart: Acts 5:3 (Ananias); 8:23 (Simon); 13:6 (Elymas); 16:16–18 (the young woman at Philippi).

The witness of the preaching and of the miracles of the disciples also forces people to discernment: "Know this, you and everyone else in Israel: It is by the name of Jesus Christ of Nazareth, whom you crucified but whom God raised from the dead, that this man stands before you healed" (Acts 4:10).

2. The Pauline Writings.

Paul uses two different verbs to designate what we call "discern": *dokimazein* ("put to the test, evaluate") and *diakrinein* (in the sense we are considering here, the word corresponds to our English "differentiate" or "judge as to worth"). Continuing the OT notion of the need for a pure faith in order to discern the call of God, Paul speaks of "evaluating" what God's will is, what is more pleasing to him (Rom. 12:2; Phil. 1:10; et al.). Believers should also evaluate themselves (1 Cor. 11:28), their works (Gal. 4:6), and their faith (2 Cor. 13:5), just as God evaluates them (1 Thess. 2:4; 1 Cor. 3:13; et al.; see also 1 Peter 1:7).

In 1 Cor. 11:29 Paul speaks of those who eat and drink judgment on themselves, "not discerning *[diakrinōn]* the body of the Lord," and he goes on to say in v. 31 that if we were to

judge ourselves as to our worth *(diekrinomen),* we would not be judged *(ekrinometha).* (For the enigmatic Rom. 14:1, one may consult the commentaries.)

3. The Johannine Writings.

Except for 1 John 4:1, which we will consider shortly, neither of the two terms characteristic of Paul occurs in the body of writings associated with the name of John. On the other hand, no other NT writings so accent the fact that the presence of Jesus forces people to discern and decide: "For judgment I have come into this world, so that the blind will see and those who see will become blind" (John 9:39). In addition, criteria are offered by which the world will be able to discern the disciples of Jesus: "By this all men will know that you are my disciples" (John 13:35). In 1 John the disciples themselves are given the signs by which they may know that they have eternal life (1 John 5:13).

4. Summary.

The presence and activity of the risen Jesus make the need for faith discernment all the more urgent, and thus the Spirit must help us know what God has given us (see 1 Cor. 2:12). This work of the Spirit will confess Jesus (1 Cor. 12:3; Rev. 19:10), will build up the community (1 Cor. 12:7, 26; 14:4), will produce genuine signs along with the peace, patience, and humility of a true disciple (Rom. 14:17–18; 2 Cor. 12:12; 1 Thess. 1:4–5), and by the constant exercise of their faculties under the influence of his gifts, he will enable the mature to discern "good and evil" (Heb. 5:14).

II. THE DISCERNMENT OF SPIRITS.

A. The Terminology.

Three NT texts speak of evaluating or discerning in the specific case of prophecy, and the word "spirit" *(pneuma)* occurs in each case. In 1 Thess. 5:19–22 Paul says, "Do not put out the Spirit's fire; do not treat prophecies with contempt. Test [*dokimazete*] everything. Hold on to the good. Avoid every kind of evil." Paul is enunciating general norms though he has prophecy in mind in a special way throughout this passage (Bruce, 125–27). In telling the Thessalonians to "evaluate" everything, he is implying that there is something of great worth in genuine prophecy.

The same two key words occur in 1 John 4:1–3. The writer tells his people not to put faith in "every spirit" but rather to "test the spirits" *(dokimazete ta pneumata),* giving as his reason "because many false prophets have gone out into the world." This same use of "spirit" *(pneuma)* to designate prophecy is found in 2 Thess. 2:2. In such cases the presupposition is that the source of what is proclaimed is spiritual but that not everything spiritual is of God. Both the source and the fruits of this spiritual impulse must be tested/evaluated: "Every spirit that acknowledges that Jesus Christ has come in the flesh is from God" (1 John 4:3). This is the criterion by which true and false prophetic spirits may be distinguished.

The verbal and conceptual constellations in the two previously considered texts throw light on the use of the phrase "discernments of spirits" found in the list of "manifestations" of the Spirit in 1 Cor. 12:8–10. Many authors have pointed to a certain logic in this list: first, the "words" of wisdom and knowledge; then "faith" and its outworking in healings and miracles; then prophecy and its control, "discernments of spirits"; then tongues and its control, interpretation. Primarily, then, the gift of discernment of spirits is the Spirit-conferred capacity to judge the origin and content of prophecy.

While Paul's immediate concern in this passage is prophecy, it is legitimate to apply his terminology to the gift of discerning the origin and content of any spiritual manifestation. Under this aspect, any of the gifts can be called a "spirit," which Paul himself does in 1 Cor. 14:12. The use of *diakrisis* here rather than words related to *dok-* was probably dictated by two reasons. First, the capacity Paul emphasizes is distinguishment and judgment rather than testing and evaluating. He retains this terminology in 1 Cor. 14:29: "Let the others discern *[diakrinetōsan]*." Second, nouns such as *dokimasia* or *dokimē* refer more to the test itself or its result rather than to the ability to evaluate. The use of the plural here ("discernments") alludes to the multiple exercise of the gift not only by one person on many occasions but also by the many persons on specific occasions.

B. The Subject and Object of Discernment.

1. The Subject of Discernment.

Discernment of spirits as a gift of the Holy Spirit resides in an individual person, yet its exercise is presumed to be collaborative as well. Thus, the instructions in 1 Thess. 5:21 and 1 John 4:1 are addressed to the whole community, and 1 Cor. 14:29 speaks of "the others" discerning what the prophets say. The local church, living by the Spirit, is able to recognize his gifts in their midst, including that of discerning spirits. Individuals who possessed this gift in varying degrees would have been expected to make a corporate judgment regarding the source and doctrinal authenticity of prophecy and other gifts. This is the most probable meaning of the enigmatic statement in 1 Cor. 14:32 that the *pneumata* (spiritual activities) of the prophets are subject to the prophets (who discern).

2. The Object of Discernment.

The answer to the question of what is discerned may be brief. As in the OT, the two primary areas of discernment are the origin of prophecy (and other spiritual manifestations) and the movements of the human heart. Discernment differs from prudence in that, although the criteria of love, service, peace, order, etc., are important corroborations of discernment, its essence lies in being able to make out the source of

spiritual activity (Martin, 18:58). Each person must accordingly judge himself/herself (1 Cor. 11:28, 31), and those who have the gift and spiritual authority must also discern those spiritual manifestations that affect the life of the community.

III. DISCERNMENT OF SPIRITS IN THE HISTORY OF THE CHURCH.

While not ignoring the role of discerning spiritual manifestations in others, most early Christian teaching on discernment of spirits dealt with identifying the source of movements within the individual heart. The possible sources are four: God, an angel, oneself, or an evil spirit. Basing themselves on the list of "thoughts" *(dialogismoi)* in Mark 7:21–22, the Christians of the first four centuries developed a very refined spiritual anthropology that has formed the basis of personal discernment to our own day (Bardy et al., 3:1247–81).

The age of enlightenment with its "closed system" of thinking tended even in religious circles to reduce discernment to prudence or character evaluation. With the abundant reappearance of spiritual manifestations, the true role of discernment has become once again apparent. Because the Spirit of God moves in the human heart, bestowing his gifts, especially that of prophecy, and because these can be counterfeited by Satan and by the human spirit, we see the need once again to pray for the gift of the discernment of spirits so that we may know "those things given to us by God" (1 Cor. 2:12).

See also GIFTS OF THE SPIRIT.

■ **Bibliography:** G. Bardy, F. Vandenbroucke, and J. Pegon, "Discernement des esprits," *Dictionnaire de spiritualité* (1957), 3:1247–81 ■ A. Bittlinger, *Gifts and Graces: A Commentary on 1 Corinthians 12–14* (1967) ■ F. F. Bruce, *1 & 2 Thessalonians* (1982) ■ J. D. G. Dunn, *Jesus and the Spirit* (1975) ■ G. D. Fee, *The First Epistle to the Corinthians* (1987) ■ J. Guillet, "Discernement des esprits dans l'Ecriture," *Dictionnaire de spiritualité* (1957), 3:1222–47 ■ A. Linford, *A Course of Study on Spiritual Gifts* (2d ed., n.d.) ■ F. Martin, "Le discernement communautaire," *Animation spirituelle de la communauté, Collection "Donum Dei," Cahiers de la CRC* (1971), 18:45–63.
■ F. Martin

DISCIPLESHIP MOVEMENT See SHEPHERDING MOVEMENT.

DISPENSATIONALISM Dispensationalism has not been part of the major theological traditions of Reformed and Wesleyan Christianity, although many of its advocates get their general orientation from one of these traditions. Nevertheless, the dispensational system has had a strong influence in the church and is widespread. It was popularized by John Nelson Darby's commentaries and has entered into millions of homes via the *Scofield Reference Bible* (1909). The system has been advocated by such prominent educational institutions as Moody Bible Institute and Dallas Theological Seminary. Lewis Sperry Chafer, the founder of Dallas Theological Seminary, claimed that his eight-volume *Systematic Theology* (1948) has the distinction of being unabridged, premillennial, and dispensational. In effect, dispensationalism is an interpretative scheme grafted onto the traditional body of Christian doctrine.

The interpretation of dispensationalism varies, but its basic assumption is that God deals with the human race in successive dispensations. According to the *Scofield Reference Bible*, "a dispensation is a period of time during which man is tested in respect to his obedience to some specific revelation of the will of God" (p. 5). Each dispensation has its point of beginning, its test, and its termination in judgment due to humanity's continual failure. Most dispensationalist interpreters identify seven dispensations: the dispensations of innocence, conscience, civil government, promise, law, grace, and the kingdom. Furthermore, dispensationalism makes a sharp distinction between Israel and the church, which represent essentially two peoples of God. The prophets of Israel did not foresee the church age, which is a "parenthetical" era.

Dispensationalism has influenced pentecostal theology, but the earliest pentecostal teachings were not tied directly to dispensationalism. From its inception, the modern pentecostal movement gave prominence to eschatology. Gerald T. Sheppard makes this point in his observation, "Pentecostals commonly thought of the twentieth-century outpouring of the Spirit as evidence of the 'latter rain' or at least as a sign of a 'last days' restoration of the Apostolic church prior to the return of Christ" (1984, 7). A strong eschatological perspective permeated the revival in 1901 in ▸Topeka, KS, and in 1906–09 at ▸Azusa Street. O. W. Orwig, who attended some of the Azusa Street meetings, recalled a decade later the principal themes of pentecostal preaching at the revival as "the teaching that the baptism in the Spirit was upon the sanctified, evidenced by speaking in tongues, however brief, as on the day of Pentecost.... The subject or doctrine, of divine healing received special attention.... Likewise was the doctrine of the premillennial coming of Christ ardently promulgated" (*The Weekly Evangel* [Mar. 18, 1986], 4).

Charles F. Parham, the leader of the pentecostal revival at Topeka, affirmed also that the prevailing mood of premillennialism was at the very heart of early pentecostalism.

Dispensationalism began to flourish with the rise of the pentecostal movement. Since pentecostals as a whole shared the premillennial vision of the future, dispensationalism with its intense emphasis on futuristic eschatology had a strong appeal to them. The statements of faith of pentecostal denominations such as the Church of God (Cleveland, TN), the Pentecostal Holiness Church, and the Assemblies of God commit them to premillennialism but not necessarily to dispensationalism. It has, however, been an easy exercise for many pentecostals to adopt essential aspects of the Scofieldian dispensational system because it provides a convenient method of organizing biblical history and teaches that it is possible to fit the full range of prophetic Scripture into something like a complicated puzzle.

Nevertheless, the marriage of the pentecostal emphasis to dispensationalism was strange in light of the dispensational assertion that the gifts of the Spirit, especially what has been called "the sensational gifts" or "sign gifts" (healing, faith, working of miracles, and tongues), were confined to the apostolic age. The dispensational teaching of the Scofieldian type that denies the possibility of a modern pentecostal experience ("cessationism") has been glossed over, with minor pentecostal adaptations, to allow for the continuation of all the spiritual gifts in the church today. Such accommodations have been made by pentecostals who saw the dispensational system as a helpful aid to emphasizing the premillennial second coming of Christ, the Rapture of the church, the seven years of the great Tribulation, the Millennium, and the cataclysmic Judgment that will mark the end of the present order.

Scofieldian dispensationalism maintains that the gifts of the Spirit, such as speaking in tongues and working of miracles, are not for the postapostolic age and that they should be forbidden because God no longer bestows such gifts. Pentecostals have taken exception to the dispensational teaching that "sign gifts" or "sensational gifts" granted to the apostolic church were temporary; nevertheless, the dispensational understanding of the church, as well as its eschatology, has influenced pentecostal theology.

For a number of years a standard textbook in a number of pentecostal Bible institutes and colleges was Myer Pearlman's *Knowing the Doctrines of the Bible* (1937). Pearlman's exposition of eschatology fits the dispensational vision of the future, but he does not make a sharp separation between Israel and the church. Contrary to dispensationalism, he sees real continuity between the congregation of Israel and the Christian church (348–49). Like Pearlman, other pentecostal writers, such as George L. Britt, Ralph M. Riggs, E. S. Williams, A. A. Ledford, and Ray H. Hughes, depend on a dispensational posture in both eschatology and ecclesiology (*Ages and Dispensations* [1949]). In agreement with the dispensational hermeneutic, Pearlman interprets some sections of the Bible as dealing with the nation of Israel and some others as being concerned with only the church. On the assumption that the church began at Pentecost, he argues against calling Israel the "church" and never describes the church as "spiritual Israel" or "new Israel."

In recent years there has been less dependency among pentecostal scholars on the dispensational system. Excellent examples of this are two books on eschatology: Stanley Horton's *The Promise of His Coming* (1967) and R. Hollis Gause's *Revelation: God's Stamp of Sovereignty on History* (1983). Both of these scholars are premillennial, but neither is dispensational. The term *dispensation* does not appear in Horton's book, and Gause affirms progressive revelation that does not make the dispensational divisions of biblical history. Nor does Gause distinguish between the church and Israel, but he sees the character of God and the character of salvation as progressively revealed.

See also DAKE, FINIS JENNINGS; ESCHATOLOGY, PENTECOSTAL PERSPECTIVES ON; SCOFIELD REFERENCE BIBLE.

■ **Bibliography:** C. W. Buxton, *What About Tomorrow?* (1974) ■ L. S. Chafer, *Systematic Theology* (1948) ■ D. P. Fuller, *Gospel and Law: Contrast or Continuum?* (1980) ■ W. C. Meloon, *We've Been Robbed* (1971) ■ C. C. Ryrie, *Dispensationalism Today* (1965) ■ G. T. Sheppard, "Pentecostals and the Hermeneutics of Dispensationalism: The Anatomy of an Uneasy Relationship," *Pneuma* (Fall 1984) ■ G. F. Taylor, *The Second Coming of Jesus* (1950).
■ F. L. Arrington

DONALD GEE CENTRE The Donald Gee Centre for Pentecostal and Charismatic Studies is an interdenominational archival resource, available (at the discretion of the trustees) to researchers. It is currently situated at Mattersey Hall, Nottinghamshire, England. The center holds original papers and rare books relating to the 20th-century outpouring of the Holy Spirit. Its areas of interest include the historical antecedents of pentecostalism, its early beginnings, the formation of denominational groups, including black groups, missions development and policy, the charismatic renewal, and restoration fellowships.   ■ W. K. Kay

DOOR OF FAITH CHURCHES OF HAWAII A small pentecostal denomination resulting from the missionary work of Mildred Johnson (later Brostek), who was sent to the Hawaiian Islands by the Pentecostal Holiness Church (PHC) in 1936. She left the PHC and established the Door of Faith in 1940 as an independent ministry. In 1999, with the 88-year-old Brostek still leading the organization, the ministry in Hawaii reported 40 churches, 3,000 members, and a Bible school. In addition, there are ordained ministers serving in Canada, Singapore, Japan, New Zealand, Indonesia, Okinawa, and Mexico. The strongest presence is in the Philippines, with some 200 Door of Faith churches. Brostek was in Honolulu when Pearl Harbor was bombed and remained during the war.

■ **Bibliography:** R. Donavan, *Her Door of Faith: The Lifestory of Mildred Johnson Brostek* (1971) ■ C. Jones, *Guide to the Study of the Pentecostal Movement* (1983).   ■ W. E. Warner

DOWIE, JOHN ALEXANDER (1847–1907). Faith healer, founder of Zion City, IL, and the Christian Catholic Church.

Dowie—who became a prominent advocate of healing—was a sickly child. When he was 13, his family migrated to Australia, where he began to earn his living. At age 20 he decided to enter the ministry and began to prepare for university. In 1868 he left Australia for Edinburgh University, where he studied at the Free Church School. After three years, Dowie returned to Australia. On Apr. 1, 1872, he accepted a call to the Congregational Church in Alma. The next year he took a church in Manly Beach. In 1875 he moved again, this time to a church in Newton, a Sydney suburb. There, he later claimed, he became convinced of the practical message of divine healing.

On May 26, 1876, Dowie married his cousin Jean. In 1878 he left the Congregational Church and launched an independent ministry, first in Sydney and later in Melbourne. After an unsuccessful try for a seat in the Australian parliament, Dowie gained notoriety for his stubborn opposition to the liquor traffic. During the 1880s he also renewed his focus on healing.

John Alexander Dowie (shown here in high-priestly robes), a strong proponent of divine healing at the end of the 19th century and the founder of Zion City, IL, as a religious community.

Dowie and his wife and their two children (William Gladstone and Esther) migrated to the U.S. in 1888. After two years of itinerant healing evangelism, which took him to many parts of the country, Dowie established a base of operations in Evanston, IL, in 1890. During the 1893 Chicago World's Fair he conducted meetings across the street from popular attractions, and his ministry began to grow as people testified to healings. He started a publication, *Leaves of Healing,* and opened a divine-healing home in Chicago. Local controversy only increased his audiences. Soon several homes and an enlarged publishing effort took shape, and Dowie began conducting services in his spacious Zion Tabernacle. In 1895 Dowie organized his followers into the Christian Catholic Church.

Intensely evangelistic, Dowie stressed consecration and holiness and welcomed participation by blacks and women. The primary focus of his work, however, was healing. Dowie insisted that those who sought his prayers relinquish all medicine and, instead, exercise faith. He also demanded that his followers abstain from use of all pork products. Stubborn and aggressive, Dowie seemed to welcome conflict: over the years, his sharp criticism alienated virtually every other significant American exponent of divine healing.

In 1900 Dowie unveiled plans for a religious community that would be molded by his own views of what a holy society should be. The community—known as Zion City and located north of Chicago on Lake Michigan—grew to approximately 6,000 persons during the next few years. Dowie, meanwhile, became increasingly eccentric. He reasserted his ʾrestorationist hopes and announced in 1901 that he was the prophesied Elijah, the Restorer. In 1904 he told his followers to anticipate the full restoration of apostolic Christianity and revealed that he had been divinely commissioned to be the first apostle of a renewed end-times church.

In Sept. 1905, as Dowie prepared to announce plans for the planting of Zions in other areas, he suffered a stroke. This followed several major confrontations with critics, first in New York during a much-heralded visit in 1903, then in Australia, where his attacks on the vices of the reigning British monarch gained international press attention. While traveling in the interests of both his health and his Zion in 1906, he lost control of his community. Individuals there had suffered severely as a result of financial mismanagement. He died in 1907, disgraced, and ignored by most of the thousands who had acclaimed him.

Dowie's end-time expectations, his message of divine healing, and his restorationist vision made him an important forerunner of pentecostalism. Many of his followers accepted pentecostal views; some became prominent leaders in a movement that regarded itself as an end-time restoration. Most pentecostal leaders with roots in Zion affiliated with the Assemblies of God. Some, however, more committed to a thoroughgoing restorationism, moved on into Oneness pentecostalism.

See also Healing in the Christian Church.

■ **Bibliography:** G. Lindsay, *John Alexander Dowie* (repr. 1980) ■ G. Wacker, "Marching to Zion," *Church History* 54 (Dec. 1985).

■ E. L. Blumhofer

DRAPER, MINNIE TINGLEY (1858–1921). Faith healer and missions executive. Born in Waquit, MA, Minnie T. Draper grew up in Ossining, NY. She never married and for a time supported herself and her mother through teaching. A Presbyterian, she faithfully attended a local church.

The strain of overwork broke Draper's health, and for four years she lived as an invalid. Physicians were consulted but could not relieve her suffering. Hearing about the doctrine of faith healing, she was anointed with oil and prayed for at ʾA. B. Simpson's Gospel Tabernacle in New York City. Miraculous healing followed, and at the same time the Lord also "definitely sanctified and anointed her with the Holy Ghost and power" (Lucas, 3). Convinced, as a result, that Christ is the Healer for every believer, she never again went to a physician or took any form of medicine.

Successful evangelistic work followed Draper's healing, and for many years she served as an associate of A. B. Simpson, assisting him in conventions held at Rock Springs, PA; New York City; and Old Orchard, ME.

Dowie's Shiloh Tabernacle (white building), which seated nearly 8,000. The smaller building (right) is the Zion radio station WCBD, which went on the air in 1923.

Prayer for the sick is what Draper is best remembered for. However, she also chaired various committees and served for several years as a member of the executive board of the ⌐Christian and Missionary Alliance (CMA) until it was reorganized in 1912.

When news of pentecostal happenings reached Draper in 1906, she was initially cautious. At the same time, however, she earnestly desired a deeper work of the Spirit in her own life. One night in her room the Lord appeared to her and "hours elapsed wherein she saw unutterable things, and when she finally came to herself, she heard her tongue talking fluently in a language she had never learned" (Lucas, 3).

Draper identified with pentecostal believers and participated in the development of several important ministry enterprises. She assisted in the organization of at least two churches: the Bethel Pentecostal Assembly, Newark, NJ (c. 1907), and the Ossining Gospel Assembly, Ossining, NY (1913). She remained in the CMA until 1913.

Draper's greatest achievements in pentecostalism resulted from her involvement with the Bethel Pentecostal Assembly of Newark. In 1910 the executive council of the Bethel Pentecostal Assembly, Inc., organized "to maintain and conduct a general evangelistic work in the State of New Jersey, in all other states of the United States and any and all foreign countries" (McGee, 4). People often referred to the council as the Bethel Board. Draper served as president of the board until her death in 1921, even though she was a member of the Ossining church.

Most of the institutions founded by the board, the Pentecostal Mission in South and Central Africa (1910) and the Bethel Bible Training School (1916), remained independent due to a restriction in the constitution and bylaws. The Newark congregation joined the Assemblies of God in 1953.

■ **Bibliography:** C. J. Lucas, "In Memoriam," *FGMH* (Apr. 1921) ▪ G. B. McGee, "Three Notable Women in Pentecostal Ministry," *AGH* 1 (1986).   ■ G. B. McGee

DUFFIELD, GUY PAYSON (1909–98). Foursquare pastor, educator, and author. Duffield was born in Hingham, MA, to evangelical Christian parents who, shortly after the birth of their son, moved to Toronto, Ont. While there, the younger Duffield was converted to Christ as a child and, at age 10, consecrated his life to Christian ministry during a missionary rally conducted by evangelist Paul Rader. He later entered L.I.F.E. Bible College in Los Angeles and graduated in 1928.

Early ministry took Duffield to Vancouver, B.C., where he served for a year at Canadian L.I.F.E. Bible College. After this his pastorates included Senlac and Evesham, Sask., and Victoria, B.C. During this time, he met and married Orpha Audrey Strong (1907–) of Rocanville, Sask. Their daughter, Darlene Starr, is married to Harold Sala, president of Guide-

lines for Living, a worldwide radio and television ministry. Together the Duffields traveled in evangelistic work and pastored in Hillsboro, OR; Bellingham, WA; Pomona, CA (1940–56); and Vancouver, B.C. (pastor of Kingsway Foursquare Church and dean of Canadian L.I.F.E. Bible College, 1956–58). He then received the call to pastor Angelus Temple in Los Angeles (1958–74) and to join the faculty of the adjacent L.I.F.E. Bible College (1958–85). In recognition of his service to the International Church of the Foursquare Gospel, L.I.F.E. Bible College conferred two honorary degrees on him (S.T.D., 1959; D.D., 1968).

Duffield's literary contributions include *Pentecostal Preaching* (1957), *Handbook of Bible Lands* (1969), and *Foundations of Pentecostal Theology* (with Nathaniel M. Van Cleave; 1983).

■ **Bibliography:** Personal correspondence, G. P. Duffield to G. B. McGee, 29 Dec., 1987, and 9 Jan., 1988.   ■ G. B. McGee

DUNCAN, SUSAN A. (1854–1935). Important early pentecostal teacher and cofounder of Elim Tabernacle in Rochester, NY. With her sisters, Hattie M. Duncan, Nellie Fell, and M. E. Work, she founded Gospel Mission in 1887. Their eldest sister, ⌐E. V. Baker, joined them in 1894, and they founded Elim Faith Home the following year. In 1901 they established a publishing house and began publishing *Trust,* which Susan Duncan edited for more than 30 years. Elim Tabernacle was established a few years later. In 1906 they founded Rochester Bible Training School, where they taught many early pentecostal leaders, including the great teacher ⌐John Wright Follette, who later joined the faculty.

Susan Duncan had charge of the work during E. V. Baker's visit to India in 1898–99 and after her sister's death in 1915. In 1924 Elim Memorial Church was founded, and by 1935 they had sent out more than 60 missionaries and had spent more than $100,000 in support of foreign missions without any solicitation of funds.

■ **Bibliography:** S. A. Duncan, *Talks about Faith* (n.d.) ▪ idem, "Incidents Connected with My Call," in E. V. Baker, *Chronicles of a Faith Life* (n.d.) ▪ "Elim Church Founder Dies," *Democrat and Chronicle* (Rochester) (Oct. 2, 1935), 13.   ■ R. M. Riss

DUNK, GILBERT T. S. (1912–97). Gilbert Dunk was converted during a crusade by ⌐George Jeffreys in Brighton, England, in 1927 and began evangelistic ministry four years later. After attending Bible school, he entered pastoral ministry with the Elim Church in Great Britain in Birmingham, the Midlands, and the Channel Islands (the latter under German occupation during WWII).

Dunk moved to New Zealand in 1952. The Pentecostal Church of N.Z. had suffered a major schism in 1946 that led to its eventual demise. The remnants of this church continued on for several years and eventually merged with the Elim Church in Great Britain. Dunk came to N.Z. to facilitate this amalgamation. The merger took place on Jan. 1, 1953, and the new Elim Church of N.Z. (Incorporated) was born. Dunk became the general superintendent of the movement (the title was adopted from the Elim Church in Great Britain). He held this office until 1962, when the title reverted to that of president, and a N.Z. layperson was elected to fill this role. Dunk later became president for a subsequent term and was also president of the short-lived N.Z. Pentecostal Fellowship, an umbrella group for N.Z. pentecostal churches in the 1960s.

The Elim movement remained one of the smallest pentecostal groups in N.Z., with only 5 small churches until the mid 1970s. It has since expanded substantially under the leadership of Pastor ˒Ian Bilby and now comprises some 50 churches. However, Dunk's experienced leadership throughout the 1950s and '60s had provided a stable base for the movement, making its later expansion possible. Dunk also became the pastor of the Wellington Elim Church, a position he held for the next 18 years. He transferred to the Christchurch assembly in the 1970s and retired to Levin. He died in 1997.

■ **Bibliography:** James E. Worsfold, *A History of the Charismatic Movements in New Zealand* (1974) ▊ Elim Church of New Zealand (Inc.), "Guidelines for Credentialled Ministers" (July 1994), 5–6.

▊ B. Knowles

DU PLESSIS, DAVID JOHANNES (1905–87).

South African-born (but naturalized American) ecumenical and international pentecostal spokesman. The oldest of nine sons of David J. and Anna C. du Plessis, he was born on Feb. 7, 1905, in a town called Twenty-four Rivers, near Cape Town at the far southwestern tip of Africa. Of Huguenot stock, his parents were religious people who became pentecostals under the influence of ˒John G. Lake and ˒Thomas Hezmalhalch. These were turn-of-the-century missionaries from ˒John Alexander Dowie's mission in Zion City, IL. They also had connections with the ˒Azusa Street Mission. David's father was a carpenter and a sometime lay preacher. In 1916 the senior Du Plessis family moved to Basutoland (since 1966 known as Lesotho), an enclave for tribal blacks. There, until the family moved to Ladybrand in 1917, the carpenter assisted missionaries in the construction of a mission compound. While there, Du Plessis, in his 12th year, was deeply impressed with the joyfulness of the blacks all about the mission compound. His conversion, as he tells it in *A Man Called Mr. Pentecost* (1977), came in 1916 during a sudden severe storm en route back to the compound from a mail run to a distant town. Water baptism came the next year, under the auspices of the Apostolic Faith Mission (AFMSA), the

David J. du Plessis, known as Mr. Pentecost, who was reared in South Africa but later moved to the U.S. His work with ecumenical groups brought both acclaim and criticism.

South African church of his parents in which he was to serve until 1947. In 1918, at about 13 years of age, he was baptized in the Holy Spirit at meetings held by English evangelist Charles Heatley in a coffin warehouse.

While Du Plessis remembered his mother as a compassionate peacemaker, he recalled his father as a stern disciplinarian. Following early pentecostal practice not limited to South Africa, the elder Du Plessis forbade his family the use of medicine and medical care, not even for plagued cattle, whose needless deaths led to a brief imprisonment (that ended when a friend paid the fine). When David du Plessis went off to Grey University in Bloemfontein for a few years of college training, his father—disturbed over the son's involvement with education—voluntarily surrendered his lay preacher's license, overwhelmed by a sense of paternal failure. In addition, because of the prohibitive distance and because he thought his son—at age 22—too young to marry, the father did not attend David's wedding and refused to welcome his bride until after the birth of their first child, when a reconciliation occurred.

In an oft-told story, when a visiting missionary asked for donkeys to use in mission work, the senior Du Plessis brought young David by the ear to the platform and presented the embryonic ecumenist as "David the Donkey," lacking a suitable animal. Characteristically, Du Plessis in later years spoke of the "D.D." given him by his father in that episode—which was in fact a sincere act of devotion on his father's part.

As a young pastor, Du Plessis was asked to speak with a woman named Anna Cornelia Jacobs, who had absented herself from church meetings over a minor misunderstanding. She was restored, but what is more, they married on Aug. 13, 1927, and their marriage lasted just short of 60 years. Seven children were born to this marriage: Anna Cornelia (1928–), Eunice Elizabeth (Mar.–Dec. 1932), David Johannes Jr. (1933–85), Philip Richelieu (1940–), Peter Louis le Roux (1944–), Matthew Kriel (1947–), and Basel Somerset (1949–). (Du Plessis's mother, wife, and a daughter were all named Anna Cornelia.) Both David and his wife became naturalized citizens of the U.S. in 1968.

The earliest ministry in the AFM found Du Plessis a teenage street preacher. At age 15 he undertook an apprenticeship in the denominational printery, a move that took him from the family home in Ladybrand to Johannesburg. His stay there was short-lived, and Du Plessis returned home to undertake college study, first at Ladybrand and later at Bloemfontein. In the mid 1920s, seeking fulfillment of his call to full-time ministry, Du Plessis variously served part-time and full-time pastoral roles (he also had a period of employment at the railway) in the cities of Benoni, DeAar, and Pretoria. He was ordained Apr. 11, 1930, at the age of 25.

By age 30 Du Plessis played a leading role in the AFM, the strongest pentecostal church in South Africa. He edited *Comforter/Trooster,* the bilingual house organ of the denomination. Placing second in the election for general secretary of the AFM in 1932, he won that spot in 1936 and kept it until he resigned in 1947 for the first steps in what was to become a global ministry.

Apart from brief trips abroad, Du Plessis remained in South Africa through the Depression years and WWII until 1947. During these years he operated the denominational bookroom and edited the denominational periodical, which had fallen on bad times. Du Plessis was active in 1935 to merge the AFM with a group known as the Full Gospel Church (in which his wife had grown up). The merger effort was abortive, and the Full Gospel group fell into a relationship with the American Church of God (Cleveland, TN)—a denominational fellowship with which Du Plessis was to spend his earliest years in America. Drawing on personal experience gained during a 1937 visit to America, Du Plessis introduced the camp meeting to his church. By 1940–41 he was involved in Bible-school work. Among his administrative accomplishments were the creation of a retirement system for ministers through the use of a mandated tithe from all ministers; he also was responsible for the purchase of a campground, the establishment of an orphanage, and the construction of denominational offices. Through the later war

years, Du Plessis led in the reorganization of the AFM constitution. The revision was published in the Mar. 1946 issue of the *Comforter.*

It was during this South African period, actually at the annual AFM conference at Johannesburg on Dec. 13–20, 1936, that from an illiterate English evangelist—who could not read road signs—Du Plessis heard a prophecy that was to guide him over the next 50 years. ▸Smith Wigglesworth had been commended to Du Plessis by British pentecostal leader ▸Donald Gee following the evangelist's successful meetings in Australia and New Zealand. Du Plessis was his interpreter for Afrikaans congregations. The prophecy itself grew over the years, and it was reinterpreted (for details, see Robinson, 85–91). An account of it was not published until 1964, though a privately printed tract by Du Plessis in 1951 referred to the prophecy. But the gist of the inspired words announced abruptly to Du Plessis by Wigglesworth was that the South African would find himself giving witness in the remote parts of the world—provided only that Du Plessis would remain obedient and faithful to the Lord. Du Plessis often recalled that the evangelist at the time specifically prayed for the continued health of the budding ecumenist.

The war's end brought travel opportunity. Already at the 1937 general council of the Assemblies of God (AG) in Memphis, TN, Du Plessis (who with others, including Donald Gee, had been invited by General Secretary ▸J. Roswell Flower) had discussed possible worldwide joint efforts of pentecostals. Du Plessis knew many pentecostals through the publications he exchanged for his own in an effort to keep up with global pentecostalism. Scandinavian pentecostals, perennial foes of any formal organization outside the local church, hosted a European conference in Stockholm in 1939 to thwart the unitive tendencies they feared.

The first ▸Pentecostal World Conference (PWC) was held in Zurich during May 1947. Du Plessis obtained a leave of absence from his AFM secretarial post and arrived a week ahead of time. Swiss pentecostal pastor ▸Leonard Steiner was the organizing secretary. When AFM leaders refused Steiner's request to extend Du Plessis's leave of absence, Du Plessis took the bold and prophetic step of resigning as their general secretary—an office he had formally held for a dozen years (1935–47). In 1947 he sent a cable to Anna with the direction to sell all and come to Basel, where Du Plessis would provide leadership in the forthcoming PWCs.

Du Plessis served as organizing secretary for the PWC for nearly a decade, from its 1949 meeting in Paris to its 1958 gathering in Toronto. He resigned after the 1952 London meeting but was requested again to serve following the 1955 Stockholm conference.

A fully supported office in Switzerland to serve the worldwide pentecostal movement did not materialize, owing to the diversity and regional interests that marked global pentecostalism. By Aug. 1948 Du Plessis left for America. There he worked to facilitate the formation of the ˈPentecostal Fellowship of North America—an event that occurred in Oct. 1948 as Du Plessis lay critically injured in a Beckley, WV, hospital—the result of a severe auto-train accident while traveling with Church of God pastor ˈPaul Walker.

Between 1949 and 1951 Du Plessis taught at Lee College, the Church of God school in Cleveland, TN. During 1952–54 Du Plessis worked with the Far East Broadcasting Company. By 1952 he had moved his family to Stamford, CT, where for a year he served as interim pastor at the Stamford Gospel Tabernacle (AG). For that reason, he affiliated in 1955 with the American AG as one of its ordained ministers (though he never relinquished his ordination with the South African AFM). Between 1956 and 1959 he lived in Dallas, TX, where he was the organizing secretary for ˈGordon Lindsay's ˈVoice of Healing Fellowship.

For Du Plessis the 1950s opened with efforts at uniting world pentecostals. As that decade closed, increasingly he became involved in the ecumenical movement. While in Stamford, he was moved to visit the offices of the World Council of Churches (WCC), uninvited and unannounced, in New York City. Hearing some hard words for Latin American pentecostals from John Mackay, president of Princeton Seminary, Du Plessis wrote a letter to Mackay, which led to the two becoming friends. Mackay was Du Plessis' gate into organized ecumenism. As president of the International Missionary Council, Mackay brought Du Plessis to the 1952 meeting at Willingen, West Germany, and had him address the 210 delegates. Probably because of Du Plessis's interviews with more than half of the global ecclesiastical representatives, most of whom had never seen a "rational pentecostal," he there earned the title "Mr. Pentecost."

At Willingen, W. A. Visser 't Hooft invited Du Plessis to the 1954 World Council Assembly at Evanston, IL. By 1959 Du Plessis was giving lectures at major theological centers—Princeton, Yale, Union, Colgate, Bossey, and others. He was received by three Roman Catholic pontiffs—John XXIII, Paul VI, and John Paul II.

Although around 1960 Du Plessis's favor rose in the ecumenical world, his ministry increasingly drew the ire of the pentecostal denominational establishment. By 1960 a changed situation in pentecostal history aggravated the uneasiness of his peers. In May of that year, ˈDennis Bennett, an Episcopal priest serving in Van Nuys, CA, declared at a Sunday morning service that he had received the baptism in the Holy Spirit and had spoken in tongues. The charismatic movement was born. Du Plessis blessed it; establishment pentecostals were in turn bewildered, angered, and hostile. Du Plessis is regarded by many as the father of the charismatic movement.

Meanwhile, the North American pentecostal establishment luxuriated in its postwar acceptance among evangelicals. In 1961 ˈThomas F. Zimmerman, who in 1959 had become general superintendent of the AG, was returned for a second year to the post of elected president of the National Association of Evangelicals.

It was an era that completed the evangelicalization of pentecostalism. In 1961 the only change (other than the rearrangement of the original 17 into 16 points) ever made to the Statement of Fundamental Truths of the AG was accomplished under Zimmerman's leadership. The added elements were evangelical accents: the Virgin Birth, deity, and sinlessness of Jesus—items too widely assumed to have been expressed when the 1916 statement was crafted.

An editorial in *United Evangelical Action* (June 1961, 28ff.), house organ of the ˈNational Association of Evangelicals (NAE), protested Du Plessis' coziness with the WCC, particularly objecting to his reputation in ecumenical circles as a spokesperson for the pentecostal movement—while in fact he had no official authority. Clearly embarrassing was the circulation of a minister of the AG, widely noted in the religious press, within World Council and National Council circles when the chief executive officer of the Assemblies of God was the elected president of the rival NAE. Out of this environment emerged a demand for Du Plessis to cease and desist from such ecumenical ministry. Du Plessis sought counsel from a hundred friends, asking advice on whether to quit the ecumenical circle. He interpreted their response to mean he should by no means forsake this emerging acceptance among ecumenists. Declining a request to withdraw, he was—in 1962—asked to surrender his credentials as an ordained minister of the AG. He retained membership, however, in the First Assembly of God, Oakland, CA, where he and his family had moved in 1954. From 1962 until 1980, when he was reinstated as an ordained AG minister, Du Plessis served as an uncredentialed and unofficial pentecostal ambassador-at-large.

This period saw Du Plessis's increasing participation in ecumenical events. While both Du Plessis and Donald Gee were invited to the WCC Third Assembly at New Delhi, Gee declined in deference to the concerns of pentecostal brethren. But Du Plessis went, revealing their contrasting styles. By invitation of Augustin Cardinal Bea, he was an invited guest at the third session of ˈVatican II (1963–65). He attended all six assemblies of the WCC, from Amsterdam (1948) to Vancouver (1983), that were convened during his lifetime.

The crown of his ecumenical achievements lay in the development of the Roman Catholic–Pentecostal ˈDialogue, one of a wide series of discussions with "separated brethren" begun as a result of Vatican II. Efforts to enter formal dialogue with the North American establishment churches of pentecostalism were unsuccessful, largely because frontier pentecostal missionary enterprises, especially in Latin America, reflected conflict between pentecostal missionaries and local Roman Catholic clerics. The churches could not politically afford to engage in friendly discussion with those who, according to distressing field reports, so strongly opposed their missionaries.

With official dialogue thus impossible, coupled with Du Plessis's rising role as "Mr. Pentecost," a proposal emerged to draw together a surrogate group of representative pentecostal leaders who would speak as pentecostals when it was not feasible to engage those who would speak for the pentecostal movement. (Initial explorations for what became the International Roman Catholic–Pentecostal Dialogue were actually made by the Reverend Ray Bringham, a charismatic leader earlier associated with the Church of God [Anderson, IN].) Benedictine monk Fr. ▸Kilian McDonnell, an authority on Protestant theology and a consultant to the Vatican's Secretariat for Promoting Christian Unity, solicited the aid of David du Plessis in constructing such a dialogue. McDonnell and Du Plessis served as cochairpersons of the first 10 sessions (1972–82), after which ▸Justus du Plessis succeeded his older brother as cochair for the pentecostal team (later, in 1992, ▸Cecil M. Robeck Jr. took that role).

At the invitation of the joint faculties of Fuller Theological Seminary in Pasadena, CA, Du Plessis formally donated his papers and personal library to the seminary. An archive was established. For the final two years of his life, Du Plessis served the seminary as Resident Consultant for Ecumenical Affairs and supervised the sorting of his papers and library. During routine gall bladder surgery in Aug. 1986, inoperable abdominal cancer was discovered. He died in 1987 at Pasadena, a week short of his 82nd birthday, and is buried with his wife, Anna (and with them the cremains of David Jr.) at Mountain View Cemetery in Altadena, CA, adjacent to Pasadena.

For all his editorial and organizing work in South Africa and with the PWC, Du Plessis—true to his pentecostal tradition—left no tightly argued theological writings. Two of his three published volumes (*Mr. Pentecost* [1977] and *Simple and Profound* [1986]) were actually written by others following extensive interviews. *The Spirit Bade Me Go* (1961, 1970) is a collection of miscellaneous writings, whose periodic revision clearly reflected historical currents in his ministry.

Du Plessis preferred to consider "speaking in tongues" a consequence—rather than "the evidence"—of the coming of the Spirit. Asked if one had to speak in tongues as a sign of the Holy Spirit's baptism, he would reply: "You must not, but you will." Gifts of healing, he taught, were given to the sick and not to the evangelists who prayed for them. The gift of interpretation, in his view, could be identified with thoughts that came after a glossolalic address. And he was never content with the jargon "message in tongues," which he repeatedly exposed as unbiblical terminology. Speaking in tongues was always addressed to God, not to humans. And more often than not, he said, it was prophecy and not "interpreta-

tion" that followed glossolalic outbursts in pentecostal assemblies. In his practical wisdom, he counseled scores of newly Spirit-baptized charismatics to stay in their churches—to the unending consternation of establishment pentecostals. He stood firm for "the ecumenicity of the Holy Spirit." He exemplified in his own life the virtues and values of forgiveness, and his simple lifestyle offered stunning contrast to the opulence of certain highly visible pentecostal televangelists.

No stranger to controversy, Du Plessis never outgrew the convictions formed in the 1920s to the 1940s that South African apartheid (which became official policy in South Africa in 1948) was a workable scheme, given social realities. Nor was he thanked by many of his pentecostal peers for favorable comment on the apparitions of Mary reported at Medjugorje in Yugoslavia—which he personally visited. Clearly his confrontational behavior often proved irksome to ecclesiastics, as does that of prophets in any age.

Even apart from his leadership in the Roman Catholic–Pentecostal ▸Dialogue, the PWC, and the charismatic movement as a whole, Du Plessis's catalytic role affected a wide range of pentecostal institutions: the ▸Full Gospel Business Men's Fellowship International, ▸Women's Aglow, the ▸Pentecostal Fellowship of North America, and the ▸Society for Pentecostal Studies. Predictably, all of these were multidenominational in character.

No one in the 20th century so effectively linked three of the major movements of the time—the pentecostal movement, the ecumenical movement, and the charismatic movement. *Time* magazine (Sept. 9, 1974, 66) reported the choice of seven editors of religious publications for the leading "shapers and shakers" of Christianity. Du Plessis was among them, along with people like Billy Graham, Hans Küng, Jürgen Moltmann, and Rosemary Radford Ruether (the editors had eliminated Cesar Chavez, Harvey Cox, Norman Vincent Peale, and ▸Oral Roberts). Kilian McDonnell spoke of Du Plessis as "a national treasure." In 1976 St. John's University in Collegeville, MN, presented to him the prized Pax Christi award, clear evidence of his high repute in Roman Catholic circles. He was the first non–Roman Catholic ever to have received (in 1983) the distinguished Benemerenti award, presented on the pope's behalf by Jan Cardinal Willebrands. In 1978 Du Plessis received an honorary doctorate from Bethany Bible College (Santa Cruz, CA). His example, his wry and rabbinic teaching style—if not his consistent logic—inspired hundreds of younger pentecostal leaders and subtly molded the emerging theology of a major force in Christendom. For the 20th century at least, he was indeed "Mr. Pentecost."

■ **Bibliography:** Though no definitive biography exists, many details are given in Martin Robinson's dissertation, "To the Ends of the Earth: The Pilgrimage of an Ecumenical Pentecostal, David J. du Plessis (1905–1987)" (U. of Birmingham [U.K.], 1987). Selected facts appear in the autobiography ("as told to Bob Slosser") *A Man Called Mr. Pentecost: David du Plessis* (1977) as well as in Du Plessis's two other published works, *The Spirit Bade Me Go* (rev. and enlarged, 1970) and *Simple and Profound* (1986).

Du Plessis's role in the Roman Catholic–Pentecostal Dialogue emerges in J. L. Sandidge, "Roman Catholic–Pentecostal Dialog: A Contribution to Christian Unity," *Pneuma* 7 (1985). Details of the first five years: A. Bittlinger, *Papst und Pfingstler: Der römisch katholisch-pfingstliche Dialog und seine ökumenische Relevanz* (1978). The second five years: J. L. Sandidge, *Roman Catholic/Pentecostal Dialog [1977–1982]: A Study in Developing Ecumenism* (1987) ■ P. D. Lee, *Pneumatological Ecclesiology in the Roman Catholic–Pentecostal Dialogue: A Catholic Reading of the Third Quinquennium* (1994) ■ see also M. Robinson, "David du Plessis: A Promise Fulfilled," and N. Horn, "South Africans and Apartheid: A Short Case Study of the Apostolic Faith Mission," in J. A. B. Jongeneel et al., eds., *Pentecost, Mission, and Ecumenism* (W. Hollenweger Festschrift) (1992).

The personal papers of David du Plessis are housed in the David J. du Plessis Center for Christian Spirituality at Fuller Theological Seminary in Pasadena, CA.   ■ R. P. Spittler

DU PLESSIS, JUSTUS TELO (1917–). Pastor and honorary secretary for Ecumenical Affairs for the Apostolic Faith Mission (AFM) of South Africa; cochairman of the Roman Catholic–Classical Pentecostal ▸Dialogue (1982–91). A descendant from the French Huguenots who settled South Africa in 1688, Justus Telo du Plessis was born in the Lesotho territory of South Africa to godly parents who became believers under the ministry of Andrew Murray. Justus du Plessis was saved at age 17 under the ministry of his eldest brother, ▸David, who would later become known as "Mr. Pentecost."

During more than 50 years of ministry, Du Plessis served as a missionary, pastor, district chairman, and member of the executive council of the AFM, the oldest and largest pentecostal church in South Africa, with a membership of approximately a half million. In 1970 Du Plessis was elected general secretary of the AFM, a position he held until his retirement in 1982. Progressive steps taken under his leadership include the establishment of a fund for higher education and the creation of the AFM pastors' pension fund. One of his most significant contributions to the church was his key role in working for a better understanding and greater acceptance of pentecostalism in South Africa. In the area of higher education, Du Plessis's role as liaison with the

Steve Durasoff, Assemblies of God missionary and educator, with Russian Orthodox priest in Rostov.

South African government allowed him to negotiate changes in educational curriculum that met the needs of churches that did not subscribe to the Calvinistic doctrines taught in state-supported schools.

Like his brother David, Justus became active in the charismatic renewal movement worldwide. He participated in the Roman Catholic–Classical Pentecostal Dialogue, from which he retired in 1991. At present (2000) he is in failing health.

■ P. H. Alexander

DUPREE, SHERRY SHERROD (1946–). Archivist and historian of African-American pentecostalism. A native of North Carolina, Sherry DuPree is the daughter of Matthew Needham Sherrod Sr. (1908–90) and Mary Elouise Heartley (1914–). She is a graduate of North Carolina Central University (B.S., 1968; M.A., 1969) and the University of Michigan (A.M.L.S., 1974; Ed.S., 1978). Early in her professional career she was an instructional media specialist at Tappan Middle School, Ann Arbor, MI (1970–76). Subsequently, she has served on the library staffs of the University of Florida (1977–83) and Santa Fe Community College in Gainesville, FL (1983–).

DuPree's research on African-American pentecostalism began when, as a librarian at the University of Florida, she was approached by a student asking for information on the pentecostal movement. At that time she realized how little had been written about African-American pentecostalism.

In 1989 DuPree edited the *Biographical Dictionary of African-American Holiness-Pentecostals 1880–1990* and, six years later, the *African-American Holiness Pentecostal Movement: An Annotated Bibliography*. She founded the DuPree African-American Pentecostal and Holiness Collection at the Schomburg Center for Research in Black Culture at the New York Public Library. DuPree also has been involved in the State of Florida's African American Steel Guitar Project. She is the recipient of the 1997 Black Achiever's Award in the religion category and served as president of the ▸Society for Pentecostal Studies for the year 2000.

Sherry DuPree is married to Herbert C. DuPree, a geographer. They have three sons: Amil, Andre, and Andrew.

■ S. M. Burgess

DURASOFF, STEVE (1922–). Missionary, educator. Steve Durasoff pastored for 11 years in the Assemblies of God (AG), earned a Ph.D. in religious education at New York University (1968), worked for the Oral Roberts

Evangelistic Association for five years, and taught at Oral Roberts University in the Department of Theology for 15 years. He has also traveled extensively in Eastern Europe and the Soviet Union as a missionary evangelist. Among his publications are *The Russian Protestants: Evangelicals in the Soviet Union, 1944–1964* (1969); *Pentecost behind the Iron Curtain* (1972); *Bright Wind of the Spirit: Pentecostalism Today* (1972); and "Communist World at Our Seaport," *PE* (July 5, 1981). Durasoff is retired and lives in Springfield, MO. ■ F. Bixler

DURHAM, WILLIAM H. (1873–1912). Dynamic leader of the early pentecostal movement and proponent of the doctrine of Christ's ▸"finished work." Originally from Kentucky, Durham joined the Baptist Church in 1891 but was not converted to Christ until seven years later while in Minnesota, where he experienced a vision of the crucified Christ. He immediately devoted himself to full-time ministry and became pastor of Chicago's North Avenue Mission in 1901. When the gifts of the Spirit became evident there in 1906, Durham visited the ▸Azusa Street Mission in Los Angeles, where he received the baptism of the Holy Spirit and spoke in tongues on Mar. 2, 1907, at which time ▸W. J. Seymour prophesied that wherever Durham preached, the Holy Spirit would fall upon the people.

When Durham returned to his church in Chicago, the pentecostal revival spread quickly through his ministry. His

William Durham (right), who pastored pentecostal churches in Chicago and Los Angeles but is best known for his teaching on the "finished work of Calvary." He is shown here with Harry Van Dusen around 1910.

overcrowded meetings lasted far into the night and sometimes until morning. Durham reported in his periodical, *The Pentecostal Testimony,* that "it was nothing to hear people at all hours of the night speaking in tongues and singing in the Spirit" (Brumback, 1961, 69). A "thick haze . . . like blue smoke" often rested on the mission. When this was present, those entering the building would fall down in the aisles (Miller, 1986, 123).

Frank Ewart (1975, 99) wrote that "thousands came to hear Durham preach, and all went away with the conviction that he was a pulpit prodigy." At one point there were as many as 25 ministers from out of town at his meetings seeking the baptism of the Holy Spirit.

Many people who later became prominent pioneers of the pentecostal movement attended Durham's meetings, including ▸A. H. Argue; ▸E. N. Bell; ▸Howard Goss; ▸Daniel Berg, founder of the Assemblies of God in Brazil; and ▸Luigi Francescon, a pioneer of the pentecostal movement in Italy. ▸Aimee Semple, before her marriage to Harold McPherson, was instantaneously healed of a broken ankle through Durham's ministry in Jan. 1910.

Durham's church soon became a leading center for the pentecostal movement worldwide. The ▸Assemblea Cristiana of Chicago, which had received the pentecostal message as a result of Durham's friendship with Luigi Francescon, became the mother church of other Italian assemblies in the U.S., Italy, and South America. F. A. Sandgren, a Norwegian elder in Durham's mission, published a Scandinavian periodical, *Folke Vennen,* resulting in several Swedish, Norwegian, and Danish pentecostal missions in Chicago. A group of Persians under the leadership of ▸Andrew Urshan also received encouragement from Durham.

Durham became well known for his repudiation of the Holiness doctrine of sanctification as a "second work of grace," arguing that the "finished work" of Christ on Calvary becomes available to the believer at the time of justification. The benefits of Calvary are therefore appropriated for sanctification over the entire period of the Christian's life, rather than at a single subsequent moment, as was believed by most pentecostals in Durham's day.

Durham went to Los Angeles with this message, and upon his return to Chicago, contracted a head cold. Returning to Los Angeles, he died of pneumonia during the summer of 1912.

See also FINISHED WORK CONTROVERSY.

■ **Bibliography:** R. M. Anderson, *Vision of the Disinherited* (1979) ■ F. Bartleman, *How Pentecost Came to Los Angeles* (2d ed., 1925) ■ C. Brumback, *Suddenly . . . from Heaven* (1961) ■ J. Colletti, "Sociological Study of Italian Pentecostals in Chicago, 1900–1930," in *Papers of the 16th Annual Meeting of the SPS* (1986) ■ F. Ewart, *The Phenomenon of Pentecost* (rev. ed., 1975) ■ S. Frodsham, *With Signs*

Following (1946) ∎ D. Hayes, *The Gift of Tongues* (1913) ∎ W. J. Hollenweger, *The Pentecostals* (1972) ∎ A. S. McPherson, *This Is That* (1919) ∎ T. W. Miller, "The Significance of A. H. Argue for Pentecostal Historiography," *Pneuma* 8 (Fall 1986).

∎ R. M. Riss

DYE, COLIN (1953–). Pastor, evangelist, teacher, senior minister of Kensington Temple, London. Dye was born in Kenya, East Africa, and moved to London for training at the Royal Ballet School and the Royal Ballet Company (1970–75). Converted in 1972, he attended Bible college after 1975 and then worked at a Christian drug rehabilitation center before becoming a church worker and then assistant pastor at Kensington Temple (KT), the most famous and largest Elim Pentecostal congregation in the city. During a pastorate in Bournemouth (1981–85), he took a bachelor of divinity degree from London University. Upon returning to London in 1985 he became associate pastor of KT under Wynne Lewis and was closely involved in the setting up of KT's satellite churches.

During this time he founded KT's International Bible Institute of London, and in 1991 he was appointed senior minister of KT. After writing *Building a City Church*, he worked to plant a network of congregations that has become the London City Church, with KT at its center. In 1998 there were 400 churches and fellowships representing 110 nationalities linked in this way, with an attendance of more than 11,000 people. Satellite broadcasting technology is a key ele-ment in the network, and services are broadcast weekly to several receiving centers in London and other parts of Europe. This technology also carries the Sword of the Spirit School of Ministry, which is accompanied by written study guides.

In 1997 KT opened a new permanent London venue for its Sunday evening services. Meanwhile, Dye has traveled extensively and developed links with churches in Scandinavia and in São Paulo, where his broadcasting experience has been put to good use. Dye's concern for Europe, however, is marked by the Euro Pentecost Conference (held in Rome in 1998), which has raised the profile of Pentecostal issues across the European Community. Missionary work concentrates on Albania, France, Benin, and Sri Lanka, where the church runs a children's home. Theologically Dye is concerned to emphasize "radical Pentecostalism," which underlines both the distinctive doctrines of the Pentecostal heritage and social action.

∎ **Bibliography:** C. Dye, *Building a City Church* (1993) ∎ idem, *Breakthrough Faith* (1995) ∎ idem, *Explaining the Church* (1996) ∎ idem, *Prayer Explosion* (1996) ∎ idem, *Living in the Presence* (1996) ∎ idem, *Revival Phenomena* (1996) ∎ idem, *It's Time to Grow* (1997) ∎ idem, *Healing Anointing* (1997) ∎ idem, *Effective Prayer* (1997) ∎ idem, *Knowing the Spirit* (1997) ∎ idem, *The Rule of God* (1997) ∎ idem, *I Will Awaken the Dawn* (1997) ∎ idem, *Something Good from Nazareth* (1997) ∎ idem, *Laying Hold of Your Inheritance* (1997) ∎ idem, *God's Provision in a Time of Lack* (1997) ∎ idem, *Ministry in the Spirit* (1998) ∎ idem, *Glory in the Church* (1998) ∎ idem, *Prayer that Gets Answers* (1998).   ∎ K. Kay

E

EASTMAN, DICK (1944–). Mission strategist and prayer leader with international evangelistic ministry. Eastman, converted in 1961, was educated at Moody Bible Institute, North Central Bible College in Minneapolis (B.A., Bible and Theology), and the University of Wisconsin (M.Sc., Journalism).

Since 1988 Eastman has been the international president of Every Home for Christ (EHC), a worldwide ministry of house-to-house evangelism whose purpose is to bring the printed gospel to every home. Under his leadership, EHC launched a major 10-year strategy in 1996 to reach the 1,739 least evangelized peoples of the world. He has also organized its *Change the World School of Prayer.* Since 1990 Eastman has served as president of the National Prayer Committee, which plans for America's annual National Day of Prayer and sponsors the Concerts of Prayer movement. Eastman's books include *No Easy Road: Inspirational Thoughts on Prayer* (1971); *The Hour That Changes the World* (1978); *A Celebration of Praise* (1984); *Living and Praying in Jesus' Name* (1988); *Love on Its Knees* (1989); *The Jericho Hour* (1994); and *Beyond Imagination: A Simple Plan to Save the World* (1997).

■ P. D. Hocken

ECCLESIASTICAL POLITY The organization, governance, and discipline of the older pentecostal denominations reflect the wide spectrum of traditional church structures of episcopalian, presbyterian, or congregational organizations. In contrast, the charismatic movement, which originated in the 1960s, has tended to retain an informal or extrachurch structure under the leadership of dominant personalities, paralleling the early-20th-century pentecostal movement.

1. The Local Church.

The early participants in the pentecostal movement were not welcome in mainline denominational churches because of the enthusiastic style of revivalistic worship and particularly because of the phenomenon of speaking in tongues. The antipathy was mutual, however, as a sense of spiritual elitism led pentecostals to condemn the "dead" denominational churches. Local units were formed in makeshift upper rooms or barnlike tabernacles under the charismatic leadership of itinerant evangelists heralding the "full gospel" of pentecostalism.

These believers perceived their churches as the restoration of NT faith and practice, based solely on the Bible. They were consistently suspicious of ecclesiastical systems, some even to the extent of refusing to organize and have a name or even a membership list. Leadership was based on charisma, both in the biblical sense and in the sociological usage of Max Weber. Many of the leaders defined themselves by the biblical terms

"apostle" or "prophet." At first nearly all the churches were staunchly independent, refusing any external guidance or discipline, believing themselves to be Spirit-led. Some still retain their autonomy and have refused to follow the general trend into regional and national associations. One early leader, ▸Charles Fox Parham, advocated local congregationalism under the guidance of elders, to the extent that he refused the invitation of ▸William J. Seymour to assist in bringing discipline to the extreme manifestations at Seymour's ▸Azusa Street Mission in Los Angeles.

The same issues that drove the pentecostals out of the mainline churches haunted them as independents. Spirit baptism produced a split-level hierarchy of superior and inferior saints: those who could not show evidence of Spirit baptism usually were not allowed leadership roles in the local organization. Ardor versus order remained a tension as moderate pastors attempted to restrain the ecstatic extremes.

These tensions burst into open conflict in the late 1940s in the ▸Latter Rain movement. Bethesda Tabernacle, Detroit, and the Wings of Healing Temple, Portland, OR, became centers that radiated the teaching of extreme congregationalism and a restoration of the apostolic ministry of laying on of hands. This apostolic succession produced a class of gifted Christians claiming superiority to the old-line pentecostals. Prophetic guidance in the hands of the laity and the deliverance derived from the confession of sin to fellow believers tended to undermine the traditional authoritarian role of the pentecostal pastor.

Local groups evolving out of the 1960s charismatic movement were also frequently beset by issues from what are known as the ▸"shepherding" or "discipleship" movement. Churches were organized into authoritarian hierarchies for purposes of guidance and spiritual discipline, with strong emphasis on the interests of the local community. This phenomenon paralleled the communalism of the "hippie" era.

The civil rights movement and women's liberation movement of the late 20th century made the pentecostal churches, like others, self-conscious about the roles of minorities and women in the local church as well as in the denominations. Most churches continue to be divided along ethnic and racial lines, although no denomination has any formal ethnic or racial limitations. Those churches that include significant minority elements usually set them apart, such as the Latin American districts of the ▸Assemblies of God (AG) or the work among racial minorities of the ▸Church of God (CG, Cleveland, TN). Minorities are infrequently selected for leadership in integrated local churches and even less frequently raised to ministerial status. Although some pentecostal churches have always ordained women, the role of women as active head pastors has declined, and, with the notable exception of ►Aimee Semple McPherson, they have not traditionally been elevated to denominational leadership positions. On the other hand, the CG is an example of the other extreme that does not even allow women to be voting members of the local church and limits their ministerial status to "exhorters," which does not permit administration of the sacraments. A similar pattern is reflected in one of the major institutions of the recent charismatic movement; Melodyland Christian Center, Anaheim, CA, will not ordain women or allow them to be elected to the governing board.

2. National Denominations.

Most pentecostal groups just after the turn of the 20th century had no polity structure outside the local church and did not require a higher authority for ministerial ordination. Fellowship among these groups was characterized by conventions, camp meetings, and six-week Bible schools. Denominationalism and ecclesiasticism were feared as the Babylon that might seduce the new movement away from its spiritual dynamism. Nevertheless, informal social structures centered on such charismatic figures as ►Charles F. Parham and ►Florence L. Crawford. Gradually regional associations were found to be beneficial. The necessity of controlling fanatical and unethical itinerant preachers required structures for credentialing a qualified clergy. Traditional ecclesiastical structures were particularly tempting because of the practice of the railroad companies of granting free passes to clergy, who were required to verify their status within a recognized religious body. Some congregations, however, favored a worldwide body of unorganized believers, led only by the Spirit, while others claimed the biblical pattern of Acts 6 and 8 to justify overseers and voting processes. These tensions caused further splintering in the fledgling groups.

The call for a national, as opposed to a regional, organization was issued in 1914 and resulted in the formation of the General Council of the AG. This call was based on the desirability of doctrinal unity, the legal advantages of chartered churches, and the efficiency of a unified missionary, publishing, and educational endeavor. Although the original Preamble and Resolution on Constitution recognized the inclusion of foreign countries, in practice the organization has followed the culturally and pragmatically established pattern of nationalism and colonialism in its polity, without attempting any scriptural justification for the denomination's correspondence to these human institutions. The organization responded to the antiestablishment sensibilities by carefully guaranteeing the autonomy of the local churches. In terms of traditional polity, the structure is a centralized presbyterian form that retains the autonomy of the local congregation. Ordination is by the presbytery, not the local body. This general pattern has also been adopted

by many other pentecostal groups, such as the ►Pentecostal Church of God (called the Pentecostal Church of God of America until 1979).

The earlier regional organizations, such as the CG and the ►Pentecostal Holiness Church (PHC), gradually expanded also into national organizations with more centralized polity based on the episcopal backgrounds of their Holiness and Wesleyan traditions. This strongly centralized pattern is also reflected in the largest black pentecostal group in the U.S., the ►Church of God in Christ. The structure reflects the strong personal leadership of the founder, ►Charles H. Mason. Similarly, the centralized structure of the ►International Church of the Foursquare Gospel results from the dominant personality of founder ►Aimee Semple McPherson.

A congregational type of polity was manifested in a 1921 revolt against the episcopal centralization of the PHC, resulting in the formation of the ►Congregational Holiness Church. This form has been a staunch characteristic of the Scandinavian pentecostal churches as well, their background reflecting the Free church's resentment of the hierarchical domination of the state church.

3. Suprachurch and Extrachurch.

Fear of an apostate, liberal ecumenism has generally prevented the pentecostals from joining the World Council of Churches. Two Chilean groups, however, Mision Iglesia Pentecostal and Iglesia Pentecostal de Chile, joined that body in 1961. Some pentecostals in the U.S. have been part of the moderate ►National Association of Evangelicals since its inception in 1942. The fear of ecclesiastical hierarchies sidetracked attempts to form an international pentecostal fellowship at Amsterdam in 1921 and at Stockholm in 1939; but at Zurich in 1947 the ►Pentecostal World Conference was formed. This in turn spawned regional and national organizations such as the ►Pentecostal Fellowship of North America (1948) and the British Pentecostal Fellowship (1948).

The ►Full Gospel Business Men's Fellowship International (1951) and the ►Fountain Trust (1964) are leading examples of charismatic organizations that are ecumenical in spirit but exist apart from the denominational structures of the churches themselves.

See also CHURCH MEMBERSHIP; CHURCH, THEOLOGY OF THE.

■ **Bibliography:** R. H. Gause, *Church of God Polity* (1958) ■ W. J. Hollenweger, *The Pentecostals* (1972) ■ K. Kendrick, *The Promise Fulfilled: A History of the Modern Pentecostal Movement* (1961) ■ J. T. Nichol, *Pentecostalism* (1966) ■ R. Quebedeaux, *The New Charismatics: The Origins, Development, and Significance of Neo-Pentecostalism* (1976). ■ D. J. Wilson

EDVARDSEN, ARIL (1938–). Norwegian evangelist with worldwide pentecostal ministry. Born and brought up in Kvinesdal in southwestern Norway, Edvardsen was converted in 1956 soon after marrying his wife, Kari. Baptized in the Spirit in 1958, Edvardsen soon began an evangelistic ministry, starting a magazine called *Troens Bevis* (Evidence of Faith) in 1961. Giving priority to the unreached and unchurched, his evangelism supports missionaries and indigenous churches.

Kvinesdal has become the center of this missionary enterprise, with camping facilities for major conferences and studios for gospel radio and television. Edvardsen's ministry has become increasingly interdenominational since the Kvinesdal conferences of 1970 and 1971, which contributed significantly to the rise of charismatic renewal in Norway. Rising tension with the Norwegian Pentecostal Assemblies led to a separation in 1976, but a reconciliation was effected in 1989. Edvardsen has held campaigns in many countries and in the 1990s reached several of the largely Muslim states of the former Soviet Union. He opened a U.S. office in Fort Lauderdale, FL, in 1983 under the name International World Ministries. Edvardsen's life and ministry are described in *Dreaming and Achieving the Impossible* (1984).

■ P. D. Hocken

ELIM FELLOWSHIP An international ecumenical and pentecostal organization serving pastors, churches, missionaries, and other Christian workers, with headquarters in Lima, NY. It began in 1933 as an informal fellowship of churches, ministers, and missionaries, originating from a nucleus of people who had been trained at the Elim Bible Institute.

The school was founded in 1924 by ▸Ivan Q. Spencer, who had attended the "Old Elim," Rochester Bible Training School operated by the ▸Duncan sisters. Before founding Elim Fellowship, Spencer had been a member of the ▸Assemblies of God (1919–24).

By 1997 the group numbered 170 affiliated churches and 814 credentialed ministers and Christian workers. A high percentage of its credential holders serve on foreign mission fields.

Spencer's original simple, interdenominational concept (rather than being another denomination) is still the guiding force at Elim. He envisioned that his ecumenical body of believers would "provide a vehicle for fellowship without imposing all of the strict controls and regulations that most denominations have developed." Service to others is stressed, and frequently missionaries go out to assist previously established national movements rather than to start new Elim ministries.

Although basically adopting the classical pentecostal statement of faith—the entire statement has fewer than 250 words—the organization is perhaps more tolerant of other beliefs and practices than most pentecostal groups. It was a charter member of the ▸Pentecostal Fellowship of North America and its successor, the ▸Pentecostal/Charismatic Churches of North America; and of the ▸National Association of Evangelicals.

Always listening for what he believed to be God's voice for guidance, Spencer began the Bible school with very little money but a lot of faith. Emphasizing missions, Spencer saw 10% of the students go into foreign service during the first decade of the school's existence.

Never content with the status quo in pentecostal experience, Spencer looked for perpetual revival and was disappointed when it was not sustained. Spencer was often criticized by outsiders when he accepted questionable prophecies and impulses that he felt came from God. Critics looked at Elim as a group that permitted and even encouraged fanaticism. Another complaint was that Spencer and others embraced the teaching of a "selective rapture" of believers; some, it was taught, would be left when Christ returned for his church. Still another belief was that of the "Manchild Company," which meant believers could have victory over death—both for the soul and for the body.

Perhaps the greatest break between Elim and other pentecostals came in 1948, when Spencer introduced the New Order of the ▸Latter Rain to the fellowship. After visiting ▸Myrtle Beall's Bethesda Temple in Detroit, Spencer was certain that the Latter Rain was the revival movement that would restore unity to the body of Christ. Spencer and other leaders later saw, however, that excesses in the movement caused deep divisions within, and criticism outside, the fellowship. He and the fellowship tried to become a moderating force and called for believers to avoid extremes.

The fellowship publishes the *Elim Herald*, which Spencer founded in 1930. Most of the churches and members are concentrated in New York and Pennsylvania. Spencer's son ▸Carlton (Ivan C.) followed his father as the fellowship's leader.

Beginning as the Elim Ministerial Fellowship (1933–47), the fellowship became Elim Missionary Assemblies in 1947 and Elim Fellowship in 1972.

■ **Bibliography:** M. Meloon, *Ivan Spencer, Willow in the Wind* (1974) ▪ "People Serving People: A Closer Look at Elim Fellowship" (n.d.).   ■ W. E. Warner

ELIM PENTECOSTAL CHURCH Founded by Welsh evangelist ▸George Jeffreys. The Elim Evangelistic Band was formed in Monoghan, Ireland, in Jan. 1915. The first church in 1916 was a former laundry in Hunter Street, Belfast. George Jeffreys drew up a statement of faith that formed the basis of the later fundamentals. The name Elim was chosen following the Welsh custom of giving churches names and also after the Elim Mission, Lythan, Lancashire. In 1919 the Elim Pentecostal Alliance was created as a property-holding body on the advice of John Leech. An advisory council was set up with Leech as president and William Henderson as secretary. By the end of 1920 there were 15 assemblies and 21 workers in Ireland. George Jeffreys preached all over Britain but did not establish his first church until 1921, at Leigh on Sea, Essex. Their headquarters were in Belfast, but in 1922 Jeffreys shifted his attention to England, joining his brother ˃Stephen at Grimsby. An aggressive evangelistic policy was adopted, and George moved to Clapham, London, from 1922 to 1924. The brothers spent five months in Canada and the U.S. in 1924, shortly after the formation of the ˃Assemblies of God of Great Britain and Ireland. They returned to Barking, London, where large crowds were attracted and many outstanding miracles of healing were witnessed. Stephen separated from his brother, who continued in Ilford and East Ham. But ˃P. S. Brewster, ˃Douglas Scott, and D. B. Gray, leader of the London Crusader Choir, joined Elim. Brewster was saved and Scott healed. A Bible school was begun at Clapham in 1925, and in Jan. 1926 the former Redemptorist Convent in Clarence Road, Clapham, was opened as the Elim Bible College.

The Elim Evangelistic Band was a closely knit company with only basic rules. These were replaced by a constitution in 1922, which was revised twice before 1929, when the Elim Foursquare Gospel Alliance (EFGA) was created. The name highlighted the distinctive tenets: Jesus Christ as Savior, Healer, Baptizer, and Coming King. In 1928 there were 70 churches; another 108 were added by 1934. In 1924 E. J. Phillips (1893–1973), pastor of Armagh, editor of *Elim Evangel,* and former Preston student, was asked to take over the administration at Clapham. The structure was modeled on the Salvation Army (E. C. Boulton and others had been Salvationists). In 1934 administrative control was transferred to an executive council of nine men, with Principal George Jeffreys having appointed three. E. J. Phillips was secretary-general. The supreme governing body was the annual ministerial conference of the EFGA. This followed the pattern of Methodism, and a deed poll was drawn up in Apr. 1934.

After 1934 George Jeffreys was less successful in Britain. He achieved spectacular results in Europe, particularly in Switzerland, where he had 12,000 converts in 1935, with a further 2,000 in two weeks in 1936. He continued his futile search for the ideal form of church government, devoting his efforts to established or affiliated churches rather than to pioneering new ones. The constant changes and agitation led to conflict with the majority of the executive board and the ministerial conference. Substantial concessions were made, but Jeffreys resigned from the Alliance in December 1939. A small group of ministers joined him and formed the Bible Pattern Church Fellowship at Nottingham in Nov. 1940.

Coming so soon after the outbreak of the war in Europe, it was a severe blow. It was a barren time, as the consequent restrictions, evacuation, and bombing, as well as the internal problems, reduced the number of churches. It left many disheartened.

In 1944 an evangelistic committee was formed, and P. S. Brewster began with a pioneer crusade in Wigan, Lancashire. This was the first of several successful efforts. The number of churches rose to 250 in 1953, reaching 300 in 1962. A group of 10 Full Gospel Testimony churches founded by ˃Fred Squire (1904–62) joined the Alliance in 1954. In 1964 a group of 21 churches in the eastern counties joined the Alliance. A proposal in 1957 to seek affiliation with the Church of God (Cleveland, TN) failed to achieve the required 75% majority by only seven votes.

E. J. Phillips retired as secretary general in 1957. In 1965 the four-acre site in Clapham was acquired by the local authority, and offices were built in Cheltenham and opened in 1968. The Bible college moved to a 30-acre site in Capal, Surrey, where it remained until its move to Nantwich, Cheshire, in 1987. The constitution has been adapted over the years to meet changing conditions. A much greater emphasis is now given to shared leadership and team ministries. A number of churches have adapted their buildings to multipurpose facilities, particularly in city areas. The rate of opening new churches has slowed, but there has been growth within many local churches, and the Elim Pentecostal Church is larger now than at any time in its history. There are more than 600 churches in Britain and nearly 9,000 worldwide. The flagship church is Kensington Temple in London, which has an attendance of 6,000 each Sunday, with another 6,000 in its branch churches.

The first missionaries went to Africa in 1920 to work with ˃W. F. P. Burton. The Elim Missionary Council was formed in 1929 (later named Elim Missionary Society, now Elim International Missions). It works in 16 countries, with an annual budget of £400,000. In 1978 nine missionaries and four children were killed in Rhodesia.

■ **Bibliography:** E. C. Boulton, *George Jeffreys: A Ministry of the Miraculous* (1928) ■ D. W. Cartwright, *The Great Evangelists* (1986) ■ W. J. Hollenweger, *The Pentecostals* (1972) ■ B. R. Wilson, *Sects and Society* (1962). ■ D. W. Cartwright

EPICLESIS (EPIKLESIS) A liturgical invocation of the Holy Spirit during the Eucharist (or Mystery) to make the elements into the body and blood of Christ, or to descend on the people so that they may profit spiritually. The earliest appearance of an epiclesis in liturgical documents is in the anaphora attributed to Addai (supposed 1st-century apostle of Edessa) and Mari, and in the *Apostolic Tradition* of Hippolytus (d. 236). Both of these early epicleses are limited to prayers for the divine Spirit to descend on the eucharistic participants, however. The first clear mention of any transformation of bread and wine into Christ's body and blood is in the mystagogical catecheses of Cyril of Jerusalem (late 4th century). In the Egyptian Anaphora of St. Serapion, there is an epiclesis asking for the descent of the Logos instead of the Spirit.

The presence of epicleses in other sacramental celebrations is attested as early as the late 2nd century by Tertullian, who speaks of sanctification of baptismal water through the Holy Spirit. Ambrose and Cyril of Jerusalem also imply baptismal epicleses. Hippolytus mentions such a prayer for the descent of the Holy Spirit on the presbyter, the deacon, and the bishop for their ministry.

■ **Bibliography:** S. M. Burgess, *The Holy Spirit: Eastern Christian Traditions* (1989) ▌ A. Chavasse, "L'épiclèse eucharistique dans les anciennes liturgies," *Mélanges de Science Religieuse* 3 (1946).
■ S. M. Burgess

EPISCOPAL RENEWAL MINISTRIES See ACTS 29 MINSITRIES.

ERICKSON, ELMER C. (1896–1980). Swedish-American evangelist. As a young boy, Erickson attended the Sister Bay Church, a Swedish Baptist church in northeastern Wisconsin, with his family. As a result of their conversion to pentecostalism in 1911, Erickson, his family, and a few church members left the church and began to conduct pentecostal meetings in their homes. Deeply influenced by the local church polity that the Sister Bay Church practiced, he remained convinced that local church autonomy was the correct biblical pattern for each local church. Erickson, who was ordained as a minister with the Assemblies of God (AG) in 1918, staunchly believed that the independent Scandinavian pentecostal churches in the area should not join the North Central District of the AG when it organized in 1922 but that these churches should remain autonomous and free from any denominational affiliation. Erickson organized a meeting in 1922 in St. Paul, MN, during which several Scandinavian pentecostal churches agreed to remain independent from the AG and to fellowship with one another under the name Independent Assemblies of God. Today these churches are under the name Fellowship of Christian Assemblies. For the rest of his life, Erickson pastored the Duluth Gospel Tabernacle, which became one of the most

influential Scandinavian pentecostal churches in the U.S. during his pastorate. For several years he was editor of the *Herald of Faith,* which for years was the leading Scandinavian pentecostal periodical in the U.S.

■ **Bibliography:** J. R. Coletti, "Lewi Pethrus: His Influence upon Scandinavian-American Pentecostalism," *Pneuma* 5 (2, 1983).
■ J. Colletti

ERVIN, HOWARD MATTHEW (1915–). Biblical scholar, author, educator, and presently professor of OT at Oral Roberts University, where he has taught for more than 35 years. A Baptist by profession since his conversion more than 60 years ago, Howard Ervin is one of the earliest academically trained voices in the modern charismatic movement. He holds an A.B. and Th.B. from Eastern Baptist Theological Seminary in Philadelphia, an M.A. in Near Eastern Studies from the Asia Institute in New York, and a B.D. from New Brunswick Theological Seminary (NJ). His Th.D. in OT was awarded by Princeton Theological Seminary, and he took postdoctoral studies at the Institute of Holy Land Studies in Jerusalem and Dropsie College for Hebrew and Cognate Learning in Philadelphia.

As a pastor, lecturer, and teacher, Ervin is recognized both in the U.S. and abroad. His participation in the International Roman Catholic–Pentecostal ►Dialogue since 1979 has done much to open ecumenical channels between these two groups, and he continues to have a burden for spiritual renewal of the whole church.

Ervin is perhaps equally well known for his writing career, which has spanned more than 30 years. His *These Are Not Drunken, As Ye Suppose* (revised in 1987 as *Spirit Baptism: A Biblical Investigation*) remains a classic exegetical defense of the pentecostal and charismatic experience of Spirit baptism. He has also penned a series of essays on the practical implications of Spirit baptism (*This Which Ye See and Hear* [1972]) and numerous articles on charismatic renewal. Another important work, *Conversion-Initiation and the Baptism in the Holy Spirit* is a refutation of James D. G. Dunn's classic *Baptism in the Holy Spirit* (1970). Dr. Ervin and his wife, Marta, who have three daughters and five grandchildren, reside in Tulsa, OK.

Howard M. Ervin, a Baptist charismatic and professor of Old Testament at Oral Roberts University.

■ **Bibliography:** Autobiographical statement supplied to this writer ▌ C. Farah Jr. and S. Durasoff, "Biographical Sketch," in P. Elbert, ed., *Essays on Apostolic Themes* (1985).
■ P. H. Alexander

ESCHATOLOGY, PENTECOSTAL PERSPECTIVES ON

For most Christians the present determines the future: they believe they will reap what they sow. But for most pentecostals the future determines the present: their view of eschatology governs their view of current events. Their interpretation of prophecy has had a very significant effect on their perception of world historical events and on their political and social response to those events. On a smaller scale, their eschatological views have affected their own history by stimulating evangelistic and missionary endeavors.

1. Theological Background.

The pentecostal views on eschatology are not uniquely pentecostal but are widely shared with fundamentalist (and many evangelical) churches. The pentecostals, however, are unique in viewing the outpouring of the Spirit as itself a fulfillment of end-time prophecy. Some anti-pentecostal authors have seen it likewise—but as satanic in origin.

a. Premillennialism. In general, pentecostal eschatology may be characterized as premillennial, expecting the second advent of Christ prior to the establishment of the millennium, the 1,000-year kingdom of Revelation 20. This may be contrasted with the dominant 19th-century postmillennial view, which foresaw the church gradually bringing about a Christian millennium, after which Christ would return as King. The medieval and modern Reformed view tended to be amillennial, viewing the millennium merely as a symbol of the church age.

b. Dispensationalism. Premillennialists may be further divided into historicist and futurist persuasions. Historicist premillennialists see the fulfillment of prophecies as occurring within the historical church age; this perspective was discredited in the mid 19th century by the Millerites. The pentecostals are overwhelmingly futurists, expecting the major fulfillment of biblical prophecies to lie in the future, and nearly all expect those fulfillments to be imminent. A variant on the futurist position, known as dispensationalism, was developed by English-born John Nelson Darby (1800–1882). He believed that history could be divided into seven eras or dispensations, in each of which God related to humanity in a different way. The era of the church is parenthetical: prophecy is silent about it. The church and Israel are viewed as two separate people of God, each with a specific role. This view was popularized in the U.S. especially by the ▸*Scofield Reference Bible* (1909) and became the view that has dominated pentecostalism.

c. Pretribulationism. Futurists may be further divided into pretribulationists and posttribulationists. Most pentecostals have followed the prevailing view of the late-19th-century prophetic conference movement, expecting the rapture, or removal, of the church prior to a time of tribulation. Some, however, continue to expect the church to remain on earth through the great tribulation until Christ returns to set up an earthly kingdom. A smaller segment envisions a rapture in the middle of the great tribulation, the midtribulationist view. The doctrine of the pretribulation rapture has allowed pentecostals to preach on the one hand a pessimistic message of impending doom with "wars and rumors of wars" as a sign of the end, while on the other hand presenting the optimistic message of "the blessed hope" of the rapture of the church.

d. Antinomianism. Most pentecostals' view of the moral issues surrounding the fulfillment of latter-day prophecies may be characterized as antinomian. Since the fulfillment of the prophecies is predestined by the determined will of God, these fulfillments are welcomed as a sign of the end and are, in the pentecostals' view, justified—not subject to ordinary measurements of God's moral laws. The end justifies the means. They have applauded the restoration of Israel, no matter what the means employed, while at the same time deploring rising crime rates and wishing to reverse the trend. Yet they view both of these phenomena as fulfillment of prophecy. The application of the principle has not been consistent. This moral problem was not new, as evidenced by Jesus' statement about his own betrayal: "The Son of Man will go as it has been decreed, but woe to that man who betrays him" (Luke 22:22).

2. Israel.

The pentecostals' perception of history has been most influenced by their premillennialist belief that the restoration of Israel to Palestine is a sure sign of the imminent return of Christ. Belief in the restoration of Israel had been an important part of Puritan theology as well as of the prophetic conference movement, but the pentecostals associated the development of modern Zionism with the era of the outpouring of the Spirit, thus producing a sense of kindredness.

Pentecostals were thrilled during WWI by the announcement of the British foreign secretary, Arthur Balfour, that Britain favored the establishment in Palestine of a home for the Jews. Just over a month later, the Turks abandoned Jerusalem to the British. The event was heralded as "the end of the times of the Gentiles." The eventual establishment of the state of Israel in 1948 and the capture of the old city of Jerusalem by the Israelis in 1967 would likewise be interpreted as marking the end of the times of the Gentiles. The whole purpose of WWI, according to some, was the freeing of the Holy Land from the Turks.

After the war Britain was given control of Palestine under a mandate from the newly established League of Nations. British leaders attempted to limit Jewish migration to Palestine, for the Balfour Declaration had also promised protection of the civil rights of non-Jews in Palestine. These limitations were severely criticized by pentecostals as violating the divine plan. In 1937, in the face of irreconcilable differences between the Arabs and the Jews, the British recommended the partitioning of the land into two separate states. This plan was criticized at first but was later reevaluated as a direct fulfillment of prophecy. Over the long haul, though, interpreters expected and cheered the prospect of the entire Holy Land being restored to Jewish autonomy in spite of the Arabic dominance in the region for centuries.

Between the world wars rumors were rampant that the Jerusalem temple was about to be rebuilt and that the Jews were preparing for the restoration of Mosaic sacrifices. (These stories also flourished after the 1967 war, and they continue to crop up.)

The Jewish-Arab rioting culminated in the British withdrawal from Palestine in 1948, and the Jews won the ensuing battles and established an independent state of Israel. The United Nations had attempted a partition of the land, but this was rejected by both parties, and the victorious Jews refused to be bound by the suggested borders. Pentecostal preachers exhorted everyone to rejoice over the failure of the partition plan, give thanks for the glorious sign of the end times, and prepare for the rapture that was, of course, even more imminent than the establishment of the earthly kingdom in Jerusalem.

It is interesting to note that prior to 1948 one major interpretation of the prophecies, following the scheme of the *Scofield Bible*, called for the Jews to be converted prior to the restoration to the land. Even after 1948 some voices continued to separate the coming religious restoration from the existing political restoration, but the overwhelming majority simply reinterpreted the prophecies after the fact when faced with the awesome reality of what they called the greatest event of the century. Even though many had been wrong in the specifics of their interpretation, the establishment of Israel greatly enhanced the credibility of the premillennialists in general.

Some moderate voices decried the Jews' treatment of the Arab refugees, lamenting that the methods were not of God even if the fulfillment of prophecy was of God. At the same time, however, they pointed out that the Jews would have been justified in taking all of the land, including that across the Jordan River, which they had not been able to do.

In 1956, in response to Arab pressures and to the Egyptian nationalization of the Suez Canal, the Israelis, in conjunction with the French and British, attacked Egypt. Under pressure from both Russia and the U.S., the Israelis were forced to withdraw. Pentecostal response was that the attack had been brash, but that, nevertheless, it was likely part of the divine plan because it would probably hasten the coming Russian attack at the Battle of Armageddon, which would occur during the great tribulation.

Israel's 1967 June War brought a more critical attitude among the wider Christian community toward Israeli expansionism. But the annexation of all of Jerusalem was enthusiastically received by the pentecostals. Former general superintendent of the ›Assemblies of God (AG) ›Ralph M. Riggs asserted that the 1967 war confirmed that God gave Palestine to the Jews. Israeli officials developed the policy of cultivating the support of the premillennialists in order to influence public opinion in their favor. Particularly useful were highly visible figures such as ›Oral Roberts, who was invited to the Holy Land and given red-carpet treatment.

Support for Israel has continued through the Yom Kippur War of 1973, the attack on Iraq in 1981, and the invasion of Lebanon in 1982. Pentecostals are admonished that it is their duty to stand behind Israel and are reassured that Israel will never be destroyed by the Arabs. This is usually accompanied by an appeal to self-interest: that the Jews are God's chosen people and that he will bless those who bless Israel. In the 1980s that support has followed the direction of rightwing fundamentalism and has become more political in nature. The appeal has gone to pentecostal congregations to sign petitions and send money for lobbyists to get the U.S. government to move its embassy to Jerusalem and thus recognize Israel's claims to territory conquered in war—which is strictly prohibited under international law. Laypersons influenced by pentecostal dispensationalism have become influential in Christian lobbies such as the American Christian Trust headed by Bobi Hromas. This group maintains a continuous prayer vigil across the street from the Israeli embassy in Washington, DC, and sends money to Israel to support Jewish settlements in the occupied West Bank.

3. Anti-Semitism.

While pentecostals have been staunch backers of Zionism, they have at the same time, ironically, been tolerant of anti-Semitism. Persecution of the Jews has been treated matter-of-factly as God's means of driving the Jews out of the lands of their dispersion back into their God-given homeland of Palestine. This was not antinomianism, however, for the perpetrators of crimes against God's chosen people would be punished, and those who blessed Israel, "the apple of his eye," would be rewarded. The victory of tiny Japan over giant Russia in 1905 was seen as a punishment for Russian persecution of the Jews. The execution of Czar Nicolas I by the Bolsheviks was God's retribution for his treatment of the Jews. In 1931 the U.S. was depicted, even as it began its slide into the Depression, as a prosperous nation being blessed by God for its kindly treatment of the Jews.

The pentecostals shared in the anti-Semitism that pervaded American culture. In the 1920s a forged document entitled the *Protocols of the Elders of Zion*, which was purportedly written by Jewish conspirators who were bent on taking over the world, was circulated. These were widely distributed by Henry Ford and were accepted as legitimate by pentecostals as well as by other premillennialists. This tended to reinforce the endemic American anti-Semitism and thus perpetuated the apathy of the church community toward the forthcoming Jewish Holocaust. When the Germans and Russians joined forces in the 1937 Nazi-Soviet pact, the binding force was simplistically viewed as anti-Semitism. It was not until WWII was over and 6 million Jews had been exterminated that the AG passed a resolution opposing anti-Semitism.

4. The Arabs.

Like most Americans, the pentecostals found little in common with the Islamic peoples, whereas the Jews shared with Western civilization the Judeo-Christian traditions. Premillennialists identified with people who at least worshiped the same God, even if they did reject his Son. But even beyond this, the pentecostals were indifferent to the existence of the native Palestinians, both Moslems and Christians. Their cavalier treatment of the likely destruction of the Moslem shrines in Jerusalem is particularly revealing of an underlying aggressiveness. At the time of the fall of Jerusalem in WWI, they were delighted by the prospect that British planes might bomb the Dome of the Rock and make way for the Jewish temple to be rebuilt. Reports of plots to destroy the shrines are usually editorialized with the observation that if the Jews do not tear them down, then God will do so with an earthquake.

As conflicts between Jews and Arabs developed in the Holy Land, the pentecostals consistently sided with the Jews. At the time of the 1936–37 disturbances, the Jews were identified as peacemakers who were trying to explain to the Arabs their ultimate intentions. When the British in 1939 attempted to restrict immigration, the pentecostal analysts observed that it did not make any difference anyway, for the whole land was eventually to belong to the Jews. In 1948 some admitted that the Jews had no rights in the land at all, but that they would return anyway, for it had been prophesied. There was criticism of the Jews' treatment of the Arabs, but that too was interpreted prophetically: the Jews were building up an antipathy that would in turn bring the great tribulation upon them. In 1956 the Suez crisis was justified because the Arabs were, after all, trespassing on the Jews' God-given land. In 1982 the invasion of Lebanon was given similar justification.

5. Russia.

Since 1917 Christianity has shared an antipathy toward communist Russia because of the militant atheism of the revolutionaries. In addition, the pentecostals have inherited an earlier, premillennialist anti-Russian attitude that stems from two sources: (1) Russian anti-Semitism and (2) the identification of Russia with "Gog" and "Magog" in Ezek. 38–39

and as a participant in the Battle of Armageddon in Rev. 16:16. More than anticommunism, and even more than anti-Russian imperialism, the pentecostals' attitude is sheer anti-Russianism. Since WWI they have persistently identified world events as always leading to an imminent Armageddon—to be preceded, of course, by their own escape from it all in the rapture.

This system predetermines that Russia will eventually attack, and therefore all peace overtures or disarmament schemes are ultimately doomed to fail. In a curious contrast to the antinomian welcome of Israel's inevitable expansion and fulfillment of her destiny, they have generally supported resistance to Russia's expansion in fulfillment of her prophetic role. No one is ever exhorted to rejoice that the Russians are coming.

Even peripheral events may take on apocalyptic significance. The 1924 Japanese Exclusion Act precluding Japanese immigration to America was interpreted as God's means of driving Japan into an alliance with Russia at Armageddon. Japan's invasion of China in 1931 and again in 1937 identified Japan as the "kings of the east" (Rev. 16:12), which would also be gathered to Armageddon. After WWII this label was given to India or China as they took over the headlines.

Between the world wars the Russian army was identified as preparing for Armageddon. And the Far East, the Near East, or Europe were all designated as places where the battle might break out. The start of WWII was depicted as leading to Armageddon; some lamented America's unholy alliance with Russia, while others perceived that the chief result of the war would be the rise of Russia to dominance.

As the Cold War developed between Russia and the U.S. after WWII, the arms race was seen as a harbinger of Armageddon. Prophetic voices were euphoric in 1948 as Russian aggression brought the Berlin Blockade and the overthrow of Czechoslovakia in the same year that Israel

Eschatological (dispensational) chart used at the Central Bible Institute, Umuahia, Nigeria (1966).

became a state. This was the peak of prophetic interest, not to be surpassed even by the occupation of Jerusalem in 1967.

The expected Armageddon became even more ominous as the Russians joined America as a nuclear power. As the nuclear arms race produced enough bombs to destroy the earth many times over, the premillennialists drew the conclusion that the Armageddon battle would be a nuclear one. But they had a unique twist to their fatalism: humanity would not be destroyed, for according to their prophetic model, many events were to transpire after Armageddon—Christ would eventually set up an earthly kingdom—so there was no need to fear the holocaust. War was certain, but so was survival. While other Christian groups attempted to be peacemakers and advocated nuclear disarmament, the pentecostals were resigned to divinely ordained war and were militantly anti-Russian and anticommunist: these were demonic forces that must be resisted in spite of their fulfillment of prophecy.

Interest waned somewhat in the era of detente, but in the 1980s it was further stimulated by Russian intervention in Afghanistan as it moved south toward Israel. Public opinion became more widely influenced by this eschatology as millions followed the teachings of popular television evangelists; almost all were premillennialists and pentecostal. Television personality ›Pat Robertson guaranteed the fulfillment of Ezekiel concerning Russia by the fall of 1982. Pentecostals claimed that President Ronald Reagan was premillennialist, as he had come under the influence of pentecostal laymen and clergymen as governor of California and then as president. These included Herb Ellingwood, George Otis, ›Harald Bredesen, and Secretary of the Interior James Watt. Critics were uneasy about having a president who believed that nuclear war was inevitable yet did not fear his own destruction. The whole idea of a nuclear deterrent to war seemed to be breaking down.

6. Europe.

The interpretation of events in Europe has been pervaded by the expectation of a latter-day revival of the Roman Empire in some form or another, to be presided over by the Antichrist. There is a variety of scenarios; a leading one identifies "Gomer" in Ezekiel 38:6 with Germany, who will form a northern confederacy with Russia. England has been identified with Ezekiel 38:13; her former colonies, including the U.S., being the "young lions."

Following WWI, the first candidate to be the revived Roman Empire was the League of Nations, a sign of the soon-to-come Armageddon. The predicted role for the league was that of defending the Jews against the Russians, Russia not being a member of the group. Mussolini's self-conscious revival of the empire, however, soon gained precedent. Italy's intervention in the Spanish Civil War in 1937 was depicted as a model for Mussolini's possible intervention

in the Middle East that would naturally lead to Armageddon. Some authors asserted that Mussolini was the Antichrist. It was more usual, though, to identify such world figures tentatively as probabilities or possibilities, the list including Hitler, Stalin, and Franklin D. Roosevelt. After WWII Hitler would be identified with the "hunters and fishers" of Jer. 16:16, whose function was to drive the Jews back to Palestine.

Prior to the Nazi-Soviet pact of 1939 it was frequently predicted that such an alliance would take place. When it did happen, the premillennialists virtually gloated in their accuracy. Then, when Hitler junked the treaty and attacked Russia in 1942, there was sheepish silence on the subject.

A flurry of apocalyptic interest accompanied WWII. In the first three months of 1941, 31 out of the 90 major articles in the AG *Pentecostal Evangel* were about prophecy and the war in Europe. After the war there was great excitement about the United Nations. Just as had been the case with its predecessor, the League of Nations, the U.N. was depicted as a forerunner of a one-world government that would be set up by the Antichrist. Students of prophecy were deeply suspicious of such organizations, especially when the goal was world peace, which the pentecostals considered to be a wild fantasy anyway.

The 1949 North Atlantic Treaty Organization (NATO), which included the U.S., was identified as a revival of the Roman Empire. Many teachers believed that the U.S. would be one of the nations destroyed at the Battle of Armageddon. Even though the church would escape all this in the rapture, this was not a teaching popular with patriotic Americans and was not stressed. The European Common Market in 1958 was also depicted as the revived Roman Empire, and its eastern counterpart, the 1955 Warsaw Treaty Organization's Council for Mutual Economic Assistance, chartered in 1959, was now seen as the great northern confederacy. Similar themes continued to be stressed among pentecostals in the 1970s and '80s. In the 1990s the expansion of the European Common Market beyond 10 members required a rewriting of details of the prophetic interpretation that had identified for many years the 10 horns of the beast in Rev. 12:3; 13:1; 17 with the 10 members of the Common Market.

7. The Pentecostal Movement.

The outpouring of the Holy Spirit is seen by pentecostals as an important sign of the end. A sense of urgency has been an important motivation for missionary endeavor and evangelism, making the pentecostals the fastest-growing segment of Christianity, which they attribute to the work of the Spirit. The terror of impending doom and the imminent blessed hope have been the heart of their evangelistic appeal. Many also believe that Christ will not return until the gospel has been preached to the ends of the earth. They have a duty, therefore, to facilitate his return by spreading the Good

News. Since the end is near, they are indifferent to social change and have rejected the reformist methods of the optimistic postmillennialists and have concentrated on "snatching brands from the fire" and letting social reforms result from humankind being born again.

While the pentecostals have interpreted the ecumenical movement as the great apostate church symbolized by Babylon, some Seventh-day Adventists have depicted the modern charismatic-pentecostal revival as the very means of unification for that ecumenical apostasy. Evaluations may vary, but the growth is undeniable. Whether that growth is due to the pentecostals' identification of nearly every current event as a sign of the end, or in spite of it, remains to be seen.

■ **Bibliography:** G. Halsell, *Prophecy and Politics: Militant Evangelists on the Road to Nuclear War* (1986) ■ W. W. Menzies, *Anointed to Serve: The Story of the Assemblies of God* (1971) ■ E. R. Sandeen, *The Roots of Fundamentalism: British and American Millenarianism 1800–1930* (1970) ■ G. T. Sheppard, "Pentecostalism and the Hermeneutics of Dispensationalism: Anatomy of an Uneasy Relationship," *Pneuma* 6 (2, 1984) ■ T. P. Weber, *Living in the Shadow of the Second Coming: American Premillennialism 1875–1925* (1979) ■ D. Wilson, *Armageddon Now! The Premillenarian Response to Russia and Israel Since 1917* (1977). ■ D. J. Wilson

ESCOBEDO, MODESTO (1889–1979).

Pioneer Assemblies of God (AG) pastor and evangelist in Mexico. He was ordained by the Latin District Council of the AG in Mexico City in 1925 and served as an evangelist and later as pastor of the AG work in Villanueva, Tampaulipas, Mexico. He pastored churches in Villanueva and Matamoros from 1925 to 1949. From 1949 to 1961 he served as a leading traveling evangelist, a presbyter, and national leader in the Mexican Assemblies of God.

■ **Bibliography:** Luisa Jeter de Walker, *Siembra y Cosecha: Reseña histórica de Las Asambleas de Dios de México y Centroamérica,* vol. 1 (1990). ■ G. Espinosa

ETHICS IN THE CLASSICAL PENTECOSTAL TRADITION

When talking about pentecostal ethics, we do well both to recognize the breadth of the topic and to take steps at the outset to limit the scope of the discussion. First, although this volume is devoted to pentecostal and charismatic movements, the fact that charismatics have their roots primarily in the Roman Catholic Church and the mainline Protestant denominations justifies not treating them here. Their approaches to moral theory and specific ethical issues generally reflect the moral teachings of the churches that form their tradition. These traditions, rich in their own right, do not offer a distinctively pentecostal approach to ethics. Second, pentecostals can now be found around the world in many cultures and among many people groups, each of which

confronts pentecostals with its own distinctive historical and contemporary ethical challenges. As a practical consequence, the specific moral responses of pentecostals in these manifold cultural settings cannot be meaningfully treated in a brief discussion; prudence dictates limiting the scope of the discussion. This will be done somewhat arbitrarily by focusing primarily on classical pentecostals in North America.

1. Moral Theory.

In the Catholic tradition, Thomas Aquinas's treatment of natural law comes quickly to mind as exemplifying what it means for a strain of Christianity to embrace a distinctive moral theory. Poised at the beginning of the 21st century, classical pentecostalism has not yet embraced a similarly compelling and clearly articulated moral theory. Put another way, there are as yet no moral theorists among classical pentecostals who (by defining a distinctive approach to moral theory to which either pentecostal clerical leaders or pentecostal scholars have felt compelled to respond) have achieved the stature comparable to the stature of Thomas Aquinas in the Catholic tradition. This fact is less indicative of outright disagreement among pentecostals than it is of the embryonic—or perhaps truncated—state of the discussion over moral theory in pentecostal circles. Holiness pentecostals, for example, have written at length about the nature, value, and role of sanctification. But beyond saying what sanctification might mean for one's outward appearance (e.g., conservative dress codes) or personal behavior (e.g., abstinence from drinking, smoking, dancing, gambling, and going to movies), they have generally drawn few moral implications. On the other hand, ►Finished Work pentecostals, such as the AG, have generally downplayed the importance of developing a comprehensive moral theory.

As a result, it is possible to sketch only in the most tentative way the main lines of a pentecostal moral theory. Given certain practices and theological commitments common to pentecostals, it is easier to say what the general features of such a theory ought to look like than to describe the specifics of any actual theory intentionally appealed to by pentecostals.

Murray Dempster, a social ethicist in the classical pentecostal tradition, has set forth several general features that, in his view, define the parameters for a pentecostal moral theory (1983, 1987). To begin with, an adequate pentecostal moral theory is, as he sees it, theocentric. This means, in part, that a clear understanding of God—particularly of his holiness and goodness—must guide one's life. But more importantly, it means that pentecostals distinguish themselves from other Christians in their view that God's Spirit resides at the center of, and enlivens, all aspects of pentecostal life—including its social, political, and economic practices, and its institutions. In addition, Dempster believes that an adequate pentecostal moral theory ought to be distinguished by its concept of the *Imago Dei,* its portrayal of what it means to be a covenant people, its prophetic tradition of social criticism, and its concern for the poor, the weak, and the disenfranchised. Elaborating on a theme first articulated by Stanley Hauerwas, Dempster also contends that an adequate pentecostal moral theory should provide a place for imagination. In his view, human imagination can be an effective instrument of God's Spirit to stimulate redemptive and transformative action in a fractured and chaotic world.

Within a network of valued relationships and activity, an ethics of imagination stimulates the moral agent in response to God's acts to reenact the human actions of liberation, justice, love, and reconciliation through a profound identification with the theological convictions and ethical norms of the biblical stories associated with God's creative power. An ethics of imagination not only aims at the reenactment of its stories, but also at the embodiment of its stories in the formation of the church as the new society (1983, 31).

Another scholar in the classical pentecostal tradition, Howard Kenyon, believes that although it is appropriate for pentecostal ethicists to call attention (as Dempster has done) to the experience of Spirit baptism, "what is equally needed is an understanding of the significance that the concept 'Age of the Spirit' has had on the Pentecostal worldview" (1988, 419). What made the early pioneers truly pentecostal was more than just the ability to speak a language they had not formally studied. What made them pentecostal was that their entire orientation was governed by the bold notion that they were living in the "Age of the Spirit" (414).

For Kenyon, this broader emphasis on the concept "Age of the Spirit" means two things in particular: (1) an adequate pentecostal moral theory must be eschatological, and (2) it must be prophetic. To be eschatological is to be future-oriented: "The final hope of the believer lies in the blessed hope, this hope that Christ will return and that the fulfillment of all promise lies in the age to come" (419). To be prophetic means to proclaim God's Word boldly and to articulate its social implications for the immediate day and age, rather than simply to foretell future events (420). (His understanding of the prophetic role of pentecostals seems close, if not identical, to Dempster's treatment of the prophetic tradition of social criticism.) Finally, Kenyon believes that an adequate pentecostal moral theory—eschatological and prophetic at its core—will embody three fundamental themes or messages that will be its points of departure for action: liberation, reconciliation, and justice (421–22).

2. Critique of Pentecostalism.

It is important to keep in mind that the features of moral theory described here are idealizations. At no time during the rise of pentecostalism have they (or any other models for pentecostal moral theory) been formally discussed and filled out in a comprehensive way (much less adopted) by the governing body of any pentecostal denomination or movement. In

a certain respect, this result is exactly what one would expect from a religious movement whose pioneers were bound by a common experience rather than a common creed.

But some scholars believe that the historical reality is actually more complex and darker than simply saying that pentecostals have not yet developed a full-bodied moral theory. Dempster, for instance, implies that pentecostalism has come perilously close to what he calls the "trivialization" and "evangelicalization" of the moral life. The moral life is "trivialized" when pentecostals diminish its profundity and weightiness by focusing narrowly on inconsequential, personal, and external behaviors. It is "evangelicalized" when they occlude or reject altogether certain distinctively pentecostal beliefs and practices and uncritically assimilate themselves into the evangelical mainstream (1983, 46, 47, nn. 65, 66). Although Dempster does not actually say that pentecostals have succumbed to these reactions, the historical evidence strongly suggests that both have occurred in varying degrees in the classical pentecostal movement.

Kenyon carries the critique further than Dempster. Identifying the AG as an example of what can go wrong with a pentecostal movement as it proceeds through various stages of institutionalization, he argues that in three areas—the status of African Americans in church membership and ministry, the role of women in ministry, and the participation of Christians in war—the AG has "developed a set of moral principles lacking the distinctiveness of a thoroughgoing Pentecostal social ethic." In its early formative years, according to Kenyon, the denomination's ethical posture was shaped by four theological emphases: the imminent return of Christ, the authority of Scripture, the present age of the Spirit, and the priority of world evangelization. He contends that of the four, only two—the authority of Scripture and the priority of world evangelization—continue to have significant impact. In his view, the AG has been "reactionary, portrayed in the denomination's ambiguous attitude toward blacks; dogmatic, demonstrated in the fellowship's mixed approach to women in ministry; and pragmatic, illustrated in the General Council's dramatic shifts in its attitudes toward participation in war" (1988, iii).

In "Pentecostals and Social Ethics," Cecil M. Robeck Jr. offers a critique of the broader pentecostal movement. He prefaces his critique with two historical observations. First, revivalism and the Holiness movement were both deeply involved in bringing about social transformation. Second, pentecostals are heirs both to revivalism and to the Holiness movement: "The spiritual and social commitments of these movements lie behind the birth of Pentecostalism" (103). Robeck believes there is ample historical evidence of this heritage of commitment to social transformation. He cites a number of examples, including A .J. Tomlinson and his ministry to the poor of Appalachia, Lilian Trasher and her orphanage for Egyptian children, Aimee Semple McPherson and her Temple Commissary, and William J. Seymour's contribution to racial equality in the church.

In Robeck's view, pentecostals have been quick to recite Jesus' well-known words when he stood at the beginning of his ministry and proclaimed his call: "The Spirit of the Lord is upon me, because he has anointed me to preach good news to the poor. He has anointed me to proclaim release to the captives and recovering of sight to the blind, to set at liberty those who are oppressed, to proclaim the acceptable year of the Lord" (Luke 4:18–19 RSV). Unfortunately, according to Robeck, although pentecostals have invoked this passage as though they were empowered to do the same things as Jesus, they have actually appropriated them only in a narrow and limited way.

> While pentecostals have ministered freely to those enduring spiritual poverty, they have often ignored the plight of the economically deprived of our society. The approach all too often has been to move away from the city, and away from the poor, and to argue that Jesus anticipated that we would always have the problem of the poor around. . . . Pentecostals have typically overlooked those who are captive to the abuses of the unjust structures of society or ideology, and at times have turned their eyes away from the plight of those who are oppressed by their fellow human beings, whether by economic, political, social, military or even religious means. (104)

Robeck believes three factors largely explain why pentecostals, the heirs of revivalism and the Holiness movement, have departed from their historical heritage of social ethics. First, the millennial perspective of pentecostals differs markedly from that of many revivalists and Holiness folk of the 19th century. Shortly before the turn of the century they changed from a postmillennial to a premillennial position. Hence, pentecostals came at a time when "evangelicals" didn't have time to think about *building* the kingdom of God. Its coming in power was imminent. Second, the rise of the old liberalism and the social gospel tended to taint pentecostal, Holiness, and evangelical involvement with issues of social justice. It became identified as a "liberal" tool and therefore as something "off-limits" to pentecostals. Third, the issue of peer pressure also came into play. As pentecostals rubbed shoulders with evangelicals, they also adopted the values and concerns of evangelicals who stood over against "liberals" who championed the social gospel (106).

3. Issues of Public Policy and Social Ethics.

It is not possible to deal, even cursorily, with all the important specific social issues and the historical and contemporary responses of the various pentecostal organizations. The following few topics have been selected because they represent particularly pressing social issues to which pentecostals have chosen (or found themselves forced) to respond.

Abortion. Like most conservative evangelicals, classical pentecostals have opposed the practice of abortion on demand. However, unlike Catholics, who also officially oppose abortion on demand, classical pentecostals are relative newcomers to the public political arena in which the debate over abortion has raged. Whereas Catholics have a long and well-established stance against the practice of abortion on demand, pentecostals did not generally begin to focus serious attention on the issue until long after the 1973 Supreme Court ruling in *Roe v. Wade*. The AG, for example, did not adopt an official position on this subject until 1985. (By comparison, its position on biblical inerrancy was adopted 15 years earlier, in 1970.) The United Pentecostal Churches International adopted a one-sentence statement in 1974, but its fuller document was not adopted until 1988. The Church of God of Prophecy addressed the issue in its general assembly of 1981 in a discussion that took account of the various theological and scientific arguments of the time. Curiously, although the assembly went on record saying "to willfully abort that life [the life of the fetus] constitutes murder," it concluded its deliberations by adopting a measure merely "advising against abortions" (Assembly Minutes, 1981, 136).

Participation in War. Early pentecostals were generally but not universally pacifist, though they engaged in little formal or systematic theorizing on the issue. Particularly prior to WWI pentecostals commonly expressed pacifist tendencies, and during WWI some were conscientious objectors. Prior to America's entry into the war in 1917 most American pentecostals were strongly opposed to war. In the years between the world wars, the pacifist position steadily weakened. By the outbreak of WWII some pentecostals endorsed the idea of Christian participation in war and declared the pacifist position unbiblical. During WWII several pentecostal denominations reiterated their traditional pacifist positions. But the official positions of organizations like the AG and the Church of God were commonly ignored by their own constituencies. Following WWII the pre–WWI pacifist tendencies continued to erode. The Church of God altered its official pacifist position in 1947 to allow its members "liberty of conscience." In 1967 the AG altered its own position (dating back to 1917) so as to allow each member to choose combatant, noncombatant, or conscientious-objector status. (See ▸Pacifism.)

Race Relations. The history of race relations in classical pentecostal circles is mixed but generally does not reflect well on pentecostals. At the Azusa Street revivals in the early part of the 20th century (1906–13), people of many races worshiped together without apparent racial discord. At the time of the revival, Azusa was described by the press as a "colored" congregation that met in a "tumble-down shack." Yet according to Robeck, "it was a church where whites, blacks, Hispanics, Asians, and others met together regularly and where from their own perspective the 'color-line' was virtually nonexistent." In the decades that followed, pentecostals generally succumbed to the prevailing views of the popular culture. Few churches were integrated; the vast majority were single-race congregations.

Despite having its roots in the South where racial discrimination and segregation were overt and widespread, the Church of God (CG, Cleveland, TN) stands as something of an exception. Since 1909 the denomination has had a number of black ministers and congregations, and none of its official policies differentiated between black and white churches or ministers until after 1920. In 1926, at the request of black ministers (probably due to prevailing social attitudes of the time), congregations were officially segregated. Forty years later, in 1966, the denomination struck down all official barriers.

If the number of racially mixed congregations and racial diversity among leaders is a sign of a denomination's commitment to racial integration, then the CGP is probably the most racially integrated pentecostal denomination in the world. "The CGP may have been the first church to defy Jim Crow laws in their worship services, and they have long opposed the Ku Klux Klan" (*Church of God of Prophecy). The CGP has not only been integrated virtually from its beginning, its current leadership structure at all levels, including the general presbytery, is fully integrated, and its worldwide membership is constituted of roughly equal representation from African Americans, whites, and Hispanics.

The AG, basically a white denomination, has struggled with racial issues (particularly relations between African Americans and whites) somewhat differently than other pentecostal denominations. On one hand, the Assemblies has never banned blacks or formally segregated its congregations. On the other hand, it did impede blacks who sought ministerial credentials, and it contributed virtually nothing to the civil rights struggle in the 1960s. In the closing quarter of the 20th century the denomination's Division of Home Missions has devoted increasing attention to inner-city ministry opportunities, but the total number of African American members and ministers remains quite small. The Hispanic population is the fastest growing ethnic group in the AG. However, most congregations with substantial Hispanic memberships are not racially or ethnically mixed, and the AG allows separate church leadership structures at the district level where Spanish- and English-speaking churches coexist in relatively close geographical proximity.

The Church of God in Christ (COGIC) is the largest black pentecostal denomination in North America. A popular belief—the so-called Sisterhood Myth—is that the COGIC is the black counterpart of the AG. But doctrinal differences that differentiate the two denominations make this popular belief untenable. Despite the fact that the COGIC experienced a major split in 1969, the church saw phenomenal growth in the 1970s and 1980s. A notable contributing factor seems to have been the friendship the denomination's leadership extended to people in the charismatic movement, something no other African-American denomination can claim (*Church of God in Christ).

The most notable single event involving racial reconciliation in pentecostal circles occurred in 1994 at an interracial convocation of pentecostal leaders, ministers, and scholars in Memphis, TN. At that time the all-white pentecostal Fellowship of North America was disbanded in favor of a racially inclusive association named the Pentecostal/Charismatic Churches of North America. During the session—called by some "the Miracle in Memphis"—leaders of predominantly white pentecostal denominations repented of the long-standing racial insensitivity and implicit racism in the denominations they represented. Unlike the all-white leadership structure of the disbanded PFNA, the leadership of the newly established PCCNA was racially balanced: six whites and six blacks and headed by Bishop Ithiel Clemmons of the Church of God in Christ. Commenting on the convocation, Vinson Synan observed, "The high point of the historic gathering was the session where a white AG pastor washed the feet of Bishop Clemmons while begging forgiveness for the sins of the past. After this Bishop Charles Blake of Los Angeles washed the feet of Thomas Trask, General Superintendent of the AG" (1997, 186).

Gender Issues. In the late-19th- and early-20th-century origins of the pentecostal movement, numerous women emerged in leadership roles, including pastoral, evangelistic, teaching, and other ministerial roles. Some women were among the important associates of early pioneers like Parham and Seymour; others headed important ministries in their own right. In general they enjoyed considerable freedom to preach and carry out other ministries in the earliest days of the movement. After 1920 women in leadership and public-ministry roles declined dramatically and continued to do so until the charismatic renewal, when in some quarters the momentum was reversed. The reasons for the decline are numerous and complex. However, one of the major reasons seems to have been the influence on pentecostals by fundamentalists, whose teachings about certain biblical passages on the role of women gained ascendancy in conservative Christian circles and eventually among pentecostals.

4. Social Norms and Mores in Daily Life and Practice.

To the extent that classical pentecostals have roots in the Holiness movement, they have been deeply affected by the social norms and mores of that movement. For example, the

AG and the CG, both historically indebted to the Holiness movement, established strong social norms (including, in many instances, standards of church membership) in their early formative years that reflect the beliefs and social expectations of the Holiness movement. These included stringent proscriptions on alcohol and tobacco use, social dancing, attendance at movies, use of cosmetics, and wearing of jewelry. It also included distinctly conservative (even austere) standards for apparel and hairstyles. Most of these social norms and mores were justified on the grounds that while spiritual and moral maturity are matters of the "inner" life, outward appearance and behavior reflect one's spiritual condition. Thus, for example, in its official statement of practical commitments, the CG cites scriptural references supporting the claim that the human body is the temple of the Holy Ghost and speaks of "glorifying God in our body." It goes on to identify numerous types of behaviors and practices that degrade the human body and thus defile the believer's relationship with God. The United Pentecostal Church International has gone so far as to adopt official position papers on several topics it deems significant: gambling, modesty, makeup, jewelry, television programs, even organized sports and technology. The AG has not formally gone to the same lengths, but it has adopted position papers regarding alcohol (complete abstinence) and gambling (gambling, whether legal or illegal, is an evil to be avoided).

Despite extensive teaching and preaching on a wide range of social norms and mores, and despite extensive admonishment by church leaders (including adopting carefully crafted position papers), most pentecostal churches have seen a steady erosion of their social norms and standards for personal conduct and appearance since WWII. The generations of pentecostals who were in their teens and twenties in the 1950s experienced enticements and pressures to conform to the popular culture that earlier generations had not faced. Some of them also expressed not only a felt need to conform to the dress styles, mannerisms, and fads adopted by their nonpentecostal peers, but also a measure of embarrassment over what they perceived as the quaint and outdated fashions of their parents' generation.

Three technological/social phenomena of the post-WWII era affected pentecostals profoundly and irrevocably: widespread access to automobiles, easy availability of handheld transistor radios, and steady arrival of televisions in homes. Automobiles granted North American young people, including pentecostal young people, the privilege of traveling places and being with people in ways not generally available to pre-WWII generations. As teen pregnancy increased in the general population, it also increased among teens from pentecostal families, who discovered comfortable, private accommodations in the backseats of their cars. Automobiles also provided convenient private places to try the alcohol and tobacco products their parents had forbidden them to use. The widespread availability of inexpensive, handheld transistor radios allowed immediate access to popular secular music. The emergence of television in the late 1940s and its widespread acceptance in American life in the 1950s affected pentecostal family and church life in ways that have yet to be fully understood. It was one thing for parents to forbid their children to attend movies (parental control, while not absolute, was generally effective); it was quite another to cope with and control viewing an electronic device (the television) that occupied a central place in the home and had the status of a prominent piece of furniture. The television, more than any other single technological invention, allowed pentecostal families to compare themselves with the popular images of family life presented by corporate marketing agents and program producers.

Having gained widespread acceptance and use in the 1990s in homes, businesses, and educational institutions, the Internet shows signs of posing an additional and somewhat different challenge than the other three technological/social phenomena already discussed. Paradoxically, although the Internet grants inexpensive, almost instantaneous access to sites around the world that people once either could not visit at all or found very expensive to visit, the Internet's primary social and moral challenge derives from the isolation it imposes on the user. Extended periods of intense isolation associated with Internet use—"cocooning"—challenge traditional pentecostal social values in at least two ways. The most obvious way is that during prolonged periods of private interactivity users can be exposed to kinds of web sites (e.g., pornographic sites) that directly contradict traditional pentecostal moral values. The less obvious but perhaps more substantial challenge is the way the Internet, more so even than television, militates against the kind of community building that has traditionally characterized pentecostal social relations.

Some pentecostal churches remain among the most conservative of any churches in North America, trying to adhere to their own long-held but gradually changing holiness standards. But increasingly large numbers of pentecostal young people—perhaps the preponderance of them today—are indistinguishable from their Gen-X peers either in personal appearance or behavior in matters once thought to be distinctive (if not defining) features of pentecostal life and practice. The social and moral challenge facing pentecostals today is whether they will be able to successfully nurture in the current generation of young people the spiritual and moral habits of the "inner life" (the original intent of the old Holiness movement) without alienating them by attempting to impose an outdated and unrecoverable code of dress and behavior.

■ **Bibliography:**

Books and Monographs. L. Christianson, *A Charismatic Approach to Social Action* (1974) ■ S. M. Fahey, *Charismatic Social Action* (1977)

■ H. N. Kenyon, "An Analysis of Ethical Issues in the History of the Assemblies of God" (diss., Baylor U., 1988) ■ H. R. Niebuhr, *Christ and Culture* (1951) ■ D. Petersen, *Not by Might nor by Power: A Pentecostal Theology of Social Concern* (1996) ■ L. J. Suenens and D. H. Camara, *Charismatic Renewal and Social Action: A Dialogue* (1979) ■ H. V. Synan, *The Holiness-Pentecostal Tradition: Charismatic Movements in the Twentieth Century* (1971, 1997).

Articles and Papers. E. Y. Alexander, "What Doth the Lord Require?: Toward a Pentecostal Theology of Social Justice," *SPS Annual Papers* (1996) ■ J. Beaman, "Pacifism and the World View of Early Pentecostalism," in *Pastoral Problems in the Pentecostal-Charismatic Movement*, ed. H. D. Hunter (1983) ■ C. Black, "The Holy Spirit and Christian Ethics," *Paraclete: A Journal of the Person and Work of the Holy Spirit* (Fall 1982) ■ M. W. Dempster, "Christian Social Concern in Pentecostal Perspective: Reformulating Pentecostal Eschatology," *JPT* 2:51–64 ■ idem, "The Church's Moral Witness," *Paraclete: A Journal of the Person and Work of the Holy Spirit* (Winter 1989) ■ idem, "Peacetime Draft Registration and Pentecostal Moral Conscience," *Agora* (Spring 1980) ■ idem, "Pentecostal Social Concern and the Biblical Mandate of Social Justice," *Pneuma* 9 (Fall 1987) ■ idem, "Responding to the Changing Official Position on Abortion within the Assemblies of God, USA," *SPS Annual Papers* (1993) ■ idem, "Soundings in the Moral Significance of Glossolalia," in *Pastoral Problems in the Pentecostal-Charismatic Movement*, ed. H. D. Hunter (1983) ■ H. Dyck, "*L'Esprit du Seigneur Est Sur Moi?* A Brief Analysis of the Social Ethics of the Pentecostal Assemblies of Canada (PAOC)," *SPS Annual Papers* (1996) ■ S. Hauerwas and S. Saye, "Domesticating the Spirit: Eldin Villafane's The Liberating Spirit: Toward an Hispanic American Pentecostal Social Ethic," *JPT* 7 (Oct. 1995) ■ P. W. Lewis, "A Pneumatological Approach to Virtue Ethics," *Asian Journal of Pentecostal Studies* 1 (1, Jan. 1998) ■ idem, "Value Formation and the Holy Spirit in the Pneumatologies of Thomas C. Oden, Jürgen Moltmann, and J. Rodman Williams," *SPS Annual Papers* (1994) ■ P. M. Moonie, "The Charismatic Renewal and Social Action: A Call to Involvement," *Zadok Centre News* 19 (July 1981) ■ C. M. Robeck Jr., "Pentecostals and Social Ethics," *Pneuma* 9 (Fall 1987) ■ E. A. Villafañe, "Pentecostal Call to Social Spirituality: Confronting Evil in Urban Society," *SPS Annual Papers* (1990) ■ idem, "The Politics of the Spirit: Reflections on a Theology of Social Transformation for the Twenty-First Century," *SPS Annual Papers* (1996). ■ M. D. Palmer

EUROPEAN PENTECOSTAL THEOLOGICAL ASSOCIATION (EPTA)

Following discussions at the Pentecostal European Conference in The Hague, the Netherlands, in 1978, EPTA was formed in 1979, in Vienna, Austria. Its stated purpose was "the promotion of Pentecostal learning, ministerial training and theological literature, and the fostering of exchange and cooperation between member institutions." Membership is either institutional (Pentecostal Bible schools and theological colleges) or individual. EPTA holds annual conferences, and the presiding officers hold office for two years.

EPTA differs from the North American Society for Pentecostal Studies (SPS) in several respects. It is strictly for pentecostals and does not include charismatics. It is more institution-oriented, addressing the concerns of pentecostal education and training colleges. Thus, papers at EPTA conferences discuss pastoral and administrative issues facing these institutions as well as strictly academic questions. EPTA also has an international and intercultural role, given the diversity of languages and cultures in Europe. In 1989 a committee was formed to assist with the development of pentecostal theological education and ministerial training in Eastern Europe; the conferences are held in Eastern Europe every third year.

The *EPTA Bulletin,* published quarterly since 1981, initially consisted of book reviews but began including scholarly articles on pentecostal topics in 1985. The format became more substantial in 1991 and its publication less frequent. It became annual in 1993, and since 1996 it has been called *Journal of the European Pentecostal Theological Association.*

■ P. D. Hocken

EUROPEAN PIETIST ROOTS OF PENTECOSTALISM

Pietism has been influential in the development of pentecostalism in both Europe and the U.S. From those two centers various emphases and concerns of Pietism have been transferred to pentecostal and charismatic movements throughout the world. To describe the influence of various expressions of Pietism within the pentecostal traditions, it is first necessary to look at the heritage of Pietism, its adaptation in the 18th-century Wesleyan revivals, and developments in late-19th- and early-20th-century European Pietism, as well as the role of American revivalism in both its Wesleyan Holiness and Keswick articulations.

What is Pietism? It has never been a monolithic movement. Pietism is ideologically and socially diverse; however, its main identifying characteristics are (1) affirmation of the possibility of a personal experience of God, beginning with a "new birth" by the Holy Spirit; (2) insistence that the experience of God has direct implications for the manner in which a Christian person may live (sanctification); (3) requirement of Christian community, a community that often understands itself to have a reformist stance against the larger social context; (4) chronologically, the designation of the particular confluence of these concerns after the development of confessional orthodoxy and before the Enlightenment, as well as groups and ideas tracing their heritage to this period; and (5) the near-exclusive use of the term for Protestant groups, although similar ideas and emphases are found among Roman Catholic and Orthodox Christians.

1. The Heritage of Pietism.

The major impetus for Pietism within the Lutheran tradition came from the work of Johann Arndt (1555–1621). Arndt edited writings of Thomas Aquinas and John Tauler, thereby making Catholic mysticism available to Lutheran believers. He contributed essays on "True Christianity," in which he insisted on the mystical union with God (new birth) and argued that Christian commitment is to result in a life of active piety, congruent with the model provided by Christ.

These emphases were picked up by many Lutheran theologians who articulated them primarily in tractates designed to edify the literate layperson and to exhort the clergy. However, it was only with Philipp Jakob Spener (1635–1705) that Pietism became a movement with defined goals. A scholarly pastor, he was well acquainted with the writings of the Reformers and counter-reformers. He concluded that it was not enough to provide doctrinal purity. The inner life of the individual was to be transformed. Spener suggested a method in *Pia Desideria* (1675) and introduced eschatological expectations as a motivational device. The method was to (1) develop Bible study sessions at which laypersons would be involved in the interpretation of Scripture; (2) implement the "priesthood of believers"; (3) give the practice of Christian truth priority over Christian dogma; and (4) develop the interior life of the Christian. Each aspect of this proposal received criticism from the more traditional Lutheran theologians.

Perhaps the most effective supporter of Spener was August Hermann Francke (1663–1727), pastor and theologian at Hamburg and then Halle. Francke's description of his conversion, emphasizing the role of the conscience, both in its unease and assurance, became paradigmatic for conversion within the Pietist movement. He argued that the soul senses the emptiness of love for the world and that it responds to the call of God with repentance that leads to conversion. This results in joy and assurance, both of which are reinforced by resisting the persecutions and temptations of the world. This understanding of conversion became central to Wesley's experience and was adapted by revivalist movements throughout Europe and North America. Francke also undertook serious and extensive efforts at social and economic reform.

One of Francke's students was Count Nikolaus Ludwig von Zinzendorf (1700–1760). Zinzendorf contributed to the survival of the movement by developing communitarian structures (Herrnhut) and critically interacting with and adapting to the Enlightenment in Germany. His critique of the Enlightenment influenced Goethe, Schleiermacher, and other German intellectuals. Zinzendorf was also more ecumenical in his understanding of the church, and this contributed to the spread of Pietist ideals beyond the confines of German Lutheranism.

Pietist *biblicism* developed in southern Germany. Johann Albrecht Bengel (1687–1752) was the most important early Pietist contributor to developing biblical studies, especially in textual criticism. His magisterial commentary on the NT, *Gnomen Novi Testament* (1742), later served as the basis for John Wesley's *Explanatory Notes upon the New Testament* (1755). It also contributed directly to pentecostal hermeneutics in Western Europe and North America.

Another Pietist emphasis, *primitivism*, developed gradually within Germany and was directly related to the issue of whether or not the group should remain in the Lutheran church. Some of the radical Pietists opted for separatism. It was Gottfried Arnold (1660–1714) who most definitively articulated the primitivist vision in *Die erste Liebe der gemeinden Jesu Christi, das ist Wahre Abbildung der ersten Christenen nach ihrem lebendigen Glauben und heiligen Leben* (1696; versions of this text are kept in print by pentecostal publishing houses in Europe). It argues that the true church is not defined by its doctrinal stance as judged by the confessional decisions but by its fidelity to the new birth by the Holy Spirit. He provided the framework for what would eventually become the standard pentecostal historiography, the "history of heresies" tradition. Primitivists have argued that the NT tradition is to be paradigmatic, and they have reevaluated many groups that have been judged heretical by the established churches, reinterpreting them as reform or renewalist movements seeking to reestablish the NT model.

2. Pietism in the Wesleyan Revivals.

Pietism influenced various aspects of English church life before 1800, including the Society of Friends (Quakers), Puritans, and Anglican theologians of the Caroline period. Each of these has influenced pentecostalism. However, the most significant channel by which Pietist concerns flowed into the pentecostal theological synthesis is that of Methodism in its various forms and derivative movements. The primary leader of the Methodist revivals was John Wesley (1703–91), who received his early theological formation from his mother, who had personal roots in the Puritan tradition, and from his father, who had studied the Caroline theologians. Wesley drew from both traditions and became attracted to German Pietism when he met a spiritually confident Moravian on a ship during a severe storm and soon after visited Herrnhut. He also adapted the insights of Spanish and French Roman Catholic mystics to articulate his vision for Christian spirituality, adding to the Pietist understanding concepts of human divinization found in 4th-century Christian writers.

Wesley's chosen theologian, John Fletcher (1729–85), was the first to use the term *baptism of the Holy Spirit* to describe the process of sanctification and the accompanying assurance of spiritual well-being. True to his Pietist heritage, he emphasized the internal spiritual changes of "new birth" and lifestyle as well as Christian responsibility for relief work and social reform. Fletcher became the Methodist theologian of choice in North America. His works were published in more editions than those of Wesley.

The Wesleyan-Fletcher theological synthesis was shaped by Pietist concerns. It developed in three primary, overlapping arenas within North America: (1) the Methodist Church, (2) the perfectionistic revivalist movements, and (3) in other denominations—a phenomenon that has been described as the "arminianizing of America" or the "Methodist century." The central concerns were those of the 17th-century German Pietists described above. Prominent evangelists and theologians included Charles G. Finney, Asa Mahan, Phoebe Palmer, James Caughey, Orange Scott, and Thomas Upham. The 1858 revival gave impetus to the Pietist concerns. D. L. Moody, William E. Boardman, Charles Cullis, Hannah Whitall Smith, Robert Pearsall Smith, George Müller, William Arthur, A. B. Simpson, S. D. Gordon, Andrew Murray, and R. A. Torrey became important exponents of the "higher Christian Life." Hannah Whitall Smith's *Christian's Secret of a Happy Life* (1875) became the standard interpretation of the spiritual life advocated by the revivalist movement.

The Smiths and Boardman were instrumental in establishing the series of meetings that became known as the Keswick movement. Because of the personal moral problems of Robert Pearsall Smith and the different cultural conditions in which Keswick initially functioned, American perfectionist expectations were separated from the doctrine of sanctification, as was Pietist social concern. Keswickian perspectives significantly influenced the Reformed wing of the American Holiness movement. As Juhuni Kuosmanen, *Heratyksen Historia* (1979); Daniel Brandt-Bessire, *Aux sources de la spiritualité pentecôtiste* (1986); and especially Donald Dayton, *The Theological Roots of Pentecostalism* (1987), have demonstrated, both Keswickian and Wesleyan perfectionist elements of the Holiness movement provided theological paradigms and leadership to the nascent American pentecostal movement.

3. Nineteenth-Century European Pietism and Pentecostalism.

The traditions of classical Pietism that have influenced pentecostalism are diverse and regionally specific. Also, the extent of direct influence is problematic, since relationships between and reading patterns of early adherents are difficult to define. Examination of several early European pentecostal periodicals indicates that American and British Holiness-Keswick authors are cited more frequently than all other traditions combined. The most frequently cited authors are W. Boardman, H. W. Smith, C. Finney, D. L. Moody, A. J. Gordon, S. D. Gordon, W. Arthur, A. B. Simpson, R. A. Torrey, J. A. Dowie, E. Irving, and A. Murray. They are used as definitive authorities on spiritual life, theology, mission, and

evangelism. Melvin Dieter, *The Holiness Revival of the Nineteenth Century* (1980), discusses the transference of American Wesleyan Holiness spirituality to Britain and the Continent as well as its transformation in that context.

However, there were important parallel or complementary traditions in Europe. In Germany, the efforts of Robert Pearsall Smith, later reinforced by R. A. Torrey, were institutionalized and indigenized in the *Heiligungsbewegung* or *Gemeinschaftsbewegung*. Leaders included T. Christlieb, E. Schrenk, C. H. Rappard, E. Modersohn, and J. Vetter. Theodor Jellinghaus (1841–1913), author of *Das vollige gegenwartige Heil durch Christum* (1880; 5th ed., 1903), and Jonathan A. B. Paul were the most important theologians. The movement later split, as chronicled in Dieter Lange, *Eine Bewegung Bricht sich Bahn* (1979), over the issue of pentecostalism; however, the popular books of the *Gemeinschaftsbewegung* writers on theology and spirituality have continued to circulate in pentecostal churches.

In Scandinavia there were other Pietist traditions. While there was significant interchange across changing political boundaries, Hans Nielsen Hauge (1771–1824) was particularly influential in Norway, while Lars Levi Laestadius (1800–61) and Peter Waldenstrom (1838–1917) were especially influential in Sweden and Finland. Methodist, Baptist, and Darbyist thought were significant throughout Europe, as was the example of the Salvation Army.

Other European Pietist figures became paradigmatic of how the pentecostal theological synthesis should be lived in Europe. Andrew Murray provided a model for theological writing, Otto Stockmeyer and A. Monod were known for preaching and pastoral skills, and J. F. Oberlin was exemplary of Pietist social analysis and social ministry. Johann Christoph Blumhardt's experiences with healing at Möttlingen provided a counterbalance to Anglo-Saxon traditions; the Bad Boll healing ministry continued by his son, Christoph Blumhardt, suggested institutional forms, as did the ministries of Friedrich and Friedrich von Bodelschwingh (father and son).

4. Conclusion.

Through these and other sources, pentecostals in North America and Europe were influenced by classical Pietist concerns. Pentecostals on both continents have continued to articulate the central foci of Pietist thought. The differences in theology and praxis are in significant measure due to the divergent expressions of Pietism encountered at crucial stages in the development of national movements.

See also HOLINESS MOVEMENT.

■ **Bibliography:** K. Aland, *Pietismus und Bibel* (1970) ■ idem, *Frommigkeit und Theologie. Gesammelte Aufsatze zum Pietismus und zur Erwekungsbewegung* (1980) ■ idem, *Geschichte des Pietismus* (1978) ■ idem, *Spener Studien* (1943) ■ idem, *Studien zur Theolo-*

gie Zinzendorfs (1962) ▪ E. Bayreuther, *Der junge Zinzendorf* (1957–61) ▪ D. Blaufuss, *Spener Arbeiten* (1980) ▪ N. Bloch-Hoell, *Pinsebevegelsen* (1956) ▪ M. Brecht, "Probleme der Pietismusforschung," *Dutch Review of Church History* 76 (1997) ▪ D. Dayton, D. Faupel, and D. D. Bundy, *The Higher Christian Life* (1985) ▪ P. Fleisch, *Die moderne Gemeinschaftsbewegung in Deutschland* (1912) ▪ idem, *Die Pfingstbewegung in Deutschland* (1957) ▪ E. Geise, *Und flicken die Netze: Dokumente zur Erweckungsgeschichte des 20. Jahrhunderts* (1976) ▪ E. Geldbach, ed., *Evangelisches Gemeindelexikon* (1978) ▪ M. Gerhardt and A. Adam, *Friedrich von Bodelschwingh,* 3 vols. (1955–58) ▪ P. Grunberg, *Philipp Jakob Spener* (1893–1906) ▪ N. Holm, *Pingstströrelsen* (1978) ▪ W. Koepp, *Johann Arndt und sein Wahres Christentum* (1959) ▪ G. Kramer, *August Hermann Francke* (1880–82) ▪ F. D. Macchia, *Spirituality and Social Liberation: The Message of the Blumhardts in the Light of Wuerttemberg Pietism* (1993) ▪ G. Malzer, *Bengel und Zinzendorf* (1968) ▪ idem, *J. A. Bengel: Leben und Werk* (1970) ▪ J. Müller-Bohn, *Entschiedende Jahrhundertwende. Geistlichgeschichtliche Beurteilung der Jahre 1895–1945. Originaldokumentation der Erweckungszeit 1895–1945* (1972) ▪ J. Ohlemacher, *Die Gemeinschaftsbewegung in Deutschland: Quellen zu ihrer Geschichte 1887–1914* (1977) ▪ A. Outler, *John Wesley* (1972) ▪ E. Peschke, *Bekehrung und Reform. Ansatz und Wurtzeln der Theologie A. H. Franckes* (1977) ▪ idem, *Studien zur Theologie A. H. Franckes* (1964–66) ▪ H. Renkewitz, *Im Gespräch mit Zinzendorfs Theologie* (1980) ▪ A. Ritschl, *Geschichte des Pietismus* (1880–86; repr. 1961) ▪ J. Sauter, *Die Theologie des Reiches Gottes beim alteren und jungeren Blumhardts* (1962) ▪ M. Scharfe, *Die Religion des Volkes* (1980) ▪ M. Schmidt, *Der Pietismus als theologische Erscheinung* (1984) ▪ idem, *Pietismus* (1972) ▪ idem, *Wiedergeburt und neuer Mensch. Gesammelte Studien zur Geschichte des Pietismus* (1969) ▪ F. E. Stoeffler, *German Pietism During the Eighteenth Century* (1973) ▪ idem, *The Rise of Evangelical Pietism* (1965) ▪ Patrick Streiff, *Jean de la Flechere ... ein Beitrag zur Geschichte des Methodismus* (1984) ▪ Henryk Ryszerd Tomaszewski, "Grupy Chrześcijańskie Typu Evangeliczno-Baptystycznego na Terenie Polski od 1858–1939" (Ph.D. diss., Warsaw, 1978) ▪ C. P. van Andel, *Gerhard Tersteegen. Leben und Werk* (1973) ▪ J. Wallmann, *P. J. Spener und die Anfänge des Pietismus* (1970).

▪ D. D. Bundy

EVANGELICALISM The NT Greek word *euangelion* has been called the richest word in the Christian vocabulary. In biblical usage, "good news" refers to the central core of the Christian message of salvation, its primary meaning to this day. Since the Protestant Reformation, however, the word *evangelical* has taken on various specialized doctrinal and denominational meanings used to define several Christian traditions.

The Reformation use of the word and its derivatives is seen in the names of several Lutheran denominations and institutions (such as the Evangelical Lutheran Church in the United States), the Evangelical and Reformed Church, and the ʾNational Association of Evangelicals (NAE). The first person to employ the word *evangelical* to denote a specific doctrinal tradition was Martin Luther, who used it to define Christians who stressed justification "by faith alone" and who used the Bible as the final authority, in contrast to the Roman Catholic ecclesiastical system, which allowed a place for tradition and good works along with faith.

In addition to the foregoing basic assumptions, Luther added the universal priesthood of believers in contrast to Roman claims for an exclusive priesthood of the ordained clergy. Therefore, Roman Catholic theologians such as Erasmus, Thomas More, and Johannes Eck labeled the Reformers "Evangelicals," a term not accepted by Luther, for he saw the evangel as the essential core of Christian truth and not restricted to any sectarian meaning.

Nonetheless, the Treaty of Westphalia in 1648, and the *Corpus Evangelicorum* of 1653 recognized the Reformers as "Evangelicals." This usage was further entrenched in 1817, when the union of Lutheran and Reformed churches in Germany referred to both groups as "evangelical."

From that time forward, the word was freely applied to all Protestants in general, with no understanding that it defined any particular tradition within Protestantism. Thus, to this day in most predominantly Catholic countries, the term *evangelical* is the popular word used to identify all Protestant Christians, regardless of any particular theological tradition within the various churches.

It was in the foregoing sense that Calvin and his followers in the Reformed tradition were also called "Evangelicals." Calvin's *Institutes,* while promoting the predestination theory for which he became famous, agreed with Luther's basic contentions concerning justification by faith, the primacy of Scripture, and the priesthood of all believers. Added to these principles was the necessity of a conscious conversion experience to settle the question of election for the individual.

This understanding brought the action words *evangelize* and *evangelization* into the Protestant lexicon as methods of bringing persons to an understanding and acceptance of their election to eternal salvation. Nowhere was this more evident than among the Puritan Reformers in England and America.

The necessity of an evangelical conversion experience was an article of faith among the American Puritan settlers of New England. They were the first major group of evangelical settlers in North America. They created many of America's first colleges, including Harvard and Yale, as ministerial training centers for preparing evangelical pastors and leaders.

After the early Puritan communities evolved into the third and fourth generations, church leaders were vexed by the large number of church members born in the church who never had undergone a conversion experience. By means of the Halfway Covenant of 1657, those citizens of Massachusetts who had never undergone a conversion experience were nonetheless allowed to be members of the churches, although without voting or ministerial rights.

This emphasis on a conversion experience became part of the American religious folklore and an essential element in the various awakenings and revivals that have swept over the nation through its history. Vivid and often emotional conversion experiences were seen as necessary to salvation, despite the various understandings of the churches regarding water baptism and the other sacraments and ordinances.

The extraordinary revivals of Jonathan Edwards in Northampton, MA, in the 1730s and the mass evangelism of George Whitefield a few decades later had as their goal the conversion of many who were already church members. The story of John Wesley before and after his Aldersgate experience in 1738 clearly demonstrated the difference between the sacramental approach he followed before Aldersgate and the evangelical approach he followed for the rest of his life.

Most historians speak of the 18th-century Wesleyan movement in England as the "evangelical revival." Wesley clearly identified himself as an evangelical although he never severed his relationship with the Anglican Church. Since Wesley, Anglicans have been classified as high-church Anglo-Catholics or low-church evangelicals in the tradition of Wesley and the Puritan Reformers. In Britain, therefore, the term *evangelical* took on a new meaning, i.e., that of a particular party within an existing church tradition.

The term also became synonymous with any Protestant who refused to countenance the liberalizing influences that continually arose within Protestant churches. Thus, the New England Unitarian movement led by William Ellery Channing, Ralph Waldo Emerson, and Theodore Parker was opposed by such evangelicals as Timothy Dwight and Nathaniel Taylor. Similarly, when Horace Bushnell promoted a new "halfway covenant" theology with his 1857 book *Christian Nurture*, it was the opposing evangelicals who held firmly to the necessity of a conversion experience.

In Europe during the same century, other forces and events further helped to define the meaning of the word *evangelical* as it applied to Protestants. In the light of a perceived new threat from Roman Catholicism and the gradual loss of a clear evangelical witness in the major Protestant bodies, a call was issued for evangelicals to meet in London in 1846. This meeting, which was led by Thomas Chalmers (Scotland), Merle D'Aubigné (Switzerland), S. S. Schmucker (U.S.), and F. Tholuck (Germany), formed the Evangelical Alliance, which was to carry the evangelical cause into the 20th century.

The Evangelical Alliance formulated a doctrinal statement whose nine affirmations placed the evangelical movement squarely in the mainstream of traditional Protestant orthodoxy. These statements affirmed: (1) the inspiration of the Bible; (2) the Trinity; (3) the depravity of man; (4) the mediation of Christ; (5) justification by faith; (6) conversion and sanctification by the Holy Spirit; (7) the return of Christ and the Final Judgment; (8) the ministry of the Word; and (9) the sacraments of baptism and the Lord's Supper.

Because the foregoing statements made more liberal members uncomfortable, the Alliance was unable to exercise a major influence in the mainline Protestant churches beyond 1900. Thereafter, the liberals went their separate way, creating their own agenda; this ultimately led to the founding of the Federal Council of Churches and the World Council of Churches. On the other hand, the conservative evangelicals moved in the direction of fundamentalism.

The 19th century also saw tremendous growth among Methodists and Baptists in England and America. This growth greatly strengthened the evangelical cause. The Methodists, who spread rapidly across the American frontier, went beyond the conversion experience common to all evangelicals to emphasize a postconversion crisis that Wesley and his followers called variously "entire sanctification," "perfect love," the "second blessing," or "Christian perfection." Along with this emphasis on inner spirituality, the Wesleyans also stressed social responsibility and reform, typified by Wesley's famous opposition to slavery.

The Methodists came to America in 1766 and were organized as a distinct denomination in 1784. After the extraordinary camp meeting at Cane Ridge, KY, in 1800, the Methodists practically preempted the camp meeting as a tool of evangelism. Throughout the century various Methodists also attempted to renew and perpetuate the teaching of second-blessing sanctification in the church. These included Timothy Merritt and Phoebe Palmer after 1830 and John Inskip with his colleagues in the National Holiness Association (NHA), formed in 1867 at the close of the Civil War.

The revivalist movement unleashed by Charles G. Finney in the middle of the century also carried the evangelical message to the cities and towns of America. Finney, America's first "professional evangelist," preached a modified perfectionism, which demonstrated the ecumenical appeal of the Holiness emphasis so dear to the heart of the Methodists. The Oberlin Theology promoted by Finney and Asa Mahan became central to the message of mainstream evangelicalism in America. This emphasis greatly moderated the hard-line Calvinism that had characterized much of American Protestant theology since the days of Jonathan Edwards.

A stream distinct from the perfectionism promoted by the Methodists and other revivalists was the fundamentalist movement that arose in the latter years of the 19th century. Arising in reaction to the liberalism in the mainline churches, the fundamentalists felt threatened by the challenges of Darwinism and other emerging sciences that seemed to constitute a threat to the biblical accounts of creation. In the latter decades of the century a theological movement known as "higher criticism" arose in Germany, which attempted to make an accommodation with these developments.

After the turn of the century, those who favored this type of accommodation began to call themselves "Modernists." Conservatives who opposed this movement were first called "Fundamentalists" in 1920, using the term made famous with the publication in 1910–15 of *The Fundamentals,* a set of 12 booklets explaining the five essential and nonnegotiable fundamentals of the faith. They included the deity of Christ, the Virgin Birth, the substitutionary atonement, the inerrancy of Scripture, and the visible return of Christ. Edited by A. C. Dixon and R. A. Torrey, they were financed by California oil millionaires Lyman and Milton Stewart.

By 1919 an umbrella organization for like-minded defenders of the orthodox faith was formed under the leadership of William Bell Riley, an aggressive Baptist pastor from Minneapolis. Called the World's Christian Fundamentals Association (WCFA), the new organization brought some focus to the movement.

The struggles that ensued between modernists and fundamentalists were especially severe among Baptists and Presbyterians, eventually resulting in splits producing the fundamentalist Bible Baptist churches and Regular Baptist churches, and the Presbyterian Church in America (later the Orthodox Presbyterian Church) founded by J. Gresham Machen.

The nadir of the fundamentalist cause was the famous "Monkey Trial" of 1925 held in Dayton, TN, where a local high school teacher, John T. Scopes, was convicted of teaching evolutionary theory in the public schools in violation of a newly passed Tennessee law. Although no less a person than William Jennings Bryan led the prosecution, the defense of Clarence Darrow succeeded in painting all fundamentalists as anti-intellectuals who opposed the march of scientific and academic progress.

Thereafter, the fundamentalists withdrew themselves from public debate and entered a separatistic world of bitter censure against all who compromised the faith. This movement toward separation included the founding of many independent Bible schools and splinter denominations. By the 1930s it seemed as if modernism had won the day in the mainline American Protestant denominations.

In the meantime, a powerful new evangelical movement was forming out of the remnants of the separatistic ►Holiness movement that had left Methodism after 1894. This was the pentecostal movement that was born in 1901 in Topeka, KS, under the leadership of former Methodist ►Charles Fox Parham. This movement, which shared most of the basic presuppositions of fundamentalism, went beyond second-blessing holiness and the five points of fundamentalism to stress the present-day exercise of the gifts of the Spirit, especially those of divine healing and speaking in tongues.

The pentecostal movement was given worldwide impetus through the ►Azusa Street Mission in Los Angeles, pastored by the black Holiness preacher ►William J. Seymour. From 1906 to 1909 thousands of Azusa Street pilgrims were baptized in the Holy Spirit and spread the pentecostal message around the world. By 1920 the movement had crystallized into three streams: (1) the Holiness pentecostals, who continued to stress a second-blessing sanctification experience; (2) the Baptistic pentecostals, who taught a finished work theology that denied the necessity of a second blessing; and (3) the ►Oneness pentecostals, who denied the doctrine of the Trinity while emphasizing a Unitarianism of the Son, Jesus Christ.

It soon became apparent that the pentecostals were something different from the fundamentalists, who thereafter reasserted the ancient theory of the cessation of the charismata. This theory denied the possibility of supernatural gifts in modern times. Warfield's 1918 anticharismatic book, *Counterfeit Miracles,* established the fundamental opposition to the rising pentecostal movement. The dispensational scheme accepted by most fundamentalists left no place for a pentecostal "Latter Rain" teaching that called for a restoration of signs and wonders in the last days before the end of the age and the second coming of Christ. In 1928 the WCFA rejected the pentecostals as "fanatical" and "unscriptural."

Until WWII the conservative evangelicals in America consisted of a dwindling and defeated minority in the mainline denominations, the splinter groups that had separated from the mainline churches, the Holiness and pentecostal churches, and the independent fundamentalist groups centering around such leaders as Bob Jones and Carl McIntire. The public image of fundamentalism was that of negative, censorious legalists who were more interested in attacking their opponents than in proclaiming a positive gospel.

In 1941 Carl McIntire attempted to bring all fundamentalists together in a new coalition that he called the American Council of Christian Churches (ACCC). He regarded this as a countermovement to the liberal Federal Council of Churches (FCC). By this time, however, there were many conservative evangelicals prepared to shed the image of the fighting fundamentalist and return to the classical evangelicalism exemplified by the Evangelical Alliance, which predated the fundamentalist controversy. Leaders in this movement were Harold J. Ockenga of Boston's Park Street Church and Carl F. H. Henry.

These men led in the creation of a new evangelical coalition that stressed the basic affirmations of fundamentalism but with a new name and image that distanced it from the unfortunate associations of the past. Against the wishes of McIntire, the new National Association of Evangelicals

(NAE) was formed in 1942. To the further chagrin of the fundamentalists, the NAE accepted the pentecostals and refused to join forces with the ACCC. The NAE thereafter became the home of a "new evangelicalism" and provided a base for the phenomenal growth of evangelical Christianity after WWII.

Giving intellectual leadership to the movement was Carl F. H. Henry, whose 1948 book, *The Uneasy Conscience of Modern Fundamentalism,* became the textbook for the new movement. By 1948 Billy Graham began crusades that soon made him the outstanding evangelist of his generation. Always working closely with the NAE, Graham helped Henry establish the central organ of the movement in 1956, the fortnightly magazine *Christianity Today.* This periodical soon became the intellectual counterweight to the liberal *Christian Century* magazine.

By the 1960s, with the fundamentalists now on the sidelines, the struggle for leadership in the churches was between the new evangelicals and the liberal establishment that still dominated the ecclesiastical machinery of most major Protestant denominations. Largely ignored were the fundamentalists, who were not taken seriously again until the rise of Jerry Falwell with his new brand of activist fundamentalism in the 1980s.

During this period, the campaigns of Graham and the growth of the pentecostal churches were contrasted with the drastic membership declines in the mainline liberal churches. Another sign of rising evangelical strength was the growth of the Southern Baptist Convention, which by 1970 surpassed the more liberal United Methodist Church to become the largest Protestant denomination in the U.S.

Evangelicalism was brought to the attention of the nation and the world with the election of Jimmy Carter—a Southern Baptist—as president of the U.S. in 1976. A committed evangelical, Carter popularized the term *born again* to a nation that had largely forgotten its evangelical heritage.

"Born-again" religion also received a boost with the rise of the charismatic movement in the mainline churches. This movement represented the incursion of pentecostalism into the older traditional churches after decades of rejection. The first neo-pentecostal to make headlines was ›Dennis Bennett, pastor of Saint Mark's Episcopal Church in Van Nuys, CA, whose 1960 experience of speaking in tongues shocked the religious establishment. Soon thousands of ministers and laypersons in all the mainline churches were speaking in tongues and attempting to stay in their churches. Encouraging them was the traveling pentecostal ecumenist ›David J. du Plessis, who advised them to "bloom where you are planted."

By 1967 the pentecostal movement had entered the Roman Catholic Church, bringing evangelicalism into previously unthinkable territory. By 1979 a Gallup poll conducted on behalf of *Christianity Today* found that 19% of the American population (44 million adults and children) considered themselves to be "pentecostal or charismatic Christians." Part of the explanation of this phenomenon was the advent of the electronic church, which saw the rise of ›Pat Robertson's Christian Broadcasting Network (CBN) to prominence as an alternative to secular television. Following Robertson's lead were such evangelical television entrepreneurs as ›Jim Bakker (PTL [Praise the Lord or People That Love] Network) and ›Paul Crouch (Trinity Broadcasting Network [TBN]).

These television ministries followed the pioneering work of Billy Graham and ›Oral Roberts, who also helped found the National Religious Broadcasters (NRB). This coalition of evangelical broadcasters arose after WWII when the Federal Council of Churches attempted to gain a monopoly on religious broadcasting in America, which would have kept the evangelicals off the air.

The election of Ronald Reagan in 1980 marked a symbolic national political triumph for the new evangelicals. Some claimed that the born-again Americans had put him in the White House. Whether true or not, it was obvious that Reagan's positions on abortion and prayer in public schools were items on the evangelical agenda. The religious right instead of the liberal religious establishment became the spiritual advisors to the president.

David Barrett's *World Christian Encyclopedia* estimates that in the U.S. in A.D. 2000 some 41 million Christians described themselves as evangelicals. The world figure in A.D. 2000 stood at 210 million. This represented a remarkable comeback for the evangelical cause from the dark days of the 1920s. By this time the evangelicals had apparently not only survived their struggles with liberalism but were thriving in a world where the liberal churches were in a state of decline.

■ **Bibliography:** G. Marsden, *Fundamentalism and American Culture* (1980) ▮ R. Quebedeaux, *The Young Evangelicals* (1974) ▮ D. Wells and J. Woodbridge, *The Evangelicals* (1977).

■ H. V. Synan

Indigenous evangelists in the Lilongue section of Nyasaland.

EVANGELISM Evangelism has been a priority among pentecostals throughout their history. The historical self-image of the major pentecostal church bodies is that they were raised up to be an instrument of evangelism in the world. Traditionally, therefore, it has been felt that to be a pentecostal is to be an evangelistic witness. Pentecostals see aggressive evangelism in the pages of the NT, and due to their high regard for the Bible and their literal interpretation of Scripture, they interpret the pentecostal experience as a mandate for evangelism in its various forms and methods.

1. Definition and Nature of Evangelism.

The term *evangelism* has a multitude of explanations and definitions. The Madras Conference of the International Missionary Council came up with some 31 definitions. The word's history from the NT reveals a twofold usage—as a noun and as a verb. The noun *euangelion*, "good news," occurs 75 times: the verb *euangelizomai*, "to announce, proclaim, or preach good news," appears 24 times. The gospel is the evangel, the Good News. Evangelism is the act of proclaiming the good news of Jesus Christ in the power and anointing of the Holy Spirit with the intention that men and women will come to put their trust in Christ for salvation and serve him in the fellowship of his church.

For pentecostals evangelism involves much more than simply proclaiming the gospel. Evangelistic proclamation is not an end in itself but a means to an end—the persuasion of sinners to accept Christ as Lord and to follow him as responsible members of a local church who in turn proclaim the Good News. Pentecostal evangelism would reject the liberal tenets of universalism that say the work of evangelism is simply to inform people that they are already saved. Neither do pentecostals believe that proclaiming only for the sake of giving objective information is sufficient. Pentecostal evangelism involves the good news of deliverance over against the bad news that humanity is dead and bound in the oppression of sin. Pentecostal evangelism therefore calls for a confrontation; it is the conveyance of truth-as-encounter. The pentecostal witness preaches for a verdict and expects results.

This is the sense in which Jesus announces his mission of evangelism under the anointing of the Holy Spirit: "The Spirit of the Lord is on me, because he has anointed me to preach good news to the poor. He has sent me to proclaim freedom for the prisoners and recovery of sight for the blind, to release the oppressed, to proclaim the year of the Lord's favor" (Luke 4:18–19).

There is, therefore, a persuasiveness and aggressiveness in pentecostal evangelism like that shown in the preaching of the apostle Paul as he seeks to persuade King Agrippa to become a believer. Paul indicates that he has been rescued in order to rescue others through evangelism. God's commission to him is central to his evangelistic testimony: "I will rescue you from your own people and from the Gentiles. I am sending you to them to open their eyes and turn them from darkness to light, and from the power of Satan to God, so that they may receive forgiveness of sins and a place among those who are sanctified by faith in me" (Acts 26:17–18).

2. Biblical/Theological Foundations for Evangelism.

Pentecostals have seen their evangelistic outreach as more than the mere extension of a religious movement or recruitment to a particular ideology or experience. From the outset of the modern pentecostal movement there was a sense of "divine destiny," the participation with God in a new work for the last days. The theological mood and atmosphere set by premillennialism and the actualization of the experiences and promises of Scripture (particularly the "outpouring" passages such as Joel 2:28–32 and Acts 2:16–21) caused pentecostals to view evangelism as an extension of the purposes of God for the world.

Pentecostals have seen redemption as the central purpose of God in Scripture and evangelism as the comprehensive method for fulfilling that purpose. Their literal biblicism has caused them to be aggressively obedient to the Great Commission passages in the Gospels. Acts 1:8 could be claimed as the golden text for their style of evangelism: "But you will receive power when the

A gospel team with house trailer at Hickory Grove, OK, in 1912.

Holy Spirit comes on you; and you will be my witnesses in Jerusalem, and in all Judea and Samaria, and to the ends of the earth."

For pentecostals, the connection of the "power" in Acts 1:8 to the evangelistic task is quite clear: only the coming of the power of the Holy Spirit to those who are witnesses for Christ makes the work of evangelism possible. In this light the "power" passages of Acts 1:8 and 2:1–4 and the "enduement" passage of Luke 24:48 have been central to pentecostal preaching and teaching on evangelism.

Therefore, evangelism, and not other spiritual gifts or manifestations, should be seen as the primary result of the baptism of the Holy Spirit and the operation of spiritual gifts. Evangelism occupies the central place in the growth of pentecostal churches. Other supernatural manifestations revolve around it. Donald Gee contended that evangelism was a natural expression of the spiritual gifts of 1 Cor. 12. In his writings he argued for a combination

A colporteur at work in a village in the Congo.

of and balance between the manifestations of spiritual gifts and evangelistic proclamation to unbelievers. He believed that if spiritual gifts could not flourish in the arena of public witness, there was something wrong with their usage (see Gee, 1932, 1963).

Theologically, evangelism cannot be limited to the work of the Holy Spirit alone. "Evangelism," says Harold John Ockenga, "must be Trinitarian if it is to be biblical." The Great Commission itself incorporates the desire and activity of the triune God in that we are to go, to teach, and to baptize all nations in the name of "the Father, and of the Son, and of the Holy Ghost" (Matt. 28:19). The Bible honors each member of the Trinity, says Ockenga, in that "the New Testament makes it clear that the Father elects, which is predestination; that the Son redeems, which is atonement; and that the Holy Spirit regenerates, which is salvation" (Henry, 2:96).

3. Motivation for Evangelism.

A sense of participation in what is central to the nature and heart of God motivates pentecostals toward evangelism. Emerging from this central desire of God for evangelism come additional facets of the pentecostals' motivation for reaching the unconverted.

First, pentecostals have understood an obedience to evangelize as one of the primary steps of obedience in Christian discipleship. Therefore, evangelism is not an end within itself once a person has been reached and led to personal belief in Christ. Immediately this new convert is urged to testify to others and to begin preaching. He or she is "saved to serve."

In early pentecostalism in particular, one finds many accounts of people who stood up to preach within a few days of their conversion. C. Peter Wagner's study of the dynamic growth in Latin American pentecostalism indicates that personal witnessing and street evangelism by the newly converted were some of the central marks of their outstanding expansion (Wagner, 1986).

Second, it has been crystal clear in the theology of pentecostal evangelism that humankind is lost and is under the judgment of eternal punishment unless reached with the good news of the gospel (Ezek. 18:4; Luke 13:3–5; Rom. 2:12; 3:23; 5:12; 6:23; 2 Thess. 1:7–8; James 1:15; 2 Peter 3:9). The doctrinal confessions of all major pentecostal organizations reflect their belief in "eternal life for the righteous and eternal punishment for the wicked," with no "second chance" salvation.

This is related to a third motivation for evangelism: the imminent return of Christ and the end of all things. There is an "eschatological urgency" inherent in evangelistic theology and practice of pentecostals. Thomas F. Zimmerman, a former general superintendent of the Assemblies of God (AG), has stated the certainty of impending doom and judgment that hangs over the world in a coming retribution that will be both universal and final. Out of this reality he says, "Men must be told!" (Henry, 2:65–66).

4. Supernatural Evangelism.

The "telling" in pentecostal evangelism, however, has involved more than verbal proclamation. Pentecostals have understood miraculous signs and wonders to be demonstrations of "the Lord working with them, and confirming the words with signs following" (Mark 16:20). This was clearly the proclamation strategy of early Christians (Rom. 15:19; 1 Cor. 2:1–5). This makes pentecostal evangelism distinctive, since it proceeds from a worldview of power leading to what Ray H. Hughes, first assistant general overseer of the Church of God (CG, Cleveland, TN), calls "supernatural evangelism" (Hughes, 1968, 63). Divine healing, for example, has been an evangelistic door opener that leads to verbal proclamation (Acts 3). For pentecostals, every healing and miracle and every spiritual manifestation or "power encounter" in exorcism becomes an "earnest" of the kingdom of God and the means whereby the message and dominion of this kingdom are actualized in the lives of people who are delivered. Pentecostal evangelists and missionaries would identify with the report of one missionary from England to Le Havre in 1930: "Every new work is opened on the ministry of Divine Healing; for without the supernatural it would be impossible to get any interest created in the gospel message" (Frodsham, 91–92).

This conviction of "God among us and working with us" is one of the key factors in the persuasive attraction of pentecostal-charismatic worship. That pentecostal worship is a key evangelistic factor has been agreed upon by both inside interpreters and outside observers of pentecostal church growth. Central to pentecostal worship is the unique style of preaching in pentecostal evangelism. It is "a Spirit-endowed preaching which is pungent and penetrating," says Hughes, who claims that there is a "miracle element" present in pentecostal preaching, making it a powerful evangelistic force (1981, 149; see also McClung, 73).

Supernatural evangelism has also been called "power evangelism," a concept first articulated in the Fuller Theological Seminary School of World Mission and popularized by ›John Wimber, a contemporary proponent of its church growth school of thought:

By power evangelism I mean a presentation of the gospel that is rational but that also transcends the rational. The explanation of the gospel comes with a demonstration of God's power through signs and wonders. Power evangelism is a spontaneous, Spirit-inspired, empowered presentation of the gospel. Power evangelism is evangelism that is preceded and undergirded by supernatural demonstrations of God's presence. (35)

5. Evangelism and the Media.

Being aggressively intent upon evangelizing every available person, pentecostals have made extensive use of ›radio and ›television for the propagation of the gospel. Pentecostal radio preachers began blanketing the U.S. with gospel broadcasts in the 1920s and 1930s. Leading denominations established departments of radio and television as the church moved into the electronic age.

One of the earliest television pioneers was ›Rex Humbard, who constructed the Cathedral of Tomorrow in Akron, OH, to televise a local worship service into America's living rooms. ›Oral Roberts moved from the tent to the tube and expertly used the medium of television to telecast his healing campaigns and television specials. By 1985 he commanded an audience of 2.5 million households.

Later the pioneers of televangelism were joined by a new breed of television evangelists. ›Pat Robertson founded the Christian Broadcasting Network (CBN) and its popular *700 Club,* which eventually drew 4.4 million viewers daily. ›Jim Bakker began his broadcast career under Robertson's tutelage and later founded the PTL Network ("Praise the Lord"). ›Jimmy Swaggart began with the radio broadcast *The Campmeeting Hour* and eventually moved to television. By mid

Iowa-Missouri preachers of the Assemblies of God, early 20th century.

A street meeting in El Salvador.

1987 Swaggart was viewed by 3.6 million viewers per day and received 40,000 letters weekly at his headquarters in Baton Rouge, LA.

Robertson's ministry pioneered televangelism as a two-way medium with the establishment of phone-in prayer lines. Annually, CBN and the PTL Network were recording hundreds of thousands of conversions and miraculous healings. This was also the pattern established in the televangelism ministry of ►Paul and Jan Crouch through the Trinity Broadcasting Network in Southern California.

Contrary to the critics of televised pentecostal preaching, there was an established effort among televangelists to bring new converts into established local churches—pentecostal, charismatic, and evangelical. In many instances, televangelism was combined with mass crusades in overseas missionary preaching and new church planting.

Eventually, televangelism was to make a wider contribution to humanitarian ministries and higher Christian education. Oral Roberts established Oral Roberts University and the City of Faith Medical Center. Swaggart funneled some $12 million dollars annually into the foreign missions enterprises of the AG and funded an international child care program to feed, clothe, educate, and heal some 250,000 children in Third World countries. In addition, he founded a Bible college for the training of evangelists, pastors, and missionaries. Robertson funded Operation Blessing, providing food

and medical attention to needy people in the U.S. and abroad. Bakker's PTL ministry opened a home for handicapped children and another for unwed mothers. Pentecostals have effectively and positively used the media as a channel to preach the gospel of salvation.

6. The Future of Evangelism.

As pentecostals and charismatics stand at the beginning of the 21st century, there does not appear to be any departure from their aggressive stance on the need to evangelize. They continue to be committed to training and deploying evangelists. They have held congresses and consultations on evangelism strategy, particularly in the great urban centers of the world. Two statements, "A Declaration at St. Louis" (1968) by the AG and "A Covenant on World Evangelism" (1983) by the CG, reveal strong sentiments of self-identity as agencies for evangelism.

■ **Bibliography:** "America's Pentecostals," *Christianity Today* (Oct. 16, 1987) ■ A. A. Biddle, "The Holy Spirit Prompting Evangelism," *Pentecostal Doctrine* (1976) ■ D. J. Bosch, *Witness to the World* (1980) ■ R. Champion, E. S. Caldwell, G. Leggett, eds., *Our Mission in Today's World* (1968) ■ S. H. Frodsham, *With Signs Following* (1946) ■ D. Gee, *Pentecost* (1932) ■ idem, *Spiritual Gifts in the Work of the Ministry Today* (1963) ■ C. F. H. Henry and W. S. Mooneyham, eds., *One Race, One Gospel, One Task,* vol. 2 (1967) ■ R. H. Hughes, *Church of God Distinctives* (1968) ■ idem, *Pentecostal Preaching* (1981) ■ A. P. Johnston, *The Battle for World Evangelism* (1978) ■ L. J. Lord, "An Unholy War in the TV Pulpits," *U.S. News & World Report* (Apr. 6, 1987) ■ L. G. McClung Jr., ed., *Azusa Street and Beyond: Pentecostal Missions and Church Growth in the Twentieth Century* (1987) ■ C. P. Wagner, *Spiritual Power and Church Growth* (1986) ■ idem, *Strategies for Church Growth* (1987) ■ J. R. Williams, *The Pentecostal Reality* (1972) ■ J. Wimber, *Power Evangelism* (1986).   ■ L. G. McClung Jr.

EVANGELISTS The term *evangelist,* though briefly mentioned in the Bible, is not specifically defined. The term comes from the Greek word *euangelistems,* "one who proclaims good news." A pentecostal evangelist has traditionally been one who devotes himself or herself entirely to a full-time itinerant ministry of preaching the gospel, especially the message of salvation and deliverance. In this regard, an evangelist is one with a specialized ministry that involves more than being a witness for Christ (a duty expected of all believers in the pentecostal-charismatic heritage).

1. Biblical Descriptions and Models.

The word "evangelist" is used only three times in the NT (Acts 21:8; Eph. 4:11; 2 Tim. 4:5). Although Philip is the only person specifically called an evangelist (Acts 21:8), other workers may have functioned in the same role: Timothy (2 Tim. 4:5), Luke (2 Cor. 8:18), Clement (Phil. 4:3), and

Epaphras (Col. 1:7; 4:12). Evangelists are seen as a gift to the church from the ascended Christ (Eph. 4:11) and have traditionally been classed with apostles and prophets as itinerant workers, in contrast to pastors and teachers who are attached to local assemblies (though this may be an imposition from church history more than an interpretation of the Scripture itself). Many pentecostal pastors, in the spirit of the young pastor Timothy, have seen themselves in a dual role of pastor-evangelist (2 Tim. 4:5). Indeed, in the history of pentecostal tradition an itinerant evangelist often established a local congregation, continued to pastor it as founding pastor, and conducted occasional revival/evangelistic crusades away from the local church base.

The composite picture of a pentecostal evangelist would identify with the lessons emerging from Philip, a NT evangelist (Acts 8).

He (or she) is one from among the people, chosen as a deacon but gifted with a preaching ministry (Acts 6:5; 8:5). The roots of most early pentecostal evangelists were from the common people of the poorer class. Most were lay preachers later ordained to the clergy.

Miracles typically follow the evangelist's preaching (8:6). Divine healing and miracles of deliverance have been emphasized in the preaching of pentecostal evangelists as inclusive in the salvation message.

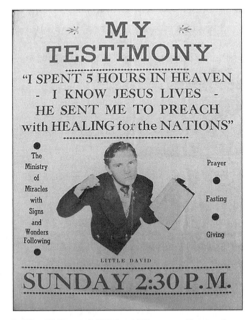

In the 1940s and 1950s child evangelists such as Marjoe Gortner and "Little David" Davillo Walker drew large crowds. Little David preached his first sermon at age 9, and at age 14 he preached for two weeks in the Royal Albert Hall, London, as well as in Paris, France.

The evangelist crosses cultural, racial, and economic barriers to preach Christ (8:5). The crowds attending the crusades of itinerant evangelists have typically been racially integrated.

The evangelist baptizes converts (8:12, 38). Evangelists have not always left this to the work of local pastors (a source of tension). Itinerant evangelists have established a "following," initially through informal literature and later through the use of the electronic media.

The evangelist is flexible, preaching from city to city, ready to follow the leading of the Holy Spirit to another place or person (8:26, 29, 40). The leading of the Holy Spirit, even to another country, has been a hallmark of traveling evangelists. Many would not limit themselves to a calendar of specific dates for a crusade but would leave the conclusion of evangelistic crusades open-ended, depending on the work of the Holy Spirit and the response of the crowds.

2. The Evangelist in Christian Tradition.
Stephen Neill has traced three main types of evangelists in the expansion of Christianity: (1) A person raised up by God to perform evangelistic ministry in a specified geographic area among a designated group of people; (2) a paid agent representing a missions society in itinerant evangelism to areas where the church or missions society has not yet been firmly established; (3) a lay preacher or pastor entrusted with the care and oversight of an existing congregation (Neill, 200).

3. Evangelists in the Pentecostal Tradition.
Pentecostal evangelists would fit into all three of Neill's classifications but would not necessarily be bound by them, particularly those among the independent "healing" evangelists with ministries of larger or more visible proportions. Menzies indicates that the pentecostal evangelists of the 1920s and 1930s had ministries that were far-reaching in their influence (170–71). Harrell traces the self-sustaining and extensive ministries of evangelists in what he calls "the healing revival (1947–58)," and "the charismatic revival (1958–74)" in *All Things Are Possible* (1975); his bibliographic essay is a valuable resource for researchers on pentecostal evangelists (240–54).

A complete listing of all names in the history of pentecostal evangelists would not be possible in this overview. No one evangelist could be said to be the prototype of all modern pentecostal evangelists. Nevertheless, a survey of the literature of pentecostalism suggests that many outstanding figures had ministries of impact during various eras. Gordon Atter has "Biographical Sketches of Pentecostal Pioneers" as a separate chapter in his review of pentecostal history (57–85). He includes persons such as ▸Frank Bartleman, W. T. Gaston, ▸Howard A. Goss, ▸C. H. Mason, ▸Claude A. McKinney, ▸Charles F. Parham, ▸W. W. Simpson, ▸A. H. Argue, Charles E. Baker, Marion Keller, ▸Alexander Boddy, ▸Stephen and

Technology in the service of the Gospel: Nigerians from northern Nigeria ready to go out with manually operated Victrola record players that allow them to play messages and Gospel songs in various regional languages.

George Jeffreys, and ˃Lewi Pethrus in his review of some 45 pentecostal pioneers from the U.S., Canada, and Great Britain. Others of note are ˃Aimee Semple McPherson, ˃Charles S. Price, ˃Smith Wigglesworth (Menzies, 170–71); ˃William F. P. Burton, ˃Edmund (Teddy) Hodgson (Whittaker, 146–98); J. W. Buckalew, ˃A. J. Tomlinson, ˃J. F. Rowlands (Conn); Edith Mae Pennington (Warner,); ˃Mary C. Moise and Maria B. Woodworth-Etter (Blumhofer, 11). Harrell's study highlights the more recent figures of ˃William M. Branham, ˃Oral Roberts, ˃Gordon Lindsay, ˃Jack Coe, ˃T. L. Osborn, ˃A. A. Allen, W. V. Grant, Don Stewart, and ˃Morris Cerullo (1975; 1985).

Typical methodologies of pentecostal evangelists have been the use of mass crusades incorporating music, testimonies, prayer for the sick, and the extensive use of publishing (tracts, magazines, and paperback pamphlets and books). Many of the early evangelists combined an itinerant preaching schedule with the planting of new churches, often "preaching them out" and turning them over to associates or an organized denomination (Menzies, 170). Many began as children, and the phenomenon of the child evangelist (or "boy preacher") was popularized in pentecostalism. "Little David" Walker and Marjoe Gortner are notable examples (Harrell, 1975, 81, 166, 233).

The message of pentecostal evangelists has been typically centered on salvation and deliverance, with a popular highlighting of divine healing. Prayer lines for the sick have been common, as well as confrontations with spiritual oppression resulting in exorcisms. In addition, evangelists have prayed

for seekers to be baptized in the Holy Spirit. Eventually, the North American healing evangelists saw their calling to move beyond their borders into the international arena (Harrell, 1975, 94; Quebedeaux, 42–47).

Many evangelists have remained independent, not allowing themselves to be "tamed" or controlled by any denomination. This has traditionally been a source of tension and has caused contempt for the ministry of the evangelist in church circles. On the other hand, nonaffiliated evangelists have often seen their work as interdependent with the mission outreaches of established church departments of home and foreign missions. Harrell notes that there has been isolation and fragmentation among the healing evangelists themselves, although some efforts have been made to form networks and associations (1975, 144). Many early independent evangelists, however, were incorporated into the polity and structure of newly formed denominations (Conn, 74).

4. Pentecostal Evangelists and the Future.

Pentecostal-charismatic trends indicate that the ministry of the itinerant evangelist will continue in the 21st century with more attention being given to integrity and accountability.

Major pentecostal denominations encourage the ministry of evangelists, holding conferences for mutual exchange and providing training for evangelistic ministry (Champion). Pentecostals have participated in interdenominational conferences designed for itinerant evangelists, such as the International Conference for Itinerant Evangelists in Amsterdam, which was attended by 4,000 evangelists in 1983 and by more than 10,000 in 2000. In addition, there continues to be an emphasis on the development of lay evangelists in the charismatic movement, and new pentecostal-charismatic evangelists are becoming prominent in the non-Western world.

See also EVANGELISM; GIFTS OF THE SPIRIT; MISSIONS, OVERSEAS.

Evangelistic service in market place, with Wesley Hurst and students near Mbeya, Tanzania (1959).

■ **Bibliography:** G. F. Atter, *The Third Force* (1962) ■ E. Blumhofer, "The Role of Women in Pentecostal Ministry," *AGH* (Spring 1985) ■ R. Champion, E. S. Caldwell, and G. Leggett, eds., *Our Mission in Today's World* (1968) ■ C. W. Conn, *Like a Mighty Army: A History of the Church of God* (1977) ■ J. D. Douglas, *The Work of an Evangelist* (1984) ■ G. P. Duffield and N. M. Van Cleave, *Foundations of Pentecostal Theology* (1983) ■ D. Gee, *The Pentecostal Movement* (1949) ■ D. E. Harrell Jr., *All Things Are Possible: The Healing and Charismatic Revivals in Modern America* (1975) ■ idem, *Oral Roberts: An American Life* (1985) ■ W. W. Menzies, *Anointed to Serve* (1971) ■ S. Neill, G. H. Anderson, and J. Goodwin, eds., *Concise Dictionary of the Christian World Mission* (1971) ■ R. Quebedeaux, *The New Charismatics* (1976) ■ W. Warner, "From the Footlights to the Light of the Cross," *AGH* (Winter 1987), 6–9, 20 ■ C. Whittaker, *Seven Pentecostal Pioneers* (1983).

■ L. G. McClung Jr.

EVANGELIZATION SOCIETY, THE (TES).

A missions agency originally connected with the Pittsburgh Bible Institute and founded by ᐳCharles Hamilton Pridgeon on Aug. 18, 1920, following prayer and the voluntary commitment on the part of several hundred people to support its work. The first board of directors (self-perpetuating) included Pridgeon as general director, Louise Shepard Pridgeon, Edgar L. Clementson, William H. Hammon, and Grace D. Dorchester. Following its inception, several couples traveled overseas as missionaries.

The purpose of the society is "the propagation of Christianity and the doing of Christian and charitable work at home and abroad in association with and supplementary to the work of the Pittsburgh Bible Institute" (Charter of the Evangelization Society, 2). With the decline of the Pittsburgh Bible Institute and the growth of TES, the latter has more recently focused on forming "branches and centers to promote prayer and the study of the word among those who will cooperate in the spread of the Gospel at home and abroad and help as He enables in its many forms of Christian activity" (Vogel to McGee, 1988).

While the earlier work of TES has come to an end in China, it currently has mission outreaches in the U.S., consisting of five churches; Zaire, with 200 churches and 55,000 members; and ministries in India and Taiwan. The work is supported by unsolicited donations, reflecting the concept of faith held by the British Christian philanthropist George Müller. The agency also ordains qualified applicants for Christian ministry. TES is evangelical and pentecostal in doctrine and has discarded Pridgeon's doctrine of universalism called the "restitution" or "reconciliation" of all things.

The headquarters office for TES is located in Gibsonia, PA. David W. Vogel currently serves as the general director. Since 1990 TES has been connected with Salem Heights Christian Life Center, a pentecostal church founded by David Vogel's son, Ralph T. Vogel.

■ **Bibliography:** H. P. Beach and C. H. Fahs, *World Missionary Atlas* (1925) ■ Charter of The Evangelization Society (n.d.) ■ E. L. Clementson, *Louise Shepard Pridgeon* (1955) ■ G. D. Clementson, *Charles Hamilton Pridgeon* (1963) ■ *The Encyclopedia of Christian Missions: The Agencies* (1967) ■ D. W. Vogel to G. B. McGee, Jan. 29, 1988 ■ "Welcome to the Evangelization Society" (n.d.).

■ G. B. McGee; B. A. Pavia

EVANS, WILLIAM IRVIN

(1887–1954). ᐳAssemblies of God (AG) educator and executive presbyter. Raised by Methodist parents, William Evans received the baptism in the

William Irvin Evans

Holy Spirit at the Missionary Training Institute in Nyack, NY. He served as pastor in Richmond, VA; Ossining, NY; and Butler, NJ. In 1917 he joined the faculty of the year-old Bethel Bible Training School in Newark, NJ, under the principalship of ᐳW. W. Simpson and then ᐳFrank M. Boyd.

When Boyd left in 1923 to head the recently formed Central Bible Institute (CBI) in Springfield, MO, Evans became principal at Bethel. In 1929 Evans, in turn, became principal at CBI when the two schools merged. He remained in dynamic leadership there a quarter century, the institution reflecting the image of the man.

■ **Bibliography:** W. I. Evans, *This River Must Flow! Selections from the Writings and Sermons of W. I. Evans* (1954). ■ D. J. Wilson

EWART, FRANK J.

(1876–1947). Pentecostal preacher and author. Born in Australia, Ewart began his ministry in the Baptist Church as a bush missionary. In 1903 he immigrated to Canada and served as pastor of a Baptist church. After he received the baptism in the Holy Spirit in 1908 he was dismissed by the Baptist organization. In 1911 he became the assistant pastor to ᐳWilliam H. Durham in Los Angeles, and when Durham died in 1912 Ewart became the pastor. In 1913 he heard ᐳR. E. McAlister preach at the Arroyo Seco camp meeting on water baptism in the name of Jesus Christ, and the following year he openly began preaching the shorter formula and rebaptizing pentecostals. Ewart was one of the

Frank J. Ewart, an influential spokesmen for the Oneness movement in its early years, and author of *The Phenomenon of Pentecost.*

first pentecostals to teach the ʾOneness of God rather than the doctrine of the Trinity. He spread the Oneness message throughout the pentecostal movement in his periodical *Meat in Due Season*. In 1919 he founded a successful church in Belvedere, CA, where he continued to pastor until his death. He is the author of at least eight books: *Jesus, the Man and Mystery* (1941), *The Name and the Book* (1936), *The New Testament Characters X-Rayed* (1945), *The Modern Rip Van Winkle* (n.d.), *The Revelation of Jesus Christ* (n.d.), and *The Phenomenon of Pentecost* (1947). He was an ordained minister of the ʾUnited Pentecostal Church.   ■ J. L. Hall

EXORCISM Although Peter Toon, in the *New International Dictionary of the Christian Church*, describes exorcism as "the practice of expelling evil spirits by means of prayer, divination, or magic" (365), pentecostal/charismatic theology would not understand the means of exorcism as being in any other source than the power of God. Instead, exorcism would be "the act of expelling evil spirits or demons by adjuration in the name of Jesus Christ and through His power" (Richardson, 5).

A review of the literature, history, and oral "stories" of pentecostalism reveals the centrality of the practice of exorcism in the expansion of the pentecostal and charismatic movements. While there is some general agreement in theology and practice, there remains a broad diversity in specific beliefs and ministries surrounding exorcism.

No clarified doctrinal statement on demonology and exorcism exists among major pentecostal bodies. Although pentecostal expositions such as Duffield and Van Cleave's *Foundations of Pentecostal Theology* (1983) are available, much of these discussions are the reworking of earlier evangelical commentaries on the subject. Like many themes in pentecostal/charismatic belief and practice, exorcism has been practiced but not formally theologized.

1. Scriptural Data.

Since the Gospels are replete with the accounts of the power of Jesus over demons, pentecostals have seen the ministry of Jesus as the biblical paradigm for the practice of exorcism. This would also be true of the work of the apostolic church in the book of Acts. Almost every pentecostal/charismatic writing on the subject will include a case study from the story of the Gerasene demoniac (Matt. 8:28–34; Mark 5:1–20; Luke 8:26–39).

In addition to the many general statements in the Gospels regarding the work of Jesus in the lives of demonized persons (see, e.g., Matt. 4:24; 8:16; Mark 1:32–34, 39; 3:11; 6:13; Luke 4:41; 6:18; 7:21), Michael Green has noted seven specific accounts of his work with individuals:

1. The man with the unclean spirit in the synagogue (Mark 1:21–28; Luke 4:31–37).
2. The blind and mute demoniac (Matt. 12:22–29; Mark 3:22–27; Luke 11:14–22).
3. The Gerasene demoniac (Matt. 8:28–34; Mark 5:1–20; Luke 8:26–39).
4. The Syrophoenician woman's daughter (Matt. 15:21–28; Mark 7:24–30).
5. The epileptic boy (Matt. 17:14–21; Mark 9:14–29; Luke 9:37–43).
6. The woman with a spirit of infirmity (Luke 13:10–17).
7. The mute demoniac (Matt. 9:32).

Along with this list, Green includes "with probability" the healing of Simon's mother-in-law (Luke 4:39), whose fever Jesus "rebuked." He notes that three incidents were deemed important enough to appear in all three Synoptics—the Beelzebub controversy, the Gerasene demoniac, and the epileptic boy (Green, 1981, 127–30).

One is impressed with the clear authority with which Jesus cast out demons. In terms of his own self-understanding of his authority and mission, Jesus most certainly believed that he was liberating the demonized completely (in other words, it was not psychological transference or unfulfilled hope). This fact was also immediately visible to observers and witnesses. Jesus gave proof of his divinity and authenticity through his actions. His language of exorcism exhibits expressions consistent with his divine authority: "He *commanded* the unclean spirit"; "Jesus *rebuked* the devil"; "He *cast out* many devils"; "He *suffered not* devils to speak" (italics mine; see Duffield and Van Cleave, 486; Conn, 104).

The deliverance ministry of exorcism continued in the early church as normative and expected. In fact, the disciples understood it as being part of the Great Commission (Mark 16:15–17). Apostolic practices and subsequent correspondence to the newly established churches evidenced exorcism as an ongoing practice (Acts 8:6–7; 16:16–18; 19:11–12; 26:18; Eph. 2:2; Col. 1:13; 2 Tim. 2:25–26; 1 John 5:18). A complete listing of Scripture references to Satan and evil spirits is found in Scanlan and Cirner.

2. Exorcism in the Christian Tradition.

There is evidence for the practice of exorcism in the Christian tradition from the time of the apostles to the present day. Harper reviews the special clerical position of "exorcist" in the historic churches and includes samples of older forms and rituals of exorcism used in church liturgy (125–27).

Mainline pentecostals and Protestant charismatics would not separate the duties of clergy and laity in the performance of exorcism. All believers share equally in the power of exorcism according to the biblical teaching of the priesthood of all believers (Mark 16:15–17; 1 Peter 2:9). Philip the deacon (Acts 6:5) was instrumental in the exorcism of demons (Acts 8:4–8). Typically, however, exorcism in pentecostal ranks has been exhibited through missionaries, pastors, and evangelists, especially those seen to have a special "deliverance" ministry.

Classical pentecostalism has generally been skeptical toward those claiming to have a specialized ministry in this area. British pentecostal George Canty expresses this attitude: "In this connection, nobody was ever given a special gift for 'exorcism,' only for discernment, as part of the protection of the Church, chiefly against false teachers with lying and deceitful doctrines of demons. Nobody manifested a ministry exclusively for dealing with demons. This would draw attention more to Satan than to Christ" (255).

Though some orders have been established in the historic churches for a special class of persons called "exorcists," this model was not incorporated into the classical pentecostal awakening or the charismatic revival.

The influence of pentecostals on evangelical thought is especially seen in the marketplace of mission and the extension of the church. Missiologists have been among the first to recognize the pentecostal contribution to world evangelization through a serious confrontation with Satan's power. This is the conclusion of Arthur F. Glasser, a respected Presbyterian missionary dean:

> Besides this, the pentecostals were willing to tackle the "dark side of the soul" and challenge the growing phenomenon of occultism, Satan worship and demon possession. Whereas IFMA [Interdenominational Foreign Missions Association] people and other noncharismatic

evangelicals (particularly the Baptists!) had found it relatively easy to expose the extravagance of the occasional charlatan, they were silenced in the presence of the pentecostals' serious confrontation of the hard realities of the spirit world. Here was a spirituality which could not be ignored. (119–20)

3. Special Issues.

a. Exorcism and Healing. The diversity of opinion regarding the source of disease (whether from demons or natural causes) and the connection between (or separation of) exorcism and healing is as broad as the number of authors one wishes to consult. There is no monolithic agreement in doctrine and practice.

For example, "There seems little doubt that every accident, misfortune, quarrel, sickness, disease, and unhappiness is the direct result of the individual work of one or more wicked spirits," says one pentecostal writer (Whyte, 27). Others, particularly from a North American middle-class perspective, would argue for a distinction between sickness from natural causes and demon-related disorders (based on an understanding of such references as Matt. 4:23–24; 8:16; Mark 1:32; Luke 7:21). Thus, as Longley believes, "We do not exorcise sickness itself, only demons who cause sickness. Prayer for the sick within various Christian ministries is totally different from casting out demons" (93).

Many pentecostal writers are careful to point out that Jesus healed diseases *and* cast out demons, citing such examples as Matt. 8:16 and Luke 13:32. In addition, mention is made of examples of healing without the notation of any presence of demons as in John 11:3–4; Phil. 2:25–27; 1 Tim. 5:23; 2 Tim. 4:20 (Duffield and Van Cleave, 487; Conn, 105; Canty, 250). Canty concludes:

> Even in Mark 16, where healing and deliverance from demons are mentioned together, they are not confused as if they were both the same thing. The language is that some would be sick and need healing, and that some would be possessed and need spirits to be cast out. Sheer lack of Scriptural suggestion about demon possession and sickness being one and the same thing obliges us to reject such a doctrine, while recognizing that the one or two cases recorded make it possible that violent possession will also (as we might expect) have effects on the body. (251)

The practice of some, therefore, "who in ministering to the sick always try to cast out a demon, is not biblical procedure" (Duffield and Van Cleave, 487). This would be Green's conclusion, who points out that in his mission charge to the Twelve, Jesus empowered them

in two respects, not one: to have authority over demons and to heal diseases (Luke 9:1–2). Demons are expelled;

diseases are healed. In other words, the Gospel writers seem to indicate that illness may be caused by direct demonic invasion though it certainly need not be. They are abundantly clear that there is a difference between healing and exorcism. (127)

While John Wimber understands this view of an "either/or" distinction as built upon Western dichotomization, he argues for a more holistic approach in dealing with sickness: "Jesus frequently spoke the same way to fevers as he did to demons, because he saw the connection between sickness and Satan" (Wimber, 100). Because of Western secularization, Wimber argues, modern Christians find it easier to compartmentalize faith and science and keep them separate. "Often, of course, there are psychological or physical explanations for illness. But more frequently than many Christians realize, the cause is demonic" (98).

b. Classifications and Terminology. Classical pentecostal writings have traditionally made a distinction between demon possession and demon influence. While allowing for demonic affliction, pentecostal commentators have been adamantly against any possibility of demon possession among believers (Duffield and Van Cleave, 487, 494–96; Conn, 105, 132; Longley, 86–90; see also the official statement of the general presbytery of the Assemblies of God, "Can Born-Again Believers Be Demon Possessed?" May 1972).

To differentiate types of demonic activity, pentecostal/charismatic writers have used a trilogy of "states of demonic control": oppression, obsession, and possession (Whyte, 29; Lindsay, 1977, 26–32; Bubeck, 83–85). Lindsay sees them in a progression and adds a fourth in the series: "oppression, depression, obsession, and possession." He views demonic activity in a number of ways and uses the terms, "attacking, harassing, and actually dominating." He includes "professing Christians" as objects of demonic offensives (1972[b], 23).

Regarding Christians, Bubeck understands "oppression" as attacks from the outside in terms of spiritual warfare. Obsession, he says, has traditionally meant the subject's "uncontrollable preoccupation" with demonic forces or phenomena.

It is something less than total commitment or ownership but is a step in that direction. A Christian who has of his own will developed overt curiosity about the occult, or in other ways has habitually given ground to Satan, may find himself demonically obsessed as traditionally defined. (84)

Possession, says Bubeck, is total control by the evil spirit as exhibited by the command of a person's will and by ownership of the person. He claims that the word *possession*, though an English expression, is not a word of the original language and agrees with classical pentecostals that

no believer can be possessed by an evil spirit in the same sense that an unbeliever can. In fact, I reject this term altogether

when talking about a believer's problem with the powers of darkness. A believer may be afflicted or even controlled in certain areas of his being, but he can never be owned or totally controlled as an unbeliever can. (85, 87–88)

In terms of classifications and terminology, says Green, Jesus made no distinction between oppression or possession: "The Greek word is *daimonizomai*, 'to be demonized,' or sometimes *echein daimonion*, 'to have a demon.' The modern distinction between oppression and possession has no basis in the Greek NT" (131).

Wimber also prefers the broader term *demonization* (187). In discussing "How Evil Spirits Affect Mankind," Scanlan and Cirner prefer the threefold classifications of "temptation, opposition, and bondage" and make no mention of "oppression, obsession, and possession" (27–36).

c. Types and Orders of Demons. Pentecostal literature, especially from the ranks of evangelists, has asserted that all demons are not alike. Pentecostals have said that the Bible speaks of many kinds of evil spirits, discerned by their manifestations or effects they have in those they afflict. Richardson says the Bible refers to spirits of fear, unclean spirits, foul spirits, spirits of error, perverse spirits, lying spirits, deceiving spirits, spirits of emulation, spirits of jealousy, spirits of whoredom, spirits of infirmity, and familiar spirits (39).

Others would add the spirit of bondage, deaf and mute spirits, and spirits of heaviness and haughtiness (Lowery, 33ff.; Garrison, 1). Lindsay devotes a chapter to this discussion ("Different Orders of Demons") and claims that certain demons are specifically adapted to afflict the bodies of people. He refers to "demons of the sense organs" (deaf and blind spirits, infirm spirits) and lying spirits that cause oppression in the brain (1972[c], 14–21).

4. Methodology and Practices.

a. Discernment. Citing biblical support for supernatural insight (1 Cor. 12:10; 1 John 4:1), pentecostal/charismatic writers have stressed the need for discernment. "We do not have to rely on a sensation or a hunch," says Green (134), and it would be dangerous to do so (Richardson, 20). Lindsay devotes a special chapter to discernment, along with a fourfold test for discernment. He, along with most others, would assert that the discernment gift, "is particularly designed to detect the presence of demons" (1972[b], 30–38).

Authors also suggest various signs of demonization. Green, for example, lists such things as an irrational and violent reaction against the name of Jesus, unnatural bondage to sexual perversion, strange behavior or moodiness, and sudden changes of voice or emotions (134–35).

b. Preparation. In some instances confrontation with a demon-possessed person is immediate and there is no time for prolonged preparation. In these instances, the long-term maturity and preparedness in the Christian readies him or her for the confrontation. In cases where there is time for preparation, fasting and praying have been held up as the primary way to ready oneself (Richardson, 21; Green, 138; Lindsay, 1972[a], 19).

Green provides a checklist of preparatory steps, including giving time to confession and prayer, claiming the victory of Christ, studying the Bible, gathering the support of a team, etc. (137–39). Harper stresses the importance of personal holiness:

> We should never go lightly into this ministry. First we should seek personal cleansing, in the same way as a surgeon will wash before an operation. We should repent of any sin, and relinquish any trust or confidence in ourselves. We must confess, if necessary, any unbelief in the power of our Lord and the authority of His word. (111)

c. Action. To cast out demons "in the name of Jesus" would indicate that it is being done under his authority and by his power. In his commission, Jesus said that his followers would drive out demons in his name (Mark 16:17; Acts 16:18). This is not to be taken as a magic formula or special ritual. Richardson notes, "Enunciating the name 'Jesus' or even claiming the protection of Christ's blood is meaningful only if the person has a genuine relationship with Jesus and exercises his position of authority that is in Christ" (25).

This should not mean, however, that we must constantly quote or repeat the name of Jesus with every act we do in his name. Duffield and Van Cleave point out that demons left people when the name of Jesus was not uttered (Acts 5:15–16; 19:11–12). The casting out of demons, they insist,

> does not require a barrage of words with voluminous repetitions of the word "Jesus" or "Christ." We have authority and can use it as "ambassadors" (2 Co 5:20), but we must avoid treating it as a magic incantation, like a piece of abracadabra or spell. When we utter "Lord Jesus Christ" it indicates that he is the Lord of the one who speaks, otherwise we are like the sons of Sceva, unknown to the spirits. (490)

A variety of methodologies are recorded in pentecostal/charismatic sources. In the NT even aprons and handkerchiefs from the hand of Paul were instrumental in exorcism (Acts 19:11–12). Some may lay hands on the demonized; others may not. There is no actual record in the Scriptures of deliverance from demons by the laying on of hands. Neither is there any mention of coughing up or spitting out demons (though this is reported in some contemporary deliverances). In addition, the Scripture does not give us any encouragement to hold conversations with demons (Duffield and Van Cleave, 490–91).

Harper (and others) state that the name or nature of the demon may be revealed and, in that case, we name the spirit when we command it to leave the person. However, the practice followed by some,

> of asking the demons for their names has no scriptural warrant. There is no instance of Jesus doing it; in Mark 5 he asked the man what his name was, and it is the man who answers, "my name is legion," although the demons would seem to have added the words "for we are many" (Mark 5:9). As for carrying on a conversation with them, this is extremely dangerous and scripturally unwarranted. (117)

Harper also emphasizes the need for "after-care" in the life of the delivered person. He speaks of filling (baptism of the Holy Spirit), healing (emotional), self-discipline, faith, and praise (119–22). Green also points out the need for encouragement and pastoral care after one has been delivered (145).

5. Exorcism and the Mission of the Church.
Green sees exorcism as a natural part of the growth and extension of the church into new areas of darkness. He refers to the commission of Jesus to the Seventy (Luke 10:19) and says that demonic opposition is to be expected when the kingdom of God is being advanced (1981, 146–47). Paul Pomerville says that the power encounter involved in exorcism has been an intentional church growth strategy among pentecostals (109).

Church growth proponents have noted that seriously dealing with demonic opposition has been one of the distinctive marks of pentecostal growth. McGavran cited exorcism as a part of the answer to his question, "What makes pentecostal churches grow?" Pentecostals, he said,

> accept the fact that most men and women today believe that demons and evil spirits (varying forms of Satan and dark thoughts) do invade them, bind them, and rule over them. Pentecostals believe that the mighty name of Jesus drives out evil spirits and heals all manner of sickness. (98)

Wagner concludes that exorcism was a key factor in the exploding growth among Latin American pentecostals (126–29), and De Wet believes that is the only way to successfully deal with the worldview of animists and the unseen spiritual resistance in the Muslim world (163–64).

See also SPIRITUAL WARFARE: A NEOCHARISMATIC PERSPECTIVE.

■ **Bibliography:** M. I. Bubeck, *The Adversary* (1975) ■ G. Canty, "Demons and Casting Out Demons," *Pentecostal Doctrine* (1976) ■ C. W. Conn, *The Anatomy of Evil* (1981) ■ C. De Wet, "The Challenge of Signs and Wonders in World Missions for the Twentieth Century," in *Azusa Street and Beyond,* ed. L. G. McClung Jr. (1986) ■ G. P. Duffield and N. M. Van Cleave, *Foundations of Pentecostal Theology* (1983) ■ M. Garrison, *How to Try a Spirit* (1976) ■ A. F. Glasser and D. A. McGavran, *Contemporary Theologies of Missions* (1983) ■ S. D. Glazier, *Perspectives on Pentecostalism: Case*

Studies from the Caribbean and Latin America (1980) ■ M. Green, *I Believe in Satan's Downfall* (1981) ■ M. Harper, *Spiritual Warfare* (1970) ■ M. L. Hodges, *A Theology of the Church and Its Mission* (1977) ■ W. J. Hollenweger, *The Pentecostals* (1972) ■ G. Lindsay, *Demon Manifestations and Delusion,* vol. 3 (1972[b]) ■ idem, *Fallen Angels and Demons,* vol. 2 (1972[a]) ■ idem, *The Ministry of Casting Out Demons* (1977) ■ idem, *The Origin of Demons and Their Orders* (1972[c]) ■ D. M. Lloyd-Jones, *The Christian Soldier* (1977) ■ idem, *The Christian Warfare* (1976) ■ A. Longley, *Christ Made Satan Useless* (n.d.) ■ T. L. Lowery, *Demon Possession* (n.d.) ■ S. E. McClelland, "Demon, Demon Possession," *EDT* (1984) ■ D. A. McGavran, "What Makes Pentecostal Churches Grow?" *Church Growth Bulletin* (1977) ■ J. T. Nichol, *Pentecostalism* (1966) ■ J. Penn-Lewis, *War on the Saints* (1977) ■ J. D. Pentecost, *Your Adversary the Devil* (1969) ■ R. Peterson, *Are Demons for Real?* (1972) ■ P. A. Pomerville, *The Third Force in Missions* (1985) ■ C. Richardson, *Exorcism: New Testament Style* (1974) ■ M. Scanlan and R. J. Cirner, *Deliverance from Evil Spirits* (1980) ■ L. J. Suenens, *Renewal and the Powers of Darkness* (1983) ■ P. Toon, "Exorcism," *NIDCC* (1974) ■ M. F. Unger, *Demons in the World Today* (1971) ■ C. P. Wagner, *Spiritual Power and Church Growth* (1986) ■ H. A. M. Whyte, *Dominion over Demons* (1974) ■ J. Wilson, *Principles of War* (1964) ■ J. Wimber, *Power Evangelism* (1986).

■ L. G. McClung Jr.

F

FAITH, GIFT OF After the two "word" gifts mentioned in 1 Cor. 12:8, Paul lists "faith" *(pistis)* as another "manifestation of the Spirit" and follows this with "charisms of healings" and "workings of [deeds] of power." Since Paul lists "faith" here as a special gift, he is describing something different from that faith by which a person is justified. This article will first study instances in which this special aspect of faith is narrated or described in the NT, discuss briefly the significance of the term in 1 Corinthians, and then proceed to consider how the charismatic gift of faith has been viewed in the history of Christianity.

1. The Charismatic Gift of Faith in the New Testament

a. In the New Testament outside 1 Corinthians 12:9. Generally, the NT uses the word *pistis* (faith) to describe that act by which people accept God's witness concerning what he has done for the human race in the life, death, and resurrection of Jesus Christ, and come to confess Jesus as Lord and to receive the effect of God's saving action for themselves. This faith is "the work of God" (John 6:29) to which the one believing agrees. As Thomas Aquinas expressed it, "Not that righteousness is merited through faith, but rather the very act of believing is itself the first act of righteousness that God works in someone. From the fact that he believes in God who makes righteous, he submits himself to God's righteousness and thus receives its effect" (*Commentary on Romans,* 4:5).

It is significant, however, that this same word *faith* is used to describe a very particular actualization of that same acceptance, trust, and knowledge in connection with mighty works of God. The synoptic Gospels, sensitive to the general NT teaching regarding saving faith, exploit the ambiguity of the Greek *sōzein* ("heal, save") to make some of the healing miracles a symbolic teaching regarding this faith. In the story of the woman with the flow of blood, the actual healing is used to symbolize the salvation of the Gentiles as Jesus makes his way to the daughter of the synagogue ruler. The Synoptics record Jesus' words as: "Your faith has healed/saved you" (Matt. 9:22/Mark 5:34/Luke 18:42; cf. Matt. 9:29); and they are taken up by Luke in regard to the healed and grateful leper (Luke 17:19), and to the forgiven and grateful woman (7:50). A similar notion, exploiting the same ambiguity, underlies Luke's report that Paul, as he looked intently at the cripple in Lystra, saw that he had "faith to be healed/saved" (Acts 14:9; see also 3:16; cf. Acts 16:31; Rom. 1:16–17; et al.). In all the above instances, *pistis* describes an inner attitude of trust, abandonment, and belief that results in the believers' healing, a symbolic expression of their salvation.

Another series of Synoptic texts present Jesus' teaching regarding the relation of *pistis* to the performance of works outside the believer. Much of this is linked to Jesus' saying about faith moving mountains, which we find in four places: in Matt. 21:21 and Mark 11:22ff. as Jesus' reply to the disciples' astonishment at the withered fig tree; in Matt. 17:20 in his reply to their question concerning their inability to cast out a demon (cf. Mark 9:29, and see the whole discussion of faith in the Marcan account); and in Luke 17:6 in response to their request for an increase in faith (Luke changes "mountain" to "sycamore tree"). The general context of this last Lucan use of the saying is forgiveness and unity among the believers, and this is reflected in the further Marcan teaching, which transposes Jesus' saying about forgiveness (see Matt. 6:14–15) and adds it to the powerful saying, "Therefore I say to you: all that you pray and ask for, believe that you have received it, and it will be done for you" (Mark 11:24/Matt. 21:22; see John 11:40). The same notions of unity, forgiveness, and the "prayer of faith" are combined in James 5:15–16.

The kind of faith described in Mark 11:24 is illustrated in the variant reading of Acts 6:8, which describes Stephen performing great wonders and signs "full of God's *faith* [text, 'grace'] and power." We can find it as well in Paul, who, after receiving a word from the Lord, told all his companions about to face shipwreck that they would not be harmed: "So keep up your courage, men, for I have faith in God that it will happen just as he told me" (Acts 27:25).

b. Pistis in 1 Corinthians 12:9. Paul is aware of the general NT tradition concerning Jesus' teaching on faith. This is evident from his allusion in 1 Cor. 13:1–3 to the saying of Jesus during his comparison of the gifts he has just mentioned (ch. 12) with love: "If I have all faith so as to move mountains, but I do not have love, I am nothing" (13:2).

The *pistis,* then, to which Paul refers in 1 Cor. 12:9 is that faith that renders someone apt to be an instrument of the Holy Spirit in performing "healing" and "works of power" *(dynameis),* and generally in praying efficaciously (see 1 John 5:14). The fact that it is listed among the other "manifestations" of the Spirit sheds an important light on Paul's concept of these manifestations or "spiritual things" *(pneumatika)* or "gifts" *(charismata).* The charismatic gift of faith is a particular intensification of that basic attitude toward God in Jesus Christ by which we accept his saving act, his authority, and his complete trustworthiness, and base our lives on his Word. It is possible to have the right relationship to God and be thus justified by the blood of Christ through faith without having the particular gift called faith: "to another faith in the same Spirit" (1 Cor. 12:9). On the other hand, it is possible to have a minimal faith, even without a great love of God (1 Cor. 13:2) and be able to move mountains. The ideal, however, is that the basic faith relationship to God be elevated so that a person goes beyond the usual boundaries of human existence and, in the power of God, lays hold of and gives human existence to God's desire to perform a particularly wonderful work that can lead to salvation. Johannes Bengel describes this gift of faith as "a most ardent and realistic *[praesentissima]* laying hold of God, most especially in regard to his will" (cited by Robertson and Plummer, 266). F. Prat (1:426) describes it thus: "an invincible confidence, founded on theological faith and assured by a supernatural instinct that God, in a given case, will manifest his power, his justice, or his mercy."

2. The Gift of Faith in the Life of the Church.

From earliest times, commentators were aware of the relation between this gift and the performing of signs and wonders. John Chrysostom says that the faith to which Paul refers in 1 Cor. 12:9 is not that regarding the articles of faith *(dogmatōn)* but miracles *(sēmeiōn)*, and that such faith is the "mother of miracles" (*PG* 61, 245). Cyril of Jerusalem first notes that the faith of others can bring about a healing. He appeals to the fact that Jesus "saw the faith" of those who brought the paralyzed man to him (Matt. 9:2/Mark 2:5/Luke 5:20), and he also cites John 11:40. He remarks in regard to the "second kind" of faith that it is not only doctrinal but also effects things beyond human power. He includes among these things the ability to contemplate God and to grasp the mystery of the universe and the history of the world. He urges his hearers, "Regard highly therefore, that faith which comes from yourself and is directed to him, that you may also receive from him that faith which effects things beyond man's power" (*Catechesis* 5, 10–11; *PG* 33, 517–20).

The gift of assured and efficacious prayer is part of the charismatic gift of faith. We see this in men such as George Müller of Bristol, who was able to care for thousands of English orphans through his prayer to God for what they needed. Another common instance of this gift is to be found in those with an authentic healing ministry. It seems that the faith of the minister of healing can be imparted to the one to be healed and enable him to reach out and "lay hold" of God's will. J. Brosch describes it this way: "Faith as a gift is essentially a tremendous assurance, received only by divine grace; an assurance which draws the supernatural into the natural world. An immovable faith such as this is particularly suited to win the weak and establish them" (cited by Bittlinger, 33). By insisting on the fact that this gift is a divine work, we can lift from the shoulders of the sick the unjust burden imposed by those who tell them that they are not healed because they "do not have enough faith." On the other hand, we should all pray as the disciples did, "Lord, increase our faith" (Luke 17:5).

■ **Bibliography:** A. Bittlinger, *Gifts and Graces: A Commentary on 1 Corinthians 12–14* (1967) ■ J. D. G. Dunn, *Jesus and the Spirit* (1975) ■ G. D. Fee, *The First Epistle to the Corinthians* (1987) ■ F. Prat, *The Theology of St. Paul* (1945) ■ A. Robertson and A. Plummer, *A Critical and Exegetical Commentary on the First Epistle of St. Paul to the Corinthians* (1914).   ■ F. Martin

FAITH CHURCHES See INTERNATIONAL CONVENTION OF FAITH CHURCHES AND MINISTERS.

FAITH HOMES Hospices for healing, especially prevalent from about 1882 until the first decade of the 20th century. One of the expressions of the ►Holiness movement of the late 19th century had been the parallel healing movement, which eventually gave rise to rest homes operated on a faith basis for the sick and terminally ill. Faith homes were often closely tied to Holiness missions and/or Bible schools operated by the same personnel and therefore became important outlets for teaching, preaching, and evangelism.

Faith homes were an important component of the Holiness milieu out of which the pentecostal movement arose. The pentecostal revival was spread by Holiness pastors and laypeople as they testified at other Holiness missions about the baptism of the Holy Spirit, the gift of unknown tongues, and the outpouring of the Holy Spirit at the Holiness mission at ►Azusa Street, Los Angeles, in 1906. Because some of these missions were associated with faith homes, it is not surprising that healing became an important aspect of the pentecostal message.

Most faith-healing homes were financed without any solicitation of funds. This method had its origins in the work of George Müller, who in 1835 began an orphanage in Bristol, England, which he financed by prayer. Every year Müller published an annual report on the income he had received and on what had been accomplished during that year, but he and his staff did not appeal for assistance even under very difficult financial conditions, believing that they were to trust God for all of the needs of the work. This method became very popular in America, not only for faith homes, but for many Holiness missions and Bible schools.

Although some of the first faith homes were for very sick patients who had nowhere else to go, many became open to others seeking healing, rest, or spiritual or material help, and to missionaries on furlough. Mrs. ►Elizabeth V. Baker wrote of Elim Faith Home in Rochester, New York:

> We take all guests alike whether rich or poor, for a limited time, longer or shorter as the Spirit directs. All sit down at the same table, and share equally in the comforts and advantages of the Home both temporal and spiritual. Immediately after breakfast, . . . all come together where an hour is taken up over the Word of God in exposition and prayer. God has especially honored this morning study of

His Word, and often the Spirit has fallen upon us in a remarkable way, sometimes holding us till dinner time. Special prayer and instruction is given each guest privately as the case requires. Hundreds have been healed in answer to prayer alone. (Baker, 63–64)

The idea for faith homes may have arisen from the establishment of a faith home by Johann Christoph Blumhardt at Bad Boll, Germany, in 1852. Blumhardt had been a Lutheran minister in nearby Möttlingen, and in 1842 one of his parishioners, a young girl named Gottlieben Dittus, was diagnosed by doctors as "demon-possessed." Blumhardt and others prayed for two years for this girl, who not only suffered from a strange nervous disorder, but in whose home numerous psychic phenomena had been observed. One day, as Blumhardt was praying with Gottlieben's sister, she heard the voice of a girl that said, "Jesus is victor." From this time onward, there was renewal on an unusual scale, and people began converging upon Möttlingen from all parts of Europe seeking healing. To accommodate them, Blumhardt opened the church manse as a faith home, where he conducted Bible studies and provided guidance and prayer at regular intervals for each patient. After Lutheran ecclesiastical authorities ordered Blumhardt to release those in the manse into the care of physicians, he resigned his church and purchased and renovated Bad Boll, a bankrupt gambling and health spa. This facility became the center of Blumhardt's ministry, which was continued for many years after his death in 1880 by his two sons and by Gottlieben Dittus.

Another important influence on the American healing movement was Dorothea Trudel of Männedorf, Switzerland, who prayed successfully for many victims of an epidemic there in 1851. People from many parts of Europe traveled to Männedorf seeking healing; she eventually opened her own home in order to minister to them. She then began acquiring additional homes as more and more people sought her help.

The first home in America was established by Charles Cullis, a physician who purchased a home in Boston for the terminally ill in 1864. He financed it on the same basis that George Müller had run his orphanages in Bristol, expanding it to include a local church, an evening school, an orphanage, and a publishing house. Within a few years Cullis became familiar with the ministry of Dorothea Trudel and in 1870 began to pray for the healing of the sick people under his care. The first person healed under Cullis was Lucy Drake, who had had an inoperable brain tumor until Cullis prayed with her. After three months there was no longer any sign of a tumor.

In 1882 other faith homes began to appear in America and England. One of the first was Bethshan Institute of Healing, opened by Mrs. Elizabeth Baxter in London, where the great South African preacher Andrew Murray was healed of a throat disorder that had threatened to end his public ministry. During the same year, Miss Carrie F. Judd founded Faith Rest Cottage in Buffalo, NY, which soon became widely recognized as a center for divine healing, prayer, and spiritual renewal. She used this facility for her extensive teaching, writing, and publishing ministries. She later married George Montgomery and moved to California, where she established the Home of Peace at Beulah Heights, near Oakland, in 1893 (►Carry Judd Montgomery).

►A. B. Simpson, inspired by these developments, opened The Home for Faith and Physical Healing in 1883 in New York City, a precursor of Berachah Home, which he established the following year with generous donations from E. G. Selchow, a businessman who had been healed at Simpson's first healing center.

By 1887 more than 30 faith homes had been established in the U.S., but many had become targets of intense criticism. In 1885, for example, a faith-cure home in St. Louis, MO, was under investigation as the result of the death of a child under its care. Until this time newspapers had given favorable publicity to the faith cure establishments, helping to spread positive public awareness of the healing movement, but later publicity became much less favorable. Healing centers were sometimes accused of viewing the use of physicians and medicines as demonstrations of lack of faith and of refusing medical aid for their patients. In response to such criticisms, A. B. Simpson wrote in 1890:

> We do believe that God heals His sick and suffering children when they can fully trust Him. At the same time we believe that no one should act precipitately or presumptuously in this matter, or abandon natural remedies unless they have an intelligent, Scriptural and unquestioning trust in Him alone and really know Him well enough to touch Him in living contact as their Healer. (Niklaus, Sawin, and Stoez, 88)

In 1894 ►John Alexander Dowie opened Divine Healing Home Number One in downtown Chicago. The Chicago commissioner of health responded by passing an ordinance requiring such homes to be attended by a licensed physician. Dowie, however, rejected the use of medical science and was arrested several times for the violation of this ordinance, but charges were eventually dropped and the ordinance declared invalid. These events generated a great deal of publicity for Dowie, who then opened two additional homes to accommodate the multitudes who flocked to Chicago for his prayers. All of these facilities were consolidated into the splendid seven-story former Imperial Hotel of Chicago, which Dowie acquired in 1896, naming it the Zion Divine Healing Home.

In 1898 ►Charles Parham opened Bethel Healing Home in Topeka, KS, "to provide home-like comforts for those who were seeking healing, while we prayed for their spiritual needs as well as their bodies. We also found Christian homes for orphan children, and work for the unemployed"

(Parham, 39). Parham used this home as the center for his ministry, publishing *The Apostolic Faith* twice a month and holding services. Two years later Parham left this home in charge of two Holiness preachers in order to visit other homes, including Dowie's in Chicago; the Eye-Opener in the same city; John Walter Malone's work in Cleveland, OH; A. B. Simpson's work, which had moved to Nyack, NY; and ˃Frank W. Sandford's Holy Ghost and Us society at Shiloh, in Durham, ME. When Parham returned he found that "the ministers I left in charge of my work had not only taken my building but most of my congregation" (Parham, 48). Parham then opened a Bible School at a mansion known as Stone's Folly, where the pentecostal movement was born in the first days of 1901.

Other faith homes in operation during this era included the Fourfold Gospel Mission at Troy, NY, established by Sara M. C. Musgrove; Arthur and Kittie Sloan's faith home in Stratford, CT; Miss Fannie Curtis's home in the same city; Mrs. Lucy Drake Osborn's Home for Incurables in Brooklyn; Miss M. F. Barker and Miss H. M. Anderson's home in Ilion, NY; J. D. Asbough's Faith Cure Home in St. Louis; the Louisville Home in Kentucky founded by J. T. Burghard; J. R. Newton's home in New York City; the Pink Cottage in Stanford, KY, founded by George O. Barnes; Mother Moise's Home in St. Louis; Beulah Rescue Home in Chicago; the Missionary Home in Alliance, OH; Mrs. S. G. Beck's Kemuel House in Germantown, PA; Miss M. H. Mossman's Faith College in Ocean Grove, NJ; Mrs. J. P. Kellogg's Home in Utica, NY; and Mrs. Dora Dudley's home in Grand Rapids, MI (Anderson, 50, 73; Cunningham, 504–5; Chappell, 99–100, 166–68).

Faith homes also became an important part of the pentecostal movement in the years following the outpouring of the Holy Spirit in 1906, especially since many of them accepted the message of Pentecost during the first few years of the revival. The experience at Elim Faith Home in Rochester, NY, may have been typical: "Later we heard about the work in Los Angeles accompanied with speaking in tongues ... but not till our convention season was there any manifest outpouring.... While the meeting was going on in the church a few had gathered in Elim Home for further waiting, and it was there the power fell" (Baker, 134–35).

See also HEALING IN THE CHRISTIAN CHURCH.

■ **Bibliography:** D. Albrecht, "Carrie Judd Montgomery: Pioneering Contributor to Three Religious Movements," *Pneuma* 8 (Fall 1986) ■ R. Anderson, *Vision of the Disinherited* (1979) ■ E. Baker, *Chronicles of a Faith Life* (n.d.) ■ E. Blumhofer, "The Christian Catholic Apostolic Church and the Apostolic Faith: A Study in the 1906 Pentecostal Revival," in C. Robeck Jr., *Charismatic Experiences in History* (1985) ■ A. Brooks, *Answers to Prayer from George Müller's Narratives* (n.d.) ■ P. Chappell, "The Divine Healing Movement in America" (Ph.D. diss., Drew U., 1983) ■ R. Cunningham, "From Holiness to Healing: The Faith Cure in America 1872–1892," *Church History* 43 (Dec. 1974) ■ D. Dayton "The Rise of the Evangelical Healing Movement in Nineteenth-Century America," *Pneuma* 4 (Spring 1982) ■ R. Niklaus, J. Sawin, and S. Stoesz, *All for Jesus* (1986) ■ S. Parham, *The Life of Charles F. Parham* (1930) ■ E. Prange, *The Gift Is Already Yours* (1980).   ■ R. M. Riss

FARICY, ROBERT (1926–). American Jesuit theologian and leader in the Catholic charismatic renewal (CCR). Ordained in 1962, Faricy became professor of spirituality at the Gregorian University, Rome, in 1971. Involved in charismatic prayer groups from 1975 on, Faricy became a member of the Italian National Service Committee in 1976. Besides the CCR, he has specialized in the theology of prayer, Christian involvement in the world, and the future of religious life. He has sought to encourage spiritual renewal among Catholic religious men and women through the renewal of their charisms of poverty, chastity, obedience, and the specific charisms of their founder or foundress. Faricy was coeditor, with Sr. Lucy Rooney, of *Renewal in the Spirit*, a newsletter for the renewal of religious life (18 issues, 1979–85). He is now professor emeritus of spiritual theology, still resident in Rome.

Faricy is the author of many books, including *The End of the Religious Life* (1983); *Medjugorje Up Close* (1986); *Seeking Jesus in Contemplation and Discernment* (1983); *Healing the Religious Life* (with S. Blackborow; 1986); *The Contemplative Way of Prayer* (with L. Rooney; 1986); *Wind and Sea Obey Him* (1988); *Lord Jesus, Teach Me to Pray* (1995); and *Your Wounds I Will Heal* (1998).   ■ P. D. Hocken

FARROW, LUCY F. (early 20th century). Pastor, evangelist, and missionary, noted for being a woman of prayer who laid hands on many who received their Pentecost during the early days of the ˃Azusa Street revival. Lucy Farrow was born in slavery in Norfolk, VA. A niece of the famous abolitionist-journalist Frederick Douglass, Farrow showed outstanding leadership qualities. She entered the pentecostal picture through contact with ˃Charles F. Parham. In 1905 she was serving as a pastor of a small Holiness church in Houston, TX, when she was engaged by Parham to work as a governess for his family that summer. William J. Seymour filled the pulpit in her absence. When she returned to Houston later that year, she had experienced speaking in tongues. While in Houston, she served as the cook for Parham's Bible school and persuaded Parham to enroll Seymour as a student.

In Feb. 1906 Seymour went to Los Angeles to serve as a pastor of a small Holiness church. Recognizing the capabilities of Lucy Farrow and of a man named J. A. Warren, he sent money to cover their fare to Los Angeles. Lucy Farrow was described as an "anointed handmaid" who not only brought the full gospel to Los Angeles but whose ministry included the laying on of hands through which "many received the Pentecost and the gift of tongues."

In Aug. 1906 Farrow made a trip to Norfolk, VA, via Houston and New Orleans. En route, she preached in Houston, sharing with the state encampment of Parham's Apostolic Faith Movement. There she laid hands on at least 25 people and many spoke in tongues. She also prayed for the sick along the way and shared her testimony. Arriving in Virginia, Farrow held a series of meetings in Portsmouth. The meetings lasted several weeks, and ultimately it was reported that 150 had received "the baptism of the Holy Ghost." About 200 were reported saved as a result of her Portsmouth campaign.

By Dec. 1906 Farrow had determined that she had a call to go as a missionary to Monrovia, Liberia, a city governed by expatriated American slaves. She sent word to Azusa, asking for replacement personnel to continue the work in Portsmouth; then she proceeded to New York. There she was joined by the G. W. Batmans; Julia W. Hutchins; Mr. and Mrs. ▸Samuel J. Mead; and the Shidelers, who were on their way from Azusa to Liberia; and Mr. F. M. Cook, who received his Pentecost when they laid hands on him. While in New York, this band of missionaries held two weeks of meetings. The Meads and Shidelers went to Benguella, Angola, while the others proceeded to Monrovia via Liverpool, England. They arrived in Liberia in late December.

Farrow settled in Johnsonville, Liberia, about 25 miles from Monrovia, where she preached and ministered until Aug. 1907. During that time she reportedly brought many into the faith. Many were sanctified and healed, and 20 received their Pentecost.

Farrow's missionary ministry was a faith venture financed largely by supporters from Azusa. Receiving direction from the Lord, as well as the necessary funds, Lucy Farrow returned to Azusa in the latter half of 1907, again by way of Virginia and the South. She held meetings in Littleton, NC, in November for an Apostolic mission there.

Upon her return to Azusa, Lucy Farrow continued to minister from a small "faith cottage back of the mission." Those who came to her there were reported to have been healed, to have been baptized in the Spirit, or to have received "a greater filling."

■ **Bibliography:** *AF* 1 (1, 1906): 1 ■ *AF* 1 (4, 1906): 3 ■ *AF* 1 (6, 1907): 8 ■ *AF* 1 (12, 1908): 4 ■ *AF* 2 (13 *[sic]*, 1908): 2 ■ "Latest Report from Our Missionaries to Africa," *AF* 1 (5, 1907): 3 ■ B. F. Lawrence, *The Apostolic Faith Restored* (1916) ■ D. J. Nelson, "For Such a Time as This: The Story of Bishop William J. Seymour and the Azusa Street Revival" (Ph.D. diss., U. of Birmingham, U.K., 1981) ■ "Pentecost in Portsmouth," *AF* 1 (4, 1906): 1 ■ "The Work in Virginia," *AF* 1 (2, 1906): 3.   ■ C. M. Robeck Jr.

FASTING Fasting, the voluntary abstaining from physical nourishment for spiritual purposes, has been practiced by modern pentecostals from the outset of the movement. Fasting is a long-standing practice in Christianity, and clearly people fasted for church revival and personal needs well before the outpouring of the Holy Spirit at ▸Azusa Street. In some regions of the world fasting was undoubtedly a part of the spiritual condition that led to the Spirit's infilling.

1. The Background of Fasting.

The pentecostal regimen of fasting is only the latest in a long history of the practice. Perceived as a form of sacrifice to God, fasting has been a constant feature of humanity's search for, and communion with, God. For a fast to be beneficial it must be made in a spirit of reverence toward God, in which the one who fasts acknowledges his or her dependence on God and worships him as Creator and Lord. Fasting is basically a quest for spiritual mastery over the sensory appetites, an elevation of thoughts to God and his will. Because fasting is a normal inclination of those who are eager to express love for God and manifest dependence on him, the pentecostal believer comes easily to accept it as a spiritual, beneficial practice.

a. The Old Testament. Fasting has an abundant record and validity in both the OT and the NT. The religious fast for specific purposes is frequently mentioned in the OT. In its strictest sense it meant going without both food and drink for a designated period of time, as mentioned by Esther to Mordecai: "Fast for me. Do not eat or drink for three days, night or day. I and my maids will fast as you do" (Esth. 4:16).

Annual fasts by the entire congregation were prominent in Hebrew religious practice. Fasting on the Day of Atonement was spoken of as a time for afflicting oneself (Lev. 16:29, 31; 23:27–32; Neh. 9:1). This indicates the earliest reason for fasting: the affliction of one's flesh so that one might be more susceptible to things of the spirit.

Zech. 8:19 mentions four annual fasts that were observed in the fourth, fifth, seventh, and tenth months of the Jewish year. These were spoken of as commemorative fasts, to be observed with joy and gladness. Esth. 9:31 refers to the origin of still another annual fast, known as Purim, which commemorated the Jews' survival in Persia.

Israel had special times of prayer, sometimes prompted by national need or calamity (Judg. 20:26; Joel 1:14). These occasions emphasize the spiritual impulse to humble oneself in times of personal distress.

Frequently, OT fasting is mentioned in connection with repentance, both national and personal. "They drew water and poured it out before the Lord. On that day they fasted and there they confessed, 'We have sinned against the Lord'" (1 Sam. 7:6; see also Deut. 9:3–4; 1 Kings 21:27; Neh. 9:1–2).

In this regard fasting might be predominantly an expression of self-punishment. While all fasting has the underlying purpose of subjugating the flesh, it is not in all instances punitive in nature.

Fasting was also a means of expressing grief: "They mourned and wept and fasted until evening for Saul and for his son Jonathan, and for the army of the Lord and the house of Israel, because they had fallen by the sword" (2 Sam. 1:12). Fasting for divine guidance was also prevalent in OT times. Moses said, "When I went up on the mountain to receive the tablets of stone ... I stayed on the mountain forty days and forty nights; I ate no bread and drank no water" (Deut. 9:9; see Exod. 8:21–23; 2 Sam. 12:16–23; 2 Chron. 20:3–4).

b. The New Testament. In the NT fasting is more sharply focused than in the OT. Of the annual fasts mentioned in the OT, only the Day of Atonement is mentioned in the NT (Acts 27:9). While fasting in the OT was only occasionally personal and specific, in the NT it is almost always so. The Pharisees, who regarded fasting as one of the three most important works of righteousness, were said to have had a set schedule of fasting (Luke 18:12). Anna was said to have fasted often (Luke 2:37).

The only recorded occasion of Jesus' fasting was during his 40 days in the wilderness (Matt. 4:1–4), and that occasion seems to have been a fast inspired by immediate events rather than a formal fast. He was apparently so intent upon his confrontation with Satan that he did not eat. Also, the fact that Satan tempted him to turn stones into bread suggests that there was no food available in the wilderness.

Jesus had much to say about fasting and assumed that his hearers fasted frequently (Matt. 6:16–18). He emphasized the personal nature of fasting on an occasion when the disciples of John the Baptist asked him, "How is it that we and the Pharisees fast, but your disciples do not fast?" (Matt. 9:14). Jesus replied that his disciples had no need to fast while he was with them but that they would fast when he was taken from them (v. 15). This reveals that formal fasting was not encouraged or expected by him but that urgent spiritual need would later bring it about.

There was much fasting by the disciples after Jesus was taken away. At times the apostles did without food because there was none available, as is strongly implied in the case of Peter (Acts 10:9–10) and Paul (2 Cor. 6:5; 11:27). But it is also clear that voluntary fasting for spiritual reasons was regarded as a worthy and pious practice. This was particularly so with regard to the selection of ministers. Jesus' extended fast in the wilderness of Judea preceded his calling of the 12 apostles. The church at Antioch fasted before the selection of Barnabas and Paul to go out as missionaries (Acts 13:2–3). Paul and Barnabas then "appointed elders for them in each church and, with prayer and fasting, committed them to the Lord" (14:23).

2. The Modern Practice.

With its strong reliance on Scripture patterns and spiritual resources, the pentecostal movement has always emphasized the appropriateness of fasting.

a. Spiritual Aspects. Pentecostals readily accept and practice physical deprivation for spiritual benefit. To begin with, fasting is so thoroughly scriptural that sincere Christians cannot neglect it. The example of Jesus and the early church was clear for those who daily endeavored to be like him. Furthermore, fasting was viewed as being linked with self-control (KJV "temperance"), which is a fruit of the Spirit (Gal. 5:23). Just as self-control is an essential part of the spiritual life, gluttony is a hindrance to it. Fasting therefore benefits spiritual well-being as a conditioning for Christian growth and an encouragement of faith and meekness. The body is the "temple of the Holy Spirit" (1 Cor. 6:19), and it must bring honor to God. Fasting rather than gluttony encourages the spiritual nature of the human temple.

Fasting is spoken of in the Scriptures as a source of spiritual power. It is contrary to natural reasoning to deplete oneself of physical energy at a time when it is needed most. But the diminished bodily strength is replaced by a spiritual energy necessary for spiritual needs.

When Jesus healed the epileptic youth after his disciples had failed to do so, they wondered at their failure. Jesus replied, "This kind does not go out except by prayer and fasting" (Matt. 17:21). The joining of prayer with fasting is mentioned in numerous places and must be regarded as a necessary part of any fast (see 2 Sam. 12:16; Acts 13:3; 14:23; 1 Cor. 7:5).

b. Practical Aspects. The pentecostal emphasis on fasting is a necessary accompaniment to the equally strong emphasis on the gifts of the Spirit, particularly the gifts of healing. Although every type of revival has been accompanied by periods of private and congregational fasting, the occurrences of healing and miracles have been especially attended by such devotion.

As in earlier Christian times, fasting among pentecostal churches has been largely voluntary, with each person free to determine whether or not to fast, and to what degree. Scheduled fasting has at times been practiced, especially in times of congregational need, e.g., the selection of pastors and other personnel, financial needs, effectiveness of ministries, and other group concerns. The practice has never been mandated, for it is viewed as a private and voluntary matter between the believer and God.

Certain errors and dangers are to be avoided in the practice of fasting. In particular, fasting can become a source of self-righteousness, as it was with the Pharisee who prayed, "God, I thank you that I am not like other men. ... I fast twice a week and give a tenth of all I get" (Luke 18:11–12). Still other people fast for self-serving purposes, such as the achieving of particular political ends or social reforms. While these may be admirable in intent, they are not the kind of fasts referred to in Scripture. (Neither is the fast [or "hunger strike"] intended to force one's will upon another.) The true fast is a sacrifice made as an act of worship to God and is certainly not an effort to obligate God to the one fasting. Fasting should not be done to demonstrate the faster's spirituality or piety. It is not for the purpose of favorably impressing either God or man. That is why Jesus called it erroneous to make any show of fasting (Matt. 6:17–18).

See also SPIRITUALITY, PENTECOSTAL AND CHARISMATIC.

■ **Bibliography:** H. A. G. Belben, "Fasting," *NBD* (1962) ■ C. W. Conn, *A Balanced Church* (1975) ■ W. W. Kelly, "Fast, Fasting," *Baker's Dictionary of Theology* (1960). ■ C. W. Conn

FAUSS, OLIVER F.

FAUSS, OLIVER F. (1898–1980). General superintendent of the ⸕United Pentecostal Church (UPC) and author. During his early childhood in Oklahoma, Fauss attended a Methodist church. After moving to Texas, he received the baptism in the Holy Spirit in 1911 and began evangelizing in 1915. In the same year he accepted water baptism in the name of Jesus Christ. He was ordained in 1917. Fauss served as the chairman of the Apostolic Church of Jesus Christ from 1928 to 1930 and as the chairman of the South Central Council of the ⸕Pentecostal Assemblies of Jesus Christ from 1930 to 1935. He became assistant general superintendent of the UPC in 1947 and served in this position until 1972. After the death of General Superintendent ⸕A. T. Morgan in 1967, Fauss served the remainder of the term. Fauss is the author of *What God Hath Wrought* (1945), *Baptism in God's Plan* (1955), and *Buy the Truth and Sell It Not* (1965). These three books were combined into one volume in 1985 under the first title.

■ **Bibliography:** A. L. Clanton, *United We Stand* (1970). ■ J. L. Hall

FEE, GORDON DONALD

FEE, GORDON DONALD (1936–). NT scholar, author, and educator. Fee's teaching career in biblical studies, which began in conjunction with receiving the Ph.D. degree in NT studies from the University of Southern California, spans more than three decades and includes stints at Southern California College (1966–69, now Vanguard University), an Assemblies of God (AG) school in Costa Mesa; Wheaton College (1969–74), Wheaton, IL; and Gordon-Conwell Theological Seminary (1974–86), South Hamilton, MA. Since 1986 he has been professor of NT at Regent College, Vancouver, B.C. He also served as dean of faculty from 1996 to 1999. Because of his passion for foreign missions as well as

his teaching, Fee has been hosted by several overseas Bible colleges and seminaries, including the Far East Advanced School of Theology (AG) in the Philippines, the East Africa School of Theology, Nairobi, and in (then) Osiek, Yugoslavia. Fee, the son of AG minister Donald Fee, is, though first and foremost a scholar, also an ordained AG minister (1959), having served pastorates in Des Moines, WA (1958–62), and (as interim) at the Magnolia Congregational Church in Magnolia, MA (1975).

Fee is internationally known and respected for his work as a NT text critic and for his work on the New International Version translation committee, which he joined in 1992. In addition to authoring countless articles in his field of specialization, he has written several books on NT studies, including *New Testament Exegesis: A Handbook for Students and Pastors* (2d ed., 1993), *1 and 2 Timothy, Titus* (New International Biblical Commentary series, 1988), *How to Read the Bible for All Its Worth* (with D. Stuart; 2d ed., 1993). Among Fee's most significant publications are his commentary on 1 Corinthians (New International Commentary, 1987). In this volume Fee's pentecostal slip showed to the larger academy for perhaps the first time, and the volume secured his place in evangelicalism as well as in the larger world of NT studies. Eventually the publisher invited him to succeed F. F. Bruce as the editor of the series. Later he also contributed *Paul's Letter to the Philippians* (1995).

What could easily be called Fee's magnum opus and his most theological work, *God's Empowering Presence: The Holy Spirit in the Letters of Paul*, appeared in 1994. Fee's convictions about the truth of the pentecostal experience coupled with his reputation as a scholar made this work perhaps the most substantial contribution to Pauline pneumatology in the 20th century. A subsequent, more popular edition of the work, *Paul, the Spirit, and the People of God* (1996) reached beyond the academic community to grassroots Christianity. Such was the impact of *God's Empowering Presence* and Fee's growing reputation among evangelicals that *Christianity Today* featured a cover story concerning Fee's view of the Holy Spirit. But his growing stature put officials of his own denomination in an uncomfortable position, especially when Fee tacitly countered AG doctrine.

While the Christians in the pew generally appreciate Fee's wrestling with what the NT has to say about the Holy Spirit, denominational powers have been less than thrilled that such a high-profile figure seemed to counter fundamental teachings. Rumblings of this storm sounded as early as 1976, when in an essay in *Pneuma*, Fee challenged the traditional pentecostal hermeneutic underlying the doctrine that Spirit baptism is distinctly subsequent to conversion. Then, in 1985, chapter 6 of the first edition of *How to Read the Bible for All Its Worth* ("Acts and Historical Precedent") was likewise regarded as an implicit threat to the pentecostal doctrine that glossolalia is the "initial physical evidence" of Spirit baptism. But denominational frustration that Fee would not toe the doctrinal line was perhaps no more evident than in the 1995 review of Fee's magisterial work on pneumatology, *God's Empowering Presence*. Oddly, this was one of the first scholarly books on pneumatology by a pentecostal to receive a hearing by those outside pentecostalism and the charismatic movement, and it would have afforded pentecostalism one of its only forays into genuine academic discussion in this area. Yet the denominational reviewer, though acknowledging the volume could be a "basis for dialogue" with evangelicals, did not really seem to know what to make of it. The denominational weekly publication *Advance* implicitly trivialized the work by assigning an unqualified reviewer. The reviewer, calling Fee's purpose "noble," proceeds to spend the majority of his time cautioning readers about four areas of the book that, in his opinion, "mainline pentecostals" would question. The review reflected little effort to understand the book on its own terms. That Fee did not espouse strict doctrinal positions when it came to the "timing of the baptism [in the Spirit]" caused the reviewer further consternation in his rather brief and unreflective remarks. Despite this quasi-official damning with faint praise, denominational churches continue to invite Fee to speak and lecture. He has visited the Assemblies of God Theological Seminary, the denominational seminary, though never for part of a formal lectureship series. His ties with the denomination might be said to be, like a mooring rope, loose, but because of his stature and integrity, secure.

Thus, within pentecostal circles, Fee is both admired and denounced. To some Fee epitomizes the heretofore oxymoron, "a pentecostal scholar." His careful regard for Scripture and his skills as an interpreter render him a voice to take seriously; moreover, his zeal behind the pulpit and his passion for the pentecostal message of the Spirit's presence in this age authenticate him to insiders and outsiders alike as one deeply committed to the pentecostal experience.

■ **Bibliography:** P. H. Alexander, "Profile: Gordon Fee," *Catalyst* 23 (1, 1996) ▮ Z. Bicket, "Review of *God's Empowering Presence: The Holy Spirit in the Letters of Paul* [by Gordon D. Fee]" *Advance* (May 1995) ▮ curriculum vitae (1999) ▮ G. D. Fee, "Baptism in the Holy Spirit: The Issue of Separability and Subsequence," *Pneuma* 7 (2, 1985) ▮ idem, *God's Empowering Presence: The Holy Spirit in the Letters of Paul* (1994) ▮ idem, "Hermeneutics and Historical Precedent," in *Perspectives on the New Pentecostalism,* ed. R. P. Spittler (1976) ▮ idem, *Paul, the Spirit, and the People of God* (1996) ▮ W. Zoba, "Father, Son, and ...," *Christianity Today* (June 17, 1996).
■ P. H. Alexander

FELLOWSHIP OF CHRISTIAN ASSEMBLIES

This organization originated during the spring of 1922 when approximately 25 Scandinavian ministers agreed to meet in St. Paul, MN, to discuss the possibility of creating an informal fellowship of autonomous local churches. About half of these ministers were pastors of independent local assemblies in the upper Midwest region. The other half were pastors in the same region that had incorporated in 1918 as a body of local independent churches under the name of Scandinavian Independent Assemblies of God. During their first year of existence, they published their own periodical called the *Sanningens Vittne,* which later became the primary periodical for all the Scandinavian assemblies in the U.S.

The gathered ministers decided to merge together as a fellowship of churches under the name Independent Assemblies of God. The basis of their unity was their belief that each local church was free to manage and direct its own affairs without being responsible to any denominational organization. The "New Order of the Latter Rain" controversy divided the fellowship in 1951. The ministers supporting the new revival separated from the fellowship and organized under the name Independent Assemblies of God, International. The other group continued under the original name until 1973, when they changed their name to Fellowship of Christian Assemblies. The fellowship has more than 300 ministers in churches in the Midwest, East Coast, West Coast, and in four Canadian provinces: Alberta, British Columbia, Ontario, and Saskatchewan.

See also INDEPENDENT ASSEMBLIES OF GOD, INTERNATIONAL.

■ **Bibliography:** J. R. Colletti, "Lewi Petrus: His Influence upon Scandinavian-American Pentecostalism," *Pneuma* 5 (2, 1983) ▮ *The Fellowship of Christian Assemblies: An Experience in Inter-church Fellowship* (1978) ▮ A. C. Piepkorn, *Profiles in Belief,* vol. 3 (1979), 154.
■ J. Colletti

FIELDS OF THE WOOD

A 216-acre biblical theme park located in Cherokee County, NC, maintained and operated by the Church of God of Prophecy (CGP). The original acreage was purchased in 1939–40 as a result of A. J. Tomlinson's desire to preserve the site that housed the events of June 13, 1903—his "rediscovery" of the NT church. The first temporary marker was erected on Nov. 15, 1940, on the site of the W. F. Bryant home. Three days later the purchased acreage was officially named Fields of the Wood by A. J. Tomlinson. This grew out of his understanding of Psalm 132:6, which was introduced to him by Grady R. Kent. Starting in 1941, a series of services memorializing similar events was initiated. The annual meetings of this nature, many of which survived into the early 1990s, were the following: June 13, 1903, the service prior to each general assembly, reenactment of the first Thanksgiving Day, and an Easter pageant. Also several tent revivals and special youth activities have been held there. Including revival participants and youth groups, approximately 135,000 people come to Fields of the Wood each year.

The designs of Fields of the Wood were first influenced by the Church of Prophecy Marker Association (CPMA), General Secretary Grady R. Kent, and Auxiliary Designer L. S. Rhodes. Commensurate with Kent's preoccupation with apocalyptic literature, the Fields of the Wood has four gates (Rev. 21). Prominent for many years was an airplane marked "Wings of Prophecy" from the White Angel Fleet, which at its peak included 100 airplanes. Growing out of A. J. Tomlinson's 1939 interpretation of Isa. 60:1, 8 (which started with Grady Kent), a connection was made with the Wright brothers' first successful flight, which occurred in the same state and in the same year that A. J. Tomlinson joined the fledgling Church of God. One large structure, now changed to

include a summary history, included a list of churches honored as related to a Holiness doctrine of perfection. One mountain slope has an enlarged version of the Ten Commandments (the letters are 4 feet by 6 feet) topped by a huge Bible (34 feet by 24 feet) opened to Matt. 22:37–40. This design, created by Rhodes, illustrates how the Law and Prophets find fulfillment in the love of God in Christ. Smaller markers record the Beatitudes, the Twenty-Third Psalm, and the Lord's Prayer. Individual marble markers describe each of the original 29 teachings and five international departments most prominent until the 1990s. Also included are a pavilion from which outdoor services are moderated and a baptismal pool.

Among the early markers is the replica of the tomb of Joseph of Arimathea, the Bethlehem star, and a large cross on one of the mountaintops that sometimes displays flags from all nations that have a CGP congregation. This theme, which moves away from the influence of Kent, was enhanced in 1986 with the introduction of a representation of Golgotha. A new gospel theater features videos, puppet ministries, and drama teams.

■ **Bibliography:** C. T. Davidson, *America's Unusual Spot* (1954) ■ P. Gillum, *These Stones Speak* (1985) ■ W. H. Phillips, "The Vision of Heritage Ministries." ■ H.D. Hunter

FIERRO, ROBERT FELIX (1916–85).
Pioneer Mexican-American pentecostal faith healer and evangelist. Affectionately known to Anglo audiences as the "burned-over Irishman," Fierro was one of the greatest Mexican-American pentecostal evangelists of this century. He graduated from the Latin American Bible Institute (LABI) of the Assemblies of God (AG) in San Diego, CA, in 1936. He was later ordained an evangelist in the Latin District Council of the AG in Northern California on Oct. 23, 1941. A few years after his ordination he founded one of the first Spanish-speaking pentecostal radio programs in the U.S., called *The Cross of Calvary,* based in Oakland, CA. His various radio ministries ran for approximately 45 years. He also founded the Latin American Evangelistic Association in the 1950s, along with a newsletter to raise money and inform people of his crusade schedule. He claimed to have preached to over a million

An artist's conception of the Fields of the Wood, a Bible theme park in Cherokee County, NC, operated by the Church of God of Prophecy.

people throughout the U.S. and especially in Latin America. He claimed that in 1956 alone over 750,000 people attended his crusades in the U.S., Mexico, and Puerto Rico, with more than 52,000 converting to his pentecostal brand of Christianity.

After controversies surrounding a personal loan from an Anglo woman and Fierro's unwillingness to submit to the Anglo interpretations of the constitution, by-laws, and policies of the General Council of the AG, he withdrew from the AG in 1961. In 1978 Fierro asked to be reinstated, a request that was warmly granted. Fierro's evangelistic zeal, fiery personality, fluency in both Spanish and English, popularity among Latinos and Anglos, as well as his acclaimed radio programs make him one of the most important bilingual and bicultural Latino pentecostal evangelists of the 20th century.

■ **Bibliography:** V. De León, *The Silent Pentecostals* (1979).
■ G. Espinosa

FINISHED WORK CONTROVERSY A major controversy in the early pentecostal movement over whether sanctification is a second definite work of grace. Except for the ▸Keswick movement in England and the ▸Christian and Missionary Alliance (CMA) in the U.S., the ▸Holiness movement of the 19th century had held the view of sanctification taught by John Wesley in his *Plain Account of Christian Perfection,* according to which there is an instantaneous experience of "entire sanctification" or "Christian perfection" distinct from the conversion experience. As former members of the Holiness movement, ▸Charles F. Parham, ▸William J. Seymour, and the other early pioneers of pentecostalism retained the Wesleyan view, modifying it by regarding the baptism of the Holy Spirit with tongues not as a third work of grace, but as a gift of power upon the sanctified life. Beginning in the late 19th century, most people within the Holiness movement had come to consider "entire sanctification" to be synonymous with "the baptism in the Holy Spirit," although they did not believe that the gift of tongues was the initial evidence of this experience. The early pentecostal leaders, however, believed that entire sanctification and Holy Spirit baptism were two separate experiences and that the latter experience was always accompanied by the gift of tongues. There were, therefore, three stages of Christian experience: conversion (or justification), entire sanctification, and the baptism of the Holy Spirit.

The finished work controversy began in 1910 when ▸William H. Durham, the renowned pastor of North Avenue Mission in Chicago, who had received the pentecostal experience at ▸Azusa Street in 1907, began criticizing the Wesleyan idea of entire sanctification. He believed that the finished work of Christ on Calvary provided not only for the forgiveness of sins but for the sanctification of the believer.

Thus, for sanctification the believer need only appropriate the benefits of the finished work of Calvary that were already received at the time of regeneration. Sanctification for Durham was a gradual process of appropriating the benefits of the finished work of Christ, not a second instantaneous work of grace subsequent to conversion. Durham therefore did not restrict the time of sanctification either to the moment of regeneration or to any other particular subsequent moment in the Christian experience. He objected to the doctrine of entire sanctification because he felt it circumvented the need for an ongoing sanctification process in the life of the Christian.

When Durham first publicly aired his views on this matter at a 1910 pentecostal convention held in Chicago, it caused considerable controversy. During the same year, however, ▸Howard Goss invited Durham to a camp meeting in Malvern, AR, where Durham was able to convince Goss and many of Parham's former followers in the southern Midwest of his views.

The following February, Durham went to Los Angeles with his message. He was refused a hearing at ▸Elmer K. Fisher's ▸Upper Room Mission, which had become a major center for the pentecostal movement. However, he went to Azusa Street Mission and, in William J. Seymour's absence, began preaching. Here "the fire began to fall at old Azusa as at the beginning" (Bartleman, 145), and these meetings soon became known as the "Second Azusa outpouring" (Valdez, 26). When Seymour returned, however, he locked Durham out of the Azusa Street Mission.

Undaunted, Durham began holding meetings at a large building on the corner of Seventh and Los Angeles streets in Los Angeles, where over 1,000 people attended the Sunday meetings, several hundred attending on weeknights. Some of the people who assisted Durham in ministry at this time were Harry Van Loon and ▸Frank J. Ewart. Ewart wrote that he found it easy to accept Durham's message, since he had believed it while still in the Baptist church (102).

After several months Durham returned to Chicago, where G. Smidt, one of the founders of the pentecostal movement in Finland, visited Durham's church and became convinced of the finished work view. Smidt returned to Finland, where considerable controversy erupted, especially since ▸T. B. Barratt, the Norwegian pioneer of pentecostalism who had considerable influence in Finland, steadfastly resisted Durham's opinions on this issue.

Durham wrote some strongly polemical articles on the finished work of Christ in the periodical he published, *The Pentecostal Testimony,* and his adversaries were just as adamant in their opposition to his views. Parham believed Durham's view to be "diabolical," as did ▸Florence Crawford, who had become a leader of the Apostolic Faith Movement in the Pacific Northwest. Other pentecostal leaders who did not accept Durham's viewpoint included ›G. B. Cashwell, ›C. H. Mason, and ›A. J. Tomlinson. These people held to the three-stage understanding of Christian experience, since they had had an experience of entire sanctification prior to being baptized in the Holy Spirit and speaking in tongues and were wary of anyone who could receive the baptism of the Spirit "on an unsanctified life" (Hollenweger, 25). These views were usually held by those who came into the pentecostal movement as Methodists, Wesleyans, Free-Will Baptists, or as members of most Holiness groups. The various Apostolic Faith groups, the Church of God (CG, Cleveland, TN), the Pentecostal Holiness Church (PHC), and other pentecostal denominations that had formerly been part of the Holiness movement therefore did not accept the teachings of Durham on sanctification.

On the other hand, pentecostals who had formerly been part of the CMA generally accepted the finished work view, because the CMA did not hold to a belief in a second work of grace after conversion. This was also true of those who had been Baptists or Presbyterians.

Although Durham died in 1912, the finished work controversy continued to rage. When ›A. A. Boddy of Sunderland, England, visited California later that year, he found that "the pentecostal people in Los Angeles were just about tired of shaking fists at one another" over this question. Here and at other important pentecostal centers he introduced a nonpartisan resolution that those involved "refrain from condemning one another on the matter" (Boddy, 6).

Nevertheless, the issues that Durham had raised continued to be a source of controversy within the early pentecostal movement. At the 1914 convention held in Hot Springs, AR, where the AG denomination was established, the opening address, delivered by ›M. M. Pinson, was entitled "The Finished Work of Calvary." Although the "Basis of Union" adopted at these meetings had no statement of faith, this keynote address set the stage for an organization that held to the finished work doctrine. From this time onward this understanding of sanctification spread rapidly, becoming the majority view among pentecostals by the end of the next decade. One of the reasons for the success of Durham's viewpoint was that many people seemed to be receiving the baptism of the Holy Spirit without first having experienced entire sanctification, despite the belief by second-work-of-grace advocates that entire sanctification was a necessary prerequisite.

The pentecostal movement remained split into two opposing camps for about 35 years over the issue of sanctification, and both sides often adopted extreme positions on the question. Those who believed in sanctification as a second work of grace began to refer to the experience of entire sanctification as an eradication of one's sinful nature, not merely a complete surrender to God. Finished work advocates, on the other hand, often minimized the need for experiential sanctification in the life of the believer, resting in the knowledge that provision for this had already been made by the death of Christ. With the closer cooperation that arose among the pentecostal groups after WWII, which resulted in the formation of such bodies as the ›Pentecostal Fellowship of North America, extremes of this kind became modified.

■ **Bibliography:** R. M. Anderson, *Vision of the Disinherited* (1979) ▮ G. Atter, *The Third Force* (3d ed., 1970) ▮ F. Bartleman, *How Pentecost Came to Los Angeles* (2d ed., 1925) ▮ E. Blumhofer, *The Assemblies of God: A Popular History* (1985) ▮ A. A. Boddy, "They Two Went On," *LRE* (Oct. 1912) ▮ C. Brumback, *Suddenly . . . from Heaven* (1961) ▮ F. Ewart, *The Phenomenon of Pentecost* (rev. ed., 1975) ▮ W. J. Hollenweger, *The Pentecostals* (1972) ▮ R. A. Larden, *Our Apostolic Heritage* (1971) ▮ W. W. Menzies, *Anointed to Serve* (1971) ▮ idem, "The Non-Wesleyan Origins of the Pentecostal Movement," in V. Synan, ed., *Aspects of Pentecostal-Charismatic Origins* (1975) ▮ A. C. Valdez Sr., *Fire on Azusa Street* (1980).
■ R. M. Riss

FINKENBINDER, FRANK O. (1898–1988). Pioneer Anglo-American Assemblies of God (AG) missionary to Puerto Rico. Although he only finished the 9th grade, he and his future wife (Aura Argetsinger) attended Beulah Heights Bible School in North Bergen, NJ. In 1920 the two were married and Frank was ordained an AG missionary to Puerto Rico. The Finkenbinders arrived in Puerto Rico in 1921, the year their son ›Paul was born, to aid the AG work already begun by ›Juan L. Lugo, Solomon and Dionisia Feliciano, and ›Francisco Ortiz Jr. A year later Finkenbinder helped the fledgling AG work legally incorporate as the ›Iglesia De Dios Pentecostal, for which he served as second president. In 1923 Finkenbinder founded the Puerto Rican AG periodical *La Evangelista Pentecostal*. In addition to their administrative work, the Finkenbinders ministered in Ponce, Santurce, and Aibonito.

Due to Aura's poor health, the Finkenbinders left Puerto Rico in 1936 and accepted a Spanish-language pastorate in New York City. A few years later, in 1941, they moved to Denver, CO, where Frank became involved in the Latin American District Council of the AG and pastored two churches. In 1950 he was selected to serve as the director of the Latin American Bible School (LABI) in Ysleta (El Paso), TX. Next to ›H. C. and Sunshine Ball and ›Alice E. Luce, Frank Finkenbinder was perhaps the most influential and important Anglo-American leader in the Latin American District Council of the AG in the 20th century.

■ **Bibliography:** V. De León, *The Silent Pentecostals* (1979) ▮ D. R. Torres, *Historia de la Iglesia de Dios Pentecostal, M.I.* (1992).
■ G. Espinosa

FINKENBINDER, PAUL EDWIN ("HERMANO PABLO")

(1921–). Famous bilingual Anglo-American radio evangelist in Latin America. Born in Santurce, Puerto Rico, to Assemblies of God (AG) missionaries ▸Frank and Aura Finkenbinder, Paul (Pablo) followed in the footsteps of his father as an evangelist to Latin America. After studying at Zion Bible Institute in Providence, RI, and Central Bible Institute of the AG in Springfield, MO, he was ordained by the AG in 1947.

Paul Finkenbinder served as a missionary in El Salvador (1943–64), where he founded Hermano Pablo Ministries, Inc. In 1955 he launched Latin American Radio Evangelism (LARE). He is perhaps most famous for his program *Un Mensaje a la Conciencia* (A Message to the Conscience), which was carried on some 1,500 radio and 300 television stations in 24 countries throughout Latin America and the Caribbean. He is also a popular syndicated columnist throughout the Spanish-speaking world.

Finkenbinder began to produce Christian television programs in El Salvador in 1960. Sources say that 100,000 people viewed the LARE telecast weekly in El Salvador. This work developed into producing Christian films that could be aired on Spanish television. Finkenbinder used Christian television as a means of reaching middle- and upper-class Latin Americans. After a conflict with the AG hierarchy over working with interdenominational organizations, Finkenbinder withdrew from the AG and began his own ministry in 1972. In 1988 he asked to be reinstated into the AG, a request that was warmly granted.

■ **Bibliography:** Stephen R. Sywulka, "Finkenbinder, Paul Edwin," in *Twentieth-Century Dictionary of Christian Biography*, ed. J. D. Douglas (1995) ■ miscellaneous papers in the AG Archives, Springfield, MO.   ■ G. Espinosa

FIRE-BAPTIZED HOLINESS CHURCH (FBHC). Founded

by ▸Benjamin Hardin Irwin of Lincoln, NE, in 1895. Beginning as a radical offshoot of the Iowa Holiness Association, the FBHC embraced Irwin's teaching of a "third blessing," beyond justification and sanctification. This "baptism of fire" was accompanied by varied shouting manifestations familiar to the camp meetings of the American frontier. Those receiving "the fire" also at times would see balls of fire or feel fire burning in their bodies.

The classical Holiness movement soon disowned Irwin and what they called "third blessingism," thus forcing the Fire-Baptized movement to follow an independent path. Irwin organized a national body in Anderson, SC, in Aug. 1898 that was called the Fire-Baptized Holiness Association (FBHA). The new church body represented regional associations in ten American states and two Canadian provinces. The headquarters of the movement was located in Olmitz, IA, where Irwin published a paper known as *Live Coals of Fire*.

Irwin spread the Fire-Baptized movement through tent campaigns in the South and Midwest. Thousands attended his crusades, which also featured divine healing for the sick. In time, Irwin added more "baptisms" in addition to the third blessing, which he named the baptisms of dynamite, lyddite, and oxidite. He also formulated a strict lifestyle for his followers that went beyond the usual Holiness dress codes of the day. Added to plain dress for women was a code that forbade Fire-Baptized men to wear neckties.

Added to these strictures were dietary prohibitions from the OT, forbidding the eating of pork and other "unclean" meats. Fire-Baptized members thus gained the pejorative name "The no-necktie, no hogmeat people."

Despite these teachings, the movement continued to grow under the charismatic leadership of its founder, who had himself appointed "general overseer" for life. This growth came to an abrupt end in 1900 when Irwin confessed to "open and gross sin" and left the movement in confusion. In many areas the church disappeared.

Remnants of the movement were held together, however, by Irwin's young assistant, ▸Joseph H. King, who moved the headquarters of the church to Royston, GA, in 1902. Under King's leadership the church abandoned the baptisms of dynamite, lyddite, and oxidite but continued to hold to a separate baptism in the Holy Ghost "and fire."

The church was radically changed in 1907 when King and most of the ministers of the church received the baptism in the Holy Spirit evidenced by speaking in tongues, as taught by ▸G. B. Cashwell, who had been to Azusa Street in 1906. In Apr. 1908 the church amended its doctrine to include the pentecostal view on tongues, thus becoming the first official pentecostal denomination in the U.S.

Because of similarities in doctrine and practice, the FBHC merged with the ▸Pentecostal Holiness Church (PHC) in Falcon, NC, in 1911. Although the FBHC was larger, the new church adopted the name of the smaller PHC.

Three branches of the FBHC remain to this day. The black branch of the church requested autonomy in 1908 and was granted a friendly separation by the parent body. This group was led by Bishop William E. Fuller, who built his denomination into a national body that today has more than 300 congregations. It is now known as the Fire-Baptized Holiness Church of God of the Americas.

A white splinter group also withdrew from the PHC in 1916 in an effort to reconstitute the original movement. A third group in Kansas never entered the pentecostal movement and is now known as the Fire-Baptized Holiness Church (Wesleyan).

■ **Bibliography:** J. Campbell, *The Pentecostal Holiness Church, 1898–1948* (1951) ■ J. and B. King, *Yet Speaketh: The Memoirs of the Late Bishop Joseph H. King* (1949) ■ V. Synan, *The Holiness-Pentecostal Tradition* (1998).   ■ H. V. Synan

FIRST CHURCH OF JESUS CHRIST (FCJC). A ›Oneness group established by H. E. Honea in 1965, with headquarters in Tullahoma, TN. Bishop Honea reported in 1986 that the group had 40 churches, 235 ministers, and about 15,000 members. The churches are located in 10 southern and midwestern states. Honea had formerly ministered in the Church of Jesus Christ. The FCJC will license ministers at age 18 and ordain at 21. In 1998 the church changed its by-laws to give women ordination rights. The FCJC's articles of faith include the generally accepted pentecostal doctrines. However, the FCJC believes that the baptism in the Holy Spirit with speaking in tongues is necessary to become a part of the kingdom of God, and it considers footwashing to be as "much a divine command as any other New Testament ordinance." The FCJC has about 75 national churches in Haiti, Jamaica, Africa, India, and the Philippines. The official periodical is *Banner of Love*.

■ **Bibliography:** "Articles of Faith and By-Laws for FCJC" (1985).
■ W. E. Warner

FISHER, ELMER KIRK (1866–1919). Early pentecostal pastor. Born in Wintersville, OH, to Methodist parents William R. Fisher and Lydia Jane (Kirk) Fisher. Fisher graduated from Moody Bible Institute and in 1894 married Clara Daisy Sanford, the daughter of Heman Howes Sanford, a professor of classical languages at Syracuse University. Early in his ministry Fisher evangelized for the Congregational Christian Church and then for the Northern Baptists. He pastored a Baptist church in Camarillo, CA (1903–5); from there he went to the First Baptist Church of Glendale, CA (1905–6). In 1906 he received the pentecostal baptism in the Spirit at the New Testament Church in Los Angeles, pastored by ›Joseph Smale. Afterward he went to ›Azusa Street and worked with ›William J. Seymour. He was left in charge there for four months while Seymour evangelized in the South. He then started the ›Upper Room Mission at 327-1/2 South Spring Street with 300 in attendance. From there he went to Mercantile Place, then Kohler Street, then Los Angeles Street. After turning the church over to his son-in-law, Harry S. Horton, he pastored a large group of Armenians in Boyle Heights for a time. Then he evangelized in Seattle and in Canada and opened a mission in Denver. He later returned to Los Angeles, where he died in the influenza epidemic on Jan. 19, 1919, and was buried from the Church of the Open Door. ›Frank Bartleman criticized Fisher because he believed in order and did not allow all to speak who thought they were moved by the Spirit. Fisher's grandsons include ›Dr. Stanley M. Horton and ›Rev. Wesley R. Steelberg of the Assemblies of God, and Dr. Robert E. Fisher of the Church of God (Cleveland, TN).

■ **Bibliography:** Interview with Harold Fisher, Nov. 13, 1986 ■ Upper Room Mission, *The Upper Room* (1909–11).
■ S. M. Horton

FLATTERY, GEORGE MANFORD (1936–). Missionary, educator, and president of the International Correspondence Institute (ICI). Born in Three Sands, OK, to George W. and Stella Flattery, Assemblies of God (AG) missionaries to Burkina Faso, West Africa. He received a B.A. from Central Bible College (1956), M.R.E. from Southwestern Baptist Theological Seminary (1958), B.A. from Southern Methodist University (1959), and Ed.D. from Southwestern Baptist Theological Seminary (1966). In 1955 he married Esther Scheuerman; they have two sons, George Warren (b. 1956) and Mark Douglas (b. 1960).

Flattery began his ministry as minister of education at Oak Cliff Assembly of God, Dallas, TX (1960–62), and later founded Calvary Chapel, Richardson, TX (1962–66). In 1967 he received appointment with the AG Division of Foreign Missions as president of the International Correspondence Institute (ICI), a bold new venture in theological education by extension. Flattery, having served as an educational consultant to the division, was a major driving force in the establishment of the new program. ICI offered a college degree program for ministerial training, as well as programs in Christian service, Christian ministry, and evangelism. In addition to other responsibilities, George and Esther Flattery hosted *World Alive*, a television program for the American audience. Through his leadership, ICI became one of the foremost programs in theological education by extension.

ICI University was merged with Berean University in 1999 to form ›Global University of the Assemblies of God, with headquarters in Springfield, MO. In that same year Flattery was named chancellor of the institution.

■ **Bibliography:** Assemblies of God Office of Information press release, Dec. 26, 1967 ■ "Berean, ICI merge to form Global University," *PE* (July 18, 1999) ■ Central Bible College Alumni Association, "Citation for George Flattery, 1977 Alumnus of the Year."
■ G. B. McGee; B. A. Pavia

FLORES, SAMUEL JOACHÍN (1937–). Second leader of the ›Light of the World Church (La Iglesia La Luz del Mundo) in Mexico. He grew up under the tutelage of his father, ›Eusebio Joachín González, and was baptized in his father's church at the age of 16. He married Eva at the age of 25 and was 27 when he succeeded his father as the spiritual leader of the Light of the World Church. As the Living Apostle for life, Samuel is both the spiritual head and international director of the church.

Under his leadership the church began to project itself outward into Mexican society and foreign countries. Stronger ties were established with the Mexican government, and a cathedral-size church and headquarters complex was built in Guadalajara. The church has witnessed remarkable growth under his leadership and has instituted a global mission program.

■ **Bibliography:** See under "Light of the World Church."

■ D. D. Bundy

FLOWER, JOSEPH JAMES ROSWELL (1888–1970), and **ALICE REYNOLDS** (1890–1991). Pioneer leaders in the Assemblies of God (AG). J. Roswell Flower (he later dropped the name "James") was born in Belleville, Canada, to George Lorenzo and Bethia Rice Flower, both members of the Methodist Church. While still a young man, Flower's parents and grandparents came into contact with followers of ʼJohn Alexander Dowie. In 1902 the family moved to Dowie's community of ʼZion City, IL. Disillusionment, however, prompted the family to move to Indianapolis, IN, where they soon identified with the ʼChristian and Missionary Alliance (CMA). The younger Flower accepted a position with the Indiana Seed Company and began to "read law" with a local attorney in preparation for a career in law.

Alice Reynolds was born to Charles Ernest and Mary Alice Reynolds in Indianapolis. Her father had been reared as a Quaker and her mother as a Methodist. After the latter received a physical healing, the spiritual tone of the family was deepened. Eventually the family became part of the local branch of the CMA, the "Gospel Tabernacle," in Indianapolis, pastored by George N. Eldridge.

When the pentecostal message came to Indianapolis in Jan. 1907 through the ministry of ʼGlenn A. Cook, it strongly impacted the congregation of the Gospel Tabernacle. As the revival continued, Flower surrendered his life to Christ (Apr.

J. Roswell Flower and Alice Reynolds Flower, leaders in the Assemblies of God from its beginnings. They founded the *Christian Evangel* (later renamed *Pentecostal Evangel*) in 1913.

14) and shortly after became active in ministry. When ʼThomas Hezmalhalch arrived, having attended the ʼAzusa Street revival in Los Angeles, Alice Reynolds received the baptism in the Holy Spirit on Easter Sunday (Mar. 31). In June, Flower attended the Pentecostal Camp Meeting in Alliance, OH, sponsored by ʼLevi R. Lupton, ʼC. A. McKinney, and ʼIvey G. Campbell. This gave him broad exposure to other early pentecostal leaders.

On his way to assist a church in Kansas City, MO, in 1908, Flower stopped at the faith home operated by "Mother" ʼMary Moise and "Mother" ʼLeonore Barnes. While there, he sought for the baptism in the Holy Spirit, reporting: "I spent a whole month there and found this period of seeking to be hard work at first. It appeared to be a battle of faith. So I went at it in that spirit." After realizing that he had to exercise faith to receive the pentecostal baptism, and following a lengthy time of prayer one day, he experienced the power of the Holy Spirit and said, "It seemed as though a great light shone around me and I was filled with holy joy and laughter" (Skoog, 2). After several months the "delayed evidence" of glossolalia came to him (ibid.).

While in Kansas City, Flower assisted (along with Fred Vogler, a later leader in the AG) A. S. Copley until 1910. During this time he and Copley issued a monthly magazine Flower had begun publishing in Indianapolis with C. T. Quinn entitled *The Pentecost* (1908–10; later changed to *Grace and Glory*). Flower served initially as foreign editor and later as associate editor. His contributions clearly demonstrate his familiarity with many personalities and facets of the emerging pentecostal movement.

J. Roswell Flower and Alice Reynolds were married in 1911. During the following year they traveled and preached in northern Indiana. Later they joined ʼD. W. Myland, a longtime friend and former leader in the CMA, and his wife in conducting services in Ohio. With the leadership of the Mylands, the Flowers assisted in the establishment of the Gibeah Bible School in Plainfield, IN. While there in 1913, several important events occurred: (1) J. Roswell began his first pastorate in neighboring Indianapolis; (2) he received ordination from the World's Faith Missionary Association; (3) the couple began publishing the *Christian Evangel* (later the *Weekly Evangel*; since 1919 the *Pentecostal Evangel*); and (4) Myland and Flower organized the Association of Christian Assemblies for interested pentecostal churches in Indiana and the surrounding states; this was a precursor to the General Council of the Assemblies of God, founded a year later.

With the organization of the AG at Hot Springs, AR, on Apr. 2–12, 1914, the group selected ʼE. N. Bell as general chairman and Flower as secretary-treasurer. After the council, the Flowers moved to Findlay, OH, to continue publishing the *Evangel*, now listed as an official periodical of the AG. With the development of the "New Issue" (ʼOneness pentecostalism) in the AG, Flower strongly argued for the orthodox view of the Trinity and played a particularly vital role in helping the organization retain that doctrinal posture.

When the AG relocated its executive offices and the printing plant to St. Louis in 1915, the Flowers moved there as well. Eventually the family moved to Stanton, MO, and Flower began an itinerant ministry, conducting "Bible conventions" in churches. Nevertheless, he maintained close contact with the AG leadership and assisted in the search for affordable property to expand the work of ›Gospel Publishing House. Flower supported Bell's recommendation of purchasing property in Springfield, MO, which has been the site of the organization's headquarters since 1918.

With the growth of the AG missions enterprise, Flower was selected to serve as the first missionary secretary-treasurer in 1919, although he had never served as a missionary. In that year, the family moved to Springfield, where he assumed his new responsibilities. Flower worked with distinction, and during his tenure in 1921 the AG adopted a significant statement defining the goals of its foreign mission effort. The office, however, was divided in 1923, and Flower received the second position of missionary treasurer. He had struggled with the financial turmoil of the missionary department during these years, and his outspoken recommendations for changes may have been responsible for the general council choosing an older man (also with no missionary experience) to become missionary secretary in 1923. Flower continued as treasurer until 1925, when he was voted out of office due to his (and ›John W. Welch's) recommendation at the council meeting that the AG adopt a constitution (ironically, it adopted one at the next gathering, in 1927).

With this turn of events, the Flowers accepted a pastorate in Scranton, PA, in 1926. While pastoring, Flower was elected as the Eastern District secretary and served in this additional capacity until 1929 when he became superintendent of the Eastern District (New York, New Jersey, Pennsylvania, and Delaware). As a result, the Flowers moved to Lititz, a suburb of Lancaster, PA. As superintendent he selected Green Lane, PA, to be the site of the annual district-sponsored camp meetings; the property that was purchased became known as "Maranatha Park." A summer Bible school at the camp site started in 1932 and became a permanent institution in 1938. It has been known through the years as Eastern Bible Institute, Northeast Bible Institute, and currently as Valley Forge Christian College located in Phoenixville, PA.

In 1931 Flower was elected to serve as the nonresident assistant general superintendent and held that position until 1935, when he was selected to serve as general secretary-treasurer (he continued as assistant superintendent until 1937); he subsequently moved with his family to Springfield, MO. When the AG established the position of general treasurer in 1947, Flower continued as general secretary until his retirement in 1959. During these years he played key roles in the development of the denomination as well as in its entry into the ›National Association of Evangelicals (NAE) and participation in the ›Pentecostal Fellowship of North America and the ›Pentecostal World Conference. While serving on the NAE's executive board in its early years, Flower became acquainted with Bob Jones Sr., well-known fundamentalist evangelist and educator. The latter, impressed by Flower's administrative work in the AG, arranged for Bob Jones College (later, University) to confer on him an honorary doctor of laws degree in 1946, a surprising event considering the normally hostile attitude of fundamentalists toward pentecostals. Flower was also a supporter of AG higher education and strongly urged the adding of a fourth year of specialized missions studies at Central Bible Institute (CBI) in 1943. An active community leader, he served on the Springfield city council from 1953 to 1961.

For many years the name J. Roswell Flower was synonymous with the AG. The significance of his multiple contributions to the denomination cannot be underestimated. In addition, his typewritten lecture notes at Central Bible Institute in 1949 entitled "History of the Assemblies of God," have proven to be a valuable source of information on the development of the organization.

Alice Reynolds Flower also made important contributions to the AG, particularly through her speaking, writing, and teaching. Her work has been widely published, and she contributed to the *Pentecostal Evangel*. Furthermore, she reared six children, five of whom were ordained in the AG and have had important ministries: ›Joseph R. Flower (former superintendent of the New York District and elected in 1975 as general secretary), Adele Flower Dalton (missionary and writer), George E. Flower (d. 1966; sometime superintendent of the Southern New England District), Suzanne F. Earle (homemaker and pastor's wife), Roswell S. Flower (d. 1941 while a student at Central Bible Institute preparing for missionary service), and David W. Flower (former superintendent of the Southern New England District and pastor).

Alice Flower's devotional writings have made a major contribution to the literature of pentecostal spirituality. They include *Love's Overflowing* (1928); *From under the Threshold* (1936); *A Barley Loaf* (1938); *Straws Tell* (1941); *The Set of Your Sails and Other Twilight Chats* (1942); *Open Windows* (1948); *Threads of Gold* (1949); *Building Her House Well* (1949); *The Home, a Divine Sanctuary* (1955); *Grace for Grace* (1961); *The Child at Church* (1962); *Springs of Refreshing* (comp. I. M. Isensee, 1975); *Along a Gently Flowing Stream* (1987); *The Altogether Lovely One* (n.d.); *Blossoms from the King's Garden* (n.d.); *The Business of Coat-Making* (n.d.); *The Out-Poured Life* (n.d.); and *What Mean Ye by These Stones?* (n.d.).

■ **Bibliography:** M. T. Boucher, "J. Roswell Flower" (unpub., 1983) ■ S. F. Earle, "Her Children Shall Call Her Blessed," *Christ's Ambassadors Herald* (May 1958) ■ A. Flower (Dalton), "This Is My Dad," *TEAM* (July–Sept. 1957) ■ A. R. Flower, *Grace for Grace* (1961) ■ J. R. Flower, "Publishing the Pentecostal Message," *AGH* 2 (Fall 1982) ■ J. R. Flower, interview by W. W. Menzies, June 26, 1967, AG Archives ■ J. Henderson, "J. Roswell Flower: An Essay on Practical Spirituality" (unpub., n.d.) ■ "J. R. Flower with Christ," *PE* (Aug. 16, 1970) ■ J. Kleeman (Newburn), "Mother Flower," *Springfield! Magazine* (May 1984) ■ G. B. McGee, *This Gospel Shall Be Preached* (1986) ■ W. W. Menzies, *Anointed to Serve* (1971) ■ S. Overstreet, "Mother Flower Remembers," *The News-Leader* (Springfield, MO) (Dec. 1, 1984), 4B ■ D. Skoog, "Soldier of Faith," *Live* (June 2, 1957).   ■ G. B. McGee

FLOWER, JOSEPH REYNOLDS (1913–). Pastor and denominational executive. Joseph Reynolds Flower was born in Indianapolis, IN, to ►J. Roswell and Alice Reynolds Flower. Reared in a devout Christian home, the younger Flower received the baptism in the Holy Spirit in 1926 during a revival conducted by William Booth-Clibburn. He later enrolled at Franklin and Marshall College in Lancaster, PA. Impacted by the ministry of ►Charles S. Price at the Ebenezer Camp near Buffalo, NY, he transferred to Central Bible Institute (College after 1965) and graduated from there in 1934. In 1940 he married Mary Jane Carpenter. They have three children: Joseph Reynolds Jr.; Mary Alice; and Paul William.

Flower began his ministry in 1934 by pastoring in Bethlehem, PA; ordination followed in 1943. He pastored and pioneered other Assemblies of God (AG) churches in Stroudsburg and Pottstown, PA; Dansville, Buffalo, and Syracuse, NY; Dover-Foxcroft, ME; and Melrose, MA. Between pastorates on two occasions he engaged in evangelistic work.

After moving to Syracuse, Flower was elected as the assistant superintendent and presbyter of the (then) New York–New Jersey District and as a sectional secretary in the same district. From 1954 until 1975 he served as superintendent of the New York District. For 10 of those years (1965–75) he represented the northeastern area of the U.S. on the denomination's executive presbytery. He served as general secretary from 1975 to 1993.

Flower has authored numerous articles for AG publications, including the *Pentecostal Evangel*. One of his most important contributions came with the writing of "Does God Deny Spiritual Manifestations and Ministry Gifts to Women?" (mimeographed, 1979).

■ **Bibliography:** A. R. Flower, *Grace for Grace* (1961) ■ W. W. Menzies, *Anointed to Serve* (1971).   ■ G. B. McGee

FOLLETTE, JOHN WRIGHT (1883–1966). Pentecostal teacher, poet, and artist. Follette was a descendant of Huguenots who first settled in the Catskill Mountains in the early 1660s. His fifth-great-grandfather, Hugo Frere, was among the 12 who established the community of New Paltz. Follette received his college and ministerial training at the New York Normal School in New Paltz, Taylor University, and Drew Theological Seminary.

Follette was raised a Methodist. In 1911, however, after receiving the baptism of the Holy Spirit, he was ordained by a council of pentecostal ministers at Elim Tabernacle, Rochester, NY. He affiliated with the Assemblies of God (AG) in 1935. Soon he became a favorite speaker at church conferences, summer Bible camps, and retreats for missionaries around the world. He also taught at Elim Bible Institute in Rochester and at Southern California Bible College (AG).

John Wright Follette

Possessing a sensitive, artistic temperament, Follette expressed himself in prose, painting, musical compositions, and especially in poetry. Being a lover of nature, he had an awareness and a keen insight into its mystical language. He once remarked, "Who can always catch and interpret the subtle and ever-changing rays of light sifting through nature or flashing from the human heart?" Spiritual truth shines through his poetry and ministers to needs at various levels, whether taken literally or allegorically.

Follette's writings include *Arrows of Truth* (1969); *The Bethany Household* (n.d.); *Broken Bread* (1957); *A Christmas Wreath: A Collection of Christmas Poems, Written One Each Year Between 1919 and 1965* (1968); *Fruit of the Land* (n.d.); *Old Corn* (1940); *Psalms, Hymns and Spiritual Songs* (a hymnal of original compositions [1968]); *Smoking Flax and Other Poems* (1936); *This Wonderful Venture Called Christian Living* (1974); and inspirational booklets in the Poured Out Wine series.

Follette died at New Paltz in 1966 following a stroke. Characteristically, he chose to make his own funeral a moment for teaching by earlier recording the sermon that was played at that time.

■ **Bibliography:** Documents provided by AG Archives ■ interview with J. H. Burgess, Jan. 21, 1988 ■ C. Schwager and S. Scribner, "A Word about the Author," in John Wright Follette, *A Christmas Wreath: A Collection of Christmas Poems, Written One Each Year Between 1919 and 1965* (1968), v–viii.   ■ S. M. Burgess

FORD, JOSEPHINE MASSYNGBAERDE (1928–). Catholic Scripture scholar. Born in Nottingham, England, Ford qualified as a nurse. Then, as an Anglican she studied theology, obtaining her Ph.D. from the University of Nottingham. Becoming a Catholic, she taught in Uganda. She moved in 1965 to the University of Notre Dame, South Bend, IN, where she was assistant professor, then associate professor, and from 1980 on professor of biblical studies. She authored the Anchor Bible volume on Revelation (1975). Ford became involved early in the ʼCatholic Charismatic Renewal, writing numerous articles and booklets, including *The Pentecostal Experience* (1970) and *Baptism in the Spirit* (1971). Soon disputing the movement's main direction, especially concerning the role of women and its relationship to Catholic sacramental life, she produced writings that were more critical, including *Which Way for Catholic Pentecostals?* (1976). Her most detailed pentecostal article, "Toward a Theology of 'Speaking in Tongues,'" is reprinted in *Speaking in Tongues: A Guide to Research on Glossolalia* (ed. W. E. Mills; 1986).

■ **Bibliography:** R. Quebedeaux, *The New Charismatics II* (1983).
■ P. D. Hocken

FORD, LOUIS HENRY (1914–95). Pastor, bishop, and public relations director for the national ʼChurch of God in Christ (COGIC). Ford was born in Clarksdale, MS, the son of Cleveland Ford Sr. In the winter of 1934, Louis Ford moved to Chicago with only 25 cents in his pocket, explaining that he heard God declare that this was his field. Later he ministered in Evanston, IL, but returned shortly to Chicago, where he began to preach on street corners. Beginning in a small storefront, his congregation moved into a tent and later to a hall on Michigan Avenue. He built the St. Paul COGIC on Wabash Street. In 1954 in Detroit, Overseer Ford was elevated to bishop by Senior Bishop ʼC. H. Mason. He succeeded Bishop J. O. Patterson as presiding international bishop of the COGIC (1990–95). In that capacity, he reopened the Saints Academy in Lexington, MS, in 1993. He understood that his mission was to return the church to prayer and fasting. On May 20, 1996, the Illinois senate approved a bill to rename the Callumet Expressway the Bishop Louis Henry Ford Memorial Freeway. He was married to Margaret Little. The Fords had two children, Charles Mason (the present pastor of St. Paul COGIC in Chicago) and Janet Grace.

■ **Bibliography:** S. DuPree, *African-American Holiness-Pentecostal Movement: An Annotated Bibliography* (1996) ■ idem, *Biographical Dictionary of African-American Holiness-Pentecostals: 1880–1990* (n.d.). ■ S. S. DuPree

FORREST, TOM (1927–). International Catholic charismatic leader and promoter of evangelism. Born in Brooklyn, NY, Forrest was ordained priest in the Redemptorist order in 1954 and worked in the Dominican Republic and then in Puerto Rico. He was baptized in the Spirit in 1971 and soon became pastor of Aguas Buenas, which then became a center for ʼCatholic Charismatic Renewal (CCR) in the Caribbean and parts of Latin America. From 1978 to 1984 he was director of the ʼInternational Catholic Charismatic Renewal Office and chairman of the associated International Council for CCR, first in Brussels and then in Rome.

Forrest, a dynamic preacher, returned to the U.S. after coordinating the worldwide retreat for priests in the Vatican in Oct. 1984. He worked again in Rome (1987–91, 1995–96) and in Washington, DC (1991–95, 1996–), launching and directing Evangelization 2000, a worldwide Catholic program to promote a decade of evangelism in preparation for the new millennium. ■ P. D. Hocken

FORSTER, ROGER T. (1933–). Church leader, evangelist, and Bible teacher in Britain. Converted to Christ as a student at Cambridge, where he graduated in mathematics (1954), Forster quickly became a zealous evangelist. His itinerant ministry (1956–69) particularly had an impact on students through university missions. From 1969 to 1974 he was associated with the Honor Oak Fellowship, led by T. Austin-Sparks, whose teaching on the cross and on organic church life had a deep impact.

The Ichthus Christian Fellowship in South-East London began in 1974 under Forster's leadership. His vision of a radical gospel message that would have an impact on all levels of society found expression as Ichthus grew into a network of local fellowships, characterized by social and racial inclusiveness (many are in the inner-city areas of London). Forster's commitment to evangelism, to *koinonia*—Christian fellowship expressed in sharing of lives—and to addressing the problems of social deprivation led to his participation in the Malaysian Consultation on Word, Kingdom, and Spirit (1994). Since the mid 1980s Forster has become an influential figure in Britain, being one of the four founders of ʼMarch for Jesus (1987), active in the Evangelical Alliance, and a regular speaker at ʼSpring Harvest. He is a leading advocate of church planting and took part in the Singapore consultation (1989) that launched ʼAD 2000.

Forster's wife, Faith (1941–), whom he married in 1965, has pioneered church planting with Roger since 1974. She is very involved in pastoring, teaching, and in prayer ministry. She has been on the executive board of the Evangelical Alliance in the U.K. since 1983 and a member of the World Evangelical Fellowship International Committee since 1991. The Forsters have three children.

■ **Bibliography:** B. Hewett, *Doing a New Thing?* (1995) ■ A. O'Sullivan, "Roger Forster and the Ichthus Christian Fellowship: The Development of a Charismatic Missiology," *Pneuma* 16 (2, 1994).   ■ P. D. Hocken

FOUNTAIN TRUST (FT). The primary service agency for charismatic renewal in Great Britain, from its formation in July 1964 until its voluntary dissolution in 1980. The Fountain Trust was formed by ‸Michael Harper, assisted by his wife and some professional friends, who became the trustees. Devised as a service agency to promote renewal in the Holy Spirit, FT had neither members nor branches but used conferences, meetings for praise and teaching, tapes, and books to spread its work. Its magazine, *Renewal,* first published in Jan. 1966, has continued under independent auspices since FT's closure.

From its inception, FT sought to service renewal in all the British churches by forming an advisory council representative of all strands in the movement. Though its thrust was more toward renewal in the historic churches, it included leaders such as ‸Arthur Wallis with nondenominational convictions. Tensions later developed between FT and the ‸House Church Movement. FT's International Conference at Guildford in 1971 was described as the charismatic movement's "coming of age" in Britain, but it attracted some criticism for including a Roman Catholic speaker. However, FT did not waver in welcoming Catholic charismatics, collaborating closely with the Catholic National Service Committee from its formation in 1973. FT had earlier engaged in periodic talks with British pentecostal leaders. In 1972 Harper was joined at FT by ‸Thomas Smail, who took over as director in 1975. Smail's theological gifts complemented Harper's talent for popular presentation, and he initiated first a theological workshop on renewal and then the magazine *Theological Renewal* (1975–83). In 1978 Smail was succeeded by an Anglican priest, Michael Barling. The agency was dissolved in 1980. The FT model of an agency seeking renewal across the churches influenced other commonwealth countries, and similar agencies were set up in Australia and New Zealand.

See also CHARISMATIC MOVEMENT.

■ **Bibliography:** E. England, *The Spirit of Renewal* (1982) ■ P. D. Hocken, *Streams of Renewal* (1986, 1997).   ■ P. D. Hocken

FOURSQUARE GOSPEL CHURCH OF CANADA The Foursquare Gospel churches of Eastern and Western Canada were originally affiliated with respectively the Eastern and Northwest districts of the ‸International Church of the Foursquare Gospel (ICFG), the parent organization with headquarters in Los Angeles, CA. A district for Western Canada was formed in 1964 with ‸Roy H. Hicks Sr. as supervisor. In 1976 the Church of the Foursquare Gospel of West-ern Canada was chartered as a provincial society. Incorporation of the Foursquare Gospel Church of Canada as a federal corporation came about in 1981, including all Canadian Foursquare Gospel churches. The current president and general supervisor is Victor F. Gardner. The church's headquarters and L.I.F.E. Bible College of Canada, a ministerial training school, are located in Burnaby, B.C.

The organization includes 39 churches, an inclusive membership of 3,063, and 103 ordained clergy. A national convention meets annually for inspiration and to address the needs of the organization. It publishes two periodicals: *Canadian Challenge* and *News and Views.*

■ **Bibliography:** C. H. Jacquet Jr., *Yearbook of American and Canadian Churches* (1999) ■ N. M. Van Cleave, *The Vine and the Branches* (1992).   ■ G. B. McGee; B. A. Pavia

FRANCESCON, LUIGI (1866–1964). Italian-American evangelist. Born in Cavasso Nuova, a province of Udine, Italy, Francescon immigrated to the U.S. and arrived on Mar. 3, 1890, in Chicago, IL, where he began to work as a mosaic artisan. In Dec. 1891 Francescon attended a service conducted by a small group of Italian Waldensians in Chicago's Railroad YMCA Hall and converted from Catholicism to Presbyterianism. Shortly afterward he became a member of the First Italian Presbyterian Church. On Aug. 25, 1907, Francescon attended a pentecostal meeting conducted by ‸William H. Durham at the North Avenue Mission and experienced the baptism in the Holy Spirit with the evidence of speaking in tongues. Durham later prophesied that Francescon was divinely called to preach the pentecostal message of Spirit baptism to the Italian people. In 1907 Francescon helped establish the first Italian-American pentecostal church, the ‸Assemblea Cristiana. In the following year, Francescon traveled to other cities in the U.S., such as Los Angeles, Philadelphia, and St. Louis, and helped establish pentecostal churches in the Italian communities. In 1909 he went to Argentina and helped establish the Italian pentecostal movement in that country, which is presently incorporated as the Iglesia Cristiana Pentecostal De Argentina. Francescon's greatest evangelistic success began in 1910 in Sao Paulo, Brazil. Out of his evangelistic efforts grew one of the largest pentecostal churches in Brazil, the Congregacioni Christiani.

■ **Bibliography:** Autobiography of Louis Francescon, untitled (privately published, June 1951) ■ G. Bongiovanni, *Pioneers of the Faith* (1971) ■ W. Hollenweger, *The Pentecostals* (1972) ■ P. Ottolini, *Storia dell' Opera Italiana* (1945).   ■ J. Colletti

FRANGIPANE, FRANCIS (1946–). Pastor of River of Life Ministries in Cedar Rapids, IA. In a vision in 1971 he saw a

Three leaders in the nondenominational charismatic churches in North America: (left to right) Francis Frangipane, Mike Bickle, and Paul Cain.

great metropolis in terrible darkness and experienced the power of light surging up from his innermost being, coursing through his hands and the hands of others. A visible splendor shone from them. As they laid hands on the multitude in darkness and prayed for them, they also received the light. This vision helped to convince him that a period of great glory and harvest awaited the church. In 1973, as pastor of a small church in Hilo, HI, during a month of prayer and fasting, he recognized his iniquity not as something he occasionally committed, but as something perpetually a part of him. He then understood why humankind needed the blood of Christ. In 1975, as a pastor in Detroit, MI, he appeared on a morning talk show in that city. For a time, he was associated with The Walk, a fellowship of churches led by John Robert Stevens. In hundreds of cities he has sought to unite pastors in prayer. By 1999 he had written 20 books, nearly 25,000 pastors were receiving his newsletter, and River of Life had a congregation of 1,400. He conducts conferences focusing on intercession and citywide prayer movements, spiritual warfare, and unity in the church.

■ **Bibliography:** F. Frangipane, *The Days of His Presence* (1995) ▪ idem, *Holiness, Truth, and the Presence of God* (1986).

■ R. M. Riss

FRODSHAM, ARTHUR W. (1869–1939).

First-generation pentecostal pastor and evangelist. The eldest brother of ▸Stanley H. Frodsham, Arthur heard early in 1909 of Stanley's baptism in the Spirit in England. Arthur immediately sought the baptism for himself, receiving both it and healing for a long-standing stomach disorder in Feb. 1909. He did evangelistic work based in Fort William, Ont., for a few years; during visits to Britain he helped with *Victory,* the journal started by his brother in Bournemouth.

After pastoring a church at Fergus, Ont., Frodsham applied in 1916 for accreditation as an ▸Assemblies of God

(AG) pastor and moved in 1918 to Fredonia, NY. In 1923 he moved to California, where he pioneered and built AG churches at Glendale (1923–30) and Manhattan Beach (1932–39), with two intervening years at Burbank. He was for some years secretary of the Southern California and Arizona District Council of the AG.   ■ P. D. Hocken

FRODSHAM, STANLEY HOWARD (1882–1969).

Writer, editor, and teacher who ministered in the pentecostal movement beginning in 1908. Wanting to become a writer, Frodsham studied hard to learn proper grammar, history, and literature at a private school in his native England.

After Frodsham's conversion in the London Young Men's Christian Association (YMCA), he spent a year in Johannesburg as the secretary for the newly formed YMCA. Then he traveled to Canada. All this time he sought for a deeper spiritual experience. Back in England in 1908 he found what he was searching for, at All Saints Church in Sunderland, when he received the baptism in the Holy Spirit.

Frodsham began his publishing ministry in 1909 when he introduced *Victory,* a monthly paper that reported on the pentecostal revivals in various parts of the world.

Following his marriage to Alice Rowlands, Frodsham took his wife to America in 1910. In 1916 he began his ministry with the General Council of the ▸Assemblies of God (AG). That year he was elected the general secretary; the next year he became the missionary treasurer; and in 1921 he was

Stanley H. Frodsham, editor of the *Pentecostal Evangel* for nearly 30 years and author of 15 books. In his later years he identified with the New Order of the Latter Rain.

elected as editor of all AG publications, which included the weekly *Pentecostal Evangel (PE)*. In addition to his writing and editing of the *PE*, he wrote for Sunday school papers and quarterlies. His first book, *The Boomerang Boy and Other Stories*, was published in 1925.

Of the 15 books Frodsham wrote, the best known is *Apostle of Faith* (1948), a biography of his friend ›Smith Wigglesworth. Another popular book is *With Signs Following* (1926, 1946). He edited another book for Wigglesworth, *Ever Increasing Faith* (1924), which also became very successful.

Frodsham left AG employment twice to take editorial positions with other organizations: The Russian Missionary Society (1920–21) and the Christian Workers' Union (1928–29). He returned each time to edit the *PE*.

In 1949 Frodsham retired as editor of all AG publications and gave up his credentials. For the next several years he ministered in ›Latter Rain circles, teaching for a time at Elim Bible Institute.

■ **Bibliography:** F. Campbell, *Stanley Frodsham, Prophet with a Pen* (1974).   ■ W. E. Warner

FROEN, HANS-JACOB (1912–). Norwegian charismatic pioneer. A pastor in the Lutheran state church, Froen had an experience of the Holy Spirit in 1938, later recognized as the "baptism," receiving a prophecy about his future ministry. Serving 31 years in the Mission to Seamen in Oslo, he was for 10 years chairman of the Evangelical Alliance of Norway. Hearing of charismatic revival in America, Froen prayed for its outbreak in Norway. Froen became the recognized leader of the movement in Norway in 1970 when he attended ›A. Edvardsen's summer camp and then spoke publicly of his experience at a Full Gospel Business Men's Fellowship International convention in Oslo. From 1971 to 1981 he directed Agape, a service agency for charismatic renewal, editing its magazine *Dypere Liv* (Deeper Life). Froen won friends by his personal warmth and evangelistic zeal, but his growing dissatisfaction with confessional Lutheran theology reduced Agape's impact on the state church.   ■ P. D. Hocken

FRUIT OF THE SPIRIT The expression "the fruit of the Spirit" appears only once in the Bible (Gal. 5:22–23) and is there defined as consisting in nine behavioral qualities: "love, joy, peace, patience, kindness, goodness, faithfulness, gentleness, and self-control." The immediate context of the phrase is Gal. 5:13–6:10, in which Paul turns from a more doctrinal discussion concerning the importance of Christ and the question of the efficacy of circumcision for his converts, and exhorts them to embrace certain ethical commitments. The nature of this hortatory section is vital for a precise appreciation of what "the fruit of the Spirit" represents here. This context shows that the phrase refers specifically to behavioral qualities to be manifested in the Christian treatment of oth-

ers, especially other Christians. Although the appeal must be responded to by individuals and although personal attitudes are obviously involved, the fruit of the Spirit is exhibited primarily in Christian interpersonal relationships and corporate life in the congregation.

1. Context.

In Gal. 5:1 Paul reminds his readers that they have been set free "for freedom," and he urges them not to allow themselves to be entrapped anew in a "yoke of slavery," the latter phrase referring to the commitment to circumcision and Torah (Law of Moses) observance promoted by Paul's opponents in Galatia. In the next several verses (5:2–12), Paul makes plain the stark alternatives for his Gentile readers: either trust in Christ as sufficient basis for standing before God, or turn from him to the futile attempt to obtain justification by observance of "the whole law."

Then, in 5:13, Paul returns to the term "freedom" *(eleutheria)* mentioned in 5:1 in order to warn the Galatians not to abuse their freedom from Torah, and to make the point that Christian freedom entails very clear obligations. Paul summarizes these obligations in two ways. First, in a clever but profound turn of phrase, Paul states that Christians have been freed in order to "serve *[douleuete]* one another in love." Then, with the Galatian preoccupation with the Torah in mind, Paul declares that "the entire law is summarized in a single command: 'love your neighbor as yourself'" (v. 14). These initial statements of the ethical section of the letter show that Paul's major concern here is to urge a practical yet radical commitment to one another. The next comment, "[But] if you keep on biting and devouring each other, watch out or you will be destroyed by each other" (v. 15), suggests that Paul's teaching here is not simply general exhortation but is apparently fired by actual problems of conflict within the Galatian churches.

Beginning in 5:16 Paul employs the Spirit/flesh contrast he uses elsewhere (cf. 3:3; 4:29; Rom. 8:1–17) to distinguish two types of life. (English translations render "flesh" *[sarx]* in a variety of ways; in Gal. 5:16–6:10 the NIV consistently translates the term by "sinful nature.") Using a variety of figures, Paul refers to the Spirit as the dynamic of the life he advocates. He exhorts the readers to "walk *[peripateite]* by the Spirit" (5:16), to be "led *[agesthe]* by the Spirit" (5:18), to "keep in step *[stoicheō]*" with the Spirit (v. 25), and to "sow to *[speirō eis]* the Spirit" (6:8). The contrast is to gratify the "desire of the flesh" (5:16), which is directly contrary to the Spirit (5:17). Those who belong to Christ have crucified the flesh with its passions and desires (5:24). Whoever "sows to the flesh" (6:8) will reap destruction. In the context of this running contrast between the flesh and the Spirit, the reference to the fruit of the Spirit is one of several figurative expressions used by Paul to connect the behavior he advocates here with the Holy Spirit.

2. The Spirit and the Christian Life in Paul.

Indeed, Paul characteristically links Christian life with the Spirit and makes the Spirit the source of the power for Christian ethical obedience. Earlier in this letter Paul has reminded the Galatian Christians that their initiation into Christian life was by the power of the Spirit (3:3) and that God gives them the Spirit freely (3:5; cf. also 4:6, "God sent the Spirit of his Son into our hearts"). Likewise, in 1 Cor. 12:13, Christians are those who have been "baptized by one Spirit into one body" and have all been "given the one Spirit to drink." In Rom. 8:9–11 Paul says that the presence of the Spirit is the assurance of all Christians (cf. 5:5), and in 8:13–14 he calls for Christians to draw upon the Spirit to "put to death" the misdeeds arising from selfish desires. Therefore, although the image of "fruit of the Spirit" is unique to Gal. 5:22, the underlying idea of the Spirit as the empowering source of Christian endeavor is an amply attested Pauline theme. Especially interesting in comparison with this passage is Rom. 14:17, where, in another passage dealing with strife in the Christian community, Paul describes the kingdom of God as involving "righteousness, peace, and joy in the Holy Spirit," qualities that are substantially paralleled in Gal. 5:22–23.

3. The Fruit Image.

Before turning to a more detailed consideration of Gal. 5:22–23, we should note that early Christian sources show a widespread reference to fruit as an image for human behavior. For example, in Phil. 1:11, Paul's prayer for the readers includes the desire that they be filled with the "fruit of righteousness." The same figure appears in James 3:18, a similar expression in Heb. 12:11. Note also Eph. 5:9, where we read of the "fruit of light" that consists in "all goodness, righteousness and truth."

The metaphor of deeds as fruit is reflected also in other places in the NT, such as 2 Peter 1:8, which warns against being "unfruitful [*akarpos*, NIV "unproductive"] in your knowledge of our Lord Jesus Christ"; Eph. 5:11, which refers to "fruitless deeds of darkness"; and Jude 12, where false teachers are described as being "without fruit." In Rom. 7:4–5, Paul contrasts his readers' preconversion way of life with their new responsibility as Christians by employing the images of bearing fruit *(karpophoreō)* formerly "for death," but now "to God." The same verb appears in Col. 1:6, where the gospel message is described as "producing fruit" everywhere it has gone, and in 1:10, where Paul prays that his readers will live a proper Christian life, "bearing fruit in every good work."

In fact, of course, the use of fruit as a metaphor for human actions is commonplace in the ancient background of the early Christians. Several OT passages reflect this imagery (e.g., Prov. 1:31; 13:2; Jer. 17:10; 21:14; Hos. 10:12–13; Amos 6:12). This is indicated also in several passages in the Gospels, such as Matt. 3:8, where the Baptist demands of his hearers "fruit in keeping with repentance," and Matt. 7:15–20, where

Jesus states of false prophets, "By their fruit you will recognize them." Certainly among the most well-known uses of the imagery is John 15:1–8, where Jesus' followers are described as "branches" who are to "bear fruit." (Although some sermonic treatments of this passage have taken the fruit to be converts made through the efforts of Christians, the image much more likely refers to the full range of Christian obedience.)

As these passages show, the "fruit" of human actions may be either good or bad and thus reveals the nature and purposes of the human actor. In the NT passages where the image is used as an ethical metaphor, the emphasis is on the moral quality of the actions (e.g., "fruit of righteousness"). In several of the passages, God is implored to enable or assist Christians to "bear fruit," indicating that the writers understand the righteous behavior referred to as at least to some degree the result of divine activity and not purely a matter of human striving. By the phrase "fruit of the Spirit," Paul certainly underscores this note, making the behavioral qualities in view in Gal. 5:22–23 emphatically the ethical manifestation of the Holy Spirit.

As indicated already, the contextual contrast in Gal. 5:13–6:10 between the "flesh" and the divine Spirit no doubt supplies the immediate reason for the appearance of the phrase

Using a chart to explain the fruit of the Spirit in a native language in Nyasaland.

in this passage. That is, the phrase "fruit of the Spirit" arises out of the ethical dualism reflected in the context. This ethical dualism removes ambiguity from the realm of human actions and makes all behavior a result either of self-oriented human desires or of the impulse supplied by the Spirit of God. However, by calling the behavior listed in 5:22–23 the "fruit of the Spirit," Paul did not mean to portray Christians as automata manipulated by the Spirit. Rather, his intention was to portray the sort of behavior that could properly be taken as evidence of God's Spirit and that could be approved and promoted in the Christian fellowship.

4. The Nature of the Fruit of the Spirit.

Certain contextual factors in Gal. 5:13–6:10 that indicate that "fruit of the Spirit" has to do here with the way Christians treat fellow believers have already been mentioned. A more detailed analysis of the two contrasting lists that constitute respectively the "works of the flesh" and the Spirit's "fruit" will further confirm and clarify this conclusion.

The items listed as springing from the "flesh" form one of several so-called vice lists in the NT. These lists overlap somewhat, but each seems fitted to its context. None of them was intended to give anything more than a representative list of evil works. For example, in 1 Cor. 6:9–11 Paul lists 10 vices characterizing the "wicked." A still longer list appears in Rom. 1:28–32 in a more global discussion of the results of human moral darkness. Comparison of the evils in Gal. 5:19–

Joy—a fruit of the Spirit—radiates from this man who is about to be baptized in Aguazul, Casanare, Colombia.

21 with these other vice lists indicates that this list tends to emphasize sins that manifest chaotic selfishness and that tear at the fabric of Christian fellowship. Note that in addition to commonly condemned vices such as "sexual immorality" *(porneia)* and associated sins ("impurity and debauchery," *akatharsia, aselgeia*) and other evils of Greco-Roman society, such as idolatry *(eidōlolatria),* "witchcraft" (or "sorceries," *pharmakeia*), drunkenness, and "orgies" *(kōmoi),* 8 of the 15 items in the list refer to attitudes and actions that violate relationships with others: "hatred, discord, jealousy, fits of rage, selfish ambition, dissensions, factions, and envy."

The Spirit desires "what is contrary to the sinful nature [flesh]" (v. 17), and the description of the Spirit's "fruit" makes this explicit, consisting in a ninefold list of interpersonal attitudes and actions that enhance Christian fellowship (cf. other lists of virtues in, e.g., Rom. 5:3–5; 2 Peter 1:5–7). The nine terms are not simply to be seen as inner attitudes or personality attributes that one seeks so as to claim a certain personal spiritual attainment or to make one in Stoic-like fashion personally immune to circumstances in life. Rather, these terms describe personal behavior essential to corporate Christian life and reflect an attitude that has others in view rather than one's own private religious aims. That is, the primary context for the fruit of the Spirit is life together in Christ, and the Spirit's fruit does not consist in passive qualities that operate within the inner world of the individual but represent very active qualities of behavior directed outwardly toward those who have been made one's "brothers." Thus, although a few of the terms (such as "self-control," *enkrateia*) have a limited similarity to the ideals of some of the Greco-Roman philosophical traditions, the intent and tenor of the list here is substantially different.

There have been attempts to find some sort of inner organization or structure in the list of nine qualities given in Gal. 5:22–23, but all such efforts convey a strong impression of weakly founded speculation. H. D. Betz, for example, offers an elaborate scheme involving three triads of concepts that descend from divine to human action (286–88). It is true that nine can yield three groups of three, but there is no hint here or anywhere else in early Christian literature that Betz's triads were recognized as fixed groups. Paul does seem to have been drawn to the use of triads, such as (with variations) the triad of "faith, hope, and love" (e.g., 1 Cor. 13:13; cf. 1 Thess. 1:3; 5:8), but the triads that Betz finds within the nine terms in Gal. 5 do not appear as such elsewhere. Paul's nine terms may well be the product of a rhetorical style that tended to speak of Christian virtues in ad hoc groupings of threes, here producing a group of terms that collectively is a threefold list of threes, but there is little indication that the list has the more fixed and detailed inner structure that Betz pictures.

It is certainly no accident that this list is headed by "love" *(agapē),* the chief virtue in early Christian ethical instruction and already twice emphasized by Paul in this passage (Gal. 5:13–14) as the essence of Christian ethical responsibility. In the NT, *agape* most commonly refers to love for other Christians and involves much more than affectionate feelings. In view of modern romanticized associations of the term, which tend to focus on the subjective, emotional experience of love, it has to be emphasized that the NT demand for Christian love always expects fulfillment in practical and tangible actions. That is, to love someone is to demonstrate active concern for that person's welfare, even in preference to one's own desires (cf., e.g., Phil. 2:1–4).

"Joy" and "peace" are elsewhere associated in Paul (Rom. 14:17; 15:13), and in numerous other references Paul says that joy is an important aspect of Christian existence. It is worth noting that these other Pauline references to joy tend to connect it with Christian fellowship in various ways. For example, Paul takes joy in his converts (Rom. 15:32; 2 Cor. 7:4; Phil. 1:4–5; 1 Thess. 2:19–20; 3:9; Philem. 7); he expects his converts to share in his joy over their fellow converts (2 Cor. 2:3; Phil. 1:25–26); he praises Macedonian Christians whose joy was manifested in generosity for the Jerusalem believers (2 Cor. 8:1–4); and he makes his joy dependent on good relations among his converts (Phil. 2:2). The joy referred to here in Gal. 5:22 accordingly fits the context where interpersonal Christian relations are the focus and therefore equals joy arising from and directed toward the Christian fellowship.

"Peace" in Paul carries overtones of his Semitic background where *shalom* involves total well-being, as indicated in the "grace and peace" salutations with which Paul opens his letters (e.g., Gal. 1:3). However, Paul also ties peace directly to Christian fellowship with God (Rom. 5:1) and with other Christians (Rom. 14:19; 1 Cor. 7:15; 14:33; 16:11). The present context suggests that the personal peace given by God's Spirit is to be manifested in the Galatians' relations with one another.

"Patience" (or "longsuffering," *makrothymia*), "kindness" (*chrēstotes,* a pun on *christos,* "Christ"?), and "gentleness" (or "humility, courtesy," *prautēs*) are all easily recognized as qualities expressed almost entirely in personal relations, but the remaining terms are also to be seen in this setting. "Goodness" *(agathōsunē)* is here probably to be taken as "generosity," doing good practically to others (cf. 6:10, where the Galatians are to "do good *[to agathon]* to all people, especially to those who belong to the family of believers"). "Faithfulness" *(pistis)* here has to do with a steadfastness toward others that grows out of confidence in God.

The last term, "self-control" *(enkrateia)* is rarely used in the NT (elsewhere only in Acts 24:25; 2 Peter 1:6; cf. also the verb form in 1 Cor. 7:9; 9:25 and the adjective in Titus 1:8) but appears more frequently in the noncanonical literature of early Greek-speaking Christianity (e.g., *1 Clement* 35:2; 62:2;

Barnabas 2:2; Polycarp, *To the Philippians* 4:2). It is also a frequent term both in Greco-Roman philosophy and in the writings of Greek-speaking Jews of the day (e.g., 4 Macc. 5:34; Jos., *Wars* 2:120, 138; *Antiq.* 8:235). Particularly in the Jewish and noncanonical Christian writings, the term is often, though not always, associated with control of one's sexual appetite. Here, however, the term probably carries a more general connotation, such as we find in its other NT uses, referring to control of one's passions, which issues in behavior that is orderly and pleasing to God.

Betz (288) suggests that the final position of "self-control" in the list gives it a certain intended prominence and that the term implies that Christian ethics is presented here as fulfilling "the central demand of Greek ethics." However, we are dealing with something different from the Stoic idea of control of one's inward responses to circumstances. In the present list, "self-control" represents a treatment of others that subordinates one's own selfish desires to the higher aim advocated in 5:13–14, to "serve one another in love." No doubt Paul's first readers would have caught the verbal echoes of Greek philosophical ideals pointed out by Betz, but careful consideration of the context indicates that here Paul gives to the term a characteristically Christian nuance that emphasizes one's behavior toward others.

A blind woman at Pandita Ramabai's Mukti Mission singing "The Joy of the Lord Is My Strength."

5. The Fruit of the Spirit and Christ.

As R. B. Hays has cogently shown, the entirety of the ethical section of Gal. (5:13–6:10) is governed by Paul's christology. Paul's exhortations to the Galatians, epitomized in 5:13b ("serve one another in love"), call for behavior that conforms to the paradigm given in Christ, whom Paul elsewhere refers to as the Son of God "who loved me and gave himself for me" (2:20). The fruit of the Spirit is to be the way of life of "those who belong to Christ Jesus" (5:24). Those who so live by the Spirit "fulfill the law of Christ" (6:2). That is, the fruit of the Spirit listed in 5:22–23 is both the product of the operation of the Holy Spirit in believers and also the manifestation of participation in Christ. Paul has already referred to the Holy Spirit as "the Spirit of his [God's] Son" (4:6). It is therefore quite fitting that the fruit of this Spirit should be behavior that reflects the "crucifixion" of selfish desires of the "flesh" (5:24), Paul's language alluding, of course, to Christ's own sacrificial death.

The fact that Christ is the foundation for and paradigm of the behavior called the fruit of the Spirit makes the connection apparent between Gal. 5:13–26 and other Pauline passages such as Rom. 13:8–14. There, as in the passage in Galatians, after emphasizing that mutual love is the central Christian obligation (13:8–10), Paul proceeds to contrast a list of similar vices to be rejected (vv. 12–13) with an opposite and wholly new type of behavior, described in simple but powerful imagery: "Rather, clothe yourselves with the Lord Jesus Christ" (v. 14). The Galatians metaphor, "fruit of the Spirit," focuses on the agency enabling Christians to conform their lives to Christ, and the ninefold definition of the spiritual fruit makes more specific than the Romans passage what Christian love for one another involves.

6. Conclusion.

Paul's reference to the "fruit of the Spirit," unique to the Galatian letter, forms part of an important section of ethical instruction often overlooked in the historical concentration on the doctrinal issues in this fiery writing and supplies Christian tradition with a memorable and evocative metaphor for understanding Christian ethics. Three things may be emphasized about this "fruit": (1) It refers to active attitudes and behavior directed toward others in the Christian fellowship and aimed at enhancing and preserving that fellowship. (2) It is not the result of mere ethical striving or of one's own spiritual exercises but is manifestation of the gift of God's Spirit allowed sway in one's life. (3) It rises from and is conformed to the sacrificial paradigm of Christ's own self-sacrifice.

See also HOLY SPIRIT, DOCTRINE OF.

■ **Bibliography:** H. D. Betz, *Galatians* (1979) ■ F. Hauck, *TDNT*, 3:614–16 ■ R. B. Hays, "Christology and Ethics in Galatians: The Law of Christ," *CBQ* 49 (1987) ■ R. Hensel, *NIDNTT*, 1:721–23.
■ L. W. Hurtado

FULLAM, EVERETT L. ("TERRY") (1930–). Episcopal priest, teacher, and conference leader. Ordained a priest in 1967, Fullam taught philosophy at the University of Rhode Island and biblical studies at Barrington College. In 1972 he became rector of St. Paul's Episcopal Church in Darien, CT. Under his leadership the parish became one of the most active Episcopal churches in the U.S., increasing Sunday attendance from 250 to 1,200 in five years.

Everett (Terry) Fullam, one of the leaders in the Episcopal Renewal Ministries.

A number of the innovations Fullam instituted at St. Paul's are now widely practiced by congregations active in spiritual renewal. Among these are the policy of moving under the headship of Jesus Christ and making decisions in unity of the Spirit; using liturgy as an outline for worship; tithing resulting from walking in a covenant with Christ; pastoral care through smaller and more intimate "shepherd" or "home" groups; and the audio- and videotaping and distribution of sermons and lectures.

Fullam's teaching ministry in parish renewal extended to both clergy and laity in all denominations worldwide. He was also the president of the executive board of Episcopal Renewal Ministries. He is retired and lives in Deltona, FL.

Fullam's publications include *Living the Lord's Prayer* (1981); *Facets of the Faith* (1982); *Your Body, God's Temple* (1984); *Riding the Wind* (1986); and *How to Walk with God* (1987).

■ **Bibliography:** B. Slosser, *Miracle in Darien* (1979).
■ C. M. Irish

FULLER, WILLIAM E. (1875–1958). Church planter and executive. William Edward Fuller was born in Mountville, SC, the son of sharecroppers. Raised as a Methodist, he was attracted to the *Holiness movement through the ministry of *B. H. Irwin and the Fire-Baptized Holiness Association, which he joined in 1897. An interracial group in its beginnings, the *Fire-Baptized Holiness Church (FBHC) elected Fuller as a member of the executive board at its national organizational meeting in Anderson, SC, in 1898. By 1900 he had organized more than 50 black FBHC congregations in South Carolina and Georgia.

In 1908 Fuller and his black colleagues petitioned the church for permission to form a separate black version of the denomination. This was granted in an amicable separation, with properties deeded over to the new church, which from 1908 to 1922 was known as the Colored Fire-Baptized Holiness Church.

In time Fuller moved the headquarters of the church to Atlanta, GA. Before his death in 1958 the church had changed its name to the ˒Fire-Baptized Holiness Church of God of the Americas and had given Fuller the title of presiding bishop. Since 1958 the church has been led by Fuller's son, Bishop W. E. Fuller Jr.

■ **Bibliography:** V. Synan, *The Old-Time Power: A History of the Pentecostal Holiness Church* (1997).

■ H. V. Synan

FULL GOSPEL BAPTIST CHURCH FELLOWSHIP See MORTON, BISHOP PAUL.

FULL GOSPEL BUSINESS MEN'S FELLOWSHIP INTERNATIONAL (FGBMFI). Interdenominational organization of charismatic laypeople. ˒Demos Shakarian, a lay leader in Southern California felt God leading him to start an organization of businessmen who could come together from all different denominations to share their faith in Christ. In 1951 he founded the first chapter of the FGBMFI. The speaker for the first meeting was ˒Oral Roberts, who had just completed a healing campaign in Los Angeles. Roberts encouraged Shakarian in his efforts and prayed at that first meeting that God would raise up a thousand chapters throughout the world and that the gospel would go forth through this organization.

The FGBMFI began with breakfast meetings held on Saturday mornings at Clifton's Cafeteria in downtown Los Angeles. However, the idea just did not seem to be working, and after the first year Shakarian was very discouraged. One Friday night he told his wife and his house guest, evangelist ˒Tommy Hicks, that he felt he must pray that God would give him an answer regarding the future of FGBMFI. While in prayer, God took Shakarian around the world in a vision and showed him humankind as dead and lifeless and then as alive and full of joy as the Spirit of God was poured out. As he saw this vision, his wife, Rose, spoke through tongues and interpretation to describe what he was seeing. The next morning at the FGBMFI meeting he received a check for $1,000, and ˒Thomas R. Nickel offered the services of his press to print a magazine for the group. Nickel was appointed editor of the magazine called *The Full Gospel Business Men's Voice.*

During the next year, eight more chapters of the FGBMFI began around the country, and the first annual convention was held in Los Angeles. The attendance at the initial meeting was about 3,000. The speakers included almost all the noted independent ministers who were associated with the healing revival: Oral Roberts, ˒Jack Coe, ˒Gordon Lindsay, ˒Raymond T. Richey, O. L. Jaggers, and Tommy Hicks.

The FGBMFI continued to grow at a startling rate. By the mid 1960s it had more than 300 chapters, with a total membership of 100,000. Growth did not stop, and in 1972 there was a membership of 300,000. By 1988 the fellowship had more than 3,000 local chapters and had spread to 87 countries.

The original vision of the FGBMFI was a nonsectarian fellowship of laity who could come together to share what God had done in their lives without any apology—even if that testimony included healing or tongues or deliverance from demonic forces. The impact of the FGBMFI on the pentecostal and charismatic movements has been considerable and not without controversy. The typical meeting, usually held in a hotel ballroom or a restaurant, was often a marked departure from the traditional pentecostal meetings of the past. The FGBMFI took the message of the power of the gospel to heal and deliver and of the baptism of the Holy Spirit from the tents to the hotels and convention centers of America. Often speakers were laymen who told of God's remarkable and miraculous intervention in their lives and businesses. They offered prayer for the sick, and many were saved, healed, and filled with the Holy Spirit in these services. This was certainly not the traditional revival meeting of the past, nor was it like any of the usual interdenominational testimony meetings. Many of the traditional ministers from pentecostal denominations could not adjust to this new approach; and although it was stressed that the FGBMFI was not a replacement for the local church, many pastors felt threatened by this open ecumenical fellowship.

The FGBMFI was in large part responsible for the rise of the teaching ministries of many of the prominent "faith teachers." The members were usually from churches that had not stressed nor taught on faith or healing or the ministry of the Holy Spirit, and so teachers like ˒Kenneth E. Hagin Sr., ˒Kenneth Copeland, and others were much in demand to teach at the regional and annual conventions.

The FGBMFI started a television program called *Good News* in the 1970s that at one time was seen in 150 cities. This half-hour program was hosted by Demos Shakarian and, like many local meetings, consisted of ordinary businessmen telling extraordinary stories about their faith in Christ.

The leader of the FGBMFI since its beginning has been Demos Shakarian. Shakarian suffered a stroke in 1984 that resulted in his taking a less active role in the day-to-day operations of the fellowship. In Mar. 1988 the board of directors voted to remove Shakarian as president but to retain him as spiritual director. He died in 1993. Demos's son Richard has taken over the leadership role.

See also CHARISMATIC MOVEMENTS.

■ **Bibliography:** B. Bird, "FGBMFI: Facing Frustrations and the Future," *Charisma* (June 1986) ■ D. E. Harrell Jr., *All Things Are Possible* (1975) ■ D. Shakarian, *The Happiest People on the Earth* (1975) ■ idem, "FGBMFI Struggles toward the Future," *Charisma* (Mar. 1988).   ■ J. R. Zeigler

FULL GOSPEL CHURCH OF GOD IN SOUTHERN AFRICA

George Bowie, a native of Scotland, migrated to the United States, where he received his Spirit baptism under the ministry of J. T. Boddy. Bowie then traveled to South Africa as a missionary of the Newark, NJ, Bethel Pentecostal Mission. Arriving in 1910, he established the Pretoria Pentecostal Mission. Eleazer Jenkins from Wales and Archibald Haig Cooper from England soon joined Bowie's missionary efforts. Cooper had first set foot in South Africa as part of the British forces fighting the Anglo-Boer War in 1901. Converted during a 1904 Gipsy Smith tent meeting, he received the baptism of the Holy Spirit in 1907. He then became an active member of the Johannesburg Apostolic Faith Mission, where ʼJohn G. Lake was serving as vice president. Subsequently, Cooper began an independent Pentecostal Mission in Middleburg, Transvaal, finally joining his work with that of Bowie in 1910. By 1913 Cooper was leader of the Pretoria Pentecostal Mission. In 1917 a division in the Pentecostal Mission led to the formation of the short-lived Church of God. Reunification in 1921 brought decentralization under the new name Full Gospel Church. On Mar. 28, 1951, the Full Gospel Church strengthened its missions and financial base by amalgamating with the ʼChurch of God in the United States (Cleveland, TN) and adopted the name ʼFull Gospel Church of God in Southern Africa (FGCOGISA). The FGCOGISA did not escape the racial tensions that have plagued the nation of South Africa. Almost from the beginning, white Pentecostals accepted racial segregation, and the church was divided into European (White), Black, Coloured, and Indian communities, with Europeans controlling the executive council. When South Africa changed national laws in 1994, the FGCOGISA was separated into the Irene Assemblies (White) and the United Assemblies (Black, Coloured, and Indian). Reunification of these two groups occurred in 1997, with a total membership of approximately 300,000. The denomination's early attempts at educational institutions were short-lived, and it was not until 1951 that the present Berean Bible Seminary was established. Colleges for other racial groups include Chaldo (Black) in Cape Town and Bethesda (Indian) in Durban as well as numerous missions schools. Addition-

ally, the denomination operates the correspondence program, Irene Theological College. The FGCOGISA remains bilingual due to the strong historical influences of both Holland and Great Britain. The headquarters are located in Irene, Transvaal. The highest governing body is the annual general council, which elects the general moderator. The denomination was a founding member of the Fellowship of Pentecostal Churches in 1977 and currently publishes *Dunamis*.

■ **Bibliography:** C. W. Conn, *Like a Mighty Army: A History of the Church of God* (1996) ■ L[emmer] du Plessis, "Pinkster Panorama: 'N Geskiedenis van die Volle Evangelie-kerk van God in Suidelieke Afrika, 1910–1983" (1984) ■ E. J. Moodley, "Pentecostal Catechesis in the Context of a Post-Apartheid South Africa: A Paradigm Change" (thesis, CG Theol. Sem., 1997) ■ A. H. Verster, "Religious Education: An Individualistic Approach to Practical Ministry" (thesis, CG Theol. Sem., 1987).   ■ D. G. Roebuck

FULL GOSPEL EVANGELISTIC ASSOCIATION

The Full Gospel Evangelistic Association (FGEA) was originally comprised of ministers who were a part of the ʼApostolic Faith (AF, Baxter Springs, KS) and were interested in forming a foreign missions outreach. The group formed the Ministerial and Missionary Alliance of the Original Trinity Apostolic Faith in 1951, but they were disfellowshiped by the AF. The year following, the group organized as the FGEA. Thus, a more progressive element within ʼCharles Parham's AF was on its own. Parham's daughter-in-law, Pauline Parham, became active in the new organization and served as the first superintendent of Midwest Bible Institute, which is sponsored by FGEA.

FGEA ordains ministers, supports foreign missions, and has an affiliation with local churches. By 1987 there were 175 ministers, 30 member churches and institutions, plus mission stations and cooperating churches.

Midwest Bible Institute was established in 1959 and began operating at Webb City, MO, the next year. The best-known instructor at the school in its formative years was the British pentecostal Charles H. E. Duncombe. The school moved to Houston, TX, in 1971. FGEA has its office on the campus.

Taking a classical pentecostal position, FGEA is Trinitarian, accepts sanctification as a "definite work of grace," believes in divine healing and health, is premillennial, and practices footwashing.

The missionary emphasis has been on Latin America, with missionaries serving in Mexico, Guatemala, and Peru. Other missionaries have been sent to Taiwan.

FGEA publishes *Full Gospel News* as its official periodical. The affiliated churches use Sunday school literature published by pentecostal publishers.

■ **Bibliography:** "By-laws, FGEA" (n.d.) ■ C. Jones, *Guide to the Study of the Pentecostal Movement* (1985) ■ "This Is Full Gospel Evangelistic Association" (brochure, 1980).   ■ W. E. Warner

FULTON, CHARLES B., JR.

FULTON, CHARLES B., JR. (1938–). President and CEO of ►Acts 29 Ministries. Born in West Palm Beach in 1938, Fulton grow up in a religious home, though his experience with God was less than intense. He attended Stetson University in DeLand, FL, where he was a prelaw and business major. During his senior year, however, he attended a Billy Graham Crusade and made a public profession of faith in Christ. After that, Fulton changed his sights and focused on becoming ordained in the Episcopal Church.

Following his graduation from Stetson and a tour of duty in the U.S. Army, Fulton enrolled in Berkeley Divinity School at Yale University and received his M.Div. in 1964. He was ordained into the diaconate in Aug. 1964 and became an Episcopal priest in December of that year.

Fulton spent the next 30 years mostly as a parish priest, integrating sound business principles with the gospel of Jesus Christ to produce flourishing, thriving churches. His parish assignments included three key spots in Florida: Palmetto, Osprey, and Jacksonville. In each Fulton saw growth in spiritual depth and attendance during his time as rector.

In 1993 Fulton was elected by the board of Episcopal Renewal Ministries to become its new president and CEO. One of his first decisions was to relocate the ministry headquarters from Evergreen, CO, to its present location in Atlanta, GA, to make it more accessible to Episcopalians across the country and around the world. In 1997 he and the board approved the change of the ministry's name to Acts 29 Ministries to reflect the Lord's call on the modern Christian's life to continue the work of the apostles in the book of Acts.

Fr. Fulton and his wife, Judy, live in Marietta, GA. They have five children and six grandchildren.   ■ D. B. DeBolt

FUNDAMENTALISM

FUNDAMENTALISM Fundamentalism refers to a movement among theologically conservative Protestant churches that reached its height in America during the 1920s and survives in resurgent post–WWII fundamentalist and evangelical churches and movements. With roots in 19th-century millenarianism, fundamentalism arose as a reaction to the liberal teachings of 19th-century higher criticism and the subsequent movement known as modernism. Fundamentalists saw themselves as defenders of orthodox Christianity against those in the churches who were attempting to accommodate the faith to the realities of the modern world.

Although an elaborate system of particular doctrines emerged from the movement, all fundamentalists stressed the verbal and inerrant inspiration of the Bible, which was seen as the final and complete authority for faith and practice. Fundamentalism also preached a rigorous lifestyle that often precluded the use of alcohol, tobacco, drugs, and attendance at places of "worldly amusement," such as the stage and, later, movie theaters.

After its zenith in the 1920s, fundamentalism and the modernist movement against which it struggled, suffered drastic declines. Fundamentalism gained its greatest attention in the famous "Monkey Trial" of 1925, in which John T. Scopes was tried for teaching the theory of evolution in the public schools of Dayton, TN. As a result of publicity surrounding this trial, fundamentalists came to be regarded as anti-intellectuals who stood in the way of social and academic progress.

Despite this perception, fundamentalism, in its more respectable form known as evangelicalism, has not only survived the negative image of the 1920s, but has flourished in the latter half of the century.

1. The Roots of the Movement.

Modern fundamentalism had its origins in the evangelical and millenarian movements of 19th-century England and America. The movement toward fundamentalism began in England in the wake of the French Revolution. When Pope Pius VI was exiled in 1798 and a new regime installed in revolutionary France, with a new calendar and the seeming overthrow of the established order, some Christians believed that they were living in the last days before the end of the age. English evangelicals thus began to seek answers for these events in biblical prophecies relating to the end times. Leaders in this pursuit were Lewis Way, an Anglican; ►Edward Irving, a Presbyterian; and John Nelson Darby, founder of the Plymouth Brethren.

In their studies, these men saw in Scripture the teaching of the imminent rapture of the church at the second coming of Christ, which would occur before the Millennium (the thousand years of peace predicted in the book of Revelation). They saw biblical prophecies concerning the return of the Jews to the Holy Land and a new outpouring of the Holy

Two of the twelve volumes of *The Fundamentals*, published between 1910 and 1915 and mailed free of charge to 250,000 ministers and laypeople by California oil millionaires Lyman and Milton Stewart.

Spirit "on all flesh," with the restoration of the charismata, as signs of the last days. They expected these signs to take place in their time. Indeed, when prophecy and glossolalia broke out in Irving's London Presbyterian congregation in 1830, he was sure that the end was near. But his Presbyterian elders felt otherwise. After being tried and expelled from the presbytery for teaching heresy concerning the person of Christ, Irving founded the ›Catholic Apostolic Church, which, along with the term *Irvingism,* became a byword among the enemies of the movement.

Darby, however, continued to popularize the teachings of the movement among his own English followers and among large groups of Americans during his several preaching tours of the U.S. One avid teacher of the new millenarian doctrines in America was William Miller of New York. He boldly predicted that the second advent of Christ would take place on or before the year 1843. His growing group of followers, which swelled to some 100,000 believers, were disappointed and scattered after the expected event failed to occur. This experience also gave Adventism a bad name, and "Millerism" became as unpopular in America as Irvingism was in Britain.

Despite the negative results of the Irving and Miller episodes, interest in the premillennial second coming of Christ continued to increase throughout the century and gained powerful allies in America before 1900. In 1872 the Niagara Bible Conferences in Ontario, Canada, stirred new support. Led by Baptists James Ingles and Adoniram J. Gordon, Presbyterian James H. Brookes, and Episcopalian William R. Nicholson, the prophetic movement began to flourish in America, centering around Bible conferences devoted to biblical prophecy.

In addition to millenarianism, these teachers included in their set of doctrines a vigorous defense of the literal, or verbal, inspiration of the Scriptures. In time, belief in the "inerrant" autographs (original manuscripts) of Scripture became a bedrock teaching of the movement. The absolute authority of Scripture provided a defense against the twin evils of modernism and Roman Catholicism, which was fast becoming the largest denomination in the U.S.

The major enemies of these teachers, however, were not the Roman Catholics but the higher critics. When the modernist movement began to gain strength under the influence of such leaders as Shailer Matthews, Charles Briggs, and A. C. McGiffert Sr., prophetic leaders saw themselves as the defenders of the faith against the German "higher critics" and their modernist American followers. By the late 1890s the millenarians had won no less a personage than Dwight L. Moody to their cause. Their greatest prizes, however, were Princeton Seminary professors Charles Hodge and Benjamin Warfield, who were destined to give important biblical and intellectual support to the movement. Although not supportive of the millenarian aspects of fundamentalism, Hodge

and Warfield stressed the inerrant authority and inspiration of the Scriptures. Their distinctive work was known as the Princeton Theology.

2. Institutionalization.

The fundamentalist movement began to crystallize after the turn of the century with the organization of the American Bible League in 1902 and the World's Christian Fundamentals Association in 1919. The latter organization came into being under the influence of the publication of a series of 12 pamphlets entitled *The Fundamentals* between 1910 and 1915. Financed and sent free of charge to 250,000 ministers and laymen by California oil millionaires Lyman and Milton Stewart, these booklets contained an exposition of the five points of the movement. They were (1) the verbal inerrancy of the Scriptures, (2) the deity and virgin birth of Christ, (3) the substitutionary atonement, (4) the physical resurrection of Christ, and (5) Christ's bodily return to earth. Edited by A. C. Dixon and R. A. Torrey, they gave the movement its popular name and distilled its distinctive theology.

In addition to these teachings, a dispensational eschatological schema called ›dispensationalism was popularized before the turn of the century. This interpretation of history and prophecy divided spiritual history into seven periods, or "dispensations," according to the differing methods of God's dealing with humankind in each period. These periods were those of (1) innocence, (2) conscience, (3) human government, (4) promise, (5) law, (6) grace, and (7) kingdom. Darby, the originator and promoter of this teaching, also popularized it in the U.S. between 1866 and 1877. In Darby's system the church age, or "age of grace," began with the birthday of the church and was destined to end with the rapture of the church at the second coming of Christ. Then the seventh dispensation, the millennial reign of Christ, or the "kingdom" age would begin.

Although fundamentalists and dispensationalists strongly supported the miracles of the Bible as one of the bedrock fundamentals of the faith, they denied the presence of miracles in modern times. Thus, they added to the dispensation of the church age a subdispensation in which the charismata ceased after the canon of Scripture was completed. The fundamentalist belief in miracles was limited to the historical fact that they had occurred in biblical times.

Buttressing this claim was the book by Warfield titled *Counterfeit Miracles* (1918), which held that not one single documented miracle had occurred since the death of the last apostle. Much of this view was based on a refusal to accept the miraculous claims of the Roman Catholic Church. This view also predisposed the fundamentalists to oppose the pentecostal movement, which had appeared at the beginning of the century.

Major dispensational leaders were A. C. Gaebelein and C. I. Scofield. The dispensational scheme was most widely publicized through the notes of the *Scofield Bible* (1909), which continued to enjoy heavy sales among evangelicals throughout the rest of the century. Despite its antimiraculous teachings, many pentecostals joined the dispensationalist camp and taught the scheme in their Bible colleges with appropriate modifications to accommodate glossolalia and divine healing.

3. The Fundamentalist Controversy with the Modernists.

While liberalism was small and ineffectual before WWI, it grew greatly in influence after the war. Although some denominations feared and opposed the new views, more and more theologians and seminaries joined the modernist ranks. Although some large Protestant denominations, such as the Southern Baptists and Missouri Synod Lutherans were largely unaffected, others, such as the Methodist and Episcopal communions, found increasing numbers of modernists in their ranks.

The outstanding liberal voice in the land was that of Harry Emerson Fosdick, pastor of New York's First Presbyterian Church (although he was a Baptist) and professor of homiletics at Union Theological Seminary. Fundamentalists found Fosdick a popular target. After preaching a controversial sermon in 1922 titled "Shall the Fundamentalists Win?" he was removed from his Presbyterian pulpit, whereupon he founded the influential Riverside Church in New York City with help from John D. Rockefeller.

Another target of the fundamentalists was the Federal Council of Churches, which by 1920 was largely under the control of the modernists. Formed in 1908, it was seen by fundamentalists to be under the control of evolutionists and higher critics. A first line of attack was to root the modernists out of the mainline Protestant denominations. In the 1920s skirmishes broke out in several churches where fundamentalists attempted to oust leading modernists and gain control of the denominational machinery. The ensuing battles resulted in the defeat of the fundamentalists, however. In their attempts to drive modernists from the northern Presbyterian and Baptist churches, the fundamentalists were themselves rejected.

The climax of the conflict between fundamentalists and modernists came in 1925 in the famous Scopes trial in Dayton, TN. Charged with teaching evolution contrary to a recently passed Tennessee law, high school teacher John T. Scopes was defended by the most famous trial lawyer in America, Clarence Darrow. Coming to aid the prosecution was the most famous fundamentalist in the land, thrice-defeated Democratic presidential candidate William Jennings Bryan, a committed Presbyterian fundamentalist.

Although Scopes lost the trial and was fined a hundred dollars, the fundamentalists lost in the court of public opinion. Because of the trial, fundamentalists were seen as anti-intellectual and were derided by the press and especially by the universities. Despite this drastic setback, fundamentalism refused to die. The strength of the movement was seen in the fact that it not only survived the Scopes trial but that it continued in a more moderate form as evangelicalism in future years.

After 1925 the fundamentalists largely abandoned the seminaries and universities to the modernists and concentrated on building Bible institutes where their faith would be safe from the glare of the liberal media and the intellectuals who, like H. L. Mencken, found fundamentalists to be easy targets to lampoon. Such schools as Moody Bible Institute in Chicago and the Bible Institute of Los Angeles (BIOLA) became havens of fundamentalist theology. Some fundamentalists left their denominations to found new ones, such as the Presbyterian Church of America (later the Orthodox Presbyterian Church), founded by J. Gresham Machen in 1936, and the General Association of Regular Baptist Churches, founded by breakaways from the Northern Baptist Convention. Others joined smaller groups, such as the Christian and Missionary Alliance and the Evangelical Free Church.

4. Controversy with Pentecostals.

An important area of influence for fundamentalism was the rising pentecostal denominations that appeared after 1906. Although disagreeing with the cessationist teaching of the dispensationalists, most pentecostals during the 1920s and 1930s thought of themselves as fundamentalists "with a difference." Especially influential to pentecostals was the teaching of the premillennial rapture of the church. The reappearance of the charismata had been closely tied to the rapture of the church from the times of Edward Irving. Pentecostals saw in the renewal of healing and tongues a sure sign of the end of the age and of the rapture of the church. The prominence given to the rapture of the church in pentecostal preaching and teaching led historian ▸Robert Mapes Anderson to the conclusion that early pentecostalism was more a Second Coming movement than a tongues movement.

The disagreement with pentecostals over miracles eventually led to a break between fundamentalists and pentecostals. Although no pentecostal groups had formally joined the World's Christian Fundamentals Association after 1919, they were formally rejected by the organization in 1928. The resolution that disfellowshiped the pentecostals stated,

Whereas the present wave of Modern pentecostalism, often referred to as the "tongues movement," and the present wave of fanatical and unscriptural healing which is sweeping over the country today, has become a menace in many churches and a real injury to sane testimony of Fundamental Christians,

Be it resolved, that this convention go on record as unreservedly opposed to Modern pentecostalism, including the speaking in unknown tongues, and the fanatical healing known as general healing in the atonement, and the perpetuation of the miraculous sign-healing of Jesus and His apostles, wherein they claim the only reason the church cannot perform these miracles is because of unbelief.

From this point on, it was impossible to classify the pentecostals as fundamentalists, although the general public then and to this day is unaware of the differences. Indeed, in many minds the pentecostals were and continue to be falsely thought of as hyperfundamentalists.

5. From Fundamentalism to Evangelicalism.

When it became clear that the fundamentalists had lost the battle for the minds of mainstream American Protestant Christianity, they withdrew more and more into a social and theological shell. Eventually a spirit of censoriousness and condemnation took over the rhetoric of the movement with leaders such as Bob Jones and Carl McIntire denouncing those who had fallen from the straight and narrow way. These and others began to build institutional bastions for future warfare in defense of the faith. In 1927 Bob Jones created his university in Cleveland, TN, not far from Dayton, where the famous trial had taken place.

In 1941 Carl McIntire founded his American Council of Christian Churches (ACCC) to counteract the influence of the Federal Council and later of the National Council of Churches. The creation of the ACCC came at a point when more moderate voices were being heard. In the emergency of WWII many conservative Christians began to fellowship together in unprecedented ways. Leaders among these men were theologian Carl F. H. Henry and Harold J. Ockenga, pastor of Boston's historic Park Street Church. A group of moderate fundamentalists, meeting in Chicago in 1943, were invited to join McIntire's group, but they were repelled by his belligerent spirit. When discussions of a possible merger began, the presence of pentecostals in the moderate group became the bone of contention that ended all hopes of union.

McIntire regarded the pentecostals as apostates with whom he could have no fellowship. He refused to accept them or other evangelicals who fellowshiped with them in his new ACCC. In a historic moment the moderates rejected the fundamentalists, accepted the pentecostals, and adopted the name ►National Association of Evangelicals. This was the final break with the discredited militancy that characterized the older fundamentalists. It marked the beginning of a new era, when evangelists such as Billy Graham would preach under the banner of evangelicalism rather than of fundamentalism. It also

marked the first time in Christian history that a charismatic movement was accepted into the mainstream of the church.

Since that time pentecostals have grown to be the majority force in the NAE, with pentecostals such as ►Thomas F. Zimmerman (Assemblies of God) and ►Ray H. Hughes (Church of God, Cleveland, TN) serving as presidents of the organization. The crusades of Billy Graham after 1948 were strongly supported by pentecostals around the world, often making up the majority of his audiences in Third World countries. For this and other reasons, Graham was denounced by Bob Jones and other fundamentalists for compromising the purity of the gospel.

6. Fundamentalism Today.

The most prominent fundamentalist of the last quarter of the century has been Jerry Falwell, whose *Old Time Gospel Hour* has taken him into the living rooms of the people of America. His brand of conservative political activism harked back to the heady days before 1925, when fundamentalism was a force to be reckoned with in American life. His "Moral Majority" is believed to have played a key role in the election of Ronald Reagan in the 1980 presidential election.

But the prime religious forces in America after WWII were evangelicalism and pentecostalism, both of which played leading roles in the religious revival of the 1950s. Paralleling the evangelistic crusades of Billy Graham were those of Oral Roberts, who introduced pentecostalism to the American public with his televised healing services under the big tent.

The growth of the pentecostal churches and the outbreak of the charismatic movement in the mainline churches left the fundamentalists far behind the attention of the American public. In the opinion of this writer, the breaks with fundamentalism in 1928 and 1943 turned out to be a blessing that freed the rising pentecostals from the dead cultural and theological baggage of a discredited movement and opened up the way for unparalleled influence and growth in the last half of the twentieth century.

See also EVANGELICALISM.

■ **Bibliography:** G. Dollar, *A History of Fundamentalism in America* (1973) ■ S. Grebstein, *The Monkey Trial: The State of Tennessee vs. John Thomas Scopes* (1960) ■ D. Hart, *Defending the Faith: J. Gresham Machen and the Crisis of Conservative Protestantism in Modern America* (1994) ■ G. Marsden, *Fundamentalism and American Culture* (1980) ■ W. Menzies, *Anointed to Serve* (1971) ■ "The Rise of Fundamentalism," *Christian History* (issue 55, vol. 16, no. 3) ■ E. Sandeen, *The Roots of Fundamentalism* (1970). ■ H. V. Synan

G

GAINES, MARGARET (1931–). Church of God (CG, Cleveland, TN) missionary. Born in Anniston, AL, to parents who had been pentecostal missionaries to Japan, Margaret Gaines was called to be a missionary in 1946 at Bible Training School (later Lee University). The special guest that week was pentecostal missionary Josephine Planter. When the CG World Missions Board expressed reluctance to send a young single woman, Gaines raised her own support and sailed for Tunisia in Apr. 1952, where she assisted Planter for one year. Soon the missions board granted her an official appointment and support.

Moving to the village of Mégrine, she opened a mission in her home. By 1957 she had enough converts to establish a church. The missions board asked her to serve in France in 1961 and then in Israel in 1964. Early work there included teaching in the Middle East Theological Institute in Jerusalem and church planting in Aboud (in what was then known as the Occupied West Bank) and Amman, Jordan. In 1970 she opened Aboud Elementary School, which continues to serve the children of Aboud.

■ **Bibliography:** C. W. Conn, *Like a Mighty Army: A History of the Church of God* (1996) ■ idem, *Where the Saints Have Trod* (1959) ■ idem, M. Gaines, *Of Like Passions* (2000) ■ idem, "Reflection on Margaret Gaines' Ministry to Tunisia, France and Israel" (paper, CG School of Theology, 1987) ■ D. G. Thompson, "Keepsakes for the Kingdom" (thesis, CG School of Theology, 1994).

■ D. G. Roebuck

GARCÍA PERAZA, JUANITA ("MITA") (1897–1970). Founder of the Mita Congregation, Inc., in Puerto Rico in 1940. A former Roman Catholic, García Peraza was born and raised in Hatillo, Puerto Rico. From a wealthy family, she used her inheritance to open up a successful department store in the city of Arecibo. Throughout the 1930s she battled gastroenteritis. She promised God that if he would cure her, she would serve him for the rest of her life. She was allegedly healed of her illness in 1940 through the prayers of a missionary. In response to her healing, she began attending an Assemblies of God church in Arecibo, Puerto Rico. She became active in the church as a prophetess and was eventually opposed by the leadership of the church.

After Juanita left the church in Arecibo, she believed God called her to form her own movement. In 1940 she founded her own denomination, the Mita Congregation, in Arecibo. She and her followers began preaching the triple message of love, liberty, and unity. In 1949 Fela González had a divine revelation in which God allegedly stated that the Holy Spirit was to be called "Mita." They believe that the Holy Spirit (Mita) embodied himself in the person of García Peraza (and now in her successor, Teófilo Vargas [Aarón]).

Members of the congregation were instructed not to associate with members of other pentecostal churches because they did not preach about "Mita." Her religion differs from other traditional forms of Christianity not only in its theology, but also in the operation of cooperatives and social service activities for its parishioners. Many of Juanita's disciples came to believe that she was God's incarnation on earth and referred to her as "Mita" and "Goddess." After her death in 1970 leadership passed to Teófilo Vargas (called Aarón). In 1978 the University Hispano Americana posthumously awarded Juanita García Peraza an honorary doctorate for her extraordinary religious and social work in Puerto Rico.

■ **Bibliography:** "Centenario del Natalicio de la Persona de Mita," *El Nuevo Dia* (July 6, 1997) ■ "'Congregation Mita': Avance de la Obra de Mita, 1940–1990," *El Nuevo Dia* (Nov. 17, 1990) ■ C. Cruz, *La Obra do Mita* (1990) ■ *Enciclopedia de Grandes Mujeres de Puerto Rico*, vol. 3 (1975): 323–24, 347–81 ■ D. T. Moore, "La Iglesia de Mita y Sus Doctrinas," *Siguiendo La Sana Doctrina* (Sept.–Oct. 1988), 96–104 ■ D. R. Tories, *Historia de la Iglesia de Dios Pentecostal, M.I.: Una Iglesia Ungida Para Hacer Misión* (1992), 126–31 ■ T. Vargas Seín [Aarón], "Denominational Statistical Information Form for the Mita Congregation" (Sept. 1997).

GARLOCK, HENRY BRUCE (1897–1985). Missionary, administrator, and pastor. The eldest child of Edmund and Jessie Garlock, Henry Garlock attended Beulah Heights Bible Training School, North Bergen, NJ (1918–20). He first preached in the Pentecostal Holiness Association (F. S. Perkins), which supported him as a missionary to Liberia (1920–23), where he married Ruth E. Trotter (1897–1997) on June 28, 1921. Ordained in the Assemblies of God (AG) in 1924, he served as missionary to Ghana (1932–36) and Malawi (1953–57) and as the first African field director (1943–53) for the AG. Garlock pastored in Atlantic City, NJ (1923–26), Colorado Springs, CO (1926–29), Wichita, KS (1929–32), and Kansas City, KS (1936–43).

■ **Bibliography:** H. B. Garlock, *Before We Kill and Eat You* (1979) ■ G. Lindsay, *Maria Woodworth-Etter, Her Life and Ministry* (1981) ■ Obituary, *PE* (July 28, 1985) ■ J. L. Sherrill, "Cannibal Talk," in *God Ventures: True Accounts of God in the Lives of Men*, ed. I. B. Harrell (1970), 13–17 ■ *Assemblies of God Ghana 1931–1981* (n.d.).

■ D. D. Bundy

GARR, ALFRED GOODRICH, SR. (1874–1944). Early pentecostal missionary, evangelist, and pastor. Alfred Goodrich Garr was born in Danville, KY, to Oliver and Josephine Garr. At age eight, during a Baptist revival meeting, "A. G." Garr was baptized and joined the church. Intense spiritual questions remained until he found peace with God at age 15. Called to the ministry, he began preaching in the hills of Kentucky. Realizing the need for academic preparation, he enrolled at Centre College, Danville, KY, and later transferred to Asbury College in Wilmore, KY. While there he met and married Lillian Anderson. Following their studies, the Garrs traveled to California to pastor the Burning Bush Mission in Los Angeles.

Hearing of the revival at the ⁀Azusa Street Mission, Garr attended and received the baptism in the Holy Spirit with speaking in tongues on June 14, 1906, thus becoming the first white pastor of any denomination to claim this experience there. His wife received the baptism shortly afterward. When his church board refused to accept his new experience and teaching, Garr resigned. A week later he felt called to India as a missionary. Announcing his intention to the Azusa participants, they immediately gave hundreds of dollars, enough to send a party of five. Garr and his family traveled to Chicago in July to meet with the Burning Bush leaders and then to Danville, VA, to prepare for passage to India. Like other Azusa Street participants, the Garrs believed that

A. G. Garr, one of the first to be baptized in the Spirit at the Azusa Street Mission, who then served as a pentecostal missionary in India and Hong Kong, beginning in 1907.

tongues speaking had equipped them to minister abroad in (previously unlearned) languages.

Arriving in Calcutta at the turn of 1907, Garr visited a conference being held for missionaries. This gathering offered him the opportunity to tell of the recent events in Los Angeles. At the invitation of Pastor C. H. Hook, he began to hold services at the historic Carey Baptist Chapel in Lal Bazaar, Calcutta, where a pentecostal revival took place. There he taught the "Bible evidence" doctrine of tongues as conceived by ⁀Charles F. Parham, stating unequivocally that without tongues one had not received the baptism in the Holy Spirit and could not be considered pentecostal. Within a few weeks, however, he modified the doctrine. While holding steadfastly to the evidential part of Parham's thesis on tongues, Garr doubted—for a pragmatic reason (he could not speak Bengali after all) as well as theological reasons—the utility of tongues for preaching. Instead, he located the source of spiritual empowerment in praying in tongues, now marveling at the "blessedness of [God's] presence when those foreign words flow from the Spirit of God through the soul and then are given back to Him in praise, in prophecy, or in worship" (1907, 43). In this regard, Garr was among the first pentecostals to challenge Parham's understanding of the utility of tongues for missionary evangelism and to forge what became the classical pentecostal understanding of the role of tongues in Spirit baptism.

Garr later ministered at ⁀Pandita Ramabai's Mukti Mission (near Poona) and also held services in Bombay and Colombo, Ceylon (Sri Lanka). Following an invitation to Hong Kong, the Garrs arrived there on Oct. 9, 1907, and began conducting services in the Congregational Board Mission. While their ministry was quite effective, the Garrs suffered personal tragedy with the death of two daughters and an associate, Maria Gardener; they also faced other difficult circumstances. Ministry in Japan followed, but they resumed their work in Hong Kong on Oct. 4, 1909. Several months later they took a year's furlough in the U.S. and returned to China on Apr. 9, 1911. After a short stay, they departed for America in Dec. 1911.

Following their return to the U.S., the Garrs traveled in evangelistic work and A. G. became well-known in pentecostal circles for his faith-healing ministry. Three years after the death of his wife in 1916 (a son, Alfred Jr., was born to them in China), he married Hanna Erickson (1919).

Garr's ministry of itinerant evangelism continued until he conducted a revival in Charlotte, NC, in 1930. Because of the tremendous response to his preaching, Garr settled there and established a church that was eventually housed in the old city auditorium; as a result, it became known as the Garr Auditorium (now Garr Memorial Church). For many years this congregation was one of the best-known pentecostal churches in the southeastern U.S. On Jan. 12, 1940, the Garr

School of Theology opened with ►Charles William Walkem as the dean; it closed in 1943, however, when many of its students entered the war effort. Following Garr's death, his wife and son pastored the church.

■ **Bibliography:** R. P. Downing, "God Works in Mysterious Ways His Wonders to Perform" (typescript; n.d.) ■ H. and A. Fritsch, eds., *Letters from Cora* (1987) ■ B. Gann, ed., *The Trailblazer: The History of Dr. A. G. Garr and the Garr Auditorium* (n.d.) ■ A. G. Garr, "Tongues, the Bible Evidence," *Cloud of Witnesses to Pentecost in India* (Sept. 1907) ■ "Good News from Danville, Va.," *AF* (Sept. 1906) ■ "In Calcutta, India," *AF* (Apr. 1907) ■ E. M. Law, *Pentecostal Mission Work in South China* (c. 1916) ■ G. B. McGee, "'Latter Rain' Falling in the East: Early-Twentieth-Century Pentecostalism in India and the Debate over Speaking in Tongues," *Church History* 68 (Sept. 1999) ■ "Pentecost in Danville, Va.," *AF* (Oct. 1906) ■ V. Synan, *The Holiness-Pentecostal Tradition* (1997).

■ G. B. McGee

GARRIGUS, ALICE BELLE (1858–1949).

The founding mother of the ►Pentecostal Assemblies of Newfoundland. Garrigus went from the U.S. to St. Johns, Nfld., as a mature woman of 52 with a clear purpose: "to preach the full gospel— Jesus as Savior, Sanctifier, Baptizer, Healer and Coming King" (Janes, 2:137). Her Full Gospel message always emphasized the subjective element of the faith but never with a hint of religious fanaticism or at the expense of personal decorum. Garrigus was a leader strong enough to control any fanatics yet sufficiently pliable to yield to the Spirit's work.

Garrigus began her labors in a simple, unpretentious setting, Bethesda Mission, which grew under her leadership to become a denomination, Bethesda Pentecostal Assemblies, later known as the Pentecostal Assemblies of Newfoundland. The church serves in both Newfoundland and Labrador, as well as in numerous mission stations around the world.

■ **Bibliography:** B. K. Janes, *The Lady Who Came,* 2 vols. (1982–83).

■ J. A. Hewett

GARR MEMORIAL CHURCH

A prominent urban pentecostal church in Charlotte, NC. ►A. G. Garr, founder of the church, had a fruitful ministry before going to Charlotte in 1930. He was pastor of a Holiness mission in Los Angeles

Alice Garrigus, who in 1910, at age 52, founded what became the Pentecostal Assemblies of Newfoundland.

in 1906 and was one of the first persons to receive the baptism of the Holy Spirit at the ►Azusa Street Mission.

Garr went in 1907 to India, expecting God to enable him to speak the language of the people, which was an early belief of how God would exercise the gift of tongues. The venture failed, however, and Garr made use of an interpreter. In 1908 he and his wife went as missionaries to Hong Kong, where they studied the Chinese language and established a strong mission station. Many missionaries who passed through Hong Kong and visited the Garr's mission continued to spread the pentecostal message throughout the Orient.

In the spring and summer of 1930, A. G. Garr and his wife, Hanna, conducted a tent revival in Charlotte, NC, that attracted citywide attention. Garr remained in the city and in 1931 established an independent church. The church purchased and rebuilt the city auditorium as its sanctuary. It was first named Garr Auditorium and is now the Garr Memorial Church.

Garr, his wife, and son, Alfred, were partners in the ministry from the beginning. Hanna Garr began a daily radio broadcast, *Morning Thought,* in 1937 and continued it for 48 years. When Garr died in 1944, she became pastor of the church, a post she held for 29 years. Alfred Garr Jr. succeeded his mother as pastor in 1973 and led the church for 14 years. He then became pastor emeritus and executive director of the church's Camp Lurecrest near Charlotte. He was succeeded as pastor by Karl D. Coke.

■ **Bibliography:** Files of the Garr Memorial Church, Charlotte, NC ■ "Garr Memorial Church Jubilee" (phonograph record of the church's music, with a historical review), 1980.

■ C. W. Conn

GAUSE, RUFUS HOLLIS (1925–).

Contemporary theologian, scholar, and professor at the ►Church of God (CG, Cleveland, TN) School of Theology. Gause attended Emmanuel College (1944), Presbyterian College (B.A., 1945), and Columbia Theological Seminary (M.Div., 1949). He later earned a Ph.D. at Emory University (1975).

In 1947 Gause began his teaching career at Lee College, where he served in the religion department until 1972. From Lee he became the first dean and director of the CG School of Theology in 1975.

Gause was president of the ►Society for Pentecostal Studies (1971–72) and a member of the board. His published works include *Church of God Polity* (1973), *Living in the Spirit* (1980), *Revelation* (1984), and *The Preaching of Paul* (1985).

■ **Bibliography:** Archives of the Church of God (Cleveland, TN).
■ C. W. Conn

GAXIOLA, MANUEL JESÚS (1927–). Key writer and leader of the Iglesia Apostólica de la Fe en Cristo Jesús (Apostolic Church of Faith in Jesus Christ) in Mexico. He was born in Guamúchil, Sinaloa, Mexico, in 1927. Gaxiola graduated from the Apostolic Theological Institute in Mexico City; the Pentecostal Bible Institute in Tupelo, MS; the University of the Americas; and from Fuller Theological Seminary in Pasadena, CA, where he earned a master's degree in missiology. He is an ordained minister in the Iglesia Apostólica and has served as a pastor, president of the denomination's national youth convention, secretary of Christian education, secretary of national and foreign missions, district bishop, and secretary general of the Iglesia Apostólica in Mexico. In addition to his leadership at the national level, he wrote an important study of the Iglesia Apostólica in Mexico called *La Serpiente y La Paloma* (1970). Since then he has earned a Ph.D. from the University of Birmingham, U.K., has served as director of CERLAM (The Center for the Study of Religion in Latin America), and as president of the ▸Society for Pentecostal Studies. ■ G. Espinosa

GEE, DONALD (1891–1966). Pastor, author, educator, conference speaker, editor, and ecumenist. Gee, son of a London sign painter (d. 1900), was converted in 1905 in Finsbury Park Congregational Church, London, through the preaching of Seth Joshua, a Methodist influenced by the Welsh revival. With his mother, Gee joined a Baptist congregation in 1912 and became a pentecostal believer in Mar. 1913. He continued his occupation as sign painter until forced to find alternative service on a farm to avoid imprisonment because of his conscientious objection to military service in WWI. In the countryside he led a small pentecostal fellowship and after the war accepted appointment (1920–30) to a small chapel in Leith, a suburb of Edinburgh. Congregational growth resulted in the building of Bonnington Toll Chapel. The events of this decade are narrated in *Bonnington Toll—and After: The Story of a First Pastorate* (1943, 1960). Gee's first involvement with the larger pentecostal movement occurred during this period as he attended the International Pentecostal Conference in Amsterdam in 1921.

A competent musician, Gee was often invited to serve as pianist or organist for large gatherings, and he produced the first *Redemption Tidings Hymn Book* (1924). He began contributing articles to pentecostal periodicals in 1922.

In 1928 Gee accepted an invitation to serve as a Bible teacher in Australia and New Zealand, where he spent seven months. On the way he wrote his first book, *Concerning Spir-*

itual Gifts (1928). Until WWII restricted his freedom to travel, Gee lectured all over the world. He taught in the Danzig Bible School and Filadelfia Bible School (Stockholm) as well as in North American camp meetings. His travel on five continents provided data for his history of pentecostalism, *Upon All Flesh* (1935), in which he argued that the pentecostal revival is a diverse worldwide movement, transcending national interest and united by a shared experience. As a teacher he was renowned for his judicious counsel and the thoughtful care with which he avoided extreme positions on issues of contention within the pentecostal movement. This tendency led to his being known as the "Apostle of Balance," a reputation that resulted in his being elected vice chairman of the British Assemblies of God (AG) (1934–44) and later chairman (1945–48).

Gee's experiences throughout the world led him to think in terms of pentecostal ecumenism and resulted in the European Pentecostal Conference at Stockholm (1939). The next conference was organized by Gee and ▸David du Plessis in Zurich (1947). At this conference Gee was appointed editor of *Pentecost* (1947–66), in which he would publish some of his most important and provocative essays. Some of these were in response to harsh criticism by pentecostals for his cooperation with the 1954 Billy Graham Evangelistic Campaign in London and for his attending the meeting of the

Donald Gee, a leader in the pentecostal movement who preached in many countries throughout the world and wrote several books on the baptism in the Spirit and spiritual gifts.

World Council of Churches' Faith and Order Commission in St. Andrews, Scotland, in 1960. Gee was invited to be an observer at the New Dehli Assembly of the World Council of Churches (1961), but because of pressure organized by American AG general superintendent ►Thomas Zimmerman at the Jerusalem ►Pentecostal World Conference, Gee was forced to decline the invitation. However, despite growing concern in his own church and in the American AG, he established and maintained contact with the leaders of the early charismatic renewal in Europe and North America.

In 1951, at age 60, Gee embarked on a career as principal of the newly reorganized Bible school of the British AG at Kenley, Surrey, near London. It was a formidable task. Funds were scarce, and critics of Bible school training within the AG were vocal. This context, while restricting Gee's freedom to travel, allowed him time for his editorial responsibilities, for extensive reading and reflection, as well as for productive years of writing.

In 1964 Gee was relieved of his position as principal. His last two years were spent with editorial work, teaching at International Bible Training Institute, and occasional lecturing. He died of heart failure on July 20, 1966, in London.

A self-educated man, Gee was a prolific author, writing more than 30 books. The number of periodical articles is formidable. From 1924 on he contributed more than 500 articles to *Redemption Tidings* alone (sometimes under the pen name "Circumspectus"). His articles appeared in nearly every pentecostal periodical around the world. Books and articles, many of which were revised and republished by Gee himself, have been translated into many languages and continue to be reprinted. His complete bibliography has not been established.

■ **Bibliography:** D. D. Bundy, "Donald Gee: The Pentecostal Leader Who Grew in Wisdom and Stature," *AGH* 12, 3 (1992) ■ J. Carter, *Donald Gee: Pentecostal Statesman* (1975) ■ D. Gee, *After Pentecost* (1945) ■ idem, *All With One Accord* (1961; repr. as *Toward Pentecostal Unity* [n.d.]) ■ idem, *Concerning Shepherds and Sheepfolds: A Series of Studies Dealing with Pastors and Assemblies* (1930; repr. 1952) ■ idem, *Concerning Spiritual Gifts* (1928; repr. 1937; rev. ed., 1972) ■ idem, *The Fruit of the Spirit: A Pentecostal Study* (n.d.) ■ idem, *Fruitful or Barren?* (1961) ■ idem, *The Glory of the Assemblies of God* (n.d.) ■ idem, *God's Grace and Power for Today: The Practical Experience of Being Filled with the Holy Ghost* (1936; repr. 1972) ■ idem, *God's Great Gift, Seven Talks Together about the Holy Spirit* (n.d.; repr. 1972) ■ idem, *Keeping in Touch: Studies in Walking in the Spirit* (1951) ■ idem, ed., *Messages Preached at the Fifth Triennial Pentecostal World Conference* (n.d.) ■ idem, *The Ministry Gifts of Christ* (n.d.) ■ idem, *The Missionary Who Stayed at Home* (n.d.) ■ idem, *Pentecost* (1932) ■ idem, *The Pentecostal Movement: A Short History and an Interpretation for British Readers* (1941) ■ idem, *The Pentecostal Movement, Including the Story of the War Years (1940–1947)* (1949) ■ idem, *Proverbs for Pentecost* (1936) ■ idem, *Spiritual Gifts in the Work of the Ministry Today* (1963) ■ idem, *Studies in Guidance* (1936; rev. ed., 1941) ■ idem, *Temptations of the Spirit-Filled Christian* (1966) ■ idem, *These Men I Knew: Personal Memories of Our Pioneers* (1980) ■ idem, *"This Is the Will of God . . .": The Bible and Sexual Problems* (1940) ■ idem, *"To the Uttermost Part": The Missionary Results of the Pentecostal Movement in the British Isles* (1932) ■ idem, *Trophimus I Left Sick: Our Problems of Divine Healing* (1952) ■ idem, *Why Pentecost?* (1944) ■ idem, *Wind and Flame: Incorporating the Former Book, The Pentecostal Movement, with Additional Chapters* (1967) ■ idem, comp. and ed., with H. W. Greenway and I. MacPherson, *World Pentecostal Conference, 1952* (1952) ■ W. J. Hollenweger, *Enthusiastisches Christentum. Die Pfingstbewegung in Geschichte und Gegenwart* (1969), 191–200 ■ English ed., *The Pentecostals* (1972), 206–17 ■ Spanish ed., *El Pentecostalismo, Historia y Doctrinas* (1976), 207–17 ■ idem, "The Pentecostal Movement and the World Council of Churches," *Ecumenical Review* 18 (1966) ■ W. K. Kay, *Inside Story: A History of the British Assemblies of God* (1990) ■ J. L. McNamee, "The Role of the Spirit in Pentecostalism: A Comparative Study" (diss., Tübingen, 1974) ■ R. Massey, *Another Springtime: Donald Gee, Pentecostal Pioneer. A Biography* (1992) ■ A. Missen, *The Sound of a Going: The Story of the Assemblies of God* (1973) ■ R. M. Ross, "Donald Gee: In Search of a Church, A Sectarian in Transition" (diss., Knox College, Toronto, 1974) ■ idem, "Donald Gee, Sectarian in Search of a Church," *Evangelical Quarterly* 50 (1978) ■ Colin Whittaker, *Seven Pentecostal Pioneers* (1983).

■ D. D. Bundy

GELPI, DONALD L. (1934–). North American Catholic charismatic theologian. Gelpi became a Jesuit as a young man and was ordained as a priest in 1964, specializing early on in theology. Spiritual concerns were prominent in his first publications, e.g., *Functional Asceticism: A Guideline for American Religious* (1966) and *Discerning the Spirit: Foundations and Futures of Religious Life* (1970). Baptized in the Spirit in 1969, Gelpi directed his mind to God's work in pentecostal blessing, writing *Pentecostalism: A Theological Viewpoint* (1971), the first systematic study of charismatic renewal by a Catholic theologian, and *Pentecostal Piety* (1972). Gelpi's later writings manifest a concern to develop a more indigenous American theology with a sound philosophical basis rooted in American experience and culture, particularly *Inculturating North American Theology: An Experiment in Foundational Method* (1988) and *The Turn to Experience in Contemporary Theology* (1994). Works reflecting both these concerns and his charismatic experience include *Charism and Sacrament: A Theology of Christian Conversion* (1976); *Experiencing God: A Theology of Human Emergence* (1978); *The Divine Mother: A Trinitarian Theology of the Holy Spirit* (1984); *Committed Worship: A Sacramental Theology for Converting Christians* (1993); and *The Conversion Experience* (1998). Gelpi is professor of historical and systematic theology at the Jesuit School of Theology, Berkeley, CA.

■ P. D. Hocken

GEREJA BETHEL INDONESIA Indonesia is the largest nation in Southeast Asia and is the world's largest Muslim country. From the early 17th century until their declaration of independence, the more than 3,000 islands comprising Indonesia were primarily under the control of the Dutch. The nation won independence in 1949. The Gereja Bethel Indonesia (GBI; Indonesian Bethel Church of God) traces its roots to Dutch-American missionaries C. Grosebeek and D. van Klaveren, who sailed for Batavia (Jakarta, Java) in January 1921. They were from the Bethel Pentecostal Temple in Seattle, WA. After some persecution and failure in Bali, a predominately Hindu region, they established a pentecostal church in Surabaya (Java). Many of their converts were in the oil business and spread the pentecostal message as they were transferred to other parts of Indonesia. In 1924 the Dutch government recognized the church that had developed from their converts as De Pinkster Gemeente in Nederlands Indië (The Pentecostal Assembly in Netherlands India). The name was changed to Pinksterkerk (Pentecostal Church) in 1937 and then to The Pentecostal Church of Indonesia in 1942 to reflect its national identity. Between 1931 and 1966, nine divisions occurred, resulting in new denominations.

Due to organizational differences and their concerns about ongoing anti-Western sentiment, Pastors Van Gessel and Ho L. Senduk left the Pentecostal Church in 1952 and formed the Gereja Bethel Injil Sepenuh (Bethel Full Gospel Church). They practiced congregational rather than centralized church government. Conversations with the Church of God (CG, Cleveland, TN) began in 1955 when missionary Dalraith N. Walker went to Indonesia. ˒Wade H. Horton also visited the country. After meeting ˒Paul H. Walker at a 1958 conference in the United States, Senduk visited Cleveland, TN, and returned to Indonesia as an ordained minister in the Church of God. This led to further visits to Indonesia by CG officials and evangelists. On February 5, 1967, the Bethel Full Gospel Church signed an amalgamation agreement with the CG, which was then signed in Cleveland, TN, on March 9, 1967.

The amalgamation was soon rejected by many in the Bethel Full Gospel Church, however. This was due, at least in part, to continuing anti-Western sentiment and disagreements regarding spending. When the Indonesian Minister of Religious Affairs ruled that Senduk did not have the right to arrange the amalgamation, Senduk claimed undue governmental interference and withdrew from the Bethel Full Gospel Church to established GBI on Oct. 6, 1970. Senduk founded the Bethel School of Evangelism, now Bethel Theological Seminary, in 1956 in order to train ministers. The present facilities were constructed in 1968 with funds raised by the Youth World Evangelism Action, a youth missions program in the United States.

The governmental polity of GBI is congregational. Pastors work together in regional ministers' councils. On the national level an overseer with five assistant overseers is responsible for particular church ministries, along with a general treasurer and a general secretary. National decisions are determined by a synod comprised of all ordained ministers. In 1996 GBI reported a membership of over 1.3 million in 2,200 churches. ˒Abraham Alex Tanusaputra pastors the Bethany congregation in Surabaya, which is recognized as the largest congregation in the CG movement with over 40,000 members in 1995. The denomination also sponsors 20 Bible schools and four seminaries.

■ **Bibliography:** C. W. Conn, *Like a Mighty Army: A History of the Church of God* (1996) ▌ J. A. Pickens, "Theological Education in Southeast Asia: A Challenge to Reach the Masses" (thesis, CG Theol. Sem., 1996) ▌ A. B. Setyobekti, "Strategies of Church Growth in GBI (Bethel Church Indonesia)" (thesis, CG Theol. Sem., 1997) ▌ A. Soerjadi, "Reflection on Indonesian Revival and Basic Applied Strategy for Christians" (thesis, CG Theol. Sem., 1980). ▌ D. G. Roebuck

GIBSON, CHRISTINE AMELIA (1879–1955). Educator and pastor. A champion of the faith principle, Christine A. Gibson headed the Zion Bible Institute, East Providence, RI, during the first 31 years of its existence. Born in British Guiana (Guyana today), she was orphaned as a small child and converted at age 21. In 1905 a series of circumstances brought her to the U.S. and to a Holiness faith home in East Providence. Soon after she became pastor of the church connected with the home, she received the pentecostal baptism while on a visit to Rochester, NY. In 1910 she married Rueben A. Gibson (d. 1924), who afterward joined her in the work in East Providence. The faith principle, the keystone in the operation of both church and home, was enshrined also in the administration of the worker training school Gibson opened the year after her husband's death. Although she died in 1955, the school continued for decades to rely on prayer rather than on advance pledges or fees. In other ways, such as the requirement that female students wear uniforms, Zion continued traditions set by its founder and other pentecostal pioneers.

■ **Bibliography:** Zion Bible Institute, *Zionian* (1974), 29–30, 36–87. ▌ C. E. Jones

GIFTS OF THE SPIRIT The Holy Spirit is called a "gift" three times in the book of Acts (2:38; 10:45; 11:17) and once specifically "the gift of God" (Acts 8:20; cf. also John 4:10). Yet this terminology (Gk. *dōrea, dōron, doma,* or *dōrema*) is *not* used in the NT to refer to the varied powers and activities of those who have received the Spirit. "Gifts" in the NT are normally either sacrifices (Matt. 5:23–24; 8:4; 15:5; 23:18–19; Luke 21:1, 4; Heb. 5:1; 8:3–4; 9:9; 11:4) or material gifts of some kind (e.g., Matt. 2:11; 7:11; Mark 7:11; Luke 11:13; Phil. 4:17; Rev. 11:10), while the singular "gift" in a more profound sense refers to salvation, righteousness, or eternal life, or even to Jesus Christ himself (see, e.g., Rom. 5:15–17; 2 Cor. 9:15; Eph. 2:8; 3:7; 4:7; Heb. 6:4; James 1:17). Only in Eph. 4:8 are "gifts" (Gk. *domata*) viewed in relation to the ministries of the church, and even here the choice of words is not Paul's own, for he is quoting from Ps. 68:18. The reference is not to a divinely given power to perform these ministries, but to the persons who perform them: apostles, prophets, evangelists, and teachers.

The more characteristic NT expressions for what Christians today call "gifts of the Spirit" are "spiritual things" (Gk. *pneumatika*), "graces" or "favors" *(charismata)*, and "showings" or "manifestations" *(phanerōseis)*. Two other terms for similar phenomena are "workings" *(energēmata)* and "ministries" *(diakoniai)*. All of these are ways of getting at what could be called the plurality of the Holy Spirit. The Spirit of God is one, according to both Jews and Christians, just as God is one, yet because the Spirit's activity was often seen in relation to individuals or specific groups, the diversity or plurality of the Spirit's power and presence was constantly in evidence. Already in the Hebrew Scriptures the Spirit of God could be viewed as plural when an author wanted to dramatize a number of different virtues, as in relation to the expected Messiah: "The Spirit of the Lord will rest on him— the Spirit of wisdom and of understanding, the Spirit of counsel and of power, the Spirit of knowledge and of the fear of the LORD" (Isa. 11:2; cf. 1 Peter 4:14). Even the word "spirit" (Gk. *pneuma*) was occasionally used in the plural, not only of evil spirits (as in the Gospels or in 1 Peter 3:19), but also of the varied activities of the Spirit of God. John, for example, sent greetings to the seven churches of Asia "from God and from *the seven spirits* before his throne" (Rev. 1:4; cf. 5:6). The author of 1 John warns his readers not to believe every spirit, but to "test the spirits to see whether they are from God, because many false prophets have gone out into the world. This is how you can recognize the Spirit of God: Every spirit that acknowledges that Jesus Christ has come in the flesh is from God, but every spirit that does not acknowledge Jesus is not from God. This is the spirit of the antichrist" (1 John 4:1–3; cf. v. 6).

The best-known statement of the apostle Paul on the subject of "spiritual gifts" (1 Cor. 12:1–11) centers on this issue of unity versus plurality. There are different "gifts" *(charismata)*, Paul writes, "but the same Spirit. There are different kinds of service *[diakoniai]*, but the same Lord. There are different kinds of working *[energēmata]*, but the same God works all of them in all men" (1 Cor. 12:5–6). The plurality or diversity in the Corinthian congregation was clear for anyone to see. What Paul does is to affirm unity in the face of this diversity. From a list of specific examples (vv. 7–11) he

concludes, "All these are the work of one and the same Spirit, and he gives them to each one, just as he determines." The varied "workings" of the Spirit of God to which Paul appeals here are "the message of wisdom," "the message of knowledge" (v. 8), "faith," "gifts of healings" (v. 9), "miraculous powers," "prophecy," "distinguishing between spirits," "speaking in different kinds of tongues," and "interpretation of tongues" (v. 10). There is no evidence that the list is intended to be systematic or exhaustive. Some items fall into pairs, such as "tongues" and "interpretation of tongues," "prophecy" and "distinguishing between spirits," "message of wisdom" and "message of knowledge," and perhaps "gifts of healings" and "miraculous powers." Yet "prophecy" and "message of wisdom" or "message of knowledge" seem to overlap, while "faith," or "faithfulness," shows no particular relationship to any other item in the list. Most of the gifts are gifts of *speech*, yet at least two (healings and miraculous powers) are gifts of *action*, and we may well suspect that there are others (cf. 1 Peter 4:11: "If anyone speaks, he should do it as one speaking the very words of God. If anyone serves, he should do it with the strength God provides"). If this is Paul's organizing principle, it is again difficult to know how "faith" is to be classified. Is it a gift of speech or of action?

Paul introduces the metaphor of the human body in 1 Cor. 12:12. He crowns his emphasis on unity with the conclusion that "we were all baptized by one Spirit into one body—whether Jews or Greeks, slave or free—and we were all given the one Spirit to drink" (v. 13). Far from being in tension, unity and diversity reinforce each other in Paul's argument. Only the recognition of the Spirit's unity can legitimize for him the Spirit's diverse expressions. Paul introduces a kind of fable in 12:14–26, in which he imagines different parts of the human body each talking about its relationship to other parts or to the body as a whole (e.g., "Because I am not a hand, I do not belong to the body," v. 15; "I don't need you!" v. 21). The application comes in vv. 27–30, where Paul again speaks explicitly of *charismata*, or "gifts": "first of all apostles, second prophets, third teachers, then miracles, also those having gifts of healing, those able to help others, those with gifts of administration, and those speaking in different kinds of tongues" (v. 28). He then asks rhetorically, "Are all apostles? Are all prophets? Are all teachers? Do all work miracles? Do all have gifts of healing? Do all speak in tongues? Do all interpret?" (vv. 29–30) . The rhetorical questions repeat in part the immediately preceding list in v. 28, which in turn invites comparison with Paul's earlier list in vv. 7–11.

The most conspicuous difference between the lists of spiritual gifts in 1 Cor. 12:7–11 and 12:28–30 is that the latter begins with three items that refer not to powers or activities but to persons of status in the ancient church: apostles, prophets, and teachers (cf. Eph. 4:11; also 2:20; 3:5). These are set off from what follows by being numbered from one to three, giving the impression that Paul has deliberately combined two types of lists, one applicable to the Christian church generally and one adapted specifically to a local congregation (in this instance Corinth). Of the six remaining items in vv. 28–30, four coincide with the list in vv. 7–11: "miracles" and "gifts of healings," "tongues" and "interpretation of tongues." The only new items introduced are references to "those able to help others" (Gk. *antilēmpseis*) and "carrying out responsibilities" *(kybernēseis)*. These are also the only two items from v. 28 that are not picked up in vv. 29–30. Paul asks, "Are all apostles? Are all prophets? Are all teachers? Do all work miracles? Do all have gifts of healing? Do all speak in tongues? Do all interpret?" The questions he does *not* ask are, "Do all do helpful deeds?" and "Do all carry out their responsibilities?"

The reason for the omission is not hard to find. The doing of helpful deeds and the carrying out of routine responsibilities in the congregation were not the sort of gifts that made others in the congregation envious. They are clearly the least "charismatic" of all the gifts in 1 Cor. 12 and may not even have been counted among the "spiritual gifts" by anyone other than Paul. Perhaps they are ministries arising out of the gift of "faith" or "faithfulness," which seemed to stand by itself in the previous list (v. 9), unrelated to the other gifts. Those who contributed to the work of the congregation by "doing helpful deeds" and "carrying out responsibilities" were probably the ones most tempted to say, "Because I am not a hand [or an eye], I do not belong to the body" (i.e., because I do not prophesy or work miracles or speak in tongues, I do not really count in the life of the congregation). Paul's purpose in 1 Cor. 12 is not to list all the varied gifts of the Spirit, much less rank them, but to attribute them all to the same Holy Spirit and to make sure that simple and humble acts of service were not overlooked in the congregation's zeal for miracles and inspired speech. This is probably the point of his rather obscure reference in vv. 22–24 to the "less honorable" or "unpresentable" parts of the human body that are "indispensable" and are consequently treated with "special honor" or "special modesty." To introduce a modern analogy, the "helpers" and "servers" in the congregation were like the coaching staff of a talented basketball team. Though they lack the speed and athletic ability of their players, their team can hardly survive without them. Paul appears to be making a case for the apparently "ungifted" helpers and even leaders in the congregation, that their gifts too might be recognized and appreciated as the work of the Spirit.

Near the end of 1 Corinthians Paul refers explicitly to "the household of Stephanas … the first converts in Achaia" as those who "devoted themselves to the service of the saints. I urge you, brothers, to submit to such as these and to everyone who joins in the work, and labors at it" (1 Cor. 16:15–16; cf. 1 Thess. 5:12–13). It is likely that already in ch. 12 he has

in mind people of this sort and wants it clearly understood that their labors too are gifts of the Spirit. This emphasis sets the stage for Paul's celebration of love in ch. 13. Love is not itself one of the spiritual gifts. No one can excuse a failure to love on the ground that "I don't have that gift"! Yet if love is the motivation of those who help and those who serve in the congregation without attracting attention to themselves, then love must govern as well the exercise of *all* the spiritual gifts. When it does, the gifts of the Spirit will be used, without jealousy or arrogance, to unify and build up the congregation, not divide or destroy it.

At the same time, Paul urges his readers to "eagerly desire the greater gifts" (12:31). He has carefully avoided specifying what the "greater gifts" are, yet in ch. 14 he pointedly ranks two of them: "Pursue love and eagerly desire the spiritual gifts, but especially that you may prophesy" (14:1). Prophecy is "greater" than speaking in tongues because it communicates meaning and therefore has the possibility of "building up" the congregation. Tongues speaking also has this possibility, but only if it is accompanied by interpretation; otherwise it divides the hearer from the speaker. Paul can say, "I thank God that I speak in tongues more than all of you," yet add almost in the same breath, "but in the church I would rather speak five intelligible words to instruct others than ten thousand words in a tongue" (14:18–19). Clearly, Paul was a "charismatic," yet the thrust of his argument in 1 Corinthians is to channel the charismatic experiences of his readers in such a way as to make them better servants to each other in the body of Christ.

In Rom. 12 he accents the gifts of helping and serving even more than in 1 Corinthians and makes no mention of tongues speaking, healing, or miracles: "We have different gifts *[charismata]*, according to the grace given us. If a man's gift is prophesying, let him use it in proportion to his faith. If it is serving, let him serve; if it is teaching, let him teach; if it is encouraging, let him encourage; if it is contributing to the needs of others, let him give generously; if it is leadership, let him govern diligently; if it is showing mercy, let him do it cheerfully" (Rom. 12:6–8). Here the giving of "leadership" and the showing of "mercy" echo the "responsibilities" and the "helpful deeds" of 1 Cor. 12. Paul then adds, in the spirit of 1 Cor. 13, "Let love be sincere. Hate what is evil; cling to what is good. Be devoted to one another in brotherly love. Honor one another above yourselves. Never be lacking in zeal, but keep your spiritual fervor, serving the Lord. Be joyful in hope, patient in affliction, faithful in prayer. Share with God's people who are in need. Practice hospitality" (Rom. 12:9–13).

The one conclusion that emerges from this survey is that the NT, and Paul in particular, defines "spiritual gifts" very broadly, encompassing both the natural and the supernatural, both the visible miraculous signs that gave evidence of the Spirit's presence at Pentecost and the deeds of love, kindness, and service that were part of the believer's obligation already in the OT and Judaism. The Holy Spirit was indeed plural as well as singular to the earliest Christians, and the wisest among them resisted all efforts to limit the Spirit's gifts to one kind of activity or one set of phenomena. Though the pentecostal and charismatic movements have strongly emphasized the gifts of tongues and prophecy in particular, they have also called the attention of the Christian church to the crucial importance of gifts of the Spirit generally and in so doing have served as an agent of renewal in the last half century.

See also DISCERNMENT OF SPIRITS, GIFT OF; FAITH, GIFT OF; GLOSSOLALIA; HEALING, GIFT OF; INTERPRETATION OF TONGUES, GIFT OF; KNOWLEDGE, WORD OF; MIRACLES, GIFT OF; PROPHECY, GIFT OF; WISDOM, WORD OF.

■ **Bibliography:** C. K. Barrett, *A Commentary on the First Epistle to the Corinthians* (repr. 1988) ■ D. Bennett, "The Gifts of the Holy Spirit," in *The Charismatic Movement*, ed. M. Hamilton (1975) ■ A. Bittlinger, *Gifts and Graces* (1967) ■ D. Bridge and D. Phypers, *Spiritual Gifts and the Church* (1973) ■ F. D. Bruner, *A Theology of the Holy Spirit* (1970) ■ D. A. Carson, *Showing the Spirit* (1987) ■ H. Conzelmann, *1 Corinthians* (1975) ■ J. D. G. Dunn, *Baptism in the Holy Spirit* (1970) ■ idem, *Jesus and the Spirit* (1975) ■ E. E. Ellis, *Prophecy and Hermeneutic in Early Christianity* (1978) ■ G. D. Fee, *The First Epistle to the Corinthians* (1987) ■ idem, *God's Empowering Presence* (1994) ■ idem, "Gifts of the Spirit," in *Dictionary of Paul and His Letters* (1993) ■ R. Y. K. Fung, "Ministry, Community and Spiritual Gifts," *Evangelical Quarterly* 56 (Jan. 1984): 3–20 ■ W. A. Grudem, *The Gift of Prophecy in 1 Corinthians* (1982) ■ J. Koenig, *Charismata: God's Gift for God's People* (1978) ■ J. W. MacGorman, *The Gifts of the Spirit* (1974) ■ R. P. Martin, *The Spirit and the Congregation: Studies in I Corinthians 12–15* (1978) ■ P. D. Opsahl, ed., *The Holy Spirit in the Life of the Church* (1978) ■ S. Schatzmann, *A Pauline Theology of Charismata* (1986) ■ S. Smalley, "Spiritual Gifts and 1 Corinthians 12–16," *JBL* 88 (1968): 427–33.

■ J. R. Michaels

GIFTS OF THE SPIRIT: NATURAL AND SUPERNATURAL

Pentecostal scholar Russ Spittler says, ▸"Glossolalia is a human phenomenon, not limited to Christianity nor even to religious behavior.... The belief that *distinguishes* the movement can only wrongly be thought of as describing the *essence* of Pentecostalism." I believe Spittler to be correct. The notion that glossolalia (or any other gift of the Spirit, including healing and precognition) is essentially "supernatural" is in my view biblically and scientifically untenable. It is biblically untenable because the lists of charismata in the NT include so-called extraordinary gifts (healing, prophecy, glossolalia) *and* so-called ordinary gifts (management, teaching, giving money to the poor, being married or unmarried [Rom. 12:6–8; 1 Cor. 7:7; 12:8–11]). Paul's criterion for a

charism is not phenomenological but functional: *pneumatikos* (spiritual), *sarkikos* (fleshly), and *physikos* (natural) are not ontological but functional terms. They do not answer the question "What is?" but "What does it do to a person or a community?" Therefore, a charism is a natural gift that is given for the common good (*pros to sympheron*, 1 Cor. 12:7), operates in an ecclesiological and christological context, and is open to judgment by the ecumenical community (1 Cor. 12:3; 14:22, 29).

Scientifically, glossolalia and other gifts have been demonstrated to be human abilities (Hollenweger) that may or may not be used in Christian spirituality. They are not abnormal, only uncommon in certain cultures. If the "laws of nature"—which are human conventions—have to be changed because of new discoveries, a theology that is based on the difference between "natural" and "supernatural" has to shift the frontier between these two realms correspondingly.

Just as music, normal speech, and the bread in the Eucharist are common gifts of creation and may be transformed in the liturgical context, so speaking in tongues and other gifts are natural gifts that many human beings may possess. Just as a cathedral is built of ordinary stones, so glossolalia and other gifts are ontologically natural and ordinary phenomena. And just as, when put together in a masterpiece, the stones in a cathedral do not change ontologically but functionally, so speaking in tongues and other gifts can become something that, like the cathedral, proclaims, "God is here."

This, however, is not the reigning understanding of the gifts of the Spirit in pentecostalism and the charismatic movement. Usually they are understood to be strictly supernatural. In certain quarters the hallmark of pentecostalism is believed to be its supernatural aspects. In order to distinguish themselves from other, identical phenomena, the gifts of the Spirit are then presented like this:

	Natural	Supernatural	
		divine	*demonic*
Glossolalia	Knowing foreign languages	Speaking in tongues in a Christian context	Speaking in tongues in a non-Christian context
Healing	Medical treatment	Healing in a Christian context	Healing in a non-Christian context
Precognition	Meteorology, other prognostic sciences	Prophecy in a Christian context	Precognition in a non-Christian context
Exorcism	[No natural equivalent]	Exorcism in a Christian context	Exorcism in a non-Christian context

The problem with this table is that it has never been established that the Bible separates reality into a natural and a supernatural realm; rather, this is a notion that has unwittingly been taken over from Thomas Aquinas. However, the modern catholic understanding of, for example, the sacraments departs from this Thomistic base. It argues functionally rather than ontologically—a thought that has been taken up by Frank Macchia in relation to glossolalia: "It is a kind of primary sacrament or *kairos* event." The pentecostals "have parted significantly from the conservative Evangelical preoccupation with subjective conversion and have been led into the vicinity of the ecumenical Lima document (BEM)" (Macchia, 63, 69–70).

This situation understandably has grave consequences for our understanding of the gifts of precognition, healing, and glossolalia in non-Christian religions. Traditionally they have been classified as demonic, a recipe for distorted relationships with people of other religions and very much in contrast to the biblical tradition. "Astrology" led the Magi to the cradle of Christ. The Persian king Cyrus, who liberated the Jews from captivity, was called an "anointed," a "Messiah," or, in Greek, "Christ" (Isa. 45:1). And Paul freely and copiously quotes from non-Christian religious sources, for instance, in the famous love chapter, 1 Cor. 13.

The Bible does not say that extraordinary healings and other gifts in a non-Christian context are *by definition* demonic—it depends very much how they are used. They only become instruments of demons *if* used for manipulative or destructive purposes. Phenomenologically there is no difference between Christian and non-Christian glossolalia or healing. Both belong to the order of creation.

This has been clearly seen by Miroslav Volf, who states,

Charisms should not be defined so narrowly as to include only ecclesial activities. The Spirit of God is active not only in the fellowship (of the church) but also through the fellowship in the world. The Spirit who is poured out upon all flesh (Acts 2:17ff.) also imparts charisms to all flesh: they are gifts given to the community, irrespective of the existing distinctions or conditions within the community. Very frequently *charismatic* is taken to mean extraordinary. Ecclesiologically this restricted understanding of charisms can be found in some pentecostal (and "charismatic") churches that identify charismatic with spectacular. A secularized form of this "supernaturalistic reduction" is found in the commonly accepted Weberian understanding of charisma as an extraordinary quality of a personality. One of the main points of the Pauline theology of charisms is to overcome this restrictive concentration on the miraculous or extraordinary. (1987, 184–85)

The Spirit of God is—as the charismatic theologian Jean-Claude Schwab says—always mediated through human media: through understanding, experience, emotions. That does not mean that God's action is, so to speak, secularized. Rather, his field of action is not reduced to human categories like "natural" and "supernatural."

■ **Bibliography:** W. J. Hollenweger, *Geist und Materie. Interkulturelle Theologie* 3 (1988) ■ F. Macchia, "Tongues as a Sign: Towards a Sacramental Understanding of the Pentecostal Experience," *Pneuma* 15 (1, 1993) ■ J. C. Schwab, "Charismes et médiations. Ou: Comment le Saint-Esprit intervient dans la vie des hommes," *Hokhma: Revue de réflexions théologiques* (Switzerland), 43 (1990) ■ M. Volf, *Work in the Spirit: Toward a Theology of Work* (1991) ■ idem, "Human Work, Divine Spirit, and New Creation: Toward a Pneumatological Understanding of Work," *Pneuma* 9 (2, Fall 1987). ■ W. J. Hollenweger

GIMENEZ, JOHN (1931–), and **ANNE (NETHERY)** (1932–). Bishop (John) and pastor (Anne) of Rock Church, Virginia Beach, VA. Born in New York City, John dropped out of school after the eighth grade and was in and out of reform school and prison from age 11 until age 31 when he was converted. He traveled in ministry nationally and internationally giving his testimony.

Anne was born in Houston, TX, and at age 14 moved with her parents to Corpus Christi, TX. She was converted in a ▸T. L. Osborn tent crusade in 1949. At age 30 she went into full-time evangelistic ministry.

John and Anne were married in 1967 and a year later established Rock Church in Norfolk, VA. Attendance reached nearly 5,000 by 1987, and the church moved to Virginia Beach.

The couple founded Rock Christian Network, Rock Ministerial Fellowship, Rock Church International Relief Agency, Rock Church Bible School, and Rock Church Academy. They also produce a weekly television program and *Rock Alive*, a daily television ministry. John was the national chairman of Washington for Jesus rallies in 1980, 1988, and 1996. He also founded the National Organization for the Advancement of Hispanics. Anne founded International Women in Leadership. Together they authored *Upon This Rock*. John has authored several books and many albums. Anne is the author of *Emerging Christian Woman, Mark Your Children for God,* and *Beyond Tradition.*

■ **Bibliography:** E. C. Martin, "Anne Gimenez: Co-Pastoring Beside Her Beloved," *Ministries* (Winter 1985–86). ■ S. Strang

GLAD TIDINGS MISSIONARY SOCIETY A ▸Latter Rain organization growing out of Glad Tidings Temple, Vancouver, B.C. At one time five churches in Canada and Washington State were associated with the Vancouver congregation, with approximately 5,000 in membership. This organization was an early participant in the New Order of the Latter Rain and was formed in 1950. Early teachings of the group can be found in the *Pastor's Pen*, by Reg Layzell and compiled by B. M. Gaglardi, dealing with the Latter Rain and God's plan and method—restoration, the laying on of hands, and an eyewitness account of the Latter Rain meetings in North Battleford, Sask., in 1948.

■ **Bibliography:** C. Jones, *Guide to the Study of the Pentecostal Movement* (1983) ▪ R. Layzell, *Pastor's Pen* (1965).

▪ W. E. Warner

GLAD TIDINGS TABERNACLE Glad Tidings Tabernacle was for many years one of the leading pentecostal congregations in the Northeast. Affiliated with the Assemblies of God (AG), the congregation was established in 1907 by Marie Burgess, a Christian worker with varied home missions experience who accepted pentecostalism in Zion City, IL, in Oct. 1906. Two months later she complied with ▸Charles Parham's wish that she bring the pentecostal message to New York.

Burgess began services in midtown Manhattan in January and met with immediate response, especially from participants in the ▸Christian and Missionary Alliance. These men and women provided a strong nucleus for the growing congregation, which dated its origins to the opening of Burgess's mission on May 5, 1907. In 1909 Burgess married ▸Robert Brown, an Irish immigrant who was a dedicated Wesleyan Methodist lay preacher before he embraced pentecostal views at Burgess's mission.

The growing congregation moved to bigger facilities, enlarged those, and finally purchased a commodious church building on 33rd Street in Manhattan. The Browns shared a strong missionary vision, and through the WWII era their congregation usually led all AG congregations in missionary giving. The congregation commissioned many workers from its own numbers. A weekly radio broadcast carried the Sunday afternoon services across the metropolitan area. Through the 1940s Glad Tidings Tabernacle functioned as a center for New York area pentecostals.

Robert Brown exerted considerable influence as a denominational presbyter and district leader. Stubborn and opinionated, he was nonetheless revered and loved. After his death in 1948 his wife continued to give leadership to the congregation, assisted by her nephew, R. Stanley Berg. By that time changing urban conditions had influenced the size and character of the congregation. When Marie Brown died in 1971, she had served the church for 63 years.

■ **Bibliography:** G. P. Gardiner and M. E. Brown, *The Origin of Glad Tidings Tabernacle* (1955). ▪ E. L. Blumhofer

GLOBAL UNIVERSITY OF THE ASSEMBLIES OF GOD
Located in Springfield, MO, Global University (GUAG) is the endorsed distance-education institution of the Assemblies of God (AG), which serves students worldwide. It offers courses in evangelism and discipleship along with courses required for ministerial credentials, A.A., B.A., and M.A. degrees. Courses are mainly distributed in print format but also include use of the Internet, CD-ROM, and video conferencing.

GUAG was formed in 1999 by a merger between Berean University and ICI University. The school is accredited and will continue to be known as ICI (International Correspondence Institute) to its overseas constituency. The president of the university is Ronald A. Iwasko.

The merged school continues to fulfill the needs of stateside correspondence training as first laid out by ▸Frank M. Boyd in 1947, when it was called the General Council Correspondence School. In 1958 the name was changed to Berean School of the Bible and included a nondegree ministerial studies program for those desiring credentials as well as college degrees. The school was renamed Berean College in 1985 and, with the addition of graduate degrees, the name was changed to Berean University in 1995.

GUAG also is carrying on the vision and purposes of the International Correspondence Institute (ICI), which was

Alice, a member of the correspondence school staff in Nigeria, c. 1965.

developed by ►George M. Flattery in 1967 to supplement the training of national ministers and lay workers overseas and to coordinate the many different correspondence programs being developed by AG missionaries around the world. After 5 years of operating from a two-room office on the campus of Central Bible College in Springfield, MO, ICI transferred its operation to Brussels, Belgium, in 1972. After three years the rented facilities became inadequate, and a new, modern, five-story building was completed in 1975 in nearby Rhode-Saint-Genèse. This building served as international headquarters for ICI from 1975 until 1991. In Aug. 1991 ICI moved its international office from Brussels to a 38,000-square-foot building it had purchased in Irving, TX, near the Dallas/Fort Worth International Airport.

In 1993 the name was changed to ICI University (ICIU) because of the growth of ICI with its different schools and centers across the globe and to reflect its development of a school of graduate studies. ICIU has provided evangelism, discipleship courses, and study materials, as well as bachelor's and master's degrees to students in 168 different nations. ICIU also operates national offices in over 160 of these countries, including countries in the former Soviet bloc. GUAG's combined operations are now located in Springfield, MO.

■ **Bibliography:** *Until the Day Dawns: The Story of International Correspondence Institute* (1987) ■ *AG-News* (May 19, 1999) ■ "Berean, ICI Merge to Form Global University," *PE* (July 18, 1999).
■ G. W. Gohr

GLOSSOLALIA The usually, but not exclusively, religious phenomenon of making sounds that constitute, or resemble, a language not known to the speaker. It is often accompanied by an excited religious psychological state, and in the pentecostal and charismatic movements it is widely and distinctively (but not universally) viewed as the certifying consequence of the baptism in the Holy Spirit.

1. Terminology.

Not used in English before 1879, the technical term *glossolalia* derives from *glōssais lalein*, a Greek phrase used in the NT meaning literally "to speak in [or 'with' or 'by'] tongues." Its inclusion in the list of spiritual gifts (*charismata*) given in 1 Cor. 12:8–10 accounts for the popular equivalent expression "the gift of tongues," though that precise phrase nowhere occurs in Scripture. A French scholar coined the term *xenoglossia* (or *xenoglossy:* French *xenoglossia*) in 1905 to describe a spiritualist medium who, in trance, wrote in modern Greek though she had no acquaintance with that language. *Xenographia*, it was later argued, would be more accurate. *Xenolalia*, a more frequent synonym of *xenoglossia*, describes glossolalia when the language spoken is identifiable as one among the over 3,000 known to occur on the globe. Two other terms describe *xenoglossia:* the

longer *xenoglossolalia* and *heteroglossolalia* ("speaking in other languages"). *Glossographia* refers to automatic writing that is inspired from a higher power but results in no known language. In recent times, scholars have coined still other words for related phenomena: *propheteialalia*, the inspired vernacular speech of the prophet; *akolalia* (perhaps better *akuolalia*), the perceived hearing of another language even when one is not spoken; *ermeneglossia*, a technical term for interpretation of tongues; *echolalia*, the agitated repetition of the words of another; *idiolect*, a glossolalic dialect peculiar to an individual. "Prayer language" as a synonym for glossolalic prayer (cf. 1 Cor. 14:14) appears to be of recent origin, made popular by pentecostal and charismatic televangelists and talk-show hosts. Fortunately, a term used late in the 2d century by Tatian, an early Christian apologist, never got picked up in the modern European languages; he used *glossomania* to refer to the insane speech of the Greek philosophers against whom he wrote (*Oration,* 3). Although the OT contains records of ecstatic religious speech, there is no Hebrew equivalent for the term *glossolalia* nor any use of the expression *glōssais lalein* in the Septuagint (the Greek translation of the OT in common use during NT times). The singular *glōssa lalein* does appear in the Septuagint, but not in reference to glossolalia.

2. Non-Christian Varieties.

Whatever its origin, glossolalia is a human phenomenon, not limited to Christianity nor even to religious behavior among humankind. *Dramatic glossolalia* occurs in television situation comedies when actors spontaneously initiate a language then put the punch line in the vernacular. No external source for such speech, neither divine nor devilish, need be imagined beyond the stage talents of the speakers. *Spiritualistic glossolalia* and related phenomena among spiritual mediums were among the first studied by psychologists near the beginning of the 20th century. Pentecostals have attributed a satanic origin to such cases, even though proof lies outside scientific methods of sociopsychological inquiry. *Pathological glossolalia* is known to medicine and psychiatry, the result of such causes as organic neurological damage, effects of drugs, or psychotic disorders. Schizophrenic disorders have furnished examples of glossolalia. Research conducted by social scientists (Malony/Lovekin, 1985) over the past two decades have corrected earlier views that all glossolalia, even and especially its Christian varieties, arose from mental illness or social and economic deprivation.

More relevant to Christian glossolalia are clearly reported cases of *pagan glossolalia*, both ancient and modern. These have varied in the degree of religiousness involved—some more or less culturally routine, others evincing marks of singular prophetic distinctiveness.

Among ancient parallels, the Delphic Oracle (Parke, 1956) is best known. Located at the city of Delphi less than

50 air miles across the Corinthian Gulf to the northwest of Corinth, the Delphic Oracle flourished in the high classical period of Greek culture (the 5th century B.C., Nehemiah's time in Israel), but its popularity had declined by NT times. Private citizens or public officials consulted the oracle in order to acquire, as they believed, divine guidance regarding particular issues like marriage decisions, business ventures, and battle strategies. An inquirer would first undergo purification rites and present sacrificial offerings. Then the inquirer would be brought into the presence of a young woman, a priestess of Apollo said to possess a "pythonic spirit" (named for the serpent said to have been slain by Apollo: such a priestess is mentioned in Acts 16:16). A male prophet of the temple received the question of the inquirer. The young priestess fell into a state of frenzied ecstasy and spoke out words that were unrecognizable. The attending priest supposedly translated these into understandable Greek of the period and presented the oracular response to the seeker of the will of the gods. The result, though often ambiguous, was taken to strengthen the intent or preference of the inquirer, who was thus led to believe the action taken reflected the divine will.

Scholars do not agree regarding what produced the ecstatic state. Researchers have variously proposed a narcotic effect from chewing leaves of a nearby tree or use of a sacred drink. Now discounted is an earlier theory of intoxicating gases that escaped from a cleft in the earth at that vicinity. Some suggest a demonic spirit. Whatever the cause, the Delphic ecstatic speech formed, not only a parallel to, but also a precedent for, the glossolalia at Corinth. It may be that the popularity of speaking in tongues at Corinth in part was fueled by a misguided Christian effort to match the speech of surrounding pagan deities.

An important study by anthropologist L. Carlyle May (1956) that predates the rise of the charismatic movement shows the widespread occurrence of *contemporary pagan, or non-Christian, glossolalia* among 20th-century cultures. Using a taxonomy of glossolalia that ranges from mumbles and grunts through esoteric priestly languages and imitations of animal speech to widely related instances of xenolalia, May shows that cases outside Christian influence have been reported in Malaysia, Indonesia, Siberia, Arctic regions, China, Japan, Korea, Arabia, and Burma, among other places. He found that it was used sparingly among American Indians but was widespread in African tribal religions. He concludes that glossolalia on the whole occurs infrequently and has not been reported to appear in whole tribal groups except where affected by Christianity. More often it produces religious leaders rather than followers, but it is by no means a necessary feature even of ecstatic religious leaders.

Reports of such cultural, pathological, and dramatic cases of glossolalia are descriptive: it does not lie within the methods of social science or historical research to conclude that any given instance of glossolalia, Christian or non-Christian, may have a divine (or devilish) origin. What exists—phenomena that appear—can be described by all observers. Observers, from their own worldview, determine what they believe is the spirit—or Spirit—that impels the glossolalist.

3. Biblical Data.

If sheer quantity of text is the measure, more is said in Scripture about glossolalia than about the Virgin Birth or the ordination of women. Roy Harrisville (1974) counts 35 references to the phenomenon in Mark, Acts, and 1 Corinthians—28 of them in 1 Corinthians, 23 of which are in ch. 14. These texts chronologically locate glossolalia from just prior to the ascension of Jesus and the first Christian Pentecost around A.D. 30, through the middle 50s at Corinth in Greece, to Paul's mission in Ephesus in Asia Minor around A.D. 60. The phenomenon therefore, as reported in NT records, spanned three decades, flourished in both Jewish (Jerusalem) and Gentile (Corinth) centers, and appeared in widely separated parts of the Mediterranean—Corinth is nearly 1,500 air miles from Jerusalem—in places that marked the eastern and western limits of Paul's missionary enterprise. If glossolalia appears with surprising infrequency over the centuries in the life of the church, that does not rise from a lack of biblical accounts of its origin.

The most frequent phrase, which appears in Mark, Acts, and 1 Corinthians puts "tongues" in the plural *glōssais lalein*. "In tongues" (or "with tongues") is the appropriate translation whether or not the preposition *en* appears. The singular, "to speak in a tongue," occasionally occurs, but only in 1 Cor. 14:2, 4, 13, 27 (where, in the KJV, "unknown" is italicized to show there is no comparable Greek word underlying the English adjective). There are "new" tongues (Mark 16:17), "tongues of men and of angels" (1 Cor. 13:1), and "other tongues" (Acts 2:4). Besides speaking in tongues, one may also "pray" in tongues (1 Cor. 14:14). The parallel structure of 1 Cor. 14:14–16 suggests that to "sing in the Spirit" and to "bless in the Spirit" also are glossolalic acts. One may even "have" (1 Cor. 14:26) a tongue. There are "kinds [species, varieties] of tongues" (1 Cor. 12:10, 28).

A large consensus among biblical scholars concludes that Mark's gospel ended at Mark 16:8. Among several alternative endings that appear in copies of NT manuscripts, Mark 16:9–20 seems to have been added to the original gospel in the late 2d century. The textual history is complicated, and conclusive proof is impossible. Accepted theories of the origins of the canonical Gospels make it clear that sayings of Jesus and stories about him circulated orally for decades before they were ever gathered into written Gospels (cf. Luke 1:1). An example appears in Acts 20:35: "Remembering the words the Lord Jesus himself said, 'It is more blessed to give than to receive'"—a saying not found in any of the four

Gospels. What is striking about the "Markan Appendix," as Mark 16:9–20 is called, is this: of all the sayings and stories of Jesus that were still circulating in the 2d century, the one that got attached to a canonical gospel distinctly reflected charismatic interests, including speaking "in new tongues." This suggests that interest in glossolalia clearly persisted into the 2d century.

Three clear occurrences of glossolalia, besides at least two other strong allusions, appear in the book of Acts. Acts 2 describes the descent of the Holy Spirit on the first Christian Day of Pentecost, a late spring Jewish holiday that earlier celebrated the agricultural harvest but later observed the harvest of Sinai, the giving of the law through Moses. On this day "they were all filled with the Holy Spirit and began to speak in other tongues as the Spirit enabled them" (v. 4). Said the listeners, "We hear them declaring the wonders of God in our own tongues!" (v. 11). This was in Jerusalem, among Jews, on a Jewish holiday. Later, yet in Palestine, but in a Gentile household, the address of Jewish leader Peter was interrupted when the Spirit fell on the foreign group. Peter's fellow Jews who had made the trip to Caesarea with him "were astonished that the gift of the Holy Spirit had been poured out even on the Gentiles. For they heard them speaking in tongues and praising God" (10:45–46). Still later, in Ephesus, a leading city in western Asia Minor, Paul met a group of people who knew only of John's baptism. After Paul laid hands on them, "the Holy Spirit came on them, and they spoke in tongues and prophesied" (19:6).

Luke's interest in the book of Acts seems to include a sort of theological geography. In his gospel, Luke took Jesus from rural Galilee to the Jewish capital of Jerusalem; likewise, in Acts he takes Paul from the Jewish center to the imperial capital of Rome. In doing so, Luke seems to mark the movement of the gospel westward by gradual stages—each characterized by the descent of the Holy Spirit—Jerusalem (Jews alone), Caesarea (Gentiles on Jewish soil), Ephesus (Gentiles in Greek territory). At each step the Holy Spirit falls and glossolalia is an accompanying feature.

"Samaria" (Acts 8:14–24)—a nation of half-Jews—could be inserted between "Jerusalem" and "Caesarea" above, but glossolalia is not mentioned. Many commentators conclude its presence, however, since there was some aspect of the episode that led the magician Simon to offer money to acquire the trick of giving the Spirit by the laying on of hands. Connections flourished in those days between magic, nonsense syllables, and popular piety.

The other place where glossolalia originally may have appeared in the text of Acts describes the effects of prayer following the safe release of Peter and John: "After they prayed, the place ... was shaken. And they were all filled with the Holy Spirit and spoke the word of God boldly" (Acts 4:31). Many NT scholars, Rudolf Bultmann among them, believe the original text may have read "... filled with the Holy Spirit and spoke in tongues." No surviving manuscript, however, preserves such a reading.

It is Paul's first letter to the Corinthians that most speaks of glossolalia. The setting of the letter is crucial to its interpretation. First Corinthians is not a zero-based treatise on spiritual gifts. Rather, it is a forceful pastoral letter sent to correct rumored wrongs in a church founded a half-dozen years earlier by the apostle Paul in Corinth, the capital city of southern Greece. Paul's unnamed successor(s) warped teachings he had left. The congregation, at least an influential and troublesome part of it, developed a distorted doctrine of Christianized human nature such that it overemphasized the spiritual side of the Christian life to the neglect even of basic morality (e.g., incest was arrogantly tolerated [1 Cor. 5:1–13]). With that mind-set, using glossolalia would attest a supposed higher spirituality.

Paul's response to the Corinthian superspirituality lay in his appeal, not to end the use of glossolalia, but to govern its use by three guidelines: (1) recognition of the diversity of charismata graciously given by the triune God (1 Cor. 12); (2) the supremacy of love, without which no charisma counts (1 Cor. 13); and (3) the priority of congregational edification over personal benefit (1 Cor. 14).

Is glossolalia at Corinth the same phenomenon that appeared in Jerusalem a quarter century earlier? Acts describes xenolalia on the Day of Pentecost (2:14). The hearing of identified languages is not mentioned in the other two instances where glossolalia is mentioned in Acts (10:46; 19:6)—though the vocal consequence consisting in "praising God" (10:46, cf. 2:11) may imply that the content of the glossolalic speech was understood. In any case, Acts is theological history—a work composed by its author freely at will. First Corinthians, by contrast, is a pastoral response in the form of a straightforward but longer-than-average letter that addresses specific problems in a particular congregation.

Glossolalia in Acts is heard as "our own languages" (2:11). Corinthian glossolalia is addressed to God—"no one understands him," and he "does not speak to men but to God" (1 Cor. 14:2). Glossolalia in Acts is an outcome of the Spirit's arrival. In Corinth it is a charisma, one among others. (Luke does not use the term *charisma* in Acts or in his Gospel: it is, except for 1 Peter 4:10, a Pauline word.) Corinthian glossolalia occurred in a settled congregation and required the companion gift of interpretation to extend its usefulness beyond the speaker. Paul, not Luke, speaks of "interpretation": there is no uninterpreted glossolalia in Acts. In Acts 2 at least, the tongues are immediately perceived as various native languages. The glossolalia of Acts seems once-for-all, at least initiatory: glossolalia at Corinth habitually recurred.

Phenomenologically, the glossolalia of Acts and 1 Corinthians may be the same. But Luke in Acts makes a theologically symbolic use of glossolalia entirely appropriate to the genre of Acts, while in 1 Corinthians the phenomenon crops up as a pastoral problem rising from overzealous charismatic piety.

A clear precedent for NT glossolalia appears in the tradition of ecstatic prophetism in the OT. Israel's prophets were given to dreams, visions, and a variety of abnormal behaviors that included broken speech. Samuel directed Saul to Gibeah and said, "You will meet a procession of prophets coming down from the high place with lyres, tambourines, flutes and harps being played before them, and they will be prophesying. The Spirit of the LORD will come upon you in power, and you will prophesy with them; and you will be changed into a different person" (1 Sam. 10:5–6). Earlier, when Moses gathered 70 elders to the meeting tent, "then the LORD came down in the cloud and spoke with him, and he took of the Spirit that was on him and put the Spirit on the seventy elders. When the Spirit rested on them, they prophesied, but they did not do so again" (Num. 11:25). Contagious ecstatic prophetism is an acknowledged part of Israel's past and an unavoidable topic in OT theology. What is striking is the nearly universal voice effects coupled with emotive experience.

In nonbiblical Jewish literature roughly contemporary with NT times, the Testament of Job 48–50 furnishes the nearest parallel to Paul's reference to "tongues of angels" (1 Cor. 13:1). Facing his impending death, Job distributed his goods among his children, saving the best—a triple stranded charismatic sash—for the three daughters. As each daughter tied one of the strands about herself, her "heart was changed" (cf. 1 Sam. 10:5–6) and she "no longer cared for earthly matters." The first daughter then spoke "ecstatically in the angelic dialect, sending up a hymn to God." The mouth of the second daughter "took on the dialect of the archons and she praised God." The third daughter "spoke ecstatically in the dialect of those on high . . . in the dialect of the cherubim." No evidence exists that Paul knew of the Testament of Job.

4. Theological Nuances.

Nearly all classical pentecostal groups adhere to the doctrine that speaking in tongues certifies the personal experience of the baptism in the Holy Spirit. Representative is the doctrinal formulation of the American Assemblies of God:

> The baptism of believers in the Holy Ghost is witnessed by the initial physical sign of speaking with other tongues as the Spirit of God gives them utterance (Acts 2:4). The speaking of tongues in this instance is the same in essence as the gift of tongues (1 Cor. 12:4–10, 28), but different in purpose and use.

Nineteenth-century Holiness groups sought to recover Wesley's emphasis on personal holiness. Donald W. Dayton

(1987) shows that over the decades of that century, Wesley's language of "pure love" and "entire sanctification" was gradually replaced by the phrase "baptism in the Holy Spirit"— commonplace among Holiness people and revivalists as the end of the 19th century drew near. A simultaneous development, it can be argued, was the shift from Wesley's "assurance" to the notion of "evidence." This exchange was doubtlessly facilitated by the rise of a popular scientism after the American Civil War. Darwin published *Origin of the Species* in 1859 and *Descent of Man* in 1871. Holiness seekers, who also resisted imported German higher criticism, opposed the "evidence" argued by the new biological and biblical sciences. Adamantly opposed to the conclusions, they may well have been captured by the method: one gets at truth by "citing evidence." This pop intellectualism accounts for the way the question was put at century's end, when Charles F. Parham's Bible school students gathered in Topeka in 1900. As he left for ministry elsewhere, Parham, founder of the Apostolic Faith Movement, charged his students to search the Scriptures and to discover the "Bible evidence" for the baptism in the Holy Spirit. The answer identified by the students gave birth to the pentecostal movement: speaking in tongues is the initial physical evidence of the baptism in the Holy Spirit.

Classical pentecostals account for the difference between Acts and 1 Corinthians by maintaining a distinction between speaking in tongues as the *evidence* of the baptism in the Holy Spirit (as the frequent outcome of the Spirit's descent in Acts) from the *gift (charisma)* of tongues mentioned in 1 Corinthians. Most pentecostals admit the difficulty of supporting the doctrine of initial evidence from 1 Corinthians. In truth, the doctrine finds its sole support from the historical precedent of the cases of the Spirit's descent in Acts 2, 10, and 19.

Not all classical pentecostals teach initial evidence. Exceptions include organized classical pentecostal churches in Scandinavia, Germany, the United Kingdom, and Latin America. Admittedly, the case for initial evidence is not as strong as that for major doctrines such as the sinfulness of humankind or the efficacy of the atonement. Yet historical precedent as a basis for belief should not be belittled. Jesus himself appealed to precedent: did not the Pharisees, chagrined that Jesus' disciples picked and ate grain on the Sabbath, recall that David "unlawfully" entered the sanctuary and ate consecrated bread? (Mark 2:23–28).

5. Historical Survey.

What counts for glossolalia in Christian history depends on how the term is defined. The technical term *glōssais lalein* (in the plural) is limited to the NT itself, until the phrase is picked up by patristic commentators citing the NT. But if ecstatic speech and written nonsense syllables are counted, then glossolalia can be sporadically located over the whole history of the church until its exponential spread in the 20th-century pentecostal and charismatic movements.

The first full generation of glossolalia is recounted in Acts: 30 years elapsed between the Jerusalem Pentecost (Acts 2, around A.D. 30) and the Ephesian descent of the Spirit (Acts 19:1–6, about A.D. 60). Over the next hundred years, little is recorded. By the third generation of the 2d century, however, the magical use of esoteric nonsense syllables occurs in Christian Gnosticism, and a prophet named Montanus (who flourished in Phrygia in central Asia Minor) announced that he had become the Paraclete. Doing combat with heretics, both Irenaeus (c. A.D. 180) and Tertullian (A.D. 207 or later: he had himself become a Montanist) offered as apologetic defense the existence in their communities of the apostolic charismata.

But for Origen in the 3d century and Augustine in the late 4th and early 5th, it is clear that charismatic phenomena, including glossolalia, were valued as marks of the birth of the church centuries earlier. Augustine made a metaphor: the church, by his day spread over the then-known world, collectively spoke in virtually all the languages of the inhabited globe. It was Augustine who established the belief, deeply held by many to the present day, that the charismata ended with the days of the apostles.

Saints through the Middle Ages are often credited with the capacity to speak in tongues, though careful historical research has to be applied to determine where such attributed endowments are little more than stylized encomium.

Neither Luther (1483–1546) nor Calvin (1509–64) reflected firsthand encounters with glossolalia. For Luther and his foes, "speaking in tongues" had to do with the Roman Mass offered in Latin: Luther said the vernacular is needed. Calvin saw the tongues of the Jerusalem pentecostal as symbolic of the inclusion in the church of non-Jews.

Persecution from Louis XIV against 17th-century French Protestants produced the French prophets of the Cevennes mountain region in southeastern France. Records describe extraordinary phenomena—trances, faints, shakings, and glossolalic sounds. Some of the Camisards, as they were known, escaped to England, where they later forced John Wesley's attention to glossolalia. Wesley (1703–91) theoretically defended the contemporary relevance of the charismata and thought kindly of the Montanists. Reactions to his own preaching included some who were "constrained to roar." While he supported deep personal experience of the sanctifying Spirit, it seems to be too much to claim Wesley was himself a glossolalic.

The 19th century opened with the Shakers well situated in upstate New York. It closed with the birth of the pentecostal movement. In the 1820s and 1830s, both among the Shakers and the followers of Edward Irving, a popular London Presbyterian pastor, glossolalia occurred repeatedly. In the 1840s glossolalia emerged with the rise of Mormons: both Joseph Smith and Brigham Young spoke in tongues. Latter-day Saint doctrinal formulations to this day include the practice.

Throughout the 19th century, the Holiness movement grew. Its pursuit of restored holiness and the "perfect love" engendered by Wesley the century before traced a shift, as Donald W. Dayton (1987) shows, in terminology from terms like "entire sanctification" and "Christian perfection" toward a rising preference for "baptism in the Holy Spirit." In the 1890s, four renowned Bible teachers who did not have Wesleyan roots—A. J. Gordon, Reuben A. Torrey, A. B. Simpson, and C. I. Scofield—wrote books that, though their preferred terminology varied, urged the fullness of the Spirit upon every believer.

The stage was thus set for the birth of the pentecostal movement. It took only the linkage of speaking in tongues with the evidence of the baptism in the Holy Spirit to bring about the pentecostal movement. That happened in the closing days of 1900 among Charles Parham's Topeka Bible School students: when glossolalia was pronounced to be the initial physical evidence of the baptism in the Holy Spirit, the classical pentecostal movement was born. The rest is history (Synan, 1971; details in this section have been drawn largely from Williams/Waldvogel, 1975).

6. Varied Explanations.

How does glossolalia occur? What are its effects and significance? Responses to these and similar queries turn on the worldview of the inquirer and the methodology adopted. Even Third World illiterate pentecostals are entitled to their uncomplicated view that God has filled them with himself and they speak in tongues under the direct drive of the Holy Spirit.

Research conducted by social scientists (Malony and Lovekin, 1985) has been the kind of inquiry most productive of theories. The earliest psychological investigations viewed glossolalia as the by-product of an unhealthy mind or a disordered personality. It has been attributed to hysteria or hypnosis, suggestion or regression. Some researchers view it as an altered state of consciousness, others as learned behavior or narcissistic self-preoccupation.

Buddhist doctrine explains xenolalia as a linguistic survivor from a prior existence. Jungian theory views glossolalia as an individual breakthrough from the collective unconscious. It has been described as the consequence of stimulation of Broca's Area in the left cerebral hemisphere and as a form of right-brain speech. It can be styled as the suspension of the rational or as a mix of a cry (anticipating death) and a laugh (celebrating birth: Hutch, 1980) or as a kind of mysticism—although glossolalia played no major role in the classical Christian mystical tradition.

Pentecostals are gratified to learn that they have been, in more recent research, accorded healthy normal personalities—if, as a whole, a bit more anxious than others. In fact, history, psychological analysis, and personal testimony converge to suggest occasional coincidence of personal or social stress and the use of glossolalia. Ongoing research will add to the common understanding of the phenomenon, but research cannot exhaust the meaning of the experience to the individual believer.

7. Evaluation.

A few summarizing and interpretive conclusions can be offered.

1. Glossolalia is a human phenomenon, not limited to Christianity nor even to religious behavior. Speaking in tongues "embraces every ecstatic oral-auditory phenomenon from speaking a language not generally known … to speaking in forceful declamations, incantations, and other verbal effusions that are more likely to be psychological-spiritual projections of inner speech than some authentic language itself" (Williams/Waldvogel, 1975, 61).

2. The impulse for glossolalia, not readily accessible to scientific determination, may rise from the speakers themselves, from a demonic spirit, or from the Holy Spirit. Even if glossolalia occurs in a balanced pentecostal environment, any one of the three sources may apply. The discernment of the community is essential. On the other hand, glossolalia of simply human origin is probably more frequent than recognized. That explains, for example, the humanities scholar who "taught himself" to speak in tongues and can do so at will.

3. It is equally wrong to conclude (1) that glossolalia did not occur between the 1st and the 20th centuries or (2) that it is a regular and predictable outcome of revivalistic religious fervor. Despite emotional excesses at the Kentucky Cane Ridge revival in the early 1800s—surely the most emotional of American awakenings, where appeared such phenomena as shaking, barking, falling, and fainting—no clear cases of glossolalia are reported. Nor do any come from the lay-led prayer revival of the 1850s. The charismatic renewal after the 1960s, on the other hand, is replete with reports of glossolalia among many quiet and controlled mainline Christians.

4. The doctrine of speaking in tongues as the initial physical evidence of the baptism of the Holy Spirit can be labeled the distinctive teaching of the pentecostal churches. But it is misguided to confuse that which *distinguishes* pentecostalism with its *essence*. The pentecostal family of Christians are, on the whole, balanced evangelical believers with a high view of Scripture, a penchant for deeply personal (but not mystical) religious experience, and a conspicuous passion for global evangelization.

5. Even deaf people speak in tongues. But this has been little studied among social scientists and, for that matter, rarely observed among pentecostals.

6. "That a phenomenon has a psychological explanation does not exclude it from being a gift of the Spirit" (McDonnell, 1976, 154). That an experience is human cannot mean it is not Christian, as the incarnation itself discloses. Given the theology of the book of Hebrews, one may conclude that

Christians in fact have a better chance of becoming truly human than non-Christians.

7. Xenolalia is at the same time the most difficult variety of glossolalia to document yet the most widely reported among global cultures.

8. Most instances of glossolalia seem not to consist in the extraordinary use of some identifiable language. The significance of glossolalia for the individual speaker may lie in its capacity to vent the inexpressible—hence the observed connection with stress. But in congregational life the good of the group exceeds that of the individual, and the companion charisma "interpretation" is required. Such interpretation need not be considered literal translation of the speech given in tongues but rather an explanation of the meaning of that glossolalic utterance for the gathered Christians. Eccentricities arise when interpretations are preserved and assigned a value above Scripture and the tradition of the local church or the Christian family of which it is a part.

9. After all self-induced and demonically originated glossolalia has been accounted for, there remains a variety—one could say a level—of encounter with the Holy Spirit, the consequence of which is speaking in tongues. The capacity for speech distinguishes human nature among living beings; it likewise differentiates—in OT theology—God from the many other gods. It is not to be wondered at that one of the finest varieties of religious experience links divine and human speech. Nor is it surprising that the result of that mix transcends rational thought.

10. Genuine Christian glossolalia is temporary, a feature of the present age between the first Christian Pentecost and the second coming of Christ. "Tongues … will be stilled" (1 Cor. 13:8); there will be no speaking in tongues in heaven. Glossolalia is therefore supremely eschatological, a broken speech for the broken body of Christ till perfection arrives.

See also BAPTISM IN THE HOLY SPIRIT; HOLY SPIRIT, DOCTRINE OF THE; INITIAL EVIDENCE; INTERPRETATION OF TONGUES, GIFT OF.

■ **Bibliography:** L. Barnett and J. P. McGregor, *Speaking in Tongues: A Scholarly Defense* (1986; independent pentecostal, voluminous but uncritical) ■ D. A. Carson, *Showing the Spirit* (1987; evangelical, noncharismatic) ■ D. Christie-Murray, *Voices from the Gods* (1978; anthropological) ■ S. D. Currie, "'Speaking in Tongues': Early Evidence outside the New Testament Bearing on '*Glōssais Lalein*,'" *Interpretation* 19 (1965) ■ G. B. Cutten, *Speaking with Tongues* (1927) ■ D. W. Dayton, *Theological Roots of Pentecostalism* (1987) ■ F. D. Goodman, *Speaking in Tongues: A Cross-Cultural Study* (1972; involves an altered state of consciousness) ■ H. Gunkel, *The Influence of the Holy Spirit* (1888; repr. 1979) ■ R. H. Gundry, "'Ecstatic Utterance' (NEB)?" *JTS* 17 (1966; actual human languages) ■ R. W. Harris, *Spoken by the Spirit* (1973; classical pentecostal collection of 75 anecdotal reports) ■ R. Harrisville, "Speaking in Tongues: A Lexicographical Study," *CBQ* 38 (1976) ■ W. H.

Horton, *The Glossolalia Phenomenon* (1966; classical pentecostal) ■ A. L. Hoy, "Public and Private Uses of the Gift of Tongues," *Paraclete* 2 (1968; classical pentecostal) ■ H. D. Hunter, *Spirit-Baptism* (1983) ■ R. A. Hutch, "The Personal Ritual of Glossolalia," *JSSR* 19 (1980) ■ C. O. Ishel, "Glossolalia and Propheteialalia: A Study of I Corinthians 14," *WTJ* 10 (1975) ■ M. T. Kelsey, *Tongue Speaking* (1964; Jungian) ■ J. P. Kildahl, *The Psychology of Speaking in Tongues* (1972; not known languages yet religiously useful) ■ E. Lombard, *De la glossolalie* (1910) ■ W. G. MacDonald, *Glossolalia in the New Testament* (n.d.; classical pentecostal) ■ A. Mackie, *The Gift of Tongues* (1921; pathological) ■ H. Malony and A. Lovekin, *Glossolalia: Behavioral Science Perspectives* (1985; reviews a century of social science research) ■ I. J. Martin, *Glossolalia in the Apostolic Church* (1960) ■ L. C. May, "A Survey of Glossolalia and Related Phenomena in Non-Christian Religions," *American Anthropologist* 58 (1956) ■ K. McDonnell, *Charismatic Renewal and the Churches* (1976; misleadingly titled, best summary of psychological research on glossolalia to 1975) ■ P. C. Miller, "In Praise of Nonsense," in A. H. Armstrong, ed., *Classical Mediterranean Spirituality* (1986; on the use of nonrational syllables in ancient magic and Gnosticism) ■ W. E. Mills, *Glossolalia: A Bibliography* (1985; over 1,150 entries and a useful, sometimes flawed, bibliographic essay) ■ idem, ed., *Speaking in Tongues: A Guide to Research on Glossolalia* (1986; mainly reprinted technical articles, exegetical, historical, psychological in perspective) ■ E. Mossiman, *Das Zungenreden* (1911) ■ H. W. Parke and E. Wormell, *History of the Delphic Oracle* (1956) ■ C. Richet, "Xenoglossia: L'écriture automatique en langues étrangères," *Proceedings of the Society for Psychical Research* 19 (1905–7) ■ J. L. Sherrill, *They Speak with Other Tongues* (1964: popular) ■ F. Stagg et al., *Glossolalia* (1967; noncharismatic Southern Baptist assessment) ■ C. G. Williams, *Tongues of the Spirit* (1981). ■ R. P. Spittler

GLOSSOLALIA: AN OUTSIDER'S PERSPECTIVE

Social psychology is "the study of the manner in which the personality, attitudes, motivations, and behavior of the individual influence and are influenced by social groups." Experiments have demonstrated that the social norms of a group have an impact not only on how the individuals in that group behave, but even to some extent how they perceive reality. In other words, any group exerts a pressure to conform, but it also provides a "frame of reference," a way of cognitively "making sense of the world" (cf. Sherif, 106).

One area of sociopsychological research is glossolalia, and a question that can be asked is, As we examine the setting in which and the method whereby an individual is first introduced to glossolalia, do we find that the setting and method affect glossolalic speech? (We must be clear that this approach deals only with the *phenomenon* of glossolalia and can say nothing about its origin or source.)

The social psychologist may theorize that exposure to persons who are already engaged in glossolalia will have a measurable impact on an initial glossolalic experience. (This hypothesis would leave out of consideration "spontaneous" glossolalists, that is, those who speak in tongues without any prior exposure to glossolalia.) As the glossolalic phenomenon is experienced in a specific social setting, the actual form of glossolalia, which includes its sociolinguistic structure and the physical manifestations that accompany it, may be shaped by an established norm that is "taught" or "caught" via an implicit social norm.

To pursue this hypothesis one would likely observe that the social format for the practice of glossolalia occurs, more often than not, during a ritual activity known as the "altar call." Kildahl provides a "typical" example of one such altar call: a man named Bill Jones, who was seeking the baptism in the Holy Spirit, remained after a church service to discuss "the gift of tongues." Jones states that once they began praying as a group the guest speaker began to "pray in tongues," and that he (Jones) felt, as he listened to the preacher praying in tongues, "as if there were an electrifying charge in the air." Jones continues his account by stating that the preacher placed his hands on Jones's head and then encouraged Jones to repeat what he (the preacher) said. As reported by Kildahl, the actual words the preacher spoke were "Aish nay gum nay tayo." Jones did as instructed and began to repeat the glossolalic sentence. After two or three recitations, however, Jones began to modify the speech by saying, "aish nay … anna gayna … ayna ganna keena … kayna geena anna nay-manna nay-manna …" (Kildahl, 3).

It would seem, then, that Jones's glossolalic speech was based on the rearrangement of certain phonemes of the speech that had first been presented to him and which he recited. However, what if a person experienced glossolalia for the first time without reciting a set formula? The response to this question could be that it is possible for a person to hear glossolalic speech from other participants and then rearrange the phonemic structure into a novel schema. For example, as a person prays during an altar call or in any setting where glossolalic speech is occurring all around, a kind of linguistic pattern may be implied without any explicit instruction. This process would be similar to the way in which all humans acquire language—through "immersion" in a language.

The evidence suggesting that glossolalia can be learned by immersion was found by linguists who discovered that individual pentecostal communities do conform to a certain pattern of glossolalic speech. For instance, Pattison examined the linguistic studies of Wolfram (1966) and Nida (1964) and concluded that glossolalic phonemes were similar to the known language of the speaker, with a further delimiting by a "restricted phonemic code" (Pattison, 79). Furthermore, Samarin records a pentecostal minister as saying that it seemed to him "that there are certain similarities of tongues and some of these words seem to be common to a number of people." The minister continued by saying that he had traveled all over the United States, Germany, and Sweden, and that "many times there [seemed] to be a few 'established patterns' among public tongue speakers." Samarin also includes the statement of an Assemblies of God minister who observed that "those under the influence of strong personalities sometimes tend to speak similarly in tongues just as they may imitate mannerisms" (Samarin, 98).

With these data serving as a guide, the social psychologists' hypothesis may be that glossolalic phonemes and patterns are directly related to modern languages, and more specifically to the language of a local group practicing glossolalia. Further, the social psychologist may propose that the arrangement of these morphemes into glossolalic "words" represents the desire of the group to conform to a sociolinguistic norm that acts as a delimiting agent in the selection of morphemes *and* in the possible combination of those morphemes into words. That is, like all human speech, glossolalic speech in pentecostal communities is shaped by an extant norm of linguistic production, whether taught explicitly or by immersion, which subsequently limits the "glosso-linguistic" possibilities within individual pentecostal communities.

Having produced a hypothesis, a social psychologist might construct an experiment that would study the linguistic structure of glossolalic speech in different parts of the world, with an emphasis on structural similarities within a linguistic community. Further, specific research could be done to analyze the claims of "spontaneous" glossolalists who believe that they acquired the speech apart from any prior exposure to the norm. The key questions in this case would be (1) Does the form of glossolalia in any way relate to a "spontaneous" glossolalist's native language? and (2) Is there a way to ascertain whether or not any linguistic modifications occurred in an individual's glossolalic speech after he or she became part of a specific glossolalic community?

See also Gifts of the Spirit: Natural and Supernatural.

■ **Bibliography:** A. M. Brower and J. L. Nye, eds., *What's Social about Social Cognition?* (1996) ■ F. Corum, *Like as of Fire: A Reprint of the Old Azusa Street Papers* (1981) ■ E. Durkheim, *The Elementary Forms of Religious Life* (repr. 1995) ■ K. Fiedler and G. R. Semin, *Applied Social Psychology* (1996) ■ R. Kidd and M. Saks, eds., *Advances in Applied Social Psychology*, vol. 1 (1980) ■ J. Kildahl, *The Psychology of Speaking in Tongues* (1972) ■ P. Mattick Jr., *Social Knowledge* (1986) ■ E. M. Pattison, "Behavioral Science Research on the Nature of Glossolalia," in *Journal of the American Scientific Affiliation* (Sept. 1968) ■ R. P. Philipchalk, *Psychology and Christianity* (1987) ■ W. Samarin, *Tongues of Men and Angels* (1972) ■ M. Sherif, *The Psychology of Social Norms* (1936) ■ D. A. Teppeiner, "Tongue Speaking: A Model," *Journal of the American Scientific Affiliation* (Mar. 1974). ■ S. F. Hopkins

GLOSSOLALIA, MANUAL In Greek, speaking in tongues (*glossais lalein, glossolalia*) clearly means speaking in languages and not in ecstatic gibberish (Horton, 1976). This definition, though clear and simple when referring to vocally articulated languages, poses a challenge to the 103 signed languages existing worldwide.

Pentecostal pastors and missionaries ministering among the deaf attest to the fact that "deaf people do speak (vocally) in tongues." However, since the early 1990s the phenomenon known as "manual glossolalia" has gained recognition. According to the testimony of a retired deaf evangelist, this experience dates as far back as the 1940s or 1950s: "Our hands would take on different shapes and movements we could not recognize, but we just assumed it was all a part of our enthusiastic praise."

Every verified instance of signed language characteristically has three basic components: (1) specific hand configurations that involve certain rules defining clear and appropriate hand shapes; (2) articulation qualities that incorporate the movements of a particular hand shape identifying the intensity of the concept being expressed; and (3) the planes of placement that help identify verbal tenses and directionals as to who is doing what action. Each signed language contains far more complex linguistic values than these three basic and consistent components.

Testimonies have been given by deaf congregations of messages in tongues, spoken in what appeared to be a foreign signed language, followed by subsequent interpretations articulated in the American Sign Language. These expressed foreign sign languages contained clearly defined hand shapes, verbal tenses, and placements. Unfortunately, reports of these experiences have been few and far between. What is currently witnessed could be defined as the infant babblings of a signed language. Most manual glossolalia speakers appear to be "saying" only one word or syllable, much like an individual whose first experience with tongues involved constantly repeating sounds such as "ba, ba, ba." This particular experience is often recognized as only the beginning of the language and certainly not the fullness thereof. Those trained in the linguistics of a signed language, when observing the manual glossolalia, could recognize appropriate hand shapes, consistent articulation patterns, and clearly identified grammatical planes. Thus the observed linguistic characteristics of manual glossolalia make it clear that they do not represent gibberish—although they do not necessarily show manual glossolalia to give expression to a complete language.

Those who would reject the possibility of manual glossolalia do so on the basis of their understanding that glossolalia must involve speaking (*lalein*). However, the difference between spoken language and signed language is *mode*, not *essence*. Both spoken and signed language are in essence symbolic representations of human thought, expressed in two modes that can be used interchangeably by those who know both. Spoken and signed glossolalia, therefore, may simply be two modes in which the "thoughts of the Spirit" are expressed.

Finally, it is difficult to preclude the possibility that manual glossolalia are valid, since, as Jesus said, "The wind blows wherever it pleases. You hear its sound, but you cannot tell where it is going. So it is with everyone born of the Spirit" (John 3:8).

■ **Bibliography:** *Ethnologue,* ed. B. F. Grimes, 13th ed. (1996) ■ S. Horton, *What the Bible says about the Holy Spirit* (1976). Websites: Summer Institute of Linguistics ■ DeafWorldWeb.

■ J. L. Smith

GONZÁLEZ, EUSEBIO (AARÓN) JOAQUÍN (1898–1964).

Founder of the ʼLight of the World Church (La Iglesia La Luz del Mundo) in Mexico. Born on Aug. 14, 1898, in Colotlán, Jalisco, Mexico, he grew up in poverty in rural Jalisco before the outbreak of the Mexican Revolution (1910–17). At the age of 17 he enlisted in the Mexican army and fought in the revolution. Toward the end of his 11-year military career, while stationed in Monterey, Joaquín was converted to ʼOneness Pentecostalism by traveling prophet evangelists José Perales and Antonio Muñoz. These evangelists, who called themselves Saul and Silas, were ministers in the ʼApostolic Church of Faith in Jesus Christ (Iglesia Apostólica de la Fe en Cristo Jesús). After his conversion, Joaquín left the military because it seemed incompatible with his new life and because the military did not allow ministers to serve in the Mexican army.

Shortly thereafter, he was instructed by God to abandon Monterrey and go to Guadalajara, Mexico, the new Holy City. He arrived on Dec. 12, 1926, and began to build what he believed to be Christ's new church on earth, La Iglesia La Luz del Mundo.

Joaquín was initially renamed "Abraham" by Saul and Silas, under whose direction he was first tutored in the Christian faith. He broke with his mentors and became associated with the Iglesia Evangélica Cristiana Espirituel Mexicano (later Iglesia Evangélica Cristiana Espirituel), which was led from 1926 by Francisco Borrego and was a sort of predecessor and then competing organization to the Iglesia Apostólica de la Fe en Cristo. Joaquín later broke with Borrego and attempted unsuccessfully to come to a mode of cooperation with Iglesia Apostólica de la Fe en Cristo. About this time Joaquín had a series of visions or dreams in which he understood God to rename him "Aarón" and give him the charge to restore the primitive NT church and lead God's new chosen people, the new spiritual Israel. Because of this name, the Iglesia La Luz del Mundo is sometimes referred to as the "Aaronista" church, and the members as "Aaronistas."

After several years of meeting in available facilities, Aarón in 1934 opened his first church building. In 1955 he purchased 35 acres of land on the east side of the city in the Hermosa Provincia section of Guadalajara. There he built the mother church of the movement and also sold land to followers at low prices so they could build their own homes.

Members of the church believe that after Aarón's death on 9 June 1964, God elected his son, ʼSamuel Joaquín Flores, to be the next Living Apostle and leader of the church.

■ **Bibliography:** See under "Light of the World Church."

■ D. D. Bundy

GOSPEL PUBLISHING HOUSE (GPH).

The publishing division of the General Council of the ʼAssemblies of God (AG). After the AG was formed at Hot Springs, AR, in Apr. 1914, ʼT. K. Leonard offered his printing facilities in Findlay, OH, as a temporary headquarters and printing plant. The name Gospel Publishing House was adopted (this name was used by an earlier company in New York). AG had assumed ownership of two periodicals: the *Christian Evangel* (later called the *Weekly Evangel,* 1915–18; *Christian Evangel,* 1918–19; and the *Pentecostal Evangel,* 1919–), and the *Word and Witness* (discontinued in 1915). The council moved to St. Louis in 1915 and then to Springfield, MO, in 1918. By this time Sunday school curriculum and books were being published along with the *Evangel.* The present plant was occupied in 1949, and other buildings were added to the complex, including a four-story administration building in 1961.

The building in St. Louis, MO, that housed the Gospel Publishing House and the Assemblies of God office in 1915–18. This photo shows the employees around 1916, with J. Roswell Flower in the center.

GPH, with more than 300 employees, operates a complete modern printing plant, producing 22 tons of books, music, periodicals, and Sunday school literature every working day. The Sunday school literature, Radiant Life curriculum, is used not only by the AG but also by other denominations. Gospel Publishing House partners with the General Council of the AG Division of Foreign Missions in distributing the Spanish curriculum Vida Nueva throughout the world. Earnings from Gospel Publishing House sales are used to help fund and operate various ministries of the General Council of the AG.

■ **Bibliography:** M. Hoover, "Origin and Structural Development of the Assemblies of God" (thesis, Southwest Missouri State U., 1968) ■ W. Menzies, *Anointed to Serve* (1971) ■ "PCPA Welcomes Three New Members," *The Round Table* (Nov.–Dec. 1986).

■ W. E. Warner

GOSS, HOWARD ARCHIBALD (1883–1964). First general superintendent of the ▸United Pentecostal Church (UPC). Converted in 1903 under the ministry of ▸Charles F. Parham, Goss attended Parham's short-term Bible school in Houston, TX, in 1905. While riding a train with other pentecostals in 1906, he received the baptism of the Holy Ghost. In the same year, Parham appointed him to be field supervisor of the Apostolic Faith Movement in Texas. After moral charges were brought against Parham in 1907, Goss separated from Parham and evangelized in Texas, Arkansas, Kansas, Iowa, Illinois, and Missouri, establishing several pentecostal churches. Goss and ▸E. N. Bell were chiefly responsible for organizing the Assemblies of God (AG) in 1914, and Goss was elected to serve on the first executive presbytery and as the person issuing credentials to ministers in the South and West. E. N. Bell rebaptized Goss in the name of Jesus Christ in 1915. After the division of the ▸Oneness ministers from the AG in 1916, Goss served on the credentials committee of the General Assembly of the Apostolic Assemblies. In 1919 he moved to Canada and established a church in Toronto, serving as its pastor until 1937. In the U.S., Goss was a member of the organizing board of presbyters for the Pentecostal Ministerial Alliance and served as the first chairman of this organization from 1925 to 1932. In 1939 he became the general superintendent of the ▸Pentecostal Church, Incorporated. At the merger that formed the UPC in 1945, Goss became the first general superintendent of the new organization and served until 1951. With his wife, Ethel, Goss wrote *The Winds of God* (1958), a history of the early years of the pentecostal revival.

■ **Bibliography:** A. L. Clanton, *United We Stand* (1970).

■ J. L. Hall

Advertisement for gospel services led by Howard and Ethel Goss, leaders in the Oneness movement, in Ottawa, Canada, in 1919.

GOURLEY, THOMAS HAMPTON (1862–1923). American pentecostal pioneer. After a dramatic conversion and healing in 1894, Gourley became a tent evangelist and traveled across the Midwest, rapidly absorbing the theology of the radical Holiness movement. In late 1906 he emerged in Seattle, WA, where amid spectacular news reports he conducted a nightly downtown revival and a daily rescue mission. As news reports and missionaries filtered out from the ▸Azusa Street Mission in Los Angeles, Gourley accepted the new pentecostal theology, and by late 1907 he began publishing one of the first pentecostal journals, the *Midnight Cry*.

Over the next few years, Gourley built a small but loyal following in the Seattle area, though he became increasingly estranged from other pentecostal leaders. In Mar. 1911 he led a band of about 150 to nearby Lopez Island, where, convinced of the imminent end of human history, they lived in a communal arrangement until 1919. During the height of

America's participation in WWI, Gourley was charged with violating the Sedition Act of 1918 for comments made in opposition to the war. He was tried and acquitted, but the publicity destroyed the Lopez Island commune. By the early 1920s Gourley had moved to St. Louis, where he affiliated with ►"Mother" Mary Moise and taught a controversial doctrine of perpetual health. He died tragically in Feb. 1923 as a result of a train wreck near Calhoun, GA.

■ **Bibliography:** James R. Goff Jr., "The Limits of Acculturation: Thomas Hampton Gourley and American Pentecostalism," *Pneuma* (18, Fall 1996) ■ Charles P. LeWarne, "'And Be Ye Separate': The Lopez Island Colony of Thomas Gourley," in *Pacific Northwest Themes: Historical Essays in Honor of Keith A. Murray,* ed. James W. Scott (1978).   ■ J. R. Goff Jr.

GRACE MINISTRIES See KANSAS CITY PROPHETS.

GRAVES, FREDERICK A. (1856–1927). Songwriter. Ordained at age 62, F. A. Graves is remembered chiefly as a gospel songwriter. Born in Williamstown, MA, "Freddie" was orphaned at nine and discovered to have epilepsy at 14. He was converted in childhood and joined the Congregational Church. At age 21, still struggling to overcome periodic seizures, Graves moved to Nobles County in southwestern Minnesota. Soon afterward, believing that he had been healed, he served briefly as an organizer and evangelist for the American Sunday School Union. Short courses in Bible and music followed in Chicago and in Northfield, MA. Upon return, Graves went to hear healing evangelist ►John Alexander Dowie (1847–1907) in Minneapolis. There, despite a relapse, he experienced permanent healing, a pivotal event in his spiritual journey and the backdrop for two long-lasting songs: "Honey in the Rock" (1895) and "He'll Never Forget to Keep Me" (1899).

Before Dowie's downfall, Graves moved his family to Zion City, IL, where he was to remain the rest of his life. Acceptance of pentecostalism enhanced his popularity, and his family's contributions to the pentecostal cause magnified his ministry. He was ordained to the ministry of the General Council of the AG in 1918. All of his children attended Central Bible Institute, Springfield, MO. Arthur Graves (1902–73) became a prominent pastor and president of Southeastern Bible College, Lakeland, FL; Carl, a missionary in Ceylon and pastor in Michigan; and Irene, wife of Myer Pearlman (1893–1943), a convert from Judaism noted as a teacher at Central Bible Institute and a writer on doctrine. (Pearlman recalled that in the first pentecostal mission service he attended in San Francisco, they had sung "Honey in the Rock.") F. A. Graves died in Zion City (population 5,000) in Jan. 1927. Nearly 1,000 people attended his funeral.

■ **Bibliography:** C. Brumback, *Suddenly . . . from Heaven* (1961) ■ F. A. Graves, *So He Made It Again* (1924) ■ I. P. Pearlman, *Myer Pearlman and His Friends* (1953).   ■ C. E. Jones

GREEN, LYNN (1948–). International leader in ►Youth With A Mission (YWAM). Born and brought up in western Colorado, Green studied electrical engineering at the University of Colorado. Giving his life to the Lord in 1969, he joined YWAM and spent two years in training and ministry in Switzerland, Afghanistan, the U.S., Northern Ireland, and England. Green assumed responsibility for YWAM in Britain from 1971 until 1989, and he became regional director for YWAM in Europe, the Middle East, and Africa in 1986.

Green was one of the founders of ►March for Jesus and is chairman of Challenge 2000, the English expression of the DAWN (Disciple a Whole Nation) movement. He has been the initiator and director of the Reconciliation Walk, mobilizing Christians to retrace in prayer the steps of the First Crusade so as to defuse 900 years of bitterness between Muslims, Jews, and Christians. Green has authored *Small Church, Big Vision* (with C. Forster; 1995).   ■ P. D. Hocken

GREENWAY, ALFRED L. (1904–84). Alfred Greenway was a key figure in the formation of the Apostolic Church of New Zealand. He was of Welsh extraction and came out from Great Britain in early 1934 to become the first superintendent of the newly established Apostolic Church in N.Z. He was inducted into the Wellington Apostolic Church as copastor with ►E. R. Weston, and this became the headquarters assembly of the new movement.

Greenway undertook considerable itinerant work, and the Apostolic Church grew rapidly under his forthright teaching ministry and energetic leadership. He visited Australia in 1936, where he met Leonard W. Coote, founder of the Japan Apostolic mission, and as a result received a call to minister in Japan. After briefly returning to N.Z., he left for Japan in 1937; pastor J. F. D. Thompson took over his superintendency in N.Z.

Greenway's ministry in Japan was cut short by WWII, and he returned to take up a pastorate in Adelaide, Australia, a position he held until 1947. He maintained contact with his N.Z. colleagues, and after returning to Wales for a time to become principal of the Apostolic Church's Bible college there, he came back to N.Z. in 1950. After a period of itinerant ministry he held pastorates in Auckland and Hamilton and opened a Bible school for the training of ministers for the Apostolic Church.

After his first wife died and he remarried, Greenway resigned from the Apostolic Church in 1961—although continuing his Bible school for several years—and took up ministry in a Presbyterian church. He eventually moved to Tauranga, where he taught in the interdenominational Faith

Bible College and pastored another Presbyterian church. He remained active in ministry until his death in 1984.

■ **Bibliography:** J. E. Worsfold, *A History of the Charismatic Movements in New Zealand* (1974).   ■ B. Knowles

GREENWOOD, CHARLES LEWIS (1891–1969). Pentecostal pioneer, evangelist, and pastor. Charles Lewis Greenwood (popularly known as "C. L.") was one of 12 children of a poor family in Melbourne, Australia. He had limited education; after a turbulent teenage period he was converted at age 19 in a Church of Christ in Footscray, Victoria.

Hearing of South Melbourne pentecostal meetings being conducted by Robert Horne, a former Methodist minister who had recently experienced glossolalia, Greenwood attended, seeking the baptism in the Holy Spirit. "After three long years," he wrote of his experience on Nov. 20, 1913, "God filled me with the Spirit."

In 1915 Greenwood married Frances Ella Reed, and in 1916 they began holding cottage meetings in their Sunshine (Melbourne) home. Some people were converted, and baptisms were performed in their bathtub. By 1925 the small group had purchased land and built a timber-framed gospel hall, to which American evangelist ▸Alfred Valdez came in March of that year. A short evangelistic campaign was organized, drawing people from all over Melbourne. Many were converted, and several hundred received the ▸baptism in the Spirit. Weekend meetings were transferred to Prahran town hall and within a year to a theater in Richmond, which was renamed Richmond Temple. A decision was made to formalize the establishment of the Pentecostal Church of Australia. In 1925 Greenwood was ordained "minister of the Gospel" of the new church, and he became its pastor in 1927, a position he was to hold for the next 40 years.

Under Greenwood's leadership the church grew strong, becoming arguably the premier pentecostal church in Australia. New branch assemblies were established in Victoria and New South Wales, and some existing congregations affiliated. In 1937 the Pentecostal Church of Australia and the Assemblies of God (AG) in Queensland amalgamated under the name the Assemblies of God in Australia, and Greenwood was elected the first commonwealth chairman.

Greenwood was primarily an evangelist. He had a passion to win souls for Christ and took every opportunity to do so. His preaching was simple and uncluttered but always focused on the need to find salvation in Jesus. This earnestness was reflected in a burning passion for worldwide missions—the first missionary sailed for India within months of the foundation of Richmond Temple.

Greenwood's ministry was marked by powerful prophetic gifts and significant healings; he often pointed to individuals in the congregation and urged them to repent of sins only they and God knew about. His preaching was lively, demonstrative, and enthusiastic. He also had a flair for administration. While members of his congregation universally praised his compassion and pastoral concern, other ministers both within and without the AG sometimes found him intractable, intolerant, and uncooperative. His contribution to the formation and ongoing development of the AG in Australia was paramount in its first quarter century of development.

■ **Bibliography:** B. Chant, *Heart of Fire* (1984) ■ P. Duncan, *Pentecost in Australia*, Sydney (n.d.) ■ C. L. Greenwood, "Life Story" (seven taped addresses, 1965) ■ D. and G. Smith, *A River Is Flowing* (1987).   ■ B. Chant

GREGORY THAUMATURGUS (c. 210–260). Bishop of Neocaesarea in Pontus, "wonderworker," and power evangelist. Gregory was born to a well-to-do pagan family in Pontus on the Black Sea and encountered Christianity at the age of 14 after his father's death. He accompanied his sister to Caesarea in Palestine, intending to go on to Beirut (Berytus) and study law there. Instead, for the next five years he became the pupil of Origen of Alexandria, who at that time was teaching in Caesarea. Shortly after returning to Pontus, Gregory became bishop of Neocaesarea.

Five biographies of Gregory (in Latin, Syriac, and Armenian) recount the miracles that earned him the name *Thaumaturgus* or "wonderworker"; Gregory of Nyssa's seems to be the most credible. It is reported that Gregory Thaumaturgus prophesied and could heal the sick. Demons were subject to him and were exorcised by his fiat. He was credited with turning back flooding rivers and drying up lakes. In one account we are told that he cast his cloak over a man and caused his death. He banished pagan gods in a heathen temple by his simple presence. Basil the Great, in his great work *On the Holy Spirit* (74), declared that Gregory should be numbered among the apostles: "By the superabundance of gifts, wrought in him by the Spirit in all power and in signs and in marvels, he was styled a second Moses by the very enemies of the church. Thus, in all that he through grace accomplished, alike by word and deed, a light seemed ever to be shining, token of the heavenly power from the unseen which followed him."

While critical scholars have "demythologized" the supernatural element in Gregory's ministry, there must have been some truth to the reports of signs and wonders that accompanied his evangelism. Gregory of Nyssa tells us that there were only 17 Christians in Neocaesarea when Gregory began his ministry there, but when he died there were only 17 who were not Christians.

■ **Bibliography:** Basil the Great, *On the Holy Spirit* ■ Gregory of Nyssa, *Panegyric on Gregory Thaumaturgus* ■ W. Telfer, "The Cultus of St. Gregory Thaumaturgus," *Harvard Theological Review* 29 (1936)

■ R. van Dam, "Hagiography and History: The Life of Gregory Thaumaturgus," *Classical Antiquity* 1 (1982).
■ S. M. Burgess

GUERRA, ELENA (1835–1914). Italian Roman Catholic nun and precursor to the Catholic Charismatic Movement. Founder of the Oblate Sisters of the Holy Spirit in Lucca, Italy, Sr. Elena Guerra wrote twelve confidential letters (1895–1903) to Pope Leo XIII requesting a renewed preaching on the Holy Spirit. She urged that the faithful rediscover life lived according to the Holy Spirit and that the Church be renewed, together with society and the very "face of the earth." She insisted that "Pentecost is not over.... It is going on in every time and in every place, because the Holy Spirit desired to give himself to all men and all who want him can always receive him."

To invoke this renewal, Sr. Elena conceived of a modern prayer movement with the same expectancy as the apostles had in the Cenacle of Jerusalem, the upper room where the first Pentecost was experienced. She referred to this modern intercession as the "Universal Cenacle"—a "union of prayer to the Holy Spirit." She called on Pope Leo XIII to unite Christians in a "unanimous and unceasing prayer to the divine Spirit ... so that the Light of the Paraclete may shine over the darkness of ignorance and error."

In response to her urging, Pope Leo XIII issued a letter, *Provida Matris Caritate* (1895), in which he asked all Catholics to celebrate a solemn novena (nine days of prayer) to the Holy Spirit, for the renewal of Christianity. In 1897 he wrote an encyclical letter on the Holy Spirit, *Divinum Illud Munus*, in which he stated that the novena was to be perpetual, done every year between the feasts of Ascension and Pentecost. On January 1, 1901 (the same day as the Pentecostal outpouring in Topeka, Kansas, USA), Pope Leo invoked the Holy Spirit by singing the hymn "Veni Creator Spiritus" on behalf of the entire Church.

Although Sr. Elena did not live to see the fulfillment of her prophetic mission, it was in part realized when Pope John XXIII called the Second Vatican Council into session, beginning in July 1962. She was the first woman beatified by John XXIII, who called her a modern-day "Apostle of the Holy Spirit."

■ **Bibliography:** D. M. Abbrescia, *Elena Guerra, Prophecy and Renewal* (1982) ■ K. Kollins, *Burning Bush: A Return to the Cenacle in Adoration and Intercession* (1999; Italian ed., 2001) ■ E. Guerra, *Rebirth in the Holy Spirit* (1985). ■ R. V. Burgess

GUILLÉN, MIGUEL (c. 1896–1971). Second president of the ▸Latin American Council of Christian Churches (Concilio Latino Americano de Iglesias Cristianas [CLADIC]) and key leader of the Latino pentecostal movement in the mid 20th century. He was converted by ▸H. C. Ball in south Texas in 1916. After a number of years in lay ministry, Miguel was ordained by the Latin American District Council of the Assemblies of God (AG) in the U.S. as a missionary to Tampico, Mexico, in 1919. Upon his return to the U.S. he became pastor of a small Spanish-speaking congregation in Port Arthur, TX (1921–23).

Guillén later joined ▸Francisco Olazábal's breakaway denomination from the AG, CLADIC. In 1933 Olazábal named him copastor of the church in Chicago. Two years later he became the superintendent of the Chicago District, and in 1936 he was named superintendent general of CLADIC, second in command after Olazábal. After Olazábal's death in 1937 there was considerable infighting over the direction of the denomination. This resulted in the fragmentation of CLADIC into a number of smaller *concilios* (councils or denominations). Guillén remained in control of the southwestern section of CLADIC. He served as president of CLADIC from 1937 to 1971. Under his leadership, CLADIC witnessed modest church growth and the establishment of CLADIC Seminary in 1954. The story of CLADIC and Guillén's life and ministry are recorded in the history he wrote, *La Historia del Concilio Latino Americano de Iglesias Cristianas*.

■ **Bibliography:** M. Guillén, *La Historia del Concilio Latino Americano de Iglesias Cristianas* (1991). ■ G. Espinosa

GUNSTONE, JOHN (1927–). One of the main teacher-leaders of the charismatic movement in the Catholic wing of the Church of England and a popular author of books on pastoral liturgy. Gunstone was one of the first Anglo-Catholics to be baptized in the Spirit (1964). His numerous writings reflect his varied ministry: as a vicar near London (1958–71); as chaplain of the Barnabas Fellowship at Whatcombe House, Dorset (1971–75); and as county ecumenical officer of Greater Manchester (1975–92). He was editor of the magazine *Healing and Wholeness* (1994–98). Gunstone's books include *Greater Things Than These* (1974), *A People for His Praise* (1978; on renewal and congregational life); *Pentecostal Anglicans* (1982); *Prayers for Healing* (1987); and *Pentecost Comes to Church: Sacraments and Spiritual Gifts* (1994). He has been a trustee of ▸Anglican Renewal Ministries since its formation in 1981. ■ P. D. Hocken

GUTI, EZEKIEL H. (1923–). Guti was born in Chiping near Mutare, Zimbabwe, in 1923. His mother was the first to share the gospel message with him. Handinawangu, as he was known at the time, experienced dramatic dreams and visions, including the vision of an angel who challenged him to serve God. After a time of spiritual indifference he spoke in tongues and was baptized in water in 1947.

Not long after this Guti moved to Highfields in Harare. Following a vision, he changed his name to Ezekiel and became a popular preacher. Because he had not been ordained, he was not permitted to preach in churches, but he traveled long distances by bicycle to preach in the countryside. Because of his radical messages about heaven and hell and because of his claim to visions, Guti was disfellowshiped by the church of which he had been a member.

For a time Guti had close fellowship with Nicholas Benghu from South Africa, but division occurred when some of the leaders working with Benghu accused him of attempting to take over their work. In May 1960 he left Highfields for Bindura. It was from that time that he dates the birth of the Zimbabwe Assemblies of God, Africa (ZAOGA). Guti states that he was opposed continually by missionaries and also by the white government in what was then Rhodesia; he bears no grudge against whites today. He moved back to Highfields, where he started the Highfields Revival Centre. Although the government did not officially recognize his work, it knew what he was doing and permitted him to continue unhindered. By 1970 there were 80 churches around the country belonging to this ministry; all had self-supporting pastors. In 1970 Guti went to the U.S., where he attended Christ for the Nations Institute, graduating in 1972.

Guti returned to Zimbabwe and married Eunor. A Bible college was established in Harare, where over 800 people have been trained for ministry. There is also an orphanage near Mutare. Phenomenal growth has occurred in the number of churches belonging to this movement as well as the number of adherents. In Harare the buildings used for Sunday gatherings were too small, so the National Sports Centre was rented for special Sunday meetings with over 10,000 in attendance. Guti says that he was going to build a huge hall, but God told him to construct buildings in different parts of the country.

Guti's followers regard him as an apostle; he teaches, preaches, prophesies, and emphasizes the need for the Christian's reliance on the work of the Holy Spirit. He continues to preach a simple message in which holy living and Christ are central. The place of healing, miracles, and exorcism are given as the reason for the continual growth of this movement. The cell principle is employed in each local church.

Churches affiliated with Guti are also found in Malawi, Zambia, Botswana, Mozambique, and other African countries. Outside Zimbabwe his movement is known as Forward in Faith. He claims over a million adherents in Zimbabwe. Guti's critics do not like what they call his autocratic approach. It is not uncommon to hear prayers addressed to God as "the God of Ezekiel." Guti responds that when OT believers prayed to "the God of Abraham," they were not worshiping Abraham, but were merely identifying with one who was God's spokesman. His followers say that what hap-

pens must be understood in the light of the African concept of respect for leaders, especially religious leaders.

■ **Bibliography:** Gayle D. Erwin, *African Apostle* (n.d.) ■ E. H. Guti, *Restoring the Purpose of True Cost of Leadership* (1994) ■ D. Maxwell, "Social and Conceptual History of Northeast Zimbabwe: 1890 to 1990" (diss., Oxford, 1994).   ■ D. Garrard

GYPSIES One of the most mysterious groups of people in the world for centuries past has been the Gypsies, also called Travellers, Bohemians, Gitanos, and finally Roma, as they have recently named themselves. For hundreds of years, nomadic Gypsy tribes have survived on the outskirts of dominant cultures in Asia, Europe, and more recently, America. They have neglected—even spurned—the practice of writing down their system of beliefs, history, or heritage. Gypsies have always maintained a strict division between themselves and non-Gypsy peoples, based on a taboo system of pollution and cleanliness. Some of the rituals of dominant religions such as Catholicism have been adopted into their customs, but the true tenets of Gypsy beliefs have remained a mystery to anthropologists and others venturing to understand their way of life.

The 20th century, however, has brought an unprecedented spiritual movement among Gypsy camps in Europe and America. Beginning in the early 1950s, evangelical pentecostalism was introduced to a small number of Gypsies, and the movement has since grown from family to family and tribe to tribe to become a major factor in nations worldwide.

The official beginning of the pentecostal revival among European Gypsies is attributed to one incident near Lisieux, France, in 1950. A Gypsy woman of the Manouche tribe, Mrs. Reinhard, was at the marketplace one day, and she was handed a tract after listening to a colporteur declare, "God still heals the sick today." She tucked the tract in her wallet as she continued her shopping. The tract remained in her wallet for many months as her caravan traveled on. Later, the caravan

A group of Roma men.

was passing by Lisieux again, and this time Mrs. Reinhard's young son was very sick. Doctors operated on him but told the woman that there was nothing else they could do. Remembering the tract about divine healing, Mrs. Reinhard had a nurse read her the address on the back page. She then went directly to the address, an Assemblies of God (AG) church. It was Sunday morning, and Mrs. Reinhard interrupted the service to request prayer for her son. The minister accompanied her to the hospital and prayed for the boy. In a few days the boy was well, and the Reinhard family accepted Christ.

News of the healing spread quickly among family and tribe members. As they traveled, they attended services at evangelical churches and continued to testify to the healing and their salvation. Among those converted within the family was a married son, Mandz, who eventually became the first Gypsy preacher.

A few years later, in 1952, Clément Le Cossec was preaching in a municipal hall in Brittany. He encountered Mandz and his wife, who wished to be baptized but had been refused by the church because they were not married according to the laws of the country. Their marriages had been performed within the tribe according to Gypsy customs, regardless of the law of the country. Le Cossec arranged for the baptism of Mandz and his wife. Seeing the spiritual needs of the growing number of Gypsy converts, Le Cossec vowed to evangelize these people who had thus far been ignored by other Christian groups and movements. One evening soon thereafter, in a basement in Brest, Brittany, about 30 Gypsies gathered for a church meeting led by Le Cossec. They prayed to receive the Holy Spirit, and as a result many began to speak in tongues.

After that incident, reports of baptism in the Spirit and speaking in tongues began to filter in from sources far and wide. In a booklet written by Le Cossec in the mid 1960s, he recounts how similar revivals were taking place simultaneously in other countries, such as Portugal, Greece, and the

A Roma campground in France, 1982. The traditional horse-drawn wagons have been replaced by trailers drawn by cars and pick-up trucks.

U.S., each unaware of what was happening in the others. In 1954 a pastor of a Gypsy church in the Greek Peloponnesus was baptized in the Spirit while praying. A group of Gypsies gathered for prayer in Portugal were baptized in the Spirit without knowing what was happening. Also around that time, the Gypsy revival in the U.S. was beginning in Grand Island, NE, and Pittsburgh, PA.

The revival in Grand Island began in March of 1954 among the members of the Mason family soon after the father, who was known as the "King of the Gypsies," had passed away. One of the man's sons, Dick Mason, gathered with his family for the funeral services. He was the only converted Christian among the family members. He had contacted AG pastor Harold D. Champlin to discuss salvation with and pray for his family. That evening the family gathered at the parsonage, and several were converted and baptized in the Holy Spirit.

In both Europe and America, word also spread of cases of miraculous healing—many compared to those performed by Jesus in the Gospels—as the pentecostal revival continued to grow. The first baptisms took place in 1952 at St. Marc's Beach near Brest, and by 1963, 6,000 had been immersed. A statistical count in 1970 showed that out of the population of 12 million Gypsies worldwide, over half had attended an evangelical service, and 47,260 had been baptized.

A major development early on in the spread of the Gypsy evangelical movement was the organization of national conventions designed to promote the revival. The first European convention took place in 1954 in Brest. Although the police opposed the massive gathering of caravans, the convention was a success, and the leaders quickly established the convention as an annual event attracting thousands of Gypsy pilgrims. Another was held two months later in Rennes, France. The Gypsies who gathered there numbered about 500.

The first national convention in the U.S. took place in Texarkana, AR, in Dec. 1964. Meetings during this convention were held in what was at the time the only active Gypsy church in America. It was referred to as "The Hill" and was built by Lawrence Young on a site where more than 300 Gypsies had set up permanent residence. Several of the most prominent early leaders of the Gypsy evangelical movement attended this convention as delegates from the Gypsy ministry in France. They included John Le Cossec, son of Clement Le Cossec; Joe Mazzu, French foreign missionary; and Robert and Stevo Demeter, French Gypsy ministers. The convention was coordinated by Patrick McLane, an AG pastor from New Jersey.

Since then, the annual conventions have become major productions, drawing thousands of Gypsy caravans carrying pilgrims from all regions. In France, a permanent center for the conventions was established at Ennordres. Leaders of the

Gypsy evangelical movement organized these conventions based on four clearly established goals: (1) to bring converts together for spiritual growth, (2) to evangelize the family and friends of converts, (3) to examine spiritual and material problems standing in the way of the movement, and (4) to witness to non-Gypsies. Camp meetings, smaller versions of the conventions, are also held on holidays such as Easter, Pentecost, and in summer months, and they also attract thousands of Gypsy pilgrims.

The movement also brought new educational needs for the Gypsies. In 1960 a group of preachers in France inaugurated short-term Bible courses, and in 1963 they established a Bible College of the Assemblies of God and admitted 10 young people. By this time the movement was considered worldwide, with evangelistic communities appearing across Europe and the U.S. In the first three decades, over 70,000 Gypsies were converted and baptized, and the numbers continued to grow. The mission now includes several periodicals, a radio station, a Bible institute, a mobile school, and special classes held at campsites.

A Roma girl.

Educational opportunities produced spiritual leaders within the Gypsy camps. By 1977 in France, 260 Gypsy ministers conducted services every week, attended by at least 30,000 Gypsies. In 1983 the number of preachers in Europe was said to be 1,200, with 600 in Spain and 400 in France, while 200,000 Gypsies attended evangelical meetings. At this time most Gypsy churches remained under the direction of the International Evangelical Gypsy Mission led by Le Cossec. Some of the larger churches, however, had become self-governing, such as the church in France, which was led by an all-Gypsy committee of seven, presided over by Djimy Myer.

The nomadic lifestyle of the Gypsies, as well as the fairly uncomplicated practice of inducting lay preachers among the Gypsy men, easily facilitated the spreading of the message from tribe to tribe. At the beginning, the movement stayed among those of the Manouche tribe in France, but soon large groups in other tribes, such as the Kalderash Romanies of Eastern Europe and the Spanish Gitanos, were being converted by traveling Gypsy ministers and at conventions. The fact that the Gypsy Evangelical Movement is such a strong intertribal movement is one of the most important aspects of its impact on Gypsy life worldwide. Unlike in the past, putting themselves in the public eye as a united group has been an advantageous technique for survival.

In the past the Gypsies have been no strangers to prejudice. Over the centuries, in many countries, edict after edict was passed in efforts to settle the Gypsies into one area or force them to move on. Anti-Gypsy racism reached its peak during the devastation of the Holocaust; after the Jews, the Gypsies were the second-largest group of victims to be slaughtered.

In the wake of this persecution has come a worldwide concern for human rights and equality, and the Gypsies have not escaped this awareness. Causes that have provided reasons to unite have shown unprecedented success among Gypsy tribes, and the Gypsy evangelical movement is one of the most notable among these.

In 1965 the International Gypsy Committee was formed in cooperation with the Gypsy Evangelical Church in order to further facilitate unity among various tribes, nations, and religions. This committee's aim was to promote the rights of the Gypsy people and end injustices inflicted by dominant cultures. In 1971 the first World Romany Congress took place, at which time delegates from 14 countries adopted the name *Rom* for all Gypsies, as well as a flag, a slogan, and an anthem. They even asserted a common heritage in the warrior classes of India, a theory that many claim remains to be proven. Representatives were established at the United Nations, the UN Human Rights Commission, and UNESCO. The fourth World Romany Congress in 1990 instigated a variety of programs involving reparations, education, culture, public relations, language, and a Gypsy encyclopedia.

The survival of the Gypsies in this century has required some radical alterations in their relations with the non-Gypsy population. Whereas in the past a secretive manner and nominal assimilation protected their lifestyle, they now have been forced to speak up and to make some assertions about their beliefs and their identities in order to claim their rights. The evangelical movement has been and continues to be a significant aid in uniting Gypsies of all nations without requiring assimilation with the dominant culture.

The worldwide Gypsy evangelical movement continues to spread today in Gypsy tribes around the world. One remarkable example of the strength of the movement is in south Serbia, between Kosovo and Bulgaria. The Orthodox Church here is aggressively antievangelical, yet the number of pentecostal Gypsies continues to grow. Serbia's only Gypsy pastor, Selim Alijevic, describes services in which 500 to 600 members attempt to fill a church building designed to hold only 300. In 1998, 20 house churches with 150 to 200 Gypsy converts were planted in nearby cities and villages. The need for churches with Gypsy ministers continues to grow. Alijevic is working hard to train leaders among the Gypsies.

The Gypsies make up about 10% of the population in Leskovac, and the growth of this movement has led to more animosity from other Serbians. Mio Stankovic, senior pastor of the pentecostal church in Leskovac, was recently named "the most dangerous man in town." Yet the Gypsy movement grows, with continued reports of miraculous healing, conversions, and baptisms in the Spirit.

■ **Bibliography:** C. M. Black, "Miracles among the Gypsies," *PE* (Oct. 23, 1977) ■ W. Cantelon, "10,000 Gypsies," *Gypsy Work Magazine*, 1 (1970) ■ H. D. Champlin, "Evangelizing the American Gypsies," *PE* (July 26, 1964) ■ T. Dixon, "Revival among Gypsies Dispels Spiritual Darkness in Serbia," *Charisma* (Mar. 1999) ■ A. Fraser, *The Gypsies* (1992) ■ C. Le Cossec, "Revival among the Gypsies" ■ idem, "The Story of How within 30 Years an Indigenous Church Has Become a Reality among the Gypsies," *Europe Pulse* 14 (1, Jan. 1983) ■ R. Lyon, "If You Were a Gypsy . . .," *PE* (Apr. 24, 1966) ■ idem, "Pentecostal Fire Burns in Gypsy Camps," *PE* (Mar. 7, 1965). ■ S. L. Thomas

H

HAGIN, KENNETH E. (1917–). Teacher, prolific author, and advocate of the "Word of Faith" (►Positive Confession) message. Born prematurely with a deformed heart, he was not expected to survive, yet he managed to function for 15 years before becoming an invalid. He reported that the following year, during a 10-minute period, his vital signs failed three times. On each occasion he witnessed the horrors of hell. This experience resulted in his conversion on Apr. 22, 1933. The following year he was healed, and he soon began a ministry as a lay preacher for a small, multidenominational country church in Texas, attended predominately by Southern Baptists. His baptism in the Holy Spirit in 1937 led him into ministry as a pentecostal in the same state, where he pastored six churches successively.

Hagin began an itinerant ministry as a Bible teacher and evangelist in 1949. During the following 14 years he had a series of eight visions of Jesus Christ, who in the third vision granted him the gift of discerning of spirits, enabling him to pray more effectively for the healing of the sick. As a result of his final vision in 1963, he set up his own office at his home in Garland, TX, for the distribution of his tapes and books. Three years later he moved to Tulsa, OK. Since 1978 the name of the ministry has been "Rhema Bible Church aka Kenneth Hagin Ministries"; it is located in Broken Arrow, a suburb of Tulsa.

Kenneth Hagin Sr., a leader in the "Word of Faith" movement and founder of the Rhema Bible Training Center, Broken Arrow, OK.

Hagin founded Rhema Bible Training Center in 1974. By early 2000, more than 16,500 students had graduated, and his daily radio program, *Faith Seminar of the Air*, was heard via more than 300 daily broadcasts in the U.S., with a shortwave audience in more than 120 other nations. At that time, more than 53 million copies of the 125 books authored by Hagin and Kenneth Hagin Jr. were in circulation, and more than 58,000 tapes were distributed each month. Hagin's monthly magazine, *The Word of Faith*, has a circulation of 540,000.

With respect to his prophetic ministry, Hagin (1972, 109) has written,

> When the word of knowledge began to operate in my life after I was filled with the Holy Ghost, I would know things supernaturally about people, places, and things. Sometimes I would know through a vision. Sometimes while I was preaching, a cloud would appear and my eyes would be opened so that I would see a vision concerning someone in the congregation.

Kenneth Hagin emphasizes the message of uncompromising faith in God's desire to bless, in every area of life, all who do not doubt him. Although he has been criticized as the leader of the "Word of Faith" and "Positive Confession" movements (Hunt, 1987, 56; McConnell, passim), his message emphasizes the need to pray only according to God's principles as found in the Judeo-Christian Scriptures.

■ **Bibliography:** K. E. Hagin, *The Art of Prayer* (1991) ■ idem, *Following God's Plan for Your Life* (1993) ■ idem, *He Gave Gifts unto Men: A Biblical Perspective of Apostles, Prophets, and Pastors* (1992) ■ idem, *How You Can Be Led by the Spirit of God* (1978) ■ idem, *I Believe in Visions* (1972) ■ idem, *I Went to Hell* (1982) ■ idem, *Love: The Way to Victory* (1994) ■ idem, *Mountain Moving Faith* (1993) ■ idem, *What to Do When Faith Seems Weak and Victory Lost* (1979) ■ D. Hunt, *Beyond Seduction* (1987) ■ D. R. McConnell, *A Different Gospel* (1988). ■ R. M. Riss

HALL, HOMER RICHARD (1920–). Healing evangelist. H. Richard Hall was born in poverty. With the influence of a pentecostal mother, he started preaching at age 14 and received ordination with the Church of God of Prophecy (CGP) at age 24. Hall reported that in 1952 God audibly told him to preach deliverance. Immediately resigning as CGP state overseer of Colorado, he left to pursue his new ministry outside denominational structures.

Hall was a small-town evangelist throughout the 1950s and for the most part remained such throughout his career. By 1972 his magazine, *The Shield of Faith* (started in 1956 as

The Healing Broadcast, then *The Healing Digest*), had a circulation of 100,000.

The United Christian Ministerial Association was established by Hall in 1956 as an organization of independent clergy and churches. In 1972 he had ordained more than 2,000 ministers. Hall worked in cooperation with pentecostal denominations but never won their support. He emphasized healing and, like ˒William Branham, whom he admired, frequently exercised the gift of ˒knowledge.

Hall identified with social outcasts and with those outside the churches, especially the youth of the rebellion of the 1960s and 1970s, by campaigning with college-age talent and attempting to relate to youth.

■ **Bibliography:** D. E. Harrell Jr., *All Things Are Possible* (1975) ■ C. E. Jones, *Guide to the Study of the Pentecostal Movement* (1983).
■ S. Shemeth

HALL, JIMMIE LOUIS ("J. L.") (1933–). Pastor, church executive, and editor. Born in James, TX, Hall was converted to Christ in 1953 before spending two years in the U. S. Army. He received a ministerial license with the United Pentecostal Church International (UPCI) in 1955 and ordination in 1964. He served pastorates in Ardmore, OK, and Wichita, KS. While in Wichita he worked as secretary/treasurer of the Kansas District before his election as district superintendent, an office he held from 1971 to 1976. During this time he also earned a B.A. at Friends University in Wichita (1961) and an M.A. at Emporia (KS) State University (1974).

With his training in journalism, the UPCI national leadership invited Hall in 1976 to become editor of UPCI Word Aflame Publications, located at the denominational headquarters in Hazelwood, MO. In 1982 he became editor-in-chief of UPCI publications, a responsibility that includes oversight of the *Pentecostal Herald,* the official voice of the UPCI, and *Forward,* a magazine for ministers. In 1980 he organized and began supervision of the UPCI Historical Center in Hazelwood. Since 1986 he has planned and promoted the biennial UPCI symposiums on Oneness Pentecostalism. He is a member of the Society for Pentecostal Studies.

Hall's many publications include numerous articles for the *Dictionary of Pentecostal and Charismatic Movements*

J. L. Hall, pastor, church executive, and editor in the United Pentecostal Church, International.

(1988) and "A Oneness Pentecostal Looks at Initial Evidence," in G. B. McGee, ed., *Initial Evidence: Historical and Biblical Perspectives on the Pentecostal Doctrine of Spirit Baptism* (1991). He has also coedited and contributed to *The Pentecostal Minister* (1991), *Doctrines of the Bible* (1993), and three collections of papers entitled *Symposium on Oneness Pentecostalism* (1986, 1990, 1991). A gracious and articulate spokesperson for the UPCI and Oneness Pentecostalism, Hall wrote *The United Pentecostal Church and the Evangelical Movement* (1990) to demonstrate the evangelical moorings of Oneness theology.

■ G. B. McGee

HAMMOND, HATTIE PHILLETTA LUDY (1907–94). Evangelist. Born and raised in Williamsport, MD, Hammond grew up in the Brethren Church with headquarters in Ashland, OH. In 1922, at age 15, she attended a pentecostal camp meeting conducted by evangelist John J. Ashcroft. Hattie was saved and baptized in the Holy Spirit at that meeting and immediately began witnessing to her teachers and classmates.

Dedicating her life to full-time ministry at age 16, Hammond began traveling on the evangelistic field and was soon asked by George Bowie to speak in Cleveland, OH; by J. Narver Gortner in Oakland, CA; by ˒Robert and Marie Brown in New York City; and by ˒E. S. Williams in Philadelphia.

Hammond was ordained by the Assemblies of God in 1927. By the 1930s she had become one of the most powerful speakers in the pentecostal movement. Promoting the

Hattie Hammond, who by the 1930s had become one of the most powerful speakers in the pentecostal movement, with a widespread evangelistic ministry.

"deeper life" teaching, she became a popular camp meeting speaker and Bible teacher. Her message was simple, inspiring total abandonment and consecration to God. She ministered all over America in colleges, conventions, Bible schools, churches of all denominations, and in more than 30 countries.

■ **Bibliography:** Handwritten diary, 1927–36 ■ interview by Wayne E. Warner (Aug. 16, 1982) ■ eulogy. ■ G. W. Gohr

HANSON, CARL M. (1865–1954).

Evangelist, pastor, church official. Born to Norwegian immigrants in Minnesota in Dec. 1865, "Daddy" Hanson was an early pentecostal pioneer in the northern Great Plains. After completing common school, he enrolled in Augsburg Seminary's college preparatory program in 1881, where he converted to Christ. He left Augsburg in 1882 before completing his first year. Hanson was healed of blood poisoning and tuberculosis and by 1895 began itinerating as a Scandinavian Free Mission evangelist. About 1896 he held services in Grafton, ND, in which a young girl spoke in tongues. Hanson sought and received this gift two years later. He moved to Minneapolis in 1900, working as a carpenter to support his ministry. Hanson associated with ►F. A. Graves's church, remaining an active evangelist. In Mar. 1905 he was jailed and fined for holding "frenzied meetings" in which he advocated tongues speech in Fergus Falls, MN. Hanson moved to Dalton, MN, where he farmed and reared 10 children with his wife, Matilda. Two daughters became missionaries, Esther M. Hanson and Anna C. Berg. On Sept. 25, 1909, he was ordained by ►William Durham in Chicago, transferring to the ►Assemblies of God (AG) in 1917. He served as the first chairman of the North Central District (AG) from 1922 to 1923. Hanson served pastorates in Chicago, and in St. Paul, Sauk Centre, and Princeton, MN. He died June 28, 1954 in Braham, MN, where he had lived since 1945.

■ **Bibliography:** "Rev. C. M. Hanson at Home with the Lord," *North Dakota District Echoes* (July–Aug. 1954) ■ "Fined $35: Evangelist Who Has Been Holding Frenzied Meetings Is Taken into Court," *Fergus Falls Daily Journal* (Mar. 11, 1905), 3. ■ D. J. Rodgers

HARGRAVE, VESSIE D. (1915–87).

Church of God (CG, Cleveland, TN) pastor, missionary, educator, administrator, and author. Born in Texas on May 28, 1915, Hargrave spent part of his early life in Mexico and developed a lifelong love for that country. Preaching from the age of 18, he began his pastoral ministry in Pine Grove, TX, in 1935. Following two other pastorates in Texas, he served as state youth and Christian education director in 1941–42.

His ministry shifted to Latin America when he was appointed social and moral director (missionary) for the CG in Mexico in 1944. The next year he became the CG superintendent of Latin America, serving in that office until appointed superintendent of Europe in 1962. From 1964 to 1968, Hargrave served as the foreign missions director of the CG, an elected position that also placed him on the denomination's general executive committee. He then filled succeeding terms as overseer of South Carolina, the Hispanic work of the eastern U.S., and Missouri.

Among Hargrave's many accomplishments, he established the International Preparatory Institute (1947–54) and encouraged the growth of *El Evangelio,* the CG's official Spanish-language publication.

■ **Bibliography:** C. W. Conn, *Like a Mighty Army: A History of the Church of God* (1996) ■ V. D. Hargrave, *The Church and World Missions* (1970) ■ idem, *Manantiales del Predicador, Volumes I–VIII* (1958–77) ■ idem, *Undaunted by Obstacles* (1960) ■ idem, "Glossolalia: Reformation to the Twentieth Century," in W. H. Horton, ed., *The Glossolalia Phenomenon* (1966) ■ C. Moree, "Vessie D. Hargrave: Undaunted by Obstacles," *Church of God Evangel* (Nov. 23, 1987). ■ D. G. Roebuck

HARPER, MICHAEL CLAUDE (1931–).

Pioneer figure in the charismatic renewal in Britain, a leader in worldwide renewal, and prolific author. Converted as an undergraduate at Cambridge, Harper was ordained a priest of the Church of England in 1956. From 1958 to 1964 he served at All Souls, Langham Place, one of London's major evangelical churches, under John Stott. In the fall of 1962 he had an enlivening and empowering experience of the Holy Spirit, receiving the gift of tongues in Aug. 1963. Harper sponsored talks by F. Maguire, ►Larry Christenson, and ►David du Plessis in 1963, and organized residential conferences at Stoke Poges in Feb. and June 1964. Publishing Christenson's booklet on tongues and his own on prophecy by the summer of 1964, he resigned from All Souls and became the first full-time general secretary of the ►Fountain Trust. The Trust embodied Harper's goals and ideals, focusing on new life in the Spirit for Christians of all churches in the context of the renewal of the body of Christ. His organizational, teaching, and writing work now multiplied, with a first trip to the U.S. in 1965 and to Australia and New Zealand in 1967. Editing the Fountain Trust's magazine, *Renewal,* from its inception in Jan. 1966, Harper changed to director in 1972, but in 1975 he resigned as director and editor to concentrate on his teaching ministry, based in Hounslow, West London, until 1981, when he moved to Haywards Heath, Sussex. Harper was a canon of Chichester Cathedral from 1984 to 1995, when he resigned his Anglican orders to join the Antiochian Greek Orthodox Church.

From the late '70s to the mid '90s, Harper's ministry was primarily international with a twofold focus: serving renewal within the Anglican Communion and promoting its ecumenical relations. The Anglican focus developed from his role as convener of a charismatic conference for Anglicans immediately before the Lambeth Conference in July 1978, which led in 1981 to the formation of ▸Sharing of Ministries Abroad (SOMA), of which he was appointed full-time international director in 1984. Harper's ecumenical service to the charismatic renewal found its principal expression in the ▸European Charismatic Consultation (ECC), formed in 1988, and the ▸International Charismatic Consultation on World Evangelization (ICCOWE), which developed from a consultation held in Singapore in 1987. Harper played key roles in the ICCOWE worldwide conference at Brighton (1991) and the ICCOWE–ECC European conference at Prague (1997).

Throughout his ministry Harper has been supported by his wife, Jeanne, herself musically gifted and for many years active in the Lydia Fellowship for women. Harper's gifts are illustrated in his steady literary output. His practical spiritual teaching is seen in *Power for the Body of Christ* (1964), *Walk in the Spirit* (1968), and *Spiritual Warfare* (1970). His narrative skills shine in *As at the Beginning* (1965), an account of pentecostal origins and the first blossoming of charismatic renewal; *None Can Guess* (1971), his own personal story; and *A New Way of Living* (1973), on the Church of the Redeemer in Houston, TX. His ability to clarify contemporary issues in the light of the gospel is seen in *Let My People Grow* (1977), *Three Sisters* (also under the title *This Is the Day;* 1979), and *The Love Affair* (1982).

Increasingly troubled by doctrinal permissiveness in the Anglican Church, which was brought to a head by the ordination of women in the Church of England, Michael and Jeanne Harper joined the Orthodox Church in Mar. 1995. Harper was soon ordained as a priest and made dean of a new Antiochian Orthodox Deanery for Great Britain. His position on women is set out in *Equal and Different* (1994); the story of his pilgrimage to Orthodoxy is told in *The True Light* (1997).

■ **Bibliography:** E. England, *The Spirit of Renewal* (n.d.) ■ P. D. Hocken, *Streams of Renewal* (1986, 1997) ■ R. Quebedeaux, *The New Charismatics II* (1983) ■ M. Robinson, *Two Winds Blowing* (n.d.).   ■ P. D. Hocken

Michael C. Harper, clergyman in the U.K. who has had a significant role in the charismatic renewal since 1962.

HARRELL, DAVID EDWIN JR. (1930–). Church historian, university professor, and writer. David Harrell is a prolific writer on religious themes, but he is best known in pentecostal and charismatic circles for his highly acclaimed *All Things Are Possible* (1975) and *Oral Roberts: An American Life* (1985), both published by Indiana University Press. He was reared in the Church of Christ but later regarded himself as nondenominational. Harrell's Vanderbilt University Ph.D. dissertation was "A Social History of the Disciples of Christ, 1800–1866," published in 1973. He also wrote *White Sects and Black Men in the Recent South* (1971); *Pat Robertson: A Personal, Religious, and Political Portrait* (1987); and *The Churches of Christ in the Twentieth Century: Homer Hailey's Personal Journey of Faith* (1999).

In addition, Harrell has contributed major articles to numerous journals. He was the senior Fulbright lecturer at the University of Allahabad, India (1976–77). He served as the director of the American Studies Research Centre in Hyderabad, India, as a Distinguished Fulbright appointment (1993–95). In 1985 Harrell was named university scholar in history and chairman of the department at the University of Alabama at Birmingham. In 1990 he joined the history department at Auburn University as the Daniel F. Breeden Eminent Scholar in the Humanities.

■ **Bibliography:** *Who's Who in America* (41st ed., 1980–81).
■ W. E. Warner

HARRIS, LEO CECIL (1920–77). Founder of Christian Revival Crusade in Australia. Son of Cecil Harris, an Apostolic Church pastor who was converted in Perth, Western Australia, under flamboyant South African evangelist, ▸F. B. Van Eyk, Leo Harris turned to the Lord through ▸C. L. Greenwood's preaching at the age of eight and immediately became a fervent evangelist, writing out texts in colored pencil and pasting them on lampposts in the neighborhood.

In 1935, at age 15, Harris was baptized in water and the next year in the Holy Spirit. He preached his first sermon at 19 and was soon shepherding his first church, a small pentecostal congregation in Ipswich, Queensland. After three short pastorates, he undertook itinerant ministry and joined his family in the Assemblies of God (AG). In 1941, in Ballarat, Victoria, Harris was convinced by Thomas Foster to accept

British Israelitism, which resulted in his leaving the AG. He launched a small magazine called *Echoes of Grace*, which later became the *National Revivalist*.

In 1944 Harris formed with a number of independent churches in New Zealand the National Revival Crusade. In early 1945 he felt a call, confirmed by a prophecy, to return to Australia. In September he conducted a series of successful meetings in Adelaide, South Australia, at the invitation of the British Israel World Federation, after which he was persuaded to remain and establish a church. On Nov. 4 he launched the National Revival Crusade in Australia. Three years later he married Belle Davey of Ballarat, Victoria. During the same year, more than 100 people were baptized in the Holy Spirit in the Adelaide meetings.

Meanwhile, Thomas Foster in Melbourne, Victoria, and Leo's father, Cecil, and brother Alan, in Brisbane, Queensland, were holding successful meetings. Other assemblies were started, particularly in Victoria. The emphasis was on a "full kingdom gospel," which combined a pentecostal emphasis on divine healing and the power of the Holy Spirit with a focus on national revival in the light of the "Israel identity."

Originally the new movement was simply a group of local churches in fellowship whose "only constitution" was the Word of God. By 1958, however, a national constitution was adopted by the majority, with some churches in Victoria dissenting and retaining their independence. By the mid 1960s, although still only numbering a few hundred, Harris's congregation was the largest pentecostal church in Australia.

In 1963 the name of the movement was changed to Christian Revival Crusade (CRC). Harris continued to exercise apostolic leadership through his preaching, his input to the growing number of pastors, and his publications. His influence was widespread and resulted in many new congregations. By the time of his death in 1977, there were 65 CRC assemblies in Australia, 8 in New Zealand, and 1 in Papua New Guinea. Twenty years later, the numbers had risen to more than 130 in Australia, more than 350 in Papua New Guinea, and others in Southeast Asia and the Pacific.

Toward the end of his life, Harris's emphasis on British Israelitism diminished markedly, and today it is no longer a CRC distinctive. He made important contributions to Australian pentecostal theology in four main areas: (1) He stressed the autonomy of the local congregation. Harris strongly resisted attempts to centralize denominational organization, though there is evidence that before his death he regretted some aspects of the constitutional structures of the CRC. (2) He taught the authority of Christ and the resultant authority of the believer. In contrast to the early pentecostal emphasis on outward signs of holiness and sanctification, Harris presented a message of grace, freedom, and victory in Christ. (3) He stressed the power of the Word of God to inspire faith. He regularly preached on divine healing and prayed for the sick,

often with significant success. (4) He developed a ministry of exorcism. There was some criticism of this by other pentecostal groups. He himself retreated from his first exaggerated ventures into this area, although the general stance he took is now widespread in Australian pentecostalism.

Harris was generally conservative in his methodology and distanced himself from emotionalism and disorderly phenomena in worship. By the end of his life he was widely esteemed for his integrity, maturity, and apostolic stature as a Christian leader.

■ **Bibliography:** Barry Chant, *Heart of Fire* (1984) ■ Dudley Cooper, *Flames of Revival* (1995) ■ Leo Harris, "Mileposts of Revival," *Impact* (#412, special memorial issue).

■ B. Chant

HARRIS, THORO (1874–1955). Black composer and publisher. A child prodigy whose compositions in the Methodist Holiness style found appreciation among pentecostals, Harris published the first of his several hymnals about 1900. His wide range of musical interests reflected his classical training and acquaintance with the church music tradition. As owner of Windsor Music Company in Chicago, he associated with well-known figures in gospel music, including Peter Bilhorn, James Rowe, and Henry Date. He is remembered for "More Abundantly" (1914), "Jesus Loves the Little Children" (1921), "All That Thrills My Soul Is Jesus" (1931), and "He's Coming Soon" (1944). He composed "Pentecost in My Soul" in 1948.

■ **Bibliography:** C. Brumback, *Suddenly . . . from Heaven* (1961) ■ P. Kerr, *Music in Evangelism* (1962) ■ F. J. Metcalf, *American Writers and Composers of Sacred Music* (1925). ■ E. A. Wilson

HARRISON, ALDA B. (1875–1959). Pioneer leader in the Church of God (CG, Cleveland, TN). The wife of a Presbyterian minister, Harrison was filled with the Holy Spirit in 1908 at the Pleasant Grove, FL, camp meeting. She became zealous in the pentecostal cause but remained faithful to her responsibilities in the Presbyterian Church. She joined the CG in 1911 and began a ministry to its young people.

When Harrison's husband moved to Cleveland, TN, she became active in youth efforts under the name of Bertie Harrison and in 1929 was instrumental in the organization of the Young Peoples Endeavor. That same year, at age 54, she began publication of a youth magazine, *The Lighted Pathway*, and personally financed the project. Until her death in 1959 Mrs. Harrison remained the inspiration of the youth movement and editor emeritus of *The Lighted Pathway*.

■ **Bibliography:** A. Harrison, *Mountain Peaks of Experience* (n.d.). ■ C. W. Conn

HARVEY, ESTHER BRAGG (1891–1986). Missionary to India. Born in Port Huron, MI, Esther Bragg was converted in a Methodist revival as a teenager and later healed of an incurable illness when some pentecostal friends prayed with her. She did mission work in the slums of Port Huron for one year before attending a small Bible school in Norwalk, OH, in 1911. There she received the baptism of the Holy Spirit and was ordained by the school in 1913. She felt a burden to go as a missionary to India and joined a group of missionaries traveling to Nawabganj, India, where she met her future husband. The group arrived on Christmas Day of 1913.

James Harvey, a soldier in the British Army, was stationed at Fazibad, a few miles from Nawabganj in 1909. He was saved on the way to India and soon felt called into missions work. He was able to buy his way out of the army in 1912 and started the mission at Nawabganj. After a short courtship, James Harvey and Esther Bragg were married in Nov. 1914 at a Methodist church in Lucknow. Receiving missionary appointment from the Assemblies of God in 1916, the Harveys established Sharannagar Mission as a home for widows and orphans and a training school for boys. Together they began publication of *Sharannagar News,* which gave testimonies of healing and reports on their mission activities in India.

After James Harvey died suddenly in 1922, the school was renamed the James Harvey Memorial School, and Esther continued to oversee the mission and the school. They had one daughter, Zaida Harvey, who was four years old at her father's death. In 1940 she married Sidney Grimmette, a Bible teacher. But after only eight months of marriage he died of cancer. Thus, they never made it to India. Esther continued alone on the mission field and retired in 1961, returning to the U.S. after 48 years of service in India.

■ **Bibliography:** J. Booze, *Into All the World* (1980) ■ E. B. Harvey, biographical sketch (1961) ■ idem, *The Faithfulness of God* (1945).   ■ G. W. Gohr

HAYFORD, JACK WILLIAMS JR. (1934–). Pastor, composer, author, educator. Hayford was born June 25, 1934, in Los Angeles. At the time of Hayford's birth his parents were not Christians, but they were soon converted at the Long Beach Foursquare Church after their baby son was healed of a serious condition that threatened his life. Hayford contracted polio a year and a half later and was again healed in answer to prayer.

From 1934 to 1938 the Hayfords lived in the Los Angeles area. After brief stays in San Luis Obispo, CA, and Anachondra, MT, the Hayford family moved in 1941 to Oakland, CA, where their young son would spend his childhood and high school years. During the years in Oakland, Hayford attended various times Methodist, Friends, Presbyterian, Foursquare, and Christian Missionary Alliance churches. He dates his conversion to Feb. 25, 1944, when he responded to an altar call at the Oakland Foursquare Church.

At the age of 16, Hayford made a commitment to pursue full-time Christian ministry. Planning to train at Nyack Bible Institute (now Nyack College) in NY, he changed his mind after attending an Oral Roberts Crusade in Oakland and decided to attend the *International Church of the Foursquare Gospel's (ICFG) L.I.F.E. Bible College in Los Angeles. After early graduation from high school, Hayford entered the college in the spring of 1952. At L.I.F.E. Bible College Hayford met Anna Marie Smith, and they married on July 4, 1954. Anna graduated with honors from L.I.F.E. in 1955, and Jack graduated with a B.Th. midterm 1956 as class valedictorian.

In the spring of 1956 Hayford preached and promoted summer youth camps for the Foursquare Great Lakes District of Churches. In June 1956 Hayford began his first pastorate in the Ft. Wayne, IN, Foursquare Church where he stayed four years. The small church the Hayfords founded remained small, never attended by more than 50 people.

Hayford returned to the Los Angeles area in June 1960 to serve as the national youth director for ICFG. In 1965 he accepted the position as dean of students for L.I.F.E. Bible College in Los Angeles, where he served until 1970. It was while serving as dean of students that Hayford was asked to be the interim pastor for a fading Foursquare congregation in Van Nuys, CA. Taking over a congregation of 18 in Mar. 1969, Hayford's ministry has turned the First Foursquare Church of Van Nuys, better known as "The Church on the Way," into one of America's megachurches with a membership of 10,000.

The Church on the Way is located on two separate campuses in the heart of urban Van Nuys in the San Fernando Valley of Los Angeles County. The congregation reflects the multicultural melting pot of Southern California with nine ethnic congregations. With a church staff of 100, The Church on the Way has birthed nearly 300 congregations and outreaches as part of its extension ministries in the last 28 years. The congregations' attendees range from the Hollywood wealthy to the urban poor. The church has a $2 million annual missionary budget that

Jack Hayford, popular speaker, composer, and pastor of the Church on the Way, Van Nuys, CA.

reaches into nearly 100 nations and sends short-term mission teams to 15–20 nations annually.

During the years of service as senior pastor of The Church on the Way, Hayford's ministry has been characterized by balance and integrity. As a communicator, his low-key, often self-effacing style, coupled with theological depth and biblical fidelity, has overcome the stereotype of the pentecostal preacher and contributed to his broad acceptance beyond pentecostal circles. In 1989 Hayford was a plenary speaker for the Lausanne II Congress on World Evangelism, the only pentecostal afforded such an honor. His wide interdenominational influence has allowed him to be a bridge builder between the pentecostal and evangelical sectors of the church. Hayford has served as one of the primary speakers for the Promise Keepers men's stadium events and was the emcee of the 1997 Washington, DC, Promise Keepers "Stand in the Gap" rally, attended by over a million men.

Hayford is a gifted musician and composer and has written over 500 hymns and songs. His composition "Majesty" has been one of the most recorded and used songs in contemporary Christian worship music. He has authored 35 books and served as general editor of *The Spirit-Filled Life Study Bible* and its related publications; his publications have sold more than 2 million copies. Hayford's media ministry distributes over 150,000 audio- and videotapes annually, with well over 3 million in circulation. In addition, his teaching ministry is broadcast on hundreds of radio and television stations.

Besides serving as dean of students at L.I.F.E. Bible College, Hayford taught at the school until 1973. While continuing to pastor The Church on the Way, he returned to the college in 1977 and served as president until 1982. Hayford completed a second bachelor's degree in 1970 from Azusa Pacific University and holds three honorary doctorates. In 1987 Hayford and The Church on the Way founded The King's College to train leaders for Christian service. In Jan. 1999 Hayford founded The King's Seminary as a graduate professional theological school, to "prepare church leadership for the 21st century."

Hayford is known as a pastor to pastors and speaks around the world to 20,000 leaders annually. In 1997, as an expansion of The King's College, Hayford founded the Jack W. Hayford School of Pastoral Nurture to further his mentoring ministry to pastoral leaders.

■ **Bibliography:** B. Anderson and R. McCarter, *25 Years of Silver Service* (1994) ▌ J. W. Hayford, *The Church on the Way* (1982) ▌ idem, *Glory on Your House* (1982) ▌ idem, *A Passion for Fullness* (1990). ■ S. D. Moore

HAYWOOD, GARFIELD THOMAS (1880–1931). Pastor, church executive, and songwriter. Haywood was born to Benjamin and Penny Haywood of Greencastle, IN. The third of nine children, he was reared in a Christian home, attending both Baptist and Methodist churches. When he was three, his parents moved to Indianapolis, where Haywood spent the remainder of his life.

Educated in the public school system in Haughville, Haywood attended through his sophomore year. During his high school years he discovered artistic talents, later selling his abilities as a cartoonist to two black weekly papers, *The Freedman* and *The Recorder*. On Feb. 11, 1902, he married Ida Howard of Owensboro, KY. They had one daughter, Fannie Ann.

News of the pentecostal revival taking place at the Azusa Street Mission arrived in Indianapolis in late 1906. It was largely through the efforts of another black man, Elder Henry Prentiss (who went from Azusa Street to Whittier, CA, where he held open-air meetings) that the scattered "pentecostals" in Indianapolis found a pastor. Henry Prentiss led Haywood into the pentecostal experience and the latter wrote to the *Apostolic Faith* newspaper to share his testimony (July–Aug. 1908, 1).

By the end of 1908 Henry Prentiss had turned the Indianapolis work over to Haywood, who continued on as its pastor. Under his leadership the congregation grew rapidly. Haywood obtained credentials with a small organization in 1911 called the ▸Pentecostal Assemblies of the World

The gifted G. T. Haywood, who as a pastor, denominational leader, composer, and editor was one of the most influential early leaders in the pentecostal movement.

(PAW). Yet his world was much wider, for he ministered in churches and camp meetings and joined in some of the early general councils of the Assemblies of God (AG), which formed in 1914. The fact that he was given the floor in an early council of the Assemblies has led some to speculate that he was a minister with that movement, an assumption that he heartily denied. Yet it does demonstrate how highly his leadership was regarded by that nearly totally white group.

Jan. 1915 was pivotal in Haywood's career; during this time Glenn A. Cook took the message known as the "New Issue," including baptism in Jesus' name, to Indianapolis. At first Haywood was reticent to accept it, but finally he received the message. Warned too late by the AG leader ▸J. Roswell Flower, Haywood was rebaptized in Jesus' name, and his congregation swiftly followed him in his action. He never faltered from that position. Between 1918 and his death on Apr. 12, 1931, G. T. Haywood served as a pastor; as field superintendent; and then — with the reorganization of the PAW in 1919, which he helped to incorporate — as general secretary. In 1922 he became executive vice chairman, and in 1923, secretary. In 1925 he was named presiding bishop when the PAW moved to an episcopal polity.

Haywood's leadership has been described as balanced, visionary, and progressive. He was a prolific writer who often illustrated his own works, e.g., *The Finest of the Wheat* (n.d.), *The Victim of the Flaming Sword* (n.d.), and *Before the Foundation of the World* (1923). He was famous for his charts and paintings, which depicted his theological understanding. Perhaps his most widely acknowledged contribution to pentecostalism was his music, which is still sung in most pentecostal congregations, including those outside the ▸Oneness movement. His spirituality is evident in such songs as "I See a Crimson Stream of Blood" and "Jesus the Son of God."

■ **Bibliography:** P. D. Dugas, compiler, *The Life and Writings of Elder G. T. Haywood* (1968) ■ M. E. Golder, *The Life and Works of Bishop Garfield Thomas Haywood (1880–1931)* (1977) ■ idem, *History of the Pentecostal Assemblies of the World* (1973) ■ C. E. Jones, *Black Holiness: A Guide to the Study of Black Participation in Wesleyan Perfectionist and Glossolalic Pentecostal Movements* (1987).
■ C. M. Robeck Jr.

HEALING, GIFT OF

At both the beginning and the end of his discussion of "manifestations" of the Spirit in 1 Cor. 12, Paul mentions "gifts of healings" (*charimata iamatōn:* 1 Cor. 12:9, 28, 30). These are the only explicit designations of this reality in the NT, but the fact of healing is frequently narrated and described in the Gospels and elsewhere. This article will deal first with a biblical view of healing in general. Then, after a brief consideration of the role of healing in Jesus' ministry and the disciples' ministries, it will proceed to a specific treatment of what is designated by the Pauline phrase "gifts of healings."

1. An Old Testament View of Healing.

Health and sickness are viewed according to the implicit or expressed anthropology of a given culture. (See Martin, 1978, and bibliography given there.) God's successive revelation to the Jews created a prophetic interpretation of reality, which, while refracted through the culture, also acted in turn upon the culture, making of it the vehicle for a revealed understanding of the human condition. The interpretation of health and sickness that we find in the OT is just such a prophetic interpretation of these realities.

a. The Experience of Health and Sickness. It is significant that there is no one word in Hebrew that means "healthy." The state of being healthy is expressed in terms that indicate vigor, life, even "being fat" (*br'*), or simply by *shalom*, which we usually translate as "peace" but which really means the presence in a person, or a relationship, of all that ought to be there. Sickness, on the other hand, is most commonly described in words derived from the root *ḥlh*, which connotes "weakness," "exhaustion," "lacking vitality," etc. The most common way of expressing the recovery of health is through the root *ḥyh*, meaning "life." To be sick is to approach that state of absolute weakness and diminution which is death, while to recover health is to receive life once again. The most awful aspect of sickness is that a human being risks coming to that state where there is no praise of God. For people of the old covenant, that was death: "The grave cannot praise you, death cannot sing your praise.... The living, the living—they praise you, as I am doing today" (Isa. 38:18).

From this point of view it is easy to understand how the "death" Adam was threatened with and that was eventually set loose in the world was linked in the Hebrew mind with sickness. Any loss of vitality indicates a certain separation from God, who is life, just as any recuperation implies a renewal of the divine presence.

In the deeply intuitive and symbolic anthropology of the OT, an experience of sickness is an experience of sin. Thus, prayers for deliverance from sickness always include an avowal of sin (Pss. 38:2–6; 39:9–12; et al.), while praise of God for such deliverance mentions forgiveness (Pss. 30:2–5; 32:1–11; 103:3; et al.). The linking of sickness/death and sin is expressed in the oldest stratum of the Yahwistic tradition now found in Gen. 2 and 3. The placing of this text at the beginning of the Torah by the inspired redactor is one more instance of the theological judgment that proposed a prophetic interpretation of all human suffering. It is not that the OT taught that every sickness was related to a personal sin; it is rather that every sick person was a physical expression of the weakness of the people who were alienated from God. Only God knows the degree of personal culpability. On the same principle, the prophets looked forward to the presence in Zion of a restored and purified people: "No one living in Zion will say, 'I am ill': and the sins of those who dwell there will be forgiven" (Isa. 33:24).

Healing, the restoration to life, is always the work of Yahweh. Asa is condemned because, when he was sick, "he did not seek help from the LORD, but only from the physicians [by implication, magicians]" (2 Chron. 16:12). It was not forbidden, however, to have recourse to those who were skillful in binding up wounds or broken bones as prophetic allusions to these actions indicate (Isa. 1:6; Ezek. 30:21; et al.). The use of herbs and other means of healing were certainly practiced (2 Kings 20:7; Isa. 38:21) and were considered part of wisdom (1 Kings 5:9–14 [Heb.]; Wisd. Sol. 7:20). In the biblical tradition, Sirach (38:1–15) praises the doctor, stating that his wisdom comes from God, that the doctor must also pray to God, and that God has provided healing herbs to be used wisely. The last line of this passage once again links sickness and sin, though the exact tenor of the expression is difficult to interpret.

Oral Roberts praying for the sick during a tent revival.

Throughout the whole history of Israel, including intertestamental times, are instances as well of charismatic healers who have a power from God to restore to life. Even in the pagan world, people instinctively turned to God, as they understood him, for healing and restoration. (For examples of biblical and extrabiblical narratives of such healings, see Martin, 1988.)

b. The Symbolic Understanding of Sickness and Healing. Very early, the OT tradition began to speak of the wholeness of the people when they were faithful to God and the debilitated state that resulted from their sins in terms of health and sickness. This type of predication was facilitated by the symbolic anthropology characteristic of a culture that expressed psychological and spiritual states in terms of the body, especially the eyes, heart, limbs, etc. (see Wolff; Lack).

The Lord's act of rescuing his people from bondage is termed a "healing" in Exod. 15:27 and Hos. 11:3. However, the people's further infidelities resulted in sickness and wounds that only God can heal (Isa. 1:5–7; 6:10; Hos. 5:13; 7:1). He promises to heal their apostasy (Jer. 3:22; Hos. 14:5). The sickness of an individual may be directly related to this illness of the people as in Jer. 17:14, or the link may be more remote, as in Pss. 30:3; 32:1–5. The symbolic use of terms relating to health and sickness is continued in the later tradition of Judaism, both in regard to the nation and to the individual (e.g., 1QH 2:8; CD 12:4; 13:9–10; b. Sanh. 101a; b. Ber. 5a; Mek. Besh. 5; Tg. Jer. 33:6; Tg. Isa. 35:1–6; 61:1–3). We may cite as one example a targumic tosephta found in connection with Gen. 22: "Our sins do not allow us to find healing . . . upon repentance depends our healing" (Grelot, 24). This mentality throws light on sayings of Jesus such as, "It is not the healthy who need a doctor, but the sick. I have not come to call the righteous, but sinners" (Mark 2:17/Luke 5:31–32; cf. Matt. 9:12–13).

2. Healing in the New Testament.

a. The Ministry of Jesus. Jesus responded to the emissaries from John the Baptist by appealing to their own experience that promises such as Isa. 35:5–6 and 61:1 were being fulfilled (Matt. 11:4–6/Luke 7:22–23.) This same view is reflected in texts such as Acts 10:38. Again, in nearly all the statements in the synoptic Gospels that summarize the activity of Jesus, healing is mentioned. Matthew frames his account of the Sermon on the Mount and the first 10 wonders wrought by Jesus with the notice that "he went throughout Galilee, teaching in their synagogues, preaching the good news of the kingdom, and healing every disease and sickness among the people" (Matt. 4:23; see 9:35). This same type of statement is repeated frequently. Some examples are Matt. 4:24–5:2; 8:16–17; 12:15–16; 15:29–31; Mark 1:32–34; 3:7–13; Luke 4:40–41; 6:17–19; et al.

Jesus, by his preaching, by his manner of life in associating with marginalized people (Matt. 9:12–13 par.; Luke 15:1–2), and by his healings and exorcisms manifested the fact that "the kingdom of God is near" (Mark 1:14 par.). The word of the Lord had described a servant, anointed by Yahweh, who would preach the good news to the poor, bind up the brokenhearted, open the eyes of those who had no vision, and comfort those who mourn (Isa. 61:1–2). In applying this promise to himself, Jesus was announcing that in his person the kingdom of God was breaking in (Luke 4:17–21). By healing from disease and casting out demons, Jesus inaugurated the kingdom and embodied it (Matt. 12:28; Luke 11:20).

The importance of this ministry can be seen in the light of the symbolic anthropology described above.

A boy with a crippled leg healed through ministry of Raymond Jimenez, Medellín, Colombia, 1969.

Through healing, Jesus was evidencing the power and compassion of God to free human beings from all aspects of the power of evil. He himself made this explicit at times (Luke 13:16), and this is intensified by the fact that the Gospels may describe someone "demon-possessed" as "healed" by the word of Jesus (see Matt. 15:22–28; cf. Mark 7:25–30; see also Luke 9:42). In addition, the healings worked by Jesus embody and symbolize that healing work by which he will heal the people of their sins and infidelity (Matt. 8:17).

b. The Healing Ministry of the Church. The healing ministry of the church is based on the apostolic commission given to the disciples during Jesus' lifetime: "He called his twelve disciples to him and gave them authority to drive out evil spirits and to heal every disease and sickness.... As you go, preach this message: 'The kingdom of heaven is near.' Heal the sick, raise the dead, cleanse those who have leprosy, drive out demons'" (Matt. 10:1, 7–8; Mark 6:7–12; Luke 9:1–6). It is obvious, then, that healing and deliverance from demonic power are integral parts of evangelization.

We see this principle at work, not only in the summary of the signs that "accompany those who believe" (Mark 16:17) and in such texts as describe the characteristics of an apostle ("signs, wonders, and miracles ... with great perseverance" [2 Cor. 12:12]), but also in the book of Acts where Luke is careful to narrate many instances of healing done by the servants of the Lord. Such actions witness to the resurrection of the Lord Jesus (4:33), and, in the symbolic nature of all Christian healing, witness as well that "Salvation/healing *(sōtēria)* is found in no one else, for there is no other name under heaven given to men by which we must be saved/healed *(sōthē-nai)*" (4:12).

As in the life of Jesus, healing and teaching are considered aspects of one activity, namely, preaching the gospel. In the Gospels are three instances where Matthew records that Jesus healed while, in parallel places, Mark speaks of teaching. Luke, in one of these, mentions both activities (Matt. 14:14/Mark 6:34/Luke 9:11; Matt. 19:2/Mark 10:1; Matt. 21:14/Mark 1:17). In the same way, after Paul had struck Elymas blind, the proconsul who saw what happened "believed, for he was amazed at the teaching about the Lord" (Acts 13:12).

The witness to the resurrection made through healing can take place in the midst of believers, as in the case of Dorcas (Acts 9:36–43) and Eutychus (Acts 20:9–12). However, the primary purpose of healing is to demonstrate tangibly God's intention and ability to lead people to the ultimate salvation, which is eternal life—i.e., the fruit of healing is conversion. This is demonstrated frequently in Acts, as can be seen in Luke's notice concerning belief recorded after a healing or a deliverance. Some examples are Acts 4:4, 31; 5:14–15; 9:35–42.

3. The Gift of Healing.

a. In the Early Community. The only explicit mention of the gift of healing, as has been noted, is found in the discussion in 1 Cor. 12:9, 28, 30 where both terms ("gift" and "healing") are in the plural. This, along with the related expression, "miraculous powers" *(energēmata dynameōn,* 1 Cor. 12:10; see v. 29) is probably meant to evoke the sense of abundance and variety in the gifts that spring from faith. The gifts of healing and of miracles are distinguished because of the particular symbolic power of healing to evidence God's action freeing humankind at every level from bondage to evil and the effects of sin.

Since the charismatic gift of faith is itself a specific intensification of the basic attitude toward God by which we are brought to salvation (▶Faith, Gift of), "gifts of healing" refers to a particular specification of the general power to preach the gospel conferred upon the whole body of believers and realized in different ways within the body.

James 5:13–16 describes an established function in the community whereby someone who is ill or weak *(asthenei)* is to call in the elders, a specific group, who are to anoint him in the name of the Lord. The prayer of faith (cf. 1 Cor. 12:9) will heal/save *(sōsei)* the ill or enervated *(kamnonta)* person, and the Lord will raise him up *(egerei,* undoubted resurrection overtones), and if the person has committed sin (see above, 1.a), it will be forgiven him. This passage does not speak of a *charisma* of healing but of a power in the community of faith expressed through its leaders. On the other hand, 1 Cor. 11:30 speaks of the weakness, sickness, and death that occur when the community does not discern the body of the Lord. This notion of individual health and sickness on every level of human existence being an embodied symbol of the whole community is a matter of experience that finds expression and confirmation in the theological anthropology already begun in the OT.

While it is easy to distinguish the charisma of healing from those healings effected by the Lord through the community's prayer of faith, the same cannot be said for the function of healing that is part of the apostolic commission to preach the gospel. In the first place, the NT restricts its accounts of healing on the part of the disciples to instances involving the well-known preachers of the gospel. We must bear in mind as well that the gifts of healing and of miracles are by their nature manifestations of God's existence and power, and they witness to Jesus. Thus, though Paul seems to have the internal life of the Corinthian community in mind (1 Cor. 12–14), he lauds even prophecy for its capacity to convict and change the unbeliever (1 Cor. 14:24).

In light of the NT presentation of healing, we may draw four conclusions: (1) The preaching of the word is itself sufficient to bring about healings; this is confirmed in modern experience. (2) Those who are sent to preach the gospel are often endowed with the gift of healing as part of their empowerment to bring people to salvation. (3) God works healings through the ministry of the elders and the prayer of faith. (4) There is a specific gift, possessed by some but not by others, that provides for healing both within and outside of the community and, in both instances, witnesses to the power of the resurrection to offset the moral and physical consequences of individual and communal sin. The writings of the early ecclesiastical fathers bear abundant witness to the presence of this gift in their communities (see Kydd).

b. Healing in the Modern Church. God heals in answer to prayer. This is sometimes in the context of the ministry of the elders within a community of faith. God also heals in order to provide an "audio-visual aid" when the gospel is being preached. Finally, God brings about healing through special charismata, and it is to this last manner of healing that we will address a few concluding remarks.

All life, vigor, and strength come to us from our Lord Jesus Christ who, as he now lives "to God," applies the restoring power of his cross to our lives. Healing is a symbolic foreshadowing of the full life to which humankind is called, "our adoptive sonship, the redemption of our bodies" (Rom. 8:23).

As healing takes place within the body of believers, we are given on the level of our existence in this world an unmistakable demonstration of that power "for us who believe," which the Father "exerted in Christ when he raised him from the dead" (see Eph. 1:19–20).

When unbelievers experience healing at the hands of Christians, they are being given a presentation of the Good News, "not simply with words, but also with power, with the Holy Spirit, and with deep conviction" (1 Thess. 1:5). Charismatic gifts of healing are qualities given to certain members of the body in and through which God demonstrates his saving power so that the response of faith will rest "not on men's wisdom, but on God's power" (1 Cor. 2:5).

In every century the Spirit has unceasingly given the gifts needed to build and protect the body of Christ. The challenge particular to the gift of healing is that it can easily be imitated or co-opted by evil powers so that what was once a demonstration of God's Good News can become a source of pride and vainglory, leading both the minister and those to whom he ministers into a state of distraction or even ruin. The possession of this gift, with which certain persons are obviously more highly and permanently endowed than others, is a concretization of God's call to a life of love, humility, and that form of ministry by which one becomes and remains the "servant of all."

"Gifts of healings" are greatly needed in our age. As we become sensitive to the unity of the human person and of the human race, we see how physical healing does more than rectify disorders of the body; it makes God present to the one healed and to all those joined to that person. As our modern

Healed of a curvature of the spine, Ines Margues, a Spanish believer, showing the braces she once needed.

understanding of the psychology of health and sickness expands, we grow to appreciate more profoundly the wisdom of the inspired theological anthropology of the Scriptures, which sees these states as symbolic embodiments of individual and societal alienation from God.

To heal a poor person of the effects of malnutrition is to reverse a process created by the structures of sin of which the person may be an innocent victim. To heal a person of AIDS is to claim the victory of the cross of Christ not only over physical disorder, but also over the very forces of death that lead to eternal ruin. To heal an angry or anxious person of heart disease or cancer is to initiate a process of reconciliation and restoration that derives from the power of the cross. To free someone from Satan's domination, gained through a life exposed to alienation and violence, is to liberate a human memory from the power of evil so that it can generate thoughts and attitudes that correspond to the truth of the gospel and become a temple in which the Father is adored in spirit and truth. In brief, healing is an essential part of preaching the gospel and of bearing witness to the reality and majesty of Jesus Christ.

See also GIFTS OF THE SPIRIT; HEALING IN THE CHRISTIAN CHURCH.

■ **Bibliography:** P. Gelot, "Une tosephta targoumique sur Genèse xxii dans un manuscrit liturgique dans la Geniza du Caire," *RÉJuiv-HJud* 16 (1957): 5–26 ■ R. Kydd, *Charismatic Gifts in the Early Church* (1984) ■ R. Lack, *La Symbolique du Livre d'Isaie* (1973) ■ F. MacNutt, *Healing* (1974) ■ F. Martin, *Narrative Parallels to the New Testament* (1988) ■ idem, "The Charismatic Renewal and Biblical Hermeneutics," in *Theological Reflections on the Charismatic Renewal,* ed. J. Haughey (1978) ■ "Pentecôtisme: Guérison," in M. Viller, ed., *Dictionnaire de spiritualité ascétique et mystique, doctrine et histoire* (1984) ■ J. and P. Sandford, *The Transformation of the Inner Man* (1982) ■ H. W. Wolff, *Anthropology of the Old Testament* (1974).

■ F. Martin

HEALING IN THE CHRISTIAN CHURCH

I. Confrontational
   A. Ante-Nicene Christianity
   B. Johann Christoph Blumhardt (1805–80)
   C. John Wimber (1933–97)

II. Intercessory
   A. Help from Beyond
   B. Brother André (1845–1937)
   C. Mary of Medjugorje

III. Reliquarial
   A. Bones of Blessing: Relics and Healing
   B. The Convulsionaries of St. Médard

IV. Incubational

   A. Männedorf—Place of Mercy
   B. The Message of Morija

V. Revelational
   A. William Branham (1909–65): Prophet of This Age?
   B. Kathryn Kuhlman (1907–76): Handmaiden of the Lord

VI. Soteriological
   A. Oral Roberts (1918–): Quintessential Pentecostal
      1. The First Pole: Certainty
      2. The Second Pole: Sovereignty

VII. Conclusion

German theologian Adolf von Harnack once observed that from the beginning Christianity felt a special responsibility to care for the sick in body. In fact, he said that Christianity was, and is, "a religion for the sick." Sanatoria, hospitals, and clinics permeating those parts of the world most deeply influenced by Christianity support his statement; so do the countless healing ministries that have marked the church throughout its history. The former reflect an approach that emphasizes the application of hard-earned knowledge to find cures for illness; the latter talks about "divine healing," the direct intervention of God to restore health. The two approaches have often been in conflict with each other, but together they have reinforced the image of Christianity as a religion of the sick.

Given what we know of the life of Jesus Christ, the church's concern with sickness ought not to be surprising. Deliverance from disease was a major part of what Jesus did. There are some 30 accounts of healing in the Gospels, involving a large but indefinite number of people. In the gospel of John, however, only 5% of the verses refer to healings. But if one focuses on the part of the Gospel of Mark that deals with only the ministry of Jesus—that is, excludes the accounts of the passion and resurrection—a full 47% of the material is devoted to Christ's healing ministry.

The healings performed by Christ encompassed a wide range of physical problems, as well as problems that were likely emotional in nature and episodes explicitly presented as arising from demonic activity. In all of this, Jesus was responding to a world that had slid into rebellion against God (Gen. 3). Among many passages, Luke 11:14–20 and John 12:31 and 14:30 make it clear that Jesus understood his healing ministry as demonstrating the defeat of Satan and influence of evil in the world. Matt. 8:16–17 serve as a summary statement: "When evening came, many who were demon-possessed were brought to him, and he drove out the spirits with a word and healed all the sick. This was to fulfill what was spoken through the prophet Isaiah: 'He took up our infirmities and carried our diseases.'"

René Latourelle, a Roman Catholic scholar who studied the miraculous in Jesus' ministry, said, "Miracles can be seen to be the visible traces of the radical change that in Jesus Christ affects human beings and the universe in which they dwell." The healings point beyond themselves to what was accomplished by Christ on a larger scale. His fundamental mission was to establish the kingdom of God on earth. This kingdom is neither a place nor a time, but rather a condition or a relationship in which people respond to God's call by focusing on doing what would please and glorify God. They find, in return, that God unstintingly gives himself to them, and this reign of God on earth was repeatedly linked to the miraculous in the gospel accounts (Matt. 4:23–24; 11:4; Mark 1:39).

Inspired by the ministry of Christ, spiritually freed by the grace of God in Christ, and empowered by the Holy Spirit who anointed Christ, the church moved into the world in the name of Christ. A part of what it has done from the beginning until now is serve as a channel for divine healing: God has miraculously restored people to health through the agency of Christians. This healing ministry has taken many forms. In fact, it is likely that a truly comprehensive study of divine healing through the church will never be written. What we are able to learn suggests that much has happened that will remain beyond our reach. It is daunting to contemplate preparing even a list of only contemporary ministries that claim to have a healing component.

However, I would argue that the approaches to healing in the church with which we are familiar can be grouped into six models. I have called them confrontational, intercessory, reliquarial, incubational, revelational, and soteriological. I constructed these models by grouping ministries on the basis of their fundamental thinking and practice in relation to healing. This is one attempt to impose some sort of order upon highly unstructured human experience. Of course, reality is not as neat as these models might suggest.

In fact, the models are not completely exclusive of each other. The healing theologies the various groups developed have not been simple. For example, occasionally one finds an idea of great importance to one group playing a supporting role in another. Referring to basic theological and practical assumptions in the study of Christian healing is useful, but oversimplification is a persistent danger.

Against this background, the study of the history of healing in the Christian church leads to five observations: (1) divine healing has continued throughout the history of the church; (2) the claims of healers and their supports are often overstated; (3) the stereotypical healer does not exist; (4) healing flows out of mystery; (5) healing can never be a proof of doctrinal correctness. These observations will be supported by an examination of the six models I have identified.

I. CONFRONTATIONAL.

This approach to healing is closely allied to the biblical picture of Jesus' ministry. Healing is part of God's shaping of the destiny of the entire universe through sending his Son to establish his reign on earth. This is a direct challenge to evil. Those taking this view insist that the challenge has been successful. The emphasis is on confrontation, victory, liberty, and healing through Christ.

A. Ante-Nicene Christianity.

The story of the church from c. A.D. 100 to c. A.D. 320 is spellbinding. The overall impression is of a lively, confident church, and this is particularly remarkable given the fact that throughout that period the church was constantly subject to persecution. Jesus had come, bringing the kingdom of God, and that kingdom had continued to thrive.

Tertullian, brilliant defender of Christianity in the early 3d century, poured scorn on the entertainment world of his time and described the joys of being a Christian by asking what greater pleasure there could be "than to find yourself trampling underfoot the gods of the Gentiles, expelling demons, effecting cures, seeking revelations, living to God? These are the pleasures, the spectacles of Christians, holy, eternal, and free."

Here is a confident man. I draw attention particularly to his reference to casting out demons and being involved in healings. From Tertullian's point of view, the power of Christ was still very present. Two of Tertullian's approximate contemporaries, Origen in the Middle East and Novatian in Rome, present the same general picture. In terms of the reliability of the reports from these three men, they are probably as trustworthy with regard to healings and exorcisms as they are with reference to other aspects of the life of the church of their time. It is likely that the inferences to be drawn from them are accurate.

The theme of demonic encounters runs through the ante-Nicene literature. Justin Martyr, philosopher turned Christian, writing in the mid 2d century, picked it up, as did Minucius Felix 50 years later, and Tertullian developed it at considerable length beyond the comments cited earlier. He argued that rather than persecuting Christians the Roman authorities should acknowledge their indebtedness for the frequent exorcisms Christians performed on their behalf. Interestingly, Tertullian was writing to living Roman officials. The strength of his argument lay in the fact that his claims could have been readily checked. The same sense of victory is found in Cyprian, Bishop of Carthage, who wrote a generation later than Tertullian. He said, "Yet these [spirits] when adjured by us are forced to go out of the bodies which they have possessed." Elsewhere he stated that demons could not remain in a person in whom the Holy Spirit dwelt through baptism. Another author from later in the 3d century, Lactantius, also supports the concept.

However, there is also another picture that emerges from both Minucius Felix and Cyprian. Both admitted that dealing with the demonic was not always simple. Cyprian pointed to spiritual deceptiveness. He also suggested that exorcisms may be brief or they may be protracted, underlining the determinative role of faith on the part of the sufferer or the degree of grace enjoyed by the healer.

More needs to be said to strengthen the impression left by earlier comments I have cited that physical healings were common. Irenaeus, 2d-century bishop of Lyons, assists here. Embroiled in controversy as he typically was, in his *Against Heresies,* he said:

> Wherefore, also, those who are in truth His [Christ's] disciples, receiving grace from Him, do in His name perform [miracles], so as to promote the welfare of other men, according to the gift which each one has received from Him.... [Some] heal the sick by laying their hands upon them, and they are made whole.

The Apostolic Tradition, reflecting Roman practice of the late 2d century and probably written by the also controversial Hippolytus, outlines procedures to be followed in the ordination of various levels of clergy. The relevant comment is, "If anyone among the laity appears to have received a gift of healing by a revelation, hands shall not be laid on him, because the matter is manifested." In other words, laying on of hands would not augment an ability that had already been made clear. The author appears to have thought that healing would not be a surprising occurrence.

Writing just a little later in his *Contra Censum,* Origen observed bluntly that Christians "perform many cures." He was calling on his detailed knowledge of the church in the Middle East, and he would certainly not discount physical healing as a real feature of Christian experience.

To round out the picture, one must acknowledge that some of these authors claimed to know of resurrections performed by Christians. Tertullian made comments that pointed in that direction, but it is Irenaeus who was most explicit. He said that raising the dead "has been frequently done in the brotherhood on account of some necessity" and elsewhere repeated that "the dead have been raised up, and remained among us for many years." Two mitigating observations may be made. First, in the late 20th century there are frequent references to "near death" experiences in which people who are judged to be clinically dead in fact retain consciousness and subsequently "come back to life." Second, R. C. Finucane has reminded us that people living in antiquity and the Middle Ages often had difficulty in determining who was truly dead.

Finally, it must be noted that the expectations of exorcisms and healings common in the church of the early centuries did not mean that Christian experience was invariably triumphant. In one of his essays entitled *Mortality,* we find Cyprian of Carthage coping with the consequences of a major plague. He was struggling to buttress the faith of his wounded flock.

Among other comments, he suggested that death through disease should be redefined. Anything so powerful as to take persons out of a corrupt and collapsing world and into heaven where family, friends, and apostles await should not be seen as complete tragedy. Although this was not ringing consolation, it may have helped someone. Clearly, Christians were not entirely insulated against the suffering common to humankind.

B. Johann Christoph Blumhardt (1805–80).

Living at a place and time far removed from those living in the ante-Nicenera, but embracing an understanding of divine healing very similar to theirs, is Johann Christoph Blumhardt. This Tübingen-educated Lutheran pastor from southern Germany not only established a reputation as an extraordinary healer, but he impacted Karl Barth to such an extent that the famous Swiss theologian identified him as one of three men whom he called "my mentors."

Blumhardt's healing ministry was set securely in a well-developed theological framework. Primary features of this system were eschatology and pneumatology, but it centered on Christology. The core of Blumhardt's theology was the phrase "Jesus is victor!" and the key scriptural passage was Matt. 12.28: "If I drive out demons by the Spirit of God, then the kingdom of God has come upon you."

For Blumhardt, Jesus had brought the kingdom of God. He had initiated a thoroughgoing spiritual revolution. Exorcisms and healings were proof that the world had come under a new spiritual order. Blumhardt thought that these miracles were reversals of God's original creative process. If God could speak something into existence out of nothingness, then he could just as easily speak something out of existence into nothingness. In this thinking, Blumhardt was at one with Justin, Tertullian, Cyprian, and others. He is a prime example of what I am calling the "confrontational" model of healing. Barth pointed out that Blumhardt's emphasis on the absolute victoriousness of Christ highlighted a concept that had escaped all of his contemporaries inside and outside the church. It was, Barth said, "the content of his own particular perception and confession."

In Blumhardt's case, this unique position is to be traced to an exorcism in which he was involved in 1843. In December of that year Gottlieben Dittus, for whom he had been praying for two years, and her sister, Katharina, were suddenly freed from a demonic presence. The deliverance was marked by Katharina's shrieking, "Jesus is victor! Jesus is victor!" Blumhardt immediately sensed the significance of the events.

The liberation of these women was a microcosmic representation of the all-encompassing work of Christ. Jesus was indeed victor over all manifestations of evil. The rest of Blumhardt's life, and most of that of his son, Christoph, was spent exploring the implications of that lesson.

While differing over significant features of the exorcism, Karl Barth accepted the fundamental interpretation. He said, "Blumhardt realized, in contrast to all older Protestantism and basically to the whole of Western Christendom, that in this name [Jesus] not just a psychic but a historical and even cosmic decision is made, and a question not only of disposition but of power is raised, which all those who confess it must face."

Barth faced that power and acknowledged, with Blumhardt, that Jesus has the capability of dealing conclusively with sin and its consequences.

Blumhardt became famous instantly. People flocked to him in hopes of healing while he developed a procedure to follow that would reflect his theology. It was quiet, calm, and confident. There were no healing services or prayer lines. He did not look for instantaneous healings, and he readily referred people to physicians. During the early period of his healing ministry in particular, the healings seem to have occurred with very little attention being paid to them. Blumhardt wanted to hold them firmly in the context of the church's full message.

In the early 1850s Blumhardt purchased a large residence in Bad Bol, east of Stuttgart, and established a *Kurhaus* (healing center). Once there, healing came very close to being the primary concern, but even then the approach was understated. Confident in Christ's power, Blumhardt created an environment of restfulness and calm. People were invited to come to the *Kurhaus* and stay as long as necessary. Payment was arranged on a sliding scale. Guests were encouraged to participate in the devotional life of the house, and the initiative in prayer for healing was left with them. Blumhardt would remain at table after meals giving people the opportunity to make appointments to meet him privately or in small groups for prayer later. There was a peacefulness to his approach to the problem of pain. He could say to sufferers, "If you are healed, it is from God. If you are not, God will give you strength to bear it." He refused to offer unwarranted assurances. It was God who healed through Jesus. Blumhardt's attitude must have had the effect of summoning people to faith, to the conviction that "Jesus is victor." Verification of claims to healing was an issue for Blumhardt as it has been for all other healers. However, both contemporary witnesses and modern students acknowledge the many reports of physical and psychological cures.

Johann Christoph Blumhardt exercised one of the best-known healing ministries of the 19th century. His emphasis on the victorious nature of the life and ministry of Christ makes him a prime example of the confrontational approach to healing. Beyond that, the fact that the ministry was set in the midst of a comprehensive and clearly articulated theology earns Blumhardt an almost unique position among those known for ministries marked by miracles. In this respect Blumhardt's closest rival might be John Wimber.

C. John Wimber (1933–97).

For almost 15 years ›John Wimber was one of the most controversial figures in North American evangelicalism. His ministry, which developed in California in the 1960s and '70s, began to get attention across the evangelical world in the early 1980s. It was a ministry emphasizing salvation, power, healing, ›exorcism, and an upbeat, soft-rock musical style in worship, and it appealed to the young.

As Wimber became better known, a polarization set in. Among others, biblical scholars Wayne Grudem and Jack Deere and psychiatrist John White joined Wimber's ›Vineyard Christian Fellowship, impressed by what they had seen. On the other hand, John Armstrong, Wallace Benn, Mark Burkill, and Roy Zuck, representative of many, went to considerable lengths to denigrate his work. At the epicenter stood Wimber himself, telling his story with warm humor, fascinating and frustrating evangelicals in the process.

Wimber appears to have been unique within the healing guild in that the results of one of his conferences (Harrogate, England, Nov. 3–6, 1986) were examined carefully by a social anthropologist. David Lewis, who had been a participant in the conference, analyzed 1,890 returned questionnaires and then interviewed 100 randomly selected respondents. Of 867 people who received prayer for physical healing, 32%, or 277, claimed that they had been healed totally or received a high degree of healing. By contrast, 50.5% of those who had requested prayer for emotional problems testified to complete healing, as did 68% of those who had prayed for deliverance from evil spirits. Of the 42% who stated they had received little or no healing, none showed any bitterness toward God or Wimber or gave any evidence of spiritual stress or disenchantment.

The concept of the kingdom of God was central to Wimber's healing ministry. In this respect he sounds much like Blumhardt, Irenaeus, and Tertullian. Jesus brought the rule and reign of God into the world in his incarnation, and it is established wherever people open their hearts to him. The "signs and wonders" to which Wimber made frequent reference serve to demonstrate the superiority of God's power over evil. They also gave birth to Wimber and Kevin Springer's "Power Trilogy"—*Power Evangelism* (1986), *Power Healing* (1987), and *Power Encounters* (1988)—to which *Power Points* was added in 1991. Wimber was definitely a representative of the confrontational model of healing.

Unique to Wimber among those with healing ministries was the degree to which he devoted attention to teaching. He did this orally during his many conferences, but he also used the books just mentioned along with booklets, audio- and videotapes, and a monthly periodical. A wide range of subjects was examined, including salvation, the Christian life, healing, deliverance from demonic activity, and then, in the later years of his ministry, prophecy. He also focused extensively on those who did not receive healing during his meetings, helping them to understand their experience. Perhaps this is why there was so little discontent among them, as noted earlier.

Wimber also showed a high level of concern for social and ethical issues, stating once that healing involved "breaking the hold of poverty and oppressive social structures." The Anaheim Vineyard, Wimber's church, gave hundreds of thousands of dollars to caring for the poor and distributed thousands of meals among the underprivileged. It also worked hard to impress its young people with the Christian responsibility to help those who are less fortunate.

Most striking in his teaching, however, was Wimber's "democratization" of healing. In the cases of most outstanding healing figures, their ministries were tied to them personally. By contrast, John Wimber launched sustained efforts to help as many believers as possible to pray for the sick effectively. He appears to have been concerned to prevent Vineyard's ministry from becoming too closely bound to himself, while at the same time coaching people in healing to a degree that has rarely, if ever, been done. However, it appears that in spite of the stir Wimber caused in charismatic and evangelical circles, he came and went with little impact on the wider society. The kingdom of God played a key role in Wimber's thinking about healing. In his ministry, as in J. C. Blumhardt's and that of much of the early church, there was the assumption that victory over all forms of evil was won by Jesus Christ. This is the foundation of a confident proclamation of healing.

II. INTERCESSORY.

The intercessory model of healing differs dramatically from the one just considered, in which the emphasis is on the victorious work of Christ, which made it possible for people to seek divine healing simply by praying to Jesus in faith. In the intercessory approach, the work of Christ is most definitely assumed, but attention shifts to special people who are commonly called "saints." They are seen as enjoying extraordinary relationships with God for various reasons, and therefore, as being able to influence God favorably on behalf of those who invoke their names. This is very much a "popular" understanding of healing, one that is "of the people." It appeared on the margins of the church, and its most striking examples usually have arisen there, far from the centers of ecclesiastical and political power.

The intercessory model of healing has been remarkably tenacious. It can be found throughout practically the whole history of the church. Taking the wide sweep of the Christian story into consideration, it has been the most common approach to healing, dominant in the Roman Catholic and Orthodox traditions. No comprehensive treatment of the Christian view of divine healing would be credible without taking it seriously.

A. Help from Beyond.

The practice of calling on someone else for help when one needs God's favor is firmly established in Christian practice. The Bible encourages Christians to ask others to pray for them in times of difficulty. Early in Christian experience, people with reputations for spirituality would have been sought out for help. An enigmatic body of material coming from the early Christian centuries helps us understand the dynamics involved.

The material makes up what is known as the New Testament Apocrypha. These documents were modeled after the canonical Gospels and the Acts of the Apostles, but for various reasons they were never judged to be inspired and therefore never became viewed as Scripture. It is the Apocryphal Acts of the Apostles (AAA) that are of particular interest here.

The AAA are full of strange, even bizarre accounts—bed bugs that took orders, dogs that talked—but they give us some sense of what was going on in the minds of ordinary Christians during the time when they were written. They function as a genre of novels, written on the margins of the church, encapsulating the world that "simple" Christians liked to think about and perhaps believed in. One modern commentator calls them "the most important witnesses to the religious ideals of a great part of the Christian race." If that is true, their historical value lies not in the details of their stories, but in what the authors unconsciously reveal about themselves and their readers.

The two most striking groups of protagonists presented in the AAA are apostles and one category of their converts, beautiful, intelligent, and profoundly spiritual women. It is given to the apostles to perform miracles and to the women to withstand persecution for their chastity and their faith. In this context, it is the ministry of the apostles that must occupy us.

The apostles were clearly the "stars" in these novels, and they healed under many circumstances. For example, in Ephesus the apostle John gathered all the women in the city who were elderly and ill into the theater and healed them en masse, igniting faith in the hearts of many. Peter raised a young man from the dead in the context of a contest to demonstrate the superiority of conflicting faiths. Thomas exorcised a demon who had troubled a woman sexually at night for five years, and he also raised a young woman from the dead after her boyfriend had killed her because she would not enter into a pact of chastity with him. In all these cases, the apostles acknowledged that the healing power came from Jesus. However, by the time the AAA were written, the apostles had come to be viewed as people who had lived truly exceptional spiritual lives, and many had become accustomed to associating the marvelous and the miraculous with them. Here is the foundation for the approach to healing that I am calling "intercessory."

The later development of this approach is intriguing. Moving beyond A.D. 320, we note, first, that in the mind of the people, healing powers came to be associated, not only with apostles, but also with other leading personalities. In fact, the most common view of healing became this "popular" view centered on superstars rather than the more Christocentric, official, confrontational understanding held by Christian leaders.

One of the greatest of this cadre of healing heroes was Martin of Tours, who lived in the 4th century. Accounts related to him show him as the agent of healing of many kinds of physical disease and as possessing remarkable exorcistic powers. Significantly, the stories of Martin's healings and exorcisms sound very much like the accounts in the AAA. For example, on occasion, when performing exorcisms, he would lock himself in a church with those who were demon possessed, and then he would lie on the floor and pray. The demons in people would begin to shriek and confess their sins while the people in whom they dwelt would be suspended upside down in midair. Martin's biographer noted their modesty was preserved by their garments remaining in place in spite of their inversion. On another occasion, Martin's name was invoked to silence a barking dog.

A second feature of the development of healing expectations beyond c. 320 is posthumous ministry. People began to believe that the ministries of these extraordinary people were not bounded by death. While on earth the saints led lives that were particularly pleasing to God. Consequently, in death they were perfectly placed in the immediate presence of God to intervene even more effectively on behalf of persons still on earth. The theological foundation for this thinking was provided primarily by Ambrose of Milan (c. 339–397) and John of Damascus (c. 675–c. 749).

The officers of the church, representing the official view of the church, joined their people in embracing this perspective. But that is not all they did. First, from at least the 4th century on, under the leadership of Basil of Caesarea, they became serious about the practice of medicine. Hospitals began to appear near various important centers. Caring for the sick began to occupy an important place beside praying for the sick. Second, they exposed the more popular view to careful analysis. Augustine led the way in this regard. He insisted that martyrs (and saints) should not be worshiped, that commemorating martyrs by holding meals at their graves was questionable, that one ought not to glory in the miraculous, and that miracles are not certificates of doctrinal purity.

When Jesus healed, there was a simplicity about it that carried over into the practice and the thinking of the church up to c. 320. However, beside or beneath that stream was another, which surfaced in the Apocryphal Acts. Ordinary Christians began to think about larger-than-life heroes whose miraculous deeds took on the aura of spectacle. In the AAA this was the apostles, but as this view of healing moved from the margins to the center of the church, the "saints" took their place beside the apostles, and not even death was a barrier. As the church moved into the Middle Ages, the vast majority of Christians assumed that miracles would come through the heavenly intercession of spiritual giants.

B. Brother André (1845–1937).

The same attitude surfaced in Montreal, Que., Canada, in the early 20th century in association with Alfred Bissette, or Brother André, a very ordinary individual. Having joined a religious order in Montreal in 1870, Brother André soon discovered that the sick were frequently enjoying extraordinary healings as a result of his intervention. Word of this began to spread; one miraculous account led to another; a flood of troubled people began to seek him out; one decision led to another, and by the time of his death a massive oratory was under construction on a wooded mountain in the center of Montreal. It would become a testimony to not only the many cures people attributed to Brother André's intervention, but to the impact he would have on the whole of Quebec culture.

Brother André was an intensely devout man. Central to his healing ministry was a conviction that wove him securely into the fabric of Quebec society—the intercession of St. Joseph could result in miraculous cures. St. Joseph had been proclaimed the patron saint of Canada in 1624 and of the entire Roman Catholic Church in 1870. Brother André was profoundly convinced of the effectiveness of this great saint's intervention. This is seen in the naming of the oratory built by his followers in honor of St. Joseph and in Brother André's use in his healing ministry of medals of St. Joseph and of oil taken from a lamp burning before a statue of St. Joseph.

The movement that grew up around Brother André, and that achieved concrete expression in the oratory (completed in 1967 at a final cost of $10 million), was built on the miraculous. No complete count of miracles seems possible. Testimony to 125 was received during the process leading up to Brother André's beatification in 1982, but the claims number into the thousands. One account is particularly interesting:

There were many eyewitnesses of the following signal wonder. A large contingent of American visitors had thronged round the doors of the office all morning. At dinner-time, Brother André returned to the rectory. He was already mounting the steps under the eyes of hundreds of pilgrims, when a man went up the steps to stop him and to show him, through the open doors of an ambulance that had forced its way amid the tumultuous crowd, a man lying on a stretcher. "Untie him and let him walk," said the Brother simply, and went on into the house without further ado. The sick man got up and walked barefooted through the madly enthusiastic crowd.

The account is useful for a number of reasons. It certainly provides a sense of what life at the oratory was like—the surging crowds, the joyous response to healing. We have no information about the actual condition from which the man suffered, but it would appear that it was serious. It also shows Brother André acting on certain knowledge that the man would be healed. He did not even wait to see what happened.

It appears that Brother André's life of prayer and devotion led him to attribute the miracles he saw to God. He repeatedly used the expression "the good God" in reference to God. However, he could also refer to the miracles as the results of the intercession of saints. Those who came to the oratory were convinced of Brother André's own effectiveness as an intercessor, but he routinely tried to divert attention to St. Joseph—"I do not cure; St. Joseph cures." He could also bring Joseph and Mary together in his thinking, saying, "When the Virgin Mary and Saint Joseph intercede together, *that pushes hard!*" (his emphasis).

There remain many questions to be asked about Brother André and St. Joseph's Oratory. Nevertheless, tourists still flock to it, and he still commands the devotion of hundreds of thousands. He is seen as a special friend of St. Joseph and of "the good God," who can speak effectively on their behalf. Occupying this role, Brother André is a prime example of the intercessory approach to healing.

C. Mary of Medjugorje.

Events occurring on a somewhat barren Bosnian plateau also illustrate the intercessory approach to healing. Since June 1981 it has been claimed that the Virgin Mary has appeared for longer or shorter periods (from just under a minute to just under an hour) to six people, in the case of three of them, every day until now (May 13, 1999). The alleged apparitions of Medjugorje have been the source of deep controversy in the Roman Catholic Church, but they have also gathered intense support. Millions of pilgrims have made the difficult trip to this Bosnian village, and the phenomenon is served by numerous web sites. Apparitions and reports of the sun seen bouncing around the sky aside, what interests us here are the reports of healings.

Miraculous healings have been part of the Medjugorjean picture from the beginning. Initially the "visionaries" would join priests after their daily apparition and pray with the laying on of hands for pilgrims who had needs. The procedure has evolved over the years, but ministry to the sick continues. The literature on Medjugorje carries many accounts of healings, and they continue to be posted on web sites today. Here, by way of illustration, is a case that involved a woman from Houston, TX. Fr. Philip Pavic gave me a copy of the file, which her family brought to Medjugorje after her healing. As a child the woman was diagnosed with myasthenia gravis,

a terminal neuromuscular disorder related to muscular dystrophy. In Nov. 1988 this young woman and her mother visited Medjugorje. During her pilgrimage, the woman came to believe she had been healed, and she discontinued her medication. When she was examined by her physician, the head of research at an institution specializing in muscular dystrophy, later that month, he confirmed her claim to healing. In the transcript of the interview, he said in part, "It's a miracle! What can I say. I'm delighted. It's a miracle."

At Medjugorje, the dominant idea about healing has been Mary's role as intercessor. One of the visionaries said that she and the others began to lay hands on the sick and pray for them because "that is part of Our Lady's message. She has often spoken of it." A priest who has been involved over the years described the procedure that was followed at one time, saying, "The evening service ends with a prayer for the sick. Many pilgrims are always on hand—some have come from the most distant places—to ask the Mother of God to intercede for them in their illnesses, asking God to heal or comfort them."

Medjugorje is still somewhat of a conundrum for the Catholic Church. There still has been no official position on the nature of the apparitions. However, the claims to the miraculous continue to mount, and the documentation supporting some of them is rather impressive. Medjugorje demonstrates that a model of healing that surfaced in the 2d century is still present among Christians at the end of the second millennium.

III. RELIQUARIAL.

A. Bones of Blessing: Relics and Healing.

Having noted that evidence for the first two models of Christian healing appeared in the early centuries of the life of the church, we turn to a third, which also surfaced then. This is the reliquarial model; the name is derived from the word *relic*. Relics can be understood as remains of saints' bodies, objects used by saints (e.g., clothing), or anything that touched saints' remains or even their tombs.

For approximately 1,000 years relics were viewed with great respect. Beginning sometime in the 3d century, as a result of popular acclaim, the church began to move toward formal inclusion of these objects in its worship. In the 8th century the Council of Nicaea (A.D. 787) and then Emperor Charlemagne elevated their liturgical and official importance.

The passage of time saw their significance increase. The insatiable thirst for relics created an atmosphere in which networks developed through which relics were "mined" in cemeteries in Rome and shipped to eager markets in northern Europe. Shrines in which some of these relics were lodged became popular destinations for pilgrims. Competition arose among some of the shrines, and raiding parties determined to steal particularly valuable relics from someone else's shrine were not uncommon.

Throughout the centuries theologians struggled to shape the devotion to relics, but they met with little success. The dilemma they faced was how to endorse the sanctity of relics and the intervention of the saints, which enjoyed such popular acclaim, without condoning attendant excesses, which could become extraordinarily bizarre. However, over the last two centuries the dilemma has evaporated. The picture has changed dramatically and interest in relics has declined sharply. It would appear that the wave of popular support, which carried them to a high water mark in the 10th century, broke up under pressure from changing societal forces.

The question remains, what made relics so important for so long over so large a geographical area? The primary answer is the miracles that were associated with them.

Ambrose, 4th-century bishop of Milan, had much to say about relics and miracles. Two bodies were exhumed and identified as those of martyrs Gervasius and Protasius. In an excited sermon, he compared what happened thereafter to what happened in the days when Christ walked on earth. With an allusion to the book of Acts, he referred to people who had been healed by the shadow of the bodies of the saints.

The next day, while preaching another sermon, Ambrose made reference to a healing of a blind man named Severus. Ambrose reported, "He cried out, saying that when he touched the hem of the martyrs' garment in which the sacred relics were covered, light was restored to him." The recovery was attributed to direct contact with the relic. This pattern occurs repeatedly in accounts of healing related to relics.

Augustine, famous bishop of Hippo, was also interested in the reliquarial approach to healing. In countering the suggestion that miracles were no longer occurring in his time, he said, "The truth is that even today miracles are being wrought in the name of Christ, sometimes through His sacraments and sometimes through the intercession of the relics of his saints." Later he added,

If I kept merely to miracles of healing and omitted all others, and if I told only those wrought by this one martyr, the glorious St. Stephen, and if I limited myself to those that happened here at Hippo and Calama, I should have to fill several volumes and, even then, I could do no more than tell those cases that have been officially recorded and attested for public reading in our churches.

This recording and attesting, in fact, is what I took care to have done, once I realized how many miracles were occurring in our own day and which were so like the miracles of old and also how wrong it would be to allow the memory of these marvels of divine power to perish from among our people. It is only two years ago that the keeping of records was begun here in Hippo, and already, at this writing, we have nearly 70 attested miracles.

Augustine did not specify the process of attestation, but it is clear that he was convinced that some effort was being made at verification and that many unusual events were taking place. Further on in the same chapter he summed up his discussion by commenting, "It is a simple fact, then, that there is no lack of miracles even in our day"—words that loom large, coming as they do from one of the great spirits and minds of the 4th and 5th centuries.

However, before accepting comments like these, even from Augustine, one must remember that his evidence would be shaped by the level of medical knowledge current at the time. They would have had some idea of what health and illness actually are, what particular symptoms mean, what degree of illness is present, what the prognoses of particular illnesses are, and what would constitute recovery. However, judged by modern medical standards, Augustine and his contemporaries obviously would have lacked the knowledge required to make accurate medical pronouncements on all of these. As a result, when viewed from our perspective, his evidence would be seriously compromised. Nevertheless, in some cases, such as the recovery of sight mentioned by Ambrose, they might have had a greater chance to identify something truly unusual.

B. The Convulsionaries of St. Médard.

The six-month period between July 1731 and Jan. 1732 produced one of the most extraordinary phenomena in Christian history—the convulsionaries of St. Médard. This movement sprang up in a small cemetery in a working-class quarter of Paris, closely connected to the life and death of an ascetic young deacon, François de Pâris. Through him it flowed into the extremely convoluted ecclesio-political world of 18th-century France.

De Pâris was a Jansenist. This was a group within the Roman Catholic Church that followed the teaching of Cornelius Jansen in giving ideas drawn from St. Augustine a much larger place in Catholic theology than the church was prepared to grant. Jansen's work was condemned as heretical in the 17th century. In the 18th century, Jansenism in France became intertwined with "Gallicanism," a party that was convinced that the French church could govern its own affairs in most matters without reference to Rome. In 1713 Jansenism was again declared heretical; this brought many who were also "Gallicans" into opposition not only to Rome, but also to Louis XIV, the king of France. This was the context in which François de Pâris lived and worked, acquiring a reputation for great holiness.

Shortly after De Pâris's death on May 1, 1727, reports began to circulate of miracles that occurred at his tomb. Many from all classes in society began to travel to the cemetery in hopes of cures. But more importantly, these miracles at the Jansenist deacon's tomb began to be promoted as proof of the correctness of both Jansenism and Gallicanism. De Pâris was launching his most effective political/theological argument posthumously.

In the summer of 1731, events in the cemetery took a surprising twist. A young woman who was placed on the tomb fell into violent seizures. When they stopped, she discovered she had received a complete healing. For the next six months convulsions were a major part of the experience of St. Médard.

Conditions in the cemetery became chaotic, and life in St. Médard virtually came to a halt as thousands plugged narrow streets, flocking to the grave of François de Pâris. In addition, De Pâris's reputation for sanctity grew. In Jan. 1732, to get control of the chaos and to minimize the damage caused by devotion to De Pâris, Louis XV closed the cemetery. The Convulsionaries became a strong underground movement, but soon the Jansenists began to distance themselves, as the extremism of the convulsions became a political liability.

The Convulsionaries are certainly one of the most exotic of Christian healing groups, and they are firmly reliquarial. The miracles for which evidence exists all occurred before the convulsions broke out, and the body of material is impressive. Between June 22, 1728, and Apr. 12, 1729, a theologian from the Sorbonne, working with the authorization of the archbishop of Paris, gathered 61 pages of carefully notarized testimony. Further evidence is found in a document submitted to the parliament in Paris by a group of clergymen in 1734. It relates to a healing claimed by Pierre Lero in 1727.

Being unable to find a cure for a severely ulcerated left leg, Lero had gone to St. Médard. A mass had been said for his healing, a woman had prayed over him, and, most significantly in the eyes of those submitting this document, a small piece of wood from De Pâris's bed was placed on his leg. Within a month his healing was complete.

This use of relics related to De Pâris was the most common feature of the miracles attributed to him. People took dirt from his grave and water from the well in the yard behind the house in which he had lived. And, of course, they clamored to touch his grave. All of these were believed to have the power to perform miracles, having been energized by the sanctity of De Pâris himself.

Events that occurred in that unpretentious quarter of Paris in the 1730s are disturbing. Certainly there is no way of determining precisely what happened in that cemetery. In fact, police stood guard, noting who came and went, but the level of disorder reached such proportions that they could not have kept track of even those developments which they could have understood. However, one historian was prepared to say, "Orthodox defenders of the faith [opponents of Jansenism and Gallicanism] had been greatly embarrassed and unsettled by the amazingly strong evidence supporting the miraculous character of many of the Paris cures"—support for the effectiveness of the reliquarial approach to healing. Perhaps in the midst of anomalies and enigmas, there were healings as well.

IV. INCUBATIONAL.

The next approach to healing is quite different from the first three. With the exception of the late Blumhardt, the accounts have implied, if not explicitly stated, that healings would typically be instantaneous. Furthermore, it has been assumed that healing flows through the agent of healing, whether personally or posthumously, whether by touch, by extension of power to objects, or by intervention. The healer stands between the source of healing and the recipient of healing. There is also a particular aura surrounding ministries where the first three approaches were dominant. It is characterized by urgency, intense emotion, and varying degrees of frenetic disorder. Most of this changes when one focuses on ministries that adopted what I call an "incubational" approach.

An incubator provides a supportive, safe environment. It is that environment that marks the next two healing ministries to be considered. The emphasis is on prayer and patience, and it results in a sense of calmness and peace. Both examples of this model come from Switzerland.

A. Männedorf—Place of Mercy.

Like St. Joseph's Oratory in Montreal, The Elim Institution in Männedorf, Switzerland, grew up around a very unpretentious person. In the case of Elim, it was Dorothea Trudel (1813–62). Having seen five men who worked in a nephew's business healed after she had prayed in 1850, Trudel found herself sought out by many who were ill. She welcomed all comers, rooting her ministry in prayer. Many passages of Scripture were used as various leaders of Elim interpreted their ministry, but the favorite for Trudel and the others was James 5:14–15.

Elim has had a challenging history. Three times in the first two decades of its life the Department of Health of the Canton of Zurich attempted to shut it down. The concern was over the lack of medical supervision in an institution that was very much like a hospital and dealt with severe mental disorders, sometimes using various restraints. On all three occasions Elim won its case, arguing from biblical passages such as James 5:14–15 and pointing out that physicians were making referrals, that people knew the nature of Elim's ministry before they came, and that there were cures. It was permitted to carry on.

The same concerns led to further action in 1900, however, and this time with success. Restrictions came into effect on July 1, 1901, forbidding Elim to admit the mentally ill. This had significant implications for Elim insofar as mental illness had been one of the primary focuses of the ministry from the outset. The redefinition this action required was one of the factors that moved Elim toward becoming the retreat center and senior residence it is now.

The two dominant characteristics of Elim's ministry were prayer and patience. Trudel set the tone for both. Motivated by passages like James 5:14–15, she set herself to pray. She would often sleep beside seriously ill women so she could pray for them through the night. During her four-times-daily Bible studies, she would have those in special need of prayer placed on each side of her so she could lay hands on both as she spoke. This commitment to prayer became a hallmark of Elim.

However, patience was probably the dominant feature. Elim was willing to accept that there may be a time lapse before a person who has been prayed for will be healed. The other healing ministries, with the exception of the later Blumhardt, were more likely to assume that healing would be instantaneous. Those who reported on the healings that occurred at Elim often pointed out that those healed had been at Elim for extended periods. The task of the staff at Elim was to pray for people and to provide a safe environment for them until they got better. One leader, writing in 1944, said that people had been at Elim for from 14 days to four and a half months before they were healed.

The testimonies about healing were strong. Of course there are problems with inadequate diagnoses, with imprecise observations with regard to recoveries, and with the lack of medical certification, but some of the claims are impressive. In a list sent to Cantonal authorities giving the names of people at Elim who suffered from various mental disorders, one leader mentioned a woman from Strasbourg. He said that she had been delirious and had been the worst case a doctor in Bern had dealt with in 19 years—"now healed." We have only this leader's word for it, but he was making the claim before scrupulous government officials. He must have been trying to be accurate, knowing that claims could be investigated.

August Bachtold (1838–1912) adds further information. He had studied theology at Basel and Tübingen, pastored a church, engaged in historical research, and ended life as an archivist. He himself received a healing (of what he does not say) while spending seven weeks at Elim. He also saw others gradually improve until they were well. He insisted that these were real healings. It would be difficult, if not impossible, to verify these claims of miraculous healings now. However, they most certainly carried weight for those who heard the reports initially.

Trudel responded to the sick in her own way, forging an approach that was truly incubational. She struggled to create a warm, supportive environment in which people could focus attention on God until such time as specific needs were met. It was this patience that gave Elim its distinctive atmosphere.

B. The Message of Morija.

"Healing . . . is rarely instantaneous. It is the fruit of persevering prayer." These words, from one of the three founders of Morija (Moriah), catches the character of their ministry. Morija and La Fraternité Chrétienne (The Christian Fraternity), which grew out of it, were founded in 1936 by Charles and Blanche de Siebenthal and Marguerite Chapuis. Morija's mission was clearly defined. Charles wrote, "The house of prayer and faith of the Christian Fraternity is open to all, without exception, for healing prayer, spiritual retreat, rest, the battle of faith, and exorcism. For everyone, it is called 'Morija,' that is, 'Chosen by the Eternal One.'" When founding Morija, the De Siebenthals and Chapuis determined that it should be a faith ministry without any regular source of income.

Over the six years after its establishment, Morija grew slowly. For an extended period the little band met early in the morning, out-of-doors in the woods. In 1942 it found a permanent home in Yverdon-les-Bains, Switzerland, and 30 years later it undertook an ambitious building program, which created an attractive complex of buildings.

As the ministry grew, Charles de Siebenthal insisted that its central concern was evangelism. However, it would be hard to argue with the claim that healing through prayer has been the dominant feature of Morija. The founders made clear that the root of this emphasis is Jesus: "He is the same yesterday, today, and forever." At the center of their commitment to healing was the belief in persevering prayer. One longtime staff member insisted that the key to Morija is determined, unrelenting prayer. The basic principle is simple: identify a need and then pray for it until God obviously responds.

People who want help are welcome to come and stay at Morija. Once they get there, they are encouraged to participate in the daily devotional periods, and they are prayed for repeatedly. James 5:13–16 serves as a kind of motto for Morija, understood as teaching the practice of persevering prayer.

This approach to praying for the sick works itself out in a distinctive organizational feature of Morija: the circle of prayer. Charles de Siebenthal thought the circle of prayer was of crucial importance to the life of the ministry, and another leader called it the Christian Fraternity's backbone. This group is made up of men and women who feel they are called to a ministry of intercession, and they respond to that call by making a vow to be faithful to that ministry. The circle of 20 to 25 people meets from 6 to 7 A.M. four days per week. This group has a history of taking prayer very seriously. On one occasion it prayed for 40 hours without a break for a person who was experiencing episodes of insanity. The result was a dramatic healing.

Many reports of healings are associated with Morija, but all are anecdotal. As a point of policy, Morija has never kept guest registrations, so there is no permanent record of who has come to Morija or for what reason. There are no medical diagnoses of illnesses. The testimonies of people claiming to have been healed refer to a wide range of problems: spinal injuries, intestinal disorders, epilepsy, blood clots, emotional illness, and demon possession.

One staff person I interviewed told of a woman who came to Morija suffering from depression. The staff member received a vision of the woman encased in a block of ice. She realized that she was being shown that prayer would remove the depression just as sun melts ice. For more than a year, those engaged in the ministry of prayer prayed continuously for the woman, and deliverance finally came. Accounts like this abound.

However, those working at Morija are not naïve. They acknowledge that not everyone is healed. Charles de Siebenthal taught that real life is to be found in the realm of the spiritual, not in material pleasure or riches, or even in perfect health. Prayer always overcomes evil, but it does not necessarily remove suffering. The goal of prayer is not to get things, but "to obtain God, himself."

Morija has many interesting features. One is the role played by women. Two of the three original leaders were female, and much of the ministry now is being carried out by a small group of older women living in residence and willingly drawing small salaries. Another is the predominant atmosphere of Morija: quiet orderliness. It is unruffled and unrushed. People really seem to believe that God is in control and that God can be trusted. The most striking feature is the emphasis on persevering prayer. "Healing ... is rarely instantaneous," but while waiting for God to heal, Morija wraps its guests in warm incubational safety.

V. REVELATIONAL.

This fifth approach to healing is much more like the first three approaches than like the previous one. Practitioners of the revelational approach came to expect that God would give them special knowledge. He would show them what needs were present or who was being healed. This is the revelational approach to healing. God reveals information upon which the healer can act.

A. William Branham (1909–65): Prophet of This Age?

Mystery, conundrum, enigma—the words all apply to William Marrion Branham. He was born in poverty, he died in controversy, and his name is known around the world. He launched a healing ministry in the U.S. in 1946 and within two years was internationally famous. He was gentle and harsh, humble and paranoid. Assessments of his life picture him as a specially appointed prophet to this age and as a mouthpiece of Satan.

Branham developed a wildly fanciful interpretation of church history, and he unleashed a withering attack on modern women. He appears to have introduced the concept of the "Serpent's Seed," an expression he applied to the descendants of Cain, who, he believed, had been conceived through

sexual intercourse between Eve and the serpent in the Garden of Eden. These people are particularly susceptible to sin. Branham thought this group was made up of doctors, lawyers, architects, and scientists. He also claimed that the West Coast would slide into the ocean, the rest of the country would be destroyed by a great explosion, and the Millennium would begin in 1977.

Branham was propelled toward his healing ministry by a remarkable vision he received on May 7, 1946. At 11 P.M. the darkened room in which he had been praying began to fill with light, and through the light a being stepped toward him. Sensing that Branham was terrified, the being said,

> Fear not. I am sent from the presence of Almighty God to tell you that your peculiar life and your misunderstood ways have been to indicate that God has sent you to take a gift of divine healing to the peoples of the world. IF YOU WILL BE SINCERE, AND CAN GET THE PEOPLE TO BELIEVE YOU, NOTHING SHALL STAND BEFORE YOUR PRAYER, NOT EVEN CANCER. (emphasis his)

Branham's work as a healer began shortly after this vision and continued until his death in 1965 as a result of a car accident. He was an innovator, employing practices that other healers would copy. Three features of his work, however, were unique to him, and all three were revelatory in nature.

The first of these were vibrations in his left hand. The angel who came to him in 1946 called this the "first pull," as in a fish pulling on a line, an image that would appeal to the outdoors man in Branham. These vibrations came as he held a hand of the sick person who came to him and enabled him

A 1948 Kansas City meeting bringing together two of the most prominent names in the salvation-healing movement, William Branham and Oral Roberts. (Left to right) Young Brown, Jack Moore, Branham, Roberts, and Gordon Lindsay.

to identify the source of the illness, that is, which spirit was behind the illness, because Branham believed that all illness and accidents were caused by evil spirits. Branham thought that the primary purpose of the vibrations was the arousing of faith in the person who came for healing rather than the actual conveying of information.

The second feature, or "pull," was Branham's "gift of ▸discernment," which came in 1949. In describing it he said, "You all know that this gift in my life is supernatural. It is a gift whereby the Holy Spirit is able to discern diseases, and thoughts of men's hearts, and other hidden things that only God could know and then reveal to me." Branham did not believe that this was like a "gift of the Spirit" that other Christians might use. He identified it with Jesus' ability to know what was in people's hearts, and he thought that its use was limited to one person in each generation. He insisted that he was absolutely passive when this gift was in operation. As a person came up to him, he would begin to see things related to him or her above them, and he would simply tell what he saw. Again, he thought the revelations were for the purpose of building faith in people. As people approached him on the platform, he would ask if they would believe that Jesus could heal them if he could reveal information about them which he could not know without divine help. Inevitably, they would say yes. He then would give the revelation and pronounce them healed, sometimes without ever touching them. ▸Walter Hollenweger, who interpreted for Branham in Europe in the 1950s, attested that he did not know of a case in which the information Branham gave was wrong.

The angel also spoke of a "third pull," but Branham never gave any indication of what it was. The third unique feature of his ministry, however, was his dependence on an angel. He did not talk about this celestial being with any consistency, but throughout the years of his greatest success he demonstrated extreme dependence on the angel's presence. He would not turn to address those coming for prayer until he was convinced the angel was with him. He relied on the angel to tell him about the people who were approaching.

It is impossible to know how many people were actually healed in Branham's meetings. The procedure he followed precluded verification. A number of people were ushered onto the platform each night. He talked to some, prayed for some, laid hands on some, and sent some on their way, telling them to go rejoicing because they were healed. There is no record of any consistent follow-up after people crossed the platform.

The sheer power of the meetings inclined people to believe everything Branham said, including all of his pronouncements of healing. Nevertheless, some independent attempts to measure Branham's success present a very different picture. Two reports claim that many who were pronounced healed in fact died of their diseases. Another

authority insisted that only a small percentage of those who sought healing actually benefited.

Whatever the accuracy of Branham's claims regarding healing, he did play an important role in 20th-century religious life. He did much to foster a widespread expectation that God could be counted on to heal miraculously.

B. Kathryn Kuhlman (1907–76): Handmaiden of the Lord.

The second example of the revelational approach to healing differs dramatically from the first. Born in Missouri, ▸Kathryn Kuhlman went into evangelism in the U.S. in 1928. After traumatic events in her personal life, she found herself near Pittsburgh with a healing ministry in 1947. She rose to fame rapidly, established another base in California, went on radio and television, and became the leading proponent of healing evangelism in the 1960s, a position she retained until her death.

The most outstanding feature of Kuhlman's ministry was her insistence on absolute dependence on the Holy Spirit. This emphasis appears to have been unique among those with healing ministries. No one before Kuhlman had highlighted the importance of the role the Holy Spirit played in healing to the degree to which she did. She insisted that she had nothing whatsoever to do with the apparent healings. Her explanation was that God performed the miracles according to his purposes and plans about which she knew absolutely nothing. The Holy Spirit then revealed to her what God had done, hence the categorization of her ministry as revelational. Her role was simply to serve as a "handmaiden," announcing what the Holy Spirit had shown her. Kuhlman's sense of dependence on the Holy Spirit was such that, similar to Branham, she would not start a "miracle service," as she called them, until she was sure she felt the "anointing" of the Spirit. The Holy Spirit was carrying on the ministry of Jesus. Regarding her services, she could say, "The Presence of the Holy Spirit has been in such abundance that by His Presence alone, sick bodies are healed, even as people wait on the outside of the building for the doors to open."

Along with many others who have had healing ministries, Kuhlman emphasized the importance of faith to healing—without it there could be no healing—but her concept of faith was much different from that of many of the others. She taught that it was something that had to be given. "Faith is not a condition of the mind. It is a divinely imparted grace to the heart." It could not be humanly generated. From here it was a short step to the most fundamental point in her healing theology: "Healing is the sovereign act of God." The responsibility for healing rests entirely with God. Humans are only his servants, helping people accept what he does.

Interestingly, Kuhlman insisted that her understanding of divine healing came exclusively from her study of the Bible and from the Holy Spirit. In fact, it is likely that she was dependent for some of her insights on ▸A. B. Simpson and ▸Aimee Semple McPherson, with their thinking being mediated through Bible schools, which she attended for short periods in the 1920s. In addition to that, her understanding of faith is remarkably similar to views held earlier by ▸Charles S. Price. In fact, in several places her vocabulary and style are so close to his that it is probable that she was borrowing from him. Why she may have suppressed this dependence is difficult to determine.

The way this theology played out in actual "miracle services" is important to note. Following the ministry of music in a service, Kuhlman would preach, emphasizing the love and faithfulness of God and encouraging people to believe in him. At least one observer has suggested that she was really preaching to herself, preparing herself to meet the demands for faith that would come later. Then, under a sense of the anointing, she would begin to announce what the Holy Spirit showed her, e.g., "Someone in the balcony just had a deaf ear opened." She would then invite whoever had received that healing to come to the platform. When the person arrived, she would help her or him share this experience with the congregation. She was an encourager and a servant, reminding people of what God could do and then announcing to them what he had done.

Kuhlman was very conscious of the need to verify miracle claims. More than any other person who had a healing ministry, she was open to medical scrutiny. She did receive negative evaluations, and again the procedure she followed got in the way of comprehensive analysis. However, most of the physicians who commented on her work were prepared to state that actual miracles had occurred. In addition to this, one of her biographers pointed out that she was very careful about what she published. She laid down a set of stringent criteria a report of a healing had to meet before it made its way into one of her books.

Numerous detailed reports of healings are available, some complete with the names of physicians who could provide certification. I contacted a woman living in Canada who had been healed of multiple sclerosis in a 1969 Pittsburgh meeting. Between then and 1995 when I interviewed her, she had experienced no recurrence of the disease. There is no way of determining what proportion of people claiming healings in Kuhlman's services were actually healed, but extraordinary things genuinely did occur.

VI. SOTERIOLOGICAL.

The last model of healing arose in the United States during the last century, championed by Episcopalians, Presbyterians, and Baptists, among others, who shared what we would call a basically evangelical theological perspective. They taught that people can be miraculously cured through the same means by which they become Christians, that is, through the atoning work of Christ. Their key idea was "healing is in the atonement." In other words, they located the attack on illness within the doctrine of salvation (soteriology). One of the proponents of this view, R. Kelso Carter, said, "the Atonement provided for the body all that it provided for the soul." The general tenor of this approach is propositional. If one could accept a particular theological concept, one could be healed. It reflects the Reformed emphasis on a rational approach to the Word.

Here the idea that healing has a soteriological base will be examined through the 20th-century tradition that has emphasized it most strongly—pentecostalism. Speaking in tongues is perhaps the most widely recognized hallmark of pentecostalism, but an emphasis on healing has also been very important right from the beginning of the movement's life early in the first decade of this century. Our window through which to view pentecostal healing will be Oral Roberts.

A. Oral Roberts (1918–): Quintessential Pentecostal.

▸Oral Roberts erupted into a healing ministry in May 1947 and kept campaigning until Dec. 1968. His services were characterized by huge tents, massive crowds, and tremendous energy. In one evening he laid hands on 9,300 people as they filed past in healing lines. He was the archetypical pentecostal healing evangelist, and he served as a model for countless other pentecostals who never became quite as famous.

In 1968 he became a United Methodist and left the campaign trail to concentrate on his television ministry and his newly founded Oral Roberts University (ORU). Thirteen years later he opened a state-of-the-art hospital in Tulsa, OK, only to have to close it in 1989 as a result of financial difficulties. He retired as president of ORU in 1993. In spite of those aspects of his ministry that others could only dream about, Roberts offers a strikingly suitable example of pentecostal healing theology, especially during the pre-ORU era. It is a theology that oscillates between two poles.

1. The First Pole: Certainty.

Early in his healing ministry, Roberts outlined his thinking on healing, saying, "The healing that Jesus brings is more than spiritual, more than mental, more than physical—it is that and more; His healing is to make us 'whole.' Health in soul, mind and body. Healthy relations, healthy attitudes, healthy habits." What he had in mind was a comprehensive improvement of one's life.

In line with part of 19th-century evangelicalism and with pentecostalism, Roberts rooted healing in the atonement, the act by which Jesus opened the way to reconciliation between God and humanity. The idea appears repeatedly in his preaching and writing. Scattered throughout are statements like, "Healing is in the atonement, therefore it includes all"; "Each one of us has a perfect right to God, and just as He will forgive all our sins, He will heal our diseases"; "Know that

God's will is to heal you"; "Turn your faith loose—now!"; "God wants to heal you now. The best time is when God is ready; He is ready now!"

It would be difficult to misunderstand all of this. Roberts's concrete statements declare that on the basis of the atonement a person can experience healing at precisely the moment when it is needed. In order to facilitate this, Roberts counseled people to seek a "point of contact," which he defines as "any point where your faith makes contact with God's power." It might be found in a sermon, in someone's laying hands on you, in touching the radio while listening to Roberts preach. He thought it was important because "it sets the time and is the point of expectation for your healing." This concept was unique to Roberts, but certainty based on the atonement is not. That is vintage pentecostalism, and it has appeared throughout the group's history.

2. The Second Pole: Sovereignty.

The first pole in Roberts' healing theology is certainty. Some pentecostals have held this position without qualification, but Roberts did not. As with most pentecostals, there is another pole in Roberts's teaching on healing—sovereignty. Roberts did not embrace either pole, but rather oscillated between them. He constantly preached certainty while interspersing asides on sovereignty.

Roberts gives the impression that he would have liked to preach the certainty of healing with the consistency of more extreme pentecostals. However, he had made observations during his ministry that he simply could not ignore. He knew that frequently people were not healed. He counseled that when that happens, one has to recognize that God has a better way. He could even talk about sickness that glorifies God, saying that sometimes God sees best not to heal, "but that gives way to a greater miracle and to serve a larger purpose."

Roberts most certainly did not like what can be seen as ambiguity. In fact, he was deeply troubled that many were not healed. His method of dealing with that reality was to explain unhealed disease in terms of God's sovereignty. As one commentator said, "He could only accept the mystery and keep trying." That is, he acknowledged the sovereignty and preached the certainty.

There have been disputes over exactly how valid claims to healings in Roberts's ministry are. Again, his methods—fast-moving healing lines involving hundreds of people—mitigated against verification. Some very compelling accounts have been recorded, and certainly thousands of believers saw him as a source of solutions to unresolvable problems.

The theology behind Roberts's ministry was one he had absorbed by listening to the preaching of his father and other older pentecostals. He did not refine that theology through consulting theologians. Any modifications he made were results of "hands-on" experience gained through an endless succession of nights under canvas. Typically, he was bold and confident, full of promise and certainty. However, the reality of disappointing failures to heal forced him to acknowledge God's sovereignty. When it came to healing, the early Roberts was the quintessential pentecostal.

VII. CONCLUSION.

It would be impossible to produce a comprehensive study of divine healing as it has appeared among Christians through the centuries. Available sources would not lead to everything that has happened, and the ministries that could be discovered would likely be staggering in number and complexity. The six models I have proposed provide a reasonably adequate entry to an extravagantly luxuriant field. Other researchers may add examples of the six models or, perhaps, add more models.

Clearly, God's direct intervention in restoring health through Christians has appeared in many forms, reflecting the ministry of Jesus himself. No patterns or formulas can be extracted from the accounts of Jesus' healings. The healings flow from God, and God keeps his own counsel. It is enough that we know that God looks with mercy on human pain.

■ **Bibliography:** V. Dawe, "The Attitude of the Ancient Church toward Sickness and Healing" (diss., Boston U., 1955) ■ C. de Siebenthal, *25 ans de marche avec Dieu (1936–1961)* (1962) ■ R. C. Finucane, *Miracles and Pilgrims: Popular Belief in Medieval England* (1977) ■ idem, "The Use and Abuse of Medieval Miracles," *History* 60 (1975) ■ D. E. Harrell Jr., *All Things Are Possible: The Healing and Charismatic Revivals in Modern America* (1975) ■ D. Ising, ed., *Johann Christoph Blumhardt: Ein Brevier* (1991) ■ M. Kelsey, *Psychology, Medicine, and Christian Healing* (1989) ■ B. R. Kreiser, *Miracles, Convulsions, and Ecclesiastical Politics in Early Eighteenth-Century Paris* (1978) ■ B. Lafrenière, CSC, *Brother André: According to Witnesses* (1990) ■ R. Latourelle, *Miracles of Jesus and the Theology of Miracles,* trans. M. J. O'Connell (1988) ■ F. D. Macchia, *Spirituality and Social Liberation: The Message of the Blumhardts in the Light of Wuerttemberg Pietism* (1993) ■ W. Warner, *Kathryn Kuhlman: The Woman behind the Miracles* (1993) ■ K. Zeller, *Dorothea Trudel von Männedorf: Ihr Leben und Wirken* (1971).   ■ R. A. N. Kydd

HEBDEN, JAMES (d. c. 1919) and **ELLEN K.** Pentecostal pioneers in Toronto, Ont. The Hebdens were involved in Christian work in Yorkshire, England, where James Hebden was a building contractor. After an abortive missionary visit to Jamaica, they arrived in Toronto in late 1904. An experience of healing raised their faith expectations, and without knowing any pentecostals, Mrs. Hebden was baptized in the Spirit in Nov. 1906; her husband received the baptism in December. The Hebden mission on Queen Street, East, was the first pentecostal assembly in Canada. Many received the baptism in the Spirit there. Several missionaries went out from this mission: the Chawners, Atters, Slagers, and

Semples [›Aimee Semple McPherson]. The Hebdens' absolute opposition to any pentecostal organization contributed to the decline of the Queen Street Mission, and in 1910 they left Toronto as missionaries to Algiers, North Africa. James Hebden died c. 1919; his wife survived him for many years.

■ **Bibliography:** T. H. Miller, "The 'Canadian' Azusa': The Hebden Mission in Toronto," *Pneuma* 8 (1, 1986).   ■ P. D. Hocken

"HERMANO PABLO" See Paul Edwin Finkenbinder.

HEZMALHALCH, THOMAS (1848–1934). Early pentecostal evangelist and missionary. Known widely as "Brother Tom," Hezmalhalch was one of the many pentecostals who went out from the ›Azusa Street Mission. An Englishman who came to the U.S. in the 1880s, he was a Holiness preacher before he was baptized in the Spirit. His name is associated with pentecostal revivals in U.S. cities, including Zion, IL; Pueblo, CO; and Indianapolis, IN.

He is perhaps best known for his ministry with ›John G. Lake in South Africa beginning in 1908. The Apostolic Faith Mission was formed there as a result of the pentecostal outpouring in that country. Several pentecostal periodicals—including *Pentecost*, *The Upper Room*, and the *Latter Rain Evangel*—kept their readers abreast of that early movement of the Spirit. Brother Tom's ministry in South Africa began after he had reached 60 years of age.

Although Hezmalhalch was not considered a great preacher by some contemporaries, his name is legendary in both the U.S. and South Africa as a man who walked in the Spirit and who had great influence in the early pentecostal movement. He even tells of picking up a poisonous viper in California to convince a taunting atheist that there is a God. This bizarre incident, however, seems to be an exception in his ministry.

In his later years Hezmalhalch stayed in the home of friends in Southern California and taught an adult class at Bethany Church, Alhambra.

■ **Bibliography:** *AF* (Los Angeles) (1906–7) ■ A. Flower, "The Ministry of 'Brother Tom,'" in W. Warner, ed., *Touched by the Fire* (1978) ■ "Gone Home," *Trooster Comforter* (May 1934).   ■ W. E. Warner

Thomas Hezmalhalch, better known as "Brother Tom," who took the pentecostal message to South Africa with John G. Lake and others in 1908.

HICKEY, MARILYN SWEITZER (1931–). Bible teacher. Born in Dalhart, TX, Hickey moved to Denver, where she attended high school. She earned a B.A. at the University of Northern Colorado. After serving as a high school teacher, she entered the ministry with her husband, Wallace. He currently is pastor of Orchard Road Christian Center in Greenwood Village, CO.

The Lord called Hickey in 1976 to "cover the earth with the Word." A Bible study class in her home paid for her first radio teaching broadcasts. Now Marilyn Hickey Ministries has expanded to 120 radio stations and some 35 television outreaches. Her magazine is read in some 200,000 homes.

In 1983 Hickey heard the Lord say, "Go to Ethiopia." She raised money to purchase Bibles and food for the hungry in Haiti, the Philippines, Bangladesh, and Honduras, as well as distributing Bibles in Iron Curtain countries.

■ **Bibliography:** D. M. Hazard, "Marilyn and Wally Hickey: They Make a Great Team," *Charisma* (Oct. 1985).   ■ S. Strang

HICKS, ROY H. (1920–). Foursquare executive and preacher. In the years that followed his graduation from ›L.I.F.E. Bible College in 1943, Roy Hicks, a native of Big Sandy, TN, became a leader in the ›International Church of the Foursquare Gospel (ICFG). In 1982 he was named general supervisor of the denomination's 1,000 congregations, a position he held until 1986. He considers his ministry as that of a prophet and teacher. As a denominational leader he frequently spoke in charismatic circles such as ›Rhema Bible Training Center and ›Christ for the Nations Institute, and in meetings conducted by the ›Full Gospel Business Men's Fellowship International. This close association with charismatic groups set him apart from most classical pentecostal officials.

Hicks is the author of 14 books, including *Faith, Use It or Lose It: The Word of Faith* (1976); *Praying beyond God's Abilities* (1977); *Instrument-Rated Christians* (1979); *Another Look at the Rapture* (1982); *Healing Your Insecurities* (1982); *Keys of the Kingdom* (1984); and *Sacred Cows and Green Pastures* (1999).

L.I.F.E. Bible College awarded Hicks an honorary D.D. degree in 1975.

■ **Bibliography:** ICFG Public Relations press release.
   ■ W. E. Warner

HICKS, TOMMY (1909–73). Missionary evangelist and faith healer. Tommy Hicks is noted for his work as an overseas evangelist. Successful on several continents in the mid 1950s, his work in Argentina in 1954 was the most outstanding of all. Because of the crowds, the revival had to be moved to the Huracane Football Stadium (seating capacity 110,000), which overflowed. The revival lasted two months; 3 million people are reported to have attended, with 300,000 decision cards filled out, many healings manifested, and 50,000 New Testaments and Bibles distributed. Hicks was well accepted in the country; the vice president was among the reported converts. The success overseas gained Hicks sustained support from the ▶Full Gospel Business Men's Fellowship International.

Hicks wrote *Manifest Deliverance for You Now!* (1952); *Capturing the Nations in the Name of the Lord* (1956); *Millions Found Christ* (1956); and *It's Closing Time* (1958).

Evangelist Tommy Hicks, who conducted huge meetings in Argentina in the early 1950s, pictured here during a meeting held in Buenos Aires.

■ **Bibliography:** D. E. Harrell Jr., *All Things Are Possible* (1975) ■ G. G. Kulbeck, *What God Hath Wrought* (1958) ■ L. Stokes, *The Great Revival in Buenos Aires* (1954).   ■ S. Shemeth

HILDEGARD OF BINGEN (1098–1179). Medieval Catholic charismatic visionary and prophet. One of the greatest Christian mystics, Hildegard founded (1136) a convent near Bingen, which became the center for the Hildegardian revival. She had visions from age 5 onward but did not divulge them until she was 42, when she experienced a calling to proclaim God's words in the Spirit. At that time she saw the heavens open, and a fiery light permeated her whole mind and inflamed her heart. Believing that she had been instructed to speak and write about what she had experienced, Hildegard recorded this experience in her *Scivias* (short for "Know the Ways of the Lord") and drew a self-portrait of the episode, in which, like the original Pentecost event, she was crowned by parted tongues of fire. Bernard of Clairvaux and those attending the Synod of Trier (1147) encouraged her to publish all that she had learned from the Holy Spirit.

Hildegard was taken seriously as a prophet by everyone, from the popes to the humblest serfs. She wrote to many prominent people (300 letters still exist), never mincing words when she considered their behavior unworthy of their calling. She went on numerous preaching missions, delivering fiery apocalyptic sermons—an exceptional role for a woman in those days. In addition, Hildegard wrote 77 hymns

of divine praise (her own poetry, which she set to music), a history of the universe, numerous theological commentaries, a book on natural history, and one on medicine. She also drew 36 multicolored "illuminations," in which her visions are vividly captured.

In one of her greatest hymns, *De Spiritu Sancto*, Hildegard speaks of the creative and re-creative work of the Holy Spirit: "Holy Spirit, making life alive, moving in all things, root of all creative being, cleansing the cosmos of every impurity, effacing guilt, anointing wounds. You are lustrous and praiseworthy life, You awaken and re-awaken everything that is." For Hildegard, God's "elect" are those who have been touched by the fiery tongues of the Spirit. This reception of the gift of the Holy Spirit is necessarily accompanied by the production of divine fruits and an ability to discern good from evil. Spiritual gifts are not limited to those listed in Isa. 11:2–3; they also encompass those mentioned in 1 Cor. 12 and elsewhere.

Hildegard's biographers provide pericopes portraying her own spiritual life. She is reported to have sung in the Spirit—to such an extent that the occasions of her singing became like concerts. Her ecstatic visions and the numerous miracles attributed to her became legendary.

■ **Bibliography:** S. Burgess, *The Holy Spirit: Medieval Roman Catholic and Reformation Traditions* (1997) ■ M. Fox, ed., *Illuminations of Hildegard of Bingen* (1985) ■ C. Hart and J. Bishop, eds., *Hildegard of Bingen: Scivias* (1990).   ■ S. M. Burgess

HINN, BENEDICTUS ("BENNY") (1952–). Evangelist and televangelist. During the 1990s, "Benny" Hinn became one of the most prominent healing evangelists. His television shows include a half-hour program, *This Is Your Day!*, which airs three times daily on Trinity Broadcastng Network (TBN), and segments from his monthly Miracle Crusades.

Hinn was born in Jaffa, Israel, to a Greek father and an Armenian mother. During his childhood his father served as the mayor of Jaffa. Although his parents were devout Greek Orthodox, Hinn's early education took place at School of the Monks, a Roman Catholic institution. During the political unrest caused by the Six Day War of 1967, the Hinn family moved to Toronto, Canada. His father quickly learned English and became a successful insurance salesman. Hinn attended a public high school and began attending services at a local charismatic Anglican congregation. He made a public confession of his faith in Christ soon afterward, in 1972. Despite his father's strong opposition to his newfound faith, Hinn devoted himself to a study of Scripture and participated in the local Jesus movement. The following year Hinn attended a ›Kathryn Kuhlman healing service in Pittsburgh, PA. While worshiping at the meeting, he heard a voice say, "My mercy is abundant to you." After witnessing three hours of healing testimonies, he thought, "I want what Kathryn Kuhlman's got." He attended a number of her meetings elsewhere and was invited to participate in a memorial service for Kuhlman in Pittsburgh in 1977, the year after she died.

From 1977 to 1981 Hinn worked with the Kuhlman ministry on a monthly basis, speaking to audiences after films were shown of Kathryn Kuhlman's services. Kuhlman became an important role model for Hinn's healing ministry. Hinn began preaching in December 1974, after experiencing another vision urging him to preach to the lost. Overcoming his fear of public speaking and a stuttering problem, Hinn began to proclaim the Word with power, and his stuttering was gone. He preached for the next five months in pentecostal churches around Toronto and slowly began to gain a following. His father and the rest of his family were converted and became part of his new ministry. His rallies soon attracted national publicity in Canada through the *Toronto Star* and the *Globe and Mail.* The Canadian Broadcasting Corporation and other stations broadcast documentaries about Hinn's crusades and his growing ministry.

Following the model of Kuhlman's meetings, Hinn rarely lays hands on individuals, but rather waits for them to come forward and testify to their experiences of healing. He is known for "blowing the anointing" as he throws his coat on people or waves his arms over crowds, and many are slain in the Spirit. In 1978 Hinn met Suzanne Harthern, the daughter of a pentecostal minister based in Orlando, FL. The following year the couple were married and Hinn began to establish an international ministry.

By 1983 the Hinns had relocated to Orlando and founded the independent, interdenominational Orlando Christian Center. Starting with a few hundred people, the church grew rapidly. By 1992 it had become a thriving megachurch on a 40-acre parcel of land and claiming over 7,000 members. Today it is World Outreach Church.

Hinn's television ministry began during the mid-1980s with the broadcast of his church's Sunday worship. The show was picked up by TBN and soon became one of the network's most popular programs. Hinn's *This Is Your Day!* show now reaches a reported audience of over 60 million homes worldwide. Hinn became a successful author in the 1990s with his first book, *Good Morning, Holy Spirit,* published by Thomas Nelson in 1990. It sold nearly a quarter of a million copies within a few months and still is on the best-seller list. He has published several other popular books, *"Rise and Be Healed!"* (1991); *The Anointing* (1992); *Lord, I Need a Miracle* (1993); *The Blood: Its Power From Genesis to Jesus to You* (1993); *Welcome, Holy Spirit* (1995); *This Is Your Day for a Miracle* (1996); *The Miracle of Healing* (1998); and *Kathryn Kuhlman: Her Spiritual Legacy and Its Impact on My Life* (1999). He has a quarterly publication called *This Is Your Day for a Miracle.* During the early 1980s the ›Word of Faith teachings of ›Hagin, ›Copeland, and others began to have an enormous impact on Hinn, as became evident in his writings and in his sermons.

By 1990 this interest caused two anticult groups, Christian Research Institute and the Watchman Fellowship, to criticize not only Hinn's theology but also his healing claims and lifestyle. The *Orlando Sentinel* printed an article exposing Hinn's opulent lifestyle. He responded through a *Publishers Weekly* article, saying "God wants all his children taken care of." He defended his expensive home as necessary for security reasons. In response to skeptics who voiced doubt concerning the claims of healings during his crusades, Hinn enlisted the services of five volunteer doctors who have worked to substantiate healing testimonies.

The criticisms of Hinn's Word of Faith religious teaching and onstage theatrics came to a head in 1993. Christian Research Institute's Hank Hanegraaff and televangelist James Robison contacted Hinn personally and warned him that his ministry would fail if he continued "in his slaughter of the innocent sheep." Hinn was deeply shaken by Robison's rebuke and promised to change his ministry's emphasis. A short time later he renounced the central elements of his faith message, including ›positive confession, the divine right to be healed, and the "health and wealth" gospel, even calling the Word of Faith teachings "New Age." As a result of Hinn's change in message and practices, he felt a need to edit out all references to Word of Faith teaching from subsequent editions of his books. In addition, he hired Dudley Hall, an associate of Robison, to help him avoid future doctrinal errors in his writing. Hinn was ordained with the Lester Sumrall Evangelistic Association at this time, but from 1994 to 1996 he affiliated with the Assemblies of God in hopes this would help him be more accountable for his teachings and ministry. That association was short-lived. Also, in 1994 Hinn made the news because of the testimony of heavyweight boxing champion Evander Holyfield, who claimed to be healed of a serious heart ailment while attending a Hinn meeting.

Hinn's television programs continue to place a strong emphasis on dramatic healing testimonials. He also conducts monthly miracle crusades around the world. Since have been located in Dallas, Texas. He has international offices in Europe, Canada, Australia, New Zealand, New Guinea, India, Fiji, and the Philippines.

■ **Bibliography:** M. Bearden, "Benny Hinn," *Publishers Weekly* (Feb. 10, 1992) ■ "Benny Hinn Speaks Out," *Charisma & Christian Life* (Aug. 1993) ■ "Benny Hinn under Fire," *Ministries Today* (March–April 1991) ■ P. Ferraiuolo, "Christian Leaders Admonish Hinn," *Christianity Today* (Aug. 16, 1993) ■ G. Fisher et al., *The Confusing World of Benny Hinn* (1993) ■ R. Frame, "Best-selling Author Admits Mistakes, Vows Changes," *Christianity Today* (Oct. 28, 1991) ■ "Holyfield Claims Miraculous Healing," *Springfield (MO) Leader & Press* (June 1994), *Assemblies of God Minister* (Sept. 30, 1994). ■ J. G. Melton, *Prime-Time Religion* (1997), 141–44

■ G. W. Gohr

HISPANIC PENTECOSTALISM The rapid growth that pentecostalism has registered in Latin America has occurred also among Hispanics/Latinos in North America, beginning early in the century and accelerating since WWII. As early as 1962, *Time* magazine referred to these vigorous, grassroots movements as "the fastest growing church in the hemisphere." The combined membership of the various pentecostal organizations in the U.S., Canada, and Puerto Rico is now estimated at 6 million adults, about 20% of the entire Hispanic/Latino population.

1. The Hispanic Pentecostals.

a. The Hispanic Peoples. Hispanic is a term that has been widely used in the press to describe the ethnically diverse peoples whose common heritage, in addition to ascribed cultural and psychological traits, includes the Spanish language and the Roman Catholic religion. Many of these same people prefer to be referred to as Latinos (Span. *latinos,* masc. plural; the feminine form *latina* is also used) or simply by the adjectival form of their country of origin (e.g., Mexican, Cuban, Argentine). These peoples include past and recent immigrants—and their descendants—from the Spanish-speaking countries of the Caribbean and Central and South America, as well as immigrants from Spain and their descendants, some of whom have lived in the Southwest since before the American Revolution. (See Table 1, p. 722.)

Hispanic culture has been perpetuated by the various peoples who have merged in Latin America since the 16th-century Spanish conquest of the New World, including the predominant native peoples, several million Africans transported during the Colonial period (1492–1822), and successive waves of European and Asian immigrants. While many American Latinos remain close to their cultural traditions, others, like actor Anthony Quinn, son of Mexican immigrants and briefly associated with pentecostals in his youth, have identified completely with North American values and lifestyles. The success of Latinos in business, the professions, politics, and the arts have made them a fixture in American culture. Popular recording artists, such as Ricky Martin and Gloria Estefan, and sports stars like Sammy Sosa demon-

strate the extent to which Latinos have become folk heroes to many Anglo as well as Hispanic youth.

The more than 30 million Hispanics in the U.S. constitute the nation's second-largest minority. A campaign to obtain a complete count of this population anticipates identifying up to 33 million in the census of the year 2000. The proportion of Hispanics in the U.S. population has increased much more rapidly than was expected 20 years ago. Since 1980 the Hispanic community has grown from 6.4% of the U.S. population to 11.3%. Besides a birth rate exceeding that of the general population, growth has come from immigration, mainly from Mexico and Central America. Economic problems in these areas, natural disasters like the devastating Hurricane Mitch in 1998, and the aspiration for a better life have resulted in continuing heavy migration northward. America's Cuban population, centered in Florida but widely dispersed and easily assimilated, now numbers more than a million persons. The 4 million Puerto Ricans, U.S. citizens who since 1952 have been a self-governing commonwealth, enjoy unrestricted access to the mainland. There are an additional 2.4 million persons of Puerto Rican origin in the U.S.

Although numerous differences distinguish the subcultures within the Hispanic population, Latinos as a whole are on the average younger, poorer, and less educated than the general population. This population is overwhelmingly urban (88%), with 45% of all Hispanics found in just six metropolitan areas: New York, Los Angeles, Miami, Chicago, San Francisco, and San Jose, CA. Increasingly, however, Hispanics are diffused throughout the U.S. Despite continued heavy immigration, more than half of all Hispanics are at least third-generation Americans. Nevertheless, Spanish, a unifying force, persists as the preferred language of about 20 million people in the U.S. Hispanic youth, who are often more conservative in respect to traditional values than their Anglo counterparts, characteristically hold on to traditional cultural features. It has been suggested that cultural conservatism and social disadvantage have contributed to the spread of pentecostalism among these groups (see ▸Sociology of Pentecostalism).

b. Implications of Hispanic Pentecostal Growth. The emergence of the Hispanic pentecostal movement has implications for both the future of American pentecostalism and the assimilation of Latino Roman Catholics into American Protestantism. Opinion polls report that while 52% of Americans and 54% of American Catholics consider religion to be "very important" to them personally, the response from Hispanics was 64%. The attraction of pentecostalism for Latinos has drawn comment from Roman Catholic spokespersons who lament the resulting loss of tradition and community solidarity. Hispanics make up more than a third of American Catholics and are expected to account for one half of all the nation's Catholics within a generation. In California and the

Southwest the proportions already exceed 50%. While an estimated 70% of American Hispanics are baptized Catholics, many fewer consider themselves to be "practicing Catholics" and, according to estimates, as few as 12% regularly attend Mass. Even Latinos who do not regularly attend Catholic services, however, may maintain an altar and traditional religious practices in their homes. An estimated 20% of Latinos are Protestants, in large part pentecostals. In recent years the Roman Catholic Church is believed to have lost an estimated 60,000 parishioners annually, while the number of pentecostal congregations appears to have doubled. New religious movements, the Jehovah's Witnesses, and Mormons together claim the remaining 10% of all Hispanics.

In the meantime, disproportionate growth has occurred among the ethnic churches of the primarily white U.S. pentecostal denominations like the Church of God (CG; Cleveland, TN) and the Assemblies of God (AG). Between 1980 and 1997, the number of Hispanic congregations in the AG grew from 1,100 to 1,723 (56.7%), while the membership grew from 93,000 to 178,017 (91.2%). In the meantime, the congregations and membership in the Anglo geographical districts increased by, respectively, 17.2% and 7.7%. In addition, approximately 10% of the Anglo AG congregations are made up of Hispanics, further increasing the denomination's Hispanic character.

The CG has also enjoyed substantial growth among its Hispanic and culturally integrated congregations. The group's U.S. Hispanic churches grew from 271 congregations and 30,000 members in 1987 to 650 churches and 44,000 members in 1999, apart from another 200 congregations and 22,000 members in Puerto Rico. The CG held its first national Hispanic convention in 1985 with only 500 delegates from five ethnic districts. Growth in all pentecostal denominations has occurred regionally, with large numbers of churches in the Southeast adding to the already wellestablished groups in California and the Southwest, the Mid-Atlantic states, and in Puerto Rico. Such sustained increases appear to have arrested the tendency of these denominations to be exclusively white and middle class. The Church of the Foursquare Gospel, the Church of God of Prophecy (CGP), and the United Pentecostals all report significant Hispanic memberships, many of them fully integrated into the Anglo ecclesiastical structures. In the CGP, Latinos hold high administrative positions in predominately non-Hispanic districts.

c. Hispanic Pentecostal Denominations. (See Table 2, p. 723) Current estimates of Hispanic pentecostal adherents in the U.S. approach 6 million, with an additional 700,000 in Puerto Rico. In addition to the predominately Anglo pentecostal churches that have organized Spanish-language branches, there are exclusively ethnic denominations such as the Iglesia Apostólica de la Fe en Cristo Jesús (IAFCJ; Apostolic Church of the Faith in Jesus Christ) in the Southwest

and the Spanish Christian Churches of the East Coast that contribute importantly to Hispanic pentecostalism. About a third of the membership of the Hispanic pentecostals in the U.S. belong to these exclusively ethnic organizations. Sometimes referred to as indigenous churches, these groups account for the vast majority of the Puerto Rican pentecostals.

The tendency for pentecostals to fragment organizationally, often attaching themselves to a charismatic leader, is an important consideration in the emergence of new movements. In addition, large numbers of independent congregations are found among Hispanics, especially in Puerto Rico and among East Cost Puerto Rican communities. An early (1960) study of the movement in New York identified 240 pentecostal congregations, half of which were not denominationally affiliated. Added to various independent churches are congregations affiliated with Latin American groups such as the Brazilian Iglesia Universal del Reino de Dios and Dios es Amor churches, groups that now have Spanish-speaking congregations in the U.S. Religious statistics sometimes include unspecified "indigenous" Protestants, usually referring to pentecostals. Elsewhere, revival centers and social outreach ministries have found a response among Hispanic youth who are sometimes former gang members and addicts who find in pentecostalism a resolute, emotionally satisfying form of Christianity.

Hispanic membership reports may omit large numbers of children, relatives, and sympathizers who take part in the activities of the church community without having advanced to communicant status. Rigid demands on personal conduct and commitment to the work of the congregation, including tithing and acceptance of the group's authority, appear to trim membership to a dedicated nucleus. Missiologists sometimes multiply the number of communicants by a factor of two or more in order to determine the total number of participants.

Pentecostal statistics must also take into account the difficulty of identifying and following memberships recruited from a population that in the past was often deeply committed to Catholic traditions and was largely excluded from the benefits of American life. Hispanic congregations have often contended with unemployment and shifting jobs, limited resources and inadequate facilities, suspicious and even hostile neighborhoods and, all too frequently, the indifference of Anglo pentecostals. Congregations are often youthful, comprised disproportionately of women and children, and lack recognition within the Hispanic community. Yet the descriptions of these organizations suggest vitality and institutional strength as well as substantial numerical growth.

d. Hispanics and Nonpentecostal Protestantism. If adverse conditions, authoritarian traditions, and expressiveness and spontaneity in religion make pentecostalism especially suited to Hispanics, perhaps these features account for the substantial minority of American Hispanics who have turned to the movement and why, in contrast, nonpentecostal Protestants have attracted relatively few Hispanics. A study by the Home Missions Council in 1930 reported that the number of Spanish-language churches was 453, representing 14 denominations with a combined membership of 28,000. The study found that no more than 2% of the Hispanic population was Protestant, and the largest grouping, the Methodists, had 10,000 members. Baptists claimed 6,500 and Presbyterians 6,700. Other major religious bodies had fewer than 10 congregations and 800 adherents each. The report, submitted by Thomas F. Coakely, concluded that the Mexican-American "is not adequately cared for either religiously or socially. The whole area [of Hispanic evangelism] is practically untouched." In contrast to other Protestant groups, according to Dr. ˒Jesse Miranda of California's Azusa Pacific University, the Hispanic sectors of pentecostalism reflect an alternative perspective of the heart over the mind. For these adherents, "the Pentecostal emphasis on the power and the freedom of the Spirit is a refreshing option. Pentecostals emphasize the participation of all believers and introduce a new type of theology that is practical and transforming."

e. Characteristics of Hispanic Pentecostals. A popular account of the rise of pentecostalism identifies features that appeal both to the masses of Latin America as well as to the Hispanic populations of the U.S. "Most adherents are poor, few of them well educated," the article revealed.

Their minister is likely to be a factory worker himself, secure in the pentecostal belief that "a man of God with a Bible in his hand has had training enough." Many pentecostals attend church every night for a two-hour service. Loud Bible readings and spontaneous testimonials are part of every service, punctuated by shouts of *"Aleluyah"* and *"Gracias a Dios."* The hymns well over a rhythmic clapping, generally accompanied by a guitar, drums, tambourines, a bass fiddle, piano, or small combo. Part of pentecostals' appeal—particularly to immigrants—is their total, emotional participation.

The writer quoted a Chicago Presbyterian pastor who commented, "When you walk into a pentecostal service, you are likely to be asked, no matter who you are, your name, where you are from, and 'Brother, do you have a word to say for us?'"

Few Hispanic pentecostal churches are static and secure. Most involve rapidly changing communities of migrant laborers or marginally employed industrial and service workers. Although congregations are generally comprised of families, most of them first-generation Protestants, members are often alienated from their extended families. Many churches are in effect family-operated missions or congregations dominated by two or three extended families linked by intermarriage. As the more successful and established members of the church find employment and housing outside the barrio, association with the church is likely to become complicated by social mobility and changing values. Where mobility and

generational differences—often in the form of loss of Spanish fluency among the younger people—are overcome, the church may lose its appeal for recent, unacculturated newcomers. In fact, leading Hispanic churches throughout the U.S. have acquired the sleek look of affluence and success, with comfortable buildings, well-dressed parishioners, and social acceptance.

2. Beginnings of Hispanic Pentecostal Churches in the United States and Puerto Rico.

a. Hispanics and the Early Pentecostals. At the ˒Azusa Street Mission in Los Angeles, focus of the 1906 West Coast revival, ethnic diversity was notable. The meetings were noticeably "free of all nationalist feeling," according to an early account. "If a Mexican or a German cannot speak English, he gets up and speaks in his own native tongue and feels quite at home, for the Spirit interprets through his face and the people say, 'Amen.' No instrument that God can use is rejected on account of color or dress or lack of education. That is why God has so built up the work."

But the successors of the short-lived Azusa Street Mission soon split along ethnic as well as doctrinal and regional lines in ways that are still reflected in the extreme diversity among Hispanic pentecostals.

"Mexicans were present at Azusa Street at an early date," writes historian ˒Robert Mapes Anderson, "and soon initiated missions of their own. Within a decade pentecostal preachers of Spanish extraction had firmly planted Pentecost among the 'floating population' of migrant Mexicans in many cities and towns from San Jose to Los Angeles to San Diego and throughout the outlying farm areas." Along the Texas border with Mexico, Oscar Nelson responded to rejection by the white community by writing, "The Lord told us, 'The white people have rejected the gospel and I will turn to the Mexicans'" (1979, 126). Reports of the AG in Texas in 1926 indicate that two-fifths of the membership was Mexican, even after a dozen or more churches had been lost in a defection. Although these congregations developed alongside Anglo churches, they largely assumed responsibility for their own work from the beginning.

The ˒Oneness controversy that divided pentecostals after 1916 also affected Hispanic churches. Early preachers Juan Navarro, Francisco F. Llorente, and ˒Marcial De La Cruz accepted the Oneness position and established churches as early as 1914, a year after the doctrine was propounded at the Arroyo Seco camp meeting. The work was taken up in 1917 by Antonio Nava, a recent Mexican immigrant, who established a congregation in Yuma, AZ, in 1919 and pastored in Calexico from 1920 to 1928. By 1925, with 23 churches scattered along the border from California to New Mexico, the group's pastors gathered in San Bernardino to organize. Only seven of the congregations had buildings, but an official name was adopted and an effort was made to establish criteria for ministerial credentials. Although the fledgling denomination suffered serious reverses in the following years, it survived to reorganize as the Asamblea Apostólica de la Fe en Cristo Jesus at the group's sixth general convention in San Bernardino in 1930. During the interim the Apostolics in Mexico continued to grow and emerge after WWII as a major source of further growth and leadership in the U.S. Although the church was separated from other pentecostals by its authoritarian rigidity as well as by its theology, it nevertheless remained effective in the postwar years. A leading study of Mexican Americans published in 1970 considered it to be "the predominant Mexican-American sect."

b. Hispanic Pentecostal Beginnings in Texas.

Of the nearly 400,000 members of Hispanic pentecostal denominations reported currently, at least two-thirds trace their origins to the work that began with ▸Henry C. Ball and his associates working in Texas, elsewhere in the Southwest, and in California. The pentecostals of Puerto Rico, including the work of the Church of God, can be traced to the efforts of ▸Juan L. Lugo, ▸Francisco Olazábal, and other ministers who were influenced also by Ball and the work he helped structure. It is thus possible by tracing the development of the early AG to indicate the origins of most of the present Hispanic pentecostal organizations.

Henry C. Ball, reared by his mother near the Mexican border, exhibited remarkable spiritual sensitivity and an affinity for Hispanic peoples while he was still a teenager. He started a Methodist church in a school in Ricardo, TX, before coming under the influence of a pentecostal preacher and affiliating with the recently organized AG in 1914. As his parish grew, Ball moved to nearby Kingsville, where his congregation shared facilities with the Anglo AG congregation. The challenge of providing instruction for new converts and guidance to new congregations brought into being by his members whose work took them to other locations, defined Ball's ministry for years to come. Within a short time a fellowship of Mexican pastors met to organize and provide suitable training for workers. By 1922 there were 50 Mexican churches in towns along the border.

During this formative period Ball was assisted by ▸Alice E. Luce, a former Anglican missionary to India who had experienced the revival that erupted in the girls' home operated by ▸Pandita Ramabai. Luce had come from Canada seeking entry to Mexico and had met Ball en route. She accompanied Sunshine Marshall, a young woman who also aspired to missionary work, in a short-lived venture in Monterrey, Nuevo Leon, from which they soon withdrew because of the hazards of the Mexican revolution then in progress. Returning to Texas, Marshall married Henry C. Ball, and Luce continued on to Los Angeles to open the pentecostal work there.

c. Hispanic Pentecostal Beginnings in California.

Alice E. Luce has been credited with being the catalyst that encouraged other workers to initiate ministry among the Hispanic peoples of California. Capable, well-educated, and committed to the task, she prepared much of the printed materials used for instruction among the early Hispanic pentecostals and encouraged formal preparation of pastors and evangelists. The school she founded in San Diego in 1926, later named the Latin American Bible Institute and located in La Puente, produced several generations of Hispanic leaders, including ▸Robert Fierro, a distinguished evangelist whose ministry became well known throughout the AG in both the U.S. and Latin America. While Luce was laying these educational foundations, the work progressed throughout the state.

Accounts of the earliest AG churches in Los Angeles revolve around several key families whose influence and resources gave the nascent work stability. Several of these leaders had previous backgrounds in other denominations and shared with Luce concern for establishing the work on a sound theological basis. From the origins of a mission at what is now Olvera Street, Los Angeles, churches were begun in Watts, Huntington Park, Santa Paula, and Irwindale. Two young Welsh brothers, Richard and ▸Ralph D. Williams, whom Luce had recruited previously for Hispanic ministry, opened churches in San Diego and took the pentecostal message to the San Joaquin Valley.

Meanwhile, the work in Northern California was emerging among the mixed communities of Mexicans, Puerto Ricans, and Portuguese in San Francisco, San Jose, and the East Bay. After a beginning in Danville, the work spread to Niles and Hayward, as Domingo Cruz, a fiery, illiterate, one-legged preacher became a legend for his persuasive preaching and his remarkable effectiveness in overcoming his handicaps. In addition to establishing strong churches and producing effective leadership, pentecostalism in Northern California gave rise to two of the most important figures among the early Hispanic pentecostals, Francisco Olazábal, the movement's leading evangelist, and Juan L. Lugo, who initiated the work in Puerto Rico.

d. Hispanic Pentecostal Beginnings in Puerto Rico and on the Atlantic Coast.

Juan L. Lugo is recognized as the pioneering missionary to Puerto Rico. Converted in Hawaii as a youth, Lugo accompanied his pastor to the mainland, where he was ordained in the AG and began his long, productive ministry. In 1917 Lugo received the promise of financial support from Bethel Church, Los Angeles, an Anglo congregation, to enable him to fulfill his vision of taking the pentecostal message to his homeland. Lugo conferred with ▸J. Roswell Flower at the AG headquarters in St. Louis, MO, en route to the East Coast, and was joined soon after his arrival in Puerto Rico by a colleague from California, Salomón Feliciano. After attempting to start a work in

Santurce, where he succeeded in reaching immigrants from St. Thomas, Lugo proceeded to Ponce, his family's home. There the missionaries gathered a sufficient following to produce an open rupture with the other evangelical pastors and to establish the judicial basis for their religious work. Within two years eight congregations had been formed, and Lugo returned to the mainland to attend the 1919 general council in Chicago. Accompanied by his bride, the daughter of a Puerto Rican physician, Lugo continued on to the Pacific Coast to visit his family, returning to Puerto Rico via Texas, where he conferred with Henry C. Ball and met a recent addition to the pentecostal ranks, Francisco Olazábal.

By 1921 the 11 churches and 600 members of the thriving work were brought under the AG. The majority adopted the name Iglesia de Dios Pentecostal (Pentecostal Church of God) in order to include the term *church (iglesia)* for clear identification in legal matters, although the group remained an integral part of the AG. A small defection occurred at the time, as some leaders chose to retain the name Asambleas de Dios for their churches. Subsequent growth under Lugo's leadership was accelerated with the addition of other missionaries, including ›Frank O. Finkenbinder, who arrived with his bride in 1921. Before his family's health forced him to leave Puerto Rico 15 years later, Finkenbinder had assisted the work to grow from a dozen churches, none of which had its own facilities, to 40 churches, most of which had permanent buildings.

This pentecostal growth in Puerto Rico led in time to the opening of churches among the Puerto Ricans of New York. By 1929, with 25 churches in Puerto Rico, Juan L. Lugo left to pastor a church in the Greenpoint district of Brooklyn. The acquisition of a former synagogue gave the congregation an identity and adequate facilities for the large church that emerged under Lugo's leadership. Within a decade more than 30 Puerto Rican pentecostal churches had come into being, as works were begun in the various Hispanic districts of metropolitan New York, and Francisco Olazábal directed much of his energies to establishing churches on the East Coast.

e. Francisco Olazábal and the Latin American Council of Christian Churches.

Francisco Olazábal stands out as the dominant figure among the early Hispanic pentecostals. A convert influenced by ›George and Carrie Judd Montgomery in California at the turn of the century, Olazábal returned to Mexico in preparation for the Methodist ministry. He later pastored briefly in El Paso and attended Moody Bible Institute, where he became acquainted with Reuben A. Torrey. As an effective Methodist evangelist and overseer of the denomination's work in Northern California, Olazábal once again was influenced by the Montgomerys in San Francisco to seek the pentecostal experience. In 1917 he accepted credentials with the AG and joined Henry C.

Ball in Texas as pastor of the church in El Paso. By 1920 his congregation had grown to 400 members. Ball sent his own associate, ›Demetrio Bazán, from San Antonio to assist Olazábal.

In 1922 Mexican ministers of the Texas–New Mexico District requested the formation of a Latin American District within the AG to give them greater voice in the administration of their churches. Ball, who had received prior notification that the proposal had been denied, responded at the 1922 meeting of the Mexican ministers in Victoria, TX, with what was taken by some ministers as an insensitive rejection of their wishes. Reportedly, about 20 pastors met in Houston the following March to secede from the General Council and to form the Latin American Council of Christian Churches (LACCC), with Francisco Olazábal as their leader.

The extraordinary work of Olazábal, and the significance of the organizational split for the future of the movement can hardly be overestimated. Considered the most effective Hispanic pentecostal minister up to that time—and perhaps since—he was referred to as the "great Aztec" by a contemporary biographer. Imposing and forthright, his superior preparation, his articulate, persuasive presentation, and his close identification with the Hispanic people and their aspirations all contributed to his remarkable influence.

Olazábal established the headquarters of the LACCC in Texas and began a ministry that soon radiated throughout the country. He traveled widely, conducting healing meetings in rented halls and establishing churches with unusual effectiveness for the next 14 years. His work in New York and Chicago led to the establishment of dozens of new churches, as did his campaigns in Los Angeles and Puerto Rico. His emphasis on evangelism and healing were combined with concern for the social needs of the Hispanic communities. By the late 1930s his organization had 50 churches and an estimated 50,000 adherents. Olazábal was apparently at the height of his career when he was killed in an automobile accident in Texas in 1937.

f. Institutionalization of the Early Revival.

The many unanswered questions regarding Olazábal's work have left much room for conjecture about what might have been had he survived or had he remained with the AG. Victor De León concluded that "the probability will always exist that had Francisco Olazábal remained with the General Council, he would have been the first Latin American superintendent of the [Hispanic] convention, and much earlier than 1939"—the date when leadership devolved to a Hispanic (1979, 30). In fact, Henry C. Ball remained prominent in the formation of the Hispanic work for the next 16 years, opening the Latin American Bible Institute in San Antonio in 1926, concurrently with the San Diego school founded by Luce; cultivating the work in Mexico and Central America in the formative stages; publishing his paper, *Luz Apostólica;* and preparing hymnals, one of which *(Himnos de Gloria)* came into general use throughout the Spanish-speaking world. Not only did Ball provide stabilizing leadership at a time when pentecostals often belittled formal preparation, but his personal influence was important in the development of a number of qualified leaders, including Rubén J. Arévalo and Juan Consejo Orozco, both of whom served as superintendents of the AG of Mexico, and Josué Cruz and Horacio Menchaca, notable in establishing the church in the U.S.

Not the least of Ball's contributions was his success in recovering some of the losses sustained by the AG with the secession of 1923 and his recruitment of able men who succeeded him in the denomination's leadership. In 1929 the Mexican convention in the AG, which had operated under the Texas–New Mexico District, was converted to the ▸Latin American District Council, with Ball serving as superintendent. At the same time the churches in Mexico were placed entirely under national control, with two of Ball's former students as superintendent for extended periods of time. In the meantime Ball's former assistant, Demetrio Bazán, had led the move to rejoin the AG the year after the defection and accepted Ball's former pastorate in Kingsville. He successively pastored in Laredo, Houston, and San Antonio before accepting the invitation to the church in Denver in 1932. In turn Bazán recruited able leadership in the Rocky Mountain states, including Augustín López, pastor of an independent congregation in Denver, and José Girón, a Presbyterian who was to succeed him as superintendent of the Latin American District in the post–WWII era. By 1937, with the approaching retirement of Henry C. Ball, Demetrio Bazán had emerged as the dominant figure in the Hispanic ministry in the U.S. His election as superintendent of the Latin American District Council of the AG in 1939 introduced a new era in the development of the Hispanic pentecostal work.

3. Development of the Movement Since World War II.

a. Hispanic Pentecostals on the East Coast and in Puerto Rico. (See Table 3, p. 223.) WWII marked the beginning of a new era for Hispanic pentecostalism in several respects. The rising tide of Puerto Rican nationalism under Governor Luis Muñoz Marín brought religious pluralism and tacit support for Protestantism. In the ensuing economic development program and the recognition of commonwealth status for the island, the pentecostal churches benefited from the assertiveness of the popular groups in demanding a larger place in Puerto Rican society. With the flood of Puerto Ricans who arrived in New York and other eastern cities, a community of 500,000 immigrants ready to adapt to American life provided a receptive field for the already established Hispanic pentecostal groups and soon engendered additional organizations.

Moreover, the influence of Olazábal in both Puerto Rico and New York had helped establish the work in the 1930s. With his death in 1937 the churches he had opened tended to fragment, creating new organizations and unleashing new leadership within the ranks of the pentecostals. When the Puerto Rican churches in the East broke with the Texas-based, Mexican-dominated LACCC the following year, a primary beneficiary was the Asamblea de Iglesias Cristianas (Assembly of Christian Churches), whose work was introduced into Puerto Rico in 1940.

Olazábal's impact on Puerto Rican pentecostalism had been notable even earlier in the formation of the Defensores de la Fe (Defenders of the Faith) that dated from his association with a former Christian and Missionary Alliance minister, Juan Francisco Rodríguez Rivera, in 1934. Rodríguez, who was influenced by the fundamentalist evangelist Gerald B. Winrod about the same time, formed a group that has been considered at least marginally pentecostal. The Defensores began work in New York in 1944 and reported 26 churches in Puerto Rico by 1948.

A third group traced to Olazábal's ministry is the Iglesia de Cristo en las Antillas (Church of Christ in the Antilles), whose emergence is not attributed to any single founder. When the ministers of this association changed its name to the Iglesia de Cristo Misionera (Missionary Church of Christ) in 1938, the original congregation separated, retaining the former name and giving rise to a new denomination. By 1980 the two churches, of approximately equal size, reported a combined total of 250 congregations and 15,000 members in Puerto Rico. Subsequently, the Iglesia de Cristo en las Antillas changed its name to the Iglesia de Cristo Universal (Universal Church of Christ).

The Iglesia Pentecostal de Jesucristo (Pentecostal Church of Christ), a group formed by a former pastor of the Iglesia de Dios Pentecostal in 1938, and the Iglesia de Dios (Church of God), organized by a group of nine pastors in 1940, further contributed to the proliferation of pentecostal organizations in Puerto Rico. The former church reported 45 churches and the latter 75 by 1980. A similar pentecostal organization, the Samaria Iglesia Evangélica (Samaria Evangelical Church) was founded by a former Catholic whose conversion in a Baptist church followed an intense spiritual struggle. Given to fasting, prayer, and the exercise of the gifts of healing and exorcism, Julio Guzman Silva, a blacksmith, formed his own church in 1941 and was the leader of an association of 25 churches by 1980.

These demonstrations of local initiative were matched by the introduction of several denominational missions in the postwar period. The Foursquare Church (Iglesia Cuadrangular) arrived in 1930, the Church of God of Prophecy

(Iglesia de Dios de la Profecía) in 1938, the CG in 1944, the Open Bible Standard Church in 1958, and the United Pentecostal Church in 1962. Of these the CG was by far the most successful, benefiting from the denomination's association with Antonio Collazo, Juan L. Lugo's son-in-law, in the years just after WWII. Collazo had separated from the Iglesia de Dios Pentecostal previously and emerged as the main influence in the new organization.

The Iglesia de Dios Pentecostal, affiliated with the General Council of the AG beginning in 1921, has continued to grow rapidly since 1945. By 1950 it registered a larger membership than any other Protestant group in Puerto Rico, with 12,000 members in the late 1940s and 100,000 according to recent estimates. In 1956 the group separated from the AG, forming an entirely autonomous organization and opening the way for a new Asambleas de Dios affiliated with the mainland denomination. The growth of the new organization, an integral district of the general council, has resulted in 179 churches and 19,000 communicant members to the present.

The Hispanic pentecostal churches on the East Coast showed the same tendency to fragment in the postwar era. While it was reported that there were about 25 such groups in 1937, a comprehensive study identified 240 in 1960. In addition to the denominations whose work began as missions, the AG, the CG, and the CGP, the Hispanic groups in the metropolitan East include the Asamblea de Iglesias Cristianas and autonomous groups fraternally linked to the Puerto Rican churches, such as the Defenders of the Faith. The congregations formerly associated with the Puerto Rican Iglesia de Dios Pentecostal are now independent of the Puerto Rican organization and are designated the Spanish Christian churches. A much smaller organization, the Damascus Christian Church, and a larger number of independents, many with names similar to the affiliated churches, make up the balance of the East Coast Hispanic pentecostal churches. There is relatively little difference operationally and doctrinally between all the local churches of these groups, although those with wider associations presumably benefit from the exchange of a larger pool of leadership and resources. These churches have moved out from their initial locations in New York City and the immediate environs. The Spanish Eastern District of the AG, for instance, reports churches in Massachusetts, Connecticut, and Rhode Island, as well as in Pennsylvania, Delaware, and Ohio, although the preponderance remain in New York and New Jersey.

b. The Asamblea Apostólica de la Fe en Cristo Jesus. The growth of the Asamblea Apostólica in the U.S. has been a major development of Hispanic pentecostalism in the postwar years. After the 1930s, when the Mexican population in the U.S. experienced little net increase and agricultural laborers were repatriated, the churches demonstrated increased awareness of the larger society and encouraged better internal organization. The Apostolic Bible Training School was organized in Hayward, CA, in 1949. Between 1950 and 1962, 42 new churches were established, and evangelists started missions in Washington, Oregon, Pennsylvania, and Florida. The group also attempted to send foreign missionaries to Central America and Italy. By 1970 the group had better defined its relationship with the Mexican Apostolics and had organized the North American churches into 13 districts, each administered by a bishop. Clearly the group represents the most conservative position of any of the pentecostal groups, retaining an episcopal hierarchy and centralized control; authoritarian pastors in the local churches; and rigid demands on tithing, dress, and conduct. Many of the pastors support themselves with secular employment, full or part-time. Holland notes that the strength of the Apostolic movement is found in the rural labor camps and in small southwestern towns that to some extent replicate the social conditions of rural Mexico (1974, 370).

c. The Latin American Churches of the Church of God (Cleveland, TN). Although the CG only organized its Hispanic work formally after WWII, the group's Central American work flourished in the 1930s. When, under the aegis of ▸Vessie Hargrave, the work was organized in 1946 under the supervision of Josué Rubio, the Hispanic work grew rapidly. Rubio promoted the church in several parts of the country, working on the West Coast, the Atlantic Coast, and in Texas. Table 4 indicates the national distribution of the denomination's Hispanic churches. Church of God congregations function autonomously, although they work under the same organizational structure as the Anglo churches. Contributions are directed exclusively for use within the administrative territory of the Hispanic churches. The CG's rapid growth makes it the second-largest Hispanic pentecostal group in the U.S.

d. The Latin American Districts of the Assemblies of God. (See Table 5.) The AG entered a new phase in its Hispanic work with the accession of leadership by Demetrio Bazán. Faced with the problems of cultural difference and distance, Bazán promoted the separation of the Spanish Eastern District from the Latin American District. In 1956 this entity was made a separate administrative unit, although the two districts continued to work under the supervision of the denomination's Home Missions Department until 1973, when they were given status equal to the church's geographical districts. At that time the Puerto Rican church was given similar status. In 1981 a seventh district was created for the largely Cuban population in the southeastern states that in the next five years grew to include 60 churches and a membership of 6,000. In 1998 the Pacific Latin American District (PLAD) was divided into separate North and South PLAD districts.

4. A Current Assessment of Hispanic Pentecostalism in the U.S.

a. Hispanic Pentecostal Initiative. Several features characterize contemporary Hispanic pentecostals. First, the movement continues to have a life of its own, the result of Hispanic initiative, even when the church operates within the framework of a predominately Anglo religious body. The growth of these congregations has come spontaneously, almost entirely as a result of their own resources, efforts, vision, and leadership.

b. Contextualized Faith. These churches flourish precisely where there is ethnic control and where ethnic cultural norms are respected. Esdras Betancourt, director of the Church of God Department of Hispanic Ministries, and other leaders of the movement have emphasized that Hispanic culture demands latitude for adapting denominational polity and customs to fit the sensibilities of their members.

c. Dynamic Leadership. Hispanics have gained recognition for their dynamic, aggressive leadership. Unwilling to wait, and demonstrating their ability to mobilize their communities, Latino pentecostal groups have caused a veritable "Hispanic panic" among Anglo pentecostals. The Assemblies of God, for example, responded to Hispanic growth and assertiveness by placing a Hispanic on its general presbytery alongside the executive officers representing the denomination's geographical regions.

d. Hispanic Diversity. Hispanics have had to contend with the many internal divisions and varying degrees of cultural conservatism within their communities. Recent immigrants often feel uncomfortable with culturally assimilated second- and third-generation Latinos, and differences in national origin, often important among Hispanics, sometimes strain relationships even within the church. Moreover, social-class differences, family backgrounds, and denominational loyalties also may divide Hispanic pentecostals. The processes of growth, development, identity, and degree of one's commitment to the larger community are all features that make the future of the Hispanic pentecostal churches dynamic and unpredictable.

e. Social Concern. Hispanic pentecostals have a strong social commitment. Conscious of their own status as an ethnic minority and the cultural gulf that has sometimes separated their communities from the larger society, Hispanics are sensitive to social disabilities and are concerned with obtaining increased opportunity. For them, pentecostalism has played a major part in their finding their own personal and community fulfillment. It is not surprising to find that they are often in the vanguard of social service and community-development programs and that this social concern has emerged directly from their pentecostal faith. The continued influx of Hispanics from Latin American churches and the growing political, economic, and cultural power of the Hispanic pentecostals will give them even greater opportunity in the future to express these concerns and to influence the character of the U.S. pentecostal movement.

5. Tables

Table 1. Percentage of Hispanics Born in the U.S. by Country of Family Origin

Mexico	61.6%
Puerto Rico	57.9%
Central and South America	39.0%
Cuba	27.3%

In Tables 2–5, Column A indicates number of congregations, Column B, number of communicants.

Table 2. Hispanic Pentecostal Denominations in the United States

	A	B
Asamblea Apostólica de la Fe en Cristo Jesús	220	80,000
Asamblea de Iglesias Cristianas	100	9,000
Latin American Council of Christian Churches	115	8,500
Spanish Christian Church	275	25,000
Total	710	122,500

Source: Estimates provided by denominational leaders and other informed observers.

Table 3. Puerto Rican Pentecostal Churches and Members

	A	B
Asambleas de Dios	198	18,000
Asamblea de Iglesias Cristianas	140	15,000
Iglesia de Cristo Misionera	395	30,000
Iglesia de Dios (Mission Board)	200	22,000
Iglesia de Dios de la Profecía	N/A	30,000
Iglesia de Dios Pentecostal	480	175,000
Iglesia Defensores de la Fe	123	12,000
Iglesia del Evangelio Cuadrangular	N/A	18,000
Others	N/A	30,000
Total	1,536	350,000

Source: Estimates provided by denominational leaders and other informed observers.

Table 4. Church of God (Cleveland, TN) Hispanic Churches
and Members by Region

	A	B
New England Hispanic	42	2,410
Northeastern Hispanic	116	11,864
Southeastern Hispanic	104	3,732
North Central Hispanic	35	2,426
East Central Hispanic	16	768
South Central Hispanic	74	4,187
Northwestern Hispanic	41	1,717
Southwestern Hispanic	62	7,449
Hispanic Churches in English-speaking districts	150	10,000
Total*	640	44,533

Source: Church of God, Department of Hispanic Ministries
*Exclusive of Hispanic members of Anglo congregations

Table 5. Assemblies of God Mainland Hispanic District
Churches and Members by Region

	A	B
Spanish Eastern	285	29,437
Southeastern Spanish	132	12,762
Midwest Latin American	58	3,743
Gulf Latin American	348	32,247
Central Latin American	126	8,167
Pacific Latin American North	186	26,000
Pacific Latin American South	224	34,000
Total*	1,367	139,586

Source: Assemblies of God headquarters, Office of the General Secretary
*Exclusive of Hispanic members of Anglo congregations

■ **Bibliography:** V. De León, *The Silent Pentecostals* (1979) ■ R. Dominguez, *Pioneros de Pentecostes* (1971) ■ L. Grebler, Morre, and Guzman, "Protestants and Mexicans," *The Mexican-American People* (1973) ■ K. Haselden, *The Death of a Myth* (1964) ■ C. Holland, *The Religious Dimension in Hispanic Los Angeles* (1974) ■ La Ruffa, "Pentecostalism in Puerto Rican Society," in S. Glacier, ed., *Perspectives on Pentecostalism in the Caribbean and Latin America* (1980) ■ J. Lugo, *Pentecostes en Puerto Rica* (1951) ■ G. B. McGee, "Pioneers of Pentecost: Alice E. Luce and Henry C. Ball," *AGH* 5 (2, 1985). ■ E. L. Wilson; J. Miranda

HITE, BENJAMIN HARRISON (1888–1948). Pentecostal preacher and leader. Born in Kentucky, Hite received the baptism in the Holy Spirit in 1912 in Nashville, TN. He evangelized in Tennessee, Arkansas, Oklahoma, Illinois, and Missouri, establishing many missions that grew into churches.

In 1921 he founded the First Pentecostal Church in St. Louis, MO, and remained pastor there until his death. He was the first chairman of the ʼPentecostal Church, Incorporated (PCI), serving from 1934 to 1939. He was then elected to serve as the superintendent of the Central District in the PCI from 1939 to 1945 and later as the superintendent of the Missouri District of the ʼUnited Pentecostal Church. He was known for his unusual ministry of healing.

■ **Bibliography:** A. L. Clanton, *United We Stand* (1970).
■ J. L. Hall

HOCKEN, PETER DUDLEY (1932–). Roman Catholic historian and theologian. Born in Brighton, Sussex, U.K., and reared as an Anglican, Peter Hocken converted to Roman Catholicism in 1954. Subsequently he studied at Oscott College, Birmingham (1958–64), and was ordained to the priesthood on Feb. 23, 1964, serving the Diocese of Northampton in pastoral work until 1968. From 1968 to 1976 he taught moral theology at Oscott College, interrupted only by his pursuit of the S.T.L. (licentiate) from the Accademia Alfonsiana in Rome (1964–71). Since 1976 he has served the Mother of God community in Gaithersburg, MD, and Northampton, U.K.

Through the years Hocken has maintained a strong ecumenical interest and has been actively involved in such interests since 1965, including membership in the Bishops' Ecumenical Commission for England and Wales (1973–76). Since 1972 he has served on the editorial board of *One in Christ*, a Roman Catholic ecumenical journal. In 1971 he became involved in the charismatic movement. This experience contributed to his Ph.D. studies undertaken at the University of Birmingham. He has authored numerous articles in both scholarly and popular journals and has been a contributor to *New Heaven? New Earth?* (1977) and *The Church Is Charismatic* (1981). His most recent publications included *Streams of Renewal* (1986) on the origins of the charismatic movement in Great Britain, and *One Lord, One Spirit, One Body* (1987) on the ecumenical grace of the charismatic movement. He served as the president of the Society for Pentecostal Studies in 1986. ■ C. M. Robeck Jr.

HODGES, MELVIN LYLE (1909–88). Author and missionary to Latin America. Melvin Hodges was born in Lynden, WA, to parents who had left the Methodist Church because of their newfound pentecostal experiences. At age 10 he was baptized in the Holy Spirit and called to the ministry. Two years later his family moved to Colorado. His father, a minister, taught him Greek at home; at age 15 Hodges pursued additional study in the language at Colorado College. In 1928 he married Lois M. Crews; they had three children. He began his ministry as an evangelist in Colorado and received ordination from the Assemblies of God (AG) in 1929. While

pastoring there, he was chosen to serve as district youth director (1931–33). After moving to Wyoming, he became the first presbyter from that state to serve the Rocky Mountain District (1933–35).

Hodges received appointment from the AG in 1935 as a missionary to Central America. Arriving in El Salvador in 1936, he assisted missionary Ralph D. Williams in Bible institute teaching. Moving to Nicaragua, he was elected as the general superintendent of the pentecostal churches and founded the Nicaraguan Bible School at Matagalpa. While there he began to redirect the church polity from a paternalistic structure, dependent on American financial assistance, to one based on indigenous church principles.

In 1945 Hodges returned to the U.S. for a brief time to edit the *Missionary Challenge,* a promotional magazine for the AG Division of Foreign Missions. During his last term in Central America (1950–53), he served as the chairman of the AG missionary fellowship for the region, superintended the work in El Salvador, and continued his Bible institute administration and teaching.

Hodges's missiological insights were strongly molded by the writings of Roland Allen. Asked by Noel Perkin to give a series of lectures at a missionary conference in 1950, he later expanded them for publication by ⸂Gospel Publishing House in 1953 under the title *The Indigenous Church.* Moody Press published an abridged edition the same year under the title *On the Mission Field: The Indigenous Church.* This was the first book on missiology published by a pentecostal; it reflects Allen's principles as well as Hodges's expertise in building indigenous churches in Central America and his pentecostal pneumatology. Since forces within pentecostalism were at that time at work to return overseas missions to a paternalistic approach, the timing of Hodges's book proved to be of crucial importance.

Gustavo Goldamez and Melvin Hodges, Assemblies of God leaders in El Salvador.

Hodges later took office as field director for Latin America and the West Indies for the AG Division of Foreign Missions in 1954. During these years his efforts to build strong evangelistic national churches contributed significantly to the spectacular church growth among pentecostals in Latin America.

After retiring from his field director's position in 1973, Hodges received appointment as professor of missions at the AG Theological Seminary; Noel Perkin Professor of World Missions in 1980; and professor emeritus in 1986. Northwest College of the AG conferred an honorary D.D. degree on him in 1974. A prolific writer, his books include *The Indigenous Church* (1953); *Build My Church* (1957); *Growth in Your Christian Ministry* (1960); *Spiritual Gifts* (1964); *When the Spirit Came* (1972); *A Guide to Church Planting* (1973); *A Theology of the Church and Its Mission: A Pentecostal Perspective* (1977); and *The Indigenous Church and the Missionary* (1978).

■ **Bibliography:** J. P. Hogan, "Breaks New Ground," *PE* (Aug. 12, 1973) ■ G. B. McGee, *This Gospel Shall Be Preached* (1986, 1989) ■ idem, "The Legacy of Melvin L. Hodges, *International Bulletin of Missionary Research* 22 (Jan. 1998) ■ *Who's Who in Religion, 1975–1976.*   ■ G. B. McGee

HODGSON, EDMUND ("TEDDY") (1898–1960).

British missionary and martyr. Born in Preston, Lancashire, he was called up in 1916 and served as a gunnery instructor. After being wounded he returned to Preston, where he became a master cabinetmaker. He sailed with ⸂James Salter to the Belgian Congo in 1920, where he used his practical skills in boat building and church construction. Barely surviving blackwater fever, he returned to England in 1923. After regaining his health he returned to the Congo in 1924, and in 1930 he carried out extensive deputation work for the Congo Evangelistic Mission (CEM).

An unspoiled man, Hodgson was greatly loved. In 1932 he married Linda Robson, but she died in 1933. In 1939 he married nurse Mollie Walshaw of Halifax; she died in 1952 at age 40.

Hodgson became field director of the CEM (later the Zaire Evangelistic Mission) in 1954 in succession to ⸂W. F. P. Burton; his last furlough was in 1958–59. Following independence from Belgian rule in June 1960 and a period of unrest, most of the CEM workers were withdrawn to Kamania for safety. When New Zealander Elton Knauf sought to return to his station at Lulungu, Hodgson accompanied him. They were both murdered on Nov. 23, 1960.

■ **Bibliography:** E. Hodgson, *Fishing for Congo Fisher Folk* (1934) ■ idem, *Out of Darkness* (1946) ■ C. Whittaker, *Seven Pentecostal Pioneers* (1983).   ■ D. W. Cartwright

HOGAN, JAMES PHILIP (1915–). Missionary and pentecostal missions executive. Born on a ranch near Olathe, CO, to Mr. and Mrs. James E. Hogan and converted as a child during a revival meeting conducted by two women evangelists, J. Philip Hogan received the baptism in the Holy Spirit a year later, in 1924. Hogan later attended Central Bible Institute (CBI; College after 1965) and graduated in 1936. He married (Mary) Virginia Lewis, daughter of Gayle F. Lewis—who was at the time superintendent of the Central District and later an Assemblies of God (AG) denominational executive—following her graduation from CBI in 1937. They have had two children: James Richard (d. 1956) and Phyllis Lynne (Hilton).

After graduation Hogan began his ministry as an evangelist. Later pastoral ministry included churches in Springfield, MO; Painesville, OH; and Detroit, MI. While in Detroit, Hogan invited Leonard Bolton, a missionary to China (L. Bolton, *China Call* [1984]), to conduct a missions convention in his church. He and his wife subsequently responded to Bolton's call for committed Christians to serve abroad as missionaries.

The AG approved the Hogans as missionaries in 1945, and they went to the University of California at Berkeley to study Chinese language and culture. Appointed to North China on Jan. 15, 1946, they sailed in Feb. 1947. Traveling to Ningpo, they ministered at the Bethel Mission founded by Nettie D. Nichols. There Hogan taught in the Bible school, led evangelistic teams, and learned the local dialect. They remained there for 18 difficult months with the threat of a Communist takeover making their situation ever more perilous. Leaving Ningpo, they went to Shanghai, where they conferred with AG missionaries Howard and Edith Osgood and the Garland Benintendises. Eventually the Hogans and Benintendises traveled to Formosa (Taiwan) for ministry. With the imminent threat of a Communist invasion of Formosa, the Benintendises, Virginia Hogan, and their children returned to the U.S. J. Philip Hogan stayed in Formosa, training a national minister and baptizing about 15 converts. After six months, conditions forced him to return home (1950). A brief pastorate followed in Florence, SC.

In 1952 Noel Perkin, director of AG foreign missions, invited Hogan to become a field representative for the promotions division of the agency. He accepted this assignment and moved his family to Springfield. Two years later he received appointment as secretary of promotions and traveled widely among AG churches and conventions promoting foreign missions. During his years in this office (1954–59) new and more effective programs were implemented to advance the cause of missions.

With the retirement of Perkin in 1959, the general council selected Hogan to become the executive director of the Division of Foreign Missions, based on the confidence he had gained among the council's ministers through his missionary

Dr. Roberto Suazo Cordova (left), the new president of Honduras, greeting Assemblies of God missionary Fernando Nieto and J. Philip Hogan (ca. 1982).

experience, preaching ministry, editorials in the *Pentecostal Evangel,* and other promotional work. With his encouragement, important and creative international ministries were developed during his administration. His commitment to indigenous church principles fostered the already growing number of overseas theological institutions (Bible institutes, Bible colleges, and advanced schools of theology) established for the training of national ministers and lay workers.

In addition to his administrative and promotional work, Hogan also served as a key strategist for the missions program. Whether with the Global Conquest initiative in 1959 or the Decade of Harvest program for the 1990s (a fraternal effort of the AG in the U.S. with national AG church organizations overseas), Hogan's imprint can be seen on the development of the missions enterprise.

Hogan's stature among evangelical and pentecostal missions executives led to his serving three terms as president of the Evangelical Foreign Missions Association (EFMA), the missionary branch of the ▸National Association of Evangelicals (NAE): 1968–70; 1976–78; 1983–85. He also served on the World Relief Corporation board of directors and various boards of directors in the AG. Hogan was the founding chairman of the World Assemblies of God Fellowship, as well as the keynote speaker at the organization's first congress on Oct. 26, 1994. In recognition of his service to AG missions, two colleges conferred honorary doctorates of divinity on him: Southern Asia Bible College, Bangalore, India (1970); and North Central Bible College, Minneapolis, MN (1975).

During Hogan's 30-year tenure, the number of AG missionaries grew from 753 (1959) to 1,464 (1987); the budget from $6,734,780 to $76,679,376; the number of overseas churches from 13,975 to 110,608; and the overseas constituents of national AG church organizations from 627,443 to 14,241,714.

■ **Bibliography:** AG Division of Foreign Missions press release ■ G. B. McGee, *This Gospel Shall Be Preached* (1986, 1989) ■ W. W. Menzies, *Anointed to Serve* (1971) ■ E. A. Wilson, *Strategy of the Spirit: J. Philip Hogan and the Growth of the Assemblies of God Worldwide 1960–1990* (1997). ■ G. B. McGee; B. A. Pavia

HOLINESS CHURCH OF NORTH CAROLINA See INTERNATIONAL PENTECOSTAL HOLINESS CHURCH.

HOLINESS MOVEMENT The pentecostal movement owes its inspiration and formation to the Wesleyan Holiness revival of the 19th century. It was born in the midst of Holiness retreat from attempts to reshape Methodist institutions to conform to the practices of camp meeting evangelists and, at the outset of the adaptation of these practices, to work among rural newcomers in the cities. The retreat, so clear in hindsight, was to many contemporaries neither inevitable nor desirable. Nor was it uniform, representing as it did the growing rift between the Eastern Methodists, who in 1867 had founded the National Camp Meeting Association for the Promotion of Holiness, and their converts, who as the years progressed increasingly dominated the affiliated state associations. The latter predominated in the independent churches and missions that appeared after 1880. And it was from this group, concerned as it was with healing, eschatology, and ecclesiology (issues outlawed for discussion by the national leaders), that most early pentecostals were drawn. Considered radicals among radicals, future glossolalists were absent from leadership in the insurgent independent group. Not one future pentecostal leader, for example, is listed as attending or endorsing the General Holiness Assembly of 1901 in Chicago, the last and most impressive move toward the creation of a comprehensive national Holiness denomination. It is not as a cohesive group within the Holiness ranks, however, that they were shut out. Rather, it is their espousal of issues deemed either controversial or heretical that placed many future pentecostals on the fringes of Christian perfectionism.

The issues that gave rise both to Holiness independence and to pentecostalism can be attributed to the aims of the original promoters of the 19th-century revival, who traced the church's malady to lack of the marks of sanctification. Other issues were secondary at best. National Holiness leaders, all of whom in the first decades were Methodists, insisted that those affiliated with it and its auxiliaries be members in good standing in some Christian body. They also required that meetings conducted by National Association workers be conducted in accordance with association regulations concerning doctrine and decorum. Agitation concerning church politics or emphasis on doctrines or experiences other than entire sanctification had no place, they said, in National Holiness meetings. An entirely sanctified membership would result in blameless conduct and peace in the church.

The die of Holiness conflict over independent churches was cast in the decade following 1880 with the birth of three bodies later known as the Church of God (Anderson, IN), the Church of God (Holiness), and the Holiness Church of California. Although church polity rather than doctrine was at issue, the emergence of these groups witnessed to the vitality of issues other than Holiness teaching in the movement and to the powerlessness of the Methodist Holiness evangelists to guide and control converts, especially in the Midwest, West, and South. All three churches conformed to strict Holiness orthodoxy. By their very existence, however, they opened the way to experimentation that both associations and independent church bodies were ill fitted to cope with. Pentecostalism became one of the chief end products.

The Holiness independents envisioned churches of saints meeting together for worship, edification, and watch care. Daniel Sidney Warner (1842–95) and John P. Brooks (1826–1915), theoreticians of the two Church of God groups, believed that the NT provided a specific plan for church government and that local congregations should be set in order according to that plan. In each place, the Church of God consisted of the wholly sanctified living out the divine command under the Scripture-mandated name. No membership roll had to be kept, for true saints recognized one another. As a human body, the local church was subject to mistakes in administration. As to its true members, however, it could never be in error. Since the Lord himself admitted those who were being saved, he alone determined who were true members. George M. Teel, theologian of the Holiness Church of California, described a church also composed solely of the entirely sanctified. Unlike the Church of God, however, the Holiness Church kept a membership roll, a feature adopted at organization by later Holiness and pentecostal bodies. Differences aside, reliance on the guidance of the Holy Spirit occupied a prominent place in the thinking of Holiness independents and so opened the avenue to experience-centeredness and Spirit guidance so often revealed in later pentecostal thought. Future pentecostals in the Holiness ranks started in this direction intellectually very soon thereafter.

Administrative difficulties attendant on the reliance of Holiness independents on Scripture and Spirit soon surfaced in the form of the so-called antiordinance heresy. Originating among the infant Church of God ranks in northern Missouri, the revolt against baptism and the Lord's Supper rapidly spread over the central and southern plains area. Based on the idea that the true believer depends on the guidance of the Holy Spirit alone, extremists came to discount even Scripture, the church, and common sense as standards of authority. Stories abounded of marriages contracted for and broken up on spiritual impulse. Faced with charismatic leaders among the new insurgents, conservative Holiness independents stood defenseless. In the years following 1881, this mode of thinking nearly destroyed the infant Texas Conference of the Free Methodist Church. Although within a decade or two the antiordinance movement died of its own excesses, its existence demonstrated the potential explosiveness of reliance on charisma, emotion, and Spirit guidance, factors inherent in the rise of pentecostalism a few years later.

Close on the heels of the antiordinance agitation arose another doctrinal novelty that appealed to a similar clientele and sprang from similar impulses. Invented by ▸Benjamin Hardin Irwin (b. 1854), an independent evangelist who operated on the fringes of the National Association, the Fire-Baptized teaching distinguished between entire sanctification and the baptism with the Holy Spirit and posited the latter as a third experience of grace. Like John Fletcher (1729–85), Wesley's colleague, Irwin regarded the sanctified Christian as the potential recipient of multiple infusions of power, the baptism of the Holy Spirit and fire being but the first. Later blessings he characterized by various explosives: dynamite, lyddite, and oxidite. Beginning in 1895 with Iowa, Irwin organized state and provincial Fire-Baptized associations wherever he preached, and these in turn became units of the ▸Fire-Baptized Holiness Association of America, formed at Anderson, SC, three years later. The life tenure granted the founder as general overseer and the baptism-of-fire doctrine both ended with exposure of Irwin's moral failings in 1900. The group's acceptance of third-work pentecostalism under his successor, ▸Joseph Hillery King (1869–1946), seven years later can be attributed partially to their earlier belief in the postsanctification experience of the baptism of the Holy Spirit and fire. Similarly, adoption of a three-work schema by the Cleveland, TN–based ▸Church of God about the same time may be attributed to the influence of this teaching. Emphasis on Spirit guidance, faith healing, and premillennialism, which pervaded these Holiness groups, remained intact after they entered the pentecostal group. The phenomenology of the experience of fire also remained. George Floyd Taylor (1881–1934), theologian and educator in the ▸Pentecostal Holiness Church with which the Fire-Baptized group merged in 1911, recalled testimonies of Irwin's followers concerning physical sensations of warmth and burning coincident with the spiritual experience. Likewise, ▸Charles Fox Parham (1873–1929), father of the doctrine of tongues as the initial physical evidence of the baptism of the Holy Spirit, had attended B. H. Irwin's meetings and, although not favorably impressed, observed the shouting and ecstatic demonstrations that accompanied the experience. At the height of the Azusa Street revival, Irwin reappeared as a pentecostal worker in Oakland and San Francisco. Apparently there was a tie between those attracted to experiences witnessed by fire and tongues.

Pentecostalism sprang not only from tensions between the established Methodist leaders of the National Holiness Association and their radical, independent Holiness brethren, but also from the commitment to Wesleyan perfectionism, which united them. Perfect love, both groups taught, was both a Methodist doctrine and a Bible doctrine. Resulting in heart purity, the experience of entire sanctification was essential not only to Methodists but to all true Christians. The Tuesday Meetings of Phoebe Palmer (1807–74) and the National Holiness camp meetings, therefore, welcomed comers from all evangelical denominations. Congregationalists, Baptists, Presbyterians, Episcopalians, Quakers, and Mennonites were accepted. Profession of a Holiness experience by non-Methodists resulted in unpredictable changes both in doctrine and in the non-Wesleyan churches to which new Holiness believers returned. As the movement expanded, Holiness believers from Methodist backgrounds increasingly taught that purity of intention and eradication of unholy desire was the essential fruit of entire sanctification, a theory taken to its extreme by the eccentric, scholarly evangelist W. B. Godbey (1833–1920). Non-Wesleyans, on the other hand, rallied around the teaching of the ▸Keswick Convention for the Promotion of Practical Holiness (from 1875 on held annually in the Lake District of northwest England) that power for Christian service was the principal fruit of sanctification and that suppression of sinful desire, not eradication of it, was the best the higher Christian life had to offer. Claiming less of a transformation than Wesleyan perfectionists, the Keswick Holiness advocates were also more tolerant of discussion of healing and eschatology. For potential pentecostalists it was a short step from the baptism of the Holy Spirit as a means of spiritual power to the acceptance of tongues as the initial witness of such a baptism. Anglican pentecostal pioneer ▸A. A. Boddy (1854–1930) early sensed the connection. He circulated his published pentecostal testimony at Keswick in 1908. In America the center most sympathetic to the Keswick teaching was Moody Bible Institute in Chicago. This city—which contributed ▸William H. Durham (1873–1912), ▸E. N. Bell (1866–1923), and ▸Andrew Urshan (1884–1967) to pentecostal leadership—was the early center of the so-called ▸finished work of Calvary teaching, which among pentecostal theologies bears the closest resemblance to Keswick. ▸A. B. Simpson (1843–1919), Presbyterian founder of the ▸Christian and Missionary Alliance, from which many early pentecostals were drawn, tried to bridge the Wesleyan Keswick chasm by saying that he taught neither eradication nor suppression, but habitation. To say the least, the situation on the edges of the National Holiness movement at the turn of the century was a fluid one, susceptible to a multitude of interpretations and methodologies beyond the scrutiny of ecclesiastical or academic critics. Anglicans like Boddy, ▸George B. Studd (1861–1946), ▸Cecil H. Polhill (1860–1938), ▸Robert Phair (1837–1931), and ▸J. Eustace Purdie (b. 1880); Presbyterians like ▸N. J. Holmes

(1847–1919); Quakers like ▸Levi Lupton (1860–1929) and ▸A. J. Tomlinson (1865–1943); and Mennonite Brethren in Christ like ▸George A. Chambers (1879–1957) all were ready to accommodate the niceties of received doctrine and tradition to new spiritual experiences.

By the turn of the century, worship patterns and mission strategies developed in Holiness cottage, camp, and band meetings, and in independent churches and missions these patterns were ripe for adoption and adaptation by the infant glossolalia-centered movement. The system of self-support that Bishop ▸William Taylor (1821–1902), a National Holiness member, developed to utilize European and American businessmen in his quasi-independent foreign missionary enterprise had evolved by the 1890s into so-called faith work, in which unsalaried young people went to the field without formal backing or advanced pledges, depending solely on faith and prayer for support. Future pentecostal strongholds in India, Chile, and West Africa grew out of the pioneer Holiness efforts of Taylor workers; ▸Willis C. Hoover (1856–1936) in Chile was the outstanding example. A corollary of this method was a trial period spent in slum or rural work at home using the faith principle as a test of the suitability of candidates for foreign service. Workers who proved themselves in this way would be given transportation to the field but no guarantee of support after arriving. A large number of independent city missions sprang up in the U.S. and Europe under this plan, which was at the height of its popularity at the time of the Topeka, Houston, and Los Angeles revivals.

Not only had the plan of organization and support been established but the content and manner of conducting worship as well. Beginning with the "Cleansing Wave" of Phoebe Palmer, a new genre of Holiness-experience songs emerged in which the whole congregation testified, shouted, and at times gave expositions of Scripture and doctrine. Destined to provide the core repertoire of the hymnodies of both Holiness and pentecostal movements for well over a half century, these songs abounded with images drawn from the Bible and John Bunyan (1628–88): the Exodus, the Promised Land, and heaven in analogies derived from the camp meeting ground, the railroad, and debt and hard times. These songs drew worshipers into sympathy one to another at the same time they were reinforcing teaching from the pulpit and creating a common doctrinal and behavioral standard.

In the 1890s both Wesleyan and Keswick Holiness advocates increasingly identified the second crisis with Pentecost, and references to the upper-room event began to appear in church names and song texts. Use of the pentecostal designation was thematic rather than dogmatic, however. Holiness people in both camps sang hymns such as "The Comforter Has Come" by Frank Bottome (1823–94) for more than a decade before it gained permanent standing in the pentecostal repertoire by repeated use at ▸Azusa Street. Between 1891 and 1911 Hope Publishing Company of Chicago issued six volumes of *Pentecostal Hymns* compiled by Henry Date. Other Holiness contributions were songbooks issued by the Pepper Publishing Company of Philadelphia, the Christian Witness Company of Chicago, the Christian Alliance Publishing Company of New York, the Pickett Publishing Company of Louisville, and the Pentecostal Mission Publishing Company of Nashville. Notable individual contributions as composer or compiler were made by A. B. Simpson, ▸F. A. Graves (1856–1927), R. Kelso Carter (1849–1926), L. L. Pickett (1859–1928), Charlie Tillman (1861–1943), ▸D. Wesley Myland (1858–1943), and ▸Herbert Buffum (1879–1939), all of whom were white; and C. P. Jones (1865–1949) and ▸Thoro Harris (1874–1955), blacks.

Due to their roots and the roots of their followers in the Holiness movement, Charles Fox Parham and ▸William J. Seymour (1870–1922) acted at Topeka, Houston, and Los Angeles in an already familiar arena. Parham, who tacitly encouraged female followers to challenge the ascetic Holiness dress code, had intimate knowledge of the independent and National Holiness movements in the Great Plains. Seymour, a black, had ties with the Revivalist people of Cincinnati and the Evening Light Saints (Church of God [Anderson, IN]) in Indiana and Louisiana. Both were familiar with Holiness inner-city missions and with Holiness communalism. Parham's Bethel Healing Home and his Bethel Bible School in Topeka were markedly similar to the World's Faith Missionary Association home in Shenandoah, IA, where ▸Clara Lum (d. 1942), an Azusa Mission worker, trained; the God's Bible School and Missionary Training Home, which Seymour visited in Cincinnati; N. J. Holmes's Altamont Bible and Missionary Institute in Greenville, SC; and the healing home in East Providence, RI, which ▸Christine Gibson (1879–1955) was to transform into Zion Bible Institute, a faith school. In the last decades of the 19th century, a Holiness language of several dialects had been formulated; it encompassed a like number of doctrinal, racial, ecclesiastical, and social constituencies. For several months in 1906, 1907, and 1908, a number of these dialects merged into a unified one in a multiracial slum mission on Azusa Street in Los Angeles. Although they were destined to separate, those Holiness people were so marked by this experience that they were permanently redirected. To the movement launched at Azusa, however, the new pentecostals brought a richly diverse inheritance of Holiness doctrine, ecclesiology, worship, and institutionalism—all of which were henceforth both to unite and divide them.

See also Black Holiness Pentecostalism; Initial Evidence.

■ **Bibliography:** R. M. Anderson, *Vision of the Disinherited* (1979) ■ J. P. Brooks, *The Divine Church* (1891) ■ C. Brumback, *Suddenly . . . from Heaven* (1961) ■ J. E. Campbell, *The Pentecostal Holiness Church, 1898–1948* (1951) ■ C. W. Conn, *Like a Mighty Army: A*

History of the Church of God (1977) ■ C. E. Cowen, *A History of the Church of God (Holiness)* (1948) ■ D. W. Dayton, *Theological Roots of Pentecostalism* (1987) ■ M. E. Dieter, *The Holiness Revival of the Nineteenth Century* (1980) ■ idem, "Wesleyan-Holiness Aspects of Pentecostal Origins: As Mediated Through the Nineteenth-Century Holiness Revival," in V. Synan, ed., *Aspects of Pentecostal-Charismatic Origins* (1975) ■ C. C. Fankhauser, "The Heritage of Faith: An Historical Evaluation of the Holiness Movement in America" (thesis, Pittsburgh [KS] State U., 1983) ■ S. H. Frodsham, *With Signs Following* (1946) ■ J. R. Goff, "Charles F. Parham and His Role in the Development of the Pentecostal Movement: A Reevaluation," *Kansas History* 7 (Fall 1984) ■ idem, "Fields White unto Harvest: Charles F. Parham and the Missionary Origins of Pentecostalism" (diss., U. of Arkansas, 1987) ■ C. E. Jones, *Perfectionist Persuasion: The Holiness Movement and American Methodism, 1867–1936* (1974) ■ idem, "Anti-Ordinance: A Proto-Pentecostal Phenomenon?" *Wesleyan Theological Journal* 25 (Fall 1990) ■ idem, "Symbol and Sign in Methodist Holiness and Pentecostal Spirituality," in Timothy Miller, ed. *America's Alternative Religions* (1995): 23–31 ■ idem, "Tongues-Speaking and the Wesleyan-Holiness Quest for Assurance of Sanctification," *Wesleyan Theological Journal* 22 (Fall 1987) ■ A. M. Kiergan, *Historical Sketches of the Revival of True Holiness and Local Church Polity from 1865–1916* (1972) ■ L. Lovett, "Black Origins of the Pentecostal Movement," in V. Synan, ed., *Aspects of Pentecostal-Charismatic Origins* (1975) ■ W. W. Menzies, *Anointed to Serve* (1971) ■ D. J. Nelson, "For Such a Time as This: The Story of Bishop William J. Seymour and the Azusa Street Revival, a Search for Pentecostal/Charismatic Roots" (diss., Birmingham U., 1981) ■ R. L. Niklaus, J. S. Sawin, and S. J. Stoesz, *All for Jesus* (1986) ■ S. E. Parham, *The Life of Charles F. Parham* (1930) ■ D. R. Rose, *Vital Holiness: A Theology of Christian Experience* (1975) ■ M. H. Schrag, "Benjamin Hardin Irwin and the Brethren in Christ," *Brethren in Christ History and Life* (Dec. 4, 1981) ■ idem, "The Spiritual Pilgrimage of the Reverend Benjamin Hardin Irwin," *Brethren in Christ History and Life* 4 (June 1981) ■ J. W. V. Smith, *The Quest for Holiness and Unity* (1980) ■ T. L. Smith, *Called unto Holiness* (1962) ■ V. Synan, *The Holiness-Pentecostal Movement in the United States* (1971) ■ idem, *The Old-Time Power: A History of the Pentecostal Holiness Church* (1973) ■ G. M. Teel, *The New Testament Church* (1901) ■ E. L. Waldvogel [Blumhofer], "The 'Overcoming Life': A Study in the Reformed Evangelical Origins of Pentecostalism" (diss., Harvard, 1977) ■ D. S. Warner, *The Church of God or, What Is the Church and What Is Not* (1902) ■ G. H. Williams and E. Waldvogel [Blumhofer], "A History of Speaking in Tongues and Related Gifts," in M. P. Hamilton, ed., *The Charismatic Movement* (1975).   ■ C. E. Jones

HOLLENWEGER, WALTER JACOB (1927–). Swiss theologian and scholar of pentecostalism and intercultural theology. Born in Antwerp, Belgium, Hollenweger became a youth leader in the Swiss Pentecostal Mission and attended the International Bible Training Institute (1948–49), Burgess

Walter J. Hollenweger, prominent analyst and historian of the pentecostal movement.

Hill, U.K., founded by Fred Squire. He studied at the University of Zurich (1955–65) and followed lectures at Basel. He received his doctorate from the University of Zurich for the 10-volume *Handbuch der Pfingstbewegung* (diss. 1966; microfilm, 1967); portions of the first volume were revised and published as *Enthusiastisches Christentum* (1969). Two additional and different versions were also published: *The Pentecostals* (1972) and *Le Pentecostalismo: Historia y doctrinas* (1976). Hollenweger served as secretary for evangelism of the World Council of Churches (1965–71) and as professor of mission at the University of Birmingham and Selly Oaks Colleges, England (1971–89). Forty-seven students received doctorates under his guidance; another 32 master's degrees were directed by him. After retirement, he served as guest professor at the Universities of Bern and Zurich (1989–92) and conducted religious services throughout German-speaking Europe, using original religious drama and music. He is an ordained clergyperson in the Swiss Reformed Church and a prolific author.

■ **Bibliography:** W. J. Hollenweger, *Ein theologisches Lesebuch* (1980) ■ idem, *Erfahrungen der Leibhaftigkeit* (1979) ■ idem, *Evangelism Today: Good News or Bone of Contention?* (1976) ■ idem, *Pentecost between Black and White* (1974) ■ idem, *Pentecostalism: Origins and Developments Worldwide* (1997) ■ idem, *Umgang mit Mythen* (1982) ■ idem, *Wie aus Grenzen Brucken werden* (1980) ■ J. A. B. Jongeneel, ed., *Pentecost, Mission and Ecumenism: Essays on Intercultural Theology*, Festschrift in Honor of Professor Walter J. Hollenweger (1992).   ■ D. D. Bundy

HOLMES, NICKELS JOHN (1847–1919). Pastor, educator, and church leader. Born in Spartanburg, SC, and trained in law at Edinburgh University, Holmes decided to enter the Presbyterian ministry and was ordained by the Enoree Presbytery in South Carolina in 1888. He served as pastor of the Second Presbyterian Church of Greenville, SC, from 1892 to 1895.

In July 1896 he received an experience of sanctification after a visit to hear D. L. Moody in Northfield, MA. After this he organized the Tabernacle Presbyterian Church, a small ▸Holiness denomination in SC. Prior to this he had begun to hold classes for young ministers on Parris Mountain near Greenville, SC. By 1898 these classes became the Holmes Bible and Missionary Institute. The school operated then—as it does now—as a "faith" school, not charging students for educational costs.

In 1907 Holmes and his entire Bible institute accepted the pentecostal message from ▸G. B. Cashwell, an ▸Azusa Street pilgrim. After speaking in tongues, Holmes and the institute continued to teach a Wesleyan theology, staunchly defending the sanctification experience as a second blessing while promoting glossolalia as ▸initial evidence of the baptism in the Holy Spirit.

In 1915 the Tabernacle churches merged with the ▸Pentecostal Holiness Church (PHC) in Canon, GA. Holmes and the institute did not join in the merger, although the school was later related to the PHC. His institution, now known as the Holmes College of the Bible, is the oldest pentecostal educational institution in the world.

■ **Bibliography:** N. Holmes, *Life Sketches and Sermons* (1920).
        ■ H. V. Synan

HOLY SPIRIT, DOCTRINE OF: THE ANCIENT FATHERS

  I. Before the Council of Nicea (A.D. 325)
    A. The Apostolic Fathers
    B. The Early Apologists
    C. The Impact of Early Heresies on Christian Pneumatology
      1. Gnostic Religions
      2. Montanism
      3. Marcionism
      4. Dynamic and Modalistic Monarchianism
    D. The Response of Later Apologists and Polemicists
      1. Irenaeus
      2. Tertullian
      3. Two Early Christian Martyrs
      4. Clement of Alexandria
      5. Origen
      6. Novatian
      7. Hippolytus
      8. Cyprian

  II. The Nicene and Post-Nicene Period (to the End of the Sixth Century)
    A. Theological Controversies and Creedal Formulae
    B. Eastern Christianity from the Fourth through the Sixth Centuries
      1. Eusebius of Caesarea
      2. Cyril of Jerusalem
      3. Didymus the Blind
      4. Athanasius
      5. John Chrysostom
      6. Basil of Caesarea
      7. Gregory of Nyssa
      8. Gregory of Nazianzen
      9. Ephrem of Syria
     10. Narsai
     11. Pseudo-Macarius
     12. Pseudo-Dionysius the Areopagite
    C. Western Christianity from the Fourth through the Sixth Centuries
      1. Hilary of Poitiers
      2. Ambrose
      3. Augustine of Hippo

I. BEFORE THE COUNCIL OF NICEA (A.D. 325).

Theological understanding of the person and work of the Holy Spirit grew slowly during the first 300 years of the Christian era. This resulted in part from the need to address significant christological questions. But it also can be attributed to the fact that during this period Christians suffered persecution, which made it all but impossible for leaders of the church to gather in a general council to resolve theological issues.

In addition, much of the apostolic awareness of the work of the Spirit seemingly was lost, partially because of a diminishing of both prophetic ministry and ecclesiastical emphasis on the gifts of the divine Spirit. This diminishing resulted from the inability of prophets and priests to find common goals for the church, from prophetic excess and abuse, and from an institutionalization process in which Spirit charismata came to be localized in the office of the bishop. The charismata were also reserved for certain truly exceptional Christians, such as those who were to be martyred, those who became confessors (suffered persecution but were not martyred), and, by the late 3d and early 4th centuries, the ascetics. By default, after the late 2d century the most prominent exercise of the charismata was to be in heretical and fringe groups, such as the Gnostics and the Montanists.

Admittedly, significant strides were made during the first three Christian centuries in conceptualizing Spirit doctrine and in pneumatological definition. For example, in the writings of Tertullian, a late-2d- early-3d-century North African father, expression is given to the distinctive personhood and work of the Spirit and to a Trinitarian understanding of God as "three in one," a concept that would eventually be adopted by the larger church in the Nicene formula. There was further definition of the salvific role of the Holy Spirit in the waters of baptism, and of his reception, first thought to occur in baptism, and later understood to be in *chrismation* (in the East) and in the laying on of hands *(baptisma Spiritus)* or confirmation (in the West). Certain of these Fathers also added significantly to the Christian conceptualization of the nature of the Godhead by more clearly defining terminology such as "Trinity" and divine "persons."

A. The Apostolic Fathers.

The earliest church fathers—sometimes called "apostolic fathers" because they were thought to have known the apostles—wrote occasional pieces that responded to local contemporary needs, rather than systematic theological treatises. Their references to the Spirit do very little to define the person and office of the divine Spirit beyond that of canonical writings. Two of them (Pseudo-Clement and the writer of the *Shepherd of Hermas*) even confuse the Holy Spirit with the Son or Word of God. Others, such as Clement of Rome and Ignatius of Antioch, speak of the Father, Son, and Spirit with a much clearer understanding of the separateness and the divine status of the Spirit.

Because prophetic ministry was still prominent in the church (according to Pseudo-Barnabas it would seem that it was even normative), the apostolic fathers were concerned to distinguish between the true and the false prophets. The *Didache* identifies false prophets as those who ask for money, stay longer than two days, and do not have "the ways of the Lord." The author of the *Shepherd of Hermas* also warns against those who use "prophecy" to collect money for themselves, give empty answers, have an earthly spirit, and attempt to gain a prominent place. The latter writer also suggests that the Holy Spirit and an evil spirit can possess a person at the same time.

Clement of Rome and Ignatius of Antioch, both bishops, claimed to be inspired, like canonical writers, by the divine Spirit to write to the churches. Both recognize the operation of spiritual gifts among average Christians, although this is tempered by their stress on the importance of obedience to the bishop. Ignatius writes to yet another bishop, Polycarp of Smyrna, encouraging him to pray that he would be deficient in nothing and might abound in all gifts. The *Martyrdom of Polycarp* is the first noncanonical work to recognize the support given by the Spirit to martyrs. It also includes the first doxology outside of Scripture in which the Holy Spirit is exalted with the Father and the Son.

B. The Early Apologists.

Struggling to defend the church against pagan Roman attacks, the apologists made the first attempt to conceptualize and interpret Christian theology with the tools of classical philosophy. They were so concerned with Christology—especially Logos theology—that they gave little place to the Holy Spirit. Perhaps because of inadequate vocabulary, but certainly because of undeveloped Trinitarian concepts, they, like certain of the apostolic fathers, used the term *spirit* to express the preexistent nature both of Christ and of the divine Third Person. They occasionally used the term to denote all three Persons.

In fairness, however, it should be pointed out that the apologists were actually experimenting with vocabulary, an effort that was to result eventually in the more adequate expression of emerging orthodox theology. For example, Theophilus is the first Christian to apply the word *Trinity* to the Godhead. Athenagoras presents the first clear-cut definition of the relationship of the Holy Spirit to the rest of the Trinity, in language that anticipates the great creedal statements of the next several centuries. (Although he labels the three as "God, Word, and Wisdom," Theophilus also refers to the Holy Spirit as "Wisdom.")

One of the tendencies of classically trained Christian apologists was to follow Platonic metaphysical systems, especially the concept of emanation, in explaining the nature of the Trinity and its interrelationships. By emanation is meant the notion that all creatures issue from the One, and eventually return to that One. In expressing the nature of the Godhead in Platonic terms, therefore, it was understandable that certain apologists, such as Justin Martyr, would introduce subordinationism—placing the Son below the Father, and the Spirit below both of the other divine persons. Another apologist of the 2d century, Tatian, argues against the integration of Neoplatonism into Christian thought, although he too seems to imply subordination, at least in the function of the divine persons. The same subordinationist tendency appears again in 3d-century Alexandria, especially in the writings of Origen, but eventually it was struck down as heresy at the councils of Nicea (325) and Constantinople (381) in the struggle against the Arians and Macedonians.

It is apparent from the early apologists that the charismata were in evidence in the 2d-century Christian community. Justin Martyr explains that the prophetic gifts exercised by OT figures had been transferred to Christian believers. Theophilus goes a step further, arguing that the ancient Greeks had been given similar gifts.

C. The Impact of Early Heresies on Christian Pneumatology.

Orthodoxy can exist and be so defined only in the presence of heresy—the teaching of the losing side in struggles with orthodoxy. In addition, there certainly is more reason for the mainstream church to formulate theological positions when it is threatened by opposition that it considers to be in error. So it was in the early church. Challenges from competing groups led mainstream polemicists to a clarification and systematization of basic doctrine.

1. Gnostic Religions.

Perhaps the most serious challenge came from Gnostic religions, which flourished from the 1st through 3d centuries A.D., some continuing well into the Middle Ages. The Gnostics agreed on several significant tenets, including a whole system of radical dualism. They understood the spirit of each human to be unalterably divine, and the body to be evil, imprisoning the spirit that had not received special revelation. Salvation to the "Christian Gnostic" was not through the sacrificial death of Christ but rather through a gift of higher knowledge through the Holy Spirit—quite different from a gospel view of redemption in which the Spirit works on the moral nature of humans rather than by merely enlightening their minds. Those individuals who recognize the presence of the divine Spirit within them were called pneumatics or the elect, whereas others less fortunate were identified with matter.

Individuals who received special knowledge were given gifts of the Spirit; but these were not to be shared with the common "ignorant" people, who lacked *gnosis*. Apparently these gifts included glossolalia, of which we have several written examples (although these may be merely barbarizations of language). It seems that Gnostic prophets abounded, and opponents were quick to point out charlatans (e.g., Irenaeus in his account of Marcus, a follower of Valentinus).

Gnostic theologies are highly complex and allegorically expressed, although little attempt is made to articulate the nature of God who is understood to be incomprehensible. Both the Son and the Spirit are viewed as emanations, which by definition subordinates them to the Father. Several times in Gnostic texts, the Holy Spirit is referred to as the divine mother. Again, Christ is said to have been born of a virgin—the Holy Spirit. Whoever becomes a Gnostic Christian is said to have gained both a father (God the Father) and a mother—the Spirit of God.

Several sacraments are present in Christian Gnosticism, including baptism, Eucharist, unction, sealing, and bridal chamber. The unction of the Holy Spirit is of a higher order than traditional sacraments, and anointing by the Spirit is valued above baptism.

It can be assumed that antagonism to the Gnostics led the mainline church to fear anyone who claimed a "special knowledge" or "revelation." Thus, the place of the prophet was diminished and more authority placed into the hands of the priest.

2. Montanism.

If Gnosticism was damaging to the influence of those who claimed prophetic gifts within the broader church, a derivative of Gnosticism in Asia Minor, Montanism, proved to be fatal. About A.D. 155, Montanus, a former priest of Cybele who had converted to Christianity, began to prophesy in his new context. His prophecies gained immediate attention, in part because of his manner of delivery—he was said to have lost control of himself; fallen into a sort of frenzy and ecstasy; raved, babbled, and uttered strange things (certain pentecostal historians take this to be glossolalia); and prophesied in a manner contrary to established custom. He was joined by two prophetesses, Maximilla and Priscilla (or Prisca), who deserted their husbands with Montanus's sanction and claimed the same prophetic gifts their founder enjoyed. (Apparently Montanist women continued to exercise a prophetic gift after the death of these three, for Tertullian, himself a convert to Montanism, tells of an early-3d-century woman who fell into ecstasy during services but did not deliver her prophetic message until the congregation had departed.)

All three of these early Montanist leaders believed that their prophecies would be God's final word to man. Montanus identified a new holy place—Pepuza in Phrygia—where Christ would return, and gathered his followers to await that event. The Montanists believed that the OT and NT were superseded by the new prophecies, which were put into written form (all of these writings soon disappeared, probably as the result of the persecution of the Montanists). The authority of the mainline Catholic Church as well as its avenues for imparting grace were rejected, to be replaced by the authority of the new prophets and a new and more demanding discipline. They practiced a perfectionist lifestyle with a new extreme of intolerant exclusiveness. The product was a legalistic requirement of additional fasting, rejection of second marriages, and promotion of other forms of self-denial and unreserved preparation for martyrdom.

Intolerance was answered by intolerance. But the mainline church was impotent to wipe out the new prophecy until it was itself legitimatized by the state. From the beginning of the 4th century, however, the Montanists suffered acute persecution by the orthodox faithful, until at last they were exterminated in the 6th century under Justinian.

Paul Tillich recognizes four effects of the victory of Christianity over Montanism: the canon was victorious against the possibility of new revelations; the traditional hierarchy was confirmed against the prophetic spirit; eschatology became less significant; and with the loss of the strict Montanist discipline, a growing laxity infected the church (Tillich, 1968, 41).

3. Marcionism.

Marcion, a wealthy shipowner from Asia Minor who moved to Rome shortly before A.D. 140, was excommunicated from the orthodox community for his radical teachings. He proceeded to form a rival religious community. His church flourished in the late 2d century to the extent that the final victor in his controversy with the mainline church was in doubt.

Marcionist teachings, like those of Gnostic religions, centered on radical dualism. Unlike the Gnostics, however, Marcion never claimed special *gnosis* and did not argue that salvation comes by knowledge as opposed to faith. He distinguished between a god of the OT—the creator of matter (which was evil)—and the God of the NT—the true God of love. As a docetist, Marcion would not allow for an Incarnation, because the very notion of a divine Redeemer participating in materiality was repugnant to him.

Rejecting the OT and much of the NT, Marcion was devoted to the writings of the apostle Paul, in large measure because of Paul's distinction between law and grace. Notwithstanding, Marcion seemingly found no place for the Holy Spirit, and this seems strange for someone so devoted to the apostle. He seems to have identified the Spirit of God with Christ, the giver of supernatural life.

Because of his success in winning converts, Marcion became the target of the leading Trinitarian writers in the early-2d- and early-3d-century church. Origen argues that Marcion could not really have been a Paulinist because of his rejection of the Paraclete. It is impossible to experience the blessings of the gospel while at the same time rejecting the gospel. Tertullian agrees, adding that Marcion quenched the Spirit by denying ecstatic prophecy. He challenged Marcion to show that there are gifts of the Spirit functioning in his church, adding that they are fully in operation within his own true Christian community.

Marcion's rejection of the Holy Spirit prompted the ablest contemporary defenders of the faith—Irenaeus, Tertullian, and Origen—to rise in support of the church's belief in the divine Third Person. In so doing, they amplified and further developed the church's doctrine of the Spirit. But they also chose to address the ongoing charismatization of the church in the late 2d century, a witness to the continued functioning of the Spirit through his gifts—a witness that might not otherwise be available.

4. Dynamic and Modalistic Monarchianism.

Certain early Christians reacted against what they considered "tritheism" in Trinitarian teachings. They stressed the "one man rule" or "monarchy" of the Father, rather than that of the Logos, whom they saw as a second god, or of a third, the Holy Spirit. These unitarians came to be known as monarchians.

Such dynamic monarchians (or adoptionists) as Theodotus of Byzantium in the West and Paul of Samosata in the East taught that Jesus was merely a man on whom the divine Spirit descended at his baptism in the Jordan River, giving him power for his messianic mission. The man Jesus was adopted and filled with the divine Logos or Spirit (qualities of God, not persons in the Godhead). But Jesus was not God.

Modalistic monarchians, such as Noetus of Smyrna, taught that God appears in different modes, in different ways. Praxeas, against whom Tertullian wrote, taught that God the Father was born through the Virgin Mary and that he, the only God, suffered and died. The leading modalistic monarchian was Sabellius of Libya; he believed that God changes masks throughout history as an actor would on the stage. He appears as the Father in his functions of creating and lawgiving; he takes on the countenance of the Son in his work of redemption; and he assumes the guise of the Spirit in his work of sanctification. The one God only *appears* to be a Trinity.

As with the threat of Marcionism, the monarchian challenge impelled leading Trinitarians such as Tertullian, Hippolytus, and Novatian to reflect further on the nature of the Godhead and to develop new terminology to better express these concepts. Certainly the challenge of heresy within the church led ultimately to a more adequate understanding of the divine "three in one."

D. The Response of Later Apologists and Polemicists.

With the writings of the apologists who defended the church against Roman persecution and of the polemicists who guarded against false teachings, the doctrine of the Holy Spirit matured significantly during the 2d and 3d centuries. Trinitarian concepts and vocabulary developed further, and the role of the Spirit in salvation was clarified. This also was the period in which the Spirit and authority were united formally. This fusion of prophetic and priestly functions was completed under Cyprian. In turn, the institutional church allowed the charismata (1 Cor. 12) to die, rendering them powerless in the hands of others. The result was that the prophetic spirit came to center in sectarian movements. These, of course, were immediately in conflict with the institutional church.

1. Irenaeus.

A disciple of Polycarp of Smyrna, Irenaeus (c. A.D. 130–202) became bishop of Lyons in Gaul. He was the most influential of all early church fathers. Recognizing the Gnostic threat, he chose to defend the young church by giving the first systematic exposition of its beliefs. In the process, he said much about the Holy Spirit.

Reacting against the Gnostic teaching of emanation, Irenaeus speaks of the Son and the Spirit as inherent in the very life of God, rather than as proceeding from the Father. His anti-Gnosticism also led him to stress the role of the Son and the Spirit (the "Word" and the "Wisdom") in creation. Furthermore, he reacted against Marcion's depreciation of the OT by emphasizing the Spirit's inspiration of christological prophecy in the OT. Gnostic teachings that Jesus merely *seemed* to take on human flesh prompted Irenaeus to emphasize the incarnation and the act of the Spirit that united the Word of God with the flesh of Jesus in the womb of Mary. This stress on the incarnation also is in reaction to the adoptionists, who argued that Jesus was merely a man until the Spirit descended on him at his baptism in the Jordan.

Irenaeus insists that humankind is redeemed by Christ through the regenerating power of the Holy Spirit, but not as the result of having received a special knowledge *(gnosis)* from God. Furthermore, the redemptive act is for all those who have faith in Christ as Savior and is not reserved for those who claim to be spiritually elite.

The bishop of Lyons recognized the ongoing operation of the Spirit in the life of the church—a recognition far beyond other writers of the 2d century, with the possible exception of Tertullian. Where the church is, there is the Spirit of God; and where the Spirit of God functions, there is the church. The Christian life is an ascent to God, and the Spirit serves as the ladder.

Irenaeus also recognizes the continued operation of charismatic gifts, including prophecy, among the brethren in his own church. He warns, however, against certain false Gnostics (especially one named Marcus) who fabricated spiritual gifts to win the favor of others, especially rich women in the congregation. The only real answer to such Gnostic novelty is for the truly spiritual person to hold to the apostolic tradition as handed down by the succession of Catholic bishops. Irenaeus's advice was to be followed by the Catholic Church, with the result that spiritual gifts soon were located in the office of the bishop and were institutionalized in the sacraments. Although the Mass became the central Spirit experience, it usually was not known as such. When the act lost its name, the breadth of its significance was gone.

2. Tertullian.

Born in Carthage c. A.D. 150, Tertullian was trained as a lawyer. In midlife he moved to Rome, where he was converted to Christianity. Later he returned to Carthage, where he began writing in support of his new faith. Attracted by the extreme asceticism of the Montanists, he broke with the Catholics in Carthage in about 207 and joined with the "New Prophecy."

The first important "pentecostal" theologian, Tertullian adds measurably to the church's understanding of the person and work of the Holy Spirit. He gives to Christianity its language of "Trinity" and of "Persons" in the Trinity. Certainly in part from his Montanist experience of the Spirit, he is able to distinguish the operation of the divine Third Person from that of the Father and the Son. They are separate in function yet one in essence. The uniqueness of the Spirit's role is demonstrated in his salvific work. Regenerated in waters of baptism, which the Spirit sanctifies, the Christian then is anointed with the Spirit by God the Father ("blessed unc-

tion" or "chrismation"). Indeed, argues Tertullian, it is these very distinctions of personhood and function in the Godhead that separate Christianity from Judaism.

Tertullian introduces in his writings a form of dispensationalism that argues that although the Spirit was poured out on the 1st-century church, it was the Montanist "New Prophets" who would be instruments in revealing the full provision of the Spirit. Spiritual insights gained through visions received by the prophets in dreams and in states of ecstasy, and the prophetic utterances that followed, become norms for his own hyperascetic teachings. He assumed that the functioning of Spirit gifts is clear evidence of the true spirituality of the Montanist movement, and he challenged the heretic Marcion to show similar evidence of the charismata.

Tertullian always felt that he was true to traditions handed down from the primitive church. As a result, he reacted against the tendency he perceived in the mainline church to live below the extraordinary ascetic requirements of the New Prophecy and to squelch or to institutionalize prophetic ministry. But admittedly, the very force of his apologetics on behalf of the message of his prophets undoubtedly accelerated the institutionalization process he wished to abort.

3. Two Early Christian Martyrs.

In A.D. 202, during the persecution by Septimius Severus, five Christians gave their lives for their faith in the arena at Carthage. These included Vivia Perpetua and her maid-servant Felicitas. Their martyrdom is recorded by an anonymous author with unmistakable Montanist leanings (perhaps Tertullian). Not only does the text suggest the importance of end-time events in the history of the church—a clear reference to the New Prophecy—but it also includes a passage describing the final moments of the two women, who face death with triumphant ecstasy (reminiscent of Polycarp of Smyrna).

The significance of this martyrology for our study is that the women's most unexpected reaction of triumphant joy is attributed to the presence of the Holy Spirit, who is understood to provide strength and comfort for those summoned to martyrdom. Here we have a recognition of the legitimate exercise of spiritual gifts by a class of believers who lived beyond the expectation of the rest of the church. This principle later would be applied to monks and virgins as well. Of course, this also implied that the charismata should not be expected to function as readily in the lives of more ordinary Christians.

4. Clement of Alexandria.

With the decline of Athens, Alexandria became the intellectual capital of the late Roman Empire. Here blends of philosophy and religious belief were common. It is understandable that certain Christian writers, trained in Neoplatonic thought, would bring their philosophic understanding to bear on Christian theology. Clement of Alexandria (d. before A.D. 216) argued that philosophy was given by God to the Greeks for the same purpose as law had been given to the Hebrews, namely, to bring them to Christ.

When referring to God, Clement depends on Neoplatonic doctrine, which makes heavy use of negative (apophatic) theology—i.e., that nothing can be said directly about God, for he cannot be defined. But Neoplatonic concepts of emanation and hierarchy are applied to the Christian Trinity. The result is more than a hint of subordination of the Son to the Father and of the Spirit to the other two divine Persons.

The Spirit's work is most important, however. Clement states that the believer is combined with regal gold (the Holy Spirit), in contrast to the Jews, who are silver, and the Greeks, who are a third element. The more the Christian becomes a true Gnostic, the closer he or she will be to the light of the Spirit. All true knowledge comes from the Spirit of God. In addition, all spiritual gifts also flow from the Spirit. The perfect man or Gnostic can be distinguished by the reception of the charismata (here Clement refers to the 1 Cor. 12 list of gifts).

5. Origen.

Origen, one of the greatest scholars of the ancient church, was born c. A.D. 185, probably in Alexandria. He became a student of Clement in the catechetical school there and eventually succeeded his mentor as head. He viewed philosophy as the prelude to an understanding of Christianity, with the Christian Scriptures as the highest object of scholarly activity.

Neoplatonism recognized God as the One, the unspeakable being from whom all other beings emanate, including intermediate beings between the One and the creatures of earth. This hierarchical concept, when applied to Christian theology, led to the subordination of the Son and the Spirit in Origen's early writings. In time, however, he seems to have become somewhat uncomfortable with this concept, and by the time he wrote his great treatise *On First Principles,* he seemed more inclined toward a recognition of the equality of members in the Godhead.

Origen struggled over whether the Spirit is to be described as "generate," like the Son, or "ingenerate," like the Father. As a consequence of these speculations, he seems to be moving toward the concept of the procession of the Spirit in his later writings, but he is lacking in the terms and definitions necessary for adequate expression of these concepts. The Spirit is associated in honor and dignity with the Father and the Son, yet his work is also distinct. The chief function of the Holy Spirit is to promote holiness among believers in Christ. He is their holiness. He turns the human mind to the things of God and assists the faithful in apprehending spiritual truth, avoiding falsehood, and promoting holiness. He leads toward spiritual maturity or perfection, although this is not gained in a moment of time but is progressive.

Origen sought to refute claims of the pagan philosopher Celsus, who had attempted to discredit the charismata exercised by individuals in the church. Spiritual gifts given to the apostles were still operating in Origen's day, although not to the same extent. Origen reports that evil spirits were expelled, healings did occur, and the future was foretold in his own church. He places considerable emphasis on the validating force of signs and wonders. These are to be exercised by those who are led by the Spirit but not by all Christians.

6. Novatian.

The 3d-century church had numerous "holiness" factions, including the Novatians, who vigorously denied the right of a priest or bishop to be reinstated if he had apostatized (or recanted the faith) in the face of persecution. The leader, Novatian, led the group out of the Catholic Church, arguing that it was contaminated by those who had been reinstated.

Novatian was the first Latin writer of the Roman Church. In his *Treatise Concerning the Trinity,* penned before his separation from the mother church, we find a description of the offices of the Spirit in the OT and the early church—a description that is as rich as the writing of any ante-Nicene father. The church is perfected and completed by the gifts of the Spirit. While Novatian demanded a higher standard of perfection among Christians in his own day, he also recognized that such holiness is the product of the operation of the Spirit through his gifts. Where the Spirit is, the church is perfect and complete.

7. Hippolytus.

Hippolytus of Rome (d. A.D. 136), a disciple of Irenaeus, was openly hostile to fringe and heretical groups. He struggled against the Gnostics, Marcionists, Montanists, and Monarchians. His purpose was to maintain tradition established in the 1st and 2d centuries. His primary work, the *Apostolic Tradition,* is our most detailed picture of the Roman church at the beginning of the 3d century. It also is a window into the exercise of spiritual gifts within the established structure of the church, though Hippolytus does not limit the operation of the Spirit to the ecclesiastical hierarchy, as Cyprian later did.

The election of the bishop was to be by Spirit-led laity and clergy alike. Hands were laid on the ordinant, and prayer was offered for the descent of the Spirit. The Holy Spirit also was poured out on the presbyter at the time of his ordination, when the bishop laid on hands and prayed. Similarly, the ordination of the deacon involved a petition for the granting of the Spirit. There was no need to lay hands on the confessor, who already had emerged triumphantly from the trials of persecution. Again, the Spirit was seen as descending on those who suffer for Christ.

If any claimed to have the gift of healing, hands did not have to be laid on them, for it would soon be apparent whether the Spirit functioned within them when they prayed for the sick. Here is clear evidence that the 3d-century church at Rome was acquainted with the gift of healing. Another important gift, according to Hippolytus, is that of teaching. The Spirit-led teacher's words would be profitable to the hearers, as the healer's would be to the sick. Hippolytus placed considerable emphasis on the Spirit's instruction through the Word at weekday-morning gatherings. So the Spirit is functioning through the hierarchy, through gifted laity, and in the assemblies of believers. This is the last generation in the West in which it would be said that the Spirit does indeed deal directly in and through the entire church.

8. Cyprian.

Cyprian, bishop of Carthage from A.D. 248 to 258, taught that the church is the indispensable ark of salvation. He also contended that the church exists only wherever the bishop is. But Cyprian also was strongly charismatic. Therefore, he contended that spiritual gifts are vested in the bishop, who has the sole claim to exercise the charismata.

With Cyprian the process of institutionalization of the prophetic element was completed. Office and charismata were now one. The sacraments had become the sole vehicle for the expression of spiritual gifts. And when gifts were no longer emphasized and the priesthood only rarely exercised the prophetic function outside the sacraments, the charismata fell into disuse. Only those who attempted to reach beyond their fellow Christians—monks, virgins, and radical fringe groups—kept the prophetic tradition alive.

II. THE NICENE AND POST-NICENE PERIOD (TO THE END OF THE SIXTH CENTURY).

A. Theological Controversies and Creedal Formulae.

The church's dark night of Roman persecution ended early in the 4th century (A.D. 303 in the West, 324 in the East). Constantine created a religious pluralism in which Christianity became one of the legitimate religions of the empire. In 381 came the final stage in the evolution of the church from persecution to dominance when Theodosius declared the empire to be solely a Christian state.

Constantine's hopes that the church would be a uniting factor in the empire soon were dashed, because Christendom itself was deeply divided. Divisive issues became even more apparent after Christians were freed from their struggle for survival. Chief among these issues was the conflict over the relationship of persons in the Trinity. Neoplatonic theories of subordination led to the Arian teaching that the Son was inferior to the Father, and it eventually led to the heresy of the Macedonians—that the Holy Spirit was inferior to both Father and Son.

Arius, an Alexandrian presbyter, declared that the Son had a separate existence from the Father. He was not consubstan-tial (of the same essence) or coeternal with the Father. Arius did not take this reasoning to its inevitable conclusion, however. Nowhere did he declare that the Spirit was not equal to the Son.

Athanasius, a deacon and secretary to the bishop of Alexandria, vigorously opposed Arius. His case was based on the soteriological principle that no half-god could accomplish the redemption of humankind. But Athanasius still did not raise the companion question of the relationship of the Holy Spirit in the Godhead.

Emperor Constantine called the First Ecumenical Council at Nicea in 325 to deal with the Arian threat. After considerable debate the council issued a creedal statement that declared that the Son is coeternal and equal in substance with the Father. Nothing like that is said about the Spirit, however. Creedal writers were content to include the statement, "And [we believe] in the Holy Ghost." Unfortunately, ecclesiastics throughout history have tended to react to present challenges to the truth rather than to anticipate areas of potential heretical growth and church division.

While Arianism officially was expelled from the empire, it reemerged in a different form in Egypt. Here a group of Arians who had come to admit the Nicene position regarding the Son refused to recognize the Spirit in the Godhead, declaring him to be the greatest of creatures. They came to be known as "trope-mongers" (tropes are metaphors) or "Tropici," because they dismissed the Scriptures that went against their position as being merely figures of speech. Their most prominent leader was the Arian bishop of Constantinople, Macedonius, hence the later name Macedonians. Athanasius also spoke of them as "enemies of the Spirit," or "Pneumatomachi."

Although several synods attempted to deal with the Macedonians, final action was not taken until the Second Ecumenical Council was summoned by Theodosius to meet at Constantinople in 381. The Macedonians were condemned, and a passage was added to the third article of the Nicene Creed "And [we believe] in the Holy Ghost" — namely, the terminology, "the Lord and Giver-of-Life, who proceedeth from the Father, who with the Father and the Son together is worshiped and glorified, who spake by the prophets." Thus, while the Constantinople addition to the Nicene Creed does not explicitly declare the deity of the Holy Spirit, it does so implicitly by requiring for him divine dignity and worship.

In declaring that the Spirit proceeds from the Father, the council rejected the Arian position. Unfortunately, this did not entirely settle the relation of the Third Person to the Trinity. There still remained the question of his relation to the Son. By the 4th century the Eastern (Greek) church already was teaching a procession from the Father *through the Son,* while the Western (Latin) church was soon to follow Augustine's position that the procession was from the Father *and the Son (filioque).* Since the early Middle Ages this has proven to be the most irreconcilable issue between Eastern and Western Christendom.

Still another theological controversy emerged in the East—the dispute over the nature of Christ and the relationship that the Holy Spirit bears to the incarnate Word. The central figure in this dispute was Nestorius, a monk at Antioch, who became patriarch of Constantinople in 428. He rejected the popular term used to describe the Virgin, *theotokos* ("bearer of God") in favor of the expression *Christotokos* ("Christbearer") or even *theodochos* ("God-receiving"). By his reasoning, the Spirit did not conceive the Logos but formed within the Virgin's womb the man who was assumed by the Word. Afterward the Spirit came down on him at baptism, glorifying him and giving him power to do miraculous works. The Spirit also gave him authority over unclean spirits and ultimately gave him the power to ascend to heaven.

Nestorius's opponents, led by Cyril of Alexandria, found in his teachings that the Logos did not truly become man and that the incarnate Son received the Spirit of God as by a superior power. In short, they accused Nestorius of radical dyophisism (two natures in Christ that were not hypostatically united). Emperor Theodosius II called the Third Ecumenical Council at Ephesus in 431 to deal with Nestorianism. Nestorius was excommunicated and deposed from his see, his teachings were condemned, and the term *theotokos* was reaffirmed. The first permanent split in the history of the church resulted.

Decisions of the Council of Ephesus proved to be of critical importance, not only to an understanding of the natures of Christ but also in its treatment of the Virgin Mary and of the Holy Spirit. Paul Tillich has observed that from the very time that the Spirit was declared to be divine (at the Council of Constantinople in 381), the divine Third Person was gradually replaced in popular piety by the Virgin Mary (Tillich, 1968, 78). Perhaps this can be explained in part by the institutionalization of the Spirit's gifts (3d century) and by the greater emphasis on his transcendence than his immanence after the Council of Constantinople (381).

But the reaffirmation of the term *theotokos* certainly played a part in the ever-increasing veneration of the Virgin in both East and West. Remember, however, that by the post-Nicene period the Virgin had become the model of how the Holy Spirit operated in human life. So Mary was now being portrayed as the earthly locus of the Spirit (later she became known as the "spouse of the Holy Spirit").

In Eastern churches the Spirit remained, and continues to be, an object of Christian piety. However, in the West, with but a few exceptions, the divine Spirit was never again to be as important for piety for the vast majority of Christians.

B. Eastern Christianity from the Fourth through the Sixth Centuries.

The earliest centers of theology in the Greek East were Alexandria and Antioch. Eusebius of Caesarea, Didymus the Blind, Athanasius, and the three Cappadocians (Basil of Caesarea, Gregory of Nyssa, and Gregory of Nazianzen) were leading figures in the Alexandrian school. Theodore of Mopsuestia and John Chrysostom belonged to the school of Antioch. Alexandrians tended to be Platonists and emphasized the allegorical-mystical interpretation popularized in the 3d century by Origen. They also emphasized the transcendence of God in which Word and Wisdom (Son and Holy Spirit) were viewed as intermediate beings between God and the world. Those in Antioch preferred Aristotle and were inclined toward a grammatical-historical explanation of Scripture

1. Eusebius of Caesarea.

The court theologian of Emperor Constantine, Eusebius (c. 260–339), was the first important Christian historian. That he was a follower of Origen is evident from his doctrine of the Trinity, in which the Son is subordinated to the Father. At the Council of Nicea he served as a mediating agent and agreed to sign the Nicene Creed, which declared the Son to be of "the same substance as the Father." Although Eusebius never became an Athanasian, he never again defended Arianism.

As a historian, Eusebius provides information on individuals who enjoyed unusual richness of life in the Spirit. One of these was a man named Quadratus, who, along with the daughters of Philip, was renowned for prophetic gifts and through whom wonderful works were accomplished by the power of the Spirit. Eusebius also tells of Melito, bishop of Sardis, who probably lived during the reign of Marcus Aurelius (161–180). Melito was known as a prophet, as a "eunuch who lived altogether in the Holy Spirit" (*Ch. Hst.* 4.26.1; 5.24.5).

Eusebius was not so kindly disposed toward the self-styled "New Prophets" or Montanists, however. He writes of Christ's distinction between true and false prophets. The Montanists were inspired by the devil, not by the Holy Spirit, he concludes (*Ch. Hst.* 5.16.4ff.). Against the Montanists, Eusebius also gathered the witness of other writers: Asterius Urbanus, Miltiades, Apollinus, and Serapion (*Ch. Hst.* 5.16.17–19.4).

Above all, Eusebius stands for unity in the body of Christ. Those who claim to be Spirit-directed and do not work toward this unity are anathema.

2. Cyril of Jerusalem.

The early church had developed a long and arduous process for preparing adult converts for baptism. They were enrolled as "catechumens" under the care and instruction of a teacher. By the 4th century, the 40 days before Easter (i.e., Lent) had been designated for the preparation of catechumens to be baptized on Easter. The 24 catechetical lectures of Cyril, bishop of Jerusalem (d. 386), were pastoral teachings aimed at these baptizands.

Because baptism is a sacrament of the Spirit, Cyril refers frequently to the divine Third Person, although he attempts to confine himself to what is said of the Spirit in Holy Writ. Anything additional is vain, even dangerous, speculation. Such was the error of the Gnostics, Montanists, and Marcionists.

Again and again Cyril refers to the grace of the Spirit as water. By water all things exist and are renewed. Cyril draws the Eastern Christian connection between the waters of creation, the waters of deliverance (Red Sea), and the waters of re-creation (the womb of Mary and the waters of baptism). In each case the Holy Spirit is the active agent.

In baptism, the Spirit is present to remit sins and to seal the believer. But he is also present to grant supernatural power, the gift of prophecy, his own presence and protection, fruit as listed in Gal. 5:22–23, and gifts of all varieties. It is interesting to note that Cyril adds the gifts of chastity, virginity, voluntary poverty, and preparation for martyrdom to scriptural lists. All spiritual gifts are antidotes for the defilement of the believer.

When the newly baptized Christian came up from the water, he or she was anointed with scented oil while receiving the laying on of hands. This was the sacrament of "chrismation," of which the "unction" or anointing was the most important part (in the Latin West the term *confirmation* developed later). The anointing balm introduces the presence of the Spirit in sanctifying power, and a life in the Spirit, which for Cyril was indescribably rich.

3. Didymus the Blind.

Born early in the 4th century, Didymus of Alexandria lost his sight when he was only four years of age. He prayed for and received inner light, which to him more than compensated for his physical handicap. His writings on the Holy Spirit include three books on the Trinity and a separate protest against Macedonianism.

Didymus depicts the Spirit as one with the Father and the Son—the same in honor, in operation, in divine nature, and in essence. The Three also share in function, though the Spirit has a unique operation. Through his unction the soul is strengthened so as to share in the life of God and is permitted to drink at the everlasting fountain. Baptism is the sacrament of the Spirit. Those who are martyred before baptism, having been washed with their own blood, are given divine redemption by the Spirit.

Among all Eastern fathers, Didymus appears closest to the Western doctrine of the *filioque* clause. According to his formula, the Spirit goes forth from the Father, is sent by the Son, but still is indivisibly one with the Person who sent him. The Spirit has no substance except that which is given him by the Son.

4. Athanasius.

The great champion of Trinitarianism, Athanasius (c. 296–373), vigorously fought Arianism—which challenged the equality of the Son to the Father—and its companion heresy, Macedonianism—which challenged the equality of the Holy Spirit to the rest of the Godhead. Present and victorious at the Council of Nicea in 325, he did not live to attend the Second Ecumenical Council at Constantinople in 381. His influence was present, however, through his writings and the work of his disciples.

Athanasius's arguments for the full deity and Godhead of the Spirit are based primarily on the Spirit's divine activity within the Trinity. He is what he does. He performs and exhibits characteristics that could be ascribed only to God. He is the effective principle in the Trinity who apportions to us what the Father accomplishes through the Son. The Spirit is the instrument of the Son in both creation and sanctification. The Spirit receives his mission from the Son, but he proceeds from the Father. There is then no statement of double procession in Athanasius's writings.

Athanasius shows that any rejection of the full divinity of the Spirit would ruin Christianity. To deny the Spirit is to deny the very agent of grace who has been provided by the Father through the Son to sinful humankind.

5. John Chrysostom.

The greatest teacher and preacher of the ancient Greek church, John Chrysostom (347–407), lived as a hermit monk for six years, rose to the office of presbyter in the church at Antioch, and in 397 was chosen patriarch of Constantinople. Because of his impassioned sermons, however, Chrysostom later was banished. He died in exile.

Chrysostom's sermons emphasize the influence of the Holy Spirit on human ethical behavior. The Spirit gives life, knowledge, and Christlikeness—which is a sign to unbelievers of the validity of the gospel. The Spirit searches the heart, helps with human infirmities, and makes intercession for the saints. It is absolutely essential that the Christian listen to the voice of the Spirit.

Obviously, Chrysostom calls for character (the fruit of the Spirit), rather than for the charismata (the extraordinary gifts). Indeed, he insists that while spiritual gifts played a vital role in the beginning of the church, they have ceased. Specifically, Chrysostom declares that tongues no longer were necessary after the church was established. In this, his reasoning is similar to that of Augustine of Hippo, a Western contemporary.

6. Basil of Caesarea.

Cappadocia, in what is now central Turkey, produced in one generation three of the greatest fathers of Eastern Christendom. These were Basil of Caesarea (Caesarea Mazaca, now Kayseri in Turkey); his brother Gregory of Nyssa; and their associate, Gregory of Nazianzen. With the Cappadocians the doctrine of the Holy Spirit was brought to a new pitch of development. From Athanasius came their desire to define the Spirit's *homoousios*—that he is of one and the same nature with the Father and the Son. From Origen came their concern to strengthen the doctrine of the three hypostases. By restricting the term *ousia* to define the Godhead as one (essence) and *hypostasis* to that wherein the Godhead is three, the Cappadocians introduced much needed clarification into Trinitarian terminology. They also added the insight that each hypostasis indwells and reciprocates with the other two. From their synthesis came the "three in one" concept that has remained the basis of orthodoxy from the time of the Council of Constantinople (381).

Basil was born c. 330 in Caesarea of Cappadocia and was trained in Greek literature, philosophy, and oratory. He was drawn to a life of Christian asceticism and founded the monastic system in Pontus. He is best known for the Basilian rule, which remains standard for Eastern ascetics even today. His monks were encouraged to be actively involved in providing relief to Christians, pagans, and Jews alike. On the outskirts of Caesarea he built a complex of buildings to house travelers, the sick, and the poor. This later was called the Basilead.

Basil came to be known as a champion of the Spirit (and eventually, "Doctor of the Holy Spirit") from his rejection of any suggestion that the divine Third Person was a created being and for his insights into the relationship of the Spirit and the church in his writings. He endeavored to mediate differences between East and West and even to win back semi-Arians to the Catholic fold. Therefore, he avoided dogmatic statements concerning the deity of the Spirit, concentrating instead on subtle indicators of that divinity. For example, he declares that the Spirit is not a creature, that he is no stranger to the divine nature, that he is intrinsically holy, one with the blessed divine nature and inseparable from the Father and the Son. The same glory, honor, and adoration must be given to all three Persons in the Godhead.

On the matter of procession, Basil is more direct. The Spirit proceeds out of God, not by generation like the Son, but as the breath of his mouth. Here then, is one of the classic Eastern Christian statements on procession.

But Basil's grasp of the full range of the Holy Spirit's work in the life of the believer is perhaps the most exceptional in the ancient world. As the Spirit is the conductor of the symphony of creation, so he is also creator of the church (again a symphony operating in the harmony of the Spirit), which sanctifies all of creation through the work of the Spirit. The church is a body composed of individual members, each of whom is assigned a particular charisma by the Spirit. Edification or life in the Spirit occurs when there is mutual cooperation of its members in the exercise and participation of the individual charismata.

The charismata are not ends in themselves but instruments of virtue. No one can possess all of the charismata. But when those gifted by God live together, they reap the fruits of sharing in the gifts of the Spirit. Ministry is a charisma of the Spirit to be exercised for the benefit of others.

Basil places earthly goods and services alongside gifts delineated by Paul under the rubric "charismata." Teachers are quickened by divine grace to provide spiritual nourishment for the hungry. Office, however, is less important to Basil than the functioning of spiritual gifts. A simple monk may spiritually lead those in high ecclesiastical position. Basil allowed a certain Musonius, who was his junior, to preside over episcopal assemblies because of his many charismata. To become a *pneumatophor*—an active receptacle, carrier, and distributor of the Holy Spirit and his gifts—it is necessary first to become detached from this life. Life in the Spirit involves spiritual freedom that is worked out in a life of self-denial, discipline, and obedience. All Christians, however, are recipients of the charisma of life, the highest of all the charismata bestowed by the Spirit.

7. Gregory of Nyssa.

The younger brother of Basil the Great, Gregory of Nyssa (b. c. 335/36) was highly studious but weak in health and shy in disposition. Against his will, he was named bishop of Nyssa by his brother. In 381 he attended the Council at Constantinople, influencing its decisions greatly and writing the additions to the Nicene Creed (including the most significant statement concerning the Holy Spirit), which were sanctioned by the council.

Gregory of Nyssa is one of the great mystics of the church. He recognized that humans are at a disadvantage in exploring the depths of the divine mystery. Notwithstanding human limitations, however, he does delve into the nature of God and particularly into the Spirit's transformation of humans into the image of God.

In defending Christianity against charges of tritheism, Gregory of Nyssa argues that when we speak of God the Father, God the Son, and God the Holy Spirit, we are not naming three Gods, for the three share a common divine essence. We are naming three Persons in the Godhead. While the Son is the Word of God, the divine Spirit is the "Breath of God." Each Person has his individual work but does not operate separately from the other two.

Each member of the Trinity must be distinguished by origin. The One is the cause; the other two are caused. The Son is directly from the Father, while the Spirit is from the Father through the Son—clearly the Eastern formula of procession.

Perhaps the most instructive of Gregory's teachings involve the sanctifying role of the Spirit in transforming humankind back to the image of God. This process can be compared to an aim of ancient teachers known as *paideia*, the training of the physical and mental faculties to produce a broad, enlightened, and mature outlook, harmoniously combined with maximum cultural development (Jaeger, 1961). This is accomplished through the sacraments or "mysteries" of the church, by participation in which the Christian grows from glory to glory in the process of "deification" (sharing in the characteristics, though not in the essence, of God).

The Spirit of God transforms common or material elements—whether water, bread, wine, or oil—through his sanctifying power, so as to transform the participant in spiritual rebirth. Water becomes the agent of re-creation, bread and wine are transformed into the body and blood of Christ, and the Spirit is bestowed by anointing with the oil of chrism.

After a person has been cleansed, the Holy Spirit comes to set that soul on fire, giving the grace of his fruit. Gregory uses the symbol of a "fertile dove" for the Spirit, and his gifts are the offspring of that dove. Grace given by the Spirit increases as a person is nurtured and grows to perfect maturity. Eventually, those who hold communion with the Spirit have the assurance that he will also quicken them for life everlasting.

Gregory of Nyssa describes such a person of the Spirit, his own saintly sister, Macrina, who lived a contemplative and rigorously ascetic existence. At the end of her life she suffered intensely, but her conversation and demeanor served to lift those around her to "heavenly sanctuaries." Even through death, her advance in perfection continued on from glory to glory in the infinite and eternal realm.

8. Gregory of Nazianzen.

A lifelong friend of Basil the Great, Gregory of Nazianzen studied in Palestine, Alexandria, and Athens before returning to his native Cappadocia. He was strongly attracted to a life of solitude but chose to live in the world under a strict ascetic rule. Basil eventually named him bishop of Sasima, and later he became archbishop of Constantinople.

Gregory's orations and homilies refer frequently to the Holy Spirit. The most important of these are his oration *On the Holy Spirit* and his sermon on Pentecost. He struggled against those who, like the Sadducees, denied the existence of the Holy Spirit and those who admitted to his existence but denied his full deity. Gregory argues that the Spirit is not contingent; that he is neither a creature nor a servant; that he is not generate or generated, but proceeds; that he is not just a second Son of God. The Spirit reveals the Son, who in turn takes us to the Father. He is the divine Person in whom we worship and through whom we pray.

Figures of speech and imagery borrowed from the world of nature are not adequate to depict relationship within the Trinity or to describe members in the Godhead. Time and again he resolves to depend on "few words" to describe the nature and work of the Spirit. He couples this economy of words with a strong distaste for irreverent inquiry, especially the tendency to become "frenzy-stricken for prying into the mystery of God" (*On the Holy Spirit*, 8).

In *The Oration on Pentecost* Gregory presents a masterly account of the supernatural work of the Spirit leading up to the climax of Pentecost. He reminds the reader of the Spirit's ongoing creativity in bringing individuals in the OT and NT to their ultimate potential in God. The Spirit turns the shepherd into a psalmist, fishermen into proclaimers of the gospel, and Saul into the apostle Paul. But such Spirit activity is not simply in the past—he was equally active in Gregory's own day. Gregory also points out that, while the divine Third Person is active in an ecclesiastical context, he is not limited to established avenues provided in the church. He works within the believer as he wills, not as humans command.

Although John baptized with water, Jesus baptizes with the Holy Spirit—and this is the perfect baptism. The Spirit moves upon the waters of baptism, thereby "deifying" the believer in baptism. And the Spirit indwells those whom he has regenerated. In *The Oration on Pentecost* Gregory presents a magnificent picture of the *koinonia* of the Spirit, especially as operating in his own life and those around him. Gregory could function fully as priest only as he lived in the Spirit. In obedience to the Spirit's beckoning, he moved, he spoke, or he was silent.

Gregory also related instances of divine healing in his time, including that of his own father and mother. He even reported that his parents had visions of his own danger during a storm at sea and prayed for his deliverance. Indeed, he confidently declared, the Holy Spirit had chosen presently to provide a wide diversity of gifts to many, bringing them together in a unity of the Spirit.

Gregory even offered a theory to explain the late development of the teaching about the Holy Spirit. He reasoned that in the OT the Father is revealed and the Son hinted at. In the NT the Son is fully revealed, the Spirit adumbrated. The era of the church has brought the doctrine of the Spirit to full development.

9. Ephrem of Syria.

Ephrem (c. 306–373), called "the Harp of the Spirit" by his fellow Syrians, has the distinction of being the only Syrian writer to be publicly recognized by the Western church. Although he was born to a Christian mother, his pagan father expelled him from his home in Nisibis when he found friends in the church. Tradition reports that Ephrem later founded a school at Edessa where he met with numerous disciples. But he is best remembered for his prolific writings, which include biblical commentaries, homilies, hymns, and odes.

Ephrem remained aloof from Greek modes of thought, never searching for precise definitions nor being preoccupied with areas that lie beyond the experience and capability of the human intellect. He believed that the nature of the Godhead, the mystery of the incarnation, the immanence of the holy in this world through the sacraments and the office of the divine Spirit, and sacred or liturgical time are beyond human probing. These subjects can be approached only by means of the languages of metaphor or symbolism and in the context of prayer and wonder. Poetry thus becomes the most appropriate tools for the practitioner of symbolic theology.

Beginning with Paul's first-Adam/second-Adam typology, Ephrem found connections between everything. What is hidden in the OT is revealed in the New, and what is revealed in this world through the sacraments points to what is for us the hiddenness of God. But symbols are more than mere pointers. They are within themselves the actual presence of what they symbolize. This is possible only in the realm of sacred or liturgical time (eternity), wherein all moments in ordinary linear time converge to a single point. The participant enters sacred time through the working of the Holy Spirit, who effects the conjunction of the two times. Therefore, baptism is seen as humanity's entry into paradise, the kingdom of heaven. Participation in the Eucharist actually is involvement with the hosts of heaven (including the saints of all ages) in the marriage supper of the Lamb. By the Spirit, the "not yet" is made into the "already." For Ephrem, the Christian life is allowing the Holy Spirit to effect this entry into sacred time at every moment of life. The Spirit also removes scales from the eyes so that the Christian can recognize the world as transfigured and the kingdom of God as existing within. The Spirit is central in this blending of earth and heaven, of time with the timeless, of known with the unknown.

The nature of the Trinity and of the interrelationships of the three Persons are ineffable. Human knowledge is merely feeble twilight to that of the angels, which in turn is but a little twinkling to the knowledge of the Spirit. Ephrem argues that the Father, the Son, and the Spirit are comprehended by their names only. On the question of how one God can be three Persons, Ephrem introduces a number of symbolic triads, the most frequently used being that of flame (Father), heat (Son), and light (Spirit). Here is a one that is three and a three that is one. Similarly, wheat is composed of the root, the stalk, and the ear; each is complete in itself yet part of the same plant.

Ephrem also articulates the doctrine of *perichoresis* or circumincession—the reciprocal being of the three Persons of the Trinity in one another. The three are blended, though not confounded; distinct, though not divided. The Spirit is not merely the love by which the Father and the Son love each other—a doctrine common in the medieval Western church. Rather, the love of one Person is common to all three. This reciprocity exists both at

Ephrem of Syria, called the "Harp of the Spirit" by his Syrian friends.

the transcendent level and in divine immanence. Every act of members in the Godhead is the work of the whole Trinity. For example, the Son is present in the Eucharist by the will of the Father and by the intervention of the Holy Spirit.

Spirit activity is apparent throughout the entire panorama of salvation, reaching in ordinary linear time from creation to the end of time. Yet it is seen in sacred or liturgical time as a single act. Thus, the Spirit's work at creation, in which he brooded or moved on the waters, is part of the same act wherein the Spirit parted the Red Sea for the children of Israel, effected the incarnation of the Son in the water-filled womb of Mary, and brings re-creation through waters of baptism to the Christian.

One of the most beautiful images that Ephrem employs is that of the pearl, which is used to give meaning to the incarnation. According to ancient mythology, the pearl is created when lightning strikes the mussel in the sea. The Spirit is the fire that enters the mussel, giving birth to Christ, the Great Pearl. He who dives for the pearl goes through the same process as the one who is baptized: first he strips, then is covered with oil (anointed), and finally dives into the water to find the pearl. Again at the Eucharist, Christ gives pearls beyond price—his body and blood—to the participant. The fire of the Spirit also descends to give the pearl at the *epiklesis* (the invocation of the Holy Spirit to come to bless the bread and wine).

Early Syrian writers conceived of the Holy Spirit as feminine. This concept began to decline during the 4th century as devotion to the person of Mary grew. Ephrem is a key transition figure because he placed equally strong emphasis on both the Mother-Spirit and on Mary. There also seems to be a similar trend among most Syrian writers to move away from seeing the dove as a symbol of the Holy Spirit, transferring this imagery also to Mary. Ephrem appears to be moving in this direction, for he relates Noah's dove to Mary.

In all Syrian baptismal services the holy oil or *myron* is poured onto the waters shortly after the *epiklesis* (or invocation) to the Holy Spirit. With the oil the Spirit imprints his marks on his followers. Oil depicts the image of Christ, the restoration of the "image of God" that Adam had spoiled. This is the mark of being separated out by God—a "hidden circumcision" and a symbol of the newly born Christian's holiness.

By the work of the Holy Spirit, the eucharistic participant is allowed to enter sacred time, though still living in historical time. The Spirit effects the transformation of the elements into the body and blood of Christ. For Ephrem, this is symbolic of the Spirit's work in the formation of Christ's body in Mary's womb, and of the miracle at Cana, when water was turned to wine. The fire of the Spirit is imparted through the eucharistic mystery; his divine warmth provides clothing for the otherwise naked. The Spirit crushes the icy bond of sin and the devil, bringing springtime to the church.

The Spirit's salvific provision is a continual source of amazement to Ephrem. But he also understands the created world as sacrament. Even everyday provisions, including food, cause him to wonder. To a person born of the Spirit and guided by his hand, it is possible to live in a continuous attitude of awe and praise as all things are rendered holy.

Ephrem recognizes that the Spirit's work is not limited to the sacramental mysteries as narrowly defined. He carefully guards against putting God in a box, recognizing that the Spirit's activities are beyond defining and spill over all boundaries of human expectation. To illustrate this, he shares several of his own experiences, which he had while reading the Bible. Thus, he reports that while reading the Genesis paradise narrative, he was filled with joy and was lifted up and transported into paradise itself. Here he learned unspeakable truths, even beyond those recorded by the writers of Scripture.

It was clear to Ephrem that one who heeds the Holy Spirit's prompting to seek divine riches rather than the transitory things of the earth will become a harp of the Spirit and a treasurer of his riches, speaking as a fountain of divine words and inwardly singing God's good will.

10. Narsai.

Narsai (413–c. 503) was the most profound and original thinker of the great church of the East (Assyrian, or the more familiar but less satisfactory name, Nestorian). He taught at and eventually headed the famed School of Edessa, which supplanted the School at Antioch as the center of radical dyophysitism (distinguishing sharply between the two natures of Christ). Like Ephrem of Syria, Narsai's Assyrian supporters styled him "the Harp of the Holy Spirit," though his enemies labeled him "the leper."

According to Narsai's homilies, the Holy Spirit is an eternal being, equal to the Father and the Son in essence and in the Godhead. The three Persons are three hypostases of fatherhood, generation, and procession in one God—a mystery hidden from all. The Spirit proceeds from the Father in a manner that is beyond searching and gives life, or re-creation, to those he has created.

Narsai teaches that at the man Jesus' baptism in the Jordan River he received the Spirit and was anointed with hidden power so that by the Spirit he was able to banish demons and heal the sick. When Jesus died on the cross, the Word did not share in his sufferings. The mortal vessel of flesh, built by the Spirit, fell, and the Spirit rent the sanctuary veil. But the second Adam arose and gave life to Adam and to his offspring.

The victorious King of Heaven then promised that he would open the treasury of the all-enriching Spirit. His disciples would be clad with the armor of the all-prevailing Spirit to engage in a contest against the evil one. Consistent with his dyophysite Christology, however, Narsai differentiates between the essence and the power of the Spirit (a distinction that Gregory Palamas later popularized in the Byzantine church). Narsai teaches that the Spirit who descended at Pentecost did not come in his essence or nature, but rather in his power.

At Pentecost the treasure of the Spirit was delivered into the hands of a new priesthood to dispense. By the laying on of hands, the priest receives the power of the Spirit so that he is enabled to perform the divine mysteries. By administering the "drug of the Spirit" in the Eucharist, the priest can purge iniquity from the mind. He nourishes the faithful with this "food of the Spirit," prepared as a living sacrifice at the table of life. He summons the divine Third Person to come down on the assembled congregation so that it might be worthy to receive the body and the blood. The Spirit causes the power of the Godhead to dwell in the bread and the wine, completing the mystery of the Lord's resurrection from the dead.

The priest also consecrates the bosom of the waters of baptism, and the Spirit bestows the adoption of sons and daughters on those who are baptized. Narsai likens the baptismal vat of water to a furnace in which the Spirit heats the weak clay that is the person. Then, instead of clay, the baptized emerges from the water recast as spiritual gold, with the hue of heavenly beings. The priest is a painter of the Spirit, without hands. The "drug of the Spirit" is in the water as in a furnace, to purify the image of men from uncleanness.

After baptism it behooves those who have sickness in their souls and iniquity in their thoughts to run to the priest continuously so as to receive this drug of the Spirit. The priest causes spiritual babes to grow with the Spirit's nourishment (the food of the bread and the drink of the wine). He calls for the Spirit to come down to give power to the elements, changing them into the body and blood of Christ.

Like so many other Eastern Christian mystics, Narsai placed great emphasis on the sense of awe and fear that must accompany the Spirit's work in the mysteries. This is the riches of the Spirit, the promise of the King that cannot be broken.

11. Pseudo-Macarius.

St. Macarius of Egypt (late 4th century?) was the spiritual hero of the Egyptian monastic community in the desert of Scete. He was famed for his virtue and life of prayer (he was said to have been in a state of continual ecstasy). By the age of 40, Macarius was exercising gifts of healing and of forecasting the future. Some of his contemporaries believed that he raised a dead man for the purpose of persuading a heretic who did not acknowledge bodily resurrection.

The 57 homilies, 20 dialogues, and other writings ascribed to Macarius have had a wide and lasting influence, not only on Eastern Christendom but also on the Western churches, even to our day. Modern scholarship, however, has seriously questioned whether these works were in fact authored by Macarius. The issue may never be settled. What is certain is that the spirituality of the writings attributed to him is consistent with the picture of Macarius as drawn by his early biographers. They present a daily anticipation of the miraculous, a dependence on divine gifts of grace to overcome demonic forces, a deep awareness of the effects of sin, a resulting life of prayer, and an ascetic lifestyle that reaches toward an extremely high ideal of perfection.

The writings of Pseudo-Macarius represent an experiential tradition of spirituality. After experiencing evil, the penitent sinner must seek an experience of grace in which there is the gradual cessation of evil. With grace abounding in a Christian's life, the virtue and the fruit of the Spirit become as perceptible to that person as sin is. The goal of the ascetic life, then, is progress in grace, and it is the Spirit of God who is the essential maker of that progress.

Pseudo-Macarius recognized the incomprehensibleness of the transcendent God. But the greatest mystery is that the Almighty chose to reveal himself as immanent to man. The Holy Spirit's power and effectual working, which is the kingdom of God on earth, was inaugurated with the advent of the Savior. Because of Christ's propitiatory sacrifice, humans can attain the heavenly kingdom. By putting off sin and putting on "the soul of the Holy Spirit," the Christian is delivered from sin and begins to grow in the Spirit's image. The Christian begins a new life in the habitation or heavenly house of the divine Spirit and puts on Christ, the Pearl of Heaven, who cannot be worn by one who has not been begotten by the Spirit.

In his treatment of the operations of the Holy Spirit, Macarius is full of awe and exaltation. God's wealth is the working of the Spirit. But the Spirit's activity is not only provision. It is also metacognition, or awareness of the divine process in oneself. As a royal treasury his gifts are beyond measure. He provides nourishment, repose, consolation, joy, delight, animation, and a spiritual investiture of untold beauty. These provisions will result in a Spirit-given inebriation that is ineffable.

Pseudo-Macarius, like so many other Eastern spirituals, describes the Spirit as unspeakable light. This was the brightness that shone in the face of Moses and the brightness that became a guiding pillar of light and cloud. This light is the life of the soul. The Christian's mind is always in heavenly flame because of the indwelling light of the Spirit. All true knowledge is revealed by the Spirit, who leaves secret and unutterable impressions in the human mind. Those who are truly led by the light of the Spirit, Pseudo-Macarius said, cannot learn from another person, but in their mind should pass, by the operation of the Spirit, into another age—that of the heavenly kingdom.

Gifts of the Spirit ("royal gifts") are given to those who ask. They are not to be sought after as ends in themselves, but rather they are dispensed by Christ to those who seek a life in him. Each person is adorned uniquely, each retaining his or her own personality and nature, though filled with the same Spirit. Such gifts are given so that the Christian can have power and can fly over all wickedness into the very air of the Godhead.

Pseudo-Macarius lays great stress on experiencing the indwelling Spirit of God. He is not satisfied with mere head knowledge and correct notions. Those who are children of God and born of the Spirit should anticipate a wide variety of experiences as part of their Spirit-led lives. There are times when they will be, as it were, entertained at a royal banquet, rejoicing with joy and inexpressible gladness. On other occasions, they will be like a bride reposing in communion with her bridegroom. At still other times, they become like angels without bodies, light and unencumbered in body. Sometimes they are like those inebriated with strong drink, being exhilarated and intoxicated with the Spirit, experiencing his divine and spiritual mysteries. On occasions they are in weeping and lamentation for the human race, being consumed by the love of the Spirit for humanity. Frequently they are fired by the Spirit with such love that, if it were possible, they would take every person—good or bad—into their own hearts. Sometimes they are humbled by the Spirit, or live in unspeakable joy, or in great quietness, with no sense of anything but spiritual pleasure. Occasionally, they are like a mighty champion who comes upon the enemy, defeating him with the heavenly weapons of the Spirit. But there are also times when the soul is instructed by grace in a kind of unspeakable understanding and wisdom, in things that are impossible to utter with tongue and speech. Having been considered worthy of such gifts, it is possible for one to advance toward perfection, being translated from glory to glory, and from joy to perfect joy.

Perhaps more than any other desert father, Pseudo-Macarius speaks to modern Christians because of his emphasis on personally experiencing the divine Spirit and on the growth toward perfection that results. His desert life also reminds the busy, modern church that true communion with God is possible only as an individual takes time to enter a quiet place for solitary prayer.

12. Pseudo-Dionysius the Areopagite.

Pseudo-Dionysius was an anonymous author who attributed his writings to Dionysius the Areopagite, a 1st-century

A.D. convert who was baptized by the apostle Paul after Paul delivered his sermon at Mars Hill in Rome (Acts 17:34). Actually Pseudo-Dionysius was a disciple of Proclus (d. 485), whom he quotes almost verbatim in one of his writings. He was himself first quoted by Severus at Constantinople in 533. His writings were composed, therefore, between 480 and 530. He obviously was Eastern—perhaps a monk with strong Neoplatonic training. But it is otherwise impossible to identify the author, who managed to dissociate himself from historical events, even from the christological controversies raging during his lifetime.

Elusive as his identity has been, Pseudo-Dionysius remained perhaps the most influential intellectual father and spiritual master of Christian contemplatives in both East and West for a thousand years.

Pseudo-Dionysius introduces the question of whether it is possible to know God. From there he develops his negative theology, declaring that the essence of God is beyond description and human understanding. What we do not know about things divine is what we know. We can affirm many of God's attributes, but this knowledge cannot reach to the essence of God, which transcends all of these qualities and is indescribable in its dynamic reality. Names applied to God in the Scriptures identify his attributes, but even these do not give us any understanding of his essence.

To acquire the boundless meaning of God's nature, which is the end to which mystical contemplation leads, demands that the soul pass beyond sense experience and the operations of the intellect into "the darkness of unknowing." Here the impressions of the senses and all preconceived ideas are set aside and all the faculties are quieted. In this darkness the soul is elevated to a vision of God as light more luminous than all the stars of the universe combined. This is a transcendent level of truth achieved through the mystical life. The realization of God's inner light, this intimate union with him in a near-identification with his eternal way of existence, is what Dionysius means by "deification" (sharing in his attributes, although not in his essence). This is the end of negative theology and of the mystical steps of purgation, illumination, and perfection.

Pseudo-Dionysius's neo-Platonic system of thought is not marked by the specifically Christian revelation of God as Father, Son, and Holy Spirit. The Godhead is attributed a Trinitarian nature only as a natural expression of its supernatural fruitfulness. Because it was untenable by the 5th and 6th centuries for a Christian to deny that a difference exists within the Trinity, Pseudo-Dionysius declared that distinctions within the Godhead are essentially whatever theologians say are differences. But it is not possible either to speak or to think of what these are, because the power of human intellect is limited.

For our purposes, Dionysius is important because of his notion of a transcendentally ineffable God who can be approached experientially beyond the bounds of sense perception and reason. Because there is no place for an immanent God in Pseudo-Dionysius's celestial world, however, his writings necessarily were reinterpreted by his spiritual descendants, beginning with Maximus Confessor. Maximus makes provision for distinctions between three divine Persons who deal in human affairs, especially in the redemptive process—a God who has chosen to be revealed in the Son by the Spirit.

C. Western Christianity from the Fourth through the Sixth Centuries.

Western Christianity was saved from much of the devastation experienced in the East, devastation that resulted from its struggles against Arianism. This was due in part to the long-established Trinitarian tradition in the West (especially the formulae of Tertullian), together with the Latin emphasis on practical, nonspeculative theology and the influence of Stoicism with its stress on divine immanence—in contrast to Eastern Neoplatonic concern with divine transcendence. To be sure, all Western theologians of this period were dependent in varying degrees on Eastern writings. But when the Arian threat in the form of Germanic invaders did come to the West, it developed its own expression of Trinitarian doctrine. Augustine of Hippo accomplished for the Latin West what Athanasius and the Cappadocians gave to the Greek East: a unique synthesis of Trinitarian doctrine.

1. Hilary of Poitiers.

Hilary, Bishop of Poitiers in Gaul, was exiled to Phrygia in Asia Minor by the Arian Emperor Constantius II. While in exile he came into contact with Eastern Christian thought, which he subsequently brought back to the West. He argued in defense of Nicene orthodoxy and Athanasius and in so doing summarized for the West the issues at stake in the Arian controversy.

Like Athanasius, Hilary championed the deity of the Spirit. The divine Third Person is at the same time the Spirit of God and the Spirit of Christ. He has the same nature as the Father and the Son. They are equal in perfection and dignity as well. The Spirit, however, remains distinct from the Father and the Son. He is a real Person within the Trinity. Yet he is beyond defining, for he is incomprehensible. It is best not to speak where Scripture is silent. Here Hilary betrays his Eastern inclinations.

On the subject of procession Hilary approached what became, with Augustine of Hippo, the Western doctrine of the *filioque*. While the Spirit proceeds from the Father through the Son, Hilary discounts any difference between receiving from the Son and proceeding from the Father. Therefore, his views are consistent with the *filioque* doctrine.

Hilary had a well-developed understanding of what pentecostals and charismatics call "life in the Spirit." The Spirit sanctifies and enlightens the believer. The Holy Spirit is God's great gift to his church. In turn, various Spirit gifts are given for edification. But in order to make full use of the great gift of the Spirit, it is essential to exercise his charismata. From Hilary's writings it is quite apparent that these were functioning in the church of his day. Hilary writes that the grace of the Spirit was revealed in a contemporary, St. Honoratus, through his prayers, his fruit, and his charismatic gifts. It is the heretics and unbelievers who lack the Spirit and consequently are led into error.

2. Ambrose.

Ambrose, bishop of Milan, was raised in Gaul. He moved to Rome, where he studied law. His success as a lawyer led to his appointment in 370 as governor of Liguria and Aemila. Four years later, with the death of the intended Arian bishop of Milan, he was elected by acclamation to the bishopric, though he was still but a catechumen. Eight days after his baptism he was consecrated bishop. Recognizing the weight of his responsibilities and his lack of theological training, Ambrose began to read heavily in the Eastern fathers—especially Athanasius, Basil, and Didymus. Like Hilary of Poitiers, therefore, he served as a carrier of the rich Eastern Christian tradition to the emerging West, laying the groundwork for his great follower, Augustine of Hippo.

Holy Scripture was for Ambrose an immense sea that does not readily reveal its secrets to the superficial observer. In order to gain a higher knowledge of God and his purpose, it is necessary to discern various layers of meaning that lie in each verse. The Holy Spirit reveals these hidden but higher truths. To a literal interpretation of Scripture, Ambrose added the allegorical, which he understood to be of a higher significance. Even the Spirit must be understood as a mystery.

Ambrose accepts the Eastern belief that water blessed by the Spirit is salvific—whether in creation, deliverance (Re[e]d Sea), the incarnation (watery womb of Mary), or baptism. The Spirit is the stream flowing from the living fount of God, which Joel promised (2:28). In turn, from the one river of the Spirit flow many streams, representing various Spirit gifts. He is the great Dispenser of God's blessing to the human race.

Together with the Father and the Son, the Spirit possesses certain divine properties, including power, creativity, life, and light. Members of the Godhead are one in substance and in operation, and one cannot be conceived of without the others. Notwithstanding, each of the three constitutes a separate Person. The Spirit has personal characteristics that indicate his personality. For example, he is said to be grieved and tempted. He also has unique functions—he reveals, he is the author of the incarnation, he descends with complete power, he gives birth to the church, he is the primary link binding Christ to his church, and he infuses his gifts to individual souls.

For Ambrose, life in the Spirit begins with the sacraments. In baptism the water, the blood, and the Spirit play essential roles. The water washes, the blood redeems, and the Spirit renews and resurrects. Baptism is closely associated with the incarnation as a watery work of re-creation.

In the Eucharist, the Spirit actualizes the mystery of salvation. Again, the incarnation, a work of the Spirit, is actualized through the Eucharist. At the same time, the Eucharist anticipates the resurrection, which also is a work of the Spirit.

In the sacrament of confirmation the Spirit seals the soul and provides his sevenfold gift. In ordination the Spirit provides power to the priest to forgive sins. Indeed, the very office of the priesthood is considered a gift of the Spirit.

Life itself is dependent on the Spirit of God. Where the Spirit is, there is life; where life is, there is the Holy Spirit. Through him the Christian can enjoy a more abundant life of holiness, purity, creativity, and conformity to the image of God.

3. Augustine of Hippo.

Certainly the greatest theologian and thinker of the ancient Western church was Augustine, bishop of Hippo. Although reared in a strong Christian home by his mother, Monica, he sowed wild oats as a youth. His indiscretions resulted in a strong consciousness of the sinful nature of humankind. With his relatively negative anthropology, Augustine, more than any other theologian, shaped Christian soteriology in the West. Augustine taught that all humans are cursed by original sin and are fallen to the extent that their wills are impaired. No one has more than a very limited capability of positively effecting his or her own salvation. Therefore Augustine placed great emphasis on Christ's propitiatory sacrifice on the cross. The primary salvific role of the Holy Spirit is to reprove of sins and then to forgive the penitent. Outside the church there is no Holy Spirit and no such forgiveness.

Unlike Eastern fathers who begin with the three divine hypostases and then proceed to the unity of God, Augustine begins with the unity of God and proceeds to the Persons. In part, Augustine's emphasis of unity over diversity in the Godhead is a reaction against his predecessor in the West, Marius Victorinus, who spoke of God as "a triple being." For Augustine, the unity of the Godhead is inseparable, and there is equality in deity. The Spirit is consubstantial and coeternal with the Father and the Son. He is the Spirit of both the Father and of the Son. Augustine concludes that the Holy Spirit is the communion of divine love between the other two divine Persons—a concept that remained central to Western Catholic pneumatology from that time onward.

Because the third divine Person is the Spirit of both the Father and the Son, it follows that he proceeds from both. In this proposition, Augustine gives definitive shape to the Western church's position, which stands in contrast with the Eastern Christian concept of single procession. After 1,500 years, this remains the primary theological difference separating Western Christians from their counterparts in the East.

In an attempt to explain distinction of operation within the Trinity, Augustine likens God's Trinitarian being to the memory, intellect, and will in the human psyche. The Holy Spirit is likened to the faculty of the human will. Therefore, the Spirit of God is the energizer who renews the human moral faculty so that humankind can obey God's law, and he is the heavenly teacher leading humanity into all truth as Christ was the great teacher while on earth. The Spirit gives to believers a love for God that aids in the pursuit of righteousness. The very presence of the Holy Spirit is God's law written in human hearts. He is the "finger of God" reaching out to touch humankind.

The church was born of the Spirit on the Day of Pentecost. When God's great gift, the Holy Spirit, was poured out on the faithful, a new law was written on human hearts—a law of love and not of fear. Since that time, the Spirit is received only in the church and with the imposition of hands. But whenever a person secedes from the church, the Spirit also withdraws.

The Spirit's operations in the church are many. The charismata are like stars in the sky, on which the babe in Christ must be contented to stare until able to look at the sun. But these gifts must be tested carefully, as one examines a pot to see whether it is cracked. If the gift or gifts give off a dull sound, they are not genuine. But if they ring full and clear, they are of God.

On several occasions Augustine explicitly states that the gift of tongues was only for the 1st-century church. Glossolalia served as a sign to the 1st-century unbeliever, but it was not to be expected in his own generation. Far more important than tongues is love, a gift of the Spirit that transcends time and circumstance.

Despite Augustine's rejection of tongues as an ongoing gift of the Spirit, he quite readily admitted to numerous contemporary miracles. He directly related certain wonders occurring in his own church at Hippo to the "gifts of healing" mentioned by Paul in 1 Cor. 12:9. While no one person seemed to possess a gift of healing, these miraculous recoveries involved divine intervention in response to the prayers of the Hippo congregation and those healed.

Augustine's impact on the medieval Catholic church and on evangelical Protestantism can hardly be overstated. His formulation of Western Trinitarian dogma, his conception of the Spirit as the love between the Father and the Son, and especially his articulation of the double procession of the Holy Spirit mark him as one of the most important pneumatological thinkers in Christian history.

■ **Bibliography:** J. L. Ash, "The Decline of Ecstatic Prophecy in the Early Church," *Theological Studies* 35 (June 1976) ■ L. Bouyer, "Charismatic Movements in History within the Church," *One in Christ* 10 (2, 1974) ■ B. L. Bresson, *Studies in Ecstasy* (1966) ■ S. M. Burgess, *The Holy Spirit: Eastern Christian Traditions* (1989) ■ idem, *The Holy Spirit: Ancient Christian Traditions* (1984) ■ idem, *Reaching Beyond: Studies in the History of Perfectionism* (1986) ■ J. P. Burns and G. M. Fagin, *The Holy Spirit* (1984) ■ Y. M.-J. Congar, *I Believe in the Holy Spirit* (1983) ■ B. de Margerie, *The Christian Trinity in History* (1982) ■ G. S. Hendry, *The Holy Spirit in Christian Theology* (1956) ■ A. I. C. Heron, *The Holy Spirit* (1983) ■ W. Jaeger, *Early Christianity and Greek Paideia* (1961) ■ B. Krivocheine, "The Holy Trinity in Greek Patristic Mystical Theology," *Sobornost* 21 (3, 1957) ■ W. Lewis, *Witnesses to the Holy Spirit: An Anthology* (1978) ■ G. McGee, ed., *Initial Evidence* (1991) ■ M. O'Carroll, *Trinitas: A Theological Encyclopedia of the Holy Trinity* (1987) ■ idem, *Veni Creator Spiritus: A Theological Encyclopedia of the Holy Spirit* (1990) ■ P. D. Opsahl, ed., *The Holy Spirit in the Life of the Church: From Biblical Times to the Present* (1978) ■ F. Stagg, E. G. Hinson, and W. E. Oates, *Glossalalia: Tongue Speaking in Biblical, Historical, and Psychological Perspective* (1967) ■ H. B. Swete, *The Holy Spirit in the Ancient Church* (1912) ■ P. Tillich, *A History of Christian Thought* (1968) ■ F. Wadid, "L'essentiel de la vie monastique: d'après les Lettres de saint Antoine," *Irenikon* 70 (3, 1987) ■ B. Ward, *Signs and Wonders: Saints, Miracles and Prayers from the 4th Century to the 14th* (1992) ■ C. Williams, *The Descent of the Dove: A Short History of the Holy Spirit in the Church* (1939) ■ G. Williams and E. Waldvogel [Blumhofer], "A History of Speaking in Tongues and Related Gifts," in M. P. Hamilton, ed., *The Charismatic Movement* (1975).

■ S. M. Burgess

HOLY SPIRIT, DOCTRINE OF: THE MEDIEVAL CHURCHES

I. Medieval Eastern Christianity
   A. *Assyrian and Non-Chalcedonian*
      1. 'Abdisho' Hazzaya
      2. Isaac of Nineveh
      3. Gregory of Narek
   B. *Byzantine (Chalcedonian)*
      1. Maximus the Confessor
      2. Photius
      3. Symeon the New Theologian
      4. Gregory Palamas

II. Medieval Roman Catholic West
   A. *The Eleventh Council of Toledo (675)*
   B. *Controversy over the Filioque*
   C. *The Scholastics*
      1. Anselm of Canterbury
      2. Peter Abelard
      3. Richard of St. Victor
      4. Peter Lombard
      5. Joachim of Fiore
      6. Thomas Aquinas
      7. Bonaventure
   D. *Catholic Women (1100–1450)*
      1. Hildegard of Bingen (1098-1179)
      2. Gertrude of Helfta (1256–1301/2)

3. Brigitta of Sweden (1302/3–73)
4. Catherine of Siena (c. 1347–80)
5. Julian of Norwich (c. 1342–after 1416)
   and Margery Kempe (c. 1373–after 1433)
   E. *Popular Piety in the Medieval Roman*
      Catholic West

III. Radical Dualism
   A. *Messalians*
   B. *Paulicians*
   C. *Bogomils*
   D. *Cathars*

I. MEDIEVAL EASTERN CHRISTIANITY.

Pneumatology has always been at the very heart of Eastern Christian theology, occupying a place much more central than in the christologically inclined West. In part this has resulted from the fact that Eastern churches from the time of the three Cappadocian fathers (Basil the Great, Gregory of Nyssa, and Gregory Nazianzen) have emphasized the uniqueness of function of the three divine hypostases, while the West, following Augustine, has tended to stress the unity of the divine nature or essence. The East, however, has balanced this concept of individuality in the Godhead by recognizing the reciprocal being (*perichoresis* or circumincession) of these hypostases in each other. No member of the triune God functions without the involvement of the other two.

Eastern pneumatology differs in emphasis as well. Because Eastern Christians have a more positive view of humanity than is found in the West, they emphasize the role of the Spirit in perfecting believers, restoring in them the image of God that was tarnished in the Fall. God the Creator re-creates humankind and all of nature. He intends for the ultimate end of humanity to be *theosis*, or "deification"—meaning that through the work of the Holy Spirit humanity becomes Godlike, sharing in divine characteristics (though not in divine essence). The West, by contrast, influenced by Tertullian and Augustine's conception of humanity's cataclysmic fall (or original sin), places greater emphasis on the sacrificial death of the Savior, with the Spirit serving as prime agent in regeneration.

Eastern and Western Christianity were divided in the early Middle Ages over the mystery of the origin or procession of the divine Spirit, and this remains the chief stumbling block in the path of their unity today. Eastern Christians almost universally declare that the Holy Spirit proceeds from the Father *through the Son*, while the West—at least since the 9th century—has argued that the Third Person issues from the Father *and the Son* (hence the *filioque* controversy).

Numerous mystics in both oriental and occidental Christendom have insisted that God can be personally experienced. Eastern Christians, however, have placed a greater emphasis on sensorial perception than have their counterparts in the West. By the Spirit, spiritual eyes are enlightened, and other senses—such as smell, taste, and touch—are quickened. Certain Eastern mystics even contend that the Spirit is higher than all the images and representations in our creation that we experience through our senses. To these mystics, God must be experienced at a level higher than natural powers can reach and human language can describe.

The East always has been inclined toward an understanding of God as transcendent. As such he is essentially unknowable and indescribable. Eastern spiritual writers, therefore, have approached these subjects by means of the language of metaphor—the use of symbolism. The symbol becomes the language of mystery, a vehicle to represent that which is other than human—of the hidden which calls out for description. Symbolic language, then, attempts to express the inexpressible as the communicator seeks to know the unknowable. It can be postulated that one of the reasons why pneumatology has remained so central a doctrine in the East is that oriental Christianity early developed a symbolic vocabulary to express both the nature and work of the Holy Spirit.

Through the centuries, Eastern Christians have also placed a greater emphasis on the gifts of the Holy Spirit—yet another means for the unknowable, infinite, and undefinable God to become known to humanity. Pre-20th-century Western Christians traditionally have understood the gifts functioning in the church as being confined to the Isa. 11:2 list (wisdom, understanding, counsel, might, knowledge, and fear of the Lord). Eastern Christians also have tended to incorporate the Pauline lists in 1 Cor. 12 (word of wisdom, word of knowledge, faith, gifts of healing, prophecy, discerning of spirits, tongues, and interpretation of tongues), Rom. 5 (peace, faith, hope, glory in tribulation, patience, experience, and love), Rom. 12 (prophecy, ministry, teaching, exhorting, giving, ruling, and showing mercy), Eph. 4 (apostles, prophets, evangelists, pastors, and teachers), and 2 Tim. 1 (power, love, and a sound mind).

Not only has Eastern Christianity operated from the expectation of a wider range of spiritual gifts, but it also has never ceased to be actively charismatic. Perhaps this has resulted from the fact that Eastern monasticism has always remained contemplative and never become active, as in the Roman church. But it also seems to have stemmed from the fact that the East never was beset with the level of clericalism found in the West. Laypeople until recent times assumed teaching and preaching ministries. Simple and unordained Eastern monks became recognized and venerated as Spirit-filled spiritual fathers and counselors. But above all, there simply has been a greater expectation of functioning charismata in the East.

The individuals described below are representative of Eastern Christianity during the Middle Ages (7th through

15th centuries). It must be remembered that after the early 8th century, Islam quickly conquered most of their homelands. Therefore, with the exception of the Byzantine Empire, which finally succumbed to the Turks in 1453, and part of the Assyrian church, which was too far east for Islam to reach, Eastern Christians fell under the dominion of the followers of Mohammed. The most creative Christian theological writings tended to cluster in the period immediately before and just after the Islamic conquest.

A. Assyrian and Non-Chalcedonian.

1. 'Abdisho' Hazzaya.

We know little about the life of 'Abdisho' Hazzaya, the great 7th-century East Syrian mystic. He wrote extensively on the nature of monastic life, on certain of the writings of Pseudo-Dionysius and Evagrius Ponticus, and about the visions of Ezekiel and of St. Gregory. In all of these works, the Holy Spirit is given a prominent place.

'Abdisho' is most concerned with the work of the Spirit in the soul of the Christian who reaches beyond toward perfection. The divine Third Person is the "treasure of life" whose power is received at baptism. Having become an heir of God, the Christian is stamped with the seal of the Spirit and is set over the treasures of the heavenly Father. Chief among these spiritual treasures is the Spirit-led rise toward perfection. The move upward from the corporeal state to purity is accomplished as the Spirit frees those in whom he dwells from human passions, entering the soul as a fiery impulse. As divine heat expands in the soul, exhaling sweet odors of a perfume that cannot be described, the person moves from darkness into light, from doubt to certainty, from the vision of corporeal things to that of intelligible things and the consciousness of the next world. Here is the kingdom of heaven, with security, peace, and joy in the Holy Spirit.

In this vision of fiery impulse or holy light, the mental faculties become intoxicated as with strong wine, and they are enraptured. The mind moves beyond thought. Mysteries and revelations that the human mind can receive spiritually only from the divine Mind are manifested. This is a sphere of incomparable light, accompanied by ecstasy and tears of joy, which flow uncontrollably. The soul is imbued with love for all of humanity, and the Spirit allows it to hear "a fine sound of glorification" that cannot be explained by human tongue.

The highest state in the rise to perfection is achieved when self is viewed, not as a material body, but only as the fire in which it is clad. The human mind that reaches this sphere of perfection has no image or likeness of itself. Instead it is swallowed up in the hidden glory of the Trinity so that it is impossible to distinguish its nature from that of holy light. The soul feeds on the Holy Spirit, and there is no need of natural food. But even at this loftiest height, 'Abdisho' reminds the reader, no one can know God's essence, which resembles neither fire nor the light of the sun.

'Abdisho' suggests that it is possible to distinguish the work of the Holy Spirit from that of a demon. The first sign of the Spirit's operation is that the love of God burns in the human heart like fire, leading to complete renunciation of the world and a love of asceticism. The second sign is the growth of true humility of the soul. The third sign is true kindness to all people—demonstrated by a gift of tears, whenever one's thoughts are extended to others. The fourth sign is true love with an ineffable vision of God as pure light. The final sign of the working of the Spirit is the illuminated vision of the mind that receives the light of the Trinity. At this stage the firmament of the heart is turned to a sapphire sky. The individual is elevated to an unutterable ecstasy from which flow spiritual speech and the gift of knowledge. Here one has a consciousness of the mysteries of future things, together with a holy smell and taste. Here one is transported into sacred or eternal time.

'Abdisho' also identifies characteristics of being led by a demon. The demon of fornication begins by heating the body, causing the mind to be perturbed and numb. These attacks of the evil one are to be countered by vigil and prostrations before the cross, walking, recitation of the Psalms, and reading.

Ultimately, one must rely on a kind of spiritual intuition as an indicator of whether a given vision is from God or the enemy. If the soul contracts and the heart is afflicted, it is caused by demons. But if peace and quietness reign over the thoughts, it is certain that God's grace is working within through his Spirit.

2. Isaac of Nineveh.

Isaac, bishop of Nineveh in the late 7th century, is representative of the mysticism that flourished in the East Syrian church during the early centuries of Islamic domination. He was strongly influenced by the heretical Syrian dualists known as Messalians (see p. 760), from whom he gained an appreciation of the spirituality of experience and of a life in the Spirit. Because of his Spirit emphasis, Isaac was something of an ecumenist, appealing to Greek Chalcedonians and Syrian non-Chalcedonians as well.

Isaac assumes that God is too hard for the intellect to grasp and scrutinize. God can be known only through spiritual knowledge, which begins with a childlike spirit that Isaac sees as part of dying to the world. Asceticism is the mother of saintliness and the beginning of spiritual knowledge. By the Spirit one lives a virtuous life, successfully struggling with passions because senses and mind are made one by the Spirit. Spiritual eyes now see the divine treasure that is hidden from the sight of the sons of flesh.

Detachment from the world results in flashes of intuition in which the soul is raised to God, enters a state of ecstasy or spiritual drunkenness, and receives the gift of tears. It is at such times that divine gifts are bestowed. Spiritual intoxication, or ecstasy, and the gift of tears are available to all who seek them, as are nightly visions, freedom from the pangs of torture, unusual warming of the body during prayer, great joy in the Holy Spirit, and wisdom and humility from the Spirit.

When a person receives the gift of the Comforter and is secretly taught by the Spirit, there is no need of material things. God's Word becomes a bottomless source of incomprehensible ecstasy and joy in God. All of God's provisions become available to the person who lives in the Spirit.

3. Gregory of Narek.

Perhaps the most outstanding figure in Armenian literature, Gregory of Narek (Grigor Narekatsi) was born in the 10th century. After losing his mother in infancy, he entered a monastery where he was educated. He was ordained a priest and lived the rest of his life in the cloister. Gregory's fame stems not only from his writings but also from the many miracles attributed to his ministry.

Gregory stresses the three-in-one relationship of the Godhead. The Trinity is inscrutable and bathed in ineffable light, inaccessible to the highest soaring of the human intellect and beyond all limits and comparisons in quality and quantity.

While sharing in the same power and substance as the Father and the Son, the Spirit also is active by himself, with unique functions. He created the law, inspired prophets, glorified the Son, and prompted the writings of the apostles.

But the Holy Spirit continues to be active in the hearts of those who hunger after God. The eyes of the redeemed become like doves as one grows in perfection. The Spirit digs up the hardened field that is the human heart of flesh and plants spiritual seed to make it productive. Then he provides "spiritual springtime." Gregory cried out for forgiveness so that he might be refashioned in the image of the Holy Spirit.

Gregory interjects numerous personal notes that suggest his heavy dependence on the Holy Spirit. He writes at the Spirit's direction and through his strength. He prays that the Spirit will be present with him when he speaks so that the church will be edified. He has come to recognize that the Spirit is the true craftsman for effectiveness of ministry and for life itself.

B. Byzantine (Chalcedonian).

1. Maximus the Confessor.

A citizen of the Byzantine Empire in the 7th century, Maximus became a champion of Orthodoxy against a wide variety of nascent heresies. Eventually he fell out of favor with the emperor and was brought to trial for his efforts. He was flogged, his tongue was plucked out, and his right hand was cut off. He died shortly thereafter (662), broken in body but not in spirit.

A prolific writer, Maximus restated and reinterpreted Pseudo-Dionysius's system, which purported to be Christian but lacked a Christocentric emphasis. Strongly influenced also by the Cappadocian fathers, he proceeded to turn apophatic or negative theology around. For him the Trinity was not simply a Christian name for the superessential Monad, but the revelation of the transcendent, dynamic, and personal reality of the Godhead. The same God is both Unity and Trinity.

God creates by his consubstantial Word and Spirit out of the infinite goodness of his essence. As created, humanity enjoyed a natural disposition toward God. The fall of Adam, however, led to ignorance about God, with accompanying self-love and disorder of the soul. The human soul was disharmonized from the body, and the unity of the entire earth with its creator was undermined.

But even human beings' sins against God did not alter the fact that mankind was created in the divine image and likeness. It remained God's purpose that humankind be re-created and united with him. Maximus calls this "deification"— the ultimate fulfilling of humanity's capacity for God, in which it is possible to share in his characteristics, though not in his essence. The agent of re-creation is the Holy Spirit, who cooperates with the life of asceticism. Life in the Spirit is the kingdom of God, in which the human mind receives clear impressions of God and is seized by divine light and love. Human deification on earth, however, is but a momentary experience—just a glimpse of the everlasting deification, which is eternal union with the triune God.

Maximus the Confessor served as a carrier to the Medieval East of the ideas of Origen, Evagrius, the Cappadocians, Cyril of Alexandria, and Pseudo-Dionysius. In so doing, he synthesized these various strands into mature Byzantine theology, preserving the unique Eastern understanding of the nature and office of the Holy Spirit. This he did with unusual eloquence, combining as successfully as any Christian writer the language of spirituality and the language of theology.

2. Photius.

Best known as the great Eastern Christian champion of single procession, Photius was born early in the 9th century and passed away near its end.

At a time when relations between Byzantium and Rome were badly strained, especially over the clashes of rival missionaries in the Balkans, Photius was called on to defend the Eastern position of the single procession of the Holy Spirit. He argued this on three grounds. First, he stated that Jesus himself declared the same in John 15:26, for he clearly indicated that the Spirit would receive "from that which is mine," meaning from the Father. Second, the decrees of Holy Synods overwhelmingly support single procession. Finally, he based his argument on the weight of support found in the church fathers. Only a few—including Augustine, Ambrose, and Jerome—had opposed this position.

Photius argued that the Spirit would have gained nothing by proceeding from the Son that he did not already possess through his procession from the Father. Double procession actually results in the heretical doctrine of subordination, which the Macedonians taught. Again, the very immutability of the hypostatic properties necessarily founders if the Spirit proceeds from the Son. Admitting to two causes in the Trinity diminishes the majesty of the monarchy. Logically, double procession results in the Spirit's being relegated to the position of grandson.

Photius's determination to have the "truth," as he understood it, won out, and the intransigence of both sides in the controversy resulted soon after his death in a final schism between East and West (1054). The tragedy is that the controversy he engaged in is still the primary theological barrier between Orthodoxy and the West, and 11 centuries later the arguments on both sides remain much the same.

3. Symeon the New Theologian.

►Symeon (949–1022) was born in Paphlagonia in Byzantine Asia Minor and was brought by his uncle to Constantinople to finish his studies. Instead, he began a life of piety, eventually becoming a monk at age 27.

When he was about 20, Symeon received his first vision of God as light. He reported that as he prayed, he was blessed with abundant tears and everywhere experienced divine light. These visions were repeated throughout his life, including the time when he served as abbot. Because of the richness of his spiritual experiences, Symeon attempted to lead other monks to a similar ongoing and direct experience of God. Many of his fellow monks revolted against his leadership, and Stephen, archbishop of Nicomedia—the chief theologian at the emperor's court—reacted strongly against his enthusiasm or charismatic approach. Eventually Stephen and other enemies succeeded in having Symeon exiled, and although he was later exonerated by the patriarch and the emperor, he remained in exile until his death.

Symeon was one of the most personal writers in Eastern Christian spirituality. He revealed as few others did his own interior experiences of the indwelling Trinity. He exposed both the ecstatic heights of spiritual life and the ascetical struggle that are essential features of Eastern Christian spirituality. Above all, he highlighted the cooperation in the Christian life of the Holy Spirit. For this he became famous both in his own day (when he was known as the one who possessed the true science of the Spirit) and in subsequent centuries, because he felt a call by the Spirit not only to preach but also to write.

According to Symeon, the Godhead—especially the quality of being both three and one—is ineffable. He often refers to the Trinity as light and the Spirit as inhabiting light.

Because God is luminous, he is able to make persons light as well. Because of this, it is possible to participate in the life of God in this present existence.

Symeon argued that the most dangerous heresy is to suggest that it is impossible to possess the same fullness of mystical graces as did the early church. It is possible, indeed absolutely essential, that a person have a direct personal mystical experience of God by seeing him, feeling him, and knowing the transcendent and ineffable one in an intimate relationship. This is the work of the Holy Spirit. Without him, humanity is dead now and eternally. With him, all of the treasure of the Trinity is made available, together with a full consciousness of the abiding and vivifying Spirit in the interior life. This life in the Spirit begins when a person is baptized in the Holy Spirit.

Water baptism is separate from baptism in the Holy Spirit. While the first confers the grace of the indwelling Trinity, the latter is a gateway to a greater conscious awareness that one lives in the presence of God through the illumination of the Holy Spirit. Baptism in the Spirit results in a greatly intensified experience (or sensation, knowledge, awareness, power) of the indwelling Trinity. It is not enough that Christians rationalize their faith; they must be consciously aware of divine life within, just as a pregnant woman is aware that new life stirs within her. They must feel the well of living water spring up in their souls. They must be aware that they possess divine light and be aware of its effects on them. Only a cadaver would not recognize the Spirit's presence within it.

Symeon's argument that it is necessary to consciously experience the Holy Spirit is based on the grounds that a person who is "deified" must experience this union with God just as God the Logos was conscious of becoming man. In addition, this awareness is like that which the Father and the Son have in their union. And so Symeon encourages others to pursue a life in the Spirit. He also continuously pleads with God for the Holy Spirit in his own life.

One must prepare for a baptism of the Holy Spirit. First the heart must be purified, for the Spirit cannot fill an unclean vessel. Then the Spirit begins a growth of meekness and humility, of compunction (awareness of one's guilt before God), and of penitence. Finally, there is the purification of many tears. No one ever receives the Spirit without constant tears. Tears shed in repentance flow into tears that issue in response to divine radiance.

Although Symeon's references to a "baptism of the Holy Spirit" and to "seeking the Spirit" remind the reader of modern pentecostal and charismatic terminology, there are significant differences. Unlike pentecostals, Symeon had no expectation that a miraculous gift of tongues would accompany the infilling of the Spirit (although he claimed to exercise tongues speech). Rather, the Spirit's reception is accompanied by the gift of tears, an intensified sense of compunction, and an intensified conscious awareness of the divine

Trinity as light dwelling within. Symeon also anticipated that the fruit of the Spirit (mentioned in Gal. 5) and other ascetical virtues would accompany the presence of the Holy Spirit, *for these also are his gifts.*

After a person receives the baptism of the Spirit, the Spirit's vivifying presence in the interior life opens the door to all divine graces (1 Cor. 2:9), which Symeon associated with *theosis,* or deification, of the Christian. These graces include reception of life through the sacraments. The Holy Spirit transforms the waters of baptism, as well as the bread and wine of the mystery, into life. The Spirit then gives new eyes to see the invisible world and works of God and new ears to hear the divine voice whenever it speaks through a human voice. As a person comes to experience the triune God as light, he or she is overcome by great spiritual joy and perception.

Symeon also prays for additional gifts of the Spirit: words of wisdom, words of knowledge, divine intelligence, direct language, strength, and power to speak. His biographer, Nicetas, tells us that he did indeed exercise these various charismata—especially gifts of knowledge, healing, and victory over demons.

Perhaps with greater fervor than any other voice in the Middle Ages, Symeon called on Christians to return to a radical living of the gospel, to the charismatic and prophetic life of the primitive church. The emphasis that he draws from Scripture on the necessity of a second baptism—that of the Spirit—is especially unique for his time. He clearly enlarged the horizons of oriental Christian spirituality and has challenged and inspired Christians in both East and West for almost a millennium.

4. Gregory Palamas.

Raised in a noble family close to the court of the Byzantine emperor, Gregory Palamas (1296–1359) entered monastic life at age 20. He is remembered for his prolonged debate with a Greek Italian "philosopher," Barlaam the Calabrian, over the issue of whether humans could directly experience God.

Barlaam rejected the claims of the Hesychasts to spiritual knowledge of God. He insisted that only a secular education providing for the acquisition of wisdom could lead to a true knowledge of God. The hesychastic practice of continually reciting the Jesus Prayer was particularly offensive to the rationalistic Barlaam.

Gregory Palamas recognized the seeming inconsistency between a belief in the absolute transcendence of God and Hesychasm, which was confident that an immanent God could indeed be known, experienced, and participated in. To him it was imperative that he find a middle ground reconciling these seeming opposites.

Palamas's solution to this dilemma was that God cannot be known, communicated with, or participated in as he is in his essence; but he can be known, communicated with, and participated in as he is in his energies. In a sense, then, God exists in two modes and is equally present in both. Humankind can participate in the divine energies by grace and thereby share the life of God and be "deified" by participation in that life. Through his energies—the uncreated light that took on flesh in Christ Jesus, and the deifying gift of the Holy Spirit—God reveals himself positively to the spiritual senses, without losing anything of his transcendence.

Humanity was created by the energy of the whole Trinity. The first human received a created body and the divine Spirit, who is an ineffable uncreated divine energy. The fall resulted in humankind's loss of the Spirit of God, and therefore the likeness of God also was lost. But the image remained untouched, though the loss of likeness resulted in a dimming and distorting of that image. So it was that in the OT period humankind could participate in divine grace only incidentally and apocalyptically but not permanently. Since the incarnation, however, grace has operated permanently and has become available for participation by humanity, if the divine Spirit is received anew.

The deifying gift of the Holy Spirit is a mysterious light that transforms into light (or transfigures) those who receive its richness so that they shine like the sun. The human mind that is overshadowed by the energy of the Holy Spirit is driven upward by the Spirit of wisdom and becomes itself entirely radiant. The saints, as a consequence, become instruments of the Holy Spirit, having received the same energy as he has. As proof of this, Palamas cited such graces as the gifts

Gregory Palamas.

of healing, miracles, foreknowledge, irrefutable wisdom, diverse tongues, interpretation of tongues, and the word of instruction as operating at times of intense mental prayer and even on occasion without prayer. Palamas lays particular emphasis on the practice of "Paul's laying on of hands" for receiving such gifts.

Through the concentration of the intellect during prayer, a person may also experience ecstasy—a condition in which human powers are elevated above their natural state, so that the individual receives a vision of divine light and is received into that light. All mental activity ceases, and union with God *(theosis)* occurs.

With Gregory Palamas the Eastern Christian tradition of experiencing the absolutely transcendent God received its most accepted theoretical explanation. Palamas more than any other Eastern writer unfolded the mystery of how the incomprehensible uncreated light chose to make himself known to created humanity through his Spirit, even to the extent of transfiguring and "deifying" those created in his image and accepting his grace.

II. MEDIEVAL ROMAN CATHOLIC WEST

Augustine's theological synthesis—which reasoned that humanity through original sin in the garden had fallen cataclysmically so as to be wholly dependent on divine grace for salvation—resulted in a highly christological emphasis in Western medieval theology. As a result, the Holy Spirit came to be understood in Roman Catholic thought as the mutual love existing between the Father and the Son and/or as the agent of Christ in redemption. The Occident, therefore, did not place as much emphasis on pneumatology in general and on the unique offices of the divine Spirit in particular, as did the Christian Orient. The Holy Spirit became "the dark side of the moon" in Western theology.

A. The Eleventh Council of Toledo (675).

Augustine's doctrine of the double procession of the Holy Spirit was added to the Nicene-Constantinople Creed at the Eleventh Council of Toledo in 675. It spoke of the Spirit as the Third Person of the Trinity, who was God coequal and consubstantial with the Father and Son, not begotten or created, but proceeding from *both the Father and the Son (filioque)*. The three Persons are inseparable in existence and operation but distinct in personal properties. The Father has eternality without birth, the Son eternality with birth, and the Holy Spirit eternality without birth but with procession.

Of particular significance to our study is the statement of double procession and the declaration that the Spirit is not distinct from the Father and the Son in operation. Both clauses are markedly different from the teachings of the Christian East.

It was thought in the West that the insertion of the *filioque* clause was decisive against Arianism. There is no rea-

son to believe that Catholic Christians had any awareness that their doctrine of double procession was an advance on earlier teaching. Little did they realize that the issue of *filioque* would remain the primary theological issue dividing East and West for the next 1,300 years.

The refusal to admit unique functions for the Spirit was also crucial—though few have recognized its importance. This was a natural outgrowth of the Western inclination to begin with the unity of the Godhead and then to move to the Persons, as opposed to the East, which begins with the unique qualities of the three divine Members and only then turns to qualities of unity. While the East places equal weight on each member of the Trinity, the Western position tends to relegate the Spirit to a position of lesser importance than the Son.

B. Controversy over the Filioque.

Controversy between East and West over the procession of the Holy Spirit erupted in the early 9th century when Charlemagne attempted to have the *filioque* inserted in the Nicene Creed. Open conflict broke out between individuals of the two persuasions, who competed as missionaries in the Balkans. Soon Photius was on the offensive, declaring that the divine Spirit proceeds from the Father alone.

Writing at the request of Pope Nicholas I, Ratramnus (d. 868) maintained that the *filioque* stemmed from the very teachings of Christ and was handed down from the apostles to the Fathers. He cited Augustine in the West, and Eastern Fathers such as Athanasius, Gregory of Nazianzus, and Didymus.

In contrast, John Scotus Erigena (c. 813–891), the greatest theologian of the Carolingian Renaissance, did not champion the *filioque*. Thoroughly Neoplatonic in orientation, Scotus taught the essential oneness of philosophy and religion. He agreed with fellow Carolingians on the unity and eternity of God. The Trinity is a threefold light, a threefold goodness, three substances in one Essence—Father, Son, and Holy Spirit—one God. However, he maintained that the Spirit proceeds from *(ex)* the Father through *(per)* the begotten Son. Furthermore, because he was a Neoplatonist, it is not surprising that he broke with fellow Carolingians such as Alcuin over the existence of evil. There is little room in Scotus's theology for the regenerative operation of the Holy Spirit.

There was no important Western theologian on the Holy Spirit in the 10th century. In 1054, however, the final schism between Eastern and Western Christendom occurred. Once again Western writers came to the defense of the *filioque* clause. Among these was Peter Damian (d. 1072), who argued that the Father, Son, and Holy Spirit are one in essence but differ from one another by their originational properties. He insisted that the *filioque* must be accepted because it is taught by Scripture and the Fathers. Quoting the creed of the Eleventh Council of Toledo, Damian stated that the Spirit proceeds from both Father and Son, but he then added that this is for the sanctification of creatures.

C. The Scholastics.

1. Anselm of Canterbury.

From the 11th century to the end of the Middle Ages, the scholastics dominated Western theology. Scholasticism was not a philosophy per se, but rather an approach to all intellectual inquiry through the use of Aristotelian logic. In the area of pneumatology, scholastics attempted to defend the double procession and to work toward a solution to the very difficult question of the precise difference between the origin of the Son and the origin of the Spirit.

Anselm (1033–1109) is the first scholastic theologian of real significance. His theology of the Holy Spirit is to be found in his *Monologion,* written c. 1070 when he was abbot of Bec, and in a treatise *De Processione Spiritus Sancti,* composed at Canterbury where he became archbishop. A rationalist by approach, Anselm on the one hand takes from Augustine of Hippo his analysis of the Spirit's activities—understanding and love. On the other hand he considers of secondary importance his great spiritual ancestor's mystical concept of the Spirit as the mutual love between the Father and the Son.

For Anselm the Holy Spirit was first and foremost the love of himself proceeding from his memory and thought. This concept results from his reasoning that the supreme Spirit is capable of an act of understanding, of remembering himself, and necessarily also of loving himself. This is seen as the basis for the existence of the divine Third Person. In this supreme Spirit, memory is the Father and understanding is the Son. It is therefore evident to Anselm that the Holy Spirit proceeds from both.

Notwithstanding, having found rationale for his position on double procession, Anselm concluded that the Trinity actually is a mystery beyond the human intellect. From this basis it can be argued that he actually ascribed to reason far more competence than can be justified, projecting his theological speculations much too far into the realm of the unknowable.

2. Peter Abelard.

One of the greatest and certainly the most controversial of the early scholastics, Abelard (1079–1142) dealt with the Trinity as his primary subject. He began with the premise that the church's creed must be tested by reason. In reacting against his first master, Roscellinus, who had tritheistic tendencies, Abelard perhaps went too far to the other extreme—that of overemphasizing the unity of the Godhead. As a result, he was soon confronted with the charge of modalism—i.e., of making Persons in the Trinity into mere modes of the divine Being. This attack was characteristic of the period (and similar to many of the attacks Abelard

inflicted on his opponents). But in this case it was not really fair, for he also insisted on the fullness of the personality of each divine Person.

Having emphasized the personal distinctions in the oneness of the Godhead, Abelard dwelt on the procession of the divine Spirit. It is the nature or distinctive character *(proprium)* of the Spirit to proceed from both Father and Son. Here Abelard drew special importance from Jesus' breathing of the Spirit upon the disciples and the witness of the church fathers. Further, he reasoned that if the Spirit is eternal, his procession from the Father and the Son also must be eternal. Therefore, he must equally be the Spirit of the Son and of the Father.

Abelard became embroiled in a theological controversy with Bernard of Clairvaux (d. 1153), who insisted that Abelard the rationalist did not give sufficient place to the cross and the atonement of Christ. At the Council of Sens (1141) Abelard was condemned for heresy and put to silence. Charges against him included allegations that he rejected the omnipotence of the Son and the Holy Spirit, that he denied the consubstantiality of the Spirit with the Father, that he denied the coequality of the Spirit with the Father and the Son, and that he denied the Father's equality with the Son and Spirit in wisdom. He died the following year. Whether or not the charges against him were justified, Abelard left a heritage that has significantly influenced Western thought in medieval and modern times.

3. Richard of St. Victor.

During the last half of the 12th century, the abbey of St. Victor in Paris was a center for intense theological discussion in a climate that combined deep spirituality and a trust in the power of reason. Richard of St. Victor (d. 1172) wrote a treatise on the Trinity in which he attempted to demonstrate by means of reason the existence of the triune Godhead, including that of the Second and Third Persons. The perfect deity has everything, including perfect love. To be charity, love must tend to another, for charity cannot exist as private love of self. Such love implies that there is one who is personally over and against that perfect presence and who is the Son. The love that is simply given is the Father. The love that gives is the Son. But there is also a Third Person: the love that receives is the Holy Spirit.

On the issue of procession, Richard argues that the Third Person proceeds both from the one who was born and from the one who cannot be born. Beginning with the one who cannot be born, there is an immediate procession, that of the Love-Son, and one that is simultaneously immediate (from the Father) and mediate (from the Son), that is the Holy Spirit.

No other being or person proceeds from the Spirit, but it is through the Spirit that God as love is given to the believer and takes root in him. The Spirit, then, is best described as the divine "gift."

Interestingly, Richard suggests that his ideas are based not merely on rational deduction, but also on spiritual experience—known in part to humanity through human experiences of love. But this does not mean that Richard presents a well-rounded and full pneumatology. He offers only a definition of the triune Godhead that probably was more convincing to his own generation than to Christians today.

4. Peter Lombard.

Having studied under Abelard at Paris and having been closely related to the theologians at St. Victor, Peter Lombard (d. 1160), bishop of Paris, created a systematic and traditional summary of the Christian faith that became a standard throughout the Middle Ages—the *Book of Sentences.* His reasoning on behalf of a Godhead that is united in essence and plural in Persons is based on an analogy to the human mind. Love naturally proceeds from pure intellect and its conception or idea. The Spirit then proceeds essentially from the Father and the Son. The Holy Spirit is the Spirit of both by virtue of proceeding from both.

The Holy Spirit loves by himself without the medium of any virtue; however, the divine Spirit also is the love by which people love God and their neighbors. In human existence the Spirit prompts acts of faith and love through the medium of virtues of faith and hope.

Peter Lombard became the great authority for medieval theological students in the West. This was not without challenge, however. Joachim of Fiore charged him with heresy, arguing that he actually had taught a quaternity in God. Lombard eventually was cleared of the charge by the Fourth Lateran Council (1215), 50 years after his death.

5. Joachim of Fiore.

Perhaps the most important prophetic figure of the Middle Ages, Joachim of Fiore (c. 1130–1202), had a series of visions that he believed helped him to understand the mysteries of Scripture and from which he developed a dispensational system that he applied to human history. He tried to show the historical concordance between the unfolding of history in the OT and NT and in the process to understand the future.

Joachim taught that human history could be divided into three overlapping time periods: the age of the Father (from creation to Christ), the age of the Son (reaching from the 9th or 7th centuries B.C. to A.D. 1260), and the age of the Spirit (from c. A.D. 500 to the end of the world). The three ages represented ongoing spiritual progress. During the age of the Spirit, humankind and the church will be perfected, and the world will be evangelized. All humans will be brought by the Holy Spirit into religious life in which they will be inspired by the love of God to despise this world and worldly things. The purified church will be under monastic leadership. The Holy Spirit will complete the teachings of Christ and impart to each one knowledge and grace to achieve perfection and to persevere in it, walking in light and truth up to the end. The

age of the Spirit, then, is to be a time of utopian perfection structured on the principles of monasticism in which the various members of Christ's mystical body will achieve great spirituality and harmony of purpose. The process of individual perfection will be completed.

A new form of free and spiritual religion will replace the obsolete ecclesiastical order, which struggles over the letter of the gospel. The spiritual person of the third age will know the truth without veil and will receive directly from the Holy Spirit all the charismatic gifts necessary for perfection.

As the institutional church will be transformed into the true spiritual church, so the kingdoms of this world will yield to the kingdom of God. This globe will then become "spiritualized," and heaven will descend upon earth.

At a certain point, however, Joachim's description of the future utopia of the Spirit seems less than clear or complete. As with most visionaries, Joachim thought he was viewing the Promised Land but was not being permitted to enter it himself.

Joachim's dreams of a third age of the Spirit are reminiscent of Montanus's dreams of a new era in which the Spirit would reveal all things. They both anticipated that the future utopia would be led by ascetics, although details are radically different. Both Montanist and Joachimite prophecies failed to materialize, and followers of both Montanus and Joachim of Fiore were harshly persecuted by the mainstream church as heretics.

6. Thomas Aquinas.

Aquinas (1224–1274) was the greatest philosopher and theologian of the medieval Western church and the "Prince of the Scholastics." He developed a synthesis of Aristotelian philosophy and Christian thought. As a rationalist, Aquinas believed that reason played an important role in understanding God and his relationship to humankind. But in delving into the nature of the Godhead and interrelationships between divine Persons, reason was limited. It was possible to reveal the unity of the divine essence through reason. But it was impossible to know rationally the distinctions of Persons in the Godhead.

Aquinas agrees with Augustine and Anselm that the Holy Spirit is the bond of love between the Father and the Son; however, he readily admits that this did not provide a sufficiently intellectual force to form a basis for organizing his treatise on the Trinity. He prefers to argue the origins of the Son and the Spirit from analogy. He begins with the premise that there are two origins in the Trinity: that of generation and that of procession. This he does by relating the intellectual acts of understanding and willing. Generation of the Son is essentially a likeness-producing act. But the Spirit proceeds by will, which is not a likeness-producing act, but instead an impulse-producing act. In sum, the Son is generated by intellect, and the Spirit proceeds by will.

On the issue of double procession, Aquinas argues that if the Spirit did not proceed from the Son, he would not be distinguished from him. As always, he deals with this question in a dialectic and highly rationalized way. The Greeks are wrong in assuming that Jesus' statement, "All that belongs to the Father is mine. That is why I said the Spirit will take from what is mine and make it known to you" (John 16:15) refers to his humanity. The words can be applied only to his divinity.

Although Thomas accepts the *per Filium* ("double procession"), he is careful to exclude any inequality in the Godhead. He also is much more concerned to affirm the unity of the hypostases than to stress their order and source of origin.

Aquinas teaches that the gift of sanctification belongs to the Holy Spirit. While the Son is the author of holiness, the divine Spirit is its sign. The Spirit makes one holy. The church is holy because the Spirit of God is present within it.

Virtues of the Christian life are strengthened by the Spirit's deep and lasting gifts (Thomas understands the Isaian list to be the permanent charismata). By spiritual gifts the believer is able to function beyond natural human means, for the mind is moved by a higher than human principle. The gifts are dispositions that make the Christian ready to grasp and follow the inspirations or promptings of the Spirit.

This is a position far removed from a purely rational moral attitude. For Aquinas morality is based on the saving and perfecting divine will, according to norms that go far beyond human reason. Gifts of the Spirit are at the service of moral and theological virtues that unite mankind to God himself ("All who are led by the Spirit are sons of God" [Rom. 8:14]).

In attempting to determine precisely how the gifts influence the practice of moral and theological virtues, Aquinas ties one gift of the Spirit and one of the beatitudes to each of the virtues. To each of these combinations he then attempts to join one of the elements of the fruit of the Spirit as listed in Gal. 5:22–23. For example, Thomas states that happiness is a great virtue—the final end of human life. Children are said to be happy because they are full of hope. The apostle Paul says that Christians are saved by hope. The Beatitudes pronounce benedictions on those who are childlike or poor in spirit. The poor in spirit are those with humility.

Aquinas distinguishes between gifts and charisms. As we have seen, gifts (Isa. 11:2–3) are permanent and are received by all Christians from the Holy Spirit, enabling them to be receptive to God. Charisms (1 Cor. 12:8–10) are temporary actions of God. For example, he distinguishes between the gift of wisdom, which is common to all individuals in a state of grace, and the charismatic gift, *sermo sapientiae*, which is extraordinary. Thomas identifies several charisms, each of which he places in a distinct category. These include revelatory or prophetic charisms—illumination, revelation, utterance under divine empowerment, and performance of miraculous signs. Speech charisms comprise tongues (preach-

ing in other languages), interpretation of speeches (not just tongues), utterance of wisdom, and knowledge. Miracles and healings are action charisms. The highest charism is prophecy, and the highest form of prophecy is illumination.

Thomas was a supernaturalist, both theologically and experientially. In centering his discussion around the manifestation of 1 Cor. 12:8–10 rather than on verses that speak of ministries and offices, he is in agreement with both modern pentecostals and most early Christian thought. Unlike pentecostals, however, Thomas believes charismata may be given by God as blessings to believers and unbelievers alike. In addition, he argues that charisms are given, not primarily to supply ecstatic experiences, as some modern pentecostals would claim, but rather to provide divine revelatory knowledge.

We have ample evidence that Thomas personally experienced the presence of God. On one occasion he reported experiencing a transport of heavenly grace while celebrating the Mass. Again, near the end of his life, he was reported to have been in an ecstatic state for almost three days.

Unfortunately, in his own time and in the centuries that followed, Thomas Aquinas has been thought of simply as a great rationalist. As a result of this unbalanced overgeneralization, his sensitive discussion of mystical themes—such as the distinction between ordinary gifts and charisms—and his experiences in the Spirit usually have been overlooked. Certainly Aquinas did provide the great medieval Western theological synthesis, and it still speaks to modern Christians who attempt to find a balance between reason and revelation, tradition and experience.

7. Bonaventure.

While Thomas Aquinas supplied a theological synthesis for Western Christendom, Bonaventure (c. 1217–74) provided a spiritual synthesis. Bonaventure was born at the time that the young Franciscan movement was beginning to gain considerable popularity. He reported being healed from a serious illness through the prayers of Francis of Assisi. This event clearly established a close bond between Bonaventure and Francis, who died in 1226.

About 1234 Bonaventure went to study at the University of Paris, and in 1243 he entered the Franciscan order. He taught for many years in Paris, eventually becoming minister general of the order. Bonaventure proved to be a moderate leader, facing various challenges to the Franciscans.

Bonaventure's spirituality combined the mysticism and negative theology of Pseudo-Dionysius with the Franciscan devotion to the humanity and passion of Christ. His overriding purpose was to portray the journey of the inner person inward and upward into the mystery of the triune God. For him, the soul's journey was a growth in the Spirit—and expansion of the heart in love and the other great virtues through the three stages of purgation, illumination, and perfection.

His doctrine of the Trinity is based on the Pseudo-Dionysian principle of the self-diffusion of God. The Father is the fountain-source of divine fecundity. Out of his boundless fecundity, the Father generates his Son, expressing himself in his perfect image, his eternal Word. This fecundity issues further in the procession of the Spirit from the Father and the Son as their mutual love and the Gift in whom all other spiritual gifts are given. In turn, all creatures emanate out of God and return to God. This doctrine of emanation is the basis of Bonaventure's understanding of rational creatures as vestiges and images of the divine in the soul's journey to God.

The crucified Christ was the center of Bonaventure's spiritual synthesis. Through the cross the charity of the Holy Spirit is nourished in devout hearts and the sevenfold grace is poured out. Then the Spirit brings devotion to the crucified Christ.

Bonaventure personally wrestled with the Spirit and received that spiritual and mystical ecstasy that gives rest to the intellect and through which natural affections pass over entirely to God. In this state the very marrow of a person is inflamed by the fire of the Holy Spirit. Aware of the importance of this mystical wisdom, Bonaventure insisted that emphasis should be on unction rather than inquiry, on inner joy rather than on the tongue, on God's gift to humanity—the Holy Spirit—rather than on words and on writing.

Bonaventure had a great reverence for Francis of Assisi and the workings of the Spirit in and through him. In his biography of Francis, the saint is portrayed as a man of the Spirit. The joy of the Spirit came over him, and he was assured that all his sins had been completely forgiven. He was rapt in ecstasy and totally absorbed in a wonderful light. In this state his heart was expanded, and he saw clearly what would transpire for him and his followers in the future.

Francis learned in prayer that the presence of the Spirit for whom he longed was granted more intimately to those who invoke him and withdraw from the noise of worldly affairs. Francis was frequently lifted up by the Spirit into ecstasy beyond human understanding (also described as being "drunk in the Spirit"). On these occasions he was unaware of time and of the place and people that he passed. But these ecstasies always brought greater devotion to the crucified Christ. For Francis, to know Christ and him crucified was a gift of the Spirit.

The Spirit led Francis in establishing the Franciscan rule. Wherever Francis went, the Spirit of the Lord was with him, giving him words of sound teaching and miracles of great power. Francis directed his efforts chiefly to the exercise of those virtues that by the inspiration of the Holy Spirit he knew most pleased God. He exercised the gifts of wisdom and knowledge, bringing hidden things to light. The spirit of prophecy also was apparent in him, for he foresaw the future and had insight into the secrets of the hearts of those around him. Whatever was hidden by man was revealed to him by

the Spirit. In short, he was so often moved upon by God that he seemed to live among others more like an angel than a human being.

Having been called by their leader to penance and gospel perfection, a large number of Francis's followers experienced the work of the same Spirit. One such disciple had been an abusive husband who opposed his wife's Christian commitment. Francis heard about this and assured her that her husband soon would be a comfort to her. She returned home to discover that the Holy Spirit had come upon her spouse, making him a new man. Thereafter, they both took the vow of celibacy, becoming followers of Francis.

Bonaventure reports that Francis lived so completely in the presence of the crucified Christ that late in life he miraculously also received the stigmata (the wounds of Christ). These remained with him to his death.

Bonaventure's formulating of the dynamics of growth in the Spirit has become one of the classical expressions of Western spirituality. In the 15th century he was given the title of Seraphic Doctor or *Doctor Devotus* (Devout Teacher) because of the extent to which he displayed the Spirit's unction in his life and writings.

D. Catholic Women (1100–1450).

As we have seen, the high Middle Ages in Europe was a significant period of mysticism, as Christians sought direct experiences with God. While men such as Bernard of Clairvaux, Bonaventure, Francis of Assisi, and Thomas Aquinas in his final years were famous for their mystical spirituality, female mystics were far more numerous at this time, although they are perhaps less familiar to most readers.

Religious women were severely restricted in the ways they could act on their vocation. Normally, they could not administer the sacraments, hear confessions, grant absolution, or preach. Their sole role was to pray for the salvation of their own soul and for others in the Christian community. Despite these obstacles, religious women such as Hildegard of Bingen, Gertrude of Helfta, Brigitta of Sweden, Catherine of Siena, Julian of Norwich, and Margery Kempe did emerge as respected leaders of the faithful. Their roles as prophets, mediators, and healers constituted the one exception to women's presumed inferiority in medieval society. They also became known for their writings, their efforts to reform the church, and as founders of new religious orders. Above all, they are remembered by their contemporaries as agents of the Holy Spirit. As one writer in A.D. 1158 put it: "In these days God made manifest his power through the frail sex, in these handmaidens whom he filled with the prophetic spirit" (*Annales palidenses* [*Monumenta Germaniae historica, scriptorum tomus* 16], 90). They wrote about the Holy Spirit; they claimed personal inspiration by the Spirit; and they often thundered against evils in both their ecclesiastical and secular societies, as had the prophets of old.

1. Hildegard of Bingen (1098–1179).

Perhaps the greatest female mystic of the Middle Ages, Hildegard (1098–1179) became abbess of a Benedictine monastery in 1136. In 1148 she founded her own convent near Bingen. Hildegard reports having had visions first at the age of five but not revealing them to others until at the age of 42 she experienced a calling to proclaim God's words in the Spirit. In a personal Pentecost event, she saw the heavens open, and a fiery and brilliant light permeated her mind and inflamed her heart. Believing that she was instructed to speak and write about what she had experienced, she proceeded to describe this vision in her *Scivias* (short for "Know the ways of the Lord") and to draw a self-portrait of her experience in which, like the original Pentecost event, she was crowned by parted tongues of fire. She was encouraged by Bernard of Clairvaux and other church leaders to accept her divine calling by publishing all that she had learned from the Holy Spirit.

Hildegard was taken seriously as a prophetess by everyone, from the popes to the humblest serfs. She wrote to many prominent people (300 letters still exist), never mincing

Self-portrait by Hildegard of Bingen, showing her reception of the Holy Spirit.

words when she considered their behavior unworthy of their calling. She went on numerous preaching missions, delivering fiery apocalyptic sermons—an exceptional role for a woman in those days. In addition, Hildegard wrote 77 hymns of divine praise (her own poetry, which she set to music), a history of the universe, numerous theological commentaries, a book on natural history, and a book on medicine. She also drew 36 multicolored "illuminations," in which her visions are vividly captured.

Hildegard placed great emphasis on the creative and re-creative work of the Holy Spirit. She also insisted that those who have experienced a personal Pentecost by being touched by the fiery tongues of the Spirit will be virtuous, with overflowing grace and an ability to discern good from evil.

In one of her greatest hymns, *De Spiritu Sancto*, Hildegard speaks of the creative and re-creative work of the Holy Spirit: "Holy Spirit, making life alive, moving in all things, root of all creative being, cleansing the cosmos of every impurity, effacing guilt, anointing wounds. You are lustrous and praiseworthy life. You awaken and re-awaken everything that is." For Hildegard, God's "elect" are those who have been touched by the fiery tongues of the Spirit. The reception of the gift of the Holy Spirit is necessarily accompanied by the production of divine fruits. In addition, the divine Third Person gives gifts in superabundance to those born of water and of the Spirit. These gifts include those enumerated in Isa. 11:1–3 and 1 Cor. 12, as well as tears and compunction from which the fruit of holiness must grow.

Hildegard's biographers provide insights into her own spiritual life. She is famous for her "concerts" or singing in the Spirit, her ecstatic visions and resulting prophecies, and her numerous miracles. But above all, she is remembered for the transparency with which she portrays her own spiritual experiences through artistic and written media.

2. Gertrude of Helfta (1256–1301/2).

Committed at the age of five to the care of the nuns of the cloister school at Helfta, Gertrude soon developed a strong devotion to the sacred heart of Christ. When she was 26, she had her first vision of Jesus, who told her that he would lead her into a more fervent life. Raptures and many additional visions followed, leading to a spirituality so intense that she was often insensible to what was happening around her.

It would be a mistake to characterize Gertrude's theology merely as Christocentric. In reality, she was devoted to the entire divine Trinity. She developed a special relationship to each person in the Godhead, characterizing the Father as wisdom, the Son as power, and the Holy Spirit as goodness or love. God is love, and to Gertrude the Holy Spirit is the love between the Father and the Son. The goodness of the Holy Spirit continually came to her despite her unworthiness, ministering with ineffable sweetness and providing for her a precious nuptial alliance with the Trinity. The Spirit's breath quickens, attracts, draws, and consumes the faithful. It also breaks down human boundaries to God's will.

Gertrude taught that the Christian may be baptized in the power of the Holy Spirit, and having received divine breath in the power of the Spirit, be free from the wiles of the enemy. Gertrude asked Christ that she be given four virtues—purity of heart, humility, tranquillity, and concord—in order to prepare a dwelling place for the Holy Spirit. Then she saw a stream of honey coming from the sacred heart of Jesus, which entirely filled her heart. This she recognized as the unction and grace of the Holy Spirit purifying her from every stain.

Of all Christian saints, Gertrude used the most encompassing definition of spiritual gifts, drawing from lists found in Isa. 11:1–3; Rom. 5:1–5; 12:6–8; 1 Cor. 12:8–10; Gal. 5:22–23; Eph. 4:8, 11–12; and 2 Tim. 1:6–7. In addition to her visions and prophecies, she is credited with numerous miracles, including the ending of a severe winter and later for the cessation of excessive rains. She also was frequently graced with compunction and divinely induced weeping. But above all, she was given fervency in love, purity of soul, patience in tribulation, and a desire to be among the wise maids as she awaited the heavenly Bridegroom.

3. Brigitta of Sweden (1302/3–73).

The most prominent medieval Scandinavian mystic, Brigitta began to experience visions and other ecstasies at the age of seven. Later she married and bore eight children. When her husband died in 1344 she retired to a life of penance and prayer. From 1345 onward she was divinely guided to travel, to send messages, to denounce evils of her day, to discern good and evil spirits, and to otherwise promote the "vineyard," as she called the kingdom of God on earth. She founded an order (later known as the Brigittines) for both nuns and monks, and ruled over both communities. Together with Catherine of Siena, Brigitta successfully campaigned to move the papacy back to Rome from Avignon at the end of the so-called Babylonian captivity of the church.

Brigitta understood the Trinity in terms of complete mutuality—a reciprocal indwelling of the three divine persons. She applied this doctrine of mutuality (*perichoresis* or circumincession) also to the relationship between Christ and his bride.

Brigitta exulted in her awareness that she had been freed from the world and had been led into "the mansion of the Holy Spirit," wherein she enjoyed continuing mutuality with the divine Trinity. Her relationship with the Holy Spirit was particularly intimate, for the Spirit dwelled in her and spoke directly to her.

In addition to her visions, Brigitta is remembered for prophecies concerning prominent church leaders and royalty. In some cases she ordered them to follow a reformed course of action. She also exercised the gift of discernment, distinguishing between good and evil spirits, and bringing deliverance to those possessed by evil forces. She taught that the divine Spirit might be given to good and wicked alike but would not continue to dwell in a sinful vessel. It is reported that she also had gifts of tears, levitation, and of "speaking the language of angels."

4. Catherine of Siena (c. 1347–80).

The 24th of 25 children of a Sienese dyer, Catherine reportedly had a vision at the age of seven in which she vowed her virginity to Christ. Subsequently, she defied efforts to make her marry. At age 20 she received the Dominican habit and gave herself to solitary contemplation. Shortly thereafter, however, she gave herself to the service of the poor and the sick. Meanwhile, her mystical experiences increased in frequency and intensity, as did her austerity. Her efforts to end the so-called Babylonian Captivity of the church (1307–77) were rewarded, in large measure because Pope Gregory XI placed great importance on prophetic voices. She was surrounded by a devoted group of supporters who were attracted to her spirituality, her ecstatic prayer life, her devotion to the blood of Christ, and her exceptional charismatic gifts.

Catherine recognized that at creation God created humans in the divine image and likeness. After humankind lost its innocence, God the Trinity reclothed it with innocence in the person of the only-begotten Son, restoring the divine image and likeness. In the Eucharist she received the "whole of God"—the warmth and light of the Spirit, the light and wisdom of the Son, and the power and strength of the Father.

Catherine came to know the divine Spirit as the very love between the Father and Son, their personal union and embrace. The Spirit also is our servant and waiter, humbly attending to every need of those who seek after God. She also depicts the Spirit as a mother who "nurses the soul at the breast of divine charity" and as the source of light and understanding for spiritual insight and true scholarship.

Heeding her Dominican call, Catherine ministered to crowds that often exceeded a thousand people. Her words burned with such effectiveness that the very person of the Holy Spirit seemed to speak through her. She taught that the Spirit intends for Christians to enlarge their love for the poor and as a result distribute their wealth to the needy.

Unlike most Western Christians of her time, Catherine did not limit her understanding of spiritual gifts to the Isa. 11:1–3 list. Nor was she convinced that spiritual gifts are intended only for a spiritual elite. She personally received gifts of celibacy, prophecy (the ability to see, in her visions, into the future), preaching, and healing the sick.

5. Julian of Norwich (c. 1342–after 1416) and Margery Kempe (c. 1373–after 1433).

We know little of the life of Julian of Norwich, the famous 14th-century English mystic. She lived as an anchoress in a cell attached to the side of a church at Norwich, England, and received her revelations on May 13, 1373, when she was 30 years old. These she recorded in her *Showings*, a significant literary achievement that earned her the title "first English woman of letters."

In explaining her revelations, Julian articulates a vision of the suffering Christ and of her own partaking in those sufferings. Her life of prayer also led her progressively toward a deeper contemplative penetration into the mysteries of the Trinity. She refers to the Trinity as uncreated love—an objective relationship between Father, Son, and Holy Spirit. Love is the substance or being of each member of the Trinity. Each divine Person may be found only in the other Persons whom he loves. Julian illustrates this divine mutuality in the Christian's life of prayer. The Father directs the will of the human soul to the will of the incarnate Son. In turn, this eternal, creative act is furthered by the "sweet, secret operation"—the sending of the Holy Spirit.

While an anchoress, Julian of Norwich received visitors and gave them counsel. One such person was Margery Kempe, a 40-year-old mother of 14 children. Margery had visions of Christ and felt compelled to break off marital relations with her husband and to live alone, in preparation for a pilgrimage by foot to Jerusalem. Margery faced criticism for this plan, as well as for the emotional outbursts and tears she experienced whenever she heard preaching about Christ's crucifixion.

Julian gave Margery real support by confirming that her emotional outbursts were a sign of the Holy Spirit's indwelling. She also taught Margery that the Spirit tends to move a soul to chasteness and makes a person stable and steadfast in the right faith. In addition, the Spirit gives tears of contrition, devotion, and compassion. When these signs are present, the Holy Spirit is in the soul.

Margery's husband released her from the obligations of marriage, and she undertook her pilgrimage to Jerusalem. Upon her return home, she discovered her husband bedridden and cared for his needs. Margery was occasionally accused of heresy because of her visions but was spared death at the stake by her high social standing, the support of esteemed men, and her tendency to check out her experiences with individuals having ecclesiastical authority.

E. Popular Piety in the Medieval Roman Catholic West.

Charismata, or gifts of the Spirit as described by Paul in 1 Cor. 12, were exercised widely in the Catholic West during the Middle Ages. But most Catholic theologians taught that it was not to be expected that they would function in all believers. These were extraordinary gifts reserved for the ministries of the most pious, and so they marked the lives of the saints. For example, certain of the saints spoke in earthly languages not their own: Dominic in German, Colette in Latin and German; Clare of Monte Falcone in French; Angelus

Clarenus in Greek; Stephen in Greek, Turkish, and Armenian; and Jean of the Cross in Arabic. Hildegard is said to have written numerous books on music, the lives of saints, medicine, and devotional subjects—all in Latin, a language completely unknown to her.

Sometimes the miracle was in the hearing of the listeners: Vincent Ferrer was understood by Greeks, Germans, Sardinians, and Hungarians as he preached in Spanish. The Spanish of Louis Bertrand was comprehended by Indian natives in the Western Hemisphere. Francis Xavier's Portuguese was understood by both Japanese and Chinese.

Known cases of ecstatic utterance in an unknown tongue are far rarer. Hildegard is said to have sung in unknown tongues to the extent that her biographer refers to these occasions as "concerts." It is reported that Francis Xavier was heard to speak the language of angels. Clare of Monte Falcone engaged in holy conversation, speaking heavenly words about heavenly things.

In at least three bulls of canonization the gift of tongues was listed among the evidences of piety that were used in support of the elevation of individuals to the status of saints: Vincent Ferrer, Francis Xavier, and Louis Bertrand. On the other hand, it is most curious that in the 11th-century *Rituale Romanorum*, speaking in and interpreting unknown languages was considered a sign of demon possession. It would seem that the orthodoxy of the individuals involved in tongues speaking determined whether the phenomenon was viewed as a sign of sainthood or of demon possession.

Numerous other charismatic gifts were apparent in the lives of the saints. For example, St. Colette enjoyed the gift of knowledge and the gift of discernment, along with a reputation for ministering healing to lepers and raising the dead. Vincent Ferrer was famous for his prophetic gift and many miracles of healing. Francis Xavier reportedly had a ministry of healing—ranging from deliverance from barrenness to relief from pain in childbirth. Louis Bertrand laid hands on the sick in a hospital, with the results that people regained their sanity and the dead were raised to life.

In his *Sounds of Wonder: A Popular History of Speaking in Tongues in the Catholic Tradition*, Eddie Ensley argues that from the 9th through the 16th centuries spontaneity of worship, improvised songs of jubilation, clapping of hands, and even dance movements were apparent in the lives not only of saints and mystics, but also of many ordinary believers. The word *jubilation* means spiritual inebriation. By the language of jubilation Ensley means going beyond ordinary speech into a transcendent language of praise, which he views as the equivalent of speaking in tongues.

Ensley also points to a high level of devotion to the Holy Spirit in the medieval Catholic West. This was a time when hymns to the Spirit, such as "Veni, Creator" ("Come, Creator Spirit") and "Veni, Sancte Spiritus" ("Come, O Holy Spirit")

were popular. Congar adds that churches were dedicated to the Holy Spirit in this period. The town of Saint-Saturnin was renamed Pont-Saint-Esprit. In the early 12th century, confraternities of the Holy Spirit, which cared for the poor and for deserted children, appeared in the Auvergne. A brotherhood of the Holy Spirit was founded in 1177 at Benevento. Hospitals and hospices under the patronage of the Spirit appeared in numerous places, especially along pilgrimage routes.

Ensley suggests that popular devotion often took the form of spontaneity in praise and the giving of self to God and in a greater docility toward the inspirations of the Spirit. Among the faithful, there was a nearly childlike credulity about things religious, including a widespread belief in miracles. Wandering preachers were amazingly similar in preaching style to modern pentecostals. Healing services were frequent. In a spirit of renewal, nobles and commoners often worked together as volunteers to build great cathedrals and other church structures. During such times miracles abounded, and it was common to hear groups singing in the Spirit, as practiced in the present-day charismatic renewal.

III. RADICAL DUALISM.

From well before the beginning of the Christian era, perhaps even as far back as the Persian prophet Zoroaster, radical dualism has reared its deterministic head. Dualism assumes the existence of two cosmic forces—one of light or good, the other of darkness or evil—which to a greater or lesser extent control each individual. Radical dualism teaches that such control is virtually complete, leaving very little, if any, free will or individual responsibility. In Christian terms, this usually has been described as the struggle within humanity between the devil and his evil spirits and God through his Holy Spirit.

Historically, radical dualism appears in Gnosticism and its offspring: Manichaeism, Messalianism, Paulicianism, Bogomilism, and Catharism. Each of these appeared sequentially in movement from East to West. Each was considered a significant threat to the established and orthodox Christian community. In part this was a threat because radical dualism reinterpreted Christian anthropology, calling attention to the divine element within the human spirit while depreciating the physical body as a prison for the spirit. This led as well to a reinterpretation of soteriology. Certain chosen individuals (a kind of "elect") claimed to receive special divine knowledge from the Holy Spirit for salvation. Other less "gifted" individuals either acquiesced or were condemned by the intolerantly exclusive dualists. In all cases, radical dualists purported to exercise spiritual gifts, but because of their rejection of commonly accepted theology—especially established means of grace such as the sacraments—they were branded as heretics and often persecuted by the mainstream church.

While it would not be fair to label the majority of modern pentecostals and charismatics as radical dualists, there are striking similarities. In most cases they do teach a cosmic struggle between the forces of good and evil. They stress the importance of a baptism in or with the Holy Spirit and of the exercise of supernatural gifts in order to be "victorious" in this conflict and to understand divine purposes, though they believe that these charismata are for all believers, not simply for an elect few. They often reject or minimize established order. These connections have not escaped certain pentecostal historians, such as B. L. Bresson, who openly identifies with historic dualists.

A. Messalians.

A sect probably originating in Edessa and in surrounding parts of Mesopotamia c. A.D. 360, the Messalians survived in the East until the 9th century. They also were known as Euchites, or "praying people," from the Greek translation of their oriental name (Aram. *mezalin*, participle of *zela*, to pray), because they placed such an emphasis on individual prayer.

Christian Messalians were radical dualists, believing that every person is possessed from birth by a personal demon. Even the body of Christ had to be purified from devils by the Logos, though through glorification Christ became like the Father. They even taught that Satan and the Holy Spirit dwelt together in the individual—probably after baptism, although this is not certain.

Water baptism, the church's traditional answer to demonic forces, did not satisfy the Messalians. The individual demon must be driven out through unceasing fervent prayer and other ascetic exercises and the reception of the Holy Spirit. The demon's departure is perceived in visual fashion by images such as smoke, black serpents, or a sow with her litter. The subsequent indwelling of the Spirit of God is perceived through sensory experiences. Sometimes the Spirit was seen to enter the soul with the appearance of an innocuous fire, and at other times the Spirit's coming is likened to sexual intercourse (Spirit baptism as intimate communion with the heavenly Bridegroom). Experiential evidence was necessary so that it was certain that the Spirit had indeed been received. The Messalians also practiced the laying on of hands for the reception of the Spirit.

The Messalians claimed prophetic gifts by which they even knew the states of departed souls and by which they could read the hearts of individuals. It was said that when they had visions of demons, some of the people danced in order to trample the evil forces that appeared to them.

As with most dualists, the Messalians had a contempt for churches. After all, had they not personally received the Holy Spirit? Were they not especially blessed, having been freed of all sins and made perfect and superior? Their orthodox enemies reported that they lived far from perfect lives, living promiscuously, dissolving legitimate marriages, and even allowing their women a high place in their communities!

Because of their religious and social counterculturalism, the Messalians were persecuted mercilessly. The movement ceased to exist in the Eastern Mediterranean world by the 9th century. It reappeared in the Balkans, however, under the name Bogomil (see below).

B. Paulicians.

The Paulicians were radical dualists who during the early Middle Ages spread throughout Asia Minor and Armenia and finally into the Balkans. It appears that they were quite diverse in theological emphasis.

Like the Messalians, the Paulicians condemned the Christian establishment and its hierarchy, questioned a large part of its sacramentally based soteriology, rejected its Mariology, refused to venerate its saints and images, and interpreted the NT in an individualistic way. However, they placed a heavier emphasis on the authority of Scriptures than did the more experientially oriented Messalians.

Byzantine Paulicians appeared more Marcionist than their Armenian brothers, distinguishing between the good God of the NT and an evil God of the OT who created the world. Because they rejected as evil all of creation, especially flesh, they taught against the incarnation and were decidedly docetic. In contrast, the Armenian Paulicians were adoptionist—stressing the humanity of Jesus.

According to *The Key of Truth*, which numerous scholars think is a handbook of Armenian Paulicians, Christ's faithful followers, who, like their Master, acquit themselves nobly, will receive the same grace of the Spirit as he. They take on themselves the same prophecy and ministry as Jesus, they preach and suffer, they yield in like manner to the Spirit as Jesus did after his baptism.

The *Key* also teaches that the Holy Spirit enters the catechumen immediately after the third handful of water is poured over his head in the Spirit's honor. The Spirit enters to exclude evil spirits. This is not a separate and distinct baptism of the Spirit, as the Messalians taught, however.

Like the Messalians, the Paulicians developed a two-class system. The spiritually adopted are set apart from common unbelievers or misbelievers who are dependent on the ineffectual infant baptism offered by the mainline church as the vehicle for elimination of original sin.

A well-known Paulician leader, Sergius Tychicus, who reformed the movement, had great evangelistic abilities and successes. Married people abandoned their spouses, and monks and nuns broke their monastic vows. But his opponents also claim that he exalted himself, even to the point of identifying himself with the Holy Spirit and offering himself to be worshiped. These charges are remarkably similar to those leveled against Mani, as well as against Paul of

Samosata, who is thought by some scholars to have been the founder of the Paulician movement.

Byzantine Paulicians remained strong and militant in their resistance to orthodoxy until the 10th century, when they were decimated and dispersed. Some of them amalgamated with the dualistic Bogomils of the Balkan Peninsula. In Armenia, Paulicianism seems to have lasted at least another century, eventually to be swamped by the rising tide of Islam.

C. Bogomils.

The Bogomils were members of a medieval Balkan sect that originated in Bulgaria but were a revival of earlier radical dualists, such as the Manichees, Messalians, and Paulicians. Their name appears to mean "beloved of God."

The Bogomils taught that the devil or Satanael was the elder of the two sons of God; he fell from his lofty position and created the visible world, including humankind. In order to escape his domination, all contact with matter and especially flesh must be avoided. The Bogomils, therefore, were especially known for their extreme asceticism; they rejected lawful marriage and maintained that reproduction of the human species was a law of the demon. They also forbade eating meat, drinking wine, and the sacraments in general. They had an aversion to baptized children. The cross was called an enemy of God, churches were material creations and therefore abodes of the devil, and icons and relics were rejected. They spurned the order of priesthood, the apostolic succession, and the Orthodox hierarchy.

The Bogomils were intolerantly exclusive. True Christianity could be found only in their own communities. Hence they claimed for themselves the sole right to the name of Christians. They alone lived "according to the Spirit."

In creation, when Satanael made Adam's body, he begged his Father to send down his Holy Spirit on Adam. Satanael agreed that humankind would belong to both of them. God agreed, and Adam came to life, with a corrupt body and a divine soul.

In Bogomilism it seems that the Son and the Spirit were not distinct hypostases but different names and emanations of the Father—two rays proceeding from the lobe of his brain. In this teaching, the Bogomils seem to resemble early Sabellianism or modalistic monarchianism.

They taught that each person was inhabited by a demon. Even Christ or the Holy Spirit could not withstand their potential to harm, since the Father had not yet deprived them of their power. In this, the Bogomils differed from the Messalians, who taught that the Holy Spirit could completely fill and dominate a person.

The Bogomils, like other dualists, believed in a distinction between the "perfect" or "chosen" on one hand and the "believer" or "hearer" on the other. An elect person was considered a receptacle of the divine Spirit and was consequently called *theotokos,* or "God-bearer," a name usually reserved for the Virgin Mary in the Orthodox Christian world. Having denied the incarnation of Jesus, it was Bogomil teaching that each of them as *theotokos* "gave birth to the Word" by teaching. They claimed to experience the Trinity personally and therefore no longer to be subject to the law, having been made incapable of sin.

Apparently the Bogomils had a rite of initiation called the baptism of Christ through the Spirit, which they distinguished from water baptism. In this rite the Spirit was invoked and the Lord's Prayer sung, while the Gospel of John was placed on the head of the initiate.

Bogomilism spread rapidly in the Balkans and even in Asia Minor in the 11th century. During the time it also passed into Italy and France, where its adherents were called Patrines or Cathari. During the 13th and 14th centuries, Bogomilism actually became the national religion of Bosnia. In the 15th century, persecution forced many into Herzegovina, which became the final bastion of Bogomilism. The movement in the Balkans eventually was wiped out or merged into Islam.

D. Cathars.

Catharism (known in France as Albigensianism) was the most powerful heresy in the medieval West. This movement seems to have grown out of Balkan Bogomilism, appearing in the West in the 12th century and growing to such threatening proportions in the 13th century that it was considered the prime object of the Inquisition. It lasted until the 14th century when it finally succumbed to intense persecution.

As with earlier dualists, the Cathars believed that the God of the OT was one of love and that he created the human soul. Therefore, humanity was in a most difficult position: the soul was spiritual and good, but the flesh was evil. So it was necessary to liberate the soul from the flesh as effectively as possible. According to the Cathars, one could escape the flesh by participating in the rite of *consolamentum* (which may have been the equivalent of the Bogomil baptisma) and by observing their system of radical asceticism, which they believed led to perfection.

The Cathars taught that water baptism was not profitable for salvation. Instead, they believed that to enter the company of their elite, the *perfecti,* it was necessary to take the *consolamentum,* or initiatory sacrament. This was a baptism with fire and the Holy Ghost, performed by the imposition of hands. Through this rite they believed that mortal sins were forgiven and the Holy Spirit was received.

Enemies of the Cathars reasoned that the *consolamentum* was called a baptism with fire because the participants were surrounded by a circle of lanterns, the fire of which was to dispel the darkness of their secret meeting place.

The preliminaries to attaining the status of *perfecti* were extremely arduous. The candidates had to be approved by the other perfect ones and had to show fitness to undertake their life by a year's probation, in which they fulfilled their fasts on every Monday, Wednesday, and Friday as well as during three penitential seasons—all on bread and water. At no time could the Catharist eat what they defined as a product of coition: meat, milk, eggs, and cheese. Fish was allowed because it was thought to be a product of the water itself, not of coition. Because sexuality formed part of Satan's creation, sexual contact in any form was strictly forbidden. If married, a candidate had to abandon his or her partner.

The Cathars who had received the *consolamentum* faced a lifetime of rigid observance of the group's precepts. They encouraged each other in their tense battle for perfection. Any breach involved the sinner once again in Satan's world and resulted in a loss of the *consolamentum.*

The Cathars rejected the Trinity in favor of a subordination of two Persons to the Father. They could not admit that Christ was God, nor could they agree to his humanity. Like most other Gnostics, they rejected the incarnation, the atoning death, and the resurrection of Jesus Christ. They believed that Jesus' mission was to convey to human prisoners of the flesh instructions for effecting an escape from the body.

■ **Bibliography:** N. Arseniev, *Mysticism and the Eastern Church* (1979) ▪ Bernard of Clairvaux, *Bernard of Clairvaux: Selected Works* (1987) ▪ P. B. T. Bilaniuk, *Theology and Economy of the Holy Spirit: An Eastern Approach* (1980) ▪ Bonaventure, *Opera omnia,* 15 vols. (1864–71) ▪ J. F. Bonnefoy, *Le Saint-Esprit et ses dons selon S. Bonaventure* (1929) ▪ B. L. Bresson, *Studies in Ecstasy* (1966) ▪ S. M. Burgess, *The Holy Spirit: Eastern Christian Traditions* (1989) ▪ idem, *The Holy Spirit: Medieval Roman Catholic and Reformed Traditions* (1997) ▪ idem, "Medieval Examples of Charismatic Piety in the Roman Catholic Church," in R. Spittler, ed., *Perspectives on the New Pentecostalism* (1966) ▪ idem, ed., *Reaching Beyond: Chapters in the History of Perfectionism* (1986) ▪ A. Butler, *Lives of the Saints,* 4 vols. (1965) ▪ Y. M.-J. Congar, *I Believe in the Holy Spirit,* 3 vols. (1983; French ed. 1979–80) ▪ G. B. Cutten, *Speaking in Tongues* (1927) ▪ I. H. Dalmais, "The Spirit of Truth and of Life. Greek Pneumatology and Latin Pneumatology: Are They Conflicting or Complementary?" *Lumen Vitae* 28 (1, 1973) ▪ J. Dupuis, "Western Christocentrism and Eastern Pneumatology," *Clergy Monthly* 35 (1971) ▪ E. Egert, *The Holy Spirit in German Literature until the End of the Twelfth Century* (1973) ▪ E. Ensley, *Sounds of Wonder: A Popular History of Speaking in Tongues in the Catholic Church* (1977) ▪ M. A. Fahey and J. Meyendorff, *Trinitarian Theology East and West* (1977) ▪ L. Gillet "A Monk of the Eastern Church", *Orthodox Spirituality: An Outline of the Orthodox Ascetical and Mystical Tradition* (1978) ▪ C. Hart and J. Bishop, trans., *Hildegard of Bingen: Scivias* (1990) ▪ G. S. Hendry, *The Holy Spirit in Christian Theology* (1956) ▪ Joachim of Fiore, *Das Reich des Heiligen Geistes* (1955) ▪ A. R. Kezel, ed., *Brigitta of Sweden: Life and Selected Revelations* (1990) ▪ R. Knox, *Enthusiasm: A*

Chapter in the History of Religion (1962) ▪ H. Küng and J. Molt-mann, *Conflicts about the Holy Spirit* (1979) ▪ W. Lewis, *Witnesses to the Holy Spirit: An Anthology* (1978) ▪ V. Lossky, *The Mystical Theology of the Eastern Church* (1976) ▪ idem, *The Vision of God* (1963) ▪ S. R. Maitland, *Facts and Documents Illustrative of the History, Doctrine, and Rites of the Ancient Albigenses and Waldenses* (1882) ▪ W. McCready, *Signs of Sanctity: Miracles in the Thought of Gregory the Great* (1989) ▪ J. Meyendorff, *Byzantine Theology: Historical Trends and Doctrinal Themes* (1974) ▪ R. Murray, *Symbols of Church Kingdom: A Study in Early Syriac Traditions* (1975) ▪ S. Noffke, *Catherine of Siena: The Dialogue* (1980) ▪ M. O'Carroll, *Trinitas: A Theological Encyclopedia of the Holy Trinity* (1987) ▪ idem, *Veni Creator Spiritus: A Theological Encyclopedia of the Holy Spirit* (1990) ▪ P. O'Leary, "The Holy Spirit in the Church in Orthodox Theology," *Irish Theological Quarterly* 46 (3, 1979) ▪ P. D. Opsahl, ed., *The Holy Spirit in the Life of the Church: From Biblical Times to the Present* (1978) ▪ R. Payne, *The Holy Fire: The Story of the Fathers of Eastern Church* (1980) ▪ J. F. Quinn, "The Role of the Holy Spirit in St. Bonaventure's Theology," *Franciscan Studies Annual* 33 (1973) ▪ M. Reeves, *Prophecy in the Later Middle Ages* (1969) ▪ H. M. B. Reid, *The Holy Spirit and the Mystics* (1925) ▪ S. Runciman, *The Medieval Manichee: A Study of the Christian Dualistic Heresy* (1947) ▪ Rupert of Deutz, *De Sancta Trinitate et operibus eius* (1971–72) ▪ D. Staniloae, "The Holy Spirit in the Theology and Life of the Orthodox Church," *Sobornost* 1 (7, 1975) ▪ E. Timiades, "The Centrality of the Holy Spirit in Orthodox Worship," *Ekklesiastikos Pharos* 60 (1–2, 1978): 317–57 ▪ C. N. Tsirpanlis, "Pneumatology in the Eastern Church," *Diakonia* 13 (1, 1978) ▪ J. Walsh, ed., *Julian of Norwich: Showings* (1978) ▪ B. Ward, *Miracles and the Medieval Mind* (1982) ▪ idem, *Signs and Wonders: Saints, Miracles and Prayers from the 4th Century to the 14th* (1992) ▪ H. Watkin-Jones, *The Holy Spirit in the Medieval Church* (1922) ▪ G. Williams and E. Waldvogel [Blumhofer], "A History of Speaking in Tongues and Related Gifts," in M. P. Hamilton, ed., *The Charismatic Movement* (1975) ▪ M. Winkworth, ed., *Gertrude of Helfta: The Herald of Divine Love* (1993).
▪ S. M. Burgess

HOLY SPIRIT, DOCTRINE OF: REFORMATION TRADITIONS

I. Magisterial Reformers
   A. *Martin Luther (1483–1546)*
   B. *Ulrich Zwingli (1484–1531)*
   C. *John Calvin (1509–64)*

II. Catholic Reformers
   A. *Ignatius of Loyola (1491–1556)*
   B. *John of Avila (1499/1500–1569)*
   C. *John of the Cross (1542–91)*

III. Radical Reformers
   A. *Thomas Müntzer (1488/9–1525)*
   B. *Menno Simons (c. 1496–1561)*

I. MAGISTERIAL REFORMERS.

Any study of the pneumatology of the Protestant Reformers should begin with the three most influential magisterial (or teaching) Reformers—Luther, Calvin, and Zwingli. For our purposes, they are especially important, because each had much to say about the Holy Spirit's person and work.

A. Martin Luther (1483–1546).

It has long been argued that the famed father of the Protestant Reformation, Martin Luther, had nothing new or distinctive to teach about the Holy Spirit, limiting the Spirit's operation to divine acts of regeneration and sanctification. In large measure this misconception has stemmed from his strong Christocentric emphasis as well as his vigorous attacks on enthusiastic contemporaries who claimed to be "people of the Spirit."

At first glance Luther does seem to follow traditional medieval Catholic pneumatology. Because of his strongly negative theology, in which he understands the Trinity to be beyond the human mind to grasp or the tongue to express, the divine Spirit's role is to search and know the deep things of God. At this point Luther adds a distinct new element, namely, that the Spirit then reveals these transcendent secrets to us through the Scriptures.

Luther defends the traditional Western church's doctrine of the *filioque*, which posits that the Holy Spirit proceeds from both the Father *and the Son*. Here he depends on John 15:26: "When the Counselor comes, whom I will send to you from the Father, the Spirit of truth who goes out from the Father, he will testify about me." Luther insists that to be sent by is synonymous with to proceed from.

In his *Spiritus Creator* (1953) Regin Prenter argues that in Luther's understanding of the divine Spirit we can find an integrating center around which the other fundamental tenets of his faith—justification by faith, law and grace, the cross, and vocation—form a constellation. According to Prenter, Luther conceives the Spirit's purpose to be bringing to humans the great treasure of Christ for the purpose of conforming them to his image, especially to his death and resurrection. This conformity to Christ begins when individuals are affected by God's law and recognize that they are justly condemned to death and hell. In this event, which Luther refers to as *Anfechtung*, or inner conflict, all self-righteousness and self-confidence are smashed.

Once given to agonized sinners, the divine Comforter makes groanings for them that cannot be uttered. He intercedes for them and sustains them in their *Anfechtung*, bringing Christ crucified and resurrected to their anguished hearts, and carrying them over into a new life (Luther refers to this as *vivificatio*). Karl Barth points out that Luther, in his *Commentary on the Epistle to the Galatians*, recognizes that conversion is accompanied by a testimony of the Holy Spirit in the experience of the believer. Barth thus demonstrates that

John Calvin is not the first Reformer to reintroduce the concept of the testimony of the Holy Spirit in the experience of the believer.

Luther contends that the Holy Spirit works outside the Scriptures and the sacraments. This leads him to oppose vigorously a variety of "enthusiasts"—including his former colleague, Andreas Bodenstein von Karlstadt, the "Three Prophets of Zwickau," and Thomas Müntzer—whom he calls *Schwärmer* and "the heavenly prophets." Luther argues that these radicals place the internal work of the Holy Spirit before the external word of Scripture. He accuses them of radical subjectivity, of seeking inward experiences rather than allowing the Holy Spirit to come to them through the Word and sacraments. He indicts them for works righteousness and for placing their own spirits above the true Spirit of God.

It is not surprising then that Luther does not emphasize spiritual gifts. Following Augustine, he argues that "new tongues" have ceased. He insists that divine healing, like all outer miracles, must be judged in the light of God's Word. In general, miracles are no longer necessary because the church was established long ago. Late in life, however, Luther seems to have altered these views. He prayed for Philip Melanchthon's healing, and this colleague was restored to health. Another friend, Friedrich Myconius, reports that God brought him back to life through Luther's healing prayer. Luther himself reported that he had brought healing to others but that he could not heal himself.

B. Ulrich Zwingli (1484–1531).

A Swiss contemporary of Luther, Ulrich Zwingli, developed a radically different pneumatology, in part because of his humanistic training and his attachment to Desiderius Erasmus. Zwingli does not limit the divine Spirit's work to the Scriptures and the sacraments. The Spirit comes to humans whenever and wherever God chooses.

Like Luther, Zwingli understands the Scriptures to be the sole norm and authority in matters of faith. Unlike Luther, Zwingli teaches that it is necessary to consult the mind of the Spirit of God before turning to Scripture. The meaning of the Scripture belongs to all those who believe in Christ and who therefore possess his Spirit. It is with the help of that Spirit that ordinary people will understand Scripture in accordance with the divine mind in the plainest way. The Christian should not stick to the bare letter of Scriptures, but rather seek the letter that is expounded by the Spirit of God. It is the Spirit who leads readers beyond literal surface meanings to deeper hidden understandings. While God has ordained that the external Word should be proclaimed, faith does not come by the external Word. Almighty God preaches in our hearts; in the process, the Spirit works in both the preacher and the hearers.

The Anabaptists went far beyond Zwingli, arguing the primacy of the inner word. Zwingli counters that they choose certain scriptural texts and ignore others. These radicals assert their own spirit over the Spirit of God. Zwingli insists that the Holy Spirit agrees in all things with Scripture and Scripture with the Spirit. The divine Third Person is not only the true author of Scripture, but also the reliable interpreter of Holy Writ. In the end, the Holy Spirit, working through the preaching of the Word, will inevitably transform all things.

Zwingli discards hierarchical structures in his Zurich parish. These he saw as hindrances to the flow of grace by the Spirit throughout the Christian body. In their place, he argued for the authority of the preacher-prophet and the magistrate. It is through the faithful ministry of the preacher-prophet that the Holy Spirit rules all.

Luther calls Zwingli an enthusiast *(Schwärmer),* insisting that he stresses the Holy Spirit rather than the Word. At the opposite pole, the Anabaptists and spiritualists contend that Zwingli does not give sufficient room for the divine Spirit to speak. In balance, it can fairly be said that Zwingli stresses the Holy Spirit without divorcing the Spirit from the Word.

C. John Calvin (1509–64).

Perhaps the most influential of all Protestant Reformers, John Calvin laid the groundwork for much of the Protestantism of the next four centuries. He is especially known for his many writings, especially the *Institutes of the Christian Religion.*

Calvin teaches that the Holy Spirit fulfills the action of the Father and the Son. Everything that God does happens through the Holy Spirit. The Spirit "sustains, quickens and vivifies all things in heaven and on earth ... in all things transfusing his vigor, and inspiring them with being, life, and motion" (*Institutes,* 1.13.14–15). The Spirit gives life, form, and efficacy to nature, which stands at the Spirit's disposal in stages of creation and re-creation.

For Calvin, as the world was first formed through the Holy Spirit, so the church is created through the activity of the Spirit in fallen humans. It is in the church that the Spirit renews the image of God in humanity, and it is there that the Spirit's judgments bring about "right order." According to Calvin's teaching, an individual's election to salvation is accomplished through the regenerating work of the Holy Spirit. Effectual "calling" consists in the preaching of the Word and in the Spirit's illumination. The Spirit sanctifies only the elect.

Faith is the decisive moment within effectual calling. It is by faith under the aegis of the Spirit that an individual apprehends divine benevolence—the electing love of God. Just as the Holy Spirit gives rise to faith in the elect, so the Spirit also enables them to persevere in it. Election, then, must be "proven" throughout the whole course of life. Calvin also speaks of the preservation of the church as a whole by the "hidden and incomprehensible power of God" (*Commentary on Daniel,* 2:44–45). The dynamic of the Spirit-formed church is very important to Calvin, as he is preoccupied with the concept of the place of the church in the history of God's restoration of order.

According to Calvin, Scripture reveals God's creative and re-creative plan. The Spirit illuminates our hearts, enabling us to discern Christ within the Word. The Word of God is made alive to the individual by the "secret testimony of the Spirit" *(testimonium Spiritus Sancti internum).* This testimony is superior to that of the church, the enthusiasts, or even reason itself, but it adds no new revelation to the word of the gospel. It merely certifies biblical truth. The Spirit's testimony also gives the witness to the sonship of the believer.

Calvin teaches that all of the genuine fruit of the Spirit (Gal. 5:22–26) are given to all Christians, regardless of their setting in time, place, or circumstance. They are to be applied to the common good of the church.

Spiritual giftings also are for the upbuilding of the entire Christian community. Calvin infers that the list of gifts in 1 Cor. 12:8–10, 28 is for his own generation. He understands that this is only a partial listing of a much greater variety of divine gifts. However, he recognizes constraints on their activity. Clearly, he is not an enthusiast. He overlooks or downplays the supernatural nature of several spiritual gifts. For example, he understands the gift of healing to be applicable only in the context of extreme unction. He condemns Catholic reports of miracles as foolish, false, and delusions of Satan. As a rule, he sees the gifts of healing, like the rest of miracles, as long vanished.

The gift of prophecy is considered by Calvin as *forth*telling, rather than *fore*telling. Prophecy is equivalent to inspired, Spirit-motivated preaching. Discernment of spirits is viewed as an ability to make piercing judgments between true and false ministers.

The gift of tongues was a means of communication given to early Christian missionaries unacquainted with foreign languages with which they had to deal. Interpreters of tongues rendered these foreign tongues into the native language. Calvin clearly rejects contemporary glossolalia. He teaches that we do not receive the Spirit so that we may speak with tongues, but for a better use—that we may believe with the heart unto righteousness. Christian life must be demonstrated by virtue rather than by the ecstatic gifts (as advocated by certain of his detractors among the Catholic and radical Reformers).

II. CATHOLIC REFORMERS.

The Catholic Reformation (or Counter-Reformation, as it was called earlier) grew from a variety of roots and developed a rich canopy formed by many strong branches. It was the product of a persistent and strong medieval piety strengthened by a new mysticism and a deep reverence for church traditions. Catholic reform found expression in the deepening of lay piety, the reform of old religious orders, and the rise of new orders that were dedicated to a revival of spiritual life and service to others. The lives and writings of three Catholic Reformers who had much to say about the person and offices of the Holy Spirit, and especially the Spirit's gifts, are highlighted in this section.

A. Ignatius of Loyola (1491–1556).

The founder of the Society of Jesus (the Jesuits), Ignatius of Loyola became a reformer after his military career was cut short by serious war injuries. He is best remembered for his attempts to reform the Roman church from within, principally by education, more frequent use of the sacraments, and preaching the gospel to the newly discovered pagan world.

By far the most important of Ignatius's extant writings is the *Spiritual Exercises,* which contains the marrow of his spirituality. The exercises begin with repentance and purification and lead to a desire to serve the kingdom of God under the standard of Christ in an ever-growing docility to the Holy Spirit. In his *Autobiography,* Ignatius narrates the steps by which his spiritual and mystical life had evolved from 1539 to 1556.

The *Spiritual Diary* is the longest and most intimate of Ignatius's writings, and it abounds with references to the Holy Spirit. Here we learn of his inexpressible intimacy with the Trinity and of his many accompanying secondary mystical phenomena. These include mystical tears, Trinitarian visions and illuminations, various kinds of locutions (God speaking to the soul), and profound mystical consolations, touches, reposes, and joys.

Ignatius's *Spiritual Exercises* contain fewer direct references to the Holy Spirit. Ignatius lived at a time when church authorities persecuted members of religious movements known as *Alumbrados,* who claimed the direct and constant inspiration of the Holy Spirit. As a consequence, Ignatius's references to the Holy Spirit are presented in a way that eliminate the possibility of an Alumbrados-like interpretation. He mentions, for example, that Elizabeth was filled with the divine Spirit, that the Spirit came upon Jesus at his baptism, and that the risen Christ gave the apostles the Holy Spirit. He also speaks of the Spirit who guides both the individual and the church; but this is expressed in the safe context of the "Rules for Thinking with the Church."

Ignatius explicitly states that God the Holy Spirit will communicate to the devout person seeking God's will. In this communication the Spirit also governs and directs the exercitant just as the Spirit governs and directs the church.

We know from both his *Autobiography* and *Spiritual Diary* that Ignatius frequently received divine communication in the form of visions. He also had "cherubic" or intellectual experiences, which included thoughts concerning the Trinity. He rejected spiritual illuminations that disturbed him, labeling them temptations from an evil spirit.

Ignatius also experienced a gift of tears—often in such abundance that he could not control himself. We are told that if he did not shed tears at least three times during Mass, he felt deprived. For Ignatius, tears signified the presence of the Holy Spirit.

Of all Ignatius's spiritual gifts and mystical experiences, perhaps the most interesting and novel was the gift of *loquela*—which can be variously translated as "speech," "language," or "discourse." This gift seems to be connected with heavenly music. Harvey D. Egan has suggested that *loquela* might be associated with today's charismatic phenomenon of sung glossolalia. Sacred music enraptured Ignatius, nourishing him both spiritually and physically. In this he is in the company of the music-loving mystics—including Hildegard of Bingen, Francis of Assisi, and Catherine of Siena—who also experienced the divine harmony as heavenly song.

B. John of Avila (1499/1500–1569).

Known for his reform of clerical life in 16th-century Spain and for founding several religious colleges, John of Avila was a famous preacher (the "Apostle of Andalusia") and mystic. Fortunately, a large number of his sermons have been preserved. Among the most penetrating are those on the Holy Spirit, including six homilies prepared for Pentecost. John's theme throughout is the importance of knowing the Holy Spirit, of being in contact with the Spirit, and of surrendering to the Spirit's impulses.

As with most mystics, John of Avila describes the Holy Spirit in apophatic terms—i.e., he does not attempt to delve deeply into the mystery of the Godhead. Clearly, the Holy Spirit is God, for only God could have healed the wound left by the ascension of Jesus. The Holy Spirit is also Christ's Spirit, the heart of Christ, and the Comforter. Beyond this, John uses such common expressions as water, wind, and breath to describe the divine Spirit, and honey to typify the sweetness of life in the Spirit. He also uses the symbols of gentle air, wine (because the Spirit will make individuals leave behind their own minds and adopt that of Christ), and milk (because the Spirit sustains the soul just as a mother nourishes and cherishes her infant). The perfume of the Spirit, John suggests, makes all other perfumes seem bitter.

John insists that no one is saved without receiving the divine Spirit. All are dead without him, like dead grass. But the Spirit chooses to come and re-create humanity, making it possible for them to demonstrate God-likeness in their daily lives.

John's asceticism is integrated into his pneumatology. He teaches that the Holy Spirit will not come to an unprepared person. First, an individual must recognize the Spirit's power and long for the Spirit's presence. Then that person must make his or her life spotless by giving to the poor and by mortifying the flesh through fasting and seclusion, thus being freed from earthly cares and all carnal desires. Finally, the petitioner must be vigilant for the arrival of the Spirit.

Because the Spirit is gentle and not obtrusive, it is possible for the petitioner to be unaware of being baptized in the Holy Spirit. John suggests several "signs" of the Spirit's coming. The recipient will feel a burning of the fire of charity and an unwavering love of God leaping within the heart. The soul will be filled with great happiness. The recipient will not give in to fleshly temptations. All fears will be gone—fear of poverty, dishonor, hunger, death, the world, and the devil.

When the Spirit comes into the human heart, all straw will be consumed. The young girl will no longer be concerned about her clothes or how to make herself attractive. She will be humble. She will no longer be interested in the swaggering young man with the sword by his side and a feather in his cap. The man will not lose his head over every pretty woman he sees, and he will not spend all of his time eating, enjoying himself, and attending to his business. Infilled Christians are disciplined and do not dwell on carnal or sensorial concerns.

The Spirit's coming will have the same effects experienced by the apostles waiting in the cenacle on the Day of Pentecost. They lost all fear; they came to life, preaching Christ with fiery eloquence. They performed many miracles, curing the sick and returning the dead to life. Above all, they were able to say with complete certainty what was the proper thing to do and what was not. They loved their neighbors as much or even more than their own brothers, for the link generated by the Spirit of God is stronger than the ties of blood.

Throughout his sermons on Pentecost, John of Avila reminds his hearers to seek the Holy Spirit. This seeking must be a lifelong discipline, for the divine Spirit will not remain with those who do not continuously submit themselves to God's grace. Christians are free people, but at the same time they willingly make themselves into slaves for Christ's sake.

C. John of the Cross (1542–91).

The famous discalced (barefoot) Carmelite reformer from Castille, John of the Cross, describes the soul in search of God, in movement toward union with him, and in struggle against the obstacles to this goal. He understands the spiritual journey as a gradual process. The first phase is life in the senses in which the soul hears and responds to the call to set out on the spiritual path (the stage of illumination). This is followed by a stage of dark night and negation (purgation), which John sees as decisive in developing a sober and genuine relationship with God. Only in the darkness do individuals learn to put their hands into the hand of God. The third phase—full union, or likeness of love—is the goal and fruit of the previous phases. This union with God is habitual, but there are moments when it is more vital, experiential, or alive, through the work of the Holy Spirit.

Being made in the image of God, the human soul has a Trinitarian character, consisting of memory, intellect, and will. The power of memory is the analogue of the Father, who is source and end of all being. The intellect mirrors the person of the Son, the image and wisdom of the Father. The will—the power by which we choose to return God's love and thus become united with the divine—is the analogue of the Holy Spirit, who is the love between the Father and the Son. The divine Spirit proceeds from the Father and the Son by way of will, for which reason, then, the Spirit is understood as bond, warmth, communicability of divine Being, and the "infinite fire of Love."

For John, the soul in mystical union is one with God in operation and loves through the Paraclete, having shared in the Spirit's spiration. This is the process by which the Spirit inhales *(aspira)* the soul into the Father and the Son. Within this union with the Godhead, the divine Spirit supernaturally and secretly teaches the soul and, in a way mysterious to it, raises it up in virtues and gifts. As individuals are purged of their sensory affections and appetites, they gain liberty of spirit in which they acquire the 9 fruits of the Holy Spirit (Gal. 5:22–23).

John often refers to anointings of the Holy Spirit. The Spirit provides sublime ointments for those espoused to the beloved, personally anointing and preparing them for the marriage that is spiritual union. Unfortunately, an individual can easily disturb and hinder these anointings of the Spirit by giving place to human senses, appetites, and knowledge, or by seeking personal satisfaction and pleasure.

At the highest level in the journey of faith, the Holy Spirit provides "spiritual" apprehensions. These include visions, revelations, locutions, and spiritual feelings. John pays special attention to the Spirit's role in granting locutions—literally, God speaking to the soul. In the process, the Spirit not only infuses wisdom into the soul but puts it in order as well, helping it to know what must be known and ignore what must be ignored, to remember what ought to be remembered and forget what ought to be forgotten.

John of the Cross resorts to an unusually rich variety of symbols when referring to the person and offices of the Holy Spirit. These include the image of water in a fountain, leaping up to life everlasting. The Spirit also is the "breath" or breeze" of God, the "juice of pomegranate," and "a wine of savory love." Finally, because of the "inner resurrection of the Spirit," the soul enjoys life unending and eternal in union with the triune God.

III. RADICAL REFORMERS.

The 16th-century Reformation involved not only the Protestant magisterial or teaching Reformers and the Catholic Reformers, but also the so-called radical Reformers. These "radicals" included nonconformists, visionaries, and other unique individuals who rebelled not just against the Roman church but against mainstream Protestant Reformers and as a consequence incurred the enmity of both major groups. The radicals were united in opposition but not in thought and action. George Williams has classified the radical Reformers into three basic groups: (1) the anabaptists, whose modern heirs are the Mennonites and the Amish; (2) the spiritualists, who have a modern counterpart in the Schwenckfelder church; and (3) the evangelical rationalists and anti-Trinitarians, the ancestors of the modern-day unitarians.

The anti-Trinitarians gave little attention to the concept of a Holy Spirit. In contrast, the person and work of the divine Third Person was central to the theologies of both anabaptists and spiritualists. Thomas Müntzer was one of the leading revolutionary spiritualists, and Menno Simons was the most important figure in anabaptism.

A. Thomas Müntzer (1488/9–1525).

At first a disciple of Martin Luther, Müntzer was diverted to the Radical Reformation by the Zwickau Prophets. He came to emphasize the "inner word" (as opposed to the "outer" or audible word), direct revelation in visions and dreams, Holy Spirit possession and guidance, abandonment of infant baptism, radical social reforms, and a belief in the millennium. He understood the apparent outpouring of the Spirit on himself and others as confirmation of the prophecy of Joel 2:27–32. During the so-called Peasants' War, Müntzer increasingly assumed a leadership role. On May 15, 1525, the peasants were routed outside Frankenhausen. He was taken captive, tortured, and beheaded.

In his writings, Müntzer contends that Christians are to experience the Holy Spirit as powerfully in postbiblical times as they did at the time of the prophets and apostles. He insists on the necessity of a baptism of the Holy Spirit. While outer baptism is not required, inner baptism—the revelatory descent of the Holy Spirit—is absolutely necessary. For Müntzer, the primary precondition to Spirit baptism is spiritual misery and despair, or inner turmoil *(Anfechtung),* and the abandoning of all worldly pleasures. Every Christian must suffer in order to become conformed to Christ. Only those who crucify their lives receive the Holy Spirit and are aware of the Spirit's indwelling. With the Spirit indwelling, the elect come into possession of the key of David, whereby they can unlock the book of seven seals, the Bible, and discern spirits. Müntzer believes that both the OT and the NT are to be interpreted according to the Spirit's promptings, rather than by bookish reasoning.

Müntzer teaches that as long as Christians have life, they should seek after signs of God's work in their lives. These signs or testimonies are communicated to God's people through spiritual gifts. They will prophesy, dream dreams, and see visions. Furthermore, they will be able to distinguish by divine revelation between the work of God and that of malignant spirits.

Thomas Müntzer's quest for an invincible faith turned him into a charismatic preacher who claimed immediate access to the will of God. He felt commissioned to transform the old creation into a new heaven and a new world—if need be, with the sword of Gideon. His Spirit-filled followers would be charged with finding the final solution to the problem of evil, and would, in the final phase of history, restore fallen creation. A godless man has no right to live if he impedes the pious; the sword must be used against those who refuse to participate in his reformation of the world through the gospel.

Müntzer proclaims that the climax of divine activity will be a total renewal of the world through the reception of the Holy Spirit. Meanwhile, the bestowal of the sevenfold gift of the Spirit (Isa. 11:2) is the goal of redemption. Among the numerous spiritual gifts he claims for himself and his followers is the reception of direct instruction from the divine Spirit in the form of visions, dreams, ecstatic utterances, and inspired exegesis.

Attacking Müntzer on his own turf, Luther declared that he had still to prove that he is of God's people by a single miracle. Müntzer responded that only a false prophet would demand miracles or boast of having the spirit of Christ.

Thomas Müntzer's death did not extinguish his dream. The "left wing" of the Reformation convulsed through several other periods of apocalyptic idealism and violence. In the end, however, the survival of the radical Reformation was based not on violence, but on the pacifistic movement begun by its greatest leader, Menno Simons.

B. Menno Simons (c. 1496–1561).

Under Menno Simons's leadership, the anabaptist movement was purged of its radical elements and gained widespread respectability. Raised by his parents to the service of the Catholic Church, Simons was ordained priest in 1524, subsequently serving two parishes until 1536. However, after reading the teachings of Luther and other Reformers, he came to doubt the Catholic dogma of transubstantiation. As a result of his subsequent searching of the Scriptures on this issue, Simons decided in 1536 to put aside church offices and join a small group of devoted evangelical anabaptist brethren, the followers of Obbe Philips. Upon hearing that his own brother was among the 300 insurgent anabaptists killed after the fall of Münster, he wrote a pamphlet against John of Leyden and his "perverted sect." Simons became a pacifist, and his followers, soon to be called Mennonites,

absorbed remnants of other anabaptist movements. During most of his remaining years, Simons and his followers suffered severe persecution, and he lived as a fugitive with a price on his head.

Simons acknowledges that the reason Christians are able to confess that the Holy Spirit is God is that they are brought to this by the Scriptures. As of old, the Holy Spirit still converts those who become part of the true church. Their minds are regenerated by the operation of the Holy Spirit (or the baptism of the Holy Spirit) after hearing the divine Word of God. Therefore, conversion does not come through water baptism. He insists that water baptism be administered only to those who have already turned to Jesus and who have been baptized with the Holy Spirit of God.

For Simons, this is just the beginning of a life directed and vivified by the divine Spirit. Via the discipline of the Spirit, the Christian is to be conformed to Christ, and conformation to Christ means becoming one with Christ's nature. The only agent for this union, which is called "salvation" or "sanctification," is the Holy Spirit. The Spirit of Christ effects, sustains, and reestablishes the full union of the Christian with the nature and the life of the Lord. The Spirit persuades believing hearts and warns them against sins and temptations. He humbles and chastises them when they have separated themselves from Christ. He nurtures the bonds of union with Christ. He makes Christ present in believers.

Simons lays special emphasis on the Spirit's anointing. He is convinced that the Spirit's unction teaches individuals how they should conduct themselves in matters of practical living. True Christians are free from bitter partisanship, hatred, and envy. They have a lovely spirit of peace, as well as pure and upright minds. They do not live for themselves, but for Christ and for their neighbors. They submit to others in humility, avoid unscriptural strife, and readily acknowledge their shortcomings. They make peace with their neighbors and heap fiery coals on the heads of their enemies.

Even in his emphasis on divine unction, Menno Simons is distinctly a biblicist. True divine unction is consistent with and based on the Bible and will bring life and light to biblical texts.

Simons sees the Holy Spirit as adorning Christians with heavenly and divine gifts. He lays special emphasis on gifts of speech, wisdom, and discernment but warns that these are never to be exercised for personal gain or authority. He believes that the divine Spirit expresses God's will through the consensus of the believing community—the local congregation. In the Holy Spirit, each member assumes responsibility for the well-being of all. When individuals distort the message of the Spirit, the united witness of other members brings recognition of error. This permits the development of a theology in which prophetic and mystical elements are held in balance.

Those who do not seek the witness of the community, says Simons, may become spiritually rebellious—and this rebellion may even extend to what Simons defines as the "sin against the Holy Spirit." A person in this condition risks being forsaken by the Spirit and continues to be totally lacking in spiritual understanding.

■ **Bibliography:** S. M. Burgess, *The Holy Spirit: Medieval Roman Catholic and Reformation Traditions* (1997) ■ J. Calvin, *Institutes of the Christian Religion* 3 vols. (1960) ■ P. de Klerk, *Calvin and the Holy Spirit: Papers and Responses Presented at the Sixth Colloquium on Calvin and Calvin Studies* (1989) ■ P. Divarkar, *Ignatius of Loyola: Spiritual Exercises and Selected Works* (1991) ■ H. Egan, *Ignatius Loyola the Mystic* (1987) ■ E. Egli, ed., *Huldreich Zwinglis Sämtliche Werke, Corpus reformatorum 88–97* (1905–) ■ P. Elbert, "Calvin and the Spiritual Gifts," *JETS* 22 (1979) ■ H.-J. Goertz and W. Klaassen, eds., *Profiles of Radical Reformers: Biographical Sketches from Thomas Müntzer to Paracelsus* (1982) ■ J. Heubach, ed., *Der Heilige Geist im Verständnis Luthers under die lutherischen Theologie* (1990) ■ H. Hillerbrand, ed., *Radical Tendencies in the Reformation: Divergent Perspectives* (1988) ■ B. Hoffman, *Luther and the Mystics* (1976) ■ John of Avila, *The Holy Ghost (Six Sermons on the Holy Spirit)* (1959) ■ W. Krusche, ed., *Das Wirken des heilgen Geistes nach Calvin* (1957) ■ P. Matheson, ed., *The Collected Works of Thomas Müntzer* (1988) ■ J. Parratt, "The Witness of the Holy Spirit: Calvin, the Puritans and St. Paul," *EQ* 41.3 (1969) ■ E. Peers, ed., *The Complete Works of Saint John of the Cross* (1974) ■ J. Pelikan and H. Lehmann, eds., *Luther's Works*, 55 vols. (1955–) ■ R. Prenter, *Spiritus Creator: Studies in Luther's Theology* (1953) ■ L. Verguin, ed., *The Complete Writings of Menno Simons* (1956) ■ G. Williams, *The Radical Reformation* (1962).

■ S. M. Burgess

HOLY SPIRIT TEACHING MISSION

HOLY SPIRIT TEACHING MISSION A charismatic teaching center that was based in Ft. Lauderdale, FL. The Holy Spirit Teaching Mission (HSTM) sponsored teaching conferences, distributed books, audio and video teaching tapes, and published *New Wine* magazine.

HSTM grew out of a Ft. Lauderdale Bible study, led by a Spirit-baptized Episcopalian, Eldon Purvis. Purvis and a group of laymen started the "Committee of Forty," which sponsored the first HSTM teaching conference in June 1963, which included charismatic speakers ˒Dennis Bennett, ˒David du Plessis, and ˒John Sherrill. Over the next few years HSTM regularly sponsored conferences in Ft. Lauderdale and in other parts of the U.S. These conferences featured many of the prominent leaders and Bible teachers of the charismatic renewal (CR).

In June 1969 HSTM began publishing *New Wine* magazine, which became the most widely circulated charismatic publication of the 1970s. The magazine was distributed free of charge in the early years and contained many high-quality, teaching-focused articles.

Purvis, a man of vision and administrative skill, wanted HSTM to become a center for the burgeoning CR. Personal problems, however, brought about Purvis's resignation in Oct. 1970. This crisis at HSTM proved catalytic in bringing together four independent charismatic Bible teachers, ˒Don Basham, ˒Bob Mumford, ˒Derek Prince, and ˒Charles Simpson, who had been regular contributors to *New Wine* magazine and teachers at HSTM conferences. The four were asked to help with the leadership problems at HSTM; and as a result of their involvement, the four men committed themselves together in mutual submission and accountability. Soon the four were the primary leaders of HSTM and major contributors to the magazine.

In Mar. 1972 HSTM changed its name to Christian Growth Ministries (CGM), believing that the new name better reflected the ministry's purpose in bringing spiritual growth to believers through Bible teaching. Over the next four years the magazine's circulation grew to over 100,000 in 140 nations. CGM discontinued teaching conferences in the fall of 1973, and the magazine, book, and tape distribution became the primary focus of the ministry. *New Wine* increasingly became the principal voice of the emerging ˒shepherding movement, led by the four teachers, who were joined by the Canadian Pentecostal ˒W. J. E. (Ern) Baxter in 1974. CGM and Ft. Lauderdale were seen as the identifiable center of the movement, and Mumford and the other teachers were sometimes referred to as the "Ft. Lauderdale Five."

In 1978 *New Wine* relocated to Mobile, AL, and CGM's name was changed to Integrity Communications (IC). The move reflected the growing leadership role of Charles Simpson in the shepherding movement. IC became the distributor of Basham's, Baxter's, Mumford's, and Simpson's books and tapes, and published the periodicals *Businessgram* and *Fathergram* in addition to *New Wine*. In 1985 IC started Hosanna Music, for distributing quarterly worship tapes, which proved enormously successful. Hosanna was sold in 1987 and became a for-profit company that continues to produce worship and music materials.

Because of financial problems with *New Wine* and a growing separation of the teachers—Prince had exited the shepherding movement in 1983—*New Wine* ceased publication with the Dec. 1986 issue. This effectively ended the shepherding movement as such. In 1987 IC was renamed Charles Simpson Ministries and publishes *Christian Conquest* magazine and distributes Simpson's books and tapes.

■ **Bibliography:** D. Basham, "Birth of a Mission," *New Wine* (Apr. 1970) ■ idem, "How It All Began," *New Wine* (June 1984) ■ "Forum," *New Wine* (Dec. 1976).   ■ S. D. Moore

HOLY TRINITY BROMPTON Anglican church founded in 1839 on Brompton Road, central London. Its vicar, the Rev. Sandy Millar, has overseen considerable growth in the church since his appointment in 1985. The Reverend Nicky Gumbel, a member of the church's ordained staff, is the author of a number of best-selling books. Holy Trinity is widely known for its charismatic renewal. It is also the home of the ▸Alpha course, now being used in over 10,000 churches in 73 countries. Alpha course, a practical introduction to the Christian faith, includes praying for the baptism with the Holy Spirit.

■ C. M. Irish

HOOVER, WILLIS COLLINS (1856–1936). Founder of pentecostalism in Chile. Hoover was born in Freeport, IL, to Methodist parents who were part of the Wesleyan/Holiness tradition. He was shaped in the Wesleyan/Holiness camp meetings in Illinois and Iowa. He received professional credentials in medicine (1884). Hoover experienced a call to serve as a missionary in South America and married Mary Louise Hilton, a graduate of the Chicago Training School for Home and Foreign Missions. Mary Hoover was also part of the Holiness movement on the edges of the Methodist Episcopal Church, and her connections to that tradition would prove crucial in the transition to pentecostalism.

Hoover did not receive initial appointment to Chile with the Methodist Episcopal Missionary Society; rather, he chose to go to Chile with support from the William Taylor Building and Transit Fund. This fund enabled self-supporting Wesleyan/Holiness missionaries to enter missionary service. ▸Taylor had initiated Methodist-related missions in Chile in 1878 as an effort to prove to the Methodist Missionary Society that self-supporting, self-governing, self-theologizing, and self-perpetuating churches would result from the work of self-supporting missionaries. He described this project as "Pauline Missions."

Hoover began his mission work in 1889 as the rector of the *Collegio Ingles* in Iquique, Chile. He quickly learned Spanish and became pastor of the first Spanish-speaking Methodist church in the area. He also developed preaching points in nearby cities. As control of the self-supporting missions in Chile by the Methodist Episcopal Mission Society became more complete, decisions about ministry in Chile were increasingly made in New York. First, all of the male missionaries were taken into the Chile District of the Cincinnati, OH, Con-

Willis C. Hoover, the "father of pentecostalism in Chile."

ference. The Chile Conference was inaugurated later. This disenfranchised the women missionaries who were working primarily in education throughout Chile and who had worked as equals with the Taylor mission. It also disenfranchised the Chilean (often part-time) assistants and evangelists. Care was also taken to appoint as new missionaries those who did not believe in self-supporting missions and who were opposed to the Holiness revivalist techniques, such as street preaching, tent meetings, open-air evangelism, and lay ministry.

Hoover prospered as a pastor and evangelist because of his abilities with Spanish and his respect for Chileans and Chilean culture. He normally served as the official translator at the Methodist Episcopal Annual Conferences. His churches grew. He was made Superintendent of the Iquique District (northern Chile) in 1897. He was appointed pastor at Valparaiso in 1902. There he used the Holiness revivalist techniques to lead the congregation into becoming the largest Protestant congregation in Chile. Visitors to Chile, including ▸A. B. Simpson, remarked on the effort to minister to the poor; others were amazed to find an American missionary living like the Chileans.

Hoover developed leadership within the congregation and formed a corps of assistant pastors who were often put in charge of small groups that would later grow into churches. However, there was significant pressure on the self-supporting missionaries who had remained affiliated with the mission after the incorporation into the mission-board system. They received significantly less financial assistance from the Methodist Missionary Society than the newer missionaries. Then efforts were made to ruin the reputation of Hoover's closest missionary friend through trumped-up charges of financial mismanagement. Hoover, however, worked to develop the congregation and to rebuild the church after the earthquake of 1906.

The strife in the Methodist Episcopal Mission led the Hoovers to search for spiritual revival in other places. In 1907 ▸Minnie Abrams, a Wesleyan/Holiness missionary in India who had resigned from the Methodist Episcopal Missionary Society to work with ▸Pandita Ramabai, sent the Hoovers a copy of her book *The Baptism of the Holy Ghost and Fire* (2d ed., Bombay, 1906). Minnie Abrams was a close friend of Mary Hoover and had been her classmate in Chicago. Mary Hoover also began corresponding with pentecostal leaders and their wives around the world, including ‣A. A. Boddy and ‣Thomas Ball Barratt as well as American pentecostal leaders. In 1909 the Hoovers experienced the pentecostal baptism of the Holy Spirit. The congregation at Valparaiso largely followed them into the experience, as did two congregations led by former Hoover assistants. At the 1909 Annual Conference of the Methodist Church there were significant expressions of pentecostal worship. The Methodist missionaries took umbrage, but Methodist Bishop Bristol reminded the angry missionaries that this type of worship was typical of the American Holiness camp meetings and defended Hoover.

Thereafter, the missionary attacks focused on Hoover's endorsement of the evangelist and prophetess Nellie Laidlaw. At the 1910 annual conference she was used as a wedge to remove Hoover from his position as district elder. After that conference, on May 1, 1910, he resigned his Methodist pastorate in Valparaiso. The Methodists had him arrested and attempted to force him to leave the country. The local magistrates freed him, and he was asked by his Chilean assistants to lead them in establishing the Methodist Pentecostal Church of Chile. This he did. Hoover received some criticism from North American pentecostals for retaining the word *Methodist* in the name of the church but was encouraged to retain it by T. B. Barratt. In 1932 conflict over a variety of issues led Hoover to participate in the establishment of another denomination, the Iglesia Evangélica Pentecostal. He led this new denomination until his death in 1936. His memories of these events are recorded in his book *Avivamiento* (1934).

■ Bibliography:

Primary Sources. W. C. Hoover, *Historia del Avivamiento Pentecostal en Chile* (Valparaiso, 1934; repr. 1948), repr. in *Historia del Avivamiento, origen y desarrollo de la Iglesia Evangélica Pentecostal* (Santiago: Eben-Ezer, 1977) ■ idem, *PE* "Apostolic Power Brings Apostolic Persecution: How God Exonerated His Servants under Trial," *LRE* (Feb. 1921) ■ idem, "Ecclesia—Church. Needed a Complete Purification of Pastors and People," *LRE* (May 1921) ■ idem, "Pentecost in Chile," *PE* (July 16, 1932) ■ idem, "The Pentecostal Revival in Chile," *PE* (July 22, and Aug. 5, 1922) ■ idem, "A Phenomenal Self-supporting Native Work: Transformed from Professional Rogues to Preachers of the Gospel," *LRE* (Jan. 1921) ■ idem, "Raised from the Dead," *PE* (Mar. 14, 1936) ■ idem, "The Remarkable Spread of Pentecost in Chile," *PE* (Jan. 5, 1918) ■ idem, "Send Me Where You Need Me," *LRE* (Dec. 1921) ■ idem, "Through Perils and Hardships to Crowning Days: The Outpouring of the Spirit in Chile," *LRE* 6 (June 1914) ■ idem, "The Wonderful Works of God in Chile," *LRE* 3 (Apr. 1911, July 1911) ■ idem, "Work in Chile," *Word and Work* (July 1911) ■ M. L. H. to Mrs. Boddy, dated Mar. 24, 1909, publ. as "South America: A Congregation Hungry for God," *Confidence* [Supplement] 2, 6 (June 1909) ■ May [*sic*] Louise Hoover, "Pentecost in Chile, South America," *The Upper Room* 1 (6, Jan. 1910).

Secondary Sources. G. F. Arms, *History of the William Taylor Self-Supporting Missions in South America* (1921) ■ D. D. Bundy, "Bishop William Taylor and Methodist Mission: A Study in Nineteenth-Century Social History," *Methodist History* 27 (4, July 1989) and 28 (1, Oct. 1989) ■ idem, "William Taylor, 1821–1902: Entrepreneurial Maverick for the Indigenous Church," in *Mission Legacies: Biographical Studies of Leaders of the Modern Missionary Movement*, ed. G. H. Anderson et al. (1995) ■ idem, "Unintended Consequences: The Methodist Episcopal Missionary Society and the Beginnings of Pentecostalism in Norway and Chile," *Missiology* 27 (1999) ■ J. T. Copplestone, *The History of Methodist Missions*, vol. 4, *Twentieth-Century Perspectives (The Methodist Episcopal Church, 1896–1939)* (1973), 589–610 ■ D. H. Talbert and A. R. Schick, *La Iglesia Metodista Pentecostal, Ayer y hoy*, 2 vols. (1987) ■ W. J. Hollenweger, "Methodism's Past is Pentecostalism's Present: A Case Study in Cultural Clash in Chile," *Methodist History* 20 (1982) ■ M. G. Hoover, "A Church Grows in Chile Because Willis Hoover Took a Stand," *AGH* 8 (3, Fall 1988) ■ idem, ed. *Willis Collins Hoover: History of the Pentecostal Revival in Chile* (2000) ■ J. A. B. Kessler, *A Study of the Older Protestant Missions and Churches in Peru and Chile, with Special Reference to the Problems of Division, Nationalism and Native Ministry* (1967) ■ C. Lalive d'Epinay, *Haven of the Masses: A Study of the Pentecostal Movement in Chile* (1969) ■ "Revival in Valparaiso, Chile," *The Upper Room* 1 (11, May 1910) ■ W. Taylor, *Our South American Cousins* (1878) ■ idem, *Story of My Life: An Account of What I Have Thought, Said and Done in My Ministry of More Than Fifty-Three Years in Christian Lands and among the Heathen*, ed. John Clark Ridpath (1895) ■ British ed.: *William Taylor of California, Bishop of Africa: An Autobiography*, rev. with preface by C. G. Moore (1897) ■ H. Tennekes, *El movimiento pentecostal en la sociedad chilena* (1985).

■ D. D. Bundy

HOPE CHAPEL

HOPE CHAPEL In 1971 Ralph Moore (‣International Church of the Foursquare Gospel) founded the first Hope Chapel in Manhattan Beach, CA, followed by Hope Chapels in Hermosa Beach, CA, and in Kaneohe, HI, where he is senior pastor. Moore's ministry now spans more than 100 churches in Hawaii, the U.S. mainland, Japan, and the South Pacific, involving more than 20,000 people. All Hope Chapels are built around cell groups, use of public facilities, community service, and personal evangelism.

■ **Bibliography:** C. P. Wagner, *The New Apostolic Churches* (1998).
■ S. M. Burgess

HORNSHUH, FRED (1884–1982). A pentecostal pioneer in the Northwest, Hornshuh evangelized and founded numerous churches for the ‣Apostolic Faith (AF, Portland) and later for the Bible Standard Mission. He was the youngest of eight children and lived on a farm in Oregon until he was 16. His parents sent him to ‣John Alexander

Dowie's Zion College for two years. In 1908 he received a degree from Willamette University.

Hornshuh was baptized in the Spirit in an AF meeting in Portland in 1909 and preached for this group for several years. Because of disagreements with the AF leadership, Hornshuh and others left to form what they called the Bible Standard Mission. In 1935 this group became a part of the Open Bible Evangelistic Association, which was later changed to ˒Open Bible Standard Churches. He founded a magazine in 1919, *Bible Standard,* which was later called *The Overcomer.*

Today Hornshuh is best known for founding the Lighthouse Temple, Eugene, OR (1919), and other churches in the Northwest, as well as what is now Eugene Bible College (1925).

■ **Bibliography:** R. Mitchell, *Heritage and Horizons* (1982).

■ W. E. Warner

HORTON, HAROLD LAWRENCE CUTHBERT (1880–1969).

British pentecostal educator and author. Horton was trained as a Methodist minister but was converted to the pentecostal tradition early in the revivals. He became a prolific author and contributed to most English-language pentecostal periodicals. Horton was very influential in the development and defense of the "initial evidence" doctrine within the British Assemblies of God in Great Britain and Ireland (AGGBI) as well as in the Assemblies of God (U.S.), where many of his essays are kept in print. He taught for most of his life at the AGGBI Bible School at Hampstead, London.

■ **Bibliography:** D. Gee, *Wind and Flame* (1967) ■ H. L. C. Horton, *Arrows of Deliverance* (n.d.) ■ idem, *The Baptism of the Holy Spirit* (1961) ■ idem, *Chords from Solomon's Song (*1937) ■ idem, *The Gifts of the Spirit* (1934; 2d ed., 1946) ■ idem, *Preaching and Homiletics* (1946, 2d ed., 1949) ■ idem, *Receiving without "Tarrying"* (n.d.) ■ idem, *The Sons of Jeshurun: Illustrating Spiritual Types and Characteristics* (1944) ■ idem, *Talks on Occupying the Land: A Challenge and a Call to Fuller Inheritance* (n.d.; repr. 1944) ■ idem, *What Is the Good of Speaking with Tongues?* (1946) ■ W. K. Kay, *Inside Story: A History of the British Assemblies of God* (1990) ■ A. Missen, *The Sound of a Going: The Story of the Assemblies of God* (1973) ■ C. Whittaker, *Seven Pentecostal Pioneers* (1983).   ■ D. D. Bundy

HORTON, STANLEY MONROE (1916–).

Author, educator, and theologian. Stanley M. Horton was born to Harry and Myrle Horton. His father was an evangelist from Owen Sound, Ont., and his mother was the daughter of ˒Elmer K. Fisher, pastor of the Upper Room Mission in Los Angeles. The younger Horton was converted and baptized in water in 1922. He received the baptism in the Holy Spirit in 1936 and felt called to a teaching ministry four years later. He was ordained by the New York–New Jersey District of the Assemblies of God in 1946 (since 1948 he has been a member of the Southern Missouri District). In 1945 he married Evelyn G. Parsons of Boston, MA. They have three children: Stanley Jr.; Edward; and Faith.

Horton received his educational training at Los Angeles City College (A.A., 1935), University of California at Berkeley (B.S., 1937), Gordon-Conwell Theological Seminary (M.Div., 1944), Harvard University (S.T.M., 1945), and Central Baptist Theological Seminary (Th.D., 1959). Additional studies were completed at the Biblical Seminary of New York (now New York Theological Seminary).

After graduating from Harvard, Horton began teaching at Metropolitan Bible Institute, North Bergen, NJ (1945–48), which he followed with a lengthy term of service at Central Bible College in Springfield, MO (1948–78). In 1978 he began teaching at the Assemblies of God Theological Seminary in the same city, where he is now professor emeritus. The seminary's board of directors awarded him the title "Distinguished Professor of Bible and Theology" in 1987 in recognition of his scholarship and long-term service to the denomination.

In 1979–80 Horton served as president of the ˒Society for Pentecostal Studies. In his extensive travel abroad Horton served as guest professor (1962) at the Near East School of Archaeology in Jerusalem and has taught classes at AG colleges and seminaries in many countries, including India, Belgium, Germany, Taiwan, the Philippines, and Singapore.

Horton has made notable contributions to the pentecostal movement and to the AG in particular through his prolific writing. For more than 25 years he authored the *Adult Teacher's Quarterly* as well as books and manuals for ˒Gospel Publishing House, the publishing arm of the AG. His books include *Into All Truth* (1955); *The Promise of His Coming* (1967; later reissued as *Welcome Back, Jesus*); *Desire Spiritual Gifts ... Earnestly* (1972); *It's Getting Late* (1975); *What the Bible Says about the Holy Spirit* (1976); *The Holy Spirit* (1979; study guide for International Correspondence Institute); *The Book of Acts* (1981); *Bible Doctrines: A Pentecostal Perspective* (with William Menzies; 1993), *Bible Prophecy: Understanding Future Events* (1995); and *Our Destiny: Biblical Teachings on the Last Things* (1996). He has also contributed chapters to *Encounters with Eternity* (1986); *Five Views on Sanctification* (1987); and *How Different Religions View Death and Afterlife* (1991). More recently, he edited *Systematic Theology: A Pentecostal Perspective* (1994); chaired the editorial committee for *The Full Life Study Bible;* and assisted in editing the *Complete Biblical Library.* He is the general editor of the Pentecostal Textbook Project. In addition to these works, he has written hundreds of articles and book reviews.

Horton became an influential writer in the AG at a time when only a few pentecostals were professionally trained at the graduate level in theology and biblical languages. Theologically, he has had a profound influence on the course of AG theology in the last five decades.

■ **Bibliography:** "A/G Editors Honor Stanley Horton for 25 Years of Writing Ministry," *PE* (Apr. 27, 1975) ▮ P. Elbert, ed., *Faces of Renewal: Studies in Honor of Stanley M. Horton* (1988) ▮ D. Jacobsen, "Knowing the Doctrines of Pentecostals," *Pentecostal Currents in American Protestantism*, ed. E. Blumhofer et al. (1999) ▮ *Who's Who in Religion* (2d ed., 1977).   ■ G. B. McGee; E. J. Gitre

HORTON, WADE HENRY (1908–). Twice general overseer of the Church of God (CG, Cleveland, TN). Horton began his ministry in 1933 and pastored churches in South Carolina, North Carolina, and Washington, DC. He is noted for his vigorous preaching on the practical aspects of Christianity.

After six years of service in world missions (1952–58) and two as state overseer of Mississippi (1960–62), Horton was called upon in 1962 to lead the denomination as its tenth general overseer. During his tenure (1962–66) the CG experienced such progress that he was returned to the office for a second tenure (1974–76), the first man to serve two separate tenures. Horton also served on the CG executive council for a total of 30 years.

Among Horton's published works are *Pentecost: Yesterday and Today* (1964); four books of sermons; and a compiled study of tongues speaking, *The Glossolalia Phenomenon* (1966).

■ **Bibliography:** Archives of the Church of God (Cleveland, TN).   ■ C. W. Conn

HOUSE CHURCH MOVEMENT (HCM). The original designation of the networks of nondenominational charismatic assemblies in Great Britain. The name HCM lasted much longer than the house fellowship patterns of its origins, but it has been widely replaced by the term *New Churches* in the 1990s. In the 1970s and 1980s the term *restoration* was widely used to describe the goals and character of the movement, but this emphasis has mostly decreased as their fellowship patterns have widened.

HCM's original thrust was the restoration of the NT church, with the fivefold ministries of Eph. 4:11, many streams emphasizing the ministry of apostles. Apostles were seen as church planters leading apostolic teams. While HCM avoided particular millenarian positions, church restoration was typically seen as preparation for the Lord's return. Christian life was presented as a radical discipleship, kingdom living, and an acceptance of the leaders' pastoral authority, which in some streams extended to the discernment of major life decisions in such areas as family, finance, career, work, and possessions. HCM assemblies have been mostly subdivided into housegroup cells for pastoral formation and deepening of mutual relationships.

HCM roots lie in a series of conferences convened by D. Lillie and ʼA. Wallis in the late 1950s and early '60s. At this stage, the emerging cluster of convictions that later characterized HCM combined a vision for the restoration of the NT church, without, at the time, any mention of apostles, and the pentecostal experience of ʼbaptism in the Spirit and the spiritual gifts. Many of the early HCM leaders were former Plymouth Brethren, expelled for their pentecostal testimony; their vision of church restoration in many ways equaled "Brethren teaching plus Pentecost." When the term *HCM* was first coined, it referred mainly to two networks now of minor importance: (1) the groups associated with South Chard, Somerset, begun by S. Purse (ex-Brethren) around 1951, and (2) the groups relating to a charismatic Holiness teacher, G. W. North, with centers particularly in the Wirral (Merseyside) and Exeter, Devon. At Chard, Purse was supported by V. Dunning, I. Andrews, and H. Greenwood.

During the 1960s, independent charismatic fellowships in Britain increased in number, helped by the ministries of men such as D. Clark, C. McAlpine, E. Trout, and A. Wallis. Some assemblies were independent on doctrinal grounds (holding to local autonomy and excluding any translocal *episcope,* such as that of D. Lillie) and others for more pragmatic reasons. A conference of about 50 invited leaders in Paignton, Devon, in 1970, entitled "Our Generation," was the first meeting together of almost all the men who later became leaders of HCM networks. Around the same time, a group of independent charismatic leaders in the London area, including ʼG. Coates, D. Mansel, J. Noble, and M. Smith, began regular meetings. From this circle came *Fulness* magazine, published from 1970 to 1982.

Early in 1972 Wallis convened a meeting of leaders to share God's vision for the end times. Six attended (ʼA. Wallis, ʼB. Jones, P. Lyne, D. Mansell, G. Perrins, and H. Thompson), and from this group (to which J. Noble was added) came unforeseen a covenant of mutual commitment. This group of 7 was soon expanded to 14, a step that many later saw as a mistake. From 1972 to 1974 there was a growing interest, first in London, then in Bradford, Yorkshire, in teachings on apostleship, eldership, and discipling. One forum for such teaching was the annual Capel Bible Week in Surrey, at which ʼE. Baxter from Fort Lauderdale, FL, spoke in 1974. This American connection led to an increased emphasis on discipleship and submission.

In 1976 the group of 14 divided, with two main blocs emerging. An attempt of Baxter to mediate failed, ending any Fort Lauderdale influence. This split marked a clear contrast between the two groups. One group, termed R1 by Walker, was more authoritative, organized, and exclusive. It was influenced especially by Jones and Wallis, most strongly represented in Bradford, and had its expression in *Restoration* magazine, begun in 1975. The other group, termed R2, was more relaxed, in some areas more permissive, and less organized. It was associated with G. Coates and J. Noble and was mostly found in the London area. Its periodical was *Fulness*.

In 1980 Jones encouraged ʼT. Virgo of Hove, Sussex, to develop an apostolic team, now known as New Frontiers, in the south of England; and in 1981 another team, known as Cornerstone, was formed under ʼT. Morton of Southampton, Hampshire, soon joined by Wallis. Key events in HCM growth were the annual Bible weeks, first the Lakes and then the Dales Bible weeks in the north, organized from Bradford (1975–86), and later the Downs Bible weeks in the south (1979–88) and the Stoneleigh Bible weeks (1991–), organized by Virgo.

While the R1-R2 distinction had a definite basis immediately after the split of 1976, it became less relevant with the formation and growth of New Frontiers (now the largest of the New Church networks in Britain) and Cornerstone, as well as the groupings that had their origin in charismatic Baptist churches that became independent and adopted a less democratic polity, notably Salt and Light (which grew out of Basingstoke, Hampshire; ʼB. Coombs and V. Gledhill); the King's Churches (under the leadership of Aldershot, Hampshire; D. Brown); and the Jesus Fellowship centered at Nether Heyford, Northamptonshire (N. Stanton). The sharp antitheses of 1976 gradually became a spectrum ranging from the more restorationist and exclusive (Covenant Ministries under Jones) through New Frontiers, Salt and Light, and Cornerstone, to the looser revivalist-cooperative patterns of Pioneer (under Coates).

In the 1980s some London leaders, especially Noble, sought to build bridges to the wider charismatic movement, in contrast to the strident antidenominationalism of *Restoration*. The other major HCM figures largely adopted an intermediate position, with fewer links to denominational charismatic renewal than Noble but, unlike Jones, taking an active part in the Evangelical Alliance and the British Charismatic Leaders Conference.

Since the late 1980s, relationships between the New Churches and other Christians in Britain have become much more cooperative, especially those with other evangelicals and charismatics. First expressed through ʼSpring Harvest, the pan-evangelical annual camps with an acceptable charismatic flavor, relationships continued through the ʼMarch for Jesus, begun by New Church leaders and expressing their ethos and creativity, and more recently through the widespread New Church use of the ʼAlpha Course of Anglican origin.

■ **Bibliography:** *Restoration* (May–June 1987) ▪ B. Hewett *Doing a New Thing?* (1995) ▪ J. V. Thurman, *New Wineskins* (1982) ▪ T. Virgo, *Restoration in the Church* (1985) ▪ A. Walker, *Restoring the Kingdom* (1985, 1988, 1998) ▪ A. Wallis, *The Radical Christian* (1981). ■ P. D. Hocken

HOUSTON, FRANK (1922–). Assemblies of God (AG) pastor and church leader in New Zealand and Australia. Houston, formerly a Salvation Army officer, became involved with Ray Bloomfield's pentecostal church in Ellerslie, Auckland. Bloomfield and Houston conducted revival meetings among rural Maori at Waiomio in Northland, which was a forerunner of the healing revival that emerged after ʼTommy Hicks' visit to N.Z. in late 1957.

In 1959 Houston became pastor of the Lower Hutt AG, a position that he was to hold for the next 18 years. He became general superintendent of the AG in 1966, and his energetic leadership and open attitude toward other pentecostal and mainstream churches were key factors in its expansion over the next 11 years.

In 1977 Houston moved to Sydney, Australia, where he established a large pentecostal church—the Christian Life Centre—which had planted nearly 20 churches in and around Sydney by 1989. The Christian Life Centre now has branches in more than 60 countries of the world.

■ **Bibliography:** H. Houston, *Being Frank: The Frank Houston Story* (1989). ■ B. Knowles

HOWARD-BROWNE, RODNEY M. (1961–). Revivalist. Converted to Christ at age 5 and baptized in the Holy Spirit at 8, he had a dream at 13 that caused him to weep for the lost. In 1979 the fire of God fell on him for three days. He began his ministry the following year with Youth for Christ in his native South Africa and Nambia.

In late 1987 Howard-Browne and his family arrived in the United States to engage in evangelistic work. Beginning in April of 1989 at Clifton Park, New York, he began to experience continuous revival during his meetings. Over the course of the following 10 years, he conducted meetings of several weeks' duration in over 350 major cities in North America, Australia, New Zealand, South Africa, England, Scotland, Wales, Holland, Germany, Hong Kong, Singapore, and the Philippines, some of them attended by tens of thousands of people. By 1995 at least 75,000 decisions for Christ had been made.

In 1996 he helped found a church called The River at Tampa Bay, FL, and in 1997, the River Bible Institute. Over the years, Howard-Browne and his family have been traveling as missionaries in North America, Australia, New Zealand, South Africa, England, Scotland, Wales, Holland, Germany, Hong Kong, Singapore, and the Philippines. His meetings have been accompanied by many phenomena similar to those that characterized the great revivals under Whitefield, Wesley, and Finney, including repentance, weeping, laughing, falling, and drunkenness in the Spirit.

■ **Bibliography:** R. M. Howard-Browne, "Look What the Lord Has Done," *Chronicles of Revival* 3 (Dec. 1998). ■ R. M. Riss

HUGHES, RAY HARRISON (1924–).

A ʾChurch of God (CG, Cleveland, TN) minister and prominent pentecostal preacher and administrator. Twice Hughes was general overseer of the CG (1972–74; 1978–82), and twice he was president of Lee College (1960–66; 1982–84). He received academic degrees from Tennessee Wesleyan College (B.A., 1963) and the University of Tennessee (M.S., 1964; Ed.D., 1966).

The son of Pastor J. H. Hughes, Ray H. Hughes began his ministry in 1941 as an evangelist of notable effectiveness. Evangelism has always been his foremost ministry, although he has been successful as pastor, state overseer, and denominational executive. He came on the national scene in 1946 as speaker at a mass rally of pentecostal youth in the Hollywood Bowl in Los Angeles. He has frequently been the featured speaker for the British pentecostal churches at Royal Albert Hall in London and for numerous other international and interdenominational meetings. He has spoken at six ʾPentecostal World Conferences, numerous ʾPentecostal Fellowship of North America (PFNA) conventions, and the ʾNational Association of Evangelicals (NAE) conferences. Hughes has served as chairman of the PFNA and president of the NAE.

Hughes's administrative ministry in the CG has included several positions; he was concurrently director of the CG radio ministry *Forward in Faith* (1960–63) and president of Lee College (1960–66).

Among Hughes's published works are *Religion on Fire* (1956), *What Is Pentecost?* (1963), *Church of God Distinctives* (1968, 1989), *The Outpouring of the Spirit* (1980), and *Pentecostal Preaching* (1981). His most popular collection of recorded sermons is *The Anointing Makes the Difference*.

Ray H. Hughes, a prominent minister in the Church of God who has also been active in interdenominational efforts such as the Pentecostal World Conference, the National Association of Evangelicals, and the Pentecostal Fellowship of North America.

■ **Bibliography:** Archives of the Church of God (Cleveland, TN) ▍ C. W. Conn, *Like a Mighty Army: A History of the Church of God* (1996) ▍ idem, *Our First 100 Years* (1986).   ■ C. W. Conn

HUMBARD, ALPHA REX EMMANUEL (1919–), and MAUDE AIMEE (1921–).

Traveling evangelists, gospel singers, pastors, and television pioneers. Born in Little Rock, AR, the son of a minister, Rex Humbard grew up in gospel work. His family traveled throughout the country pioneering churches and conducting revival crusades. When his family moved their musical ministry to Dallas, TX, Humbard met Maude Aimee Jones. Rex and Maude Aimee married in 1942 and set out together on the road with Rex's family. In 1952, after a successful meeting in Akron, OH, he decided to leave his family's ministry and remain in Akron to build a church. One of the notable successes in establishing the work was the series of meetings held with ʾKathryn Kuhlman. Humbard had a vision for the role of television in gospel ministry and built the Cathedral of Tomorrow to accommodate his weekly telecasts. A large network of television stations carried his Sunday morning services in the late '60s and early '70s. In 1973 Humbard became involved in controversy because of questionable investments. The aura of scandal hung over his ministry for several years.

Although Rex Humbard came from a pentecostal background, he did not emphasize the baptism of the Holy Spirit in his ministry. The following statement was made by the director of public relations for his church: "The Cathedral of Tomorrow is not Pentecostal; neither is the pastor or any of the staff. Neither are we affiliated with any Pentecostal organization, and the magazine is not slanted at the Pentecostal message at any time. We are an interdenominational evangelistic church" (Harrell, 192). The above statement should not be interpreted to mean that the church was anticharismatic, but rather that it was determined to avoid controversy. Prayer for the sick and anointing with oil were a regular part of the service, but the stress was always on the message of salvation. It was a formula that worked with a great deal of success.

Maude Aimee began singing at the age of nine and has had a long career as a successful gospel singer. She was a featured soloist on the Humbards' weekly telecast. In addition she accepted the responsibility of raising a family and occasionally preaching. The Humbards have been considered pioneers in the field of Christian television and have served as role models for many of the ministry couples now seen on television.

■ **Bibliography:** D. E. Harrell Jr., *All Things Are Possible* (1975) ▍ R. Humbard, *Miracles in My Life* (1971).   ■ J. R. Zeigler

HUMBURG, EMIL (1874–1965).

German pentecostal leader. After two years' ministry in the newly established

Gemeinschaft (Holiness society) in Mülheim-Ruhr, Humburg became leader on the death of its pastor in 1907. Welcoming the pentecostal message, he attended conferences at Hamburg (Dec. 1908) and Sunderland, England (June 1909), receiving the baptism in the Spirit in the summer of 1909. As pastor of the largest pentecostal assembly in Germany, Humburg was with ˒J. Paul and others in the forefront of defense against the ˒Berlin Declaration, becoming one of the main writers and the publisher of the German movement. In 1911 he became president of the *Hauptbrudertag* (senior pastors' conference), a position he held until 1957. In 1913 he became the first president of the ˒Mülheim Association. Humburg carried a major burden in the difficulties facing the German assemblies after the two world wars and made an unsuccessful attempt in 1934 to get the Berlin Declaration withdrawn.

■ **Bibliography:** C. H. Krust, *50 Jahre Deutsche Pfingstbewegung* (1958).					■ P. D. Hocken

HURST, WESLEY ROBINSON (1922–87). Pastor and missionary. Hurst was born in Mineral, IL, to Rev. and Mrs. Wesley R. Hurst Sr., pastors in the Christian Advent Church who later joined the Assemblies of God (AG). Reared in Minnesota and Nebraska, Hurst later attended North Central Bible College and graduated in 1943 (B.A. in 1978). In the same year he married June Van Dover. He held pastorates in Bruce and Britton, SD; Tulsa, OK; and Kalispell, MT. He also spent three and a half years in itinerant evangelism. Feeling called to overseas missions work in the late 1940s, the Hursts received appointment with the AG and traveled to Tanganyika (later Tanzania) in 1953. Organizing the pentecostal believers he found there, Hurst opened a Bible institute at Mbeya and contributed to the founding of the Tanzanian AG.

After seven years (1960) the Hurst family returned to the U.S., and Wesley became the secretary of promotions for the AG Division of Foreign Missions. Ten years later he succeeded ˒Maynard L. Ketcham as field director for the Far East. In this capacity Hurst focused on training national church leaders, providing advanced ministerial education through the Far East Advanced School of Theology (FEAST; now Asia Pacific Theological Seminary [APTS]), using advanced media technology in spreading the gospel and promoting the development of the Assemblies of God Asian Mission Association (AGAMA), a network of Asian AG national church organizations working together to evangelize the region. For his contributions to missions, Northwest College of the AG conferred an honorary D.D. degree on him in 1981. He died in 1987, shortly after dedicating the new facilities for APTS in Baguio City, Philippines. He is survived by his wife and three children: Judy Mitchell, Wesley Randall Hurst, and Jhan Hurst.

■ **Bibliography:** "He Dared to Dream," *Mountain Movers* (Apr. 1987) ▮ "Wesley R. Hurst with Christ," *PE* (Mar. 1, 1987).
					■ G. B. McGee

IGLESIA DE CRISTO MISIONERA One of several Puerto Rican Pentecostal denominations. The group began as the Iglesia de Cristo en las Antillas (Church of Christ in the Antilles) as a result of ›Francisco Olazábal's campaign in Puerto Rico in 1934. Within a few months 12 churches in the northeastern part of the island organized a general council. In Mar. 1938 the group changed its name to the Iglesia de Cristo Misionera (Missionary Church of Christ) in order to be more inclusive. The dominant personality during the early years was Florentino Figueroa Rosa, who held the position of general supervisor for more than 25 years, beginning in 1940. The group reported 81 congregations in Puerto Rico with 13,300 members. A remnant that retained the name Iglesia de Cristo en las Antillas after 1938 has also grown substantially.

■ **Bibliography:** D. Barrett et al., *World Christian Encyclopedia* (2001) ■ E. Carver, "Showcase for God: A Study of Evangelical Church Growth in Puerto Rico" (thesis, Fuller Theol. Sem., 1972) ■ D. Moore, *Puerto Rico Para Cristo* (1969).   ■ E. A. Wilson

IGLESIA DE DIOS PENTECOSTAL DE PUERTO RICO

In 1912 American pentecostal missionaries en route to the Orient stopped in Hawaii long enough to make several converts among Puerto Ricans living at the government experimental station near Honolulu. As a result, a congregation was organized with Francisco D. Ortiz Sr. as pastor.

In 1916 one of the members who had gone to California to work, Juan L. Lugo, felt called to return to Puerto Rico as a missionary. He was soon joined by other homeward-bound members of the Hawaiian congregation, including the pastor. The work grew rapidly. A street meeting in Ponce provided a nucleus for the first congregation. After four years there were 8 churches; after five years, 13. In 1921 a convention met in Arecibo and formed the Iglesia de Dios Pentecostal de Puerto Rico (IDPPR), which incorporated the next year.

En route from California to Puerto Rico, Lugo stopped over in St. Louis, where he met the secretary of the newly formed General Council of the Assemblies of God (AG). Consequently, until 1947, when it was refused the status of a domestic district, the Puerto Rican group considered itself part of the AG fellowship. The years of uncertain relations that followed coincided with the migration of many islanders to the continental U.S., particularly to New York. Organization of stateside churches followed.

In 1955 the American AG proposed the union it had refused eight years earlier, only to be rejected this time by the Puerto Rican brethren. The next year the IDPPR formally announced its independence and granted practical autonomy to its New York area churches under the name ›Concilio Latino-Americano de la Iglesia de Dios Pentecostal de New York. It retained, however, jurisdiction over other mainland work. In 1970 it reported 207 churches and 30,000 members in Puerto Rico.

■ **Bibliography:** A. C. Piepkorn, *Profiles in Belief,* vol. 3 (1979).
■ C. E. Jones

ILUNGA, NGOI WA MBUYA KALULWA (JONATHAN)

(c. 1905–). Ilunga Jonathan is the present executive officer of the ›Pentecostal Community of Congo (PCC), the largest pentecostal denomination in the south-central area of Congo/Kinshasa. He was born c. 1905 in the district of Kayeye, Katanga, Congo. He was among the first converts to the Christian faith in his area and soon became a leader and teacher in the primary school at Kabondo-Dianda when Garfield Vale was resident missionary of the Congo Evangelistic Mission.

Ilunga was well-known for his itinerant ministry and was promoted to senior station pastor at the coal-mining town of Luena, where he worked until 1960. Prior to Congo's independence on June 30, 1960, he was chosen by a group of Congolese pastors and missionaries of the Congo Evangelistic Mission (the former name of PCC) to become the legal representative (executive officer) of the PCC to succeed the missionary representative Harold Womersley.

During the years of civil war that followed, the country was divided to such an extent that he was unable to fulfill his responsibilities. However, as soon as a semblance of order was restored he moved to Kamina, from where he has led the church since. In 1973–74 he attended the International Bible Training Institute at Burgess Hill in England.

Ilunga was the executive officer of the PCC at a time when phenomenal spontaneous growth was taking place. He still maintains his official position; in spite of his advanced age, he has enjoyed remarkable health. His entourage, including his sons, is responsible for most important decisions; this has lead to considerable discontent on the part of many pastors. Bureaucracy and autocracy have caused many splits in the community, which is estimated to have 2,500–3,000 assemblies and 500,000 adherents. Although the administrative offices for the Community are still at Kamina, Ilunga now resides in Lubumbashi. He is known in the Church of Christ (the umbrella organization to which all Protestant churches have to belong by government decree) at Kinshasa as the *doyen,* or elder, a term of respect, and was granted the

"Order of the Leopard" for his services to the state by the late President Mobutu Sese Seko.

■ **Bibliography:** D. J. Garrard, "The History of the Congo Evangelistic Mission/Communauté Pentecôtiste au Zaïre from 1915 to 1982" (diss., Aberdeen, 1983).   ■ D. J. Garrard

INDEPENDENT ASSEMBLIES OF GOD INTERNATIONAL

The Independent Assemblies of God International shared a common history with the ˒Fellowship of Christian Assemblies until 1951; the two groups were united under the name Independent Assemblies of God. The "New Order of the ˒Latter Rain" controversy that began in 1947 divided the two groups. In Oct. 1949 ministers of the Independent Assemblies of God met at the Philadelphia Church in Chicago for their annual meeting.

The two groups were already divided. The larger group argued that the Latter Rain movement supported unscriptural teachings and practices, such as the casual way in which spiritual gifts and prophecies were given by the laying on of hands and the belief in the restoration of apostles and prophets. The smaller group led by Andrew W. Rasmussen supported these teachings and practices.

By the time the annual meeting of 1951 convened, the rift had become permanent. The pro–Latter Rain group decided to separate from the other body and organize themselves under their present name. Their headquarters currently are located in Santa Ana, CA, under the administration of Philip A. Rasmussen. More than 1,800 ministers were listed in its 1986 ministerial handbook.

See also Fellowship of Christian Assemblies.

■ **Bibliography:** J. Colletti, "Lewi Pethrus: His Influence upon Scandinavian-American Pentecostalism," *Pneuma* 5 (2, Fall 1983) ■ A. C. Piepkorn, *Profiles in Belief,* vol. 3 (1979).

■ J. Colletti

INDEPENDENT EVANGELICAL CHURCH (Iglesia Evangélica Independiente).

The Independent Evangelical Church (IEC) was an outgrowth of the work begun by the Swedish pentecostal missionaries ˒Axel and Ester Andersson in San Luis Potosí in 1921. This church was supported by the Swedish Filadelfia Church in Stockholm, Sweden, until 1946. Since then it has developed into a completely indigenous Mexican pentecostal denomination with its own authentic traditions. It has managed to weather a number of internal divisions and has had its share of martyrs. This version of Mexican pentecostalism tends to be more ethically and socially conservative than other forms. The IEC has witnessed solid growth through the years, growing from approximately 50,000 to 60,000 members in 1965 to an estimated 727 congregations and more than 160,000 adherents in 1993.

■ **Bibliography:** Patrick Johnstone, *Operation World* (1993) ■ Marvin J. Penton, "Mexico's Reformation: A History of Mexican Protestantism," Ph.D. diss., Iowa (1965).   ■ G. Espinosa

INDEPENDENT PENTECOSTAL EVANGELICAL CHURCH MOVEMENT (Movimiento Iglesia Evangélica Pentecostés Independiente [MIEPI]).

MIEPI was founded by Valente Aponte González in the early 1930s as a breakaway from the ˒Church of God in the Republic of Mexico (Iglesia de Dios en la República Mexicana), which itself was the result of a schism in the ˒Assemblies of God in Mexico. Known for its sectarianism and hostility to outsiders, MIEPI is one of the most interesting indigenous pentecostal denominations in Mexico. Unlike most other pentecostal churches, but like the ˒Light of the World Church (Iglesia La Luz del Mundo), it believes that it is the one true church. They stress the "one body of Christ," which they interpret to be themselves. They were, for example, openly hostile to one of Billy Graham's crusades in Mexico in the 1960s and in the past have refused to participate in the Pentecostal Fraternal Association in Mexico (Asociación Fraternal de Iglesias Pentecostales en la República de México), an organization that includes most, though not all, of the indigenous and foreign pentecostal denominations in Mexico.

Some scholars have suggested that its sectarianism has been shaped by its heavy emphasis on *personalismo* (strong charismatic personalities). This was evident in Valente González's strict control over the church, his emphasis on doctrinal uniformity, and his practice of excommunicating dissidents and moral offenders. After González's death, "Sister" Febe Flores became the secretary and director of the church and its official magazine, *El Consejero Fiel* (Faithful Counselor).

The movement has seen rapid growth throughout the latter part of the 20th century. Between 1961 and 1970, it grew from 70 ministers and 12,500 adherents to more than 600 churches and 40,000 adherents. In the early 1990s MIEPI had an estimated 1,500 congregations and 85,500 adherents throughout Mexico.

■ **Bibliography:** D. Barrett, *World Christian Encyclopedia* (1982) ■ P. Johnstone, *Operation World* (1993) ■ M. J. Penton, "Mexico's Reformation: A History of Mexican Protestantism," Ph.D. diss., Iowa (1965).   ■ G. Espinosa

INDIAN PENTECOSTAL CHURCH OF GOD

The origins of the Indian Pentecostal Church of God (IPC) are closely tied to the founder, the Rev. Dr. ˒K. E. Abraham, born on Mar. 1, 1899, to a Syrian Orthodox Christian family in Kerala. Converted and baptized in 1915, he became active in the Brethren movement and conducted meetings in various places in Kerala. In 1921 he married a pentecostal woman, and in 1924 he received the baptism of the Holy Spirit and became an active church planter.

During this time he came in contact with the American missionary Robert F. Cook of the Church of God (Cleveland, TN). They worked together until 1930, when they separated over issues of independence of the Indian churches and the question of voluntary versus paid mission workers. K. E. Abraham preferred a system of volunteer workers. Until today the IPC has no salary system—all support comes from the local church. A Bible school was begun in 1930. In 1934 the name was changed from South Indian Pentecostal Church to the Indian Pentecostal Church of God.

The ministry spread outside Kerala. M. K. Chacko went to Delhi, Kurien Thomas to Ittarsi, K. T. Thomas and Captain Samuel to North India, and Pastors P. M. Samuel and P. T. Chacko to Andhra Pradesh. By 1974 there were 450 self-supporting churches in Andhra and 900 churches throughout India. Some 90% of the converts are reported to be from a Hindu background. By 1997 IPC had more than 3,000 local churches in India, including 1,700 in Kerala, 700 in Andhra, 210 in Tamil Nadu, 70 in Karnataka, and smaller numbers of churches in Maharashtra, Madhya Pradesh, and several regions of North India and the North East.

IPC is considered the largest indigenous pentecostal movement in India. It continues to grow at the average rate of one new church per week. Dedicated young people, trained in the Bible school, are sent to unevangelized fields and are the key to this continued expansion. IPC congregations are found overseas in the Gulf States, U.S., Canada, and Australia. Organizational structure consists of regional councils and a general council over all. The denomination is served by Hebron Bible College, Salem Bible College, and nine affiliated Bible schools, the Bahya Kerala Mission Board, the Pentecostal Young People's Association, a women's auxiliary, and various publications.

The IPC central working office is at Hebronpuram, Kumbanad, Kerala, but the registered office is at Eluru, West Godavari District, Andhra Pradesh. According to its Memorandum of Association and Constitution, "The Indian Pentecostal Church is a group of indigenous independent Churches established in several parts of India having no foreign mission control but enjoying the spiritual fellowship of all pentecostal groups of the same doctrine found all over the world." IPC did not refuse foreign assistance. In 1938 a place of worship was built in Trivandrum with financial help from churches in Sweden.

K. E. Abraham believed that ministry could progress better without foreign missionary domination. Self-supporting churches should be led by self-sacrificing national ministers. Local churches should manage their own affairs and hold their own property. "For evangelism to be effective, Churches in Asia, must, of necessity, be indigenous and independent—

independent Christian Churches in independent India." The IPC is an important example of Christian nationalism in India prior to India's independence. The IPC thus challenged the Assemblies of God and Church of God, which were of missionary origins in India.

In 1935 a North-South split occurred between believers from Trivandrum ("South") and members from Central Travancore ("North"). A temporary reunion took place in 1950, but soon IPC divided into two. From this division emerged the Sharon Pentecostal Fellowship and other independent movements.

The founder toured several countries and conducted meetings in several denominations. He was especially well received in Sweden and other Scandinavian countries and was awarded an honorary D.D. degree in the U.S. He died at Kumbanad, Kerala, in Dec. 1974, at the age of 75.

■ **Bibliography:** S. Abraham, "A Critical Evaluation of the Indian Pentecostal Church of God—Its Origin and Development in Kerala" (thesis, Serampore U., 1990) ▌ IPC, "A Handbook of the Indian Pentecostal Church of God" (1994) ▌ S. Mathew, "Biblical Leadership: A Theology of Servanthood for the Church in India" (thesis, Fuller, 1989) ▌ A. T. Pothen, "The Indian Pentecostal Church of God and Its Contribution to Church Growth" (thesis, Fuller, 1988) ▌ Saju, *Kerala Penthecosthu Charithram. Kottayam* (1994) ▌ P. J. Titus "IPC Movement in Andhra Pradesh" (unpub. paper, 1997) ▌ H. G. Verghese, *K. E. Abraham: An Apostle from Modern India* (1974).   ■ R. E. Hedlund

INDIGENOUS CHURCHES The exceptional growth of the church in the non-Western world during the 20th century has been characterized by a diversity of localized cultural expressions. As Paul Hiebert (1996) states, "The emergence of independent churches around the world expressing indigenous forms of Christianity is undermining the equation of Christianity with Western culture." Social accommodation and cultural assimilation of the Christian faith are part of an essential, ongoing process everywhere. Wherever the Gospel goes, it takes root in the local culture. Indigenous movements are demonstrations of what Lamin Sanneh (1991) calls the "translatability" of the gospel.

Africa leads the way in sheer numbers of independent churches and denominations that are neither Catholic, Orthodox, nor Protestant, but distinctly African. The ▸African Initiated Churches (AIC) today comprise a distinct component of African Christianity. Most African Christians will be members of AIC congregations in the first part of the 21st century.

The distinctive African experience finds parallels in Asia and Latin America. The emergence of grassroots churches and ecclesial base communities are expressions of a vigorous Latin American indigenous spirituality. Similar expressions can be found in every region of the world where Christianity has taken firm root, either as culturally adapted Great Tradition denominational Christianity or as marginal "fringe" groups of the Little Tradition. (In religious studies, the Great Tradition consists of the major streams of the Christian tradition [Catholic, Orthodox, Protestant]. Alongside the institutional religion of the Great Tradition may be found the popular "folk" religion of the Little Tradition.) In North America the Great Tradition consists of Baptists, Mennonites, and Methodists—denominations considered "sects" in Europe—as well as Catholics, Lutherans, and Presbyterians. Pentecostals were looked upon as sectarian when they emerged at the beginning of the 20th century but have entered the mainstream of church life in North America and are in the process of doing so in South America and other regions of the world, including Asia.

Andrew Walls (1990) has remarked that the greatest missionary achievement of the 19th century was the Christianizing of the U.S. The missionary spread of this indigenous Christianity resulted in other local expressions of Christianity in Africa, Oceania, Latin America, and Asia.

This article briefly surveys, by way of illustration, the indigenous churches in Asia in general and India in particular. The bibliography also covers other continents.

1. Asia.

In Asia the adaptation of the gospel proceeds in a vast plurality of cultures, languages, and competing ideologies. "The Church by inculturating itself becomes part of a culture." Contextualization or inculturation is an integral part of the process of Christianization. The Christian message is being incarnated in each segment of the Asian diversity. The gospel not only transforms persons and cultures, it is itself culturally transformed in the process. The genius of the gospel is that it is not tied to any one human culture. Sanneh speaks of this "translatability" as the "source of the success of Christianity across cultures."

Autonomous indigenous church movements are a worldwide phenomenon. Asian incarnations of the gospel are embodied in various indigenous movements of the continent. The Assembly Hall and the True Jesus Church are two contrasting indigenous church movements in Taiwan. Both are "churches of the soil belonging to the Chinese and served entirely by the Chinese." In addition to these two indigenous denominations, Taiwan has a large number of Independent "local" churches with no outside affiliation or mission relationships. In the Philippines, the Iglesia Ni Cristo, spurned by "Great Tradition" Protestants and Catholics as a heretical sect, has become the largest independent church in Asia—larger than any single Protestant denomination in the Philippines and twice the size of the largest African Independent Church. In contrast to much of the present independent church movement in India, the Iglesia is not a "charismatic" church. There is no emphasis on healing, spiritual manifestations, or special revelations. The Bible is central, but the founder claimed special insight and authority for interpreting the Bible which sets the Iglesia apart from all other churches.

Other Asian countries also manifest indigenous church movements. Japan has its Spirit of Jesus Church, which grew to the second largest Protestant church in less than 20 years in the postwar period, stressing lay witness and house meetings. In Korea, where Christianity entered the core of Korean culture, Christianity came to be identified with nationalism. Korea, which has been styled a land of explosive church growth, has produced the world's largest Christian congregations. Korean Christianity is predominantly Presbyterian, but according to Connor it is more Confucian than Presbyterian. Outwardly Western in ornate basilicas with pipe organs and vested choirs, Korean Christianity has its own distinctive indigenous forms, including a proliferation of breakaway Presbyterian denominations and other local expressions.

The case of China is a fascinating study in subalterneity. Cut off and under persecution for 40 years, the church in China has become

Man in Congo teaching God's Word to his family.

fully indigenous and during the past two decades has experienced explosive growth. The reason for the growth, according to Covell, is the very "Chinese-ness" of the church, especially the fact that they no longer have any foreign connections. In parts of China where there were few Christians during the missionary era, today tens of thousands of Christians are reported. While the visible church disappeared under the Cultural Revolution, the Christian faith survived in small house-group meetings. House churches had also been characteristic of earlier, prerevolutionary indigenous movements such as the True Jesus Church, the Little Flock, the Independent Church, and the Jesus Family. Under repression, the house churches proved flexible and became the training ground for an emerging lay leadership of the indigenous Chinese church.

Coming closer to India, the entire church in Nepal is an indigenous church that has emerged within the past 50 years through Nepali initiative, despite persecution and repression. The Nepali church is completely indigenous with no foreign missionary connections.

2. India.

In India the earliest example of an indigenous Christian movement is found in six Syrian Christian denominations, all of which claim and accept the tradition that St. Thomas the apostle founded Christianity in India. These include the Orthodox Syrian Church (in two sections), the Independent Syrian Church of Malabar (Kunnamkulam Diocese), the Mar Thoma Church, the Malankara (Syrian Rite) Catholic Church, the (Chaldean) Church of the East, and the St. Thomas Evangelical Church (two factions) as well as a section of the Church of South India. The St. Thomas Christians are purely indigenous and Indian in culture, loyalty, faith, and tradition. The Mar Thoma Syrian Evangelistic Association, founded in 1888, is an indication of the vigor and vitality of the tradition. Its 180 mission stations, run on the pattern of ashrams, engage in various forms of service among the lower castes throughout India. Their history, uniqueness, and influence make the St. Thomas Christians most significant for the study of indigenous Christianity.

A number of religious revitalization movements occurred during the 19th century in Kerala. An indigenous Christian Revival Movement was founded by Justus Joseph, a Brahmin convert. The Revival Church in 1881 became Yuomayam. Completely separate from any Christian denomination, it now considered itself the fulfillment of Christianity and all religions. After the death of the founder in 1887, the movement declined under his successors (his son and his brothers), then dwindled to a few persons in a few locations. This movement was the product of ferment created by the translation and publication of the Bible in Malayalam. The founder was always regarded as Christian; his lyrics and hymns can be found in the hymnals of the Syrian church. A century ago his was an example of contextualization.

It is to be expected that a number of independent movements should be found in Kerala, the traditional home of Christianity in India. Among them are numerous indigenous pentecostal movements. The largest is the ▸Indian Pentecostal Church of God, begun by ▸K. E. Abraham around 1930.

Tamil Nadu also has a large number of independent church movements. In Tirunelveli a schism took place at Nazareth in 1857, led by one Arumainayagam Sattampillai. A church building was erected after the pattern of a Jewish temple. A number of OT practices were incorporated, such as observing Passover, worship on the seventh day, washing feet and legs before worship, and offering frankincense. Some Hindu rites were accepted, as well as Hindu marriage law and inheritance law. After Sattampillai's death the church split, declined from 6,000, then dwindled and died. Thangaraj (1971) records that the split occurred when the founder donned high-priestly garments and decreed that the church should offer animal sacrifices. The community reacted vehemently, and most of the members separated to form the Hindu Christian Community. This community still exists today known as the Indian Church of the Only Saviour. The historic cause of the original schism—conflict with the foreign missionaries—led to a strong nationalistic spirit "rejecting all Western and missionary influence." Its worship has been described as a combination of Jewish and

The cross rising from the lotus blossom, symbolizing Christianity rising from native Indian traditions. The image is hand painted on a leaf, an indication that poor Third World artists use whatever is available to them.

Christian practices and appears "more Indian than the worship in other churches," with the singing of South Indian classical tunes by a congregation standing with folded hands.

Madras and Tamil Nadu have experienced numerous breakaway movements and independent church activities. Caplan (1983) makes the interesting observation that "theologians display an almost palpable reluctance to engage the beliefs and practices of ordinary Hindus"—but it is this folk-religion perspective that is addressed by the popular Christianity prevalent today in a large number of pentecostal and other South Indian independent churches.

The ➤Apostolic Christian Assembly is one of the prominent indigenous church bodies of Madras. Worship is bilingual (Tamil and English), but it incorporates a number of features familiar to Hindus and in harmony with Tamil religious tradition. The main church at Purasawalkam has a membership of 12,500 (1996–97). There are 144 branch churches in India with a total of 17,600 believers. The Apostolic Christian Assembly is a vibrant model of a South Indian indigenous church.

Another indigenous model is the Laymen's Evangelical Fellowship begun in Madras in 1935 by N. Daniel, whose life has been described as a sequel to that of Sadhu Sundar Singh. Today the Laymen's Evangelical Fellowship (LEF) is led by the eldest son of N. Daniel, Joshua Daniel, who is senior pastor at the headquarters church. About 3,000 attend the Sunday morning services conducted in English, Tamil, and Telugu. There are 30 worship centers in Madras City with a total membership of about 10,000. A growing missionary vision has led to establishing more than 400 main Fellowship Centres spread across Andhra Pradesh, Tamil Nadu, and several North India and northeastern states. With several satellite centers around each of the main centers, LEF has become a significant denomination in India.

Madras has numerous independent churches, both pentecostal and nonpentecostal. Probably more than Madras, Andhra Pradesh is the main center of indigenous Christian movements in India today. Among these stand the Assemblies of Bakht Singh, who began his ministry in Madras among the various denominational churches where he stressed the importance of the Bible as the Word of God. The first assembly, Jehovah Shammah, began at Madras in 1941 as a "true testimony" for the Lord among people "dissatisfied with the denominational churches." Today assemblies are found in many parts of India, from Kalimpong to Kanyakumari, but especially in Andhra Pradesh. The main center is in Hyderabad, at Hebron, which is also the resting place of the Bakht Singh. Statistical information is difficult to obtain, but the assemblies are widely dispersed in India, especially in Andhra Pradesh. In addition, a large number of independent assemblies and churches have spun off that have no present relationship with the assemblies of Bakht Singh.

Other well-known indigenous church movements of Andhra include the Bible Mission of Fr. M. Devadas as well as the movement around Subba Rao, the Christ-centered Hindu healer. The latter (which was studied by Kaj Baago and others) appears to have largely dissipated since the death of Subba Rao. The Bible Mission (well described in a Birmingham thesis by P. Solomon Raj) is active and vigorous, with a large annual convention attracting more than 20,000 at Guntur. The published writings of the founder are available in English translation.

Andhra has numerous indigenous pentecostal churches and other denominations. Among them the Andhra branch of the Indian Pentecostal Church of God is prominent. Today there are hundreds of IPC churches in the major centers of Andhra Pradesh. Hyderabad has a fellowship of 75 different Full Gospel groups as well as other churches of indigenous origins.

Throughout coastal Andhra numerous indigenous pentecostal and other independent church movements are found, such as the Gospel Band at Chirala. Another is the Independent Christian Believers Gospel Fellowship at Ramachandrapuram in East Godavari. At Panguluru it was the India Fellowship of Bible Churches. Vizag is reportedly the home of several movements, including 1,000 house churches. Bheemunipatnam is the headquarters of the New Testament Church in India founded by P. J. Titus, who also heads the COTR Seminary. Vijayawada has its Gospel Association of India and other indigenous movements. Rajahmundry, Guntur, Visakapatnam, and Vijayawada all are hubs of independent church life; the full extent is yet to be ascertained and the implications considered. Whatever else may be shown, it is evident that indigenous Christianity is much more vigorous in Andhra than government and other statistics would indicate.

Indigenous churches are found in various regions of India. In Bombay the New Life Fellowship is an example of an Indian urban movement that began in 1968 and by 1994 had grown to 1,450 house churches in Bombay and more than 2,000 throughout India. Other independent movements in Bombay include the Cornerstone Fellowship and the City of the Lord Church, as well as other ministries among poor and downtrodden peoples.

In a recent study, 3 out of 10 urban churches studied in Pune appear to be indigenous in character. One is a trilingual charismatic house fellowship of mostly young adults. Another is an independent charismatic fellowship of 250 members, with converts from Hindu, Muslim, and Sindhi backgrounds. The third is a Brethren-style group of 120 worshipers. Three-hour services seem to be characteristic of these lively Pune churches.

The Agape Fellowship group of churches flourishes throughout Punjab as well as in some neighboring states. (It is not without significance that Punjab was an area of Dalit conversion movements in which subaltern communities sought a social-religious identity not dependent on the elite and privileged.)

In North Gujarat, an Isupanthi movement discards caste but retains its original cultural identity and avoids a separate political or civic identity. The converts are neither deculturized nor denationalized.

Indigenization of the faith is a topic of ongoing debate in historic Catholic and Protestant churches. Indigeneity is a natural quality of the independent churches of the Little Tradition. Expressions of faith are found not only in worship styles but in the lives of the worshipers. The indigenous churches are making an impact on the larger society in India today. David Barrett postulates that at present India may have several hundred independent church movements and that these may mushroom in the next 10 or 20 years.

Christianity has proven to be culturally translatable. Christ is found in an Indian robe in Indian churches of the Little Tradition.

■ Bibliography:

General. K. Baago, *Pioneers of Indigenous Christianity* (1969) ■ D. Barrett, ed., *World Christian Encyclopedia* (1982) ■ L. Brown, *The Indian Christians of St. Thomas* (repr. 1990) ■ L. Caplan, *Religion and Power: Essays on the Christian Community in Madras* (1989) ■ S. K. Chatterji, "Indigenous Christianity and Counter-Culture," *R & S* 36 (4, Dec. 1989) ■ P. G. Hiebert, *Anthropological Reflections on Missiological Issues* (1994) ■ idem, "Missiological Education for a Global Era," in *Missiological Education for the 21st Century,* eds. J. D. Woodberry, C. Van Engen, and E. J. Elliston (1996) ■ W. J. Hollenweger, *The Pentecostals* (1972) ■ J. Massey, "Christianity and Culture: Their Relationship in the 19th and 20th Centuries in Punjab" *R & S* 36 (4, Dec. 1989) ■ S. Rajamanickam, *Roberto de Nobili on Indian Customs: An Introduction by S. Rajamanickam and Translation of His Information, a Report about Some Indian Social Customs* (1989) ■ L. Sanneh, *Translating the Message: The Missionary Impact on Culture* (1991) ■ M. Singer, *When a Great Tradition Modernizes: An Anthropological Approach to Indian Civilization* (1972).

African Independent Churches. D. B. Barrett, *Schism and Renewal in Africa: An Analysis of Six Thousand Contemporary Religious Movements* (1968) ■ V. E. W. Hayward, ed., *African Independent Church Movements* (1963) ■ G. Oosthuizen, *Afro-Christian Religions* (1979) ■ idem, *The Healer-Prophet in Afro-Christian Churches* (1992) ■ idem, *The Pentecostal Penetration of the Indian Community in South Africa* (1975) ■ idem, "Indigenous Christianity and the Future of the Church in South Africa," *International Bulletin of Missionary Research* (Jan. 1997) ■ H. W. Turner, *History of an African Independent Church I: The Church of the Lord (Aladura)* (1967).

Asia. D. H. Adeney, *China: The Church's Long March* (1988) ■ N. Braun, *Laity Mobilized: Reflections on Church Growth in Japan and Other Lands* (1971) ■ J. H. Conner, "When Culture Leaves Contextualized Christianity Behind," *Missiology* (Jan. 1991) ■ R. Covell, *Mission Impossible* (1990) ■ R. Khatry, "The Church in Nepal," in *Church in Asia Today,* ed. Saphir Athyal (1996) ■ T. Lambert, *The Resurrection of the Chinese Church* (1991) ■ C. Perry, *A Biographical History of the Church in Nepal* (1989) ■ A. J. Swanson, *Taiwan: Mainline versus Independent Church Growth, A Study in Contrasts* (1970) ■ A. L. Tuggy, *Iglesia Ni Cristo: A Study in Independent Church Dynamics* (1976).

India. K. Baago, *The Movement around Subba Rao: A Study of the Hindu-Christian Movement around K. Subba Rao in Andhra Pradesh* (1968) ■ Y. Bandela, "The Gospel Association of India" (unpub. ms., Fuller, 1974) ■ D. W. Bennett, "Perspectives of Biblical Pastoral Leadership: A Case Study of Ten Churches in Pune, India" (diss., Fuller, 1990) ■ L. Caplan, "Popular Christianity in Urban South India," *R & S* 30 (2, June 1983) ■ J. Daniel, *Another Daniel* (1980) ■ K. Devasahayam, "The Bible Mission," *R & S* 29 (1, Mar. 1982) ■ R. E. Hedlund, "Church Planting in Selected Indian Cities" in *Evangelization and Church Growth Issues from the Asian Context* (1992) ■ W. Hoerschelmann, *Christliche Gurus: Darstellung von Selbstverständnis und Funktion indigenen Christseins durch unabhängige, charismatisch geführte Gruppen in Südindien* (1977) ■ J. C. Kurundamannil, "Yuomayam: A Messianic Movement in Kerala, India" (diss., Fuller, 1978) ■ Julius Lipner, "A Modern Indian Christian Response," in *Modern Indian Responses to Religious Pluralism,* ed. Harold G. Coward (1987) ■ J. Mattam, "Indian Attempts towards a Solution to the Problems of Conversion," in *Mission and Conversion: A Reappraisal,* ed. J. Mattam and S. Kim (1996) ■ S. S. Pillai, *Strategy to Reach Greater Madras* (1996) ■ R. R. Rajamani, *Monsoon Daybreak* (1971) ■ J. Saldanha, "Patterns of Conversion in Indian Mission History," in *Mission and Conversion: A Reappraisal,* ed. J. Mattam and S. Kim (1996) ■ Edwin Samuel, ed., *In the Day of Thy Power: Compiled from the Messages of Bro. R. R. Rajamani and Bro. Bakht Singh* (repr. 1983) ■ P. S. Raj, *A Christian Folk Religion in India: A Study of the Small Church Movement in Andhra Pradesh, with a Special Reference to the Bible Mission of Devadas* (1986) ■ M. T. Thangaraj, "The History and Teachings of the Hindu Christian Community Commonly Called Nattu Sabai in Tirunelveli," *Indian Church History Review* 5 (1, June 1971) ■ J. C. B. Webster, *The Dalit Christians: A History* (1994) ■ P. Younger, "Hindu-Christian Worship Settings in South India," in *Hindu-Christian Dialogue: Perspectives and Encounters,* ed. Harold Coward (1990).

Pacific Region. G. W. Trompf, ed., *The Gospel Is Not Western: Black Theologies from the Southwest Pacific* (1987).

North American Indigenous Christianity and Churches. J. A. Carpenter and W. R. Shenk, eds., *Earthen Vessels: American Evangelicals and Foreign Missions, 1880–1980* (1990) ■ D. W. Dayton and R. K. Johnston, eds., *The Variety of American Evangelicalism* (1991) ■ M. A. Noll, N. O. Hatch, G. M. Marsden, D. F. Wells, and J. D. Woodbridge, eds., *Eerdmans' Handbook to Christianity in America* (1983) ■ R. E. Osborn, *The Spirit of American Christianity* (1958) ■ B. L. Shelley, *The Gospel and the American Dream* (1989) ■ A. F. Walls, "The American Dimension in the History of the Missionary Movement," in Carpenter and Shenk, *Earthen Vessels.*

Latin American Grassroots Churches. C. L. Berg Jr. and P. E. Pretiz, "Latin America's Fifth Wave of Protestant Churches," *International Bulletin of Missionary Research* (Oct. 1996) ■ M. Berg and P. Pretiz, *The Gospel People* (1992) ■ idem, *Spontaneous Combustion: Grass-Roots Christianity, Latin American Style* (1996) ■ E. Nida, *Understanding Latin Americans* (1974) ■ C. Nunez, E. Antonio, and W. D. Taylor, *Crisis and Hope in Latin America: An Evangelical Perspective* (rev. ed., 1996) ■ E. A. Wilson, "Identity, Community, and Status: The Legacy of the Central American Pentecostal Pioneers," in Carpenter and Shenk, eds., *Earthen Vessels: American Evangelicals and Foreign Missions, 1880–1980* (1990).   ■ R. E. Hedlund

INGRAM, JAMES HENRY (1893–1981). A missionary leader of the Church of God (CG, Cleveland, TN) for 50 years. Ingram served as a missionary ambassador and traveled to many countries rather than serving in only one. His earliest missions work was in Bermuda in 1921. Following several assignments to the British colony and later missions work in the U.S., Ingram began the CG missions endeavor in Mexico, where he served from 1932 to 1943. In the course of his Mexican ministry, he also opened works in Panama, El Salvador, Costa Rica, and Argentina.

Ingram's most notable work was his Golden Jubilee World Tour in 1936 to celebrate the 50th anniversary of the CG, during which he brought numerous independent congregations into the denomination. The missions in China and India proved to be fruitful fields for the pentecostal message. His efforts led to the establishment of strong pentecostal works in more than a dozen other countries.

A prolific writer, Ingram aroused the awareness of the CG to its missionary responsibility and emphasized the needs of the world. A compilation of his missionary writings, *Around the World with the Gospel Light*, was published in 1937.

Long after most men decline in activity, Ingram continued his worldwide ministry. Even past age 80 he traveled widely and nurtured those fields he had opened to the message of Pentecost. He died in California in 1981 at age 88.

■ **Bibliography:** C. W. Conn, *Where the Saints Have Trod* (1959) ■ P. Humphrey, *J. H. Ingram—Missionary Dean* (1966).
■ C. W. Conn

INITIAL EVIDENCE The doctrine of initial evidence is the chief doctrinal distinctive of classical pentecostalism. Pentecostals have used a variety of expressions to describe the relationship of tongues speech to baptism in the Holy Spirit, including "Bible evidence," "initial gift," "only evidence," "first evidence," "initial sign," and "initial evidence." The earliest known reference to the latter surfaces in doctrinal statements of the ▸Pentecostal Holiness Church and the ▸Fire-Baptized Holiness Church in 1908. Gradually this term became dominant, with some adapting it to "initial physical evidence," to

highlight that baptism in the Holy Spirit involves a vocal utterance that occurs in conjunction with the spiritual dimension of the experience. To understand the historical progress of the doctrine, six stages will be considered, followed by a discussion of its significance: (1) developments before 1900; (2) Spirit baptism according to Charles F. Parham; (3) adaptation of the Parham thesis; (4) expositions before 1960; (5) early challenges to the doctrine; and (6) later challenges and expositions.

1. Developments Before 1900.
Contrary to the notion that certain gifts of the Holy Spirit, notably tongues, interpretation, prophecy, healings, and miracles had necessarily ceased with the age of the apostles, recent historians have traced their ongoing role in the process of conversion-initiation in the life of the churches into the early medieval period. In these and later centuries, reports of spiritual phenomena among Christian mystics (e.g., Hildegard of Bingen) and various fringe groups (e.g., Montanists, Prophets of the Cevennes [Camisards]) sometimes mentioned ecstatic utterances such as speaking in tongues. Pentecostal apologists cited these precedents to demonstrate that manifestations of tongues continued throughout church history (e.g., B. F. Lawrence, *The Apostolic Faith Restored* [1916], 32–51; S. H. Frodsham, *With Signs Following* [rev. ed., 1946], 253–62).

To classical pentecostals, the doctrine of speaking in tongues as the initial evidence of the baptism in the Holy Spirit had disappeared with the apostolic age. Not until the turn of the 20th century did believers rediscover and reinstate the doctrine due to the end times "outpouring" of the Spirit as foretold in Joel 2:28–29. From their vantage point, this paralleled Martin Luther's recovery of the doctrine of justification by faith, John Wesley's teaching on Christian perfection, and the efforts of Johann Christoph Blumhardt, Dorothea Trüdel, ▸A. B. Simpson, and others in the restoration of belief in divine healing through the atoning work of Jesus Christ (e.g., A. J. Tomlinson, *The Last Great Conflict* [1913], 136–37).

The theological roots of the doctrine can be found in the soil of pietism and evangelicalism and more immediately in the 19th-century charismatic revival in Scotland and England led by ▸Edward Irving and in the Holiness movement and radical evangelicals' expectation of the restoration of the gift of tongues. Belief in the premillennial return of Christ and longing for the recovery of the supernatural empowerment that had invigorated the early church were coupled together in the thinking of Irving, a prominent Scottish pastor in London. Reports of the charismata, especially speaking in tongues, first appeared under his ministry in 1830. More than any other figure, he became identified with belief in the availability of the gifts of the Holy Spirit. To Irving, speaking in tongues signified the "standing sign" of the church's inheritance won through the redemptive work of Jesus Christ. Therefore, God intended for every believer to receive this introductory and continuing evidence of supernatural empowerment ("The Church, with Her Endowment of Holiness and Power," in *The Collected Writings of Edward Irving in Five Volumes,* ed. G. Carlyle [1864], 5:449–506).

Irving saw tongues speech as the confirmation of the church's pentecostal infilling (Acts 2:4) and saw the potential of xenolalia (i.e., intelligible known languages) miraculously aiding missionaries in preaching the gospel in the mission lands. Although having previously recommended radical proposals for the conduct of missions (*Missionaries after the Apostolical School* [1825]), he did not encourage the use of tongues for this purpose. Nonetheless, in one noteworthy instance, Mary Campbell, a prominent participant in the revival, claimed that she had received the Turkish language and that of Palau Island in the South Pacific to equip her to evangelize these people groups.

While many dismissed the importance of Irving after his untimely death in 1834, save for his having demonstrated the inherent dangers of dabbling in religious enthusiasm, his restorationist vision and the stories of the revival lived on to inspire others on both sides of the Atlantic (e.g., A. Dallimore, *Forerunner of the Charismatic Movement* [1983]). Pentecostals found a recent precedent for their own experiences of tongues, but they seemed unaware of Irving's belief in its evidential value. Yet a hint of this appears in a brief comment made by ▸Charles Parham: "We have found . . . that the Irvingites, a sect that arose under the teachings of Irving . . . during the last century, received not only the eight recorded gifts of 1 Cor. 12, but also the speaking in other tongues, which the Holy Ghost reserved as the evidence of His oncoming" (*A Voice Crying in the Wilderness* [2d ed., 1910], 29). In later years apologists Bernard L. Bresson (*Studies in Ecstasy* [1966]) and W. H. Turner (*Pentecost and Tongues* [2d ed., 1968]) discovered that Irving had taught a form of initial evidence and used this information to substantiate a doctrinal model.

Interest in the baptism and gifts of the Holy Spirit also flourished in the Wesleyan and ▸Keswickian ("Higher Life") camps of the Holiness movement, whose origins can be found in the teachings of John Wesley, John Fletcher, Phoebe Palmer, Charles G. Finney, William E. Boardman, and others. Wesleyan Holiness preachers told the faithful that the "second blessing"—a crisis experience of sanctification (i.e., a perfection of motives and desires), separable from conversion—would instantaneously eradicate their sinful dispositions and elevate them to a new plateau of Christian living. Higher Life advocates, sharing belief in a second work of grace but avoiding the "sinless perfection" of the Wesleyans, preferred to look at it as "full consecration" that empowered them for victorious living and evangelism. By the end of the century, both camps had chosen to use pentecostal imagery

from the NT to describe the experience. Whether viewed as "sinless perfection" or "full consecration," it signified the post-conversion baptism in the Holy Spirit, believed to be identical in nature to that received by the disciples on the Day of Pentecost and elsewhere in the book of Acts.

An empowered life marked by "perfect love" and spiritual fruitfulness revealed the inward evidence of Spirit baptism; conformity to biblical proscriptions and avoidance of certain cultural taboos provided a measure of outward verification. In the early 1890s, however, the issue over evidence reached a new peak of discussion. The radical Holiness preacher ▸Benjamin Hardin Irwin caused an uproar when he added a third work of grace, different in nature from the second work of sanctification. From his perspective, sanctification cleansed the believer from "inbred sin" in preparation for the "baptism of fire" (Matt. 3:11) that brought enablement for Christian witness. This three-stage approach to conversion-initiation naturally raised the subject of how the evidence of the third work differed from that of the second. Since mainline Wesleyan Holiness leaders taught that empowerment came with sanctification, they condemned Irwin's teaching as the "third blessing heresy." Nevertheless, "fire-baptized" theology became part of the vital groundwork for the pentecostal movement.

Another formative influence came in the latter part of the century as radical evangelicals in the Protestant missions movement longed for the restoration of apostolic power in "signs and wonders" (Acts 5:12) to expedite gospel proclamation. Given the slow pace of conversions overseas and the nearness of Christ's return, they wondered how the Great Commission could be achieved in such a short time. Radical evangelical missionaries who desired to begin preaching as soon as they arrived on their respective mission fields became frustrated when language study required several years before they could gain enough fluency. Beginning at least by the 1880s, some speculated that with mustering sufficient faith, God might enable them to "speak with new tongues" (Mark 16:17) in order to bypass the nuisance of language school. Thus, by the close of the century, the possible restoration of the gift of tongues (xenolalia) for missionary evangelism had generated interest for over two decades.

2. Spirit Baptism According to Charles F. Parham.

The central figure in the birth of pentecostal theology was the midwestern Holiness preacher Charles F. Parham, who had apparently been influenced by Irwin's fire-baptized theology, as well as the teachings of ▸Frank W. Sandford, a visionary mission leader and founder of the Holy Ghost and Us Bible School at Shiloh, ME. It is also noteworthy that Parham had read with great interest the story of M. Jennie Glassey, a young woman who testified to having received several West African dialects in preparation for missionary service, and printed an excerpt of it in his *Apostolic Faith* (Topeka) (May 3, 1899, 5). His synthesis of Holiness and faith-healing theology, premillennial eschatology, zeal for world evangelization, and anticipation of the divine bestowal of foreign languages became fully formed by late fall of 1900. Proof of the authenticity of the doctrine came with a revival at his Bethel Bible School in Topeka, KS, in early Jan. 1901. He then announced that by the power of the Spirit he and his students had spoken in Spanish, French, Italian, Norwegian, Swedish, German, Bulgarian, Russian, Hungarian, "Bohemian," "Chinese," and Japanese.

In his analysis of Spirit baptism, Parham believed that tongues signified the outpouring of the Holy Spirit, verified the reception of Spirit baptism, and provided linguistic expertise for God's elite band of end-times missionaries. Though pentecostalism had no predominant founder or father figure, he receives credit for this fundamental teaching, since he made the theological link between Spirit baptism and tongues that became the hallmark of classical pentecostal theology. Yet a number of his beliefs proved to be controversial even to pentecostals, such as the annihilation of the wicked at the final judgment, which they rejected. On another point, he argued that Spirit-baptized believers—the "bride of Christ," those "sealed" by the Holy Spirit unto the "day of redemption" (2 Cor. 1:21–22; Eph. 1:13; 4:30), would alone be taken in the "rapture" of the church (1 Thess. 4:13–17); pentecostals generally discarded this as well. Nevertheless, the latter teaching highlighted a basic issue that has challenged pentecostal theologians through the years: the unique difference of the Spirit's work in a Christian who speaks in tongues from one who does not.

In regard to theological methodology, Parham and most early pentecostals applied a ‣"restorationist hermeneutic" to derive the doctrine of initial evidence from the life of the NT church, much as other restorationists had done in varying degrees with their own distinctive beliefs. Examples can be found in the required communal lifestyle in the ecclesiology of the Hutterites, certain teachings of the restoration movement in America, and Holiness views of Spirit baptism. While traditional Protestant method prioritized, using explicit statements from the biblical text for building doctrine, pentecostals appealed to a direct implication obtained from scriptural narrative. Luke the evangelist, in his choice and arrangement of materials in Acts, wrote with a clear theological intent. The recorded "pattern" of Spirit baptisms portrays the experience as distinct from regeneration and plainly accompanied by glossolalia in three instances: the Day of Pentecost (Acts 2:4), the account of Cornelius and other Gentiles (10:44–48), and the Ephesian believers (19:1–7). Corroborating data also comes from two allusions to tongues: the Samaritan revival (8:4–19) and the experience of Paul (9:1–19). Therefore, baptism in the Holy Spirit not only depicted the spirituality of the early church but established the norm of speaking in tongues for all believers. Though citations of biblical passages to support this teaching have not been limited to the book of Acts (e.g., Mark 16:17; John 20:22), the use of Acts has been indispensable. At the same time, this individual dimension was not to be confused with the expression of the gift of tongues in corporate worship (1 Cor. 14).

The most extensive presentation of pentecostal pneumatology in the earliest years of the movement, *The Spirit and the Bride* (1907), came from the pen of ‣George F. Taylor. It follows the Holiness-pentecostal threefold makeup of conversion-initiation, the linguistic function of tongues, and the "sealing" of the bride of Christ. Like other pentecostals, Taylor pointed to the ‣dispensational significance of baptism in the Holy Spirit, arguing that a new age had dawned and their encounter with the Spirit marked the beginning of the end times: "The early rain began on the Day of Pentecost, and the first manifestation was speaking with other tongues as the Spirit gave utterance, and then followed the healing of the sick, casting out devils, etc. So it would only be natural to expect that in the latter rain Pentecost [it] should be repeated and followed by the same manifestation" (*The Spirit and the Bride* [1907], 91). Another significant exposition of the dispensational theme appeared with ‣D. Wesley Myland's popular *Latter Rain Covenant* (1910), although it lacks a clear endorsement of tongues as initial evidence.

To confirm the soundness of the doctrine, several leaders set up experiments. Speakers preached to audiences on the baptism in the Holy Spirit without announcing that tongues would occur with the reception of the Spirit. In both instances, seekers spoke in tongues. The two best-known "test cases" took place in San Antonio, TX, in 1907 and Pittsburgh, PA, in 1921 (E. E. Goss, *The Winds of God* [rev. ed., 1977], 104; W. W. Menzies, *Anointed to Serve* [1971], 126n.).

3. Adaptation of the Parham Thesis.

The theology of Spirit baptism taught by Charles Parham appears to have reigned largely uncontested for the first eight years of the movement. In the periodical literature, pentecostals did not connect speaking in tongues with prayer before 1907, at least on the North American scene. However, as early as 1906 some began to have misgivings about the value of xenolalic tongues for missions but without doubting their credibility as intelligible languages. Pentecostal missionaries found they had to learn foreign languages. Reliable testimony of their preaching *at will* in their newfound languages and being understood by their hearers could not be found. A period of theological reflection then commenced in which pentecostals sought for a better biblical understanding of the role of tongues, increasingly viewed as glossolalia (simply unrecognized languages) rather than xenolalia.

‣Alfred G. Garr, one of the earliest pentecostal missionaries, played a key part in the modification of Parham's "Bible evidence" teaching. After the ‣Azusa Street revival (1906–9) in Los Angeles, where he had been instructed in the doctrine and baptized in the Spirit, he arrived in Calcutta, India, at the turn of 1907, only to find that he could not speak in what he thought was Bengali after all. For pragmatic and theological reasons, he altered the doctrine within a few weeks but retained tongues as essential to baptism in the Holy Spirit. Though still the "tongues of men and of angels" (1 Cor. 13:1), glossolalia now denoted the Spirit praying through the believer to God in worship and intercession (1 Cor. 14:2): "It is the sweetest joy and the greatest pleasure to the soul when God comes upon one in all one's unworthiness and begins Himself to speak in His language. Oh! The blessedness of His presence when those foreign words flow from the Spirit of God through the soul and then are given back to Him in praise, in prophecy, or in worship" ("Tongues, the Bible Evidence," *Cloud of Witnesses to Pentecost in India* [Sept. 1907], 43). Garr may have been the first to propose this redefinition in print, but others soon shared this conviction. To them, tongues speech still remained the source of divine power for Christian witness and the gateway to the exercise of the nine gifts of the Spirit (1 Cor. 12:8–10). Adopted by the majority of pentecostals, this modification underscored their belief in the transforming power of the experience, fundamental zeal for evangelism and missions, and pragmatism about the means for world evangelization.

Pentecostals also asserted that glossolalia signified a new dimension of the reign of Christ within the heart that brought an enduement of power for an "overcoming" life in the Spirit. ›John Wright Follette, an early spiritual master, wrote, "Many in Pentecost today seem to have missed the idea or purpose of the latter rain and instead of falling into line with God for a deeper life, ripening, maturing, and drying [as grain for the harvest], they are occupied with the incidentals. These incidentals ['manifestations and gifts'] are all very essential but only to the end—growth." At Spirit baptism, he declared,

> the heart is warmed into a generous love and yielding and pouring out of life for the needy race. Then there are prayers, groanings, and intercessions in the Spirit. Why? Because the purpose of God has gripped the heart, and hence the soul lives for that one end—the fulfillment of God's purpose and maturity.... The work He is doing is mystical, intricate, and spiritual. He is transforming us and making us like Christ, that we may share with Him in the age to come." (J. W. Follette, *Arrows of Truth* [1969], 132, 134)

Not surprisingly, early pentecostals often described the effects of Spirit baptism in ways that naturally resembled the Holiness and "Higher Life" traits of the sanctified and empowered life. In a typical exposition, ›A. A. Boddy cited five benefits:

(1) Wondrous joy that the Spirit has thus sealed the believer unto the day of redemption. It is something very real. (2) An increase in the believer's personal love of the Lord Jesus. (3) A new interest in the word of God. The Bible becomes very precious and its messages very real. (4) A love to the souls for whom Christ has died and a desire to bring them to Him. (5) The soon coming of the Lord is now often laid upon the believer's heart. ("Speaking in Tongues: What Is It?" *Confidence* [May 1910], 100; cf., F. L. Arrington, *Christian Doctrine* [1994], 3:77–84)

Unexpectedly, certainty about the actual meaning of tongues declined after the general demise of belief in their linguistic utility. For example, pentecostals often pointed to the predictive statement of Isa. 28:11 ("For with stammering lips and another tongue will [the LORD] speak to this people" [KJV]) that Paul quotes in 1 Cor. 14:21. Some proposed that this referred to the exercise of xenolalic tongues for gospel witness to unconverted hearers; illustrations frequently came from happenings in worship settings (Frodsham, *With Signs Following*, 229–52). While similar to the Parham thesis, this idea differed in that the tongues were still unknown to the speaker. Inadvertently, it raised new questions about the function of the gifts of tongues and interpretation in such circumstances (W. F. Carothers, "The Gift of Interpretation," *Latter Rain Evangel (LRE)* [Oct. 1910], 7–10).

Another adaptation came a few years later with the emergence of the "Jesus Name," or ›Oneness, movement (1913–) within pentecostalism, which adopted a non-Trinitarian view of the Godhead and taught that water baptism must be done in the name of Jesus Christ, the redemptive name of God revealed in the NT. To Oneness Christians this represented the final restoration of the doctrine of salvation and practices of the early church. In terms of the Acts narrative, the case rested on Peter's exhortation to observers on the Day of Pentecost to be baptized in Jesus' name (Acts 2:38) and the application of this formula in 8:16; 10:48; and 19:5.

Many Oneness pentecostals, especially those who left the General Council of the ›Assemblies of God (AG) in 1916 and started several agencies that later merged to form the ›United Pentecostal Church International in 1945, challenged the two-stage conversion-initiation theology of the AG and the three-stage approach of the Holiness pentecostals. Accordingly, baptism in the Holy Spirit completes the conversion process instead of serving as a separate enduement with power. This one-stage experience involves faith, repentance, water baptism in the name of Jesus, and the infilling of the Holy Spirit marked by speaking in tongues (D. K. Bernard, *The New Birth* [1984]). From this standpoint, they embraced the historic Reformed position that made salvation synonymous with Spirit baptism. Finally, Oneness believers kept the classical pentecostal insistence on tongues along with the modification made by

Garr and others that glossolalia largely comprised prayer in the Spirit, except for the operation of the gift of tongues in corporate worship.

4. Expositions Before 1960.

One of the most perceptive proponents of initial evidence was ►Daniel W. Kerr, who championed the doctrine at the 1918 general council meeting of the AG and wrote several articles in the *Pentecostal Evangel (PE)* to refute arguments against it. In his study of the NT, Kerr observed that the gospel writers had "selected" their materials from the available data. For example, the apostle John authored his gospel to confirm believers in the truth about Jesus Christ as the Son of God. Following a similar methodology, Luke chose materials to draw attention to the outpouring of the Holy Spirit on the church and the baptism of individual believers:

> What is [Luke's] purpose? No doubt, his purpose is to show that what Jesus promised He hath so fulfilled. He says, "they that believe shall speak in other tongues." The 120 believed and, therefore, they spake in other tongues as the Spirit gave them utterance. We also believe, and we speak in other tongues as the Spirit gives utterance. ("The Bible Evidence of the Baptism with the Holy Ghost," *PE* [Aug. 11, 1923], 3)

This represented the most striking characteristic of Luke's theology of the Spirit in Acts: the biblical text clearly shows that whether in Acts 2, 10, or 19, tongues accompanied Spirit baptism. Not only did Kerr offer the most refined hermeneutical defense of the doctrine by an early pentecostal, but his means of interpretation predated the work of evangelical redaction critics by several decades.

Reflecting on the finding of this neglected biblical teaching, Kerr expressed gratitude for the truths that had been regained by Luther, Wesley, Blumhardt, Trüdel, and Simpson. Sharing the restorationist vision of other pentecostals, he concluded,

> During the past few years God has enabled us to discover and recover this wonderful truth concerning the Baptism in the Spirit as it was given at the beginning. Thus we have all that the others got, and we got this too. We see all they see, but they don't see what we see. ("The Basis of Our Distinctive Testimony," *PE* [Sept. 2, 1922], 4)

Other attempts at defending the validity of the "pattern" proved less effective. ►Stanley H. Frodsham appealed to the "law of threefold mention" ("triplication") found in George Mackinlay's *Recent Discoveries in St. Luke's Writings* (1921). Some turned to the so-called "law of first occurrence" or "first mention" (see J. E. Hartill, *Principles of Biblical Interpretation* [1947], 70−72); for an illustration of this approach, see H. W. Steinberg, "Initial Evidence of the Baptism in the Holy Spirit," in *Conference on the Holy Spirit Digest*, ed. G. Jones (1983), 1:37−41.

For decades to come, pentecostal teachers followed in the wake of Parham, Kerr, and others. Publications by prominent advocates included Joseph H. King (*From Passover to Pentecost* [1911]), ►Garfield T. Haywood (*The Birth of the Spirit in the Days of the Apostles* [n.d.]), Frank Lindblad (*The Spirit Which Is from God* [1928]), ►Donald Gee (*Pentecost* [1932]), ►Paul H. Walker (*The Baptism with the Holy Ghost and the Evidence* [c. 1935]), ►Myer Pearlman (*Knowing the Doctrines of the Bible* [1937]), ►Carl Brumback (*What Meaneth This?* [1947]), and ►Harold Horton (*The Baptism in the Holy Spirit* [1956]).

Other contributions came with books by W. H. Turner (*Pentecost and Tongues* [1939, 1968]) and Robert Chandler Dalton (*Tongues Like as of Fire* [1945]), both originally prepared as master's theses. ►Wade H. Horton edited a scholarly collection of historical and pastoral essays on the doctrine in *The Glossolalia Phenomenon* (1966). Bernard L. Bresson provided an extensive survey of charismatic phenomena in church history in his *Studies in Ecstasy* (1966), written to defend the classical pentecostal teaching on Spirit baptism. These publications marked the gradual emergence of a pentecostal academy. (Bresson's inquiry was later superseded in scope and interpretation by the three-volume study of Stanley M. Burgess entitled *The Holy Spirit: Ancient Christian Traditions* [1984]; *Eastern Christian Traditions* [1989]; *Medieval Roman Catholic and Reformation Traditions* [1997].)

5. Early Challenges to the Doctrine.

Historians of pentecostalism have suggested that disagreement about the nature of sanctification drew the first theological line between pentecostals: the "finished work of Calvary" controversy that erupted in 1910. While this and the later quarrel over Oneness theology (1913−) forged the identities of pentecostal denominations, the first actual division arose over the doctrine of initial evidence and began in late 1906. It centered on the question, "Should the accounts of tongues speech in Acts be understood to mean that glossolalia is indispensable to baptism in the Holy Spirit?" Those who saw tongues in Acts and 1 Corinthians as serving the same purpose often struggled with making tongues a litmus test. Because of the sovereign dispensing of the gifts (1 Cor. 12:7−11), they hesitated to make an ironclad connection.

Since pentecostalism in India began in mid 1906 independently of Parham's theology and events in North America, it is significant that the foremost leader, ►Minnie F. Abrams, believed that baptism in the Holy Spirit brought the power and gifts of the Spirit, usually involving but not necessarily requiring glossolalia (*The Baptism in the Holy Ghost and Fire* [2d ed., 1906]). She noted that Joel's prediction mentioned more than one feature of the Spirit's power. Nonetheless, she said that "as a rule" believers would speak in tongues when they were baptized or shortly thereafter ("The Object of the Baptism in the Holy Spirit," *LRE* [May 1911],

8–11). The Parham thesis later reached the subcontinent through the pages of the *Apostolic Faith* (Los Angeles), published by the Apostolic Faith Mission on Azusa Street, and with the arrival of Alfred and Lillian Garr.

Certain pentecostal leaders in North America also questioned the imperative of tongues. On the North American scene these included ►William Hamner Piper, pastor of the Stone Church in Chicago and editor of the *LRE,* and later ►William J. Seymour, pastor of the Apostolic Faith Mission on Azusa Street in Los Angeles. The best-known pentecostal to oppose the doctrine was ►Fred F. Bosworth, an early leader in the AG, who eventually objected to the organization's commitment to initial evidence. Determining that he could no longer continue his association in good conscience, he resigned before its general council meeting in 1918, which reaffirmed the doctrine as "our distinctive testimony." In his booklet *Do All Speak with Tongues?* (n.d.), Bosworth unequivocally declared initial evidence to be an error for several reasons, including: (1) tongues speech in both Acts and 1 Cor. 12 and 14 represents the gift of tongues; (2) no explicit statement can be found in the NT to support the doctrine; and (3) none of the greatest soul-winners (e.g., Charles G. Finney) ever spoke in tongues and yet were filled with the Holy Spirit.

Neither did all North American pentecostal denominations recognize the doctrine. While it became uniform in white organizations (e.g., AG, ►Church of God [Cleveland, TN], ►Church of God of Prophecy, ►International Church of the Foursquare Gospel, ►International Pentecostal Holiness Church, ►Open Bible Standard Churches, ►Pentecostal Assemblies of Canada, ►Pentecostal Church of God, ►United Pentecostal Church International, and their overseas constituencies), some African-American pentecostal bodies rejected it. The ►Church of God in Christ (COGIC), led by Charles H. Mason, originally endorsed the doctrine; however, many leaders and members concluded that dancing and shouting could be of equal value. For the ►United Holy Church of America, tongues represented one of the spiritual gifts that came with baptism in the Holy Spirit. On the other hand, several black Oneness denominations have upheld the doctrine of initial evidence: the ►Bible Way Church Worldwide, Church of Our Lord Jesus Christ of the Apostolic Faith, and ►Pentecostal Assemblies of the World.

In England the ►Elim Pentecostal Church founded by ►George Jeffreys considered both tongues and prophecy as evidences. On the European continent, leaders such as ►Jonathan Paul in Germany and ►Gerrit R. Polman in the Netherlands doubted the absolute need for tongues. In South America the Pentecostal Methodist Church founded by ►Willis C. Hoover did not formally adopt the doctrine and considered the "holy dance" to be as important as tongues.

In a related development, division took place within the ►Christian and Missionary Alliance (CMA) founded by ►A. B. Simpson. In the early 1890s a flurry of interest in xenolalic tongues for missionary evangelism had risen within the ranks. Wishing to avoid the "dangers" of the Irvingite movement, the CMA convention in Oct. 1892 encouraged the faithful to pray that the Spirit would assist missionaries in acquiring the necessary foreign languages, a move that left a measure of ambiguity about how this would be accomplished. Although Simpson sympathized with the possibility that God might actually bestow intelligible languages if a person had sufficient faith, he condemned the opinion of some that missionaries had an obligation before God to claim this promise (Mark 16:17). In several published articles during these years, he wrestled with the purpose of tongues but with the application to missions rather than Spirit baptism in view (e.g., "Connection between Supernatural Gifts and the World's Evangelization," *Christian Alliance and Missionary Weekly (CAMW)* [Oct. 7 and 14, 1892], 226–27).

When several branches of the CMA reported occurrences of tongues speech in 1907, Simpson once more faced the problem of how tongues related to the life and mission of the church. He disagreed with those who insisted on its role in baptism in the Holy Spirit. With the Pauline lens of 1 Cor. 12 and 14, he looked at the phenomenon in Acts as the gift of tongues; as a result, he declared that no one gift of the Spirit could be entertained as proof of Spirit baptism. Among those who experienced glossolalia, some chose to follow Simpson's lead (e.g., Robert A. Jaffray, "'Speaking in Tongues'—Some Words of Kindly Counsel," *CAMW* [Mar. 13, 1909], 395–96, 406), while others left (e.g., Daniel W. Kerr). A sizable number of pentecostals withdrew over the next 10 years, with many of them joining and having a formative influence on the AG and its adherence to initial evidence.

Neither the leaders nor the church bodies cited above disparaged speaking in tongues but variously considered the possibility of exceptions, the evidential superiority of love over tongues, the equal weight of other gifts and manifestations, or in some instances the acceptance of the Pauline definition of tongues for the Acts narrative. At times the entire discussion—obviously a sophisticated matter about proper biblical interpretation—must have appeared confusing to the faithful. Given how freely early pentecostals used the term "gift of tongues" to describe any occasion of speaking in tongues, it should come as no surprise that they sometimes wondered if tongues speech required the gift of interpretation for the private exercise of glossolalia.

Regardless of the objections, the doctrine became the majority position among pentecostals due to (1) their strong conviction about the theological importance of the Acts narrative; (2) their own testimonies of Spirit baptism that identified them with the early Christians and confirmed the truth of the teaching; (3) influential editorials and articles in pentecostal periodicals; (4) books, booklets, and tracts (e.g., ▸A. S. McPherson, *This Is That* [1919]); and (5) the development of denominations that adopted creedal statements to ensure doctrinal uniformity. With the decision of the AG, the largest body of organized pentecostals, to uphold the doctrine in 1918, the period of its evolution had ostensibly ended. Notwithstanding, to prevent the erosion of the doctrine and pentecostal spirituality in later years, the denomination began to require that ministers annually reaffirm their fidelity to initial evidence.

6. Later Challenges and Expositions.

In the postwar period, pentecostals increasingly pursued graduate education in biblical studies, theology, and church history. The timing of the emergence of pentecostal scholarship proved fortuitous because new challenges faced the doctrine of initial evidence. Important scholarly works published since 1970 have not only questioned the underlying foundation of baptism in the Spirit as a separable experience from regeneration, but pentecostals' understanding of Luke's theological intent in Acts as well. Well-known scholars who have disputed the classical pentecostal view include James D. G. Dunn (*Baptism in the Holy Spirit* [1970]), Frederick Dale Bruner (*A Theology of the Holy Spirit* [1970]), and more recently Max Turner (*The Holy Spirit and Spiritual Gifts* [rev. ed., 1996]). Pentecostal scholar ▸Gordon D. Fee has expressed similar concerns (*Gospel and Spirit* [1991]; *God's Empowering Presence* [1994]), while a leading churchman, ▸Jack W. Hayford, has called for a modified position on initial evidence (*The Beauty of Spiritual Language* [1992]). The issues have hardly been new, but the responses have demanded a higher level of exegetical and theological expertise than obtainable in previous years. Expositions by earlier pentecostals, though ahead of their time in recognizing the value of biblical narrative, remained limited due to their focus on Acts rather than the larger Lucan corpus and by a dispensationally circumscribed concept of the kingdom of God.

Recent pentecostal NT scholars have appealed to a broader framework of biblical theology to articulate the doctrine, chief among them Roger Stronstad (*The Charismatic Theology of St. Luke* [1984]; *Spirit, Scripture and Theology* [1995]) and Robert P. Menzies (*Empowered for Witness* [1994]). Representative shorter studies include Ben C. Aker, "New Directions in Lucan Theology: Reflections on Luke 3:21–22 and Some Implications," in *Faces of Renewal*, ed. P. Elbert (1988), 108–27; and Mathew S. Clark, "Initial Evidence: A Southern African Perspective," *Asian Journal of Pentecostal Studies* 1 (July 1998): 203–17. Anthony D. Palma's *Baptism in the Holy Spirit* (1999), which addresses initial evidence, comes from a larger forthcoming work on pentecostal

pneumatology. In the progress of the doctrine, charismatic theologians have made significant contributions, notably ▸J. Rodman Williams (*Renewal Theology* [1996]); and ▸Howard M. Ervin (*These Are Not Drunken, as Ye Suppose* [1968]; *Conversion-Initiation and the Baptism in the Holy Spirit* [1984]). ▸Peter Hocken has provided helpful insights on the meaning of Spirit baptism in *The Glory and the Shame* (1994).

Pentecostal systematic theologians have explored the doctrine of Spirit baptism, with some also investigating the role of tongues in the spirituality of the believer, including Simon Chan, *Spiritual Theology* (1998) and "The Language Game of Glossolalia, or Making Sense of the 'Initial Evidence,' " in *Pentecostalism in Context,* ed. W. Ma and R. P. Menzies [1997]); Harold D. Hunter (*Spirit-Baptism* [1983]); Steven J. Land (*Pentecostal Spirituality* [1993]); Frank D. Macchia, "Sighs Too Deep for Words: Toward a Theology of Glossolalia," *Journal of Pentecostal Theology* 1 (Oct. 1992): 47–73, and "The Struggle for Global Witness: Shifting Paradigms in Pentecostal Theology," in *The Globalization of Pentecostalism,* ed. M. W. Dempster et al. (1999); F. P. Möller (*The Work of the Holy Spirit in the Life of the Believers* [1997]); Jon Ruthven, "Charismatic Theology and Biblical Emphases," *Evangelical Quarterly* 69 (July 1997): 217–36; John W. Wyckoff, "The Baptism in the Holy Spirit," in *Systematic Theology,* rev. ed., ed. S. M. Horton (1995), and *The Prophethood of All Believers* (1999). ▸Eldin Villafañe, a theologian and social ethicist, has presented the social implications of a Hispanic pentecostal understanding of the Spirit in *The Liberating Spirit* (1993).

Historians as well as exegetes wrote chapters for *Initial Evidence* (1991), edited by Gary B. McGee. A perceptive historical essay on the pentecostal baptism can be found in Edith L. Blumhofer's introduction to her *Pentecost in My Soul* (1989). Studies on various aspects of the doctrine have appeared in *Pneuma: The Journal of the Society for Pentecostal Studies, EPTA Bulletin, Paraclete, Journal of Pentecostal Theology, Asian Journal of Pentecostal Studies,* and *Australasian Pentecostal Studies,* among other academic publications.

7. Significance.

From a historical perspective, Charles F. Parham's linking of speaking in tongues with Spirit baptism laid much of the theological foundation for the pentecostal movement. It clearly set pentecostals apart from their Wesleyan Holiness and Higher Life counterparts, noted for their own accentuation of the Spirit-filled life, by insisting that every Christian should seek for the charismatic experience of tongues speech. It further distinguished them from mainline Christians. After mid-century, however, pentecostals left their isolation to become more closely associated with evangelicals. In the process the differences between them gradually blurred, and for various reasons Spirit baptism and tongues declined among classical pentecostals. At risk was the core feature of pentecostal spirituality that first-generation pentecostals had experienced and ardently propagated.

Despite the early disappointment with xenolalia, the apparently easy transition to glossolalia reflected the underlying eschatological and missionary ethos that has endured within pentecostalism. To the faithful, the doctrine of initial evidence not only depicts the NT teaching on Spirit baptism but serves to highlight that Christians should seek the same empowerment that characterized believers in the book of Acts. Glossolalia offers a spiritual dimension that brings an increased perception of the Spirit's ministry less accessible otherwise. (Although pentecostals have differed at times about whether or not exceptions to tongues speech can occur at Spirit baptisms, they have largely agreed on the exceptional value of glossolalia for the Spirit-filled life.) In the words of Roger Stronstad:

> This outpouring of the Spirit of prophecy in the contemporary pentecostal/charismatic renewal restores important NT realities. For example, the baptizing/filling with the Holy Spirit restores the immediacy of God's presence to his people. In other words, the formerly transcendent God becomes immanent in the conscious experience of his people.... Further, there is a new hunger for the Word of God and a new existential understanding of God's Word. Finally, and more directly related to the age-old purpose for the gift of the Spirit, the baptizing/filling with the Spirit restores the Spirit's empowering in witness. Thus, pentecostals/charismatics witness as prophets by works which are empowered by the Spirit and by words which are inspired by the Spirit. ("The Prophethood of All Believers: A Study in Luke's Charismatic Theology," in *Pentecostalism in Context*, ed. W. Ma and R. P. Menzies [1997], 75)

Undoubtedly, this dynamic has accounted for much of the remarkable growth of pentecostalism, the most vibrant and unexpected development in 20th-century Christianity.

The interpretation of Acts by those who have supported the doctrine has directly challenged the methodology of scholars who have elevated the importance of didactic literature (e.g., Paul's epistles) above biblical narratives for doctrinal formulations. As the 20th century progressed, a growing appreciation of the diversity of literary genres has led to a greater recognition of the complementary theologies of Luke and Paul, as well as other biblical writers. According to William W. Menzies, "Seen together, Lucan and Pauline theology furnish for us a richer picture of life in the Spirit than either alone! It is this larger reality that supplies ... a theological setting, an 'analogy of faith' for the life, experience, and belief of the early church, which may indeed aid in understanding particular passages of Scripture" ("The Methodology of Pentecostal Theology: An Essay on Hermeneutics," in *Essays on Apostolic Themes*, ed. P. Elbert [1985], 12). By applying a restorationist hermeneutic, pentecostals stand in a long line of Christians who have looked to the life of the early church for theological truth that brings spiritual renewal.

■ **Bibliography:** E. L. Blumhofer, *Restoring the Faith: The Assemblies of God, Pentecostalism, and American Culture* (1993) ▮ D. W. Dayton, *Theological Roots of Pentecostalism* (1987) ▮ M. W. Dempster, B. D. Klaus, D. Petersen, eds., *The Globalization of Pentecostalism* (1999) ▮ P. Elbert, ed., *Essays on Apostolic Themes: Studies in Honor of Howard M. Ervin* (1985) ▮ J. R. Goff Jr., *Fields White unto Harvest: Charles F. Parham and the Missionary Origins of Pentecostalism* (1988) ▮ H. I. Lederle, *Treasures Old and New: Interpretations of "Spirit-Baptism" in the Charismatic Renewal Movement* (1988) ▮ W. Ma and R. P. Menzies, eds., *Pentecostalism in Context: Essays in Honor of William W. Menzies* (1997) ▮ L. E. Martin, ed., *The Topeka Outpouring of 1901* (1997) ▮ K. McDonnell and G. T. Montague, *Christian Initiation and Baptism in the Holy Spirit* (1991) ▮ G. B. McGee, ed., *Initial Evidence: Historical and Biblical Perspectives on the Pentecostal Doctrine of Spirit Baptism* (1991) ▮ idem, "'Latter Rain' Falling in the East: Early 20th-Century Pentecostalism in India and the Debate over Speaking in Tongues," *Church History* 68 (Sept. 1999) ▮ idem, "Looking for a 'Short-Cut' to Language Preparation: Radical Evangelicals, Missions, and the Gift of Tongues," *International Bulletin of Missionary Research* (forthcoming) ▮ C. W. Nienkirchen, *A. B. Simpson and the Pentecostal Movement* (1992) ▮ V. Synan, *The Old-Time Power: A History of the Pentecostal Holiness Church* (rev. ed., 1998) ▮ idem, "The Role of Tongues as Initial Evidence," in *Spirit and Renewal,* ed. M. W. Wilson (1994) ▮ C. van der Laan, "The Proceedings of the Leaders' Meetings (1908–1911) and of the International Pentecostal Council (1912–1914)," *Pneuma* 10 (Spring 1988).   ■ G. B. McGee

INTEGRITY COMMUNICATIONS See HOLY SPIRIT TEACHING MISSION.

INTERDENOMINATIONAL CHRISTIAN CHURCH (Iglesia Cristiana Inter-denominacional). Also known as the Portales Church, this Mexican quasi-pentecostal denomination was founded in 1926 when a group of evangelical Protestant Christians banded together to form an interdenominational church. Josué Mejia Fernández is considered the key founder of the church. His mystical experiences with God and his creative evangelistic techniques attracted hundreds of Mexicanos throughout Mexico. He regularly used drama to attract and evangelize people. The denomination's stress on personal holiness, salvation, divine healing, and mystical experiences with God place it very close to the pentecostal and particularly the charismatic movements in Mexico today. Most of the ministers are apprenticed, and in 1965 there were an estimated 500 churches throughout Mexico. A unique aspect of this church is its use of "patrons" or mature Christians who nurture and instruct younger Christians in the faith. This tradition may have been shaped by the Catholic *compadrazgo* (godparent) tradition in Mexico.

This church has been more open to Mexican Catholic practices and attitudes than have most Mexican pentecostal denominations. Despite their more tolerant attitudes, they are very critical of "Catholic vices" and preach regularly against the Roman Catholic Church and its traditions. Statistics for the denomination are hard to come by. In 1961 it was estimated that the Portales church numbered some 30,000 adherents. By the early 1980s it claimed approximately 500 congregations and some 50,000 adherents throughout Mexico.

■ **Bibliography:** David Barrett, *World Christian Encyclopedia* (1982) ■ Marvin J. Penton, "Mexico's Reformation: A History of Mexican Protestantism," Ph.D. diss., Iowa (1965). ■ G. Espinosa

INTERNATIONAL CATHOLIC CHARISMATIC RENEWAL SERVICES

Originally called the International Communication Office (ICO), and then International Catholic Charismatic Renewal Office (ICCRO), the International Catholic Charismatic Renewal Services (ICCRS) serves the ▸Catholic charismatic renewal (CCR) worldwide. ICCRS was set up by the U.S. National Service Committee in Oct. 1972. ICO, with ▸R. Martin as director in Ann Arbor, MI, began as a service from North America, with greater numbers, resources, and experience than CCR elsewhere.

From its modest beginnings as ICO in Ann Arbor to its current incarnation as ICCRO in Rome, Italy, with an international staff drawing on worldwide resources, the organization passed through several stages: the removal of the ICO office and staff to Brussels, Belgium, in 1976 at the invitation of ▸Cardinal Suenens; the formation of an international council for ICO in 1978 with nine members representing all continents; the replacement of R. Martin by ▸T. Forrest as director at the end of 1978 and his regular visitation of all parts of the world; and the removal of the ICO office from Brussels to Rome in 1981, followed immediately by the change of name to ICCRO.

The contribution of ICCRO–ICCRS to international CCR has been primarily through: (1) the work and travels of the full-time staff, particularly F. Mascarenhas (India; director 1981–87) and K. Metz (U.S.; 1987–94); (2) the organization of international conferences—e.g., general conferences in Rome and in Dublin, Ireland (1975, 1978), leaders' conferences (1973, 1975, 1978, 1981, 1984, 1987, 1989), and an international retreat for priests in the Vatican (1984); (3) a newsletter, originally *ICO Newsletter* (monthly; first issued July 1975), then the bimonthly *International Newsletter Serving the Charismatic Renewal in the Catholic Church* (1978–90), *ICCRO Newsletter* (1990–93), and *ICCRS Newsletter* (1993–); (4) the channeling of aid from wealth-

ier countries to CCR in the Third World; and (5) an emphasis on evangelism.

Links between ICCRO and the Catholic hierarchy were first assured through Cardinal Suenens at the request of Paul VI and, since Suenens' retirement, more formally through Bishops P. Cordes (1984–95) and S. Rylko (1995) of the Council for the Laity (the Vatican department assigned responsibility for CCR). In Sept. 1993 ICCRO became ICCRS, as the Vatican officially recognized this body and approved its canonical statutes.

See also CATHOLIC CHARISMATIC RENEWAL.

■ P. D. Hocken

INTERNATIONAL CHARISMATIC CONSULTATION ON WORLD EVANGELIZATION

(ICCOWE) An international and interdenominational body of leaders in the worldwide ▸charismatic movement. The first impulse for such a body came from a meeting of ▸Michael Harper, ▸Tom Forrest, and ▸Larry Christenson in 1983. Meetings with leaders of other church renewal networks led to two consultations in Singapore (1987, 1988) and a prayer vigil in Jerusalem in 1989.

Before Singapore the pentecostals and nondenominationals were included as a distinct stream. In 1988 a consultative council was formed, with an executive committee of six (two Catholics, two Protestants, two pentecostal/charismatics). From an early stage the group embraced Forrest's vision of a decade of evangelization preparing for the year 2000. At the Jerusalem meeting the decision was made to hold a major international conference at Brighton, England, in July 1991.

The Brighton conference, on the theme "That the World May Believe," attracted 3,000 participants from 100 countries, a smaller number than originally hoped, but it provided an important boost to interchurch cooperation in evangelism. A theological section provided an important first-time meeting of international scholars; many of the papers are in *All Together in One Place* (ed. H. D. Hunter and P. D. Hocken, 1993).

The Brighton themes of evangelization, renewal, and unity were pursued at two consultations: Luray, VA (1992), and Port Dickson, Malaysia (1994), and at a major conference in Prague, Czech Republic, in Sept. 1997. The Prague conference on the theme "Building Bridges, Breaking Barriers" gathered for the first time some Orthodox leaders with charismatics from historic and new churches. The ICCOWE secretariat, based in Haywards Heath, U.K., produces an occasional bulletin, *ICCOWE Link*.

■ **Bibliography:** M. Harper, "ICCOWE: What It Is and How It Started," *Pneuma* 16 (2, 1994) ■ E. Mellen, P. Hocken, C. B. Johns, "Charismatics at Brighton," *Ecumenical Trends* 21 (3, Mar. 1992).

■ P. D. Hocken

INTERNATIONAL CHURCH OF THE FOURSQUARE GOSPEL

The International Church of the Foursquare Gospel (ICFG) was founded by the gifted evangelist ▸Aimee Semple McPherson on Jan. 1, 1923, with the opening of ▸Angelus Temple, and incorporated Dec. 30, 1927.

"Sister," as the founder was affectionately called, entered the ministry with her husband, Robert Semple, as a relatively young convert. Ordained together by William H. Durham on Jan. 2, 1909, the Semples pastored, worked in the Full Gospel Assembly in Chicago, and aided Durham in evangelistic meetings during 1909–10. In mid 1910 the couple began a term as missionaries in China. Robert Semple's untimely death in Aug. 1910 brought that dream to an end. Aimee returned to the U.S. with the couple's newly born infant daughter, Roberta. Aimee remarried in late 1911, to Harold Stewart McPherson. Following the birth of their son, Rolf, the couple embarked on an evangelistic ministry.

Beginning in 1915, "Sister" ministered in Ontario, Canada, then in 1916–18 conducted a series of tent revivals along the East Coast from Maine to Florida. She purchased a "gospel auto" on which she painted slogans, such as "Jesus is coming soon—get ready." Her sermons were enthusiastically received, her message clear and simple; her method was broadly appealing and, as a result, her reputation increased and her crowds grew.

In June 1917 Sister McPherson began to publish *The Bridal Call* (since 1964 *The Foursquare Advance*), a monthly magazine with articles she authored. This magazine, as well as her participation as an editor with the New England pentecostal monthly *Word and Work* helped to broaden her appeal and solidify a supportive constituency. By 1918 she had begun a series of transcontinental evangelistic campaigns in a number of major U.S. cities. She also embarked on a successful international campaign to Australia (1922), where she held meetings in Melbourne, Sidney, and Adelaide.

The name "Foursquare" was derived from an experience Sister McPherson had in her July 1922 Oakland, CA, crusade. There, in a moment of "divine inspiration" while preaching on Ezekiel's vision (Ezek. 1:4–10) of the four cherubim with four faces, which she understood to typify the fourfold ministry of Christ, she declared it to stand for "The Foursquare Gospel." The four cardinal doctrines of "Foursquare" were all descriptive of Jesus Christ. He was identified as "Savior," "Baptizer with the Holy Spirit," "Physician and Healer," and "Coming King." These four emphases were already present in the 19th-century Holiness movement, especially in the work of ▸A. B. Simpson, who in 1890 had authored a book called *The Four-fold Gospel*. Simpson had identified Christ as Savior, Sanctifier, Healer, and Coming King, but these themes were uniquely appropriated, "pentecostalized," and popularized by "Sister." She formed the Echo Park Evangelistic Association and solicited the signatures of hundreds, regardless of denomination, who would preach these points.

McPherson's transcontinental trips led to broad-based support in many denominations. Along the way these people contributed thousands of dollars, making possible the building of the denomination's parent organization, Angelus Temple. It was originally intended as a building where "Sister" would hold evangelistic meetings while she was in town, while its pulpit would be shared with other evangelists when she was away. But her adherents in Los Angeles soon encouraged her to settle there. Under the auspices of the Echo Park Evangelistic Association, the temple was constructed, and the evangelistic association became responsible for the buildings and grounds.

To the temple were added the prayer tower (Feb. 1923); the radio station KFSG (Kall Four Square Gospel, Feb. 1924); a five-story building housing the Lighthouse of International Foursquare Evangelism (L.I.F.E.) Bible College (Jan. 1926), founded in Mar. 1923 to train pastors, evangelists, and missionaries; a denominational bookstore, Ye Foursquare Book Shoppe (1927); and the Angelus Temple Commissary (Sept. 1927). Students who graduated from L.I.F.E. formed branch churches referred to as Foursquare Gospel Lighthouses. By 1927 it was clear that a new corporation was needed, and in December it was formally incorporated as the Church of the Foursquare Gospel.

Aimee Semple McPherson served as founder and president of the organization until her death on Sept. 27, 1944. During her lifetime, Angelus Temple continued to function as the centerpiece of the denomination while it gained nationwide prominence. From its pulpit the gospel was proclaimed by McPherson as many as 21 times weekly. She was also actively involved in local community causes, and during the Depression more than 1.5 million needy individuals were helped through the temple commissary. The constant drain on the financial resources of Angelus Temple to meet the needs of the ministry, especially of the commissary, led to a severe financial crisis in the mid 1930s. The help of ▸Giles N. Knight was solicited, and by the end of the 1930s the movement was financially sound and fully prepared to face the future.

During the 1920s and 1930s, the organization of the fellowship was carefully established. Sister McPherson was designated president for life, and a board of directors was brought into existence. It included John Goben, Mae Waldron Emmel, Harriet A. Jordan, Herman Reitz, T. A. Overgard, and James Abbott. A general supervisor and various supervisors were appointed to manage regional or district affairs. The board, the district supervisors, and five other individuals were elected from a missionary cabinet by the convention body at its annual meeting to serve in an advisory capacity to the president and board.

The doctrinal position of the ICFG is found in its declaration of faith, penned by its founder. It is Trinitarian with respect to the Godhead and progressive in its view of sanctification, exhorting the Foursquare faithful to "live and walk in the Spirit moment by moment, under the precious blood of the Lamb." On the baptism of the Holy Spirit, the Declaration of Faith teaches that "the believer may have every reason to expect His [the Spirit's] incoming to be after the same manner as that in . . . Bible days" and supports that position with references to John 14:16, 17; Acts 1:5, 8; 2:4; 8:17; 10:44–47; 19:6; and 1 Cor. 3:16. Little separates the doctrinal position of the ICFG from that of the Assemblies of God except for minor nuances.

At the time of Sister McPherson's death in 1944, ˒Rolf McPherson, her son, who for several years had carried administrative responsibilities alongside his mother, became president of the organization for life "unless or until he should desire to resign or retire." Aimee had left a legacy of more than 400 churches in North America; 200 mission stations; and 22,000 church members, more than 3,000 of whom had graduated from L.I.F.E. and received ministerial credentials. The presidency of "Doctor" McPherson, as Rolf is most often referred to, is one that has brought accelerated growth to the ICFG around the world. According to figures released in Jan. 1988, Foursquare had grown by the end of 1986 to include 1,250 churches in the U.S. and a total of 15,051 worldwide. It ministers in 59 countries, supporting 141 missionaries, and gives over 4.1 million dollars to missions annually. It claimed 383,774 new converts in 1986, bringing its total membership in the U.S. to 188,757, with a worldwide total membership of 1.1 million. Denominational assets rose to nearly $479 million.

Rolf McPherson's leadership has also been typified by action in which the ICFG has reached beyond itself and interacted with other pentecostals and the larger evangelical world in a positive way. During the 1940s, Rolf McPherson brought the ICFG into membership in the ˒Pentecostal Fellowship of North America and enrolled the denomination in the ˒Pentecostal World Conference. Howard P. Courtney played significant roles in both groups. Due to concerns that some evangelicals had regarding Foursquare, the ICFG was not among the first pentecostal groups to join the ˒National Association of Evangelicals (NAE). Yet in 1952 McPherson successfully led the fellowship into that association, where it has played an important role, especially through commission representation. Since joining the NAE, the ICFG has also taken membership in the National Religious Broadcasters.

The year 1987 was an important one for ICFG history. Rather than remaining in office for life, President McPherson announced his retirement. In a series of meetings that followed, John R. Holland was nominated and ratified as president-elect of the fellowship. In Feb. 1988 he moved into ICFG headquarters to work alongside McPherson until "Doctor" officially retired on May 31, 1988. Thus, Holland became president at that time, elected to a four-year term. For the first time since its founding, the ICFG is being led by someone outside the McPherson family. Holland has been a minister and/or supervisor in the ICFG both in the U.S. and Canada since 1953.

The future of the ICFG is a bright one, thanks to those who have led it to its present position. The movement shows particular vigor in California, Oregon, Washington, and the Great Lakes region, especially Illinois. It has proven itself to be innovative on the mission field and is among the fastest-growing denominations in the world, especially in Brazil, the Philippines, Colombia, and Nigeria. The ICFG supports nearly 60 Bible schools, and in North America L.I.F.E. Bible College has been joined by L.I.F.E. of Canada and L.I.F.E. Bible College East, Christiansburg, VA.

Foursquare continues with its long-held vision for helping the poor. Work in the commissary goes on unabated. The ICFG has also participated in disaster-relief programs all over the world, supported in large part by its women's organization, United Foursquare Women. It continues to recognize a significant role for women in ministry, with over 40% of its ministerial rolls consisting of women. It is also producing a number of vital churches. Among its best-known congregations is The Church on the Way in Van Nuys, CA, served by ˒Jack Hayford.

■ **Bibliography:** Articles of Incorporation and Bylaws of the International Church of the Foursquare Gospel (1985) ■ P. Damboriena, *Tongues as of Fire* (1969) ■ "'Doctor'—A Doer That Worketh," *Foursquare World Advance* (1988) ■ C. Duarte, "Historical Resume of the International Church of the Foursquare Gospel" (1979) ■ "80 Facts You Should Know Concerning the Decade of Destiny in the 1980s" (n.d.) ■ "Foursquare Gospel Church Joins N.A.E.," *United Evangelical Action* 11 (1952) ■ J. W. Hayford, *The Church on the Way* (1982) ■ "International Church of the Foursquare Gospel—A History of Spiritual Achievement," *Congressional Record-House* (Feb. 5, 1973), H 712 ■ A. S. McPherson, *Aimee* (1979) ■ idem, *The Story of My Life* (1973) ■ idem, *This Is That* (1919, 1921, 1923) ■ "Meet the Hollands," *Foursquare World Advance* 24 (1988) ■ J. Montgomery, *Fire in the Philippines* (rev. ed., 1975) ■ V. Synan, *The Twentieth-Century Pentecostal Explosion* (1987) ■ R. Williams, "The Selection of a President," *Foursquare World Advance* (1987), 21, 23.

■ C. M. Robeck Jr.

INTERNATIONAL CONVENTION OF FAITH CHURCHES AND MINISTERS Established in 1979, the Tulsa-based International Convention of Faith Churches and Ministers consists of more than 800 pastors and congregations committed to the word of faith (so-called "name it, claim it") teaching of its most prominent founding members: Doyle

Harrison; ˒Kenneth Hagin Sr.; ˒Kenneth Copeland; ˒Frederick K. C. Price; Norvel Hayes; ˒Charles Capps; Jerry J. Savelle; and ˒John H. Osteen. Dependent on ideas first promulgated by ˒E. W. Kenyon (1867–1948), they head large churches in Tulsa, Fort Worth, Houston, Los Angeles, and Cleveland, TN. All teach that the faithful can rightfully possess things from God after having publicly confessed them. Television ministries and publishing are principal means of spreading the message, dissemination of which has brought strong reactions from other charismatic leaders. The official organ is the *International Faith Report*. Papers issued by individual members—such as Hagin's *Word of Faith* (Tulsa), Price's *Ever Increasing Faith Messenger* (Los Angeles), and Copeland's *Believer's Voice of Victory* (Fort Worth)—and the Tulsa-based Harrison House, a book publishing firm founded in 1975, also serve the International Convention constituency. Schools serving the movement are the Rhema Bible Training Center (Tulsa, OK) and the Crenshaw Christian Center School of Ministry (Los Angeles).

■ **Bibliography:** C. E. Jones, *The Charismatic Movement: A Guide to the Study of Neo-Pentecostalism with an Emphasis on Anglo-American Sources* (1995) ■ C. Farah, *From the Pinnacle of the Temple* (1979) ■ J. G. Melton, *Encyclopedia of American Religions* (1987) ■ V. Synan, "Faith Formula Fuels Charismatic Controversy," *Christianity Today* 24 (Dec. 12, 1980). ■ C. E. Jones

INTERNATIONAL CORRESPONDENCE INSTITUTE See GLOBAL UNIVERSITY OF THE ASSEMBLIES OF GOD.

INTERNATIONAL EVANGELISM CRUSADES A fellowship that grants ministerial credentials, charters churches, and operates International Theological Seminary (ITS) in Northridge, CA. Frank E. Stranges, who attended North Central Bible College (˒Assemblies of God), founded International Evangelism Crusades (IEC) in 1959 and ITS in 1976. He is president of both and serves as pastor of a local church in Northridge, the IEC Christian Center. In 1967 Stranges founded the National Investigations Committee on Unidentified Flying Objects (NICUFO) and has published books on the subject. IEC's statement of faith is similar to that of other pentecostal groups. In 1999 IEC numbered 16,000 members and 2,000 credentialed ministers worldwide. In the U.S. the fellowship claims 2,400 members and 60 chartered churches. ITS operates with four academic sessions each year and has attracted 25 to 30 Korean students for each session.

■ **Bibliography:** IEC, ITS Catalog (1985) ■ IEC Newsletter (1986). ■ W. E Warner

INTERNATIONAL MINISTERIAL ASSOCIATION (IMA). A ˒Oneness ministerial and church fellowship organized in

1954 by W. E. Kidson and other ministers who withdrew from the ˒United Pentecostal Church and other Oneness bodies. In 1999 the association had 120 affiliated churches in the U.S. and 1,250 ministers worldwide. Paul W. Todd, Homosassa, FL, serves as chairman. Rick Van Hoose, Evansville, IN, a former chairman, is editor of the association's magazine, *Herald of Truth*. The headquarters for the group is in St. Louis. IMA is also affiliated with the Apostolic World Christian Fellowship, South Bend, IN.

■ **Bibliography:** IMA Constitution (1987). ■ W. E. Warner

INTERNATIONAL PENTECOSTAL-CHARISMATIC SCHOLARLY ASSOCIATIONS Six continents around the world have established at least one academic society committed to the study of the extended pentecostal family. The oldest such group is the ˒Society for Pentecostal Studies in North America. Occasional academic groups have been formed in connection with the ˒Pentecostal World Conference (PWC) since 1995, the ˒International Charismatic Consultation on World Evangelization (ICCOWE), sponsor of Brighton '91, and the ˒North American Renewal Service Committee (NARSC) at Orlando '95. A formal request to form a pentecostal group at the American Academy of Religion (AAR) was denied in 1984, while the Charismatic Themes in Luke-Acts Study Group currently meets in conjunction with the national meeting of the Evangelical Theological Society (ETS).

1. Africa.

Centre for Pentecostal and Charismatic Studies. The Association of Evangelicals of Africa is led by long-term general secretary Tukundoh Adeyemo, a charismatic from Nairobi, Kenya. Annual conferences address topics such as AIDS and the role of women in Africa. The group publishes a paper titled *Afroscope*. The Centre for Pentecostal and Charismatic Studies in Accra, Ghana, is maintained by E. Kingsley Larbi.

Pentecostal Theological Association of Southern Africa. Short-lived attempts to bring together pentecostal scholars in South Africa include the Society for Pentecostal Theology. Chaired by Willie J. Wessels on the faculty of the University of South Africa, this group produced in 1992 a journal titled *Pneumatikos*. The Relevant Pentecostals earlier published a significant document by the same name and a journal named *Azusa*. Chairs included Pravinand Maharaj and Japie Lapoorta. In June 1998 the Pentecostal Theological Association of Southern Africa was organized in Johannesburg. Mathew Clark, chair, announced an international conference early in 2000 and a newsletter. Dennis Erasmus serves as secretary with Christo van den Berg (publications), Francois Möller (ecumenism), and Pieter Grabe.

2. Asia.

Asia Charismatic Theological Association (ACTA). Birthed during the 15th ▸Pentecostal World Conference meeting in Singapore in 1989, an organizational meeting of the Asia Charismatic Theological Association (ACTA) was held in the home of Canon James Wong with ▸Vinson Synan as advisor. On Nov. 13–20, 1994, the Charismatic Fellowship of Asia gathered some 6,000 delegates from all over Asia at the Philippine International Convention Center in Manila, which changed the acronym to mean Christ for Asia Movement. ACTA held sessions hosted by the Asian Seminary of Christian Ministries a day before the general congress. The executive board for ACTA chosen at that time was Tissa Weerasingha, Canon James Wong, John Kayser, Miguel Alvarez, and Bambang H. Widjaja. As of 1998 this group is no longer active.

Asia Pacific Theological Association (APTA). Headed by Abraham Visca, the second conference was Sept. 20–23, 1993, in Hong Kong. Asia Pacific Theological Seminary (APTS) Press published *Spirit, Scripture and Theology: A Pentecostal Perspective* by Roger Stronstad.

The Theological Commission of the Asia Pacific Theological Association of the Assemblies of God held its First Annual Theological Forum at the Asia Pacific Theological Seminary, Feb. 4–6, 1997. The featured speaker was Vinson Synan. Others who delivered papers included Young-Hoon Lee, "Yoido Full Gospel Church and the Movement of the Spirit in Korea"; Wonsuk Ma, "First Waver Look at the Third Wave: Lower Level Power Encounter"; Paul W. Lewis, "Pneumatological Approach to Virtue Ethics."

The *Asian Journal of Pentecostal Studies* is sponsored by APTS and APTA. The first issue was released in 1997. All issues are available on the Internet. William M. Menzies, chancellor of APTS, serves as editor, while Wonsuk Ma, academic dean of APTS, serves as associate editor.

International Theological Conferences on Holy Spirit—Korea. The annual International Theological Conference on the Holy Spirit hosted by the International Theological Institute (ITI) of Yoido Full Gospel Church is a one-day affair where papers on selected themes from various theological traditions in Korea are presented. The 1997 theme was "Sanctification of a Christian in the Work of the Holy Spirit." The venue was Yonsei University of Seoul, and the featured speaker was Jerry Horner. Previous international speakers include ▸J. Rodman Williams and Harvey Cox. In 1999 this conference was held at the headquarters of the Yoido Full Gospel Church. The papers, most in Korean, are published each year by the ITI.

Conference of Pentecostal Theologians—India. This group held a conference May 21–23, 1998, at the New Life Bible College. Convener Paulson Pulikottil brought together papers on Asian theology, feminism, and pneumatology. The May 25–27, 1999, conference in Banglore on pentecostal hermeneutics, spirituality, and ethics was coordinated by M. Stephen. This group brought together many who had been part of the Pentecostal Society for Theological Studies led by Isaac V. Mathew.

Korean Pentecostal Society. This academic body was organized Oct. 31, 1997, and is led by Young-Hoon Lee. Publication of the *Journal of Korean Pentecostal Theology* started in 1998. It is published in Korean by the Han Sae Institute for Pentecostal Studies. The second meeting was held in conjunction with the Asian Pentecostal Society. Yeol Soo Eim, Samwhan Kim, and Samwhan Lee made presentations on behalf of the Korean Pentecostal Society.

Asian Pentecostal Society. The organizational meeting held during the 18th Pentecostal World Conference held Sept. 22–25, 1998, at the Yoido Full Gospel Church elected Wonsuk Ma as president, Miguel Alvarez as first vice president, Paulson Pulikottil as second vice president, and Yeol Soo Eim as secretary-treasurer.

The first annual meeting of the Asian Pentecostal Society converged with the second meeting of the Korean Pentecostal Society. The meeting was held May 21, 1999, at the Gospel Theological Seminary, Daejon City, Korea. Paper presenters include Wonsuk Ma, Miguel Alvarez, David Daniels, and Jean-Daniel Plüss in addition to three presenters from the Korean Pentecostal Society. The Gospel Theological Seminary started publication of a journal titled *The Spirit & Church* in Nov. 1999. The second meeting of the Asian Pentecostal Society was slated for Aug. 2000 at the Asian Seminary of Christian Ministries in Manila, Philippines.

3. Europe.

European Pentecostal and Charismatic Research Association (EPCRA). Organized by David Bundy and led by Jean-Daniel Plüss, the first meeting of the European Pentecostal and Charismatic Research Association was held in 1981 at the Catholic University of Louvain. Normally held in alternating years, the 1995 meeting was jointly held with the Society for Pentecostal Studies, and in 1997 it was joined with the ▸International Charismatic Consultation on World Evangelization (ICCOWE) and European Charismatic Consultation (ECC) conference and called Prague '97. The most frequently featured speaker at EPCRA meetings is Walter J. Hollenweger.

Papers published from these occasional conferences have been published in the Peter Lang series "Intercultural History of Christianity," edited by Jan A. B. Jongeneel, and in the *European Pentecostal Theological Association Bulletin*. Papers from the 1999 conference will be published in the series *Perspektiven der Weltmission*.

European Pentecostal Theological Association (EPTA). The European Pentecostal Theological Association (EPTA) has hosted annual conferences since 1978 and publishes the *Journal of the European Pentecostal Theological Association (JEPTA).* Although EPTA conferences have focused on Bible school administrators, in July 1998 the conference brought together Max Turner, James Dunn, and David Pawson to present papers on Spirit baptism.

Pentecostal and Charismatic Research Fellowship. On Dec. 7, 1996, the first annual conference of the Pentecostal and Charismatic Research Fellowship was held at Regents Theological College, U.K., under the leadership of Keith Warrington and Neil Hudson, both lecturers at the college. The title of the conference was "Pentecostal Paradigms," the invited speakers being Faith Forster, Nigel Wright, David Allen, Max Turner, and John Smyth.

4. Latin America.

Encuentro Pentecostal Latinoamericana (EPLA). In Oct. 1971 the "First Encounter" of Unidad Pentecostal Latinoamericana was celebrated in Buenos Aires, and in 1978 pentecostals met again in Oaxtepec, Mexico, responding to the convocation for the creation of a Latin American Assembly of Churches. Pentecostals participated massively in the founding of the Consejo Latinoamericano de Iglesias (CLAI). Three pentecostals were part of the first board of directors of CLAI—Gabriel Vaccaro, Enrique Chávez, and Roger Cabezas. Further encounters were held in 1978 in Venezuela and in 1979 in Colombia. From 1979 to 1983 Norberto Saracco led the Fraternidad de Pentecostales Latinoamericanos.

In Jan. 1988 Marta Palma, a member of the Iglesia Pentecostal de Chile and the Latin American secretary for the WCC's Commission on Inter-Church Aid, Refugee, and World Service (CICARWS), took the initiative to gather a number of pentecostals in Salvador, Brazil. These and subsequent conferences have been called together under the name Encuentro Pentecostal Latinoamericana (EPLA). Subsequent meetings convened in Indaiatuba, Brazil, then Havana, Cuba, followed by Buenos Aires, Argentina (1989); Santiago, Chile (1990); San Pablo, Brazil (1992); and again Cuba (1998). On Aug. 10–14, 1992, the 1er Encuentro de Mujeres Pentecostales was held in San José, Costa Rica.

The 1990 theme was *Libro Pentecostalismo y Liberacion.* Papers were edited by Carmelo Alvarez and published by DEI in Costa Rica under the title *Pentecostalismo y Liberacion.* Here the Comisión Evangélica Pentecostal Latinoamericana (CEPLA) was formed, which is led by Bishop Gamaliel Lugo of the Unión Evangélica Pentecostal Venezuela. A joint meeting with the Society for Pentecostal Studies (SPS) convened Nov. 11–13, 1993, in Guadalajara,

Mexico. Papers around the theme *Hasta los Fines de la Tierra* were distributed as bound copies together with SPS papers.

5. Oceania.

Association of Pentecostal and Charismatic Bible Colleges of Australasia (PCBC). The Association of Pentecostal and Charismatic Bible Colleges of Australasia (PCBC) has offered annual conferences led by Barry Chant since 1991. The papers of these conferences are published in the *PCBC Journal.* Since 1999 Southern Cross College has published the *Australasian Pentecostal Studies,* edited by Scott Stephens and Mark Hutchinson.

Fellowship for Pentecostal Studies in Aotearnoa, New Zealand. Warren Hight is secretary of this fledgling body.

■ **Bibliography:** C. Alvarez, ed., *Pentecostalismo y Liberacion: Una experiencia latinoamericana* (1992) ■ *Comisión Evangélica Pentecostal Latinoamerica: Proceso de Unidad y Cooperacion Pentecostal en America Latina, 1960–1992* (1992) ■ O. Ortega, "Ecumenism of the Spirit," in *In the Power of the Spirit: The Pentecostal Challenge to Historical Churches in Latin America,* ed. B. Smith and D. A. Smith (1996).
                                                      ■ H. D. Hunter

INTERNATIONAL PENTECOSTAL CHURCH OF CHRIST

(IPCC). A Wesleyan pentecostal organization that is the result of a 1976 amalgamation between the International Pentecostal Assemblies and the Pentecostal Church of Christ. The two groups trace their history to the early outpouring of the Holy Spirit in this century. The IPCC has its headquarters in London, OH.

1. International Pentecostal Assemblies.

Holiness preacher ►G. B. Cashwell went to Los Angeles in 1906 because he had heard about the ►Azusa Street revival. He returned to his North Carolina home baptized in the Spirit and eager to spread the message throughout the South. Many believed and also received the experience, including a group in Atlanta. A new pentecostal church was established there in the fall of 1907, and Cashwell founded a pentecostal paper, the *Bridegroom's Messenger.* Later the *Pentecostal Holiness Advocate* stated that Cashwell intended the paper "to take care of the Pentecostal work of the South" (Synan, 127). Mrs. E. A. Sexton became Cashwell's associate editor and later editor.

In 1919 Paul and Hattie Barth, who were pastors of the church in Atlanta, founded Beulah Heights Bible School. The Atlanta church and a few pentecostal churches in the Southeast founded the Association of Pentecostal Assemblies (APA) in 1921. An amalgamation took place in 1936 when the APA and the International Pentecostal Church joined forces, calling the new group the International Pentecostal Assemblies (IPA). The IPA continued publishing the

Bridegroom's Messenger and operating Beulah Heights. The first chairman of IPA was John W. Pitcher of Baltimore.

2. Pentecostal Church of Christ.

John Stroup, who was an elder in the Methodist Church in South Solon, OH, received the baptism in the Holy Spirit in 1908. He ministered in the Ohio Valley between 1913 and 1917, and in May 1917 he invited ministers and church representatives to meet at Advance (now Flatwoods), KY. There they organized the Pentecostal Church of Christ (PCC), with Stroup as the bishop.

For six years, beginning in 1928, two other groups were associated with the PCC. They were the United Pentecostal Association of Conneaut, OH, and the Full Gospel Pentecostal Church of Maryland. Both groups had withdrawn by 1934.

Beginning in 1923 the *Pentecostal Witness* was the official publication for the PCC. It consolidated with the *Bridegroom's Messenger* in 1974 when the trial merger began.

3. The Merger of IPA and PCC.

At a general conference in London, OH, Aug. 10, 1976, the two groups voted to merge and become the IPCC. Chester I. Miller, who served as PCC's general overseer, became the leader of the new organization. Clyde M. Hughes succeeded Miller as general overseer in 1990.

IPCC operates Beulah Heights College in Atlanta, GA. In 1999 IPCC reported 70 churches in the U.S., 163 ministers, and 5,311 members. Missionaries serve in several countries.

IPCC was a member of the old *Pentecostal Fellowship of North America and joined the *Pentecostal/Charismatic Churches of North America when it formed in 1994. Its statement of faith is similar to that of other Wesleyan pentecostal groups that belong to the Pentecostal/Charismatic Churches of North America.

■ **Bibliography:** The *Bridegroom's Messenger* and the *Pentecostal Witness* ■ Minutes of the IPCC (1984, 1985 supplement) ■ Statement of Faith of IPCC (n.d.) ■ V. Synan, *The Holiness-Pentecostal Movement in the United States* (1971).

■ W. E. Warner

INTERNATIONAL PENTECOSTAL COUNCIL A consultative body of pentecostal leaders, mostly European, that met four times during its short existence (1912–14). The council was formed during the Sunderland, England, convention at the end of May 1912. It had no formal membership, but the main European leaders who took the initiative in its formation invited visiting American leaders to participate (*J. H. King was a signatory to the May 1912 statement).

The council was formed "to protect this [pentecostal] work from wrong teaching, or false teachers." This concern found expression in its rejection of teachers claiming direct divine inspiration in a way that denied any need for discernment by fellow Christians (1912); in warning against itinerant teachers without credentials from other assemblies as well as repudiating a teaching on the "eunuch life" (1913); and in denouncing the placing of inspired divine messages on the same level as Holy Scripture (1914).

Probably more important than the warnings against deviations were two positive statements made by IPC, one on the "Baptism of the Holy Ghost and Fire" (May 1912) and "Declaration" (Dec. 1912). (A third declaration mostly sought to refute the anti-pentecostal allegations in *War on the Saints* by J. Penn-Lewis and E. Roberts [May 1913].)

The first statement was brief, manifesting a clear concern to issue a statement on the baptism of the Holy Ghost that all leaders could sign. It speaks of the baptism in terms of the Holy Spirit indwelling the believer in his fullness "and is always borne witness to by the fruit of the Spirit and the outward manifestation, so that we may receive the same gift as the disciples on the Day of Pentecost."

The concern for unity in the movement, especially championed by *A. A. Boddy and *T. B. Barratt, is clear in the Amsterdam Declaration of Dec. 1912: the "present outpouring … we consider to have been granted … in these last days … for the edifying and perfecting of the Body of Christ, and its preparation for the 'rapture.'" It also reflects the strong concern for holiness of life, emphasized by *Jonathan Paul, stating that there often has to be a progressive entrance into the fullness of blessing implied in this baptism. All true deepening is a work of the Holy Spirit and cannot be effected by "merely human or self-originated efforts."

The IPC witnesses to the unusually close fellowship and warm friendship existing among the first major European pentecostal leaders, especially Boddy, Barratt, Paul, and *Gerrit Polman. It is one of the tragedies of pentecostal history that this international communion was interrupted by the outbreak of WWI and never fully recovered.

■ **Bibliography:** *Confidence* (June and Dec. 1912; July 1913; June 1914) ■ C. van der Laan, "The Proceedings of the Leaders' Meetings (1908–1911) and of the International Pentecostal Council (1912–1914)," *EPTA Bulletin* 6 (3, 1987).

■ P. D. Hocken

INTERNATIONAL PENTECOSTAL HOLINESS CHURCH The International Pentecostal Holiness Church (IPHC) is one of the oldest and largest pentecostal denominations in the U.S. With roots in the 19th-century *Holiness movement, it was formed before the advent of the pentecostal movement. Directly influenced by the *Azusa Street revival, it was one of the first organized denominations to adopt a pentecostal statement of faith.

The roots of the church lie in the National Holiness Association movement with beginnings in Vineland, NJ, in 1867.

The western part of the church had its origins in the Iowa Holiness Association, which began in 1879, while the eastern part began its existence in 1896 as the North Carolina Holiness Association. The original impulse of these movements was the attempt to revive the Wesleyan experience of entire sanctification.

The present church represents the merger of three groups: the Fire-Baptized Holiness Church, the Holiness Church of North Carolina, and the Tabernacle Pentecostal Church. All three of these were Wesleyan groups that accepted the pentecostal revival after 1906.

1. The Fire-Baptized Holiness Church.

The oldest of the three groups was the ᐧFire-Baptized Holiness Church (FBHC), which was founded by ᐧBenjamin Hardin Irwin as the Iowa Fire-Baptized Holiness Association in Olmitz, IA, in 1895. Before entering the Baptist ministry, Irwin had practiced law in Lincoln, NE. After his conversion in 1879 he came under the ministry of preachers in the Iowa Holiness Association, becoming in his words, a "John Wesley Methodist." He soon joined the Wesleyan Methodist Church and began a ministry of tent evangelism featuring divine healing. After a study of Wesley and Wesley's colleague, John Fletcher, Irwin sought for and received an experience that Fletcher referred to as a "baptism of burning love." It then became Irwin's contention that after the "second blessing" of entire sanctification, there was a "third blessing" for all the sanctified, called the "baptism of fire."

This teaching set Irwin and his followers apart from the mainline Holiness leaders, who denounced it as the "third blessing heresy." In addition to the "fire" experience, Irwin required his people to follow OT dietary rules against eating pork and insisted on a strict dress code, which, in addition to the usual Holiness code for women's dress, forbade men to wear neckties. To detractors, Irwin's followers were called the "no ties, no hog-meat" people. Worship in fire-baptized meetings was characterized by shouting and dancing before the Lord.

By 1898 the Fire-Baptized movement had spread to eight states and two Canadian provinces. In August of that year, a national organization was established in Anderson, SC, with Irwin designated as general overseer for life. He also began the publication of a periodical called *Live Coals of Fire*. The church grew rapidly under the dynamic preaching of its founder until 1890 when Irwin resigned from the church after confessing to "open and gross sin." His young assistant, ᐧJoseph H. King, of Georgia took over the church and attempted to hold it together after Irwin's fall.

2. The Holiness Church of North Carolina.

The Holiness Church of North Carolina (HCNC) had its beginning in the same period under the leadership of ᐧAmbrose Blackman Crumpler, a North Carolina Methodist preacher who was sanctified under the ministry of Beverly

Carradine in 1890 while living in Missouri. In 1896 he moved back to North Carolina, determined to bring the Holiness movement to his native state. After organizing the North Carolina Holiness Association in Magnolia, NC, in 1897, he began a ministry of tent evangelism featuring sanctification and divine healing.

By 1898 Crumpler began to organize independent congregations to shepherd his converts, although he was still an ordained Methodist minister. The first church to bear the pentecostal Holiness name was organized in Goldsboro, NC, on Nov. 4, 1898. He also began publication of a periodical for the association known as *The Holiness Advocate*. His fiery preaching and disregard for church polity caused controversy among North Carolina Methodists.

In 1899 near Elizabeth City, NC, Crumpler was tried on charges of violating Rule 301 of the Methodist Discipline, which forbade evangelists to preach in a local parish without an invitation of the local pastor. Although he was acquitted, Crumpler decided to organize a separate denomination, which he called the Pentecostal Holiness Church of North Carolina (PHCNC). This transpired in Fayetteville in 1900. The PHCNC adopted a "discipline" based on the Holiness Church of Donelsonville, GA. Crumpler's new church was identical in doctrine and government to the Church of the Nazarene, which was forming at the same time.

In 1901 the church voted to drop the word *pentecostal* from its name. This was done because many members identified themselves as pentecostal rather than bearing the "reproach" of the word "Holiness." In this period the word *pentecostal* did not denote tongues speaking but was widely used as a synonym for the Holiness experience.

3. The Tabernacle Pentecostal Church.

The third group that ultimately merged to form the church was the Tabernacle Pentecostal Church (TPC), which began in South Carolina in 1898 under the leadership of ᐧNickles John Holmes. A Presbyterian pastor trained at the University of Edinburgh, Holmes had practiced law before entering the ministry. In 1896, while pastor of the Second Presbyterian Church of Greenville, SC, he traveled to Northfield, MA, where he accepted the second blessing teaching of D. L. Moody.

Due to pressure from the Enoree presbytery concerning his teachings on sanctification, Holmes left the Presbyterian Church in 1898 to found an independent congregation in Greenville as well as a Bible college on Parris Mountain outside the city. Other churches following his lead formed the Brewerton Presbyterian churches, mostly in South Carolina. These congregations later changed their name to TPC.

All three of these small Holiness groups joined the ranks of the pentecostal movement after 1906 under the ministry of ᐧGaston Barnabas Cashwell, a minister in Crumpler's

North Carolina church. Traveling to ʼAzusa Street in 1906, Cashwell returned to Dunn, NC, to open a pentecostal revival in December. By 1908 all three churches had accepted the pentecostal "initial evidence" teaching that glossolalia was the necessary first sign of the baptism in the Holy Spirit.

By the end of 1907 practically all the ministers of the three tiny denominations had not only received the tongues-attested baptism but had led their congregations to accept the new experience and teaching. King and Holmes quickly experienced glossolalia, but Crumpler refused to accept the new movement. In Jan. 1908, when it became apparent that his church had become pentecostal, Crumpler left the denomination he had founded and returned to the Methodist Church. In Jan. 1908, under Cashwell's leadership, the HCNC adopted a pentecostal article of faith requiring all ministers and members to accept the doctrine. In 1909 it changed its name to Pentecostal Holiness Church (PHC).

The FBHC also adopted a similar article in Apr. 1908, with the understanding that tongues was the reality that the church had been seeking under Irwin's "fire-baptism" teaching. Holmes and the school and churches under his influence also accepted the new teaching.

4. Mergers.

Now with similar doctrines and experiences, the leaders of the FBHC and the PHC began negotiations in 1909 to merge the two churches. Sentiment soon arose in favor of a merger, since both churches operated in the same territory and had shared fellowship for many years. On Jan. 31, 1911, the merger took place in the camp-meeting village of Falcon, NC. At the time of the merger, the FBHC was the larger of the two groups. Altogether the membership of the united churches was about 2,000.

In 1915, in the village of Canon, GA, the TPC merged with the PHC. Although the Holmes Bible and Missionary Institute did not join in the merger, the school became the major center for training pastors and missionaries for the church. By the 1940s Holmes Bible College became directly related to the church.

The theology of the church was typical of the Holiness pentecostal groups that represented the first wave of American pentecostalism. The church's teachings were distilled in its five "cardinal doctrines": justification by faith; sanctification as a second definite work of grace; the baptism in the Holy Spirit evidenced by speaking in tongues; divine healing in the atonement; and the imminent, premillennial second coming of Christ.

The government of the church reflected its Methodist roots. The highest governmental body was the general conference, which met quadrennially, while the licensing, ordination, and assigning of pastors was the province of the regional, annual conferences. In 1937 the general superintendent was given the honorary title of bishop. Beginning in the 1960s, the church moved toward a modified congregational polity in contrast to the centralized episcopacy that characterized the early years. In 1975 it changed its name to International Pentecostal Holiness Church.

5. Growth and Development.

In the years after the mergers, the church developed several institutions, mainly under the leadership of ʼGeorge Floyd Taylor, who served as general superintendent from 1913 to 1917. In 1917 Taylor inaugurated the official organ of the church, known as the *Pentecostal Holiness Advocate*, and in 1919 he became the founder and first president of the Franklin Springs Institute, located near Athens, GA. This in time developed into Emmanuel College, the first liberal arts college owned by the denomination. Also, in 1919 Taylor sold to the church his privately owned Sunday school literature business, which ultimately became known as Advocate Press.

The foreign missions program of the church began in 1909, when the first missionary was sent to Hong Kong, China. A second field was opened in India in 1910, while the first missionary to South Africa went out in 1913. Other fields were opened in South America by the 1930s.

The church suffered its only schism in 1920, when Watson Sorrow and Hugh Bowling, leaders in the Georgia Conference, objected to the general teaching in the church that the use of medicine or doctors was an admission of a lack of faith in divine healing. Those following Bowling and Sorrow left the denomination in 1921 to found the ʼCongregational Holiness Church, which accepted medicine as well as prayer. In time this church planted congregations in the southeastern U.S.

The IPHC grew slowly during the 1920s and 1930s under the longtime leadership of Joseph H. King, who served as head of the church from 1917 until his death in 1946 (with the exception of the years 1941–45, when Dan T. Muse served as chairman of the general board).

The church moved outward in the years following WWII. One influence in bringing pentecostals together was the healing-deliverance crusades of the era led by IPHC evangelist Oral Roberts. For the first time, pastors of the various pentecostal bodies cooperated in these crusades, becoming better acquainted with one another. Also, the exigencies of WWII had demonstrated the need for closer cooperation between the churches.

In 1943 the IPHC, along with several other sister pentecostal bodies, joined the ʼNational Association of Evangelicals (NAE) as charter members. Building on relationships created in the lobbies of the NAE, the IPHC became one of the founders of the ʼPentecostal Fellowship of North America (PFNA) when it was formed in Des Moines, IA, in 1948. After the ʼPentecostal World Conference (PWC) was formed in Zurich, Switzerland, in 1947, the church also played an active part in the triennial Pentecostal World Conferences that followed. A leader in building these relationships was ▸Bishop J. A. Synan, who headed the church from 1950 to 1969.

This spirit of pentecostal ecumenism also led the church to form affiliations with the Iglesia Metodista Pentecostal de Chile (MPC) in 1967 and the Igreja Metodista Wesleyana do Brasil in 1984. In the U.S., affiliations were also formed with the predominantly black Original United Holy Church in 1977 as well as with the Congregational Holiness and Pentecostal Freewill Baptist Churches in 1980.

The post–WWII era was also a period of tension within the church over the ministry of Oral Roberts, a member of the East Oklahoma Conference, who gained national prominence for his healing crusades after 1948. Roberts' opponents in the church included Paul F. Beacham, longtime president of Holmes Bible College, and H. T. Spence, editor of *The Advocate*. Roberts' friends were able to win acceptance for his ministry in the 1953 general conference when his friend Oscar Moore was elected bishop. Roberts also gained new respect and acceptance within the church after his positive reception at the Berlin Congress of 1966. The new Oral Roberts University, which opened in 1965, was staffed largely by IPHC people. Many of his friends in the church were puzzled when he left the denomination in 1969 to become a United Methodist.

Like most American classical pentecostal bodies, the church experienced mixed reactions to the charismatic movement in the traditional Christian churches after 1960. A leading voice encouraging fellowship with the charismatics was ▸Vinson Synan (son of Bishop J. A. Synan), who led the New Orleans Charismatic Congresses in 1986 and 1987.

The growth of the IPHC over the years was steady but not spectacular. The size of the church in the U.S. by decade was as follows: 1920: 6,000; 1930: 12,000; 1940: 22,000; 1950: 40,000; 1960: 53,000; 1970: 70,000; 1980: 110,000; 1990: 125,000; 1998: 170,000. With the accession of the Chilean and Brazilian churches, the worldwide statistics of the church soared in the 1960s and 1980s. By 1998 the world constituency of the church stood at 2.7 million members (including affiliates). By the end of the 1980s the church had missions work in 81 nations and had plans to expand into other areas of the world.

■ **Bibliography:** A. Beacham Jr., *A Brief History of the Pentecostal Holiness Church* (1983) ■ J. Campbell, *The Pentecostal Holiness Church, 1898–1948* (1951) ■ H. V. Synan, *The Old-Time Power: A History of the Pentecostal Holiness Church* (rev. ed., 1998).

■ H. V. Synan

INTERNATIONAL PENTECOSTAL PRESS ASSOCIATION (IPPA). Founded in 1967 by pentecostal journalists in cooperation with the ▸Pentecostal World Conference

(PWC). Member periodicals are not required to belong to the PWC but are to remain in sympathy with that organization's goals and statement of faith. Purposes include: to meet and encourage cooperation among members, to gather and disseminate information of the pentecostal movement, and to promote excellence in the journalistic profession. A general meeting of IPPA is conducted in association with the triennial meeting of the PWC. Continental chapters meet annually. IPPA publishes a quarterly newsletter and the *World Directory of Pentecostal Periodicals*. Scholarships are awarded to deserving students, with some preference given to Third World applicants.

■ **Bibliography:** IPPA Constitution and Bylaws (rev. 1976) ■ *Pentecost: International Report* (quarterly).   ■ W. E. Warner

INTERPRETATION OF TONGUES, GIFT OF The spiritual gift *(charisma)* by which one so endowed makes clear to the congregation the unintelligible utterance of one who has spoken in tongues. This gift, and not speaking in tongues as often stated, appears at the end of three lists of charismata (1 Cor. 12:10, 30; 14:26), not because it is least valued, but because of its necessarily close relation to glossolalia—which it follows immediately in all these places.

Interpretation *(hermeneia)* itself is a charismatic gift, no less extraordinary than any other charisma. The overall corrective pastoral advice given by Paul in 1 Cor. 12–14 calls for the elimination of uninterpreted glossolalia in the congregation (14:5). For this reason, those who speak in tongues should pray for the ability to interpret (v. 13). But a different person may interpret (v. 27). Since it can be determined if an interpreter is present (v. 28), this charisma may habitually reside with certain persons known for such ability. Not all are interpreters (12:30). Speakers in tongues should not exercise their gift but speak to themselves if no interpreter is present (14:28). Interpretation shares with prophecy the end result of an uplifting message that bears meaning for the whole congregation. Coupled with speaking in tongues, the double event gains a sign value when unbelievers are present (v. 22).

According to Acts 2:6–8, 11, the speaking in tongues that occurred on the first Christian Day of Pentecost was heard by the gathered Jewish pilgrims in their own native dialects. No interpretation was necessary, nor is any interpretation of tongues reported in Acts 10:46 or 19:6. Acts knows of no gift of interpretation. Both *interpretation* (in the sense of a charismatic gift) and *charisma* are Paul's words, not Luke's. Luke does use the *hermeneia* cluster of words in a noncharismatic sense, to indicate translation from one language to another, for example, "Tabitha (which, when translated, is Dorcas)" (Acts 9:36).

In the patristic and Reformation eras, interpretation was understood narrowly as "translation," because the Fathers and the Reformers generally understood speaking in tongues to mean using foreign languages, after the model of Acts 2. In the early pentecostal movement newly Spirit-baptized believers undertook overseas missionary ventures, convinced that speaking in tongues would be God's way of equipping them for that task without language study. Early pentecostal leader Charles F. Parham never relinquished that view of the purpose of glossolalia. By 1910 W. F. Carothers found it necessary to write an article cautioning his pentecostal peers against construing interpretation as a means of personal or group guidance. Classical pentecostal teachers over most of the 20th century have viewed interpretation as a rendering of the essence of the glossolalic utterance in the vernacular. Individual pentecostal teachers developed nuances: (1) expecting the interpretation to match in length or patterns of intonation the glossolalic utterance it translates; or (2) insisting that the interpretation must, like speaking in tongues, be addressed "to God" (1 Cor. 14:2) and therefore be a prayer (these might also teach that any interpretation that began, "Thus saith the Lord ..." was thereby out of order). But these views seem needlessly restrictive. Among the new charismatics, especially in Roman Catholic charismatic groups organized as communities, prophecy rather than "tongues and interpretation" prevails—with Pauline warrant.

Both social scientists and theologians have focused on glossolalia, surely the most studied charisma, to the neglect of interpretation. In the rare instances where speaking in tongues issued in the use of an identifiable language, interpretation expectedly would be translation. But the idea of *hermeneia* is broader, ranging from "speech" that expresses what is unclear, through "translation" that exchanges from one language to another, to "commentary" that explains or interprets" (Robinson, 1964). In all uses of the word the movement from obscurity or unintelligibility to clarity of expression prevails. Thiselton (1979), considering the way the word cluster "interpretation" is used by Philo and Josephus (near-contemporaries of Paul), concludes that the gift of interpretation means "to put into words, to say it articulately." He assumes that glossolalia is ecstatic speech. Behm (1964, 1:665) says that the gift of the interpretation of tongues consists in "the conversion of what is unintelligible into what is intelligible and therefore an explanation of the spiritual movement which fills the ecstatic."

It is not necessary to look for one-to-one correspondences between a glossolalic speech and its interpretation. It is enough to acknowledge that for the uplift of the gathered church the Holy Spirit who moves one to broken speech moves another (or the same one) to clarify what the Spirit says to the church at that time.

■ **Bibliography:** D. Basham, *A Handbook on Tongues, Interpretations and Prophecy* (1971) ■ J. Behm, " *hermeneia*, etc." *TDNT* 2:661–66 (NT word cluster for "interpretation") ■ E. Best, "The Interpretation of Tongues," *SJT* 28 (1975) (discusses what to make of glossolalia for today) ■ W. F. Carothers, "The Gift of Interpretation: Is It Intended to Be a Means of Guidance?" *LRE* (Chicago) (Oct. 1910) ■ D. G. Dunn, "The Responsible Congregation (1 Cor. 14:26–40)," in L. de Lorenzi, ed., *Charisma und Agape* (1983) ■ D. Gee, *Concerning Spiritual Gifts* (1949; repr. 1980) ■ W. Grudem, "A Response to G. Dautzenberg on 1 Cor. 12:10," *Biblische Zeitschrift* 22 (1978) (rejects Dunn's proposal that "discernment of spirits" should rather be translated "interpreting the revelations of the Spirit") ■ A. L. Hoy, "The Gift of Interpretation," *Paraclete* 3 (1969) (classical pentecostal view) ■ W. Peremans, "Les hermeneis dans l'Egypte greco-romaine," in G. Grimm, ed., *Das römisch-byzantinische Ägypten: Akten des internationalen Symposiums 26.–30. Sept. 1978 in Trier* (1983) ■ J. Robinson and H. B. Cobb, eds., *The New Hermeneutic* (1964) ■ A. C. Thiselton, "The 'Interpretation' of Tongues: A New Suggestion in the Light of Greek Usage in Philo and Josephus," *JTS* 30 (1979) ■ H. Weder, "Die Gabe der *hermeneia* (1 Cor. 12 und 14)," in H. F. Geisser and W. Mostert, eds., *Wirkungen hermeneutischer Theologie* (1983). ■ R. P. Spittler

IRISH, CHARLES MANNING (1929–). A leader in the charismatic movement within the Episcopal Church, and former national coordinator of Episcopal Renewal Ministries. A veteran of the Korean War, Irish was in business for 10 years prior to entering the ministry. He graduated from Bexley Hall Seminary to become vicar of St. Luke's Mission in Bath, OH, in 1969. Following a charismatic experience in 1970, Fr. Irish led St. Luke's, a small five-year-old congregation, into becoming a nationally known charismatic parish of 1,200. He attended the first Episcopal charismatic clergy conference in 1973 and two years later was recruited to the national board of the Episcopal Charismatic Fellowship. In 1978 he was elected its national coordinator and editor of *Acts 29*. Under the new name, Episcopal Renewal Ministries (a

Charles M. Irish, national coordinator of Episcopal Renewal Ministries, celebrating the Eucharist at the 1983 ERM National Priests' Conference.

name later changed to ˺Acts 29) headquarters were moved in 1986 to Fairfax, VA, where he directed the work full-time until 1992. He returned to St. Luke's, where he continues as an associate. He is the author of numerous articles and one book, *Back to the Upper Room* (1993). Theologically he teaches the baptism in the Holy Spirit as a definite experience subsequent to conversion. His leadership focuses on spiritual renewal in the historic churches, giving particular attention to the practical aspects of parish renewal and ministry of the laity.   ■ D. A. Reed

IRVING, EDWARD (1792–1834). Scottish-Presbyterian pastor, theologian, considered a founder of the ˺Catholic Apostolic Church, also known as Irvingites. Irving studied mathematics at the University of Edinburgh (ages 13–17). He taught briefly at Haddington and later at Kirkcaldy. Interest in theology persisted, and by following lectures at the university, Irving passed his theological examinations in 1815 and was licensed to preach by the presbytery of Kirkcaldy. In 1818, after difficulties in the parish, he returned to the university to study science and linguistics in anticipation of missionary service in Persia. However, he became the assistant to Dr. Thomas Chalmers at St. John's Glasgow (1819). After three difficult years, he was ordained in Annam Presbytery (1822) and became minister to a small congregation in London. In London he quickly achieved recognition and published a series of sermons, *For the Oracles of God, Four Orations; For Judgement to Come, an Argument in Nine Parts* (1823). The church became too small to accommodate the crowds, and a new church was built in Regent Square.

Influenced by the ideas of Samuel Taylor Coleridge and Thomas Carlyle, Irving became convinced that he was to function as a prophet and priest. His study of the biblical accounts of the early church persuaded him that since the fivefold offices of apostles, prophets, evangelists, pastors, and teachers had been abandoned, the Holy Spirit had, as a result, left the church to its own devices. This conviction was reinforced and provided with an interpretative key by the millenarian and apocalyptic views espoused by Henry Drummond (1786–1860), a wealthy banker with whom Irving became closely associated after 1825. A group for the study of spiritual concerns, sponsored by Drummond at Albury, his estate in Surrey, had a significant influence on Irving, who became its leader. In 1825 Irving preached on "Babylon," developing these ideas and predicting the end of the world. These sermons were published as *Babylon and Infidelity Foredoomed by God* (1826). He also published, with an extensive introduction, an apocalyptic treatise written by a Spanish Jesuit, M. Lacunza, *The Coming of the Messiah in Glory and Majesty* (1827), and a three-volume set of *Sermons, Lectures, and Occasional Discourses* (1828).

In the latter, along with his apocalyptic views, Irving began to publish his ideas on the liturgy and Christology. His apocalyptic dualism resulted in a view of the incarnation quite out of keeping with Presbyterian theology. At this time, prayer groups were established to seek a new outpouring of the Holy Spirit, and many were led, by Irving's assistant, Alexander Scott, to seek the charismata described in the NT as part of early Christian spirituality. Anticipation was increased during Irving's preaching tours to Scotland in 1828 and 1829. In early 1830, parishioners near Glasgow began to experience charismata, especially glossolalia, and understood these in light of Irving's analysis. A delegation from Albury was sent to investigate and concluded that the manifestations were indeed of divine origin.

The general presbytery of the London area called Irving to account for his christological views expressed in *The Orthodox and Catholic Doctrine of Christ's Human Nature* (1830). Meanwhile, the Albury groups began to experience glossolalia and prophetic utterances. By early 1831 many in Irving's church and other churches throughout Britain had begun to prophesy and speak in tongues. In Oct. 1831 the practice of these charismata had become part of the worship in Irving's church. He considered them to be of divine origin and revelatory. Irving was censured by the London Presbytery in 1832 for violating liturgical regulations by allowing women and men not properly ordained to speak in the services. He was expelled from his pulpit on Apr. 26, 1832, and led about 800 members from the Regent Street church to form the first congregation of what would become the Catholic Apostolic Church. Irving's status as a clergyman in the Church of Scotland was removed by the presbytery of Anna on Mar. 13, 1833. On returning to London, Irving found himself relegated to a minor role in his congregation because he himself had received no charismata.

As the form of the new church took shape, Irving was recognized as an "angel," while Drummond, Cardale, and Taplin were declared "apostles." It was a conscious decision to remove Irving from his position of leadership within the movement. The members in London were divided into seven churches. Finally, in an effort to further remove him from the center of power, Irving was sent by the "apostles" to Glasgow in 1834, where he died and was buried in the cathedral.

After Irving's death the development of the organization continued. In 1835 the collegium of apostles was brought to 12. Reshaping of the liturgy according to J. B. Cardale's understanding of early Christian practice resulted in the gradual assimilation of Roman Catholic and Orthodox liturgical elements and architecture. Prophecy became less functional, and after the publication of Cardale's *Prophesying and the Ministry of the Prophet in the Christian Church* (1868), it virtually ceased in British churches. In the Netherlands and Germany the tradition remained "enthusiastic" longer; under the leadership of T. Carlyle and other dissidents, continental apostles were chosen and the movement became indigenized as the Neu-Apostolische Gemeinde.

Irving and his church became important features of pentecostal historiography as historical precedents were sought for revivals with emphasis on the charismata, especially glossolalia. It is evident from early periodical articles that the Irving phenomenon became an interpretative grid by which pentecostal theologians came to understand and evaluate their own experience. This historiography has been continued by writers such as J. Nichol, *The Pentecostals* (1966); D. Gee, *Wind and Flame* (1967); V. Synan, *The Holiness-Pentecostal Movement* (1971); and J. Kuosmanen, *Heratyksen Historia* (1979). The best analysis of the significance of Irving for pentecostals is by D. Brandt-Bessire, *Aux sources de la spiritualité pentecôtiste* (1986).

See also WEST OF SCOTLAND REVIVAL.

■ Bibliography:

On Irving:

Works. E. Irving, *Collected Works*, 5 vols., ed. G. Carlyle (1864–65). **Dictionaries.** A. Algermissen, "Irving," *LThK* 5 (1960) ■ *Dictionary of National Biography* (1891–92), 10:489–93 ■ J. D. Douglas, "Irving, Edward," *NIDCC* (1974) ■ T. Kolde, "Irving, Edward," *NSHERK* (1910), 7:33–34 ■ *New Catholic Encyclopedia* (1967), 7:660 ■ *ODCC* (1957), 702. **Studies.** T. Carlyle, *Reminiscences* (1932) ■ A. Dallimore, *Forerunner of the Charismatic Movement: The Life of Edward Irving* (1983) ■ A. L. Drummond, *Edward Irving and His Circle* (1937) ■ W. Jones, *Biographical Sketch of Rev. Edward Irving* (1835) ■ D. Ker, *Observations on Mrs. Oliphant's Life of Edward Irving* (1863) ■ T. Kolde, *Edward Irving* (1901) ■ O. W. Oliphant, *The Life of Edward Irving, Illustrated by His Journals and Correspondence* (1862; 2d ed., 1865) ■ J. C. Root, *Edward Irving, Man, Preacher, Poet* (1912) ■ P. E. Shaw, *The Catholic Apostolic Church* (1946) ■ G. Strachen, *The Pentecostal Theology of Edward Irving* (1973). ■ H. C. Whitley, *Blinded Eagle* (1955).

On the Catholic Apostolic Church:

Dictionaries. K. Algermissen, "Katholisch-Apostolische Gemeinden," *LThK* 6 (1961): 73–74 ■ A. Humbert, "Irvingiens," *DThC* 7 (2, 1923): 2566–70 ■ T. Kolde, "Catholic Apostolic Church," *NSHERK* (1908) 2:457–59 ■ W. Lohff, "Irvingianismus," *LThK* 5 (1950): 771–72 ■ *ODCC* (1957), 251 ■ J. G. Simpson, "Irving and the Catholic Apostolic Church," *Encyclopedia of Religion and Ethics* (1914), 422–28 ■ T. C. F. Stunt, "Catholic Apostolic Church," *NIDCC* (1974), 203–4. **Studies.** D. Allen, "A Belated Bouquet: A Tribute to Edward Irving (1792–1834)," *Expository Times* 103 (1992) ■ idem, "Regent Square Revisited: Edward Irving—Precursor of the Pentecostal Movement," *JEPTA* 17 (1997) ■ idem, "The Significance of Edward Irving (1792–1834)," *Paraclete* 22 (1988) ■ S. J. Andrews, *God's Revelation of Himself to Men* (1886) ■ R. A. Davenport, *Albury Apostles* (1970) ■ D. Dorries, "Nineteenth Century British Christological Controversy, Centering upon Edward Irving's Doctrine of Christ's Human Nature" (diss., Edinburgh, 1987) ■ O. Eggenberger, *Die neuapostolische Gemeinde* (1953) ■ K. Kandtmann, *Die Neu-Irvingianer* (1907) ■ G. W. P. McFarlane, *Christ and the Spirit: The Doctrine of the Incarnation According to Edward Irving* (1996) ■ D. MacLeod, "The Doctrine of the Incarnation in Scottish Theology: Edward Irving," *Scottish Bulletin of Evangelical Theology* 9 (1991) ■ W. S. Merricks, "Edward Irving: The Forgotten Giant," *Evangelical Quarterly* 59 (1987) ■ E. Miller, *The History and Doctrines of Irvingism* (1878) ■ H. M. Prior, *My Experience of the Catholic Apostolic Church* (1880) ■ J. Purves, "The Interaction of Christology and Pneumatology in the Soteriology of Edward Irving," *Pneuma* 14 (1992) ■ J. Robert, *Catholiques-apostoliques et neo-apostoliques* (1960) ■ Kenneth W. Stevenson, "The Catholic Apostolic Church: Its History and Its Eucharist," *Studia Liturgica* 13 (1979) ■ A. Weber, *Die Katholisch-apostolischen Gemeinden* (1978). ■ **D. D. Bundy**

IRWIN, BENJAMIN HARDIN (b. 1854). Holiness preacher and church executive. Born near Mercer, MO. In 1863 the Irwin family moved to Tecumseh, NE, where Benjamin early acquired an interest in law. After becoming a lawyer, Irwin practiced law in Tecumseh until 1879, when he was converted in a Baptist church. He soon became a preacher and pastor in his local church.

By 1891 Irwin received a sanctification experience through the ministry of preachers in the Iowa Holiness Association. He then immersed himself in the writings of Wesley, Fletcher, and other Methodist leaders. Though he described himself as a "John Wesley Methodist," Irwin was especially impressed with John Fletcher's idea of a "baptism of burning love," which he felt came after the experience of entire sanctification.

From 1892 to 1895 Irwin served as a traveling evangelist in the Wesleyan Methodist church, holding meetings in Kansas, Nebraska, and Iowa. Many of his meetings were in Brethren in Christ congregations. His ministry was radically changed in 1895, when he experienced a "baptism of fire" in Enid, OK. In short order he began to teach a "third blessing" called "the fire" and began organizing ▶Fire-Baptized Holiness Associations (FBHA) where he went. The first one was organized in Iowa in 1895.

By 1896 Irwin was preaching tent revivals in Georgia, South Carolina, and Canada, organizing associations as he went. In Aug. 1898 he organized an international FBHA in Anderson, SC, with regional associations in eight states and two Canadian provinces. He also began publication of a periodical, *Live Coals of Fire*.

The teachings of the new church included a strict external holiness code as well as adherence to the dietary laws of the OT. Furthermore, he began to encourage his followers to seek further experiences that he called the baptisms of dynamite, lyddite, and oxidite. The mainstream of the Holiness movement, however, rejected his teachings as the "third blessing heresy."

In 1900 Irwin fell from the leadership of the church after confessing to "open and gross sin," after which leadership passed on to his young assistant, ˃Joseph H. King. In 1907–8 the church accepted pentecostalism and became one of the first denominations to teach officially the "initial evidence" theory of the baptism in the Holy Spirit.

In 1911 the major stream of the movement merged with the ˃Pentecostal Holiness Church (PHC) in Falcon, NC, to form the present PHC. The black members of the movement separated in 1908 under the leadership of ˃William E. Fuller and continue to this day as the ˃Fire-Baptized Holiness Church of God of the Americas.

Irwin's career after 1900 is largely unknown. Irwin's letters to the ˃Azusa Street paper, *Apostolic Faith*, indicate that he became a pentecostal after 1906.

See also HOLINESS MOVEMENT.

■ **Bibliography:** J. Campbell, *Pentecostal Holiness Church, 1898–1948* (1950) ■ M. Schrag, "The Spiritual Pilgrimage of the Reverend Benjamin Hardin Irwin," *Brethren in Christ History and Life* 4 (June 1, 1981): 3–29 ■ H. V. Synan, *Old-Time Power* (1998).

■ H. V. Synan

IRWIN, DAVID KENT (1931–84). Pentecostal missiologist-scholar. David Irwin was born in 1931 in Kansas City, MO. He married Myrtle Deborah Selness in 1952. They had three sons: Paul Maurice, Philip Wesley, and Daniel Kent. Irwin attended Central Bible College (Diploma in Theology, 1952); Southern California College (B.A., 1962); Chapman College (M.A. in Psychology and Counseling, 1974); the University of Missouri–Columbia (M.A. in Cultural Anthropology, 1981); and was working on a D.Miss. at the time of his death. An ordained Assemblies of God (AG) minister, Irwin pastored in Maryville, MO (1952–54); Clark, MO (1954–57); and Beaumont, CA (1957–59). In 1959 he became a missionary to Egypt, where he served as administration chaplain at the Assiut Orphanage until 1962. He joined the faculty of Malawi Bible Institute, Dedza, Malawi, in 1962, and became foreign-missions editor for the

Pentecostal missiologist-scholar David Irwin.

AG from 1970 to 1975. Irwin served as professor of cultural anthropology at the AG Theological Seminary from 1975 until his death.

As a scholar, Irwin was active in cross-cultural ethnographic studies, applied missiological strategies, and ecological/environmental photography. His greatest concern, however, was to minister to the Islamic world. As a result, he began the Center for Ministry to Muslims in 1982. In 1984 Irwin was tragically killed in an automobile accident. In his memory, his family, North Central Bible College, and the AG Division of Foreign Missions established an endowment fund that sponsors the David Irwin Chair of Islamic Studies in Minneapolis, MN.

■ **Bibliography:** *Dictionary of International Biography* 16 (1980), 388 ■ *International Who's Who of Intellectuals* 4 (1982), 543 ■ interview with Deborah Irwin, Nov. 9, 1998 ■ *Men of Achievement* 7 (1980), 292.

■ S. M. Burgess

ITALIAN PENTECOSTAL CHURCH OF CANADA Ministering to Italians in Canada, this small group originated in 1912 when several members of an Italian Presbyterian Church in Hamilton, Ont., formed a mission, Chiesa Cristiana Italiana Independente. The next year the mission became pentecostal after several members received the baptism in the Holy Spirit. Other Italian congregations sprang up in other cities as a result of the mission's evangelistic efforts. Early leaders of the Italian Pentecostal Church of Canada (IPCC) included Luigi Ippolito, Ferdinand Zaffato, and Giuseppe DiStaulo. Although the group had operated for more than 40 years, it did not apply for a provincial charter until 1958; it was granted the next year.

IPCC is closely associated with the ˃Pentecostal Assemblies of Canada, with identical beliefs, but has retained its identity to minister to Italians. The group is also associated with the ˃Christian Church of North America and the Assemblies of God of Italy and was a member of the ˃Pentecostal Fellowship of North America until the latter's demise. Headquarters are in Montreal. *Evangel Voice* is published every three months in Italian and English.

■ **Bibliography:** D. Ippolito, "Origin and History of the IPCC" (1986). ■ W. E. Warner

JACKSON, RAY, SR. (1903?–90). Pentecostal leader in New Zealand. Ray Jackson Sr. and his family were members of Bethel Temple, a large pentecostal church in Seattle, WA, led by W. H. Offiler. They were sent as "Bethel Temple" missionaries to Japan and Indonesia in the 1930s. Jackson briefly visited New Zealand in 1942 as part of an evacuation convoy back to the U.S. and returned three years later to work with the Pentecostal Church of New Zealand. His teachings, however, provoked a secession from that church the following year and laid the foundations for the movement that later evolved into the New Life Churches of New Zealand (NLCNZ). Jackson was also responsible for introducing the teachings of the ▸Latter Rain movement to N.Z. in 1948–49.

Following his shift to Australia in 1950, Jackson opened a Bible school in Sydney in 1952, and many of the early leaders of the NLCNZ came from this particular body of students. Jackson's connections with the NLCNZ became more tenuous after the mid 1950s. Nevertheless, his doctrinal emphasis and "Latter Rain" insistence on the autonomy of the local church remained characteristic of this movement. Jackson's churches in Australia (the Associated Mission Churches of Australia) were always a more sectarian group than their counterparts in N.Z. and failed to achieve any significant growth or influence.

■ **Bibliography:** B. Chant, *Heart of Fire* (1973) ■ B. Knowles, "For the Sake of the Name: A History of the 'New Life Churches' from 1942 to 1965" (thesis, U. of Otago, 1988) ■ idem, "Some Aspects of the History of the New Life Churches of New Zealand 1960–1990" (diss., U. of Otago, 1994) ■ R. M. Riss, *Latter Rain: The Latter Rain Movement of 1948 and the Mid-Twentieth-Century Evangelical Awakening* (1987).   ■ B. Knowles

JACOBS, CINDY (1951–). Teacher-intercessor. The daughter of a Southern Baptist pastor, raised in Texas, Cindy first heard God's call in 1960 and was a zealous Christian as a teenager. In 1973 she married Mike Jacobs; they have two children. In the early 1980s Cindy Jacobs heard God calling her to go to the nations. After she and her husband wrestled with this call, they were led to found Generals of Intercession (GI), an international ministry promoting intercession and spiritual warfare against demonic forces.

Cindy is president and Mike CEO of GI, which has moved its offices to Colorado Springs. Cindy has been organizing an army of prayer warriors, working closely with ▸C. Peter Wagner, ▸John Dawson, and Ed Silvoso. Her teaching and prayer ministry takes her to all continents; Latin America is a place of frequent outreach. She has become an international director of ▸Women's Aglow, a convener of the Spiritual Warfare Network, and is involved in the ▸AD 2000 Prayer Track as well as being on the board of directors for ▸March for Jesus USA. Cindy Jacobs' books include *Possessing the Gates of the Enemy* (1991) and *Voice of God and Women of Destiny* (1998).

■ **Bibliography:** A. Kiesling "The Lady Is a General" *Charisma* (3, 1994).   ■ P. D. Hocken

JACOBS, SAM G. (1938–). Leader in ▸Catholic charismatic renewal (CCR) in the U.S. and diocesan bishop. Born in Greenwood, MS, Jacobs was ordained priest for the diocese of Lafayette in 1964. He served as an associate pastor in Rayne, LA (1964–70), and as pastor/campus minister at McNeese State University Catholic parish (1970–81). During that time, Jacobs became the bishop's liaison for CCR in his diocese (1978) and a member of the National Advisory Committee for the CCR (1978). When the new diocese of Lake Charles was formed in 1981, he became a pastor at Big Lake, LA (1981–86), and then vocation director for the new diocese (1986–89). Jacobs was a member of the National Service Committee for CCR in 1982–93 and was its chair in 1987–93.

In 1989 Jacobs was named bishop of Alexandria-Shreveport, LA, the first leader in CCR in the U.S. to be made a diocesan bishop. He is chair of the U.S. bishops' ad hoc committee on the charismatic renewal (1992–).

          ■ P. D. Hocken

JAKES, THOMAS D., SR. (1957–). Charismatic televangelist, pastor, and prolific author. Born on June 9, 1957, in South Charleston, WV, T. D. Jakes graduated from Center Business College in 1972 and received the D.Min. degree in 1995. Raised as a Baptist, he was filled with the Holy Spirit in a storefront ▸Apostolic church. From 1976 to 1982 he was employed in business and industry. Meanwhile, in 1980, he became part-time pastor of Greater Emanuel Temple of Faith in Montgomery, WV, with 10 members. In 1982 he assumed the full-time pastorate of Greater Temple of Faith and began a local radio ministry, *The Master's Plan*. In 1983 Jakes held his first Bible conference.

In 1990 Jakes moved his ministry to South Charleston, WV. In 1992 he first preached his most popular sermon, "Woman, Thou Art Loosed," addressing hurting women. The following year, his first book, *Woman, Thou are Loosed,* was released, and he began a weekly television broadcast, *Get Ready with T. D. Jakes,* on Trinity Broadcasting Network

(TBN) and Black Entertainment Television (BET). Meanwhile, his congregation had grown to nearly 1,000 persons of all races. In 1995–96 Jakes hosted the nationally syndicated *Get Ready* program on radio.

In 1996 Jakes moved his own family and 50 other families from West Virginia to Dallas, TX, where he established The Potter's House. Within three years this multiracial, nondenominational church has grown to over 17,000 members. Jakes has addressed the evils of racism and the need to help outcasts assimilate into society. Within the Potter's House are programs for the homeless, prostitutes, the illiterate, drug and alcohol abusers, and those with AIDS. Jakes is host of *The Potter's House,* nationally broadcast four times weekly on TBN and BET. He is the author of 19 books. Jakes is married to Serita Ann Jamison (1981). They have three children: Cora, Sarah, and T. D. Jr.

■ **Bibliography:** K. Walker, "Thunder from Heaven," *Charisma* (1996). ■ S. M. Burgess; J. Zeigler

JARAMILLO, DIEGO (1933–). Major leader in the ▸Catholic charismatic renewal (CCR) in Latin America. A native of Colombia, Jaramillo joined the Eudist Congregation (Congregation of Jesus and Mary, founded by St. John Eudes in the 17th century) and was ordained a priest. He has served as a professor at the major seminaries of Cali and Bogota in Colombia and as rector of the Eudist seminary at Usaquén. He first came into contact with CCR in 1967, and in 1971 he was named associate director of El Minuto de Dios, a communitarian network of social and pastoral initiatives in Bogota. On the formation in 1973 of the Encuentro Carismatico Catolico Latin-Americano (ECCLA), the overall CCR meetings for Latin America, Jaramillo became its coordinator and soon became director of the CCR center in Bogota and editor of the Colombian CCR magazine *Fuego,* all housed by the El Minuto de Dios Community. He became a member of the ICCRO council in 1978 and was its president in 1987–90. ■ P. D. Hocken

JEFFREYS, GEORGE (1889–1962). Founder and leader of the Elim Foursquare Gospel Alliance (▸Elim Pentecostal Church). George Jeffreys, the sixth of eight sons of miner Thomas Jeffreys and his wife Kezia, was born in Nantyffylon, Maesteg, Wales, Feb. 28, 1889. The family belonged to the Welsh Independent (Congregational) church. Together with older brother ▸Stephen, George was converted Nov. 20, 1904, at Siloh Chapel, under the preaching of minister Glassnant Jones. George was working at the Co-operative Stores, and his brother Stephen was a coal miner. A sister, four brothers, and their father had all died. George was frail in health; he suffered from a speech impediment and showed the beginnings of facial paralysis.

When pentecostalism was introduced to Wales in early 1908, George and Stephen were opposed to the movement. However, Stephen's son, Edward, was baptized in the Spirit and spoke in tongues while on holiday, and uncle and father sought the experience. George was baptized by immersion in the Llynfi River in Apr. 1911. He was also baptized in the Spirit and healed. Joining a small group of pentecostals, he began preaching. In Sept. 1912 he applied to the ▸Pentecostal Missionary Union and was sent to Preston to train under ▸Thomas Myerscough. He was "set apart for the ministry by the Independent Apostolic Church known as Emmanuel Christ Church . . . , Maesteg, 13 November 1912."

In Jan. 1913 Stephen requested George's help in a mission he was conducting near Swansea. Following this success the brothers went on to mid-Wales and then to London before George was requested to return to Preston to complete his training. In May he was invited by ▸A. A. Boddy to speak at the Sunderland Convention. He stayed on to hold special meetings for the vicar. A visitor from Ireland who heard George preach invited him for meetings and enclosed the fare. Meetings were advertised in Monaghan, but when it was learned that Jeffreys was pentecostal, the owners of the hall canceled the booking. In Jan. 1915 George met a group of men in Monaghan, and they formed the Elim Evangelistic Band. George was left a sum of money in a will and was advised to register his group, which took the name Elim Pentecostal Alliance. He traveled extensively in Britain after establishing his first church in Belfast in 1916. Confining his church-building work to Ireland, he established his first English work in 1921. Joined by Stephen, he went to Grimsby and Hull before moving to London in 1922. In 1924 they spent five months in Canada and the U.S. On their return they were together for a time in London before Stephen went on his own. George then embarked on a sustained period of evangelistic activity lasting 10 years, until 1934. Everywhere there were huge crowds, dozens of healings, thousands of converts. From Plymouth to Dundee, from Swansea to Rochester, churches were established. The most successful crusade in Birmingham recorded 10,000 converts. Without support from other churches, usually with only a handful at the start, he went from place to place and within a short time established flourishing new churches.

George was not satisfied that he had found the right method of church government (though the rules were all made by him). He began to bring in one change after another. Setting up an annual ministerial conference in 1933, he constantly agitated for change. Finally, in 1939, after granting major concessions, the ministerial conference rejected his demands, and he resigned. He was asked to stay but finally resigned definitively in Nov. 1940 and founded the Bible-Pattern Church Fellowship in Nottingham. This was a congregational group, and for a time there was

George Jeffreys (left) and Stephen Jeffreys, founders of the Elim Pentecostal Church and considered England's greatest evangelists since Wesley and Whitefield.

considerable antagonism between the two groups. George himself was a sick man, and though he continued to hold campaign meetings, he was never again to achieve the success of former years.

Not only in Britain but in mainland Europe, Jeffreys was a great success. In Switzerland he had 14,000 converts (1934–36). He visited Sweden several times and was the chief preacher in the great European Pentecostal Conference in Stockholm in June 1939. From Holland in 1922 to France in 1950, his ministry was widely accepted. Though the later years left Jeffreys increasingly isolated, he was for 10 years the greatest evangelist produced in Britain since Whitefield or John Wesley. He died quietly among friends in his Clapham home on Jan. 26, 1962.

■ **Bibliography:** E. C. W. Boulton, *George Jeffreys—A Ministry of the Miraculous* (1928) ■ D. W. Cartwright, *The Great Evangelists* (1986) ■ A. W. Edsor, *George Jeffreys: Man of God* (1964) ■ W. J. Hollenweger, *The Pentecostals* (1972) ■ R. Landau, *God Is My Adventure* (1935) ■ Bryan J. Wilson, *Sects and Society* (1961).
                                        ■ D. W. Cartwright

JEFFREYS, STEPHEN (1876–1943). British pentecostal evangelist. Third of eight sons of miner Thomas Jeffreys and his wife, Kezia. He spent 24 years as a coal miner (1889–1912). Jeffreys was a member of Siloh Independent Chapel, Maesteg, Wales, where he played in the flute band; he was converted there on Nov. 20, 1904, during the height of the Welsh revival.

In 1898 Jeffreys married Elizabeth Lewis, daughter of Joseph Lewis, deacon at Siloh and a miner. They had three daughters and one son, Edward (1899–1974), founder of Bethel Evangelistic Society, who eventually became an Anglican minister. Stephen was a simple, lovable man who delighted in preaching. Without theological training and having only a few sermons, he was thrust into evangelistic work through the recommendation of his brother, ►George, who asked him to preach at Cwmtwrch near Swansea, Wales, in Oct. 1912. A further visit in December extended to a seven-week mission in which there were 130 converts in the small village. He had to telegraph his brother at the Preston Bible School to ask for his assistance. With very favorable coverage in *The Life of Faith* (a magazine, edited by Jessie Penn-Lewis and F. B. Meyer, which attempted to eradicate Holiness and pentecostal influences from Great Britain), Stephen left the mine. In response to many requests, the brothers went on to mid-Wales and from there to London for meetings. Later in 1913 Stephen preached in a Llanelly Baptist church and stayed on, accepting the pastorate of Island Place Mission.

In July 1914 a vision occurred while Jeffreys was preaching. The face of a lamb appeared on the wall of the mission and then changed to the face of the Man of Sorrows. Hundreds witnessed this vision. It was widely reported by the local press and created considerable interest. Stephen was frequently away, preaching, though remaining pastor there until 1920. Meetings in Dowlais were so successful that a building was rented and then purchased, and Stephen became pastor.

Joining his brother George's Elim Evangelistic Band, he still continued to preach wherever he could.

In 1924 Stephen went with George and three others on a five-month tour of Canada and the U.S. On their return he left Dowlais (Nov. 1924) and was engaged as a full-time evangelist in London. These arrangements were short-lived, and early in 1926 he went off independently. The newly formed Assemblies of God of Britain and Ireland (AGGBI) invited him to hold meetings, and for the next three years he traveled extensively in pioneering churches.

In Bedford, Bishop Auckland, Bury, Chesterfield, Doncaster, Dover, Manchester, Sunderland, and many other places, Jeffreys established or strengthened assemblies. Outstanding miracles were witnessed. People sometimes stood in line all night to obtain seats. At Sunderland mounted police were needed to control the crowds. Jeffreys' work dramatically changed the character of the AGGBI and its rate of growth. He established many churches and inspired others to do the same. By the middle of 1928 he became the object of a totally unjustified attack by a hostile section of the press; he ignored this and went on preaching. After meetings in Newcastle he left for the U.S., where he drew large crowds at Springfield, MO, and Los Angeles. From there he went on to New Zealand, where he remained until going on to Australia for a few meetings before visiting South Africa.

On Jeffreys's return his health began to deteriorate, and he became increasingly incapacitated. His wife died in 1941, and he went to live with his daughter May in Porthcawl, Wales. He lived his last eight years in quiet seclusion. He preached his last sermon a few weeks before his death on Nov. 17, 1943. He was indeed a beloved evangelist. In Bishop Auckland four brothers who were converted became ministers in the AGGBI. In Manchester ▸J. N. Parr left business to become a full-time pastor of his greatly enlarged congregation following Jeffreys's mission. Jeffreys was happy to move on to the next place and could not turn down any offer to preach.

See also WELSH REVIVAL.

■ **Bibliography:** A. Adams, *Stephen Jeffreys* (1928) ■ W. J. Adams, *Miracles of Today* (1927) ■ D. W. Cartwright, *The Great Evangelist* (1986) ■ E. Jeffreys, *Stephen Jeffreys—Beloved Evangelist* (1946) ■ C. Whittaker, *Seven Pentecostal Pioneers* (1983).
                                                                                    ■ D. W. Cartwright

JENKINS, LEROY (1935–). Tent evangelist and faith healer. Jenkins's ministry began with the spectacular healing of his almost completely severed arm in an ▸A. A. Allen tent meeting in Atlanta, GA, in May 1960. Jenkins recounts in his autobiography, *How I Met the Master* (n.d.), that he had run from a divine call his entire life and considered the accident that injured his arm to be divine judgment. Immediately following his healing Jenkins began to preach and pray

for the sick with what was considered to be great success. With the help of the business manager of the deceased Jack Coe, he was able to obtain Coe's 10,000-seat tent and to hold meetings with great success all over the country throughout the 1960s.

Although for a short period of time Jenkins attended a Presbyterian church, he was raised by his mother in a pentecostal atmosphere and declared himself to be "thoroughly Pentecostal in belief and doctrine." Jenkins's ministry was known for his "fantastic miracles," but they were not enough to keep him from trouble. Jenkins was divorced from his wife and was arrested several times in cases involving drugs and alcohol. Jenkins began a new phase by founding "The Church of the What's Happening Now" in Columbus, OH, in the early 1970s. Jenkins had moved completely away from his early pentecostal roots, but he still found a following for his unique brand of religion.   ■ J. R. Zeigler

JERNIGAN, JOHN C. (1900–1980). The fifth general overseer of the Church of God (CG, Cleveland, TN). A Tennessee native, Jernigan was converted in 1921, entered the CG Bible Training School, and began preaching before the year ended. He pastored churches in Tennessee, Texas, and Illinois before he was assigned to a state overseership in 1926. An effective administrator, he was elected general overseer in 1944, a position he held for four years. As general overseer he not only served his denomination but also helped organize the ▸Pentecostal Fellowship of North America (PFNA) in 1948. He was chairman of the constitution committee in 1948 and the first president of the PFNA (1948–50).

Jernigan published numerous sermon outlines and other books; among them are his autobiography, *From the Gambling Den to the Pulpit* (1927) and *Advice to Ministers* (1948).

■ **Bibliography:** Archives of the Church of God (Cleveland, TN) ■ C. W. Conn, *Like a Mighty Army: A History of the Church of God* (rev. ed., 1977).   ■ C. W. Conn

JESUS ONLY See ONENESS PENTECOSTALISM.

JEYARAJ, YESUDIAN (1929–). Prominent Indian AG leader who was born Jan. 15, 1929, in Colombo, Ceylon, to Kurubathan Yesudian and Thangama Jeyaraj. His father was employed by the British government and the Foreign Bible Society. Young Jeyaraj's early education came at Nazareth Christian School in Tirunelveli, Tamil Nadu State. With the rapidly expanding pentecostal work among the Tamils, Jeyaraj traveled with missionaries Robert and Doris Edwards as their interpreter. Meanwhile, he studied with the Berean Bible School through correspondence. In 1951–54 he attended Tamil Bible College in Madurai, where he later became a teacher.

Yesudian Jeyaraj, elected the first general superintendent of the General Council of the AG in India.

In 1952 Jeyaraj married Rajamma Matthew (1929–91). They had five children. Jeyaraj became a pentecostal minister in 1949 and was ordained by the AG in 1957. In 1955 he moved to Shencottah (Sengottai), where he pastored. In 1956 an industrial school was begun in Shencottah, training young men and women in technical skills. To date more than 2,500 have graduated.

Jeyaraj became Tamil District Secretary in 1957 and subsequently served as general superintendent of South India AG (1958–61, 1962–98). During this time of administrative work, he helped to develop and oversee more than 800 churches in Tamil Nadu, as well as to found Trinity Bible School for women in Shencottah, two high schools, five elementary schools, and two matriculation schools. In 1995 Jeyaraj was elected the first general superintendent of the General Council of the Assemblies of God of India.

■ **Bibliography:** D. Edwards, *Good Fight* (n.d.) ▪ J. Kruger, *To Light a Candle* (n.d.).   ■ H. V. Sullivan

JOHN XXIII See VATICAN II.

JOHN PAUL II AND THE CATHOLIC CHARISMATIC RENEWAL

When Pope John Paul II assumed the chair of St. Peter in 1978, he inherited a Catholic charismatic movement that had grown rapidly since its beginnings in the late 1960s. The hierarchy had initiated a process of bringing the movement under greater institutional control years earlier by actively encouraging clerical participation and appointing formal liaisons in most dioceses to facilitate communication between charismatics and bishops. By 1975 Pope Paul VI had endorsed the movement and appointed Belgian Cardinal ▸Léon-Joseph Suenens to oversee its development. Essentially, the magisterium had adopted a spirit of openness to the charismatic movement, which Catholics prefer to call a "renewal."

John Paul II did not deviate significantly from his predecessor's handling of the Catholic charismatic renewal (CCR). In Dec. 1978 he formally asked Cardinal Suenens to continue guiding the CCR as the episcopal advisor to the International Catholic Charismatic Renewal Office (ICCRO). Suenens continued in this role until his resignation in 1982, when John Paul appointed the vice president of the Pontifical Council for the Laity, Bishop Paul Cordes (now archbishop), to oversee the CCR. While Cordes did not personally identify with the CCR to the degree that Suenens had, he proved a strong advocate for the movement and continued to ingratiate the CCR to the Holy See in the years that followed.

During his pontificate, John Paul II has taken several steps, both symbolic and substantive, to illustrate his support for the CCR. A meeting with leaders of the ICCRO in Dec. 1979 was the first of many regular appointments that the international leaders were to have with the pope. It was John Paul's own initiative that brought the headquarters of the ICCRO from Brussels to Rome, symbolizing its close connections to the heart of the church's mission. In 1993, after eight years of consultation, the ICCRO was officially recognized by the Vatican and changed its name to the ▸International Catholic Charismatic Renewal Services (ICCRS). Also, John Paul selected a charismatic priest, Fr. ▸Raniero Cantalamessa O.F.M.Cap., to be the official preacher to the papal household. Finally, in Nov. 1995 the Pontifical Council for the Laity officially recognized the ▸Catholic Fraternity of Covenant Communities and Fellowships, an international organization of Catholics belonging to ecumenical charismatic communities. This recognition, John Paul said in a message to Catholic charismatics on Nov. 9, 1996, was an expression of the church's "appreciation for the Fraternity's goals and methods" while also serving as a means of strengthening the Fraternity's "ecclesial identity."

In the same 1996 message, John Paul II alluded to a document being prepared by the Pontifical Council for the Laity that would further articulate the role of charismatics in the church and identify the marks of authentic gifts of the Spirit. Drafts of this document were made, but disagreements regarding revisions made by the Congregation for the Doctrine of the Faith led to its being pulled by Archbishop Cordes. The document to which John Paul referred in 1996 has not been officially released.

Much of John Paul II's enthusiasm for the CCR stems from the role the Holy Spirit has played in his own spirituality. As a schoolboy, his father taught John Paul the Prayer of the Holy Spirit, and he has recited it daily since then (Ranaghan, 7). His 1986 encyclical, *Dominum et Vivificantem: On the Holy Spirit in the Life of the Church and the World*, exemplified his recognition of the Spirit's centrality to the church. Furthermore, he has addressed the topic of charisms multiple times in his Wednesday audiences and on other occasions throughout his pontificate. At the June 14, 2000, general audience, John Paul quoted from the Report of the Third Five Years (1985–89) of Catholic-Pentecostal Dialogue: "Koinonia is the work of God and has a markedly Trinitarian character. Initiation in the Trinitarian koinonia has its point of departure in Baptism, by means of faith, through Christ, in the Spirit. The means that the Spirit has given to sustain koinonia are the Word, the minister, the sacraments, and charisma" (par. 31).

John Paul II's support for the CCR, though strong, has been tempered by his realization of the potential challenges to magisterial authority that come with laypeople feeling empowered by the Holy Spirit. Thus, in nearly all of his statements regarding the CCR, John Paul refers to the necessity of maintaining unity with the church, guarding against

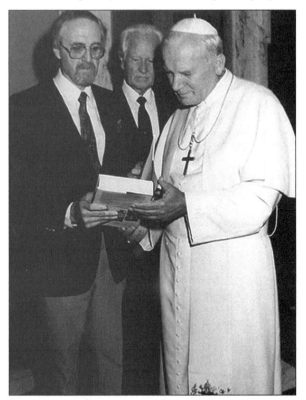

Pope John Paul II receiving a copy of the original *Dictionary of Pentecostal and Charismatic Movements* from Jerry Sandidge. In the background is the Rev. Justus du Plessis.

fideism, having an active parish life, as well as recognizing the need for charisms to benefit the whole church. His 1988 Apostolic Exhortation to the laity, *Christifideles Laici*, made explicit that "no charism dispenses a person from reference and submission to the Pastors of the Church" (ch. 2, par. 24). In no area has the pope felt the need to reiterate this more than with regard to ecumenical dialogue. While the ecumenical nature of the CCR has been judged by John Paul to be more blessing than curse, all calls for Catholic charismatic participation in dialogue with both ⁁neo-pentecostals and classical pentecostals include the words *genuine* or *authentic* to describe such ecumenism. These words imply a steadfast Catholic commitment to the authority of the Holy See as the *sine qua non* of any ecumenical dialogue. [The *Declaration Dominus Iesus: On the Unicity and Salvific Universality of Jesus Christ and the Church*, written by Cardinal Ratzinger at the behest of John Paul II (2000), similarly appears to represent a cautionary delimiting of the extent to which the church can be allowed to engage in ecumenical dialogue—Ed.]

With few exceptions, John Paul II has not been disappointed by the CCR. Evangelization has been a central theme of his papacy, and the CCR has been vital to this mission. The renewal is credited with promoting increases in priestly vocations and lay activism. Charismatics have proven a force for theological conservatism, mirroring John Paul II's own tendencies, particularly in relation to birth control, abortion, and the role of women in the church (Csordas, 7). Devotion to Mary, often regarded as the first charismatic, has been a visible feature of the CCR, and many charismatics have been vocal in their support of John Paul's efforts to recognize Mary as coredemptrix. Moreover, though charismatic Catholicism and social activism are not mutually exclusive, the CCR's conservative flavor has made the movement an effective tool in John Paul II's struggle against liberation theology. Finally, with large numbers of Latino Catholics converting to evangelical and pentecostal forms of Protestantism, the CCR may provide the sense of spirituality that many Latino Catholics believe to be lacking in the Roman Catholic Church (Deck, 409–39). These are some of the reasons why John Paul II has been eager to promote the CCR.

See also CATHOLIC CHARISMATIC RENEWAL.

■ **Bibliography:** R. J. Bord and J. E. Faulkner, *The Catholic Charismatics: The Anatomy of a Modern Religious Movement* (1983) ▮ D. Cole, "Current Pentecostal/Ecumenical Tensions," *Ecumenical Trends* 24 (May 1995) ▮ P. J. Cordes, *Call to Holiness: Reflections on the Catholic Charismatic Renewal* (1997) ▮ T. J. Csordas, *Language, Charisma, and Creativity: The Ritual Life of a Religious Movement* (1997) ▮ A. F. Deck, "The Challenge of Evangelical/Pentecostal Christianity to Hispanic Catholicism," in J. P. Dolan and A. F. Deck, eds., *Hispanic Catholic Culture in the United States: Issues and Concerns* (1994) ▮ J. Duin, "At 25, Charismatics Hope They Can Renew

Their Renewal," *National Catholic Reporter* 28 (May 29, 1992) ▪ W. Levada, "The Charism of Cardinal Suenens," *Origins: CNS Documentary Service* 26 (June 20, 1996) ▪ J. Manney, "The People's Movement at Age 25," *New Covenant* 26 (July 1996) ▪ K. McDonnell, *Open the Windows: The Popes and Charismatic Renewal* (1989) ▪ idem, "The Death of Mythologies: The Classical Pentecostal/Roman Catholic Dialogue," *America* 172 (Mar. 25, 1995) ▪ M. McGuire, *Pentecostal Catholics: Power, Charisma, and Order in a Religious Movement* (1982) ▪ R. J. Pettey, *In His Footsteps: The Priest and the Catholic Charismatic Renewal* (1977) ▪ "Pope Encourages Catholic Charismatics," *The Tablet* 247 (Sept. 25, 1993) ▪ K. Ranaghan, "Appointment in Rome," *New Covenant* 9 (Mar. 1980).

▪ C. R. Prentiss

JOHNSON, BERNHARD, JR. (1931–95). Missionary to Brazil and evangelist. Bernhard Johnson Jr. was born in California and taken to Brazil (1940) by his parents, Rev. and Mrs. Bernhard Johnson Sr., who were Assemblies of God (AG) missionaries to Minas Gerais in Brazil for 20 years. His father was stoned many times for his testimony. Bernhard Jr., an American AG missionary for 38 years, obtained his training at Gammon Institute in Brazil and at Central Bible College in Springfield, MO. He married Doris in 1952. Their marriage produced one daughter and two sons. Johnson was ordained in 1954 and became a missionary to Brazil in 1957.

Johnson established a fivefold ministry: Good News crusades, biblical and theological education, Children of Brazil Outreach (COBO), media, and health care. Rom. 1:16 provided him with the emphasis on evangelism—"I am not ashamed of the gospel, because it is the power of God for the salvation of everyone who believes." He led 1.8 million people to Christ.

He was mainly known for his Good News crusades, which were accompanied by signs and wonders. A crusade lasted up to eight days and had a daily attendance of 1,500 to 200,000. This represented as much as 90% of the population of the city where the crusade was held. The people who accepted Christ at these crusades numbered between 305 and 13,500. Furthermore, between 12% and 72% of those who accepted Christ were established in churches a year later. Johnson conducted approximately eight crusades a year between 1967 and 1991. As a result of the Decade of Harvest, he directed roughly 13 crusades a year from 1991 until he died. Having conveyed the salvation message in 31 countries on six continents—South America, Europe, Asia, Africa, Australia, and North America—via crusades, his influence was global. Like his parents, Johnson had his life threatened due to testifying for Christ. A gunshot whizzed past his head during a crusade.

Although the crusades emphasized the salvation message, many people were baptized in the Spirit, healed, and/or delivered during the crusades. The blind and deaf were healed. Cripples carried their crutches and wheelchairs above their heads when they left some crusades. A woman dying of cancer and in a coma for 30 days was healed and living three and one-half years later. A lady had seven demons cast out of her and was still a strong Christian five and one-half years later. A middle-aged lady experienced a short leg growing 8 inches during a crusade.

Bernhard formed a crusade team of 25 Brazilians. Part of the team was responsible for six to eight months of preparatory work at each crusade site, which included conducting counselor training classes, establishing prayer groups, advertising, and distributing flyers. Some of the team followed up each crusade by organizing visitation of each new convert and distribution of literature. Thus, the team was at each crusade site from 8 to 12 months.

The biblical and theological education founded by Johnson in Brazil consisted of Brazil Extension School of Theology (BEST) in 1979, Brazil Advanced School of Theology (BAST) in 1982, Bible Institute of Campinas in 1984, Theological Graduate School of the AG in 1989, and Rio de Janeiro Pentecostal Bible Institute in 1993. BEST had a four-year program with 32 subjects taught in a cycle, one course at a time for 6 weeks each. The courses were taught by trained teachers at 365 church campuses. At Johnson's death, 14,200 students were enrolled in BEST. BEST graduated between 800 to 1,000 students each year. Each BEST student had to be actively engaged in ministry.

Children of Brazil Outreach (COBO) was founded in 1982. Initially, the program was started to meet the food, clothing, educational, dental, and medical needs of street children. The needs of 7,000 children have been met in 42 private schools established by COBO in 11 states of Brazil. The success of the private COBO schools in decreasing negative behavior was noted by the public schools. They asked COBO to teach Bible in the public schools. At Johnson's death, 96,000 children were being taught the Bible by 191 evangelical teachers in 230 public schools weekly. *The Children's Bible Reader,* containing a four-page weekly lesson for four years, had almost been completed in 1995 in order to facilitate this Bible education in the public schools. Kids Krusades became a part of the COBO program, with as many as 3,000 children accepting Christ at a crusade.

Other Bernhard Johnson Ministries included weekly national radio and TV programs (*Words of Life, Good News,* and *Bernhard Johnson Presents*); publication of Bernhard's book, *Divine Healing: A Touch from God;* and Health Care Ministries Clinics, which provided both physical and spiritual assistance.

After Johnson's death, his wife, Doris, and his third-generation missionary son, Terrence Bernhard Johnson, took over many of his responsibilities.

▪ **Bibliography:** B. Braithwaite, "Over 12,000 Saved in Bernhard Johnson Crusade in Rio," *PE* (Oct. 7, 1984) ▪ Division of Foreign

Missions of the Assemblies of God, "Call to Prayer: November Emphasis: Brazil," *Mountain Movers* (Oct. 1989) ∎ J. D. Douglas, *The Work of an Evangelist* (1984) ∎ "Focus on Bernhard Johnson," *Council Today* (Aug. 11, 1985) ∎ T. Gibbs, "Bernhard Johnson Presents," *PE* (Oct. 26, 1980) ∎ B. Johnson, "Good News Crusades and the Brazilian Revival," *Advance* 18 (Mar. 1982) ∎ idem, "'Reverend Johnson . . . What's Your Gimmick?'" *PE* (Apr. 14, 1974) ∎ idem, "The Stretcher Was Empty!" *Mountain Movers* 23 (1981) ∎ idem, "What Jesus Said Before He Left," *PE* (May 18, 1975) ∎ D. P. Johnson, "Boas Novas (Good News)," *PE* (July 2, 1967) ∎ S. Montgomery, "Missionary-Evangelist Reports 1,050 Accept Christ in Brazil," *PE* (Oct. 25, 1987) ∎ G. Royer, "Instruction for New Converts," *PE* (Oct. 26, 1980) ∎ L. Triplett, "The 'Best' Bible School Training in Latin America," *PE* (Sept. 17, 1978) ∎ P. C. Zintner, "Divine Healing: A Touch from God," *PE* (Oct. 27, 1996).
∎ E. B. Robinson

JOHNSON, JOSEPH J. (1943–). Leader of the Lutheran renewal. Johnson received the empowering of the Holy Spirit in 1962 at the age of 19 while he was a student at Concordia College. Lutheran evangelist ˃Herbert Mjorud prayed for him, and he received the gift of tongues. He started a charismatic prayer group in which he prayed for other students to be filled with the Spirit and to begin prophesying. Johnson served as an intern pastor in Oslo, Norway, 1968–70. He graduated from Luther Seminary in 1971 and received the D.Min. from Fuller Seminary in 1991.

Johnson has been senior pastor of a charismatic congregation, Grace Lutheran Church, Show Low, AZ, since 1978. In 1984–89 Johnson served on the board of the Association of Christian Therapists. He teaches at the Lutheran Renewal Conference as well as at many seminars in Lutheran churches in the United States, Canada, and Norway, emphasizing a healing ministry. He has been a member of the International Lutheran Renewal Board since 1989. ∎ P. Anderson

JONES, BRYN (1940–). Prominent leader in the ˃House Church Movement in Great Britain. Born near Swansea, Wales, the son of a miner, Jones was converted in 1957 and baptized in the Spirit one year later at a pentecostal church. He studied at the Bible College of Wales (1958–61) and then pioneered several churches in Guyana (1963–66). From 1968 on, Jones pastored an independent church in Bradford (U.K.). He received a vision for the "restoration" of the NT church and was one of a group of nondenominational leaders who covenanted together in 1972. After pastoring a church in St. Louis, MO, from 1978 to 1983, Jones became the leading apostle in the Harvestime network, later renamed Covenant Ministries International, originally based in Bradford but since 1991 located near Coventry. Jones has retained his restorationist emphasis, while this has been declining in other new church networks. He has also had a stronger emphasis

on social transformation, and in 1990 he obtained an M.A. in Peace Studies at Bradford University.

∎ **Bibliography:** B. Hewett, *Doing a New Thing?* (1995) ∎ A. Walker, *Restoring the Kingdom* (rev. ed., 1998).
∎ P. D. Hocken

JONES, CHARLES EDWIN (1932–). Librarian, archivist, bibliographer, and historian. Born in Kansas City, MO, Jones received his education at the Bethany-Peniel College (OK) and the Universities of Michigan (M.A.L.S., 1955) and Wisconsin (M.S., 1960; Ph.D., 1968). He has worked as librarian and archivist (Nazarene Theological Seminary, Park College, University of Michigan, and Brown University) and as professor of history (Houghton College).

Jones's dissertation, "Perfectionist Persuasion: A Social Profile of the National Holiness Movement within American Methodism, 1867–1936" (published in 1974 with the subtitle *The Holiness Movement and American Methodism, 1867–1936*), provides a backdrop for understanding the sociological and ecclesiological bases for the rise of the pentecostal movement. His bibliographical publications—*A Guide to the Study of the Holiness Movement* (1974), *A Guide to the Study of the Pentecostal Movement* (1983), and *Black Holiness: A Guide to the Study of Black Participation in Wesleyan Perfectionist and Glossolalic Pentecostal Movements* (1987)—have made significant contributions to the study of those movements. *The Charismatic Movement: A Guide to the Study of Neo-Pentecostalism with Emphasis on Anglo-American Sources* (2 vols., 1995) has pulled together a disparate literature and provided a scholarly base from which to study the tradition.

∎ **Bibliography:** C. E. Jones, *Perfectionist Persuasion: The Holiness Movement within American Methodism (1867–1936)* (1974) ∎ *Contemporary Authors* ∎ Library and Information Professionals *(1988).*
∎ D. D. Bundy

JONES, OZRO THURSTON, SR. (1891–1972). Pastor, evangelist, youth educator, bishop of Pennsylvania, and successor to Bishop ˃C. Mason as senior bishop of the ˃Church of God in Christ. He confessed salvation under the ministry of the late Elder Justus Bowe in 1912. In 1914 he was appointed as the first leader of the National Youth Department of the denomination. Through his profound preaching ministry he established several congregations in the Midwest and South, having conducted integrated revivals in Coffeeville, KS, as early as 1917. He held the distinction of being one of the five original bishops consecrated in 1933 by Bishop Mason and was the last to succumb. He is best remembered as a peerless and profound gospel preacher (he addressed the Pentecostal World Conference in Toronto in 1958), a pioneering educator of youth, a family-oriented

Christian with a godly character. He was married to Neanza Williams of St. Louis, MO, who bore him six children.

■ L. Lovett

JONES, THEA F. (1920–). Healing evangelist. The faith healing ministry of T. F. Jones was incorporated as Thea Jones Evangelistic Association in Cleveland, TN, in 1949. In 1954 Jones bought the Philadelphia Metropolitan Opera House and started a church. By the mid 1970s the church claimed membership of 6,000 with an inclusive membership of more than 22,000.

Jones's books include *Miracles, Signs and Wonders: Compiled from the Ecclesiastical History of Eusebius* (n.d.); *Mistakes of Satan* (n.d.); *What's in the Manger?* (n.d.); *Miracles in My Life* (n.d.); and *Mr. Jones Goes to Town* (n.d.).

■ **Bibliography:** C. E. Jones, *A Guide to the Study of the Pentecostal Movement* (1983). ■ S. Shemeth

JOYNER, RICK (1949–). Founder and executive director of Morning Star Publications and Ministries in Charlotte, NC. Originally from Raleigh, NC, he was born again of the Spirit in 1971. He was a professional pilot and business owner but had a vision in 1982 that resulted in the founding of Morning Star Publications in 1985; he entered full-time ministry in 1987. As a result of a three-part vision in 1987 and 1988, he authored *The Harvest* (1989). In 1988 he launched the *Morning Star Prophetic Newsletter,* and in 1991 he founded *Morning Star Journal.* In a Feb. 1989 feature article in the former, he related a vision he had regarding John Wimber and the Vineyard, according to which "something was going to be born out of the movement which was greater than anything I had ever prophetically seen before." By 1999 he had written 19 books and numerous articles.

■ **Bibliography:** R. Joyner, *The Call* (1999) ■ idem, *The Final Quest* (1996). ■ R. M. Riss

JUNGKUNTZ, THEODORE (1932–). Lutheran theologian and author. Jungkuntz is perhaps best known for giving strong theological direction to the Lutheran charismatic movement. He received a Th.D. from Erlangen University, once the leading center of confessional Lutheran theology in Germany. In 1968 he became involved in the charismatic movement while teaching theology at Valparaiso University in Indiana.

Jungkuntz articulated a theology that demonstrated the consistency of charismatic renewal with the Lutheran confessions. He authored several books and numerous articles dealing with the two themes of the Lutheran confessions and charismatic theology. He was a major contributor to *Welcome, Holy Spirit* (1987), a pastoral and theological perspective on

charismatic renewal, prepared by an international Lutheran charismatic theological consultation.

In 1984 Jungkuntz became pastor of Cross and Resurrection Lutheran Church, a congregation associated with the Word of God, an ecumenical Christian community in Ann Arbor, MI.

■ **Bibliography:** L. Christenson, ed., *Welcome, Holy Spirit* (1987) ■ T. Jungkuntz, *Confirmation and the Charismata* (1983) ■ idem, *Formulators of the Formula of Concord: Four Architects of Lutheran Unity* (1977) ■ idem, *A Lutheran Charismatic Catechism* (1979).

■ L. Christenson

JUNK, THOMAS (early 20th century). Twentieth-century evangelist and missionary. Earliest records place Junk at the ▸Azusa Street Mission early in the revival. A German-American, Junk and his wife accompanied ▸Florence Crawford and four others on an evangelistic tour of Oakland, CA, in Aug. 1906, moving north through Salem, OR, and into Seattle. There Junk reported moderate success in bringing the pentecostal revival. He established and preached at a small, racially integrated storefront pentecostal mission on Seventh Avenue in Seattle. ▸T. B. Barratt cites a testimony given by a young Jewish convert, Lewis Rudner, in *The Household of God,* that describes a service in which Thomas Junk and others recited a number of Scriptures and sang songs in Hebrew as a manifestation of the gift of tongues. As a result, the man was converted.

Toward the end of 1908 or the beginning of 1909 Mrs. Junk died. Thomas Junk went to Tsao-Hsien, Shantung, in northern China, where he served as a missionary for several years. His letters indicated that his ministry was focused on new-convert evangelism, punctuated with healings, miracles, and exorcisms. North China was frought with famine during his time there. He collected a following of deserted children and provided them with food, clothing, and the gospel. The Stone Church of Chicago and the Upper Room Mission in Los Angeles supported Junk's ministry in China.

■ **Bibliography:** *AF* 1 (3, 1906): 1, 3, 4 ■ 1 (4, 1906): 3 ■ 1 (5, 1907): 3 ■ T. B. Barratt, *In the Days of the Latter Rain* (rev. 1928; repr. 1985), 167–69 ■ *LRE* 2 (7, 1910): 12 ■ 2 (10, 1910): 14 ■ 3 (6, 1911): 14 ■ 3 (12, 1911): 12 ■ "Slow to Arrive," *Daily Oregon Statesman,* Salem, OR (Oct. 10, 1906) ■ *The Upper Room* 1 (6, 1910): 5 ■ 1 (10, 1910): 6 ■ 1 (11, 1910): 8 ■ 2 (3, 1910): 6, 8 ■ 2 (5, 1911): 5. ■ C. M. Robeck Jr.

JUSTER, DANIEL C. (1947–). Messianic Jewish leader and scholar. Juster has a B.A. in Philosophy of Religion from Wheaton College; a M.Div. from McCormick Seminary, Chicago, and a Th.D. from New Covenant International Seminary, New Zealand.

Ordained a Presbyterian minister, Juster was called in 1972 to pastor the first Hebrew Christian church in Chicago within the United Presbyterian Church. At that time, Juster was wrestling theologically with the relationship between Israel and the church, which led to his increasing identification with the messianic Jewish movement. In 1977 he was called to pastor Beth Messiah Congregation in Rockville, MD, the first messianic Jewish congregation in the greater Washington area. By this time Juster was convinced of the rightness of forming messianic congregations, maintaining a Jewish identity, and living a Jewish lifestyle. In 1979 he was instrumental in the formation of the ▸Union of Messianic Jewish Congregations, of which he became president (1979–86).

Juster has been one of the foremost scholars in the messianic Jewish movement and has authored numerous books, of which the most influential have been *Growing to Maturity: A Messianic Jewish Guide* (1982, 1985, 1987); *Israel, the Church and the Last Days* (with Keith Intrater; 1990); *Jewish Roots* (1995); and *The Irrevocable Calling* (1996). Juster is the founder of Messiah Biblical Institute and director of Tikkun Ministries, an organization dedicated to the restoration of Israel and the church. Tikkun Ministries has associated pastors and congregations in Israel, Brazil, and Korea.

■ **Bibliography:** D. A. Rausch, *Messianic Judaism* (1982).
                                                          ■ P. D. Hocken

K

KANSAS CITY CONFERENCE The first general ecumenical gathering of pentecostals and charismatics from the mainline denominations in North America took place July 20–24, 1977, in Kansas City, MO. Since most of the American denominational charismatic renewal groups conducted annual conferences, it was decided that all of them would meet together at the same time and place. The format called for a general conference that would safeguard the identity of the sponsoring groups while giving expression to a common unity of purpose in the plenary sessions. Denominational gatherings were held in the mornings in various locations around the city, and common workshops were offered in the afternoons. In the evenings all the separate groups came together as one in Arrowhead Stadium.

Kansas City was in reality a conference of conferences. The supporting groups included Catholic charismatics, Episcopalians, Baptists, Methodists, Presbyterians, Lutherans, pentecostals, Mennonites, messianic Jews, and persons from several nondenominational streams. Serving as chairman for the conference was ▸Kevin Ranaghan, a leader of the Roman Catholic People of Praise Community in South Bend, IN. One-half of all registrants were Roman Catholics.

The conference theme was "Jesus Is Lord," a phrase that summarized the basic doctrinal ground for the unprecedented unity and cooperation displayed in the meeting. This theme was stressed by the keynote speakers, which included ▸Bob Mumford, ▸Larry Christenson, Kevin Ranaghan, and James Forbes.

The most memorable prophecy given to the conference followed the refrain "Mourn and weep, for the body of my Son is broken." Many messages called for the reconciliation of the churches. Major churchmen who participated in the conference were Léon-Joseph Cardinal ▸Suenens, primate of Belgium and papal liaison to the Catholic charismatic renewal; Bishop ▸J. O. Patterson, presiding bishop of the Church of God in Christ; and ▸Thomas F. Zimmerman, general superintendent of the ▸Assemblies of God.

The conference followed the "three streams" approach, put forth by ▸Ralph Martin, that the major sources of the renewal consisted of (1) the classical pentecostal churches, (2) the mainline Protestant charismatic movements, and (3) the Catholic charismatic movement. Thus, the conference was organized around leadership representing these elements, with an executive committee made up of Ranaghan (Catholic), Christenson (Lutheran), and ▸Vinson Synan (pentecostal).

The larger planning committee was composed of leaders from the foregoing three streams. They were composed of: Ranaghan, Christenson, and Synan, along with ▸Nelson Litwiller (Mennonite), Carlton Spencer (pentecostal), ▸Brick Bradford (Presbyterian), Bob Hawn (Episcopalian), Roy Lamberth (Baptist), David Stern (messianic Jewish), ▸Howard Courtney (pentecostal), Ken Pagard (Baptist), and Robert Frost (nondenominational).

The Kansas City Conference was the largest ecumenical conference in the history of the nation, with some 50,000 registered for the sessions. The next decade saw the greatest growth of charismatics and pentecostals in North America and the world in the history of the movement. At the time of the Kansas City Conference there were an estimated 50 million pentecostals and charismatics in the world. By the time of the next ecumenical conference in New Orleans in 1987 that number had surpassed the 200 million mark.

The Kansas City Conference was important in that it demonstrated a unity never before seen in the pentecostal-charismatic movement. The songs and intense worship experienced in Kansas City spread rapidly to all sectors of the renewal around the world.

See also CHARISMATIC MOVEMENT.

■ **Bibliography:** D. Manual, *Like a Mighty River* (1977) ▍ V. Synan, *In the Latter Days* (1984). ■ H. V. Synan

KANSAS CITY FELLOWSHIP See KANSAS CITY PROPHETS.

KANSAS CITY PROPHETS The Kansas City prophets are a group of individuals that includes ▸Mike Bickle, Paul Cain, John Paul Jackson, and others associated with the Kansas City Fellowship (KCF; now Metro Christian Fellowship), in Kansas City, MO.

In 1982 Mike Bickle began a church in Kansas City, MO, after receiving a prophecy that he would "raise up a work that will touch the ends of the earth." The church grew rapidly, and a parachurch organization, Grace Ministries, which represented several men engaged in itinerant, prophetic ministries, was established in 1986.

Beginning in 1987 Paul Cain became one of the main spokesmen of the KCF, a church based on the ▸Latter Rain theology. Cain is seen by many supporters of today's renewal movements as a modern-day apostle or prophet. In the 1950s Cain traveled with and was influenced by ▸William Branham, whom he called "the greatest prophet that ever lived." He promotes Branham's Manifest Sons of God teachings, also known as Joel's Army, which has caused Al Dager, Hank Hanegraaff, and others to label this group as heretical.

In Jan. 1990 Ernest Gruen, a charismatic pastor in Kansas City for 27 years, released a 233-page document listing erroneous prophecies and teachings of the Kansas City prophets. To combat these accusations, ►John Wimber stepped in, offering himself and the ►Vineyard Movement as a "covering" to the KCF and the prophets. Wimber said that he would deal with any errors that might have originated from the KCF. One of these was a lack of accountability for prophecies. Bob Jones, one of the group's foremost prophets, was removed from public ministry on the basis of various charges. Wimber also expressed a great respect for Cain and acknowledged that Cain was a gifted prophet. Since that time Paul Cain has prophesied that an earthshaking outpouring of revival will occur in the last days, which will include mass healings of Christians.

The church split with the Vineyard in 1996 after the Vineyard and the Toronto Airport Church parted ways. It is currently known as the Metro Christian Fellowship (MCF). The Kansas City prophets continue to promote Latter Rain teachings and are deeply involved in the ►Toronto Blessing Movement, where many of their prophecies are promoted. Prophetic messages and powerful manifestations are evident in their meetings. Paul Cain and ►Rick Joyner together produce *The Morning Star Prophetic Bulletin*, which reports on their activities. MCF also manages a Bible training center, a Christian school, and various outreach ministries.

■ **Bibliography:** A. Dagger, "The Restoration of Apostles and Prophets and the Kansas City–Vineyard Connection," *Media Spotlight* (1990) ▮ J. L. Grady, "Kansas City Churches Mend Rift," *Charisma* (Sept. 1995) ▮ M. Maudlin, "Seers in the Heartland," *Christianity Today* (Jan. 14, 1991) ▮ D. Pytches, *Some Said It Thundered* (1991) .   ■ G. W. Gohr

KASEMAN, JIM (1943–). Pastor, evangelist, and founder of the ►Association of Faith Churches and Ministries. Although successful by human standards—a college graduate and officer in the Army National Guard, married, and the father of five children—it was not until after Jim Kaseman was "born again" at a small Bible study in 1972 that he was delivered from the torment of his alcoholism and his frequent thoughts of suicide. In 1975 Kaseman answered a small ad in a magazine and soon enrolled in the first class of Rhema Bible Training Center in Tulsa, OK. After graduating from Rhema, he moved to Willmar, MN, where he pastored a small church. Eight months into his pastorate he felt the Lord leading him into a traveling ministry, and by 1979 Kaseman had helped found 27 churches in North and South Dakota and Minnesota. Then, through a remarkable set of circumstances, Kaseman found himself invited to Finland to spread the message of faith. In 1978 he founded the Association of Faith Churches and Ministries. In 1982 God spoke to him to translate 27 books by ►Kenneth E. Hagin Sr. into the Russ-

ian language. By 1988 over a million books had been translated, printed, and smuggled into the Soviet Union for distribution. In 1998 Kaseman started a church and training center in Calgary, Alb., Canada.

■ **Bibliography:** J. Kaseman, *The Jim Kaseman Story* (1983).
          ■ J. R. Zeigler

KAYEMBE, MICHEL (c. 1945–). Kayembe wa Dikonda, or Kayemba Michel as he is known to all, trained in law at the National University of Congo/Zaire, Kinshasa Campus, but after his studies was sent to Manono in Shaba as the managing director of a tin mine, Zaïre Etain. During this time, ►Ronald Monot was church planting in the area and led Kayembe to Christ. The latter was filled with the Holy Spirit and, after he moved to Lubumbashi, became an elder at Viens et Vois.

In 1985 Kayembe moved to Kinshasa for business purposes. Through contacts he became aware of the work of the ►Full Gospel Business Men's Fellowship International (FGBMFI) and within a short time began to plant chapters in Zaire/Congo. His influence in business and political circles is such that Kayembe gains audience with governors and members of Parliament. Many non-Christian businessmen and politicians have become Christians as a result of this outreach.

Kayembe is a favorite speaker at Full Gospel functions throughout the Francophone region of Central Africa, of which he is now overseer. Since he started working with FGBMFI in 1985, there is hardly a city of any size in the Congo/Kinshasa that does not have a chapter. He has also been responsible for planting chapters in adjoining countries. Kayembe is a man of great Christian integrity and zeal; during his leadership he has had opportunity to witness to the late President Mobutu Sese Seko.

■ **Bibliography:** *Contact Zaire*, pub. of the Zaire Evangelistic Mission ▮ D. J. Garrard, unpub. priv. papers.   ■ D. J. Garrard

KELLAR, NANCY (1940–). Teacher and leader in the ►Catholic charismatic renewal (CCR). Born and raised in Manhattan, NY, Nancy Kellar joined the Sisters of Charity in 1960 and became actively involved in CCR in 1970. With Fr. Jim Ferry she founded the first House of Prayer in CCR at Convent Station, NJ, in 1971. In 1975 she founded, with Sr. Marjorie Walsh, a charismatic prayer house at Scarsdale, NY. Serving as a "Traveling Timothy" for the ►National Service Committee (NSC), she became a popular teacher in the movement.

A member of the NSC from 1984 to 1994, Kellar was elected the North American representative on the ►ICCRO Council in 1992. In 1995 Kellar became the first woman to serve as director of the ICCRS office in Rome, opening up her teaching ministry worldwide. In 1996 ICCRS divided the director's responsibilities in Rome, freeing Kellar for a new position of service coordinator of the ICCRS teaching ministry. She now pursues this teaching and networking role from her original base in New York State. She has been a member of the ▸North American Renewal Service Committee since 1985 and vice chair since 1993.

■ P. D. Hocken

KELLER, OTTO C. (1888–1942) and **MARIAN (WELLER)** (1889–1953). Missionaries to Tanzania and Kenya. A Canadian from Parry Sound, Ont., Marian Weller was raised in the Church of England. She graduated from the Normal Training School and began her career as a schoolteacher. After attending some evangelistic meetings, she made a renewed commitment to God and was baptized by immersion. Later, in 1909, she received the baptism of the Holy Spirit and began to feel a call to missionary service. Soon afterward Rev. Robert J. Craig recommended she attend the Rochester (NY) Bible Training School before going into missionary work. While attending the school, Marian met and married her first husband, Karl Wittick, a Baptist minister and fellow student.

The Witticks left for Tanganyika (Tanzania) in Oct. 1913 as independent pentecostal missionaries. After three months on the field, Karl died from poison in their water supply. Marian also became ill from the water, but she recovered and remained on the field to supervise the building of a mission in Tanganyika.

In 1914 Marian was joined by several workers, including Otto C. Keller, an American pentecostal missionary. Marian and Otto were married in 1918 and began a work together in British East Africa (Kenya). In 1924, to receive government recognition for their mission, the Kellers needed the backing of a chartered organization. They gained affiliation with the ▸Pentecostal Assemblies of Canada (PAOC), and over the next two decades several missionaries from Canada joined them in their work. Their missionary society, with headquarters in Nairobi, Kenya, became known as the Pentecostal Assemblies of God (affiliated with the PAOC). With hundreds of national pastors in Kenya today, the legacy of the Kellers is evident in the strong national church with indigenous leadership.

Otto Keller passed away in 1942, and Marian carried on the ministry until 1946, when she retired and other missionaries came to take over. She lived the last years of her life in Victoria, B.C.

■ **Bibliography:** M. Keller, *Twenty Years in Africa* (1933) ■ G. McGee, "Keller, Otto C. and Marian (Weller)," *Biographical Dictionary of Christian Missions,* ed. G. H. Anderson (1998).

■ G. W. Gohr

KENDRICK, GRAHAM (1950–). One of the world's most respected worship leaders and songwriters. Born in Northamptonshire, England, Kendrick, the son of a Baptist minister, began writing songs as a teenager for a Christian band in which he played. Trained as a teacher, he launched out as a singer/songwriter in 1972. Through ▸Clive Calver, he became musical director of Youth for Christ and contributed to Spring Harvest, the large annual Christian convention in England.

Since 1984 Kendrick has been a leader of the Ichthus Christian Fellowship under ▸Roger Forster, writing his first marching songs for praise marches that were part of Ichthus's evangelistic strategy. This led to Kendrick's role as one of the founders of ▸March for Jesus, along with Forster, ▸Gerald Coates, and ▸Lynn Green. Among his best-known songs are "The Servant King," "Shine Jesus Shine," "Meekness and Majesty," and "Knowing You." His books include *Worship* (1984), *Shine Jesus Shine* (1992), and *Awaking Our Cities for God: A Guide to Prayer-Walking* (with S. Hawthorne; 1994).

■ P. D. Hocken

KENDRICK, KLAUDE (1917–). Assemblies of God (AG) minister, educator, educational administrator, and writer. Kendrick was born in Arizona and later graduated from Southwestern Assemblies of God College (at that time located in Enid, OK) in 1938. He completed the B.A. at Texas Wesleyan College in 1945, the M.A. at Texas Christian University in 1948, and the Ph.D. at the University of Texas in 1959. His graduate studies concentrated on history and college administration.

Kendrick served Southwestern AG College as instructor, dean of men, business manager, and finally vice president (1940–55). From 1955 to 1960 he served Evangel College, Springfield, MO, as academic dean and president. In 1960 he returned to Southwestern, where he was president until 1965. In 1965 he joined Texas Wesleyan College as chairman of the division of social sciences, serving until 1977. From 1977 to 1979 he was academic dean of Southern California College.

Since Kendrick's formal retirement in 1977, he has accepted a number of challenging assignments at various churches and educational institutions. For two years he was responsible for upgrading the Far East Advanced School of Theology in Baguio, Philippines, to the graduate level. During that assignment he served as the school's president for more than a year. Subsequently, he assisted AG schools in Singapore, Malaysia, Fiji, and most recently in Bulgaria.

Kendrick is married and has two children. He has written numerous articles and books, chief among them *The Promise Fulfilled* (1961), a history of the modern pentecostal movement.

■ **Bibliography:** Interview with author (Feb. 1999) ■ vita supplied by Klaude Kendrick (Feb. 1988).

■ S. M. Burgess

KENNEDY, MILDRED ("MINNIE") (1862–1947). Mother of ►Aimee Semple McPherson. Orphaned at age 12, "Minnie" was reared by Salvationists and became heavily involved in that movement. She became the second wife of a widower, James Morgan Kennedy (1836–1921), and at first she did not accept Aimee's involvement in pentecostalism, but she soon changed her mind. After the death of Aimee's husband, ►Robert Semple, Minnie spent the fall and winter months in New York City involved with the Salvation Army and providing moral support to her daughter. Moving back to Ingersoll, Ont., she provided support to Aimee, who by this time had begun an active evangelistic ministry along the East Coast and up into Canada.

When Aimee settled in Los Angeles, Minnie also moved there. Both mother and daughter were legally responsible for the Echo Park Evangelistic Association. "Mother," as she was called, showed remarkable skills in providing the primary financial and business leadership to the association in its early days. When Aimee disappeared in May 1926, Minnie was in charge of the business conducted at the temple, and after initial reports of Aimee's apparent drowning, Minnie sent a telegram to ►George Jeffreys, inviting him to come immediately to conduct meetings. He could not come, and within days Aimee reappeared.

After a decade as a widow, Mother Kennedy remarried on June 28, 1931, to Guy Edward Hudson. The courtship was short, the marriage unanticipated. Shortly after their wedding, charges of bigamy were filed against Hudson by another woman. The marriage to Minnie was annulled less than a month after it had been entered. Later that year the bigamy charges lapsed and Hudson obtained a "quickie" divorce in Las Vegas. Minnie met him there, and they were remarried. On July 4, 1932, she announced a separation; divorce followed in Nov. 1932.

As with many mother-daughter relationships, it was not always easy for these two very strong women to see things alike. The newspapers reported a deep rift between them, with such spectacular headlines as "Police Guarding Aimee from 'Ma,'" and much was made of a broken nose, which Minnie was quoted as having received in an altercation with Aimee. To what extent the rift was real is difficult to assess, but when Aimee's daughter, Roberta, disagreed with Aimee on certain elements of temple administration in 1937, Minnie sided with Roberta in the ensuing highly publicized court scene. The least that may be said following that incident is that mother and daughter continued to drift apart.

Following Aimee's death in 1944, Minnie declined into relative obscurity. She never fully recovered from the effects of an automobile accident in early 1947 and died on Nov. 23, 1947, in Hermosa Beach, CA.

■ **Bibliography:** D. Cartwright, *The Great Evangelists* (1986) ■ "Police Guarding Aimee from 'Ma,'" *San Francisco Chronicle* (Sept. 3, 1930) ■ L. Thomas, *Storming Heaven* (1970).

                                  ■ C. M. Robeck Jr.

KENYON, ESSEK WILLIAM (1867–1948). Evangelist, pastor, educator, and author. Born in upstate New York, Kenyon preached his first sermon at a Methodist church in Amsterdam, NY, at age 19. After attending various schools and pastoring several churches in New England, he founded Dudley Bible Institute in Dudley, MA, a faith venture he financed with proceeds from his evangelistic meetings in Canada, Chicago, and many parts of the Northeast, where thousands of conversions and healings were reported. The school soon moved to Spencer, MA, and was renamed Bethel Bible Institute; he continued as president for 25 years. The school later moved to Providence, RI, and became Providence Bible Institute.

In 1923 Kenyon founded Figueroa Independent Baptist Church in downtown Los Angeles, where he became a pioneer in radio evangelism with broadcasts from KNX every morning. After doing a few broadcasts from Tacoma, WA, in 1931, he began a daily program from KJR in Seattle, *Kenyon's Church of the Air*, which led to the founding of a church there of the same name, later known as New Covenant Baptist Church.

Kenyon later devoted himself more fully to itinerant ministry and writing. His 16 books have enjoyed extensive circulation and influence. Although he was not a pentecostal, his work *The Wonderful Name of Jesus* (1927) was widely read among Oneness pentecostals (Reed, 1975, 160–62). His writings have had a broad acceptance in the Deeper Life and charismatic movements. Various aspects of his theology later became an important influence on such diverse people as ►W. J. "Ern" Baxter,

E. W. Kenyon, Bible teacher and author who has had an important influence on the "word of faith" branch of the pentecostal movement.

ʿF. F. Bosworth, David Nunn, ʿT. L. Osborn, ʿJimmy Swaggart, and many others (Gossett and Kenyon, 1977, 3). Kenyon's writings also became seminal for the ministries of ʿKenneth Hagin, ʿKenneth Copeland, Don Gossett, Charles Capps, and others in the Word of Faith (ʿPositive Confession) movement.

Although Kenyon has been criticized for holding to a form of Gnosticism, the similarities between Kenyon's theology and the Gnostic system are only superficial. Although Kenyon held that Jesus died both spiritually and physically (1964, 135–37), the ancient Christian Gnostics held that Jesus did not die physically; some even maintained that Jesus himself was in need of redemption. For Gnostics, redemption involved deliverance from the world and from the physical body, all matter being inherently evil. Kenyon, on the other hand (1964, 97–106), believed in the physical resurrection of Christ, the redemption of the physical bodies of believers, the centrality of the incarnation, the necessity of the Virgin Birth, and the importance of the preexistence of Christ, all of which were antithetical to the central tenets of Gnosticism.

[For a critical analysis of Kenyon's views, see ʿPositive Confession Theology.—Ed.]

■ **Bibliography:** D. Gossett and E. W. Kenyon, *The Power of the Positive Confession of God's Word* (1977) ■ R. K. Housworth, letter to R. M. Riss (Feb. 26, 1988) ■ D. Hunt, *Beyond Seduction* (1987) ■ E. W. Kenyon, *The Father and His Family* (1964) ■ R. Kenyon [Housworth], "He Is at Rest," repr. from *Herald of Life* (Apr. 1948) ■ D. R. McConnell, *A Different Gospel* (1988) ■ J. A. Matta, *The Born Again Jesus of the Word-Faith Teaching* (1987) ■ D. Reed, "Aspects of the Origins of Oneness Pentecostalism," in H. V. Synan, ed., *Aspects of Pentecostal-Charismatic Origins* (1975).
                                                        ■ R. M. Riss

KERR, CECIL (1936–), and **MYRTLE** (1936–). Leaders in ministry of reconciliation in Northern Ireland. Born in Ulster, Cecil Kerr committed his life to Christ at the age of 15 and was ordained to the ministry in the Church of Ireland in 1960. Soon married to Myrtle, an Anglican from the Irish republic, Cecil served in Coleraine and then in a Belfast school before becoming chaplain to Queen's University in 1965. Baptized in the Spirit through contact with American Episcopalians from Houston, TX, the Kerrs felt led to form a community center for reconciliation between Protestants and Catholics in the power of the Spirit, founding the Christian Renewal Centre at Rostrevor in 1974 with an ecumenical staff living a shared life. Though centered in Ireland, the Kerrs' witness to repentance and reconciliation has also taken them to South Africa and Israel. Cecil Kerr's books include *Power to Love* (1976) and *The Way of Peace* (1990).
                                                        ■ P. D. Hocken

KERR, DANIEL WARREN (1856–1927). Pioneer pastor and educator. Daniel W. Kerr is representative of a number of seasoned clergy drawn into the pentecostal movement in its infancy. A native of Center County, PA, he was founder of two Bible institutes—Southern California Bible School (1920) and Central Bible Institute (1922)—and an early executive presbyter of the General Council of the Assemblies of God (AG). From 1911 to 1919 he was pastor of the large Pentecostal Church of Cleveland, OH. Previous to this Kerr had served in Illinois and Ohio under the Evangelical Association and the ʿChristian and Missionary Alliance (CMA).

In 1907 while pastor at Dayton, Kerr and his wife, Mattie, received the pentecostal experience while attending the Beulah Park camp meeting east of Cleveland. Transferred four years later to the CMA church in Cleveland, they found a largely pentecostal congregation ready to declare its independence. After eight years he resigned from this congregation to move to California. Venerated by the AG as a pastor and schoolman, Kerr died in 1927 at age 71 in Springfield, MO.

■ **Bibliography:** C. Brumback, *Suddenly . . . from Heaven* (1961) ■ J. R. Evans, "With Christ Which Is Far Better," *PE* (Apr. 16, 1927).
                                                        ■ C. E. Jones

KESWICK HIGHER LIFE MOVEMENT This renewalist tradition takes its name from an English village that has been the site of annual conventions devoted to the cultivation of the "higher Christian life" since 1875.

1. The History of Keswick.

From the early decades of the 19th century, evangelists from the American Holiness movement became regular features of British church life. These men and women, as well as their publications, stirred interest in the Spirit-filled life. W. E. Boardman's *The Higher Christian Life* (1859) was especially influential. Robert Pearsall Smith contributed *Holiness through Faith* (1870) and *Walk in the Light* (1873). His wife, Hannah Whitall Smith, wrote *The Christian's Secret of a Happy Life* (1875).

During 1873 the Smiths and Boardman were in England and became involved in a series of sessions for clergy and laity focusing on the "higher life." In 1874 W. Cowper-Temple hosted a meeting of about 100 persons at his Broadlands estate, chaired by R. P. Smith, including Theodore Monod, George MacDonald, and Amanda Smith. Aug. 1874 saw another meeting at Oxford. Speakers included the Smiths, Theodore Monod, Otto Stockmayer, Evan Hopkins, Asa Mahan, and W. E. Boardman. The Oxford Conference had significant influence on the Continent, and what became "Keswickian" in England is known as the "Oxford movement" in the rest of Europe. The proceedings were published as *Account of the Union Meeting for the Promotion of Scriptural Holiness* (1875).

Brighton was the site of another meeting led by the Smiths (May 29–June 7, 1875) with speakers such as Mahan, Hopkins, and T. Monod. The proceedings of Brighton were published as *Record of the Convention for the Promotion of Scriptural Holiness* (1875). Smith also began a periodical, *The Christian's Pathway to Power* (1874–78), which became *The Life of Faith* (1878–), the official organ of the Keswick convention.

T. D. Harford-Battersby and Robert Wilson invited the Smiths to conduct a "Union Meeting for the Promotion of Practical Holiness" at Keswick (June 29–July 6, 1875). Smith withdrew from evangelistic work before the meeting, and its leadership fell to Battersby. The conventions at Keswick became annual events and served as the model for similar conferences through the world, many of which bear the name "Keswick."

2. The Development of a Theological Tradition.

A product of the American Holiness movement, the Keswick Convention soon developed an indigenous tradition. Keswick theologians rejected the absolutizing of sanctification by the parent movement (during the late 19th and early 20th century), which was often expressed in terms of "sinless perfection" by radical American preachers. However, they retained the emphasis that a normative Christian life is characterized by "fullness of the Spirit." It is this, they argued, that gives power for living a consistent Christian life. Keswickians teach that reception of "fullness of the Spirit" is a definite act of faith, distinct from but usually coincident with regeneration. The actualization of this power usually develops throughout the Christian life. The experience provides for victory over temptation and sin but does not result in the eradication of tendencies to sin. For times of special need, "fillings" of the Holy Spirit are available. "Fullness" and "fillings" are to be sought by all Christians following the biblical paradigms.

3. The Influence of Keswick.

Jessie Penn-Lewis's *The Awakening in Wales* (1905) indicated that the Welsh revival had its roots in Keswick, a thesis accepted by most historians. The teaching of Keswick found its way to the Continent through the efforts of O. Stockmayer, T. Monod, R. A. Torrey, R. P. Smith, T. Jellinghaus, E. Modersohn, and others. On the Continent it achieved its most permanent form in the German Holiness movement. One of the influential authors and preachers of this group, ᐅJ. Paul, became a founder of the German pentecostal movement. ᐅA. A. Boddy, English pentecostal leader, also attended Keswick, and through his influence and that of his periodical *Confidence*, a Keswickian understanding of "baptism of the Holy Spirit" (and therefore of the evidence for the reception of the Spirit) became normative for most pentecostal movements.

ᐅA. B. Simpson, founder of the ᐅChristian and Missionary Alliance (CMA), influenced by A. J. Gordon and W. E. Boardman, adopted a Keswickian understanding of sanctification. Simpson's *Fulness of Jesus* (1890) and the work by CMA theologian G. P. Pardington, *The Crisis of the Deeper Life* (1906), articulate this perspective. Simpson was attracted to the pentecostal understanding of "baptism in the Holy Spirit" but apparently did not experience glossolalia. His theological treatise *The Four-Fold Gospel* (1925), organized around the doctrine of Christ as Savior, Sanctifier, Healer, and Coming King, became a paradigm for early North American pentecostal theological formulations. Other Keswick theologians, such as H. A. Ironside and W. Graham Scroggie, became opponents of pentecostalism.

See also HOLINESS MOVEMENT.

■ **Bibliography:** S. Barabas, *So Great Salvation* (1952) ▮ D. Brandt-Bessire, *Aux sources de la spiritualité pentecôtiste* (1986) ▮ D. D. Bundy, *Keswick: A Bibliographic Introduction to the Higher Life Movements* (1975; repr. 1986) ▮ idem, "Between the Réveil and Pentecostalism: The Wesleyan/Holiness Tradition in Belgium and The Netherlands," *Asbury Theological Journal* 51 (2, 1996) ▮ idem, "Keswick and the Experience of Evangelical Piety," in *Modern Christian Revivals*, ed. E. L. Blumhofer and R. Balmer (1993) ▮ D. Dayton, *The Theological Roots of Pentecostalism* (1987) ▮ D. A. Ekholm, "Theological Roots of the Keswick Movement: William Boardman, Robert Pearsall Smith and the Doctrine of the 'Higher Christian Life'" (diss., Basel, 1992) ▮ J. R. McQuilkin, "The Keswick Perspective," in *Five Views on Sanctification*, ed. M. Dieter et al. (1987) ▮ G. Marsden, *Fundamentalism and American Culture: The Shaping of Twentieth-Century Evangelism 1870–1925* (1980) ▮ I. M. Randall, "Old Time Power: Relationships between Pentecostalism and Evangelical Spirituality in England," *Pneuma* 19 (1997). ■ D. D. Bundy

KETCHAM, MAYNARD L. (1905–93). Missionary to India. Maynard L. Ketcham lost his father when he was five months old. His godly mother raised him in the Methodist Church. When Ketcham was five years old, Fanny Simpson, a missionary to India, came to their church and laid hands on him and claimed him as a missionary to India.

Shortly after entering Massachusetts Institute of Technology (MIT) with a strong desire to become an engineer, Ketcham left to attend Beulah Heights Bible Training School in North Bergen, NJ, and later Taylor University. Following graduation, he taught at Beulah Heights, where he met his future wife, Gladys Koch. They were married in 1928 and have had three children—Jimmy, who died of polio; David; and Marjorie.

Ketcham left in 1926 to take over the mission station at Behar, India, that had been established by Simpson. He was ordained with the ᐅAssemblies of God (AG) in 1927 and established the Door of Hope Orphanage at Puruila and pioneered churches throughout Bangladesh and India.

At the beginning of his second term in India, Ketcham was elected superintendent of the AG of North India and also chairman of the North India Field Fellowship and later as general secretary of the All-India Pentecostal Fellowship. He held this position until he moved to Springfield, MO, to assume responsibilities as field secretary for Southern Asia in 1951. Ketcham was eventually made field secretary for the Far East in 1955. In Korea he helped initiate training for national workers. Under his direction the Evangelistic Center in Seoul, Korea, was organized and built. Today this church is the largest in the world and is pastored by ▸Paul Y. Cho. The Ketchams have been made honorary lifetime pastors of that church.

After retiring from his position as field secretary for the Far East in 1970, Ketcham became an instructor for the missions departments of Central Bible College and Evangel College in Springfield, MO. Later Ketcham worked as an elder to PTL Ministries and became an advisor for PTL Prison Ministries. He also was involved in the prison ministries program of the AG chaplaincy department.

■ **Bibliography:** "Dear Uncle Maynard," *PE* (Feb. 26, 1984) ■ M. L. Ketcham, *Pentecost in the Ganges Delta* (1945) ■ idem, *Tigers That Talk* (1979) ■ M. L. Ketcham, interview with D. Womack, Mar. 3, 1970, Office of Promotions, AG Division of Foreign Missions.   ■ S. Shemeth

KING, JOSEPH HILLERY (1869–1946). A founder and the first bishop of the ▸Pentecostal Holiness Church (PHC). Born in Anderson County, SC, to a family of poor sharecroppers as one of 11 children, he moved with his family to Franklin County, GA, in 1882. In 1885, on his 16th birthday, King was converted in a Holiness-oriented Methodist camp meeting in Carnesville, GA. Later, on Oct. 23, 1885, he received the "second blessing" of entire sanctification. Soon afterward he felt a call to preach and to assist in several local revivals. His first application for a Methodist exhorter's license was denied due to lack of education.

In 1890, after serving a short term in the U.S. Army, King married Willie Irene King. This marriage soon ended in divorce, however, since his new wife had no intention of being the wife of a Holiness minister. Because of his convictions against divorce and remarriage, King vowed to remain celibate as long as his first wife lived. In 1891 he was licensed to preach in the Georgia Conference of the Methodist Episcopal Church (the northern branch of Methodism) and was assigned as pastor of the Rock Spring–Walton circuit near his home. He also served several other charges at this time. He was assigned in 1895 to the Lookout Mountain circuit near Chattanooga. Because of his thirst

for knowledge, he decided to attend the U. S. Grant University School of Theology. Despite his lack of prior education, he graduated in 1897.

While in Chattanooga, King became disenchanted with the increasingly negative policy of the Methodist Church toward the Holiness movement. He also came in contact with ▸Benjamin Hardin Irwin's ▸Fire-Baptized Holiness Association (FBHA), which promised a third experience after sanctification called "the fire." After receiving this experience and graduating from the university, he joined Irwin's group in 1897. When Irwin formed a national movement in Anderson, SC, in 1898, King was one of the charter members.

After the Anderson convention, Irwin sent King to Toronto, Canada, where he pastored a local congregation and led in planting churches in eastern Canada. In 1900 Irwin called King to the church's headquarters in Iowa to assist in editing the denominational journal, *Live Coals of Fire.* Soon after King's arrival, Irwin left the church in disgrace after confessing to "open and gross sin." The 31-year-old King then became general overseer of the badly demoralized church. In prayer, he was assured that the FBHA would survive and that he would die as its leader.

By 1902 King had not only succeeded in holding remnants of the church together but had moved the headquarters to Royston, GA, near his family home. He then led the church in dropping the word "Association" from its name and adding the word "Church" (FBHC). For five years the growth of the church was slow, until the pentecostal movement reached the church through the ministry of ▸G. B. Cashwell, a preacher from the ▸Holiness Church of North Carolina, who had been to Azusa Street in 1906 and experienced glossolalia. Most of King's preachers received the pentecostal experience in Cashwell's historic meeting in Dunn, NC, in Jan. 1907. The next month, King invited Cashwell to preach the pentecostal message in his FBHC congregation in Toccoa, GA. After some theological struggles, King accepted the experience and spoke in tongues himself in Cashwell's meeting.

King immediately led the church in adopting a pentecostal statement of faith; this was done in Jan. 1908. Thus, the FBHC became the first denomination to embrace pentecostalism officially. King and his followers thereupon agreed that the tongues-tested baptism was the reality they had been seeking in the earlier "baptism of fire" experience.

Pentecostalism injected such new life into the movement that King was kept busy developing new institutions for the now-growing denomination. In 1909 he moved his center of activities to Falcon, NC, where he founded the monthly *Apostolic Evangel* and a new orphanage for the church.

In 1911 King took a two-year trip around the world in the interest of world missions. On this trip he preached for ▸Thomas Ball Barratt in Oslo, Norway, and for Canon Harford-Battersby in Sunderland, England. While he was away on the world tour, the FBHC merged with the PHC (the smaller group) in Falcon, NC, to form the present Pentecostal Holiness Church. Because he was away, King was not chosen to head the newly united church but was elected assistant general superintendent in charge of world missions. For four years he pastored the Memphis, TN, church while heading the world missions department.

King was elected general superintendent of the church in 1917, a position he was to hold for the rest of his life (with the exception of the years 1941–45 when Dan T. Muse was elected chairman). In 1920, after learning of the death of his first wife, he married Blanche Leon King, a teacher in the new Franklin Springs Institute near his home in Royston. They had four children: Easter Lily; Joseph Jr.; Virginia; and Mary Ann. In 1937 King was given the honorary title of bishop.

King's chief theological contribution was his 1911 book *From Passover to Pentecost,* which gave classic expression to the Holiness-pentecostal teachings of the early pentecostals. Over the years it became required reading for the ministers of the church.

When Bishop King died in Anderson, SC, in 1946, he still held the chairman's position that he had inherited in 1900. At the time of his passing, the PHC had grown to include 26,000 members in 700 churches in the U.S., with hundreds of churches on foreign mission fields.

■ **Bibliography:** J. Campbell, *The Pentecostal Holiness Church, 1898–1948* (1951) ■ J. King and B. King, *Yet Speaketh: The Memoirs of the Late Bishop Joseph H. King* (1949).   ■ H. V. Synan

KNIGHT, CECIL BRIGHAM (1925–).

The 15th general overseer of the Church of God (CG, Cleveland, TN). A native of Alabama, Cecil B. Knight began his ministry in 1944 and pastored churches in Mississippi, Alabama, and Florida before being assigned to youth and Christian education work in 1956. Along with these assignments he also served as ►Pentecostal Fellowship of North America youth commission secretary. He earned degrees from the University of Southern Mississippi (B.S., 1948) and Butler University (M.A., 1968). His work in Christian education produced the book *Keeping the Sunday School Alive* (1959).

Knight's two-year tenure as general overseer (1976–78) was followed by four years as president of the Church of God Theological Seminary (1978–82). He was the first full-time head of the young institution. In 1982 he was reelected to his denomination's executive committee but resigned that post and returned to the seminary's presidency, where he led in attaining academic and theological accreditation of the seminary.

■ **Bibliography:** Archives of the Church of God (Cleveland, TN).   ■ C. W. Conn

KNIGHT, GILES N. (d. 1968).

Minister, administrator, and personal manager for ►Aimee Semple McPherson from 1936 to 1944. Knight was a faithful member of the ►Angelus Temple staff and one of the first two persons awarded an honorary D.D. degree from ►L.I.F.E. Bible College. In 1936 it became obvious that the Angelus Temple commissary, while meeting great needs in the area, was causing a substantial drain on the financial resources of the congregation. Threatened by foreclosure on certain temple properties, McPherson named Knight to the post of assistant business manager on July 10, 1936. He was given the responsibility of placing the temple on a "cash basis." Knight's appointment and subsequent hard-line fiscal policies led to some friction with Aimee's daughter, Roberta Semple (who had previously held Knight's position); Harriet Jordan, dean of the college; and Rheba Crawford, associate pastor. Ultimately, "Sister" threw her support totally to Knight, who through hard work and extensive fund-raising activities was able to retire the temple's indebtedness by 1938. During these and subsequent years he managed Aimee's personal schedule as well. Knight held the position of vice president and secretary-treasurer of Angelus Temple, L.I.F.E., and the Echo Park Evangelistic Association until he was succeeded by Rolf McPherson on Feb. 1, 1944. Giles Knight died on July 13, 1968, in Santa Barbara, CA.

■ **Bibliography:** A. S. McPherson, *Aimee Semple McPherson: The Story of My Life* (1973) ■ L. Thomas, *Storming Heaven* (1970).   ■ C. M. Robeck Jr.

KNOWLEDGE, WORD OF

The actual phrase "word of knowledge" (NIV "message of knowledge"; *logos gnōseōs*) is found only once in the NT, as the second in the list of nine manifestations of the Spirit in 1 Cor. 12:7–10. To grasp its significance, we will first consider the NT notion of knowledge in general, then the word of knowledge in particular, and finally, some ancient and modern applications of the term to aspects of church life.

1. "Knowledge" in the New Testament.

(For OT and intertestamental background, see bibliography under Schütz and Bultmann). The word *gnōsis* ("knowledge") occurs 29 times in the NT, 21 of which are in the recognized Pauline writings (16 times in 1 and 2 Corinthians). The correlate *epignōsis* occurs 20 times, mostly in the Pauline literature but never in the Corinthian correspondence. The verb form *ginōskein* is found 221 times, mostly in the Johannine writings (82 times), while *epiginōskein* occurs 44 times (Acts, 13 times; Pauline writings, 12 times; never in Johannine literature). Most of the theologically significant occurrences of these words occur in John and Paul, with John using the verb form exclusively (as he does for *pisteuein* [except for 1 John 5:4]) and Paul making use of the substantive form as well as the verb.

a. Johannine Usage. While exploiting and transposing the rich OT notion of the "knowledge of God," John distinguishes that act by which one comes to know God or the things of God *(ginōskein)* from the fact of possessing knowledge *(eidenai;* see de la Potterie). Eternal life is coming to know God and growing in that knowledge of him as well as of Jesus Christ, whom he has sent (John 7:3). In the better Greek variant reading of John 14:7, Jesus tells Philip, "If you knew me, you will know my Father; and from now on you do know him and have seen him." Those who have really seen Jesus, that is, come to know him, have begun to see and know the Father. Such knowledge is the fruit of faith: "We believe and know that you are the Holy One of God" (John 6:69).

b. Pauline Usage. (1) *General.* The Fourth Gospel and the Johannine writings in general are but an intensification of movements of thought begun much earlier in the Christian community. The overall Pauline use of words related to the root *gnō* is a good illustration of this, though the distinction between this root and the other root expressing knowledge *(id)* is not developed as in John.

Paul speaks of an "ignorance of God" (1 Cor. 15:34; see 1 Peter 2:15; also Acts 17:30; Eph. 4:18; 1 Peter 1:14) and of the Gentiles who "have no knowledge of God" *(eidotes*—Gal. 4:8; 1 Thess. 4:5; 2 Thess. 1:8; cf. LXX Ps. 78:6). He asserts in the tradition of the OT that God can be known through his works (Rom. 1:19ff.; cf. Job 12:7–9; Wisd. Sol. 13:1–9); and that it is precious to know the will of God (Hos. 4:6; Mal. 2:7; Rom. 12:2; Phil. 1:9; Col. 1:9), to walk in the way that pleases him, and to come to know him (Col. 1:10; see Eph. 1:17). Important as it is to know God, however, it is more important to be known by him (1 Cor. 8:3; 13:12; Gal. 4:9; esp. Rom. 8:29) and to be in awe of his wisdom and knowledge (Rom. 11:33).

For Paul, all that was promised in the old covenant is transcendently fulfilled in "knowing Christ" (Phil. 3:8, 10) in whom are hidden all the treasures of wisdom and knowledge (Col. 2:3; see Philem. 6), and on whose face shines the light of the new creation, giving knowledge of God's glory (2 Cor. 4:6). This consideration of Paul's teaching on knowledge is in keeping with the teaching of the Christian community at large. This same teaching is retained but receives particular accent in what is termed his First Letter to the Corinthians.

(2) *In the Corinthian Correspondence.* The density of the occurrence of the word *gnōsis* in the Corinthian correspondence noted above (10 times in 1 Corinthians alone) indicates that Paul is dealing with a problem whose particular shading and choice of vocabulary is due to the situation at Corinth. He begins by complimenting the Corinthians for being rich in "all your speaking and in all your knowledge" (1 Cor. 1:5) but continues by finding fault with them because their community is riddled by "divisions" (1:10). Realizing that their divisions arise from fleshly thinking about divine

relatives, he proposes as a remedy the "message of the cross" (1:18) and goes on to speak of the nature of true wisdom, describing it as the result of God's revelatory action through the Spirit (2:10), expressed not in "words taught us by human wisdom but in words taught by the Spirit" (2:13).

Paul returns to the theme of "knowledge" in his discussion of meat offered to idols (1 Cor. 8:1–13). His ironic use of the term allows us to see that one particular instance of fleshly thinking at Corinth was the Corinthians' pride in having "knowledge" regarding the spiritual forces in this world and the manner in which these find expression in idols. This knowledge makes them superior to pagans and weaker Christians but, as Paul points out, it only puffs them up since it does not lead to love and service (8:1).

2. The Word of Knowledge.

Finally, in chapter 12 Paul arrives at another source of pride and division among the Corinthians: their misunderstanding of charismatic gifts and their exaggerated esteem for the more dramatic of these gifts. Here his response is first to point to the Trinitarian source of all Christian charisms, services, and forms of work and then to give a list of manifestations of the one and same Spirit. The first two are described this way: "To one there is given through the Spirit the [word] of wisdom, to another the [word] of knowledge by means of the same Spirit" (12:8).

Two things must be noted here. First, the accent is on the notion of "word" (NIV "message"). This corresponds to the twofold compliment in chapter 1 as well as to the distinction between words of human wisdom and those taught by the Spirit in 1 Cor. 2:13, and to the distinction between "word" and "knowledge" made in 2 Cor. 11:6. The gift is the capacity to express verbally either wisdom or knowledge. Commentators as diverse as Chrysostom (*Homily 29 on 1 Corinthians,* PG 61, 245); Aquinas (*In Primam ad Corinthios 12,* lect. 2); Robertson and Plummer (265); Allo (325); and Fee (592–93) have noted this.

Second, Paul is making a distinction in descending order. Wisdom is named first and is "through the Spirit," thus accenting the fact that both content and expression are the direct work of the Spirit through both revelation and *logos,* respectively. Knowledge is named second and is "by means of the same Spirit." Its content may or may not be the result of revelation and seems to have to do with "knowledge of creatures as they reveal God's plan" (Aquinas) or "Christian insight into the realities of Christian existence here and now and its practical consequences" (Pearson, 42). Paul is talking about the charismatic capacity to communicate this insight and thus seems to be touching on certain aspects of teaching. This has been frequently suggested.

In the other occurrences of the word *gnōsis* in his discussion of spiritual gifts, Paul does not restrict himself to a meaning for it that is distinct from wisdom. Thus, in 13:2

he describes the result of prophecy as knowing "all mysteries [refer to 2:7, 10] and all knowledge." His long consideration of knowledge in 13:8–12 certainly uses the term generically, as does his mention of speaking "either by *[en]* revelation, or by knowledge, or by prophesying, or by teaching" (14:6 NKJV). In another context (Rom. 15:14), Paul seems to divide the gifts into "knowledge" and "power" in much the same way as 1 Peter 4:11 divides them into "speaking" and "serving."

Given this diversity of reference and yet occasional distinction between wisdom and knowledge, we may say that when Paul draws a difference, wisdom refers to divinely conferred revelational understanding of God and his plan of salvation while knowledge refers to an understanding of the practical working out of that plan here and now. We may then define the gift of "word of knowledge" as being the charismatically endowed capacity to express some aspect of God's plan as it is at work in creation here and now, revealing something of God.

3. The Word of Knowledge in Tradition.

Tradition often reflects the fluid use of the term *gnōsis* that we have noted in Paul (Dupont), often extending this to include the phrase "word of knowledge." For instance, Origen linked both the word of wisdom and the word of knowledge to the understanding of Scripture (*On Principles* 1:8; *PG* 11:119), while Diadochus of Photike taught that *gnōsis* described experiential, transforming knowledge of God and *sophia* referred to the gift of being able to teach divine things (*One Hundred Chapters*, 9; *Sources Chrétiennes*, 5bis, 88ff.). Because of the Gnostic heresy, this type of terminology became infrequent.

In our own day, a very special gift, that of knowing what God is doing at this moment in another's soul or body, or of knowing the secrets of another's heart (the ancients' *kardiagnōsis*), is often described as a "word of knowledge." This gift is particularly common among pentecostals and those involved in the charismatic movement. The existence of the gift and its divine origin and fruit are unquestionable. (See bibliography under Madre and Linford.)

The word of knowledge serves a valuable purpose, since by revealing to one person what God is doing in another person, God stirs up faith and allows someone to reach out more firmly for the gifts of healing, consolation, etc., that he is offering. In such contexts, the word of knowledge works in close harmony with the charismatic ›gift of faith.

If the definition given above of the "word of knowledge" is accepted, then this modern use has a certain basis in Scripture. In strictly Pauline terminology, the gift could perhaps better be classified as a type of revelation (1 Cor. 14:30) pertaining to prophecy (1 Cor. 14:24–25). It might also be termed a certain type of discernment.

See also GIFTS OF THE SPIRIT.

■ **Bibliography:** E. B. Allo, *Saint Pau: Première Epître aux Corinthièns* (1956) ▪ R. Bultmann, "Ginōskō," *TDNT* (1964), 1:689–718 ▪ I. de la Potterie, "Oida et ginōskō, les deux modes de la connaissance dans le quatrième Evangile," *Bib* 40 (1959): 709–25 ▪ J. Dupont, *Gnosis: La Connaissance Religieuse dans les Epitres de Saint Paul* (2d ed., 1960) ▪ A. Linford, *A Course of Study on Spiritual Gifts* (n.d.) ▪ P. Madre, *Le Charisme de Connaissance* (2d ed., 1985) ▪ B. Pearson, *The Pneumatikos-Psychikos Terminology in 1 Corinthians*, SBL diss., 12 (1973) ▪ A. Robertson and A. Plummer, *A Critical and Exegetical Commentary on the First Epistle of St. Paul to the Corinthians* (2d ed., 1914) ▪ E. Schütz, "Knowledge," *NIDNTT* (1971), 2:390–409.   ■ F. Martin

KOLLINS, KIM CATHERINE-MARIE (1943–). Teacher-leader in the ›Catholic charismatic renewal (CCR) in Europe. Born in Michigan, Kollins was baptized in the Spirit

Kim Collins, teacher and leader in the Catholic Charismatic Renewal in Europe.

in a nondenominational center in Florida in 1978. Sensing a call to ministry in 1980, her evangelistic ministry quickly spread to classical pentecostal churches in the U.S. and then unexpectedly in late 1981 to Catholic charismatics in France. At the Pentecost over Europe Conference in Strasbourg (1982), Kollins heard the words "Unite my church" that have since been a key to her ministry. She ministered increasingly in Catholic circles, especially in France and Germany; she became a Catholic in 1984 and joined the community of Lion of Juda (now the Beatitudes). She made her home in Kelkheim, Germany, and became a prominent figure in German CCR. She is currently cochair of the ›European Charismatic Consultation and a member of the executive committee of the ›International Charismatic Consultation on World Evangelization. Her story is told in *It's Only the Beginning* (1989). Kollins is the author of *Burning Bush: A Return to the Cenacle in Adoration and Intercession* (revised from the Italian *Roveto ardente: Un ritorno al cenacolo nell'adorazione e intercessione*, 1999).   ■ P. D. HOCKEN

KRAMAR, MARILYNN (1939–). Founder of ›Charisma in Missions and the Latino pentecostal movement in the Roman Catholic Church in the U.S. and Latin America. A fifth-generation pentecostal, Kramar was born the daughter of an Assemblies of God (AG) minister in Los Angeles, CA, in 1939. A few years after she joined the pentecostal movement in 1954, she and her husband, Glenn, attended

Central Bible Institute (CBI) and worked at AG headquarters in Springfield, MO. They left CBI in 1961 and in 1967 went to Colombia as AG missionaries. In 1968 Marilynn was licensed as an AG missionary-evangelist. She and her husband served as the last nonnational superintendents of the AG work in Colombia from 1967 to 1970.

While in Colombia the Kramars began ecumenical dialogue with the Roman Catholic hierarchy. It was through these dialogues and ecumenical work with Roman Catholic priests and nuns that the Kramars became interested in Roman Catholicism. After they returned to the U.S. in 1972, they continued to dialogue with Roman Catholic priests in Los Angeles. Experiencing personally the results of Vatican II and the deep spirituality of the many Catholic priests and nuns they had met in Colombia and Los Angeles, the Kramars resigned from the AG, having received a special calling by God to become Roman Catholics.

Shortly after joining the Roman Catholic Church they put their evangelistic training and skills they had learned in the AG to use for the Roman Catholic Church by founding Charisma in Missions (a Catholic international missionary evangelization society) in Dec. 1972. With the support and blessing of Timothy Cardinal Manning of the Archdiocese of Los Angeles, Charisma in Missions began holding evangelistic and renewal services in the Spanish-speaking community throughout California and throughout Latin America. From 1972 to 1997 Marilynn Kramar estimates that Charisma in Missions touched the lives of over 1 million Latino Catholics in the United States alone. In 1997 there were over 70,000 U.S. Latinos on her Charisma in Missions mailing list and 220 Spanish-speaking prayer assemblies (which she estimates average between 70 and 120 people) in the Archdiocese of Los Angeles alone. In addition to Charisma in Missions evangelistic ministries, Kramar has developed CharisBooks, CharisPublications, CharisMedia, and CharisTapes; the latter provides Spanish charismatic music and videotapes and audiotapes of Charisma in Missions conferences. She is a highly sought-after speaker and evangelist, not only in the U.S., but also in Latin America. Charisma in Missions has been blessed by Archdiocese of Los Angeles and is located in the heart of East Los Angeles. Marilynn Kramar is rightly considered the "Mother" of the Latino pentecostal movement in the Roman Catholic Church in the United States.

■ **Bibliography:** "Charisma in Missions" (videotape, n.d.) ■ M. Kramar, *Charisma in Missions: Catholic Missionary Evangelization Society* (n.d.) ■ idem, with Robert C. Larson, *The Marilynn Kramar Story: Joy Comes in the Morning* (1990). ■ G. Espinosa

KUHLMAN, KATHRYN (1907–76). The world's most widely known female evangelist. After completing the tenth grade—all that was offered—Kathryn Kuhlman began her ministry at age 16, assisting her sister and brother-in-law. She was soon on her own, itinerating in Idaho, Utah, and Colorado, finally settling down in Denver in 1933 in the Kuhlman Revival Tabernacle. By 1935 she had established the 2,000-seat Denver Revival Tabernacle. She effectively used the media and established an influential radio ministry. Her marriage to an evangelist, who divorced his wife to marry Kuhlman, destroyed her Denver ministry. They continued to evangelize, but apparently after about six years—she was silent on the subject—she left him and started over again on her own.

In 1946 in Franklin, PA, a woman was suddenly healed of a tumor during one of Kuhlman's services. This became typical of the "miracle services." Kuhlman would call out the specific disorder that was being cured in a certain area of the auditorium, and it would be received by the appropriate individual. She again developed a daily radio ministry. In 1948 she moved to Pittsburgh, which remained her headquarters as she held regular services in Carnegie Hall and the First Presbyterian Church. She was catapulted toward national fame by a seven-page laudatory article in *Redbook* magazine.

From California in 1965 came the insistent invitation of Ralph Wilkerson of Anaheim Christian Center (later ►Melodyland). Kuhlman began services at the Pasadena Civic Auditorium, which seated 2,500, but later moved to the Los Angeles Shrine Auditorium, where for 10 years she regularly

Kathryn Kuhlman, one of North America's best-known evangelists during the 1960s and 1970s.

filled the 7,000 seats. She also continued the Pittsburgh meetings while expanding into television, producing more than 500 telecasts for the CBS network. In 1972 she received the first honorary doctorate awarded by Oral Roberts University.

It was not until the mid 1960s that Kuhlman became particularly identified with the charismatic movement. The older pentecostals out of the Holiness tradition found her twice suspect: she was a divorcee, and she did not satisfy them by giving testimony in her ministry to any personal experience of speaking in tongues. (She did not permit tongues in the regular course of the miracle services.)

Kuhlman objected to the appellation "faith healer" and gave the credit to the power of the Holy Spirit. Believing that gifts of healing were for the sick, the only gift she claimed, if any at all, was that of "faith" or "the word of knowledge" (1 Cor. 12:8–9). She had no explanation of why some were healed and some not, but she emphasized that the greater miracle was the regeneration of the new birth and always referred to herself as an evangelist.

Apart from the well-documented healings, the most sensational phenomenon associated with Kuhlman was people "going under the power" (sometimes referred to as ▶"slain in the Spirit"), or falling, when she prayed for them. This sometimes happened to dozens at a time and occasionally hundreds.

Kuhlman was an incessant worker and gave meticulous attention to every detail of her services; everything had to be first-class. Conducting them herself, she was on her feet from four to five hours at a time. A strikingly tall redhead and elegant dresser, she was very dramatic in gesture and consciously deliberate in speech. Her friend and biographer Jamie Buckingham admitted, "She loved her expensive clothes, precious jewels, luxury hotels, and first-class travel" (247). She was a star, even until her death just short of her 70th birthday.

■ **Bibliography:** J. Buckingham, *Daughter of Destiny: Kathryn Kuhlman . . . Her Story* (1976) ■ H. K. Hosier, *Kathryn Kuhlman: The Life She Led, the Legacy She Left* (1976).   ■ D. J. Wilson

KUZMIČ, PETER (1946–).

Author, educator, pastor, and church planter. Born into a pentecostal pastor's home in Nuskova (Slovenia), Yugoslavia. His theological studies were taken at a pentecostal Bible school in Erzhausen, West Germany (1970); B.A., Southern California College (1971); M.A., Wheaton College (1972); Dr. Theol., Catholic Faculty of Theology, University of Zagreb (1981).

Kuzmič is the former pastor of two churches and was secretary of the governing body of Kristova Pentecostal Crkva, the organization for pentecostal churches in former Yugoslavia. He is cofounder and director of Biblijsko Teoloki Institut in Osijek, Croatia. In 1987 he gained recognition from the Assemblies of God (AG) Division of Foreign Missions as an "approved minister abroad," while remaining in his native country.

An authority on Christianity and Marxism, Kuzmič has participated in many theological conferences and seminars in Western and Eastern Europe, India, Burma, the Philippines, South and Central Africa, and the U.S. He serves as chairman of the theological commission of the World Evangelical Fellowship; member of the executive committee of the Fellowship of European Evangelical Theologians; member of the Lausanne Committee for World Evangelization; and adjunct professor at the AG Theological Seminary, Springfield, MO, and Fuller Theological Seminary, Pasadena, CA.

His broader ecumenical work has taken him to the Sixth Assembly of the World Council of Churches, Vancouver, B.C. (1983), and the Roman Catholic/Pentecostal Dialogue (1985). In addition to numerous journal and magazine articles, Kuzmič wrote a major study on the influence of Slavic Bible translations on Slavic literature, language, and culture, as well as *The Gospel of John* (1974, a study guide for the International Correspondence Institute [▶Global University]) and a book on biblical hermeneutics. He is the editor of *Izvori,* a Christian monthly in Croatian. Since 1993 Kuzmič has been the Paul E. and Eva B. Toms Distinguished Professor of World Missions and European Studies at Gordon-Conwell Theological Seminary.

See also PART I: EUROPE, EASTERN.

■ **Bibliography:** "The Church within Socialism" (interview with Peter Kuzmič) *World Evangelization* (June 1987) ■ P. Kuzmič, "BTI: A School with a Purpose," *PE* (May 31, 1987) ■ idem, "Evangelical Witness in Eastern Europe," *Serving Our Generation* (1980).
                                                            ■ J. L. Sandidge

L

LAKE, JOHN GRAHAM (1870–1935). Faith healer, missionary, and pastor. John G. Lake was ordained to the Methodist ministry at the age of 21 but chose a career in business rather than the appointment he was offered. Lake became a very successful businessman, founding a newspaper and then moving into real estate and finally into the insurance business. Although he was offered a $50,000-per-year guarantee to be the manager of an insurance trust, Lake felt that God was dealing with him to devote all of his energy to preaching the gospel.

The breakthrough of God into Lake's life centered around several remarkable healings in his family, culminating in the instantaneous healing of his wife from tuberculosis under the ministry of *John Alexander Dowie in 1898. After experiencing these healings, Lake became associated with Dowie's ministry and served as an elder in the Zion Catholic Apostolic Church. Later, after leaving Dowie, Lake became involved in ministry at night while continuing in his business activities in the daytime. Lake sought God for the baptism in the Holy Spirit, and after nine months of seeking, Lake felt the power of God come upon him in answer to his prayers.

Shortly after receiving the baptism in the Holy Spirit in 1907, Lake felt God directing him to Africa. He left his job and distributed his funds and set out for Africa in faith that

God would supply his family's needs. Lake, his wife and their seven children, and four other adults arrived in South Africa in the spring of 1908. The party of missionaries found that God had gone before them and prepared the way. A lady met them at the boat and provided them with a house because the Lord had spoken to her to provide for his servants. Unfortunately, these miraculous provisions did not continue. The people thought that the missionaries were rich Americans, and so while Lake and his party poured all of their resources into the work, they were often without sufficient food to feed themselves.

Mrs. Lake died in Dec. 1908 while Lake was away on a preaching trip. It has been suggested that she died of overwork and malnutrition. Her death was a severe blow to Lake, and although he continued to minister in Africa for four more years, he was often stricken with loneliness, which eventually caused his return to the U.S. After returning to the States, Lake married Florence Switzer in 1913 and settled in Spokane, WA, a year later.

It is estimated that during the next five or six years thousands of healings occurred through Lake's ministry. He moved to Portland, OR, in May 1920 and started a work similar to his work in Spokane. Lake's health did not allow him to complete his vision of a chain of healing institutions throughout the country, and he died of a stroke in 1935.

■ **Bibliography:** J. G. Lake, *The Astounding Diary of Dr. John G. Lake* (1987) ▌ idem, *Spiritual Hunger and Other Sermons* (1987) ▌ G. Lindsay, *John G. Lake—Apostle to Africa* (1981).

■ J. R. Zeigler

LANCASTER, SARAH JANE (JEANNIE) (1858–1934). Founder of Apostolic Faith Mission in Australia. Born Sarah Jane Murrell in Williamstown, Victoria, and brought up as a Methodist, Lancaster was founder of the first pentecostal congregation in Australia. At age 21 she married Alfred Lancaster; they had seven children. At age 44, as a member of the York Street Mission Hall in Ballarat (near Melbourne), she was challenged to study the biblical teaching on divine healing. Four years later, in 1906, she received a pentecostal booklet from England, and on Apr. 2, 1908, she was baptized in the Holy Spirit and spoke in tongues.

She began to conduct pentecostal meetings, and the following year she and some friends bought a Temperance Hall in Queensberry Street, North Melbourne, renamed it Good News Hall (GNH), and opened it on New Year's Eve 1909. The small but flourishing church held a regular program of meetings on Sundays and during the week, including an annual Easter footwashing service. Lancaster, called

John G. Lake, who helped establish the Apostolic Faith Mission during missionary service in South Africa and later started churches and healing centers in the northwestern U.S.

"Mother" or "Mummy" by her admiring congregation, was gracious and caring, with real compassion for the poor and needy. During the Depression years she spearheaded extensive welfare work among the poor and needy, providing free meals for over 100 men daily, and clothing, soap, shoes, and health care where possible.

In 1901 Lancaster began publication of a magazine called *Good News*, which was printed at GNH and distributed widely. In 1921 she invited English pentecostal evangelist ʼSmith Wigglesworth to Melbourne, followed the next year by the colorful ʼAimee Semple McPherson. McPherson dissociated herself from GNH in order to reach a wider audience.

In 1926 the South African ʼF. B. Van Eyk joined GNH, which was renamed the Apostolic Faith Mission in 1928. Van Eyk's flamboyant methods and persuasive preaching drew large crowds wherever he went, and a number of new churches were established.

Lancaster was a zealous evangelist. Services were held by the mission all over Australia; regular outreach programs were conducted at the annual Melbourne Show, where thousands of leaflets were distributed. By 1928 more than 20 new congregations had been established. Lancaster strongly believed in male leadership, and although in 1923 she formally handed over leadership to men, she continued to be the driving force behind the movement. Her encouragement of other women led to new churches being opened in Western Australia and Queensland by women such as Edie Anstis, Florrie Mortomore, and Annie Dennis.

Lancaster was remarkably innovative, willing to pioneer new ideas and creative methods of ministry. This was both her strength and her weakness; she derived some unorthodox positions from her personal Bible study. She held a non-Trinitarian view of the Godhead and believed in conditional immortality, views that led to her being ostracized from the Christian community at large. Widowed when she was 71, she married Richard Hocking, two years her senior, on June 15, 1932. She died on Mar. 6, 1934. Although the movement she started eventually foundered, most of its adherents joined more orthodox pentecostal congregations, and her influence is still widespread today.

■ **Bibliography:** B. Chant, *Heart of Fire* (1984) ■ P. Duncan, *Pentecost in Australia* (n.d.) ■ D. and G. Smith, *A River Is Flowing* (1987).   ■ B. Chant

LATIN AMERICAN DISTRICT COUNCIL OF THE ASSEMBLIES OF GOD IN THE U.S.A.

The Spanish-speaking branch of the Anglo-dominated General Council of the Assemblies of God (AG) in the U.S. The Latin American District Council of the AG (LADCAG) traces its roots to ʼHenry C. Ball in south Texas. In 1916 H. C. Ball

founded the first church in Ricardo, and then in Kingsville, TX. That same year he founded *La Luz Apostólica (The Apostolic Light)*, a Spanish-language magazine. Ball was joined in his pioneering evangelistic efforts by ʼRodolfo Orozco, Sunshine Marshall (later Ball), ʼAlice E. Luce, ʼFrancisco Olazábal, ʼJuan L. Lugo, ʼFrank Finkenbinder, ʼDemetrio and Nellie Bazán, ʼGeorge and Francisca Blaisdell, and Francisco Natividad Nevárez. The first "Mexican Convention" was held in Kingsville, TX, in 1918. That same year, Alice E. Luce went to California where she set up a church (El Aposento Alto) in the Mexican Plaza in downtown Los Angeles. Luce was later joined in her pioneer evangelistic efforts by Francisco and Natividad Nevárez and George and Francisca Blaisdell. By the time of the fourth Mexican Convention in 1920, there were more than 500 communicant members in Texas, California, Arizona, New Mexico, Colorado, and Northern Mexico.

These early pioneers recognized the need for a women's support group and for a means to raise funds for foreign missions. In partial response to these needs, Francisca Blaisdell founded the Dorcas women's organization in 1922 in Agua Prieta, Sonora, Mexico. Three years later the Women's Missionary Council (Concilio Misionero Femenil) was developed in the U.S. under the leadership of Sunshine Ball in San Antonio, TX. The Women's Missionary Council has played an important role, not only in raising money for foreign missions, but also as a women's support organization. In 1917 H. C. Ball and A. E. Luce were joined in their evangelistic efforts by Francisco Olazábal. He was a tremendous preacher and perhaps the greatest Latino healing evangelist of the 20th century. His evangelistic crusades attracted hundreds of Latinos to the AG.

While Ball, Luce, and Olazábal pioneered the AG work in the U.S. Southwest, Juan L. Lugo pioneered the work in Puerto Rico. After being converted in Hawaii in 1913, Lugo went to California, where he worked as a migrant laborer by day and as an evangelist at night. Lugo claims that in 1916 God gave him a vision to take the pentecostal message to Puerto Rico. Later that year Lugo landed in Puerto Rico and pioneered the work on the island along with Francisco and Panchito Ortiz, Solomon and Dionisia Feliciano, Lena Howe, and Frank and Aura Finkenbinder. From the outset, the Puerto Rican pentecostal work was an indigenous work, with some help from a few Anglo-American missionaries. The work incorporated in 1921 as the Pentecostal Church of God of Puerto Rico (Iglesia de Dios Pentecostal de Puerto Rico) and by 1927 had an estimated 1,300 adherents attending 37 congregations all over the island. A year later they sent Tómas Alvarez to begin a work among the Puerto Rican diaspora in New York City.

In 1930 the "Mexican Convention" was changed to the Latin American District Council of the AG in the U.S. Separate districts were formed for the U.S., Mexico, Central America, and the eastern U.S. (including Puerto Rico). Recognizing the need for ministerial training, Alice E. Luce and H. C. Ball in 1926 founded Latin American Bible Institutes (LABIs) in San Diego, CA, and San Antonio, TX. The growing need for Spanish-language literature for pastors, Bible institutes, Sunday schools, and evangelistic crusades prompted the creation of Editorial Vida in 1947, which became the Spanish literature division of the ˒Gospel Publishing House of the AG.

The strong and visionary leadership of Anglo leaders such as H. C. Ball and Alice E. Luce also had drawbacks. There have been two major schisms in the LADCAG. The first schism came in 1923 when Francisco Olazábal left the AG because the "gringos have control." Shortly thereafter, Olazábal formed what is now known as the Latin American Council of Christian Churches (CLADIC).

The second major schism took place in 1956, after the General Council of the AG, which had in 1947 denied the request made by their Puerto Rican brethren to be an organic district in the U.S., as opposed to a foreign indigenous national district, reversed its decision. But at this point the Puerto Rican branch of the AG decided to become its own independent autonomous denomination. The Pentecostal Church of God, M.I., as it is known today, is the largest pentecostal denomination on the island, numbering over 112,000 adherents.

Despite the two schisms, the LADCAG witnessed tremendous growth in the mid 20th century. By 1935 there were 174 ministers, 80 congregations, and approximately 4,500 adherents in the U.S. and Puerto Rico. The most rapid growth took place after H. C. Ball stepped down and the leadership was handed over to Demetrio Bazán, who served as the second district superintendent from 1939 to 1958. By 1960 there were 600 ministers, 325 churches, and 20,000 members. In the period 1960–66, the AG witnessed phenomenal growth in the Latino community, where today there are more than 1,740 Latino churches and over 290,000 adherents, making it the largest Latino pentecostal denomination in the U.S. and Puerto Rico.

Unlike many other Latino pentecostal denominations, the LADCAG has had strong and stable leadership that presides over seven regional districts in the U.S. and Puerto Rico. Their doctrinal beliefs are identical to the larger general council of the AG. They actively encourage the spiritual gifts and believe speaking in tongues is the initial physical evidence of the baptism in the Holy Spirit (1 Cor. 12, 14). This Trinitarian pentecostal movement also ordains women to the pastoral ministry and believes that Jesus Christ will return any day to set up his millennial kingdom on earth. Like almost every other Latino pentecostal denomination in the Americas, they also hold to the inerrancy and infallibility of the Bible, the Virgin Birth, Christ's divinity and substitutionary

atonement, and his bodily resurrection. Although they place a heavy emphasis on holy living, they do not have a strict dress code and do not require women to wear a head covering during worship services. Women are allowed to cut their hair and wear modest jewelry and cosmetics, in sharp contrast to most Oneness pentecostal groups.

■ **Bibliography:** G. Espinosa, "Borderland Religion: Los Angeles and the Origins of the Latino Pentecostal Movement in the U.S., Mexico, and Puerto Rico, 1906–1946" (Ph.D. diss., U. of Calif.-Santa Barbara, 1998) ■ C. Holland, *The Religious Dimension of Hispanic Los Angeles* (1974) ■ Office of the Statistician, General Council of the AG, Springfield, MO, 1997.   ■ G. Espinosa

LATTER RAIN MOVEMENT A pentecostal movement of the mid 20th century that, along with the parallel healing movement of that era, became an important component of the post–WWII evangelical awakening. Although highly controversial, the "New Order of the Latter Rain," as it was called by its opponents, bore certain similarities to the early pentecostal movement that originated at ˒Azusa Street, Los Angeles, in 1906. While its impact was on a small scale, its effects were nevertheless felt worldwide, and it became one of several catalysts for the charismatic movement of the 1960s and 1970s.

The movement was characterized by many reports of healings and other miraculous phenomena, in contrast to the preceding decade, which was described by pentecostals as a time of spiritual dryness and lack of God's presence. It stressed the imminence of the premillennial return of Jesus Christ, preceded by an outpouring of God's Spirit, which was expected in accordance with the "former rain" and the "latter rain" of Joel 2:28 (KJV). This was interpreted as a dual prophecy of the Day of Pentecost as described in Acts 2 and of the outpouring of the Holy Spirit that was to immediately precede the coming of the Lord. There was an emphasis on spiritual gifts, which were to be received by the laying on of hands, in contrast to the old pentecostal practice of "tarrying" for the Holy Spirit that had become widespread during the years prior to the revival.

Some of the influence precipitating the Latter Rain includes (1) ˒William Branham, who exercised the laying on of hands in his healing ministry; (2) healing evangelist Franklin Hall's emphasis on fasting and prayer; (3) the church government format in use by the Independent Assemblies of God, which stressed the autonomy of the local church; and (4) the emphasis on the "new thing" of Isa. 43:19 (KJV), which had found its way into the movement years after it was stressed during the meetings of the early pentecostal revival at the turn of the century.

The Latter Rain movement originated at Sharon Orphanage and Schools in North Battleford, Sask., Canada, as a spark igniting an explosion of revival among many pentecostals. It spread quickly throughout North America and many places around the world.

The president of Sharon's "Global Missions" was George Hawtin, who had been a pastor of the ▸Pentecostal Assemblies of Canada (PAOC) and had founded Bethel Bible Institute in Star City, Sask., in 1935. Two years later the institute moved to Saskatoon, and it became PAOC property in 1945 in order to achieve full PAOC recognition. Disputes between Hawtin and PAOC officials led to Hawtin's resignation under pressure in 1947; another Bethel teacher, P. G. Hunt, resigned in sympathy.

In the fall of 1947 Hawtin and Hunt joined Herrick Holt of the North Battleford, Sask., Church of the Foursquare Gospel in an independent work that Holt had already established. Milford Kirkpatrick joined them as global missions secretary, while George Hawtin's brother, Ern, came as a member of the faculty. During this time, the students began to gather to study the Word of God, with fasting and praying. According to Ern Hawtin, on Feb. 12, 1948, God moved into their midst in a

> strange new manner. Some students were under the power of God on the floor, others were kneeling in adoration and worship before the Lord. The anointing deepened until the awe of God was upon everyone. The Lord spoke to one of the brethren, "Go and lay hands upon a certain student and pray for him." While he was in doubt and contemplation, one of the sisters who had been under the power of God went to the brother saying the same words and naming the identical student for whom he was to pray. He went in obedience, and a revelation was given concerning the student's life and future ministry. After this a long prophecy was given with minute details concerning the great thing God was about to do. The pattern for the revival and many details concerning it were given. (Hawtin, 1949, 3)

After they had spent a day searching the Scriptures, it seemed on Feb. 14 "that all Heaven broke loose upon our souls and heaven above came down to greet us" (G. Hawtin, 1950, 2). Ern Hawtin wrote, "Soon a visible manifestation of gifts was received when candidates were prayed over, and many as a result began to be healed, as gifts of healing were received" (E. Hawtin, 1949, 3). As people became aware of these events, they flocked to North Battleford from all parts of North America and many parts of the world to the camp-meeting conventions at Sharon publicized by *The Sharon Star*. Before long, the teachers from Sharon began receiving invitations to minister throughout North America.

At the invitation of Reg Layzell in Vancouver, B.C., George and Ern Hawtin held meetings at Glad Tidings Temple during Nov. 14–18, 1948. ▸Myrtle D. Beall, pastor of Bethesda Missionary Temple in Detroit, MI, traveled

2,500 miles by car to attend these meetings and returned to her church to spark revival there, attracting people from all parts of the country, including ▸Ivan and ▸Carlton Spencer (the founder of Elim Bible Institute and his son). They had been in attendance at the Zion Evangelistic Fellowship in Providence, RI, for a Pentecostal Prayer Fellowship gathering in Dec. 1948 when a latecomer arrived and shared "what he had heard of a visitation in Detroit." Ivan Spencer and his wife went to Detroit within a few days and returned to ignite revival at Elim Bible Institute.

Mrs. Beall wrote a letter describing the revival at Bethesda to ▸Stanley Frodsham, who had been a pioneer of the early pentecostal movement, a leader of the ▸Assemblies of God denomination in the U.S., and the editor of the *Pentecostal Evangel*, its official periodical, for 28 years. As a result of this letter, he went to Mrs. Beall's church in Jan. 1949, where "he was moved deeply by scenes of people under great conviction of sin, making confession and finding peace" (Menzies, 1971, 232).

In Feb. 1949 Thomas Wyatt of Portland, OR, invited the Hawtin party to his church, Wings of Healing Temple, where George Hawtin and Milford Kirkpatrick ministered to 90 preachers from almost every part of North America. One of the pastors attending was A. Earl Lee of Los Angeles, CA, whose church became a center of revival soon after he returned.

By 1949 the North Battleford brethren were becoming less central to the movement, and leadership began to emerge in other circles, partly as a result of tendencies toward sectarianism among the former. This was one of the reasons that the Latter Rain soon became anathema among many denominational pentecostals. However, such pentecostal stalwarts as ▸Lewi Pethrus of Sweden continued to endorse the movement. As leaders of the Apostolic Church, Elim Bible Institute in New York State, and Bethesda Missionary Temple in Detroit continued to move in the revival, the movement progressed with lasting effects.

One of the most important publications of the Latter Rain movement was *The Feast of Tabernacles* by George Warnock, which later came to be republished by Bill Britton of Springfield, MO, and was widely disseminated during the next several decades. The thesis of Warnock's book was that although the Feast of Passover was fulfilled in the death of Christ and although the Feast of Pentecost had had its fulfillment in the outpouring of the Holy Spirit on the Day of Pentecost, the third of Israel's great feasts, the Feast of Tabernacles, is yet to be fulfilled. Those involved in the Latter Rain revival felt that this and many other insights into the Word of God had been given by the Holy Spirit within the context of the 1948 revival by prophetic revelation. This "blaze of prophetic light" was not restricted to the penetration of mysteries within the Bible but included the "unveiling of peoples' lives and hearts through the agency of the Spirit of God" working through the laying on of the hands of "prophets and apostles of His choosing." While many people received renewed faith and hope with respect to their gifts and callings as a result of prophetic ministry of this type, there were a few people whose faith had become shipwrecked, perhaps after receiving the laying on of hands with prophecy from inexperienced people or from others who may have engaged in these practices with mixed motives. The controversy that raged as a result of these problems served to discredit the entire movement in the eyes of most of the major pentecostal denominations, including PAOC, the AG in the U.S., the ˒Pentecostal Holiness Church (PHC), and the ˒Apostolic Church. Many experienced pastors were dropped from the rolls of these and other bodies for their involvement in the Latter Rain movement. At the third annual convention of the ˒Pentecostal Fellowship of North America (PFNA) in 1950, for example, Ivan Q. Spencer resigned under pressure from membership in the PFNA board of administration. He discovered later that the Elim Missionary Assemblies had been dropped from the list of associates because Spencer and this group of churches, which he represented, were actively involved in the Latter Rain movement.

Stanley Frodsham was also active in the movement. In a letter to his daughter, Faith Campbell (May 7, 1949), he wrote that it was inappropriate to associate "this new revival which God is so graciously sending, where so many souls are being saved, where so many lives are being transformed, where God is so graciously restoring the gifts of the Spirit, with the fanatical movements of the past 40 years." In 1949, under pressure and eligible to retire, Frodsham resigned from the editorship of the *Pentecostal Evangel* and withdrew his name as an ordained minister of the AG.

While there was not a general acceptance of the doctrines and practices of the Latter Rain within the denominational churches, there was a significant extent to which they were received outside of the major pentecostal denominations. Many hundreds of "revival churches" became visible, particularly in North America, during the Latter Rain revival, not a few of which had been in existence prior to the revival. Most of these churches were independent and autonomous, and many became mother churches to numerous others that were established or nurtured by members of the mother church.

There were many other similarities between the early pentecostal movement and the 1948 Latter Rain revival, both of which were known as the "Latter Rain movement." Both arose during a time of spontaneous evangelical awakening, and both were characterized by a strong expectation of the imminent coming of Christ. Both employed the laying on of hands for the impartation of gifts of the Spirit, and both reported the supernatural occurrence of "heavenly singing"

by "Spirit-filled" congregations, the sounds of which were likened to the sounds of a great pipe organ. Both recognized the existence of present-day apostles, prophets, evangelists, pastors, and teachers, and both were characterized by widespread repentance and "brokenness" before the Lord. People such as Stanley Frodsham, who had been present at both revivals, often remarked that there was the same strong atmosphere of the presence of the Lord in both cases.

Both movements were also severely criticized by the denominations of which they were originally a part. Walter J. Hollenweger (1965–67, 02a.02.144, 758) has observed that the institutional pentecostal denominations at this time began to experience anew what had come about at the inception of their own movement, but this time from the opposite standpoint: that of the conservative denominations that they had criticized at the time of their own inception.

The churches either spawned or influenced by the Latter Rain were usually independent assemblies with little or no central organization, and for this reason the extent of the influence of the Latter Rain was not always fully evident. However, many of those involved in the Latter Rain carried on and developed principles that had arisen in the late 1940s, becoming a vital part of the charismatic renewal in the 1960s and 1970s. Marion Meloon wrote of a blind woman on the staff of Elim Bible Institute, Rita Kelligan, who, at a convention in 1949, developed a gift of setting psalms to music, "giving us the rich heritage that forms part of the charismatic renewal worship today" (1974, 160). Some of the other distinctive beliefs and practices of the Latter Rain that found their way into the charismatic renewal were the "foundational ministries" of Eph. 4:11, tabernacle teaching, the Feast of Tabernacles, and the "foundational truths" of Heb. 6:1–2.

The influence of the Latter Rain on the charismatic renewal of the 1960s and 1970s can also be seen in the continuity of many of the institutions of the Latter Rain with those of the charismatic movement. For example, *Logos Journal,* one of the most widely circulated magazines of the charismatic renewal, grew out of an earlier publication, *Herald of Faith/Harvest Time,* edited by ˒Joseph Mattsson-Boze and ˒Gerald Derstine. Mattsson-Boze played an important part in the 1948 Latter Rain revival, and Gerald Derstine was associated for several years with J. Preston Eby, who had been forced to resign from the PHC in 1956 due to his Latter Rain teaching and practice.

Other important components of the charismatic renewal also had roots in the 1948 Latter Rain revival, including John Poole's church in Philadelphia, which had been pastored by his father, Fred C. Poole, who had been very active in the Latter Rain movement until his death in 1963. The Elim Missionary Assemblies, a fellowship of churches closely associated with Elim Bible Institute, located first in Hornell, NY, and later in Lima, NY, also helped to carry on the beliefs and practices of the Latter Rain into the charismatic movement. The same was true of the Bethesda Missionary Temple in Detroit, where ›James Lee Beall succeeded his mother, Myrtle Beall, as pastor. The ›Independent Assemblies of God International, a loose fellowship of several hundred churches of Scandinavian origin, also served to carry on the principles of the Latter Rain after a serious split over this issue in 1949 with the ›Fellowship of Christian Assemblies, of which it had been a part.

J. Preston Eby succinctly stated a major emphasis of the Latter Rain when he made reference to preparation for the coming outpouring of the Holy Spirit

> which shall finally bring the FULLNESS, a company of overcoming Sons of God who have come to the measure of the stature of the fullness of Christ to actually dethrone Satan, casting him out of the heavenlies, and finally binding him in the earthlies, bringing the hope of deliverance and life to all the families of the earth. This … great work of the Spirit shall usher a people into full redemption—free from the curse, sin, sickness, death and carnality. (1976, 10)

■ **Bibliography:** G. F. Atter, *The Student's Handbook: Cults and Heresies* (1963) ■ F. Campbell, *Stanley Frodsham: Prophet with a Pen* (1974) ■ W. Cathcart, *To Glory from "Gloom"* (n.d.) ■ J. P. Eby, "The Battle of Armageddon, Part IV" (1976) ■ M. Gaglardi, *The Pastor's Pen, Early Revival Writings of Pastor Reg Layzell* (1965) ■ E. Hawtin, "How This Revival Began," *The Sharon Star* (Aug. 1, 1949) ■ G. Hawtin, "The Church—Which Is His Body," *The Sharon Star* (Mar. 1, 1950) ■ T. Holdcroft, "The New Order of the Latter Rain," *Pneuma* 2 (Fall 1980) ■ W. J. Hollenweger, *Handbuch der Pfingstbewegung*, 10 vols. (1965–67) ■ M. E. Kirkpatrick, *The 1948 Revival and Now* (n.d.) ■ M. Meloon, *Ivan Spencer: Willow in the Wind* (1974) ■ W. W. Menzies, *Anointed to Serve: The Story of the Assemblies of God* (1971) ■ A. W. Rasmussen, *The Last Chapter* (1973) ■ R. M. Riss, *Latter Rain* (1987) ■ idem, "The Latter Rain Movement of 1948," *Pneuma* 4 (Spring 1982). ■ R. M. Riss

LAURENTIN, RENÉ

LAURENTIN, RENÉ (1917–). Well-known Catholic scholar and church journalist. Born in Tours, France, Laurentin's seminary studies were interrupted by WWII, during which he spent five years as a prisoner of war in Germany; he was later awarded the Croix de Guerre and the Légion d'Honneur.

Ordained as priest in 1946, Laurentin pursued his studies as a biblical exegete with a particular interest in Mary, the mother of Jesus. He obtained his Litt.D. from the Sorbonne (1952) and his D. Theol. from the Institut Catholique in Paris (1953). Besides his exegetical study *Structure et Théologie de Luc 1–11* (1956), Laurentin became the premier Catholic authority on Marian apparitions, editing seven volumes of documents on Lourdes (on which he also wrote a six-volume history) and several recent books on the Marian apparitions that have been reported since 1981 in Medjugorje in Bosnia-Herzegovina. His major exegetical study, *The Truth of Christmas beyond the Myths: The Gospels of the Infancy of Christ*, appeared in English translation in 1986. He became professor of theology at the Catholic University of Angers, France, in 1952.

Laurentin served as a consultant to the preparatory commission for Vatican II and was later appointed a theological expert at the council. During the council, his gift for informed theological journalism found expression in a series of books on the council and on the episcopal synods that followed. In addition, Laurentin has written about the lives of several modern French saints.

Laurentin's ability to keep in touch with significant new developments in the Roman Catholic Church brought him in contact with the Catholic charismatic renewal (CCR) as early as 1967, though it was 1970 before he had firsthand experience during a visit to the U.S. His interest and personal experience of blessing led to his books *Catholic Pentecostalism* (1977) and *Miracles in El Paso* (1982). Laurentin has spoken at major CCR conferences and is a respected voice supporting the movement. His book on the Holy Spirit, *L'Esprit Saint Cet Inconnu* (*The Unknown Holy Spirit*, 1997), contains a section on charismatic renewal and recent currents.

■ P. D. Hocken

LAUSTER, HERMAN

LAUSTER, HERMAN (1901–64). Founder of the Church of God (CG, Cleveland, TN) in Germany. Born in Stuttgart, Germany, Lauster came from a staunch Lutheran family. In 1926 he and his bride, Lydia, emigrated from Germany to Grasonville, MD, where he became a merchant. He was converted in 1930 and filled with the Holy Spirit in 1934. He united with the CG and in 1936 went back to Germany as a pentecostal missionary.

Nazi control of Germany made Lauster's efforts difficult, but three churches were secretly established in the Swabian region. In 1938 Lauster came to the unfavorable attention of the Nazis and was imprisoned in Welsheim Prison. Nevertheless, seven new churches were established during WWII. Lauster survived the war and its aftermath. He died in 1964 while preaching at a U.S. servicemen's retreat in Berchtesgaden, Bavaria.

■ **Bibliography:** C. W. Conn, *Like a Mighty Army: A History of the Church of God* (rev. 1977) ■ B. Lauster, *Herman Lauster—One Man and God* (1967). ■ C. W. Conn

LAW, TERRY

LAW, TERRY (1943–). Evangelist, missionary, and speaker. Law is a prominent influence in missions in Poland, Russia, and several other countries. He has led international missionary teams into 40 countries and extensively supports the evangelistic work of nationals in Russia and Poland. Through unusual providence, he has met with several world leaders and has been able to minister in places historically inaccessible to Christian influence. His organization, World Compassion, has distributed over 17 million pieces of Christian literature in the former Soviet Union. He also has done extensive Bible distribution in China. His mission work is characterized by teaching about worship, providing humanitarian aid and literature, and divine healing.

Law graduated from Oral Roberts University and lives in Tulsa, OK, where he oversees Terry Law Ministries and World Compassion. He is active across the U.S. as a public speaker and teacher. He has published several books and articles and numerous teaching tapes on subjects related to worship, spiritual warfare, and discipleship. His book *The Truth about Angels* has been widely read by charismatics and pentecostals of many denominational backgrounds.

Evangelist and missionary Terry Law.

■ **Bibliography:** T. Law, *The Truth About Angels* (1984) ▌ idem, "How to Silence Satan," *The Psalmist* (Apr.–May 1992) ▌ idem, "Launching Our Weapons," *New Wine* (Aug. 1984).

■ D. J. Hedges

LAWRENCE, BENNETT FREEMAN (b. 1890). An early pentecostal preacher in the Midwest. He was associated in evangelism efforts with his mother-in-law, "Mother" ▸Mary Barnes, ▸J. Roswell Flower, Fred Vogler, and others as early as 1908. He was a charter member of the ▸Assemblies of God and was elected assistant secretary at the second general council in the fall of 1914. After he united with the ▸Oneness movement in 1916, little more was heard of him. He is best known for the first history of the pentecostal movement, *The Apostolic Faith Restored* (1916).

■ **Bibliography:** C. Brumback, *Suddenly ... from Heaven* (1961) ▌ B. Lawrence, *The Apostolic Faith Restored* (1916).

■ W. E. Warner

LAYING ON OF HANDS The laying on of hands in the pentecostal and charismatic traditions includes three principal areas: the healing of the sick, the impartation of the Holy Spirit, and various practices of commissioning.

1. Healing.

From the beginning of the pentecostal movement there has been strong emphasis on divine healing. The "full gospel," according to pentecostals, includes healing as one of its components. The doctrinal statement of the Pentecostal Fellowship of North America (PFNA) contains the affirmation:

"We believe that the full gospel includes ... healing of the body." In connection with healing, the laying on of hands is commonly practiced.

Biblical basis for laying on of hands in relation to healing is drawn from numerous NT accounts. Jesus himself often laid hands on people for healing. In an early statement about his ministry we read, "The people brought to Jesus all who had various kinds of sickness, and laying his hands on each one, he healed them" (Luke 4:40). Particularly in the Gospel of Mark there are many references to Jesus' use of hands in healing, e.g., to take by the hand (Peter's feverish mother-in-law [1:31]; Jairus's dead daughter [5:41]; a demonized boy [9:27]), to touch (a leper [1:41]; a deaf mute [7:33]), as well as to lay hands on (various sick people [6:5]). Through manual contact there was a transference of spiritual physical vitality from Jesus to those needing healing. This continues in the book of Acts. Peter took a lame beggar by the hand, and he was healed (3:7). Tabitha was raised from the dead, and Peter, taking her by the hand, lifted her up (9:40–41). Even handkerchiefs and aprons that had touched Paul's body were used to heal the sick (19:12), and on the island of Malta Paul laid hands on Publius's father so that he was made well (28:7–8). In addition to these accounts about Jesus, Peter, and Paul, we have the words of Mark 16 regarding believers: "these signs will accompany those who believe. In my name ... they will place their hands on sick people, and they will get well" (vv. 17–18).

Pentecostals, accordingly, view the laying on of hands for healing to continue as a practice available in principle to all believers. They see no reason to assume that such a practice should be limited to the early church: it is to continue with "those who believe" through the ages. Further, healing will happen, as Jesus said, "in my name," not in the name or authority of the one who lays hands. So pentecostals from the earliest days have made use of laying on of hands (manual contact of whatever kind) in the name of Jesus for the healing of the sick. The pentecostal conviction about healing, however, is by no means limited to the laying on of hands. Jesus himself and the apostles often healed by simply a word spoken. Likewise, those today in the pentecostal and charismatic movements in various ways may pronounce healing in Jesus' name without any physical touch. However, the value of personal contact through hands is strongly emphasized.

2. The Impartation of the Holy Spirit.

Pentecostals also recognize a close connection between laying on of hands and the gift of the Holy Spirit. For those who have come to faith, there is frequently the laying on of hands to receive the Holy Spirit.

Scriptural basis for this practice is drawn primarily from the book of Acts. In the account of the Samaritans, after Philip had proclaimed the gospel and baptized them, Peter and John came down from Jerusalem and laid hands on them to receive the Holy Spirit: "Peter and John placed their hands on them, and they received the Holy Spirit" (8:17). Some three days after Saul of Tarsus had recognized Jesus as Lord, Ananias went to Saul (Paul) and "placing his hands on Saul" declared both Paul's healing from temporary blindness and his being filled with the Holy Spirit (9:17). Paul himself many years later ministered to a number of disciples in Ephesus. They came to faith in Jesus, were baptized in his name, and thereafter "when Paul placed his hands on them, the Holy Spirit came on them" (19:6). In these accounts, receiving, being filled with, and coming on refer essentially to the same activity—the impartation of the Spirit. The laying on of hands was done in immediate conjunction with all three.

The experience of Agnes Ozman that initiated the pentecostal movement occurred through the laying on of hands. She was a student at Charles Parham's Bethel Bible College in Topeka, KS. According to one account it happened thus:

About 7:00 P.M. [Jan. 1, 1901] when meditating in her devotions, Agnes Ozman was reminded that believers in the NT church were "baptized in the Spirit" on several occasions when hands were laid on them. Acting on an impulse when Parham had returned [from a brief mission], she asked Parham to lay hands upon her in biblical fashion. Refusing the request at first, he finally relented and said a short prayer as he laid hands on her. According to Miss Ozman's own testimony: "It was as his hands were laid upon my head that the Holy Spirit fell upon me and I began to speak in tongues glorifying God." (Kendrick, 1961, 52–53)

It is quite interesting that the first laying on of hands that began the pentecostal revival was done reluctantly!

Pentecostals also affirm, however, that frequently the Holy Spirit is received without the laying on of hands. God sovereignly moves without making use of any human medium. Scriptural basis for this is seen in the accounts of the first coming of the Spirit in Jerusalem and the later outpouring in Caesarea. On the Day of Pentecost those who had been waiting in Jerusalem were "all ... filled with the Holy Spirit" (2:4). Hands obviously could not have been laid, because these persons were the first to receive. At Caesarea some time later while Peter was still preaching the gospel to the centurion and his friends, the Holy Spirit suddenly "came on all who heard the message" (10:44). There was neither need nor opportunity for the laying on of hands.

A Presbyterian minister and early charismatic, James H. Brown, speaks of how "there came a day and hour when the Spirit of God invaded our small Saturday evening prayer group, where we met to pray for the Sunday worship service. Literally, the Spirit fell! He electrified everyone in the room!" (Jensen, 1962, 6). In this testimony, typical of many in the movement of the Spirit, there is no reference whatever to laying on of hands: God simply "invaded"!

In the Catholic charismatic renewal (CCR) an important concern has been that of relating the laying on of hands in the sacrament of confirmation to baptism in the Holy Spirit. According to official Catholic teaching, when the bishop lays hands on one of the confirmed, the Holy Spirit is given for the person's inner strengthening and outward witness. Thus, confirmation is sometimes called "the pentecostal sacrament." How then does this sacrament, said to objectively give the Holy Spirit, relate to laying on of hands practiced by believers in general who pray for people to receive the Holy Spirit? Catholic charismatics have differentiated between sacramental laying on of hands and laying on of hands in the charismatic movement in various ways. Some view the latter as a prayer for the one confirmed that he will have "full docility" to the grace received in the sacrament (Gelpi, 1971, 179–83). In somewhat similar vein others have spoken of baptism in the Spirit as the release of the power of the Spirit already given in sacramental confirmation. Through this additional laying on of hands wherein Spirit baptism occurs, one experiences "the effects of confirmation" (Clark, 1969, 15). Still another approach is that of placing less stress on the sacrament of confirmation as actually giving the Holy Spirit and viewing it rather as "an offer" that needs to be personally accepted (Muhlen, 1978, 141, 203). In this last case, the emphasis has moved from sacramental laying on of hands as an objective medium of Spirit baptism to an offer of that which has yet to be received. Presumably, a later laying on of hands when a person is open in faith could be the occasion for the actual reception of the Holy Spirit.

There clearly is need in the church at large for a better understanding of the relationship between laying on of

Sam Klingler praying for a young man in a tent crusade in Pita, Peru, in 1995.

hands and the gift of the Holy Spirit. The book of Hebrews speaks of the laying on of hands as an elementary doctrine that we should go beyond: "Let us leave the elementary teachings about Christ and go on to maturity, not laying again the foundation of repentance from acts that lead to death, and of faith in God, instruction about baptisms, the laying on of hands, the resurrection of the dead, and eternal judgment" (6:1–2). Since in these verses laying on of hands most likely refers to the impartation of the Holy Spirit, we can hardly "go on to maturity" without some basic reconsideration. If Catholics tend to overemphasize the sacramental, many Protestants have little or no comprehension of what is at stake. Pentecostals here have much to contribute by their closer approximation of laying on of hands to the NT practice.

3. Commissioning.

Pentecostals, like many other bodies of Christians, practice laying on of hands for commissioning (ordaining, appointing). According to Acts 6:5–6, seven men were chosen by the Jerusalem believers to serve ("deacon") tables, and thereafter the apostles prayed and laid their hands on them. Some years later prophets and teachers in the Antioch church, after fasting and praying, laid hands on Paul and Barnabas and sent them off (13:1–3). During one of their missionary journeys Paul and Barnabas appointed (literally, "chose by stretching out the hand") elders in a number of churches (14:23). The pentecostal practice of commissioning persons with the laying on of hands is in general accord with these NT examples. Pentecostals, however, do not view any

Le Chee Leong being ordained by the laying on of hands at the Annual General Council of Malaysian Assemblies of God (1970).

such practice as sacramental, that is, that imposition of hands in and of itself imparts some special grace for ministry.

In relation to ordination, many nonpentecostal churches also make use of some statements of Paul to Timothy about hands laid on him. Paul refers first to this laying on of hands as being done by the body of elders: "Do not neglect your gift, which was given you through a prophetic message when the body of elders [or "presbytery," KJV] laid their hands on you" (1 Tim. 4:14). In his second letter Paul admonishes Timothy: "I remind you to fan into flame the gift of God, which is in you through the laying on of my hands" (2 Tim. 1:6). Both of these declarations to Timothy are frequently utilized, especially in ordaining persons by the laying on of hands to the gospel ministry.

Pentecostals, while commonly following a similar practice, lay a larger stress on the prophetic side. Though hands are involved, the more important aspect is the gift (*charisma*—"spiritual gift") bestowed by prophetic utterance. Paul not only speaks of this utterance in 1 Tim. 4:14 but also earlier refers to "the prophecies once made about you [Timothy], so that by following them you may fight the good fight" (1:18). In accordance with Paul's emphasis on prophecy, some pentecostal bodies are primarily concerned about what is declared by the body of elders (or presbytery). Through such prophecy accompanied by the laying on of hands, the candidate to be commissioned is basically equipped for his further ministry in the body of Christ.

See also HEALING, GIFT OF; HEALING IN THE CHRISTIAN CHURCH.

■ **Bibliography:** S. B. Clark, *Confirmation and the "Baptism of the Holy Spirit"* (1969) ■ D. L. Gelpi, *Pentecostalism: A Theological Viewpoint* (1971) ■ J. Jensen, ed., *Presbyterians and the Baptism of the Holy Spirit* (1962) ■ K. Kendrick, *The Promise Fulfilled* (1961) ■ E. Lohse, *TDNT*, 9:431–34 ■ H. Muhlen, *A Charismatic Theology* (1978) ■ E. D. O'Connor, *The Laying On of Hands* (1969) ■ D. Prince, *Laying On of Hands* (n.d.) ■ H. G. Schütz, *NIDNTT* 2:150–52 ■ J. R. Williams, *The Gift of the Holy Spirit Today* (1980).

■ J. R. Williams

LEA, LARRY (1950–). Founder and pastor of Church on the Rock, Rockwall, TX. The son of a wealthy Texas businessman, Lea was converted to Christ at age 17 while in a psychiatric ward. After graduating from Dallas Baptist College in 1972, he became youth minister of Beverly Hills Baptist Church in Dallas and began attending Southwestern Baptist Theological Seminary in Fort Worth. After answering a call to faithful and extensive prayer, Lea established an independent charismatic work, Church on the Rock, in 1980. By 1987 the church had grown from 13 members to over 11,000. He became vice president and dean of theological and spiritual affairs at Oral Roberts University in 1986, continuing with his pastoral responsibilities in Rockwall. Heavily influenced by ᐥPaul Yonggi Cho of South Korea, he has emphasized the need for prayer and obedience in the Christian life.

Lea's numerous publications include *Could You Not Tarry One Hour?* (1987); *The Hearing Ear: Learning to Listen to God* (1988); *The Weapons of your Warfare* (1989); *Wisdom: Don't Live Life without It* (1990); *Highest Calling: Serving in the Royal Priesthood* (1991); and *Releasing the Prayer Anointing* (1996). ◼ R. M. Riss

LEBEAU, PAUL (1925–). Belgian Jesuit theologian. Lebeau studied in the U.S. from 1954 to 1958, when his interest in ecumenism was first kindled. His active involvement in the charismatic renewal began early in 1974, and he was soon invited to become theological advisor to ᐥCardinal Suenens in relation to the latter's responsibility for Catholic charismatic renewal. Lebeau joined the faculty at Lumen Vitae, Brussels, in 1974 and in 1982 became president of the Institut d'E-tudes Théologiques, also in Brussels. He was cochairman with ᐥT. Smail of the European Charismatic Leaders Conferences in 1976, 1978, and 1980, playing a significant role with his linguistic ability and irenic manner. Specializing in ecclesiology and concerned about the social impact of the renewal, Lebeau's writings are available only in article form, mostly in French (*Theological Renewal* contains two items in English). ◼ P. D. Hocken

LEE, FLAVIUS JOSEPHUS (1875–1928). The second general overseer of the Church of God (CG, Cleveland, TN). Born in Cleveland, TN, Lee was deeply religious even as a youth and was choir director of the local Baptist church. On Aug. 28, 1908, he was filled with the Holy Spirit in a revival conducted by ᐥA. J. Tomlinson, pastor of the local CG. The experience changed Lee's life, and he soon became a minister of deep piety and great effectiveness.

In 1909 Tomlinson was elected to the newly created office of general overseer and Lee became his companion in labor. In 1911 Lee succeeded Tomlinson as pastor of the local church and in 1913 was appointed overseer of Tennessee. Soon he was second only to Tomlinson in influence in the CG. In 1922 he succeeded Tomlinson as superintendent of the recently established (1918) Bible Training School. That post also placed Lee on the newly created executive committee.

In 1923 a growing dissatisfaction with Tomlinson's autocratic leadership led to his removal from the office of general overseer. The CG, through its council of 12, selected Lee to fill the vacated office. The five years of Lee's overseership were difficult, but steady growth and expansion continued. He led the CG away from the external fanaticism that threatened pentecostalism in the southeastern U.S. at that time. Lee's ministry was cut short by his death of cancer in 1928.

Flavius J. Lee, described by Church of God historian Charles W. Conn as "a singularly pious man and effective teacher," elected general overseer following the dismissal of A. J. Tomlinson. Lee College (now Lee University) was named for him.

Having consistently preached divine healing as scriptural truth, he declined medical treatment during his illness.

Lee's writings included *Demonology* (c. 1925), an unpublished diary, and a posthumously published book of sermons (1929). In 1947 the CG renamed its oldest college, Lee College, in his honor.

◼ **Bibliography:** C. W. Conn, *Like a Mighty Army: A History of the Church of God* (rev. 1977) ◼ F. J. Lee, unpublished diary ◼ Mrs. F. J. Lee, *Life Sketch and Sermons of F. J. Lee* (1929). ◼ C. W. Conn

LEE, YONG-DO (1901–33). Early Korean Methodist charismatic. Lee was born on Apr. 6, 1901, in Hwanghae province in North Korea. He was imprisoned four times between 1919 and 1924 and spent more than three years in detention because of his activities for the national independence against the Japanese occupation of the Korean peninsula. After that he entered Hyup Sung Seminary, a Methodist institution, in the spring of 1924. Unfortunately, he was diagnosed to be in the terminal stage of tuberculosis and was told to quit seminary in the winter of 1925. However, he had two consecutive mystical experiences, on Christmas Eve of 1928 and on the morning of Jan. 4, 1929, which became the source of his revival movement. From this time until his death in Oct. 1933 he traveled around the country and made every effort to evangelize it through the repentance movement. Lee criticized the lethargic church of Korea and emphasized its need for a revival. He suggested three keys to a true revival of the Korean church: repentance, prayer, and love. He was convinced of the power of prayer and prayed with all his power and might. He started a new style of revival meeting that was mystical and indigenous to the Korean people. This style was quite different from the Great Revival of 1907 that had been led by foreign missionaries. He emphasized mystical union with Christ as well as unconditional and undiscriminating love. His marvelous success in many revival meetings led him to be attacked and misunderstood, largely by jealous pastors. He was an outstanding activist and reformer, but his unconditional love lacked theological reflection, which hindered him from discerning the faults of his followers. In Mar. 1933 he was ordered by the Methodist Church, to which he had belonged from the first, to stop his ministry. He was later involved with the "Jesus Church," in June 1933. On Oct. 2, 1933, he died of pulmonary tuberculosis. In 1999 the general meeting of the Korean Methodist Church decided to rehabilitate him.

■ **Bibliography:** J.-H. Byun, *Biography of Yong-Do Lee* (1993) ■ idem, ed., *Articles Related to Yong-Do Lee* (1993) ■ idem, ed., *Diary of Yong-Do Lee* (1993)■ Y.-H. Lee, *The Holy Spirit Movement in Korea: Its Historical and Doctrinal Development* (diss., Temple U., 1996).   ■ Y.-H. Lee

LENSCH, RODNEY (1934–). Pioneer itinerant teacher in the Lutheran charismatic movement. Lensch graduated in 1959 from Concordia Seminary, Springfield, IL, a seminary of the Lutheran Church–Missouri Synod (LC–MS). Seven years later, while serving in his second LC–MS congregation, he experienced the baptism with the Holy Spirit. When called to testify before synod officials, he elected to resign from his call rather than cause divisions, though he had not been faulted theologically.

After leaving the congregation, Lensch took up a traveling ministry as a conference speaker and counselor to pastors and congregations, living first in St. Louis, MO, and later in St. Paul, MN, where he helped initiate the annual International Lutheran Conference on the Holy Spirit.

He moved to Albany, NY, in 1983 to affiliate with Our Savior's Lutheran Church, the mother church for charismatic renewal in LC–MS. He continued his traveling ministry in the U.S. and also in Australia and Brazil. In 1987 Lensch helped form a charismatic advocacy group within the LC–MS, Renewal in Missouri (RIM). Since 1990 he has been focusing primarily on a writing ministry, publishing among others *Theocratic Church Government* (1996) and a "prophetic autobiography," *Be All Thy Graces Now Outpoured* (1998).

See also LUTHERAN CHARISMATICS.

■ **Bibliography:** L. Christenson, ed., *Welcome, Holy Spirit* (1987) ■ R. Lensch, *Fundamentals of the Spirit-Filled Life,* Course 1 (1974) ■ idem, *My Personal Pentecost* (1968).   ■ L. Christenson

LEONARD, THOMAS KING (1861–1946). Pastor and executive presbyter of the ʼAssemblies of God (AG). Miraculously healed of tuberculosis as a young man, he soon felt a calling into the ministry. He was ordained by the Christian Church in 1901 and pastored three small Christian Churches in and near Findlay, OH. He received the baptism of the Holy Spirit in 1906 at a meeting conducted by ʼC. A. McKinney. He then became convinced that pentecosts should have a permanent home in Findlay, so he sold his farm and purchased an old saloon, which he converted into a church. The first services were held in Mar. 1907. As early as 1912 he began calling his church "Assembly of God." Leonard also began a print shop and started a Bible school in the upstairs part of the building.

When the AG was founded in Apr. 1914, Leonard was elected to the first executive presbytery. He also proposed that the church body call itself the "Assemblies of God" and establish its first headquarters at Findlay. The AG headquarters and printing operation were located in Findlay for six months before relocating to St. Louis, MO, in Jan. 1915.

Reportedly, in 1917 Leonard's Gospel School in Findlay merged with Andrew Fraser's Mount Tabor Bible School in Chicago. He later reopened the school, and after discussion with ʼAimee Semple McPherson, he made plans for it to be recognized by the ʼInternational Church of the Foursquare Gospel (ICFG). He visited ʼAngelus Temple in 1928 to seek affiliation, but apparently neither Leonard or his school ever joined the ICFG. Leonard continued to pastor his church in Findlay, but from 1929 to 1938 he was an independent minister. He was reinstated with the AG in 1938 and retired from pastoring in 1941.

■ **Bibliography:** ■ H. Davidson, comp. "Summary of T. K. Leonard's Activities in the Central District" (1989) ■ T. K. Leonard, ministerial file, Flower Pentecostal Heritage Center ■ P. C. Taylor, "T. K. Leonard and the Pentecostal Mission," *A/G Heritage* (Winter 1994–95), 23–25 ■ *The Vineyard* (1983).   ■ G. W. Gohr

LEWER, ALFRED (d. 1924). Pioneer British missionary to the Tibetan border of China. Born in London, he was a member of the Congregational Church and a close friend of ʼDonald Gee. Together they joined A. E. Saxby's (1873–1960) Baptist Church. Baptized in the Spirit in Sept. 1913, Lewer spent a short time in the ʼPentecostal Missionary Union (PMU) Training Home, Hackney. In Oct. 1915 he sailed with W. J. Boyd and David Lee to serve with the PMU. In spite of his limited education he became very proficient in the difficult Chinese language. He endeared himself to the people, sharing their food, sleeping out-of-doors, and settling their disputes.

Known affectionately as "Brother Alf," his labors were truly apostolic. In 1916 he married Mary Buckwalter of

Philadelphia. By stages they moved to the borders of Tibet but later settled in Wei Hsi, an important town on the main route from southwest China, near Burma (Myanmar). Forays into the surrounding areas met with considerable success among the Lisu people. Though a strong swimmer, Lewer tragically drowned crossing the swollen Mekong River in Sept. 1924.

■ **Bibliography:** D. Gee, *Alfred G. Lewer* (1928) ■ idem, *These Men I Knew* (1980).   ■ D. W. Cartwright

LEWIS, GAYLE F. (1898–1979).

A pastor and administrator in the General Council of the ˈAssemblies of God (AG). He became general superintendent at the death of ˈWesley R. Steelberg in 1952 but was returned to the position of assistant superintendent in 1953.

As a Methodist, Lewis received the pentecostal experience and a call into the ministry. He attended Rochester (NY) Bible Training School and then pastored at Austinburg, OH, beginning in 1921. From 1930 to 1945 he was the superintendent of the old Central District of the AG. In 1945 he was elected as an assistant general superintendent. Among other duties at the national headquarters (1945–65) he directed the ˈGospel Publishing House and the home missions department. He was active in the ˈPentecostal Fellowship of North America, the ˈNational Association of Evangelicals, and the ˈPentecostal World Conference.

■ **Bibliography:** "Gayle F. Lewis, 1898–1979," *PE* (Oct. 21, 1979).   ■ W. E. Warner

LIDMAN, SVEN (1882–1960).

Swedish author, pentecostal theologian, editor. The child of wealthy and highly educated parents, Sven Lidman received a classical education. He was graduated from the University of Uppsala in 1901 with a degree in law. After military service (1901–3) he attempted to return to the study of law but was unsuccessful as a student; he returned several years later to briefly study Italian. Lidman went to Stockholm and published a series of critically acclaimed novels and collections of poetry. By 1920, 13 titles had appeared including *Pasiphaë* (1904), *Primavera* (1905), *Källorna* (1906), *Imperia* and *Elden och altaret* (both in 1907), as well as *Härskare* and *Thure-Gabriel Silfverstååhl* (both in 1910). These and scores of essays established him as perhaps Sweden's most prominent author. The works explored religious and family issues, sexuality, and the inner workings of the human mind and conscience. He was also the editor (1916–18) of the activist magazine *Svensk Lösen.*

In 1920 Lidman published an annotated translation of Augustine's *Confessions.* In the introduction to this volume it is clear that he was involved in a deep religious struggle. The translation is passionate and engaging. Augustine had in some ways become his mentor. A while later he came into contact with Lewi Pethrus, and in 1921 Lidman received Christian baptism at the *Filadelfiaförsamling* in Stockholm. He then became editor (1922) of the Swedish pentecostal periodical *Evangelii Härold,* a post he held until 1948.

Lidman was a popular preacher for the pentecostal movement. Many of his sermons were originally published in *Evangelii Härold,* initially under the editorship of Pethrus. These were gathered and published as book-length collections that began with *Bryggan hållor* (1923) and ended with *Stjärnan som tändes på nytt* (1950), a total of 18 volumes.

By 1948 Lewi Pethrus could no longer tolerate an independent, popular, talented voice that might compete with him for influence in the Swedish pentecostal movement. Lidman was removed from the editorship of *Evangelii Härold* and banned from speaking in the congregations over which Pethrus maintained de facto control. Lidman became a member of an independent pentecostal church in Stockholm. This conflict provoked a crisis of faith, not only in Lidman, but also in his family, several of whom have written novels or exposés about life in the pentecostal movement and the role of Pethrus.

Lidman spent nearly a decade writing his four-volume autobiography. The volumes entitled *Gossen i grottan* (1952), *Lågan och lindansaren* (1952), *Mandoms möda* (1954) and *Vällust och vedergällning* (1957) were a triumph of the genre. They and Lidman's other writings have produced an extensive critical and analytical literature.

■ **Bibliography:** Z. Åberg, *Ur Sven Lidmans Skrifter. Valda stycken samlade och utgivna till hans sextiofemårsdag* (1947) ■ *Europeiska Pingstkonferensen I Stockholm, den 5–12 juni 1939* (1939) ■ R. Hentzel, *Boken om Sven Lidman* (1952) ■ C.-E. Sahlberg, *Pingströrelsen och tidningen Dagen—från sekt till kristet samhälle, 1907–63* (1977) ■ G. E. Söderholm, *Den Svenska Pingstväckelsens Historia, 1907–1927,* 2 vols. (1929) ■ H. Sundberg, *Sven Lidman om människan och Gud, en innehållsanalytisk undersökning* (1996) ■ A. Sundstedt, *Pingstväckelsen—dess uppkomst och första utvecklingsskede* (1967) ■ idem, *Pingstväckelsen—en världväckelse* (1973) ■ idem, *Pingstväckelsen och dess genombrott* (1971) ■ idem, *Pingstväckelsen och dess utbredning* (1972) ■ idem, *Pingstväckelsen—och dess vidare utveckling* (1971).   ■ D. D. Bundy

L.I.F.E. BIBLE COLLEGE

Lighthouse of International Foursquare Evangelism (L.I.F.E.) Bible College was founded by the ˈInternational Church of the Foursquare Gospel in 1923 in Los Angeles to train pastors, evangelists, and missionaries. The college is now in San Demas, CA.

Mt. Vernon Bible College, founded in 1957 in Mt. Vernon, OH, became L.I.F.E. Bible College East when it moved to Christiansburg, VA. L.I.F.E. Bible College Canada, founded in 1928 in Vancouver, B.C., merged with Pacific Bible College in 1997 to form Pacific Life Bible College in Surrey, B.C.

LIFE IN THE SPIRIT SEMINARS (LSS). A practical course of preparation for receiving the ˃baptism in the Spirit.

Unlike the origins of the pentecostal movement, in which those seeking "the baptism" customarily tarried in persistent prayer like the apostles in Jerusalem, the beginnings of the ˃charismatic movement were characterized by seekers being "prayed over" by having hands imposed to receive the baptism of the Spirit.

LSS as a means of preparing people for this "praying over" were first devised in the Word of God community in Ann Arbor, MI, some six months after the community's founding in the fall of 1967. The Word of God seminars were first published in 1971, with a small booklet for participants and a larger book, the *Team Manual*, with detailed guidance for the team conducting the seminars. In the following eight years, 130,000 copies of the *Team Manual* were printed and circulated throughout the English-speaking world, predominantly among Roman Catholics.

LSS were primarily developed for use in prayer groups, many of which lacked experienced leadership. Aware of the dangers of a superficial experience when there was little preparatory teaching and no clear repentance for sin, the authors sought to provide simple and practical instruction. The objectives are spelled out in ˃Stephen Clark's introduction to the 1971 and 1973 editions. In many ways LSS represented a popular exploitation of a genre of spiritual formation long familiar in the Catholic tradition, applied to the situation of the ˃Catholic charismatic renewal.

The original LSS involved two introductory sessions for explanation and sign-up and then seven seminars (God's Love, Salvation, The New Life, Receiving God's Gift, Praying for Baptism in the Holy Spirit, Growth, and Transformation in Christ). Some Catholics were uncomfortable with the seminars' lack of reference to sacramental initiation. So in 1979 a separate Catholic edition was produced as an alternative to the original, which is now called the ecumenical edition. However, the Catholic edition purposely avoided much sacramental explanation, seeing LSS as a retreat situation in which doctrinal explanation can distract from repentance for sin and turning to Jesus in faith. This sacramental and Catholic concern led two nuns, Srs. Burle and Plankenhorn of St. Louis, to produce alternative seminars: *You Will Receive Power* (1977). Most of the European courses follow this more doctrinal emphasis and give fewer instructions on the "how to" aspects: P. Philippe *Afin que vous portiez beaucoup de fruits* (That Ye May Bear Much Fruit; 1977); H. Mühlen, *A Charismatic Theology* (1978); D. Grasso, *Vivere nello Spirito* (Living in the Spirit; 1980). The Anglican course *Saints Alive!* by J. Finney and F. Lawson (1982) was also promoted by some Catholics.

In retrospect, LSS, aiming at bringing alive the faith of churchgoers with minimal spiritual experience, presumed a general acquaintance with basic Christian doctrine. The need for courses of initiation and formation is as great as before, but more recent ones presume less knowledge on the part of the participants. In the 1990s the ˃Alpha Course from ˃Holy Trinity Brompton, London, which is explicitly directed toward the unchurched, is becoming the most widely used introductory program in many countries.

See also CATHOLIC CHARISMATIC RENEWAL.

■ **Bibliography:** P. Hocken, *Clergy Review* (Nov. 1980), 404–8.

■ P. D. Hocken

LIGHT OF THE WORLD CHURCH (IGLESIA LA LUZ DEL MUNDO). Founded in Guadalajara, Mexico, by ˃Eusebio (Aarón) Joaquín González in 1926. After serving in the Mexican military for eleven years (1915-26), Joaquín was converted by ˃Oneness Pentecostal prophet evangelists José Perales and Antonio Muñioz (called Saul and Silas) of the Apostolic Church of Faith in Jesus Christ, who renamed him "Abraham." This practice of renaming remains a practice of La Luz del Mundo.

According to La Luz del Mundo tradition, shortly after Joaquín was converted, he had a number of revelations from God that stated that his new name would be "Aarón" and that he would reestablish the primitive church as described in the NT book of Acts. Through these revelations God also ordered him to leave Monterrey for Guadalajara, Mexico, where he would reestablish the "chosen people" of God.

En route, on foot, to Guadalajara, Aarón—who referred to himself as "El Siervo [the servant]"—evangelized, was said to have performed various miracles, and was persecuted and imprisoned. On December 12, 1926, he arrived in Guadalajara and began preaching in front of the Catholic cathedral in the neighborhood of San Juan de Dios. At this stage La Luz del Mundo was loosely affiliated with the Iglesia Evangélica Cristiana Espirituel Mexicano (later Iglesia Evangélica Cristiana Espirituel), led from 1926 by Francisco Borrego, a sort of predecessor and then competing organization to the Iglesia Apostólica de la Fe en Cristo. Important in the background of these developments were an Irish missionary (Joseph Stewart) and Swedish missionaries (Ester and ˃Axel Andersson). In 1932 the Apostolic Church and the fledgling Light of the World Church broke off formal relations with each other after a failed attempt to unite the two Oneness organizations. For the first few years the congregation met in various locales. In 1934 Aarón opened his first church building. In 1955 he purchased 35 acres of land on the eastside of the city in the Hermosa Provincia section of Guadalajara. There he built the mother church of the movement and also sold land to followers at low prices so they could build their own homes.

After Aarón's death in 1964, his mantle as God's "living apostle on earth" was passed on to his son, ᐳSamuel Joaquín Flores, who was then 27 years old. The church has been profoundly shaped by these two charismatic leaders.

La Luz del Mundo has been active in international missions since the 1950s. The church began sending out a significant number of missionaries in the early 1960s to Costa Rica, El Salvador, Honduras, and Guatemala. Samuel Joaquín Flores has fostered the emphasis on foreign missions, and by 1997 there were congregations in 28 countries. The church began work in the U.S. in the 1950s, and by 1995 there were at least 45 congregations scattered throughout the U.S., especially in Texas and California. The largest congregation in the U.S. is in East Los Angeles. Although the movement was born in Mexico and has attracted a predominantly Latin American constituency, its goal is to spread its understanding of Christianity around the world. It avoids relationships with other religious traditions, including the other Oneness churches.

La Luz del Mundo holds to many Oneness pentecostal beliefs and attitudes. It claims to be Trinitarian in theology, but like the Oneness churches, it does not use the term "persons" to refer to God, Christ, and the Holy Spirit. One significant difference from the other pentecostal churches is the role of the "living apostle." The church teaches that God has given the true church a "living apostle" who speaks the truth of God to the believers. The two "living apostles" have, to the present, been Eusebio (Aarón) Joaquín González and Samuel Joachín Flores.

The biggest celebration in the Light of the World Church is the Holy Supper (*Santa Cena*), held every August 14 in Guadalajara, Mexico; all members of the church are strongly encouraged to attend. Guadalajara has become an international pilgrimage center for the denomination. As many as 100,000 pilgrims attend the annual weeklong celebration surrounding the Holy Supper. The original church building has been expanded several times. In the mid-1980s a new administrative complex and cathedral church seating over 12,000 people were built in Guadalajara.

The church has good relations with the Mexican government and celebrates all national Mexican holidays, although it is very anti-Catholic. The Light of the World Church received a big boost to its national public image in Mexico when Monseignor Rafaél Rodríguez Guillén and Father Joaquín Juárez Ubaldo (late 1990s) left the Catholic church and joined the Light of the World church. These converts have gone on speaking tours throughout Mexico, denouncing corruption in the Roman Catholic Church.

The "living apostle on earth," or "servant," is the head of the church, followed by pastors, all of whom are considered evangelists. The "living apostle" selects and ordains the pastors, based on the information putatively given to him by God and by other pastors. Pastoral formation and education are based on an internship model. Musical instruments are prohibited, and all singing is a cappella. The highest office women can serve in is that of deaconess, although women have been instrumental in the founding of many congregations. The church prohibits women from cutting their hair and wearing jewelry, cosmetics, or pants. During worship services men sit on the left side of the sanctuary and women on the right. Their strict social ethic prohibits smoking, stealing, dancing, attending movies, cursing, and drinking hard liquor.

Despite its rigorous holiness ethic, the church has experienced solid growth throughout the 20th century. Although exact statistics are hard to come by, the church claims to have gone from 75,000 adherents in 1972 to over 1,200 congregations and about 1.5 million adherents around the world in 1996. The mother church in Guadalajara may have as many as 25,000 members. One of the church's few publications is a small booklet, *Conocereis la Verdad* (Guadalajara, n.d.) that attempted to respond to the research of Manuel Jesús Gaxiola y Gaxiola in *La Serpiente y la Palorna* (1970). Also published is *Revista Luz del Mundo,* of which at least eight fascicles came into print, beginning in 1983.

The church has experienced only one major schism, which occurred in 1942 when José Maria González left La Luz del Mundo, taking 25 pastors and 400 members with him. These founded El Buen Pastor, a denomination that has also grown significantly and has been involved in extensive missionary work in Central America and the Caribbean. El Buen Pastor shares most of its theology and ecclesiology with La Luz del Mundo, including the concept of prophetic leadership.

■ **Bibliography:** R. de la Torre, *Los hijos de la luz: Discurso, identidad, y poder en La Luz del Mundo* (1995) ■ M. J. Gaxiola y Gaxiola, *La Serpiente y la Palorna* (1970; 2d ed. 1994) ■ K. D. Gill, *Toward a Contextualized Theology of the Third World* (1994) ■ R. S. Greenway, "The 'Luz del Mundo' Movement in Mexico," *Missiology* 1(1973) ■ R. R. Guillén, "De Monseñor Rafaél Rodríguez Guillén a Monseñor Javier Lozano Barragán: Porqué soy miembro de La Luz del Mundo," *Editorial Concepto* 5 (Feb. 1997) ■ P. F. Loret de Mola, "Origins, Development and Perspectives of La Luz del Mundo Church," *Religion* (1995) ■ L. Rodolfo and M. Quiroz, *Alternativa religiosa en Guadalajara: Una aproximación al estudio de las Iglesias Evangélicas* (1990) ■ L.A. and L.E. Rene Renteria Solis, *La Luz del Mundo: Historia de la Igiesia Crisdana, Vida y Obra del Apostol Aaron Joaquin* (1997). ■ D. D. Bundy

LINDSAY, GORDON (1906–73), and **FREDA THERESA** (1916–). Leaders of the healing movement, publishers, editors, founders and directors of ˈChrist for the Nations Institute.

Gordon Lindsay's parents were members of ˈJ. A. Dowie's Zion City, IL, communitarian experiment when he was born. The bankruptcy of that city forced the family west, where they temporarily became participants in the communitarian experiment of ˈFinis Yoakum at Pisgah Grande, CA. When this community also failed because of leadership and financial problems, the family moved to Oregon. Lindsay attended high school in Portland, OR, where he was converted in a meeting at which ˈCharles F. Parham preached. He came under the influence of ˈJohn G. Lake, former resident of Zion City, missionary to South Africa, and founder of the Divine Healing missions in Spokane, WA, and Portland, OR. Lindsay joined the healing and evangelistic campaigns of Lake, traveling throughout California and the southern states. Lindsay began his own ministry in California as pastor of small churches in Avenal and San Fernando.

Lindsay returned to Portland, where he and Freda Schimpf were married in the Foursquare Gospel Church. When WWII began, travel restrictions and financial concerns caused the Lindsays to accept a pastorate in Ashland, OR. In 1947 Lindsay resigned from the church to become manager of the ˈWilliam Branham campaigns. In an effort to report and publicize those campaigns, Lindsay published the first issue of the ˈVoice of Healing in Apr. 1948 (1948–57; called *World-Wide Revival*, Mar. 1958 to Aug. 1959; renamed *Christ for the Nations*, 1967–). Lindsay's decision to report on other revivalist healing campaigns caused Branham to break relations with his manager in 1948.

Thereafter, Lindsay used the periodical to facilitate healing movement efforts, report the results of meetings, and discuss the theological significance of the healing ministries of a large number of evangelists. Itineraries of individual evangelists were published, and in return individuals adhered to the loose set of guidelines established for the Voice of Healing organization.

In addition to publishing activities, Lindsay organized conventions of healing evangelists. These were held in Dallas (1949) and Kansas City (1950). The intent was to coordinate the activities of the evangelists, prevent misunderstandings, and avoid conflict with the established pentecostal churches. Eventually, many of the healing evangelists found it more lucrative to establish their own magazines and to avoid tacit endorsement of their competition. The number of healing evangelists participating in Voice of Healing activities decreased.

In 1956 Lindsay established Winning the Nations Crusade, which, on the model of ˈT. L. Osborne's Native Church Crusades, sent "deliverance teams" on missions throughout the world. Later Lindsay would develop his own Native Church Crusade (1961), which has supplied resources to Third World church-controlled building programs. Remark-

ably, this money has been provided with no requirements for allegiance or submission to the American organization.

Recognizing the need for literature articulating the theology and history of the healing and charismatic movements, Lindsay became a prolific author and historian of the healing movement. He wrote more than 250 books and pamphlets in addition to the continuous flow of articles for the *Voice of Healing*. Through the Native Literature Work, millions of volumes were published and circulated throughout the world. He also established a radio program and, together with W. A. Raiford, organized the Full Gospel Fellowship of Churches and Ministers International (Sept. 1962; first convention, St. Louis, June 1963). Their hope was that this organization could provide leadership and structure to the charismatic movement. The effort could not compete with the already established Full Gospel Business Men's Fellowship International. However, Gordon and Freda Lindsay have made major contributions to interdenominational and interconfessional understanding among pentecostals and charismatics.

Prior to 1966 these ministries functioned under the aegis of the Dallas-based Voice of Healing, Inc. In 1966 the headquarters were relocated to Dallas Christian Center. The various projects were reorganized and in 1967 renamed ˈChrist for the Nations, Inc. Seminars dealing with ministry and theological and missiological issues became popular. In 1970 Christ for the Nations Institute (CFNI) opened under the direction of Lindsay, who devoted the last three years of his life to establishing this center of theological and spiritual formation for the charismatic and pentecostal movements. Lindsay died on Apr. 1, 1973, while seated on the platform during the Sunday afternoon worship service at CFNI.

Freda Lindsay was elected president of CFNI, and the real growth of that institution came under her leadership.

■ **Bibliography:** D. E. Harrell Jr., *All Things Are Possible: The Healing and Charismatic Movements in Modern America* (1975) ■ F. Lindsay, *Freda* (1987) ■ idem, *My Diary's Secrets* (1976) ■ G. Lindsay, *All about the Gifts of the Spirit* (1962) ■ idem, *The Chaos of Psychics*, 4 vols. (1970) ■ idem, *Crusade for World Fellowship* (n.d.) ■ idem, *Gifts of the Spirit*, 4 vols. (n.d.) ■ idem, *God's Master Key to Success and Prosperity* (1959) ■ idem, *The House the Lord Built* (n.d.) ■ idem, *John G. Lake—Apostle to Africa* (n.d.) ■ idem, *The John G. Lake Sermons* (1949) ■ idem, *The Life of John Alexander Dowie* (1951) ■ idem, *Men Who Heard from Heaven* (1953) ■ idem, *Miracles in the Bible*, 7 vols. (n.d.) ■ idem, *Sorcery in America*, 3 vols. (1971) ■ idem, *William Branham: A Man Sent from God* (1948) ■ idem, *The World Today in Prophecy* (1953).   ■ D. D. Bundy

LITWILLER, NELSON (1898–1986). Mennonite missionary, bishop, and charismatic leader. Nelson Litwiller was born, reared, and educated as a Mennonite and remained one until

Nelson Litwiller. The cover photo of this winter 1987 issue of *Empowered*, the magazine of the Mennonite Renewal Services, was taken at the Festival of the Holy Spirit, Goshen, IN, 1972.

his death. He graduated with a B.A. from Goshen College and a B.D. from Bethany Biblical Seminary (1925).

In 1925 Litwiller was ordained by the College Mennonite Church, Goshen, IN. With his wife, Ada Ramseyer (married 1919), he served from 1925 until 1956 under the Mennonite Board of Missions in Argentina. In 1947 he was appointed a bishop in the church. As a missionary to Uruguay from 1956 to 1967, Litwiller founded the Montevideo Mennonite Seminary, which he served as president for 10 years.

In June 1970 Litwiller attended several midweek prayer meetings led by ˒Kevin Ranaghan at St. Joseph's high school in South Bend, IN. During a time of special prayer, he was baptized in the Holy Spirit.

From that time until shortly before he succumbed to cancer, Litwiller was intensely active in efforts to bring reconciliation and unity, first between traditional Mennonites and Mennonites who were embracing the pentecostal experience, and then among Protestants and Catholics, evangelicals and pentecostals. In 1975 he helped establish Mennonite Renewal Services. His zeal helped make the 1977 Kansas City Conference on the Holy Spirit a reality. He envisioned the 1986 and 1987 New Orleans Congresses on World Evangelization and the Holy Spirit.

■ **Bibliography:** G. Derstine, "Nelson Litwiller (1898–1986)," *Charisma* 12 (Jan. 6, 1987) ■ N. Litwiller, "Revitalized Retirement," *My Personal Pentecost*, ed. R. S. Koch and M. Koch (1977) ■ "Litwiller Honored at New Orleans '86," *Empowered* 5 (1, 1987) ■ "Remembering the Bishop," *Chariscenter USA Newsletter* 12 (2, 1987).   ■ J. A. Hewett

LLORENTE, FRANCISCO (1890–1928). Founder of the Oneness pentecostal movement among Latinos and of the ˒Apostolic Assembly of Faith in Christ Jesus, Inc. (Asamblea Apostólica de la Fe in Cristo Jesús, Inc). Born in Acapulco, Guerrero, Mexico, in 1890, Llorente traveled to San Diego, CA, in 1912, where he was converted to pentecostalism by former Azusa Street participant Juan Navarro Martínez. Shortly thereafter he was ordained an evangelist and began preaching among Mexican migrant laborers. In 1914 he converted Marcial de la Cruz, who with himself and Juan Navarro Martínez began preaching the Apostolic message throughout Southern California. Through their preaching they established small churches in Colton, San Bernardino, Riverside, Los Angeles, and Watts. In contrast to Anglo and black Oneness pentecostals, Llorente and his followers prohibited women's ordination and required women to wear a head covering during public worship services. In 1917 Llorente began pastoring an Apostolic Assembly church in the Mexican district of downtown Los Angeles. A few years later, in 1925, he took over the pastorate of the Apostolic Assembly church in National City, CA. That same year, the burgeoning Apostolic Assembly organized its first annual national convention in San Bernardino, CA. At this meeting Llorente was elected "pastor general," or presiding bishop of the Apostolic Assembly, in which capacity he served until his untimely death in 1928. Under his leadership, the Apostolic Assembly grew from 2 congregations in 1914 to 15 by 1925. His creative and visionary leadership laid a solid foundation on which subsequent Apostolic leaders built throughout the 20th century.

■ **Bibliography:** B. Cantú, *Historia de la Asamblea Apostólica de la Fe in Cristo Jesús, 1916–1966* (1966) ■ C. Holland, *The Religious Dimension in Hispanic Los Angeles* (1974).   ■ G. Espinosa

LOGOS INTERNATIONAL FELLOWSHIP, INC. A charismatic publisher, founded in 1966 by Dan Malachuk, that distributed an estimated 45 million books worldwide. By 1981, however, Logos International Fellowship (LIF) filed for bankruptcy on indebtedness that exceeded $5 million.

In 1965 Malachuk, president of a retail jewelry business in Plainfield, NJ, obtained U.S. publishing rights to a series of lectures written by former spiritualist medium Raphael Gasson of England. It was published as *The Challenging Counterfeit* (c. 1966). Malachuk then asked ˒Jamie Buckingham to work with ˒Nicky Cruz, a ˒Teen Challenge convert, on a book entitled *Run, Baby, Run* (1968), which sold more than 8 million copies. Then came other very successful titles, including books by Merlin Carothers (*Prison to Praise* [1970], etc.) and ›Dennis Bennett's *Nine O'Clock in the Morning* (1970) and *The Holy Spirit and You* (with Rita Bennett, 1971). Other best-sellers quickly followed. By the mid 1970s some 50 books a year were being published. The *Logos Journal* soon became popular among pentecostals and charismatics and within three years boasted nearly 50,000 subscribers.

Logos later became LIF, a nonprofit organization, and listed several well-known personalities on its board of directors, including ›David du Plessis, Gen. Ralph Haines, Dennis Bennett, Jamie Buckingham, and others. LIF also sponsored conferences on the Holy Spirit.

Malachuk created a biweekly newspaper, the *National Courier*, but it became a financial burden and all but destroyed LIF. The staff was headed by Bob Slosser, formerly with the *New York Times*. Former staffer Jamie Buckingham later described it as "an incredibly exciting and expensive operation." The *Courier's* circulation of nearly 100,000 was far below what it needed to break even. In an attempt to keep the paper operating, Malachuk began borrowing money for LIF—about $5 million from several hundred individuals.

The *Courier* ceased publication in 1977, and its indebtedness became a heavy load for LIF to shoulder. Authors were told that the company would pay royalties later. By 1981 more cuts were made in an attempt to save LIF. The *Logos Journal* went the way of the *Courier*. The prosperity theme of many successful best-selling LIF titles seemed to have a hollow ring.

LIF finally filed for bankruptcy in 1981, thus leaving many creditors, investors, and authors without much hope of ever recovering their money. Part of the LIF operation was taken over by Bridge Publishing, whose president, Raymond Stanbury, hoped to make restitution for the LIF indebtedness.

Following LIF's closing, Malachuk moved to Peterborough, NH, and founded Inspirational Publishing Services, a subsidy publisher.

■ **Bibliography:** BP [Bridge Publishing] Newsletter (Mar. 1982) ▮ J. Buckingham, "End of an Era: Final Chapter of the Logos Saga," *Charisma* (Dec. 1981) ▮ D. Malachuk, letter to Logos authors (Dec. 13, 1979).   ■ W. E. Warner

LOPEZ, ABUNDIO L. and **ROSA** (c. 1880s–1920s). Pioneer pentecostal evangelists and Azusa Street participants. They were two of the first Latino converts to pentecostalism in the Americas. They began attending the Azusa Street revivals in Los Angeles less than two months after the revivals began in Apr. 1906. Abundio claimed to have been baptized in the Holy Spirit at the Apostolic Faith Mission on June 5, 1906. Their conversion and work among Mexicans is noted in the second edition of *The Apostolic Faith* newsletter. Shortly after Abundio and Rosa began attending the Azusa Street revivals, they conducted open-air evangelistic crusades in the Mexican Plaza District in downtown Los Angeles. They continued to faithfully attend the Azusa Street revivals from 1906 to 1909 and spread the pentecostal message throughout Mexican barrios and migrant labor camps all over Southern California. Abundio's important work among Mexicans was recognized by the Azusa Street Mission and William J. Seymour, who ordained him to the ministry in 1909. Nothing is known about their later life or ministry.

■ **Bibliography:** G. Espinosa, "Borderland Religion: Los Angeles and the Origins of the Latino Pentecostal Movement in the U.S., Mexico, and Puerto Rico, 1906–1946" (Ph.D. diss., U. of Calif.-Santa Barbara, 1998).   ■ G. Espinosa

LUCE, ALICE EVELINE (1873–1955). Indigenous-church pioneer and educator. With a French Protestant (Huguenot) ancestry, Alice Eveline Luce was born in Cheltenham, England. Her father, the Reverend J. J. Luce, served as vicar of St. Nicholas Church (Anglican) in Gloucester, England. She was converted to Christ at age 10 and felt a strong inclination to the Christian ministry. Following high school she was educated at the Cheltenham Ladies' College and later studied nursing and theology.

Luce's intense desire for ministry led her to journey in 1896 to India as a missionary under appointment with the Church Missionary Society (CMS). She settled in Azimgarh, United Provinces, and worked in a school there and among women isolated in harems.

With the emergence of the pentecostal movement early in this century, news of the baptism in the Holy Spirit finally reached Luce in India. Hearing of two women who had received this experience, she visited them to find out more about this baptism. Convinced that this was from God, she prayed until she received it (c. 1910).

Before long, Luce became ill from drinking contaminated water. After a period of convalescence she returned home in 1912. In the following year the CMS loaned her to the Zenana Bible and Medical Mission (now known as the Bible and Medical Missionary Fellowship). Secretarial work with this agency required her to move to Vancouver, B.C., Canada. In 1914 she resigned from the CMS on medical grounds.

While serving in Canada, Luce felt called of God to go to Mexico as a missionary. The Mexican Revolution, however, altered her plans, and eventually she moved to Texas. It was there that she became acquainted with ›Henry C. Ball, Sunshine Marshall, ›Mack M. Pinson, and Lloyd Baker. This association with other pentecostal believers led to her ordination in 1915 by Pinson into the newly organized General Council of the Assemblies of God (AG).

Two years later Luce and Sunshine Marshall traveled to Monterrey, Mexico, for missionary work. Because of the Revolution, however, they were forced to return to the U.S. After this disappointment, Luce moved to Los Angeles to begin evangelistic work among the Hispanics living in that city.

Realizing that the best way to evangelize the Hispanic population was through training pastors and evangelists, she founded the Berean Bible Institute in 1926 in San Diego and served there until her death in 1955. The school is currently known as Latin American Bible Institute and is located in La Puente, CA.

The significance of Alice E. Luce in the history of the AG and Hispanic evangelism is threefold. First, her efforts at Bible institute training prepared the way for many young people to minister effectively to their own people. Luce's second area of influence was her many publications. In the first 20 years of the Bible institute where she served, most of the curricular materials (books and notes) were prepared by her. ˃Gospel Publishing House published three of her books: *The Messenger and His Message* (1925), *The Little Flock in the Last Days* (1927), and *Pictures of Pentecost* (n.d.). Other Latin American institutes also used her materials. Luce's literary output was enormous. She also regularly contributed to the *Apostolic Light* published by ˃Henry C. Ball. Writing in English for Gospel Publishing House, she wrote lesson comments for intermediate and senior Sunday school teachers' quarterlies for many years.

The articulation of a missionary strategy for the AG is Luce's third contribution and explains the direction of her ministry. Early in 1921, before the general council met, Luce contributed a series of three articles to the *Pentecostal Evangel* entitled "Paul's Missionary Methods." This represented the first exposition of indigenous church principles to ever appear in that publication, although brief references to them had been made before. Luce articulated principles aimed at the establishment of self-supporting, self-governing, and self-propagating NT churches, having been influenced by the publication of Roland Allen's *Missionary Methods: St. Paul's or Ours?* (1912). As a pentecostal, however, Luce went beyond Allen in her view of NT evangelism. Luce believed that apostolic methods would be followed by the power and demonstration of the Holy Spirit.

Alice Luce, who went as a missionary to India in 1896, became a pentecostal in 1910, and devoted the rest of her life to writing, missions, and training others.

A clear attitude of humility is apparent in these three significant articles. The picture of NT ministry is the servanthood of Jesus Christ. Luce noted that the unconverted can easily sense an attitude of cultural or racial superiority on the part of pentecostal missionaries if such a feeling exists. While foreign leadership may be necessary for a time, this must be based on greater experience or spirituality, not on nationality. Luce believed that this attitude of humility and obedience to the Holy Spirit would serve as a model to the converts and young ministers. Consequently, when they follow in the same footsteps, their ministries will bear much fruit because they are following the NT pattern.

■ **Bibliography:** V. De León, *The Silent Pentecostals* (1979) ▊ A. E. Luce, "Paul's Missionary Methods," *PE* (Jan. 8, 1921) ▊ G. B. McGee, "Pioneers of Pentecost: Alice E. Luce and Henry C. Ball," *AGH* 2 (1985) ▊ *PE* (Jan. 22, 1921) ▊ *PE* (Feb. 5, 1921).

■ G. B. McGee

LUGO, JUAN L. (1890–1984). Pioneer pentecostal missionary in Puerto Rico. A Puerto Rican living in Hawaii early in the century, Lugo was converted in 1913 and soon began ministry in California in company with his pastor, ˃Frank Ortiz. Lugo was ordained by the ˃Assemblies of God (AG) in San Jose, CA, in 1916 and felt a call to evangelize his homeland. He received assistance from Bethel Church in Los Angeles and left the same year for the Atlantic coast, conferring en route with ˃J. Roswell Flower in St. Louis and ˃Robert Brown in New York. After an initial effort in Santurce, Lugo continued to Ponce, his family home, where he was met by Salomon Feliciano, with whom he had worked in California. The several congregations that emerged from these efforts affiliated with the AG in 1921, with Lugo serving as executive head. After a profitable decade of expanding work, Lugo began ministry in New York City, establishing a church in a former synagogue. He returned to Puerto Rico to start a Bible institute in 1937 and resided permanently in New York after 1940. Lugo's wife, Isabel, from a socially established Catholic family, has been credited with having contributed much to the couple's ministerial success.

■ **Bibliography:** V. De León, *The Silent Pentecostals* (1979) ▊ R. Dominguez, *Pioneros de Pentecostes* (1971), 1:55–122 ▊ J. Lugo,

Pentecostes en Puerto Rico (1951) ■ D. Moore, *Puerto Rico Para Cristo* (1969).   ■ E. A. Wilson

LUKUSA, LUVUNGU ALBERT (1952–). Pastor of Viens et Vois Assembly of the ▸Pentecostal Community of Congo in Lubumbashi, Congo Democratic Republic; he comes from Mbuji Mayi in the Kasai province. Lukusa holds a degree from the National University (Lubumbashi Campus) and served for a number of years as part of the leadership team at Viens et Vois until Pastor Kiluba wa Kiluba withdrew in 1986.

He has given strong leadership to this large French-speaking assembly begun by ▸Ronald Jean Monot in 1977. Under Lukusa's leadership the growth of several large churches in the Lubumbashi suburbs have been encouraged. Elders from the pastoral team at Viens et Vois have become leaders of newly planted churches in this city with a population of over a million inhabitants. The membership of the central church exceeds 5,000, and the church facility is unable to accommodate all members in its multiple Sunday services, in spite of several expansions.

Lukusa is a popular speaker at conventions. He has ministered to congregations in Zambia and South Africa. He is well known for his practical and clear pentecostal teaching ministry and has spoken out clearly against tribalism in the church.

■ **Bibliography:** *Contact Congo,* magazine of the Zaire Evangelistic Mission, 736 (Mar. 1998) ■ D. J. Garrard, unpub. private papers.
      ■ D. J. Garrard

LUM, CLARA E. (d. 1946). Participant in the Azusa Street revival and editor. Lum played a significant role in widely publicizing the events of the Azusa Street revival in 1906–8.

Formerly a servant in the home of Charles F. Parham, Lum was "sanctified and anointed" about 1897. She arrived at Azusa Street in 1906 seeking the "baptism"; after receiving it she stayed to help in a secretarial capacity. Clara regularly exercised the gifts of tongues and interpretation of tongues and was featured in worship services at the mission, where she read testimonies from those who wrote in. She recorded in shorthand testimonies and "messages in tongues" given at Azusa and then published them in *The Apostolic Faith.*

In an early scandal Lum was accused of taking "French leave" of the mission in 1908, purloining the newspaper and its mailing lists. She relocated in Portland, OR, where she continued to publish *The Apostolic Faith* for Florence Crawford's fledgling group. An explanation that may be understood as an apology for taking the paper with her was printed in *The Apostolic Faith* (21 [May–June 1909], 2).

Local records indicate that Clara Lum had relatives in the Portland area. A brother, William, lived in Portland, and a

sister, Mrs. Mary Brooks, resided in Waldport, OR. Clara never married and lived in no fewer than 15 Portland locations. Her primary stability seems to have been derived from her work with the Apostolic Faith. In 1909 she reported her occupation as a teacher at the Apostolic Faith school. Later she was listed as an editor (1911–13), as an editor of a children's paper (1916–17), and as a stenographer (1918–36) or typist (1938, 1941). Clara apparently retired to Gresham, a suburb of Portland, in the mid 1940s. She died there on Dec. 15, 1946.

■ **Bibliography:** *AF* 1 (4, 1906): 3 ■ 1 (6, 1907): 8 ■ *AF* (Portland) 21 (May–June, 1909): 2 ■ *The Bridegroom's Messenger* 1:3 (Dec. 1907) ■ F. T. Corum, *Like as of Fire* (1981), preface ■ *Oregon Journal* (Dec. 18, 1946), 22 ■ *The Oregonian* (Dec. 18, 1946), 20 ■ Portland City Directory (1909–44) ■ C. W. Shumway, "A Study of the 'Gift of Tongues'" (A.B. thesis, U. of S. Calif., 1914).
      ■ C. M. Robeck Jr.

LUPTON, LEVI RAKESTRAW (1860–1929). Evangelist and missions advocate, Lupton was born near Beloit, OH, to devout Quaker parents. Years later in a business venture Lupton and his wife, Laura, and others moved westward and founded the village of Lupton, MI. In 1885 he professed to having been converted, sanctified, and called to the ministry. The East Goshen Monthly Meeting (a local church) ordained Lupton when he returned to Ohio. In 1896, while attending the annual conference of the Ohio Yearly Meeting of Friends, he reported a physical healing.

Evangelistic ministry followed, reflecting Lupton's Wesleyan Holiness theology and belief in "faith healing." In 1900 he conducted revival services in Alliance, OH, that culminated in the organization of the First Friends Church. To expedite his interest in foreign missions, Lupton and his associates later founded the World Evangelization Company (1904), a periodical called *The New Acts* (1904–10), and the Missionary Home (1905), which functioned as a Bible institute and camp-meeting site. All were located near Alliance. These ventures were all short-lived: in 1906 Lupton's year-old African mission died; he stopped printing his newspaper and dismissed classes, primarily for lack of funds. These parachurch ministries, as well as Lupton's careless financial practices, generated tension within the Ohio Yearly Meeting.

Unfulfilled expectations were rekindled, however, when a pentecostal revival under the leadership of ▸Ivey Campbell occurred at ▸C. A. McKinney's Union Gospel Mission in Akron, OH. Lupton and his supporters attended. Upon his return to Alliance, Lupton held services, hoping for such a revival there. He subsequently received the baptism in the Holy Spirit on Dec. 30, 1906; his wife claimed that "a halo lit upon his brow." On Feb. 9, 1907, the Damascus Quarterly

Meeting (the local district) dismissed Lupton for disloyalty and refusal to abandon independent ministries. (The controversy over glossolalia was side-stepped.) The "tongues issue" persisted among Holiness Friends; however, the movement suffered a severe blow, because, to no small degree, it had been intimately associated with the failed Lupton.

With C. A. McKinney and Ivey Campbell, Lupton envisioned Alliance as "the headquarters for this gracious Pentecostal movement in this part of the country." As a result, he sponsored a camp meeting in June 1907 that had a major impact on the pentecostal movement's development in Ohio and the Northeast. Speakers included ›Frank Bartleman, A. S. Copley, W. A. Cramer, and ›Joseph H. King. More than 700 people attended from 21 states and Canada; among those in attendance were George Fisher, ›J. Roswell Flower, and Alice C. Wood. Significantly, the camp meeting was interracial in composition. At the close Lupton and several others organized the Apostolic Evangelization Company, with him as director carrying the title "the Apostle Levi." Little came of this effort.

At the 1908 camp meeting the participants adopted a "missionary manifesto" urging the formation of a mission agency—the first of its kind among pentecostals. Realization of this goal came about the following year when the (American) Pentecostal Missionary Union was established, modeled after an agency with the same name founded in England in early 1909.

From 1907 to 1910, Lupton traveled widely as a popular speaker in pentecostal circles, perhaps becoming the movement's most articulate advocate of foreign missions. Unfortunately, his ministry, the institutions he founded, and the Pentecostal Missionary Union collapsed in Dec. 1910 after he confessed to adultery. Because of this embarrassment, later pentecostal writers, notably Bartleman, Flower, and King, referred to the 1907 camp meeting but refused to mention Lupton by name, thus effectively eliminating his memory and contributions for many years. Nevertheless, C. E. McPherson, a local newspaper reporter in Alliance, wrote his biography entitled *Life of Levi R. Lupton* (1911), ostensibly the first biography written about an early pentecostal leader.

■ **Bibliography:** T. D. Hamm, *The Rise of Modernist Quakerism, 1895–1907* (1988) ■ G. B. McGee, "Levi Lupton: A Forgotten Pioneer of Early Pentecostalism," *Faces of Renewal*, ed. P. Elbert (1988) ■ C. E. McPherson, *Life of Levi R. Lupton* (1911) ■ W. M. Smith, *Chapters from the New Acts* (n.d.).

■ G. B. McGee; E. J. Gitre

LUTHERAN CHARISMATICS In the summer and fall of 1961 small groups of Lutherans in scattered locations in the U.S. began to have what later came to be known as "charismatic experiences." These initial experiences were often sparked by ecumenical contacts, principally with Episcopalians. By mid 1962 Lutheran charismatics began to meet and correspond with one another.

1. The American Lutheran Church (ALC).

Most of those affected at the outset were from the ALC, located principally in Minnesota, Montana, Southern California, Illinois, and North Dakota. ›Herbert Mjorud, an ALC evangelist, became a prominent exponent of charismatic renewal and was instrumental in the initial spread of the movement. Other early participants who remained visible in the leadership of the movement included ›Larry Christenson, ›Dick and Betty Denny, James Hanson, ›Morris Vaagenes, and George Voeks.

The initial response in the ALC was one of cautious interest. A study commission was appointed to look into the matter of speaking in tongues. A team consisting of psychiatrist Paul Qualben, clinical psychologist John Kildahl, and NT theologian Lowell Satre visited Zion Lutheran Church in Glendive, MT, and Trinity Lutheran Church in San Pedro, CA, where they interviewed and tested members who had experienced speaking in tongues. They found some convictions among those interviewed which they deemed un-Lutheran, such as equating "Spirit-filled" with speaking in tongues. On the other hand, they noted beneficial results in the personal lives and dedication of those who had entered into charismatic experience. The study commission published a report in 1963 that discouraged speaking in tongues in public gatherings but allowed it in one's private devotions. In 1972 Paul Qualben reported on their research in a seminar at Wartburg Seminary in Dubuque, IA. "We had two preconceptions when we went to these congregations," he said. "We expected to encounter people who were emotionally unstable, and we expected the phenomenon to be short-lived. We were wrong on both counts. The people we interviewed were a normal cross-section of a Lutheran congregation, and today, 10 years later, the movement is still growing."

2. The Lutheran Church–Missouri Synod (LC–MS).

In the mid 1960s some LC-MS pastors entered into similar experiences. These included Robert Heil, ›Theodore Jungkuntz, ›Rodney Lensch, Donald Matzat, ›Herbert Mirly, Donald Pfotenhauer, ›Erwin Prange, and ›Delbert Rossin.

The Commission on Theology and Church Relations produced two reports on the charismatic movement, one in 1972, another in 1977. The reports were generally cool toward the movement. They suggested that charismatic gifts were primarily for the apostolic age, though they did not disallow them.

Nevertheless, the movement continued to grow in LC–MS circles. LC–MS congregations, such as Faith Lutheran

Church in Geneva, IL, and Resurrection Lutheran Church in Charlotte, NC, became prominently associated with the renewal and exerted considerable influence both inside and beyond the LC–MS.

Renewal in Missouri (RIM) began its ministry in 1987 after three informal dialogues held between renewal pastors and LC–MS officials from 1984 to 1986. RIM attempted to address questions such as "Who speaks for such a varied movement, and how can we relate to it?" and "What do LC–MS charismatics really believe? There seems to be such a wide range of positions held by them." In addition, the original 53 founders and associations of RIM decided to become "vulnerably visible" as they attempted to bring to the synod a more balanced view concerning the Holy Spirit and spiritual gifts.

RIM and the Missouri Synod are working together to foster "Bold witness, dynamic worship, and vibrant faith." Currently 617 pastors are either involved in renewal or have stated they are supportive. RIM has conducted two national conferences, 12 district-wide Pastors' Renewal Seminars, and a variety of leadership institutes.

3. The Lutheran Church in America (LCA).

The LCA had fewer participants in the renewal than the ALC or LC–MS, but by the late 1960s prominent LCA pastors like Paul Swedberg in Minneapolis and Glen Pearson in York, PA, together with their congregations, were openly identified with charismatic renewal.

In 1974 the LCA produced a pastoral perspective on charismatic renewal that was generally more positive toward the movement than any previous Lutheran statement.

4. Growth.

The growth of the Lutheran charismatic movement in the U.S. during the 1960s was more widespread than most people realized. Even those involved in the movement were surprised when, with little publicity or fanfare, the first International Lutheran Conference on the Holy Spirit drew more than 9,000 people to Minneapolis in 1972. This conference became an annual event and a focal point for renewal, with increasing attendance throughout the 1970s.

The movement grew significantly during the 1970s. By the middle of the decade it was conservatively estimated that about 10% of the Lutherans in the U.S., clergy as well as laity, identified with the charismatic movement. A relatively small number of Lutheran congregations—fewer than 20 in 1975, about 80 by 1986—could be described as "charismatic" in the sense of identifying visibly with this renewal and integrating the charismatic dimension into the total life of their church. A larger number of congregations, however, were significantly influenced by charismatic renewal. By the mid 1970s there was scarcely a Lutheran congregation in the country that did not have some members who were charismatic. Lutherans

were the third-largest group represented when an ecumenical charismatic congress was held in Kansas City in 1977, drawing more than 50,000 people.

The leadership of the renewal in the U.S. developed in clusters of regional leaders who met annually, and in the International Lutheran Renewal Center (ILRC) located in St. Paul, MN. The ILRC sponsored conferences, publications, leaders' meetings, congregational and community renewal events, and theological research. Larry Christenson served as director of the center, with Dick Denny, ▸W. Dennis Pederson, and Delbert Rossin coordinating various aspects of the center's ministry.

Larry Christenson stepped down as director of the ILRC in 1995, and ▸Paul Anderson, who had worked with him in San Pedro, CA, took his place. Anderson has focused primarily on the North American scene of Lutheran renewal. A more open climate exists between evangelical Lutherans and Lutheran charismatics, due in part to ecumenical ministries such as Promise Keepers.

The influence of Lutheran renewal waned in the late 1980s and early 1990s, but it has begun to grow again in all streams of Lutheranism, not only in the Evangelical Lutheran Church of America, the largest Lutheran body in America, formed in 1987 through a merger, and in the Lutheran Church–Missouri Synod, but also in smaller Lutheran bodies.

In the fall of 1997 the International Charismatic Consultation on World Evangelization (ICCOWE) held a conference in Prague. Thirty-five Lutheran delegates were represented, primarily from Europe and the U.S. The Lutheran participants met together during the conference and discussed the feasibility of an International Lutheran Leaders' Network, which was later launched to facilitate communication among Lutheran charismatics throughout the world.

5. Theological Perspective.

ILRC coordinated the work of a 32-member international Lutheran theological consultation that produced *Welcome, Holy Spirit: A Study of Charismatic Renewal in the Church* (1987). It dealt with a broad range of issues and was the most comprehensive theological work to come out of the charismatic movement. On the sensitive issue of baptism with the Holy Spirit they struck a mediating position. The biblical material is clear enough: John the Baptist prophesied that Jesus would baptize his followers with the Holy Spirit; Jesus confirmed it; believers in the early church experienced it. The term is used in reference to two events in Acts: Pentecost and the outpouring of the Spirit in the household of Cornelius.

However, theological explanations about the coming of the Spirit had come to sharp disagreement here. The pentecostal view saw baptism with the Spirit as a "second blessing" by which someone who has already received salvation is

Lutherans gather for a worship service at a charismatic conference.

empowered for service. The sacramental and evangelical views took exception to this interpretation. They held that baptism with the Spirit was either identical with or invariably happened along with water baptism or salvation. Thus, every believer has been baptized with the Spirit.

The Lutheran consultation recognized that the case is hard to resolve on purely exegetical grounds. Neither in the Gospels, where it is used prophetically, nor in Acts, where it is used descriptively, is the term precisely defined; and its use in Acts is somewhat ambiguous. It is difficult to make Pentecost out to be a salvation event for the disciples. Jesus' words to them in Acts 1:4–8 speak not in terms of salvation but rather in terms of power for witness. Jesus' expression "you shall be baptized with the Holy Spirit" (1:5) is not a reference to baptism with water, since the disciples were not baptized at Pentecost when the promise was fulfilled. It was rather a metaphorical expression denoting the experience that the disciples would have of being filled with the Holy Spirit and manifesting it in a demonstrable way. That was exactly what happened to those who were gathered together on Pentecost: "And they were all filled with the Holy Spirit and began to speak in other tongues as the Spirit gave them utterance" (2:4). On the other hand, the primary interpretation the apostles in Jerusalem put on what had happened in the household of Cornelius was that it was a salvation event (11:18).

"Baptized with the Holy Spirit," despite its presence in the NT, is terminology that was little used in the history of the church until the advent of the Holiness and pentecostal movements. Even in the later writings of the NT it does not occur. Luke himself gives greater weight to the term *filled with the Spirit.*

In the 20th century, however, through the pentecostal and charismatic movements, the term *baptism with the Holy Spirit* broke on the scene with dramatic results. The Lutheran consultation noted that to give disproportionate emphasis to a teaching or a term that has relatively little biblical or historical weight could lead to distortion.

The Lutheran consultation contended, however, that the term should not be abandoned or neglected. They noted that some mainline churches with venerable theological traditions tended to acknowledge the vitality and growth of pentecostal Christianity while at the same time belittling its exegesis and theology generally and its doctrine of baptism with the Spirit in particular. They allowed that it would be theoretically possible for the Spirit to enliven the life and worship and witness of pentecostals, prosper their missionary endeavors in an unprecedented way, yet make little headway with them in regard to their understanding of Scripture and their theology. Authentic experience can be inaccurately assessed and explained. But they suggested that to make such a judgment in regard to a movement with the scope and significance and history of worldwide pentecostalism would be audacious. They warranted that the Spirit might want to correct some aspects of pentecostal teaching; a second wave of pentecostalism in the 20th century, the charismatic movement, could be the Spirit's occasion for addressing some new questions to pentecostal theology. But they pointed out that it might equally be the Spirit's occasion for Catholics and Protestants to give more respectful consideration to the exegesis and theology of pentecostals.

In considering the coming and the working of the Holy Spirit in the post-Pentecost Christian community, the Lutheran consultation found it instructive to study the NT, especially the historical sections, from a perspective of the Spirit's strategy. They observed that there are a number of basic factors or elements that Scripture links to the coming of the Spirit. The way that they occur, however, suggests a discriminating and varied use of the different factors—sovereign and often surprising strategies that the Holy Spirit employs to accomplish particular objectives. This approach suggested a fresh way of looking not only at the biblical material but also at some of the traditional systematic approaches to the topic.

The Lutheran consultation considered the three systematic approaches to the coming of the Spirit that are prominent in the church today: the sacramental, the evangelical, and the pentecostal. Simply stated, the sacramental approach teaches that the Holy Spirit is given in water baptism. The evangelical approach links the gift of the Spirit to regeneration; you receive the Holy Spirit when you are born again. The pentecostal approach says that you receive the Holy Spirit when you are baptized with the Holy Spirit, an event that happens subsequent to regeneration.

They proposed neither an alternative systematic nor a critique of systems already on the scene but simply a different way of looking at the reality of the Spirit's coming—a way that gives perhaps greater attention to the sovereign strategy of the Spirit in varying situations.

They found that a strategic approach to the coming of the Spirit answers to the realistic way in which the NT presents the kingdom of God and the kingdom of this world in conflict with one another. It helps identify fundamental truths in the scriptural revelation yet recognizes that the Spirit is sovereign in applying these truths to specific situations.

In considering baptism with the Spirit strategically, they saw that it answered to the need for a signal outpouring of the Spirit's power to initiate or renew witness and ministry. In Acts, both times the term occurs it describes a dramatic initial outpouring of the Spirit. The history of the pentecostal and charismatic movements tended to echo this: A key factor in the spread of the movements was the widely shared personal experience of an outpouring of the Spirit. For many, perhaps most, this initiated a new sense of the Spirit's presence and power for life and ministry.

The experience was commonly accompanied by a manifest demonstration of the Spirit's presence through charismatic gifts, and this they found was also consistent with the scriptural witness. In the theology of Luke, the experience of being filled with the Holy Spirit consistently resulted in a manifest demonstration of the Spirit's presence, usually in the form of exalted speech—they spoke in tongues (Acts 2:4; 10:46; 19:6), prophesied (19:6), extolled God (10:46), spoke the Word of God with boldness (4:31); or it was accompanied by a supernatural sign—a healing (9:17–18), a divine judgment (13:9–11), or a rapturous vision (7:55).

To state that such events, or such charisms, are "not necessary" in terms of systematic theology, the consultation said, would miss the point. They recognized that a specific outpouring of the Spirit with the manifestation of spiritual gifts is not "necessary" either for salvation or for fruitful ministry. One could argue the case both from Scripture and history—systematically. (One would have but to mention a handful of prominent and universally respected movements or believers outside the pentecostal tradition to make the point.) But, they pointed out, that would be like saying, "It is not necessary that an air strike precede an infantry engagement in order for a battle to be won." However, if the commander has planned things that way, then another kind of necessity comes into play: the necessity of paying heed to the commander's strategy.

Given the worldwide spread and witness of the pentecostal and charismatic movements, and given a history of more than 80 years, the Lutheran consultation contended that the church as a whole must consider questions not only of exegesis and systematic theology but also of the Spirit's strategy. They recognized that nonpentecostals might not agree with some aspects of the pentecostal way of explaining the coming of the Spirit. They allowed that pentecostals and charismatics might have oversystematized their own perception and experience of the Holy Spirit. But they acknowledged that pentecostals have accurately perceived the Spirit's strategy: God is calling believers to receive a personal outpouring of the Holy Spirit; he is calling them to be filled with the Holy Spirit in a way and to a degree that they have not done before.

The Lutheran consultation observed that one of the great misconceptions that circulates around discussions of the Holy Spirit is the notion that we have everything that we state in our doctrines. That, they said, is like claiming a victory on the battlefield because one has a textbook on military strategy. The strategy of the Spirit is calling the church to experience more of what the doctrines talk about—to go beyond an intellectual belief in the Third Person of the Trinity to a demonstration of the Spirit and power; to extend our expectation of the Spirit's working to the horizons of Scripture. They did not see this happening simply through reasserting traditional doctrines of the Holy Spirit. They saw it calling for an obedient response to the strategy of the Spirit: a personal encounter with Jesus, who fills followers with the Holy Spirit.

Whether one understands this as an appropriation of something already received (sacramental, evangelical) or a receiving of something promised (pentecostal), the strategy of the Spirit, the consultation concluded, would be served: The Spirit would be poured out, believers would talk about the Holy Spirit with a new sense of reality, they would walk in a new dimension of his reality and power, and the Lord's people would register gains against the powers that oppose the gospel.

See also CHARISMATIC MOVEMENT.

■ **Bibliography:** L. Christenson, *The Charismatic Renewal Among Lutherans* (1985) ■ idem, *Welcome, Holy Spirit* (1987) ■ E. Jorstad, *Bold in the Spirit* (1974) ■ K. McDonnell, ed., *Presence, Power, Praise—Documents on the Charismatic Renewal*, vols. 1–3 (1980) ■ D. Matzat, *Serving the Renewal* (1978) ■ P. Opsahl, ed., *The Holy Spirit in the Life of the Church* (1978).

Denominational Reports. "Anointing and Healing," LCA/USA, 1962 ▮ "The Charismatic Movement and Lutheran Theology," LC–MS/USA, 1972 ▮ "The Charismatic Movement in the Lutheran Church in America: A Pastoral Perspective," LCA/USA, 1974 ▮ "Christian Faith and the Ministry of Healing" ALC/USA, 1965 ▮ "Guidelines," ALC/USA, 1973 ▮ "The Lutheran Church and the Charismatic Movement: Guidelines for Congregations and Pastors," LC–MS/USA, 1977 ▮ "The Lutheran Church of Australia and Lutheran Charismatic Renewal," Feb. 1977 ▮ "Policy Statement Regarding the Neo-Pentecostal Movement," LC–MS/USA, 1975 ▮ "Report of the Lutheran Council in the United States," Lutheran Council, USA, 1978 ▮ "A Report on Glossolalia," ALC/USA, 1963 ▮ "A Statement with Regard to Speaking in Tongues," ALC/USA, 1964. ▮ L. Christenson; P. Anderson

M

McALISTER, HARVEY (1892–1978). Canadian pastor and evangelist. The brother of ›R. E. McAlister and a signer of the ›Pentecostal Assemblies of Canada charter in 1919, Harvey McAlister has been called the "delightful expositor of divine healing." McAlister taught school before his ordination in 1913. He pastored churches in Toronto, Winnipeg, and Calgary before embarking on a teaching ministry that eventually took him to 50 countries. He emphasized signs and wonders in his meetings, combining exposition with an evangelistic appeal. In a career that lasted almost 70 years, he preached a six-week meeting in Hong Kong at age 75.

■ **Bibliography:** C. Brumback, *Suddenly . . . from Heaven* (1961) ■ G. G. Kulbeck, *What God Hath Wrought* (1958) ■ W. Menzies, *Anointed to Serve* (1961) ■ "With the Lord," *Pentecostal Testimony* 60 (1, 1979). ■ E. A. Wilson

McALISTER, ROBERT EDWARD (1880–1953). Pastor and executive officer of the ›Pentecostal Assemblies of Canada. R. E. McAlister is considered to have made strategic administrative contributions during the denomination's formative years. Reared in a Presbyterian family, he briefly attended Bible school in Cincinnati before entering evangelistic work in western Canada. He was a participant in the ›Azusa Street meetings in Los Angeles in 1906, returning to Canada as an enthusiastic pentecostal. He established churches in Westmeath and Ottawa, Ont. He pastored London Gospel Temple, London, Ont., for almost 20 years (1920–39). In 1919 he joined with several other ministers to charter the Pentecostal Assemblies of Canada, with the intention of receiving government recognition and providing a fellowship where "everyone would speak the same thing." He served as secretary and treasurer of the new organization (1919–32) and as editor of the *Pentecostal Testimony*. He is remembered for his competent, untiring efforts to advance the new movement. A persuasive debater and inspiring expositor, it was said that he was able to "frame resolutions in such clear-cut language as to end all debate."

■ **Bibliography:** C. Brumback, *Suddenly . . . from Heaven* (1961) ■ S. Frodsham, *With Signs Following* (1941) ■ G. G. Kulbeck, *What God Hath Wrought* (1958) ■ W. E. McAlister, "Called Home," *Pentecostal Testimony* 34 (11, 1953). ■ E. A. Wilson

McCAULEY, RAY (1949–). Major church leader in South Africa. Ray McCauley was born again in 1969 at a time when he had won bodybuilding titles in South Africa. He studied at Rhema Bible Training Center, Tulsa, OK (1978–79), and then began the Rhema Bible Church with meetings in his parents' home. In 1981 he bought a warehouse capable of seating 2,000; and in 1985 a new 5,000-seat auditorium in Randburg (outside Johannesburg) was dedicated by Kenneth Hagin. By early 1999 the Rhema Church had grown to 16,000 members, 33 full-time pastors, and a full-time staff of 650, who serve not only the multiracial congregation, but also four orphanages and two hospitals for the poor. McCauley is the president of the International Federation of Christian Churches (IFCC), which represents several hundred churches and ministries in Southern Africa, and in 1991 he was elected president of the Pentecostal Charismatic Fellowship of South Africa. McCauley played a significant role in the peace process and in the sociopolitical changes in South Africa. In 1991 he was elected to the facilitating committee involved in the peace talks, and he helped to plan the historic Peace Accord signed by the political leaders. In 1992 he was involved in efforts to bring peace and reconciliation following massacres in Boipatong and Bisho. In 1994 he lent Rhema's support to the country's first multiracial elections. He initiated Operation Mercy–Rwanda in 1994 and a nationwide Stop Crime campaign in 1995. McCauley married Lynda in 1976. They have one son and an adopted daughter. He has written *Faith That Fights for a Nation* (1992), *Power and Passion* (1996), and a biography, *Destined to Win* (1986). ■ P. D. Hocken

McCLAIN, SAMUEL C. (1889–1969). U.S. pentecostal preacher, educator, author, and leader. Born in Georgia, McClain was converted in a Baptist church in Arkansas in 1903. After he received the Holy Spirit in 1912 he conducted prayer meetings. Ordination followed in 1914, and he accepted baptism in the name of Jesus Christ in 1916. He conducted revivals in Arkansas, Kansas, Oklahoma, Texas, and New Mexico, establishing several churches. He pastored in Arkansas, Texas, New Mexico, Mississippi, and Idaho. McClain taught in a Bible school in Eureka Springs, AR (1918–20), and in the Pentecostal Bible Institute in Tupelo, MS (1947–50). From 1921 to 1925 he served as Arkansas state overseer in the Pentecostal Assemblies of the World and as a presbyter for the Texas District of the ›Pentecostal Church, Incorporated (PCI; 1934–35). He edited *The Apostolic Herald*, the official periodical of the PCI, from 1937 to 1940 and wrote *Student's Handbook of Facts in Church History* (1965).

■ **Bibliography:** A. L. Clanton, *United We Stand* (1970). ■ J. L. Hall

McDONNELL, KILIAN (1921–). Roman Catholic theologian of the Order of St. Benedict. McDonnell was educated in public schools, graduating from high school in Velva, ND, in 1940. McDonnell entered Benedictine monastic life at St. John's Abbey in Collegeville, MN, in Aug. 1945. He received his B.A. from the Benedictine St. John's University in Collegeville in 1947 and undertook graduate work in liturgy at Notre Dame in 1948 and in library science at Catholic University of America, Washington, DC, in 1949. He was ordained to the Roman Catholic priesthood in 1951 and served in parish work in Hastings and Detroit Lakes, MN, for four years.

McDonnell's pursuit of theological studies led to the licentiate in theology at the University of Ottawa in Ontario, Canada, in 1960. After receiving that degree he pursued research at several German, Swiss, French, and British universities and ecumenical institutes through 1964, when he obtained the S.T.D. from the Theology Faculty of Trier, Germany. Known early as a Calvin scholar (a major work was *John Calvin, The Church and the Eucharist* [1967]), McDonnell's sights broadened to include extensive work in ecumenical issues as well as pentecostal and charismatic research. He has served as professor of theology in the graduate school of St. John's University.

Killian McDonnell, one of the foremost scholars of the Catholic charismatic movement.

In 1967 McDonnell became the founder and executive director of the Institute for Ecumenical and Cultural Research. He served as the president of its board for a time beginning in 1973, when a new director was named. Housed on the campus of St. John's, the center is designed to bring people together for dialogue and to conduct research on subjects with cross-disciplinary and ecumenical implications. Among the early figures he invited to study at the institute were renewal leaders ˒Arnold Bittlinger, ˒Larry Christenson, and ˒J. Rodman Williams.

McDonnell's commitment to issues bearing on Christian unity have led him to serve on national consultations between Roman Catholics and Presbyterians, Lutherans, and Southern Baptists. On the international level he has engaged in meetings with the World Council of Churches and in consultation with the United Council (Presbyterians and Congregationalists), Disciples of Christ, and Methodists; and for nearly 15 years he has cochaired the Roman Catholic–Pentecostal ˒Dialogue beside ˒David (and now ˒Justus) du Plessis. In 1983 he received the *Pro Pontifice et Ecclesia*, a papal award for his work on ecumenism, and the following year St. John's University granted him the *Pax Christi* award for work done in the same field.

McDonnell's interest in the pentecostal and charismatic renewal movements has led to a stream of literature on the subject from his hand. It was he who first coined the term *classical pentecostalism* to refer to that which was present in the pentecostal churches founded since 1900 and to distinguish it from charismatic renewal in the historic churches. At the suggestion of ˒Cardinal Suenens in 1973, he was the principal author of the first attempt to explain the renewal in a document that had international significance, the "Statement of the Theological Basis of the Catholic Charismatic Renewal."

The following year he was the principal author of the first Malines Document titled "Theological and Pastoral Orientations on the Catholic Charismatic Renewal." These documents established him as a primary interpreter of the Roman Catholic charismatic renewal and as an informal liaison to the Vatican (1974–85), and formally for the National Service Committee of Catholic Charismatic Renewal and American Catholic Bishops. In this latter capacity his hand may be seen in the formal statements issued by this committee.

McDonnell has combined pastoral concern with theological precision, enabling him to bring scholarship and the renewal into contact with each other. His own *Charismatic Renewal and the Churches* (1976) brought new levels of "responsibility" to tongues speakers with its assessment of all the pertinent psychological studies to date. In 1978 his book *The Charismatic Renewal and Ecumenism* attempted to outline an ecumenical theology with guidelines for implementation. His magnum opus to date, however, is the massive, three-volume, edited work entitled *Presence, Power, Praise* (1980), in which he collected, often translated, and contextualized over a hundred documents issued by Protestant and Roman Catholic churches between 1973 and 1980 on the charismatic renewal.

His most recent publications include *Open the Windows: The Popes and Charismatic Renewal* (1989); *Christian Initiation and Baptism in the Holy Spirit: Evidence from the First Eight Centuries* (with George T. Montague; 1991); *Toward a New Pentecost, for a New Evangelization* (1993); and *The Baptism of Jesus in the Jordan: The Trinitarian and Cosmic Order of Salvation* (1996).   ■ C. M. Robeck Jr.

MACEDO, EDIR (1945–). Bishop in the Igreja Universal do Reino de Deus (Church of the Universal Reign of God), Brazil. Bishop Edir Macedo Bezerra was born in 1945 in the city of Rio das Flores, Brazil. He grew up in a Catholic family but with some contact with Umbamda. He attended university in Rio de Janeiro, where he majored in mathematics and worked for the Brazilian lottery to finance his studies. He experienced conversion in a pentecostal meeting and joined a pentecostal congregation called Casa de Bençōes. For a time he pastored a pentecostal congregation in Rio de Janeiro called Nova Vida.

In 1977 he had a vision or dream in which God told him to begin a new church using the name Igreja Universal do Reino de Deus. He began with a small congregation, but the movement grew quickly. The church also developed an aggressive missionary posture. It has established churches in Portugal, Mozambique, Angola, Indonesia, the U.S., and numerous other countries throughout Latin America and Europe. The style has been to develop congregations, buy significant buildings (for example, a historic church in downtown Lisbon, Portugal), and attract even more people. Statistics present difficult problems in all traditions, but according to 1997 church statistics, there are about 6 million adherents in about 1,500 congregations and numerous preaching points. Other observers place the membership at between 1.5 and 2 million.

The Igreja Universal has grown quickly because of its theology and its approach to communication. Under Macedo's leadership, which is highly centralized, the church invested significant funds and energy in electronic media. It became the first Brazilian pentecostal church and first non-Catholic religious tradition to have a prominent profile on television on both a national and international scale. This has not been without its problems, since it has attracted the jealousy and anger of competitors; and it has made occasional indiscretions into national news, as in 1995 when an evangelist physically desecrated a Brazilian national religious symbol on live television. Despite, or perhaps aided by, the controversies, the Igreja Universal has become a significant element of Brazilian popular culture. Its carefully designed, strategically placed buildings are frequently found embedded in advertising as well as in commercial, popular tourist art. Demographically, the church appeals especially to persons from middle- and upper-middle-class backgrounds.

The theology of the Igreja Universal accepts the traditional pentecostal theology with its emphasis on the work of the Holy Spirit but focuses firmly on healing, exorcism, and personal transformation. Observers from both the traditional pentecostal and Catholic traditions have criticized the approach as being too close to the African-Brazilian traditional religious understanding of healing. However, Macedo's publications and sermons on television suggest that the understanding of healing and exorcism is grounded in a reading of the Bible that sees Jesus using healing and exorcism as means to gain people's attention, to demonstrate the power of the "kingdom of God," and to establish a basis for sanctifica-

tion. The church has particular requirements about monies (usually U.S. dollars) given as tithes and offerings as well as in exchange for services of exorcism and healing. Macedo and other authors of the church deserve careful analysis as creative pentecostal theologians.

Bishop Macedo is a prolific author. His books generally go through multiple editions and printings. Many of them have sold between 250,000 and 350,000 copies. These are published through the Igreja Universal do Reino de Deus publishing house, Editora Gráfica Universal, in Rio de Janeiro. Prices are kept low and production quality is high.

■ **Bibliography:** E. Macedo, *Aliança com Deus* (2d ed., 1993) ■ idem, *Apocalipse hoje* (5th ed., 1993) ■ idem, *O avivamento do Espírito de Deus* (1986) ■ idem, *Cárater de Deus* (1986) ■ idem, *O Espíritu Santo* (4th ed., 1992) ■ idem, *A Libertação da teologia* (9th ed., 1993) ■ idem, *Mensagens* (1995) ■ idem, *Nos Passos de Jesus* (1986; 12th ed., 1995) ■ idem, *As obras de carne e os frutos do Espírto* (1986) ■ idem, *Orixás cabocols e guias—Deuses ou demônios?* (1990) ■ idem, *Pecado e arrependimento* (1986) ■ idem, *O poder sobrenatural de fé* (3d ed., 1991) ■ idem, *Vida con Abundácia* (12th ed., 1993) ■ A. Ruuth, *Igreja Universal do Reino de Deus: Gudsrikets Universella Kyrka—en brasiliansk kyrkobildning. Resumen: Iglesia Universal del Reino de Dios* (1995).　　　　■ D. D. Bundy

McGEE, GARY BLAIR (1945–). A prominent authority on the history of pentecostal missions and missiology and long-time professor of church history at the Assemblies of God Theological Seminary, Springfield, MO. McGee (B.A., Central Bible College; M.A.R., Concordia Seminary; M.A., Southwest Missouri State University; Ph.D., Saint Louis University) first earned international recognition as one of the two principal editors of the *Dictionary of Pentecostal and Charismatic Movements* (1988).

Gary McGee, a prominent historian of pentecostal missions and missiology.

Among his many writings must be noted *This Gospel Shall Be Preached: A History and Theology of Assemblies of God Foreign Missions* (1986, 1989); *Initial Evidence: Historical and Biblical Perspectives on the Pentecostal Doctrine of Spirit Baptism* (1991); *How Sweet the Sound: God's Grace for Suffering Christians* (1994); and *Signs and Wonders in Ministry Today* (1996). Numerous dictionary articles, essays for Festschriften, and journal compositions round out McGee's scholarly publications. Denominational readers became familiar with McGee as a frequent contributor to the *Pentecostal Evangel, Assemblies of God Heritage, Enrichment,* and *Paraclete.*

McGee has traveled extensively, including teaching stints at Continental Theological Seminary in Belgium, Romanian Bible Institute in Romania, Southern Asia Bible College in India, and Asia Centre for Evangelism and Missions in Singapore. He holds editorships at the *International Bulletin of Missionary Research* and *Pneuma: The Journal of the Society for Pentecostal Studies,* and he serves on the dissertation series committee of the American Society of Missiology. The fall of 1992 saw him at Yale Divinity School as a research fellow and as a senior mission scholar-in-residence at the Overseas Ministries Study Center. Active since 1990 in the Pentecostal–Roman Catholic ▸Dialogue, McGee is known for being a balanced scholar, able to articulate convincingly his own points of view while understanding and respecting those of others.

Among those who chronicle the history of missions, McGee emerges as arguably one of the most articulate voices in pentecostal missions history and praxis of the 20th century. Through his writing, research, teaching, and lecturing he has aided the entire pentecostal movement in better understanding itself, its motives, and its invaluable heritage.

■ P. H. Alexander

McKENNA, BRIEGE (1946–).

Catholic charismatic sister with healing ministry. Born and brought up in Northern Ireland, McKenna, after determined persistence, entered the Poor Clare nuns at age 15. She soon developed crippling rheumatoid arthritis, which led her superiors to send her in 1967 to their convent in Tampa, FL. At a charismatic retreat in Dec. 1970 she was dramatically healed and baptized in the Spirit. Six months later, on Pentecost 1970, McKenna heard an inner voice say, "You have my gift of healing; go use it." Later that year she heard a call to minister to and intercede for priests. McKenna now works with Fr. Kevin Scallon of Dublin, Ireland, in ministry to priests, especially conducting "Intercession for Priests" retreats. Her life and ministry are described in her book *Miracles Do Happen* (1987).

■ P. D. Hocken

McKINNEY, CLAUDE ADAMS (1873–1940).

Pastor and evangelist. Born in Oil City, PA, McKinney received his early education in Long Island, NY. Saved in a Methodist church, he became involved in church work and singing gospel songs. He also helped with Salvation Army street meetings, where he met Elizabeth Ream ("Libby") Sawyer. Claude and Libby attended ▸A. B. Simpson's Bible institute in New York and served as missionaries to the Belgian Congo with the ▸Christian and Missionary Alliance (CMA), where they were married in 1897.

At the suggestion of A. B. Simpson, the McKinneys moved to Akron, OH, and started the Union Gospel Mission to minister to the destitute of the city. Claude was ordained by the CMA in 1902.

Soon after hearing about the pentecostal outpouring at the ▸Azusa Street Mission in Los Angeles, McKinney received the baptism of the Holy Spirit in late 1906. He began evangelizing in various places in Ohio and withdrew from the CMA in 1908. He organized the Pentecostal Church at Akron in 1914. He was ordained by the Assemblies of God in 1918 and helped in forming the Central District of the AG. He personally founded several churches in Ohio and in all likelihood is the father of Pentecost in Ohio, as he influenced other important leaders such as ▸T. K. Leonard.

■ **Bibliography:** N. Sparlin, *Our Heritage: First Assembly of God* (1965) ▪ *The Vineyard* (1983).   ■ G. W. Gohr

MacKNIGHT, JAMES MONTGOMERY (1930–).

Pastor and administrator. MacKnight was born in Campbellton, N.B. He graduated from Eastern Pentecostal Bible College in 1953 and was ordained in Apr. 1955 by the Pentecostal Assemblies of Canada (PAOC). MacKnight pastored several churches in Ontario: Verona, Belleville, Oshawa (King Street), and Ottawa (Bethel). He served three years as senior evangelist of Canada for Christ Crusades. From 1978 to 1982 he was pastor of Central Pentecostal Tabernacle in Edmonton, Alb.

MacKnight was elected general superintendent of the PAOC in 1982. During his 14-year term of office he spearheaded a forward thrust in church planting and church growth in Canada and in target cities around the world. Recognized as a world leader in pentecostal circles, he has ministered extensively in Canada and the U.S. at conferences, camp meetings, conventions, and other types of special services. Having retired as superintendent, he is currently serving a pastorate in his denomination in Canada. He also serves as vice chairman of the Pentecostal World Conference.

■ **Bibliography:** Biographical sketch (Apr. 1986) ▪ *The Pentecostal Testimony* (Jan. 1983), 2 ▪ Pentecostal World Conference website (1999).   ■ G. W. Gohr

MacNUTT, FRANCIS SCOTT (1925–).

Priest and faith healer. Born in St. Louis, MO, MacNutt received his B.A. at Harvard, M.F.A. at Catholic University of America, and Ph.D. at Aquinas Institute of Theology. Ordained to the Catholic priesthood in 1956, he was elected president of the Catholic Homiletic Society and later was founding editor of its magazine, *Preaching.* In 1967 he received the baptism in the Holy Spirit at a retreat in Tennessee and became active in reintroducing the message of Christ's healing power in the Roman Catholic Church as well as among charismatic groups. He was a pioneer in the charismatic renewal in foreign lands, particularly in Latin America among priests and other church leaders.

In 1980 MacNutt married Judith Sewell, whom he had met five years earlier while she was working as a missionary in Jerusalem. This resulted in an automatic excommunication from the Catholic Church (now lifted), as well as his leaving a number of positions, such as being a member of the ᐧNational Service Committee of the Catholic charismatic movement.

Both MacNutt and his wife are now giving conferences to a wide number of Christian groups, ranging from the Toronto Airport Church to the National Catholic Conference at Notre Dame. In 1987, at the invitation of the Episcopal bishop of northern Florida, they moved Christian Healing Ministries, a center where people come for healing prayer, to Jacksonville, FL. At present they are working with medical doctors on research verifying the effects of prayer for healing. MacNutt has written *Healing* (1974), *Power to Heal* (1977), *The Prayer that Heals* (1981), *Overcome by the Spirit* (1990), and *Deliverance from Evil Spirits* (1995), and has coauthored with Judith *Praying for Your Unborn Child* (1988).

■ **Bibliography:** C. R. Morris, *American Catholic* (1997), 398–400 ▌ J. Pugh, "Francis MacNutt: Catholic in Exile," *Charisma* (Nov. 1983). ■ S. Strang

McPHERSON, AIMEE SEMPLE (1890–1944).

Gifted missionary, evangelist, editor, author, and founder of the International Church of the Foursquare Gospel (ICFG).

Born Aimee Elizabeth Kennedy on Oct. 9, 1890, on a small farm near Ingersoll, Ont., Canada, to James Morgan Kennedy (1836–1921) and his second wife, ᐧMildred ("Minnie") Pearce Kennedy (1862–1947), she was reared in a Christian home. Her father, a farmer and bridge builder, was a Methodist organist and choir director who taught his young daughter to play the piano and organ, while her mother, orphaned at age 12, had been reared by Salvationists. Aimee was a good student, whose faith was shaken for a time by exposure in her local high school to teaching on the theory of evolution.

During the winter months of 1907–8, ᐧRobert James Semple, a pentecostal evangelist, held storefront meetings in an attempt to establish a work in Ingersoll. It was there that Aimee made a firm commitment of faith. On Aug. 12, 1908, Robert Semple and Aimee Kennedy were married in a simple Salvation Army ceremony performed in the apple orchard of Aimee's parents' home, "Kozy Kot."

Following their honeymoon, the couple settled for a short time in Stratford, Ont., then went to London, Ont., where they pioneered a church. By Jan. 1909 they had moved to Chicago. Robert and Aimee Semple were ordained by ᐧWilliam H. Durham on Jan. 2, 1909. For several months the couple accompanied Durham on evangelistic tours in the northern U.S. and Canada.

From their courtship days, the couple was determined to serve as "faith" missionaries in China. Departing from Chicago in 1910, they left for China with a stop at Semple's home near Belfast, Ireland, and a visit in London; then they traveled on through the Suez Canal. They arrived in Hong Kong in June 1910 and were immediately immersed in language study and literature distribution. Within weeks of their arrival, Robert Semple contracted malaria and died on Aug. 19, 1910, leaving Aimee a widow before her 20th birthday. With few financial resources, Aimee stayed in Hong Kong until after the birth of the Semples' daughter, Roberta Star, on Sept. 17, 1910.

Aimee returned to New York City that fall, where she was joined by her mother, Minnie. She worked with the Salvation Army, serving lunch in a Rescue Mission, then collecting money in Broadway theater lobbies. While in the city, she met Harold Stewart McPherson (1890–1968). After a brief courtship the couple went to Chicago with Roberta in tow. They were married on Oct. 24, 1911, in a simple parsonage ceremony.

While living in Chicago, Aimee again became active in church work, but within a year the couple moved to Providence, RI, where their son ᐧRolf Potter Kennedy McPherson was born on Mar. 23, 1913. After a time Aimee returned to Canada with the children and became actively involved in ministry. Harold followed her, and for a time the two ministered together. Harold acted as the advance man, obtaining the necessary site permits and the tents needed to make possible the evangelistic meetings in which Aimee preached. In 1917 Aimee began to publish *The Bridal Call,* a monthly magazine in which she wrote many articles on the basic essence of her teachings. This move helped to solidify a constituency of followers, especially along the eastern seaboard. But the evangelistic activity of the McPhersons was difficult, and it took its toll on both of them. Ultimately, Harold McPherson left the evangelistic party, returning to Rhode Island. The couple was divorced in Aug. 1921.

In 1919 Aimee received ordination with the Assemblies of God (AG) as an "evangelist." She held these credentials until Jan. 5, 1922, when she returned her fellowship papers to General Council chairman ᐧE. N. Bell. While her recent divorce might have posed some problems, it was actually the issue of property ownership that sparked her resignation. Bell responded to her concerns by holding out the possibility that were she to acknowledge that the tabernacle then under construction, ᐧAngelus Temple, was not held in her name, the executive committee would look favorably on her continuation in the AG. She chose not to do so and parted from the AG without prejudice.

Denominational loyalties were lightly held in those days, especially in Holiness and pentecostal circles. It comes as no surprise, then, that while Aimee had credentials with the AG, because of her popularity she was granted credentials by others, even when she did not seek them herself. In Dec. 1920, for instance, she received membership in the Philadelphia-based C. C. Hancock Memorial Church of the Methodist Episcopal Church. That same day she was licensed as an exhorter with the Methodist Episcopal Church. Her ministry continued through the Midwest, to St. Louis and Wichita, back to Denver, then on to California. There, on Mar. 27, 1922, she was ordained by the First Baptist Church in San Jose, again at their encouragement. This ordination was a controversial one that was never ratified by the larger Baptist association. Her ability to appeal broadly across denominational lines was rare among early pentecostals. Her meetings were always interdenominational or ecumenical. They were supported by many people and pastors within historic mainline churches. Her vision was interdenominational from the start, and the cornerstone of Angelus Temple was inscribed to read that the temple was dedicated to "the cause of interdenominational and world-wide evangelism."

In Los Angeles the evangelist looked for a suitable place to preach. She decided in 1921 to build her own and, purchasing the property near Echo Park, designed and built Angelus Temple. She crisscrossed the nation raising funds and proclaiming the gospel. In 1922 she even held an evangelistic tour in Australia. By Jan. 1, 1923, when the 5,300-seat temple was dedicated, it was clear that she needed to settle down and pastor her growing flock. The ICFG was born that day, although its formal incorporation did not come until Dec. 1927.

The 1920s were important years for "Sister," as she came to be known. She continued to write and publish her own works. First came such works as *This Is That* (1919, 1921, 1923), her initial autobiography, then *Divine Healing Sermons* (n.d.) and *The Second Coming of Christ* (1921). The year 1922 brought her inspiration for "The Foursquare Gospel" in the midst of a sermon on Ezek. 1:4–10, which she preached in Oakland, CA. Jesus Christ was preached henceforth as Savior, Baptizer in the Holy Spirit, Healer, and Coming King. She preached her first radio sermon that same

Aimee Semple McPherson, the gifted and flamboyant founder of the International Church of the Foursquare Gospel and of Angelus Temple in Los Angeles.

year and in 1924 opened radio station KFSG in Los Angeles, which is still operated at the ICFG. She was the first woman to receive an FCC license to operate a radio station. She envisioned sending out other evangelists, but she saw the need for training, and in 1923 she established the Lighthouse for International Foursquare Evangelism (L.I.F.E.) Bible College. The early 1920s saw her investing in foreign missions as well, and in 1927 she opened the Angelus Temple Commissary.

McPherson captured the imagination of the lower classes while she captivated the hearts of many in the middle and upper classes. Her commissary met the physical needs of over 1.5 million people during the Depression, regardless of race, creed, or color. She fought for higher wages and greater benefits for police and firefighters and railed against organized crime. Her vision provided an expanded role for pentecostal women to engage in ministry. Many Foursquare Gospel Lighthouses were pioneered and pastored by women for whom she became the role model. Black evangelist Emma Cotton was encouraged by McPherson to establish the church that would ultimately become the formidable Crouch Temple of the Church of God in Christ. McPherson also led Angelus Temple to engage in disaster relief efforts when earthquakes hit Southern California.

But the latter 1920s were difficult years. McPherson preached sometimes more than 20 times weekly while also overseeing her burgeoning work. In May 1926 she had become a highly publicized international figure when she suddenly disappeared, apparently drowned off Venice Beach while swimming. A month later she was found in Mexico, with a story of her kidnapping by some people who feigned to need her help. Rumors spread, and she was embroiled in controversy about an alleged affair in Carmel, CA, with a former employee, Kenneth Ormiston. A grand jury investigated her, but while it was not in session, the district attorney charged her with the obstruction of justice and suborning perjury. Ordered to stand trial, she was ridiculed daily from pulpit to press. Ultimately, the charges were dropped for lack of evidence, and the district attorney became personally embroiled in his own legal dilemma. McPherson authored her account of things in *In the Service of the King* (1927); shortly thereafter an unauthorized biography, *Sister Aimee* (1931), was written by N. B. Mavity. In some minds the issue was never settled, and books and TV reconstructions have not left much to the imagination. But Aimee was much more resilient than is often acknowledged, and Angelus Temple and Foursquare people proved to be loyal to her during this critical time.

The 1930s brought their share of problems too. McPherson suffered a nervous breakdown in 1930 and entered an ill-fated marriage to David L. Hutton on Sept. 13, 1931. The vision of the commissary brought with it an increasing indebtedness and threatened to force the work of Foursquare into bankruptcy. But again she persevered, and the work continued to prosper through her hard choices and gifted capabilities.

During the 1930s, Aimee took advantage of opportunities to expand the ministry. In spite of some trouble with the loyalties of a few of her associates, she consolidated the work of the temple with a few well-chosen appointments. Among them was ▸Giles Knight, a minister and administrator who helped put the organization on solid financial footing. In 1934 she engaged in several widely publicized public debates, arguing with avowed atheist Charles Lee Smith about the existence of God, and in North Little Rock, AK, she engaged in debate with Elder Ben M. Bogard on the subject of the continuation/cessation of miracles and divine healing. Issues such as the efforts of the higher critics, modernism, and evolution led her to pen the statement "What's the Matter?" in 1928. These issues remained problematic in her portrayal of the larger church throughout the 1930s.

Always one who enjoyed music, as early as 1923 Aimee had published the *Tabernacle Revivalist,* including her own composition "Former and Latter Rain" and her own selection of responsive readings covering the four cardinal doctrines she preached. In the 1930s came *Four-Square Melodies,* including more of her compositions. To this volume she appended the Apostles' Creed, the Ten Commandments, and additional readings from the Psalms. In 1937 she published her Foursquare Hymnal with a supplement featuring 64 of her own compositions as well as those of other pentecostals, including ▸Thoro Harris and ▸C. W. Walkem. This work was revised in 1957. In all, she wrote some 180 songs, many of which have never been published. She composed, with the aid of arranger Walkem, seven full-length sacred operas, including *The Bells of Bethlehem, Regem Adorate,* and *The Crimson Road.* Several of her works were also released as sheet music in arrangements for use by soloists and choirs.

A 1936 trip around the world resulted in her plea *Give Me My Own God* (1936), published in a revised format from London under the title *I View the World* (1937). Her travels reinforced her concerns about Hitler, Mussolini, and Stalin, and she spoke often of them and the danger they held for world peace. When war finally materialized, she actively participated in raising money for war bonds and drew many illustrations from the conflagration for her vividly illustrated,

partially acted sermons. She also did much to popularize a restorationist view of church history with her vision the "Dispensation of the Holy Ghost" repeatedly shared in her very popular sermon "Lost and Restored." During the 1930s this was reinforced through an annual "Cavalcade of Christianity" and other similar productions on the Angelus Temple platform or in the Shrine Auditorium of Los Angeles.

During WWII Aimee paid special attention to military personnel who visited Angelus Temple, inviting them to the platform and giving them Bibles. She continued to hold evangelistic meetings around the U.S. and in Canada, though on a sharply reduced scale. She did much to demonstrate Foursquare loyalty to the war effort and sent her magazine, the *Foursquare Crusader,* to army camps. In 1943 she was able to take a vacation in Mexico, but while there she contracted a tropical fever that sometimes left her incapacitated for weeks.

In 1944, perhaps for the first time recognizing her own physical limitations, "Sister" named Rolf McPherson vice president of Foursquare. She also called ▸Howard Courtney to serve alongside him in the national office as general supervisor and director of foreign missions. These were among the last appointments she made. During Sept. 1944, she began a crusade in the Oakland, CA, Civic Auditorium. She preached a sermon the evening of Sept. 26. That night she went to bed and was found the following day, dead from what was described as "shock and respiratory failure" following an apparently accidental overdose of a medical prescription. She was buried in Forest Lawn Cemetery in Glendale, CA, on Oct. 9, 1944, in one of the largest funerals ever held in Los Angeles.

The impact of the life and ministry of Aimee Semple McPherson is a significant one by all accounts. She was a colorful, sometimes controversial, figure. But she was also an extremely gifted communicator and organizer; a competent musician; a prolific writer; in many ways a servant of the people, especially the poor; and an instiller of vision who challenged her followers to trust in Jesus Christ, "the same yesterday, today, and forever" (Heb. 13:8), a theme prominently displayed in many Foursquare churches today. She was undoubtedly the most prominent woman leader pentecostalism has produced to date.

■ **Bibliography:** R. Bahr, *Least of All Saints: The Story of Aimee Semple McPherson* (1979) ▮ O. Coats, "The Ordination of Mrs. McPherson," *Moody Monthly* 22 (1922): 1026–27 ▮ R. L. Cox, *Bogard-McPherson Debate* (n.d.) ▮ idem, *There Is a God Debate* (n.d.) ▮ idem, *The Verdict Is In* (1983) ▮ R. L. Cox, comp., *The Four-Square Gospel* (1969) ▮ T. B. Cox, *Getting "It"* (1927) ▮ J. D. Goben, *"Aimee" the Gospel Gold Digger!* (1932) ▮ A. S. McPherson, *Aimee: Life Story of Aimee Semple McPherson* (1979) ▮ idem, *Aimee Semple McPherson: The Story of My Life* (1973) ▮ idem, *Give Me My Own God* (1936) ▮ idem, *I View the World* (1937) ▮ idem, *In the Service of the King*

(1927) ■ idem, *The Story of My Life* (1951) ■ idem, *This Is That* (1919, 1921, 1923) ■ A. S. McPherson, sermons: *Divine Healing Sermons* (n.d.) ■ idem, *Fire from on High* (1969) ■ idem, *The Foursquare Gospel* (1946) ■ idem, *The Holy Spirit* (1931) ■ idem, *The Second Coming of Christ* (1921) ■ idem, *When the Fig Tree Putteth Forth Her Leaves* (n.d.) ■ correspondence: A. S. McPherson to E. N. Bell (Jan. 5, 1922) ■ E. N. Bell to A. S. McPherson (Feb. 2, 1922) ■ A. S. McPherson to Bro. Welch and Bro. Bell (Mar. 28, 1922) ■ C. H. Magee, *Antics of Aimee: The Poetical Tale of a Kidnapped Female* (1926) ■ N. B. Mavity, *Sister Aimee* (1931) ■ R. P. Shuler, "McPhersonism" (n.d.) ■ idem, "Miss X" (n.d.) ■ L. Thomas, *Storming Heaven* (1970) ■ idem, *The Vanishing Evangelist* (1959).

■ C. M. Robeck Jr.

McPHERSON, ROLF KENNEDY (1913–). Pastor, administrator, and denominational executive. McPherson was born Rolf Potter (Kennedy) McPherson on Mar. 23, 1913, in Providence, RI, to Harold Stewart McPherson and ˺Aimee Elizabeth (Kennedy) Semple McPherson. On July 21, 1931, he was married to Lorna Dee Smith. The couple had two daughters, Kay Sterling (b. 1932) and Marleen Beth (1932–61).

In 1933 McPherson graduated from the Southern California Radio Institute. He has used his media experience to develop several Foursquare video productions. He attended L.I.F.E. Bible College in 1933–34. Ordained to the ministry in 1940, he served as editor of the Foursquare magazine from 1940 to 1943.

Early in 1944 McPherson was named vice president of the ˺International Church of the Foursquare Gospel (ICFG) and aided his ailing mother, Aimee, in her last year of leadership. Upon her death in Sept. 1944, he assumed the presidency of the ICFG. His administrative acumen and financial skills helped to build the denomination from 492 churches in 1944 to 12,628 churches in 1986, serving 1.1 million members and adherents worldwide. During his tenure as president, the denomination took membership in the National Association of Evangelicals and in the Pentecostal Fellowship of North America (now Pentecostal-Charismatic Churches of North America). McPherson has served on the administrative boards of both of these organizations. On May 31, 1988, McPherson retired from the presidency and was succeeded by John R. Holland. McPherson continued to serve on various boards of the church.

Since 1993, when his wife died, McPherson has continued to keep daily office hours at the headquarters building of the ICFG, responding to correspondence on behalf of the church and serving as an unofficial resource to a range of boards and programs of Angelus Temple and the ICFG, now led by Paul Risser. McPherson also continues to hold the title President of the Echo Park Evangelistic Association and The Church of the Foursquare Gospel, though both are now inactive corporations. In 1997 McPherson married Evangeline Carmichael.

■ **Bibliography:** *Who's Who in America* (1976–77) ■ "Foursquare Gospel Church Joins NAE," *United Evangelical Action* (May 1, 1952). ■ C. M. Robeck Jr.

MAINSE, DAVID (1936–). Canadian radio and television personality. Mainse was born in Campbells Bay, Que., the son of a missionary to Egypt. He was educated at Eastern Pentecostal Bible College and ordained in the ˺Pentecostal Assemblies of Canada.

Mainse pastored churches in eastern Canada, and in 1962, while at Pembroke, he began a television ministry that grew into Crossroads Christian Communications (CCC). *Crossroads* came to be released on 150 master and satellite stations by 1976. He resigned from the pastorate in 1970 to concentrate on TV and evangelistic endeavors across Canada.

Mainse is host of the popular one-hour *100 Huntley Street* telecast, which started in 1962 as a 15-minute program following the late news. The program is now seen across Canada and in parts of the United States.

Christian programming inspired and birthed by CCC is now seen in at least 50 countries. A TV broadcast school provides training in TV production and has graduates serving in 65 countries. In 1992 CCC moved to Burlington, Ont.

■ **Bibliography:** D. Mainse, *100 Huntley Street* (1983).

■ S. Strang

MALACHUK, DANIEL (1922–). Founder of charismatic religious publishing company ˺Logos International (1966), which published books, the *Logos Journal*, and the *National Courier* newspaper. In his youth Malachuk was a member of the famous Glad Tidings Tabernacle in New York City.

Malachuk led Logos to become the world's largest charismatic book publisher before it went bankrupt in 1981. He was an international director of the ˺Full Gospel Business Men's Fellowship and was a founding regent of Oral Roberts University. He was director of several overseas spiritual renewal conferences, including the World Conference on the Holy Spirit, Jerusalem (1974).

Malachuk founded a subsidy publishing company after Logos went bankrupt, and he is the author of *Stained Glass Religion—Who Needs It?* and coauthor of *Prophecy in Action*.

■ **Bibliography:** J. Buckingham, "End of an Era, Final Chapter of the Logos Saga," *Charisma* (Dec. 1981). ■ W. E. Warner

MALLORY, ARENIA CORNELIA (1905–77). Educator, teacher, church parliamentarian, and college president in the ˺Church of God in Christ (COGIC). In Oct. 1926, in response to a request of Bishop ▸Charles H. Mason, Mallory caught a Jim Crow train to begin her assignment as the new head of Saints Industrial and Literary School in Lexington, MS (COGIC). She established the first high school and band for African Americans in Holmes County. She attempted to integrate her school faculty long before the Supreme Court legalized integration, but she was repudiated by a mob. She organized a singing group called the Harmonizers, who traveled the entire U.S. in recruitment and fundraising efforts. During the Kennedy administration, she served as manpower specialist and consultant for the U.S. Department of Labor. More than anyone in COGIC's history, she was distinguished by the scores of leaders she influenced. She was a protégée of Mary Mcleod Bethune and was the church's most distinguished educator.

■ **Bibliography:** C. E. Jones, *Black Holiness: A Guide to the Study of Black Participation in Wesleyan Perfectionist and Glossolalic Pentecostal Movements* (1987).   ■ L. Lovett

MARANATHA CAMPUS MINISTRIES, INTERNATIONAL (MCMI).

A collegiate campus ministry founded by ▸Robert T. ("Bob") Weiner and his wife Rose in Paducah, KY, following a successful evangelistic effort with high school students in 1972. Later in that same year they established their first campus church at Murray State University, Murray, KY.

The goal of the organization focused on reaching collegians around the world with the gospel. As they were won to Christ, MCMI discipled them through the establishment of churches on or near college and university campuses, known as Maranatha Christian churches. These churches developed full-fledged programs with children's ministries, Bible training classes, community involvement, etc., but retained their evangelistic outreach to the nearby campuses.

Weiner combined the Jesus Movement's zeal with a radical, "in-your-face" discipleship. Not surprisingly, MCMI was not without its opponents. Although evangelical and charismatic in theology, MCMI created controversy—if not for its intense discipleship and charismatic exuberance, certainly for its '70s-style political activism. The movement nonetheless continued to thrive. Within a decade after its founding, MCMI had established 52 fellowships; seven years later there were 70 congregations in 22 nations.

As a denomination, MCMI conducted regional, national, and international conferences, the Maranatha Satellite Prayer Network (MSPN), the Maranatha Leadership Institute, *The Forerunner* (a newspaper), and other literature. The international office was located in Gainesville, FL, and the staff worked under the direction of an executive board. Weiner served as president from 1972 to 1989.

Strain on the organizational structure and on its founder led MCMI's board to restructure the highly centralized "federation" in 1989, which essentially disbanded the denomination.

■ **Bibliography:** "A Team of Cult Watchers Challenge a Growing Campus Ministry," *Christianity Today* (Aug. 10, 1984) ■ "Maranatha Ministries: Why Bob and Rose Weiner Disciple College Students," *Charisma* (May 1982) ■ "Bob Weiner: New Wineskins for the '90s," *Charisma* (May 1990).   ■ E. J. Gitre

MARCH FOR JESUS

City-based marches of praise and intercession for all believers in Jesus Christ. March for Jesus (MFJ) was initiated in 1987 by four charismatic leaders in Britain: ▸G. Coates, ▸R. Forster, L. Green, and ▸K. Kendrick. The concept of praise marches in city streets developed through the efforts of Ichthus Fellowship and ▸Youth With A Mission to plant a church in Soho, Central London, in the mid 1980s. The first MFJ was held in the City of London on May 25, 1987, with nearly 15,000 participants, a figure that increased to 55,000 in 1988. From the start, MFJ made use of Kendrick's "Make Way" praise songs, written to be public proclamations of Christian faith. While other issues have been strictly excluded from MFJ, it has developed an intercessory and evangelistic strategy, expressed in the handbook *Prayerwalking* by G. Kendrick and J. Houghton (1990). The MFJ Vision Statement reads: "To see churches united in public worship of the Lord Jesus Christ and working together to impact their city with praise, prayer, and proclamation." The first citywide MFJ in the U.S. took place in Austin, TX, in Mar. 1991 with 15,000 Christians from 120 churches, with Tom Pelton of Austin becoming the MFJ U.S. coordinator. The first global MFJ took place in June 1994; it brought together 9 million believers in 178 nations, with an estimated 1.5 million marching in 550 cities in the U.S. Though many cities stage an annual march, global MFJs are now taking place every two years; the largest in 1996 was in São Paolo, Brazil, with 2 million marchers.

■ **Bibliography:** G. Coates, R. Forster, L. Green, G. Kendrick, *March for Jesus* (1992).   ■ P. D. Hocken

MARSHALL, SARAH CATHERINE WOOD (1914–83).

American author. Born in Johnson City, TN, Catherine Wood was the daughter of a Presbyterian minister. In 1936 she married Peter Marshall, also a Presbyterian minister and later chaplain of the U.S. Senate.

From Mar. 1943 until the summer of 1945 she was bedridden with tuberculosis. One night in a vision she felt a sense of Christ's healing presence. She trusted God for her healing and soon recovered.

When Catherine's first husband died of a heart attack in Jan. 1949, she began her literary career by collecting his sermons in *Mr. Jones, Meet the Master*. She wrote his biography, the best-selling *A Man Called Peter*, in 1951 and *Christy* in 1967. She was named "Woman of the Year" by the Women's National Press Club in 1953 and continued to gain worldwide attention because of her writings.

Marshall served as woman's editor for *Christian Herald* magazine from 1958 to 1960. She married Leonard Earl LeSourd, executive editor of *Guideposts*, in 1959 and became an editor of the magazine in 1961. In 1975 Marshall and LeSourd joined popular writers Elizabeth and John Sherrill to found Chosen Books, a publisher of inspirational literature. She died in Boynton Beach, FL.

■ **Bibliography:** *Biography Index* (1997) ■ *Contemporary Authors Online* (1999) ■ J. Melton, *Religious Leaders of America* (1991).
■ G. W. Gohr

MARTIN, R. FRANCIS (1930–). Catholic Scripture scholar and leader in the ˄Catholic Charismatic Renewal (CCR). Born Robert Martin in New York City, he took the name Francis when entering the Cistercian abbey at Spencer, MA, in 1950. He was ordained a priest in 1956 and was sent to study Scripture in Rome. Martin taught Scripture at Spencer (1961–65) and then at Madonna House Community, Combermere, Ont. (1965–71). He did further studies in Rome (1971–76), was a visiting professor at the Ecole

Francis Martin, S.J., a Catholic charismatic New Testament scholar, who was baptized in the Spirit in 1968 and has been a leader in the renewal.

Biblique in Jerusalem, and gained his doctorate at the Pontifical Biblical Institute in Rome in 1978.

Martin was baptized in the Spirit in 1968 following a visit to Combermere by two young men from Ann Arbor, MI. During his years in Rome and Jerusalem, he was active in the CCR, acquiring a reputation as a dynamic teacher who combined the scholarly with the spiritual. Martin is a brilliant linguist and became known to CCR leaders in many countries through his translation work at the CCR International Conference in Rome in 1975. In those years he published three books that led to many conference talks: *Touching God* (1975), *Footprints of God* (1976), and *The Songs of God's People* (1978).

In 1979 Martin moved to the Mother of God Community in Gaithersburg, MD. He has taught Scripture at the University of Steubenville, OH, and at academic institutions in Washington, DC, and has been a major speaker at the Conference for Priests and Deacons held at Steubenville since 1975. More recent works include *Baptism in the Holy Spirit* (1986), *Stories Comparable to New Testament Narratives* (1988), and *The Feminist Question* (1994).

■ P. D. Hocken

MARTIN, RALPH (1942–). Prominent lay leader in the Catholic Charismatic Renewal (CCR). Having a conversion experience through a Cursillo retreat just before graduating with a degree in philosophy from Notre Dame in 1964, Martin worked with Stephen Clark on the national secretariat of the Cursillo movement (1964–70). He was baptized in the Spirit in the spring of 1967 after hearing of the "Duquesne weekend" (˄Catholic charismatic renewal).

In Nov. 1967 Martin and three colleagues began the prayer meeting at Ann Arbor, MI, that grew into the Word of God community. He was closely associated with Word of God's outreach, was the first editor of *New Covenant* (1971–75), directed Servant Ministries (1980–90), and was a leader in the Sword of the Spirit, an international community formed by Word of God and other communities (1982–90). Martin has been one of the most respected leaders in the CCR. As well as serving on the ˄National Service Committee (1970–75), he contributed to its international expansion, becoming the first director of the International Communications Office (1975–79), moving with the office to Brussels to work more closely with ˄Cardinal Suenens. Since the Word of God's distancing itself from the Sword of the Spirit in 1990, Martin's wider ministry continues under the umbrella of Renewal Ministries.

Martin's role has been important as both teacher and prophet. He has constantly stressed the call to repentance for sin, the demands of the holiness of God upon his people, and the importance of basic Christian orthodoxy, giving striking prophecies in St. Peter's, Rome, in 1975 and at the ˄Kansas City Conference in 1977.

Since 1983 this message has been spread through F.I.R.E. (with ʼJohn Bertolucci, ʼMichael Scanlan, and ʼAnn Shields), as well as through his weekly television program *The Choices We Face*. His publications include *Unless the Lord Build the House* (1971); *Hungry for God* (1974); *Fire on the Earth* (1975); *Husbands, Wives, Parents, Children* (1978); *A Crisis of Truth* (1982); *The Return of the Lord* (1983); *Called to Holiness* (1988); *The Catholic Church at the End of an Age* (1994); and *Is Jesus Coming Soon?* (1997).   ■ P. D. Hocken

MARXISM AND PENTECOSTALISM The following is based mainly on the works of Peter Kuzmič, probably the best-informed pentecostal theologian on Marxism. He has discovered that the topic of Marxism generates in pentecostal and charismatic circles "more heat than light," and he agrees with Paul Tillich: Marx's name "has become so potent a political and semi-religious symbol, divine or demonic, that whatever you say about him will be used against you by fanatics on both sides" (Tillich, 906). Kuzmič is aware that dogmatic Marxism is dead. "Even if the process were reversible by the use of military power, the people would not take it any longer. Where all of this will lead is impossible to predict" (144).

In Kuzmič's opinion, Marxism is neither monolithic, nor is it—as is sometimes said—neutral science. Christians must know that Marxism and Christianity are "actually relatives, relatives historically and philosophically at odds with each other." "Nicolai Berdyaev argued that communism and Christianity are rival religions, and William Temple explained the similarity of Christian and Marxist social ideas by pronouncing the latter a Christian heresy" (147).

For pentecostals it is particularly important to realize that Friedrich Engels started as a born-again, evangelical Christian. He found that his individualistic and supernatural Christianity was too superficial to cope with the evils of the beginning capitalist and industrial era. Karl Marx also had religious roots, which can be seen in the fact that on many pages he quotes the Bible (in the translation of Luther, which is only detectable in the German original text for readers whose ears are attuned to the language and cadences of Luther's Bible, for neither Marx nor Engels acknowledged their quotations from the Bible). It is also interesting that the famous Communist Manifesto was originally called a "Confession of Faith." There are many more parallels between the Christian church and the Communist party, between Christianity and Communism, the decisive difference being that for Christianity truth is never in our hands; it is always in God's hand, that is, ahead of us (see Hollenweger).

It is also to be noted that probably one of the best books on Jesus was written by a Marxist philosopher, Milan Machově. In this book, Machově destroys many of the facile sociological theories of our time, especially in relation to the resurrection of Jesus. In fact, he says there is only one expla-

nation for the resurrection of Jesus. And that explanation is "God." However, since this concept is not available to Machově, he must leave the question open. This, it seems to me, is a much more honest atheistic approach than many of the modern and superficial "explanations" of the resurrection.

In Eastern Europe, pentecostals had to learn to distinguish between "dogmatic" (rigid, inflexible, bureaucratic, consistently anti-Christian) and "nondogmatic" (humanist, tolerant, philosophically open for dialogue) Marxism. We also must differentiate between Marxism where it is in power, where it is a marginal or emerging force, and where it is outlawed and thus underground (see on this Mojzes).

Both Marxism and pentecostalism understand truth as something that happens. Truth is not something that simply exists but rather something that emerges. Both are therefore in opposition to objectivism and idealism.

> The perception that Christianity [or pentecostalism for that matter] and Marxism are irreconcilable enemies which can meet only on a battle-ground has enormous destructive potential for the international community and the future of humanity. This crusader mentality is a betrayal of the Gospel, for it reduces the Christian faith to a politico-ideological force. It may also be a distortion of Marxism.... While in the East, Christian truth and values are officially opposed, in the West they are often verbally honored while practically they are ignored or even totally rejected.... Christianity is not the official ideology of the West and capitalism is not the economic theory of biblical faith. Old extreme positions must go: Christianity should no longer be identified with anti-communism nor should Marxism be reduced to militant atheism. (Kuzmič, 152–53)

For pentecostals, however, it is imperative to discover that Marxist criticism of religion—with all its stereotypes, abuse of science, and false propaganda

> is not all wrong, and we have come to acknowledge that the rise and spread of Western and Marxist atheism is proportionately related to the shrinking credibility of the institutional Church.... We must humbly acknowledge that religion was frequently used as a manipulative tool of the powerful and mighty, often serving as an ideological screen to justify the actions of powerful oppressors to pacify the poor and exploited. White-washing unjust wars, justifying economic injustices and blatant exploitation, and smoke-screening racial discrimination are only some of the obvious evils that the church has practiced for ages.... The Pentecostals as "the church of the working class" and as a movement of the "whole/full gospel," are in a unique position to overcome this criticism and other Marxist prejudices and stereotypes. (Kuzmič, 161)

This differentiated picture of Marxism, to which one would have to add the voices of some Latin American pentecostals (▸Social Justice and the Pentecostal/Charismatic Movement) and some South African pentecostal authors, would probably be used by some as proof that the "Marxist-Communist onslaught on South Africa . . . clothes itself with a religious cloak. . . . It is even prepared to pose as 'Pentecostal'" (Möller, 20). To this I can only add: Why is it then that one has to be a Communist to fight apartheid in South Africa and economic exploitation in Latin America? Cannot pentecostals also do and say something intelligent against these evils?

■ **Bibliography:** W. J. Hollenweger, *Marxist and Kimbanquist Mission: A Comparison* (1973) ▪ idem, "Efficiency and Human Values: A Theological Action-Research-Report on Co-Decision in Industry," *Expository Times* 86 (8, May 1975) ▪ idem, "Karl Marx (1818–1883) and His Confession of Faith," *Expository Times* 84 (5, Feb. 1973) ▪ idem, "Marxist Ethics," *Expository Times* 85 (10, July 1974) ▪ P. Kuzmič, "Pentecostals Respond to Marxism," in M. A. Dempster, R. D. Klaus, and D. Peterson, eds., *Called and Empowered: Global Mission in Pentecostal Perspective* (1991) ▪ also in *EPTA Bulletin* 9 (1, 1990) ▪ M. Machově, *A Marxist Looks at Jesus* (1976) ▪ P. Mojzes, ed., *Varieties of Christian-Marxist Dialogue* (1978) ▪ F. P. Möller, *Church and Politics: A Pentecostal View of the South African Situation* (1988) ▪ P. Tillich, "How Much Truth Is There in Karl Marx?" *Christian Century* (Sept. 8, 1949).

■ W. J. Hollenweger

MARY AND THE HOLY SPIRIT In popular terms Mary, the mother of Jesus, has been described as the "first pentecostal." Commenting on Laurentin's treatment of Mary as the model charismatic, Carluer states: "In this portrait of Mary the author defines her essentially as the prototype of the charismatic. It is a portrait that in its broad outline is quite acceptable to an evangelical Christian" (Carluer, 74). The epithet "charismatic," or Spirit-filled, is rooted in the biblical tradition. Matthew (1:18–25) and Luke (1:26–38), both writing independently, know a tradition about Mary's virginal conception of Jesus through the Spirit. This "virginal conception" should be carefully distinguished from "virginal birth," which would indicate that Mary's hymen was not broken when she delivered her baby; this mythological feature is found only in the apocryphal NT. Luke portrays Mary conceiving Jesus through the "overshadowing" of the Holy Spirit. The verbs used are *eperchesthai* ("come upon") and *episkiazein* ("overshadow"). *Eperchesthai* is also used of the Spirit's coming on those assembled in the upper room on the Day of Pentecost (Acts 1:8), but Luke may also have in mind Isa. 32:15: "until the Spirit is poured upon us from on high." The verb *episkiazein* (cf. the transfiguration of Jesus [Matt. 17:5; Mark 9:7; Luke 9:34; Acts 5:15]) means "to cover." It is used to describe

God's presence under the symbol of the cloud over the tabernacle (Ex. 40:35 [29]) and of his powerful protection of the chosen people (Pss. 91:4 [90:4]; 140:7 [139:8]). The Spirit's power both implements a unique form of procreation through Mary and bestows on Mary's Son a special character.

From a literary point of view, Luke's account is constructed according to the OT birth announcement narrative, but the unique feature is found in the virginity of Mary. However, the annunciation pericope itself is primarily christological, not mariological; it emphasizes Jesus' human origin as well as his divine nature. The subject of Mary's biological virginity was debated very little for 1,600 years (A.D. 200–1800) but has emerged as a matter of discussion in the Roman Catholic Church since Vatican II. The position is, perhaps, best summarized in the *Dutch Catechism* (1967): "They [Matthew and Luke] proclaim that this birth does not depend on what men can do of themselves—infinitely less so than in other human births. That is the deepest meaning of the article of faith, 'born of the Virgin Mary'" (74–75).

Scholars have recognized that the NT makes no explicit connection between the divinity of Jesus and his virginal conception. However, Mary is addressed as the one "highly favored." In pentecostal terms, the blood of the Lamb finds its origin in Mary and, while she is informed that Jesus will be a successor of King David, she is also told that he will be called "great" (a title usually predicated of God) and "Son of the Highest." The annunciation pericope itself bears some close affinity to the Palestinian Aramaic text from Qumran Cave 4 (4QpsDan Aa).

1. He will be great (cf. Luke 1:32).
2. He will be called Son of the Highest (cf. Luke 1:32).
3. He will be called Son of God (cf. Luke 1:35).
4. He will reign . . . forever (cf. Luke 1:33).
5. [He] will come upon you (cf. Luke 1:35) (see Fitzmyer, 1973–74).

Luke also presents Mary as the "handmaid of the Lord" (1:38 KJV), and he shows her as a true disciple, a member of the eschatological family of Jesus who hears the Word of God and believes (cf. 8:19–21). She is, therefore, the model who receives the Spirit's abundant blessing (cf. 1:45). She may also have been present with the other men and women disciples at the Last Supper.

This aspect of Mary as disciple is also expressed in the Gospel of John in two pericopes. In the first (2:1–12) Mary requests Jesus to assist at the marriage feast at Cana, where the wine has run out and where Jesus performs his first sign, the changing of water into wine; v. 12 shows Mary as a disciple following Jesus to Capernaum after the wedding feast. In the second (19:25–30) John presents Mary as standing at the foot of the cross *(para tō staurō)* in contrast to the women in the synoptic tradition who stand at a distance *(apo makrothen).* She stands there in the capacity of a disciple closely united to Jesus carrying his cross. Jesus commends her to the disciple John, and John to Mary. This Johannine scene contains profound symbolism; in the "hour" of Jesus, Mary in the person of John receives the commission (role) of maternal, spiritual care for the postresurrection community. Mary and John are seen as representatives of a small community of believing disciples who persevere in the hour of trial. Mary may also symbolize Israel, who gives birth to the Christian community. This emotive scene occurs just before Jesus bows his head and transmits the Spirit (v. 30; there is a Johannine play on the word *paradidomi*). Thus, the Spirit begets Jesus' eschatological family at the foot of the cross. Mary seems to have been an important person for the Johannine community.

Mary is also closely associated with the Holy Spirit, for Luke specifically mentions that she and other women were present in the upper room with the apostles prior to the descent of the Holy Spirit on the Feast of Pentecost. Mary is the only person to be mentioned by name on this occasion, except for the 11 apostles. Thus, Luke, as well as John, presents Mary as a member of the believing Christian community after the resurrection. The coming of the Spirit at the time of Jesus' conception was a foreshadowing of the coming of the Spirit upon the entire community on Pentecost. Thus, Mary is regarded as one of the first to receive the "baptism in the Spirit" even prior to Pentecost.

Mary has been linked closely to the charismatic renewal within the Catholic church, although more enthusiastically so in France and Canada than in the U.S.

The ▸Catholic charismatic renewal focuses on "Mary's Spirit-animated presence in the communion of saints" and Mary as the model of the church in a way that is "truly biblical and ecumenical" (Laurentin, 194). Mary is also seen as the model of Christians who are baptized in the Spirit. Suenens says, "Mary is the one who, beyond all others, has been sanctified, the daughter of Sion visited by the Spirit, who, moreover, in her response to the angel showed herself to be moved by the Spirit at a depth unique to herself" (199). Mary is also the model of the charismatic life in that she exercised the charisma of prophecy when she recited the Magnificat (Luke 1:45–56); because she is a woman of prayer and reflection on the mysteries of God (2:19, 51); as a teacher (the Orthodox Church calls her the "fiery chariot of the Word"); and, according to Catholic tradition, on account of her assumption into heaven like Elijah the prophet and Enoch. She also is associated with many miracles, healings, and private revelations. But she is regarded by some moderns as a "liberation theologian." Gutierrez asserts, "The Magnificat ... is one of the NT texts which contains great implications both as regards liberation and the political sphere" (207; see also Ford, 1983).

Most important, however, Mary is seen by Roman Catholics to possess the epitome of the fruits of the Spirit (Gal. 5:23). This is really the implicit biblical background to the greatly misunderstood doctrine of the immaculate conception of Mary's soul (Ford, 1973). In the Catholic title *Mater Misericordiae* (Mother of Compassion), Mary is also venerated as the protector and intercessor for all the poor and troubled of the world. Thus, she is associated with social consciousness. Montague says, "The experience of Mary is one of the most precious gifts of the Spirit. She is a charism of the Spirit in person. From her we learn to believe more purely, to discern the Spirit more clearly, to listen to the Word more intently, and to wait more creatively the hour of the Lord's coming" (98).

See also CATHOLIC CHARISMATIC RENEWAL.

■ **Bibliography:** R. E. Brown, *The Virginal Conception of the Bodily Resurrection* (1973), 21–28 ■ idem, "Croyons-vous au Saint-Esprit?" *Cahiers marial* 90 (Nov. 15, 1973 [special issue on Mary]) ■ idem, "Luke's Description of the Virginal Conception," *TS* 35 (1974) ■ R. E. Brown et al., eds., *Mary in the New Testament* (1978), 105–34 ■ J. Y. Carluer, "Un livre courageux Pentecôte chez les catholiques!" *Experiences* 16 (8, 1974) ■ D. Daube, *The New Testament and Rabbinic Judaism* (1957) ■ G. J. M. M. Farrell and G. W. Kosicki, C.S.B., *The Spirit and The Bride Say "Come!": Mary's Role in the New Pentecost* (1981) ■ J. A. Fitzmyer, "The Contribution of Qumran Aramaic to the Study of the New Testament," *NTS* (1973–74), esp. 391–94 ■ idem, "The Virginal Conception of Jesus in the New Testament," *TS* 34 (1973) ■ J. M. Ford, *My Enemy Is My Guest: Luke and Violence* (1983) ■ idem, "Our Lady and the Ministry of Women in the Church," *Marian Studies* 23 (1972) ■ G. Gutierrez, *Theology of Liberation: History, Politics and Salvation*, trans. and ed. Caridad Inda and John Eagleson (1973) ■ R. Laurentin, *Catholic Pentecostalism, an In-depth Report on the Charismatic Renewal*, trans. M. J. O'Connell (1977) ■ J. McHugh *The Mother of Jesus in the New Testament* (1975) ■ G. T. Montague, *Riding the Wind: Learning the Ways of the Spirit* (1974) ■ L. Pfaller and J. Alberts, *Mary Is Pentecost: A Fresh Look at Mary from a Charismatic Viewpoint* (1973) ■ L. Suenens, *A New Pentecost?* (1974).   ■ J. M. Ford

MASCARENHAS, FIORELLO (1944–). Catholic charismatic leader from India. Mascarenhas was baptized in the Spirit in 1972 while studying for ordination as a Jesuit. Ordained priest in 1975, Fr. Fio first became a chaplain to university students, then founder-director of the Catholic Charismatic Bible Institute in Bombay. He was the first chairman of the Indian National Service Team (NST) for ▸Catholic Charismatic Renewal. He became director of the International Catholic Charismatic Renewal Office from 1981 and chairman of the ICCRO council (1984–87). On his return to India, Fr. Fio became pastor of the Holy Family parish in Mumbai (Bombay), and again chair of the NST.

He is currently rector of St. Peter's parish and liaison for CCR in the archdiocese of Mumbai. Fr. Fio has led retreats for bishops and priests as well as for lay leaders in 75 countries. He has authored *Biblical Spirituality for All* (1991), *CCR Leaders Handbook* (1996), *The Holy Spirit* (with R. R. Silvano, 1998), and *God's Best Ideas* (1999).   ■ P. D. Hocken

MASON, CHARLES HARRISON (1866–1961).

Founder of the Church of God in Christ (COGIC). One of the most significant figures in the rise and spread of the modern pentecostal movement, Mason was born Sept. 8, 1866, on Prior Farm just outside of Memphis, in an area that is today the town of Bartlett, TN. His parents, Jerry and Eliza Mason, former slaves, were members of the Missionary Baptist Church, a source of strength for them in the distressing times that followed the Civil War.

As a young boy Mason was religious in bent. He often joined his mother and her neighbors in prayer. Mason said he prayed earnestly that God would give to him "above all things a religion like the one he had heard about from the old slaves and seen demonstrated in their lives" (Mason, 6). It was this yearning for the God of his forebears that became the dynamic of his life.

When Charles was 12 years old, a yellow-fever epidemic forced Jerry Mason and his family to leave the Memphis area for Plumersville, AR, where they lived on John Watson's plantation as tenant farmers. The plague claimed Jerry Mason's life in 1879. During those fearful and difficult days the younger Mason worked hard and had little chance for schooling.

In 1880, just before his 14th birthday, Mason fell ill with chills and fever. His mother despaired of his life. However, in an astounding turn of events, he was miraculously healed on the first Sunday in Sept. 1880. He and his mother went to the Mt. Olive Baptist Church near Plumersville, where the pastor, Mason's half-brother, the Rev. I. S. Nelson, baptized him in an atmosphere of praise and thanksgiving. Mason went throughout the area of southern Arkansas as a lay preacher, giving his testimony and working with souls on the mourners' bench, especially during the summer camp meetings.

Mason was licensed and ordained in 1891 at Preston, AR, but held back from full-time ministry to marry Alice Saxton, a beautiful daughter of his mother's closest friend. To his greatest disappointment and distress, she bitterly opposed his ministerial plans. She divorced him after two years and later remarried. Mason fell into such grief and despair that it is said that at times Satan even tempted him to take his own life (Lee, 5).

The year 1893 marked a crucial turning point in Mason's life. Following his heartrending divorce, Mason was determined to get an education. That same year Meyer and Brothers of Chicago published a significant and widely read volume: *An Autobiography: The Story of the Lord's Dealing with Mrs. Amanda Smith, The Coloured Evangelist.* That autobiography deeply impressed Mason as it did many blacks throughout the nation, especially in the South. Amanda Smith (1839–1915), a disciple of John Inskip, became one of the most influential, widely traveled, and respected black Holiness evangelists of the 19th century. Her life story swept many blacks into the Holiness movement, including Mason.

After reading Smith's autobiography, Mason claimed the grace of divine sanctification and at Preston, AR, preached his first sermon on the subject of Holiness. He chose as his text 2 Tim. 2:3–4, which begins, "Thou therefore endure hardness, as a good soldier of Jesus Christ" (KJV). This sermon stayed with him throughout his life.

On Nov. 1, 1893, Mason entered Arkansas Baptist College, founded by Dr. E. C. Morris, pastor of Centennial Baptist Church at Helena, AR, and president of the Arkansas Baptist State Convention. Mason was deeply disturbed by the new higher criticism that Dr. C. L. Fisher, a top graduate of Morgan Park Seminary (now the University of Chicago Divinity School) had brought to Arkansas Baptist College. He had both hermeneutical and cultural suspicions of the methods, philosophy, and curriculum at the college. He came to the personal conclusion that for him the school

Charles H. Mason, cofounder and long-time leader of the Church of God in Christ, who was baptized in the Spirit at Azusa Street in 1906.

would be of no help in his task of preserving the vitality of slave religion. He left there in Jan. 1894.

In 1895 Mason met and soon became friends with Charles Price Jones, newly elected pastor of the Mt. Helms Baptist Church at Jackson, MS. Jones was a graduate of Arkansas Baptist College. Like Mason, Jones had come under the influence of the Holiness movement and in 1894 claimed the experience of sanctification while pastoring Tabernacle Baptist Church at Selma, AL. By preaching sanctification as a second definite work of grace subsequent to conversion, Mason and Jones caused no small stir among black Baptists. From 1896 to 1899 the Holiness conventions, revivals, and periodicals of Mason and Jones split the Baptists and, in a few cases, the Methodist churches, causing the development of independent "sanctified" or "holiness" congregations and associations. Mason, Jones, and their colleagues met with vehement opposition and were eventually expelled from the Baptist churches (the National Baptist Convention). After much praying and studying of Scripture in search of future direction for these independent "sanctified" congregations, Mason, while walking along a certain street in Little Rock, AR, received the revelation of a name, the Church of God in Christ (1 Thess. 2:14; 2 Thess. 1:1). Thus, in 1897 a major new black denomination was born. From the 17th through the 19th centuries, most blacks had encountered Christianity under the aegis of Baptist or Methodist churches. Mason and Jones changed the religious landscape in the black community and broadened the black religious experience. Through the dynamic preaching of Mason and the prolific writings and hymnology of Jones, Sanctified or Holiness churches sprang up throughout the South and Southwest bearing the COGIC name.

As the new work progressed, Mason continued to seek a more complete consecration of his life. During the latter half of 1906, he received reports of the pentecostal revival in Los Angeles. He traveled to California, and under the ministry of ›W. J. Seymour, Mason received the baptism of the Holy Spirit and spoke in tongues. After some five weeks in Los Angeles, Mason returned to Memphis and Jackson, eager to share his additional experience of the Lord with his brethren. However, when he presented his pentecostal message to the church, both he and his message were rejected. After days and nights of intensive debate, Mason and Jones separated, and the church split. Those who agreed with Mason met in Sept. 1907 to reorganize the COGIC. They elected C. H. Mason as general overseer and appointed D. J. Young, Mason's constant companion, as editor of the new periodical, *The Whole Truth*.

By ordaining ministers of all races, Mason performed an unusually important service to the early-20th-century pentecostal movement. He appears to have been the only early convert who came from a legally incorporated church body and who could thus ordain persons whose status as clergymen was recognized by civil authorities. This recognition allowed clergy to perform marriages and carry out other ministerial functions having legal consequences and entitled them to certain economic advantages, such as the right to obtain reduced clergy rates on railroads. As a result, scores of white ministers sought ordination at the hand of Mason. Large numbers obtained credentials carrying the name COGIC. In the years 1909–14, there were as many white COGIC churches as there were black, all carrying Mason's credentials and incorporation. Ironically, Mason, who viewed his lifelong task as one of simply preserving the "spiritual essence" and the "prayer tradition" of the black religious experience, found himself in a unique and pivotal historical position.

By 1913 it had become increasingly clear that as pentecostals moved toward denominationalism, they would follow the segregating practices of American culture. The color line that had been washed away in the blood of Jesus at the ›Azusa Street revival reappeared.

On Dec. 20, 1913, elders ›E. N. Bell and ›H. A. Goss issued a call to convene a general council of "all pentecostal saints and Churches of God in Christ" to meet the following April at Hot Springs. This invitation went only to the white saints. E. N. Bell's periodical, *Word and Witness,* was not distributed in the black religious community. On the first week in Apr. 1914 Mason traveled to the Hot Springs convention to invoke God's blessings on the newly formed General Council of the Assemblies of God (AG). He preached on Thursday night to more than 400 white pentecostal preachers (with one black—›G. T. Haywood of Indianapolis, who would become the leader of a new body called the ›Pentecostal Assemblies of the World).

Despite this new racial separation, Mason maintained a warm fellowship with the white pentecostals. He preached at their conventions, maintained a strong fellowship with ›A. J. Tomlinson of the ›Church of God (CG, Cleveland, TN) and ›J. H. King of the ›Pentecostal Holiness Church (PHC, Franklin Springs, GA). In 1952 he was the elder statesman attending the Pentecostal World Conference at London, England.

The Federal Bureau of Investigation (FBI) developed a file on C. H. Mason because of his pacifism and interracialism. In 1918 some white followers of Mason in Los Angeles were identified as being of German extraction. Mason was jailed at Lexington, MS, for allegedly preaching against the war, although he sold bonds to help the war effort. William B. Holt, one of the white brethren targeted by the FBI as suspicious, was a lawyer and former Nazarene preacher. He traveled to Lexington and posted a $2,000 cash bond for Mason's release.

A reference from the 1918 FBI report is instructive. After quoting from one of Mason's tracts, it comments, "It is clear that Mason and his followers felt it to be of far reaching significance that one of the great religious movements of the 20th century was founded by a member of the African race."

Later scholars have echoed the same conclusion as the FBI report. Dr. Gayraud Wilmore, a most careful and respected scholar, says, "This movement begun by C. H. Mason and W. J. Seymour at the turn of the century, has been one of the most powerful expressions of Black religion in the world" (Wilmore, 210–13). Wilmore's assessment is supported by Yale historian Sidney Ahlstrom, who observed that the lives of W. J. Seymour and C. H. Mason personify a process by which black piety exerted its greatest direct influence on American religious history (Ahlstrom, 1059–60).

Mason led the COGIC until his death in 1961. Under his leadership the church experienced phenomenal growth. Thousands of Mason's followers, migrating from south to north and from southwest to far west, carried his teachings and evangelistic spirit to virtually every major city in America. At his death in 1961 the COGIC, which had begun in a gin house at Lexington, MS, claimed some 5,500 congregations and 482,679 members. At least 10 other church bodies owed their origins to Mason's church. Since his death the church has continued its rapid growth. Mason stamped his personality on his church far more emphatically than any other Holiness leader. He lived to see the COGIC become a major denomination and one of the largest pentecostal bodies in the world, with a graduate seminary to its credit. Mason traces the church's phenomenal growth to a covenant-promise that the Lord had given him. He died at age 95 in Harper's Hospital, Detroit, MI, on Nov. 17, 1961. Martin Luther King Jr. preached his last sermon from Mason's pulpit—Mason Temple, headquarters of the COGIC in Memphis, TN, where Mason's remains are entombed.

See also Black Holiness-Pentecostalism.

■ **Bibliography:** S. E. Ahlstrom, *A Religious History of the American People* (1972) ■ I. Clemmons, ed., *Profile of a Churchman: The Life of Otha M. Kelly in the Church of God in Christ* (1976) ■ O. B. Cobbins, *History of the Church of Christ (Holiness), U.S.A., 1895–1965* (1966) ■ L. J. Cornelius, *The Pioneer History of the Church of God in Christ Compiled* (1975) ■ J. Courts, *The History and Life of Elder C. H. Mason, Chief Apostle, and His Co-laborers* (1920) ■ C. T. Gilkes, "Cultural Constituencies in Conflict: Religion, Community, Reorganization and the Rise of the Saints, 1890–1925," *Association of Black Sociologists and the Society for the Study of Social Problems* (1983) ■ C. E. Jones, *Black Holiness: A Guide to the Study of Black Participation in Wesleyan Perfectionist and Glossolalic Pentecostal Movements* (1987) ■ E. Lee, *C. H. Mason, A Man Greatly Used of God* (1967) ■ L. Lovett, "Aspects of the Spiritual Legacy of the Church of God in Christ: Ecumenical Implications," *Midstream* 24 (4, 1985) ■ M. E. Mason, *The History and Life Work of Elder C. H. Mason and His Co-Laborers* (1934) ■ D. J. Nelson, *A Brief History of the Church of God in Christ* (1984) ■ A. W. Peagues, *Our Baptist Ministers and Schools* (1892), 18–21 ■ C. H. Pleas, *Fifty Years of Achievement, The Church of God in Christ* (1957) ■ V. Synan, "The Quiet Rise of Black Pentecostals," *Charisma* 11 (June 1986) ■ G. S. Wilmore, *Black Religion and Black Radicalism* (1972).   ■ I. C. Clemmons

MATTSSON-BOZE, JOSEPH D. (1905–88). Swedish-American missionary and evangelist. Joseph Boze was born in Marstrand, Bohuslan, Sweden. As a young man, Boze converted from the Mission Covenant Church to pentecostalism and soon became a copastor of one of Sweden's leading pentecostal churches, the Smyrna Assembly of Gothenburg. He came to the U.S. after receiving an invitation to pastor Chicago's leading Scandinavian pentecostal church, the *Filadelfia-Forsamlinger,* in 1933. From 1943 to 1970 Boze was the editor of the prominent Scandinavian-American pentecostal periodical, the *Herald of Faith.* In the late 1940s he became a well-known proponent of the New Order of the ▸Latter Rain revival. He resigned his pastorate in Chicago in 1958 and for the next 20 years traveled as an evangelist, holding crusades in such countries as Honduras, India, Kenya, Singapore, Spain, Thailand, and Yugoslavia. Even while living in the U.S., Boze was a dominant figure in Sweden's pentecostal movement. He was responsible for bringing such notable evangelists to Sweden as ▸William Branham, William Freeman, and ▸Kathryn Kuhlman.

■ **Bibliography:** Personal papers of Joseph Mattsson-Boze, David J. du Plessis Archives, Fuller Theological Seminary Library, Pasadena, CA ■ *Trons Harold* 5 (3, Mar. 1936): 11–12.   ■ J. Colletti

MEAD, SAMUEL J. (1849–1936), and **ARDELLA (KNAPP)** (1843–1934). Missionaries to Africa. Having been farmers in Vermont, in 1885 the Meads and their niece Bertha traveled as pioneer Methodist Episcopal missionaries—as members of the original "Pioneer Forty"—to Angola under Bishop ▸William Taylor's direction. In Malange the Meads assisted Taylor in opening one of his most successful African missions. Taylor believed missions work should be self-supported, and the Malange station was operated along these lines. The Meads, with their own finances, purchased some 300 acres of land to farm. The work was arduous, and the trials were many. More than a few died, including the Meads' niece, Bertha.

Samuel's responsibilities included evangelizing the lost, teaching school, and supervising the large farm. Having no children, the couple adopted several African children. Bishop Taylor wrote of the Meads in his book *The Flaming Torch in Darkest Africa* (1898): "If there were a thousand such trainers such as Samuel Mead and his wife, Ardella, there would in a few years be 20,000 native evangelists and pastors in Africa under the leadership of our all-conquering King."

Feeling a lack of spiritual power, the Meads returned to the U.S. in 1904 and were seeking for a deeper work of God in their lives. Claiming to have been led by God to settle in Los Angeles, they began attending the revival services at the ᐳAzusa Street Apostolic Faith Mission in 1906 and received the baptism in the Holy Spirit. *The Apostolic Faith*, a newspaper published by the mission's leaders, reported that the Meads identified several African dialects being spoken by some who were experiencing glossolalia. Soon thereafter the Meads, along with other early pentecostal missionaries, returned to Africa from Los Angeles. In 1909 they retired from the Methodist Board of Foreign Missions and settled in California.

■ **Bibliography:** W. C. Barclay, *Widening Horizons, 1845–1895: History of Methodist Missions* (1957) ■ A. A. Boddy, "Some Los Angeles Friends," *Confidence* (Nov. 1912) ■ A. K. Mead, "Sister Mead's Baptism," *AF* (Nov. 1906) ■ S. J. Mead, "From a Missionary to Africa," *AF* (Sept. 1906).

■ G. B. McGee; E. J. Gitre

MEARES, JOHN L. (1920–). Pentecostal leader with inner-city ministry. Born in Largo, FL, of pentecostal parents, Meares graduated from Lee College, Cleveland, TN, in 1944 and married Mary Lee Bell. After pastoring a Church of God (Cleveland, TN) in Memphis, TN, Meares heard a call to Washington, DC, in 1955 and began his ministry in a tent meeting in a black area of the city. He immediately established a worship center for his new congregation. He first leased a building and in 1957 bought a theater on Georgia Avenue and renamed it the Washington Revival Center.

In 1967 Meares sensed a call to deepen his ministry beyond a revival-healing work to an emphasis on teaching and worship, and from more random evangelism to the formation of a church to minister unto the Lord. In 1975 the present Evangel Temple was opened on Rhode Island Avenue, N.E.

In the 1970s Meares developed a practical interest in the church and church formation, which led to closer relationships with John McTernan (Rome, Italy), Robert McAlister (Rio de Janeiro, Brazil), and ᐳEarl Paulk (Decatur, GA). Out of this came a legal corporation, The International Evangelical Church; the spiritual fellowship The International Communion of Charismatic Churches; and Meares' own consecration as bishop in 1982.

Perhaps Meares' greatest contribution has been in interracial reconciliation between black and white Christians. In Washington, DC, the city council proclaimed the week of Evangel Temple's 30th anniversary in 1985 "Evangel Temple/Bishop John L. Meares Week" in recognition of this ministry. This reconciling emphasis spread nationally through the

Inner City (later National) Pastors' Conferences held 1984–93. Meares, long a close friend of ᐳDavid du Plessis, was a core committee member in the ᐳDialogue between Roman Catholics and classical pentecostals (1972–82). Bishop Meares retired as senior pastor of Evangel Temple in 1989.

■ **Bibliography:** *Evangel Temple's 30th Anniversary Historical Journal* (1985). ■ P. D. Hocken

MELODYLAND CHRISTIAN CENTER A large Christian center in Anaheim, CA, pastored by ᐳRalph A. Wilkerson. In 1961 Wilkerson began a ministry with 28 people in the growing Orange County area, and by 1964 a 750-seat church had been built. However, even with three morning services the facilities became overcrowded. Youth rallies on a monthly basis, frequent charismatic conferences, and varied interdenominational activities began to call for still larger accommodations. In 1969 the Melodyland Theater complex near Disneyland became available for purchase, and Wilkerson's congregation purchased the 3,600-seat theater at a bankruptcy sale and converted it into Melodyland Christian Center. Before long the number of people attending the multiple Sunday services at Melodyland was between 10,000 and 15,000. As an extension of Melodyland in 1972 a delinquency prevention center (Melodyland Hotline) with 24-hour coverage for troubled youth, dope addicts, suicidals, etc., was incorporated and began to serve an ever-increasing number of people. In 1973, in conjunction with Melodyland Christian Center, the Melodyland School of Theology was founded, and within a few years it was training hundreds of students from across the U.S. and from many foreign countries to serve in various kinds of Christian ministry. In 1976 Melodyland High School and later Melodyland Christian College were instituted to serve the growing needs for education within a genuinely Christian context. Melodyland Christian Center has continued to expand its facilities by adding buildings to serve educational and other purposes.

In the history of the modern charismatic movement, Melodyland Christian Center will probably be best remembered for annual charismatic clinics. Melodyland became known as an international crossroads of the movement, attracting speakers of many denominations. People came from around the world to participate in the clinics. The charismatic movement remains indebted to Ralph Wilkerson for his vision and energy in making possible these memorable occasions.

Over the past decade Melodyland has experienced a comeback, with fresh vision and new initiatives. These include a feeding program in Bonginkosi, Khayelitsha, Cape Town, South Africa. In 1999 Ralph Wilkerson retired from the pastorate to resume evangelistic work. He was succeeded as senior pastor by Neville McDonald.

■ **Bibliography:** "Coast Clinic Held by Charismatics," *New York Times* (Aug. 26, 1973), 30 ■ "Melodyland Makes a Comeback," *Charisma* (Aug. 1987) ■ J. N. Vaughn, *The World's Twenty Largest Churches* (1984).   ■ J. R. Williams

MEMPHIS MIRACLE See ASSEMBLIES OF GOD (sec. V.E, "Racial Reconciliation").

MENNONITE CHARISMATICS Contemporary charismatic forces were first felt among Mennonites in the U.S. in the 1950s. In 1954 ▸Gerald Derstine, a Mennonite minister and missionary to Native Americans on a Minnesota reservation, was baptized by the Holy Spirit. Others in his small congregation and throughout the reservation experienced a number of spiritual signs, including glossolalia and slayings in the spirit. Derstine recorded the events in his writings and spoke of them openly as a "visitation by God to the Mennonites." Upon learning about his experiences, Derstine's local church conference in Pennsylvania called him home from the field to answer questions. According to Derstine, the board of bishops asked him to denounce these experiences as unchristian. When he refused to do so, he was stripped of his status as minister in the Mennonite Church (MC). He then moved to Florida to establish the independent Gospel Crusade, later known as Gospel Crusade World Wide Ministries.

Derstine's removal was the precursor to extensive debates within the larger MC (one of the two main Mennonite denominations in the U.S.) about the theological and social correctness of charismatic beliefs and practices. In the 1950s many officials and laypeople viewed the experience of spiritual signs accompanying Holy Spirit baptism as potentially damaging to the community's unity and principles. As it was, the charismatic movement was one of a number of non-Mennonite religious movements that were disrupting insular, sectarian Mennonite communities. The charismatic movement encouraged several tenets in particular that were potentially problematic for the Mennonite Church, including a more personalistic (as opposed to communalistic) definition of spiritual experience and authority, and worship styles foreign to those traditionally found in Mennonite congregations. Most importantly, the charismatic movement was built on—and encouraged—the kind of ecumenical interactions that much Mennonite history and theology were wary of.

In marked contrast, the General Conference of the Mennonite Church (GC; the second large Mennonite denomination) did not perceive charismatic expression as a threat. Historically less conservative than the Mennonite Church, and hence less concerned with sectarian and identity issues, GC leadership was open to those adopting charismatic expression. In most cases they welcomed Mennonites who had been baptized in the Spirit with apparently little contention. (Nevertheless, at present fewer GC Mennonites than MC Mennonites consider themselves charismatic—see below.)

Despite the warning Derstine's local church board gave to other charismatics, MC missionaries returning from the field sometimes spoke of their own charismatic experiences. Throughout the 1960s, individuals who had encountered renewal led others in receiving baptism in the Spirit, often in private homes. During this period most Mennonite charismatics continued to participate in Mennonite congregations, even as they also began to attend a growing number of paradenominational charismatic services and groups, such as ▸Full Gospel Business Men's International and ▸Women's Aglow. Only in the late 1960s did these isolated cases of charismatic conversion give way to larger and more public renewal services and expression.

In the early 1970s two MC colleges, Eastern Mennonite College (VA) and Goshen College (IN) held large, successful charismatic renewal services on their campuses within the structure of yearly "spiritual renewal week." The great outpouring of devotion that came from these meetings encouraged a group of Mennonite charismatic leaders to set up national renewal meetings in 1974 and 1975. These meetings, sponsored locally by Mennonite congregations, typically took place in public parks to accommodate the thousands of Mennonites and others who attended. Local conference boards began to commission formal responses to the charismatic movement's claims and its most prevalent signs of speaking in tongues and ecstatic worship.

In spite of the increasingly positive responses to the charismatic movement at both the conference and individual level in the 1970s, many local congregations remained resistant to the changes that the movement engendered in people filled with the Spirit. Nevertheless, the positive responses encouraged charismatic Mennonites to become more vocal within their local churches. In 1971 debate raged on the pages of the church magazine *Gospel Herald* over the godliness of speaking in tongues, the spiritual value (or lack thereof) of both traditional and Spirit-filled Mennonite services, community, and authority.

In a number of communities, charismatic Mennonites formed congregations independent of the Mennonite church, often relying on resources and contacts from parachurch organizations. Such independent charismatic churches attracted large numbers of non-Mennonite charismatics as well, and many quickly lost much of their distinctive Mennonite flavor. Noting this attrition with some alarm, prominent Mennonite charismatics, including ▸Nelson Litwiller and R. Herbert Minnich, joined together in 1975 to found Mennonite Renewal Services (MRS), based in Goshen, IN. MRS promoted charismatic renewal within the denomination, hoping to circumvent the exodus of charismatic

Mennonites who sought fellowship and guidance from non-Mennonite sources.

The strong negative and positive responses to the charismatic movement led MC officials to engage in systematic reflection on the church's official position. After several years of consultations and congregational study groups, the denomination published a formal statement that was affirmed by the MC General Assembly in 1976. This watershed document weighed the value of personal spiritual renewal in the balance of the importance of community life, noting both positive contributions and weaknesses of the movement toward that goal. Above all, it articulated an Anabaptist position on the baptism of the Spirit: While it stressed its value, the authors stated that no one sign or set of signs could establish its occurrence (or lack thereof). Writing for the MRS magazine *Empowered* in 1983, Daniel Yutzy echoed this view, stating that "difficulty, severe testing or spiritual challenge may be a more typical consequence of the baptism [than tongues or other signs associated with the movement].... Each one has a unique and personal set of experiences with the baptism."

This document and the general agreement among Mennonite charismatics that the baptism of the Spirit was not marked by any sign or spiritual gift in particular mitigated what might have been a full-scale schism of charismatics from the MC. Marking the end of the most contentious period, Gerald Derstine was reinstated as a minister in his home conference in 1977. At the same time, the document sidestepped issues that would continue to prove most difficult for many mainstream Mennonite congregations to resolve, namely, the place of more free-flowing, spontaneous worship within the traditional form of Mennonite church services.

In the 1980s a number of new Mennonite congregations with openly charismatic emphasis gained the support of local and national conferences. These churches are marked by the acceptance and practice of spiritual gifts within the church (including anointing, faith healings, prophetic words, and speaking in tongues) and strong emphasis on evangelism and missionary work. Most such congregations maintain their strongest connections with the MC through missions boards and evangelistic work. In addition, these congregations also tend to have more established ties with non-Mennonite charismatic and evangelistic groups than most other Mennonite churches. The growth of these congregations denotes an important change in the relations between Mennonites and charismatics, toward more open acceptance and accommodation. A 1989 survey of members of Mennonite congregations found that 5–10% of Mennonites consider themselves to be "strongly involved," and another 10–15% "somewhat involved" in charismatic activities. (The percentage of involvement is clearly higher in the MC than in the GC, where long-standing conflict over the movement did not

occur.) As a further sign, MRS closed its doors in 1996 after several attempts at restructuring. According to its founders, MRS had fulfilled its goals and was no longer needed as an additional organization to promote renewal within the church.

One of the most intriguing outcomes of the movement's inroads into the Mennonite community is the degree to which charismatic forms and styles now appear as normal within mainstream Mennonite practice. The team of sociologists who found that only 10–15% of all Mennonites say that they participate at all in charismatic or Spirit-filled activities also discovered that almost half of all Mennonites claim the baptism of the Spirit. J. Howard Kauffman suggests that this may denote Mennonites' lack of awareness of the more "standard" meaning of Holy Spirit baptism. However, it may also denote a turn to a Mennonite or Anabaptist definition of charismatic renewal that takes root in the specifics of Mennonite history and theology.

Historian Kenneth Davis argues that early Anabaptist and Mennonite founders were charismatic, even though they did not give any special significance to ecstatic experiences. Others have noted the numerous, though often isolated, experiences and debates over glossolalia, slayings in the spirit, and the like in Mennonite history. On several occasions such events sparked movements that formed new denominations through schisms, including the Evangelical Mennonite Church and the Mennonite Brethren in Christ in the first half of the 20th century. Other groups and communities, notably Reba Place Fellowship (Evanston, IL), have successfully integrated notions of communal living, nonhierarchical church authority, and other Anabaptist principles with Holy Spirit renewal, providing clear-cut examples of another way in which Mennonite charismatic interaction takes place. In 1989 theologian Harold E. Bauman published a widely heralded book that articulated a specifically Mennonite understanding of the connections between Mennonite and charismatic theology.

The notion that Mennonite charismatics have formed a specifically Mennonite form of charismatic renewal is backed to a degree by some of Kauffman's other findings. For instance, Mennonites who engage in charismatic practice look very similar to their noncharismatic counterparts when comparing their adherence to standard Anabaptist theological principles, including views on race relations, social welfare, and the separation of church and state. Nevertheless, a tension continues, as charismatics are also somewhat less likely to espouse pacifism and more likely to oppose the ordination of women, marking their connections to mainstream evangelical and charismatic theological positions. Charismatic Mennonites nevertheless are more likely than mainstream Mennonites to be highly involved in spiritual disciplines of all kinds, including regular church participation, devotional practices such as prayer, and stewardship.

In the summer of 1995 Duane Yoder reported (*Empowered* [Spring–Summer, 1995]: 3) that in the past 10 years the MRS had developed local renewal networks that included prophetic and apostolic leaders. A number of congregations began shifting to "cell congregations." In an open letter to the "Empowered Network," however, he stated the conclusion that "the time for the denominational renewal networks, as we have known them, is coming to a close."

■ **Bibliography:** H. E. Bauman, *Presence and Power: Releasing the Holy Spirit in Your Life* (1989) ■ C. Bender, "A Radical Reformulation: Mennonites in the Age of the Spirit" (MS, Lancaster [PA] Mennonite Historical Society, 1991) ■ K. R. Davis, "Anabaptism as a Charismatic Movement," *Mennonite Quarterly Review* 53 (3, 1979) ■ G. Derstine, *Visitation of God to the Mennonites* (1954) ■ *Empowered* (1983–89) ■ J. H. Kauffman, "Mennonite Charismatics: Are They Any Different?" *Mennonite Quarterly Review* 70 (4, 1996) ■ R. S. Koch, *My Personal Pentecost* (1977) ■ Mennonite Church, General Assembly, *The Holy Spirit and the Life of the Church* (1976) ■ Reba Place Fellowship, "An Introduction to Reba Place Fellowship" (1978) ■ D. Yutzy, "The Baptism with the Spirit," *Empowered* 1 (1, 1983).   ■ C. Bender

MENZIES, WILLIAM WATSON (1931–). ▸Assemblies of God (AG) pastor, educator, missionary, and author. Menzies was born to Sophie B. and William E. Menzies. He married Doris L. Dresselhaus in 1955; they have two sons, Glen Wesley (1956) and Robert Paul (1958). After completing a B.A. at Central Bible College, Springfield, MO (1952), William Menzies earned both a second B.A. and an M.A. at Wheaton (IL) College. He earned a Ph.D. in American church history at the University of Iowa in 1968. Ordained in 1956, he founded or pastored churches in Michigan and Iowa (1954–58, 1963–64). As an educator he taught at three schools of the AG in Springfield, MO: Central Bible College (1958–70), Evangel College (1970–80; 1987–), and the AG Theological Seminary (1980–84).

At the AG headquarters in the same city, Menzies also served on numerous denominational committees—often in the role of theological advisor—and edited the denominational youth magazine. He wrote the commissioned denominational history of the AG, *Anointed to Serve* (1971)—an adaptation of his doctoral thesis. In 1970 Menzies cofounded (with ▸Vinson Synan and Horace Ward) the ▸Society for Pentecostal Studies. He was its first president and the first

William W. Menzies, who, among many other accomplishments, cofounded the Society for Pentecostal Studies and was the first editor of its journal, *Pneuma*.

editor of its journal, *Pneuma* (1979–83).

Long interested in missions education, Menzies lectured and traveled extensively in the U.S., Europe, South America, Scandinavia, and countries within and upon the Pacific rim. Since at least 1972 he has had a formative influence on the Far East Advanced School of Theology (since 1898 known as the Asia Pacific Theological Seminary) in Baguio, Philippines, and served as that school's president (1984–85; 1988–96); he became its chancellor in 1996. From 1985 to 1987 he was vice president for academic affairs at California Theological Seminary, Fresno. As a respected interpreter of pentecostal theology, he participated in the Lausanne Consultation (1984) and serves on its subsequent committees. In 1986 he was named a consulting editor for *Christianity Today*. His other writings, besides many articles and reviews, include *Understanding the Times of Christ* (1971), *Understanding Our Doctrine* (1970), *Philippians: The Joyful Life* (1981), *Bible Doctrines: A Pentecostal Perspective* (1993), and *Spirit and Power* (and R. Menzies; 2000). See also W. Ma and P. R. Menzies, eds., *Pentecostalism in Context: Essays in Honor of William W. Menzies* (1997).   ■ R. P. Spittler

MESSIANIC JUDAISM

1. History.

Jewish believers in Jesus have reflected their Jewish roots as part of their new covenant faith in limited ways throughout history. However, it was not until the 19th century that their efforts produced significant institutions. The Hebrew Christian Alliance of Great Britain formed in the 1860s, an American Alliance in 1915, and an International Alliance in 1925. These organizations provided membership and fellowship for individual Jewish believers.

Various perspectives were held among Alliance members concerning Jewish lifestyle. In general, the majority did not live a significantly Jewish life, either by the calendar of Judaism or by other Jewish observances. However, a notable minority argued for a Hebrew Christianity that would be both congregationally based and Hebraic in worship and liturgy. Most noteworthy in this regard was Mark John Levy, the general secretary of the Hebrew Christian Alliance of America (HCAA), who even convinced the Episcopal denomination of his position. Ironically, the HCAA rejected his position.

Other significant leaders and trends should also be noted. Theodore Lukey edited *The Messianic Jew* in Eastern Europe at the turn of the century. Jacob Rabinowitz planted a famous messianic synagogue in Kishinev, Moldova, in the late 19th century. Before his adoption of dispensational theology, A. C. Gaebelein, a noted American theologian, forcefully argued for messianic Judaism. His journal, *Our Hope*, edited with Ernest Stroeker, put forth this case (Rausch, 1979, 94–99, 212–62).

In 1921 a converted tailor, David Bronstein, founded the Peniel Community Center in Chicago. Bronstein completed Moody Bible Institute and McCormick Theological Seminary and was ordained as a Presbyterian minister. He was to have a marked effect on Jewish outreach. In 1934 Bronstein founded the First Hebrew Christian Church in Chicago (Presbyterian). Bronstein was also able to win many of his family members to his faith. His brother-in-law, Jacob Peltz, became general secretary of the American Alliance. Morris Kaminskey, another brother-in-law, started a similar congregation in Toronto under Anglican auspices. The Presbyterian church also established congregations in Los Angeles, Baltimore, and Philadelphia (Bronstein, 1947).

Jewish missions in America and Europe also experienced significant growth during this period. Some mission work, both then and to this day, resulted in congregations. Mission policies on congregations have varied.

The late 1960s and early 1970s produced new beginnings in the movement toward messianic Jewish congregations. Manny Brotman, in the mid 1960s, came in contact with many of the old Alliance leaders and with the Chicago work of David Bronstein Sr. (Bronstein was succeeded by Morris Kaminskey, who was in turn succeeded by Larry Rich, later the HCAA general secretary.) While in Chicago, Brotman founded the Young Hebrew Christian Alliance (YHCA). He greatly influenced young Jewish believers in a messianic Jewish direction. Joel Chernoff was part of the new YHCA. He, with Rick Coghill, became a significant influence for messianic music, forming the noted musical team Lamb. The influence of the youth eventually persuaded the late Martin Chernoff, saved under the ministry of Morris Kaminskey in Toronto, to move his congregation in Cincinnati in a messianic Jewish direction (1971) (Rausch, 102–11).

The Jews for Jesus outreach under Moishe Rosen also raised Jewish consciousness among Jewish followers of Jesus. Literature and Jewish gospel music exemplified by the Liberated Wailing Wall proclaimed that one could be a Jew for Jesus. (The Jesus Movement brought a significant harvest of Jewish people into new covenant faith, and some of these found their way into the messianic Jewish world. The impact of the charismatic roots of these young Jewish believers was felt on the movement. Jews for Jesus adopted the style of the Jesus Movement for Jewish evangelism.)

Others during the early 1970s also began to move in a messianic Jewish direction. This included Daniel Juster, under whose leadership Bronstein's Chicago congregation became Adat ha Tikvah (1974); and Beth Messiah Congregation in Rockville, MD, founded by Paul Liberman, Sid Roth, and Sandra Sheskin, first pastored by Manny Brotman (1973–75) and later by Juster (1978–86, 1988–present). Herb Links also took his Presbyterian-related group in a messianic Jewish direction. It became Beth Messiah, Philadelphia (1973). During this period, John Fischer and Mike Becker founded B'nai Maccabim in the North Chicago suburbs. Dr. James Hutchin, Wheaton College chaplain, wrote a significant Ph.D. dissertation, "The Case for Messianic Judaism," for Fuller Theological Seminary. He also became involved in the planting of messianic Jewish congregations.

Members of these congregations swelled the ranks of the HCAA. In 1975 their numbers provided the votes to change the name of the organization to the Messianic Jewish Alliance of America (MJAA). This was a clear affirmation of new messianic Jewish directions.

A significant move toward messianic Judaism was also taking place in works related to the Assemblies of God (AG). Ray Gannon and Phil Goble founded Beth Immanuel in the Los Angeles area (1971). Gannon went on to establish Beth Immanuel on Long Island, and Goble, congregations in Miami, Fort Lauderdale, and northern New Jersey. These men were influenced by the indigenous concepts of Fuller Seminary's School of World Mission (Goble and Gannon, 1975).

In the late 1970s attempts were made by several leaders to form a union—the Union of Messianic Jewish Congregations (UMJC). This union included 19 congregations at its inception (1979) and includes almost 90 as of this writing (2000). Conferences, leadership training, planting of congregations, and development of materials have been important services of this fellowship.

During the first years of the UMJC there was serious conflict between the UMJC and the MJAA, whose board from 1979 on was no longer in favor of the formation of a Union. Some of this had to do with issues of polity and the meaning of a superstructure for accountability of leaders and congregations. The battle did eventually become very intense and produced a division in the movement that lasted for 15 years. Accusations were traded far and wide. With many congregations joining the UMJC, the MJAA decided to form its own association of congregations, but one with a looser government. In 1984 the International Alliance of Messianic Congregations and Synagogues (IAMCS) was formed. In the midst of this tension, the UMJC formed an affiliated individual organization called the Association of Messianic

Believers. Its suborganization, the Association of Messianic Jewish Believers, was given affiliation with the Hebrew Christian Alliance so that the U.S. became the only nation with two affiliated associations. The sentiment of the International Alliance during these years was more favorable toward the Union. In the early 1990s the leaders of the UMJC and the MJAA experienced what they considered a move of the Holy Spirit that softened hearts for reconciliation. Both organizations had continued to grow. It was clear that neither would supersede the other. Both counted more than 80 member congregations. The reconciliation was deep and real. Joint minimum standards for leaders, for handling difficulties between congregations in the respective organizations, and even joint conferences were a fruit of the reconciliation. This new unity also enabled cooperation together in other projects such as the Toward Jerusalem Council II project. This is a movement of prayer to see the position of the church with regard to the Jewish life of Jesus reversed. Such leaders as ▸John Dawson, ▸Peter Hocken (Roman Catholic), Brian Cox (Episcopal), Don Finto, and Olin Griffin have joined this effort from the world of the church along with messianic Jewish leaders from the UMJC and the MJAA.

The messianic Jewish movement continued to grow in important ways in the 1990s. As part of the continuing recognition of the messianic Jewish congregational movement, the International Hebrew Christian Alliance, based in England, changed its name to the International Messianic Jewish Alliance (IMJA). Later its international offices were moved to Virginia Beach, VA, under David Sadaca, its general secretary. Before his death, Harcourt Samuel, for many years the real spiritual leader of the International and British Alliances, visited the UMJC annual conference in America and affirmed the messianic Jewish movement. This led to greater openness and change on the international level (IHCA). Joel Chernoff was elected president and Rich Nichol vice president of the IHCA (1998). Chernoff is a leader in the MJAA and its general secretary, and Nichol is a former president of the UMJC.

In addition, the messianic Jewish movement spurred new, tighter organizations that reflected what Peter Wagner calls postdenominational Christianity. The UMJC and the MJAA are broad umbrella organizations for messianic Jews and congregations of many different types (charismatic and non-charismatic, more and less traditional in Jewish practice). In the early 1980s the leaders of Beth Messiah Congregation (Daniel Juster, Andrew [Eitan] Shishkoff, and Keith [Asher] Intrater) were influenced by the new types of apostolic movements that were becoming common in the U.S. and in many other countries. An association of congregations planted in relationship to Beth Messiah Congregation was formed, which mostly networked groups in the Mid-Atlantic states. With the sending of Intrater and Shishkoff to Israel, the

association grew and became known as Tikkun Ministries. Tikkun sponsored a sending agency as well as a network of congregations in the U.S., which numbers 19 congregations. The association is committed to fivefold ministry leadership and the full expression of the Holy Spirit gifts. Since 1984 it also sponsors Messiah Biblical Institute and Graduate School of Theology.

In the early 1990s Jonathan Bernis, messianic Rabbi of Sh'ma Israel congregation in Rochester, NY, called together 10 national leaders in the messianic Jewish movement for three days of fasting and prayer for the movement. During this time of prayer, Jonathan shared his vision for evangelistic music festivals in Russia. He started an organization called Hear O Israel for these festivals, the first of which was held in St. Petersburg. Festivals were also held in Moscow and Odessa. The results were astonishing, with thousands attending each festival, half being of Jewish descent and thousands making first-time professions of faith. Several congregations have been planted as a result. Most of them formed a new apostolic stream under Hear O Israel. This is a stream oriented to all the gifts and the power of the Spirit. In addition, a jointly sponsored Bible school (Messianic Jewish Bible School, led by Wayne Wilkes) was formed by Hear O Israel,

Messianic Jews in Jerusalem.

Tikkun Ministries (Daniel Juster), God's Grace Foundation (Roger West), B'nai Maccabim Congregation in Chicago (Mike Becker), and Shady Grove Church in Dallas (Olen Griffin). A new campus was also planted in Budapest (1998). Other organizations are also seeing significant planting success in Russia.

Ray Gannon, in cooperation with the AG and King of Kings congregation in Jerusalem planted a Bible college in Israel to train leaders for messianic Jewish congregations in Israel. The Israel movement is also growing significantly. Its present director is Asher Intrater. It has been given full autonomy by the AG and is now governed fully by messianic Jews in Israel.

In addition, after many failed attempts, a messianic Jewish Alliance of Israel has been formed. This alliance is affiliated with the IMJA. It has unified the messianic Jewish believers in the land and sponsored many celebrations for feasts, drawing over 1,000 Jewish believers.

2. Philosophy.

Those who identify themselves primarily as messianic Jews vary in philosophy. The following description of common elements reflects predominant viewpoints. Messianic Jews affirm classical evangelical doctrines but express these doctrines in more Judaic terms. Messianic Jews also believe in the value of planting messianic Jewish congregations as a home for Jews and Gentiles who desire a Jewishly rooted expression of their faith. These congregations reflect a corporate Jewish lifestyle greatly furthering the goal of fostering a new covenant people movement in the Jewish community. By maintaining connections to their people, messianic Jews have natural opportunities to share their faith. Furthermore, messianic Jews believe they are called by God to maintain a biblically rooted Jewish life (Juster, 157–90; Rausch, 1981, 117–42).

A variety of opinions may be found on the place of the Law in this lifestyle. The basic consensus is that the Law has continuing value in its universal moral principles (2 Tim. 3:16–17). Also, the Law is seen as a focus for defining Jewish lifestyle since it provides the roots of Jewish life in the memory maintained by feasts and other observances. Yet all must be celebrated with regard to Yeshua's (Jesus') fulfillment in a new covenant context (UMJC, "The Place of the Law," 1983). New publications presenting the messianic Jewish view continue to be published (e.g., Juster, *Israel, the Church and the Last Days; The Irrevocable Calling;* Shiffman, *The Return of the Remnant;* Berkowitz, *Torah Rediscovered* [1996]).

Messianic Jews are predominantly charismatic in orientation. The gifts of the Spirit are seen as important for accomplishing God's work. This emphasis is connected with the conviction that convincing Jewish people of the claims of Jesus will require a supernatural demonstration of God's kingdom.

Messianic Jews are usually Zionist. Some believe that Jewish people have a right to their land under standards of justice and mercy. Others see the present regathering to the land as the fulfillment of the biblical promise to Israel. Some see the present regathering as a stage of God's working to eventually bring the promised fulfillment after Israel's repentance with regard to accepting Jesus as the Messiah. All hope for Israel's ultimate salvation and reingrafting (Rom. 11).

The messianic Jewish movement continues to grow, with more than 200 identifiable groups in North America, dozens in Israel, dozens in Russia, and congregations in most countries with a significant Jewish population. Growing ministries continue under Ilan Zamir, the messianic Jewish Alliance of Israel, Asher Intrater, The Israel School of the Bible, Ari and Shira Sorko-Ram Maoz, Eitan Shishkoff, Ohalai Rachamim, David Lazarus, Beth Immanuel, and many more.

■ **Bibliography:** D. Bronstein Jr., *Peniel Portrait* (1947) ■ P. Goble and R. Gannon, *Everything You Need to Grow a Messianic Synagogue* (1975) ■ D. C. Juster, *Jewish Roots* (1986) ■ P. Liberman, *The Fig Tree Blossoms* (1976) ■ D. Rausch, *Messianic Judaism, Its History, Theology, and Polity* (1981) ■ idem, *Zionism in Early American Fundamentalism* (1979) ■ M. Schiffman, *The Return of the Remnant* (1991) ■ D. Stern, *The Messianic Jewish Manifesto* (1988).

■ D. C. Juster

METRO CHRISTIAN FELLOWSHIP See KANSAS CITY PROPHETS.

METROPOLITAN CHURCH ASSOCIATION (BURNING BUSH). The Metropolitan Church Association (MCA) was founded in 1894 by hotel owner Edwin L. Harvey (1865–1926) and banker Marmaduke (Duke) M. Farson (1863–1929). Initially a mission congregation of the Rock River Conference of the Methodist Episcopal Church (MEC), the MCA emerged as an important center for the Holiness movement in Chicago. It attracted nearly 1,000 Sunday school pupils and 200 adults by the time it separated from the MEC in 1899. The MCA's insistence that physical manifestations, especially jumping, were regular features of authentic worship resulted in the common practice of referring to MCA members as "jumpers."

In the fall of 1900 Farson hired Seth C. Rees, a Quaker who was president of the International Apostolic Holiness Union, a union of Holiness people committed to premillennial eschatology, to assume leadership of the MCA ministry in Chicago. Engaging in a threefold strategy of highly publicized noon meetings in the heart of Chicago's financial district, evening meetings in select neighborhoods, and Salvation Army–style missions to the poor and homeless, Rees took Chicago by storm. In early March a scheduled two-week evangelistic campaign started a revival that attracted front-page coverage in Chicago newspapers. Within three months an estimated 2,200 people, including ▸Glenn Cooke, had experienced salvation.

In December the MCA opened a campaign in Boston that was one of the most successful in Rees' evangelistic career. In May of 1902 the MCA established a periodical, *The Burning Bush*. Adopting features commonly associated with mass-circulation periodicals, the *Burning Bush* became a religious expression of the "muckraking" journalism of the early 20th century. Employing a professional cartoonist, the *Burning Bush* used caricature and publication of private correspondence in a never-ending war against the wealthy, prominent evangelists, established denominations, and alleged Holiness compromisers. Although marked by considerable controversy, the MCA attracted the adherence of several colorful religious figures, such as Alma White, founder of the Pillar of Fire and the nation's first female bishop, Susan Fogg, an eccentric African-American preacher, and Bud Robinson, a folksy Texan who contributed significantly to the rapid early growth of the Church of the Nazarene.

Especially significant was the MCA's role in the origins of pentecostalism. In Apr. 1906 ▸A. G. Garr, an MCA evangelist, led part of the MCA's Los Angeles mission to Seymour's Azusa Street Mission. Following his experience of pentecostal baptism (Garr is believed to have been the first white person to speak in tongues at Azusa Street), Garr returned to Chicago and then to Danville, VA, where he had headed an MCA mission, to spread the pentecostal message. Later he traveled to the MCA mission in India. Although disappointed with his inability to speak local languages, Garr would spend the remainder of his life as a healing evangelist, spreading the message of Pentecost in the U.S. and around the world.

Bitter critics of pentecostalism, the MCA firmly believed that their early attacks on pentecostalism, especially reports of Charles F. Parham's arrest on sodomy charges in San Antonio, TX, played an important role in the Holiness movement's rejection of pentecostalism.

Undoubtedly the most controversial feature of the MCA was its rejection of private property. Organizing intentional communities in Waukesha, WI, and Bullard, TX, the MCA, with over 1,000 residents, was one of the largest communal societies in American history. Experiencing a steady decline after WWI, the Burning Bush Movement gradually evolved into a conventional evangelical religious body. Having abandoned the remaining features of communalism, the MCA sold its Waukesha property in 1956. Although the MCA continues to publish the *Burning Bush* and operates a church in Milwaukee, WI, its continued vitality is as an indigenous international movement with over 50,000 members in India and churches in South Africa, Swaziland, and Mexico.

■ **Bibliography:** W. Kostlevy, "Nor Silver, Nor Gold: The Burning Bush Movement and the Communatarian Holiness Vision" (diss., Notre Dame, 1996). ■ W. Kostlevy

MEYER, JOYCE (1943–). Televangelist and prolific author. Meyer was raised in Appalachia by an abusive father, leaving her with anger and hatred toward men. At the age of 18 she left home. Shortly thereafter she entered into a disastrous marriage that endured 20 separations in five years. Twice she was abandoned, eventually living in a rooming house and subsisting on junk food. Finally, after the birth of a son, David, her husband deserted her for good. A month later Joyce met Dave Meyer, already a Spirit-filled Lutheran, whom she married in 1967.

Although converted at age nine, Meyer became convinced that the only way to be saved was never to do wrong again. She continued to be frustrated until 1976, when she pleaded with God for help. Soon after, she felt touched by the Holy Spirit with a spirit of rejoicing and a positive purpose for her life. She immediately began teaching Bible classes. In 1980 Meyer initiated the *Life in the Word* radio broadcast, which is now heard on more than 250 radio stations nationwide. In 1993 her popular 30-minute *Life in the Word* television program was released. She is the author of 30 books and a library of tapes. In 1991 she formed Hand of Hope, the ministry's missionary arm, which is directed by her son, David.

Meyer makes no apologies for her absence of formal theological schooling. She is living proof of how God revolutionizes lives, and the richness of her schooling with the Holy Spirit has touched a multitude of lives, especially those needing emotional healing. Joyce and Dave have three other children: Laura, Sandra, and Danny.

■ **Bibliography:** K. Walker, "The Preacher Who Tells It Like It Is," *Charisma* (Nov. 1998). ■ S. M. Burgess; J. Zeigler

MIRACLES, GIFT OF The term "operations/workings of powerful deeds" *(energēmata dynameōn)* occurs fifth in a list of manifestations of the Holy Spirit in 1 Cor. 12:7–10. A shorter form of the same expression ("powerful deeds," *dynameis)* is found in Paul's resume of the list in 1 Cor. 12:28–29. The plural form is used most probably to evoke the notion of variety and abundance, as is the case with the corresponding terminology concerning healing: "gifts of healing" *(charismata iamatōn;* 1 Cor. 12:9, 28, 30).

The root *dyn* connotes "ability, capacity, power" (see Grundmann). It is sometimes used in the Septuagint as a translation of the Hebrew root *gbr* when this refers to the power of God to effect his will (1 Chron. 29:11; Job 12:13; Pss. 54:1; 145:12). The frequency with which the term *dynamis* is employed to denote a powerful deed or "miracle" in the NT probably reflects intertestamental usage. As witness to this, we may point to the frequency with which the Hebrew word *gbrh* in the Qumran literature (1QH 1:35; 4:28–29; 11:3; et al.) refers to the wonderful and powerful works of God. In a saying of Jesus belonging to what Mussner (19) terms "the oldest tradition of the gospels," we find this prophetic condemnation of Korazin, Bethsaida, and Capernaum: "If the miracles *(dynameis)* that were performed in you had been performed in Tyre and Sidon/Sodom" (Matt. 11:21, 23; Luke 10:13). The notion that God's powerful works were being performed to lead people to repent and understand his intentions is found frequently in the NT: Matt. 7:22; 13:54, 58; Mark 6:2, 5; Luke 19:37; Acts 2:22; 8:13; 10:38; 19:11; 2 Cor. 12:12; Gal. 3:5; Heb. 2:4; 6:5.

The fact that, in the Corinthian lists, "miracles" are distinguished from "healings" is probably due to the special ability of healing miracles to symbolize and communicate the saving power of God (ˋHealing, Gift of). On other occasions *dynamis* is a generic term that includes acts of healing. In Mark 6:2 we encounter the reaction to Jesus on the part of his fellow townsmen: "What's this wisdom that has been given him, that he even does miracles!" Mark then goes on to report, "He could not do any miracles *(dynamin)* there, except lay his hands on a few sick people and heal them" (Mark 6:5; Matt. 13:54, 58).

The fact that Paul himself lists "miracles" alongside the common OT expression "signs and wonders" in 2 Cor. 12:12 (see also Acts 2:22; Heb. 2:4), entitles us to think that *dynameis* may be a generic term to him as well. Certainly the multiplication of food, the power over weather and other cosmic forces, some forms of exorcism, and the like should be classified as "miracles," but such realities do not exhaust the possibilities. We have seen that healing itself can be considered a demonstration of power. Other indications as well point to a broader understanding of what Paul may mean by such expressions as we find in Gal. 3:5: "Does God give you his Spirit and work miracles [*energon dynameis;* note resemblance to 1 Cor. 12:10] among you because you observe the law, or because you believe what you heard?"

Miracles may refer to any aspect of the divine activity by which people are "cut to the heart" (Acts 2:37), a lifetime of habit patterns of sin are erased, spiritual blindness is overcome in an instant, physical and moral healing takes place as the gospel is preached, and enemies are both touched and brought to the Lord. This is what Paul refers to when he says that he preached in such a way that the Corinthians' faith "might not rest on men's wisdom, but on God's power" (1 Cor. 2:5), or when he refers to his assurance concerning God's choice of the Thessalonians because "our gospel came to you not simply with words, but also with power, with the Holy Spirit and with deep conviction" (1 Thess. 1:5).

The charismatic gift designated in 1 Cor. 12 refers to a particular spiritual endowment by which a person is able to demonstrate God's justifying and saving power, and to manifest the lordship of Jesus Christ over the whole universe by bringing about physical and moral effects that clearly transcend the power of merely human resources. Though many of these effects may be imitated and indeed co-opted by Satan, the criteria for discerning God's activity are clearly given in the NT (ˋDiscernment of Spirits, Gift of). One of the surest signs that God is the source of the event is that the working of miracles proceed from and lead to faith. The Christian community in every age has need of this precious gift in order that faith might grow both in extension and depth.

■ **Bibliography:** A. Bittlinger, *Gifts and Graces: A Commentary on 1 Corinthians 12–14* (1973) ▌ J. D. G. Dunn, *Jesus and the Spirit: A Study of the Religious and Charismatic Experience of Jesus and the First Christians as Reflected in the New Testament* (1975) ▌ W. Grundmann, *"dynamai/dynamis"* in *TDNT* 2 (1964) ▌ R. Latourelle, *The Miracles of Jesus and the Theology of Miracles* (1988) ▌ R. Laurentin, *Miracles in El Paso?* (1982) ▌ F. Mussner, *The Miracles of Jesus* (1970) ▌ H. Van Der Loos, *The Miracles of Jesus* (1965).   ■ F. Martin

MIRANDA, JESSE (1937–). Important Mexican-American Assemblies of God (AG) leader and speaker. Born in Albuquerque, NM, on Apr. 9, 1937. Miranda studied at the Latin American Bible Institute (LABI), Southern California College (B.A.), Talbot Theological Seminary (M.R.E.), California State University, Fullerton (M.Ed.), Fuller Theological Seminary (D.Min.), and the University of Southern California (1978). He has served as a pastor (1957–59) and as secretary-treasurer (1973–78), assistant superintendent (1980–84), and superintendent (1984–92) of the Latin American District Council of the AG in the U.S. He has also worked at the LABI in La Puente, CA (1959–73) and as professor of urban ministry at Azusa Pacific University. He has written articles for the *Dictionary of Christianity in America, Apuntes, Christianity Today,* and the Promise Keepers men's movement in the U.S. He published *The Christian Church in Ministry* (1980), which has since been translated into six languages. In addition to his scholarly publications and work in the AG, he has served as the president of Alianza de Ministerios Evangélicos Nacionales (AMEN) and as consulting editor of *Christianity Today.* He has also worked with the Lausanne Committee on World Evangelization. Miranda is considered one of the leading Latino pentecostal and Protestant church leaders in the U.S. in the late 20th century.   ■ G. Espinosa

MIRLY, HERBERT H. (1918–). Leader of Lutheran renewal (ˋLutheran Charismatics). After completing ministerial training at Concordia Seminary (1945), Mirly served as pastor of four congregations of the Lutheran Church–Missouri Synod in Illinois and Pennsylvania for 19 years before accepting the call as executive secretary for the Council of Lutheran Churches in St. Louis and editor of the *St. Louis Lutheran*. It was during this ministry that he first became aware of Lutheran pastors who had experienced what they called "the baptism of the Holy Spirit." Shortly thereafter his wife, Dolores, and their daughter, Rebecca, experienced Spirit baptism. After becoming pastor of Resurrection Lutheran Church in Charlotte, NC, Mirly asked for and received his baptism in the Spirit.

Resurrection Church had only about 50 people attending worship when Mirly introduced a contemporary worship service. During the next seven years it grew to 1,500 members and has started satellite churches in three adjacent communities. Since 1985 Herb and Dolores Mirly have ministered a message of Spirit renewal to Missouri Synod churches throughout the southeastern U.S. They have two daughters.

■ P. Anderson

MISSIOLOGY: PENTECOSTAL AND CHARISMATIC

I. Characteristics of Pentecostal Mission Praxis

II. A Pentecostal and Charismatic Theology of Mission
   A. The Quest for a Pentecostal Missiology
   B. The Roots and Main Themes of Pentecostal Theology of Mission
   C. The Distinctives of Mission Theologies of the Charismatic Movements

III. Mission, Evangelization, and Social Concern

IV. Impending Challenges
   A. Evangelization and Proselytism
   B. Common Witness and the Issue of Christian Unity in Mission
   C. Relation to Other Religions
   D. Other Challenges

The pentecostal movement is the most rapidly growing missionary movement in the world; furthermore, "a growth of from zero to 400 million in 90 years is unprecedented in the whole of church history" (Hollenweger, 1996, 4). Pentecostalism and evangelization can be seen almost as synonyms as the 1989 constitution of the Assemblies of God (AG) (U.S.) states: "The priority for reason-for-being of the Assemblies of God is to be an agency for evangelizing the world."

Pentecostalism and the charismatic movement are a global, multicultural phenomenon (Poewe, 1994). According to David Barrett's calculations, pentecostals and charismatics are found on every continent and in every country, among almost all cultural and sociological groups of the human

mosaic (Barrett, 2000). As with other growing churches, so also pentecostal and charismatic churches are growing fastest in the Two-Thirds countries (Patte, 1991). This article focuses on pentecostal missiology and treats distinctive charismatic contributions separately.

I. CHARACTERISTICS OF PENTECOSTAL MISSION PRAXIS.

According to G. McClung (U.S.), seven factors are characteristic of pentecostal missions (he includes the charismatic movements, but it is safer to apply these characteristics only to classical pentecostal missions). Pentecostal missions are (1) experiential and relational; (2) expressly biblical with a high view of inspiration; (3) extremely urgent in nature; (4) "focused, yet diversified": they prioritize evangelization but not to the exclusion of social concern; (5) aggressive and bold in their approach; (6) interdependent (both among various pentecostal/charismatic groups and in relation to older churches and their mission endeavors); and (7) unpredictable as to the future.

Similar kinds of characterizations have been proposed by others (e.g., Van der Laan, 1986; Kärkkäinen, 1998), who have suggested these factors: naïve biblicism and eschatology, individualism, total commitment, pragmatism, flexibility, a place for emotions, personal testimonies, establishment of indigenous churches as a goal of missions, demonstration of the power of the Spirit, and participation of all believers.

In recent decades pentecostals have enthusiastically employed mission strategies of evangelicals, such as those of the church growth movement. Pentecostals have also profited from developments of contextualization theory; in fact, before the term *contextualization* was coined, pentecostals did much of it by introducing local music styles in worship services and in building churches that did not look like churches.

The indigenous church principle, as revealed by the title of M. Hodges' classic *The Indigenous Church* (1953), has been a high priority from the beginning. This was, paradoxically, helped by the lack of funding, especially in the beginning decades of pentecostal missions when a considerable number of missionaries went overseas without any pledged support. The "faith missions" principle (Fiedler, 1997) was enthusiastically adopted by many pioneers, both because of the biblical support of the idea and because of an intensive expectation of the Second Coming, but it soon gave way to a more traditional mission praxis.

Pentecostals have been pragmatists in their approach to mission. Consequently, flexibility in choosing methods, strategies, and structures (or lack thereof!) has been a hallmark of pentecostal missiology. In their mission and church structures, pentecostals embrace all the possible variations, from episcopal (e.g., former Eastern Europe, Africa) to presbyterian (mainly English-speaking world) to polities emphasizing the total autonomy of local churches (Scandinavian pentecostals and their mission fields, e.g., in some Latin American countries).

Pentecostal evangelization and mission praxis has also given birth to numerous more or less independent organizations, as well as numerous personal ministries, often led by a strong, charismatic evangelist.

Along with participation in the AD 2000 and Beyond Movement, pentecostal and charismatic Christians in the 1990s have focused on reaching the people living in the so-called 10/40 window.

In recent years an enthusiastic use of mass media in evangelization has been characteristic of pentecostals.

II. A PENTECOSTAL AND CHARISMATIC THEOLOGY OF MISSION.

A. The Quest for a Pentecostal Missiology.

Pentecostals have been more "doers" than "thinkers" in the area of mission. They have given experience a privileged place, not just in missiology, but also in spirituality and in their approach to Scripture interpretation. Therefore, a distinctively *pentecostal* theology of mission is still in the making. Pentecostals were generally so busy with their practical mission and evangelism that they did not bother themselves with writing missiological treatises or academic theological studies.

The first treatise appeared in 1953. *The Indigenous Church*, written by the most noted pentecostal missiologist of the previous generation, Melvin L. Hodges, and its sequels, *Theology of the Church and Its Mission* (1977) and *The Indigenous Church and the Missionary* (1978), followed the paths explored by evangelicals in mission theology and social action. In 1985 Paul A. Pomerville's *The Third Force in Missions* developed a pentecostal missiology that creatively injected a pentecostal view of the dynamic work of the Holy Spirit into an evangelical interpretation of the kingdom of God. Larry D. Pate's *From Every People* (1989) focused on the growing Two-Thirds World missions movement. None of these works, however, produced much *theology* of mission.

A major compendium on pentecostal missiology, touching on crucial issues of theology of mission as well, was published in 1991 under the title *Called and Empowered: Pentecostal Mission in Global Perspective*. The authors represent a truly global group of pentecostal theologians. This shows that a new generation of pentecostal missiologists is ready to tackle impending issues of missions, such as the biblical basis of mis-

sion, social justice, and the challenge of contextualization. Douglas Petersen's *Not by Might, Nor by Power: A Pentecostal Theology of Social Concern in Latin America* (1996) is the most comprehensive theological statement on social justice.

Pentecostals have produced several historically oriented monographs and studies on mission strategies and church growth (e.g., McGee and McClung). Increasing numbers of studies on mission and mission theology have been produced by W. Hollenweger and his Birmingham University (U.K.) students, many of whom come from pentecostal or charismatic backgrounds (for a presentation of topics, see Hollenweger 1991).

B. The Roots and Main Themes of Pentecostal Theology of Mission.

Two traditions have shaped the pentecostal view of mission: an inherited evangelical-conservative agenda and the ethos of the Holiness movements and other revival movements of the earlier century.

It was quite natural for pentecostals (despite some of the prejudices of evangelicals) to align themselves with evangelicals, since the conciliar ecumenical movement seemed too liberal both theologically and in its mission agenda. Evangelical-conservative mission theology has had a strong influence, starting with a classic book by a missiologist of an earlier generation, Roland Allen, whose *Missionary Methods: St. Paul's or Ours?* (originally 1912), though reflecting views of a sacramental tradition (Anglican), has been widely read by pentecostals until the present time.

Sunday school teachers in 1938 in what was then the Belgian Congo. Note the white Jesus and the romanticized setting in this Western Sunday school picture.

A strong pentecostal presence in the evangelical Lausanne movement with the highly influential "Lausanne Covenant" has further shaped pentecostals' view of mission.

Both pentecostals and evangelicals share conservative doctrinal views regarding the inspiration and authority of the Bible, the lostness of humankind without Christ, and justification by faith, as well as priority of evangelism over social action. From evangelical-conservatives, pentecostals also inherited the insistence on the necessity of conversion and emphasis on an individual's salvation experience. Pentecostals consequently came to stress the importance of "crisis" experience rather than "growth" experience in conversion.

Roots in the 19th-century Holiness movements and in other revival movements gave birth to pentecostalism's eschatological, premillennial atmosphere. "So intensely did they expect the Second Coming of Christ that envisioning an additional decade—or even another century—for evangelization would have been inconceivable" (McGee, 1993, 42). If it is true that eschatology is the "mother of theology," it is certainly true that eschatology has been the "mother of pentecostal missiology" (Faupel, 1996). But when the end did not come, pentecostals easily adopted the missionary methods of other Protestants.

The most distinctive, and most hotly disputed, pentecostal doctrine and experience, that of Spirit baptism, combined with strong eschatological fervor, nourished the beginning days of pentecostal missions. As early as 1908, ʾJ. R. Flower, one of the pioneers, contended that "carrying the gospel to hungry souls in this and other lands is but a natural result of receiving the baptism of the Holy Ghost."

From the beginning, some, though not all, pentecostals started teaching the doctrine of speaking in tongues as ʾinitial (physical) evidence of the reception of the baptism with the Holy Spirit. This belief was soon linked with world mission. In the first years of the movement, there was even an unwarranted optimism that speaking in tongues *(xenolalia)*, a form of glossolalia in which existing human languages previously unknown to the speaker could be spoken, would be given by the Holy Spirit to help finish the evangelization of the world before the imminent return of Christ. Of course, very soon it was found that the theory did not work and it was abandoned.

Even after the rejection of the expectation of the fulfillment of the missionary commandment by a supernatural gift of tongues, the primary mission "strategy" has been the baptism in the Holy Spirit as empowerment for witness and service (Acts 1:8). Pentecostals have been known for "the radical strategy in modern missions" (McGee, 1997). There are enough recorded instances of miracles, "signs and wonders," in various mission fields to support the thesis that supernatural power has been a crucial dimension of pentecostal mission. This view of the continuing presence of God's power naturally sets pentecostalism in conflict with the heritage of ʾdispensationalism, which holds that miracles and wonders ceased with the era of the apostles (Sheppard, 1984).

The belief that Spirit baptism equips every believer, men and women alike, for ministry reveals the leveling influence of modern pentecostalism and the key to its rapid growth. Mission and evangelization are both the right and the responsibility of every believer. Even where this ideal is not fulfilled, the mind-set is there. The role of women missionaries has been extraordinarily significant in pentecostal missions (Cavaness, 1994). Since pentecostals have emphasized the divine power in doing mission, their approach often has been faith-filled positivism, even triumphalism.

Emerging pentecostal academic scholarship has reflected especially on Lukan studies, also with a view to mission (Lopez, 1997; Menzies, 1991; Penney, 1997). For pentecostals, Luke's distinctive pneumatology speaks for a prophetic community empowered by the Spirit for missionary service. Another theologically helpful orientation has been offered by the Kingdom of God theology, the contributions of which will be considered in Section III below.

C. The Distinctives of Mission Theologies of the Charismatic Movements.

Charismatic Christianity until recently has been called "the sleeping giant of world mission" (McGee, 1993, 44). The 1990s were called by the leaders of the movement a decade of evangelization. D. Shibley's *A Force in the Earth: The Charismatic Renewal and World Evangelism* (1989) and E. Pousson's *Spreading the Flame* (1992) are perhaps the most comprehensive missiological presentations of the charismatic movements. Their focus, though, is in history, biography, and strategy rather than on a distinctive theology of mission.

The most sophisticated theological reflection in the charismatic renewal in general and in charismatic mission in particular is offered by theologians from a Roman Catholic background. A recent compendium, entitled *John Paul II and the New Evangelization* (1995), provides some interesting perspectives on the topic, both by Catholics and by others. Promoting evangelization on an international scale is the purpose of "Evangelizacion 2000" in Rome, led by Fr. ʾT. Forrest, C.S.S.R. The most distinctive contribution of the Catholic charismatic movement on missions is its emphasis on the integral relation of evangelization and sacraments (e.g., McDonnell, 1995[b]). Furthermore, along the incarnational principle (John 1:14 et al.) of Catholicism, the charismatic theology underlines a holistic view of humanity and the world. Still another distinctive is the much more prominent role of liturgy and worship. Catholic charismatics have already launched several important evangelistic programs and training schools.

The ʾInternational Charismatic Consultation on World Evangelization (ICCOWE), led by Eastern Orthodox priest

Michael Harper, is a venue for charismatic and pentecostal theologians from various denominations to further world evangelization through prayer and study. The approximately 70-member advisory council has wide global representation of both theologians and missionary leaders (Harper, 1994). The ›North American Congress on the Holy Spirit and World Evangelization is another example of a charismatic network for mission.

A consultation on charismatic theology sponsored by the WCC in Geneva in 1980 produced a landmark document, *The Church Is Charismatic* (Bittlinger, ed., 1981). While mission was not the focus, some interesting developments from a missiological viewpoint were offered. A summary of a theological group, compiled by Hollenweger (1981, 21–28), suggested that there are three major orientations to the Spirit's role in the world: (1) the Spirit—an ecclesiological approach: the Spirit works for the unity and united witness of all churches; (2) the Spirit—a cosmological approach: the Spirit renews creation and bestows fullness of life that encompasses physical healing and healing of social relationships as well; (3) the Spirit—a sacramental approach: the Spirit is mediated through personal conversion, baptism, confirmation, and ordination as sacramental theologies renew their focus on the Spirit.

Dutch Reformed missiologist J. A. B. Jongeneel, coming from a pentecostal background, has extensively studied the role of the Spirit in mission. Jongeneel takes his lead from a "missionary pneumatology" of R. Allen. Oddly enough, pentecostals have not much used Allen's two definitive works on the Spirit, *Pentecost and the World: The Revelation of the Holy Spirit in the "Acts of the Apostles"* (1917), and *Mission Activities Considered in Relation to the Manifestation of the Spirit* (1930), that have informed other confessions about the Spirit. Jongeneel shows that the origin of mission is in the movement of the Holy Spirit as the Spirit sends the church into the world. The same movement equips the church to accomplish its mission. Jongeneel, much more than classical pentecostals, highlights the role of the fruit of the Spirit along with the gifts of the Spirit. He also sees the critical role of experience of the Spirit, Spirit baptism, although balance is needed.

Anglican charismatic Andrew M. Lord of the U.K. has recently outlined a "Mission Eschatology: A Framework for Mission in the Spirit" (1997), with a view toward a holistic, hope-filled approach to mission. Following NT theologian O. Cullman and others, Lord contends that "the missionary work of the Church is the eschatological foretaste of the kingdom" (112). He suggests seven dimensions of a genuine charismatic mission agenda: Jesus' lordship, healing, justice, unity-in-diversity of the people of God, freedom of creation, praise and worship, and fellowship. Lord also reminds us that the inbreaking of the Spirit takes place in the context of a spiritual battle. For a holistic mission, there is no opposition between evangelism and social concern.

Charismatics have followed pentecostals in emphasizing signs and wonders. In fact, some charismatics, especially the so-called ›third wave (Wagner, 1988), have come to highlight the role of healings and exorcisms in a more visible way. Among others, John Wimber's book on *Power Evangelism* (1986) and C. Peter Wagner's flood of books on spiritual warfare, especially on "territorial spirits," have disseminated ideas throughout the global charismatic movement. These ideas have received enthusiastic acceptance, especially in animistic contexts (Asia, Africa) and in Latin America, but they have also come under critical questioning. A pronounced theology of the kingdom of God has been outlined as a framework for most of these writings.

What are differences and differing emphases in relation to classical pentecostalism? First, mainline charismatics have been more open to the challenge of social justice, perhaps because most of their churches have been. Second, their interpretation of Scripture has been less fundamentalistic, and thus there has been more flexibility for contextualization into specific contexts (including the Western world). Third, because most charismatics live in sacramental churches, they have been able to integrate evangelization into sacraments, even if they don't fully resolve the dilemma.

III. MISSION, EVANGELIZATION, AND SOCIAL CONCERN.

One of the most common criticisms of pentecostal missions, voiced especially by Latin American and African observers, is its alleged lack of social concern. Both Marxist and Catholic writers have sometimes attributed the growth of the movement to foreign resources and leadership. They have further assumed that pentecostals are indifferent to, and even obstructionist in their attitudes toward, the fundamental issues of social injustice, repression, discrimination, corruption, and poverty.

One persistent misunderstanding among observers of pentecostalism has tended to confuse the issue. The earlier generation of sociologically oriented observers of pentecostalism tended to regard the birth and appeal of the movement in terms of social deprivation theory. This view basically suggests that all religious movements, including pentecostalism, develop as a result of individuals or groups feeling disadvantaged. This model, however, has been unable to explain why pentecostalism has also appealed to social classes other than the lower ones. Contrary to deprivation theories, it has been argued that pentecostalism and other such movements were both cause and effect of social change (Gerlach and Hine, 1970).

If the social deprivation theory has been incorrect in its explanation of the growth of pentecostalism, another common misconception among observers of the movement is that pentecostals are indifferent to social issues. This misconception has come under similar attack by the growing pentecostal literature on social ethics, social justice, and social concern in general. D. Petersen (1996), referring specifically to the Latin American context, notes that pentecostalism, rather than being just a movement "for the people" is actually "a social program" in itself. Pentecostals do not generally have written statements as to the "preferential option for the poor," because most pentecostal churches are "churches of the poor."

Although pentecostal mission focuses on evangelization, it is not to the exclusion of social concern and never has been. Holistic mission has been part of pentecostal mission work. In fact, pentecostals have worked with the poor for social renewal in unobtrusive ways and have initiated major social reform programs and institutions.

In the formative years of the movement, many pentecostals' eschatological fervor blurred the meaning of social improvement. Why invest in a world that was believed would fade away? The recent pentecostal theology of social concern, however, argues that the eschatological undergirding does not necessarily lead to such a pessimistic attitude toward social ethics. Although tension among pentecostals still continues between those with a view that emphasizes the "other-worldliness" of the eschatological hope and those with a view toward improvement of the present, for most pentecostals, eschatological hope has brought with it optimism about the work they are doing.

P. Kuzmič (1985) of the former Yugoslavia argues that the view that the doctrine of the impending premillennial return of Christ paralyzes efforts for social improvement is more a Western, cultural-theological creation based on conservative (American) political positions rather than on a clear reading of Scripture. His colleague, M. Volf (1990), has argued that when Christians create history that is compatible with the kingdom of God, such projects have eschatological significance: what is valid will remain.

It is precisely this view of the kingdom of God that has informed pentecostal social thinking during the last decade. NT exegete G. Fee (1991) has been in the vanguard of those introducing pentecostals to the concept of the kingdom of God. God brings his future reign to the present with the proclamation of "good news to the poor" everywhere. According to Fee, the "final consummation, our glorious future, has been guaranteed . . . by the resurrection of our Lord. But meanwhile, until that future has come in its fullness, we are to be the people of the future in the present age, who continue the proclamation of the kingdom as good news to the poor" (17). The eschatological kingdom has a normative moral structure reflective of God's own ethical character. Pentecostals believe that when Christians are empowered with the Spirit of God, they are equipped to do "kingdom works" in the midst of human suffering and plight.

M. W. Dempster (1991) has argued that there are three interrelated areas in a genuine pentecostal ministry: (1) the *kerygmatic* ministry, which proclaims the kingdom in spoken word; (2) the *koinoniac* ministry, which demonstrates the kingdom in social witness; and (3) the *diakonic* ministry, which manifests the kingdom in moral deeds. To attain this requires pentecostals to read the Bible in a "liberation style," in line with the hermeneutical circle, the concept of which some pentecostal missiologists have borrowed from more liberal liberation theologians.

One of the key issues of social justice in the modern world, the racial question, has definite roots in the birth of the pentecostal movement. In the formative years of the movement the Azusa Street Mission was essentially a black church despite the number of whites initially in attendance, and thus it attained a more universal character than was typical of other churches of that time. The short history of pentecostalism, however, reflects prejudices, racial segregation, and negative attitudes similar to those that have existed in the rest of the churches. Very soon white pentecostals separated themselves from the black and "colored," and separate constituencies were formed.

In the U.S. context, it was not until 1994 that white and black pentecostal organizations coalesced to celebrate the "Memphis Miracle." Recently, some pentecostals in the former Eastern Europe (Volf, 1995), Asia (Chan, 1994), the U.S. (Robeck, 1996), and South Africa (Horn, 1994) have expressed their concerns over this racial division as working against the paradigm of Pentecost, where people of various nationalities were united.

Along with racial unity, the first pentecostals were born with the idea of pacifism. A literal reading of the Bible and an enthusiasm caused by the wonder of God's Spirit uniting people of different origins in worship in the same community caused pentecostals to regard war as belonging to the "old age." However, most pentecostals soon came to embrace the ideology of the majority of their societies, accepting legitimate warfare. During the last decade there have been calls to revive the early pacifistic ethos (Shuman, 1996).

Generally, though not always, pentecostals have been reluctant to take part in political actions to further their social concerns. This is not necessarily because of a lack of political dimension but rather because of an alternative way of seeing their mission. Pentecostal theologians of social concern would argue that pentecostals have created their own alternative institutions that function as instruments of human justice. They will also question the definition of social concern that includes only political, state, and civil categories as the exclusive means of being involved in the improvement of society.

IV. IMPENDING CHALLENGES.

A. Evangelization and Proselytism.

Pentecostals have often been accused of proselytism because of their zeal for evangelization. Often pentecostals have gone out to evangelize without identifying the difference between Christians of other churches, especially Roman Catholic and Orthodox churches, and persons without a meaningful relationship to any church. The biblical mandate to evangelize, combined with the eschatological urgency to finish the task, have prevented pentecostals from showing concern for the issue of proselytism until the last decade or so.

The long-standing international dialogue with the Roman Catholic Church has encouraged pentecostals to address the issue of proselytism *(Final Report 1991–1997)*. C. M. Robeck (1996), the pentecostal cochair, admits freely that proselytism is a blight on the veracity of the Christian message and on the effectiveness of Christian mission.

More often than not the term *proselytism* is defined *for* pentecostals (and evangelicals) rather than *with* them. When pentecostals are criticized for proselytism, they are often left wondering if, in the older churches' judgment, there exists any place for evangelization.

Pentecostals are also having problems with the Eastern Orthodox Church. What pentecostals (and other evangelicals) consider a legitimate mission to Russia and to other former Eastern European countries, is considered by Orthodox (and Catholic) churches in the area to be illegitimate and culturally damaging proselytism. Orthodox churches generally still hold to the idea of "territorial occupation of Orthodox countries" and cultures and tend to see evangelists from other countries as violent intruders financed by foreign money.

To help both pentecostals and other churches avoid the danger of proselytism, Robeck (1997) suggests that they begin to take one another seriously. Unilateral actions that violate others do not communicate community. Name-calling and making accusations to third parties without first addressing the perceived offender in a direct and loving manner are inappropriate behaviors.

B. Common Witness and the Issue of Christian Unity in Mission.

Although it is not always acknowledged, it was the modern missionary movement in the beginning of the 20th century that gave birth to organized forms of seeking Christian unity (such as the WCC). Most pentecostals entertain serious doubts about, and even hostility toward, ecumenism, although pentecostalism arose as an ecumenical revival movement within historic churches. The pioneers' original purpose was not to form a separate movement, but to be a catalyst for reform, to revitalize existing churches through the outbreak of the experience and power of the Spirit. Very soon pentecostals were bluntly rejected, some of them even persecuted. The older churches did not heed their message, which actually was twofold: to the world, the call for repentance, and to the churches, the call for revitalization.

What can a movement do in a situation like this? It can deny its own reason for existence and mission or follow the path other revival movements have taken throughout the history of Christianity by starting all over again, by proclaiming the message of repentance and forming new churches.

What are the prospects for any sort of common witness joining pentecostals and other Christians? Much depends on how one defines terms like *evangelization, common witness, proselytism,* and so on. The issues are further complicated by the fact that these definitions are intertwined with issues of soteriology and ecclesiology. For example, conversion for pentecostals is usually a sudden crisis experience, while more sacramentally oriented churches understand conversion to be a long process, initiated and sustained in the community of faith. Before any meaningful exchange is possible, a common vocabulary is needed and must be worked out by all parties.

Helpful precedents exist. The discussions between Roman Catholics and evangelicals have paved the way, although pentecostals have not been officially part of the team but have rather participated as individual representatives ("Evangelicals and Catholics Together," 1994).

The Catholic cochairperson of the Roman Catholic–Pentecostal Dialogue, ▸K. McDonnell (1995[a]), has contended that the experience of Jesus Christ is the point of departure: the theological basis of common witness is found in Jesus Christ, the Absolute Witness. He also names a host of other biblical truths that join pentecostals with Catholics and other Christians.

Furthermore, at the grassroots level, pentecostals have participated in common prayer groups, social projects in various mission fields, and in large-scale evangelistic campaigns led by evangelists (Billy Graham, Luis Palau, ▸Reinhard Bonnke) who try to include Christians from pentecostal/charismatic, Catholic, and various Protestant communities.

Buddhist priests and Islamic leaders invited to the opening of the Krabi Good News Crusade in Thailand to discuss how their religious faith can strengthen the Thai people's loyalty to Thailand.

C. Relation to Other Religions.

One of the questions facing all Christians in general, and pentecostal/charismatic Christians in particular, is the relationship to followers of other religions and/or atheists; technically this is known as the issue of "theology of religions." Basically, three options have been proposed: (1) exclusivism: there is no salvation outside the church and not much common ground (the traditional view); (2) inclusivism: salvation can be found in other religions too (the liberal view); (3) a mediating position: although other religions have salvific elements, it is only in Jesus Christ that the "fullness of salvation" can be found (the official Catholic view after ▸Vatican II). Pentecostal/charismatics have identified themselves with the first option and naturally so when we take into consideration the inherited fundamentalist and evangelical-conservative heritage.

Not until the long-standing dialogue with the Roman Catholic Church started in 1972 had pentecostals even thought seriously about the issue. The dialogue revealed that most pentecostals oppose the idea of salvific elements outside the church, although the belief in the preparatory work of the Spirit in the hearts of men and women to hear the gospel is mutually acknowledged *(Final Report 1991–1997).*

Recently, evangelical-charismatic theologian C. Pinnock has suggested that "one might expect the pentecostals to develop a Spirit-oriented theology of mission and world religions because of their openness to religious experience, their sensitivity to the oppressed of the Third World where they have experienced much of their growth, and their awareness of the ways of the Spirit as well as dogma" (1996, 274).

The global presence of pentecostal-charismatic Christianity, the privileged place of the Spirit and experience in their theology, and the growing internationalization of mission all challenge pentecostals and charismatics to deepen their understanding of the role of the Spirit in the world (Yong, 1998).

D. Other Challenges.

Pentecostals have several other questions to consider at the beginning of the third millennium. For example, in pentecostal ecclesiology, how is the church and its ministry understood, and how does it relate to mission, proselytism, common witness, and so on? Another question to consider is the pentecostal/charismatic understanding of "power," particularly the uses and abuses of spiritual power with regard to healing and "power encounter." There are also the issues of contextualization to consider in the pentecostal/charismatic view of spirits, ancestors, and other culture-tied practices in any given culture. (Hollenweger, 1997, offers provocative examples from Asia, Africa, and the Americas of some of the most controversial contextualizations on the fringes of pentecostalism.) Finally, there is the view of culture in which pentecostals have tended to focus on individual conversion and have either neglected cultural transformation or rejected cultures as "sinful" from the outset.

■ **Bibliography:** M. F. Abrahams, *The Baptism of the Holy Ghost and Fire* (2d ed., 1906) ■ L. Ahonen, *Missions Growth: A Case Study on Finnish Free Foreign Missions* (1984) ■ S. Aigbe, "Cultural Mandate, Evangelistic Mandate, Prophetic Mandate ... Of These the Greatest Is ...?" *Missiology* (1991) ■ A. H. Anderson, *Bazalwane: African Pentecostals in South Africa* (1992) ■ idem, *Moya—The Holy Spirit in African Context* (1992) ■ K. Asamoah-Gyadu "'Missionaries without Robes': Lay Charismatic Fellowships and the Evangelization of Ghana," *Pneuma* 19 (2, 1997) ■ *Asian Journal of Pentecostal Studies* (1988–) (contains essays on missiology from Asian perspectives) ■ D. Barrett, "Annual Statistical Table on Global Mission," in each January issue of *IBMR* ■ idem, "The Twentieth-Century Pentecostal/Charismatic Renewal in the Holy Spirit, with Its Goal of World Evangelization," *IBMR* 12 (3, 1988) ■ J. P. Bastian, "The Metamorphosis of Latin American Protestant Groups: A Sociohistorical Perspective," *Latin American Research Review* 2 (1993) ■ A. Bittlinger, ed., *The Church is Charismatic* (1995) ■ idem, "The Significance of Charismatic Experience for the Mission of the Church," *IRM* 75 (298, 1986) ■ D. Bundy, "Pentecostal Mission to Brazil: The Case of the Norwegian G. L. Pettersen," *Norsk tidskrift for misjon* 47 (1993) ■ idem, "Swedish Pentecostal Mission Theory and Practice to 1930: Foundational Values in Conflict," *Mission Studies* 14 (1 and 2, 1997) ■ B. Cavaness, "God Calling Women in Assemblies of God Missions," *Pneuma* 16 (1994) ■ S. Chan, "Asian Pentecostalism, Social Concern and the Ethics of Conformism," *Transformation* 11 (1, 1994) ■ E. Cleary and H. Stewart-Gambino, eds., *Power, Politics and Pentecostals in Latin America* (1996) ■ *Consultation with Pentecostal Churches in the Americas, San Jose, Costa Rica* (WCC, 1996) ■ *Consultation with Pentecostal Churches, Lima, Peru* (WCC, 1994) ■ H. Cox, *Fire from Heaven: The Rise of Pentecostal Spirituality and the Reshaping of Religion in the Twenty-First Century* (1995) [contains area studies] ■ idem, "Christian Social Concern in Pentecostal Perspective: Reformulating Pentecostal Eschatology," *JPT* 2 (1993) ■ M. Dempster, "The Church's Moral Witness: A Study on Glossolalia in Luke's Theology," *Paraclete* 23 (1989) ■ idem, "'Crossing Border': Arguments Used by Early American Pentecostals in Support of the Global Character of Pacifism," *EPTA Bulletin* 10 (2, 1991) ■ idem, "Pentecostal Social Concern and the Biblical Mandate of Social Justice," *Pneuma* 9 (2, 1987) ■ M. Dempster, B. D. Klaus, and D. Petersen, eds., *Called and Empowered: Global Mission in Pentecostal Perspective* (1991) ■ idem, *The Globalization of Pentecostalism* (1998) ■ "Evangelicals and Catholics Together: The Christian Mission in the Third Millennium," *First Things* 43 (1994) ■ *Evangelization, Proselytism and Common Witness*, Final Report of the International Roman Catholic–Pentecostal Dialogue 1991–1997 ■ W. Faupel, *The Everlasting Gospel: The Significance of Eschatology in the Development of Pentecostal Theology* (1996) ■ G. Fee, "The Kingdom of God and the Church's Global Mission," in *Called and Empowered*, ed. M. Dempster, B. D. Klaus, and D. Petersen (1991) ■ K. Fiedler, *The Story of Faith Missions* (1997) ■ H. Foltz,

"Moving Towards a Charismatic Theology of Missions," in *Probing Pentecostalism* (1987) ∎ L. Gerlach, and V. H. Hine, *People, Power, Change: Movements of Social Transformation* (1970) ∎ R. Gerloff, "Mission from the Perspective of the Impoverished and Excluded: The African Diaspora in the United Kingdom and Europe," *Mission Studies* 13 (1, 1996) ∎ S. D. Glazier, ed., *Perspectives on Pentecostalism: Case Studies from the Caribbean and Latin America* (1980) ∎ James R. Goff, *Fields White unto Harvest: Charles F. Parham and the Missionary Origin of Pentecostalism* (1988) ∎ S. J. Grenz, "Toward an Evangelical Theology of the Religions," *Journal of Ecumenical Studies* 31 (1 and 2, 1994) ∎ M. Harper, "ICCOWE: What Is It and How It Started," *Pneuma* 16 (2, 1994) ∎ I. Hexham, "Beyond the Myth of Apartheid: Charismatic Christianity and the Future of Afrikanes Religion," in *Religion and the Future*, ed. G. Pillay (1992) ∎ W. Hollenweger, *Pentecostalism: Origins and Developments Worldwide* (1998) [both 1998 and 1972 contain globally representative area studies of pentecostalism] ∎ idem, *The Pentecostals* (1972) ∎ idem, "From Azusa Street to Toronto Phenomenon," *Concilium* 3 (1996) ∎ idem, "Mission Perspectives for the Nineties," *IRM* 30 (319, 1991) ∎ idem, "Towards a Church Renewed and United in the Spirit," in *The Church Is Charismatic*, ed. A. Bittlinger (1981) ∎ J. Nico Horn, "After Apartheid: Reflections on Church Mission in the Changing Social and Political Context of South Africa," *Transformation* 11 (1, 1994) ∎ T. M. Johnson, "Global Plans in the Pentecostal/Charismatic Tradition and the Challenge of the Unevangelized World," in *Pentecost, Mission and Ecumenism*, ed. J. A. B. Jongeneel et al. (1992) ∎ J. A. B. Jongeneel, "Ecumenical, Evangelical and Pentecostal/Charismatic Views on Mission as a Movement of the Holy Spirit," in *Pentecost, Mission and Ecumenism*, ed. J. A. B. Jongeneel et al. (1992) ∎ V. M. Kärkkäinen, "From the Ends of the Earth to the Ends of the Earth: An Analysis of the Factors Contributing to the Growth of the Finnish Pentecostal Mission," *EPTA Journal* 19 (1998) ∎ B. D. Klaus, "The Mission of the Church," in *Systematic Theology*, ed. Stanley Horton (1995) ∎ C. Kraft, "Allegiance, Truth and Power Encounters in Christian Witness," in *Pentecost, Mission and Ecumenism*, ed. J. A. B. Jongeneel et al. (1992) ∎ P. Kuzmič, "History and Eschatology: Evangelical Views," in *Word and Deed: Evangelism and Social Responsibility*, ed. B. Nicholls (1985) ∎ J. P. LaPoorta, *Unity or Division? The Unity Struggle of the Black Churches within the Apostolic Faith Mission of South Africa* (1997) ∎ H. I. Lederle, "The Spirit of Unity—A Discomforting Comforter: Some Reflections on the Holy Spirit, Ecumenism and the Pentecostal-Charismatic Movements," *Ecumenical Review* 42 (1990) ∎ Dario Lopez, "The Liberating Mission of Jesus: A Reading of the Gospel of Luke in a Missiological Key," *Transformation* 14 (3, 1997) ∎ H. Lord, "Mission Eschatology: A Framework for Mission in the Spirit," *JPT* 11 (1997) ∎ J. Ma, "A Comparison of Two Worldviews: Kankna-Ey and Pentecostal," in *Pentecostalism in Context*, ed. W. Ma and R. Menzies (1997) ∎ W. Ma, "A 'First Waver' Looks at the 'Third Wave': A Pentecostal Reflection on Charles Kraft's Power Encounter Terminology," *Pneuma* 19 (2, 1997) ∎ idem, "Toward an Asian Pentecostal Theology," *AJPS* 1 (1, 1998) ∎ F. Macchia, *Spirituality and Social Liberation: The Message of the Blumhardts in the Light of Württemberg Pietism, with Implications to Pentecostal Theology* (1993) ∎ L. G. McClung, *Azusa Street and Beyond: Pentecostal Missions and Church Growth in the Twentieth Century* (1986) ∎ idem, "From Bridges (McGavran 1955) to Waves (Wagner 1988): Pentecostals and the Church Growth Movement," *Pneuma* 7 (1, 1985) ∎ idem, "Pentecostal/Charismatic Perspectives on a Missiology for the Twenty-First Century," *Pneuma* 16 (1, 1994) ∎ idem, "Pentecostal/Charismatic Perspectives on Missiological Education," in *Missiological Education for the 21st Century*, ed. J. D. Woodberry et al. (1996) ∎ idem, "The Pentecostal 'Trunk' Must Learn from Its 'Branches,'" *Evangelical Missions Quarterly* 29 (1, 1993) ∎ idem, "Theology and Strategy of Pentecostal Missions," *IBMR* 12 (1, 1988) ∎ K. McDonnell, "Can Classical Pentecostals and Roman Catholics Engage in Common Witness?" *JPT* 7 (1995[a]) ∎ idem, "Evangelization and the Experience of Initiation in the Early Church," in *John Paul II and the New Evangelization*, ed. R. Martin and P. Williamson (1995[b]) ∎ G. B. McGee, *This Gospel Shall Be Preached: A History and Theology of Assemblies of God Foreign Missions to 1959* (1986; vol. 2, 1989) ∎ idem, "The Azusa Street Revival and Twentieth-Century Missions," *IBMR* 12 (2, 1988) ∎ idem, "Pentecostal and Charismatic Missions," in *Toward the Twenty-First Century in Christian Mission* (1993) ∎ idem, "Pentecostal Mission Strategies: A Historical Review," *Missionalia* 20 (1, 1992) ∎ idem, "Pentecostal Phenomena and Revivals in India: Implications for Indigenous Church Leadership," *IBMR* 20 (3, 1996) ∎ idem, "The Radical Strategy in Modern Missions: The Linkage of Paranormal Phenomena with Evangelism," in *The Holy Spirit and Mission Dynamics*, ed. C. D. McDonnell (1997) ∎ I. MacRobert, *The Black Roots and White Racism of Early Pentecostalism in the USA* (1988) ∎ D. Martin, *Forbidden Revolutions: Pentecostalism in Latin America, Catholicism in Eastern Europe* (1996) ∎ R. Menzies, *The Development of Early Christian Pneumatology with Special Reference to Luke–Acts* (1991) ∎ R. E. Mosher, *Pentecostalism and Inculturation in Chile* (diss., Rome, 1995) ∎ M. R. Mullins, "The Empire Strikes Back: Korean Pentecostal Mission to Japan," *Japanese Religion* 17 (3, 1992) ∎ L. D. Pate, "Pentecostal Missions from the Two-Thirds World," in M. Dempster, B. D. Klaus, and D. Petersen, eds., *Called and Empowered: Global Mission in Pentecostal Perspective* (1991) ∎ J. M. Penney, *The Missionary Emphasis of Lukan Pneumatology* (1997) ∎ D. Peterson, *Not by Might, Nor by Power: A Pentecostal Theology of Social Concern in Latin America* (1996) ∎ C. H. Pinnock, "Evangelism and Other Living Faiths: An Evangelical Charismatic Perspective," in *All Together in One Place*, ed. P. C. Hocken and H. D. Hunter (1993) ∎ idem, *Flame of Love: A Theology of the Holy Spirit* (1996) ∎ *Pneuma* 16 (1, 1994) (dedicated to missiological issues) ∎ *Pneuma* 16 (2, 1994) (focuses on charismatic renewal, also with a view to mission) ∎ K. Poewe, ed., *Charismatic Christianity as a Global Culture* (1994) ∎ P. A. Pomerville, *The Third Force in Missions* (1985) ∎ E. Pousson, *Spreading the Flame: Charismatic Churches and Missions Today* (1992) ∎ C. M. Robeck, "Evangelization or Proselytism of Hispanics? A Pentecostal Perspective," *Journal of Hispanic/Latino Theology* 4 (4, 1997) ∎ idem, "Mission and the Issue of Proselytism," *IBMR* 20 (1,

1996) ▪ idem, "Racial Reconciliation at Memphis: Some Personal Reflections," *Pneuma* 18 (1, 1996) ▪ idem, "The Social Concern of Early American Pentecostalism," in *Pentecost, Mission and Ecumenism*, ed. J. A. B. Jongeneel et al. (1992) ▪ E. Rommen, ed., *Spiritual Power and Missions: Raising the Issue*, EMS Series 3 (1995) ▪ A. M. Sanchez-Walsh, "Latino Pentecostalism: A Bibliographic Introduction," *Evangelical Studies Bulletin* 15 (1998) ▪ J. Sepúlveda, "Reflections on the Pentecostal Contribution to the Mission of the Church in the Latin America," *JPT* 1 (1992) ▪ G. Sheppard, "Pentecostals and the Hermeneutics of Dispensationalism: The Anatomy of an Uneasy Relationship," *Pneuma* 6 (2, 1984) ▪ D. Shibley, *A Force in the Earth: The Charismatic Renewal and World Evangelization* (1989) ▪ J. Shuman, "Pentecost and the End of Patriotism: A Call for the Restoration of Pacifism among Pentecostal Christians," *JPT* 9 (1996) ▪ R. J. Spittler, "Implicit Values in Pentecostal Mission," *Missiology* 16 (1988) ▪ V. Synan, "AD 2000 Together, a Pentecostal/Charismatic Explosion," in *The Countdown Has Begun: The Story of the Global Consultation on AD 2000*, ed. J. Gary and O. Gary (1989) ▪ idem, *The Spirit Said "Grow"* (1992) ▪ P. N. Van Der Laan, "Dynamics in Pentecostal Mission: A Dutch Perspective," *IRM* 75 (298, 1986) ▪ Eldin Villafañe, *The Liberating Spirit: Toward an Hispanic American Pentecostal Social Ethic* (1992) ▪ M. Volf, *Exclusion and Embrace: A Theological Exploration of Identity, Otherness, and Reconciliation* (1996) ▪ idem, "Fishing in the Neighbor's Pond: Mission and Proselytism in Eastern Europe," *IBMR* 20 (1, 1986) ▪ C. P. Wagner, *The Third Wave of the Holy Spirit* (1988) ▪ C. P. Wagner and F. D. Pennoyer, eds., *Wrestling with Dark Angels: Toward a Deeper Understanding of the Supernatural Forces in Spiritual Warfare* (1990) ▪ G. F. Wessels, "Charismatic Christian Congregations and Social Justice: A South African Perspective," *Missionalia* 25 (3, 1997) ▪ E. Wilson, *Strategy of the Spirit: J. Philip Hogan and the Growth of the Assemblies of God Worldwide 1969–1990* (1998) ▪ idem, "Toward a Latin American Pentecostal Political Praxis," *Transformation* 14 (1, 1997) ▪ A. Yong, "'Not Knowing Where the Wind Blows …': On Envisioning a Pentecostal/Charismatic Theology of Religions," in *Purity and Power: Revisioning the Holiness & Pentecostal/Charismatic Movements for the Twenty-First Century* (1998) ▪ B. W. Yoo, *Korean Pentecostalism: Its History and Theology* (1988) ▪ T. F. Zimmerman, "Evangelism and Eschatological Imperatives," in *One Race, One Gospel, One Task*, ed. C. F. H. Henry and S. Mooneyham, vol. 2 (1967).   ▪ V. M. Kärkkäinen

MISSIONARY CHURCH OF CHRIST See IGLESIA DE CRISTO MISIONERA.

MISSIONARY CONFERENCE, THE A nondenominational conference of missionaries called by the General Council of the Assemblies of God (AG) "to include every person in Pentecost who was interested in missions, regardless of their affiliation, to discuss better cooperation, in the home and foreign fields, better facilities for carrying on missionary work, and above all, to raise the standard of missions to the place it should rightfully hold in the heart and mind of every Chris-

tian" ("First Conference of Pentecostal Missionaries," 13). As a matter of convenience, the first conference followed the general council meeting at St. Louis in Sept. 1917. ˒John W. Welch, chairman of the AG, assured the conference that it was independent and not subject to general council legislation; nevertheless, the latter would welcome suggestions that would advance the cause of missions. Thirty missionaries attended, including Christian Schoonmaker, Fannie Simpson, Nettie D. Nichols, Ivan Kauffman, C. W. Doney, Blanche Appleby, ˒H. C. Ball, Charles C. Personeus, and Florence Murcutt. The conference chose S. A. Jamieson to be the chairman and Anna C. Reiff as the secretary. Various issues were addressed, notably the use of native workers, the need for missionary rest homes in the U.S., and additional financial support. Ten resolutions were passed, with the last one declaring the Missionary Conference to be a permanent organization.

The conference normally continued to follow the meetings of the general council while retaining its independent status. Later officers included ˒Daniel W. Kerr as chairman and Zella Reynolds, sister of ˒Alice Reynolds Flower, as secretary.

The significance of the organization centered on the need to provide guidelines for the burgeoning missionary enterprise. Conferences provided opportunities for missionaries to receive inspiration, express their needs to pastors and general council officers, and pass helpful resolutions. In addition, laypersons received information about conditions abroad and the challenge to be faithful in giving. The close association of the general council to an undenominational organization also reflects the state of early pentecostal ecumenicity.

Due to the positive relationships developed at the gatherings, many independent missionaries joined the AG. Consequently, the Missionary Conference eventually outlived its usefulness, and the last meeting was held in 1921.

See also MISSIONS, OVERSEAS.

▪ **Bibliography:** G. B. McGee, *This Gospel Shall Be Preached* (1986) ▪ A. C. Reiff, "First Conference of Pentecostal Missionaries," *LRE* (Oct. 1917).   ▪ G. B. McGee

MISSIONS, OVERSEAS (NORTH AMERICAN PENTECOSTAL)

I. The Pentecostal Missions Movement
   A. *Historical Context*
   B. *Pentecostal Missions Begin*
      1. The Topeka Revival (1901)
      2. The Fargo (ND)—Moorehead (MN) Revival (1904)
      3. The Azusa Street Revival (1906–9)
   C. *Early Missionaries*
      1. Three Groups
      2. Women Missionaries

    D. *Effectiveness*
    E. *Early Attempts at Organization*

II. The Emergence of Pentecostal Mission Agencies after 1910
    A. *The Need for Organization*
    B. *North American Agencies*
       1. Pentecostal Mission in South and Central Africa
       2. General Council of the Assemblies of God
       3. Pentecostal Assemblies of Canada
       4. International Pentecostal Holiness Church
       5. Church of God (Cleveland, TN)
       6. Russian and Eastern European Mission
       7. Other Agencies
    C. *Oneness Agencies*
    D. *Cooperation and Ecumenicity*

III. Increased Cooperation

IV. Pentecostal Missiology
    A. *Early Missiological Perspectives*
    B. *William Taylor*
    C. *A. B. Simpson and the CMA*
    D. *Roland Allen*
    E. *Melvin L. Hodges*
    F. *Publications*
    G. *Historical Perspectives*

V. Missions Education

VI. Independent Ministries

VII. Significance

I. THE PENTECOSTAL MISSIONS MOVEMENT.

A. Historical Context.

The origins of the Protestant missionary movement can be traced to the spiritual awakenings of the 17th and 18th centuries, which produced Pietism, Moravianism, the Great Awakening, and the Wesleyan revival in England. Kenneth Scott Latourette noted that this evangelical strain within Protestantism "made much of the transformation of the individual through the Christian gospel and it also gave rise to many efforts for the elimination of social ills and for the collective betterment of mankind" (1941, 4:65).

In the 19th century the Western colonial powers raced to build overseas empires, undergirded by presuppositions of their own cultural and racial superiority and propelled by new means of transportation. At the same time, many devout Christians followed the summons of the Great Commission (Matt. 28:19–20) and traveled abroad as missionaries. This evangelical trend in missions was reinforced by the revival campaigns of Dwight L. Moody, among others, the organi-

zation of the Student Volunteer Movement for Foreign Missions (1888), and the rise of the independent faith missions. As a result, there developed the widest expansion of Christianity since the time of the ancient Christian church began to occur in the late 19th century.

Millennial expectations figured heavily into the missionary movement. The postmillennial vision of an emerging kingdom of God on earth through the propagation of the gospel and the establishment of human institutions (schools, orphanages, hospitals, etc.) held the loyalty of Christian denominations and missionaries during most of the century. A shift occurred in the last decades, however, when premillennial teaching (in both its dispensational and nondispensational forms) rapidly gained widespread popularity. This perspective, reflecting a pessimistic appraisal of human progress, anticipated an imminent return of Christ prior to the establishment of his millennial kingdom on earth.

The growing acceptance of premillennialism extended into the Holiness movement, among Wesleyans (George D. Watson, W. B. Godbey, et al.) as well as "higher life" teachers with Reformed-Keswick sympathies (A. J. Gordon, A. B. Simpson, et al.). In their view, Christians were living in "the last days" (Joel 2:28–32), and the evangelization of the heathen required a mighty outpouring of the Holy Spirit to accomplish that objective. Simpson expressed this concern to the membership of the Christian and Missionary Alliance (CMA) by saying, "We believe God wants us to deeply realize our special calling as a distinct spiritual and missionary agency in these last days.... May the Holy Spirit help us to behold the vision, to receive anew the great commission, and then go forth in the power of a new baptism of the Holy Ghost to make it real" (Simpson, 1900, 32). Many shared this concern as the end of the century approached. The preaching, publications, schools, and sometimes mission agencies that such leaders founded or supported, exercised a profound influence on the later pentecostal missionary movement.

With the slow pace of conversions overseas, radical evangelicals searched for ways to expedite gospel proclamation in the few remaining days, months, or years before Christ's return. Since formal language study would often require several years before a missionary had sufficient fluency to preach, some considered that God might bestow intelligible languages according to the promise of Mark 16:17 (KJV): "And these signs shall follow them that believe ... they shall speak with new tongues." This meant that with sufficient faith, missionaries could receive languages and bypass the nuisance of formal study and immediately begin preaching when they arrived on the mission fields.

This discussion became widespread in radical evangelical circles after 1880. In the following two decades, missionaries who expected to receive languages directly from God included Cecil H. Polhill, Arthur T. Polhill, and C. T. Studd, members of the famous "Cambridge Seven" (U.K.); members of the "Kansas-Sudan Movement" (U.S.); William W. Simpson and William Christie (U.S.); Walter S. and Frances Black (Canada); and M. Jennie Glassey (U.S.), among others. Glassey's testimony of receiving several African dialects in 1895, as well as the theological and missiological teachings of Frank W. Sandford, helped Charles F. Parham conclude in the fall of 1900 that speaking in tongues would not only provide the "Bible evidence" of the postconversionary baptism in the Holy Spirit, but also speed missionary evangelism.

B. Pentecostal Missions Begin.

1. The Topeka Revival (1901).

A revival on Jan. 1, 1901, at Charles F. Parham's Bethel Bible School in Topeka, KS, gave rise to modern pentecostalism. Parham believed that the glossolalia (speaking in tongues) that he and many of his students experienced was specifically xenolalia (speaking of actual foreign languages). Thus, the Spirit's linguistic provision with dynamic power would afford an unparalleled missionary advance before Christ's return. Parham's linkage of the baptism in the Holy Spirit to glossolalia also laid the foundation for classical pentecostalism's belief in "initial evidence."

Surprisingly, the Topeka revival produced no foreign missionaries. Perhaps the hopes for sending missionaries waned amid the persecution and discouragement that followed. Notwithstanding, spiritual awakenings and missionary zeal have long been associated on the American religious scene, and Topeka ultimately proved to be no exception. Its actual impact on world missions can be found in the results of the later revivals that it spawned, notably the Azusa Street revival in Los Angeles, CA.

2. The Fargo (ND)—Moorhead (MN) Revival (1904).

In 1904 a pentecostal revival emphasizing baptism in the Holy Spirit as empowerment for evangelism occurred among Swedish-Americans in the Fargo-Moorhead area on the border of North Dakota and Minnesota. In all likelihood, the revival arose from the pietism of Swedish immigrants. The first to speak in tongues was Augusta Johnson. In late 1904 Mary Johnson and Ida Andersson departed for Durban, South Africa, apparently the first missionaries of the pentecostal movement.

3. The Azusa Street Revival (1906–9).

Sparked by news of the Welsh revival and more directly by the ministry of William J. Seymour, a black Holiness preacher and former student of Parham's at his Bible school in Houston, TX, the Azusa Street revival significantly contributed to internationalizing the greatest spiritual awakening of the 20th century. Through the influence of Azusa and other pentecostal revivals, millions at home and overseas have entered the ranks of the Christian church, representing an almost unprecedented expansion of the Christian faith. To understand its importance, four aspects of the Azusa Street revival must be considered.

First, the participants at Azusa Street (Seymour, Frank Bartleman, Florence L. Crawford, Alfred ["A. G."] Garr, et al.), considered their newfound languages to be the languages of the world, reflecting Parham's xenolalic perspective. *The Apostolic Faith,* a newspaper published occasionally from 1906 to 1908 by the revival's leadership, reported, "God is solving the missionary problem, sending out new-tongued missionaries ... without purse or scrib *[sic]*, and the Lord is going before them preparing the way" (*Apostolic Faith* [Nov. 1906], 2). While this view was widely shared by other contemporary pentecostals, it soon became apparent that glossolalia did not equip people to preach in other languages, although Parham himself never flinched in his belief to the contrary.

Second, those who attended the revival services believed that the apostolic "signs and wonders" that had characterized the

The first Pentecostal missionaries from the Northwest to the Orient in 1907. The leader is M. L. Ryan (seated in center, second row).

advance of the early Christians in the book of Acts had been restored. This pneumatological emphasis, while rejected by outsiders, underscored a reliance on the leading of the Holy Spirit to the point of representing a unique posture toward the Christian world mission. Indeed, pentecostals' wholesale return to the apostolic pattern of 1st-century Christianity was without parallel on the missionary landscape.

Third, the enthusiasm for world evangelization prompted a dispersion of new missionaries. Although the leaders of Azusa constituted a credentials committee and issued licenses for missionaries and evangelists, they did not organize a mission agency. This conceivably reflects their concerns about the urgency of the hour, reluctance to rely on the support of a human agency (reflecting the "faith" principle held by the British Christian philanthropist George Müller and the missiology of William Taylor), naïveté about conditions overseas, and the desire to be directed completely by the Spirit. Thus, most of the early missionaries traveled abroad on "faith" (without pledged support) and with their perceived new languages for overseas preaching. The records also indicate that all pentecostals—whether men or women, clergy or laity, blacks or whites, could be called to foreign missions.

Alfred G. ("A. G.") Garr, pastor of the Burning Bush Mission in Los Angeles, and his wife, Lillian, both of whom had received the pentecostal baptism at the Azusa Street Mission in June 1906, sailed for India (and eventually Hong Kong) several months later. They were among the first and best-known pentecostals to leave Azusa for "the regions beyond." Others included Louise Condit and Lucy M. Leatherman (Jerusalem), Lucy Farrow (Africa), Lizzie Fraser (India), Samuel J. and Ardella K. Mead (veteran Methodist missionaries who returned to Africa), Henry M. Turney (South Africa), and Ansel and Etta Post (Egypt). Generally speaking, the early missionaries traveled to the traditional sites of Protestant endeavor: Africa, the Middle East, India, and China. This dispersion represents the concern among the Azusa Street participants for world evangelization, as well as the leveling effect of the revival.

The publication and widespread distribution across North America of the newspaper *The Apostolic Faith* carried the teachings and news of the revival, testimonials from around the country, and reports from missionaries. Numerous pentecostal publications assisted in the dissemination of this information as well.

Fourth, the interracial and intercultural features of the revival highlighted vital aspects of the ministry of the Holy Spirit, notably the purification, empowerment, and reconciliation of believers. The predicted eschatological "outpouring" of the Spirit that began on the Day of Pentecost was given not only to the "sons" and "daughters," but to the "servants" and "handmaids" (Joel 2:28–29 [KJV]) as well. In so doing, the Spirit conferred dignity and gifts on the poor and oppressed; this also explains why pentecostalism has been easily indigenized in many parts of the world. Thus, the leadership of Seymour, son of former slaves, and the unusual interracial makeup of the revival have inspired pentecostals and other Christians in North America (e.g., African Americans) and around the world (e.g., people of color in the Republic of South Africa) who have felt the sting of racial prejudice and other forms of oppression.

Other revivals also significantly influenced the missionary effort. Revivals occurred in, among other places, Indianapolis, IN; Alliance, Akron, and Cleveland, OH; Rochester and Nyack, NY; Dunn, NC; Portland, OR; Memphis, TN; Houston, TX; and Toronto and Winnipeg, Canada. Parham's revival in Zion City, IL, resulted in the journey of John G. Lake and Thomas Hezmalhalch (who had attended Azusa Street) to South Africa in 1908, after which they contributed to the founding of the Apostolic Faith Mission. A revival in Spokane, WA, triggered by news of the happenings at the Azusa Mission, produced several parties of missionaries who left the Pacific Northwest in 1907 for Japan, China, India, Africa, and Scandinavia; these included M. L. Ryan, H. L. and Emma Lawler, Will Colyar, Rosa Pittman Downing, Cora Fritsch Falkner, Edward Reilly, E. May Law, and Bertha Milligan.

Influential personalities touched by the Azusa Street revival included Thomas B. Barratt, who received the baptism in the Holy Spirit while visiting New York City. He returned to Norway with the new message and eventually carried it to England, Sweden, and other European countries; pentecostal missionaries from these countries soon traveled overseas. Others who developed international ministries include Cecil H. Polhill, founder of the Pentecostal Missionary Union in Great Britain (1909), the first successful pentecostal missions agency to be established; Minnie T. Draper, one of the founders of the Pentecostal Mission in South and Central Africa (1910); William F. P. Burton and James Salter, founders of the Congo Evangelistic Mission (1915); Luigi Francescon, missionary to Argentina (1909) and Brazil; Daniel Berg and Gunnar Vingren, missionaries to Brazil (1910); and G. R. Polman, organizer of the Pentecostal Mission Alliance in the Netherlands (1920). The pentecostal movement in India began in 1906, independently of events in North America and Europe. Limited evidence suggests that other contemporary indigenous pentecostal revivals occurred overseas without the influence of the Azusa Mission.

From North America alone, approximately 200 pentecostal missionaries had traveled overseas by 1910. Their travels, needs, and triumphs were heralded to the members of the burgeoning movement by means of early pentecostal periodicals such as the *Apostolic Faith* (Los Angeles, 1906), *Bridegroom's Messenger* (1907), *Word and Witness* (1907), *Latter Rain Evangel* (1908), *New Acts* (1904), *Pentecost* (1908), *Evening*

Light and Church of God Evangel (1910), *Christian Evangel* (1913), *Pentecostal Holiness Advocate* (1917), and *Word and Work* (1879). In addition, the editors received funds from readers and distributed them to the designated missionaries.

C. Early Missionaries.

1. Three Groups.

At least three different groups of missionaries went overseas. The first were those who felt called but who, because of their eschatology, belief in xenolalia, and adherence to the faith principle, ventured abroad without adequate financial resources or an understanding of the history, culture, or language of the people to whom they wished to minister. They shared their testimonies, often attempting to proselytize other Protestant missionaries to the newfound pentecostal blessing. Their attempts to convert non-Christians were limited by lack of preparation.

The second group was composed of veteran missionaries who received the baptism in the Holy Spirit and joined the pentecostal movement. These individuals brought maturity and respectability to the movement, though they often faced hardships after leaving their parent agencies. Numbered among them were Minnie F. Abrams (Methodist), H. A. Baker (Christian Church), Susan Easton (Women's Union Missionary Society of America), J. C. Lehman (independent Holiness), Max Wood Moorhead (Presbyterian), William W. Simpson (CMA), Christian Schoonmaker (CMA), Samuel J. Mead (Methodist), and Alice C. Wood (Friends and CMA).

The graduates of Bible institutes formed the third group of missionaries. Undoubtedly, the school with the most influence on pentecostal missions before 1920 (among the small minority of missionaries who had received such training) was A. B. Simpson's Missionary Training Institute at Nyack, NY. Before long, however, distinctively pentecostal Bible institutes appeared (either founded as pentecostal schools or having become so later) such as the Altamont Bible and Missionary Institute (later Holmes College of the Bible), Paris Mountain, SC (1898); Missionary Training Home, Alliance, OH (1905); Rochester Bible Training School, Rochester, NY (1906); Findley Bible and Missionary Training School, Findley, OH (c. 1907); Beulah Heights Bible and Missionary Training School, North Bergen, NJ (1912); Bethel Bible Training School, Newark, NJ (1916); Bible Training School (later Lee University), Cleveland, TN (1918); Glad Tidings Bible Institute (later Bethany College), San Francisco, CA (1919); Southern California Bible School (later Vanguard University of Southern California), Los Angeles, CA (1920); Central Bible Institute (later Central Bible College), Springfield, MO (1922); Evangelistic and Missionary Training Institute (later Lighthouse of International Foursquare Evangelism, now L.I.F.E. Bible College),

Los Angeles, CA (1923); Zion Bible Institute in East Providence, RI (1924); and Canadian Pentecostal Bible College, Winnipeg, Manitoba (1925). The training these schools provided in Bible instruction and spirituality, though generally lacking in formal missiological studies, prepared a committed force of missionaries who eventually brought stability to the overseas endeavors of the movement.

2. Women Missionaries.

The extensive role of women in pentecostal missions reflects that of the Protestant missions movement in general. Pentecostal women maintained that the Lord had called them to serve overseas, having been assured by Peter's statement on the Day of Pentecost, "Even on my servants, both men and women, I [God] will pour out my Spirit in those days, and they will prophesy" (Acts 2:18 [NIV]). While sometimes denied full ministerial opportunities at home, women found considerable liberty to preach, evangelize, teach, and administer charitable institutions abroad.

Throughout most, if not all, of the history of pentecostal missions, married and single women missionaries have constituted a majority. The achievements of married women have been substantial (e.g., Maria W. Atkinson [CG], Louise Jeter Walker [AG], and Jean Firth [ICFG]). The number of single women serving as missionaries, however, has steadily declined, at least in the denominational agencies. Nevertheless, their impact on the development of national churches and charitable institutions is without dispute. Single women like Lillian Trasher (General Council of the Assemblies of God [GCAG]), Nellie Hendrickson (PAOC), Lucille Jenkins (Mitchell) (OBSC), and Marie Stephany (AG) made notable contributions. Minnie F. Abrams, a missionary to India, founded the only women's pentecostal mission agency, the Bezaleel Evangelistic Mission (c. 1910). Other prominent women, including Elizabeth V. Baker, Marie Burgess Brown, Florence L. Crawford, Minnie T. Draper, Alice Bell Garrigus, Christine Gibson, Aimee Semple McPherson, Carrie Judd Montgomery, Virginia E. Moss, Avis Swiger, and Etta H. Wormser, while not serving as missionaries (with the exception of McPherson), impacted pentecostal missions through the institutions they founded (schools, mission agencies, denominations) or served.

D. Effectiveness.

The general impact of the earliest missionaries appears to have been short-lived and disappointing. Disillusionment quickly crept in because of the harsh realities they faced, their inability to communicate with the people, financial instability, and lack of preparation.

Observers within the movement began to notice the deficiencies as early as 1906. A. B. Simpson, an outsider, referred in 1908 to these early missionaries as "unhappy victims of some honest but mistaken impression" (Simpson, 1908, 11–12).

MISSIONS OVERSEAS

American women teaching child evangelism in Argentina (Feb. 18, 1969).

Noel Perkin and J. R. Flower on their way to the Congo (date unknown).

Richard Exley of Tulsa, OK, evangelizing a Jamaican boy (Oct. 1983).

Ruth Vassar, daughter of missionaries Ted and Estelle Vassar, in native Maharastran dress in Poona, West India (c. 1941).

Karen and Dale Preiser, distributors for VIDA publications, displaying books in Haiti (Dec. 15, 1981).

Although Simpson accurately described the failures of some (and there was a high turnover rate before 1920), there were those who persevered: among others, Paul and Nellie Bettex, the Henry M. Turneys, and E. May Law.

Despite later pronouncements that described this seminal period of pentecostal missions (1906–20) as a "golden era," such was not the case. The death toll in certain fields was staggering. In some cases missionaries refused vaccination for epidemics due to their steadfast belief in faith healing. Some, such as T. J. McIntosh, traveled around the world (twice between 1907 and 1909) without settling down to do permanent mission work. Despite the problems, however, the number of pentecostals volunteering for foreign service continued to increase each year; permanent works were gradually established and converts gained.

E. Early Attempts at Organization.

Perceptive leaders recognized that the lack of accountability, financial stability, legal recognition, and long-range strategy produced problems that needed to be addressed. The earliest attempt on the part of American pentecostals to organize a mission agency took place in Alliance, OH, at the close of the Pentecostal Camp Meeting in 1907—a meeting organized by Levi R. Lupton, Ivey Campbell, and Claude A. McKinney. The proposed Apostolic Evangelization Association, however, failed to materialize.

At the next annual camp meeting the participants issued a "Pentecostal Manifesto," which laid the groundwork for an agency. Nevertheless, this did not transpire until 1909, when the Pentecostal Missionary Union (PMU) in the U.S. became a reality, with Lupton as its president. The manifesto and the later organization of the PMU called for missionary preparation in the form of Bible training and practical ministerial experience, reflecting a mature level of thinking. Concerns that the missionary have a definite call, adequate legal recognition, and the confidence of a local church point to major problems that Lupton and his associates faced. In a short time, the PMU endorsed and partially supported 75 missionaries. It is notable that the structural authority of the agency was minimal. Early pentecostal missionaries tended to be staunchly independent, "living by faith," and receiving financial assistance from many sources. The PMU collapsed in Dec. 1910 with Lupton's public confession of moral failure. It had also become the target of antiorganizational sentiments. A parallel attempt in 1909 to establish a PMU in Canada failed.

Providing the model and inspiration for these efforts was the successful Pentecostal Missionary Union (PMU) founded in Great Britain in Jan. 1909 by Cecil H. Polhill, one of the original "Cambridge Seven" of athletic and missionary fame. Having been a missionary on the Tibetan border with the China Inland Mission (CIM), Polhill received the pentecostal baptism in Los Angeles in 1908. With the establishment of the PMU, modeled after the CIM, he served as its president for many years. In 1924 the PMU was integrated into the newly formed Assemblies of God in Great Britain and Ireland.

II. THE EMERGENCE OF PENTECOSTAL MISSION AGENCIES AFTER 1910.

A. The Need for Organization.

The failure of the American PMU did not erase the need for addressing the problems of the enterprise. The inability to purchase property in certain countries because of lack of legal recognition, the occasional practice of acquiring property under the name of a recognized Protestant mission board, the inadequate and often inequitable funding of missionaries, and the unfortunate turnover in personnel continued to cause alarm. By 1913 Anna C. Reiff, the successor to William H. Piper as editor of the *Latter Rain Evangel*, began to address "the missionary problem." Specifically she questioned whether every believer received the "George Müller call" to faith living and argued that missionaries needed regular assistance from believers at home. The costs of their basic needs left no available funds to open new works in their mission areas. For the welfare of the missionaries Reiff appealed to pentecostals to reach the middle ground between the organizational restrictions of mission boards and total independence.

B. North American Agencies.

1. Pentecostal Mission in South and Central Africa (PMSCA).

The first major pentecostal mission agency in America to be established following the debacle of the PMU was the Pentecostal Mission in South and Central Africa (1910), founded by the independent executive council of the Bethel Pentecostal Assembly, Newark, NJ, "to maintain and conduct a general evangelistic work in the State of New Jersey, in all other States of the United States and any and all foreign countries" (Beach and Fahs, eds., 1925, 24). Begun by members of the Ossining, NY, Gospel Assembly—notably Minnie T. Draper (1857–1921)—and the Bethel Pentecostal Assembly in Newark (both independent but cooperating congregations), the "Bethel Board" sponsored works in Liberia, the Union of South Africa (later the Republic of South Africa), Swaziland, Portuguese East Africa (later Mozambique), and Venezuela. For a short time, it served as the legal umbrella for William F. P. Burton's Congo Evangelistic Mission (U.K.). Draper directed the affairs of the agency until her death in 1921.

This agency, funded by wealthy pentecostals who were members of the board and by generous offerings from the supporting churches, invested its monies in a trust fund to gain additional revenue. By 1925 the Pentecostal Mission had an income of $30,150, making it second only in size and financial underpinnings to the GCAG. With the collapse of the stock market in 1929, the trust fund suffered a serious blow and the agency's activities declined. Many of its missionaries—including Fred Burke, Anna Richards Scoble, and the Edgar Pettengers—transferred to the GCAG. The PMSCA churches in South Africa eventually became known as the Full Gospel Church. A merger in 1951 with the Church of God (Cleveland, TN) resulted in a change of name to Full Gospel Church of God.

2. General Council of the Assemblies of God.

The next major agency to appear came with the organization of the GCAG at Hot Springs, AR, in 1914. Its executive presbytery also functioned as a "missionary presbytery." In the following months approximately 30 missionaries became affiliated. From the beginning, the new organization concentrated on world evangelization as one of its primary objectives; by 1920 giving had reached $90,812.40 (representing a 43% increase over the previous year).

With the growing responsibilities of the executive presbytery, the missionary department was established in 1919 with J. Roswell Flower as secretary-treasurer. At this time, the department served largely as a distribution center for funds designated for specific missionaries; undesignated monies were allocated equally. It exercised little authority over missionary personnel and did not provide strategic planning for the global effort.

AG missions turned an important corner in 1927 with the permanent appointment of Noel Perkin as missionary secretary to superintend the responsibilities of the department and the overseas personnel. His past missionary experience in Argentina, rapport with pastors, bookkeeping skills, and gentle manner contributed to the maturing of GCAG missions. In 1931 he published the first *Missionary Manual*, containing policies and missiological perspectives. Promotion of missions became an important priority as did the need for establishing a solid financial base to cover administrative expenses.

Noteworthy early missionaries included Blanche R. Appleby (China), the Alfred A. Blakeneys (India), the Henry B. Garlocks (Africa), the Carl F. Juergensens (Japan), the Maynard L. Ketchams (India), Juan L. Lugo (Puerto Rico), Nettie D. Nichols (China), the Nicholas Nikoloffs (Eastern Europe), the Victor G. Plymires (China, Tibet), Lillian Trasher (Egypt), the Ralph D. Williamses (Central America), the Arthur E. Wilsons (Burkina Faso), and Anna Ziese (China).

3. Pentecostal Assemblies of Canada (PAOC).

Canada felt the impact of the Azusa Street revival through the ministry of Robert E. McAlister, who received the baptism in the Holy Spirit in Los Angeles in 1906. An important revival also occurred in Winnipeg through the ministry of A. H. Argue, who received the pentecostal baptism at the

Arriving at Matroe Mission, Liberia, in Dec. 1947.

North Avenue Mission in Chicago. Without external influence, however, Mrs. ›Ellen Hebden received the same experience in Nov. 1906. In Toronto she and her husband, James, directed the Hebden Mission, which in that region became the "Canadian Azusa." These revivals played key roles in sending missionaries, including the Charles W. Chawners (South Africa), the Thomas Hindles (Mongolia), the Arthur Atters (China), the Otto Kellers (East Africa), and the Alex Lindsays (India).

Since many of the Canadian pentecostal churches were initially linked to the American GCAG, practical considerations (including problems distinct to Canadian missionary efforts) finally led to the friendly separation and incorporation of the PAOC in 1922.

4. International Pentecostal Holiness Church (IPHC).

Among Holiness bodies that entered the pentecostal movement, the Pentecostal Holiness Church (PHC) was the first to establish a "missionary board" at its Fayetteville, NC, convention in 1904. Two years later, T. J. McIntosh became the first missionary to receive support but did not travel overseas under the auspices of the church. Within a short time the Fire-Baptized Holiness Church and the Tabernacle Pentecostal Church, both of which later amalgamated with the PHC (1911, 1915), sent out missionaries as well. Bishop Joseph H. King's world tour of pentecostal missions (1909–12) helped to enlist independent missionaries into the church.

While the PHC (later the International Pentecostal Holiness Church [IPHC]) experienced rapid turnover in missionary personnel during the early years, the denomination nevertheless witnessed continued growth abroad. Notable missionaries included Lucy Jones (China), the W. H. Turners (China), and the African Americans Kenneth and Geraldine Spooner (Africa).

5. Church of God (Cleveland, TN) (CG).

The CG traces the beginning of its missions effort to the trip of R. M. and Ida Evans to the Bahamas in 1910. Evans, an elderly former Methodist minister, achieved some success, but after great personal sacrifice he and his wife had to return to the U.S. because of lack of financial support.

CG missions grew slowly during this period because of the disruptions of the war, no plan of regular support (reflecting the socioeconomic conditions of the church members), and the church split of 1923. Notwithstanding, some missionaries did travel abroad without assurance of consistent financial provision. These included Sam C. Perry (Cuba), the Peter N. Johnsons (China), and the P. F. Branewalls and J. F. Carscaddens (French West Africa).

A missions board was appointed in 1926, but stability and steady growth did not begin until the 1930s. During these years, J. H. Ingram, the missions overseer of California and Arizona, became a powerful force for missions in the denomination through his worldwide travels. Ingram contacted many independent pentecostal missionaries and encouraged them to unite with the CG. Thus, important mission works founded by pioneer missionaries quickly expanded the scope of the church's mission responsibilities; these included the efforts of Maria W. Atkinson (Mexico), Robert F. Cook (India), and Herman Lauster (Germany), among others.

6. Russian and Eastern European Mission (REEM).

The REEM was organized in Chicago in 1927. It had roots in the Eastern European activities of missionaries Nicholas Nikoloff, Gustave H. Schmidt, and Paul B. Peterson. In the following year the agency established in Danzig (Gdansk), Poland, a field office to supervise the work in Eastern Europe as well as a Bible institute for the training of ministers. The Bible institute paid large dividends by preparing young men for the ministry (Poles, Hungarians, Yugoslavs, Bulgarians, Russians, et al.). Through the evangelistic work of its missionaries and the graduates of the school, REEM reported 80,000 converts in Eastern Europe and Russia by the time of WWII. Its activities were published in the *Gospel Call*, the official voice of the agency.

From 1927 to 1940 REEM maintained close ties with the GCAG by sharing personnel and mutual support. Its refusal, however, to amalgamate with the GCAG, as well as differences over financial policies and its gradual departure from a distinctively pentecostal theology, led the GCAG to sever the relationship in 1940. Eventually, REEM changed its name to Eastern European Mission and later to Eurovision, before becoming part of the Slavic Gospel Association.

7. Other Agencies.

The number of mission agencies and denominations increased as pentecostals recognized that the goal of world evangelization required coordination, regular financial support, and promotion. Such organizations included the Apos-

tolic Faith Movement (Portland, OR), begun by Florence L. Crawford in 1907 (first missionary sent in 1911); National and International Pentecostal Missionary Union, founded by Philip Wittich in 1914 (later it became part of the International Pentecostal Church of Christ); Pentecostal Church of God (1919); The Evangelization Society (TES) of the Pittsburgh Bible Institute, founded by Charles Hamilton Pridgeon in 1920; Church of God of Prophecy (CGP, 1923); Pentecostal Assemblies of Newfoundland, pioneered by Alice Belle Garrigus and organized in 1925; Church of God in Christ (COGIC), founded by Charles H. Mason and C. P. Jones in 1897 (first Home and Foreign Missions Board in 1925); International Church of the Foursquare Gospel (ICFG), established by Aimee Semple McPherson in 1927; Christian Church of North America (CCNA; its mission agency was founded in 1929); Elim Fellowship (1933, originally Elim Ministerial Fellowship, later Elim Missionary Assemblies); and Open Bible Standard Churches (OBSC), formed by the merger of the Open Bible Evangelistic Association and the Bible Standard Churches in 1935.

C. Oneness Agencies.

The entry of the "New Issue" (the Oneness view of the Trinity) into the pentecostal movement in 1913 created new divisions and ultimately led to a split within the GCAG in 1916. While a considerable number of ministers left the GCAG, the impact on the missionary personnel appears to have been minimal, although the controversy did arise on some foreign fields, notably China.

As a result, several Oneness organizations came into existence. Like other pentecostals, they shared the same concerns for world evangelization. Two months after the schism within the GCAG, a large group of Oneness believers gathered in Eureka Springs, AR, and formed the General Assembly of the Apostolic Assemblies (GAAA). *The Blessed Truth*, edited by D. C. O. Opperman, the newly elected chairman, was designated the official voice of the organization. The membership voted that missionary funds should be sent to Opperman, who would then distribute them to the missionaries. Seven missionaries were named on the ministerial list.

The GAAA was short-lived, however, and merged around 1918 with the largely African-American (and Oneness) Pentecostal Assemblies of the World (PAW), which had been formed in 1907. Andrew D. Urshan, a former missionary to Persia (later Iran), received an appointment as foreign missionary secretary in 1923.

Dissatisfaction with the PAW led to a division along racial lines, and three new white organizations came into existence. One gathering of ministers founded the Pentecostal Ministerial Alliance (PMA) in 1925 and expressed the usual concerns about missions. To administer the foreign missions department, Edgar C. Steinberg, a former missionary to China, was chosen to serve as the first missionary secretary-treasurer in 1927. The 17 missionaries listed on the roster as receiving some or all of their support from this agency included O. W. Coote (Japan), the C. M. Hensleys (China), the A. J. Holmeses (Liberia), and Dorothy McCarty (India).

A second group of ministers organized the Emmanuel's Church in Jesus Christ in 1925. Urshan was selected as its foreign missions secretary, and every church was requested to send regular monthly support. Ten missionaries received assistance, some of whom also received monies from PMA. A third constituency from PAW began the Apostolic Church of Jesus Christ (ACJC) in 1925.

The continuing disunity among Oneness believers distressed many people and resulted in the merger of ACJC and part of the remaining white constituency of PAW in 1932 to form the Pentecostal Assemblies of Jesus Christ. The new denomination supported 20 missionaries and adopted a nine-point missions policy.

A further development came in 1932 when the PMA changed its name to the Pentecostal Church, Incorporated (PCI). During that decade missions giving increased dramatically, and 26 missionaries received support. In 1944 the PC adopted a comprehensive missions policy.

While many had left the PAW to form new Oneness organizations, the blacks and some whites therein remained separate and retained the original name. After years of instability, PAW appointed a foreign missions board, and the work achieved some progress under the direction of Bishop Earl Parchia.

D. Cooperation and Ecumenicity.

An early ecumenical endeavor on the home front emerged from the GCAG in 1917 when it called for a nondenominational conference of missionaries to address the needs of the pentecostal mission enterprise. Known as the Missionary Conference, its first meeting took place following the GCAG meeting at St. Louis in the same year. Although independent, officers of the latter attended its sessions and welcomed suggestions. The conferences continued to follow meetings of the general council until the last meeting in 1921, when it was perceived that the body had outlived its usefulness. Many of the missionaries who participated eventually affiliated with the GCAG.

Cooperation abroad sometimes characterized the early (Trinitarian) pentecostal missionaries for several reasons. First, many shared the ideal of unity among Spirit-baptized believers. Second, the relatively small numbers of pentecostal missionaries in any given country fostered fellowship among those of like faith. Third, with the belief in Christ's imminent return, coupled with the relative youth and limitations of pentecostal mission agencies, many missionaries did not perceive themselves as overseas representatives of particular church organizations. Thus, for spiritual and practical reasons

they were willing in certain instances to form fellowships to provide direction to their efforts. The Pentecostal Interior Mission in Liberia, representing all the missionaries there, was a notable example of such cooperation. A similar attempt occurred in India but collapsed with the untimely death of Christian Schoonmaker. The Truth Bible Institute in Beijing, China, represented another such venture. In the same spirit of cooperation and mutual concern, the GCAG organized the Scandinavian Missionary Relief Fund during WWII to assist more than one hundred Norwegian and Swedish pentecostal missionaries in China, Argentina, and Brazil who had been cut off from their regular sources of income.

With the growing size of mission agencies, the missionaries became more closely linked to others who had been sent out by the same organization; consequently, they became less familiar with pentecostal missionaries from other organizations. In reference to training, a growing number of missionaries received Bible institute training and hence grew in denominational loyalty. The ever-increasing demands for financial assistance also required them to broaden their base of support beyond a few congregations, thus gradually requiring extensive itineration when they were home on furlough. With these changes, missionaries forged stronger ties to their sending agencies.

In the U.S., denominationalism continued to splinter the pentecostal movement, setting the stage for increased isolation among the leaders. Generally there was little contact between pentecostal mission boards in the U.S. until after WWII. However, the fraternal relationships between the GCAG and the PAOC, and between the GCAG and REEM, were notable exceptions.

Although pentecostals experienced considerable isolation from other Christians before WWII, the GCAG joined the Foreign Missions Conference of North America in 1920. While GCAG leaders decried the growing theological liberalism within some missions agencies in the conference, they nevertheless profited from the practical assistance that came with membership.

III. INCREASED COOPERATION.

A major turn of events came with the founding of the National Association of Evangelicals (NAE) in 1942 and the willingness of its leadership to include pentecostal denominations. Consequently, pentecostal executives came into contact with one another, and their interest in fellowship played an important role in the formation of the Pentecostal World Conference (PWC, 1947) and the Pentecostal Fellowship of North America (PFNA, 1948); the latter was transformed into the Pentecostal/Charismatic Churches of North America (PCCNA) in 1994. The PFNA adopted seven criteria for cooperation in missions and promised to promote spiritual fellowship and coordination of overseas efforts. However, since the PWC and the PFNA (PCCNA) do not have any legislative powers but serve only to promote consultation and goodwill, their actual impact on mission policies has been virtually nonexistent. After the establishment of the NAE, its mission arm, the Evangelical Foreign Missions Association (EFMA), later the Evangelical Fellowship of Mission Agencies, commenced operation in 1945. The GCAG, CG, OBSC, and IPHC became charter members (the CCNA and ICFG joined later). With this affiliation, pentecostals gained broader exposure to each other's mission programs and those of other evangelical agencies. Notwithstanding, a formal caucus of pentecostal mission agencies has never developed.

The relationship with the EFMA proved to be difficult during its early years. Citing the resentment expressed by some members against pentecostal representation, the unproven benefits of association, and the cost of contributions, the GCAG withdrew in 1950. Three years later, at the urging of Clyde W. Taylor, the executive secretary, they rejoined. Since then the connection has been cordial and positive. Noel Perkin, director of GCAG foreign missions from 1927 until 1959, became the first pentecostal to serve as EFMA president in 1959–60. His successor as GCAG missions director, J. Philip Hogan, served three terms as EFMA president.

IV. PENTECOSTAL MISSIOLOGY.

A. Early Missiological Perspectives.

Early pentecostals often referred to four Scripture passages that articulated their mission to the world: Matt. 24:14, 28:19-20; Mark 16:15–18; and Acts 1:8. The Great Commission of Jesus, the promise of apostolic power to accompany proclamation, and the imminent return of Christ provided the motivation for the growing dispersion of missionaries. Hence, the pentecostals aimed to convert the heathen to Christianity as quickly as possible.

Not all pentecostals accepted Parham's xenolalic interpretation of glossolalia. In *The Baptism of the Holy Ghost and Fire,* an important early treatise by Minnie F. Abrams, the author noted that when one receives Spirit baptism, "the fire of God's love will so burn within you that you will desire the salvation of souls ... and realize that He to whom all power is given has imparted some of that power to you, sufficient to do all that He has called you to do" (1906, 44). To Abrams, the baptism in the Holy Spirit brought a deeper relationship with Christ and filled the believer with love for the lost. Consequently, "when those anointed to preach the gospel are bold enough to accept and exercise the gifts of the Spirit, and to do the signs and miracles authorized in the word of God, in three years time the gospel will spread more rapidly and bring more under its power, than it has in the past 300 years" (ibid., 72–73). In a similar vein, J. Roswell Flower, later a founding

father and missionary secretary of the GCAG, wrote in 1908: "The baptism of the Holy Ghost does not consist in simply speaking in tongues.... It fills our souls with the love of God for lost humanity, and makes us much more willing to leave home, friends, and all to work in His vineyard, even if it be far away among the heathen" (cited in McGee, 1986, 45). As pentecostals found the xenolalic interpretation of tongues to be inaccurate, they focused on the value of glossolalia as praise and intercessory prayer in the spirit, as the source of spiritual power.

Through the years pentecostal publications have contained thousands of accounts of healings, exorcisms, and deliverances from chemical addictions; many of these testimonies to the miraculous came from foreign lands as a result of gospel proclamation. Missionaries have attested their willingness to confront evil powers due to the spiritual dynamic of the baptism in the Holy Spirit.

B. William Taylor.

Radical evangelicals and early pentecostals received inspiration from the mission policies and writings of William Taylor, the well-known Methodist missionary bishop for Africa (1884–96). Taylor's endeavors in South America, India, and Africa centered on establishing self-supporting, self-propagating, and self-governing national Methodist Episcopal church bodies free from dependence on the Methodist Mission Board in New York City. This practice, along with his recruitment and appointment of self-supporting missionaries, generated severe tensions with the board. He explained his theory of missions in *Pauline Methods of Missionary Work* (1879).

Taylor's difficulties with the Methodist Mission Board, successful endeavors on three continents, and his own colorful experiences in ministry made him a folk hero to many radical Methodist, Holiness, and later pentecostal missionaries. His ministry inspired the Free Methodist Vivian Dake, founder of Pentecost Bands, and A. B. Simpson, founder of the CMA. He had a profound impact on the course of Chilean pentecostalism and the missionary expansion of European pentecostalism through his influence on Thomas B. Barratt. Two of the missionaries who participated in the Azusa Street revival, Samuel and Ardella Mead, were Methodist Episcopal missionaries and part of Taylor's "Pioneer Forty" who went to Angola in 1885.

C. A. B. Simpson and the CMA.

Since some early pastors and missionaries received training at Simpson's Missionary Training Institute at Nyack, NY, the first Bible institute in America, the CMA had a marked influence on the development of pentecostal missions, especially that of the GCAG (the largest pentecostal mission agency). At least three areas of influence are detectable. First, the Bible institute program at Nyack, which focused attention more on spiritual than on academic training, became the pattern for the Bethel Bible Training Institute at Newark, NJ (1916); Southern California Bible School, Highland Park, CA (1921); and Central Bible Institute, Springfield, MO (1922), all three begun by former members of the CMA. The various emphases on missions at Nyack were repeated at Bethel, Southern California, Central, and elsewhere. Many of their students became pentecostal missionaries.

Since the early missionaries rarely had college or university training (there were notable exceptions), the pentecostals readily adopted the Bible institute approach for theological training. Shorter than the traditional program of ministerial preparation, it offered students an intensely biblical education, a dynamic spiritual atmosphere through daily chapel services and prayer meetings, and a speedier entry into the ministry. A former CMA pastor, David Wesley Myland, who joined the ranks of the pentecostal movement, echoed Simpson's concerns by stating that he "would rather see one person baptized in the Holy Ghost and fire, dead in love with God's Word, reading it day and night and praying the heathen through to salvation than to see a score of missionaries go out with only intellectual equipment" (1911, 71).

The emphasis on the Christian life of faith represents a second influence of Simpson's; its roots, however, extend beyond him to George Müller and leaders in the late-19th-century faith-healing movement. Müller's philanthropic enterprises in England exemplified the benefits of the faith life and God's miraculous provision. Without his publicly mentioning his needs, finances and material assistance were always forthcoming. Simpson urged CMA missionaries to trust God for their needs since they traveled abroad without fixed salaries; he did, however, encourage the membership to contribute regularly.

Similarly, Simpson believed that the benefits of Christ's atonement extend beyond the spiritual to the physical nature of humankind. Missionaries, therefore, should exercise faith for their own healing and pray for the sick. The healing of diseases and other manifestations of divine power would then propel the success of Christian missions. Simpson's missionaries usually shunned medicines and vaccines. The early pentecostal missionaries, some directly influenced by him, usually

Roland Allen, an Anglican missionary to China, who unwittingly exerted a profound influence on pentecostal missions through his writings, particularly *Missionary Methods: St. Paul's or Ours?*

held the same view. They easily linked prayer for the sick with the work of the Spirit. As was true of the CMA, the pentecostals suffered the loss of some missionaries (e.g., Christian Schoonmaker, a GCAG missionary to India [formerly with the CMA], died from smallpox in 1919, having refused inoculation).

The missiological perspectives taught at Nyack represent the third influence on pentecostals. Rooted in the writings of Rufus Anderson, Henry Venn, and William Taylor, the strategy of building strong national churches overseas through application of indigenous church principles received new attention at the turn of the century. These principles, expressed succinctly in the "three selfs" (self-propagating, self-supporting, self-governing), were in part popularized through the publication of *The Planting and Development of Missionary Churches* (1886) by John L. Nevius, a Presbyterian missionary to China. Students at Nyack studied the teachings of Nevius.

D. Roland Allen.

For decades many pentecostal missionaries followed the paternalistic practices of the established Protestant denominations. When Christ did not return as expected, they naturally followed the lead of others to consolidate their work. Missionaries often lived on "mission compounds," operating charitable institutions such as orphanages and schools and retaining tight control over local pastors and evangelists by paying them with funds raised in North America. Although the missionaries cherished their freedom to be directed personally by the Holy Spirit, their paternalism in some instances actually stifled the building of strong national churches, ironically denying national ministers the opportunity of exercising gifts of leadership (1 Cor. 12:28) for the superintendence of their churches. As time passed, many, but not all, pentecostals moved away from paternalism to plan and work for the development of indigenous church organizations.

The high-Anglican missionary to North China, Roland Allen, reflecting the missiological perspectives of Anderson, Venn, and Nevius, proved to be the most powerful influence in the development of pentecostal missiology. With the publication of his books *Missionary Methods: St. Paul's or Ours?* (1912) and *The Spontaneous Expansion of the*

Church and the Causes Which Hinder It (1927), Allen unwittingly shaped the future course of pentecostal missions. Through these books several key individuals were able to mold a new generation of missionaries. Allen's emphasis on the Pauline methods of church planting, as seen in the book of Acts, naturally appealed to the pentecostals who believed that the dynamic power ("signs and wonders") of the NT church had been restored.

Alice E. Luce, a former missionary to India with the Church Missionary Society and later to Hispanics in America, may have been the first pentecostal exponent of Allen's teachings. His first book made a deep impression on her while she was still in India. Later, as a GCAG missionary, she wrote a series of articles for the *Pentecostal Evangel* in 1921; these articles helped set the stage for the denomination's strong endorsement of indigenous church principles at its general council gathering later that year. Through these articles, Luce advocated Allen's perspectives on church planting. Foreign leadership may be necessary for a time, but it cannot be based on attitudes of racial or cultural superiority. Such guidance must be founded on greater experience and spiritual maturity. Missionary leadership should model humility and obedience to the Holy Spirit if younger national ministers are to be properly trained to take their places.

While Luce approved of Allen's methods, her pentecostal theology led her to believe that apostolic methods of evangelism and church planting would be followed by the power and demonstration of the Holy Spirit. She challenged her readers by asking, "When we go forth to preach the Full Gospel [salvation, baptism in the Holy Spirit, divine healing, second coming of Christ], are we going to expect an experience like that of the denominational missionaries, or shall we look for the signs to follow?" (*Pentecostal Evangel* [Jan. 22, 1921], 6). Luce had a particularly strong influence on Ralph D. Williams and Henry C. Ball, both indigenous-church pioneers among Latin Americans. Another influential voice supporting these methods within GCAG missions was that of Noel Perkin. As director, he urged missionary candidates to familiarize themselves with Allen's books before going overseas.

E. Melvin L. Hodges.

One missionary who followed Perkin's advice was Melvin L. Hodges, an AG missionary to Central America and later field director for Latin America and the West Indies. Upon arriving in Central America in 1936, he began working with Ralph D. Williams to put indigenous principles into effect.

In 1953 the Gospel Publishing House published *The Indigenous Church*, written by Hodges. A series of lectures at the 1950 Missionary Conference in Springfield, MO, provided the basis for the book. When Moody Press gained permission to reprint an abridged edition of the book under the title *On the Mission Field: The Indigenous Church* (1953), it gained wider publicity. The book proved to be the most significant work on mission strategy and theology that the pentecostal movement had produced. In 11 chapters Hodges discussed the nature of a NT church and its implementation. Relying on his experiences in working with national church organizations, he also explained how to change an existing paternalistic structure into an indigenous one. To a considerable extent, Hodges repeated the methods advocated by Anderson, Venn, Nevius, and particularly Allen. The book's uniqueness consisted in its practical nature and fusion of indigenous principles with pentecostal theology. He asserted that "the faith which Pentecostal people have in the ability of the Holy Spirit to give spiritual gifts and supernatural abilities to the common people ... has raised up a host of lay preachers and leaders of unusual spiritual ability—not unlike the rugged fishermen who first followed the Lord" (Hodges, 1953, 132). The application of Hodges' teachings has played a major role in the spectacular spread of pentecostalism overseas.

F. Publications.

The need for mission education in the home churches prompted the GCAG to publish *Our World Witness* (1963) by Noel Perkin and John Garlock, and the CG to publish *The Church and World Missions* (1970) by Vessie D. Hargrave. The prolific Melvin L. Hodges continued to contribute books on missiology and church growth, including *Build My Church* (1957), *Growth in Your Christian Ministry* (1960), *A Guide to Church Planting* (1973), *A Theology of the Church and Its Mission* (1977), and *The Indigenous Church and the Missionary* (1978). When *On the Mission Field* was published by Moody Press and later articles were published in edited works and journals (e.g., "A Pentecostal's View of Mission Strategy," *International Review of Missions* 57 [July 1968]: 304–10), Hodges became the first pentecostal to publish on missiology outside of denominational publications.

A strategy of pentecostal missions appeared with *Breaking the Stained-Glass Barrier* (1973) by David A. Womack, a former GCAG missionary to Latin America. A CG perspective on mission appeared in the same year with *Unto the Uttermost* (1973) by Wade H. Horton.

A significant pentecostal missiology appeared in *The Third Force in Missions* (1985) by Paul A. Pomerville, formerly a GCAG missionary. Pomerville notes that the lack of emphasis in evangelical missions on the work of the Holy Spirit can be traced to the rationalistic impact of Protestant scholasticism through its overidentification of the Spirit with the written Word and an abhorrence of personal "experience" as a factor in spiritual authority. Accordingly, he states that "as a renewal movement, emphasizing a neglected dimension of the Holy Spirit's ministry, pentecostalism sets the subtle influence of post-Reformation scholasticism in bold relief. It is at this point that pentecostalism functions as a 'corrective' in contemporary missions" (Pomerville, 1985, 79).

Pomerville also maintains that the NT theology of the kingdom of God lays the groundwork for properly understanding the outpouring of the Spirit both then and now. The proclamation of the gospel, coupled with the dynamic work of the Spirit, should characterize the extension of God's kingdom before the return of Christ. This should form the heart of pentecostal missiology. Although he praises George Eldon Ladd (*The Presence of the Future*, 1974) for his insights on the kingdom of God, he faults him for not adequately addressing the work of the Spirit that must accompany it. This emphasis on nondispensational premillennialism also reflects a trend in pentecostal theology away from the specially adapted dispensationalism that has been popular in pentecostalism from its beginning.

A valuable resource for the study of pentecostal missions and church growth is *Azusa Street and Beyond* (1986), edited by L. Grant McClung Jr., a former CG missionary to Europe. Recent discussions on various aspects of pentecostal missiology have included *Called & Empowered: Global Mission in Pentecostal Perspective* (1991) and *The Globalization of Pentecostalism: A Religion Made to Travel* (1999), both books edited by Murray W. Dempster, Byron D. Klaus, and Douglas Petersen.

Significant work on issues related to the mission of the church took place during the fourth Quinquennium of the international Roman Catholic and Classical Pentecostal Dialogue. Since pentecostalism has flourished in historically Roman Catholic countries, the final report reflects progress in addressing the thorny issue of proselytizing: "evangelization, proselytism and common witness: the report from the fourth phase of the international dialogue 1990–1997 between the Roman Catholic Church and some classical pentecostal churches and leaders" (1998).

G. Historical Perspectives.

Early pentecostal literature reflects a strong triumphalism, no doubt caused by its restorationist impulse. The same statement on the place of pentecostal missions in the history of the church appears in two early missions documents: the GCAG *Missionary Manual* (1931) and repeated in Horace McCracken's *History of Church of God Missions* (1943). The original author of the statement (probably Noel Perkin), stated that the Lord's pentecostal missionary movement began on the Day of Pentecost. Led and energized by the Holy Spirit, it spawned a remarkable expansion of the Christian faith until the close of the 1st century. At that time people rejected the Spirit's leadership, and the movement halted; the Dark Ages followed. Although the Reformation brought partial restoration, it failed to complete its task. With the "outpouring of the Spirit" in 1901, "the Lord's Pentecostal missionary movement was resumed" (*Missionary Manual*, 1931, 7).

This restorationist interpretation of history actually says more about the contemporary feelings of isolation and rejection by other Christians that the pentecostals experienced than it does about the course of church history. With the growing alignment of denominational (Trinitarian) pentecostals with evangelicals (NAE, etc.) in the 1940s, later histories and manuals made little or no reference to it. Valuable surveys of the pentecostal movement addressing its history and missions expansion include Bennett F. Lawrence, *The Apostolic Faith Restored* (1916); Stanley H. Frodsham, *With Signs Following* (rev. ed., 1946); Donald Gee, *To the Uttermost Part* (c. 1932), and *The Pentecostal Movement* (rev. ed., 1949); and Gordon F. Atter, *The Third Force* (1962).

Pentecostal missionaries realized from the earliest years that they had to maintain contact with publications such as *Apostolic Faith, Bridegroom's Messenger*, and *Latter Rain Evangel* to publicize their ministries and inform the readers of their needs. Hence, letters from missionaries, frequently containing accounts of healings and deliverances, abound in these periodicals. However, historical treatments of the enterprise from the earliest period are rare; a notable exception is E. May Law's *Pentecostal Mission Work in South China* (c. 1916). As missions agencies (independent and denominational) grew in size and sophistication, they increasingly produced their own magazines to highlight their activities, sometimes including references to the role of pentecostal missions in the history of the church. Independent missions agencies sponsored such publications as *The Gospel Call* (REEM), *The Record of Faith* (TES), and *Full Gospel Missionary Herald* (PMSCA). Denominational publications such as the *Church of God Evangel* (CG), *Pentecostal Evangel* (GCAG), and the *Bridal Call Foursquare* (ICFG) included sections devoted to missions. Later they produced magazines to focus entirely on missions (e.g., the GCAG *Missionary Challenge* [1944]). In addition, the GCAG Department of Foreign Missions developed a series of booklets in the 1930s and 1940s describing the work of its missionaries on various fields (e.g., Jacob J. Mueller, *With Our Missionaries in North India* [1937]; Arthur E. Wilson, *A Visit to Mosi Land, French West Africa* [c. 1932]; and H. C. Ball and A. E. Luce, *Glimpses of Our Latin American Work in the United States and Mexico* [1940]). These contain valuable historical accounts for tracing the development of the work.

Missionary biographies and autobiographies began to appear, especially in the 1930s. These accounts served to promote the cause of missions and provide more information and personal details about the work of individuals (e.g., Marion Keller, *Twenty Years in Africa: 1913–1933* [n.d.]; Stanley H. Frodsham, *Wholly for God* [1934]; and Helen I. Gustavson, *Tsinan, China: The Opening of an Effectual Door* [1941]).

Broader and more scholarly historical treatments of pentecostal missions appeared later in denominational histories (e.g., Joseph E. Campbell, *The Pentecostal Holiness Church: 1898–1948* [1951]) or in studies of the entire movement (e.g., Nils Bloch-Hoell, *The Pentecostal Movement* [1964]; Prudencio Damboriena, S.J., *Tongues as of Fire* [1969]; and Walter J. Hollenweger, *The Pentecostals* [1972]). These proved to be especially helpful, because historians of Christian missions have until recently given only scant attention to the pentecostal movement. Studies on overseas church growth have also been helpful in interpreting its progress and importance (e.g., Arno W. Enns, *Man, Milieu and Mission in Argentina* [1971]).

The first history devoted entirely to an agency's program appeared with Horace McCracken's *History of Church of God Missions* (1943); this was surpassed in scope and detail by Charles W. Conn's *Where the Saints Have Trod* (1959). Historical treatments of AG missions have included Serena M. Hodges, ed., *Look on the Fields* (1956). Major histories of AG missions began to appear with the publication of *Making Many Rich* (1955) by Elizabeth A. Galley Wilson; *The Silent Pentecostals* (1979) by Victor De León; and the two-volume *This Gospel Shall Be Preached: A History and Theology of Assemblies of God Foreign Missions* (1986, 1989) by Gary B. McGee; and Everett A. Wilson, *Strategy of the Spirit: J. Philip Hogan and the Growth of the Assemblies of God Worldwide, 1960–1990* (1997). In a promising development, pentecostals in the Two-Thirds World countries have begun writing their own histories (e.g., Fred G. Abeysekera, *History of the Assemblies of God in Singapore, 1928–1992* [1992]).

V. MISSIONS EDUCATION.

Curricular offerings in missiology were slim in early pentecostal Bible institutes. When Central Bible Institute (CBI), Springfield, MO, opened in 1922, it offered one course in missions, "Missions and Missionaries," which covered the history of Christian missions, the present efforts of pentecostal missionaries, and "home missionary" work as well (McGee, 1986, 88). The recognition that specialized training would enhance the success of missionaries developed in the 1940s. The GCAG offered an advanced course of study at CBI beginning in 1944. With the founding of the American Association of Bible Colleges in 1947, pentecostal schools began to offer four-year baccalaureate programs, and majors in mission studies soon appeared.

Graduate and seminary training in missions began to appear in the 1970s. These institutions, some offering advanced degrees in missiology, include Oral Roberts University (1965), Assemblies of God Theological Seminary (1973), Church of God Theological Seminary (1975), Regent University (1977), and the graduate school of Vanguard University of Southern California (1983).

VI. INDEPENDENT MINISTRIES.

Since the beginning of pentecostal missions, there has been a strong current of independence. The antiorganizational sentiments of many missionaries reflected the painful rejection by former denominations over their newfound spirituality, as well as their intense desire to live by faith and be led totally by the Spirit in their ministries. Thus, relying on individuals and supporting congregations, independent pentecostal missionaries have continued in ministry for many years, some with considerable success. Their number, the scope of their ministries, and the success they have achieved is nevertheless difficult to ascertain.

While the fears of many were allayed by the benefits of joining with pentecostal agencies (e.g., the personnel in the Missionary Conference who joined the AG), the tension between independence and structure has continued to the present. Although the denominational agencies place high value on team work and have believed that the Spirit can work through committees and boards as well as individuals, the desire to be directed personally by the Spirit lies at the core of pentecostal concerns.

Over the years various individual and group initiatives have surfaced to promote effective overseas evangelism without the strictures of denominational boards. These include the efforts of the faith-healing evangelists in overseas crusades in the 1950s and 1960s (e.g., M. A. Daoud, Tommy Hicks, and Morris Cerullo). T. L. Osborn, another evangelist, began the Association for Native Evangelism in 1953. Gordon Lindsay's foreign missions efforts were advertised through the pages of his *Voice of Healing* magazine, known later as *Christ for the Nations;* his Christ for the Nations Institute in Dallas, TX, and its sister schools overseas, have trained many missionaries. Another important ministry is Youth With A Mission (YWAM), founded by Loren Cunningham. Of particular note in supporting charitable endeavors overseas has been Mission of Mercy with headquarters in Colorado Springs, CO.

In some instances, independent missionaries have been supported by networks of churches, such as the Fellowship of Christian Assemblies (1922) and the Independent Assemblies of God (1922), which reflect their Scandinavian origins and the congregational influence of Swedish pentecostalism. Their approach to missiology can be found in many countries (e.g., Brazil and Africa) where Swedish missionaries and others holding to congregational church polity have ministered. At times tensions have emerged on fields between agencies that promote national church organizations and Bible institutes for training clergy and advocates of the local congregation as the primary base for missions and education.

VII. SIGNIFICANCE.

Pentecostal missions arose within the theological and missiological milieu of radical evangelicalism, whose proponents anticipated the restoration of the apostolic power of the early church to bring closure to the Great Commission before the imminent and premillennial return of Jesus Christ. While some radical evangelicals continued to pray for the sick and exorcise demons well into the 20th century, the contrast in spirituality between evangelical and pentecostal missionaries became more apparent as the former recoiled from identification with pentecostal practices. Pentecostals continued to emphasize the importance of baptism in the Holy Spirit, the restoration of the gifts of the Holy Spirit for the life and mission of the church, and the strategic purpose of miracles in evangelism.

Their approach to evangelism found a warm response among many peoples whose worldviews recognized the possibility of "power encounters" in the spiritual realm to break satanic bondage. Furthermore, with the belief that the Holy Spirit confers gifts on individuals for ministry, pentecostalism has been easily contextualized and has quickly raised up indigenous charismatic leaders. As a result, significant church growth has taken place in many countries (e.g., Brazil, Chile, Korea, South Africa) among both denominational pentecostals and independent pentecostals and charismatics.

The pentecostal movement in its various forms has challenged Christians of many backgrounds to review their understanding of the role of the Holy Spirit in the Christian world mission. The emphasis on the power of the Holy Spirit, the indigenization of pentecostalism, and the pragmatism of pentecostal missions, dynamics shared by Euro-American and the rapidly increasing numbers of Third World pentecostal missionaries, have made pentecostalism the most dynamic force in evangelization today.

■ **Bibliography:** M. F. Abrams, *The Baptism of the Holy Ghost and Fire* (2d ed., 1906) ■ B. C. Aker et al., eds., *Signs and Wonders in Ministry Today* (1996) ■ D. H. Bays, "Indigenous Protestant Churches in China, 1900–1937: A Pentecostal Case Study," in *Indigenous Responses to Western Christianity,* ed. S. Kaplan (1995) ■ idem, "The Protestant Missionary Establishment and the Pentecostal Movement," in *Pentecostal Currents in American Protestantism,* ed. E. L. Blumhofer et al. (1999) ■ H. P. Beach and C. H. Fahs, eds., *World Missionary Atlas* (1925) ■ D. Bundy, "Swedish Pentecostal Mission Theory and Practice to 1930: Foundational Values in Conflict," *Mission Studies: Journal of the International Association for Mission Studies* 14 (1 and 2, 27 and 28) (1997): 147–74 ■ idem, "William Taylor 1821–1902," in *Mission Legacies,* ed. G. H. Anderson et al. (1994) ■ B. Cavaness, "God Calling: Women in Assemblies of God Missions," *JSPS* 16 (Spring 1994): 49–62 ■ A. W. Clanton and C. E. Clanton, *United We Stand: A History of Oneness Organizations* (2d ed., 1995) ■ M. Dempster et al., eds., *Called and Empowered: Global Mission in Pentecostal Perspective* (1991) ■ idem, *The Globalization of Pentecostalism* (1999) ■ Yeol Soo Eim, "The World Wide Expansion of the Foursquare Church," D.Miss. diss., Fuller Theol. Sem., 1986 ■ J. R. Goff Jr., *Fields White unto Harvest: Charles F. Parham and the Missionary Origins of Pentecostalism* (1988) ■ M. L. Hodges,

The Indigenous Church (1953) ■ W. J. Hollenweger, *Pentecostalism: Origins and Developments Worldwide* (1997) ■ P. Humphrey [Scarborough], *J. H. Ingram: Missionary Dean* (1966) ■ J. A. B. Jongeneel, ed., *Pentecost, Mission and Ecumenism: Essays on Intercultural Theology* (1992) ■ V-M. Kärkkäinen, *Ad Ultimum Terrae: Evangelization, Proselytism and Common Witness in the Roman Catholic Pentecostal Dialogue* (1999) ■ K. S. Latourette, *A History of the Expansion of Christianity,* 4 (1941) ■ A. E. Luce, "Paul's Missionary Methods" (pt. 3), *PE* (Feb. 5, 1921), 6–7 ■ W. Ma et al., eds., *Pentecostalism in Context: Essays in Honor of William W. Menzies* (1997) ■ L. G. McClung Jr., ed., *Azusa Street and Beyond: Pentecostal Missions and Church Growth in the Twentieth Century* (1986) ■ idem, "Pentecostal/Charismatic Perspectives on a Missiology for the Twenty-First Century," *JSPS* 16 (Spring 1994): 11–21 ■ K. McDonnell, "Pentecostals and Catholics on Evangelism and Sheep-Stealing," *America* (Mar. 6, 1999), 11–14 ■ G. B. McGee, *This Gospel Shall Be Preached: A History and Theology of Assemblies of God Foreign Missions to 1959* (1986) ■ idem, *This Gospel Shall Be Preached: A History and Theology of Assemblies of God Missions Since 1959* (1989) ■ idem, "Historical Perspectives on Pentecostal Missionaries in Situations of Conflict and Violence," *Missiology: An International Review* 20 (Jan. 1992): 33–43 ■ idem, "Pentecostal Strategies for Global Mission: A Historical Assessment," in *Called and Empowered: Global Mission in Pentecostal Perspective,* ed. M. W. Dempster et al. (1991) ■ idem, "The Radical Strategy in Modern Mission: The Linkage of Paranormal Phenomena with Evangelism," in *The Holy Spirit and Mission Dynamics,* ed. C. D. McConnell (1997) ■ T. W. Miller, *Canadian Pentecostals: A History of the Pentecostal Assemblies of Canada* (1994) ■ *Missionary Manual* (1931) ■ R. B. Mitchell and L. M. Mitchell, *Heritage and Harvests: The History of International Ministries of Open Bible Standard Churches* (1995) ■ D. W. Myland, *The Latter Rain Covenant and Pentecostal Power* (2d ed., 1911) ■ D. Petersen, *Not by Might Nor by Power: A Pentecostal Theology of Social Concern in Latin America* (1996) ■ L. S. Vaccaro de Petrella, "The Tension between Evangelism and Social Action in the Pentecostal Movement," *IRM* 75 (Jan. 1986): 34–38 ■ K. Poewe, ed., *Charismatic Christianity as a Global Culture* (1994) ■ P. A. Pomerville, *The Third Force in Missions* (1985) ■ E. K. Pousson, *Spreading the Flame: Charismatic Churches and Missions Today* (1992) ■ idem, "A 'Great Century' of Pentecostal/Charismatic Renewal in Missions," *Pneuma* 16 (Spring 1994): 81–100 ■ C. M. Robeck Jr., "The Assemblies of God and Ecumenical Cooperation: 1920–1965," in *Pentecostalism in Context: Essays in Honor of William W. Menzies,* ed. W. Ma et al. (1997) ■ idem, "Evangelization or Proselytism of Hispanics? A Pentecostal Perspective," *JHLT* 4:4 (1997): 42–64 ■ D. J. Rodgers, "Spirit of the Plains: North Dakotan Pentecostalism's Roots in Immigrant Pietism and the Holiness Movement" (1997) ■ T. Salzer, "The Danzig Gdanska Institute of the Bible," *AG Heritage* 8 (Fall 1988): 8–11, 18–19 ■ idem, 8 (Winter 1988–89): 10–13, 17–18 ■ A. B. Simpson, *Annual Report of the Superintendent and Board of Managers,* May 4, 1900 ■ idem, *The Eleventh Annual Report of the Christian and Missionary Alliance,* May 27, 1908 ■ I. A. Whitt,

"Developing a Pentecostal Missiology in the Canadian Context (1867–1944)" (D.Miss. diss., Fuller Theol. Sem., 1994) ∎ E. A. Wilson, *Strategy of the Spirit: J. Philip Hogan and the Growth of the Assemblies of God Worldwide, 1960–1990* (1997).   ∎ G. B. McGee

MITA CONGREGATION, INC.

MITA CONGREGATION, INC. (La Congregación Mita, Inc.). Founded in Puerto Rico in 1940 by Juanita García Peraza. Peraza was born into a wealthy family in Hatillo, Puerto Rico, in 1897. In 1940 Juanita's doctors informed her that the painful illness she had been battling for eight years was now terminal. She then turned to God, promising that if he healed her, she would dedicate her entire life to serving him. A short time later she met a pentecostal missionary who prayed for her and, according to Mita tradition, she was healed. After her healing she had contact with a pentecostal church in Arecibo.

Peraza ran into trouble when she began accusing parishioners and even the pastor of sin. This prompted the church to expel her. She left the church with 11 followers (including Teófilo Vargas Seín, who was to become president of the group after Peraza's death) and began the Mita Congregation in 1940. It was incorporated in 1957 when it numbered approximately 2,000 members. Mita Congregation claims to be based on the same principle as the primitive church. They believe in the Bible and preach the triple message of love, liberty, and unity. What distinguishes them from other forms of charismatic Christianity is the central place they give to Mita. According to Mita tradition, the name Mita means the "Spirit of Life" and was revealed to Peraza as well as to her followers as the new name for the Holy Spirit and herself. They believe that Mita's name is the fulfillment of a number of prophecies, which they believe teach that the Holy Spirit would return with a new name (Isa. 52:6, 62:2; John 14:16; Rev. 2:17; 3:12). They identify Juanita Peraza with Mita and believe that God chose her body to be the dwelling place of the Holy Spirit. The result is a nontraditional notion of the Trinity (God, Christ, Holy Spirit/Mita/García Peraza). They place a heavy emphasis on divine healing, music, prophecy, words of knowledge, and other manifestations of the Spirit. The two sources of revelation are the Bible and Mita (whose spirit now rests on Aarón Vargas, García Peraza's successor). Mita and Aarón are considered living prophets. Salvation is earned by a combination of faith in God and obedience to Mita and the Congregation's teaching. They believe that they are the one true church of God. Their theology has shaped their social ethic, which stresses abstinence from alcohol, smoking, and political involvement.

The Mita Congregation sponsors a number of social programs for the poor as well as drug and alcohol rehabilitation programs. In addition, they also sponsor youth programs, the Mita Band and Choir, a school, banks, cooperatives, a senior citizens home, and other programs and businesses. They do not have a professional, paid clergy. Church leaders are appointed by Vargas as lay leaders. To help cover the costs of the growing movement, members began to create small businesses near the church. They formed Hermanos Mita, Inc. (Mita Brothers, Inc.) and started a market, bazaar, bakery, cafe, hardware store, travel agency, shoe store, furniture store, and restaurant. They also opened a credit cooperative for church members.

In 1948, after members of the Mita Church began migrating to New York, Juanita (Mita) and Nicolás Tosado made a trip to New York and organized a church there. Later they also opened churches in Chicago, Philadelphia, and Washington, DC. Mita's work spread overseas to the Dominican Republic in 1963 and Columbia in 1969.

Juanita (Mita) died in 1970 at the age of 72. Her followers built a mausoleum in her honor in Hato Rey. After her death, control of the church was divided between two leaders: Teófilo Vargas Seín (Aarón), who became the president of the group, and Nicolás Tosado (Amós), who became vice president. In 1970 Nicolás Tosado (Amós) left the Mita Congregation and three years later moved to New York, where he and his followers formed their own church, called the People of Amós (Pueblo de Amós). His work has spread to other cities throughout the U.S. and into El Salvador, Guatemala, and Puerto Rico.

The Mita Congregation, Inc., under Vargas's leadership, continued to expand throughout the '80s and '90s into countries such as Haiti, Mexico, Venezuela, and Costa Rica. Today there are an estimated 48,000 adherents attending 43 churches in 11 countries throughout the world, including 1,500 adherents in the United States, 10,000 in the Dominican Republic, 15,000 in Puerto Rico, and 20,000 in Columbia. They began work in Mexico City, Puebla, and Acapulco in the 1980s. In 1990, at a cost of $5.8 million, they built a new 6,000-seat church in Puerto Rico.

∎ **Bibliography:** "Centenario del Natalicio de la Persona de Mita," *El Nuevo Dia* (July 6, 1997) ∎ "'Congregation Mita': Avance de la Obra de Mita, 1940–1990," *El Nuevo Dia* (Nov. 17, 1990) ∎ C. Cruz, *La Obra de Mita* (1990) ∎ *Enciclopedia de Grandes Mujeres de Puerto Rico*, vol. 3 (1975), 323–24, 347–81 ∎ D. T. Moore, "La Iglesia de Mita y Sus Doctrinas," *Siguiendo La Sana Doctrina* (Sept.–Oct. 1988) ∎ Teófilo Vargas Seín (Aarón), "Denominational Statistical Information Form for the Mita Congregation" (Sept. 1997) ∎ D. R. Torres, *Historia De La Iglesia De Dios Pentecostal, M.I.: Una Iglesia Ungida Para Hacer Misión* (1992), 126–31.

MITCHELL, ROBERT BRYANT

MITCHELL, ROBERT BRYANT (1905–97). Administrator, educator, and missionary leader for ▸Open Bible Standard Churches (OBSC). He was the eldest of the six A. E. Mitchell children, all of whom followed their parents into the ministry. He graduated from the Bible Institute of Los

Angeles in 1924 and attended UCLA to prepare for a medical career but transferred to ⸱L.I.F.E. Bible College and prepared for the ministry. Following ordination with the ⸱International Church of the Foursquare Gospel (ICFG) in 1929, he founded three churches in the Midwest and taught at two ICFG schools. Along with 32 other ministers, he withdrew in 1932 to form the Open Bible Evangelistic Association (later OBSC). He served as dean of Open Bible College (1935–53), general chairman of OBSC (1953–67), missionary director of OBSC (1967–73), and part-time instructor at Eugene Bible College (1975–79). He also served as chairman of the ⸱Pentecostal Fellowship of North America (1967–68) and on committees of the ⸱National Association of Evangelicals. He wrote the official history of OBSC, *Heritage and Horizons* (1982), and he and his wife, Lucille, wrote *Heritage and Harvests* (1995), the history of OBSC missions.

■ **Bibliography:** R. E. Smith, "R. B. Mitchell, a Man for All Time," *Message of the Open Bible* (Jan.–Feb. 1998).
■ W. E. Warner

MITTON, MICHAEL (1953–). Teacher-leader in Anglican renewal in England. Mitton earned a B.A. in theology from Exeter University and was ordained priest in 1979. He served as vicar of St. Chad's, Kidderminster (1982–89). From 1989–97 he was director of Anglican Renewal Ministries (ARM) while at the same time editing *Anglicans for Renewal* and its theological supplement *Skepsis*. Mitton not only promoted charismatic renewal but also helped renewal to be understood and welcomed within the Anglican structures. He was also coordinator of the various Anglican renewal agencies around the world and a member of the ⸱SOMA international executive board, traveling to many countries. Since 1997 Mitten is deputy director of the Acorn Christian Healing Trust and national coordinator of the Christian Listener project. Mitton's books include *Requiem Healing* (with Russ Parker, 1991); *The Sounds of God* (1993); *The Heart of Toronto* (1995); and *Restoring the Woven Cord* (1995, U.S. title *The Soul of Celtic Christianity*). He is editor of *The Way of Renewal,* a report on renewal from the Board of Mission of the Church of England General Synod. ■ P. D. Hocken

MJORUD, HERBERT (1910–). Pioneer exponent of charismatic renewal among Lutherans. In 1962 Mjorud received the gift of tongues during a visit to the Episcopal parish of ⸱Dennis Bennett, in Seattle, WA. He was serving as an evangelist for the American Lutheran Church (ALC) at the time. He had earlier experienced miraculous healings while serving a congregation in Anchorage, AK.

Mjorud began to include a charismatic message in his evangelistic meetings, which led to controversy. When his six-year term as an evangelist with the ALC expired, his call was not renewed. He formed his own evangelistic association and continued to hold meetings throughout the U.S. In 1968 he began a series of around-the-world evangelistic tours, with a particular concentration of work in Sri Lanka, where he was instrumental in starting two Bible schools. Key elements of his personal experience, pastoral concern, and theological perspective are summed up in the books and articles he authored.

Mjorud was healed of cancer in 1981 after he had been sent home to die.

■ **Bibliography:** L. Christenson, ed., *Welcome, Holy Spirit* (1987) ■ H. Mjorud, *Dare to Believe* (1975) ■ idem, *Fighting Cancer with Christ* (1983) ■ idem, *What's Baptism All About?* (1979).
■ L. Christenson

MOHAN, DAVID (1948–). Assemblies of God (AG) evangelist and pastor of Indian megachurch. David Mohan was converted, baptized, and filled with the Holy Spirit in Tuticorin, Tamil Nadu, India, in 1968. Subsequently, he received his B.A. from Pope College in Sawyerputam, Tamil Nadu, and the B.R.E. from Southern Asia Bible College in Bangalore in 1971. He began his ministry in 1973 at Mambalam in Chennai (formerly Madras). The New Life AG started with seven members. His congregation grew to 400, but a cyclone destroyed New Life Church facilities. Shortly thereafter, property was purchased on the main road at Little Mount, Chennai, where New Life Church is still located. Initially, they met in a thatched church shed, which was consumed by fire. A permanent facility then was erected, seating 5,000.

Thereafter, New Life Church grew rapidly. In 1989, 2,500 were in attendance. The church grew to 3,000 in 1990, and an extension was added to the facilities. By 1999, over 15,000 were attending five Sunday services. In addition, New Life operates 1,050 care cell groups of 7 to 12 believers. (Mohan credits these groups with the church's phenomenal growth.) The church also supports 40 indigenous missionaries across Southern Asia and has mothered more than 120 churches in the city of Chennai over the past two decades. More than 40 pastors have been sent out from New Life. In addition, the church sponsors a "National Highway Scheme," planting churches by conducting crusades in important towns and villages along national highways.

Mohan and his wife, Getzial, have three children, Chadwick Samuel, Benjamin Clifford, and Merlin Jemima.

■ **Bibliography:** D. Stewart Sr. "Fire of the Spirit Burning in South India," *PE* (Nov. 8, 1998) ■ Interview with Chadwick Samuel Mohan, October 1999. ■ S. M. Burgess

MOISE, MARY GILL ("MOTHER") (1850–1930). A pioneer in pentecostal social ministry in St. Louis, MO.

"Mother" Moise began her mission work under Episcopal bishop Daniel S. Tuttle. About 1907 she united with pentecostals and operated her home of mercy. Her home was called a ▸"faith home" and practiced an open-door policy for wayward girls, drunks, prostitutes, and other social outcasts. The home was also used as a Bible training center for future preachers. Early pentecostals traveling through St. Louis always found a welcome. Her work with homeless girls won for her a first prize in the 1904 World's Fair.

Moise accepted rebaptism in the name of Jesus, which placed her and the work in the ▸Oneness branch of pentecostalism. She also accepted the belief that Christians need never die. At her death a St. Louis newspaper called her "one of the most widely known mission workers in the country."

■ **Bibliography:** W. Warner, "Mother Mary Moise of St. Louis," *AGH* (Spring 1986). ■ W. E. Warner

MONOT, RONALD JEAN (1943–). Born at Bukavu (Congo Democratic Republic) of Brethren missionary parents in 1943, Monot was brought up in the Congo. He did his schooling in Lubumbashi and in Switzerland, from where he prepared to return to the Congo as a missionary. He was baptized in the Holy Spirit prior to going to the Congo in the mid 1960s but still planned to work with the Christian Brethren Assemblies in Lubumbashi. Once in the Congo, this caused a considerable stir, and he was asked to leave the Brethren. He became affiliated with the Congo Evangelistic Mission and continued to evangelize in cooperation with the Pentecostal Community of Congo.

Monot was primarily an evangelist and church planter. He planted churches at Kiambi among the pygmies (Bambote) and undertook evangelistic journeys throughout the Katanga, East and West Kasai, and parts of the Kivu. He traveled with national helpers, such as Felix Dyabupemba, many of whom became responsible for the churches Monot planted. Monot believed that the influence of the French language was a vital factor in the evangelization of the larger cities of the Kasai and the Katanga, where many civil servants and students gathered from other regions in the Congo and did not speak the local languages fluently. He was the first to plant French-language churches at important centers like Mbuji Mayi, Lusambo, and lastly at Lubumbashi. From these cities churches have grown at phenomenal rates so that, while in 1973 there were few if any pentecostal churches in the Kasai, today it is difficult to find a town of any size that does not have a pentecostal church. Monot would spend several months in a center before leaving the church in national hands and then move elsewhere. He emphasized baptism in the Holy Spirit and the gifts of the Spirit in the life of every believer and would often spend extended periods of time in prayer and fasting before deciding upon which cities and centers would be targeted for church plants.

In 1977 Monot moved from Kamina to Lubumbashi, where he planted the French-speaking assembly Viens et Vois. He later established a center intended for the training of evangelists at Ruashi, where today there is an Advanced School of Theology (three-year degree course) and an assembly with over 1,500 members, Centre Evangélique d'Eau Vive. Since 1990 Monot lives in Geneva, where he pastors an Assemblies of God church.

■ **Bibliography:** *Contact Zaire,* magazine of the Zaire Evangelistic Mission (Now Congo) ▪ D. J. Garrard "The History of the Congo Evangelistic Mission/Communauté Pentecôtiste au Zaïre from 1915 to 1982" (diss., Aberdeen, 1983). ▪ D. J. Garrard

MONTAGUE, GEORGE T. (1929–). Leader-theologian in the ▸Catholic charismatic renewal and biblical scholar. Montague joined the Marianist order as a young man, was ordained as priest in 1958, and completed his doctoral dissertation on Paul in 1960. Baptized in the Spirit in 1970, he soon became a popular speaker at charismatic conferences. His personal testimony is given in *Riding the Wind* (1974), and his charismatic experience is combined with biblical scholarship in *The Spirit and His Gifts* (1974) and *The Holy Spirit: Growth of a Biblical Tradition* (1976). Montague served on the National Service Committee for Catholic charismatic renewal (1978–82).

Montague has held responsible positions in academic and ecclesiastical circles. He was closely associated with the *Catholic Biblical Quarterly* (general editor, 1973–75) and was president of the Catholic Biblical Association (1977–78). He also served as seminary rector and university professor in St. Louis, MO, and Toronto, Ont. His other books include *Maturing in Christ* (1964), *Building Christ's Body* (1975), and *Mark: Good News for Hard Times* (1981).

Montague was director of novices for the Marianists in Katmandu, Nepal (1982–88), and has since been on the faculty of St. Mary's University, San Antonio, TX. He is coauthor (with ▸K. McDonnell) of *Christian Initiation and Baptism in the Holy Spirit* (1990). ■ P. D. Hocken

MONTANISM (mid 1st to 6th century A.D.). An early Christian group with pentecostal-like traits, including belief in spirit-possession, an imminent parousia, and the leadership of women, as well as the practice of prophecy and glossolalia (the latter is disputed). The founder, Montanus, a former priest of Cybele, was converted to Christianity in about A.D. 155 and continued to prophesy in his new context. An anonymous opponent reported that Montanus lost control of himself, falling into "a sort of frenzy and ecstasy" in which "he raved and began to babble and utter strange things, prophesying in a manner contrary to the constant custom of the church handed down by tradition from the beginning" (Eusebius, *Church History* 5.16.7). Montanus identified a new place, Pepuza in Phrygia, where the parousia was to occur, a new age of the Spirit, a new authority (their prophecy), a new church polity (prophetic leadership), and a new and more demanding level of asceticism and intolerant exclusivism. He declared his words to be a "New Prophecy"—the fulfilling of Jesus' promise of the coming of the Paraclete (John 14:12–18).

Montanus soon was joined by Maximilla and Priscilla (or Prisca), two women who deserted their husbands with Montanus's approval and claimed to possess a prophetic charisma similar to that of their leader. All three of these New Prophets believed that their prophecies were to be the final word of God to humanity, superseding the authority of the OT and NT. They taught that the Holy Spirit still was fully operational in the church.

Opposition to the Montanists resulted in part from their insistence on a new and more radical asceticism, which they practiced in preparation for the parousia. Second marriages were prohibited and even marriage itself. Strict fasting, unreserved preparation for martyrdom, and separation from the world also were expected of the "pneumatic," or spiritual. The adoption of this perfectionist lifestyle led not only to legalism but also to a spirit of intolerant exclusivism. Montanists attacked the mainline church for its laxity and for not exercising spiritual gifts.

In A.D. 206 the Montanists won a powerful convert, the esteemed theologian Tertullian, who appears to have been attracted to the group by its extreme asceticism and apocalypticism. Tertullian does not seem to have completely identified with the movement's founders, and he may have changed Montanism as much as it changed him. While he approved of ecstatic prophetic speech, there is no hint that he accepted the excesses that had characterized the utterances of Montanus and his two priestesses. For example, he tells of a woman who fell into ecstasy during the church service but did not communicate her revelation until the congregation had departed. In addition, Tertullian held to the fullness of the Spirit in the apostolic period, in direct contrast to the claims of the early Phrygian Montanists.

Montanist intolerance was met with intolerance. Once the Edict of Milan (A.D. 313) provided freedom of worship to mainline Christians, they in turn sought to stamp out religious dissent, including fringe groups such as the Montanists. An edict of Constantine deprived the Montanists of their places of worship and forbade their religious meetings. The movement finally disappeared in the 6th century when Emperor Justinian forced the remaining Montanists to gather their wives and children together into their places of worship.

These buildings and their occupants subsequently perished in fires set by imperial command.

Modern pentecostals who have identified with the Montanists have forgotten that the founders of the New Prophecy were not biblicists and that they were much more radically ascetic than 20th-century people of the Spirit. Perhaps it would be more useful to correlate the evolution of modern pentecostal groups to changes that occurred in Montanism over the course of its five centuries of existence.

■ **Bibliography:** G. N. Bonwetsch, *Die Geschichte des Montanismus* (1881) ■ S. M. Burgess, "Montanist and Patristic Perfectionism," in *Reaching Beyond: Chapters in the History of Perfectionism* (1986) ■ P. de Labriolle, *Les Sources de l'histoire du montanisme* (1913) ■ Didymus of Alexandria, *De trinitate* 3.41 ■ Epiphanius, *Haereses* 48 ■ idem, *Panarion* 43.2 ■ Eusebius, *Church History* 5.7.4, 5.16.7, 5.18.2 ■ E. Huber, *Women and the Authority of Inspiration: A Reexamination of Two Prophetic Movements from a Contemporary Feminist Perspective* (1985) ■ D. Rankin, *Tertullian and the Church* (1995) ■ Tertullian, *Against Praxeas* 1 ■ idem, *On Monogamy* 4.14 ■ idem, *On the Veiling of Virgins* 9 ■ idem, *A Treatise on the Soul* 9.

■ S. M. Burgess

MONTGOMERY, CARRIE JUDD

MONTGOMERY, CARRIE JUDD (1858–1946). A minister-teacher, writer, editor, director of ▸faith homes, and social worker whose ministry spanned more than 65 years. Worldwide, Carrie Judd Montgomery was best known for her *Triumphs of Faith: A Monthly Journal Devoted to Faith Healing and to the Promotion of Christian Holiness*. Her religious associations included the Episcopal Church, the Holiness healing movement, the ▸Christian and Missionary Alliance (CMA), the Salvation Army, and the pentecostal movement. Always interested in building bridges between diverse groups, she operated several transdenominational ministries.

1. The Early Years and Her Healing.

Reared in an Episcopal home in Buffalo, NY, where piety was practiced daily, Carrie Judd was one of eight children. At the age of 11 she made a spiritual commitment and was later confirmed at the Episcopal Church. Two of the Judd children died of tuberculosis, and Carrie was not well. While attending the Buffalo Normal School, she suffered a fall that forced her to drop out of school. She became an invalid and was not expected to live. Through the ministry of a black woman, Mrs. Edward Mix, Carrie was healed, and her story was told in the *Buffalo Commercial Advertiser* on Oct. 20, 1880.

Judd later wrote a book, *The Prayer of Faith* (1880), which gave her testimony and encouraged others to believe for healing. ▸A. B. Simpson read the book and later developed a lifelong friendship with her. Her miraculous healing also brought her into the leadership circle of the growing faith movement. In addition to Simpson, Montgomery shared the faith-healing platform with Charles Cullis, W. E. Boardman, ►Maria B. Woodworth-Etter, and Mrs. Michael Baxter of Bethshan, London.

2. Publications.

Judd's first literary effort was published when she was 15. A Buffalo newspaper published a poem she had written and then published others. Also as a teen she began working in the office of a health magazine, an experience that would help prepare her for the publishing phase of her life. In addition to her book *The Prayer of Faith,* she wrote her autobiography, *Under His Wings* (c. 1936), and other books, including *Secrets of Victory* (1921), *Heart Melody* (c. 1922), and *The Life of Praise.* Her biggest literary output, however, was *Triumphs of Faith,* a magazine she founded in 1881 and edited for 65 years. The magazine bridged the Holiness and pentecostal movements, and its pages provided a nonsectarian forum for a variety of denominations to express concern and teachings on common themes that greatly influenced the healing movement, social work, and worldwide missions.

3. Early Ministry.

Although it was unusual to hear women speak in public during the 1880s, the timid Carrie Judd began to give her testimony of healing. She received a good response among Holiness believers, and she began to speak at conventions that A. B. Simpson sponsored. In 1885 William E. Boardman invited Judd to speak at his healing convention in London, but she was unable to accept the invitation. When the ►Christian and Missionary Alliance (CMA) was organized in 1885, Judd was named recording secretary of the board. Even though she later was associated with the Salvation Army and the pentecostal movement, she maintained strong ties with the CMA.

The room in which Montgomery was confined during her illness became a faith sanctuary, a place where people could pray. Then a weekly meeting began in her home. Soon Faith Rest Cottage was established in Buffalo, where the sick could receive comfort, encouragement, prayer, and teaching. The home was one of several established across the country in the late 19th century by people who believed in divine healing.

4. Ministry in the West.

After ministering in the East during the 1880s, Judd moved to Oakland, CA, in 1890. That spring she married a wealthy businessman, George S. Montgomery, who owned property in an area near Oakland called Beulah (later Beulah Heights). Here the Montgomerys established the Home of Peace in 1893 in a big, three-story Victorian house, which is still being used by the organization. The Home of Peace was destined to have a far greater outreach than the Buffalo home. Various ministries were established as the Montgomerys saw the need. An orphanage was operated from 1895 to 1908. An average of 50 to 100 children were in the home. The Salvation Army took over its operation in 1908. Shalom Training School was established in 1894 to train missionary candidates.

Foreign mission work was always a priority with the Montgomerys. They made missionary trips and welcomed missionaries to stay at the Home of Peace while they were on furlough. Support for the missionaries was channeled through Home of Peace, and freight was shipped from the facilities. Missionaries from a hundred societies have used the home and its services.

Montgomery organized a CMA church the first year she lived in Oakland. Since the early CMA was a loosely organized fellowship of believers rather than strictly a denomination, the Montgomerys also joined the Salvation Army and were active for several years. They also organized the People's Mission in San Francisco but turned it over to the Salvation Army after the death of the director. Land at Beulah Heights was donated to the Salvation Army for a rescue home for girls.

Another parachurch project was the campground called "Elim Groves" at Cazadera. Notable pentecostal and nonpentecostal leaders ministered there.

George and Carrie Judd Montgomery (shown here with their daughter, Faith Berry, in about 1907), who were a team for four decades, she as a minister and editor and he as a supporting husband and businessman.

5. Involvement in the Pentecostal Movement.

Always interested in a deeper spiritual experience, Montgomery became aware of the pentecostal revival and began to pray for the baptism in the Holy Spirit. She received the experience at the home of a friend in Chicago in 1908. Due in part to her image as a moderate pentecostal, Montgomery maintained relationships with nonpentecostals, including A. B. Simpson and other Alliance leaders. Following a missionary trip around the world in 1909, she ministered in two of Simpson's services and spoke at four other CMA conventions. Several CMA ministers were influenced to seek a pentecostal experience, including ʾD. W. Kerr and ʾJohn Salmon.

After her baptism in the Spirit, Montgomery began publishing articles about the pentecostal outpouring around the world. Her emphasis on holiness in *Triumphs of Faith* shifted to that of power, but she never neglected holiness and divine healing themes.

One of the points that helped Montgomery maintain credibility with her nonpentecostal friends was her position on speaking in tongues. She highly valued her own experience but believed some people in the pentecostal movement had given tongues too prominent a place in the church. Her emphasis was on unity and love. She was a charter member of the General Council of the ʾAssemblies of God.

After Montgomery's death in 1946, the organization continued publishing *Triumphs of Faith* as a ministry to missionaries into the 1970s.

■ **Bibliography:** D. Albrecht, "The Life and Ministry of Carrie Judd Montgomery," (research paper, Western Evangelical Sem., 1984) ■ C. Judd, *The Prayer of Faith* (1880) ■ C. Montgomery, *Under His Wings* (1936) ■ R. Niklaus, J. Sawin, and S. Stoesz, *All for Jesus* (1986) ■ "With Christ," *PE* (July 26, 1946).

■ W. E. Warner

MONTGOMERY, GRANVILLE HARRISON (1903–66).

ʾPentecostal Holiness Church (PHC) pastor, superintendent, evangelist, and editor. Best known as editor of ʾOral Roberts' publications (1952–61). Born into poverty in the coal-mining community of Merrimac, VA, Montgomery left school at age 12 to work in the mines to supplement his family's income after his father's death. He was converted in 1918 after two women founded a PHC nearby. He was issued a PHC license when he was 16 and later graduated from Holmes Bible and Missionary Institute (later Holmes Bible College). He also taught for a year at this school.

During the 1920s and 1930s Montgomery pastored in the South and East. In 1937 he began devoting his time to writing and evangelism, becoming the editor of the *Pentecostal Holiness Advocate* (1937–49). During part of this period he also served as editor for all PHC publications, managed the PHC publishing house, and was superintendent of evangelism.

Oral Roberts, who was himself a member of the denomination at the time, hired Montgomery to edit his publications in 1952. During the nearly 10 years with Roberts, Montgomery wrote most of Roberts' many books. He also left the PHC during this time and joined the ʾOpen Bible Standard Churches.

After leaving Roberts in 1961, Montgomery edited *The Christian Challenge,* published by ʾJack Coe's widow, Juanita. A series of critical articles he wrote on some of the practices in the salvation-healing movement and published in the *Challenge* created friction with some of his pentecostal friends.

In 1963 Montgomery joined the staff of Defenders of the Christian Faith (founded by Gerald B. Winrod) and became editor and president, which he remained until his death. Defenders published his biography, *This Man Montgomery,* edited by M. L. Flowers, in 1964.

Three of Montgomery's seven children were born deaf. One of these, Paula, ministered to the deaf in Jamaica. His son William is an ʾAssemblies of God (AG) minister, and his daughter Bonnie is married to an AG minister.

In addition to ghost-written books, Montgomery wrote *Practical Holiness* (n.d.); *After Armageddon—What?* (n.d.); *The History of Defenders of the Christian Faith* (1965); and several others. He also founded *The Christian Challenge* magazine in the late 1940s (this name was later used on the Coe publication).

■ **Bibliography:** M. L. Flowers, *This Man Montgomery* (1964).

■ W. E. Warner

MOORE, JENNIE EVANS (1883–1936).

Evangelist and pastor. A gifted, cheerful black woman of high intellect, Jennie E. Moore worked as a maid and lived at 217 N. ʾBonnie Brae Street in Los Angeles. She attended the ʾSeymour-led cottage prayer meetings across the street during the spring of 1906. On Monday, Apr. 9, 1906, she became the first woman in Los Angeles to speak in tongues. She also played the piano, an instrument for which she claimed to have no prior training, and sang in tongues under the inspiration of the Spirit on that occasion. The following Sunday morning (Easter), she worshiped with her regular congregation, the First New Testament Church. After the sermon by Pastor ʾJoseph Smale, she shared her testimony and spoke in tongues. Reaction was quick and mixed, but many of those present accompanied her that week to the newly opened mission on Azusa Street.

From the beginning, Jennie was active at the ʾAzusa Street Mission, where she continued to share her testimony, exhort, and lead in singing. A capable evangelist in her own right, she itinerated in 1907–8 with two other women between Los Angeles and Chicago, where they visited William Durham's mission. While there, she wrote letters home in glowing terms of what a "blessed place" it was.

On May 13, 1908, Jennie married William J. Seymour in a simple ceremony in Los Angeles. The couple are reported to have adopted a daughter. They lived on the second floor of the Azusa Street Mission, where they continued to minister. In 1915 Jennie was listed as one of the trustees of the mission. Following Seymour's death in 1922, Jennie stayed on as pastor. By 1935 her health had deteriorated to the extent that she was hospitalized. She died on July 2, 1936.

■ **Bibliography:** *AF* 1 (8, 1907): 3 ■ 1 (12, 1908): 1 ■ *Confidence* 5 (10, 1912): 232–34 ■ ibid., 5 (11, 1912): 244–45 ■ D. J. Nelson, "For Such a Time as This" (Ph.D. diss., Birmingham, 1981) ■ C. W. Shumway, "Study of 'The Gift of Tongues,'" (A.B. thesis, U. of S. Calif., 1914).   ■ C. M. Robeck Jr.

MOORHEAD, MAX WOOD (1862–1937). Missionary, publisher, educator. Moorhead was born in Erie, PA, on Dec. 7, 1862, and reared an Episcopalian. A bank clerk ambitious for wealth and influence, he converted to Christ at age 21. He attended Amherst College from 1885 to 1889 but did not graduate. At Amherst he overcame doubts about Christ's atonement, struggling with, but finally rejecting, agnosticism. He dedicated his life to missionary service at D. L. Moody's 1886 Northfield Conference. Although there are no existing records of Moorhead having attended Union Theological Seminary in New York City, his name appears on the list of student delegates representing the institution at the first international convention of the Student Volunteer Movement for Foreign Missions in 1891. He went to India as a missionary under the Presbyterian board.

By 1897 in Bombay, Moorhead came to believe divine healing is in Christ's atonement. After earnestly praying for revival for a year, Moorhead attended services in Calcutta conducted in Jan. 1907 by ˒A. G. Garr, the first missionary sent out from the ˒Azusa Street revival in Los Angeles, CA. Moorhead accepted Garr's teaching that tongues were the "Bible evidence" of Spirit baptism and experienced this evidence himself in Mar. 1907. He became an independent itinerant evangelist. To herald the recovery of the gift of tongues, which Moorhead believed would be as widely accepted as healing, he published a free periodical with worldwide circulation, *Cloud of Witnesses to Pentecost in India* (1907–c. 1910). He published an endorsement of an ill-fated prophecy of Ceylon's destruction by July 1908, repudiating the prediction after its nonfulfillment. After spending 13 years as a missionary in India, Moorhead ministered and taught in England. During WWI he was imprisoned for several months as a German spy due to his objection to patriotic war fervor. Upon release he came to America. Moorhead spent his later years teaching at various schools, including Howard Carter's Bible School in London; Beulah Heights Missionary and Bible Training School, North Bergen, NJ; Buddington

Memorial Bible School, Chicago; and his last post, Elim Bible School, Hornell, NY. Moorhead believed himself to be a "manifest son of God," having "victory over death," which caused confusion for like-minded Elim ministers when he suddenly died on May 2, 1937.

■ **Bibliography:** M. W. Moorhead, "A Personal Testimony," *Cloud of Witnesses to Pentecost in India* (Sept. 1907) ■ Obituary, *Elim Pentecostal Herald* (May 1937), 6–7.   ■ D. J. Rodgers

MORGAN, ARTHUR THEODORE (1901–67). General superintendent of the ˒United Pentecostal Church (UPC) from 1951 to 1967. Although born in Texas, Morgan grew to adulthood in Louisiana. In 1929 he was ordained in the ˒Pentecostal Assemblies of the World but later joined the Pentecostal Ministerial Alliance. He pastored in Louisiana and Texas. In 1944–45 he served as the superintendent of the South Central District of the ˒Pentecostal Church, Inc. Morgan also served as secretary-treasurer of the Texas District of the UPC from 1945 to 1951, when he was elected as general superintendent, a position he held until his death.

■ **Bibliography:** A. L. Clanton, *United We Stand* (1970).
                                                    ■ J. L. Hall

MORGAN HOWARD, CONCEPCIÓN (CHONITA) (1898–1983). Pioneer Mexican-American pentecostal woman evangelist, pastor, and women's leader in the U.S. and Mexico. Born to an Anglo father (Morgan) and Mexican mother, Chonita was converted to pentecostalism in the small mining town of San Jose de las Playitas, Sonora, Mexico. Not long after her conversion in 1913 she felt called to the ministry and went out with some other Mexican converts on horseback to spread the pentecostal message to neighboring Sonoran *pueblos*. She eventually traveled to California, where she came under the influence of George S. Montgomery, who had attended the Azusa Street revival in 1907 and was responsible for bringing the pentecostal work to San Jose de las Playitas.

Chonita began evangelistic work in the U.S. around 1915. In 1919 she met and married a young Anglo pentecostal preacher named Lloyd Howard, who was pastoring a small group of Mexicans in the border town of Pirtleville, AZ. In 1926 the Assemblies of God recognized her evangelistic talent and ordained her an evangelist to the Mexicans living along the Arizona-Mexican border. Chonita served as the second president (Sunshine Ball was the first—1927–40) of the Women's Missionary Council (Concilio Misionero Feminil) from 1941 to 1962 and was responsible for instigating important projects such as Plan Mundial (World Ministries) to raise funds for foreign missionaries and the Home for the Aged Project. The Women's

Missionary Council saw tremendous growth under her talented and creative leadership. From 1966 to 1968 she pastored Betel Asamblea de Dios in Douglas, AZ. Chonita conducted pioneer evangelistic work in California, Arizona, New Mexico, and Sonora, Mexico, from 1915 to 1968. Her 53-year pioneer ministry touched the lives of thousands of Mexican Americans and Mexicans and helped establish the pentecostal work among Latinos on both sides of the U.S.–Mexican border.

■ **Bibliography:** G. Espinosa, "'Your Daughters Shall Prophesy': A Comparative Study of Women's Roles in the Latino Assemblies of God and the Apostolic Assembly," in *Women and Twentieth-Century Protestantism*, ed. M. L. Bendroth and V. L. Brereton (1998). ■ G. Espinosa

MORROW, PETER (1930–), and **ANNE** (1939–). Peter Morrow is an Australian-born former Anglican high school art teacher. Following his conversion to pentecostalism, he was a student in ▸Ray Jackson's Bible school in 1952 and later engaged in informal evangelistic work for some years in Australia, New Zealand, and the U.S. On his return to N.Z. in the late 1950s, Morrow assisted ▸Rob Wheeler and ▸A. S. Worley in their evangelistic campaigns, particularly in the initial follow-up of converts. He moved to Christchurch, N.Z., in late 1962 to take over the pastorate of the newly formed Christchurch Revival Centre (later renamed Christchurch New Life Centre). Morrow's open attitude toward other churches enabled him to have considerable influence on the nascent charismatic movement in the late 1960s. This was through teaching meetings, such as those held at "Adullam's Cave" (a coffee bar run by his church), and personal contact. By the late 1970s, Morrow's congregation had grown to more than 1,000, making it one of the largest pentecostal churches in New Zealand.

Anne Morrow's ministry alongside her husband has also contributed to this growth. She has taken a strong leadership role in women's issues. In particular, she organized and led the 1977 "Save Our Homes Campaign" (a conservative Christian convention intended to provide a balance to what was perceived as destructive radical feminism). She also coordinated the New Life Churches' responses to the 1984 "Forums on the United Nations Convention of the Elimination of All Forms of Discrimination against Women" and acted as spokesperson for these responses. She has led the movement toward greater recognition of women's ministry roles in the New Life Churches.

Peter Morrow was also spokesperson for the South Island New Life Churches. This senior role, together with his international standing as a conference speaker, led to his recognition as an "apostle" by the movement in 1987. Morrow has suffered ill health in recent years, largely due to a savage attack (which nearly cost him his life) by a machete-wielding former psychiatric patient.

■ **Bibliography:** B. Knowles, "For the Sake of the Name: A History of the 'New Life Churches' from 1942 to 1965" (thesis, U. of Otago, 1988) ■ idem, "Some Aspects of the History of the New Life Churches of New Zealand 1960–1990" (diss., U. of Otago, 1994). ■ B. Knowles

MORTON, PAUL S., JR. (1950–). Baptist charismatic pastor. Paul Sylvester Morton was born in Windsor, Ont., Canada, on July 30, 1950. He is the son of the late Bishop C. L. and Matilda E. Morton. As a boy he demonstrated a special musical talent, singing with his brothers. He attended St. Clair College in Windsor. In 1967 he felt called to preach. In 1972 he moved to New Orleans, LA, where he assumed the position of assistant pastor to Percy Simpson at the Greater St. Stephen Missionary Baptist Church. Subsequently, he graduated from Union Baptist Seminary of Louisiana.

In 1974 Percy Simpson died accidentally, and Paul S. Morton was installed as pastor the following year. Phenomenal growth followed, culminating in the building of a 4,000-seat sanctuary in 1992. Morton officiates at five services per Sunday in two locations. Greater St. Stephen Full Gospel Baptist Church now has more than 18,000 active members.

In 1993 Morton was elevated to bishop. Subsequently, he founded the Full Gospel Baptist Church Fellowship and serves as presiding bishop. Morton also is president of the Greater St. Stephen Full Gospel Baptist College of Ministry and Theological Seminary.

Morton has a daily radio broadcast, *Striving for Excellence*, and several local television broadcasts as well as a nationally televised program aired Sunday mornings on Black Entertainment Television (BET). His many books include *It's Time for the Outpouring; What Is the Full Gospel Baptist Church?* and *Why Kingdoms Fall.* He also has recorded five albums with the Greater St. Stephen Mass Choir. Morton is married to Debra Brown (1977). They have three children: Jasmine, Paul Jr., and Christiann. ■ S. M. Burgess; J. Zeigler

MORTON, TONY (1950–). Teacher, apostle, founder of Cornerstone Ministries (now known as c.net). Born in Liverpool and raised in a non-Christian context, he became a Christian while studying in London in 1967, after which he studied Spanish and theology at Southampton University. He was first introduced to the church in a Reformed context and was then baptized in the Spirit in 1970. After a period in advertising and public relations, he trained as a teacher.

During this time Morton and his wife, Hannah, helped establish what is now the 1,000-member Community

Church Southampton, founded in 1982. This fast-growing church became a center for spiritual life, laying emphasis on fellowship, worship, and prayer. ʼArthur Wallis joined the team to further establish it and remained on the team for the rest of his life. Morton was considerably influenced by Wallis's teaching on revival and prayer, which has become a central focus for the church.

The Cornerstone team was established in 1982 to plant contemporary and powerful churches. By 1997 there were 35 churches in the U.K. In Southampton an innovative and flexible approach to church life has produced, among other things, a youth congregation and a conscious decision to plant culturally relevant congregations in capital cities, including Johannesburg, Brussels, Mumbai (Bombay), and London. Altogether more than 15 nations have been impacted.

Morton's books include *Covenant People* (1986), *Developing Prophets and Prophecy in the Local Church* (1992), and *Leadership Skills Course*, a training manual.

■ W. K. Kay

MOSS, VIRGINIA E. (1875–1919). Pastor and educator.
With a great-grandmother who had been a country preacher and a mother active in Woman's Christian Temperance Union crusades in the mid 1870s, the idea of feminine involvement in preaching and social work was not new to Virginia E. Moss.

Born in Susquehanna, PA, Moss suffered from frail health and various ailments her entire life. With her husband, she moved in 1899 to the Newark, NJ, area, where most of her ministry activities eventually took place, particularly in North Bergen.

A fall on ice when Moss was 13 years old left her with permanent spinal damage. By 1904 paralysis had spread from her waist to her feet. In that year she received a complete healing from this condition. With the healing came a consecration to Christian service. Her testimony was warmly received by many, but not by the pastor and members of the local Methodist church to which she belonged. Home prayer meetings with other believers led to the opening of the Door of Hope Mission on Feb. 7, 1906. Although emphasizing evangelism and faith healing, the mission also cared for wayward women.

Upon reading in a West Coast publication, *The Triumphs of Faith*, published by Carrie Judd Montgomery, that the "latter rain" was falling, Moss began to seek a deeper work of the Holy Spirit. She and several others traveled to Nyack in the summer of 1907 because "there a meeting was being held for the purpose of seeking God, and the baptism of the Holy Ghost and fire, and speaking in tongues." One member of their party received the baptism in the Spirit and spoke in tongues at the meeting. After this, others at the Door of Hope Mission sought for the pentecostal baptism and con-

sequently spoke in tongues, which Moss also received after the Nyack visit. Nightly services were held through 1908 to assist other seekers; outstanding healings were also recorded.

Moss felt led to open a "rest home" (ʼFaith Homes) in 1909. This ministry, as well as her mission, enlarged in 1910 when property was purchased in North Bergen. There the work proceeded as the Beulah Heights Assembly.

A view of the world in need of the gospel was never far from Moss's thoughts. Her mother had been called to go to India but never went. Remorse over this failure haunted the mother, but the daughter determined to aid the cause of world evangelization. She recounted that the Lord spoke to her and said, "I want witnesses of my Word and Spirit to go forth from a Missionary Training School at Beulah." Aware that many pentecostals viewed formal theological education with suspicion, since the baptism in the Spirit supposedly made this unnecessary, she nevertheless heeded Paul's admonition to Timothy: "Study to shew thyself approved unto God …" (2 Tim. 2:15 KJV) and opened the Beulah Heights Bible and Missionary Training School in 1912.

Many early graduates of this school distinguished themselves in Assemblies of God (AG) foreign missions. Two later field directors, ʼHenry B. Garlock (Africa) and ʼMaynard L. Ketcham (India and the Far East) attended this school. Other notable graduates included Edgar Barrick (India), ʼFrank Finkenbinder (Latin America), John Juergensen (Japan), Lillian Merian Riggs (Africa), Marie Stephany (North China), and Fred Burke (South Africa).

Virginia "Mother" Moss died in 1919 after directing the school for 7 years and the church for 13. The church and school eventually became closely linked to the AG for several years. Later the school was renamed the Metropolitan Bible Institute and was operated by the New York–New Jersey District of the AG for several years.

■ **Bibliography:** G. B. McGee, "Three Notable Women in Pentecostal Ministry," *AGH* 1 (1986) ■ V. E. Moss, *Following the Shepherd* (1919).   ■ G. B. McGee

MOUNT SINAI HOLY CHURCH OF AMERICA
Founded in 1924 by ʼIda Robinson, pastor in the ʼUnited Holy Church, as a pentecostal denomination giving full rights to women as bishops and elders. The predominantly black denomination has grown from its beginnings in Philadelphia to more than 120 churches in 16 states and the District of Columbia, with foreign missions in Cuba and Guyana, a nursing home, and a farm/retreat center. Central to the life of Mount Sinai are (1) the convocation—the annual meeting of bishops, ministers, and delegates who oversee organization, doctrine, and appointments; (2) doctrine, based on the Apostles' Creed, with special emphasis on the life of Christ (his virgin birth, miracles, crucifixion, resurrection, and sec-

ond coming), the baptism of the Holy Spirit as a gift of God upon a sanctified life, and the tribulation and great white throne judgment; (3) the ordinances of baptism, communion, footwashing, blessing of children, and tithing, along with emphasis on marriage with strict prohibitions against divorce and remarriage; and (4) the standard, a set of rules governing principles of holy conduct, including prohibitions against alcohol, tobacco, artificial adornings, secret societies, and arms-bearing in military service.

■ **Bibliography:** A. Fauset, *Black Gods of the Metropolis* (1944) ■ M. M. Fisher, "Organized Religion and the Cults," *Crisis* 44 (Jan. 1937) ■ C. Gilkes, "The Roles of Church and Community Mothers," *Journal of Feminist Studies in Religion* 2 (1, 1986) ■ *The Manual of the Mount Sinai Holy Church* (1984) ■ J. Ratliffe, "The Enabling of a Local Pentecostal Congregation to Rethink the Role of Women in the Church" (D.Min. thesis, Interdenominational Theological Center, Atlanta, GA, 1976) ■ H. D. Trulear, "Reshaping Black Pastoral Theology: The Vision of Ida B. Robinson," *Journal of Religious Thought* 48 (1989).   ■ H. D. Trulear

MÜHLEN, HERIBERT (1927–). One of the most prominent Catholic theologians to be renewed in the Spirit. Ordained in 1955, Mühlen was professor of dogmatics at Paderborn (Germany, 1964–97). Author of two major works on the Holy Spirit, *Una Mystica Persona* (1964) and *Der Heilige Geist als Person* (1969), Mühlen experienced the Spirit through his contact with pentecostals at the Catholic-Pentecostal ›Dialogue, in which he participated (1972–77, 1985–86). From the mid 1970s until the late 1980s Mühlen was the foremost leader of Charismatische Gemeinde Erneuerung (Charismatic Parish Renewal; CGE) in the Catholic Church in West Germany. He advocated a form of renewal fully integrated into the church's pastoral structures and differentiated from the worldwide Catholic charismatic renewal. He has been coeditor of *Erneuerung in Kirche und Gesellschaft (Renewal in Church and Society)* since its foundation in 1977. In 1990 Mühlen distanced himself from the CGE and founded a new organization called Credo, for which he wrote a handbook entitled *Neu mit Gott* (1990).

Mühlen has written extensively on the Spirit's role in the renewal of church life. Only *A Charismatic Theology* (1978) and a few articles are available in English, e.g., in *One in Christ* and *Theological Renewal*.   ■ P. D. Hocken

MÜLHEIM ASSOCIATION (MA). The oldest segment of German pentecostalism. The Mülheim Association, the Christliche Gemeinschaftsverband GmbH Mülheim/Ruhr, was formed when the pentecostal issue, especially the gift of tongues, split the Gemeinschaftsbewegung, the network of Holiness groupings within the state churches. Though MA was formed in 1913, Mülheim had been the site of annual pentecostal conferences since 1907 and was the home base of MA's first president, ›Emil Humburg. From the start, MA was an interdenominational movement, rather like the Christian and Missionary Alliance, with member fellowships from the state churches (Lutheran and Reformed), such as those of E. Edel and C. O. Voget, and from free assemblies; the MA thus included both pedobaptists and practitioners of believer's baptism. Its most respected teacher was ›J. Paul.

MA never defined itself against other traditions, and thus (unusual for a pentecostal group) some congregations upheld the historic creeds as well as the Lutheran Augsburg Confession. Despite this ecumenicity, MA was even more firmly rejected by German evangelicals in the ›Berlin Declaration than the pentecostal movement in other countries. MA affirms all the spiritual gifts without requiring glossolalia as initial evidence for baptism in the Spirit. Holiness of life is a major emphasis, continuing a Keswick-type emphasis on victory over sin. MA published *Pfingstgrüsse* monthly from 1909; it was renamed *Grüsse aus dem Heiligtum* in 1919, and is now known as *Heilszeugnisse (Testimonies of Grace)*. MA, which has increasingly become a form of independent free church, has been open to some ecumenical contacts since 1967. Membership has declined over the years and now totals 3,180 committed members.

See also EUROPEAN PENTECOSTALISM.

■ **Bibliography:** W. J. Hollenweger, *The Pentecostals* (1972) ■ idem, "'Touching' and 'Thinking' the Spirit: Some Aspects of European Charismatics" in R. P. Spittler, ed., *Perspectives on the New Pentecostalism* (1976) ■ C. Krust, *50 Jahre Deutsche Pfingstbewegung* (1976) ■ idem, *Was wir glauben, lehren und bekennen* (1963).   ■ P. D. Hocken

MULUNGO, LAURENTINO (1922–). Born in 1922 in Mozambique into a Muslim family, Mulungo was converted to Christ in 1936 and was one of the few believers left by the Canadian missionary ›Austin Chawner at Maputo. His joyful, Contagious, and positive spirit has helped sustain him through many trials, including six years of imprisonment under the Communist regime in Mozambique. This same spirit has endeared him to many thousands of the people of Mozambique. He attributes any success to prayer and complete reliance on the Lord. He has traveled extensively in ministry, especially in Mozambique, and has also visited a number of countries in Africa and Europe.

During the years of the war for independence against the Portuguese and the civil war that followed, Mulungo traveled constantly on country roads frequented by rebel soldiers, and when warned of the dangers, he responded that everyone needed to be ministered to. In Maputo alone he has 38,000 believers in his church. He began to implement the cell-group concept many years ago, and today there are at least 106 such groups under the leadership of Mulungo's team. Some of the groups are large and would normally be considered churches (he does not restrict the size of a cell to any particular number). Apart from cell groups Mulungo also has a number of churches. In Maputo all those from the cell groups gather on the first Sunday of each month at the main church for a communion service. The building is of a warehouse type and is packed wall to wall with people. Those who cannot enter press in on the outside. Although most evangelism is through the cell groups, it is apparent that these services are themselves tools for evangelism, and it is not unusual to see 60 new converts at one of these Sunday meetings. Mulungo continues to be active after 59 years in ministry.

■ **Bibliography:** D. J. Garrard, unpub. private papers (including e-mail from Bill Mercer, PAOC missionary, Maputo, Mozambique, Apr. 10, 1998). ■ D. J. Garrard

MUMFORD, BERNARD C., JR. (BOB) (1930–). Bible teacher, author. Mumford was born Dec. 29, 1930, in Steubenville, OH. At age 12 he was converted to Christ at a Church of the Nazarene revival meeting in Roanoke, VA, but soon fell away and was, as he described it, "in a backslidden state for twelve years." Mumford joined the navy and recommitted his life to Christ at an Assemblies of God (AG) church in Atlantic City, NJ, while home on leave in 1954.

After his discharge from the navy, Mumford attended a small AG Bible college and graduated in 1959. While in college Mumford married Judith. The Mumfords spent the year after graduation in the Medical Missionary Training Institute in Toronto, Ont. Ordained as an AG minister, Mumford briefly served as an evangelist and pastored for two years a small church in Kane, PA. In 1963 Mumford began teaching at the Elim Bible Institute in NY State, and over the next three years he served as academic dean and dean of men. After hearing pentecostal ecumenist David du Plessis speak at the college, Mumford felt a profound call to minister transdenominationally.

In 1966 Mumford left Elim to attend the Episcopal Reformed Seminary in Philadelphia. During his years in seminary, Mumford began to travel, ministering for ▸Full Gospel Business Men's Fellowship International (FGBMFI), World Missionary Assistance Plan (World MAP), the ▸Holy Spirit Teaching Mission (HSTM), and other charismatic conferences. While in seminary he also pastored briefly in Wilmington, DE. He graduated from seminary in 1969 and moved to Southern California, where he taught a weekly Bible class at ▸Melodyland Christian Center that was attended by hundreds. In 1970 Eldon Purvis of HSTM invited Mumford to move to Ft. Lauderdale to be a part of a team of charismatic leaders.

Mumford became formally associated with ▸Don Basham, ▸Derek Prince, and ▸Charles Simpson in 1970, and with Canadian pentecostal leader ▸Ern Baxter in 1974. Together the five men became leaders of the controversial ▸shepherding movement. Mumford's popularity made him the celebrity leader of the movement, and he more than any other was the target of criticism during the shepherding controversy.

Mumford, considered by many "a Bible teacher of real genius," was in demand as a speaker in the heyday of the charismatic renewal. He continued to be a popular charismatic speaker during the 1970s, delivering a plenary-session message at the 1977 Kansas City Conference on Charismatic Renewal in the Churches that inspired more than 20 minutes of continuous praise to God.

Mumford remained associated with the shepherding movement until its dissolution at the end of 1986. Mumford continues his teaching and writing ministry, LifeChangers, from Raleigh, NC.

■ **Bibliography:** B. Ghezzi, "Bob Mumford after Discipleship," *Charisma* (Aug. 1987) ■ B. Mumford, *Focusing on Present Issues* (1979) ■ idem, "Mumford: Application, Not Doctrine Was Flawed," *Christianity Today* (Mar. 1990). ■ S. D. Moore

MURRAY, GEORGE A. (c. 1860–1909), and **ANNIE** (d. 1912). Pentecostal pioneers in Toronto, Ont. Natives of Dundee, Scotland, and married in 1889, the Murrays both suffered from lifelong handicaps, George being lame in both feet and Annie blind in both eyes. Hearing God's call, they went as missionaries to Palestine in 1890, initially unsponsored but later associated with the ▸Christian and Missionary Alliance. Moving to Toronto in 1904, the Murrays were baptized in the Spirit soon after "Pentecost" arrived in the city, and they opened a pentecostal mission at Concord and Hepbourne.

Teachers of ▸Keswick-type Holiness doctrine, they were committed to pentecostal unity, and George became secretary of the United Pentecostal Missions of Toronto, a voluntary association that organized the citywide convention in Oct. 1908. After George's death in Aug. 1909, Annie responded to a call to India, where she served in Bombay from 1910 until her death in 1912. ■ P. D. Hocken

MUSIC, PENTECOSTAL AND CHARISMATIC

I. The Roots of Pentecostal-Charismatic Music
   A. *Biblical Influences*
      1. Old Testament Practices
      2. New Testament Practices
   B. *Historical-Musical Influences*
      1. Reform and Revival
      2. Early American Music
      3. The Gospel Hymn

II. The Tradition Develops
  A. *The New Hymnals*
  B. *Choral Music and Chorus Singing*
  C. *Music Education*

III. Expansion and New Directions
  A. *Contemporary Christian Music*
  B. *The Charismatic Renewal*
  C. *Blended Worship*

IV. Coming of Age
  A. *Organization of Music Ministry*
  B. *Music Education*
  C. *Music and Media*
  D. *Toward the Future*

The pentecostal movement has long been distinguished for the important role it gives to music in all aspects of the lives of its adherents. Fervent, spiritual singing is and has been typical of the pentecostal-charismatic tradition of worship. The value of music for the worship, evangelism, education, and nurture of the church has emerged as a major emphasis of the movement. Music occupies a vital place in the religious experience of typical pentecostal-charismatic believers, expressing a wide range of economic, political, and social values; styles of worship; and musical tastes.

Music can be a powerful influence when it is performed by devout believers and anointed by the presence of the Holy Spirit. This spiritual approach, encompassing a variety of music types and styles, is an identifying characteristic of music associated with the pentecostal-charismatic tradition

Hymn singing in Texas, 1915.

and has its basis in both the Bible and historical church traditions.

I. THE ROOTS OF PENTECOSTAL-CHARISMATIC MUSIC.

The roots of music representing the pentecostal-charismatic tradition run deep and strong. They are firmly embedded in scriptural practices yet influenced by the historical traditions of Christian church music. From the beginning of the 20th century, music of the pentecostal tradition has emphasized a heartfelt, sincere, and enthusiastic approach to singing and instrumental performance. Early revival meetings typically saw worshipers caught up in the exuberant and spirited singing of gospel hymns. Their singing was joyful in spirit and consisted primarily of congregational expressions of praise and testimony. Often the singing was a capella or accompanied only by guitar or pump organ. It was spontaneous, exuberant, and sometimes included "singing in tongues." Music was part of the believers' church experience before, during, and after the service. Early accounts tell of singing, praising, hand clapping, shouting, and even dancing unto the Lord.

Following what they believed to be the NT model, early pentecostal believers placed little emphasis on ritual and ceremony in worship. Adherents of such bodies as the Assemblies of God (AG), Church of God (CG), Pentecostal Holiness Church (PHC), Church of God of Prophecy (CGP), International Church of the Foursquare Gospel (ICFG), Church of God in Christ (COGIC), Pentecostal Assemblies of Canada (PAOC), and more recently, charismatic groups developing within the traditional denominations, believe worship to be primarily a matter of the heart and personally oriented. They have developed an attitude of freedom in worship that they perceive to have existed in the early church.

The movement has emphasized congregational participation through singing and performing a variety of types and styles of music. Most important, perhaps, this tradition recognizes the work of the Holy Spirit in guiding and influencing the experience of the individual in both corporate and private worship. The importance of singing and performing with the aid and direction of the Holy Spirit is a central aspect of pentecostal-charismatic music.

This attitude quite naturally leads to musical expression and ministry that tends to be less liturgical and formal in its organization and practice than many Christian church traditions. Music comes to be more subjective in its expression, and it is demonstrably emotional in its style of performance. Consequently, pentecostal-charismatic music has some characteristic qualities in both sound and concept that distinguish it from other eras and practices of both liturgical and evangelical traditions.

A. Biblical Influences.

The importance of music in the life of believers can be seen throughout Scripture. Music is an integral part of the universe, born in the heart of God (Job 38:7; Isa. 14:7; 44:23). Scripture reveals that God created music, both sacred and secular, and established it as part of the total lifestyle of his people (Ex. 15:1–21; Josh. 6:4–5).

In addition, God provided for the use of music in the worship and the training programs of the temple and tabernacle (2 Chron. 5:11–14; Pss. 100:1–2; 150).

Finally, God designed and established music as a specialized ministry within the church, to be well organized and spiritually administered (1 Chron. 16:1–10; 2 Chron. 29:25–28). An analysis of musical interests and practices within the pentecostal-charismatic movement reveals a significant influence of these biblical models on the organization of programs, manner of performance in worship, and acceptance of diversity of style.

1. Old Testament Practices.

The role of music in ministry and praise and worship, both vocal and instrumental, is modeled in the OT. Music was intended not only for religious functions but also for secular purposes, such as call to battle, celebration, work activities, and social life.

The music and worship of the tabernacle and temple provide organizational models for music ministry, including emphasis on congregational singing, prominent use of choirs and special singers, and love and appreciation of instrumental music (1 Chron. 16:37–42; 25:1–6; 2 Chron. 5:11–14).

Perhaps the most significant OT influence is the importance placed on singing psalms and other Scriptures. This practice has enjoyed immense popularity, especially in pentecostal-charismatic music from 1970 to the present. Yet the earliest pentecostals used the various psalters that were popular during the late 19th century along with traditional hymnals. In addition, they made liberal use of various kinds of musical instruments. The rise of singing psalms and Scripture songs, as well as the rebirth of dance in worship, in the charismatic movement is directly attributed to OT examples. And this resurgence of singing choruses and Scripture songs, along with spontaneous, exuberant worship has spread widely in nonpentecostal settings, in large part because of the influence of the pentecostal-charismatic movement.

2. New Testament Practices.

In the earliest years of pentecostalism, music was a vital and expected part of church life and ministry, home, street meetings, jail services, and even work activity (Conn, 1977, 109, 158, 180, 196). The heavy dependence of the pentecostal-charismatic tradition on the NT for doctrine and lifestyle also helped to shape its beliefs and ideas concerning the use of music.

Variety in music forms and tastes is a strong characteristic of the pentecostal-charismatic tradition that derives from the NT. The gospel hymn, traditional hymn, chorus, gospel song, and Scripture song are all part of the repertory enjoyed by congregations and individuals. The acceptance of diversity can be most attributed perhaps to Paul's writings to the Colossians and Ephesians, in which he suggests at least three different song types or texts. In Col. 3:16 (KJV) the apostle writes, "Let the word of Christ dwell in you richly in all wisdom; teaching and admonishing one another in psalms and hymns and spiritual songs, singing with grace in your hearts to the Lord." Music historians have corroborated the early Christian practice of using song types other than OT psalms (Reese, 1940). Even the earliest music services of the AG, CG, and PHC churches used a variety of song types. Spontaneous songs, psalms, gospel hymns, and later gospel songs and praise choruses all gained common use and popularity.

This appreciation and tolerance of different music styles also applied to performance. Using guitars, rhythm instruments, and keyboards together with various combinations of traditional band and orchestral instruments has become the norm. The AG music program had been particularly distinctive in its use of musical instruments in the church. Instrumental music combined with solo, group, and eventually choral singing all came to be accepted components to supplement the fervent, enthusiastic congregational singing so typical of the movement. This inclusiveness continues today as a prominent feature of pentecostal-charismatic music.

The psalm represents inspired text given by God to humanity to express various themes and emotions. The hymn embodies the believer's expression of praise, thanksgiving, and

The music band of the Truth Bible Institute in China.

prayer to God. The gospel song offers to the believer and nonbeliever alike a vehicle for testimony and prophecy. These comprise the basic elements for developing a rich and satisfying music ministry in the pentecostal-charismatic tradition. Chorus singing, Scripture songs, praise, and dance are elements that evolved later out of this background.

The manner of singing—spirited, enthusiastic, jubilant, with purpose—so typical of pentecostal music during the entire history of the movement is also perceived to be based on biblical example. In 1 Cor. 14:15 (KJV), Paul encourages edification of the church through singing: "I will sing with the spirit, and I will sing with the understanding also." These two concepts—spiritual or spirited singing, and communicative or impactive singing—can be described as a double-stranded thread that weaves through the entire fabric of pentecostal-charismatic music.

Music and singing that call for the performer's involvement emotionally and physically, while making provision for the prompting, directing, and moving of the Holy Spirit, are thought to be both necessary and good. Yet it is also deemed necessary that music effectively communicate the text, its message, and its meaning in their intellectual dimension. Above all, emphasis is on the anointing of the Holy Spirit, and for many this includes "singing in tongues."

B. Historical-Musical Influences.

Numerous musical styles, approaches, and practices of the past have influenced pentecostal-charismatic music, but it is music most directly associated with evangelical reform that has had the greatest impact. Church music from A.D. 300 to 1500 is important primarily in relation to the significance it had for music born out of the Protestant Reformation.

1. Reform and Revival.

Out of the Reformation came an understanding of the importance of the effective use of hymns for worship and for individual and corporate expression of doctrine and faith. Martin Luther's contribution through his chorales is fundamental to the development of hymn singing in the evangelical movement. Even so, the psalter long remained the basic songbook of the reform movement, while the hymn achieved popularity and widespread use more slowly.

Hymn singing became the most popular form of musical expression by the mid 18th century. But the emerging pentecostals in the early 20th century used gospel hymns and psalters along with the traditional hymnals. Describing CG meetings of the early 1900s, C. W. Conn writes that "the meetings were begun with singing, without musical accompaniment unless some person with a guitar happened to bring his instrument along. Such hymns as 'Amazing Grace,' 'Blessed Assurance,' 'At the Cross,' and 'What a Friend We Have in Jesus' were invariably sung, for what is now properly called 'gospel singing' was unknown" (1977, 19). This descrip-

Marimba Band Ecos Cristianos (Christian Echos), Guatemala.

tion applies not just to meetings held in the South but also to practices on the West Coast and in middle America. During this time some use was also made of folk music, spirituals, and simple choruses.

The influence of Luther's thought can be seen not only in the popularity of hymn singing but in the importance placed on music training. This emphasis was reflected in a fondness for presenting weeklong singing schools to develop music-reading skills and to teach new songs. This practice is in vogue today, particularly in rural areas in the southern U.S. Such schools are also enjoyed by nonpentecostals of various denominations.

The works of Isaac Watts, noted English hymn writer of the 18th century, have exerted tremendous influence on the music of evangelicals of the late 18th and 19th centuries and, subsequently, the pentecostal movement of the 20th century. Several of Watts' hymns are favorites in pentecostal-charismatic churches today: "When I Survey the Wondrous Cross," "At the Cross," "O God, Our Help in Ages Past," and "Joy to the World" continue to be sung with conviction and frequency.

The hymns of John and Charles Wesley and the widespread influence of the Wesleyan revival also hold great significance for the Holiness and pentecostal traditions. Typical hymns from Charles Wesley's prolific pen that are still sung today include "Hark the Herald Angels Sing," "Love Divine All Loves Excelling," and "O for a Thousand Tongues to Sing." Charles Wesley's hymns were more personal and intimate than those of Watts. John Wesley was concerned that singing be at the same time spiritual and of good musical quality. His instructions to the congregation included admonishments to "Sing all, sing lustily, sing modestly, sing in time, and above all, sing spiritually" (Reynolds, 1963, 55–56).

2. Early American Music.

The psalms and hymns brought to America by the colonists exerted a direct influence on pentecostal-charismatic music, as did the development of singing schools, which were a popular part of American music in the late 17th and early 18th centuries (Alford, 1967, 43–46). Music associated with the great revival movements of the 18th and 19th centuries, especially the popularity of the folk-oriented hymn (which came to be known as the camp meeting or revival spiritual) also had far-reaching effects on pentecostal-charismatic music.

Black music and Negro spirituals were a major part of these revivals and camp meetings, creating a repertory and tradition that not only influenced white pentecostals from traditional denominations but also provided the basis for much of the rich music expressions of American black pentecostals today. Churches like the COGIC are renowned for their great choirs, soloists, impressive congregational singing, and upbeat instrumental music, all of which have become a major part of the music scene in the 20th century.

The writing of Lowell Mason, Thomas Hastings, George Root, William Bradbury, and Isaac Woodbury continued to expand the popularity and importance of hymns while developing a new form known as the Sunday school song, which is still popular in pentecostal-charismatic churches.

Then there was the shape-note system of music notation, a purely American tradition of music notation and an approach to singing that has strong historical significance. It became the primary vehicle in development of a new form of music composition and style of singing that has flourished in the pentecostal movement since the early 20th century. The work of Andrew Law in the *Music Primer* and Smith and Little in *The Easy Instructor* effectively launched the shape-note tradition in this country.

"The basis of the system was the providing of a simple method of visually identifying the pitch of the note by a particular note shape. These shapes then represented certain pitches, and the singer could find the pitch through the visual shape rather than actually reading the music" (Alford, 1967,

Gospel trio, Malawi.

46). The system began with a four-way—fa, so, la, mi—approach that gave way to a new seven-shape system. Each shape represents one note of the diatonic scale. This system of notation and publishing became extremely popular and influential; it provided an opportunity for development and dissemination of the gospel or "convention song."

3. The Gospel Hymn.

Clearly the gospel hymn occupies a place of great importance in any description of pentecostal-charismatic music. Its value and appropriateness are described by Robert M. Stevenson: "Gospel hymnody has the distinction of being America's most typical contribution to Christian song. . . . Its very obviousness has been its strength. . . . In an age when religion must win mass approval in order to survive, in an age when religion must at least win a majority vote, . . . gospel hymnody is inevitable" (1953, 162).

The gospel hymn (song of testimony) exists in several forms. E. S. Lorenz perhaps best defines the gospel hymn as "a sacred folk song, free in form, emotional in character, devout in attitude, evangelistic in purpose and spirit" (1923, 342). This is an apt description of a form that was to have lasting influence on music of the pentecostal movement.

Along with traditional publishers, several pentecostal denominations joined the early rush to publish these newly popular gospel or convention songs in collections. By the third decade of the 20th century, these collections, or "convention" songbooks, were in wide use in churches, revival meetings, camp meetings, and conventions. Local church choirs made much use of them, and their popularity eventually led to a period of dominance of this form in the pentecostal-charismatic movement. The gospel hymn also encouraged singing by special choirs and groups rather than just by a congregation.

Publishers in the AG (Gospel Publishing House; Melody Music), PHC (Advocate Press), and the CG (Tennessee Music and Printing; Pathway Press) joined with other prominent gospel hymn publishers such as Stamps-Baxter Music, Vaughan Music, and Hartford Music in producing hundreds of collections that spread this type of song and approach to singing throughout the movement. Tennessee Music and Printing Company of the CG has emerged as the single largest producer of gospel hymn collections.

Popular pentecostal writers of gospel hymns during the first four decades of the 20th century included Otis L. McCoy ("I'm on the Battlefield"), Vep Ellis ("Have Faith in God"), Cleavant Derricks ("When God Dips His Love in My Heart"), and ▸Herbert Buffum ("Lift Me Up above the Shadows" and "He Abides"). These were preceded in the genre before the pentecostal era by prominent writers and composers of the late 19th century, e.g., Ira D. Sankey ("I Am Praying for You"); Fanny Crosby ("Blessed Assurance" and "Near the Cross"); William Bradbury ("He Leadeth Me");

James Rowe ("Love Lifted Me"); W. J. Kirkpatrick ("The Comforter Has Come"); and Charles Gabriel ("Send the Light").

Twentieth-century writers whose works are familiar to the pentecostal-charismatic movement have included Norman J. Clayton, John W. Peterson, Thomas A. Dorsey, Charles Weigle, George Schuler, Charles Bartlett, Charles Wycuff, Bill and Gloria Gaither, Albert Brumley, Joe Parks, Ralph Carmichael, Lanny Wolfe, Jack Hayford, Bennie Triplett (CG), Mark Harris (CG), Geron Davis, and Twila Paris (AG).

While the gospel hymn has not had a significant role in the charismatic movement, it has an essential place in the development of music in the pentecostal tradition. Its popularity and influence among a broad spectrum of pentecostal believers are immeasurable.

Denton Alford concludes that "Pentecostal musicians, ministers and believers attach great importance to the use and value of the gospel song in the religious lives of 20th-century Christians. While Pentecostal church music has always encompassed . . . hymns and psalms . . . the very nature of the Pentecostal outreach and ministry has lent itself to an emphasis on the gospel hymn or gospel song" (1967, 49).

II. THE TRADITION DEVELOPS.

The prominence of music in the pentecostal-charismatic movement can be gauged by the time devoted to singing and instrumental music in worship. It is not unusual for up to two-thirds of worship services to be given to music performance. Moreover, music is used in the sanctuary and in the home with equal fervor.

By the 1930s a new style of music called the gospel song had gained prominence. Songs tended to tell the story of redemption—"Oh, Happy Day," "A New Name in Glory"— or announce the second coming of Christ and the joys of an eternity spent in heaven—"When I Take My Vacation in Heaven," "When I Make My Last Move," and "I'll Fly Away." Many songs related experiences of the perceived joys

Singers at the Pacific Area Conference in Suva, Fiji, 1970.

or hardships of the Christian life—"We'll Soon Be Done with Troubles and Trials," "I've Got That Old Time Religion in My Heart," and "Victory in Jesus." Texts were often more experientially oriented than praise or worship related.

The emergence of gospel music and the increasing emphasis placed on training also produced teachers of great renown, such as Homer Rodeheaver, Virgil Stamps, Adgar Pace, and Otis McCoy.

The popularity of the all-male gospel quartet began in the early 1930s and lasted well into the '50s. There seemed to be a particular liking for the timbre of the male voice in the genre of gospel music. These quartets sang in churches, schools, singing conventions, and revivals, and later on radio and television. Their singing style and their music gained immediate acceptance among pentecostals in America, particularly the AG, CG, CGP, PHC, and PAOC. Many of the featured soloists were pentecostals and included such people as James Blackwood, Connor B. Hall, and J. D. Sumner. Eva LeFevre was one of the few female soloists featured with these quartets. Later the quartets developed recording and concert careers, moving out of the churches and onto the stage. Hundreds of groups formed during that era, some of the most prominent being the Blackwood Brothers, the Homeland Harmony Quartet, the Statesmen, and the Singing LeFevres.

For a time, gospel music became primary in the pentecostal-charismatic movement, almost to the exclusion of other forms. This emphasis lasted until the 1950s, when a return to a more middle-of-the-road flavor became the trend.

A. The New Hymnals.

In an effort to become more balanced and retain the best of past traditions while exploring the fresh and new, mainstream pentecostal denominations returned to using hymns, gospel hymns, and other musical forms during the 1950s. Several denominational publishers exerted leadership by compiling, editing, and publishing hymnals for their constituencies.

While these efforts did not produce hymnals of the traditional variety, they did culminate in some noteworthy collections that contain traditional hymns, gospel songs, and music for special occasions and choirs. A popular publication of this type was the *Church Hymnal,* published in 1951 by Tennessee Music and Printing Company of the CG. This hymnal is heavily weighted toward gospel songs, and it has remained popular since its inception, with more than 5 million copies in print. It is used not only by pentecostals but also by churches of many other denominations. The *Foursquare Hymnal,* published in 1957 by the ICFG, and *The Gospel Hymnal,* published in 1973 by Advocate Press of the PHC, are other examples of this type.

Hymns of Glorious Praise, published in 1969 by Gospel Publishing House of the AG, and *Hymns of the Spirit,* published in 1969 by Pathway Press of the CG, are examples of more traditional hymnals. *Singing His Praise,* published in 1991 by the AG, is the most recent example of a pentecostal hymnal.

The broadening musical tastes and interests in the pentecostal-charismatic movement affected repertory, style, and content. Hymn singing witnessed a new prominence, and congregational participation in worship through singing was emphasized once again.

B. Choral Music and Chorus Singing.

During most of the first half of the 20th century, pentecostal congregations were known as singing churches. Congregational singing and participation in worship were identifying characteristics until the 1940s. By this time, due to influences already mentioned, congregational music diminished in favor of performances by soloists and special groups. This trend lasted until the 1960s, when greater balance between congregational singing and choral singing developed.

The '60s ushered in a time of effective use of church choirs, encouraged by the enhancement of choirs and music departments in denominational colleges and Bible training schools. Choral singing fueled the development of local-church sanctuary choirs, youth choirs, and children's choirs and other specialized groups (e.g., camp-meeting choirs and ministers' choirs). In addition, denominational publishers and music departments began publishing choral octavos and collections prominently featuring the compositions and arrangements of pentecostal musicians such as Cyril McClellan, Hope Collins, and Ralph Carmichael of the AG, and Delton Alford of the CG.

Another development was the rise of chorus singing. Fresh, new melodies and texts combined with a simple compositional form to provide an ideal vehicle for corporate and personal praise and worship through music. This development was to blossom a decade or more later and be expressed in the exuberant Scripture and praise songs of the charismatic movement.

C. Music Education.

Of great significance to the music explosion occurring in the pentecostal-charismatic movement during the '60s and '70s was the contribution of colleges and Bible schools of the traditional pentecostal denominations. While the singing school, church music school, and Bible school had always exerted influence in music training, these two decades witnessed an intensified impact of education on music, particularly in institutions of higher learning. These schools were now training not only

A Tommy Barnett album, from the days before Christian music became a part of popular culture.

singers and instrumentalists, but also ministers of music, choral and band directors, and arrangers and composers. Evangel College, Central Bible College, and Southern California College (AG); Lee College (CG); Emmanuel College (PHC); and L.I.F.E. Bible College (ICFG) increased efforts to educate Christian men and women for greater effectiveness through music ministry.

This trend has since grown and enlarged in scope, and today's pentecostal music and musicians still reflect this influence.

III. EXPANSION AND NEW DIRECTIONS.

Beginning in the mid 1960s, there has been rapid growth and development of music as the pentecostal-charismatic revival has grown to worldwide proportions. The U.S. has also witnessed, with the appearance of the megachurches, huge and sophisticated music programs and the opportunity for unprecedented acceptance by the nonpentecostal Christian community. Pentecostal churches are no longer only on "the other side of the tracks," and their influence is growing. The dynamic growth and tension produced by the historical pentecostal-charismatic continuum has exerted considerable influence on pentecostal-charismatic music.

A. Contemporary Christian Music.

Pentecostal musicians have always considered themselves to be contemporary—that is, worshiping through music styles created in their own particular era. In each decade of this century, the music was certainly reflective of contemporary styles: gospel singing, piano styles reminiscent of jazz, popular singing of the quartets, and so on. However, from the mid 1950s to the late '60s, young people in particular became increasingly restless, because what they were hearing in church had little in common with the music they were listening to elsewhere.

Ralph Carmichael, one of the first to notice and respond to this point of alienation between youth and the church, was a popular and talented composer-arranger with roots in the AG. Through his music he attempted to build a bridge between the generations and introduced new styles of music together with "new" instruments, such as drum sets, electric guitars, electric keyboards, and sophisticated electronic sound systems. Herein lies the birth of what is called today contemporary Christian music (CCM). CCM has had far-reaching effects on the entire Christian church, not without stirring controversy and arousing resistance.

The late 1960s ushered in a time (much like the early pentecostal revival) when music was taken out of the church and shared with the world beyond through street services, outdoor concerts, coffee house performances, and the like. Attempts were made to take the message of Jesus anywhere people would listen. Christian bands, vocal groups, soloists, and recording artists came into prominence; many of the writers, arrangers, and star performers were pentecostal-charismatic in background.

Traditions, beliefs, musical tastes, and demographics have all led to the highly pluralistic music ministry found in the pentecostal-charismatic movement today, so much so that an acceptance of "new" and innovative approaches has virtually become the norm.

A few of the major CCM influences important to an understanding of the state of music in the pentecostal-charismatic movement of the 1980s and 1990s include: (1) youth musicals and religious folk music, early 1960s; (2) music of the Jesus Movement, late '60s, early '70s; (3) folk, gospel, and popular artists of the 1950s–'70s; (4) crossover music and middle-of-the-road, easy-listening music, late '70s and '80s; (5) emergence of Christian rock music, late '70s and '80s; (6) popularity of singing choruses and Scripture songs, '60s–'80s; and (7) influence of Christian artists and writers using popular musical forms and ideas such as rock, rap, alternative, jazz, country, and fusion.

Prominent songwriters, some of whom are pentecostal, who made noteworthy contributions during this time include Bill and Gloria Gaither, Andrae Crouch (COGC), Lanny Wolfe (UPC), David Binion (CG), Jack Hayford (ICFG), Steven Curtis Chapman, Kirk Franklin, Michael W. Smith, Mark Harris (CG), and Twila Paris (AG). Artists and groups, many of whom come from the pentecostal-charismatic tradition, who have or have had an impact on CCM include George Beverly Shea, the Cathedrals, Evie Tornquist, Sandi Patti, Amy Grant, the Bill Gaither Trio, Phil Driscoll, Mylon LeFevre, Petra, Steve Taylor, Walter Hawkins, the Imperials, Carman, 4 Him, Point of Grace, BeBe and CeCe Winans, Shirley Cease, Ron Kenoly, and Alvin Slaughter.

B. The Charismatic Renewal.

The charismatic renewal of the mid 20th century has brought about a revival of emphasis on praise and worship in American religious life. Freedom in worship, joyful singing, both vocal and physical expressions of praise, instrumental accompaniment of singing, and acceptance of a wide variety of music styles are all characteristic of this renewal.

As in the early days of the pentecostal revival, it is not unusual to find

"Old-Time Power"—a traditional pentecostal hymn.

charismatic worshipers singing, shouting, clapping hands, leaping, and dancing before the Lord as they offer him sincere praise and thanksgiving. Yet among some classical pentecostals there is discomfort with the freshness and exuberance found in the music of the charismatics. Concern is expressed about dancing, marching, chanting, and frequent clapping of hands; however, there are those who remember when it was usual and expected to find traditional pentecostal believers also dancing before the Lord, happily participating in "Jericho marches" and "singing in the Spirit."

Music contributions of note relating to the charismatic renewal include: (1) the importance of singing psalms and Scripture songs; (2) heavy use of music for praise and worship, not only in the sanctuary but also in conferences, festivals, small groups, home churches, and in private; (3) use of musical instruments, both formally and informally; (4) a return to emphasis on spirited congregational singing, featuring praise leaders rather than choirs; (5) use of spontaneous and choreographed dance and pageantry; (6) use of drama, mime, and hand-signing; and (7) emphasis on the prophetic role of the musician.

C. Blended Worship.

The 1990s witnessed rapid growth and change in the pentecostal/charismatic churches in both worship and music. The emergence of megachurches, multicultural churches, urban and inner-city ministries, and the "revival explosion" all created a need for a more diverse and blended approach. New paradigms for the worship and revival experience created opportunity for diversification, inclusion and assimilation of styles, forms, and expressions of music in the life of the believer.

Key influences in the development of blended music and a blended multicultural worship include the Brownsville, FL, revival (AG), Christian television networks, renewed emphasis on praise and worship, and contemporary Christian music groups such as the Brooklyn Tabernacle Choir (NY), Christ Church Choir (TN), and Saints in Praise (CA; COGIC).

IV. COMING OF AGE.

The first century of music in the pentecostal-charismatic movement has culminated in the development of a strong, biblically based, experientially oriented ministry that draws from many traditions and styles. Pentecostal-charismatic music can be said to have come of age through the development of music traditions by classical pentecostals, the charismatic infusion of new perspectives, and the response to the popularity and acceptance of contemporary Christian music. It is not only thriving and surviving but also exerting influence on music ministry ideals of other traditions. This maturity can be seen in several particular areas of influence.

A. Organization of Music Ministry.

Churches and denominations within the pentecostal-charismatic movement have begun to develop and organize music ministries of substance with programs that effectively use music in worship, evangelism, education, and Christian growth. The liturgy of the pentecostal-charismatic worship service itself has developed more meaningfully. Larger churches have begun to develop impressive, sophisticated music ministries with graded choral programs, instrumental and orchestral programs, music schools and academies of the arts, production of musicals, cantatas, and pageants featuring music.

Some denominations have also begun to sponsor general programs and departments of music (e.g., CG, AG, CGP) to effectively meet the growing needs of music ministry.

B. Music Education.

Church music schools, conferences, seminars, and festivals are constantly being developed in all corners of the pentecostal-charismatic movement to provide avenues for effective training. Denominational institutions of higher learning have been joined by independent schools within the tradition in producing music degree programs for the development of performers, composer-arrangers, music ministers, and professionals who are competent musically yet sensitive to pentecostal-charismatic distinctives. Institutions of notable achievement include Evangel University and Central Bible College (AG), Lee University (CG), Patten College (AG), Emmanuel College (PHC), and Oral Roberts University (independent).

Denominational and independent publishers have contributed to the impact of education by providing music resources. Music publishers of influence include Pathway Music and SpiritSound Music Group (both CG), Melody Music and Radiant Music (both AG), and a number of independents: Hosanna-Integrity Music, Lexicon-Light Music, Maranatha, Vineyard, and Word.

C. Music and Media.

Opportunities for music outreach through media ministries are abundant, and pentecostal-charismatic churches often use music as a part of their media ministries. Formats have changed and expanded in relation to the technology of the time.

Radio broadcasting has long been a popular endeavor for pentecostal-charismatic ministers and churches. The format and quality of the broadcast often depends on the type of church or ministry it represents. Practically all pentecostal denominations have been or are involved in radio broadcast-

Music ministry in El Salvador.

ing. The list of individual or church-related radio broadcasts is virtually endless, and coverages vary from local stations, to powerful regional stations, to worldwide efforts via networks and satellites.

When television replaced radio as the most influential medium of communication during the mid 20th century, evangelicals and later pentecostal-charismatics seized the opportunity to speak directly to the public. By the 1970s, pentecostal-charismatic preaching and music were reaching across America and around the world. The decades of the 1960s–1980s have prominently featured independent television ministries, including prominent figures in the pentecostal-charismatic movement, e.g., Oral Roberts, Pat Robertson (*The 700 Club*), Paul and Jan Crouch (PTL), Kenneth Copeland, and Rod Parsley.

While the denominations as such have not enjoyed equal success in their television efforts, there is a growing trend for individual congregations to produce television outreach locally and regionally. The advent of nationwide cable systems featuring religious programming almost exclusively, together with satellite broadcasting and link-up capabilities for international outreach, have made global impact through television broadcasting possible. Music is a vital ingredient in all these efforts.

D. Toward the Future.

While the past produced challenge, success, adversity, and triumph, and the present signals maturity and stability of impressive dimensions, the future holds the greatest possibilities for music ministry.

The time has come for development of a total music ministry that will serve the spiritual, emotional, aesthetic, and educational needs of the pentecostal-charismatic movement. Such a ministry concept will recognize contributions of the past while encouraging acceptance of new ideas and efforts. It will emphasize education and training in music both in preparation and performance and provide organized programs denominationally and locally. Finally, it will always recognize and promote excellent and proficient performance of religious music without lessening the importance of the spiritual dimension that must accompany music offered in praise and service to God.

■ **Bibliography:** D. L. Alford, *Music in the Pentecostal Church* (1967) ■ R. Allen and G. Borror, *Worship: Rediscovering the Missing Jewel* (1982) ■ A. E. Bailey, *The Gospel in Hymns* (1950) ■ G. Barna, *User-Friendly Churches* (1991) ■ L. S. Blackwell, *Wings of the Dove: The Story of Gospel Music in America* (1978) ■ L. Boschman, *The Rebirth of Music* (1980) ■ C. Brumback, *What Meaneth This?* (1947) ■ J. Burt and D. Allen, *History of Gospel Music* (1971) ■ G. Chase, *America's Music* (1955) ■ C. W. Conn, *Like a Mighty Army: A History of the Church of God* (1977) ■ D. P. Ellsworth, *Christian Music in Contemporary Witness* (1979) ■ C. L. Etheringston, *Protestant Worship Music* (1962) ■ D. J. Grout, *A History of Western Music* (1960) ■ W. J. Hollenweger, *The Pentecostals* (1972) ■ L. Hooper, *Church Music in Transition* (1963) ■ A. Z. Idelsohn, *Jewish Music* (1967) ■ G. P. Jackson, *The Story of the Sacred Harp* (1944) ■ P. Kerr, *Music in Evangelism* (1952) ■ C. B. Knight, ed., *Pentecostal Worship* (1974) ■ E. S. Lorenz, *Church Music: What a Minister Should Know about It* (1923) ■ A. C. Lovelace and W. C. Rice, *Music and Worship in the Church* (rev. ed., 1976) ■ J. T. Nichol, *Pentecostalism* (1966) ■ K. W. Osbeck, *The Ministry of Music* (1961) ■ B. Owens, *The Magnetic Music of Ministry* (1996) ■ G. Reese, *Music in the Middle Ages* (1940) ■ W. J. Reynolds, *A Survey of Christian Hymnody* (1963) ■ P. Scholes, ed., *Oxford Companion to Music* (1950) ■ B. Sorge, *Exploring Worship* (1987) ■ R. M. Stevenson, *Patterns of Protestant Church Music* (1953) ■ E. L. Thomas, *Music in Christian Education* (1953) ■ P. L. Walker, *The Ministry of Church and Pastor* (1965) ■ F. L. Whittlesey, *A Comprehensive Program of Church Music* (1957).
■ D. L. Alford

MYERSCOUGH, THOMAS (1858–1932). British estate agent, Bible school leader, and missionary secretary. Converted in 1874, Myerscough was leader of a group of Bible students associated with the Brethren in Preston, Lancashire. First introduced to pentecostal teaching at nearby Lytham, he was baptized in the Spirit at the Sunderland Convention in 1909. His gifts as a Bible teacher were recognized, and his Bible class work developed into the ᐟPentecostal Missionary Union (PMU) Bible School (1911–14). Among its students were ᐟW. F. P. Burton, E. J. Phillips (1893–1973), ᐟJames Salter, R. E. Darragh (1886–1959), and ᐟGeorge Jeffreys. These were formative years, and Myerscough's sound teaching had a lasting impact on his students. He took an active part in the PMU and served on its council. He was a founding member of the Assemblies of God of Great Britain and Ireland and was a member of its executive council from 1924. He was the first secretary-treasurer of the Congo Evangelistic Mission until his death in Mar. 1932, when his son succeeded him. He was pastor of the Preston Assembly and a great promoter of missionary work.

■ **Bibliography:** *Confidence* 58 (Jan. 1913): 5–6 ■ D. Gee, *Showers of Blessing*, vol. 4 (1910) ■ idem, *These Men I Knew* (1980).
■ D. W. Cartwright

MYLAND, DAVID WESLEY (1858–1943). Evangelist, pastor, author, and Bible school teacher. Myland, Canadian born, grew up in a log cabin close to Cleveland, OH. He received four years of training to be a Methodist preacher. During his lifetime, Myland was miraculously healed seven times when close to death. As a result, he preached healing in addition to the Holiness doctrine of crisis sanctification. Since the Methodists did not approve the teaching of healing, he became associated with the ᐟChristian and Missionary Alliance (CMA) in 1890.

While with the CMA, Myland wrote hymns, coauthored a hymnal with James M. Kirk, and was part of the Ohio Quartet. He also held three positions with the Ohio District of the CMA: secretary (1894), superintendent (1898–1904), and evangelist (1910). During one of his evangelistic meetings, he appeared with D. L. Moody. Additionally, Myland operated El Shaddai, a home for rest and healing, in Cleveland for three years; and he pastored a CMA church in Columbus, OH (1904–12). He also published the *Christian Messenger*, a paper devoted to the fourfold gospel: salvation, sanctification, healing, and Second Coming.

Myland's theology changed after he sought and received the baptism in the Spirit and experienced his seventh healing in Nov. 1906, having heard about the outpouring of the Spirit

David Wesley Myland (pictured with his wife), an early and prominent leader in the Christian and Missionary Alliance but later identified with the pentecostal movement.

at ▸Azusa Street seven months earlier. Immediately Myland began preaching the pentecostal message until 1912, when the CMA officially broke with pentecostalism over the issue of tongues. This resulted in Myland and 24 other pastors leaving the organization.

During 1906–19, Myland had a major writing ministry. He wrote the first pentecostal hymn, "The Latter Rain" (1906); three pentecostal hymnals (1907, 1911, 1919); and the first definitive pentecostal theology that was widely distributed, the *Latter Rain Covenant* (1910). When Myland wrote this book, he used two hermeneutical principles: translating Scripture from the original language and interpreting Scripture by Scripture under the illumination of the Holy Spirit. This led him to view Scripture passages as having three possible interpretations: historical, spiritual, and dispensational; or, in other words, literal, typological, and prophetical. Thus, he interpreted the early and latter rains referred to in Deut. 11:13–15 as literally meaning the spring and autumn rains; typologically meaning justification of the believer and baptism in the Spirit; and prophetically meaning baptism in the Spirit and the second coming of Christ. His understanding of the last dispensation differed from the standard dispensational interpretation. Myland justified the use of the gifts of the Spirit before the second coming of Christ, while the dispensationalists used it to deny the use of the gifts of the Spirit during the church age.

Myland was also concerned about Christians being overcomers so that they might be raptured during the first resurrection. His theology of the rapture was pretribulational and premillennial (cf. Myland, *The Revelation of Jesus Christ* [1911]).

Upon leaving the CMA, Myland became a leader in the pentecostal movement. His ministerial experience and prior writing gave him the credentials he needed to found and teach at the Gibeah Bible School in Plainfield, IN, among former CMA people (1912–14). While at Gibeah he taught (1912–13) and ordained ▸J. Roswell Flower and Alice Reynolds Flower (1913), who were involved in establishing the Assemblies of God (AG). Myland was also a weekly contributor to the *Christian Evangel*, which was edited by J. Roswell Flower and later became the *Pentecostal Evangel*, the official organ of the AG. While in Plainfield, Myland formed the Association of Christian Assemblies and became its general superintendent (1913–14). The organization disbanded in 1914.

Myland did not accompany Flower to the organizational meeting in Hot Springs, AR, in Apr. 1914 of the General Council of the AG, nor did he affiliate with it. Apparently he was not ready to commit himself to a pentecostal organization and wanted to maintain contact with the CMA. Since Myland was held in such high esteem by the early leaders of the AG, he undoubtedly would have been one of the major leaders if he had affiliated.

After leaving Plainfield, Myland continued to teach. He founded and taught at Ebenezer Bible Institute in Chicago (1915–18). Gibeah and Ebenezer, however, closed their doors for various reasons when Myland left them. Next he taught at Beulah Heights Bible Institute in Atlanta (1918–20) and became the first chairman of the board of trustees for the institute. It is known today as Beulah Heights Bible College.

Myland continued his administrative ministry as the first chairman (1919–20) of the general council for the Apostolic Christian Association, which incorporated on Oct. 29, 1919, in Atlanta, GA. This association later merged with what is now the ▸International Pentecostal Church of Christ. While in Atlanta, Myland associated with Paul and Elizabeth Barth, who continued the work when he left. The Barth family was instrumental in publishing the *Bridegroom's Messenger*.

After leaving Atlanta, Myland pastored churches until he was 83 years old, in Philadelphia, PA; Jackson, Redford, and Detroit, MI; and Toledo, Van Wert, and Columbus, OH. At least one of these congregations was black.

In Van Wert, Myland opened another El Shaddai, a school and a home for healing (1932–33). He continued to write hymns, manuscripts, and letters. One of these letters refutes the doctrine of eternal security (1933). The last 10 years of his life were spent in Columbus, pioneering a new church and preaching in established churches. Interestingly enough, he maintained his credentials with the Methodist church through all of these changes in his religious career.

■ **Bibliography:** "Annual Report of Alliance: 1905–1906" (unpub., 1906) ■ "Apostolic Christian Association," *Bridegroom's Messenger* 13 (Nov.–Dec. 1919) ■ J. K. Butcher, "The Holiness and Pentecostal Labors of David Wesley Myland, 1890–1918" (thesis, Dallas Theol. Sem., 1982) ■ "CMA Board of Managers Minutes: April, 1898" (unpub., 1898) ■ "CMA Board of Managers Minutes: June 4, 1910" (unpub., 1910) ■ R. B. Eckvall, H. M. Schuman, and A. C. Smead, *After Fifty Years* (1939) ■ D. W. Faupel, "The Function of 'Models' in the Interpretation of Pentecostal Thought," *Pneuma* 2 (1980) ■ A. R. Flower, *Grace for Grace* (1961) ■ C. E. Jones, *A Guide to the Study of the Pentecostal Movement* (1983) ■ W. W. Menzies, *Anointed to Serve* (1971) ■ "Minutes of the General Council of the Assemblies of God, Hot Springs, Arkansas: April 2–12, 1914" (unpub., 1914) ■ S. Murray, "Minutes of Board of Trustees of Beulah Heights Bible Institute" (unpub., 1918) ■ D. W. Myland, *The Latter Rain Covenant* (1910) ■ idem, *The Revelation of Jesus Christ* (1911) ■ idem, "Philadelphia Assembly" (church advertisement, c. 1920) ■ idem, "Special Services at the Glory Barn" (announcement, 1930).

Letters. Myland to Beloved in Christ Jesus (Dec. 18, 1932) ■ Myland to Elder in Christ Jesus (Sept. 16, 1930) ■ Myland to Gordon (May 5, 1933; Apr. 18, 1938; May 31, 1941; June 30, 1941) ■ Myland to Palmer (Dec. 23, 1927) ■ Myland to Sister in Christ (Jan. 24, 1933). ■ E. B. Robinson

N

NAICKOMPARAMBIL, MATHEW (1947–). Catholic charismatic healing evangelist in India. Born in Kerala, Mathew Naickomparambil was baptized in the Spirit in the early 1970s on his own, before the ▸Catholic charismatic renewal was known in India. He entered the seminary of the Vincentian order for service in the Syro-Malabar rite and was ordained priest in 1976, after which he received many gifts of the Spirit. In 1978 the first healing occurred through his ministry, and a few years later he began to have frequent visions. On Jan. 1, 1987, Naickomparambil was led simply to proclaim the Word of God rather than to counsel and minister individually, which led to daily proclamation of the Word at what became known as the Potta Evangelization Retreat, north of Cochin. In 1990 the Vincentian order bought a nearby hospital in Muringoor, near Chalakudy, to form the Divine Retreat Centre, with structured weeklong programs, mostly led by Naickomparambil. Vast crowds, including many non-Christians, flock to Muringoor, about 15,000 each week, and up to 150,000 at their five-day conventions. Good news and healing conventions are held by Naickomparambil and his associates in parishes all over Kerala. He first visited the U.S. in 1992 and ministered at healing conferences then and on subsequent visits.

■ **Bibliography:** J. Duin, "India's 'Billy Graham' Is Catholic" *Charisma* (Nov. 1994).　　　　　■ P. D. Hocken

Mathew Naickomparambil with Mother Teresa.

NATIONAL ASSOCIATION OF EVANGELICALS (NAE). An association of evangelical, Holiness, and pentecostal individuals, local churches, and denominations, formed in 1942 to provide visibility and advocacy for the concerns of conservative Christians in the U.S. Its membership in 1999 was about 6.8 million. The chart shows the 10 largest groups in 1999.

Assemblies of God	2,494,574
Church of God (Cleveland, TN)	753,230
Church of the Nazarene	619,576
Salvation Army	453,150
Christian and Missionary Alliance	328,078
Presbyterian Church in America	279,549
International Church of the Foursquare Gospel	231,522
Conservative Baptist Association	200,000
International Pentecostal Holiness Church	170,382
Baptist General Conference	134,795

From its inception, this group has been distinguishable from the smaller, highly vocal, and often strident organization of fundamentalists organized in 1940 by Carl McIntire, the American Council of Christian Churches (ACCC; 1999 membership nearly 2 million). The NAE is fundamental in its doctrinal commitment yet more inclusive and less sectarian than the ACCC. For many it also provided a conservative alternative to the Federal Council of Churches of Christ in America (FCCCA)—succeeded by the now 52-million–member National Council of Churches of Christ in the U.S. (NCC)—whose theological and political agenda seemed to represent exclusively the concerns of more liberal Protestants. The NAE was unique in that it did not wish to condemn these other ecumenical agencies but rather to occupy territory between them.

To describe the NAE in ecumenical terms may, at first glance, seem odd. Most of its members view genuine Christian unity as spiritual unity and champion the doctrine of an invisible church. They tend to shy away from any contact with the formal "ecumenical movement." Yet the NAE provides cross-denominational fellowship, shares common doctrinal and social agendas, and raises a visible voice that is demonstrative of the Christian character and commitments of those involved. These factors are indicative of its basically ecumenical nature. The two most significant differences between what is normally identified as the "ecumenical movement" and the NAE are (1) the list of candidates that are welcomed into membership, and (2) the NAE's unwillingness to date to enter into church unity talks that envision some form of visible unity other than cooperation on a social or political agenda.

In many ways the NAE could be termed the brainchild of ▸James Elwin Wright. In 1929 he had launched the New England Fellowship (NEF) to bring a modicum of cohesiveness to isolated conservative Christians who felt lonely in the seemingly theologically hostile and dominantly Roman Catholic world of New England. The NEF was highly successful from its inception, recruiting cooperation from a broad spectrum of fundamentalist and evangelical groups, among them pentecostals. Wright was proactive in his recruitment of pentecostals in this venture, a fact that was not always appreciated in many fundamentalist circles.

The NEF organized a range of activities and events for its constituency, including camps, seminars, Bible studies, and a series of radio programs. From 1937 to 1939 Wright traveled the U.S., taking the pulse of American evangelicalism. By 1939 he began to share with people like Harold John Ockenga, pastor of the famed Park Street Church in Boston, and other church and denominational leaders around the country, his dream of a similar organization on a national scale. Wright visited many leaders personally during those years and continued to include pentecostals as he had done in the NEF.

A National Conference for United Action among Evangelicals was convened in St. Louis, MO, Apr. 7–9, 1942. Its purpose was to discuss the necessity of founding a "front" to represent the concerns of evangelical organizations before various governmental agencies; the need for a kind of "clearing house" for items of common interest and concern; and a concern to provide a visible means to demonstrate before an otherwise unbelieving world the determination of many to stand against the forces of unbelief and apostasy. Several pentecostal groups showed immediate interest in this proposal, including the Pentecostal Holiness Church (PHC), ▸Open Bible Standard Churches (OBSC), the ▸Church of God (Cleveland, TN; CG), and the ▸Assemblies of God (AG). Of the 150 delegates present at this meeting, about 10% were pentecostals.

In spite of early pentecostal interest in the NAE, full participation did not come easily. Pentecostals were chary of the positive response they were given by these "Calvinists," and, as ▸J. R. Flower noted, some pentecostals kept their "fingers crossed" lest they lose this "good fortune." Harold Ockenga did much to alleviate pentecostal fears, arguing repeatedly that pentecostals and Holiness groups such as the Free Methodists and the Nazarenes should have an equal voice with others who called themselves evangelical.

For many the issue of pentecostal participation peaked in Apr. 1944, when Carl McIntire published several articles in his paper, the *Christian Beacon,* repudiating pentecostals. "Tongues," his paper claimed, "is one of the great signs of the apostasy." The real gift of tongues had long since ceased to exist. McIntire announced his willingness to merge the ACCC into the NAE *if* the NAE would, among other things, "get rid of the … tongues groups."

Flower wondered aloud whether the NAE had hurt its chances of representing evangelical Christians in the U.S. by including pentecostals in their numbers. But Ockenga reassured him that the course was set and that pentecostals would participate. As late as 1947 Ockenga was still defending that decision. By then, pentecostals were committed to stay. Flower, with ▸E. S. Williams's encouragement, had led the AG into the organization. ▸G. H. Montgomery had urged participation in the NAE by the Pentecostal Holiness Church. ▸Frank Smith, Gerald Crooks, ▸R. Bryant Mitchell, and Roy E. Southard led the OBSC into the NAE, and the CG took its cue from ▸J. H. Walker, ▸Earl P. Paulk, E. L. Simmons, ▸M. P. Cross, and E. C. Clark. Since its founding meetings, other pentecostal groups, including the ▸Christian Church of North America, ▸Church of God of the Mountain Assembly, ▸Elim Fellowship, ▸International Church of the Foursquare Gospel (ICFG), ▸International Pentecostal Church of Christ (IPCC), ▸Pentecostal Church of God (PCG), and the ▸Pentecostal Free Will Baptist Church (PFWBC) have joined the NAE.

While pentecostals were in the minority of NAE membership in the 1940s and 1950s, their rapid growth since then has moved them into the majority position. According to 1999 figures on the roughly 6.8 million members in the NAE, nearly 3.8 million are pentecostal. Of the 49 member groups, 12 are pentecostal. The AG constitutes 37% of the NAE's total membership, and the composite pentecostal membership constitutes 56% of the organization. At a significant level, then, the NAE could be said to represent pentecostal thinking.

Pentecostal participation on the various commissions of the NAE, including the commissions on the chaplaincy, churchmen, stewardship, and women has been evident through the years. Similarly, pentecostals have served as convention coordinators in recent years. Still, of the 30 presidents (now chairs) who have led the NAE, only five have been pentecostals. ▸Thomas F. Zimmerman served two terms as president in 1960 and 1961 while holding the position of general superintendent of the AG. Bishop J. Floyd Williams, general superintendent of the PHC, was elected to a two-year term in 1980–81. ▸Ray H. Hughes, first assistant general overseer of the CG, served as president in 1986–87. Don Argue, president of North Central College of the Assemblies of God, held the office in 1992–93.

In 1994 longtime executive director Billy Melvin retired from leadership of the NAE after 28 years in that position.

The NAE took the opportunity to rewrite its bylaws. A new office of president replaced the office of executive director, the senior ongoing staff position. The earlier office of president, which had been a biennially elected position, was succeeded by the position of chairman. In Dec. 1994 Don Argue of the Assemblies of God was hired by the NAE to become the first pentecostal to hold the office of president, a position he held until Apr. 1998. That same year, R. Lamar Vest of the Church of God was elected chairman of the organization, a position he held until 2000.

Dr. Argue functioned as a transitional president for the organization. His presidency was marked by several contributions. First, he did much to lift the national and international profile of the NAE. He made public appearances with Roman Catholic and Orthodox leaders as well as with the general secretary of the National Council of Churches. He worked closely with the Washington, DC, office to establish the NAE as a politically significant voice. He attempted to move the NAE from an organization that was publicly identified with the religious right and the Republican Party to one that was able to offer leadership to a range of conservative and moderate evangelical Christians in both political parties.

Second, Argue helped to raise the plight of persecuted Christians in the minds of many around the globe. His work in this and other areas led to the publication of the NAE's important "An Evangelical Manifesto." He was appointed to the U.S. State Department's Advisory Committee on Religious Freedom Abroad and as part of that committee he traveled for three weeks throughout China with several American religious leaders. They met with government and Communist Party leaders to discuss the issue of religious freedom. Argue's contributions in this area also contributed to President Clinton's appointment of an ambassador at large to work on issues of religious freedom and religious persecution.

Third, Argue attempted to bring about a degree of racial reconciliation in the larger evangelical community. Although other pentecostal groups have joined the NAE, as of 1999 the NAE has still had only one black or Hispanic pentecostal denomination as member, though some other black pentecostals have participated in the National Black Evangelical Association (NBEA) founded in Los Angeles, CA, in 1963.

While Argue may have received some impetus to work toward racial reconciliation from pentecostals who had helped in the formation of the Pentecostal/Charismatic Churches of North America in 1994, he is surely to be remembered for his work attempts to reach out to the NBEA. Argue and the NAE also worked with Zondervan Publishing House to develop literature designed to facilitate greater communication between congregations of different races and to work toward racial reconciliation within churches. Approximately 10,000 churches wrote in for these materials.

The NAE publishes *United Evangelical Action* six times annually, with articles addressing a variety of socially relevant issues. Recent topics have included medical ethics, nuclear war, liberation theology, the sanctuary movement, evangelicals in the mainline, racism, and pornography. Occasionally it publishes articles that highlight pentecostal works or articles by pentecostal authors. *Washington Insight*, a regular newsletter, has done much to inform NAE members of "evangelical concerns and the federal government," encouraging active participation by evangelicals and pentecostals in political concerns. Most recently it has addressed the issue of the sexual trafficking of women and children.

The pentecostal groups that have joined the NAE have benefited in several ways. First, they have gained visibility and respectability that they sought from their evangelical peers. Formerly viewed as sectarians, they are now often addressed as bona fide Christian denominations.

Second, pentecostal concerns that were shared by other Christians now have a greater hearing in the church, and through cooperation with the NAE membership, pentecostals have a larger voice in the public arena.

Third, pentecostals inevitably came to the place where they recognized the need for dialogue with one another. Out of this recognition, the pentecostals who were NAE members formed the ▸Pentecostal Fellowship of North America (PFNA) in 1948. That entity was dissolved in 1994 and was replaced by the interracial ▸Pentecostal/Charismatic Churches of North America (PCCNA).

Fourth, membership in the NAE has contributed to the broadening, or "evangelicalization," of those pentecostal groups that have participated as well as to the "pentecostalization" of those evangelicals who were at one time markedly anti-pentecostal. This is most noticeable in their changing worship style and music.

While pentecostals have gained through participation in the NAE, they have also lost some things. The evangelicalization of pentecostals has brought them into dialogue with evangelical Christians, but this interaction has been at the risk of certain pentecostal distinctives. First, most pentecostals were pacifists prior to WWII. Evangelism on military bases was allowed, and sometimes supported, but pentecostal military chaplains were nonexistent, and pentecostals were discouraged from serving in the military, especially in combatant roles. The NAE first gave pentecostals entrée to the military through its Chaplain's Commission. By the Vietnam era the AG, as one representative group, had rewritten its position on military service. It no longer declared that as a fellowship it could not "participate in war and armed resistance which involves the actual destruction of human life" in accordance with Scripture, but left the decision to the individual. This allowed the fellowship to identify more clearly with the NAE members whose traditions, for the most part, had not shared a pacifist past. More often than not, many still identify with the political right and have been hard on those with whom they have disagreed.

Second, and less overt, is the movement away from support for women in ministry. Some pentecostals have never ordained women; others have. At the very least, women have traditionally played a more significant role in ministry within the pentecostal tradition than they have in the larger evangelical tradition. But as evangelical values have been adopted by pentecostals, the role of women in ministry has suffered.

Third, the doctrinal concerns of evangelicals have become the doctrinal concerns of pentecostals. Some pentecostal groups have rewritten their statements of faith, and others have imported such "evangelical" issues as "inerrancy" into their theological arenas for the first time.

Fourth, taking membership in the NAE has meant that pentecostals have stood in solidarity with the NAE in its suspicion of the ecumenical movement as embodied in the World and National Councils of Churches. Thus pentecostals have effectively been cut off from meaningful interaction with the conciliar sector of the church, in part to maintain a position acceptable to other NAE member denominations, but at the expense of forfeited witness.

On balance, the NAE has aided many pentecostal concerns. Pentecostal missions have been represented in the Evangelical Foreign Missions Association (EFMA), a group formed from within the missions committee of the NAE in 1945. The AG, CG, OBSC, and PHC were all charter members. Likewise, the National Religious Broadcasters (NRB) was formed in 1944 because of NAE concerns "to safeguard free and complete access to the broadcast media." Pentecostals have also benefited significantly from the work of the NRB as pentecostal evangelists have pioneered the field of televangelism.

A number of challenges still lie ahead for the NAE due to the cultural shifts that are currently occurring around the world. It has had some success in modernizing itself in recent years, as is evidenced from its informative website. Yet, like many other institutions at the end of the 20th century, it will need to continue its search for a meaningful and relevant purpose in a changing world. What clear purpose will it serve in the 21st century? How best can it represent the churches that brought it into existence when their own denominational impact and loyalties seem to be on the decline? Will it be able to overcome the temptation to withdraw from engagement in a more secularized and pluralistic setting? Will it be able to recruit the kind of leadership it will need from those who are not white, male, and aging? Only the future will tell. In early 2000, the NAE headquarters moved from Carol Stream, IL, to Glendora, CA.

■ **Bibliography:** J. Carpenter, "From Fundamentalism to the New Evangelical Coalition," in G. Marsden, ed., *Evangelicalism and Modern America* (1984) ■ idem, "The Fundamental Leaven and the Rise of an Evangelical United Front," in L. Sweet, ed., *The Evangelical Tradition in America* (1984) ■ "China Mission: More Than 'Ping-Pong' Diplomacy," *Christianity Today* (July 13, 1998) ■ E. C. Clark, "Chicago Conventional Evangelicals," *Church of God Evangel* (May 29, 1943) ■ C. W. Conn, *Like a Mighty Army, Moves the Church of God* (1955) ■ Constitution and By-Laws of the General Council of the Assemblies of God 1939, 1987 ■ "Foursquare Gospel Church Joins NAE," *United Evangelical Action* 11 (May 1, 1952) ■ J. W. Kennedy, "NAE Rethinks Mission: Departing Leader Calls for Better Use of Resources," *Christianity Today* (Apr. 27, 1998) ■ E. W. Lindner, ed., *Yearbook of American & Canadian Churches* (1999) ■ G. Marsden, *Reforming Fundamentalism* (1987) ■ W. H. Menzies, *Anointed to Serve* (1971) ■ R. B. Mitchell, *Heritage and Horizons: The History of Open Bible Standard Churches* (1982) ■ G. H. Montgomery, "Does United Evangelical Action Include Pentecostal Holiness?" *Pentecostal Holiness Advocate* 27 (4, May 27, 1943) ■ J. D. Murch, *Cooperation without Compromise: A History of the National Association of Evangelicals* (1956) ■ idem, *Evangelical Action! A Report of the Organization of the National Association of Evangelicals for United Action* (1942) ■ H. J. Ockenga, "The 'Pentecostal' Bogey," *United Evangelical Action* 6 (1, 1947) ■ "Ockenga Disavows Barnhouse's Speech at NAE Convention," "Tongues," and W. O. J. Garman, "Analysis of National Association Convention and Constituency," in *Christian Beacon* 9 (2, Apr. 27, 1944) ■ C. M. Robeck Jr., "The Assemblies of God and Ecumenical Cooperation: 1920–1965," in W. Ma and R. Menzies, eds., *Pentecostalism in Context: Essays in Honor of William W. Menzies,* Journal of Pentecostal Theology Supplement Series 11 (1997) ■ R. Robins, "A Chronology of Peace: Attitudes toward War and Peace in the Assemblies of God: 1914–1918," *Pneuma* 6 (1984) ■ B. L. Shelley, *Evangelicalism in America* (1967) ■ V. Synan, *The Old-Time Power: A History of the Pentecostal Holiness Church* (1973) ■ Correspondence located in the AG Archives in Springfield, MO, including J. R. Flower to H. J. Ockenga, June 1, 1943 ■ July 5, 1943 ■ May 4, 1944 ■ H. J. Ockenga to J. R. Flower, May 28, 1943 ■ May 22, 1944.

■ C. M. Robeck Jr.

NATIONAL GAY PENTECOSTAL ALLIANCE The National Gay Pentecostal Alliance (NGPA) is an Apostolic, or ‣Oneness, pentecostal denomination with a special outreach to the lesbian and gay community. After William H. Carey was excommunicated from the United Pentecostal Church in 1979, he decided to start a church and support group as a means of reaching out to lesbians and gays. On July 28, 1980, Carey and a Sister Schwarz signed papers creating the Gay Pentecostal Alliance in Schenectady, NY. The word National was added to the name, and the federal government formally recognized NGPA as a denomination the following year. The first ordination service was held in Omaha, NE, in 1981. The church is administered by two presbyters appointed by district elders. Current presbyters are William Carey and LaDonna C. Briggs. In the U.S., NGPA operates churches in New York, South Carolina, Georgia,

Michigan, Illinois, Arkansas, Louisiana, Nebraska, and Nevada. Affiliated churches are also located in Canada, Indonesia, Italy, South Africa, Russia, and the Ukraine. NGPA headquarters are located in Ferndale, MI, and a bimonthly newsletter, *The Apostolic Voice,* is published in Schenectady, NY. A Russian-language edition, *Apostolsky Golos,* is also published bimonthly. Ministerial training classes are taught through Pentecostal Bible Institute in Schenectady, and correspondence courses are also available.

■ **Bibliography:** *Pentecostal Coalition for Human Rights Newsletters* (1981) ■ National Gay Pentecostal Alliance web page (Nov. 1999).
■ G. W. Gohr

NATIONAL SERVICE COMMITTEE (NSC). See Charismatic Renewal Services.

NATIVE AMERICAN PENTECOSTALS The Native Americans, or American Indians, comprise hundreds of culturally and linguistically distinct groups who came to the Americas in numerous waves of migration, by way of the Bering Strait land bridge as well as through island hopping across the Pacific Ocean. Thus, when Europeans arrived in the New World, they confronted not one monolithic culture, but many mutually independent cultures spread out across the continent.

Three factors have served to reduce the numbers of these tribes significantly over the years: wars of conquest, disease, and assimilation. Today there are approximately 540 federally recognized tribes numbering nearly 3 million. They live primarily on Indian reservations and in urban enclaves.

The earliest known pentecostal outreach to Native Americans was that of Ernest and Ethel Marshall, who set out to establish an ►Assemblies of God (AG) church in San Carlos, AZ, tribal headquarters of the San Carlos Apache reservation in 1936. It is evident that by at least 1947 there were Apaches attending the church who had received the baptism in the Holy Spirit with speaking in tongues.

Charles Lee, a young Navajo artist who was already a Christian, was visiting a friend in San Carlos that summer and tells of his experience. "At my friend's home, I heard his mother praying and speaking in tongues. But what impressed me most was the consistency and enthusiasm of my friend's family and others who attended the Assembly of God church in San Carlos."

Lee had previously been associated with a Zia Pueblo artist in New Mexico who had ties with the ►Oneness movement, a pentecostal movement that rejects Trinitarianism as being tritheism (a belief in three gods). This artist had been ostracized from his tribe because of his glossolalic experience.

During his visit to San Carlos, Lee became ill. "A nurse took my temperature and it was 103 degrees. I was so sick I could hardly move." The family summoned their pastor,

Ethel Marshall, to pray for a miracle of healing. "She read from the book of James about anointing the sick with oil and praying for healing. Then she put some oil on my forehead and prayed that God would heal me. I was healed instantly."

Lee reports that later in the year he was given the opportunity to return to San Carlos to provide artistic illustrations for a book. "I was not interested in the money I would get for the book illustrations," says Lee. "I was just happy to have an excuse to get back to that church." It was on New Year's Day 1948 that Lee attended a service that would forever change the course of his life.

The sermon text was Isa. 6, in which the Lord asks Isaiah, "Whom shall I send and who will go for us?" "I knew the Lord was speaking to me," says Lee. "I knew God was calling me to the ministry, but I also was certain that I had to have the baptism of the Holy Spirit if I was going to be a minister of the gospel." On Jan. 12, 1948, Charles Lee was baptized by immersion (he had previously been sprinkled), and at 7:00 that evening he was filled with the Holy Spirit and spoke in tongues.

The account of Charles Lee's experience is important because of his subsequent ministry. In 1953 Lee founded Mesa View AG in his home region of Shiprock, NM, in the Four Corners area of the Navajo reservation. He served as pastor of the church for 36 years and later taught at American Indian Bible College. At one time Lee's congregation was the largest AG church in New Mexico. Hundreds of Native Americans have received the baptism in the Holy Spirit through his influence.

Since the San Carlos church was planted in 1936 the pentecostal message has produced Native American churches and adherents in virtually every significant Native American population center. *The Native American Christian Community: A Directory of Indian, Aleut, and Eskimo Churches,* compiled by R. Pierce Beaver in 1979, lists 217 Native American churches that are clearly identified as pentecostal.

By far the most significant pentecostal groups with ministry to Native Americans have been independent groups and the AG. Beaver states that "the independent church is overwhelmingly a phenomenon of Navajoland." David Scates identifies 76 indigenous pentecostal "camp" churches in his 1981 book *Why Navajo Churches Are Growing.*

These churches, which began around 1960, developed around charismatic clan leaders. The movement had several points of origin on the Navajo reservation and was noted by anthropologist William H. Hodge, who wrote an article "Navajo Pentecostalism" in *The Anthropological Quarterly* (37 [3]). According to Scates, the impact of this movement exceeds these statistics. Perhaps 50% of the Navajo people have come under the tents of the Navajo pentecostal preachers and many hear the gospel preached in an understandable and culturally relevant manner for the first time. Some of these were Christians from mission churches and others were converted in these meetings and then incorporated into mission churches where they had family ties. Others were incorporated into the indigenous camp churches that resulted from these beginnings.

Beaver lists another 217 Native American churches that are the product of missionary activities representing classical pentecostal groups. Of these, 182 are AG, of which 68 are in Arizona and New Mexico, including 40 Navajo congregations. Twenty-seven are in Alaska, 10 in North Carolina (all indigenous Lumbee congregations), and 10 in Washington. Other states with AG Native American churches are California, Colorado, Florida, Georgia, Idaho, Michigan, Minnesota, Montana, New Jersey, Nevada, New York, North Dakota, Oklahoma, Oregon, Texas, Wisconsin, and Wyoming.

The ˒Pentecostal Church of God lists 31 churches, 15 of which are in Arizona and New Mexico, and the ˒Church of God (Cleveland, TN) lists four churches in four different states.

The primary concern of the Native American pentecostal church today is leadership formation and the transition from a largely missions-dependent entity to self-governance, self-propagation, and self-determination. In 1995 the Native American Fellowship was formed, which is pentecostal. Native Americans from many different pentecostal persuasions participate in this fellowship, although the leadership is entirely AG. The fellowship publishes a quarterly magazine called *The Native Pentecostal News* and sponsors an annual convocation of Christian Indian leaders.

The pentecostal message came to Navajo Charles Lee through a white missionary. Now that same message is being proclaimed by Native American pastors and evangelists in a culturally relevant way.   ■ D. J. Moore

NAVA, ANTONIO CASTAÑEDA (1892–1999). Key pioneer of the Oneness pentecostal movement among Latinos in the U.S. and a founder of the ˒Apostolic Assembly of Faith in Jesus Christ, Inc. (Asamblea Apostólica de la Fe en Cristo Jesús, Inc.). Of humble origins from Durango, Mexico, Nava immigrated to Southern California in the wake of the Mexican Revolution as a migrant field worker and was converted to Oneness pentecostalism by ˒Marcial de la Cruz in 1916. Shortly after his conversion he was baptized in the name of Jesus Christ by an Anglo-American named Brookhart in Los Angeles. That same year, Francisco Llorente, Marcial de la Cruz, and the newly converted Nava founded what later became known as the Apostolic Assembly of the Faith in Jesus Christ, Inc. This was the first Spanish-speaking Oneness pentecostal denomination in the U.S. Nava was ordained to the ministry on Apr. 26, 1918, in San Bernardino, CA, by the Pentecostal Assemblies of the World, a black Oneness pentecostal denomination. He went on to found and pastor churches in Yuma, AZ (1918–19);

Calexico, CA (1921–28); Zaragoza, Baja California (1921); Mexicali, Baja California (1922); and Los Angeles, CA (1935–64). Nava served as presiding bishop of the Apostolic Assembly in 1929–50 and 1963–66. He was instrumental in helping the Apostolic Assembly break its ministerial ties with the Pentecostal Assemblies of the World. Nava married Delores Ochoa in 1933, and together they raised eight children. His creative leadership, fiery preaching, pioneer evangelistic work among migrant Mexican farm workers, and longevity made him famous in the Spanish-speaking Oneness pentecostal movement in the U.S. and Mexico.

■ **Bibliography:** B. Cantú, *Historia de la Asamblea Apostólica de la Fe en Cristo Jesús, 1916–1966* (1966) ▮ C. Holland, *The Religious Dimension in Hispanic Los Angeles* (1974).   ■ G. Espinosa

NELSON, PETER CHRISTOPHER (1868–1942). Evangelist and educator. Born in Denmark, Nelson immigrated with his family to the U.S. in 1872. He felt called to the ministry at a youthful age and enrolled at Denison University in 1890 to begin preparation. He married Myrtle Garmong in 1893 and completed his bachelor's degree in 1897. In 1899 he entered Rochester Theological Seminary, where he studied under Augustus H. Strong. After completing his studies, Nelson entered the Baptist ministry, engaging in evangelism and pastoring; he also worked with the YMCA during

P. C. Nelson, an immigrant to the U.S. from Denmark, who became a minister, first as a Baptist and then as a pentecostal. He founded Southwestern Bible School in Enid, OK (now Southwestern Assemblies of God College, Waxahachie, TX).

WWI. Following the war, he was called to pastor the Conley Memorial Baptist Church in Detroit.

Nelson embraced pentecostalism in 1920. Because his congregation refused to accept his new doctrines on faith healing and the baptism in the Holy Spirit, he resigned and spent seven years in evangelistic ministry. Settling in Enid, OK, in 1927, he founded a church and opened Southwestern Bible School. These initiatives prompted him to affiliate with the Assemblies of God. Traveling widely in the promotion of the school, Nelson became well known for his pulpit ministry. His contribution to pentecostal education was expanded by the publication of his writings: *The Young Minister's Guide* (1932), *Bible Doctrines* (1934), *Life of Paul* (1939), *Does Christ Heal Today?* (1941), *Word Studies* (1941), *The Baptism in the Holy Spirit* (1942), and *The Letters of Paul* (1945). He translated Eric Lund's *Hermeneutics* from Spanish into English in 1934.

In 1941 Nelson negotiated for the merger of Southwestern Bible School and South Central Bible Institute in Fort Worth, TX, to form Southwestern Bible Institute (now Southwestern Assemblies of God College). Two years later it moved to Waxahachie, TX, to occupy the former campus of Trinity University. Nelson died shortly before the move.

Soviet neocharismatic evangelist gives call to repent during outdoor crusade in Odessa.

■ **Bibliography:** K. Kendrick, "A Pioneer Pentecostal Educator," *AGH* 2 (Spring 1982) ■ P. C. Nelson, "Autobiography of P. C. Nelson," Enid, OK (typewritten, 1928).   ■ G. B. McGee

NEOCHARISMATICS In the 1980s the various groups in the renewal were categorized as belonging to either the first wave (classical pentecostals), the second wave (charismatics in the historic mainline churches), or the ▸third wave (nonpentecostal, noncharismatic, mainstream church renewal); the third wave was also referred to as "neo-pentecostals." In recent years, however, the amazing growth of independent and postdenominational groups throughout the world has required a revision in this classification scheme (Hollenweger, 1997; Barrett and Johnson, 2000).

The so-called third wave should be viewed as part of a broader category, "neocharismatics," which includes the vast numbers of independent and indigenous churches and groups that cannot be classified as either pentecostal or charismatic. These are Christian bodies with pentecostal-like experiences that have no traditional pentecostal or charismatic denominational connections (and sometimes only very slender—if any—historical connections). Their greatest concentrations of strength are in the prophetic African independent churches, in Asia—especially the house-church movement in China—and in Latin American countries, especially Brazil. Furthermore, the label "neocharismatic" also includes what are called churches of the ▸New Apostolic Reformation. Barrett and Johnson discovered that the neocharismatics actually outnumber all pentecostals and charismatics com-

bined (see the section on global statistics, pp. 284–302; see also the introduction, p. xvii).

■ **Bibliography:** D. Barrett and T. Johnson, *World Christian Encyclopedia* (2000) ■ W. J. Hollenweger, *Pentecostalism* (1997).
          ■ S. M. Burgess

NEO-PENTECOSTALS See Neocharismatics.

NEW APOSTOLIC CHURCH An independent church movement that originated in Germany in 1863. It is characterized by apostolic church government, including the functioning of the fourfold gift ministries of Eph. 4:11—apostle, prophet, evangelist, pastor-teacher. Since 1960 the New Apostolic Church (NAC) has experienced significant growth internationally.

The roots of the NAC go back to noted London pastor ▸Edward Irving and his endorsement of the expression of spiritual gifts (1 Cor. 12:8–10) in the modern church, as well as his belief in the restoration of apostolic church government. After Irving was ousted from his Regent Square Church in 1832, hundreds followed him in the establishment of an independent body called the Newman Street Church. This church became a haven for ministers and laity who had become disillusioned with denominational opposition to the supernatural activity of the Holy Spirit. Six other churches affiliated with Newman Street to form the London Council. With Irving's premature death in 1834, leadership of the new movement was assumed by men who were being placed in the role of apostle. By 1835 the final number of apostles were chosen, the 12 completing the "apostolic college." The movement formally organized, assuming the name ▸Catholic Apostolic Church (CAC).

A prominent apostle of the CAC, Henry Drummond (1786–1860), invited the 12 apostles, along with seven prophets, to retreat to his Albury rural estate for a year of prayer, study, and planning in order to determine the future shape of the church. One of their conclusions was to apportion Christendom into 12 territories, with each apostle assuming responsibility for one portion. The apostles agreed to live within their territory for a three-and-a-half-year period, learning of its culture and religious traditions, and bearing witness of their vision of a unified Christendom under apostolic authority. New churches sprang up in various countries as a result of this mission. None of the apostles was more successful in representing the CAC overseas than Thomas Carlyle (1803–55), apostle to Germany. By the time of Carlyle's death in 1855, the church had taken firm root in that country. By 1860 the need for local apostles in Germany was desperate. Prophet Heinrich Geyer's calling of two new apostles in 1860 was vetoed by the English apostles. They remained unbending in their conviction that 12 was the absolute and final number of apostles until the second coming of Christ. They also held that even the deceased apostles should not be replaced.

In 1862 prophet Geyer called out another new apostle, again resulting in censorship from England. But this time respected Hamburg bishop Friedrich Schwartz (1815–95) and his congregation stood with Geyer against the headquarters at Albury. When English apostle Francis Woodhouse (1805–1901) excommunicated Geyer, Schwartz, the Hamburg congregation, and everyone else supporting the "alien" apostleship, the ousted Germans were faced with the option of forming a new organization.

The New Order of apostles, later incorporated as the New Apostolic Church, identify 1863 as the official year of their birth. Differences with the mother church, the CAC, had become irreconcilable. Most significant for the future of the NAC was their conviction that the number of apostles should be unlimited. As the NAS continued to ordain new apostles in keeping with their growth, the CAC was facing decline. After the last of the Albury apostles, Woodhouse, died in 1901, there was no provision for the future ordination of priests, so today only a remnant of the CAC membership survives.

Yet the original vision, with roots in Edward Irving's London prayer meetings of the 1830s, found a continuing link to the future through the NAC. The NAC also abolished the elaborate liturgical practices and clerical vestments carried over from the CAC. The leadership believed that the former practices detracted from the desired simplicity of the divine services. This move allowed the NAC to appeal to a broader constituency, contributing to its capacity to expand. The movement was further centralized and unified in 1895, when the office of chief apostle was added.

During the 1960s and '70s, through the efforts of chief apostle Walter Schmidt, the NAC reached its highest rate of international growth. Since 1980, Zurich, Switzerland, has become the world headquarters of the movement. This allows leaders of the church the freedom to travel internationally under the auspices of a politically neutral country. In the 1990s the NAC is approaching 16 million members in approximately 60,000 congregations worldwide. The number of apostles has reached nearly 300.

The NAC is a thriving church today, with a colorful ancestry of charismatic expression and apostolic restoration, rooted in Irving's London revival of the 1830s. The origins of the NAC thus predate the beginnings of the pentecostal revival in the U.S. (Azusa Street, 1906) by more than 70 years. Some evidence even suggests that the British-German revival may have played a role in the origins of American pentecostalism. For example, ▸Parham mentions Irving in a sermon preached in Kansas City just 21 days after ▸Agnes Ozman's Spirit baptism: "... the Irvingites, a sect that arose under the teachings of Irving, a Scotchman, during the last century, received not only the eight recorded gifts of 1 Cor. 12, but also the speaking in other tongues, which the Holy Ghost reserved as the evidence of His oncoming" (*A Voice Crying in the Wilderness*, 1902, 29). ▸Alexander Dowie was influenced profoundly by Irving: "A greater and mightier man of God never stood upon this earth" (*Leaves of Healing*, 15:433). A. J. Gordon, Kelso Carter, Horace Bushnell, and others wrote of Irving and his teachings prior to 1901. (For a summary of possible connections, see Kent Griffin, "On Trial for the Baptism of the Holy Spirit," Resource [Pentecostal Assemblies of Canada], 2 [4], 17–20.)

The penetration of Edward Irving's writings and teachings into 19th-century America, as well as the vigorous expansion into North America of both the CAC and the NAC during the latter half of the century, represent possible directions for fruitful scholarly inquiry. But setting aside possible causal connections, it is noteworthy in itself that two radically diverse traditions of pentecostal expression have coexisted side by side to the present day.

■ **Bibliography:** C. W. Boase, *Supplementary Narrative to the Elijah Ministry* (1870) ■ J. B. Cardale, *The Character of Our Present Testimony and Work* (1865) ■ T. Carlyle, *A Short History of the Apostolic Work* (1851) ■ D. W. Dorries, "Edward Irving and the 'Standing Sign' of Spirit Baptism," in G. B. McGee, ed., *Initial Evidence* (1991) ■ T. Dowglass, *A Chronicle of Certain Events* (1852) ■ H. Drummond, *A Brief Account of the Commencement of the Lord's Work to Restore His Church* (1851) ■ C. G. Flegg, *Gathered under Apostles* (1992) ■ M. Kraus, *Completion Work in the New Apostolic Church* (1978) ■ E. Miller, *The History and Doctrines of Irvingism*, vols. 1, 2 (1878) ■ S. Newman-Norton, ed., *The Hamburg Schism* (1974) ■ Mrs. M. O. W. Oliphant, *The Life of Edward Irving* (1862) ■ G. Rockenfelder, ed., *History of the New Apostolic Church* (1970)

■ G. Standring, *Albury and The Catholic Apostolic Church* (1985) ■ B. Wallace, personal conversations (1988–98) ■ Apostle Weinmann, *History of the Kingdom of God* (1971) ■ F. W. Woodhouse, *A Narrative of Events affecting the Position and Prospects of the Whole Christian Church* (1847). ■ D. W. Dorries

NEW APOSTOLIC REFORMATION The New Apostolic Reformation is an extraordinary renewal movement at the close of the 20th century that is, to a significant extent, changing the shape of Protestant Christianity around the world. For almost 500 years Christian churches have largely functioned within traditional denominational structures of one kind or another. Particularly in the 1990s, but with roots going back for almost a century, new forms and operational procedures began to emerge in areas such as local church government, interchurch relationships, financing, evangelism, missions, prayer, leadership selection and training, the role of supernatural power, worship, and other important aspects of church life.

Some of these changes are being seen within denominations themselves, but for the most part they are taking the form of loosely structured apostolic networks. In virtually every region of the world these new apostolic churches constitute one of the fastest-growing segments of Christianity. The three major components of the historical roots of the New Apostolic Reformation are (1) the African Independent Churches, which began in the early 1900s as a reaction against the serious lack of contextualization in the traditional mission churches; (2) the Chinese House Church Movement, which began building momentum in the late 1970s and may now embrace nearly 10% of the Chinese population; and (3) the Latin American grassroots churches, so identified by researchers Mike Berg and Paul Pretiz, which, probably since the early 1980s, now include a disproportionate number of the largest and most dynamic churches in Latin America. In the U.S. the majority of the churches and networks of churches that would be included in the New Apostolic Reformation would be those that have previously self-identified as "independent charismatics." Nevertheless, a smaller number of apostolic churches would see themselves as noncharismatic or traditional evangelical in theology and style.

The most radical of the differences between the new apostolic churches and traditional denominationally based Christianity has to do with leadership. The locus of trust for directional leadership centers much more on individuals in new apostolic churches, whereas in traditional churches it centers mainly on groups. This is true of local church government, where the pastor is seen as the leader, not simply as an employee of the church. Traditionally, the final word in local churches has been with the congregation or a board elected by the congregation. It is also true of translocal government, with individual apostles rather than presbyteries or annual conferences or cabinets or districts or conventions in the top decision-making and vision-casting position.

The New Apostolic Churches, in which 18 leaders in the New Apostolic Reformation describe their movements.

Literature on new apostolic churches is expanding rapidly. The three top books at this writing are *Churchquake! The Explosive Dynamics of the New Apostolic Reformation* by C. Peter Wagner (1999), which is the first textbook in the field; *Reinventing American Protestantism* by Donald E. Miller (1997), a sociologically oriented report of Vineyard Christian Fellowship, Calvary Chapel, and Hope Chapel; and *The New Apostolic Churches,* edited by C. Peter Wagner, in which 18 apostolic leaders describe their own movements. The three best books on the gift and office of apostle are *Apostles and the Emerging Apostolic Movement* by David Cannistraci (1998), *Apostles, Prophets and the Coming Moves of God* by Bill Hamon (1997), and *Moving in the Apostolic* by John Eckhardt (1999).

See also NEOCHARISMATICS.

■ C. Peter Wagner

NEW CHURCHES See NEW APOSTOLIC REFORMATION.

NICHOL, JOHN THOMAS (1928–2000). Historian and educator. Born in Dorchester, MA, Nichol (originally Nykiel) is the son of John and Felixa Nykiel. He married Dorothy Marie Jashinsky on Aug. 30, 1952. Nichol received his A.B. from Gordon College (1949) and his A.M. (1953) and Ph.D. (1965) degrees from Boston University. He also earned S.T.B. (1953) and S.T.M. (1954) degrees from Harvard University. Nichol has served on the faculties of Gordon College, New England College of Pharmacy, and Bentley College. In 1971 he was appointed vice president for academic affairs and dean of faculties at Bentley College, Waltham, MA.

Nichol's book *Pentecostalism* was published in 1966. This sympathetic treatment chronicled the movement's proliferation and problems in America at a time when the emerging charismatic movement made its message timely. This book, published by a major publisher (Harper and Row), marked the beginning of a new scholarly interest in American pentecostalism.

Nichol has also written on business and religion, as well as on Christianity in his parents' native Poland.

■ E. L. Blumhofer

NICKEL, THOMAS ROY (1900–1993). Founder and for 10 years editor of the *Full Gospel Business Men's Voice.* Born and raised in Missouri, Nickel graduated from Southwest Missouri State College (now University) and had a long and varied career in journalism before moving to California during WWII. Early in 1953 he felt impressed to attend a Los Angeles meeting of the fledgling ▸Full Gospel Business Men's Fellowship International, where he offered his press and services to ▸Demos Shakarian, the organization's founder and president. Nickel was immediately appointed to edit and publish a magazine. The *Voice's* initial circulation of 5,000 grew to 250,000 by 1962 and proved a significant factor in the growth of the organization and the charismatic movement. On leaving the magazine in 1962, Nickel founded another one called *Testimony.* He has written three books and hundreds of articles.

■ **Bibliography:** *Full Gospel Business Men's Voice* (Feb. 1953), 2 ■ J. Sherrill, *The Happiest People on Earth* (1975).   ■ L. F. Wilson

NIKOLOFF, NICHOLAS (1900–1964). Pastor, educator, and missionary to Eastern Europe. Nicholas Nikoloff was born to Greek Orthodox parents in Bulgaria. His mother had been educated at an American college, and through her influence he attended a Protestant church in Bourgas. He was converted in 1914 while reading a Bible he had purchased. Five years later he began to study law at the University of Sofia. When ▸Ivan Voronaev passed through Bulgaria on his way to evangelize in Russia, Nikoloff learned of the baptism in the Holy Spirit.

Immigrating to the U.S. in 1920, Nikoloff attended college in New York City and received the baptism in the Holy Spirit under the ministry of ▸Robert and Marie Brown at Glad Tidings Tabernacle. He pastored several churches in New York and New Jersey and at the same time attended Bethel Bible Training School in Newark, NJ, graduating in 1924. He then taught at the school until 1926.

Feeling called of God to return to Bulgaria, Nikoloff and his American-born wife, Martha, spent five years (1926–31) evangelizing and pastoring in Bourgas. He also served as the first superintendent of the Evangelical Pentecostal Churches in Bulgaria. From 1935 to 1938 he worked as principal of the Biblical Institute in Danzig (now Gdansk, Poland). While

there, he assisted in the training of young people who went back to various Eastern European countries to preach the gospel. He returned to Bulgaria in 1939 to evangelize and teach.

With the coming of WWII, Nikoloff returned to the U.S. and served as president of Metropolitan Bible Institute, North Bergen, NJ (1941–50), and New England Bible Institute, Framingham, MA (1950–52). In 1952 he joined the faculty of Central Bible Institute of Springfield, MO, where he served (chairman of the Department of Religious Education in 1954; the Bible department beginning in 1956) until his retirement in 1961 due to ill health.

During his years in the U.S., Nikoloff earned the B.R.E. and M.R.E. degrees from the Biblical Seminary in New York (now New York Theological Seminary). In 1956 he completed the Ph.D. from New York University. In recognition of his scholastic record, he received the University's Founders Day Certificate of Achievement.

Nikoloff's publications included two Bulgarian church magazines, several books and tracts, and a songbook in that language. He also worked for five years (1954–59) as the editor of the Sunday school quarterly *Youth Teacher* at ▸Gospel

Nicholas and Martha Nikoloff, early pentecostal missionaries to Eastern Europe, especially to Bulgaria.

Publishing House. The Nikoloffs had three children: a daughter born in Danzig, who died at an early age; another daughter, Natalie (Eliott); and a son, Dr. Paul H. Nichols.

Nicholas Nikoloff made important contributions to the development of the pentecostal churches in Bulgaria, the advance of pentecostalism in Eastern Europe and the Soviet Union, and the training of AG ministers and missionaries.

■ **Bibliography:** "Martha Nikoloff, a Life Committed to Ministry," *Onward* (May 1988) ▮ N. Nikoloff, *Report on Europe* (1943) ▮ idem, "The Signs Follow in Bulgaria," *PE* (June 25, 1932) ▮ "Nicholas Nikoloff with the Lord," *PE* (Dec. 13, 1964) ▮ T. Salzer, "The Danzig Gdanska Instytut Biblijny: Its History and Impact" (unpublished, 1988).   ■ G. B. McGee

NONDENOMINATIONAL PENTECOSTAL AND CHARISMATIC CHURCHES

It is almost impossible to tabulate the number of nondenominational charismatic churches in the U.S. In 1980 a Gallup poll for *Christianity Today* reported that 19% of all adult Americans (more than 29 million) considered themselves to be pentecostal or charismatic Christians. In 1999 missiologist David Barrett estimated that there were as many as 72 million charismatics and pentecostals in the U.S. Some of these belong to mainline denominations; others attend independent charismatic churches.

Some pentecostal churches have remained independent since the early days of the movement for a variety of reasons, including church splits or the fact that the pastors were asked to leave a denomination. But the independent charismatic church did not really appear until the late 1970s, and it did not truly come into its own until the 1990s. The early charismatic movement—which was affected by ministries such as the Oral Roberts Evangelistic Association, ▸Full Gospel Business Men's Fellowship, and television ministries such as the Christian Broadcasting Network and Trinity Broadcasting Network—was often seen as an attempt to fill an emotional, experiential vacuum left in American Christendom, which had become more liberal and rationalistic.

Many early charismatics were once Catholics or members of mainline Protestant churches and often describe their former churches as formal, cold, or dead, while they perceive their charismatic churches as free, warm, and alive. However, many of the new charismatics do not feel comfortable in the classical pentecostal denominations, partly for cultural reasons, such as the preoccupation with the avoidance of "worldly dress." But more often the leadership of the church was turned off by the church politics they saw in the denomination.

In addition, many of the fast-growing churches with large budgets and large staffs often were controlled by the family of the founder of the church, and life was less complicated if denominations were not involved. Though not as legalistic as yesterday's pentecostals, today's charismatics consider it inap-propriate to indulge in the use of tobacco, alcoholic beverages, or drugs. In some quarters the use of wine in moderation is not condemned; in others total abstinence from any form of alcohol is advocated.

The matter of divorce, which tends to put some pentecostals into a "second-class" status, is less of a problem in most charismatic churches, because hard-and-fast rules were not adopted years ago when divorce was not such a common circumstance. Generally speaking, converts are accepted in whatever marital state they find themselves at the time of their conversion. Divorce for a converted person is frowned upon as a sin, but a convert who happens to be divorced is welcomed into the body without reservation. Some churches offer support groups or classes for divorced persons, and others provide counsel for those considering remarriage.

Generally, there is no outright condemnation for members attending motion pictures, plays, sporting events, musical concerts, and the like. However, most charismatics find themselves so involved in a wide variety of church activities that they have little time for secular entertainment.

The one trait that marks charismatics is their exuberance in worship: They raise their hands and sometimes clap or wave in time to the music as they sing choruses. The lyrics for their choruses are usually displayed by overhead projection on a wall or screen or are sung from memory, and they sing heartily. They seldom rely on hymnals. Many of the choruses are based on biblical passages, often from the psalms.

Some churches have spontaneous praise as well as dancing in time to music, but this dancing could not be compared with what takes place on a dance floor. Other churches have praise-dance groups that have learned Hebrew dance patterns and "dance before the Lord" while the congregation watches and worships with them.

Most charismatic churches have choirs and employ musical instruments—from a few guitars and a drummer to full orchestras. Vocal soloists, ensembles, and choirs often sing with commercially produced accompaniment tracks.

In vocal worship, some churches make a distinction between praise and "high praise"—the former being expressed aloud in the common language, the latter being uttered in unknown tongues, sometimes called "singing in the Spirit." While classical pentecostals practice praying aloud (sometimes called praying in concert), charismatics emphasize praising aloud, often accompanied by hand clapping. To many, the charismatic congregation's contributions to the church are a new awareness of the gifts of the Holy Spirit as a ministry to the life of the church, new devotional techniques for public and private worship (not just tongues), exercise of "body life," and an emphasis on discipleship.

When pentecostal believers were forced out of the mainline denominations in the early 20th century, they formed independent churches that tended to hold denominations suspect. Many remained as independent entities, but some nevertheless formed "fellowships" and avoided using the term *denomination*. This was the case with the General Council of the Assemblies of God. In some respects this parallels what has occurred in the charismatic renewal in recent years. The Church of God (Cleveland, TN), founded before the turn of the century as a Holiness denomination, simply accepted the baptism of the Holy Spirit as an authentic biblical experience. Something similar to this took place in the 1960s in several denominations after respected clergy and laity testified to speaking in tongues. In several instances denominations appointed committees to study the biblical validity of the phenomenon, and favorable reports were adopted along with guidelines about charismatic manifestations.

When the ›neo-pentecostal or charismatic movement began in the 1950s and became full-blown in the 1960s, at first many neo-pentecostals stayed in their churches. ›David du Plessis was one leader who encouraged them to do this. "There is no doubt the Holy Spirit is hard at work at bringing unity," he said. "Dialogue is becoming more and more acceptable."

Some congregations, such as ›Terry Fullam's St. Paul's Episcopal Church in Darien, CT, and ›Morris Vaagenes' North Heights Lutheran Church in Roseville, MN, became known as "charismatic parishes."

Yet other charismatics, such as ›Jamie Buckingham from Melbourne, FL, and Ken Sumrall from Pensacola, FL, were forced to withdraw from their denominations because of their newfound charismatic experiences.

Most of the ministers and their congregations preferred to remain independent rather than to affiliate with the classical pentecostal denominations. And most also wanted to avoid starting new denominations because of the stigma they identified with denominations. Yet the charismatics typically were not loners. Most emphasized the unity of believers, and they sought out other charismatics for fellowship. To fan the flames of renewal, charismatic conferences and meetings were sponsored with names such as Camps Farthest Out and National Leadership Conference.

Slowly, new groups began to form, often based on personal relationships between ministers. Among the first to emerge in the early 1970s were groups affiliated with ›Derek Prince, ›Bernard "Bob" Mumford, ›Charles Simpson, ›Don Basham, and later ›W. J. "Ern" Baxter. In 1975 these men called a "Shepherds' Conference" in Kansas City, MO. Some saw this as the forming of a new charismatic denomination, and the matter was hotly debated that year. Those men maintained that they were not starting a denomination, and they held to this so firmly that their group of churches never really became a strong force within the charismatic renewal and finally disintegrated in late 1986.

After a few years there were so many nondenominational charismatics that when the historic 1977 Conference on Charismatic Renewal in the Christian Churches was held in

Kansas City, the nondenominationals were allowed to hold their own meetings while the denominational charismatics (Roman Catholics, Lutherans, Episcopalians, and so on) were holding theirs. In fact, there were two nondenominational meetings—one was for the Prince-Mumford-Simpson-Basham group (which went under a number of different names through the years), and the other for the nondenominationals who did not want to be affiliated with those men. (The discipleship controversy was raging around the ›shepherding movement at this time.)

When the nondenominational ministers formed their own congregations, they found they had to take on some of the trappings of a denomination in order to qualify for non-profit status by the Internal Revenue Service (IRS). They had to form nonprofit corporations. (The IRS expects churches to have a distinct legal existence, a recognized creed and form of worship, a definite and distinctive ecclesiastical government, a formal code of doctrine and discipline, a distinct religious history, a membership not associated with another church denomination, a complete organization of ordained ministers ministering to their congregations, ordained ministers who were selected after completing a prescribed course of study, a literature of its own, established places of worship, regular congregations, regular religious services, Sunday schools for religious instruction of the young, and schools for the preparation of its ministers.)

Few, if any, churches could satisfy all of these criteria, but organizations meeting a preponderance of these items clearly could be recognized by the IRS as a church. In their efforts to satisfy IRS scrutiny, attempts to form single independent local churches sometimes grew into mini-denominations. At times, IRS audits—or the fear of the audits—caused independent charismatic churches to add ministries, such as Bible schools, that were not their original intent.

Some charismatic churches—especially the larger ones—were so totally dominated by a strong pastor—who in some instances had almost unlimited control over the finances—that several of these churches came under scrutiny by the IRS. So in the 1970s some "fellowships" were formed that served as umbrella organizations to some of these nondenominational groups that wished to be affiliated and to add legitimacy in the eyes of the IRS. The ›International Convention of Faith Churches and Ministries in Arlington, TX, with approximately 1,100 ministers, and Liberty Fellowship in Birmingham, AL, which in 1999 listed 35 churches and 215 pastors, were formed in this era.

At the same time, younger men were beginning their own ministries. Some of these set about to recapture certain aspects of church life and mission that others deemphasized. These young ministers formed what they called "New Testament" churches according to what they considered to be the biblical blueprint. Some of these churches are informally linked to each other. Pastors establishing new churches look to existing churches for oversight, although there is an absence of legal or formal ties such as exist in a denomination.

Black pentecostals also have many large, independent charismatic churches. They provide theological conservatism and political-social radicalism that will both challenge and contribute to the development of evangelism. One of the largest charismatic churches pastored by a black minister is Crenshaw Christian Center, which occupies the old Pepperdine University Campus in Los Angeles. Its pastor, ʼFrederick K. C. Price, also conducts a nationwide television ministry.

Other charismatics have developed "Christian centers" on a congregationalist community-church model that, at least in the beginning stages, seeks to do without buildings and sometimes has a very informal sacramental practice. Typical of these structures are the neocharismatic missions of the Jews, which tend to form charismatic messianic synagogues with a loose relationship with one another ʼMessianic Judaism).

In the early 1980s, hundreds of new churches were started by eager young pastors who had been trained at the new charismatic institutions such as ʼRhema Bible Training Center in Tulsa, OK; ʼChrist for the Nations Institute in Dallas; or a host of smaller Bible schools affiliated with churches.

By 1984 there were so many of these nondenominational congregations that the Pentagon recognized them so they could send chaplains to the military. Founded by James Ammerman of Dallas, a former chaplain, the Chaplaincy of Full Gospel Churches estimates that more than 140,000 independent charismatic churches have been started since 1960, which is, they say, a very conservative estimate. In 1999 Ammerman represented roughly 7.5 million people in approximately 1,294 independent charismatic churches.

In Ammerman's 1999 listings are 134 "fellowships," some of which have the trappings of a denomination and some of which are merely umbrella organizations. Ammerman estimates that there are at least 3 million believers in independent churches that are not affiliated with his group. In 1999 the group had placed 56 chaplains in the army, 12 in the navy, 9 in the air force, 62 in the National Guard reserves, 43 in prisons, and 38 in hospitals.

Even though many fellowships had formed, few, if any, used the word *charismatic* in their titles, and almost all were unknown other than by the pastors or churches with whom they were affiliated. Then in 1986 Oral Roberts founded the Charismatic Bible Ministries (CBM) as a fellowship. Later the word *International* was added to the name. Roberts invited 77 men and women as trustees who represented a virtual Who's Who of the nondenominational charismatic segment of the pentecostal/charismatic movement. Within a year more than 2,000 had joined. In 1999 it had almost 6,000 members, including lay ministers.

The trustees adopted a statement of purpose: "The purpose of the fellowship is to provide a broad range of spiritual,

educational and professional benefits to ministers who choose to participate. The foremost benefit is mutual fellowship—spiritual enrichment during conferences, sharing of methods, revelations, prophecies, and teachings in the fullness of the Holy Spirit; and personal encouragement from one minister to another."

Though it advances specific goals, ICBM is not a denomination. It is neither opposed to church denominations nor does it discourage its members from involvement in their respective or independent groups.

But much more than networks or fellowships or denominations, the dynamic of these pentecostal/charismatic churches is the element of the supernatural—the gifts of the Holy Spirit and miracles being available to everyone. It is not the fact that a church is independent or part of a denomination that is emphasized; it is the fact that the people who worship in that church experience a consciousness of God's presence. In that presence they worship him, not in a distant formal manner, but with awareness that he actually is present.

In the 1990s the charismatic megachurch became more common. Ted Haggard, a graduate of Oral Roberts University, began New Life Church in Colorado Springs, CO, in 1984; in 1999 it had more than 7,000 members. Keith Butler, whose roots were in the Church of God in Christ, broke from his denomination and formed Word of Faith International Christian Center, a predominantly black church in Detroit, which in 1999 had 15,000 members. Butler also pastors a 1,300-member church in Atlanta and a 350-member church in Phoenix. Dennis Leonard's Heritage Christian Center in Denver had grown to 11,000 members in 1999, while Don Meares' Evangel Church in suburban Washington, DC, had a membership of 3,000.

Also in the 1990s, charismatic ministers who believed they lacked a system of accountability but did not want the rigid structure of a denomination began to form loose networks of churches, often called fellowships. By 1999 there were hundreds of these networks, often headed by a visionary leader sometimes referred to as an apostle. Ché Ahn, a Korean-American pastor based in Los Angeles, heads a network called Harvest International Ministries, which in 1999 represented 300 churches. ʼJohn Arnott, who was formerly associated with the Vineyard Movement, heads a network of churches known as Partners in Harvest. Observers predict that as these networks mature and experience growth, they could possibly become the denominations of tomorrow.

See also CHARISMATIC MOVEMENT.

■ **Bibliography:** J. Guinn "Church Audits under the Tax Reform Act," *Ministries Today* (Sept./Oct. 1986) ■ L. Howard, "Humble Young Men, Enormous New Churches," *Charisma* (Sept. 1984) ■ K. S. Kantzer "The Charismatics among Us," *Christianity Today* (Feb. 22, 1980) ■ D. Roberts, "They Call Him Mr. Pentecost," *Charisma* (Nov./Dec. 1978) ■ S. Strang, "The Ever-Increasing Faith of Fred Price," *Charisma* (May 1985) ■ idem, "Groundwork Set for New Ministry," *Charisma* (Sept. 1986).   ■ S. Strang

NORTH AMERICAN CONGRESSES ON THE HOLY SPIRIT AND WORLD EVANGELIZATION

The first North American Congress on the Holy Spirit and World Evangelization was held in New Orleans on Oct. 8–11, 1986. More than 7,000 leaders from a total of 40 denominations and church groups attended the conference. The theme of the conference was a challenge to work together for the evangelization of the world. One of the main speakers was ▸John Wimber, who also led three workshops on ▸"Signs and Wonders." Roman Catholic leader ▸Tom Forrest urged the group to unite in the belief that "Jesus Christ is Lord." Honored at this meeting for their contributions were ▸Oral Roberts, ▸Demos Shakarian, ▸David du Plessis, and Mennonite renewal leader ▸Nelson Litwiller. Two denominational renewal groups were formed at this meeting, one of Southern Baptists and the other a mix of the Churches of Christ, the Christian Church, and the Disciples of Christ.

The second congress, with up to 35,000 registrants and perhaps as many as 40,000 in attendance, was a general conference that, unlike the first one, was open to the public and held in New Orleans on July 22–26, 1987. The theme of this conference seemed to be a call to personal holiness and commitment to evangelization. Participants had their choice of 110 different workshops, such as "God's Call to the Single Adult," "Messianic Worship in the Local Congregation," "Discovering Your Ministry in the Body of Christ," and "Spiritual Warfare." Workshop leaders included ▸James Robison, Ken Sumrall, ▸Michael Scanlan, ▸Anne Gimenez, Shirley Boone, Charles and Francis Hunter, ▸Dennis Bennett, ▸Marilyn Hickey, ▸Charles Simpson, and John Meares.

Chairman ▸Vinson Synan reported that 3,500 to 5,000 persons went to the prayer room each night in response to the altar call. Many of these were first-time converts. Responding to a call to change New Orleans, over 10,000 participants gathered for a parade in the port area on the Mississippi River. It was the largest parade in New Orleans' history, with the exception of Mardi Gras.

One of the most remarkable moments occurred when German evangelist ▸Reinhard Bonnke gave an altar call for salvation and one-third of those present stood to their feet. He repeated the call and more stood! David Sklrenko Sr., a Roman Catholic, suggested that Bonnke's call could have been understood by Roman Catholics as a "renewing of Christian vows" rather than as a first-time commitment. Many remarkable healings were reported under Bonnke's ministry as well.

Synan remarked, "This Conference brought evangelization into the thinking of the charismatic renewal. Where evangelization has never before been a big part of the charismatic experience, now it will become the major thrust of the renewal."

A world congress with 25,000 in attendance was held in 1990 in Indianapolis.

■ **Bibliography:** S. Lawson, "The Big Charismatic Get-Together," *Charisma* (Sept. 1987) ■ idem, "Focus on Miracles and Evangelism," *Charisma* (June 1987) ■ idem, "Leaders Unite in New Orleans," *Charisma* (Dec. 1986).   ■ J. R. Zeigler

NORTH AMERICAN RENEWAL SERVICE COMMITTEE

(NARSC). Steering committee for the North American Congresses on the Holy Spirit and World Evangelization. After the meeting on the Holy Spirit held in Kansas City in 1977, there was talk of another national meeting. On May 6–7, 1985, 32 Christian leaders met in St. Louis, MO, to discuss plans for a national conference. ▸Vinson Synan, assistant general superintendent of the ▸Pentecostal Holiness Church, served as chairman of the group. The decision was made to hold a national leadership conference in New Orleans in 1986 and a general North American conference in New Orleans in 1987. Conferences were also held in Indianapolis (1990) and Orlando (1995), and one is planned for 2000. ▸Kevin Ranaghan, chairman of the Kansas City meeting and serving on the steering committee of the NARSC, said one of the goals of the NARSC was to emphasize the role of the Holy Spirit in world evangelization. He added, "[We want to show] that we are people who are depending on the power of the Holy Spirit in Christian life and the power of the Holy Spirit in spiritual gifts."

■ **Bibliography:** S. Haggerty, "Kansas City 2," *Charisma* (July 1985).   ■ J. R. Zeigler

NORTON, ALBERT

(d. 1923). Missionary in India. A university-trained minister from Chicago, Norton was an early proponent of faith missions. He exhibited tenacity and self-sacrifice in reaching the Kurkus of central India. He collaborated with ▸Pandita Ramabai in famine relief in 1899 and was on hand to witness the outpouring that occurred at her nearby Mukti Mission in 1905. A similar revival with pentecostal phenomena was experienced at his home for boys.

■ **Bibliography:** F. J. Ewart, *The Phenomenon of Pentecost* (1947) ■ S. Frodsham, *With Signs Following* (1941) ■ B. F. Lawrence, "Apostolic Faith Restored," published serially in *Weekly Evangel* (Apr. 1, 1916) ■ C. Montgomery, *Under His Wings* (1936) ■ J. E. Norton, "In Memorium of Albert Norton," *LRE* (Apr. 1924).
                              ■ E. A. Wilson

O

O'CONNOR, EDWARD DENNIS (1922–). Prominent priest-theologian in the early stages of the Catholic charismatic renewal. O'Connor entered the Holy Cross Congregation in 1939 and was ordained priest in 1948. He taught theology at the University of Notre Dame from 1952, becoming an associate professor of theology. O'Connor was one of the first priests to receive the baptism in the Spirit in 1967. His book *The Pentecostal Movement in the Catholic Church* (1971) describes the origins at Notre Dame, interpreting them within a Catholic framework. In the first years of the movement O'Connor wrote several pamphlets on charismatic topics and theological articles, mostly concerning ecclesiology and the spiritual life. He served on the National Service Committee from 1970 to 1973, when he resigned due to his unease with its attitude toward church authority. O'Connor, who still participates in charismatic prayer meetings, has edited *Perspectives on Charismatic Renewal* (1975) and authored *Pope Paul and the Spirit* (1978).

■ P. D. Hocken

OLAZÁBAL, FRANCISCO (1886–1937). Hispanic evangelist. Considered to have been the most effective Hispanic preacher of the early pentecostal movement, Mexican-born Olazábal was converted in San Francisco under the influence of ▸George and Carrie Judd Montgomery about 1900. He completed studies at the Methodist seminary in San Luis Potosí, Mexico, and had brief pastorates before returning to the U.S. to enter Moody Bible Institute, where he met R. A. Torrey. His ministry with the Methodist Church reached its height during WWI, when he pastored a congregation in Los Angeles and was given oversight of churches in northern California. His reacquaintance with the Montgomerys—who in the meantime had become pentecostal—led to his own baptism and his affiliation with the Assemblies of God in 1917.

In 1923, having grown restive within the predominantly Anglo organization, he led a group of disaffected pastors in forming the Latin American Council of Christian Churches (LACCC). In the following 14 years he conducted numerous well-attended crusades in California, Texas, the Midwest, and Puerto Rico, and on the East Coast. Known affectionately as "El Azteca," the well-educated, physically imposing, and unusually effective evangelist dominated his devoted following. By 1937, when he met an untimely death in an auto accident, the LACCC numbered an estimated 150 churches with 50,000 adherents in Puerto Rico, New York, Chicago, Texas, and California.

■ **Bibliography:** H. C. Ball, "De los Primeros Cincuenta Años de las Asambleas de Dios Latinas," *La Luz Apostólica* 50 (9, 1966) ■ V. De León, *The Silent Pentecostals* (1979) ■ R. Domínguez, *Pioneros de Pentecostés* (1971) ■ C. L. Holland, *The Religious Dimensions in Hispanic Los Angeles* (1974). ■ E. A. Wilson

ONENESS PENTECOSTALISM A religious movement that emerged in 1914 within the ▸Assemblies of God (AG) stream of the early American pentecostal revival, challenging the traditional Trinitarian doctrine and baptismal practice with a modalistic view of God, a doctrine of the name of Jesus, and an insistence upon rebaptism in the name of the Lord Jesus Christ. It took on organizational form in 1917 as a result of expulsion from the AG. Originally called the "New Issue" or "Jesus Only," by 1930 the movement's self-designation was "Jesus Name," "Apostolic," or "Oneness" pentecostalism (OP).

1. Origins.

In its distinctive teachings as well as those doctrines held in common with its AG parent, OP is an inheritor of 19th-century revivalism, and in particular the non-Wesleyan or ▸Keswick Holiness movement. As a form of evangelical experiential religion, the Holiness movement emphasized the importance of divine power in the life of the Christian, an experience that came to be called the "Higher Life" or the baptism of the Holy Spirit. This was accompanied by a Jesus-centered piety in which the name Jesus was the object of devotion. For many, the name itself became a source of spiritual power. As the virgin birth and deity of Christ came under attack by the liberalism of the day, some evangelical apologists turned to a biblical study of the names of God in the OT to demonstrate that Jesus was the God of the old covenant.

As the earliest Oneness leaders developed a distinctive doctrine of the name of Jesus, they were influenced heavily by the writings of such Higher Life advocates as Arno C. Gaebelein, A. J. Gordon, William Phillips Hall, ▸Essek W. Kenyon, and ▸A. B. Simpson, as well as the Presbyterian writer J. Monro Gibson.

The New Issue, however, emerged within the leadership that spearheaded the first doctrinal schism within the early pentecostal movement, the "finished work of Calvary" teaching of Chicago pastor and evangelist ▸William Durham. It was a radical extension of Durham's mission, which was to shift the focus from a pneumatological preoccupation with multiple experiences (conversion, sanctification, baptism of the Holy Spirit) to the "simple gospel" that focuses all grace in Christ's atoning work. This christological move not only formed the doctrinal foundation of the non-Wesleyan pente-costal stream, especially the AG, it also sowed the seeds of a radical Christocentric alternative that reasoned that, if there is only one name (Jesus) to be used in baptism, that name must be given by God in biblical revelation, and it must reflect the radical unity of God's being. The New Issue pioneers had been disciples of Durham and had continued to promote the fin-ished work message following his death in 1912. Among them were ▸Frank Ewart, ▸Garfield T. Haywood, ▸R. E. McAlister, ▸Franklin Small, and ▸Andrew Urshan.

2. Beginnings.

The initial impetus for the Oneness movement occurred in Apr. 1913 at a highly publicized international pentecostal camp meeting in Arroyo Seco, outside Los Angeles. The moment came in a baptismal sermon by Canadian evangel-ist R. E. McAlister, in which he proposed that the reason the apostles baptized in the name of the Lord Jesus Christ (vari-ations in Acts) instead of the triune name commanded by Jesus (Matt. 28:19) was that they understood "Lord-Jesus-Christ" to be the christological equivalent of "Father-Son-Holy Spirit."

An otherwise little-known figure, John G. Scheppe, med-itated on McAlister's explanation throughout that night. In the early hours of the morning he ran through the camp shouting that God had revealed to him the truth of baptism in the name of the Lord Jesus Christ.

Although the initial "revelation" made little immediate impact, McAlister's sermon had a lasting effect on a friend and fellow worker, Frank J. Ewart. Australian by birth and a former Baptist minister, Ewart had come into the pentecostal experience while pastoring in Canada. In 1911 he became an associate at Seventh Street Mission in Los Angeles under William Durham.

Following the 1913 camp meeting, Ewart continued to minister in Los Angeles while privately studying the bap-tismal question raised by McAlister. One year later he was ready to act. He erected a tent in the town of Belvedere out-side Los Angeles and preached his first public sermon on Acts 2:38 on Apr. 15, 1914. He was joined by ▸Glenn A. Cook, another prominent evangelist, and together they bap-tized each other in a baptismal tank set up in the tent. While other early pentecostals had been baptized in the name of Jesus, notably Howard Goss and Andrew Urshan, this was the first public baptism to be carried out with a theologically consistent rationale. As the first theologian of the New Issue, Ewart's particular contribution was a modalistic view of God and a theology of the name of Jesus.

The new doctrine spread rapidly through evangelistic tours and Ewart's new publication, *Meat in Due Season*, which had an international circulation. The message was quickly planted in the Midwest by Glenn Cook in the early months of 1915. The result was a number of baptisms at Mother ▸Mary Barnes' Faith Home in St. Louis. It was here that ▸J. Roswell Flower, himself a convert of Cook and leader in the newly formed AG, first heard but strongly resisted the doctrine.

Cook proceeded on to Indianapolis, where he successfully won over another prominent leader, L. V. Roberts, and his entire congregation. More significant for the future was the recruitment of the popular black preacher Garfield T. Hay-wood, who was baptized with 465 members of his thriving congregation. Haywood had been part of Durham's inner cir-cle and a strong advocate of the ▸finished work teaching. His conversion was strategic as he wielded wide influence nation-ally as an evangelist and preacher, even though he did not officially hold credentials with the AG. His influence even-tually resulted in large numbers of black pentecostals joining the Oneness ranks.

By the spring of 1915 the new movement was making dramatic inroads in the fledgling AG fellowship. Louisiana lost all 12 of its ministers. Advances were being made across Canada through the efforts of R. E. McAlister, the conver-sion of ▸Franklin Small (a pentecostal leader from Win-nipeg), and numerous American evangelists.

As the New Issue spread, controversy intensified. A lead-ing figure in the debate was ▸E. N. Bell, member of the exec-utive presbytery of the AG and editor of its two magazines, *Weekly Evangel* and *Word and Witness*. His assistant editor was Flower, already an opponent and soon to be the movement's staunchest opponent. Throughout the spring of 1915 Bell published articles and editorials denouncing the New Issue. Although he accepted baptism in the name of Jesus Christ as a valid alternative, he opposed any requirement to be rebaptized. Yet in his writings he remained cordial and con-ciliatory.

The summer brought a change in Bell. At an AG camp meeting in Jackson, TN, under the strain of conscience or fatigue, he requested to be rebaptized by Roberts. This appar-ent defection stunned many and precipitated confusion throughout the fellowship. In the fall Bell absented himself from the headquarters for the remainder of the year, leaving Flower in charge of the editorial work.

In articles that Bell then wrote, but strictly edited by Flower, it is clear that his spiritual affections centered on the centrality of Jesus Christ and the significance of the name "Lord." In a portion edited out, he defended his personal con-viction in the validity of baptism in the name of the Lord Jesus Christ but continued to maintain that rebaptism was unnecessary. He denounced contention and factionalism, rec-ommended freedom in baptismal practice, discouraged rebaptism, and admonished preachers to refrain from pro-moting their preference without expressed permission of the host pastor. This and his firm Trinitarian belief served to restrain him from enlisting in the new movement.

The rapid and aggressive spread of the New Issue, Bell's rebaptism, and the growing confusion within the AG ranks thrust Flower into the center of the controversy as defender of the Trinitarian cause. Sensing the urgency to reverse the tide, he sought permission to call the 3d general council for Oct. 1–10, 1915, in St. Louis. The stated purpose was to address the new teaching. Once assembled, attention was concentrated on an examination of the baptismal formulae. Although no consensus was reached, the council called for neutrality, liberality, and respect for the rights of conscience for both ministers and local congregations. It denounced aspects of the new teaching on God and Christ as being in variance with Scripture.

The coming months were intended as a trial period to ease tensions. But little effort was made to follow the guidelines of the 3d council. New Issue advocates continued to evangelize aggressively within the fellowship. The Trinitarian faction reacted with increasing hostility and intensified its attacks on the movement.

As antagonism mounted, the agenda for the 4th council in the fall of 1916 was set to settle the matter. The Trinitarians entered the meeting in control of the key positions and committees. The committee to draft a doctrinal statement was solidly Trinitarian, including Bell, who by then was back in full favor with the council leadership.

Although the council at its inception in 1914 had disavowed any intention to create an organization "that legislates or forms laws and articles of faith" (*Council Minutes*, 1914, 4), the 4th council was faced with the unpleasant task of setting doctrinal limits. The result was a 17-point "Statement of Fundamental Truths" that included a strongly worded section affirming the historic doctrine of the Trinity (*Council Minutes*, 1916). With the adoption of the statement, 156 of the 585 ministers were instantly barred from membership, and with them numerous congregations.

3. Organizational Development.

Amid rumors of its demise, the disenfranchised company of dissidents reappeared within months to ensure for itself a future. Leaders such as ᵉHoward Goss, H. G. Rogers, and ᵉD. C. O. Opperman, who less than three years earlier had been in the forefront of forming the AG, called for an organizational meeting on Dec. 28, 1916, in Eureka Springs, AR. Six days later the General Assembly of Apostolic Assemblies (GAAA) came into being, with a membership of 154 ministers, missionaries, elders, deacons, and evangelists.

The life of the GAAA, however, was brief. Most ministers needed an organization that was legally authorized to issue credentials. But with the impending involvement of the United States in WWI, it was soon discovered that the GAAA had been formed too late to authorize ministerial exemption from military service.

A small pentecostal organization with an active legal charter was soon found. The ᵉPentecostal Assemblies of the World (PAW) originated as a loose fellowship in 1907 in the Los Angeles area. Haywood had held credentials since 1911, and undoubtedly through his good efforts a merger was negotiated by Jan. 1918 in St. Louis under the charter of the PAW.

By the following year three publications already in existence were officially recognized: Ewart's *Meat in Due Season*, Haywood's *Voice in the Wilderness*, and Opperman's *The Blessed Truth*.

Prominent early Oneness leaders varied in their relationship to the PAW. Ewart was listed in the membership of both the GAAA and PAW, but he held no official position, and his name disappeared from the rolls by 1920. Although he later held credentials with other organizations, he devoted his energy to pastoring in Belvedere, CA, teaching, and writing.

Franklin Small from Winnipeg converted to the New Issue in 1915. He held credentials with the PAW for the purpose of fellowship but also became a charter member of the ᵉPentecostal Assemblies of Canada (PAOC) in 1917. He promoted the Oneness message through his magazine *Living Waters*. In 1921 he formed a Canadian organization, the ᵉApostolic Church of Pentecost (ACOP), to promote the Oneness movement in western Canada. The ACOP is distinctive in that it permits membership to those who adhere to the doctrine of the Trinity and holds to the Calvinistic doctrine of the "eternal security" of the believer.

ᵉAndrew Urshan, a Persian immigrant, was a prominent evangelist and missionary with the AG until 1919. He had been baptized in the name of Jesus and continued the same practice in his ministry since 1911. After the schism in 1916 he came under increasing suspicion for holding views sympathetic to the New Issue. But it was not until 1919 that he finally affiliated with the PAW. He advanced the new doctrine through evangelism and the publication of his periodical, *The Witness of God*.

G. T. Haywood was wide-ranging in his influence as a preacher, teacher, hymn writer, artist, organizational leader, and periodical publisher. He was an outspoken advocate of racial integration within the PAW. His doctrinal teaching and leadership continued to inspire the black Oneness movement long after his death in 1931. He held various positions within the PAW, including presiding bishop.

The vision of a racially integrated body gradually eroded between 1920 and 1924. Haywood's influence and the moving of the PAW headquarters to Indianapolis resulted in the blacks increasing sufficiently in number until they soon became the majority in the North. Given the South's segregation laws, conventions were held in the North. Financial limitations prevented large numbers of the white southern majority to attend. In 1921 the southern constituency held a

Bible conference in Little Rock, AR, which had the effect of both unifying the white members and deepening the rift between them and the northern blacks.

The whites argued pragmatically that an integrated organization was a barrier to the spread of the movement in the South. However, their racist attitudes were exposed in complaints that a black official, Haywood (then general secretary), was signing ministerial credentials for the white ministers. A compromise resolution in 1923—to allow T. C. Davis, a black, and Howard Goss, a white, to sign certificates for those who requested—failed to stem the tide of disunity.

The whites entered the 1924 General Conference with a proposal that two racially separate administrations be formed under one umbrella organization. With its failure to meet the approval of the blacks, the majority of whites withdrew from the PAW, cutting its rolls by over 50%. The schism left a legacy of bitterness on both sides. It was regarded as a special affront to the black members who had struggled to maintain the racial unity of the fragile organization.

The years 1924–31 were slow and struggling for both sides. The names and number of members in the PAW remained virtually unchanged. While the whites grew faster, differences within their ranks resulted in the formation of three groups in 1925, based in part on regional concentration.

One group formed in Tennessee as The Pentecostal Ministerial Alliance (PMA). Baptistic influences were evident organizationally in its congregational polity and doctrinally in its understanding that one is born again at conversion. In 1932 it changed its name to ʾPentecostal Church, Incorporated (PCI).

Another group formed in the Houston area as Emmanuel's Church in Jesus Christ (ECJC), representing the tri-state region of Louisiana, Oklahoma, and Texas. It managed to merge in 1927 with the Apostolic Church of Jesus Christ (ACJC), a third group that had formed earlier in St. Louis. Theologically, many of its members embraced an alternative teaching that to be born again one must undergo water baptism in Jesus' name and receive the baptism with the Holy Spirit.

This period was one of fragmentation, failed attempts to reunify, and little numerical growth. Finally, a large unity conference of all Oneness groups was held in Columbus, OH, in Sept. 1931 to explore the possibility of reunification. From that meeting came a flurry of negotiations, with both white organizations approaching the PAW. The PMA's proposal, which included a separate administration system, failed in the negotiation stage.

The offer by the ACJC of a racially balanced, integrated system quickly won the support of many PAW leaders. A swift merger was achieved by Nov. 1931 under a new name, The ʾPentecostal Assemblies of Jesus Christ (PAJC). The speed with which the leaders negotiated the merger, however,

soon became a source of suspicion on the part of some black leaders in the PAW. They feared that insincerity and opportunism were the motives prompting the white negotiators.

The charges, the compromise to change the name of the organization, and the abandonment of the episcopal form of government (which the PAW had practiced since 1925) were sufficient reasons for ministers like Samuel Grimes, E. F. Akers, and A. W. Lewis to take action. The original PAW charter was salvaged from obscurity just before its expiration date. A meeting to reorganize was called in Dayton, OH, and the old organization reemerged under the leadership of Grimes.

The continuing PAJC was soon fraught with racial tension. Due to the selection of the southern city of Tulsa, OK, as the site of the 1937 general convention, black ministers were confronted with segregated accommodations. This indignity motivated most of the ministers who had supported the new experiment to return to the PAW. Sufficient pain and disillusionment came with the experience to discourage any serious attempt at a merger in the future.

A persistent drive for unity continued between the two white organizations, the PAJC and PCI. One unsuccessful attempt was made in 1936. In 1941 a significant schism occurred when L. R. Ooten from Indiana led nearly 1,000 ministers from the tri-state region of Indiana, Ohio, and West Virginia out of the PAJC to form the Apostolic Ministerial Alliance.

In 1945 the two organizations finally negotiated a merger to form the largest Oneness organization, the ʾUnited Pentecostal Church Incorporated (UPCI). Creating a ministerial strength of nearly 1,800 ministers and over 900 congregations, the union was built on a delicate compromise over the theological interpretation of the new birth. All agreed on the practice of baptism in Jesus' name and the pentecostal experience of the baptism of the Holy Spirit according to Acts 2:38. But they could not agree that this pattern constitutes the new birth. The compromise called on each member to refrain from promoting one position if it threatened the unity of the fellowship. The compromise succeeded in maintaining the structural unity of the new body, with the exception of two major defections in later years. Eventually the segment that identified Acts 2:38 with the new birth increased sufficiently in numerical growth that it finally gained control of most of the leadership positions. The UPCI is by far the largest Oneness organization. It maintains an aggressive evangelistic program, operates its own publishing house, and supports nine Bible schools in the U.S. and Canada.

Although much of its doctrine and organizational structure are similar to those of the AG, there are differences. Due in part to the Wesleyan Holiness influence of certain early Oneness leaders, the UPCI maintains a more centralized form of church government. It expects a higher degree of conformity to its code of conduct and allegiance to the organizational fellowship. There are restrictions on the public fellowshiping of any minister or group that has been formerly dismissed from the UPCI for doctrinal or moral cause. Its doctrine of sanctification is consistent with that of the AG, the Keswickian view that holiness is a progressive work in the life of the believer and perfection is unattainable in this life. In practice, however, it reflects strong Wesleyan Holiness influences and perceives itself to be part of the Holiness pentecostal tradition. Specified religious customs are set forth as a standard of holiness that serve to separate adherents from the world. The two customs that distinguish the UPCI from many other groups are the injunction for women not to cut their hair (see 1 Cor. 11) and the ruling against clergy owning a television.

The PAW has continued to be a predominantly black organization since 1931. Although whites are a small minority, an intentional policy of racial integration is maintained. White representation is encouraged at all levels, including the office of presiding bishop. The PAW continues a high degree of commitment to an episcopal polity.

Most black Oneness groups trace their origin directly or indirectly to the PAW. Haywood's abiding influence is evident in the fact that there has been little variance from his core doctrinal teachings. Most disputes and splits have occurred over leadership, divorce and remarriage, and the use of wine in communion.

The growing institutionalization of the movement and a desire for a larger expression of unity among the smaller organizations led in 1971 to the formation of the Apostolic World Christian Fellowship (AWCF). The original vision came from Worthy Rowe, a pastor in South Bend, IN. Invitations were extended to official heads of organizations, which resulted in eight groups being represented at the first meeting. Organizationally, the AWCF continues to be an association of Oneness organizations that respects the sovereignty of each. Voting rights are granted only to organizational officials, though independent clergy are encouraged to attend.

The UPCI refused to participate from the outset due to Rowe's association with a doctrinal deviation taught by his father, G. B. Rowe. The latter had held official positions in the early PAW, PAJC, and UPC, but was finally dismissed from the UPCI in the early 1950s for refusal to abandon his commitment to a form of adoptionist Christology. Worthy, having never publicly renounced his father's views, has continued under the ban. The UPCI has extended the fellowship ban to the AWCF under a policy of guilt by association, not only over Rowe's leadership, but also because of the presence of a small number of ministers or groups who in the past had either split or were dismissed from the UPCI.

Isolated from pan-pentecostal organizations such as the Pentecostal World Fellowship and the Pentecostal and Charismatic Churches of North America, Oneness groups from around the world find in the AWCF a vehicle for demonstrating unity, assessing numerical strength, and coordinating evangelistic efforts. It currently represents 153 Oneness organizations worldwide with an estimated membership of 3.5 million.

Like the pentecostal movement in general, a small segment of Oneness believers is invisible or can be found on the fringes. Hundreds of independent churches affiliate with no organization. Beliefs that are essentially Oneness can be found among approximately two dozen small Sabbatarian groups. Some are Yahwist groups devoted to the Sacred Name of Yahweh, water baptism in the name of Jesus or Yahshua, and a modalistic view of God. And some snake-handling sects in West Virginia, Tennessee, and Kentucky hold to a form of Oneness belief and practice.

The Oneness stream of pentecostalism has experienced remarkable growth since the 1960s in both North America and the Third World. The UPCI now claims a global membership of 2.3 million, and the worldwide Oneness movement is estimated to have at least 14 million followers in over 425 organizations (see T. French).

4. Theology.

a. A Theology of the Name. Historically OP is part of the modern pentecostal movement, rooted in the millenarian and restorationist impulses of late-19th-century evangelical religion. Many of its beliefs and practices can be traced to these origins.

OP also represents the perennial possibility for latent themes and concepts in Scripture to be rediscovered and adapted to a new context. It is particularly evident in the manner in which distinctively OT Jewish themes and interests were displaced by the advance of Gentile Christianity in the early church. NT scholar Richard Longenecker observes how this pattern influenced the early christological disputes:

> In reaction to the direction that the crystalization *[sic]* of thought in mainstream Christianity was taking, some undoubtedly latched onto earlier titles which they felt were being ignored and certain perspectives which they considered illegitimately relegated to an inferior position in the structure of Christian thought. (*The Christology of Early Jewish Christianity*, 153)

In OP's distinctive doctrines of God, Christ, and Christian initiation, the primitivist influence is exhibited in the claim to have rediscovered the apostolic truth and power of the nature and name of God. OP also reflects the sectarian tendency to place all other doctrines at the service of the primary "discovery," and by it to define the group's relationship to all other Christian bodies.

The specifically Jewish characteristics of the Oneness doctrine of God are the belief that the name reveals God's true nature, that God is without internal differentiation, and that God "dwells" in tabernacle, temple, and in particular in God's revealed name.

Oneness Christology extends this Jewish concept of divine "dwelling" in a name to the name Jesus, thereby making the name of Jesus a central christological affirmation of his deity rather than his humanity. When interpreted in terms of the two-nature theory of later centuries, OP reflects the Nestorian tendency to separate the two natures in Christ.

The theology of the name takes on significance for the believer when that person invokes the name of Jesus in water baptism. By so doing the initiate is united with the crucified and risen Lord (Rom. 6:6). In the Christian life, the name of Jesus is a source of divine protection against evil forces, an instrument of spiritual power to manifest the signs of the kingdom, and the cause of religious persecution by those who resist Jesus and his mission.

b. *The Name and the Nature of God.* The heart of Oneness theology is the belief that God has revealed himself through his name beginning in the OT. The name is more than a human designation for divine reality. It is God's chosen means for revealing his presence, character, and purpose, and for making possible the divine-human encounter (Ex. 33:18–19). Although the OT records various names for God, usually to designate divine attributes, the name Yahweh (YHWH) holds a special place as the name by which God is known in revelation. The singularity of this name affirms and substantiates the belief in the radical unity of God's nature. In the words of Frank Ewart, "The unity of God is sustained by the absolute unity or oneness of His name" (*The Revelation of Jesus Christ*, 21). Treating Yahweh as a proper name prepares the way for a theology of the name of Jesus, the NT name given by God as a means of self-revelation and salvation.

The radical unity of God is affirmed in the *Shema* (Deut. 6:4) and other passages that state God's oneness, leading Oneness writers such as David Bernard to claim for OP the designation "Christian Monotheism" (*The Oneness of God*, 13).

Oneness theology builds its alternative to the Trinitarian doctrine of God on three principles. First, the nature of God is understood as a simple dialectic of transcendence and immanence. The only distinction within the Godhead is otherness and communicability. In the NT it is expressed as Spirit and Word, or, in personal categories, as Father and Son. The oneness of God is preserved in God's transcendence, God's threeness in revelation. In contrast to Trinitarian theology, the divine threefold reality exists only in revelation.

Second, the "personhood" of God is reserved for God's immanent and incarnate presence in Jesus, while "Spirit" designates God in transcendent otherness. Unaware of the complexity of traditional Trinitarian language, OP interprets "person" according to the modern definition of a corporal human being. This explains the Oneness charge that Trinitarians are crypto-tritheists. To describe the transcendence of God as "Spirit," however, does not imply that God is an impersonal force. The character of personhood is preserved in the name that embodies and reveals God. This "Spirit-Person" dialectic is the principle by which Oneness theology understands the incarnation. It is the one Spirit, the full-undifferentiated Deity, not the Second Person of the Trinity, who becomes incarnate in the human person from Nazareth. In Oneness terms, the Father (deity) indwells the Son (humanity).

Third, the threefold divine reality is expressed as three "manifestations" of the one Spirit in the person of Jesus. Based on the christological hymn in 1 Tim. 3:16, the term "manifestation" (cf. KJV) implies self-revelation, not the character of being-itself. As a form of modalism, it preserves the radical monarchy of God and affirms a triune revelation. Believing mistakenly that Trinitarianism implies divine existence in three *separate* and distinct centers of consciousness or persons, OP argues that the whole essential Godhead, not just one divine person, is present in Jesus (see Col. 2:9).

Some Oneness writers prefer the more functional term *offices* to *manifestations*. But its lack of biblical reference and personal connotation make it less appealing to most Oneness representatives.

The Oneness interpretation of the traditional "us" passages in the OT (e.g., Gen. 1:26; 3:22), which some Trinitarians interpret as dialogue among the members of the Trinity, varies with authors. Gordon Magee argues that God is speaking to angels (*Is Jesus in the Godhead or Is the Godhead in Jesus?* 26). John Paterson, who holds a variant position that the Word was a distinct reality within the Godhead before the incarnation, believes that God was conversing with the Word, "the embodiment of the invisible God" (*God in Christ Jesus*, 39). Embodiment here refers to a divine hypostatic reality within the divine being. The plural name Elohim is generally understood to refer to a plurality of attributes or majesty, not persons.

Like Trinitarians, analogies are used by Oneness writers to illustrate their understanding of the tri-unity of God. These include the triune nature of humanity as body, soul, and spirit; a man as son, husband, and father; a tree with roots, branches, and sap; a light ray giving illumination, warmth, and power; fire that also provides light, heat, and power. The Oneness selection of analogies, however, is weak, since Trinitarian apologists over the centuries have drawn upon the same analogies.

The three manifestations of Father, Son, and Holy Spirit function in much the same way as persons do in Trinitarian theology. Personality is attributable to all three. The difference is that for OPs there is only one divine being who is revealed as Father *in* the Son and as Spirit *through* the Son.

The theological center is Christocentric in that as a human being Jesus *is* the Son, and as Spirit (i.e., in his deity) he reveals, indeed, *is* the Father, and sends, indeed *is*, the Holy Spirit as the Spirit of the risen Jesus who indwells the believer. Because God is one, the Father, Son, and Holy Spirit are all present in the manifestation of each (in traditional Trinitarian language, a *perichoresis*).

OP is a form of modalism, which, unlike Sabellianism, affirms the presence of all three manifestations simultaneously, rather than in successive epochs of salvation history. While OP language is occasionally similar to the doctrine of the economic Trinity, it is insufficiently developed to warrant identification with it.

It can also be argued that OP overcomes the traditional charge against Sabellianism, namely, that since the three *persona* or masks are restricted to God-in-revelation, there is no theological necessity that they reveal the inner and true nature of God. God, in this scheme, could be essentially other than what is revealed in the *persona*. OP, on the other hand, upholds a radical Christocentrism that concentrates the three manifestations in the historical reality of Jesus. More important, the person of Jesus as revelation is bound to the being of God by means of the name of Jesus, the name that bears within it the very nature of God and is given as God's "proper name" in the New Testament.

c. *The Name and Christology*. The most distinctive aspect of Oneness Christology, and fundamental to it, is its understanding of the name of Jesus. Since Jesus etymologically embodies the name Yahweh (meaning "Yahweh is salvation") and is the name given by the angel to Mary, Jesus is treated as the proper name of God for the new covenant era. It reveals the identity of Jesus in his deity and describes his mission as Savior (see Matt. 1:21; Luke 1:31; John 5:43; Acts 4:12; Phil. 2:9–11; Heb. 1:4).

In the compound name "Lord Jesus Christ," the name of Jesus is treated with few exceptions as the revelational name, with "Lord" and "Christ" functioning as descriptive titles that distinguish this Jesus from all others by that name. Rather than it being a reference to his humanity, as in the traditional interpretation, the name uniquely bears the stamp of divinity.

Jewish Christian characteristics are evident in Oneness Christology. To the Hebrew *Shema* (Deut. 6:4), a favorite passage of OPs for defending the radical unity of God, is added the supporting NT text, "In him dwelleth all the fulness of the Godhead bodily" (Col. 2:9 KJV). This text is used to counter the incipient tritheism that is perceived to diminish the full revelation of God in Christ. OPs argue that if only one Person in the Godhead becomes incarnate, then Jesus is neither the full revelation of deity nor the revelation of the full deity. It leads ultimately to an unwarranted subordination of Jesus in his deity. OPs desire to elevate him to

his rightful place in the Godhead and in his mission to the world.

Two metaphors drawn from Jewish Christian roots that are significant for Oneness Christology are "dwelling" and "glory." The more prominent one is "dwelling," taken primarily from Col. 2:9. Recalling the Jewish experience of God's dwelling temporarily in localized places, God now dwells permanently in the human tabernacle of Jesus. This fits well with OP's fundamental principle of one undifferentiated Spirit indwelling the one human person. In Father-Son terminology, the Father is the divine Spirit who indwells the human Son. In his deity Jesus is Father; in his humanity, Son. Yet the Father continues in transcendence after the incarnation as does the divine Logos in Trinitarian theology.

Complementary to the dwelling metaphor is that of "glory." Like the glory tradition in pre–NT Hellenistic Judaism, Oneness theology emphasizes such NT terms as "manifestation" (1 Tim. 3:16), "image" (Heb. 1:3), "form" (Phil. 2:7), and "face" (2 Cor. 4:10). They are all used to express the divine-human reality in terms of the Spirit-person dialectic. In Christ the hidden God becomes manifest. He who is without form takes on the form of a servant. The invisible one reveals himself as in a mirror, Christ being the true and perfect image. The OT theophanies are temporary preincarnate manifestations that anticipate the future permanent binding of God to the human flesh of Jesus.

The preexistence of Christ is developed in three stages. To protect the monarchy of God, the first stage is the mind and thought of God in God's utter transcendent, undifferentiated being that exists from eternity. Prior to the creation of the world, God had a plan. It is only as the thought of God, as God's eternal plan to create the world, that Christ preexisted.

From solitary thought emerges the second stage of divine expression. The creative and redemptive activity of God reveals God as Logos. *Spirit* defines God in God's eternal being; *Word* is God-in-relation or God-in-time. Although not a distinct hypostasis within the Godhead, the Word is both a coming forth from God and God in God-self. The Word is everything that can be implied by personification without affirming a second personality within the divine being.

The third stage is the divine self-disclosure in the incarnation. God as Spirit exists without form or differentiation. When God assumes form, God is present in full essential being. As the form of God, Jesus is the preexistent Word. But in his full deity he is the essential Godhead. In his incarnation Christ's deity is the one Spirit (Father) who proceeds from eternity, through the Word, into the human form of Jesus (Son).

The sonship of Jesus begins with his birth. As human the Son is subordinate to the Father. In his deity there can be no subordination or inferiority of status. So while both natures are affirmed, a deliberate distinction between them must be maintained, reflecting the characteristic tendency in Jewish Christian thought to preserve the integrity of the divine transcendence.

The two natures in Christ are revealed in his human existence by acts that can be attributed to either his deity or humanity. While some writers follow a strand of early fundamentalist teaching, especially the writings of Essek Kenyon, that the deity (the Father) abandoned the human Jesus on the cross, Bernard affirms the permanence of the union (see *The Oneness View of Jesus Christ*) at every point in his life and death.

Oneness theology generally teaches that the sonship, being human, will cease in the eschaton. With the mediatorial work of Christ completed, he will return to the form in which he existed prior to the creation, or simply be known as the Almighty God. The humanity and sonship ultimately become dispensable in order that Christ may ultimately reign as the Lord of glory. The Trinitarian doctrine of eternal differentiation between Father and Son is replaced by a functional and temporal sonship.

d. *The Name and the Christian.* The theology of the name is a fundamentally practical one and finds its raison d'être in the life of the Christian. Both historically and theologically the quintessential moment in the appropriation of the name is the rite of water baptism. The paradigmatic text for Christian initiation is not the familiar John 3:16, but Acts 2:38: "Repent, and be baptized every one of you in the name of Jesus Christ for the remission of sins, and ye shall receive the gift of the Holy Ghost" (KJV). This text forms the basis of a unique three-stage soteriology that blends a conversionist theology, the pentecostal doctrine of Spirit baptism, and the Oneness teaching of the name of Jesus.

Repentance, the first stage, is defined as faith acting in obedience. Repentance and obedience are the active elements in faith, without which salvation cannot be appropriated. Rejecting the conversionist axiom that the disposition of a heart turned toward God is sufficient for salvation (or, "only believe"), OP anticipates in the obedient act of repentance a willingness to take the second step of obedience—baptism in the name of Jesus.

As a test of true obedience, this second stage is the moment of binding the name of Jesus to the convert. Although consistent with its theology of the name, the demand for rebaptism remains a major point of contention with other Christian bodies. The third stage, receiving the Holy Spirit, is understood according to the traditional pentecostal pattern of Spirit baptism accompanied by speaking in tongues.

Exegetically, the invocation of the name of Jesus in baptism according to Acts 2:38 is harmonized with the Trinitarian baptismal formula in Matt. 28:19 by hermeneutically differentiating between "name" and "titles." Since Jesus is the one proper name of God given in revelation for the new covenant age, "Father, Son and Holy Spirit" are reduced to descriptive titles. The singular form of "name" in Matt. 28:19 points forward to Jesus as the one name of the Father, Son, and Spirit. Consequently, OPs argue that Matt. 28:19 is the dominical commission to baptize in the one name (Jesus) of the Father, Son, and Holy Spirit. Acts provides the formula and the apostolic enactment.

Oneness soteriology, however, has been divided from the beginning into two main schools of thought. One view holds to the Reformed evangelical tradition of the AG, which identifies the new birth with the act of conversion and confession of faith in Jesus Christ as Savior. Baptism in the name of Jesus conforms the believer more fully to the Apostolic pattern of Christian initiation; and Spirit baptism is a subsequent experience of empowering for witness (Acts 1:8). Early representatives of this position are Ewart and Small (see also Kenneth Reeves, *The Great Commission Re-Examined*). Fundamental elements exist within this view, especially a common understanding of the new birth, which readily helps identify OPs with the wider evangelical-pentecostal community.

The other, more misunderstood and less tolerated, view redefines the new birth by incorporating both water and Spirit baptism as constituent elements. It hermeneutically harmonizes Jesus' words to Nicodemus that one must be born of water and Spirit (John 3:5) with Acts 2:38 as a command to baptize in the name of Jesus and receive the pentecostal experience of Spirit baptism. By adapting the traditional interpretation of Col. 2:11–13 (that baptism is the new covenant rite of circumcision) and Rom. 6:6 (that baptism identifies one with Christ in his redemptive work), the divinely chosen means by which a believer receives cleansing from sin is baptism in the name of Jesus. The emphasis on baptism "for the remission of sins" (Acts 2:38) leads many to conclude that OP teaches a form of baptismal regeneration. Its rejoinder, however, is that, to be efficacious, baptism must be accompanied by active faith and executed in the name of Jesus. As Haywood put it, "To be saved by water baptism, it must be administered in the name of Jesus" (*Birth of the Spirit*, 24).

Pneumatologically, by incorporating the Acts 2:38 promise of the Spirit into the theological construct of the new birth, this stream shifts the initial coming of the Spirit from its traditional location in the conversion experience to the pentecostal moment of Spirit baptism. In other words, one is neither born again nor receives the Spirit apart from the pentecostal experience of Spirit baptism.

G. T. Haywood and Andrew Urshan are the original architects of this distinctive Oneness teaching on the new birth, and they gave it its most articulate rendering (see Haywood, *The Birth of the Spirit and the Mystery of the Godhead* [n.d.] and Urshan, *The Doctrine of the New Birth or the Perfect Way to Eternal Life* [1921]). The doctrine is a mutation of the Wesleyan emphasis on "full" salvation, comprising various elements in the process of Christian initiation. In its current expression, however, it collapses a complex understanding of salvation into a conversionist definition of the new birth. It combines the common evangelical belief that one must be born again to be saved with its own rendering of Acts 2:38 as necessary for the new birth. The ecumenical offense is the implication that Trinitarian Christians are not born again and therefore are not inheritors of the kingdom.

Views of other Christians vary. The evangelical-Reformed stream recognizes as born again all those who confess Jesus as Savior, while only Oneness believers enjoy the benefits of the "full" gospel. An unspecified judgment rests upon those who hear but reject the message.

The "new birth" stream has more difficulty in that by definition Trinitarian Christians are not born again. Various efforts are made to circumvent the problem: (1) a recognition that spiritual life begins at conception, not birth; (2) all Trinitarians, OT saints, and the righteous people of other faiths who walk in all the light they have and persevere when persecuted will ultimately be saved, while Oneness believers will enter the kingdom in a secret resurrection called the rapture; (3) Trinitarians represent those worshipers in the temple precincts who were present but relegated to the "outer court of the Gentiles." By recognizing that others outside the Oneness paradigm of the new birth will be reconciled to God, a total break with the wider Christian community is avoided.

Serious consideration of the status of other Christians, however, remains a lacuna in Oneness theology. Its sectarian spirit and two-tier classification of Christians engenders mistrust and discourages relations with other Christians.

OP comprises the third and most isolated stream of the modern pentecostal movement. While it shares a common religious heritage with and embraces much of traditional pentecostal theology, OP stands outside the accepted canons of orthodoxy by its rejection of the doctrine of the Trinity and Trinitarian baptism. Unlike cults that claim for themselves exclusive rights to salvation, OP is obliged to acknowledge its own evangelical and pentecostal roots and experience. Therefore, the classification of the Oneness movement as a cult by some evangelical apologists is reductionistic and must be challenged. OP is best described as a heterodox expression of Christianity whose relationship to the wider Christian community is at present ambivalent. While some representatives remain relatively isolated, others actively participate in wider Christian enterprises, including the ▸Society for Pentecostal Studies.

As the Oneness movement matures, it will need to address the theological and spiritual virtues that bind it to its evangelical-pentecostal roots. Trinitarian Christians, likewise, will be increasingly challenged to listen with patience to a growing presence among them that has not followed the way of the cult but whose commitments at present are not readily accommodated within the historic Christian tradition.

■ **Bibliography:** D. Bernard, *The New Birth* (1984) ■ idem, *The Oneness of God* (1983) ■ G. Boyd, *Oneness Pentecostals and the Trinity* (1992) ■ A. Clanton, *United We Stand—A History of Oneness Organizations* (1970) ■ R. Del Colle, "Oneness and Trinity: A Preliminary Proposal for Dialogue with Oneness Pentecostalism," *JPT* 10 (1997) ■ F. Ewart, *The Revelation of Jesus Christ* (n.d.) ■ T. French, "Oneness Pentecostalism in Global Perspective: History, Theology, and Expansion of the Oneness Pentecostal Movement" (thesis, Wheaton College, 1998) ■ R. Gerloff, *A Plea for British Black Theologies* (1992) ■ K. Gill, *Toward a Contextualized Theology for the Third World* (1994) ■ M. Golder, *History of the Pentecostal Assemblies of the World* (1973) ■ G. T. Haywood, *The Birth of the Spirit and the Mystery of the Godhead* (n.d.) ■ D. Reed, "Aspects of the Origins of Oneness Pentecostalism," in *Aspects of Pentecostal-Charismatic Origins*, ed. V. Synan (1975) ■ idem, "Oneness Pentecostalism: Problems and Possibilities for Pentecostal Theology," *JPT* 11 (1997) ■ idem, "Origins and Development of the Theology of Oneness Pentecostalism in the United States" (diss., Boston U., 1978) ■ F. Small, *Living Waters—A Sure Guide for Your Faith* (n.d.) ■ J. Tyson, *The Early Pentecostal Revival: History of Twentieth-Century Pentecostals and the Pentecostal Assemblies of the World, 1901–30* (1992) ■ A. Urshan, *The Doctrine of the New Birth or the Perfect Way to Eternal Life* (1921) ■ Amos Yong, "Oneness and Trinity: The Theological and Ecumenical Implications of Creation *Ex Nihilo* for an Intra-Pentecostal Dispute," *Pneuma* 19 (1, 1997).

■ D. A. Reed

ONGMAN, JOHN (1845–1931). Swedish mission organizer and theorist. Born in Oviken, Jämtlands, Sweden, Ongman accepted believer's baptism (1864) and received a call to preach (1869). He immigrated to the U.S., where he served as a pastor in Pietist Swedish Baptist churches in St. Paul, MN, and Chicago. In Chicago he studied in the Swedish section of the Baptist Theological Union Seminary. He returned to Sweden in 1889, where he founded the ▸Örebro Mission (1892) and the Örebro Mission School (1908). He was influenced by the German and American Holiness Movements, ▸A. B. Simpson, and Charles G. Finney. He published through the Örebro Mission Press *(Örebro Missionsförening Förlag)* translations of the works of German and American Holiness writers, writings that became very important in defining the ecclesiology and spirituality of the Swedish pentecostal movement.

When the pentecostal movement began in Sweden in 1907, Ongman accepted the "charismatic gifts," although he remained independent of the pentecostal churches as they organized. When the Baptist churches in Sweden forced ▸Lewi Pethrus out of the Baptist Union, Ongman and the Örebro Mission did not follow their example. Many students in the Mission School became pentecostal missionaries, including ▸Axel Andersson (Mexico) as well as Ongman's son, ▸Paul, who became head of the pentecostal Filadelfia

Mission. Ongman hired pentecostal theologians and mission theorists to teach at his school.

■ **Bibliography:** C. Th. Lundström and J. Magnuson, *Skördemän och skördefält* (1925) ■ J. Magnuson, *John Ongman: En levnadsteckning* (1932) ■ idem et al., *50 år i ord och bild, 1892–1942. Jubileumsskrift för Örebro Missionsförening* (1942) ■ idem, *Och Herren verkade* (1945) ■ idem, *Örebro Missionsskola 1908–1958* (1958) ■ J. Ongman, *Samlade Skrifter*, 3 vols. (1931, 1934) ■ P. Ongman and C. Andin, *I den elfte timmen: överblick Örebro Missionsförenings evangelistverksamhet* (1917) ■ *Örebromissionen 75 år, ". . . men Gud gav växten"* (1967) ■ *Örebro Missionsskola 1908–1933. Minnesskrift* (1933) ■ *Örebro Missionsskola 75 år* (1983) ■ G. Westin, *Svenska Baptistsamfundet, 1887–1914. Den baptistiska organisationsdualismens uppkomst* (1965). ■ D. D. Bundy

ONGMAN, PAUL (1885–1957). Swedish pentecostal mission leader, mission theorist, author. Paul Ongman was born in St. Paul, MN, the son of John Ongman and Minnie Eriksson Ongman. He immigrated to Sweden when his parents moved back home in 1889. After graduating from university in 1908, Ongman became professor at the Örebro Mission School (1908–22). From 1900 to 1921 he was a member of the Baptist Union but became a pentecostal in 1921.

Ongman became a traveling evangelist (1922–24) and then pastor at the Tabor Pentecostal Church (Stockholm). He served as mission secretary of the Filadelfia Mission of the Swedish pentecostal movement (1930–45). In that office he had a major role in defining Swedish pentecostal mission theory and practice as well as in the selection and deployment of Swedish (and other Scandinavian) missionaries throughout the world.

■ **Bibliography:** D. D. Bundy, "Swedish Pentecostal Mission Theory and Practice to 1930: Foundational Values in Conflict," *Mission Studies* 14 (1997) ■ J. Magnuson et al., *Örebro Missionsskola 1908–1958* (1958) ■ *Örebromissionen 75 år, ". . . men Gud gav växten"* (1967) ■ *Örebro Missionsskola 1908–1933. Minnesskrift* (1933) ■ *Örebro Missionsskola 75 år* (1983) ■ P. Ongman, *Krigsnöd och kampglädje* (1939) ■ idem, *Skugga och verklighet* (1933) ■ idem, "Yttre missionens möte," *Trettioårshögtiden. Tall, hållna vid Filadelfiaförsamlingens i Stockholm jubileumsmöten de 30 aug.–2. sept. 1940* (1940) ■ idem, with C. Andin, *I den elfte timmen: överblick Örebro Missionsförenings evangelistverksamhet* (1917) ■ A. Sundstedt, *Pingstväckelsen*, 5 vols. (1969–73). ■ D. D. Bundy

OPEN BIBLE STANDARD CHURCHES, INC. A pentecostal denomination that traces its lineage to the ▸Azusa Street revival by way of the ▸Apostolic Faith (AF) (Portland) and the pentecostal revivals in the Midwest. Headquarters for the Trinitarian ▸"finished work" group is in Des Moines, IA.

In 1998 the Open Bible Standard Churches (OBSC) numbered 377 affiliated and fellowshiping churches in the U.S. An additional 894 interdenominational congregations existed in 36 other countries. The 2,161 credentialed ministers worldwide served a constituency of nearly 100,000.

1. Northwest Element—Bible Standard Conference (BSC) (1919–35).

An AF (Portland) minister, ▸Fred Hornshuh, was a successful church planter along the Pacific coast, especially in the Northwest. But he and a few other ministers became disenchanted with certain AF policies: (1) the exclusiveness of the group, which forbade fellowship with other pentecostal groups; (2) the unkind treatment of those with whom they differed; (3) the requirement that divorced and remarried people should renounce their present marriage and return to their first mate; (4) the centralized form of government, which among other things required ministers to attend the three-month camp meeting; and (5) feminine domination (i.e., ▸Florence Crawford). A break in 1919 brought about a new organization that was first called the Bible Standard Mission (later Conference).

Hornshuh had started a dynamic church (later called Lighthouse Temple) in Eugene, OR, in 1913, which was the first pentecostal church in the area. Following the break with the AF, Hornshuh began publishing the *Bible Standard* magazine. What is now Eugene Bible College was founded in 1925 as Bible Standard Theological School. Hornshuh and his small band of ministers and laymen took the pentecostal message to many cities and communities in the Northwest.

2. Open Bible Evangelistic Association (OBEA) (1932–35).

OBEA, like the BSC, was a split from another pentecostal group—also formed by a woman—▸Aimee Semple McPherson's ▸International Church of the Foursquare Gospel (ICFG).

In 1927 a small Des Moines pentecostal group headed by John Goben invited Mrs. McPherson to the city for widely promoted meetings. She returned the next year, and many conversions and healings were reported. As a result, three congregations were organized and united with the ICFG.

When Goben took a position with Mrs. McPherson's work in California, he arranged for Willard H. Pope to take his place in Des Moines. ▸John R. Richey later succeeded Pope, and other young Foursquare couples followed Richey to pioneer churches in the Midwest.

In 1930 the Midwest group began to question the wisdom of ICFG's episcopal plan of holding church property. There was no change, however. Then in 1931 Mrs. McPherson, who was divorced, married David L. Hutton. The next year the ministers in the Midwest voted to withdraw from ICFG and subsequently formed OBEA.

Both groups—OBEA and Hornshuh's BSC—were formed in reaction to policies that their parent organizations legislated.

3. Amalgamation.

Recognizing their similar doctrinal beliefs and visions, the BSC and the OBEA united forces in 1935. The new name—a combination of the two—was adopted: Open Bible Standard Evangelistic Association. A total of 210 ministers made up the new association. The name was changed to the present OBSC in 1940.

Despite the fact that the BSC in its beginning had started in the Holiness wing of the pentecostal movement and the OBEA had accepted the "finished work" position, this was not an issue by 1935. BSC had also practiced footwashing, but it likewise was not an issue in the amalgamation.

The doctrinal statement adopted was similar to that of the General Council of the ⭑Assemblies of God (AG), ICFG, and other Trinitarian "finished work" pentecostal groups. These beliefs include salvation by faith, healing in the atonement, the pretribulation rapture of the church, and speaking in tongues as the initial physical evidence of the baptism in the Holy Spirit.

The local church is ruled by the congregation, calling its own pastor, electing its own officials, and having a voice in the divisional and national conferences. There are five U.S. divisions: Pacific, Midwest, Central, Eastern, and Southeastern. The denomination meets biennially in a general conference. An elected general board of directors conducts the business of the organization.

The denomination operates Eugene Bible College in Eugene, OR, a four-year accredited program with an enrollment of over 200. The school also offers correspondence courses that give the constituency additional opportunities to receive Bible training. Extension sites in other states began in 1999.

Additionally, more than 9,000 students in 23 countries participate in INSTE, a local church-based discipleship/leadership training program in five languages.

Message of the Open Bible is the official monthly magazine. The *Overcomer* is published quarterly for youth. In the past, the denomination published a Sunday school curriculum, but in recent years it has been relying on other publishers to fill this need.

The OBSC is a member of the ⭑National Association of Evangelicals, the ⭑Pentecostal/Charismatic Churches of North America, and the ⭑Pentecostal World Conference.

The AG in the late 1950s made a formal invitation for the OBSC to unite with them. However, the OBSC chose to remain a separate organization.

A charter member and former superintendent of the Midwest group, ⭑R. Bryant Mitchell, is the author of the

414-page official history, *Heritage and Horizons* (1982), published by the denomination.

■ **Bibliography:** R. Mitchell, *Heritage and Horizons* (1982) ▮ R. Mitchell and L. Mitchell, *Heritage and Harvests* (1995) ▮ "Policies and Principles of OBSC" (1985).   ■ E. Warner

OPPERMAN, DANIEL CHARLES OWEN (1872–1926).

Evangelist and educator. Daniel Charles Owen Opperman was born on July 13, 1872, in Clinton Township, Elkhart County, IN. His family moved to Nevada, MO, in 1881 and settled in Florida in 1884. In 1884 Opperman had a conversion experience. He was a member of the German Baptist Brethren. After his father's death in 1887, his mother and four children returned to Indiana, settling in Goshen. Opperman did farm work and studied. In 1893 he enrolled in a Brethren college in Mt. Morris, IL. He later studied for one year at Manchester College in North Manchester, IN. From May 23 until July 6, 1899, Opperman was enrolled at Moody Bible Institute.

While a student at Moody, Opperman began attending ⭑John Alexander Dowie's Zion City. He joined Dowie's Christian Catholic Church and eventually directed Zion City's education program. On Mar. 10, 1900, Opperman married Ella Syler. Their son, Daniel Paul, was born on Jan. 22, 1901. Ella died a week later. A bout with tuberculosis resulted in Opperman's move to Texas, where he met Charles Parham in 1906. Opperman became a pentecostal evangelist before experiencing Spirit baptism (which he did on Jan. 13, 1908,

Daniel Opperman, best remembered in the pentecostal movement for his efforts in education. He was one of the organizers of the Assemblies of God but later helped form a Oneness organization.

in Belton, TX). He married Hattie Ruth Allen near Rogers, TX, on July 22, 1907. A son, Joseph, was born to this union.

Opperman's prior teaching experience prompted his recognition as an educator, and he conducted numerous short-term Bible institutes that served early pentecostal needs. A founding member of the Assemblies of God and an executive presbyter (1914–15), Opperman withdrew in 1916 to become chairman of a fledgling ▸Oneness association, the General Assembly of Apostolic Assemblies, with headquarters in Eureka Springs, AR. During his years in Oneness pentecostal leadership, Opperman edited *The Blessed Truth* and became a pastor in Lodi, CA. He died in a car-train accident in Baldwin Park, CA, on Sept. 15, 1926.

■ **Bibliography:** G. P. Gardiner, "Out of Zion . . . into All the World," *Bread of Life* (Feb. 1983) ■ D. C. O. Opperman, "Journal," unpub. ms., AG Archives.   ■ E. L. Blumhofer

ORDINANCES, PENTECOSTAL

This article focuses on what traditional pentecostalism has labeled "ordinances" (although it must be kept in mind that classical pentecostals are far from uniform, even in the fundamentals). Since Protestant charismatics and Roman Catholic charismatics have generally accepted the sacramental traditions of their respective heritage, these traditions will not be covered. Independent Protestant charismatics are excluded, although many of these groups have not inherited their understanding of ordinances from a parent group.

1. The Words "Sacrament" and "Ordinance."

The terms "sacrament" and "ordinance" can have the same basic meaning, yet some pentecostals have deliberately spurned the word "sacrament" because it seemed to imply a self-contained efficacy, independent of the participant's faith. That is an unnecessary conclusion; using "sacrament" will be important because it functions to identify only water baptism and the Lord's Supper as sacraments and footwashing as something less. In this context a sacrament refers to those external rites directed by Scripture and observed by the gathered people of God.

"Sacrament" will be used here in a cognitive/symbolic way, rather than in the causal way that might suggest that salvation is conveyed *ex opere operato,* through the administration of the sacrament. On the one hand, if there is no faith on the part of the recipient, there is no sacrament. On the other hand, the administration of the sacraments should not be the sole prerogative of the ordained ministry. The practice of denominationally licensed ministers administering the sacraments seems biblically allowable but not mandatory.

2. Water Baptism.

The biblical imagery for baptism probably extends into the ancient Hebrew religious and ceremonial lustrations in which water was the medium for cleansing from the defilement of sin. It would seem axiomatic to say that North American pentecostals consider water the appropriate element for the ceremony, yet it does not seem theologically inappropriate to suggest that another liquid would be appropriate, especially under certain conditions that limit the availability of water.

All major pentecostal denominations in the U.S. practice water baptism by immersion (some even break ice in rivers to immerse the candidate), but some pentecostals in South America and Eastern Europe officially sanction sprinkling. Some pentecostals in South Africa practice triple immersions. Pentecostals have been so emphatic about water baptism being a response to faith that most—with notable exceptions like the Pentecostal Methodist Church of Chile—not only reject pedobaptism (although not "infant salvation") and sometimes lack urgency in performing the rite, but some have insisted on rebaptism if a person was baptized as an infant or sprinkled as an adult. Furthermore, some groups counsel rebaptism if a person "backslides" and then is "saved again." Oneness pentecostalism reflects a departure from the Trinitarian formulas used by other pentecostal groups. Counted among their number are those who theologically link faith and repentance with water baptism in the name of the Lord Jesus Christ by immersion and initial-evidence Spirit baptism. As to the matter of water baptism actually incorporating the initiate into the body of Christ, North American (Trinitarian) pentecostalism has tended to tie the indwelling of the Holy Spirit to union with Christ and thereby consider the believer united to the entire body of Christ.

The early pentecostal preference in the U.S. for immersion may lie as much in the continuity of the demonstrative nature of regular worship services as in their finding scriptural support for the practice. There was a general dearth of serious inquiry into the subject, and an overall consensus on the subject was lacking. The NT term translated "to baptize"

Baptism in Salisbury, Rhodesia (now Harare, Zimbabwe).

Water baptism in Lake Atitlan, Guatemala.

(baptizō), and specific texts such as Acts 8:39, seem to encourage immersion. But Scripture taken in its entirety does not preclude the appropriateness of sprinkling or pouring.

The crucial concern in the sacrament of baptism is the subject. To those committed to the cognitive view of the sacraments, no proxy faith is sufficient. Pentecostals have a natural inclination to hold in juxtaposition the understanding of faith as an intellectual assent to pertinent propositions and an obedient walk of the believer in an attitude of trust and commitment. Fortunately, most advocates of causal sacramentalism, specifically proponents of baptismal regeneration, expect to move recipients past the ceremony to a full and complete allegiance to the gospel. The NT does not envision such a thing as an unbaptized Christian, and a sense of urgency should undergird this sacrament.

3. The Eucharist.

The Synoptic accounts and the Pauline elaborations describe Jesus as instituting this sacrament. The elements used in the original Last Supper probably included unleavened bread and fermented wine. Pioneer pentecostals in the U.S., when unable to locate unleavened bread, introduced

various substitutes. Most pentecostals, however, have been quite adamant in their refusal to partake of fermented wine. A primary concern here is that to use fermented wine would not only contravene a doctrine of total abstinence of such things, but it would provide a working premise for alcoholism. Emerging pentecostal scholarship and international pentecostal practice have challenged this point of view.

In the socioeconomic stratum and cultural climate of early pentecostalism, it was easier to deny any possible connection to the dreaded practice of drinking intoxicating beverages. At the same time, the historical reality of the first Eucharist need not be denied nor pressed too far. It seems that the early church's use of unleavened bread and fermented wine was something of a historical accident. That is, these elements are not intrinsic to the ceremony but were incorporated because of the historical situation. The process of distilling intoxicating drinks has changed since the 1st century, but the biblical mandate prohibiting drunkenness has not. Again, it is not theologically necessary to insist on the fruit of the vine, but it is encouraged by apostolic precedent.

Other things are not as value laden for Western pentecostals, such as the posture of the body, the manner of the breaking of the bread, the use of a table, or an incorporated liturgy. Pentecostals in countries dominated by Greek Orthodox churches evidence this influence by insisting on kneeling or standing while engaged in intense prayer that easily breaks into glossolalic utterances. In years past it often seemed that enthusiastic worship was the supremely important catalyst. Pentecostals have insisted on all endorsed candidates (ruling out infants and adult unbelievers) partaking of both elements while recalling the death of Jesus and experiencing his presence. Pentecostals typically do not see the Eucharist as a source of forgiveness of sins but expect a state of reconciliation as a precondition. Perhaps owing to a fear of compromising the uniqueness of the death of Christ on the cross, the concept of sacrifice related to the Lord's Supper is largely underdeveloped in pentecostalism. Intercommunion among pentecostal groups is usually not problematic.

4. Footwashing.

The Johannine account of the Lord's Supper includes a scene not found in the Synoptics. Because the story (John 13:1–17) recounts Jesus' washing the disciples' feet at the same occasion as the "first Eucharist" (cf. 1 Tim. 5:10), some have viewed footwashing as an ordinance and have insisted that it should always follow the observance of the Lord's Supper. Some pentecostal groups have practiced footwashing as an ordinance. Such an insistence wrongly infers a moral necessity in Jesus' actions that should be applied only to water baptism and the Eucharist.

This object lesson in humility, as portrayed by Christ, is not an extraneous rite. It can be engaged in with full confidence that the participating Christian community has taken a positive step toward realizing *koinonia*. The ceremony can draw attention to Christian servitude, while at the same time demonstrating publicly that Christian commitment transcends societal barriers of race, nationality, gender, and social class.

See also CHURCH, THEOLOGY OF THE; SACRAMENTS.

■ **Bibliography:** H. D. Hunter, "Reflections by a Pentecostalist on Aspects of BEM," *Journal of Ecumenical Studies* 29 (3/4, Summer/Fall 1992) ■ C. M. Robeck Jr. and J. L. Sandidge, "The Ecclesiology of Koinonia and Baptism: A Pentecostal Perspective," *Journal of Ecumenical Studies* 27 (3, Summer 1990) ■ J. C. Thomas, *Footwashing in John 13 and the Johannine Community* (1991).
■ H. D. Hunter

ÖREBRO MISSION AND ÖREBRO MISSION SCHOOL

The Örebro Mission was founded in 1892 by ►John Ongman in Örebro, Sweden, as a ministry of the local Baptist congregation of which Ongman was minister. It quickly became a major sending agency for Swedish and Norwegian Baptists. By 1908 a need was felt to establish a center for educating prospective missionaries. The Örebro Mission Training School was established with Ongman as rector. When pentecostalism arrived in Sweden from Norway in 1908, Ongman and the school accepted the pentecostal theology and liturgy but remained independent of all pentecostal organizations. Among the pentecostal mission theorists and leaders who taught at Örebro Mission School were Karl Andin, Rikard Fris, and ►Paul Ongman. Many pentecostal missionaries received training at the school. It is now Örebro Theological Seminary.

■ **Bibliography:** *100 år i ord och bild: Örebromissionen, 1892-1992* (1992) ■ J. Magnuson, *John Ongman: En levnadsteckning* (1932) ■ idem et al., *50 år i ord och bild, 1892–1942. Jubileumsskrift för Örebro Missionsförening* (1942) ■ idem, *Och Herren verkade* (1945) ■ idem, *Örebro Missionsskola 1908–1958* (1958) ■ P. Ongman and C. Andin, *I den elfte timmen: överblick Örebro Missionsförenings evangelistverksamhet* (1917) ■ *Örebromissionen 75 år, ". . . men Gud gav växten"* (1967) ■ *Örebro Missionsskola 1908–1933. Minnesskrift* (1933) ■ *Örebro Missionsskola 75 år* (1983).
■ D. D. Bundy

OROZCO, RODOLFO O. (1891–1991).

Considered by many to be the father of the Assemblies of God (AG) movement in Mexico. Born in Nuevo León, Mexico, Orozco emigrated to the U.S. as a migrant agricultural laborer. He was converted in an Anglo-American pentecostal church in Pasadena, TX, in 1915. That same year he purchased a house in Houston, TX, and organized one of the first Mexican pentecostal churches in that state. Later that year Henry C. Ball asked Orozco to join his fledgling AG work in evangelizing the Mexican population in Texas. Orozco accepted the offer and began conducting evangelistic work throughout the state. Three years later, in 1918, he was ordained an evangelist by the Latin American District Council of the AG in San Antonio, TX. In Aug. 1922 his wife died of tuberculosis. His own bout with tuberculosis, along with his wife's death, had a devastating impact on Orozco, who decided to return to his hometown of Monterrey, Mexico. Once in Monterrey, he met two Mexican pentecostals who asked him to lead a Bible study and worship service. Orozco agreed and that same year founded one of the first AG churches in Mexico. Prompted by the need for larger facilities, he directed the construction of Templo Christiano El Salvador de Asambleas de Dios in 1928. Orozco went on to pastor this church for 65 years while at the same time spreading the pentecostal message throughout Mexico.

Not long after the AG work in Mexico became independent of the work in the U.S., in 1929, Orozco helped found the periodical *Gavillas Doradas* in 1932. In 1940 he founded Alba Institute, perhaps the first all-women's Pentecostal Bible Institute in Mexico. In addition to founding a Bible institute, Orozco also helped plant four daughter churches and served as the second general superintendent of the AG work in Mexico (1931–40). Orozco continued in his 90s to copastor with his son-in-law the church he founded. The work Orozco began in 1922 with Templo Cristiano in Monterrey has blossomed into over 105 churches throughout the state of Nuevo León in the 1990s.

■ **Bibliography:** G. Espinosa, "Borderland Religion: Los Angeles and the Origins of the Latino Pentecostal Movement in the U.S., Mexico, and Puerto Rico, 1900–1945" (Ph.D. diss., U. of Calif.–Santa Barbara, 1998) ■ I. González V., *Templo Cristiano El Salvador Asambleas de Dios, 70 Aniversario Cronicas* (1992).
■ G. Espinosa

ORTIZ, FRANCISCO D. (c. 1878–1922).

Pioneer Puerto Rican pentecostal evangelist and pastor. Born in Puerto Rico, Ortiz migrated to Hawaii, where he worked in the sugarcane fields. In 1911 a group of pentecostal missionaries from the Azusa Street revivals in California stopped off on Oahu, HI, on their way to China and Japan. While on Oahu, the missionaries began evangelistic work among Puerto Rican migrant field laborers working at the experimental agricultural station set up by the U.S. government. The Azusa Street missionaries converted a number of Puerto Rican field workers at the station, including Francisco D. Ortiz. On Nov. 15, 1911, they ordained Ortiz and asked him to shepherd the small flock of recently converted Puerto Rican pentecostals. He served in this capacity until 1913, when he, along with his son Panchito and Juan L. Lugo, set sail for San Francisco. Francisco conducted evangelistic work among Mexican migrant laborers throughout central and northern California. In 1916 he was ordained in the Assemblies of God (AG) and became the associate pastor of the San Jose AG church. A few years later he traveled to Puerto Rico and provided important leadership to the fledgling AG work on the island. Francisco Ortiz Sr. was joined in his evangelistic efforts by his son Francisco Jr. ("Panchito"). Panchito, along with his wife Santitos, were key in spreading the pentecostal message throughout California and Puerto Rico. Before his untimely death in 1922 he founded the first pentecostal periodical on the island, *Nuevas De Salvación (News of Salvation).*

■ **Bibliography:** G. Espinosa, "Borderland Religion: Los Angeles and the Origins of the Latino Pentecostal Movement in the U.S., Mexico, and Puerto Rico, 1906–1946" (Ph.D. diss., U. of Calif.–Santa Barbara, 1998). ■ G. Espinosa

ORTIZ, JUAN CARLOS (1934–). Argentine evangelist and conference speaker. Ortiz's unique ministry, which emphasizes Christian unity and biblical truth rather than conventionality, began with the Assemblies of God. He was secretary of the ▶Tommy Hicks meetings in Buenos Aires in 1954 and gained prominence as pastor of the city's Hidalgo church. Increasingly well known in Latin America, he extended his ministry to the U.S. through association with various leaders of the charismatic renewal. As Ortiz's provocative messages brought him recognition, his sometimes iconoclastic style and fellowship with Catholics and mainline Protestants alienated him from his denominational colleagues. He has spoken in settings as diverse as Lutheran churches, a Trappist monastery, and the Latin American Mission Church in San Jose, Costa Rica. He was a vocal figure in the Lausanne Congress on World Evangelization in 1974 and has subsequently worked with evangelicals, promoting interagency coordination. His most widely read book, *Disciple,* appeared in 1975.

Subsequently, four other books by Ortiz have been published: *Cry of the Human Heart* (1977); *Living with Jesus Today* (1982); *God Is Closer Than You Think* (1992); and *Disciple: A Handbook for New Believers* (1995).

■ **Bibliography:** J. E. Orr, *Evangelical Awakenings in Latin America* (1978) ■ J. C. Ortiz, "Just Getting 'Fatter' Isn't Growth," *Eternity* 26 (15, 1975) ■ idem, "When Is Jesus with You?" *Christian Life* 44 (7, 1982) ■ C. Peter Wagner, *Look Out! The Pentecostals Are Coming* (1973). ■ E. A. Wilson

OSBORN, TOMMY LEE (1923–). Missionary, healing evangelist, pastor, and author. Born on an Oklahoma farm, T. L. Osborn was converted to Christ at age 12 and was called to preach at age 14. The following year he assisted E. M. Dillard with revivals in Arkansas, Oklahoma, and California, where he met Daisy Washburn (1924–) in 1940 and married her the following year.

In 1941 the Osborns went into the Kiamichi Mountains of Oklahoma as evangelists. They soon returned to California, where they itinerated for two years before pioneering a new work, Montaville Tabernacle, in Portland, OR.

The Osborns went to India in 1945 as missionaries. While there, T. L. contracted typhoid fever and their infant son struggled with cholera and amoebic dysentery. The following year they returned to the U.S. to pastor the Full Gospel church of McMinnville, OR.

T. L. heard Hattie Hammond at a camp meeting in Brooks, OR, preaching on "Seeing Jesus." The next morning he was awakened with a vision of Jesus Christ that changed his life. In Sept. 1947 the Osborns returned to the pastorate of Montaville Tabernacle. Soon afterward ▶William Branham conducted a healing campaign in Portland's Civic Auditorium, where Osborn observed a young girl's deliverance when Branham prayed, "Thou deaf and dumb spirit, I adjure thee in Jesus' name, leave the child." When Branham snapped his fingers, she heard and spoke perfectly. Osborn said, "When I witnessed this, there seemed to be a thousand voices speaking to me at once, all in one accord saying over and over, 'You can do that'" (Oct. 1949, 9).

After many days of prayer and fasting, Osborn and his wife began a ministry as healing evangelists in the spring of 1948. Early the following year they reported from Jamaica, "The people are so hungry … they eat the Word like starving birds" (Osborn, Feb. 1949, 14). Scores of healings were reported, with hundreds of conversions. The Osborns returned to the U.S. for highly successful campaigns in Flint, MI, with William Branham and ▶F. F. Bosworth; in Detroit with Bosworth and Benham; and in Pennsylvania, Tennessee, and Texas with ▶Gordon Lindsay.

The following year Osborn reported over 18,000 conversions within 12 days in Puerto Rico, and 50,000 in Camaguey, Cuba, in Jan. 1951. In 1952 thousands more came to Christ in Punto Fijo, Venezuela, before police arrested Osborn for "witchcraft" after many reports of healings had been received by physicians and Roman Catholic priests. In Guatemala City, during a political upheaval in Feb. and Mar. 1953, another 50,000 people were brought to Christ.

In 1953 Osborn formed the Association for Native Evangelism to facilitate the spreading of the gospel by trained nationals. This program, financed by many different denominations, has produced about 400 new self-supporting indigenous churches every year since it began. By 1964 the Osborns had ministered in over 40 countries, with startling successes in Kenya, Indonesia, Formosa, Japan, Java, Holland, Chile, Switzerland, and elsewhere.

Osborn's ministry is characterized by flexibility. In an effort to reach youth in the late 1960s, he grew a beard and modified his wardrobe and vocabulary. Recently, the Osborns have emphasized that Daisy has functioned as a minister in her own right, serving as president of the Osborn Foundation, international editor of *Faith Digest* magazine, and director of overseas evangelism.

The Osborn Foundation maintains headquarters in Tulsa, OK, with international branches in major cities throughout the world, and has produced tapes, films, and printed literature in more than 80 languages, reaching many millions worldwide.

■ **Bibliography:** D. Graham, "DMO: Directing the Action of National Evangelism Worldwide," *Faith Digest* 24 (July 1979) ■ D. E. Harrell Jr., *All Things Are Possible* (1975) ■ T. L. Osborn, "From the Island of Jamaica," *Elim Pentecostal Herald* (Feb. 1949) ■ idem, "My Life Story and Call to the Healing Ministry," *Voice of Healing* (Sept. 1949; Oct. 1949) ■ idem, *Young in Faith* (1964).
                                                                        ■ R. M. Riss

OSCHOFFA, SAMUEL BILEÓU JOSEPH (1909–85). Pastor, prophet, and founder of the ▸Celestial Church of Christ (CCC) Worldwide, an African charismatic movement. Born and nurtured in Porto Novo (Benin Republic) of Nigerian parentage, he was brought up in a polygamous household and was the only surviving child of his family. His birth was linked to a covenant his father made with God, hence the biblical name "Samuel" and the Yoruba name "Bileóu," which connotes "a special gift of God." In fulfillment of his father's vow, he received catechetical training under the Methodist mission but later abandoned it and took up carpentry. Oschoffa thus had little or no formal education. By 1946 he had become an ebony and timber merchant.

Oschoffa claimed to have had a visionary experience on May 23, 1947, while marooned in the Toffin forest in search of timber. In the vision he was commissioned to found a church charged with "cleansing the world." Consequently, he started to carry out healing miracles, the first being the healing of a canoe paddler in the same forest. What started as a small group has grown today to about 2,500 parishes worldwide with a membership of several million. CCC is expanding most rapidly in Nigeria. Oschoffa was regarded as an embodiment of simplicity and humility, one endowed with supernatural qualities, who displayed remarkable charisma before his followers. As spiritual/administrative head, he was vested with the "sole, ultimate and unchallengeable authority" on all matters affecting the church. Members referred to Oschoffa as *Papa*, which shows how he was respected and treated as a father figure. He died on Sept. 10, 1985, and was accorded an elaborate burial in Imeko (Nigeria). The anniversary of Oschoffa's death has become institutionalized in CCC as an annual ritual, while his mausoleum at the Celestial City in Imeko became the "New Jerusalem," an annual pilgrimage center. Oschoffa was succeeded by ▸Alexander A. A. Bada.

■ **Bibliography:** A. U. Adogame, "Celestial Church of Christ: The Politics of Cultural Identity in a West African Prophetic-Charismatic Movement" (diss., Bayreuth, Germany, 1997) ■ *Celestial Church of Christ Constitution* (Nigeria Diocese) (rev. ed., 1980) ■ O. Obafemi, *Pastor S. B. J. Oshoffa: God's 20th-Century Gift to Africa*, (1986) ■ S. O. Odeyemi, *The Coming of Oshoffa and the Birth of Celestial Church of Christ* (1992).   ■ A. U. Adogame

OSTEEN, JOHN HILLERY (1921–99). Interdenominational pastor and broadcaster. Born in Paris, TX, Osteen received his B.A. from John Brown University and an M.R.E. from Northern Baptist Theological Seminary. He was ordained as a Southern Baptist minister in 1942 and served as assistant pastor of a church in San Diego, CA, and as pastor of churches in Hamlin, Baytown, and Houston, TX. In 1958, while pastor at Hibbard Memorial Baptist Church in Houston, Osteen was baptized in the Holy Spirit. About that time, his daughter, who was born with a birth injury, was healed. This ushered Osteen into a healing ministry.

Osteen established Lakewood Baptist Church, Houston, TX, with about 150 members. Now known as Lakewood Church (interdenominational), with a membership of thousands, the church places strong emphasis on world missions and has touched 111 nations. They have national and international television ministries carried on various local networks and on the Fox Family satellite network. Osteen was publisher and author of 30 books. After his unexpected death in Jan. 1999, his family and Lakewood Church are continuing his vision of "Reaching the Unreached and Telling the Untold."

■ **Bibliography:** "Runners Up," *Charisma* (Aug. 1985).
                                                                        ■ S. Strang

OTTOLINI, PIETRO (1870–1962). Italian-American evangelist. Ottolini was born in Pescaglia, a city in the province of Lucca, Italy. At age 21 Ottolini immigrated to the U.S., arriving in Chicago on Sept. 11, 1891. In 1900 he converted from Catholicism and became a member of Chicago's First Italian Presbyterian Church. In 1907 he became a pentecostal after receiving the baptism in the Holy Spirit with the evidence of speaking in tongues during a meeting conducted by ▸William H. Durham at the North Avenue Mission. During the next few years, Ottolini served as an elder in the ▸Assemblea Cristiana. He traveled to New York in 1908 and helped to establish pentecostal churches among the Italian communities in Buffalo, Holley, and New York City. Beginning in 1910, Ottolini made several trips to northern and southern Italy and helped establish the first pentecostal churches in those regions. In 1917 he moved his family to St. Louis and established the Italian Evangelical Church. He spent the rest of his life supporting the churches he helped establish and lived in St. Louis until his death.

■ **Bibliography:** "Biography of Peter Ottolini," personal papers of Anthony DeGregorio, Du Plessis Center Archives, Fuller Theological Seminary Library, Pasadena, CA ■ R. Bracco, *Risveglio Pentecostale in Italia* (n.d.) ■ L. DeCaro, *Our Heritage: The Christian Church of North America* (1977) ■ P. Ottolini, *The Life and Mission of Peter Ottolini* (n.d.) ■ idem, *Storia dell'Opera Italiana* (1945).

■ J. Colletti

OZMAN, AGNES NEVADA (1870–1937). Evangelist. Agnes Ozman was assured a place in pentecostal history when she became the first to speak in tongues at ▸Charles Parham's Bethel Bible College in Topeka, KS. Despite conflicting accounts about her expectations and the sequence of events, her experience is usually credited with establishing the validity of Parham's assertion that tongues speech evidenced Spirit baptism.

Ozman was born in Albany, WI, on Sept. 15, 1870. She grew up in rural Nebraska, where she attended a Methodist Episcopal church. A participant in various nondenominational settings as well, she eventually espoused both premillennialism and healing. In 1892 she enrolled for the winter term at T. C. Horton's Bible school in St. Paul, MN. In 1894 she moved to New York to continue her training at A. B. Simpson's training institute. Unsettled and driven by the need to pursue spiritual reality, she served briefly as a city missionary in Kansas City. From there she went, in the fall of 1900, to Parham's school in Topeka.

After Ozman's tongues experience in 1901, she returned to city missionary work. In Lincoln in 1906 she heard about pentecostalism, related her earlier experience, and identified with the emerging movement. In 1911 she married pentecostal preacher Philemon LaBerge. The two traveled about the country holding meetings wherever possible. In 1917

Agnes N. Ozman, the first person to speak in tongues at Charles F. Parham's Bethel Bible College in Topeka, KS, in 1901. This picture was taken in 1937, the year of her death.

LaBerge affiliated with the Assemblies of God, receiving credentials as an evangelist. Agnes died in Los Angeles on Nov. 29, 1937.

■ **Bibliography:** E. L. Blumhofer, *The Assemblies of God,* 2 vols. (1989) ■ A. O. LaBerge, *What God Hath Wrought* (n.d.).

■ E. L. Blumhofer

P

PACIFISM The literature of early pentecostals indicates that they were generally, but not universally, pacifist. Pentecostal history is characterized over the years by a declining pacifism that basically corresponded to the trends in public opinion in the population at large.

Little attempt was made at theorizing about pacifism in any systematic way. The limited pacifist tendencies reflected the prevailing premillennialist eschatology. Because most pentecostals believed that the end times would feature wars and rumors of wars, there was no active pacifism that tried to prevent war—only a passive type that prevented the individual Christian from participating in war or, if conscripted, from killing. The moderating influence undermining the initial pacifism has usually been the belief that the power of the established government was divinely ordained and that, therefore, the Christian was to support the government's decision to go to war. There was little discussion of the traditional differentiation of just and unjust wars.

1. Before World War I.

The pacifist elements in pentecostalism may be accounted for by the roots of the movement—particularly in the Holiness churches, but also in the evangelical and Pietist traditions. Significant pacifist strains may be found in the Church of the Nazarene, Free Methodist Church, and Wesleyan Methodists. Evangelicals were influenced by such dominant personalities as leader Alexander Campbell of the Disciples of Christ, who was an absolute pacifist, and revivalist Dwight L. Moody, who identified himself with ▸Quaker concepts and was a conscientious objector in the Civil War. ▸John Alexander Dowie, the founder of ▸Zion City, IL, did not allow soldiers into membership. Two thousand of his American followers would become pentecostals, as well as some in Holland, Switzerland, and the Republic of South Africa.

Early pentecostal leaders expressed their pacifism even before the crisis situation engendered by the outbreak of WWI. ▸Charles Fox Parham had married a Quaker and claimed that for 20 years prior to the war he had taught that true Christians should not go to war. He believed at the same time, however, that peace conferences were hopeless. In 1912–14, ▸Frank Bartleman taught in Europe in opposition to the developing war spirit there. Shortly after WWI he published a tract, "Christian Citizenship," which forbade Christians' going to war. In response to the Boer War, the British pentecostal preacher Arthur Sydney Booth-Clibborn wrote a pacifist book, *Blood against Blood,* which was touted in 1915 by the *Weekly Evangel* of the ▸Assemblies of God (AG).

2. World War I.

The outbreak of WWI created a crisis for the fledgling pentecostal movement on both sides of the Atlantic. Independent congregations and recently formed denominations had difficulty establishing themselves in government eyes as organized religions that could qualify their members as exempt from military service because their organization was opposed to war—or at least exempt from combatant service because their church opposed killing.

▸Donald Gee, who later was to become chairman of the British AG, was a conscientious objector and was exempted to do farm labor. He continued to promote pacifism longer than any other major pentecostal leader. Some British pentecostals were sent to prison for their pacifist stands. ▸Howard Carter was imprisoned, whereas ▸John Carter was exempted.

Prior to U.S. entry into the war in 1917, it appeared that most American pentecostals were adamantly opposed to war. Frank Bartleman, writing in the *Weekly Evangel,* opposed U.S. support of Britain's involvement. Upon entry of the U.S. into the war, the passage of the Espionage and Sedition Acts made it a crime to obstruct recruiting or to cause someone to refuse duty in the military services. This generally produced the development of a more moderate position, advocating noncombatant service rather than conscientious objection to war altogether. The AG in 1917 officially declared its opposition to participation in war that involved the destruction of human life, basing its position on scriptural precepts, "Follow peace," "Love your enemies," and "Thou shalt not kill." Although this was defined as a historical Quaker position, the organization claimed that it did not discourage enlistment of people whose conscientious principles were not involved. In the same year, the ▸Church of God (CG, Cleveland, TN) took a position against its members going to war. The ▸Church of God in Christ (COGIC) also reflected a pacifist position, and its founder, Bishop ▸Charles H. Mason, was jailed and accused of being a German sympathizer. Similar positions were indicated in pentecostal churches in Russia, Germany, Switzerland, and Canada.

To what extent the pacifist leadership influenced the rank-and-file members is impossible to know. There is indication of opposition to the prevailing pacifist tendency. S. A. Jamieson, one of the founding fathers of the AG, opposed the pacifist point of view, and Bartleman complained that "one dare not pray publicly in a meeting for God's saints in prison [conscientious objectors] without being assailed by a torrent of abuse."

In the total American population, 20,873 men claimed noncombatant status, but only 3,989 persisted in their position after induction. Of these, 450 were sent to prison, 17 of them pentecostals. Out of one group of 1,000 of these inductees in camps, 13 were listed as pentecostal, another 20 were probably members of the COGIC, and some others were from smaller sects that also may have been pentecostal.

3. Between the World Wars.

Between the world wars the pacifist position continued to erode among pentecostals. Some did continue to preach absolute pacifism. Frank Bartleman published a tract, "War and the Christian," boldly asserting, "A 'War Church' is a Harlot Church." But the Russian pentecostals who had held a pacifist line during the 1917 revolution modified that stance in 1927, advising members to serve in the armed forces. This transition did, however, produce objections within the AG that threatened to withdraw support. The AG at this time was under the influence of ›Stanley H. Frodsham, editor of the *Pentecostal Evangel* (1921–48), whose pacifism was derived from a general withdrawal from the affairs of this world. The trend, though, lay with the thinking of ›Eudorus N. Bell, chairman of the General Council in 1914 and again from 1920 to 1923, who hinted at a just war philosophy by insisting that a soldier who killed in battle was not a murderer but a vehicle of justice. Thus, the way of the combatant was justified. In 1928 the CG moderated its 1917 attitude "against members going to war" to "against members going to war in combatant service."

In a 1930 article in the *Pentecostal Evangel (PE)* the British leader Donald Gee lamented the lack of teaching on war and continued to reassert the view that conscientious objection was the only option open to the Christian. But his moderation was reflected in a call for tolerance of those who believed otherwise. Britain's ›Elim Pentecostal churches continued an antiwar attitude in the 1930s; but as war came, James McWhirter of that denomination declared pacifism itself to be the unbiblical position.

4. World War II.

The beginning of WWII in 1939 again brought the issues to the forefront. AG general superintendent ›Ernest S. Williams encouraged Christians to request noncombatant status and recommended the statement developed by New York's Broadway Tabernacle: "I cannot reconcile the way of Christ with the way of war." Williams did not approve, however, of the belief that a person who killed in battle was a murderer. The beginning of conscription brought an immediate response in the *PE*, reasserting the pacifist position adopted in 1917 and restated in the 1927 AG constitution. This statement was far afield from the value system of the denomination as a whole; the AG would claim 50,000 men in the armed services, including wholesale enlistments. The CG also maintained a pacifist position; but, likewise, few of its young men complied.

Although the ›Pentecostal Holiness Church (PHC) apparently had never adopted a pacifist statement, at the beginning of the war it favored isolation; but when war came, the church gave total support to the war effort, sending thousands of men to fight. Chief Bishop ›Dan T. Muse condemned all protest to the war and said that those who refused to register for the draft were dishonoring God.

With so many men under arms, the pentecostals appropriated their due proportion of chaplain positions in the armed services. The beginning of the pentecostal chaplaincy may be seen as the tacit admission of the transition from pacifism to nonpacifism within the movement. The AG had 34 appointments by 1944, and the PHC received a total of 12. This chaplain's lobby within the AG would become a major force after the war to change the denomination's official position so as to conform to practice.

Selective Service records show a total of 11,950 conscientious objectors in WWII. Of these, only 131 are listed as pentecostals of various hues.

5. After World War II.

At the end of WWII the CG altered its official pacifist position to allow liberty of conscience of its members to be combatants, noncombatants, or conscientious objectors. This has generally become the position of most American pentecostals. In the Korean War and Vietnam War, pentecostals rarely sought noncombatant or conscientious objector status.

Amazingly, in 1947 a committee reported to the General Council of the AG that after due consideration no change was necessary in the statement of the denomination. But in 1957 the scriptural reference of "Thou shalt not kill" was dropped without comment from the supporting statements on military service. In 1961 the executive presbytery of the AG blocked publication in the *PE* of an article advocating conscientious objection to war. As the popular romanticism of the general population leaned in the direction of antinuclear views and opposition to the Vietnam War, the conservatism of the AG toughened, finally culminating in the 1967 statement allowing each member to choose combatant, noncombatant, or conscientious objector status.

This development may be contrasted, however, with a growing antimilitarism in the postwar German and British pentecostal churches, the British leadership strongly supporting the banning of atomic weapons. But the general American trend may further be illustrated by the defeat of a resolution by the AG in 1981 that would have supported the establishment of a World Peace Tax Fund. The fund would have allowed those opposed to military spending to allocate their taxes to peaceful resources.

Thus, while some pentecostals retained residues of the general pacifism of an earlier era, others had even gone beyond nonpacifism and had hardened into an antipacifist position, continuing to merely reflect, rather than to instruct, public opinion.

See also QUAKERS.

■ **Bibliography:** R. M. Anderson, *Vision of the Disinherited* (1979) ▮ J. Beaman, "Pentecostal Pacifism: The Origin, Development, and Rejection of Pacific Belief among Pentecostals" (thesis, North American Bapt. Sem., 1982) ▮ W. J. Hollenweger, *The Pentecostals* (1972) ▮ W. W. Menzies, *Anointed to Serve: The Story of the Assemblies of God* (1971) ▮ R. Robins, "A Chronology of Peace: Attitudes toward War and Peace in the Assemblies of God: 1914–1918," *Pneuma* 6 (1, 1984).   ■ D. J. Wilson

PARHAM, CHARLES FOX (1873–1929). American pentecostal pioneer and author. Parham formulated classical pentecostal theology in Topeka, KS, in 1901 and thus deserves recognition as founder of the pentecostal movement. Born amid a panorama of religious ideas and persuasions, he connected the basic tenets that later defined the movement: evangelical-style conversion, sanctification, divine healing, premillennialism, and the eschatological return of Holy Spirit power evidenced by glossolalia. Parham's efforts gave pentecostalism a definable theological corpus and instilled within the movement a fervent missionary emphasis. Believing that glossolalia was actually xenolalia (known foreign language), he surmised that the gift of Holy Spirit power foreshadowed a period of unequaled missions activity. This end-time revival would mark the conclusion of the present church age and herald the return of a triumphant Christ. With his student-disciples, Parham launched the first sustained period of pentecostal growth; through his influence, others later made his ideas a global phenomenon.

Born in Muscatine, IA, on June 4, 1873, Parham fought an early struggle for survival. As an infant he suffered a virus (probably encephalitis) that weakened his childhood constitution and permanently stunted his growth. After moving with his parents to Cheney, KS, in 1878, Parham endured, beginning at age nine, an even greater physical malady. He was stricken with rheumatic fever—a condition that plagued him throughout his life despite long periods of remission. With the first bout of rheumatic fever, he felt a call to the ministry and began imitating revival preachers he had seen. Because of his weakened physical condition, he spent much of his childhood performing light farm chores in the presence of his deeply religious mother. When she died in 1885, Parham vowed to meet her in heaven. He was converted shortly thereafter and became active in the local Congregational church.

In 1890 Parham entered Southwest Kansas College and for three years struggled with his studies and his call to preach. Survival after a particularly severe attack of rheumatic fever in 1891 convinced him to reaffirm his ministerial call and also left him with a firm belief in the doctrine of divine healing. In 1893 he quit school to assume a supply pastorate of a Methodist church. Enamored with the theology of the Holiness movement and spurred by his college experience with divine healing, Parham left the Methodist Church in 1895 to assume an independent ministry. The following year he married Sarah Thistlethwaite, and together in 1898 they founded the Bethel Healing Home in Topeka. The home offered lodging and faith training for individuals seeking a divine cure. Parham's ministry in Topeka also included publication of a bimonthly Holiness journal, the *Apostolic Faith*, and some interest in rescue missions for the city's homeless.

In the summer of 1900 Parham embarked on a tour of Holiness religious centers. The focus of his 12-week journey was ▸Frank W. Sandford's Holiness commune in Shiloh, ME. Impressed with the emphasis throughout the Holiness movement on a "latter rain" outpouring of the Holy Spirit, Parham sought for himself a greater personal manifestation of this power. Through Sandford, he heard isolated reports of xenolalic tongues among missionaries. Privately he drew great significance from the discovery. Convinced that Christ's premillennial return would occur on the heels of a worldwide revival, Parham viewed xenolalic tongues as proof of Spirit baptism, since it made all recipients instant missionaries. The emergence of large numbers of divinely trained mission

Charles F. Parham, who at one time pastored a Methodist church in Kansas, then founded the Bible school in Topeka, KS, where the pentecostal movement in North America began in 1901.

workers and the example of apostolic power restored in the last days would prompt the start of the expected global revival.

Parham returned to Topeka in Sept. 1900 and optimistically secured quarters for a Bible school to prepare prospective missionaries for the outpouring of Holy Spirit power. In an elaborate old mansion on the edge of town, he taught his students the essentials of Holiness doctrine and challenged them to search for the true evidence of Holy Spirit reception. He strategically directed them to the account of Acts 2 where xenolalic tongues sparked the initial phase of Christian growth, and on Jan. 1, 1901, one of Parham's students (ˑAgnes Ozman) experienced the expected blessing and sign. During the next few days, Parham and about half of his student body of 34 were likewise baptized. Parham followed the Topeka revival with an ambitious effort to spread what he now believed was the true "apostolic faith." By April, however, his plan was dashed. Negative publicity and marginal numbers quelled the initial enthusiasm, and Parham spent the next few years in relative obscurity. He continued to proclaim pentecostal doctrine, however, and kept a small core of followers.

Parham's Apostolic Faith movement (AF) received a renewed thrust with the outbreak of revival in Galena, KS, in late 1903. There the message of the pentecostal baptism fused with divine healing to create a mass outpouring of support in the boom towns of the lead and zinc mining district. Newspaper coverage generated widespread interest, and Parham quickly garnered several thousand converts. On the strength of this success he invaded Texas early in 1905 and established a string of AF churches centered in the growing suburbs of Houston. In Dec. 1905 Parham launched another Bible school effort to train missionary evangelists. The Houston Bible school prompted further growth as Parham's disciples fanned out into the rural sections of Texas. Most significant in this 10-week training session was the attendance for several weeks of ˑWilliam J. Seymour, a black Holiness evangelist. Seymour subsequently carried the new message to Los Angeles, where through the ˑAzusa Street revival he succeeded in winning increased numbers of pentecostal converts.

By mid 1906 Parham was at the height of his popularity and enjoyed between 8,000 and 10,000 followers. The previous year he had resumed publication of the *Apostolic Faith*—now decisively pentecostal in theology. He also launched a program of organization to link his scattered flock and to monitor the success of the impending missionary revival. Naming himself "Projector," he formulated a loosely constructed federation of assemblies to promote increased evangelical activity. Unfortunately for Parham, events of the next year would prevent him from successfully establishing this organizational agenda. Late in 1906 he turned his attention to the opportunity of securing faction-riddled Zion City, IL, as a pentecostal capital. Despite an amazing growth rate and

good press coverage, Parham's forces failed to win control of Zion from ˑJohn Alexander Dowie's heir apparent, Wilbur Glenn Voliva. The strategic shift toward Zion also prevented him from visiting Seymour's revival in Los Angeles until late in October, by which time the revival had begun to assume its own separate identity. Parham's belated attempt to harness the religious enthusiasm and establish his own authority created a backlash, and he was forced to establish a rival mission. Meanwhile, Voliva's forces in Zion consolidated to stifle his influence there. By the end of 1906 Parham's position as leader of the movement was left seriously in doubt.

The final blow to Parham's prominence came in the summer of 1907, when he was arrested in San Antonio, TX, on a charge of sodomy. The details of the case are extremely sketchy and filled with innuendo and rumor. It is clear, however, that questions about Parham's reputation surfaced late in 1906—precisely the period in which his collapse as pentecostal leader began. All charges were dropped by Texas authorities without explanation, and most of the damaging press came from the religious publications of Parham's opponent, Wilbur Voliva. Parham himself refused extensive comment on the charges, expecting his followers simply to accept that the whole affair had been an elaborate frame. In the end the debacle ruined any impact that he might have retained over the growing pentecostal movement. Marred by scandal, he spent the final two decades of his life alienated from the bulk of the movement he had begun. From a base in Baxter Springs, KS, he retained a core of only several thousand followers, although his nationwide revival efforts touched many more. At the time of Parham's death in 1929, he was almost unknown among the developing second generation of the pentecostal denominations. Yet to no one individual did the movement owe a greater debt.

Parham's contributions to pentecostalism included the crucial definition of tongues as initial evidence and the particularly acute level of "latter rain" millenarianism. Tongues as evidence provided pentecostals with an identity significantly different from that of the Holiness movement by making Holy Spirit baptism a demonstrable experience. The missionary emphasis engendered by the perceived millenarian function of xenolalic tongues, despite the fading of that dream after 1908, played a crucial role in the growth of pentecostalism around the world. In addition, Parham contributed as one of the movements most prolific authors. He edited the *Apostolic Faith* with varying regularity throughout his ministry (Topeka, KS, 1899–1900; Melrose, KS, and Houston, TX, 1905–6; Baxter Springs, KS, 1910–17, 1925–29) and published two books: *Kol Kare Bomidbar: A Voice Crying in the Wilderness* (1902) and *The Everlasting Gospel* (c. 1919).

See also APOSTOLIC FAITH MOVEMENT, ORIGINS; APOSTOLIC FAITH (BAXTER SPRINGS, KANSAS); AZUSA STREET REVIVAL; CLASSICAL PENTECOSTALISM.

■ **Bibliography:** R. Anderson, *Vision of the Disinherited* (1979) ■ J. Goff, *Fields White unto Harvest* (1988) ■ D. Nelson, "For Such a Time as This" (Ph.D. diss., U. of Birmingham, 1981) ■ S. Parham, *The Life of Charles F. Parham* (1930).   ■ J. R. Goff Jr.

PARISH RENEWAL COUNCIL An interchurch organization formed by denominational renewal fellowships for the promotion of congregational renewal in the Holy Spirit. In informal discussions at a meeting of the Charismatic Concerns Committee at Glencoe, MO, several denominational leaders from mainline Protestant churches expressed their concern that congregational renewal, where they saw the movement's future, was being neglected. One reason was that the focus of its largest segments, the Roman Catholic and the nondenominational, was elsewhere. So in Sept. 1980, 10 leaders from four renewal fellowships met at Aurora, IL, seeking how to cooperate so as "to open the local churches to the ministry of the Holy Spirit." As a result, some 60 leaders came together at Tulsa, OK, in Jan. 1981 to form the Parish Renewal Council (PRC).

The aims of PRC were "to centralize some of the charismatic renewal activities for parish pastors, priests, lay leaders and to cooperate with church denominational leaders." The five groups initially forming PRC were the Presbyterian Charismatic Communion, Lutheran Charismatic Renewal Services, Episcopal Renewal Ministries, United Methodist Renewal Services Fellowship, and the Fellowship of Charismatic Christians in the United Church of Christ. The American Baptist Charismatic Fellowship joined PRC in 1983 and Mennonite Renewal Services in 1985. PRC had an executive committee with two representatives from each member fellowship.

In fact, many of the functions originally envisaged for PRC did not materialize, such as the sponsoring of regional and national parish renewal conferences and the publication of theological-biblical position papers and treatises. An evaluation of its role was undertaken by the PRC executive committee in 1984, and one of its goals was specified as identifying and highlighting those congregations that could be labeled as "lighthouse renewal groups." In fact, the PRC concept remained more attractive than it was immediately practical, and the meetings ended in 1985 without any formal dissolution.   ■ P. D. Hocken

PARR, JOHN NELSON (1886–1976). Leader in the Assemblies of God of Great Britain and Ireland (AGGBI). Converted in 1904, Parr's early association was with the Methodist Church and Star Hall Holiness, Manchester. Introduced to pentecostal teaching when a friend visited Sunderland, he was baptized in the Spirit in 1910. In 1917, while holding a senior position in a large factory, he became part-time pastor of a small pentecostal church. At the end of the war he continued to pastor the assembly. He took a leading part in the formation of the AGGBI in 1924. He was chairman–general secretary (1924–32) and first editor of *Redemption Tidings* from 1924 on. False accusations were made against him (later withdrawn), and he resigned and joined ▸Fred Squire (1904–62) in the Full Gospel Testimony, serving as general superintendent.

Parr's ministry was continued in Manchester, and a crusade by ▸Stephen Jeffreys in 1927 brought in hundreds of new converts. Parr resigned his position at the factory and built up a large assembly. He opened Bethshan Tabernacle in 1928 and later enlarged it. He continued there until his retirement in 1964 at the age of 78. Energetic and pugnacious, he took up radio work at age 69. He was active to the last as a soul winner.

■ **Bibliography:** J. N. Parr, *Incredible* (1972).
          ■ D. W. Cartwright

PATHWAY PRESS The trade division, particularly for book publication, of the Church of God (CG, Cleveland, TN) Publishing House. Other divisions of the firm are Tennessee Music and Printing Company and local Pathway Bookstores, which are located in a half-dozen cities in the southeastern U.S.

The CG began its publishing ministry in 1910 with a weekly journal, *Church of God Evangel,* which has been published continuously ever since; it is now a biweekly journal. In 1917 the CG established its own printing plant for production of its Sunday school literature. In 1929 a youth magazine, *The Lighted Pathway,* was begun. Other materials and publications featuring every aspect of Christian ministry have been added to the literary output. Recently, an elaborate program for improving students' cognitive abilities has been added. Pathway Press is one of the larger denominational publishing houses in the U.S.

■ **Bibliography:** C. W. Conn, *The Evangel Reader* (1958).
          ■ C. W. Conn

PATTERSON, GILBERT EARL (1939–). Church of God in Christ (COGIC) pastor and bishop. Patterson was born in Humboldt, TN, to Bishop W. A. Patterson Sr. and Mary L. Williams Patterson. Converted under his father's ministry at Holy Temple COGIC in Memphis, he was filled with the Holy Spirit in 1956 at New Jerusalem COGIC in Detroit. He became a licensed minister in 1957 and was ordained the following year. He was the first member of the provisional board of the International Youth Congress and served for 11 years on the National Evangelist Board under the late Bishop L. C. Page. In 1969 Patterson founded his first church. In 1988 he was appointed over the Fourth Ecclesiastical

Jurisdiction of Tennessee. Currently, he is pastor of two churches in Memphis with a combined membership of over 20,000. He also has a nationwide television ministry and serves on the general board of COGIC. He is married to Louis Dowdy Patterson.

■ **Bibliography:** S. DuPree, *African-American Holiness-Pentecostal Movement: An Annotated Bibliography* (1996) ■ idem, *Biographical Dictionary of African-American Holiness-Pentecostals: 1880–1990* (n.d.).   ■ S. S. DuPree

PAUL, JONATHAN ANTON ALEXANDER (1853–1931).

German pentecostal leader and author. After graduating from the Studium der Theologie in Griefswald, Paul pastored in Pommeren from 1880. He was active in the Gnadauer Verband (a revivalist group within the state church), in youth work, and in social action concerns, including industrial missions and ministry to railway workers. He wrote and preached extensively about "full salvation," drawing upon the Pietist and Anglo-Saxon revivalist traditions; and in 1907, after a visit to Oslo, he became a pentecostal believer. Attacked by the Gnadauer Verband in the infamous ▸Berlin Declaration, Paul became a founder of the Mülheim pentecostal movement. A prolific writer, he edited several periodicals, including *Heiligung, Lied des Lammes, Pfingstgrüsse,* and *Heilszeugnisse.* A skillful poet, many of his works are included in the Mülheim hymnal, *Pfingstjubel.* He (with five others) provided the first modern German-language translation of the NT, *Das Neue Testament in der Sprache der Gegenwart* (1914).

■ **Bibliography:**

Selected Works. J. A. A. Paul, *Ihr werdet die Kraft des Heiligen Geistes empfangen, ein Zeugnis von der Taufe mit dem Heiligen Geist und Feuer* (1896), Swedish trans. *Andeopet* (1906) ■ idem, *Siegreiches Leben durch das Blut Jesu* (n.d.) ■ idem, *Unsere Botschaft an die Kranken* (n.d.) ■ idem, *Was ist die Pfingstbewegung?* (n.d.) ■ idem, *Wie ich in die Pfingstbewegung kam* (n.d.) ■ idem, *Zur Daimonenfrage, Ein Wort zur Verständigung* (n.d.).

Selected Secondary Literature. P. Fleisch, *Die Geschichte der deutschen Gemeinschaftsbewegung bis zum Auftreten des Zungenredens (1875–1907)* (1912; repr. 1985) ■ idem, *Die Pfingstebewegung in Deutschland* (1957) ■ idem, "Paul, Jonathan," *RGG,* 2, 4 ■ E. Geise, *Jonathan Paul, Ein Knecht Jesu Christi* (2d ed, 1965) ■ E. Geldbach, "Paul Jonathan," *Evangelisches Gemeindelexikon* (1978), 398–99 ■ C. H. Krust, *50 Jahre Deutsche Pfingstbewegung, Mülheimer Richtung* (1958) ■ D. Lange, *Eine Bewegung bricht zich Bahn* (1979) ■ S. Schönheit, *Der Aufbruch der Pfingstbewegung, 1906–1910* (1981) ■ C. van der Laan, "The Proceedings of the Leader's Meetings (1908–1911) and of the International Pentecostal Council (1912–1914)," *EPTA Bulletin* 6 (1987).   ■ D. D. Bundy

PAULK, EARL PEARLY, JR. (1927–). Televangelist, pastor, and archbishop. Bishop Earl P. Paulk Jr. grew up in a classical pentecostal family, the son of Earl P. Paulk Sr., a former assistant general overseer of the Church of God (CG, Cleveland, TN). His grandfather, Elisha Paulk, was a Freewill Baptist preacher.

Paulk was called to the ministry and began preaching at age 17 in Greenville, SC. Two years later he became the state Sunday school and youth director for South Carolina (CG); later he pastored the Hemphill Church of God in Atlanta, GA (now known as Mount Paran Church of God). Paulk earned a B.A. at Furman University in 1947 and completed the M.Div. at the Candler School of Theology of Emory University in 1952.

In 1960 Paulk and his brother Don founded the Gospel Harvester Church in Atlanta's inner city. The church moved to the suburbs in 1973 and became known as Chapel Hill Harvester Church. The church has grown to more than 10,000 with 20 full-time pastors. The church also developed ministries for unwed mothers, homosexuals, prisoners, and those with chemical addictions. It runs Cathedral Academy, a K–12 school in Decatur, GA, with an enrollment of about 350.

Paulk has become well-known for his "kingdom message" through his preaching, the monthly publication of *Thy Kingdom Come,* and his many books. The latter include: *The Divine Runner* (1978), *Satan Unmasked* (1984), *The Wounded Body of Christ* (1985), *Sex Is God's Idea* (1985), *Thrust in the Sickle and Reap* (1986), *The Prophetic Community* (1995), *Offspring* (1996), and *The Blood* (1996). His autobiography is entitled *The Provoker* (1986).

Earl Paulk Jr., pastor of the Chapel Hill Harvester Church in Atlanta, GA.

In 1982 Paulk was named to the office of bishop in the International Communion of Charismatic Churches.

■ L. G. McClung Jr.

PAWSON, DAVID (1930–). British Bible teacher with international ministry. After leaving school at 16 and working on the land, Pawson obtained a B.Sc. in Agriculture (Durham) and later an M.A. in Theology (Cambridge). He was in the Methodist ministry for 12 years before serving as pastor of two Baptist churches: Chalfont St Peter, Buckinghamshire, (1961–68), and the Millmead Centre, Guildford (1968–79). Since the beginning of his own charismatic experience in 1964, Pawson has seen evangelicals and charismatics as needing each other, a position argued in *Fourth Wave* (1993). Since 1979 his teaching ministry has become full-time and more international, mostly to church leaders and to men of all denominations. His lucid expository teaching has led to a vast output of audio- and videocassettes (the former reaching 120 countries). Many of the topics he consistently addresses are now treated in his books: *The Normal Christian Birth* (1989); *When Jesus Returns* (1995); *Once Saved, Always Saved?* (1996); and *Jesus Baptizes in One Holy Spirit* (1997). Pawson has never been afraid of tackling controversial topics, as in *Leadership Is Male* (1988) and *The Road to Hell* (1992). He has long had a great love for Israel and the Jewish people and has been a strong opponent of the view that the church has replaced Israel.

■ P. D. Hocken

PAYNE, LEANNE (1932–). Teacher and minister of inner healing. Like ▸Agnes Sanford, Payne was led into the healing ministry through a personal healing, and she experienced a filling with the Holy Spirit and other spiritual gifts some time before receiving the gift of tongues. Her first contact with charismatic renewal was in 1963 with R. Winkler of Wheaton, IL. Payne, an Episcopalian, emphasizes the indwelling presence of Christ and the importance of rooting healing ministry in a strong Trinitarian theology. This concern led to her first book, *Real Presence: The Holy Spirit in the Works of C. S. Lewis* (1979). Payne, who founded Pastoral Care Ministries in Milwaukee, WI, in 1982 (located in Wheaton, IL, since 1993), emphasizes gender identity as vital for human wholeness and the importance of restoring the church's Jewish roots. Her other books include *The Broken Image: Restoring Personal Wholeness Through Healing Prayer* (1981); *The Healing of the Homosexual* (1984); *Crisis in Masculinity* (1985); *The Healing Presence* (1989); *Restoring the Christian Soul* (1991); and *Listening Prayer* (1994).

■ P. D. Hocken

PEARLMAN, MYER (1898–1943). Educator and author. Born into a Jewish family in Edinburgh, Scotland, he moved with his family to Birmingham, England, at age seven. He received his common-school training at the Birmingham Hebrew School and excelled in his studies. At age 14 he mastered the French language on his own and later used this knowledge to act as an interpreter for the U.S. Army in France during WWI. He immigrated to New York City in 1915 and enlisted in the Army Medical Corps when he was 19. After the war he moved to California. While passing by Glad Tidings Mission in San Francisco, he felt drawn inside, where the people were singing "Honey in the Rock," composed by ▸F. A. Graves. After several months of attending meetings at the church, Pearlman was converted to Christianity and received the baptism of the Holy Spirit. He graduated from Central Bible Institute, Springfield, MO, in 1925 and was asked to join the faculty. In 1927 he married one of his pupils, Irene Graves, daughter of F. A. Graves.

Pearlman taught a variety of courses, but his forte was synthesis classes on the OT and NT. The Pearlman Memorial Library on the campus of Central Bible College was dedicated to him in 1944 as a lasting token of appreciation from the students.

In addition to his teaching career, Pearlman for many years prepared the *Adult Teacher's Quarterly* as well as the *Adult Student's Quarterly* for Gospel Publishing House. During WWII he also edited *Reveille,* a devotional publication geared to American servicemen. He is best remembered for his monumental outline of theology called *Knowing the Doctrines of the Bible* (1937). He also wrote *Seeing the Story of the Bible* (1930); *Why We Believe the Bible Is God's Book* (1931); *The Life and Teachings of Christ* (1935); *Through the Bible Book by Book* (1935); *The Heavenly Gift* (1935); *The Minister's Service Book* (1941); *Daniel Speaks Today* (1943); and several other books. His books have been translated into Hindustani, Portuguese, Arabic, Italian, Spanish, and other languages. Overwork caused his health to break at a comparatively early age.

■ **Bibliography:** I. P. Pearlman, *Myer Pearlman and His Friends* (1953) ▌ "Myer Pearlman's Own Story," *AGH* (Winter 1989–90).

■ G. W. Gohr

PEARSON, CARLTON DEMETRIUS (1953–). Evangelist, pastor, and prominent leader in the charismatic movement. Pastor of Higher Dimensions Family Church in Tulsa ,OK. He is the overseeing bishop of more than 500 churches and ministries through the Azusa Interdenominational Fellowship and conducts a national ministry of television evangelism and conferences.

Pearson was born in Otay, CA, near the border of Mexico, where he grew up in poverty and hardship. He was saved and began preaching at age five. In his teen years he was mentored by Bishop J. A. Blake of San Diego. He has become one of the most influential leaders of the charismatic movement and a national leader in the racial integration of the church.

While attending Oral Roberts University, Pearson founded the Souls of Fire music ministry that appeared on ˒Oral Roberts's prime-time television broadcasts and traveled extensively with Oral Roberts as an associate evangelist. In 1982 he founded Higher Dimensions Family Church in Tulsa with his longtime friend Gary McIntosh, carrying out a long-cherished vision for an integrated charismatic congregation. The church has grown to over 5,000 members, with several significant affiliate ministries. The most prominent of these ministries is Azusa Interdenominational Fellowship, a national association of churches and ministries, which in 1997 hosted its first international conference in Durban, South Africa.

Pearson's ministries include substantial benevolence in feeding the poor, providing assistance to families and unwed mothers, and child day care. He has also established a national music ministry that produces many successful gospel music recordings.

Pearson's current television program is *Sunday Night Live* and is seen across the U.S. and in Canada and Europe. He has published many books and pamphlets.

Bishop Carlton Pearson, a prominent leader in the charismatic movement and overseer of more than 500 churches and ministries through the Azusa Interdenominational Fellowship.

■ **Bibliography:** C. Chappell, "Azusa: Bridge between Races and Denominations," *The Oklahoma Eagle* (Apr. 14, 1994) ■ E. Parker, *Carlton Demetrius Pearson* (1992) ■ C. Pearson, *Crisis at the Crossroads* (1989) ■ idem, *Every Single One of You* (1994) ■ idem, *Is There a Man in the House?* (1996).   ■ D. J. Hedges

PEDERSON, W. DENNIS (1938–92). A leader in the Lutheran charismatic movement who combined gifts of teaching and administration with a broad missionary vision. Pederson graduated from Augsburg Theological Seminary, Minneapolis, in 1963, and received the D.Min. from the Jesuit School of Theology in Berkeley in 1978. He served as a principal staff assistant to the governor of Minnesota 1971–75. Having experienced a personal spiritual renewal during Holy Week 1972, Pederson began relating to other Lutheran charismatics the following August at the first International Lutheran Conference on the Holy Spirit in Minneapolis.

Pederson returned to the active ordained ministry in 1975 as minister of evangelism and education in a Lutheran congregation in California. In 1978 he was called as an associate pastor and administrator to North Heights Lutheran Church, St. Paul, MN, one of the leading Lutheran charismatic churches in the country.

Together with senior pastor ˒Morris Vaagenes, he cofounded the International Lutheran Center for Church Renewal as a ministry of North Heights Lutheran Church (1980), which merged with Lutheran Charismatic Renewal Services in 1983 to form the International Lutheran Renewal Center (ILRC). Pederson became coordinator of ILRC's international ministries, traveling extensively abroad and helping to develop a worldwide network of relationships among Lutheran charismatic leaders. Pederson died in 1992 in a plane crash.

See also LUTHERAN CHARISMATICS.

■ **Bibliography:** L. Christenson, ed., *Welcome, Holy Spirit* (1987).

■ L. Christenson

PENDLETON, WILLIAM H. (b. 1847). Early pentecostal pastor. Pendleton was born in Arkansas. Married in 1866, he and his wife, Sarah, had 13 children. A Civil War veteran, Pendleton embraced "second work" teaching while a Baptist deacon in 1879. In an 1893 Downey, CA, camp meeting of the Holiness churches, he experienced "full sanctification." Recognized as a Holiness church minister from 1895 on, he became pastor of the Los Angeles Holiness Church. A frequent and popular camp-meeting speaker, Pendleton was elected to the denominational board of elders (1898). During the summer of 1906 he attended Azusa Street, after which he became the focus of controversy in the Holiness church because he experienced and taught baptism in the Spirit evidenced by tongues as subsequent to sanctification. Defrocked (Aug. 27, 1906), he and 28 members moved to the Eighth and Maple mission, where he succeeded ˒Frank Bartleman as pastor through 1910. As late as 1913 he was listed as pastor at a pentecostal assembly at 1162 East 43d in Los Angeles.

■ **Bibliography:** F. Bartleman, *How Pentecost Came to Los Angeles* (1925) ■ J. M. Washburn, *History and Reminiscences of the Holiness Church Work in Southern California and Arizona* (1912).

■ C. M. Robeck Jr.

PENSACOLA REVIVAL See BROWNSVILLE REVIVAL.

PENTECOST, FEAST OF The Feast of Pentecost, commemorated in the church as the day on which the Holy Spirit descended (Acts 2) in fulfillment of the promise of Jesus (John 16:7, 13; Acts 1:4, 14), is traditionally recognized as the birth of the church as an institution.

Pentecost, meaning 50, is the Greek name for the OT Feast of Weeks, since this festival occurred on the 50th day (seven weeks) after Passover. Along with the feasts of Passover and Tabernacles, Pentecost was one of the three annual pilgrimage feasts for the Jews. A harvest festival, it marked the beginning of the time when the people brought their offerings of firstfruits. Lev. 23:15–21 provides the most detailed account of the ritual observed during the feast. The observance is also known as the Feast of Ingathering (Ex. 23:16) and Day of Firstfruits (Num. 28:26).

In Judith 6:17–21 (c. 100 B.C.), Pentecost is the feast of covenant renewal, an understanding also reflected within the Qumran community. After the destruction of the temple in Jerusalem in A.D. 70, Jews celebrated Pentecost to commemorate the giving of the Law at Sinai.

The coming of the Holy Spirit on the Day of Pentecost (Acts 2) implies the passing of the old system of worship, as well as the climax and fulfillment of the promises that system foreshadowed. For the church, Pentecost has become a time to celebrate God's bestowal of the gift of the Spirit. "Pentecostals" are modern Christians who believe in the possibility of receiving the same experience of the Holy Spirit as the apostles on the Day of Pentecost (Acts 1:1–4).

■ **Bibliography:** H. L. Bosman, "Feast of Weeks," *NIDOTTE* (1977) ▮ R. de Vaux, *Ancient Israel,* 2 vols. (1961) ▮ J. D. G. Dunn, "Pentecost, Feast of," *NIDNTT* (1976) ▮ C. Feinberg, "Pentecost," *ZPEB* (1976) ▮ D. A. Garrett, "Feasts and Festivals of Israel," *EDBibT* (1996) ▮ S. Gilmour, "Easter and Pentecost," *JBL* 81 (1962) ▮ E. Lohse, *"Pentemcostem," TDNT* (1968) ▮ H. Schauss, *The Jewish Festivals* (1938).   ■ T. Powell

PENTECOSTAL ASSEMBLIES OF CANADA

Part of the fastest-growing religious groupings in the country, the Pentecostal Assemblies of Canada (PAOC) has been characterized both by stability and by vision leading to aggressive evangelistic outreach. This becomes obvious as one traces the denomination's history through four periods.

1. Beginnings (1906–25).

Within months of the outpouring of the Spirit at ⌐Azusa Street in Los Angeles, pentecostalism had taken root in Canada. By 1910 it had spread to both coasts, with comparatively large concentrations in Toronto and Winnipeg. In the early decades of the century, the prairie provinces had the largest proportions of pentecostals relative to their population size. Not coincidentally these provinces also had the largest proportions of immigrants from the U.S. It has often been observed that throughout the history of the country, Canadian sectarianism has been fundamentally American (U.S.) in nature, and in no case has this been truer than for PAOC. Alongside American brethren, Canadian pentecostals had dynamic Christian experiences focusing simultaneously on Christ and the Holy Spirit.

The first attempt to create an organization among Canadian pentecostals occurred in the East in 1909, but it collapsed in the face of intense opposition. Nine years later a decision was made to form the PAOC and then to join the ⌐Pentecostal Assemblies of the World (PAOW), an American body. The PAOC received its charter on May 17, 1919, but the PAOW was never contacted.

In 1919 pentecostals in Saskatchewan and Alberta, as yet not officially attached to the PAOC, joined the Assemblies of God (AG) of the U.S. The general superintendent of the AG, J. W. Welch, was present at the conference at which this decision was made, and another American, Hugh Cadwalder, was elected district superintendent.

One year later the PAOC itself decided to join the AG. This was particularly significant, for the PAOC had been "Jesus Only" (⌐Oneness pentecostalism) when it received its charter. By this decision it repudiated that stance. This act brought most Canadian pentecostals into membership with the AG. Some even held ministerial credentials with both the American and the Canadian groups, since the PAOC continued to exist as a separate entity. It also united most Canadian pentecostals, because as a part of the action, those from the West had joined the PAOC.

It also precipitated the first major split in Canadian pentecostalism. One of the group's charter members, ⌐Frank

Orthodox icon of the Feast of Pentecost.

Small from Winnipeg, regarded the move away from the Jesus Only position as an unwarranted compromise. After having been dropped from the ranks of the PAOC, Small founded the ►Apostolic Church of Pentecost in 1921. Again, among its charter members were prominent American Oneness pentecostals.

The organizational relationship between the AG and the PAOC persisted until 1925, when the PAOC asked to be released from the AG, primarily because of differences over missionary policy. The request was granted, leading to an amiable parting.

While these organizational discussions were going on, the PAOC was continuing to experience growth. In 1920 it established a national paper, *The Pentecostal Testimony*, and it articulated a centralized missionary policy to facilitate the overseas evangelism that had already been carried on by Canadian pentecostals for 12 years. During this period the PAOC attracted strong leadership. Some, like ►G. A. Chambers, ►A. G. Ward, R. L. Dutaud, J. C. Ball, and F. M. Bellsmith, came from other denominations, while others, for example, ►A. H. Argue and C. E. Baker, left business to assume prominent positions. The contribution made by these people cannot be overestimated. First and foremost, it was their religious experiences, their understanding of Scripture, and their life experience that defined the nature of the emerging movement. They gave it their priorities and formulated its doctrine. They also exemplified its view of spirituality. The explicit emphases they expressed have changed little since 1920. In short, they established the ideological framework in which the PAOC and its members would grow and develop.

In spite of strong American roots, the PAOC achieved an autonomous Canadian identity. It also made significant strides in defining itself doctrinally. By 1925 it had clearly made a place for itself among Canadian religious groups.

2. Consolidation (1926–51).

Leadership at the beginning of the period of consolidation was provided by the same men who had been involved in the creation of the group. In 1925, however, several additional men who had had active ministries in other denominations came into the PAOC. Three were Presbyterian, one a Methodist, and one an Anglican. All were in the West, one in Saskatchewan and the others in Manitoba. They contributed significantly to the shape the PAOC acquired.

The concern that had dominated Canadian pentecostalism from its beginning—the evangelization of the lost—continued to preoccupy it. *The Pentecostal Testimony* carried articles stressing the importance of evangelism. By Dec. 1951 it had also carried more than 150 reports of evangelistic meetings. These reports were careful to give statistics regarding the number of people who had been converted, healed, or baptized in the Holy Spirit. This was vital information, serving both as an encouragement and as a stimulus. Large evan-

gelistic campaigns carried on by prominent personalities were also a feature. ►Aimee Semple McPherson, ►Charles Price, ►Harvey McAlister, and Lorne Fox were active across the country. The same burden for the lost motivated international missionary service. By 1927 Canadian pentecostals were supporting missionaries on five fields. The fundamental concerns of the PAOC remained intact, but around them changes were occurring.

Economic growth went hand in hand with the denomination's numerical growth. Pentecostals were acquiring the financial resources vital to carrying out their ministry. A somewhat crude comparison of denominational receipts makes this apparent. In a 12-month period in 1927 to 1928, the PAOC received $71,000, but from Jan. to Sept. 1952, it took in $530,000. Through its national periodical, the PAOC began to offer advice to its members with regard to financial planning. "Annuity bonds" and "wills" became topics of articles for the first time in 1928.

More money also meant better and larger facilities. In 1927 the church in Kitchener, Ont., erected a building that seated 800, and one year later Calvary Temple in Winnipeg bought the First Baptist Church, which accommodated 1,500 people. Growth in the denomination was obvious.

During this same period, the PAOC also became active in theological education. The motivation throughout was to prepare people, both men and women, for ministry. The first efforts were concentrated on short-term schools. In 1925 Canadian Pentecostal Bible College opened in Winnipeg, with ►J. Eustace Purdie as principal. Purdie was an Anglican minister who had recently been baptized in the Holy Spirit, and he held this post until his retirement in 1950. During his tenure, he trained a generation of leaders for the denomination.

The organizational structure also grew, and this, too, came about in the pursuit of basic objectives. In 1935 General Secretary A. G. Ward wrote:

I feel we must not fail to recognize that as a movement grows numerically and new departments are opened up, of necessity it must be carried on in the most efficient business-like way. We have certainly outgrown some of our former policies and methods of conducting affairs, and now we must either make the necessary changes and improvements or be forced into retrogression.

In this spirit, pentecostals turned their hands to creating a structure. In the 1920s, district conferences and attending organizations began to appear, and in the 1930s and 1940s, national departments were added. Along with many others, the prominent figure involved in this process was ►D. N. Buntain. Basic priorities—evangelism and the ministry of the Holy Spirit—were retained. However, important and far-reaching changes were taking place in the PAOC, and not everyone was comfortable with what was happening.

In the 1940s, the *Pentecostal Testimony* began to carry articles with titles like "The Love of Many Waxen Cold," "Is Pentecost Doomed to Defeat?" and "Is Pentecost Passing?" G. A. Chambers, the denomination's first general superintendent, said, "We have not only turned aside, but have stepped down to the level of other religious bodies who long ago lost the anointing. . . ." The PAOC was experiencing something of an identity crisis. In the light of this it is not surprising that the PAOC was wracked by another major split in 1947–48. One of its leaders, George Hawtin, said:

> The Great Pentecostal revival of the 20th century was no sooner under way than we, like all our predecessors, began to divide ourselves up into denominational groups. We like all others before us set up our fences, and made our statement as to what we believed, making it impossible to go on to the next glory and the next revelation of truth.

This new movement began in Saskatchewan and was known as "The ▸Latter Rain" or "The Sharon Movement." It placed particular emphasis on the gifts of the Spirit and on fasting, and it developed its own missionary arm, Global Outreach. Faced with this challenge, about half of the PAOC churches in Saskatchewan, as well as proportionally smaller numbers elsewhere in western Canada, left the denomination and "went Latter Rain."

3. Growth (1952–78).

Having passed through a particularly turbulent period, the PAOC moved into several decades of strong growth. The most important concern in the collective mind of the denomination continued to be evangelism, but at the same time the PAOC took its place among other Canadian denominations. Several features make this obvious.

Economically, the PAOC continued to experience significant gains. In the 1950s this led to some attempt to rationalize and to understand the implications. In that decade, the *Pentecostal Testimony* carried articles that promoted private enterprise and investment and that showed how money could be used to further denominational objectives. Two decades later a national stewardship department was created in order to provide investment counseling and estate planning.

The stronger financial base also provided the resources necessary for aggressive building programs. Two examples are Central Tabernacle in Edmonton, built in 1972 with a seating capacity of 2,000, and Winnipeg's Calvary Temple, capable of accommodating 2,500 and completed in 1974.

A second feature marking increasing maturity within the PAOC is a developing social awareness. Some members of the denomination have held public office. One, Sam Jenkins, served as president of the Marine Workers and Boilermakers Union of the Canadian Coalition of Laborers. Another, Everett Wood, held a seat for the socialist New Democratic Party in the legislative assembly of Saskatchewan for 16 years.

For most of that time he was a member of the cabinet. Others have represented right-of-center political parties.

Philanthropy has also been an important part of PAOC ministry. This was expressed through a home for girls, a major regional hospital, and numerous senior citizens' residences. The first of these residences appeared in 1942, but as the denomination aged, they became common in connection with major churches. A number of PAOC churches were also active in the late 1970s in the relocation of Vietnamese refugees. Local committees found accommodations; provided food, clothing, and furniture; and arranged language training and employment for the refugees.

Educationally, the PAOC underwent significant changes. With the rest of the population of Canada, but at a slower pace, general educational levels rose within the denomination. There was an increasing number of university graduates and professionals within its membership. Theological colleges (the PAOC operated five in the 1970s, one in French and four in English) have been a part of this trend. One entered into an association with a Lutheran seminary, which enabled it to offer an M.Div. degree.

In the midst of economic, social, and educational developments, the PAOC has retained its intense interest in evangelism. During the 1950s it began to experience some difficulties with large campaigns that led to a refocusing of energy. A number of programs were created among youth. Ambassadors in Mission and Team Canada have both conducted direct evangelism on streets and in parks in connection with major events such as the 1976 Olympics in Montreal. Meanwhile the denomination developed national programs such as Canada for Christ, which organized crusades for widely recognized evangelists, and Pentecostal Assemblies Church Expansion, which attempted to teach church-growth principles. In 1976 these and other programs were amalgamated and came to be known as the Department of National Spiritual Life and Evangelism.

4. Development (1978–2000).

The last two decades of the century were a challenge for the PAOC, as for other religious groups. Facing deepening spiritual interest in the general population of Canada, matched with a growing disenchantment with organized religion, the PAOC worked to maintain trajectories established much earlier in its history. Evangelism and church planting were kept to the fore. In 1984 General Superintendent James MacKnight set before the fellowship the goal of 75 new assemblies in two years. By 1986, 102 had been established. In 1987 MacKnight chaired the first Congress on Pentecostal Leadership; a second was held in 1993. These major policy and planning meetings were held to ensure that the PAOC approached the millennium "on track."

Challenges in the 1980s made it apparent that the organization of the PAOC would have to be reviewed. This was undertaken in the 1990s and continued through the decade as leaders searched for more efficient means of managing resources. Elected to office in 1996, General Superintendent William Morrow has carried this forward with vigor. Departments at the national office were restructured and reduced in number, and a new regional district was created by grouping together all of the predominantly French-language churches in Quebec.

Part of the review focused on education. By the mid 1990s the number of colleges the PAOC operated had increased to six and dropped again to five as another French institution was established and then the two French colleges were amalgamated. All four of the English-language schools achieved accreditation or candidate status with the Accrediting Association of Bible Colleges (AABC) by the early 1990s, and toward the end of the decade tentative steps were being taken toward graduate studies. Initiatives were put in place to ensure that students at the PAOC's colleges were receiving the training necessary to minister effectively in the 21st century.

Conclusion.

At the beginning of the new millennium, the PAOC finds itself in a demanding situation. It is ministering in a pluralistic society in which residual Christian values appear to be weakening, yet signs of effectiveness can be seen. Some churches are growing strongly in suburban areas, and others have been planted in the difficult surroundings of inner cities.

The number of ethnic churches is growing, and many other assemblies are successfully multiracial. Leadership is engaged in a process of redefining or removing any structural obstacles in the way of the PAOC's pursuit of its mandate of evangelization at home and abroad.

The major challenge the PAOC faces is internal. How will it cope with the fact that it is now one denomination among others? How will it mobilize growing human and economic resources to continue its reach for objectives it has held dear throughout its history?

■ **Bibliography:** G. F. Atter, *The Third Force* (1970) ■ G. G. Kulbeck, *What God Hath Wrought* (1958) ■ T. W. Miller, *Canadian Pentecostals: A History of the Pentecostal Assemblies of Canada* (1994) ■ E. A. Peters, *The Contribution to Education by the Pentecostal Assemblies of Canada* (1970).   ■ R. A. N. Kydd

PENTECOSTAL ASSEMBLIES OF JESUS CHRIST Formed in 1931 as an attempt to return to the original interracial fellowship that marked ▸Oneness pentecostalism. At the initial stages of pentecostal organization, all Oneness pentecostals were affiliated with the multiracial ▸Pentecostal Assemblies of the World (PAW). In 1924 many white constituents, citing increased effectiveness in world evangelism, withdrew to form the ▸Pentecostal Church, Incorporated (PCI).

The remaining membership of the PAW then affiliated with the Apostolic Church of Jesus Christ in 1931, forming the Pentecostal Assemblies of Jesus Christ (PAJC) in an ill-fated attempt to restore interracial harmony. Within weeks, black followers of Bishop Samuel Grimes met in Dayton, OH, to decide to continue the PAW under the old charter. Following a decision to hold the 1937 conference in Tulsa, OK (a city with segregated facilities), most of the blacks who had remained in the PAJC returned to the PAW. In 1945, since there was virtually no doctrinal difference and great congruity in constituency, the PAJC merged with the PCI to form the United Pentecostal Church, which is the largest of the Oneness pentecostal bodies.

■ **Bibliography:** J. G. Melton, ed., *The Encyclopedia of American Religions*, vol. 1 (1989) ■ J. T. Nichol, *Pentecostalism* (1966).
          ■ B. M. Stout

PENTECOSTAL ASSEMBLIES OF NEWFOUNDLAND

The expansion of pentecostalism to Newfoundland and Labrador is traced to the ministry of Alice Belle Garrigus, a pentecostal evangelist from Boston, MA. She opened the Bethesda Mission (later Bethesda Pentecostal Church) in St. John's, Nfld., on Easter Sunday in 1911. As the pentecostal revival spread, more converts were gained and churches were established. By 1925 the numbers had increased sufficiently to gain legal recognition from the provincial government. For the next five years it was known as the Bethesda Pentecostal Assemblies, becoming the Pentecostal Assemblies of Newfoundland (PAON) in 1930. Using a coastal vessel, *The Gospel Messenger*, PAON began its ministry outreach to Labrador two years later.

Since Newfoundland and Labrador constituted a dominion separate from Canada in the British Commonwealth until 1949, PAON developed independently of the ▸Pentecostal Assemblies of Canada. Nevertheless, they share a common statement of faith and work closely in overseas missions and in the governance of Eastern Pentecostal Bible College in Peterborough, Ont. A unique distinctive of PAON is the large school system it sponsors, maintaining both elementary and high schools. Denominational educational rights were uniformly established in the Constitution of Canada in Sept. 1987, thereby giving PAON all the educational rights that had been in place for other denominations since Newfoundland became part of Canada in 1949. A. Earl Batstone has served as general superintendent since 1996.

PAON maintains an official monthly magazine, *Good Tidings*, with a circulation of 8,000. It also operates the Religious Book and Bible House. It maintains significant ministries to students on the campus of Memorial University of Newfoundland and to various residential institutions through the office of the Chaplain for Institutions. The official denominational ministerial training college is Eastern Pentecostal Bible College in Peterborough, Ont.

The 1991 national census showed pentecostals in Newfoundland numbering 40,100. PAON lists 141 churches in Newfoundland and Labrador as of Aug. 1, 1997.

■ **Bibliography:** B. K. Janes, *The Lady Who Came* (1982) ▮ idem, *The Lady Who Stayed* (1982) ▮ C. E. Jones, *A Guide to the Study of the Pentecostal Movement* (1983) ▮ R. D. King, ed., *Good Tidings* (1935–) ▮ A. C. Piepkorn, *Profiles in Belief*, 3 vols. (1979).

■ J. A. Hewett

PENTECOSTAL ASSEMBLIES OF THE WORLD

One of the oldest interracial Oneness pentecostal organizations. An outgrowth of the ⌐Azusa Street revival, it held its first recorded meeting in 1907 in Los Angeles. J. J. Frazee from Portland, OR, was both first secretary and general secretary from 1912 to 1916. ⌐G. T. Haywood, prominent black Oneness leader from Indianapolis, held credentials since 1911. In 1918, with the assistance of Haywood, the Pentecostal Assemblies of the World (PAW) expanded its numbers by absorbing the fledgling General Assembly of Apostolic Assemblies (GAAA). This group had formed a year earlier when the "New Issue"/Oneness ministers and congregations were expelled from the AG. The GAAA was seeking a chartered organization that could provide ministerial exemption from military duty.

Following incorporation in 1919, the number of black members increased dramatically in the northern region, largely due to Haywood's influence. Although the PAW was fully integrated, racial tension with the southern white members finally led to a schism in 1924. The Pentecostal Assemblies of the World (PAW) reorganized under an episcopal polity, electing Haywood as first presiding bishop, a position he held until his death in 1931.

The whites splintered into three groups. An unstable merger was accomplished in 1931 between the PAW and one group, the Apostolic Church of Jesus Christ (ACJC), forming the ⌐Pentecostal Assemblies of Jesus Christ (PAJC). Concern over the change of name, abandonment of the episcopal polity, and lack of trust resulted in the reconstitution of the PAW, with Samuel Grimes of New York City as its presiding bishop. The interracial experiment of the PAJC collapsed in 1937, and most black members returned to the PAW.

Predominantly black, the PAW is conscientiously integrated at every level of the organization. It has suffered only one schism since 1931. This occurred under the leadership of one of its bishops, S. N. Hancock, in 1957, as the result of a power struggle.

The PAW adheres strictly to the Oneness "new birth" teaching of Haywood, practices footwashing, advocates the use of wine in communion, and permits divorce and remarriage in the case of adultery or separation by an unsaved partner. Headquarters are in Indianapolis. In 1997 its recorded worldwide membership was 1 million in 1,800 U.S. and 2,400 foreign congregations. It is represented in every state and on every continent, with its strongest works in Africa, Asia, the Caribbean, and Latin America.

■ **Bibliography:** T. French, "Oneness Pentecostalism in Global Perspective" (thesis, Wheaton College, 1998) ▮ M. Golder, *History of the Pentecostal Assemblies of the World* (1973) ▮ J. Tyson, *The Early Pentecostal Revival: History of Twentieth-Century Pentecostals and The Pentecostal Assemblies of the World, 1901–30* (1992).

■ D. A. Reed

PENTECOSTAL/CHARISMATIC CHURCHES OF NORTH AMERICA

See PENTECOSTAL FELLOWSHIP OF NORTH AMERICA.

PENTECOSTAL CHURCH, INCORPORATED

The all-white Pentecostal Ministerial Alliance was organized at St. Louis, MO, Nov. 3, 1925, in the wake of the breakup of the biracial ⌐Pentecostal Assemblies of the World. Race, not doctrine, was the issue. The 1926–27 roll contained 222 names. Although membership was restricted to clergy, fellowship soon developed among churches served by members. In 1932 the adoption of a new name—The Pentecostal Church, Incorporated—and of a plan for district and local church government established a milestone on the road to denominational order. That destination was reached at St. Louis 13 years later, when the Pentecostal Church, Incorporated, claimed 175 congregations and 810 ministers. In 1945 it merged with the ⌐Pentecostal Assemblies of Jesus Christ to form the ⌐United Pentecostal Church, International.

■ **Bibliography:** A. L. Clanton, *United We Stand* (1970) ▮ C. E. Jones, *Black Holiness: A Guide to the Study of Black Participation in Wesleyan Perfectionist and Glossolalic Pentecostal Movements* (1987) ▮ idem, *The Charismatic Movement: A Guide to the Study of Neo-Pentecostalism with an Emphasis on Anglo-American Sources* (1995).

■ C. E. Jones

PENTECOSTAL CHURCH OF GOD

(PCG). A baptistic pentecostal organization with headquarters in Joplin, MO, that probably owes its existence to the fact that the General Council of the ⌐Assemblies of God (AG) adopted a statement of faith in 1916. A group of pentecostals who shared beliefs similar to those of the AG but were fearful of any type of rigid statement met in Dec. 1919 under the leadership of former AG executive presbyter, ⌐John C. Sinclair, and formed the Pentecostal Assemblies of the U.S.A.

Other ministers who were at one time associated with the AG included A. D. and Violet McClure, Eugene N. Hastie,

C. A. McKinney, Cyrus B. Fockler, Will C. Trotter, and later, Frank Lindblad. Another minister, William E. Kirschke, served as national youth leader with the Pentecostal Young People's Association from 1937 to 1939 and later was a prominent Sunday school leader in the AG.

Sinclair came to the U.S. from Scotland when he was a youth. He was associated with the Holiness movement before receiving the baptism in the Holy Spirit while pastoring a church in Chicago. It has been reported that Sinclair was the first to receive the pentecostal experience in Chicago (Moon, 138).

A layman, George C. Brinkman, became the first secretary of the PCG and donated his paper, *The Pentecostal Herald,* to the new organization.

A name change, from the Pentecostal Assemblies of the U.S.A. to the Pentecostal Church of God, was effected in 1922 when the church went through a financial and leadership struggle. A second name change came in 1934, when the group added "of America" to distinguish it from a local church in Kansas City. The PCG offices and publishing interests were in Chicago until 1927, when they were moved to Ottumwa, IA. From Iowa the group moved to Kansas City in 1934 and then to the present headquarters in Joplin, MO, in 1951. Finally, in 1979, the name was changed to Pentecostal Church of God, Incorporated.

The PCG doctrinal statement, an instrument that the founding fathers were careful not to include in 1919, was deemed essential by 1933. It is similar to the AG statement and other pentecostal baptistic statements.

The PCG's greatest period of growth came during the 1940s, when the number of churches and ministers doubled. During the late 1940s, however, the Northwest District was decimated by the New Order of the ˈLatter Rain. Most of the churches and the district superintendent joined the new movement. By 1955 that district gained new churches and members to offset the loss to the Latter Rain.

Although work among the American Indian tribes has been strong for many years, foreign mission efforts had been somewhat neglected until recent years. This can be seen by the fact that it was not until 1949 that the church saw the need for a full-time foreign missions administrator and a board of directors—even though the world missions department was established in 1932. By 1999 PCG missions had established 4,963 churches and 57 Bible schools in 50 countries.

Local churches, which practice the congregational form of government, are located in 47 states. The U.S. is divided into 40 districts. On the 80th anniversary in 1999, the annual report showed a total of 1,237 U.S. churches, 4,963 churches outside the U.S., a worldwide constituency of 600,000, and 5,700 ministers worldwide.

The PCG owns and operates the Messenger Publishing House in Joplin, which publishes the *Pentecostal Messenger,* the official periodical since 1927, and *The Spirit*. Other departments are Christian Education, Home Missions/Evangelism, Youth Ministries (formerly Pentecostal Young Peoples Association [PYPA]), Women's Ministries (formerly Pentecostal Ladies Auxiliary), King's Men Fellowship, and Senior Christian Fellowship. In 1999 the PCG had three military chaplains on active duty.

The PCG's first Bible school was Pentecostal Bible Institute, founded in 1946, in Gilroy, CA. Southern Bible College was opened in 1958 in Houston; it was moved to Joplin, MO, in 1987 and renamed Messenger College.

The general superintendent to serve the longest (1953–75) was R. Dennis Heard. He was born in Arkansas but moved with his family to California, where he became involved with the PCG. He was a pastor and district official and was active in PYPA leadership. Heard led the PCG into the ˈNational Association of Evangelicals, the ˈPentecostal Fellowship of North America, and the Pentecostal Congress. PCG is a member of the ˈPentecostal/Charismatic Churches of North America. Roy M. Chappell followed Heard as superintendent, followed by James D. Gee in 1987.

■ **Bibliography:** "Facts of Interest about the PCG" (1985) ▌ C. Jones, *Guide to the Study of the Pentecostal Movement* (1983) ▌ K. Kendrick, *The Promise Fulfilled* (1961) ▌ E. Moon, *The Pentecostal Church* (1966) ▌ "PCG General Constitution and Bylaws" (1984) ▌ "Presenting the PCG World Ministries" (n.d.) ▌ 1999 Annual Report. ■ W. E. Warner

PENTECOSTAL COALITION FOR HUMAN RIGHTS

(PCHR). A support and political-action organization for racial and sexual minorities within pentecostal churches, with a strong emphasis on homosexual rights. Formed in Jan. 1981 by ˈJames S. Tinney, a professor at Howard University and at that time a minister in the ˈChurch of God in Christ (COGIC), its founding signaled a growing social concern for human rights within pentecostal circles. From the beginning, PCHR had a largely black following; its novelty was its devotion to liberation movements of all types, especially homosexual rights. The organization was formed to combat the Moral Majority, Christian Voice, Religious Roundtable, and other "extremist groups." PCHR sought to secure these rights not only in the civil arena but also by pressing pentecostal churches to acknowledge confessed homosexuals as full participants in the body of Christ. This latter crusade caused PCHR to be identified almost exclusively with the gay-rights issue and the political activism of its founder. Chapters were organized in Washington, DC; Portland, OR; and Los Angeles, with regional representatives in four other cities. Most pentecostal leaders saw PCHR as a foreboding development. A national magazine (*Logos Journal* [May–June 1981], 4) urged Tinney's excommunication, and COGIC dutifully responded. Seventeen PCHR protesters bearing signs and banners picketed Sunday services in front of Temple Church of God in Christ, the headquarters for Bishop Samuel Kelsey, who had expelled Tinney. During its confrontational years, PCHR became the first group to picket a pentecostal church, to stage demonstrations at pentecostal conferences, to secure homosexual-oriented advertising on a gospel radio station (WYCB–AM), and to successfully challenge licensing and programming of radio and TV stations carrying antigay pentecostal preaching. In 1982 PCHR conducted the first "City-wide Lesbian and Gay Revival." Eventually the founding chapter developed into the organization of Faith Temple, an independent pentecostal church in Washington, DC, comprised mostly of black homosexuals. The strength of this group dissipated after Tinney was excommunicated from the ministry of COGIC because of his advocacy of homosexuality. The coalition had a further setback when its founder died of AIDS in 1988. More recently PCHR has become less strident, focusing more on education and counseling through its publications, a telephone hotline, and the *Pentecostal Coalition for Human Rights Newsletter,* produced since 1981. PCHR also conducts dialogues with clergy groups around concerns such as pastoral counseling for homosexuals and ministry to persons with AIDS.

■ **Bibliography:** "Coalition to Press for Human Rights among Pentecostals," Religious News Service (Mar. 5, 1981) ■ H. Hostetler, "Dealing with Immorality among the Saints," *Logos Journal* (May–June 1981) ■ C. E. Jones, *The Charismatic Movement* (1995), 555 ■ *Pentecostal Coalition for Human Rights Newsletters* (1981) ■ G. Sheppard, "James Tinney's PCHR Versus Jerry Falwell's Moral Majority," *Agora* 4 (1981) ■ D. Willingham, "Pentecostal Gay Rights?" *Church of God Evangel* (Aug. 10, 1981).   ■ G. W. Gohr

PENTECOSTAL COMMUNITY OF THE CONGO

One of the largest pentecostal denominations in Congo today, founded by ex-slaves from Congo. Between 1870 and 1900 slavery was still being practiced in Angola. Emancipation made it more difficult to send them to the Americas, and many remained in Angola. A number of these, among them Luban and Songye slaves from Congo, were evangelized by the American Board of Commissioners for Foreign Missions, the Board of Missions of the Presbyterian Church of Canada, and the Brethren Missions in the Bie area.

Among the first groups to return to Congo was one led by Shalumbo a Musongye, who had been taken slave as a youth. The group found its way to Mwanza, where ▸W. F. P. Burton and his fellow missionary ▸James Salter were evangelizing. The second group came from Kisamba in Angola and had spent some time with the Methodists in the border area, inquiring as to the whereabouts of their homes before returning to the Congo interior. These men, although at first hesitant about the pentecostal doctrine of the baptism in the Holy Spirit, were all baptized in what Burton called a "Luban Pentecost," when 160 people experienced this infilling and spoke in tongues in 1920. This group included 34 ex-slaves, all of whom evangelized and planted churches in the areas where they eventually settled. (These areas included the entire core region of what later fell under the responsibility of the Congo Evangelistic Mission.) Those best known because of the contribution they made were Shalumbo, Ngoloma, and Mutombo Kusomba Shimioni. Shalumbo founded churches among the Basongye in what is today the East Kasai province as well as among the Luba of the Katanga; he was a born leader with a persuasive personality. Ngoloma from the Kinkondja area moved to his home area at Kipamba, where he founded churches and had considerable influence on the local chief. Mutombo Kusomba Shimioni evangelized among the cannibals of the Kabombwe area and later became senior pastor of the Kabongo region. The impact of these men in their own areas in confronting witchcraft and preaching the gospel was such that it made possible the opening up of the entire region for the evangelization that followed and later resulted in the Pentecostal Community of the Congo, one of the largest pentecostal denominations in Congo today.

■ **Bibliography:** W. F. P. Burton, *God Working with Them* (1933) ■ idem, *When God Changes a Man* (1937) ■ Congo Evangelistic Mission Report No. 3 (1924) and No. 68 (1937) ■ J. Duffy, *A Question of Slavery* (1967) ■ D. J. Garrard, "The History of the Congo Evangelistic Mission/Communauté Pentecôtiste au Zaïre from 1915 to 1982" (diss., Aberdeen, 1983).   ■ D. Garrard

PENTECOSTAL CONFERENCE OF NORTH AMERICAN KERALITES

During the 1960s and 1970s, an increasing number of Asian Indians migrated to America due to relaxed immigration laws. Many of these immigrants were pentecostals from Kerala, the pentecostal capital of India, who came as a result of their connections with missionaries. Others came as students or as family members of Indian nurses who were recruited by U.S. hospitals to meet the shortage of nurses. Most of these immigrants settled in cities in the East and South of the U.S. A corresponding trend took place in Canada.

The Indian pentecostals started churches of their own all across the U.S. and in the major cities of Canada. By 1983 these churches felt a strong need for fellowship and mutual support for their faith and life in the West. The result was the birth of the Pentecostal Conference of North American Keralites.

The first conference took place in Oklahoma City in the summer of 1983. It was organized by Oommen Abraham, son of ʾK. E. Abraham, founder of the indigenous India Pentecostal Church. About 300 people attended this conference. The conference met a need so great that it steadily grew in attendance. The 17th conference (1999) took place in Somerset, NJ, and was attended by 7,000 people, while the 18th conference in Oklahoma City attracted 4,500.

Denominational leaders and revival speakers from Asia and North America speak at these conferences. The youth sessions attract thousands of young Keralite pentecostals. Frequent speakers at these conferences from the U.S. include academics of Indian origin, Eazhamkulam Samkutty of Southern University, Baton Rouge, LA, and Thomson K. Mathew and C. T. Lukutty, both of Oral Roberts University.

■ **Bibliography:** R. Vakathanam, ed., *Tenth Anniversary Souvenir of North American Conference of Pentecostal Keralites* (1992) ▌ S. George, ed., *Fifteenth Anniversary Souvenir of NACPK* (1997).

■ T. K. Mathew

PENTECOSTAL FELLOWSHIP OF NORTH AMERICA

(PFNA). A fellowship of 24 pentecostal groups, founded in 1948, that met annually to promote fellowship and to demonstrate unity among pentecostals. Recognizing that it had failed to attract any except white pentecostal groups, the board of administration initiated a series of meetings with African Americans beginning in 1992. The result was that the PFNA voted to disband in Oct. 1994—on its 46th anniversary—and make room for the multiracial organization, ʾPentecostal/Charismatic Churches of North America (PCCNA).

1. History.

Ironically, it took the formation of the ʾNational Association of Evangelicals (NAE) in 1942 to bring pentecostals together. Some pentecostals had proposed unity meetings in the 1920s, but nothing of substance resulted. When pentecostals got acquainted in NAE meetings, they began to think seriously about a fellowship among themselves. Then when the ʾPentecostal World Conference (PWC) was created in 1947 at Zurich, Switzerland, a challenge was thrown out to North American pentecostals to work toward a cooperative fellowship.

The first visible sign of pentecostal cooperation came on May 7, 1948, in Chicago, following the annual NAE meeting. Twenty-four leaders of eight pentecostal groups met in an exploratory conference concerning unity. Nobody was interested in an amalgamation of denominations, but it was determined that the groups would benefit in numerous foreign and domestic areas from a fellowship of pentecostal organizations.

A second exploratory meeting in Chicago later that year attracted 27 leaders from 12 denominations. ʾNoel Perkin,

secretary for the foreign missions department of the ʾAssemblies of God (AG), told the group that the denominations represented did not have to create fellowship but had to recognize that it already existed. He also suggested the name Pentecostal Fellowship of North America.

An important part of the second meeting was the appointment of a committee to draw up articles of the fellowship. The four selected for the committee were ʾJ. Roswell Flower (AG), E. J. Fulton (ʾOpen Bible Standard Churches), Herman D. Mitzner (ʾInternational Church of the Foursquare Gospel), and H. L. Chesser (ʾChurch of God, Cleveland, TN). Their job was not particularly difficult, because they simply modified the NAE statement of faith with a pentecostal paragraph and brought it back to the body.

The PFNA was organized at Des Moines, IA, Oct. 26–28, 1948. One of the speakers was an evangelist who was then beginning to gain national attention, ʾOral Roberts.

2. Objectives.

With the exceptions of an expansion of the first paragraph and the insertion of "endeavoring" in paragraph 4, the objectives of the PFNA adopted in 1948 remained unchanged:

1. To provide a vehicle of expression and coordination of efforts in matters common to all member bodies, including missionary and evangelistic efforts throughout the world.
2. To demonstrate to the world the essential unity of Spirit-baptized believers, fulfilling the prayer of the Lord Jesus "that they all may be one" (John 17:21).
3. To provide services to its constituents that will enable them to accomplish more quickly and efficiently their responsibility for the speedy evangelization of the world.
4. To encourage the principles of comity for the nurture of the body of Christ, endeavoring to keep the unity of the Spirit until we all come to the unity of the faith.

Although the PFNA was not a legislative body, it issued throughout its history resolutions involving political, religious, or social actions. In 1951 a resolution was prepared protesting the Universal Military Training Program. Other resolutions included showing support for the charismatic movement (1965) and encouraging pentecostal youth to consider public school teaching as a career (1964).

A ʾOneness leader, ʾHoward A. Goss, represented the ʾUnited Pentecostal Church at the second exploratory meeting in Chicago in 1948. His group, however, became ineligible for membership as soon as the doctrinal statement—with its Trinitarian paragraph—was adopted. The brief statement permits any pentecostal group to belong as long as they are Trinitarian and otherwise orthodox.

3. Structures.

The PFNA operated with a board of administration with representation of member bodies. The board met in the spring to plan fall meetings and to conduct other business relating to the fellowship and the PWC. Beginning with the organizational meeting in 1948, the annual meeting was hosted by a number of American and Canadian cities.

For several years the PFNA encouraged local churches to establish chapters in key cities, but by 1966 only 37 chapters were operating. One former official stated that a great deal of enthusiasm was shown in the early years, as local chapters united churches for the purpose of sponsoring evangelistic meetings and other special events. But apparently local churches eventually preferred to remain independent of united efforts, much to the consternation of the denominational leaders. Eventually the local chapter idea died from a lack of interest.

Other committees that have functioned included those on youth, foreign missions, radio, and women's ministries. A quarterly, *PFNA News,* was printed for the organization by the AG.

Having never established a permanent office or salaried employees, the PFNA records remained with whoever was secretary at the time. In 1982 the records were deposited in the AG Archives for safekeeping and to be made available to PFNA members and researchers.

See also PENTECOSTAL WORLD CONFERENCE; PENTE-COSTAL/CHARISMATIC CHURCHES OF NORTH AMERICA.

■ **Bibliography:** E. Blumhofer, *The Assemblies of God* (1989) ■ W. Menzies, *Anointed to Serve* (1971) ■ Minutes, PFNA Board of Administration and Annual Meetings (1948–) ■ *PFNA News* (1960–94).   ■ W. E. Warner

PENTECOSTAL FIRE-BAPTIZED HOLINESS CHURCH OF GOD OF THE AMERICAS See FIRE-BAPTIZED HOLINESS CHURCH.

PENTECOSTAL FREE-WILL BAPTIST CHURCH (PFWBC).

A large segment of the Free-Will Baptist Church that became pentecostal in experience and doctrine. In 1855 a group of seven congregations in North Carolina who believed in freedom of the will and instantaneous sanctification formed the Camp Fear Conference of the Free-Will Baptist Church. Later, in 1907, the Camp Fear Conference adopted pentecostal views on the baptism of the Holy Spirit. The Pentecostal Free-Will Baptist Church was thus an existing conference that embraced Pentecostal doctrine and experience. As the work spread, additional conferences were formed: Wilmington in 1908, New River in 1911, and a South Carolina conference in 1912. These four united into a general conference in 1943.

The general conference organized under the name PFWBC in 1959. The church had 7,000 members, 135 churches, and 180 ministers. Herbert Carter was elected general overseer. (The South Carolina Conference declined to organize with the North Carolina conferences and became the Free-Will Baptist Church of the Pentecostal Faith.) In 1960 the organization established headquarters in Dunn, NC, and initiated an official journal, *The Messenger.*

The PFWBC has now expanded into Virginia, Georgia, and Florida, and it has missions in India, the Philippines, Mexico, Nicaragua, Venezuela, and Puerto Rico. In 1971 it established Heritage Bible College in Dunn. Don Sauls became the second general superintendent in 1984; he was succeeded by Preston Heath in 1996.

■ **Bibliography:** H. Carter, *History of the Pentecostal Free-Will Baptist Church* (1978) ■ *Faith and Practices of the Pentecostal Free-Will Baptist Church* (1977).   ■ C. W. Conn

PENTECOSTAL HOLINESS CHURCH See INTERNATIONAL PENTECOSTAL HOLINESS CHURCH.

PENTECOSTAL HOLINESS CHURCH OF CANADA

The Pentecostal Holiness Church (PHC) was one of the first pentecostal denominations to minister in the dominion of Canada. First organized as the Fire-Baptized Holiness Association by B. H. Irwin, the church had conventions in Ontario and Manitoba when the denomination was formed in Anderson, SC, in 1898. Canadian "ruling elders" included Oliver Fluke of Ontario and Albert E. Robinson of Manitoba.

Early congregations included the Evangelistic Centre in Toronto, founded by George Fisher in 1906, and the Apostolic Faith Mission congregation in Vancouver, B.C., begun by George S. Paul in 1907.

In 1926 the Ontario Conference of the PHC was organized in Toronto by E. D. Reeves. The high-water mark for the denomination was reached in the 1930s, when the Evangelistic Centre Church of Toronto, pastored by O. E. Sproull, was for a time the largest pentecostal congregation in the nation.

The western portion of the church was begun in 1938 as the Pacific Coast Missionary Society, a group of churches with roots in the ʼApostolic Faith Mission of Portland, OR. In 1942 these churches merged with the Pentecostal Holiness Church.

For many years the PHC of Canada was listed as part of the American denomination. This was changed in 1971 when the PHC was legally chartered as a Canadian church. The first Canadian general superintendent was Bishop Harry Nunn. Today the Canadian PHC consists of 33 congregations in three conferences located in Ontario, British Columbia, and Nova Scotia.

■ **Bibliography:** V. Synan, *The Old-Time Power: A History of the Pentecostal Holiness Church* (rev. ed., 1998).   ■ H. V. Synan

PENTECOSTAL MISSION IN SOUTH AND CENTRAL AFRICA (PMSCA).

An early pentecostal missions agency founded in 1910 by the executive council of the Bethel Pentecostal Assembly of Newark, NJ (often referred to as the "Bethel Board") "to maintain and conduct a general evangelistic work in the State of New Jersey, and in all other States of the United States and any and all foreign countries" (Beach and Fahs, 24). By 1925 PMSCA had a budget of $30,150 and supported missionaries in Liberia, the Republic of South Africa, Swaziland, Mozambique, Mexico, and Venezuela. A separate field council directed the activities in South Africa. The organization promoted its work by publishing the *South and Central African Pentecostal Herald* (1917); the publication was later renamed the *Full Gospel Missionary Herald* (1921). The executive council also directed the affairs of the Bethel Pentecostal Assembly and sponsored the Bethel Bible Training School (1916–29).

Members of the council included ›Minnie T. Draper, president and, for many years, an associate of ›A. B. Simpson in the ›Christian and Missionary Alliance; Joseph R. Potter; Mr. and Mrs. Lewis B. Heath; Mary S. Stone; Eleanor B. Schoenborn; and Christian J. Lucas. Several members were wealthy and invested their contributions in a trust fund that helped to support the foreign endeavors. The Bethel Bible Training School served as a recruiting ground for its overseas endeavors. Missionaries to Africa with the agency included George and Eleanor Bowie, Fred Burke, Ernest Hooper, Edgar and Mabel Pettenger, Ralph and Lillian Riggs, and Anna Richards Scoble.

When the stock market crashed in 1929 the trust fund suffered a serious setback, and much of the missionary work was curtailed. A proposed amalgamation with the Assemblies of God (AG) in the same year never occurred. Many of the missionaries eventually affiliated with the AG and made significant contributions. Among American pentecostal missions agencies before 1929, the PMSCA was second only to the AG in the size and financial underpinnings of its operation.

The churches founded by the PMSCA missionaries merged with the Churches of God in South Africa (a group of breakaway congregations from the PMSCA that organized in 1917 at Pretoria) at the Kroonstad Conference in 1920 to become "one body, the Church cemented together through the love and sacrifice of Jesus Christ" and took the name Full Gospel Church (FGC). The first constitution for the new body was ratified at Bloemfontein on Apr. 19, 1922. The relationship granting joint jurisdiction of the FGC to the executive council of the Bethel Pentecostal Assembly ended in 1933. In 1951 the FGC amalgamated with the Church of God (Cleveland, TN) and changed its name to ›Full Gospel Church of God in Southern Africa. In 1997 the church reported 958 churches, 2,000 workers, 4 Bible schools and 2 theological schools, and some 350,000 members.

■ **Bibliography:** R. S. Armstrong, "The Get Acquainted Page," *LRE* (July 1936) ■ H. P. Beach and C. H. Fahs, eds., *World Missionary Atlas* (1925), 24 ■ C. W. Conn, *Like a Mighty Army: A History of the Church of God* (2d ed., 1977) ■ "Editorials," *Full Gospel Missionary Herald* (Jan. 1921) ■ G. B. McGee, *This Gospel Shall Be Preached* (1986) ■ E. L. Schoenborn, "Reports from Other Lands," *Full Gospel Missionary Herald* (Jan. 1921) ■ D. W. Slocumb, comp., *Leaders in World Evangelism* (1985) ■ A. Thompson, "The Full Gospel Church of God—South Africa," *World Pentecost* (3, 1972).   ■ G. B. McGee

PENTECOSTAL MISSIONARY UNION (PMU).

The first pentecostal missionary agency, the PMU was formed in Great Britain under the leadership of ›C. Polhill. The Pentecostal Missionary Union of Great Britain and Ireland, formed in Jan. 1909, reflected Polhill's passion for world mission, the strong missionary thrust among early pentecostals, and the availability of missionaries expelled from other societies for the pentecostal witness.

1. PMU Council.

The PMU was administered by a council of between 4 and 10 members. Throughout the PMU's 16-year history, the role of President C. Polhill was dominant because of his missionary experience, his administrative expertise, his social standing, and, not least, his money. Membership over the years included many well-known pioneers in the movement in Britain, including ›A. A. Boddy, E. W. Moser, ›T. Myerscough, ›S. Wigglesworth, and a Mrs. Crisp, first principal of the PMU training home for women. The handwritten PMU minute books at Nottingham are the most important resource, giving a full picture of the human problems not mentioned in the encouraging reports regularly published in *Confidence* and *Flames of Fire*.

2. Doctrine.

The PMU required that all candidates had received the baptism of the Holy Spirit and were sincere in professing the fundamentals of the evangelical faith. The "Principles" specify those truths, adding that candidates "be able to have fellowship with all believers holding these fundamental truths, even if widely differing in their judgment as to points of church government," a point later applied to the practice of water baptism. At least three council members were asked to resign for holding extreme views.

3. Training Homes.

The PMU opened two training homes in London, one for young men, the other for young women. The superintendency of the men's home presented a constant problem, as few of Polhill's nominees lived up to expectations and were acceptable to the pentecostal grassroots. The interlude when the council asked T. Myerscough in Preston to train the male students (among whom were ›W. F. P. Burton, ›G. Jeffreys, and E. J. Phillips) was perhaps its peak period, at least until the final years under H. Carter.

4. Missionaries.

The first PMU missionaries went to India (1909) and China (1910). China was the preferred mission field, due to Polhill's commitment and connections. Thus, almost all candidates from the London training homes went to China, while most in India were formerly with nonpentecostal societies. From 1911 on, the Chinese work was based in the city of Yunnanfu (Kunming) in the southwest, with a hope of eventually penetrating Tibet. By 1915 there were 18 PMU missionaries in China, six in India, and one new arrival in Africa in the Belgian Congo. Later a field was opened in Brazil.

The PMU minutes reveal the constant problems posed by the missionaries. Many were the instances of independence and lack of discipline, such as the incurring of expenses without reference to the council, impulsive journeys, disregard of the council's rules about engagement and marriage (a two-year period was required on the field before engagement), and reliance on undiscerned prophetic messages. Other difficulties arose from death and ill health caused by the rigors of an alien climate.

Polhill made strenuous efforts to provide oversight both in India and in China. In 1911 a question was added to the application form: "Are you willing to work in harmony with those who may be placed over you in the Lord?" At one stage there was talk of the Irish barrister John Leech going to India as superintendent, but no appointment was ever made, despite a decision in 1915 not to send any more members to India until a superintendent had been found. In China attempts were made through Polhill's contacts with other missionary societies, especially the China Inland Mission and the Christian and Missionary Alliance, to have their leader oversee newly arrived PMU missionaries, though this did not generally work well in practice. Only in 1921 was a superintendent appointed for China, William Boyd, who had gone out in 1915. A greater stability appeared at that time, with much heroic groundwork being done by, for example, ›A. Lewer, who tragically drowned on the Burma-China border in 1924.

5. Support.

The official principles of the PMU stated: "The Mission is supported entirely by the free will offerings of the Lord's people." These donations were listed at the end of each issue of *Confidence*. However, Polhill's personal generosity was always important. His numerous donations were always for specific projects (e.g., the lease of the women's training home, some travel costs to the mission field, students' vacation expenses). In the PMU's last years, however, there was a worsening shortage of funds caused by an increasing number of missionaries and a growing lack of confidence in the PMU on the part of the pentecostal assemblies in Britain. This reflected a widening gap between the educated Anglican patriots, Polhill and Boddy, and the rank-and-file working-class pentecostals, who included many conscientious objectors to military service.

6. The End.

The formation of the ›Assemblies of God of Great Britain and Ireland (AGGBI) in 1925 came at a natural time for Polhill's retirement and for the PMU to become the missionary arm of the new group. During 1925 the PMU council included five nominees from AGGBI, and from 1926 it was replaced by the Assemblies' Home Missionary Reference Council, on which E. Moser and T. H. Mundell remained.

■ **Bibliography:** D. Gee, *Wind and Flame* (1967).

■ P. D. Hocken

PENTECOSTAL WORLD CONFERENCE (PWC). A triennial, international, ecumenical gathering of pentecostals, first convened in 1947.

Known through 1958 as the World Pentecostal Conference, it has been incorrectly identified in literature under the names World Conference of International Pentecostal Churches, World Federation of Pentecostal Churches, and World Pentecostal Fellowship. In the 1961 meeting it was identified for the first time as the Pentecostal World Conference. Its purposes include the promotion of *spiritual* fellowship among pentecostals, regardless of denominational affiliation or the lack of it; demonstration to the world of the "essential unity of Spirit-baptized believers" in fulfillment of John 17:21; promotion of courtesy, mutual understanding, and scriptural purity among the various pentecostal groups; maintenance of those pentecostal truths "most surely believed among us"; and cooperation on items of mutual concern in fulfilling the Great Commission.

The beginnings of the pentecostal movement in the 20th century found a widespread hope among its adherents that the pentecostal renewal would sweep over the churches, producing a new and visible unity among all Christians in answer to Jesus' prayer (John 17:21). Hopes were soon turned to frustration when divisions emerged over issues of polity, doctrine, mores, and personalities. In spite of the divisions, there was a growing concern that some differences could be ignored for the sake of common witness in worship. Hence, the earliest days of pentecostalism in the U.S. saw camp meetings emerge with national and international invitations for pentecostals of all stripes to attend.

As the pentecostal movement matured, groups like the General Council of the Assemblies of God (1914) emerged, seeking to coordinate efforts on such issues as missions, publications, and education. In Europe Alexander A. Boddy, rector of All Saints Church in Sunderland, England, began as early as 1908 the Sunderland Conference, which the next year was renamed International Conference. The Hamburg Conference, held in Germany in 1908, also brought many international pentecostal leaders together. These conferences were soon joined by others in Mülheim and Zurich.

In 1911 Thomas B. Barratt issued "An Urgent Call for Charity and Unity," in which he proposed an international pentecostal union or alliance. While his proposal was not accepted initially, it did not fall on deaf ears. In June 1912 a Consultative International Pentecostal Council emerged from the Sunderland Convention, and by December a full-fledged Consultative Council was held in Amsterdam to provide advisory counsel to the pentecostal movement. Additional meetings of the International Advisory Council were held in Sunderland in May of 1913 and 1914. The beginning of WWI brought an end to such councils.

In 1920 invitations to an International Pentecostal Convention to be held in Jan. 1921 in Amsterdam were sent out by Mr. and Mrs. ˈG. R. Polman. Pentecostals from Britain, Scandinavia, Germany, and Switzerland attended. A tendency toward a preaching of the cross *(theologia crucis)* by the Germans and a triumphalistic critique by the Scandinavians led to some division, but as Donald Gee reported, participants generally were able to rise above their differences.

In the U.S. the vision for unity among pentecostals fell to two provocative pentecostal leaders. ˈFrank Bartleman repeatedly rebuked pentecostals in his writings for their divisiveness, and he consistently exhorted them to greater unity. After all, he wrote, "the Spirit is laboring for the unity of believers today, for the 'one body,' that the prayer of Jesus may be answered, 'that they all may be one that the world may believe.'"

Warren F. Carothers, originally affiliated with ˈCharles F. Parham and the ˈApostolic Faith Movement, joined the Assemblies of God (AG) in 1914, and in 1921 he was instrumental in the passage of the resolution by the General Council of the AG on "World-Wide Cooperation." He was appointed to a committee whose purpose was to encourage an "ecumenical union of Pentecostal believers." That committee moved too slowly for Carothers, and shortly thereafter he withdrew from the AG, establishing a committee of his own. He convened unity conferences in St. Louis, MO, in Oct. 1922; Chicago, IL, in Nov. 1923; and Owensboro, KY, in July 1924. The committee published a periodical, *The Herald of the Church*, to spread its message. Carothers' vision survived for more than a decade, but by 1934 it had foundered.

In 1937 the General Council of the AG (U.S.) invited pentecostal leaders from around the world to attend its general council. These leaders decided to call a World Conference in London during 1940. May 1939 saw a Pentecostal

Unity Conference in London among several British pentecostal groups, while a second one was convened in Jan. 1940. The most significant conference of that period was held June 5–12, 1939, in Stockholm. It came as the suggestion of ˈDonald Gee and was given form by ˈLewi Pethrus. Delegates from nearly 20 countries were present, and as many as 8,000 people attended some meetings. Its primary value lay in personal fellowship, encouragement, and the opportunity to share a variety of viewpoints without formally adopting them as policy.

WWII put an end to the hope of a PWC in 1940 but did little to dampen pentecostal interests in greater cooperation with each other. In the U.S. pentecostals found unanticipated acceptance in the ˈNational Association of Evangelicals (NAE). Four pentecostal denominations joined the NAE in 1942. Others soon joined with them, although certain independent pentecostals criticized these groups for entering into a formal organization. Emerging from the pentecostal membership of the NAE was the ˈPentecostal Fellowship of North America (PFNA) in Oct. 1948.

On the European side, interest in a worldwide conference was the logical outgrowth of the highly successful 1939 European Pentecostal Conference in Stockholm. Following a preliminary meeting in Sept. 1946 in Paris, it was decided that such a World Pentecostal Conference would be convened in Zurich, Switzerland, May 4–9, 1947, with Leonard Steiner acting as the organizing secretary. This was the first of what later became a regular triennial event. Subsequent meetings have been held in Paris (1949), London (1952), Stockholm (1955), Toronto (1958), Jerusalem (1961), Helsinki (1964), Rio de Janeiro (1967), Dallas (1970), Seoul (1973), London (1976), Vancouver (1979), Nairobi (1982), and Zurich (1985). Kuala Lumpur was chosen as the site for a conference in 1988, but due to administrative difficulties and other competing events, that conference was postponed until the following year. The site was moved, and conferences resumed in Singapore (1989), Oslo (1992), Jerusalem (1995), and Seoul (1998). The PWC has selected Los Angeles (2001), Johannesburg (2004), and a city in Australia (2007) as its venues in the opening years of the new century.

Organizers for the first PWC hoped that it might become a fellowship of pentecostal groups that could provide a worldwide perspective on what God was doing in the pentecostal revival, implement relief efforts in a postwar Europe, and coordinate missionary and evangelistic efforts throughout the world. While some of these agenda items were enacted (e.g., the establishment of an office in Basel to coordinate relief efforts), it soon became apparent that it would not be possible to organize the World Pentecostal Fellowship on anything like denominational lines. Issues of polity, especially among Scandinavian and American independent pentecostals, proved too rigid for such an organization. Thus, the 1947 meeting has at times been called a failure. Yet this conference did provide an item of singular importance to the pentecostal revival. It was agreed that there should be a worldwide pentecostal missionary magazine edited by Donald Gee on behalf of this and any future PWC.

Donald Gee's assignment gave him free rein to speak to the issues he believed were crucial to the pentecostal movement. To guarantee objectivity and freedom, he was "to be answerable to God alone." He kept at the task until his death on July 20, 1966, having edited and published 77 issues of *Pentecost*. In nearly all of these issues Gee penned an editorial in which he reflected on the state of the pentecostal movement and its role in the church. His insight and wisdom, his breadth of knowledge, and his humility were carefully blended in these editorials as he assessed the critical issues facing pentecostalism. Indeed, so successful was he in this regard that his biographer, Brian Ross, described the inside back cover where Gee's editorial normally appeared as "the most openly honest and perceptive pages in all Pentecostal literature."

Following the death of Donald Gee, the PWC sought a new editor. In 1970 ›Percy S. Brewster (›Elim Pentecostal Church) became the editor of the newly titled *World Pentecost*. He was succeeded in Dec. 1978 by Eric C. Dando (AOG in Great Britain and Ireland). With the death of Dando in Apr. 1983, the task was passed to ›Jakob Zopfi (Swiss Pentecostal Mission). Beginning in 1987 *World Pentecost* experimented with a multilingual (English-German, then English-German-French) format before returning to an English-language format. The magazine provided news items on pentecostals around the world, as well as historical articles, sermons by leading pentecostal figures, and news concerning the PWC. Yet its editorials frequently lacked the significance that Donald Gee's had. In 1999 the magazine ceased publication, while the leadership of the PWC studies its utility as well as the feasibility of producing an alternative means of communication, such as an internet website.

The meetings of the PWC are planned and coordinated by an elected secretary and advisory committee. The advisory committee, a group of approximately 25 and the most diverse and truly representative group in the conference, is responsible for site, theme, and speaker selection. A six-person presidium is also elected at each gathering, including the chairperson and vice chairperson. Members of the presidium are expected to chair the various sessions of the conference. Since their inception, the positions of secretary and chair of the conferences have been dominated by Americans, British, Swiss, and Swedish members. In 1967 A. P. Vasconcelos, general superintendent of the AG in Brazil, served a term as secretary, coordinating the meeting in Rio de Janeiro, and in 1958 Canadian W. E. McAlister, general superintendent of

the Pentecostal Assemblies of Canada (PAOC), chaired the meeting in Toronto.

During the first two decades of its existence, the chair of the advisory committee was shared by L. Steiner (Switzerland), D. Gee (England), L. Pethrus (Sweden), W. E. McAlister (Canada), ›H. P. Courtney (U.S.), and ›T. F. Zimmerman (U.S.). Zimmerman, former general superintendent of the AG (U.S.), chaired the PWC from 1967 until 1989, with the exception of 1970, when P. S. Brewster was elected to the office for a one-year term. Zimmerman was succeeded by ›R. H. Hughes (U.S.). In 1998 ›T. L. Trask (U.S.) was elected chair of the PWC. Since 1973 the editor of *World Pentecost* has also served as secretary to the conference.

Through the years, the PWC has functioned remarkably well in providing an international ecumenical witness in worship. Its themes have been edifying or challenging to the pentecostal movement as a whole, and only rarely, such as in 1961, have some speakers attempted to politicize them, using their speeches as a forum to bring what they perceived to be dissidents or maverick pentecostals (e.g., ›David J. du Plessis) into line. The diversity of the conference leadership in its early years was capable of including a broad agenda from the top down. Undoubtedly, the fact that only two men, T. F. Zimmerman and R. H. Hughes, have chaired the conference almost without interruption from 1967, and the fact that the editor of *World Pentecost* has served as secretary since 1973, have added a measure of stability to the PWC.

Dangers in this policy, however, are equally obvious. First, it has centralized power in a single individual, the chairperson, or a small number of individuals (including the secretary/editor), who control the agenda for the duration of their tenure. Second, in light of the fact that the majority of pentecostals live in the Two-Thirds World and the chairperson, with the exception of only one year, has been a European or a North American, has detracted from the ability of the conference and its agenda to be truly representative of *world* pentecostalism. Third, it runs the risk of hampering younger pentecostal leaders, especially from non-Western nations, from obtaining a worldwide forum in the pentecostal movement. Fourth, until leadership is more representative of the pentecostal movement as a whole, including younger people and women, the PWC runs the risk of being perceived as "inbred" and determined to maintain the status quo.

The PWC still faces a number of challenges. First, early leaders such as Donald Gee and David du Plessis had hoped to see the PWC embrace, or at least take seriously, the charismatic renewal among the historic churches. When ›Paul (David) Yonggi Cho resigned as a member of the advisory committee in 1986, he was still encouraging the PWC to open its doors to the charismatic renewal. By the end of the century, the PWC had continued to ignore these calls, and as a result, the PWC has lost an opportunity for wider global impact.

Second, in a world of declining resources and a movement of limited financial resources, many people who might benefit from attending the conferences have been unable to do so. Thus, competition from regional and national conferences have proven to be strong factors that have reduced the impact of the PWC to a shadow of what many of its designers had hoped it might become.

Third, the domination of the PWC by leaders from Europe and the U.S. has tended, at times, to make the more or less frequently homogeneous American and European agendas the agenda of an otherwise diverse world movement. The politics of the West, both secular and ecclesiastical, have tended to dominate what might otherwise contribute to creative tension and conversation within the pentecostal movement.

Fourth, at the beginning of the 21st century, the PWC still does not have a clear sense of its raison d'être. The fact that it is merely capable of providing a forum for fellowship and incapable of providing a forum in which the worldwide pentecostal movement might undertake business leads to two outcomes. It tends to turn the meetings of the conference into back-slapping shows in which one tradition dominates the entire program and only celebrities are invited to play a public role. It also prevents the pentecostal movement from projecting a unified voice in world affairs and the affairs of the global church.

At the dawn of the new century, then, the PWC finds itself struggling to know who it is or what its reason for existing should be. As long as these factors remain unclear, it will continue to decline in importance and effectiveness, except as a stage for the status quo.

■ **Bibliography:** J. M. Boze, "Human Organizations or Divine Administration," *Herald of Faith* 14 (2, Feb. 1949) ■ "Can There Be Real Unity in the Pentecostal Movement in the United States? Some Suggestions," *Herald of Faith* 14 (5, May 1949) ■ W. F. Carothers, *The Herald of the Church* 1 (1925): 3 ■ D. J. du Plessis, *A Brief History of the World Pentecostal Fellowship* (c. 1951) ■ H. A. Fischer, *Progress of Pentecostal Fellowship* (1952) ■ D. Gee, ed., *Pentecost: A Review of World-Wide Pentecostal Missionary and Revival News* (1947–1966) ■ idem, *Wind and Flame* (1941, 1947; rev. 1967) ■ Y. C. Han, "18th Pentecostal World Conference," *World Pentecost* 55 (Winter 1998) ■ W. J. Hollenweger, *The Pentecostals* (1972) ■ idem, *Pentecostalism* (1997) ■ R. H. Hughes, "Pentecostal Leadership," *World Pentecost* 37 (Summer 1993) ■ "Introducing the Pentecostal World Conference," *World Pentecost* 46 (Autumn 1995) ■ K. Kendrick, *The Promise Fulfilled* (1961) ■ W. W. Menzies, *Anointed to Serve* (1971) ■ L. Pethrus, "No Pentecostal World Organization," *Herald of Faith* 12 (July 1947) ■ C. M. Robeck Jr., "The Assemblies of God and Ecumenical Cooperation, 1920–1965," in W. Ma and R. P. Menzies, eds., *Pentecostalism in Context: Essays in Honor of William W. Menzies* (1997) ■ B. R. Ross, "Donald Gee: Sectarian in Search of a Church," *Evangelical Quarterly* 50 (1978) ■ L. F. Sumrall, "International Pentecostal Conference in Switzerland," *Pentecostal Evangel* (May 31 and June 7, 1947) ■ C. van der Laan, "The

Proceedings of the Leaders' Meetings (1908–1911) and of the International Pentecostal Council (1912–1914)," *EPTA Bulletin* 6 (3, 1987) and *Pneuma* 10 (1, 1988) ■ E. S. Williams, "Fellowship in the Will of God: Pentecostal Bodies Consolidate?" *Herald of Faith* 13 (10, Oct. 1948) ■ "Thomas F. Zimmerman: A Pentecostal Statesman Par Excellence," *World Pentecost* 28 (Spring 1991) ■ J. Zopfi, "By My Spirit: Hope for a Changing World," *World Pentecost* 34 (Autumn 1992) ■ idem, "From Jerusalem … to All People," *World Pentecost* 47 (Winter 1996). ■ C. M. Robeck Jr.

PERIODICALS

I. Introduction: Focus of Publications
   A. *Evangelism*
   B. *Indoctrination*
   C. *Introduction of Distinctives*
   D. *Inspirational Literature*
   E. *Promotion*
   F. *Leadership Helps*

II. Publications of the Pentecostal Movement
   A. *Early Publications*
   B. *Recent Publications*

III. Publications of the Salvation-Healing Movement
   A. *The Rise of the Movement*
   B. *A Flood of Publications*

IV. Publications of the Charismatic Movement
   A. *The Origin of the Movement*
   B. *Segments within the Charismatic Movement*
   C. *New Periodicals*

V. Summary

The pentecostal and charismatic movements, like other religious organizations, have looked at the printed page as perhaps the most effective medium to reach not only their own constituencies but also prospective converts. Numerous accounts are documented in these movements' literature of people who have been either converted and/or inspired through periodicals, tracts, books, or other printed matter. This was especially true during the first half of the 20th century when there was no television and only limited use of radio. With the advent of digital products, anything that can be produced on the printed page can also be put on computer discs, CD-Roms, and the Internet for even wider distribution.

I. INTRODUCTION: FOCUS OF PUBLICATIONS.

The focus of the print media can be divided into six broad categories with additional specialized use as needed.

A. Evangelism.

This has been an emphasis in pentecostal publications from the very beginning of the movement. It can be seen in the later charismatic movement's publications as well. The strong missions programs of early pentecostals are one indication that their main objective was to convert non-Christians, not just to convert believers to pentecostalism.

B. Indoctrination.

Most early leaders in the pentecostal and charismatic movement came from denominations that relied on the printed page to indoctrinate their church members. Such a heritage influenced them later to incorporate similar publishing strategies within their own budding ministries. Both movements have utilized indoctrinational tactics in Sunday school literature, curriculum design, and other publications.

C. Introduction of Distinctives.

In addition to publishing materials dealing with evangelical-fundamental doctrines, pentecostals and charismatics use the printed medium to introduce their distinctive doctrines and practices: physical healing, sanctification, baptism in the Spirit, gifts of the Spirit, feet washing, and other doctrines and practices.

D. Inspirational Literature.

Personal testimonies and other inspirational accounts have long been a means to attract others or encourage the faithful. Often these accounts are given at a local church during a "testimony" service, but the more important use of inspirational stories has been through the printed page.

E. Promotion.

Missionary work, especially among classical pentecostals, has been promoted in periodicals almost from the beginning of the movement. The accounts not only served to attract additional missionaries to the "regions beyond" but also to raise support. Periodicals are used to promote various meetings and programs.

F. Leadership Helps.

Early pentecostals, for the most part, were not well educated. Therefore, leaders who did benefit from a good education saw the need for ongoing leadership training programs. This has included published leadership training courses and, in more recent times, audio and video training courses. Some denominations select a book—or assign a writer to produce a book on a certain subject—and then add an instructor's manual so that the material can be taught to Sunday school teachers and other church leaders.

Many of the publications produced by the pentecostal-charismatic movement are being preserved in denominational and college archives, independent ministries' collections, and even some state libraries and historical societies. The Oral Roberts University collection is probably the most extensive available on the charismatic and salvation-healing movements. Two other important independent sources are the Billy Graham Center Archives at Wheaton College and the David J. du Plessis Center for Christian Spirituality at Fuller Theological Seminary. Serious researchers should also consult the extensive bibliographical works by Charles Edwin Jones.

Researchers and collectors, however, are aware that many publications produced by pentecostals are rare if available at all. Many of the publications were not kept, thus leaving gaps in the documentation of some early pentecostal groups. The charismatic movement is young in comparison, which makes it easier to find its publications. The focus of this article will be on the older pentecostal movement (and its salvation-healing offshoot) and the charismatic movement, and will examine the various publications and how they were used.

II. PUBLICATIONS OF THE PENTECOSTAL MOVEMENT.

A. Early Publications.

The modern pentecostal movement's origins are generally traced to Charles F. Parham's Bethel Bible College in Topeka, KS, in 1901. Numerous stories were told of people around the world who read about the outpouring of the Spirit and later outpourings in other cities and communities. The first publicity on the pentecostal gatherings came from the secular press—although these reports were usually derogatory. It was not long, however, before various individuals and ministries that had accepted the pentecostal message began to publish their own periodicals and other literature.

Some of the periodicals that appeared on the scene during the first ten years of the revival predated the pentecostal outpourings—they simply made room for their new pentecostal doctrines. When the editors became pentecostal, so did the periodicals. Four examples are Parham's *Apostolic Faith* (1899), J. M. Pike's *The Way of Faith* (1890), Samuel G. Otis's *Word and Work* (1879), and Carrie Judd Montgomery's *The Triumphs of Faith* (1881).

By the end of 1908 J. Roswell Flower listed 21 pentecostal papers in an "Apostolic Faith Directory" published in his monthly *The Pentecost* (1908). Of the 21, 14 were published in the U.S. Also included in the directory were missionaries, missions (local churches), missionary societies, and three songbook publishers:

The Pentecost (1908), Indianapolis, Indiana. J. Roswell Flower.
The New Acts (1904), Alliance, Ohio. Levi R. Lupton.
Household of God (1905), Dayton, Ohio.
Good Tidings (1908), Dayton, Ohio.
The Bridegroom's Messenger (1907), Atlanta, Georgia. G. B. Cashwell and E. A. Sexton.
The Apostolic Witness (1908), Dallas, Oregon.
Trust (1902), Rochester, New York.
The Apostolic Faith (1899), Houston, Texas. C. F. Parham.
The Apostolic Faith (1906), Portland, Oregon. Florence Crawford.

The Pentecostal Record and Outlook (1908), Spokane, Washington. H. R. Bursell.

God's Latter Rain, Johannesburg, South Africa.

The Apostolic Standard, Doxey, Oklahoma.

The Christian Assembly, Cincinnati, Ohio.

The Midnight Cry (1908), Seattle, Washington.

The Latter Rain, Watertown, New York. J. E. Sanders.

The Spirit of Truth, Hants, England. W. L. Lake.

Confidence (1908), Sunderland, England. A. A. Boddy.

The Cloud of Witnesses, Bombay, India. Max Wood Moorehead.

Pentecostal Truths (Chinese), Hong Kong. Mok Lai Chi.

The Apostolic Light (c. 1904), Yokohama, Japan. M. L. Ryan.

Spade Regen, Amsterdam, Netherlands. G. R. Polman.

Early pentecostal evangelist A. H. Argue was publishing the *Apostolic Messenger* in 1908 when he too listed the above titles but added the following (reprinted in the July 1934 issue of *Word and Work*):

The Promise of the Father, Jerusalem (English and Arabic).

Word and Work, Framingham, Mass.

Apostolic Rivers of Living Water, New Haven, Conn.

Liberty and Gladness, Edinburgh, Scotland.

Pentecost in the Twin Cities, Minneapolis.

The Intercessary Missionary, Fort Wayne, Ind.

The Promise, Toronto.

Christiana, Norway.

The Pentecostal Trumpet, Denver.

Byposter, Norway.

Apostolic Banner, San Marcail, New Mexico.

The Way of Faith, Columbia, S.C.

Truth, Spokane, Wash.

The Reign of Christ, Cairo, Egypt.

Some of the publications were free while others carried a nominal subscription fee (usually 50 cents a year). Publishers who charged a subscription fee reasoned that it was the only way they could continue the publications. Other publishers, who offered their papers free, with an occasional low-key request for financial support, believed that the gospel and the pentecostal message should be offered without charge, citing biblical reasons for their positions. Flower's own *The Pentecost* was offered at a subscription fee; but when he turned it over to A. S. Copley in 1910, Copley changed the name to *Grace and Glory* and offered it free. Eighty-nine years later it was still being published as a free publication in Mountain Grove, MO.

It is obvious that publishers of early pentecostal papers did not use their publications to make money. Many of them apologized for the nominal charge, and some of the free publications failed because of a lack of financial support. The publishers honestly believed their papers were divinely ordained; and when they failed, it was not the publisher's fault, the readers simply "missed God" by failing to support the endeavor.

When early pentecostal organizations were formed, they either created their own periodicals or accepted existing ones. *The Christian Evangel* (1913) and the *Word and Witness* (c. 1911), which were given to the Assemblies of God in 1914, are examples of the latter. Another example of a group picking up an existing periodical is Florence Crawford's *Apostolic Faith* in Portland, OR. She moved to Portland in 1906 and by 1908 had taken over the *Apostolic Faith* paper, which was started by William J. Seymour and the Azusa Street Mission in Los Angeles. (Some have pointed at evidence that indicates the takeover was without Seymour's knowledge.) The paper was renamed *The Light of Hope* in 1965.

One of the early papers to be founded as a pentecostal periodical was G. B. Cashwell's *The Bridegroom's Messenger* in 1907; it is still being published by the International Pentecostal Church of Christ. Two others are *The Evening Light and Church of God Evangel* (now called *Church of God Evangel* and published in Cleveland, TN), founded in 1910, and the *Pentecostal Holiness Advocate*, which was founded in 1917 and continues to be published by the Pentecostal Holiness Church.

Many of the periodicals had limited circulation while others claimed unusually wide coverage for such young enterprises. Seymour claimed by the end of 1907 that his *Apostolic Faith* boasted a 40,000 press run. A year later, after Florence Crawford became the publisher and the paper moved to Portland, the circulation jumped to 80,000. It seems reasonable to assume, however, that the high circulation of the *Apostolic Faith* was an exception to the rule for early pentecostal periodicals.

Many periodicals began in local churches, but most of them either were discontinued or combined with other periodicals. The *Latter Rain Evangel,* which was started by William H. Piper and his Stone Church in Chicago (1908),

Academic journals published during the late 20th century, dealing with a variety of aspects of and reflecting the coming of age of the pentecostal and charismatic movements.

surprisingly continued as a local church publication for more than 30 years. Piper, who had at one time been an assistant to John Alexander Dowie, picked up ideas for a quality publication from Dowie's *Leaves of Healing*. Probably the most astute move Piper made was to hire Dowie's former secretary, Anna C. Reiff, as the editor of the *Latter Rain Evangel*. This monthly magazine carried news of missionaries, revival meetings, sermons, and articles. The magazine merged with the *Gospel Call* in 1939.

Aimee Semple McPherson very early saw the value of the printed page. She began her *Bridal Call* magazine in 1917, and it became one of the most attractive religious magazines of its day. After her death, the *Bridal Call* and the *Crusader* were combined and became the *Foursquare Magazine* (now *Foursquare Advance*).

Because the early pentecostal publications were mailed to subscribers around the world, and not just for local readership, their purposes are of concern. In the beginning the primary purpose was to spread the news about the Latter Rain, or the baptism in the Holy Spirit. Pentecostals could not expect favorable treatment in secular and nonpentecostal periodicals, so out of necessity, to promote and preserve the revival, they started their own.

As the revival continued, different views and misunderstandings arose, creating a need for defining some of the doctrinal points. Just because, at the turn of the century, two preachers spoke in tongues was no assurance that they agreed on the finer points of doctrines and practices.

Therefore, numerous articles were published on various views within the movement. The first major difference came over the doctrine of sanctification. Parham and Seymour, with their Holiness background, believed that nobody received the baptism in the Spirit until he or she had been converted and sanctified. William H. Durham began teaching a progressive sanctification, which was known as the "finished work," rather than an instantaneous experience. The end result was the same: Believers were baptized in the Spirit and spoke in tongues, but the route to that experience was on two different roads.

Parham and Seymour (and later Florence Crawford in Portland) used their papers, both of which were called *Apostolic Faith*, to promote their particular ideas on sanctification and the baptism in the Holy Spirit. Durham countered with the "finished work" teaching in his *The Pentecostal Testimony* (1907).

Later other major differences argued in pentecostal papers, tracts, and books included the correct mode of water baptism (which led to the great Trinitarian-Oneness debate) and the initial evidence controversy (whether or not speaking in tongues was the exclusive evidence of the baptism in the Holy Spirit). Small differences, though perhaps not small in the eyes of the proponents, included outward holiness practices, washing of the saints' feet, use of the gifts of the Spirit, separation from the world, snake handling, eating pork, pacifism, church organizations, local church polity, women's rights in the gospel, and countless other "essentials."

The arguments presented in the early periodicals were hardly friendly, charitable debates. A good example of intolerance is Parham's reaction to Durham's finished work teaching. Parham wrote in the July 1912 issue of *Apostolic Faith* that either Durham or he himself was wrong about the issue. Parham prayed that God would smite the one who was in error. Durham's death six months later seemed to satisfy Parham and perhaps other Wesleyan pentecostals that God had indeed spoken.

Another major issue, the Trinitarian and Oneness controversy, erupted in 1915. Three papers used to promote the Oneness side of the issue were G. T. Haywood's *Voice Crying in the Wilderness* (1910), Frank Ewart's *Meat in Due Season* (1914), and David Lee Floyd's (later D. C. Opperman's) *Blessed Truth* (1915). The *Christian Evangel* and the *Word and Witness* stood by the Trinitarian view during the controversy.

With all of the different doctrines that were being taught (many of which came by "revelation," according to the proponents), it is no wonder that publications became the most effective means to present "correct" interpretations.

The *Christian Evangel* was also a pacesetter in the publishing of Sunday school lesson materials. J. Roswell and Alice R. Flower presented a pentecostal slant to the International Sunday School Lessons for their readers. Started in 1913, the *Evangel* later became known as the *Weekly Evangel* when the Assemblies of God (AG) moved to St. Louis and discovered another *Christian Evangel* being published there. The name was changed back to the *Christian Evangel* when the denomination moved to Springfield, MO. In 1919 the magazine became known as the *Pentecostal Evangel*.

In comparison to an editor today who operates with the latest state-of-the-art word-processing equipment and who never sees the press unless he or she wants to, early editors frequently wore many hats. They often wrote the articles, set type, ran the press, mailed the finished product, and even repaired the press when it broke down. Ironically, with all of the primitive production methods used in the first half of the 20th century, editors in some cases had a shorter lead time than editors of modern times. What took two to three weeks in the early years might take six weeks today.

Most libraries early in the 20th century looked at the pentecostal publications as "fly-by-night" operations and as unimportant for their collections. Consequently, there are few extant full collections of pentecostal publications. One paper, Seymour's *Apostolic Faith* (1906–8), was reprinted as *Like as of Fire*, and later as *The Azusa Street Papers*. Many of the lesser-known periodicals are cited in books and other publications but are difficult to find today.

The list is long of people who were influenced by the early publications. Seymour's *Apostolic Faith* became the most prominent paper in the early months of the Azusa Street outpouring. Numerous people were brought into the pentecostal movement by first reading the *Apostolic Faith*, including Thomas Ball Barratt, A. H. Argue, C. A. McKinney, and J. H. King, just to name a few.

B. Recent Publications.

In recent years the classical pentecostal groups have maintained an "official organ" and have added specialized periodicals designed to promote various church departments and interests: publications for women, men, youth, history buffs, ministers, Sunday school teachers, home and foreign missionaries, and others.

Most of the groups have also published books, tracts, Sunday school curricula, and other material. Some are producing curricula for the growing Christian school movement. The smaller pentecostal groups find that purchasing curricula and other material from large publishers is more practical than publishing their own. One large publisher who serves many smaller groups and independent churches, Gospel Publishing House, avoids certain controversial subjects so that more groups will be able to use the materials.

Agora, an independent journal published largely by AG ministers and teachers survived for five years (1977–82). This publication gave authors opportunity to write articles that never would be published in the church-sponsored publications due to their controversial character or critical views. Lack of finances and writers (the publisher claimed denominational officials threatened writers with loss of ministerial credentials if they contributed) ended this journal's short and controversial life.

III. PUBLICATIONS OF THE SALVATION-HEALING MOVEMENT.

A. The Rise of the Movement.

The salvation-healing movement, popularly associated with an evangelist and a huge tent and beginning in the late 1940s and running for about the next 20 years, brought to the American scene a phenomenon that created either uncritical acclaim or total repudiation. It all depends on whether one reads the evangelists' periodicals or the local newspaper. And in the pentecostal movement it would be argued by some that the movement was responsible for church growth; others, however, claimed that the excitement and big crowds created little lasting results.

This is the movement that gave America such healing luminaries as Oral Roberts, William Branham, A. A. Allen, Jack Coe, and dozens of others of less notoriety. Each of them, to survive, needed publications, often gaudy and filled with claims of healing and deliverance from demons, finan-

cial curses, and other calamities. By 1960, however, only a handful of salvation-healing evangelists were able to attract the crowds of the heyday years. Some of them had taken pastorates, some had gone into other ministries, at least two (Allen and Roberts) had founded a college and a university, and still others had dropped out of the ministry.

Although the salvation-healing movement peaked during the 1950s, several key evangelists are credited with breaking ground for the success of this period. These include John Alexander Dowie, John G. Lake, Maria B. Woodworth-Etter, Aimee Semple McPherson, Raymond T. Richey, F. F. Bosworth, Smith Wigglesworth, and Charles S. Price. Like their successors, these pioneers used periodicals, tracts, and books to report healings, to promote their meetings, to keep in touch with their supporters, and to build faith.

Historian David Edwin Harrell Jr. considers Charles S. Price the most influential for later salvation-healing evangelists. A former Congregational minister who became a pentecostal under the ministry of Aimee Semple McPherson, Price left a pastorate in Lodi, CA, for the nomadic life of an evangelist in 1922. He was well educated and was a professional master of ceremonies and speaker on chautauqua circuits. And unlike his successors with their big staffs, in later years Price would often lead his own song service before preaching. An associate said Price felt more comfortable if he had full control over the meetings.

Golden Grain, a monthly periodical that Price started in 1925, carried his sermons, news of his meetings, and healing testimonies. Considered an extremely modest man by the standards set by some of the later flamboyant evangelists, Price seldom published his own photograph in *Golden Grain.* Although Price remained independent during his years with the salvation-healing movement, he conducted many campaigns in AG churches and camp meetings. (Price family members donated issues of *Golden Grain,* healing cards used in meetings, copies of his books, and a newspaper clipping scrapbook to the Assemblies of God Archives [Flower Pentecostal Heritage Center].)

The story of Joseph Conlee, a minister-turned-atheist, who returned to Christ during the gold rush in Alaska, was told many times in sermons by Price and published in tract and magazine form as "The Cabin on the 40 Mile." Price also wrote several books, including *The Story of My Life* (1935).

Price's death in 1947 did not end the *Golden Grain.* Lorne Fox, who was healed in a Price meeting in 1923, was associate editor for several years. The same year Price died also saw the rise of two men who would become the giants of the salvation-healing movement—William Branham and Oral Roberts. Their appearance signaled the beginning of other large ministries. Healing tents were soon common in every major city in America, and little-known evangelists began preaching to thousands and praying for the sick. It was the beginning of a new era.

B. A Flood of Publications.

With the great number of tent evangelists moving from city to city, the need for printed materials became evident, and some kind of coordination was needed. The man to fill the need was Gordon Lindsay, an AG pastor who traced his spiritual heritage to the likes of John Alexander Dowie, John G. Lake, and Charles F. Parham. He used his writing and organizational skills to publicize the dozens of campaigns taking place simultaneously across the country. Lindsay formed the Voice of Healing and began publishing a magazine with the same name. Many of the evangelists united with Lindsay and were pleased to see reports of their meetings published in the *Voice of Healing* (1948). Others, like Oral Roberts, remained independent and published their own periodicals and other literature.

One of the reasons Lindsay's *Voice of Healing* and other periodicals came on the scene is that denominational editors, operating on official policy, gave very little publicity to the evangelists. Denominational officials generally shunned the high-flying tent evangelists because of the often wild and undocumented healing claims and questionable practices.

Secular newspapers and magazines often covered the tent meetings, but reporters who knew little about pentecostal worship and practices saw an Elmer Gantry in every evangelist. Their stories reflected that suspicion. At times, however, the critical reporting only increased interest, drawing thousands to the meetings.

Pentecost (1947), the official publication of the Pentecostal World Conference, was more sympathetic to the healing evangelists than were many of the denominational publications. One reason is that Donald Gee, the English pentecostal teacher and writer, was the editor. His lifelong plea for unity among believers kept him open to any who were orthodox and moral. After Gee's death in 1966, *Pentecost* was replaced by *World Pentecost* (1971).

In addition to periodicals published by the evangelists, scores of books and tracts were published. It was an unusual evangelist who did not publish his own story. Other books dealt with exercising faith for everything from physical healings to raising the dead. Demonology and financial prosperity were two other popular topics. Since few established publishers would accept book manuscripts from the evangelists, the individual ministries became book publishers. They would hire a printer to produce the books, and then they would sell them in the meetings. The books would also be offered on the radio and television or in publications as a premium for an offering.

Publications produced by the salvation-healing ministries served their purposes in encouraging faith and promoting the ministries. Without this important medium, much of the movement's momentum would have been lost.

IV. PUBLICATIONS OF THE CHARISMATIC MOVEMENT.

A. The Origin of the Movement.

The charismatic movement received its early thrust in the 1960s after Episcopalian ʾDennis Bennett was baptized in the Holy Spirit. Since that experience in a Van Nuys, CA, church, the movement has expanded throughout the world. Not the least of the reasons given for this phenomenon are the periodicals, books, and other literature of the charismatics. And just as the *Apostolic Faith* and similar publications created a hunger in the lives of believers around the world at the turn of the century, so a new batch of publications whetted the spiritual appetites of a new generation.

Whereas pentecostal denominational publications primarily focus on people and events within their own fellowships, or at least on those who have a doctrinal and lifestyle affinity with their own, the new independent charismatic publications reached to believers of all charismatic groups. Along with this freedom and openness came risks and vulnerability—publishing articles or literature by or about people whose accounts were not fully documented or who lacked spiritual maturity. The freedom of the independent publications and the restrictions imposed on the denominational publications in the 1960s and 1970s gave readers the impression that the latter were ingrown and lacked a vision for any spiritual happenings outside their own denominational barriers.

The way pentecostals after 1960 began to look at the charismatic renewal was similar to the cautious attitude mainline denominational publications took early in this century regarding the pentecostal renewal. However, the pentecostals of the 1960s were more sympathetic than the mainline denominations were 60 years before. Countless stories were recounted of how the early pentecostals were kicked out of the mainline denominations whenever they embraced the doctrines of speaking in tongues, spiritual gifts, and physical healing.

The charismatics, beginning in the early 1960s, had their critics, and many of them were asked to leave their churches. But others were permitted to stay, and in many cases the churches became pentecostal, or as they preferred to be called, charismatic or ʾneo-pentecostal.

Denominational publications even published favorable, or at least objective, articles about the renewal. Unofficial denominational periodicals and other literature began to appear, giving the movement respectability, something early pentecostals found difficult to obtain.

The pentecostal movement publicly acknowledged the charismatic renewal as a genuine spiritual happening but grew increasingly wary of some of the charismatic claims and activities. Along with the cautious approval by the pentecostals came a division in their ranks; some advised the charismatics to leave their old-line denominations and join the existing pentecostal congregations, while others urged them to stay in their own groups and thus influence noncharismatics toward spiritual renewal.

One influential voice among the pentecostals that urged charismatics to leave their noncharismatic churches was evangelist *Jimmy Swaggart. He focused especially on Roman Catholic charismatics, urging them to leave their church and join Protestant congregations, preferably classical pentecostal congregations.

B. Segments within the Charismatic Movement.

Before looking at the periodicals and other literature of the charismatic movement, it is important to examine the various segments within the movement. The first group includes denominational congregations that became charismatic, following the lead of their minister, and were permitted to remain in the organization. Dennis Bennett's St. Luke's Episcopal Church in Seattle is one such example. A second group of charismatics represent independent churches that were formed by leaders who had been baptized in the Holy Spirit but who were no longer allowed to remain in their denomination. A third group, alluded to above, is made up of Catholic charismatics, those who basically want to add the charismatic teachings and experiences to their traditions. Still a fourth element among charismatics, which developed in the 1970s, is the "Word" or "Faith" (*Positive Confession) groups. These groups have been spearheaded by such strong leaders as *Kenneth Hagin, *Derek Prince, *Kenneth Copeland, Fred Price, and others. Leadership of the latter has come from both classical and neo-pentecostal traditions.

There are in addition many divisions within the above four charismatic groups, created by certain worship styles and practices (worship dancing, particular uses of the gifts of the Spirit, and other distinctives) and by doctrinal points (including shepherding, financial prosperity, demon exorcism, healing, etc.). Another division is created when charismatic scholars emphasize a scholarly treatment of the renewal rather than an emotional experience.

One fellowship that tried to bridge the entire pentecostal-charismatic renewal, with considerable success, has been the Full Gospel Business Men's Fellowship International (FGBMFI). This organization, with its roots in classical pentecostal traditions, recognized its ability to draw various groups together and had an important impact on these believers. The same can be said of Women's Aglow, a counterpart to the FGBMFI. Both groups can be described as experience oriented. Since the 1970s the Society for Pentecostal Studies (SPS) has been successful in attracting scholars from various wings of the pentecostal and charismatic traditions. The association publishes *Pneuma: Journal of the Society for Pentecostal Studies,* as a semiannual journal.

C. New Periodicals.

Just as in the early years of the pentecostal movement, the charismatic groups soon began to publish their own periodicals and literature. With little to hold themselves together except their new experiences, charismatic groups began to publish various small periodicals. Many of these periodicals reported testimonials of people who had been baptized in the Spirit. Some of the more serious began to define the theology.

It was not until 1971 that any one magazine was able to speak for and to the majority of charismatic groups that were springing up worldwide. That magazine was the *Logos Journal,* established in 1971 by Daniel Malachuk. He had been reared in a classical pentecostal church, the famous Glad Tidings Tabernacle (AG) in New York. The *Journal,* edited in the beginning by Alden West, filled the need for a magazine that ministered to charismatics and as an evangelism tool for the noncharismatic. It also became an important promotional medium for Malachuk's new charismatic book publishing venture. Almost overnight, from a small operation in Malachuk's kitchen, Logos Fellowship International (LFI) became the leading publisher of charismatic books, far surpassing the output of classical pentecostal book publishers. LFI was soon publishing as many as fifty books a year.

Logos's meteoric rise to fame among charismatics ended dramatically in 1981 when the company filed for Chapter XI in the U.S. Bankruptcy Court of New Jersey. It was the painful end of an important publishing venture of the charismatic movement. Others would pick up the spoils and carry on the exciting publishing idea that the risk-taking Malachuk created with his first book published in 1968.

The *Logos Journal* actually had its beginning with a previous magazine consolidation. Joseph Mattsson-Boze's *Herald of Faith* and charismatic Mennonite Gerald Derstine's *Harvest Time* had merged in 1970 as *Herald of Faith, Harvest Time.* Malachuk reached an agreement with the publishers to take over the periodical in 1971, renaming it the *Logos Journal.* Given a new burst of energy and a broader base, the *Journal* soon reached many parts of the world and all segments of the pentecostal-charismatic movement. Within three years the *Journal* had nearly 50,000 subscribers.

With an aggressive publisher, a professional editorial staff, and some of the biggest charismatic names contributing articles, the *Journal* became the most important periodical of the renewal. Readers could expect a balance of personal testimonies, news from charismatic circles, and the treatment of important doctrinal subjects. The effort was somewhat successful in helping to stabilize an often fluctuating renewal movement.

Ironically, the medium that gave LFI and the charismatic movement such wide exposure also became its downfall. In 1975 Malachuk announced that God had led him into starting the *National Courier,* a biweekly newspaper. The *Courier* folded in 1977, leaving the company deep in debt, an indebtedness that caused it to collapse four years later.

In 1981 the *Journal's* circulation dropped to 20,000. Like other aspects of the LFI venture, the *Journal's* life ended with the Sept./Oct. 1981 issue.

Benefiting most from the *Journal's* failure was *Charisma,* a magazine started by Stephen Strang and sponsored by Calvary Assembly of God in Winter Park, FL. Begun in 1975 as a competitor to the *Journal, Charisma* took over the *Journal's* subscription list when it closed.

Strang, who later became the sole owner of *Charisma,* started a church leader's magazine, *Ministries Today.* He later bought *Christian Life* magazine, which also included the *Christian Bookseller* trade magazine and the Creation House book publishing division. (*Christian Life* merged with *Charisma* in 1987 to become *Charisma and Christian Life.*) By 1987 Strang Communications Company, now in Lake Mary, FL, was considered one of the most influential and important publishing companies in the charismatic movement. Strang's editorial latitude embraces the entire pentecostal-charismatic segment of the Christian church, giving him a strong base of operation.

Although it was not strictly a charismatic publication, *Christian Life,* with charismatic founder-editor Bob Walker, became an important medium in reporting activities in the movement beginning in the 1960s. Articles telling of spiritual renewal in various denominational churches established this interdenominational magazine as a voice in the renewal. Readers learned of the charismatic experiences of such leaders as Dennis Bennett, James Brown, Howard Ervin, Don Basham, Jean Stone, John Osteen, and others. Because of its sympathy toward the renewal, *Christian Life* suffered losses in subscriptions among noncharismatics but gained new subscribers among believers who were interested in the movement.

The *Full Gospel Business Men's Voice,* begun in 1953, despite its masculine laity focus, was an important publication in the renewal. Dedicated men in local FGBMFI chapters spread the word through the magazine by distributing it in doctors' offices, bus stations, churches, and wherever else reading material would be picked up. Published testimonies of men in various walks of life helped spread the news of the renewal to church and nonchurch men alike. In recent years the organization has fallen on difficult times and has given way to Promise Keepers as the impact organization for men.

Thomas R. Nickel, who was the founding editor of the FGBMFI *Voice,* left the organization in 1962 and founded the Great Commission International. He also established *Testimony* (1962), a magazine similar in appearance to *Voice.*

Divine Voice, a leading Catholic charismatic journal published in Chalakudy, Kerala, South India.

Christian Growth Ministries, Fort Lauderdale, FL (later called Integrity Communications, Mobile, AL), published *New Wine* magazine (1969–86). Four ministers from varied backgrounds sponsored the publication: Derek Prince, Bernard "Bob" Mumford, Don Basham, and Charles Simpson. Controversy surrounded this organization, primarily because of the shepherding movement and teachings on demon possession of believers. Integrity Communications was dissolved at the end of 1986, and the ministers involved began their own independent ministries. Charles Simpson remained in Mobile and formed a new organization but retained the name Integrity Communications. He publishes a bimonthly magazine, *Christian Conquest* (1987).

Another ministry that bridges the pentecostal-charismatic movement is the work of Oral Roberts. Originally from the Pentecostal Holiness Church, Roberts later joined the Methodist Church. Although his tent meetings in the salvation-healing era were sponsored primarily by classical pentecostals, he later moved into charismatic circles with no apparent loss of following. His *Abundant Life* magazine (called *Healing Waters* [1947–53]; *America's Healing Magazine* [1953–55]; *Healing* [1956]; and *Abundant Life* [1956–]) appeals to most segments of the renewal besides his old following in the pentecostal movement. *Abundant Life* and his *Daily Blessing* devotional magazine are used to promote Oral Roberts University and other Roberts ministries, with a heavy emphasis on "seed faith" giving.

Among the magazines established to appeal to specific denominations within the renewal were *Trinity* and *New*

Covenant. Founded in 1961 and surviving for only a short time, *Trinity* was published by Episcopalians. *New Covenant*, which began in 1969, is a magazine published for Roman Catholic charismatics. Other denominations are represented in the renewal with magazine and book publishing interests.

V. SUMMARY.

The movements cited in this article—pentecostal, salvation-healing, and charismatic—are interwoven in theology and in many practices. Much of the theology of healing, deliverance, speaking in tongues, gifts of the Spirit, etc., used in the salvation-healing and charismatic movements has been borrowed from classical pentecostalism.

It is no wonder then that publications from each of the traditions reflect similar concerns. Each of them looks at the printed page as an important tool to evangelize, indoctrinate, introduce distinctives, inspire, promote their ministries, and offer leadership helps. Both movements owe much of their success to periodicals and to other publications.

See also BIBLIOGRAPHY AND HISTORIOGRAPHY OF PENTECOSTALISM (U.S.).

■ **Bibliography:** R. Anderson, *Vision of the Disinherited* (1979) ■ D. Harrell Jr., *All Things Are Possible* (1975) ■ C. Jones, *Black Holiness: A Guide to the Study of Black Participation in the Wesleyan Perfectionist and Glossolalic Pentecostal Movement* (1987) ■ idem, *The Charismatic Movement: A Guide to the Study of Neo-Pentecostalism with Emphasis on Anglo-American Sources* (forthcoming) ■ idem, *Guide to the Study of the Pentecostal Movement* (1983) ■ K. Kendrick, *The Promise Fulfilled* (1961) ■ K. McDonnell, *Catholic Pentecostalism* (1970) ■ J. Nichols, *Pentecostalism* (1966) ■ C. M. Robeck Jr., "The Decade (1973–1982) in Pentecostal-Charismatic Literature: A Bibliographic Essay," Fuller Theological Seminary, *Theology, News, and Notes* (Mar. 1983) ■ V. Synan, *The Holiness-Pentecostal Movement in the United States* (1971).   ■ W. E. Warner

PERKIN, NOEL (1893–1979). Missions executive. Born in England, Perkin grew up in the Wesleyan Methodist Church. Perkin's initial interest in dentistry changed to banking, and he accepted a position with the Bank of Montreal in Canada, eventually working at the branch office in Toronto. While there, he came into contact with the ►Christian and Missionary Alliance (CMA), whose teaching strongly influenced him. He later identified with ►Christian Schoonmaker and others who left the CMA because of their pentecostal theology. Ordained in 1918, he left for Argentina and served there for three years with Harry L. Turner, a later president of the CMA.

In 1921 Perkin returned to Canada and subsequently entered the U.S. While visiting the Rochester Bible Training School in Rochester, NY, he met and married Ora Blanchard. They had five children. Perkin served two pastorates in western New York (1922–26) before he joined the Assemblies of God (AG) headquarters staff in Springfield, MO. Given the

permanent appointment as missionary secretary in 1927, he served until his retirement in 1959.

Perkin exerted a profound influence on the development of AG foreign missions. During his long tenure, the first Missionary Manual (1931) was produced; the administrative structure grew; promotional activities expanded; and the number of missionary personnel, overseas converts, and foreign Bible institutes dramatically increased. He was instrumental in changing the missions department from an agency that largely distributed funds to one that provided leadership and planning to the entire missions enterprise. At the same time, his fervor and gentle demeanor assured the supporting constituency that the spiritual objectives of the effort remained at the forefront.

Perkin's impact also can be detected in the orientation toward establishing indigenous churches abroad. Perkin was strongly influenced by the writings of Roland Allen. In turn he encouraged the missionaries, notably ►Melvin L. Hodges, to study them as well. His missiological perspectives can be found in *Our World Witness* (1963), coauthored with John Garlock.

By the time of Perkin's retirement in 1959, the AG had become a leader in the Christian world mission. In the same year he was elected to a one-year term as president of the Evangelical Foreign Missions Association, the first pentecostal to hold the office.

■ **Bibliography:** G. B. McGee, *This Gospel Shall Be Preached* (1986) ■ I. Spence, *Mr. Missions* (n.d.).   ■ G. B. McGee

PERRY, SAMUEL CLEMENT (1875–1960). Perry joined the ►Church of God (CG, Cleveland, TN) on May 28, 1909, at the Pleasant Grove Camp Meeting in Florida. He immediately assisted in the church's evangelism efforts and is believed to have been the first pentecostal to preach in Cuba during a visit in 1910. Perry assisted in beginning the *Church of God Evangel* and in drafting the first church teachings. He was appointed one of the first state overseers and became one of the first members of the council of elders. Perry ministered in the CG until May 14, 1919, when he was excluded from the council and his credentials were revoked for disagreeing with the church's financial system. He then ministered independently before joining the ►Assembly of God (AG) on Jan. 22, 1923. During this affiliation he was instrumental in organizing the AG in Florida and served as district assistant superintendent in 1926.

In 1934 Perry returned to the Church of God, again rising to prominence in the denomination and serving on the board of directors for the Bible Training School before withdrawing from the movement on Jan. 8, 1940. Later, as an independent minister, he pastored the Pentecostal Tabernacle in Miami and published the periodical *A Call to Prayer*. Perry died in 1960.

■ **Bibliography:** The Assemblies of God of Peninsular Florida Presents Its Chronicle of the Past Fifty Years, 1925–1975 (1975) ■ *Church of God Evangel* (1910–19) ■ C. W. Conn, *Like a Mighty Army: A History of the Church of God* (1996) ■ Minutes of the Church of God General Assembly, 1910–1919, Dixon Pentecostal Research Center, Cleveland, TN ■ "Sam C. Perry" file, Dixon Pentecostal Research Center, Cleveland, TN.　　　　■ D. G. Roebuck

PERRY, TROY DEROY (1940–). Founder of Universal Fellowship of Metropolitan Community Churches (UFMCC), a mostly homosexual denomination. Troy Perry was the oldest of five children born into a Southern family of pioneer stock in Tallahassee, FL, in 1940. His father was killed in an auto accident when Troy was a teenager. He was granted his first license to preach at age 15 by a Southern Baptist church in Winter Haven, FL. At age 18 he married and became the pastor of a Church of God of Prophecy (CGP) congregation in Joliet, IL. He briefly served as assistant state overseer of Florida for the Emmanuel Holiness Church. He attended Moody Bible Institute (1960–61) and pastored CGP congregations in Chicago and Santa Ana, CA. After five years of marriage and two children, his marriage ended in divorce in 1963 due to his homosexuality, and he was excommunicated from his church. He served two years in the U.S. Army.

Afterward he decided to start a Christian church that would minister to homosexuals. The first service was held in his Los Angeles home on Oct. 6, 1968. He called the organization the Metropolitan Community Church (⸍Universal Fellowship of Metropolitan Community Churches [UFMCC]). After holding services in several locations, a new building was dedicated in Mar. 1971 with a packed congregation. The Los Angeles church had over 800 attendees by 1972. In Oct. 1973 Perry stepped down as pastor of the Los Angeles congregation to devote himself full-time to the concerns of the expanding denomination. Arrested numerous times, he led a sit-in at the 1972 Democratic National Convention and a public fast on federal property in Los Angeles for 16 days to draw attention to the movement's goals. He became a member of the board of directors of the National Gay Task Force in 1977 and the Gay Rights National Lobby in 1981. A 1987 decision by the U.S. attorney general gave Perry's group the right to minister in all federal prisons. He has been invited to the White House on several occasions to address issues related to gays, hate crimes, and AIDS. He has continued to be a leader in gay and lesbian political struggles, seeking to promote a National Gay Rights Bill. Perry holds an honorary D.Min. from Samaritan College, a seminary operated by the UFMCC. He is the author of *The Lord is My Shepherd and He Knows I'm Gay* (with C. Lucas, 1972), *Don't Be Afraid Anymore* (1990), and *Profiles in Gay and Lesbian Courage* (1991). He is a contributing editor of *Is Gay Good?* (1971) and the subject of another book, *Our God Too* (1974). As moderator of the UFMCC he travels widely and oversees more than 300 churches in the U.S. as well as congregations in several foreign countries. He serves as host of a 30-minute Internet cybercast program called "Out, Gifted and Blessed." Perry's home and headquarters are in Hollywood, CA.

■ **Bibliography:** *Contemporary Authors* (1983) ■ R. M. Enroth and G. E. Jamison, *The Gay Church* (1974) ■ T. D. Perry and C. Lucas, *The Lord Is My Shepherd and He Knows I'm Gay* (1972) ■ Troy D. Perry web page (Nov. 1999) ■ *Who's Who in Religion* (1985) ■ *Yearbook of American and Canadian Churches* (1999), 167.

■ G. W. Gohr

PERSECUTION Malicious and destructive acts against a people because of their religious beliefs and practices. Jesus spoke of an innate hatred that exists in the world toward spiritual people: "If the world hates you, keep in mind that it hated me first. If you belonged to the world, it would love you as its own. As it is, you do not belong to the world, but I have chosen you out of the world. That is why the world hates you" (John 15:18–19). This hostility is rooted in the contrast between the world and Christ. Because it hated him, it follows that it will also hate those who are like him. It is inescapable that a tension exists between Christ-likeness and world-likeness, a tension that results in hostility toward those who have renounced the world for Christ.

1. The Apostolic Church.

Paul, speaking of the hostility he endured, made this observation: "Everyone who wants to live a godly life in Christ Jesus will be persecuted" (2 Tim. 3:11–12). Paul could understand this inevitable hostility because of his own early hatred of Christians. At least six times in his writings he recounts or alludes to his persecution of the church, most extensively in his words to King Agrippa: "On the authority of the chief priests I put many of the saints in prison, and when they were put to death, I cast my vote against them. Many a time I went from one synagogue to another to have them punished, and I tried to force them to blaspheme. In my obsession against them, I even went to foreign cities to persecute them" (Acts 26:9–11).

Paul recognized persecution to be a senseless, obsessive, violent reaction to something one does not understand or accept. This violence can be transposed into a belief that it is the right and proper reaction to its object: "I too was convinced that I ought to ... oppose the name of Jesus of Nazareth" (Acts 26:9). Jesus said, "They will put you out of the synagogue; in fact, a time is coming when anyone who kills you will think he is offering a service to God" (John 16:2). Such delusion explains why a man's enemies can be even the members of his own household (Matt. 10:36). It was in such light that the early Christians understood the hostility of the world. Because they were different from the world, the world was suspicious of them and did them harm.

2. The Plain People.

In the same way, the followers of Christ have suffered through the centuries, sometimes at the hands of ungodly persons and sometimes at the hands of those who thought of themselves as servants of God. The greatest outbreaks of persecution have been directed toward those whose religious beliefs are in sharpest contrast to their time. The greater the contrast between the church and the world, whether in belief, appearance, or practice, the greater the antagonism. This was the unmistakable case with such groups as the Amish in Switzerland, the Waldenses in Italy, and the Shakers in England. These plain-dressed, nonpolitical, gentle folk were so harassed in their homelands that they took refuge in America.

3. Persecution of Pentecostals.

As the pentecostal movement arose at the turn of this century and spread around the world, it encountered opposition and hostility everywhere. The pentecostal people were distinct from the world in several ways: They were gentle in nature, nonpolitical, plain of dress, and assertive in their faith. So the world was hostile toward them. The persecution of pentecostals in America in the early years was particularly spiteful and virulent, equaled or surpassed only by the violence that drove the Mormons from Illinois to Utah in 1844.

a. America. When the early Holiness people of North Carolina and Tennessee received the baptism in the Holy Spirit in 1896, what was at first only ridicule and scorn among their detractors burst into physical violence. The Holiness people were expelled from the churches of their birth and barred from the schoolhouse where they first worshiped. When the people built churches of their own, these were torched and dynamited; their homes became targets of vandalism and destruction by fire, gunshot, and stoning.

The people themselves were physically abused. The men were beaten with clubs and stones, flogged with horsewhips, and sometimes even ambushed and shot. The women suffered less, but the water springs and wells were polluted and poisoned, regional tradespeople refused them provisions, and the children were subjected to verbal abuse from teachers and physical abuse by fellow students. It was an extended period of relentless persecution, with the persecutors vowing to stamp out the belief in sanctification and Holy Spirit baptism.

In the forefront of the atrocities was a branch of the Ku Klux Klan called the "Night Raiders," a hooded mob that spread violence and mayhem across the countryside. The Ku Klux Klan, a vigilante group that arose during the Reconstruction days after the Civil War, set themselves against everything unlike themselves in race, religion, politics, or moral values. The pentecostal people became prime targets of their prejudice and punishment. The hooded assailants would descend upon a victim's home, drag him far away into the woods, tie his upstretched arms to a limb of a tree, and flog him into unconsciousness. Then they cut the thongs and let him fall to the ground. When the victim regained consciousness, he made his way back home as best he could.

Similar hostility was encountered as the pentecostal revival spread from town to town and state to state. As late as the 1930s there were incidents of flogging, not always in the rural mountains, but often in sophisticated and metropolitan areas.

Fire, too, has been widely used to hinder or discourage the spread of the gospel. The pentecostal journals of the 1910s and 1920s constantly printed reports of burned churches, homes, and gospel tents. Typical is a *Church of God Evangel* account in 1910 of how three evangelists were falsely arrested in Alabama:

> They marched us out from our tent and up the street to the stone jail.... Immediately they left the jail and returned to the tent, cut it down, and set fire to it. While the flames were ascending, we were in the iron cells praising God that we were counted worthy to suffer shame for His sake.

That seems to have been the positive spirit with which the people faced all opposition and violence. They regarded the early apostles as their examples of how to meet persecution. The apostles were flogged and ordered not to speak in the name of Jesus, yet they rejoiced "because they were counted worthy of suffering disgrace for the Name. Day after day, in the temple courts and from house to house, they never stopped teaching and proclaiming the good news that Jesus is the Christ" (Acts 5:41–42).

It was commonplace in some areas for pentecostal people to be waylaid on their way to or from worship, or for their churches to be vandalized, or for the ministers to be arrested as disturbers of the peace or on other trumped-up charges. The most widespread abuse was slander or calumny, such as reports that the pentecostal people caused fits by the use of powders, or that their worship was orgiastic or even orgasmic in nature or effect. A favorite way of slurring the pentecostals was to call them "holy roller," a

Houssein Moodman, Iranian pentecostal minister, martyred by hanging.

tired old epithet that has long been used to insult people who are emotional in their worship.

b. Worldwide. Hostility toward the pentecostal revival has taken various forms during the past 75 years but usually at a personal or community level rather than as a state or national policy. Pentecostalism in America has never faced the official opposition or prohibition that earlier Christians suffered. In other lands, especially in non-Christian or even non-Protestant lands, there have been, and still are, times of well-organized persecution of pentecostals. The opposition in most communist countries has been relentless and widespread. There were sizable pentecostal missions in China before WWII that have now disappeared. In Russia the pentecostal Christians have demonstrated a remarkable durability in the face of danger. The plight of some pentecostals in Russia was dramatized in 1978 when seven members took refuge in the American embassy in Moscow, fleeing from state-sponsored persecution. The group of seven remained in the embassy for four years, during which time other believers tried without success to join them. When their endeavors to immigrate to America failed, the people were left with an uncertain future in their homeland.

The evidence suggests that believers in such places as the former Soviet Union and Warsaw Pact countries resorted to the age-old practice of worshiping under cover. They believe that that is the caution advised by Jesus when he said, "I am sending you out like sheep among wolves. Therefore be as shrewd as snakes and as innocent as doves" (Matt. 10:16). Another example was Nazi Germany, especially from 1936 to 1945, when the pentecostal churches worshiped mainly in homes and out of sight of the Gestapo. In Spain before 1967 the pentecostal believers were in constant danger of exposure and punishment. Some of the ministers moved from town to town in order to escape official hostility and punishment. In 1967 there was a change in national policy that recognized evangelical churches in Spain and permitted them to operate openly.

c. Violence in Christian Countries. Even in countries where there is no state or religious policy that discriminates against particular beliefs, there have been incidents of persecution that seemed to be sanctioned by official authority. For instance, in 1933 and 1934 missionary ▸Maria Atkinson of Mexico was slandered and maligned as "a dope peddler passing as an American missionary, a witch, as a hypnotist using her glasses to make people do odd things, an immoral devil-possessed old woman fostering a spirit of fornication." Bending to such accusations from newspapers and antagonistic pulpits, the governor of Sonora ordered the pentecostal churches closed. The people worshiped in secret until the closure was rescinded.

A worse outrage occurred in Veracruz in 1944 when a mob destroyed the church property, including several homes, of the La Gloria congregation. With some police reportedly encouraging the mayhem, the mob raped, flogged, and stabbed the people. Some of the church members fled to the hills and woods, where they hid in caves and underbrush and ate roots and wild fruit. Nine persons were killed or died during the persecution. The Mexican government struck hard against the crime and punished its perpetrators. Wide publicity was given to the incident, and the victims were restored to their community with full religious liberty.

d. Contemporary. The persecution of pentecostals has not resulted in death as frequently as it did for some earlier Christians. Yet it has happened often enough to remind us of the hatred that is possible toward those who are different from the world. In revolutionary lands, such as certain Latin American countries during the past decade, entire congregations have been abducted and killed. While no statistics are available, it is known that in the 1980s hundreds of believers were held hostage or were killed. Church buildings have been confiscated as political meeting places or burned to the ground. Because they are of the common people, without political or material strength, the pentecostals are at constant risk in volatile situations.

In June 1978 a brutal mob set upon a mission compound of the Elim Pentecostal Church in Ruangwa, Rhodesia, and killed 13 men, women, and children. The victims were all European missionary teachers. In mourning its dead, the Elim Church called upon its people to "seek as never before to promote the gospel of Jesus Christ in our land and beyond our land across the world."

This was the spirit of Paul, who was "convinced that neither life nor death, neither angels nor demons, neither the present nor the future, nor any powers, neither height nor depth, nor anything else in all creation, will be able to separate us from the love of God that is in Christ Jesus our Lord" (Rom. 8:38–39).

During the last decades of the 20th century, pentecostals experienced greater persecution, especially in countries dominated by fundamentalist Muslims (such as Iraq, Iran, Indonesia, and Pakistan) and fundamentalist Hindus (India).

■ **Bibliography:** C. Brumback, *Suddenly . . . from Heaven* (1961) ■ C. W. Conn, *The Evangel Reader* (1958) ■ idem, *Like a Mighty Army: A History of the Church of God* (1996) ■ idem, *Where the Saints Have Trod* (1959) ■ Periodical files of the Pentecostal Research Center (Cleveland, TN). ■ C. W. Conn

PETERSON, PAUL BERNHARD (1895–1978). Cofounder of the ▸Russian and Eastern European Mission (REEM). Born in Chicago on Feb. 11, 1895, Paul was the oldest child of G. Edward and Bengta (Svenson) Peterson. As a young man he heard continuous reports about the mass conversions taking place in Russia. Gripped by the reports, Peterson decided to become one of the organizers and eventually a trustee of the Russian Missionary Society when it decided to move its headquarters from Philadelphia to Chicago in 1920. While working for the society, he decided to devote his life to the evangelization of Russia and the Eastern European countries. Under the society's auspices, Peterson and his wife, Signe E. Anderson, whom he married in 1922, left Chicago in 1924 to serve as missionaries in Poland and Latvia. Upon his return to America, he cofounded the REEM with ▸G. Herbert Schmidt and a Chicago businessperson in Chicago in 1927. He was immediately appointed the organization's general secretary and elected its president in 1931. He served in that capacity until his death. Peterson spent the rest of his life traveling across the world for the purpose of acquainting people with the needs and opportunities for evangelism in Russia and Eastern Europe. He made several trips throughout the U.S., Asia, and Europe. At times he also visited Russia and Eastern Europe. During the war years he appealed to people throughout the world to send parcels of food and clothing to Russia and Eastern Europe. In 1952 Peterson moved to Pasadena, CA, after the decision was made to relocate the headquarters of the Eastern European Mission to Pasadena (earlier, "Russian" had been dropped from its title). While in Pasadena, Peterson directed the mission's evangelistic efforts into Western Europe as well. Germany, Greece, and the Netherlands were three countries in which workers were supported. He also helped develop Bible correspondence courses, the publication of Christian literature, and radio broadcasts as means of evangelization. Peterson lived in Pasadena until his death on Dec. 8, 1978.

■ **Bibliography:** "He Served His Generation by the Will of God," *Gospel Call* (Jan.–Feb. 1979) ■ G. B. McGee, *This Gospel Shall Be Preached* (1986) ■ P. B. Peterson, *History of the First Fifty Years (1927–1977) of the Eastern European Mission* (n.d.).

■ J. Colletti

PETHRUS, PETRUS LEWI (1884–1974). Swedish pastor and international pentecostal leader. The son of a factory worker, Pethrus grew up in the Baptist Church. He was baptized at age 15. After several years as a factory worker himself, Pethrus became an evangelist (1902–4) and attended Bethel Seminary in Stockholm (1905–6). He was elected pastor of the Baptist Church in Lidkoping (1906–11) and of Filadelfia Church, Stockholm (1911).

Pethrus, attracted by reports of the Sunderland and Oslo revivals, journeyed to Oslo, where in 1907, under the guidance of ▸T. B. Barratt, he became a pentecostal. His congregation also accepted the pentecostal message, as did numerous other churches in Sweden. In 1913 the Swedish Baptist Convention expelled Pethrus and his entire congregation from the convention, ostensibly because they practiced open communion but in reality because of their pentecostal

theology and liturgy. Despite the schism, Pethrus continued to be influenced by his Baptist heritage and would, for example, insist upon Baptist ecclesiology as the pattern for Swedish pentecostal polity.

The structure of the Swedish pentecostal movement was officially egalitarian, but Pethrus was, in actuality, its leader. He determined the priorities of the movement, represented it to the international movement, and determined the careers of individuals within the church. He could tolerate no competition to his leadership and forced talented individuals such as Sven Lidman (journalist) and A. P. Franklin (missiologist) to work outside the movement. He also caused Allan Tornburg, pastor and theologian, to lose the race for a seat in Parliament by declaring, on the eve of the election, that pentecostals should not be in politics.

On the other hand, Pethrus encouraged a number of daring enterprises. He founded the Filadelfia Church Rescue Mission (1911); the Filadelfia Publishing House (1912); the Filadelfia Bible School (1915); the periodical *Evangelii Härold* (1916–); the Kaggeholms Folkhogskola (a secondary school) (1942); a national daily newspaper, *Dagen* (1945–); a savings bank, Allmanna Spar-och Kreditkassen (1952); and a worldwide radio network, I.B.R.A. Radio (1955).

Pethrus was also a prolific author. His first book, *Jesus Kommer* (1912) was the first publication of the Förlaget Filadelfia (Filadelfia Publishing House). His collected writings comprise 10 volumes, not counting his five-volume memoirs and a number of books written after 1956. He also

Lewi Pethrus, Swedish pentecostal leader whose holistic vision for the Christian life won him an international hearing.

contributed widely to periodical publications. His books and essays have been translated into many languages.

As pastor, Pethrus led his own congregation to become the largest in the pentecostal world (until c. 1975) and the pentecostal movement in Sweden to become the largest Free Church in Sweden, primarily by his ability to relate the church to all aspects of life. His holistic vision for the Christian life and the moderation, dignity, and realism of his expectations of spiritual development won him a hearing throughout Europe, North America, and the Third World. He demonstrated to the pentecostal world that the movement did not have to be alienated from the national culture of which it is a part.

Pethrus, after initial reservations about international cooperation, hosted the 1939 World Pentecostal Conference with 20 nations represented and would thereafter be active in pentecostal ecumenism. He remained pastor at Filadelfia, Stockholm, until his retirement in 1958 and was active in the movement until his death in 1974.

■ **Bibliography:** B. Andstrom, *Lewi Pethrus* (1966) ■ N. Bloch-Hoell, *Pinsebevegelsen, en undersøkelse av pinsebevegelsens tilblivelse . . .* (1956, partial English trans., *The Pentecostal Movement* [1964]) ■ D. D. Bundy, "Swedish Pentecostal Mission Theory and Practice to 1930: Foundational Values in Discussion," *Mission Studies* 14 (1997) ■ B. Carlsson, *Organizations and Decision Procedures within the Swedish Pentecostal Movements* (1978) ■ C.-G. Carlsson, *Människan, samhället och Gud: Grunddrag ii Lewi Pethrus kristendomsuppfattning* (1990) ■ en arbetsbok (1968) ■ W. J. Hollenweger, *Handbuch der Pfingstbewegung* (diss., Zurich, 1966) ■ A. Holmberg, *Lewi Pethrus, rätt man på rätt plats rätt tid* (1976) ■ J. Kallmark, ed., *Så minns vi Lewi Pethrus* (1984) ■ S. Lidman, *Vildaasnor och paadrivare* ■ A. Lindberg, *Förkunnarna och deras utbildning: Utbildningsfrågan inom Pingströrelsen, Lewi Pethrus ideologiska roll och de kvinnliga förkunnarnas situation* (1991) ■ L. Pethrus, *Memoarer,* 5 vols. (1953–56) ■ idem, *Samlade Skrifter,* 10 vols. (1958–59) ■ R. Struble, *Den Samfundsfria Församlingen och de karismatiska gå vorna och tjänsterna. Den Svenska Pingstrockelsen Församlingssyn* 1907–1947 (1982) ■ A. Sundsted, *Pingstvackelsen,* 5 vols. (1969–73).

■ D. D. Bundy

PETTS, DAVID (1939–). British preacher, teacher, educator, and author. Brought up in a Baptist family, Petts first heard about the baptism in the Holy Spirit when he met some pentecostals in Switzerland in 1958. He was baptized in the Spirit a few weeks before going to Oxford University in September 1959.

While at Oxford, he played a major role in the founding of the Students' Pentecostal Fellowship, of which he later became traveling secretary, and for several years was used in leading students in British and American universities into the baptism in the Spirit. After 16 years of pastoral work at Colchester and Basingstoke (Assemblies of God [AG]), he became in 1978 principal of Mattersey Hall (AG Bible college), a post which he still holds. His wife, Eileen, became the college matron.

In addition to his M.A. (Oxford 1967) he has earned an M.Th. (1987) and a Ph.D. (1993) from the University of Nottingham. His thesis, titled *Healing and the Atonement,* argues against the view commonly held in pentecostalism that Christ died for our sicknesses in the same way that he died for our sins. Healing may be understood to be in the atonement, however, both indirectly and ultimately—indirectly because we receive the Spirit because of the atonement and healing is a gift of the Spirit, and ultimately because the final outworking of Christ's victory on the cross will be manifest at the Parousia, when Christians will receive incorruptible bodies.

Petts is a founding member of the European Pentecostal Theological Association and is currently its president. He is chairman of the Association of Bible College Principals, vice-chairman of the Pentecostal European Fellowship, a member of the Advisory Committee to the World Pentecostal Conference, and chairman of the Executive Council of Assemblies of God in Great Britain and Ireland.

His written works include *Be Filled with the Spirit* (1966), *Receive Power* (1974), *The Dynamic Difference* (1978), *Themes from the Major Prophets* (1978), *You'd Better Believe It* (1991), and *The Holy Spirit: An Introduction* (1998).

■ W. K. Kay

PHAIR, ROBERT (1837–1931). Canadian clergyman and archdeacon. Born in County Tyrone, Ireland, Phair experienced an evangelical conversion in 1859 in his homeland. This launched him into a life of deep devotion to Christ. Two years later he enrolled at the Church Missionary Society (CMS) college at Islington in England in preparation for ministry in Canada, where he began what would be a 48-year ministry among the native people.

Ordained first to the diaconate in 1864, then to the priesthood in 1866, Phair began his ministry with an appointment to the area that would be the scene of most of his life's work, northwestern Ontario, part of the extremely rugged Canadian Shield. His diary for 1887 reveals the privations that his ministry sometimes entailed. It tells of him tramping through heavy snow in subzero temperatures and sleeping in an overcrowded tepee in order to pray with a dying chief.

In 1888 Phair was appointed archdeacon of Islington and superintendent and secretary of the CMS in the diocese of Rupert's Land—a position he filled until his retirement in 1912. Following this, he traveled extensively in the Far East, Britain, and North America, holding Bible conferences and preaching, often through interpreters.

Phair was baptized in the Spirit shortly after 1907 in Winnipeg, Man. Without compromising his position in the Anglican Church, he frequently appeared among pentecostal leaders. In 1912 he attended meetings in Dallas, and in 1915 he was at a convention in London, England.

Since there were no official positions in Canadian pentecostalism until 1919, when Phair was 82, he never held office or credentials. His prime contribution was probably made through lending counsel. Documentation does not permit greater precision. It is likely that he also added credibility. When pentecostals spoke of him, they always did so with great respect, being careful to use his title.

■ **Bibliography:** T. C. B. Boon, *The Anglican Church from the Bay to the Rockies: A History of the Ecclesiastical Province of Rupert's Land and Its Dioceses from 1820 to 1950* (1962).   ■ R. A. N. Kydd

PHILIPPINES FOR JESUS MOVEMENT The Philippines for Jesus Movement (PJM) is an umbrella organization for more than 4,000 independent charismatic fellowships and churches in the Philippines. Established on Dec. 10, 1983, the first leader, ►Eddie C. Villanueva, had a specific vision for the nation: If God's people do not rise up for the cause of the Lord, the nation will lose its spiritual, ethical, economic, and political strength. Since its establishment, PJM has hosted prayer rallies to raise the level of Christian concern and has taken Christian positions on issues relative to political, economic, and moral topics. Their activities include the Rally Against Suppression of Freedom to Preach the Word of God (1989, at the Senate Building, Manila); the Rally Against Gambling and Other Vices (1989, at Manila City Hall); "The Nation's Return to Morality" Prayer Rally (1990); and the Prayer Rally Against a Bloc Voting Bill (1995, at the Senate Building in Manila). In achieving their goals, PJM has effectively used print, radio, and TV. The majority of non-Catholic, independent charismatic groups form the membership of PJM.   ■ W. Ma

PHILLIPS, EVERETT L. (1905–88). Pioneer missionary to Nigeria. Phillips, born in Kentucky, was influenced by missionaries as a youth. After attending Central Bible Institute he married Dorothy Prohaska in 1932. They had one son, Don (d. 1985), who also became a missionary.

The Phillipses traveled as pioneer ministers to Nigeria in response to a call by a group of Spirit-filled Nigerians in 1940. They soon opened a Bible school that became the ►Assemblies of God (AG) Divinity School and is the largest AG school there today. They also started printing notes and lessons and began a women's program in the churches. In 1943 the Phillipses were prevented from returning to Nigeria following a furlough, because Everett had developed a heart problem. Before returning to Nigeria in 1951 Phillips

served as pastor and vice president of the Great Lakes Bible Institute and as assistant superintendent of the Illinois District. Upon returning to Nigeria, he served as superintendent of the Nigerian AG and assisted in founding 120 churches.

In 1954 Phillips was appointed field director for Africa. He retired from that position in 1971 and pastored a church in Venice, FL, later settling in Springfield, MO.

■ **Bibliography:** AG Office of Information, media release (Feb. 1988) ▌ "Everett L. Phillips with Christ," *PE* (Mar. 6, 1988) ▌ "God Had a Man," *PE* (Feb. 28, 1971) ▌ W. E. Warner, "The Ministry of Everett and Dorothy Phillips in Nigeria, Africa," taped interview (Oct. 3, 1980).   ■ S. Shemeth

PIKE, JOHN MARTIN (1840–1932). Pastor, author, editor, and publisher. A native of Newfoundland, Pike came to the U.S., where he became an important figure in the Holiness movement. Settling in Columbia, SC, he was associated with the Methodist Episcopal Church, South, but was broadly supportive of a variety of Holiness ventures. The Christian and Missionary Alliance credits Pike with making it possible for them to enter South Carolina through his Oliver Gospel Mission. For several years he provided space for ►Nickels J. Holmes' Bible institute. In addition, Pike wrote for a variety of Holiness periodicals, including ►Carrie Judd Montgomery's *Triumphs of Faith*, and he contributed to works such as *Jesus Only: A Full Salvation Year Book*, published by God's Revivalist Office in Cincinnati.

Pike's prominence in pentecostalism is derived largely from his publishing work. Beginning in 1890 and extending through 1931, he published *The Way of Faith*, a weekly periodical of devotional articles, news items, and testimonies designed to provide advocacy for biblical holiness, divine healing, and the second "personal" coming of Christ. When the pentecostal revival broke out in Los Angeles in Apr. 1906, one of Pike's frequent contributors, Frank Bartleman, kept Pike's subscribers informed of its progress with a series of firsthand reports. Pike was greatly impressed with the movement, and he too wrote articles that were supportive of it.

The publishing interests of Pike went beyond his periodical. He was also instrumental in publishing a number of devotional paperback books, such as Holiness author Mary Mabette Anderson's *Lights and Shadows of the Life in Canaan* (1906). With the emergence of the pentecostal revival, Pike published Frank Bartleman's first autobiography, *My Story: "The Latter Rain"* (1909), and collected correspondence between Dr. Lilian B. Yeomans and her mother, Dr. Amelia Yeomans, in *Pentecostal Papers* (n.d.). This latter work provided careful reflection on the meaning of the pentecostal experience for these women.

J. M. Pike remained in Columbia, SC, most of his life; he died there May 16, 1932.

■ **Bibliography:** C. E. Jones, *Guide to the Study of the Pentecostal Movement* (1983) ■ *The Ninth Annual Report of the Christian and Missionary Alliance* (1906) ■ J. M. Pike, "The Bride of the Lamb," *TF* 21 (7, 1901) ■ idem, "Needed: Much Waiting upon God," *TF* 28 (8, 1908) ■ idem, "One Taken—the Other Left," *TF* 34 (10, 1914) ■ idem, "Pentecostal Movement," *TF* 30 (11, 1910) ■ idem, "Rivers of Living Water," *TF* 30 (12, 1910) ■ V. Synan, *The Holiness-Pentecostal Movement in the United States* (1971).
■ C. M. Robeck Jr.

PINSON, MACK M. (1873–1953). Early pentecostal evangelist and pastor. Pinson's important contribution to the pentecostal movement was in the South prior to 1920. Reared on cotton farms in Georgia, Pinson was one of seven children. His parents were not practicing Christians, and his father deserted the family. The death of his sister while giving birth had a lasting effect on Mack—or M. M., as he is better known—when she asked each family member to meet her in heaven. He was converted in 1893, when he was 20, in a Missionary Baptist church revival. He met some Holiness people but disputed their teaching; later, however, he had a deep spiritual experience, which he was told was the baptism in the Spirit. He felt a call to preach and soon began holding meetings.

Pinson met J. O. McClurkan, president of the Pentecostal Mission Bible and Literary Institute, a holiness school in Nashville. He began attending the school in 1902, was ordained in 1903, and remained with the organization until shortly after he was baptized in the Holy Spirit in 1907. (This school is now Trevecca College, a Nazarene school.) During his years with the mission, Pinson held very successful meetings throughout the South. Later, after being baptized in the Spirit, he went back to some of the same towns and cities to preach the pentecostal message.

Pinson's contact with pentecostals came in 1907 when he went to Birmingham to hear ˃G. B. Cashwell, who was spreading the pentecostal teaching following his ˃Azusa Street Mission experience. Pinson, however, had trouble accepting the new message. When Cashwell went to Memphis, Pinson went along. While seeking for the baptism in the Spirit in Memphis, he attended ˃C. H. Mason's Church of God in Christ. Mason too had just returned from the Azusa Street Mission and had turned his Holiness church into a pentecostal fellowship. After seeking for some time, Pinson was baptized in the Spirit while praying in bed. His friend, H. G. Rodgers, was kneeling at the bed, and he too received the experience. The two later organized several pentecostal churches in the South.

After Pinson's Memphis experience, he returned to Birmingham, where he ministered with Cashwell and others. He became a "corresponding editor" for the *Bridegroom's Messenger,* a paper Cashwell had founded in Atlanta.

Through the influence of ˃William Durham and others, Pinson accepted the Baptist view of sanctification in 1910, or the ˃"finished work," as it was called. When the editor of the *Bridegroom's Messenger,* Mrs. E. A. Sexton, wanted to change Pinson's "finished work" articles that he was submitting, he founded his own paper, the *Word and Witness,* in Nashville. He later consolidated this paper with ˃E. N. Bell's *Apostolic Faith,* retaining the name *Word and Witness.* Bell, who was a pastor in Malvern, AR, became editor; Pinson, because of his itinerant ministry, became a field correspondent. Many of his insightful reports and often sharp articles can be found in the paper.

Few people of the early years of the pentecostal movement had doubts where Pinson stood on social and doctrinal issues. Although reared in the South, he was sympathetic to blacks, even trying to integrate a meeting in the South. He signed "the call" for the General Council of the ˃Assemblies of God (AG) organizational meeting and was selected as the keynote speaker and as an executive presbyter. When the ˃Oneness issue surfaced, Pinson played an important role for the AG in slowing down the rebaptizing of believers.

Pinson studied Spanish and ministered along the Mexican border and pastored churches. After 1920 his influence waned in the AG. When he became inactive in his later years, he returned his credentials to the AG, the organization he helped to found.

■ **Bibliography:** C. Brumback, *Suddenly . . . from Heaven* (1961) ■ Correspondence between M. Pinson and J. Flower (1949–51, in AG Archives) ■ R. Leverett, "M. M. Pinson and the Pentecostal Mission, 1902–07," *AGH* (Fall 1984) ■ W. Menzies, *Anointed to Serve* (1971) ■ M. Pinson, "Sketch of the Life and Ministry of Mack M. Pinson" (1949) ■ R. Spence, *The First Fifty Years, The Story of the Assemblies of God in Alabama* (1965, excerpts reprinted in *AGH* [Fall 1984]).
■ W. E. Warner

PIPER, WILLIAM HAMNER (1868–1911). Influential early pentecostal pastor and editor. Born in Lydia, MD, on June 8, 1868, Piper was ordained in the Brethren Church in Philadelphia in 1893. On Dec. 29, 1912, he married Lydia Markley. The next year, he identified with ˃John Alexander Dowie's newly formed Christian Catholic Church. Two years before, he had experienced healing, and he fully embraced Dowie's radical stance on faith. His wife too had been healed under Dowie's ministries, of paralysis in one leg, which had also been shorter than the other. Dowie had publicized her story in his *Leaves of Healing,* and she had frequently given public testimony to her healing. Lydia Piper was one of the better-known members of Zion. One of the first group of six elders Dowie ordained as his assistants, Piper served Dowie's movement as an overseer. When Dowie opened his community, Zion City, IL, for settlement in 1901, Piper became one of its most influential and prominent citizens.

In 1906, disillusioned with events in Zion, Piper left the movement and moved to Chicago. On Dec. 9, 1906, he opened the Stone Church, where he preached a message similar to Dowie's, though shorn of apostolic pretensions. Most of his congregation were Chicago area people who had formerly associated with Zion. Prejudiced against the pentecostalism that had further divided Zion City's citizens in the fall of 1906, Piper purposely excluded pentecostal teaching from his church.

By the spring of 1907, with attendance down significantly, Piper decided that his opposition to pentecostalism was adversely affecting his ministry. He invited three former Dowie followers who had accepted pentecostal teaching to present their message in his pulpit in late June 1907. The congregation responded positively and readily identified with pentecostal worship patterns. Attendance increased dramatically, and the church became a prominent center, noted for its pentecostal conventions, missionary focus, and ongoing revival emphasis. Piper fully endorsed the pentecostal view of Spirit baptism as endowment with power for service; he refused, however, to be dogmatic about evidential tongues. Lydia Piper was among the first in the Stone Church to receive Spirit baptism (July 1907); her husband received the experience in Feb. 1908.

In Oct. 1908 the church began publishing *The Latter Rain Evangel,* a monthly magazine that circulated pentecostal teaching and news among a broad, far-flung constituency. Edited first by Piper and then by his former assistant, Anna Reiff, the *Evangel* greatly extended the Stone Church's visibility and stature throughout the movement. The church also published other tracts, pamphlets, and books that offered teaching about the movement's emphases. Probably the most influential of these was ▸D. Wesley Myland's *The Latter Rain Covenant* (1910).

On Dec. 29, 1911 (his 15th wedding anniversary), the 43-year-old Piper died unexpectedly after a brief illness. His wife served as pastor of the Stone Church until 1914, when she moved the family to California for two years. After 10 more years in Chicago, she returned to the West Coast, where she taught briefly at the Bible school that later became Southern California College. She died on Jan. 15, 1949. The Pipers had six children: Ruth, William, Theodore, Irene, Dorothy, and Esther.

Under new leadership, the Stone Church affiliated with the General Council of the Assemblies of God. Its commodious facilities accommodated the second and seventh general councils.

■ **Bibliography:** "Asleep in Jesus," *LRE* (Jan. 1912) ■ G. P. Gardiner, "Out of Zion . . . into All the World," *Bread of Life* (Apr., May 1982) ■ *LRE* (Oct. 1908).   ■ E. L. Blumhofer

PISGAH HOME MOVEMENT Founded c. 1895 by ▸Finis Ewing Yoakum, M.D. The Pisgah Home Movement reached its peak between 1911 and 1914. Yoakum, originally from Texas, had attended half a dozen colleges and had been a member of at least one medical school faculty. After receiving a miraculous healing in his own body after a near-fatal accident, he began to seek ways to bring health and healing to those who were unable to afford it.

Headquartered in Highland Park, CA, Yoakum established a variety of outreach ministries in the greater Los Angeles basin that were financed totally by faith. These efforts he named "Pisgah," after the mountain where Moses stood to view the Promised Land (Num. 21:20; 23:14; Deut. 3:27; 4:49; 34:1). Among them was Pisgah Home, 6044 Echo Street, Highland Park. In 1911 it provided regular housing for 175 workers and stable indigents and made provision for an average of 9,000 clean beds and 18,000 meals monthly to the urban homeless, the poor, and the social outcasts, including alcoholics, drug addicts, and prostitutes. Each week Yoakum sent his workers into the city distributing nickels (the price of trolley fare to Pisgah) so that these people could come to Pisgah Home and Tabernacle. There they received two free meals and spent the day in evangelistic and healing services where Dr. Yoakum preached. They sang from *Pisgah Home Songs,* a book of hymns selected and published by ▸Stanley H. Frodsham. At the end of the day, those who wished were allowed to continue at the home, while the others were given another nickel to return to Los Angeles.

Dr. Yoakum established a "free" Pisgah store at the corner of Avenue 58 and Benner Street. It was a two-story concrete block structure a short distance from Pisgah Home. Staffed entirely by volunteers, it served as a distribution center for donated clothing and food as well as used clothing and food items prepared or grown by residents of the various Pisgah projects.

Near the store, on a hill called Mount Ararat (symbolic of a new beginning) at 140 Hayes Avenue, Yoakum constructed Pisgah Ark, a wooden frame structure, as a haven for recovering prostitutes, drug addicts, and alcoholic women. Housing about two dozen, including the staff of matrons, it provided serene accommodations and a rigorous schedule of work and disciplined Bible study.

Seventeen miles from the Highland Park campus, Yoakum purchased a 24-acre plot near Lankershim Boulevard in North Hollywood. Known as Pisgah Gardens, it was designed to provide rehabilitative exercise and fresh air to those with tuberculosis and other diseases for whom it was thought some exercise would be useful. This acreage was dotted with small dwellings and tents and housed a small orphanage between 1913 and 1914. Three-fourths of this property was under cultivation, and the vegetables and fruit raised and dried there were distributed through the Pisgah free store, cooked for the "inmates" of the various Pisgah endeavors in the form of vegetarian stews, or distributed freely to the poor.

On Mar. 14, 1914, Yoakum exchanged the Pisgah Ark and Garden properties for a 3,225-acre parcel of land about 40 miles north of Los Angeles, near Chatsworth. Known as Pisgah Grande, it was established as a Utopian-like community that would house a number of Pisgah enterprises, including the ones uprooted in the purchase. Cattle were raised, fruit trees were planted, some gardening was undertaken, and tents were set up or small red brick cottages were constructed to house the workers. By 1916 about 130 workers called it home. A longer-term Pisgah Bible School was established there under the direction of William C. Stevens; this drew a number of younger people to the community. Plans were made to establish a home for the feeble-minded and insane, a cancer treatment center, and a home for illegitimate children. The death of Dr. Yoakum in 1920 brought the development scheme to a halt.

C. M. White, a close friend of Yoakum, incorporated Pisgah at that time, enabling it to continue operation. During the 1930s, property was obtained in the San Bernardino Mountains, but in 1943 it was sold because it was not easily managed year-round. Property was purchased at a lower altitude, 10 miles from San Bernardino. In 1947 a 500-acre farm parcel near Pikesville, TN, was donated to the Pisgah Home Movement. Today the tabernacle in Highland Park is called Christ Faith Mission. It continues to minister to the alcoholic and addicted, although the city has recently put restrictions on those it can serve. Pisgah maintains a Mountain Home at 7220 Sierra Highway in the Antelope Valley near Pisgah Grande, operating it as a camp-meeting center. A small community also flourishes on the Tennessee site.

■ **Bibliography:** *Confidence* 5 (11, Nov. 1912): 248–51, 255–58 ■ 7 (5, May 1914): 92 ■ J. Creek, *Footprints of a Human Life* (1949) ■ *Dictionary of American Biography* (1936), 20:611–12 ■ *Pisgah Journal* 48 (1, Mar. 1962) ■ *Word and Work* 33 (Sept. 1911), 260–68.
■ C. M. Robeck Jr.

PLYMIRE, VICTOR GUY (1881–1956). Missionary to Tibet and China. Plymire was born to Christian parents in Loganville, PA. In 1897, at age 16, he consecrated his life to God at a street meeting and began attending the Christian and Missionary Alliance (CMA) church. At first he found work with an electrical construction company, but God began to call him into full-time Christian service. Plymire attended the Missionary Training Institute at Nyack, NY, and was ordained by the CMA. He pioneered several churches in the U.S. before he felt impressed to apply for missionary service.

In 1908 Plymire was accepted as a missionary and traveled to northwest China in order to gain access for ministry in Tibet. He married missionary Grace Harkless in 1919. The couple faced many struggles and hardships in Tibet, but Plymire was determined to serve the Lord at any cost. Sixteen years passed before he had the joy of baptizing his first convert.

After returning home on furlough in 1920, Plymire received the baptism of the Spirit in Lancaster, PA. He was ordained by the Assemblies of God (AG) in 1922 and was appointed to serve again in Tibet. During his long ministry, Plymire faced enormous hardships in preaching the gospel on his treks across Tibet. An autobiographical account of his early ministry can be found in *Pioneering in Tibet* (1931) and in his diary, letters, and other papers. In 1927 his wife and baby son died of smallpox. The following year, Plymire married Ruth Weidman, also a missionary to China. The Plymires continued to minister in Tibet and China until 1949, when China was closed to missions. They returned to the U.S., serving churches in Ohio and Missouri. Ruth Plymire served as a missionary to Taiwan from 1959 until she retired in 1970.

■ **Bibliography:** G. McGee, "Plymire, Victor Guy," in *Biographical Dictionary of Christian Missions*, ed. G. H. Anderson (1998) ■ D. Plymire, *High Adventure in Tibet* (1959) ■ V. Plymire, *Pioneering in Tibet* (1931).
■ G. W. Gohr

POLHILL, CECIL H. (1860–1938). First major promoter of pentecostal missions. Polhill was one of the "Cambridge Seven" who went out as missionaries with the China Inland Mission (CIM) in 1885. After years on the Tibetan border, Polhill returned home on doctors' orders in 1900 and was soon invited to join the CIM council. He inherited the family estate near Bedford in 1903 and was widowed in 1904. Returning from a trip to China, he was baptized in the Spirit in Los Angeles early in 1908. Soon making common cause with fellow Anglican ►A. A. Boddy, Polhill used his social position and finances to promote the nascent pentecostal movement through prayer meetings in several London locations and through regular conferences.

His consuming interest was the salvation of the lost through missionary work, especially in China. After urging this cause at the Hamburg conference in Dec. 1908, Polhill and Boddy took immediate steps to form the ►Pentecostal Missionary Union for Great Britain and Ireland (PMU), of which Polhill soon became the president. He was instrumental in the establishment of missionary training homes for both men and women, and, because of his experience, emphasized the practical over the theoretical. Polhill, a disciplined man, inspired respect rather than love and undoubtedly endured ridicule by the upper class for his pentecostal witness and contacts. Although continuing to preside at the annual London conferences each Pentecost, Polhill, as the years passed, devoted himself more exclusively to the missionary task. He paid several visits to PMU missionaries in the Far East, the last one in 1924. When PMU was integrated into the newly formed 'Assemblies of God in Great Britain and Ireland in 1925, Polhill went into retirement. His publication *Fragments of Flame* became *Flames of Fire* in 1911 and ended with the demise of PMU in 1926.

■ **Bibliography:** D. Gee, *Wind and Flame* (1967) ■ P. Hocken, "Cecil H. Polhill—Pentecostal Layman," *Pneuma* 2 (1988).
■ P. D. Hocken

POLMAN, GERRIT ROELOF (1868–1932). Founder of the Dutch pentecostal movement. Polman began ministry in the Salvation Army under the direction of Arthur S. Booth-Clibborn, through whom he made contact with the 'Dowie movement in Zion City, IL, which he visited c. 1904. He returned to found a Dowie Zionist center in Amsterdam. Influenced by the Welsh revival and reports of the 'Azusa Street revival, the group became pentecostal in 1907. Polman published the periodical *Spade Regen* (1908–31) and hosted the International Pentecostal Conference, Jan. 9–16, 1921.

■ **Bibliography:** H. Bakker, *Stroomingen en sekten van onzen tijd* (1924), 161–68 ■ D. D. Bundy, "Between the Réveil and Pentecostalism: The Wesleyan/Holiness Tradition in Belgium and the Netherlands," *Asbury Theological Journal* 51 (2, 1996) ■ idem, "Pentecostalism in Belgium," *Pneuma* 8 (1986) ■ W. J. Hollenweger, "Handbuch der Pfingstbewegung" (diss., Zurich, 1966) ■ C. van der Laan, *Sectarian against His Will: Gerrit Roelof Polman and the Birth of Pentecostalism in the Netherlands* (1991) ■ idem, *De Spade Regen: Geboorte en groei van de Pinksterbeweging in Nederland, 1907–1930* (1989) ■ idem, "The Pentecostal Movement in Holland: Its Origin and Its International Position," *Pneuma* 5 (1983) ■ idem, "The Theology of Gerrit Polman: Dutch Pentecostal Pioneer," *EPTA Bulletin* 8 (1989) ■ idem and P. N. van der Laan, *Pinksteren in beweging* (1982) ■ *Vijfenzeventig Jaar Pinkstergemeente Immanuel* (n.d.) ■ G. A. Wumkes, *De Pinksterbeweging voornamelijk in Nederland* (1916). ■ D. D. Bundy

POSITIVE CONFESSION THEOLOGY An alternative title for "faith-formula theology" or "prosperity doctrine" espoused by the "Word-Faith" or "Word of Faith" movement and promulgated by several contemporary televangelists under the leadership and inspiration of 'Essek William Kenyon (1867–1948). The phrase "positive confession" may be legitimately interpreted in several ways. Most significantly of all, the phrase "positive confession" refers quite literally to bringing into existence what we state with our mouth, since faith is a confession (hence the term *Word-Faith* or *Word of Faith*). This perspective, embraced by Kenyon and his disciples in their relatively new biblical-theological emphasis, regarded the

value of the power of the tongue as a key to the confession theory. Since Kenyon's demise in 1948, several "word ministries," including such personalities as 'Kenneth Hagin, 'Kenneth Copeland, 'Charles Capps, 'Frederick K. C. Price, and others have mined the teachings of their revered teacher.

Conceptually, the views espoused by E. W. Kenyon can be traced to his exposure to metaphysical ideas derived from attendance at Emerson College of Oratory in Boston, a spawning ground for New Thought philosophical ideas. The major tenets of the New Thought movement are health or healing, abundance or prosperity, wealth, and happiness.

New Thought philosophy can be traced to Phineas P. Quimby (1802–66), whose ideas gained prominence toward the close of the last century. Quimby studied spiritism, occultism, hypnosis, and other aspects of parapsychology. It was Quimby who was said to have healed Mary Baker Patterson Eddy, the founder of Christian Science, in 1862. He attempted to make witchcraft credible by the use of scientific language. It appears that Eddy borrowed the term Christian Science from Quimby, along with his theoretical formulations, and these became the basis for the Mind Science cult she founded. Quimby labeled his formulation the science of Christ. From Quimby, 'William Branham, E. W. Kenyon, and 'John G. Lake, a view of God emerged that is currently espoused by Hagin, Copeland, Capps, and Price.

John G. Lake asserted, "Man is not a separate creation detached from God, he is part of God Himself.... God intends us to be gods. The inner man is the real governor, the true man that Jesus said was a god." Bishop 'Earl Paulk of Atlanta recently wrote, "Just as dogs have puppies and cats have kittens, so God has little gods. Until we comprehend that we are little gods and we begin to act like little gods, we cannot manifest the Kingdom of God." Copeland further asserted, "You impart humanity into a child that's born of you. Because you are a human, you have imparted the nature of humanity into that born child. That child wasn't born a whale. It was born a human. Well, now, you don't have a God in you. You are one." The origin of this view is derived from the words of the serpent in Gen. 3:4.

This emphasis in the Positive Confession movement, its critics contend, raises humankind to God's level and thereby creates a false pride that generates the belief that humans can save themselves from disaster by claiming their "divine right." The logical conclusion then is that we can purge the earth of sickness, sin, and even the "demon of poverty." This theological claim has a universal appeal because of its promise of humanistic plans to change history. This form of godism appears to be the basis of faith for Positive Confession adherents who attempt to use their "divine right" to manipulate the Divine. "Now you live in the present tense." "He is what he says he is, and you are what he says you are!" "His Word cannot lie, and you hold fast to that word in your confession."

E. W. Kenyon went beyond the scientific shamanism of the New Thought movement when he first taught "the positive confession of the Word of God." But he did not go so far as to espouse that "faith is a confession," therefore "what I confess, I possess," or to assert that we can "create reality with the words of our mouths." Such confession creates "now faith."

The disciples of Kenyon speak of prosperity as a "divine right" and have formulated laws of prosperity to be rehearsed daily by persons seeking health and wealth. Positive Confessionism, according to its critics, is rooted in an "easy believism" with no grounding or fundamental point of reference. Its doctrinal formulations are rooted in a strained biblicism without an object of faith, often placing an undue stress upon gifts rather than on the fruit of a believer.

The "rhema" doctrine is the primary key to Positive Confession theology. Rom. 10:8 is its primary passage. In its classical Greek usage, the word *rhema* has to do with stating something specifically. The major premise of rhema doctrine is that whatever is spoken by faith becomes immediately inspired and therefore dynamic in the particular situation or event to which it is addressed. Kenyon held that there are two kinds of knowledge, revelation or faith knowledge and sense knowledge. Revelation knowledge is "the knowledge that deals with things that the senses cannot discover or know without assistance from revelation knowledge." Revelation knowledge, for Kenyon and Positive Confession adherents, is the realm above sense knowledge. Kenyon's use of the category of revelation knowledge appears to be apologetic and calls the uninitiated into a true and higher knowledge of God.

Faith formula theology for Charles Farah has Gnostic tendencies, and its revelation doctrine is informed by its presuppositions. This revelation or "higher knowledge" becomes the hermeneutical principle by which adherents either discount or destroy traditional biblical themes of suffering, cross bearing, self-sacrifice, poverty, and martyrdom.

The basic Scriptures used by Positive Confession adherents to give credence to the rhema doctrine are Prov. 6:2; Rom. 10:8; 4:17; and 3 John 2. But critics of Positive Confession contend that these Scriptures are used improperly. To be "ensnared by the words of your mouth" in Prov. 6:2 has reference to a financial transaction that involves a security deposit within a contractual relationship. Rom. 4:17 and 10:8 are usually taken out of context and strained to mean that anyone can "call those things which be not as though they were." By the blessings of Abraham, adherents "nullify the curse of Adam and enter in almost all of the kingdom benefits before the kingdom has fully come." However, Rom. 4:17 is a description of Abraham's faith, specifically, not ours. Rom. 10:8, when read apart from its connection with vv. 9–11, loses its true meaning. The passages cited refer primarily to the truth that comprises the message of salvation as proclaimed in the apostolic tradition. Such truths must be

believed and relied on and confessed if salvation is to be realized, as v. 13 indicates. The context is about special faith given to us. It is obtained as a divine gift and not attained as an acquired skill. It is like grace, an offer in the righteousness of God. Such "faith comes by hearing the Word of God" (v. 17). Third John 2 is a formal greeting and not a promise; neither can it be evoked as God's will for all believers to be "healthy and prosperous."

Thus, the problem that opponents see in the rhema interpretation is a biased selection of biblical passages, often without due regard for their context. The self-defined phrase "confessing the Word of God" takes precedence over hermeneutical principles and rules for biblical interpretation. This approach not only does violence to the text but forces the NT linguistic data into artificial categories that the biblical authors themselves could not affirm. The rhema doctrinal premise (that whatever is spoken by faith becomes immediately inspired in the situation addressed) has a tendency to confuse want and need. The easy believism of the Positive Confession movement appears to be grounded in *fides qua* (i.e., how Jesus believed) rather than *fides quae* (i.e., Jesus as the object of faith). Authentic biblical faith reveals the former but is always grounded in the latter, Jesus as the object of faith. Indeed, to grasp biblical faith, one must move beyond a mere mind-over-matter wish or belief and examine the Hebraic meaning of faith, which stresses firmness, reliability, or steadfastness. The power or efficacy of faith for right relationship with God is never to be found or sought in the act itself but rather in that to which one holds firm by believing. God must be the object of our faith—never our ego wishes or selfish wants.

Those who disagree with Positive Confession theology point out that as Christians we are urged in Luke 12:22 not to worry about our basic needs, which are already included in the divine providential plan. Those who are preoccupied with life's basic necessities are said to be persons of little faith, for it is "after such things that the Gentiles seek," says Jesus. Christians of all walks are urged to grasp more fully the notion that faith does not always secure from God everything we desire, but it does get from God everything he wants us to have, and there is a fundamental difference. In the NT, faith is active; it is a "response term" that presumes the initiative of the grace of God. Within the Christian faith the biblical meaning of the noun and the associated verb "to believe" denotes the criterion of right relationship with God: (1) In the NT it appears that love is given primacy over faith, especially in the Pauline literature. Positive Confessionists reverse this emphasis. The true evidence of the arrival and sign of the kingdom is indeed based on the presence and evidence of love (John 13:34–35). "By this shall all men know that you are my disciples, if you have love one to another." Faith is never presented as a tool to manipulate God for our selfish ends, and nowhere in the teachings of Jesus does it receive primacy. (2) Paul, in the hymn of love in 1 Cor. 13, assigns primacy to love as the greatest of faith, hope, and love. Love was indeed the balancing ideal between ecstasy and order for the gifted and the nongifted. (3) At the very core of our being is the need to be loved by the one who created us for his glory and who alone as perfect love can totally satisfy our deepest needs. It is God's liberating love that breaks the shackles forged by the demonic powers of oppression, thus releasing us to become all we were meant to be in God.

■ **Bibliography:** C. S. Braden, *Spirits in Rebellion: The Rise and Development of New Thought* (1966) ■ C. Capps, *How to Have Faith in Your Faith* (1986) ■ idem, *Seedtime and Harvest* (1986) ■ idem, *The Tongue—A Creative Force* (1976) ■ P. Y. Cho, *The Fourth Dimension* (1979) ■ G. Copeland, *God's Will Is Prosperity* (1978) ■ K. Copeland, *The Force of Faith* (1981) ■ idem, *The Power of The Tongue* (1980) ■ idem, "Questions and Answers" in *Believer's Voice of Victory* (June 1986) ■ C. Farah Jr., "A Critical Analysis: The Roots and Fruits of Faith-Formula Theology," *Pneuma* (Fall 1980) ■ G. D. Fee, "The Gospel of Prosperity—An Alien Gospel," *Reformation Today* (Nov.–Dec. 1984) ■ K. Hagin Sr., *Having Faith in Your Faith* (1980) ■ idem, *How to Write Your Own Ticket with God* (1979) ■ idem, *New Thresholds of Faith* (1974) ■ idem, *Plead Your Case* (1985) ■ idem, *Right and Wrong Thinking* (1966) ■ idem, *The Word of Faith* (1984) ■ idem, *Words* (1979) ■ idem, *You Can Have What You Say* (1980) ■ D. Hunt, *Beyond Seduction* (1987) ■ D. Hunt and J. A. McMahon, *The Seduction of Christianity* (1985) ■ E. W. Kenyon, *Jesus the Healer* (1943) ■ idem, *The Two Kinds of Faith: Faith's Secrets Revealed* (1942) ■ idem, *What Happened from the Cross to the Throne?* (1945) ■ E. W. Kenyon and D. Gossett, *The Positive Confession of the Word of God* (1981) ■ G. Lindsay, *Spiritual Hunger, The God-men and Other Sermons by Dr. John G. Lake* (1976) ■ D. R. McConnell, *A Different Gospel* (1988) ■ E. Paulk, *Satan Unmasked* (1984) ■ F. Price, *Faith, Foolishness or Presumption?* (1979) ■ idem, *How Faith Works* (1976).   ■ L. Lovett

POST, ANSEL HOWARD (d. 1931). Early pentecostal missionary. After 30 years as a Baptist minister, Post came into contact with the ▸Azusa Street revival while living in Los Angeles, CA. In 1906 he received the baptism in the Holy Spirit and then propagated the new pentecostal message with other believers in nearby Pasadena.

Citizens of Pasadena did not welcome Post, however, nor the members of what was derogatorily called the Household of God "sect." They began holding meetings in a tent but were forced out by the town officials and police. They then attempted a move into a permanent structure, but again the residents of the neighborhood objected. Persecution persisted. In 1907 Post began traveling abroad, spreading the news about the revival. His travels took him to South Africa, England, Wales, India, and Ceylon (Sri Lanka).

In 1910, at age 60, Post and his wife, Etta, began ministry in Egypt as independent pentecostal missionaries. Six years later they officially affiliated with the fledgling Assemblies of God. His ministry there focused on evangelism, church planting, and the promotion of pentecostal revivals. He worked tirelessly to establish pockets of pentecostalism and to build "mission houses" for the believers. He also supported Lillian Trasher's orphanage. He died on the field.

■ **Bibliography:** "Head of Sect Is Disturbed," *Pasadena Daily News* (July 13, 1906) ■ "Household Is on Move Again," *Pasadena Daily News* (July 18, 1906) ■ "In Memoriam," *PE* (Aug. 15, 1931) ■ S. Malek, "A Story from the Beginnings of the Assemblies of God in Egypt" (unpub. ms., 1984) ■ L. Martin, ed., *The Holy Ghost Revival on Azusa Street: The True Believers* (1998) ■ A. H. Post, "Testimony of a Minister," *AF* (Jan. 1907).
■ E. J. Gitre

PRANGE, ERWIN (1917–). Lutheran charismatic leader with a widely recognized ministry of deliverance and counseling. Prange graduated from Concordia Seminary, St. Louis, MO, in 1954. He served ghetto parishes of the Lutheran Church–Missouri Synod (LC–MS) in New York and Baltimore for most of the next 18 years.

Prange pursued extensive graduate and postgraduate studies in psychology and counseling in the 1960s. While serving in his second LC–MS parish, he experienced the infilling of the Holy Spirit and spoke in tongues (1963). In 1976 he moved to St. Paul, MN, and became an associate pastor at North Heights Lutheran Church, one of the leading charismatic churches in the American Lutheran Church (ALC). Prange developed the most extensive and well-known ministry of deliverance and counseling in the Lutheran charismatic movement. Key elements of his personal experience, pastoral concern, and theological perspective are contained in a substantial number of books and articles written by Prange.

■ **Bibliography:** L. Christenson, ed., *Welcome, Holy Spirit* (1987) ■ E. Prange, *The Gift Is Already Yours* (1973) ■ idem, *How to Pray for Your Children* (1979) ■ idem, *A Time for Intercession* (1979) ■ idem, *A Time to Grow* (1976).
■ L. Christenson

PRAYER MOUNTAINS See SOUTH KOREA.

PRAYER TOWERS A place set aside for prayer, either for oneself or for specific needs of others. Numerous organizations, individuals, Bible schools, and local churches have designated rooms or buildings for prayer. Often these places are built on a second floor or higher.

Symbolically, the prayer tower idea probably comes from at least two scriptural accounts of people who prayed in places that were higher than the ground floor. When Elijah stayed with the widow and her son (1 Kings 17), he stayed in an upper room. There Elijah prayed life back into the dead son. A second upper room, of course, was the one referred to in Acts 2, in which the 120 prayed and waited for the Day of Pentecost. Another symbolic idea is a watchtower on a city wall. People in prayer can think of themselves as "watchmen."

Through the centuries believers have set aside places of prayer, sometimes in upper rooms or towers and other places of solitude. Since pentecostals and charismatics believe in waiting on God for the baptism in the Spirit and for healing, prayer towers and other places set aside for prayer seem natural.

►Carrie Judd Montgomery set aside a prayer room in an unused parlor in her parents' home in the 1880s after she read an article on the subject in a Christian magazine. Sanford's work at Shiloh, ME, featured a prayer tower, as did other 19th-century ministries. ►Charles F. Parham followed the examples of others after he moved his Bible school into Stone's Folly, an unfinished mansion in Topeka, KS. One of the domes of the mansion was converted into a prayer tower. An early pentecostal mission in Los Angeles was called the Upper Room Mission. Later ►Aimee Semple McPherson had an upper room built in her ►Angelus Temple. Believers could seek for the pentecostal experience or pray for other needs around the clock.

The best-known prayer tower of recent years has been the ultramodern, 200-foot structure on the Oral Roberts University campus. Built in 1967, this tower is manned 24 hours a day by employees of the Abundant Life Prayer Group. The employees answer several thousand calls each month from people asking for prayer. The Upper Room at ►Jim Bakker's defunct Heritage USA was designed for visitors to pray and receive prayer, and callers could call the Upper Room staff for

prayer. In the 1990s the ►Assemblies of God in Springfield, MO, created the National Prayer Center, where volunteers pray for callers. Other groups have established similar centers, making contacts through telephone, Internet, and newsletters.

■ **Bibliography:** K. Kendrick, *The Promise Fulfilled* (1961) ■ Promotional materials from the International Church of the Foursquare Gospel and Oral Roberts University.   ■ W. E. Warner

PRESBYTERIAN AND REFORMED CHARISMATICS

Despite a natural tension between a theology believed and a faith experienced, Christians in the Presbyterian and Reformed tradition have often been pioneers in movements of the Holy Spirit within the body of Christ.

John Calvin, who is referred to as the father of Reformed theology, has been called by many the theologian of the Holy Spirit in the Protestant Reformation. He had much to say about the person and work of the Holy Spirit in his classic *Institutes of the Christian Religion*. In his theology he sought a balance between the written Word and the Holy Spirit and emphasized the Christian's absolute need for the power of the Holy Spirit in order to live a life of righteousness in Christ, to which the heavenly Father has called all Christians.

It is true that Calvin intimated that the "extraordinary" gifts of the Holy Spirit had ceased. He attributed this to the facts that God did not want them further abused on the one hand and that Christians lacked the faith to appropriate them on the other. Unfortunately, Professor Benjamin B. Warfield of Princeton Theological Seminary in the late 19th century went a step further by stating that the "extraordinary" gifts had ceased with the apostles. This view quenched the Holy Spirit in the lives of numerous clergy who in turn influenced their church members.

History does record that periodically the Holy Spirit has used Presbyterians as pioneers in renewal and revival movements, enabling them to move from the theological to the experiential. Occasionally this has led to an upheaval or division within congregations and to resistance or caution by presbyteries. It may even lead to the formation of a new denomination.

A case in point occurred when the Holy Spirit moved mightily among Presbyterians living in the Cumberland Mountains of Tennessee. Ninety years ahead of the pentecostal movement, these Presbyterians were experiencing "the New Testament baptism of the Holy Spirit," as church historian B. W. McDonnald described it in his book *History of the Cumberland Presbyterian Church*. The preachers of the emerging Cumberland Presbyterian Church in the early 1800s were convinced that it was essential for the clergy to seek an endowment of Holy Spirit power before embarking upon their ministry.

The prayer tower at Oral Roberts University, Tulsa, OK.

When the neo-pentecostal, or charismatic, movement began in the mainline churches in the U.S. after WWII, the Presbyterians were again in the forefront of renewal. The first well-known Presbyterian pastor to experience speaking in tongues and healing to remain in his church was ˄James Brown, pastor of the Upper Octorara United Presbyterian Church near Parkesburg, just outside of Philadelphia, PA. About 1957 Brown was baptized with the Holy Spirit. Perplexed as to what course of action he should follow, Brown asked ˄David du Plessis for advice. "Stay in your church and renew it" was the answer. This Brown determined to do.

Brown's decision was to conduct traditional Presbyterian worship in the regular Sunday services but to have neo-pentecostal worship in informal Saturday evening sessions in the sanctuary. This strategy worked for more than 20 years with a minimum of friction. In time the Saturday services attracted hundreds of enthusiastic worshipers each week, with the little country church jammed with as many as 600 people. Thousands of clergy and laity were baptized in the Holy Spirit in these services.

These events were taking place in the late 1950s, before the more famous events in Van Nuys, CA, surrounding the ministry of ˄Dennis Bennett. For several years prior to 1960, Brown had the largest charismatic prayer meeting in the U.S. In 1977 he retired after 37 years in the same pastorate, an early success story of the renewal movement.

In May 1966 Brown and five other Presbyterian charismatic ministers took an important step. They organized the Charismatic Communion of Presbyterian Ministers, which later took the name Presbyterian Charismatic Communion (PCC) in order to include the laity. This was the first charismatic organization to be formed in a mainline denomination. ˄George C. "Brick" Bradford was chosen from among the six as the general secretary, a position he holds today. In one year the new group had 125 Presbyterian ministers on its rolls, and in a short time hundreds of pastors and laypersons joined forces in this well-organized ministry.

Not long after this move, Bradford and the PCC were confronted with a landmark case that tested the place of the gifts of the Spirit in the Presbyterian system. This case arose because of a dispute concerning the ministry of Robert C. Whitaker, pastor of the First Presbyterian Church, Chandler, AZ, near Phoenix.

In 1962 Whitaker had been baptized in the Holy Spirit and had seen the Holy Spirit slowly but surely revolutionize his ministry and the ministry of the Chandler church. By 1967 a number of his members had experienced the power of the Holy Spirit in their lives. Also, like James Brown's church, no tongues or laying on of hands were practiced in the regular services of the church. However, in home prayer meetings revival broke out.

In 1967 a small group of dissenting elders was able to persuade the presbytery of Phoenix to appoint an administrative commission to investigate Whitaker's ministry and the use of the gifts of the Holy Spirit within the life of the congregation. When Whitaker refused to take a vow to stop speaking in tongues, praying for the sick, and casting out demons, the presbytery removed him as pastor of the Chandler church. Rather than accepting this decision, he decided to appeal to the Synod of Arizona on grounds that the verdict was contrary to Scripture and violated his conscience according to a provision within the Book of Order of the United Presbyterian Church.

In Feb. 1968, when the appeal failed, Whitaker was faced with accepting the decision or appealing it further. Giving strong counsel and aid to Whitaker was a leading figure in world Presbyterianism, the late John A. Mackay, president emeritus of Princeton Theological Seminary. Both Mackay and Bradford strongly encouraged Whitaker to continue the fight. As providence would have it, Brick Bradford had been a lawyer before entering the ministry and offered his services as counsel for the plaintiff.

Bradford added a third reason for appealing to the Permanent Judicial Commission of the General Assembly, the highest court of the United Presbyterian Church. He argued that no lower judicatory (presbytery or synod) could add vows to the ordination vows set forth in the church constitution. In May 1968 *The Reverend Robert C. Whitaker vs. The Synod of Arizona* was decided in favor of Whitaker.

It was a great moral victory for all charismatics in the mainline churches. But the victory did not end with the successful appeal. As a result of the Whitaker case, every Presbyterian minister was protected from arbitrary removal by a presbytery from his or her pastorate on grounds of involvement in the charismatic renewal. Because the case did not rule on the theological implications, the 180th General Assembly (1968) ordered a theological study to be made on the question of tongues, healing, exorcism, and the neo-pentecostal movement in general.

The study commissioned by the general assembly was the first and possibly the most thorough one ever done by a major denomination. The members of the commission were made up of persons versed in theology, psychology, psychiatry, pastoral ministry, and ecclesiology. The report was so groundbreaking and comprehensive that it served as a model for many other denominational reports in the years that followed. Again the Presbyterians were pioneers in renewal.

The exegetical sections of the report, while rejecting a separate experience of Holy Spirit baptism, did allow for the exercise of spiritual gifts in the contemporary church as long as they did not lead to disorder and division.

A set of guidelines was offered for Presbyterians who were considered neo-pentecostal and for those who were not, with a view toward keeping peace in the churches. Overall the report was positive in its exegetical, psychological, and pastoral sections. The report's guidelines were adopted overwhelmingly, and the *Report on the Work of the Holy Spirit* as a whole was received by the 182nd General Assembly of the United Presbyterian Church in 1970. It has been the official policy of the church since that time.

Throughout the 1970s the renewal moved ahead with ever-increasing force. In Hollywood's First Presbyterian Church, one of the largest in the world, more than 600 members were said to be speaking in tongues. Such prominent Presbyterian leaders as Senior Pastor Louis Evans of the National Presbyterian Church in Washington, D.C., and his wife, Colleen Townsend Evans, and the late ►Catherine Marshall and her husband, Leonard LeSourd, have been openly active in the movement. Robert L. Wise, Reformed Church in America pastor, is another well-known figure in the renewal.

An important addition to the movement came in 1965, when ►J. Rodman Williams was baptized in the Holy Spirit while serving as professor of systematic theology at the Austin Presbyterian Theological Seminary in Texas. Already an able and well-known theologian among Presbyterians, Williams added serious theological depth to the charismatic movement as a whole. In later years he made significant contributions through his books and teaching positions at Melodyland School of Theology and the Graduate School of Theology at CBN University. Presbyterian Charles Farah served the renewal in a similar fashion from his teaching position at Oral Roberts University as professor of theology.

In 1984 the name was changed to Presbyterian and Reformed Renewal Ministries International (PRRMI). By 1986 PRRMI had close to 1,000 clergy members out of the 3,000 to 3,500 who had been baptized in the Holy Spirit. The total membership of the group is about 3,500 contributing members. This relatively small group is representative of some 250,000 charismatics in the Presbyterian and Reformed churches in the U.S. PRRMI (now PRMI) has members in 26 Presbyterian and Reformed denominations scattered throughout 42 nations.

■ **Bibliography:** H. Berkhof, *The Doctrine of the Holy Spirit* (1964) ■ B. Bradford, *Releasing the Power of the Holy Spirit* (1983) ■ idem, *Report on the Work of the Holy Spirit* (1970) ■ J. R. Williams, *The Era of the Spirit* (1971).   ■ H. V. Synan

PRICE, CHARLES SYDNEY (1887–1947). Pentecostal evangelist, pastor, and teacher. He commanded deep respect as one of the greatest teachers of the early pentecostal movement. Originally from Britain, Price was trained in law at Wesley College, Oxford, and emigrated to Canada. He later had a conversion experience at a Free Methodist mission in Spokane, WA, and attracted the attention of Dr. Henry I.

Rasmus, who convinced him to enter the ministry. When Price was invited to a pentecostal prayer meeting shortly after the outpouring of the Spirit at ►Azusa Street, another minister dissuaded him and successfully convinced him to study the works of modernism instead. Although he gradually gained prestige within the Columbia River Conference of the Methodist Church, he became disenchanted with the Methodist episcopal system, becoming pastor of a Congregational church in Valdez, AK.

During WWI he attained popularity as a public speaker at theaters in San Francisco, selling war bonds. He later became pastor of the First Congregational Church in Lodi, CA. In early 1920 some members of his church began attending ►Aimee Semple McPherson's meetings in San Jose. They convinced him to go, but he intended to discredit them, until "a masterful message came from the lips of the evangelist and my modernistic theology was punctured until it looked like a sieve" (Price, 1944, 34–35). On the third night he answered the altar call. He was later baptized in the Spirit at "tarrying meetings" held at a Baptist church in San Jose pastored by Dr. William Keeny Towner, who had sponsored

Charles S. Price, who was pastoring a Congregational church in Lodi, CA, when he was baptized in the Spirit at an Aimee Semple McPherson meeting. He then launched his own evangelistic ministry.

McPherson's meetings. Price returned to his church at Lodi, where "the power of God commenced to fall" (Price, 1944, 45). When denominational officials began to interfere, he started an independent church, Lodi Bethel Temple.

In 1922 Price began itinerating as an evangelist, holding meetings in Oregon and British Columbia. Several miraculous healings in Victoria became well publicized. During the following year, meetings in Vancouver attracted 250,000 people over the course of three weeks. Price later held meetings in Calgary and Edmonton, where people smashed windows to gain admittance after the 12,000 seats at the ice arena were taken. At the amphitheater in Winnipeg, Man., Price had to climb through a kitchen window to get into the building. Later meetings were held in Toronto, Minneapolis, Duluth, St. Louis, and Belleville, IL. One thousand conversions per day were reported during the last 10 days of the Belleville campaign.

In 1926 Price began publishing his periodical, *Golden Grain*. Continuing his itinerant ministry in the Pacific Northwest, he began to find it necessary to construct tabernacles in which to hold his meetings.

By 1944 Price had preached in Sweden, Norway, England, Egypt, Palestine, Turkey, Syria, Lebanon, Italy, and other parts of Europe, as well as in many additional places throughout the U.S. and Canada.

■ **Bibliography:** C. S. Price, *The Real Faith* (new ed., 1972) ■ idem, *The Story of My Life* (3d ed., 1944).   ■ R. M. Riss

PRICE, FREDERICK KENNETH CERCIE (1932–).

Pastor and television evangelist. Price was born in Santa Monica, CA, and was reared in a Jehovah's Witness environment. He married Betty Ruth Scott in 1953; they have four children.

Converted at a tent crusade in 1953, Price entered the Christian ministry in 1955. During his first 17 years of ministry, he belonged to four denominations; he was assistant pastor at Mt. Sinai Baptist Church, Los Angeles (1955–57); pastor of the African Methodist Episcopal Church, Val Verde, CA (1957–59); and pastor of ▸Christian Missionary Alliance West Washington Community Church, Los Angeles (1965–73). He received the baptism of the Holy Spirit in 1970 and soon began to develop a "faith" ministry.

In 1973 Price founded an independent church in Los Angeles called Crenshaw Christian Center. Price was ordained by ▸Kenneth Hagin Ministries in 1975. In 1981 the congregation moved to 32 acres that formerly housed Pepperdine University. In 1989 he completed a new worship center called the Faithdome at a cost of over $10 million. The multiracial congregation now exceeds 15,000 and continues to reach out to the Los Angeles community. Price began a nationally broadcast television ministry in 1978 called *Ever Increasing Faith*, which is featured on more than 125 stations

in the U.S. and abroad. In 1982 he began teaching his faith message in crusades and conferences all across the U.S.

Price is the author of more than 30 books relating to the Holy Spirit and faith, including *Is Healing for All?* (1976); *How Faith Works* (1976); *The Holy Spirit—the Missing Ingredient: My Personal Testimony* (1978); *Faith, Foolishness or Presumption?* (1979); *Marriage and the Family: Practical Insight for Family Living* (1988); *Living in the Realm of the Spirit* (1989); *Prosperity on God's Terms* (1990); and *Practical Suggestions for a Successful Ministry* (1991).

■ **Bibliography:** V. B. Lowe, "Frederick Price: The Making of a Ministry," *Religious Broadcasting* (Feb. 1987) ■ J. G. Melton, *Prime-Time Religion* (1997), 265–66 ■ F. Price, *The Holy Spirit: the Missing Ingredient* (1978) ■ *Who's Who in America* (48th ed., 1994) ■ *Who's Who in Religion* (1992).   ■ G. W. Gohr

PRIDGEON, CHARLES HAMILTON (1863–1932).

Pastor, educator, and missions executive. Pridgeon was born in Baltimore, MD, and educated at Lafayette College (B.A., 1886; M.A., 1889) and Princeton Theological Seminary (graduated 1889). Further studies took him to Free Church College and United Presbyterian College, Edinburgh, Scotland; the University of Leipzig; and Worcester University.

Pridgeon was ordained to the Presbyterian ministry and pastored in Canonsburg, PA (1890–1901). In 1892 he sought the fullness of the Holy Spirit; this proved to be a turning point in his ministry. Later contact with ▸A. B. Simpson led to his invitation to address the ▸Christian and Missionary Alliance (CMA) convention at Old Orchard campground in Maine. While there, he met Louise Shepard (d. 1928), whom he married in 1901; they had one daughter. Conflict over Pridgeon's preaching on faith healing led to his withdrawal from the Presbyterian church in the same year.

Moving to Pittsburgh, Pridgeon founded the Wylie Avenue Church in Dec. 1901. Soon following he established the Pittsburgh Bible Institute (c. 1902). The doctrines taught at the school strongly reflected those of the CMA. In 1908–9 he traveled overseas to investigate possible sites for ministry. This trip resulted in the dispatching of missionaries to China. Later Pridgeon founded the Evangelization Society of the Pittsburgh Bible Institute (1920), which placed missionaries in India and Africa as well. His other efforts included an orphanage, open-air evangelism, a hospital ministry, a printing plant, and publication of the *Record of Faith*.

In the winter of 1920 Pridgeon went to Dayton, OH, to attend a revival conducted by ▸Aimee Semple McPherson. Stirred by what he saw, he returned home and urged the students to pray for the baptism in the Holy Spirit. A remarkable revival began the following April with more than 1,500 persons receiving the pentecostal baptism in the following two to three years.

Beginning in 1918 Pridgeon generated controversy with his teaching that hell is not eternal. He explained his views in *Is Hell Eternal; or Will God's Plan Fail?* To him it was a place of limited duration required by the sins of humankind. After purification, humanity could discover the love of God. The terms used to describe this form of universalism included the "restitution" or "reconciliation" of all things, and "Pridgeonism." The "Pridgeon doctrine" was condemned as heretical by the General Council of the Assemblies of God in 1925.

■ **Bibliography:** G. D. Clementson, *Charles Hamilton Pridgeon* (1963) ▪ idem, *Louise Shepard Pridgeon* (1955) ▪ Combined Minutes of the General Council of the Assemblies of God, 1914–25 ▪ W. W. Menzies, *Anointed to Serve* (1971) ▪ idem, "The Non-Wesleyan Origins of the Pentecostal Movement," in *Aspects of Pentecostal-Charismatic Origins*, ed. V. Synan (1975) ▪ C. H. Pridgeon, *Is Hell Eternal; or Will God's Plan Fail?* (3d ed., 1931) ▪ "Pridgeon, Charles Hamilton," *Who Was Who in America*, vol. 1: 1897–1942 ▪ "Pridgeonism," *The Pentecostal Testimony* (Nov. 1923). ■ G. B. McGee

PRINCE, PETER DEREK V. (1915–). Bible teacher and author. Derek Prince was born to British parents on Aug. 14, 1915, in Bangalore, India, living there until his mother returned him to Sussex, England, where he lived with his grandparents. Prince excelled academically through his secondary and college education, studying at Cambridge University, where he specialized in philosophy. In 1940 he was elected a fellow at King's College, Cambridge.

WWII interrupted Prince's academic career, and in July 1941, while serving in the army, he was converted to Christianity. Stationed in Jerusalem, Prince met Lydia Christianson, and after leaving the army, they were married in Feb. 1946. Prince returned to England in 1949 and for eight years pastored a small pentecostal church in central London. He then went to Kenya in 1957 to lead a teacher training college. In 1963 he immigrated to the U.S. and began traveling and teaching widely during the 1960s. He moved to Ft. Lauderdale in early 1968 from the Chicago area.

In 1976 Prince associated with three other Bible teachers: ▸Don Basham, ▸Bob Mumford, and ▸Charles Simpson. With Canadian pentecostal Ern Baxter, who joined them in 1974, they became the principal leaders of the shepherding movement, a controversial expression of the charismatic renewal in the 1970s. Prince's first wife, Lydia, died in 1975.

Prince's 1976 book, *Discipleship, Shepherding, and Commitment,* was a concise biblical statement of the shepherding movement's distinctive teachings. Over time Prince became uncomfortable with some of those teachings. In 1978 he had a disagreement with the other leaders over his plans for remarriage. Though finally agreeing to Prince's marriage to Ruth Baker in 1978, an ongoing strain remained. In 1983

Prince withdrew from the shepherding movement for what he described as doctrinal reasons.

Prince was a very popular yet controversial Bible teacher in the charismatic renewal because of his emphasis on deliverance from demonic powers in believers. His emphasis on the Holy Spirit's power along with his reserved, unemotional, and logical teaching manner created a unique blend.

Prince continues (2001) his worldwide ministry from Charlotte, NC.

■ **Bibliography:** D. Prince, *Discipleship, Shepherding, and Commitment* (1976) ▪ idem, *Jubilee 1995 Celebration: 50th Year in Ministry* (1995). ■ S. D. Moore

PROPHECY, GIFT OF

I. Prophetic Speech in the Ancient World
  A. *Near Eastern Prophecy Outside Israel*
  B. *Greek and Roman Prophetic Activity*
  C. *Prophecy in Israel*

II. Prophecy in the New Testament
  A. *A Pauline Perspective*
  B. *A Lukan Perspective*
  C. *Prophecy and the Gospel Writers*

III. The Gift of Prophecy in Church History
  A. *The Early Church*
  B. *The Middle Ages*
  C. *Reformation and Post-Reformation Understandings*

IV. Prophecy in Contemporary Understanding
  A. *True and False Prophecy*
  B. *Limits of Prophetic Authority*

One of several charisms or "gifts" *(charismata)* of the Holy Spirit mentioned by Paul in 1 Cor. 12:10 and elsewhere. Prophecy (Gk. *prophētia*) has been alternatively identified as (1) an oracle, spontaneously inspired by the Holy Spirit and spoken in a specific situation; (2) a form of expositional preaching from the biblical text; or (3) a public pronouncement of a moral or ethical nature that confronts society. The commonly held understanding of prophecy as a predictive word of future events, and therefore as foreknowledge, has ancient precedence, but it does not provide an adequate basis for understanding this gift. Prophecy more commonly includes a component of "forthtelling," or the conveyance of a message with or without the predictive element. Pentecostal and charismatic Christians tend to emphasize the nature of prophecy as spontaneous, though many allow for prophetic gifts to function in "anointed" preaching and in some "inspired" social commentary.

The history of prophetic claims is an ancient and diverse one, limited neither to the church nor to the people of Israel. Prophetic claims are common in ancient Near Eastern (G. A. Guillaume; R. Wilson) and Far Eastern religions (H. H. Rowley), in Greek and Roman religious life (J. Fontenrose; H. W. Parke; D. E. W. Wormell), and in contemporary non-Christian religions such as Islam (F. Rahman), as well as in the Christian context. Even within the larger "Christian" context, spontaneous prophetic claims arise from groups as diverse as Roman Catholics, Seventh-day Adventists, Mormons, and pentecostals. Thus, the biblical discussions of prophets, prophecy, and prophetic activity should be viewed within this larger historical, religious, and cultural context. Although non-Jewish and non-Christian claims to prophetic activity do not fit the Pauline criteria for genuine manifestations of the gift of prophecy, a look at these claims to spirit possession, their content, and their methodology provides many parallels to Jewish and Christian claims and may nonetheless help us understand the nature of genuine prophetic activity.

I. PROPHETIC SPEECH IN THE ANCIENT WORLD.

A. Near Eastern Prophecy Outside Israel.

Prophetic activity in ancient Near Eastern society has been observed as early as the 19th century B.C. It took various forms but was often associated with the use of omens, and it more clearly followed the pattern of divination. In Mesopotamian society, events were observed in such a way that though they might not be seen as having a causal relationship to one another, yet they were understood to have some relationship due at least to a shared proximity of moment. The recurrence of one such event was then thought to have some relationship to the repetition of the other. If an owl flew overhead and someone's home burned down, the next time an owl was seen to fly overhead, it might be predicted that some destructive event would soon transpire.

Mesopotamian prophetic specialists or diviners banded together into schools or guilds. Entrance into such a guild was both competitive and selective. Following initiatory rites the diviner *(bārû)* was then taught such things as the use of dice, divination of oil as it was spread upon water, interpretation of dreams, the examination of the entrails of sacrificial animals, and other "arts" commonly used in the trade. While it is clear that many similar methods were used in Israel, such as the casting of lots (1 Sam. 14:41–42) or the interpretation of dreams (Gen. 40:5–8; 41:1–8; Dan. 2:1–11), some of these "arts" were clearly understood to be forms of divination, which was expressly forbidden (Deut. 18:10–11). It is not at all clear whether Israel's own prophetic guilds borrowed any of these methods directly from their Mesopotamian neighbors; rather, it appears that these methods developed independently.

In Mesopotamia, the preferred method of divination and of predicting the future was that of examination of an animal's liver. By the Babylonian period there was a sophisticated system for interpreting the meaning of various liver configurations. Ezekiel told his hearers that the Babylonian king would engage in the casting of lots, the consulting of idols, and the examination of livers (Ezek. 21:21–23) in order to determine the future of Jerusalem. Still, those who had sworn allegiance to him would interpret it as a false omen.

The Mari Letters give further evidence of "prophetic" activity in that region of the Near East. The "answerers" or *špilus* served a variety of localized cultic deities. Their utterances were quite rational but not particularly profound. Often they involved personal requests on behalf of the deity, requests that, if fulfilled, would improve the personal situation of the *špilu*. Alongside the *špilu* was the *muhhû*, one who entered into a sometimes violent form of trance or ecstasy and gave an oracle, sometimes while in the trance and sometimes later. In the cases of both the *špilu* and the *muhhû*, their oracles were often submitted to testing and scrutiny by still other forms of divination.

The Assyrians provided a parallel to the Israelite "seer" in the person of the *šabrû*. The messages from the *šabrû* were derived from visions or dreams, sometimes providing reassurance in times of peril. One example from the reign of Assurbanipal involved a prayer to the goddess Ishtar or Arbela just prior to an attack. It was recorded that she appeared to the *šabrû* with words of encouragement for the king.

On the whole, divination and prophetic, even apocalyptic, activity were present throughout the Near East and running both prior to and concurrent with Israel's own prophetic activity. Israel's prophetic activity, however, claimed to be unique, for it was derived solely from Yahweh, Israel's God.

B. Greek and Roman Prophetic Activity.

As early as the 8th century B.C., Homer mentioned the existence of prophetic activity in Pythea or Delphi, as well as at Dodona. Prophetic activity in the Greek world was generally associated with Zeus (at Dodona), and with Apollo (at Delphi). As was the case of Abram's God, who was at one point associated with the oak tree at Moreh (Gen. 12:6), so Zeus was associated with an oak at Dodona, and Apollo with a laurelwood at Delphi. The Greek deity Zeus, who controlled storms and was thought to be the supreme god in a pantheon of gods, and the god Apollo, who was largely a pastoral and agricultural deity, were most commonly addressed and invoked at Dodona and Delphi.

Plutarch (*Obsolescence of Oracles* 414B) observed that of the two cities noted for their prophetic activity, Delphi was not only the more ancient, it was also the more famous. For a time it was closely associated with the activity of a serpent who was, according to Greek mythology, originally the guardian of the Oracles of Delphi but was killed by Apollo.

Herodotus, a Greek historian writing in the 5th century B.C., gives an idea of how widespread prophetic activity was in this region when he mentions oracles in Delphi, Abae in Phocia, Dodona, Amphriaraus, Trophonius, Branchidae in the Milesian country, and Ammon in Libya (*Histories* 1.46). It is also known that oracles were delivered at such ancient sites as Olympia, Patara, Argos, and Agamemnon. Herodotus wrote during the apex of Delphic activity, while Plutarch (c. A.D. 50–120), a biographer and philosopher, wrote of Delphi during its decline.

At the height of Delphic activity, multitudes kept two prophetesses fully employed, with a third one in reserve to accommodate any overflow business (Plutarch, *Obsolescence of Oracles* 414B). Those who prophesied at Delphi were young virgins who, Plutarch maintained, were of ordinary birth and experience. They had no prior training, no technical skill, and no previously demonstrated talents that enabled them to prophesy (*Oracles at Delphi* 405C). These young women, however, were alternatively described as servants to their god (*tētheōsynestin*), as prophetesses (*prophētisin*), and as mantics (*mantia*).

The method by which these women performed their religious function involved their willingness to act as intermediaries between the god and a paying customer who sought information. Strabo (*Geography* 9.3.5) reports that they entered a cave from which gases were emitted. There they sat upon a tripod, received these gases into their bodies, and began to "prophesy." Plutarch says that at such times it was actually the god who entered their bodies and prompted "their utterances, employing their mouths and voices as instruments" (*Obsolescence of Oracles* 414E). Plutarch, who idealized this activity as involving divine possession, was concerned that the populace, however, was more interested in the winds, vapors, exhalations, and the external wonders than they were in the god who spoke.

In the early days of professional prophetism at Delphi, it was claimed that these virgins prophesied in metered verse. (See, e.g., Herodotus, *Histories* 1.47, which contains an oracle given in hexameter verse.) By Plutarch's day, metered verse was extremely rare. Simple statements needing interpretation were the norm. Thus, at times the young girl, who acted as the intermediary, was described as having a mantic power by which she foretold the future, but it was also necessary to have an oracular interpreter called a "prophet" (*prophetes*), who stood by her to help those who had made inquiry understand the meaning of her response. This relationship between the inspired speaker and the interpreter may provide a helpful parallel to the relationship between the gift of tongues and the interpretation of tongues as it was described by Paul in 1 Cor. 12 and 14. This is even more

probable in the cases where the virgin spoke unintelligible speech while possessed.

Plutarch argued that the inspiration of the young girls came from gods *(theia)* and demigods *(daimonios)* and that each intermediary or girl responded to her possession by them in different ways. In one highly publicized case, a girl went unwillingly to do the job. When she was possessed by Apollo, Plutarch said, she was as one who had a change of voice. She acted like a "laboring ship." She became hysterical, screamed, and threw herself to the ground, and within a few days she was dead (*Obsolescence of Oracles* 438A). This more or less uncontrollable behavior, however, was not typical of Delphic prophetic activity.

As one might imagine, the inquiries brought to these prophetesses were relatively uncomplicated questions on matters of daily life. Questions of whether or when to embark on a trip, how to invest money, and whether or whom one ought to marry were very common. Examples of such inquiry have been found inscribed on lead strips at the sites of the caves where the inquiry was made. The community of the Coragraeans, for instance, inquired during the late 5th century, "To what god or hero by making sacrifice and prayer [may we] dwell in the fairest and best way both now and in time to come?" Others, such as one Callicrates, were concerned with things closer to their own personal well-being. Callicrates requested that the prophetess ask "the god whether I will have offspring from Mike whom I have by remaining with her and praying to which of the gods." Questions concerning illness and healing were addressed to the god in this way as well, as in the case of Leontios, who consulted the oracle "concerning his son Leon whether there will be recovery from the disease on his breast which seizes him" (Parke).

On occasion, consultations were made to two prophetesses to determine whether the answers were true to the facts and consistent with each other. Herodotus records that Croesus, king of Lydia, made simultaneous inquiry of both Greek and Libyan oracles to determine whether he should engage in battle with the Persians. The *test of consistency* was applied to these oracles. A second test that was commonly applied was the *test of fulfillment*. If the word of the prophetess came true, it was judged to have been divinely sent. A third test was also used by Croesus. Through a messenger he asked each oracle what he had done at a specific hour. At that time he had cut up a tortoise and a lamb, then boiled them in a covered bronze caldron. Only by *revelation*, he argued, could they respond rightly, and by this means he acknowledged that genuine divination had been made only at Delphi (Herodotus, *Histories* 1.46–48).

The NT suggests that such activity was widespread at the time of Jesus and his disciples. Paul and Silas were harassed in Philippi by a slave girl who "earned a great deal of money for her owners, by fortune-telling" (*manteuomenē*, Acts

16:16). Paul recognized that this was accomplished by means of a spirit of divination, literally, a pythian spirit *(pneuma pythōna)*, and he exorcised it.

The fathers of the church were unanimous in their condemnation of these prophetic activities in Greek and Roman religion. Justin Martyr *(Apology* 1.18, 44, 56) saw the source of their inspiration as demonic. Origen reached the same conclusion in his work *Against Celsus* (7.7.3–4), because, he noted, the divine Spirit does not put a person into such "a state of ecstasy and madness that she loses control of herself," nor would the divine Spirit fill her mind and cloud her judgment with darkness. Tertullian concluded that Croesus' question of what he was cooking had been answered by means of revelation, but it was by means of demonic revelation *(Apology* 1.22), not divine revelation. In spite of this condemnation, many patterns exist in Greek and Roman prophetic activity, and these patterns help to shed light on similar ones that may be observed in the gift of prophecy as it is described in Scripture and employed in the church.

C. Prophecy in Israel.

Usually when we think of prophecy, we think of a predictive word about something that will take place in the future. When we think of prophets, our minds typically picture the literary prophets of Israel who gave us so many of the OT books. While both of these images are helpful in describing prophecy, the basic concept of prophecy as it is found in the canonical writings of Israel is quite simple. The experience of Moses and Aaron described in Ex. 4:10–16 (cf. 7:1–2) provides an early and paradigmatic understanding of prophecy. This passage indicates that *the prophet is essentially a person who speaks on behalf of another.*

God asked Moses to speak to Pharaoh about the release of the people of Israel. Moses declined God's request on grounds that he had a speech impediment. God then directed Moses to enlist the help of Aaron to convey the message. Thus, before Pharaoh, Moses would appear as God *('elohim)*, while Aaron would act as the "mouth" or the "prophet" *(nabi')*. Moses would give Aaron the message that Aaron would deliver to Pharaoh.

From such a description several observations can be made. First, the person who prophesies is not the inventor of the words to be spoken. That person is merely the conveyor of the message. Aaron spoke what Moses told him to speak, and no more. The message was Moses' message, though the precise words used to convey it were Aaron's words. Second, in this paradigm there is no confusion between the person who speaks the message and the person whose message is spoken. There is a discrete prophetic consciousness that can be clearly articulated. God gives the word. The prophet speaks. Moses gave Aaron the message and was likened by Pharaoh to God. Aaron delivered the message and was likened to the prophet. Third, the person who acts as the prophet does so only when conveying the message that has been given to him or her. Every word spoken by Aaron during his lifetime was clearly not to be considered as having equal importance with the specific thoughts or words that Moses gave him to speak to Pharaoh. Only the message that God gave to Moses and which Moses gave to Aaron from God were prophetically important.

In 1 Samuel, two texts provide additional information that helps further to define this gift. The first, 1 Sam. 9:6–9, describes Saul's entrance into the land of Zuph when he was searching for his father's lost donkeys. He was told that Samuel, a man devoted to the service of Yahweh, was there. Saul sought him out to ascertain where the herd could be found. The editor of this passage provides an interesting side note for the reader. Those who were currently called "prophets" *(nabi')*, he wrote, had formerly been called "seers" *(ro'eh)*. This emphasis on the prophet as a "seer" suggests a connection between prophecy, dreams, and visions.

Visions continued to play a significant role in the oracles of the literary prophets (cf. Isa. 6:1ff.; Ezek. 1:1ff.; 8:1ff.; Amos 7:1–9). Dreams were sometimes also used (cf. Jer. 23:25). At other times prophets heard the voice of Yahweh while pondering the significance of current events (such as the locust invasion, drought, and brush fires, which Joel [1:1–2:11] saw as harbingers of the Day of the Lord) or while studying simple everyday acts, such as Jeremiah's encounter with the potter who formed the clay (18:1ff.). Yet it appears that the earliest claims to prophetic activity involved some ability to interpret dreams or visions.

In the second text, 1 Sam. 10:6, Samuel anointed Saul on behalf of Yahweh to be a prince over Israel. Samuel told Saul that when Saul came to Gibeah of God, he would meet a band of prophets prophesying with musical accompaniment and that when he did so, the Spirit of the Lord would fall upon Saul, and he would prophesy and "be changed into a different person."

At other times also prophecy was given to the accompaniment of music. It should come as no surprise when we note the relationship of singing to prophesying (1 Chron. 25:1, 3, 6) or the prophetic forms of some of Israel's hymns, the Psalms (cf. Pss. 50; 60; 89:19–37). The Pauline encouragement for Christians to sing "spiritual songs" (Eph. 5:18–19; Col. 3:16) may also have a prophetic component to it.

In the OT there were those who banded together into prophetic schools. Amos denied that he was either a prophet or the "son of a prophet" (7:14), that is, he was not a member of any professional prophetic guild or school.

A connection to some form of "ecstatic" experience might also be derived from the statement that Saul would "be changed into a different person." Samuel's own prophecy of this was fulfilled in vv. 9–12 to such an extent that the origin of the proverb "Is Saul also among the prophets?" was understood to have arisen here. The ecstatic elements of a trance-like state, Saul's lying prostrate on the ground while prophesying, and his seeming obliviousness to his own "nakedness," might be described as extreme in the light of later Pauline reflection on the subject of prophecy, but, nonetheless, they may be observed in this text. Such "ecstatic" activity ultimately led to the description of a prophet as a "man of the Spirit" or an inspired "maniac" (Hos. 9:7) and may also lie behind the imagery suggested by the prophet as one on whom Yahweh's hand has been placed (Ezek. 3:14–16; 8:1–4).

Prophecy in the OT, then, shows great diversity. At times it comes almost silently in thoughts, visions, or dreams. On other occasions it comes quite forcefully, in a moment of significant emotion, reminiscent of drunkenness. In Moses' day it came to a limited group of elders, two of whom caused such a stir by their behavior that even Joshua attempted to have them silenced (Num. 11:24–29). The prophets of Baal also created a commotion on Mount Carmel when they shouted and engaged in self-flagellation (1 Kings 19:28–29).

Prophecy was taken seriously, whether it was announced on someone's inquiry (1 Kings 22:5–6), or at God's initiative, such as in the case of Moses and Aaron's confrontation with Pharaoh. It was treated with great care whether it was given to an individual (1 Sam. 12:1–15) or was proclaimed to a crowd gathered in a sacred place (Amos 7:10–13), though at times the message being announced cut to the hearts of those who listened.

Prophetic words were also tested. Sometimes they were predictive (cf. Jer. 31:27ff.) and therefore subject to tests of fulfillment, while on other occasions they were prescriptive (Hag. 1:1–12) and thus were tested on the basis of existing revelation or other grounds. In cases where these oracles proved to be false, the prophet's credibility was to be doubted, and the so-called prophet was to be ignored (Deut. 18:15–22) or even put to death (13:1–5). The bottom line, however, was that genuine prophecy was given by Yahweh to certain individuals, to be spoken as an inspired word on behalf of Yahweh. Moses wished that all of God's people could prophesy (Num. 11:29), and Joel promised that it would finally happen when the Spirit was poured out upon all flesh (Joel 2:28–29).

In the OT and certain intertestamental literature, both apocryphal and pseudepigraphic, there are several passages that appear to suggest that the prophetic Spirit ceased to function for a period of time. In Ps. 74:9, for instance, there appears a lament that "we are given no miraculous signs; no prophets are left, and none of us knows how long this will be." Similarly, when the Maccabees recaptured the temple from the Greeks, they dismantled the altar that had been profaned, and they set the stones aside "until there should come a prophet to tell them what to do with them" (1 Macc. 4:46). At first glance these passages seem to affirm the silence of the prophetic voice, but David Aune has demonstrated the complexity of the times, noting that there were others who

prophesied simultaneously with these claims. Furthermore, Ps. 74:9 probably refers to the fact that the temple prophets at the close of the Solomonic temple period (586 B.C.) had lost credibility in the eyes of the psalmist. Similarly, the Maccabees were probably looking for a specific type of cultic prophet to provide inspired leadership.

The intertestamental period did, however, make a substantial contribution to prophetism in the form of apocalyptic. While it is not precisely the same as prophecy, it is very clearly related to it. The term *apocalypse* is derived from the Greek term *apokalypsis,* meaning "revelation" or "disclosure." Thus, the NT book of Revelation is often called the Apocalypse of John. The term *apocalyptic eschatology* is often used to describe a system of religious beliefs related to a specific type of millenarianism that was present during that period of time. There was even a social movement known as "apocalypticism," which was motivated by these phenomena.

Most clearly related to the gift of prophecy, though, is the appearance of a genre of literature known as apocalyptic literature. The single OT book of this type and the earliest of the apocalypses is Daniel. There are many noncanonical works that emerged during this time, however—many of them pseudonymous (e.g., 1 and 2 Enoch, Apocalypse of Abraham). Their writers and readers took their revelations seriously. Commonly these apocalyptic works were based on "visions" that the writer claims to have experienced. These visions were often, though not always, interpreted by an angel or some other heavenly being, and the author of the apocalypse dutifully recorded the vision and its interpretation in the apocalyptic work. Often these visions were recorded as transcendent realities within a theoretical framework of history, using a high degree of symbolism (e.g., numerology).

II. PROPHECY IN THE NEW TESTAMENT.

A. A Pauline Perspective.

Paul speaks of prophecy on several occasions, and it is he who first labeled it among the *charismata,* the gifts of the Holy Spirit. As a manifestation of God's grace *(charis),* it is to be uttered in faith (Rom. 12:6). While the prophet is mentioned as one of God's gifts to the church (Eph. 4:11), it is in the long exposition of 1 Cor. 12–14 that we get the clearest understanding of Paul's thought on the subject.

Like Moses, Paul had a wish that all might prophesy, and repeatedly he exhorted his readers to desire or seek this gift (1 Cor. 14:1, 5, 39). Yet he always viewed prophetic activity as but one manifestation of God's varied grace within the body of Christ, which contained a rich diversity of such manifestations. While it might be the potential for *all* to prophesy, since each Christian possessed the Spirit (Rom. 8:9) and the Spirit was the bestower of this gift (1 Cor. 12:8–11), Paul's metaphor of the body of Christ suggests that he anticipated that only *some* people would be given this gift for use within that body. His rhetorical question in 1 Cor. 12:29, "Are all prophets?" which clearly anticipates a negative response, serves further to underscore this observation. It may also be noted that there are no gender restrictions placed on this gift (1 Cor. 11:5). In each Pauline passage in which prophecy is mentioned (1 Cor. 12–14; Rom. 12; and Eph. 4), it is simply listed in relation to the metaphor of the body of Christ.

Paul was clearly concerned that the exercise of this gift be of benefit to the church. Prophecy had its limitations, of course. It was described as both imperfect and, ultimately, temporary (1 Cor. 13:8). It would disappear when "the perfect" had come. But in the meantime, its purposes were clearly articulated in 1 Cor. 14:3. There were three clearly identifiable purposes: edification, exhortation, and comfort. To put it another way, prophecy was to build up, encourage, and/or console the people of God. While its primary functions aided the believer (14:22), this gift could also hold an evangelistic and/or an ethical edge. Paul noted that an unbeliever who happened to come into the assembly where this gift was manifest might recognize the presence of God and be convicted of the reality of his or her own sinfulness. The result would be that this person, too, might come to worship God (14:24–25). Jesus' own prophetic character was recognized in much this same way by the woman at the well (John 4:9) as she moved from distrust to faith.

Paul argued that in order to provide the body of Christ with clear benefit, prophecy needs to be used according to general guidelines whose aim it is to guarantee a properly functioning body. First and foremost among these guidelines was a recognition that the proper use of this gift was to serve as a reflection of the Giver. Since God is a God of peace and order, the use of this gift should be consistent with that fact. If it seeks to call attention to itself or to the person who claims to possess it, it denies the character of God (1 Cor. 14:26–33).

Second, it is a gift that is sovereignly bestowed by the Spirit of God (12:11). As such, and consistent with the OT pattern, some people would be given this gift while others would not. Paul's contention was, however, that such diversity contributes to the body's smooth functioning, which includes the orderly proclamation of prophetic oracles. How was this to be done?

Whenever the congregation gathered, Paul argued, prophetic leadership was to be shared. Each person with a prophetic word was to be given a turn. But he was not to control the floor; rather, preference was to be given to others through whom God might choose to speak (14:29–31). As Paul described the use of this gift, he did so in a very matter-of-fact way. It was simply a means for the Holy Spirit to convey a message from God to his people through an inspired intermediary. It came in the language of those who

heard it, enabling the gift to provide edification to the congregation (14:6).

The orderliness with which this gift was to be used is equally significant. Paul clearly did not define prophecy as some form of wild-eyed ecstatic phenomenon. The speaker had final control over how the prophetic word was proclaimed. The spirits of the prophets, he wrote, are subject to the prophets (14:32). Those who prophesy are not out of control, driven into some ecstatic frenzy, nor are they so "Spirit-possessed" that their personality is lost in the "divine." The speaker is human and totally in control of his or her ability to speak. Prophets may begin to speak or cease from speaking at their own initiative (14:30). There can be no legitimate claim that the Spirit has "overcome" them, forcing them to act.

Paul also recommended that the congregation even recognize a limited role for prophetic utterances that would be allowed in a given service. He suggested that two or three persons be allowed to speak (14:29) before testing. It is clear that this gift of prophecy, while very significant for the life of the congregation, should be only one component of the Christian meeting, not the whole meeting. Room should be left for a variety of other Spirit-inspired contributions; a hymn, a word of instruction, a revelation, even a tongue and its interpretation (14:26). Prophecy was not to dominate, nor was it to have an independent authority.

To guarantee that the prophetic offerings were indeed the mind of the Holy Spirit, Paul noted that an assessment needed to be made. It was an assessment of *what was spoken* (content) more than it was an assessment of *the person who spoke* (medium). In his instructions written to the Thessalonian Christians, Paul had already exhorted the church not to quench the Spirit or to despise prophesying. Instead, he had offered the advice to *test* it *(dokimazete),* accepting what was good in it while avoiding what was not (1 Thess. 5:19–22). In that context his words were addressed to the entire congregation, not merely to a specific group of prophets within it.

In 1 Cor. 14:29 Paul stated that the weighing or testing *(diakrinetōsan)* of the prophetic oracles was to be undertaken by the "others." It is possible to argue that the "others" to whom Paul refers here are other specially equipped "prophets" within the congregation. Indeed, this is a very popular interpretation of this passage. But if this injunction in 14:29 is read in the light of Paul's words to the Thessalonian Christians, the pool of "testers" is broadened to include members from throughout the congregation. The "others" may well be the rest of the congregation, including the other "prophets." This interpretation is also possible from the text, provides more consistency with Paul's overall argument, and allows for a wider dimension of the Spirit's activity in the whole congregation.

For Paul the gift of the discerning of spirits *(diakriseis pneumatōn)* is repeatedly understood to have a complementary relationship to the gift of prophecy (1 Cor. 12:10; 1 Thess. 5:20–21) in much the same way that the gift of tongues is complemented by the gift of the interpretation of tongues. Yet the metaphor of the body of Christ governs Paul's observation that the sovereign work of the Spirit is to grant the ability to test to whomever God may choose to give it, not merely to certain "prophets."

Paul is convinced that the community is best protected and edified by testing prophetic claims. So strongly does he hold to this belief that he describes his guidelines for the proper use of the gift of prophecy as being a "command of the Lord" (1 Cor. 14:37). In Paul's teaching, then, the Spirit inspires the prophetic utterance, demands that it be tested, and provides through the community of faith the means to determine its trustworthiness. Those who wish to speak but who refuse to allow for such testing may, like those in the OT, safely be ignored (14:38) by the Christian community.

B. A Lukan Perspective.

In the second volume that Luke addressed to Theophilus (cf. Luke 1:1–4; Acts 1:1–5), Luke provides examples of genuine Christian prophecy and mentions pagan "prophetic" practices. In Acts 16:16–18 he records an incident with some parallels to the prophetic phenomena prevalent in the Apollo or Pythian cult at Delphi (cf. section I.B above, Greek and Roman Prophetic Activity). In Philippi there was a slave girl who worked by divining, or telling fortunes. She followed Paul and Silas, crying, "These men are servants of the Most High God, who are telling you the way to be saved" (16:17). After repeated encounters with her, Paul became annoyed. What she proclaimed was true, but Paul apparently recognized the demonic origin of her words, and he spoke to the spirit within her, saying, "In the name of Jesus Christ I command you to come out of her!" Implicitly, at least, Luke is obviously in agreement with Paul. Prophecy needs to be tested, since some oracles, even those with what appears to be acceptable or truthful content, can be demonically inspired.

Luke also recorded two striking incidents of genuine Christian prophecy. In each case, the prophet was Agabus, though the incidents were separated by some 12 intervening years. The first took place in Antioch. There Agabus stood up and signified, or foretold *(esēmanen)*, by the Spirit that a famine was coming over all the earth (Acts 11:27–30). His prophecy was accepted by Luke as genuine on the grounds that it was fulfilled when Claudius was Caesar (11:28). The question can be raised, however, How did the Christians at Antioch know that it was genuine? Luke does not provide the answer to that question, but for them not to act until after the famine would have been not to take advantage of the warning. Thus, it appears that at times prophecy has value within specific limits of time and space. It has context speci-

ficity, and the ability to test the prophetic gift adequately also lies within that context. The Christian community in Antioch had to act when it discerned that God was actually speaking through Agabus. It is probable that Agabus's word was accepted simply because there were those in Antioch who exercised the ability to discern spirits.

It is equally clear that Agabus's warning, while a part of what the church has come to recognize as Scripture, has no similar hold on the action of the contemporary church. The famine had come and gone. But the Christians whom Agabus addressed in the first century apparently believed the prediction to be genuine, for they acted according to their ability to provide a relief offering for those who would feel the results of the famine the most, their brothers and sisters in Judea. For today's church, Agabus's prophecy must be understood against a different hermeneutical construct; it merely provides instruction and example for such truths as how God provides for the needs of people, how generous the congregation at Antioch was, or how the gift of prophecy functioned in a specific situation.

The second illustration from the prophetic ministry of Agabus took place in Caesarea (Acts 21:10–14). According to 20:22–23, Paul believed that the Holy Spirit was directing him to go to Jerusalem. A problem arose in that as he proceeded along his journey the Holy Spirit also told him (presumably by a word of prophecy) that he would undergo imprisonment and suffering. After sailing from Asia Minor, he landed in the coastal town of Tyre, where, Luke notes, certain Christians told Paul "through the Spirit" *(dia tou pneumatos)* that he was *not* to go to Jerusalem (21:4). Paul had to make a decision. Would he continue the trip or stop it altogether? He chose to continue. When Paul traveled to Caesarea, the hometown of Philip the evangelist and his four virgin daughters who had the ability to prophesy, he and his companions were met by Agabus, who had come from Jerusalem.

In this instance, the actions of Agabus are reminiscent of those of the OT prophets. He not only *spoke* a prophetic word, he also *illustrated* the word by means of a "symbolic action," a graphic picture that, when acted out, made the same point as the spoken oracle (cf. Jer. 13:1–11; 27:1–28:17; Isa. 20:2–6). In this case, Agabus took Paul's belt and bound his own hands and feet with it. Then he proclaimed: "The Holy Spirit says, 'In this way the Jews of Jerusalem will bind the owner of this belt and will hand him over to the Gentiles'" (Acts 21:11). It is clear that this particular oracle was given in a *form* that is similar to many found in the OT. Among the OT prophets, a frequently cited introduction, or "messenger formula," included the words "Thus saith the Lord." Agabus used the same basic form, but it was the Lord the Spirit who spoke. Thus, the "messenger formula" was transformed from "Thus saith the Lord" to "Thus says the Holy Spirit" or "The Holy Spirit says."

What is even clearer from this passage is that here a genuine oracle from God is subject to interpretation and is therefore in need of testing and application. The Christians at Caesarea clearly understood this to be a prophetic warning that Paul should stop his journey. On the other hand, Paul was still determined to follow his initial direction, that he was to go to Jerusalem even if it meant his death. The people understood it to mean, "Paul, don't go!" Paul apparently understood it to mean, "Go, but be prepared for suffering." After extensive discussion as to its meaning, Luke records that those who had confronted and challenged Paul, finally, perhaps even reluctantly, gave in and prayed that the Lord's will would be done (Acts 21:14).

By using concrete examples from everyday life, Luke has provided a series of pictures that reveal much about the gift of prophecy. While false prophecy or divination comes from other spirits, genuine prophecy comes from the Holy Spirit. It may have a predictive element at times, such as in the prophecies of Agabus, though this is not always the case. Prophecy needs assessment and demands application. It is possible for the whole Christian community to misunderstand a genuine prophetic word. It is important, then, to seek clarity on God's will on each occasion when the gift of prophecy is manifest.

One final passage in Acts shows that Peter and Luke understood the breadth that is possible in prophetic speech. In short, they shared the perspective on prophecy that has been noted in Ex. 4. In Acts 2:16–18 Peter declared that when the 120 spoke in tongues on the Day of Pentecost, a clear indication that the Holy Spirit had come, the prophecy of Joel (2:28–29) had been fulfilled. In Joel 2, however, there is no reference to speaking in tongues. What there is, is a reference to the ability to prophesy. Evidently, then, the ability to speak in tongues, the ecstatic activity that led some in the multitude to charge the 120 with public drunkenness, was understood first by Peter, then by many in the multitude, to be a form of "prophetic" speech. This allowed Peter to appeal to Joel in the way he did. It is clear that in one sense Luke, like Paul, distinguished the ability to speak in tongues from the ability to prophesy. Yet in another sense, Luke, in particular, agreed with Peter and the long-standing picture of the OT that prophecy at its most basic level is nothing less than inspired speech given by God through an individual.

C. Prophecy and the Gospel Writers.

Two people who serve in transitional roles between Israel and the church are John the Baptist and Jesus. Each of them is understood to have a prophetic role, John a more focused one, and Jesus, a more paradigmatic one. It is clear that the gospel writers wish to establish John the Baptist as a prophet in continuity with the church. Repeatedly they refer to him as a prophet (e.g., Luke 1:76; 7:26/Matt. 11:9; John 1:21, 25), and the people around John are said to have understood that he was a prophet (e.g., Mark 11:32/Matt. 21:26/Luke 20:6; Matt. 14:5).

A look at John's life finds him "filled with the Holy Spirit even from birth" (Luke 1:15). The angel Gabriel who appeared to Zechariah before John's birth predicted that John's task would be one of bringing people back to God, and in the power of Elijah before him he would prepare the way for the Lord (1:16–17). Thus, John preached near the Jordan, addressing multitudes as a "brood of vipers." His message was one of repentance and forgiveness (Matt. 3:7–10/Luke 3:7–9; Mark 1:4–5). Furthermore, he pointed the way to the one who would follow him, the one who would both purge and baptize with the Holy Spirit and fire (Matt. 3:11–12/Luke 3:16–17; Mark 1:7–8). While the form of John's message as recorded in the Gospels is not identical to the prophetic forms in the OT, a number of parallels exist, especially with Amos's admonition (Amos 5:4–5) and Jeremiah's "summons to flee" (Jer. 4:4–5; 6:1; 50:8–10). More significantly, John the Baptist stands firmly within the prophetic-apocalyptic stream, preaching an imminent divine intervention in history ("the ax is already at the root of the tree" [Matt. 3:10/Luke 3:9]) with an eschatological judgment in response to Israel's wickedness.

R. B. Y. Scott has helped to differentiate between prophecy as it occurred in the OT and preaching as it was carried on in the NT. If the ministry of John the Baptist is studied, the initial reaction might be that he was preaching, not prophesying. But in the NT, preaching (kēussō) always includes the announcement of Good News. Prophecy, on the other hand, merely declares the urgency of belief in and obedience to the declaration of God's will and purpose. With this as a working definition, we can clearly understand that John the Baptist served in a prophetic role.

If some understood John the Baptist to be Elijah redivivus, or the eschatological prophet (John 1:21), people see Jesus in much the same light (Mark 8:27–28/Matt. 16:13–14/Luke 9:18–19; Luke 7:16). Luke in particular develops the prophetic role of Jesus, pointing toward the inevitable fate of prophets who from the first are not acceptable in their hometowns (Luke 4:24) and ultimately are persecuted (Matt. 5:11–12/Luke 6:22–23) or even put to death (Matt. 23:37–39/Luke 13:34–35). But John also repeatedly depicts Jesus as a prophet (e.g., John 4:19; 6:14–15; 7:40; 9:17).

What John the Baptist, as well as Jesus, suggests for those who exercise the gift of prophecy is that they have a somewhat angular fit within church and society. They are not always warmly regarded, nor are their words readily received. Indeed, many who know them may ultimately reject them, precisely because they are prophets. On the other hand, simply because someone claims to be a prophet is no reason to accept everything he or she says. Jesus warned his own disciples on several occasions that false prophets would arise, parading as part of the church. They might appear to be harmless, but in reality they are bent on destruction of the flock (Matt. 7:15; 24:11, 24).

Jesus' concern was apparent in that he noted that such individuals would ultimately be rejected from entering the kingdom of heaven because (1) they were not known by him and (2) they were evildoers. Indeed, he warned his disciples beforehand (Matt. 24:24), he told them to be on guard for those who would lead them astray (v. 4), and he taught them that the false prophet ultimately produces evil fruit (Matt. 7:16–20). Jesus, then, taught that his followers should assess the fruit of those who claim prophetic authority to be sure that it is good. For the church, the norm for "good fruit" lies in Jesus, who is described for us in the apostolic writings, Scripture.

John is the only gospel writer to have written on the role of the Spirit as Paraclete. He incorporated the teachings of Jesus on the Spirit in a series of what have become known as "Paraclete Sayings" (John 14:16–17, 26; 15:26–27; 16:7–15). These sayings make clear the ongoing role of the Spirit among the followers of Christ. The term *paraclete* is related to the term *exhortation (paraklēsis),* whose verbal form means literally "to stand beside," or "to act as an advocate." When Paul wrote on the gift of prophecy, he used this term to describe one purpose of the gift (1 Cor. 14:3). According to Jesus, the Paraclete brings things to the remembrance of his followers (John 14:26), bears witness to Christ (15:26), and guides his followers into all truth (16:13). Indeed, the Paraclete, or Holy Spirit, conveys the mind of Christ to the church.

John also understood himself as functioning within the prophetic tradition of the church. He was well aware that there were many false prophets in the world (1 John 4:1), so he argued that all prophetic words should be tested. Yet he was confident of the genuineness of his own prophetic experience as when "on the Lord's Day [he] was in the Spirit *[en pneumati]* " (Rev. 1:10). What he experienced while "in the Spirit" he proclaimed as a "prophecy," but he also used the terms *revelation* and *apocalypse* (1:10) to describe it, thereby demonstrating his own continuity in the prophetic-apocalyptic tradition.

III. THE GIFT OF PROPHECY IN CHURCH HISTORY.

A. The Early Church.

Within the first several centuries A.D. the church was no stranger to continuing prophetic activity. Room was made within the church structure for prophets to function on both itinerant and local levels. Indeed, the writer to the Ephesians understood them to be foundational to the church (Eph. 2:20), for they received the mystery of Christ that the Gentiles were, through Christ, made "heirs together with Israel, members together of one body" (3:6).

One important 1st-century writing, the *Didache* (c. A.D. 90), was concerned with both types of prophetic activity,

although it appears that the predominant prophetic activity within the communities that accepted the tradition of the *Didache* was an itinerant ministry (*Did.* 10.7; 11:1–12; but see 13:1–7). Following Jesus' admonition to assess the fruit of the "prophet," the writer of the *Didache* instructed his readers to disregard anyone who benefited financially from his or her own prophetic activity. This was particularly true of itinerants. Those who settled down in a particular Christian community, however, were to be supported for their contribution to the spiritual welfare of the community.

The early 2d century reveals the claims that Ignatius, bishop of Antioch, made regarding his own experience with this gift (Ignatius, *Epistle* 7:1–2). While preaching to the congregation at Philadelphia on one occasion, he claimed that the Holy Spirit spoke through him, revealing a problem of disunity within that congregation. Ignatius maintained that until that point in his sermon he had been unaware of the problem, and its exposure in his sermon led to its ultimate resolution.

The *Shepherd of Hermas,* a devotional work most probably originating in Rome in the first third of the 2d century included a series of visions and provided guidelines for distinguishing between true and false prophetic claims (*Herm. Man.* 11). The esteem with which this work was held in the life of the church varied. Irenaeus (*Against Heresies* 4.20.2) called it *hēgraphē* or *scriptura,* a term usually reserved for the canonical writings, although there is some ambiguity attached to Irenaeus's meaning when he used this term. Clement of Alexandria cited the work repeatedly in his *Stromata* (cf. 1.1.1; 1.85.4; 2.3.4; 4.74.4; et al.). Similarly, there is a marked resemblance between portions of Hermas and the visions found in the *Passion of Perpetua and Felicitas* (cf. *Passion* 4.6–7 and *Herm. Vis.* 4.1.4–8). Tertullian, on the other hand, found it offensive because he believed it was lenient on those who had lapsed from the faith during times of persecution (*On Modesty* 10.12). Still, it was believed to provide good devotional food for thought by much of the church, including those who framed the Muratorian canon.

Hermas was particularly concerned for the impact that so-called prophets had on the newly committed Christian, the young, and the spiritually immature. Like the writer of the *Didache* and Jesus before him, he advocated the test of "good fruit." Those who function as false prophets, he argued, are bold and shameless. Some are motivated by power, others by money. He notably singled out those who prophesy on the fringe of a congregation, unnoticed or disregarded by the larger body. He argued against the usefulness of privately given "personal" prophecies. Typically they were nothing more than "empty words" that often left the immature at the mercy of the false prophet (*Herm. Man.* 11).

Competition between at least three different groups for recognition and acceptance of their prophetic claims was intense during this early period. On the one side were those who embraced one or another brand of Gnosticism. Gnostics highlighted exclusive revelation claims as authoritative. Typically they judged the traditions of the apostles to be imperfect (Irenaeus, *Against Heresies* 1.13.6; 1.25.2; 3.12.12; Tertullian, *Prescription against Heretics* 23.1). They held up their own visions and prophecies as being not only indicative of a legitimate and vibrant spirituality, but an authoritative one as well (Hippolytus, *Refutation of All Heresies* 6.37; 7.26; 10.26).

The Montanists, too, believed in the continuation of prophetic phenomena. Originating in Asia Minor in the last half of the 2d century, they held considerable strength in Phrygia and later in North Africa. Problematic though they were, recent scholarship suggests that these believers were essentially orthodox in theology (Hippolytus, *Refutation of All Heresies* 8.12; Epiphanius, *Panarion* 48.1; Jerome, *Epistle* 41.3). Their tendencies toward asceticism and apocalypticism, however, often brought them into conflict with church leaders.

Tertullian (*On Monogamy* 4.1; 2.2) found in the Paraclete saying of John 16:12–13 ample justification for even the ascetic claims of this prophetic movement. From this passage he argued that through continuing prophetic activity, the Holy Spirit reveals to the church the mind of Christ little by little. The disciples had been unable to accept and process adequately everything that Jesus had intended for them to hear. Thus, by means of a form of progressive apostolic tradition found in Scripture and the *regula fidei,* or "rule of faith" (Tertullian, *On Monogamy* 2.2–3), the church had opportunity to accept or reject what the Spirit had revealed to the church in the form of visions and prophecies.

To be sure, excesses were found in some Montanist prophecies. It appears that some predicted the imminent return of Christ, perhaps with setting dates for that event (Epiphanius, *Heresies* 48.2), while others pointed to Pepuza, a city in Asia Minor, as the New Jerusalem (Eusebius, *Ecclesiastical History* 5.18.1). Most, however, were understood as providing guidance in specific situations (Tertullian, *On Flight in Persecution* 9.4) or as providing supplementary support for certain teachings thought already to be evident in Scripture (cf. Tertullian, *On Modesty* 21.7; *On Chastity* 10.5; *On the Resurrection of the Flesh* 11.2). The most substantial problem associated with Montanist prophecy was the question of authority. How far did it legitimately extend, and what relationship did it have to the official church authorities of the day?

The third group that claimed the activity of prophetic gifts were the orthodox themselves. The *Didache* clearly fell within this context, as did the *Shepherd of Hermas.* Irenaeus (*Against Heresies* 5.6.1) noted the existence of genuine prophecies in his day and spoke against those who rejected the gift (*Demonstrations of the Apostolic Preaching* 99). In the East, Origen, who lived in Alexandria (203–231), then moved to Caesarea (232–253), had little time for either Pythian or Montanist claims. He rejected all forms of ecstasy *(ekstasia),* frenzy *(maniken),* or trance as signs of genuine prophetic activity. Yet he did believe in the genuineness of some prophetic claims. As Origen taught it, prophecy came at a moment of revelation in which the prophet saw things clearly and was then able to communicate the profound truths of Christian doctrine revealed by the Holy Spirit, truths that had been received in that moment (*Against Celsus* 7.3). It helped to provide biblical understanding and spiritual growth to the Christian community. Thus, Origen appears to have been the first Christian writer to identify the gift with a form of exposition on the biblical text. The revealed understanding of the text was a prophetic word.

Prophecy, dreams, and visions found a unique place in the life of many early martyrs, as well as within the life of the much-persecuted North African church. Indeed, because of the presence of the martyr Perpetua; the advocate of Montanism, Tertullian; and the charismatic bishop Cyprian, the North African church seems to have been more actively involved in such activities than any other church of the 3d century.

At least four categories of prophetic revelations may be found in writings that originated from the church at Carthage at that time. First among these is the fact that many individuals received ecclesiastical appointment or confirmation of an appointment by this means (Cyprian, *Epistles* 39.1, 4; 40; 48.4; 63.1; 66.5, 10). That this practice was widespread may be observed from the fact that more than 30 other people joined Cyprian in one appointment made by this means (Cyprian, *Epistle* 70).

Second, were the many visions/prophecies that were given to provide comfort to the Confessors, those who had already been tried for their faith and were either awaiting sentencing, serving a sentence, or awaiting their execution (Cyprian, *Epistles* 6.1–2; 10.4; 58.1; 78.1–2). Indeed, the persecuted church understood the ability of an individual to make a confession before the magistrates to be a fulfillment of Jesus' promise that at such a time as they were persecuted, the Holy Spirit would provide them with a prophetic response (Matt. 10:19–20; Mark 13:9–13; Luke 12:11–12; 21:11–19). Thus, there appears to have been a close relationship between prophecy and martyrdom.

Third, there were those times when visions and prophecies provided personal guidance or direction. Cyprian claimed to have been directed into hiding by the Lord (Cyprian, *Epistle* 16.4, 7) at the time of a severe persecution about A.D. 252. During a later persecution, in A.D. 257, Cyprian received another revelation that allegedly foretold of his martyrdom (*Life and Passion of Cyprian* 7), thereby enabling him to set his house in order.

At times, appeals to such revelations were also used to provide direction to a congregation. Such a usage of revelatory claims does raise questions of discernment and the possibility of improper manipulation of the gullible (cf. von Harnack), but the claim still remains. On at least four occasions Cyprian provided leadership and exhortation to the congregations over which he presided as bishop by appealing to prophetic claims (*Epistle* 11.1–4) that exhorted the churches to unity in a time of deep conflict.

In spite of the widespread character of the gift of prophecy, it did lose some of its spontaneity as time progressed. Adolf von Harnack saw that fact as in some way related to the formation of the biblical canon. David Hill and David Aune have suggested that prophetic phenomena came into disrepute by their association with such sects as the Montanists and the rise of a class of more "rational" theologians and teachers. James Ash has argued that the decline in the prophetic gifts was due to the identification of these gifts with those in church leadership and especially with the bishop. Undoubtedly, there are elements of truth in each of these explanations. Indeed, only by a movement from the spontaneous to an emphasis on the formalized did it become possible for Chrysostom (*Homily* 29 on 1 Cor. 12:1–2) to plead ignorance of what Paul meant when he wrote about spiritual gifts, because they "no longer take place." Still, prophetic gifts were present even in the more routine aspects and offices of a maturing church. It is also possible to identify them outside the church's formal structure.

B. The Middle Ages.

In the church of the Middle Ages, much of divine activity was viewed as operating within the bounds of official ecclesiastical structure. Prophetic activity was not limited to the formal structure by any means, for there were numerous outbursts of a more spontaneous nature among many, especially those who had embraced monastic life. This was true even more in the East than in the West. There were also many others to whom charismatic abilities were attributed and who were ultimately canonized by official church action as "saints," in part because of these abilities. On the whole, however, there is clear evidence that the regular church understood the *charismata* as being present in a more or less routine way with the order of Christian leadership. As early as Basil of Caesarea (A.D. 330–379), those called to Christian leadership were assumed to stand in the prophetic tradition.

Thomas Aquinas, a leading scholastic theologian of the medieval church (A.D. 1225–74), did much not only to systematize Catholic thinking in his day, but he has been a primary factor within Roman Catholic thinking ever since. Among his works were *De Veritate* and his multifaceted *Summa Theologiae*, in which he addressed the nature and working of the gift of prophecy at some length (2a 2ae. 171–75).

Arguing from an Aristotelian philosophical base, Thomas attempted to show the usefulness of this gift for the church. He understood it to be a charism or gratuitous gift (*gratias gratis datae*) given by God. It was, he argued, but one of several gifts including the words of knowledge and of wisdom, faith, and the discernment of spirits that could be subsumed under the broader category of "prophecy," because each of these shared a form of "prophetic revelation." Prophetic revelation not only involves prediction of future human events but also discloses contemporary divine realities (*res divinas;* 2a 2ae. 171, *Prol.*). Thus, for Thomas the prophet becomes a mediator of divine revelation, who through this gift instructs people in "whatever is necessary for salvation" (*De Veritate,* 12, a.2c).

The person who receives such a gift is divinely chosen, since it is a charism of grace (*De Veritate,* 2a 2ae. 172, a3a). It is given to those whom God determines are best suited to receive it. Thus, it is sometimes given to those who, humanly speaking, appear to be immature. The granting of this gift comes independently of sanctification or spiritual maturity. The best and deepest use of this gift, however, may be enhanced by sanctification since this gift requires the maximum elevation of the mind (*maxima meatis elevatio*) to things contemplative and spiritual. This "elevation" of the mind to see things that God chooses to uncover or disclose is hampered when things of the flesh such as passions (*passionum*) or a preoccupation with externalities (*exteriorum*) enter into the picture (2a 2ae. 172, a5d).

As for the method by which prophetic revelation occurs, Aquinas believed it is principally through the mind. The prophet's mind (*mens*) is moved (*movetus*) by the Holy Spirit in the same way a defective instrument is moved by its first cause. Thus, the Holy Spirit moves the prophet's mind in such a way as to perceive or apprehend, speak, or act. At times, all three of these outcomes could result from the Spirit's movement. And while it is possible that the prophet might understand all that transpires in this way, it is not necessarily the case that this will be so, for there is a possibility that the prophet's own knowledge will be defective.

Thomas also held that there were both true and false prophecies and that demons were capable of inspiring false prophecy. While a true prophet inspired by the Spirit of truth (*Spiritu veritatis*) could prophesy without a trace of falsehood, the false prophet, instructed by the spirit of falsehood, would intermingle truth with falsehood. Thus, ultimately the prophecy given by the false prophet was false prophecy.

C. Reformation and Post-Reformation Understandings.

The issue of prophecy was an important factor during the Reformation. About 1529 Martin Luther penned his famous hymn "A Mighty Fortress Is Our God," in which he affirmed that "the Spirit and the gifts are ours." He believed in the priesthood of believers and the presence of *charismata* in his day. Yet he was troubled both by Roman abuses and what he perceived to be the subjective excesses of the so-called heavenly prophets. In Luther's thinking, "when Paul or the other apostles interpreted the Old Testament, their interpretation was prophecy" (*On Joel* 2:28). Furthermore, he seemed to place all "who can expound the Scriptures and ably interpret and teach the difficult books" as prophesying (*On Zechariah* [preface]).

Martin Luther, however, disagreed violently with the claims of the Zwickau prophets led by Thomas Münzer. He believed that their expositions and their signs were "worthless" (*On Joel* 2:28). Similarly, Luther's former colleague Andreas Karlstadt became known as a "heavenly prophet" after he defected from Luther. In 1525 Luther wrote of Karlstadt's interpretations of Scripture as "false prophecies," and he warned the churches against them. As a means of responding to these false "prophecies," Luther urged the readers of his work *Against the Heavenly Prophets* to pray for a "right understanding" of God's Word, and he exhorted them to stand guard against false prophetic claims.

John Calvin held a position on the gift of prophecy that was similar to that of Martin Luther. He noted that all the ancient prophecies and divine oracles were concluded in Christ and the gospel. Thus, the canon appears to have entered into Calvin's understanding as the ultimate or final word spoken to the church. Further prophetic activity was limited to a clearer understanding of this final word. In his *Commentary on Romans* (12:5) he said, "Prophecy . . . is simply the right understanding of Scripture and the particular gift of expounding it." Clearly, though, emphasis was placed on the prophetic as something that did not occur spontaneously but, like Origen's position, was more akin to the concept of illumination. It did not seem to be fresh revelation but primarily correct understanding and application of existing revelation.

If the Protestant Reformation and its leaders brought about renewal in the church, they also made it possible for a resurgence of more or less independent prophetic claims. During the late 17th and early 18th centuries, Christians in Cevennes raised a considerable stir by making prophetic claims. "Prophetic" manifestations were particularly common among younger people, male and female, who, upon entering into trances, recited extended passages of Scripture, preached sermons, and indicted those who listened, sometimes addressing specific individuals.

Other prophetic phenomena can be traced in groups that were largely marginal to mainstream Christianity. The Quakers preserved a more or less radical notion of the Spirit through experiences of the Inner Light. Others who made prophetic claims included the Ranters, an English extremist group, and the Shakers. In both cases they adopted unorthodox, even heretical, positions. Perhaps the most significant

movement to claim spontaneous prophetic inspiration during the early 19th century was that associated with Church of Scotland minister Edward Irving. Unfortunately, his adoption of an aberrant Christology led to his being deposed from Church of Scotland ranks. He later became associated with the Holy Catholic Apostolic Church, where a variety of *charismata* were welcome. For the most part, however, the gift of prophecy since the Reformation has been closely identified with preaching. It is only as the Holiness movement drew toward the end of the 19th century that the issues of spontaneous inspiration began to reemerge.

IV. PROPHECY IN CONTEMPORARY UNDERSTANDING.

Within the pentecostal-charismatic movements, the gift of prophecy has held a significant place. It was present in the earliest pentecostal and charismatic meetings, and it continues to play an important role in the contemporary experience of these renewal movements. Discussion most frequently revolves around two basic issues. They are the question of (1) how to distinguish genuine oracles from false ones and (2) what authority contemporary oracles have in light of a closed canon of Scripture.

A. True and False Prophecy.

It is clear from Scripture that prophecy is meant to be understood as a gift that is inspired by God through the Holy Spirit; granted to individuals for purposes of edification, exhortation, and comfort; and intended to communicate the mind of God. But for someone to claim that he or she is speaking on behalf of God makes the issue of discerning between true and false claims a critical one. The early Christian community was undoubtedly faced with this problem when it attempted to determine the limits of apostolic and prophetic claims, especially as questions of *regulae fidei* (rules of faith) and canon emerged. Modern discussions on the nature of canon and how it functioned in the earliest Christian community, then, may be informative here.

Questions were raised then, as they should be now, as to what relationship contemporary prophetic claims had to accepted apostolic tradition. Today the major link with the apostles and their teachings is the NT, just as the writings of the OT played an authoritative role in the apostles' lives and provided a link for them with the people of God who had preceded them. Thus, Scripture becomes the key by which contemporary "prophets" and prophecies may be assessed. Questions of how well prophetic claims contribute to the stability of the Christian community or challenge it within the limits of the apostolic faith and tradition and how widely adaptable such utterances are for the whole Christian community are equally significant. Mere personal claims to ecstatic experience and self-reported tales of visionary activity prove fruitless as sources of authentication for prophetic authority.

With Scripture as the norm, at least three basic criteria emerge that may aid the community in the assessment of prophetic claims. There may be more, but these three are found repeatedly in Scripture and in the workings of the church. They include an assessment of the person who prophesies, reflection on the process by which the prophecy is transmitted, and an evaluation of its content.

Guidelines on who may prophesy in a Christian meeting vary. Within those churches that view it solely as Christian preaching, the answer lies in the preacher or exhorter. Within a large congregation, testing is sometimes accomplished in advance by having the would-be "prophet" pass the word before authorized elders or "prophets" or, within a Roman Catholic setting, before the priest. On other occasions, people may be allowed to speak from the floor, and the whole group is given opportunity to weigh the words. Yet in each case it is usually understood that those who speak are part of the community of faith, and thus they come under the authority of the community and its canon, Scripture, or else the person has been referred by another community whose judgment is trusted. Hence, the problems raised by prophetic claims made by strangers or by non-Christians are greatly reduced.

The test of methodology is equally helpful. Paul argued that God is a God of peace and order, and as such the use of charismata should reflect God's nature (1 Cor. 14:32–39). In addition, Scripture repeatedly recommends and invites testing to occur (Deut. 13:1–3; Matt. 7:15–23; 1 Thess. 5:19–22). Indeed, Paul noted that the Holy Spirit provides a testing charism, the discerning of spirits, for just such a purpose. Hence, those who are disruptive; who refuse to submit to community orders or its canon, Scripture; who refuse to be tested; or who place themselves in a position of authority beyond the ability of the community to provide testing, are to be ignored (1 Cor. 14:29–33a, 37–38).

Often the most helpful test may focus on what is actually said. If Scripture is normative within the Christian community, then one does not anticipate that a contemporary prophetic statement will contradict it. In the postapostolic age many prophetic claims were rejected simply because they were inconsistent with the apostolic tradition as it was found in the apostolic or NT writings and various *regulae fidei*. Perhaps the most notable of these were the many Gnostic claims that sought a legitimate place in the Christian community by alleging new revelations or personal visitations from one apostle who attempted to undermine the authority of other apostles (e.g., *Apocalypse of James* [C.G. 1.1.2]) or to generate the new teachings said to supersede the prior teachings of those in the biblical tradition (e.g., *Apocalypse of John* [C.G. 2.1.13]; Irenaeus *Against Heresies* [1.10.1–2]).

In recent years prophetic claims have had more to do with personal guidance than with predictions of the future and more to say to local congregations than to the larger church. There are exceptions to this, such as the numerous "prophe-

cies" that have been recorded and widely circulated in magazines and newsletters in charismatic renewal circles. David Wilkerson's book *The Vision* is one that is clearly meant to convey a predictive word to the larger church. Although Wilkerson has denied prophetic status, the reader of his *Vision* is hard pressed to reach the same conclusion. Care must be exercised in accepting a word of prediction in that a test of fulfillment must ultimately be invoked, and great damage and disillusionment may occur if it is ultimately found to be false. Likewise, the circulation of written prophecies can be confusing, since some will ultimately treat them with some form of an ongoing canonical status. Joseph Smith's alleged revelation that produced the *Book of Mormon* and the esteem with which certain writings of Ellen G. White are held provide significant examples.

B. Limits of Prophetic Authority.

The second issue is related to the first one. Given that the Christian community recognizes the need to test prophetic claims, and given that there exist within the body of Christ the necessary gifts and people to make possible an assessment of these claims, how far does prophetic authority extend? Many within the Reformed and dispensational camps suggest that the issue is easily resolved. Appeal is made to Heb. 1:1–2 to demonstrate that all genuine prophetic authority has ceased, since God has given the ultimate Word to humankind in the person of Jesus Christ. This passage is then used as a key to 1 Cor. 13:10 to argue that "the perfect" has come in Jesus Christ and that therefore prophecies have ceased. Prophetic activity is understood to have reached its apex in Jesus and in those through whom he revealed his will, the NT apostles and prophets. Thus, the NT writings are understood to be the final prophetic words given through human beings, with the gifts of prophecy generally understood to have ceased around the end of the 2d century (cf. Warfield) or at the time in which the NT canon was formally recognized.

This position provides the church with protection from Mormon or pentecostal claims today, but it seems necessarily to avoid a great deal of historical data. Similarly it tends to move 1 Cor. 13:10 outside the immediate context of 1 Cor. 13 for interpretation. The immediate context seems to suggest that "the perfect" *(to teleion)* to which Paul makes reference is the parousia. The parallels that exist between this critical passage and the obviously eschatological reference found in 1 John 3:2 are significant.

The majority of the church, however, has never argued that prophecy ceased upon the deaths of the apostles or with the completion of the NT canon. A review of historical data appears to demonstrate that prophecy became more or less routine, was captured by the episcopacy, and was used in a way that further established the authority of the episcopacy. This position has found its ultimate form in the Roman Catholic doctrine of papal infallibility, where *ex cathedra* statements are made. Still, this act has been infrequently invoked, and all such pronouncements following the teaching of Paul are subject to scrutiny by the Roman magisterium before acceptance.

In spite of apparent attempts to limit the prophetic spirit—by the adoption of a theological system that in essence rules all later utterances as illegitimate prophetic claims, by anticipating that all legitimate claims originate within the episcopacy, or by removing the potentially spontaneous character of this gift by defining it as did Luther and Calvin as a form of expository preaching or teaching—the spontaneous character of this gift has been demonstrated frequently in the church in a variety of sects and cults. But this fact brings the discussion back to the beginning. What is the limit of prophetic authority? Within the Christian tradition it must be limited by the teachings of Scripture as understood by the members of the community of faith as they seek to submit themselves one to another and to live under the guidance of Scripture as the ultimate written authority in all matters of faith and practice.

The renewal of interest in the gift of prophecy speaks well for the church at the end of the 20th century. While some are occupied with debates on whether early Christian prophets later "created" prophetic statements attributed to Jesus, others argue that the prophetic vocation holds great importance for the ecumenical vision of the church for the future. Insofar as Christians listen for the voice of God, discern what is that voice, and act upon it, this *charisma* will be of profit to the whole church as it faces the challenge of a new millennium.

See also GIFTS OF THE SPIRIT.

■ **Bibliography:** A. Aubert, ed. *Prophets in the Church* (1968) ■ D. E. Aune, *Prophecy in Early Christianity and the Ancient Mediterranean World* (1983) ■ M. Bickle, *Growing in the Prophetic* (1996) ■ J. Blenkinsopp, *A History of Prophecy in Israel* (1983) ■ M. Bockmuehl, *Revelation and Mystery in Ancient Judaism and Pauline Christianity* (1997) ■ E. M. Boring, *Sayings of the Risen Christ: Christian Prophecy in the Synoptic Tradition* (1982) ■ S. M. Burgess, *The Spirit and the Church: Antiquity* (1984) ■ R. P. Carroll, *When Prophecy Failed* (1979) ■ A. H. Chroust, "Inspiration in Ancient Greece," in E. D. O'Connor, ed., *Perspective on Charismatic Renewal* (1975) ■ R. E. Clements, *Prophecy and Covenant* (1965) ■ R. Coggins, A. Phillips, and M. Knibb, eds., *Israel's Prophetic Tradition* (1982) ■ J. L. Crenshaw, *Prophetic Conflict: Its Effect upon Israelite Religion* (1971) ■ T. M. Crone, *Early Christian Prophecy: A Study of Its Origin and Function* (1973) ■ G. Dautzenberg, *Urchristliche Prophetie* (1975) ■ A. B. Davidson, *Old Testament Prophecy* (1904) ■ E. Ellis, *Prophecy and Hermeneutic in Early Christianity* (1978) ■ J. Fontenrose, *The Delphic Oracle: Its Responses and Operations* (1978) ■ C. Forbes, *Prophecy and Inspired Speech in Early Christianity and Its Hellenistic Environment* (1995) ■ C. Garrett, *Spirit Possession and Popular Religion: From the Camisards to the Shakers* (1987) ■ D. Gee, *Concerning Spiritual Gifts* (rev. ed., 1980) ■ T. W. Gillespie, *The First Theologians: A Study in Early Christian Prophecy* (1994) ■ W. A. Grudem, *The Gift of Prophecy in 1 Corinthians* (1982) ■ idem, *The Gift of Prophecy in the New Testament and Today* (1988) ■ A. Guillaume, *Prophecy and Divination* (1938) ■ H. A. Guy, *New Testament Prophecy: Its Origin and Significance* (1947) ■ A. J. Heschel, *The Prophets*, 2 vols. (1962) ■ D. Hill, *New Testament Prophecy* (1979) ■ H. Horton, *The Gifts of the Spirit* (1971) ■ E. C. Huber, *Women and the Authority of Inspiration* (1985) ■ A. R. Johnson, *The Cultic Prophet in Ancient Israel* (1944, 1962) ■ C. Klein, *The Psychological Pattern of Old Testament Prophecy* (1956) ■ K. Koch, *The Prophets*, 2 vols. (1983, 1984) ■ T. A. Kselman, *Miracles and Prophecies in Nineteenth-Century France* (1983) ■ R. A. N. Kydd, *Charismatic Gifts in the Early Church* (1984) ■ G. W. H. Lampe, "Martyrdom and Inspiration," in W. Horbury, *Suffering and Martyrdom in the New Testament* (1981) ■ R. E. Lerner, *The Powers of Prophecy* (1983) ■ J. Lindblom, *Prophecy in Ancient Israel* (1973) ■ U. B. Müller, *Prophetie und Predigt im Neuen Testament* (1975) ■ N. I. Nidiokwere, *Prophecy and Revolution: The Role of Prophets in the Independent African Churches and in Biblical Tradition* (1981) ■ J. Panagopoulos, *He Ekklesia tôn prophetikôn: To prophetikon charisma en te Ekklesia tôn duo prôtôn aiônôn* (1979) ■ idem, *Prophetic Vocation in the New Testament Today* (1977) ■ H. W. Parke, *The Oracles of Zeus* (1967) ■ H. W. Parke and D. E. W. Wormell, *The Delphic Oracle*, 2 vols. (1956) ■ D. L. Peterson, *The Roles of Israel's Prophets* (1981) ■ D. Potter, *Prophets and Emperors: Human and Divine Authority from Augustus to Theodosius* (1994) ■ J. R. Pridie, *The Spiritual Gifts* (1921) ■ F. Rahman, *Prophecy in Islam: Philosophy and Orthodoxy* (1958; repr. 1979) ■ K. Rahner, *Visions and Prophecies* (1983) ■ J. Reiling, *Hermas and Christian Prophecy* (1973) ■ C. M. Robeck Jr., *Prophecy in Carthage: Perpetua, Tertullian, and Cyprian* (1992) ■ idem, "Canon, Regulae Fidei, and Continuing Revelation in the Early Church," in J. E. Bradley and R. A. Muller, eds., *Church, Word and Spirit* (1987) ■ idem, "The Gift of Prophecy in Acts and Paul, Parts I & II," in *Studia Biblica et Theologica* (1975) ■ idem, "Written Prophecies: A Question of Authority," *Pneuma* 2 (2, 1980) ■ H. W. Robinson, *Inspiration and Revelation in the Old Testament* (1946; repr. 1967) ■ T. H. Robinson, *Prophecy and the Prophets in Ancient Israel* (1923, 1953; repr. 1967) ■ F. Rousseau, *L'Apocalypse et le Milieu Prophétique du Nouveau Testament* (1971) ■ C. Rowland, *The Open Heaven: A Study of Apocalyptic in Judaism and Early Christianity* ■ H. H. Rowley, "The Nature of Old Testament Prophecy in the Light of Recent Study," in H. H. Rowley, *The Servant of the Lord* (1952, 1965) ■ D. S. Russell, *The Method and Message of Jewish Apocalyptic* (1964) ■ R. B. Y. Scott, *The Relevance of the Prophets* (1944) ■ C. Westermann, *Prophetic Oracles of Salvation in the Old Testament* (1991) ■ R. R. Wilson, *Prophecy and Society in Ancient Israel* (1980) ■ A. C. Wire, *The Corinthian Women Prophets: A Reconstruction through Paul's Rhetoric* (1990) ■ H. W. Wolff, *Confrontations with Prophets* (1983) ■ B. Yocum, *Prophecy: Exercising the Prophetic Gifts of the Spirit in the Church Today* (1976) ■ E. J. Young, *My Servants the Prophets* (1952).   ■ C. M. Robeck Jr.

PULKINGHAM, WILLIAM GRAHAM (1926–93). Episcopal priest. Ordained in 1958, William G. Pulkingham became rector of the Church of the Redeemer in Houston, TX, in 1963. The poverty of the slum district and the futility of ministry there drove him to seek the power of the Holy Spirit. Under his leadership, committed families moved into the neighborhood, eventually rejuvenating worship and parish life. Their common life soon became an inspiration for others seeking such relationships in their own church settings.

In 1972 Pulkingham moved to England and later founded Community of Celebration, which was based on Cumbrae Island. Its extension ministry, the Fisherfolk, traveled worldwide teaching folk arts in worship. Hymns and liturgical settings developed by the Fisherfolk and Pulkingham's gifted wife, Betty, have contributed significantly to modern Christian community worship. In 1985 the Community of Celebration moved to Aliquippa, PA.

■ **Bibliography:** M. Durran, *The Wind at the Door* (1986) ▉ W. Pulkingham, *Gathered for Power* (1972) ▉ idem, *They Left Their Nets* (1973).   ■ C. M. Irish

PURDIE, JAMES EUSTACE (1880–1977). Canadian churchman and educator. Having graduated in 1907 from Wycliffe College, an Anglican seminary in Toronto, Purdie immediately launched into a successful ministry in the Anglican church in Canada, serving parishes in Manitoba, New Brunswick, and Saskatchewan from 1907 to 1922. He was baptized in the Holy Spirit in 1919 in the midst of his tenure in one of these. After a brief ministry in Philadelphia in a Reformed Episcopal church in 1925, he was invited to become the founding principal of Canadian Pentecostal Bible College to be situated in Winnipeg, Man., the first full-time Bible school to be operated by the ▸Pentecostal Assemblies of Canada (PAOC). Purdie held this position until his retirement in 1950. Following retirement, he continued to minister widely within the PAOC, but he also maintained ties with the Anglican Church. He preached and assisted at communion in a parish in Winnipeg until as late as 1975.

Purdie's outstanding contribution was theological. He modeled his college's curriculum after that of Wycliffe College, insisting on a thorough understanding of doctrine and emphasizing church history along with biblical studies. "Pastoralia" was also important, with stress being placed on preaching and conducting worship services. His work is widely credited with providing the foundation for the theological stability enjoyed by the PAOC.

The other major theme of Purdie's ministry was evangelism. As a young Anglican, he held outdoor services and saw rapid growth in his parishes. He also organized evangelistic missions and Bible conferences.

■ **Bibliography:** K. R. Davis, "Purdie, James Eustace," *NIDCC* (1974) ▉ R. A. N. Kydd, "The Contribution of Denominationally Trained Clergymen to the Emerging Pentecostal Movement in Canada," *Pneuma* 5 (1983) ▉ idem, "Pentecostals, Charismatics, and the Canadian Denominations," *Eglise et Théologie* 13 (1982) ▉ B. R. Ross, "The Emergence of Theological Education within the Pentecostal Assemblies of Canada" (thesis, U. of Toronto, 1971) ▉ idem, "James Eustace Purdie: The Story of Pentecostal Theological Education," *Journal of the Canadian Church Historical Society* 17 (1975).   ■ R. A. N. Kydd

PYTCHES, DAVID (1931–). International Anglican renewal teacher. Ordained as a priest in 1956, Pytches volunteered for service with the South American Missionary Society and went out with his wife, Mary, to Chile in 1959. In 1969 Mary was baptized in the Spirit on the boat returning to Chile; this led Pytches to seek the same experience, which followed some months later. In 1970 he became suffragan bishop, and in 1972, bishop of Chile, Bolivia, and Peru. Some of Pytches' experiences of renewal as bishop are described in "The Spirit and Evangelism" in *Bishops' Move* (ed. ▸M. Harper [1978]). Pytches resigned as bishop in Latin America in 1976, becoming vicar of St. Andrew's, Chorleywood, Hertfordshire, England (1977–96). The Pytcheses' experience of the miraculous in Latin America had prepared them for the ▸"signs and wonders" teaching of ▸John Wimber and for later phenomena, such as those associated with Kansas City and with Toronto. Pytches' book *Spiritual Gifts in the Local Church* (1985—U.K. title *Come, Holy Spirit*), which almost acquired textbook status among Anglican charismatics, was followed by *Some Say It Thundered: A Personal Encounter with the Kansas City Prophets* (1991). Mary Pytches' book on inner healing, *Set My People Free* (1987), complements her husband's earlier work.   ■ P. D. Hocken

Q

QUAKERS (SOCIETY OF FRIENDS) The Society of Friends was founded by George Fox (1624–90) in the context of radical English Puritanism during the turbulent Interregnum period (1649–60). In early adulthood Fox began a search for spiritual reality. He went from minister to minister to find answers to the spiritual longing in his heart. In every case the advice offered did not satisfy him. After four years as a "seeker," Fox heard a voice speak to him, telling him that God alone could communicate to him in his condition.

In 1647 Fox began preaching. He was followed by a group of enthusiasts, numbering in the thousands by the mid 1650s. Brought to trial for his attacks on the ordained clergy, he told the judge that the latter should tremble at the Word of God, and the justice then called Fox "a Quaker"—a name that has remained. Persecution continued but only served to strengthen the movement.

The Quakers believed that every true Christian minister, whether ordained or lay, was endowed by the Holy Spirit. Christ is revealed by the "inner word" of God, or "inner voice," which is given directly to human hearts by the Spirit of God. Hereby the Christian's relationship to God, the nature of Christian doctrine, and the correct interpretation of Scripture are revealed. The "outer word," or Scripture, apart from the revelation of the Holy Spirit, has no necessary relation to spiritual enlightenment.

The Quaker distinction between the "inner" and the "outer" words was a reaction against the biblicism to which most Puritans had fallen prey by Fox's time. In his view, the Puritans left out the fundamental element in spiritual enlightenment, the experience of the Holy Spirit. For Fox, experiential knowledge of the Holy Spirit was the only basis for true Christianity. In turn, the Puritans denied the Quaker doctrine of the Spirit with assertions of the priority of Scripture, which they equated with the Word of God.

Fox argued that a true revelation from God could not contradict Scripture. According to his own experience, the Holy Spirit speaks according to Scripture. Revelation leads to an understanding of Scripture. Scripture corroborates and interprets one's prior spiritual experience.

Because of their dependence on the Holy Spirit for direct inspiration, Quakers developed a unique form of corporate worship. Sitting in silence, they waited for God to speak through one or more of them. Because any or all present could be moved upon by the Spirit of God, there was no need for clergy.

Early Quaker literature records visions, healings, prophecies, and a power from God that they likened to 1st-century Pentecost. There is even evidence of tongues speech among them. Fox eventually discouraged such ecstatic utterances, and glossolalia died out among the Quakers.

The Quakers speak to modern pentecostals and charismatics in a variety of ways. They certainly provided antecedents for the current concepts of "life in the Spirit." They faced the issue of the relationship between the divine Spirit and Scripture in opposition to Puritanism, just as 20th-century pentecostals have been forced to deal with the same issue raised by biblicists in evangelical and fundamentalist camps. Quakers even provided arguments for early pentecostals who tended to be strongly pacifistic.

See also EUROPEAN PIETISTIC ROOTS OF PENTECOSTALISM; PACIFISM.

■ **Bibliography:** J. L. Ash Jr., "Oh No, It Is Not the Scriptures!" *Quaker History* 63 (Aug. 1974) ■ H. Barbour and A. O. Roberts, *Early Quaker Writings 1650–1700* (1973) ■ B. L. Bresson, *Studies in Ecstasy* (1966) ■ R. M. Jones, *Spiritual Reformers in the Sixteenth and Seventeenth Centuries* (1914) ■ R. A. Knox, *Enthusiasm* (1950).

■ S. M. Burgess

QUEBEDEAUX, RICHARD ANTHONY (1944–). Author of numerous books about evangelicals. Quebedeaux was born in Los Angeles, CA. After obtaining his B.A. and M.A. degrees from the University of California at Los Angeles, he received an S.T.B. from Harvard Divinity School in 1968 and a Ph.D. from Oxford in 1975. A member of the United Church of Christ, Quebedeaux served as a consultant on church renewal for the United Church Board for Homeland Ministries before accepting appointment as a consultant at the Unification Theological Seminary in Barrytown, NY. He became a senior consultant at the New Ecumenical Research Association in Barrytown in 1980.

Much of Quebedeaux's published work examines, from a sociological perspective, subjects related to pentecostalism. While his books *The Young Evangelicals* (1974) and *The Worldly Evangelicals* (1978) deal with trends in the broader evangelical culture, his studies of the charismatic movement, *The New Charismatics* (1976) and *The New Charismatics II* (1983), account in cultural terms for the emergence and evolution of a broad renewal movement.

■ E. L. Blumhofer

R

RADIO Pentecostals recognized the evangelism and teaching potential of radio shortly after commercial stations began to be licensed in 1920. Despite the growing popularity of Christian television, radio continues to be an effective medium for proclaiming the gospel worldwide. By 1999 *The Directory of Religious Broadcasting* listed 1,223 full-time and 254 part-time radio stations that carried Christian programming. That figure was up 107 from 1987 (report in *DCPM*). The directory also lists nearly 700 radio, TV, and video program producers in the U.S.

Classical pentecostals, "Word" or "Faith" groups (►Positive Confession Theology), and the salvation-healing evangelists of the 1950s have used radio regionally and nationally. Few charismatics, however, have been known to develop radio ministries. Several ministries that use primarily television as their means of preaching the gospel began with radio.

1. History.

After radio was made available for preaching the gospel, ministers soon learned that effective communication with people by radio outside their sanctuaries required a different style. With a live audience, the preacher uses gestures, facial expressions, and other movements. On radio he or she is limited to content and voice quality. Consequently, some preachers never successfully made the transition. Producing the program and obtaining air time is not so difficult, but communicating with listeners is critical. As Robert W. Sarnoff, a pioneer in radio and president of Radio Corporation of America, said: "To communicate anything you must first have an audience; and second, you must have its attention." Gaining an audience and getting its attention has been the goal of gospel broadcasters ever since Calvary Episcopal Church, Pittsburgh, aired what is thought to have been the first broadcast church service on Jan. 2, 1921.

It is no surprise that the flamboyant ►Aimee Semple McPherson is said to have been one of the first women to preach on radio in 1922. This well-known pentecostal also built one of the first commercial stations, KFSG, at ►Angelus Temple in Los Angeles in 1924. Apparently the first gospel station was licensed to the National Presbyterian Church, Washington, DC, in 1922. Some of the first well-known evangelical radio preachers included John Zoller, Paul Rader, R. R. Brown, Charles E. Fuller, Donald Grey Barnhouse, Walter A. Maier, Paul Myers, J. Harold Smith, and John Roach Straton.

In addition to McPherson, other pentecostals went on the air in the beginning years of commercial radio. ►F. F. Bosworth developed a radio ministry that supplemented his citywide salvation-healing meetings. Pastors across the country were broadcasting over local radio stations during the 1920s. These included Richard and Adele Carmichael, parents of musician Ralph Carmichael.

Robert Craig, founder of Glad Tidings Temple (Assemblies of God), San Francisco, and what is now Bethany College, established KGTT in 1925. In neighboring San Jose, First Baptist Church—which had experienced a great pentecostal revival under McPherson's ministry in 1921—bought the existing KQW in 1925.

During the early years of radio not all pentecostals accepted the medium as a viable method for preaching the gospel. Some looked at "the air" as the devil's territory, not to be used. Broadcasting the gospel on radio, which was also being used for worldly entertainment, was also thought by some to compromise the gospel—a criticism later leveled against television ministries.

During the era of the salvation-healing movement beginning in the late 1940s, several evangelists used radio. Oral Roberts gained a faithful following on his *Healing Waters* program. One of the longest-running programs was ►A. A. Allen's 15-minute daily broadcast. Allen's protégé, R. W. Schambach, has used radio as well. The Voice of Healing, directed by ►Gordon Lindsay, sponsored a radio broadcast, as did ►Kathryn Kuhlman. With a few exceptions, listeners to the salvation-healing programs usually heard on-location taped broadcasts rather than studio-produced programs. What the programs lacked in quality, they made up in drama, excitement, and expectancy.

2. Objectives of the Broadcasters.

Evangelicals began to use radio in the 1920s as an evangelism and teaching tool. But they soon recognized other important purposes. A morning worship service on radio reached believers who were unable to attend because of sickness or for other reasons. Gospel music programs became popular, and later talk shows and news programs were developed to communicate the gospel and to inform listeners on important issues.

Pentecostals added another reason for broadcasting. They began praying for the sick on the air and mailing prayer cloths to persons who requested them. ►Oral Roberts urged listeners to touch their radios as a "point of contact" and then to "release [their] faith."

Some preachers began to use what they called the ►"word of knowledge" on the air to declare that a person in the audience was receiving healing for a particular need. Other speakers spoke in tongues on their broadcasts. These practices have had both critics and supporters. Criticism has also been leveled at broadcasters who use radio time for raising money rather than for preaching the gospel.

Radio—and later television—has been a medium to promote the local church. Countless people have been attracted to a local church by radio, and many of them have been converted and become members.

3. Radio's Vast Coverage.

Almost anywhere in America one can turn on a radio and hear a gospel program coming from one of the 1,477 stations broadcasting religious programs. Several producers release their programs on hundreds of outlets daily. For example, ▸Kenneth Hagin's *Faith Seminar of the Air* is aired on more than 300 stations. On some stations he might be followed by ▸Kenneth Copeland's *Believer's Voice of Victory* or another of the scores of daily programs being produced today. Three weekly programs sponsored by pentecostal denominations also have wide coverage: The ▸Church of God (Cleveland, TN), sponsors *Forward in Faith;* the ▸United Pentecostal Church produces *Harvestime;* and the ▸Assemblies of God produced *Revivaltime* from 1950 to 1995, with as many as 600 stations airing the program. For 25 years ▸C. M. Ward was the voice of *Revivaltime,* with Dan Betzer succeeding him. A short-lived program, *MasterPlan,* followed *Revivaltime.* Betzer broadcasts a two-minute program, *ByLine.* In 1999 Dr. Richard Dobbins began a counseling broadcast, *From This Day Forward.*

Missionary radio has been used for nearly 70 years. Clarence Jones and Reuben Larson established HCJB in Quito, Ecuador, in 1931. After WWII, Paul Freed built Trans World Radio at Monte Carlo. Three pentecostals—Robert Bowman, John C. Broger, and William J. Roberts—built a network of powerful stations in the Far East, which they called the Far East Broadcasting Company. These missionary stations produce their own programs with the help of missionaries and nationals. They also sell time to selected U.S. producers.

Many of the pentecostal broadcasters belong to the National Religious Broadcasters (NRB), a 1,100-member association that was formed in 1944. The association publishes *NRB Magazine* (formerly *Religious Broadcasting*) and an annual directory of radio and television stations, programs, producers, and others involved in gospel broadcasting. NRB has established principles and guidelines for fund-raising, accounting, and financial reporting. NRB offices are in Manassas, VA.

4. Gospel Radio's Future.

As indicated by the growing number of radio stations that broadcast the gospel and an increasing number of radio receivers, the future looks extremely bright. In 1952 Americans owned 105 million radios. By 1986 that figure had jumped to nearly 500 million.

It has been estimated that 90% of the world listens to radio or watches television every day. Gospel-radio producers know that quality programs targeted at a specific market—whether over U.S. stations or powerful missionary stations abroad—will have an audience. Gospel radio is an important outreach of the kingdom, reaching into hospital rooms, behind prison walls, into homes and vehicles, behind the Bamboo Curtain, and into portable receivers everywhere.

See also EVANGELISM.

■ **Bibliography:** B. Armstrong, ed., *Directory of Religious Broadcasting* (annual) ▪ D. Buss and A. Glasser, *Giving Wings to the Gospel* ▪ *NRB Magazine* ▪ *Religious Broadcasting* (magazine) ▪ S. Siedell, *Gospel Radio: A 20th-Century Tool for a 20th-Century Challenge* (1971). ■ W. E. Warner

Rev. Yamada preaching on the radio program *Word of Grace* in Japan, July 1959.

RAMABAI, SARASVATI MARY (PANDITA) (c. 1858–1922). Indian social reformer, scholar, educator, visionary, diplomat, Christian saint, and pentecostal pioneer. As a young woman, Ramabai bridged the human-rights teachings from the ancient Vedas to late-19th-century Hindu practices. Her search for an alternate spirituality was energized by unjust religious, political, and economic practices—particularly gender issues, such as lack of education, inadequate health care, child marriages, and harsh practices toward widows. These she described in *The High Caste Hindu Woman* (1887). Eventually her search for equity, compassion, a discipline for life, and a hope for the hereafter led her to the Christian church and a personal relationship with Jesus Christ. It also led her to found a community of deliverance and care at Mukti in Maharastra State in western India. It was at Mukti that disposed women and children experienced one of the greatest outpourings of the Holy Spirit in modern times.

Pandita Ramabai of India—social reformer, scholar, educator, visionary, diplomat, Christian saint, and pentecostal pioneer.

Young Ramabai was a consummate scholar. Her Brahmin father, Ananata Shastri, a learned social reformer, defied his culture by teaching her to read and write Sanskrit. By the age of 12 she memorized 18,000 Sanskrit verses of the Puranas. She became fluent in Sanskrit, Kanarese, Hindi, Bengali, Marathi, English, Hebrew, and Greek.

In 1877 a great famine struck India. Within a few months, Ramabai's father, mother, and elder sister died of starvation. Ramabai and her brother practiced the life of holy pilgrims, walking about 4,000 miles, often quoting extensive Sanskrit selections. Hindu *pandits* (scholars; also *pundits*) in Calcutta were so impressed with the remarkable Ramabai that they extended an invitation to her in 1878 for further study. They also bestowed on her the honorifics *Pandita* (= Pandit) and *Sarasvati* (the name of the Hindu goddess of wisdom).

While in Calcutta, Ramabai first came into contact with Christians, their Bible, and Bipin Behari Medhvi, who was to become her husband. Medhvi, from a Sudra caste, was educated at a mission school and later became a Bengali lawyer. (The Sudra is the lowest of the four castes, or social categories, of Hindu society; the Brahmin, to which Pandita's father belonged, the highest.) While in Bengal, Ramabai was baptized in water, joining the despised Christian community—to her husband's chagrin. In 1882, after three years of marriage, Ramabai was widowed, leaving her with an infant daughter, Mano.

Soon afterward Ramabai and her daughter returned to Maharastra State. Late in 1882 Ramabai presented the case of dispossessed Indian women to the Hunter Commission. The transcript of this meeting so moved Queen Victoria that she established women's hospitals throughout India, as well as training the first women physicians on the subcontinent. This also led to the establishment of the Arya Mahila Samaj, where teachers were trained to teach women. In 1883 Ramabai and her daughter arrived in England, where Ramabai began studies to become a teacher. At this time she joined the Church of England.

On trips to the underprivileged areas of London, Ramabai was moved by the Christian compassion and love extended to unfortunate women and children. She learned to distinguish between institutional Christianity and the "religion of Jesus Christ." At the invitation of the American Episcopal Church in 1886, she traveled to the U.S., where she formed the Ramabai Association, which later sponsored her school for child widows at Mukti.

After returning to India, Ramabai pressed her agenda of social reform. She was among the first to recommend (Dec. 1889) the adoption of Hindi, with the Devnagri script, as the national language of India. Her first home for widows, the Sharada Sadam, was begun in 1889 in Bombay (Mumbai), moving to Poona (Pune) in 1895. In addition, a trust fund was set up to develop the newly acquired farm at Khedgaon—the Mukti Sadan. Great famines and outbreaks of the bubonic plague hastened the move to Khedgaon in 1900, and with that move came the enlargement of her vision for dispossessed women and children. The Mukti Sadan became an ashram based on the Tolstoyan model of a self-sufficient community. It continued to grow, with new buildings, supportive industries, institutional support services, and religious outreach. With continued famines, additional widows and orphans came from Madhya Pradesh and the Gujarat. Bubonic plague also brought death to many of Poona's residents. Under these conditions, the news of hope at Mukti for child widows and orphans swept across India. By the turn of the century, overseas missionaries arrived to serve at Mukti, assisting Pandita Ramabai.

By 1890 Ramabai had been marginalized by most Indian social reformers, who argued that her agenda was too radical. In reality, this was in large part a consequence of her conversion to Christianity. It also was alleged that she had become "anglicized"—even taking the Christian name Mary. Many of her former associates and friends shunned her or withdrew their daughters from her day school. Accused of trying to turn their daughters from Hinduism to Christianity, she maintained her social vision for the women of India—a goal that was fully consistent with her Christian testimony and purposes. Ramabai only became bolder in her zeal to help

India's women. In addition to Mukti, she established orphanages in several villages, and a home for prostitutes, where they were sheltered, educated, and taught Christian doctrine.

In Jan. 1905 Pandita Ramabai issued a call for prayer; 550 women met twice daily for intercessory prayer. By June, 30 young women went out to preach the gospel in the villages. On June 29, 1905, evidence of an outpouring of the Holy Spirit was reported, when several were "slain in the Spirit" and others experienced a burning sensation said to evidence their baptism in the Holy Ghost "and fire."

This revival continued into 1906, when participants also experienced glossolalia. Several of the missionaries at Mukti, including ›Minnie Abrams and ›Albert Norton, also received Spirit-baptism. Ramabai reported that the Mukti girls prayed for more than 29,000 individuals by name daily. The burden of their prayers was that they be baptized with the Holy Spirit and with fire, and, as a consequence, might become true and faithful witnesses for Christ.

As the revival continued in 1907, Ramabai wrote:

I have seen not only the most ignorant of our people coming under the power of revival, but the most refined and very highly educated English men and women, who have given their lives for God's service in this country, coming under the power of God, so that they lose all control over their bodies, and are shaken like reeds, stammering words in various unknown tongues as the Spirit teaches them to speak, and gradually get to a place where they are in unbroken communion with God.

Numerous miracles are attributed to Ramabai's ministry. One involves finding water on the Mukti farm. She told the well diggers where to begin. After a day of digging, there was no water. They told Ramabai that there was no water at this place. But she was resolute, insisting that they continue digging at the same place on the following day. The laborers left their tools and returned to their abodes complaining about the futility of their efforts. Ramabai spent the night in prayer. When the laborers returned in the morning, there was so much water in the hole that they could not locate their tools. All proclaimed this to be a modern miracle.

The Mukti mission expanded in outreach to include the blind; preschool education; a comprehensive school curriculum that combined cultural activities with academics; a hospital with an outpatient department; vocational and industrial support services, including sewing, printing presses, textile weaving, basket work, and a bookstore. Meanwhile, Ramabai directed her scholarship toward a full translation of the Bible in the Marathi language.

Pandita Ramabai is remembered as one of the most amazing women of modern times. A rare blend of social concern, compassion, scholarship, and administrative skills, she also stands as one of the principal modern pentecostal pioneers.

The government of India acknowledged her remarkable life in 1989 by issuing a postage stamp bearing her likeness.

■ **Bibliography:** M. Abrams, *The Baptism of the Holy Ghost and Fire* (1906) ■ C. Butler, *Pandita Ramabai Sarasvati, Pioneer in the Movement for the Education of the Child-widow in India* (1922) ■ U. Chakravarti, *Rewriting History: the Life and Times of Pandita Ramabai* (1998) ■ P. Chappell, *Pandita Ramabai: A Great Life in Indian Missions* (n.d.) ■ R. Kumar, *The History of Doing: An Illustrated Account of Movements for Women's Rights and Feminism in India 1800–1990* (1993) ■ P. Ramabai, *The High Caste Hindu Woman* (1887) ■ idem, *Mukti Prayer-Bell* (1904–13) ■ idem, *A Testimony of Our Inexhaustible Treasure* (11th ed., 1992) ■ B. Underhill, *Pandita Ramabai: Pioneer* (repr. 1986).   ■ R. V. Burgess

RANAGHAN, KEVIN MATHERS (1940–), and **DOROTHY** (1942–). Leaders in the ›Catholic charismatic renewal (CCR) since its inception in early 1967. The Ranaghans soon became widely known through their book *Catholic Pentecostals* (1969), which has served as a standard introduction to the renewal and was later updated under the title *Catholic Pentecostals Today*. The Ranaghans, who married in 1966 and have six children, have been members of the People of Praise, an ecumenical covenant community in South Bend, IN, since its beginning in 1971.

Kevin Ranaghan has been a key figure in the organization and planning of many national and international conferences in the CCR. He served on the National Service Committee (NSC) from 1970 to 1985 as executive director and as a delegate to the ›International Catholic Charismatic Renewal Office (ICCRO, now ICCRS) from 1978 to 1984 and again since 1990. He also served as chairperson of the ›Kansas City Conference (1977) and is a member of the ›International Catholic Consultation on World Evangelism (ICCOWE) executive committee. Dorothy Ranaghan has also served on the NSC (1978–84) and edited the NSC's *Newsletter* (1983–90).

Both Ranaghans have degrees in theology, Dorothy an M.A. (Notre Dame, 1966) and Kevin an M.A. (1964) and Ph.D. (1974), with a dissertation on "Rites of Initiation in Representative Pentecostal Churches in the United States, 1901–1972." As teachers, writers, and conference speakers, both have become prominent public figures in the CCR. Other writings include K. and D. Ranaghan, eds., *As the Spirit Leads Us* (1971); K. Ranaghan, *The Lord, the Spirit and the Church* (1973) and *Renew the Face of the Earth* (1982); D. Ranaghan, *A Day in Thy Courts* (1986).

See also CATHOLIC CHARISMATIC RENEWAL.

■ **Bibliography:** F. Lilly, "Kevin Ranaghan and Renewal," *Charisma* (Apr. 1980) ■ E. D. O'Connor, *The Pentecostal Movement in the Catholic Church* (1971).   ■ P. D. Hocken

RESTORATIONISM IN CLASSICAL PENTECOSTALISM

Restorationism is a complex of ideas that, though implicit in and common to all of Protestantism, is much more influential in some groups than in others. It is essentially synonymous with primitivism. The basic belief behind restorationism is that something went very wrong very early in the history of the Christian church, so that the simple and biblical teaching and practice of the apostles was gradually corrupted through the addition of pagan ceremonies (including the development of formal liturgies and sacramentalism), Greek philosophies, riches and honors stemming from the patronage of the wealthy, and the lust for political power on the part of ecclesiastical officials (expressed especially through the papacy and other similar episcopal offices). In restorationist thought, the result of these corruptions is that the Roman Catholic Church of the Middle Ages was only a shadow of its former spiritual self, while it had grown materially rich and politically powerful. The other side of the equation is the belief that the restoration of the church to NT standards began with the Protestant Reformation of the 16th century and proceeded in successive waves up to the present, in preparation for the return of Christ to earth.

Classical pentecostals are one group among whom restorationist themes have been prominent; this was especially true in the early history of pentecostalism. In fact, many early pentecostals agreed with Daniel W. Kerr's statement that the pentecostal movement was "the climax of the process of ... recovery of truth since John Wickliffe [sic] gave us the Bible" (Kerr, 3–4). H. S. Maltby stated the restorationist scheme rather succinctly when he voiced something of a restorationistic litany:

> During the Reformation God used Martin Luther and others to restore to the world the doctrine of justification by faith. Rom. 5:1. Later on the Lord used the Wesleys and others in the great holiness movement to restore the gospel of sanctification by faith. Acts 26:18. Later still he used various ones to restore the gospel of Divine healing by faith (Jas. 5:14, 15), and the gospel of Jesus's second coming. Acts 1:11. Now the Lord is using many witnesses in the great pentecostal movement to restore the gospel of the baptism with the Holy Ghost and fire (Luke 3:16; Acts 1:5) with signs following. Mark 16:17, 18; Acts 2:4, 10:44–46, 19:6, 1:1–28:31. Thank God, we now have preachers of the whole gospel. (Maltby, 82–83)

Grant Wacker has suggested that three kinds of primitivism, or restorationism, were operative in early pentecostalism. The first is *philosophical* primitivism, exemplified by the common belief that the Bible had dropped straight from the hands of God to earth. The second is *historical* primitivism, the belief that their movement had indeed recreated apostolic Christianity. The third is *ethical* primitivism, the compulsion to repeat the forms and practices of the NT church (1988, 197–200).

Perhaps the most classic statement of restorationist theology by an early pentecostal leader was ▶Aimee Semple McPherson's 1917 sermon "Lost and Restored," which she claimed as a divine revelation. Picturing the church as a tree and using the prophetic images of agricultural blight and recovery in Joel 1–2, she detailed the fall of the church after the apostolic age in successive stages ("That which the palmerworm hath left hath the locust eaten; and that which the locust hath left hath the cankerworm eaten ..." [1:4 KJV]), to its complete corruption in the Middle Ages. Characterizing it as the "Dark Ages," she lamented:

> No wonder they are called the Dark Ages. Ah! dark indeed is the night without Jesus. ... Men and women groping in this darkness tried to win their way to Heaven by doing penance, by locking themselves up in dungeons, walking over red hot plowshares in their bare feet, and inflicting unnamable tortures upon themselves and upon one another, blindly trying by some work or deed to pay the debt that had already been paid on Calvary's rugged cross. (1989, 18)

McPherson then detailed the church's gradual restoration to apostolic standards ("I will restore to you the years that the locust hath eaten, the cankerworm, and the caterpillar, and the palmerworm, my great army which I sent among you" [Joel 2:25 KJV]), beginning with the writings of Luther and the influence of the Reformers, continuing through Wesley and the Holiness movement, and culminating with the pentecostal movement of her own lifetime. She boldly proclaimed, "The nine gifts and fruits of the Spirit ... are again being restored to the tree" (ibid., 26). In a similar manner, A. J. Tomlinson identified pentecostalism as the "last great reformation" (1913, 187).

Another biblical motif from the prophet Joel that was used popularly by early pentecostals is that of the "latter rain" (2:23). Given its definitive articulation by D. Wesley Myland in his *The Latter Rain Covenant and Pentecostal Power* (1910), the latter rain ideology contended that the history of the church was analogous to the rainfall patterns in Palestine. The first Christian Pentecost described in Acts 2 with the descent of the Holy Spirit typified the "early rain" of Palestine's agricultural season, followed by the long dry period of Christianity's corruption during the Middle Ages. The pentecostal revival of the early 20th century was therefore indicative of the latter rain, causing a ripening of the crop of humanity just before the harvest, or end of divine dealings with humanity (1910, 8ff.).

The genius of the latter rain concept, as Dayton contends, is that it pulls together the pentecostal "Foursquare Gospel" of Christ as Savior, Baptizer in the Holy Spirit, Healer, and Coming King into a workable whole. If the pentecostal movement signaled the beginning of the latter rain, the suddenness of the appearances of spectacular signs as speaking in tongues and healing only make sense. These are divinely ordained signs for the end of the age, when God is restoring the church to its apostolic character. So the latter rain argument weds eschatology to soteriology and spiritual manifestations (Dayton 1987, 28; Ware, 174).

Furthermore, pentecostals in the early 20th century also used the latter rain argument as an apologetic for their movement. When rebuked by nonpentecostals for practices that had not been typical of the Holiness and evangelical revivals, pentecostals merely claimed that their movement was a recovery of the Christianity of the 1st century. The long drought from apostolic times to the present with regard to the occurrence of the spectacular spiritual manifestations taking place in the pentecostal movement was viewed as part of God's dispensational plan for the ages. In true restorationist fashion, they claimed that their movement was the restoration of apostolic Christianity precisely because it seemed to have no immediate precedent (Dayton, 1991, 47).

As implied in the latter rain ideology, the restorationist perception of early pentecostals was closely linked to premillennial eschatological expectations. Anderson has argued that early pentecostal emphasis on restoration and eschatology offered a sense of hope and spiritual victory to the predominantly poor and underprivileged members of pentecostal congregations (96). Likewise, Faupel has contended that the pentecostal message was "proclaimed by the movement to the nations as a warning of impending judgment, and to the church as an announcement of the approaching Bridegroom" (42). The renewal of the gifts and graces of the Holy Spirit as manifested in the pentecostal movement were therefore viewed as the sign that God's work in the church was nearing an end and that Christ's return was thus imminent.

The most obvious and direct roots for early pentecostal restorationism are to be found in its primary theological ancestor—the Holiness movement. Although restorationist themes were almost always expressed in a more implicit fashion in the Holiness movement and rarely operated as a formal or independent theological construct, the large-scale exchange of ideas and personnel from the Holiness movement into early pentecostalism is unmistakable. For instance, the popular latter rain concept described above is found in the writings of Holiness authors such as George D. Watson (n.d., 70) and A. B. Simpson (214), who has been correctly described as "proto-pentecostal" for his ideological continuity with pentecostalism at several points (Nienkirchen, ch. 1). Furthermore, the almost complete absence of the latter rain terminology and concept in the writings of non-Holiness evangelicals of the era, such as Dwight L. Moody, J. Wilbur Chapman, and Reuben A.

Torrey, force one to the conclusion that the most obvious and immediate source for pentecostal restorationism was Holiness restorationism.

Another clear link between early pentecostal restorationism and that found in the Holiness movement is seen in the flow of people who became early pentecostal leaders after prior experience in the Holiness movement. As Nienkirchen has shown, numerous early pentecostal leaders were personally influenced by the ministry of A. B. Simpson, who was the first to formulate the concept of the fourfold (later foursquare) gospel of Christ as Savior, Sanctifier, Healer, and Coming King. Many of these same individuals later defected from Simpson's Christian and Missionary Alliance to join the fledgling pentecostal organizations (Nienkirchen, ch. 2). Furthermore, it should be noted that all of the early pentecostal leaders who wrote about their movement in notably restorationist terms (˃Frank Bartleman, ˃D. Wesley Myland, ˃George F. Taylor, and ˃A. J. Tomlinson) came from Holiness backgrounds (Ware, 180–81).

An alternative view of pentecostal restorationism is given in Edith Blumhofer's *Restoring the Faith* (1993). Focusing rather on the non-Holiness evangelicals of the late 19th and early 20th centuries, she shows how some aspects of early pentecostalism, most notably its eschatology, received equal input from non-Holiness sources. Her more persuasive argument, however, lies in showing how the original restorationist fervor of early pentecostalism has changed slowly over the course of the last century to become much more affirmative toward, and accommodating to, the surrounding culture, and is in fact in danger of losing the distinctiveness of its witness (259–60).

A later development in restorationism among pentecostals was the ˃Latter Rain movement of the late 1940s and 1950s. Begun by George and Ernest Hatwin and Percy Hunt of the ˃Pentecostal Assemblies of Canada in 1947, the Latter Rain movement soon spread and included some of the largest pentecostal congregations, such as the Bethesda Missionary Temple in Detroit. Bethesda pastor ˃Myrtle Beall and other Latter Rain leaders claimed that the pentecostal revival of the early 20th century had been only the early rain of Joel chapter 2, and that their revival was now the prophesied latter rain. This perception reinforced their outsider mentality and gave them a sense of conflict with everyone outside their "faithful remnant."

Prominent in the Latter Rain movement was a renewal of the use of the spectacular gifts, such as tongues and prophecy, and especially notable were the gift of healing and slaying in the Spirit. It was closely paralleled by the healing revival led by notable personalities such as ˃William Branham and ˃Oral Roberts. The implied condescension by Latter Rain advocates toward pentecostal church bodies who were moving through the inevitable processes of professionalization and institutionalization, however, was not received well (Blumhofer, 211, 218–19).

Another more recent development in pentecostal restorationism has been the House Church Movement, which began among a loose network of charismatic assemblies in Great Britain. With its beginnings in the conferences held in Britain in the late 1950s and early 1960s, it featured an emphasis on the restoration of the NT church. In some respects it was paralleled in the U.S. in the 1970s by the Christian Growth Ministries, centered in Fort Lauderdale, FL (›Shepherding Movement). Rather than the traditional emphases on the baptism of the Holy Spirit and spiritual gifts, however, this movement emphasized the role of the biblical office of apostle and models of radical discipleship that sometimes included rigid authority structures and financial commitments (Strang, 14ff.).

Finally, Wacker has noted that pentecostalism has flourished because two differing impulses have perennially warred for the mastery of its soul. Those two impulses are the *primitivist* and the *pragmatic*. The primitivist impulse is the "powerfully destructive urge to smash all human-made traditions in order to return to a 1st-century world where the Holy Spirit alone reigned." The pragmatic impulse, in contrast, is the "eagerness to do whatever was necessary in order to accomplish the movement's purposes" (1995, 142). Pentecostalism has succeeded institutionally, says Wacker, due to a delicate balancing of these two impulses. The primitive impulse has offered certitude to pentecostals concerning the truthfulness of their theological claims about the supernatural, while the pragmatic impulse has stabilized the movement by preventing its adherents from "squandering their energies in ecstatic excess" (157). Whatever the case, pentecostalism is certainly one of the most notable and successful restorationist movements in modern Christianity.

■ **Bibliography:** R. M. Anderson, *Vision of the Disinherited* (1979) ■ F. Bartleman, *How Pentecost Came to Los Angeles* (1925) ■ E. L. Blumhofer, *Restoring the Faith* (1993) ■ J. P. Brooks, *The Divine Church* (1891) ■ D. W. Dayton, "The Limits of Evangelicalism," in *The Variety of American Evangelicalism*, ed. D. W. Dayton and R. K. Johnston (1991) ■ idem, *Theological Roots of Pentecostalism* (1987) ■ D. W. Faupel, *The Everlasting Gospel* (1996) ■ D. W. Kerr, "The Selfsame Thing," *Trust* 13 (8, Aug. 1914) ■ A. S. McPherson, *Lost and Restored, and Other Sermons* (1989) ■ H. S. Maltby, *The Reasonableness of Hell* (1913), 82–83 ■ D. W. Myland, *The Latter-Rain Covenant and Pentecostal Power* (1910) ■ C. W. Nienkirchen, *A. B. Simpson and the Pentecostal Movement* (1992) ■ A. B. Simpson, *The Gospel of the Kingdom* (1890) ■ S. Strang, "The Discipleship Controversy Three Years Later," *Charisma* (Sept. 1978) ■ A. J. Tomlinson, *The Last Great Conflict* (1913) ■ G. Wacker, "Playing for Keeps," in *The American Quest for the Primitive Church*, ed. R. T. Hughes (1988) ■ idem, "Searching for Eden with a Satellite Dish," in *The Primitive Church in the Modern World*, ed. R. T. Hughes (1995) ■ S. L. Ware, *Restoring the New Testament Church* (1998) ■ D. S. Warner and H. M. Riggle, *The Cleansing of the Sanctuary* (1903) ■ G. D. Watson, *Types of the Holy Spirit* (n.d.).   ■ S. L. Ware

RHEMA MINISTERIAL ASSOCIATION INTERNATIONAL See KENNETH HAGIN.

RICHEY, JOHN R. (1899–1984), and LOUISE H. (1894–1986).

Founders of the Open Bible Evangelistic Association (OBEA) in 1932. Beginning their ministry with ›Aimee Semple McPherson and the ›International Church of the Foursquare Gospel (ICFG) in Southern California, John and Louise Richey were transferred to Des Moines in 1928, where John became the ICFG leader for the Midwest. He pastored two thriving churches in Des Moines simultaneously and started a Bible school. His vigorous leadership and evangelistic preaching helped establish pentecostal churches in the area.

When 32 ministers withdrew from ICFG in 1932 and formed OBEA, Richey became their chairman and later was elected first chairman of ›Open Bible Standard Churches (1935–38). He was related to E. N. and ›Raymond T. Richey of the Assemblies of God.

Louise H. Richey was healed of a goiter in 1918 under the ministry of ›Maria B. Woodworth-Etter and later attended L.I.F.E. Bible College, where she met her husband. They were copastors and coevangelists for nearly 60 years.

■ **Bibliography:** R. Mitchell, *Heritage and Horizons* (1982).
■ W. E. Warner

RICHEY, RAYMOND THEODORE (1893–1968).

World-famous healing evangelist. Born into a devout family in Illinois, Richey led a life of dissipation during his adolescence, until his eyesight began to fail due to a serious boyhood injury. In 1911 he surrendered his life to Christ after his eyes were healed at meetings held by Arch P. Collins in Fort Worth, TX. A few years later his father, E. N. Richey, was called to a pastorate in Houston, and Raymond became assistant pastor.

During WWI, Raymond established the United Prayer and Workers' League for the distribution of literature. Near an army camp in Houston he erected a tabernacle where hundreds were converted to Christ. While ministering to the dying during the influenza epidemic, Richey contracted tuberculosis. He went to Southern California, where he received a miraculous healing in Sept. 1919.

A year later Richey intended to assist Warren Collins of Fort Worth, TX, with meetings in Hattiesburg, MS. After all of the arrangements had been made, Collins canceled, and Richey held meetings on his own, praying for the sick. This

Raymond T. Richey, who experienced miraculous healings himself and began conducting salvation-healing meetings in the 1920s.

marked the beginning of his ministry as a healing evangelist, which took him to huge city auditoriums in all parts of the U.S. In the spring of 1923, in Tulsa, OK, there were 11,000 reported conversions. Those who were healed paraded through the streets with "a truck piled high with discarded crutches" (Richey, 1925, 107).

During WWII, Richey traveled with a large tent of red, white, and blue stripes, holding meetings for members of the armed forces, thousands of whom professed conversion. After his father's death in 1945, Richey returned to Houston to pastor Evangelistic Temple. In the 1950s he continued his traveling ministry, going to Central and South America in 1951, and Germany, Switzerland, Japan, and Korea in 1957–58.

■ **Bibliography:** T. R. Nickel, "Evang. Raymond T. Richey Now Is with His Lord," *Testimony* 23 (Second Quarter 1968) ■ "Raymond T. Richey Back from Europe," *Voice of Healing* (Dec. 1957) ■ E. M. Richey, *What God Hath Wrought* (1925).   ■ R. M. Riss

RIGGS, RALPH MEREDITH (1895–1971). Pastor, missionary, educator, author, and administrator. Ralph Riggs was born in Coal Creek, TN, to a physician father and devout mother who moved the family to Hattiesburg, MS, to enable her children to attend a Holiness academy. Riggs was converted at age 10, and four years later he was baptized in the Holy Spirit. While still in his teens, he came in contact with many of the early pentecostal leaders, including three future general superintendents of the ▸Assemblies of God (AG). Consequently, he attended that denomination's formational meeting at Hot Springs, AR, in 1914, and remained with the AG for the rest of his life.

Riggs had planned to study architecture, but believing that he was called to the ministry, he enrolled in the Rochester Bible Training School in Rochester, NY. On completion of the two-year course in 1916, he was ordained and became pastor of a Syracuse church. Three years later, under the auspices of the Pentecostal Mission, he went to South Africa, where he met and married another missionary, Lillian Merian. After three years of ministry in the cities, the Riggses moved into the northern Transvaal, often traveling by donkey cart. The difficult living conditions, exacerbated by the failure of promised support, took their toll, forcing the family, which now included two daughters, Merian and Venda, to return home in 1925.

Riggs returned to his former pastorate in Syracuse for a year, followed by pastorates at Ossining, NY, and Newark, NJ. While in Newark he also taught at Bethel Bible Training School and in 1929 moved with it to Springfield, MO. For the next 30 years Springfield was to be his home, but after only two years he left the classroom to serve as pastor of Central Assembly, which was regarded as the denominational headquarters church. It flourished during his eight years of ministry, and several daughter churches were founded. In recognition of his leadership, Riggs was made district superintendent of the Southern Missouri District. Four years later he was elected to national office as assistant general superintendent and, after eight years, as general superintendent.

During Riggs' six-year tenure as the leader of the AG, much was accomplished, including major construction projects at the administrative headquarters and at Central Bible Institute. Though he had various responsibilities, Riggs was best known for his service to education. He served on the first

Ralph M. Riggs and Pastor Anyosisye in Mwankeja, Tanzania, in 1958.

board of the American Association of Bible Colleges and worked to strengthen each of his denomination's nine colleges. Under his leadership, Evangel College, a denominational liberal arts school, was created and located in Springfield. In recognition of his contribution to higher education, he was awarded an honorary doctorate.

On leaving office, Riggs moved to Santa Cruz, CA, where he returned to the classroom for nine years before retiring as professor emeritus at Bethany Bible College. Five of his books have been published, including *The Spirit Himself* (1949) and *A Successful Pastor* (c. 1931).

■ **Bibliography:** C. Brumback, *Suddenly . . . from Heaven* (1971) ■ "With Christ," *PE* (Feb. 21, 1971) ■ "With the Lord," *Glad Tidings* (Mar. 1971). ■ L. F. Wilson

ROBECK, CECIL MELVIN, JR. (1945–). American pentecostal clergyman, historian, and ecumenist. Born on Mar. 16, 1945, in San Jose, CA, the first of five sons, to parents who both have been ministers of the ▸Assemblies of God (AG). His father, Cecil M. Robeck, was ordained in 1946 and served churches in Bellevue, WA; San Leandro, CA; and Las Vegas, NV. His mother, née Berdetta Mae Manley, was licensed in 1941 by the AG. She herself—before marriage—founded a church in Saucilito, CA, besides serving as a pastoral associate, a Bible school instructor, and an itinerant evangelist. Both parents, at different times, graduated from Glad Tidings Bible Institute in San Francisco before it became Bethany Bible College (1955) and then Bethany College (1991). In 1969 Robeck married Patsy Jolene Gibbs, a registered nurse. They have four sons.

Earning first an A.A. degree at San Jose City College (1967), Robeck completed a B.S. (1970) at Bethany Bible College—on whose board he later served. Virtually all of Robeck's professional and clerical life has been based at Fuller Seminary, to which he first came as a student in the fall of 1970 (M.Div., 1973; Ph.D., 1985), and where he has been ever since. For five years (1973–78) he served as a teaching assistant to Glenn W. Barker, and for a brief period he was a research assistant for George E. Ladd. A skilled administrator, he filled a variety of leadership roles in admissions, student services, and academic services, culminating in service as assistant, and then associate, dean of the School of Theology—all these between 1974 and 1992. Periodically, he chaired the theology division. Beginning in 1981 Robeck taught courses in NT and covered the full range of church history at Fuller. In 1997 he was advanced to a full professor in church history and ecumenics. Since 1996 he has directed the ▸David du Plessis Center for Christian Spirituality at Fuller.

During his teaching career, Robeck has published over 130 articles, reviews, and editorials and has given dozens of invited lectures. For eight years (1984–92) he edited *Pneuma: The Journal of the Society for Pentecostal Studies.*

It is Robeck's role as the century's leading pentecostal ecumenist that will secure for him a permanent place in North American religious history. As the successor to pentecostal ecumenical statesmen ▸Donald Gee and ▸David du Plessis, Robeck has since 1992 served, along with Fr. ▸Kilian McDonnell, OSB, as cochairman of the International Roman Catholic/Pentecostal ▸Dialogue. Unlike other post–▸Vatican II dialogues, where Catholic discussants engage existing global bodies of church families, the Roman Catholic/Pentecostal Dialogue draws from unofficial sources for pentecostal representation—a contrivance of David du Plessis when no pentecostal organization would accept the offer. Even the global and loosely knit ▸Pentecostal World Fellowship has been steadfastly reluctant to participate in anything ecumenical. Much pentecostal teaching and preaching fears ecumenism as a dreaded manifestation of last-day ecclesiastical apostasy. Such fear abounds in Robeck's own denomination, the AG, from representatives of which—though not from all—he has endured no small hostility. Such opposition has also arisen from the frontline Roman Catholic/pentecostal encounter on the mission frontiers in Latin America, where hostilities between local pentecostal ministers and Roman Catholic priests are sharp. Unlike David du Plessis before him, Robeck keeps his ecclesiastical superiors fully informed of his ecumenical activities, supplying them with copies of all relevant papers and documents.

Beyond the Roman Catholic/Pentecostal Dialogue, Robeck cochairs the Los Angeles regional Evangelical–Roman Catholic Dialogue, and he has served on the Faith and Order Commission of the World Council of Churches along with other WCC units. He has served similarly with the National Council of Churches. These contacts have led to participation in such widely diverse groups and conclaves as the Secretaries of Christian World Communions, the World Alliance of Reformed Churches, the International Eucharist Congress (1995), and the North American Academy of Ecumenists, which, in 1997, elected him president. The National Conference of Catholic Bishops named him as a theological expert for interpretation of papal actions to the media. His interracial conciliation interests are exemplified in his participation in the "Memphis Miracle" (1994). Those interests continue in his coeditorship (with Harold Hunter) of *Reconciliation,* a magazine for the Pentecostal/Charismatic Churches of North America—the Memphis successor to the now defunct ▸Pentecostal Fellowship of North America. The same cross-racial concern appeared earlier when he joined an international group of signatories to the 1991 document titled "A Declaration of Solidarity with the Relevant Pentecostal Witness in South Africa." Robeck is also a long-standing member and former president of the ▸Society for Pentecostal Studies.   ■ R. P Spittler

ROBERSON, LIZZIE (1860–1945). First national supervisor of women in the ▸Church of God in Christ. While serving as matron of women at Dermott Arkansas College, Roberson was exposed to the message of Charles H. Mason, who was conducting revivals in that city. Upon recommendation of Lillian Brooks Coffey, Lizzie Roberson was invited by Elder Mason to assist in organizing the women's department of the denomination. Not only did Roberson lay the foundation for the women's department for the denomination, she also organized several auxiliaries, such as the Bible Band, sewing circle, and the Home and Foreign Mission. She was distinguished by her gifted teaching ministry. Her daughter, Ida Baker, eventually became the secretary of the Home and Foreign Mission department. Lizzie Roberson's brilliance as an organizer was foundational to the work of women in the denomination and set the pace for years to come.

■ L. Lovett

ROBERTS, GRANVILLE ORAL (1918–). America's premier healing evangelist. Born in Pontotoc County, OK, Roberts was reared in abject poverty, the son of a ▸Pentecostal Holiness preacher. At age 17 he was diagnosed with tuberculosis and was bedridden for more than five months. In July 1935,

Oral Roberts, best-known healing evangelist in North America and the founder of Oral Roberts University.

under the ministry of evangelist George W. Moncey, he was healed of both tuberculosis and stuttering. The following two years he served an apprenticeship under his father in evangelistic ministry. Ordained by the Pentecostal Holiness Church in 1936, he quickly became one of the outstanding young ministers in the denomination. Between 1941 and 1947 he served four pastorates.

In 1947 Roberts launched a healing ministry with his first citywide campaign in Enid, OK. The same year he published his first book on healing, *If You Need Healing—Do These Things!;* took the message of healing to the radio airwaves; started his own monthly magazine, *Healing Waters;* and established his ministry headquarters in Tulsa, OK. The following year he began crisscrossing America with the largest portable tent ever used to promote the gospel. Eventually his "tent cathedral" would seat crowds of over 12,500.

Roberts' success in healing evangelism thrust him to the leadership of a generation of dynamic revivalists who took the message of divine healing around the world after 1947. His ecumenical crusades were instrumental in the revitalization of pentecostalism in the post–WWII era. He was also influential in the formation of the ▸Full Gospel Business Men's Fellowship International in 1951 and was a leading figure in laying the foundation for the modern charismatic movement. Roberts' most significant impact on American Christianity came in 1955, when he initiated a national weekly television program that took his healing crusades inside the homes of millions who had never been exposed to the healing message. Through this program the healing message was literally lifted from the pentecostal subculture of American Christianity to its widest audience in history. By 1980 a Gallup Poll revealed that Roberts' name was recognized by a phenomenal 84 percent of the American public, and historian Vinson Synan observed that Roberts was considered the most prominent pentecostal in the world.

Between 1947 and 1968 Roberts conducted more than 300 major crusades, personally praying for millions of people. By the mid 1950s his healing message was broadcast on more than 500 radio stations, and for almost 30 years his Sunday morning television program was the number one syndicated religious program in the nation. His monthly magazine, renamed *Abundant Life* in 1956, reached a circulation of over a million; his devotional magazine, *Daily Blessing,* exceeded a quarter million subscribers; and his monthly column was featured in 674 newspapers. By the 1980s more than 15 million copies of his 88 books were in circulation, and his yearly mail from supporters exceeded 5 million letters.

Indicative of his growing acceptance by mainline denominations, Roberts was invited in 1966 to be a participant in Billy Graham's Berlin Congress on World Evangelism, transferred his religious affiliation to the United Methodist Church in 1968, and began an ambitious television outreach in 1969 with prime-time religious variety shows. The success of the prime-time programming was remarkable, reaching as many as 64 million viewers. This led Edward Fiske, religious editor of the *New York Times,* to declare that Roberts commanded more personal loyalty in the 1970s than any minister in America.

In 1965 Roberts opened a coeducational liberal arts college in Tulsa. Receiving regional accreditation in a record six years, Oral Roberts University became a major institution when seven graduate colleges were added between 1975 and 1978: Medicine, Nursing, Dentistry, Law, Business, Education, and Theology. The university has an average enrollment of 4,600 students. Dedicated in 1967 by Billy Graham, it is considered the premier charismatic university in America. Adjacent to the university Roberts established a 450-resident retirement center in 1966.

The apex of Roberts' ministry came with the opening in 1981 of the $250 million City of Faith Medical and Research Center. The complex consisted of a 30-story hospital, 60-story medical center, and 20-story research facility. The philosophy of the center was to merge prayer and medicine, the supernatural and natural, in the treatment of the whole person. In conjunction with the medical school, doctors were being prepared to serve as medical missionaries around the world.

The medical school proved to be such a financial drain on the institution that it was forced to close in 1989. The university struggled to continue operations, and Roberts was forced to adopt a series of cutbacks to remain afloat.

In Jan. 1993, after his 75th birthday, Roberts was elected chancellor of the university, and his son, Richard, was elected the second president of Oral Roberts University by the board of regents. Oral Roberts and his wife, Evelyn, relocated to Southern California as he limited his involvement in the operation of the school.

In the fall of 1993 Roberts suffered a near-fatal heart attack. Although his heart stopped several times, his doctors were pleased to report that he had suffered no permanent damage and had made a good recovery. Roberts resumed an active speaking schedule for the next six years, traveling extensively as he started the Golden Eagle Broadcasting Network. He also remained actively involved in the International Charismatic Bible Ministries, a group he founded in 1986 as a way to provide fellowship for ministerial leaders. In Feb. 1999 Roberts again suffered heart trouble and thus received a pacemaker. He made a slow recovery, cutting back on his schedule of speaking engagements.

Theologically Roberts is a classical pentecostal who maintains that speaking in tongues is normative for every believer. His trademark, however, has been essentially an upbeat message of hope. The whole thesis of his ministry has been that God is a good God and that he wills to heal and prosper his people (3 John 2).

See also HEALING MOVEMENTS.

■ **Bibliography:** R. Frame, "Did Oral Roberts Go Too Far?" *Christianity Today* [Feb. 20, 1987] ■ D. Harrell Jr., *All Things Are Possible* (1975) ■ idem, *Oral Roberts: An American Life* (1985) ■ E. Roberts, *His Darling Wife, Evelyn Roberts* (1976) ■ E. M. Roberts, *Our Ministry and Our Son Oral* (1960) ■ O. Roberts, *The Call* (1972) ■ idem, *My Story* (1961) ■ idem, *Oral Roberts's Life Story* (1952) ■ idem, "The Media Have Had Their Say. Now the Truth . . . ," *Abundant Life* [Sept.–Oct. 1987]) ■ W. Robinson, *Oral* (1976).

■ P. G. Chappell

ROBERTS, H. V. (HARRY) (1889–1954). Harry Roberts was the son of ▸Henry Roberts and worked together with his father in pentecostal mission work in several different settings, particularly in the New Zealand Evangelical Mission (NZEM), of which his father was the missioner. Harry Roberts was zealously involved in the ▸Smith Wigglesworth campaigns in 1922 and 1923–24, where he received the baptism of the Spirit. When the NZEM became the Pentecostal Church of New Zealand (PCNZ) after Wigglesworth's campaigns, Roberts was appointed, as was his father, as an elder of the new movement by ▸A. C. Valdez Sr. He was elected chairman of its annual conference in 1924 and 1926 and became general secretary of the movement following its restructuring in 1934. He eventually succeeded his father as superintendent of the movement upon the latter's retirement in 1941. Roberts led the fight against the issue of rebaptism in "the Name" that had split the PCNZ in 1946 (▸Oneness pentecostalism). When the remnants of this movement

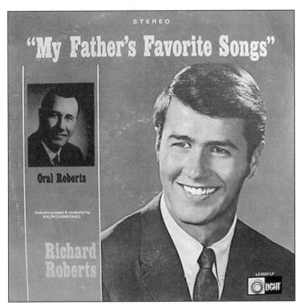

An early record album by Richard Roberts.

merged with the Elim Church of Great Britain in 1952, Roberts was elected chairman of the new Elim Church of N.Z., Inc. He wrote a number of books and pamphlets, including an eye-witness account of the Smith Wigglesworth campaigns.

■ **Bibliography:** H. V. Roberts, *New Zealand's Greatest Revival* (1951) ▐ James E. Worsfold, *A History of the Charismatic Movements in New Zealand* (1974).   ■ B. Knowles

ROBERTS, HENRY (1864–1949). Henry Roberts was effectively the pioneer of pentecostalism in New Zealand. He was converted during the Wellington campaign of English evangelist Henry Varley in 1879, and later helped in the development of evangelical work in the city. After ministering for a number of years in independent "helping hand" type missions, he set up the United Christian Mission in 1898. This group emphasized the need for the infilling of the Holy Spirit—although this appears to have been a Holiness rather than a pentecostal emphasis—and by 1900 had built a meeting hall. Roberts then identified himself with the teachings of ▸John Alexander Dowie, and the mission was renamed Zion Tabernacle but closed down the following year.

After this Roberts returned to street preaching and organizing prayer meetings for revival. Later he became the missioner of the Wellington City Mission (Pentecostal) and worked with ▸Smith Wigglesworth in his pioneer pentecostal campaigns in N.Z. After Wigglesworth's Wellington campaign, this mission changed its name to the New Zealand Evangelical Mission and eventually became the Pentecostal Church of New Zealand in 1924. Wigglesworth's missions were followed up by those of ▸A. C. Valdez Sr., who selected Henry Roberts and four others as elders of the new movement. Roberts had previously been ordained by Smith Wigglesworth and was appointed as its first general superintendent. He held this position until 1941, when he passed his office on to his son ▸H. V. (Harry) Roberts. His grandson, Charles Bilby, and his great-grandson, ▸Ian Bilby, became leading figures in the Elim Church of New Zealand.

■ **Bibliography:** H. V. Roberts, *New Zealand's Greatest Revival* (1951) ▐ J. E. Worsfold, *A History of the Charismatic Movements in New Zealand* (1974).   ■ B. Knowles

ROBERTS, RICHARD (1948–). Faith healer and televangelist. Richard Roberts is the third child of ▸Oral and Evelyn Roberts, and although he accepted Christ as a child during one of his father's crusades, he did not turn his life over to God until after he enrolled at Oral Roberts University. Married at age 19 to a fellow singer in his father's ministry, Richard gave up his ambitions to be a night-club singer. His first marriage ended in divorce in 1978. Richard married

Lindsay Salem in 1980, and together they began to seek God for a healing ministry. Richard began to see results in his prayers for the sick as he began to call out healings given to him through the ▸"word of knowledge." In Sept. 1984 the daily hour-long television program *Richard Roberts Live* began with a Christian talk show format, and many healings were reported on the program. The program was shortened to a half-hour as part of the cutbacks required because of the financial drain on the ministry. Roberts also serves as president of the Oral Roberts Evangelistic Association.

Upon his father's promotion to chancellor in Jan. 1993, Richard Roberts was elected president and CEO of Oral Roberts University by the school's board of regents. He inherited a debt of some $42 million. Richard Roberts proved to be a good administrator and managed to significantly improve the financial position of the university in the first few years of his tenure. Enrollment has risen under his leadership, and the university has successfully passed a number of accreditation challenges. Theologically the school has shown strong support for the "Word of Faith" message (▸Positive Confession) under his leadership, thus providing a noted academic resource for that growing movement.

In Sept. 1997 Richard and Lindsay Roberts launched an hour-long live television show devoted to healing ministry five days a week in prime time. Starting on 20 stations, the program grew in two years to over 200 stations and has proved to be a vehicle to bring healing to many. The show is

Richard Roberts, who succeeded his father as president of Oral Roberts University and has, with his wife, Lindsay, a primetime television program devoted to healing.

broadcast live via the Internet and features live call-in testimonies as well.

■ **Bibliography:** R. Roberts, *He's the God of a Second Chance* (1985) ▮ idem and S. Andrews, *Ashes to Gold* (1987).   ■ J. R. Zeigler

ROBERTS, THOM (1902–83). Much-loved Welsh evangelist in France. Brought up in the ▸Welsh revival, Thomas Roberts was sent to France by the ▸Apostolic Church in 1926. Uncomfortable with Apostolic exclusivism but retaining his pentecostal convictions, he became pastor of an independent Reformed church in Paris in 1936. His friendship with ▸L. Dallière and his involvement in the ▸Union de Prière shaped the direction of his life's work. Roberts, a man of deep prayer, increasingly longed for revival, the integration of Israel, and the reconciliation of divided Christians. Thrilled by news of the charismatic renewal from America, Roberts entered the most important part of his ministry as an evangelist-teacher whose ministry was welcomed by Protestants and Catholics alike. He became a key figure in the annual Porte Ouverte Conventions near Chalon from 1971 on. His vision of a European convocation in the Spirit took flesh in "Pentecost over Europe" at Strasbourg in 1982.

■ **Bibliography:** "Thomas Roberts," Supplement to *Tychique*, no. 59.   ■ P. D. Hocken

ROBERTSON, MARION GORDON ("PAT") (1930–). Religious broadcaster, politician, businessman, and the founder of the Christian Broadcasting Network (CBN). Born Mar. 22, 1930, in Lexington, VA, Pat Robertson is the son of the late U.S. Senator A. Willis Robertson and the late Gladys Churchill Robertson. He is a graduate of Washington and Lee University (B.A., 1950), Yale University Law School (J.D., 1955), and New York Theological Seminary (M.Div., 1959). He served as a first lieutenant in the U.S. Marine Corps (1950–52). Robertson married Adelia ("Dede") Elmer in 1954. They have four children: Timothy, Elizabeth, Gordon, and Ann. Pat was an ordained Southern Baptist clergyman (1961–87).

The turning point in Robertson's life, according to his own testimony, was a day in New York in 1956 when he accepted Jesus Christ as his Savior ("I passed from death into life"). Later, while in seminary, Robertson was baptized in the Holy Spirit and for a time served as associate to Harald Bredesen, charismatic pastor of the Reformed Church in Mount Vernon, NY.

Robertson moved from New York to Portsmouth, VA, in 1959, and with initial capital of $70 bought a defunct UHF television station. Since that time Robertson has built the worldwide Christian Broadcasting Network (CBN). His flagship weekday television program, *The 700 Club*, has been on the air continuously since 1966 and is viewed daily by approximately 1 million people. This program currently airs three times a day on the Fox Family Channel cable network. In a year viewers of *The 700 Club* log some 2 million prayer calls with 250 prayer counselors manning phones to pray for callers. Since 1982 CBN's Middle East Television station in southern Lebanon has provided daily outreach to Israel and surrounding countries. It is estimated that more than 90 countries around the world are being touched regularly by CBN. CBN is now a sprawling complex of Williamsburg-style buildings on approximately 700 acres in Virginia Beach and Chesapeake with an annual operating budget of more than $200 million and more than 1,000 employees worldwide.

In 1977 Pat Robertson founded CBN (now Regent) University on the CBN campus. Beginning with a graduate School of Communications, the university now also includes the graduate Schools of Education, Counseling, Business, Divinity, Communications, Law, and the Center of Leadership Studies. Regent has been given full accreditation by the Southern Association of Colleges and Schools. The stated mission of the university is to bring biblical truth to bear on every discipline in every area of life.

Another outreach of CBN is Operation Blessing International (OBI), which, beginning in 1978, has become one of America's largest private organizations helping those in need. OBI provides short-term medical, hunger, and disaster relief

Pat Robertson, founder of CBN and Regent University in Virginia Beach, VA.

and development assistance to economically challenged people in the U.S. and overseas.

In Sept. 1986 Robertson announced his intention to run for the presidency of the U.S. if 3 million registered voters signed petitions by Sept. 1987 to support his candidacy financially and with prayer. That intent was realized in 1988, when Robertson unsuccessfully sought the Republican nomination.

CBN's international mission is to spread the gospel throughout the world by means of mass media, primarily television broadcasts. CBN's most recent international project, World Reach, was launched in the fall of 1995. The goal of CBN World Reach was to see 500 million new believers into God's kingdom as we entered the new millennium.

Robertson is the author of 10 books, including *The Turning Tide, The New Millennium, The New World Order*, and his most recent release, a book of fiction, *The End of the Age. The Secret Kingdom* was on the *New York Times* best-seller list in 1983 and, according to *Time* magazine, was the number one religious book in America in 1984. Robertson is past president of the prestigious Council on National Policy. In 1982 he served on President Ronald Reagan's Task Force on Victims of Crime.   ■ J. R. Williams

ROBINSON, ALBERT ERNEST (1877–1950).

As a layman, Albert Robinson was a charter member of the ▸Pentecostal Holiness Church (PHC) and was that organization's first general secretary (1911–25). He was a member of the general board of administration during his latter years.

A Canadian by birth, Robinson became acquainted with members of the ▸Fire-Baptized Holiness Church following his conversion while serving as a printer in their literature ministry. Later he began a long friendship with ▸Joseph H. King, who would become the bishop of the PHC. His publishing work included the printing of *Live Coals of Fire, Apostolic Evangel, The Pentecostal Holiness Advocate*, and PHC Sunday school literature. He also wrote and published a magazine, *The Apologist*. His book *A Layman and the Book* (1936) was required reading for PHC ministers.

■ **Bibliography:** C. Bradshaw, *Profiles of Faith* (1984).
■ W. E. Warner

ROBINSON, IDA (1891–1946).

Black female evangelist. Born in Georgia, Ida Robinson came to Philadelphia in 1917, assuming the pastorate of a small mission. In 1924, while fasting and praying, she received a vision from God to "come out on Mt. Sinai and loose the women." She subsequently organized the ▸Mt. Sinai Holy Church of America, which gave full clerical and episcopal rights to women. As first bishop of Mt. Sinai, she conducted revivals from New York to Florida and established a network of churches where men and women had equal access to leadership. Bishop

Robinson based her claim for full clerical rights for women on four biblical premises: (1) God created male and female in his own image and gave them both dominion before forming them as distinctly sexual beings; (2) the role of women in announcing the resurrection of Jesus; (3) the relationship of the Virgin Mary to Jesus ("If Mary could carry the Word of God in her womb, then I can carry the Word of God on my lips"); and (4) the equality of male and female in the body of Christ.

■ **Bibliography:** A. Fauset, *Black Gods of the Metropolis* (1944) ■ P. Jones, "A Minority Report: Black Pentecostal Women," *Spirit* 1 (2, 1977) ■ *The Manual of the Mount Sinai Holy Church* (1984) ■ R. Ruether, ed., *Women in American Religion*, vol. 3 (1986) ■ H. Trulear, "Reshaping Black Pastoral Theology: The Vision of Ida B. Robinson," *Journal of Religious Thought* 48 (1989) ■ idem, "There's a Bright Side Somewhere," *Journal of the Afro-American Historical and Genealogical Society* 2 (8, 1987).
■ H. D. Trulear

ROBISON, JAMES (1943–).

Televangelist. Born in Houston, TX, Robison spent much of his formative years living with foster parents, Herbert and Katie Hale. Hale was pastor of Memorial Baptist Church in Pasadena, TX, where Robison was saved at age 15.

Called to preach in 1961, Robison attended East Texas Baptist College in Marshall, TX, and married Betty Freeman in Feb. 1963. While pursuing his ministerial studies, he began to preach in a number of large Baptist churches in the South, including W. A. Criswell's First Baptist Church in Dallas. His heavy schedule of guest preaching forced him to drop out of Bible college in 1964. Robison began holding citywide crusades that drew record crowds in stadiums across the U.S.

Billy Graham was so impressed by Robison's dynamic preaching that he encouraged him to broadcast his message on television, and soon he became known as a televangelist, developing the James Robison Evangelistic Association in Fort Worth, TX. In his early ministry he endorsed issues central to fundamentalism, taking firm stands against the feminist movement, homosexuality, evolution, and secular humanism.

Robison's television ministry went national in 1979 with a prime-time series of 15 weekly programs that were aired in 200 large cities. Robison's regular show, *James Robison, Man with a Message*, ranked 11th on the Arbitron ratings in Feb. 1980.

In 1981, after a prayer session with a friend, Milton Green, Robison reported personal deliverance from demons that had plagued him for close to 15 years. He was healed of a number of bodily ailments and received a new zeal to serve God. Soon afterward his wife and three children each received physical healing. After these incidents Robison began to emphasize love and Christian unity, along with teaching on healing of the sick, deliverance from demons, and the gifts of the Holy Spirit. Despite his refusal to label himself a charismatic, this new emphasis brought him into conflict with the Southern Baptist Convention, so he broke off fellowship with his Euless (TX) Baptist Church. His television programs changed to a charismatic format and continued to be as popular as ever.

After a series of missionary travels around the world in the early 1990s, Robison felt a need to minister to the physical needs of people as well as the spiritual needs. That change in emphasis was reflected in 1992 by his ministry's name change to LIFE Outreach International, an evangelistic and humanitarian organization that ministers to needy children and adults around the world through relief efforts, the building of orphanages, and evangelism. Robison also produces *Life Today*, a daily television talk show aired on over 120 stations in the United States and Canada.

Among Robison's most popular books are *A New Beginning, The Right Mate, My Father's Face, Winning the Real War, The Spirit World,* and *Living in Holy Spirit Power.*

■ **Bibliography:** J. K. Hadden, *Prime Time Preachers* (1981), 42–43 ■ J. G. Melton, *Prime-Time Religion* (1997), 292–95 ■ J. Robison, *Thank God, I'm Free: The James Robison Story* (1988) ■ K. Walker, "A Heart for Broken People," *Charisma & Christian Life* (Aug. 1997).   ■ G. W. Gohr

ROSADO, LEONCIA ROSSEAU ("MAMA LEO")

(1912–). Pioneer Puerto Rican pentecostal pastor in New York City and cofounder of the Damascus Christian Church. Born on Apr. 11, 1912, in Toa Alta, Puerto Rico, Leoncia was converted during a pentecostal crusade on the island in 1932. Under the tutelage of her pastor, Vicente Ortiz, she began preaching to youth throughout the island. Prompted by a vision from God in 1935, she immigrated to New York City, where she began working as an evangelist alongside Francisco Olazábal's Latin American Council of Christian Churches (CLADIC). After Olazábal's death, CLADIC split into a number of *concilios* (councils or denominations), one of which Leoncia and her husband founded in New York City. Her husband, Francisco Rosado, became the first bishop of the newly formed Damascus Christian Church in 1939. As the new *concilio* grew, she began targeting drug addicts, prostitutes, alcoholics, and other social outcasts in New York City and in the Puerto Rican community. Her pioneer work among social outcasts in the barrio earned her the title "Mama Leo" by those to whom she ministered. Her work with drug addicts and alcoholics was carried out through the Damascus Christian Youth Crusade, which she and her husband founded in 1957. This ministry, which was a combination youth ministry and drug rehabilitation program, served as an early model for Christian social outreach programs in

the barrio that would later be replicated by Latino and Anglo denominations and churches throughout the U.S. Her work with social outcasts has attracted the attention of New York State leaders like former Governor Rockefeller. At 85 years of age she was still actively pastoring in the New York City metropolitan area. Her creative urban ministry, dynamic preaching, and powerful spiritual experiences have made "Mama Leo" a legend in her own time.

■ **Bibliography:** V. Sánchez Korrol, "In Search of Unconventional Women: Histories of Puerto Rican Women in Religious Vocations before Mid-Century," in *Barrios and Borderlands: Cultures of Latinos and Latinas in the United States,* ed. D. L. Daly Heyck (1994) ■ E. Villafañe, *The Liberating Spirit: Toward an Hispanic American Pentecostal Social Ethic* (1993).   ■ G. Espinosa

ROSSIN, DELBERT (1932–). Pastor in the Lutheran Church–Missouri Synod (LC–MS) who became the most widely recognized spokesman and leader of the charismatic movement in that denomination. He graduated from Concordia Seminary, St. Louis, MO, in 1963. In 1966 he experienced the baptism with the Holy Spirit and shared with his congregation (Faith Lutheran, Geneva, IL) what had happened to him. The congregation prospered as it incorporated the charismatic message into its life and structure. After building a strong charismatic congregation in Geneva, Rossin began to spend time traveling to counsel with other pastors and congregations who wanted to move into charismatic renewal. He and his congregation became articulate exponents of charismatic renewal among Lutherans.

Rossin's strong emphasis on worship and his program for training elders attracted particular notice. He was widely sought as a counselor, teacher, and worship leader. He was one of the founding members of the International Lutheran Conference on the Holy Spirit (1972). In 1985 his congregation released him to serve more than half time as coordinator of pastoral and parish renewal with the International Lutheran Renewal Center in St. Paul, MN, where at present he serves as vice president. Rossin is director of Renewal in Missouri, a fellowship of 600 LC–MS pastors working together for renewal in that Lutheran body. He and his wife, Beverly, have three children.

■ **Bibliography:** L. Christenson, ed., *Welcome, Holy Spirit* (1987).   ■ L. Christenson

ROWLANDS, JOHN FRANCES

ROWLANDS, JOHN FRANCES (1909–80). Missionary, pastor, denominational leader, author, and editor. J. F. Rowlands was born in a devout Quaker family in Bristol, England. His family came into contact with the pentecostal message in 1922 while visiting relatives in South Africa. Remaining in South Africa, Rowlands received the baptism of the Holy Spirit in 1925 under the ministry of Durban pastor A. H. Cooper. That same year, Rowlands began his ministry to Indians whose families had migrated to South Africa during the 19th century as sugarcane workers. His first service to the Indians was on July 26, 1925, in Pietermaritzburg. By 1931 the work had moved to Durban, where Rowlands established Bethesda Temple as his headquarters. From Durban, the Bethesda ministry spread throughout South Africa, successful in large part because an otherwise oppressed people found a place to integrate their Indian culture and their Christian faith. The Bethesda ministry affiliated with the Full Gospel Church (later ►Full Gospel Church of God in Southern Africa) in 1931. Rowlands founded a Bible school in 1933 and built Bethesda Bible College in 1975. He began publishing the monthly *Moving Waters* in 1940, which became an international voice for the ministry. Among his publications are *Why, Oh Why?*; *Let's Call Him Boya*; and *Upper Springs: Sermons from the Sanctuary*.

■ **Bibliography:** C. W. Conn, *Like a Mighty Army: A History of the Church of God* (1996) ■ I. G. L. du Plessis, "Pinkster Panorama: 'N Geskiedenis van die Volle Evangelie-kerk vand God in Suidelieke Afrika, 1910–1983" (1984) ■ "Graphic Bethesdaland Golden Jubilee Celebrations, Special Commemorative Supplement" (1981, Dixon

J. F. Rowlands, who in 1925 began to minister to Indian immigrants in South Africa.

Pentecostal Research Center, Cleveland, TN) ■ E. J. Moodley, "Pentecostal Catechesis in the Context of a Post-Apartheid South Africa: A Paradigm Change" (thesis, CG Theol. Sem., 1997).

■ D. G. Roebuck

RUESGA, DAVID (1898–1960). Pioneer Mexican pentecostal evangelist and founder of the Church of God in the Republic of Mexico (Iglesia de Dios en la República Mexicana). Born in Michoacán, Mexico, Ruesga, after studying in a school for Catholic priests, rode with Pancho Villa during the Mexican Revolution. After the Revolution, Ruesga and his wife, Raquel, immigrated to the United States to work in the film industry. After a near-death experience Ruesga became a Christian and claimed that God had miraculously healed him. In 1920 the Ruesgas returned to Mexico, where they began to preach the pentecostal message throughout Mexico City. About this time they came into contact with Anna Sanders, a Danish Assemblies of God (AG) missionary in Mexico City. In 1923 they organized what was perhaps the first AG church in the city in the Plaza de la Concepción Tepisqueuca. Within five years Ruesga claimed that his church had more than 1,000 members, which made it one of the largest Protestant churches in the country at that time.

In 1925 he was ordained by H. C. Ball and the Latin American District Council of the AG in the U.S., after which he worked as a very successful AG evangelist and minister in Mexico City until 1931. His church and evangelistic work quickly gave birth to a number of other churches throughout Mexico. Ruesga led his fledgling movement into the AG. His leadership qualities and personal charisma were two of the primary reasons that he was named the first superintendent of the General Council of the AG in Mexico in 1929. Then in 1931, after several years of quietly suppressing his negative feelings toward the influence of Anglo-American AG leadership in Mexico, he and a number of disgruntled followers left the AG and formed the Church of God in the Republic of Mexico. They took a significant number of followers and churches with them. His decision to leave the AG in Mexico split the work in that country and greatly weakened it. This led Rodolfo Orozco and Modesto Escobedo to suspend his ordination credentials. In 1940 Ruesga led his church into a union with the U.S.-based Church of God (CG, Cleveland, TN), only to break off ties and reestablish his own independent pentecostal denomination in 1946. The movement he founded is one of the largest indigenous pentecostal denominations in Mexico today, again named the Church of God in the Republic of Mexico. By the early 1990s there were an estimated 625 congregations and 150,000 adherents throughout Mexico.

■ **Bibliography:** G. Espinosa, "Borderland Religion: Los Angeles and the Origins of the Latino Pentecostal Movement in the U.S.,

Mexico, and Puerto Rico, 1906–1946" (Ph.D. diss., U. of Calif.–Santa Barbara, 1998) ■ P. Johnstone, *Operation World* (1993) ■ L. Scott, *Salt of the Earth: A Socio-Political History of Mexico City Evangelical Protestants (1964–1991)* (1991). ■ G. Espinosa

RUMSEY, MARY (18??–19??).

Mary Rumsey, the first pentecostal missionary to Korea, was baptized in the Holy Spirit at ʼAzusa Street in 1907, at which time she received a call to spread the pentecostal message to Korea and Japan. For several years she prepared herself for the mission by studying at the Elim Bible Institute in Rochester, NY.

Mary Rumsey, the first pentecostal missionary to Korea.

In 1928 Rumsey arrived in Inchon, Korea, and began her ministry in a Salvation Army hospital and home for missionaries. Her first years in Korea were difficult, and growth was slow. Her first congregation was known as the Subbingo Pentecostal Church and was located in Seoul. In 1938, after 10 years of intensive labor, the pentecostals had ordained new pastors and changed the name of their church to the Chosun Pentecostal Church and Mission Center. By 1940 this church had spawned five other congregations pastored by Koreans. The most important Korean leader in this period was Sung Han Park, who had attended a Bible school in Japan before returning to Korea to work with Rumsey.

During this time the Japanese occupied Korea, making life difficult for all Christians. The years during WWII and the Korean War (1950–52) were especially difficult for the fledgling church. For most of this period Rumsey was forced to return to the U.S., but the churches survived.

Just after the Korean War, at the urging of Rumsey, the Chosun Pentecostal Churches were turned over to the ʼAssemblies of God (AG). This was done in 1953 under the direction of AG missionary Abner Chestnut. Soon afterward the AG planted a Bible school in Seoul. One of the first students to attend was ʼPaul Yonggi Cho, a recent convert from Buddhism. In time the seeds planted by Rumsey and Cho blossomed into the largest Christian congregation in the world, the Yoido Full Gospel Church in Seoul.

■ **Bibliography:** Y. H. Lee, "The Holy Spirit Movement in Korea," *Journal of Soon Shin University* 4 (Dec. 1993) ■ J.-Y. Moon, ed., *Korean Assemblies of God: 30th Anniversary* (1981) ■ V. Synan, "The International Ministry of Dr. David Yonggi Cho," in *The Holy Spirit and the Church: A Collection of Scholarly Papers in Celebration of the 40th Anniversary of Dr. Yonggi Cho's Ministry* (1996).

■ H. V. Synan

RUSSIAN AND EASTERN EUROPEAN MISSION

A missionary society organized in 1927 under the name Russian and Eastern European Mission (REEM; later changed to Eastern European Mission [EEM]). Its founder, ʼPaul Bernhard Peterson, felt personally challenged to evangelize Russia after hearing reports of mass conversions of Russians to Protestantism after the country's revolution in 1917. While in Chicago, Peterson came into contact with E. W. Olson, a Russian missionary who was supported by the Swedish Baptist General Conference, and William Fetler, director of the Russian Missionary Society (RMS). The dedication of these persons to the evangelization of Russia motivated Peterson to do the same. He first became involved by becoming a trustee of RMS after it decided to move its headquarters from Philadelphia to Chicago in 1920. Two years later the society decided to support Peterson as a full-time missionary; he left for Eastern Europe in 1924 and remained there until 1926.

As a result of his missionary work, Peterson decided to organize a new missionary society shortly after he returned to the U.S. After gaining additional support, the REEM was founded in the spring of 1927. ʼG. Herbert Schmidt, who had previously served as a missionary in Poland, was chosen to establish a headquarters in Eastern Europe, and Peterson worked as general secretary of the Chicago office, which was designated as the mission's international headquarters.

In the summer of 1928 Schmidt was able to establish field headquarters for the mission in Danzig (now Gdansk), Poland. In 1930 the agency supported N. J. Poysti as a missionary in Manchuria and eastern Siberia. As a result of the Japanese occupation of Manchuria, Poysti returned to the U.S. in 1935. Shortly afterward, he established a local headquarters in New York City, where he began publishing a periodical in the Russian language known as *The Way of Faith* and began broadcasting a weekly radio program in Russian. Under the direction of these persons, EEM began to serve as an interdenominational society that supported foreign and national missionaries in the Soviet Union and Eastern Europe. Prior to WWII, EEM struggled to establish itself in the Soviet Union. Until 1928 there was considerable freedom to evangelize in Soviet Russia, but under the antireligious law of 1929, however, religious conditions radically changed. By 1930 all of EEM's missionaries in the Soviet Union were arrested and either imprisoned or exiled. It was not until after WWII that the agency was able to evangelize again in the Soviet Union.

During the 1930s, the organization met with better success in Poland. It began a Bible school in Danzig and conducted short-term Bible courses in neighboring areas for students from surrounding countries, such as Romania, Lithuania, Bulgaria, Yugoslavia, Hungary, and Latvia. The Bible school remained open until shortly before WWII.

For many years EEM had worked closely with the Assemblies of God (AG) Department of Foreign Missions, sharing personnel and providing mutual support for the work in Europe and Russia. This relationship ended in 1940, however, over AG dissatisfaction with REEM financial policies, its move away from a distinctly pentecostal posture theologically, and related problems.

The outbreak of the war greatly affected the entire operation in Eastern Europe. All of its foreign missionaries were forced to return to America, and the organization lost contact with its national workers as well. Forced out of Europe, EEM decided to focus its ministry on Russians and Eastern Europeans living in western Canada and the southern half of South America. It undertook the support of missionaries and evangelists who helped to establish churches in these areas. During this time Poysti conducted a weekly radio broadcast in Russian to the Slavic people in Ecuador and its surrounding countries.

Beginning in 1945 the agency began its refugee ministry by sending food and clothing to various camps that were established to help displaced persons uprooted from their homes as a result of the war. As its relief work expanded, EEM began to support many evangelists who ministered in the camps. In 1953 it established a center in West Berlin to provide material and spiritual aid to those persons who fled East Berlin to seek resettlement in the West. The center remained open until the wall was erected in 1961.

Since the 1950s, EEM has extended its ministries in Western Europe. The organization has also established offices near Amsterdam, Athens, Munich, and Vienna. From its center near Amsterdam, EEM has helped to evangelize the Netherlands through Bible correspondence courses, radio broadcasting, and the establishment of coffee houses. Near Munich other coffee houses were established. In Athens EEM has published Sunday school materials for children and adults. It has also founded a conference center and a retirement home. EEM directs several of its evangelistic programs to Eastern Europe from near Vienna. It has continued to supply Christian literature and relief supplies to churches and organizations in Bulgaria, Poland, Romania, and Yugoslavia. In Poland EEM conducts weekly radio broadcasts known as "The Voice of the Gospel from Warsaw." It conducts six weekly programs from other countries that are broadcast to the Soviet Union; it has also continued to supply the Soviet people with Bibles. Since 1985 EEM has conducted short-term outreach opportunities to Eastern Europe and the Soviet Union for persons interested in relief and Christian literature distribution. Since 1987 the international headquarters for Eurovision (formerly EEM), which had moved from Chicago to Pasadena, CA, in 1952, is located in Claremont, CA.

■ **Bibliography:** G. B. McGee, *This Gospel Shall Be Preached* (1986) ■ P. B. Peterson, *History of the First Fifty Years (1927–1977) of the Eastern European Mission* (n.d.).   ■ J. Colletti

S

SACRAMENTS Since there are no common answers to questions concerning the nature, number, or efficacy of the sacraments, it is necessary that this article offer the answers of a particular Christian confession. The understanding of sacraments that will be presented here is that of the Roman Catholic Church.

The word *sacrament* is the English equivalent of the Latin *sacramentum,* which, in early Christian Latin, was the common translation of the Greek *mystērion,* "mystery." The NT writers, especially Paul, identified the "mystery" as God's hidden plan of salvation for all, finally and definitively revealed in Christ. Indeed, Jesus Christ was himself identified as the sacrament, or visible manifestation, of the Father's mysterious will with regard to humanity.

The Latin Fathers used the term *sacramentum* to refer to various things that in one sense or another were manifestations or symbols of saving grace. Thus, the religious rites were seen as symbols of the mysteries of Christ's life, death, and resurrection. In the course of time, in Western theology, the term came to be used more exclusively of those acts of Christian worship that were understood to be not only symbolic, but in some way efficacious of the grace that they signified. It was only at the Council of Trent that the Catholic Church definitively declared the number of such sacraments to be seven, identifying them as baptism, confirmation, Eucharist, penance, holy orders, matrimony, and the anointing of the sick.

Catholics believe that in each of these liturgical actions, the church, as Christ's body, is in a special way united to its head as the High Priest who eternally offers himself to the Father on our behalf. Each of the sacraments is seen as a uniquely efficacious sign of Christ's power, as the risen Lord, to confer the fruits of his sacrifice on those who believe in him. Christ himself is understood to have instituted the seven sacraments and to be the principal agent of the effects they bring about.

While in each case there is a human minister, and in most of the sacraments the minister is required to have been duly ordained in order to represent both Christ and the church in this liturgical act, the effectiveness of the sacraments does not depend on the faith or holiness of the minister, since in these acts of the church it is Christ himself who confers grace through the agency of his Spirit. However, it is required that the minister intend to do what the church does in celebrating the sacraments.

On the other hand, the effectiveness of the sacraments to confer the gift of the Spirit does depend on the faith of the recipients and on their being properly disposed to receive such grace. Lack of faith or refusal to renounce grave sin would prevent a sacrament from having its intended effects. However, in the case of the baptism of infants, Catholics, relying on an ancient Christian tradition, hold that the faith of the church and the intention of the parents to bring up the child as a Christian justify the belief that the infant receives the saving grace of Christ at baptism without being able to make an act of personal faith at that time. Of course he or she must make such an act of faith when capable of it, and the special occasions for this confession of faith will be at the reception of confirmation and the Eucharist, which complete that person's Christian initiation. By these sacraments, which symbolize Christ's death and resurrection and the outpouring of the Spirit at Pentecost, new Christians are brought into a saving encounter with Christ in his mysteries and begin to enjoy the life of grace that is their fruit. Their incorporation into Christ is also their incorporation into his body, the church, initiating them into the priesthood of the faithful and enabling them to live the Christian life and to take an active part in the public worship of the church.

The principal actions in which the faithful exercise their baptismal priesthood are the celebrations of the other sacraments. Chief among these is the celebration of the Eucharist, in which Christ's sacrifice of himself for the world's salvation is symbolized by the offering of bread and wine, which are transformed by the power of the Holy Spirit into the body and blood of Christ. Catholics believe that Christ becomes truly present in the Eucharist as the High Priest who offers himself to the Father and joins the church to himself in the sacramental offering of this same unique, eternal sacrifice. By receiving the Eucharist in Holy Communion, the faithful become more deeply one body with Christ and with one another.

A Pentecostal wedding in Haiti.

CHURCHES AND SANCTUARIES AROUND THE WORLD

Nigeria

Yugoslavia

Mexico

Tonga

Marshall Islands

Costa Rica

Hong Kong

China

Malawi

While the sacraments of initiation confer the grace to live up to the demands of Christian life, human failure to correspond with grace results in sin, which involves the need of reconciliation with the Lord and with the church. Such reconciliation calls for repentance on the part of the sinner, and also an action on the part of the church, since Christ entrusted to his disciples the power to forgive sin in his name (cf. John 20:23). Catholics understand the exercise of this power to be a sacrament, symbolizing and effecting the pardon that Christ himself offers to the repentant sinner.

Liturgical initiation into two states of life that are especially vital to the life of the church and also involve a particular need of grace—marriage and ministry—is also understood to have sacramental efficacy. In holy matrimony the partners themselves are the ministers of the sacrament, which consists in the marriage covenant by which they bind themselves to one another in Christ. Ordination to the diaconate, the priesthood, or the episcopate is also a sacrament, of which the bishop is the only valid minister. This sacrament, like baptism and confirmation, is believed to have a permanent effect distinct from sanctifying grace and is traditionally spoken of as a "character." The most common interpretation of this is the one given by St. Thomas Aquinas, who saw it as a participation in the priesthood of Christ, which is shared, in different ways, by the baptized, the confirmed, and the ordained.

The seventh sacrament is the anointing of the sick, which for a long time was seen as a preparation for death but has recently been again recognized in its true nature as symbolic of Christ's ministry of healing of both spiritual and physical ills.

See also CHURCH, THEOLOGY OF THE; ORDINANCES, PENTECOSTAL.

■ **Bibliography:** J. Martos, *The Catholic Sacraments* (1984) ■ K. B. Osborne, *Sacramental Theology: A General Introduction* (1988) ■ K. Rahner, *The Church and the Sacraments* (1963) ■ E. Schillebeeckx, *Christ: The Sacrament of the Encounter with God* (1963).

■ F. A. Sullivan

SALMON, JOHN (1831–1918). Born in Glasgow, Scotland, John Salmon spent 10 years of his youth at sea, during which time he was converted to faith in Jesus Christ (1854). Serving in Canada, first as a Methodist and later as a Congregationalist minister, he became interested in divine healing in the 1880s; he was healed in 1885 of a kidney disease at an ▸A. B. Simpson convention. Salmon was present in 1887 at the formation of the Christian Alliance, becoming a vice president. He was the founding father of the Christian and Missionary Alliance in Canada and founding pastor of Bethany Church in Toronto. At an Alliance convention in Ohio in 1907, Salmon received the gift of tongues, and he

became for some years a proponent of the pentecostal baptism. He retired to California in 1911, where he experienced some disillusionment with pentecostal developments.

■ **Bibliography:** L. Reynolds, *Footprints* (1982).

■ P. D. Hocken

SALTER, JAMES (1890–1972). British pioneer missionary and cofounder of the Congo Evangelistic Mission. Born in Preston, he was associated with Thomas Myerscough's Bible school and the ▸Pentecostal Missionary Union. He sailed for Africa in May 1915 to join his friend ▸William F. P. Burton. They arrived together in the Belgian Congo in September. One of their party died en route, and Salter survived attacks of malaria and blackwater fever. In 1919 he returned to Britain and visited a number of pentecostal churches and met many of their leaders. Salter and Burton formed the Congo Evangelistic Mission after the Whitsun Convention at Kingsway Hall, London. Headquarters were established at Preston with ▸Thomas Myerscough as secretary-treasurer. "Jimmy" Salter became home director. He returned to the Congo in 1920, accompanied by several recruits, including Alice Wigglesworth, daughter of ▸Smith Wigglesworth. Salter married her; she stayed in the Congo only two years. The Salters spent much of their time traveling with Wigglesworth. Salter served on the executive council of the ▸Assemblies of God in Great Britain and Ireland and was chairman of their conference. He returned to the Congo regularly, sometimes for long periods. Loving, gracious, and wise, cautious and brave, he was given the Congolese nickname Inabanza, which means "wise counselor."

■ **Bibliography:** C. C. Whittaker, *Seven Pentecostal Pioneers* (1983).

■ D. W. Cartwright

SAMUEL, SAINT (c. 1885–1934). Evangelist and convocation worship leader in the ▸Church of God in Christ. Samuel was converted under the ministry of Bishop ▸Charles H. Mason in a revival conducted at Norfolk, VA, in 1907. While some details of his life are sketchy, he was married and held pastorates in Memphis, TN; Rockingham, NC; and Norfolk, VA. Through him God wrought special miracles, and he also distinguished himself as a worship leader at the national convocations in Memphis. Many believers were blessed as they watched Samuel literally "wrestle the devil." He would stamp his feet and make a weird noise as though he were chasing an animal and then begin to rebuke Satan. His rebukes were, "Get out of here, you fool," "On your way to hell," "God rebuke you," "God is your boss," or "I'll get the Boss on you." After his death, many reported that they heard him singing in the Spirit his favorite song, "My Soul Loves Jesus," and saw him entering the funeral service.

■ **Bibliography:** C. E. Jones, *Black Holiness: A Guide to the Study of Black Participation in Wesleyan Perfectionist and Glossolalic Pentecostal Movements* (1987). ■ L. Lovett

SANDERS, ANNA (1869–1955). Pioneer Assemblies of God (AG) minister and missionary to Mexico and Cuba. Originally from Denmark, Sanders emigrated to Canada and then to the U.S., where she was later ordained a missionary by the Latin American District Council of the AG in San Antonio, TX, in 1927. After a vision in which she believed God called her to work as a missionary in Mexico, she began a lifelong career as a foreign missionary. Although she was ordained in 1927, she actually began missionary work in Mexico City in 1921, when she was 52 years old and did not know any Spanish. In Mexico City she met ➤David and Raquel Ruesga. The three founded the first permanent AG work in that city. Sanders served as a missionary in Mexico City (1921–30, 1940–47); Havana, Cuba (1931–36); Texas (1931, 1936–40); and Merida, Mexico (1948–50). While in the U.S. she taught at the Latin American Bible Institute in Texas from 1936 to 1940. The work she helped found in Mexico City served as a major catalyst in the development of the AG work throughout Mexico. She is considered one of the key founders of the AG in Mexico.

■ **Bibliography:** V. De León, *The Silent Pentecostals* (1979) ■ G. Espinosa, "Borderland Religion: Los Angeles and the Origins of the Latino Pentecostal Movement in the U.S., Mexico, and Puerto Rico, 1906–1946" (Ph.D. diss., U. of Calif.–Santa Barbara, 1998) ■ L. Jeter de Walker, *Siembra y Cosecha: Reseña histórica do las Asembleas de Dios de México y Centroamérica,* vol. 1 (1990). ■ G. Espinosa

SANDFORD, FRANK (1862–1948). Author, publisher, pastor, evangelist, Bible school founder, and utopian visionary who played a pivotal role in the training of many Holiness people who would later become pentecostals, among them ➤C. F. Parham and ➤A. J. Tomlinson. Born in Bowdomham, ME, Sandford received his primary education at Nichols Latin School in Lewiston. He was converted on Feb. 29, 1880.

Upon graduation from Bates College (1886), Sandford entered Cobb Divinity School. The following year he dropped out of seminary, claiming that it did not satisfy his "intense spiritual hunger," and he became pastor of the Free Baptist church in Topsham. That first summer he was influenced heavily by Hannah Whitall Smith's *The Christian's Secret of a Happy Life,* which seemed to satisfy the "craving" of his soul. His congregation grew rapidly.

In 1890 Sandford moved to a second pastorate in Grand Falls (Somersworth), NH. While there, he attended Methodist meetings on the campgrounds of Old Orchard, ME, and accepted the Holiness teaching on sanctification. Contact with the Christian Alliance led him to a belief in divine healing as well. He attended summer schools led by D. L. Moody in Northfield, ME, and as a result entered the Student Volunteer Movement. With T. H. Stacey, a pastor from Auburn, ME, and a denominational executive, Sandford traveled the globe and became convinced that current missionary efforts were so fruitless that he could no longer be bound by a single denomination and that the final work of God on earth would include the separation of humanity into two groups: Christ's and antichrist's, through the use of "signs, wonders, and mighty deeds."

Toward the end of his second pastorate, Sandford married Helen C. Kinney, who had served as a Christian Alliance missionary in Japan, following in her parents' footsteps. They left Great Falls and traveled to Texas, New York, and New Jersey, finally settling in Lancaster, ME.

Sandford recounted the years 1893–99 as his "journey back to apostolic life and power," and he wrote of them in *Seven Years with God* (1900; repr. 1957). During this time, he founded the Holy Ghost and Us Bible School, held evangelistic crusades, studied divine healing, and edited and published a periodical initially called *Tongues of Fire* (1894). His concern for the unreached led him to claim divine direction when, in a project financed by faith and built in large part with student labor, he constructed a large, white, Victorian structure named Shiloh, complete with turrets, towers, and flags, on a hilltop near Durham, ME. From here, the gospel would go throughout the world as students, steeped in faith, evangelism, and divine healing went forth. In the meantime this project attracted a large following, many of whom moved to the area. By 1904 some 600 residents who had donated all they owned to Shiloh were living together in community. Still, all was not well at Shiloh, for rumors flew concerning Sandford's authoritarian rule and abusive discipline.

Sandford's missionary concern led in 1905 to the purchase of a schooner, the *Coronet,* and a barkentine, the *Kingdom,* for use in worldwide evangelization. It was this enterprise that brought about Sandford's downfall. In June 1911, while on a missionary trip, the *Kingdom* was wrecked off the African coast. All personnel were placed on board the *Coronet.* Sandford was on board, providing leadership and waiting on God for direction. A series of bad decisions compounded the predicament of those on board, and by the time they reached Portland, ME, on Oct. 21, 1911, several had died from lack of food and water, and others were nearly dead. By Nov. 1 a total of nine had died.

Sandford was soon plagued by renewed reports of his iron rule and disciplinary measures. He was arrested and charged with manslaughter. His trial began on Dec. 1, 1911, and he was convicted and sentenced to a 10-year term in the federal penitentiary in Atlanta, GA. Sandford constantly maintained that God had directed him in all that he did, but he never fully recovered from this blow. Bartleman, for instance, classed him with J. A. Dowie as a spiritual charlatan who "severely abused and fleeced the flock of God" and came "to a most disreputable and execrable end." Released early from prison, Sandford lived in semiretirement until 1948, when he died at age 85.

The Shiloh movement continues to the present, with headquarters in Dublin, NH. It has kept many of Sandford's works in print through its own Kingdom Press.

■ **Bibliography:** F. Bartleman, "All Things in Common," *Confidence* 6 (4, 1918) ▌ H. F. Day, "The Saints of Shiloh," *Leslie's Monthly Magazine* (Apr. 1905) ▌ W. C. Hiss, "Shiloh: Frank W. Sandford and the Kingdom: 1893–1948" (Ph.D. diss., Tufts U., 1978) ▌ F. S. Murray, *The Sublimity of Faith: The Life and Work of Frank W. Sandford* (1981) ▌ S. Nelson, *Fair, Clear, and Terrible: The Story of Shiloh* (1989) ▌ F. W. Sandford, *The Art of War for the Christian Soldier* (1904; repr. 1966) ▌ A. L. White, "The Tragic Voyage of the Shiloh Schooner 'Coronet,'" *Down East* (May 1974) ▌ E. P. Woodward, "Sandfordism: An Exposure," *The Safeguard and Armory* 6 (Jan. 3, 1902).　　　　　■ C. M. Robeck Jr.

SANDIDGE, JERRY L. (1939–92).

Pentecostal missionary-scholar and ecumenist. Sandidge was born on Nov. 16, 1939, in Tulsa, OK, the youngest child of Frank and Hazel Sandidge. He felt a call to the ministry at the age of 9 and preached his first sermon when he was 12. He was married to Pat Hite on Aug. 15, 1959; one son, Jay, was born in 1975.

Sandidge attended Central Bible College (B.A., 1961; M.A., 1964), the University of Missouri–Columbia (M.Ed., 1968), and the Catholic University of Leuven, Belgium (M.A., 1976; Ph.D., 1985). He was ordained in 1963 by the Assemblies of God (AG), serving churches in St. Louis, MO, and Memphis, TN, before joining the Sunday school and youth departments at the AG headquarters in Springfield, MO. From 1971 until 1982, Sandidge was a missionary in Belgium, where he taught at Continental Bible College (Brussels) and founded University Action, a pentecostal ministry to university students in Europe. Subsequently, he served on the faculties of Central Bible College, the AG Theological Seminary, Oral Roberts University, and Regent University (Virginia Beach, VA). In 1988 he became senior pastor of Evangel Temple, Springfield, MO.

While in Europe, Sandidge became involved in the International Roman Catholic/Pentecostal ʼDialogue and eventually was elected secretary of the steering committee. He frequently was a representative to the European Charismatic Leaders Conference, as well as a delegate to the National Council of Churches and a speaker at the World Council of Churches (Geneva). His heart burned with the need for unity in the body of Christ, and he participated in interfaith dialogues until the time of his death. At a time when ecumenism was viewed negatively by most pentecostals, Jerry Sandidge was a leading ecumenist, standing courageously against ecclesiastics who distrusted and openly opposed him.

■ **Bibliography:** J. Sandidge, "The Origin and Development of the Catholic Charismatic Movement in Belgium" (M.A. thesis, Leuven, 1976) ▌ idem, "Roman Catholic-Pentecostal Dialogue (1977–1982): A Study in Developing Ecumenism" (Ph.D. diss., Leuven, 1985).　　　　　　　　　■ S. M. Burgess

SANDRU, TRANDAFIR (1924–98).

Author, educator, and leader of the Apostolic Church of God of Romania. Sandru was converted and baptized in water in 1941 and received the baptism in the Holy Spirit in 1942. He served the church as a lay minister from the age of 21, when he was elected as general secretary of the clandestine ACG. Sandru was ordained in 1953 and served as pastor in two churches of Bucharest. During his early pastoral work he completed his studies at the University of Bucharest and received a degree in ancient history in 1956. Communist authorities revoked Sandru's ministerial credentials in 1958, but he was reinstated in 1963, when Christian leaders and organizations from the Western world came in contact with him. Because of his bold stand, the authorities discontinued his ministry for a second time (1965–68).

After being reinstated in 1968 as pastor, Sandru devoted most of his time to the training of ministers. He conducted short-term training courses for pastors between 1974 and 1976. In 1976 he established the Seminarul Teologic Pentecostal of Bucharest, an undergraduate school that was upgraded to a university-level institution in 1992 and is known as the Institutul Teologic Penticostal–Bucuresti (The Pentecostal Theological Institute–Bucharest). Sandru served as its president. In the fall of 1997 the PTI had a total enrollment of 63 full-time students and 310 correspondence students.

Sandru was also known as the most prolific pentecostal writer of Romania. Stimulated by the great need for theological books in Romanian language, he started his literary activity in 1976 and authored 12 books in various fields: *A Pastor's Guide* (1976); *The Life and Teaching of Apostle Paul* (1977); *Pneumatology: The Person and the Work of the Holy Spirit* (1979); *The Pentecostal Apostolic Church of God in Romania* (Romanian ed., 1982; English ed., 1983); *Evangelology: The Life, Activity and Teaching of Jesus Christ* (1986); *The Biblical Doctrines of the Church* (1989); *The Pentecostal Church in the History of Christianity* (1992); *The Dogmatics of the Pentecostal Apostolic Church of God* (1993); *Pages from the History of a Local Church* (1994); *The Christian Church: Development and Spirituality* (1995); *The Lord's Wars* (1996); and *The Pentecostal Revival in Romania* (1997). For his theological activity and leadership, Sandru in 1992 received an honorary doctorate from the Church of God School of Theology, Cleveland, TN.

Sandru served the ACG as vice president (1948) and secretary-general (1945–46, 1949–50, 1951–56, 1986–94). He also edited the denominational magazines *Vestitorul Evangheliei* (*The Gospel Herald*, 1945–48) and *Buletinul Cultului Penticostal* (*Bulletin of the Pentecostal Denomination*, 1968–86).

■ **Bibliography:** D. D. Bundy. "The Roumanian Pentecostal Church in Recent Literature," *Pneuma* 7 (1985) ▮ idem, "Tandafir Sandru, Biserica Crestina: Evolutie si spiritualitate," *Pneuma* 18 (1996) ▮ T. Sandru, *Biserica Penticostala in Istoria Crestinismului* (1992).   ■ J. F. Tipei

SANFORD, AGNES MARY (1897–1982). Pioneer in healing ministry. The child of Presbyterian missionaries, Agnes White spent her youth in China, except for her college years, which she spent in the U.S. She married an Episcopal priest, Edgar Sanford, in 1923, and they returned to the U.S. in 1925.

Mrs. Sanford's interest in healing developed after she was healed of long-standing depression. Studying the Scriptures, she discovered that she had a gift of healing. Her wider ministry began when her first book, *The Healing Light,* was published in 1947 and became a best-seller. Around 1953–54 Sanford experienced a definite empowering of the Holy Spirit and then received the gift of tongues after contact with some pentecostals. In 1955 the Sanfords launched the School of Pastoral Care, which held residential conferences for clergy, their wives, and medical personnel on the ministry of healing. These continued after her husband's death in 1960.

Though Sanford never spoke in public of the pentecostal experience, she frequently did so in private, urging discretion on the recipients, many of them clergy. Through contacts in the Schools of Pastoral Care, Camps Farthest Out, and the Order of St. Luke, Sanford was one of the foremost promoters of renewal in the Holy Spirit within the historic churches in the English-speaking world. Her teaching had a sacramental dimension that gave a greater place to natural processes than evangelical and pentecostal healing ministries, presenting God's healing work as following the laws of nature and positive thinking. Sanford was the major pioneer in ministry for the healing of memories, which for her was all one with the forgiveness of sin. Her other major books include *Behold Your God* (1958), *The Healing Gifts of the Spirit* (1966), *The Healing Power of the Bible* (1969), and her autobiography, *Sealed Orders* (1972).

■ **Bibliography:** J. T. Connelly, "Neo-Pentecostalism: the Charismatic Revival in the Mainline Protestant and Roman Catholic Churches of the United States, 1960–1971" (Ph.D. diss., U. of Chicago, 1977).   ■ P. D. Hocken

SAVELLE, JERRY (1946–). Charismatic evangelist and author. Ordained by ▸Kenneth Copeland, Savelle is a leading figure in the Word of Faith movement (▸Positive Confession). With headquarters in Crowley, TX, Jerry Savelle Ministries International (JSMI) has outreach ministries in over 50 countries, including Australia, Kenya, South Africa, Tanzania, and the United Kingdom. In 1994 Savelle founded the JSMI Bible Institute and School of World Evangelism in Crowley.

Savelle is the author of numerous books, including *In the Footsteps of a Prophet* (1999), which tells the story of Kenneth Copeland's meetings in Savelle's hometown in 1969 that launched Savelle's ministry. Savelle also is author of *Turning Your Adversity into Victory* (c. 1994) and *Honoring Your Heritage of Faith: Why God Wants You to Develop and Perpetuate a Life of Faith* (c. 1995).

In 1966 Jerry Savelle was married to Carolyn, who shares in his global ministry.   ■ S. M. Burgess; J. Zeigler

SCADDEN, CECIL C. H. (1891–1964). Cecil Scadden influenced a number of different pentecostal groups in New Zealand. He was a representative at the Dec. 1924 convention, following the ▸Smith Wigglesworth campaigns, that resulted in the establishing of the Pentecostal Church of New Zealand (PCNZ). Two years later he was lay pastor of a Palmerston North church with links to the movement and a member of the leadership team at the 1926 convention in New Plymouth.

However, controversy over the constitutional format of the PCNZ led to the secession of a number of leaders, including Scadden and ▸A. C. Valdez Sr., in early 1927. The Assemblies of God (AGNZ) was established as a result, and Scadden's Palmerston North church became the first of its congregations to be organized in N.Z. Others followed, and 12 assemblies were registered at the inaugural meeting in Mar. 1927. Scadden held several leadership roles in the AGNZ, serving as secretary-treasurer from 1928 on, as a member of the executive committee throughout the 1930s, and as vice chairman of the movement from 1934 on. He also set up the first AGNZ bookshop in N.Z. and was editor of the movement's official magazine, the *New Zealand Evangel*. In 1934 he moved to Onehunga, Auckland, where he took over the principalship of a self-supporting AGNZ Bible school. By 1938, however, Scadden had left the AGNZ and for a short while pastored an independent congregation in Onehunga known as the Full Gospel Mission. This group then affiliated with the Auckland City Apostolic Church, and Scadden became a pastor in that movement the following year. He rose rapidly in the ranks of the Apostolic Church, was ordained as an apostle in 1940, and in 1942 was appointed to its N.Z. executive committee and to the office of dominion secretary. Scadden served in pastorates in Christchurch and Auckland—where his congregation was the then-largest Apostolic church in the country—and in Hastings.

■ **Bibliography:** J. E. Worsfold, *A History of the Charismatic Movements in New Zealand* (1974) ■ idem, *The Reverend Gilbert and Mrs Alice White* (1994).   ■ B. Knowles

SCANDINAVIAN MISSIONS TO LATIN AMERICA The

Churches in Norway, Sweden, and Finland were involved early in the support of missions in Latin America. This support took several forms: (1) financial and moral support for missionaries of Scandinavian descent who found their way to Latin America, usually via the U.S. or Great Britain, and began communicating with one of the churches in Scandinavia; (2) support for persons sent from either a large congregation or through one of the more centralized mission sending programs; (3) moral support for indigenous churches in Latin America; (4) the directing of economic and social development aid to communities in which there are pentecostal congregations; and (5) IBRA Radio, which has covered the continent of South America for decades.

Scandinavian pentecostal mission has touched much of Latin America, from Mexico to Argentina and Chile. It has been especially formative for Brazil, Mexico, Chile, and Argentina. Elsewhere the ecclesiology of the Swedish pentecostals has also frequently been adopted. Scandinavian missionaries and aid organizations quietly supported indigenous denominations. Such was the case in the Brazilian denomination Brazil para Cristo, with headquarters in São Paolo, where a Swedish pentecostal missionary worked quite anonymously to stabilize the structure of a ministry after a crisis. This has been a recurring pattern throughout the continent. Missionaries such as G. Leonard Pettersen (supported by Swedish and Norwegian congregations) worked under the direction of Brazilian leaders or planted churches in outlying areas and turned them over to Brazilian pastors, with minimal non-Brazilian financial support.

Scandinavian contacts with Latin America began in 1909 with the arrival of Birger Johnson in Argentina, sent from a Norwegian pentecostal congregation in New York. He soon began publishing reports in *Byposten* and *Korsets Seier*. In 1910 ►T. B. Barratt began a correspondence with ►Willis Hoover in Chile, and Hoover came to agree with Barratt on congregational polity as an improvement on their Methodist experience. In 1910 Daniel Berg and Gunnar Vingren arrived in Brazil and, from 1912 on, received support from Sweden. The Assembleias de Deus do Brasil is an outgrowth of their work. Axel and Esther Andersson arrived in Mexico in 1919, and from their ministry evolved several large denominations including about 15,000 congregations and regular preaching sites. By 1930 there were Swedish pentecostal missionaries in Argentina, Bolivia, Brazil, and Mexico. Brazil received the most attention.

In 1930, after a major debate over mission theory within the Swedish pentecostal church, Lewi Pethrus made a historic trip to Brazil to reinforce the traditional Swedish mission theory and ecclesiology. He informed missionaries, clergy, and laity alike that the churches in Brazil with ties to the Swedish pentecostal churches were independent of and equal to the Scandinavian mother churches. He insisted that each was responsible for its own growth, foreign mission, finances, and theological reflection. The Swedish churches, he averred, were to aid the Brazilian churches but not control them. Swedish pentecostal missionaries have served in Argentina, Bolivia, Brazil, Chile, Colombia (IBRA Radio), Equador, Guatemala, Honduras, Mexico, Panama, Peru, and Uruguay. Missionaries from the Brazilian church have served across the continent and in North America and Europe.

The Swedish-language Finnish Pentecostal Churches began mission work in South America before WWII, with missionaries in Argentina (1935). After the war came efforts in Brazil and Bolivia. Finnish-speaking Finnish pentecostal missionaries have served in Bolivia, Equador, Uruguay, Peru, and Mexico. Norwegian pentecostal missionaries went to Argentina, Bolivia, Brazil, Chile, Colombia, Paraguay, Tobago, and Trinidad.

Economic and social development work has long been an essential component of all Scandinavian pentecostal mission efforts. In Sweden, a separate organization, the Pentecostal Missionary Union was developed to fund, execute, and evaluate these efforts. The history and philosophy of the Swedish pentecostal developmental mission work was discussed by Åke Boberg et al., *Från vision till verklighet: 15 år med Pingstmissionens U-landshjälp* (n.d.). Studies and evaluations of some of these projects in Latin America have resulted in book-length analyses, including Jan-Åke Alvarsson, *Skola för de allra fattigaste? Utvärdering av gymnasieskolan Buenas Nuevas i Cochabamba, Bolivia* (1989); idem, *Utvärdering av Jordbruksproject i Tartagal, Argentina* (1993); and Margareta Mobergh and Francisco Pereyra, *Utvärdering av Barnhemsprojektet i Ituzaingó, Argentina* (1994).

IBRA Radio has been an influential factor in pentecostal development throughout Latin America. Transmission sites are located in 26 cities in eight Latin American countries (Argentina, Bolivia, Brazil, Chile, Honduras, Paraguay, Peru, and Uruguay). The headquarters are in Bogota, Colombia. On the history and mission of IBRA Radio, see Eskil Johansson, *IBRA Radio: Radiomission—Varför?* (n.d.); idem, ed., *IBRA Radio 30 år. International Broadcasting Association* (1985); and idem, *Radion blev mitt liv* (1990).

■ **Bibliography:**

Unpublished, Archival, and Periodical Sources. Material about Scandinavian mission and Latin America can be found in *Byposten, Korsets Seier, Korsets Seger, Korsets Budskap, Ristin Voitto, Herren Kommer, Evangelii Härold, Julens Härold, Dagen, Petrus,* and other periodicals. Yearbooks are essential for tracing developments and changes of address. Relevant Brazilian periodicals include *Boa Semente* and *Mensageiro de Paz*. Archival resources are found in several congregations in Oslo, Stockholm, Göteborg, Helsinki, and other cities, as well as at the central offices of the national pentecostal mission organizations in Oslo, Stockholm, and Helsinki. There are resources at the national libraries and archives of each country, as well as in the university libraries at Oslo, Uppsala, Helsinki, and Åbo. The most important collection of published materials is at the Pentecostal Information Center, Kaggeholm, Ekerö, near Stockholm. From 1990, Scandinavian periodical literature related to pentecostal mission may be found in the index *Missio Nordica*.

General Mission and Pentecostal Histories. W. Hollenweger, *El Pentecostalismo, historia y doctrina* (1976) ∎ idem, *Enthusiastisches Christentum: Die Pfingstbewegung in Geschichte und Gegenwart* (1969) ∎ idem, *Handbuch der Pfingstbewegung*, 10 vols. (1966; microfilm, 1967) ∎ idem, *The Pentecostals: The Charismatic Movement in the Churches* (1972) ∎ K. T. Palosuo, T. Ruolanen, and E. Vaananen, *Suomalainen kehitysyhteistyo ja lahetystyo 1977* (Helsinki, 1977) ∎ K. B. Westman et al., *Nordisk Missionshistorie* (1950) [published in all Scandinavian languages].

Finland. [*Suomen Vapaa Ulkolähetys* = Finnish Free Foreign Mission and *Finlands Svenska Pingstmission* = Finnish Swedish Pentecostal Mission] L. K. Ahonen, *Suomen helluntaiheräryksen historia* (1994) ∎ E. J. Anturi, "Helluntaiheräryksen toiminnen tarastelua," in K. Anturi et al., *Helluntaiherätys tänään* (1986) ∎ A. Hämäläinen, ed., *Kaikkeen maailman 1929–1989: 60 vuotta helluntaiseurahuntien lähetystyöyä* (1989) ∎ A. Herberts, *I Kärlekens tjänst: Finlands Svenska Pingstmission under 70 år* (1994) ∎ R. Kanto, *Pingströrelsen i Svenskfinland* (1994).

Norway. [*Norsk Pinsevennes ytre misjon* = Norwegian Pentecostal Foreign Mission] Erling Andressen, *Blandt indianere og katolikker i Argentina* (1935) ∎ D. D. Bundy, "Pentecostal Missions to Brazil: The Case of the Norwegian G. L. Pettersen," *Norsk tidskrift for misjon* 47(1993) ∎ K. Juul, *Til Jordens ender: Norsk pinsemisjon gjennom 50 år* (1960) ∎ O. Nilsen, . . . *og Herren virket med: Pinsebevegelsen gjennom 75 år* (1981) ∎ idem, *Ut i all verden: Pinsevennenes ytre misjon i 75 år* (1984) ∎ P. A. Pedersen, *Blandt indianere i Chaco* (1970) ∎ G. L. Pettersen, *Blant folkeslag i Sør-Amerika* (1947) ∎ idem, *Pinse over grensene* (1989) ∎ idem, *Sør-Amerika, framtidens kontinent* (1966) ∎ M. Ski, *Fram til Urkristendommen: Pinsevekkelsen gjennom 50 år*, 3 vols. (1956–59) ∎ I. M. Witzøe, ed., *De Aapene Døre: Norges Frie Evangelishke Hedningemissions argeider og virke gjennom 10 aar* (1925).

Sweden. [*Svensk Fria Missionen* = Swedish Free Mission] J.-Å. Alvarsson, *Dela som syskon: Att förmedla evangeliet över kulturgränserna* (1992) ∎ *Apostolisk väckelse i Brasilien* (1934) ∎ D. Berg, *Men, störst av allt . . .* (1992) ∎ Å. Boberg, *Svensk Pingstmission* (1990) ∎ D. D. Bundy, "Swedish Pentecostal Mission Theory and Practice to 1930: Foundational Values in Discussion," *Mission Studies* 14 (1997) ∎ idem, "Swedish Pentecostal Missions: The Case of Axel Andersson in Mexico," in *To the Ends of the Earth* (23d Annual Meeting of the Society for Pentecostal Studies, 1993), with Spanish version ∎ B. Carlsson, *Organisationer och Beslutsprocessor inom Pingströrelsen* (1990) ∎ E. Cohen, *Simon Lundgren e a Obra Missionária no Brasil* (1986) ∎

E. Conde, *Historia das Assembleias de Deus no Brasil* (1960) ∎ A. de Almeida, *Historia das Assembleias de Deus no Brasil* (1982) ∎ P. Franklin, *Bland pingstvänner och övergivna helgonbilder i Sydamerika* (1927) ∎ Z. B. Macalão, *Traços da vid Paulo Leivas Macalão* (1986) ∎ O. Nelson, *Aventyr i Sydamerika* (Stockholm, 1955) ∎ G. E. Söderholm, *Den Svenska Pingstväckelsens Historia, 1907–1927*, 2 vols. (1929) ∎ idem, *Den Svenska Pingstväckelsens spridning utom och inom Sverige* (1933) ∎ A. Sundstedt, *Pingstväckelsen—dess uppkomst och första utvecklingsskede* (1967) ∎ idem, *Pingstväckelsen—en världväckelse* (1973) ∎ idem, *Pingstväckelsen och dess genombrott* (1971) ∎ idem, *Pingstväckelsen och dess utbredning* (1972) ∎ idem, *Pingstväckelsen—och dess vidare utveckling* (1971) ∎ M. and N. Taranger, *Brasiliansk mosaik* (1965) ∎ A. Törnberg, *Från Amazonas till La Plata* (1956) ∎ I. Vingren, *Det började I Pará: Svensk Pingstmission I Brasilien* (1994) ∎ idem, *Pionjärens dagbok* (1968).

∎ D. D. Bundy

SCANLAN, MICHAEL (1931–). Prominent figure in the ▸Catholic charismatic renewal (CCR). A qualified lawyer, admitted to the bar of New York State in 1956, Scanlan entered the Third Order Regular Franciscans in 1957. Ordained priest in 1964, he immediately became dean at the College of Steubenville, OH. Appointed rector of St. Francis' Seminary, Loretto, PA, in 1969, he was baptized in the Spirit there that fall following a talk by two visiting Catholic leaders.

Scanlan's main contributions to charismatic renewal among Catholics have been as president at Steubenville; as a prominent preacher-teacher; as promoter-organizer of Steubenville conferences; and as a member of renewal committees. Of these, the first is probably the most significant. Returning to Steubenville in 1974, Scanlan transformed a small Catholic college into a thriving university (achieving university status in 1980) with a reputation for Christian orthodoxy and a strong, Spirit-filled campus life. As a regular speaker at renewal conferences in the U.S. and elsewhere, Scanlan was already a recognized preacher when, in 1983, he joined ▸Ralph Martin, ▸John Bertolucci, and ▸Ann Shields in F.I.R.E., which held rallies in major cities (preaching faith, intercession, repentance, and evangelism). Scanlan has pioneered annual residential conferences at Steubenville for priests and deacons (since 1975), for youth (since 1982), and for prayer-group leaders (since 1983). He was for some years a member of the National Service Committee for CCR, being chairman from 1976 to 1978. He was a member of the Servants of Christ the King community in Steubenville until 1991; the community was then part of the Sword of the Spirit (see ▸Charismatic Communities), of which Scanlan was a leader. Among Scanlan's published books are *The Power in Penance* (1972), *Inner Healing* (1974), *And Their Eyes Were Opened* (with A. Shields, 1976), *Deliverance from Evil Spirits* (with R. Cirner; 1980), and *Let the Fire Fall* (1986), an autobiography.

∎ P. D. Hocken

SCHAEPE, JOHN G. (1870–1939). The person credited with receiving the initial revelation concerning the Oneness doctrine and baptism in Jesus' name. Schaepe was reared in a German Lutheran home, one of at least three children. At age 14 he left home, taking a job aboard a ship. He spent the next five years sailing to South American ports. Deserting ship in Argentina when he was 18, John worked his way to the Pampas, where he learned to ride horses, herd cattle, and qualify as a cowboy and bronco-buster. After a time in Argentina he came to the U.S. and worked on the ranges of Wyoming and Montana; he became a fugitive from justice because of his constant brawling and fled to Hawaii.

In 1903, shortly after arriving in Hawaii, Schaepe was unable to find work. Instead, he found his way toward the Honolulu waterfront, where he intended to mug a passing sea captain with the aid of his .38-caliber pistol. What he found was a Salvation Army mission into which he was drawn by the music. There he heard testimonies that made him desire "a better way of living." He returned to his hotel room, where he was converted, and then quickly joined the Salvation Army.

Schaepe stated in his testimony that God "baptized me with the Holy Spirit" on Feb. 23, 1906, and that he spoke in Chinese, Japanese, and Korean. This would place his experience prior to the Azusa Street revival. It is probable, however, that it was actually in 1907 when he received his "baptism," since he was apparently working in Southern California, breaking horses, at the time the revival broke in Los Angeles.

The occasion for Schaepe's now famous revelation was a sermon delivered by ▸Robert E. McAlister in Apr. 1913 at the Apostolic Faith World-Wide Camp Meeting held in Arroyo Seco, outside of Los Angeles. McAlister observed that in the book of Acts the apostles always baptized the newly converted "in the name of Jesus Christ." He emphasized that the Matt. 28:19 Trinitarian formula was not used. John Schaepe was sufficiently inspired by the message that he spent the entire night in prayer. Toward morning this "would-be preacher" raced through the camp shouting out his revelation on the power of Jesus' name. Many of the campers began to study the issue. Some, including ▸Frank J. Ewart, came to accept it, were rebaptized, and began to share their beliefs from the pulpit. Out of these beginnings came the Oneness pentecostal churches.

In 1917 Schaepe was living just blocks from the Arroyo Seco campground; he remained in that general area until his death.

■ **Bibliography:** A. Clanton, *United We Stand* (1970), 15–16 ■ F. Foster, *Think It Not Strange* (1965), 52 ■ W. Menzies, *Anointed to Serve* (1971), 111–12 ■ Obituary, *Los Angeles Times* (Feb. 23, 1939), I–28 ■ J. Schaepe, "A Remarkable Testimony," *Meat in Due Season* 1 (Aug. 21, 1917) ■ V. Synan, *The Holiness-Pentecostal Movement in the United States* (1971), 154 ■ W. Warner, "The 1913 Worldwide Camp Meeting," *AGH* 3 (1, 1983).   ■ C. M. Robeck Jr.

SCHLINK, BASILEA (1904–2001). Cofoundress of the Evangelical Sisterhood of Mary and prolific author. Born Klara Schlink and brought up in Brunswick, Germany, she had a conversion experience in 1922 and thereafter saw her life in terms of Christian service. Schlink experienced the years from the early 1920s as a divine preparation for her later call; beginning in 1931 she developed a close association with her friend Erika Madauss (1904–99). In 1945, in the ruins of Darmstadt, Schlink and Madauss witnessed a revival, including a manifestation of the spiritual gifts among the girls in their Bible study, in which repentance was a key factor. From this revival grew the Sisterhood of Mary, an Evangelical Protestant community consecrated to a faith-life of simplicity and celibacy for love of Jesus. Together Schlink and Madauss (now known as Mothers Basilea and Martyria) led the Mary Sisters in a life characterized by faith in God's call, promise, and provision.

Schlink played a leading role in responding to a call to purchase a 22-acre site near Darmstadt in 1955, which was renamed Canaan. With funds and materials trusted for in faith without solicitation, the basic plan for Canaan was completed in 1963, with chapels, a home for the aged and infirm, and a retreat house. Schlink has also helped to found branches of the Sisterhood in many different countries, including one in Phoenix, AZ. She has written approximately 100 books and booklets, concentrating on the themes of God's call to repentance, the dire spiritual need of the modern world, divine judgment and mercy, the bridal love of Jesus, and the role of Israel. Schlink's own life is told in *I Found the Key to the Heart of God* (1975), and the experiences of the sisterhood are found in *Realities of Faith* (1966). Other important books include *Israel—My Chosen People* (1963; rev. 1987), *Repentance: The Joy Filled Life* (1968), *For Jerusalem's Sake I Will Not Rest* (1969), *Ruled by the Spirit* (1970), *My All for Him* (1972), *The Unseen World of Angels and Demons* (1986), *Patmos: When the Heavens Opened* (1976), and *Mary, the Mother of Jesus* (1986). Schlink's books have been translated into more than 60 languages, and she has also written many songs.

■ **Bibliography:** *A Celebration of God's Unfailing Love: Evangelical Sisterhood of Mary 1947–1997* (1997).   ■ P. D. Hocken

SCHMIDT, GUSTAV HERBERT (1891–1958). Missionary to Eastern Europe. Born in Annapol, Wolynia, Russia, to Jacob and Wilhelmine Schmidt, the younger Schmidt attended a public school in Russia from 1898 to 1905. He was converted to Christ in 1908 and received the baptism in the Holy Spirit two or three years later. He continued his education by attending business college in Berlin, Germany, and then immigrated to the U.S., where he attended the Rochester Bible Training School in Rochester, NY (1915–18).

In 1919 Schmidt received appointment as an Assemblies of God (AG) missionary to Poland and arrived there in 1920. He immediately engaged in relief work and evangelism. Success followed quickly, with Schmidt baptizing a hundred converts within four months. After several years of ministry there, he recognized the need to establish a Bible institute for the training of ministers. Returning to the U.S. in 1925, he asked the AG for permission to start such a school; they declined due to heavy financial pressures for other missions projects.

In the following year, he met C. W. Swanson, a California businessman, who financed the publication of *The Gospel Call of Russia* to publicize the ministry and needs of Eastern Europe. In 1927 he met Paul B. Peterson, a former missionary to Russia, and together they organized the ▸Russian and Eastern European Mission (REEM) to extend their ministry in this region of Europe; it worked in close collaboration with the AG until 1940. Schmidt's publication became the official voice of REEM; the title was later shortened to *The Gospel Call*.

Schmidt returned to Poland in 1929, and on Mar. 2, 1930, the Danzig Instytut Biblijny opened in the Free City of Danzig (Gdansk), the first pentecostal Bible institute in Eastern Europe. He served as dean until he was followed in this capacity by ▸Nicholas Nikoloff in 1935. With the increase of Nazi sympathies in Danzig and the approach of the war, the Bible school was closed in 1938. After the war broke out, Schmidt was imprisoned for six months by the Nazis for his pentecostal beliefs but escaped incarceration in a concentration camp in 1941 because of his American citizenship. To escape from the Gestapo he stowed away on a Swedish ship departing from Danzig, leaving his family behind. After arriving in Sweden, the American legation requested that Schmidt return to America. In a desire to help his family still in Germany, he decided to stay in Sweden, where he was declared a refugee and placed under house arrest. During his three-year stay (1943–46), Schmidt wrote a number of works, including *Songs in the Night* (the story of his escape from Danzig), *God unto Death, God in My Life, God Finds Ways*, and *The Journey Home*. After the war the family was reunited and returned to America, where Schmidt continued in ministry. He died in 1958 while on a preaching tour of Germany.

■ **Bibliography:** "Application for Endorsement as Missionary" (1919) ▮ "G. H. Schmidt Dies in Germany," *PE* (July 13, 1958) ▮ T. Salzer, "The Danzig Gdanska Instytut Biblijny: Its History and Impact" (unpub., 1988) ▮ W. Warner, "A Refugee in Sweden," *AGH* 12 (Spring 1992).   ■ G. B. McGee; B. A. Pavia

SCHOONMAKER, CHRISTIAN H. (1881–1919). Missionary to India. Schoonmaker, who was born in New York, was one of the first American Assemblies of God (AG) missionaries to India and the first chairman of the Indian AG, established in 1918 at Saharanpur, India. He intended for the Indian AG to include all the pentecostal groups, but it was disbanded shortly after he died in 1919.

Schoonmaker's religious heritage included a Methodist mother; working for the Salvation Army; being trained in the Christian and Missionary Alliance (CMA) school in Nyack, NY; and attending a convention where people received the baptism in the Spirit. When he became a missionary to India in 1907, he preached that people should wait for the baptism in the Spirit, which he received in 1908. Schoonmaker had a vision of Christ, facilitated others receiving the baptism in the Spirit, discerned spirits, was sensitive to the Spirit's leading, and had a healing ministry. He was ordained by the American AG and returned to India in 1917 despite the diseases his family had experienced in India. He died of smallpox, having refused the vaccination because of his faith. Following his death, his wife, Violet, continued working as a missionary; five of their six children became missionaries to India.

Christian Schoonmaker, a pioneer missionary to India for the Christian and Missionary Alliance. After he received the baptism in the Holy Spirit, he led other Alliance missionaries into this experience.

■ **Bibliography:** C. H. Schoonmaker, "God's Estimate of a Heathen Soul. What Is Yours?" *LRE* 10 (1917) ■ V. Schoonmaker, *A Man Who Loved the Will of God* (c. 1959).   ■ E. B. Robinson

SCOFIELD REFERENCE BIBLE Highly influential, ▸dispensationally oriented edition of the Bible named after its editor, Cyrus Ingerson Scofield (1843–1921). Initially begun in 1900, *The Scofield Reference Bible (SRB)* was first published by Oxford University Press in 1909. Scofield was aided by an eight-member group of editorial consultants on both the first edition (1909) and the "New and Improved Edition" (1917). Copyrights were reissued in 1937 and in 1945.

In 1954, at the invitation of Oxford University Press, a committee of nine men under the editorial guidance of E. Schuyler English began revising the *SRB,* and in 1967 an edition entitled *The New Scofield Reference Bible* was released. The *NSRB* reflected, among other things,

> some important word changes in the text to help the reader;... revision of many of the introductions to the books of the Bible ...; more sub-headings; clarification of some footnotes, deletion of others, and the addition of many new notes; more marginal references; an entirely new chronology [Ussher's chronology was omitted]; a new index;... a concordance.

Despite new editorial leadership, the dispensational character of its predecessor remained substantially intact.

Scofield's own spiritual roots went back to his conversion in 1879. Within three years (1882) he had accepted a Congregational pastorate in Dallas, TX. Soon afterward, under the tutelage of Presbyterian minister J. H. Brookes, Scofield was exposed to and highly taken with the writings of John Nelson Darby (1800–82) and other Plymouth Brethren. Although lacking any formal theological training, Scofield began his writing career with a book called *Rightly Dividing the Word of Truth* (1885) and *The Comprehensive Bible Correspondence Course* (1896). These laid the groundwork for his most significant work, the *SRB.* Scofield also penned a collection of essays entitled *Addresses on Prophecy* (1900) and a little-known volume on the doctrine of the Holy Spirit (1906), which was reissued in 1973 by Baker Book House under the title *A Mighty Wind: Plain Papers on the Doctrine of the Holy Spirit.*

The impact of the *SRB* on the pentecostal and charismatic movements in this country can scarcely be understated despite attempts to show that pentecostals were not originally dispensational (Sheppard, 1984). Many of the over 2 million copies that were sold or given away fell into the eager hands of members of both movements. Pentecostals were affected early and directly. Some charismatics, however, as was often the case with theological issues, accepted dispensationalism by default as part of the theological package accompanying the baptism in the Holy Spirit. Other, more progressive, charismatic groups chose another route. (The ▸Vineyard Christian Fellowship, for example, tacitly rejects dispensationalism and opts for an eschatology based more on G. E. Ladd's "already-not yet" perspective.)

Dispensationalism denies that spiritual gifts are valid under the present dispensation (e.g., see Scofield's notes on 1 Cor. 14: "Tongues and the sign gifts are to cease"; cf. Walvoord, *The Holy Spirit* [1954]), but that did not stop pentecostal pioneers from using its framework. Among pentecostal denominations, Scofield's premillennial, pretribulational brand of dispensationalism rode the coattails of 19th-century fundamentalism and soon nearly became dogma.

Pentecostal publications such as ▸Frank M. Boyd's *Ages and Dispensations* (1955) found it "an easy exercise to adapt the teaching and literature of Scofieldian dispensationalism to the Pentecostal emphasis.... the dispensational motif, given a proper Pentecostal baptism, [was seen] as a helpful aid in underscoring the importance of the doctrine of the second coming of Christ" (Menzies, 1971, 328–29). ▸P. C. Nelson, in *Bible Doctrines* (1934, 1948, 1961, 1969, 1971), a series of studies on the Statement of Fundamental Truths adopted by the Assemblies of God (AG), stated that readers who "wish to go deeper into the subject [of Israel's return to Palestine] will do well to read Blackstone's *Jesus Is Coming,*" which was virtually a dispensationalist primer. The more recent trend, however, is away from dispensational categories (Menzies, 1971, 328–29; but cf. Menzies in Synan, 1975, 85), although as recently as the 1970s dispensationalist John G. Hall (*God's Dispensational and Prophetic Plan,* 1972) was invited to speak at Central Bible College, the flagship Bible college of the AG. The *Book of Doctrine* (Church of God [Cleveland, TN]), published in 1922, is another clear reflection of Scofield's influence in pentecostal circles (see p. 144; cf. the more recent *This We Believe* [1963] by CG author J. L. Slay).

See also DISPENSATIONALISM.

■ **Bibliography:** *Book of Doctrines* (1922) ■ F. M. Boyd, *Ages and Dispensations* (1955) ■ W. E. Cox, *An Examination of Dispensationalism* (1979) ■ W. N. Kerr, "Scofield, Cyrus Ingerson," *EDT* ■ G. N. Kraus, *Dispensationalism in America* (1958) ■ D. MacPherson, *The Great Rapture Hoax* (1983) ■ F. C. Masserano, "A Study of Worship Forms in the Assemblies of God Denomination" (Th.M. thesis, Princeton, 1966) ■ W. C. Meloon, *We've Been Robbed* (1971) ■ W. Menzies, *Anointed to Serve: The Story of the Assemblies of God* (1971) ■ P. C. Nelson, *Bible Doctrines* (1971) ■ C. I. Scofield, *A Mighty Wind: Plain Papers on the Doctrine of the Holy Spirit* (1906; repr. 1973) ■ idem, ed., *The New Scofield Reference Bible* (1967) ■ idem, ed., *The Scofield Reference Bible* (1909, 1917, 1937, 1945) ■ G. Sheppard, "Pentecostals and the Hermeneutics of Dispensationalism: The Anatomy of an Uneasy Relationship," *Pneuma* 6 (2, 1984)

■ J. L. Slay, *This We Believe* (1963) ■ V. Synan, ed., *Aspects of Pentecostal-Charismatic Origins* (1975).

　　　　　　　　　　　　　　　　　　■ P. H. Alexander

SCOTT, DOUGLAS R. (1900–1967). Pioneer pentecostal apostle in France. Born in Ilford, Essex, Scott was brought up in a religious family, and from his adolescence attended a Congregational church. Although talented at sports and music, Scott had been troubled in soul for some years. He finally was converted in 1925 when he heard a Polish pentecostal student, A. Bergholc, preach about the cross. Some months later he was baptized in the Spirit after the laying on of hands by ˒George Jeffreys and being healed of a speech impediment. Convinced that the Lord had empowered him to bring the word of salvation to others, he soon shared the ˒Elim emphasis on healing signs and wonders to demonstrate the truth of the gospel to the unconverted. Scott threw himself into evangelistic work with complete dedication, gaining experience in street meetings and door-to-door evangelism.

Hearing the call of the Lord to missionary work, Scott arranged to visit Le Havre, France, to learn the language before traveling to Africa. In Le Havre, at the Ruban Bleu mission of ˒Helene Biolley in 1927, Scott began preaching in his limited French, and some remarkable healings occurred. Urged to return, Scott sought the Lord and received confirmation through prophecy. In 1929 he married Clarice Weston, gave up his job, and in Jan. 1930 the Scotts arrived in Le Havre. From this point on, Scott became God's instrument for establishing the pentecostal movement in France. Through missions and campaigns, initially in Normandy and then in southern Belgium (through contact with H. de Worm) and in western Switzerland and southeastern France, Scott initiated revival with numerous conversions. He decisively influenced the men who became key figures in the French Assemblies of God, including P. Nicolle, and was the catalyst in the 1932 Ardèche revival, bringing the pentecostal experience to L. Dallière and other Reformed pastors. Besides spending the war years in the Congo, the Scotts were also called to French North Africa, where they evangelized in 1952–56. Between 1946 and 1952, Scott labored particularly in Perpignan and Carcassonne in southwestern France.

Scott's enormous impact on French pentecostalism cannot be explained alone by his undoubted dedication, which showed most clearly in his last years while he suffered from a deteriorating heart condition. He was recognized as a man of the Spirit who always sought the Lord's guidance before he acted. He was noted for the directness of his preaching, his ability to make the Scriptures live, his humor, and his compassion for people's burdens. He mirrored an apostle's care for the churches he had founded. If one phrase catches Scott's personality, it might be *"Une église qui ne missione pas démissionne"* ("A church that does not evangelize hands in its resignation").

■ **Bibliography:** G. R. Stotts, *Le Pentecôtisme au pays de Voltaire* (1981).

　　　　　　　　　　　　　　　　　　■ P. D. Hocken

SEMINARIES AND GRADUATE SCHOOLS The last third of the 20th century will be noted for a maturing of the pentecostal movement on the subject of education in general and of theological education in particular. During that period, the movement began to offer a variety of graduate programs. Some survived their introduction; others did not. By the fall of 2000, however, over 1,600 students were enrolled in nine graduate schools or programs offered within the pentecostal and charismatic movements in North America.

Much of early pentecostalism was ambivalent toward education. Theological education was often treated with outright contempt, most probably because of two related factors. First, the pentecostal renewal did not begin among the highly educated nor within the theological seminaries of the day. It began at the grassroots in small local churches and prayer meetings. Second, those who became pentecostals in the early days of the movement believed that the general tenor of things in most historic churches and especially in their seminaries undercut the working of God and deprived the people of God's truth. Seminaries were viewed as preoccupied with the intellectual and as having little regard for experience. As such, those with theological degrees such as the doctor of divinity (D.D.) were sometimes nicknamed "Dumb Dogs," and theological seminaries became theological "cemeteries."

Yet pentecostals did appreciate and recognize the need for some formal training. Sometimes that took the form of younger people attaching themselves to a local pastor or evangelist in a mentoring relationship. This ultimately led to a series of short-term Bible schools. In a few cases, the "instructor" waited upon God for direction and inspiration and "taught" the class by means of "prophecies" or "interpretations" to utterances in tongues. More frequently, the *Scofield Reference Bible* was adopted as the sole or primary text to which students were given a more or less verse-by-verse exposition.

Initially these schools lasted for six to eight weeks and were run by such men as D. C. O. Opperman or C. F. Parham. These short-term schools, which tended to move from place to place, were soon replaced by longer-term schools, Bible institutes such as those of N. J. Holmes (Greenville, SC) or T. K. Leonard (Findlay, OH), which charged little tuition and were run almost entirely on a "faith" basis. Teachers were drawn from the ranks of successful evangelists and pastors who brought a topical, systematic, or expositional approach to the text.

As the movement entered its second generation, some of the early matriarchs and patriarchs had begun to die. That meant finding ways to collect and share their stories and experiences for the edification of the next generation of pentecostals. At the same time, pentecostals attempted to relate to the Bible institute movement in fundamentalism. As a result, pentecostals also established two-year Bible institutes.

In Mar. 1923 Aimee Semple McPherson founded the Lighthouse of International Foursquare Evangelism, better known as L.I.F.E. Bible College, which eventually offered a three-year course of study leading to the bachelor of theology (Th.B.) degree. By 1936 she had clearly moved ahead of her peers by offering a doctor of theology (Th.D.) degree program. It required a high school diploma and a four-year course of study, one more than the Th.B., including four years of Greek and a 20,000-word thesis. In later years the Greek requirement was reduced to three years and a one-year Hebrew requirement was added. The Th.D. was last advertised in 1948, but by 1955 it had produced 40 graduates. While the degree ultimately did not measure up to the rigor of accredited Th.D. programs elsewhere, it nonetheless pointed the way toward higher academic standards for pentecostals.

During the 1940s and 1950s, most other pentecostal Bible institutes followed the leading of their fundamentalist and evangelical peers adopting three- and four-year programs and expanded their schools to become Bible colleges. Many received accreditation from the conservative American Association of Bible Colleges (AABC). A few of the more "progressive" sought regional accreditation. A few shed the name "Bible" and attempted to become fully functional liberal arts colleges whose purpose it was to prepare pentecostal young people for ministry in the arts and science professions without having to face the full force of a "secular" education.

In the Assemblies of God (AG), movement toward a fifth-year B.Th. degree was made at the 1947 general council. The 1945 general council had authorized Central Bible Institute (CBI) to "provide a Full Theological Seminary Course" in addition to the Bible Institute course "as progress and growth" demanded. By 1947 the demand had been identified, and CBI was authorized to offer a fifth-year course beginning in 1949. A 155-semester-hour B.Th. was advertised in the 1948–49 catalog, and the school became known as Central Bible Institute and Seminary (Central Bible College after 1965). By 1957 it had dropped the name "seminary" and established a graduate school of religion. It offered an M.A. in religion degree, designed to provide "advanced but terminal training" for the "mature student" following the normal Bible college course. Northwest Bible College (now Northwest College of the AG) followed suit in 1958 with the establishment of a graduate division offering an M.A. in theology degree.

When the AABC registered concern that the M.A. was a degree that fell under the jurisdiction of the American Association of Theological Schools (AATS, now the ATS), the standard accreditation agency for seminaries, Northwest College withdrew its offer of the M.A. and replaced it with the

following year with a five-year bachelor of theology (Th.B.) degree. Central Bible College, however, continued to offer the M.A. in religion through 1966 when it seemed that the AG would, indeed, establish a seminary.

In 1963 pentecostal healing evangelist Oral Roberts opened a university in Tulsa, OK, under his own name and financed by his ministry. It was the first pentecostal university, and it caught the attention of Donald Gee in *Pentecost* magazine. He wrote that early pentecostal leaders had justifiably feared an "arid intellectualism" that had damaged many churches out of which these leaders had come. But, he noted, fear "drove them too far." He exhorted his readers to ever-higher academic standards on the condition that the "Holy Spirit is honored" and prescribed that those who wished to place academic degrees after their names should earn them by "hard work in a reputable place of learning."

Two years later Oral Roberts added to his university a short-lived Graduate School of Theology. Announced first in 1963, it opened its doors with 29 students on Sept. 7, 1965. Under the leadership of Roberts' longtime friend, R. O. Corvin of the Pentecostal Holiness Church, this program provided an opportunity to study theology at the graduate level within the pentecostal tradition, but theoretically, at least, not under the auspices of any single pentecostal denomination. A series of governance, administrative, and personality problems quickly developed, however, and this attempt failed in 1969.

It was the largely black Church of God in Christ (COGIC) that actually launched the first successful and fully accredited theological seminary in American pentecostal history. Intentionally ecumenical from its inception in Sept. 1970, the Charles H. Mason Theological Seminary, under the leadership of founding president-dean Leonard Lovett, brought pentecostal students into the mainstream of theological education. The COGIC established its seminary with the larger six-school consortium of black seminaries in Atlanta, GA, known as the Interdenominational Theological Center (ITC). Dr. Robert Franklin, a minister in the COGIC, is the current president of the ITC, which is accredited by the ATS and the regional Southern Association of Colleges and Schools (SACS). Students at Mason Seminary may pursue a variety of M.A. (Christian education, church music), M.Div., and doctoral (D.Min., Th.D. in pastoral counseling) degrees, sharing a common theological curriculum, classrooms, and faculty with the other member schools of the ITC. They receive from Mason a variety of student services as well as specific course offerings that are distinctive to the history, theology, and polity of the COGIC. Since its opening, the seminary has graduated more than 100 students.

The charismatic renewal was running at full steam when in the autumn of 1973 Melodyland Christian Center in Anaheim, CA, under the leadership of Pastor Ralph Wilkerson, established the Melodyland School of Theology. With Presbyterian J. Rodman Williams as its president, a board of regents, and a faculty that drew heavily from the range of charismatic and pentecostal leadership, the school held great promise of becoming a key training institution for mainline and pentecostal students who identified with the renewal. It received candidate status with the regional accreditation body in 1977, the Western Association of Schools and Colleges (WASC). It also received associate membership with the ATS. Melodyland offered the M.A. and M.Div. degrees and by 1979 boasted a student body of 218 drawn from 38 states and 21 denominations. It also enrolled more than 70 students from independent charismatic churches.

The academic year 1978–79 brought a series of reversals to this institution that ultimately led to its demise. Questions of its financial integrity and soundness, problems in the governance of the institution in relation to Melodyland Christian Center, and questions of theological orthodoxy were all raised. The latter, raised by Wilkerson, Dr. Walter Martin, and Dr. John W. Montgomery, ultimately proved to be the school's undoing. When the faculty was asked to sign a statement of faith that included an "inerrancy of Scripture" clause designed by these three men, many of its members resigned in protest. Most of the school's better students transferred to other seminaries in an attempt to salvage their academic investment. By 1981 the school had ceased to function in any viable way as a graduate school and had changed its name to the American Christian Theological Seminary. By the mid 1980s it ceased to exist.

In 1961 the General Council of the Assemblies of God authorized the executive presbytery and the board of education to establish a graduate school of theology "as soon as it was deemed feasible." Significant in the discussion was whether to call it a "graduate school of theology" or a "seminary." Because of concern for the feelings of many older pentecostals, it became known as the Assemblies of God Graduate School (AGGS) and opened Sept. 4, 1973, in Springfield, MO.

Initially housed in the headquarters complex of the AG, this theological venture expanded under the watchful eye of denominational leadership. Offering the M.A. and M.Div. degrees in biblical studies, Christian education, and missions, the school moved quickly to receive regional accreditation from the North Central Association of Colleges and Schools (NCACS) and received associate status with the ATS. With its 1984 accreditation review came a recommendation that AGGS change its name to reflect more accurately its mission. As a result, in Aug. 1984 it became the Assemblies of God Theological Seminary (AGTS). In 1987 H. Glynn Hall was appointed its first full-time president. He was succeeded

by Dr. Del Tarr, who served as president from 1990 until 1999.

Tarr may be credited with making a number of sweeping advances in the seminary. He convinced the ministers and churches of the AG to commit the funding necessary to provide a new building for the seminary. The facility was constructed adjacent to Evangel University and occupied in Aug. 1997. It includes the William J. Seymour Chapel and the Cordas C. Burnett Library, with over 80,000 volumes, adequate office and classroom space, and a large multipurpose foyer that features a life-sized bronze statue of Jesus washing Peter's feet.

During Tarr's tenure, the seminary received full accreditation with the ATS and developed a range of programs with courses now offered at a half-dozen extension sites. Currently it offers the M.A. in theological studies, Christian ministries, counseling, and intercultural ministries, and the M.Div. and D.Min. degrees. In recent years, the practical theology department has served an increasing number of pastors, district officers, educators, and missionaries in the D. Min. program, in which nearly 90 students are currently enrolled. Overall enrollment at the seminary in 1999–2000 was 342 students.

In 1999 Dr. Byron Klaus became the third full-time president of the seminary. His ministry experience, innovative style, and personal investment in younger pastors and leaders have given him wide acceptance not only among seminary presidents in the U.S. and Canada but also in AG churches. He faces two difficult tasks in the foreseeable future. First, he must continue to develop relationships with AG leaders that will result in a genuine exchange of ideas between the faculty and them. This need has been made visible most notably through recent, unwarranted criticisms lodged against the pentecostal academy, especially its historians, and published in *Enrichment*, the denomination's magazine for leaders. Second, he will need to gain adequate funding to free up the faculty to engage in the necessary theological reflection, quality research, and publication designed to facilitate dialogue, teaching, and the development of an informed pentecostal leadership.

Global University of the AG is the result of a partnership developed between Berean University and the International Correspondence Institute (ICI) in April 2000. It seeks to offer distance-learning opportunities and nontraditional master's-level degrees to mature adults. This educational enterprise is the successor to the older General Council Correspondence School that had its origins in the 1940s. It offers a range of coursework through audio- and videotapes, lecture outlines, reading and study guides, and independent learning suggestions made by "mentor/instructors." Its staff includes an impressive array of technological minds, though most of its online courses are available at the undergraduate level.

Under the leadership of Ron Iwasko, Global University, with new facilities in Springfield, MO, offers the M.A. in biblical studies, in ministerial studies (with concentrations available in leadership, missions, or education), and in Christian counseling. Only the counseling degree has a residence requirement. Students are required to complete their practicum units under the auspices of EMERGE Ministries, Inc., in Akron, OH, as well as a supervised internship in an approved agency near their home. Accreditation for studies completed through Berean University is received from the accrediting commission of the Distance Education and Training Council (DETC). Their ultimate goal is to achieve regional accreditation for their programs.

On Sept. 1, 1975, the Church of God (CG, Cleveland, TN) became the third classical pentecostal denomination to open its own school of theology. Housed initially in rented facilities, in 1980 it occupied a newly designed and built facility in Cleveland, TN, adjacent to properties of the CG headquarters building. To this facility was added the Thurman J. Curtsinger Ministry Center in 1995. The School of Theology, renamed the Church of God Theological Seminary (CGTS) in 1997, shares library facilities with the denomination's Lee University, which also acts as a recruitment base for the school. In 1984 the School of Theology received accreditation from the SACS, and in 1987 ATS granted candidate status to the school. It was fully accredited by the ATS in 1992. During the 1999–2000 year, 248 students enrolled in its M.A. (Christian formation and discipleship, and church ministry), and M.Div. programs. It currently offers courses at two off-campus sites, one of which is in Puerto Rico, and has preliminary approval to offer the D.Min.

Dr. Donald Walker has served as president of CGTS since Aug. 1998. Aided by academic dean Steve Land, he has

Women graduates of Faith Theological Seminary, Manakala, Kerala, India, in January 2000.

brought financial stability and academic integrity to the institution. He has also been able to stave off a serious takeover bid by Lee University. In late 2000 Walker announced the seminary's fourth endowed chair, given in honor of a CG leader who has invested his life in a range of ministries—the Dr. John D. Nichols Endowed Chair of Benevolence, Compassion and Care.

The CGTS faculty may be the most focused North American pentecostal faculty to date. They have developed a consistent pentecostal theological basis for their work. They offer ministerial development that emphasizes Scripture on the one hand and a Wesleyan-pentecostal heritage on the other. They have pioneered the *Journal of Pentecostal Theology* and its supplemental monograph series. Each January the seminary provides in-service training to the overseers of the CG, thereby demonstrating a practical way of maintaining communication between theological educators and denominational leaders who, in other cases, find themselves at odds with one another.

After a six-year hiatus, a new attempt was made to establish a graduate school of theology at Oral Roberts University (ORU) in 1975. With United Methodist James Buskirk at the helm as dean, the faculty was more broadly mainline than in the previous attempt. The school sought to be broadly inclusive, choosing the terms "catholic, evangelical, reformed, and charismatic" to describe its philosophy of education, but clearly attempting to integrate elements of a classical theological education into the theological grid of Oral Roberts, with an interest in the whole person, "body, mind, and spirit."

This second attempt by ORU has proved to be more successful than the first. The school currently offers the M.A. in Christian education, missions, Christian counseling, practical theology, biblical literature, and theology/historical studies. It also offers the M.Div. and D.Min. degrees. During the 1980s and 1990s, ORU encountered substantial problems, including questions of governance, financial stability, and identity, as well as morale problems among faculty and staff, with a high turnover rate. They were further compounded by the ever-present scrutiny and seemingly arbitrary and capricious funding decisions of the president, Oral Roberts. During the mid to late 1980s, the School of Theology underwent two name changes and received a new dean, Larry Lea, who attempted to turn it into a School of Theology and Missions with an emphasis on practical ministry in signs and wonders.

The 1990s brought the retirement of Oral Roberts and the naming of Richard Roberts to succeed him as president. Richard Roberts' entry onto the scene brought greater fiscal stability to the institution. Dr. Paul G. Chapell was hired to serve as academic dean, a position he held through the late 1990s before moving to Southern California. The current academic dean is Dr. Jerry Horner. During the 1999–2000 academic year, the student body numbered 454.

In 1977 televangelist Pat Robertson unveiled his vision for graduate charismatic education in the form of CBN University (now Regent University) located in Virginia Beach, VA. The project received accreditation from SACS in 1984 and offered master's degrees in five areas of specialization. The College of Theology and Ministry was divided into two schools featuring the same faculty. The School of Biblical Studies was intent on developing Bible knowledge and hermeneutical skills. It offered the M.A. degree in biblical studies and encouraged its students to pursue further academic work. The School of Ministry brought an integrative structure to equip for ministry. In this latter school the M.Div. and an assortment of M.A. degrees could be pursued.

Today the theological schools have been renamed, and graduate theological studies may be pursued in the Regent University School of Divinity. The School of Divinity offers the M.A. in practical theology, including concentrations in worship studies/worship for renewal, missiology, and biblical studies. Students may choose from five areas of concentration in the biblical studies program. Two of the M.A. degrees (practical theology and biblical studies with a concentration in English Bible) are available through the School of Divinity's distance-education program, though the ATS requires that some of the program be taken in a limited residential model (one-week modules). Students must also attend a nine-day Spiritual Formation Seminar the summer before entry into these programs, but they may pursue the remainder of the degree with a "cohort-based" education community. The School of Divinity also offers the M.Div. in practical theology and in missiology, as well as the D.Min. degree in the area of leadership and renewal. Dr. Vinson Synan, Dean of the School of Divinity, is currently exploring a possible Ph.D. in the field of leadership.

CBN seeks to be both interdisciplinary and contemporary, interacting with and transforming contemporary culture. It is housed in an open area on a well-planned campus featuring finely furnished facilities with high-tech, state-of-the-art equipment available only at a well-financed institution. Enrollment during the 1999–2000 academic year reached 289 students.

Vanguard University, known until 1998 as Southern California College, in Costa Mesa, a successful liberal arts college of the AG, entered the graduate market in 1983 with the establishment of a well-designed graduate studies program. Offering a WASC-accredited M.A. degree in religion, the program offers concentrations in biblical studies and in church leadership, providing a background to pastoral ministry or to further study. The university is currently led by president Murray W. Dempster.

The California Theological Seminary was formed in 1984 in Fresno, CA. An educational experiment of the People's Church in Fresno, the seminary has hopes of bringing

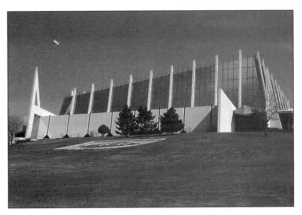

Christ's Chapel at Oral Roberts University, Tulsa, OK.

together scholars from a variety of pentecostal denominations. By 1988 the faculty included members from the AG and the CG. Under the leadership of Del Tarr, the seminary attempted to provide a multidenominational, charismatic approach to academic training for ministry, which was anthropologically and culturally sensitive to the needs of the Third World. Its strength was its global vision. In 1987 it formed a relationship with the Asia Theological Centre for Evangelism and Missions (ATCEM) in Singapore. Ultimately, however, the isolated location of CTS was a factor against the school, which closed its doors in 1990 due to low enrollment, financial difficulties, and governance issues. Its students were granted credit for their work by the AGTS, where Dr. Del Tarr had become president.

During the 1980s, televangelist Jimmy Swaggart began the Jimmy Swaggart Theological Seminary (JSTS), located in Baton Rouge, LA, near Swaggart's World Ministry Center. Unabashedly conservative, its outlook stood, in contrast to that of CBN, over against contemporary culture. It was considered to be the "advanced academic training division" of Swaggart's multifaceted ministry and was widely advertised as standing on the "cutting edge" of world evangelization by incorporating and perpetuating Swaggart's principles of "inerrancy, Pentecostal distinctives, and worldwide evangelism."

JSTS opened with great fanfare in the autumn of 1988, offering the M.A. and M.Div. degrees. Its programs were focused on practical "hands-on" experience, but their academic components were restricted by such tone-setting requirements as a course called "Dispensational Theology." An emphasis was planned to provide a variety of team-taught interdisciplinary courses. The seminary became a victim of the moral crisis surrounding Jimmy Swaggart, however, when Swaggart was stripped of his credentials with the AG and those faculty members who held AG credentials were required to resign their positions immediately or forfeit their own good standing in the AG. Thus, many on the faculty became innocent victims of the crisis.

The newest addition to graduate education in the pentecostal movement comes in the form of The King's College and Seminary. Dr. Jack W. Hayford founded The King's Institute in 1987 and expanded it to become The King's College in 1996. The following year it was officially incorporated, and the seminary was opened in Jan. 1999. Dr. Paul G. Chapell serves as executive vice president and chief academic officer, and the board of trustees has drawn membership from several pentecostal/charismatic groups.

While the school is quite new, it has made headway toward establishing itself as a potentially important West Coast addition to pentecostal theological education. In Aug. 2000 it received candidacy status with the AABC and Transnational Association of Christian Colleges and Schools (TRACS) and intends to pursue both regional and ATS accreditation as soon as feasible. The college and seminary together boast a library of 127,000 volumes, a student body of 409, with 138 students enrolled in the seminary. The seminary offers the M.Div. degree, as well as an M.A. in practical theology, and beginning in Oct. 2000 it began the D.Min. degree. It is taking an aggressive stance on continuing education and offers a variety of distance learning courses. As chancellor, Jack Hayford continues to play a substantial role in the institution's forward momentum, connecting it with his concerns for pastoral leadership and his School of Pastoral Nurture. The seminary has already announced its first endowed chair, the Pat Robertson Chair of Pneumatology, though the board has yet to locate its first incumbent.

One of the more interesting new schools in the U.S. is the arrival of the Bethesda Christian University, with its undergraduate and seminary programs. It was originally founded in 1976 in Pasadena, CA, as Full Gospel Central Bible College, moving to Whittier in 1980. Since 1995 it has been located in Anaheim. It was part of the larger vision of chancellor *David (Paul) Yonggi Cho and the Yoido Full Gospel Church. Under the presidency of the gifted and energetic Dr. Young-Hoon Lee, the undergraduate program has received candidate status with the AABC. The school's primary purpose is to serve the large Southern California population of Korean-speaking students and pastors as well as other Korean Americans with academic programs marked by pentecostal spirituality. Currently it offers the M.A. in religion and the M.Div. degree to approximately 45 students.

Nine overtly pentecostal-charismatic alternatives are available in graduate education in the U.S. today. Several evangelical seminaries, such as Gordon-Conwell Theological Seminary (South Hamilton, MA) and Fuller Theological Seminary (Pasadena, CA), which has several pentecostal and charismatic faculty members and is the home of the David J. du Plessis Center for Christian Spirituality (housing the personal papers of du Plessis and other pentecostal leaders), provide pentecostal and charismatic students with a variety of options that represent quite different emphases, foci, and commitments to academic excellence and freedom of inquiry. See also BIBLE INSTITUTES, COLLEGES, UNIVERSITIES.

■ **Bibliography:** Assemblies of God Graduate School Catalog, 1978–80 ■ AGTS 1986–88 Catalog ■ Berean University of the Assemblies of God, 1996 Catalog ■ Bethesda Christian University 2000–2001 Catalog ■ J. K. Bridges, "The Full Consummation of the Baptism in the Holy Spirit," *Enrichment* 5 (4, Fall 2000) ■ CBN University, Graduate Catalog, 1987–88 ■ Church of God School of Theology Catalog, 1985–87 and 1987–88 ■ D. Gee, "Bible Schools Become Bible 'Colleges,'" *Pentecost* 74 (Dec. 1965–Feb. 1966) ■ D.E. Harrell Jr., *Oral Roberts: An American Life* (1985) ■ Jimmy Swaggart Theological Seminary Academic Catalog, 1988–89 ■ "Jimmy Swaggart Theological Seminary Mission: Philosophy, Objectives, and Distinctives," *The Evangelist* 19 (Dec. 12, 1987) ■ The King's College and Seminary, 2000–2001 Catalog ■ "Melodyland Lingers: Is the Song Ended?" *CT* 23 (6, 1978) ■ Melodyland School of Theology Catalog, 1980–1982 ■ Oral Roberts University: Graduate and Professional Schools, 1984–85 and 1985–86 ■ ORU Academic Programs Catalog, 1986–88 ■ Southern California College, 1984–86 Graduate Studies Bulletin ■ K. Yurica, "Dissonance Jars the Melodyland Harmony," *CT* 23 (5, 1978).

■ C. M. Robeck Jr.

SEMPLE, ROBERT JAMES (1881–1910). Evangelist and missionary. Semple was born to Scotch-Irish parents who ran the general store near Magherafelt, 30 miles from Belfast, Northern Ireland. One of five children, including two brothers (Samuel and William) and two sisters (Marion and Maggie), Robert was reared in a Presbyterian family. At age 17 he immigrated to the U.S., landing first in New York, where he was employed in a variety of menial jobs—dishwasher, street and hallway sweep—and later as clothing salesman. In a short time he moved to Chicago, where he was employed at the Marshall Field Department Store. While there, Semple entered the fledgling pentecostal movement through a small storefront mission, most probably that of *William H. Durham. By late 1907 Semple, a six-foot-six-inch, handsome and eloquent speaker, had launched into an evangelistic ministry, first in Toronto, then in Ingersoll near Salford, where he met Aimee Elizabeth Kennedy. From there he went to Stratford. Returning to Ingersoll, where he had held meetings through the winter of 1908, Robert Semple married Aimee on Aug. 12, 1908, in a ceremony conducted by Lt.-Col. John D. Sharp of the Salvation Army. Following their honeymoon, they returned to Stratford, where Robert worked as a boilermaker in a locomotive factory during the day and preached in the evening. Next they moved to London, Ont., where they pioneered a church, then on to

Robert J. Semple, evangelist and missionary who served in China for only a few months before dying of malaria in 1910. His wife, Aimee, later became better known as Aimee Semple McPherson.

Chicago, where on Jan. 2, 1909, Robert Semple was ordained by William H. Durham.

The Semples remained with Durham at the North Avenue Mission for several months of teaching and service. They accompanied him on evangelistic tours in Findlay, OH, and in several Canadian towns. The couple had anticipated a full-time ministry of faith as missionaries in China, and the Italians at Durham's mission provided their initial financial backing. Leaving Chicago in 1910, they again ministered in Canada, then sailed on the *Empress of Ireland* from St. John's, N.B., to Liverpool, England. They went north to Belfast, where Robert Semple held a three-week evangelistic crusade. Aimee reported 40 converts to pentecostalism there, and the mayor of Belfast met Semple, giving him the key to the city. From Ireland, the Semples journeyed to London for a one-week stay with ˃Cecil Polhill.

The Semples sailed from London to Hong Kong by way of the Suez Canal, stopping at a number of ports on the way, where they kept abreast of the many pentecostal news reports. Arriving in Hong Kong, they were plunged into a foreign culture and climate that soon took its toll. Robert engaged in literature distribution and preached through an interpreter. The couple also immersed themselves in Cantonese language study. On a trip to Macao, Robert contracted malaria. He was returned to Hong Kong by steamer and transferred to an English sanitarium, where he died on Aug. 19, 1910, shortly after their second wedding anniversary. Robert Semple was buried in the Happy Valley Cemetery in Hong Kong. Aimee

gave birth to their daughter, Roberta Star Semple, just six weeks later, on Sept. 17, 1910.

■ **Bibliography:** G. G. Kulbeck, *What God Hath Wrought* (1958) ▉ A. S. McPherson, *In the Service of the King* (1927) ▉ idem, *The Story of My Life* (1951) ▉ idem, *This Is That* (1919) ▉ N. B. Mavity, *Sister Aimee* (1931).   ■ C. M. Robeck Jr.

SEPÚLVEDA, CARLOS (1905–96). Pioneer Puerto Rican pentecostal pastor and founder of the Assembly of Christian Churches, Inc. (Concilio Asamblea de Iglesias Cristianas, Inc. [AIC]). Sepúlveda was born in Rincon, Puerto Rico, in 1905. He was raised in a very religious home, where his mother was a devout Catholic and his father a spiritist. He converted to Protestantism at the age of 12 and later attended the Evangelical Seminary in Puerto Rico, where he graduated with honors. After seminary he studied at the Interamerican University in San Germán. He was ordained a Presbyterian minister and pastored churches in Puerto Rico in the early 1930s. In 1934 he went to New York City, where he met Francisco Olazábal and decided to join the burgeoning pentecostal movement. Sepúlveda went on evangelistic healing crusades with Olazábal throughout the southwestern U.S., New York City, and Puerto Rico in the mid 1930s. He also served as a pastor in New York City; East Los Angeles; Nogalas, AZ; Playa de Ponce, PR; and El Paso, TX. After Olazábal's death in 1937, the leadership of the ˃Latin American Council of Christian Churches (Concilio Latino Americano de Iglesias Cristianas [CLADIC]) leadership fell into considerable infighting. Out of this conflict emerged a number of concilios (councils or denominations), including Sepúlveda's AIC in 1938. Sepúlveda moved back to New York City, where he pastored a church and led the AIC from 1939 to 1974. While in New York, he influenced and at times nurtured important Puerto Rican pentecostal leaders such as Juan L. Lugo, Ricardo Tañon, Leoncia Rosado ("Mama Leo"), Abelardo Berríos, Adolfo Carrión, and many others. Under Sepúlveda's leadership, the AIC founded two Bible institutes, one in New York City, the other in Los Angeles. He also went on speaking tours throughout Puerto Rico, the Dominican Republic, Canada, Mexico, Haiti, Guatemala, Nicaragua, Columbia, and Argentina. By the 1980s the AIC had grown to over 250 churches and 14,000 adherents in the U.S., Puerto Rico, and Latin America.

■ **Bibliography:** S. Díaz and D. Sepúlveda, *En el Umbral de la Gloria* (1996).   ■ G. Espinosa

SERAPHIM OF SAROV (1759–1833). Russian Orthodox charismatic leader. Seraphim was born in Kurst in Central Russia, the son of a building contractor. When Seraphim was 10 years old he fell ill, but it is reported that he was healed when he had a vision of the Virgin Mary. At age 19 he entered a monastery, where he studied the writings of Eastern Christian spirituals (spiritual fathers). In 1780 he again fell ill and once again experienced divine healing. He was ordained shortly thereafter. From 1794 to 1804 he retreated to the woods, living by the Pachomian rule (the monastic rule established by St. Pachomius c. A.D. 300) and eating only grasses and vegetables he grew. He was left a hunchback after being attacked by brigands. Again he experienced a spiritual rapture. He remained semi-secluded until 1825, when at age 66 he entered the final period of his life, that of *staretz,* or elder, in which he devoted himself to suffering humanity.

Numerous people reportedly were healed by Seraphim's prayers. Apparently, he knew the needs of his supplicants before they told him, and his words were accepted as prophetic by the faithful. One such case was revealed in his conversation with Nicholas Motovilov in Nov. 1831, when Seraphim reported that God had revealed to him Nicholas's desire to know the goal of the Christian life. Seraphim informed the pious Nicholas that the true end of the Christian life is the acquisition of the Holy Spirit. The Spirit must be sought through prayer. One must pray until God the Holy Spirit descends; then the recipient must be silent in the divine presence.

Motovilov inquired how it is possible to know that the Holy Spirit is present in a person. Seraphim in turn asked why his visitor was not looking at him. Motovilov responded that he could not, because Seraphim's face and eyes were brighter than the sun and, therefore, he was dazzled. Seraphim informed his visitor that he also was shining in the same transfigured manner and that Motovilov would not have been able to see Seraphim as such had he not received the fullness of the Spirit. Seraphim's "evidence" for a baptism in the Spirit, then, is a transfiguration experience—being transformed, while still in the flesh, into divine light. To the Eastern mystic, this is the process by which *theosis,* or deification, is achieved. The Holy Spirit, then, is the divine agent who returns humanity to the image of God.

■ **Bibliography:** S. M. Burgess, *The Holy Spirit: Eastern Christian Traditions* (1989) ■ A. F. Dobbie-Bateman, trans., *St. Seraphim of Sarov: Concerning the Aim of the Christian Life* (1936) ■ P. Evdokimov, "St. Seraphim of Sarov: An Icon of Orthodox Spirituality," *The Ecumenical Review* 15:3 (1963) ■ V. Zander, *St. Seraphim of Sarov* (1975).

■ S. M. Burgess

St. Seraphim

SERPENT HANDLING The practice of endangering one's health by committing dangerous feats is not new to church history. Predecessors paralleling classical pentecostals who were so engaged included the following: Madam Guyon (17th century), the Camisards (early 18th century), and the Convulsionaries (18th century). The origin of serpent handling among classical pentecostals centers around the person of George Went Hensley. His 1910 Spirit baptism was accomplished in a Church of God (CG, Cleveland, TN) congregation. He became quite interested in Mark 16:18, and while praying on White Oak Mountain he told the Lord to let him find a serpent if it was God's will to handle it. Soon he noticed a timber rattler, which he handled without difficulty then and at the next church service. Hensley eventually brought this practice to the local Church of God in Cleveland, TN, with the approval of A. J. Tomlinson. Hensley joined the CG in 1912, and the resultant problems led A. J. Tomlinson, in his 1917 annual address, to say that handling serpents and fire were acceptable "under the proper conditions" but that such experiences were not "a test of salvation." In the meantime, a sister denomination that was losing members to the CG, the Pentecostal Holiness Church, denounced all such behavior as "fanaticisms." By 1922 Hensley was no longer a member of the CG.

Handling serpents can range from wrapping these poisonous creatures around necks, stuffing them into shirts, rubbing them over faces, or walking on them with bare feet, and then throwing them to a fellow worshiper.

Practitioners of serpent handling also engage in other potentially life-threatening stunts, such as drinking poison or handling fire. The strychnine or other poison that is drunk usually is diluted but is still lethal. The fire can come from self-made fire bombs and is applied directly to any exposed portion of the body. The majority of those who actually do these things are men. The practice became so widespread that by the late 1930s some states—Kentucky, Georgia, Virginia, Tennessee, North Carolina, and Alabama—started passing legislation prohibiting such activity. By the 1940s the practitioners received national attention through the coverage of magazines like *Newsweek* and *Time* along with the *New York Times*. Outside observers were surprised to learn that very few people had died from snakebites despite the fact that some communicants had been bitten several times. Steven Kane counts 61 deaths from snakebites between 1934 and 1978 and 5 from drinking strychnine.

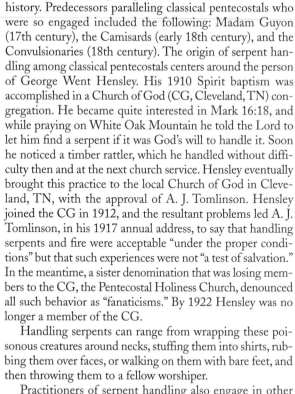

The use of fire resulted in some physical harm, but apparently no deaths were recorded. Typically most incidents of these practices leave the person without a bite or singed hairs and free from pain or harm. In the earliest years it was the scoffers who brought snakes to meetings, but more recently the practitioners of serpent handling hunt for snakes between April and September. No deaths have been reported as a result of these annual hunts. Once captured, the snakes are fed and bathed regularly.

The devotees—a sizable portion of whom are Oneness pentecostals—of serpent handling, fire contact, and strychnine drinking are adamant that these things are commanded in Scripture. Passages like Ex. 4:2–4; Job 26:13; Luke 10:19; and Acts 28:3–5 are used along with the suggestion that John 20:30 implies that Jesus himself handled venomous serpents. The principal text is Mark 16:18, and none of these people know, or would believe, that this is almost certainly not part of the original text of the Gospel of Mark. Their doctrine of the "anointing" means that they refuse to do any of these things without the perceived direct intervention from God. Usually the "anointing" is thought to be present in the midst of a demonstrative worship service that includes loud music, tongues speech, and physical agitations. When someone is bitten and dies, one of the following explanations may be offered: (1) The anointing was not present. This is a primary concern about the distraction of having photographers present and about insincere practitioners. (2) Such deaths prove to outsiders that the snakes have not been defanged—some have handled deadly Indian cobras. (3) God wills their death.

A church member testing his faith by handling a poisonous snake during a revival meeting at the Holiness Church of God in Jesus' Name, Kingston, GA. This church and others like it hold that believers are commanded to handle snakes according to Mark 16:8.

It could be a punishment, and others add that their refusal to use medicine that could have saved them brings glory to God. Sometimes snakes are handled at the funeral of the one who died from a snakebite.

Despite the ridicule of fellow Christians and the laws passed against these practices, they continue to this day. The number of adherents is not large, and they are from the lower spectrum of the socioeconomic ladder and are geographically centered in the Appalachians. These practices are not sanctioned by any international pentecostal denomination.

■ **Bibliography:** *Appalachian Journal* 1 (Spring 1974): 255–62 ▌T. Burton, *Serpent-Handling Believers* (1993) ▌K. W. Carden and R. W. Pelton, *The Persecuted Prophets* (1976) ▌"Holy Ghost People" (n.d.) ▌S. M. Kane, "Snake Handlers of Southern Appalachia" (1979) ▌D. L. Kimbrough, *Taking Up Serpents: Snake Handlers of Eastern Kentucky* (1995) ▌D. V. McCauley, *Appalachian Mountain Religion: A History* (1995). ■ H. D. Hunter

SEYMOUR, WILLIAM JOSEPH (1870–1922). Pastor of the Apostolic Faith Mission, 312 Azusa Street, Los Angeles, CA, during the ▶Azusa Street revival of 1906–9.

William J. Seymour was born May 2, 1870, in Centerville, LA, a small town in St. Mary's Parish, about 80 miles southwest of New Orleans, between Bayou Teche and the Gulf Coast. The region was noted for its sugarcane plantations, the dominance of Roman Catholics, the presence of syncretistic expressions of religion such as voodoo, a heavily Cajun culture, and the home of the Knights of the White Camellias, a white supremacist group patterned after the Ku Klux Klan.

Seymour was the eldest son of Simon and Phillis [Salabar] Seymour. His father, born c. 1841, was a brick maker, a trade that was frequently attached to the processing of sugarcane. His mother was born c. 1845. Both of them had been slaves, but during Reconstruction they worked hard to support their growing family. William J. Seymour's siblings included a younger brother, Simon Jr., born in 1872; a second brother, Amos, born in 1875; and an unnamed sister, born in May 1880. That same year, the census report for the region reveals that William and Simon Seymour were both enrolled in school and that William J. Seymour had already learned to read.

Little is known of Seymour's youth. The destruction of the 1890 census in a major fire makes it virtually impossible to reconstruct this time of his life (1881–93) apart from generalizations. What we do know is that by mid 1894 William J. Seymour could be found in Indianapolis, IN. How he came to be there is more difficult to assess. Demographic and migration studies suggest that most likely he went there seeking employment. Indianapolis, however, was not overly friendly to African Americans at the time. While it was a city along the path of the famed Underground Railroad, blacks were forced to register with the state from the 1850s onward. By the 1920s Indianapolis would become a major center for the Ku Klux Klan. Seymour arrived there in the middle of this period of growing racial concerns.

William J. Seymour, one of the most influential and respected early pentecostal leaders. He moved to California after listening to the teaching of Charles F. Parham in Houston and played a key role in the Azusa Street revival and the development of the pentecostal movement.

Initially, Seymour took up residence at 127-1/2 Indiana Avenue (1895), but later lived at 309 Bird (1898–99). Both locations, now nonexistent, stood within the borders of the city's historic black community, just north of the capitol. Seymour served as a waiter at three different hotels during this period: the Bates House (built 1852–closed 1901), the Denison Hotel (built 1880–closed 1920), and the Grand Hotel (built 1873–closed 1937). All three were prominent, upscale hotels, and Seymour's movement from rural Louisiana to early employment at these hotels shortly after arriving in Indianapolis suggests that he had help, either from friends or from family members who had preceded him in the region.

We know nothing of Seymour's exposure to Christianity in Louisiana. The dominant faith in the region was Roman Catholic, though Centerville boasted a Presbyterian church and the Methodists had worked there for a time. Information gleaned from an interview with C. W. Shumway, and recorded in a 1914 thesis for the University of Southern California, makes it clear that Seymour was converted in a "colored Methodist Episcopal Church" in Indianapolis, where he became a member for a period of time. The identity of this congregation is still a matter of debate. After a short tenure with the Methodists, Seymour left, allegedly because they were neither "premillennial" nor did they endorse "special 'revelations.'"

Mother ▸Emma L. Cotton, a leading African-American pastor in Los Angeles who had attended the Azusa Street Mission in its earliest years, claimed that Seymour subsequently affiliated with the Evening Light Saints (ELS), today's Church of God (Anderson, IN), under whose ministry he was "saved and sanctified." Seymour's commitment to premillennialism and "special revelation" would have fared no better among the ELS, however, than it did among the Methodists. The ELS were amillennial, and their magazine *The Gospel Trumpet* would later condemn Seymour's work in Los Angeles as "deception, and not an operation of the Holy Spirit."

Seymour left Indianapolis most probably in late 1899 or early 1900 and moved to Cincinnati, OH. He shared the theological commitments of Martin Wells Knapp, who directed God's Bible School and Missionary Training Home in Cincinnati. Oral tradition suggests that Seymour attended this school, though other than the fragmentary summary of Seymour's life available in Shumway's thesis, substantive documentation of his tenure in Cincinnati is still lacking. Seymour's testimony to Shumway notes that while he was in Cincinnati he contracted smallpox and lost his sight in one eye. Seymour connected this event with God's judgment on him for not entering the ministry earlier.

It appears that Seymour next went to the Houston area, most likely in 1902 or 1903, apparently to reconnect with family members. Shortly after his arrival, Seymour began to hold evangelistic meetings both in Texas and in Louisiana. Elder C. C. Carhee remembered him as holding meetings in Lake Charles, LA, during this period. In 1904 or 1905 Seymour claimed to have received a "special revelation" by which he was directed to go to Jackson, MS, to receive further spiritual direction from a "well-known colored clergyman." That man was, in all likelihood, Charles Price Jones, arguably the single most significant African-American, Wesleyan-Holiness leader in the South at that time, and a close friend of ›Charles Harrison Mason. Jones and Mason had founded the ›Church of God in Christ (COGIC).

Seymour returned to the Houston area in 1905, where, in August of that year, Mrs. ›Lucy Farrow, an African-American widow and the founder of a small black congregation, handed the reins of leadership over to him. She would spend the next several months as a governess, tending to the needs of the ›Charles Fox Parham family. Thus, Seymour clearly had the confidence of the African-American, Wesleyan-Holiness community.

In late 1905 Charles Parham returned to the Houston area, accompanied by a number of followers and by Lucy Farrow. Farrow encouraged Seymour to study with Parham and learn of the baptism in the Holy Spirit at his Bible school located at 503 Rusk Avenue in Brunner, TX. Despite local Jim Crow laws, Parham made space for Seymour, allegedly seating his white students within the classroom and allowing Seymour to listen from a hallway. But Parham also accompanied Seymour into the African-American community, where the two men preached. Seymour continued his affiliation with Parham's work in Brunner from Nov. 1905 through early Feb. 1906, during which time he integrated his Wesleyan-Holiness theological system with Parham's teaching on the baptism in the Spirit including the Bible evidence of speaking in other tongues.

In early Feb. 1906 Seymour received an invitation "from the colored people of the City of Los Angeles," to take the pastorate of a small Holiness mission in Los Angeles that had been founded by Julia W. Hutchins. Parham claims that he advised Seymour to stay in Houston, but Seymour decided to take the position in Los Angeles in spite of Parham's advice. Seymour arrived in Los Angeles on Feb. 22, 1906. He would be remembered 25 years later in the black community of Los Angeles as a man "with a 'mission' to found a church composed of members of all races."

Seymour's entry into the work begun by Mrs. Hutchins was not easy. After preaching what he had learned in Houston, he found himself locked out of the building. Mrs. Hutchins, who had founded this congregation so that she could gain church planting and pastoral experience before serving as a Holiness Church missionary in Africa, was, like many in the Holiness movement, not convinced of the legitimacy of his message. Seymour was forced to turn to Mr.

Edward Lee, a member of Mrs. Hutchins's flock who provided Seymour with housing. Lee, in turn, invited him to minister in a small Bible study being conducted at the home of Richard and Ruth Asberry at 214 (now 216) North ›Bonnie Brae Street. Seymour led the Bible study until mid Apr. 1906.

While Seymour had not yet experienced baptism in the Holy Spirit with the "Bible evidence" of speaking in tongues as defined by Parham, he continued to teach it. On Apr. 9, 1906, several members of the Bible study began to speak in other tongues. The excitement generated by this discovery quickly attracted a curious but sympathetic crowd. Seymour was forced to find a more suitable space to continue his work among these people. They rented, then moved their meetings to, a vacant building, the former sanctuary of Stevens African Methodist Episcopal [AME] Church (now First AME Church) at 312 Azusa Street about Apr. 15. Seymour and his followers began what would become a three-year revival that would impact the world.

Seymour preached regularly at the ›Azusa Street Mission, though preaching was not always the focal point of his leadership. While he could preach for an hour or more, his sermons were frequently no more than short exhortations. Besides, many services during this period included three or four such sermons by different people. Seymour's style compared favorably to the classic "call and response" antiphonal preaching style found elsewhere in the African-American tradition. A number of articles that were likely first delivered as "sermons" were published in the mission's newspaper, *The Apostolic Faith*. Some are signed, while study of the language and style of others suggests that some anonymous entries may be attributed to him as well.

Like others in the African-American tradition as a whole, Seymour cited Isaiah more frequently than any other book in the Bible. He also preached from Luke 4:18–19, another favorite text among African Americans. ›Glenn Cook claimed that every time Seymour preached, he quoted from Mark 16 and Acts 2:4.

Local news reporters frequently ridiculed Seymour's preaching. One reporter described a 20-minute exhortation by Seymour as nothing more than "a jumble of Scripture and shouting" predicting "pestilence and trouble" on earth with "hellfire and a lake of burning brimstone" for those who did not join the believers at the mission. His hermeneutical approach was largely a literal one, and Scripture provided the ultimate norm for all that he undertook or exhorted his followers to seek.

Charles F. Parham visited Seymour's mission in Oct. 1906 and claimed that he was disgusted with what he observed. He described Seymour's work as consisting of "animalisms," nothing more than "trances, falling under the power, holy-rolling-dancing-jumping, shaking, jabbering, chattering, wind-sucking and giving vent to meaningless sounds and noises as practiced by the Negroes of the Southland." In spite of these criticisms, which suggest that Seymour and his congregation were to a great extent indebted to the broader domain of African-American religion, Parham saw the potential of Seymour's work for himself. Parham moved to take over Seymour's work, explaining that it was merely an extension of his own work but gone awry.

Seymour's followers immediately rebuffed Parham. They forced him to retreat from the mission, a fact that the Holiness critic Alma White quickly exploited in her own paper. Parham was forced to change his tactics. Instead of wresting control of the mission from Seymour outright, he determined to plant a competing congregation within five blocks of the Azusa Street Mission. Parham's followers joined him in advertising that they would conduct "dignified religious services … along proper and profound Christian lines" in opposition to the brand of "religious anarchy which marks the Los Angeles Azusa Street meetings" led by Seymour.

Seymour survived this attack. His followers continued to describe him as a meek man and as a man of prayer. He prayed fervently, with his head frequently bowed within his pulpit, while others prayed, sang, or exhorted the faithful around him. He allowed many of his critics time to speak to his congregation. He made himself vulnerable, and when others started churches near the mission that competed directly with his own, he often advertised their services in his paper. Seymour attempted to move the theological ideal of a priesthood of all believers from a theory into a reality. He allowed for experimentation and growth, and while he was gentle, gracious, self-effacing, and for the most part soft-spoken, he provided circumspect correction as it was needed.

Seymour surrounded himself with a capable, interracial staff of women and men, many of whom volunteered their time. He conducted "leaders" meetings on Monday mornings. These meetings served as times of prayer, of building mutual support, of teaching, and as strategy sessions. The revival he led required planning and forethought. His administrative skills have not yet been adequately explored. The mission sponsored outreach meetings in surrounding communities, large-scale baptismal services at the beach in San Pedro, and the more or less regular publication of a newspaper with as many as 50,000 readers and subscribers worldwide. It commissioned missionaries and evangelists and ran a rescue mission in Los Angeles. Seymour clearly helped to define this interracial mission and its message.

On May 13, 1908, Seymour married ►Jennie Evans Moore, originally a member of the Asberry home Bible study, and now a member of Seymour's mission. Edward S. Lee conducted the service. Jennie became a trusted partner in ministry, often preaching at the mission, generally overseeing things when Seymour was absent, and occasionally trav-

eling on his behalf. The couple made their home upstairs in a small apartment over the mission. At least two sources suggest that the couple had a daughter who later became part of the COGIC, but thus far, no documentation has been found to support this claim.

The upstairs space at the mission was often shared with other boarders who contributed to the work of the mission in return for a room. The 1910 census shows six other adults and four children who called this space their home. Following Seymour's death in 1922, Jennie Evans Moore Seymour would continue to act as pastor of the congregation and live in the mission until at least 1931.

Seymour's marriage to Jennie Evans Moore created a bit of controversy and apparently provided the impetus for ►Clara Lum, editor of the mission's paper, *The Apostolic Faith*, to take all but the local mailing list and move the paper to Portland, OR. She went to work there for another of Seymour's former parishioners, Mrs. ►Florence Crawford. This move irreparably crippled Seymour's ability to become the leading national or international figure in the newly burgeoning pentecostal movement. There is evidence from 1915 to suggest that he hoped to lead the movement in the development of other congregations, rescue missions, foreign missions, primary and secondary schools, even colleges, universities, and schools of theology.

Seymour attempted to recover *The Apostolic Faith* newspaper, first by talking with Crawford and Lum. When that proved ineffective, he sent several of his members, including his wife, to Portland to incorporate the Apostolic Faith Mission, Portland, OR, as an extension of the work in Los Angeles. Using their newly issued articles of incorporation as "proof" that the Los Angeles Mission was the owner of the paper, Seymour's entourage attempted to persuade the postmaster of Portland that the letters and funds derived from the paper now being mailed from Portland by Crawford and Lum should be redirected to Los Angeles. Their attempt failed. The postmaster sided with Crawford, whose local mission, while still unincorporated, constituted sufficient evidence to block Seymour's attempt to recapture *The Apostolic Faith*. Seymour's corporation in Oregon would lie dormant until 1921, when Florence Crawford, her son, and another trustee simply filed amended articles and took the existing corporation for their own work.

From 1907 through at least 1919, Seymour traveled widely throughout the United States. He made trips throughout California and to Alabama, Illinois, Indiana, Ohio, Oregon, Tennessee, Texas, and Virginia. He held evangelistic meetings, baptized new converts, and "set aside" or appointed leaders in a far-reaching fellowship of pastors who were willing to work with him. During one of his trips in 1911, Mrs. Seymour invited ►William H. Durham to preach a series of services at the mission. Durham, believing that

Seymour was not capable of leading the revival any longer, used the opportunity to lobby for control of the mission. Seymour's early return set the stage for an explosive conflict that exposed Durham's plot. Seymour managed to regain control of the mission only when he and his supporters on the board of trustees locked the doors against Durham. Durham retreated, only to found another competing congregation just blocks away.

In 1915 Seymour published a 95-page book titled *The Doctrines and Disciplines of the Azusa Street Apostolic Faith Mission of Los Angeles, Cal.* for use by members of the mission. Much of it is derived verbatim from the *Doctrines and Discipline* of a variety of Methodist organizations, including the AME church that had originally built the building on Azusa Street.

Seymour's *Doctrines and Discipline* includes most of Wesley's abridged version of the "Thirty-Nine Articles of Religion" of the Anglican Church adopted in 1563 by a convocation and again in 1571 by the English Parliament. Still, Seymour revealed his own theological concerns by replacing or making subtle changes to some of the 24 remaining articles. To this work Seymour added a preface, an "apostolic address," which explains his own intentions regarding the mission, a copy of an amended constitution, and a number of paragraphs designed to serve apologetic purposes for the mission. Key among the theological concerns he raised in this volume were his rejoinders against soul sleep, annihilationism, spiritualism, baptism in Jesus' name, triple immersion baptism, and the observance of Saturday as the Sabbath. He opposed those who insisted on speaking in tongues as the "Bible evidence" of baptism in the Spirit without an equal insistence that the speaker manifest the fruit of the Spirit. And he argued theologically against racism. On the moral and ethical level, Seymour condemned free loveism, adultery, spiritual marriages, marriages to unbelievers, marital separations and divorce, the exchange of the "holy kiss" across gender lines, and "artificial dancing." He also gave practical advice on how to deal with the rising tide of racism.

Seymour was clearly hurt by attempts that had been made by people such as Parham and Durham to take over the church he had founded on Azusa Street. Clara Lum and Florence Crawford had inflicted pain by walking away with what he believed to be *his* newspaper and mailing lists. He may have felt that people such as ▸Frank Bartleman, ▸William Pendleton, ▸Elmer Fisher, and Thomas Attebury had hurt the revival to some extent by siphoning off many of his parishioners to form congregations of their own. The local press certainly portrayed them as divisive. The fact that he was not invited to participate in any formal way in the 1913 Arroyo Seco Camp meeting that convened under the name of the Apostolic Faith may have contributed further to his pain. Finally, the defection of Glenn Cook, his former business manager, first to Durham's work and then to the ▸Oneness cause, surely played a role in his feelings of rejection.

Arguments have been made regarding the role that racism may have played in these cases, but the fact that all of the people who were involved in these things were white seems clearly to have contributed to Seymour's personal reflections on racism. In several places, his *Doctrines and Discipline* addresses his pain over what he viewed as racist attitudes and racially inspired actions.

As a result of his experience with racism, Seymour requested that from 1915 onward all officers of the church had to be people of color, and he formalized this request in a constitutional change. He viewed this action as a concession to the racial problems that were growing throughout American society at the time, but he looked forward to the day when such restrictions would no longer be necessary. He continued to welcome whites to participate in the life of the congregation, and he challenged the "colored" members of his congregation not to stoop to the level of racial prejudice and discrimination, but to continue to "love our white brethren."

In spite of Seymour's continuing goodwill toward all people and his willingness to continue to serve as pastor and, from 1915 on, as bishop of the Apostolic Faith Mission he had founded in California, his congregation continued to dwindle until it was simply one more small African-American congregation in Los Angeles. He perceived himself as someone who ultimately had been rejected by the people he had been called to serve, and feelings of inadequacy attended his later years. On Sept. 28, 1922, Seymour died from a heart attack. He is buried at the Evergreen Cemetery in East Los Angeles.

■ **Bibliography:** "Apostolic Faith People Here Again," *Whittier Daily News* (Dec. 13, 1906), 1 ■ "Brother Seymour Called Home," *The Pentecostal Herald* (Chicago, IL), 9:12, no. 97 (Oct. 1, 1922), 1, 4 ■ I. C. Clemmons, *Bishop C. H. Mason and the Roots of the Church of God in Christ* (1996), 41–59 ■ J. T. Connelly, "William J. Seymour," in C. H. Lippy, ed., *Twentieth-Century Shapers of American Popular Religion* (1989) ■ Mother Cotton, "Inside Story of the Outpouring of the Holy Spirit (Azusa Street, April 1906)," *Message of the "Apostolic Faith,"* 1 (1, Apr. 1936) ■ "Death of W. J. Seymour," *The Voice in the Wilderness* 2 (13, Oct. 1922) ■ "Home-Going of Rev. W. J. Seymore [sic]," *Bridegroom's Messenger* 16, no. 241 (Nov.–Dec. 1922) ■ I. MacRobert, *The Black Roots and White Racism of Early Pentecostalism in the U.S.A.* (1988) ■ idem, "The Black Roots of Pentecostalism," in J. A. B. Jongeneel, ed., *Pentecost, Mission and Ecumenism: Essays on Intercultural Theology: Festschrift in Honour of Professor Walter J. Hollenweger* (1992) ■ L. Martin, *In the Beginning* (1994), 117–19 ■ D. J. Nelson, "The Black Face of Church Renewal: The Meaning of a Charismatic Explosion," in P. Elbert, ed. *Faces of Renewal: Studies in Honor of Stanley M. Horton* (1988) ■ idem, "For Such a Time as This: The Story of Bishop William J. Seymour and the Azusa Street Revival" (diss., U. of Birmingham [U.K.], 1981) ▪ C. M. Robeck Jr., "William J. Seymour and 'The Bible Evidence'," in G. B. McGee, ed., *Initial Evidence: Historical and Biblical Perspectives on the Pentecostal Doctrine of Spirit Baptism* (1991) ▪ C. J. Sanders, *Saints in Exile: The Holiness-Pentecostal Experience in African American Religion and Culture* (1996), 27–32 ▪ W. J. Seymour, *The Doctrines and Discipline of the Azusa Street Apostolic Faith Mission* (1915) ▪ C. W. Shumway, "A Study of 'The Gift of Tongues'" (A.B. thesis, U. of S. Calif., 1914) ▪ idem, "A Critical History of Glossolalia" (diss., Boston U., 1919) ▪ V. Synan, *Holiness-Pentecostal Movement in the United States* (1971) ▪ J. Tinney, "William J. Seymour: Father of Modern-Day Pentecostalism," *Journal of the Interdenominational Theological Center* 4 (1, Fall 1976; later published in R. Burkett and R. Newman, eds., *Black Apostles* [1978], and as "Who Was William J. Seymour?" in J. S. Tinney and S. N. Short, eds., *In the Tradition of William J. Seymour: Essays Commemorating the Dedication of Seymour House at Howard University* [1978]) ▪ A. White, *Demons and Tongues* (1919).   ▪ C. M. Robeck Jr.

SHAKARIAN, DEMOS (1913–93). Dairy farmer and founder of the ʾFull Gospel Business Men's Fellowship International (FGBMFI). Shakarian is of Armenian descent. His family escaped the Armenian holocaust due to a warning from a pentecostal prophet whom God had raised up to warn the Armenian people of disaster that would come upon them.

Demos Shakarian, a successful California dairyman who, with encouragement from Oral Roberts, founded the Full Gospel Business Men's Fellowship International in 1951.

The Shakarian family heeded the words of the prophet and fled to America. Shakarian grew up in the Armenian Pentecostal Church and gave his heart to God as a young man. When he experienced the baptism of the Holy Spirit in 1926 at age 13, he also received a healing for his impaired hearing.

In 1933 Shakarian married Rose Gabrielian in a traditionally arranged Armenian wedding. Since their wedding, Rose and Demos have devoted their lives to serving God in any way they could and felt led to sponsor revival meetings to bring the message of Jesus to their community. During this time Shakarian became friends with ʾDr. Charles S. Price through the remarkable healing of Shakarian's sister, who had been severely injured in an automobile accident and was not expected to live. (Price laid hands on Shakarian's sister, and as her body shook for 20 minutes under the power of God, her shattered pelvis was healed. The next morning new X-rays revealed a completely restored pelvis in place of the crushed and dislocated one of the day before.)

As God prospered the Shakarians through their dairy farm (one of the largest private dairies in the world), Shakarian continued to support and work in revival meetings. In 1951, after helping set up ʾOral Roberts' Los Angeles crusade, he told Roberts of his feeling that God was leading him to start a group called the Full Gospel Business Men's Fellowship International. Roberts agreed to attend the first meeting of the group, held at Clifton's cafeteria in downtown Los Angeles, and prayed an anointed prayer that called for this group to be a mighty force for the spread of the gospel. However, Shakarian experienced a year of frustration until, in a night of prayer, God gave him a vision of the work God would do in the world through this group. As he led meetings, God would direct him to the individuals he should call upon to give testimony. As businessmen told the story of how God was working in their lives and businesses, many of their friends were converted and the goal of sharing Christ in an organization of businessmen was realized. The FGBMFI has spread the message of the fullness of the Spirit and the truth of divine healing as well as the message of salvation. The FGBMFI has grown to have chapters in 160 countries. In 1984 Shakarian suffered a stroke that left him with some impairment, but he continued in an advisory capacity ubtil his death in 1993. His son Richard has taken over the leadership of FGBMFI.

▪ **Bibliography:** B. Bird, "The Legacy of Demos Shakarian," *Charisma* (June 1986) ▪ D. Shakarian, *The Happiest People on Earth* (1975).   ▪ J. R. Zeigler

SHAKERS The followers of Ann Lee (1736–81), who emigrated from England to Watervliet, NY, with eight sympathizers in 1774. The Shakers introduced a version of millenarian perfectionism within a communal setting. The

An old engraving showing the Shakers at their dance of worship, from which their name was derived. In their dances they "shook off sin" and "trampled evil underfoot" to rid themselves of sexual desire.

wife of a blacksmith in Manchester, Lee was the mother of four children, all of whom died in infancy. Her subsequent emotional distress found relief in religious enthusiasm. She was deeply influenced by radical Quakers and by French Camisard prophets, and she concluded that she was the second appearing of Christ. A concomitant interest in an end-times restoration of spiritual gifts to the church resulted in her espousal of healing and tongues.

In 1787 Lee organized her followers as the United Society of Believers in Christ's Second Appearing. Given her own unhappy marriage, it is hardly surprising that she taught them that the source of evil was the sex act and that Christians who coveted perfection should eliminate greed, pride, and sex. By regulating every minute detail of daily existence, substituting communal property for private possessions, and enjoining celibacy, Shaker communities responded to these issues.

The Shakers generally gained adherents during periods of local revival, when they challenged converts with their call to perfection. After 1787 the spontaneity and enthusiasm that marked religious gatherings under Ann Lee yielded to systematized doctrine and elaborate regulation under the supervision of Lee's successor, Joseph Meacham. As awakenings spread across the northern states after the Revolutionary War, the Shakers experienced rapid growth. They moved westward to reap a harvest from the revivals that focused in Cane Ridge, KY. By 1825 there were Shaker communities in Ohio, Indiana, and Kentucky, as well as in New England and New York. Membership surged to approximately 6,000. For several

years after 1837, spiritualism flourished in Shaker settings. The waning of revival fervor and internal tensions combined to discourage further growth. The prosperous Shaker communities merged until only one active but dying community remains.

During Lee's lifetime, Shaker services resembled early Quaker gatherings. Visitors reported that spiritual gifts operated and that these gifts validated the message of Christ's second appearing. Reports of signs, visions, prophecies, and gifts attracted the curious and convinced some; others considered Lee's personal dealings compellingly persuasive.

Lee's message was essentially ›restorationist: The primitive church had lost the gifts, but an end-time restoration had been promised. It was being realized in the 1780s. After Lee's death, religious enthusiasm was channeled into ritualistic dance, and tongues speech was confined to "quick meetings" held during the Christmas holiday season.

■ **Bibliography:** E. D. Andrews, *The People Called Shakers* (1953) ▌ G. H. Williams and E. L. Waldvogel [Blumhofer], "Speaking in Tongues and Related Gifts," in *The Charismatic Movement,* ed. M. Hamilton (1975).

■ E. L. Blumhofer

SHARING OF MINISTRIES ABROAD (SOMA). SOMA began in 1978 at the first Anglican Conference on Spiritual Renewal held in Canterbury, U.K. Leaders gathered from 25 countries believed that the Lord was directing them to share the blessings and power of the Holy Spirit with the body of Christ worldwide. Canon ›Michael Harper left his ministry at the ›Fountain Trust to accept leadership of SOMA as its executive director. SOMA's international council included ›Bill Burnett, ›Everett L. Fullam, and ›Charles M. Irish.

The leaders' vision for SOMA was a fresh approach to overseas mission. They envisioned one part of the body of Christ sharing with another so as to empower the local church to do God's work among its own people. As a first step, a series of international conferences were organized; they were held in Singapore in 1981; Limuru, Kenya, in 1983; and Suva, Fiji, in 1984. A second step was the sending out of clergy and lay teams, at its own expense, to minister in various countries in the context of short-term missions. SOMA then developed affiliated organizations in the U.S., Canada, and Far East. SOMA is continuing its ministry into the 21st century.   ■ C. M. Irish

SHEPHERDING MOVEMENT An influential and controversial expression of the charismatic renewal that emerged as a distinct nondenominational movement in 1974. The shepherding movement, also known as the discipleship movement, developed in response to the increasing independence among many charismatic Christians who were leaving their denominational churches and joining independent churches and prayer groups. It also grew in response to the highly individualistic and subjective spirituality of many charismatics.

The shepherding movement taught that every believer needed to submit to a "shepherd" or pastoral leader. This relationship was seen as essential for developing spiritual maturity and required a definite commitment to a "personal pastor." The movement also taught that all pastors and leaders needed to be personally submitted to another leader to foster accountability. These emphases were seen by critics as an attempt to create a kind of takeover of the independent charismatics, creating a pyramid-like chain of command with the shepherding leaders at the top.

The movement grew out of the association in Oct. 1970 of four popular charismatic Bible teachers: ▸Don Basham, an ordained Disciples of Christ minister; ▸Bernard (Bob) Mumford, originally ordained through the Assemblies of God; ▸Derek Prince, a philosopher turned pentecostal; and ▸Charles Simpson, a former Southern Baptist. All four leaders were frequent contributors to *New Wine* magazine, published by the ▸Holy Spirit Teaching Mission (HSTM), a charismatic teaching center in Ft. Lauderdale, FL. When problems developed that brought about the resignation of HSTM's founder, Eldon Purvis, the four were asked to help

the HSTM survive the crisis, and in doing so, they decided to join together for their own accountability and submission.

From 1970 through 1972 the four Bible teachers became increasingly involved with *New Wine* magazine, which was becoming the most widely circulated charismatic publication in the U.S. In Mar. 1972 HSTM, *New Wine*'s publisher, changed its name to Christian Growth Ministries (CGM). *New Wine* soon became the primary public voice of the four teachers' ministries; they were the principal contributors to the magazine and participants in CGM-sponsored teaching conferences. During these years, Basham, Mumford, Prince, and Simpson were developing in seminal form teachings on authority, submission, pastoral care, and discipleship that would later characterize the shepherding movement.

Three "Shepherds" conferences helped catalyze the emergence of the movement. The first was a Mar. 1973 conference held in Leesburg, FL. Expecting 75 charismatic pastors and lay leaders, the conference drew, by word of mouth, an attendance of over 450. The second, in June 1974, held at Montreat, NC, drew over 1,700 pastors and leaders. It was at this conference that Canadian pentecostal W. J. E. (Ern) Baxter associated himself with Basham, Mumford, Prince, and Simpson. Together they became known to many as the "Ft. Lauderdale Five." The 1975 National Men's Shepherds Conference, held in Kansas City, was the first nationally advertised conference and was attended by 4,700 charismatic leaders and pastors.

Through these conferences and regular articles in *New Wine* magazine, the teaching on shepherding and discipleship drew many leaders into the emerging movement, as men started submitting themselves to Mumford and the other four. In 1974 and 1975, a national network of churches and prayer groups was established, led by those submitted to the five.

The churches in this network were nontraditionally structured, with an emphasis on small cell groups or house churches. These cell groups were led by lay "shepherds," who in turn were submitted to a lead pastor, who was submitted to one of the five principal leaders or an appointed representative. The churches and groups associated with shepherding strongly emphasized the teachings on pastoral care and discipleship. The churches also stressed the importance of commitment, loyalty, and servanthood among believers. At its zenith, some 100,000 adherents were directly involved in this association. The association of churches and pastors was always said to be based on relationship, not on formal organization. Mumford and the other four always denied critics' allegations that the shepherding leaders were attempting to form a charismatic denomination.

The five principal leaders in Integrity Communications: (left to right) Ern Baxter, Derek Prince, Charles Simpson, Don Basham, and Bob Mumford.

The popularity and considerable gifts of the five teachers, their committed and talented constituency, and their skill and use of media through audio- and videotapes, books, and *New Wine* magazine all contributed to the movement's influence far beyond those directly linked to the five key leaders. This wide influence in the broader charismatic renewal gave rise to heated controversy over the movement's teaching on authority and submission, and translocal pastoral care—the "shepherding controversy" or "discipleship controversy."

The controversy came to full fury and public debate in 1975 when Christian Broadcasting Network (CBN) founder ⮞Pat Robertson began to denounce the shepherding teachings on television through *The 700 Club*. For what he called "cultic" excesses, Robertson forbade Mumford and the others to appear on CBN-affiliated radio or TV stations and ordered that all CBN tapes of the teachers be immediately erased. Robertson further wrote an open letter to Bob Mumford in June 1975, charging that Mumford and the others were controlling the lives of their followers through overuse of spiritual authority.

At about the same time, ⮞Full Gospel Businessmen's Fellowship International (FGBMFI) founder ⮞Demos Shakarian joined the controversy by forbidding the five teachers or any teaching on shepherding or discipleship in any FGBMFI chapter. Also, in September 1975, charismatic healing evangelist ⮞Kathryn Kuhlman publicly stated that the shepherding movement could "bring absolute destruction to the great charismatic movement." Kuhlman later refused to share the platform with Bob Mumford at the 1975 Jerusalem Holy Spirit Conference if he was allowed to participate. In response, Mumford withdrew from the conference. The intensity of the controversy was reflected in various pentecostal/charismatic publications, an article in the *New York Times*, and a cover-page headline in the evangelical magazine *Christianity Today*.

To deal with the growing controversy, a special ad-hoc charismatic leaders' meeting was convened in Aug. 1975 in Minneapolis, bringing together many prominent denominational and independent charismatic leaders. These included the five shepherding teachers and Pat Robertson, ⮞Dennis Bennett, ⮞Harald Bredeson, ⮞Larry Christenson, ⮞Dan Malachuk, and ⮞Kevin Ranaghan. "The shoot-out at the Curtis Hotel," as the meeting became known, was heated, with accusations flying back and forth, and accomplished little toward reconciliation and understanding. Subsequent meetings in Ann Arbor, MI, in Dec. 1975 and at the annual Charismatic Leaders Conference in Mar. 1976 did help bring some understanding as the shepherding leaders made a mild apology for any problems their teachings had caused. At the Mar. 1976 meeting in Oklahoma City, a Charismatic Concerns Committee was established to try to deal with future concerns and controversies among charismatics.

While the charismatic leaders' meetings helped calm the controversy somewhat, tensions between shepherding leaders and in particular the independent charismatics continued. These tensions forced the creation of two separate tracks at the 1977 Kansas City Conference on Charismatic Renewal in the Churches for independent nondenominational charismatics. The shepherding track was attended by more than 9,000, while the other group had some 1,500 at their subconference. The former was the second-largest group in attendance, behind the Catholic charismatics with 25,000. The Kansas City Conference was a high-water mark for the shepherding movement.

Momentum and growth continued for the shepherding movement in 1977 as more leaders and churches associated with Mumford and the other leaders. Men's conferences around the nation drew many thousands. Despite this growth, the controversy simmered among charismatics and pentecostals.

The shepherding movement's distinctive doctrines continued to develop. The theology of "covenant relationship," with a distinct ecclesiological dimension, became the unique and central doctrine of the movement. To the shepherding leaders, a believer's relationship with God is rooted in God's covenant love demonstrated by Christ's sacrificial death. Consequently, believers were to commit themselves with the same kind of self-sacrificial love and loyalty to their leaders and to other believers. Some viewed covenant relationship as a lifelong commitment.

The movement stressed the need for male leadership; women were not to have governmental roles in the church. The family was viewed as the most basic unit in church life, and the role of fathers was emphasized. The movement also held high expectations for its committed members who were asked to tithe, to be fully involved in church life, and to submit all areas of their lives to the counsel of a shepherd-pastor.

A strong emphasis was put on a fivefold pattern for the church office-ministries from Eph. 4:11–12. The movement taught that apostles and prophets were present-day translocal ministers; at the invitation of local churches, apostles and prophets could exercise governmental authority. The movement practiced translocal pastoral care. The five teachers pastored other leaders around the United States who then pastored other leaders.

Despite momentum and growth, internal conflicts challenged the cohesion of the movement. The five key leaders were strong personalities who always maintained their own independent ministries. Their diverse backgrounds and ministries created, at times, practical and theological differences. Charles Simpson, the most gifted administrator and pastor of the five, began to take on an increasing leadership role in the late 1970s. In 1978 CGM was renamed Integrity Communications, and the publication of *New Wine* moved from Ft.

Lauderdale to Simpson's base in Mobile, AL. By 1981 Basham, Baxter, and Mumford were with Simpson in Mobile; only Prince still remained in Ft. Lauderdale. In 1980 the five teachers nearly separated over internal conflicts but were held together by Simpson's influence. The internal problems were fueled by accusations of abuse of spiritual authority within the movement. Mumford and Simpson, in particular, were traveling the nation to try to deal with associated churches in crisis. By 1980 many leaders and their followers were leaving the movement.

Derek Prince quietly withdrew from the shepherding movement in 1983 and made his exit public in 1984, no longer able to support the movement's belief in pastoral care for every believer and the concept of translocal pastoral care for leaders. The remaining four teachers held together until late 1986, when financial problems with *New Wine* magazine and continuing differences among the four led to the decision to cease publication of the magazine with the Dec. 1986 issue. At the same time, Simpson and the others dissolved their formal relationship, in effect ending their association and the shepherding movement.

Simpson remains the primary leader of the movement's remnant that prefers to be called the Covenant Movement, holding that covenant relationship is the unifying doctrine of those who continue in association. In 1987 Simpson and others established the Fellowship of Covenant Ministers and Churches that has carried on, in a moderated form, many of the central themes of the shepherding movement. In 1987 Integrity Communications changed its name to Charles Simpson Ministries; Simpson now pastors Covenant Church of Mobile, AL.

After the movement dissolved, Basham moved to Ohio, and Baxter and Mumford moved to different parts of California. Basham died in 1989 and Baxter died in 1993. Mumford continues his teaching and writing ministry from Raleigh, NC, through his ministry, Lifechangers. Prince's ministry is now based in Charlotte, NC.

■ **Bibliography:** "An Important Announcement to Our New Wine Family," *New Wine* (Feb. 1979) ■ D. Basham, "How It All Began," *New Wine* (June 1984) ■ "Forum," *New Wine* (Dec. 1976) ■ K. McDonnell, "Seven Documents on the Discipleship Question," in *Presence, Power, Praise: Documents on the Charismatic Renewal,* 3 vols., ed. K. McDonnell (1980) ■ S. D. Moore, The Sheperding Movement: History, Controversy, Ecclesiology (2001) ■ D. Prince, *Discipleship, Shepherding, Commitment* (1976) ■ S. Strang, "The Discipleship Controversy Three Years Later," *Charisma* (Sept. 1978). ■ S. D. Moore

SHERRILL, JOHN LEWIS (1923–), and **ELIZABETH** (1928–). Authors and ghostwriters for several charismatic best-sellers. The Sherrills were married in 1947 and worked as freelance writers for some years. John was senior editor for *Guideposts* from 1951 to 1969. Around 1961 he contacted ▸Harald Bredesen for a possible article but realized that the resurgence of glossolalia in the 20th century required a book. During its writing, Sherrill, an Episcopalian, was himself baptized in the Spirit. The resulting book, *They Speak with Other Tongues* (1964), with its autobiographical element, became a best-seller. Possibly even more influential in the charismatic movement was *The Cross and the Switchblade* (1963), on which the Sherrills worked with ▸David Wilkerson. They also collaborated on Brother Andrew's *God's Smuggler* (1967) and Corrie ten Boom's *The Hiding Place* (1975). Elizabeth has also acted as editor for other well-known authors, such as Catherine Marshall and Charles Colson.

■ **Bibliography:** "John and Elizabeth Sherrill Tell Their Own Story," *Charisma* (Sept. 1985). ■ P. D. Hocken

SHIELDS, ANN ELIZABETH (1939–). Popular teacher in ▸Catholic charismatic renewal. Professed as a Sister of Mercy in 1960, Sr. Ann was baptized in the Spirit in Jan. 1971. A frequent speaker at national and international conferences, she has a gift for simple and challenging presentation. She was a member of the National Service Committee (1978–84) and has coauthored (with M. Scanlan) *And Their Eyes Were Opened: Encountering Jesus in the Sacraments* (1976). She has also written *Fire in My Heart* (1988) and several booklets. A member of the ▸F.I.R.E. team since its inception in 1983, Shields began working in 1993 for Renewal Ministries, a Catholic evangelistic association led by ▸Ralph Martin, editing their newsletter, cohosting the weekly television program *The Choices We Face,* and hosting a daily radio program, *Food for the Journey.* She is Superior of the Servants of God's Love, a canonically established Catholic charismatic religious community in the diocese of Lansing, MI. ■ P. D. Hocken

SHLEMON-RYAN, BARBARA LEAHY (1936–). Catholic charismatic evangelist. Born in Canton, OH, Barbara Leahy obtained a diploma in nursing in 1957 and married Ben Shlemon the same year. Mother of 5 children and now grandmother of 10, she was one of the first Catholics to receive the baptism in the Spirit, which happened at Trinity Episcopal Church, Wheaton, IL, in Mar. 1965. Barbara Shlemon developed a healing ministry with ▸F. MacNutt and later the Linn brothers. A founding member of the Association of Christian Therapists in 1976, she became editor of the *Journal of Christian Healing* (1977–80). In 1980 Barbara Shlemon cofounded a House of Prayer in Clearwater, FL. In 1988 she relocated to Southern California, founding Beloved Ministry, an evangelistic outreach sponsoring retreats, conferences, and seminars on Christian healing. She was divorced in 1987 and married Tim Ryan in 1992. She is the author of

Healing Prayer (1976); *To Heal as Jesus Healed* (with D. and M. Linn; 1978); *Healing the Hidden Self* (1982); *Living Each Day by the Power of Faith* (1986); and *Healing the Wounds of Divorce* (1989).   ■ P. D. Hocken

SIBERIAN SEVEN A pentecostal *cause célèbre* of five years' duration ended happily on June 28, 1983, when 16 members of the Vashchenko family (five of whom had spent all of the preceding five years in the U.S. embassy in Moscow) were reunited in Israel. Still in the Soviet Union, but soon to be granted exit visas also, were Maria Chmykhalov and her son, Timofei. These members of two peasant families of Chernogorsk in Siberia (who came to be known as the Siberian Seven) had been for many years at the forefront of a struggle with Soviet bureaucrats for religious freedom. In 1963 Augustina Vashchenko (her husband then in his third year of confinement in a labor camp) joined 31 other pentecostals in requesting exit visas from the U.S. embassy in Moscow. Powerless to comply, embassy officials persuaded the petitioners to return home. Fifteen years of persecution (labor camp, prison, job discrimination, and forced relocation) followed. Not knowing that to emigrate a Soviet citizen must have a formal invitation from a close relative abroad, they tried again on June 27, 1978. Denied, the seven fled into the U.S. embassy and refused to leave. (One Vashchenko son was arrested in the process and imprisoned.) Notoriety gained for them by news coverage and interested groups in the West resulted in standing invitations to the U.S., Canada, the U.K., and Sweden. Numerous appeals to the American government to put pressure on the Soviet authorities proved fruitless, as did hearings in 1981 and 1982 by the U.S. Senate and House of Representatives. The breaking of the deadlock came from the seven themselves. On Dec. 25, 1982, Mrs. Vashchenko and her daughter, Lidiya, went on a hunger strike. Hospitalized, Lidiya agreed to return to Chernogorsk, where she successfully applied for an exit visa. Once she was in Israel, the others decided to follow a similar course.

■ **Bibliography:** T. Chmykhalov, *The Last Christian: The Release of the Siberian Seven* (1986) ■ idem, *Release!* (1984) ■ J. Pollock, *The Siberian Seven* (1979) ■ U.S. Congress. House Judiciary Committee. *Siberian Seven Hearing, December 16, 1982* (1983) ■ U.S. Congress. Senate Judiciary Committee. *Relief of Seven Soviet Pentecostals Hearing, November 19, 1981* (1982) ■ L. Vashchenko, *Cry Freedom* (1987).   ■ C. E. Jones

SIGNS AND WONDERS

I. The First Eighteen Centuries
    A. *Issues of Cessationism and Hagiography*
    B. *The Ancient Church*
    C. *The Medieval Church*
    D. *The Reformation Era*
    E. *The Seventeenth and Eighteenth Centuries*

II. The Last Two Centuries
    A. *The Nineteenth Century*
    B. *The Twentieth Century*

I. THE FIRST EIGHTEEN CENTURIES.

A. *Issues of Cessationism and Hagiography.*

The emergence of pentecostalism in the 20th century has raised a variety of long-neglected questions. Among these is whether miraculous manifestations of the Holy Spirit, so apparent in the 1st-century church, disappeared or declined thereafter. A corollary issue is the relationship of the miraculous to the church's mission of evangelism.

For very different reasons, two groups of Christian scholars have argued the disappearance of the supernatural after the 1st century A.D. B. B. Warfield, late-19th-century Princeton theologian, and other cessationists insist that pentecostalism faded out of existence by A.D. 100, once the apostolic church had been founded and the canon had been written. The same conclusions have been reached by many pentecostal writers who argue from Joel 2:23, which refers to a "former" and a "latter rain." According to this view, the Holy Spirit was poured out on expectant believers in both the 1st and the 20th centuries, but the church was not graced with miracles, signs, wonders, and other charismatic gifts during the 1,800-year interim.

As a result, most Christians are unaware that pentecostalism in most of its forms actually has existed throughout Christian history in both Eastern and Western churches as well as among heretical and fringe Christian movements, and that on numerous occasions signs and wonders have been directly connected with successful evangelism.

Hagiographers (biographers of the saints) agree that miracles, signs, and wonders did not cease with the conclusion of the 1st century A.D. It has been their role to document several miracles in the lives of each candidate for sainthood. Unfortunately, most hagiographers have written uncritically, with the result that modern scholars frequently have dismissed such lives of the saints as legendary. On balance, however, it must be recognized that there have been several occasions in the history of the church's expansion that have been linked to miracles, signs, and wonders. Perhaps it is time for scholars to take a second look at such moments. Even if one dismisses the entire history of signs and wonders, it seems fair to assume that pious Christians through the centuries have believed these reports and have responded with renewed evangelical fervor.

B. *The Ancient Church.*

At the end of the 1st century, both Clement, bishop of Rome, and Ignatius, bishop of Antioch, documented the continued operation of prophetic gifts. Shortly thereafter, writers of the *Didache* and the *Shepherd of Hermas* witnessed so much charismatic activity that they found it necessary to distinguish between true and false prophets. At about the same time, the writer of *Pseudo-Barnabas* suggested that prophetic ministry is normative in the church.

In the mid 2d century, Justin Martyr argued that God had withdrawn the Spirit of prophecy and miracles from the Jews and had transferred it to the church as proof of her continued divine favor.

Similarly, Irenaeus of Lyon described the gifts of prophecy, discernment of spirits, and exorcism in his Gallic church, and even mentioned that individuals had been raised from the dead. He warned against certain false Gnostics who fabricated spiritual gifts to win favor with the naïve. In the late 2d century, Hippolytus of Rome, in his *Apostolic Tradition,* offered that there is no need to lay hands on laity who already exercise a gift of healing.

At the end of the 2d century, Tertullian of Carthage speaks of the great pleasures to be found in expelling demons, affecting cures, and seeking revelations. After his conversion to Montanism early in the 3d century, Tertullian insisted that the "New Prophets" would be instruments in revealing the full provision of the Spirit. He provides a short case study of a "sister" who experiences revelations and ecstatic visions, speaks with angels, and reports on what she has seen to church leaders. Tertullian challenges the heretic, Marcion, to show evidence on his side for such spiritual giftings.

In the 3d century, Origen of Alexandria responded to the deceased (but still formidable) opponent of the church, the philosopher Celsus, who had sought to refute the authenticity of Christian claims. One of Origen's primary arguments is that healings, exorcisms, and validating signs and wonders continue to be experienced in the church of his own day. Just as miracles and wonders added to the credibility of 1st-century apostles, so they continue to draw unbelievers into the Christian fold.

Gregory Thaumaturgus (c. 210–260), a student of Origen for five years in Caesarea in Palestine, returned to his native Neocaesarea in Pontus to become a power evangelist there. We are told that he prophesied, healed the sick, took dominion over demons, and exorcised them by his command. He is remembered for a wide range of signs and wonders—some of which seem incredible to modern scholars. One of his students, Basil the Great, declared that Gregory should be numbered among the apostles. When he returned to his homeland, there were only 17 Christians in Neocaesarea; when he died, there were only 17 there who were not Christians.

In his life of Antony of the Desert (251?–356), Athanasius describes the prototype of charismatic desert saints who experienced ministries of healing and discernment of spirits as well as signs and wonders. Clairvoyant, charismatic, and constantly at war with evil spirits, Antony's ministry was felt by those who came to learn from him, and healing

or deliverance was experienced even by those who waited outside his cell and did not come into his immediate presence.

It is clear that the early church was less pentecostal after the first three centuries. In part, this seems to have been a reaction against fanatical prophets, such as the Montanists (2d–6th centuries) and the Messalians (4th–9th centuries). At the same time, the institutional church began to localize charismatic gifts in the bishop's office, attempting to combine the roles of prophet with those of priest.

By the 4th century, John Chrysostom in the East and Augustine of Hippo in the West declared that glossolalia has ceased. At the same time, however, Augustine in his *City of God* reports contemporary divine healings and other miracles. These he links directly to the conversion of pagans.

C. The Medieval Church.

From the late 6th century, Gregory the Great (Pope Gregory I) provided some of the clearest evidence available that the miraculous was not only anticipated but experienced frequently. He understood that miracles were necessary in his own time for the conversion of pagans and the transformation of heretics. In his biographies of contemporary saints (including Benedict of Nursia), Gregory attempted to provide documentation through eyewitness accounts of a wide variety of miracles, including healings of various ailments, raising of the dead to life, exorcisms of evil spirits, foretelling of the future, and deliverance from danger. He directly correlates miracles accompanying the missionary enterprise of Augustine of Canterbury and his companions to the conversion of the Anglo-Saxons.

Throughout the centuries, Eastern Christians have placed special emphasis on spiritual giftings and have demonstrated a higher expectation of functioning charismata, with accompanying signs and wonders, than in the West. Perhaps the most famous Eastern charismatic was ▸Symeon the New Theologian (A.D. 949–1022). He reports his most intimate spiritual experiences, which include a "baptism in the Holy Spirit" accompanied by gifts of copious tears, compunction, and visions of God as light. In the process, Symeon served as a prophetic agent of renewal, calling on Christians to return to a radical living of the gospel, to the charismatic and prophetic life of the primitive church.

Numerous Eastern saints exercised gifts of healing, including Athanasius, early-14th-century patriarch of Constantinople, who became famous during his lifetime for bringing deliverance to those possessed by evil spirits, the blind, the incontinent, the deaf and dumb, and those afflicted with cancer. Even after his death it was reported that the ill were cured when praying at his grave.

Gregory Palamas (1296–1359) emphasized the laying on of hands for reception of the gifts of healing, miracles, foreknowledge, irrefutable wisdom, diverse tongues, and interpretation of tongues. He also reported ecstasies and visions of divine light.

In the medieval Roman Catholic Church there were signs of charismatic vitality in the lives and writings of such important figures as Bernard of Clairvaux, Bonaventure, and Thomas Aquinas. The sermons of Thomas Aquinas frequently were confirmed by miracles, and he often experienced ecstasy, especially in the last months of his life. Spiritual gifts were even more important to apocalyptic writers, such as Rubert of Deutz (c. 1075–1129/30) and Joachim of Fiore (c. 1132–1202).

Bonaventure reported that Francis of Assisi, while an unskilled speaker, was empowered by the Holy Spirit while ministering. Wherever he went, his sermons were accompanied with miracles of great power, including prophecy, casting out devils, and healing the sick. As a result, his hearers paid attention to what he said "as if an angel of the Lord was speaking."

Vincent Ferrer (1350–1419), a Spirit-filled Dominican missionary, drew huge crowds when he preached. Everywhere his ministry was accompanied by remarkable miracles, including healings and raising the dead, and great numbers were converted. One of his biographers estimates the number of Jews converted during his ministry at 25,000. In the kingdom of Granada alone, it is reported that 8,000 Muslims were baptized because of his power evangelism.

The medieval Roman Church clearly was male-dominated. It is amazing, therefore, that prophetic women play so prominent a role. The most famous of these, ▸Hildegard of Bingen (1098–1179), experienced ecstatic visions (which she painted for future generations to experience!), gifts of tears and compunction, wisdom, knowledge, and prophecy. Numerous miracles are attributed to her. She also is reported to have sung "concerts" in the Spirit and to have written entire books in unknown languages. Because of her prophetic and preaching ministry, Hildegard, together with several other medieval women, had a significant impact on reforming the medieval church.

In his *Sounds of Wonder: A Popular History of Speaking in Tongues in the Catholic Tradition*, Eddie Ensley contends that, from the 9th through the 16th centuries, spontaneity of worship, improvised songs of jubilation, clapping of hands, and even dance movements were apparent in the lives of many ordinary believers. The word *jubilation* means spiritual inebriation, a transcendent language of praise, which Ensley views as the equivalent of speaking in tongues. Wandering preachers were amazingly similar in preaching style to modern pentecostals. Healing services were frequent, with miracles abounding. It also was common to hear group-singing in the Spirit.

D. The Reformation Era.
Mainline Protestant Reformers such as Luther, Zwingli, and Calvin did not place the same positive emphasis on spiritual giftings and miracles as did certain radical and Catholic Reformers, who occasionally reported their own ecstatic and prophetic experiences. Many of the radical Reformers emphasized the "inner voice" of the Spirit and looked for guidance to contemporary spiritual revelations and visions. Among the most famous (or infamous) were the prophets of Zwickau, Andreas Bodenstein von Carlstadt, and Thomas Müntzer. Müntzer emphasized the "inner word" of the Spirit, direct revelation in visions and dreams, Holy Spirit possession and guidance, as well as radical social reforms and the soon-coming millennium. He insisted that Christians were to experience the Holy Spirit as powerfully in the 16th century as they did at the time of the prophets and apostles. Above all, Müntzer held to the necessity of a baptism of the Holy Spirit, whereby the elect can discern spirits and unlock biblical mysteries.

Sixteenth-century Catholic Reformers also experienced charismatic graces. For example, Ignatius Loyola, founder of the Society of Jesus (the Jesuits), frequently received divine communication in visions. He also experienced a gift of tears—often in such abundance that he could not control himself, and the gift of *loquela*, which a few modern scholars associate with today's charismatic phenomenon of sung glossolalia.

E. The Seventeenth and Eighteenth Centuries.
In the 17th century, pentecostalism could be found among several Christian fringe groups, most important among them the Religious Society of Friends (the Quakers) and the Prophets of the Cevennes (the Camisards). The Quakers' central doctrine is the "inner light/word," with the divine Spirit speaking directly to the human mind. Early Quaker literature records visions, healings, and prophecies, which they liken to the Day of Pentecost. There is even evidence of tongues speech among them, although George Fox, their founder, eventually discourages such ecstatic utterances.

The Camisards were French Protestant resistance fighters who claimed to be directly inspired by the Holy Spirit. Most notable is the enthusiasm of their young children, who prophesied at very early ages. The Camisards were seized by ecstatic inspiration, during which they uttered strange and often amazing things, and spoke in languages of which they had no knowledge.

Twenty years after the Camisards were dispersed in 1710, a similar enthusiasm broke out among the Jansenists, a radically Augustinian movement in the Roman Catholic Church. Jansenists were known for their signs and wonders, spiritual dancing, healings, and prophetic utterances.

The Moravian Brethren are remembered for their strong missionary efforts and their emotionally expressive worship and fervent prayer services. In turn, their opponents maligned them for reviving the Montanist practices of convulsive heavings and speaking in tongues.

During the First Great Awakening, Jonathan Edwards (1703–58) found it necessary to distinguish between human enthusiasm and genuine workings of the Spirit. He points out that tears, trembling, groans, loud outcries, religious "noise," and ecstasies are not necessarily evidence of the Spirit's operation.

The founder of Methodism, John Wesley (1703–91) introduced into Protestantism an awareness of the Spirit's operation in all of human experience unlike any other in Western Christianity at the time. While Wesley was not personally given to enthusiastic religion, he was very tolerant of followers who claimed dreams, visions, healings, and revelations, and of earlier prophetic groups such as the Montanists, whom he described as "real, scriptural Christians."

II. THE LAST TWO CENTURIES.

During the course of the last two centuries, Euro-American philosophers and theologians have discussed the credibility of biblical miracles and the possibility of postbiblical miracles. At least four major opinions have been advanced: (1) miracles cannot occur in a closed universe, and the biblical accounts of miracles are mythological (e.g., T. H. Huxley, *Hume* [1879]); (2) miracles happened in the biblical period but ceased with the apostles (cessationism; e.g., B. B. Warfield, *Counterfeit Miracles* [1918]); (3) miracles may potentially take place on mission fields but only at the initial entry of the Christian faith (e.g., J. Warneck, *The Living Christ and Dying Heathenism*, 3d ed. [n.d.]); (4) believers should seek for miracles in the "last days" (Acts 2:17–20), before the return of Christ, for the well-being of the faithful and to accompany gospel proclamation (e.g., A. J. Gordon, *The Ministry of Healing, or Miracle Cures in All Ages* [1882]). The following discussion focuses on radical evangelicals of the last category who highlighted the role of miraculous interventions in missions (such as physical healings, exorcisms, etc.).

The quandary over how to bring closure to the Great Commission pressed radical evangelicals, usually those holding to a premillennial eschatology, to daringly seek for the restoration of apostolic power in "signs and wonders" (Acts 5:12) in order to expedite the preaching of the gospel before the imminent coming of Christ. Their case rested on the prediction of the OT prophet Joel that God would "pour out" the Holy Spirit with miraculous power in the "last days" (Joel 2:28–29). With the slow pace of conversions overseas (only 3.6 million Protestant communicants and adherents by 1900 [H. P. Beach, *A Geography and Atlas of Protestant Missions*, 1906, 2:19]), the hope of demonstrations of divine power seemed to promise that the dynamics that propelled early Christian growth could be duplicated in their own day. Not since the time of the ancient church had so much attention been placed on the supernatural component of evangelism.

From this emerged a blueprint for end-times evangelism—the "radical strategy," a uniquely pneumatological approach to mission, adapted in various ways to the present. For some this meant praying for physical healings and power to exorcise demons; others added the possibility of receiving known human languages for missionary preaching, thus giving rise in part to the pentecostal movement; and still others sought to "bind the strong man" (Satan and/or demons) in the cosmic struggle for the salvation of humankind. Because radical evangelicals have questioned traditional and seemingly less effective means of winning converts, their interest in the ministry of the Holy Spirit has moved the expectancy of signs and wonders from the periphery of the Christian world mission to the fore.

A. The Nineteenth Century.

Observers of the missions scene who compared the methods of their day with the simplicity of NT evangelism wondered aloud if the adoption of "apostolic methods" might bring greater success. As early as 1824, the recommendation sparked controversy at a conference of the London Missionary Society. There, six years before a charismatic movement would begin in England under his influence, Presbyterian pastor Edward Irving proposed a return to the apostolic pattern and declared that missionaries should ideally follow the model initiated by Jesus in Matt. 10:9–10. Though sharply criticized for suggesting such an outrageous departure from conventional practice, Irving gained a hearing and his addresses were published as *Missionaries after the Apostolical School* (1825), perhaps the earliest missiological treatise of the century to address the subject.

At the same time, many looked to spiritual awakenings to reform society and provide the personnel and spiritual empowerment necessary to accomplish the Great Commission (Matt. 28:18–20). Johannes Warneck recorded that from the 1860s the Indonesian Christian community increased after the appearance of "pentecostal" phenomena: dreams, visions, signs in the heavens, and several instances where missionaries (e.g., Ludwig Nommensen) unwittingly drank poison given by their enemies and remained unharmed (Mark 16:18). Convinced they had served their purpose, Warneck concluded that miracles were no longer needed. Others, however, disagreed and argued for their continuing necessity, including Edward Irving, Theodore Christlieb (German theologian and historian of missions), Thomas Erskine (Scottish lay theologian), and George Müller, a well-known philanthropist whose vibrant faith for God's provision at his orphan homes in Bristol, England, modeled the idealized "faith life" for many Christians. Müller inspired the growing number of independent "faith" missionaries. Although not remembered for advocacy of signs and wonders, his perspectives on faith and the remarkable answers to his prayers helped lay the theoretical basis.

Due to the slow progress of medical science and the cries of the terminally ill, radical evangelicals such as Charles C.

Cullis, ›A. B. Simpson, A. J. Gordon, ›Carrie Judd Montgomery, and ›John Alexander Dowie examined scriptural promises of healing (e.g., Isa. 53:4–5; Jas. 5:13–16) and inspired the evangelical faith-healing movement in America. Their teachings subsequently opened the door to miracles wider, since all of the charismatic gifts might too be restored (1 Cor. 12:10). Nevertheless, for those who expected miracles of healing to occur in their ministries, the actual application brought mixed results. Despite thousands of testimonies to remarkable physical healings, some earnest seekers died because of their refusal to take medicine.

›Frank W. Sandford was an even more controversial figure than most of the above. At his Holy Ghost and Us Bible School at Shiloh, ME, he organized The World's Evangelization Crusade on Apostolic Principles. In accentuating the cosmic dimension of "spiritual warfare" in confronting the powers of darkness on mission fields, he later purchased a schooner and barkentine and led his followers on cruises around the world, praying as they passed the coastline of each country that God would release his power for its conversion.

Arthur E. Street, a Presbyterian missionary to Hainan, China, believed that prayerful intercession could bind the "strongman" (the evil spirit ruling over each country, such as the "prince of China") and provided the formula for successful evangelism (Matt. 12:29). Street's popular booklet, *Intercessory Foreign Missionaries*, published by the Student Volunteer Movement for Foreign Mission and other agencies, underwent many printings. Nearly a century later, some pentecostals, and especially independent charismatics, ›third wave, and ›New Apostolic Reformation enthusiasts advanced a similar approach to ›spiritual warfare to bring the nations under the dominion of God through binding the "territorial spirits."

Some radical evangelicals proposed that according to Jesus' promise in Mark 16:17, God would bestow intelligible human languages on missionaries. This would enable them to bypass formal language study to begin preaching immediately after arriving on their fields, since little time remained for evangelization. With sufficient faith, missionaries just might be enabled by God to "speak with new tongues" (Mark 16:17 [AV]), that is, receive the necessary language(s) as a direct gift from above.

This prospect had surfaced as early as 1830, when a charismatic movement began in Scotland and several spoke in tongues. An early participant, Mary Campbell, reported that she had received the Turkish language and the language of the Palau island group in the Pacific Ocean to equip her to preach to these peoples. Later in the century A. B. Simpson considered the possible reappearance of the gift of tongues and referred to actual occurrences in India and Africa. Others shared this optimism, including several members of the celebrated "Cambridge Seven" of athletic fame in England (C. T. Studd, and ›Cecil H. and Arthur Polhill), who arrived

in China in 1885 to serve with the China Inland Mission; members of the Kansas-Sudan movement, who sailed to Sierra Leone in 1890; missionaries of the Christian and Missionary Alliance (CMA) (William W. Simpson and William Christie), who reached China in 1892; and independent missionaries Walter S. and Frances Black and M. Jennie Glassey, who left North America for Africa in 1896.

B. The Twentieth Century.

›Charles F. Parham, a midwestern Holiness preacher, read an abridged account of Glassey's story and reflected on its implications for mission. In 1900 he announced that a "Bro. and Sister Hamaker" lodged at his headquarters in Topeka, KS, and were praying to receive the necessary language before they proceeded to the mission field. During the summer, Parham journeyed to Shiloh, ME, where he heard speaking in tongues for the first time at Sandford's school. He became convinced that glossolalia represented crucial evidence of the baptism in the Holy Spirit and that its utility for missionary evangelism held the key to world evangelization. In this way, he forged the link between tongues and Spirit baptism that became the doctrinal hallmark of classical pentecostalism.

In Jan. 1901 Parham and his students at Bethel Bible School in Topeka prayed for the fulfillment of Joel's prophecy. Discussion about the gift of tongues had stirred interest among many radical evangelicals for over two decades, and Parham's disciples believed that the outpouring of the Spirit would form them as God's special company of empowered missionaries in the end times. Participants testified, as did the faithful at the ›Azusa Street revival (1906–9) in Los Angeles, CA, and elsewhere, that God had given them the languages of the world.

Yet evidence that pentecostals preached at will in their newfound languages and were actually understood by their hearers proved difficult to find. By late 1906 and 1907, though still believing that tongues signified intelligible languages or those of angels (1 Cor. 13:1), they began reviewing the Scriptures to obtain a better understanding. Most came to recognize that glossolalia constituted worship and intercession in the Spirit (Rom. 8:26; 1 Cor. 14:2), which in turn furnished the believer with spiritual power. Notwithstanding, the original ideal lived on. During a controversial revival in the late 1940s known as the "New Order of the ›Latter Rain," the notion of the Holy Spirit conferring languages for preaching surfaced once more to capture the imagination of a small contingent of pentecostals.

Anticipation of miracles continued in the ranks of evangelicals, but with more caution and less fanfare than pentecostals accorded them. Cessationism, controversy over the "tongues movement" and faith healing, and fears of subjective religious experience produced hesitations that until recently have generally kept them from seeking signs and wonders. Still, healings, exorcisms, and other extraordinary events happened in the ministries of missionaries in the CMA, World Gospel Mission, Church of the Nazarene, Missionary Church Association, Overseas Missionary Fellowship, Presbyterian Church (U.S.A.), Southern Baptist Convention, Unevangelized Field Mission, and Worldwide Evangelization Crusade, among other organizations.

Missiologist J. Herbert Kane reflected on the importance of miracles for mission while serving with the China Inland Mission (now Overseas Missionary Fellowship) during the late 1930s and 1940s. Though doubting the need for miracles in lands where Christianity had become the dominant faith, he concluded, "there is a need for miracles in heathen lands, where from time immemorial the powers of darkness have held undisputed sway, and where the poor benighted people have been held in cruel bondage for one hundred generations." Reflecting on the growth of the church on the Fowyang field, he noted that "hundreds of our finest Christians ... entered the Christian fold by way of the miracle gate. They were driven to Christ not by a sense of sin, but by a sense of need. The latter usually precedes the former, though not always." Such needs could be "a parent with a sick child, a husband with a demon-possessed wife, a woman with an opium-smoking husband, a widow bowed down by oppression, a soldier with an infected foot, an aged father with an unfilial son, a bandit serving a prison term" (J. Herbert Kane, *Twofold Growth* [1947], 105–6). Other missionaries noted for praying for the sick and exorcising demons included Herbert Pakenham-Walsh, Anglican Bishop of Assam, and John L. Nevius and Jonathan Goforth, Presbyterian missionaries in China.

Controversy has naturally followed radical evangelicals as they have reformulated the radical strategy. Currently, debate swirls over claims that another missiological paradigm shift has begun, one noted for "strategic-level spiritual warfare" and "spiritual mapping." Shying away from identification with classical pentecostals and charismatics, missiologists such as ›Charles H. Kraft, ›C. Peter Wagner, and Timothy M. Warner adjusted the strategy yet once more.

The attention to spiritual gifts and "power encounters" with evil forces in the spiritual realm has proven to be unusually helpful in evangelizing peoples with non-Western worldviews. At the same time, it has contributed to the gradual "pentecostalization" of much of Third World Christianity in worship and ministry. Nevertheless, the focus on miracles has sometimes obscured the importance of other vital aspects of mission. In addition, some practitioners have failed to adequately consider the sovereignty of God in regard to the expectancy of miracles or the believer's security in Christ when experiencing satanic oppression.

Ministry in signs and wonders continues with great fervor in many regions of the world among a broad scope of Christians, from the global witness of Singaporean believers; to the hundreds of missionaries sent around the world by the Yoido Full Gospel Church of Seoul, Korea, pastored by ›David Yonggi Cho; to Brazilian pentecostal missionaries evangelizing in North America and Angola; and to the endeavors of Lutheran charismatics in Ethiopia. It is also significant that while Vatican II impacted the course of Roman Catholic missions with its concern for ministry to the poor, the Catholic charismatic renewal added emphasis on signs and wonders, as illustrated by the activities of evangelizers in many places such as West Africa, Kerala State in South India, and the Philippines.

The prospect of supernatural interventions in missions during the "last days" also characterized the labors of Seventh-Day Adventist missionaries in the 19th and early 20th centuries, believers historically excluded from the ranks of mainstream Christians. Reports of gospel proclamation and miracles in the history of their missions—the accounts of "special providence," deserve serious consideration.

■ **Bibliography:**

To 1800. B. L. Bresson, *Studies in Ecstasy* (1966) ■ C. Brown, *Miracles and the Critical Mind* (1984) ■ S. M. Burgess, *The Holy Spirit: Ancient Christian Traditions* (1984) ■ idem, *The Holy Spirit: Eastern Christian Traditions* (1989) ■ idem, *The Holy Spirit: Medieval Roman Catholic and Reformation Traditions* (1997) ■ E. Ensley, *Sounds of Wonder: A Popular History of Speaking in Tongues in the Catholic Tradition* (1977) ■ R. Knox, *Enthusiasm* (1950) ■ H. Remus, *Pagan-Christian Conflict over Miracles in the Second Century* (1983) ■ J. Ruthven, *On the Cessation of the Charismata: The Protestant Polemic on Postbiblical Miracles* (1993) ■ A-M. Talbot, *Faith Healing in Late Byzantium* (1983) ■ B. Ward, *Miracles and the Medieval Mind* (1982), ■ idem, *Signs and Wonders: Saints, Miracles and Prayers from the 4th Century to the 14th* (1992).

Nineteenth and Twentieth Centuries. P. G. Chappell, "The Divine Healing Movement in America" (diss., Drew U., 1983) ■ J. R. Goff Jr., *Fields White unto Harvest: Charles F. Parham and the Missionary Origins of Pentecostalism* (1988) ■ C. H. Kraft, *Christianity with Power* (1989) ■ R. A. N. Kydd, *Healing through the Centuries: Models of Understanding* (1988) ■ R. Martin and P. Williamson, eds., *John Paul II and the New Evangelization* (1995) ■ G. B. McGee, "Looking for a 'Short-Cut' to Language Preparation: Radical Evangelicals, Missions, and the Gift of Tongues," *International Bulletin of Missionary Research* (forthcoming) ■ idem, "The Radical Strategy in Modern Mission: The Linkage of Paranormal Phenomena with Evangelism," in *The Holy Spirit and Mission Dynamics,* ed. C. D. McConnell (1997) ■ R. B. Mullin, *Miracles and the Modern Religious Imagination* (1996) ■ J. L. Nevius, *Demon Possession and Allied Themes* (1896) ■ P. A. Pomerville, *The Third Force in Missions* (1985) ■ E. Rommen, ed., *Spiritual Power and Missions* (1995) ■ W. A. Spicer, *Miracles of Modern Missions* (1926) ■ C. P. Wagner, *The Third Wave of the Holy Spirit* (1988) ■ idem, *Confronting the Powers* (1996) ■ J. Wimber and K. Springer, *Power Evangelism* (2d ed., 1992). ■ S. M. Burgess; G. B. McGee

SIMPSON, ALBERT BENJAMIN (1843–1919). Founder of the ▸Christian and Missionary Alliance (CMA) in 1897. Simpson was born in 1843 at Bayview, Prince Edward Island. Following his graduation in 1865 from Knox College in Toronto, Ont., Simpson was ordained into the Presbyterian ministry and served churches in Hamilton, Ont. (1865–73); Louisville, KY (1874–79); and New York City (1879–81). He resigned as pastor of Thirteenth Street Presbyterian Church in New York City in 1881 to establish an independent church, later named the Gospel Tabernacle, for the purpose of evangelizing the unchurched masses of New York City.

Simpson's spiritual journey and beliefs were crystallized in the term *Fourfold Gospel*, which he coined to exalt Christ as Savior, Sanctifier, Healer, and Coming King. He was simultaneously a revivalist preacher, a Holiness prophet of the "deeper" or "higher Christian life" (▸Keswick Higher Life Movement), a promoter of world missions, an eschatological speculator, and a theological synthesizer. Not surprisingly, his theology, spirituality, ministry, and polity became an inspiration to many in the pentecostal movement who had in the late 19th century sat by and drunk from some of the same streams of spiritual awakening in which Simpson himself had been refreshed.

The ideological continuity between Simpson's doctrines and those espoused by early pentecostals can be established at several points. His ▸restorationist interpretation of the evolution of church history since the Protestant Reformation underscored a conviction that the present age would conclude with the days of the "latter rain," which had already begun to "sprinkle" in Simpson's own time. This anticipated outpouring of the Holy Spirit would be accompanied by supernatural manifestations of the Spirit, such as tongues, miracles, and prophecy, reminiscent of the "early rain" at Pentecost (Acts 2). He exhorted believers to pray for those special evidences of divine power typical of past revivals.

Simpson adamantly opposed any ▸dispensational notion that the gifts of the Holy Spirit had necessarily ceased with the close of the apostolic age. On the basis of Joel 2 and 1 Cor. 12, he contended that the gifts of the Holy Spirit were to continue in the church until the Second Advent. Prior to the outbreak of the ▸Azusa Street revival in 1906, Simpson acknowledged the value of the gift of tongues in the church as "an expression of lofty spiritual feeling and intense moving of the heart," not-

A. B. Simpson, founder of the Christian and Missionary Alliance, who was open to the pentecostal movement but remained a critic of the "initial evidence doctrine."

ing also that it was mentioned last in Paul's list of charismata and seemed most prone to abuse. He described the nature of tongues as both known and unknown languages, but he rejected the prevalent popular misconception that the gift could be expected by missionaries for the purpose of preaching the gospel to the heathen.

For Simpson, the book of Acts depicted church life as God intended it to be throughout all ages of church history. Like pentecostals who followed him, he was fully prepared to use the standard of spiritual life portrayed in Acts as the existential norm by which to measure the shortcomings of the church in his own time. He asserted that an openness to the supernatural quality of Christian life as exhibited by the early apostolic church was the only prevention against a deterioration into "conventional formalism."

In his writings, Simpson foreshadowed the pentecostal hermeneutical practice of deriving doctrinal truth from the narrative accounts of Acts. Though he rejected as unbiblical the ▸"initial evidence doctrine," Simpson nevertheless made full use of the classical proof texts of pentecostalism (Acts 2, 8, 19) to substantiate his claim that regeneration and the baptism of the Holy Spirit were two distinct events in the life of the believer. The Samaritans and the Ephesian disciples provided support for his two-step model of Christian initiation.

The entire Simpson corpus testifies uniformly to his conception of Spirit baptism as occurring subsequently to regeneration. Spurred on by the reading of W. E. Boardman's *The Higher Christian Life* (1858), Simpson received the baptism of the Spirit in 1874 during his second pastorate in Louisville, KY. He variously termed Spirit baptism a "second blessing," "crisis sanctification," "the anointing," "the sealing," "receiving the Holy Spirit," "the fullness of the Spirit," and "the indwelling of Christ."

Simpson made several criticisms of the pentecostal movement in "Special Revival Movements," a report he delivered to the CMA general council in 1908. He charged that the "initial evidence doctrine" spawned a preoccupation with spiritual manifestations rather than cultivating a devotion to God and tended to reduce evangelistic zeal. Moreover, those professing the pentecostal baptism had allegedly divided CMA branches, thereby reducing missionary contributions. He observed that on the foreign field some inexperienced missionaries naïvely assumed that they would receive tongues as a substitute for language study. Finally, in his address, Simpson noted a style of "prophetic authority" within the movement that resembled "the Romish confessional" or "spiritualism." Despite the drawbacks of pentecostalism, Simpson remained open to the movement that had produced impressive spiritual fruit where stable leadership had emerged.

A diary kept by Simpson from 1907 to 1916 discloses that the pentecostal movement prompted him to make "a new claim for a Mighty Baptism of the Holy Spirit in His complete fullness embracing all the gifts and graces of the Spirit." He could not, however, testify to having received tongues or similar gifts as had several of his friends. As both a forerunner of pentecostalism and a seeker of the pentecostal baptism with tongues, he remained a critic of the "initial evidence doctrine" to the end of his life.

■ **Bibliography:** D. J. Evearitt, *Body and Soul: Evangelism and the Social Concern of A. B. Simpson* (1994) ■ C. M. Glass, "Mysticism and Contemplation in the Life and Teaching of Albert Benjamin Simpson" (diss., Marquette, 1997) ■ D. Hartzfeld and C. Nienkirchen, eds., *The Birth of a Vision* (1986) ■ C. W. Nienkirchen, *A. B. Simpson and the Pentecostal Movement* (1992) ■ D. R. Reid, "'Jesus Only': The Early Life and Presbyterian Ministry of Albert Benjamin Simpson, 1843–1881" (diss., Queen's U., 1994).

■ C. Nienkirchen

SIMPSON, CHARLES VERNON (1937–). Pastor, Bible teacher, author.

Born in New Orleans on Apr. 6, 1937, the son of a Southern Baptist minister. In 1942 his family moved to the Mobile, AL, area, where he was raised. Simpson's entire childhood experience was centered around the church, and he was converted in 1951. As a teenager, Simpson responded to a call from God to pastoral ministry, and in 1957, at the age of 20, he began his ministry at Bayview Heights Baptist Church in Mobile. While pastoring, he commuted weekly to William Carey College in Hattiesburg, MS, and after graduating attended New Orleans Baptist Seminary for two years. In 1960 he married Carolyn.

Simpson experienced Spirit baptism in 1964. Ken Sumrall, a fellow Southern Baptist pastor and friend of Simpson's, was instrumental in introducing Simpson to a charismatic understanding of the Holy Spirit. Within a year, Simpson's church became charismatic, and for the next several years the church struggled to stay in the Southern Baptist Convention, enduring much scrutiny from the denomination. Simpson's Bible teaching gifts, along with his warm manner and dry wit, made him a popular charismatic speaker. In the late 1960s, while still pastoring in Mobile, Simpson traveled extensively, teaching at charismatic conferences and meetings, particularly for the ›Full Gospel Business Men's Fellowship International and the ›Holy Spirit Teaching Mission (HSTM).

In 1971 Simpson resigned from his pastorate and moved to Hollywood, FL, near Ft. Lauderdale. Simpson's move was influenced by his 1970 association with Bible teachers ›Don

Basham, ›Bob Mumford, and ›Derek Prince. From this association came the controversial shepherding movement. The four were joined in 1974 by ›W. J. E. (Ern) Baxter.

In July 1973 Simpson moved from Ft. Lauderdale to Gautier, MS, in part because a growing number of leaders in the area were looking to Simpson for pastoral leadership. With this move Simpson became senior pastor of Gulf Coast Fellowship, an association of existing churches, several of which were house churches. In Dec. 1976 Simpson moved back to Mobile, which became the new center of Gulf Coast Fellowship. Simpson's pastoral and leadership gifting was apparent as the church grew to over 1,200 members by 1982. The church with its cell-group structure was a model for other shepherding churches.

Over the years 1976 to 1981, Simpson became more involved in leading the shepherding movement. *New Wine* magazine, the movement's principal publication, moved to Mobile in 1978. By 1981 Basham, Baxter, and Mumford had joined Simpson in Mobile.

Simpson's emphasis on pastoral care greatly influenced the development of the distinctive pastoral approach of the shepherding movement. Simpson's book *The Challenge to Care* (1986) describes his pastoral philosophy. Since the shepherding movement disbanded in 1986, Simpson has continued to pastor the same church, now named Covenant Church of Mobile. Simpson also continues to teach and travel from his Mobile base through Charles Simpson Ministries.

■ **Bibliography:** "Reflections on a Lifetime of Discipleship: An Interview with Charles Simpson," *People of Destiny* (Mar. 1985) ■ C. V. Simpson, *The Challenge to Care* (1986) ■ idem, *Covenant and the Kingdom* (1995). ■ S. D. Moore

SIMPSON, WILLIAM WALLACE (1869–1961). Pioneer missionary to China.

Born in White County, TN, Simpson (no relation to ›A. B. Simpson) attended an academy of the Congregational Church. He surrendered his life to Christ in 1881 and ministered in a rural area of the state. Preparing on one occasion to preach on Mark 16:15, he was personally confronted with the challenge of overseas evangelism and decided to pursue that objective. He attended A. B. Simpson's New York Missionary Training College (later Nyack College) in 1891; the following year he headed for the Far East with other missionaries of the ›Christian and Missionary Alliance (CMA). Receiving instructions and encouragement from J. Hudson Taylor, Simpson and William Christie headed for Tibet—considered by many to be the "uttermost" part of the world. At the same time, they asked God to give them the Tibetan language for preaching the gospel (Mark 16:17).

In Dec. 1895 Simpson married Otilia Ekvall, an appointed CMA missionary to China. From this union came two daughters and a son, William Ekvall Simpson (1901–

32), who later was killed while serving as a missionary on the China-Tibet border.

Attending a convention of missionaries in Taochow, China, in 1912, Simpson received the baptism in the Holy Spirit and spoke in tongues. Due to his uncompromising belief that the evidence for baptism in the Spirit was glossolalia, tension mounted between him and the other missionaries, as well as with the officials of the CMA, particularly Robert H. Glover. Simpson returned to the U.S. in 1915 due to his wife's poor health and his stance on the pentecostal baptism. In that same year, he was forced to resign from the CMA and subsequently joined the Assemblies of God (AG). Prevented from returning to China because of his wife's deteriorating health, he accepted the post of principal at the recently established Bethel Bible Training School at Newark, NJ, in 1916. Following the death of his wife, he resigned his post and returned to China. In 1925 he married Martha Merrill, also a missionary; they had six children.

Over the years, Simpson evangelized in all of the provinces of China with the exception of the seven in the southern part; he also ministered in Tibet, Mongolia, and Manchuria. He preferred to travel on foot for much of his ministry. An advocate of indigenous-church principles, he assisted in the training of national clergy by teaching in Bible institutes, including the Truth Bible Institute in Peking (Beijing), China. Simpson took great interest in forming eschatological interpretations of contemporary events, often approaching the bizarre in speculation.

After WWII Simpson returned to China, but he retired to the U.S. following the Communist takeover in 1949. He continued to promote foreign missions until his death.

During his lifetime, Simpson became one of the best-known missionaries of the pentecostal movement. His legacy included the converts from his frontline evangelism, the Chinese clergy he trained, and his courageous example of endurance in the face of discouraging circumstances.

■ **Bibliography:** G. F. Atter, *The Third Force* (2d ed., 1965) ▮ N. Blan, *Rugged Mountains* (n.d.) ▮ W. W. Simpson, *Evangelizing in West China* (n.d.) ▮ idem, "Letter from Shanghai, China," *Christian and Missionary Alliance Weekly* (July 1, 1892).
■ G. B. McGee; B. A. Pavia

SINCLAIR, JOHN CHALMERS (1863–1936). Early pentecostal pastor. The career of John C. Sinclair of Chicago

illustrates the priority many early pentecostals gave to ecclesiastical independence. Born in Lydster, Scotland, Sinclair immigrated as a youth to the U.S., settling in Wisconsin. There he met and married a fellow Presbyterian, Mary E. Bie. Before the turn of the century, the Sinclairs moved to Chicago, where he was employed by the U.S. Steel Corporation. In Chicago he accepted the Wesleyan Holiness teaching and was called and ordained to the ministry. In 1907, as pastor of an independent church at 328 West 63d Street, Sinclair was reported to be the first person in Chicago to claim the pentecostal experience. Destined to spend most of his life as an independent, he was a participant in two early attempts at organizational unity. In 1914 he was one of three members added to the original executive presbytery of the Assemblies of God following the first general council meeting in Hot Springs, AK; however, he soon withdrew. Five years later, as pastor of the Christian Apostolic Assembly of Chicago, he served as first general chairman of the Pentecostal Assemblies of the U.S. (parent to the ▸Pentecostal Church of God), but again withdrew. In both cases, fear of latent denominationalism appears to have been the cause. With Chicago as home base, Sinclair traveled widely in his last years. He died at La Porte, IN, in 1936 and is buried in Chicago. His daughter,

John Chalmers Sinclair, early pentecostal pastor and first general chairman of the Pentecostal Assemblies of the U.S.

Dorothy, was wife of the prominent evangelist John H. Bostrom (1899–1974).

■ **Bibliography:** C. Brumback, *Suddenly . . . from Heaven* (1961) ▮ E. L. Moon, *The Pentecostal Church* (1966).   ■ C. E. Jones

SISSON, ELIZABETH (1843–1934). Missionary, writer, evangelist, and church planter. Elizabeth Sisson was born the second of three sisters to New England whaling captain William Sisson and Elizabeth (Hempstead) Sisson. She was converted in 1863 in New London, CT, where she joined the Second Congregational Church. Her interest in ministry came early, and in an autobiographical account she describes sitting in an Episcopal ordination service wishing she were a man so that she could be ordained. Later, while meditating on that service, she had a vision of Christ, whom she described as the Great Bishop, who said, "I have ordained you." Her response from that time on was that "all human ordination shriveled into utter insignificance."

Under the influence of W. S. Boardman, Sisson received sanctification. In 1871 she left the U.S. to serve in India as a missionary for the American Board of Commissioners for

Foreign Missions, where she ministered largely among the Hindu population with occasional incursions among Moslems as well.

Stricken with severe illness, Sisson was forced to leave India for a period of recuperation in a healing home in London. In 1887 she returned to the U.S. and took up a teaching and writing ministry. During this period she was associated with Carrie Judd Montgomery and became the associate editor of *Triumphs of Faith*. In the fall of 1889 the two women went to San Francisco, where Carrie became engaged to George H. Montgomery. During this time, Sisson attended the tent meetings held by ˒Maria B. Woodworth-Etter in Oakland. At one meeting a prophecy was given that predicted the destruction of San Francisco and Oakland by a tidal wave. Sisson, along with many others, believed and propagated the prophecy, which proved to be false, and because of this "error in judgment," her reputation was heavily damaged. She resigned her post with the *Triumphs of Faith* and for a time "sank into obscurity."

Sisson returned to New England, where she received her pentecostal baptism at Old Orchard, ME. In the early days of the pentecostal outpouring, Sisson, who never married, traveled across Canada and throughout the U.S., often accompanied by her sister, Charlotte W. Sisson. She made an evangelistic tour to the British Isles in 1908, spent four months ministering with ˒F. F. Bosworth in Dallas (1915), and ministered in Detroit for a period during that same year. She became affiliated with the fledgling Assemblies of God, from which she received credentials in Dec. 1917 at age 74.

A prolific writer and conference speaker, Sisson used her home at 17 Jay Street in New London, CT, as her headquarters. Elizabeth's articles were published regularly in *Word and Work* (Framingham, MA), *Confidence* (Sunderland, U.K.), *The Latter Rain Evangel* (Chicago, IL), *The Weekly Evangel* (St. Louis, MO), *The Pentecostal Evangel* (Springfield, MO), and *Triumphs of Faith* (Oakland, CA). Many of these were simultaneously published in tract form.

■ **Bibliography:** "At Rest," *TF* 54 (10, 1934) ■ E. Sisson, "The Envelope," *Confidence* 10 (8, 1915) ■ idem, *Foregleams of Glory* (1912) ■ idem, "Four Years' Continuous Revival," *Confidence* 8 (4, 1915) ■ idem, "God's Prayer House," *TF* 28 (10, 1908) ■ idem, "The Holy Ghost and Fire," *LRE* 1 (8, 1909) ■ idem, "Kept by the Power of God," *Confidence* 8 (9, 1915) ■ idem, "The Lord's Healing," *LRE* 1 (7, 1909) ■ idem, "Miss Sisson's Miraculous Healing," *Confidence* 3 (2, 1909) ■ idem, "Miss Sisson's Restoration," *Confidence* 2 (1, 1909).   ■ C. M. Robeck Jr.

SIZELOVE, RACHEL ARTAMISSIE (1864–1941). Evangelist. A former Free Methodist evangelist, Rachel A. Sizelove introduced the pentecostal teaching in Springfield, MO, and foresaw that place as a pentecostal center. In May 1907, after receiving the baptism of the Holy Spirit the preceding July at the ˒Azusa Street Mission in Los Angeles, she returned to Springfield, where her sister and her mother then lived. Commissioned by the Azusa workers, she and ˒Lucy Farrow, a black woman en route to Liberia as a missionary, traveled together as far as Dallas. The first convert of her cottage meetings in Missouri was her sister, Lillie Corum, mother of the future pentecostal editor Fred Tice Corum (1900–1982).

When Sizelove returned to Springfield six years later, the nucleus gathered in 1907 had become a thriving congregation. She recorded that during this second visit, "One afternoon there appeared before me a beautiful, bubbling, sparkling fountain in the heart of the city of Springfield. It sprang up gradually, but irresistibly, and began to flow toward the East and toward the West, toward the North and toward the South, until the whole land was deluged with living water." Although the General Council of the Assemblies of God was not to be formed for yet another year and was not to establish offices in Springfield for yet another five years, she and many others regarded the selection of Springfield as the headquarters site as the fulfillment of prophecy. A native of Marengo, IN, Rachel Sizelove lived most of her adult life in Southern California. She died in Long Beach in 1941.

■ **Bibliography:** C. Brumback, *Suddenly ... from Heaven* (1961) ■ F. T. Corum, *Like as of Fire* (1981) ■ R. A. Sizelove, *A Sparkling Fountain for the Whole Earth* (n.d.).   ■ C. E. Jones

SLAIN IN THE SPIRIT A relatively modern expression denoting a religious phenomenon in which an individual falls down, the cause being attributed to the Holy Spirit. The phenomenon is known within modern pentecostalism and charismatic renewal under various names, including "falling under the power," "overcome by the Spirit," and "resting in the Spirit."

Within the discipline of the sociology of religion, "slain in the Spirit" might fall under the general rubric of "possession trance"; however, sociologists have paid little specific attention to what is recognized in pentecostal and charismatic circles as a distinct, identifiable experience (see, e.g., Bourguignon, 1973, 1976). It is generally acknowledged that the source of the experience can, in addition to God, be a purely human response to autosuggestion, group "peer pressure," or simply a desire to experience the phenomenon. Furthermore, although the nomenclature may not have been in place for very long, it is generally recognized that the phenomenon (or something closely akin to it) has occurred throughout the history of the church; indeed, sociologists would insist that it is common to many religions (i.e., the possession trance).

Defenders of the legitimacy of the experience as distinctly Christian point to similar examples of the phenomenon prior to the modern pentecostal and charismatic movements. For example, one could point to similarities between being "slain in the Spirit" and the experience of Perpetua at her martyrdom, who was "roused from what seemed like sleep, so completely had she been in the Spirit and in ecstasy" (*The Passion of Perpetua and Felicitas*, 20). Or, one might, as MacNutt does, see in an account of a 14th-century Dominican monk an allusion to being slain in the Spirit (MacNutt, 1978, 194–95).

It is perhaps more popular to see the phenomenon of being slain in the Spirit as an accompaniment to great Protestant revivals. John Wesley's *Journal* tells of people who during his preaching "were struck to the ground and lay there groaning" (Knox, 1950, 472, citing Wesley's *Journal*, 118). Methodist circuit-rider Peter Cartwright's preaching was also accompanied by listeners falling under the power. Similar results accompanied George Whitefield's preaching and are also attested in the writings of Jonathan Edwards (ibid., 526, 529, 530). Charles G. Finney's *Autobiography* recounts episodes in which people could not move or speak, in one instance for 16 hours (Wessel, 1977 repr., 58).

The one person most associated with the phenomenon in early pentecostalism is ›Maria B. Woodworth-Etter. However, it is noteworthy that people were experiencing being slain in the Spirit in her evangelistic meetings several years prior to her participation in the pentecostal movement. Thus, an 1890 copy of the *St. Louis Post-Dispatch* contains an artist's rendering of people "under the power" at her meeting (Warner, 1986, 144). Indeed, perhaps more than anything else, this phenomenon characterized her meetings. One account in the Sept. 25, 1885, issue of the Muncie, IN, *Daily News* tells of "Dozens lying around pale and unconscious, rigid, and lifeless as though in death" (ibid., 55). In her own account of Muncie she says that many of the infidels and scoffers "were the first to fall under the slaying power of God" (Woodworth-Etter, 1984 ed., 69). She also speaks of large audiences in which "hundreds of people were struck down by the power" (Warner, 1986, 229). It seems as if the pentecostal-charismatic association of slain in the Spirit with particular personalities stems from Woodworth-Etter more than any other person.

The modern pentecostal and charismatic movements particularly associate being slain in the Spirit with the ministries of ›Kathryn Kuhlman, ›Kenneth Hagin Sr., and Charles and Frances Hunter. Kuhlman was perhaps the one most responsible for the entrance of the practice of slaying in the Spirit, principally because her meetings were so characterized by the phenomenon (Buckingham, 1976, 40, 41, 224–29).

Characteristics of the "blessing" of being "slain in the Spirit" include a loss of feeling or control; sometimes those who fall under the power reportedly feel no pain, even if they bump their heads on the way down should "catchers" fail to do their job. On many occasions the experience is accompanied by tongues speech; at other times laughing, weeping, or praising God are manifest.

During earlier revivals the experience "struck down" (and converted) many of the "convicted," the "scoffers," and the "mockers," but in modern pentecostalism and charismatic circles the experience is a spiritual one that should be sought. Almost all see the experience as deeply spiritual in nature, and afterward a general euphoria is present.

The length of time people are "under" varies. Usually the experience lasts from a few seconds to several minutes, though on some occasions it is reported to last for hours. One undocumented story about Maria Woodworth-Etter asserts that she "stood like a statue for three days and three nights" (Hagin, 1980, 5).

Almost all would see the experience in a positive way—at least initially. Some aberrant, negative examples of being slain in the Spirit do exist, however. Kenneth Hagin relates that his wife and a coworker, both of whom had questioned his authority, were unable to approach him without falling down under the power. Hagin interpreted this as a kind of "touch not the Lord's anointed" lesson (McConnell, 1988). Such a judgmental, personal "use" of "slaying in the Spirit" is unprecedented.

An entire battalion of Scripture proof texts is enlisted to support the legitimacy of the phenomenon, although Scripture plainly offers no support for the phenomenon as something to be expected in the normal Christian life. Passages appealed to from the OT include the following: In Gen. 15:12–21 Abram is said to have been overcome by a "deep sleep," at which time God spoke to him about the future of his descendants. Num. 24:4 tells of one who "falls prostrate, and whose eyes are opened" (the text makes clear that this is a visionary experience). Another passage appealed to is 1 Sam. 19:20, where Saul's men are sent to capture David. They come upon "a group of prophets prophesying, with Samuel standing there as their leader." That Samuel is "standing" is seen to imply that the prophets were "slain in the Spirit"; the text goes on to say that the Spirit came upon Saul's men. Likewise, the visionary experiences of Ezekiel the prophet are viewed as times when he was slain in the Spirit (cf. Ezek. 1:28, Ezekiel "fell facedown"; Ezek. 2:1 says "Son of man, *stand up on your feet*" [italics mine]).

But the NT receives the most attention. Two passages, Matt. 17:1–6 and 28:1–4, are said to justify the phenomenon. In 17:6 the disciples "fell facedown" at the voice of God, and in 28:1–4 the tomb guards "shook and became like dead men" at the appearance of the angel of the Lord. Both Matthean texts refer to instances of fear. One is clearly a normal response of awe-struck worship (17:6 *[epi prosopon auton]*) while the other is probably simply a figurative way of saying the guards were "petrified." Even if the guards were "slain," their experience is entirely secondary to the story and did not have any redemptive value as far as the text is concerned.

Perhaps foremost in support of the phenomenon is John 18:1–6. In that passage Jesus replies to the officers from the chief priests and Pharisees who come to seize him, and at his word "they drew back and fell to the ground." There is no mention of the Spirit here, and John portrays no relationship between Spirit, power, and Jesus. The text remains enigmatic, especially since John offers neither explanation for, nor effect of, their fall. Obviously they were not converted, because they proceeded to arrest Jesus.

Of course Acts 9:4 and 26:14, the accounts of Paul's conversion, are thought to be Paul's experience of being slain in the Spirit. The text offers no phenomenological explanation for the event, and none should be expected. In terms of resembling the modern experience, one finds close parallels. However, Luke in no way intimates that this is normal; in fact, it is the uniqueness of the event that prompts Luke to recount it three times. It is certainly legitimate to discern here a genuine spiritual experience similar to the modern phenomenon in description but distinct in purpose.

Paul's remembrance (if indeed 2 Cor. 12:2 is autobiographical) tells of "a man in Christ who ... was caught up to the third heaven." While this is appealed to as evidence that Paul experienced being slain in the Spirit, there is simply not enough data to justify the conclusion that the "third heaven" and the state of being slain in the Spirit are identical.

The evidence for the phenomenon of being "slain in the Spirit" is thus inconclusive. From an experiential standpoint it is unquestionable that through the centuries Christians have experienced a psychophysical phenomenon in which people fall down; moreover, they have attributed the experience to God. It is equally unquestionable that there is no biblical evidence for the experience as normative in Christian life.

■ **Bibliography:** E. Bourguignon, *Possession* (1976) ■ idem, *Religion, Altered States of Consciousness, and Social Change* (1973) ■ J. Buckingham, *Daughter of Destiny* (1976) ■ K. Hagin, *Why Do People Fall under the Power?* (1980) ■ R. Knox, *Enthusiasm* (1950) ■ D. McConnell, *A Different Gospel* (1988) ■ F. MacNutt, *Healing* (1974) ■ idem, *The Power to Heal* (1977) ■ W. Warner, *The Woman Evangelist* (1986) ■ H. Wessel, ed., *Autobiography of Charles G. Finney* (1908; repr. 1984) ■ M. Woodworth-Etter, *Miracles, Signs and Wonders* (1916; abr. and repr. 1977). ■ P. H. Alexander

SMAIL, THOMAS A. (1928–). Teacher and theologian. Smail studied under Karl Barth for a year and was ordained in the Church of Scotland in 1953. Baptized in the Spirit through the ministry of Dennis Bennett in 1965, he served as pastor in Northern Ireland (1968–72). Smail then became general secretary of the ʼFountain Trust, taking over editorship of *Renewal* in 1975. A gifted expositor with a rigorous theological mind, Smail edited all 25 issues of *Theological Renewal* (1975–83). Ordained an Anglican priest in 1979, he left Fountain Trust to become vice principal at St. John's College, Nottingham, in 1980.

Smail has been critical of mindless enthusiasm, emphasizing especially in his editorials in *Theological Renewal* the Trinitarian character of all Christian life and demanding a solid theological basis for spiritual renewal in the church. Smail was rector of Sanderstead, Surrey (1985–94). He has authored *Reflected Glory* (1975), *The Forgotten Father* (1980), and *The Giving Gift* (1988). The latter corrects his earlier view of subordination of the Spirit to the Son into a model of two-way coordination and interaction.

■ **Bibliography:** N. Wright, "The Charismatic Theology of Thomas Smail," *EPTA Bulletin* 16 (1996). ■ P. D. Hocken

SMALE, JOSEPH (1867–1926). Los Angeles, CA, pastor. Son of John and Ann (Stephens) Smale, Joseph Smale was born in England and received his theological education at Spurgeon's College in London. At the age of 21 he entered the Baptist ministry, in which he remained for most of his life. His earliest ministry experience was obtained in street meetings in London and in a three-year pastorate at Ryde on the Isle of Wight. He was married to Esther Isabelle (1879–1958).

At age 24 Smale immigrated to the U.S., taking a Baptist pastorate in Prescott, AZ. In c. 1895 he moved to the Los Angeles area, where he became the pastor of First Baptist Church located at 725 South Flower.

When news about the Welsh revival came to Los Angeles, Smale was interested enough to travel to Wales to visit Evans Roberts and observe the revival firsthand. Upon his return to Los Angeles, he began home prayer meetings and 19 weeks of protracted meetings in anticipation of a similar outpouring of the Holy Spirit. Many "spiritual workers" from a variety of denominational backgrounds were attracted to Smale's church, but the spontaneity of worship sought by Smale was not accepted by the church leaders. Smale withdrew to establish First New Testament Church in Burbank Hall, 542 S. Main Street, Los Angeles, in early 1906.

On Easter Sunday 1906, the First New Testament Church experienced its first incident of speaking in tongues. The speaker was ʼJennie Moore, the future wife of ʼWilliam J. Seymour. At first Smale was reticent to accept tongues. A dozen or more of his followers moved to Azusa Street, but by June 22 Smale had invited his people back with a promise to allow full freedom in the Spirit. Some returned, and for a time this congregation prospered. Those who did not return joined one of four other pentecostal missions existing in Los Angeles by Oct. 1906.

Smale and his congregation were the subject of two articles in the *Los Angeles Daily Times* during July 1906. The congregation was described as racially mixed, including the poor as well as the prosperous. Dr. Henry Sheridan Keyes, president of the Emergency and General Hospital in Los Angeles, featured in one of these articles, was one of Smale's regular parishioners. Services were well attended, and people stood along the walls and in the entry rather than leaving. Manifestations such as speaking in tongues, jumping, "slayings in the Spirit," and shouting were common. Meetings often ran all night. It was at First New Testament Church that ▸Elmer K. Fisher received his pentecostal experience. Soon after, he founded the ▸Upper Room Mission.

Smale is said to have written an 18-page apology for the pentecostal movement titled *A Tract for the Times* (Shumway). He lived at 1249 South Bonnie Brae and continued to serve First New Testament Church for several years. Although he was a Baptist, he was active in Holiness circles too, appearing with ▸Carrie Judd Montgomery and several others on the docket of speakers who addressed a four-day convention of the Christian Alliance held at Trinity Methodist Church South on Grand Avenue in Dec. 1906 or Jan. 1907.

While Smale allowed others to manifest the gift of tongues in his services and to seek for the fullness of the Spirit in his presence, he never "received the 'baptism' with 'speaking in tongues.'" This fact led ▸Frank Bartleman to describe him as God's "Moses" for pentecostalism, an obvious reference to Moses' inability to cross into the Promised Land. This may also have led to Smale's disillusionment with the pentecostal movement, against whose abuses he wrote in Jan. 1907. He continued to serve as the pastor of First New Testament Church for several years but ultimately founded Grace Baptist Church, of which he was pastor at the time of his death.

Following a lengthy illness, Smale died on Sept. 16, 1926, leaving behind his wife and a daughter, Esther Grace.

■ **Bibliography:** F. Bartleman, *How Pentecost Came to Los Angeles* (1925) ▮ B. F. Lawrence, *The Apostolic Faith Restored* (1916) ▮ C. W. Shumway, "Queer Gift Given Many," *Los Angeles Daily Times* (July 22, 1906) ▮ idem, "Rolling on Floor in Smale's Church," *Los Angeles Daily Times* (July 14, 1906) ▮ idem, "A Study of 'the Gift of Tongues,'" (A.B. thesis, U. of S. Calif., 1914) ▮ A. S. Worrell, "Christian Alliance Convention," *TF* 27 (1, 1907) ▮ idem, "The Gift of Tongues," *Living Truths* 7 (1, 1907) ▮ idem, "The Movements in Los Angeles, California," *TF* 26 (12, 1906) ▮ idem, "Rites for Churchman Tomorrow," *Los Angeles Daily Times* (Sept. 18, 1926).
■ C. M. Robeck Jr.

SMALL, FRANKLIN (1873–1961). Canadian pastor, editor, and administrator. Born at Revenna near Collingwood, Ont.,

he was one of the first in Winnipeg to receive the baptism of the Holy Spirit, in 1907. He soon became assistant pastor to ▸A. H. Argue in Winnipeg, Ont. He attended the Worldwide Camp Meeting at Los Angeles in 1913 and was ordained by the American Assemblies of God in 1914. He then became one of the seven charter members of the ▸Pentecostal Assemblies of Canada (PAOC) in 1917.

In 1921 Small severed his connections with the PAOC due to doctrinal differences on water baptism. He promoted the ▸"Jesus Only" view and that year founded the ▸Apostolic Church of Pentecost of Canada, Incorporated (ACPC) and served as the first moderator. In 1953 the Evangelical Churches of Pentecost, which included many believers in the triunity of the Godhead, merged with the ACPC, resulting in tolerance of both views of the Godhead. Current headquarters of the ACPC are located in Calgary, Alb.

Small pastored Zion Apostolic Church in Winnipeg for the last 29 years of his life. He wrote a history of the Winnipeg Revival of 1916–26 and was the author of *Living Waters: A Sure Guide for Your Faith*. He also edited *Living Waters, The Apostolic Church Advocate,* and *The Beacon,* early pentecostal periodicals published in Winnipeg.

■ **Bibliography:** G. F. Atter, *The Third Force* (3d ed., 1970), 76 ▮ R. A. Larden, *Our Apostolic Heritage* (1971), 25–35, 92–97.
■ G. W. Gohr

SMITH, CAMPBELL BANNERMAN (1900–61). Canadian pastor and administrator. Born at Eganville, near Pembroke, Ont., Smith came into contact with the pentecostal movement during the winter of 1924 and was soon converted and filled with the Holy Spirit. He left his career as bank manager to follow a call to the ministry. He entered the Pentecostal Bible College in Winnipeg in the fall of 1926 and also became secretary and bookkeeper of the college. He was ordained in 1928. In July 1928 he married Beulah Argue, daughter of ▸A. H. Argue.

During his lifetime, Smith served pastorates in Saskatoon, Sask.; Ottawa and Toronto, Ont.; and Victoria, B.C. He was twice president of Eastern Pentecostal Bible College (1940–44, 1958–61). He was also superintendent of the Eastern Ontario District of the ▸Pentecostal Assemblies of Canada before serving as general superintendent (1944–52).

Smith was killed in an automobile accident near Napanee, Ont., in 1961.

■ **Bibliography:** G. F. Atter, *The Third Force* (3d ed., 1970), 77 ▮ "Rev. C. B. Smith," *Pentecostal Testimony* (Mar. 1962).
■ G. W. Gohr

SMITH, CHARLES ("CHUCK") (1927–). Pastor and youth leader. Charles Smith was reared in pentecostal churches by

Christian parents. After high school he attended junior college in Santa Ana, CA, and then studied at L.I.F.E. Bible College in Los Angeles. Upon his graduation from L.I.F.E., Smith was ordained by the ▸International Church of the Foursquare Gospel (ICFG). He held pastorates in Prescott and Tucson, AZ, then in several locations in Southern California. In the early 1960s he opened his home to small Bible study groups. His simple, clear, and practical messages met the needs of those who attended, and he soon led a half-dozen such burgeoning groups. He was asked in 1965 to serve as associate pastor of a struggling congregation in Costa Mesa, CA, called Calvary Chapel. Three years later the congregation moved to a former Lutheran church in Newport Beach and later purchased 11 acres in Costa Mesa, where it remains today.

Under the leadership of Chuck Smith, ▸Calvary Chapel became famous for its biblical teaching, balanced use of charismata, evangelistic fervor, social concern for "hippies" and drug users, and willingness to accept the misunderstood and unloved of society. Smith became the center of national attention in the early 1970s with his mass beach baptisms in Corona del Mar and has been acknowledged as a prominent leader in the Jesus People movement of those years. Today he continues to serve as pastor of Calvary Chapel, which has grown to 35,000 members. Smith and his wife, Kay, have four children.

■ **Bibliography:** R. Enroth et al., *The Jesus People* (1972), esp. chap. 4 ▪ C. Smith, *Charisma vs. Charismania* (1983) ▪ C. Smith with H. Steven, *The Reproducers: New Life for Thousands* (1972).
                                                                    ▪ C. M. Robeck Jr.

SMITH, FRANK W. (1909–97). A charter member of the ▸Open Bible Standard Churches (OBSC), long-time pastor, and denominational leader. Getting his pentecostal start in the First Baptist Church, San Jose, CA, Frank Smith went to ▸L.I.F.E. Bible College and then pastored his first church, a Foursquare Gospel congregation in West Hollywood. Moving to Des Moines, IA, he pastored in the city for the next 42 years, retiring in 1976.

In addition to Smith's pastorates in Iowa, he served in several administrative capacities, including president of Open Bible College and divisional and general superintendent of OBSC; he taught at the college for 20 years. Active in the ▸National Association of Evangelicals, he was the Midwest section president for three years and a member of the general board and executive committee for 30 years. He also served as president of the ▸Pentecostal Fellowship of North America. He is the author of *Pentecostal Positives* (1967).

■ **Bibliography:** R. Mitchell, *Heritage and Horizons* (1982).
                                                                    ▪ W. E. Warner

SNAKE HANDLING See SERPENT HANDLING.

SOCIAL JUSTICE AND THE PENTECOSTAL/CHARISMATIC MOVEMENT The pentecostal/charismatic movement is one of the few global religions with an international network of information. Its churches are found in regions where the Eastern Orthodox churches are dominant, in the Western secularized world, as well as in Latin American, African, Chinese, and other cultures. Through its missionaries and journalists it has access to these "contextualized pentecostalisms." From them it can learn that there is not just one pentecostal blueprint for approaching cultural, political, and social problems.

One might expect that international and regional pentecostal organizations, such as the Assemblies of God, the Church of God, the Pentecostal/Charismatic Churches of North America, the Encuentro Pentecostal Latinoamericana, the Pentecostal European Conference, and the World Pentecostal Conference would eagerly listen to these different voices, noting the social and cultural differences of these pentecostalisms and looking for a common message in all these particular cultures. The official awareness of this diversity and its implications, however, is minimal. The insight that Western pentecostalism—like all other pentecostalisms—represents a syncretism between regional cultures and the gospel is only just emerging. By and large, one's own particular form of pentecostalism is viewed as the universal one.

This problem emerges in particular when European and North American pentecostals are faced with pentecostals in Latin America who value major elements of liberation theology; who supported the Sandinista government in Nicaragua; who aided socialist president Salvador Allende's rise to power in Chile (Gaxiola-Gaxiola); who hold and value membership in the WCC (Robeck); or who, when in the past were faced with the Italian "irregular" pentecostals, often voted for the Communist party. For whom else could they have voted—the *Democrazia Cristiana* who was largely responsible for the pentecostals' harassment in the past? (Hollenweger, 1988, 260).

But these issues are hardly ever discussed at pentecostal conferences. European and North American pentecostals usually find contact with ecumenical and social ethical theology questionable. (There are important exceptions, such as ▸Peter Kuzmič and Miroslav Volf, two ex-Yugoslav pentecostal theologians who are prepared to learn even from Marxism—a fact that is astonishing only to those who have no clear concept of Marxian thinking.)

For example, at the World Pentecostal Conference (Dallas, TX, 1971) the leader of the Russian pentecostals reported on the revivals in the then Soviet Union. No mention was made of the statements of the pentecostal leaders against the revivals as reported in the pentecostal periodicals. (These statements were undoubtedly enforced, since the revivals had sometimes an anti-Soviet flavor.) The only one who protested was Michael Wurmbrand, who brought up what had been printed in the periodicals. The pentecostals simply drowned his protest—by singing (*Wort und Geist,* Jan. 1971).

Another example: The Swiss/German periodical *Wort und Geist* (May 1973) published a report on a boycott appeal of the WCC, in which its member churches were asked to sell shares of companies that had investments in the apartheid economy of South Africa. The periodical commented, "Economical boycott is only another step in the direction of an Anti-Spirit crusade." There was no question of asking the South African sister churches for their opinion! In response to the "Relevant Pentecostal Witness" (c. 1990), in which South African pentecostals repented for their appeasement policy, a number of European pentecostals stated:

> We regret that we did not speak out courageously and consistently against apartheid and the political oppression and economic exploitation that this immoral system has caused for our brothers and sisters in South Africa. We also acknowledge our uncritical attitude in accepting the information disseminated by the media without independently verifying the facts about the ongoing struggle of the Church in the South African situation. (*Transformation* 9 [1, Jan.–Mar. 1992]: 32–33; and *EPTA Bulletin* 10 [1, 1991]: 34–35)

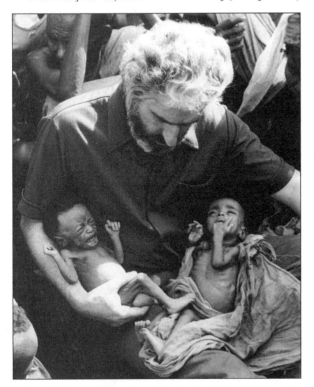

Dr. Tony Atkins holding malnourished twins in Ebnet, Ethiopia, in 1982.

A similar statement against racism in the U.S. was published by North American pentecostals ("Racial Reconciliation Manifesto," *PE* [Dec. 11, 1994]). So it seems that pentecostals can understand the issue of global social justice—but they usually come late, when the battle is already over.

The last point makes clear, however, that Americans do not have to go overseas to find interesting and contradicting statements. (Europeans have thus far not grasped this marvelous opportunity, in spite of the presence in Europe of very interesting pentecostal communities from Asia, Africa, and Latin America.) God has sent them the problem much nearer to home by way of ever-growing Hispanic communities in the U.S. In 1981 the Hispanic pentecostals in the U.S. signed the "Riverside Manifesto," demanding more cultural and political rights for Hispanics.

The leading Hispanic pentecostal, Eldin Villafañe, even stated that the controversial Reis Lopez-Tijerina "represents that 'spirit' of the oppressed among Hispanic pentecostals that see the Gospel's concern for social justice and wholistic liberation." He saw in the struggle for land "not only a political question." For him it is also "a spiritual mission of justice" (Villafañe, 97).

Some of these issues have been taken up by white U.S. pentecostals. In 1991 Murray A. Dempster, Byron D. Klaus, and Douglas Petersen published a remarkable volume of missiological essays, *Called and Empowered: Global Mission in Pentecostal Perspective.* They addressed the fact that "Pentecostal missiological literature has not kept pace with the explosive growth of the Pentecostal churches worldwide" (xii). They said that the "roots of our conviction about the global mission of the church are to be found in Jesus' proclamation of the kingdom of God" (Fee, ibid., 7). Christian social ethics does not mean "preaching Christian social action," but it means "making the truth visible," the truth that Jesus has come to preach liberty to the captives. That means among other things that the political powers must be desacralized by strategic noncooperation. "To be relevant, theology simply must respond to the questions that the poor are asking" (Peterson, ibid., 47). That does not mean that pentecostals accept the mainly Roman Catholic theology of liberation in its entirety. They criticize in particular that "the Catholic Church opts for the poor because it is not a church of the poor. Pentecostal churches do not opt for the poor because they are already a poor people's church, and that is why the poor are opting for them" (Maríz, 138).

The Hispanic pentecostal Samuel Solivan goes much further. He judges evangelical orthodoxy to be sterile because it allegorizes the topic of the poor and must therefore be reactionary. Liberation theology as taught in many American universities is not much better. Liberation theologians are not in contact with those about whom they speak. Instead of involving themselves with the poor, they speak about them and do not have a clue of the potential of hope and innovation among the poor pentecostals.

Solivan also criticizes the academic "coherence syndrome" in both the liberal and the evangelical camps. So-called coherent systematic theology is incongruent with the reality of the Hispanics, who see the luxury and waste around them—including among certain pentecostals and charismatics. Hispanics do not need a doctrine of the "inerrancy of Scripture" (in this they go along with early German pentecostalism). This doctrine was only introduced to please the National Association of Evangelicals and has made pentecostals "theological ventriloquists."

Carmelo A. Alvarez, Murray Dempster, and in particular Juan Sepúlveda oppose the "Manichaean" reading of the Bible of many Western pentecostals. In contrast they opt for a "materiality of salvation" (Volf), which applies the insights of the gospel also to the institutional forms of sin. It is no longer acceptable to them that the Holy Spirit is only interested in that which happens in the bedroom and not in what happens in the boardroom! However, in order to be effective, this critique must develop alternative economic institutions, such as economic enterprises that are not solely based on the capitalist model.

There is some hope that this is going to happen. But that will create tensions between those pentecostals who—by conforming to the dominant capitalist worldview—have become rich and powerful. In some countries (e.g., Guatemala), pentecostals are divided on this very issue. The rich members of a charismatic prayer group belong in this country largely to the neocharismatic moneyed aristocracy. They hold their prayer meetings in exclusive hotels and actively support police terror and torture. That means that in certain cases they are supporting the torture of their own brothers in the faith, the poor pentecostals. These charismatics declare their aim to be freedom for big business and suppression of social protest through an authoritarian state. All this is biblically camouflaged as the fight of the good

Children at an orphanage in Mexico.

against the evil. That "the evil" can also be their own brothers and sisters in the faith who happen to be on the other side of the social divide is a particularly cruel irony of this story. That is why the poor pentecostals in this country have begun to organize themselves and even accept political mandates. "God demands from us a prophetic stance," they say (Schäfer, Smith).

It is sad that such problems are not discussed in the popular pentecostal literature nor at the large charismatic and pentecostal conferences. I do not, however, want to give the impression that pentecostals are worse than other churches. In fact, their contribution to social action is impressive. They fight violence against women, build schools, combat drunkenness, and offer the poor and silenced people a language. However, I believe that pentecostals can do better than the mainline churches if they do not close their ears to the cries of their suffering fellow-pentecostals. So far the dialogue between the "pentecostal elites and the pentecostal poor" has not taken place. Nevertheless, there are important beginnings.

I have deliberately concentrated in this article on pentecostal social ethical thinking. How this pentecostal thinking is related to worldwide ecumenical thinking (a relationship I consider to be vital) is a question I must leave to a future generation of pentecostal scholars.

■ **Bibliography:** Most of the source material is available in W. J. Hollenweger, *Pentecostalism: Origins and Developments Worldwide* (1997) ▌ See also A. C. Alvarez, *Pentecostalismo y liberación: Una experiencia latinoamericana* (1992) ■ M. A. Dempster, B. D. Klaus, and D. Petersen, eds., *Called and Empowered: Global Mission in Pentecostal Perspective* (1991) ▌ G. Fee, "The Kingdom of God and the Church's Global Mission," in M. A. Dempster et al., *Called and Empowered* ▌ M. J. Gaxiola-Gaxiola, "Latin American Pentecostalism: A Mosaic within a Mosaic," *Pneuma 13* (2, 1991) ▌ W. J. Hollenweger, *The Pentecostals* (1988) ▌ idem, "The Pentecostal Elites and the Pentecostal Poor: A Missed Dialogue?" in K. Poewe,

Aftermath of an earthquake in Valdivia, Chile, 1960.

ed., *Charismatic Christianity as a Global Culture* (1994) ■ P. Kuzmič, "Pentecostals Respond to Marxism," in M. A. Dempster et al., *Called and Empowered* (also in *EPTA Bulletin* 9 [1, 1990]) ■ C. L. Maríz, *Coping with Poverty: Pentecostal and Christian Base Communities in Brazil* (1994). ■ D. Peterson, "The Kingdom of God and the Hermeneutical Circle: Pentecostal Praxis in the Third World," in Dempster et al., *Called and Empowered: Global Mission in Pentecostal Perspective* (1991) ■ C. M. Robeck, "Southern Religion with a Latin Accent," *Pneuma* 13 (2, 1991) ■ H. Schäfer, ". . . und erlöse uns von dem Bösen. Zur politischen Funktion des Fundamentalismus in Mittelamerika," in U. Birnstein, ed., *"Gottes einzige Antwort . . ." Christlicher Fundamentalismus als Herausforderung an Kirche und Gesellschaft* (1990) ■ J. Sepúlveda, "Pentecostal Theology in the Context of the Struggle of Life," in D. Kirkpatrick, ed., *Faith Born in the Struggle of Life* (1988) ■ D. Smith, "Coming of Age: A Reflection on Pentecostals, Politics and Popular Religion in Guatemala," *Pneuma* 13 (2, 1991) ■ S. Solivan, *The Spirit Pathos and Liberation: Toward an Hispanic Pentecostal Theology* (1998) ■ E. Villafañe, *The Liberating Spirit: Toward an Hispanic, American Pentecostal Social Ethic* (1993) ■ M. Volf, *Work in the Spirit: Toward a Theology of Work* (1991) ■ idem, "Materiality of Salvation: An Investigation in the Soteriologies of Liberation and Pentecostal Theologies," *Journal of Ecumenical Studies* 26 (3, 1989). ■ W. J. Hollenweger

SOCIETY FOR PENTECOSTAL STUDIES

SOCIETY FOR PENTECOSTAL STUDIES (SPS). Following WWII the American pentecostal movement clearly established itself among evangelicals—perhaps largely due to the statesmanship of ▸Thomas F. Zimmerman as the chief executive officer of the Assemblies of God (AG) for over a quarter century. By the 1950s, teachers in classical pentecostal schools were often trained at evangelical institutions such as Wheaton College, Gordon-Conwell Theological Seminary (South Hamilton, MA), and Fuller Theological Seminary (Pasadena, CA). With the precedent of the Evangelical Theological Society, established in 1949, it was natural to expect a similar organization among emerging pentecostal scholars. Discussions through the 1960s, when pentecostal teachers increasingly undertook university doctorates, are known to have occurred among such persons as ▸J. Robert Ashcroft, ▸R. O. Corvin, ▸Klaude Kendrick, ▸John T. Nichol, Nicholas Tavani, and others. But the founding of the SPS occurred under the leadership of ▸William W. Menzies, ▸Vinson Synan, and Horace Ward at a dinner held on Nov. 6, 1970, in conjunction with the ninth ▸Pentecostal World Conference meeting in Dallas, TX. Of the 139 persons who attended, 108 signed on as charter members. Menzies was elected the first president, and Synan became the initial secretary. An occasional newsletter has appeared at least once each year since 1971. By 1978 the need for a journal was felt. Twice yearly since the spring of 1979, *Pneuma: The Journal of the Society for Pentecostal Studies* has been published. One of the few learned periodicals to arise within the pentecostal movement, *Pneuma*, by the end of 1998, was received at 184

libraries on six continents. At the same time the membership of SPS numbered more than 350 additional scholars (mainly pentecostal and charismatic), teachers, pastors, writers, denominational executives, and students. In its early years, the SPS sought to maintain close connection with the Pentecostal World Conference and with the ▸Pentecostal Fellowship of North America (PFNA). But the varying purposes of these organizations did not lead to a fruitful relationship. Besides, interest in the society had arisen among charismatic scholars who did not subscribe to the precise theological views of the North American pentecostal establishment. At its 1982 meeting the SPS took action that had the effect of opening leadership positions to persons other than members of a classical pentecostal denomination. Within a few years a striking series of "firsts" occurred in the presidency of the organization, an office held for a year: the first charismatic (J. Rodman Williams, a Presbyterian theologian, 1985), the first Roman Catholic (Fr. Peter Hocken, 1986), the first woman (Edith Waldvogel Blumhofer, 1987), the first non-American (Ronald Kydd, of Canada, 1988), the first nonpentecostal (Donald Dayton, a Wesleyan, 1989), and the first representative from the Jesus' Name sector of classical pentecostalism (Manuel Gaxiola-Gaxiola, of Mexico, 1990). Regularly, the SPS has held an annual meeting featuring invited papers and, at times, planned discussions. Mostly such papers have related to historical and theological themes of interest to emerging theologians in the pentecostal and charismatic movements. The more neutral and exploratory character of an academic society, where members function as individuals and not as representatives of their denomination, has on occasion permitted unprecedented advance in intrapentecostal fellowship. Notable in this regard was the participation of ▸Oneness pentecostals in the third annual meeting held in 1973 at Cleveland, TN, which focused on the distinctives of that sector of the movement. Not since the Oneness (or "Jesus Only") issue resulted in the withdrawal of a fourth of the ministers from the AG in 1916 had such an encounter between establishment pentecostals and their shunned siblings occurred. In 1987 the SPS voted to affiliate with the Council of Societies for the Study of Religion, an umbrella organization of academic societies in the U.S. Recent annual meetings have raised for review themes of ethnic reconciliation within classical pentecostalism, where African American origins markedly apply. About to conclude its first generation, the SPS faces a delicate balance between its growing acceptance among scholarly and ecumenical circles and its mixed reception on the part of the classical pentecostal establishment.

■ **Bibliography:** Official SPS archives at Fuller Seminary, Pasadena, CA ■ C. M. Robeck Jr., "The Society for Pentecostal Studies," *Ecumenical Trends* (Feb. 14, 1985). ■ Among scholarly outcomes of the SPS are two bibliographies: D. W. Faupel, *The*

American Pentecostal Movement (1972) ▪ W. Mills, *Speaking in Tongues: A Classified Bibliography* (1974) ▪ and three edited collections of papers read at annual meetings: C. M. Robeck Jr., ed., *Charismatic Experiences in History* (1985) ▪ R. Spittler, ed., *Perspectives on the New Pentecostalism* (1976) ▪ V. Synan, ed., *Aspects of Pentecostal-Charismatic Origins* (1975)　　　▪ R. P. Spittler

SOCIOLOGY OF BRITISH PENTECOSTAL AND CHARISMATIC MOVEMENTS

1. Theory.

Attempts to apply sociological theories to the pentecostal and charismatic movements have been fraught with difficulty, because until recently such theories tended to ignore the views of participants in the interpretation of their own experiences. This is particularly so in the case of theories that presume that the contents of human consciousness are generated almost entirely by the economic or social forms of life (Marx, Durkheim). Where God is assumed to be a reflection of society, for example, and to have a merely symbolic existence, pentecostals rightly feel that sociology has engaged in intellectual imperialism and that religious interpretations of sociology are as valid as sociological interpretations of religion. Indeed, Milbank (1990) goes so far as to see social theories as "anti-theologies in disguise" and as a form of heresy.

Intermediate positions in such heated debate are hard to maintain. Certainly, the rejection of all-embracing sociological theories may be part of the general rejection of any single account of human existence, of any metanarrative, and this leads to the fragmentation of intellectual life and the condition of postmodernism where subjectivity is the natural state of affairs (Sampson, 1994). The sociological account of the pentecostal and charismatic movements in the U.K. offered in this article makes use of sociological concepts rather than sociological theories. It deploys concepts that apply to descriptions of society rather than to descriptions of individuals, and it tries to draw general conclusions on the basis of such empirical evidence as is available.

That said, some of the concepts are explanatory and so function like theories. For example, religions have been seen as operating within a social marketplace and as offering consumers the spiritual goods they want. Consumers, it is assumed, will accept those goods, provided that the personal and intellectual cost is not too high (Stark and Bainbridge, 1985; Iannaccone, 1990, 1992). If the same spiritual goods are offered elsewhere at a lower price, consumers will move their custom down the road. Such a conception of religion translates the benefits of the pentecostal and charismatic movements into economic terms and operates as a metaphor or allegory. It does not do more than offer an incomplete, and possibly misleading, account of religion.

Similarly, pentecostal and charismatic activity has been characterized as relating to contemporary culture and

thought in a threefold way. It is *antimodern* in its dislike of critical and liberal theology, *modern* in its appeal to reason in organization and apologetics, and *postmodern* in its openness to subjective, expressive experience (Hunt, Hamilton, and Walter, 1997). Such an analysis shows how pentecostal and charismatic churches may be understood and offers us a way of thinking about their future development. One or other of these reactions to modernity may predominate in the churches, but in any event, they cannot avoid the influence of cultural change.

An older categorization of Christian groups distinguishes between sects, denominations, and churches (Troeltsch, 1931). In general, these terms are defined by the attitude their adherents show to the rest of society. *Sects* are inward looking and against the prevailing society and are, in addition, convinced that they and only they know the way of salvation. *Denominations* are less hostile to society and willing to accept that other groups along with themselves know how to be saved. *Churches* tend to have less well-defined boundaries and membership criteria and identify themselves with society (e.g., the Church of England). Although this categorization is useful, it is not without its critics or variants (Wilson, 1976, 1982). The older pentecostal churches may be thought of as denominations. The newer charismatic groups might repudiate this label, although in a strictly sociological sense it probably fits.

Where sociological theory turns to the study of society pure and simple, its explanations are more compelling. The notion that society in the West has been subject to a long and pervasive process of secularization is hard to deny. The place of religious institutions in society has been weakened. The practice of religious observance has been reduced. The use of religious ideas and language has become less widespread (Bruce, 1995[a], 1995[b]). Yet even this theory has been disputed. It has been said that religion has not been reduced but simply displaced. Where once religion was shaped by powerful institutions and social norms, it now has been relegated to the private realm and merged with folklore and superstition (Glock and Bellah, 1976; Crippen, 1988; Davie, 1994).

The concept of social stratification, where society is divided into various levels according to their economic or political power, is expressed in classes or socioeconomic groups, each with its own value system. The classes or groups at the top are usually better educated (since education is the ladder by which one moves up in society) and therefore more open to change. These ideas may be applied to pentecostal churches. What social level are they most akin to, and is this reflected in their attitudes toward change? In brief, are pentecostals and charismatics generally recruited from lower social classes, and does this explain their theological and social conservatism? Or may pentecostals and charismatics be differentiated in class terms?

2. Data.

The best available data has been collected by Kay (1999), who surveyed all pentecostal ministers resident in the U.K. from the Apostolic Church (AC), Assemblies of God in Great Britain and Ireland (AGGBI), the Church of God (CG), and the Elim Pentecostal Church (EPC). The results, based on 930 ministers (a 56% response rate), distinguish between these denominations on the basis of (1) the age distribution of their ministers, (2) the educational levels of ministers, (3) their economic welfare, and (4) the size and growth of their congregations.

In general, EPC is the youngest, best educated, best provided for financially, and has the largest congregations. AC is the oldest, least well educated, least well paid, and has the smallest congregations. AGGBI and CG fall in between. This said, there is considerable diversity within all four groups.

The tables below illustrate these points.

Table 1. Education

Denomination	No formal training for ministry (%)	Theology degree (%)
AC	69	11
AG	45	10
EPC	14	9
CG	14	12

Table 2. Financial Provision

Denomination	Weekly take-home pay less than £200 (%)	Weekly take-home pay more than £300 (%)	No pension scheme/plan (%)
AC	76	11	11
AG	62	16	39
EPC	38	20	16
CG	66	11	23

Table 3. Congregational Size

Denomination	Fewer than 100 adults in Sunday morning congregation (%)	More than 200 adults in Sunday morning congregation (%)
AC	92	4
AG	71	11
EPC	67	14
CG	81	9

Table 4. Congregational Growth in the Past 12 Months

Denomination	None (%)	By 11–20% (%)
AC	26	6
AG	16	11
EPC	18	12
CG	19	12

Table 5. Age of Ministers

Denomination	Under 50 (%)	Over 60 (%)
AC	29	28
AG	54	21
EPC	69	10
CG	40	25

During the period when these data were collected, the take-home pay of the average male in the U.K. was approximately £260 per week. Thus, although the comparison is inexact because of the allowances ministers often receive, the indication is that the majority were paid significantly less than secular employees. When this is coupled with the lack of an occupational pension (especially in the AG, where local church autonomy militates against centralized provision of finance), it is clear that many ministers are living in economically reduced circumstances.

The table below, however, shows that EPC ministers, and to a lesser extent AGGBI ministers, are more likely to be in step with the rest of society than the AC and CG cohort. In terms of cinema attendance and drinking of alcohol, EPC and AGGBI have more liberal attitudes and beliefs. As it happens, EPC also has the youngest and best-paid ministers with higher educational levels. Moreover, unlike CG, which has roots in the U.S., the EPC is largely based in the U.K.

Table 6. Cultural Alienation

Item	AC (%)	AG (%)	EPC (%)	CG (%)
Christians should not attend the cinema	44	18	11	58
Christians should not drink alcoholic beverages	57	43	35	67
I approve of the Toronto Blessing (laughing in the Spirit)	46	58	76	27
I believe that God made the world in six 24-hour days	67	70	56	63

Numbers indicate percentage of ministers in agreement with statement.

Comparable data are not available for charismatic churches or New Churches (›New Apostolic Reformation). The clear impression of commentators, however, is that they are more middle-class in their composition and outlook (Thompson, 1996; Walker, 1985, 1997). The evidence for this is found in the ratio of income to size of constituency and in anecdotal information about levels of remuneration awarded to ministers in apostolic teams. Moreover, charismatic churches tend to flourish in locations where house prices are higher and tend to have had their beginnings in the southern, less industrial parts of England. Whereas the pentecostal congregations, especially AGGBI, still show traces of their northern origins in the old heartlands of Methodism, the charismatic churches were in the first instance often recruited from among southern disaffected Baptists. In this respect studies on the social geography of English religion and on the historical background of religious dissent are still relevant (Gay, 1968; Martin, 1967; Bruce, 1995[a]). Charismatic congregations in the 1980s, when they grew exceptionally rapidly, certainly showed evidence of being younger than pentecostal denominations and of being socially more at ease with cultural norms. Cinema attendance and the drinking of alcohol would almost without exception be acceptable to charismatics.

3. Conclusion

If religion is seen in terms of a marketplace, then the data might be said to support the analogy. The EPC is attractive to consumers and appears not to ask them to pay too high a price in terms of the entertainments and amusements they must forego.

If religion is seen in the light of its reaction to modernity, then, again, the EPC offers an acceptance of the postmodern expressiveness of the Toronto Blessing while, at the same time, providing modernity in terms of its well-run organization. AGGBI is similar, though its organizational structure has been through a period of difficulty. The two other classical pentecostal churches, AC and CG, are less willing to accept the Toronto Blessing, and AC has the worst pattern of growth.

Again, if religion is seen as a trajectory from sect-like attitudes to church-like attitudes, both EPC and AGGBI provide evidence of these kinds of changes. They show an acceptance of cultural values, and this acceptance is likely to be maintained, since their ministers are younger than those in AC and CG.

As for the economic status of their ministers, pentecostal churches are largely in the lower classes, though such a finding can hardly be thought to explain the conservative theological attitudes they hold, since many of these ministers entered pentecostal ministry precisely *because* they held conservative theological attitudes. In other words, theological conservatism preceded socioeconomic status. As far as the recruitment of pentecostal ministers is concerned, there are no comparative data available here. In a comparison with charismatic ministers, however, the evidence is equivocal:

Charismatics tend to be more liberal in their social attitudes to cinema and drinking alcohol but more conservative in their willingness to accept ministerial authority.

Thus, though sociological concepts offer a nontheological way of looking at churches, they do not reveal the whole picture. They suggest possible outcomes and trajectories as social and religious trends move one way and another. They allow predictions to be made on the basis of demographics (thus EPC looks most likely to grow in the future because of its younger ministers and its present state of health) and on the basis of the relationship between religion and society. If any religious group is going to grow, it must either recruit new members or retain the children of its members, or both. In order to do the first, there must be an interface between religious group and society to allow newcomers to pass through the invisible barrier between the two. In order to do the second, it must appeal to young people by communicating with them and offering them an identity they want. When such conditions occur, the balance between modernity and postmodernity (or expressiveness) is about right. This is particularly so since other data (Barker, Halman, and Vloet, 1993) indicate that the generation of Europeans born after 1945, not having been disciplined by war and recession, value liberty and self-expression more than duty and restraint. Pentecostal and charismatic groups that hope to appeal to the young must find a way to speak to their needs and their priorities.

The work of Wuthnow (1993), drawing on a North American context, sees the religious right (among whom pentecostals and many charismatics would be counted) as continuing to concentrate on family values, middle-class schooling, and other social issues, but doing so without centralized organization. The religious environment in the U.K. is different from that found in North America. Though pentecostal and charismatic groups are theologically conservative, they are adventurous in other ways; they tend not to be fundamentalist in attitude. Most are affiliated with the Evangelical Alliance, which expresses and orchestrates their social concerns. Where Wuthnow's analysis may be apt, however, is in the matter of identity. The larger cities of Britain are becoming increasingly multiracial and cosmopolitan. Here Christianity offers an identity that can be added to ethnic and racial identities, allowing individuals a multiple image of themselves. Pentecostal and charismatic churches may thus expect both to offer anchorage within British society to ethnic groups and to benefit from their contributions in the realm of worship and evangelism.

■ **Bibliography:** D. Barker, L. Halman, and A. Vloet, *The European Values Study 1981–1990* (1993) ■ S. Bruce, *Religion in Modern Britain* (1995[a]) ■ idem, "The Truth about Religion in Britain," *Journal for the Scientific Study of Religion* 34 (4, 1995[b]) ■ T. Crippen, "New and Old Gods in the Modern World: Towards a Theory of Religious Transformation," *Social Forces* 67 (2, 1988) ■ G. Davie,

Religion in Britain Since 1945: Believing without Belonging (1994) ■ J. Gay, "Some Aspects of the Social Geography of Religion in England: The Roman Catholics and the Mormons," in *A Sociological Yearbook of Religion in Britain*, ed. D. Martin (1968) ■ C. Y. Glock and R. N. Bellah, eds., *The New Religious Consciousness* (1976) ■ S. Hunt, M. Hamilton, and T. Walter, "Introduction" and "Tongues, Toronto and the Millennium," in *Charismatic Christianity: Sociological Perspectives,* ed. S. Hunt, M. Hamilton, and T. Walter (1997) ■ L. R. Iannaccone, "Religious Markets and the Economics of Religion, *Social Compass* 39 (1, 1992) ■ idem, "Religious Practice: A Human Capital Approach," *Journal for the Scientific Study of Religion* 29 (1990) ■ W. K. Kay, *Pentecostals in Britain* (1999) ■ D. Martin, *A Sociology of English Religion* (1967) ■ J. Milbank, *Theology and Social Theory: Beyond Secular Reason* (1990) ■ P. Sampson, "The Rise of Postmodernity," in *Faith and Modernity,* ed. P. Sampson, V. Samuel, and C. Sugden (1994) ■ R. Stark and W. Bainbridge, *The Future of Religion* (1985) ■ M. J. Thompson, "An Illustrated Theology of Churches and 'Sects'" (diss., Canterbury, 1996) ■ E. Troeltsch, *The Social Teachings of the Christian Churches* (1931) ■ A. Walker, *Restoring the Kingdom* (1985) ■ idem, "Thoroughly Modern: Sociological Reflections on the Charismatic Movement at the End of the Twentieth Century," in *Charismatic Christianity: Sociological Perspectives,* ed. S. Hunt, M. Hamilton, and T. Walter (1997) ■ B. Wilson, *Contemporary Transformations of Religion* (1976) ■ idem, *Religion in Sociological Perspective* (1982) ■ R. Wuthnow, *Christianity in the 21st Century* (1993).   ■ W. K. Kay

SOCIOLOGY OF WORLD PENTECOSTALISM

The pentecostal movement has been international since its inception. Certainly, so far as the numbers of adherents are concerned, the pentecostal movement is international. Pentecostals in the nonindustrialized parts of the world outnumber those in the industrialized nations two to one. Worldwide, "classical pentecostals" (as distinct from charismatics and neocharismatics—see part II in this volume) numbered more than 65 million in the year 2000. Regardless of which number is taken, it is clear that pentecostalism has become both the largest and the fastest-growing Protestant tradition in the world. In fact, the world's largest church, the Yoido Full Gospel Church, of which ▸David (Paul) Yonggi Cho is the pastor, is a pentecostal church in Seoul, Korea, and has over 240,000 people attending worship services each week. At the same time that the numerical growth of pentecostalism is emphasized, one should remember that Gary McGee (1994) cautions pentecostals that the triumph is not in the numbers but rather in a pentecostal witness that speaks to the social needs of the world.

Nevertheless, both the international nature of the movement and the history of international pentecostalism have been somewhat ignored until recently by all but a few scholars of pentecostalism. Pomerville (1985); McClung (1986); Dempster, Klaus, and Petersen (1999, 1991); and Hollenweger (1997) are among those who have documented this

neglect. During the past decade, however, an increasing number of studies have appeared that emphatically demonstrate the international nature of the movement. Prominent among those who have produced these works have been Martin (1990), Stoll (1990), Synan (1992), Cox (1995), and Hollenweger (1997). In addition, Poewe (1994) and Dempster, Klaus, and Petersen (1999, 1991) have edited books in which several researchers have underscored the rapid growth and spiritual impact of pentecostalism. Also, Burgess and McGee (1988) included a number of articles that discuss the international appeal of pentecostalism. Further, several authors in Cleary and Stewart-Gambing's edited volume (1997), as well as Chesnut (1997) in a separate work, explore a variety of themes that attempt to show and explain the appeal of pentecostalism in Latin America.

In addition, *Pneuma,* the *Journal of Pentecostal Theology,* the *Asian Journal of Pentecostal Studies,* and *The Journal of the European Pentecostal Theological Association* have been at the forefront in publishing studies and book reviews that document the international character of pentecostalism.

Much of the academic scholarship on pentecostalism outside the United States has focused on Latin America. However, there is increasing evidence from scholarly, popular, and anecdotal sources that in Europe, in Asia outside of Japan, and in sub-Saharan Africa the pentecostal movement is flourishing as well (Synan, 1992; Poewe, 1994; Hollenweger, 1997; Dempster et al., 1999). At the same time, a body of scholarship exists that challenges pentecostals to look closely at religious practices not commonly called pentecostal, or even Christian, but that appeal to some of the same social groups as do the pentecostals. For example, Martey (1993) focuses on the cultural and liberating aspects of African religion, while Matibag (1996) delves into the narrative roots of Afro-Cuban religions. Likewise, Perez y Mena (1998), in his studies of Caribbean spirituality and its manifestations in the United States, suggests that in the Caribbean countries the characteristics of the Afro-Latin religions have been disguised or hidden from church leaders and thus have not been well understood. As people from the Caribbean have migrated to the U.S., however, the practices have become more open and accessible to nonpractitioners. There is evidence that some of the religious practices of the Afro-Latin religions have been incorporated into pentecostal as well as Catholic worship, if not into their theologies. Studies such as these raise questions about the fact that scholars and church leaders have tended to dismiss religious activities that may be outside the paradigm of their own experiences.

1. Sociology of Religion.

According to Roberts (1995, 3), the sociology of religion focuses on religious groups and institutions (their formation, maintenance, and demise), on the behavior of individuals within those groups (social processes that affect conversion, ritual behavior), and on conflicts between religious groups (Catholic versus Protestant, Christian versus Moslem, mainline denomination versus cult).

The sociology of religion begins with the assumption that the manifestation of religion is the result of social processes. This viewpoint has been predominant since the early development of sociology, when many of the sociologists attempted to explain all things of a social nature with one, or at least a small number of, theoretical formulations and attempted to locate the cause of all human behavior, including religious behavior, within sociocultural structures.

Several social and intellectual trends have influenced the development of the sociology of religion. First, during the latter decades of the 19th century into the first two decades of the 20th, evolutionary theories were used to explain variations in social structure. Second, positivism was offered as a corrective to the "failed" evolutionary theories and took a bifurcated, or even a trifurcated, route. One route produced the *psychology of religion*. Another produced the *sociology of religion*. The third route is the *anthropology of religion*, which is linked with the study of the culture, symbols, and ideology of religion. (See Shepperd, *DPCM*, 1988, 794–99, for a more detailed presentation of the theoretical background of the sociology of religion.)

This article will view pentecostalism as a religious movement engaged in by persons attempting to make sense of, and thus bring cognitive order to, a complex and sometimes hostile world. It is defined as a social *movement*, rather than as a social group, or even as a social institution, because the boundaries and the membership of those who define themselves as pentecostal, charismatic, neo-pentecostal, or neocharismatic are amorphous. A social movement, according to Turner and Killian, (1957, 308) is

a collectivity acting with some continuity to promote a change or resist a change in the society or group of which it is a part. As a collectivity, a movement is a group with indefinite and shifting membership, with leadership whose position is determined more by the informal response of the members than by formal procedures for legitimating authority.

While many groups can be defined as pentecostal or charismatic, the category also includes persons who are members of groups not commonly defined as such. In addition, it can include those who are not members of any identifiable religious group, but who share the experiences and worldview of those who are pentecostal or charismatic. Thus, an important assumption made here is that the pentecostal movement is a blending together of a number of social, racial, economic, and national groups, as well as diverse religious and intellectual traditions (Nichol, 1971; Poewe, 1994; Cerillo, 1997). In the developing countries of the world, the result is a hybrid religiosity not entirely comparable to North American or European religious practices. What makes analysis so difficult—whether it is sociological, theological, hermeneutical, or uses some other methodological tool—is that there is no "pure" pentecostal model. When one asks, "What is pentecostal or charismatic," the answer depends partly on who provides the answer (Faupel, 1993; Johns, 1995; Robeck, 1993). This reality suggests a need for a methodology that can incorporate how people express their religious and spiritual feelings, beliefs, and practices in their own words and lives, in addition to other investigative methodologies that might be used.

The sociology of pentecostalism, then, is the application of the theories and methodologies of sociology in an attempt to understand and explain the social dynamics whereby pentecostals have been able to define themselves and the world from a distinctive pentecostal perspective.

I will look at four different approaches to the study of pentecostalism as an international social movement: (1) modernization and secularization, (2) relative deprivation, (3) symbolic interaction theory, and (4) globalization. While it is not uncommon for researchers to combine arguments from a variety of approaches, they will be separated here for heuristic, if not for theoretical reasons.

2. Modernization and Secularization.

Modernization is the process whereby a society changes from a premodern preindustrial economy to a modern industrial economy. It includes increased urbanization, workers shifting from agriculture to industry, increased literacy, and increased opportunities for political participation. In addition, the basis of knowledge changes from traditional to scientific (Smelser, 1966). Further, there is an increase in individuation accompanied by an increase in anomie (according to Durkheim) and alienation (according to Marx).

Modernization is often accompanied by secularization, that is, by a separation of religious and social institutions, by ideological and cultural differentiation, and by a decline in religiosity (Martin, 1978, 3). Martin further suggests that the level of interest in the work of the Holy Spirit by clergy and educated laypersons in the mainline (nonpentecostal) churches is another of the indicators of secularization (1978, 280).

According to Martin, while modernization refers to social change and the specialization of social institutions, secularization, on the other hand, refers to the level of commitment individuals have to the religious institutions and the impact these institutions have on the totality of identity. That is, modernization refers to the social, while secularization refers to the cultural. The basic theoretical linkage between modernization and secularization is that as modernizing societies become diverse, or pluralistic, people become less religious—that is, people tend to rely on institutions other than religion to meet their needs and solve their problems.

Despite much theorizing and empirical work, debates continue as to whether secularization is a necessary consequence of modernization or whether these are separate and independent processes.

During much of the history of sociology, sociologists who have studied religion have, for the most part, accepted the secularization thesis. On the other hand, some sociologists, such as Greeley (1995, 199), point out that the empirical evidence does not support the notion of secularization; people continue to be religious while at the same time becoming modern. Others, in particular, Stark, Bainbridge, Finck, and Iannaccone, offer a rational-choice explanation of religion as an alternative or corrective to the "modernization is pluralism is secularization" thesis. Rational-choice theory is a market-type explanation and is based on the argument that as the number of religious choices increase, participation in religious activities also increase. Iannaccone (1992, 123) writes,

> Religious "consumers" are said to "shop" for churches much as they shop for cars; weighing costs and benefits, and seeking the highest return on their spiritual investment. Religious "producers," erstwhile clergy, struggle to provide a "commodity" at least as attractive as their competitors'. Religion is advertised and marketed, produced and consumed, demanded and supplied.

Proponents of rational choice theory further argue that as modernization occurs, official, traditional, and mainline religions decline, which opens the market for new or outside religious movements. The new religions give people choices that they would not have with official or traditional or mainline religions.

3. Relative Deprivation.

An explanation used to explain the dynamics of pentecostalism by a number of researchers is that of relative deprivation. Anderson (1979) found the argument to be persuasive in his now classic study of the pentecostal movement, and other researchers have adopted the notion. The theory assumes that people and groups make comparisons about their own social progress relative to that of other persons and groups. According to Davies (1962), it is not the people at the bottom of the socioeconomic pyramid who feel the relative effects of deprivation; it is those who expect to rise but don't, or if they do, do so more slowly than others.

While the notion of relative deprivation has been popular in explaining certain kinds of social movements, the theory gains explanatory strength when linked with cognitive dissonance theory. For example, in his study of the antecedents of conflict and change, Davies proposed that when reversals follow progress, or the promise of progress, then the possibilities for dissonance increase. In his discussion of the concept he introduced three decades earlier, Festinger (1980) argued that when people experience situations or feelings that are inconsistent with their beliefs, they most likely will change their beliefs in order to reconcile the incon-

sistency or dissonance. If, for example, people believe that hard work leads to success, then, when they work hard and success does not ensue, or when they see that others seem to be succeeding with the same amount or even less work, they change their belief in the value of hard work. Although examples of many different possibilities and behaviors may be evident in some pentecostal groups, most researchers using this approach tend to focus their analysis on those who change their attitudes about the relevancy of hard work and shift their attention to heavenly rewards. This is often defined as the inappropriate response of an unhealthy personality to a real social problem.

In a variation of relative deprivation theory, Smelser (1963), in what he calls "value-added theory," has preferred to focus on the social structural context of the determinants, or stages, of collective behavior. The stages are (1) structural conduciveness, (2) structural strain, (3) growth and spread of a generalized belief, (4) precipitating factors, (5) mobilization for action, and (6) weakened social controls. He hypothesizes that each stage adds value to the previous stages. While it is difficult to say that each stage must follow in sequence, Smelser argues that each must be present for a social movement to develop.

Questions remain, however, about how this theory may apply in specific situations. For example, Smith (1994), Levine and Stoll (1997), and Burdick (1993), in separate studies, use relative deprivation to argue that a lack of opportunity for social mobility in Latin America may cause pentecostals to seek secular social redress. What is it that prompts one group to adopt a religious interpretation of its situation and another group, in a similar social situation, to engage in a riot or participate in a revolution or to seek to bring about social change through political activism? Relative deprivation theory, by itself, is unable to explain why there is a discrepancy between the reality and the stereotype of pentecostal social involvement. Montgomery (1993), in describing the growth of the African-American church in the South after the American Civil War, writes, "To look upon African-American religion as 'otherworldly' as opposed to 'thisworldly' imposes a far greater separation of the two worlds than black folk generally made" (344). Likewise, Calhoun-Brown's (1998) research on the multidimensionality of black subjective religiosity "contradict[s] the expectation that otherworldly orientations direct people away from this-worldly concerns" (433). The same point is made by Wilson (1986), when, in his description of pentecostals in general, he writes, "[d]espite the stereotypes, pentecostals are not passive and otherworldly" (87). Also, Miller (1996), in his critique of deprivation theory, contends that the variations and schisms that have occurred within the pentecostal movement cannot be explained by theories that are based on social sources alone, and he argues for a combination religious interpretation and dynamic social-movement theory. He writes that "the religious claims of the pentecostal adherents were not taken seriously" (113) by social science researchers who attempted to locate the sources of pentecostalism in deviant social or personality structures (or sometimes in both).

Pentecostalism emerged partially out of the Holiness heritage, a marginalized movement within Methodism, and partially out of the ʼKeswick renewalist tradition that emphasizes sanctification (Bundy, 1988; Dayton, 1987). The Holiness movement stresses the doctrines of free will and the universality of the grace of God as expressed in the human activities associated with holy living. Pentecostalism blends elements of the two in a theology that has, as it main points, salvation, baptism in the Spirit, divine healing, and the second coming of Christ. Hollenweger (1997, 269ff.) adds that because of the influence of black pentecostals, in particular William J. Seymour and Charles H. Mason, two additional doctrinal points were included: (1) the breakdown of racial, gender, and economic barriers as a result of the power of the Holy Spirit, and (2) an emphasis on the oral or narrative elements of worship. Daniels (1999) stresses the ethics of racial harmony when he links the spiritual, religious, and social diversity that came together to form early-20th-century pentecostalism. Thus, pentecostalism can best be seen as a restorative, rather than as a revolutionary, movement. As a restorative movement, pentecostalism brings biblical concerns to problems of daily living, attempting to achieve what its adherents have defined is its rightful place in the succession of religious social movements. When the focus is on the religious experience rather than on the social origins of its adherents, relative deprivation loses much of its explanatory power.

This does not mean that the impact and nature of the social structure and the effects of marginalization can be ignored. Pentecostalism has attracted poor and marginalized people since its modern inception. The movement had its origins among the lower and the lower-middle classes, and the pentecostal movement began at a time when a significant proportion of people in the U.S. and Western Europe were lower and lower-middle class. In addition, it was a time when the economy of the developed nations was growing rapidly with the expansion of industrialization. The circumstances were those of structural, not social mobility, and the majority of people were likely to be marginalized at some points in their lives. This situation primarily affected young adults, recent urban residents, the uneducated, the new immigrants. Further, the urban migration of rural residents and the entrance of new immigrants threatened the position of those who were already in the cities and who were struggling to make ends meet. These were people who worked hard, who lived good lives, but who were not getting ahead economically. As a result, it is possible they experienced dissonance as a result of marginalization. While marginality and relative deprivation are part of the definition of both structural and social mobility, they are also part of the historical reality of classical pentecostalism in the U.S. and Western Europe. However, one cannot assume that historical correlation is causation.

Furthermore, the concept of relative deprivation is an inadequate explanation for the rapid spread of pentecostalism in the Two-Thirds World where the majority of both pentecostals and nonpentecostals are poor. It also does not satisfactorily explain the increase in the numbers of neo-pentecostals and neocharismatics, who do not have the same social origins as classical pentecostals; rather, according to Fichter (1976) and McGuire (1975), they are more likely to have middle-class origins (see also Cleary, 1999).

4. Symbolic Interaction Theory.

Symbolic interaction theory, a variation of pragmatic philosophy, is based on the work of George Herbert Mead, Charles Horton Cooley, and Herbert Blumer, and makes several assumptions about social reality. (1) Social reality is created by humans as a response to, and in dynamic interaction with, a specific social context or situation. (2) Humans in interaction and agreement with one another create society. (3) Human behavior is created through the perception and then the definition of a specific situation. (4) Human interaction requires the shared and agreed upon definitions of symbols. Lofland and Stark (1965), in a much cited report, used Smelser's model in their study of the recruitment and conversion practices of the *Doomsday Cult*, later identified as the Unification Church (Moonies.) They hypothesized that the value-added stages act as a funnel, screening out people as they move through the stages. In a follow-up study of the changes that occurred in the ways in which the Unification Church recruits potential members, Lofland (1977) reinterpreted his earlier findings from the vantage point of symbolic-interaction theory. In his reinterpretation of his data and conclusions of his previous research, Lofland suggested that Smelser's value-added stages could be divided into two categories: (1) predisposing conditions, and (2) situational contingencies. *Predisposing conditions* are characteristics of people prior to their contact with a group such as the Unification Church. They include social strain or tension, a tendency to define this strain or tension from a religious perspective, and a dissatisfaction with conventional religions coupled with a pattern of switching from church to church.

Situational contingencies refer to the aspects of the social situation after contact has been made with the group. These include a turning point in life, having at least one friend who is a member of the group, a weakening of family ties and nongroup friendships, and intense interaction with cult members.

Lofland's ideas have had their supporters and critics. For example, David Snow and Cynthia Phillips (1980) modified Lofland's categories in their study of conversion to *Nicheron Soshu* Buddhism and argued that different groups with different philosophies may attract people with different characteristics. However, they conclude that there are at least two prerequisites to conversion, both of which may be universal in their application: (1) there must be close emotional or affective bonds with a member of the group prior to joining, and (2) if the new recruit stays in the group, there must be intense interaction and involvement with group members after joining.

Snow defines situational contingencies and their interpretation as "collective action frames." For example, Snow et al. (1986) and Snow and Benford (1992) use the idea of "collective action frames" to define how people adjust and thus make sense of dissonant social situations. These collective action frames are sets of beliefs that justify, both to oneself and to others, one's participation in a movement.

Smilde (1998) uses the notion of collective action frames to show that lower-class pentecostals in Venezuela, when faced with lack of mobility opportunity, are likely to interpret their situations as a result of supernatural agency. The middle- and upper-middle-class pentecostals may bifurcate, with one group remaining pentecostal but becoming more conservative, while the other group joins the progressive, ecumenical, nonpentecostal churches.

Margaret Poloma, in a rich body of research on pentecostals, charismatics, and neocharismatics, has used collective action frames to conceptual advantage. For example, in her study of the Assemblies of God (AG), Poloma writes that "the Assemblies of God is currently experiencing vitality and growth because of its ability to encourage personal participation in charisma without jeopardizing its organizational structure" (1989, 11). Thus, for the individuals involved, the action frame is the charisma, or move of the Spirit. For the denomination, on the other hand, the action frame is the organizational structure, defined as a result of the ministry of the Spirit.

Poloma shows how the AG has managed to regulate the tension between the charismatic and the institutional, the problem noted by Weber as "the routinization of charisma," that is, the tendency of groups to institutionalize the dynamic aspects of the group.

In a series of articles, Poloma explores the major components of the ▸Toronto Blessing, an experience in which people break into laughter, make animal sounds, fall into a trance, speak in tongues, as well as engage in other behaviors. In an article in *Pneuma* (1998), she uses questionnaires and regression analysis in an attempt to measure the relationships among these manifestations as well as divine healing, empowerment, and service. Poloma concludes that those who have experienced the "blessing" are more likely to bless others, that is, are more likely to get involved in service to others.

Poloma (1999) continues her investigation by focusing on the manifestations, metaphors, and myths of the Toronto Blessing. By manifestations she means such phenomena as animal sounds, spirit drunkenness, and laughter. Metaphors are the ways in which people use narratives to construct social

reality. Poloma sees the pentecostal movement as "a drama that is being invigorated by the newest waves of renewal" (1999, 381). As drama, it moves the stage of reality from the premodern to the modern to the postmodern stages of history and creates an alternative myth comprised of the pentecostal/charismatic definition of the whole person. The Toronto Blessing offers a "creative response to both the straightjacket of modernism and the abyss of postmodernism" (382).

Those who use the symbolic interaction approach use a variety of data gathering techniques, including questionnaires, participant observation, and in-depth interviews in order to both analyze and allow participants to explain their own motives and rationale for joining and remaining in the groups they join. Emphasis is placed on the symbolic explanation, that is, on the language used—both verbal and nonverbal. Symbolic interaction theory helps explain the construction of social realities through communication processes. For example, when people join religious groups, the theory suggests ways in which people define their experiences and thus make sense of what they perceive is happening. However, the theory does not adequately allow generalizations from one experience to another. One needs other, more structural explanations.

5. Globalization.

As scholars in the industrialized nations of the world (re)discovered the developing world, the theoretical inadequacies of explanations based both on modernization and on relative deprivation theories have become increasingly apparent. (1) Modernization, secularization, and relative deprivation are concepts theoretically linked to social Darwinism of the 19th century. (2) They assume that societies follow a narrow model of development, based primarily on the evolutionary route taken by Western Europe and the United States. (3) They minimize the role of power, the presence and control of natural resources, and the historically early control of trade relationships among societies of the world. (4) They tend to locate the reasons for lack of development either as a fault of individuals themselves or of the developing nations. (5) They tend to ignore the historical antecedents of economic, social, and religious movements.

For example, Tilly, in his historical studies of revolutionary activities, finds little correlation between economic inequalities and participation in protest movements. However, he does find that during periods of governmental repression, participation in protest movements is likely to increase. Following this line of reasoning, Miller writes that, "it could be that those who participate in pentecostalism are actively seeking power to change their situation whether it be religious or social" (1996, 114).

As a result of the work of Immanuel Wallerstein, some researchers have begun to focus on the global nature of the world system. In this model, the world is defined in terms of economic relationships, with a core of industrialized, wealthy nations, a semiperiphery of industrializing nations, and a periphery of poorer nations. The relationship among the nations is a trade relationship based on capitalism and economic imperialism.

As the rich, core nations attempt to increase production, consumption is held down by low wages and restrictions on governmental spending. This means that at the same time that rich nations get richer, poor nations get poorer. Poorer nations then may establish coalitions to prevent any single rich nation from dominating the world. However, the core nations also work to prevent coalitions. Some Asian and Latin American nations have prospered while several African nations that have resources and trained workers have suffered, ostensibly through the joint efforts of businesses and governments in the core nations.

Wallerstein suggests that two types of resistance can result. In the core nations, the working class may organize to protest low wages, the transfer of manufacturing jobs to periphery nations, and the import of foreign-made goods. Accommodation may also be the result. This can occur when the working classes join political or religious groups that promise to return the core nation to some golden age from the past or promise some future glory. In the peripheral nations, the resistance can take the form of violence against domination by the core countries. Accommodation may take the form of participation in religious protest movements, such as those provided by liberation theology or pentecostalism.

Globalization of the economy can produce, not only the transfer of economic goods, but also the transfer of ideological and cultural goods, such as technology, political ideas, and religion, even when there is local opposition to outside cultural influence. Local variations of the production process, from the manufacturing of shoes to the manufacturing of religious institutions, can and do occur. This view would define the local indigenous peoples and religions and their syncretization with the North American, European, and Eastern variants of religion as using available imported materials to create a uniquely local religious product.

In the world-system view, the emergence and growth of groups such as pentecostals in the semiperiphery and periphery nations is an example of both resistance and accommodation. It is resistance in that it is rebellion against the established church, the established government, and the established economic order. It is accommodation to the extent that energies and resources are channeled into religious activities rather than into political protest or revolutionary activities.

In an attempt to provide a more Weberian and thus a multidimensional component to Wallerstein's neo-Marxist approach to globalization, Robertson has brought the individual back into the theoretical formula. As a result, according to Dawson (1998), Robertson's idea of globalization incorporates both the secularization thesis of modernization and the recognition that religion continues to persist in the modern world. In Robertson's view, religion is both a cause and a result of globalization. Religion is a *causal factor* to the extent that it is an international phenomenon in which the barriers of tradition and privilege are broken down. Religion is a *result* to the extent that the world economy and world culture also are relatively unlimited by national boundaries.

Two possible religious scenarios can emerge. In one, revitalization movements such as pentecostalism, which promise restoration, is a possibility. In another potentiality, innovative movements, such as those provided by some of the cults, promise a new and different redistribution of spiritual rewards. Most religious movements, regardless of whether they are restorative or innovative, like most newly established businesses, fail. A few, however, grow, and by doing so alter the relationship between social structure and the individual.

Pentecostalism has found fertile ground and has grown in a global culture. A number of questions remain, among them, Is pentecostalism a part of the global economy and culture, or is it a reaction against it? Just as the global nature of the world economy has altered the distribution of economic goods in both developed and developing countries, so the global nature of pentecostalism has altered the distribution of both religious and social power. Jungja Ma writes, "The drive for economic growth has permanently altered the basic social structure, work ethic, and fundamental mindset of the people" (1999, 189). The movement of religious professionals in the form of missionaries and evangelists from the developed world to the developing world is no longer the normal movement. Nor do theologies flow in one direction. Globalization means that evangelistic activities and religious ideas flow in both directions. Nevertheless, economic and cultural imperialism can and does continue to exist. Multinational corporations attempt to control governments in the developed nations. Thus, multinational corporations have a strongly vested interest in the types of governments that control the developing nations, so that relations between nations are influenced, if not controlled, by multinational corporations, sometimes forcing popularly elected governments out of office. As a result, the corporations may try to influence both the religious and political orientations of their workers. This policy is not always successful, however, as Ma (1999) emphasizes is the case in Asia. In Latin America, pentecostals have supported governments not satisfactory to the U.S. in Chile, Nicaragua, Cuba, El Salvador, Guatemala, Argentina, and Brazil, to name a few. In some cases, the governments have been toppled as a result of actions taken by the U.S., actions often approved by U.S. pentecostals, who are likely to be more conservative than pentecostals outside the U.S.

This demonstrates a dichotomy between U.S. pentecostals and pentecostals in Latin America. For example, in an analysis of survey data, Smith and Haas (1997), in their study of revolutionary evangelicals in Nicaragua, note that Protestants do not differ significantly from Catholics in their political opinions. Evangelical Protestants, however, the majority of whom are pentecostal, were more likely than Catholics to vote for the Sandinista revolutionary candidates in 1990. Smith and Haas theorize that such support for left-wing political candidates by evangelicals and pentecostals is a reflection of marginalized social class positions and is similar to studies that found that, in Chile (Steigenga and Coleman, 1995), Protestants supported the Allende government more than did Catholics. Aguilar and associates (1993) found a similar situation in El Salvador. The situation is interesting, considering Cleary's words: "Reflections on pentecostals in Latin America shows central practices and beliefs which set pentecostals there apart from most Catholics and from other Protestants" (1999, 143).

Pentecostals themselves are attempting to make sense out of the changes that are occurring around the world and are attempting to establish the parameters of what Pluss calls "an open-ended global culture" (1999, 179), by which he means a culture of humility, of listening, of respect, and love. Presumably, a global pentecostal culture would be critical of a global market system (Cox, 1999). An overriding question continues to be, How can a global pentecostalism reject a world market system if that system is already in operation? What kinds of prophetic voice and action are open to pentecostals?

Part of the answer lies in the kinds of social response made by pentecostals around the world. Education programs have been started in areas where local governments have not been able to provide enough schools for students who want them. Often the education programs include other fundamental social services, such as providing health care, clothing, and food, not only for the students, but also for the students' families. Petersen (1996) discusses one of the more successful programs in the world, Latin America ChildCare. According to Petersen, LACC had 67,487 children in 261 primary and secondary schools in 18 countries in 1993 (1996, 153). While LACC has done its work without much recognition, it is a remarkable example of how pentecostals can help meet social needs for both its constituents as well as nonadherents.

In addition to helping provide social and educational resources for marginalized people, pentecostals have taken seriously the plight of women and have been one of the largest groups in the world to systematically provide opportunities for education, advancement, and achievement for females. As a result, upward mobility of families has partly been through the actions of women, and this has been fostered and encouraged by pentecostals (Powers, 1999).

See also MARXISM AND PENTECOSTALISM; SOCIAL JUSTICE AND THE PENTECOSTAL/CHARISMATIC MOVEMENT.

■ **Bibliography:** R. M. Anderson, *Vision of the Disinherited: The Making of American Pentecostalism* (1979) ■ A. H. Anderson and W. J. Hollenweger, eds., *Pentecostals after a Century: Global Perspectives on a Movement in Transition* (1999) ■ D. Barrett, *World Christian Encyclopedia* (2000) ■ A. Billingsley, *Mighty Like a River: The Black Church and Social Reform* (1999) ■ S. M. Burgess and G. B. McGee, eds., *DPCM* (1988) ■ A. Calhoun-Brown, "While Marching to Zion: Otherworldliness and Racial Empowerment in the Black Community," *Journal for the Scientific Study of Religion* 37 (3, 1998) ■ A. Cerillo Jr., "Interpretive Approaches to the History of American Pentecostal Origins," *Pneuma* 19 (Spring 1997) ■ R. A. Chesnut, *Born Again: The Pentecostal Boom and the Pathogens of Poverty* (1997) ■ E. L. Cleary and H. Steward-Gambing, eds., *Power, Politics, and Pentecostals in Latin America* (1997) ■ R. Collins, *The Sociology of Philosophies: A Global Theory of Intellectual Change* (1998) ■ H. G. Cox, *Fire from Heaven: The Rise of Pentecostal Spirituality and the Reshaping of Religion in the Twenty-First Century* (1995) ■ idem, 1993, "Personal Reflections on Pentecostalism," *Pneuma* 15 (Spring 1993) ■ D. M. Cupial, "Renewal among Catholics in Poland" *Pneuma* 16 (Fall 1994) ■ J. Davies, "Toward a Theory of Revolution," *American Sociological Review* 27 (1, 1962) ■ L. Dawson, "The Cultural Significance of New Religious Movements and Globalization: A Theoretical Prolegomenon," *Journal for the Scientific Study of Religion* 37 (4, 1998) ■ M. W. Dempster, B. D. Klaus, and D. Petersen, eds., *Called and Empowered: Global Missions in Pentecostal Perspective* (1991) ■ idem, *Globalization and Pentecostalism* (1999) ■ M. Eliade, "Pentecostal and Charismatic Christianity," in *The Encyclopedia of Religion* (1987), 11:229–35 ■ D. W. Faupel, "Whither Pentecostalism?" *Pneuma* 15 (Spring 1993) ■ L. Festinger, *Retrospections on Social Psychology* (1980) ■ J. Fichter, *The Catholic Cult of the Paraclete* (1975) ■ P. Freston, "Pentecostalism in Latin America: Characteristics and Controversies," *Social Compass* 45 (9, 1998) ■ A. Greeley, *Religious Change in America* (1989) ■ idem, ed., *Sociology and Religion: A Collection of Readings* (1995) ■ R. N. Gwynne and C. Kay, eds., *Latin America Transformed: Globalization and Modernity* (1999) ■ R. I. J. Hackett, "New Directions and Connections for African and Asian Charismatics," *Pneuma* 18 (Spring 1996) ■ R. Hempelmann, "The Charismatic Movement in German Protestantism," *Pneuma* 16 (Fall 1994) ■ P. Hocken, "The Charismatic Movement in the United States," *Pneuma* 16 (Fall 1994) ■ W. J. Hollenweger, *The Pentecostals* (1988) ■ idem, *Pentecostalism: Origins and Developments Worldwide* (1997) ■ S. Hunt, M. Hamilton, and T. Walker, *Charismatic Christianity: Sociological Perspectives* (1997) ■ H. D. Hunter and P. Hocken, eds., *All Together in One Place: Theological Papers from the Brighton Conference on World Evangelization* (1993) ■ L. R. Iannaccone, "Religious Markets and the Economics of Religion, *Social Compass* 39 (1, 1992) ■ C. B. Johns, "The Adolescence of Pentecostalism: In Search of a Legitimate Sectarian Identity," *Pneuma* 17 (Spring 1995) ■ J. Lofland, *Doomsday Cult: A Study of Conversion, Proselytization, and Maintenance of Faith* (1966)

■ idem, "'Becoming a World-Saver' Revisited," in J. T. Richardson, ed., *Conversion Careers: In and Out of the New Religions* (1977) ■ J. Lofland and N. Skonovd, "Patterns of Conversion," in Eileen Barker, ed., *Of Gods and Men: New Religious Movements in the West* (1983) ■ J. Lofland and R. Stark, "Becoming a World-Saver: A Theory of Conversion to a Deviant Perspective," *American Sociological Review* 30 (1965) ■ L. G. McClung, ed., *Azusa Street and Beyond: Pentecostal Missions and Church Growth in the Twentieth Century* (1986) ■ G. B. McGee, "Pentecostal Missiology: Moving Beyond Triumphalism to Face the Issues," *Pneuma* 16 (Fall 1994) ■ M. McGuire, "Toward a Sociological Interpretation of the Catholic Pentecostal Movement," *Review of Religious Research* (1975) ■ E. Martey, *African Theology: Inculturation and Liberation* (1993) ■ D. Martin, *Forbidden Revolutions: Pentecostalism in Latin America* (1996) ■ idem, *A General Theory of Secularization* (1978) ■ idem, *Tongues of Fire: The Explosion of Protestantism in Latin America* (1990) ■ E. Matibag, *Afro-Cuban Religious Experience: Cultural Reflections in Narrative* (1996) ■ A. G. Miller, "Pentecostalism as a Social Movement: Beyond the Theory of Deprivation," *Journal of Pentecostal Theology* 9 (1996) ■ J. Moltmann and K.-J. Kuschel, eds., *Pentecostal Movements in Ecumenical Challenge* (1996) ■ W. E. Montgomery, *Under Their Own Vine and Fig Tree: The African-American Church in the South 1865–1900* (1993) ■ J. T. Nichol, *The Pentecostals* (1971) ■ C. Omenyo, "The Charismatic Renewal Movement in Ghana," *Pneuma* 16 (Fall 1994) ■ D. Petersen, *Not By Might, Nor By Power: A Pentecostal Theology of Social Concern in Latin America* (1996) ■ idem, "The Formation of Popular, National, Autonomous Pentecostal Churches in Central America," *Pneuma* 16 (Spring 1994) ■ K. Poewe, ed., *Charismatic Christianity in a Global Culture* (1994) ■ M. M. Poloma, *The Assemblies of God at the Crossroads: Charisma and Institutional Dilemmas* (1989) ■ idem, *The Charismatic Movement: Is There a New Pentecost?* (1982[a]) ■ idem, "Charisma, Institutionalization and Social Change," *Pneuma* 17 (Fall 1995) ■ idem, "Inspecting the Fruit of the 'Toronto Blessing': A Sociological Perspective," *Pneuma* 20 (Spring 1998) ■ idem, "The 'Toronto Blessing' in Postmodern Society: Manifestations, Metaphor and Myth," in *The Globalization of Pentecostalism: A Religion Made to Travel*, ed. M. W. Dempster, B. D. Klaus, and D. Petersen (1999) ■ idem, "Toward a Christian Sociological Perspective: Religious Values, Theory and Methodology," *Sociological Analysis* (Summer 1982[b]) ■ M. M. Poloma and G. H. Gallup Jr., *Varieties of Prayer: A Survey Report* (1991) ■ M. M. Poloma and L. F. Hoelter, "The 'Toronto Blessing': A Holistic Model of Healing," *Journal for the Scientific Study of Religion* 37 (2, 1998) ■ P. A. Pomerville, *Third Force in Missions: A Pentecostal Contribution to Contemporary Mission Theology* (1985) ■ C. M. Robeck Jr., "Taking Stock of Pentecostalism: The Personal Reflections of a Retiring Editor," *Pneuma* 15 (Spring 1993) ■ K. A. Roberts, *Religion in Sociological Perspective* (1995) ■ R. Robertson, "After Nostalgia? Wilful Nostalgia and the Phases of Globalization, " in *Theories of Modernity and Postmodernity*, ed. B. S. Turner (1990[c]) ■ idem, "Globality, Global Culture and Images of World Order," in *Social Change and Modernity*, ed. H. Haferkamp and N. J. Smelser (1990[b]) ■ idem, "The Globalization Paradigm: Thinking Globally," in *Religion and the Social Order: New Directions in Theory and Research*, ed. D. G. Bromley (1990[a]) ■ idem, "A New Perspective on Religion and Secularization in the Global Context," in *Secularization and Fundamentalism Reconsidered*, ed. J. K. Hadden and A. Shupe (1989) ■ T. Rush, "Covenant Communities in the United States," *Pneuma* 16 (Fall 1994) ■ J. W. Shepperd, "Sociology of Pentecostalism," in *Dictionary of Pentecostal and Charismatic Movements*, ed. S. M. Burgess and G. B. McGee (1988) ■ N. J. Smelser, *Theory of Collective Behavior* (1963) ■ idem, "The Modernization of Social Relations, in *Modernization*, ed. M. Weiner (1966) ■ D. A. Smilde, "'Letting God Govern': Supernatural Agency in the Venezuelan Pentecostal Approach to Social Change," *Sociology of Religion* 59 (1998) ■ B. H. Smith, *Religious Politics in Latin America: Pentecostal vs. Catholic* (1998) ■ C. Smith and L. A. Haas, "Revolutionary Evangelicals in Nicaragua: Political Opportunity, Class Interests, and Religious Identity," *Journal for the Scientific Study of Religion* 36 (3, 1997) ■ D. A. Snow and R. D. Benford, "Master Frames and Cycles of Protest," in A. D. Morris and C. M. Mueller, eds., *Frontiers in Social Movement Theory* (1992) ■ D. A. Snow, R. Burke, S. Worden, and R. D. Benford, "Frame Alignment Processes, Micromobilization, and Movement Participation," *American Sociological Review* 51 (1986) ■ D. A. Snow and R. Machalek, "Second Thoughts on the Presumed Fragility of Unconventional Beliefs," in Eileen Barker, ed., *Of Gods and Men: New Religious Movements in the West* (1983) ■ D. A. Snow and C. L. Phillips, "The Lofland-Stark Conversion Model: A Critical Reassessment," *Social Problems* (Apr. 1980) ■ R. Stark and W. S. Bainbridge, *The Future of Religion: Secularization, Revival, and Cult Formation* (1985) ■ idem, *Religion, Deviance, and Social Control* (1997) ■ D. Stoll, *Is Latin America Turning Protestant?* (1990) ■ V. Synan, *The Holiness-Pentecostal Tradition: Charismatic Movements in the Twentieth Century* (1997) ■ C. Tilly, *Citizenship, Identity and Social History* (1996) ■ idem, *Durable Inequality* (1998) ■ idem, *European Revolutions, 1492–1992* (1993) ■ idem, *From Mobilization to Revolution* (1978) ■ R. H. Turner and L. M. Killian, *Collective Behavior* (1957) ■ R. Van Rossem, "The World System Paradigm as General Theory of Development: A Cross-National Test," *American Sociological Review* 61(June 1996) ■ A. Vervoorn, *Re-Orient: Change in Asian Societies* (1999) ■ A. Walker, "Pentecostal Power: The 'Charismatic Renewal Movement' and the Politics of Pentecostal Experience," in Eileen Barker, ed., *Of Gods and Men: New Religious Movements in the West* (1983) ■ I. M. Wallerstein, *Africa and the Modern World* (1986) ■ idem, *The End of the World as We Know It: Social Science for the Twenty-First Century* (1999) ■ idem, *The Modern World-System: Capitalist Agriculture and the Origins of the European World-Economy in the Sixteenth Century* (1976) ■ idem, *The Modern World-System III: The Second Era of Great Expansion of the Capitalist World-Economy, 1730–1840s* (1989) ■ idem, *The Politics of the World-Economy: The States, the Movements and the Civilizations* (1984) ■ idem, *World Inequality* (1996) ■ G. Waugh, "The Charismatic Movement in Australia" *Pneuma* 16 (Fall 1994) ■ E. Wilson, "Passion and Power: A Profile of Emergent Latin American Pentecostalism," in *Called and Empowered: Global Missions in Pentecostal Perspective*, ed. M. W. Dempster, B. D. Klaus, and D. Peterson (1991).   ■ J. W. Shepperd

SPENCER, IVAN CARLTON (1914–). Educator, church executive. Son of ▸Ivan Quay Spencer (1888–1970), who founded Elim Bible Institute (EBI) and ▸Elim Fellowship (EF). Carlton Spencer succeeded his father as head of both the school and the church. A native of West Burlington (Bradford County), PA, Carlton graduated from the EBI, then moved to Hornell, NY, in 1933 and was ordained to the ministry by the Elim Ministerial Fellowship (now EF) two years later. He served the school as instructor from 1938 to 1949, as president from 1949 to 1982, and as chairman of the board of trustees from 1982 to the present. He was general chairman of the fellowship, based in Lima, NY, from 1954 to 1984, and was a member of the administrative board of the ▸National Association of Evangelicals from 1948 to 1984 and of the ▸Pentecostal Fellowship of North America from 1961 to 1984.

Upon retirement as head of the EF, Carlton Spencer became first president of a new sister organization: Elim Fellowship of Evangelical Churches and Ministers, also based in Lima. Under his leadership, the EBI and EF spearheaded acceptance of the ▸Latter Rain, charismatic, and discipling movements among older pentecostals. In 1977 Spencer served on the planning committee for the first Conference on the Charismatic Renewal in the Christian Churches in Kansas City.

■ **Bibliography:** C. E. Jones, *Guide to the Study of the Pentecostal Movement* (1983) ■ D. Manuel, *Like a Mighty River* (1977).
■ C. E. Jones

SPENCER, IVAN QUAY (1888–1970). President of Elim Bible Institute and founder of ▸Elim Fellowship. Reared on a farm in the Allegheny foothills of northern Pennsylvania, Ivan Spencer grew up in the Methodist Church. From early childhood he had an interest in spiritual things. Converted at age 21, he immediately felt the call to preach. He was licensed by the Methodist Episcopal Church. For a short time he attended Wyoming Seminary near Scranton, PA, but left school when he was stricken with typhoid fever. While returning home on the train, he was instantly healed.

Spencer soon found work with a farmer in Macedon, NY, who encouraged him to visit the nearby Elim Tabernacle in Rochester, sponsored by the ▸Duncan Sisters. After visiting the church, he enrolled in the Rochester Bible Training School, which was connected with the church, in the fall of 1911. The next year Spencer received the baptism of the Holy Spirit. In 1913 he graduated from the school and was married to fellow student Minnie Back.

For the first years of their marriage, Spencer farmed and did evangelistic work. He received ordination with the Elim Tabernacle Church in 1915. He held a Methodist pastorate in upstate New York for a short time. In 1919 Spencer joined the Assemblies of God and pioneered a church at Hornell, NY.

During the summer of 1924 Spencer opened Elim Bible Institute at Endwell, NY, to train pentecostal ministers. Intending for this new school to carry the mantle of the Rochester Bible Training School, which had closed, the Duncan sisters then invited Spencer to move his school to Rochester in 1927. Disagreement arose, however, over the school's affiliations, and Elim Bible Institute moved to Red Creek, NY, in 1928. Here Spencer began editing the *Elim Pentecostal Herald* (now called *Elim Herald*) in Jan. 1931. By 1932 the school moved into larger facilities at Hornell, NY.

In the following year, the Elim Ministerial Fellowship was founded as an agency to grant ministerial credentials. During the 1940s Ivan Spencer and Elim Bible Institute were closely associated with the New Order of the ▸Latter Rain. The school moved again in 1951 to Lima, NY, where it now occupies the campus of the old Genesee Wesleyan Seminary. The Elim Ministerial Fellowship was expanded and became the Elim Missionary Assemblies in 1947; since 1972 it has been called Elim Fellowship.

Spencer attended the constitutional convention of the ▸National Association of Evangelicals in May 1943. He also served on the board of administration for the ▸Pentecostal Fellowship of North America at its inception in 1948. In 1960 Spencer's son ▸(Ivan) Carlton took over as fellowship chairman and as president of the school.

■ **Bibliography:** M. Meloon, *Ivan Spencer: Willow in the Wind* (1974).
■ G. W. Gohr

SPIRITUAL WARFARE: A NEOCHARISMATIC PERSPECTIVE Spiritual warfare is a topic that is both biblical and contemporary. The apostle Paul said, "For our struggle is not against flesh and blood, but against the rulers, against the authorities, against the powers of this dark world and against the spiritual forces of evil in the heavenly realms" (Eph. 6:12). Whether it is the temptation in the garden (Gen. 3), the constant conflict between Yahweh and the various gods of Israel's neighbors (Baal, Ashteroth, Chemosh, etc.) over the allegiance of Israel (e.g., Josh. 24:14–24), the discussion between God and Satan over Job (Job 1), the hindrance by the "Prince of Persia" of the answer to Daniel's prayer (Dan. 10:13), the temptations of Jesus by Satan (Luke 4:1–13), or the various references in Acts (e.g., 16:16–18; 19:11–20), the Epistles (e.g., 1 Cor. 10:18–21; 2 Cor. 10:4–5; 1 Peter 5:8; 1 John 3:8) and Revelation (e.g., Rev. 2–3), Scripture clearly portrays human life as lived in a context of continual warfare between the kingdom of God and the kingdom of Satan.

Jesus treated Satan and demonic forces as real foes, frequently casting out demons and thus setting people free whom he called "prisoners" and "oppressed" (Luke 4:18).

Such language is warfare language. Furthermore, he calls Satan "the prince of this world" (John 14:30), but according to John, his work will result in the destruction of Satan's works (e.g., 1 John 3:8) and, according to the author of Hebrews, of Satan himself (Heb. 2:14). In a similar vein, Paul refers to Satan as "the god of this age" who "has blinded the minds of unbelievers, so that they cannot see the light of the gospel of the glory of Christ" (2 Cor. 4:4), and John says, "The whole world is under the control of the evil one" (1 John 5:19). These, too, are images that point to the need for warfare on the part of God's forces to defeat the enemy.

But Jesus came "to destroy the devil's work" (1 John 3:8) and gives his followers "power and authority to drive out all demons and to cure diseases" (Luke 9:1–2) and to do the works that he himself had done while on earth (John 14:12). Unfortunately, pastors, missionaries, and others who seek to minister in the name of Jesus Christ have usually been blinded by a Western worldview that ignores this facet of biblical teaching and social concern.

1. Prayer and Obedience in Spiritual Warfare.

Certain principles govern the way spiritual power operates in the universe (see Kraft 1994). Among them is the scriptural fact that there is a very close relationship between what goes on in human life and what goes on in the spirit realm. We note that, at least on some occasions, Satan seeks, and sometimes obtains, special permission from God to disrupt human lives (e.g., Job 1; Luke 22:31–32). We learn, then, from Dan. 10:13 (an answer to prayer delayed by a demonic being) and 2 Cor. 4:4 (blinding unbelievers) that the enemy can sometimes be successful in thwarting God's plans.

The other side of the warfare motif in Scripture shows, however, that humans can do things that thwart the enemy's plans, such as prayer and other acts of obedience to God. Since the relationship between the spirit and human worlds is very close, it becomes clear that whatever is done in the human world has great implications in the spirit world. One of the rules seems to be that when humans honor and obey a spirit being, that being is enabled to do more of what it wants to in the human arena. Thus, when people obey God, God is able to do more of his will among humans than otherwise would be possible. Conversely, when people obey Satan, Satan is enabled to do more of his will.

Prayer, then, along with fasting, repentance, forgiveness, righteousness, and every other human attitude and behavior that stands in obedience to God can be seen as acts of war and means of enabling God to accomplish his plans in the human realm. When we pray as Jesus taught us to pray (Matt. 6:9–13), we are partnering with God to enable him to defeat the enemy and to do his will in our lives.

The term *prayer* is, however, used to label several different kinds of obedience to God. When we pray, we ask for things as Jesus commanded us to do (John 15:7; 16:24), we confess

our sins (1 John 1:9), we thank God (Eph. 5:20), and we intercede for others (as Jesus did in John 17:1–26). There are, however, two other types of activity usually referred to as prayer that, along with intercession, are especially related to spiritual warfare. These are what I call "intimacy prayer" and "authority prayer" (Kraft 1997, 49–52).

Intimacy prayer is what Jesus practiced when he went off to deserted places to spend time alone with the Father (e.g., Matt. 14:23; Luke 6:12; 9:28). This type of prayer is basically being with God in fellowship, conversation, and listening to him for direction. This is then what Jesus said is necessary between him and us if we are to bear the fruit he expects us to bear (John 15:1–17).

Authority prayer should not, I believe, be called prayer, though we regularly speak of praying for healing or deliverance. This is, rather, the taking of Jesus' authority over conditions that are against God's will and asserting his power against that of the enemy. When we follow Jesus' example and command demons to release their grip and to leave a person, we are asserting the authority Jesus gave us (Luke 9:1) to do his will in freeing that person. Likewise, we assert his authority in healing people, blessing people or objects, breaking the enemy's power over objects or places, and so forth. Most of what is discussed below assumes that this kind of "praying" will be used to wage the warfare we are called to wage against our enemy.

2. Animism vs. God-Given Authority.

Most of the world practices what anthropologists and missiologists call "animism." This is the belief, and the practices that go with that belief, that the world is full of spirits that can hurt us unless we are careful to appease them. The dangerous spirits need to be watched and kept happy. Most animists believe that evil spirits can inhabit material objects and places such as certain mountains (e.g., the OT "high places"), trees, statues (e.g., idols), rocks (e.g., the Ka'aba in Mecca), rivers (e.g., the Ganges), territories, fetishes, charms, and any other thing or place that is dedicated to spirits. Animists also believe in magic and the ability of at least certain people to convey power via curses, blessings, spells, and the like.

Many Westerners, unacquainted with animism, have difficulty with the fact that the Bible recognizes the validity of the power and the power techniques practiced by animists and that it teaches us to use similar techniques based on similar principles. Much of what God does and endorses looks on the surface like what animists do.

The reason why animism and Christianity look so similar is that the basic difference between them and us is not the presence or absence of power, but the *source* of that power. In areas such as healing, dedicating and blessing, for example, we and they have the capability of doing essentially the same things, but the source of their power is Satan while ours is God.

	Animism	God-Given Authority
Power	Believed to be contained in people and objects.	God conveys his power through people and objects.
Need (in order to utilize spiritual power)	Felt need to learn how to manipulate spirit power through magic or authority over spirits.	We are to submit to God and learn to work with him in the exercise of power and authority from him.
Ontology (what is really going on)	Power from Satan: he is the one who manipulates.	Power from God: he empowers and uses us.
God	God is good but distant, therefore ignore him.	God is good, therefore relate to him. He is close to and involved with us.
Spirits	They can hurt us, therefore appease them.	They are defeated, therefore assert God's authority over them.
People	Victims of capricious spirits who never escape from being victims.	People are captives, but we can assert Jesus' authority to free them.
Cost	Those who receive power from Satan suffer great tragedy later.	Those who work with God experience love and power throughout life.
Hope	No hope.	God wins.

The chart above shows many of the contrasts between animism and God-given authority. Note that the primary expressions of each of these areas look very similar at the surface level. It is in the underlying power and motivations that they differ. The weapons of our warfare are the same as those employed by the counterfeiter, Satan, but the source of the power by which we use these weapons and the source of our authority to use these weapons is God.

3. Gods, Idols, and Divination.

Our concern to wage spiritual warfare effectively must take into account the strong negative pronouncements by God concerning compromise with other gods, idols, and the ways in which their power is engaged. The Bible, both OT and NT, is clear that the worship of any god but the true God is not permitted (e.g., Ex. 20:3, 5; 1 John 5:21). Perhaps the clearest indication of what God feels about his people having relationships with other gods is found in the accounts of God's wrath after Israel turned to worshiping the golden calf at Mount Sinai (Ex. 32) and the god of Moab at Peor (Num. 25).

Several other practices are also forbidden to God's people and given as the reasons why God gave his people the right to drive out the inhabitants of Palestine; in Deut. 18:9–13 several of these things are listed and called "detestable ways" or "disgusting practices": sacrificing children, divination, looking for omens, using spells or charms, and consulting spirits of the dead.

Thus it is clear that many common pagan practices involving spiritual power are forbidden. God does not tolerate appeasing pagan gods or spirits or seeking information (through, e.g., shamans, fortune-tellers, tarot cards, horoscopes), health, wealth, or blessing from them. We are to war against such practices, especially among those who claim to have committed themselves to God.

4. Power Encounters.

An important part of the discussion of spiritual warfare is the concept of "power encounter," reminiscent of the scriptural encounters between Moses and Pharaoh (Ex. 7–12) and between Elijah and the prophets of Baal (1 Kings 18). Current theorists (e.g., Wimber, Wagner, Kraft) see the concept of power encounter as virtually synonymous with the concept of spiritual warfare, agreeing that healing and deliverance from demons are power encounters. They see Jesus' ministry as one large power encounter that includes numerous smaller power encounters in which, through healing and deliverance, he freed people from the power of Satan. It is argued that these encounters qualify as genuine power encounters since they involve the pitting of the power of God to bring freedom against the power of Satan to keep people in bondage.

Power-oriented people require power proof, not simply reasoning, if they are to be convinced (Tippett, 1971, 81). The

Green Zembe, Sunday school superintendent, and his class taking a "Jericho March" around the grounds in Rhodesia (Zimbabwe) in 1968.

value and validity of an approach to evangelism that involves power confrontations is widely accepted today in missiological thinking and practice, since it is recognized that most of the peoples of the world today (including an increasing number of Westerners) are, like the Israelites of Jesus day, power oriented.

5. Three Crucial Dimensions.

Spiritual power in Scripture is never an end in itself. The aim of power encounters is freedom. And this *power-freedom* dimension, discussed above, provides the basis from which the Christian can operate in two other crucial dimensions: the *allegiance-relationship* dimension and the *truth-understanding* dimension. These dimensions are highlighted by Jesus in Luke 9:11, where, after the Twelve had returned from their first teaching and healing excursion, a large crowd had gathered and Jesus "welcomed them [relationship], spoke to them about the Kingdom of God [truth], and healed those who needed it [power]."

The most important of these dimensions is the *allegiance-relationship dimension*. When Jesus' followers came back from a power-filled excursion into the towns and villages of Galilee, reporting with excitement that "even the demons submit to us in your name" (Luke 10:17), Jesus cautioned them and pointed them to something more important: our relationship with the God who provides the power. This relationship, resulting in our names being written in heaven (Luke 10:20) should, according to Jesus, be a greater cause of rejoicing than even our power over demons. So, in focusing on the very important spiritual power dimension, we must be careful not to deemphasize or neglect all the love and other fruits of the Spirit that flow from the allegiance-relationship dimension.

Nor dare we neglect what I am calling the *truth-understanding dimension*. Jesus spent most of his time teaching and demonstrating and leading his followers into truth. But, contrary to Western understandings of truth, this is to be an experienced truth, not simply an intellectual truth. John 8:32 means "you will know the truth [experientially], and the truth will set you free." This truth-understanding dimension is, according to John 8:31, based on obedience to Jesus within the relationship. And all bearing of fruit, including the fruit of spiritual power, is dependent, according to John 15:1–17, on our abiding in a close relationship with Christ.

We are, then, to encounter people and the enemy in appropriate ways with a balance of allegiance, truth, and power encounters. Any approach to Christianity and to spiritual warfare that neglects or ignores any of these three dimensions is incomplete and unbalanced.

6. Levels of Spiritual Warfare.

Scripture focuses on at least two levels of spiritual warfare. The lower level is what I call "ground-level warfare." The

upper level is ordinarily known as "cosmic-level warfare" (called "strategic-level warfare" by Wagner [1996, 19–20]).

When Jesus and the apostles cast demons out of people, they were engaged in ground-level combat, while Elijah's confrontation with Baal (1 Kings 18) and Moses' confrontation with the gods of Egypt (Ex. 7–11) involved cosmic-level warfare. Note, however, that cosmic-level warfare has a ground-level dimension. For it is the human representatives of the cosmic gods that engage in the humanly visible part of the battle. Though it is not as obvious, ground-level warfare also has an invisible cosmic dimension, for the ground-level demons are under the authority of cosmic-level spirits and, ultimately, of Satan himself (a cosmic-level being).

Ground-level warfare involves dealing with the spirits that inhabit people (demons). Indwelling spirits or demons may be of at least three kinds: (1) family spirits, gaining their power through the dedication of successive generations of children to them, are usually the most powerful of the ground-level demons; (2) occult spirits (e.g., those of non-Christian religions, New Age, Freemasonry), gaining their power through invitation, are usually (though not always) stronger than the ordinary demons; (3) "ordinary" demons, e.g., those attached to such things as anger, fear, lust, death, and homosexuality. The strength of all ground-level demons is calibrated to the amount of spiritual and emotional "garbage" in the person, and they are all weakened by dealing with those problems and dispatched in the same way (see Kraft, 1992, 1993).

Cosmic-level warfare involves dealing with at least five kinds of higher-level spirits: (1) territorial spirits over cities, regions, and nations, such as those mentioned in Dan. 10:13, 21 (called "prince of Persia" and "prince of Greece"); (2) institutional spirits such as those assigned to churches, governments, educational institutions, occult organizations (e.g., Scientology, Freemasonry, Mormonism), non-Christian religions (e.g., the gods of Hinduism, Buddhism, animism); (3)

A public renunciation of worship, which follows a profession of salvation, but precedes water baptism for a new Taiwanese convert receives water baptism. The pastor assists in removing an incense pot and other paraphernalia from an idol shelf in the home.

the spirits assigned to oversee and encourage special functions, including vices such as prostitution, abortion, homosexuality, gambling, pornography, war, music, cults, and the like; (4) spirits assigned to such things as objects, buildings, and other spaces as well as nonmaterial entities such as rituals and music; and (5) ancestral spirits, assigned to work with specific families, portraying themselves as ancestors. These spirits working at cosmic level are tightly connected to ground-level family spirits (see below) that dwell within the members of a family.

Ground-Level Warfare. An important issue to deal with in every society is ground-level demonization. We should not call this "demon possession," since this term is not a proper translation of the Greek terms that simply mean "have a demon." So, to be true to the Greek and to refrain from giving the impression that the enemy has more power than he in fact has, we use the term *demonized* to speak of demons living inside a person.

Jesus frequently encountered and cast out ground-level demons (Mark 1:23–26, 34; 3:10–12; 5:1–20; Matt. 9:32–33; Luke 8:2). Experience shows that demons can live in Christians as well as in non-Christians. The explanation seems to be that at conversion our human spirit is made clean both of sin and of demons (if any). Our soul and body, however, need continual attention to root out sin and, if we should be hosting demons, to gain freedom from them (see Kraft, 1992).

Demons can live in people only if they have legal rights granted by what I have called spiritual and emotional "garbage." Such garbage consists of rights given through dedication; through inheritance; through invitation by the person or one in authority over the person; through participation in occult organizations or non-Christian religions with accompanying vows and dedications; through the person wallowing in sin (e.g., adultery, homosexuality, gambling, drunkenness) or holding onto such attitudes as anger, bitterness, and unforgiveness; through curses (including self-curses); through murder or attempted murder (including abortion and attempted suicide) and other similar ways (see Kraft, 1992). We have found that when we first deal with the garbage in demonized people, we can then deal with the demons easily and effectively without violence (see Kraft, 1993).

Demons work at ground level in ways appropriate to the society in which they are working. They adapt their approach to the problems and concerns most prominent in any given society.

Contrary to what many assume, the major focus of ground-level warfare has to be on what the enemy attempts to do within us rather than outside of us. Our experience with several thousand clients leads us to conclude that Satan's primary concern at ground level is to knock people down in their relationships—with self, with God, and with others.

Often the most vicious attacks are on *self-image.* Prominent in the lives of a majority of our clients is a deep sense of unworthiness, often escalated to self-hate. These people usually have been believing enemy lies concerning who they are, why they are here, and the inferiority of their past, present, and future attempts to master the game of life. Such feelings get reinforced throughout life as the person, under pressure from the enemy, focuses on and remembers his or her failures while allowing the memory of successes to fade out of focus. The result is a very low self-image, often in spite of significant accomplishments and a solid relationship with Jesus Christ.

In addition to our enemy's attempts to disrupt our relationship with the self, he gives great attention to the disruption of *relationships with others.* Satan knows that the more he disrupts human relationships, the more damage he can do to God's masterpiece and to God's plans for us. Demons are also assigned to disrupt our relationship with God. We were made for this relationship, and from Satan's first attack on Adam and Eve's intimacy with God to the present, he and his angels have worked full-time to prevent (2 Cor. 4:4) or hinder our closeness with our Creator.

Cosmic-Level Warfare. Cosmic-level spirits are apparently in charge of ground-level spirits, assigning them to people and supervising them as they carry out their assignments in people or do their tempting and harassing of people from the outside. Ground-level demons consistently speak of their "assignments," implying that they are under the authority of higher-level satanic beings. I believe these to be cosmic-level spirits that Paul refers to as "the powers of this dark world and . . . the spiritual forces of evil in the heavenly realms" (Eph. 6:12). Though few biblical scholars doubt the existence of such higher-level spirits, there is a good bit of controversy over what, if anything, we are to do about them, since this matter is not fully addressed in Scripture.

7. Spiritual Mapping.

An important spiritual warfare technique is called "spiritual mapping." This is an approach to discerning and identifying cosmic-level spirits and the areas, institutions, vices, objects, etc., that they are over as a step toward developing strategies to oppose and defeat them. (See Otis, 1991; Dawson, 1989; Silvoso, 1994; Wagner, 1992.)

Dealing with Spirits Indwelling Objects, Buildings, Rituals. One category of cosmic-level spirits is assigned to trees, bodies of water, tools, or household or other objects through dedication of these objects to a given god or spirit. Such spirits are also assigned to rituals, certain music, and other nonmaterial entities through dedication. It is well known that certain musical groups in Western countries are openly committed to Satan and their music dedicated to him. Games such as Dungeons and Dragons, and probably certain movies are also dedicated to Satan. The dedication of artistic productions, often to be used for religious purposes, has been the custom of many of the world's peoples for centuries. People regularly become demonized through contact with such nonmaterial, demonically infested entities.

8. Ancestors.

As mentioned above, I believe ancestor cults to be satanic adaptations to culture carried out through demonic deception. People in every society, especially those that are strongly family-oriented, are greatly concerned over what happens to their loved ones when they die. What a stroke of genius on the part of Satan to convince people that their loved ones are still alive (true) and that they continue to actively participate in human life (false)! By so doing, demons are able to work freely, disguised as ancestors.

Among the arguments advanced suggesting that ancestors are really conscious of what is going on in human life and present to influence it, is the interpretation of the passage concerning King Saul's excursion to the "witch of Endor" (1 Sam. 28:3–19). This account, however, and the fact that at the transfiguration Moses and Elijah appeared to Jesus (Luke 9:28–31), are best interpreted as specific times when God allowed deceased people to return for specific purposes, though the witch of Endor incident may have been satanic deceit. These events should in no way be interpreted to indicate the possibility that ancestors are conscious of and interacting with human life. More to the point is the statement in Heb. 12:1 that "we are surrounded by such a great cloud of witnesses." Although this verse may mean that the deceased are able to watch us, it gives no indication that they can participate in human life.

9. Reincarnation.

A demon once responded to a question about reincarnation, "We know people's lives in detail. It's easy for us to simply tell people someone else's life as if it was their own past life." This is how demons fool Westerners into believing things—such as reincarnation—that are novel to the Western mind. Since Scripture clearly says that "man is destined to die once, and after that to face judgment" (Heb. 9:27), there is no scriptural allowance for anyone to be reborn into another earthly existence. God has created each of us unique and eternal. The battle over reincarnation, as with ancestor practices, is primarily a battle for the truth in opposition to Satan's lies. A first step toward winning such a truth encounter, however, is usually a power encounter to rid the person of demonic squatters who are perpetuating lies from within the person.

Conclusion.

In whatever aspect of spiritual warfare we are engaged, we are to seek to experience Jesus and the power of his resurrection (Phil. 3:10), learning what the enemy's schemes are

(2 Cor. 2:11), and waging against him the "good fight" (2 Tim. 4:7). Equipping us to defeat the enemy, Jesus, our Leader in spiritual warfare, gives us the "power and authority to drive out all demons and to cure diseases" (Luke 9:1; Matt. 10:8), promises that "anyone who has faith in me will do what I have been doing" (John 14:12), sends us into the world as the Father sent him (John 20:21), and plans to "crush Satan under [our] feet" (Rom. 16:20).

■ **Bibliography:** N. Anderson, *The Bondage Breaker* (1990) ■ C. Arnold, *Three Crucial Questions about Spiritual Warfare* (1997) ■ M. Bubeck, *The Adversary* (1975) ■ idem, *Overcoming the Adversary* (1984) ■ J. Dawson, *Taking Our Cities for God* (1989) ■ C. F. Dickason, *Demon Possession and the Christian* (1987) ■ D. Hunt and T. A. McMahon, *The Seduction of Christianity* (1985) ■ J. Kallas, *The Satanward View* (1966) ■ G. D. Kinnaman, *Overcoming the Dominion of Darkness* (1990) ■ C. H. Kraft, *Behind Enemy Lines* (1994) ■ idem, *Christianity with Power* (1989) ■ idem, *Deep Wounds, Deep Healing* (1993) ■ idem, *Defeating Dark Angels* (1992) ■ idem, *I Give You Authority* (1997) ■ M. G. Kraft, *Understanding Spiritual Power* (1995) ■ E. Murphy, *Handbook for Spiritual Warfare* (1992) ■ G. Otis Jr., *The Last of the Giants* (1991) ■ J. Penn-Lewis, *War on the Saints* (9th ed., 1973) ■ E. Rommen, ed., *Spiritual Power and Missions* (1995) ■ D. Sherman, *Spiritual Warfare for Every Christian* (1990) ■ E. Silvoso, *That None Should Perish* (1994) ■ A. R. Tippett, *Introduction to Missiology* (1987) ■ idem, *People Movements in Southern Polynesia* (1971) ■ C. P. Wagner, *Confronting the Powers* (1996) ■ idem, *Engaging the Enemy* (1991) ■ idem, *Warfare Prayer* (1992) ■ T. Warner, *Spiritual Warfare* (1991) ■ T. White, *The Believer's Guide to Spiritual Warfare* (1990). ■ C. H. Kraft

SPIRITUALITY, PENTECOSTAL AND CHARISMATIC

Spirituality refers to a cluster of acts and sentiments that are informed by the beliefs and values that characterize a specific religious community. *Liturgy* describes what all members of a community do together when assembled for worship. *Theology* defines systematized, ordinarily written, reflections on religious experience. *Spirituality*, by contrast, focuses on the pietistic habits of ordinary individuals. The vagueness and elasticity of the word *spirituality* rise in large part from the wide variety in which worshipers express themselves, even in a single religious communion.

Spirituality as the *gestalt* of piety is, however, not native to the pentecostal tradition. Pentecostals more easily use the adjective *spiritual* than they do the abstract noun. They more easily speak of persons than of deeds or manners, as spiritual (or unspiritual). In the far less frequent times when "spirituality" *is* used in ordinary pentecostal conversation, it applies not to what people do but to how religious they are. Statements like the following are typical: "Of course she can teach the class; she's very spiritual." "I'm greatly impressed by the new pastor's spirituality; he's deep in the Lord, a real man of

God." In pentecostal usage, spirituality admits of degrees. "Consecrated" and "consecration" are close synonyms (no doubt acquired from the Pentateuchal vocabulary of ritual sacrifice in the KJV, with antecedents in the Holiness movement), but these terms are now archaic in the pentecostal tradition and seem not to have been picked up at all in the charismatic movement.

This article describes facets of pentecostal and charismatic spirituality, chiefly as expressed in the North American context, and with an effort to observe nuances in practice between pentecostals and charismatics where that can be done. There is a geography of spirituality: this analysis needs adjustment for other cultures.

Five *implicit values* govern pentecostal spirituality:

1. By far the most pervasive is the worth accorded to individual *experience*. Included are not only religious feeling, but also emotions of joy or sorrow. Pentecostals consider personal experience the arena of true religion. The point is well made by Lesslie Newbigin in *Household of God* (1954), where he describes three broad approaches to Christian realities. (1) Protestants view religion as belief, orthodoxy, doctrinal assent—a matter of the intellect. (2) The Catholic churches (he includes highly liturgical Protestant groups, not merely the Roman Catholic Church) think rather in terms of obedience, participation, and religious acts. (3) Members of the pentecostal churches—not at all limited to the classical pentecostal churches, about which he says he knew little when he wrote—achieve religious satisfaction through personal experience, and this always brings an emphasis on the Holy Spirit. Classical pentecostals are of the third variety, and charismatics in the mainstream churches add a significant experiential component to the traditional intellectual or volitional character of their various Christian traditions.

The bent toward emotional experience among pentecostals may account in part for occasional moral failure among them, since religious and sexual experience are among the deepest of human experiences. But there is little concrete evidence to suggest that moral failure among pentecostals exceeds that in any other Christian tradition—except in visibility, given the prominence of pentecostal ministers among the televangelists.

Ministerial ineptitude, doctrinal deviation, divergent mores—these and more can long be tolerated or even forgiven if profound personal experience prevails, known usually from shared personal testimony. A quoted aphorism often heard in pentecostal circles runs this way: "The person with an experience is never at the mercy of another person with a doctrine." Of course such an emphasis lays pentecostal piety open to charges of individualism, narcissism, or elitism. But most are only barely conscious of these charges and would hardly consider them faults if they were aware of them. Pentecostals and charismatics say, "You have to experience it for yourself." "God has no grandchildren," pentecostal leader ▶David du Plessis tirelessly insisted—meaning you cannot hand on to another your own experience of God. Seekers must always find God in their own experience.

2. *Orality* as a fundamental quality of pentecostal piety has been emphasized especially by Walter Hollenweger (1983, 1986). No one can rightly appreciate pentecostal spirituality merely by reading what pentecostals have written. Approaching their fourth generation, pentecostals are only now beginning to produce substantial theological literature. They write tracts and simple studies for purposes of evangelism. Their first scholars have been historians tempted by triumphalist apologetic. Expected behaviors like avoidance of gambling or alcoholic beverages might go entirely unwritten. Nonetheless, by a lively oral tradition a newcomer soon learns.

As classical pentecostalism moves from a sect to a church, the subculture will of course become more literary. It is likely that the astonishing success of pentecostalism in Third World evangelization, as well as in nonliterate cultures, can in large part be attributed to a shared reliance on the spoken word.

3. *Spontaneity* is prized in pentecostal piety. The Holy Spirit guides worship and leads each believer, and the Spirit moves unpredictably (John 3:8). All the members expect anyone of the local assembly to follow the Spirit's leading and to do so at once. Hence, printed orders of service for public worship are not provided—though something of the sort can now be found in large metropolitan pentecostal churches, but only in the hands of the organist, the pianist, and the supervising minister. Church bulletins, increasingly used, usually contain the week's announcements and only rarely give an order of service. In small-group prayer meetings the leaders and the Spirit are in charge. Usually such gatherings give much time for "waiting on God," and no one is offended—indeed, the leader may be cheered by perceived progress—if someone leads out in a prayer, a Scripture reading, or a musical chorus that everyone knows by heart. Long pauses, as in

Worship during youth camp in Singapore.

the Quaker tradition, are uncommon in pentecostal spirituality, for pentecostals do not consider silence a virtue (Baer, 1976; Malz, 1985).

The mix of spontaneity with the unpredictable and sometimes uncontrolled urges of the Spirit call for the best resources of pastoral guidance. From time to time, if leadership in worship sags, Pauline fears of perceived madness (1 Cor. 14:23) are warranted.

4. *Otherworldliness* is a fading value among North American pentecostals, given the upward slope of their economic progress and the surrounding cultural affluence. Mainline charismatics, mostly from upper-middle-class circles, less clearly reflect otherworldliness though they share with pentecostals the sort of simple dualism otherworldliness implies. "This world is not my home" is heard less frequently now among pentecostals, and it would be unimaginable among most charismatics. The social and economic deprivation of the earlier pentecostals no doubt accented the contrast between their own straits and the pearly gates and golden streets of heaven.

Yet pentecostal otherworldliness reflects an authentic biblical motif, one more Johannine (1 John 2:15–17, 19; 4:4–6) than Pauline (1 Cor. 5:9–10). Such an outlook controls pentecostal cosmology: the *real* world is the eternal one, "up there" in heaven. It informs their eschatology: Christ will at any moment return to set at right what is wrong. It accounts for the unripened social conscience of pentecostals linked with their worldly pessimism: "The world and its desires pass away" (1 John 2:17). Among them, social justice is a part of eschatological hope, far less so a part of the church's mission. Cultural pessimism makes the correction of social ills inappropriate as a feature of any contemporary ecclesiastical agenda and accounts for earlier pentecostal mores; their women were not to use cosmetics, since it is the business of the church to "come out from them and be separate" (2 Cor. 6:14–7:1; cf. Isa. 52:11). They were not to engage in worldly activities—mixed swimming, theater attendance, card playing. Most available photos of William J. Seymour, the Azusa Street pastor, show him without a tie, which by many early pentecostals was thought "worldly." Otherworldliness linked with experiential individualism makes it nearly impossible for pentecostals to comprehend the notion of structural or systemic evil—except to say that the devil controls unredeemed human society.

5. Finally, a commitment to *biblical authority* characterizes both the pentecostal and the charismatic sectors of the church. It is important to distinguish biblical *authority* from biblical *inspiration*. Pentecostal discussions about biblical inerrancy provide a case study in theology as learned behavior. It is the authoritative role of Scripture that more naturally characterizes pentecostalism than intricate arguments about the inerrant quality of the biblical text. Yet when the question was raised by evangelical neighbors, pentecostals readily joined the more conservative inerrantist party—a logical deduction from the divinely originated written Word of God. This important nuance finds illustration in the doctrinal formulation of the American Assemblies of God. When this formulation was first produced in 1916, its opening statement concerning Scripture read this way: "The Bible is the inspired Word of God, a revelation from God to man, the infallible rule of faith and conduct, and is superior to conscience and reason, but not contrary to reason (2 Tim. 3:15, 16; 1 Pet. 2:2)." In 1961 the Assemblies of God sealed its postwar acceptance among evangelicals by retrofitting the statement on Scripture so as to read, "The Scriptures, both the Old and New Testaments, are verbally inspired of God and are the revelation of God to man, the infallible authoritative rule of faith and conduct (2 Tim. 3:15–17; 1 Thess. 2:13; 2 Pet. 1:21)." Noteworthy is the insertion of the word "verbally" ("verbal inspiration" was an evangelical catchword at the time) and the unexplained deletion of the marvelous phrase "... superior to conscience and reason, but not contrary to reason." A clear mark of a classical pentecostal is the ubiquitous presence of a Bible in hand, well marked.

The lofty regard for biblical authority, coupled with an inclination to take the words of Scripture at face value, illuminates both beliefs and practices that occur within pentecostalism. The emergence of the doctrinal curio present in the ▶"Jesus' Name" or "Jesus Only" species of (Oneness) pentecostalism, a neglected sister to establishment pentecostalism, which shuns the group, presents a case in point. Denial of the Trinity, assertion that "Jesus" is God's true name and is himself the one God, and rebaptism "in the name of Jesus only"— all these emerge from the plain fact that in every place where water baptism is mentioned in the book of Acts the biblical text specifies that the baptism was "in the name of Jesus." Similarly, if speaking in tongues is described in Scripture as an acknowledged and approved part of Christianity, pentecostals can see no good reason to eliminate it from contemporary spirituality. Indeed, they think it their providential role in history to restore to the church that long-neglected "experience."

Many of the marginal eccentricities of pentecostalism, both what the pentecostals believe and what they experience, can be understood as contemporized forms of biblical precedents. These include out-of-the-body experiences (2 Cor. 12:2–3), visits by angels (Gen. 6:7–12; Acts 5:17–20), hearing an audible voice (1 Sam. 3:2–9; Acts 9:4), visionary tours of heaven or hell (Rev. 1:11; 4:1—all remarkably similar to a species of apocalyptic literature common in sectarian Judaism during NT times). Even miraculous Spirit transport (Acts 8:39–40; cf. Gen. 5:24) can readily be found in the literature of pentecostal testimony or on the pentecostal and charismatic television talk shows—where orality and experience easily converge.

Beliefs such as the prosperity teaching (Christians should be wealthy because God is) or positive confession (the believer participates in God's creative authority: say it, aloud and with faith, and you'll have it) draw from the same biblical sources, though invariably with a highly selective hermeneutic.

These five implicit values—experience, orality, spontaneity, otherworldliness, and biblical authority—combine variously to yield a constellation of characteristic practices found in pentecostal and/or charismatic spirituality quite apart from the central features of speaking in tongues, the baptism in the Holy Spirit, and prayer for divine healing. The style of *prayer and praise* is instructive. Quite usual is collective oral prayer, all praying at once, mostly vernacular or mostly glossolalic or some mix of the two. This pattern expresses the personal experience of each. Such collective group prayer is usually cued by a leader, but it can emerge spontaneously—in which cases glossolalia often predominates. On the whole, collective prayer in pentecostal services is louder and more emotionally expressive than in charismatic circles. ▸*Fasting* often accompanies prayer, but it is rarely mandated for congregations.

The *raising of hands* in joint or individual prayer reflects literal response to biblical precedents (Ex. 17:11–12) and commands (1 Tim. 2:8). One or two hands may be used. Pentecostals are more likely to extend the arms fully upward, palms forward. Charismatics, again more restrained, often extend arms from the waist, with bent elbows, palms upward.

Proxy prayer appears in charismatic small groups. It hardly ever occurred in earlier classical pentecostalism, but it appears increasingly in contemporary pentecostalism as a learned technique acquired from charismatics. There is no biblical precedent for the action nor any injunction against it. An interested third party sits on a chair in the midst of the gathered Christians. The ▸*laying on of hands* might be done by all present in groups of up to 6 to 10 members or by a spontaneously assembled representative delegation of two or three persons. The idea is that prayer here is offered on behalf of an identified person not present and quite possibly not interested in the prayers offered. In some instances, more often in charismatic than in pentecostal groups, hands will not be laid fully on the persons who are objects of prayer but intentionally held five or six inches above the shoulders; the reason for this, if not social discretion, is unclear.

In both pentecostal and charismatic circles, leading ministers may ask gathered congregation members to extend their arms toward a person or a group during prayer. This serves as a sort of collective, symbolic laying on of hands. Finally, some pentecostal televangelists ask viewers to touch the television set as a "point of contact." *Touch* is an important, though largely unrecognized, feature of pentecostal and charismatic spirituality. "He touched me," they gratefully sing, or in hope: "Reach out and touch the Lord as he goes by" (cf. Mark 5:25–34). Laying on of hands frequently accompanies prayer for the pentecostal baptism in the Holy Spirit. But there is no universal requirement for this practice among pentecostals and charismatics, probably because of the clear precedent at Acts 10:44–45, when the Holy Spirit fell on those gathered at the household of Cornelius while Peter was still speaking—with no laying on of hands.

Expressive personal experience occurs when an individual pentecostal believer engages in ▸*dancing in the Spirit.* Always individually done, never in couples, always unplanned and never scheduled, at almost any point in the service—during hymns or during the sermon, a believer so moved will leave the seat and move up and down the aisles of the church, eyes often closed, arms usually uplifted—lost in abandon to the worship of God. This practice more often appears among black pentecostals, where usually purer forms of pentecostal worship survive. Some charismatics have intentionally inserted liturgical dance into planned services, but "scheduled" and "liturgical" dance would be twice embarrassing to classical pentecostals—on grounds both of their preference for spontaneity and their Johannine avoidance of "dance" as worldly entertainment. Only "dancing in the Spirit" has legitimacy among pentecostals: Was it not David himself who "danced before the LORD with all his might" as the Scriptures say (2 Sam. 6:14)?

Like dancing in the Spirit, which would be unlikely (but not impossible) if alone in prayer, some features of pentecostal spirituality appear only in corporate settings. The most colorful and lively of these is a *Jericho march,* so named from the march of the children of Israel seven times around the city of Jericho till the walls fell down (Josh. 6:1–27). In an atmosphere of high enthusiasm, a congregant may rise and make for the aisles, possibly inviting others to join. Around the perimeter of the place of assembly they go, gathering more worshipers till a full column is formed. Quite possibly many in the congregation who are able and willing join in as do the platform ministers. During the march, there is much singing, maybe some shouting (as happened also in the Bible, and at the bidding of the leader: Josh. 6:10, 16, 20). The whole affair might last as long as an hour or two, and it might even displace the preaching. Afterward the marchers return to their seats and the service goes on. At times a Jericho march begins with one person dancing in the Spirit, who is joined by another, then another, till the whole group is caught up. The corporate jubilation and joy of the Jericho march, which is always spontaneous and unrehearsed, affords stunning contrast to routine liturgies denounced regularly by the pentecostals—who never thought it wrong for worship to be fun. Anything like a Jericho march among upper-class charismatics would suggest classical pentecostal influence.

The most likely scene for a Jericho march is the *camp meeting*. Begun by Kentucky Presbyterians in the early 1800s and used widely among the 19th-century Holiness churches, this venerable remnant of the frontier still widely appears among North American classical pentecostals (but not among charismatics, who have moved to metropolitan four-star hotel ballrooms). "Camp meetings," with a bit of forgivable metaphor, now occur at velvet-seated, multimillion-dollar pentecostal megachurches. As recently as the 1950s tents were used. Later simple cabins were constructed. But these are now being upgraded to year-round cottages. A large wooden "tabernacle" seating up to 3,000 would be the center of activity. Bare earthen floors covered with straw or with sweet-smelling wood chips from a nearby sawmill have been replaced increasingly by poured concrete. There might be a morning Bible teacher and an evening evangelist. The camp might run one or two weeks, sometimes longer, with a succession of ministers and campers. Red checkerboard tablecloths are draped over long tables where, when the bell rings—a bell rescued from some decaying rural church—all queue up for tasty meals in common, prepared by the industrious laywomen of the camp. Afternoons allow peaceful walks through the surrounding country woods setting, or, for some adventurous boys, a trip to a not-too-distant swimming hole.

Camp meetings of the last century were also frequent settings for the pentecostal "wave offering" (after Lev. 23:9–10, 20–21 and similar references, with a permitted hermeneutical wink). At the direction of the leading minister, men and women would retrieve from purse or pocket a fresh hand-

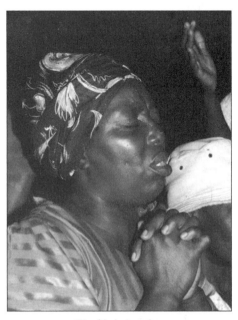

Worship in Jamaica.

kerchief and, to the accompaniment of hearty singing, "present a wave offering to the Lord." Battlefield imagery prevailed, and the crowd waved, not in surrender, but to welcome symbolically the Coming King until whose impending arrival they would sing with triumphant resolve:

> "Hold the fort, for I am coming!"
> Jesus signals still:
> Wave the answer back to heaven,
>   "By Thy grace we will!"

For many pentecostals the summer camp meetings were the occasions when they were baptized in the Spirit, perhaps also being baptized in water at a nearby creek. *Altar services* at the camps could go on through the night, yielding fresh testimonies of deepened personal experience with the Lord that might be given in the services the next day. Pentecostal services often end, unnervingly to the unaccustomed, with people going in two directions: some toward the altar for prayer, others out the rear door.

Public pentecostal services, whether at a camp meeting or a local church, form the occasions for other practices common to pentecostal spirituality. One of those that occurred from the beginning was *"falling under the power,"* being ►"slain in the Spirit"—a virtual faint, almost always supine, sometimes accompanied by soft glossolalic prayer, sometimes conspicuously silent, sometimes with arms fully raised from the lying position accompanied with loud prayer. In this posture many early pentecostals received the baptism in the Holy Spirit and, for the first time, spoke in tongues. In later pentecostalism, "falling under the power" came to be associated with certain ministers credited with having a gift that led to the phenomenon. (It flourished under ►Kathryn Kuhlman as early as the mid and late 1940s, for example.) This practice occurs also among charismatics, who have renamed it "resting in the Spirit" to escape the militaristic imagery.

Expressiveness among pentecostals and, to a lesser degree, among charismatics makes a playful appearance in the use of what may be called *sacred expletives*—happy exclamations like "Glory to God!" "Hallelujah!" "Thank you, Jesus!" often sprinkled through pentecostal rhetoric. These are at points comparable to the "yeas" heard at ball games, yet they have their origin in experiential piety.

A *word of* ►*knowledge* may occur in the public gatherings of either pentecostals or charismatics. Going beyond the strict exegetical demands of the listed spiritual gift of that name (1 Cor. 12:8, but cf. 14:26; John 1:48–50), these Christians allow that a minister (a word of knowledge "could happen to any believer," but certain ministers regularly use the gift) may be told by God certain information about one or more people present at a meeting. Several variant settings have emerged. A minister so gifted may describe a medical disorder or a specific ailment and say that if that sufferer will identify himself

The 1983 Norwood crusade in Jamaica.

or herself, God will heal the condition. In certain charismatic Roman Catholic circles, a different sociology has been observed. A lay congregant will rise, describe a hazy vision including the gender and approximate age of a person, then describe a condition of need not limited to physical ills, and then be seated. The clustered group leaders (plural leadership is characteristic of Roman Catholic prayer group leadership) may ask for self-identification and suggest a group nearby gather for immediate prayer.

In one regrettable case in the late 1980s an eager evangelist fraudulently "aided" the Spirit through use of a tiny radio receiver in his ear tuned to a concealed transmitter operated by his wife, who interviewed unknowing attendees and fed the information to her husband. Such a ruse cannot fully account for the surprising accuracy of these "words of knowledge." But misuse or abuse of the gift is an occupational hazard in pentecostal spirituality.

The authority of biblical precedent (Acts 19:12) also lies behind the long use in pentecostalism (not observed among charismatics) of *anointed prayer cloths*. In a local church a concerned family member might present a handkerchief after describing someone in particular need. Following congregational prayer, as part of a regular service (or, perhaps, private prayer with the pastor, and maybe with the elders also) the sponsor carries the cloth to the needy one in hopeful imitation of the biblical precedent. Pentecostal evangelists, in a few unfortunate instances, have huckstered anointed prayer cloths available through the mail "for a gift of a minimum of [so many] dollars to the ministry."

Biblical precedent and command (Mark 16:18; Acts 28:3–6) lie behind the bizarre practice among certain isolated

pentecostal congregations in the Appalachians where ▸*serpent handling* is practiced (La Barre, 1962). Deaths still occur. The practice is often accompanied by intentional *drinking of poison*—strychnine, usually—again "because the Bible says we should do it" (Mark 16:18, a passage regarded by a large majority of biblical scholars as a 2d-century addition to the original gospel but present in the KJV most familiar to classical pentecostals). Organized pentecostalism deplores these practices, and the charismatics only read about them.

Of course, pentecostals and charismatics *speak in tongues*, both in corporate gatherings and in private prayer. Charismatics as a whole are less emotional in their use of ▸*glossolalia*. The noise level and the appearance of possession vary widely with the broad cultural differences among pentecostals. Even the deaf speak in tongues, though that is rarely observed and has gone virtually unnoticed in research.

Holy laughter occurred in early pentecostalism. A believer, ordinarily praying at the altar, may fall into spasms of laughter, lasting minutes or upwards of an hour. This is understood as an expression of joy in the Lord. There is no social pressure to generate or repeat the experience, and it is rare today.

Prayer for *divine* ▸*healing* regularly marks pentecostal and charismatic services. Charismatic mainstreamers, given their backgrounds, more realistically regard suffering. Wise pentecostal pastors deal regularly with failed healings, the consequence of an imbalanced call, often via the one-way electronic church, for "faith": "overbelief" is a constant threat in pentecostal spirituality (Parker, 1980).

Leg-lengthening, the act of bringing a person's shorter leg to the length of the other, when both are extended, gives the appearance of an instant miracle. The practice seems to have originated after WWII, and perhaps most instances of it occur among independent charismatics. But it also appears in some "third wave" or neocharismatic pentecostalized evangelical prayer groups.

▸*Exorcisms* are not frequent anywhere, but they are serious and demanding when they occur. They most often take place among those independent pentecostals and charismatics who foster a sort of *pandemonism*—a belief that not only sins but faults and even bad habits are caused by demons, which must be expelled. Such environments on the distant margins of organized pentecostalism at times generate bizarre practices. In a Central California valley in the early 1970s attendees at independent pentecostal meetings, where much was made of demons as the cause of life's ills, were asked to bring small brown paper bags to the services. At the right moment, the evangelist directed them to cough and spit into the bag—producing an exorcism by expectoration.

Dreams and, especially, *visions* give another example of the power of biblical example (Acts 9:10–18). One sector of the charismatic movement, a sector that could be called the "The Jungian school" (Agnes Sanford popularized the

Part of a group of 200 converts in Zimbabwe, kneeling in the grass while dedicating their lives to Christ.

approach) takes dreams very seriously and finds in the intricate psychological writings of Carl Jung a theoretic basis (Kelsey, 1964, 1968). *Inner healing* was an understandable development that emerged out of this school. Classical pentecostals, on the other hand, are suspicious of psychology and with it such "inner healing." They neither need nor want any theory for a practice that is already found in the Bible (Acts 16:9–10), and among them visions outnumber dreams, neither of which are frequent, however. Some report visionary trips to heaven (or hell) and back, and itinerant ministries are born of such experiences.

All these may seem a curious conglomeration of practices cited as features of spirituality. But each springs from the values listed earlier. Pentecostals and charismatics are Christians who value the Bible highly, take their commitment with utmost seriousness, prizing the spontaneity of life in the Spirit and conveying all of this through oral testimonies and "sharing." They are members of a Christian subculture whose burgeoning numbers already exceed the total membership of Protestantism and who, in the third millennium, are expected to predominate in the new church of the Southern Hemisphere.

■ **Bibliography:** R. A. Baer Jr., "Quaker Silence, Catholic Liturgy, and Pentecostal Science—Some Functional Similarities," in R. P. Spittler, ed., *Perspectives on the New Pentecostalism* (1976) ■ W. Benn and M. Burkill, "A Theological and Pastoral Critique of the Teachings of John Wimber," *Churchman* 101 (1987) ■ K. Brown, *Holy Ground, Too: The Camp Meeting Family Tree* (1997) ■ E. Coppin, *Slain in the Spirit: Fact or Fiction?* (1976) ■ D. Covington, *Salvation on Sand Mountain: Snake Handling and Redemption in Southern Appalachia* (1995) ■ H. Cox, *Fire from Heaven: The Rise of Pentecostal Spirituality and the Reshaping of Religion in the Twenty-First Century* (1995) ■ R. Cummings, *Gethsemane* (1944) ■ C. Farah, *From the Pinnacle of the Temple* (n.d.; charismatic critique of the "positive confession" movement) ■ J. W. Follette, *Broken Bread* (1957) ■ S. Frodsham, *Spirit-Filled, -Led, and -Taught* (n.d.) ■ D. Gee, *After Pentecost* (1945) ■ idem, *Concerning Spiritual Gifts* (1937) ■ idem, *The Fruit of the Spirit* (1928) ■ idem, *Keeping in Touch* (1951) ■ idem, *The Ministry Gifts of Christ* (1930) ■ idem, *Pentecost* (1932) ■ idem, *Trophimus I Left Sick: Our Problems of Divine Healing* (1952) ■ J. Gunstone, *The Charismatic Prayer Group: A Handbook* (1976) ■ W. J. Hollenweger, "Pentecostal Research: Problems and Promises," in Charles E. Jones, *A Guide to the Study of the Pentecostal Movement,* vol. 1 (1983), vii–ix ■ idem, "Pentecostals and the Charismatic Movement," in C. Jones et al., eds., *The Study of Spirituality* (1986) ■ D. Hunt and T. A. McMahon, *Seduction of Christianity* (1985) ■ C. A. Johnston, *The Frontier Camp Meeting* (1955) ■ M. Kelsey, *Dreams: The Dark Speech of the Spirit* (1968) ■ idem, *Tongue Speaking* (1964) ■ W. LaBarre, *They Shall Take Up Serpents: Psychology of the Southern Snake Handling Cult* (1962) ■ S. Land, *Pentecostal Spirituality: A Passion for the Kingdom* (1993; use with review by Harvey Cox in *JPT* 5 [1994]) ■ D. N. Malz, "Joyful Noise and Reverent Silence: The Significance of Noise in Pentecostal Worship," in D. Tannen and M. Saville-Truike, eds., *Perspectives on Silence* (1985) ■ D. McConnell, *A Different Gospel* (1988) ■ F. McNutt, *Healing* (1974) ■ idem, *Overcome by the Spirit* (1998; on "resting" or "falling" in the Spirit) ■ L. Newbigin, *The Household of God* (1954) ■ L. Parker as told to D. Tanner, *We Let Our Son Die* (1980) ■ M. Pearlman, *The Heavenly Gift* (1935) ■ C. M. Robeck Jr., "Growing Up Pentecostal," *Theology News and Notes* (Pasadena, CA) 35 (Mar. 1988) ■ A. Sanford, *The Healing Gifts of the Spirit* (1966) ■ R. P. Spittler, "Scripture and the Theological Enterprise: View from a Big Canoe," in R. K. Johnston, ed., *The Use of the Bible in Theology: Evangelical Options* (1985) ■ D. Wilkerson, with J. and E. Sherrill, *The Cross and the Switchblade* (1963) ■ R. Wise, ed., *The Church Divided: The Holy Spirit and a Spirit of Seduction* (1986).

■ R. P. Spittler

SPITTLER, RUSSELL PAUL (1931–). New Testament scholar, theologian, and academic administrator. "Russ" Spittler was reared in the Assemblies of God (AG) in Pittsburgh, PA. He began his ministerial education at Southeastern College (Lakeland, FL), where he received a diploma in 1953.

He continued work in the field of religion at Florida Southern College (A.B., 1954). Before pursuing masters-level theological degrees at Wheaton College Graduate School (M.A., 1957) and Gordon-Conwell Theological Seminary (B.D., 1958), he married Bobbie Watson in 1955.

Spittler began his teaching career as a member of the faculty of Central Bible College in Springfield, MO (1958–62). While employed there, he was ordained by the AG and served as a book editor for ⸢Gospel Publishing House. Spittler began his military service as a U.S. Naval Reserve Chaplain in 1963 and attended the U.S. Naval Chaplains' School in Newport, RI (1965). He skillfully wove together a life of academic pursuits, compelling classroom performance, and pastoral ministry in the military while teaching at Central Bible College. In 1965 he returned to the Boston area, where he undertook study toward a Ph.D at Harvard University. For two years he pursued his work in New Testament and early Christian origins, while teaching denominational standards as an adjunct at Gordon-Conwell.

In 1967 Spittler moved to Southern California College, where he served on the New Testament faculty (1967–76) while writing his dissertation on the pseudepigraphal *Testament of Job*. Spittler's translation of and notes on the *Testament of Job* are now the standard in his field of study. He received his degree in 1971.

NT scholar Russell P. Spittler, now provost and vice president for academic affairs at Fuller Theological Seminary, Pasadena, CA.

The 1970s were years in which Spittler was active within the AG academic sphere, but he was also sought out to provide guidance to those within the broader charismatic renewal. While serving at Southern California College, Spittler was invited to participate in the newly formed International Roman Catholic–Pentecostal ⸢Dialogue. He participated during the first Quinquennium, in 1972 and again in 1974. As a professor of New Testament, Spittler was soon drafted to serve as department chair before becoming academic dean at the college (1973–76). His academic expertise, sound wisdom, and close proximity to ⸢Melodyland School of Theology made him a natural to serve on the board of regents during the peak of that school's short but vital life (1974–81). He also became a regular feature at the Glencoe meetings—annual events that brought pentecostals and charismatics together for prayer and planning.

Spittler attended the founding meeting of the Society for Pentecostal Studies (SPS) and in 1973 served as president of SPS. The papers presented at that meeting became one of the few collections from SPS that were formally published. He edited the volume that attempted to set forth *Perspectives on the New Pentecostalism* (1976).

Spittler's participation in SPS has been formative for scores of younger scholars. He provided a thoughtful model of the churchman-scholar when he served as a columnist for the cutting-edge and often controversial *Agora*, a magazine of opinion published by leading pentecostal thinkers. He has laid out many potential dissertation projects that he believed were important for pentecostal scholars to pursue, and a quick survey of those projects will demonstrate something of the profound effect he has had on American pentecostal scholarship. During the early 1990s, he served as secretary of SPS, and his seasoned administrative hand placed SPS on a sound financial and administrative footing.

In 1973 Spittler was invited to teach a course on AG polity at Fuller Theological Seminary. He was invited back to serve Fuller as associate dean for academic systems in the School of Theology (1976–86). In 1986 he became founding director of the ⸢David J. du Plessis Center for Christian Spirituality at Fuller. He worked closely with ⸢Du Plessis, making sure that the Du Plessis vision that encompassed pentecostalism, charismatic renewal, and ecumenism was given proper attention. He began to dabble in issues surrounding pentecostal spirituality, and since 1986 has become a leading expert in the field.

In 1993 Spittler returned full-time to the classroom as professor of New Testament. Specializing in the spirituality found in 1 Corinthians and the epistle to the Hebrews, he has trained a generation of pastors and church leaders from a variety of traditions in the values he found in these books.

During the summer of 1996, a major change in the administration of Fuller Theological Seminary opened up a new challenge to Spittler. He was drafted to serve as the provost and vice president for academic affairs, overseeing all academic programs in the three schools on the Pasadena campus of the seminary, as well as the various extended educational opportunities on a variety of other campuses around the world.

In 1993 Spittler was appointed a corresponding editor of *Christianity Today*. In recent years the AG has used him to meet a range of needs in the fields of education and theological development. He is the author of several books and articles, among them *Cults and Isms* (1962); *God the Father* (1976); *The Church* (1977); and "The Testament of Job," in J. H. Charlesworth, ed., *The Old Testament Pseudepigrapha*, 2 vols. (1983).   ■ C. M. Robeck Jr.

SQUIRE, FREDERICK HENRY (1904–62). British pastor, evangelist, and educator. While serving as a pastor in England's nascent Assemblies of God (Assemblies of God in Great Britain and Ireland [AGGBI]), Squire felt called to enter itinerant evangelism. Leaving his pastorate in Kirkby-in-Ashfield, England, in 1932, he headed out on the itineration trail.

A successful revival campaign in Northampton prompted him to conduct, with his Full Gospel Testimony Revival Party, campaigns throughout the South Midlands and elsewhere. In these meetings, Squire emphasized conversion, yet divine healing also took center stage. Reports of healings circulated throughout the area, drawing considerable crowds. These campaigns contributed to pentecostalism's development in Britain: in their wake numerous congregations were birthed.

The Full Gospel Testimony's (FGT) headquarters was first located at Southend, but after the war moved to Leamington. Most of those fledgling congregations associated with the AGGBI; however, the FGT became its own separate entity with Squire as its president for life. The *Full Gospel Testimony* (1935–52) served as its official paper. Throughout, Squire maintained considerable control over FGT's churches, which conflicted with the AGGBI's insistence on local autonomy. In 1938 a split occurred. Less than two decades later, in the early 1950s, the FGT disbanded, and most of the churches merged with the AGGBI or Elim Pentecostal Church.

After WWII Squire organized extensive relief work, especially in the Netherlands, which brought recognition to the pentecostal movement in Europe. He founded the International Bible Training Institute in 1947, for which he is perhaps best known. The school was first located in Leamington but later moved to Burgess Hill, where it has endured as a nondenominational institution. The school attracts students from Europe and around the world and has educated many pentecostal leaders, including the current general superintendent of the Assemblies of God in Italy, ▸Francesco Toppi.

■ **Bibliography:** D. Allen, "Signs and Wonders: The Origins, Growth, Development and Significance of Assemblies of God in Great Britain and Ireland 1900–1980" (Ph.D. diss., U. of London, 1990) ▪ D. Gee, *Wind and Flame* (1967) ▪ F. H. Squire, *Operation Relief* (n.d.).   ■ E. J. Gitre

STANPHILL, IRA (1914–93). ▸Assemblies of God minister, singer, and gospel songwriter. His contribution to gospel music, both in style and writing, is immense. He wrote more than 500 songs, including "Mansion over the Hilltop," "Suppertime," "Follow Me," "He Washed My Eyes with Tears," "Room at the Cross," "We'll Talk It Over," "You Can Have a Song in the Night," and "I Know Who Holds Tomorrow." Many of his songs were written as a result of deep personal trials, including divorce in his first marriage and later the death of his first wife. "Suppertime" was popularized by former Louisiana Governor Jimmie Davis; "Room at the Cross" has been heard for many years as a theme for the weekly *Revivaltime* broadcast. Stanphill was inducted into the Gospel Music Hall of Fame in 1981. His candid autobiography, *This Side of Heaven* (1983), gives the stories behind the writing of many of his more popular songs.

■ **Bibliography:** G. Gohr, "This Side of Heaven," *AGH* (Summer 1994).   ■ W. E. Warner

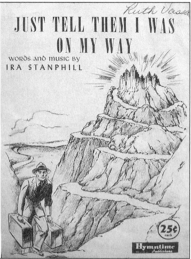

Sheet music of two of Ira Stanphill's best-loved songs.

STARK, EDMOND F. (1913–39). First Church of God (CG, Cleveland, TN) missionary to Angola. Stark, a native of Oklahoma, married Pearl Pickel, a former missionary to China and Liberia, who accompanied him to Angola in 1938. In Angola they went to Quanza Sol, a district where there were no Christians, no Bibles, and no schools. In Mar. 1939 Stark was stricken with malaria and died. The nearest missionary was two days away, and death came so suddenly that help never reached him. His death, however, had a dramatic effect on the missionary impulse of the CG. Eventually his work was salvaged and continued by others who were inspired by his sacrifice.

■ **Bibliography:** C. W. Conn, *Like a Mighty Army: A History of the Church of God* (1996) ■ idem, *Where the Saints Have Trod* (1959).
                                                                            ■ C. W. Conn

STEELBERG, WESLEY ROWLAND (1902–52). A boy preacher who grew up to become the general superintendent of the General Council of the ▸Assemblies of God (AG) (1949–52). Wesley Steelberg's parents had emigrated from Sweden. At the age of six he suffered from spinal meningitis and was given up to die but was healed.

Steelberg was converted in a small pentecostal church in Denver and later received the baptism in the Holy Spirit. After the family moved to Los Angeles, he began preaching at age 16 and was ordained the next year. He married Ruth Fisher, daughter of ▸Elmer Fisher, pastor of the Upper Room Mission in Los Angeles.

While pastoring in California, Steelberg helped organize what later became Christ's Ambassadors, the youth organization of the AG. He was the speaker for *Sermons in Song* and *Revivaltime* radio programs while he was general superintendent. He died after suffering a heart attack while ministering in Wales. Mrs. Steelberg later married ▸Howard Carter, former general superintendent of the Assemblies of God in Great Britain and Ireland.

■ **Bibliography:** "All for Jesus," *PE* (Aug. 10, 1952) ■ "Brother Steelberg Is with the Lord," *PE* (July 27, 1952) ■ L. Sumrall, *All for Jesus: The Life of Wesley R. Steelberg* (1955).   ■ W. E. Warner

STEIDEL, FLORENCE (1897–1962). Missionary to Liberia, nurse, and founder of a leper colony. Steidel was born in Illinois and raised in the Ozark Mountains of Arkansas and Missouri. During a vision and a dream one day in 1924, she was called to help the sick and dying in Africa and was shown the home in Liberia in which she would later live. She prepared for this call by obtaining nurses' training at Missouri Baptist Hospital (1924–28) and attending Southern Baptist Theological Seminary (1929–31). While staying at Mizpah Missionary Home (Assemblies of God [AG]) in New York,

New Hope Town, a leper colony founded by Florence Steidel in Liberia in 1947.

Steidel became acquainted with AG missionaries and received the baptism in the Spirit in 1934. She obtained a missionary appointment with the AG in 1935 and later studied at Central Bible College (CBC) when home on furlough in 1944. Upon arriving in 1935 at her first missionary assignment, a girls' school in Palipo, Liberia, Steidel immediately recognized the home of her 1924 dream. She knew she was where God called her. She worked for 12 years in this girls' school, which had been moved to Newaka, Liberia, before she started her leper colony.

Steidel is remembered for her work at New Hope Town, the leper colony she founded in 1947 with $100 and the labor

Mrs. Garlock, Florence Steidel, and Lettie Lewis at the entrance to New Hope Town.

of lepers. Over the next 15 years she oversaw the construction of 70 permanent buildings and the planting of 2,500 rubber trees to help the colony become self-sufficient. In addition, she was responsible in 1956 for the building of an 18-mile road connecting the colony to the nearest government road. New Hope Town housed and medically treated more than 800 lepers. It also had separate housing and educational facilities for the lepers' children who had not contracted leprosy. Usually it took four years for the people to be cured of their leprosy. Each year 100 were given "symptom free certificates," indicating that they had been symptom free for a year. Services were held each morning in a 1,000-seat chapel. Before people left New Hope Town, 90% had been saved and many had received the baptism in the Spirit.

Steidel built a Bible school in 1961; by 1962, 71 students were preparing for ministry. The development of New Hope Town was complicated by 380 inches of rain per year, by its inaccessibility, and by 50 tribal languages being spoken in the colony. Steidel received two honors for her work: Knight Official of the Humane Order of African Redemption, awarded by William V. S. Tubman, president of the Republic of Liberia, in 1957; and CBC Alumna of the Year in 1960.

■ **Bibliography:** R. F. Brock, "Florence Steidel, a Devoted Worker Who Gave Lepers New Hope," *PE* (May 27, 1962) ■ C. Carmichael, *New Hope Leprosy Mission* (c. 1959) ■ I. Spence, *These Are My People: Florence Steidel* (1961) ■ I. Winehouse, *The Assemblies of God: A Popular Survey* (1959).   ■ E. B. Robinson

STEINER, LEONHARD (1903–92).

Major figure in Swiss pentecostalism. Converted as a young man, Steiner heard a call to the ministry in 1923 and was baptized in the Spirit. He was a preacher in the Swiss Pentecostal Mission from 1927. Steiner founded the Basel assembly in 1929 and in 1945 became editor of *Verheissung des Vaters (Promise of the Father)* and missions secretary. He was led to convene the first Pentecostal World Conference in Zurich in 1947 and was unanimously elected its chairman. From 1939 on, Steiner rejected the two-stage view of new birth and Spirit baptism with the sign of tongues. One of the most ecumenical among European pentecostal leaders, he was chairman of a 1966 consultation between representatives of the World Council of Churches and some European pentecostals. Steiner is the author of *Mit Folgenden Zeichen (With Signs Following)*, a study of pentecostal history and doctrine published in 1954 but not reprinted due to his changed attitude toward the healing evangelists.   ■ P. D. Hocken

STEPHANOU, EUSEBIUS A. (1924–).

Charismatic priest of the Greek Orthodox Church. Stephanou was born in Fond du Lac, WI, in 1924, the son and grandson of priests. He graduated from high school in Detroit, MI, in 1942; received a B.A. degree from the University of Michigan; earned a B.D. from Holy Cross Greek Orthodox Seminary in Brookline, MA; received the S.T.M. from Nashotah House Seminary, Nashotah, WI; and earned a Th.D. from the General Theological Seminary, New York City. He took postdoctoral studies at the University of Athens, Greece.

Ordained a priest in Greece in 1953, Stephanou pastored Greek Orthodox churches in Ann Arbor, MI; Woburn, MA; Canton, OH; Chicago, IL; and Fort Wayne, IN. From 1955 to 1962 he served on the faculty of Holy Cross Greek Orthodox Seminary as professor of theology. He later taught in the department of theology at Notre Dame University as visiting professor (1967–68).

In 1968 Stephanou founded the Logos Ministry for Orthodox Renewal and began publication of the *Logos* monthly periodical. At that time he embarked on an itinerant ministry of evangelism among Orthodox Christians in the U.S. and abroad, including such countries as Greece, Australia, Cyprus, and Kenya. Increasingly aware of the dichotomy between orthodoxy in doctrine and orthodoxy in actual practice, he sensed a calling from God for reevangelization of Orthodox Christians.

In 1972 Stephanou received the baptism in the Holy Spirit, having been introduced to the charismatic renewal by fellow Orthodox priest Athanasius Emmert. Thereafter he has been actively involved in the Holy Spirit renewal. He soon was recognized inside and outside his church as a leader in the Orthodox charismatic renewal. Not only did he continue to publish the *Logos* magazine, but he also sponsored the first five annual Orthodox charismatic conferences between 1972 and 1978, and then again in 1986 and 1987. His communications center was located in Fort Wayne, IN, until 1988 when he relocated in Destin, FL.

Stephanou's ministry of evangelism has stressed an end-time message of salvation, healing, and deliverance. He has attempted to demonstrate to the worldwide Orthodox community that the charismatic renewal can find a natural home in the Orthodox Church, because it is the church par excellence that has been intrinsically charismatic for almost two millennia.

Stephanou's evangelical and prophetic outreach has met with misunderstanding and even the open opposition of the official Orthodox Church. He has been placed under suspension off and on since 1968. In 1986 he was notified that proceedings were in progress for the purpose of his defrocking; however, the petition of the Greek Orthodox Archdiocese of North and South America was turned down by the Ecumenical Patriarchate of Constantinople.

While numerous Orthodox priests have recanted their charismatic theology and practice, Eusebius Stephanou has courageously and vigorously continued his attempts to bring the renewal of the Holy Spirit to the Orthodox Church. In 1989 he opened the Orthodox Renewal Center of St. Symeon the New Theologian in Destin, FL, where he conducts an ongoing charismatic ministry and sponsors renewal conferences, a press, a journal *(The Orthodox Evangelist)*, as well as missions endeavors. A branch of the St. Symeon's Ministry has been operating in Kenya, East Africa, for several years.

Stephanou has authored *Belief and Practice in the Orthodox Church* (1965), *Charismatic Renewal in the Orthodox Church*

(1976), *The Worldwide Outpouring of the Holy Spirit* (in Greek) (1976), *Charisma and Gnosis in Orthodox Thought* (n.d.), *Desolation and Restoration in the Orthodox Church* (1977), *Pathway to Orthodox Renewal* (1978), *World Orthodoxy in Crisis* (1980), and *Renewal Pains in the Orthodox Church* (1982). He is also the author of numerous articles on the charismatic movement and historical pneumatology.

■ **Bibliography:** "Archdiocese Seeks to Defrock Priest," *The Greek Star: The Voice of Chicago's Hellenic Community* (May 15, 1986) ■ "'Charismatic' Priest May Be Defrocked," *The Illuminator: The Newspaper of the Greek Orthodox Diocese of Pittsburgh* 7 (56, 1986) ■ E. Stephanou, "End of Thirty Years" and "What Are We Doing to the Church?" *The Orthodox Evangelist* 30 (6, Nov. 1997) ■ Curriculum vitae supplied by Eusebius Stephanou ■ Letter from E. A. Stephanou to Rt. Rev. Philotheos, Titular Bishop of Meloa, Greek Orthodox Archdiocese, Mar. 27, 1987.   ■ S. M. Burgess

STEWART, LEON OTTO (1929–). Pastor, editor, and denominational official. Stewart was born in Pineville, FL, to two pioneer pentecostal pastors, John Wesley and Susie Ann (Allen) Stewart. Reared in Florida and Alabama, Stewart attended Holmes College of the Bible, Greenville, SC. In 1952 he graduated with a Th.B. degree and was also ordained. In that same year, he married Donna Dooley.

Although his eyesight failed early in ministry, Stewart successfully pastored Pentecostal Holiness churches in Alabama, Mississippi, and Virginia. From 1960 to 1969 he served as conference superintendent for the Alabama Conference of the ▸International Pentecostal Holiness Church (IPHC).

In 1969 Stewart was elected assistant general superintendent and held this position until 1981, when he became general superintendent (1981–89). During these years as a national officer of IPHC, he worked variously as general director of the following departments: Superannuation, Loan Fund, Publications, World Intercessory Network (WIN), Armed Forces, Archives, Men's Fellowship, Video, Home and Family Life, and Evangelism.

While general superintendent, Stewart carried the honorary title of "bishop." His administration brought tranquillity and renewed confidence in the national leadership of the IPHC, following several years of turmoil. He served on the board of administration and executive committee of the ▸National Association of Evangelicals. Additionally, under his tenure the IPHC initiated an ambitious church growth and evangelism program called Target 2000.

Stewart's editorial responsibilities have included *Prep,* a Sunday school teaching magazine for youth (1961–74); *Witness,* a publication of the Department of Evangelism (1974–81); and *Advocate,* the official voice of IPHC (1981–89). He also authored *Too Late* (1958), a religious novel.

In recognition of his leadership, Stewart has received honorary doctorates from several institutions, including a doctor of letters from Southern Nazarene University in Bethany, OK.

After leaving office, Stewart served as the president of Southwestern College of Christian Ministries in Oklahoma City, OK, for one year. Since 1991 he has pastored in Pineview, AL.

■ **Bibliography:** L. Stewart to E. Gitre (June 12, 1999) ■ V. Synan, *Old Time Power* (1998) ■ *Who's Who in Religion* (3d ed., 1985).   ■ E. J. Gitre

STRANG, STEPHEN EDWARD (1951–). Magazine editor, publisher, reporter, and entrepreneur. Stephen Strang was born to A. Edward and Amy Alice Strang in Springfield, MO. The family later moved to Florida, where the younger Strang attended the University of Florida College of Journalism. Prior to his graduation with a B.S. degree in 1973, he won the prestigious William Randolph Hearst Foundation Journalism Award. In 1972 he married Joy Ferrell; they have two sons, Cameron and Chandler.

After graduating from college, Strang landed a job as a reporter for *The Orlando Sentinel* (then called *Sentinel Star*). During his career as a reporter, Strang envisaged a Christian magazine as a forum for sharing his faith with people outside the church. He pitched the idea to the leadership of the church where he was a member, Calvary Assembly of God in Winter Park, FL, asking them to underwrite the first six issues for $15,000. They agreed, and *Charisma* was born.

Beginning as a church magazine with only 420 subscribers, *Charisma* gained a national audience of some 50,000 subscribers during the next five years. Initially Strang edited the magazine on a part-time basis; a year later, in 1976, he quit his job with the local newspaper to work full-time for *Charisma.* The relationship with Calvary Assembly of God ended on June 1, 1981, when the church's leadership allowed him to form a corporation to purchase the magazine. Since the founding of *Charisma* magazine, it has become one of the most influential publications among charismatic Christians.

With incorporation came other publishing enterprises by the newly formed Strang Communications Company. *Ministries Today,* a quarterly for ministers and church leaders, began in 1983 (current circulation 30,000). Three years later Strang Communications acquired *Christian Life, Christian Bookseller* (renamed *Christian Retailing* in 1986), and Creation House books from Robert Walker. *Christian Life* was merged with *Charisma* in the spring of 1987, making it one of the most widely read Christian magazines in America, with a paid circulation of over 225,000 subscribers in 121 countries; it is also published quarterly in Spanish as *Vida Cristiana.*

Strang Communications continues to expand and diversify. In 1990 Strang started *CharismaLife Publishers* to provide Christian education materials as well as multimedia resources for children and youth. Four years later, in conjunction with the Promise Keepers men's movement, he started another publication, *New Man;* within two years that publication had 350,000 subscriptions. In 1995 he formed a partnership with Trinity Broadcasting Network and started a program called *Charisma Now!,* which has a weekly magazine format. Strang Communications has since launched into the Internet market, hosting more than 40 ministries. And in 1999 Strang started *Inspirational Giftware,* a spin-off of *Christian Retailing,* to serve the gift industry.

Strang, his company, and its periodicals have been nominated for and have won numerous awards, from his alma mater, from business organizations, and from trade associations. He has served on the board of the Florida Magazine Association, is president of Christian Life Missions, and serves as trustee of the International Charismatic Bible Ministries.

An active and influential voice in the charismatic movement, Strang has promoted racial reconciliation and ecumenicity. He supported and promoted the "Memphis Miracle," which was seen as a watershed event for racial reconciliation within pentecostalism. He has likewise promoted unity between classical pentecostals and the charismatic movement, in all its diversity, particularly through his editorial direction at *Charisma.* Reconciliation has since moved him beyond the African-American community into other ethnic and minority groups, evidenced by the publication of *Charisma* in several international editions.

■ **Bibliography:** "Biography for Stephen Strang," strang web site (June 1999) ▪ S. Strang, "A Call for Cooperation," *Charisma* (Sept. 1985) ▪ idem, "One Small Step," *Charisma* (June 1981) ▪ Communication from S. Strang to E. Gitre, June 21, 1999.
■ E. J. Gitre

STRATON, WARREN BADENOCH (1907–66). Artist, sculptor, architect, violin-maker, and minister. The son of John R. Straton, pastor of Calvary Baptist Church in New York City, Warren Straton began to draw seriously before the age of 6. By age 11 he was selling paintings in New York galleries, and at 18 he sold statuary at Tiffany's. He studied at the Art Students League, the Beaux Arts Institute of Design, Cooper Union in New York, the University of Rochester, and in Italy.

His architectural achievements include designing the Nelson Tower and the Chrysler Building in New York City. He worked on the Pennsylvania state capitol building and the Department of Justice Building in Washington, DC. He sculpted the eagles for Arlington Memorial Bridge in Washington, DC, and the eagles for the American embassy in

Paris, France. Among his many outstanding murals are the hands of God reaching out to humankind and encircling the universe (for Oral Roberts) and Christ of the Apocalypse riding a white horse (Assemblies of God [AG] Headquarters Building).

Straton also was known as a violin-maker and restorer, following the patterns of Stradivari and Guarnieri. He developed a varnish that he believed to be an exact reproduction of that used by Stradivari. In addition, he restored numerous valuable 16th- and 17th-century paintings to their original beauty.

Straton was ordained by the AG and pastored in Rochester, NY, for 23 years. For 9 years he was head of the art department at Evangel College, Springfield, MO. He also served on the Oral Roberts University faculty and on the faculty of the American Academy in Rome. He died in an automobile accident on Apr. 18, 1966.

■ **Bibliography:** J. Fairfield, *Known Violinmakers* (1942) ▪ "Rev. Straton Dies in Crash," *Springfield [MO] Daily News* (Apr. 19, 1966).
■ S. M. Burgess

STUDD, GEORGE B. (1859–1945). The second of the three cricket-playing Studd brothers. Though George Studd had become a Christian while at Eton, he made a full commitment during an extended visit with his brother C. T. in China 10 years later. He helped build Peniel Hall, a Holiness church in Los Angeles, and by 1907 accepted the pentecostal message. He taught a Bible class at the ʳAzusa Street Mission, and in 1913 he helped organize the Worldwide Camp Meeting at Arroyo Seco, outside of Los Angeles. He later accepted the ʳOneness doctrine and worked with its early leaders, although he continued to fellowship with Trinitarian pentecostals. His great passion was missions, and he supported and corresponded with many missionaries. He gradually gave away his inherited fortune and lived very modestly.

■ **Bibliography:** F. Ewart, *The Phenomenon of Pentecost* (1975) ▪ N. Grubb, *C. T. Studd, Cricketer and Pioneer* (1933).
■ L. F. Wilson

SUENENS, LÉON-JOSEPH (1904–96). Roman Catholic cardinal, theologian, and author. Suenens studied at the Pontifical Gregorian University (Rome) and was ordained in Malines, Belgium (1927), where he taught philosophy until 1939. During the Nazi occupation (1940–45), he was vice rector of the University of Louvain (Leuven), and from 1945 to 1961 auxiliary bishop of Malines. In 1961 he was appointed archbishop of Malines-Brussels (until 1979). He was made cardinal in 1962 by Pope John XXIII.

An astute and persuasive politician and member of the commission that prepared the agenda for Vatican II, Suenens became an initiator and leader of the reform movement that

Léon-Joseph Cardinal Suenens, prelate, theologian, and author in Belgium who was influential at the Second Vatican Council.

dominated the council. He urged developing lay charismata and ecumenical cooperation in issues of social and humanitarian concern. He also urged that the church adapt, without compromising essential doctrines, to modern culture.

In 1972 and 1973 Suenens first came into contact with the ⸬Catholic charismatic renewal (CCR) in the U.S. and visited Notre Dame. He hosted a conference at Malines that attempted to evaluate the CCR and provided *Theological and Pastoral Guidelines on the Catholic Charismatic Renewal* (1974). He invited two American CCR leaders, ⸬Ralph Martin and ⸬Stephen Clark, to develop a CCR International Information Office in Brussels (it was later moved to Rome). Suenens became concerned about trends in the CCR, especially its tendency to act independently of the church. Thus, concerned about its parachurch qualities, he decreed (c. 1976) that in Belgium only priests could lead prayer groups, and he developed his ideas concerning the importance of complete integration of the CCR into the ecclesial structure of the church.

Selected English translations of Suenens' works include: *The Gospel to Every Creature* (1957), *Mary, the Mother of God* (1959), *Christian Life Day by Day* (1964), *Theology of the Apostolate* (1954), *The Right View of Moral Rearmament* (1954), *Love and Control* (1962), *The Church in Dialogue* (1965), *Coresponsibility in the Church* (1968), *The Future of the Christian Church* (1970), *A New Pentecost?* (1975), *Come, Holy Spirit* (1976), *Ways of the Spirit* (1976), *Essays on Renewal* (1977), *Your God?* (1977), *Ecumenism and Charismatic Renewal* (1978), *Charismatic Renewal and Social Action* (1979), *Open*

the Frontiers (1980), and *Renewal and the Powers of Darkness* (1983).

■ **Bibliography:** R. J. Bord and J. E. Faulkner, *The Catholic Charismatics* (1983) ■ D. D. Bundy, "Charismatic Renewal in Belgium: A Bibliographical Essay," *EPTA Bulletin* 5 (1986) ■ *Contemporary Authors*, 61–64 (1976) ■ *Current Biography Yearbook, 1965* ■ Death notice, *Christianity Today* 40 (June 17, 1996) ■ E. Hamilton, *Suenens, A Portrait* (1975) ■ *International Who's Who 1986–1987* ■ P. Lesourd and J. Ramiz, *Léon Josef Cardinal Suenens* (1964) ■ J. L. Sandidge, "Origin and Development of the Catholic Charismatic Movement in Belgium" (M.R.S.C. thesis, Leuven, 1976) ■ K. Wittstadt, "Leon-Joseph Kardinal Suenens und e II. Vatikanische Konzil," in *Glaube und Prozess*, ed. E. Klinger and K. Wittstadt (1984).   ■ D. D. Bundy

SULLIVAN, FRANCIS A., S.J. (1922–). Prominent Catholic charismatic leader and scholar. Born in Boston in 1922, Sullivan graduated from high school and entered the Jesuit novitiate in 1938. In 1945 he earned the M.A. in philosophy (Boston College) and in 1948 the M.A. in classics (Fordham University). In 1951 he was ordained priest. In 1956 he received a doctorate in sacred theology (Gregorian University, Rome). Sullivan served as professor of theology at the Gregorian from 1956 to 1992 and as dean of the faculty of theology from 1964 to 1970. From 1970 until 1992 Sullivan was a member of the *Lumen Christi* prayer group of charismatic renewal. Since 1992 he has been professor emeritus, Gregorian University; adjunct professor of theology, Boston College; and chaplain of the Cenacle prayer group of charismatic renewal at Boston College.

Among his many books is *Charisms and Charismatic Renewal* (1982). His published articles concerning the pentecostal movement and charismatic renewal include "The Pentecostal Movement," *Gregorianum* 53 (1972); "Baptism in the Holy Spirit: A Catholic Interpretation of the Pentecostal Experience" *Gregorianum* 55 (1974); "The Ecclesiological Context of the Charismatic Renewal," in K. McDonnell, ed., *The Holy Spirit and Power* (1975); "Speaking in Tongues," *Lumen Vitae* 31 (1976); "The Role of Tradition," in J. Haughey, ed., *Theological Reflections on the Charismatic Renewal* (1978); "Pentecôtisme," in *Dictionnaire de Spiritualité* XII (1984); and "Catholic Charismatic Renewal," in *Dictionary of Pentecostal and Charismatic Movements* (1988).   ■ S. M. Burgess

SUMRALL, LESTER FRANK (1913–). Missionary, pastor, and broadcaster. Sumrall was born in New Orleans, LA. He began preaching at age 17, just three weeks after being miraculously cured of tuberculosis. At age 19 he founded a church in Green Forest, AR, and was ordained by the Assemblies of God (AG). In 1934 he began to travel abroad, preaching in

Tahiti, New Zealand, and Australia, where he established a church in Brisbane. He traveled with ▸Howard Carter through Indonesia, French Indo-China, Tibet, China, Mongolia, Korea, Siberia, Russia, Poland, Germany, France, and Scandinavia.

On a trip to South America Sumrall met Louise Layman, a Canadian missionary to Argentina. A year later they were married in London, Ont. On their honeymoon they evangelized in Nova Scotia, other parts of Canada, the Caribbean Islands, and South America.

The Sumralls spent several years in the Philippines. After a successful evangelistic effort with crowds that newspapers estimated at 50,000 and thousands of conversions, Sumrall founded in Manila what remains today the largest church in the Philippines, with more than 24,000 members.

In 1963 the Sumralls moved to South Bend, IN, where Lester served as pastor. The church, now called Christian Center Cathedral of Praise, has expanded three times and currently seats 3,500.

In the meantime, Sumrall separated from the AG and founded Lester Sumrall Evangelistic Association (LeSEA), World Harvest Bible College (now merged with Indiana Christian University), and *World Harvest Magazine.*

Sumrall ventured into broadcasting with a vision to bring millions to salvation in Christ. He first established WHME, an FM radio station, in 1968. Between 1972 and 1997, LeSEA also bought television stations in Indianapolis, South Bend, New Orleans, Honolulu, Tulsa, Denver, and Colorado Springs. Established in 1985, World Harvest Radio International now has five short-wave transmitters with the capacity to reach 100% of the world's population.

In 1987 Sumrall was called to feed hungry people around the world. Since 1988 LeSEA Global Feed the Hungry (FTH), headquartered in South Bend, IN, has provided over 65 million pounds of emergency relief supplies to people in more than 50 nations.

Sumrall is the author of more than a hundred books, including *Gifts and Ministries of the Holy Spirit* (1982), *Faith to Change the World* (1983), *Dominion Is Yours* (n.d.), *My Story to His Glory* (n.d.), *God's Blueprint for a Happy Home* (1995), and *Commanding Spirits of Jehovah* (1996).

■ **Bibliography:** F. Lily, "Lester Sumrall: Cathedral of Praise," *Charisma* (Nov. 1985).   ■ S. Strang

SUNSHINE REVIVAL (1925). Birthplace of the pentecostal Church of Australia (later called the Assemblies of God in Australia). In 1916 ▸C. L. Greenwood established a small church in Sunshine, Victoria. In 1925 the American evangelist ▸A. C. Valdez visited the new church, and by the beginning of April, a full program of meetings was under way. There were tarrying meetings on Mondays, Tuesdays,

Wednesdays, and Saturdays; evangelistic services on Thursday and Saturday nights; and two services on Sundays. Within a few nights, crowds began to attend. People stood outside, unable to gain admittance. As Greenwood recalled,

> During this campaign the power of God was manifested in a wonderful way: sinners were converted, many believers were baptised in the Holy Spirit, and the power of God fell at every meeting. Soon the news spread that the Lord was pouring out His Spirit in Sunshine, and people came from near and far. Night after night the church was packed, the altar lined, and Christians from all denominations were baptised in the Holy Spirit. Trains from Melbourne were crowded. As they traveled, people sang favorite hymns, and some were converted.

Valdez claimed that people woke up in the middle of the night and were told to go to Sunshine. Some folks were so overcome that they lay on the floor for hours at a time. Visions and revelations were reported. On occasion there were demonic manifestations as people were liberated from oppression. The most common testimony was that of speaking in tongues. Some people had difficulty standing on their feet and had to be assisted to the railway station. Others lingered so long in prayer that they missed the last train. Fortunately, the brick room at the rear of the hall was relatively sound-proof, for there was plenty of shouting, crying, tongues speaking, and singing.

In the 12 months after the campaign began, some 400 people were baptized in the Holy Spirit. Valdez's original instruction to attendees was to remain faithful members of their home churches. However, the hostile reaction many received from their denominations compelled him to rethink his stance. Ultimately, he established the Pentecostal Church of Australia. It was advertised as propagating "the fourfold truth of the New Testament, salvation, Holy Ghost baptism, divine healing and the second coming of Christ."

Late in 1925, the Richmond Theatre at 343 Bridge Road, Richmond, was purchased and became Richmond Temple—still recognized as a leading pentecostal center in Melbourne. By 1926 several hundred people were attending the new church, a Bible training institute was started, missionaries were being sent out, and a full program of meetings was scheduled.

Compared with the huge crowds that had flocked to hear Reuben Torrey in 1902 or Wilbur Chapman in 1909 and 1912, the Sunshine/Prahran gatherings were almost minuscule. Yet for those concerned, and for broader Australian pentecostalism, they were highly significant. They marked the beginning of pentecostal denominationalism in Australia and the emergence of an identifiable pentecostal movement, and they relocated pentecostal revival in the mainstream of evangelical theology. Historically, the Sunshine revival was the legitimate child of the marriage of evangelicalism and enthusiasm.

■ **Bibliography:** Barry Chant, *Heart of Fire* (1984) ■ *Richmond Temple Souvenir* (1939) ■ D. and G. Smith, *A River Is Flowing: A History of the Assemblies of God in Australia* (1987).

■ B. Chant

SWAGGART, JIMMY LEE (1935–). Evangelist, televangelist. Born in Ferriday, LA, Swaggart began attending an Assembly of God (AG) church and was converted and baptized in the Holy Spirit by age eight. He married Francis Anderson at age 17 and shortly thereafter began preaching on a street corner in Mangham, LA. By age 22 he had begun an itinerant preaching ministry. His early fame spread in part because of his association with his cousin, rock and roll performer Jerry Lee Lewis. Through a burgeoning crusade ministry and successful use of radio and television, Swaggart became a major pentecostal leader in the 1980s.

As a young minister, Swaggart was ordained by the AG and pastored a church for a short time with his father. His passion for evangelism led him back into itinerant ministry. He soon established himself as a successful evangelist. By 1964 he was holding regular crusades and camp meetings with a large number of AG churches. In 1969 he began broadcasting his fiery brand of preaching and singing on radio. Income produced from donations and music recordings afforded a cycle of expansion that led to national influence. In 1972 he switched from local church meetings to Billy Graham–style crusades in city auditoriums, sponsored by local church leaders.

In 1973 Swaggart found a more effective medium in television. He soon dropped his 550-station radio broadcasts and focused exclusively on television evangelism. In 1981 he softened his image as a hostile and excessively emotional

Float of "Ministerio Jimmy Swaggart" in parade in Guatemala, celebrating the 50th anniversary of Assemblies of God (1991).

preacher to become more acceptable to mainstream Americans. His new approach was extremely successful. He developed a popular new television program, featuring his gospel music talent and a less offensive preaching style.

Swaggart's remarkable following was rooted in fundamentalistic Christian values. While the core of his supporters were pentecostal, he also had a wide following of Protestants and Roman Catholics. As his audience grew he began a local church, Family Worship Center; a college, Jimmy Swaggart Bible College; and published a monthly magazine, *The Evangelist*.

On the verge of starting his own pentecostal fellowship that might have threatened the ranks of the AG, rumors surfaced, with evidence, regarding Swaggart's involvement in sexual misconduct. The ensuing scandal led to a loss of credibility and severe financial problems for Swaggart's organization. Although Swaggart confessed that the charges were true and claimed repentance, he refused to accept rehabilitative discipline from his denomination. He was subsequently defrocked by the AG in Apr. 1988.

After disassociating himself from the AG, Swaggart's ministry struggled to survive. Swaggart's son, Donnie, and his spouse, Frances, moved into visible leadership of the ministry to avert the crisis. Within months after the confession, Swaggart proclaimed himself restored and returned to ministry, but with greatly reduced influence. The television ministry and Bible college were particularly devastated by major losses in popularity and financial support. The Family Worship Center eventually dropped in attendance to around 500, and the Bible College nearly folded. The television ministry was eventually dropped by most stations. By 1990 it appeared Swaggart's ministry was about to terminate.

During the next several years rumors continued to plague Swaggart's reputation with allegations of sexual misconduct and questionable financial dealings. Swaggart's financial survival was allegedly being accomplished through the transfer of ministry assets into real estate holdings sheltered by his tax exempt organization and other questionable dealings. In 1998, despite the severity and duration of his problems, Swaggart appeared to be able to survive. He was even launching a modest television comeback. Though his influence had greatly diminished, he was able to hold on to substantial resources for operation and to maintain a core of loyal supporters.

■ **Bibliography:** J. Camp, "Rich in Disgrace: Salvation of an Empire," interview, *CNN/Time Impact* (May 3, 1998) ■ B. Stout, "Jimmy Lee Swaggart," in *DPCM* (2d printing with corr., 1989).

■ D. Hedges

SWEET, HENRY CHARLES (1866–1960). Canadian pastor and educator. Having begun ministry in 1887 in southern

Manitoba among Baptists and the Salvation Army, Sweet went on to have a remarkably diverse career. He pastored Baptist and Presbyterian churches across western Canada, and at the conclusion of his ministry he was serving a black African Methodist Episcopal church in Winnipeg. For brief periods he was principal of a Presbyterian residential school for native children in Saskatchewan and headed up a nondenominational, evangelical Bible school in Winnipeg.

Sweet is further distinguished by his education. Having completed a nondegree program at Crozer Theological Seminary in 1897, he graduated with a B.A. from the University of Manitoba in 1906. He returned to Crozer, where he earned a B.D. in 1925, and then at age 60 attended Evangelical Theological College in Dallas (later Dallas Theological Seminary), from which he graduated with the Th.D. degree in 1928.

While Sweet never officially held ministerial credentials with any pentecostal body, he was on the faculty of Western Pentecostal Bible College, under the auspices of the ʼPentecostal Assemblies of Canada (PAOC) from 1931 to 1950, with a gap of several years from the late 1930s until 1943. While there, he taught Bible and homiletics.

The most interesting period of Sweet's association with the pentecostals followed immediately upon his first becoming involved with the movement in 1916. During these years, he was prominent in pentecostal missions in Winnipeg. While there, he made contact with ʼFranklin Small, the founder of the Apostolic Church of Pentecost of Canada, a Oneness denomination. When that group applied for a federal charter in 1921, Sweet was among the signatories. Coming from an unusually strong academic background and from a ministry that spanned racial and denominational lines, Sweet helped shape pentecostalism in western Canada.

■ **Bibliography:** *First Baptist Church, Moose Jaw: Souvenir of the Fiftieth Anniversary* (1933) ■ E. Hildebrandt, *A History of Winnipeg Bible Institute and College from 1925–1960* (1965) ■ R. A. N. Kydd, "H. C. Sweet: Canadian Churchman," *Journal of the Canadian Church Historical Society* 20 (1978) ■ "'Sweet' Memories," *The Portal* (1949).   ■ R. A. N. Kydd

SYMEON THE NEW THEOLOGIAN (949–1022). Medieval Eastern charismatic spiritual (spiritual father). Born in Galatia in Asia Minor, Symeon was the son of Byzantine provincial nobles. He entered a monastery, the Stoudion, at an early age, and soon after he gained full monastic status he was elected abbot of the monastery at Saint Mamas, where he struggled against the prevailing state of physical and spiritual decay. As a result, he came into conflict with a dissident party of monks within his community and with the ecclesiastical hierarchy.

Symeon taught that all Christians must return to a radical living of the gospel and must directly experience God as

divine Trinity. He fought vigorously against the teaching that the church of his day could not have the same spiritual graces as the church in the time of the apostles. According to his testimony, Symeon's devout prayers and desire to participate in the life of God in this present human existence culminated in an ongoing series of mystical, charismatic experiences. He experienced numerous visions of God as light, with accompanying gifts of tears and compunction or remorse for sins.

Like modern pentecostals and charismatics, Symeon distinguished between baptism in water and a baptism in the Holy Spirit. He reasoned that the divine Spirit was present in every baptized Christian but that it was possible to experience a fuller possession of the Spirit. The second stage of the Christian life is Spirit baptism with accompanying gifts of tears and compunction, an experience that greatly intensifies awareness of the indwelling Trinity and lays the groundwork for true holiness.

The evidence that Symeon offers for the Spirit-filled life is far broader than the modern pentecostal "initial evidence" of tongues, although he may have been glossolalic. It more closely resembles that of many modern charismatics. He stands as one of the greatest in a long history of renovators in Orthodox churches who have reminded Christians that the very essence of life itself is the "acquisition of the Holy Spirit of God."

See also THE HOLY SPIRIT, DOCTRINE OF: THE MEDIEVAL CHURCHES; SERAPHIM OF SAROV.

■ **Bibliography:** S. M. Burgess, *The Holy Spirit: Eastern Christian Traditions* (1989), 53–65 ■ idem, ed., *Reaching Beyond: Chapters in the History of Perfectionism* (1986) ■ C. J. deCatanzaro, ed., *Symeon the New Theologian: The Discourses* (1980) ■ G. A. Maloney, *Symeon the New Theologian: The Mystic of Fire and Light* (1975), ch. 2 ■ P. Thompson, "A Prayer to God of St. Symeon the New Theologian," *Sobornost,* n.s. (6, June 1936).   ■ S. M. Burgess

SYNAN, HAROLD VINSON (1934–). American pentecostal church executive and author. He was born the twin of Vernon, sons of ʼJoseph A. and Minnis E. Synan—the father having served a quarter century as bishop of the ʼPentecostal Holiness Church (PHC). In 1960 Vinson married Carol Lee Fuqua. They have four children: Mary C. (1961); Virginia L. (1963); Harold Vinson Jr. (1966); and Joseph A. III (1968). Following a B.A. at the University of Richmond (1958), he completed an M.A. (1964) and a Ph.D. (1967) in American social and intellectual history at the University of Georgia.

Ordained in 1954 by the PHC, Synan pastored churches in Virginia (1956–62) and Georgia (1967–74)—the latter while teaching at Emmanuel College, Franklin Springs, GA. During this time, he was a cofounder (with ʼWilliam W. Menzies and Horace Ward in 1970) of the ʼSociety for Pentecostal Studies, and he also wrote his most substantial work,

Vinson Synan, pentecostal scholar who is also a leader in the charismatic movement.

The Holiness-Pentecostal Movement in the United States (1971), revised as *The Holiness-Pentecostal Tradition: Charismatic Movements in the Twentieth Century* (1997), as well as histories of his college (*Emmanuel College* [1968]) and his denomination (*The Old-Time Power: A History of the Pentecostal Holiness Church* [1973]).

Synan was general secretary of the PHC from 1973 to 1977, assistant general superintendent from 1977 to 1981, and director of evangelism from 1981 to 1986—a dozen years in classical pentecostal denominational leadership. Participation in the International Roman Catholic–Pentecostal *Dialogue in 1973 (core member, 1976–81) foreshadowed his later ecumenical and charismatic leadership. Since 1986 he has chaired the New Orleans Congresses on the Holy Spirit and World Evangelization—which have attracted up to 40,000 charismatics and have deepened cooperation and understanding between pentecostals and charismatics. In 1994 Synan became dean of the divinity school at Regent University, Virginia Beach, VA.

His later writings, though more popular in style, reflect a fine historical sense coupled with a readable style. These include *Charismatic Bridges* (1974), *Aspects of Pentecostal Origins* (1975), *Azusa Street* (1980), *In the Latter Days* (1984), *The Twentieth-Century Pentecostal Explosion* (1987), and *The Century of the Holy Spirit: 100 Years of Pentecostal and Charismatic Renewal* (2001).   ■ R. P. Spittler

SYNAN, JOSEPH ALEXANDER (1905–84). Church planter and bishop of the *Pentecostal Holiness Church

(PHC). Synan was born in Tazewell County, VA, the second of 13 children born to Thomas and Maude Synan. His marriage to Minnis Evelyn Perdue in 1926 produced seven children. Called to preach as a youth, he joined a local Methodist church that promised to send him to college to study for the ministry. His plans changed in 1921 when he was converted in a tent revival near Fredericksburg, VA, and joined a nearby Pentecostal Holiness congregation.

After being ordained in the Baltimore Conference of the PHC in 1926, Synan planted several churches in the Tidewater area of Virginia. In 1934 he was elected superintendent of the Eastern Virginia Conference. In 1945 he was elected general superintendent, a position he held for 24 years. From 1950 to 1969 he served as the presiding chairman and bishop of the PHC.

A leader in ecumenical relations, J. A. Synan was one of the founding fathers of the *National Association of Evangelicals (NAE) in 1943 and of the *Pentecostal Fellowship of North America (PFNA) in 1948. In 1967 he negotiated an affiliation between the PHC and the Pentecostal Methodist Church of Chile.

During Synan's chairmanship, the PHC grew from 30,000 to 67,000 members in the U.S.

■ **Bibliography:** V. Synan, *The Old-Time Power: A History of the Pentecostal Holiness Church* (rev. ed., 1998).   ■ H. V. Synan

Joseph A. Synan, who was ordained a minister in the Pentecostal Holiness Church in 1926 and served the denomination as general superintendent for 24 years.

T

TABERNACLE PENTECOSTAL CHURCH See INTERNATIONAL PENTECOSTAL HOLINESS CHURCH.

TAITINGER, ROBERT W. (1927–). General superintendent (1969–82) of the Pentecostal Assemblies of Canada (PAOC). Taitinger pastored the Central Pentecostal Tabernacle, Edmonton, Alb., for 13 years (1955–68) before his election to the leadership of the PAOC at the age of 41. Converted at age 12, he took up ministry upon completing high school and succeeded D. N. Buntain in his Edmonton pastorate at the age of 28. He served on the faculty of the Canadian Northwest Bible Institute and was chairman of the Pentecostal Fellowship of North America (1972–74). An enthusiastic supporter of foreign missions, his congregation led PAOC missions giving for 15 years.

Robert W. Taitinger, who served the Pentecostal Assemblies of Canada as general superintendent for 13 years.

■ **Bibliography:** "General Officers Leave Executive Posts," *Pentecostal Testimony* 63 (12, 1982) ▌ R. W. Taitinger, "Sixty Years in the Marketplace," *Pentecostal Testimony* 59 (11, 1978).

■ E. A. Wilson

TAÑON, RICARDO (1904–). Pioneer Puerto Rican pentecostal pastor in New York City. He was born in Comerio, PR, and migrated to New York City in 1929. It was there, in 1934, that he was converted to pentecostalism in Spanish Harlem under the preaching of Mexican pentecostal evangelist Eleuterio Paz. Although he only finished 4th grade, he later attended and graduated from the Spanish American Bible Institute in New York City in 1938. In 1943 he stopped working as an elevator attendant and accepted the pastorate of a small storefront church in the Bronx, the Iglesia Cristiana Juan 3:16, with 12 members. By the 1970s Tañon's church was the largest Spanish-speaking Protestant church in the U.S., with between 1,800 and 2,000 members. In addition to leading his own church, he also planted 17 new Iglesia Cristiana Juan 3:16 churches

throughout New York City, New England, and Latin America. He is considered one of the key founders of Latino pentecostalism in New York City. Gordon-Conwell Theological Seminary honored his lifelong ministry with an honorary D.D. degree in 1977. The story of his life and ministry are recorded in his biography, *El Poder y La Gloria De Dios: Ricardo Tañon.*

■ **Bibliography:** R. Sánchez et al., *Ricardo Tañon: "El Poder y La Gloria de Dios"* (1980) ▌ E. Villafañe, *The Liberating Spirit: Toward an Hispanic American Pentecostal Social Ethic* (1993).

■ G. Espinosa

TANUSAPUTRA, ABRAHAM ALEX (1941–). Gereja Bethel Indonesia (Indonesian Bethel Church of God) pastor, college president, denomination administrator, and author. Tanusaputra was born on June 1, 1941, in Mojokerto, East Java, Indonesia. He was converted in 1965 following an accident in which he ran over a small boy while testing a new sports car. Fearing for his life because of an angry mob, Tanusaputra prayed all night in a nearby church. The boy was healed, Tanusaputra was converted and called into the ministry, and the wrath of the mob was averted. Following his conversion, Tanusaputra evangelized, planted churches, and served as director of the Asian Evangelistic Fellowship for Indonesia. Locating in Surabaya (Java) in 1976, he planted the Bethany congregation, which grew from a membership of 7 to over 40,000 by 1995. This local congregation has planted more than 100 churches in Indonesia, China, Singapore, and Australia. In 1978 Tanusaputra founded Bethany Christian Institute, now known as Bethany Theological College. He has also served as an assistant overseer of Gereja Bethel. He has authored two books: *Dipulihkan (Restored)* and *Batu Penjuru (Cornerstone).*

■ **Bibliography:** C. W. Conn, *Like a Mighty Army: A History of the Church of God* (1996) ▌ "Indonesia Pastor: Called to Be Discipler," *Cleveland Daily Banner* (Dec. 10, 1995) ▌ Lee College Commencement Program (Dec. 1995).

■ D. G. Roebuck

TARDIF, EMILIEN (1928–99). Leading healing evangelist in the Catholic charismatic renewal. Born in Quebec, Tardif joined the Sacred Heart Fathers and in 1956 went as a missionary to the Dominican Republic, where in the mid '60s he became head of his order there. Sent back to Canada with acute tuberculosis in 1973, Tardif was healed when prayed over by members of a charismatic prayer group. Returning to the Dominican Republic, he bore witness to his healing, and many extraordinary healings took place. Since 1975 Tardif had preached and ministered on every continent, especially in French- and Spanish-speaking countries. His ministry was often attended by enormous crowds and regularly accompanied by sensational cures, some narrated in Tardif's *Jesus Is the Messiah* (with J. H. Prado Flores; 1992). He has also given many retreats for fellow Catholic priests. Tardif's witness is given in *Jésus a Fait de Mot un Temoin* (1984), translated into English as *Jesus Lives Today!*   ■ P. D. Hocken

TATE, MARY MAGDALENA (1871–1930). Chief overseer, chief apostle, president, and founder of the Latter Day Church of the Foundation of True Holiness and Sanctification. Mary Tate is recognized as the first black woman church founder within the Holiness movement in the U.S. (c. 1899). The church was formally organized in 1908 in Greenville, AL. She served as general overseer of the church from 1903 until her death in Dec. 1930 in Nashville, TN. After her death, no woman was called "Mother" in this church, out of respect for the founder.

In 1931 three leaders were named to replace Mother Tate. Each represented a "dominion" within the U.S. The largest dominion today is the Keith Dominion, also known as the House of God the Church of the Living God, the Pillar and Ground of Truth without Controversy. Bishop J. C. Elliot from Sarasota, FL, is the chief overseer.

Mother Mary Magdalena Tate, the first black woman church founder in the Holiness movement in the U.S.

The Lewis Dominion, known as the Church of the Living God, the Pillar and Ground of Truth, is the smallest of the three dominions and is headed by chief overseer Bishop Helen Middleton Lewis. Her son, Bishop Meharry Lewis, is the administrative assistant from Tuskegee, AL. The third or Jewell Dominion is led by Bishop Geraldine D. Manning and has its headquarters in Indianapolis, IN.

All three dominions are noted for Hawaiian steel guitar music, a musical tradition carried over from Mother Tate's ministry. The Keith Dominion has the Campbell Brothers from Rochester, NY; Henry Nelson from Long Island, NY; and Aubrey Ghent from Florida. The Jewell Dominion has Sonny Treadway from Florida. "The Father of the Steel Guitar" is Willie Claude Eason from St. Petersburg, FL. Each dominion has a distinct sound.

■ **Bibliography:** S. DuPree, *African-American Holiness-Pentecostal Movement: An Annotated Bibliography* (1996) ■ idem, *Biographical Dictionary of African-American Holiness-Pentecostals* (n.d.) ■ G. Manning, *World Within, World Without: A Liberating View* (thesis, Wesley Theological Seminary, 1996).   ■ S. S. DuPree

TAYLOR, GEORGE FLOYD (1881–1934). Church leader, educator, and author. One of the early leaders of the ▸Pentecostal Holiness Church (PHC), George Floyd Taylor was born in Duplin County, NC, near the town of Magnolia. Afflicted from birth with a palsy-like condition, Taylor accomplished much in spite of his physical handicap.

A member of the Methodist Episcopal Church, South, Taylor was swept into the Holiness movement in 1903 under the ministry of ▸A. B. Crumpler. In that same year he was licensed to preach in the ▸Holiness Church of North Carolina (the Pentecostal Holiness Church after 1908). His interest in education led him to found the Bethel Holiness School in Rose Hill, NC, in 1903. Four years later he founded the Falcon Holiness School near Dunn, NC, which he headed from 1907 to 1916. While in Falcon, he began in 1913 the publication of a line of pentecostal Sunday school literature that was later bought by the PHC.

When the pentecostal movement swept the South under the ministry of ▸G. B. Cashwell (1862–1916), Taylor was one of the first ministers to speak in tongues in the Dunn meeting of 1907. His defense of the new pentecostal experience, *The Spirit and the Bride*, appeared in September 1907 in ringing support of the new pentecostal experience. This was possibly the first book-length defense of pentecostalism ever published. In the debates over speaking in tongues that shook the PHC in 1908, Taylor's staunch stand for the "initial evidence" theory helped swing the PHC into the growing pentecostal movement.

In 1913 Taylor was elected general superintendent of the PHC, a position he held for two years. In 1917 he became the founding editor of the official voice of the church, the *Pentecostal Holiness Advocate*. A talented writer, Taylor continued to write and edit the Sunday school literature while editing the *Advocate*. In 1919 he was called on to serve as the founding president of the Franklin Springs Institute (FSI) located in Franklin County, GA. At first a high school and Bible college, the school became Emmanuel College in 1933.

In 1928 Taylor resigned as president of FSI and moved back to North Carolina, where he earned an M.A. degree in history at the University of North Carolina at Chapel Hill. After a trip to the Holy Land in 1929, he published *A Tour of Bible Lands*. His last years were spent as a faculty member at Emmanuel College.

■ **Bibliography:** V. Synan, *Emmanuel College: The First Fifty Years* (1968).　　　　　　　　　■ H. V. Synan

TAYLOR, WILLIAM (1821–1902). Wesleyan/Holiness Methodist Episcopal missionary, mission theorist, and prolific author. Taylor developed an approach to missionary work inspired by his experiences as a missionary who established congregations in California (1849–56), Africa (1866; 1884–96), the Caribbean (1867–68), India (1870–75), and Latin America (1878–84). He also did evangelistic work in Australia, New Zealand, Sri Lanka, and England. On the basis of his experience in California and South Africa, he became convinced that the submissive colonial church model had no future. He developed (1866) the theory of "Pauline Missions."

The central theme of the theory was that the congregations resulting from mission efforts were equal with the older mission-sending churches and that they should be, from the beginning, self-supporting, self-governing, and self-propagating. He argued that Western culture and thought were not privileged as forms for Christian theological reflection and insisted that converts to Christianity be entrusted to the care of the Holy Spirit and be empowered to do theological reflection in their cultural forms and language immediately. Second, he was convinced that missionaries should live as their hosts and without support from North America or Europe. Missionaries should either adopt a country and live respectfully in the host culture, or they should preach the gospel and move on, as did the apostle Paul and William Taylor. The most complete statement of this theory was *Pauline Methods of Missionary Work* (1879), but it was discussed widely in most Methodist and Holiness periodicals between 1879 and 1910. Taylor's own life and ministry became the model for mission; the embodiment of the theory was in the biography.

After being forced by the Methodist Episcopal Missionary Society to cease functioning as a missionary in 1875, Taylor went to Latin America to establish self-supporting missions on a continent where earlier Methodist mission

efforts were generally unsuccessful. He established churches in Panama, Equador, Peru, Bolivia, and Chile. Seeing the need for more "self-supporting" missionaries, he established a sending agency, the Building and Transit Fund, for helping Wesleyan/Holiness missionaries get to the mission field, where they were to be self-supporting. Among those who went to the mission field as "Taylor missionaries" were Mary Louise and ▸Willis C. Hoover (Chile) and the ▸Mead family (Angola). It was the Mead family who at the ▸Azusa Apostolic Faith Mission revival first identified glossolalia as real languages. The Hoovers were forced out of the Methodist Episcopal Church (1910) and established the Methodist Pentecostal Church of Chile.

Taylor was the primary mission theorist for early pentecostalism, especially in Scandinavia. ▸Thomas Ball Barratt and ▸Lewi Pethrus both studied Taylor and found him a resource in arguing against the traditional form of "mission boards" as modeled by the American and British established traditions. In early pentecostal writings it is sometimes argued (as did Barratt) that the success of Taylor's mission efforts indicated that he must have experienced pentecostal "baptism in the Holy Spirit." Taylor's empowerment of African indigenous clergy has also been suggested as a source of African nationalism and of the ▸African Initiated Churches.

■ **Bibliography:** D. D. Bundy, "Bishop William Taylor and the Methodist Mission Board," *Methodist History* 27 (4, July 1989) and 28 (1, Oct. 1989) ■ idem, "Swedish Pentecostal Mission Theory to 1930: Foundational Values in Conflict," *Mission Studies* 14 (1997) ■ idem, "Unintended Consequences: The Methodist Mission Society and the Beginnings of Pentecostalism in Norway and Chile," *Missiology* 27 (1999) ■ idem, "William Taylor, 1821–1902: Entrepreneurial Maverick for the Indigenous Church," in *Mission Legacies: Biographical Studies of Leaders of the Modern Missionary Movement*, ed. G. Anderson et al. (1994) ■ G. A. Gustafson, *En Apostlagestalt på missionsfält ... eller William Taylor lif och värksamhet* (1898) ■ W. Hoover, *Historia del Avivamiento* (1934; repr. 1977) ■ W. G. Mills, "The Taylor Revival of 1866 and the Roots of African Nationalism in the Cape Colony," *Journal of Religion in Africa* 8 (1976) ■ J. Paul, *The Soul Digger: or The Life and Times of William Taylor* (1928) ■ W. Taylor, *Story of My Life: An Account of What I Have Thought, Said and Done in My Ministry of More Than Fifty-Three Years in Christian Lands and among the Heathen*, ed. John Ridpath (1897).

　　　　　　　　　■ D. D. Bundy

TEEN CHALLENGE An evangelistic program started by ▸David Wilkerson, a young preacher from Philipsburg, PA, who went to New York City (NYC) with a burning desire to share Christ with youth in trouble. What started as an evangelistic ministry to NYC gang members in 1958 has grown to a worldwide ministry aimed at reaching teenagers and young adults caught up in drugs, alcohol, and other life-controlling problems.

From its first days, the Teen Challenge ministry was supported by offerings received from churches where Wilkerson's story was told. The late Reginald Yake, pastor of the Assembly of God in Irvington, NJ, a suburb of NYC, told Wilkerson that it was the responsibility of the local churches to raise the needed money to carry on his work. Subsequently, 200 ministers in the NYC area were invited to meet at Glad Tidings Tabernacle, Manhattan, NY (R. Stanley Berg, pastor), to determine how the new youth ministry could be supported. Twenty ministers responded to the invitation. When asked what it would take to keep him on the street full-time, Wilkerson stated that he needed 100 dollars per week. Each minister pledged that his church would contribute five dollars weekly.

From the 20 ministers present for that initial Dec. 1958 meeting, a central committee of nine men was selected to form the first board of directors of Teen Age Evangelism, as the organization was originally known. R. Stanley Berg was made committee chairman; Frank M. Reynolds, secretary; and Paul DiLena, treasurer.

In those early days Teen Age Evangelism aimed to inspire and organize Christian youth to do street evangelism. Converts were directed to local churches to be discipled in the Word of God and in Christian living. Focus at the end of the first decade of ministry continued to be on NYC street gangs. *Nicky Cruz's dramatic conversion inspired and expanded the Teen Challenge ministry. *The Cross and the Switchblade* (1963) by David Wilkerson sets forth the dramatic way the Holy Spirit directed the early years of this ministry.

As workers shared their faith on the streets, they came in frequent contact with drug addicts, regarded by everyone as hopeless cases. Following one of the NYC street meetings, Ralph, a young man who had been a heroin addict for three years, approached the intrepid youth minister and asked if "he could have that too," with reference to the salvation about which he just had heard, so evident in the lives of the workers. Not recognizing that Ralph was a drug addict, Wilkerson assured Ralph that he could experience new life in Christ. He then prayed for Ralph that he might receive Christ as Savior. The next day Ralph was back with the testimony that he had not had any heroin for 24 hours and was not having any withdrawal pains. Ralph became an instant evangelist to other drug addicts, telling the youth that he had found the answer to their drug problems.

Drug addicts began flocking to Wilkerson's services and were led to Christ. Many of these addicts suffered no withdrawal pains. Ministry to drug addicts brought excitement to the Teen Challenge organization—at last there was an answer to the epidemic drug problem. News of what was transpiring in NYC spread across the country. Invitations for Wilkerson to speak in meetings came from many churches and groups.

Between 1960 and 1962 Teen Challenge ministries branched out from NYC to other cities facing the same gang and drug problems—Chicago, Los Angeles, San Francisco, Boston, and Philadelphia. Teen Challenge workers were recruited from Bible institutes and colleges and from churches to help with new centers. Christian workers planned, sacrificed, and prayed, looking for an immediate sweep of the Holy Spirit to revolutionize their cities.

The success of the evangelistic outreach in the urban areas was clearly evident in those first years. A serious problem was also evident—many drug addicts and gang members, after receiving deliverance, were returning after a few weeks to their old ways. That truth brought soul searching, much prayer, and a complete reevaluation of the evangelism methods used by Teen Challenge. Why were the new Christians not succeeding? It was found, first of all, that few churches to which the converts were directed were willing and able to work with these people. It further became apparent that new converts did not have basic skills to handle all the adjustments they needed to make—housing, jobs, pressures of old relationships, legal entanglements, and other changes. When asked what would help them most, converts requested help in getting away from their environment temporarily, where they could learn how to be Christians.

In Aug. 1961 a committee was appointed to develop an adequate program and to find a suitable place for meeting the obvious need. On the committee were David Wilkerson, Frank M. Reynolds, and Reginald Yake. They recommended the development of a five-to-eight-month program in a rural setting. They further recommended that a productive farm be purchased. Buildings would be constructed to meet the needs. Land in Rehrersburg, PA, was purchased in June 1962 from Arthur Graybill, on which the Teen Challenge Training Center was to be constructed and developed. Reynolds became superintendent of the center in August of that year. He was charged with overseeing the construction of the first buildings and of developing the Christian growth training program.

This was the beginning of what has been considered one of the most successful drug rehabilitation programs. The primary goal of the program was to teach new converts how to live disciplined Christian lives. Four key truths have provided the foundation for Teen Challenge ministry to drug addicts and other troubled youths: (1) there is hope; (2) sin is the problem; (3) Jesus Christ can change your life; and (4) the power of the Holy Spirit is essential for consistent Christian living. The first students at the Rehrersburg Training Center came from New York, Chicago, Boston, Los Angeles, San Francisco, and Philadelphia. Originally these new Christians stayed three weeks at the Teen Challenge center in one of these cities before going to the Training Center at Rehrersburg.

Rapid expansion of the ministry came as Teen Challenge centers opened across the nation. Since Wilkerson did not desire to be responsible for the administration and funding of all those ministries, each center became an autonomous unit, operating with its respective board of directors. In 1963 it was decided that Teen Challenge should come under the general supervision of the national Division of Home Missions of the General Council of the Assemblies of God, with specific supervision given to district councils. Teen Challenge has worked interdenominationally and intradenominationally; people of various denominations have served on local boards and staff. The one source of unity is the belief that students should seek the baptism of the Holy Spirit with the evidence of speaking in other tongues.

Many Teen Challenge centers have developed ministry programs to inner-city children, including drug prevention seminars for schools. Teen Challenge has also helped start 28 churches, most in inner-city areas.

In 1969 Howard Foltz, Teen Challenge director in Dallas–Fort Worth, felt called to develop a Teen Challenge program in Europe. The same basic principles were followed. In 1972 teams of Teen Challenge staff members and graduates were sent to Vietnam under contract with the U.S. Department of Defense. They were effective in assisting military personnel with drug abuse problems.

By 1999 more than 120 Teen Challenge centers had been established in the U.S. and 250 centers were operating worldwide.

■ **Bibliography:** F. M. Reynolds, "Teen Challenge at the Quarter-Century Mark," *PE* (June 19, 1983) ■ Additional information from the minutes of Teen Challenge board meetings and from personal records of F. M. Reynolds ■ D. Wilkerson, *The Cross and the Switchblade* (1963).   ■ F. M. Reynolds

TELEVISION Television, as an evolving media in the second half of the 20th century, played a major role in the growth and influence of the charismatic and pentecostal movements. Charismatic and pentecostal preachers successfully used television to broadcast crusades, teaching, music, and entertainment programs, and to raise funds and build national organizations. Observations from five decades of religious broadcasting indicate that charismatics and pentecostals have been comparatively successful in the use of television. In fact, no other segment of Christianity has employed television for evangelism and religious influence as successfully as charismatics and pentecostals. This may be true in part because of the distinctly spontaneous nature of charismatic ministries and the apparent ability of certain charismatic leaders to organize and maintain adequate resources to support broadcast ministries. The overall result has been that television has taken both the best and the worst of charismatic and pentecostal Christianity into the home of virtually every family in America.

In 1954 ▸Oral Roberts began to pioneer the use of television for charismatic ministry by broadcasting his tent crusades nationally. His bold preaching and live broadcasts of his unique ministry with healing lines brought instant national attention to the new wave of charismatic ministry beginning to sweep the country. In the 1960s Roberts produced a more conventional Sunday morning variety program that eventually became the number one syndicated religious program in the nation. Based on this success, he began an ambitious effort in 1969 to provide a similar type program on prime-time television, using Hollywood celebrities to draw an even bigger audience. His following eventually grew to 64 million viewers. The program served as a tremendous resource for developing a national following and for recruiting students and raising funds for Oral Roberts University. Edward Fiske of the *New York Times* said that Roberts commanded more loyalty in the 1970s than any minister in America. By the mid 1990s, after protracted difficulties in trying to establish the City of Faith medical center, Roberts' broadcasting activities had become substantially reduced. In 1997, after turning over the presidency of Oral Roberts University to his son, ▸Richard Roberts, Oral introduced a new phase of television ministry called Golden Eagle Broadcasting. This new television endeavor, cosponsored by several of Roberts' successful charismatic broadcasting associates—including ▸Kenneth Copeland, Billy Joe Daugherty, ▸Kenneth Hagin Jr., Jesse Duplantis, ▸Jerry Savelle, Creflo Dollar, ▸Marilyn Hickey, and several others—offered programming produced by these broadcasters and their sponsoring ministries. Another significant development in the Roberts broadcast legacy occurred in 1997, when Richard Roberts began a nightly broadcast, *Something Good: America's Hour of Healing*. The format for the program was a new approach to live "call-in" healing ministry. The program was broadcast by more than 200 stations by 1999.

Singers on PTL Thailand.

A different approach to television was taken by charismatic evangelist ˒Pat Robertson, who began his influence in television ministry in 1959 through the purchase of a defunct UHF local station in Portsmouth, VA. Robertson developed his daily flagship program, *The 700 Club*, and raised substantial funds through the now-famous approach of recruiting viewers to join as partners with a monthly pledge. Buying up additional stations in key markets and eventually securing a state-of-the-art satellite delivery system, Robertson developed the most successful Christian television enterprise then in existence. Under the name of the Christian Broadcast Network (CBN), the nonprofit religious corporation became a major force in cable television, with 30 million subscribers interested in a Christian alternative to the secular networks. Robertson used a variety of formats, including prime-time specials, news and political programs, children's programs, animation, and a short-lived soap opera, *One Life to Live*. In 1988 Robertson's political interests and substantial television following enabled him to launch a significant but unsuccessful presidential campaign. In 1989 CBN dropped its nonprofit and religious status and became The Family Channel, a commercial stock-owned corporation. A series of additional changes involving major financial restructuring in the mid '90s led to a majority stock sale to entertainment and news media magnate Rupert Murdoch for a reported 1.5 billion dollars in 1997.

The Trinity Broadcast Network (TBN) was billed in 1999 as "The Largest Christian Television Network in the World." Committed to total Christian programming, TBN established ownership and operation of more than 750 stations across the U.S. and throughout Europe, Central and South America, Africa, and many other parts of the world. The estimated annual budget in 1999 was approximately $100 million. Founded in Santa Ana, CA, in 1973 in rented studios by ˒Paul Crouch and ˒Jim Bakker, and later moved to Costa Mesa, TBN had become the major television network influence of charismatic and pentecostal Christianity at the end of the 1990s. Also notable was Jim Bakker's Praise the Lord Network (PTL) based in Charlotte, NC. This network grew into a $172 million empire at its peak in 1987, centered on a Christian theme park, Heritage USA. The network tumbled that same year in a sex and money scandal; Jim Bakker resigned due to what he called an attempted hostile takeover by an unnamed fellow pentecostal evangelist who was later alleged to be ˒Jimmy Swaggart. Swaggart, a fiery Baton Rouge preacher, who ran his own television empire, was soon thereafter dethroned by his own admitted sexual misconduct.

Also notable among charismatic television broadcasters were ˒Kathryn Kuhlman, who in the 1950s and 1960s produced more than 500 telecasts of her healing crusades for the CBS network; ˒Rex Humbard from the Cathedral of Tomorrow in Akron, OH, who broadcast in the late 1960s and early 1970s with his wife, Maude Aimee, and a large musical family; ˒Kenneth Copeland and his wife, Gloria, of Fort Worth, TX; Robert Tilton of Dallas, TX, with his *Success in Life* broadcast popular in the 1980s and early 1990s; ˒Jack Hayford and the broadcast of services from the Church on The Way in Van Nuys, CA; ˒Marilyn Hickey from Denver, CO, with her popular Bible teaching program and crusades; ˒Joyce Myers from Fenton, MO, with her Bible teaching program *Life in the Word;* ˒James Robison, a former Baptist evangelist in Dallas, TX; John Hagee in San Antonio, TX; Rod Parsley in Columbus, OH; and Benny Hinn in Orlando, FL, who broadcast his highly successful healing crusades.

Television has exposed the best and worst of charismatic and pentecostal Christianity to the national public through five decades of broadcasting that mark the evolution of the medium. The best broadcasts associated with the movement would include the early efforts of Oral Roberts and Kathryn Kuhlman to bring America into the crusade tent through live television. Those early broadcasts of prayer lines, healings, and speaking in tongues did more to raise the awareness of the American public concerning the nature of charismatic Christianity than any other medium and helped position the movement more as mainstream. Oral Roberts' well-produced weekly and prime-time variety programs, incorporating major celebrities and quality programming, which ran for three decades substantially reinforced this positive image. Also contributing to the positive image was Pat Robertson's daily broadcast of the news-type talk show *The 700 Club*. During the 1970s and 1980s this program made a major contribution to establishing a more mainstream image for charismatics and pentecostals.

The worst broadcasts—those producing the most negative images of charismatic and pentecostal Christianity—would certainly include the reported scandals involving Jim Bakker and Jimmy Swaggart. Listed also would be those of less prominent figures such as Peter Popof, accused of faking supernatural revelations through use of a concealed radio earphone; Robert Tilton, whose extravagant lifestyle and alleged discarding of unread prayer requests (after removing donations) in an open trash bin cost him his ministry; Larry Lea, whose house burned, leading to faked destitution as a fundraising ploy while concealing another elaborate residence; and several other scandals of lesser significance. These highly publicized scandals did considerable damage to the image and reputation of charismatic and pentecostal ministries everywhere. The impression of charismatic and pentecostal Christianity as conveyed through television at the end of the 20th century is a rather unsettled mixture of good and bad.

As for the future of charismatic and pentecostal television, only one of the three charismatic television networks that achieved significance (CBN, PTL, and TBN) remains: TBN. It is obvious that this remaining network, which continues to grow and increase in influence, will be a major factor in the next decade and beyond. The overall direction of charismatic and pentecostal broadcasting at the end of the century appears to move toward filling of the air waves with programming mostly of the local and regional variety, of poor or marginal quality. If this continues—and it appears that it will—the positive image of pentecostals and charismatics in society will not be enhanced and may, in fact, erode the credibility established by earlier broadcasting efforts. On the other hand, the impact on society at large appears to be relatively small; fundraising rhetoric notwithstanding, religious television appears to reach mostly the converted and have little evangelistic impact. It would seem most valuable to the future of the movement for charismatics and pentecostals to make a concerted effort to explore new approaches to broadcasting that make more effective use of the medium.

■ **Bibliography:** J. Buckingham, *Daughter of Destiny: Kathryn Kuhlman . . . Her Story* (1976) ▮ M. K. Evans, "Where Miracles Are a Way of Life," *Christian Life* (May 1983) ▮ "Fresh Out of Miracles," *Newsweek* (May 11, 1987) ▮ Golden Eagle Broadcasting website (Sept. 14, 1999) ▮ D. Harrell Jr., *Oral Roberts: An American Life (1985)* ▮ D. M. Hazzard, "Marilyn and Wally Hickey: They Make a Great Team," *Charisma* (Oct. 1985) ▮ R. Humbard, *Miracles in My Life* (1971) ▮ "Jim Bakker May Try to Revive Televangelist Career," *Detroit News* (June 12, 1999) ▮ C. McGraw and K. Christensen, "Television Has Built TBN into a Power," *The Orange County Register* (May 31, 1998) ▮ O. Roberts, *The Call* (1971) ▮ B. Spring, "Pat Robertson for President?" *Christianity Today* (Nov. 8, 1985).

                                              ■ D. J. Hedges

THEOLOGY, PENTECOSTAL

I. Theological Method
   A. *The Significance of Nonacademic Theology*
   B. *Hermeneutics and Bible Doctrines*
   C. *The Question of Theological Loci*
   D. *Contextualization*

II. Theological Issues
   A. *The Godhead and the Christ of the Full Gospel*
   B. *Regeneration, Sanctification, and Spirit Baptism*
   C. *Water Baptism and Spirit Baptism*
   D. *Speaking in Tongues*
   E. *Divine Healing*
   F. *The Gifted Congregation*
   G. *Revisioning Eschatology*

III. Conclusion

The diversity of global pentecostalism makes it impossible to speak of "a" pentecostal theology, especially since a full-blown theology of the Christian faith from a classical pentecostal perspective has not yet been written. But there are certain common threads of theological concern among pentecostals that are worth exploring. In what follows, we will attempt to explore a number of major directions of thought involved in the ongoing task of theological reflection among pentecostals.

I. Theological Method.

A. The Significance of Nonacademic Theology.

Pentecostals have always favored testimonies, choruses, and prayers over intellectual or critical reflection as the means by which to interpret the gospel. Walter Hollenweger maintains that pentecostals, coming primarily from black, non-Western roots have accented oral tradition, visions, dreams, and the dance as the primary means by which to interpret the gospel theologically. This non-Western root of the movement joined with the catholic spirituality channeled through Wesley to give pentecostalism its ecumenical significance. Hollenweger calls his approach to understanding pentecostalism *realgeschichtlich,* since it focuses on the actual experiences of pentecostal communities and the dramatic and oral means of expressing and understanding them. He distinguishes this approach from the more conceptual method, which is *idealgeschichtlich* and focuses attention on the doctrines used by pentecostal churches to conceptualize the experiences that find more direct and authentic expression through forms of communication such as the testimony and the dance (Hollenweger, 1989).

We will have occasion to question the secondary role assigned to conceptual doctrine in the above understanding of pentecostal theology. And, although Hollenweger's preference for the term "oral" as a description of pentecostal theology may be helpful in some ways for distinguishing grassroots pentecostal theology on a global level from the more academic theological methods, the term proves to be too restrictive to include forms of expression such as the dance or the written testimony. As explained below, I prefer the term *nonacademic* theology, following Karl Barth's description of Blumhardt's narrative and devotional theology in contrast to the methodical systematic theology of Friedrich Schleiermacher.

Important to note at this juncture, however, is that the so-called nonacademic theology of pentecostals has not necessarily precluded disciplined exegetical work and theological reflection within the various theological *loci*. Such disciplined exegesis and systematic theological reflection are significant, since nonacademic theology is not generally consciously critical, contextual, or methodical in its approach. Many pentecostals agree that the more rational exegetical and theological approaches to the gospel should still have a place in the development of various pentecostal theologies.

Such rational approaches to theology, however, do not negate the significance of the nonacademic theologizing among pentecostals and similar free-church movements; nonacademic narrative and dramatic theologizing can offer a significant voice in the current theological climate. The older modernist problem of history, faced so insightfully by Ernst Troeltsch—namely, how to speak of one gospel in the context of the vicissitudes of history and the diversification of tradition—is now being expanded and intensified to include the challenges inherent in the complexities of social context and cultural pluralism. The collapse of colonialism has given rise to a new appreciation for the uniqueness and significance of approaches to theology that do not follow the European or dominant North American models and systems of thought. In such an era of diversification and pluralism, many are now becoming interested in a way of theologizing that is responsive to the unique experiences of various communities of faith, especially those that have been culturally marginalized without much access to academic citadels of learning, scientific methods, or literary analysis. As pentecostal theologian Cheryl Bridges-Johns has noted, there is an opportunity in this postmodern pluralism for many marginalized believers, especially from among the pentecostals, to bring their experiences and ways of theologizing to the table of theological discourse as respected partners in dialogue (Bridges-Johns, 1997).

For such reasons, there are those who feel that the understanding of pentecostal theology as a grassroots and devotional interpretation of the gospel is extremely relevant to the current theological climate. After all, the science of systematic theology as we came to know it in the 20th century dates back largely to the work of Schleiermacher, the 19th-century progenitor of modern Protestant theology. As Karl Barth said in reference to the German Pietist Johann Blumhardt, there has always existed prior to, and alongside, this scientific or rationally systematic theology a "nonacademic" theology that takes the form of prayers, commentaries, devotions, and disputations (Barth, 1947, 588). The most creative pentecostal theological discourse can be included as a more-or-less popular form of a nonacademic theological genre.

B. Hermeneutics and Bible Doctrines.

Pentecostal theology has not been simply an attempt to interpret religious experience through a story, a song, or a dance. Pentecostals have inherited from their evangelical forebears a devotion to Scripture. For all of its advantages and limitations, theology for pentecostals from the beginning has been a biblical theology, though not generally one that has consciously utilized critical methodologies. The experiences they expressed and interpreted orally and dramatically were formed in the context of the "strange new world of the Bible." For pentecostals, theology means clarifying the message of Scripture in service to the fellowship and evangelistic mission of the church. Traditional forms of biblical theology have tended in the past, therefore, to be more popular among academically trained pentecostals than the more abstract or philosophically oriented constructive or systematic theology. Even to this day, the Assemblies of God Theological Seminary, the only U.S. seminary of the world's largest pentecostal denomination, does not have a chair of systematic theology, nor are any courses in this subject required for the seminary's degree programs, including the Master of Theological Studies. Interestingly, the seminary does require courses in biblical theology.

The advantage of this preference for a biblical theology lies in the possibility of a fresh approach to certain doctrines that have for centuries been excessively burdened by dogmatic concerns. As Harold Hunter noted, "The Pentecostal Movement's universal predilection for oral narrative and praxis is not incidentally related to the belief that pneumatic experience subject to extensive analysis can become entombed in layers of theological formulas which do not stimulate the faithful" (Hunter, 1996, 19–20). For example, though a full-blown pentecostal pneumatology has not yet been written, it might be interesting to see how this could be done in a way that transcends the burden of merely filling out the elaborate and complex doctrines of the Trinity and the church. As we will note, such an observation is not meant as a denial of the need for pentecostals to include in their discourse on pneumatology reflection that is responsive to these and other areas of doctrinal concern. But pneumatology has been neglected historically, particularly in the West, because it has functioned merely as the servant to other, more prominent, doctrines. A biblical theological method might be able to open up fresh concerns and directions for pneumatology that have not figured prominently in the history of the doctrine.

But something more than a biblical theology is required for such a pentecostal theology of the Spirit. A biblical theology of the Spirit must also be consciously critical and contextual if it is to offer a fresh approach to Scripture in a way that speaks to people in the world today. Michael Welker's recent pneumatology, *God the Spirit* (1994), might serve as a model for pentecostals who are more attracted to a biblical than to a systematic theology. Welker engages in a consciously contextual and theological reading of various biblical traditions with regard to the doctrine of the Spirit and consequently uncovers fresh pneumatological themes that have been neglected in the history of dogma. He does not discuss the Trinity or the church in his book, in order to liberate pneumatology from servitude to these towering doctrines.

This preference for biblical theology among pentecostals is due in part to the fact that pentecostalism is "restorationist," with the goal of recovering the full life of the Spirit experienced by the churches of the apostles and depicted for us in the NT. The pentecostals do not regard the apostles as constituting a spiritual "aristocracy" whose experience of the

Spirit was allegedly different in kind, and not only in degree, from that which may be had in the churches of succeeding generations. The experience of the Spirit depicted in the Bible, especially in the book of Acts, is for all Christians of all generations, because the same Spirit involved in the events and words of the text is alive in the church today, and the Jesus whom the Spirit anointed and to whom the Spirit bears witness is "the same, yesterday, today, and forever." There is for pentecostals a certain "present-tenseness" to the events and words of the Bible, so that what happened then, happens now, and what was promised then inspires assurance and hope in every Christian today. Reading the text becomes an event of the Spirit, in which the reader is transformed and made to experience what the Bible puts forth as living truth.

Thus, the pentecostals inherited a kind of "biblicism," in the sense that they believed themselves capable of entering and living in the world of the Bible through the ministry of the Spirit without the need for consciously engaging the hermeneutical difficulties of reading an ancient text from a modern situation. It is important to note that pentecostals were therefore not part of the fundamentalist/modernist debate concerning the validity and limits of historical criticism. While the fundamentalists were concerned with the factual inerrancy of the text and the methods proper to uncovering the true historical intention of the biblical author, pentecostals were seeking to spiritually discern the meaning of a text for their daily lives.

Consequently, the fundamentalists have historically been the most severe antagonists of the pentecostal movement, in part because of the basic dependence of pentecostals on contemporary experience of God's revealed presence and Word, rather than on "objective" scientific method in their interpretation of Scripture. Many pentecostals, particularly in the U.S., have worked hard over the decades to gain the acceptance of these fundamentalists, who were the more ecclesiastically and socially established siblings in the faith, by following them in their struggle to narrowly define the limits and results of historical method. Gerald Sheppard has shown that these pentecostals became over time at best awkward imitators of fundamentalist arguments concerning the historical/factual inerrancy of the biblical text and the methods allowable for uncovering authorial intent (Sheppard, 1978).

But this passion for the scientifically verifiable accuracy of the text did not arise from the ways in which pentecostals actually engaged the text. Scriptural interpretation was not primarily an academic exercise for them. As Finnish pentecostal theologian Veli-Matti Kärkkäinen noted, the fellowship and worship of the church forms the hermeneutical context for interpreting the Scripture for pentecostals (Kärkkäinen, 1997, 5, 20). The truth and authority of the Bible for pentecostals have always been spiritually discerned,

especially in the community of faith empowered by the gifts of the Spirit and "anointed" preaching. Such truth and authority of Scripture are not dependent primarily on scientific method, which was the modernist passion—whether it be fundamentalist or liberal—but on the experience of the Spirit in the context of the kerygmatic, koinoniac, and doxological functions of the church, the "discourse community" of faith. For this reason, some have called pentecostals "submodern" or "paramodern."

By basing the context of theological reflection fundamentally in the worship of the church, pentecostals imply a theological method similar to Geoffrey Wainwright's attempt, in his magnum opus *Doxology: The Praise of God in Worship, Doctrine, and Life* (1980), to make the worship of the church the center of theological reflection. Wainwright allows for a mutual illumination between doctrine and worship as well as between worship and praxis. But recently, pentecostals have tended to prefer the term "spirituality" over worship as the primary locus of theological reflection, in order to include both worship and practical living in the hermeneutical context. Thus, pentecostal theologian Simon Chan bases theology in spirituality. He reminds his readers that prior to the enlightenment all theology was regarded as spiritual. It was to be based in prayer and directed to the glory of God (Chan, 1998, 16). Similarly, Steven J. Land has written a prolegomenon to a pentecostal theology in which spirituality is regarded as the foundation of theology because it is in the formation of the sanctified and empowered life in the light of the coming kingdom that fundamental beliefs are forged as authentic expressions of faith and meaningful sources of guidance for future living. Though much more robustly eschatological than Chan's theology, Land's book shares Chan's concern to root theology fundamentally in prayer (Land, 1993). It is debatable whether or not pentecostals have commonly placed as much weight on daily living as on worship as the primary context for interpreting the Scriptures. Given the neglect in pentecostal theology of attention to secular context, it may be that Wainwright's desire to place doxology or worship at the core of both theological reflection and praxis may best fulfill the most common direction of pentecostal theologizing, especially since pentecostals seldom consciously reflect on their praxis. Besides, pentecostal life largely feeds theological reflection in the form of testimonies given to the glory of God in worship.

Of course, pentecostals today who may rightly seek to be consciously contextual beyond the walls of the church in their interpretation of Scripture will be confronted with the problem of reading an ancient text from a contemporary social and cultural context. They will then need to wrestle with the problem of determining the place and goal of historical method within the exegetical task. It is to be hoped that the pentecostals will not confine themselves to the historical methods of the fundamentalists or liberals and will not neglect the place of spiritual discernment in the interpretive process, regardless of how ambiguous or simplistic such a pietistic reading of the text might seem. As Russell Spittler commented, "I am not at all prepared to say that such simple pietistic use of Scripture is defective; it is not so much wrong as limited" (Spittler, 1985, 75). Karl Barth's passion for encountering the living Christ as the chief subject matter of the text and the related desire to place scientific and other interpretive methods in the service of this act of hearing by the Spirit of God might provide pentecostals with a way beyond the limitation of a nonacademic reading of the biblical text.

Unfortunately, many pentecostals have depended on the fundamentalists for more than hermeneutical priorities. When pentecostals in the U.S. organized Bible schools for the training of ministers to be ordained in the churches, the need arose for textbooks that would summarize the truths of Scripture. They turned to the fundamentalists for such doctrinal texts, in part because of the social and ecclesiastical proximity of pentecostals to their fundamentalist antagonists, but also because of the high view of the authority of Scripture and the high regard for certain cardinal doctrinal truths shared with the fundamentalists. Consequently, the pentecostals made their initial move toward biblical theology, not in the traditional sense of critically determining the unique themes of biblical authors or texts, but as "Bible doctrines" understood simply as a thematic organization of Scriptures. Though systematic, these were not systematic theologies in the commonly understood sense of creating a cogent vision of the Christian faith by systematically reflecting on the various *loci* in the context of the scriptural witness, the history of the Christian tradition, and a particular contemporary ecclesiastical and/or cultural context. P. C. Nelson's *Bible Doctrines* (1947) and E. S. Williams's (mistakenly titled) *Systematic Theology* (1953) are classic examples of this genre of theology as Bible doctrines. Such works were characteristically abstract and encyclopedic in nature, with little or no appeal to experience through testimony or devotional reflection. Throughout the process of developing Bible doctrines, the more experiential and oral theologizing continued among pentecostals through testimonies, sermons, and devotions, without any recognition of the fact that there existed tension between this way of doing theology and the emerging "Bible doctrines" genre.

More recent pentecostal reflection on hermeneutics reveals some of the diversity experienced outside the pentecostal movement. A number of pentecostal scholars and teachers, especially from the Bible colleges of major pentecostal denominations, seem quite content, snuggled securely in the nest of a rather narrow range of historical and linguistic investigations into the biblical text (some nest there rather uncomfortably but dutifully for vocational and economic reasons). Others, particularly in the context of academic societies such as the SPS and the European Pentecostal/Charismatic Research Association, are exploring ways of approaching Scripture that engage the full range of problems posed by historical criticism but that also move beyond these problems to literary and canonical approaches to understanding the nature of the biblical text and the task of exegesis. How this work will influence emerging pentecostal theologies and preaching, only time will tell. Future work is needed in bringing together in dialogue hermeneutical, theological, and practical discussions among pentecostal academics.

C. The Question of Theological Loci.

Swiss pentecostal theologian Jean-Daniel Plüss stated concerning the development of pentecostal theology, "In the beginning there was an experience and a testimony; then came an explanation in the form of a theological construct" (Plüss, 1993, 191). In affirming this statement it is also important to note that the theological construct was not entirely the innovation of pentecostal experience and testimony. It was already present in pre-pentecostal forms, about to be reconfigured in the context of experience and testimony, and exercising an influence on the nature of them both. The relationship between experience and doctrine is, therefore, complex. Ever since the publication of George Lindbeck's, *The Nature and Purpose of Doctrine* (1984), many have questioned the possibility of having and expressing one's faith experience totally apart from the fundamental influence of doctrine. It can be said that doctrine provides the structure within which a community experiences God and grants that community the "grammar" necessary to express it. Such insights support the legitimacy of inquiring into the doctrinal framework that gave pentecostal testimonies and dances their cogency and direction as expressions of evangelical faith.

Donald Dayton's work *The Theological Roots of Pentecostalism* (1988), represented a groundbreaking inquiry into the theological *loci* or areas of doctrinal concern that gave pentecostal theology its original framework and grammar. Dayton determined that pentecostalism took from its background in the Holiness movement a fourfold devotion to Jesus Christ as Savior, Spirit Baptizer, Healer, and Coming King (fivefold if one discusses sanctification apart from salvation and Spirit baptism). What was unique about pentecostal theology was not just Spirit baptism or speaking in tongues. Not even the four themes of salvation, Spirit baptism, healing, and eschatology that made up the "full Gospel" were unique in themselves, since they were borrowed individually from the Holiness movement and other evangelical strands of influence. What was unique was how these themes formed a "gestalt" of devotion in the Spirit to Jesus that reconfigured evangelical piety and gave pentecostalism its christological center as well as its theological cogency and direction.

David William Faupel's work *The Everlasting Gospel* (1996) seeks to argue that eschatology was not just one of the elements of a fourfold gospel for pentecostals but rather the driving force and horizon of all other elements. The full gospel becomes an end-time herald, driven to the four corners of the earth by believers empowered with a proliferation of gifts, such as tongues and healing, and the pentecostal movement emerges as an end-time missionary fellowship in service to Jesus as the Coming King. As noted below, James Dunn has rightly stated that this belief in such a proliferation of the spiritual gifts makes the empowerment and significance of the laity an important pentecostal distinctive (Dunn, 1985). In this empowered Christian force, Jesus as the Coming King functions as the Savior, Spirit Baptizer, and Healer.

Steven J. Land's theology weds the Wesleyan godly affections with the christological/eschatological center of pentecostal theology noted by Faupel in order to speak of these affections as "apocalyptic passions." In Land's theological vision, the Wesleyan christocentric understanding of the sanctified life gains a stronger pneumatological and eschatological direction. Land thereby attempts to keep pentecostalism closely tied to its Wesleyan roots without neglecting the radical eschatological direction that the movement took in its break with its Wesleyan heritage (Land, 1993).

The fourfold gospel is important for understanding the origins and enduring accents of emerging pentecostal theologies. The Christ that occupies the center of pentecostal theology is not an abstract or ideological principle, but the living Christ who still accomplishes the will of the Father through the power of the Spirit today. The living Christ as the center for theological reflection is not consistent with ideological and dogmatic responses but rather with those that are dialogical and humble. After all, no theology can claim to fully capture the essence of the living Christ without promoting an arrogance that borders on blasphemy. Understanding the living Christ as the center of theology encourages a theological reflection that is potentially pluralistic and ecumenical, since no single cultural or ecclesiastical perspective can capture Christ in his fullness. Yet pentecostal theology has a potential for a clearly defined christological and biblical criterion. Especially in the context of the vast ambiguity and distortion often associated with language concerning the Spirit in today's world, it is urgent that pentecostals clarify, in solidarity with a host of other Christian traditions, a pneumatology that is Christ-centered, devoted to the diverse witness of Scripture, and faithful to the ministry of the kingdom of God that was realized decisively in the person and work of Jesus of Nazareth and continues on today through the ministry of the exalted Christ and the Holy Spirit.

But this full gospel also reveals the current limits of pentecostal theology. Such a framework alone is potentially Christomonistic (in which devotion to Christ defines every other area of theological concern) and dominated by a concern with the way of salvation. Excluded (or reduced to subordinate status) is the fatherhood of God, election, creation, Trinity, Scripture, and church. Without a fundamental place for these doctrines, even Christology and pneumatology will suffer a lack of development. As John Christopher Thomas noted in his presidential address at the SPS in 1998, a pentecostal theology true to its roots will need to regard seriously the fivefold gospel (in which he included Jesus as Sanctifier), so that such a theology becomes inconceivable apart from a reflection on the gospel and service to the mission implied therein. But pentecostal theology cannot be confined to this paradigm if it is to speak to a broader configuration of *loci*.

D. Contextualization.

The *loci* of the full gospel are significant for understanding the origins and development of pentecostal theology. But, as implied above, the living Christ at the heart of the full gospel cannot be confined to just these *loci* and is bound to be experienced uniquely in cultural contexts very different from those involved in the early growth of pentecostalism. During the 1960s and 1970s, many classical pentecostals were faced with a kind of ecclesiastical culture shock when they discovered renewal movements that resembled features of pentecostal worship and spirituality, but within the very mainline churches that were considered to be opponents of the pentecostal revival and that were regarded as being very different from pentecostalism theologically and culturally.

While the charismatic movement was still Protestant and largely pentecostal in theology, it represented no serious challenge to classical pentecostals. But when the movement reached the Catholic Church, pentecostals were faced with an ecumenical challenge. As Vinson Synan remarked after his first experience at a Catholic charismatic service, "They were singing 'our' songs and exercising 'our' gifts. It was more than I could take" (Synan, 1974). Sacramental spirituality and church renewal suddenly provided the theological contexts for interpreting the experience of the Spirit in place of the eschatological passion and the search for revival cultivated among the pentecostals. Most charismatics did not mine pentecostal literature or testimonies for insights, since they mistakenly defined classical pentecostals as fundamentalists with nothing substantial to offer theologically or ecumenically. But their presence did provide pentecostals (especially in the U.S.) with an ecumenical challenge beyond that which the evangelicals had offered (Macchia, 1996). Pentecostal ecumenical contacts have exceeded the earlier influence of the charismatic movement. Certain pentecostal groups in Latin America, Europe, and South Korea belong to interdenominational ecumenical councils. Conversations are taking place between the pentecostals and the Roman Catholic Church, the World Alliance of Reformed Churches, and the

National Council of Christian Churches (U.S.). Only time will tell what impact such ecumenical contacts will have on developing pentecostal theologies.

The rapid growth of pentecostal movements outside the U.S. was bound to raise the issue of the contextualization of pentecostal experience with a sense of urgency. Hollenweger refers to a "responsible syncretism" that involves the adaptation to an indigenous culture by a pentecostal movement without contradicting its essence and life as a movement of Christian affirmation, which implies that *contextualization* would be a more appropriate term for describing this process than *syncretism*. Harvey Cox (1995) has provided an interesting response to global pentecostalism that deals with the same issue of pentecostal contextualization and diversity. Hollenweger and Cox are both convinced that pentecostal movements tend to incarnate themselves into their various cultures, producing a cultural and theological diversity within pentecostalism that may present future theologians of the movement with creative ecumenical challenges. As Cecil M. Robeck has remarked, pentecostalism is multicultural and ecumenical, though much of the movement does not yet realize it (Robeck, 1993).

Pentecostal theologians have already begun to deal consciously with the issue of contextualization. In separate essays, Korean pentecostal theologians Wonsuk Ma (1998) and Julie Ma (1997) have written on the unique characteristics of pentecostal communities in Korea and the Philippines respectively. Wonsuk noted that pentecostalism in Korea did not originally flourish as an eschatological movement due to the this-worldly and materialistic orientation of indigenous folk religions. Similarly, Julie found the tendency among pentecostal communities in the Philippines to adapt the pentecostal focus on healing and miraculous spiritual gifts to the shamanistic folk religions there. A similar immanent pneumatology exists in forms of African pentecostalism. There is potential in such contexts for a creation pneumatology that affirms God's presence in the material and communal aspects of life, such as one finds in the pneumatologies of Clark Pinnock (1996) and Jürgen Moltmann (1992). As I point out below, pentecostalism has always held to a "material" understanding of salvation and its blessings. But there is also the threat of materialism, as we have seen in the so-called health-and-wealth gospel in the U.S. In tension with such materialism are pentecostalism's Christocentric and eschatological orientations, which imply theological themes critical of a one-sided emphasis on material blessing and power against threatening forces in life. Certainly the way of the cross implies a gospel that would not advocate a health-and-wealth message independent of the priority of striving for justice and mercy in the world of human relationships.

In certain parts of the world, such as Africa and Asia, the relationship between the wisdom and the guidance of the ancestors and the work of the Spirit has been questioned by pentecostals. Harvey Cox implies that a potentially positive relationship is conceivable, though he admits that the majority of pentecostals would disagree (Cox, 1995, ch. 11). Wonsuk Ma, for example, wrote negatively of an identification of the voices of wise ancestors and the voice of the Spirit such as was advocated by Reformed theologian Hyun-Kyung Chung (presently of Union Theological Seminary in New York) during her presentation at the 1991 world assembly of the World Council of Churches in Canberra. She redefined the ancestral voices as the voices of victimized spirits in history that cry out for justice and claimed that "we experience the Holy Spirit through these victimized spirits" (W. Ma, 1998, 6). Perhaps a connection between such ancestral voices and the Holy Spirit can be achieved among pentecostals in Africa and Asia by following the lead of some in ecumenical conversations on this issue in identifying Christ as the chief ancestor and the one to whom the Spirit bears fundamental witness in whatever wisdom may be gleaned from ancestral voices. The Spirit speaks through victimized spirits only in their role of pointing toward the liberation story of Jesus.

Clearly the original pentecostal Christocentric pneumatology can be of help in guiding pentecostal contextualization. From such a point of departure one may justifiably question the reference of Korean scholar Boo-woong Yoo to any spiritual movement in Korea as essentially "pentecostal" (1988). This ambiguous usage of the terms *Spirit* and *pentecostal* provoked critical responses from Wonsuk Ma and Kyung-bae Min (W. Ma, 1998, 4). Such conscious efforts at critically discerning the contextualization of the pentecostal message are urgently needed. All world Christian bodies are diverse and pluralistic and face the challenges of contextualization. But the emphasis on pneumatic experience and the lack of a developed theological and liturgical tradition within pentecostalism make the challenges of contextualization especially urgent. This urgency is intensified by the fact that most pentecostals are not consciously contextual outside of the walls of the church nor consistently discerning in their integration of the pentecostal *kerygma* and elements of indigenous cultures. Hopefully there will be greater international exchange among pentecostal bodies in the future so that pentecostals might be able to bless each other in their efforts to proclaim a biblical and Christian *kerygma* that is true to pentecostal distinctives and open to diverse expressions.

II. Theological Issues.

A. The Godhead and the Christ of the Full Gospel.

The christological concentration of the pentecostal full gospel was bound to raise the issue of the Trinitarian structure of the Christian confession and theological *loci*. A concentration on Christ inevitably raises the question of his relationship to the one who has sent him and to the one who has anointed him for service and now bears witness to his person and work. There is an inherent Trinitarian structure to the gospel that involves a threefold work of God, traditionally described as Creator (Father), Redeemer (Son), and Giver of Life (Spirit). All pentecostals have agreed to some kind of a Trinitarian structure to God's self-disclosure, though not all would agree to embracing it as Trinitarian in the classical sense of involving intradivine personal relations. The Oneness wing of the pentecostal movement has rejected classical Trinitarian theology. Especially outside the U.S., Oneness pentecostals have not severed all links with other pentecostal and evangelical bodies. The challenge inherent in this fact involves ecumenical conversations between sibling pentecostal groups that hold very different views of "apostolic" faith concerning the nature of God.

The debate over the nature of the Godhead (initially termed the "New Issue") had its roots in the famous 1913 pentecostal camp meeting held for a month in Los Angeles under the powerful preaching of Maria Wordworth-Etter. There John G. Scheppe was provoked by the statement of R. E. McAlister during a baptismal service that the early apostles only baptized converts in Jesus' name and not in the formula of the Trinity. Scheppe became convinced that the power of the water-baptism experience was communicated through the name of Jesus, a conviction that eventually galvanized support among a number of pentecostals within the young Assemblies of God movement. David Reed, a leading authority on Oneness pentecostal history and theology, has noted that the original issue probably had its impetus as a new revelation concerning the significance of the name of Jesus in legitimating Christian baptism as the context in which the believer ritually accepts the gospel of Jesus Christ and the power of God unto salvation. The Christocentric piety of early pentecostalism, as well as the tendency of pentecostals to find patterns in the book of Acts for depicting apostolic experience and practice, led to the Oneness focus on the name of Jesus in baptism and its significance for the believer's initiation to the Christian faith (Reed, 1975).

It was only later, largely through the work of Frank Ewart, that a comparison between Acts 2:38 and the baptismal formula of Matt. 28:18 led to the conclusion among those who baptized in Jesus' name that the Trinitarian designations of Father, Son, and Spirit were merely functional descriptions of the self-disclosure of the one God in the human person of Jesus. Hence, the two texts were harmonized by making "Jesus" the name of the "Father, Son, and Spirit," which means theologically that the name of Jesus is symbolic of God's nature and of God's diverse involvement among us for our redemption. The monarchian understanding of God, supported by this harmonization of baptismal texts, evolved from an understanding of God's redemptive act through the powerful name of Jesus, especially as received in the context of water baptism (Reed, 1975).

There are misunderstandings on both sides of the Trinitarian/Oneness pentecostal division that will hopefully be replaced by bridges of understanding through ongoing conversations such as those that have already occurred recently at meetings of the SPS. For example, Trinitarian faith is not in its classical form tritheistic and does involve the OT teaching concerning the Oneness of God. Also, Trinitarian pentecostals grant at least a certain amount of significance to the name of Jesus as symbolic of the divine lordship and redemptive act, though this is a neglected biblical teaching that the Oneness pentecostals have rediscovered. On the other hand, Oneness pentecostals do not deny the person of the Father, but in fact emphasize the Father as the Almighty God revealed in the Son whom they regard as the human person of Jesus. This one God, the Father, revealed in Jesus can also be called the Spirit if one is referring to God's transcendent nature or to God's presence among us representing Christ (as "Holy Spirit").

Also to be recognized is the implicitly Trinitarian language that structures Oneness beliefs and experience of God. The articles of faith of the United Pentecostal Church state:

> We believe in one everliving, eternal God: infinite in power, Holy in nature, attributes and purpose; and possessing absolute, indivisible deity. This one true God has revealed Himself as Father, through His Son, in redemption; and as the Holy Spirit, by emanation.

Though not yet explicitly Trinitarian, this language does imply a certain threefold complexity to God's being that corresponds to the complexity of the divine involvement in redemption. To begin with, Oneness pentecostals can be heard maintaining that, even though the "fullness" of the Godhead was revealed in Jesus, God was still omnipresent. This distinction between a "transcendent" and all-encompassing presence of God and the God present and revealed in Jesus is then further complicated at times in an implicitly Trinitarian direction. For example, a reference was made in 1919 by A. D. Urshan to a "mysterious, inexplicable, incomprehensible threeness" to God and in 1971 by Kenneth Reeves to a "multi-intelligence" and even an "internal communication" in God. Others have described a preincarnate Word of God revealing God's immanent presence that becomes incarnated in Christ (Reed, 1975, 151–52).

Though theological reflection on the border between Trinitarian and Oneness pentecostals is relatively recent, some fruitful directions are beginning to emerge. David Reed has recently appealed to the diversity of the Christian faith from its ancient forms onward in order to caution against applying the term *heresy* to Oneness pentecostals (1995, 3ff.). He further maintains that it is possible to affirm insights central to the Oneness vision that are part of the earliest Christian witness, and which in fact deepen our own understanding of Jesus in the light of the whole biblical account (25).

Reed refers specifically to the early Jewish theology of God's name and of the early preference revealed in the book of Acts for baptism into the name of Jesus (13ff.). The Oneness pentecostals can help to enrich the diverse Christian witness today, since they point Christians to aspects of the early, diverse witness to Jesus that have been neglected in the developed theology of the West.

In searching for common ground between Trinitarian and Oneness pentecostals, Catholic theologian Ralph Del Colle focuses on the Spirit-baptismal experience among believers of the exalted Christ as the self-disclosure of the Father in the power of the Spirit. Undergirding this experience is a pneumatological Christology in which Jesus of Nazareth functions as the incarnate presence of the Father's self-disclosure through the dynamic working of the Spirit. Del Colle avoids using the term *persons* for describing this complex activity of God in Christ but centers instead on the experience and worship of Christ shared by all pentecostals. Though not all pentecostals would draw explicitly Trinitarian conclusions from their spirituality, they all share the same experience and praise of the Father through the glorified Christ in the Spirit, which is a rich source of common commitment to the Christian faith (Del Colle, 1997).

But one must still deal with the issue of "immanent" Trinitarian relations. Pentecostal theologian Amos Yong discusses the view of his mentor, R. C. Neville, that God's relational self-distinctions began with creation, God's original act of self-giving, as a form of Trinitarian theology that needs to be taken seriously. Though a Trinitarian, Yong suggests that reading these self-distinctions (Father, Son, and Spirit) back into God's eternal being is not necessary for a common Trinitarian/Oneness understanding of the divine involvement in history for redemption. Consequently, Yong wishes to open the door for substantial agreement among all pentecostals concerning the Trinitarian involvement of God in history. The Trinitarian and Oneness pentecostal disagreement over the eternal being of God need not form a barrier to their unity in the faith (Yong, 1997). To carry Yong's conversation further, it would be helpful to explore certain related issues such as the freedom of God (how can we speak of God's freedom apart from the divine act of creation?) and the authenticity of revelation (is a threefold revelation of God as Father, Son, and Spirit true to God's eternal being if this revelation does not in some way correspond to distinctions within God's eternal life?).

As Reed has noted, the key issue, it seems, for Oneness pentecostals is the preservation of the idea that Christ is the "full" revelation of this God whose Oneness is nevertheless inexplicably complex. Oneness pentecostals wish to reject the idea that Jesus only revealed a single person (a divine Son) within a Godhead that includes other persons. Jesus was the "fullness" of the Godhead in bodily form (Reed, 1974, 148). On a practical level, what is being guaranteed for Oneness pentecostals is the trustworthiness of the name of Jesus as the only means by which the power of God in fullness to save can be received. There is no possibility of other deities or divine "persons" that may be regarded as equally, or even more, significant than the One revealed in Jesus as the locus of God's redemptive activity. At stake is the power of the name of Jesus to channel the fullness of divine redemption.

With this emphasis on the divine fullness in Christ, Oneness pentecostals reacted to a distorted notion of the Trinity as a kind of tritheistic union of divine intelligences. Important to note is that this distorted view of the Trinity actually has roots in popular Christian piety and theology. A significant distortion of classical Trinitarian formulations took place in the translation of the term *hypostases* (persons) into the contemporary language of personalistic individualism. Of course, many Trinitarians would agree that the idea of Jesus as merely revealing one individual divine intelligence among others is a notion that is problematic at best. What is needed is for Trinitarian pentecostals to clarify their notion of divine "persons" so as to reject the individualistic understandings of that term popular in the West. As is well known, Karl Barth attempted to do this by rejecting the term *persons* in his discussion of the Trinity in favor of the term *modes of existence*. In a similar direction, Karl Rahner preferred the term *distinct manners of subsisting*. Following the leads of Barth and Rahner, the newer Trinitarian theologies would subordinate essentialist language (e.g., hypostasis) to relational and functional categories, which for many have implications for God's transcendent, inner life, as well as the realm of God's self-giving and self-disclosure.

Within more recent Trinitarian thinking, those holding to the social doctrine of the Trinity will find it more difficult to dialogue with Oneness pentecostals and will be more easily stereotyped as tritheists. A notable example is Miroslav Volf's provocative study on the analogous relationship between the Trinity and the church, especially since he writes from the context of his background in Croatian pentecostalism. Volf follows his mentor, Jürgen Moltmann, in advocating a social doctrine of the Trinity in which the unity of the divine persons is secured through the doctrine of *perichoresis* (the persons being "in" one another). He links this understanding of the Trinity as a society or fellowship of persons with a free-church and charismatic ecclesiology that is characterized as a fellowship of believers and not an authoritative hierarchy. In such a church fellowship, each believer, as a bearer of the Spirit, is vital to the existence and ministry of the church (Volf, 1998). Volf's theology would most likely be understood as tritheistic by most Oneness pentecostals.

Yet Volf's book does provide an interesting way of exploring the implications in Oneness theology for dealing with the analogy, implied in texts on spiritual gifts (1 Cor. 12:4–6; Eph. 4:4–6), between the divine self-disclosure as Father, Jesus (Lord), and Spirit, and the nature of the church. Perhaps a christological analogy for the church might be a point of departure for a Oneness/Trinitarian dialogue on the church and God's triunity. In such a point of departure the focus would not be on God as a society or fellowship of persons but on the implications of God's self-disclosure in Christ for the nature of relationships in the church. Indeed, the important monotheistic roots of Christianity seem to be sacrificed by the social doctrine of the Trinity. Though pentecostal theologian Simon Chan sees some value in the social analogy between God and creation or church, he warns against an "over-trinitarianizing" of God "at the expense of the equally true monotheistic conception." One can understand the importance of Chan's warning in the light of the pantheistic and animistic threats that are present in the contexts from which he writes (Chan, 1998, 28).

The Oneness concern for viewing Jesus as the locus of the redemptive activity of God in fullness can also be an important point of dialogue between Trinitarian and Oneness pentecostals. The Christ of *logos* Christology in the West has tended to lack divine "fullness," though for reasons somewhat more complex than those commonly isolated by Oneness authors. The rather limited focus historically on the nature of the *logos* in relation to the nature of the Father (Nicea) or of Jesus' human "flesh" (Chalcedon) tended to eclipse the biblical focus on Jesus' experience of the Holy Spirit, particularly in sonship (wrongly abandoned to the adoptionists and later to the shortsighted treatment of theological liberals) or in charismatic calling and servanthood. As a result, Christology has historically lacked Trinitarian fullness and has focused on the incarnate logos to the near exclusion of the more Jewish and Oneness understanding of Jesus as the locus of the Spirit's dwelling and charismatic empowerment.

At stake in this neglect is the authentic humanity of Jesus. Indeed, if the incarnate *logos* did not cancel out Jesus' genuine humanity, then Jesus would naturally be utterly dependent on the Spirit for his experience of sonship and servanthood, allowing him to become the paradigmatic child and servant of God. And what is the meaning of "incarnation" without the reality of the Spirit to unite the *logos* with the person of Jesus and with the experience and ministry of Jesus in the world? Of course, Christology in the West has never restricted the nature of Christ to one individual divine person, separate from the Father and the Spirit, as the Oneness pentecostals usually suggest. But the Oneness pentecostals are right in assuming that the fullness of the divine life surfaced in the Christ event and exercised a decisive influence on the faith of the NT. This Oneness concern for

the fullness of the divine life revealed in Jesus can still represent a point of departure in Christology that Trinitarian pentecostals can take seriously, though for somewhat different reasons than those commonly isolated by Oneness pentecostals. Hence, this entire topic can be an illuminating point of discussion for both sides of the Trinitarian/Oneness discussion.

Barriers will undoubtedly remain. Since Oneness pentecostals regard Jesus' role as the "Son" as merely descriptive of his human activity, they share a Nestorian tendency to separate the human from the divine activity in Jesus. This Nestorian Christology serves to locate the relation between the Father and the Son in the realm of Christology (Jesus as the merely human Son relates to the divine) rather than in the Godhead, as in classical Christian theology (between the divine persons of the Father and the Son). Unexplored is the significance of Jesus' sonship for revealing, not only his authentic humanity, but also the very nature of God as humble and self-sacrificial. The intradivine relation of Father and Son, in which the human Jesus is made to play an integral role, reveals for Trinitarians the complex nature of God in both lordship and servanthood. At stake is the full identification of God with Jesus' humanity and human actions, including his weakness, anguish, and act of suffering and death on the cross (fulfilling what Barth called the "humanity of God"). God is, after all, the "crucified God."

It is tempting to say that Oneness pentecostals wish to preserve the fullness of God as revealed in Jesus, while Trinitarian pentecostals, in their rejection of Nestorian Christology, implicitly want to preserve the fullness of Jesus as revelatory of God. The former offers a Christology that promises to involve humanity in the fullness of the divine life, while the latter promises to involve God in the fullness of human life. These dual concerns can form the basis for fruitful exchange and dialogue between Trinitarian and Oneness pentecostals.

Though the issues are serious, both Oneness and Trinitarian pentecostals can find commonality in their devotion to the Father through Jesus in the power of the Spirit, as Ralph Del Colle has suggested. Oneness pentecostal theologian Manuel Gaxiola refers to the Trinitarian statement of the Lausanne Pact ("We believe in one God: Father, Son, and Spirit") as a possible confessional common ground for cooperative work between Oneness and Trinitarian pentecostals in associations like the Pentecostal/Charismatic Fellowship of North America (PCCNA; Gaxiola, 1996, 127). The Oneness pentecostals are currently barred from membership due to the association's allegiance to a Trinitarian statement of faith drawn from the National Association of Evangelicals. Pentecostals of the PCCNA will be challenged to reconsider the nature of their political and ecclesiastical allegiances (Macchia, 1995).

B. Regeneration, Sanctification, and Spirit Baptism.

The pentecostal full gospel includes a concern for the regeneration of the individual but also for the dynamic experiences of holiness and "the baptism in the Holy Spirit," understood as empowerment for witness and enhanced charismatic spirituality, involving also heightened praise and an intense awareness of the divine presence. The order and relationship of these three categories—regeneration, sanctification, and Spirit baptism—have represented points of tension and debate in the history of the pentecostal movement. But at the base of the debates is a fundamental devotion to an experience of God that is life-transforming. There can be no question about the fact that the pentecostals inherited from their Holiness and revivalistic roots a dominant concern for the transformation or conversion of the individual life. They have thus attempted in their own way to guard against a view of Christianity as simply a system of dogma, a liturgical practice, or an institutional reality. Though these aspects of Christianity are unavoidable and significant within certain limits, they are not sufficient unless they are involved in Christian formation.

The pentecostal emphasis on individual crisis experience upholds the value and unique giftedness of the individual person as well as the power of the grace of God, which can be magnified at significant points in a person's life to open up new possibilities of experience and service. But there is a need to develop pentecostal formation without neglecting the sacraments of the church, the social consequences of discipleship, and gradual growth through daily spiritual discipline. In general, however, there is potential in the accents of pentecostal spirituality for developing a theology that is nourished by, and in service to, Christian discipleship.

The difficulty involved in relating regeneration to Spirit baptism within a general vision of the spiritual life has to do with the pentecostal doctrine of "subsequence." This doctrine tends to separate dramatic moments in the spiritual life (conversion, sanctification, and Spirit baptism for Holiness pentecostals, and regeneration and Spirit baptism for "baptistic" pentecostals) and even to view them as different stages in one's achievement of the "higher life." A tendency to view the spiritual life as a series of separate, disconnected experiences is typical of revivalism. The doctrine of subsequence also goes back to Joseph Fletcher's understanding of entire sanctification as a crisis experience, termed a Spirit baptism, which was understood as subsequent to, and distinct from, conversion. The scholarship on Wesley indicates that Wesley himself did not teach this doctrine, although he did not forbid his colleague, Fletcher, to do so.

The milieu of revivalism in the U.S., in which Fletcher's doctrine of subsequence flourished, opened the door for other aspects of the spiritual life to be made subsequent to, and distinct from, regeneration. Under the influence of an accent on empowerment for service popularized by the British Keswick revivals, Charles Parham was the first to regard Spirit baptism, understood as empowerment for witness, as a yet third experience, subsequent to both regeneration and sanctification. The order of the three steps of regeneration, sanctification, and Spirit baptism was questioned by converts who entered pentecostalism from outside the Holiness movement, strictly defined, and without Fletcher's understanding of entire sanctification as an experience subsequent to regeneration. The debate erupted early on between pentecostals who embraced entire sanctification as an experience subsequent to regeneration and preparatory for charismatic spirituality and empowerment (Spirit baptism), and those who viewed sanctification as a "finished work" of Christ on the cross and the legacy of all Christians by virtue of regeneration. Those in this latter category only expected two crisis experiences: regeneration and charismatic empowerment (Spirit baptism). This two-step order was understood by Holiness pentecostals as promoting empowerment without holiness. Despite such differences, the pentecostal understanding of subsequence with reference to Spirit baptism was distinctly pentecostal in the early years of the movement and would remain the dominant view of pentecostalism, especially in the U.S.

The weight that many pentecostals place on Spirit baptism (and others on sanctification as well) as an experience distinct from conversion calls into question the theological significance of regeneration. The need is urgent for pentecostals to develop a theology of regeneration to fulfill their concern for personal transformation. Pentecostals have resisted the notion that the entire Christian life is somehow contained in Christian initiation and is simply yet to be realized or actualized in future experiences. As Henry Lederlie has shown, the understanding of Spirit baptism as the actualization of that which is given in initiation is the dominant view in charismatic circles (Lederlie, 1988, 105–6). The eschatological and revivalistic orientation of most pentecostals, however, make them prone to see the Christian life as a series of significant breakthroughs that lead into genuinely new dimensions of identification with Christ. But this orientation raises the question of the continuity of Christian identity, which should connect these spiritual breakthroughs. Are not at least the seeds of all that occurs in future experiences of God already implicit in one's initial identification with Christ through the Spirit, making the regenerative life the overall context for all of our experiences with God? Can regeneration be so distinct from empowerment for service that we can speak of these as separate experiences? Is there not an integral, inseparable connection between faith and vocation? Even if pentecostals feel compelled to reject the understanding of the spiritual life as merely the "actualization" of that which occurred at initiation to the faith, should they not at least speak of spiritual breakthroughs as the "fulfillment" of that which is given in initiation?

Nonpentecostal NT scholars James Dunn and Dale Bruner called into question the exegetical support for the doctrine of subsequence in 1970. Harold Hunter produced the first thorough biblical theology of Spirit baptism from a pentecostal perspective in response to Dunn and Bruner. Hunter defended the biblical foundation for the popular notion of subsequence, but he also supported the biblical basis for questioning it. Though he saw the possibility of distinguishing Spirit baptism from initiation in the Lukan and possibly even in the Pauline witness, he concluded that both the Johannine and Pauline views of the experience of the Spirit are continuous without a distinction between successive "stages" in the spiritual life (Hunter, 1983).

Not all pentecostals have agreed that this kind of diversity exists in the biblical witness concerning the reception of the Spirit. Many classical pentecostals today would agree with charismatic theologian J. Rodman Williams that a distinction between regeneration and Spirit baptism is foundational to the entire NT witness (Williams, 1990, 2:182–85). On the other hand, not all pentecostals worldwide believe the doctrine of subsequence with regard to Spirit baptism to be biblical. The sacramental stream of the Oneness pentecostal movement sees Spirit baptism as integral to a complex of events that is understood under the heading of regeneration. Some German pentecostals have rejected the doctrine of subsequence, and Chilean pentecostal theologian Juan Sepúlveda has argued that the doctrine is not essential to his pentecostal heritage (Sepúlveda, 1996). Pentecostal exegete Gordon Fee has maintained that pentecostals exegete their experience of charismatic renewal into the biblical text and wrongly define Spirit baptism apart from regeneration (Fee, 1985, 88–89). Russell Spittler would agree, even calling the doctrine of subsequence a "non-issue." Pentecostals were not interested in establishing a new dogma of the *ordo salutis*, but they have a hope that weary or largely inactive Christians can be renewed (Spittler, 1983, 43).

More recently, Roger Stronstad (1988) and Robert Menzies (1994) have used the method of biblical theology to criticize a reading of a typically Pauline soteriological concern into a Lukan charismatic pneumatology. Luke's notion of Spirit baptism is allegedly "charismatic" and not soteriological, concerned with the empowerment of believers for prophetic witness and missions and not with one's prior initiation by the Spirit into the life of faith. This argument is not new, though it represents only a minority voice in the scholarship on Acts. Hermann Gunkel distinguished between the Lukan "post-faith" reception of the Spirit that is directed toward charismatic phenomena, especially speaking in tongues, and the Pauline reception of the Spirit as "pre-faith," initiating people into the life of faith in Christ

(Gunkel, 1888; repr. 1979, 17). More recently, theologian Hans Küng remarked that the reception of the Spirit for Luke is not fundamental and determinative for faith as it is for Paul but is directed instead toward the accomplishment of various works for God (Küng, 1967, 165).

Though such arguments, if accepted outside of pentecostal scholarship, have generally been used to reveal the somewhat deficient nature of Lukan pneumatology, which is in need of elaboration and perhaps even correction by Paul, they have served to aid a number of pentecostals in their distinction between Spirit baptism and regeneration. Does Luke's understanding of Spirit baptism have a soteriological concern? Even if one agrees with Stronstad and Menzies that it does, what is yet to be discussed is how Spirit baptism is to be related to initiation from the vantage point of an integrated biblical and systematic theology. Pentecostal scholar Gordon Anderson has proposed placing greater weight on regeneration as the source of the fullness of charismatic life that emerges in the experience of the believer through Spirit baptism. Spirit baptism would thus fulfill in the experience of the believer what is present already among all believers, since all believers are charismatic (1993). This less radical understanding of subsequence helps pentecostals to resist the temptation of elitism that accompanies their understanding of Spirit baptism. The stress on crisis experience also needs to be located more explicitly in a life of spiritual discipline and gradual formation in order to grant continuity to the Christian life. As Steve Land remarked, the Christian life should be described as "a crisis-development process which moves forward, not passively, but passionately" (1993, 33).

One can understand how believers who suddenly become charismatically aware and active in the church can view this awakening as a new stage in the spiritual life, a kind of second "conversion," quite distinct from one's initiation to faith in Christ. The 19th-century Pietist and social activist Christoph Blumhardt once remarked that one must convert twice: once from the world to God, but then a second time from God back to the world to serve the kingdom of God. There is no question that many Christians who occupy the pews of our churches today sorely require this "second conversion." Perhaps the impetus behind the doctrine of Spirit baptism as a "second conversion," so to speak, from devotion to God to devotion to others in the fullness of charismatic spirituality and service has just such a pastoral and missionary concern behind it. The challenge is how to explain more fully theologically such a dramatic experience of charismatic renewal.

The challenge also extends to relating Spirit baptism to sanctification. Early pentecostals associated Spirit baptism with the end-time proliferation of charismatic gifts and empowerment to spread the gospel to the four corners of the earth. Speaking in tongues (commonly understood as xenolalia) was considered vital as the means by which this gospel would be understood in the many languages of the world. The *Apostolic Faith* stated plainly, "The baptism with the Holy Ghost makes you a witness to the uttermost parts of the earth. It gives you the power to speak in the languages of the nations" (Dec. 1906, 2). Through Spirit baptism, the Spirit would come upon the people of God in a special way in order to use them as living oracles of God's will in these latter days. It was this miraculous activity of the Spirit that led the early pentecostals to distinguish Spirit baptism from sanctification, for in the former the Spirit uses the believer to "speak for himself" (e.g., *Apostolic Faith* 1 [3, Nov. 1906], 4).

Yet, the early literature itself does not remain true to such narrow categorizations. In the sermons and testimonies of early pentecostals, sanctification was often described in a way that included empowerment for witness, and Spirit baptism was often defined as effecting a passion for the holy life. For example, Stanley Frodsham wrote in 1917 (*Weekly Evangel*, Feb. 3) that sanctification involved a "life of fearless service," without remarking that boldness in service is essential also to Spirit baptism according to pentecostals (in reference, for example, to Luke 24:49 and Acts 4:31). E. N. Bell wrote in 1914 (*Christian Evangel*, Sept. 19) that the baptism in the Holy Spirit "fills us with divine love." He failed to add that this understanding of Spirit baptism as a process of being transformed by the love of God is also the classic Wesleyan understanding of sanctification!

Likewise, though the biblical witness does not make charismatic empowerment absolutely dependent on maturity in personal holiness (note, for example, the Samson narrative), neither does Scripture separate them. The Pauline exhortations assume that the empowerment and gifts of the Spirit are inconceivable apart from the work of the Spirit in inspiring in us the very love and image of Christ (1 Cor. 12–14; Eph. 4). As Cecil M. Robeck has shown, pentecostal pioneer William J. Seymour made love and holiness the essential evidences of the Spirit's empowering work in and through the lives of believers (Robeck, 1991). Perhaps pentecostals need to work toward viewing Spirit baptism as "vocational sanctification" (David Lim), in which the sanctifying grace of God moves believers into the oft-neglected realms of dynamic witness, charismatic service, and a heightened awareness of divine presence in praise. Indeed, there is a need, in general, to arrive at a more integral understanding of conversion, sanctification, and charismatic spirituality/empowerment that does not separate these dimensions of spirituality into distinct stages but nevertheless recognizes the theological distinctions between them, as well as the need for all Christians to consciously seek to experience all of these areas of the life of faith. What Steven J. Land wrote about entire sanctification in the Holiness pentecostal tradition applies to Spirit baptism as well:

The fundamental issues in relation to entire sanctification . . . are not those of subsequence or eradication; rather, the central concern ought to be the kind or measure of love appropriate or adequate to one who does "so love" the world. Nothing but a wholehearted love is adequate to God's self-giving in Christ. (1992, 34)

C. Water Baptism and Spirit Baptism.

The nature and form of water baptism, especially the relationship between water and Spirit baptism, are debated issues in NT scholarship and among the various church bodies of world Christianity. Despite the popularity of believer's baptism through submersion in pentecostalism, pentecostals globally range across the entire spectrum of practices and beliefs concerning water baptism. What is clear from the previous discussion is that most pentecostals would assume a kind of dualism between the baptisms of water and Spirit. The notable exception would be the Oneness pentecostals, the sacramental wing of which connects water and Spirit baptism in an overall conversion complex that includes repentance, faith, water baptism, and Spirit baptism. Of course, pentecostals would resist formalizing Spirit baptism in the context of water baptism, since such formalization does not adequately account for the implications in the Acts narrative concerning the sovereignty of the Spirit in the event of Spirit baptism and the charismatic nature of Spirit baptism as a conscious and demonstrable experience.

Pentecostals have biblical grounds for resisting a formalization of Spirit baptism through the rite of baptism in water. With the possible exception of Acts 19, Spirit baptism does not occur in the context of water baptism in any of the six accounts recorded in the book of Acts (chs. 2, 4, 8, 9, 10, 19). The references to water baptism in the NT epistles are relatively sparse, even (surprisingly) in the pastoral epistles, and one is not always sure as to whether or not some of the references are metaphorical. Yet Paul appeals to water baptism when urging Christians to recognize their unity (Gal. 3:28) or call to righteousness (Rom. 6). The drinking of the Spirit is connected to a "baptism by the Spirit" in 1 Cor. 12:13 in language that parallels the probable reference to water baptism in Gal. 3:28. There are significant implications in the NT that water baptism is integral to the individual's identification with Christ in the Spirit and may be more significant to regeneration and the empowerment of the Spirit than most pentecostals assume theologically—"theologically," because the majority of pentecostals who argue for a simplistically symbolic interpretation of believer's baptism and who separate baptism radically from regeneration, sanctification, and Spirit baptism, often experience the rite quite differently. Note Walter Hollenweger's description of a typical water baptism among Swiss pentecostals:

On five o'clock on Sunday morning the pentecostals gather at a bathing place on the shore of Lake Zurich. While the candidates for baptism change, the congregation sings. The pastor appears in white tennis clothes, wearing a white tie, while those to be baptized wear long flowing white robes. Before the assembled congregation they are asked, "Do you believe in the Lord Jesus Christ, as the Son of the living God? Have you broken every ungodly link with the world, and with every known sin . . . so that now, freed from a bad conscience through the sprinkling of your heart with the precious blood of Christ, you now wish to come to the bodily cleansing with pure water? Will you give yourself through baptism to be crucified to the world in the death of Jesus, and to die to sin? Will you . . . place the interests of the Kingdom of God in all circumstances and in every place above your own earthly interests?" (1988, 390–91).

After the baptismal candidates agree, each is baptized in water. Hollenweger continues, "The congregation sings and sometimes there is speaking in tongues" (ibid). What seems clear from the above description is that pentecostals tend to experience baptism as a rite of passage in one's identification with Christ and as an event of the Holy Spirit, regardless of what their theology may advocate. The same can be said of the Eucharist and, for a number of pentecostals, footwashing as well. What remains is for pentecostals to rethink their understanding of Spirit baptism so as to tie it more closely to water baptism and the other sacraments of the church.

D. Speaking in Tongues.

Pentecostal scholarship has come a long way toward understanding pentecostal distinctives since James Tinney's argument in 1978 that the only pentecostal distinctive was speaking in tongues. As noted above, it can no longer be assumed that pentecostal distinctives can be reduced to speaking in tongues. Yet tongues were an important distinctive at the beginning of the pentecostal movement. As noted above, pentecostals commonly assumed early on that tongues were integral to the latter-day restoration of apostolic power to share the gospel quickly with people of all nations before the end comes. The conviction at Azusa Street was that this global witness was inspired by God, first among the lowly and oppressed of the earth, for even a "little orphaned colored girl" received the commission to share the goodness of God in the languages of other nations (*Apostolic Faith* 1 [1, Sept. 1906], 1).

This socially and ecumenically relevant understanding of tongues fit in well with the deeper notion of Spirit baptism held by some at the Azusa Street revival as a unifying force among oppressed peoples. For example, a certain "Indian preacher" was reported to have addressed a racially mixed gathering, including Native Americans, whites, and a "colored brother," stating that God had willed for them to become "one great spiritual family." The report ended with the significant conclusion: "Tell me . . . can you have a better understanding of the two works of grace and the baptism in the Holy Ghost?" (*Apostolic Faith* 1 [5, Jan. 1907], 3). Though not all who were involved in the Azusa Street revival would adopt or remain true to such an ecumenical vision, tongues served implicitly to dismantle the privileges of the rich and the educated and to allow the poor and devalued of society to contribute meaningfully to the latter-day witness of the Spirit of God to the coming kingdom. Spirit baptism was understood at Azusa Street in a "glossocentric" way (Sepúlveda, 1996), but this glossocentricity was potentially constructive and positive in its implications, whatever its limitations would prove to be.

Soon it became obvious, however, that tongues could not be used to preach in foreign lands. It also became obvious that tongues were not described as bearing this function in the NT, as Jenny Everts has shown (Everts, 1994). In the decades following the beginnings of pentecostalism, the more Pauline notion of tongues as an in-depth prayer language for self-edification or a congregational gift, usually interpreted among pentecostals as a prophetic message, came to dominate the pentecostal understanding of tongues. Though xenolalia (tongues as foreign languages) did not pass completely from pentecostal testimonies, glossolalia as a transcendent form of speech or a "heavenly language" came to represent the most common understanding of tongues.

This trend is understandable, since tongues in the NT and in the ongoing life of the church have an enduring role to play in the spiritual lives of believers and churches in that tongues represent more than a supernatural capability to bear witness to God in an unlearned human language. Paul defines glossolalia as a mysterious speech that is only meant for God in an individual's private prayers (1 Cor. 14:2, 3, 14–15, 18). This definition scarcely fits xenolalia, since, as is evident in Acts 2, this language miracle is obviously directed to those who know the foreign language. Furthermore, it is difficult to fathom how tongues edify the self in private prayer (1 Cor. 14:3, 14–15) if the one who prays merely speaks to God in a human language that has never been learned. Surely something that arises more profoundly from the depths of the soul than a xenolalic miracle is implied here. And, as Gordon Fee has noted, if tongues were merely known languages foreign to the speaker, it seems strange that Paul would have referred to them analogously as foreign languages in 1 Cor. 14:10–11 (1997, 32). It is small wonder that some pentecostals, such as J. W. Carothers (1906), were hesitant from the beginning of the movement to view tongues as xenolalia.

Clearly, if tongues speaking is to enhance the ongoing charismatic and devotional life of the church, it must meet pentecostals on a level deeper than their current cognitive or linguistic capabilities. The edification of self and congregation is for the purpose of building up believers into the image of Christ. They are thus edified in order to form a solidarity with Christ in his mission through the Spirit to liberate and redeem the creation. Growth in solidarity with Christ is not simply a source of comfort and joy but also of anguish and complaint. Human weakness and protest as a context for understanding glossolalia is described eloquently by black pentecostal pioneer Charles Mason, who described his experience of tongues as a moment of solidarity with Jesus on the cross "groaning" for the redemption of the world (*Apostolic Faith* [Feb.–Mar. 1907], 7).

Hispanic pentecostal theologian Samuel Solivan wrote a theology that has as its center the cry of suffering and complaint, of which tongues are an integral part, which causes the people of God to remain dissatisfied with the status quo and eager to be vessels of the kingdom of God in our midst (Solivan, 1993). Similarly, Harvey Cox could write of the "primal speech" of tongues that overthrows the "tyranny of words" in worship and gives expression to a pain and a yearning for redemption that are too deep for words (Cox, 1995, ch. 4). As such, tongues reveal the limits of human speech to capture and express the mystery of God's redemptive presence in the midst of a suffering creation. Such an understanding of tongues holds a number of theological implications for personal piety and corporate worship. Paul's insistence that the mind is unfruitful during tongues fits well with the groanings that cannot be uttered in response to human weakness in prayer, "for we do not know how to pray" (Rom. 8:26; 1 Cor. 14:14–15). Rather than tongues being a sign of escape from this world into heights of glory, they are expressions of strength in weakness, as Gordon Fee has shown (Fee, 1997). Tongues symbolize the capacity to experience the firstfruits of the kingdom-to-come in the midst of our groaning with the suffering creation. They bring to ultimate expression the struggle that is essential to all prayer, namely, trying to put into words what is deeper than words. They express the pain and the joy of this struggle.

As Frank D. Macchia noted, the eschatological context for tongues as an in-depth response to God is also implied by Luke. The tongues of Pentecost were part of an awesome theophany of end-time signs and wonders (sound of a mighty wind, flames of fire) that foreshadowed the ultimate theophany at God's final appearance (with blood, fire, and billows of smoke) as Redeemer of the entire cosmos (new creation) (Acts 2:1–4, 19–20). As such, tongues hold potential for renewing a sense of awe and wonder in the presence of God that is so vital to a vibrant worship and personal piety. As an unclassifiable language, tongues point to God's final self-disclosure and, therefore, resist efforts to make idols of our worship, religious language, and theological systems. Tongues push the Christian forward to greater vistas of insight and commitment. They imply a dismantling of culturally defined and self-serving idols and open recipients up to the voice of God in new and unexpected ways. As such, tongues can imply a movement out of comfort zones in openness to the voices of the powerless and the victims of evil and injustice in our society (Macchia, 1992).

Tongues as groaning are not just personal or communal, but also global. Tongues clearly symbolize the crossing of cultural barriers in the united witness of the people of God, described by Luke and celebrated at Azusa Street. True, the assumption of those at Azusa Street that tongues functioned to aid in the latter-day spreading of the gospel needed to be abandoned and replaced by deeper insights into the role of tongues as in-depth communion with God. It is possible, however, that pentecostals have thrown out the baby with the bath water, so to speak, by abandoning altogether the global, intercultural, and missionary vision implied in the early understanding of tongues as the "Bible evidence" of Spirit baptism at Azusa Street. One could imagine the theological implications of that early vision of tongues as the "Bible evidence" of the Spirit baptism that was poured out in these latter days, especially among the poor and lowly, to enhance the church's capacity to share the goodness of God across cultural and national boundaries.

Of course, modern pentecostals cannot imagine that they can leap easily across cultural boundaries, especially since the churches described in the book of Acts struggled greatly to do so and with less than perfect results. But do not the groans too deep for words push one beyond the limits of cultural boundaries, so that one might bless, and be blessed by, people from very different backgrounds? Do tongues not expose these limits and how they shape one's worship and theology? Do they not reveal that these limits ultimately need not define one? Whether they be xenolalia or glossolalia, do not tongues locate one already in that final chorus of people from all nations and tongues that will praise God one day at the throne of grace (Rev. 5:9–10)?

Pentecostals have generally not understood very well the various theological implications of tongues speech, leaving a great deal of ambiguity in many minds as to why this mystical prayer is so significant for believers. Frequently, those who analyzed pentecostalism from the outside were quick to interpret such ambiguity in less than positive ways. Because of their glossolalic spirituality, pentecostals were regarded early on as demonically inspired or pathological, although later more tolerantly as "deprived" or "dependent" on authority. Christians who have offered such theological and psychological evaluations of pentecostal glossolalia needed to consider more seriously the fact that such evaluations have been made toward aspects of their own spirituality by critics of religion in general. Indeed, is there any religious experience that is not ambiguous and vulnerable to psychologically unhealthy and even "demonic" influences?

Christians who judged tongues negatively also needed to consider that the tongues speakers of the 1st-century churches can be judged in exactly the same way. Scholars of glossolalia, such as William Samarin, have done much to show that glossolalia (like most forms of Christian spirituality) cannot be attached to any single description or personality type. Their meaning depends on their context and their function (Samarin, 1972). They can participate in a diversity of symbols to inspire a truth value that transforms a community of faith into living witnesses of the very nature and will of God (Yong, 1998), or they can simply represent a playful response to God as our loving Father (Chan, 1997). They can also function "sacramentally" in bringing to verbal expression the grace of God that encounters believers in Spirit baptism (Macchia, 1993). Many other functions can be served as well.

Not long after the origin of pentecostalism, when the understanding of tongues as the miraculous ability to spread the gospel to all nations was quickly abandoned, the doctrine of tongues as the initial evidence of Spirit baptism lost much of its theological meaning. Instead of a sign that God was empowering the church to leap over national and cultural boundaries to share the gospel before the end comes, tongues became the initial sign that one had received a heightened emotional experience. Initial evidence became a dogma that sought to guarantee the reception of Spirit baptism. Though glossolalia itself was an important feature of pentecostal spirituality globally, the initial-evidence doctrine was largely enforced in North American pentecostalism. Pentecostals from other countries were sometimes surprised to learn of the doctrine upon visiting the U.S.

The dogma of initial evidence as it has been defended is not without its difficulties. The doctrine has been based on a "pattern" in Acts in which tongues are implied by their frequent occurrence to be the sign that always accompanied the experience of Spirit baptism. Passages in Acts where tongues were not mentioned (Acts 4, 8, 9) were explained in such a way as to make it reasonable to assume that tongues were indeed present in such events. The interpreter is then not basing his theology of initial evidence so much on the text of Acts as on the assumed nature of the historical events that lie behind the text and are implied in the text. But what the text of Acts implies theologically about tongues and their rich relationship to the experience of Spirit baptism was left largely unexplored. Then there is the issue of Paul's understanding of tongues. Though pentecostals also paid considerable attention to Paul's teaching on tongues, scholars have yet to analyze sufficiently the preference Paul had for prophecy in the fellowship of believers and the superiority of love over all of the gifts as the indispensable consequence and characteristic of the Spirit's work.

It is important to note that not all denominational leaders in U.S. pentecostalism held to the rigid form of the initial-evidence doctrine described above. Joseph Roswell Flower, a virtual pillar of the AG, stated that he was baptized in the Holy Spirit months before he actually spoke in tongues and that he spoke in tongues without seeking to do so. In fact, he was not even aware that he had done so until someone informed him of it afterward (*Pentecostal Evangel* [Jan. 21, 1933], 2ff.). He reasoned later, in a tract entitled *Is It Necessary to Speak in an Unknown Tongue?* (n.d., 7), that the Spirit-baptismal experience is not received according to the "full manifestation" implied in the apostolic pattern provided in Acts until one speaks in tongues. This argument shifts the focus away from tongues as the necessary accompaniment of the Spirit-baptismal event to tongues as the ideal or full biblical expression of what occurs in Spirit baptism.

In support of the focus on tongues in the initial-evidence doctrine, Luke does seem fascinated with the miracle of speech involved in tongues and features it prominently in Acts 2 and 10 (pivotal places in the book) to indicate in advance what God intends to do historically through Spirit baptism in uniting the people of God across cultural boundaries in the missionary work of the Spirit of God. If this is true, people of all denominations can see in tongues a form of expression that fulfills what Luke indicates God wants to accomplish ecumenically through Spirit baptism. New possibilities would emerge for the initial-evidence doctrine if denominational pentecostals would pursue Flower's theological direction.

E. Divine Healing.

Divine healing has functioned as an important distinctive of pentecostalism from the beginnings of the movement. Belief in the miraculous healing of the body goes back to the 19th-century Holiness movement. One historian contends that by the 1870s the healing movement "was a force to contend with in all major evangelical denominations" (R. Cunningham, 1974, 499). In the U.S., Alexander Dowie was an important figure for mediating the central importance of divine healing for pentecostalism. He underscored healing as part of the "signs and wonders" that accompany the work of the Spirit. Another, more christologically based, view of healing among revivalists that communicated its central importance for the gospel was tied to the victory of Christ in the atonement. Through the atonement, Christ, as *Christus Victor*, wrought redemption for both soul and body. From such an influence, pentecostals implicitly held an understanding of redemption that broke with the one-sided focus on penance and the forgiveness of sins typical of the Christian theological legacy in the West since the Middle Ages. The *Christus Victor* understanding of the work of the cross, heralded as the "classical" theory of the atonement by Swedish Lutheran theologian Gustav Aulén (1950), and the belief in the healing of the body as an aspect of this victory, implicitly restored to the gospel a broader base in social liberation and in the restoration of creation.

As pentecostals from German-speaking Europe occasionally note, the roots for such a broad-based theology of healing can be found in the message of the German Pietists Johann and Christoph Blumhardt. Johann Blumhardt had a vast influence on the 19th-century Protestant churches in Germany and Switzerland through his linking of the breaking in of the kingdom of God with the divine healing of the body. He prayed over an extended period of time for the healing of Gottlieben Dittus, a young woman from his parish who suffered from psychological and physical maladies understood by Blumhardt to have been attached to demonic torment and possession. At the close of the prayer "battle" *(Kampf)* the parting spirit proclaimed Jesus as victor *(Sieger)* over the forces of darkness, which became the focal point of Blumhardt's doctrine of the liberating and healing effects of the kingdom of God in the world. A revival followed that had crowds of believers passing through the church and the pastor's home daily for several months.

Blumhardt came to see the healing and the revival as evidence that the kingdom of God cannot be confined to the inner recesses of the human heart nor even to Christian fellowship and doing good. The kingdom is to come in power to transform Christians in soul and body and to make visible changes in the conditions of life. Such a tangible breaking in of the kingdom of God certainly includes spirituality, fellowship, and good works, but it comes through the divine initiative and fulfillment. Blumhardt's piety therefore was one of "action in waiting" on God *(Warten und Eilen,* "waiting and hurrying"). For Blumhardt, the healing of the body was only a foretaste of the healing of creation, and believers are to presently "groan" and yearn for such cosmic liberation from suffering. Johann's son, Christoph, took his father's message of healing and the kingdom of God in the direction of social change. The divine-healing doctrine lay behind his becoming a social activist as a member of the German Social Democratic Party, a radical socialist party of the German workers (Macchia, *Spirituality and Social Liberation,* 1993).

The Blumhardts thus left a theological legacy for Pietism as well as for both the Holiness and the pentecostal movements for understanding divine healing that still requires further discussion and exploration. All too often, there are those who advocate miraculous forms of healing but neglect the human, social, and cosmic dimensions of the healing process. Others stress these natural dimensions of healing without a proper focus on miraculous signs of God's involvement in healing, especially on a personal level. Those who stress natural forms of healing also need to stress the need to wait on the divine initiative and to hope for the divine fulfillment of the healing process. The Blumhardts can provide guidance beyond such an impasse between the miraculous and the naturalistic understandings of healing. Furthermore, the Blumhardts provide inspiration for passionately resisting sickness and death with the promises of the gospel, without presuming that individuals can initiate or fulfill such healing work at will through faith, confession, or other pious initiatives.

Those who sought to distance themselves from the young pentecostal movement tended to abandon the divine-healing doctrine. There had already been growing criticisms of this doctrine among those affected by Holiness and other revival movements at about the time that the pentecostal movement began. Perhaps the early pentecostals joined the movement out of a dissatisfaction with the decline of belief in divine healing within their own denominations. In any case, pentecostalism soon became a haven for those who wished to keep the divine-healing movement alive. The growing pentecostal denominations embraced the divine-healing doctrine, but through the decades it was the healing evangelists who brought the message of healing to the masses. Aimee Semple McPherson, William Branham, Oral Roberts, and A. A. Allen were among the key figures in promoting the vast ecumenical appeal of this healing ministry. Sometimes independent-minded and extreme in their emphases, these figures received a mixed response from the pentecostal denominational leadership.

The possible excesses in the belief in divine healing caused certain denominations to think through the doctrine more carefully. The AG, for example, drafted a position paper ("Divine Healing: An Integral Part of the Gospel," adopted Aug. 20, 1974) that affirmed the doctrine as an aspect of the full gospel and a promise for all Christians today. But the paper also cautioned against presuming that physical healing is a guarantee for those who have the faith, and it located the doctrine in the eschatological context of the resurrection, which is the ultimate fulfillment of healing.

Within such cautious doctrinal reflection, pentecostals have boldly made divine healing an aspect of their "full gospel," rooting healing in the victory of Christ on the cross and in the latter rain of the Spirit that came to restore the full power of the cross and the resurrection over the forces of sin and darkness through the mission of the church. The place pentecostals give to healing has implications for an understanding of the gospel that is not restricted to the forgiveness of sins or the reconciliation of the "soul" to God, but extends also to the liberation and redemption of human society and the entire cosmos. Miroslav Volf wrote of the "material" view of salvation that pentecostals hold in common with liberation theology. Though these movements might seem to be very different from each other, they both understand salvation as corporeal and holistic (Volf, 1989). Similarly, Cheryl Bridges-Johns elaborated on the pentecostal worldview implied in its healing doctrine, which she describes as "transrational" and therefore holistic. She writes, "For pentecostals, truth is not limited to reason. The spectrum of knowledge includes cognition, affection and behavior, each of which is fused to the other two" (Bridges-Johns, 1996, 47). She also notes that there is a spirit-body correspondence in pentecostal theology that has social implications, for "even the most weak and despised are worthy to become tabernacles of God's glory" (49).

Three developments are needed for pentecostals to draw out the theologically holistic implications of their healing doctrine. First, pentecostals need to relate pneumatology beyond the confines of the individual Christian life and the fellowship of the church to the renewal of the entire creation and the transformation of culture and society. As the Blumhardts maintained, pneumatology must have broad cosmic and historical dimensions to be fully biblical. Pneumatology must not be confined to the realm of the miraculous but also be expanded to include God's providential work through natural processes and efforts. Since poverty is a leading cause of disease and death in the world, should not a healing ministry include a fight against the social causes of poverty? Though the medical field is far from perfect, is God not involved in the wisdom and goodness effected in this area of healing? Can the church neglect this vast area of healing in its own healing ministry?

Second, as pentecostal theologians such as Michael Dusing (1996) and Michael Adams (1996) have shown, a pentecostal theology of healing must not neglect a theology of suffering, in which our faith and hope for healing are qualified by our capacity to comfort those who are not healed in this life. But many healing evangelists do not have their focus on those who suffer unavoidably and innocently. These evangelists all too often target their message exclusively toward those who simply capitulate to sickness and disease and accept them as consequences of the divine will for humanity. Such evangelists respond with a resounding "No!" to this resignation and call upon the church to accept nothing less than the healing promised in the gospel. Those who suffer innocently and unavoidably can leave the meetings of such evangelists empty-handed and filled with self-condemnation.

This is not to deny the partial legitimacy of the healing evangelist's resounding "No!" to sickness. As Dorothea Solle has shown in her book *Leiden* (*Suffering*, 1973), the voices of protest against suffering and its causes are needed to prevent our theologies of comfort and acceptance from becoming masochistic. Indeed, the secular medical community has been more committed to fighting sickness and suffering than has the church. One can wonder how true the church is to the ministry of Jesus and the apostles if it only seeks to comfort those who are sick and weak. The Blumhardts have taught us that comfort for those who are not healed must not arise from resignation to the status quo but from a resistance to it and a groaning for the final redemption to come.

But such yearning and working for healing in the broader contexts of society and creation will represent forms of protest that reveal the narrow limitations in the resounding "No!" offered by many of the most visible healing evangelists. Healing in pentecostalism tends to be confined to the individual life, which makes it relatively easy for the robust and healthy healing evangelist to offer himself or herself as proof that the promises of healing have already been fulfilled and can be fully claimed in the here and now. Such illusions of realized eschatology when it comes to healing cannot be so easily maintained once the problem of sickness and suffering is recognized as having much broader and more complex social, global, and cosmic dimensions.

Last, drawing out the implications in pentecostalism for a holistic theology of healing must not neglect the place that pentecostals have given the demonic in their healing ministries and theologies. As noted above, the understanding of the atonement most basic to the gospel in the NT is that of Jesus as victor over the forces of darkness. In the atonement, Christ destroyed "him who holds the power of death—that is, the devil" (Heb. 2:14–15), and "disarmed the powers and authorities ... triumphing over them in the cross" (Col. 2:15). The relatively scarce attention given to the demonic in the OT and the focus there on the sovereignty of God are qualified in the NT with an additional focus on the resistance of the forces of darkness to God's reign. The reign of God, therefore, is involved in dynamic conflict with the ultimate enemies of humankind, bringing victory in Christ and the mission of the Spirit in both the church and the world and moving redemption toward final, eschatological fulfillment in the parousia.

The importance the Gospels place on Jesus' exorcisms in the breaking in of the kingdom of God in his ministry (e.g., Mark 1:23–28; 5:1–20; 7:24–30; 9:14–29), as well as the charge that Jesus was casting out demons through the power of Satan (Matt. 12:27–28), are evidences that the defeat of the forces of darkness was considered essential to the gospel and to the early church's healing ministry. Jesus stated succinctly, "If I cast out demons by the Spirit of God, then the kingdom of God has come upon you" (Matt. 12:28). The churches were empowered by the Spirit to follow in Jesus' ministry of going about "doing good and healing all who were under the power of the devil" (Acts 10:38).

Jesus' exorcisms, and later those among his followers, were not only acts of personal deliverance and healing, but social acts as well. Those deemed possessed of demons were social outcasts who had their essential humanity stripped from them. In casting out the demons, Jesus and his followers restored the humanity to those who were possessed and granted them entry once more into a meaningful social life. It is, in part, for this reason that Jesus gave the warning of apostasy to those who regarded his deliverance ministry to be demonic (Matt. 12:27–28). If apostasy can be found at all, it would be found among those who have drifted so far from the faith that they can find no joy in the restoration of authentic humanity to these most dehumanized persons and would even demonize such liberating activity toward self-serving ends.

Paul Tillich has done much to restore the category of the "demonic" as a legitimate aspect of the confession and theology of the church. Though he dealt with this area only metaphorically, he did capture the ultimate threat to essential humanity that the category of the demonic adequately symbolizes (Tillich, 1936). Yet pentecostals must be cautious about the place they give to the demonic in their healing ministries and theologies and not follow the fascination with the demonic realm so prevalent in contemporary culture. "Deliverance ministries" sometimes place such a focus on the demonic that deliverance is more a matter of possessing hidden knowledge of the demonic realm (a kind of secret gnosis) than of the victory of Christ through the Spirit. Demons are named, located, categorized, and bound through elaborate prayers. Yet the development of such esoteric knowledge and activity with regard to the demonic cannot be found in the Scriptures. The focus must be on Christ and the liberty found in the gospel, for it is only there that the true nature of darkness can be understood for what it really is by way of contrast. "Resist the devil and he will flee from you" (James 4:7) seems to be fitting advice. Karl Barth (*CD*, 4/3, 168–71) captured best the scriptural response to the demonic when he wrote that he would give the demonic realm only a "quick, sharp glance." The glance would be quick because he lingers only by Christ and his gospel, yet it must also be sharp because the demonic realm must never be taken lightly (Macchia, *Satan and Demons*, 1994).

Furthermore, pentecostals must be cautious not to slip into a radically dualistic worldview in which anything outside of their more-or-less narrow understanding of orthodoxy and virtue is considered demonic. There is a vast and ambiguous realm of human thought and action that cannot simply be described as either demonic or divine. The human realm can by the grace of God bear witness to God but never without weakness and error. And those who are of other faiths or who have no conscious faith may be more effective as vessels of the kingdom of God than many within the church. Furthermore, the demonic can often be served by ideas and actions that masquerade as angels of light among us. Racism and sexism of the worst kinds have hidden under the guises of religious or patriotic causes.

Much further work is needed among pentecostal theologians toward a theology of healing that preserves the place granted healing within pentecostalism while also challenging certain extreme or questionable tendencies that will need to be examined more thoroughly from the contexts of biblical exegesis, theological reflection, and ecumenical conversations.

F. The Gifted Congregation.

Pentecostals were convinced from the beginning that they were involved in a latter rain of the Spirit that included a proliferation of miraculous gifts needed to restore the church to apostolic power. This pneumatological point of departure for understanding the nature of the church in the modern world cried out for ecclesiological reflection. The fact is, however, that ecclesiology is one of the most neglected doctrines in pentecostalism, which is illustrated by the absence of a chapter on the church in E. S. Williams's three-volume *Systematic Theology*. Even the formation of pentecostal denominations was done for practical rather than theological reasons, namely, the need for ministerial credentials to protect against rogue itinerant preachers, the need for the accreditation of missionaries, and some central organization for the distribution of missionary funds.

James Dunn has argued that the pentecostal distinctive that will be a significant challenge to contemporary ecclesiology lies in the emphasis of pentecostalism on spiritual gifts. This emphasis has the potential of empowering the laity to take their rightful place as ministers of the gospel alongside the professional clergy in the one work of the ministry (Dunn, 1983). David Lim as well sees the pentecostal movement as fulfilling the Lutheran notion of the priesthood of believers because of its accent on the proliferation of spiritual gifts in the church (Lim, 1991). Roger Stronstad feels that the pentecostals go beyond the priesthood to the "prophethood" of believers because of the role of the gifts in inspiring empowered witness among an army of prophets, a Lukan notion of the church that is lacking in the ecclesiology of the classical Reformation (Stronstad, 1995). As noted above, Miroslav Volf wrote in a similar vein of the need to see the proliferation of the gifts as a foundation for an ecclesiology as a mutual fellowship of believers in which every believer is regarded as a bearer of the Spirit and a minister for God (Volf, 1998). The theological implications for ecclesiology in the doctrine of spiritual gifts is an area of theological concern that requires further exploration by pentecostals. James Dunn rightly points out that the limited scope of gifts usually emphasized by pentecostals (the miraculous gifts listed in 1 Cor. 12, for example) hinders the full realization of this distinctive in pentecostal fellowships.

Pentecostals need to cultivate a much broader range of gifts that would include secular and social callings (e.g., Rom. 12:7–8) as well as the more miraculous and spiritual manifestations listed in 1 Cor. 12. The gifts would not only include social ministries of the church but also secular vocations from among the laity. Volf has written of the need to develop a theology of secular vocation that would transcend Luther's christological foundation to include a pneumatological vision that focuses on spiritual gifts. Using the gifts as a model for secular vocation would be more responsive to the realities of changing and developing professions such as one now has in a postmodern media culture. It would also help believers to integrate their personal life vocations with the ministry of the church (Volf, 1988).

Throughout their history "from sect to church," pentecostals harbored the vision of themselves as essentially a movement gifted by the Holy Spirit in the latter days to help prepare the world for the coming of the kingdom of God. Such a vision needs to be applied critically to their sometimes hierarchical and patriarchal institutional development as established church denominations. Is such an ecclesiastical development consistent with the early pentecostal vision of the church as an end-time missionary fellowship, structured and ordered by the liberating and empowering grace of God? At the same time, can this early vision be sustained and revised in the service of prophetic criticism toward society and the churches, including pentecostal institutional structures and priorities? Can pentecostals start again to be the blessing to the church and the world that they hoped to be at the beginning?

We live in an age that seems so very graceless. A vision of the church as a graced community of believers can bear witness to the light. The NT supports an ongoing diversification of gifts as individual believers increasingly become involved in the ministry of the church (Eph. 4; 1 Cor. 12). In such a diversification, each believer is dignified and honored as being a vessel of the one Spirit in the one task of glorifying Christ and building up the church into his image. The gifted contributions of all believers are needed to help the church experience Christ in his fullness (Eph. 4:12–13). The love of Christ will serve as the criterion for judging when these tasks are fulfilled and when they are not. A "charismania" that sees spectacular gifts as an end in themselves will not do. Yet God will often grace believers with manifestations and ministries that transcend the ordinary and the mundane in order to free them from structures and routines and to expose them to more liberating alternatives. Lim rightly characterizes the gifts of the Spirit as "incarnational" because they occur where the divine self-giving uses the realm of the human and the natural to accomplish God's will (Lim, 1991, ch. 1).

G. Revisioning Eschatology.

Pentecostalism was born with the conviction that the pentecostals were on the cutting edge of the near fulfillment of the kingdom of God. Nearly a century has passed since that conviction was born, and pentecostals have had to rethink their eschatology. The eschatological passion began to wane as pentecostals, especially (though not exclusively) white pentecostals in the U.S., began to move into the middle class. The conviction that "this world is not my home" was largely discarded in favor of a health-and-wealth message that promoted a self-centered concern for prosperity. A number of

pentecostals are calling for a revisioning of eschatological passion that preserves a legitimate desire for the coming of the kingdom of God in righteousness and justice but without the triumphalist and escapist tendencies of earlier convictions.

The first challenge involved in revisioning pentecostal eschatological passion relates to the dependence of many early pentecostals on dispensationalism. The pentecostal flirtation with dispensationalism was to be expected, since it was the overwhelmingly dominant eschatological vision of the fundamentalist world to which pentecostalism was so intimately connected. But pentecostals did not fully understand what dispensationalism implied hermeneutically. Gerald Sheppard has shown that early pentecostals adopted the dispensationalist philosophy of history but without the ecclesiological and hermeneutical assumptions that undergirded it. In time, many of the pentecostals adopted these as well, without understanding the "uneasy relationship" they were creating with typically pentecostal distinctives (Sheppard, 1984). For example, pentecostals, as noted above, read the Bible in a way that allows the text to speak directly to them and to their experience of God. This approach to Scripture does not fit well with a dispensationalist fragmentation of Scripture into different covenants and historical dispensations, so that the OT and much of the Gospels relate directly only to Israel and to the fulfillment of God's covenant with this nation in the millennium. Furthermore, pentecostals viewed the age of the church, especially the book of Acts and the 20th century, as the era of the Spirit foretold in the OT (e.g., Joel 2:28–29) and by John the Baptist (e.g., Matt. 3), and not, as the dispensationalists held, as a hiatus between promise and fulfillment with regard to the nation Israel. While still granting Israel a relationship with God that is not dependent entirely on the church, pentecostals are obligated to continue to rethink their dependence on a dispensationalist eschatology.

The second problem has to do with the pentecostal adoption of an eschatological orientation that was radically apocalyptic and dualistic in a chronological sense. The age to come and this present age were regarded as radically discontinuous. There was not much potential in this eschatological orientation for a positive understanding of the role of the Spirit in creation, culture, or society. Pentecostals need to recognize the difficulties that such an eschatological emphasis creates for Christian ecological concern or social action. Pentecostals have participated in a premillennial approach to Bible prophecy that foresees an inexorable decline in social morality and living conditions until Jesus miraculously ushers in the peace and justice of the kingdom of God. Paul Hanson has argued in his book *The Dawn of Apocalyptic* (1979) that such an apocalyptic eschatology developed in ancient Israel from the experience of exile and the related loss of hope in the prophetic vision of God's salvific and restorationist actions in history. For many pentecostals, apocalypticism arose from the hope that God will bring in salvation miraculously at the close of history, leaving little room for granting value to actions in history for social justice and healing. Martin Buber has added that apocalyptic eschatology is fatalistic and seeks to predict the end-time flow of events in advance, thus removing the prophetic responsibility to shape the future by God's grace in positive ways (Buber, 1956).

This apocalyptic eschatology also affected how pentecostals understood the mission of the church in the world. There can be little doubt that pentecostals have tended to limit their concern for the world merely to saving souls from the fires of hell. Pentecostal theologians Murray Dempster (1993) and Doug Peterson (1996) have noted that pentecostals have increasingly become involved in social and political change. But they also admit that apocalyptic eschatology, such as that which is treasured among pentecostals, implies a very pessimistic view of the capacity of secular social institutions and political strategies for changing the world into a more just and peaceful environment. Pentecostals have tended to establish their own institutional means for dealing with social problems and to limit the social action of the churches to short-term pastoral care of suffering persons. As helpful as these means of social action have been, they lack the concern to transform the existing structures of society.

Pentecostals are facing a genuine challenge to revise their eschatology so that it will retain its social relevance but discard its escapist tendencies. It is necessary to note and to build on what is positive about an apocalyptic eschatology. First, one can note a strong moral and ethical consciousness that accompanies eschatological passion among pentecostals that can be developed in the direction of social awareness and action. A helpful illustration from Pietism may be found among the Korntalers of Southern Germany. In his analysis of the 19th-century German Pietist village Korntal (near Stuttgart), Walter Hollenweger elaborately describes its fanatical eschatological passion. The workers would place their coats on the east side of the fields so that if the Lord should return they could head for Jerusalem without first running in the opposite direction. Parents would put their children to bed at night with foreheads and wrists covered in case the forces of Antichrist break in and attempt to place the mark of the beast on the children. Yet, as Hollenweger also notes, this village had a strong sense of responsibility toward the weak and the suffering. The workers of the village agreed to take only so much of their earnings for their own families, donating the rest toward the village homes for orphans, the sick, and the homeless. After all, if the time is so short on this earth, only that which is most important is really worth living for (Hollenweger, 1982, 189ff.). In a similar vein, pentecostal theologian Doug Petersen (1996, 109) accurately observes that among pentecostal communities in Latin America, "moral living is an expected characteristic in the present because one wants to be ready at any moment for an eschatological end."

Potential also exists in a pentecostal apocalyptic eschatology for prophetic criticism of the powers that be. The final judgment could be quite significant for a contemporary social ethic. After all, if God is the final Judge, then all penultimate human judgments can be radically called into question and God's judgment given priority. If in the incarnation and the cross God identifies with humanity, especially with the poor and the oppressed, then humanity is granted a dignity and a worth that no human powers can negate. Human efforts to strip any group of people of their human dignity and worth are relativized and negated by the eschatological judgment of God inaugurated in Christ, a judgment that affirms human dignity and condemns human forces of oppression and death. In a similar vein, Wolfhart Pannenberg wrote of the "critical function" of apocalyptic eschatology toward any ultimate claims made by current social ideologies (Pannenberg, 1984). The kingdom-to-come reveals all such claims as idolatrous and oppressive. There is an "eschatological reservation" to all judgments this side of eternity. The people of God are free to draw on the wisdom of any secular source in standing for social justice and healing but are bound in loyalty to the kingdom of God and of Christ alone.

To enhance pentecostal social action, there is a need for both an apocalyptic criticism and a constructive prophetic vision for history in pentecostal eschatology. Of course, pentecostal social criticism can be one-sided and paralyzing if the related boldness for witness does not involve a constructive engagement in social and political change. As noted above, Steve Land wants to root the pentecostal passion for the kingdom in the transformation of affections that is the legacy of Wesleyan spirituality. If eschatological passion represents godly affections, the potential exists for developing a spirituality that includes a passion for social justice and healing. Murray Dempster has attempted a "revisioning" of pentecostal eschatology that is more specifically hermeneutical in concern. He notes that the kingdom ethic of Jesus, along with its foundation in the call for justice in the OT prophets, was channeled to the apostolic communities through the transfer of the Spirit to the church at Pentecost. The inauguration of God's reign introduces a criticism of the systems of the world but also inspires its own embodiment among communities of Christians who bear witness to the kingdom of God in the world through the power of the Spirit of Christ (Dempster, 1993).

One could add that the theme of the kingdom of God alone is not adequate to revision pentecostal eschatology. Moltmann also suggests a "new creation" motif, since kingdom theologies have tended to be merely historical and political in orientation (Moltmann, 1996, 132ff.). But the category of the kingdom is an extremely helpful point of departure for an eschatology that is apocalyptic without negating prophetic responsibility to transform the world in the here and now. Hispanic pentecostal theologian Eldin Villafañe has written a social ethic that sets forth the beginnings of such a prophetic social ethic among pentecostals (Villafañe, 1993).

III. Conclusion.

The challenge of writing a full-blown pentecostal theology is still before us. What becomes clear from the research to date is that large areas of theological concern have not yet been consciously or methodically explored by pentecostals in a way that is consistent with their origins and diverse historical ethos as a Christian movement. In addition, pentecostal theology has rarely been consciously contextual. Traditionally, the world of the biblical text as experienced within a spiritually gifted congregation has been thought to provide the context in which pentecostals reflected theologically for the people of God. The gospel that stands at the center of this koinoniac and doxological context of theology for pentecostals is the "full gospel," which has not been occupied fundamentally by an idea but a by a person—Jesus. The living figure of Jesus as Savior, Sanctifier, Spirit Baptizer, Healer, and Coming King is the core of pentecostal theological reflection, meaning that pentecostal theology, to be true to itself, would not be ideological or dogmatic but dialogical and humble, open to legitimate pluralism. At stake from such a center of concern is the ongoing validity of Jesus' experience of the Spirit for the expectations of the churches today with regard to Jesus' ministry among them and through them to the world. This is a promising point of departure for future reflection.

■ **Bibliography:** M. Adams, "Hope in the Midst of Hurt: Towards a Pentecostal Theology of Suffering," (SPS, 1996) ■ G. Anderson, "Baptism in the Holy Spirit, Initial Evidence, and a New Model," *Paraclete* (Fall 1993) ■ G. Aulén, *Christus Victor* (1950) ■ Karl Barth, *Geschichte des Protestantismus im 19. Jahrhundert* (1947) ■ C. Bridges-Johns, "Meeting God in the Margins: Ministry among Modernity's Refugees" (lecture, Graduate Theol. Union, Oct. 1997) ■ D. Bruner, *A Theology of the Holy Spirit* (1970) ■ M. Buber, "Prophecy, Apocalyptic, and Historical Hour (1957)," in *On the Bible: Eighteen Studies*, ed., N. N. Glatzer (1982) ■ S. Chan, "The Language Game of Glossolalia," in *Pentecostalism in Context*, ed. W. Ma and R. P. Menzies (1997) ■ idem, *Spiritual Theology* (1998): 80–95 ■ H. Cox, *Fire from Heaven* (1995) ■ R. Cunningham, "From Holiness to Healing: The Faith Cure in America: 1872–1892," *Church History* (Dec. 1974) ■ D. Dayton, *The Theological Roots of Pentecostalism* (1988) ■ R. Del Colle, "Oneness and Trinity: A Preliminary Proposal for Dialogue with Oneness Pentecostalism," *JPT* (Apr. 1997) ■ M. Dempster, "Christian Social Concern in Pentecostal Perspective: Reformulating Pentecostal Eschatology," *JPT* (Apr. 1993) ■ J. Dunn, *Baptism in the Holy Spirit*

(1970) ■ idem, "Ministry and the Ministry: The Charismatic Renewal's Challenge to Traditional Ecclesiology," in *Charismatic Experiences in History*, ed. C. M. Robeck (1975) ■ M. Dusing, "Toward a Pentecostal Theology of Physical Suffering," (SPS, 1996) ■ J. Everts, "Tongues or Languages? Contextual Consistency in the Translation of Acts 2," *JPT* (Apr. 1994) ■ D. W. Faupel, *The Everlasting Gospel* (1996) ■ G. Fee, "Baptism in the Holy Spirit: The Issue of Separability and Subsequence," *Pneuma* (Fall 1985) ■ idem, "Toward a Pauline Theology of Glossolalia," in *Pentecostalism in Context* (1997) ■ M. Gaxiola, "Reverberations from Memphis," *Pneuma* (Spring 1996) ■ H. Gunkel, *The Influence of the Holy Spirit* (repr. 1979) ■ P. Hanson, *The Dawn of Apocalyptic* (1979) ■ W. Hollenweger, *The Pentecostals* (repr. 1988) ■ idem, "Der Parusiemythos: Das Beispiel der Korntaler Brudergemeinde," in *Umgang mit Mythen, Interkulturelle Theologie* 2 (1982) ■ idem, "Priorities in Pentecostal Research: Historiography, Missiology, Hermeneutics and Pneumatology," in *Experiences of the Spirit*, ed., J. A. B. Jongeneel (1989) ■ H. Hunter, *Spirit Baptism* (1983) ■ V.-M. Kärkkäinen, "*Spiritus Ubi Vult Spirat*: Pneumatology in Roman Catholic/Pentecostal Dialogue," *Ekumeniikan Jatkokoulutusseminaari* (Apr. 1997) ■ H. Küng, *The Church* (1967) ■ S. J. Land, *Pentecostal Spirituality: A Passion for the Kingdom* (1991) ■ idem, "A Passion for the Kingdom: Revisioning Pentecostal Spirituality," *JPT* (Oct. 1992) ■ H. Lederlie, *Treasures Old and New* (1988) ■ G. Lindbeck, *The Nature and Purpose of Doctrine* (1984) ■ J. Ma, "A Comparison of Two Worldviews: Kankana-Ey and Pentecostal," in *Pentecostalism in Context*, ed. W. Ma and R. Menzies (1997) ■ W. Ma, "The Korean Pentecostal Movement: Retrospect and Prospect for the New Century," Lecture, Hansei U., Korea (Nov. 1996) ■ F. D. Macchia, *Spirituality and Social Liberation: The Message of the Blumhardts in the Light of Wuerttemberg Pietism* (1993) ■ idem, "From Azusa to Memphis: Evaluating the Racial Reconciliation Dialogue among Pentecostals," *Pneuma* (Fall 1995) ■ idem, "God Present in a Confused Situation: The Mixed Influence of the Charismatic Movement on Classical Pentecostalism," *Pneuma* (Spring 1996) ■ idem, "Groans Too Deep for Words: Towards a Theology of Glossolalia," *JPT* (Oct. 1992) ■ idem, "Satan and Demons," in *Systematic Theology*, ed. S. Horton (rev. ed., 1995) ■ idem, "Tongues as a Sign: Towards a Sacramental Understanding of Pentecostal Experience," *Pneuma* (Spring 1993) ■ R. Menzies, *Empowered for Witness: The Spirit in Luke-Acts* (1994) ■ J. Moltmann, *The Spirit of Life: A Universal Affirmation* (1992) ■ P. C. Nelson, *Bible Doctrines* (1947) ■ W. Pannenberg, "Constructive and Critical Functions of Christian Eschatology," *HTR* (Apr. 1984) ■ D. Peterson, *Not by Might nor by Power* (1996) ■ C. Pinnock, *Flame of Love* (1996) ■ J.-D. Plüss, "Azusa and Other Myths: The Long and Winding Road from Experience to Stated Belief and Back," *Pneuma* (Fall 1993) ■ D. Reed, "Aspects of the Origins of Oneness Pentecostalism," in *Aspects of Pentecostal-Charismatic Origins*, ed. V. Synan (1975) ■ idem, "Oneness Pentecostalism: Problem and Possibilities for Pentecostal Theology," *Orlando '95: Congress on the Holy Spirit and World Evangelization* (July 1989) ■ C. M. Robeck, "Taking Stock of Pentecostalism: The

Personal Reflections of a Retiring Editor," *Pneuma* (Spring 1993) ■ idem, "William J. Seymour and the 'Bible Evidence,'" in *Initial Evidence,* ed. G. McGee (1991) ■ W. Samarin, *Tongues of Men and Angels* (1972) ■ J. Sepúlveda, "Born Again, Baptism and the Spirit: A Pentecostal Perspective," in *Pentecostal Movements as an Ecumenical Challenge,* ed. J. Moltmann and K-J Kuschel (Concilium, 1996/3) ■ G. Sheppard, "Word and Spirit: Scripture in Pentecostal Tradition," *Agora,* Pt. 1 and 2 (Spring/Summer 1978) ■ idem, "Hermeneutics and Dispensationalism: Anatomy of an Uneasy Relationship," *Pneuma* (Fall 1984) ■ S. Solivan, "Orthopathos: Prolegomenon for a HispanicAmerican Theology" (diss., Union Theol. Sem., NY, 1993) ■ R. Spittler, "Suggested Areas for Further Research in Pentecostal Studies," *Pneuma* (Fall 1983) ■ R. Stronstad, *Charismatic Theology of St. Luke* (1988) ■ idem, "Affirming Diversity: God's People as a Diversity of Prophets," 1994 Presidential Address, SPS ■ J. C. Thomas, "Pentecostal Theology in the Twenty-First Century," 1998 Presidential Address, SPS ■ P. Tillich, *Interpretation of History* (1936) ■ J. Tinney, "Exclusivist Tendencies in Pentecostal Self-Definition: A Critique from Black Theology," SPS (1978) ■ M. Volf, *After Our Likeness: The Church in the Image of the Trinity* (1998) ■ idem, *Zukunft der Arbeit, Arbeit der Zukunft* (1988) ■ G. Wainwright, *Doxology: The Praise of God in Worship, Doctrine, and Life* (1980) ■ M. Welker, *God the Spirit* (1994) ■ E. S. Williams, *Systematic Theology,* 3 vols. (1953) ■ J. R. Williams, *Renewal Theology,* vol. 2 (1990) ■ A. Yong, "Oneness and the Trinity: The Theological and Ecumenical Implications of Creation Ex Nihilo for an Intra-Pentecostal Dispute," *Pneuma* (Spring 1997) ■ idem, "Tongues of Fire in the Pentecostal Imagination: The Truth of Glossolalia in Light of R. C. Neville's Theory of Religious Symbolism," *JPT* (Apr. 1998) ■ B.-W. Yoo, *Pentecostalism: Its History and Theology* (1988).

■ F. D. Macchia

THIRD WAVE The term *third wave* is used to designate a movement that is similar to the pentecostal movement (first wave) and charismatic movement (second wave) but has what its constituents perceive as some fairly important differences. It is composed largely of evangelical Christians who, while applauding and supporting the work of the Holy Spirit in the first two waves, have chosen not to be identified with either. The desire of those in the third wave is to experience the power of the Holy Spirit in healing the sick, casting out demons, receiving prophecies, and participating in other charismatic-type manifestations without disturbing the current philosophy of ministry governing their congregations.

Some distinctives include:

1. Belief that the baptism of the Holy Spirit occurs at conversion (1 Cor. 12:13) rather than as a second work of grace subsequent to the new birth.
2. Expectation of multiple fillings of the Holy Spirit subsequent to the new birth, some of which may closely resemble what others call "baptism in the Holy Spirit."
3. A low-key acceptance of tongues as one of many NT spiritual gifts that God gives to some and not to others. Speaking in tongues is not considered the initial physical validation of a certain spiritual experience but rather a gift used by some for ministry or prayer language.
4. Ministry under the power and anointing of the Holy Spirit as the portal of entrance into the third wave rather than a spiritual experience as is typical of the first two waves. The context of ministry is most commonly a body of believers rather than individual activities such as those of a faith healer.
5. Avoidance of divisiveness at almost any cost. Compromise in areas such as raising of hands in worship, public tongues, methods of prayer for the sick, and others is cordially accepted in order to maintain harmony with those not in the third wave. Semantics become important, with terms such as "charismatic" and "Spirit-filled" being rejected because of their alleged implication that those who are so labeled form a sort of spiritual elite of first-class as over against second-class Christians.

The third wave became prominent around 1980, with the term itself being coined in 1983 by Peter Wagner. [In recent years it has become clear that the third wave should be viewed as part of a broader category, ►"neocharismatic," that includes the vast numbers of independent and indigenous churches and groups worldwide that cannot be classified as either pentecostal or charismatic. These are Christian bodies with pentecostal-like experiences that have no traditional pentecostal or charismatic denominational connections. See Introduction, p. xvii.]

■ **Bibliography:** V. Synan, *In the Latter Days* (1984), 136–39 ■ C. P. Wagner, "A Third Wave?" *Pastoral Renewal* (July–Aug. 1983) ■ idem, "The Third Wave," *Christian Life* (Sept. 1984).

■ C. P. Wagner

THISTLETHWAITE, LILIAN T. (1873–1939). American pentecostal pioneer. Under the direction of her brother-in-law, ►Charles F. Parham, Lilian Thistlethwaite pioneered many of the earliest pentecostal churches in the American Midwest following the ►Topeka revival of Jan. 1901. In Mar. 1906 Parham named her the first "general secretary of the Apostolic Faith Movement." As a result, she became the first woman to serve in an official leadership position in a pentecostal organization. Thistlethwaite also contributed one of the most detailed accounts of the Topeka revival in "The Wonderful History of the Latter Rain" (in S. Parham, 1930, 57–68).

■ **Bibliography:** J. Goff, *Fields White Unto Harvest* (1988) ■ S. Parham, *The Life of Charles F. Parham* (1930).   ■ J. R. Goff Jr.

THOMPSON, FRANK CHARLES (1858–1940). Compiler of the *Thompson Chain Reference Bible*. Thompson was born in Elmira, NY. He attended classes at Boston University School of Theology as a "special student" (1884–86), without ever enrolling in a regular program of study. Rutherford College in North Carolina later conferred an honorary D.D. degree on him. Thompson and his wife, Laura, were the parents of two daughters.

Thompson became a licensed Methodist preacher in 1879 and joined the Genesee (NY) Conference. After serving numerous parishes, he served as associate pastor of Asbury Methodist Church in Rochester, NY (1911–23).

The origin of the reference Bible dates back to Thompson's pastoral work in Genesee, where he recognized the need for a quality reference Bible. After church members expressed admiration for the quality of his marginal references in his Oxford Wide Margin Bible (KJV), several offered to underwrite its publication. This resulted in the formation of the Chain Reference Bible Publishing Company. The first edition appeared in 1908 but proved to be slow in gaining market exposure. In 1914 B. B. Kirkbride, a student at Cotner College and a Bible salesman during the summer, became familiar with it while working for a Nebraska firm. Impressed with the volume, he offered to sell a minimum of 3,000 per year for Thompson. The offer was accepted, and the sales surpassed the goal.

Originally Thompson's Bible contained only the text and marginal references; other items, such as the concordance, the outline of the books, and the maps of Paul's journeys (prepared by Laura Thompson) came later as a result of suggestions from customers. The B. B. Kirkbride Bible Company, with headquarters in Indianapolis, IN, emerged in 1915 from the agreement with Thompson and has offered the reference Bible as its sole product. Since that time approximately 3 million copies have been sold. It has also proved to be a favorite among pentecostal believers. During Thompson's lifetime, the volume went through two revisions (1929, 1934).

While living in Rochester, Thompson warmly supported ▸Aimee Semple McPherson's divine-healing crusade there in 1921. Following his retirement from the Rochester church, Thompson and his wife moved to California. Although Thompson was an "old-fashioned Methodist" and never became a pentecostal, Aimee Semple McPherson admired his reference Bible and endorsed it in *The Bridal Call Foursquare.* Consequently, she invited him to teach at L.I.F.E.

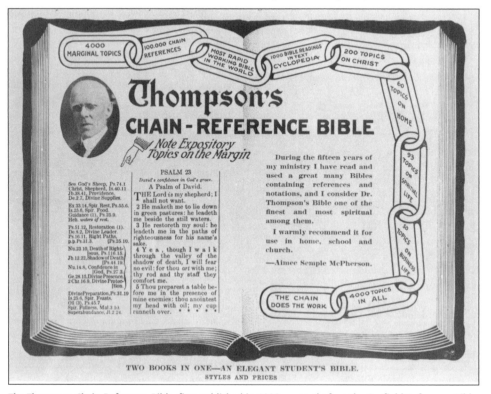

The Thompson Chain Reference Bible, first published in 1908, a year before the Scofield Reference Bible. This advertisement appeared in Aimee Semple McPherson's Bridal Call in 1924.

Bible College (c. 1924–c. 1931), where he also held the title of honorary dean.

Thompson's other publications included *Barriers to Eden* (c. 1939) and *Bob's Hike to the Holy City* (n.d.).

■ **Bibliography:** A. Alhand to G. B. McGee (Dec. 17, 1987) ■ S. Baker to G. B. McGee (Dec. 21, 1987) ■ "A Brief History of the 'Thompson Chain-Reference Bible' and the Publisher, the B. B. Kirkbride Bible Company, Inc." (n.d.) ■ "Dr. Thompson Passes at 82 in California," *Rochester Democrat and Chronicle* (May 5, 1940) ■ R. B. Mitchell to G. B. McGee (Nov. 14, 1987) ■ A. Sorenson, "People in Progress: B. B. Kirkbride Bible Co., Inc.," *Bookstore Journal* (Nov. 1984) ■ F. C. Thompson, "A Great Revival Campaign," *The Bridal Call* (Dec. 1921).   ■ G. B. McGee

TINNEY, JAMES STEVEN (1942–88). Editor and historian. A native of Kansas City, MO, Tinney focused his efforts as a historian of pentecostalism on two themes: blackness and homosexuality. He was ordained to the ministry at age 18 but worked mostly as a teacher and journalist. He served as editor of the *Washington Afro-American* (1974–75) and of *Spirit: a Journal of Issues Incident to Black Pentecostalism* (1977–79). The final issue of the latter consisted of a bibliography on the black movement. In these years Tinney emerged as a leading contender for the black origins of the pentecostal movement, holding the black William J. Seymour (1870–1922), not the white Charles F. Parham (1873–1929), to be the real founder. Sympathetic articles on pentecostal homosexuals elicited sharp reactions from others in the movement. In 1980 he organized the ▸Pentecostal Coalition for Human Rights, a support group for racial and sexual minorities that includes lesbians and gays. In 1982 he founded Faith Temple, a predominantly black gay church in Washington, DC. He also served on the journalism faculty at Howard University. He died on June 12, 1988.

■ **Bibliography:** *Spirit* (Washington), 1–3 (2, 1977–79).
                    ■ C. E. Jones

TOMLINSON, AMBROSE JESSUP (1865–1943). Ambrose Jessup Tomlinson was born on Sept. 22, 1865, near Westfield, IN, to Milton and Delilah Tomlinson. He was anemic at birth but exhibited unusual stamina throughout his life. His Quaker grandparents actively opposed slavery. His paternal grandfather, Robert Tomlinson, also denounced war and capital punishment. In other respects, his earliest years typified the life of a farm boy from Westfield. Through these years none in his immediate family were much involved with church services or related activities. He described a spiritual experience at age 12 (he heard his name called three times), but when he attended Westfield Academy he concentrated on athletics and drama. During these high school days a

number of his classmates professed Christian commitment as a result of a revival, but he refused to follow their example. He then became consumed with politics, and it was only after almost being hit by lightning that, as a new groom, he turned to the Scriptures and, at age 24, made allegiance to the gospel. He soon applied to his life the doctrine of divine healing that he learned first from a Carrie Judd Montgomery tract.

Ambrose became busily engaged in Sunday school work and contributed to the growth of a nearby Quaker congregation. Before long he became acquainted with J. B. Mitchell, who had been converted under the ministry of Charles G. Finney and had attended Oberlin College. Through this contact and travel with Mitchell, Ambrose learned firsthand about the Oberlin views on sanctification, missions, and the distribution of clothes and Bibles to the poor. Within a few years his travels introduced him to the ministries of Stephen Merritt, D. L. Moody, H. C. Morrison, ▸Ida Robinson, ▸A. B. Simpson, George D. Watson, N. Taylor, and others. One of his neighbors in Westfield, Seth Rees, would serve with M. N. Knapp as coeditor of *God's Revivalist*.

Tomlinson committed himself to colportage work for the American Bible Society and the American Tract Society. Starting in 1899, he centered his activities in Culberson, NC, where he organized, on Apr. 9, 1900, an orphanage and published an 18-page monthly religious paper called *Samson's*

A. J. Tomlinson, who was elected the first general overseer of the Church of God (Cleveland, TN) and held the position until removed from office by the denomination in 1923. His work and the congregations that remained loyal to him were then labeled the Tomlinson Church of God (now known as the Church of God of Prophecy).

Foxes. The paper, published from 1901 to 1902, featured articles and news from the Holiness movement and the healing movement and appeals to assist the needy. Tomlinson's approach produced considerable hostilities from the upper class in North Carolina, and in 1901 he made his way to Frank W. Sandford's Shiloh in Maine. He had been water baptized in 1897 by a "Brother Gleason" in Maine and reportedly in 1901 by Stephen Merritt in New York. However, as a result of his time at the Holy Ghost and Us Bible School, he was baptized again by Sandford. On Oct. 1, 1901, Tomlinson joined the fledgling group who identified themselves as "The Church of the Living God for the Evangelization of the World, Gathering of Israel, New Order of Things at the Close of the Gentile Age."

Tomlinson's most far-reaching commitment came out of a relationship with some Holiness adherents in western North Carolina. Richard Spurling Jr., Frank Porter, and W. F. Bryant organized in May 1902 a small band as the Holiness Church at Camp Creek. A. J. Tomlinson had at least four or five years of contact with Holiness people in the area. After a time of intense prayer near the Bryant home on the morning of June 13, 1903, he joined the group with the proclamation that this was the Church of God of the Bible. His leadership ability is shown in that he was then elected pastor of the church, while Spurling and Bryant turned to evangelism. By 1904 Tomlinson was pastor of three out of the four affiliated congregations and edited, with M. S. Lemons, a periodical titled *The Way.* This publication lasted at least one year, used original biblical languages, and centered on Holiness thought. Tomlinson himself was an avid reader of magazines like *Evangelical Visitor, Tongues of Fire, The Mountain Missionary, The Way of Faith, God's Revivalist,* and *The Bible Advocate,* and he was familiar with the writings of George Foxe, George Müller, David Brainerd, the ante-Nicene Fathers, and the church history of Eusebius. He was himself a prolific writer, as evidenced in his journal started in 1899, his daily church book record, his pocket memorandum, his 1913 book entitled *Last Great Conflict,* and his numerous articles in the official church publication and elsewhere.

By the end of 1904 the A. J. Tomlinson family was living in Cleveland, TN (population just under 5,000). The local church was set in order in Cleveland by late 1906 after a revival held by M. S. Lemons, Sister McCanless, and Tomlinson (who had conducted meetings there prior to this). For some time Tomlinson served this church as pastor and Sunday school superintendent, although he also traveled extensively.

When the affiliated churches convened in Jan. 1906 for what was considered the first general assembly, Tomlinson served as moderator and clerk. He penned these words as an addendum to the minutes: "We hope and trust that no person or body of people will ever use these minutes, or any part

of them, as articles of faith upon which to establish a sect or denomination." The name Church of God (CG) was adopted the next year, even though Tomlinson knew the name was in use among Warnerian and Winebrennerian churches. At the fourth annual meeting, Tomlinson not only served again as the conference moderator and clerk but was elected as the primary leader. The original title of general moderator was changed to general overseer at the next annual meeting. After the general overseer's annual address, the testimony of the prominent leaders, and various interpreted tongues messages, the general assembly of 1914 unanimously made Tomlinson's selection as general overseer permanent.

In Jan. 1907 Tomlinson became "more fully awakened" about the fledgling pentecostal movement. The result was that he preached the emerging doctrine of Spirit baptism with tongues-speech as the initial evidence during the assembly that year. Several received this experience, but as he preached this throughout the year, he joined the seekers at the altar for the very thing he had just prescribed. In June of that year Tomlinson and M. S. Lemons went to Birmingham, AL, in an attempt to meet with ›G. B. Cashwell. They met instead with ›M. M. Pinson. In 1908 Cashwell came to Cleveland and preached a sermon at the conclusion of the CG general assembly. During Cashwell's Sunday morning service, Jan. 12, 1908, Tomlinson spontaneously uttered what

Bishop A. J. Tomlinson in the 1930s, addressing those gathered for the assembly of what is now known as the Church of God of Prophecy.

he judged to be 10 different languages. From Aug. 11 to Oct. 14 of that year, Tomlinson preached a revival in Cleveland that resulted in 258 recorded spiritual "experiences" and 106 new church members. The next year, Tomlinson's Spirit-baptism doctrine was challenged by his assistant pastor, John B. Goins, and by a few members, all of whom would depart because of their opposition to his view on initial evidence.

For the next 14 years Tomlinson not only traveled widely, holding revivals and camp meetings and organizing new churches, he also either initiated or at least was a key player in the development of the principal ministries of the CG. From 1908 to 1910 he served as corresponding editor for Cashwell's *Bridegroom's Messenger*. The first issue of *The Evening Light and Church of God Evangel*, dated Mar. 1, 1910, rolled off the presses, with Tomlinson as editor (he later added the *Faithful Standard*). The first publishing house was built in 1913, with Tomlinson's prodding. His first international campaign began in Feb. 1911 in the Bahamas, where he had been preceded by one year by CG minister R. M. Evans, who helped fund the return of Edmund and Rebecca Barr to the Bahamas in 1909.

In the various general assemblies Tomlinson was always a prime mover in doctrinal considerations (including the foundational 29 teachings). At many assemblies he stood and responded to various questions and, starting in 1911, initiated annual addresses, which served as a platform to engage the body theologically. He used his 1917 annual address to bring attention to the need for an institution to train workers. Thus, a Bible training school opened in Cleveland on Jan. 1, 1918, with Tomlinson as superintendent. In Tomlinson's 1919 annual address he brought to the general assembly the need for sponsoring an orphanage. The first home opened on Dec. 17, 1920, in Cleveland.

Tomlinson's leadership was also marked by an interest in treating all races fairly. Not only had his activist grandparents taken part in the Underground Railroad, he had at least two African-American families as close neighbors in Westfield, which hosted a "colored campmeeting" every summer. He met ˃Charles H. Mason on more than one occasion and shared with him the concern to break racial barriers. Tomlinson tried to incorporate all races into the CG; nevertheless, there was an exodus of blacks in 1921. After that, Tomlinson's work moved his church toward racial egalitarianism. He was like-minded on the ministry of women, although he did not support women as participants in business meetings or sharing the full rights of ordination. However, he constantly wrote in support of female ministers and utilized them in strategic church positions.

A full account cannot be given here of the 1922–23 controversy between Tomlinson and the council of elders. Tomlinson was central in 1916–17 in forming this group of 12. However, the result of the various complications was that

Tomlinson, at age 59, started over with between 2,000 and 3,000 adherents. The courts exonerated Tomlinson of financial wrongdoing and decreed that his organization should be called Tomlinson Church of God in nonreligious matters. The group never used this name but preferred "Church of God, over which A. J. Tomlinson is General Overseer." At the time of his death on Oct. 2, 1943, the ˃Church of God of Prophecy, as it would be designated by the courts in 1952, had a membership of just under 32,000. Three of Tomlinson's four children survived him in death. ˃Milton Ambrose succeeded his father as the duly chosen general overseer of the CGP. ˃Homer Aubrey left the church and formed his own organization.

■ **Bibliography:** L. Duggar, *A. J. Tomlinson* (1964) ■ D. D. Preston, *The Era of A. J. Tomlinson* (1984) ■ R. G. Robins, "Plainfolk Modernist: The Radical Holiness World of A. J. Tomlinson" (diss., Duke, 1999) ■ A. J. Tomlinson, *God's Twentieth-Century Pioneer* (1962) ■ idem, *Historical Notes* (1970), originally published in 1943 under the title *A. J. Tomlinson: God's Anointed—Prophet of Wisdom* ■ idem, *Last Great Conflict* (1913) ■ idem, "Diary" (1899–1943), the original is in the Library of Congress ■ H. A. Tomlinson, *Diary of A. J. Tomlinson*, 3 vols. (1949–55).   ■ H. D. Hunter

TOMLINSON, HOMER AUBREY (1892–1968). General overseer, Church of God (Queens, NY). The oldest son of ˃A. J. Tomlinson, Homer Aubrey Tomlinson was born in Westfield, IN. Homer grew up with the Church of God (CG, Cleveland, TN), and was influenced in various ways by his father's ministry of leadership. Knowing the hardships endemic to a minister's life and seeing pentecostals experience persecution, Homer was not interested in joining the ministry. In 1913, after two years at the University of Tennessee and a year of teaching school, he went to Indianapolis, entering a career in advertising. By 1916 he was in New York, where he opened a small advertising agency.

During a 1919 ˃Aimee Semple McPherson tent service, Tomlinson met Marie Wunch, and they were married two months later. He served in the military during WWI. Tomlinson also accepted considerable publishing responsibilities on behalf of his father, including the *Evangel* and the *Faithful Standard*. Later he composed religious dramas and gospel songs. In 1923 Tomlinson entered the ministry to aid his father, who was starting over, founding what later became the ˃Church of God of Prophecy (CGP). He expected to succeed his father as head of the CGP, but when that did not materialize in 1943, he struck out on his own, still using the name Church of God (Queens, NY). (Exact figures of the membership, then and through the years, have been wanting. The numbers [e.g., 30 million] released by Tomlinson were inclusive of his projected spiritual domain and do not relate to any actual denominational allegiance. It seems that actual

Homer Tomlinson, who announced himself "King of the World," standing in his robes and crown in the Colosseum in Rome.

membership through all the years would, at best, be in the hundreds with most of the constituency coming initially from the Church of God of Prophecy.)

Tomlinson is best remembered for his activities between 1954 and 1966. He repeated a coronation service in the capitals of 101 nations (including Russia and Israel). Typically, after his arrival in a capital city he notified the press, went to some public area wearing a scarlet academic robe, displayed his inflatable plastic globe, crowned himself, suspended the flag from his neck, and took his seat on the portable "throne." He then removed the flag and addressed the audience, always promising some form of peace or prosperity. By his reckoning, his visit to Ghana ended a year-long drought there, while his presence in the Congo halted an uprising and massacre. Revolutions in Guatemala, Costa Rica, and Haiti were said to have stopped abruptly with his arrival. He reportedly headed off a war between the Arabs and the Israelis, and he flew over Korea in Dec. 1952 to lay the groundwork for the end of that war. Only two capitals refused his ceremony: those of the U.S. and Vietnam. This, he said, explained the tragedy of the prolonged Vietnam War. He further claimed ownership of the land of Druze, while also accepting credit for President Roosevelt's welfare programs and the 1940s European Famine Relief Effort. In 1952, 1960, 1964, and 1968 he ran as a Theocratic Party candidate for president of the U.S. His platform pro-

posed uniting church and state; abolishing taxes and substituting tithing; stopping all divorce, gambling, and use of liquor, narcotics, and tobacco; and promoting racial equality. He desired to create two new cabinet posts: secretary of righteousness and secretary of the Holy Bible. He selected prominent Catholics, Protestants from various denominations, and Jews as his cabinet officers for his projected presidency. Also, he lectured in many prominent universities in the U.S.

In all of this, Tomlinson remained good humored and aware that only a small band of followers gave him credit for these and other things (note his use of Josh. 1:3). The wide media coverage of his activities and the long list of his publications drew regular attention to his point of view, but it was usually treated with derision if not outright opposition. His response was that his claim to power could come from humility and not pride. Yet his surrealistic *Shout of the King* moves well beyond reality when he claims to have been with the Wright brothers when they invented the airplane and to have become personal friends with the likes of Eisenhower and Roosevelt.

At home, however, Tomlinson sustained a quality relationship with his immediate family. Tomlinson's wife disbelieved many of his exaggerations, and their two sons and some of the grandchildren have held positions in the established community (both sons are retired railroad executives, and one grandson is an M.D.). Homer A. Tomlinson died on Dec. 4, 1968, in his home, and his position of general overseer was assumed by his designated successor, Voy M. Bullen, who worked out of his home in Huntsville, AL. The group is now led by Bishop Danny R. Patrick out of Scottsville, KY.

■ **Bibliography:** *The Church of God Book of Doctrines: 1903 to 1970* (1970) ■ R. H. Huff, "The Preacher Who Wanted to Be President," *Liberty* (6, 1978) ■ Interview with Voy Bullen in Huntsville, AL (Feb. 26, 1981), and subsequent correspondence ■ H. A. Tomlinson, *Diary of A. J. Tomlinson*, 3 vols. (1949–55) ■ idem, *Shout of the King* (1968) ■ W. Whitworth, "Profiles: Bishop Homer A. Tomlinson," *The New Yorker* (Sept. 24, 1966).   ■ H. D. Hunter

TOMLINSON, MILTON AMBROSE (1906–95). General overseer, Church of God of Prophecy. Milton Ambrose Tomlinson was born Oct. 19, 1906, in Cleveland, TN, the last child of A. J. and Mary Jane Tomlinson. His early years featured mostly the effects of various facets of his father's ministry. Teenage "Tony" exhibited some mischievousness, and he did not give up old friends after the controversy of 1923 (ᐧA. J. Tomlinson). He worked at Herald Publishing Company after he completed high school. In 1927 he was converted, sanctified, and baptized in the Spirit, and he joined the ᐧChurch of God of Prophecy (as it is known since 1952). The next year he married Ina Mae Turner. For 10 years he served the local church as youth leader and treasurer/clerk, and he was a member of the Tabernacle Brass Band. On Oct. 17, 1932, he was ordained as a deacon. Following the general assembly of 1942 he began serving as pastor in Henderson, KY.

After the death of A. J. Tomlinson, the 39 state and national overseers who could travel to Cleveland met to select an interim general overseer. Some candidates were discussed, but the choice was unanimous after a tongues message was interpreted to refer to Milton Tomlinson. By acclamation, on Sept. 15, 1944, the next general assembly enthusiastically endorsed him as the new general overseer. There seemed to be several reasons why many people (including Milton Tomlinson and his wife) had not envisioned Tomlinson as a general overseer. Part of this must have been the contrast between father and son: the father a dynamic preacher, gifted organizer, and prolific writer; the son self-effacing and deliberate in speech. Although Milton's call to the ministry was real, it was recent, and he had no experience in the work of the world headquarters. He began as general overseer on Oct. 7, 1943, and was ordained a bishop on Oct. 13, 1943. His ordination included the laying on of hands by a field secretary and a state overseer and his own signature on the bishop's license. Later sermons by numerous church leaders turned typology into allegory by paralleling Milton to Joshua and predicting his death and/or completion of the church's work by 1983.

Most of Tomlinson's views were molded by his father's last decade. His irenic spirit was displayed in that, while some around him used an exclusive ecclesiology to proselytize, such was not his practice. In his later years he demonstrated some willingness to encourage dialogue between different Christian traditions. Until his late seventies Tomlinson kept up a local-church assignment in addition to transporting people to church and helping various ones in need. He resigned as general overseer of the Church of God of Prophecy in 1990, thus ending one of the longest such tenures in North American pentecostal history. M. A. Tomlinson passed away on Apr. 26, 1995.

■ **Bibliography:** M. A. Tomlinson, *Basic Bible Briefs* (1961) ■ idem, *The Glorious Church of God* (1968) ■ Various interviews with M. A. Tomlinson, 1976–90.   ■ H. D. Hunter

Milton A. Tomlinson, who in 1943 succeeded his father, A. J. Tomlinson, as general overseer of the Tomlinson Church of God (now Church of God of Prophecy).

TOPEKA REVIVAL The revival in Topeka, KS, in early 1901 marked the birth of the pentecostal movement. The manifestation of glossolalia on a dozen and a half students at the Bethel Bible School solidified the unique theological tenet of pentecostalism that tongues speech provides the initial evidence of the baptism of the Holy Spirit. The reception also implanted a fervent millenarian belief that pentecostal gifts marked the imminent return of Christ and promised worldwide revival during the last years before the dawn of the tribulation period.

The Topeka outbreak was a product of the ministry of ᐧCharles F. Parham. By 1900 Parham accepted a variety of theological speculations promulgated by Holiness evangelists. Nothing impressed him more than the concept of apostolic power as a sign of history's final generation. Drawing from several isolated reports of xenolalia, Parham decided that this phenomenon gave full evidence of an end-time baptism of the Holy Spirit because it promised the utilitarian method for a global revival. Spirit-filled believers could fan out and preach the gospel message without the painstaking process of learning a new language.

On this premise Parham established the Bethel Bible School in Oct. 1900 in the Stone mansion, a rented—though elaborately designed—structure on the outskirts of Topeka. He organized the school as a missionary training center but kept quiet about his conclusions on missionary xenolalia. Rather, Parham instructed his 34 students in Holiness theology and then, in late December, challenged them to search for the true evidence of the end-time spiritual outpouring. Strategically, he pointed them to Acts 2, where tongues speech clearly accompanied the dawn of apostolic power in the early church.

Much of the story of the initial outbreak of Pentecost at Topeka is obscured by the incongruity of two conflicting accounts. Parham recalled that, to his amazement, all his students agreed independently that tongues were the only "indisputable proof " of the end-time Holy Spirit baptism. At the students' New Year's Eve service in 1900, ⟩Agnes Ozman requested that Parham lay hands on her and pray specifically that she receive this baptism with the "biblical sign." Parham reported that after a brief prayer "a halo seemed to surround her head and face, and she began speaking in the Chinese language, and was unable to speak English for three days" (Parham, 1930, 52–53). Ozman, however, dated the experience to the evening of Jan. 1, 1901, and recalled nothing about the student consensus. She recalled, "I did not know that I would talk with tongues when I received the Baptism," and claimed to find biblical support for the phenomenon only *after* the experience (LaBerge, 1921, 28–29). Both agreed that at a service several days later Parham and about half the students were likewise empowered.

The two accounts cannot be totally reconciled, but a couple of things are clear. In his earliest recounting, Parham dated the initial outbreak to New Year's Day, thus confirming Ozman's timetable (Parham, 1902, 34). On the more important question of ideological origins, Parham's xenolalic theory provided the foundation for the belief in tongues as initial evidence. He led his students to an expectation of their unique role in an end-time global revival. Ozman was, like the other students, deeply interested in foreign missions and duly impressed when her tongues speech was "confirmed" by a local Bohemian who claimed to understand her words perfectly.

Publicity concerning the revival emerged a week after the initial outbreak when reporters were alerted by Stanley Riggins, a student who defected in opposition to the new doctrine. News reports centering on the strange tongues generated attention as far away as St. Louis. Late in January, Parham and a handful of Spirit-filled students set out for Kansas City, intent on establishing a string of missionary posts in major cities across the Northeast. After only marginal results and facing an acute shortage of funds, Parham postponed further campaigns in mid-February. Undaunted by the setback, he planned and publicized a summer camp meeting for Holiness evangelists nationwide, expecting "thousands" to visit the Bible school and adopt his new pentecostal plank. Tragedy struck in March, however, and ended the optimism that poor turnouts and belittling news reports had failed to dampen. Parham's one-year-old son suddenly became ill and died. Shortly thereafter the Bible school was lost when Stone mansion was sold to a new owner, and Parham and his students were forced off the premises. New quarters in the city were secured briefly, but by the end of the summer the school closed and the initial wave of pentecostal optimism ended.

An unfinished mansion in Topeka, KS, known as "Stone's Folly," that became the home of Charles F. Parham's Bible school in 1900. It was here that Agnes Ozman spoke in tongues on January 1, 1901.

Parham moved his family to Kansas City and spent the next two years in evangelistic work. Though he kept a small band of followers in Topeka and Kansas City, it was not until late in 1903 that he achieved a level of sustained growth. Nevertheless, the theological concept of tongues as evidence and xenolalia as an end-time missions tool remained a solid part of his ministerial efforts after Topeka. From those optimistic, yet humble, beginnings would rise the pentecostal movement of the 20th century.

See also APOSTOLIC FAITH MOVEMENT, ORIGINS.

■ **Bibliography:** J. Goff, *Fields White unto Harvest* (1988) ■ A. LaBerge, *What God Hath Wrought* (1921) ■ C. Parham, *Voice Crying in the Wilderness* (1902) ■ S. Parham, *The Life of Charles F. Parham* (1930).   ■ J. R. Goff Jr.

TOPPI, FRANCESCO (1928–). Italian pastor, evangelist, educator, and church official. Born in Rome, Italy, Toppi worked as a public accountant and later attended the International Bible Training Institute in Burgess Hill, England, directed by ▸Frederick Squire. In 1959 he married Anna Maria Ferretti.

Toppi began his ministry in 1949 with the Italian Assemblies of God (Assembles di Dio d'Italia, ADI) and received ordination in the same year. He engaged in evangelistic work in Southern Italy (1950–53) and evangelistic and pastoral work in Turin (1953–59). He became a member of the executive presbytery of the denomination in 1954. With the founding of the Italian Bible Institute in Rome in 1953, he was appointed secretary-treasurer for the school and also taught there.

Since 1978 Toppi has served as the general superintendent of the ADI, which now claims 168,000 members, 1,100 churches, 490 pastors, and various other entities, such as radio stations, an orphanage, and three senior citizens' homes.

The ADI was a persecuted church during Toppi's childhood. Not until 1959 did it receive official recognition from the Italian government. Throughout his administration, Toppi has worked diligently in this area. In 1988, at the helm of ADI, he negotiated with the government for full legal recognition, which among other things allowed pastors the right to visit hospitals and prisons as clergy, full accreditation for the Italian Bible Institute, and the ADI the right to collect tax-deductible offerings.

Toppi is also the senior pastor of Rome's largest Protestant church, which has over 800 members.

■ **Bibliography:** Curriculum vitae ■ "Pentecostals in Italy Given Government Approval to Evangelize after 80 Years of Limited Freedom," *PE* (Apr. 19, 1987) ■ T. Perretti to E. J. Gitre (July 5, 1999).
                                    ■ G. B. McGee; E. J. Gitre

TORONTO BLESSING The term *Toronto Blessing* is somewhat of a misnomer. It was coined by the British media after the unusual, revival-like manifestations experienced at the Toronto Airport Vineyard (TAV) were apparently carried by a visitor from Canada to the Anglican Parish Church of Holy Trinity Brompton (widely known as HTB) in central London. Although this original appellation is widely used by both those inside and outside the renewal, many involved in this religious social movement now prefer to refer to it as the "Father's Blessing." As Toronto Airport Christian Fellowship's pastor, John Arnott, noted in the introduction to his book *The Father's Blessing,* this outpouring comes from the Father and is not confined to Toronto.

Yet the Toronto Airport Christian Fellowship (originally the Toronto Airport Vineyard) will go down in history as the epicenter of this wave of the movement of the Spirit. It is from humble beginnings at a small church of some 300 persons, located in a small strip mall just outside Toronto's Pearson International Airport, that the shocks emanating from a revival meeting reverberated around the world. The nightly renewal meetings, originally scheduled for Jan. 20–24, 1994, continued uninterrupted since (except for Mondays) and were still going on as of October 2000, more than six years later. The congregation at the Toronto Airport Christian Fellowship has leveled off at around 2,000 regular attendees, with weeknight crowds having thinned to about 250 to 300. Thousands of pilgrims from around the world are still showing up each week, with about 500 attending nightly on weekends during "non-conference" times. Toronto's influence continues worldwide (Sprechner, 1998; Wies, 1998). Visitors and itinerant speakers have now carried the fire (to use a popular renewal metaphor) to scores of countries on all continents.

The Blessing came to the attention of the media when it was transported to ▸Holy Trinity Brompton in Knightsbridge, central London, in May 1994 through Eleanor Mumford, a Vineyard pastor's wife who had visited the Toronto site (Roberts, 1994). HTB, indirectly and inadvertently, became a catalyst for another major stream of the current Spirit movement in North America when Steve Hill, a seasoned ▸Assemblies of God (AG) evangelist, received the Blessing at HTB (Hill, 1997; Poloma, 1998). He in turn was instrumental in the "Pensacola Outpouring" or ▸"Brownsville Revival" that began on Father's Day of 1995.

1. The Beginning.

In 1986, while John and Carol Arnott were pastoring a church in Stratford, Ont., John reportedly "felt called" to plant another church in Toronto. By 1991 they were able to turn the Stratford church over to the associate pastor and to begin pastoring the Toronto church full-time. Many of the early efforts in the newly planted church were devoted to counseling, inner healing, and deliverance, and, as Arnott

(1998, 4) describes it, "Somehow battling the darkness had become our focus rather than dispelling it with light. Inadvertently, the devil had become too big, and God, too small!"

Reportedly spiritually "dry" from the intensive and long personal ministry, John and Carol Arnott began to see other powerfully anointed ministries in action and prayed that they might be similarly empowered. Responding to what they believed was the word of God spoken to them, they began to spend their mornings in prayer and to interact with others who were specially anointed. Their search took them to the revival in Argentina in Nov. 1993 and to attending meetings with many of the Argentinean evangelists. It was there that Claudio Freidzon, an AG evangelist, singled John out from the crowd, asking him "Do you want the anointing?" As he gave an affirmative response, John reported something "clicking" in his heart. He later reported, "I received more of the Holy Spirit's anointing and power, by faith."

Meanwhile, a ▸Vineyard pastor from St. Louis, MO, Randy Clark, was experiencing a blessing of his own through a series of meetings held by evangelist ▸Rodney Howard-Browne in Tulsa. When Arnott heard about Clark's encounter with the Holy Spirit at Howard-Browne's camp meetings, he invited Clark to come to preach four meetings at what was then the TAV. Clark came on Jan. 20, 1994, and the unexpected happened to the approximately 120 persons gathered there. As Arnott (1998, 5) reports: "It hadn't occurred to us that God would throw a massive party where people would laugh, roll, cry and become so empowered that emotional hurts from childhood would just lift off. Some people were so overcome physically by God's power that they had to be carried out." Unknown to them, the seeming pandemonium experienced on these and subsequent nights had precedents in early American revivals and in earlier church history (see Chevreau, 1994; Hyatt, 1996; Riss, 1997; Synan, 1997).

The Toronto Blessing, or "Father's Blessing," is a bona fide new religious movement that can be viewed through the lenses of the patterned stages that mark social movements (Mauss, 1975). The Toronto Blessing has experienced emergence, coalescence, organization, as well as signs of decline on the North American continent. What follows is a perspective on the Toronto Blessing, by a participant observer, in the framework known as "natural-history theory of social movements."

2. A Natural-History Perspective.

When I first began doing sociological research on the Toronto Blessing in late 1994, it was still in its charismatic moment. There was the freshness of a collective excitement that readily bound visitors from around the world together. Regardless of the music group or the speaker in this nameless-faceless stage of the renewal, people flocked to Toronto from all over the world to experience the Blessing. Many visitors were not only struck by the unusual physical manifesta-

tions that were commonplace—not only on the church premises but also in nearby hotels and restaurants patronized by the pilgrims—but also by the unity of the persons gathered from all over the world. Historical ethnic enemies repented and reached out to one another as they worshiped together and experienced afresh the Father's love. Reports of inner healing from bitterness and resentment and healing of relationships (especially marital problems) were commonplace.

The charismatic movement of the 1960s and '70s had fallen upon lean years for many full-gospel Christians of the 1980s and '90s, and the Toronto Blessing seemed to offer them spiritual refreshing. Respondents to a 1995 survey I conducted on nearly 1,000 visitors to the Toronto church confirmed this impression. Approximately half of those who filled out the questionnaires indicated that they had come to Toronto feeling "spiritual dryness and great discouragement," but most left reporting great refreshing. Nearly 9 out of 10 respondents indicated that they were "more in love with Jesus now then I have ever been in my life," and that they had "come to know the Father's love in new ways." The fresh experience of God's love carried over into relationships, especially marital ones, where 88 percent of married respondents indicated a greater love for their spouses as a result of the Blessing. This experience of refreshing (as the renewal came to be called in Great Britain) seemed to have lasting consequences. A follow-up survey of the original respondents conducted in 1997, two years after the original data was collected, demonstrated similar figures (Poloma, 1996, 1997[b]).

During the earliest stage of the movement there was, to use a Durkheimian phrase, a collective effervescence that produced not only a sense of solidarity but also provided the collective excitement that is vital for the launching of a social movement. As is common with social movements, it did not take long for the Blessing to shift from the emergence stage to the coalescence stage (Blumer, 1969; Mauss, 1975). As it coalesces, a movement must seek to define itself as it seeks a strategy for appealing to the public and for dealing with criticism that inevitably arises. What emerges is an ideology or a set of "theoretically articulated propositions about social reality" (Berger, Berger, and Kellner, 1973, 159). This development of ideology and changes in its formulation are stages that can be observed during the life history of a social movement. In the emergence stage of the Blessing movement, the leaders were free to acknowledge that they "didn't have a clue" about what God was doing through the strange physical manifestations of deep belly-laughing, uncontrollable weeping, intense screaming and shouting, spiritual drunkenness, wild jerking and shaking, and, most controversial, the "animal sounds." As they began the necessary task of defining and strategizing, tension increased between the Association of Vineyard Churches (AVC), the denomination with which the TAV was affiliated. (It is significant that the publication of John Arnott's book *The Father's Blessing,* which sought to explain some of the more controversial manifestations, became the proverbial straw that broke the camel's back, leading to the ouster of the Toronto church from the Vineyard.) Although the Vineyard grew in the midst of controversy with its democratization of "signs and wonders" in the 1980s and enjoyed similar revival-like manifestations well into the early 1990s, the AVC was further along the path of emergence and coalescence. Some sectors sought to distance the AVC from its charismatic moment and especially from the fresh Toronto Blessing that was beginning its global spread. Tension between the old move and the newer move was both an asset and a liability.

Some Vineyards, including well-attended conferences at the Anaheim, CA, Vineyard, had experienced the same manifestations that occurred later in Toronto (see White, 1988). In fact, at least one major renewal leader, Che Ahn of Harvest Rock Church in Pasadena, CA, reported having first experienced the Blessing at the Anaheim Vineyard in early 1994, just about the time the renewal first broke out in Toronto. The AVC thus provided a ready plausibility structure for the unusual physical manifestations. Affiliation with AVC was an asset in that the Toronto church at first enjoyed the support and guidance of many within the parent denomination (see Poloma, 1997[b]). In sharing some of the responsibility for the movement, in providing a model and ideology, and even in its cautioning against certain activities, the affiliation with AVC may have helped to protect the charisma of the Toronto Blessing by providing a socially constructed postmodern grid to frame the Blessing. The alliance between the Toronto church and AVC, however, became increasingly strained as the TAV became the newest charismatic wave, seemingly overshadowing the parent denomination.

When TAV was ousted by the AVC in Dec. 1995, its direction seemed to change quickly. Within weeks TAV—now the Toronto Airport Christian Fellowship (TACF)—began laying the foundation for increased organization or bureaucratization, the third stage in the natural history process for a social movement. TACF embarked on television and radio ministries, acquired three large buildings, increased the size of its staff, established new alliances (Friends in Harvest), launched a new denomination (Partners in Harvest), and established an international network (International Renewal Network). These structural and environmental changes were accompanied by ideological changes that reflect somewhat of a decline in the Toronto Blessing as a social movement—the fourth and final step in the evolutionary natural history model.

It is important to note that the transition of the Blessing from emergence to decline does not mean that the social movement is no longer viable. "Decline" refers rather to a qualitative change reflected in a loss of the inherent dynamics of a movement. Many people within the movement may not perceive the decline; they may even see this stage as an era of success, since many of the movement's goals seemingly are being realized, but it is success at the expense of conforming to existent social patterns that may quench charisma. The social movement takes on characteristics of a "movement organization," in which the structures that are in place to promote the renewal paradoxically have become forces that have sapped the freshness found during its emergence stage. Numerous ministries have been birthed to promote the renewal, and others embraced the renewal with the potentially new market it provided for existent ministries. The freshness of the "nameless-faceless" movement that was carried by word of mouth (and the Internet) with a simple message of God's love and his desire to "romance" his church, however, became more dependent on well-planned and promoted conferences with newly emergent renewal personalities that attract registrants. Subtle pressures are on these new prophets and apostles to predict and lead the movement into fresh waters and new power (second "waves," or "winds," to use renewal metaphors; see Poloma 1997[b] for a discussion of the Toronto Blessing's move from charisma to institutionalization).

At the time of this writing, the Toronto Blessing is at crossroads. From the beginning, John Arnott recognized the futility and danger of trying to control the movement. His strategy seemingly was to nurture the Blessing's spread throughout the world, encouraging it to adapt to different cultures and denominations that embraced it. A review of Internet sites in early 1998 quickly revealed that more activity seems to be going on internationally than in North America, with its main itinerant speakers being more likely to be involved in ministry outside the U.S. and Canada than within it. Meanwhile, churches that were "flowing with the river" (to use another renewal metaphor) find that the current has slowed considerably. There are fewer local renewal services, and some of the former renewal sites that made the news during the earliest days of the Blessing are but distant memories. An occasional new face with a fresh story emerges to replace some of the older ones in drawing the faithful remnant and in attracting some new followers to experience the Blessing.

With few exceptions, the renewal was embraced primarily by independent charismatic churches and pentecostals. The faltering charismatic movement in the mainline churches took only passing note of the Blessing. As it has developed into a "movement organization" in its progression from the emergent and coalescing stages, the leaders and promoters of the Blessing are notably the leaders of independent churches and newer, loosely formed networks that have emerged from the renewal. (Many pentecostals, particularly in the U.S., feel a greater affinity with the form the renewal has taken at the Brownsville AG in Pensacola, which, despite its spiritual tie to Toronto through HTB, has its own history.) Particularly noteworthy is the newer emphasis on some 'Latter Rain teachings, including the restoration of a fivefold ministry and the imminence of the Second Coming. Despite the talk about and desire for unity among all Christians that is believed essential to get the church ready for the coming of Christ, signs of unity and cooperation have been realized largely among those who accept a Latter Rain eschatology. The attempt to embrace all cultures, ethnic groups, and Christian denominations has met with only limited success. With the message of the renewal losing much of its early simplicity and developing a more particularistic style, it is difficult to see how it can break out of the religious enclave in which it now finds itself.

3. Where Is It Going?

Sociologists, including this one, have not been known for their prophetic ability, so it is with some trepidation that I attempt to predict the outcome of the Toronto Blessing. If history is any teacher, it would appear that the Toronto Blessing has traveled its course as an emergent social movement and is now a contributor to the restructuring of American Protestantism with newly emergent networks possibly becoming some new denominations of the future. It provides the most recent example of how North America continues to be a "land of religious revivals" that are regularly sparked due to the "factor of ambiguity." According to sociologist Edward Tiryakian (1979), there is a tension between the rationalistic, this-worldly orientation of Protestantism and an equally strong evangelical, Christocentric current that produces fertile ground for religious revival. The Toronto Blessing has come, revitalized some segments of the charismatic-pentecostal movement, and is now struggling to recapture the early charisma that drew thousands to Toronto for "another drink" of the Spirit. History suggests that it has run its course, and only time will reveal its lasting impact.

The natural history of a social movement may be described as a journey from a fluid charismatic movement toward institutionalization and decline—from seemingly charismatic disorder to organizational order. To rephrase a common assertion of earlier renewal days, the sides that the seemingly strange Blessing have "knocked out of the God box" constructed by believers are now being reconstructed with predictable form. What has been described by Richter (1996) as "charismatic mysticism," which in the past adopted the "inarticulate meta-language of glossolalia" and now embraced "the non-verbal Toronto Blessing" as a response to postmodernity, is increasingly adopting the language of the independent Latter Rain movement with militant end-time metaphors to replace the romantic love metaphors of its emergence stage. Despite protests about and denunciation of religion and old wineskins, the lure of and acceptance by the independent stream of the pentecostal-charismatic movement is quenching the "mystical" and nurturing the "religious" elements found in the Blessing.

Yet I would not have predicted the showers of a Toronto Blessing during the charismatic drought of the 1980s and early 1990s. And even as I write of this predictable move from charisma to institutionalization, the sparks from the Toronto Blessing continue to torch new fires, some of which are in mainline churches (including the large Roman Catholic sector). Much of this new fire is being experienced outside of North America but some of it within. The pentecostal-charismatic movement has experienced fresh fire, wind, and waves in North America several times during the past 50 years—through Latter Rain and the healing movement of the late 1940s, the charismatic movement of the 1960s and 1970s, the so-called third wave of John Wimber's early Vineyard movement, and most recently through the various streams of the 1990s "renewal/revival" in which the Toronto blessing has been central. The sociologist in me is skeptical about the fire's ability to become a blazing flame that engulfs the entire world, as its proponents claim it will, but the charismatic Christian in me has seen with her own eyes the fruits of, and experienced in her own spirit a refreshing from, the Toronto Blessing. The final chapter of the narrative on the Blessing may provide a very different ending than the one predicted by sociological theory.

■ **Bibliography:** J. Arnott, *The Father's Blessing* (1995) ■ idem, "The Toronto Blessing: What Is It?" *Spread the Fire* (1998 Anniversary Issue) ■ P. L. Berger, B. Berger, and H. Kellner, *The Homeless Mind: Modernization and Consciousness* (1973) ■ H. Blumer, "Collective Behavior," in *Principles of Sociology*, ed. A. McClung Lee (1969) ■ G. Chevreau, *Catch the Fire* (1994) ■ S. Hill, *The Pursuit of Revival* (1997) ■ E. Hyatt, *2000 Years of Charismatic Christianity* (1996) ■ A. Mauss, *Social Problems as Social Movements* (1975) ■ M. M. Poloma, *Inspecting the Fruit: A 1997 Sociological Assessment of the Blessing* (1997[a]) ■ idem, *The Toronto Report* (1996) ■ idem, "'The Spirit Movement in North America at the Millennium: From Azusa Street to Toronto, Pensacola, and Beyond," *Journal of Pentecostal Theology* (1998) ■ idem, "'The Toronto Blessing': Charisma, Institutionalization and Revival," *Journal for the Scientific Study of Religion* 36 (2, June 1997[b]) ■ P. Richter, "Charismatic Mysticism: A Sociological Analysis of the 'Toronto Blessing,'" in *The Nature of Religious Language: A Colloquium*, ed. S. E. Porter (1996) ■ R. and K. Riss, *Images of Revival* (1997) ■ D. Roberts, *The "Toronto" Blessing* (1994) ■ J. Sprechner, "All in God's Time: How the 'Toronto Blessing' Came to Pass," *Spread the Fire* (1998 Anniversary Issue) ■ V. Synan, *The Holiness-Pentecostal Tradition: Charismatic Movements in the Twentieth Century* (1997) ■ E. A. Tiryakian, "The United States as a Religious Phenomenon," in A. M. Greeley, *Sociology and Religion* (1995) ■ J. Weis, "The River Is Still Flowing," *Second Wind: A Voice of Renewal* (Winter 1998) ■ J. White, *When the Spirit Comes with Power* (1988).   ■ M. M. Poloma

TRASHER, LILLIAN HUNT (1887–1961). Missionary to Egypt. Lillian Trasher was born in Florida to a successful businessman and an educated mother. When young, she committed her life to Roman Catholicism. In her late teens, after reading the Bible and attending Bible studies at a newly converted friend's house, she knelt and prayed and knew she had met God.

At age 18 Trasher left for God's Bible School in Cincinnati, OH, for one term and subsequently went to work at an orphanage in NC. After a few months, she left for Altamont Bible School in SC, where she was baptized in the Holy Spirit and began a successful pastorate of a pentecostal church. Despite the success, she left the church to accompany an evangelist and then returned to the orphanage.

During the evangelistic tour, Trasher became engaged to Tom Jordan. Because of her call to Africa as a missionary and her fiancé's lack of interest in missions, she broke the engagement 10 days before the wedding date. That same year, 1910, she left for Africa in the face of her family's strong disapproval. Her sister went with her to take care of her and later proved to be an invaluable asset amid severe persecution. The Lord gave Lillian a verse (Acts 7:34) as she prayed in her cabin before setting sail that verified her calling to Egypt.

As Trasher cared for a starving baby after watching its mother die, she realized that her earlier training at the orphanage was all part of God's plan. She rented a house and started an orphanage in Assiout, Egypt (230 miles south of Cairo). Within one year, and with the help of Egyptian and American friends, eight children were supported in the home. She capitalized on the Egyptian belief that giving to the poor brings healing more quickly. The Egyptian government also helped her. She realized the effectiveness of prayer and that God was her source.

Lillian Trasher at the orphanage in Assiout, Egypt, with military and government leaders, who supported her efforts.

Trasher was ordained with the Church of God (Cleveland, TN) in 1912. In 1916, after five years, she had 50 children at her orphanage. On a trip to America she was impressed by the giving and prayers of the ▸Assembly of God (AG) constituency and as a result became part of that organization in 1919.

Over the years, many of the children reared at the orphanage were sought after as wives and workers. Some returned to the orphanage if they became pregnant or if they lost their jobs. Trasher delivered hundreds of babies; most of the girls were promptly named Lillian. She loved to be called Mamma. Her dedication kept her working from 1929 until 1954 without a furlough. In 1955 her family numbered 1,200. She became known worldwide.

"Mamma Lillian" was buried at the site of her orphanage, which today consists of 13 main buildings on 12 acres, housing about 650 children, widows, and blind women. Today it is known as the Lillian Trasher Memorial Orphanage.

"I believe that when she dies, in spite of the fact she is a woman and a Christian, God will take her directly to paradise." This statement, representative of her reputation in Egypt, is the highest of compliments—especially when coming from a Moslem official (Crouch, 7).

■ **Bibliography:** J. Beatty, "Nile Mother," *AGH* 4 (Winter 1984–85) ▪ J. Booze, *Into All the World* (1980) ▪ P. Crouch, "Why They Called Her the Greatest Woman in Egypt," *AGH* 4 (Winter 1984–85) ▪ B. P. Howell, *Lady on a Donkey* (1960) ▪ N. Perkin, ed., *Light along the Nile* (1942) ▪ *Letters from Lillian* (1983).   ■ S. Shemeth

"Mamma Lillian" in 1952 with a few of her children.

TRASK, THOMAS E. (1936–). General superintendent, Assemblies of God (AG) in the U.S. Born on Mar. 23, 1936, in Brainerd, MN, Trask attended North Central Bible College (Minneapolis), where he graduated in 1956. He was ordained by the AG in 1958. Trask served 25 years as a pastor, most notably at Brightmoor Tabernacle in Southfield, MI (1976–88). While in Michigan, he served as assistant superintendent of the AG Michigan District, followed by three years as superintendent.

In 1988 Trask was elected general treasurer of the AG. In 1993 he succeeded ˒G. Raymond Carlson as general superintendent. He has been a very influential chief executive, certainly ranking as the most powerful since ˒Thomas F. Zimmerman. He spearheaded a reorganization of the AG headquarters operation and numerous constitution and bylaw changes in the administrative handbook. Above all, he will be remembered for his strong emphasis on Spirit baptism as the key to revival and on revival as the key to church growth.

Thomas Trask, general superintendent of the Assemblies of God in the U.S.

Trask currently serves on the boards of the AG Theological Seminary, Central Bible College, and Evangel University. He is chairman of the ˒Pentecostal World Conference, a member of the board of administration of the ˒National Association of Evangelicals, and a member of the board of directors of the National Religious Broadcasters. He also cochairs the Pentecostal/Charismatic Churches of North America.

Trask has coauthored a number of books, including *Back to the Altar, Back to the Word, The Battle* (on spiritual warfare), *The Blessing* (on the power of the Holy Spirit today), *The Choice* (concerning God's vision for the new millennium), and *The Fruit of the Spirit.*

Trask and his wife, Shirley, have a daughter (Kim Mullen), and three sons (Bradley, Todd, and Tom).

■ S. M. Burgess

TRIPLETT, LOREN OTIS, JR. (1926–). Missionary and pentecostal missions executive. Born in San Jose, CA, Triplett grew up in California, Michigan, and Oregon. He was the son of Assemblies of God (AG) ministers L. Otis and Gladys (Behnke) Triplett. After graduating from Glad Tidings Bible Institute (now Bethany College) in 1946, he began his ministry as an assistant pastor at Red Bluff, CA, in 1946. He also served a short time as an evangelist. He married Mildred Johnson of Newburg, OR, in 1949 and was ordained by the AG in 1950. They have four children.

From 1947 to 1953 Triplett pastored churches in Oregon and Nebraska before serving as a missionary to Nicaragua from 1954 to 1966. He became assistant superintendent of the AG in Nicaragua and director of the Nicaraguan Bible Institute.

From 1966 to 1973 Triplett was manager of Life Publishers in Miami, FL. While in this capacity, he edited *Poder,* a monthly magazine serving the churches in Latin America. He served as field director for Latin America and the Caribbean for the AG Division of Foreign Missions from 1973 to 1989. He succeeded ˒J. Philip Hogan as executive director of the Division of Foreign Missions in 1990 and served in that capacity until his retirement in 1997. He has contributed articles to a number of different missionary and religious publications.

■ **Bibliography:** Missionary file in AG Division of Foreign Missions ■ Personal data sheet, AG Office of Public Relations (1980) ■ *Who's Who in America* (52d ed., 1998).   ■ G. W. Gohr

TUCKER, J. W. (1915–64). Missionary martyr. J. W. Tucker served as a missionary in the Belgian Congo (Zaire) for more than 25 years. During the latter part of his service there, rebel forces were attempting to overthrow what was then the New Republic of Congo. Tucker, a white American, was considered a threat to the rebel cause and was imprisoned and eventually beaten to death. At the time, Tucker's wife, Angeline, and their three children were also in great danger, but the rebels spared their lives. J. W. Tucker remains one of the outstanding missionary martyrs of the Assemblies of God.

■ **Bibliography:** A. Tucker, *He Is in Heaven* (1965).

■ F. Bixler

TUGWELL, SIMON (1943–). English Catholic authority on traditional, especially Dominican, spirituality. Brought up as an Anglican, Tugwell became a Catholic at Oxford University. He entered the Dominican order in 1965. In the late 1960s he had some experience of spiritual gifts after contact with British pentecostals. Before the ˒Catholic charismatic renewal developed in Britain, Tugwell helped many Catholics to benefit from the experience of pentecostal churches. His book *Did You Receive the Spirit?* (1972; rev. 1979) illustrated the life of the Spirit from the riches of patristic and medieval sources; widely acclaimed, it became for many their first introduction to things pentecostal. Tugwell never identified himself with organized charismatic renewal and, after some further writings on glossolalia, e.g., in *Prayer* (1974) and *New Heaven? New Earth?* (1976), has not pursued such topics since. He has taught theology in Norway and Rome and is currently a professor at the Angelicum in Rome.

■ P. D. Hocken

TURNEY, HENRY MICHAEL (1850–1920). Early pentecostal missionary. Turney was born to Irish Catholic parents in Louisville, KY. He later became an alcoholic, but his life changed when he was converted to Christ. In 1897 he received an experience of sanctification. While doing evangelistic work in Alaska in 1906, he heard about the ˒Azusa Street revival in Los Angeles. Leaving for California, he arrived at the Azusa Street Mission on Oct. 5, 1906, and received the baptism in the Holy Spirit the following night.

Shortly after his experience at Azusa Street, Turney established an Apostolic Faith mission in San Jose, CA. In February 1907 he married Anna E. Arian (d. 1954), and they departed for ministry in Hawaii. Returning to the U.S., he preached in pentecostal churches across the country before sailing to England in 1908. After several months the Turneys sailed for South Africa and arrived in 1909. Along with Hanna James they began ministering in the Pretoria district and in 1911 opened a mission station in eastern Transvaal. They later became closely linked to the Assemblies of God (AG) in the U.S., registering a number of South African pentecostal churches under the AG name in 1917. At approximately the same time, they affiliated with the American AG.

■ **Bibliography:** H. M. Turney, "Alaska Brother Proves Acts 1:8," *The Apostolic Faith* (Dec. 1906) ▮ idem, "Article VIII.—Letter from H. M. Turney of South Africa," *Weekly Evangel* 17 (June 1916) ▮ P. Watt, *From Africa's Soil: The Story of the Assemblies of God in Southern Africa* (1992).   ■ G. B. McGee; B. A. Pavia

TYSON, TOMMY (1922–). Pastor and evangelist. Tommy Tyson was born in Farmville, NC, and was educated at Duke University (B.A.) and Duke Divinity School (M.Div.).

Tyson had a profound new-birth experience in 1947 and responded to a call to preach in 1948. After serving six years as a pastor in the North Carolina annual conference of the United Methodist Church (UMC), he received appointment as an approved evangelist through that body. It was largely through the witness and life of J. Rufus Moseley that Tyson was led into the experience of the baptism in the Holy Spirit in 1952 while serving as a UMC pastor. From 1965 to 1968 he served as director of spiritual life at the newly founded Oral Roberts University, an appointment approved by the bishop of the North Carolina Conference.

Most of Tyson's ministry as an evangelist has been in the work of church renewal at denominational, interdenominational, and ecumenical levels. Now retired, Tyson and his wife, Frances, live in Chapel Hill, NC, at the Aqueduct, a Christian-growth conference center.   ■ S. Strang

U

UNDERWOOD, B. E. (1925–99). Bernard Edward Underwood was born in Bluefield, WV, in 1925 into the home of a Pentecostal Holiness Church pastor. He was ordained in the Virginia Conference in 1944. While pastoring churches in Virginia and West Virginia, he was called on to serve as conference youth director and Christian education director. He served two terms as superintendent of the Virginia conference (1964–78).

Underwood's work as a general official of the ⸙International Pentecostal Holiness Church (IPHC) began when he was elected assistant general superintendent in 1965, at which time he was appointed to serve as director of church institutions. His longest tenure was as director of world missions (1969–73 and 1977–89). When the 21st general conference convened in Oklahoma City in 1989, vice chairman B. E. Underwood was elected to the bishop's chair.

During his tenure as IPHC general superintendent (1989–97), Bishop Underwood initiated a paradigm shift in the denomination. In Oct. 1994 the church decided to move away from the "hierarchical model" to a "networking model," in which power did not flow down from the top but upward from the basic unit of the denomination, the local church. The local church and the pastor were henceforth to have "primacy" in the structures of the church. Replacing the "International Headquarters" with a "Resource Development Center" was one of the immediate changes. The *International Pentecostal Holiness Advocate,* which had been the official journal of the church since 1917, was replaced in 1997 by *IssacharFile.* In Aug. 1996, at the Northwood Temple Church in Fayetteville, NC, Bishop Underwood led a "solemn assembly," which called for repentance of sins like racism, male domination, and spiritual pride. His single most important book continues to be *Spiritual Gifts: Ministries and Manifestations.*

Underwood was active in the ⸙National Association of Evangelicals (NAE), the ⸙Pentecostal World Conference (PWC), and the ⸙North American Renewal Service Committee (NARSC). One of his most significant contributions, however, was leading the ⸙Pentecostal Fellowship of North America (PFNA) into dissolving itself so that a new entity, the ⸙Pentecostal Charismatic Churches of North American (PCCNA), could emerge. Underwood cochaired the defining Memphis event in Oct. 1994 with ⸙Church of God in Christ bishop ⸙Ithiel Clemmons.

■ **Bibliography:** V. Synan, "Memphis 1994: Miracle and Mandate," *Reconciliation* 1 (Summer 1998) ■ idem, *Old-Time Power: A Centennial History of the International Pentecostal Holiness Church* (1998) ■ B. E. Underwood, "The Memphis Miracle," *Legacy* 4 (July 1997). ■ H. D. Hunter

UNION DE PRIÈRE (UP). An association formed in 1946 under the leadership of Louis Dallière among those touched by the Ardèche revival in the Reformed church in France in the 1930s. Though not using the term, the UP was the pioneer "charismatic" body, with baptism in the Spirit and the spiritual gifts being received and exercised with a firm commitment to a historic church tradition. UP's charter specifies four intercessory concerns: the revival of the churches through the conversion of souls, the salvation of the Jewish people, the visible unity of the body of Christ, and the return of Jesus Christ and the resurrection of the dead. An official accord was reached between the UP and the French Reformed Church in 1972.

■ **Bibliography:** W. J. Hollenweger, "'Touching' and 'Thinking' the Spirit: Some Aspects of European Charismatics," in *Perspectives on the New Pentecostalism,* ed. R. P. Spittler (1970) ■ J. Thoorens, "L'union de prière de Charmes-sur-Rhône" (diss., Institut Catholique de Paris). ■ P. D. Hocken

UNION OF MESSIANIC JEWISH CONGREGATIONS

The Union of Messianic Jewish Congregations (UMJC) is a transdenominational fellowship of almost 90 Messianic Jewish congregations. The fellowship consists of 7 Assemblies of God (AG)–related congregations, one Presbyterian-related congregation, and more than 80 nonaffiliated congregations.

The UMJC was formed to serve the needs of the increasing number of Messianic Jewish congregations. These congregations are homes for Jews and Gentiles who appreciate a Jewishly rooted expression of their new covenant faith.

The recent roots of this movement can be traced to the establishment of Hebrew Christian churches in the past decades, the Messianic Jewish orientation of Manny Brotman in the mid 1960s, and the establishment of several Messianic congregations in the early 1970s. Some Hebrew Christian congregations reoriented themselves to the new Jewish directions (Adat ha Tikvah, formerly the First Hebrew Christian Church, under Daniel Juster [1974]; Beth Messiah, Philadelphia, under Herb Links [1971]; and Beth Messiah, Cincinnati, under Martin Chernoff). New congregations included Beth Messiah, Washington, DC, founded by Paul Liberman, Sid Roth, and Sandra Sheskin, and first pastored by Manny Brotman (1973); Beth Immanuel in Encino, CA, under Ray Gannon and Phil Goble (1971) (Goble, 1975); and B'nai Maccabim, in Highland Park, IL (Rausch, 1981, 99–108), under John Fischer (1975).

The desire began to grow among several congregations for a mutual affiliation. In 1976 James Hutchins of B'nai

Maccabim and Daniel Juster of Adat ha Tikveh asked the Messianic Jewish Alliance of America (MJAA), an organization for individuals of Jewish birth, to consider affiliation for congregations. The MJAA board noted the need for such an affiliation but stated that it should be formed separately from the Alliance (Minutes of Mar. 1976 MJAA board meeting). It stated that it would look favorably on the formation of the union. Due to a change in board composition after the 1979 MJAA elections and the convictions of the new majority on the board, this position was reversed.

In 1976 Manny Brotman and Jim Hutchins sought to form a union of congregations. This effort received little response and was halted. In 1978 invitations were sent by the two Chicago-area congregations to all known Messianic Jewish congregations in North America to discuss the possible formation of a union. This meeting was followed up by a spring 1979 meeting in which there was almost unanimous agreement to form a union. A brief incorporation meeting took place in July 1979 in Mechanicsburg, PA. Nineteen of the 22 known congregations joined (Juster, 1986, 148–55).

Since that time the UMJC has fostered many services, including a program for establishing new congregations, the development and publication of educational materials, leadership training courses and seminars (the UMJC Yeshiva), national and regional conferences, pastoral fellowships, and a program for ordination for those without other adequate sources of credentials. The UMJC maintains doctrinal and moral standards as agreed upon by its constituents.

Most UMJC members are charismatic in orientation. However, in more recent years, due to the increasing number of members without a charismatic orientation, the UMJC has decided that it would be wise to be conservative in the expression of spiritual gifts at public gatherings.

The government of the UMJC is by delegate representation, with most congregations sending their head pastor (rabbi) and another leader. These delegates elect a four-member executive board. The board appoints committee chairpersons and regional coordinators subject to delegate approval. A general secretary may be appointed, who is an appointed member of the executive board and would oversee the daily operations of the organization. In addition, the UMJC has a presidents' advisory committee made up of all past presidents of the UMJC.

See also MESSIANIC JUDAISM.

■ **Bibliography:** P. Goble and R. Gannon, *Everything You Need to Grow a Messianic Synagogue* (1975) ■ D. Juster, *Jewish Roots* (1986) ■ P. Liberman, *The Fig Tree Blossoms* (1976) ■ D. Rausch, *Messianic Judaism: Its History, Theology, and Polity* (1981) ■ M. Shiffman, *The Return of the Remnant* (1990).   ■ D. C. Juster

UNITED CHURCH OF CHRIST, FELLOWSHIP OF CHARISMATIC CHRISTIANS IN THE

The Fellowship of Charismatic Christians in the United Church of Christ (FCC/UCC) began when 73 members of the United Church of Christ (UCC) attending the 1977 Conference on Charismatic Renewal in the Christian Churches (Kansas City) decided to address the need for "a denominational nationwide fellowship for those who were interested in the charismatic renewal" (FCC/UCC pamphlet, n.d.). With every intention of remaining in the church, the FCC/UCC organized in the winter of 1977–78 to strengthen and encourage those who had a "charismatic experience" within the UCC religious tradition.

Programs of the FCC/UCC include: Acts Alive, a three-weekend lay-witness event designed to be experienced over a two- or three-year period within the local congregation; Ekklesia, a follow-up program to Acts Alive, wherein selected "pilot" churches provide further teaching, research, and development for renewal; *Focus,* a newspaper containing articles, book reviews, announcements, and other renewal information; mailings of reprint and resource materials; correspondence with pastors and laity seeking information concerning the renewal; and liaison relationships with the Office of Church Life and Leadership in the UCC.

FCC/UCC is now called Focus Renewal Ministries in the United Church of Christ. Vernon Stoop Jr. is the director of services.

Other visionary agenda are being pursued, including exploring "varieties of future growth opportunities such as developing renewal seminars, establishing Christian Healing Centers, developing apostolic ministries, exploring ways to assist in the placement of pastors, developing a book treatise on renewal and encouraging the formation of FCC/UCC … regional representatives" (*Focus* 12 [9, 1987]: 2).

■ **Bibliography:** "Fellowship of Charismatic Christians in the United Christian Church," pamphlet, n.d.   ■ J. A. Hewett

UNITED HOLY CHURCH OF AMERICA

During the late 19th century, the Holiness movement spread among blacks in the South. In 1886 one group met in Method, NC, and from that meeting arose the United Holy Church of America. Referring to themselves as the Holy People, the movement spread throughout the state. In 1894 many gathered in Durham for the first convocation of Holy People in North Carolina. Then, in 1900, this and several other Holiness associations met together to form the Holy People of North Carolina and Virginia, with Elder L. M. Mason of Goldsboro, NC, as president. Expansion dictated the adoption in 1916 of the name United Holy Church of America. Although Mason was the first president, and other church fathers such as H. L. Fisher, G. J. Branch, and J. D. Diggs gave great form and direction to the movement, church doctrine claims "no earthly founder," pointing rather to the initiative of Jesus Christ by the Holy Spirit.

The church is organized around a Holy Convocation structure, meeting in convocation by districts as well as holding an annual convocation for the whole church. Church doctrine includes strong emphasis on sanctification as a second work of grace and the baptism of the Holy Spirit as empowerment for service. The church teaches that speaking in tongues is one of the spiritual gifts that comes with Spirit baptism but is not necessarily the initial evidence.

Over the years, three schisms have taken place, resulting in new denominations that maintain basically the same structures and beliefs as the mother church. The first schism resulted in the formation of the ›Mount Sinai Holy Church in Philadelphia in 1924. The second yielded the Mount Calvary Holy Church in Boston in 1929. The third group, the Original United Holy Church, International, was formed in 1977 and maintains headquarters at its United Christian College at Goldsboro. Interestingly, relations between the groups have remained amicable even amid the schisms. Membership in the United Holy Church is estimated to be between 30,000 and 40,000, primarily along the East Coast. The church maintains ministries in England, the West Indies, Liberia, and the Philippines.

■ **Bibliography:** H. L. Fisher, *The History of the United Holy Church of America, Inc.* (1945), repr. in *The Holiness Union* (1979) ■ J. A. Forbes, "A Ministry of Hope from a Double Minority," *Theological Education* 9 (4, 1973) ■ C. W. Gregory, *The History of the United Holy Church of America, Inc., 1886–1986* (1986) ■ A. W. Lawson, *The Doctrine of the United Holy Church of America, Inc.* (1980) ■ C. E. Lincoln and L. Mumiya, *The Black Church in the African American Experience* (1990) ■ L. Lovett, "Black Holiness Pentecostalism: Implications for Social Transformation" (diss., Emory, 1979) ■ A. Paris, *Black Pentecostalism: Southern Religion in an Urban World* (1982) ■ J. Shopshire, "A Socio-Historical Characterization of the Black Pentecostal Movement in America" (diss., Northwestern U., 1975) ■ J. Tinney, "New Missions Thrust for the United Holy Church," *Washington Afro-American* (Sept. 22, 1973) ■ idem, "Prospects of Black Pentecostalism: An Emerging Third World Religion," in D. J. Jones and W. H. Matthews, *The Black Church: A Community Resource* (1977) ■ W. C. Turner, "The United Holy Church of America: A Study in Black Holiness-Pentecostalism" (diss., Duke, 1984).   ■ H. D. Trulear

UNITED HOUSE OF PRAYER FOR ALL PEOPLE, CHURCH ON THE ROCK OF THE APOSTOLIC CHURCH

The first House of Prayer (HP) was founded by Charles Emmanuel "Sweet Daddy" Grace (1881–1961) in West Wareham, MA, in 1924. A native of the Cape Verde Islands, Grace immigrated to the U.S. in 1903; he worked in a variety of jobs while beginning his career as a Holiness preacher. Soon after founding the first HP, he began traveling extensively, particularly in the Southeast, and established HPs in leading cities, including New York, Philadelphia, Atlanta, Baltimore, and Washington, DC. Typically, these HPs were located in economically depressed neighborhoods and ministered to the poor.

HP centers hold daily meetings; Sunday meetings last all day. Emotional exuberance, ecstatic dancing, falling in trances, expressive singing, and glossolalia are all hallmarks of HP services, as are frequent collections, preaching, and testimonies. Members are encouraged to uphold strict Holiness moral codes—no drinking, dancing, attending movie theaters, etc.

Criticisms have been leveled at the organization for its excessive veneration of the founder. Though never claiming to be God, Grace seems not to have discouraged this veneration. A whirlwind of controversy followed him, and he was no stranger to the courtroom. Although most charges ended in acquittals, the IRS dogged Grace for tax evasion. When he died in 1960, they estimated his worth at almost $6 million dollars, his properties spanning 14 states.

Walter McCullough, known to the members as "Sweet Daddy Grace" McCullough, took charge of the denomination's leadership. With his ascendancy, a split occurred within the ranks, leading to the organization of the True Grace Memorial House of Prayer. A judge ordered a second election, which McCullough won. At the time of this split, 137 churches, with an approximate membership of 27,500, remained with McCullough. Under his leadership, the Washington, DC–based denomination established a ministerial school in Richmond, VA. He also brought stability by improving administration and by replacing the constitution and bylaws. Bishop S. C. Madison now presides.

■ **Bibliography:** J. O. Hodges, "Charles Manuel 'Sweet Daddy' Grace," *20th Century Shapers of American Popular Religion*, ed. C. H. Lippy (1989) ■ J. W. Robinson, "A Song, a Shout, and a Prayer," *The Black Experience in Religion*, ed. C. E. Lincoln (1974) ■ *Yearbook of American and Canadian Church 1998* (1998).   ■ E. J. Gitre

UNITED METHODIST CHARISMATICS

1. Methodists in the Early Pentecostal Movement.

Methodists and Wesleyan Holiness proponents were heavily involved in the early pentecostal movement. ›Charles F. Parham was a Methodist minister, as were ›T. B. Barratt of Norway, Johannes Van Kesteren of Belgium, and ›Harold Horton of England. Entire denominations and/or congregations became pentecostal during the early decades of the pentecostal movement in Chile, Germany, Great Britain, India, Norway, Sweden, and the U.S. Many features of pentecostal theology and spirituality were borrowed or adapted from the heritage of Methodism and its derivative movements, the Wesleyan Holiness and Keswick Higher Life traditions.

2. Development of the Charismatic Movement in the United Methodist Church, U.S.

After the institutionalization of the pentecostal movement there is no published record of Methodist charismatics until ▸Tommy Tyson's 1952 experience of baptism of the Holy Spirit. Tyson, pastor of Bethany Methodist Church in Durham, NC, was encouraged by Bishop Paul Garber to remain within the church. Tyson was appointed conference evangelist in 1954 and became a national leader of the charismatic renewal, both within Methodism and in other denominations. He later became friends with ▸Oral Roberts and served as director of religious life at Oral Roberts University.

Many Methodist charismatics of the 1950s and 1960s became involved in ▸Full Gospel Business Men's Fellowship International (FGBMFI) activities. That organization published a volume of testimonies of pastors, laymen, and a district superintendent (Jolly Harper, Shreveport, LA), *The Methodists and the Baptism of the Holy Spirit* (1963). *Voice*, the FGBMFI magazine, was influential. Another important instrument of communication was the periodical *He Is Able* (1961–78). This "journal dedicated to aid the revival of the Ministry of Healing in the Methodist Church" was edited by James and Virginia Johnson in Chattanooga, TN.

Oral Roberts, longtime pentecostal Holiness evangelist, became a United Methodist (UM) in 1968, first as a member of Boston Avenue UM Church (Tulsa) and, by transfer, as an ordained elder in the Oklahoma Conference. He recruited Methodist faculty for the university, including James Buskirk, dean of the Graduate School of Theology (1976–84), Methodist bishop Mack Stokes, Bob Stamps, and Robert Tuttle. Oral Roberts University achieved recognition as a seminary for training UM clergy. Through Roberts' involvement, the charismatic movement in the UM Church achieved recognition and an element of respectability. During 1984 to 1986, however, most Methodists were fired from the School of Theology and the school lost the recognition of the UM University senate in 1986.

Because of the increased numbers of charismatic Methodist clergy and the controversies over the function of glossolalia in Christian spirituality, concern was raised as to the role of charismatics in the church. At the 1972 general conference, the Western Pennsylvania Conference presented a memorial (petition) requesting that a position statement be prepared on the charismatic renewal. This was referred to the Board of Discipleship, where a task force prepared a report that was presented to the 1976 general conference (Portland, OR).

The task force consisted of D. Cottrill, T. P. Williams, Maxie Dunnam, Horace Weaver, and ▸R. Whetstone. They presented a three-part document (*Daily Christian Advocate*

[Apr. 27, 1976], 50–59). Part one was a paper written by Robert Tuttle (then associate professor at Fuller Theological Seminary), "The Charismatic Movement: Its Historical Base and Wesleyan Framework." This brief essay traced the roots of the charismatic movement back through pentecostalism and Wesleyan Holiness revivalism to Wesley. Part two was an essay by Ross Whetstone, "The Search for Christian Experience in a Sociocultural Revolution." Whetstone, a former Salvation Army officer, argued that the charismatic movement would continue to provide "a most attractive and authentic expression of the Christian life" and that the church should accept and minister to those persons. Part three was a set of guidelines adapted from the 1970 Report of the Special Committee on the Work of the Holy Spirit of the United Presbyterian Church in the United States of America. The task force urged that the report be read in light of the study guide entitled *The Holy Spirit and Christian Experience* (1975) produced by Bishop Mack Stokes at the request of the general conference in 1972.

The guidelines were adopted, with some amendment, by the general conference on May 1, 1976. One amendment made explicit that "the inference that the one who does not speak in tongues is guilty of withholding a full surrender of self to the will and purpose of God can be divisive among the Methodists." The essays by Tuttle and Whetstone were not adopted but were "commended to the church as background to the 'Guidelines.'" The guidelines, with the essays appended, have been published as *Guidelines: The United Methodist Church and the Charismatic Movement* (1976).

3. The United Methodist Renewal Service Fellowship (UMRSF).

Whetstone was on the planning committee of the Kansas City Charismatic Conference (1977). About a thousand Methodists attended. At this conference the UMRSF was organized, with Whetstone as director. Whetstone became editor of *Manna* (1977–), a magazine publishing doctrinal, historical, and news items. A periodical for leaders in the renewal, *Manna Ministries Notes* (1977–) is also edited by Whetstone. Since 1979, each year an "Aldersgate Conference" sponsored by UMRSF has drawn 2,000 to 3,000 people. The UMRSF also coordinates Methodist involvement in national charismatic conferences. The institutional stance of the UMRSF has been cooperative and positive. This resulted in official recognition by the UM board of discipleship, with offices provided at UM headquarters in Nashville (since 1980).

4. Methodist Charismatic Renewal in Great Britain.

One of the first pastors of the Methodist Church of Great Britain to become involved in the charismatic renewal was Charles J. Clarke, pastor at Halesowen. His awareness of a need for personal renewal by the Holy Spirit developed through reading Wesley and, especially, S. Chadwick, *The Way to Pentecost* (1932). He joined the Methodist Revival

Fellowship (MRF) but found his model for ministry and spirituality through contacts with local pentecostal pastors. Clarke experienced the "baptism of the Holy Spirit" in 1963, and his magazine, *Quest* ([Oct. 1961–Dec. 1965], merged with *Renewal,* published by the ʾFountain Trust), became the unofficial link between Methodist charismatics. In 1964 he participated with ʾDavid du Plessis in the Stoke Poge meeting of British charismatic leaders, organized by ʾMichael Harper. Clarke's relationships in the MRF provided a context for telling about his experience. Increasing numbers of Methodist charismatics created a need for a distinctively Methodist information bulletin, and Clarke started another periodical, the *Newsletter for Methodists Interested in the Charismatic Renewal* (1968–72), which later merged with *Dunamis.*

The MRF remained the primary forum for recruitment until Feb. 1970, when Dr. Leslie Davison, general secretary of the home missions department, began holding prayer meetings in his London office. In July 1970 he organized a colloquium at Lutton Industrial College, and a year later he recounted his experience at Harper's First International Conference on the Holy Spirit at Guildford. These lectures were published as *Pathway to Power* (1971). Davison was abetted in his renewalist efforts by Methodist layman Lord Rank, treasurer of the home missions department.

William R. Davies and Ross Peart founded *Dunamis* (Sept. 1972–), which prints articles on doctrinal matters as well as testimonies and information about the network of charismatic groups and conferences. They published a booklet, *The Charismatic Movement and Methodism* (1973), that sought to place the renewal in the center of the Methodist tradition.

The spread of and controversy about the charismatic renewal made it necessary for the Methodist Church to examine the phenomenon. The Faith and Order Committee of the Methodist Conference prepared a report (1974) that articulated positive contributions as well as concerns. Another study, published as a pamphlet, *The Impact of Charismatic Renewal on Methodism* (1976), was undertaken by the Commission on Evangelism of the home missions division. It found that *Dunamis* had a readership of about 10,000, including 250 Methodist ministers; that most participants in the renewal were already committed Christians; and it reiterated the concerns, raised in the 1974 report, about theological terminology and the psychological stability of adherents.

■ **Bibliography:** P. C. Bennett, "Charismatic Movements in the Church: Bridges or Wedges?" (D.Min. diss., Wesley Theol. Sem., 1996) ■ J. T. Connelly, "Neo-Pentecostalism: The Charismatic Revival in the Mainline Protestant and Roman Catholic Churches in the United States 1960–1971" (Ph.D. diss., U. of Chicago, 1977) ■ M. T. Girolimon, "'The Charismatic Wiggle': United Methodism's Twentieth-Century Neo-Pentecostal Impulses," *Pneuma* 17 (1995) ■ D. E. Harrell Jr., *Oral Roberts: An American Life* (1985) ■ J. Hinton, "Oral Roberts and the Heart of British Methodism," *Renewal* (Apr.–May 1970) ■ P. Hocken, *Streams of Renewal* (1986) ■ W. J. Hollenweger, "Methodism's Past in Pentecostalism's Present: A Case Study of Cultural Clash in Chile," *Methodist History* 20 (1982) ■ E. G. Hunt, ed., *The Holy Spirit in Today's Church: A Handbook of the New Pentecostalism* (1973) ■ "An Interview with Tommy Tyson, Evangelist," *Your Church* (Nov.–Dec. 1973), 10–28 ■ K. Kinghorn, *Fresh Wind of the Spirit* (1975) ■ idem, *Gifts of the Spirit* (1976) ■ K. McDonnell, *Presence, Power, Praise* (1980) ■ A. Outler, *Evangelism in the Wesleyan Spirit* (1971) ■ R. Quebedeaux, *The New Charismatics* (1976) ■ idem, *The New Charismatics II* (1983) ■ E. Robb, *Observations on the Charismatic Movement* (1972) ■ J. H. S. Stevens, "Charismatic Hymnody in the Light of Early Methodist Hymnody," *Studia Liturgica* 27 (1997).   ■ D. D. Bundy

UNITED PENTECOSTAL CHURCH, INTERNATIONAL

(UPC). The United Pentecostal Church (UPC) was formed in 1945 by the merger of two ʾOneness pentecostal organizations, the ʾPentecostal Church, Incorporated (PCI), and the ʾPentecostal Assemblies of Jesus Christ (PAJC). Its roots, however, are traced to the pentecostal revival that began in 1901.

A. The Pentecostal Revival.

On Oct. 15, 1900, ʾCharles Fox Parham opened Bethel Bible College in ʾTopeka, KS. After the examinations at the end of the first term, Parham asked the students to study the Bible for the evidence of the baptism of the Holy Spirit. On Jan. 1, 1901, the students reported that the biblical evidence was speaking in tongues as the Spirit gave the utterance.

Parham did not readily accept their discovery, but at the request of one of the students, ʾAgnes N. Ozman, he reluctantly laid his hands in prayer upon her, and she began speaking in tongues (Parham, 1930, 52). Two days later, when Parham returned from preaching in a local church, he found 12 student ministers, including his wife, speaking in tongues. Parham felt such a holy presence that he knelt in prayer and received the Holy Spirit with the evidence of speaking in tongues.

Although Parham and his group received publicity in newspapers in Topeka, Kansas City, Lawrence, KS, and other cities such as St. Louis, MO, the pentecostal movement—called Apostolic Faith at that time—did not grow rapidly. It was not until the fall of 1903 that the movement really began to spread. At the invitation of Mary Arthur and her husband, Parham held a revival in Galena, KS, in which more than 800 were converted and baptized, and hundreds were filled with the Holy Spirit (Parham, 1930, 92). Howard Goss, later a pentecostal leader, was among those converted and baptized (Goss, 1958, 36).

In the fall of 1905 Parham opened a short-term Bible school in Houston, TX. Among the students were ʾHoward

Goss and ►William J. Seymour, a black Holiness minister living in Houston, who later became the leader of the revival at the ►Azusa Street Mission in Los Angeles. Although Goss had not received the baptism in the Holy Spirit, he came to Houston to help spread the Apostolic Faith message. In Apr. 1906 he was filled with the Holy Spirit as he and other student workers rode the train from Orchard to Alvin, TX (Goss, 1958, 76–81).

When the school ended in the early spring of 1906, the students spread the message to neighboring towns in the Houston area, establishing pentecostal congregations in several communities. By the summer of 1906 several thousand people in Texas had been converted to the Apostolic Faith movement.

From the revivals in Kansas and Texas, the Apostolic Faith movement grew from a few people in 1901 to about 13,000 by 1906 and to about 25,000 by 1908. But it was the revival at the Azusa Street Mission from 1906 to 1909 that spread the pentecostal experience around the world.

In Feb. or Mar. 1906 William J. Seymour arrived in Los Angeles to bring the message of the Holy Spirit to the city. The revival began on Apr. 9 when Jennie Moore, a young woman who later married Seymour, received the Holy Spirit (*AF* [Dec. 1906], 1). Three days later Seymour and several others were filled with the Spirit. Within a week (by Apr. 19) they had rented an old two-story frame building on Azusa Street in the downtown industrial area of Los Angeles, cleared away a place on the bottom floor, and began to hold services (*AF* [May 1908], 1). To this humble place ministers and laity flocked to receive the Holy Spirit, and they took the experience and the news with them to spread the pentecostal movement across North America and overseas.

B. Early Pentecostal Organizations.

From 1901 until 1907 the pentecostal movement was led by Parham. In Aug. 1906 Parham, in his first efforts to organize the movement, appointed W. F. Carothers to be the general field director for the U.S. and Howard A. Goss to be the field director of the rapidly growing pentecostal revival in Texas (Goss, 1958, 97). After Parham was arrested for a moral offense, the organized structure crumbled and Goss resigned his position (Goss, 1958, 123–24).

Goss, however, remained a leader among the pentecostals. From 1907 to 1914 he established churches in Texas and Arkansas and evangelized in Arkansas, Kansas, Illinois, and Iowa. He preached at ►William H. Durham's North Avenue Mission in Chicago and accepted Durham's message on the "finished work of Calvary." In 1908 he met ►E. N. Bell at a convention in Houston, and during the following winter he handed the pastorate of the large church he had pioneered in Malvern, AR, to Bell. He also turned over the paper he edited, *The Apostolic Faith,* to Bell, who merged it with the *Word and Witness* in 1910 (Goss, 1958, 202–3).

Goss was probably the prime mover for organizing the General Council of the Assemblies of God (AG) in 1914 (Anderson, 1979, 167). In 1910 he and others worked out an arrangement with ►C. H. Mason to obtain ministerial licenses with his organization, the Church of God in Christ, for legal recognition (Brumback, 1961, 154). In 1912 Goss became acquainted with H. G. Rodgers and his group in Alabama and solicited their support. In late 1913 he persuaded E. N. Bell, ►D. C. O. Opperman, and others to issue the call for ministers to attend a conference to form an organization for pentecostals. This conference, held in Hot Springs, AR, where Goss was the host pastor, organized the AG. Goss, Bell, and Opperman were chosen, along with others, to be officials in the new organization, and from this beginning the AG has grown to be a large and respected organization.

C. Doctrinal Issues.

The first doctrinal division in the pentecostal movement came when William H. Durham preached what came to be known as the "finished work" doctrine. Although Durham had earlier embraced the "second work" view, he came to believe that the act of sanctification is accomplished at the time of conversion and that it continues toward perfection throughout a person's life. By 1912 most of the independent pentecostal ministers had accepted Durham's teaching (Ewart, 1975, 200). The AG, and later the UPC, were formed by ministers who believed the finished work message.

The second doctrinal issue to divide the pentecostal movement had its beginning in 1913 at the Arroyo Seco World Wide Camp Meeting near Los Angeles. Ministering at a baptismal service, ►R. E. McAlister noted that the church in the book of Acts always baptized in the name of Jesus Christ and not in the traditional formula, "in the name of the Father, and of the Son, and of the Holy Ghost." His observation immediately stirred the interest of many pentecostal ministers, including ►Frank J. Ewart (Ewart, 1975, 105–6).

During the next several months, Ewart searched the Bible for the answer to the apparent conflict between the command Jesus gave in Matt. 28:19 and the formula used by the church in the book of Acts. He noted that without exception the baptismal formula administered in Acts was "in the name of Jesus Christ" or "in the name of the Lord Jesus" (Acts 2:38; 8:16; 10:48; 19:5; 22:16). Moreover, the baptismal references in the Epistles supported the apostolic formula and not the traditional formula.

By the spring of 1914, Ewart reached the conclusion that the singular "name" in Matt. 28:19 was Jesus Christ. He came to believe that the one true God who had revealed himself as Father, in the Son, and as the Holy Spirit was none other than Jesus Christ. To support this view, he pointed to Col. 2:9, which states that in Jesus dwells all the fullness of the Godhead bodily.

Ewart explained his discovery to other pentecostal ministers; some of them rejected his teaching, but others enthusiastically embraced it. On Apr. 15, 1914, Ewart rebaptized ►Glenn A. Cook, his assistant and a veteran evangelist of the Azusa Street Mission, in the name of Jesus Christ, and Cook rebaptized Ewart. This one act set in motion an issue that would divide the pentecostal movement between the Trinitarians and the Jesus' Name, or Oneness, believers.

Although Parham had apparently used the Jesus' Name formula as early as 1903 (Foster, 1981, 98), and ►A. D. Urshan began baptizing converts in the name of Jesus in 1910 (Urshan, 1967, 169), no issue was raised about the practice until Ewart began rebaptizing pentecostals in the name of Jesus Christ.

After Ewart and Cook were rebaptized, they rebaptized thousands of pentecostals with the shorter formula. Pentecostals from the West Coast flocked to Ewart's church in Belvedere, CA, to be baptized in the name of Jesus Christ. Cook, who had brought the pentecostal message to the Midwest in 1907, returned to Oklahoma, Missouri, and Indiana in Jan. 1915 preaching water baptism in the name of Jesus Christ. He rebaptized hundreds of pentecostals in the name of Jesus Christ, including ►Leanore ("Mother") Barnes and her staff in St. Louis, and ►Garfield Thomas Haywood and about 500 members of the large pentecostal church he pastored in Indianapolis.

After Cook's successful tour in the Midwest, the leaders of the newly formed AG, including E. N. Bell, ►J. R. Flower, and Howard Goss, readily denounced the "New Issue" (Menzies, 1971, 114). Writing in the July 17, 1915, issue of *Word and Witness,* Flower expressed his opinion that the matter was only a fad and would soon fade away on its own. Bell had earlier expressed the same view in the June 12 issue (Brumback, 1961, 195). But their expectations were shattered by the middle of 1915. Indeed, by the time the general council was held in St. Louis in Oct. 1915, it appeared that the entire AG organization might embrace baptism in the name of Jesus Christ.

An unsettling event for the leaders was Bell's rebaptism during a camp meeting in Jackson, TN, in Aug. 1915. Joining him were many other ministers, including H. G. Rodgers, and hundreds of church members. Later that summer Bell rebaptized Goss in a meeting in Arkansas. When the general council convened in October, the list of prominent pentecostal leaders that had been rebaptized had grown to include not only Bell, Goss, Ewart, Cook, Haywood, and Rodgers, but also ►R. E. McAlister, ►D. C. O. Opperman, ►George B. Studd, Harvey Shearer, L. C. Hall, ►B. F. Lawrence, Harry Van Loon, L. V. Roberts, and Frank Small (Menzies, 1971, 115).

Many Trinitarian ministers feared that the "Jesus' Only" message, a name derived from the shorter baptismal formula, would become the doctrinal position of the AG. The overwhelming majority of the ministers still believed in the traditional formula, but the matter had to be handled with tact, since so many of the leaders had embraced the Jesus' Name formula. The "New Issue" was debated at the general council in 1915. E. N. Bell and G. T. Haywood were chosen to argue on the side for water baptism in the name of Jesus Christ, and A. P. Collins and Jacob Miller were chosen to present the view for using the traditional formula, "in the name of the Father, and of the Son, and of the Holy Ghost" (Brumback, 1961, 201).

The general council in 1915 took no official action on the matter of water baptism, and it was the general feeling that time for prayer and study should be given to the matter. It is significant, however, that all Oneness leaders were replaced with confirmed Trinitarians on the executive presbytery (Anderson, 1979, 179). While the Trinitarians wanted time to strengthen their position, they attempted to impose a period of silence on the Jesus' Name ministers (Anderson, 1979, 179). During the year before the next general council, the leadership of ►J. W. Welch, J. R. Flower, and ►M. M. Pinson successfully regained some of the ministers who had accepted the Jesus' Name formula. Their most important victory was the winning back of Bell to the Trinitarian position.

By the time the general council convened in St. Louis in Oct. 1916, the majority had effectively organized to force the Oneness ministers to accept the Trinitarian formula or to leave the organization. The leaders appointed a committee of staunch Trinitarians to draw up a "Statement of Fundamental Truths." This statement embraced the traditional formula and made the doctrine of the Trinity a basis for membership.

In spite of the protests by the Oneness ministers that passing the Statement of Fundamental Truths was a violation of the organizational charter that rejected the formulation of a creed or any statement of faith other than the Bible itself, each item of the statement was passed by a majority vote. The council also charged the chairman and secretary with the responsibility of annually renewing ministerial credentials to ensure conformity to the new Statement of Fundamental Truths.

The passing of the statement effectively forced the withdrawal of about one-fourth of the ministers from the AG. Some of the ministers withdrew not because of the doctrinal issue, but because they compared the harsh actions against the Oneness faction with the way they were treated by the Holiness organizations a few years earlier. After the council the list of ordained ministers in the AG fell from 585 to 429.

D. The Oneness Ministers Organize.

In Jan. 1917 a group of Oneness ministers meeting in St. Louis formed the General Assembly of the Apostolic Assemblies. The officers chosen were D. C. O. Opperman, general chairman; Lee Floyd, secretary; Howard A. Goss, credential committee; and H. G. Rodgers, member of credential committee. This organization lasted only a year, however, since the government would not grant military exemption or railroad discount fares to the ministers in the young organization.

In Jan. 1918 the General Assembly of the Apostolic Assemblies merged with the ▸Pentecostal Assemblies of the World, a pentecostal organization that began in Los Angeles in 1906 (Golder, 1973, 31). The merger effected a reorganization of the Pentecostal Assemblies of the World with new officers: J. J. Frazee, general chairman; D. C. O. Opperman, secretary; and Howard A. Goss, treasurer. By its next conference in Oct. 1918, Edward W. Doak had become general chairman, and W. E. Booth-Clibborn had become the secretary. In Jan. 1919 the headquarters of the Pentecostal Assemblies of the World was moved from Portland, OR, to Indianapolis, IN, and the organization was incorporated in the state of Indiana. E. W. Doak remained as general overseer, and G. T. Haywood became general secretary.

For the first few years this racially integrated organization functioned smoothly, but by 1921 racial tension became evident. Southern white ministers complained about the conferences always being held in the North to accommodate the blacks due to the social prejudices in the South. Since travel was not easy, the black ministers were usually in a majority at the conferences. Some abuse by both races added to the tension.

E. Division and Mergers.

In spite of efforts by ministers of both races, misunderstandings continued to grow until in the fall of 1924 a division came on racial lines. Most of the white ministers withdrew to form a white organization, but by the end of 1925 they had formed three organizations.

In Feb. 1925 a group of white ministers met in Jackson, TN, to form the Pentecostal Ministerial Alliance. They chose L. C. Hall as general chairman and Goss as secretary-treasurer. Later, in 1932, the name of this organization was changed to ▸Pentecostal Church, Incorporated (PCI).

Many ministers who felt that the Pentecostal Ministerial Alliance was only a ministerial organization and that it did not properly recognize the status of churches met in Houston, TX, in Oct. 1925 to organize the Emmanuel's Church in Jesus Christ, with W. T. Lyons as chairman and G. C. Stroud as secretary. O. F. Fauss was the third member of the board.

Between Feb. and Nov. 1925 a third group organized under the name of Apostolic Church of Jesus Christ, with headquarters in St. Louis. Under the leadership of W. H. Whittington, this group held its first conference in Apr. 1926 to draw up a statement of doctrine.

Most ministers were not satisfied with the division among Oneness believers. From the outset they sought for a way to unite again all groups into one organization. Many of their attempts failed, but there were successes. The first merger occurred in 1928 between the Emmanuel's Church of Jesus Christ and the Apostolic Church of Jesus Christ, using the latter's name except changing "Church" to "Churches." O. F. Fauss was chosen as chairman, W. H. Whittington as secretary, and E. D. Browning as treasurer.

The next merger took place in 1932. The Apostolic Churches of Jesus Christ merged with the Pentecostal Assemblies of the World, once again creating a racially integrated organization. The new organization was named the ▸Pentecostal Assemblies of Jesus Christ (PAJC). This merger was not accepted by all the black ministers, however, and they continued under the charter of the Pentecostal Assemblies of the World.

F. The United Pentecostal Church.

The UPC was formed in 1945 by the merger of the PAJC and the PCI. Many Oneness believers felt that this union fulfilled a dream of many years.

In the spring of 1945 a committee composed of members from both organizations met twice in St. Louis to work toward an agreement on the proposed merger. The leaders carefully explored various potential problems and found acceptable solutions. The most difficult question had to do with the new birth. While most Oneness ministers identified the new birth with Acts 2:38, others did not take such a firm view.

The solution came when W. T. Witherspoon, chairman of the PAJC, retired to a private room and wrote the Fundamental Doctrine Statement, which was readily accepted by all. The statement reads:

> The basic and fundamental doctrine of this organization shall be the Bible standard of full salvation, which is repentance, baptism in water by immersion in the name of the Lord Jesus Christ, and the baptism of the Holy Spirit with the initial sign of speaking with other tongues as the Spirit gives utterance. We shall endeavor to keep the unity of the Spirit until we all come into the unity of the faith, at the same time admonishing all brethren that they should not contend for their different views to the disunity of the body.

This statement, later amended to include the phrase "for the remission of sins" after the clause on water baptism, remains the basic doctrine of the UPC.

At the merger conference, the ministers elected officers from both former organizations: Howard A. Goss, general superintendent; ▸W. T. Witherspoon, assistant general superintendent; ▸Stanley W. Chambers, secretary-treasurer; T. R. Dungan, assistant general secretary-treasurer; and Wynn T. Stairs, foreign mission secretary. M. J. Wolff became the editor of the *Pentecostal Herald*, the official voice of the organization. The united organization had about 1,800 ministers and more than 700 churches.

1. Organizational Ministries.

The UPC has experienced rapid growth since 1945. Its first headquarters building in St. Louis was enlarged immediately after the merger. A larger building was purchased in 1952; it was enlarged in 1954. In 1970 a two-story headquarters building was constructed at 8855 Dunn Road, in Hazelwood, MO. In 1983 a third floor was added to this building to provide additional office space.

The UPC sponsors missionaries and national workers in 136 nations on six continents. In 1998 it had 484 missionaries under appointment. The annual foreign missionary budget was more than $18 million for 1998 (annual reports to general conference, 1998).

The organization has operated a publishing house since 1945; it publishes tracts, books, church supplies, and since 1970 a complete curriculum of Sunday school materials for all ages and grade levels. In 1998 it had more than 165 books in print under the imprint of Word Aflame Press. The organization also publishes nine national periodicals, including the *Pentecostal Herald,* its official organ.

Among the endorsed institutions of the UPC are seven Bible colleges, an orphanage, a rehabilitation center for boys, and a ministry to those addicted to alcohol and other drugs. The organization maintains a heritage center in its headquarters building, operates a chaplaincy ministry to penal institutions, and provides endorsement of chaplains to the military. It also assists ministries for evangelizing ethnic groups in the U.S. and Canada.

2. Doctrines and Beliefs.

Since the UPC emerged from the Holiness movement of the 19th century and the pentecostal revival that began during the early years of this century, its doctrinal views reflect many of the beliefs of the Holiness-pentecostal movement, with the exception of the "second work of grace," the historic doctrine of the Trinity, and the traditional Trinitarian formula in water baptism. It embraces the pentecostal view that speaking in tongues is the initial sign of receiving the Holy Spirit. It shares the hope of the second coming of Jesus Christ, the rapture of the church, the resurrection of the dead, the judgment and eternal punishment of the wicked, the Millennium, and the eternal bliss of the redeemed.

The UPC also holds a fundamental view of the Bible: "The Bible is the only God-given authority which man possesses; therefore all doctrine, faith, hope, and all instructions for the church must be based upon and harmonize with the Bible" (Manual of the United Pentecostal Church, 19). It rejects all extrabiblical revelations and writings and accepts church creeds and articles of faith only as the thinking of men.

The distinctive beliefs of the UPC center on a non-Trinitarian view of God and on the practice of water baptism in the name of Jesus Christ. It holds that the Trinitarian concept is not an adequate explanation of God's revelation of himself as the Father, in the Son, and as the Holy Spirit, and that an emphasis on separate eternal persons in the Godhead tends toward tritheism.

In contradistinction to the doctrine of the Trinity, the UPC holds to a Oneness view of God. The one God who revealed himself in the OT as Jehovah also revealed himself in his Son, Jesus Christ. Thus, Jesus Christ was and is absolute deity; he was the one true God manifested in flesh, and in him dwells all the fullness of the Godhead bodily. Moreover, the Holy Spirit is God with us and in us. Thus, God is manifested as Father in creation and as the Father of the Son, in the Son for our redemption, and as the Holy Spirit in our regeneration.

At the same time, Oneness believers hold to the full humanity of Jesus Christ. He was God of very God, but he was also man. God was manifest in flesh; he took upon himself human nature. As the Son of God, Jesus died for our sins, was raised by God, and was exalted to a position of power—as Lord and Christ (Acts 2:36). The man Christ Jesus is our mediator and advocate. His humanity did not detract from his deity, nor did his deity detract from his humanity. He was both God and man.

Since Jesus Christ is the redemptive name of God revealed in the NT economy of salvation, it is through this name that salvation and blessings are appropriated by and bestowed upon believers (Matt. 1:21; Luke 24:47; John 1:12; 20:31; Acts 2:38; 3:16; 4:12). As the name of God in redemption, Jesus is the singular name of God manifested as Father, in the Son, and as the Holy Spirit. For this reason, the apostles and early Christians baptized in the singular name of Jesus Christ or Lord Jesus and not in the titles of Father, Son, and Holy Spirit (Acts 2:38; 8:16; 10:48; 19:5; 22:16; Rom. 6:3–4; 1 Cor. 1:13–15; Gal. 3:27; Col. 2:12).

The UPC holds that water baptism by immersion in the name of Jesus Christ is a command, not an option, and that it has to do with the remission of sins. It does not believe, however, in baptismal regeneration.

Salvation is held to be by grace through faith in Jesus Christ, not by works: it is by faith in Jesus Christ that sinners are justified. At the same time, sinners must believe the gospel; they are commanded to repent of their sins and to be baptized in water; and they are promised the gift of the Holy Spirit. The UPC believes that these various aspects of faith and obedience work together in God's grace to reconcile us to God.

The members of the UPC observe the communion service and practice the ordinance of footwashing.

Although the matter is left to the conscience of each member, the official position of the UPC in regard to military service is conscientious objection to killing. They accept, however, noncombatant military service.

The members of the UPC hold to a standard of conduct and dress similar to that held by pentecostals during the early years of this century. They shun movies, worldly sports and amusements, dancing, public swimming, immodest dress, and wearing makeup and jewelry. Women are taught not to cut their hair, and men are taught to wear short hair. The organization stresses and supports the family as God's primary institution and teaches that the church is God's redemptive fellowship for all believers.

3. Church Government.

The basic governmental structure is congregational, with each local church autonomous in the conduct of its business. The organization embraces a modified presbyterian structure in that ministers meet in sectional, district, and general conferences or assemblies to elect officials and to conduct business. Only ministers are allowed to vote and to participate in business at these conferences.

Much of the business of the organization is conducted by officials, boards, and committees. A general superintendent, two assistant general superintendents, a secretary-treasurer, divisional directors, district superintendents, and executive presbyters are members of the general board of presbyters, the highest authority under the general conference. An executive board, consisting of members from the general board, conducts necessary business between meetings of the general board.

In 1945 Howard A. Goss was elected as the first general superintendent. In 1951 ˈArthur T. Morgan was elected general superintendent and served until his sudden death in 1967. ˈOliver F. Fauss was chosen to fill the unexpired term, until Jan. 1968. ˈStanley W. Chambers was elected as general superintendent and served until 1977, when ˈNathaniel A. Urshan, the present general superintendent, was elected.

The headquarters building in Hazelwood, MO, houses offices for its general officials and the Pentecostal Publishing House. In addition to church administration, the work is organized into divisions: foreign missions, home missions, Sunday school, editorial, education, youth, ladies, Harvestime (radio), and publishing.

The basic structure of the UPC has changed little during its history. As the organization has grown, more districts have been organized and divisional operations expanded. In the years since the merger, the home missions, youth, ladies, education, and Harvestime divisions have been formed.

In 1998 the UPC reported 3,861 churches, 8,219 ministers, a Sunday school attendance of 422,137, and an estimated constituency of more than 600,000 in the U.S. and Canada. In the rest of the world, it reported 21,407 churches and preaching points and 1,979,141 constituents (annual reports to general conference, 1998).

■ **Bibliography:** R. M. Anderson, *Vision of the Disinherited* (1979) ■ C. Brumback, *Suddenly . . . from Heaven* (1961) ■ A. L. Clanton, *United We Stand* (1970) ■ F. T. Corum, *Like as of Fire* (1981) ■ F. J. Ewart, *The Phenomenon of Pentecost* (1975) ■ F. J. Foster, *Their Story: 20th Century Pentecostals* (1981) ■ M. E. Golder, *History of the Pentecostal Assemblies of the World* (1973) ■ E. E. Goss, *Winds of God* (1958) ■ W. W. Menzies, *Anointed to Serve* (1971) ■ C. F. Parham, *Voice Crying in the Wilderness* (1902) ■ S. E. Parham, *The Life of Charles F. Parham* (1930) ■ A. D. Urshan, *Life of Andrew Bar David Urshan* (1967).   ■ J. L. Hall

UNIVERSAL CHURCH OF THE KINGDOM OF GOD

Founded by Bishop Edir Macedo (1945–) in 1977. Macedo was from a small-town, lower-middle-class family in the state of Rio in Brazil. After moving to the city, he began work in a state lottery, rising to an administrative office. During that time he attended college but did not complete his course of studies. At age 33 he converted to pentecostalism. Macedo and four other individuals founded their own brand of pentecostalism and converted a funeral parlor in a Rio de Janeiro suburb into their first church. In 1981 he and another founder consecrated themselves bishops. From 1986 to 1989 Macedo lived in the U.S., where he began setting up Universal churches in the Latino community.

After Macedo returned to Brazil in 1989, he purchased TV Record, Brazil's fifth-largest television network, and began promoting his brand of pentecostalism on TV. This new platform immediately thrust him and the Universal Church (UC) into the political arena, where they have been active ever since. Macedo was jailed on charges of fraud in 1992, but due to the political pressure put on the authorities by the UC, he was released only 12 days later.

The UC is like most other brands of pentecostalism in Latin America in its heavy stress on the spiritual gifts. They especially emphasize healing, exorcisms, prayer, family, liberation, and prosperity. Services are offered almost every day. The UC tends to be more lax on women's comportment and is not as strict as most other Latin American forms of pentecostalism. The UC preaches a prosperity gospel that teaches that faithful Christians should expect to be rewarded with spiritual, physical, and material blessings in this life. The UC began their work in the U.S. in the 1980s. By 1997 they had at least 25 churches throughout the U.S., with an estimated 6,000 to 10,000 followers. In California alone there are at least 20 UCs. One church, which meets in the Million Dollar Theater in downtown Los Angeles, has a membership of over 1,500. The UC newspaper ¡*PARE de Sufrir!* (Stop Suffering!) has an estimated monthly print run of 50,000 copies. The paper is full of personal testimonies of how God has changed people's lives and biting editorials about the corruption of the Roman Catholic Church. The UC also runs its own radio and television programs in Los Angeles, CA. Two bishops live in the U.S. and supervise the church's work there. The Brazil-based Universal Church is quickly moving into the Latino community in the U.S. It represents a new, vital, and powerful form of Latin American prosperity teaching that is bound to see continued growth throughout the 21st century.

■ **Bibliography:** P. Freston, "Pentecostalism in Brazil: A Brief History," *Religion* (1995) ■ "Universal Church of the Kingdom of God," *¡PARE de Sufrir!* 7 (Mar. 1997).   ■ G. Espinosa

UNIVERSAL FELLOWSHIP OF METROPOLITAN COMMUNITY CHURCHES

The Universal Fellowship of Metropolitan Community Churches (UFMCC) was founded Oct. 6, 1968, by Rev. ►Troy D. Perry in Los Angeles as an organization that would minister to homosexuals and others who felt discriminated against in traditional churches. The UFMCC has been described as a "fundamental Pentecostal" organization. It is strong in the U.S. South and West, but in the last 30 years it has grown to encompass a worldwide constituency. With its headquarters now in Hollywood, CA, the fellowship has grown to include congregations throughout the world, including such places as Canada, Mexico, Puerto Rico, Philippines, Argentina, Nigeria, Australia, New Zealand, South Africa, Germany, and Russia. The group is Trinitarian and accepts the Bible as the divinely inspired Word of God.

The fellowship has two sacraments, baptism and Holy Communion, as well as a number of traditionally recognized rites such as ordination. Some local congregations are charismatic, but the denomination is broadly ecumenical. A 1987 decision by the U.S. attorney general gave the UFMCC rights to minister in all federal prisons. The UFMCC is a champion for civil and human rights across the globe. In the mid 1990s it made an effort to end the ban on lesbians and gays in the U.S. military. It also has worked to promote a national gay rights bill. Membership in the United States was 46,000 in 1996 with approximately 350 congregations worldwide. After an earthquake in 1994 destroyed the Metropolitan Community Church of Los Angeles, the mother church of the UFMCC movement, a new global headquarters and spiritual center were erected in West Hollywood and dedicated in 1999. The five-story UFMCC World Center houses the Los Angeles congregation, administrative offices, a visitors' center, a crisis intervention center, and Samaritan College, a school for training men and women for the ministry, with extension centers in other countries. UFMCC's publications include a monthly newsletter, *Keeping in Touch,* and the UFMCC E-Mail News Service.

■ **Bibliography:** R. M. Enroth and G. E. Jamison, *The Gay Church* (1974) ■ C. E. Jones, *The Charismatic Movement* (1995), 710 ■ *Yearbook of American and Canadian Churches* (1999) ■ UFMCC web page (Nov. 1999).   ■ G. W. Gohr

UPPER ROOM MISSION Founded in the fall of 1906, this pentecostal mission, located at 327-1/2 South Spring Street in Los Angeles, CA, became for several years the "strongest" mission in town. Established by the former pastor of the First Baptist Church in Glendale, ►Elmer Kirk Fisher, the mission was formed with the help of several families from Glendale as well as many of the white people who were originally at the Azusa Street Mission. In Feb. 1911, when ►William Durham came to Los Angeles from Chicago seeking to preach, he went first to the Upper Room Mission. Fisher did not allow him to preach, however, because of his views on sanctification. Durham then went to the Azusa Street Mission.

The Upper Room was located on the second floor of an office building. Poorly ventilated, it consisted of a 300-seat auditorium, three small apartments, and several tiny rooms that served as offices. The motto adopted by the congregation was "Exalt Jesus Christ; Honor the Holy Ghost."

Worship services were held three times each Sunday (11:00 A.M., 3:00 P.M., and 7:30 P.M.). Each Monday evening a group of German-speaking pentecostals, who were considered part of the congregation, held services of their own in the facility. Bible studies—generally surveys of such books as Acts, Romans, Daniel, and Hebrews—were conducted from 11:00 A.M. until 1:00 P.M. every Tuesday through Friday. On each of those days, there also were evening meetings beginning at 7:30. The last week of the month was set aside to conduct baptismal services (Wednesday) and to celebrate the Lord's Supper (Thursday). Baptismal services were generally held near Terminal Island in the Los Angeles harbor and were attended by hundreds.

In addition to the meetings held at the main facility on Spring Street, people from the mission gathered each evening and conducted two or three street meetings in Los Angeles, often targeting bars and the red-light district. At times the youth group led such meetings in neighboring Glendale.

The impact of the Upper Room may be assessed partially by the number of missionaries and missionary projects it helped to support. This was documented in the more or less monthly publication of the mission, begun in June 1909 and jointly edited by Elmer K. Fisher and ►George B. Studd. The latter did most of the editorial work. Like many of the early pentecostal periodicals, *The Upper Room,* as it was called, printed articles that had already appeared in other pentecostal publications, letters from missionaries, responses to the paper, personal testimonies, and articles by the staff. The periodical ran at least through May 1911.

Tongues as the "Bible evidence" of baptism in the Spirit was very important to this mission. Azusa appears to have been more fluid on the subject and in 1915 rejected the idea completely, coming to view tongues as a sign or gift that might follow the baptism. Fisher, however, repeatedly kept the issue before his readers.

■ **Bibliography:** C. Brumback, *Suddenly ... from Heaven* (1961) ■ W. Frodsham, "A Pentecostal Journey in Canada, British Columbia, and the Western States," *Confidence* 4 (6, 1911) ■ *The Upper Room* 1 (1, 1909) ■ 2 (5, 1911), 1.

■ C. M. Robeck Jr.

URQUHART, COLIN (1940–).

Teacher and author with an international ministry. Ordained an Anglican priest in 1964, Colin Urquhart was baptized in the Spirit early in his ministry at St. Hugh's Church, Lewsey, Luton (1970–76). Since 1976 he has concentrated on an international teaching and healing ministry that has been centered since 1978 in the interdenominational Bethany Fellowship. Urquhart's ministry, focusing on "kingdom faith," has increasingly crossed church boundaries, leading in 1980 to the founding of Kingdom Faith Ministries. In 1984 he founded, with Bob Gordon, Roffey Place Christian Training Centre, near Horsham, Sussex, where the emphases were spiritual and practical more than academic. When Gordon left in 1989, Urquhart moved into Roffey Place. In 1992 he formed Kingdom Faith Church in Horsham, with two other churches since added. Urquhart's story is told in *When the Spirit Comes* (1974), *Faith for the Future* (1982), and *From Mercy to Majesty* (1995). He has authored several best-sellers, including *Anything You Ask* (1978), *The Positive Kingdom* (1985), *Receive Your Healing* (1986), *My Dear Child* (1990), *My Dear Son* (1992), *The Truth That Sets You Free* (1993), *Your Personal Bible* (1994), and *Friends of Jesus* (1997). His wife, Caroline, has authored *His God, My God* (1983).

■ **Bibliography:** J. Peters, *Colin Urquhart* (1994).

■ P. D. Hocken

URSHAN, ANDREW DAVID (1884–1967).

Pentecostal preacher, missionary, and author. The oldest son of a Presbyterian pastor in Iran, Urshan immigrated to the U.S. in 1901. While living in Chicago, he received the Holy Spirit in 1908 and established a Persian mission. He was ordained by ▸William Durham in 1910. In 1914 Urshan returned to Iran as a missionary. During WWI he became a refugee in Russia for several months during 1915 and 1916, establishing pentecostal churches in Tiflis, Armaear, and Leningrad. It was at Leningrad that he was baptized in the name of Jesus Christ. Urshan served as foreign missions secretary in the

Andrew D. Urshan, a native of Persia who returned to his native land as a pentecostal during the early years of the movement. He later embraced the Oneness teaching.

▸Pentecostal Assemblies of the World in 1923. In 1925 he became a founding member of Emmanuel's Church of Jesus Christ, serving as its first foreign missions secretary. Beginning in 1917, Urshan published the periodical *The Witness of God.* He is the author of several books, including *The Life of Andrew D. Urshan* (n.d.), *The Almighty God in the Lord Jesus Christ* (1919), *My Study of Modern Pentecostals* (n.d.), *Apostolic Faith Doctrine of the New Birth* (n.d), *Timely Messages of Comfort* (1918), *The Supreme Need of the Hour* (1923), *Timely Messages of Warning* (1917), and *The Doctrine of Redemption of the Body* (1925). He was known as "the Persian Evangelist."

■ **Bibliography:** A. L. Clanton, *United We Stand* (1970).

■ J. L. Hall

URSHAN, NATHANIEL ANDREW (1920–).

General superintendent of the ▸United Pentecostal Church, International (UPCI; 1978–). The son of ▸Andrew D. Urshan, he was born in Minnesota but spent his early years in several other states. Urshan began evangelizing in 1941 and later pastored in New York City before he accepted the pastorate of Calvary Tabernacle in Indianapolis, IN. He continued to pastor this large and influential church until 1979. In 1961 Urshan became the speaker on *Harvestime,* the radio program

Nataniel A. Urshan, general superintendent of the United Pentecostal Church, International.

of the UPC. He served as assistant general superintendent of the UPC from 1972 to 1977. In 1978 he was elected to the office of general superintendent of the UPC and continues to serve in that position.   ■ J. L. Hall

UTTERBACH, CLINTON (1931–), and **SARAH** (1937–). Pastors of the Redeeming Love Christian Center, one of the largest (2,600), predominantly black, independent charismatic congregations on the East Coast. "Clint," an accomplished musician and composer and former director of the Utterbach Concert Ensemble, along with his wife, Sarah, a former corporate executive, came under the teaching of ˃Kenneth Copeland. Through his assistance, they attended Rhema Bible Training Center. While at Rhema, they also traveled with ˃Kenneth Hagin as part of his crusade team. In 1980 they founded Redeeming Love Christian Center in their home. The congregation moved to Teaneck, NJ, in 1982 before settling in its present location in 1985 in Nanuet, NY. The Utterbachs also operate a national broadcast, a preschool learning center, and a music ministry. Their central message is "the authority of the believer" based on a covenant relationship with God through the new birth. The Utterbachs' ministry features an emphasis on biblical teaching, total prosperity (spiritual, mental, physical, financial, and social), ordinances of baptism and the Lord's Supper, the acceptance of women in ministry, and a witness for strong family life modeled on their own marriage.

■ **Bibliography:** K. Dow, "Nanuet Church Gets Message across in Style," *Rockland County Journal-News* (June 2, 1987) ■ C. Utterbach, "Heirs to the Promise," *Horizons Unlimited* 1 (1987) ■ S. Utterbach, "Heirs Can Afford to Wait," *Horizons Unlimited* 1 (1987).   ■ H. D. Trulear

V

VAAGENES, MORRIS G. C., JR. (1929–). Senior pastor of North Heights Lutheran Church (American Lutheran Church), St. Paul, MN, a congregation prominently identified with the ▸Lutheran charismatic movement. Vaagenes graduated from Augsburg Theological Seminary, Minneapolis, in 1954. He received the D.Min. from Luther-Northwestern Seminary, St. Paul, in 1979.

Vaagenes and his wife served as missionaries in Madagascar until a health problem with one of their children forced them to return to the U.S. In 1961 he was called to North Heights, a congregation with a few hundred members. He and his wife experienced the baptism with the Holy Spirit in 1962. His weekly Bible study became a gathering place for the nascent charismatic renewal in the Minneapolis–St. Paul area.

The congregation grew dramatically in a major expression of charismatic renewal among Lutherans in that area as well as internationally, with the annual International Institute on Church Renewal and the two-year program of the International Lay Ministry Training Center.

By the mid 1980s the North Heights congregation had grown to more than 4,000 members and worshiped at two sites—Roseville and Arden Hills. By 1998 North Heights had over 7,000 members. Vaagenes edits two publications designed to inspire spiritual renewal: *A Call to Renewal* and *Lutheran Renewal International*. He founded a Lutheran Bible School, Lay Ministry Training Center International, and a television program, *Renewal International*. He and his wife, Bonnie, have four children.

■ **Bibliography:** L. Christenson, ed., *Welcome, Holy Spirit* (1987).
■ L. Christenson

VALDEZ, A. C., SR. (1896–1988). Evangelist and missionary. A. C. Valdez Sr. attended the historic ▸Azusa Street meetings as a boy in 1906–9. The Valdez family was Roman Catholic, having been influenced by a Franciscan style of Catholicism that believed in the gifts of the Spirit, including speaking in tongues (Valdez, 22). The Valdez family embraced the outpouring of the Spirit at Azusa Street and became part of the revival that resulted from those meetings. Ordained by a mission in Long Beach, CA, in 1916, Valdez moved quickly from part-time ministry into a long, fruitful life of preaching the gospel around the world. Together with his son, A. C. Valdez Jr., he held campaigns in South America, Australia, New Zealand, India, China, Japan, the South Sea Islands, and Hawaii. After the death of his first wife he continued his evangelistic ministry and frequently preached

for his son at his successful church, Milwaukee Evangelistic Temple. After the death of his son, Valdez continued his ministry and appeared on *The 700 Club* and the *PTL Club*, telling of his early experiences in the founding of the pentecostal movement.

■ **Bibliography:** A. C. Valdez Sr., *Fire on Azusa Street* (1980).
■ J. R. Zeigler

VALENZUELA, ROMANITA CARBAJAL DE (c. 1914). Pioneer Mexican Oneness pentecostal woman evangelist and founder of La Iglesia Apostólica de la Fe en Cristo Jesús (Apostolic Church of Faith in Jesus Christ) in Mexico. She was converted and baptized in the name of Jesus in 1912 in Los Angeles, CA. She may have attended the Spanish Apostolic Faith Mission, located on North Hill Street in Los Angeles and pastored by a G. Valenzuela. There is little reason to doubt that she had either heard about or actually visited the famous Apostolic Faith Mission where the Azusa Street revivals were still flickering on and off until 1913. In 1914 Carbajal felt called to take the pentecostal message back to her family in Villa Aldama, Chihuahua, Mexico. Despite the dangers of the Mexican Revolution, she traveled back home and quickly converted 12 members of her family and planted a church. In Nov. 1914 she led them into the baptism of the Holy Spirit. Upon receiving notice that her husband wanted her to return home to Los Angeles, she sought out and converted a Methodist pastor to the Oneness doctrine. Under Carbajal's prompting, the former Methodist pastor took over the fledgling flock of Mexican pentecostals before Carbajal returned to Los Angeles. Carbajal's work quickly spread to the neighboring states of Chihuahua, Durango, Coahuila, and other states in Mexico, so that by 1932 there were over 26 congregations and 800 members throughout the country. Carbajal clearly exercised the prophetic gifts of evangelism, church planting, and shepherding. Her courageous spirit and prophetic vision for evangelizing her family and Mexico clearly resonates with many other prophetic women in early pentecostalism. Carbajal rightly deserves to be called the "Mother" of Oneness pentecostalism in Mexico.

■ **Bibliography:** G. Espinosa, "'Your Daughters Shall Prophesy': A Comparative Study of Women's Roles in the Latino Assemblies of God and the Apostolic Assembly," in *Women and Twentieth-Century Protestantism*, ed. M. L. Bendroth and V. L. Brereton (1998).
■ G. Espinosa

VAN CLEAVE, NATHANIEL MOORE (1907–). Foursquare pastor, educator, and executive. He was born to Herbert Roland and Elsie Chase Van Cleave in Fort Smith, AR. He studied at L.I.F.E. Bible College (Th.D., 1943), Los Angeles Baptist Theological Seminary, and the extension division of the University of California. Van Cleave was ordained in the ▸International Church of the Foursquare Gospel (ICFG) in 1929 and married Lois Standlee the following year; they have two children. Pastoral ministry began in 1930 in Lamar, CO, and continued later in Van Nuys, CA; Decatur, IL; Pasadena and Long Beach, CA; and Portland, OR. From 1943 to 1949 he was a missionary to the West Indies. At different times he also served on the faculty of L.I.F.E. Bible College, including a year as president of the school (1976–77). He received the status of professor emeritus in 1985.

Van Cleave's executive responsibilities in the ICFG included that of district supervisor (1954–60, 1968–76), interim general supervisor (1981, 1986), board of directors member (1976–80), and missionary cabinet member (1954–88). He also served on the board of regents of L.I.F.E. Bible College (1976–87). For his service to the denomination, the latter conferred an honorary D.D. on him in 1970.

Van Cleave's publications include *Handbook of Preaching* (1943), *Foundations of Pentecostal Theology* (with Guy P. Duffield; 1983), and *The Vine and the Branches* (1992).

■ **Bibliography:** Resume supplied to this writer ▮ *Who's Who in Religion* (3d ed., 1985). ■ G. B. McGee; B. A. Pavia

VAN DUSEN, HENRY PITNEY (1897–1975). Theologian and seminary president. The appearance of "The Third Force in Christendom," by Henry P. Van Dusen, in the June 9, 1958, issue of *Life* magazine sent waves of self-affirmation into the pentecostal world. In it, the president of the liberal Union Theological Seminary (NY) described in highly complimentary terms mission successes of pentecostal, Holiness, Adventist, and Church of Christ groups. Unused to such praise from outsiders, pentecostals eagerly adopted "Third Force" as being particularly applicable to them. In 1962 the Canadian pentecostal Gordon F. Atter even used the phrase as the title of his general history of the world movement. Secular historians such as William McLoughlin were less sure of its applicability, however. A Presbyterian, Van Dusen devoted his entire career to theological education.

■ **Bibliography:** G. F. Atter, *The Third Force* (1962) ▮ W. G. McLoughlin, "Is There a Third Force in Christendom?" *Daedalus* 96 (Winter 1967) ▮ H. P. Van Dusen, "The Third Force in Christendom," *Life* 44 (June 9, 1958). ■ C. E. Jones

VAN EYK, FREDERICK BARNABAS (1895–1939). Evangelist and church planter (Apostolic Faith Mission [AFM] in Australia). Van Eyk was converted in South Africa and became an evangelist in the AFM. In 1926 he migrated to Australia with his wife, Cecilia, and their four children. After successful rallies in Perth, Western Australia, he went to Adelaide, where there were crowded meetings, many healings, and a baptismal service in the Torrens River attended by 1,000 people. Van Eyk continued on to Victoria, where he ministered with considerable success in rural areas. He was fearless and audacious in confronting sickness and disease, willingly praying for the most impossible cases, and sometimes even announcing in advance that particular people would be healed. After a visit to New Zealand, Van Eyk persuaded ▸Jeannie (Sarah Jane) Lancaster that the Good News Hall congregation and its few satellite churches should combine under the name Apostolic Faith Mission (1927).

Meanwhile, Van Eyk continued to travel. He became known for his uninhibited presentation of the gospel—he walked, leaped, waved his handkerchief, sang, evicted interjectors, entertained, and debated with unbelievers at open air meetings. Because of the strength of his approach, he was particularly persuasive with men. At the same time, his preaching content was substantial and his doctrines were thorough. He was also a talented musician and vocalist. In 1927 the Church of Christ pastor in Maryborough, Queensland, with about 40 of his members, joined the AFM. Other mainline denominational ministers followed this example. In Perth, Brisbane, Rockhampton (Queensland), and Cairns there were many healings, Spirit baptisms, and water baptisms.

Around this time, Cecilia, who was resident in Melbourne, suffered a mental breakdown and returned to South Africa. In 1928, in Toowoomba (near Brisbane), Van Eyk's association with one of the young women in the church was felt to be inappropriate, and he was asked to discontinue his ministry until he was reunited with his wife. Van Eyk protested his integrity but left Queensland.

In 1929 Van Eyk began preaching again in the mining town of Cessnock, New South Wales, in the midst of industrial unrest. He began in typically audacious fashion by singing to and addressing a miners' union meeting. He then launched a formal campaign, and some 15% of the population attended nightly; there were 700 conversions, 73 people were baptized in one service, and many were healed and baptized in the Holy Spirit. There was also strong reaction from the local clergy when Van Eyk set up a church. This was the beginning of the Foursquare Church in Australia. Within a few years several Foursquare churches were operating in New South Wales and Queensland, including Lithgow (near Sydney), where, again, many healings and baptisms took place. Van Eyk launched the *Elim Foursquare Gospel Express* in May 1932. He did finally return to South Africa but divorced his wife and then married the young lady from Toowoomba. Within a few months, while hunting, he was bitten by a tse-tse fly and contracted trypanosomiasis. Because of his belief in divine healing, he refused medication. He died on Dec. 21, 1939, at age 44.

Van Eyk's preaching was Christ-centered and evangelical. He also emphasized the baptism in the Holy Spirit and the second coming of Christ. His ministry to the sick was effective and beneficial. He was successful in planting churches and fearless in his ministry. Many of his hearers testified they had never heard more powerful or convincing preaching. The tragedy lay in his failure to avoid the indiscretion that ultimately discredited his standing in Australia.

■ **Bibliography:** B. Chant, *Heart of Fire* (1984).   ■ B. Chant

VASSAR, THEODORE ROOSEVELT (1909–75). Minister
and missionary. Ted Vassar was born in Tryon, OK, the son of Dr. John Alexander and Lenora Isabelle (Scott) Vassar. He graduated in 1930 from Southwestern Bible School (later Southwestern Assemblies of God [AG] College) in Enid, OK, where he studied under ►P. C. Nelson. Two years later Vassar married Freddie Estelle Barnett (1912–80), a flamboyant woman evangelist with a "call to India."

After pastoring AG churches in Texas and Oklahoma, the Vassars became missionaries to Maharashtra State, India, in 1937. Following their first term of service in Pune, they were

Ted and Estelle Vassar, missionaries to India. Ted Vassar was known as a "thinking pentecostal" who emphasized the importance of exercising creative and cognitive gifts in Christian service.

placed in charge of the Boys' Orphanage, a farming project, and an elementary school in Junnar. Vassar also served as superintendent of the South India District Council of the AG, although he labored to make the Indian church self-supporting and self-governing. It was his vision that those under his care be encouraged into full-time ministry. He was not disappointed, as dozens of orphans followed him into Christian service, among them Benjamin Shinde (late professor at Southern Asia Bible College, Bangalore) and Solomon Wasker (missionary to the province of Assam and pastor in Bombay).

The Vassars returned to the United States in 1952, pastoring several churches in Texas. Ted Vassar had a ministry to youth and a ministry of teaching, balancing evangelism with social action. He was known as a "thinking pentecostal," emphasizing the importance of exercising creative and cognitive gifts in Christian service.

Five children were born to the Vassars: Bobby Joe (1935–37), Ruth Lenora [Burgess] (1939–), Theodore Roosevelt Jr. (1943–94), Helen Elizabeth [Sullivan] (1945–), and Rose Marie (1948). Two children, Bobby Joe and Rose Marie, died on the mission field from disease.

■ **Bibliography:** R. V. Burgess, "Obeying the Great Commission: The Acts of Obedience of Ted and Estelle Vassar" (unpub., 1983) ■ Interviews with R. V. Burgess and H. E. Sullivan, Mar.–Apr. 1988.
■ S. M. Burgess

VATICAN II

1. Description.

The Second Vatican Council is the 21st of the councils that the Catholic Church reckons as "ecumenical"—that is, as councils of the universal church. Of these 21 councils, 8 took place in the first millennium before the split between Eastern and Western Christianity; 10 were councils of the pre-Reformation Western church, and 3 of the post-Reformation Roman Catholic Church.

Vatican II was by far the most global of these councils, for it brought together about 2,400 Catholic bishops from every continent and from practically every country in the world. Every Catholic bishop, whether of the Latin rite or of one of the Eastern rites, whether actually in charge of a diocese or not, was invited to take part with full voting rights. Along with the bishops, about 100 general superiors of the religious orders of men (such as the Benedictines, Franciscans, and Jesuits) also participated with full voting rights.

The new approach to the ecumenical movement that Pope John XXIII intended the council to take was already shown prior to the opening of the council in his establishment of the Vatican Secretariat for Promoting Christian Unity and in the invitation extended to the other Christian churches and church federations to send their delegates as official observers to the council. The number of such delegated observers increased from 49, representing 17 churches or federations during the first period of the council, to 99, representing 28 churches or federations in the final period. These observers were invited to attend all the sessions of the council, were given all the documents distributed to the bishops, and had many opportunities to meet the bishops and discuss the matter before the council with them in various formal and informal meetings.

2. Chronology.

Pope John XXIII's surprise announcement of his intention to summon an ecumenical council was made on Jan. 25, 1959. Within the following year the various preparatory commissions were established, and all the Catholic bishops, heads of religious orders, and faculties of theology were requested to submit their proposals regarding a possible agenda for the council. In July 1962 invitations went out to the other Christian churches to send delegates as official observers.

The solemn opening of the council took place on Oct. 11, 1962. The first period ended on Dec. 8 without the promulgation of any completed document. Perhaps the most significant feature of that first period was the manifestation of the fact that a large majority of the bishops were dissatisfied with the work that had been done by the preparatory commissions. It became evident that a new, more progressive approach to many questions would be taken by the new commissions that had been established by the council, along with the help of the theologians whom the bishops had brought to Rome as their advisors. These commissions worked not only during the periods when the council was in session but during the intervals as well.

Pope John XXIII lived to see only the first period of the council that he had summoned. His death on June 3, 1963, had the effect of automatically suspending the council. However, the first official act of his successor, Pope Paul VI, was to announce that the work of the council should go forward.

The second period lasted from Sept. 29 to Dec. 4, 1963, and concluded with the promulgation of the Constitution on the Sacred Liturgy and the Decree on the Instruments of Social Communication. This period was largely taken up with the discussion of the draft of the document on the church—the one generally considered the most basic document of the council and certainly the one that was most keenly debated. Consensus was reached through the process of taking a distinct vote on every crucial paragraph of the text.

The third period, from Sept. 14 to Nov. 21, 1964, closed with the promulgation of three important documents, all having to do with Catholic doctrine about the church: the Dogmatic Constitution on the Church, the Decree on Ecumenism, and the Decree on the Eastern Catholic Churches.

During the course of the fourth and final period, from Sept. 14 to Dec. 8, 1965, the remaining 11 documents were promulgated: on Oct. 28 the Decree on the Bishop's Pastoral Office, the Decree on the Renewal of Religious Life, the Decree on Priestly Formation, the Declaration on Christian Education, and the Declaration on the Relationship of the Church to the Non-Christian Religions. On Nov. 18 the Dogmatic Constitution on Divine Revelation and the Decree on the Apostolate of the Laity were promulgated, followed on Dec. 7 by the Declaration on Religious Freedom, the Decree on the Ministry and Life of Priests, and the Pastoral Constitution on the Church in the Modern World.

A few days before the solemn close of the council, a "Prayer Service for Promoting Christian Unity" was held, with the participation of the observers from the other Christian communities, along with Pope Paul VI and the whole assembly of the council.

3. Doctrine.

As it would be impossible, within the limits of this article, to give even a brief summary of the contents of the 16 documents produced by Vatican II, I shall only indicate some of the highlights of the documents that would be of most interest to the readers of this dictionary.

a. The Dogmatic Constitution on the Church. While two documents of Vatican II are entitled "Dogmatic Constitutions," in neither of them did the council define any doctrine as a "dogma of faith"—an action that would have had the effect of condemning the contrary doctrine as heretical. Following the direction that Pope John XXIII gave to the council in his opening address, in which he called for a council whose exercise of its teaching authority would be "predominantly pastoral in character," the council sought to express Catholic doctrine positively, in language that would be better adapted to a modern mentality, rather than to condemn contrary points of view.

In contrast to what had been the typical Catholic description of the church as a hierarchically structured society, Vatican II began by presenting the church as a mystery of faith, having its origin in the mystery of the Trinity. Various aspects of this mystery were then illustrated by the multiple images that are found in Scripture, in recognition of the impossibility of adequately expressing the nature of the church in any one description of it. A highly significant change was made in the text when the previous assertion of identity between the Church of Christ and the Roman Catholic Church was dropped in favor of saying that the Church of Christ subsists in the Catholic Church, while many elements of sanctification and truth are found outside its visible structure. This decision led the way to a more explicit recognition of the ecclesiastical reality of the other Christian communities, in the Decree on Ecumenism.

While previous Catholic ecclesiology had stressed the notion of the church as the "mystical body of Christ," Vatican II preferred the equally biblical concept of the church as "people of God," thus putting a stronger accent on the historical reality of the church as a body of people who had to struggle with weakness and sin on their pilgrim way to the kingdom of God. It is also significant that the chapter on the church as people of God comes before the chapter on the hierarchical structure of the church. The main achievement of this chapter was to clarify the role of bishops: determining that they receive their offices of ruling and teaching not from the pope, but by their sacramental ordination to the episcopate, and that they constitute a body or "college" that shares with the pope the pastoral care of the universal church. The "Synod of Bishops" that now meets every three years to discuss matters of concern to the whole church is one fruit of the doctrine of episcopal collegiality established by Vatican II.

b. The Dogmatic Constitution on Divine Revelation. After an introductory chapter on the nature of revelation and the response of faith, the major portion of this document is devoted to the question of the ways in which this revelation is handed on in the church. Here the first question that needed to be clarified was whether tradition is rightly seen as a source of revelation, distinct from Holy Scripture. The answer of Vatican II, which in fact is also the answer of the Council of Trent, is that there is but one source of revelation: the gospel itself, which was handed on by the apostles both in writing and by their preaching and example. "Now what was handed on by the apostles includes everything which contributes to the holiness of life, and the increase in faith of the People of God; and so the church, in her teaching, life and worship, perpetuates and hands on to all generations all that she herself is, all that she believes." Hence, while sacred Scripture is the Word of God, inasmuch as this Word was put in writing under divine inspiration, the Word of God is also handed on in the faith and life of the church, where there can also be authentic growth in the understanding of what God has revealed.

The greater part of this document (four of its six chapters) can be described as an instruction addressed to the Catholic faithful as to how they should esteem, read, and understand the Bible. While insisting that the Bible must be interpreted in the light of the church's faith, it also recognizes the important contributions that modern biblical scholarship can make to our grasp of the authentic meaning of the sacred text.

c. The Decree on Ecumenism. The Decree on Ecumenism is the official declaration of the Catholic church's decision to participate fully in the modern ecumenical movement. It begins with the recognition that this movement, which began among the "separated brethren" and was "fostered by the grace of the Holy Spirit." It goes on to admit that men of both sides were to blame for the developments that have led to the disunity of the Christian people and that all are called to repentance as the first step toward reunion. Going beyond the admission of the presence of "elements of sanctification and truth" outside the limits of the Catholic Church, the decree recognizes that the "sacred actions of the Christian religion" that are carried out in other churches can truly engender a life of holiness and lead to salvation. From this the conclusion is drawn that these separated churches and communities as such are being used by the Holy Spirit as means of grace and salvation for their adherents. This positive assessment of the salvific role of the other churches is balanced by the assertion that it is only the Catholic Church that is believed to possess the fullness of the means of grace and that it is in the Catholic Church that the unity that Christ gave to the church has been preserved, as an endowment that the church can never lose.

d. The Declaration on Religious Liberty. The Declaration on Religious Liberty is the only document of the council that has a subtitle spelling out the limits of the question that it treats. This subtitle reads, "On the rights of the person and communities to social and civil liberty in religious matters." The essential teaching of this document is that the dignity of the human person requires that every person be free from coercion on the part of any human power whatever, in such wise that no one is to be forced to act in a manner contrary to his or her religious beliefs, or to be restrained from acting in accordance with his or her beliefs, provided that the just requirements of public order are observed. Since this declaration is addressed to the whole world, its primary argument is one that ought to appeal to all people, whatever their religious beliefs. However, in the second part of the document, it is shown how consonant this teaching is with the fundamental tenet of Christian faith that the act of faith must be a free response of man to God.

There can be no doubt that this declaration is the fruit of a development of Catholic thinking with regard to the rightful exercise of religious liberty to non-Catholics in countries where Catholicism enjoys special legal recognition as the religion of the great majority of the people. The position of Vatican II is clearly stated in the following sentence: "If, in view of peculiar circumstances obtaining among certain peoples, special legal recognition is given in the constitutional order of society to one religious body, it is at the same time imperative that the right of all citizens and religious bodies to religious freedom should be recognized and made effective in practice." Later on a frank admission of past failure to observe this principle is made: "In the life of the People of God as it has made its pilgrim way through the vicissitudes of human history, there have at times appeared ways of acting which were less in accord with the spirit of the gospel and even opposed to it." Here we see a practical fruit of a fundamental choice made earlier by the council, to view the church not as a "perfect society," but as a "pilgrim people of God."

See also CATHOLIC CHARISMATIC RENEWAL; CHARISMATIC MOVEMENT; DIALOGUE, ROMAN CATHOLIC AND CLASSICAL PENTECOSTAL.

■ **Bibliography:** W. M. Abbott, ed., *The Documents of Vatican II* (1966) ▪ A. Flannery, ed., *Vatican Council II: Constitutions, Decrees, Declarations* (1975) ▪ R. Latourelle, ed., *Vatican II: Assessment and Perspectives*, 3 vols. (1988–89) ▪ H. Vorgrimler, ed., *Commentary on the Documents of Vatican II*, 5 vols. (1967–69). ▪ F. A. Sullivan

VERHOEF, W. W. (1928–). Pioneer leader in the charismatic movement in Holland. While a theological student in the Dutch Reformed Church in 1951, Verhoef was baptized in the Spirit as he was prayed over by a faith healer. Associating briefly with a movement known as Stromen van Kracht (Streams of Power), Verhoef began his own charismatic monthly, *Vuur (Fire)*, in Mar. 1957, when his former colleagues started to rebaptize. As editor, he sought to promote charismatic renewal within the historic churches on an ecumenical basis and soon had wide representation on the editorial board, including a Catholic priest as early as 1964. In 1972 *Vuur* with Verhoef became one of the main elements in the Charismatische Werkgemeenschap Nederland (Dutch Charismatic Working Fellowship). Verhoef's contribution in Holland has been important through his leadership of national conventions; his sponsoring of days of theological reflection; and his writings, none of which are available in English.

■ **Bibliography:** C. and P. van der Laan, *Pinksteren in Beweging* (1982). ▪ P. D. Hocken

VERNAUD, JACQUES (1932–). Vernaud was born at Albert Schweitzer's mission station in Lambaréné, Gabon, on Nov. 9, 1932, of Swiss nationality. His father had been converted through the ministry of the renowned Indian holy man Sadhu Sundar Singh and had worked in Gabon with the French Reformed Church Mission since 1930. Through the ministry of ▸George Jeffreys he was baptized in the Holy Spirit in 1934. His mother was instantaneously healed of heart trouble at the same time. In 1936 Vernaud's father was used of God in a pentecostal revival in Gabon. Because of this, he was forced to leave the French Reformed Church Mission. Consequently, Jacques Vernaud grew up in a pentecostal family and went to Bible College at the International Bible Training Institute in Burgess Hill, Sussex, England.

After his training Vernaud went as a missionary to Gabon with the French Assemblies of God (AG) in 1955; it was there he met Johanna, a Dutch nurse working with the same mission. They were married and have three daughters. Soon after their marriage the French mission requested that they go to the Republic of the Congo (Congo/Brazzaville). They moved there in May 1961, becoming the first pentecostals in this former French colony. Vernaud preached in many of the towns and villages but decided to finally settle in Brazzaville in June 1962. The president at the time was the Catholic priest Fulbert Youlu, who was not in favor of Protestant churches, and the request for government authorization to allow the AG to work in the Congo was rejected. Vernaud was in the Congo during the days of the revolution, and it became very difficult to work there.

In the meantime Vernaud had been in contact with interested individuals in the Congo Democratic Republic (Congo/Kinshasa) across the Congo River who had invited him to visit the capital (at that time still Leopoldville). Alphonse Futa, an elder in a Baptist Church in Kinshasa, had come into the pentecostal experience through the healing of one of his children. Vernaud made frequent crossings from Brazzaville to Kinshasa, and as the work in Kinshasa grew, he decided to move permanently (1965). At that point the French AG felt that they were no longer able to support the Vernauds, since they did not want to commence a work in Congo/Kinshasa. Johanna's nursing expertise became their sole means of support for six years until the Vernaud family and the work in Kinshasa was adopted by the AG–U.S., which already had a work in the eastern part of the country. During that time 16 churches were planted in Kinshasa and many more in the inland villages. Vernaud and Futa worked together and traveled widely holding crusades and opening new pentecostal churches. The crowds had not heard the message of the gospel, nor that of healing, but many were healed.

In 1969 Tommy L. Osborn was invited by Vernaud for a crusade. Again there were many healings; this crusade had a great impact on Kinshasa. Vernaud was the organizer and Osborn's interpreter. It was after this time that the pentecostal work in Kinshasa really began to grow. So great was the response that Vernaud continued holding meetings for another two weeks in order to do the follow-up and make sure that the converts were introduced to a local church. Six new churches were opened across the city as a result of the crusade. Since that time the pentecostal message has had a great impact on many churches and other denominations.

Vernaud continued to evangelize in a big tent he took to many different places for crusades. His travels took him as far south as Kananga in the West Kasai province. Pressure from the umbrella Protestant group, The Church of Christ, introduced a politicized regime in the churches that became very antagonistic to missions and white missionaries in particular. As a consequence Vernaud soon found himself in conflict with national AG leaders. On several occasions he was accused before the state and thought that he would have to leave the country. In 1984 he decided that the only way he could continue to work in Kinshasa was to plant a church and pastor in the capital. A site was chosen in the district known as *La Borne*. On Apr. 29, 1984, 25 people gathered at the first meeting. Today this is most likely the largest Protestant church in Central Africa, with an estimated 15,000 members. Here Vernaud concentrates on training people for the continued vision of the church involved in social, educational, and medical work as well as evangelism. During the 1997 overthrow of the Mobutu regime, when citizens of Kinshasa were under continual threat by armed soldiers and many homes were pillaged and thousands of people lost their lives, the Vernauds were the only AG missionaries in the entire country to remain. Vernaud plans to continue ministry in Kinshasa for the foreseeable future.

■ **Bibliography:** P. Calzada, *Racontez ses merveilles: 40 ans de mission* (1997) ▊ D. J. Garrard, unpublished private papers ▊ R. J. Monot to D. J. Garrard (Apr. 3, 1998) ▊ J. Vernaud to D. J.Garrard (May 13, 1998).   ■ D. J. Garrard

VICTORY OUTREACH INTERNATIONAL

VICTORY OUTREACH INTERNATIONAL Pentecostal/charismatic denomination founded by ▸Sonny Arguinzoni in 1967 in East Los Angeles, CA. After being converted by Nicky Cruz and David Wilkerson in New York City, Arguinzoni felt called to the ministry. In 1962 he left New York City to attend the Latin American Bible Institute (LABI) of the Assemblies of God (AG) in La Puente, CA. While at LABI he met and married Julie Rivera and began working with Teen Challenge in Los Angeles. After recognizing that most ex-drug addicts, gang members, and social outcasts did not fit and were not welcomed in the typical Protestant churches of his day, he decided to create a church for people rejected by the larger society. In 1967 Arguinzoni and his followers purchased a small church in the Boyle Heights section of East Los Angeles and began what developed into Victory Outreach International (VOI). It has grown from a single church in 1967 to more than 210 churches and 350 rehabilitation homes throughout the U.S., Latin America, Europe, Africa, and Asia in 1997. Approximately 350 pastors and evangelists serve throughout the U.S. and around the world. VOI has six major forms of ministry: (1) churches, (2) drug rehabilitation homes for men and women, (3) prison ministry, (4) a television program entitled *Treasures Out of Darkness*, (5) children's homes, and (6) drug and gang prevention crusades. Between 1967 and 1997, VOI claims, more than 127,000 men and women have participated in their rehabilitation homes, and they have ministered to more than 1.7 million prisoners in the U.S. and around the world. VOI estimates that the 10,900 gang prevention outreach rallies and drama events they produce annually minister to over 2 million people throughout the

U.S. and world. At these events they have distributed approximately 20 million pieces of evangelistic and anti-crime literature since VOI was founded in 1967. They truly are an "outreach" ministry. VOI publishes *G.A.N.G.* [God's Anointed Now Generation] *Life* magazine. Although VOI is interracial, a majority of its members are of Mexican, Puerto Rican, black, or Latin American heritage. VOI opened a Bible school at their international headquarters in La Puente, CA; Victory Outreach School of Ministry now has over 275 enrolled students. While most VOI churches tend to be between 100 and 300 members, some are quite large, and Sonny Arguinzoni's church in La Puente has more than 4,000 members. VOI is unique in that it specifically targets the inner city, drug addicts, ex-prisoners, gang members, alcoholics, homosexuals, prostitutes, and other social outcasts. Its aggressive outreach programs, conservative theology (they do not ordain women to the ministry), and active lay ministry contribute to its otherworldly message of salvation in Jesus Christ.

■ **Bibliography:** S. Arguinzoni, *Internalizing the Vision* (1995) ▊ idem, *Sonny* (1987) ▊ idem, *Treasures out of Darkness* (1991).   ■ G. Espinosa

VIENS ET VOIS

VIENS ET VOIS Viens et Vois (Come and See), founded in 1977 by ▸Ronald Jean Monot, was the first French-speaking church of any denomination in the center of the city of Lubumbashi, Democratic Republic of Congo. (*Viens et Vois* is also the title of a publication of the French Assemblies of God.) Monot managed to procure what previously had been a factory in a building adjacent to the main street in the center of town. After renovations the building seated more than 1,000 people. Meetings began with a handful, but soon the numbers increased. Felix Dyabupemba, who had long been a collaborator with Monot and who had previously been the pastor of the church planted in Mbuji Mayi (East Kasai Province) during Monot's crusades there, was intimately involved in the evangelism. Meetings were held in French with Swahili interpretation of the sermons and announcements. Worship included songs in French as well as Swahili and other Congolese languages such as Tshiluba and Lingala. Because the church was Francophone, many government officials from other regions of the country who did not speak Swahili began to attend the services. This mix of French and Swahili has continued until the present day.

Once the group of believers had grown, Monot began to choose those who demonstrated ministry gifts and formed a pastoral team with Dyabupemba as the head elder. The congregation grew steadily over the years in spite of a number of setbacks. In 1984 Dyabupemba was disciplined for misconduct and Kiluba wa Kiluba became pastor. However, after a brief period he became involved in his own evangelistic ministry and left Viens et Vois with the blessing of the church. In 1987 ʼAlbert Lukusa Luvungu, who had been on the eldership team since 1980, became pastor and has guided the church since that time. The church facilities were expanded, but the number of those attending kept growing, so that it became necessary to have three services on a Sunday in order to fit in all the worshipers.

At the same time daughter assemblies were started to take the overflow in various parts of the city. Bin Baruani, one of the elders, became the pastor of a new church in the district known as Ali Lac. By 1998 Viens et Vois had planted four other assemblies in Lubumbashi, with over 6,000 members between them.

The church has sent its members to participate in conventions throughout Congo as well as neighboring countries including Zambia and South Africa. Recently it has been greatly influenced by the ʼFaith movement doctrines through its contacts with the Rhema church in South Africa.

The influence of Viens et Vois extends far beyond Congo, because Monot emphasized the importance of pastoral and ministerial training. A number of those who had been part of this pastoral oversight have moved away from Congo. Men like Martin Mutyebele, a former employee of the state mining company, moved to Belgium. He began meetings in Brussels and now leads one of the largest Protestant churches in that country in association with the Church of God (Cleveland, TN). Gédéon Monga, who had worked closely with Monot both as an interpreter and companion, moved to Belgium to complete a doctorate and is today pastor of a large Protestant church near Liège. ʼMichel Kayembe was also part of the eldership before moving to Kinshasa, where he became involved with the ʼFull Gospel Business Men's Fellowship. He has since become a resident in the U.S. and commutes regularly from there to Kinshasa. The influence of Viens et Vois continues to make itself felt especially through its open declaration of the gospel and its contacts with believers in government.   ■ D. J. Garrard

VILLAFAÑE, ELDIN (1940–). Leading pentecostal scholar and church leader in the U.S. Born in Santa Isabel, PR, in 1940, he grew up in New York City. He is an ordained Assemblies of God (AG) minister and past presbyter of the Spanish Eastern District Council of the AG. He attended and then worked as minister of education in the famous Iglesia Cristiana Juan 3:16 in the Bronx, which at the time, with 1,800–2,000 members, was the largest Spanish-speaking Protestant church in the U.S. He received a B.A. from Central Bible College of the AG (1969), an M.A. from Wheaton College School of Theology (1970), and a Ph.D. in social ethics from Boston University (1989). In 1976, while working on his Ph.D., he was appointed professor of Christian social ethics at Gordon-Conwell Theological Seminary.

Eddie Villaneuva, Hispanic American scholar.

Villafañe is the founder and past director (1976–90) of the Center for Urban Ministerial Education (CUME), one of the premier urban ministerial educational centers in the U.S., sponsored by Gordon-Conwell. The center offers seminary training for urban pastors and church leaders in English, Spanish, Portuguese, French (for Haitians), and American sign language. The center serves approximately 300 students a year, representing 150 churches, 40 denominations, and 22 nationalities. It offers diplomas and M.A. and M.Div. degrees in urban ministries. From 1990 to 1993 Villafañe served Gordon-Conwell Seminary as associate dean for urban and multicultural affairs. He won a $2.27 million grant from the PEW Charitable Trust to create and direct the Contextualized Urban Theological Education Enablement Program (CUTEEP). He has served as president of SPL and La Comunidad of Hispanic American Scholars of Theology and Religion. He is the author of *The Liberating Spirit: Towards an Hispanic-American Pentecostal Social Ethic* (1993) and *Seek the Peace of the City: Reflections on Urban Ministry* (1995). In addition to his two published books, he has written 35 articles and has lectured across the nation on urban ministry, social ethics, pentecostalism, and the Latino experience in the U.S. From 1990 to 1996, Villafañe cotaught a number of courses on pentecostalism and urban ministry with Dr. Harvey Cox at the Harvard Divinity School. In 1998 Villafañe served as the Luce Lecturer in Urban Ministry at the Harvard Divinity School. He is one of the first pentecostal scholars to write in depth about urban ministry and the Latino pentecostal experience in the U.S. and Latin America.

■ **Bibliography:** G. Espinosa, interview with Eldin Villafañe, Oct. 1997.   ■ G. Espinosa

VILLANUEVA, EDDIE C. (1946–). The founding pastor of the Jesus Is the Lord Church, which has close to 500 congregations in the Philippines and overseas. A former communist activist, Villanueva experienced the power of the Holy Spirit and received a call for ministry while serving as a professor at Polytechnic University of the Philippines. In the mid 1980s, Ralph Mahony, a famous Christian statesman, visited the Philippines to conduct a crusade. One evening, with more than 25,000 people gathered, he pronounced prophetic messages regarding Villanueva's ministry instead of his expected preaching. Villanueva is also the founder of the ▸Philippines for Jesus Movement, an umbrella organization for non-Catholic, independent charismatic fellowships and churches in the Philippines with more than 4,000 member churches. He has an extensive TV and radio ministry throughout the nation, and he has brought Christian—and particularly pentecostal—convictions into the political, economic, and moral dimensions of Filipino society. He envisions the Philippines to be the "America of Asia," that is, exemplifying characteristics of economic strength and missionary commitment. Villanueva is perhaps best referred to as "an apostle to the nations" and "a prophet of God for the Philippines."

■ **Bibliography:** M. Wourms, *The JIL Love Story: The Church without a Roof* (1992).

■ W. Ma

VINEYARD CHRISTIAN FELLOWSHIP Vineyard Christian Fellowship refers to a group of more than 500 churches founded by ▸John Wimber, pastor of the central church of the organization, Vineyard Christian Fellowship of Anaheim, CA. The church, which reported a peak membership of 5,000 in 1987, was started by Wimber's wife, Carol, in a home fellowship meeting in Oct. 1976. The first public service was held in May 1977 under the name of Calvary Chapel of Yorba Linda, CA, with John Wimber as pastor. It remained associated with ▸Chuck Smith's ▸Calvary Chapel fellowship until 1983, when Wimber decided to join a group of six churches called "Vineyards," led by Kenn Gulliksen.

The churches are affiliated organizationally under the Association of Vineyard Churches, established in 1985 and led by Wimber's successor, Todd Hunter.

Vineyard Ministries International is an umbrella organization that supervises and coordinates Vineyard ministries internationally through seminars, books, tapes, and other resources.

■ **Bibliography:** K. N. Springer, "Applying the Gifts to Everyday Life," *Charisma* (Sept. 1985) ■ T. Stafford, "Testing the Wine from John Wimber's Vineyard," *Christianity Today* (Aug. 8, 1986) ■ C. P. Wagner, ed., *Signs and Wonders Today* (1987) ■ C. Wimber, "A Hunger for God," in *Riding the Third Wave*, ed. J. Wimber and K. Springer (1987) ■ *The Winepress* (1987).   ■ C. P. Wagner

VINGREN, ADOLF GUNNAR (1879–1933). Swedish pentecostal missionary. Vingren was born in Ostra Husby Parish, Ostergotland, Sweden. In 1897 Vingren became a member of the Swedish Baptist movement after he was baptized in a church in Wraka, Smaland. He came to the U.S. in 1903, and while living with his uncle in Kansas, he worked as a laborer until 1905, when he decided to attend the Swedish Department of the University of Chicago Divinity School. Upon graduation in 1909 he became the pastor of a Swedish Baptist church in Menominee, MI.

Shortly afterward, while visiting Sweden, Vingren came into contact with the country's pentecostal movement. Upon his return to Chicago he attended a pentecostal conference sponsored by the First Swedish Baptist Church and converted to pentecostalism. Vingren traveled back to Michigan, resigned from his pastorate, and returned to Chicago. While in Chicago, Vingren attended several pentecostal churches, including ▸William H. Durham's North Avenue Mission and the Svenska Pingst Forsamlingen, Chicago's first Scandinavian pentecostal church.

During the summer of 1910 Vingren accepted the pastorate of a Swedish Baptist church in South Bend, IN. During a Saturday evening prayer meeting, Adolf Uldine, a member of the church, prophesied to Vingren that he should go to Para and preach about Jesus. Shortly afterward, Uldine gave the same prophecy to Daniel Berg, whom Vingren had met a year earlier in Chicago. After finding out that Para was in Brazil, Vingren and Berg returned to Chicago and were dedicated as missionaries by Durham at the North Avenue Mission. They also visited the Svenska Pingst Forsamlingen and received nearly $400 from the church to help finance their trip to Brazil.

Together, Vingren and Berg left the U.S. on Nov. 4 and arrived in Brazil two weeks later. After finding a Baptist church, they were invited to attend the church and live in the pastor's home. They were soon asked to leave the church, however, because of their pentecostal preaching. Vingren and Berg, who were now living on their own, conducted evening services for the 18 church members who had also left the Baptist church. Less than a year later these persons decided to organize a church called the Apostolic Faith Mission in the home of Henrique Albuquerque at Rua Siqueira Mendes in the neighborhood of Cidade Velha. They elected Vingren as their pastor. When church members began to meet in the new home of Albuquerque at 224 Sao Jeronimo Avenue, they officially registered themselves as a church called the Assembly of God. From this small congregation grew the Assemblies of God, presently the largest Protestant denomination in Brazil.

During the next 18 years, Vingren often went to Sweden and the U.S. to enlist support for his ministry in Brazil. He also traveled along the East Coast of Brazil to support the growing number of pentecostal churches that had developed in this region's cities. In 1930 Vingren became very weak as a result of stomach cancer. He returned to Sweden in the fall of 1932 and died the following spring.

■ **Bibliography:** W. J. Hollenweger, *The Pentecostals* (1972) ▮ I. Vingren, *Pionjarens dagbok* (1968).   ▮ J. Colletti

VINYARD, RICHARD (1913–89). Faith healer and ▸*Voice of Healing* evangelist. Richard Vinyard was an ▸Assemblies of God pastor during the first great ▸William Branham crusade (1948) in Kansas City. Branham's ministry caused such a stir that Vinyard overheard two young men in Sunday school speculating as to why Pastor Vinyard was not used of God in the same way as Branham. This stirred the heart of Vinyard to speak to the boys, and in response to their question as to why he didn't do the same things as "Brother Branham," he had to confess, "I was not where I should be with God." Vinyard set himself to seek God, and after a period of several months he was awakened by God at 4:00 one morning and told that from that day on he would have a ministry of healing. Vinyard told the story to his church the next Sunday, and several were healed. This was the beginning of many years of fruitful ministry not only in the U.S. but in many foreign lands as well. Vinyard also served on the staff of *Voice of Healing* for several years during its early days.

■ **Bibliography:** G. Lindsay, "The Story of the Great Restoration Revival—Part IV," *World-wide Revival* (June 1958).
                    ▮ J. R. Zeigler

VIRGO, TERRY (1940–). Prominent leader among the New Churches (formerly known as ▸House Churches) in Britain. Virgo, baptized in the Spirit in 1962, studied at London Bible College; his Reformed convictions were influenced by Martyn Lloyd-Jones. After pastoring a church in Seaford, Sussex, for 10 years, Virgo returned to the Brighton area to form the Clarendon Church in 1980 (Clarendon was renamed Christ the King and moved to nearby Brighton in 1993). Virgo has pursued his vision of church restoration, forming an apostolic team that oversees New Frontiers, the largest of the New Church networks in Britain, and promoting the Downs Bible Weeks (1979–88) and later the Stoneleigh Bible Weeks (1991–).

Virgo spent two years in Columbia, MO (1993–95), leading the Christian Fellowship of Columbia and gathering 12 other churches into a network of fellowship. He has been a strong supporter of the ▸"signs and wonders" message of ▸John Wimber and of the ▸Toronto Blessing in a framework of church planting, revival, and restoration. His books include *Restoration in the Church* (1985) and *A People Prepared* (1996).

■ **Bibliography:** B. Hewett, *Doing a New Thing?* (1995) ▮ A. Walker, *Restoring the Kingdom* (1988).   ▮ P. D. Hocken

VOICE OF HEALING From Apr. 1948 until May 1967, when the magazine *Voice of Healing* (*VoH*) changed its name to *Christ for the Nations* (vol. 20, no. 2), ▸Gordon Lindsay labored as its founder, editor, and director.

VoH began as a promotional tool for the ▸William Branham revival meetings. No sooner had the first issue appeared, however, than Branham announced his retirement from active campaigning, leaving Lindsay with many subscriptions for a magazine that had unexpectedly lost its chief reason for being.

About the same time, other evangelists who were engaged in deliverance ministries began requesting coverage in *VoH,* which Lindsay chose to grant. During the next 10 years *VoH* became the primary voice of the worldwide salvation healing revivals, featuring the crusades and schedules of numerous evangelists and publishing photographs and documented accounts of miracles that occurred in these services (healings of the blind, deaf, crippled, and those with other ailments).

Though Lindsay was himself an Assemblies of God (AG) minister before entering the publishing field, his magazine was not intended as a promotion of that, or any other, denomination. Neither did the subscribers of *VoH* represent an organized denomination. Instead, "The avowed purpose of *Voice of Healing* from the beginning [was] not to become a denomination but to serve all groups. We ordained no ministers but encouraged them to remain in their own organizations and be a blessing there, but at the same time, ministering to, and recognizing the whole body of Christ" (*VoH* 10 [1, 1957]: 2). This explicit affirmation of an ecumenical spirit permeated *VoH* through the 1950s and well into the 1960s.

Rather than a denomination, *VoH* was, first, a magazine and, second, a loosely knit fellowship of evangelists who shared the following characteristics: They had a mature healing ministry, accepted and subscribed to the articles of *VoH*'s constitution, had personal character that was above reproach, practiced the ideals of *VoH*'s fellowship, labored for unity among God's people, were willing and helpful in cultivating the circulation of *VoH,* and they were evangelists—not pastors (*VoH* 5 [3, 1952]: 2).

Though *VoH* began as a fellowship of American evangelists ministering in the U.S., a growing awareness of and commitment to foreign mission needs came to dominate the magazine in the late 1950s. By Feb. 1958 Lindsay announced that *VoH* was changing its name with the next issue to *World-Wide Revival*, a move intended to reflect more fully the scope of the organization's worldwide activities. Though that name lasted only through July 1958, the foreign mission emphasis took over the magazine, while that of the American evangelists on the local campaign trail gradually disappeared.

During the late 1950s and early 1960s, ›Tommy Hicks, ›R. W. Culpepper, David Nunn, ›Morris Cerullo, and others associated with *VoH* circled the world with their message of salvation in Jesus with attendant miracles of healing and deliverance. Reports concerning their crusades provided the bulk of many of those issues.

On the same page of that Feb. 1958 issue of *VoH*, Lindsay reported that he and other evangelists were "joining forces in an all out move for world-evangelization." Lindsay's own contributions to that effort came through several programs. He reviewed them in "The Story of the Winning the Nations Crusade" (*VoH* 19 [6, 1966]: 2–4, 14).

The Winning the Nations Crusade, as his work of world evangelism was known, had as its centerpiece an effort to raise monies that would establish funds to sponsor indigenous revival centers and churches (cf. *VoH* 10 [1, 1957]: 7). *VoH* contributed monies to a fund that in turn loaned these monies to a developing congregation for church building. The latter repaid the money interest free, which funds were again circulated. This effort, coupled with the Native Church Crusade (see *VoH* 17 [6, 1964]: 3, 15), had by 1966 established or supported some 1,200 native churches. *VoH* reported the commissioning of some 1,500 native evangelists since 1953.

The Holy Land Crusade was the second important ministry of *VoH*. Since 1959 gospel teams had traversed Israel distributing messianic literature (some 170,000 books in 1965 alone).

Lindsay early recognized the importance of the written word for evangelization. Between 1954 and 1966, through the "Native Literature Crusade" and his world literature program, *VoH* distributed millions of pieces of gospel literature, including more than one hundred of Lindsay's own titles (some having a circulation of 50,000–100,000 copies). In 1965 alone about 1 million books printed in a dozen languages and concerning a host of evangelical topics were distributed.

Finally, *VoH* sponsored international evangelistic radio programs. A more notable work was that in Central America, begun in 1957, with ›Paul Finkenbinder. Christ for the Nations reported that his ministry was being carried over several hundred radio stations in Central America, with 10,000 program releases per month.

The first issue of *Christ for the Nations* (20 [2, 1967]: 2) carried an editorial in which Lindsay wrote: "Divine healing is the means, and *Christ for the Nations* is the objective—and has been our objective from the beginning. Truly our call is to put the Gospel before all nations."

■ **Bibliography:** G. Lindsay, ed., *The Voice of Healing* 1–20 (1948–67).   ■ J. A. Hewett

VOLF, MIROSLAV (1956–). Prominent theologian and writer. Born Sept. 25, 1956, Volf received his B.A. from the Evangelical-Theological Faculty, Osijek, Croatia (1977); the M.A. from Fuller Theological Seminary, Pasadena, CA (1979); and the Dr.Theol. (1986) and Dr.Theol.Habil. (1994) from the University of Tübingen. He has served as professor of systematic theology both on the Evangelical-Theological Faculty, Osijek, Croatia, and at Fuller Theological Seminary. Currently he is Henry B. Wright Professor of Theology, Yale Divinity School, New Haven, CT.

Volf is the author of nine books, including *Work in the Spirit: Toward a Theology of Work* (1991); *Exclusion and Embrace: A Theological Exploration of Identity, Otherness, and Reconciliation* (1996); and *After Our Likeness: The Church as an Image of the Triune God* (1998). He is editor of *A Passion for God's Reign: Theology, Christian Learning, and the Christian Self* (1998); and coeditor of *Gerechtigkeit, Geist und Schoepfung: Die Oxford-Erklaerung zur Frage von Glaube und Wirtschaft* (1992); *The Future of Theology: Essays in Honor of Jürgen Moltmann* (1996); and *A Spacious Heart: Essays on Identity and Togetherness* (1997). Among his many articles are "Human Work, Divine Spirit, and New Creation: Toward a Pneumatological Understanding of Work," *Pneuma* 9 (1987); "Materiality of Salvation: An Investigation in the Soteriologies of Liberation and Pentecostal Theologies," *JES* 26 (1989); "The Church as a Prophetic Community and a Sign of Hope," *European Journal of Theology* 2 (1993); and "'The Trinity Is Our Social Program': The Doctrine of the Trinity and the Shape of Social Engagement," *Modern Theology* 14 (3, 1998).

Miroslav Volf married Dr. Judith Gundry in 1981. He is a member of the PCUSA (Presbyterian Church U.S.A.).   ■ S. M. Burgess

VORONAEV, IVAN EFIMOVICH (1886–?). Russian pentecostal missionary. Voronaev was born in the province of Orenburg in central Russia. As a young man Voronaev served as a Cossack under the Tsar before his conversion in 1908. Shortly afterward, he served as a Baptist pastor in the Siberian cities of Irkutsk and Krasnoyarsk. During a period of severe persecution of Protestants by the state church, Voronaev left Russia for the U.S. He first settled in San Francisco and became a pastor of the Russian Baptist Church. Three

Ivan Voronaev, Russian pentecostal pastor and missionary, who was imprisoned for his faith.

years later he accepted an invitation to pastor the Russian Baptist Church in New York City. While there, he converted to pentecostalism. As a result, Voronaev resigned from his pastorate and founded the first Russian pentecostal church in New York City. He soon felt a deep conviction for his homeland and decided to return to Russia in 1920. There he helped establish several pentecostal churches. Under the antireligious law of 1929, Voronaev was arrested and spent most of the rest of his life in prison.

■ **Bibliography:** S. Durasoff, *Bright Wind of the Spirit: Pentecostalism Today* (1972) ▌ W. J. Hollenweger, *The Pentecostals* (1977) ▌ P. Voronaeff, *My Life in Soviet Russia* (1969).   ■ J. Colletti

VOUGA, OSCAR (1903–78). Pentecostal preacher and leader. Born in Missouri in a Presbyterian home, Vouga moved to California in 1921 and was converted to the pentecostal movement in 1924. He held pastorates in Idaho, Alabama, Texas, Tennessee, Georgia, and Canada. Later responsibilities included being the general secretary of the Pentecostal Church, Incorporated (1944–45), and editor of its official organ, *The Apostolic Herald* (1943–45). In 1945 Vouga served as the secretary for the joint committee, general board, and general conference that formed the ▸United Pentecostal Church (UPC). He was the assistant general superintendent of the UPC (1949–62) and its foreign missions director (1963–69). He is the author of *Our Gospel Message* (1967).

■ **Bibliography:** A. L. Clanton, *United We Stand* (1970).   ■ J. L. Hall

W

WACKER, GRANT (1945–). Historian of American pentecostalism. Wacker's parents and maternal grandparents were Assemblies of God (AG) ministers and missionaries. A graduate of Stanford and Harvard, Wacker taught at the University of North Carolina, Notre Dame, and the National Humanities Center. Since 1992 he has taught American religious history at Duke University Divinity School.

In 1995 Wacker served as president of the SPS. In 1997 he became a senior editor of *Church History: Studies in Christianity and Culture*. Wacker has published articles about early pentecostal history in various academic journals, including *Church History, Harvard Theological Review, Journal of American History, Journal of Ecclesiastical History*, and *Pneuma: Journal of the Society for Pentecostal Studies*. His most recent book is *Heaven Below: Early Pentecostalism and American Culture* (2001). A layman, Wacker is a member of Orange United Methodist Church in Chapel Hill, NC.　■ E. Blumhofer

WAGNER, CHARLES PETER (1930–). Missionary, educator, author, and church-growth authority. C. Peter Wagner was born in New York City to C. Graham and Mary Wagner. In 1950 he married Doris Mueller; they have three children. Wagner earned degrees at Rutgers University (B.S., summa cum laude, 1952; Phi Beta Kappa), Fuller Theological Seminary (M.Div., 1955), Princeton Theological Seminary (Th.M., 1962), Fuller Theological Seminary School of World Mission (M.A. in Missiology, 1968), and University of Southern California (Ph.D. in Social Ethics, 1977).

Ordained to the ministry in 1955 by the Conservative Congregational Christian Conference, Wagner and his wife traveled to Bolivia for missionary service under the South America Mission and Andes Evangelical Mission (now SIM International). During those years he served as a professor at George Allan Theological Seminary, Cochabamba (1962–71), and as associate general director of the Andes Evangelical Mission (1964–71).

Having studied under church-growth specialist Donald A. McGavran, Wagner joined the faculty of Fuller Theological Seminary School of World Mission in 1971 as McGavran's understudy. He has served at Fuller as vice president of the Charles E. Fuller Institute for Evangelism and Church Growth (1971–79) and as professor in the School of World Mission (1971–99). In 1984 he was appointed the first Donald A. McGavran Professor of Church Growth. He also designed and taught, with John Wimber, the controversial course MC510, "Signs and Wonders."

When the Lausanne Committee for World Evangelization was formed in 1974, Wagner became a charter member. For seven years he served on its executive committee. He was the first chairperson of the Lausanne Strategy Working Group, which focused on reaching unreached peoples. With Edward R. Dayton he initiated and coedited the first three *Unreached Peoples* annuals.

In 1985 Wagner became the founding president of the North American Society for Church Growth. Wagner also coined the phrase "third wave" to describe noncharismatic evangelicals who believe that signs and wonders of the Holy Spirit will accompany the proclamation of the gospel. Wagner's status as an authority on worldwide church growth, which has often highlighted the growth of pentecostals and charismatics, can be traced to his own work in Latin America, research, and frequent travels. He also coordinates the AD 2000 United Prayer Track and the International Spiritual Warfare Network. In 1999, along with George Otis Jr. and Ted Haggard, Wagner cofounded the World Prayer Center in Colorado Springs, which he also directs. He is also dean of the Colorado Springs extension site of Fuller Seminary.

A prolific writer, Wagner has contributed many magazine and journal articles. His books include *Latin American Theology: Radical or Evangelical?* (1970); *Frontiers in Missionary Strategy* (1972); *Look Out! The Pentecostals Are Coming* (1973; later retitled *What Are We Missing?*); *Your Church Can Grow: Seven Vital Signs of a Healthy Church* (1976); *Your Spiritual Gifts Can Help Your Church Grow* (1979); *Church Growth and the Whole Gospel* (1981); *On the Crest of the Wave: Becoming a World Christian* (1983); *Leading Your Church to Growth: The Secret of Pastor/People Partnership in Dynamic Church Growth* (1984); *Strategies for Church Growth: Tools for Planning Evangelism and Missions* (1987); *Signs and Wonders Today* (ed.; rev. ed., 1987); *Wrestling with Dark Angels* (1990); *Warfare Prayer* (1992); *Blazing the Way: A New Look at Acts* (1995); *Confronting the Powers* (1996); and *New Apostolic Churches* (1998).

■ **Bibliography:** Curriculum vitae supplied to this writer ■ "Testing the Wine from John Wimber's Vineyard," *Christianity Today* (Aug. 8, 1986) ■ *Who's Who in Religion* (3d ed., 1985) ■ The World Prayer Center, website (July 13, 1999).

　　　　　　　　　　　　　　　　■ G. B. McGee; B. A. Pavia

WALDVOGEL, HANS R. (1893–1969). Pastor and founder of *The Bread of Life*. A native of Switzerland, Waldvogel was the son of Adam and Anna Waldvogel. Adam was a German Baptist minister who immigrated with his family of two sons and four daughters to Chicago in 1908. The children followed their father into ministry: both sons became pentecostal pastors; two daughters married German Baptist pastors, and one served as a full-time pentecostal church staff member.

Waldvogel came into contact with the Zion Faith Homes in 1919. He attended services there and was deeply influenced by two of the leaders of that independent pentecostal center, Eugene Brooks and Martha Wing Robinson. The Zion Faith Homes did not accept evidential tongues. The leaders also looked askance at the ongoing "denominationalizing" of pentecostalism. They stressed instead a Christocentric experiential piety similar to that espoused by ▸A. B. Simpson, adding the practice of spiritual gifts and replacing premillennialism with an amillennial stress on the presence of God's kingdom within believers. They preserved a strong emphasis on divine healing, rooted in their participation with Zion's founder, ▸John Alexander Dowie.

Hans R. Waldvogel, a leader among German pentecostals in the U.S., who pastored the Ridgewood Pentecostal Church and founded the *Bread of Life* magazine.

After training for the ministry by working under a pastor in Kenosha, WI, Waldvogel accepted a call to a small German pentecostal mission in Brooklyn, NY, in 1925. In time he transformed it into a thriving center of German pentecostal outreaches known as the Ridgewood Pentecostal Church. Located in a predominantly German neighborhood in Brooklyn, the congregation soon added English services and supported aggressive evangelism, which resulted in the opening of other congregations around the city. From 1947 Waldvogel increasingly left pastoral responsibilities to his brother, Gottfried (a graduate of the ▸Christian and Missionary Alliance's Nyack College in its institute days), and his nephew, Edwin Waldvogel. He traveled as an evangelist in Germany, Switzerland, and Austria, where he conducted large tent campaigns that both helped establish new congregations and nurtured war-devastated older groups.

In the U.S. Waldvogel not only gave leadership to a network of independent pentecostal congregations but also preached weekly on a half-hour German radio program; founded a monthly periodical, *The Bread of Life,* which extended the pentecostal emphases of the early Zion Faith Home leaders to others interested in the "deeper" life; established a camp in upstate New York; and led a faith home in Woodhaven, NY.   ■ E. L. Blumhofer

WALKEM, CHARLES WILLIAM (d. 1982). Musician, pastor, teacher, and author. During the 1930s and 1940s, Walkem collaborated with ▸Aimee Semple McPherson, arranging

much of her music, "setting down the strains at her dictation." Walkem's musical career spanned three decades, beginning in the 1920s and continuing long after the death of McPherson in 1944. A number of his arrangements may be found in the *Foursquare Hymnal* (1937). He was particularly used to help write and arrange songs for L.I.F.E. Bible College, such as "Long Live LIFE" (1945) and "L.I.F.E., I Love You" (1946), and to edit and arrange many of the tunes in McPherson's sacred operas, such as "Bells of Bethlehem."

In 1931 Walkem accompanied Aimee Semple McPherson and her entourage in a trip around the world as she recuperated from a breakdown brought on by overwork. During this period they worked together on her sacred operas. Upon their arrival in New York, he acted as the family spokesperson, indicating to members of the press that she was still too ill to handle the fatigue of a press interview.

Ordained by the ▸International Church of the Foursquare Gospel, Walkem was used widely as a speaker and teacher. A "self-made scholar," he was the author of a number of smaller pamphlets on theological subjects. He held an honorary D.D. from L.I.F.E. Bible College (1943) and served on the faculty from 1930 to 1978.

■ **Bibliography:** S. F. Middlebrook, *Preaching from a Pentecostal Perspective* (1970) ▪ "Poet of the Piano," *Foursquare World Advance* (Jan.–Feb. 1983) ▪ L. Thomas, *Storming Heaven* (1970).

■ C. M. Robeck Jr.

WALKER, JOHN HERBERT, JR. (1928–88). Missionary and educator of the Church of God (CG, Cleveland, TN). The son of ▸J. H. Walker Sr., a veteran pentecostal leader, J. Herbert Walker Jr. grew up in the pentecostal movement. He earned academic degrees at Vanderbilt (B.A., 1947), George Peabody College (M.A., 1953), Vanderbilt School of Religion (M.Div., 1955), and the University of Tennessee (Ph.D., 1967).

Walker and his wife, Lucille, were missionaries to Haiti from 1947 to 1952. He then was an administrator for Latin America (1955–57), Europe, the Middle East (1970–76), and Church of God World Missions (1980–84). He served as executive director (1984–88). In the area of education Walker was academic dean and professor of sociology at Lee College (1957–70) and coordinator of education for missions

(1976–80). His literary works include *Haiti* (1950) and *God's Living Room* (1971).

■ **Bibliography:** Archives of the Church of God (Cleveland, TN) ■ C. W. Conn, *Where the Saints Have Trod* (1959).

■ C. W. Conn

WALKER, JOHN HERBERT, SR. (1900–1976). Fourth general overseer of the Church of God (CG, Cleveland, TN) and a pentecostal minister and leader for more than 50 years. A native of Louisiana, Walker began his ministry in the CG in 1922. After serving as president of Lee College (1930–35), Walker was elected general overseer at the age of 35, the youngest man ever chosen, and served for nine years (1935–44). His other executive positions were editor-in-chief of CG publications (1946–48) and director of CG world missions (1948–52).

Walker was a member of the constitution committee of the ▸National Association of Evangelicals in 1942 and the ▸Pentecostal World Conference in 1949. He was a strong voice in bringing the pentecostal movement to its present role of leadership and cooperation in the evangelical world.

■ **Bibliography:** Archives of the Church of God (Cleveland, TN) ■ C. W. Conn, *Like a Mighty Army: A History of the Church of God* (rev. 1977).   ■ C. W. Conn

WALKER, PAUL HAVEN (1901–75). A pentecostal pioneer from North Dakota, whose ministry in the Church of God (CG, Cleveland, TN) and the pentecostal world spanned 56 years. In 1919 Walker began a new field ministry that established churches in Maryland, North Dakota, South Dakota, and Minnesota. His later ministry as state overseer and executive missions secretary of the CG (1952–58) was largely administrative. He led in establishing churches in 10 mission fields in Latin America, Europe, and Asia.

Active in worldwide pentecostal ministry, Walker was a member of the ▸Pentecostal World Conference advisory board (1955–58) and the Evangelical Foreign Missions Association. He produced two books: *The Baptism with the Holy Ghost and the Evidence* (c. 1935) and his autobiography, *Paths of a Pioneer* (1971).

■ **Bibliography:** C. W. Conn, *Our First 100 Years* (1986) ■ P. H. Walker, *Paths of a Pioneer* (1971).   ■ C. W. Conn

WALKER, PAUL LAVERNE (1932–). Twentieth general overseer of the Church of God (CG, Cleveland, TN) and senior pastor of the Mt. Paran Church of God in Atlanta, GA. Born in Minot, ND, the son of pentecostal pioneer Paul H. Walker, he holds degrees from Lee University, Presbyterian College (B.A., 1953), Emory University (B.D., 1964), and Georgia State University (M.Ed., 1970; Ph.D., 1972).

During the 1950s, Walker pastored churches in South Carolina and Florida and in 1960 became pastor of the 565-member Mt. Paran congregation. Walker's ministry was highly successful: in 1987 the church had 6,432 members in multiple sanctuaries.

Walker is a staff member of the Atlanta Counseling Center and a prominent speaker at interdenominational conferences. Among his published books are *The Ministry of Church and Pastor* (1965), *Counseling Youth* (1967), *Knowing the Future* (1976), *Understanding the Bible and Science* (1976), *Courage for Crisis Living* (1978), and *How to Keep Your Joy* (1987).

In 1996 Walker was elected from his long pastorate in Atlanta to the general overseership of the CG. He served in that capacity until 2000.

■ **Bibliography:** Church of God Archives at Lee University (Cleveland, TN) ■ Files of the Mt. Paran Church of God (Atlanta).   ■ C. W. Conn

WALKER, ROBERT ALANDER (1912–). Magazine editor, author, and publisher. Born in Syracuse, NY, Walker married Jean Browning Clements in 1937. After earning a B.S. (1936) and M.S. (1941) from Northwestern University, Walker became the founder and editor of *HIS Magazine*, published by Inter-Varsity Christian Fellowship (1941–43). He was an assistant professor of journalism at Wheaton College (1941–51) and served in various capacities at Scripture Press Foundation (1939–56).

From 1939 to 1943 Walker took the helm as editor of the *Sunday School Promoter* published by Scripture Press. Within a few years he began publishing the magazine in a *Reader's Digest*–size format and changed the name to *Christian Life*. It was a monthly magazine with a strong emphasis on spiritual renewal aimed at the evangelical Christian community. In addition to testimonies of evangelicals, the magazine began carrying news of the charismatic renewal around the world in the 1960s.

Walker also served as director and sales manager for Scripture Press Ministries in Chicago (1945–56) and chief executive officer of Christian Life Missions, Inc., in Wheaton, IL (1956–86), which was the publisher of *Christian Life, Christian Bookseller,* and Creation House books. Walker continued as editor of *Christian Life* until Dec. 1986, when Christian Life Missions sold out to Strang Communications Company. Subsequently, *Christian Life* magazine merged with *Charisma* in the spring of 1987, and *Christian Bookseller* became *Christian Retailing*. Walker currently is editor emeritus for *Charisma*.

Walker has authored several books, including *A New Song* (with Pat Boone, 1970), *Finger Licking Good* (with Col. Harland Sanders, 1975), *The Successful Writer and Editor* (1979), and *Leads and Story Openings* (1984).

Other notable accomplishments include the launching of an international Sunday school contest and introducing personality profiles to the Christian reading public. Walker married Barbara Melin in 1995. They have homes in Wheaton, IL, and in Boca Raton, FL. The Robert Walker Scholarship Fund helps young Christians called into the ministry of Christian journalism.

■ **Bibliography:** J. Franzen, "History and Accomplishments of Robert Walker" (online, 1996) ■ *Who's Who in America* (46th ed., 1990–91) ■ *Who's Who in Religion* (1977).   ■ G. W. Gohr

WALLIS, ARTHUR R. (1923–88). Major figure in the ⸾House Church Movement in Great Britain. From a Plymouth Brethren background, Wallis began to pray and fast for revival in the early 1950s and soon experienced the Spirit's power. Influenced by G. H. Lang and D. Lillie, he developed a vision for the restoration of the NT church. Wallis served with Lillie as a convener of the Devon conferences (1958, 1961, 1962). Wallis experienced a growing interest in spiritual gifts and received the gift of tongues in 1962, which led to his exclusion from Brethren assemblies during his New Zealand tour (1963–64). Between 1965 and 1972 Wallis worked both with the ⸾Fountain Trust and with leaders who believed that renewal must lead to reformation and restoration of the church. Covenanting with a group of these men in 1972, Wallis became a major teacher and father figure in the "restorationist" movement, centered in the city of Bradford. His major books are *In the Day of Thy Power* (1956, repr. as *Rain from Heaven*), *God's Chosen Fast* (1968), *Pray in the Spirit* (1970), and *The Radical Christian* (1981).

■ **Bibliography:** P. Hocken, *Streams of Renewal* (1986, 1997) ■ A. Walker, *Restoring the Kingdom* (1985, 1988) ■ J. Wallis, *Arthur Wallis: Radical Christian* (1991).   ■ P. D. Hocken

WALTON, JOHN (1934–). Leader in the New Life Churches of New Zealand (NLCNZ). Walton was originally a member of the Exclusive Brethren but was expelled for heresy in 1969 after becoming involved with the charismatic movement. He then attended a Baptist church that in the mid 1970s became a "New Life" church. He rose rapidly through the ranks of the NLCNZ and contributed to its progress toward a more structured movement. This resulted in the recognition of ⸾Rob Wheeler and ⸾Peter Morrow as "apostolic leaders" at its 1987 annual conference. Walton replaced Rob Wheeler as one of the two leaders of the movement in 1989. By the early 1990s Walton was the sole head of the NLCNZ (Morrow, like Wheeler before him, resigned due to failing health).

■ **Bibliography:** B. Knowles, "Some Aspects of the History of the New Life Churches of New Zealand 1960–1990" (diss., U. of

Otago, 1994) ■ M. Toomer, "National Church Leader 'Walks with His People,'" *Challenge Weekly* (May 8, 1996).   ■ B. Knowles

WANNENMACHER, JOSEPH PAUL (1895–1989), and **HELEN (INNES)** (1890–1985). Pioneer Assemblies of God (AG) pastors. Helen Innes was born in Cincinnati, OH, and moved with her family to John Alexander Dowie's Zion City, IL, in 1901. She was baptized by Dowie when she was nine. Receiving a scholarship to Chicago University, she graduated with a teaching degree in 1915. While on a visit to Zion City in 1915 she attended a service at the Zion Faith Home and received salvation. Soon afterward she received the baptism of the Holy Spirit and later decided to move to the ⸾faith homes to train for Christian work. She ministered in the faith homes for six years, helping to establish pentecostal missions in nearby Kenosha, WI, and Waukegan, IL. While at the Zion faith homes, she met Joseph Wannenmacher, her future husband, who was preparing for the ministry.

Joseph Wannenmacher was born to a German Catholic family in Hungary. At his urging, his family immigrated to Milwaukee, WI, in 1909. He found work as a mechanic and then as foreman of a tool shop. When he became afflicted with tuberculosis in his foot, he was forced to change professions. He then took up music for a livelihood. For a time, Wannenmacher turned to Christian Science for a possible cure for his condition. Then in 1917 he attended a German pentecostal mission in Milwaukee pastored by Hugo Ulrich. There he received salvation, immediate healing of his affliction, and soon afterward the baptism of the Holy Spirit. Saved and filled with the Spirit, he began playing the violin and giving his testimony everywhere he went.

Immediately after their marriage in 1921, Joseph and Helen pioneered a Hungarian mission that became known as the Full Gospel Church (now Calvary Assembly of God) of Milwaukee, WI. They were both ordained by the AG in 1923. The Wannenmachers published Hungarian literature and began conducting Hungarian and English services in the same building. From 1934 to 1944 Joseph Wannenmacher served as assistant superintendent of the Wisconsin–Northern Michigan District of the AG. They formed a Hungarian Branch of the AG and served as its first superintendent from 1944 to 1957. He made nine evangelistic trips to Eastern Europe. After WWII Wannenmacher ministered and helped with relief work in Austria and Germany. He also ministered in Hungary, Romania, Lithuania, and Yugoslavia, preaching at a number of camps for displaced persons. Probably his most significant contribution to the Eastern Europeans was the compilation and distribution of thousands of copies of a paperback German hymnal that was widely used in evangelistic outreach as well as in the churches.

The Wannenmachers ministered for more than 60 years in Milwaukee, shepherding Calvary Assembly and pioneering at least six other assemblies in the Milwaukee metropolitan area. Helen was copastor; she also was a noted retreat speaker and wrote monthly columns for the *Bread of Life* magazine. Beginning in 1962, Joseph Wannenmacher served as pastor emeritus of Calvary Assembly of God in Milwaukee. Their three children, John, Philip, and Lois (Graber) all have been involved in AG ministries.

■ **Bibliography:** *Bread of Life* (Nov. 1985), 5–7 ■ G. Gohr, "Two Pioneers of Pentecost in Milwaukee," *AGH* (Spring 1989) ■ "When God's Love Came In," *PE* (Oct. 29, 1949).   ■ G. W. Gohr

WARD, CHARLES MORSE (1909–96). Evangelist. For 25 years the speaker on *Revivaltime,* the radio outreach of the Assemblies of God (AG), Ward also served as president of Bethany Bible College.

In 1929 Ward graduated from Central Bible Institute in Springfield, MO. His father, A. G. Ward, had served as general secretary of the ▸Pentecostal Assemblies of Canada and as pastor of Central Assembly in Springfield, MO.

After graduation C. M. Ward served as a pastor, editor, and evangelist in Canada. For several years he taught at North Central Bible College in Minneapolis, MN, and served in missionary promotional work.

In 1945 Ward began a nine-year term as pastor of the Full Gospel Tabernacle in Bakersfield, CA. His successful ministry there was the basis for his appointment as speaker for *Revivaltime* on the ABC radio network.

From 1953 to 1978, C. M. Ward, the speaker for the Assemblies of God radio program *Revivaltime* from 1953 to 1978.

Over the next 25 years Ward preached 1,306 radio sermons, which were published in annual volumes. He also wrote hundreds of booklets, articles, and tracts to complement the ministry of *Revivaltime.*

While still serving as the speaker for *Revivaltime,* Ward was elected as president of Bethany Bible College in 1973. Always controversial, Ward stirred feelings with the publication of his autobiography in 1976.

■ **Bibliography:** *Revivaltime Pulpit* (published by *Revivaltime*) ■ C. M. Ward with Doug Wead, *The C. M. Ward Story* (1976).
                                                                    ■ B. M. Stout

WARE, R. KENNETH (1917–). Pentecostal missionary in France. In his youth Ware had a speech impediment, which was healed during a campaign of ▸Smith Wigglesworth, who told him, "This tongue will preach the gospel." Ordained in 1935 in Switzerland, his mother's homeland, Ware ministered in Toulon, France, until 1943. With his wife, Suzy, a pentecostal of Jewish background, whom he married in 1942, Ware ministered to Jewish refugees. The Wares escaped to Switzerland from the German occupation in 1943, returning to Paris in 1948. Receiving ▸Assemblies of God (AG [U.S.]) ministerial approval in 1953, Ware specialized in producing written materials and for a time had printing equipment in his home. He initiated a Sunday school program in 1960 and served on the committee that produced the Colombe Bible (1978). In 1981 he took over direction of the *Centre de Formation Biblique* of the French AG at Bièvres, near Paris, a position he was forced to relinquish due to illness in 1985.
                                                                    ■ P. D. Hocken

WARNER, WAYNE EARL (1933–). Pastor, editor, and archivist. Born June 4, 1933, in Wendling, OR, the son of Harry E. and Ethel (Bowers) Warner. After serving as a personnel sergeant in the U.S. Army (1953–55), he attended Eugene Technical School (1956–58). In 1958 he married Evangeline Joy Mitchell, daughter of ▸R. Bryant Mitchell, who was general superintendent of the ▸Open Bible Standard Churches (OBSC) (1953–67). He is the father of three grown children, Lori Mentze, Avonna Schirman, and Lolisa Collins.

After receiving a diploma from Eugene Bible College in 1961, Warner was ordained by the OBSC in 1963. He pastored Open Bible churches in Yacolt, WA (1962–63), and Perryton, TX (1963–64). While pastoring an Open Bible church in Hopedale, IL (1964–68), he also was editor of the *Mackinaw Valley News,* Minier, IL (1964–68). Warner became book editor of the Gospel Publishing House in Springfield, MO, in 1968 and received ordination with the Assemblies of God (AG) that same year. He later took courses at Drury College (1969–70).

Wayne Warner, director of the Assemblies of God Archives, now called the Flower Pentecostal Heritage Center.

Since 1980 Warner has been the director of the AG Archives, now called the Flower Pentecostal Heritage Center. In 1981 he began editing a quarterly publication for the archives called *Assemblies of God Heritage.* He also writes a weekly historical column for the *Pentecostal Evangel* called "Looking Back." Warner is active in the SPS and is a good resource on early pentecostalism and AG history.

Warner is the author or editor of the following works: *Good Morning, Lord: Devotions for Servicemen* (1971); *1000 Stories and Quotations of Famous People* (1972); the series *Faith, Hope, Love* (1975); *Letters to Tony* (1975); *Touched by the Fire* (1978); *The Woman Evangelist: The Life and Times of Charismatic Evangelist Maria B. Woodworth-Etter* (1986); *Kathryn Kuhlman: The Woman Behind the Miracles* (1993); *The Anointing of His Spirit* (1994); *Only Believe!* (1996); and *The Essential Smith Wigglesworth* (1999). He has also contributed numerous articles to the *Pentecostal Evangel, Enrichment, Christian Education Counselor,* and other publications.

Warner is a member of the Missouri Writer's Guild and has served as its president (1974–76). He married Patsy Creek in 1994, and in 1996 he was selected by Eugene Bible College to receive its annual alumni award with honorary membership in Delta Epsilon Chi, the honor society for the Accrediting Association of Bible Colleges. He is listed in *Contemporary Authors* and *Who's Who in Religion.*

■ **Bibliography:** *Contemporary Authors Online* (1999) ▪ *Who's Who in Religion* (1977).   ■ G. W. Gohr

WATSON, DAVID C. K. (1933–84). Renewal leader with perhaps the greatest spiritual impact on Britain to date. The archbishop of Canterbury visited David Watson on his deathbed to thank him for his contribution to the Church of England. His first appointment under John Collins at St. Mark's, Gillingham (1959–62), was an important preparation for his baptism in the Spirit while serving in Cambridge (1962–65). In 1965, after taking over St. Cuthbert's, York, which was destined for closure, Watson developed team ministry and strong teaching programs, necessitating a move to a larger church, St. Michael-le-Belfrey, in 1973.

Watson was a gifted evangelist who had a major impact in student milieus through the many university missions he led. In York he encouraged the creative arts in worship and used gifted Christian artists in his evangelistic teams. Watson broadened from a commitment to evangelical churchmanship to being strongly committed to the Spirit's work across all the churches, lessening barriers between Protestants and Catholics. In his later years, his friendship with ▸John Wimber opened many Anglicans to Wimber's teaching.

Watson married Anne in 1964. His autobiography, *You Are My God* (1983), reveals the importance of his marriage for his ministry and is unusually open about the trials they experienced together. Watson moved to London in 1982 to concentrate on a wider teaching ministry but was soon taken ill. The account of his struggle with cancer, *Fear No Evil,* published just after his death, was an instant best-seller. Other books include *My God Is Real* (1970); *One in the Spirit* (1973); *Anyone There?* (1979); *Discipleship* (1981); and two volumes in an evangelical series, *I Believe in Evangelism* (1976) and *I Believe in the Church* (1978).

■ **Bibliography:** E. England, *The Spirit of Renewal* (1982) ▪ idem, ed., *David Watson: A Portrait by His Friends* (1985) ▪ T. Saunders and H. Sansom, *David Watson: A Biography* (1992).

■ P. D. Hocken

WEINER, ROBERT THOMAS (1948–). Church planter, author, evangelist. Born in Chicago, IL, the grandson of a Jewish rabbi, Weiner converted to faith in Jesus Christ. He attended Trinity College before joining the U.S. Air Force, where he served as the chaplain's assistant. While stationed in Southern California, Weiner received the baptism in the Holy Spirit in the home of baseball player and Christian leader Albie Pearson and became the youth pastor of a growing Assemblies of God (AG) church. In 1972 Weiner and his wife, Rose, founded ▸Maranatha Campus Ministries in Paducah, KY, after leading a revival there among high school students. By the time Weiner resigned in 1989, the ministry had founded churches in 16 nations and had established ministries on 150 college campuses. Under Weiner's leadership Maranatha established several successful ministries, including Champions for Christ, Reel to Real Ministries, The Providence Foundation, and the *Forerunner* newspaper, as well as ordaining hundreds of full-time ministers.

Maranatha dissolved into several different organizations following his resignation.

In 1991 Weiner started Christian Youth International and headquartered the ministry in Moscow, Russia. Through his training conferences 200,000 Russian students received Bibles, and an estimated 370 cell churches were formed in the nations of the former Soviet Union during the first few years after communist rule. Weiner closed the Moscow office in 1996. In 1993, together with AIMS (Accelerating International Mission Strategies), Weiner founded China Harvest to get Bibles and training to the growing Chinese church.

■ S. Strang

WELCH, JOHN WILLIAM (1858–1939). Pastor, church executive, and educator. J. W. Welch gave maturity and dignity to the General Council of the Assemblies of God (AG) in its early years. An original executive presbyter and general chairman (1915–20 and 1923–25), the staunchly trinitarian Welch proved himself during the "New Issue" crisis. Both times he succeeded E. N. Bell (1866–1923) as presiding officer. Born in Seneca, NY, he spent many years as an organizer for the American Sunday School Union and as an evangelist for the Christian and Missionary Alliance (CMA). He was ordained by the latter at age 41. Assignment by the CMA in 1910 as superintendent in Oklahoma brought him into contact with A. B. Cox, pioneer pentecostal evangelist, at Muskogee. Similarities between the AG and the CMA may be attributed in part to Welch's leadership in the formative years. Pentecostal ministry included pastorates at Galena, KS; Essex, MO; and Modesto, CA. In 1915 he served a brief stint as editor of the *Christian Evangel* in St. Louis. Following a year as teacher at the Glad Tidings Bible Institute in San Francisco, Welch became president of Central Bible Institute in 1931. He died in Springfield, MO, on July 14, 1939, at age 80.

■ **Bibliography:** C. Brumback, *Suddenly . . . from Heaven* (1961) ▌ "Brother Welch Promoted to Higher Service," *PE* (July 29, 1939).

■ C. E. Jones

WELSH REVIVAL The 1904–5 revival in Wales, commonly known as the Welsh revival, was in fact one of a series of spiritual awakenings that occurred in Wales during the late 19th and early 20th centuries. In the historiography the 1904–5 revival has become the most important of these awakenings. The revival had a significant impact on pentecostalism, not only because of the converts of the revival who became pentecostal, but also because the story of the events, including what was interpreted as glossolalia (the ancient Welsh *hywl* chant), provided precedent and warrant for pentecostal liturgy and theology. Because of the coverage in the international religious press, many early pentecostal writers were aware of the Welsh revival, and some were directly influenced by it. Many other early pentecostal writers, as well as modern historians of pentecostalism, mention the Welsh revival and interpret it as a forerunner of pentecostalism.

The Welsh revival owed its beginnings to three Welsh revivalists: Seth Joshua, Joseph Jenkins, and Evan Roberts. Joshua was a member of the Forward Movement, a radical Holiness parachurch tradition. Jenkins was a minister and evangelist in the Calvinistic Methodist Church, much influenced by the Forward Movement. The most important leader of the revival was Evan Roberts (1878–1951), born at Loughor, Wales, a miner and a member of the Calvinistic Methodist Church of Moriah. These three men knew each other and cooperated in ministry.

After receiving a call to preach, Roberts went to Newcastle Emlyn in Sept. 1904 to enter preparatory school. He dropped out of school in late October of that same year to enter the revivalistic ministry. With some of his colleagues, he returned to Moriah. Prayer meetings and services led to conversions and ecstatic responses to the spiritual phenomena. The revival used traditional Welsh cultural forms to express religious experiences. Accounts of the revival were printed in the major Welsh newspapers. The revival spread throughout Wales, and by the end of 1904 there were at least 32,000 converts in South Wales. It spread also through the Welsh diaspora in Europe, Latin America, and North America. Soon it crossed ethnic lines, and revivals developed in many countries

Evan Roberts, leader of the Welsh revival of 1905, an enigmatic figure who later distanced himself from the revival.

of Europe, as well as in Africa, Australia, China, and India. Each area touched by the revivals experienced social change as well as spiritual renewal. No effort was made to organize the results of these revivals. Converts were welcomed into the congregations of various denominations, as had been the case during earlier revivals.

By Feb. 1905 opposition to the revival began, both in the traditionalist camp and among evangelicals who were embarrassed by the unruly nature and demonstrative spirituality of the revival. Much of the criticism focused on Roberts, who was "a prophetic type, hypersensitive, nervous, and not a particularly good speaker." But he had an intuitive sense for what was happening in his audience. Some considered him to have telepathic abilities. He was also subjective in his analyses and judgments. Even a sympathetic observer (Henri Bois) concluded, "Everything that comes from his subconscious is regarded by Roberts as the guidance of the Spirit, while everything that comes from reason or from the good advice of his friends is human counsel." Peter Price, distinctly hostile, put it more strongly. He accused Roberts of acting as though he was a fourth person in the Trinity. "He does not conduct himself like one who is led by the Spirit, but as one who leads the Spirit" (Hollenweger, 176–85).

Various persons claimed to have initiated the Welsh revival. Jessie Penn-Lewis claimed that it started in the ▸Keswick revivals conducted under her auspices in Wales. F. B. Meyer, also associated with the Keswick movement, asserted that he had initiated the revival. Both claims were immediately denied by the Welsh. Ironically, Penn-Lewis and Meyer were instrumental in repressing the ecstatic manifestations of the revival—"singing in the Spirit," loud spontaneous prayer, and prophecy—and in effect stopping the revival. Penn-Lewis took control of Evan Roberts, censoring his mail and keeping him from the public (Roberts lived in the Penn-Lewis home for several decades). Meyer, who was offended by the Wesleyan Holiness influences both at Keswick and in the Welsh revival, worked at distancing Keswick from the Holiness "enthusiasm" and to repress it in Wales. Interest in revival continued but, leaderless, this particular revival had come to an end. Later Penn-Lewis wrote *War on the Saints*, in which she attributed the ecstatic manifestations of the revival to demonic influences. Evan Roberts' name was listed as an author to add authority to the book.

> The acknowledged leader of the [Welsh revival] movement, Evan Roberts, remained an enigma right up to the time of his death.... By his own decision he withdrew into silence and carried out no further public work for the gospel. The revival disappeared, and has made those valleys in Wales almost inaccessible to any further divine visitation. The faithful of Wales have nostalgia for the past, but unfortunately nothing else. (D. Gee, *Elim Evangel* [1933], quoted in Hollenweger, 183)

Nevertheless, the Welsh revival prepared the way for the pentecostal movement a few years later. One direct connection between the two is found in the person of ▸A. A. Boddy, who visited Wales during the Welsh revival and later became one of the most important leaders of pentecostalism in England. Other early British pentecostal leaders were known as "Children of the Welsh revival." Wales became a major center of pentecostal revival, and Welsh pentecostal revivalists contributed significantly to the development of early pentecostalism in Britain and beyond.

■ **Bibliography:**
Selected Works. R. M. Anderson, *Vision of the Disinherited* (1979) ■ M. N. Garrard, *Mrs. Penn-Lewis: A Memoir* (1930) ■ W. J. Hollenweger, *Enthusiastisches Christentum: Die Pfingstbewegung in Geschichte und Gegenwart* (1969) ■ idem, *Handbuch der Pfingstbewegung,* 10 vols. (1966) ■ idem, *El Pentecostalismo, historia y doctrina* (1976) ■ idem, *The Pentecostals: The Charismatic Movement in the Churches* (1972) ■ B. P. Jones, *An Instrument of Revival: The Complete Life of Evan Roberts, 1878–1951* (1995) ■ idem, *Voices of the Welsh Revival* (1967) ■ E. Jones, *The Welsh Revival of 1904* (1969) ■ H. E. Lewis, *With Christ among the Miners* (1907) ■ J. V. Morgan, *The Welsh Religious Revival, 1904–1905* (1909) ■ J. Penn-Lewis in collaboration with E. Roberts, *War on the Saints: A Text Book on the Work of Deceiving Spirits among the Children of God and the Way of Deliverance* (1912) ■ D. M. Phillips, *Evan Roberts: The Great Welsh Revivalist and His Work* (1906) ■ H. Williams, *The Romance of the Forward Movement of the Presbyterian Church* (1965) ■ *Y Diwygiad a'r Diwygwyr: hanes toriad gwawr Diwygiad 1904–05* (1906).

Selected Pentecostal Works. T. B. Barratt, "Den Store Vaekkelse i Wales," *Byposten* 2 (2, 14 Jan. 1905) ■ idem, *When the Fire Fell and An Outline of My Life* (1927; repr. in *The Work of T. B. Barratt,* 1985) ■ D. D. Bundy, "Spiritual Advice to a Seeker: Letters to T. B. Barratt from Azusa Street, 1906," *Pneuma* 14 (1992; edition of letter from Barratt to E. Roberts) ■ D. Gee, *The Pentecostal Movement* (1941) ■ idem, *Wind and Flame* (1967) ■ W. Kay, *Inside Story: A History of the British Assemblies of God* (1990) ■ J. Kuosmanen, *Herätyksen Historia* (1979) ■ M. Ski, *Fram til Urkristendommen: Pinsevekkelsen gjennom 50 år,* vol. 1 (1956) ■ G. E. Söderholm, *Den Svenska Pingstväckelsens Historia, 1907–1927,* 2 vols. (1929) ■ L. Steiner, *Mit folgenden Zeichen: Eine Darstellung der Pfingstbewegung* (1954) ■ A. Sundstedt, *Pingstväckelsen-dess uppkomst och första utvecklingsskede* (1967) ■ J. E. Worsfold, *The Origins of the Apostolic Church in Great Britain* (1991).

■ D. D. Bundy

WESLEYAN HOLINESS CHARISMATIC FELLOWSHIP
Persons within the charismatic renewal whose ecclesiastical parentage is traced to John Wesley (but who are typically not United Methodists) have formed the Wesleyan Holiness Charismatic Fellowship (WHCF), also known as Fellowship of Charismatic Nazarenes. Wilbur Jackson is

chairman, and Stan Puliam is secretary. Membership is largely from the Nazarene, Wesleyan, Free Methodist, Church of God (Anderson, IN), and Salvation Army churches.

A review of the list of participants in recent WHCF activities shows that members are frequently "former Nazarene," or "former Free Methodist," etc. This observation helps the reader understand the stated purpose of the fellowship: to be "an information and communications link, a hand of fellowship and support to those who have been 'disfellowshiped' from former ties or who feel alone in their new walk" (*Newsletter*, 1987, 1). WHCF additionally seeks to foster understanding and dialogue between Wesleyan charismatics and denominational leadership in the light of differences of experiences.

The particular spiritual experience to which the leadership within the various Wesleyan family of churches has been closed or resistant is the ability to speak and worship God in tongues as the Spirit gives utterance.

See also CHARISMATIC MOVEMENT.

■ **Bibliography:** W. Jackson, "The Wesleyans and the Charismatic Movement," lecture at the 1986 New Orleans Leaders Congress, the WHCF sessions ■ H. A. Snyder, *The Divided Flame: Wesleyans and the Charismatic Renewal* (1986) ■ idem, "Wesleyans and Charismatics—Tensions vs. Cooperation," lecture at the 1986 New Orleans Leaders Congress, the WHCF sessions ■ *WHCF Newsletter* (Spring 1987). ■ J. A. Hewett

WEST OF SCOTLAND REVIVAL (1830). A revival in the Gareloch region of Scotland in the 1830s, highlighted by charismatic manifestations. Like other classic revivals, this movement evidenced numerous conversions. A distinguishing feature that set this revival apart from others was the prominence of the supernatural gifts of the Holy Spirit. During 1830–33, the religious world of Britain was both shocked and fascinated by this charismatic revival that predated the pentecostal movement in the U.S. by more than 70 years.

1. Background.

Laypersons were the chief actors for the duration of this revival, although the initial inspiration and theological foundation were contributed by various ministers of the Church of Scotland. For instance, the preaching of John McLeod Campbell (1800–1872), pastor of the Rhu (formerly Row) parish, had a powerful impact on the entire region. His sermons focused on God's fatherly love for all people, demonstrated supremely in the gift of his Son Jesus, and proved to be a refreshing contrast to the rigid Scottish Calvinism of that time, which tended to produce a sense of unworthiness among the people. Under Campbell's ministry, many felt a sense of joyful liberty and expectation of blessing. Others were drawn to the gospel for the first time. One chronicler

reports that "thousands were converted" during Campbell's five years of pastoring the Rhu parish.

Another instigator of revival was Campbell's young assistant, A. J. Scott (1805–66). Scott was convinced that the cessation of the supernatural gifts of the Spirit in the church was not the result of God's design but of a lack of faith among God's people. He encouraged people throughout the region to exhibit faith for the restoration of spiritual gifts to the modern church. He also made a theological distinction between conversion and the baptism in the Spirit, and he taught and counseled Christians to expect a baptism of God's power.

Edward Irving (1792–1834) was another Scottish minister who played a major role in revival preparation, even though his pastorate was located in distant London, England. A noted and controversial minister, Irving returned to his native Scotland in the summers of 1828 and 1829 as a guest preacher in the Rhu and Roseneath parishes. His sermons, in which he established the implications of the doctrine of the incarnation for our identification with the life of Christ and his ministry, were well received Also, Irving's proclamation of Christ's second coming created a sense of anticipation of things to come.

2. Spontaneous Beginnings: The Gareloch and Port Glasgow.

Even with the profound influences exerted on the people of the area by the ministries of Campbell, Scott, and Irving, no one could have predicted the events of 1830 that sparked the West of Scotland revival. Humble laypersons of the Macdonald and Campbell (no relation to John McLeod Campbell) families surfaced from virtual anonymity to spearhead a movement that would capture the attention of all of Britain.

Twin brothers James and George Macdonald (1800–1835; both died in the same year), shipbuilders living with their three sisters in Port Glasgow on the banks of the Clyde River, often ferried across the Clyde to experience the ministry of John McLeod Campbell in neighboring Rhu. The family was also well acquainted with the ministries and teachings of both Scott and Irving. One of the sisters, Margaret, while suffering from a terminal illness, also was beset by spiritual struggles. In 1830, however, she experienced spiritual awakening and peace, and she began to have visions and to prophesy.

On Apr. 14, 1830, although weak and ill, Margaret prophesied to her brothers, "There will be a mighty baptism of the Spirit this day." James responded with the confession, "I've got it." He promptly made his way to Margaret's bedside, startling her with the strong command, "In the name of Jesus of Nazareth, arise up and walk." Repeating the command, he took her hand to help her from her bed. As Margaret made the effort to arise, her body was healed instantly.

Not finished, James Macdonald was inspired to take further action. He penned a letter, addressed to a family friend, Mary Campbell (1806–39), who was bedridden and dying of a lung disease. Mary had lost her younger sister, Isabella (1807–27), at the age of 20, just two years before, and doctors held out no hope for Mary. Isabella, who was known as a woman of prayer and insight into the things of the Spirit, had left a spiritual legacy for Mary to follow. Mary shared her sister's keen spiritual sensitivity, adding to it a penetrating theological mind. By 1830 she was convinced that the miraculous ministry of Christ was possible for all believers.

On Feb. 1 she experienced a spiritual "trance," followed on Mar. 28 by an expression of the gift of unknown tongues. These experiences encouraged her to believe for her physical healing, although her condition continued to worsen. Then came the letter from James Macdonald, received on Apr. 15. Not only did James relate the report of Margaret's healing, but he boldly commanded Mary to rise from her bed and walk. The impact of James's written words were life-changing for Mary, as she relates. "I felt as if I had been lifted from off the earth, and all my diseases taken from off me at the voice of Christ. I was verily made in a moment to stand upon my feet, leap and walk, sing and rejoice."

Mary Campbell ferried from her Garelochhead home to Post Glasgow to share her marvelous news with the Macdonalds. They celebrated and worshiped. Others joined them, and prayer services at the home began to be held on a daily basis. By Apr. 18 James and George joined Mary as recipients of the gift of tongues. Among their group, the gift of interpretation of tongues and prophecy began to be exercised. In one of the early meetings, which did not dismiss until 6 A.M., four persons were converted. Within a few days, Mary returned to her home on the Gareloch to convene daily services there.

News of Margaret and Mary's miraculous healings, along with other expressions of the charismata, quickly spread throughout the Gareloch region and beyond. People interested in witnessing firsthand these unusual events began to migrate to the area. The Macdonalds and the Campbells opened their homes to these visitors. Similar prayer meetings opened up in nearby Scottish towns and cities, such as Edinburgh, Glasgow, Musselburgh, Greenock, Rhu, and Roseneath. Mary Campbell soon found her Garelochhead home to be too small to accommodate the growing numbers of service attendees and found temporary lodging in Helensburgh that was more suitable for larger gatherings.

3. Absence of Clergy.

Where were the clergy as the attention of the religious world suddenly focused on these humble laypersons and the meetings being held in their homes? Campbell attended some of the initial prayer meetings, lending his credibility to the early stages of the revival. Yet not being the pastor of either Mary Campbell (parish of Roseneath) or the Macdonalds (parish of Port Glasgow), he did not assume a supervisory role over the meetings or their proceedings. To the contrary, he gradually distanced himself from the movement, perhaps not wanting his name associated with it. This development is not difficult to understand in light of the opposition from his presbytery that had arisen over his doctrinal commitment to "unlimited atonement." Had he closely associated himself with the controversial charismata, his denominational officials likely would have gained further leverage against him. In May 1831 Campbell's case reached the general assembly of the Church of Scotland. In a decision that later would bring a measure of shame on the Church of Scotland, Campbell was stripped of his ordination and ousted from his pastoral position in the Rhu parish. Over the next three years, Campbell engaged in a traveling ministry before settling in Glasgow with an independent congregation. Although Campbell never opposed the notion of supernatural gifts in the modern church, he chose not to associate himself with the Gareloch manifestations nor with the next phase of revival as it spread to England.

A. J. Scott had vacated the region almost two years before the 1830 outbreak of manifestations. He accepted Edward Irving's invitation to move to London to be his pastoral assistant after Irving's 1828 visit to the region. As news of the 1830 manifestations reached London, Scott closely followed the developments. His influence on the Campbell and Macdonald families was well known, so his noticeable silence about the manifestations is not easy to explain. The most obvious answer is that Scott did not want to give cause for additional consequences in his heated battle with the Church of Scotland. Scott had left Irving to pastor his own church, but he was facing official censure due to denominational differences. That battle ended in defeat as the same general assembly of 1831 that deposed Campbell also revoked Scott's ministerial license. As a result, Scott's future pastoral labors and his work in higher education took place outside the auspices of the Church of Scotland.

4. Irving's Acceptance.

Without the blessing of Campbell or Scott, the Gareloch revival at least gained the support and endorsement of Edward Irving from distant London. When reports of revival reached London, a six-member delegation of persons closely associated with Irving's church made its way to the West of Scotland to investigate. After weeks of observation, mostly of the Macdonald meetings, the delegation returned home with a favorable recommendation. Irving took the team's positive report to heart. Even more convincing to him were the personal letters he received from Mary Campbell. Her letters revealed that Irving's own doctrine of Christ's true humanity had been the key to her confidence to appropriate supernatural empowerment.

5. London Spotlight.

The recognition that Irving's Christology played a role in the outbreak of the charismata had a profound affect on Irving and caused him to shift his personal ministry agenda in the direction of preparing his own church for a revival of the Spirit's empowerment. Therefore, the ultimate impact of Irving's support on the events in the west of Scotland was to divert attention away from the Gareloch to a new center of revival in Irving's London church. The charismata first broke out in the early morning prayer services. When they spread to the regular Sunday services of his 2,000-member church, controversy ensued. Irving's refusal to censure the expression of spiritual gifts led to his ejection from the pastorate of the church he had built. A homeless congregation of several hundred members followed Irving to the streets and eventually formed the locus of a new church on Newman Street. Irving's Newman Street Church became a haven for both laity and church leaders who identified with the charismatic expression of worship. The revival in London contrasted with the West of Scotland revival in that events in London developed within the context of ecclesiastical relationships and pastoral oversight. An ecclesiastical framework for the expression of the charismata represented a unique experiment in Protestant church history.

The London revival also distinguished itself from the West of Scotland and other revivals in that it advocated a restoration to Christendom of the ancient form of apostolic church government. Irving himself did not aspire to apostleship, preferring the offices of pastor, evangelist, and prophet. Yet by 1833 the first apostles had been appointed out of Newman Street (John Cardale [1802–79] and Henry Drummond [1786–1860]). Irving's commanding presence, however, made it difficult for the apostles to lead. As six other area churches affiliated with Newman Street in their identification with the charismata and a London council was formed, it was Irving and not the apostles who presided. Only Irving's untimely death in 1834 released the apostles to assume leadership of the expanding movement. A final "apostolic college" of 12 men had been chosen by 1835.

Without Irving, the base of operations shifted to Drummond's country estate in rural Albury, south of London. Forming an organization named the ►Catholic Apostolic Church (CAC), the movement mobilized internationally to spread their message of apostolic restoration. High-church liturgy and structure dominated the movement, a departure from the spontaneity of Irving's Newman Street Church. The CAC sought to minimize the seminal role of Irving, seeking to disassociate itself from the label "Irvingite." Yet Edward Irving had been the catalyst primarily responsible for bringing theological and ecclesiastical solidification to the effort of recovering the biblical experiences of Spirit baptism, spiritual gifts, signs and wonders, and apostolic church government.

6. Mary Campbell.

Meanwhile, back in Scotland, the continuation of momentum was dependent on the roles of key figures. Mary Campbell burned with a passion to see the church ministering supernaturally as Jesus had in his earthly ministry. She sought to set an example for others. On one occasion Mary announced publicly that she was going to pray for the miraculous recovery of a lame boy. At the designated time, thousands jammed the streets and lined the banks of the Gareloch to catch a glimpse of the event. After praying, she commanded the boy to walk. Casting aside his crutches, he began to limp across the street. The crowd burst into applause, having witnessed an obvious miracle. Although the boy continued to limp, he was able to walk and proceeded to walk the several miles home without assistance. The crowd stayed to listen as Mary led in singing, preaching, and exhorting the people. Boats lingered on the waters nearby, as rumor had it that Mary's next exploit would be to walk on the water. Mary had no such intention. Yet her boldness to demonstrate her faith made a deep impression on the people of the region, and her fame was widespread.

Visitors flocked to Mary's temporary residence in Helensburgh throughout the summer of 1830, hoping to witness the charismata in action. One such visitor, a young businessman from Edinburgh, was reluctant to leave. A special relationship blossomed between him and Mary. In 1831, Mary Campbell became Mary Caird. That same year, William Rennie Caird (1802–94) and his young bride departed to London to become catalysts for the revival that was igniting in Irving's church. When the apostles formed the CAC, the Cairds were in the forefront of this new experiment. As the movement expanded internationally, the Cairds assumed the role of evangelists, effectively ministering both in North America and Europe. Mary's dynamic ministry was halted abruptly by her untimely death in 1839 as she and William were laboring on Austrian soil. She is buried in Strasbourg.

7. The Macdonalds.

When Mary Caird departed from the Gareloch in 1831, revival activity was focused solely on the Macdonald family, who were also affected by the shifting tide of events developing in London. Margaret Macdonald, as a prophetess, was a key revival figure. One of the members of the London delegation investigating the outbreak of revival, Robert Norton (1807–83), took a special interest in Margaret. Margaret married Robert, and they relocated to Albury as the CAC was developing. Robert had been a medical doctor but became a pastor with the new movement. Probably his most important contribution was his role as historian. He chronicled the Scotland, London, and Albury phases of the revival and lent apologetic credence to the development of the CAC.

Without Margaret's presence, the Macdonald brothers shouldered the burden of leadership for the continuing revival in the west of Scotland. James and George held daily prayer meetings, sometimes holding services in other homes or even outdoors, as well as in their own home in Port Glasgow. James's preaching once held the attention of over 1,000 persons who stood in a driving rain to hear his message. Conversions to Christ were frequent in their meetings, and manifestations of the charismata were the distinguishing features. The Macdonalds ministered the baptism of the Spirit to people, teaching that speaking in tongues is both a sign of Spirit baptism and a devotional prayer language for personal edification.

The Macdonalds closely followed news of revival activity in London and the experiment in apostolic government in the CAC. They rejected, however, attempts by the leaders of the new church to bring their ministry under apostolic authority. The CAC saw this as a rejection of God's authority and sought to discredit the ministry of the Macdonalds. But the Macdonalds continued their meetings with regularity for three years until revival intensity began to decline.

In 1835 sickness claimed the lives of these gallant charismatic pioneers. They left a mark on their region that would be long remembered. Even among those who kept their distance from the charismata, their regard for the character of the Macdonald brothers was unquestioned, largely because the Macdonalds risked their lives ministering to the sick and dying during an outbreak of the deadly cholera disease. When other ministers fled the region, James and George could be found in homes and hospitals sharing Christ's love with the needy.

8. Assessment.

This three-year revival in the west of Scotland cannot be found in most history books, not even those focusing on revival movements. The scope of its influence has yet to be measured fully. This revival patterned various teachings and experiences of the Spirit's charismata long before these practices gained widespread acceptance in the 20th-century pentecostal and charismatic movements. The Scottish revival spawned two centers of revival: Irving's London ministry and the CAC, both of which exerted worldwide and lasting influence in the spread of charismatic expression in the church's life and worship. Only recently has evidence emerged to support a direct connection between Irving's teaching and the advent of North American pentecostalism (see ►New Apostolic Church [NAC]). Both the CAC and her "separated brethren," the NAC, penetrated North America with missionaries during much of the 19th century. With Irving being the father and theological founder of both movements, his name and writings would have been recognized widely by representatives of various Christian groups. All this was decades before the Azusa Street revival in 1906. More direct links to pentecostalism may yet be discovered as these phases of the movement receive more scholarly attention.

■ **Bibliography:** W. W. Andrews, *Edward Irving: A Review* (1900) ■ C. W. Boase, *Supplementary Narrative to the Elijah Ministry* (1870) ■ J. M. Campbell, *Reminiscences and Reflections* (1873) ■ J. B. Cardale, "On the Extraordinary Manifestations in Port Glasgow," *The Morning Watch* (1830) ■ T. Carlyle (apostle), *A Short History of the Apostolic Work* (1851) ■ D. W. Dorries, "Edward Irving and the 'Standing Sign' of Spirit Baptism," in G. B. McGee, ed., *Initial Evidence* (1991) ■ idem, "Nineteenth-Century British Christological Controversy, Centering upon Edward Irving's Doctrine of Christ's Human Nature" (Ph.D. diss., Aberdeen, 1988) ■ H. Drummond, *A Brief Account of the Commencement of the Lord's Work to Restore His Church* (1851) ■ C. G. Flegg, *Gathered under Apostles* (1992) ■ E. Irving, "Facts Connected with Recent Manifestations of Spiritual Gifts," *Fraser's Magazine* (1832) ■ P. Newell, "A. J. Scott and His Circle" (Ph.D. diss., Edinburgh, 1981) ■ R. Norton, *Memoirs of James and George Macdonald of Port-Glasgow* (1840) ■ A. J. Scott, *Neglected Truths* (1830) ■ G. Strachan, *The Pentecostal Theology of Edward Irving* (1988).   ■ D. W. Dorries

WESTON, EDWARD (NED) R. (1883–1947).

Edward R. Weston played a significant role in the early development of the Pentecostal Church of New Zealand, and later of the Apostolic Church as well. He was born of an Exclusive-Brethren family in Ireland and was converted at age 15. Two years later his family moved to London, where Weston made a practice of preaching in the open air at Hyde Park Corner. This did much to mold his forthright speaking style and his ability to communicate at the level of his hearers.

He emigrated to N.Z. in 1913 and became a Baptist minister, serving churches in Berhampore (Wellington), Takapuna, Tauranga, and Mosgiel. He received the baptism of the Spirit in 1922 and was strongly supportive of ►Smith Wigglesworth's two campaigns in 1922 and 1924. Weston later became pastor of the Wellington South branch of the New Zealand Evangelical Mission (later renamed the Pentecostal Church of New Zealand [PCNZ]). He was an exceptionally gifted Bible scholar and teacher, and he did much to formulate the doctrinal standards of the PCNZ. He eventually became chairman of the movement in 1931 but seceded with his congregation to join the Apostolic Church (AC) following its arrival in N.Z. in late 1933. His congregation in Newtown thus effectively became the first AC congregation in N.Z. Weston did much to establish the AC in N.Z., helping to set up seven new congregations in the first five months of 1934.

Weston moved to Australia in 1937, where he held several pastorates and became principal of the Apostolic Ministers' Training Center in Melbourne. Differences of opinion over constitutional issues led him to resign from the AC in 1943 and form an independent pentecostal congregation. Nevertheless, the esteem in which he was held was such that fellowship with his former Apostolic colleagues remained strong, and senior Apostolic ministers took part in his funeral in 1947.

■ **Bibliography:** J. E. Worsfold, *A History of the Charismatic Movements in New Zealand* (1974) ■ idem, *The Reverend and Mrs. Edward and Eily Weston* (1994).   ■ B. Knowles

WHEATON, ELIZABETH RYDER (1844–1923).

Social reformer and evangelist. Elizabeth Ryder was born to John and Mary Van Nest Ryder in Wayne County, OH. Her parents, both Christians, died by the time she was five years of age. At the death of her mother, Elizabeth was separated from her siblings and was not reunited with her brothers (J. M. and Emanuel) and her sister (Lida Ryder Hoffman) until 1902.

At first Elizabeth was placed in a foster home where she remained until the family moved away. Subsequently, she was reared by her grandparents. As a child she worshiped among the Methodists. Later she would describe her commitment to Christianity at this time as "normal."

At age 18 Elizabeth married J. A. Wheaton. They had one son, but within two years of their marriage both her husband and their infant son had died. Elizabeth's self-acknowledged conversion came in the wake of their deaths. In the years that followed, she heard of "holiness" and "the baptism of the Holy Spirit for service." She began to attend a Holiness church some distance from her home. It was there that she received her "sanctification." On Nov. 11, 1883, she claimed to have received a vision of Jesus in which she was asked to follow him. Thus she began her prison ministry.

Mother Wheaton, as she was frequently called, was known primarily as a prison evangelist, although she was also engaged in rescue work. She was not attached to any single denomination but ministered frequently in street meetings, especially in front of bars and houses of prostitution, on railroad cars, in Peniel Missions, and in various Crittenden rescue centers. From 1895 on, she made the Missionary Training Home in Tabor, IA, under the supervision of Elder Weavers, her home address.

For a time Wheaton was accompanied and assisted by a Mrs. Hattie Worcester Kelly. In later years Mother Wheaton continued her independent faith venture alone, ministering to those in state and federal prisons in nearly every state and territory of the U.S., and in Canada and Mexico. She carried numerous letters of reference, signed by governors and wardens alike. Her reputation was widely known, and she is said to have become such a well-known figure on the railroads that she was frequently allowed to travel at no charge.

Mother Wheaton was a featured speaker at the semiannual camp meeting of the Holiness Church in Southern California in Apr. 1905, where she told of her work in the slums and prisons and engaged in altar work among the seekers present.

In the spring of 1906 Wheaton was a guest in the ʼFrank Bartleman home, accompanying him to meetings at the cottage on ʼBonnie Brae Street and an all night prayer meeting at ʼJoseph Smale's First New Testament Church. She also went with Frank Bartleman on his first visit to the Apostolic Faith Mission on ʼAzusa Street. It was later reported in *The Apostolic Faith* that she had come "tarrying for her Pentecost." By Jan. 1907, at age 62, Henry McLain reported that Wheaton had gone to a meeting in Clearwater, CA, where she "was baptized with the Holy Spirit and spoke in two languages."

Always interested in foreign missions, Mother Wheaton made two trips to Europe. She was jailed in Edinburgh, Scotland, for holding a street meeting.

In her declining years, Mother Wheaton was unable to continue her heavy travel schedule. She suffered both physical and emotional trauma and was ultimately confined to her home in Tabor, IA. A letter she wrote just six weeks before her death indicates that she was lonely and living in anticipation of her imminent death. She died on July 28, 1923, at the Faith Home in Tabor, IA.

■ **Bibliography:** F. Bartleman, *How Pentecost Came to Los Angeles* (1925; repr. 1985) ■ "A Nationally Known Prison Worker Died Here Saturday," *Beacon-Enterprise* (Tabor, IA) 42 (31, 1923) ■ J. M. Washburn, *History and Reminiscences of the Holiness Church Work in Southern California and Arizona* (1912; repr. 1985) ■ E. R. Wheaton, *Prisons and Prayer or A Labor of Love* (1906).

■ C. M. Robeck Jr.

WHEELER, ROB (1932–).

Rob Wheeler's career spans the entire history of the New Life Churches of New Zealand (NLCNZ). He was a member of ʼRay Jackson's Bethel Chapel in Auckland from 1946 on and attended Jackson's 1951 Bible school in Sydney, Australia. Wheeler returned to N.Z. in June 1953, initially taking over the pastorate of the Auckland church and becoming pastor of the Tauranga Upper Room Fellowship the following year. He resigned in late 1957 to begin itinerant tent-crusade evangelism, modeled on the pattern of ʼOral Roberts and others in the U.S. The success of these campaigns led to the creation of a group of independent pentecostal churches that eventually evolved into the NLCNZ.

Wheeler also conducted numerous short-term evening Bible schools to provide Christian workers for these new churches. In 1964 he became pastor of the newly founded Auckland Christian Fellowship in Epsom, Auckland. In the 1980s Wheeler became increasingly involved in political issues and unsuccessfully stood for the Mount Albert seat in the 1987 general election. Wheeler was recognized as an apostle in the NLCNZ at their 1987 annual pastors' convention, but he resigned this role two years later due to ill health.

■ **Bibliography:** B. Knowles, "For the Sake of the Name: A History of the 'New Life Churches' from 1942 to 1965" (thesis, U. of

Otago, 1988) ▮ idem, "Some Aspects of the History of the New Life Churches of New Zealand 1960–1990" (diss., U. of Otago, 1994) ▮ B. Rudman, "For God and National, *New Zealand Listener* (Mar. 28, 1987) ▮ S. Stratford, "Christians Awake! Join the National Party, Save New Zealand," *Metro* (Nov. 1986) ▮ "Treasures of Grace: God Holds the Copyright," *Bible Deliverance* (Feb. 1961).

■ B. Knowles

WHETSTONE, ROSS (1919–). Pastor, educator, and Methodist charismatic leader. Ross Whetstone was a leader in organizing the United Methodist Renewal Service Fellowship (UMRSF) in 1977. At that time he held the Ruth Jones Cadwallader Chair of Evangelism at Scarritt College in Nashville (*Manna* [Dec. 1977]: 1). This is "a group of United Methodist Christians [who are] seeking to glorify Christ and serve his Body, the church, in all ministries which relate to renewal by the power of His Spirit" (*Manna* [Dec. 1987]: 3). He has served as the executive director of UMRSF and editor of *Manna*, the agency's newsletter.

After his baptism in the Holy Spirit (1937), Whetstone became active in the Salvation Army. He joined in 1938 and was commissioned an officer in 1939. In 1950 he transferred his ordination to the Central New York Conference of the Methodist Church. During the early 1950s he completed theological studies, first attending Pennsylvania State College at Mansfield and then Colgate-Rochester Divinity School. After several local pastorates in Pennsylvania and New York, he joined the national board of evangelism of the United Methodist Church (UMC) (1957) as leader for the Contact Teleministry movement. He then became assistant general secretary for the evangelism section in the UMC.

■ **Bibliography:** P. Guinn, "Ross Whetstone: Forty Years of Miracles," *Manna* 4 (4, Oct. 1980) ▮ R. Whetstone, ed., *Manna* 10 (2, 3, 4, 1987).   ■ J. A. Hewett

WHITE, KENT (1860–1940). Minister, evangelist, teacher, editor, and author. Born in Beverly, Randolf County, VA (later WV) to Francis Marion and Elizabeth (Buckley) White. Reared on a farm, Kent was educated in local schools. From 1882 on he attended courses at the University of Denver. On a trip through Montana in Mar. 1883 White preached to a Methodist congregation normally served by another pastor. There he met Mollie Alma Bridwell, whom he married in Denver, CO, on Dec. 21, 1887. Ordained a deacon (1889) and later an elder (1891) in the Colorado Methodist conference, White pioneered several churches and served as pastor in Lamar and Morrison. His connection with the Methodists was severed in 1902 when he identified with the fruit of his wife's evangelistic labor, known pejoratively as the "Holy Jumpers." This group organized in 1902 under the name Pillar of Fire.

The paths of the Whites repeatedly crossed those of pentecostals prior to 1909. During this period, White accepted the pentecostal teaching and embraced its experience, while Alma rejected glossolalia. It was this doctrinal difference between Alma and Kent that became the excuse for their separation in 1909. Kent identified with the Apostolic Faith, then in 1922 he moved to England, where he served as an Apostolic Faith pastor and teacher until 1939. Returning to Denver in 1939, he died there the following year. White was the author of *The Word of God Coming Again* (1919) and *The Hostel of the Good Shepherd* (1938), as well as numerous articles.

■ **Bibliography:** A. White, *Demons and Tongues* (1910) ▮ idem, *My Heart and My Husband* (1923) ▮ idem, *National Cyclopedia of American Biography* (194?), 35:152 ▮ idem, *The Story of My Life* (1921).   ■ C. M. Robeck Jr.

WHITEHEAD, CHARLES (1942–). Prominent lay leader in the ▸Catholic charismatic renewal (CCR). Whitehead obtained a B.A. in history from Durham University, U.K., in 1965. Charles, brought up Catholic, and his wife Sue, brought up Anglican, came to living faith through contact with local Baptists in 1975. Whitehead, a successful businessman in the paper and pulp industry, has given increasing time to the charismatic renewal since the mid 1980s, though he was the managing director of paper companies from 1980 to 1995 and is chairman of the Institute of Paper in the U.K. (1996–).

Whitehead joined the National Service Committee of Catholic Charismatic Renewal in England and Wales in 1981, becoming chairman in 1986. In 1989 he joined the ICCRO (now ▸International Catholic Charismatic Renewal Services) council in Rome, becoming president in 1990. In this international position, Whitehead has played an important role as a strong witness to the work of the Holy Spirit and as a trusted facilitator and advisor. His gift for popular teaching is seen in his book *Pentecost Is for Living* (1993).   ■ P. D. Hocken

WIERWILLE, VICTOR PAUL (1916–85). Organization executive. Founder of The Way International, Victor Paul Wierwille is significant to the history of pentecostalism because of his routinization of glossolalia. From 1941 to 1957 he served as a pastor in the Evangelical and Reformed Church, a body later merged into the United Church of Christ. Early in his ministry Wierwille began a radio Bible study successively called the *Vesper Chimes*, *The Chimes Hour*, and *The Chimes Hour Youth Caravan*, which provided the foundation later for the Power for Abundant Living course and for The Way International. In 1951 he experienced tongues through the ministry of pentecostal evangelist J. E. Stiles, who claimed to have developed a technique for inducing the gift. Two years later Wierwille inaugurated his 12-session course, which culminated in students being taught to speak in tongues. In 1957 he established the headquarters of The Way, an organization often considered cult-like, for nurturing converts, on the farm near New Knoxville, OH, where he had been born. He died there in 1985 at age 68. At that time The Way International claimed more than 30,000 adherents. It is thought that membership has since declined, with no more than 20,000 in 1995 and around 10,000 in 2000.

■ **Bibliography:** W. J. Cummins, *The Living Word Speaks* (1981) ■ J. A. MacCollam, *The Way of Victor Paul Wierwille* (1978) ■ R. L. Sumner, *Jesus Christ Is God* (1983).   ■ C. E. Jones

WIGGLESWORTH, SMITH

(1859–1947). English evangelist known throughout many parts of the world for his strong faith and legendary answers to prayer. An indication of Wigglesworth's continued popularity is the fact that no fewer than six books by or about him are in print—three of which were first published in the 1980s. What makes his life more unusual than most of the healing evangelists of the 20th century is that he was hardly known outside of his hometown until he was 48. That was in 1907, when he received the pentecostal experience at Sunderland under the ministry of ▸A. A. and ▸Mary Boddy. Until that happened he was operating a plumbing business in Bradford and assisting his wife Polly in a mission. He had been an aggressive personal evangelist but did little preaching.

Born to a very poor family, Wigglesworth was deprived of an education because he had to help support his family from the time he was six. As a consequence, he never learned to read well until he was an adult. Later he claimed he never read anything but the Bible. He would not take credit for two books, *Ever Increasing Faith* (c. 1924) and *Faith That Prevails* (1938), explaining that others had taken his sermons in shorthand and published them.

Wigglesworth's healing ministry began before he was baptized in the Spirit. He received healing from a ruptured appendix and wrote later that God gave him great faith for people suffering with appendicitis. He would usually conclude a sermon by praying for the sick, regardless of what text he had taken.

Wigglesworth's wife, Polly, died about the time his ministry began to broaden. He was soon preaching in other countries, becoming one of the better-known evangelists in the pentecostal movement. His daughter, Alice Salter, who was a missionary to Africa, frequently accompanied him on his international trips.

Wigglesworth was often accused of being rough on the people who came for prayer. It was claimed that he would strike a sick person with his fist; a person suffering from

Smith Wigglesworth, a plumber with a limited formal education, who, after being baptized in the Spirit in 1907, became a noted pentecostal evangelist.

stomach problems might receive prayer along with a sharp hit to the afflicted area. Others who were crippled were ordered to run across the platform after he prayed for them. Criticism came from such leaders as ▸E. S. Williams, former general superintendent of the General Council of the ▸Assemblies of God. Close associates, however, told of Wigglesworth's compassion for suffering people, often praying and weeping over requests he had received.

Wigglesworth's ministry centered on salvation for the unconverted, healing for the sick, and a call to believers to be baptized in the Holy Spirit. ▸Donald Gee, in reporting Wigglesworth's death in 1947, wrote that a "unique ministry, a gift of Christ to His church, has been taken from the worldwide Pentecostal Movement. He died in the harness—nearly 88 years of age."

■ **Bibliography:** "Awaiting the Resurrection," *PE* (Apr. 5, 1947) ■ S. Frodsham, *Smith Wigglesworth: Apostle of Faith* (1948) ■ W. Warner, taped interview with E. S. Williams, AG Archives (1979).   ■ W. E. Warner

WILKERSON, DAVID RAY

(1931–). Founder of Teen Challenge and evangelist. David Wilkerson was born and reared in a pentecostal home under the influence of pentecostal preaching by both his parents, Kenneth and Ann

Wilkerson, and his grandfather, Jay Wilkerson. He attended Central Bible Institute (now College) from 1951 to 1952. He and his wife Gwen have four children.

Wilkerson started his ministry in a traditional way by pastoring a small church in Philipsburg, PA. Yet he was innovative in that he produced a television program from the Assemblies of God (AG) church in Philipsburg at a time when many pentecostal and Holiness people were questioning whether or not it was worldly for Spirit-filled Christians to own or watch a television.

The dramatic story of Wilkerson's launch into a worldwide ministry is well told in the book *The Cross and the Switchblade* (1963). His faith in the Bible as the Word of God has been the balance wheel that has guided him in some unusual areas of ministry. His prayer life has been the place where God has been able to get his attention, when no one else could persuade him.

During a prayer vigil in 1958 Wilkerson's attention was drawn to an article in *Life* magazine. The story graphically depicted the murder trial of seven young men who had killed a crippled boy, Michael Farmer. As he looked at the artist's drawing of these seven young men sitting in the courtroom, he did not see seven ruthless murderers; he saw scared young men. He asked himself if they had ever heard the story of Jesus.

Led by the Holy Spirit, Wilkerson went to New York City to try to talk to the seven young men. He was told he would have to get permission from the trial judge. Unable to contact the judge, he again was told to attend court and ask to speak to the judge in his chambers. This led to his being ejected from the courtroom and getting his picture on the front page of the *New York Daily News* (Mar. 1, 1958). Although Wilkerson was unable to talk with these young men personally, the experience was used by God to begin his ministry to the gangs on the streets of New York. The picture in the newspaper became a passport to the gangs. The gangs welcomed him as "the guy the cops don't like," and Wilkerson seized the opportunity to witness to them. The success of his street evangelism led to the founding of the ▶Teen Challenge ministry with close ties to the AG. Wilkerson was appointed executive director of this New York City ministry in 1958 and continues to the present to hold this position. Many of the new converts were drug addicts and alcoholics, so Wilkerson established a home in Brooklyn where these young men and women could receive intensive discipleship training.

Many graduates of Teen Challenge chose to enter full-time Christian ministry. They often faced difficulty being accepted into established Bible colleges, so in 1966 Wilkerson established Teen Challenge Bible Institute, Rhinebeck, NY, to provide Bible school education for those completing the Teen Challenge program.

The growth of the Teen Challenge ministry and its spread across the U.S. and overseas brought about an ever-increasing public exposure in all media to Wilkerson and his message. The bold stance he took on the "born again" experience and being filled with the Holy Spirit with the evidence of speaking in tongues caused a stir in the church world. The beginning of the charismatic movement in many circles, both Roman Catholic and Protestant, was sparked by *The Cross and the Switchblade*.

Students and teachers at Duquesne University read about speaking in tongues in *The Cross and the Switchblade*. A hunger was created for this experience that could transform their lives. As a result, the modern "outpouring" of the Holy Spirit among Roman Catholics traces back to Duquesne University. By 1969, 42 ministers in the United Methodist Church in the Western Conference in Pennsylvania had testified to the experience of speaking in tongues. They described *The Cross and the Switchblade* as the key in creating a hunger for a personal encounter with the Holy Spirit.

The widespread popularity of Wilkerson's book resulted in many invitations for him to preach to a wide spectrum of inter- and intra-denominational circles. His ministry soon expanded to preaching at citywide crusades across America and Canada. In 1972 Wilkerson established World Challenge to coordinate his ministry outside of New York City. Through World Challenge he expanded his citywide crusades, summer street evangelism, and missionary outreach. He has assisted in starting numerous Teen Challenge centers in countries around the world. Wilkerson has been a prolific writer in calling the church to the work of evangelism and in spreading the prophetic message of repentance and holiness (19 books by 1985). World Challenge also produced several movies on evangelism and prophetic themes. In 1987 David Wilkerson; his brother, Don Wilkerson; and Robert Philips founded Times Square Church in New York City. He resigned from the AG in the same year.

Wilkerson's books include *The Cross and the Switchblade* (1963), *Twelve Angels from Hell* (1966), *The Little People* (1966), *Hey, Preach . . . You're Coming Through!* (1968), *Rebel's Bible* (1970), *The Untapped Generation* (1971), *Suicide* (1978), *A Final Warning* (1991), *Set Thy Trumpet to Thy Mouth* (1993).   ■ F. M. Reynolds

WILKERSON, RALPH A. (1927–). The founder and pastor of ▶Melodyland Christian Center. Born in 1927 to Benjamin and Lela Wilkerson in Ponca City, OK, Wilkerson graduated from Tulsa University and was ordained by the Assemblies of God in 1948. He married Allene Work; they have two daughters, Angela and Debi. Wilkerson is the author of several books: *Loneliness: The World's Number One Killer* (1978); *The Redwoods* (1977); *Success from Stress* (1978);

Satellites of the Spirit (1978); *ESP or HSP?* (1978); and *Beyond and Back* (1977). For the last of these Wilkerson received a Religion in Media (RIM) award in 1977. In that same year he received an honorary doctorate from Oral Roberts University.

Ralph Wilkerson expanded the outreach of Melodyland Christian Center to include a delinquency prevention center (24-hour hotline), a school of theology, and a Christian high school and college. For many years he sponsored the annual Melodyland Charismatic Clinics that featured speakers from many denominations and attracted people from around the world. In June 1999 Wilkerson retired as senior pastor at Melodyland Christian Center to become an evangelist.

◼ J. R. Williams

WILLANS, JEAN STONE (1924–). Important figure in the origins of the charismatic movement. In 1959 Jean Stone was a high-church Episcopalian, belonging to St. Mark's Church, Van Nuys, CA. That fall she was baptized in the Spirit and joined a group of parishioners likewise touched by God, including the rector, ˃Dennis Bennett. After Bennett announced his experience and then resigned (Apr. 1960), Stone was responsible for the national publicity in *Newsweek* and *Time*. In 1960 she founded the ˃Blessed Trinity Society, which published numerous leaflets and pamphlets and, beginning in 1961, a quarterly magazine, *Trinity*, the first nonpentecostal journal in America devoted to this new move of the Spirit. With others in the society, Stone organized conferences called "Christian Advances" in the Pacific Coast states. With ˃Harald Bredesen she was responsible for the term *charismatic renewal* being used to designate the new movement.

Between 1960 and 1965 Stone was an indefatigable promoter of charismatic renewal in the historic churches. Vigorous and determined, with a directness of approach, she traveled frequently, including a brief visit to Britain in 1964. Stone's influence in America declined in 1966 with the cessation of *Trinity* magazine, which was linked to financial troubles outside Stone's control, and to her divorce and subsequent marriage to Richard Willans.

The Willanses then moved to the Far East, settling in Hong Kong in 1968. They founded the Society of Stephen, led an ecumenical prayer group, and assisted with the beginning of Catholic charismatic renewal in Hong Kong. They ministered in particular to drug addicts and had close association with the work of Jackie Pullinger. The Willanses returned to Altadena, CA, in 1983. Jean Stone Willans's account of her charismatic experience was published in *The Acts of the Green Apples* (1973, rev. 1995). In 1995 the Hong Kong government honored the Willanses for their ministry with a memorial plaque in Kowloon. Influenced by the Convergence Movement, Jean (1998) and Richard (1997) have

been ordained bishops by an archbishop with orders from the Eastern Church of St. Thomas Christians.

See also BLESSED TRINITY SOCIETY.

◼ P. D. Hocken

WILLIAMS, ERNEST SWING (1885–1981). Pastor, denominational executive, and author. Born in 1885 in San Bernardino, CA, Williams entered the home of Christian parents who were charter members of the First Holiness Church in that city (his middle name was derived from James R. Swing, the president of the Southern California and Arizona Holiness Association at the time of his birth). His father was a carpenter who supplemented the family income through odd jobs. Because of the poor economic situation, Williams's education was at first limited to grammar school. Later, when the family moved to Santa Ana in 1899, he attended business school for a time.

In 1904 Williams made a commitment to Christ. Shortly thereafter he and a friend decided to enroll in a "Holiness school in Chicago." They got as far as Denver, where he worked on a ranch. His mother wrote weekly; she told him of the ˃Azusa Street revival, and in the fall of 1906 Williams went to the mission on Azusa Street, where, on Oct. 2, 1906, he received his pentecostal experience.

Almost immediately Williams was drawn toward ministry. He continued to attend the Azusa Street Mission, telling Pastor ˃William J. Seymour that he wanted to enter the ministry. In his timidity, he interpreted Seymour's silence as not affirming his call. For a time he was "defeated," but during the first camp meeting of Azusa in Aug. 1907, Williams was asked to accept the leadership of an Apostolic Faith mission in San Francisco. He was soon ordained and remained in San Francisco for two years. Following a short pastorate in Colorado Springs, he returned to the West Coast, where he engaged from 1909 to 1911 in evangelistic work. In 1911 he married Laura O. Jacobson, from Portland, OR.

The Williamses moved eastward, conducting meetings in Kentucky and Indiana, and in 1912 they accepted a two-year pastorate in Conneaut, OH. The couple then went to Bradford, a town in the mountains of Pennsylvania. While there, Williams read of the founding meeting of the Assemblies of God (AG) in Hot Springs, AR (Apr. 1914). He wrote, asking to be enrolled in this new general council. Late that same year he was recognized as an ordained minister with the AG.

Williams's early years of ministry were difficult, filled with hardships and self-denial. He was invited in 1917 to serve as pastor of Bethel Pentecostal Assembly in Newark, NJ, a significant pentecostal church in the region.

In 1920 Williams became pastor of Highway Mission Tabernacle in Philadelphia. The congregation was small at first, but it grew rapidly, purchased an old Presbyterian church building, and expanded it with a large balcony. The year 1920 also brought him into the position of executive presbyter for the Eastern District of the AG. For a decade Williams and his wife remained as pastors of Highway Tabernacle, but his exposure as an executive presbyter in the East and as general presbyter for the new movement, as well as his election to the executive presbytery of the denomination in 1927, led to nationwide exposure.

The 1929 general council of the AG elected Williams to the office of general superintendent for the denomination, and the following October he left Philadelphia and moved to Springfield, MO, where he served until 1949. Membership in the AG tripled under his leadership, as did the number of churches and ordained ministers. Missionary giving expanded, and new mission fields were opened.

Williams's term as general superintendent was marked by the Great Depression of the 1930s. He provided a strong sense of stability for the denomination during those years. It was he who led the AG, cautiously at first, into association with the ᵀNational Association of Evangelicals in 1943. He helped pioneer the Radio Department, establishing *Sermons in Song*, a 15-minute weekly radio broadcast, for which he began preaching on Jan. 6, 1946. He guided the AG into dialogue with other world and American pentecostals, participating in the initial meetings of the ᵀPentecostal World Conference and giving the keynote address at the first convention of the ᵀPentecostal Fellowship of North America (1949).

Upon Williams's retirement from the office of general superintendent, he taught at Central Bible Institute for seven years and served as its academic dean for a year. He continued to speak and to write.

Throughout his ministry, Williams had submitted short synopses of his sermons for publication in the *Pentecostal Evangel*, the denomination's weekly publication. Later he wrote several books, including the first systematic theology by a pentecostal. Williams also had a weekly question-and-answer column in the *Evangel*. Many of these questions and answers, like those of the first general superintendent, ᵀE. N. Bell, were collected and published in book form by ᵀGospel Publishing House.

Laura Williams died on Feb. 26, 1980, and Ernest S. Williams spent his remaining months in Maranatha Village, an AG retirement center in Springfield, MO.

■ **Bibliography:** "Long-Time General Council Leader with Christ," *PE* (Dec. 13, 1981) ■ "Memories of Azusa Street Mission,"

PE (Apr. 4, 1966) ■ W. Menzies, *Anointed to Serve* (1971) ■ D. D. Merrifield, ed., "The Life Story of Reverend Ernest S. Williams" (unpub., 1980) ■ "Pentecostal Origins: James S. Tinney Interviews E. S. Williams," *Agora* (Winter 1979) ■ E. S. Williams, *Encouragement to Faith* (1946) ■ idem, *A Faithful Minister* (1941) ■ idem, *Not I but Christ* (1939) ■ idem, *Questions and Answers on Faith and Practice* (1963) ■ idem, *Systematic Theology*, 3 vols. (1935) ■ idem, *Temptation and Triumph* (n.d.) ■ idem, *Your Questions Answered* (1968).

■ C. M. Robeck Jr.

WILLIAMS, J. RODMAN (1918–). Presbyterian charismatic theologian and educator. Born Aug. 21, 1918, to John Rodman and Odessa Lee (Medford) Williams in Clyde, NC. Williams received the A.B. from Davidson College (NC) in 1939, graduating Phi Beta Kappa. He earned his B.D. (1943) and Th.M. (1944) at Union Theological Seminary (VA), was ordained in the Presbyterian Church of the U.S. (1943), and served as a U.S. marine chaplain (1944–46). He later earned the Ph.D. in philosophy of religion at Columbia University and Union Theological Seminary (New York City, 1954).

J. Rodman Williams, a Presbyterian pastor and seminary educator who was an early participant in the charismatic renewal. Among his writings is *Renewal Theology*, a systematic theology from a charismatic perspective.

In 1949 Williams married Johanna Servaas and was appointed associate professor of philosophy at Beloit College (WI), where he served until 1952. Thereafter he was pastor of First Presbyterian Church, Rockford, IL (1952–59), then professor of systematic theology at Austin Presbyterian Seminary (1959–72). As an early participant in charismatic renewal, he played an active role, becoming president of the International Presbyterian Charismatic Communion. In 1972 he became the founding president and professor of theology at ᵀMelodyland School of Theology in Anaheim, CA. During that time he participated in the International Roman Catholic-Pentecostal ᵀDialogue.

Currently Williams serves as professor of theology at the Regent (formerly CBN) University School of Divinity in Virginia Beach, VA. In 1985 he served as president of the Society for Pentecostal Studies. Among his many publications are *The Era of the Spirit* (1971), *The Pentecostal Reality* (1972), and *The Gift of the Holy Spirit Today* (1980). Between 1988 and 1992, Williams completed work on his three-volume *Renewal Theology*, a major study in systematic theology from a charismatic perspective (reissued in one volume, 1996).

■ C. M. Robeck Jr.

WILLIAMS, RALPH DARBY (1902–82). Pioneer missionary to Latin America. Williams was born in Sudbrook, Monmouthshire, England. He was converted and baptized in the Holy Spirit during a pentecostal revival in 1919. Later he and his brother Richard (d. 1931; see L. J. Walker, *Peruvian Gold*, 1985, 56) traveled to the U.S. and graduated from Glad Tidings Bible Institute (later Bethany Bible College) in 1924, where he studied the missiology of Roland Allen. A year later he was ordained by the Assemblies of God (AG) and married fellow student Jewyl Stoddard (d. 1976); they had four children.

Before leaving England, *Alice E. Luce, an indigenous church pioneer among Mexican-Americans, had visited Ralph and Richard Williams and encouraged them to consider becoming missionaries to Latin America. Later Ralph and his brother received appointments (1926) as AG missionaries and assisted Luce in her church and in the Berean Bible Institute (later Latin American Bible Institute) in San Diego, CA. Ralph served as associate pastor and instructor in the school.

After teaching briefly in Mexico City, the Williamses arrived in El Salvador in 1929 as the first AG missionaries to that country and contributed to the organization and guidance of the pentecostals there. A constitution was approved in 1930 that placed the churches on an indigenous footing. Ralph Williams also established a Bible institute in 1931 and introduced, with Francisco R. Arbizu, the "Reglamento" ("Standard for Doctrine and Conduct") for church members and pastors.

After a furlough to the U.S., Williams returned to El Salvador in 1936 with *Melvin L. Hodges and his wife Lois, newly appointed missionaries to Central America. In the following year Williams built Bethel Church and Bethel Bible Institute in Santa Ana, El Salvador. Election as field superintendent for Central America followed in 1940 and considerably increased the scope of his work. During his ministry, the number of churches grew from 12 to more than 400 in the region. Later activities took Williams to Nicaragua, Costa Rica, Honduras, Guatemala, Mexico, Venezuela, Colombia, Panama, Cuba, Puerto Rico, and the Spanish Eastern District of the AG. He married Lois Alma Stewart in 1976 and returned to the U.S. to work at the office of Program of Applied Christian Education (PACE), an AG educational agency that provides advanced training for ministers in Latin America.

Williams's contribution to foreign missions lay in his application of indigenous-church principles for the building of strong national churches and in pioneering quality educational training for national pastors and leaders. His Bible institute program in El Salvador became a model for other such institutions throughout Latin America.

■ **Bibliography:** J. A. Carpenter and W. R. Shenk, *Earthen Vessels: American Evangelicals and Foreign Missions, 1880–1980* (1990)

▌ E. L. Cleary and H. W. Stewart-Gambino, eds., *Power, Politics, and Pentecostals in Latin America* (1997) ▌ G. B. McGee, *This Gospel Shall Be Preached* (1986) ▌ idem, "Missionaries with Christ," *PE* (July 25, 1982) ▌ R. D. Williams, memoirs (unpub., 1981).
                                                  ■ G. B. McGee; B. A. Pavia

WILSON, FREDERICK A. (1909–82). Fred Wilson was converted under the ministry of Congregationalist evangelist Lionel Fletcher in the 1920s and water baptized by Pastor Joseph Kemp at the prominent Baptist Tabernacle in Auckland. Wilson was influenced by the pentecostal ministry of *A. H. Dallimore in 1932, becoming convinced of the reality of the baptism in the Spirit and drawn to the British-Israel doctrine. He received the baptism of the Spirit the following year. After a successful period in the clothing business, he became in 1946 the pioneer minister of a small mission in Avondale, Auckland, that ultimately became the Church of Christ (Foursquare Gospel) New Zealand. Although this church was less charismatic than other pentecostal groups and had somewhat puritanical and separatist practices, stressing separation from the world and the wearing of head coverings by women in church, it spread rapidly. By 1951 it had built a church in neighboring Mount Roskill and continued to attract more than 1,000 people to its services throughout the 1960s. The church appears to have relaxed its puritanism to some extent, and by 1985 its facilities included a gymnasium, library, bookshop, and youth camp. It had also opened branches in other suburbs of Auckland and in Osaka, Japan.

■ **Bibliography:** James E. Worsfold, *A History of the Charismatic Movements in New Zealand* (1974).   ■ B. Knowles

WIMBER, JOHN (1934–98). Founding pastor of the *Vineyard Christian Fellowship of Anaheim, CA, and president of Vineyard Ministries International. Born and raised in a non-Christian home, he developed a successful career in the music industry. A dramatic conversion experience in 1963 drew him into a commitment to full-time Christian service. After graduation from Azusa Pacific University, Wimber was recorded (ordained) in 1970 by the California Yearly Meeting of Friends and served as copastor of the Yorba Linda Friends Church for five years.

In 1975 Wimber joined *C. Peter Wagner of the Fuller Evangelistic Association in pioneering the Charles E. Fuller Institute of Evangelism and Church Growth. In his role as church growth consultant, he worked with hundreds of churches across the denominational spectrum.

Wimber left Fuller to establish the Anaheim Vineyard in 1977. Soon afterward he and his congregation began praying for the sick and, after an agonizing period of ineffectiveness, began seeing dramatic results. This launched Wimber, a gifted leader and public speaker, into a renowned national

John Wimber, founding pastor of the Vineyard Christian Fellowship of Anaheim, CA, and president of Vineyard Ministries International.

and international "signs and wonders" ministry that has had a profound effect on tens of thousands of charismatics and noncharismatics alike. Meanwhile his church grew to 5,000, and he sparked an aggressive church-planting effort that now includes more than 500 churches affiliated with the Association of Vineyard churches. Wimber continued leading the ministries affiliated with Vineyard until his death in 1998.

Wimber lectured with Wagner in the Fuller Theological Seminary Doctor of Ministry program, beginning in 1975. He first introduced a lecture, "Signs, Wonders and Church Growth," in 1981. Then, from 1982 to 1985, he taught a full course in the Fuller School of World Mission, "The Miraculous and Church Growth," which became not only the most popular course in the seminary's history but also the most controversial.

■ **Bibliography:** E. Gibbs, "My Friend John Wimber," in *Signs and Wonders Today*, ed. C. Peter Wagner (1987) ■ K. N. Springer, "Applying the Gift to Everyday Life," *Charisma* (Sept. 1985) ■ T. Stafford, "Testing the Wine from John Wimber's Vineyard," *Christianity Today* (Aug. 8, 1986) ■ J. Wimber, *Power Healing* (1987) ■ J. Wimber with K. Springer, *Power Evangelism* (1986).

■ C. P. Wagner

WINSETT, ROGER EMMET (1876–1952). A popular songwriter and songbook publisher in the early years of the pentecostal movement. Winsett's own compositions included

"In the Great Triumphant Morning," "The Message of His Coming," and others, but he is best known for the many songbooks he published during the first half of the 20th century. He obtained rights to hundreds of songs, including "In the City Where the Lamb Is the Light," "Look to the Lamb of God," "Joy Unspeakable," "Victory," "Victory Ahead," and "Living by Faith."

The R. E. Winsett Music Company was later purchased by Sacred Music Company.   ■ W. E. Warner

WISDOM, WORD OF Word of wisdom (Gk. *logos sophia*) is one of several charismata; mentioned by Paul only in 1 Cor. 12:8. The fact that Paul does not elaborate on the use of this charism or provide further definition of its character has left it open to a variety of interpretations. In pentecostal circles it has been commonly understood to be a word of revelation given by the Holy Spirit to provide wisdom to the Christian community at a particular time of need, often applying scriptural wisdom to the situation. It may best be understood by looking at the larger wisdom tradition of Israel in general, then by studying the concept of wisdom as it appears within the context of 1 Corinthians.

In the tradition of Israel, wisdom played an important role. This may be observed by studying the various forms that it took in the literature of the nation. It was present in the preaching of Qoheleth and in the extended poetry of Job. It appeared often in the pithy one- and two-line proverbs, and it was both personified and highly praised in Proverbs 8. Wisdom made its appearance in other OT writings as well. The Spirit or *rûaḥ* of God was believed to have provided wisdom, literally, to have made "wise-hearted" (*el kol ḥomkmê lemb*) those who made clothes for members of the Aaronic priesthood (Ex. 28:3). Joshua was said to have received the spirit of wisdom through the laying on of hands (Deut. 34:9), and it was anticipated that the messianic figure would also receive the spirit of wisdom (Isa. 11:2).

In addition there are several references that connect the subject of wisdom (Heb. *ḥomkma*) to that of the *rûaḥ* of God. One example occurs in Gen. 41, where we are told that Pharaoh dreamed a dream in which seven gaunt cows had devoured seven healthy ones, and seven thin stalks of grain had swallowed up seven healthy ones. His own court magicians and wise men were unable to interpret it for him. Joseph was summoned. He told Pharaoh that God would give him the answer. He went on to interpret the dream as meaning that seven abundant years of crop production would be followed by seven lean years and to recommend that Pharaoh appoint a discerning and wise person to oversee Egypt's agricultural production during the good years to ensure survival in the lean ones.

Pharaoh acknowledged the wisdom of the plan. He asked his own court officials, "Can we find anyone like this man, one in whom is the Spirit of God *[rûaḥ 'elohîm]?*" Turning back to Joseph, Pharaoh continued, "Since God has made all this known to you, there is no one so discerning and wise *[wᵉhakam]* as you" (Gen. 41:38–39). Thus, the *rûaḥ* was recognized as being with Joseph. Wisdom was identified within a specific situation, given to a particular end. The interpretation of the dream, with its application to Egypt's need, provided also the revelation of wisdom made known by God. The result was not only that Egypt was saved through the systematic storage of grain but that ultimately it proved to be God's means for preserving the Abrahamic line.

The prophet Daniel was also skilled in wisdom, endowed with knowledge, and capable of understanding visions and dreams (Dan. 1:4, 17). God was the source of Daniel's wisdom, for he acknowledged that God

> gives wisdom to the wise
> and knowledge to the discerning.
> He reveals deep and hidden things;
> He knows what lies in darkness (2:21–22).

In Nebuchadnezzar's second year as regent over Babylon, the king had a dream that none of his wise men could discern or interpret. Daniel, concerned that the king had overreacted by sending forth an order to destroy all his men, rallied three of his friends to pray that God would reveal the dream and its meaning to him. The answer came in the form of a vision, and the "mystery" was revealed. Daniel informed Nebuchadnezzar that God had given him the key. He advised, "This mystery has been revealed to me, not because I have greater wisdom *(homkma)* than other living men, but so that you, O king, may know the interpretation and that you may understand what went through your mind" (Dan. 2:30). After Daniel told him the dream and its interpretation, the king declared, "Surely, your God is God of gods and Lord of kings, and a revealer of mysteries, for you were able to reveal this mystery" (2:47).

Later Nebuchadnezzar issued a decree in which he spelled out that his own wise men (4:6 [MT 4:3]) had been unable to reveal either the dream or its meaning but that Daniel, in whom the king identified what he called the "Spirit of the gods" *(rûaḥ 'elohîm,* 4:8–9 [MT 4:5–6]), was able to do both. Once again, the idea of wisdom, the presence of the *rûaḥ* or Spirit, and the fact of revelation are all present. The word itself is specific and interpretive in nature, and it ultimately led to Nebuchadnezzar's recognition that Daniel's God is indeed God.

The term "wisdom" (Gk. *sophia*) is an important one for the apostle Paul; and it is with him that we meet the charism. It appears in the Pauline corpus 28 times, of which 17 are found in 1 Corinthians, the majority of which occur in 1:18–4:21. Paul stood squarely within the tradition of the Hebrews and was well versed in both Jewish and Greek views of wisdom. In the Corinthian situation, however, it is almost certain that he takes on the terms "knowledge" and "wisdom" from a group of the Corinthians themselves. This leads him, in his first letter to Corinth, to distinguish between two types of wisdom: human wisdom, or the wisdom of the "wise," and the wisdom of God.

The wisdom of the "wise" is a form of wisdom that is an intellectual accomplishment pursued especially by the Gentiles (1 Cor. 1:22). The acquisition of this worldly wisdom was considered to be a status symbol (1:26–27). Before God, however, it appears as a foolish quest (1:20; 3:19), a human attainment that falls below even the "foolishness" of God (1:25). Humanity has sought to know God. They have pursued salvation through the attainment of wisdom, but through the divine plan people have been unable to know God in this way (1:21). Their "wisdom" has been of a speculative nature. Ultimately, God will destroy the wisdom of the "wise" (1:19). It seems clear that Paul was not disparaging the intellectual attainment of wisdom per se but the acquisition of wisdom, which was thought to be inherently salvific. Such humanly derived wisdom was ultimately doomed to failure and would not transcend the ages (2:6).

In contrast to human wisdom, the wisdom of God was described as a secret and hidden wisdom (2:7) that goes uncomprehended by the natural human being (2:13–16) as well as by demonic powers (2:8). This wisdom is revealed *(apekalypsen* [cf. Eph. 3:3–6]) by the Spirit (2:10). It is related to the plan of salvation (2:7, 9), and it has its origin in the mind of God (2:11) from eternity past (2:7). Its purpose is the glorification of God's people (2:7), and it involves the impartation or interpretation *(synkrinontes)*—perhaps more literally, "making a judgment by means of comparison" of spiritual truth, to those who possess the Spirit (2:12–13). Thus the utterance or word of wisdom comes through the Spirit in such a way as to proclaim Christ, the wisdom of God, crucified.

Isaiah wrote that the Spirit of wisdom *(rûaḥ homkma)* would come upon the shoot of the stump of Jesse (Isa. 11:2). Hence, both testaments perceive the source of God's wisdom to be the Spirit. In Isaiah's prophecy this bestowal of wisdom would, among other things, enable the messianic figure to rule with righteousness (11:4–5). He would also assemble the outcasts of Israel (v. 12), recover a remnant (v. 11), and destroy their enemies (vv. 14–16). In short, the concepts that Paul mentions as being present in Jesus (1 Cor. 1:30), including wisdom, righteousness, sanctification, and redemption, may have their background in this Isa. 11 prophecy. It appears that the wisdom of God is provided so that God's people may have direction within the ongoing plan of God. It is a form of spiritual guidance. Thus the suggestion of James (1:5) that those who lack wisdom should ask God for it may apply to the general category of wisdom as a way of life so prevalent among the people of Israel and the wisdom of tradition, but it may also take on a special significance in relationship to utterances of wisdom that may be requested to fill a specific need.

In 1 Cor. 12:8 Paul calls this charism a "word" *(logos)*, "message," or "utterance" of wisdom. The connection between wisdom and *logos* in the form of "wise words," or "wisdom characterized by word (rhetoric)" may be all that Paul means by this construction as some have suggested. Yet the fact that *logos* appears in the same way with knowledge raises the distinct possibility that Paul has in mind a *specific type* of utterance. It is a word, revealed by God, providing direction from the wisdom of God, which may interpret a situation and enable a congregation to move in accordance with the will of God in light of the plan of salvation. Not all Christians are given this gift, since it is sovereignly distributed by the Holy Spirit (12:11) for the community welfare (12:7–8).

In the postapostolic era, the word of wisdom continued to be accepted as a legitimate charism. Justin Martyr *(Dialog with Trypho* 87) relied on Isa. 11:2 to explain the continuing spirit of wisdom in the church. Origen worked with the Pauline catalog of gifts in 1 Cor. 12 to argue that the charismata there were listed in descending order of value to the life of the church. The word of wisdom, which Origen described as possessing an intuitive or transrational *(themoremma)* character *(On Prayer* 25:2), was singled out as God's greatest gift *(Comm. on Matt.* 3). Through it, prophets spoke *(Exhort. to Mart.* 8), and the more intelligent Christians came to understand the "spiritual significance" of Scripture *(On First Prin.* Pref. 8). This enabled them to be Bible teachers *(Ag. Celsus* 1:44; *Comm. on Matt.* 15:37; 16:13).

Origen's observations that Paul gave a hierarchy of charisms in 1 Cor. 12:8–10, as well as his connection of the word of wisdom with the prophet and with the teacher are common in the church today. The weakness in the theory of hierarchy in this particular catalog of gifts, however, is that it fails to take seriously all other Pauline catalogs of gifts (Rom. 12:6–8; 1 Cor. 12:28–30; Eph. 4:11) as being either legitimate catalogs or as listing legitimate charisms.

The connection of words of wisdom with prophecy or the view that words of wisdom are a form of prophetic speech is a common one. Jesus told his disciples that when they were brought before those who would persecute them, he would give them words (lit. "a mouth" *[stoma]*) *and* wisdom *(sophia)* to respond (Luke 21:15; Matt. 10:19–20). Early Christians viewed these words alternately as prophetic words and words of wisdom (e.g., *Cyprian, Ep.* 10.4; 57.4; 58.5; 76.5; 81.1). Such manifestations and more particularly those utterances that revealed the mind of God in specific ways are often denied as having validity since the completion of the canon (Unger, Baxter) or are tolerated with ambivalence, leaning toward condemnation (Bridge and Phypers).

Fears motivating such arguments are real, since the understanding of this charism as a form of prophetic speech must include the claims of the Mormon "prophet" Joseph Smith, who allegedly received a "word of wisdom" in 1833 on the evils of tobacco, wine, and hot drinks such as coffee *(Doc. & Cov.* 89). Questions are raised relating to the infallibility of such utterances and their relationship to Scripture, as well as to the role that a completed Christian canon might play in testing. Within the mainstream of pentecostalism, Harold Horton comes closest to Smith by arguing that the word of wisdom is a word of revelation concerning God's purpose for people, things, or events in the future. This definition is broad enough to include even Smith's utterances, and in the opinion of this author, provides inadequate safeguards.

The connection of this gift with teaching is a more mediating one. In this regard Griffiths has rendered *logos* as "teaching," so that what results is a "teaching of wisdom" derived from Scripture. Close to this, but clearly more spontaneous in its orientation, is Donald Gee's contention that a "word of wisdom" is a revelation that occurs when one preaches or teaches Christ and the cross, and the hearts of the hearers "burn" within them. It approaches the Calvinist concept of an inner testimony of the Spirit, the Wesleyan concept of illumination, and the Barthian concept in which Scripture becomes the Word of God to those who hear God speak as it is proclaimed.

See also GIFTS OF THE SPIRIT.

■ **Bibliography:** R. E. Baxter, *Gifts of the Spirit* (1983) ■ A. Bittlinger, *Gifts and Graces* (1967; repr. 1972) ■ D. Bridge and D. Phypers, *Spiritual Gifts and the Church* (1973) ■ E. E. Ellis, *Prophecy and Hermeneutic in Early Christianity: New Testament Essays* (1978), 45–62 ■ G. D. Fee, *The First Epistle to the Corinthians* (1987) ■ D. Gee, *Concerning Spiritual Gifts* (rev. 1980) ■ M. Griffiths, *Grace Gifts* (1978) ■ G. Holmes, "The Word of Wisdom," in G. Jones, ed., *Conference on the Holy Spirit Digest* (1983), 1:216–20 ■ H. Horton, *The Gifts of the Spirit* (1934; repr. 1971) ■ K. C. Kinghorn, *Gifts of the Spirit* (1976) ■ J. Randall, *Wisdom Instructs Her Children: The Power of the Spirit and the Word* (1971) ■ M. F. Unger, *The Baptism and Gifts of the Holy Spirit* (1978). ■ C. M. Robeck Jr.

WITHERSPOON, WILLIAM THOMAS (1880–1947).

Pentecostal preacher and leader. Born in Pennsylvania in a home that was not religious, Witherspoon joined a Methodist church after his marriage. Later he worshiped with the Christian and Missionary Alliance, but when he received the baptism of the Holy Spirit in 1912, his fellowship with this group ended. He founded Apostolic Gospel Church in Columbus, OH, in 1914 and served as the pastor of this church until his death. In 1932 Witherspoon became the first foreign missionary chairman of the ►Pentecostal Assemblies of Jesus Christ (PAJC). He was elected general chairman of the PAJC in 1938 and served until the merger that formed the ⸢United Pentecostal Church (UPC) in 1945. He was the first assistant general superintendent of the UPC, serving from 1945 until his death.

■ **Bibliography:** A. L. Clanton, *United We Stand* (1970).

                                                                                          ■ J. L. Hall

WOMEN, ROLE OF The history of women's roles in pentecostal and charismatic movements is complex and contradictory. On the one hand, the pentecostal tradition has often appeared far more open to women's preaching and leadership than have more mainstream Protestant churches such as the Presbyterians or Episcopalians. On the other hand, male pentecostal leaders have just as often drastically narrowed the boundaries within which their female counterparts may speak and act in positions of authority, so that pentecostalism has come to be perceived as far more conservative than mainline Protestantism on gender issues. A careful, balanced historical account is needed to understand how these rival narratives actually fit into the broader picture.

Such an account will not simply attend to the "great female leaders" of the tradition, for these exceptions tell us little or nothing about the ways in which women's roles were bounded for the majority of participants. Nor should such an account solely emphasize the theological discourse through which women were told to keep silent in the churches and submit to male authority, since women's practical activities often expanded well beyond these prescriptions. Both endeavors—learning about female leaders and analyzing ideology—are, of course, important and necessary instruments of historical revision, but they are not ends in themselves. What is also needed, as a vital complement to these other explorations, is attention to the voices of ordinary pentecostal women, including the kinds of prayers they uttered, the poetry and hymnody they composed, and the narratives of suffering and healing they related to fellow travelers across the land. Through these texts we may inch our way closer to an understanding of women's varied experiences within the pentecostal tradition.

1. The Nineteenth-Century Background.

In the 18th century, numerous dissenting churches on the American continent had allowed women to pray and testify during worship services, but with the birth of the new nation they "traded their early egalitarianism for greater political power and influence" (Brekus, 8). In the early years of the 19th century, groups like the Methodists, inspired by John Wesley (1703–91), continued to let women who felt called to preach become exhorters, testifying in public to what they believed God had done in their own lives and urging others to surrender and be converted. These women were very often revered, even by those not accustomed to women's public

speech: Jarena Lee, of the African Methodist Episcopal Church, spoke hundreds of times to both black and white congregants, for instance, while a Methodist clergyman wrote that Sally Schulyer's "gift in prayer, at all times, surpassed all I ever heard, of man or woman" (Brekus, 127). Yet the 1830s and 1840s also brought renewed controversy over female preaching and public female speech in general, and women were increasingly ordered to "keep silence in the churches" according to Paul's dictum in 1 Cor. 14:34–35.

The Holiness movement retained a greater openness to women's leadership, due in part to the key figure of Phoebe Palmer. Palmer herself helped inspire and lead the movement through her "Tuesday Meetings for the Promotion of Holiness" in New York City between 1835 and 1874, as well as her voluminous tracts, periodicals, and books such as *The Way of Holiness, Faith and Its Effects,* and *Promise of the Father.* Palmer's advocacy of the "shorter way" to sanctification than Wesley had elaborated held significant appeal for readers and pilgrims seeking holiness, while she earned wide acclaim as a public speaker and teacher. Though Palmer was not in favor of women preaching, she herself was a spiritual model for women and men alike. The same was true of her British counterpart, Hannah Whitall Smith, author of *The Christian's Secret of a Happy Life* (1875) and an important leader in the Keswick movement.

In general, of course, pious women of the 19th century were expected to remain within the sphere of hearth and home, in line with the "ideology of domesticity" that Victorian-era Americans held so dear. The icon of the visionary female exhorter, buttressed by female role models found in Scripture, did not fare very well next to that of the dutiful wife and mother who read the Bible to her children in scenes of domestic bliss. Women filled the pews—outnumbering men in virtually all Protestant churches—and were critical to the success of religious life as a whole, but they were increasingly prohibited access to the pulpit and banned from speaking publicly in church at all. Exceptions such as Lucy Drake, Elizabeth Mix, and ⸢Carrie Judd Montgomery, all of whom headed important healing ministries that reached a broad public, did not, however much favorable publicity they received, alter the status quo of ordinary women. Women's religious roles were vital but ever pushed to the margins, often invisible outside the arena of home prayer meetings, sickrooms, and devotional literature.

2. Early Pentecostalism.

Women were conspicuously present at the early-20th-century events now considered to mark the beginnings of the modern pentecostal movement. ⸢Agnes Ozman's receipt of Spirit baptism on Jan. 1, 1901, accompanied by speaking in tongues, has been retold over and over again as the moment of pentecostalism's "birth" at ⸢Charles F. Parham's Bethel Bible College in Topeka, KS. ⸢Lucy Farrow, head of a black

Holiness mission in Houston, worked with ›William J. Seymour in the early days of the ›Azusa Street revival and spread the evidential doctrine of tongues far and wide as an evangelist and missionary. ›Florence L. Crawford, Mabel Smith, ›Ivey Campbell, and ›Rachel A. Sizelove, among others, traveled to the Azusa Mission and became well-known evangelists and preachers, spreading the pentecostal doctrine far and wide. Countless lesser-known women also contributed to the local revivals that took place around the country and were celebrated for their work.

Such work was sanctioned in part because of the doctrinal emphasis on the third person of the Trinity, which enabled pentecostals to view ministerial authority as rooted in the movement of the Spirit rather than in clerical office. Instead of "Keep silence in the churches," the central scriptural passage was "Your sons and your daughters shall prophesy," from the book of Joel. Furthermore, as an article in the *Apostolic Faith* proclaimed in 1906, God was looking for as many as would help him in these final days:

> God does not need a great theological preacher that can give nothing but theological chips and shavings to the people. He can pick up a worm and thrash a mountain. He takes the weak things to confound the mighty. He is picking up pebble stones from the street and polishing them for his work. He is even using children to preach His Gospel. A young sister, 14 years old, was saved, sanctified and baptized with the Holy Ghost and went out, taking a band of

First Assembly of God, Hong Kong, night Bible class (1974).

workers with her, and led a revival in which one hundred and ninety souls were saved. (*AF* [Los Angeles] 1 [2, Oct. 1906], 3)

The urgency of early pentecostalism, grounded in eschatological convictions about the imminent apocalypse and the need for fervent evangelization beforehand, meant that every voice should be raised to heaven in prayer and directed to sinners in need of repentance and conversion. All efforts were needed to that end, giving women a crucial role within the movement.

This role did not, however, encompass ministerial authority, nor did the outpourings of the Spirit abolish the command for women to be submissive to men. Pentecostals allowed for women to minister because the Spirit-filled prophetess was the voice of God rather than the holder of an ecclesial office. But as pentecostals recognized that tongues were more often "unknown" than known human languages, and as pentecostals increasingly understood that not all Christians are called to be full-time ministers, they began to move away from an emphasis on the Holy Spirit as the primary qualification of ministry toward the addition of other qualifications. They augmented the image of egalitarianism in the upper room under the anointing of the Holy Spirit with images of church officers ordained by human authority figures. With less emphasis on tongues as a sign of ministerial authority, other evidences of a calling became necessary. This was especially so among those who participated in denominational life.

3. Ordination Controversies and Resolutions.

a. The Assemblies of God. The tension that exists within pentecostalism regarding the ordination of women has been and remains especially evident in the General Council of the Assemblies of God (AG). A reading of early issues of the *Christian Evangel* and *Pentecostal Evangel* reveals that editor and leader ›E. N. Bell opposed the idea of women performing any sacerdotal function connected with the authority of the ordained office. Bell agreed that women had the right to prophesy as the mouthpiece of God but could not fill a governmental office. According to Bell,

> There is no instance of any women being put in a place of *authority to rule*, govern or teach in an authoritative sense, that is, by the authority of their office, anywhere in the New Testament. When one speaks as a prophet, he speaks with the authority of God, but when one speaks as an apostle, he speaks with the authority of an apostle.... No woman has been known to have been appointed by the Lord as an elder or an apostle, or to any position where ruling with authority is inferred. (Bell, 2)

Thus, Bell could support women being ordained as evangelists or missionaries but not as elders (pastors).

Bell's view became prominent in the AG. Active women pastors were present at the organizational meeting of the 1914 general council of the AG, but that council voted that while women could prophesy, they could not serve as pastors. Although the general council and major periodicals discouraged ordaining women as pastors, congregational polity allowed the boundaries of women's sphere to remain somewhat fluid. Already-established female pastors or those women who could gain support because of a dynamic and charismatic ministry sometimes succeeded despite opposition. This was true of course of ˅Aimee Semple McPherson until she withdrew from the AG in 1922. Additionally, numerous women worked side by side with their husbands, even though in many cases the woman was the prominent minister. One example of this was ˅Marie Burgess Brown in New York.

The ordination question came to a head in the AG in the 1930s. In 1931 the general council resolved that women could only be ordained as evangelists and that their certificates must omit the rights to "bury the dead, administer ordinances of the church and perform the rite of marriage, when such acts are necessary." Thus, the argument that women should do these pastoral functions in the last days because of the urgency of the times was effectively silenced. Although the rights to officiate the ordinances "when such acts are necessary" were restored to women in 1935, the patterns of limitation continued to be generally accepted.

As with most pentecostal denominations, the AG experienced the cultural changes of post–WWII America. The reality of women entering the workforce in increasing numbers collided with the appeal of middle-class America, growing fear regarding the loss of the family, and the threat of imperial Communism. Simultaneously, the AG and other pentecostal denominations welcomed fellowship with evangelical groups such as the ˅National Association of Evangelicals—evangelicals who more often than not restricted the roles of women in the churches. All of this resulted in an increased emphasis on women at home with families and a decreased emphasis on women in the pulpit. Combined with a loss of urgency regarding the second coming of Christ, like other pentecostal denominations, the AG increasingly resolved the tension between institution and charisma with an increasingly male ministry.

b. The Church of God. Unlike the AG, the Church of God (CG) traces its history back to 1886, prior to the emergence of a pentecostal movement at the turn of the 20th century. Rooted in the Baptist tradition while also being influenced by radical Holiness elements, the Church of God has never allowed the ordination of women. Operating as baptistic congregations under the name Christian Union, the Church of God likely licensed women prior to 1900. Movement toward a centralized and episcopal form of government led to specific limitations on the roles of women, however. In 1908 the

First Assembly of God, Hong Kong, night Bible class (1974).Nigerian Bible school wives receive training for their role in husbands' ministries.

Church of God agreed to allow for deaconesses. This position was reversed the very next year when the General Assembly determined that there was no NT example of the ordination of women. Since the diaconate was an ordained office in the church, women could be considered deaconesses only by virtue of marriage to a deacon. In recognition of the fact that women were preaching the gospel, the assembly agreed to provide an evangelist's license both to men who were not eligible for ordination and to women who were ministering the Word. From that time, women have been licensed by the CG but excluded from any ordination. By 1910 General Overseer A. J. Tomlinson had defined "church" as "government." This allowed him to argue that women could preach in public assembly but not participate in any governmental activity, due to Paul's injunction to keep silent in the church.

The rights of licensed women ministers have varied, however. By 1914, limits on the rights and responsibilities of women evangelists were clearly codified. Although women were allowed to pastor churches, when necessary, they were limited to preaching functions. Female pastors had to secure a male minister to baptize converts, receive members into the church, officiate in the Lord's Supper, solemnize marriages, and any other practice that required governmental authority. These restrictions were removed in 1990 when the assembly granted women all the rights of licensed male ministers with the exception of the possibility of ordination. Such revisions seem to reflect a growing acceptance among pentecostal denominations of the changes regarding women's roles in American culture.

c. African-American Churches. Strong charismatic leaders with lengthy tenures have generally founded African-American churches. Thus, these denominations have primarily responded to questions regarding the ordination of women according to the views of their founders.

The largest African-American pentecostal denomination, the Church of God in Christ (COGIC), has prohibited women from being ordained and serving as pastors. With

Baptist roots, founder Charles Harrison Mason created two primary means of service for women. For the most part, women serve in the Women's Work department with local, regional, and national church mothers coordinating the work of the department. Interestingly, the first national church mother, Lizzie Robinson, was identified as "general overseer" of the Women's Work, and many church mothers have been involved in informal ministerial training, in large part because women were often more educated than men. In addition to the highly organized and effective Women's Work, the COGIC licenses women to serve as evangelists and missionaries. Such licensing is done by the male episcopate with the approval of the appropriate church mother.

Although the COGIC officially prohibits women from being ordained and serving as pastors, some highly visible violations of this policy, such as the ordination of Sandra Crouch in 1998, may indicate new possibilities for the future.

Women have founded other African-American denominations, which have chosen to grant full ordination to women. ▸Mary Magdalena Lewis Tate founded the Church of the Living God, the Pillar and Ground of Truth in 1908. Ordained as a bishop, Mother Tate served as general overseer, president, and apostle elder. In 1924 Pastor ▸Ida Robinson left the United Holy Church of America after a vision in which she was directed to "come out on Mt. Sinai and loose the women." She founded the ▸Mt. Sinai Holy Church of America with full rights for women including the episcopate. Unlike many denominations founded by women, other women have succeeded the founder as bishop.

d. The Charismatic Movement. The diversity of denominational traditions and the inclusion of many independent congregations make discussion of any aspect of the charismatic movement difficult. Although women have excelled among those mainline denominations that have opened their doors to the ordination of women, it remains difficult for women to find congregations that prefer a female pastor. Despite this fact, growing numbers of women have left their classical pentecostal denominations for mainline churches that have both a place for the ordination of women and a sizable renewal movement.

Like the pentecostal movement, the charismatic movement reflects continued tension between the presence of prophesying daughters and Victorian readings of Scripture. Periodicals such as *New Wine* magazine and authors such as ▸Larry Christenson frequently discuss issues of submission and authority in ways that emphasize men as protectors or "covering" for women in both the home and church. Yet, with or without the benefits of ordination, women continue

to rise up as preachers and pastors, especially those who are media savvy.

4. Prayer, Worship, and Devotion.

If women's "roles" in pentecostalism referred only to positions of authority, then this story would read as a narrow account of limited opportunity, regression, and disempowerment for women. If, however, we mean by women's roles the vast and varied contributions that women have made to the tradition, including but not exclusively defined in terms of official authority, then there is yet much more to say. Indeed, much of pentecostalism's patent appeal for women has been the female networks that have offered spiritual sustenance by means of Bible study, hymn singing, testimony, and earnest communal prayer. Attention to the language and practice of pentecostal women's religious devotion is crucial for understanding the ways in which women without access to sanctioned leadership roles have nonetheless been important actors in pentecostal history, shaping the tradition and reconfiguring both theological and testimonial forms to accord with their own concerns about home and family life, their experiences of grief and loneliness, and their understanding of healing.

Denominational periodicals such as the *Church of God Evangel* (started in 1910), the *Pentecostal Holiness Advocate* (started in 1917), and the *Whole Truth* (started in 1907) devoted considerable space to sections called "Testimonies and Requests for Prayer." In the case of the first two periodicals especially, far more contributions from women were printed than from men. Women's printed narratives centered

**Women's Missionary Council, Hong Kong, 1954.
(Center: Mrs. Ralph Cobb)**

on two basic emotional themes: sorrow and joy. Both testimonies and prayer requests articulated the ravages of physical and spiritual pain, while also professing complete trust that relief was on its way, to be bestowed by a beneficent God. In their own words, women asserted the trials of their lives, sometimes perceived as the "cost" of following Jesus; the sense of isolation from religious community; and laments of emotional distance from a husband who remained unsaved. Pentecostal women struggled to praise God in the midst of their despondency, without denying the reality of suffering here on earth. Most intimated that they had essentially given up hope in this world of "gloom and woe," counting instead on a world of happiness beyond, a "home beyond this veil of tears."

Praying for wayward husbands, derelict children, licentious neighbors, and their own struggle with sin gave pentecostal women a way to redeem their suffering and find meaning in daily experiences of pain. The world seemed to mock them every day, whether for their beliefs or for their modest pentecostal attire. As one woman wrote to the *Advocate*, "People think I am crazy for not partaking of everything of this world, and not dressing and acting like the world, but we know we are peculiar people, and we are not of the world." Women who could not be leaders in the churches could take pride in the jeers of outsiders, openly counting themselves as martyrs for the faith and soldiers of the cross. This role encompassed taking on suffering and transforming it into a blessing, praying for and consoling others in their pain, and remaining vigilantly on guard against the lure of cheap pleasures such as jewelry, alcohol, and vain flirtations. It was, their faith assured them, the most important role they could possibly play as Christian women in a wicked, fallen world.

To the end of fulfilling this role, many women gathered themselves into communities of pentecostal sisters, or "prayer bands," which met regularly to pray over multitudes of prayer requests. This was a practice that reached deep into the Christian tradition, of course, and also one that allowed women some measure of autonomy and leadership. Berta Maxwell of the ▸Pentecostal Holiness Church was a well-known figure in the 1930s for her thriving prayer group in Falcon, NC, and female participants wrote regularly to the *Advocate* to express their gratitude for her work. Maxwell herself wrote frequently to the same periodical, assuring the sick and lonely that their prayer requests were heeded, as in this 1935 excerpt:

> On each Thursday afternoon the meeting of Mizpeh Prayer Band is held at Falcon, N.C., at four o'clock. At this hour letters with requests are read, and we pray for each one separately. After all written requests are prayed for, other requests are presented, and we pray for them one by one. We then read the requests printed in *The Advocate*, and pray for each one separately. We also pray for any others we hear of needing help, far or near. (*Advocate* [May 23, 1935], 7)

Women's Missionary Council, Tonga, 1971.

Maxwell's letter confirmed that no matter how isolated individual readers might be, all were embraced by the prayers of Christian women. Women who involved themselves in such a prayer band were surely convinced that their prayers made a difference in other people's lives.

This tradition of women meeting together for prayer and fellowship would later be carried on in such independent charismatic groups as ▸Women's Aglow Fellowship, not to mention countless local prayer groups housed in churches and homes. Here, no matter how silent women may have been forced to be during official worship services in pentecostal and charismatic church sanctuaries, they have been encouraged to speak about their lives and pray aloud for others in need of assurance and relief. Here they may even shout out whatever has been pent up in their hearts as "prayer warriors" taking on the whole dominion of Satan and his minions. Here women have also found spaces wherein to act in leadership positions, counseling other women in need and perhaps occupying positions as officers or board members of a local women's prayer group. Authority, they have discovered, can reside as easily outside the churches as within them.

Pentecostal women have also found sustenance in roles of intimate fellowship with God, perceiving themselves quite literally as God's daughters. Unlike Christian traditions that have moved away from this kind of intimacy or that conceptualize God only in abstract, transcendent terms, pentecostalism has continued to cultivate a relational sense of the divine that may, in fact, have special implications for women. God and Jesus, separately and together, have been felt as living, immediate presences by pentecostals, conversing with their beloved children on the most ordinary of subjects and acting as sympathetic, affectionate companions to them in their times of loneliness. God, as Father, can stand in as the "Daddy" that a woman may never have had, whether due to neglect or abandonment. Often enough, moreover, pentecostal women have interpreted Jesus quite literally as a lover, husband, or intimate friend, cultivating a daily relationship with him replete with the same risks and possibilities of earthly relationships: misunderstanding, loss of trust, forgiveness, and renewal. Importantly, this interpretation of divine relationships sets a standard by which human relationships can be measured, along with techniques by which they might be improved. The opportunities provided by the roles of God's daughter, lover, and companion have comprised a vital fount of pentecostalism's appeal and satisfaction for women: a source of love received as well as bestowed.

The devotional rhythms of pentecostalism, in which worshipers strive to feel healed, inwardly transformed, and outwardly set free from suffering through the power of the Holy Spirit, have had important consequences for women throughout this century of pentecostal expansion. In the early decades, as women recounted stories of illness and death, unsaved loved ones, a husband's neglect or even desertion, a son's call to war, and personal despair, they sought solace from women who could understand what they were going through and who would pray for them, even as they sought comfort from God. In later decades, especially since the 1970s, pentecostal and charismatic women have been no less in need of their sisters than before, even as they have become ever more explicit about physical or sexual abuse, parental or personal alcoholism, depression and other mental illnesses, delinquent children, and other trials.

5. Conclusions.

The history of women's roles in pentecostalism is not one but many stories, stories that are interlocking yet contradictory and that together lead to ambivalent results. Pentecostal leaders have utilized women in leadership positions when necessary or convenient, then have heatedly restricted their

Young Cakchiquel women volunteering to make the daily ration of tortillas for Bible students.

opportunities in order to protect men's power. Women have asserted their call to preach, prophesy, and pray in public but then have remained in congregations where they are told to keep silent and be submissive to authoritative male leaders. Pentecostal scholars have struggled to interpret the tradition as one that is egalitarian at its core (in terms not only of gender but of race as well) and corrupted by fallen men; but there is little evidence available to the social historian for corroborating such an assertion. Theological prescriptions and social prejudices have been welded together until they are all but inextricable, with little indication that women's position within pentecostalism has improved over 100 years. If anything, the tradition's major spokesmen seem to have increasingly belittled women's capacity for leadership and entrenched their own structures of power.

Such continuing hostility to women's leadership, especially in the wake of second-wave feminism, has not provoked the kind of widespread indignation among pentecostal women that has occurred in mainline Protestant denominations. There, decades of activism among women as well as men have enabled women to step up from the second-class status they once occupied into full opportunities for ordination and clerical leadership as they feel called (Nesbitt). Most pentecostal women do not have such resources at their disposal: many, if not the majority, believe feminism is evil and either interpret the Bible as mandating female submission to male authority or quietly oppose this interpretation while remaining loyal to their tradition. Church leadership is not their most pressing issue, certainly not in comparison to saving souls. If change is to come regarding women's roles in pentecostalism, it will surely come gradually.

Meanwhile, pentecostal women remain as actively involved as ever in the other roles that they believe God wants them to fill, praying for personal, social, and international issues to be resolved and rejoicing in their intimate relationship with Jesus. They do not doubt that their work as Christian women matters in the world, nor that they are working to bring about a new heaven and a new earth. Prayer warriors all, they are marching into the new millennium armed for battle with all who would wreak havoc on the divine purpose to which God has called them.

■ **Bibliography:** E. N. Bell, "Women Elders," *Christian Evangel* (Aug. 15, 1914) ■ E. Blumhofer, "The Role of Women in the Assemblies of God." *AGH* 6 (Spring 1986) ■ C. A. Brekus, *Strangers and Pilgrims: Female Preaching in America, 1740–1845* (1998) ■ A. Butler, "Sisters Doing It for Everyone: The Women's Work of the Church of God in Christ, 1912–1945" (paper, AAR, 1996) ■ N. F. Cott, *The Bonds of Womanhood: "Woman's Sphere" in New England, 1780–1835* (2d ed., 1997) ■ C. R. Dirksen, "Let Your Women Keep Silence," in D. N. Bowdle, ed., *The Promise and the Power: Essays on the Motivations, Developments, and Prospects of the Ministries of the*

Church of God (1980) ■ R. M. Griffith, "'Joy Unspeakable and Full of Glory': The Vocabulary of Pious Emotion in the Narratives of American Pentecostal Women, 1910–1945," in P. N. Stearns and J. Lewis, eds., *An Emotional History of the United States* (1998) ■ E. J. Lawless, *Handmaidens of the Lord: Pentecostal Women Preachers and Traditional Religion* (1988) ■ L. G. Murphy, J. G. Melton, and G. L. Ward, *Encyclopedia of African American Religions* (1993) ■ P. D. Nesbitt, *Feminization of the Clergy in America: Occupational and Organizational Perspectives* (1997) ■ M. M. Poloma, *The Assemblies of God at the Crossroads: Charisma and Institutional Dilemmas* (1980) ■ D. Roebuck, "Limiting Liberty: The Church of God and Women Ministers, 1886–1996" (diss., Vanderbilt, 1996).

■ R. M. Griffith; D. Roebuck

WOMEN'S AGLOW FELLOWSHIP INTERNATIONAL

Women's Aglow Fellowship International (WAFI) is an interdenominational organization of charismatic Christian women centered on prayer and evangelization. WAFI was founded in 1967 as the Full Gospel Women's Fellowship, established by four women in Seattle, WA, whose husbands were active leaders in the ▸Full Gospel Business Men's Fellowship. Both groups were outgrowths of the healing and charismatic movements within Protestant and Catholic churches, and they correspondingly emphasized practices and doctrines such as Spirit baptism, glossolalia, prophecy, and healing prayer. Throughout its history the women's group has been held together by local worship meetings and Bible studies, as well as larger (regional, national, and even international) retreats and conferences. In 1995 WAFI claimed an American membership of 18,828 women, with an estimated 20,000 more throughout the world.

In 1969 the Full Gospel Women's Fellowship began publishing a quarterly newsletter for participants and prospective members, a digest-sized collection of testimonies, Bible lessons, instructions for evangelizing, and notices of charismatic prayer meetings in the Seattle area. They named this newsletter *Aglow*, from Rom. 12:11, "Be aglow and burning with the Spirit" (AMPLIFIED). This vehicle spurred rapid growth of the organization around the United States, and in 1972 the group was reincorporated as the nonprofit WAFI. At the group's first international conference in 1974, there were up to 1,000 people in attendance from 25 states, the Netherlands, Mexico, Canada, and Nigeria. Along with WAFI's subscription list of 75,000, the publications department had also begun to produce books, audiotapes, and Bible studies for charismatic Christian women.

Most of WAFI's American constituents in the early days were white, middle-class homemakers, and the group's published literature strongly emphasized women's domestic roles as wives and mothers. This emphasis was certainly in keeping with the conservative values of the charismatic movement of the time, but the message conflicted with the women's liberation movement that had also emerged during the 1960s. WAFI authors frequently denounced feminists for dismantling traditional gender hierarchies and scorning the notion that women's highest vocation is in the home. Many of them even claimed to be "former feminists" whose marriages were only saved by renewed commitment to the principle of wifely submission to male authority. Though a concept central to WAFI women's self-perception, it was clearly very difficult to live out, as evidenced in the large number of stories aimed at encouraging their readers to see the beneficial effects of submitting to their husbands.

In fact, one of the most widely published WAFI Bible studies, *God's Daughter*, heavily stressed this theme when it was first published in 1974. Acknowledging how much easier it is for women to yield to the lordship of Jesus than to that of their husbands, author Eadie Goodboy (a WAFI staff member) assured her readers that submission did not mean servitude, nor did it imply that a woman should be a "doormat." Rather, she affirmed that Christian women could experience true liberation through submission, that if they rejected the "role-reversal so common in society today" they could find "service and creativity in our God-ordained roles" as wives, mothers, and homemakers. Christian joy for women was a product not simply of surrendering to God's will but of submitting to the authority of one's husband, whether he was Christian or not.

This message extolling wifely submission and domesticity fit well with the "family values" campaigns increasingly waged during the 1970s and supported by President Ronald Reagan in the 1980s, visible in such arenas as Anita Bryant's public war against homosexuality, Jerry Falwell's powerful Moral Majority, Beverly LaHaye's Concerned Women for America, Phyllis Schlafly's battle against the Equal Rights Amendment, and James Dobson's Focus on the Family empire. Unlike these leaders and organizations, however, WAFI was not a political organization and refrained from issuing public statements on issues like abortion and the ERA. Nonetheless, the group experienced substantial growth during the formative years of the New Christian Right, and many of its members, aging along with the organization, have undoubtedly been part of that movement as well.

At the same time, WAFI can be strongly differentiated from these other movements because of the centrality of spiritual devotion in the group's ongoing existence. Women from local chapters often get together for informal Bible studies or times of small-group prayer. Larger meetings have long been organized along the lines of a pentecostal or charismatic worship service, beginning with "praise and worship" music, then moving into testimonies, Scripture reading, offerings, a sermon, and a time for healing prayer. The prayer segment of the meetings often lasts a full hour or more and is clearly the most important time for many of the women who attend.

Like others who have believed in healing prayer during this century and before, WAFI women have prayed for multiple types of healings, including relief from physical illness, mental distress, depression, alcoholism, and abuse. Indeed, since the mid 1980s, WAFI has taken an increasingly therapeutic turn, as meetings came to feel as much like recovery groups as worship meetings. Just as subjects like incest and addiction received growing attention in American popular culture, so too did such topics rise to the fore in WAFI meetings and published literature. Images of squeaky clean families, glued together by joyously submissive supermoms, were replaced by dark tales of incest-ridden childhoods, alcoholic parents, and unfaithful husbands. No longer were women expected to submit cheerfully to such indignities, but they were urged to seek psychiatric help and, if necessary, divorce as well. Jesus, always Savior and Friend to WAFI women, was increasingly imagined as a replacement father for women whose own fathers had abandoned them and as a replacement husband for divorced, widowed, or unhappily married women. Along with Bible studies, worship services, retreats, and conferences, WAFI established official support groups for women in need, promoted as Christ-centered alternatives to secular twelve-step groups like Alcoholics Anonymous.

WAFI's breathless growth during the 1970s slowed somewhat in the 1980s and peaked in the early 1990s, under the leadership of long-standing president Jane Hansen. While continuing to attract women in other parts of the world, WAFI's attraction for its traditional constituency of white middle-class women has definitely waned and its American numbers declined. WAFI leaders claim this trend as a strange kind of success for them, in that there are now more openings for women's leadership within the churches than there once were—hence, fewer women are now entering WAFI in search of leadership positions. There are undoubtedly less sanguine reasons for the numerical decline, such as the felt distance between the high echelons of the national leadership and the ordinary women of the local fellowships. Seattle administrators are sometimes perceived as out of touch with ordinary women, too busy jetsetting around the world to make home visits, dressing expensively, even gaudily, as they preside over yearly conferences while still issuing heartfelt appeals for increased sacrificial giving. Retaining a strong loyalty to their local chapters, many WAFI women are simply uninterested in the administrative challenges of maintaining the group's membership and expanding its ministries.

Despite its image as a white woman's organization, WAFI has been increasingly successful at attracting middle-class women of color as the national leadership in Seattle has focused energy on racial reconciliation. In part, this growing commitment to healing racism can be attributed to the growing international membership of the organization and the visible presence of women of color at international conferences.

Members and leaders who are Native American and African American have spoken bluntly to their white sisters about the latter's responsibility for rectifying past wrongs, and some impressive gains seem to have been made in this area. This shift is consonant with a broader shift in American evangelical culture, as groups as diverse as the Christian Coalition, Southern Baptist Convention, and Promise Keepers have made race issues a central platform.

References to homemakers have also sharply declined in the 1990s, as demographic shifts among the WAFI membership have made visible increasing numbers of single mothers and working women. Now, rather than hearing cheerful proclamations of wifely submission, one is more likely to hear stories about healing from divorce. WAFI women are also just beginning to speak in term of "mutual submission" between husbands and wives, an emphasis far more in keeping with the values of modern Americans, Christian and non-Christian alike. References to a one-sided notion of wifely submission have dropped out of sight in the literature, replaced with a supple egalitarianism. How much this shift has been directly influenced by American feminism is debatable (WAFI women themselves see no influence at all), but WAFI women have clearly come to stand on common ground with many feminists, whether either party acknowledges this commonality or not.

Drawing in new members has proven very difficult in WAFI's recent history. Unlike the early years, WAFI's potential members in the United States now have many other options, as evangelicals inspired by the men's group Promise Keepers have forged parallel women's groups such as Chosen Women, Promise Reapers, Praise Keepers, and Women of Faith. These newer fellowships are theologically looser than WAFI and draw a younger clientele. Participants do not yet have the kinds of ambivalent feelings toward their leaders that many WAFI women have come to feel toward theirs. Realistic about their diminished appeal among younger American women, WAFI's energies have visibly shifted, global evangelization taking precedence over local growth. The story of WAFI's future almost certainly lies in Africa, Asia, and Latin America more than North America; but whether this global growth portends further imperialistic expansion of American Christianity or the genuine internationalization of WAFI itself remains, for now, an open question.

Whatever WAFI's future holds, it is clear that this organization has been a significant vehicle for charismatic and pentecostal women for more than three decades and that its history beautifully illustrates the trajectory of American charismatic/pentecostal culture during that time. In many ways WAFI has much more in common with modern American culture—"the world" that they profess to despise—than with the early-20th-century pentecostalism that they claim as their heritage. At the same time, they have injected women's voices and concerns into what has always been, with very few exceptions, a tradition led and dominated by men, and for this service WAFI's place in pentecostal history is assured.

■ **Bibliography:** R. M. Griffith, *God's Daughters: Evangelical Women and the Power of Submission* (1997) ■ S. M. Setta, "Healing in Suburbia: The Women's Aglow Fellowship," *Journal of Religious Studies* 12 (2, 1986).   ■ R. M. Griffith

WONGSAK, JOSEPH C. (1955–). Pioneer church planter in Thailand. Born into a Chinese-Thai family, Wongsak was intelligent and studious as a young man and won a government scholarship to Monash University, Melbourne, Australia, in 1973 to study economics and political science. Evangelized by a student from Singapore, Wongsak gave his life to Christ and joined the Waverly Christian Fellowship. In 1976 he heard God's call to return to Thailand and plant churches in each district of the nation by the year 2000. Together with his Thai wife, Rojana, whom he met in Melbourne, Wongsak returned to Thailand in 1981 with a Ph.D. What became the Hope of Bangkok Church began in a hospital classroom in 1981, leading to a process of forming disciples. In 1985 Wongsak founded the Thailand Bible Seminary and started a church in Northern Thailand. By 1997 there were more than 800 Hope of God churches covering most districts of Thailand, with 40 in 13 other countries. The Hope of God churches emphasize covenant relationships and discipleship formation, as well as operating centers and clinics to serve the poor.

■ **Bibliography:** C. Peter Wagner, ed., *New Apostolic Churches* (1998), 271–73.   ■ P. D. Hocken

WOODWORTH-ETTER, MARIA BEULAH (1844–1924). One of the best-known and most successful itinerant evangelists at the turn of the century. Although often controversial because of her emphasis on the power of the Holy Spirit and faith healing, Maria B. Woodworth-Etter ministered with the Winebrenner (German Reformed) Churches of God (CG) for 20 years (1884–1904). Even later when she was in her 60s and 70s she was one of the most popular evangelists on the sawdust trail.

Much of Woodworth-Etter's popularity and notoriety—which carried over into the pentecostal movement—can be traced to the practice of faith healing and other charismatic gifts she began to employ in meetings in about 1885. Those features attracted an estimated 25,000 people to a camp meeting near Alexandria, IN, in 1885. Newspapers gave varied reports of her exploits, usually calling attention to the trances (or being ▶"slain in the Spirit") and general pandemonium but not failing to notice the many conversions usu-

ally registered in every meeting. (See Warner, 1986, for numerous newspaper quotes from coast to coast.) In most cities where she conducted her 19th-century meetings— some as long as five months—newspaper editors were caught up by the huge crowds, the excitement, and a woman in the pulpit; they regarded her meetings as the biggest news story at the time. Generous front-page coverage, which was often critical and satirical, was common. Woodworth-Etter, however, took it all in stride, even after the editorial broadsides, and after being arrested and charged with obtaining money under false pretenses in one city and practicing medicine without a license in another.

Woodworth-Etter never lost sight of her "call" to preach, which she said God gave to her when she was a child. Her preaching netted conversions (as many as 500 a week in 1885), planted churches, and spread Holiness teaching in the 19th century and pentecostalism in the 20th. She became probably the best-known Holiness preacher to embrace

A poster advertising a 1922 meeting in Ottumwa, IA, led by Maria B. Woodworth-Etter, who began praying for the sick in her 1880s meetings.

pentecostalism. Her contribution to women's rights in the ministry would be difficult to measure, but it must be immense. Ironically, historians outside of the pentecostal movement have largely ignored Woodworth-Etter's contribution to revival movements in America.

1. Early Life and Preaching.

Born Maria Beulah Underwood near Lisbon, OH, in 1844, she was one of eight children. Their father died when Maria was 12, so she dropped out of school to help her mother. A Dr. Belding (possibly Warren A. Belding) conducted a revival meeting at the Lisbon Christian Church when Maria was 13. She was converted and baptized and felt a call to the ministry even though she knew her church did not have women preachers.

Later Woodworth-Etter's disastrous marriage to P. H. Woodworth and the rearing of her six children made a preaching career highly unlikely. In a series of deep sorrows, the Woodworths lost five of their six children to illnesses. In 1879, when Maria was 35, she attended a Friends revival meeting and renewed her spiritual commitment. Soon she began having success in preaching local revivals, and those successes launched her into a lifelong itinerant ministry. Apparently her first church association was with the United Brethren, but she joined the Churches of God (Winebrenner) in 1884. Her attitude throughout her career was ecumenical, however, even accepting an invitation from the Reorganized Church of Jesus Christ of Latter-Day Saints to preach in Nebraska in 1920.

2. Nineteenth-Century Mass Evangelism.

Woodworth-Etter's meetings took on gigantic proportions beginning in 1885, after she had been preaching for about five years. When she opened a campaign in Hartford City, IN, in January, the crowds poured in from miles around, and soon no building in town could hold them. As many as 20 reporters attended and filed stories. Even the *New York Times* took notice and published stories. Conversions and trances became popular. Lawyers and doctors joined the common people at the once despised "mourner's bench." Hartford City was only the beginning of exciting meetings—somewhat of a Woodworth-Etter prototype—which made her a household name throughout the Midwest and beyond. Some amazing accounts of healings and conversions were frequently reported in newspaper stories and later repeated in Woodworth-Etter's journal-type books.

During the 19th century, Woodworth-Etter preached a subsequent spiritual experience that she called "the power." This was often accompanied by a trance and a vision that could go on for hours. She regarded this phenomenon as the same as that experienced by the apostle Peter in Joppa (Acts 10). She often went into trances herself during a service, standing like a statue for an hour or more with her hands raised while the service continued. As would be expected, the trances drew much criticism in and outside the church. She was soon dubbed the "trance evangelist." Later she was called the "priestess of divine healing" and the "voodoo priestess." A frequent charge was that she hypnotized the people. Two doctors in St. Louis tried to have her committed as insane during a meeting she conducted there in 1890.

Woodworth-Etter undoubtedly picked up bits and pieces of her theology from Finney, Mahan, Simpson, Boardman, and other 19th-century ministers and theologians. She did not originate the teachings and practices but certainly popularized them through her mass meetings and many books.

The gift of prophecy operated in her meetings from the beginning, Woodworth-Etter claimed. Possibly the best-known prophecy, and one she never reported in her books, was that the San Francisco Bay area would be destroyed by an earthquake and tidal wave in 1890. Newspapers said that about 1,000 people fled to the hills because of the prophecy.

In 1891 Woodworth-Etter divorced P. H. Woodworth, charging him with adultery. He died the next year. She married Samuel Etter in 1902 and so hyphenated her two last names.

3. The Pentecostal Movement.

Woodworth-Etter's involvement with the pentecostal movement on a major scale began in 1912, at age 68, in Dallas, where ˃F. F. Bosworth had founded a church. He invited her to conduct a meeting, which ran from July until December. The meeting was momentous for both Woodworth-Etter and the pentecostal movement (not to speak of the boost it gave to Bosworth's local church). It gave Woodworth-Etter a national platform as a pentecostal heavyweight, inasmuch as many important leaders in the movement from all over the country were attracted to the meeting. Pentecostalism and Woodworth-Etter received favorable publicity through published reports in the movement's periodicals as far away as England. The next spring Woodworth-Etter was the main speaker at the Worldwide Camp Meeting in Los Angeles.

With the exception of ˃Charles F. Parham, ˃Frank J. Ewart, and a few others, it appears that most early pentecostals looked at Woodworth-Etter as a godsend to the movement and accepted her uncritically. They knew about her legendary 19th-century ministry and were certain that she would have success in the pentecostal movement. From eyewitnesses and published reports, it appears that the movement was not disappointed with her ministry.

Although Woodworth-Etter claimed that people spoke in tongues in her meetings from the beginning, this claim never was documented. In looking back on her own ministry after the pentecostal movement began, she equated her subsequent experience of the 1880s as the baptism in the Holy Spirit, but she does not claim to have spoken in tongues in the early years. Her particular brand of Holiness, however, put her in a vanguard that helped usher in the pentecostal movement.

In 1918 Woodworth-Etter established a local church in Indianapolis. She was the pastor but continued to conduct meetings in the Midwest during the last six years of her life. That church is now the large Lakeview Christian Center.

In examining Woodworth-Etter's 40-plus years as a Holiness-pentecostal preacher, primarily as an evangelist, one is amazed at what she was able to accomplish as a woman between 1880 and 1924. She was organizing and preaching huge campaigns with little or no local church backing, 30 to 40 years before women could vote in national elections. She took salvation, faith healing, and a subsequent spiritual experience of power to the masses. Amazingly, her 8,000-seat tent, which she began to use in 1889, was often too small to hold the seekers, the faithful, the curious, and the usual troublemakers. And her Holiness star kept rising, right into the fledgling pentecostal movement.

Maria B. Woodworth-Etter was no theologian, but in the words of D. William Faupel, she was "a monumental figure in terms of spreading the pentecostal message" (Warner, 1986, 175).

■ **Bibliography:** W. Warner, *The Woman Evangelist* (1986) ■ idem, "Indiana's Forgotten Women on the Sawdust Trail," *Indianapolis Star* (Sept. 16, 1984) ■ idem, "Maria B. Woodworth-Etter and the Early Pentecostal Movement," *AGH* (Winter 1986–87) ■ idem, "Maria B. Woodworth-Etter, A Powerful Voice in the Pentecostal Vanguard," *Enrichment* (Winter 1999) ■ M. Woodworth-Etter, *Signs and Wonders* (1916; repr. 1980).   ■ W. E. Warner

WOON MONG RA (1914–). Influential conference speaker, educator, prayer-mountain founder, author, revival preacher, Christian businessman, editor, and publisher.

Woon was born in North Korea. In 1935 he dropped out of Waseda University in Japan. He wanted to find the real meaning of life and went to Yongmun Mountain. Amid this quest, in 1942 he heard a voice from heaven and spent time in prayer, fasting, and meditating on the Scripture at Yongmun Mountain. This led him to establish Aehyangsook, which means "a community for establishing a country of love." He tried to awaken the farmers from their ignorance and planted one church in each village. He was ordained as an elder in the Methodist Church.

Woon began the prayer-mountain movement in Korea in the 1940s. Since he began his Christian life by listening to the voice from heaven, he began to emphasize the experiential dimension of the Christian faith and encouraged people to pray, making Yongmun Prayer Mountain a place of prayer all year round. Since that time he has regularly held open-air prayer meetings at Yongmun Prayer Mountain in the mid-

dle of August, drawing crowds of more than 10,000. The outpouring of the Holy Spirit has been tremendous, with many signs and wonders following the meetings. Those who were trained spiritually at Yongmun Prayer mountain were sent to other parts of the country and established similar prayer mountains. More than two-thirds of the prayer mountains in Korea were established by Woon's disciples.

Woon, a Spirit-filled revival preacher, traveled to the four corners of the Korean peninsula igniting revival fires. He used various methods to spread the pentecostal message, including literature. He wrote more than 50 books, published three different magazines and newspapers in English and Korean, and ran the publication office called Aehyangsook. He also used educational institutions as one of his channels. He established the Gideon Bible College and Theological Seminary, Yongmun Mountain Covenant, Gideon Bible Institute, and Yongmun Minister Training Institute. These institutions have trained thousands of pentecostal preachers. He also established Aehyangwon for orphans and established a church for the mentally ill. In 1979 he established the Jesus Pentecostal Holiness Church in Korea and was ordained its bishop.

Woon has been persecuted a great deal. Under the Japanese regime he was put into prison several times. His controversial theology was condemned as heresy by the Jesus Presbyterian Church. Since he never received any formal theological training, his theology is mixed with oriental philosophies. In fact, he recognizes Buddha and Confucius as OT prophets. Also, based on 1 Peter 3:19, he claims that the dead spirit has one more opportunity to be saved.

■ **Bibliography:** Suh Young Na, "The Church in Korea and Hospitable Exclusivism in Light of the Thought of Bishop Woon Mong Ra" (diss., 1997) ■ Woon Mong Ra, *The Holy Spirit I Have Experienced and a Half Century of Its Movement* (1990) ■ idem, *I Would Have Liked to Live Nor to Die* (1986) ■ C. W. Park, "Why do the People Visit Prayer Mountain?" *Pastoral Monthly* 215 (July 1995).   ■ Y. S. Eim

WORLD COUNCIL OF CHURCHES While the origins of the World Council of Churches (WCC) are rooted in the 19th century, the WCC was formed Aug. 22, 1948, in Amsterdam, the Netherlands. The World Missionary Conference held in Edinburgh, Scotland, in 1910 played a very significant role in the birth of the modern "ecumenical movement." The original impetus was to bring unity of witness among Western churches working on the mission frontiers of the world. Several years later the first Life and Work world conference was held in Stockholm, Sweden (1925), followed by the first Faith and Order world conference in Lausanne, Switzerland (1927). Representatives from Life and Work and from Faith and Order came together in 1948 to form the WCC. The International Missionary Conference (IMC), formed in 1921 as a descendant of the 1910 Edinburgh Conference, would ultimately join forces with the WCC at its third assembly, held in New Delhi (1961).

Work on the WCC had begun as early as Aug. 29–Sept. 1, 1938, when a group of 48 friends, who crossed various denominational lines, came together to discuss the possibility of building bridges between the churches, especially in Europe. Together, they formed the Provisional Committee of the World Council of Churches. They bought property in Geneva at 17 Route de Malagnor and opened a provisional office. The encroachment of Adolf Hitler across Europe ultimately forced them to put their plans on hold until well after the end of WWII.

Immediately following the war, Europe was in a shambles. Children had been orphaned, families had been separated, churches had been destroyed, and people were cold and hungry. Churches, especially in the U.S., reached across the Atlantic in an attempt to lift postwar Europe from the ashes. Only when the healing of Europe had begun was it possible for the WCC to come into being. By that time there was considerable interest in the idea, not only in Europe but also in the U.S. When the WCC was finally formed, it made it clear to all interested parties that its basis for membership would include the mandatory confession of "the Lord Jesus Christ as God and Savior according to the Scriptures" and an explicit commitment that all who joined would agree to "seek to fulfil together their common calling to the glory of God, Father, Son, and Holy Spirit." They would become a fellowship of churches, working together on issues of common concern.

Fundamentalist Christian groups in the U.S. refused to cooperate with the WCC or the National Council of the Churches of Christ in the United States of America (est. 1950). Driven by eschatological visions of a "superchurch" that would ultimately give way to the Antichrist, they established a "rival ecumenical machine." It was known as the American Council of Christian Churches (ACCC, 1941). It was soon followed by the formation of an International Council of Christian Churches (ICCC, 1948). These groups were heatedly opposed to the WCC, but they also refused to accept pentecostals in their organizations. A more moderate group, also opposed to the WCC but in less outspoken ways, was the ➤National Association of Evangelicals (NAE, 1942), which classical pentecostal denominations were allowed to join. As a result, several pentecostal denominations became charter members. A World Evangelical Fellowship (WEF) was ultimately formed, and many evangelical and pentecostal churches quickly joined it.

Pentecostals were often skeptical of the WCC, in spite of its stated basis for membership, fearing that it compromised on fundamental doctrines. In spite of this fear, there were signs of openness to the ecumenical movement on the part of several important pentecostal figures. ➤David J. du Plessis

(1905–87) and ➤Donald Gee (1891–1966) were pentecostal leaders who urged their brethren to become involved in various meetings of the WCC. Gee frequently used his position as editor of *Pentecost*, the official organ of the ➤Pentecostal World Conference (PWC), to speak up in favor of ecumenical engagement by pentecostals. ➤J. Roswell Flower, general secretary of the Assemblies of God (AG) in the U.S. and acting secretary for the PWC, and Du Plessis attended the Second Assembly of the WCC in Evanston, IL, in 1954. Flower attended as an official observer, and Du Plessis as an appointee of WCC general secretary W. A. Visser 't Hooft, to coordinate all press interviews for nonEnglish-speaking delegates. In 1960 both Du Plessis and Gee attended two sessions of the WCC's Commission on Faith and Order in St. Andrews, Scotland. Du Plessis also attended the Third Assembly of the WCC in New Delhi and was listed in the program as an "observer ... personally invited."

The overriding opinion of pentecostals, however, was to confuse contact with compromise. Publicly they feared that the WCC would become a "superchurch," with power to eliminate their testimony and hand them over to Rome. They had not read the famous "Toronto Statement" adopted by the WCC in 1950 that shunned such ideas. They worried about whether or not the basis for membership, though rooted in the requirement of a common confession of Jesus as Lord and Savior, was really based on a "lowest common denominator" theology, and that therefore "liberalism" and the "social gospel" would dominate the WCC agenda. In spite of this public assessment, pentecostal leaders in the AG were secretly building relationships with the WCC behind the scenes. During its first decade, the Division of Foreign Missions of the AG was actively involved with a number of ecumenical programs with the Foreign Missions Conference of North America and the International Missionary Conference. These groups ultimately would become the missionary arm of the NCCCUSA and the WCC respectively. These relationships were further strengthened by AG cooperation with the Provisional Committee of the WCC and the opening of offices in the same building as the NCCCUSA in New York. Much of this came to a halt, however, when ➤Thomas F. Zimmerman, newly elected as general superintendent of the AG, chairperson for the PWC, and president of the NAE, and David du Plessis clashed over their respective roles on the world ecclesiastical stage.

In 1961 Du Plessis lost his credentials with the AG. Over the next several years Zimmerman engineered passage of a resolution that was adopted in 1965. That resolution, reaffirmed as late as 1997, spoke in strong opposition to what it termed the "ecumenical movement." The bylaws of the AG now read in part: "The General Council of the Assemblies of God disapproves of ministers or churches participating in any of the modern ecumenical organizations on a local, national, or international level in such a manner as to promote the Ecumenical Movement." Although the statement does not mention the WCC, it was clearly directed toward the WCC as well as the NCCCUSA. Of the major pentecostal denominations in the U.S., only the AG has incorporated such a statement into its constitution and bylaws, although some other pentecostal groups (in the U.S.) are little more sympathetic toward the WCC than is the AG.

Not all pentecostals took such a negative stance on the WCC. At the third assembly in New Delhi, for instance, two small Chilean pentecostal denominations joined the WCC—the first pentecostal groups to do so: La Iglesia Pentecostal de Chile and Misión Iglesia Pentecostal. These pentecostal groups reported that the reason they had not joined the WCC sooner was that they had been misinformed about the organization by other pentecostals. On his first visit to Latin America, Lesslie Newbigin saw the division between evangelicals (the vast majority of whom are pentecostals) and the historic churches. He realized that "evangelical Christianity in this vast continent had been founded on a negation. Not the beauty of the Gospel but the horror of Rome seemed to be the deepest motive." Of his visit Newbigin said, "When one begins by exalting a negative it is very difficult to get out of that posture" (1985, 184). Augusto E. Fernandez Arlt has contended that the reasons the pentecostals from Chile joined the WCC had more to do with the relief they received following the 1960 earthquake than with any theological reasons. He is partially correct, for relief workers from the WCC assisted in the moral and financial rebuilding of the country, and pentecostals were beneficiaries of their work. But these pentecostal churches also argue that for the first time they felt that they had become part of the global church.

The two pentecostal groups in question were uniquely Chilean in their origin, their leadership, and their financial structure, and must be classed among the "autochthonous" pentecostal churches of the world. No North American or European mission board founded them, nor have they ever been dependent on such boards to meet their needs. Arlt reports that the significance of these groups joining the WCC shows the openness of the World Council and the opportunity for other Latin American pentecostal churches to consider membership. It was possible for these two groups to associate with the council without losing their authenticity as pentecostals.

Through the years other pentecostal denominations have joined them in the WCC. In 2000, the Missão Evangelica Pentecostal de Angola, the International Evangelical Church (U.S.), the Iglesia de Misiones Pentecostalies Libres de Chile, and the Iglesia de Dios (Argentina), led by Bishop Gabriel O. Vaccaro, all hold one or another level of membership in the WCC. For a time La Igreja Evangelica Pentecostal "O Brasil para Christo" held membership but left the WCC when their founder, Manuel de Mello, died suddenly and left them without a clear rationale for their membership. Pentecostal interests in the U.S.S.R. were represented at the WCC through their membership in the Union of Evangelical Christian Baptists of the U.S.S.R., which they were required to join during the rule of Joseph Stalin. With the coming of *glasnost/perestroika*, however, they withdrew from the Baptist Union to form their own Pentecostal Union and left the WCC. Others would include as pentecostal churches in the WCC such African Indigenous Churches (AICs) as the Eglise du Christ sur la Terre par le Prophète Simon Kimbangu in Zaire, the African Church of the Holy Spirit (Kenya), the African Israel Church, Nineveh (Kenya), the Church of the Lord Aladura (Nigeria), and the Eglise Evangélique du Congo.

As early as 1972 Barry Till noted in *The Churches Search for Unity*, "As far as pentecostal membership [in the WCC] is concerned, the absence of the great majority of the Pentecostalist churches is a serious matter, a weakness second only to the official absence of Rome" (284–85). The possibility for better relations between pentecostals and the WCC, though often shunned by both parties, came about through the birth of the charismatic movement in the 1960s.

In Aug. 1980 the Central Committee of the WCC adopted a four-point recommendation made by the subunit on Renewal and Congregational Life. Its recommendations regarding the charismatic renewal came as a result of an important task-force meeting in West Germany (1978) and a theological consultation in Bossey, Switzerland (1980), that investigated the renewal and its implications for all the churches. The result has been an ongoing interest in the worldwide charismatic renewal by the WCC leadership. Subsequently, several books dealing with the pentecostal and charismatic movements have been published by the WCC, as well as many articles in *The Ecumenical Review* and *International Review of Mission*.

The more or less evangelical orientation within the WCC has been apparent since its inception, but it has become especially noticeable since the 6th assembly in Vancouver (1983) and the growing strength of member churches from the Two-Thirds World. This bent was reflected in its general secretary, Emilio Castro, his openness to pentecostals, and his concern for world evangelization. It was Emilio Castro who recommended the title of the 7th assembly in Canberra, Australia (1991), be "Come Holy Spirit." The Central Committee added the clause "Renew the Whole Creation." During this important assembly, pentecostal and charismatic churches received considerable attention. In the end the WCC adopted 10 recommendations that would lead to greater interaction between the WCC and pentecostals.

Following the Canberra assembly, the WCC opened an office in Geneva for Church and Ecumenical Relations and hired Hubert van Beek to staff it. His primary job description involves building relationships between the WCC and evangelical, pentecostal, and AICs. To this end, he has supported the work of Marta Palma, a Chilean pentecostal and WCC staff member who serves the interests of pentecostals and the WCC in Latin America. As early as 1971 the WCC had aided certain encounters between interested pentecostals in meetings known as Encuentro Pentecostal Latinoamericano (EPLA). That work continues in Latin America, but van Beek has also convened a number of regional conferences with pentecostal leaders and representatives of WCC member churches (e.g., Lima, Peru [1994]; San Jose, Costa Rica [1996]; Bossey, Switzerland [1997]; etc.) and has attended and participated in meetings of the ▸Society for Pentecostal Studies as well as the European Pentecostal-Charismatic Research Association.

Through the years the WCC has also sought to build bridges with pentecostal groups by inviting individuals to participate in its assemblies, conferences, and consultations. The Plenary Commission on Faith and Order invited ▸Cecil M. Robeck Jr. to serve as an advisor to its 1989 meeting in Budapest, Hungary, and then asked him to serve as a pentecostal delegate, with voice and vote on the commission between assemblies in 1991–98. Following the 8th assembly in Harare, Zimbabwe (Dec. 1998), he was elected to the Plenary Commission through 2006 and was elected to serve as an advisor to the Standing Commission on Faith and Order, which functions as the executive committee for the Plenary Commission. Robeck also offered a course on "Global Pentecostalism and the Ecumenical Challenge" at the Ecumenical Institute in Bossey, Switzerland, operated by the WCC, on Mar. 5–11, 2001. It was the first course taught by a pentecostal at that institution. Other pentecostals who have repeatedly participated in WCC consultations and assemblies have included such scholars as Harold Hunter (U.S.), Cheryl Bridges Johns (U.S.), Veli-Matti Kärkkäinen (Finland), Simon Chan (Singapore), Juan Sepulveda (Chile), Japie Lapoorta (South Africa), and David Daniels (U.S.).

The Harare assembly also proved pivotal for pentecostal-WCC relations. It approved the formation of a Joint Working Group to work more formally on interests shared between pentecostals and the WCC. This group is patterned in some ways after the Joint Working Group that represents interests shared between the Roman Catholic Church and the WCC. Both groups report internally at the highest levels of the WCC. Since the assembly, the pentecostal group has been renamed the Joint Consultative Group, because it does not represent a specific denomination but rather a complex movement of churches. It was convened for the first time in Hautecombe, France, on June 20–24, 2000, with a pentecostal team drawn from Europe, Africa, Asia, Latin and North America. What the future holds for pentecostal-WCC relations in an increasingly secularized world in which the church is increasingly marginalized is yet to be seen, but interest seems to be increasing.

■ **Bibliography:** A. E. F. Arlt, "The Significance of the Chilean Pentecostals' Admission to the World Council of Churches," *International Review of Missions* 51 (1962) ■ A. Bittlinger, ed., *The Church Is Charismatic* (1981) ■ K. Bridston, "Faith and Order: 1960," *Lutheran World* 8 (1960) ■ D. T. Cole, "Pentecostal Koinonia: An Emerging Ecumenical Ecclesiology among Pentecostals" (diss., Fuller Theol. Sem., 1998) ■ R. Davis, *Locusts and Wild Honey* (1978) ■ M. de Mello, "Participation Is Everything," *International Review of Mission,* 60 (238, Apr. 1971) ■ C. L. d'Epinay, *Haven of the Masses: A Study of the Pentecostal Movement in Chile* (1969) ■ D. P. Gaines, *The World Council of Churches* (1966) ■ D. Gee, "Amsterdam and Pentecost," *Pentecost* 6 (Dec. 1948) ■ idem, "Contact Is Not Compromise," *Pentecost* 53 (Sept.–Nov. 1960) ■ idem, "Missions and Prophets," *Pentecost* 10 (Dec. 1949) ■ idem, "Pentecost and Evanston," *Pentecost* 30 (Dec. 1954) ■ idem, "Pentecostals at New Delhi," *Pentecost* 59 (Mar.-May 1962) ■ P. Hocken, *Streams of Renewal* (1986) ■ W. J. Hollenweger, "Towards an Intercultural History of Christianity," *International Review of Missions* 76 (Oct. 1987) ■ idem, *Pentecostalism: Origins and Development Worldwide* (1997) ■ D. T. Irvin, *Hearing Many Voices: Dialogue and Diversity in the Ecumenical Movement* (1994) ■ D. Kessler, ed., *Together on the Way* (1999) ■ M. Kinnamon, ed., *Signs of the Spirit* (1991) ■ H. Martin, *Beginning at Edinburgh* (1960) ■ J. Moltmann and K.-J. Kuschel, eds., *Pentecostal Movements as an Ecumenical Challenge* (1996) ■ L. Newbigin, *Unfinished Agenda* (1985) ■ C. M. Robeck Jr., "The Assemblies of God and Ecumenical Cooperation: 1920–1965," in W. Ma and R. P. Menzies, eds., *Pentecostalism in Context: Essays in Honor of William W. Menzies* (1997) ■ idem, "The New Ecumenism," in M. Stackhouse, T. Dearborn, and S. Paeth, eds., *The Local Church in a Global Era: Reflections for a New Century* (2000) ■ idem, "A Pentecostal Assessment of 'Towards a Common Understanding and Vision' of the WCC," *Midstream: The Ecumenical Movement Today* 37 (1, 1998) ■ idem, "A Pentecostal Looks at the World Council of Churches," *The Ecumenical Review,* 47 (1, 1995) ■ idem, "Pentecostal Perspectives on the Ecumenical Challenge" (paper, AAR, 1984) ■ idem, "A Pentecostal Reflects on Canberra," in B. J. Nicholls and B. R. Ro, eds., *Beyond Canberra: Evangelical Responses to Contemporary Ecumenical Issues* (1993) ■ idem, "Pentecostals and Ecumenism in a Pluralistic World," in M. W. Dempster, B. Klaus, and D. Petersen, eds., *The Globalization of Pentecostalism: A Religion Made to Travel* (1999) ■ idem, "Some Reflections from a Pentecostal/Evangelical Perspective," in A. Falconer, ed., *Faith and Order in Moshi: The 1996 Commission Meeting* (1998) ■ idem, "Taking Stock of Pentecostalism: The Personal Reflections of a Retiring Editor," *Pneuma* 15 (1, 1993) ■ M. Robinson, "To the Ends of the Earth—The Pilgrimage of an Ecumenical Pentecostal, David J. du Plessis (1905–1987)" (diss., U. of Birmingham [U.K.], 1987) ■

R. Rouse and S. Neill, eds., *A History of the Ecumenical Movement 1517–1948* (1954) ▮ B. Till, *The Churches Search for Unity* (1972) ▮ H. van Beek, ed., *Consultation with Pentecostal Churches* (1994) ▮ idem, ed., *Consultation with Pentecostals in the Americas* (1996) ▮ A. J. van der Bent, *What in the World Is the World Council of Churches?* (1978, 1981) ▮ W. A. Visser 't Hooft, *The Genesis and Formation of the World Council of Churches* (1982) ▮ idem, *Has the Ecumenical Movement a Future?* (1974) ▮ World Council of Churches Yearbook: 2000. ■ C. M. Robeck Jr.; J. L. Sandidge

WORLEY, A. S. (1921–). An independent pentecostal evangelist from Walhalla, SC, Worley was invited to come to New Zealand to conduct healing campaigns. Worley arrived in late 1959 and conducted a number of campaigns over the next 12 months. He had considerable influence on the new generation of healing evangelists then emerging in N.Z. Worley's ministry in N.Z. was notable for the healings that took place, particularly the filling of people's teeth as a sign of the power of God. His most significant contribution, however, was his highly successful campaign in Timaru in June and July 1960. The Timaru revival ignited a wave of healing evangelism in the South Island and led to unprecedented pentecostal growth in N.Z. The New Life Churches, for example, grew tenfold (from 6 to more than 60 churches) during the five-year period 1960 to 1965. This expansion is directly attributable to the ministries of Worley and of the evangelists he inspired during his time in N.Z.

■ **Bibliography:** R. E. Grice, *Apostle to the Nations: An Authorised Biography of A. S. Worley, a Man of Faith and Miracles* (n.d. [1990]) ▮ B. Knowles, "For the Sake of the Name: A History of the 'New Life Churches' from 1942 to 1965" (thesis, U. of Otago, 1988) ▮ idem, "Some Aspects of the History of the New Life Churches of New Zealand 1960–1990" (diss., U. of Otago, 1994). ■ B. Knowles

WORRELL, ADOLPHUS SPALDING (1831–1908). Well-known Baptist scholar, teacher, editor, evangelist, and—in later life—a seeker for the baptism in the Spirit at the ▸Azusa Street Mission. After Worrell's death in 1908 the *Louisville Courier-Journal* ran a full-column obituary, "Divine Healer to the Last," which described him as something of an eccentric but godly man who refused any kind of medical help for the stomach cancer that took his life.

Educated at Mercer University, Worrell was regarded as a Greek scholar in the 19th century, and he devoted much of his early career to teaching. He was also president of Mt. Pleasant College in Missouri. During the Civil War he was a captain for the Confederate forces and then became a Baptist evangelist. In the 1890s he was an editor for the *Western Recorder,* the Kentucky Baptist paper. He later published his own periodical, *The Gospel Witness.* In 1903 he completed a translation of the NT, the *Worrell New Testament,* which is still being published by ▸Gospel Publishing House.

Worrell had been in the ministry for nearly 40 years by 1891 when, he reported, he had a spiritual experience in which Christ was revealed to him and "enthroned in his heart as permanent Ruler thereof" *(Didactic and Devotional Poems).* After personally investigating the pentecostal movement, he wrote "An Open Letter to the Opposers of This Pentecostal Movement," in which he—while not accepting everything that was going on under the name of pentecostal—attempted to reason with people who had formed negative opinions of the movement.

■ **Bibliography:** "Divine Healer to the Last," *Louisville Courier-Journal* (Aug. 1, 1908) ▮ *The Western Recorder* (1890s) ▮ A. Worrell, *Didactic and Devotional Poems* (1906) ▮ idem, "An Open Letter to the Opposers of This Pentecostal Movement," *Triumphs of Faith* (Nov. 1907; repr. in *AGH* [Spring 1992]). ■ W. E. Warner

WORSHIP Worship, in the general sense, refers to piety or spirituality. In the more specific, or narrow, sense, it refers to the form or style of expression of piety or spirituality and is a public witness to the union of God and humanity. An early pentecostal educator and minister, M. E. Collins (*Worship,* 7), defined worship as "the act of expressing profound love, appreciation, reverence, and devotion to a thing, person or God." Defined in this way, worship is a social, or human, choice to help remind the believer of God's presence and provision. In this article, worship will be viewed in the narrow sense by which Collins defined it, that is, as an expression of piety and spirituality. Focus will be chiefly on the contributions of the Lutheran, Reformed, Free Church, Anglican, Quaker, and Methodist worship traditions as background to pentecostal worship.

Two phrases can sum up the Protestant tradition: justification by faith and the priesthood of all believers (Bartlett).

Worship service in a Liberian pentecostal church, June 29, 1967.

The appropriate social response to these notions is thanksgiving. As a result, two ordinances, or observances, are common as praise, celebration, or thanksgiving to most Protestant groups. Baptism and initiation is carried over from the Roman Catholic practice of baptism and confirmation. The observance of the Lord's Supper replaced the Mass as a distinctive ordinance of worship. The Lord's Supper is generally seen as a memorial of thanksgiving to the saving work in Christ. To a Protestant, the elements are a reminder of the death and resurrection of Christ and are not assumed by most to be a sacrifice. In the observance of both baptism and the Lord's Supper, the believer offers her or his life as a sacrifice to Christ. The vows of initiation, whether they are taken in baptism or in sharing the Lord's Supper, are renewed on a regular basis in some Protestant denominations. In addition, wedding and funeral services can be included within the category of worship.

1. Lutheran.

Lutheran worship is strongly conservative and formal (White). Martin Luther initially wanted to reform the Catholic Church rather than establish an alternative worship experience. At the same time, many of his innovations were drastic for the times and provided the model for a significant portion of Protestant liturgical worship. For example, Luther emphasized the sacraments but was the first prominent leader to point out that the sacraments were not sacrificial.

The Lord's Supper for Luther contained the physical and spiritual presence of Christ in the worship service, but he also believed that preaching should be the center of the service. In addition, music and the visual arts have been emphasized in Lutheran worship. Many of the well-known hymns sung by the different denominations were written by Lutheran hymn writers, and composers have provided the Western world with standards of excellence.

2. Reformed.

John Calvin is largely responsible for the pattern of the Reformed worship service and has had considerable impact on other Protestant churches, most notably in the simplicity of style and in the lack of liturgy (Bartlett; tenZythoff). Through the influence of Luther and Calvin, the preaching of the Word on each Lord's Day gradually became the central focus of Protestant worship. Calvin thought the Catholic worship style was too passive and allowed the worshiper to entertain stray thoughts. In order for worship to have the desired effect, i.e., to produce a change in the lives of believers, Calvin argued that believers had to play an active part in the worship experience by meditation, reflection, and self-examination. This was possible only if the Scriptures were available in the believers' language and if preaching was done under the anointing of the Holy Spirit so as to engage the minds of believers. As the saving work of grace came to be understood as the work of the Holy Spirit, preaching was seen to be the expression of the uttered word of God as revealed through the words of Scripture. As each believer is a priest, each has access to God through the Word, as revealed by the Holy Spirit, rather than through the sacraments. Calvin thought that the Lord's Supper should be observed no more often than once a month lest it lose its symbolic significance, which, for Calvin, was its chief significance.

Calvin encouraged singing because singing also required active engagement by the worshiper. Calvin saw music as being both a symbolic aid to help focus the believer's mind on Christ and thus an aid in worship, and as an expression of worship in its own right. Public prayer, for Calvin, was also an aid to worship and should be spontaneous rather than written, and patterned after the NT prayers.

3. Free Church.

The Free Church tradition contributed two specific expressions to Protestant worship (Mead). First, the autonomy of the local congregation meant that no form of expression became standard. Second, an emphasis on the authority of the Word of God as the model for worship precluded prayerbooks and liturgy.

There are three general categories of Free Church tradition: the Anabaptist, the Puritan, and the Disciples of Christ (White; Hughes). The Anabaptist movement began as a resistance to official churches. As a result, the form of worship was simple, with a great deal of local variation. Some stressed singing; others stressed the Lord's Supper. All limited baptism to believers.

The Puritans believed that worship should include only what Scripture allowed. No liturgy or ceremony was included, and some opposed the recitation of the Lord's Prayer. In contrast to the Anabaptists, however, they practiced infant baptism.

The Disciples of Christ are a product of the American frontier revivals, and, in contrast to the Puritans, they attempt to avoid all that Scripture avoided. Systematic theology and formal creeds receive less emphasis, while preaching receives

Praising God during evangelistic crusade in Honduras (1988).

greater emphasis as a result. Disciples of Christ reject infant baptism as unscriptural but give the Lord's Supper central place in the worship experience.

4. Anglican.

The Anglican tradition of worship revolves around the 1549 edition of the *Book of Common Prayer* by Thomas Cranmer and its later revisions. The congregation participates in worship by reciting Scriptures, prayers, and readings. Initially, hymns and the Lord's Supper were excluded but were added later, although some conservatives among Anglicans are still opposed to both.

5. Quaker.

The Quaker contribution to worship has been the removal of sermons, public prayers, and hymns from the service (Flew). Even Scripture is considered less important than the voice of the Holy Spirit, who provides an inner light within each worshiper. Emphasis is placed on corporate worship, or meeting, where each person waits patiently and quietly for the Holy Spirit to speak to him or her; when this happens, the individual tells the others what the Spirit revealed. While the Quakers stress the work of the Holy Spirit in revealing inner light, they do not believe in the outward manifestation of the baptism of the Holy Spirit, such as glossolalia, which most modern Quakers view as disruptive. In addition, Quakers stress the equality of all believers, with no categorization by gender, racial, or income differences.

6. Methodist.

The Methodist worship style is a pragmatic blend of several traditions (Hughes). Under the influence of John and Charles Wesley, Methodism began as a renewal movement within the Anglican Church and included elements from Moravian worship, Puritan evangelicalism, and Reformed preaching. The worship experience included hymns set to popular music, informal preaching, and spontaneous prayer.

In the U.S., due to the influence of Bishop Francis Asbury, the formal, liturgical contribution of the Anglican tradition was dropped, while preaching, hymn singing, and spontaneous prayer were underscored. For ceremonies such as baptisms, weddings, funerals, and some other special observances, aspects of the *Book of Common Prayer* have been retained (White).

The Methodists were instrumental in the revival movements of the 19th century and represented a distinctively American religious movement. The Methodists emphasized hymns in the revival meetings and involved the worshipers as active, joyous participants rather than as mere observers.

7. Pentecostal.

Pentecostal worship is an eclectic amalgamation of a variety of traditions, reflecting, to some extent, the denominational origins of its adherents. Some congregations maintain a significant form of liturgical worship, while others appear, at least to the outsider, to have no coherent pattern or order of worship. All, however, are characterized by an attitude of allowing the Holy Spirit to lead, an attitude that means pentecostal worship tends to be less structured than that of other groups, even of those groups with which it shares similarities. Historically, pentecostal worship style is linked to the frontier revivals conducted primarily by Methodists, Disciples of Christ, and Baptists in 19th-century America (Mead).

The pentecostal churches that were organized during the first decades of the 20th century place emphasis on the work of the Holy Spirit in worship. The central focus of the service is not the sermon or the music, but the moving of the Holy Spirit. There is the expectation that God will minister in love to the worshiper through the agency of the Holy Spirit (Collins). Normally, the service will stop for the moving of the Holy Spirit, usually expressed through glossolalia.

Some of the larger pentecostal and charismatic churches have developed specialized worship leaders, such as song leaders, who not only select songs but actively participate in the worship experience, being sensitive to the needs of those who are present. The altar service, a holdover from the frontier revival meetings, has become an institutionalized part of the service in some churches. Many churches have specific

Jamaican women worshiping.

Worship at the Truth Bible Institute, Beijing, China.

persons designated as altar workers. The practice can vary from having mature Christians in the congregation pray and counsel those who come forward, to having a volunteer staff of lay "prayer counselors," led either by another volunteer or by a staff member of the church (Collins).

Since the early 1960s there has been dramatic increase in the numbers of charismatics in the historical or mainline denominations, including the Catholic Church. Usually designated charismatics or neo-pentecostals, these enthusiasts are developing a new style of worship that combines both glossolalia and the traditional worship style of the denomination in which they are centered. This certainly is one of the more interesting trends in modern expressions of worship (Randall).

While most pentecostal worship services have only recently begun to be racially integrated again, blacks have shared leadership from the beginning of the modern pentecostal movement, taking an active part in the historical pentecostal revivals. As a result, black influence can be seen in preaching style and in music, both of which play significant roles in pentecostal worship (Patterson et al.; Synan, 1997).

As a result of the many possible combinations of worship styles, people with different worship needs are able to find the style most appropriate to them. People from different traditions now are being brought together in meaningful worship experiences. The isolation of traditional pentecostals is being penetrated, and the number of pentecostals around the world is increasing. In short, pentecostals and neo-pentecostals are discovering that God can be worshiped in a variety of ways; Christians thereby may live a life energized by the Holy Spirit (Synan, 1987).

See also MUSIC, PENTECOSTAL AND CHARISMATIC; SPIRITUALITY, PENTECOSTAL AND CHARISMATIC.

■ **Bibliography:** J. V. Bartlett "Worship (Christian)" in J. Hastings, ed., *Encyclopedia of Religion and Ethics* (1925), 12:762–76 ■ G. Collins, *Innovative Approaches to Counseling* (1986) ■ M. E. Collins, *Worship* (n.d.) ■ R. N. Flew, *The Ideas of Perfection in Christian Theology* (1934) ■ J. W. Fowler, *Faith Development and Pastoral Care* (1987) ■ R. T. Hughes, "Christian Primitivism as Perfectionism: From Anabaptists to Pentecostals," in S. M. Burgess, ed., *Reaching Beyond: Chapters in the History of Perfectionism* (1986) ■ S. Mead, *The Lively Experiment* (1963) ■ J. O. Patterson, *History and Formative Years of the Church of God in Christ with Excerpts from the Life and Writings of C. H. Mason* (1969) ■ C. Randall, "The Importance of the Pentecostal and Holiness Churches in the Ecumenical Movement," *Pneuma* (Spring 1987) ■ V. Synan, *The Holiness-Pentecostal Movement* (1971, 1997) ■ idem, "Pentecostalism: Varieties and Contributions," *Pneuma* (Spring 1987) ■ G. J. tenZythoff, "The Non-Perfectionism of John Calvin," in S. M. Burgess, ed., *Reaching Beyond: Chapters in the History of Perfectionism* (1986) ■ J. F. White, *Christian Worship in Transition* (1976).   ■ J. W. Shepperd

WRIGHT, JAMES ELWIN (1890–1973). Minister, real estate developer, religious executive, and author. Wright was born in Corinth, VT, to Joel Adams and Mary Melissa (Goodwin) Wright, and was married to Florence Daisy Dunkling in 1911. They had one daughter, Muriel Virginia (Evans). For a time Wright entered the ministry, having received a theological education at the Missionary Training Institute (▶Christian and Missionary Alliance) at Nyack, NY, in 1921. His strengths, however, lay in his organizational skills and his ability to work one-on-one.

Working as a real estate developer in New England, Wright attached himself to Park Street Church in Boston. During the 1920s, he sought to establish an organization that would provide a unified identity and voice to conservative Christians in New England. His New England Fellowship, formed in 1929, quickly gained a broad following, including pentecostals; it brought together over a thousand churches in its first five years of existence.

Wright began a nationwide trip in 1937 to test the feasibility of a similar organization on the national level. By 1939 he was openly promoting the idea, and in Apr. 1942 he called a National Conference for United Action Among Evangelicals to be convened in St. Louis, MO. This meeting gave birth to the ▶National Association of Evangelicals (NAE).

From its inception, Wright helped to include pentecostals in the NAE, often at considerable personal expense. He remained with the NAE as executive secretary of the commission on international relations (1948–57). In 1951 he became cosecretary to the World Evangelical Fellowship. He authored *The Old Fashioned Revival Hour* (1940; rev. 1942), *Evangelical Action!* (1942), and *Manna in the Morning* (1943). In his later years he made his home in Rumney Depot, NH, while maintaining an office in Boston.

■ **Bibliography:** J. Carpenter, "The Fundamentalist Leaven and the Rise of an Evangelical United Front," in L. I. Sweet, *The Evan-*

gelical Tradition in America (1984) ■ G. M. Marsden, *Reforming Fundamentalism* (1987) ■ J. D. Murch, *Co-Operation without Compromise* (1956) ■ *Who's Who in America*, 1958–59.

■ C. M. Robeck Jr.

WYATT, THOMAS (1891–1964). Evangelist and radio speaker. Reared in hardship and deprivation in Jasper County, IA, Wyatt left school at age 11 when his father became a semi-invalid. After his conversion in the Methodist church at Ira, IA, he had a near-death experience. While in an 18-hour coma, he heard the words, "I am the Lord that healeth thee." After his recovery he began a Midwestern healing ministry that even attracted the attention of *Look* magazine (Nov. 23, 1937).

In that same year Wyatt moved to Portland, OR, where he established a ministry that continued for 22 years. *Wings of Healing*, his pioneer radio healing ministry, was first heard on Mother's Day in 1942. By June 21, 1953, his broadcasts were carried on both the ABC network and 552 Mutual Broadcasting Company stations. In July 1957 he began "Global Frontiers Telecast," an expansion of an intensely patriotic, anticommunist campaign begun in 1954 (*March of Faith* 9 [7, 1954]: 14–15; 9 [8, 1954]: 14–15). Round-the-world short-wave radio broadcasts began in 1959.

A 1953 evangelistic and healing crusade in West Africa prompted the establishment in Portland of Bethesda World Training Center (Bethesda Bible Institute had been established in 1947). From this school Wyatt sent forth "Gospel invasion teams" on an international level as an evangelistic effort and patriotic American resistance to the spread of communism. The ministry established new headquarters in the Embassy Building, Los Angeles, in Oct. 1959.

During 1962–63, Wyatt conducted numerous evangelistic tours of America. A massive heart attack felled him on Dec. 9, 1962. After recovering, he reestablished his fast pace. He continued his preaching tours, speaking against threats from world communism, militant atheism, and apathy and indifference in the church (see "Report on 'World Crisis Conference,'" *March of Faith* 18 [10, 1963]).

Struck down again in Nov. 1963, he still continued his radio ministry. He died peacefully in his sleep on Apr. 19, 1964.

■ **Bibliography:** *A Memorial Tribute to Thomas Wyatt—A Man of Vision* (1964) ■ B. Miller, *Grappling with Destiny* (1962) ■ T. Wyatt, *Give Me This Mountain* (n.d.) ■ T. Wyatt, ed., *The March of Faith* (1946–; continued after his death by his wife, Evelyn).

■ J. A. Hewett

Y

YEOMANS, LILIAN BARBARA (1861–1942). Faith healer. Born in Calgary, Alb., the eldest of three daughters. Both parents were medical doctors. Lilian Yeomans was reared in a Christian home, attending Sunday school and church regularly. During the Civil War her family moved to the U.S., where her father served as a surgeon for the U.S. Army. This led to Lilian's interest in a medical career. Ultimately she graduated with a M.D. degree from the University of Michigan and returned to Canada, where she went into practice in partnership with her mother, Amelia Le Sueur Yeomans, as a physician and surgeon.

To manage the stress from her heavy practice she began to rely on drugs, among them morphine and chloral hydrate. She soon became addicted to morphine. When she showed signs of advanced addiction, she attempted all known medical cures, including a detoxification program at the Keeley Gold Cure Institute. That proved to be ineffective, and she was placed in a sanitarium for nervous diseases. She traveled from Winnipeg to New York City, where she also attempted a cure through Christian Science practitioners. That, too, proved to be ineffective, and she began to read her Bible. Her healing came on Jan. 12, 1898, under the ministry of ▸John Alexander Dowie.

In true Holiness fashion, Lilian sought a crisis experience of sanctification; she claimed to have received it in Sept. 1907. That same night she also spoke in tongues. Over the next several months she wrote a variety of letters to her mother and other acquaintances, which were subsequently published in the *Way of Faith,* and separately under the title of *Pentecostal Letters,* which was compiled by her mother. These letters outline her understanding of speaking in tongues and her feelings about the value of the pentecostal experience. She encouraged her mother, who had been the vice president of the Canadian Woman's Christian Temperance Union and president of that country's Suffrage Club, to ask God for the experience; she received it in Jan. 1908. Lilian Yeomans later held evangelistic meetings throughout the U.S. and Canada. She attempted to pioneer pentecostal works, especially in Alberta.

In Yeomans' later years she settled in Manhattan Beach, CA. She served on the faculty of L.I.F.E. Bible College under ▸Aimee Semple McPherson, where she taught courses on divine healing and church history. She authored several devotional books and works on healing, all of which were published between her 65th and 81st years. In 1940, at the age of 80, she was still conducting evangelistic meetings. In 1941, at the encouragement of her friend ▸Carrie Judd Montgomery, she published a short book of her sister's works titled *Gold of Ophir: Spiritual Songs Given through Amy Yeomans.* Yeomans died on Dec. 9, 1942, and is buried in Forest Lawn Cemetery, Glendale, CA.

■ **Bibliography:** L. B. Yeomans, *Balm of Gilead* (1935) ▮ idem, *Divine Healing Diamonds* (1933) ▮ idem, *Healing from Heaven* (1926) ▮ idem, *The Hiding Place* (1940) ▮ idem, *Resurrection Rays* (1930) ▮ idem, *The Royal Road to Health-ville* (1938) ▮ idem, *The Upper Room* 1 (1910): 3.   ■ C. M. Robeck Jr.

YOAKUM, FINIS EWING (1851–1920). Faith healer and social reformer. A medical doctor who practiced in Texas, Colorado, and California, Finis Yoakum gave up his lucrative career (he reportedly earned $18,000 per month) after a personal healing in order to found the Pisgah Home Movement. His parents were Franklin and Narcissa (Teague) Yoakum; his father was a country physician in Texas who later became a minister with the Cumberland Presbyterian Church and served as the president of their college in Larissa, TX. Finis and his wife, Mary, whom he married in 1873, had three sons and twin daughters.

Yoakum studied at Larissa College as well as at another college, in the Dallas–Fort Worth area. Ultimately, he graduated with the M.D. degree from the Hospital College of Medicine in Louisville, KY, on June 16, 1885. Following medical school he specialized in neurological disorders and finally occupied the chair of mental diseases on the faculty of Gross Medical College in Denver, CO.

On the evening of July 18, 1894, while on his way to organize a class leader's association for the Methodist Church, he was struck by a buggy driven by a drunken man. A piece of metal pierced his back, broke several ribs, and caused internal hemorrhaging. A medical assessment of his injuries predicted that they would be fatal. Plagued by infection for several months, he moved to Los Angeles, hoping to gain relief. There, on Feb. 5, 1895, he was prayed for by W. C. Stevens of the Christian Alliance, at which time he began a remarkable recovery, nearly doubling his weight within three months. On July 2, 1895, he was awarded a license to practice medicine in California.

That year, Dr. Yoakum received a vision directing him toward a mission to the needy. While Yoakum continued to hold his medical certification until his death, he closed his formal medical practice, moved out of his house into a tent, and adopted the habit of wearing secondhand clothes. He built a tabernacle that doubled as a dormitory in Arroyo Seco between Los Angeles and Pasadena, and vowed to spend the remainder of his life serving the chronically ill, poor, destitute, and social outcasts.

While in the Los Angeles area, he associated with the Holiness churches, frequently speaking on divine healing at their camp meetings and annual gatherings between 1901 and 1904. When the ‣Azusa Street revival broke out in 1906, Yoakum visited the mission. He spoke in tongues as early as 1902, and he wrote of this continuing experience in 1911. He maintained a cordial, even supportive, relationship with the fledgling pentecostal movement but never identified himself closely with it. This lack of close identification led to criticism of him by ‣E. N. Bell, who warned his readers that Yoakum was not really "pentecostal."

Yoakum held regular healing services for several years at 1 P.M. on Mondays at the Spring Street Mission and at 1 P.M. on Thursdays at the assembly on Eighth and Maple. He held Sunday services at his tabernacle and conducted other services on his properties in what would later become North Hollywood. When he was not on his Pisgah properties, he could be found most days in an office suite between 10 A.M. and 1 P.M. in downtown Los Angeles, where he laid hands on, and prayed for, the sick and needy who sought him out. He distributed handkerchiefs or prayer cloths.

From 1907 on Yoakum began a wider public ministry that reached its peak between 1911 and 1914. In addition to his own periodical, *Pisgah,* his work was widely publicized by ‣Carrie Judd Montgomery in *Triumphs of Faith,* by ‣A. A. Boddy in *Confidence,* by ‣William Hamner Piper in the *Latter Rain Evangel,* and by Samuel Otis in *Word and Work.* During these years he engaged in a public speaking ministry throughout the U.S., Canada, and Great Britain.

Yoakum was a controversial figure throughout the latter part of his life. He was the object of a love-hate relationship with the city of Los Angeles, because his ministry attracted indigents to the city from other areas of the country, yet the city was happy to send many of their own to him for care. He also encountered criticism because he refused to make his financial books available for public scrutiny. His comment was that those who did not trust him should not give and those who gave should trust him. Finally, he alienated some because he received ordination as a "bishop" from a self-appointed bishop in the East.

Yoakum was compared by some to ‣John Alexander Dowie, for in 1914 he purchased a 3,225-acre parcel in Lime Valley, northeast of Los Angeles, where he intended to establish a utopian center under the name of Pisgah Grande. His death from a heart attack in 1920 left that work unfinished.

See also PISGAH HOME MOVEMENT.

■ **Bibliography:** A. A. Boddy, "Dr. Yoakum's Work at Los Angeles," *Confidence* 5 (11, 1912) ▥ "Founder of Pisgah Dies," *Los Angeles Daily Times* 2 (Aug. 19, 1920) ▥ "Some Information," *Work and Witness* (Dec. 20, 1913) ▥ P. D. Smith, *He Is Just the Same Today* (1931). ■ C. M. Robeck Jr.

YOUTH WITH A MISSION A nondenominational parachurch organization whose purpose is to provide Christian service and to evangelize the world with youth. It had its origin in a vision given to a young Assembly of God (AG) Bible college student, Loren Cunningham, in 1956. The vision consisted of waves of youth going ashore on every continent in the world to evangelize. Cunningham began Youth With A Mission (YWAM) in his parents' California home in Dec. 1960. He incorporated YWAM in the summer of 1961 and became its director. His first two missionaries went to a Liberian leper colony as vocational volunteers (1961–62). He sought for YWAM to be accepted as part of the foreign missions effort of the AG (1961). AG responded by offering him a position in the AG international headquarters; however, in 1964, after 146 young YWAMers had spent eight weeks in the Bahama Islands winning 6,000 souls, AG officials and Cunningham were unable to agree on a structure for YWAM. Cunningham never responded to the job offer, gave up his AG ministerial credentials, and developed YWAM as an interdenominational evangelistic ministry that included street meetings, door-to-door evangelism, music, drama, urban evangelism, Olympic evangelism, and mercy service.

The structure established by Cunningham consists of two legal corporations. The first of these operates four mercy ships. The second corporation consists of four regions that are divided and subdivided into areas, nations, and districts. The four field offices are located in Tyler, TX; Harpenden, U.K. (two field offices); and Canberra, Australia. Each region has its own council; however, authority is decentralized and located in more than 670 autonomous centers in 142 countries. Each center has its own separate funding, constitution, bylaws, board, incorporation, and IRS clearance.

The operation of YWAM is unified by an international council consisting of a board of seven men and an annual strategy conference. There are 35 international offices. One is in Belo Horizonte, Brazil, where James Stier, the former president, is located. A second office is in Auckland, N.Z., where Frank Naea, the current president, whose term started Sept. 2000, is located. A third office is located in Lausanne, Switzerland, where Loren Cunningham, the founder and international chairman is located. The Pacific and Asia Christian University (PACU) founded in Kailua-Kona, HI, has become the University of the Nations, with seven campuses in six countries. There are no salaried employees in this structure; instead, each person must raise his or her own funding, even though YWAM has no definite ties with any specific denomination.

Currently, YWAM sends over 50,000 short-term (2–3 months) volunteers out each summer to do evangelistic work; has over 11,500 full-time workers; has more than 240 Discipleship Training Schools (DTS) with a five-month curriculum; offers college degrees at the University of the Nations in such areas as Christian ministries, communication, counseling, and education; and owns four mercy ships that provide medical and engineering services, deliver relief and emergency supplies, and do discipleship training and evangelism. Thus far, YWAM has ministered in every one of the more than 220 present-day countries on earth.

In 1976 YWAM–Austria became interested in working with charismatic Catholics. Gradually this interest provided the impetus to start providing Catholics with discipleship training. This work with Catholics has expanded from Austria to Poland, Ireland, Germany, England, U.S., Uganda, Ghana, Philippines, Columbia, and New Zealand. The Roman Catholics have responded by forming the International Catholic Program for Evangelization (ICPE), which is an adaptation of YWAM's DTS.

■ **Bibliography:** "Abused Teen Who Killed Dad Sentenced to YWAM Work," *Charisma* 9 (1984) ■ M. A. Berry, ed., *The Great Commission Handbook 1988 Edition* (1987) ■ A. Butcher, "YWAM April 1999 News Release," YWAM Web Site (Apr. 1999) ■ L. Cunningham, "Chronology of Steps of YWAM's Relationship with Springfield," director's report (c. Sept. 1962) ■ L. Cunningham and J. Rogers, *Is That Really You, God? Hearing the Voice of God* (1984) ■ D. M. Cupial, "Renewal among Catholics in Poland," *Pneuma* 16 (Fall 1994) ■ G. Dryden, YWAM researcher, telephone interview by author, Aug. 19, 1999 ■ R. Grant, "Olympic Challenge," *Charisma* 9 (1984) ■ P. Hocken, "Youth With A Mission," *Pneuma* 16 (Fall 1994) ■ B. Joffe, "Man with a Mission," *Charisma* 11 (1985) ■ University of the Nations International Home Page (Feb. 1999) ■ R. M. Wilson, *God's Guerrillas: Youth With A Mission* (1971) ■ "World Christian Bookstore, a ministry of Youth With A Mission," YWAM Web Site (June 1999).   ■ E. B. Robinson

Z

ZAIRE EVANGELISTIC MISSION Originally founded as the Congo Evangelistic Mission by ▸William F. P. Burton and ▸James Salter. Burton was a student at the ▸Pentecostal Missionary Union (PMU) Bible School, Preston, Lancashire. Due to sail for Africa with James McNiell, he was in disagreement with leaders of the PMU and sailed alone in Mar. 1914. Joined later by his friend "Jimmy" Salter, they journeyed together with two others to the Belgian Congo, arriving there in Sept. 1915. Taking the name Pentecostal Mission, they were for a time part of the Pentecostal Mission in South and Central Africa. Burton become their legal representative.

With the continuation of the war in Europe, the only help came from the U.S. Burton went to South Africa in 1918 and returned with four helpers, including Hettie Trollip, whom he married. Salter returned to Britain for Easter 1919. Traveling extensively, he had a great impact and gathered several new workers, including Cyril Taylor, a final-year medical student from Cambridge; Smith Wigglesworth's daughter, Alice, whom Salter married; and ▸Edmund Hodgson from Preston.

Following the Kingsway Convention in Whitsun 1919, at which many of the leaders were present, the Congo Evangelistic Mission was established, with offices in Preston. A. E. Saxby (1873–1960) was chosen president and ▸Thomas Myerscough, secretary-treasurer. Burton became field director and Salter became home director. Support and personnel came from the ▸Elim Pentecostal churches and from independent churches and the Assemblies of God.

F. D. Johnstone, a former Preston student and worker in the Congo since 1914, joined the group with his wife. Fevers and dysentery struck many times, and some fourteen workers died, while others were compelled to return incapacitated. In spite of the difficulties, the work expanded. In total, some 189 missionaries served on the field. In addition there were many national workers, from a total of 25 in 1925 to 578 in 1960. In 1960 there was a staff of 80 at 13 stations; 65 were Europeans. There were 40,000 registered believers in 950 assemblies.

Independence from Belgian rule in June 1960 saw a period of civil unrest when many believers were killed. The missionaries were withdrawn for a time; but New Zealander Elton Knauf and E. Hodgson returned when conditions were still unsettled and were killed in Nov. 1960.

See also Part I: Congo, Democratic Republic of (section I.A).

■ **Bibliography:** W. Burton, *God Working with Them* (1933) ■ M. W. Moorhead, *Missionary Pioneering in the Congo Forests* (1922) ■ H. Womersley, *Congo Miracle* (1974).   ■ D. W. Cartwright

ZIMMERMAN, THOMAS FLETCHER (1912–91). Assemblies of God (AG) minister and administrator. Thomas F. Zimmerman was born in Indianapolis, IN, the son of Thomas Fletcher and Carrie D. (Kenagy) Zimmerman. He was converted at the age of seven, at approximately the time his mother was healed of tuberculosis; he experienced the pentecostal baptism of the Holy Spirit four years later. While still in high school, Zimmerman felt called into full-time gospel ministry, initially intending to go as a missionary to China.

After a year at Indiana University, which he left because of family financial pressures, Zimmerman worked for a printing business. In 1928 he became assistant pastor to John Price of Indianapolis, whose daughter he married five years later. He was ordained by the AG in 1936 and pastored AG churches in Kokomo, IN (1933); Harrodsburg, IN (1934); South Bend, IN (1935–39); Granite City, IL (1939–42); Springfield, MO (1943–47); and Cleveland, OH (1951–52). From 1941 to 1943 he served as assistant superintendent, Illinois District of the AG; from 1943 to 1947 as assistant superintendent, Southern Missouri District of the AG; and from 1949 to 1951 as secretary-treasurer, Southern Missouri District of the AG.

The radio department of the AG was born in 1945, and Zimmerman was chosen as its director. From 1946 to 1949 he was narrator of a 15-minute weekly program, *Sermons in Song*. Because of his interest in radio evangelism, he also was among the founders of the National Religious Broadcasters, an organization he served both as vice president and president.

Thomas Zimmerman and Burt Webb in Nigeria, 1959.

In 1953 Zimmerman became an assistant general superintendent of the AG, and at the general council meeting at San Antonio in 1959 he assumed the chief leadership role, a position he retained until 1985. During his 26 years as general superintendent, the AG experienced phenomenal growth, doubling in numbers of members, adherents, and ministers. By 1985 the AG had 11 accredited colleges (he served on the boards of directors of Central Bible College and Evangel College, Springfield, MO), and the AG Theological Seminary (originally the AG Graduate School) had been founded, with Zimmerman serving as president from 1973 to 1985. Maranatha Village retirement complex also originated under his leadership, and he was chairman of its board of directors from 1976 to 1985.

Zimmerman's strong influence has been felt outside the AG as well. He was the first pentecostal to be elected as president of the ▸National Association of Evangelicals, which the AG joined in 1942. He also served as a member of the executive committee, Lausanne Committee for World Evangelization; as president, Lausanne Committee for World Evangelization—U.S.A.; as chairman of the ▸Pentecostal Fellowship of North America; and as a member of the board of managers, American Bible Society, since 1967. He also has served with the international advisory committee of the ▸Pentecostal World Conference as chairman for the past six conferences: 1970 in Dallas, TX; 1973 in Seoul, Korea; 1976 in London; 1979 in Vancouver, B.C.; 1982 in Nairobi, Kenya; and 1985 in Geneva, Switzerland.

Thomas Zimmerman was known for his personal charisma and drive, his exceptionally strong leadership style (although this occasionally has been controversial), and his prominent level of participation in the life of his church and community.

■ **Bibliography:** C. Brumback, *Suddenly . . . from Heaven* (1961) ■ W. W. Menzies, *Anointed to Serve* (1971) ■ Minutes of the General Council of the Assemblies of God (esp. 1959ff.) ■ "No Regrets for AG's Shepherd," *The Springfield News-Leader* (Sept. 8, 1985), E1, E6 ■ *Who's Who in America* (1975ff.) ■ *Who's Who in Religion* (1976). ■ S. M. Burgess

ZION CITY See DOWIE, JOHN ALEXANDER.

ZION EVANGELISTIC FELLOWSHIP Established in 1935, the Zion Evangelistic Fellowship brought together independent churches in at least a half-dozen northeastern states. ▸Christine A. Gibson (1879–1955), the founder, designed it as an agency for life service of graduates of Zion Bible Institute, East Providence, RI, which she headed, and as means of enlisting financial and prayer support for the school and foreign missions.

In 1953 the 96 congregations in the fellowship had a combined membership of 10,000. Most of the 22 missionaries it then endorsed were working in Africa. Teachings were similar to those of the AG. In 1956, a year after Gibson's death, the Zion Evangelistic Fellowship was dissolved. Shortly thereafter former members in New Hampshire and Maine formed the Apostolic Challenge, a ministerial fellowship similar to the original organization.

■ **Bibliography:** R. Crayne, *Pentecostal Handbook* (1986) ■ R. L. Moore, "Handbook of Pentecostal Denominations in the United States" (M.A. thesis, Pasadena College, 1954). ■ C. E. Jones

ZOPFI, JAKOB (1932–). Swiss pentecostal pastor and evangelist. Born in Switzerland, Zopfi was educated at Elim Bible College in London, England, and graduated in 1959. He began his ministry as pastor of the Swiss Pentecostal Mission in Basel (1961–65) and was ordained in 1964. That same year he married his wife, Sylvia; they have two sons and one daughter. After leaving the pastorate, Zopfi engaged in evangelistic ministry. During that period, he also taught at the Bible School in Gunten/Emmetten, Switzerland.

Throughout Zopfi's extensive ministry, he has been a leader in the European pentecostal movement. Since 1967 he has, at one time or another, been involved in or been a leader within the following organizations: Pentecostal Assemblies of Switzerland (SPM), Pentecostal European Conference (PEK/EPF), which later became the Pentecostal European Fellowship (PEF), the Swiss Evangelical Alliance (SEA), the Federation of Pentecostal Churches of Switzerland (BPF), and most recently the ▸Pentecostal World Conference (PWC). Since 1973 he has been the general superintendent of the SPM.

Zopfi's editorial responsibilities have included *Wort und Geist* (formerly *Verheissung des Vaters*) and the official publication of the PWC, *World Pentecost*. Additionally, he has edited several books, including *Schwarmgeist* (1976); *Prophetie und Endzeit* (1982); *Auf alles Fleisch* (a study of pentecostal history, 1985); *Jesus—Maszstab in allem*, 2 vols. (1991, 1993); and *Wer die Amsel nicht hört* (1997).

■ **Bibliography:** Curriculum vitae ■ Assemblies of God Office of Public Relations, personal data sheet. ■ E. J. Gitre

Pentecostal and Charismatic Timeline

Pentecostalism in most of its forms has existed throughout Christian history in both Eastern and Western churches.

First Century A.D.	• Pentecost, when the Holy Spirit came upon the disciples—ten days after Jesus ascended into heaven—and they began exhibiting miraculous manifestations, including glossolalia, discernment of spirits, prophecies, and gifts of healing. Immediately afterward they begin to spread the gospel throughout the known world.
	• Around A.D. 96, Clement, bishop of Rome, and Ignatius, bishop of Antioch, document the continued operation of prophetic gifts.
	• Writers of the *Didache* and the *Shepherd of Hermas* witness so much charismatic activity they find it necessary to distinguish between true and false prophets. At about the same time, the writer of *Pseudo-Barnabas* suggests prophetic ministry is normative in the church.
Second Century A.D.	• Justin Martyr argues that God has withdrawn the Spirit of prophecy and miracles from the Jews and has transferred it to the church as proof of her continued divine favor.
	• Irenaeus of Lyon describes the gifts of prophecy, discernment of spirits, and exorcism in his Gallic church, and even mentions that individuals have been raised from the dead. He warns against certain false Gnostics who fabricate spiritual gifts to win favor with the naïve.
	• Hippolytus of Rome, in his *Apostolic Tradition*, offers that there is no need to lay hands on laity who already exercise a gift of healing.
	• Tertullian of Carthage speaks of the great pleasures to be found in expelling demons, affecting cures, and seeking revelations.
Third Century A.D.	• Tertullian insists that the "New Prophets" (Montanists) will be instruments in revealing the full provision of the Spirit. He provides a short case study of a "sister" who experiences revelations and ecstatic visions, speaks with angels, and reports on what she has seen to church leaders.
	• Origen of Alexandria says healings, exorcisms, and validating signs and wonders continue to be experienced in the church. Just as miracles and

(Third Century A.D. continued)	wonders added to the credibility of 1st-century apostles, so they continue to draw unbelievers into the Christian fold.
	• Gregory Thaumaturgus, an evangelist in Neocaesarea, prophesies, heals the sick, takes dominion over demons, and exorcises them by his command. He is remembered for a wide range of signs and wonders—some of which seem incredible to modern scholars. One of his students, Basil the Great, declares that Gregory should be numbered among the apostles.
	• Athanasius' *Antony of the Desert* (251?–356) describes the prototype of charismatic desert saints who experience ministries of healing and discernment of spirits as well as signs and wonders.
Fourth Century A.D.	• Augustine, in *The City of God*, reports contemporary divine healings and other miracles. These he links directly to the conversion of pagans.
	• The heretical Messalians (c. 360–800) teach that everyone is possessed by a personal demon, driven out only by prayer and the reception of the Holy Spirit. They practice laying on of hands for this Spirit baptism.
Sixth Century A.D.	• Gregory the Great (Pope Gregory I), in his biographies of contemporary saints (including Benedict of Nursia), attempts to provide documentation through eyewitness accounts of a wide variety of miracles, including healings of various ailments, raising of the dead to life, exorcisms of evil spirits, foretelling of the future, and deliverance from danger. He directly correlates miracles accompanying the missionary enterprise of Augustine of Canterbury and his companions to the conversion of the Anglo-Saxons.
Tenth–Eleventh Centuries A.D.	• Symeon the New Theologian (949–1022), perhaps the most famous Eastern charismatic Christian, reports his most intimate spiritual experiences, which include a "baptism in the Holy Spirit" accompanied by gifts of copious tears, compunction, and visions of God as light.
Twelfth–Fourteenth Centuries A.D.	• Hildegard of Bingen (1098–1179), experiences ecstatic visions (which she painted) and gifts of tears and compunction, wisdom, knowledge, and prophecy. Numerous miracles are attributed to her. She also is reported to have sung "concerts" in the Spirit and to have written entire books in unknown languages. Because of her prophetic and preaching ministry, Hildegard, together with several other medieval women, have a significant impact on reforming the medieval church.

(Twelfth–Fourteenth Centuries A.D. continued)	• Numerous Eastern saints exercise gifts of healing, including Athanasius, patriarch of Constantinople (early 14th century), who becomes famous during his lifetime for bringing deliverance to those possessed by evil spirits, the blind, the incontinent, the deaf and dumb, and those afflicted with cancer. Even after his death it is reported that the ill are cured when praying at his grave.
	• Gregory Palamas (1296–1359) emphasizes the laying on of hands for receiving the gifts of healing, miracles, foreknowledge, irrefutable wisdom, diverse tongues, and interpretation of tongues. He also reports ecstasies and visions of divine light.
	• The Roman Catholic Church shows signs of charismatic vitality in the lives and writings of such important figures as Bernard of Clairvaux, Bonaventure, and Thomas Aquinas. The sermons of Thomas Aquinas are frequently confirmed by miracles, and he often experiences ecstasy, especially in the last months of his life. Spiritual gifts are even more important to apocalyptic writers such as Rubert of Deutz (c. 1075–1129/30) and Joachim of Fiore (c. 1132–1202).
	• Bonaventure reports that Francis of Assisi, while an unskilled speaker, is empowered by the Holy Spirit while ministering. Wherever he goes, his sermons are accompanied with miracles of great power, including prophecy, casting out devils, and healing the sick. As a result, his hearers pay attention to what he says "as if an angel of the Lord was speaking."
	• Vincent Ferrer (1350–1419), a Spirit-filled Dominican missionary, draws huge crowds when he preaches. Everywhere his ministry is accompanied by remarkable miracles, including healings and raising the dead.
Sixteenth Century A.D.	• Catholic Reformer Thomas Müntzer emphasizes the "inner word" of the Spirit, direct revelation in visions and dreams, Holy Spirit possession and guidance, as well as radical social reforms and an imminent Millennium. He insists that Christians are to experience the Holy Spirit as powerfully in the 16th century as in the time of the prophets and apostles. Above all, Müntzer holds to the necessity of a baptism of the Holy Spirit, whereby the elect can discern spirits and unlock biblical mysteries.
	• Ignatius Loyola, founder of the Society of Jesus (the Jesuits), frequently receives divine communication in visions. He also experiences a gift of tears—often in such abundance that he cannot control himself—and the gift of *loquela*, which a few modern scholars associate with today's charismatic phenomenon of sung glossolalia.

Seventeenth Century A.D.	• The central doctrine of the Religious Society of Friends (the Quakers) is the "inner light/word," with the divine Spirit speaking directly to the human mind. Early Quaker literature records visions, healings, and prophecies, which they liken to the Day of Pentecost. There is even evidence of tongues speech among them, although George Fox, their founder, eventually discourages such ecstatic utterances.
	• The Prophets of the Cevennes (the Camisards), French Protestant resistance fighters, claim to be directly inspired by the Holy Spirit. Most notable is the enthusiasm of their young children, who prophesy at very early ages. The Camisards are seized by ecstatic inspiration, during which they utter strange and often amazing things, and speak in languages of which they have no knowledge.
	• Jansenists, belonging to a radical Augustinian movement in the Roman Catholic Church from 1640 to 1801, become known for their signs and wonders, spiritual dancing, healings, and prophetic utterances. Some reportedly speak in unknown tongues and understand foreign languages in which they are addressed.
Eighteenth Century A.D.	• The Moravian Brethren emphasize strong missionary efforts, emotionally expressive worship, and fervent prayer services.
	• During the First Great Awakening, Jonathan Edwards (1703–58) finds it necessary to distinguish between human enthusiasm and genuine workings of the Spirit. He points out that tears, trembling, groans, loud outcries, religious "noise," and ecstasies are not necessarily evidence of the Spirit's operation.
	• John Wesley, the founder of Methodism (1703–91), introduces into Protestantism an awareness of the Spirit's operation in all of human experience unlike any other in Western Christianity at the time. While Wesley is not personally given to enthusiastic religion, he is very tolerant of followers who claim dreams, visions, healings, and revelations, and of earlier prophetic groups such as the Montanists, whom he describes as "real, scriptural Christians."
	• The "Awakened," a Lutheran revivalistic movement in Finland, begins in 1796 with a sudden outpouring of the Holy Spirit, accompanied by such observable signs as visions and glossolalia. This renewal continues into the 20th century.
	• Seraphim of Sarov (1759–1833), the Russian Orthodox charismatic leader, asserts that the goal of the Christian life is the reception of the Holy Spirit. Seraphim's "evidence" for a baptism of the Holy Spirit is a transfiguration experience—being transformed, while still in the flesh, into divine light. Seraphim also is remembered for a gift of healing.

Nineteenth Century A.D.	• At a conference of the London Missionary Society in 1824, six years before a charismatic movement would begin in England under his influence, Presbyterian pastor Edward Irving proposes a return to the apostolic pattern and declares that missionaries should ideally follow the model initiated by Jesus in Matthew 10:9–10. Though sharply criticized for suggesting such an outrageous departure from conventional practice, Irving gains a hearing and his addresses are published as *Missionaries after the Apostolical School* (1825), perhaps the earliest missiological treatise of the century to address the subject. • The West of Scotland revival (1830) features a variety of spiritual giftings, including prophesy, healings, glossolalia, and interpretation of tongues. This renewal is led by laity. • Pentecostal phenomena, including glossolalia, are reported among South Indian Christians in Travancore and Madras State in the 1860s and 1870s. • Johannes Warneck records that from the 1860s the Indonesian Christian community increased after the appearance of "pentecostal" phenomena: dreams, visions, signs in the heavens, and several instances where missionaries (e.g., Ludwig Nommensen) unwittingly drank poison given by their enemies and remained unharmed. • Edward Irving, Theodore Christlieb (German theologian and historian of missions), Thomas Erskine (Scottish lay theologian), and George Müller argue for the continuing necessity of miracles. • Müller, a well-known philanthropist, whose vibrant faith for God's provision at his orphan homes in Bristol, England, modeled the idealized "faith life" for many Christians, inspires the growing number of independent "faith" missionaries. Although he is not remembered for advocacy of signs and wonders, his perspectives on faith and the remarkable answers to his prayers help lay the theoretical basis. • Due to the slow progress of medical science and the cries of the terminally ill, radical evangelicals such as Charles C. Cullis, A. B. Simpson, A. J. Gordon, Carrie Judd Montgomery, and John Alexander Dowie examine scriptural promises of healing and inspire the evangelical faith-healing movement in America. Their teachings subsequently open the door wider to miracles, since all of the charismatic gifts might too be restored. • Frank W. Sandford, at his Holy Ghost and Us Bible School at Shiloh, ME, organizes the World's Evangelization Crusade on Apostolic Principles. In accentuating the cosmic dimension of "spiritual warfare" in confronting the powers of darkness on mission fields, he later purchases a schooner and barkentine and leads his followers on cruises around the world, praying as they pass the coastline of each country that God would release his power for its conversion.

(Nineteenth Century A.D. continued)	• Arthur E. Street, a Presbyterian missionary to Hainan, China, believes that prayerful intercession could bind the "strongman" (the evil spirit ruling over each country, such as the "prince of China"), and he provides the formula for successful evangelism. Street's popular booklet *Intercessory Foreign Missionaries* is published by the Student Volunteer Movement for Foreign Mission and other agencies. Nearly a century later, some pentecostals and especially independent charismatics, third wave, and New Apostolic Reformation enthusiasts advance a similar approach to spiritual warfare to bring the nations under the dominion of God through binding the "territorial spirits."
	• Some radical evangelicals propose that according to Jesus' promise in Mark 16:17, God would bestow intelligible human languages on missionaries. This would enable them to bypass formal language study to begin preaching immediately after arriving on their fields, since little time remained for evangelization. Mary Campbell, a participant in a charismatic movement in Scotland, reports that she has received the Turkish language and the language of the Palau island group in the Pacific Ocean to equip her to preach to these peoples.
	• National Holiness Association is founded in Vineland, NJ, in 1867.
	• Isaiah Reed forms the largest holiness association in America, the Iowa Holiness Association, in 1879.
	• Church of God (Cleveland, TN) is founded in 1886.
	• A. B. Simpson, founder of the Christian and Missionary Alliance (CMA), considers the possible reappearance of the gift of tongues and refers to actual occurrences in India and Africa. Others share this optimism, including several members of the celebrated "Cambridge Seven" of athletic fame in England (C. T. Studd, and Cecil H. and Arthur Polhill), who arrived in China in 1885 to serve with the China Inland Mission; members of the Kansas-Sudan movement, who sailed to Sierra Leone in 1890; missionaries of the CMA (William W. Simpson and William Christie), who reached China in 1892; and independent missionaries Walter S. and Frances Black and M. Jennie Glassey, who left North America for Africa in 1896.
	• It is reported that by the end of the 19th century, approximately 900,000 African Christians have experienced pentecostal-like phenomena.
Twentieth Century A.D.	• Charles F. Parham, a midwestern Holiness preacher, reads an abridged account of Glassey's story and reflects on its implications for mission. In 1900 he announces that a "Bro. and Sister Hamaker" were lodged at his headquarters in Topeka, KS, and were praying to receive the necessary language before they proceeded to the mission field. During the summer,

(Twentieth Century A.D. continued)

Parham journeys to Shiloh, ME, where he hears speaking in tongues for the first time at Sandford's school. He becomes convinced that glossolalia represents crucial evidence of the baptism in the Holy Spirit and that its utility for missionary evangelism holds the key to world evangelization. In this way he forges the link between tongues and Spirit baptism that becomes the doctrinal hallmark of classical pentecostalism.

- In Jan. 1901 Parham and his students at Bethel Bible School in Topeka pray for the fulfillment of Joel's prophecy: that God would "pour out" the Holy Spirit with miraculous power in the "last days." Agnes Ozman speaks in tongues. Discussion about the gift of tongues had stirred interest among many radical evangelicals for over two decades, and Parham's disciples believe the outpouring of the Spirit will form them as God's special company of empowered missionaries in the end times. Participants testify that God had given them the languages of the world.

- In 1905 William Seymour accepts Charles Parham's pentecostal message.

- Under Seymour's leadership, the Azusa Street Revival (1906–13) in Los Angeles becomes the first significant outburst of pentecostal fervor in America.

- The Holy Spirit is poured out on orphan girls at Pandita Ramabai's Mukti Mission in Western India (1905–6). This revival results in miracles, healings, spiritual gifts (including glossolalia), and a powerful social outreach to India's poor and destitute.

- The Church of God in Christ is founded in 1907.

- In 1909 Florence Crawford founds the Apostolic Faith Church in Portland, OR.

- W. H. Durham begins the "Finished Work" movement in Chicago.

- The International Pentecostal Holiness Church is founded in 1911 as a merger of earlier pentecostal groups.

- The Assemblies of God, the largest classical pentecostal denomination, is founded in Hot Springs, AR, in 1914.

- The Oneness Movement splits the Assemblies of God in 1916.

- The Church of God of Prophecy is founded in 1923.

- Aimee Semple McPherson forms International Church of the Foursquare Gospel in Los Angeles in 1927.

- Several mergers in 1945 produce the oneness United Pentecostal Church (MO).

- Dennis Bennett of the Episcopal Church in Van Nuys, CA, is credited with beginning the charismatic movement in 1959.

(Twentieth Century A.D. continued)	• The Catholic Charismatic Renewal begins in 1967, simultaneously in both Duquesne University, Pittsburgh, and Bogota, Colombia.
	• Large numbers of neocharismatic, indigenous, and independent churches emerge around the world. By 2000, neocharismatic groups have more than 286 million members and adherents.
	• The Toronto Blessing phenomenon (neocharismatic) begins in 1994, with a similar outpouring in Pensacola, FL (classical pentecostal), in 1995.
	• By mid-2000, the total in pentecostal and charismatic renewal has grown to over 523 million.

Picture Sources

Ahonen, Lauri 256

Assemblies of God, Division of Foreign Missions 6, 7, 9, 13, 23, 36, 40, 41, 59, 61, 65, 83, 87, 89, 91, 97, 107, 110, 112, 116, 133, 142, 147, 148, 170, 173, 174 (2), 176, 177, 181, 182, 204, 208, 215, 218, 221, 223, 232, 241, 242, 244, 245, 258, 265, 269, 271, 357, 361, 375, 376, 377, 378, 379, 425, 436, 449b, 470, 522, 535, 603, 614, 618, 620, 622a, 622b, 649, 650, 669, 683, 684, 685, 696, 697, 724, 725, 780, 810, 835, 836, 873, 878, 882, 890, 892, 913, 914, 915, 916, 919, 928, 947, 948a, 984, 1016, 1022b, 1033, 1034–1035, 1077, 1078a, 1078b, 1093, 1094, 1097, 1100, 1101, 1102, 1105a, 1106b, 1110, 1118, 1153a, 1153b, 1176, 1204, 1205, 1206, 1207, 1208, 1218, 1219, 1220, 1225

Assemblies of God, Flower Pentecostal Heritage Center 255, 257, 326, 331, 339, 346, 348, 365, 366, 368, 369, 437, 438, 439, 440, 441, 444b, 451a, 457, 553, 554, 560a, 564, 586, 587, 589, 594, 617, 619, 624, 642, 647b, 660, 661, 662, 678, 679, 688b, 712, 826, 828, 845, 865, 896, 905, 912, 927, 931, 946, 952, 955, 986, 997, 1022a, 1031, 1043, 1054, 1071, 1148, 1180, 1182, 1185, 1211

Assemblies of God, Gospel Publishing House 374, 442, 525, 887, 920

Assemblies of God, National Youth Ministries 382

Barrett, David & Todd Johnson 301

Bundy, David 449

Burgess Archives 119, 120, 123, 125, 136, 139, 306, 313, 314, 329, 352, 353, 363, 373, 417, 450, 461, 512, 567, 569, 621, 623, 644, 647a, 651, 655, 713, 741, 752, 781, 811, 825, 917, 918, 922, 961, 976, 981, 995, 1017, 1025, 1048, 1049, 1052, 1104, 1171, 1186, 1217

Cartwright, Desmond 690, 730, 808, 1187, 1195

Chariscenter 853, 857, 861, 1109

Christ for the Nations 708

Christian and Missionary Alliance 524, 1069

Church of God, Archives of the Hal Bernard Dixon, Jr., Pentecostal Research Center 30, 62, 203, 209, 531, 536, 539, 558, 560b, 571, 771, 837, 948b, 1030, 1143, 1144

Church of God in Christ, 304

Church of God of Prophecy 637, 1147

Church on the Way 687

Cooley, Robert 561

DuPree, Sherry 1115

Durasoff, Steven 593

Episcopal Renewal Ministries 307, 370, 652, 802

Ernst, Manfred 100, 101

Full Gospel Business Men's Voice 713, 1058

Hall, J. L. 688a

Harper, Michael 478

Hedges, D. J. 572, 834, 960

Hocken, Peter 460, 462, 463

Hoover, Mario 770

International Church of the Foursquare Gospel 1051, 1142

International Lutheran Renewal Center 523, 849

International Pentecostal Holiness Church 693, 1111a, 1111b

Irwin, Deborah 805

Kenyon's Gospel Publishing Society 819

McGee, Gary B. 854

Mennonite Renewal Services 843

Menzies, William 871

Moore, S. David 692, 1050

New Covenant Magazine 480

Oral Roberts Evangelistic Association 600, 695, 1024, 1026

Paulk, Earl 956

Pentecostal Assemblies of Canada 1114

Presbyterian and Reformed Renewal Ministries 444, 1198

Religious News Service Photo/Wide World 1053, 1059, 1146

Robertson, Marion Gordon ("Pat") 1027

Spittler, Russell 1103

Trask, Thomas 1154

United Pentecostal Church International 1167a, 1167b

Vineyard Ministries International 1200

Wagner, C. Peter 930

Woods, Daniel 340

Index of Personal Names

A

Abbott, J., 793
'Abdisho' Hazzaya, 748–49
Abel, M., 232
Abelard, P., 753–54
Abell, T. D., 386
Abeysekera, F. G., 899
Abhayaratna, O., 252
Abraham, K. E., 122, 123, 305, 778–79, 781, 968
Abraham, T. S., 305
Abrams, A., 55
Abrams, M. F., 55, 120, 121–22, 124, 305–6, 387, 391, 771, 788, 888, 895, 1018
Abrogena, D., 202
Acena, B. P., 201
Acevedo, E., 176
Adams, E. M., 553
Adams, F., 70
Adams, H., 78
Adams, J. A. D., 308
Adams, L., 78
Adams, M., 1136
Adewale, A. J., 416
Adini-Abala, A., 72, 76, 308–9
Adler, R., 476, 504
Aeschliman, D. R., 232
Affuso, M., 136
Ahn, C., 507, 1151
Ahn, S. O., 245, 309–10
Aho, E., 412
Ahone, P., 183
Ahonen, E., 104, 412
Ahonen, L. K., 411
Ainsley, E., 170
Aker, B. C., 790
Akeredolu, J. L., 416
Akers, E. F., 939
Alamo, T., 310–11
Albano, P., 136
Albert, R., 75
Alcantara, R., 201
Alcuin, W., 568
Alexander, G. P., 122
Alexander, H. E., 105
Alexander, J., 347
Alexander, N., 560
Alexandru, I., 215
Alford, D., 917
Allen, A. A., 203, 311–12, 313, 336, 622, 809, 978, 1015, 1135

Allen, D., 797
Allen, R., 421, 724, 845, 878, 896–97
Alt, M. A., 129–30
Alton, W. D., 210
Alufurai, A., 226
Alungwa, M., 152
Alvarez, C., 797, 1078
Álvarez, E., 78
Alvarez, M., 202, 796
Álvarez-Pérez, C., 211
Alvarsson, J.-A., 410
Alvino, G., 137
Amande, D., 180
Amaya, F., 176
Ambrose, 745–46
Amisi, P., 70
Ammerman, J., 934
Amundsen, D. W., 388
Anacondia, C., 149
Ancellotti, A., 139, 496
Anderson, C. P., 170, 223
Anderson, F., 34
Anderson, M., 70
Anderson, P., 848
Anderson, P. R., 66, 313
Anderson, R., 400, 403, 896
Anderson, R. M., 383, 412, 657, 717
Anderson, R. P., 313
Anderson, T., 34
Andersson, A., 47, 165, 177, 314, 778, 840, 944
Andersson, I., 887
Andin, A., 409
Andin, K., 949
Andreas, P., 200
Andreassen, E., 34
Andreassen, M., 34
Andréasson, E., 410
Ang, L. Y., 171
Ange, D., 508
Ankerberg, J., 353
Annacondia, C., 24, 25, 161, 500, 512
Anselm of Canterbury, 753
Anturi, E. J., 411
Appleby, B., 885, 892
Appleby, R., 497
Aquinas, T., 755–56
Arbouet, R., 116
Arce, R., 412
Are, B., 19
Arevalo, R., 341
Arévalo, R., 176
Argañaras, R., 140, 502

Argue, A. H., 48, 331, 594, 621, 892, 962, 978, 1075
Argue, D., 923–24
Argue, W., 331
Argue, Z., 331
Arguinzoni, S., 331–32, 1175
Armstrong, G., 67
Armstrong, H. W., 154
Armstrong, J., 701
Armstrong, M., 26
Armstrong, R., 480
Arndt, J., 611
Arnold, G., 611
Arnold, R. L., 332
Arnott, J., 332, 502, 552, 934, 1149–51
Arons, E., 186
Aroolappen, J. C., 118, 119
Arthur, M., 328
Arthur, W., 96, 612
Asare, C. A., 16
Asberry, R., 344, 346, 437–38, 1055
Asbough, J. D., 632
Aschoff, F., 332–33, 509
Ashcroft, J. J., 688
Ashcroft, J. R., 1079
Ashimolowo, M., 45
Ashmore, L., 171
Aspelind, J., 47
Assibey, T., 511
Athanasius, 738–39, 1063
Atkinson, M. W., 177, 343, 888, 893, 985
Attebury, T., 1057
Atter, A., 892
Atter, G. F., 898
Aucher, J. W., 82
Augustine of Hippo, 746
Aulén, G., 1134
Austin-Broos, D., 141, 143, 145
Austin-Sparks, T., 645
Awet, D., 267
Awrey, D., 98, 124, 344

B

Ba, Z., 183
Babajide, D. O., 416
Baba-Lwamba, I., 73
Bachtold, A., 707
Backman, E. L., 571
Bada, A. A. A., 351, 951
Baedeker, F., 89
Bafoungissa, J. B., 76
Bailey, A. L., 536
Baker, C. E., 621, 962

Baker, D. H., 171, 225
Baker, E. V., 351–52, 375, 389, 390, 391, 394, 396, 588, 630–31, 888
Baker, H. A., 352, 888
Baker, J., 479
Baker, L., 844
Baker, S., 278
Bakker, J. O., 352–54, 456, 488, 565, 616, 1119
Bakker, T. F., 352–54, 565
Balangui, C., 202
Balca, J., 90
Ball, H. C., 77, 176. 341, 354, 381, 432, 682, 718, 720, 829, 830, 844, 845, 885, 897, 898, 949
Ball, J. C., 962
Balogun, J. O., 416
Baltzell, D., 327
Banaga, E., 203
Bang, J. P., 410
Bangau, P. A., 172
Banks, J. G., 478
Banton, A., 27
Baraghine, T., 70
Barker, E., 199
Barker, F., 199
Barker, G. W., 1023
Barling, M., 646
Barnes, G. O., 632
Barnes, L. O., 364, 642, 1162
Barnes, M., 937
Barnett, T., 917
Barnhouse, D. G., 1015
Barr, E. S., 29–30, 364–65, 533, 1145
Barr, R., 29–30, 364–65, 533, 1145
Barratt, T. B., 23, 55, 65, 80, 88, 89, 92, 96–97, 103, 104, 109, 117, 123, 176, 193, 222, 258, 280, 365–66, 390, 406, 409, 411, 418, 436, 524, 546, 638, 771, 798, 814, 822, 877, 888, 972, 978, 986, 1040, 1116, 1158
Barrett, D., 24, 126, 384, 407, 416, 417, 501, 555, 783, 932
Barrick, E., 909
Barth, K., 701, 1120, 1121, 1123, 1127, 1137
Barth, P., 797, 921
Bartleman, F., 98, 105, 124, 346, 347, 348, 366, 386, 387, 389, 391, 392, 393, 406, 457, 621, 641, 847, 887, 953, 954, 960, 972, 988, 1020, 1037–38, 1057, 1075, 1193
Bartlett, C., 916
Barton, D., 527
Basham, D. W., 367, 478, 484, 769, 911, 933, 981, 999, 1060–62, 1070
Basil of Caesarea, 739–40
Basombrio, E., 413

Bastian, J. P., 157
Batman, G. W., 348, 632
Battermann, H., 151, 152, 267
Battley, D., 513
Bauman, H. E., 870
Baumert, N., 367, 493, 549
Baxter, W. J., 189, 367–68, 484, 631, 769, 774, 819, 911, 933, 1060–62, 1070
Bays, D., 389
Bazán, D., 368, 719, 720, 722, 829
Bázan, M. T., 368
Beall, J. L., 368, 488, 833
Beall, M. D., 368–69, 598, 831, 833, 1020
Beane, J. S., 382
Beardsmore, J. W., 70
Beatrice, F., 297
Beaty, J. M., 116
Beaver, R. P., 926
Bebbington, D. W., 387
Beckenham, C., 154
Becker, M., 872, 874
Becker, W., 492
Beckham, W. J., 502
Bednar, M., 94
Beijersbergen, A., 186
Beling, D., 249
Beling, J. G., 251
Bell, E. N., 333, 334, 335, 369, 424, 537, 553, 560, 594, 642, 679, 728, 856, 866, 937–38, 954, 989, 1161, 1162, 1204–5
Bell, J. W., 143, 146
Bellingham, A., 234
Bello, M., 82
Bellsmith, F. M., 962
Bemal, C., 462
Bender, G. F., 65, 279, 280
Bengel, J. A., 611
Benn, W., 701
Bennett, D., 435, 477, 479, 483, 484, 490, 572, 616, 769, 844, 902, 935, 979, 980, 981, 996, 1061, 1074, 1197
Bennett, D. J., 28, 49, 190, 225, 295, 306, 369–70, 383
Bennett, R., 369–70
Bensley, M., 188
Berends, K. O., 387, 389
Berg, A., 71
Berg, D., 39, 165, 208, 370–71, 418, 594, 888, 1177
Berg, G. E., 122–23, 347, 348
Berg, M., 159, 930
Berg, R. S., 669, 1117
Bergholc, A., 1045
Berkhof, H., 494
Berly, D., 493
Bernal, C., 513

Bernard, D. K., 387, 787
Bernis, J., 504, 873
Bernsten, B., 348
Berntsen, B., 59–60, 60
Berntz-Lanz, O., 53
Berríos, A., 1051
Bertolucci, J., 371, 862, 1041
Betancourt, Á., 82
Bettex, P., 371–72, 891
Betzer, D., 1016
Beyer, H., 414
Bhengu, N. B. H., 169, 231, 372
Bialiks, G. S., 22
Bially, G., 23, 279, 280, 493
Bickle, M., 417, 502, 507, 816
Biesbrouck, J., 32, 494, 496
Bilbrough, D., 503
Bilby, I., 417, 589, 1026
Bilhorn, P., 691
Binas, R. G., 204
Binion, D., 918
Biolley, H., 105–6, 417–18, 1045
Bissette, A., 703–4
Bittlinger, A., 408, 418, 490, 492, 497, 548, 577, 853
Bitton, D., 396, 397
Björk, O. L., 418–19
Bjorner, A. L., 419
Bjorner, S., 365
Bjørner, S., 80
Blachnicki, F., 495
Black, D., 492
Black, M., 48
Black, S. A., 146
Black, W. S., 887, 1067
Blackaby, H., 364
Blacker, J., 28
Blackwood, J., 916
Blaisdell, F. D., 432
Blaisdell, G., 341
Blake, J. A., 959
Blakeney, A., 352, 892
Blakeney, J., 67, 69
Blanco, A., 78
Blattner, E., 280
Blaxland, G., 28
Bliss, G., 8
Bliss, M., 8
Bloch-Hoell, N. E., 407, 435, 899
Bloomfield, R., 188, 435–36
Blue, K., 29
Blumhardt, J. C., 492, 612, 631, 700–701, 1121, 1130, 1135
Blumhofer, E., 384–85, 386, 387, 389, 400, 403, 404–5, 408, 436, 1079
Boardman, W. E., 421, 612, 785, 820, 821, 905, 1069, 1071
Boberg, Å., 410

Bochian, P., 92, 93, 212, 215, 216, 324, 436, 547
Boddy, A. A., 97, 193, 258, 295, 347, 391, 417, 436–37, 454, 456, 489, 546, 621, 639, 728, 771, 798, 807, 821, 972, 991, 1195, 1223
Boddy, J. T., 654
Boddy, M., 96, 97, 437, 1195
Bododea, I., 91, 324
Bododea, J., 213, 214
Bodor, E., 92, 212, 214, 215
Boesak, A., 431
Bogard, B. M., 858
Bogue, G., 28
Bolton, L., 181, 725
Bonaventure, 756–57, 1064
Bond, B., 274
Bongartz, S., 169
Bonhoeffer, D., 419
Bonino, J. M., 157
Bonnin, E., 567, 568
Bonnke, R. W. G., 25, 29, 111, 114, 131, 137, 155, 170, 231, 232, 233, 268, 275, 438–39, 882, 935
Boone, P., 149, 441
Boone, S., 935
Boosahda, W., 504, 557
Booth-Clibborn, A. S., 953, 1163
Booth-Clibborn, W., 258, 448
Booy, A., 138
Boris, I., 151
Borrego, F., 176
Bosch, D., 233, 431
Bosch, J. C., 567
Bosworth, F. F., 334, 346, 439–40, 789, 820, 950, 978, 1015, 1072
Bottome, F., 728
Boudenwijse, B., 414
Boulton, E. C. W., 323
Bourgeois, P., 460
Bowdle, D. N., 385
Bowe, J., 426, 813
Bowie, G., 67, 228, 264, 654, 970
Bowler, A., 274
Bowling, H., 558
Bowman, R., 1016
Boyd, F. M., 335, 524, 623, 669, 1044
Boyd, W. J., 838, 971
Boyer, P., 388
Bracco, R., 135
Bradbury, W., 915
Bradford, G. C., 440, 481, 816, 996
Bradin, G., 90, 93, 213–14, 215, 216, 324
Brainerd, D., 1144
Branch, G. J., 1157
Branco, P., 209
Branding, H. W., 440
Brandt-Bessire, D., 258, 612

Branewall, P. F., 893
Branham, W. M., 84, 111, 251, 330, 336, 363, 367, 439, 440–41, 477, 622, 688, 708–9, 830, 842, 867, 950, 978, 992, 1020, 1135, 1178
Brannen, F., 154
Brant, R., 484
Braseth, E., 344
Braxton, S. L., 441
Bredesen, H., 441–42, 478, 481, 498, 572, 604, 1061, 1197
Brelsford, G. S., 6
Brémond, A., 493
Brengle, E., 201
Brenkus, J., 94
Brereton, A., 70
Bresson, B. L., 785, 788
Brewster, P. S., 442, 547, 599, 973
Bridges-Johns, C., 1121, 1135–36, 1216
Briem, E., 406, 409
Briggs, C., 656
Briggs, L. C., 925
Bright, J., 535
Brigitta of Sweden, 758
Bringham, R., 503, 576
Brinkman, G. C., 966
Britt, G. L., 585
Brittain, B. E., 442–43
Britton, B., 443, 831
Britton, F. M., 443, 457, 558
Brofeldt, P., 103, 104
Broger, J. C., 1016
Bronstein, D., 872
Broocks, R., 504, 507
Brookes, J. H., 656, 1044
Brooks, J. P., 421, 727
Brostek, M., 586
Brotman, M., 872, 1156, 1157
Brouwer, S., 408, 414
Brown, D., 153, 774
Brown, E., 8
Brown, J., 49, 478, 481, 981, 996
Brown, J. H., 444, 835
Brown, K. D., 431
Brown, M., 131, 446
Brown, M. B., 348, 888, 1205
Brown, R., 444, 669, 688
Brown, R. R., 1015
Brown, V. R., 445
Browning, E. D., 1163
Brumback, C., 393, 397–98, 447, 524, 788
Brumley, A., 916
Brummett, A. W., 154
Bruner, F. D., 362, 447, 790, 1130
Bruns, M., 272
Brusco, E., 166
Bryan, D., 272

Bryan, W. J., 615, 657
Bryant, D., 227
Bryant, J., 447
Bryant, S. N., 543
Bryant, W. F., 530, 1144
Brynhildsen, J., 70
Buai, R., 183
Buber, M., 1138
Bucamupaka, E., 47
Buchanan, W. A., 447–48
Bücher, J., 227
Buchtik, J., 277
Buchwalter, A., 181
Buciaga, C., 341
Buckalew, J. W., 30, 622
Buckingham, J. W., 363, 448, 843, 844, 933
Budean, P., 213
Budeanu, P., 90, 324
Buffum, H., 448, 728, 915
Bull, A. D., 266
Bundy, D. D., 98, 165, 409, 413, 448–49, 547, 796
Buntain, D. M., 449, 962, 1114
Buntain, D. N., 48, 251, 449–50
Buntain, M., 124
Burciaga, C., 176, 450
Burgess, J. H., 122–23, 352, 450
Burgess, S. M., 140, 788
Burghard, J. T., 632
Burke, F., 169, 909, 970
Burke, J., 498
Burkill, M., 701
Burnett, B., 450–51, 485
Burr, B., 22, 54, 70
Burton, W. F. P., 67, 340, 416, 451, 561, 599, 622, 888, 891, 920, 967, 971, 1036, 1225
Busby, R., 130
Bush, L., 501
Bush, M., 151
Bushnell, H., 614, 929
Buskirk, J., 1048, 1159
Bustamante, M., 341
Bustgaard, A., 153
Buström, S., 208
Buthelezi, M., 431
Butler, H., 69
Butler, K., 934
Butler, T., 503
Byrd, R., 201
Byrd, V., 451–52

C

Caballeros, H., 513
Cabezas, R., 797
Cabrera, O., 24–25, 161, 512
Cabrera, P., 82

Cabrera, R. D., 278
Cadwalder, H., 48, 961
Cain, P., 417, 816, 817
Caird, M., 1191
Calderon, A. D., 176
Caldwell, W., 251
Calisi, M., 139, 509, 559
Callaway, H., 229–30
Calley, M., 143
Calver, C., 453–54, 818
Calvin, J., 541, 764–65, 995, 1010, 1064, 1218
Campbell, I. G., 454, 642, 846–47, 891, 1204
Campbell, J. E., 898
Campbell, J. M., 1189
Campbell, M., 1067, 1190
Campos, E. C., 56
Candelaria, J., 206
Cannistraci, D., 930
Cannon, K. G., 431
Canova, P., 412
Cantalamessa, R., 140, 454, 496, 810
Cantel, M., 454–55
Cantelon, W., 151, 152
Cantú, B., 455
Cantwell, M., 151
Capps, C. E., 455, 795, 820, 992
Car, 21
Cardale, J., 459, 803, 1191
Cárdenas, E., 199
Carey, W. H., 925
Carhee, C. C., 1055
Carlson, G., 455, 1154
Carlson, G. R., 337, 455–56
Carlyle, T., 459, 803, 804, 929
Carmichael, R., 916, 917, 1015
Carmichael, S., 428
Carothers, J. W., 1132
Carothers, M., 844
Carothers, W. F., 326, 328, 346, 546, 972, 1161
Carrasco, D., 199–200
Carríon, A., 1051
Carscaddens, J. F., 893
Carter, A. H., 171, 340, 456, 953, 1105, 1110
Carter, J., 340, 456–57, 616, 953
Carter, K., 929
Carter, R. K., 710, 728
Cartwright, P., 1073
Cary, L., 202
Cary, L. R., 244
Casanova, M., 497
Case, H., 78
Cashwell, G. B., 347, 363, 393, 457–58, 566, 639, 640, 730, 797, 799–800, 822, 976, 989, 1115, 1144

Cassidy, M., 233
Castellanos, C., 513
Castillo, G., 56
Castren, H., 103
Castro, E., 160, 1215
Castro, L., 211
Castro, P., 201
Catargiu, V., 214
Cathcart, W., 27, 458
Catherine of Siena, 758–59
Caudle, B. H., 201
Caughey, J., 612
Cavnar, J., 482
Cawston, A., 123
Cease, S., 918
CeauXescu, N., 216
Cerillo, A., Jr., 387, 388
Cerillo, M., 131
Cerullo, M., 25, 472, 567, 622, 899, 1179
Cerullo, R., 201
Ceuta, I., 325
Chacko, M. K., 779
Chacko, P. T., 779
Chadwick, S., 552, 1159
Chafer, L. S., 585
Chalke, S., 508
Chalmers, T., 614
Chambers, G. A., 48, 472, 728, 962, 963
Chambers, N., 532
Chambers, S. W., 472, 1163, 1165
Champion, R., 334
Champlin, H. D., 684
Chan, S., 1216
Chandler, T., 190
Channing, W. E., 614
Chanter, H. V., 323
Chapell, P. G., 1048, 1050
Chapman, J. W., 1020
Chapman, M. W., 123
Chapman, S. C., 918
Chappell, R. M., 966
Chavda, M., 72, 507, 520
Chávez, E., 797
Chawner, C. A., 180, 520, 910
Chawner, C. W., 180, 228, 892
Chernoff, D., 504, 520–21
Chernoff, J., 873
Chernoff, M., 872, 1156
Cherry, F. S., 425
Cherry, J., 507
Cheshier, I., 422
Chesnut, A. B., 244
Chesser, H. L., 521, 968
Chikane, F., 231
Chikhwaza, L., 170
Chinguwo, R., 169
Chirelli, E., 113
Chit, M., 182

Chmykhalov, M., 1063
Cho, D. Y., 29, 137, 148–49, 155, 234, 237, 242, 244, 502, 503, 521–22, 528, 822, 837, 973, 1050, 1068, 1083
Choi, B. S., 240
Choi, J.-S., 148, 522
Chole, D., 152
Christenson, L. D., 418, 480, 483, 490, 517, 522–23, 549, 572, 689, 792, 816, 847, 853, 1061, 1206
Christian, J., 422
Christian, W., 422, 543
Christiansen, J., 280
Christie, W., 887, 1070
Christlieb, T., 612, 1066
Chrysostom, J., 739, 1063
Chui B. I., 225, 512
Chung, Y. K., 155
Clanton, A. L., 385
Clark, D., 353, 773
Clark, E. C., 923
Clark, E. W., 34
Clark, G., 312, 506
Clark, I. G., 551–52
Clark, M. S., 790
Clark, R., 552
Clark, S., 568, 1109
Clark, S. B., 460–61, 463, 465, 473, 482, 484, 494, 552, 840
Clark, T., 246
Clarke, C. J., 490, 491, 552–53, 1159–60
Clarke, F., 151
Clarke, K., 498
Clasue, K., 223
Clayton, N. J., 916
Cleage, A., 429
Cleary, E. L., 157
Clement of Alexandria, 735
Clementson, E. L., 623
Clemmons, I. C., 385, 401, 402, 403, 554, 555
Clifford, W., 249–50, 251
Coady, A. R., 188, 556
Coates, G., 45, 491, 508, 556, 773, 818, 860
Cochrane, R. H., 370
Codreanu, T., 216
Coe, J., 336, 554, 556–57, 622, 653, 906, 978
Coffey, L. B., 536
Coffin, W. S., 269
Coghill, R., 872
Cohen, E., 412
Cohen, R., 504
Cojocaru, P., 214
Cole, B., 270
Coleridge, S. T., 803
Collazo, A., 210, 721

Colletti, J., 386, 572
Collins, A. P., 333, 334, 354, 537, 1021
Collins, G., 421
Collins, H., 917
Collins, J., 490, 1186
Collins, P., 188, 528
Colyar, W., 888
Conatser, H., 557
Conde, C. B., 205
Conde, E., 412
Condit, L., 888
Cone, C., 430
Cone, J. H., 429–31
Congar, Y., 494, 549
Conlee, J., 978
Conn, C. W., 48, 385, 389, 397–98, 558, 899, 914
Connelly, J. C., 384
Conrad, P., 81
Constantine, 736–37
Conté, L., 113
Cook, F. M., 632
Cook, G. A., 347, 424, 559–60, 642, 694, 937, 1055, 1057, 1162
Cook, J., 194
Cook, R. F., 122–23, 532, 560–61, 779, 893
Cook, R. G., 560
Cooke, G., 874
Cooley, C. H., 1086
Cooley, R. E., 561
Coombe, J., 26
Coombs, B., 45, 490, 550, 561–62, 774
Cooper, A. A., 228
Cooper, A. H., 1030
Cooper, H., 654
Coote, O. W., 894
Coots, L. W., 147
Copeland, K., 237, 427, 484, 488, 562, 653, 714, 795, 820, 919, 980, 992, 1016, 1039, 1118, 1119
Copeland, M. S., 431
Coplan, D. B., 228
Copley, A. S., 642, 847
Corbett, D. J., 245
Cordes, P., 792
Corpuz, R. D., 203
Correll, N. L., 562
Correll, S., 78
Cortese, A. G., 562–63
Cortez, F., 202
Corum, F. T., 389, 1072
Corvin, R. O., 563, 1079
Cotton, E., 391, 395, 396, 563, 1054
Cottrill, D., 1159
Couchman, R., 199
Courtney, H. P., 563–64, 816, 858, 973
Courts, J., 536

Cousen, C., 490, 495, 550, 564
Cowper-Temple, W., 820
Cox, B., 873
Cox, H., 12, 157, 796, 1125, 1133, 1176
Crabtree, J., 529
Cragin, C., 34, 83, 199
Cragin, H. W., 34, 83, 199
Craig, R., 377, 1015
Cramer, W. A., 847
Crandahl, M., 272
Crawford, F. L., 48, 327, 334, 347, 387, 564–65, 597, 638, 814, 887, 888, 893, 945, 976, 977, 1056, 1057, 1204
Crawford, R. R., 565
Creech, J., 403
Crews, M., 385
Cristallo, R., 137
Criswell, W. A., 1028
Crociani, B., 138
Croft, J., 520
Cronje, C., 233
Crooks, G., 923
Crosby, F., 915
Cross, C., 70, 154
Cross, M. P., 565, 923
Crouch, A., 565, 918
Crouch, P. F., 565, 616, 620, 919, 1119
Crumpler, A. B., 457, 566, 799, 1115
Crumpton, D., 231, 511
Cruz, N., 566–67, 843, 1117, 1175
Cullis, C., 612, 631
Culpepper, R. W., 567, 1179
Cummings, R. W., 567
Cunningham, L., 567, 1223
Cunningham, R., 334
Cunningham, R. J., 388
Cupertino, J., 466
Curry, J. H., 533
Curtis, F., 632
Cyprian, 736
Cyril of Jerusalem, 738

D

Da Costa, J. P., 208
Dager, A., 816
Dagys, J., 277
Dahlqvist, E., 264
Dai, D., 260
Dai, K., 182
Dake, F. J., 569
Da Lapa, J., 497
Dallière, L., 489, 493, 516, 569–70, 1027, 1045
Dallimore, A. H., 570, 1199
Dallmayer, H., 109
Dalton, A. F., 643
Dalton, R. C., 788
Damboriena, P., 899

Damian, P., 753
Dando, E. C., 973
Daneel, I., 238
Daneel, M. L., 416
Daniel, D., 511
Daniel, J., 782
Daniel, N., 782
Daniel, P., 511
Daniels, D., 234, 385, 401, 796, 1216
Danielsson, E., 103, 104, 150–51
Daoud, M. A., 899
Darby, J. N., 345, 584, 601, 655–56, 1044
Darell-Huckerby, C., 146
Darling, A., 498
Darragh, R. E., 920
Darrow, C., 615, 657
Da Silva, B., 41, 251
Date, H., 691, 728
D'Aubigné, M., 614
Daugherty, B. J., 571–72, 1118
Daugherty, M. L., 386
Davies, W., 491, 1160
Davis, G., 916
Davis, H., 83
Davis, K., 870
Davis, T. C., 939
Davis, W. E., 123
Davison, L., 1160
Dawson, H., 547
Dawson, J., 503, 573, 806, 873
Dayton, D. W., 387, 389, 399–400, 400, 401, 573, 612, 673, 674, 1079, 1123
Dayton, E. R., 1181
Deacon, J., 151
De Almeida, A., 412
De Alwis, A., 248–50
Dean, B., 248
Dean, M., 7
De Andreis, G., 508
De Caro, L., 386
De Castro y Hernández, F., 82
DeCelles, P., 463, 473
De Costa Barata, A., 208
De Fante, V., Sr., 202
De Gruchy, J. W., 431
De Hass, M., 237
De Hernández, M. B., 277
Deiros, P., 24, 25
Delabilière, C. E. D., 258
De la Cruz, M., 573, 717, 927
Del Campo, C., 55
Del Colle, R., 1127, 1128
De León, V., 386, 899
Delk, J., 396
Del Mundo, L., 176
De Lopez, A., 346
De Los Reyes, A., 512

Del Rosso, A., 136
DelTurco, J., 526
De Mattos, J., 208
De Meesterk, F. L., 32
De Mello, L., 40
De Mello, M., 40
Demeter, R., 684
De Monléon, A., 474, 493, 494, 549
De Moraes, Z., 38
Dempster, M. W., 388, 605, 606, 790, 881, 898, 1077, 1078, 1138
De Nascimento, J., 497
Denison, E., 202
Denny, D., 847, 848
Denny, R., 574
Denton, W., 201
De Pâris, F., 705–6
De Pieri, L., 140
D'Epinay, C. L., 159, 160, 412
De Rougemont, F., 258, 489
Derr, P., 267
Derricks, C., 915
Derstine, G., 484, 487, 574–75, 832, 869, 980
De Siebenthal, C., 707–8
De Silva, J. J. B., 248, 249
Devadas, M., 782
De Valenzuela, R., 175, 323
Devin, R., 130
DeVito, R., 277
De Walker, L. J., 78, 82
De Worm, H. T., 489, 569–70
Díaz, D. G., 176
Dickinson, J., 76
Dickson, A. S., 458
Didymus the Blind, 738
Dieter, M., 493, 612
Diggs, J. D., 1157
DiLena, P., 1117
DiOrio, R. A., 487, 582
Di Prizio, G., 496, 498
DiStaulo, G., 805
Dittert, H., 110
Dittus, G., 1135
Divine, M. J., 426
Dixon, A. C., 614, 615, 656
Dixon, H. B., Jr., 330
Dixon, P., 45, 556
Doak, E. W., 1163
Dobbins, R., 1016
Dobson, J., 1209
Dodzweit, A., 72, 308
Dollar, C., 1118
Domoutchief, C., 106
Donald, K. G., 123
Doney, C. W., 7, 885
Dorchester, G. D., 623
Dorsey, T. A., 916

Dortch, R., 353
Dougherty, E., 498
Douglas, J. E., Sr., 313
Dowie, J. A., 26, 58, 184, 187, 227, 228, 230, 257, 308, 387, 439, 444, 454, 524, 538, 541, 569, 586–87, 612, 631, 642, 680, 772, 828, 842, 946, 953, 977, 978, 979, 989, 992, 1026, 1038, 1067, 1134, 1223
Downing, R. P., 888
Doyal, G., 248
Drake, L., 631, 632, 1203
Draper, M. T., 587–88, 888, 891, 970
Dreher, A., 89
Dreher, J., 89
Driscoll, P., 918
Driver, E. R., 423
Droogers, A., 414
Drummond, H., 459, 803, 929, 1191
Dubb, A. A., 416
Dubose, D. J., 537
Dudley, D., 632
Duffield, G. P., 547, 588
Duncan, F., 26, 1091
Duncan, H. M., 351, 352
Duncan, P., 26, 28, 536, 1091
Duncan, S. A., 351, 352, 396, 588
Duncombe, C. H. E., 654
Dungan, T. R., 1163
Dunk, G. T. S., 588–89
Dunn, G., 201
Dunn, J. D. G., 790, 797, 1124, 1130, 1137
Dunnam, M., 1159
Duplantis, J., 1118
Du Plessis, D. J., 28, 32, 141, 148, 190, 234, 257, 330, 336–37, 383, 407, 441, 477–78, 481, 484, 490, 493, 494, 496, 499, 554, 572–73, 576–78, 589–92, 616, 662, 689, 769, 844, 853, 933, 935, 973, 996, 1023, 1050, 1103, 1214
Du Plessis, J. T., 593, 853
Dupont, M., 502
Dupree, S. S., 385, 386, 593
Dupret, P., 113
Durasoff, S., 383, 593–94
Durham, W. H., 333, 334, 347, 348, 368, 371, 387, 391, 393, 424, 526, 528, 594, 623, 638, 646, 689, 728, 793, 856, 906, 936, 951, 977, 989, 1050–51, 1056–57, 1161, 1167, 1177
Dusing, M. L., 547, 1136
Dutaud, R. L., 962
Duvall, R., 386
Dwight, T., 614
Dyabupemba, F., 1175
Dye, C., 595

E

Eady, C. S., 123
Eames, R., 274
East, R., 491
Eastman, D., 596
Easton, S. C., 121, 888
Eby, J. P., 832, 833
Eck, J., 613
Ecke, K., 489
Eckhardt, J., 507, 930
Edel, E., 910
Edel, R. F., 492
Edmund, H., 203
Edvardsen, A., 268, 496, 598
Edwards, J., 42, 615, 1066, 1073
Edwards, R., 123, 809
Eerola, E. W., 412
Efimovich, I., 91
Eggleton, H., 272
Eichorn, A., 114
Eim, Y. S., 796
Eirikson, A., 117
Eiseland, N. L., 389
Eivers, M., 502
Ekanayaka, R., 252
Ekanyu, J., 274
Ekman, U., 509
Elbert, P., 790
Elder, M., 151
Eldridge, G., 347, 642
Eliya, N., 248
Ellenberger, P., 113
Ellingwood, H., 604
Ellis, J. B., 532
Ellis, V., 915
Emerson, R. W., 614
Emiau, S. P., 274
Emmanuel, A., 20
Emmel, M. W., 793
Emmert, A., 295
Endersen, A., 81
Eneas, A., 30
Eneas, W. V., 30
Engineer, M., 124
Engstrom, T. W., 101
Enns, A. W., 899
Ephrem of Syria, 741–42
Epstein, D. M., 386
Erasmus, D., 795
Erickson, A., 200
Erickson, C., 201
Erickson, E. C., 600
Erickson, L., 199
Ericsson, E., 117
Erigena, J. S., 753
Erola, W., 182
Erskine, T., 1066

Ervin, H. M., 363, 483, 546, 600, 790, 981
Escobedo, M., 341, 537, 605, 1030
Esperanza, R. C., 201
Espinosa, E., 503
Espinosa, G., 401
Espinosa, R., 83
Esselbach, F., 32
Esselbach-Whiting, A., 32
Estevens, E., 78
Etim, E., 416
Eugene, T. M., 431
Eusebius of Caesarea, 738
Evans, G., 136
Evans, I. V., 30, 893
Evans, L., 997
Evans, R. M., 30, 533, 893, 1145
Evans, W. I., 335, 377, 524, 623
Everts, J., 1132
Ewald, T. W., 306
Ewart, F. J., 389, 391, 424, 560, 623–24,
    638, 937, 941, 977, 1042, 1126, 1161–
    62, 1212

F

Fabian, A., 95
Falkner, C. F., 888
Falley, J., 85
Falley, M., 85
Fallon, R. H., 26
Falvo, D. S., 140
Falwell, J., 353, 616, 658, 1209
Faricy, R., 496, 632
Farina, D., 526
Farmer, L., 83
Farrell, G., 246
Farrow, L., 347, 632–33, 888, 1055,
    1072, 1203–4
Farson, M. M., 874
Faught, J. H., 49
Faupel, D. W., 383, 387, 1124
Fauss, O. F., 635, 1165
Faux, W. M., 122
Fedotov, I., 219
Fee, G. D., 635–36, 790, 881, 1130,
    1132, 1133
Felder, C. H., 431
Feliciano, E., 82
Feliciano, J., 82
Feliciano, S., 82, 639
Felix, H., 54
Fell, N. A., 351
Fellingham, D., 45, 503
Fenken, P., 180–81
Fernández, J. M., 791
Ferrer, V., 1064
Fetler, R., 89, 1031
Fetler, W., 88, 89, 1031
Fichtenbauer, J., 505, 559

Fierro, R. F., 637–38
Filho, C. F. D., 513
Filmalter, J., 511
Finke, B., 500
Finkenbinder, F. O., 209, 639, 719, 829,
    909, 1179
Finkenbinder, P. E., 640
Finney, C. G., 345, 421, 612, 785, 944,
    1073, 1143
Finney, J., 491, 840
Finstrom, D., 280
Finto, D., 873
Fiorese, V., 138
Firth, J., 66, 888
Fischer, J., 872, 1156
Fischer, J.-D., 493
Fish, S., 182
Fisher, C. L., 865
Fisher, E. K., 347, 638, 641, 772, 1057,
    1075, 1105, 1166
Fisher, F. S., 542
Fisher, G., 969
Fisher, H. L., 422, 1157
Fisher, R. E., 641
Fiske, E., 1024
Fitts, B., 503
Fitzgerald, M., 117
Flattery, G. M., 641, 669–70
Fleisch, P., 407
Fletcher, J., 611–12, 727, 785, 1129
Fletcher, M. P., 507
Flint, M., 352
Flood, G., 34
Flora, C. B., 166
Flores, J. P., 502
Flores, L., 83
Flores, S. J., 641–42, 841
Flower, A. R., 642–43, 885, 977
Flower, D. W., 643
Flower, G. E., 643
Flower, J. R., 334, 335, 336, 337, 368,
    397, 590, 642–43, 644, 694, 719, 834,
    845, 847, 879, 892, 895, 921, 923,
    937, 968, 975, 976, 1134, 1162, 1214
Flower, M. L., 906
Floyd, D. L., 977
Fluke, O., 969
Flynn, T., 492
Fockler, C. B., 966
Fogg, S., 875
Foglio, D., 139
Foh, N. K., 171
Follette, J. W., 588, 644, 787
Fonn, T., 124
Fontaine T., A., 414
Forbes, J. A., 427, 430, 485, 816
Ford, J. M., 463, 645
Ford, L. H., 537, 645

Forest, D., 152
Forrest, T., 461–62, 498, 502, 645, 792,
    879, 935
Forster, F., 45, 797
Forster, R. T., 45, 508, 645, 818, 860
Forteza, F., 568
Fortunato, F. P., 526
Fosdick, H. E., 657
Foss, K., 509
Fosseus, H., 496
Foster, R., 518–19, 558–59
Foster, T., 690–91
Fotescu, L., 216
Fox, G., 1014, 1144
Fox, L., 69, 962
Fox, T., 174
Francescon, L., 39, 134, 165, 526, 594,
    646, 888
Francesconi, L., 23
Francke, A. H., 611
Frangipane, F., 503, 507, 646–47
Franklin, K., 918
Franklin, R., 537
Franks, W. R., 30
Fraser, A., 838
Fraser, L., 888
Frazee, J. J., 423, 965, 1163
Frazen, C., 149
Frazier, E. F., 420
Fredriksson, K., 34
Fredriksson, M., 34
Freeman, W., 867
Freidzon, C., 161
French, C. E., 210
French, C. F., 82
Frey, C., 151
Frey, W. C., 306
Frías, P., 414
Friedzon, C., 512
Frigerio, A., 412–13
Fris, R., 409, 949
Fritsch, C., 59
Frodsham, A. W., 647
Frodsham, S. H., 97, 334, 372, 391, 395,
    396, 406, 528, 572, 647–48, 788, 831,
    898
Froen, H.-J., 496, 648
Fromke, D. V., 561
Frost, R., 508, 816
Frutiger, C., 113
Fulford, W. H., 422
Fullam, E. L., 307, 652
Fullam, T., 933
Fuller, C. E., 1015
Fuller, W. E., 421, 423, 640, 652–53, 805
Fulton, C. B., Jr., 307, 655
Fulton, E. J., 968
Futa, A., 71

G

Gabriel, C., 916
Gabriel, M., 205
Gadberry, A., 83
Gaebelein, A. C., 656, 872, 936
Gagaka, J. B., 153
Gaglardi, B. M., 669
Gaines, M., 659
Gaither, B., 916, 918
Galilea W., C., 57
Gamanywa, S., 268
Gambino, H. S., 157
Gamboa, T., 573
Gannon, R., 872, 874, 1156
Ganuza, J. M., 412
Garber, P., 1159
Garcia-Herreros, R., 498
García Peraza, J., 659
Gardner, L., 121
Gardner, V. F., 646
Garlock, H. B., 659, 892, 909
Garlock, J., 897
Garr, A. G., 59, 60, 121, 124, 152, 248, 306, 348, 660–61, 786–87, 875, 888, 907
Garr, L., 59, 121
Garrard, D., 69
Garrard-Burnett, V., 157
Garrett, D., 188, 503
Garrigues, J.-M., 494
Garrigus, A. B., 48, 524, 661, 888, 893, 964
Garsulao, C., 201
Gartner, B., 496
Gashagari, A., 47, 220
Gaston, W. T., 334, 621
Gaudet, V., 139, 493, 496
Gaukroger, S., 491, 508
Gause, R. H., 585–86, 661
Gaxiola, M. J., 408, 662, 1079, 1128
GaXpar, V., 214
Gay, R., 503
Gbenakou, H., 113
Geddie, J., 194
Gee, D., 26, 27, 91, 92, 98, 104, 105, 258, 323, 330, 340, 341, 389, 407, 454, 547, 572, 586, 590, 618, 662–63, 788, 838, 898, 953, 954, 972, 973, 979, 1023, 1046, 1195, 1202
Gelpi, D. L., 663
Gerdine, J. L., 240
Gerlach, L., 158, 165, 389
Gerloff, R., 408
Gerner, K., 492
Gerometta, O. A., 412
Gertrude of Helfta, 758
Getaway, S., 114

Geyer, H., 929
Gheroghe, I., 215
Giant, J., 431
Gibson, C. A., 664, 729, 888, 1226
Gifford, P., 17, 237, 408, 414
Gih, A., 269
Gikonyo, P., 153
Gilkes, C. T., 431
Gill, D. M., 387
Gill, K., 409
Gillett, D., 491
Gillquist, P., 558–59
Gimenez, A., 668, 935
Giménez, H. A., 24, 25
Gimenez, J., 668
Giminez, H., 512
Ginn, M., 122
Girón, J., 720
Gislason, E., 117
Gitonga, A., 154
Glardon, C., 258
Glasser, A. F., 625
Glassey, J., 400, 1067
Glassey, M. J., 785, 887
Glazier, S. D., 157
Gledhill, V., 774
Gleiss, P., 493
Glennon, J., 28
Glover, K., 26
Glover, R. H., 1071
Goben, J., 793, 945
Goble, P., 872, 1156
Godbey, W. B., 728, 886
Goff, H. H., 457
Goff, J. R., Jr., 386, 387, 400, 404
Goforth, J., 1068
Göhner, P., 274
Göhner, S., 274
Gohr, G., 329
Goins, J. B., 1145
Golder, M. E., 385
Gonzales, E., 513, 678
Gonzales, M., 202
González, A., 78
González, E. J., 641, 840–41
González, F. H., 81–82
González, J., 278
Gonzalez, J. M., 176
González, K., 78
González, V. A., 778
Goodwin, B., 430
Goodwin, F. L., 307
Gordon, A. J., 351, 376, 408, 656, 821, 886, 929, 936, 1067
Gordon, B., 1167
Gordon, S. D., 612
Gorietti, U. N., 135
Goss, E. E., 391, 424

Goss, H. A., 326, 333, 391, 394, 395, 537, 594, 621, 638, 679, 866, 938, 968, 1160–61, 1162–63
Gossett, D., 820
Gourley, T. H., 387, 679–80
Goursat, P., 493
Grace, E., 1158
Graham, B., 15, 101, 188, 232, 330, 332, 417, 522, 554, 592, 616, 658, 882, 1024
Graham, J., 490
Graham, L., 353
Graham, P., 143
Graner, L., 122
Grant, A., 918
Grant, W. B., 490
Grant, W. V., 567, 622
Grasso, D., 496
Graves, C., 250, 251
Graves, F. A., 680, 689, 728, 959
Gravina G., A., 280
Gray, D. B., 599
Green, L., 52, 503, 508, 680, 818, 860
Green, M., 491
Greenaway, C. E., 216
Greenway, A. L., 680–81
Greenwood, C. L., 26, 27, 681, 1110
Greenwood, H., 496
Gregerson, D., 109, 193
Gregory of Narek, 749
Gregory of Nazianzen, 740–41
Gregory of Nyssa, 740
Gregory T., 681
Grier, W. D., 248
Griffin, K., 929
Griffin, O., 873, 874
Griffith, R. M., 387
Griffith, T. A., 52
Grimes, S., 939, 964
Groesbeek, C., 127–31
Grondal, H., 496
Gros, J., 388
Grossman, S., 492
Grothaus, C., 151, 264
Groves, A. N., 118
Groza, P., 215
Gruen, E., 487, 817
Guerekozoungbo, C., 54
Guerra, E., 682
Guerreiro, J. D. C., 180
Guillén, M., 341, 381, 557, 682
Gulbrandsn, P., 193
Gulyas, S., 216
Gumbel, N., 312, 501
Gungu, C., 151
Gunstone, J., 315, 490, 682
Gustafsson, A., 34
Gustafsson, F., 34

Gustafsson, O., 237
Gustavson, H. I., 898
Guti, E. H., 682–83

H

Hackett, T., 97
Hagee, J., 1119
Hagemeier, R., 71
Hagemeier, S., 71
Hager, C. R., 59
Haggard, T., 934
Hagin, K., 427, 1073, 1118
Hagin, K. E., 237, 455, 484, 488, 562,
    571, 653, 687, 714, 795, 817, 820,
    980, 992, 998, 1016
Hahn, J., 353
Haines, R., 844
Hale, F. A., 354
Hall, C. B., 916
Hall, D., 714
Hall, H. R., 687–88
Hall, J. L., 688
Hall, L. C., 1162
Hall, M. W., 538
Hall, R. B., 306
Hall, W. P., 936
Halldorf, D., 71
Hallesby, O., 496
Halstead, C. R., 52
Hämäläinen, A., 411
Hamilton, M. P., 355
Hammon, W. H., 623
Hammond, H. P. L., 688–89, 950
Hamon, B., 930
Han, Y. C., 244, 245
Hancock, S. N., 965
Hanegraaff, H., 446, 714, 816
Hang, T. T., 171
Hansen, E., 270, 415
Hanson, C. M., 689
Hanson, G., 60
Hanson, J., 847
Hanson, P., 1138
Hardie, R. A., 239
Härdstedt, J., 208
Hare, T. R., 315
Harford-Battersby, T. D., 821
Hargrave, V. D., 198, 689, 722, 897
Harper, M., 28, 29, 190, 295, 473, 490,
    495, 497, 548, 550, 646, 792, 880,
    1013, 1059, 1160
Harper, M. C., 689–90
Harrell, D. E., Jr., 386, 388, 690, 978
Harris, C. W., 424
Harris, L. C., 27, 445, 458, 690–91
Harris, M., 916, 918
Harris, T., 691, 728, 858
Harris, W. W., 13

Harrison, A. B., 532, 691
Harrison, B., 562
Harrison, D., 795
Harrisville, R., 671
Harry, M., 495
Hartman, L. L., 78–79
Hartman, P., 78–79
Harvey, E. B., 692
Harvey, E. L., 528, 874
Haskins, G. W., 314
Hasmatali, E. D., 52, 272
Hastie, E. N., 965
Hastings, T., 915
Hatchett, E. I., 171
Hathaway, B., 514
Hathaway, W. G., 547
Hatwin, G., 1020
Hauge, H. N., 612
Haughey, J., 463, 517
Hawkins, R. B., 31
Hawkins, W., 918
Hawksley, G., 70, 154
Hawn, R. H., Sr., 306, 816
Hawthorne, A. J., 424
Hawtin, G., 48, 831
Hayes, D. L., 431
Hayes, N., 795
Hayes, S., 230
Hayford, J., 916, 918, 1119
Hayford, J. W., 189, 692, 790, 1050
Hays, R. B., 652
Haywood, G. T., 48, 387, 389, 406, 423,
    560, 693–94, 788, 937, 938, 943, 965,
    977, 1162, 1163
Healy, P., 204
Heard, R. D., 966
Heath, L. B., 970
Hebden, E., 48, 711–12, 892
Hebden, J., 48, 711–12
Hébrard, M., 474
Heddle, E., 490
Hedin, S.-G., 256
Heeterby, A., 99
Heil, B., 487
Heil, R., 847
Heinerborg, K. E., 257
Heinonen, E., 104
Hemmingway, D., 275
Henderson, N., 151
Henderson, W., 599
Hendrickson, N., 151, 888
Henry, C. F. H., 616, 658
Hensley, C. M., 894
Hensley, G. W., 1052
Herbert, G., 91
Herberts, A., 412
Herman, H., 133, 201
Hernández, F., 210

Hernández, J. I., 176
Herndon, B., 76
Herndon, L., 76
Herne, J. V., 116
Herrmans, A. A., 103
Herschell, K., 113
Herskovits, M. J., 420
Hervas, J., 567
Hess, D., 37
Hess, R., 60
Heward-Mills, D., 510
Hewitt, J., 458
Heywood, R. S., 120
Hezmalhalch, T., 58, 227, 346, 348, 642,
    712, 888
Hickey, M. S., 712, 935, 1118, 1119
Hicks, R. H., Sr., 646, 712
Hicks, T., 24, 111, 188, 363, 554, 653,
    713, 774, 899, 950, 1179
Hickson, J. M., 28
Hidalgo, R. Z., 200, 412
Hiebert, P., 779
Higton, T., 491
Hilary of Poitiers, 745
Hildegard of Bingen, 713, 757–58, 1064
Hilgert, A., 151
Hill, A., 121
Hill, R., 431
Hillary, D., 251
Himitian, J., 498
Hindle, T., 892
Hine, V. H., 389
Hinn, B., 149, 713–14, 1119
Hippolytus, 736
Hirsch, T., 312
Hite, B. H., 723
Ho, D., 181
Hobart, B., 28
Hocken, P. D., 140, 384, 549, 723–24,
    792, 873, 1079
Hodge, C., 656
Hodges, E. F., 323
Hodges, M. L., 78, 200, 546, 547, 724,
    877, 878, 897, 982, 1199
Hodges, S. M., 899
Hodgson, E., 68, 622, 725, 1225
Hodgson, J., 228
Hoekendijk, K., 185, 254, 490
Hoffman, S., 268
Hogan, J. P., 216, 337, 725–26, 895, 1154
Holland, J. R., 794
Holleman, C., 123
Hollenweger, W. J., 98, 140, 227, 258,
    385, 402, 406, 408, 412, 435, 440,
    709, 729–30, 796, 832, 878, 880, 899,
    1120, 1131–32, 1138
Holloway, G., 202, 205
Holmes, A. J., 894

Holmes, N. J., 728, 730, 799, 988, 1045
Holmström, A., 47
Holt, W. B., 423
Honea, H. E., 641
Honomou, E., 113
Hooft, V., 572
Hook, C. H., 121, 660
Hooper, E., 970
Hoover, M. L., 55
Hoover, W. C., 23, 55–56, 198, 199, 305, 728, 770–71, 789, 1040, 1116
Hopkins, E., 820
Horner, J., 796, 1048
Hornshuh, F., 772, 945
Horst, F., 201
Horsthuis, J. H., 186
Horton, H. L. C., 340, 547, 772, 788, 1158, 1202
Horton, S. M., 389, 547, 585–86, 641, 772–73, 790
Horton, T. C., 952
Horton, W. H., 664, 773, 788, 897
Hortsman, H., 129
Houck, M., 248
Houfe, E., 490
Hounshell, J., 239
Houston, F., 27, 188, 190, 436, 774
Howard, D., 476
Howard, H., 123
Howard, T., 559
Howard-Browne, R. M., 552, 774–75, 1150
Howell, I., 136
Howell, J. H., 385
Hoyle, L., 315, 491
Hoyt, T., Jr., 431
Hromas, B., 602
Huamán P., S. A., 412
Huat, T. J., 171
Hubbard, D. A., 572
Hudson, G. E., 819
Hudson, H., 143
Hudson, N., 797
Hughes, P. E., 490
Hughes, R. H., 585, 619, 775, 923, 973
Hughes, R. T., 387, 388, 404
Huh, H., 242, 243, 244
Huizer, G., 414
Humbard, A. R. E., 499, 619, 775–76, 1119
Humbard, M. A., 775–76
Humburg, E., 97, 109, 776, 910
Hunston, R., 547
Hunt, I., 188
Hunt, P., 48, 1020
Hunter, C., 484, 935, 1073
Hunter, H. D., 790, 792, 1121, 1130, 1216

Hunter, T., 1177
Hunter, W. L., 200
Hurlburt, J. R., 199
Hurst, W. R., 267, 776
Hutchin, J., 872
Hutchins, J. W., 345, 348, 437, 632, 1055, 1156
Hutchinson, M., 797
Hutchinson, W. O., 322
Hutton, D. L., 858, 945

I

Idosa, B., 234
Igana, J. D. N., 108
Ignatius of Loyola, 765–66
Ihalainen, H., 71
Ikonen, J., 224
Ilawan, G., 202
Ilunga, J., 68, 69, 777–78
Immanuel, B., 874
Ingles, J., 656
Ingram, J. H., 23, 30, 31, 33, 52, 116, 177, 210, 343, 532, 784, 893
Innvaer, R. O., 411
Inskip, J. S., 119, 422, 614, 865
Intrater, A., 873, 874
Ippolito, L., 805
Irangi, S., 151
Ireland, R., 39
Irenaeus, 734, 1063
Irish, C. M., 307, 802–3
Irving, E., 118, 398, 459, 612, 655, 657, 784–85, 803–4, 928, 929, 1066, 1189, 1190, 1191
Irwin, B. H., 344, 400, 423, 640, 652, 727, 785, 799, 804–5, 822, 969
Irwin, D. K., 805
Isaac of Nineveh, 749
Ito, A., 147
Iverson, D., 503, 507
Iwasko, R., 1048
IzbaXa, A., 214

J

Jacks, G., 188
Jackson, C., 223
Jackson, J., 487
Jackson, J. P., 502, 816
Jackson, M. E. J., 387
Jackson, R., 28, 188, 556, 806, 908, 1193
Jackson, R. A., 244
Jacobs, C., 503, 806
Jacobs, S. G., 806
Jacobsen, D., 387
Jacobson, A., 272
Jaffray, R. A., 60, 789
Jagelman, I., 28
Jaggers, O. L., 653

Jakes, T. D., 806–7
Jakob, M., 493
Jamieson, E., 31, 52
Jamieson, R. J., 31, 33, 52, 53, 272
Jamieson, S. A., 335, 885, 953
Jansa, B., 494
Jaramillo, D., 498, 499, 513, 807
Jaramillo, U., 499
Javier, E., 204
Javier, V., 205
Jeffreys, G., 32, 108, 340, 442, 588, 598–99, 621–22, 789, 807–8, 920, 971, 1045, 1174
Jeffreys, S., 621–22, 807, 808–9, 957
Jellinghaus, T., 612, 821
Jenkins, E., 228, 654
Jenkins, J., 1187
Jenkins, L., 809, 888
Jenkins, S., 49, 963
Jernigan, J. C., 809
Jeske, O., 92
Jeter, H., 77, 78
Jeter, J. A., 422, 535
Jeurgensen, C. F., 147
Jeurgensen, J., 147
Jeyaraj, Y., 809–10
Jiloveanu, I., 91
Jiloveanu, J., 215
Jimenez, R., 696
Jing D., 63
Joachim of Fiore, 754–55
Joaquín, E., 176
Johannesson, J.-E., 410
Johansen, G., 198
Johanson, M.-L., 208
Johansson, P., 154
Johansson, S., 247
John, A. J., 123
John, P. V., 123
John of Avila, 766–67
John of the Cross, 767
John Paul II, Pope, 139, 162, 454, 461, 465, 495, 496, 519, 578, 579, 591, 810–11
Johnson, A. G., 97
Johnson, A. J., 418
Johnson, B., 23, 34, 425, 812
Johnson, E., 223
Johnson, H. A., 176, 240
Johnson, J. J., 813
Johnson, L. E., 201
Johnson, M., 586, 887
Johnson, P. N., 893
Johnson, S. C., 424, 543, 544
Johnson, T. M., 417
Johnston, R. K., 388
Johnston, T., 154
Johnstone, F. D., 1225

John XXIII, Pope, 1171–72
Jones, A., 421
Jones, B., 45, 491, 502, 550, 643, 658, 676, 773, 813, 817
Jones, C. E., 382, 383, 385, 407, 416, 813
Jones, C. P., 421, 422, 426, 535, 728, 866, 893, 1055
Jones, J. P., 120
Jones, K., 45
Jones, L., 91, 892
Jones, O. T., 536–37, 813–14
Jones, T. F., 814
Jones, T. J., 340
Jones, W. R., 430
Jongeneel, J. A. B., 388, 409, 796, 880
Jordan, F. W., 389
Jordan, H. A., 793
Jorgensen, J.-P., 496
Joseph, J., 119, 781
Joseph, J. A., 31
Joseph, P., 115
Joshua, S., 1187
Joyfitch, P., 250
Joyner, R., 502, 507, 814, 817
Judd, C. F., 631
Judson, A., 181
Juergensen, C. F., 892
Juergensen, J., 909
Julian of Norwich, 759
Jungkuntz, T., 481, 549, 814, 847
Junk, T., 60, 346, 348, 814
Juster, D. C., 504, 814–15, 872, 873, 874, 1156, 1157
Juul, K., 411

K

Kabila, L., 70
Kagarama, J., 275
Kairo, P., 266
Kaiser, R., 251
Kakobe, Z., 268
Kalambule, L. E. R., 169
Kalau, E., 177
Kaluzi, J., 265
Kameta, M., 267
Kaminskey, M., 872
Kammensjö, A., 410
Kamsteeg, F., 414
Kane, J. H., 1068
Kane, S., 1052
Kanto, R., 412
Kardec, A., 37
Kärkkäinen, V.-M., 579, 1122, 1216
Kaseman, J., 342, 817
Katau, E., 177
Kauffman, I., 885
Kauffman, J. H., 870
Kayembe, M., 74, 817

Kayo, J., 275
Kayumba, E., 68
Kebede, S., 87
Keifer, R., 460
Kellar, N., 817–18
Keller, M., 621, 818, 898
Keller, O. C., 151, 818, 892
Kellogg, J. P., 632
Kelly, J. P., 507
Kelty, H., 77
Kelty, M., 77
Kempe, M., 759
Kendrick, G., 45, 387, 503, 508, 818
Kendrick, K., 384, 396, 399, 818, 860, 1079
Kennedy, M., 819, 856
Kenoly, R., 918
Kent, G. R., 538, 636–37
Kenyon, E. W., 440, 562, 795, 819–20, 936, 992
Kenyon, H. N., 385, 606
Kerr, C., 475, 492, 820
Kerr, D. W., 335, 788, 820, 885, 906, 1019
Kerr, M., 820
Kessler, J. A. B., 412
Keswick, G., 26, 436
Ketcham, M., 124, 182, 776, 821–22, 892, 909
Kettunen, H., 270, 415
Kham, H. L., 182
Ki Dong Kim, 512
Kidula, M., 152
Kifwame, K., 69
Kiguru, S., 152
Kikuchi, R., 147
Kikuyama, K., 147
Kil, S. J., 240
Kildahl, J., 847
Kill, E., 412
Killingbeck, R., 187
Kiloba, U., 68
Kilola, M., 267
Kilpatrick, J., 445–46, 502
Kim, C., 242
Kim, D., 245, 507
Kim, I. D., 240
Kim Sun Do, 512
Kinderman, G., 214
King, B. L., 390
King, C. V., 364
King, J. H., 97, 98, 124, 457, 553, 640, 727, 788, 798, 799, 800, 805, 822–23, 847, 866, 892, 978, 1028
King, M. L., Jr., 428, 537, 555
Kinsey, L., 532
Kirk, J. M., 920
Kirkpatrick, M., 831

Kirkpatrick, W. J., 916
Kirschke, W. E., 966
Kita, K. E., 172
Kivikangas, V., 411
Kjellås, R., 198
Kjellberg, A., 47
Klahr, P., 205
Klaus, B., 388, 547, 898, 1047, 1077
Klaver, P., 184
Klemin, R., 25
Kluzit, J. P., 82, 116
Kluzit, S., 116
Knapp, M. W., 1054
Knauff, E., 68
Knight, C. B., 823
Knight, G. N., 823, 858
Knight, K., 121
Knoch, O., 493
Knowles, M., 239
Knutas, M., 246
Kobo, J., 511
Kohl, H., 251
Kolini, M., 220
Kolisang, M., 232
Koller, J., 493
Kollins, K. C., 825
Komanapalli, E., 125
Komant, E., 220
Komont, E., 152
Kong M. Y., 171, 224–25
Koo, L., 171
Kopfermann, W., 493, 509
Kopittke, C. S., 279
Korneliussen, T., 275
Kossila, E., 224
Koukola, G., 76
Kourouma, H. D., 114
Kowae, W., 269
Koy, J. A., 102
Kraan, K. J., 185
Kraft, C. H., 1068
Kramar, M., 472, 825–26
Kreider, L., 507
Kristinsson, H., 117
Krohns, D., 180
Kubuabola, R. I., 102
Kuhlman, K., 209, 232, 330, 389, 484, 499, 572, 709–10, 714, 775, 826–27, 867, 1015, 1061, 1073, 1119
Kumuyi, W. F., 15, 16, 18, 510, 574
Kundalawa, B., 252
Küng, H., 592
Kunjummen, C., 123
Kuosmanen, J., 411, 612
Kusmin, P., 152
Küttner, G., 494
Kuzmic, P., 89, 90, 94, 546, 827, 862, 881, 1076

Kwak, B. J., 244
Kydd, R., 1079

L

Labanchi, E., 136
Labang, F., 204
LaBarre, W., 386
LaBerge, A., 389
Lacombe, J. D. B., 116
Ladd, G. E., 898, 1023
Laestadius, L. L., 612
Lafitte, M., 493
Lagar, J. R., 23
Lagasca, E. B., 203
Lagdameo, A. N., 207
LaHaye, B., 1209
Lai, W., 154
Lake, J. G., 27, 58, 227, 346, 348, 570,
    654, 712, 828, 842, 888, 978, 979, 992
Lalou, M., 20
Lamah, J., 114
Lamb, W., 26
Lamberth, R., 816
Lan, L. S., 171
Lancaster, J., 26, 547
Lancaster, S. J., 447, 828–29
Land, S. J., 790, 1122, 1130, 1131
Landeo, C., 199
Landero, V., 497
Landi, E., 136
Lang, G. H., 121, 550, 1184
Lang, P., 796
Lang, W. C., 171
Lange, D., 612
Lange, J., 463
Langstaff, A., 29
Lapasaran, N. J., 205
Lapka, J., 170
Lapoorta, J., 1216
Larsen, A., 80, 395
Larsen, M., 489
Larsen, V., 65–66
Larson, L., 279
Larson, R., 1016
Larsson, B., 410
Lastimosa, T., 202
Latimer, S. W., 116, 532
Latourelle, R., 699
Latto, T. T., 48
Lattu, P., 104
Laurentin, R., 494, 549, 833, 863
Lauster, H., 532, 833, 893
Law, A., 915
Law, E. M., 888, 891, 898
Law, I., 130
Law, M., 59
Law, T., 833–34
Lawler, B., 60

Lawler, H. L., 60, 888
Lawless, E. J., 387
Lawrence, B. F., 364, 389, 391, 393, 834,
    898, 1162
Lawrence, R. C., 424
Lawson, F., 491, 840
Lawson, K. C., 424
Lawson, R. C., 543
Layzell, R., 669, 831
Lazaro, E., 267
Lazarus, D., 874
Lea, L., 363, 836–37, 1048, 1119
Leach, J., 315
Leatherman, L., 23, 348, 888
Lebeau, P., 494, 497, 549, 837
Le Cossec, C., 493, 684
Le Cossec, J., 685
Ledbetter, J. W., 537
Lederlie, H., 1129
Ledford, A. A., 585
Lee, A., 1058–59
Lee, B., 244
Lee, C., 926, 927
Lee, D., 838
Lee, E. S., 345, 437–38
Lee, F. J., 532, 837
Lee, J., 423, 1203
Lee, W. P. K., 224
Lee, Y. D., 240, 837–38
Lee, Y.-H., 796, 1050
Leech, J., 97, 599, 971
LeFevre, E., 914
LeFevre, M., 916
Lehman, J. C., 888
Lehmann, D., 16, 17
Lehtinen, K., 510
Lemay, H., 507
Lemons, M. S., 530, 1144
Leng, L. S., 171
Lensch, R., 481, 838, 847
Lentink, W. J., 547
Leonard, B. J., 385
Leonard, D., 934
Leonard, T. K., 334, 678, 838, 855, 1045
Le Page, D., 169
Lerch, J., 214
Le Roux, P. L., 227–28
Levy, M. J., 870–71
Lewer, A., 838–39, 971
Lewini, A., 248, 249, 395
Lewis, A. C., 52
Lewis, A. W., 939
Lewis, D., 701
Lewis, F. E., 425
Lewis, G. F., 337, 839
Lewis, J. L., 1111
Lewis, M., 479
Lewis, P. W., 796

Lewis, W. C., 425
Liberman, P., 872, 1156
Liddle, J., 70
Lidman, S., 839
Lier, H. C., 496
Liga, N., 512
Lightfoot, J. B., 436
Ligon, B., 487
Lilli, S., 138
Lillie, D., 489, 549–50, 773, 1184
Lim, D., 1131, 1137
Lim, P., 171
Lincoln, C. E., 385, 430
Lindbeck, G., 1123
Lindblad, F., 788, 966
Linderholm, E., 409–10
Lindgren, A. B., 70, 71, 264
Lindkvist, J. A., 103
Lindquist, F. J., 456
Lindsay, A., 892
Lindsay, F. T., 841–42
Lindsay, G., 111, 209, 227, 336, 380, 388,
    441, 477, 523, 591, 622, 653, 708,
    841–42, 899, 950, 979, 1015, 1178–
    79
Lindskog, A., 219
Lines, B., 75, 76
Links, H., 872, 1156
Linn, D., 484, 1062
Lippy, C. H., 383, 400, 404
Lisle, G., 142
List, P., 154
Litwiller, N., 816, 842–43, 869, 935
Livingstone, D., 70
Llewellyn, J. S., 146
Llorente, F., 321, 573, 717, 843
Loggia, G., 136
Lokken, I., 180
Lombard, P., 754
Lombardi, G., 23, 134, 527
Long, C., 430
Long, K., 251
Loos, C. F., 251
Lopes, E., 208
López, A., 720
Lopez, A. L., 844
López, L., 321
Lopez, R., 844
Lopez-Tijerina, R., 1077
Lord, A. M., 880
Lorente, F., 175
Lorenz, E. S., 915
Lorenzen, A., 81
Lovekin, A. A., 389
Lovett, L., 385, 398, 402, 426, 430, 1046
Low, D., 172
Lowe, C. W., 348
Lowell, H., 560

Lowery, B., 138
Lowney, E., 422
Lowo, M., 69
Lubele, S., 265
Lucas, C. J., 970
Lucas, K., 70
Luce, A. E., 121, 176, 341, 354, 381, 387, 639, 718, 829, 830, 844–45, 897, 898, 1199
Luce, E. A., 121
Lucien, I., 75, 76
Lugo, J. L., 81, 209, 210, 381, 432, 639, 719, 777, 829, 845, 892, 949, 1051
Lukey, T., 872
Lukusa, L. A., 846
Lum, C. E., 347, 729, 846, 1056, 1057
Lundgren, K.-E., 410
Lupande, E. Y., 70
Lupton, L. R., 454, 642, 728, 846–47, 891
Lutchmann, P., 231, 232
Luther, M., 613, 763–64, 784, 914, 1009–10, 1064, 1218
Luvungu, A. L., 1176
Lyne, P., 773
Lynn, J., 266
Lyons, W. T., 1163

M

Ma, J., 1125
Ma, W., 388, 790, 796, 1125
Maasbach, J., 185
McAlister, H., 201, 852, 962
McAlister, R. E., 48, 424, 623, 852, 868, 892, 937, 1042, 1126, 1161, 1162
McAlister, W. E., 973
McAlpin, B., 28
McAlpine, C., 189–90, 490, 773
Macaulay, R., 234
Macauley, J., 87
Macauley, P., 87
McBain, D., 44, 490
McBride, J., 151
McCabe, J., 458
McCarty, D., 894
McCauley, D. V., 385
McCauley, E., 346, 348
McCauley, R., 511, 852
Macchia, F. D., 384, 668, 790, 1133
McClain, S. C., 852
McClellan, C., 917
McClung, L. G., Jr., 127, 898
McClure, A. D., 965
McClurkan, J. O., 989
McCoy, O. L., 915, 916
McCracken, H., 898, 899
McCraw, D., 28
McCullough, W., 1158

McDonald, G., 820
Macdonald, J., 1190–92
McDonald, N., 868
McDonnell, K., 140, 384, 388, 389, 403, 418, 465, 507, 517, 549, 576–77, 578, 579, 592, 853, 882, 1023
McDonough, E., 487, 582
MacDougall, B., 488
Macedo, E., 40, 209, 853–54, 1165
McGavran, D., 546, 1181
McGeady, J., 492
McGee, G. B., 127, 140, 385, 389, 400, 790, 854–55, 899, 1083
McGiffert, A. C., Sr., 656
McGlothen, M. C., 536
McGuire, M. B., 384
Machado, A. R., 208
McHaffey, D. S., 124
Machel, S., 180
Machen, J. G., 615, 657
Machove, M., 862
MacInnes, D., 490, 491
McIntire, C., 615, 658, 922, 923
McIntosh, T. J., 59, 60, 891, 892
Mackay, J. A., 481, 572, 591, 996
McKee, D., 492
McKenna, B., 487, 855
McKinney, C. A., 454, 621, 642, 838, 846–47, 855, 891, 966, 978
McKinney, J., 464
McKinney, L. O., 171, 223
Mackish, R., 94, 216
Macklin, J., 536
MacKnight, J. M., 855, 963
Mackreill, T., 169
McLain, H., 1193
McLane, P., 684
McLean, E. L., 78
McLean, H., 60
MacLean, L., 18
McLean, S., 60
McLoughlin, W. G., 386, 1170
McNabb, M., 521
McNeill, J., 28
McNiell, J., 1225
MacNutt, F. S., 484, 498, 855–56, 1062
McPherson, A. S., 26, 59, 78, 90, 213, 314, 330, 331, 374, 376, 386, 389, 390, 396, 524, 528, 554, 563, 594, 597, 622, 790, 793–94, 819, 823, 829, 838, 856–58, 888, 893, 945, 962, 977, 978, 995, 997, 998, 1015, 1019, 1046, 1050, 1135, 1142, 1145, 1182, 1205, 1222
McPherson, R., 245, 310, 564, 794, 856, 859
MacRobert, I., 385, 402–3
McTernan, J., 137–38, 868

Madsen, O., 509
Mafadi, J., 229
Magee, G., 941
Maguire, F., 479
Mahan, A., 345, 612, 615, 820
Mahaney, C. J., 487, 507, 550
Mahoney, R., 170, 268
Maier, W. A., 1015
Mainse, D., 484, 488, 859
Mak, B., 270
Mäkelä, J., 415
Malachuk, D., 483, 485, 843–44, 859, 980–81, 1061
Malcolm X, 428
Mallory, A. C., 536, 859–60
Malone, J. W., 632
Maloney, H. N., 389
Maltby, H. S., 1019
Mamiya, L., 385
Manikai, M., 72
Maninen, V., 411
Manley, W. F., 345, 346, 347
Manni, M., 140
Manninen, E., 104
Manning, F., 166
Manning, G., 1115
Manning, T., 473
Mansel, D., 773
Mantladi, J., 229
Manwo, L., 187
Maoz, A., 874
Marchand, J. A. G., 412
Marcion, 733
Marcoux, M., 568
Maréchal, M., 72, 76, 108
Margues, I., 697
Mariz, C., 41, 166
Mark, J., 6
Marker, G., 342
Marnham, C., 312
Marsden, G. M., 399
Marshall, C., 997
Marshall, E., 926
Marshall, J., 26
Marshall, J. H., 31, 52
Marshall, S. C. W., 829, 844, 860–61
Marthurin, R., 116
Martin, C. J., 431
Martin, D., 157, 160, 414
Martin, F., 496
Martin, G., 66
Martin, J., 431
Martin, L., 389, 497
Martin, O. L., 387
Martin, R., 384, 460–61, 462, 463, 465, 473, 475, 482, 484, 494, 507, 508, 552, 792, 816, 861–62, 1041, 1109
Martín, R., 82

Martin, R. F., 861
Martin, W., 521, 1047
Martinez, A., 177, 412
Martinez, F., 208
Martínez, J. N., 843
Martinez, S., 139
Martini, C. M., 139
Martins, J. A. C., 21–22
Marx, K., 862
Masaoay, B., 204
Mascarenhas, F., 792, 864–65
Mason, C. H., 347, 387, 403, 423–26,
    535–37, 537, 543, 553, 560, 597, 621,
    639, 645, 813, 860, 865–67, 893, 953,
    989, 1036, 1055, 1086, 1133, 1145,
    1161
Mason, L. M., 422, 915, 1157
Massey, R. E., 124
Mast, E., 151
Mast, M., 105
Matache, D., 213
Mateo, D., 82
Matheney, D., 155
Mattheis, R., 180
Matthew, D., 550
Matthews, S., 45, 656
Mattson-Boze, J., 257, 572, 980
Mattsson, A.-L., 85
Mattsson, S., 85
Mattsson-Boze, J. D., 832, 867
Matzat, D., 481, 847
Maunde, M. S., 169
Mavity, N. B., 857
Mawambe, T., 72
Maximus the Confessor, 749–50
Maxwell, B., 1207
May, L. C., 671
May, S., 122
Mayala, L., 268
Mayer, E., 109
Mayer, M., 151
Mayo, M. F., 347
Mazzu, J., 684
Mazzucco, M., 23, 278
Mbatha, P., 231
Mbete, P., 232
Mbiti, J., 431
Mbwanga, G., 70
Meacham, J., 1059
Mead, A., 867–68, 895
Mead, G. H., 1086
Mead, S. J., 347, 632, 867–68, 888
Meadows, P., 453
Meares, D., 934
Meares, J., 488, 868, 935
Mederlet, E., 492
Medina, C. S., 342
Meeking, B., 576

Mehr, H. H., 8
Meikle, J., 151
Melendez, E., 570
Mella, O., 414
Melton, J. G., 385
Melvin, B., 923
Mencken, H. L., 657
Menna, L., 23
Menzies, R. P., 388, 790, 1130
Menzies, W. W., 384, 387, 400, 791, 796,
    870, 1079, 1112
Mercer, B., 180
Meredith, E. H., 243
Merritt, S., 1143
Merritt, T., 614
Messias, P., 278
Messner, R., 353
Metz, K., 792
Meyer, B., 15
Meyer, E., 110, 151
Meyer, F. B., 345, 1188
Meyer, J., 875
Meyer, L. R., 305
Mgweno, A., 266
Mials, G. A., 422
Middlestaeds, R., 267
Mihok, E., 90
Mikongo, D. E., 71
Millar, S., 501, 770
Miller, C. I., 798
Miller, D. E., 384, 930
Miller, D. R., 160
Miller, E., 498
Miller, R. E., 24
Miller, T. W., 385
Miller, W., 656
Milligan, B., 59, 888
Mills, W. E., 383, 389
Minalainen, L.-R., 415
Minay, J., 198
Minnich, R. H., 869
Mintern, R. A., 26
Miranda, D., 40
Miranda, J., 717, 876
Miriam, M. H., 85
Mirly, H. H., 847, 876–77
Mitchell, A., 272
Mitchell, J. B., 1143
Mitchell, R. B., 385, 901–2, 923, 946,
    1185
Mitchell, R. C., 416
Mitchell, W., 185
Mitten, M., 315
Mitton, M., 508, 902
Mitzner, H. D., 968
Mix, E., 1203
Mjorud, H., 480, 496, 813, 847, 902
M'molecha, M., 70

Mobergh, M., 410
Modersohn, E., 612, 821
Moggs, T., 97
Mogoba, M. S., 431
Mohammed, 6, 10
Mohan, D., 123, 902
Moise, M. G., 364, 622, 632, 642, 902–3
Mok L. C., 59
Molina, S., 78, 204
Moll, G., 493
Möller, F. P., 416, 790
Moltmann, J., 592, 1125, 1127
Mömmö, S., 265
Monaghan, P., 559
Monbuleau, D., 113
Monga, G., 1176
Monod, A., 612
Monod, P., 54
Monod, T., 820, 821
Monot, R. J., 846, 903, 1175
Montague, G. T., 507, 903
Montgomery, C. J., 210, 345–46, 347,
    387, 389, 396, 557, 719, 904–6, 909,
    936, 975, 988, 995, 1067, 1072, 1075,
    1143, 1203, 1222, 1223
Montgomery, G. H., 719, 905, 906, 907,
    923, 936
Montgomery, J., 501
Montgomery, J. W., 1047
Montt, J. E. R., 159, 162
Moodman, H., 984
Moody, D. L., 28, 96, 292, 376, 400, 612,
    656, 730, 886, 907, 920, 953, 1020,
    1037, 1143
Moomau, A., 60
Mooneyham, T. D., 22
Moore, B. S., 147, 431
Moore, J. E., 345, 346, 347, 382, 438,
    708, 906–7, 1056, 1074
Moore, R., 771–72
Moorhead, M. W., 121, 888, 907
Mora, A., 200
Mora, V. M., 56
More, T., 613
Moreno, J., 278
Morgan, A. T., 635, 907, 1165
Morgan, D., 154, 388
Morgan Howard, C., 907–8
Moroco, F., 83
Morphew, D., 234, 238, 511
Morris, E. C., 865
Morris, J. B., 154
Morrison, B., 352
Morrison, G., 86
Morrison, H. C., 1143
Morrison, J. C., 181
Morrison, V., 266, 274
Morrow, P., 188, 190, 908, 1184

Morrow, W., 964
Morton, C. M., 211
Morton, I., 146
Morton, K., 146
Morton, P. S., 427, 506, 908
Morton, T., 45, 774, 908–9
Mosala, I. J., 431
Moseley, J. R., 1155
Moser, E. W., 970
Moss, V. E., 909
Mossman, M. H., 632
Motessi, A., 498
Mpayo, Y., 267
Muela, K., 69
Mueller, I., 266
Mueller, J. J., 898
Mugabe, H., 180
Mühlen, H., 492–93, 509, 549, 840, 910
Muhoz, G., 537
Mukombi, K., 69
Muldoon, R., 189
Muller, D., 511
Müller, G., 351, 612, 623, 630, 888, 896, 1066, 1144
Muller, R., 190
Mullin, R. B., 388
Mulungo, L., 180, 910–11
Mumford, B. C., 367, 484, 769, 816, 911, 933, 981, 999, 1060–62, 1070
Munch, M., 509
Mung, D. S., 183
Munida, A., 203
Muñoz, A., 678, 840
Muñoz, R., 82
Munro, M., 151
Müntzer, T., 767–68
Murai, J., 149
Murashkov, I., 217
Murcutt, F., 885
Murphy, L. G., 385
Murray, A., 228, 234, 612, 631, 911
Murray, B. D., 542
Murray, G. A., 911
Murrell, S. J., 26, 206
Muse, D. T., 823, 954
Musgrove, S. M. C., 632
Mushunganya, M., 71
Musisi, G., 510
Mussolini, B., 527
Mwalili, S., 153
Mwambipile, R., 267
Mwatha, S., 154
Myers, J., 550, 1119
Myers, N., 528
Myers, P., 1015
Myerscough, T., 807, 920, 970, 971, 1036, 1225

Myland, D. W., 375, 376, 389, 642, 728, 786, 896, 920–21, 990, 1019, 1020

N

Naea, F., 1223
Nahimana, E., 47
Naickomparambil, M., 125, 512, 922
Nardi, L., 140
Narsai, 742–43
Naude, B., 233
Nava, A. C., 321, 387, 927
Navarrette, F., 412
Navarro, A., 499–500
Navarro, J., 321, 717
Ndagora, R., 71
Ndjongue, G., 108
Ndondo, K., 71
Ndovi, S., 510
Nee, W., 561
Neighbour, R., 502
Nelson, D. J., 386, 402
Nelson, O., 717
Nelson, P. C., 377, 927–28, 1123, 1171
Nelson, W., 306
Neville, R. C., 1127
Nevius, J. L., 896, 1068
Newbigin, L., 550
Newington, D., 180
Newsome, I. S., 431
Newton, J. R., 632
Ngagassi, H., 266
Ngon, L. S., 171
Ngouabi, M., 75
N'gouwa, J. B., 108
Ngume, R., 154
Nichol, J. T., 383, 400, 404, 408, 930–31, 1079
Nichol, R., 873
Nicholle, A., 213
Nichols, N. D., 725, 885, 892
Nicholson, W. R., 656
Nickel, T. R., 477, 653, 931, 981
Nicolas, J. H., 549
Nicolle, A., 216
Nicolle, P., 1045
Nida, E., 159, 160
Nienkirchen, C. W., 387
Nieves, R., 78
Nikitin, I., 95
Nikoloff, M., 91
Nikoloff, N., 91–92, 892, 893, 931–32, 1043
Nilsén, K., 34
Nilsen, O., 411
Nilsén, R., 34
Nilson, J., 267
Nishimoto, R., 270, 415
Nitsch, V., 214

Noad, M. G., 70
Noble, J., 492, 773, 774
Nodor, D., 508
Noll, M. A., 387, 408
Nordmoen, B., 198
Norton, A., 121, 935, 1018
Norton, R., 1191
Norton, R. C., 32
Norton, W., 121
Novak, J., 90
Novatian, 736
Nsanzurwimo, J., 220
Ntigahera, F., 47
Ntsikana, 228
Numbers, R. L., 388
Nunn, D., 567, 820, 1179
Nunn, H., 969
Nuutinen, P., 104
Nyerere, J., 268
Nyström, S., 247, 256
Nzishura, S., 47

O

Obaldo, S., 201
Oberlin, J. F., 612
Obonyo, J., 154
Obote, M., 273
Obu, O. O., 443
Ockenga, H. J., 616, 618, 658, 923
O'Connor, E. D., 549, 936
Odeleke, B., 19
Oden, T., 559
Odongo, R., 152
Odulami, S., 14
Offiler, W. H., 127
Ojo, J. O., 416
Okafor, V., 114
Okello, T., 275
Okonkwo, M., 510
Olai, G., 410
Olazábal, F., 176, 210, 342, 387, 557, 682, 719, 720–21, 777, 829, 830, 936, 1051
Ollé, J., 72, 75, 76, 108
Olsberg, N., 572
Olsen, G., 201
Olsen, W., 153
Olson, E. W., 1031
Olson, I., 280
Olson, S., 500, 513
Oman, A., 68
Omara, J., 274
Omese, J., 275
Ong, R., 225
Ongman, J., 314, 409, 411, 489, 944–45, 949
Ongman, P., 409, 418, 944, 945, 949
Ontermaa, V., 412

Ooshuisen, G. C., 230
Oosthuizen, G. C., 416
Ooten, L. R., 939
Opperman, D. C. O., 333, 335, 375, 537, 938, 946–47, 977, 1045, 1161, 1163
Origen, 735–36, 1063
Orlebar, M., 121
Ormiston, K., 857
Orozco, J., 341
Orozco, R. O., 176, 341, 381, 450, 537, 829, 949, 1030
Orr, J. E., 88
Ortega, R., 175
Ortiz, F., Jr., 639, 845, 949–50
Ortiz, F., Sr., 777, 949–50
Ortiz, J. C., 484–85, 498, 500, 950
Ortiz, L., 78, 79
Ortiz, V., 1029
Orwig, O. W., 395, 585
Osagiede, E., 20
Osborn, L. D., 632
Osborn, T. L., 15, 24, 71–72, 78, 111, 131, 152, 155, 185, 201, 275, 308, 477, 554, 622, 668, 820, 842, 950–51, 1174
Oschoffa, S. B., 12–13, 951
Oshoffa, S. B. J., 467
Ossa, M., 414
Osteen, J. H., 363, 484, 795, 951, 981
Osterberg, A., 346, 347
Osterberg, L., 347
Ostins-Kipushya, A., 73
Østreng, A., 193
Otabil, M., 427
Otang, M., 151
Otis, G., 604
Otis, S. G., 528, 975
Otsuki, T., 150
Otteno, E., 152
Ottolini, P., 134, 526, 527, 951
Oumarbarry, A., 114
Overgard, T. A., 793
Owen, H., 490
Owen, M., 557
Owens, C., 537
Owino, A., 152
Ozman, A. N., 346, 524, 553, 952, 956, 1148, 1160, 1203

P

Pace, A., 916
Padgett, C. M., 30
Pae, B. K., 243, 244
Pagard, K., 483, 816
Page, A. T., 99
Page, E. M., 536
Page, L., 99, 957
Paglia, C., 526
Pähl, E., 494

Paino, P., 507
Pakarinen, K., 343
Pakenham-Walsh, H., 1068
Palamas, G., 751–52, 1063–64
Palau, L., 101, 882
Palma, A. D., 790
Palma, M., 797
Palmer, P., 55, 612, 614, 727, 785, 1203
Palmer, W., 55
Palmertz, G., 47
Pannenberg, W., 1138
Panozza, A., 139
Panzo, F., 22
Parchia, E., 894
Parham, C. F., 121, 227, 228, 326–27, 327–28, 330, 333, 334, 345, 346, 347, 374, 386, 389, 391, 393, 394, 396, 400, 439, 444, 524, 537, 545, 553, 585, 597, 615, 621, 631–32, 632, 638, 654, 660, 669, 679, 729, 784, 785–786, 790, 802, 846, 887, 929, 946, 952, 953, 955–56, 972, 975, 977, 979, 995, 1037, 1045, 1055, 1067, 1129, 1141, 1143, 1147–49, 1160–61, 1203, 1212
Parham, R., 326
Parham, S., 326, 390
Paris, A. E., 386
Paris, T., 916, 918
Park, G., 244
Park, S.-S., 243, 244
Parker, C. L., 340
Parker, J., 246
Parker, T., 614
Parkinson, J. M., 146
Parks, J., 916
Parks, J. H., 543
Parks, N., 543
Parmentier, M., 186
Parr, J. N., 91, 340, 957
Parry, I., 70
Parsley, R., 919, 1119
Parsons, T. M., 243
Pastor, B., 512
Pate, L. D., 878
Paterson, J., 941
Pates, D. W., 181
Paton, A., 238
Paton, N., 238
Patrick, L. C., 536
Patterson, G. E., 957–58
Patterson, J., 275, 645
Patterson, J. O., 426, 537, 816
Patterson, W. W., 129
Patti, S., 918
Paul, G. S., 969
Paul, J. A. A., 88, 96, 97, 109, 110, 258, 371, 489, 776, 789, 798, 821, 910, 958
Paul, J. A. B., 612

Paul, R., 224, 248, 249
Paulk, E. P., 488, 868, 923, 958–59
Paul VI, Pope, 139, 465, 568
Pavéz, V., Jr., 56
Pavic, P., 704
Pawson, D., 490, 516, 797, 959
Payne, J., 424
Payne, L., 487, 959
Pearlman, M., 335, 585, 788, 959
Pearson, C. D., 959–60
Pearson, M., 476, 504
Peart, R., 491, 1160
Pederson, W. D., 848, 960
Peltz, J., 871, 872
Pemberton, R., 52
Pendleton, W. H., 347, 366, 960, 1057
Pennington, E. M., 622
Penn-Lewis, J., 798, 1188
Perales, J., 678, 840
Peraza, J. G., 901
Pereyra, F., 410
Pérez, J. C., 176
Perini, P., 502
Perkin, N., 214, 335, 336, 337, 724, 725, 892, 895, 897, 898, 968, 982
Perón, J., 24
Perpetua, V., 735
Perrault, J., 82
Perrault, L., 77, 82, 116
Perri, G., 138
Perrins, G., 550, 773
Perron, J., 347
Perruc, R., 247
Perry, S. C., 77, 78, 893, 982
Perry, T. D., 983, 1166
Personeus, C. C., 885
Pesare, O., 139
Petersen, D., 166, 878, 881, 898, 1077, 1138
Peterson, D., 388
Peterson, J. W., 916
Peterson, P. B., 214, 893, 985–86, 1031
Pethrus, L., 39, 88, 104, 222, 255, 257, 280, 340, 365, 407, 409, 410, 419, 496, 547, 572, 622, 831, 839, 944, 972, 973, 986–87
Petree, J., 498
Petrelli, G., 136
Petrelli, J., 526
Pettenger, E., 970
Pettersen, L., 34, 1040
Pettersen, R., 34
Petts, D., 341, 987
Pettyjohn, A. W., 202
Pétursson, P., 412
Pfaler, V., 104
Pfotenhauer, D., 481, 847
Phair, R., 728, 987–88

Philippe, P., 840
Phillips, E. J., 340, 599, 920, 971
Phillips, E. L., 988
Phillips, W. T., 329, 424
Photius, 750
Piccolo, G., 137
Pickett, L. L., 728
Piepkorn, A. C., 383
Pierce, T. B., 570
Pierson, A. T., 408
Pike, E., 511
Pike, J. M., 457, 975, 988
Pillay, G., 227, 232
Pina, J. A., 180
Pinder, S. B., 30
Pinheiro, J., 208
Pinnock, C., 517, 559, 883, 1125
Pinson, M. M., 333, 334, 457, 537, 639,
    844, 989, 1144, 1162
Piper, W. H., 348, 444, 546, 789, 891,
    976, 989–90, 1223
Pipkin, P., 201
Píriz, A., 277
Pitt, O., 199, 200
Pittman, R., 59
Pius, IX, Pope, 37
Plummer, W., 528
Plüss, J.-D., 98, 258, 796, 1123
Plymire, V. G., 892, 991
Poewe, K., 232, 408
Poggenpoel, F. P., 416
Polanen, G., 254
Polhill, A. T., 886, 970–71, 1051, 1067
Polhill, C. H., 60, 97, 489, 728, 886, 888,
    991–92, 1067
Polman, G. R., 32, 97, 184, 258, 437,
    546, 789, 798, 888, 972, 992
Polmann, R. G., 106
Poloma, M., 384, 385, 388
Pomerville, P. A., 878, 897
Poole, F. C., 832
Poole, J., 832
Pope, W. H., 945
Popof, P., 1119
Popov, H., 92
Porada, F., 202
Porrello, L., 138
Porter, F., 1144
Porter, W., 155
Poseins, R., 267
Pospisil, W., 124
Post, A. H., 6, 98, 346, 348, 888, 994
Potma, C. T., 32
Potter, J., 169, 970
Pöysti, M., 104
Poysti, N., 224
Pöysti, N., 104
Poysti, N. J., 1031

Prado, C., 22
Prange, E., 847, 994
Prentiss, H., 693
Preston, D. D., 547
Pretiz, P., 159, 930
Pretorius, P., 181
Priam, G., 52
Price, C. S., 331, 449, 622, 644, 962, 978,
    997–98, 1058
Price, F. K. C., 795, 934, 980, 992, 998
Price, P., 1188
Pride, F., 490–91
Pridgeon, C. H., 623, 893, 998–99
Pridgeon, L. S., 623
Prince, D., 367, 478, 484, 520, 769, 911,
    933, 980, 981, 1060–62, 1070
Prince, P. D. V., 999
Pringle, P., 527–28
Pritchard, L., 149
Prosch, K., 503
Pseudo-Dionysius, 744–45
Pseudo-Macarius, 743–44
Pugh, P., 277
Puhakainen, A., 104
Pulikottil, P., 796
Pulkingham, W. G., 473, 483, 1013
Pumayallim, S. A. H., 200
Purdie, J. E., 48, 728, 962, 1013
Purvis, E., 769, 911
Pylkkänen, V., 104
Pytches, D., 489, 491, 498, 504, 1013

Q

Quebedeaux, R., 384, 485, 1014
Quimby, P. P., 992
Quinn, C. T., 642
Quiñones, S. F., 81, 209
Quiroga, G., 65

R

Ra, W. M., 241–43, 245–46
Raassina, H., 269
Raatikainen, A., 412
Rabe, R., 110
Rabinowitz, J., 872
Rabuka, S., 102
Rachamim, O., 874
Rader, P., 439, 588, 1015
Radford, L., 8, 121
Radstock, G., 89
Raem, H.-A., 579
Rahm, H., 498
Rahman, M., 410
Rahneff, P. S., 213
Rahner, K., 549, 1127
Raiford, W. A., 842
Ramabai, S. M., 55, 120, 123, 176, 305,
    410, 660, 771, 935, 1016–18

Ramankutty, P., 123
Ramirez, D., 401
Ranaghan, D., 1018, 1061
Ranaghan, K. M., 383, 463, 473, 484,
    816, 843, 935, 1018
Randall, B., 363
Randall, H. E., 6–7
Rappard, C. H., 612
Raroha, D., 90–91
Rasmus, H. I., 997
Rasmussen, A. W., 778
Ratramnus, 753
Rauch, G., 482
Rawlings, J., 19
Rawlyk, G. A., 387
Raymer, D., 86
Read, W., 160
Reagan, R., 604, 616, 658, 1209
Rebner, G., 494
Reed, D. A., 387, 1126, 1127
Rees, G., 275
Rees, S. C., 874–75
Reeves, E. D., 969
Régimbal, J.-P., 493
Reichel, A., 28
Reid, P., 508
Reiff, A. C., 885, 891
Reilly, E., 888
Reimers, A., 488
Reineker, R., 251
Reitz, H., 793
Renshaw, A., 154
Rethmeier, C., 503
Reuss, A. D., 258
Reyes, R., 77
Reynolds, F. M., 1117
Reynolds, Z., 885
Rhee, C.-J., 245
Rhenius, C. T. E., 118
Rhodes, L. S., 637
Riak, L., 183
Ribeiro, B., 208
Ricciardiello, R., 136
Rich, L., 872
Richard of St. Victor, 754
Richards, E., 185
Richards, N., 45, 503
Richardson, A., 70
Richardson, J. C., 385
Richey, E. N., 354
Richey, J. R., 945, 1021
Richey, L. H., 1021
Richey, R. T., 653, 978, 1021–22
Richter, C., 494
Ridings, R., 503
Ridley, J., 28
Rietdijk, J., 32
Riggs, L. M., 909, 970

Riggs, M., 431
Riggs, R. M., 335, 337, 352, 389, 585, 602, 970, 1022–23
Riley, B., 22
Riley, D., 22
Riley, W. B., 615
Ringeltaube, W. T., 118
Rios, A. M., 570
Riss, R. M., 387
Rivas, F., 455
Rivas, J., 176
Rivera, J. F. R., 210, 720
Rivero, J. C., 82
Rivers, M. M., 536
Robeck, C. M., Jr., 383, 386–87, 388, 446, 575, 579, 606, 607, 882, 1023–24, 1125, 1131, 1216
Roberson, L. W., 536, 1024
Robert, D., 114
Roberts, B., 160
Roberts, E., 193, 294, 322, 345, 798, 1187–88
Roberts, F., 231, 234, 399
Roberts, H., 417, 1026
Roberts, H. V., 417, 1025–26
Roberts, J. D., 429, 430
Roberts, L. V., 560, 937, 1162
Roberts, O., 15, 111, 131, 188, 201, 224, 330, 336, 379, 386, 389, 390, 441, 477, 554, 563, 571, 592, 602, 616, 619, 620, 622, 653, 695, 708, 710–11, 801, 906, 919, 934, 935, 960, 968, 978, 981, 1015, 1020, 1024–25, 1046, 1058, 1118, 1135, 1159, 1193
Roberts, R., 275, 1026–27, 1048
Roberts, T., 105, 106, 493, 497, 516, 1027
Roberts, W. J., 1016
Roberts, W. M., 536
Robertson, C., 446
Robertson, P., 101, 353, 363, 380, 390, 441, 484, 488, 604, 616, 619, 620, 919, 1027–28, 1049, 1061, 1119
Robins, R. G., 387
Robinson, A. E., 969, 1028
Robinson, B., 875
Robinson, I., 387, 425, 909, 1028, 1143, 1206
Robinson, J., 69
Robinson, R., 487
Robison, J., 363, 487, 714, 935, 1028–29, 1119
Rockefeller, J. D., 657
Rodeheaver, H., 916
Rodgers, H. G., 457, 537, 560, 989, 1162
Rodriguez, B., 322
Rodríguez, E., 77
Rodríguez, F., 77
Roebert, E., 234, 511

Roebuck, D. G., 387
Rogers, H. G., 938
Rohloff, I., 568
Roininen, A., 85
Roininen, K., 85
Roisko, E., 411
Rojas, I., 176
Rolim, F. C., 412
Romeo, A., 137
Romeo, M., 137
Ronchi, G., 138
Root, G., 915
Ros, H., 274
Rosa, F. F., 777
Rosado, L. R., 570, 1029, 1051
Rosario, A., 82
Rose, J., 170
Rose, S. D., 408, 414
Rosen, M., 872
Rosenving, H. P., 81
Ross, B., 973
Rossin, D., 481, 506, 847, 848, 1029
Rotaru, F., 90, 212
Roth, K., 151
Roth, S., 872, 1156
Rothgeb, R., 223
Rothgeb, W., 223
Rouhomäki, J., 415
Row, R., 172
Rowe, J., 691, 916
Rowe, W. A. C., 547
Rowlands, J. A., 231
Rowlands, J. F., 231, 232, 622, 1029–30
Rowling, W., 189
Rubens, D., 116
Rubin, T., 232
Rubio, B., 176
Rubio, J., 722
Rudner, L., 814
Ruesga, D., 176, 341–42, 537, 1030, 1037
Ruether, R. R., 592
Ruff, P. R., 258
Ruibal, J. C., 499, 513
Ruis, D., 503
Rumsey, M., 239, 243, 1031
Ruotsalainen, P., 343
Rush, C., 421
Rush, T., 384
Russell, N. R., 146
Ruthven, J., 790
Rutten, B., 86
Rutten, L., 267
Rutten, V., 86, 87
Ruuth, A., 412
Rwechungura, F., 267
Ryakhovsky, S., 95
Ryan, M. L., 59, 60, 888

Ryder, F. L., 23, 31, 53
Rylko, S., 792

S

Sadaca, D., 873
Safu, M., 147
Sagatwa, L., 220
Saginario, C., 526
Sagne, J.-C., 494
Sahib, P., 104
Salamba, S., 152
Salinas, M. U., 56
Salmenkivi, A., 415
Salmon, J., 906, 1036
Salmon, T., 234
Salter, J., 67, 451, 725, 888, 920, 967, 1036, 1225
Samarin, W. J., 389, 1134
Sambou, N., 113
Sampedro, F., 414
Samuel, A. C., 123
Samuel, H., 873
Samuel, K. J., 512
Samuel, P. M., 779
Samuel, S., 1036
Samuel, V. V., 170
San, L. N., 183
Sánchez, J., 82, 199
Sanders, A., 77, 176, 341, 1037
Sanders, C. J., 385, 431
Sandford, F. W., 328, 387, 394, 400, 538, 632, 785, 955, 1037–38, 1067
Sandgren, F. A., 594
Sandidge, J., 98, 577, 578, 579, 1038
Sandru, T., 212–13, 325, 1038–39
Sandwith, W. H., 97
Sanford, A. M., 28, 295, 478, 487, 959, 1039
Sankey, I. D., 915
Sanneh, L., 779
Santagada, O. D., 412
Santana, B. C., 210
Saraswati, P. R., 119
Sardaczuk, W., 94
Sargent, W. L., 347
Sarnoff, R. W., 1015
Satirio, J., 513
Savedra, P., 280
Savelle, J., 155, 795, 1039, 1118
Saxby, A. E., 838
Saxby, W., 347
Scadden, C. C. H., 1039
Scallon, K., 855
Scanlan, M., 371, 484, 862, 935, 1041
Schaaf, R., 152
Schaepe, J. G., 1042
Schambach, R. W., 1015
Schatzmann, S., 258

Scheel, I., 151
Scheppe, J. G., 937, 1126
Schlabach, T. F., 388
Schlafly, P., 1209
Schlink, B., 489, 1042
Schmid, E., 246
Schmidt, C., 91
Schmidt, G. H., 214, 893, 1031, 1042–43
Schmidt, W., 411
Schmucker, S. S., 614
Schneider, H., 492, 512
Schniewindhaus, J., 494
Schober, H., 110
Schoenborn, E. B., 970
Scholfield, B., 28
Schoonenberg, P., 494
Schoonmaker, C. H., 121, 888, 896, 1043
Schrenk, E., 612
Schuler, G., 916
Schuler, R., 15
Schuyler, S., 1203
Schwartz, F., 929
Scism, E. L., 123, 124
Scism, H. E., 100, 124
Scism, S., 124
Scoble, A. R., 970
Scofield, C. I., 162, 656, 1044
Scopes, J. T., 615, 655, 657
Scott, A. J., 1189, 1190
Scott, C. W. H., 352
Scott, D., 70, 105, 106, 258, 493, 569, 599, 1045
Scott, F. K., 278
Scott, J. L., 535
Scott, O., 612
Scott, R. B. Y., 1006
Scott, R. J., 347
Sears, T. A., 146
Seehuus, C. M., 193
Seevaratnam, J., 171
Seín, T. V., 901
Selassie, H., 85
Selchow, E. G., 631
Semple, A., 59, 1050
Semple, R. J., 59, 819, 856, 1050–51
Senduk, L., 533, 664
Sengulane, D., 511
Sepulveda, J., 1216
Sepúlveda, J., 57, 414, 1051, 1078
Sequiera, M., 208
Serafini, P., 140
Seraphim of Sarov, 1051–52
Severin, A., 34
Severin, R., 34
Severus, S., 735
Sexton, E. A., 989
Seymour, W. J., 121, 327, 328, 344, 345–47, 348–49, 366, 386, 391, 395, 396,

402, 422, 423, 437–38, 457, 535, 546, 553, 559, 615, 632, 638, 641, 729, 789, 866, 887, 906–7, 956, 976, 977, 1053–57, 1074, 1086, 1098, 1131, 1143, 1161, 1197, 1204
Shadare, J. B., 14
Shakarian, D., 441, 477, 554, 653, 931, 935, 1058, 1061
Sharp, J. D., 1050
Shaw, S. B., 345
Shea, G. B., 918
Sheard, J. D., 536
Shearer, H., 1162
Sheppard, G. T., 585
Sherrill, E., 1062
Sherrill, J. L., 139, 383, 441, 460, 490, 769, 1062
Sheskin, S., 872, 1156
Shibley, D., 879
Shields, A. E., 862, 1041, 1062
Shija, E., 410
Shishkoff, E., 873, 874
Shlemon-Ryan, B. L., 481, 484, 487, 498, 1062–63
Shorten, R., 230
Showall, W., 382
Shumway, C. W., 391
Sibomana, J., 220
Siburian, R., 130
Sickler, B., 152, 268, 275
Siebers, H., 414
Siemens, C., 52
Siemens, R., 151
Sievers, E., 511
Silcox, A., 543
Silva, J. G., 211, 721
Silvestre, G. L., 82
Silvoso, E., 161, 503, 806
Simat, E., 123
Simmon, D. M., 387
Simmons, E. E., 146
Simmons, E. L., 923
Simonfalvi, L., 510
Simons, M., 768–69
Simpson, A. B., 55, 96, 376, 387, 400, 523–24, 587, 612, 621, 631, 632, 710, 728, 770, 789, 821, 855, 886, 895–96, 904, 905, 906, 936, 944, 970, 998, 1020, 1036, 1067, 1069–70, 1143, 1182
Simpson, C. V., 363, 367, 488, 550, 769, 911, 933, 935, 981, 999, 1060–62, 1070
Simpson, F., 124, 885
Simpson, G. E., 385
Simpson, W. W., 60, 623, 887, 888, 1070–71
Sinaga, D., 130

Sinclair, J. C., 554, 965, 1071
Singer, H. B., 385
Singer, M., 385
Singh, S. S., 248
Sisson, E., 98, 1071–72
Sizelove, R. A., 1072, 1204
Ski, M., 411
Skinner, G., 274
Skinner, J., 151
Sladden, D., 492
Slaughter, A., 918
Slay, J. A., 244
Sloan, A., 632
Slosser, B., 441, 844
Sly, L. B., 278
Smail, T. A., 491, 492, 497, 548, 646, 837, 1074
Smale, J., 345, 347, 366, 641, 906, 1074–75, 1193
Small, F., 48, 325, 937, 938, 961–62, 1075, 1112, 1162
Smet, W., 32
Smidt, C. E., 384
Smidt, G., 103, 104
Smith, A., 820, 865
Smith, A. B., 422
Smith, B., 474
Smith, C., 453, 1075–76, 1177
Smith, C. B., 1075
Smith, C. L., 858
Smith, E. D., 425
Smith, F. W., 923, 1076
Smith, G., 82, 116
Smith, H. G., 210
Smith, H. W., 612, 820
Smith, J., 292
Smith, J. H., 1015
Smith, L., 34, 422
Smith, M., 773, 1204
Smith, M. W., 918
Smith, O. J., 439
Smith, R., 143, 228
Smith, R. P., 96, 257, 612, 820, 821
Smith, T., 529
Smith, V., 34
Smolchuck, F., 386
Smyth, J., 797
Snipes, H. C., 422
Snyder, H., 559
Sobrepeña, D., 204
Söderlund, Å., 275
Söderlund, G. E., 410
Soininen, V., 103
Solís, P., 277
Solivan, S., 1077–78
Solle, D., 1136
Somerville, R. S., 539
Somoza, D., 498

Sorbo, E., 122
Sorenson, P., 24
Sorrow, W., 557–58
Sosa, E., 280
Southard, R. E., 923
Sozi, P., 511
Speaks, J., 431
Specter, H., 116
Spencer, I. C., 572, 816, 831, 1091
Spencer, I. Q., 352, 377, 598, 831, 1091
Spencer, J. M., 386
Spener, P. J., 611
Spengler, E., 152
Spittler, R. P., 383, 384, 388, 389, 547, 561, 667, 1102–4, 1123
Spooner, K., 892
Springer, K., 701
Sproull, O. E., 969
Spurling, R. G., Jr., 530, 545, 1144
Squire, F. H., 599, 957, 1104, 1149
Stacey, T. H., 1037
Stafford, G., 182
Stafford, I. S., 536
Stahl, F. J., 229
Stählberg, T., 208, 247
Stairs, W. T., 1163
Stamps, B., 1159
Stamps, V., 916
Stankovic, M., 686
Stanphill, I., 1104
Stanton, N., 44, 774
Stapleton, R. C., 484
Stark, E. F., 21, 1105
Stark, P. M., 21–22
Steelberg, W. R., 337, 641, 839, 1105
Stehn, G., 92, 212
Steidel, F., 1105–6
Steinberg, E. C., 893
Steiner, L., 92, 105, 258, 407, 972, 973, 1106
Stenbäck, C. G., 496
Stenersby, O., 153
Stephanou, E. A., 487, 1106–7
Stephany, M., 888, 909
Stephens, S., 797
Stern, D., 816
Sternall, R. E., 524
Stevens, J. R., 647
Stevenson, R. M., 915
Stewart, D., 203, 312, 622
Stewart, G., 69
Stewart, J. H., 459
Stewart, L. O., 1107
Stewart, M., 615
Stewart-Gambino, H., 167
Stibbe, M., 43
Stier, J., 1223
Stiles, J. E., 1195

Stockhowe, G. W., Jr., 306
Stockmayer, O., 121, 820, 821
Stockmeyer, O., 612
Stoddart, T., 123
Stokes, L. B., 24, 77
Stokes, M., 1159
Stoll, D., 157, 160, 165, 414
Stone, C., 138
Stone, J., 385, 479, 490, 981
Stone, M. S., 970
Stoop, V., 1157
Strang, S. E., 488, 981, 1107–8
Stranges, F. E., 795
Straton, J. R., 1015, 1108
Straton, W. B., 1108
Street, A. E., 1067
Strobhar, W. N., 427
Strong, A., 274, 928
Stronstad, R., 790, 791, 1130
Struble, G., 153
Stubbs, J., 254
Studd, C. T., 886, 1067, 1108
Studd, G. B., 728, 1108, 1162, 1166
Suede, E., 201
Suenens, L.-J., 32, 460, 464–65, 485, 494, 549, 792, 810, 853, 861, 1108–9
Suh, Y., 242
Sullivan, F. A., 139, 384, 496, 549, 1109
Sumner, J. D., 916
Sumrall, K., 363, 487, 507, 933, 935, 1070
Sumrall, L. F., 1109–10
Sundaram, M. K. S., 322
Sundkler, B., 227, 230–31, 416
Sundram, G., 322
Sundstedt, A., 410, 412
Sung, J., 129, 131, 225, 269, 415
Suurmond, J.-J., 548
Svanstedt, E., 314
Swaggart, J. L., 353, 374, 380, 456, 499, 569, 619, 620, 820, 1049, 1111, 1119
Swallen, W. L., 240
Swanson, A., 261
Swanson, C. W., 91, 213–14, 1043
Swedberg, P., 848
Sweet, H. C., 48, 1111–12
Swing, J. R., 1197
Symeon the New Theologian, 750–51, 1063, 1112
Synan, H. V., 91, 140, 384, 385, 386, 387, 389, 398, 399, 446, 489, 796, 801, 870, 935, 1049, 1079, 1112–13, 1124
Synan, J. A., 801, 816, 1113

T

Taatikainen, A., 152
Tadeu, J., 509
Taitinger, R. W., 1114

Tañon, R., 1051, 1114
Tanusaputra, A. A., 664, 1114
Tapani, K., 411
Taponen, H., 412
Tardif, E., 498, 1114–15
Tarerner, S., 202
Tarr, D., 1047, 1049
Tate, A. E., 266
Tate, M. L. E., 425, 1206
Tate, M. M., 1115
Tavani, N., 1079
Tay, M., 512
Taylor, C., 28, 386, 527, 528, 895
Taylor, G. F., 387, 389, 457, 558, 566, 727, 786, 800, 1020, 1115–16
Taylor, J. H., 305, 1070
Taylor, M., 492
Taylor, N., 614, 1143
Taylor, S., 918
Taylor, W., 55, 65, 198, 199, 365, 409, 411, 418, 728, 770, 867, 888, 895, 896, 1116
Teel, G. M., 727
Tejima, I., 149
Telle, A., 109, 193
Telman, H., 90
Telman, K., 90
Ten Boom, Corrie, 330
Tendero, E., 204
Tertullian, 734–35, 1063
Thannie, G., 20
Thamauturgus, Gregory, 1063
Thayer, C., 154
Thayer, F., 154
Thigpen, P., 385, 476
Thistlethwaite, L. T., 1141
Thobois, J., 493
Tholuck, F., 614
Thomas, C. D., 171
Thomas, J. C., 1124
Thomas, K., 779
Thomas, K. T., 779
Thomas, L., 386
Thomas, P. J., 123
Thomas, R., 499
Thomas, W., 136
Thomas, W. R., 136
Thomas, Z. R., 146
Thommen, K., 119
Thompson, A., 245
Thompson, F. C., 1142–43
Thompson, H., 773
Thompson, J. F. D., 680
Thompson, L., 19
Thoms, H., 169
Thomson, D. P., 492
Tichenor, R., 464, 486
Tierney, M., 492

Tile, N., 230
Till, B., 1215
Tillich, P., 862, 1137
Tillman, C., 728
Tilton, R., 1119
Tinney, J. S., 385, 402, 430, 966–67, 1143
Tipei, P. R., 216
Tippett, B., 169
Tipton, J. M., 521
Titus, P. J., 782
Tjwan, O. N., 129
Tjwan, T. H., 130
Toaspern, P., 494
Todd, P. W., 795
Tollefsen, G., 70, 264
Tollefsen, O., 264
Tomczak, L., 487
Tomlinson, A. J., 30, 387, 389, 391, 394, 395, 457, 530, 531, 532, 538, 539, 541–42, 543, 545, 553, 606, 622, 637, 639, 728, 837, 1020, 1037, 1052, 1143–45
Tomlinson, H. A., 390, 1145–46
Tomlinson, M. A., 539–42, 1145, 1147
Tommasello, L., 137
Tommek, H., 492
Toon, P., 624
Toppi, F., 135, 1149
Torrey, A., 246
Torrey, R. A., 28, 96, 109, 400, 408, 421, 612, 615, 656, 719, 821, 1020, 1110
Tosado, J., 901
Tosado, N., 901
Tosetto, M., 526
Toulis, N. R., 141, 144
Touré, M., 114
Touré, S., 113, 114
Towner, W. K., 997–98
Townes, E., 431
Traettino, G., 136, 138, 139, 509
Trasher, L. H., 7, 330, 533, 606, 888, 892, 1153
Trask, B., 182
Trask, R., 182
Trask, T. E., 338, 446, 973, 1154
Traustason, V. L., 117
Triplett, B., 916
Triplett, L. O., 1154
Troeltsch, E., 1121
Trotter, W. C., 966
Trout, E., 490, 773
Trudel, D., 631
Truschel, P., 54
Tsige, H., 87
Tucker, J. W., 69–70, 1154
Tuckwell, S., 384
Tugwell, S., 491, 1154–55
Tumusiime, J., 275

Turnbull, A., 323
Turnbull, R., 116
Turner, D., 272
Turner, H., 407
Turner, H. W., 416
Turner, J. M., 124
Turner, M., 428, 790, 797
Turner, W. C., 385
Turner, W. H., 785, 788, 892
Turney, H. M., 888, 891, 1155
Turney, R. M., 228
Tuthill, H. G., 391, 394
Tuttle, D. S., 903
Tuttle, R., 1159
Tutu, D., 233, 431
Tweedie, J., 508
Tyson, J. L., 385
Tyson, T., 478, 498, 1155, 1159

U

Uchimura, K., 149
Udd, M., 169
Udd, R., 169
Ukaegbu, J., 511
Umwari, S., 152
Underwood, B. E., 554, 555, 1156
Upham, T., 612
Urquhart, C., 491, 1167
Urshan, A. D., 146, 389, 406, 594, 728, 893, 938, 943, 1126, 1167
Urshan, N. A., 1165, 1167–68
Utterbach, C., 1168
Utterbach, S., 1168

V

Vaagenes, M. G. C., 847, 933, 960, 1169
Vaccaro, G., 797
Vailea, L., 272
Valdez, A. C., Jr., 1025, 1026, 1169
Valdez, A. C., Sr., 27, 187, 201, 224, 251, 567, 681, 1039, 1110, 1169
Valdez, D., 78
Valdez, N. B. C., 205
Vale, G., 70
Valenzuela, R. C. D., 1169
Valenzuella, G., 347
Vamvu, A., 213
Van Beek, H., 1216
Van Cleave, N. M., 547, 1170
Van Dam, W. C., 185, 494
Van den Brink, J. E., 185
Van den Dries, P., 185
Vanderbijl, S. A. A., 170
Vanderbout, E., 201
Van der Westhuizen, N., 234
Van der Woude, P., 184
Van Dusen, H. P., 572, 1170
Van Eyk, F. B., 26, 27, 448, 829, 1170–71

Van Galoen, L., 32
Van Gessel, G., 128, 130, 664
Van Hoften, A., 32
Van Hoose, R., 795
Van Kesteren, J., 32, 1158
Van Klaveren, D., 127–28, 130–31
Van Kracht, S., 185
Van Loon, H., 638, 1162
Van Loon, W., 129
Van Niekerk, F., 511
Van Nimwigen, J., 254
Vanzandt, J. C., 406
Vargas, J., 211
Vargas, T., 659
Varghese, T. M., 124
Varick, J., 421
Varonaeff, K., 91
Vasconcelos, A. P., 973
Vásquez, E., 82
Vásquez, F., 280
Vasquez, M. A., 401
Vassallo, M., 140
Vassar, T. R., 123, 1171
Vatanen, T., 412
Vaters, P., 151
Vaurula, R., 412
Veenhof, J., 494
Vega, G., 513
Velarde, M., 206
Venn, H., 896
Venter, B., 232
Verhoef, W., 185, 186, 494, 548, 1174
Vernaud, G., 108
Vernaud, J., 71–72, 75, 308, 1174–75
Vessey, L., 243
Vest, R. L., 924
Vetter, J., 89, 612
Vetter, N., 184
Veum, H., 264
Vidal, P., 280
Videla, J., 278
Viksten, M., 152
Villafañe, E., 790, 1077, 1176
Villanueva, E. C., 205, 504, 512, 988, 1176, 1177
Vingren, A. G., 39, 165, 208, 370, 418, 888, 1177–78
Vinnichek, J., 92
Vinyard, R., 1178
Virgo, T., 45, 508, 550, 774, 1178
Voeks, G., 847
Vogel, D. W., 623
Vogel, R. T., 623
Voget, C. O., 110, 489, 910
Volf, M., 517, 546, 548, 550–51, 668, 881, 1127–28, 1135, 1137, 1179
Voliva, W., 956
Von Bodelschwingh, F., 612

Von Harnack, A., 698
Von Herder, J. G., 229
Von Zinzendorf, N. L., 611
Voronaev, I. E., 217–18, 931, 1179–80
Vouga, O., 1180
Vrancken, P., 32

W

Wacker, G., 383, 387, 388, 389, 400, 403–4, 1019, 1181
Wadam, J., 182
Wagley, C., 39, 40
Wagner, C. P., 415, 488, 503, 618, 806, 930, 1068, 1181, 1199
Wagner, P., 25, 137, 149, 873, 1141
Wahlsten, J., 247
Wainwright, G., 1122
Waite, M., 514
Wakutompwa, B. M., 68
Waldenstrom, P., 612
Waldman, M., 504
Waldvogel, H. R., 279, 387, 1181–82
Walkem, C. W., 661, 858, 1182
Walker, A., 28, 431
Walker, B., 981
Walker, D., 1048
Walker, J. H., Jr., 532, 923, 1182–83
Walker, J. H., Sr., 1183
Walker, L. J., 888
Walker, M., 175
Walker, P. H., 664, 788, 1183
Walker, P. L., 1183
Walker, R. A., 479, 1183–84
Walker, T., 491
Walker, W., 163
Wallace, M., 415, 560
Wallerstein, I., 1087
Wallis, A., 189–90, 489, 490, 550, 646, 773, 909, 1184
Walls, A., 780
Walsh, M., 817
Walsh, V., 507
Walther, G., 352
Walton, J., 1184
Wanigasekera, D. E. D., 248
Wannenmacher, J., 90, 214, 1184–85
Ward, A. G., 472, 962
Ward, C. M., 1016, 1185
Ward, G. L., 385
Ward, H., 870, 1079, 1112
Ward, R. J., 121
Ware, R. K., 1185
Warfield, B., 656, 995, 1063
Warneck, J., 1066
Warner, D. S., 727
Warner, T. M., 1068
Warner, W. E., 386, 387, 389, 1185–86
Warren, J. A., 632

Warrington, K., 797
Washington, B. T., 419
Washington, J., 429
Watson, D. C. K., 490, 1186
Watson, G. D., 886, 1020, 1143
Watt, J., 604
Watt, P., 416
Watts, I., 914
Weaver, C. D., 388
Weaver, H., 1159
Weaver, P., 341
Webb, B., 1225
Webber, R., 504, 558–59
Weber, M., 596
Weech, E. W., 30
Weeks, P., 504
Weems, R. J., 431
Weerasinghe, T., 252
Wegner, A. W., 65
Wegner, E., 65
Wei, I., 63
Wei, P., 63, 261
Weigle, C., 916
Weiner, R. T., 484, 507, 860, 1186–87
Weist, M., 120
Welbourn, F., 238
Welch, J. W., 334, 643, 885, 961, 1162, 1187
Welker, M., 1121
Wendland, E., 169
Wentland, G., 266
Wereldzending, J. M., 32
Werlinder, G., 47
Werlinder, V., 47
Wesley, C., 914
Wesley, J., 292, 300, 506, 611, 614, 784, 785, 914, 1066, 1073, 1129, 1188
Wessels, W. J., 795
West, C., 431
West, R., 874
Westcott, H., 29
Westman, K. B., 409
Weston, E. R., 1192
Wheaton, E. R., 347, 1193
Wheeler, R., 188, 189, 556, 908, 1184, 1193
Whetstone, R., 1159, 1194
Whitaker, R., 481, 996
White, A., 391, 875, 1056
White, C. M., 991
White, D., 152
White, G., 188
White, J., 29
White, K., 387, 1194
White, M. C., 239
White, N., 188
White, R. H., 422
White, S., 559

Whitefield, G., 1073
Whitehead, C., 491, 1194
Whittington, W. H., 1163
Whittley, L., 536
Wickliffe, J., 1019
Wickramaratna, C., 249
Wickramaratna, J. S., 248, 249, 251
Widdecombe, M., 491
Wierwille, V. P., 1194–95
Wiggins, H., 27
Wigglesworth, S., 26, 97, 106, 187, 251, 258, 308, 323, 330, 418, 437, 447, 564, 590, 622, 648, 829, 970, 978, 1025, 1026, 1036, 1039, 1185, 1195, 1225
Wiklund, E., 264
Wilans, J. S., 435
Wilder, R. P., 119
Wildrianne, J. P., 216
Wiles, P., 138
Wiley, O., 346, 347
Wilhelmsen, K., 272
Wilkerson, D., 139, 190, 209, 460, 481, 490, 566, 1116–18, 1175, 1195–96
Wilkerson, R. A., 484, 826, 868, 1047, 1196–97
Wilkes, W., 873
Willans, J. S., 1197
Willebrands, J., 572, 576–77
Willems, E., 39, 159, 160, 412
Willenegger, R., 258
William, D., 427
Williams, A., 114
Williams, D. P., 322, 323, 538, 545
Williams, D. S., 431
Williams, E. S., 218, 335, 336, 547, 585, 688, 923, 954, 1123, 1137, 1195, 1197–98
Williams, J. C., 279
Williams, J. F., 923
Williams, J. R., 384, 418, 481, 493, 497, 550, 790, 796, 853, 997, 1047, 1079, 1130, 1198
Williams, M., 22, 32, 201, 382
Williams, M. D., 386
Williams, N. D., 16, 19
Williams, P. W., 383, 400, 404, 421
Williams, R. D., 719, 892, 897, 1199
Williams, R. F., 426
Williams, S. E., 543
Williams, T. P., 1159
Williamson, R., 487
Wilmore, G., 430, 431, 867
Wilson, A. E., 892, 898
Wilson, B., 160, 412
Wilson, D., 388
Wilson, E. A., 166, 388, 899
Wilson, E. A. G., 899

Wilson, F. A., 1199
Wilson, R., 821
Wimber, J., 29, 417, 453, 488, 493, 502, 507, 508, 619, 626, 701–2, 814, 817, 880, 935, 1013, 1152, 1177, 1181, 1186, 1199–1200
Wimbush, V., 431
Winberg, A., 47
Winberg, T., 47
Winchester, C. W., 351
Winger, A., 280
Winkler, R., 295, 478, 479, 959
Winn, F., 59
Winrod, G. B., 906
Winsett, R. E., 1200
Wise, R., 557, 997
Witherspoon, W. T., 146, 1163, 1202–3
Wittich, P., 893
Wittick, K., 151, 264, 352
Wittick, M., 151, 264
Wolfe, L., 916, 918
Wolff, M. J., 1163
Womack, D. A., 338, 897
Womble, J., 154
Womersley, D., 69
Womersley, H., 69, 777
Wong, J., 512, 796
Wongsak, J. C., 270, 1211
Wonsak, J. A., 415
Wood, A., 23, 48, 77, 279, 888
Wood, B., 48
Wood, E., 963
Woodbury, I., 915
Woodhall, R., 407
Woodhouse, F., 929
Woods, I., 514

Woodson, C. E., 420
Woodward, G., 50
Woodworth, F., 78
Woodworth, M., 78
Woodworth-Etter, M. B., 330, 331, 386, 387, 390, 396, 418, 439, 622, 978, 1072, 1073, 1126, 1211–13
Woon, M. R., 1213
Work, M. E., 351
Worku, Y., 86
Worley, A. S., 188, 556, 908, 1217
Wormser, E. H., 888
Worrell, A. S., 347, 1217
Wortman, M., 23
Wright, B., 487
Wright, H., 113
Wright, J. E., 923, 1220
Wright, N., 491, 551, 797
Wyatt, T., 1221
Wyckoff, J. W., 790
Wycuff, C., 916

X

Xavier, F., 126
Xunea, I., 214

Y

Yake, R., 1117
Yang, J., 262
Yeomans, L. B., 389, 1222
Yépez, H. C., 83
Yerima, G., 54
Yew, L. C., 171
Yli-Vainio, N., 104, 495
Yoakum, F. E., 842, 990–91, 1222–23
Yong, A., 1127

Yoo, B.-W., 409, 1125
Yoo, J., 243
Yoon, S. D., 244
York, L., 87
York, P., 87
Young, J. D., 422, 535
Young, P., 171
Youngrin, P., 50
Yrjölä, T., 104
Yumiyama, K., 147

Z

Zabrodsky, B., 487
Zaccardi, G., 135
Zaffato, F., 805
Zaiss, H., 111, 185
Zamir, I., 874
Zamora, S., 199
Zampino, P., 476, 504
Zaphlishny, D., 91
Zeissler, C., 201
Zelman, J., 90
Zhang B., 261
Zhang L., 261
Zhidkov, J., 219
Zhidkov, M., 92
Ziese, A., 352, 892
Zimmerman, T. F., 337, 485, 554, 591, 618, 658, 663, 923, 973, 1079, 1154, 1214, 1225–26
Zoller, J., 1015
Zopfi, J., 1226
Zuck, R., 701
Zulu, A., 231, 233
Zum Felde, B., 151
Zwingli, U., 764, 1064

Index of Countries and Regions

A

Afghanistan, 3, 10–11
Africa, Central, 3–4
Africa, East, 4–5, 511
Africa, North, 5–11, 415–16
Africa, West, 11–20, 309, 510–11
Albania, 21
Algeria, 7–8, 21
America, Latin, 157–67, 413–15, 497–98, 512–13, 715–23, 797, 829–30, 1040–41
America, North, 48–51, 277, 382–409, 477–89, 505–8, 525–27, 715–23, 926–27, 935
American Samoa, 21
Andorra, 21
Angola, 21–22
Anguilla, 22
Antigua, 23
Arabian Peninsula, the, 9
Argentina, 23–25, 161, 498, 512
Armenia, 26
Aruba, 26
Australia, 26–29, 513, 528, 1110–11
Austria, 29
Azerbaijan, 29

B

Bahamas, 29–31
Bahrain, 9, 31
Bangladesh, 31
Barbados, 31
Belgium, 32–33, 494
Belize, 33, 161
Belorussia, 33
Benin, 33
Bermuda, 33
Bhutan, 34
Bolivia, 34–35, 161
Bosnia-Herzegovina, 35
Botswana, 35
Bougainville, 35
Brazil, 35–42, 161, 497, 513
Britain. *see* Great Britain
British Indian Ocean, 46
British Virgin Islands, 46
Brunei, 46
Bulgaria, 46
Burkina Faso, 46
Burma. *see* Myanmar
Burundi, 47

C

Cambodia, 47
Cameroon, 47
Canada, 48–51, 325–26, 507–8, 542–43, 1149–52
Cape Verde, 51
Caribbean Islands, 51–53
Cayman Islands, 53
Central African Republic, 53–54
Chad, 54
Channel Islands, 54
Chile, 55–58, 161–62, 498
China, 58–64, 512, 780–81
Christmas Island, 65
Cocos Islands, 65
Colombia, 65–66, 162, 497–98
Comoros, 66
Congo, Democratic Republic of, 67–76
Cook Islands, 76–77
Costa Rica, 77, 162
Croatia, 77
Cuba, 77–79, 162
Cyprus, 80
Czech Republic, 80, 495

D

Denmark, 80–81, 222, 495, 509
Djibouti, 81
Dominica, 81
Dominican Republic, 81–83, 162

E

Ecuador, 83–84, 162
Egypt, 6–7, 84
El Salvador, 84, 162
England, 42–46, 96–98
Equatorial Guinea, 84
Eritrea, 84–85
Estonia, 85
Ethiopia, 85–88
Europe, Eastern, 88–96, 494–96, 509–11, 797–98, 862–63, 1031–32
Europe, Western, 96–98, 490–94, 496–97, 508–9, 797–98, 862–63

F

Faeroe Islands, 99
Falkland Islands, 99
Fiji, 99–102
Finland, 103–5, 222, 343, 411–12, 495–96, 509
France, 105–7, 493–94, 509

French Guiana, 107
French Polynesia, 107–8

G

Gabon, 108
Gambia, 108
Georgia, 108
Germany, 88–96, 96–98, 109–11, 492–93, 494–95, 509, 928–29
Ghana, 12, 111, 510
Gibraltar, 111
Great Britain, 42–46, 96–98, 315, 322–23, 340–41, 459–60, 490–92, 508, 549–50, 1080–83
Greece, 112, 1000–1002
Greenland, 112
Grenada, 112
Guadeloupe, 112
Guam, 112
Guatemala, 112, 162–63
Guinea, Republic of, 113–15
Guinea-Bissau, 115
Guyana, 115

H

Haiti, 115–17
Honduras, 117, 163
Hungary, 117, 495, 510

I

Iceland, 117–18, 222
India, 118–26, 512, 778–79, 781–83
Indonesia, 126–31
Iran, 9, 132
Iraq, 9, 132
Ireland, 132, 508
Isle of Man, 132
Israel, 8, 132, 1002–3
Italy, 132–41, 496, 508–9
Ivory Coast, 141

J

Jamaica, 141–47
Japan, 147–50, 780
Jordan, 8, 150

K

Kanaky, 186–87
Kazakhstan, 150
Keeling Islands, 65
Kenya, 4–5, 150–55
Kirghizia, 156
Kiribati, 156
Kuwait, 9, 156

L

Laos, 156
Latin America, 157–67, 413–15, 497–98, 512–13, 715–23, 797, 829–30, 1040–41
Latvia, 168
Lebanon, 8, 168
Lesotho, 168
Liberia, 168
Libya, 7–8, 168
Liechtenstein, 168
Lithuania, 168
Luxembourg, 168

M

Macedonia, 168
Madagascar, 168
Malawi, 3, 169–70
Malaysia, 170–73
Maldives, 173
Mali, 173
Malta, 173
Marshall Islands, 173–75
Martinique, 175
Mauritania, 7–8, 175
Mauritius, 175
Mayotte, 175
Melanesia, 194–96
Mexico, 163, 175–78, 323–24, 341–42, 537–38
Micronesia, 178–79, 194–96
Middle East, the, 5–11
Moldavia, 179
Monaco, 179
Mongolia, 179
Montserrat, 179
Morocco, 7–8, 179
Mozambique, 180–81
Myanmar, 181–83

N

Namibia, 183
Nauru, 184
Nepal, 184
Netherlands, the, 184–86, 494
Netherlands Antilles, 186
New Caledonia, 186–87
New Zealand, 187–92, 513–14, 527–28
Nicaragua, 163, 192
Niger, 192
Nigeria, 12, 192, 443, 467–69, 510–11
Niue Island, 192
Norfolk Island, 192
North America, 48–51, 277, 382–409, 477–89, 505–8, 525–27, 715–23, 926–27, 935
Northern Cyprus, 192

Northern Mariana Islands, 192
North Korea, 192
Norway, 88–96, 193, 222, 411, 509

O

Oman, 9, 194

P

Pacific Islands, 194–96
Pakistan, 10, 196
Palau, 196
Palestine, 196
Panama, 163, 197
Papua New Guinea, 197
Paraguay, 163, 198
Peru, 163, 198–200
Philippines, 201–7, 512, 988
Pitcairn Island, 207
Poland, 207, 495, 510
Polynesia, 194–96
Portugal, 208–9, 496–97, 509
Puerto Rico, 209–11

Q

Qatar, 9, 211

R

Réunion, 211
Romania, 212–17, 324–25
Russia, 88–96, 217–19, 495, 510, 1031–32
Rwanda, 219–20

S

Sahara, 221
Saint Helena, 221
Saint Kitts and Nevis, 221
Saint Lucia, 221
Saint Pierre and Miquelon, 221
Saint Vincent, 221
Samoa, 221–22
San Marino, 222
Sao Tome and Principe, 222
Saudi Arabia, 9, 222
Scandinavia, 222, 409–12, 495–96, 509, 1040–41
Scotland, 42–46
Senegal, 222
Seychelles, 223
Sierra Leone, 223
Singapore, 223–25, 512
Slovakia, 225
Slovenia, 226
Solomon Islands, 226
Somalia, 227
Somaliland, 227
South Africa, 12, 227–38, 511
South Korea, 239–46, 511–12, 780

Spain, 247, 496–97
Spanish North Africa, 247
Sri Lanka, 248–53
Sudan, 7, 253
Suriname, 253–55
Svalbard and Jan Mayen, 255
Swaziland, 255
Sweden, 88–96, 222, 255–57, 409–11, 496, 509
Switzerland, 257–59
Syria, 9–10, 259

T

Taiwan, 259–64
Tajikistan, 264
Tanzania, 4–5, 264–69
Thailand, 269–70, 415
Timor, 271
Togo, 271
Tokelau Islands, 271
Tonga, 271–72
Trinidad and Tobago, 272–73
Tunisia, 7–8, 273
Turkey, 10, 273
Turkmenistan, 273
Turks and Caicos Islands, 273
Tuvalu, 273

U

Uganda, 4–5, 273–76
Ukraine, 277
United Arab Emirates, 9, 277
United Kingdom. *see* Great Britain
United States of America, 277, 312, 314–15, 321–22, 326–29, 344–50, 382–409, 445–46, 453, 505–7, 550, 926–27
Uruguay, 163–64, 277–78
Uzbekistan, 278

V

Vanuatu, 279
Venezuela, 164, 279–81
Vietnam, 281
Virgin Islands of the U.S., 281

W

Wallis and Futuna Islands, 281
Western Samoa, 221–22

Y

Yemen, 9, 281
Yugoslavia, 281

Z

Zambia, 3, 282
Zimbabwe, 3, 282

Index of Groups and Associations

A

Action Apostolique Africaine (AAA), 54
Action Missionnaire, 75
Acts 29 Ministries, 306–8, 655
A Fe Apostólica, 39
Africa Enterprise, 233
African Apostolic Action, 54
African Independent Churches, 230, 296
African indigenous pentecostals/charismatics, 296
African Initiated Churches (AICs), 230, 309
African Methodist Episcopal Church (AME), 421, 447, 451, 996
All Australia Conference, 27
All for Christ Church, 203
Alliance for Evangelism, 128
Alliance of Christian Churches (ACC), 312
All-Union Council of Evangelical Christians—Baptists (AUCECB), 93
American Academy of Religion (AAR), 795
American Association of Bible Colleges (AABC), 378–79
American Baptist Charismatic Renewal, 312–13
American Board of Commissioners for Foreign Missions (ABCFM), 59
American Council of Christian Churches (ACCC), 615–16, 920
American Evangelistic Association (AEA), 313
Anabaptists, 1216
Anglican Church, 5, 14, 16, 28, 50, 120, 190, 225, 231, 273, 295, 437, 450–51, 614, 1011, 1184, 1217
Anglican Renewal Ministries (ARM), 43, 315, 900
Animism, 315–18
Antiochian Evangelical Orthodox Mission (AEOM), 558–59
Apostles Gospel Outreach Fellowship International (AGOFI), 100–101
Apostolado da Oração, 41
Apostolic Assembly of Faith in Jesus Christ (AAFCJ), 321–22, 455, 573, 843, 925
Apostolic Christian Assembly (India) (ACA), 322, 782
Apostolic Church (AC), 27, 43, 80, 146, 279, 322–23, 418
Apostolic Church in Australia, 458
Apostolic Church in Czechoslovakia, 93
Apostolic Church in Italy (CAI), 136
Apostolic Church of Faith in Jesus Christ, 323–24, 1167
Apostolic Church of God of Romania (ACG), 324–25, 436, 1036–37
Apostolic Church of New Zealand, 680–81
Apostolic Church of Pentecost (ACOP), 48
Apostolic Church of Pentecost of Canada, 325
Apostolic Faith, 326–27, 333, 564, 772
Apostolic Faith Mission (AFM), 3, 27, 48, 327, 344, 448, 1051–55, 1168–69, 1191
Apostolic Faith Mission of South Africa (AFMSA), 589–90, 593

Apostolic Overcoming Holy Church of God, 329
Apostolic pentecostals, 294
Apostolic World Christian Fellowship (AWCF), 938
Asamblea Apostólica de la Fe en Cristo Jesus, 721–22
Asamblea Cristiana, 25
Asamblea Cristiana Cultural, 25
Asamblea Cristiana de Argentina, 25
Asambleas de Dios, 25, 162
Asambleas de Dios de Bolivia, 34
Asia Charismatic Theological Association (ACTA), 796
Asian Christian Charismatic Fellowship, 205
Asian Pentecostal Society, 796
Asia Pacific Theological Association (APTA), 796
Asociación Evangelísta Mensaje de Salvacón, 24
Asociación Evangélistica Mensaje de Salvación, 25
Assemblea Cristiana, 134, 333, 594
Assembleas de Dios de México (ADM), 176
Assemblee di Dio in Italia (ADI), 133–35
Assemblées de Dieu de Guinée (AG–Guinea), 113
Assemblées de Dieu du Gabon (AG–Gabon), 108
Assembleia de Deus Pentecostal de Angola, 22
Assembleias de Deus, 39, 40
Assembleias de Deus de Portugal, 208–9
Assemblies of God (AG), 8, 21, 22, 23, 30, 34, 39, 60, 69–70, 77–78, 82, 83, 99, 113, 130–31, 146, 147, 169, 181–82, 198, 199–200, 222, 226, 247, 271–72, 277, 333–40, 544, 596–97, 722, 890, 921, 1182–83
Assemblies of God (AG)–U.S. Missions Department, 22, 776
Assemblies of God in Australia, 27
Assemblies of God in Calcutta, 449
Assemblies of God in France (AG–France), 75, 105–6, 113, 187
Assemblies of God in Great Britain and Ireland (AGGBI), 43, 70, 340–41, 456, 772, 809, 955, 1102
Assemblies of God in Italy (AG–Italy), 133–35
Assemblies of God in Malaysia, 170–71
Assemblies of God in Mexico, 341–42, 450
Assemblies of God in New Zealand, 435–36
Assemblies of God in Puerto Rico, 659
Assemblies of God in the Marshall Islands, 174–75
Assemblies of God of Ceylon, 249–50, 251
Assemblies of God of Myanmar, 182
Assemblies of the Lord Jesus Christ, 342
Assembly Hall Churches, 64
Assembly of Christian Churches (ACC), 342
Associated Pentecostal Churches of New Zealand (APCNZ), 189, 551–52
L'Association des Églises de Pentecôte du Rwanda (ADEPR), 220
Association of Evangelicals of Africa, 795
Association of Faith Churches and Ministries (AFCM), 342, 817
Association of International Mission Services (AIMS), 342–43

Association of Pentecostal and Charismatic Bible Colleges of Australasia (PCBC), 797
Association of Pentecostal Churches of Rwanda (ADEPR), 220
Awakened, 343
Azusa Street Mission, 6, 97, 105, 120, 122, 124, 127, 344–49, 366, 422, 454, 457, 553, 560, 563, 641, 712, 717, 730, 798, 814, 844, 846, 855, 887–88, 888, 904–5, 995, 1106, 1153, 1167, 6660

B

Baptist Church, 24, 54, 120, 142, 363–64, 369, 448, 480, 483, 506, 615
Baptist pentecostals, 293–94, 363–64
Belgian Christian Pentecostal Fellowship Elim, 32
Belgian Gospel Mission, 32
Belgische Christelijke Pinkstergemeenschap Elim, 32
Berlin Mission Society, 229–30
Bethel Church, 114
Bethel Full Gospel Church of Indonesia, 533
Bethelite Mission, 31
Bible Overte, 114
Bible Standard Conference (BSC), 943
Bible Way Churches of Our Lord Jesus Christ, 382
Black American pentecostals/charismatics, 297
Black Holiness pentecostalism (BHP), 419–28
Blessed Trinity Society, 435, 441–42
Bond van Evangelisatie, 128
Bonnie Brae Street Cottage, 437–38, 904, 1191
Bread of Life Fellowship, 205
British Missionary Council, 458
Broederschap van Vlaamse Pinkstergemeenten, 32
Brotherhood of Flemish Pentecostal Churches, 32
Brotherhood of the Cross and Star (BCS), 443
Bukot Non Jesus Church, 175
Bulgarian Evangelical Pentecostal Union, 94–95

C

Calvary Chapel, 453
Calvary Life Assemblies, 28
Calvinists, 765, 1216
Camps Farthest Out, 28
Campus Christian Fellowship, 15
Campus Crusade for Christ, 226
Catholic Apostolic Church (CAC), 459, 656, 803, 926–27
Catholic charismatic renewal (CCR), 32, 40–41, 124–25, 139–40, 186, 190–91, 206–7, 252, 295, 367, 371, 454, 460–67, 473–74, 481–83, 552, 632, 645, 806–7, 810–11, 817, 825, 853, 861, 864–65, 901, 920, 1016, 1039, 1060, 1107, 1112–13, 1192
Catholic Fraternity of Charismatic Covenant Communities and Fellowships (CFCCCF), 476
Celestial Church of Christ (CCC), 12–13, 14, 351, 467–72, 949
Center for the Study of Religion in Latin America (CER-LAM), 662
Center for Urban Ministerial Education (CUME), 1174
Central African Evangelical Cooperation, 54
Ceylon Pentecostal Mission (CPM), 123, 170, 224, 249, 250–51

Charisma in Missions, 472–73, 825
Charismatic Bible Ministries (CBM), 488, 932
Charismatic communities, 473–76
Charismatic Episcopal Church (CEC), 476, 559
Charismatic movement, xix, 44, 204–5, 211, 246, 291, 294–95, 477–519
Charismatic Renewal Services (CRS), 519–20
Charismatic Work Fellowship the Netherlands (CWN), 185–86
Chi Alpha, 521
Chiesa Apostolica Italiana, 136–37
Chiesa Cristiana, 138
Chiesa Cristiana Pentecostale Italiana (CCPI), 135–36
Chiesa di Dio, 137
Chiesa Evangelica della Riconciliazione, 138
Chiesa Evangelica Internazionale, 137–38
Chiese Elim in Italia, 137
Chiese Evangeliche della Valle del Sele, 136
Child Evangelism Fellowship, 226
Children of Brazil Outreach (COBO), 812
China Inland Mission (CIM), 60, 989
Chosen Pentecostal Church, 243–44
Christ Apostolic Church, 14, 19
Christ Apostolic Church, Bethel, 20
Christ for the Nations (CFN), 25, 116, 147, 523, 842
Christian Action Faith Ministry International, 16
Christian and Missionary Alliance (CMA), 23, 59–61, 113, 120, 279, 333, 439, 523–25, 588, 638–39, 642, 821, 893–94, 902–4, 918–19, 980, 989, 996, 1041, 1067–68, 1068–69
Christian Assembly, 333
Christian Association of Nigeria, 19
Christian Broadcasting Network (CBN), 380, 616, 619, 1025–26, 1117
Christian Church (Disciples of Christ) (CCDC), 211
Christian Church of North America (CCNA), 525–27
Christian City Churches International, 28, 29, 527–28
Christian Faith Ministries International, 19
Christian Growth Ministries (CGM), 484, 528, 769–70
Christian Interdenominational Fellowship (CIF), 231
Christian Life Centres, 27, 29
Christian Mission Fellowship (CMF), 101
Christian Outreach Centres, 28, 29, 100, 226, 528
Christian Revival Crusade (CRC), 27, 691
Christians Baptized with the Holy Spirit (CBHS), 213, 215–16
Christian Worker's Union (CWU), 528
Christian Youth International, 1185
Christ's Church Fellowship (CCF), 528–29
Christ to the Philippines, 203
Church Growth International, 522
Church Missionary Society (CMS), 844, 985
Church of Christ, 27
Church of God, Jerusalem Acres, 538–39
Church of God by Faith (CGF), 535
Church of God (Cleveland, TN), 21, 23, 28, 30, 31, 33, 43, 48, 51, 82, 83, 100, 116, 137, 143, 146, 154, 156, 183, 198, 200, 202, 210, 244–45, 268, 272, 278, 343, 521, 530–34, 538,

544, 596–97, 689, 775, 823, 833, 891, 921, 956, 980, 1046, 1103, 1151, 1180–81
Church of God (Cleveland, TN) in Canada, 534–35
Church of God in Christ (COGIC), 115, 421, 422–24, 426–27, 535–37, 555, 560, 563, 565, 645, 813, 859–60, 865–67, 955–56, 1022, 1034, 1044, 1203–4
Church of God in Korea (CGK), 244–45
Church of God in the Republic of Mexico, 537–38
Church of God Mission International, 16
Church of God of Congo (EDC), 75–76
Church of God of Prophecy (CGP), 30, 116, 143, 210, 245, 539–42, 544, 687, 1143
Church of God of Prophecy in Canada (CGPC), 542–43
Church of God of the Mountain Assembly (CGMA), 543
Church of Melanesia (COM), 226
Church of Our Lord Jesus Christ of the Apostolic Faith, 543
Church of Scotland, 120
Church of the Foursquare Gospel in Korea (ICFG), 245
Church of the Foursquare Gospel in the Philippines (CFGP), 202–3
Church of the Living God, Christian Workers for Fellowship (CLGCWFF), 543–44
Church of the Lord Jesus Christ of the Apostolic Faith, 544
Church of the Pentecost Bible Training Center, 18
Church of the Twelve Apostles, 20
Classical pentecostals, xviii–xix, 293, 553–55, 576
Comisión Evangélica Pentecostal Latinoamericana (CEPLA), 797
Commonwealth Bible College, 27
Communauté des Eglises de Pentecôte au Burundi (CEPBU), 47
Communauté Pentecôtiste du Congo, 68–69, 71–72
Communion of Evangelical Episcopal Churches (CEEC), 557, 559
Community of Jesus (CJ), 475
Community of Pentecostal Churches of Burundi, 47
Concilio Latino-Americano de Iglesias Cristianas (CLAIC), 557, 682
Concilio Latino-Americano de la Iglesia de Dios Pentecostal de New York, 557
Confederation of Reformed Churches of French Polynesia, 107–8
Conference of Pentecostal Theologians—India, 796
Congo Evangelistic Mission (CEM), 67–69, 725
Congo Protestant Council, 67
Congregação Cristã, 39
Congregational Holiness Church (CHC), 557–58
Congregazioni Cristiane Pentecostali (CCP), 135
Conseil Protestant du Congo, 67
Consejo Latinoamericano de Iglesias (CLAI), 797
Convergence movement, 504, 558–59
Coopération Evangélique Centrafricaine, 54
Coopération Evangélique dans le Monde, 54
Coptic Orthodox Church, 6
Cornerstone Ministries (c.net), 45
Corporación Evangélica de Vitacura, 24
Couples for Christ (CFC), 207
ʼovenant Ministries International, 45

Creole religion, 141–43
Crossroads Christian Communications (CCC), 859
Cult Awareness Network (CAN), 311
Cursillo movement, 281, 567–68

D

Damascus Christian Churches, Inc., 570
Darlinghurst Baptist Church, 26
Deeper Christian Life Mission, 15, 16, 18, 239, 574
Deima Church, 20
Denominational pentecostals, 293
De Pinkster Gemeente in Nederlandsch Indie, 129
Deus é Amor, 40
Disciples of Christ, 1216–17
Door of Faith Churches of Hawaii, 586
Dualism, 760–62
Durban Christian Centre, 231–32, 234, 236–37
Dutch Full Gospel Assemblies, 32
Dutch Missionary Society, 127
Dutch Reformed Church, 228, 233

E

Eastern European Mission (EEM), 1029–30
Eglise Evangélique de Pentecôte, 108
Eglise Pentecôtiste Alleluia, 113
Eglises Baptistes, 54
Eglises de Dieu du Congo, 75–76
Eglise Shekina, 114
Eglises Unies de Pentecôte du Rwanda, 220
Église Vivante, 220
Eglishe Unie du Saint-Esprit, 47
Elim Church International (ECI), 47, 154
Elim Church of New Zealand (ECNZ), 188, 589
Elim Fellowship (EF), 87, 1089
Elim Foursquare Gospel Alliance (EFGA), 442, 599, 807
Elim Foursquare Gospel Alliance of Uganda (EFGA), 275
Elim Pentecostal Church (EPC), 43, 598–99
Elim Pentecostal Church of Kenya, 154
Elim Pentecostal Church of Rwanda (EPER), 220
Elim Pentecostal Church Tanzania (KEPT), 266
Elim Pentecostal Fellowship Uganda, 275
El Shaddai, 206
Emmanuel's Church in Jesus Christ (ECJC), 937
Empowered Ministries (EM), 507
Encuentro Carismatico Catolico Latin-Americano (ECCLA), 462, 499
Encuentro Pentecostal Latinoamericana (EPLA), 797
Episcopal Church, 482–83, 505–6, 652, 802–3
Episcopal Renewal Ministries (ERM), 307, 370
Ethiopian Hewot Berhan Church (EHBC), 86
Ethiopian Orthodox Church, 87
European Pentecostal and Charismatic Research Association (EPCRA), 796
European Pentecostal-Charismatic Research Association (EPCRA), 98
European Pentecostal Fellowship (EPF), 98
European Pentecostal Theological Association (EPTA), 98, 610, 797

Evangelica Assembleia de Deus de Moçambique, 180
Evangelical Alliance, 42
Evangelical Assemblies of God of Mozambique, 180
Evangelical Churches of Pentecost (ECOP), 49
Evangelical Church of Croatia, 90
Evangelical Church of Germany (EKD), 333
Evangelical Cooperation in the World, 54
Evangelical Fellowship of Fiji (EFF), 101–2
Evangelical Foreign Missions Association (EFMA), 923
Evangelicalism, 613–16, 658
Evangelical Mission of Vista Alegre, 22
Evangelical Orthodox Church (EOC), 558–59
Evangelical Reconciliation Church, 138
Evangelical Theological Society (ETS), 795
Evangelists, 617–22
Evangelization Society, the (TES), 623
Every Home for Christ (EHC), 101, 226, 596

F

Faith Tabernacle Church, 14
Far East Missionary Society, 223
Federal Council of Churches (FCC), 616, 657
Fédération des Eglises de Réveil, 76
Federation of Free Pentecostal Churches, 438
Federation of Revival Churches, 76
Fellowship of Christian Assemblies, 50, 636
Fellowship of Covenant Ministers and Conferences (FCMC), 488
Filadelfia Church, 255–56, 314
Filipino Assemblies of God of the First Born, 202
Finlands Svensk Pingstmission, 34
Finnish Free Foreign Mission (FFFM), 71, 84–86, 104, 224, 265, 269, 277
Finnish Free Pentecostal Mission, 34
Fire-Baptized Holiness Church (FBHC), 423, 443, 640, 652–53, 727, 799, 804, 822–23
First Church of Jesus Christ (FCJC), 641
Flower Pentecostal Heritage Center, 1184
Fondación Visión de Futuro, 24
Fountain Trust (FT), 646, 689
Foursquare Church of Myanmar, 183
Foursquare Gospel Church of Canada (FGCOC), 49, 73, 646
Franklin Springs College, 25
Fraternité Evangélique Pentecôte en Afrique du Congo, 72
Free Churches, 110–11, 1216–17
Free Pentecostal Fellowship in Kenya (FPFK), 153
Free-Will Baptist Church of the Pentecostal Faith (FWBPF), 363
French Reformed Church, 108, 569
Friends First, 233
Full Gospel Assemblies, 184
Full Gospel Believers Church, 86
Full Gospel Bible Fellowship (FGBF), 268
Full Gospel Business Men's Fellowship International (FGBMFI), 16, 28, 32, 74, 102, 126, 172, 178, 225, 231, 247, 367, 441, 472, 477, 554, 597, 653–54, 817, 859, 909, 929, 1022, 1056, 1068, 1157
Full Gospel Church, 3, 28, 148, 155, 169, 269, 1028

Full Gospel Churches of Kenya (FGCK), 152–53
Full Gospel Church of Eritrea, 85
Full Gospel Church of God in Southern Africa (FGCOGISA), 654
Full Gospel Church of South Africa, 532
Full Gospel Evangelistic Association (FGEA), 327, 654
Full Gospel Mission, 138
Fundamentalism, 655–58
Future Christian City Church, 28

G

Gemeinschaftsbewegung (GB), 109
Generals of Intercession (GI), 806
Geraja Bethel Indonesia, 130
Gereja Bethel Indonesia, 533, 664, 1112
Gereja Pentekosta di Indonesia (GPDI), 129–30
Glad Tidings Missionary Society, 668–69
Glad Tidings Tabernacle, 444, 669, 929
Gnostics, 732
Good News Hall (GNH), 26, 27, 828–29
Good News Training Institute, 18
Gospel Crusade, Inc., 575
Gospel Publishing House (GPH), 678–79
Greek Orthodox Church, 213, 1104–5
Ground Level, 45
Gypsies, 683–86

H

Hebrew Christian Alliance of America (HCAA), 871–72
Higher life movement, 553, 820–21
Hispanic pentecostalism, 715–23
Holiness Church of North Carolina (HCNC), 799
Holiness movement, 96, 293, 418, 421–22, 448, 542, 553, 566, 615, 632–33, 726–29, 798–801, 953–54, 958, 1018, 1035–36, 1141–43, 1191, 1220
Holiness Pentecostal Church, 203
Holmes Bible College, 24–25
Holy Alamo Christian Church, Consecrated (HACCC), 310
Holy Ecclesia of Jesus, 150
Holy Spirit Teaching Mission (HSTM), 769–70, 909, 1068
Holy Spirit Renewal Ministries (HSRM), 313
Holy Trinity Brompton (HTB), 43
Hope Chapel, 771–72
Hope of Bangkok Church, 270
House Church Movement (HCM), 44, 64, 556, 773–74, 813, 1176–77, 1182
House of Prayer, 443

I

Ichthus Fellowship, 45, 645, 818
Iglesia Cristiana Pentecostal De Argentina, 646
Iglesia Cristiana Pentecostal de Cuba, 79
Iglesia de Cristo Misionera, 777
Iglesia de Dios, 78, 162–65, 278
Iglesia de Dios de la Profecia (Profesía), 25, 159, 210
Iglesia de Dios en el Paraguay, 198
Iglesia de Dios en la República Mexicana, 177–78, 537–38
Iglesia de Dios Pentecostal, 24, 209–10

Iglesia de Dios Pentecostal de Puerto Rico, 777
Iglesia de la Biblia Abierta de Cuba, 78–79
Iglesia del Evangelio Cuadrangular, 25, 34, 66, 78, 278
Iglesia del Evangelio Quadrangular, 210
Iglesia Evangélica Filadelfia, 247
Iglesia Evangélica Pentecostal, 23, 78
Iglesia La Luz del Mundo, 641, 678, 840–41
Iglesia Metodista Pentecostal (IMP), 55–57
Iglesia Pentecostal Brasilera, 35
Iglesia Pentecostal de Argentina, 25
Iglesia Pentecostal de Chile, 56
Iglesia Pentecostal Sueca, 34
Iglesia Pentecostal Unida, 34, 65–66, 79, 278
Iglesia Santa Pentecostes, 25
Iglesia Wesleyana Nacional, 24
Igreja Evangélica Pentecostal de Angola, 22
Igreja Universal del Reino de Deus (IURD), 40, 853–54
Independent African Churches (IACs), 12–14
Independent Assemblies of God (IAG), 169, 778
Independent Evangelical Church, 778
Independent Pentecostal Evangelical Church Movement
    (MIEPI), 778
Indian Pentecostal Church of God (IPC), 122–23, 305, 778–
    79, 781
Indigenous churches, 779–83
Integrity Communications (IC), 769
Interdenominational Christian Church, 791–92
International Catholic Charismatic Renewal Services (ICCRS),
    792, 817–18
International Charismatic Consultation of World Evangeliza-
    tion (ICCOWE), 541, 690, 792, 795
International Church of the Foursquare Gospel (ICFG), 34, 66,
    78, 83, 185, 310, 314–15, 529, 564, 646, 692, 793–94, 838,
    856–59, 1019, 1074, 1168, 1180
International Communion of Charismatic Churches, 488
International Convention of Faith Churches and Ministers,
    794–95
International Correspondence Institute (ICI), 641
International Evangelical Church, 137–38
International Evangelism Crusades, 795
International Ministerial Association (IMA), 795
International Pentecostal-Charismatic Scholarly Associations,
    795–97
International Pentecostal Church of Christ (IPCC), 278, 797–
    98
International Pentecostal Conference, 365
International Pentecostal Council (IPC), 98, 798
International Pentecostal Holiness Church (IPHC), 154, 798–
    801, 890, 1105, 1154
International Pentecostal Press Association (IPPA), 801
International Theological Conferences on Holy Spirit—Korea,
    796
Invisible Church (Durban), 233–34
Islam, 16, 19, 85, 127. see also Muslims
Italian Apostolic Church, 136–37
Italian Elim Churches, 137
Italian Pentecostal Christian Church (CCPI), 135–36
Italian Pentecostal Church of Canada (IPCC), 805

J

Japan Evangelical Association (JEA), 148
Jerry Savell Ministries International, 155
Jesus Army, 44–45
"Jesus Christ Is Lord" Churches, 138
Jesus Christ Saves Global Outreach, 205
Jesus for Africa, 232
Jesus Is the Lord Church, 1175
Jesus Is the Lord Fellowship, 205
Jesus People, 138, 453
Jesus Reigns Ministries, 205
Jews for Jesus, 872
Joweto Project, 232–33

K

Kanisa La Elim Pentekoste Tanzania (KEPT), 266
Kansas City prophets, 816–17
Kensington Temple (KT), 43, 595
Kenya Assemblies of God (KAG), 153–54
Keswick Higher Life Movement, 820–21
Kimbanguism, 74
Kingsway International Christian Centre (KICC), 45
Kiribati Protestant Church (KPC), 156
Koinonia Foundation, 232
Korean Assemblies of God (KAG), 244
Korean Pentecostal Church, 244
Korean Pentecostal Holiness Church (PHCK), 245–46
Korean Pentecostal Society, 796

L

Laestadians, 103
Lamb of God community, 475
Latin American Bible Institute (LABI), 332, 354, 637, 639
Latin American Churches of the Church of God, 722
Latin American Council of Christian Churches
    (LACCC/CLADIC), 210, 682, 719–20, 934, 1027, 1049
Latin American District Council of the Assemblies of God
    (LADCAG), 368, 829–30
Latin American Radio Evangelism (LARE), 640
Latin Encounter, 472–73
Latter Rain movement, 28, 48, 172, 188, 336, 369, 443, 830–33,
    1018
Legião de Maria, 41
Legion of Christ's Witnesses, 230–31
Lewi Pethrus Foundation, 117, 257
Life in the Spirit Seminars (LSS), 840
Lighthouse of International Foursquare Evangelism (L.I.F.E.),
    376, 379, 692–93, 712, 823, 839–40
Light of the World Church, 641, 678, 840–41
Lillian Trasher Memorial Orphanage, 7
Living Church, 220
Living Water Unlimited Church, 19
Living Way Church, 251–52
Logos International Fellowship, Inc., 843–44
London Missionary Society, 120, 372
Love of Christ fellowship, 205
Lower Hutt Church of Christ, 445

Lutheran Church, 87, 103, 109, 120, 197, 313, 332–33, 343, 441, 455, 480–81, 483, 506, 522–23, 549, 574, 611, 763–64, 813, 814, 838, 847–51, 876–77, 900, 958, 992, 1027, 1167, 1216

M

Mana Egreja Crista, xx, 125
Maranatha Campus Ministries, International (MCMI), 860, 1184
March for Jesus (MFJ), 43, 188–89, 573, 860
Marcionism, 733
Margaya Fellowship, 252
Marxism, 862–63
Masonic Order, 37
Melodyland Christian Center, 868, 909, 1194–95
Mennonite charismatics, 869–71
Messianic Jewish Alliance of America (MJAA), 521, 873
Messianic Judaism, 297, 504–5, 520–21, 814–15, 871–74
Methodist Church, 24, 44, 55, 103, 120, 142, 191, 194, 239, 443, 506, 614–15, 837–38, 1153, 1156–58, 1192, 1217
Methodist Episcopal Church, 55, 770–71, 996
Methodist Revival Fellowship (MRF), 1157–58
Metro Christian Fellowship (MCF), 417
Metropolitan Church Association (Burning Bush), 874–75
Miracle Life Fellowship, 203
Miracle Revival Fellowship, 311
Misión Iglesia Pentecostal, 24
Misión Wesleyana National, 56
Missão Evangélica de Vista Alegre, 22
Missionary Aviation Fellowship, 28
Missionary Conference, the, 885
Mission Evangélique de Pentecôte (MEP), 108
Mission Libre Suédoise, 47
Mission Pentecostal, 25
Mita Congregation, Inc., 899
Monarchianism, 733–34
Montanism, 732–33, 901–2
Morning Star Publications and Ministries, 814
Mount Sinai Holy Church of America, 907–8, 1026
Mukti Mission, 120, 122, 305, 351, 660, 1016
Mülheim Association (MA), 908
Mulu Wengel, 86
Muslims, 4–5, 6–11, 113, 115, 276, 297. see also Islam
Myalism, 142

N

National Association of Evangelicals (NAE), 336, 338, 378, 456, 532, 541, 565, 613, 616, 643, 775, 920–23, 966, 970
National Council of Churches of Christ, 336
National Gay Pentecostal Alliance (NGPA), 923–24
National Initiative for Reconciliation (NIR), 233
National Religious Broadcasters (NRB), 923
National Revival Crusade, 27, 691
National Service Committee (NSC), 462, 464, 817
Native American Pentecostals, 924–25
Neo-apostolics, 298
Neocharismatics, 25, 125, 291, 296, 298–99, 926
New Apostolic Church (NAC), 459, 926–27

New Apostolic Reformation, 927
New Churches, 44–45, 1176–77
New England Fellowship (NEF), 921, 1218
New Frontiers International, 44, 45
New Life Churches of New Zealand (NLCNZ), 556, 782, 806, 900, 906, 1182, 1191, 1215
New Testament Church of God, 28, 31, 33, 154
New Zealand Evangelical Mission (NZEM), 1023–24
Nigerian Jesus Women Prayer and Ministry, 20
Nondenominational Pentecostal and Charismatic churches, 930–32
Non-white indigenous neocharismatics, 296
North American Congresses on the Holy Spirit and World Evangelization, 933
North American Renewal Service Committee (NARSC), 541, 795, 933
North American Society for Church Growth, 1179
Norwegian Free Churches Missions, 70

O

Ondas de Amor y Paz, 24, 25
Oneness Pentecostalism, 48, 62, 65, 128, 129, 143, 159, 163, 187–88, 270, 280, 294, 321–22, 329, 364, 440–41, 447, 559–60, 624, 641, 717–18, 834, 891–92, 934–42, 1160–61
Open Bible Faith Fellowship, 50
Open Bible Evangelistic Association (OBEA), 943–44, 1019, 1074
Open Bible Standard Church (OBSC), 51, 52, 78–79, 114, 146, 210, 272, 278, 899–900, 921, 943–44, 1183
Open Door, the, 54
Oral Roberts University, 25
Örebro Mission, 34, 280, 942, 947
Organization of the Islamic Conference, 19
Original Church of God (OCG), 535
Original Gospel movement, 149
Orthodox charismatics, 295

P

Pacific Missionary Aviation (PMA), 178–79
Pacifism, 951–53
Parish Renewal Council, 955
Pathway Press, 955
Pentecostal and Charismatic Research Fellowship, 797
Pentecostal Apostolic Church of God (PACG), 215–16
Pentecostal Assemblies of Canada (PAOC), 23, 31, 48–49, 51, 78, 86–87, 113, 151–52, 180, 220, 270, 274, 331, 449–50, 472, 520, 818, 852, 855, 890, 959–62, 1011, 1073, 1112
Pentecostal Assemblies of God (PAG), 151–52, 266–67
Pentecostal Assemblies of God—Uganda, 274
Pentecostal Assemblies of Jesus Christ (PAJC), 962, 1158, 1200–1201
Pentecostal Assemblies of Newfoundland, 661, 962–63
Pentecostal Assemblies of Switzerland (SPM), 1224
Pentecostal Assemblies of the West Indies (PAWI), 52
Pentecostal Assemblies of the World (PAOW), 51, 175, 423, 560, 694, 891–92, 936–38, 962, 963, 1165
Pentecostal Assembly of Jesus Christ, 65, 66
Pentecostal Association of Ghana, 18

Pentecostal/Charismatic Churches of North America (PCCNA), 14–19, 541, 555, 598, 922
Pentecostal Christian Congregations (CCP), 135
Pentecostal Church, Inc., 723, 963, 1158
Pentecostal Churches of Uganda (PCU), 275
Pentecostal Church in Dutch East India, 129
Pentecostal Church of Australia (PCA), 27, 681, 1108
Pentecostal Church of God (PCG), 529, 597, 963–64
Pentecostal Church of Iceland (PCI), 117
Pentecostal Church of Indonesia, 129
Pentecostal Church of Malaya (PCM), 170
Pentecostal Church of New Zealand (PCNZ), 187–89, 308, 417, 445, 1037, 1190
Pentecostal Church of Poland, 94
Pentecostal Coalition for Human Rights (PCHR), 964–65, 1141
Pentecostal Community of Congo (CEPCO), 68–69, 71–72, 777–78, 965
Pentecostal Conference of North American Keralites, 965–66
Pentecostal European Conference (PEK/EPF), 1224
Pentecostal European Fellowship (PEF), 1224
Pentecostal Evangelical Brotherhood in Africa: Congo (FEPACO), 72
Pentecostal Evangelical Church, 108
Pentecostal Evangelical Fellowship of Africa (PEFA), 268
Pentecostal Evangelistic Fellowship of Africa (PEFA), 47, 152
Pentecostal Fellowship of North America (PFNA), 336, 541, 554, 558, 598, 643, 775, 922, 966–67
Pentecostal Foreign Mission of Norway (PYM), 153
Pentecostal Free-Will Baptist Church (PFWBC), 363, 967
Pentecostal Friends (PF), 103
Pentecostal Gospel Temple, 143
Pentecostal Hallelujah Church, 113
Pentecostal Holiness Church (PHC), 61, 123, 124, 162, 266, 457, 563, 566, 586, 597, 730, 805, 822–23, 904, 921, 1026, 1110–11, 1113–14
Pentecostal Holiness Church (PHC) of Canada, 967
Pentecostal Missionary Union (PMU), 60, 365, 968–69, 989–90, 1034, 1223
Pentecostal Mission in South and Central Africa (PMSCA), 889–90
Pentecostal Mission of Central and South Africa, 264
Pentecostal Revival (PR), 80–81
Pentecostal Theological Association of Southern Africa, 795
Pentecostal World Conference (PWC), 969–72, 1021, 1224
Pentecostal World Conferences (PWC), 98, 104, 336, 456, 541, 554, 590, 597, 643, 775, 795
People of Praise, 475
People's Mission, 264
Philippine Council of Evangelical Churches (PCEC), 201, 204
Philippines for Jesus Movement (PJM), 201, 986
Pietism, 109, 371, 610–12
Pilgrim Holiness Church, 52
Pillar of Fire, 1192
Pinsevennenes Ytre Misjon, 34
Pioneer, 45
Pisgah Home Movement, 988–89, 1220–21
Plumbline, 45

Porte Ouverte, La (PO), 54
Positive Confession movement, 455, 990–92, 1037
Postpentecostals, 292
Power Pentecost Church, 19–20
Prayer groups, 74, 139–40, 502–3
Prayer mountain movement, 240–43, 260–61
Prepentecostals, 292
Presbyterian Church, 120, 121, 191, 240, 440, 444, 481, 506, 815, 993–95, 1196
Primera Iglesia Pentecostal de Cuba, 78
Prophetic Independent Churches, 12–14
Protestant charismatics, 295, 486–87, 548–49, 591–92
Puritans, 1216

Q

Quakers (Society of Friends), 1012, 1217

R

Reba Place Fellowship (RPF), 475
Redeemed Gospel Church (RGC), 154–55
Redeeming Love Christian Center, 1166
Renewal in the Holy Spirit (RNS), 139–40
Renewal Ministries Australia (ARMA), 29
Restoration Church, 220
Restorationism, 44, 1017–19
Revival Centre Church, 223–24
Rhema Church, 226, 234, 852
Roman Catholic Church, 16, 21, 22, 36, 38, 44, 49–50, 73, 140–41, 156, 172, 194, 197, 206–7, 254, 481–83, 507, 549, 567–68, 576–82, 591–92, 682, 765–67, 810–11, 853, 861, 1106–7, 1169–72
Romanian Pentecostal Church, 93
Russian and Eastern European Mission (REEM), 91–92, 94, 213–15, 891, 983–84, 1029–30
Russian Missionary Society (RMS), 89
Russian Orthodox Church, 95, 217
Russian Union of Christians of the Evangelical Faith (RUCEF), 95

S

Salt and Light Ministries, 45, 561–62
Salvation Army, 254, 1041, 1110
Scandinavian missions, 1038
Schweizerische Pfingstmission, 53, 258
Scripture Union, 15
Sele Valley Evangelical Churches, 136
Serpent handlers, 1050–51
Servants of the Light community, 475
Shakers, 1056–57
Sharing of Ministries Abroad (SOMA), 451, 690, 1057–58
Shepherding movement, 1058–60
Shiloah Apostolic Church, 143
Sidang Injil Borneo church (SIB), 172–73
Society for Pentecostal Studies (SPS), 661, 772, 795, 1077
South African Assemblies of God (SAAG), 372
Spirit Churches, 12–14
Spiritism, 37–38
Spirit of Jesus Church, 149–50

Spiritual Renewal Seminars, 225
Spring Harvest, 42–43
St. Andrew's Chorleywood (SAC), 43
St. Francis Association for Catholic Evangelism (FACE), 371
Student Christian Movement, 15
Svenska Fria Mission, 23, 34, 47, 86, 264–66
Swedish Free Churches Missions, 70–71, 153, 219, 264–66, 269–70
Swedish Pentecostal Mission, 176–77
Swiss Evangelical Alliance (SEA), 1224
Swiss Pentecostal Mission (SPM), 53, 258

T

Tabernacle of Glory, 172
Tabernacle Pentecostal Church (TPC), 799–800
Tabor College, 29
Taiwan Assemblies of God (AG), 260
Tanzanian Assemblies of God (TAG), 267
Teen Challenge, 247, 565, 567, 1114–16
Temple Trust, 29
Third wave ministries, 25, 125, 291, 489, 1139
Three-Self Reform Movement (TSRM), 63
Tiumphant Church Ministries, 203
Tokaikolo Christian Fellowship (TCF), 272
Topeka Revival, 120, 887, 1139, 1145–47
Toronto Blessing Movement, 817, 1147–50
Trinity Broadcasting Network (TBN), 565, 713–14, 1117
True Jesus Church, 63, 64, 261–63, 270, 780

U

Umoja wa Makanisa ya Pentekoste, 265–66
L'Union des Eglises Evangéliques Elim en République Centrafricane, 53
Unión des las Asambleas de Dios (UAD), 23, 24
Union of Elim Evangelical Churches in the Central African Republic, 53
Union of Evangelical Christians and Baptists (UECB), 219
Union of Flemish Pentecostal Churches, 32
Union of Messianic Jewish Congregations (UMJC), 872–73, 1154–55
United Church of Christ, Fellowship of Charismatic Christians in the, 1155
United Church of the Holy Spirit, 47
United Holy Church of America, 51, 52, 422, 907, 1155–56
United House of Prayer for All People, Church on the Rock of the Apostolic Church (HP), 1156
United Methodist Charismatics, 1156–58
United Methodist Renewal Service Fellowship (UMRSF), 1192
United Pentecostal Churches of Rwanda, 220
United Pentecostal Church of Myanmar, 182–83
United Pentecostal Church (UPC), 25, 28, 30, 34, 50, 53, 66, 83, 100, 123, 143, 146, 155, 175, 182, 200, 247, 270, 278, 440, 472, 635, 679, 688, 723, 905, 1158–63

United States Conference of Catholic Bishops (USCCB), 464
Uniting Church, 28
Universal Church of the Kingdom of God (UC), 1163–64
Universal Fellowship of Metropolitan Community Churches (UFMCC), 981, 1164
Universal Pentecostal Church, 203
Upper Room Mission, 1164

V

Valley Road Pentecostal Church, 152
Vatican II, 1169–72
Verbond van Vlaamse Pinkstergemeenten, 32
Victory Outreach International, 331–32, 1173
Viens et Vois, 1173–74
Vineyard Christian Fellowship, 50, 259, 417, 488, 1175, 1197–98
Voice of Healing, 472, 556, 1176
Volksmission, 264

W

Waverly Christian Family Centre, 29
Waves of Love and Peace, 24, 25
Way International, The, 1192–93
Welsh Revival, 88–89, 105, 345, 351–52, 418, 1025, 1185–86
Wesleyan Holiness Charismatic Fellowship (WHCF), 52, 611–12, 1114, 1186–87
West of Scotland Revival, 1187–90
Women's Aglow Fellowship International (WAFI), 25, 573, 1207–9
Word for the World, 204, 205
Word of Faith Movement, 455, 687, 714, 990–92, 1037
Word of God community, 473, 475
Work of Christ community, 475
World Alliance of Reformed Churches (WARC), 575
World Council of Churches (WCC), 56, 662–63, 1211–14
World Horizon Mission, 117
World Miracle Bible Church, 16
World Vision, 102, 226
Wycliffe Bible Translators, 226

Y

Young Men's Christian Association (YMCA), 63, 119, 120, 647
Young Messianic Jewish Alliance of America, 521
Young People's Endeavor (YPE), 565
Young Women's Christian Association (YWCA), 120
Youth for Christ, 207
Youth Mission Training Institute (YMTI), 310
Youth With A Mission (YWAM), 28, 102, 107, 247, 380, 573, 680, 1221–22

Z

Zimbabwe Assemblies of God, Africa (ZAOGA), 683
Zion Evangelistic Fellowship, 1224
Zionist Churches, 12–14
Zulu Zionist Church, 12

Index of Publications

A

Abundant Life (Roberts, O.), 981, 1024

Acts 29 (Acts 29 Ministries), 802

Adullam News, The (Baker, H. A.), 352

Adult Teacher's Quarterly (Assemblies of God), 772, 959

After Our Likeness (Volf, M.), 517, 548, 550

Again (Antiochian Evangelical Orthodox Mission), 559

AG Heritage, 449

Aglow (Women's Aglow Fellowship International), 1209

Agora (Assemblies of God), 978, 1103

Alleluja (Catholic Charismatic Renewal), 496

Alpha Manual (Holy Trinity, Brompton), 312

America's Healing Magazine (Roberts, O.), 981

Anchor Bible Dictionary, The, 449

Anglicans for Renewal (Anglican Renewal Ministries), 43, 315, 486, 491, 902

Apologist, The (Robinson, A. E.), 1024

Apostolic Banner, 976

Apostolic Evangel (Fire-Baptized Holiness Association), 822

Apostolic Faith, The (Azusa Street Mission), 59–60, 97, 120, 228, 326, 327–28, 347, 375, 394–95, 559, 565, 693, 805, 844, 846, 868, 887, 888, 898, 955–56, 975, 976, 977, 978, 979, 1056, 1161, 1193

Apostolic Faith Report (Apostolic Faith), 327, 977

Apostolic Herald, The (Pentecostal Church, Inc.), 852

Apostolic Herald (Chiesa Apostolica in Italia), 136

Apostolic Light (AG–Latin American District Council), 347, 354, 829, 976

Apostolic Messenger (Argue, A. H.), 976

Apostolic Rivers of Living Water, 976

Apostolic Witness (Assemblies of the Lord Jesus Christ), 342, 975

Asian Journal of Pentecostal Studies (Asia Pacific Theological Association), 790, 796

Assemblies of God Heritage (Assemblies of God), 855, 1186

Australasian Pentecostal Studies (Southern Cross College), 790, 797

Australian Evangel, The (Buchanan, W. A.), 448

Azusa (Relevant Pentecostals), 795

B

Baptism in the Holy Ghost and Fire, The (Abrams, M. F.), 55, 120, 121, 305, 771, 788, 895

Baptism of the Holy Ghost, The (Mahan, A.), 345, 421

Bible Advocate, The, 1144

Bible Standard (Open Bible Standard Churches), 772

Biographical Dictionary of African-American, Holiness-Pentecostals (DuPree, S. S.), 386, 593

Bishop C. H. Mason and the Roots of the Church of God in Christ (Clemmons, I. C.), 385, 555

Blackwell's Dictionary of Evangelical Biography, 449

Blessed Truth, The (General Assembly of the Apostolic Assemblies), 893, 938, 947

Boa Semente (Casa Publicadora das Assembleias de Deus), 208

Bolletin de la Confraternidad de Las Asembleas de Dios de Sud America, Zona Sur (AG–U. S.), 24

Bombay Guardian (Mumbai), 120

Bratskii Vestnik (Union of Evangelical Christians and Baptists), 218, 219

Bridal Call, The (International Church of the Foursquare Gospel), 793, 856, 898, 977, 1142

Bridegroom's Messenger (Cashwell, G. B.), 457, 797–98, 888, 898, 921, 975, 976, 989, 1145

Bulletin of the American Schools of Oriental Research, 561

Bulletin of the Near East Archaeological Society, 561

Bulletin of the Pentecostal Church (Pentecostal Apostolic Church of God), 215

Bulletin voor Charismatische Theologie (Charismatic Work Fellowship the Netherlands), 186, 494

Burning Bush (Metropolitan Church Association), 875

Byposten (Barratt, T. B.), 193, 365, 976

C

Call to Renewal, A (Lutheran renewal movement), 1169

Cantos de Alegria (Casa Publicadora das Assembleias de Deus), 208

Catholic Biblical Quarterly, 449

Catholic Charismatic (Lange, J.), 463, 474

Catholic Pentecostals (Ranaghan, K., and D. Ranaghan), 383, 484, 493

CCF Viewpoints (Christ's Church Fellowship), 529

Charisma and Christian Life, 364, 385

Charisma (Calvary Assembly of God), 981, 1107–8, 1183

Charisma (Jesus-Haus), 493

Charismatische Gemeinde Erneuerung (Catholic Charismatic Renewal), 492

Chile Pentecostal, 199

Chinese Recorder, 55

Christ for the Nations (Christ for the Nations Institute), 523, 842, 899, 1179

Christiana, 976

Christian Alliance and Missionary Weekly (Christian and Missionary Alliance), 789

Christian Assembly, The, 976

Christian Century, 403

Christian Challenge (Coe Foundation), 556, 906

Christian Conquest (Simpson, C.), 981

Christian Evangel (Assemblies of God), 642, 678, 888, 921, 976, 977, 1204

Christian Initiation and Baptism in the Holy Spirit (McDonnell, K., and G. T. Montague), 465, 507, 517

Christianity Today, 384, 485, 489, 561, 616, 635, 871, 876, 932, 1061

Christian Life (Scripture Press), 981, 1183

Christian Messenger (Christian and Missionary Alliance), 920

Christian Patriot (Chennai), 120

Christian's Pathway to Power, The (Keswick Higher Life Movement), 821

Christians Today (Istituto Biblico Italiano), 135

Chronicle of Higher Education, The, 534

Church History (Society for Pentecostal Studies), 1181

Church Is Charismatic, The (Bittlinger, A.), 292, 418

Churchman, The, 490

Church of God Evangel (Church of God), 30, 531, 533, 558, 898, 956, 982, 1206

Cloud of Witnesses to Pentecost in India (Moorhead, M. W.), 907, 976

Come and You Will See (Rinnovamento nello Spirito Santo), 139

Comforter/Trooster (Apostolic Faith Mission), 590

Confidence (Azusa Street Revival), 306, 366, 437, 546, 971, 976, 1223

Contact-Congo (Zaire/Congo Evangelistic Mission), 4

Coros de Alegria (Casa Publicadora das Assembleias de Deus), 208

Cristiani oggi (Istituto Biblico Italiano), 135

Cross and the Switchblade, The (Wilkerson, D.), 139, 190, 460, 481, 490, 566, 1062, 1196

Cuvantul Adevarului (Apostolic Church of God of Romania), 325

D

Dagen (Swedish Pentecostal Mission), 256

Daily Blessing (Roberts, O.), 981, 1024

Dake's Annotated Reference Bible (Dake, F. J.), 570

Day, The (Swedish Pentecostal Mission), 256

Deeper Life (Agape), 648

Dictionary of Pentecostal and Charismatic Movements, 449, 486, 688, 854

Dictionary of Religion in America, 449

Dictionary of South African Biography (Beyers, C. J.), 227

Divine Power (Ceylon Pentecostal Mission), 251

Documents of Mechelen (International Catholic Renewal Office), 32

Dunamis (Full Gospel Church of God in Southern Africa), 654

Dunamis (Methodist), 44, 491, 1160

Dypere Liv (Agape), 648

E

Echoes of Grace (British Israelitism), 691

El Consejero Fiel (Independent Pentecostal Evangelical Church Movement), 778

El Evangelio (Church of God), 200, 689

Elim Evangel (Elim–U. K.), 4, 5

Elim Herald (Elim Fellowship), 598, 1091

Elim Year Book (Elim–U. K.), 5

Empowered (Mennonite Charismatics), 871

Encyclopedia of African American Religions (Murphy, L. G., et al.), 385

Encyclopedia of Early Christianity, 449

Encyclopedia of the American Religious Experience (Lippy, C. H., and P. W. Williams), 383

Encyclopedia of World Christianity, The (Barrett, D. B.), 3, 269

En Mission Avec Eux (AG–France), 4

Enrichment, 855

EPTA Bulletin (European Pentecostal Theological Association), 98, 409, 449, 547, 610, 790, 797, 1077

Erneuerung in Kirche und Gesellschaft (Catholic Charismatic Renewal), 493, 910

European Pentecostal Theological Association Bulletin (EPCRA), 796

Evangelical Studies Bulletin, 383

Evangelical Visitor, 1144

Evangeliebladet (Apostolic Church), 80

Evangelii Härold (Swedish Free Churches), 5, 256, 839, 986

Evangelist, The (Swaggart, J. L.), 1111

Evangelist (Union of Christians of Evangelical Faith), 218

Evangel Voice (Italian Pentecostal Church of Canada), 805

Evening Light and Church of God Evangel, The (Church of God), 30, 888, 976, 1145

Evidence of Faith (Edvardsen, A.), 598

Expositor Dominical (Casa Publicadora das Assembleias de Deus), 208

F

Faithful Counselor (Independent Pentecostal Evangelical Church Movement), 778

Faithful Standard (Church of God), 1145

Fanning the Flame (Catholic Charismatic Renewal), 507

Fellowship Magazine (Charismatic Renewal Movement), 486

Feu et Lumière (Lion de Juda/Beatitudes community), 494

Fiel (Assembleas de Dios), 247

Field Focus (AG–U. S. Division of Foreign Missions), 5

Filadelfia-Forsamlinger (Mattsson-Boze, J. D.), 867

Final Frontiers (Association of International Mission Services), 5

Forerunner, The (Maranatha Campus Ministries, International), 860

Forward (United Pentecostal Church International), 688

Foursquare Advance, The (International Church of the Foursquare Gospel), 793, 977

Foursquare Crusader (International Church of the Foursquare Gospel), 858, 977

Full Gospel Men's Voice, The (Full Gospel Business Men's Fellowship International), 653, 931, 981

Full Gospel Missionary Herald (Pentecostal Mission in South and Central Africa), 898, 970

Full Gospel News (Full Gospel Evangelistic Association), 327, 654

Full Gospel Testimony, The (Full Gospel Testimony), 1104

G

G.A.N.G. (God's Anointed Now Generation) *Life* (Victory Outreach International), 1175

Gavillas Doradas (AG–Mexico), 341, 949

Gemeinde Erneuerung (Evangelical Church in Germany), 509

Gesú Risorto (Comunità Gesú Risorto), 140

Go-Between, The (Scottish Episcopal Renewal Fellowship), 492

God's Latter Rain (Latter Rain Movement), 976

God's Revivalist (Church of God), 1143, 1144

Golden Grain (Price, C. S.), 978

Golden Sheaves (AG–Mexico), 341

Good News (Good News Hall), 26, 447, 829

Good Tidings (Pentecostal Assemblies of Newfoundland), 964, 975

Gospel Call of Russia, The (Russian and Eastern European Mission), 91, 898, 977, 1043
Gospel Herald (Mennonite Charismatics), 869
Gospel Messenger (Congregational Holiness Church), 558
Gospel Trumpet, The (Evening Light Saints), 1054
Grace and Glory (Assemblies of God), 642, 976
Grain of Mustard Seed, The (Chiese Evangeliche della Valle del Sele), 136
Grüsse aus dem Heiligtum (Mülheim Association), 910
Guideposts (Sherrill, J. L.), 1062

H

Harvest Messenger (Africa Harvest 2000), 5
Healing and Wholeness (Anglican Renewal), 682
Healing Digest, The (Church of God of Prophecy), 688
Healing Waters (Roberts, O.), 981
Heiligung (Mülheim Association), 956
Heilszeugnisse (Mülheim Association), 910, 956
He Is Able (Methodist Church), 1159
Herald of Deliverance (Apostolic Christian Assembly), 322
Herald of Faith/Harvest Time (Latter Rain Movement), 832, 867, 980
Herald of Healing (Voice of Healing), 556
Herald of the Church, The (Assemblies of God), 972
Herald of the Gospel (Swedish Free Churches), 5, 256
HIS Magazine (Walker, R. A.), 1183
Hokhma, 259
Holiness-Pentecostal Movement in the United States, The (Synan, H. V.), 383, 399, 539, 804, 1113
Holiness-Pentecostal Tradition, The (Synan, H. V.), 292, 383, 384
Holy Spirit, The (True Jesus Church), 261
Holy Spirit and the Power, The (McDonnell, K.), 384, 549
Household of God, 975

I

ICCOWE Link (International Charismatic Consultation on World Evangelism), 792
ICCRO (see *ICCRS*)
ICCRS International Newsletter (International Catholic Charismatic Renewal Services), 499, 792
ICO Newsletter (International Catholic Charismatic Renewal Services), 792
Il est Vivant! (Emmanuel), 493
Il granel di sapene (Chiese Evangeliche della Valle del Sele), 136
Il Regno di Dio, 135
India Alliance (Christian and Missionary Alliance), 120
Indian Witness (Lucknow and Calcutta), 120, 121
Intecessary Missionary, The, 976
International Bulletin of Missionary Research, 384, 417, 855
International Faith Report (International Convention of Faith Churches and Ministers), 795
International Review of Missions, 449, 897, 1215
In the Latter Days (Synan, H. V.), 383, 384
Introduction to Life (Ceylon Pentecostal Mission), 251

J

Jesus vive é o Senhor (Comunidade Emanuel), 513
Journal of Christian Healing (Association of Christian Therapists), 1062

Journal of Educational Sociology, 561
Journal of Korean Pentecostal Theology (Han Sae Institute), 796
Journal of Pentecostal Theology (Church of God Theological Seminary), 790, 1046
Journal of the American Academy of Religion, 401
Journal of the European Pentecostal Theological Association, The, 98
Joy (AG–U. K.), 4

K

Kädenojennus (Lutheran charismatic church), 509
Keeping in Touch (Universal Fellowship of Metropolitan Community Churches), 1166
Kingdom of God, The, 135
Koinonia (Catholic Charismatic Renewal), 497
Korsets Seier (Barratt, T. B.), 23, 103, 365

L

La Evangelista Pentecostal (AG–Puerto Rico), 639
La Forza della Verità (Iniziativa di Comunione nel Rinnovamento Carismatico Cattolico), 509
La Luz Apostólica (AG–Latin American District Council), 347, 354, 829
L'Araldo Apostolico (Chiesa Apostolica in Italia), 136
Latter Rain, The (Latter Rain Movement), 888, 976
Latter Rain Evangel (Apostolic Faith Mission), 712, 787, 891, 898, 976, 990, 1223
La Voce (Rinnovamento Carismatico Servi di Cristo Vivo), 140
Leader's Touch (AG–U. S. Division of Foreign Missions), 5
Leaves of Healing (Dowie, J. A.), 977, 989
Le Muséon, 449
Liberty and Gladness, 976
Lied des Lammes (Mülheim Association), 956
Life of Faith, The (Keswick Higher Life Movement), 821
Lighted Pathway, The (Church of God), 532, 558, 691, 956
Light of Hope, The (Azusa Street Mission), 976
Like a Mighty Army (Conn, C. W.), 385, 558
Live Coals of Fire (Fire-Baptized Holiness Church), 640, 799, 804, 822
Logos Journal (Logos International), 485, 832, 844, 859, 966, 980, 1106
Lutheran Renewal International (Lutheran renewal movement), 1169
Luz del Mundo (Iglesia Evangélica Filadelfia), 247

M

Manna Ministries Notes (United Methodist Renewal Service Fellowship), 1159
Manna (United Methodist Renewal Service Fellowship), 1159, 1194
Maran Atha (Pentecostal Revival), 80
Meat in Due Season (Oneness Pentecostalism), 937, 938
Message of the Open Bible (Open Bible Standard Churches), 946
Message to the People of South Africa, The (South African Council of Churches), 451
Messenger, The (Pentecostal Free-Will Baptist Church), 969
Midnight Cry (Azusa Street Mission), 679, 976
Ministries Today (Buckingham, J. W.), 448, 476, 981, 1107
Miracle Magazine (Allen, A. A.), 311

Missiology, 449

Missionary Challenge (AG–Division of Foreign Missions), 724, 898

Missions Banaret (Örebro Mission), 419

Morning Star Journal (Joyner, R.), 502, 507, 814

Morning Star Prophetic Bulletin (Joyner, R.), 817

Morning Star Prophetic Newsletter (Joyner, R.), 814

Mountain Missionary, The, 1144

Moving Waters (Full Gospel Church of God in Southern Africa), 1030

N

Nairobi Pentecostal Bible College Newsletter (Nairobi Pentecostal Bible College), 5

National Catholic Reporter, 461

National Courier, The (Logos International Fellowship), 844, 981

National Geographic (National Geographic Society), 38

National Revivalist (British Israelitism), 691

New Acts, The (World Evangelization Company), 846, 888, 975

New Covenant (Catholic Charismatic Renewal), 462, 463, 464, 485, 519–20, 861, 981

New Creation (Catholic Charismatic Renewal), 492

New Encyclopedia of Archaeological Excavations in the Holy Land, 561

Newsletter for Methodists Interested in Charismatic Renewal (Methodist Revival Fellowship), 490, 553, 1160

New Strait Times, The, 172

New Way of Living, A (Harper, M.), 473, 548

New Wine (Holy Spirit Teaching Mission), 367, 484, 485, 769–70, 981, 1060, 1061–62, 1206

New Zealand Evangel (AG–New Zealand), 1039

Nine O'Clock in the Morning (Bennett, D.), 225, 383, 484

Novas de Alegria (Casa Publicadora das Assembleias de Deus), 208

NRB Magazine (National Religious Broadcasters), 1016

O

One in Christ (Roman Catholic Church), 577, 578

Operation World, 3, 507

Our 16 Doctrines (AG–U. S.), 339

Our Hope (Messianic Judaism), 872

Our Life Together (First Baptist Church, Chula Vista, CA), 483

Our Sunday Visitor, 461

Overcomer, The (Open Bible Standard Churches), 772, 946

Oxford Encyclopedia of Archaeology in the Near East, 561

P

Paraclete, 790, 855

PCBC Journal (Association of Pentecostal and Charismatic Bible Colleges of Australasia), 797

Pensieri dal–l'Alto (Missione del Pieno Evangelo), 138

Pentecost, The (Assemblies of God), 642, 662, 1046

Pentecostal Coalition for Human Rights Newsletter (Pentecostal Coalition for Human Rights), 967

Pentecostal Currents in American Protestantism (Blumhofer, E., et al.), 383, 384

Pentecostal Echoes (Coe Foundation), 556

Pentecostal Evangel (AG–U. S.), 5, 92, 331, 334, 335, 369, 642, 643, 644, 678, 831, 832, 855, 897, 898, 921, 977, 1186, 1198, 1204

Pentecostal Herald (Pentecostal Church of God), 966, 1163

Pentecostal Herald (United Pentecostal Church International), 688

Pentecostal Holiness Advocate (Pentecostal Holiness Church), 457, 566, 797, 799, 800, 888, 906, 976, 1107, 1156, 1206–7

Pentecostal Messenger (Pentecostal Church of God), 966

Pentecostal Record and Outlook, The (Bursell, H. R.), 976

Pentecostal Revival (Istituto Biblico Italiano), 135

Pentecostal Testimony, The (Pentecostal Assemblies of Canada), 5, 334, 594, 638, 852, 962–63, 977

Pentecostal Trumpet, 976

Pentecostal Truths (Mok Lai Chi), 976

Pentecostal Witness (Pentecostal Church of Christ), 798

Pentecost (Apostolic Faith Mission), 712, 888, 973

Pentecost in the Twin Cities, 976

Pentecôte (AG–France), 4

People of Destiny (House Church Movement), 488

People's Mouthpiece, The (Apostolic Overcoming Holy Church of God), 329

Pfingstgrüsse (Mülheim Association), 910, 956

PFNA News (Pentecostal Fellowship of North America), 969

1971 Plan for Union (National Council of Churches), 191

Pneuma: Journal of the Society for Pentecostal Studies (Society for Pentecostal Studies), 383, 384, 414, 449, 497, 579, 635, 790, 855, 871, 1023, 1079, 1083, 1181

Pneumatikos (Society for Pentecostal Theology), 795

Post Express Wired, 19

Preaching (Catholic Homiletic Society), 855

Promise, The, 976

Promise of the Father, The (Steiner, L.), 976, 1106

Prontuário das Assembleias de Deus (Casa Publicadora das Assembleias de Deus), 208

Q

Questions and Answers (Gospel Publishing House), 369

R

Reconciliation (Pentecostal/Charismatic Churches of North America), 555, 1023

Record of Faith, The (Pridgeon, C. H.), 898, 990

Redemption Tidings (AG–U. K.), 4, 457, 663, 956

Reflections (Chiesa Apostolica in Italia), 136

Reign of Christ, The, 976

Religious Studies Review, 449

Renewal (Fountain Trust), 43, 553, 689

Renewal in the Spirit (Catholic Charismatic Renewal), 632

Renewal Journal (Australian Charismatic churches), 53

Resource (PAOC Overseas Missions Department), 5

Restoration (Robison, J.), 487

Restoration (U.K.), 488, 491, 550

Restoring the Faith (Blumhofer, E.), 383, 384, 436

Reveille (Pearlman, M.), 959

Revista Avivamento (Casa Publicadora das Assembleias de Deus), 208

Riches of Grace (Apostolic Church), 323

Riflessioni (Chiesa Apostolica in Italia), 136
Rinnovamento nello Spirito Santo (Rinnovamento nello Spirito Santo), 139, 496, 509
Risuscito (Comunità Maria), 496
Risveglio Pentecostale (Istituto Biblico Italiano), 135
Rundbrief für Charismatische Erneuerung in der Katholischen Kirche (Catholic Charismatic Renewal), 493

S

Saints Alive (Anglican Church), 315, 486, 491, 840
Samson's Foxes (Church of God), 1144–45
Sanningens Vittne (Fellowship of Christian Assemblies), 636
Scofield Reference Bible (Oxford University Press), 345, 570, 584, 585, 1044, 1045
Serviteur de Dieu (AG–France), 4
Sharannagar News (Harvey, E. B.), 692
Shield of Faith, The (Church of God of Prophecy), 688
Small Voice, The (Charismatic Renewal Movement), 486
South and Central African Pentecostal Herald (PMSCA), 970
Spade Regen (Polman, G. R.), 976
Spirit: A Journal of Issues Incident to Black Pentecostalism (Tinney, J. S.), 1143
Spirit, The (Pentecostal Church of God), 966
Spirit Alive Missions (Presbyterian Church U.S.A.), 486
Spirit Bade Me Go, The (Du Plessis, D.), 383, 481, 592
Spirit and Church, The (Gospel Theological Seminary), 796
Spirit of Truth, The (Lake, W. L.), 976
St. Louis Lutheran (Lutheran Charismatics), 877
Streams of Living Water (Foster, R.), 518, 559
Sunday School Promoter (Scripture Press), 1183
Sunday School Study Manual (Istituto Biblico Italiano), 135
Sursum Corda (Charismatic Episcopal Church), 476
Svensk Lösen (Lidman, S.), 839

T

Tempi di Restaurazione (Chiesa Evangelica della Riconciliazione), 138
Theological Education, 561
Theological Investigations, 549
Theological Renewal (Foundation Trust), 491, 548, 646, 837
Theology of the Holy Spirit, A (Brunner, F. D.), 362, 447
They Speak with Other Tongues (Sherrill, J.), 139, 383, 460, 481, 490, 1062
Through Analogy to Reality (Apostolic Church), 547
Tongues of Fire (Anglican Renewal Ministries), 486, 1032, 1144
Transformation, 1077
Treasures Old and New (Communion of Evangelical Episcopal Churches), 557
Trinity (Blessed Trinity Society), 370, 435, 479, 480, 981
Triumphs of Faith (Montgomery, C. J.), 904, 906, 909, 975, 988, 1072, 1223
Troens Bevis (Edvardsen, A.), 598
Truth, 976
Tychique (Chemin Neuf), 493–94

U

United Evangelical Action (National Association of Evangelicals), 591, 924
Upper Room, The (Upper Room Mission), 712, 1166

V

Venite e Vedrete (Rinnovamento nello Spirito Santo), 139
Verheissung des Vaters (Steiner, L.), 976, 1106
Victory (Assemblies of God), 647
Vine, The (Risen Christ community), 492
Vision, The (Coates, G.), 556
Vision of the Disinherited (Anderson, R. M.), 313, 383
Vision Speaks, The (Church of God, Jerusalem Acres), 538
Voice (Full Gospel Business Men's Fellowship International), 477, 479, 480, 1159
Voice in the Wilderness (Oneness Pentecostalism), 938
Voice of Healing (Lindsay, G.), 311, 441, 523, 567, 842, 899, 979, 1178–79
Volle Evangelie Koerier (Brotherhood of Full Gospel Assemblies), 184
Vuur (Verhoef, W.), 185, 186, 490, 548, 1174

W

WARC Update (World Alliance of Reformed Churches), 575
Washington Afro-American (Tinney, J. S.), 1143
Way, The (Tomlinson, A. J.), 1144
Way of Faith, The (Pike, J. M.), 110, 366, 457, 975, 976, 988, 1144, 1222
Way of Faith, The (Poysti, N. J.), 1031
Weekly Evangel (AG–U. S.), 369, 585, 642, 678, 937, 953
Welcome, Holy Spirit (Christenson, L.), 517, 549, 814
Wesleyan Theological Journal, 449
Where Do We Go from Here? (Cell churches), 502
Whole Truth, The (Church of God in Christ), 537, 866, 1206
Whole Truth, The (Church of the Lord Jesus Christ of the Apostolic Faith), 544
Witness of God, The (Oneness Pentecostalism), 938
Word Among Us, The (Mother of God Community), 486
Word and Witness (AG–U. S.), 333, 369, 375, 678, 866, 888, 937, 989, 1161, 1162
Word and Work (Christian Worker's Union), 366, 528, 793, 888, 975, 976, 1223
Word of Faith, The (Positive Confession), 687
World Christian Encyclopedia (Barratt, D. B.), 3, 269, 293, 294, 302, 384
World Churches Handbook (Brierley, P.), 3, 268
World Directory of Pentecostal Periodicals (International Pentecostal Press Association), 801
World Harvest Magazine (Lester Sumrall Evangelistic Association), 1110
World Pentecost (Pentecostal World Conference), 973, 979, 1226
Wort und Geist (Zopfi, J.), 1077, 1226

Y

Yearbook of American and Canadian Churches, 535
Yearbook of the Pentecostal Movement, The (Pentecostal Movement Information Center), 257

General Index

A

animism, 7, 315–18, 1092–93

anointing the sick, 17, 160, 249, 318, 364, 424, 524, 536, 776, 870, 926, 1033, 1036

apostolic churches, 169, 175–76, 187, 214, 294, 298, 321–29, 459, 928–30, 983–84

archives, 270, 329–31

authority, spiritual/ecclesiastical, 104, 484, 1098–99

B

baptism in the Holy Spirit, xxi, 44, 59, 60, 68, 109, 196, 206, 212, 218, 305–6, 321, 340, 349, 354–63, 422–23, 479–81, 785–86, 1129–32. *See also* Holy Spirit

baptism in water. *See* sacraments/ordinances

biblical criticism, 237–38, 338, 367, 418, 1122

biblicism, 262, 611, 617, 877, 993, 1014, 1122

bibliography/historiography, xvii, 270, 382–417, 898–99

C

charismatic movement, xv–xvi, xix, 291, 294–95, 336–37, 363–64, 477-519, 995–97, 1158–60

  see individual country/region

  African American, 506-507

  Africa, xviii, 12-13, 14-17, 113-14, 230-35, 500-501, 510-11

  and Acts 29 ministries, 306–8

  and nondenominational churches, 932–34

  Anglican, 295

  Asia, 28-29, 64, 124-5, 171-72, 183, 189-91, 204-7, 225, 226, 246, 252, 272, 511-12

  Baptist, xxii

  Catholic, 460–67

  communities, 476–76

  Europe, 32-33, 44, 98, 139-40, 185-86, 489–97, 508-10

  Latin America, 40-41, 66, 158-59, 211, 497-500, 512-13

  Lutheran, 847–51

  Mennonite, xxii, 869–71

  Methodist, 1158–60

  North America, 49-50, 477–89, 507-8

  Oceana 513-14

  Orthodox, 295, 1106-7

  Presbyterian & Reformed, 995–97

  statistics, 284–85, 286–89

  theology, 17, 465–66, 548–50

charisms. *See* gifts of the Spirit

churches

  and cell theology, 46, 502, 902

  and congruence, 262–63

  convergence movement, 558–59

  independent African, 12–14, 230, 309

  indigenous, 779–83

  prepentecostal, 292–93

classical pentecostalism, xv–xvi, xviii–xix, 43, 47–50, 55–56, 134–35, 184–85, 187–88, 286–91, 293, 553–55, 1019–21

  see individual country/region

  and black holiness pentecostals, 419–28

  and ethics, 606–7

  hispanic, 715–23

  theology, 544–48

  versus charismatics, xxi-xxii, 515–17

communism, 88, 92, 94, 145, 212–19, 324–25, 862–63, 1205, 1221. *See also* socialism

controversies, 121, 213, 340–41, 353, 443, 592, 596–97, 638–39, 657–58, 784–91, 830–33, 874–75, 1204–6

D

demonology, 15, 17, 196, 240

  and demon possession, 159, 308, 624–27, 1101, 1136–37

denominations. *See also* charismatic movement; neocharismatic; Unitarianism/Oneness pentecostalism

  and black holiness pentecostals, 419–28

  and ecclesiastical polity, 597

  Catholic postcharismatic, 295

  Hispanic, 715–23

  mainline postcharismatic, 294–95, 486

  nondenominational, 487-88, 930–33

  pentecostal, 293–94, 546

  postpentecostal, 292

  prepentecostal, 292

  renewal, 299–301

dialogue, 138, 418, 575–82, 882

discernment of spirits, 291, 582–84, 765, 876, 1009, 1064

Dispensationalism, 137, 584–86, 601, 734, 879, 898, 1044, 1138

doctrine. *See* theology

E

ecstasy, 144, 195, 343, 433, 571, 671, 732–33, 735, 743, 748–749, 752, 756, 904, 1000, 1002, 1008, 1065

ecumenical movement, xxii, 23, 40, 498–99, 816, 894, 1171–74

education, 69, 73, 86–87, 117–18, 180, 256–57, 325, 335, 337, 338–39, 372–74, 533–34, 899. *See also* schools; teachers

  and black holiness pentecostalism, 426

  in the African churches, 17–18

enculturation, 262–63, 420

eschatology, 37, 601–5, 1138–40

ethics, 12, 19, 25, 431, 605–9, 1086

evangelicalism, xxii. *See also* fundamentalism

evangelism, 87, 128–9, 131, 170, 201, 233, 261, 285, 312, 501–2, 617–21

evangelists, 621–22

experience, religious, 199, 206, 211, 240–41, 306, 309, 1097, 1129

F

faith, 629–31, 696, 825, 1033

faith healing, 149, 209, 312, 324, 351, 401, 630, 727, 785, 891, 896, 899, 946, 978–79, 1067, 1134–37, 1212–13, 1231
fasting, 14, 183, 240, 250, 310, 510–11, 633–35, 766, 904, 1099
feminism and feminist theology, 166, 430–31, 1208, 1210
finished work controversy, 638-39
fruit of the Spirit, 447, 455, 634, 648–52, 1057
fundamentalism, 217–19, 262–63, 613–16, 658

G

gifts of the Spirit, xvii, xviii, xix, xx, 62, 88, 160, 206, 239–43, 318, 358, 570–71, 629–30, 664–668, 801–2, 1137–38, 1200–1202. *See also* discernment of spirits, faith, faith healing, glossolalia (tongues), interpretation of tongues, knowledge (word of), miracles (gift of), prophecy, wisdom (word of)
glossolalia, xviii, xix, 17, 59, 60, 121, 143, 206, 217, 305, 328, 334, 340, 343, 349, 358–59, 667, 670–78, 787–91, 801–2, 1101, 1132–34
Gypsies, 10, 683–86

H

heresy and heretics, 88, 656, 727, 732, 734, 736, 750–51, 754, 759, 762, 862, 1080, 1126, 1213
heritage and history, 12, 715, 879, 944, 947, 975, 979, 1007–9, 1064, 1086, 1210–11
hermeneutics, 262–63, 1121–23
historiography. *See* bibliography/historiography
Holiness/perfectionism, 143, 293, 296, 311, 345, 421–22, 640, 726–29, 798–801, 1020
Holy Spirit. *See also* baptism in Holy Spirit
    and black holiness pentecostals, 421
    blasphemy against, 432–35
    history of, 354–55
    indwelling of, 16, 673
    theology of, 51, 361–62, 548, 549, 730–69, 834–36
hymnology. *See* music

I

indigenization, xvii, xx, 14, 84, 149–50, 261–63, 783, 900
indwelling of the Holy Spirit, 16, 355, 547, 743, 744, 750–51, 758, 759, 761, 768, 798, 942, 947, 1094, 1095, 1112
initial evidence, 784-91
initiation rites, Christian, 196, 1036
inspiration, 323, 541, 545, 614, 656, 734, 756, 766, 793, 877, 879, 885, 891, 895, 1002, 1010, 1014, 1045, 1065, 1098, 1173, 1189
interpretation of tongues, 801-2

J

Jesus Christ, 359–60, 652, 695–96, 1033, 1125–31
Judaism, relationship to pentecostalism, 8, 149, 297, 504–5, 538, 601–3, 871–74, 1156–57

K
knowledge, word of

L

laity, 40–41, 460, 464, 489, 510, 576, 596, 625, 653, 700, 848, 996, 1190

Latter Rain, 830-33
laying on of hands/imposition of hands, 143, 144, 834–36
liberation theology, 40–41, 429–31, 1076, 1077, 1088
liturgy, 482–83, 559
    African, 14–15, 16–17

M

marriage and divorce, 18, 43, 207, 377, 382, 540–41, 551, 717, 727, 733, 761, 767, 1036, 1205, 1209
martyrs, 9, 10–11, 93, 274. *See also* persecution
Mary, the Virgin, 863–64
mind and spirit, 518, 584, 760, 1048, 1095
ministries
    military, 534
    radio, 25, 82, 152, 179, 193, 206, 222, 247, 256, 444, 1015–16
    television, 8, 64, 179, 193, 222, 276, 353, 371, 619–20, 1118–20
    women in, 13, 19–20, 121–22, 129–30, 144, 250, 310, 314–15, 335, 352, 425, 888, 925, 1061
miracles, 72, 267, 268, 276, 308, 317, 328, 344, 351, 694–711, 875–76
missiology, 533, 547, 855, 877–83, 895–97
missions, 769–70, 885–900, 925, 949, 970–71, 1031–32, 1040, 1166, 1225
music, 16, 144, 183, 196, 565, 911–20
Muslims or Islam, 7–8, 10, 113, 114–15, 127, 203, 276, 805

N

nationalism, 39, 158–59, 199
Native Americans, 352, 926–27
neocharismatics, xv–xvi, xvii, xix–xx, xxi, 41–42, 125, 137–39, 158–59, 285, 286–89, 291, 296, 298–99, 928
    see individual country/region
non-pentecostal Christians, xv–xvi, 43–44, 49–50, 196, 273, 293–95, 482–83, 655–58, 1217–20

O

Orthodox charismatics, 295, 1051–52, 1106-7, 1112

P

pacificism and peace, 651, 924, 953–55
pentecostalism. *See* classical pentecostalism
periodicals and journals, 974–82, 1107–8
persecution, 55–56, 63–64, 66, 92–93, 125, 133–34, 198, 243–44, 252, 274, 284, 371, 866–67, 924, 983–85. *See also* martyrs
    and black holiness pentecostalism, 423–24
philosophy and theology, 37, 372–73, 393, 395–96, 410, 505, 731–32, 735, 753, 755, 874, 1040, 1048, 1086–87, 1138, 1141
pluralism, 45, 338, 405, 542, 665, 720, 736, 780, 918, 925, 964, 1084–85, 1121, 1124–25, 1140
pneumatology, 51, 361–62, 548, 549, 730–69
polemics, 237
politics, 19, 37, 41, 56–57, 74, 94–95, 166–67, 261, 881
polity, church/ecclesiology, 39, 164–65, 188, 200, 254, 342, 409, 410, 426–27, 529–30, 546, 547, 558, 596–97, 664, 694,

722, 724, 726, 774, 799–800, 872, 899, 904, 939, 940, 965, 971–72, 977, 1040, 1205
poverty, 10, 18, 39–40, 57, 145, 241, 284, 311, 386, 468, 501, 607, 702, 992, 1136
prayer, 14, 74, 205, 240–43, 347–48, 502–3, 1092, 1206–8
preaching, 18, 50, 241, 270, 314–15, 316, 438, 447–48
prophecy and prophets, xvii, 11–12, 12–13, 176, 241, 344, 502, 666, 803, 999–1012
prosperity, 29, 41–42, 237–38

R

racism and racial issues, xviii, 231, 232–33, 237, 347, 349, 421, 429–31, 924, 939–40, 1057
radio ministries, 25, 82, 152, 179, 193, 206, 222, 247, 256, 444, 1015–16
reconciliation, 140–41, 189, 233, 254, 339–40, 429–30, 924
relationship of pentecostals/charismatics to other major religions, 29, 45–46, 61–62, 66, 87–88, 99–100, 106, 140–41, 252, 313, 464–65, 883
relationship of pentecostals/charismatics to others in renewal, 16–17, 49, 99–102, 155, 165
religious education. *See* education
religious freedom, 84, 134, 219, 1031–32, 1063, 1173–74
religious life, 276, 469, 472
research, 329–31, 572–73, 586, 1079
resting in the Spirit. *See* slain in the Spirit
revivals, 24–25, 27, 55, 80–81, 88–89, 118–21, 164–65, 239–40, 280, 336, 337–38, 343, 445–46, 521, 1110–11, 1147–49, 1187–88, 1189–92
rituals, 130, 143, 150, 316–17, 468–69
roots of pentecostal and charismatic Christianity, 88–91, 96–97, 103–4, 109–11, 184–85, 193, 257–58, 530–32, 610–12, 1160–65

S

sacraments/ordinances, 947–49, 1033, 1036, 1129–32
    baptism in water, 143, 149, 196, 360–61
saints, 144, 319, 328, 344, 347, 357, 392, 404, 466, 529, 544, 596, 674, 703–5, 727, 752, 759–60, 866, 977, 983, 1009, 1064, 1228–29
scholarly associations. *See* research
schools, 18, 34, 58, 81, 86, 117–18, 122–23, 190, 220, 267, 305, 335, 354, 372–81, 839–40, 1045–50. *See also* education; teachers
science, 37, 237–38, 543, 626, 632, 862, 1066–67, 1231
secularism, 134, 346, 376, 380, 395, 398, 414, 432, 446, 467, 492, 495, 509, 521, 539, 565, 578, 609, 616, 626, 668, 751, 913, 925, 1084–85
sexuality, 14, 29, 40, 145, 189, 507, 763, 967, 1028, 1059, 1094–96, 1097, 1209
shamanism, 148–50, 316, 993, 1093, 1123
shepherding, 49, 252, 367, 475, 484, 488, 550, 596, 769–70, 911, 933, 981, 999, 1060–62, 1070
signs and wonders, xvii, xx, 488–89, 1063–68
slain in the Spirit, 225, 338, 346, 438, 827, 1018, 1072–74, 1211
slavery, 37, 141–42, 419–21
social concerns and social justice, 17, 18, 38–39, 41, 117, 124, 133–34, 145, 160, 166, 189, 232–35, 309, 315, 431, 607–8, 881, 966–67, 1076–78

social customs, 194, 608–9
    and taboos, 14, 16–17, 316, 317, 529, 530, 542, 683, 785
social gospel, 234–35, 251, 607
socialism, 110, 145, 181, 862–63. *See also* communism
sociology, 57, 195–96, 1080–89
soteriology, 710–11, 746, 760, 761, 882, 943, 1020
spirituality, 11–12, 37-38, 73, 161, 315-17, 634, 1096–102
statistics, xv
    continental, 3–20, 286–88
    country, 3–282, 296–98
    global, 284–302
suffering, 20, 142, 145, 154, 284, 423, 428–30, 468, 631, 694–95, 700, 708, 759, 881, 993, 1005–6, 1052, 1078, 1101, 1128, 1133, 1136–39, 1195, 1203, 1207–8
supernatural, the, 18, 62, 127, 131, 217, 239–41, 262, 267, 268, 274, 290–91, 324, 349, 359, 378, 390–93, 398, 403–4, 503, 517, 615, 619, 626, 630, 665, 667–68, 739–40, 745, 760, 784–85, 832, 850, 879, 897, 928, 934, 1189–90
superstitions, 131, 229, 420, 499
syncretism, 38, 260–61, 510, 1076, 1125

T

teachers, 65, 276, 305. *See also* education; schools
television ministries, 8, 64, 179, 193, 222, 276, 353, 371, 619–20, 1118–20
theology
    and evangelicalism, 614–15
    and evangelism, 617–18
    and faith, 517–18
    and theologians, 263, 334, 367, 785–90
    black, 428–32
    charismatic, 17, 465–66, 548–50
    education (*See* education)
    issues in, xviii, xx, xxi, 60–61, 114–15, 213, 215, 339
    of the Holy Spirit, 51, 361–62, 549, 730–69, 834–36
    oneness, 940–44
    pentecostal, 544–48, 1120–40
    positive confession, 992–94
    sources and origins, 80–81, 460–61, 466, 473–74, 490–91, 515–16
third wave, xvii, 286–87, 296, 298, 1141
tolerance and conviction, 36, 121, 134, 213, 237, 325, 338, 420, 956, 1075, 1077
tongues. *See* glossolalia.
tradition, 173, 1217–20
    in the African churches, 13–14, 18–19
    Indian, 130
Trinity, the, xviii, 37, 143, 334, 554, 615, 732–34, 735, 737, 738, 740–42, 1125–28, 1164

U

Unitarianism/Oneness pentecostalism, 47, 65, 89, 129, 175, 187–88, 294, 296, 297, 787, 893–94, 934–42, 1125–28, 1162–63, 1164

V

visions and dreams, 8, 14, 308–9, 316, 1101–2

W

war
    and ethics, 607
    Persian Gulf, 8
    spiritual, 502–3, 1091–96
    World War I, 30, 89–92, 97–98, 103, 110
    World War II, 5, 21, 61, 92–94, 103–4, 110, 554–55
wealth. *See* prosperity
wisdom, word of, 1200-1202

women
    in the church, xviii–xix, 13, 19–20, 121–22, 129–30, 144, 250, 310, 314–15, 335, 352, 425, 888, 925, 1061, 1203–8, 1209–11
    in the home and society, 19–20, 144, 322, 324, 342, 1203–4
    worship, xvii, xix, 16–17, 131, 183, 322, 346, 469, 540, 599–600, 932, 1206–8, 1217–20

We want to hear from you. Please send your comments about this book to us in care of the address below. Thank you.

GRAND RAPIDS, MICHIGAN 49530 USA

WWW.ZONDERVAN.COM